GUINNESS
WORLD RECORDS™

14ᵀᴴ EDITION

Acknowledgements

Editor
David Roberts

Chief Consultant / Contributor
Dave McAleer

Assistant Editor
James Bradley

Desk Editor
Mary Novakovich

Design
Maria Centorino
David Sterne

Proofreader
Andy Gregory

Writers
Bruno MacDonald
Dave Jennings

Picture Research
Betty Halvagi
Beverley Hadfield

Pre-Production Manager
Patricia Langton

Vice President – Media
Ian Castello-Cortes

With thanks to:
Louise Wilson, Neil Hayes, everyone at Slice, Phil Matcham at CIN, Steve Haberfield, Michael Heatley, Brian Southall, James Rigg, Andrzej Michalski, Rob Hackett, Ross Carter, Martin Downham, Janet Jones, BusinessAge magazine, Malcolm Connah, Richard M White, Steve Earnshaw, Steve Hampson, Russtti Gaynor, Robin Clarke, Derek Christie, Simon Belofsky, Andy Brobbin, Kevin Ennis, Allan Hollings, Graham Betts, Lloyd Eckert, Neil Thompson, Richard Lambeth.

Communicate with The Guinness Book of British Hit Singles by writing to Guinness World Records, 338 Euston Road, London NW1 3BD. Alternatively, email

editor@14th.britishhitsingles.com

If you would like an opportunity to contribute votes for your favourite singles to register in our all-time Top 100 Singles Chart, turn to the last page in this book.

Contents

Chart Watching

Dave McAleer reveals the stats and facts behind the last chart year of the 20th century

The official last year of the 20th century was a record breaker. There were more No.1 singles than ever before and an unprecedented number of solo female singers topped the chart. Westlife **increased their two-year tally of No.1s to seven and** Eminem **proved that rappers could rack up hit after hit. Teenagers** Craig David, Britney Spears, Billie Piper **and** LeAnn Rimes **sold stacks of singles, and a group that split 30 years earlier sold more albums than anyone else.**

Only Bob the Builder's chart-topper did not enter in that position; before that there was a staggering 42 records that did and none of these managed to hold the top spot longer than three weeks. For the first time, people expected a new No.1 every week and record companies, with their aggressive marketing tactics, rarely disappointed them. Despite the fact that most No.1s were seldom even "eight-day wonders", the tabloids still made much of such chart battles as Victoria Beckham vs Spiller, or Westlife vs Bob the Builder – both of these being won by the underdogs. It's worth pointing out that entries at No.1 are still almost unknown in every other country. Despite the glut of chart-toppers, the year's most successful singles included a 600,000-selling No.2 by The Baha Men (who proved that records can go up as well as down) and a record by US country group Lonestar, which failed to crack the Top 20 but amazingly out-performed every other chart entry.

British acts increased their share of the year's Top 100 singles to 44 per cent, which meant that European acts lost a little of the ground they gained last year. In this chart, male soloists managed 13 slots, 21 singles were by female soloists (one third being British) and female vocalists were predominant on 31 of the 66 records by groups or duos. Trance and garage music were very successful in 2000; pop, dance and R&B / hip hop together accounted for 90 per cent of singles sales, while rock music hit an all-time low (unlike in the US where it enjoyed a very healthy comeback).

Eight singles passed the half-million mark in the UK, compared with 20 in each of the previous two years. There were 65 fewer entries in the Top 75 than last year but the number of records debuting in the Top 10 passed the 200 mark for only the second time. Entries in the Top 10 used to be rare, now six a week is not unusual. Only 11 per cent of Top 75 chart entries managed a 10-week chart stay and more than 50 per cent did not stay longer than a fortnight.

Comparisons with the US market were again quite startling. Across the Atlantic the average hit spent more than 11 weeks in the Top 20, whereas in the UK it was fewer than three! Despite this, the actual sales of hit singles here were higher than in the US where, on occasion, the No.1 sold fewer than 40,000 copies. Thankfully, UK singles fared better in the US than last year (their worst year since 1960), with Westlife, BBMak, Sting, Sonique and Samantha Mumba making Top 20 visits. Both markets had record album sales and both saw dramatic drops in singles sales. In the US singles plummeted 36 per cent (after a 25 per cent drop last year), while in the UK they were down by 17.5 per cent. These figures make interesting reading when one considers that an estimated 1.5 billion blank CDRs were sold worldwide, and that the number of people regularly using the major internet music downloading site Napster rose 500 per cent between February and August to 6.7 million, and that company boasted 1.39 billion downloads in September alone!

Outsiders could be forgiven for thinking that these statistics suggest the hit single has fallen from favour. But that is far from the case as it is clear that the attraction of hit singles has, if anything, increased. The growth of interest in Napster, MP3.com, Peoplesound and other similar operations may have affected sales, but they have helped to increase music fans' awareness of countless tracks and acts that otherwise they may never have discovered. Perhaps now is the time for chart compilers to consider adding some download elements into their calculations, as this will better indicate which tracks are really the most popular. The album chart already includes a proportion of downloads and, if this innovation were introduced for singles, it would probably help to slow down the chart.

In this year's book we have included several new features which we hope will be welcomed. For the first time, in this first year of the century, we include a 42 page fact-packed trivia trip looking at every No.1 of the past, extended biographies for the Top 10 artists, plus the real names of literally hundreds of Top 10 hitmakers.

It is impossible to prophesise what the next 12 months will bring; after all, who would have would have thought that the last No.1 of the 20th century and the biggest selling single of 2000 would be secured by a nine-inch builder! However, it's most unlikely that in 2001 either Space or Odyssey will score No.1s, and almost certain that we will be in for another record-breaking year on the world's fastest moving and most exciting chart.

Chart Milestones

The official UK charts used to compile The Guinness Book of British Hit Singles have altered in size and format on a number of occasions. Here are the major changes since the chart began in 1952.

14 NOVEMBER 1952
First chart was a Top 12 compiled for the New Musical Express

1 OCTOBER 1954
NME chart becomes a Top 20

30 DECEMBER 1955
NME chart becomes a Top 25 but for one week only

13 APRIL 1956
Top 30 established

26 FEBRUARY 1960
Last NME Top 30 used by Guinness Book of British Hit Singles

10 MARCH 1960
Week ending 5 March data inaugurates the first Record Retailer chart used in this book

3 JANUARY 1963
Top 50 now independently audited

13 FEBRUARY 1969
Top 50 now compiled for Record Retailer and the BBC by British Market Research Bureau

6 FEBRUARY 1971
Postal strike responsible for limiting the chart to a Top 40 for seven weeks

27 MARCH 1971
Top 50 resumes

6 JANUARY 1973
Top 30 only, for one week

22 DECEMBER 1973
Top 30 only, for one week

JULY 1977
First edition of The Guinness Book of British Hit Singles hits the shops

6 MAY 1978
Top 75 begins

8 JANUARY 1983
Chart compilation taken over by Gallup

DECEMBER 1992
The chart, produced in association with the BPI and BARD, becomes the copyright of Chart Information Network Co Ltd, or CIN for short. Gallup's compilation is based on a minimum of 500 record outlets incorporating vinyl, cassette and CD singles

12 FEBRUARY 1994
Chart compilation taken over by Millward Brown and the sample of record outlets is increased to more than 1,000

30 DECEMBER 2000
Last Top 75 singles chart of the 20th century is incorporated into this current edition of Guinness British Hit Singles

A final note about the way in which the chart information is recorded in this book. Establishing an "official" chart in pop's young days proved difficult among all the competition. When this book was first published in 1977, the choice of which chart to use was not an easy one. It is possible to argue that the Record Retailer chart, in the very beginning, was not the most widely accepted. As a result, one question is regularly raised when referring to the Beatles' chart history. The Record Retailer chart, and consequently this book, listed a peak chart position of No.2 for 'Please Please Me' in 1963. Virtually every other chart at the time shows this as the Beatles' first chart-topper, but our chart choice was proved to be correct as, by the mid 1960s, Record Retailer (now Music Week) had been generally accepted by the music industry as the official UK chart.

Pop Quiz Top Tips

We don't like to boast, but the fact is that this book you're looking at is the bible for pop quiz players and quizmasters. If you memorised every fact in your Guinness Book of British Hit Singles, your pop knowledge would be unbeatable. The only snag is that by the time you'd done it, our next edition would be out and you'd probably have lost all your friends.

Fortunately, you don't have to go quite that far – not even if you're one of that dedicated body of men and women for whom answering questions about music is a way of life. For most of us, pop quizzes are an occasional diversion at the local pub, club or with like-minded groups of people on the internet, but there are those for whom they are a kind of profession. Frighteningly dedicated teams of "anoraks" are known to travel the pub circuit, moving from quiz to quiz, accumulating prize money and yet more knowledge. The compilers of pop quizzes have to take account of both kinds of player, the likely age range of their audience, and a whole lot of other variables.

But there are some pieces of advice that can be regarded as universal and, after quizzing a few quiz players and presenters, we offer these tips:

ASKING THE QUESTIONS:

So you've decided that anything Chris Tarrant can do, you can do better. You want to compile the questions and be in the spotlight. Then we suggest:

1. **First, foremost and always: GET YOUR FACTS RIGHT**. You've got this book, so make use of it, and save yourself the hideous embarrassment of having to admit to being wrong in public. Why not take your Guinness Book of British Hit Singles with you to the venue, so you can produce it triumphantly should anyone dispute an answer?

2. **Make the scoring system as simple as possible** – and if it is more complex than one point per correct answer, then try to make sure that everyone understands the rules before you begin.

3. **Make sure that everyone can hear you**. You need to do a soundcheck before you start your quiz just like a band needs to do one before a gig – particularly given the inadequacies and eccentricities of many pub PA systems. Far better to spend a minute or so ensuring that those tucked away in the far corners of the venue can hear you than to spend much of the evening repeating questions.

4. **Mark the answers yourself, or have a trusted assistant to do it**. Getting the teams to swap answer sheets can lead to arguments, which could turn nasty if you're running a big-prize quiz. People can get their opponents' scores wrong either in order to cheat or just out of honest drunken incompetence. And while you're at it…

5. **Mark the answers after every round**. This adds to the excitement, as people get to find out how well (or not) they're doing. It also avoids putting everyone through a long, nerve-jangling wait at the end, and minimises the opportunities for people to employ the simplest cheat of all: that old classroom favourite, the casual peek at your neighbour's answers.

6. **Ban the use of mobile phones during the quiz**. Firstly because they break everyone's concentration, and secondly because hardcore quiz devotees have been known to try to phone a friend to get an answer – or even to have someone on standby outside the venue with a copy of this book!

7. **Keep inserting the word "hit" into the question**. This will stress the fact that you're talking about the best-known version of a song, and so avoid any danger of sad obsessives rushing up to inform you that your answer refers to a cover version, and that the original was recorded between 5pm and 6:30pm on 11 June 1966 by the seminal Arkansas garage band The In Breed.

8. **Beware of questions involving years, particularly those that ask the audience to specify in which year a song was a hit**. Many a Christmas hit could justifiably be said to have been a hit in two years; Mud's "Lonely This Christmas", for instance, hit the top in 1974 but actually stayed at No.1 into 1975 – and re-entered the chart in 1985. Many a record has finally hit the chart long after its first release, so even if you own

the single, the date on its label isn't necessarily the year in which it was a hit. And anyway, let's face it, "What year did X have a hit with Y?" is a boring question.

9. **Remember that your audience has come to play a pop quiz, not to listen to your enthralling banter**. Too many quizmasters let their egos get in the way of the entertainment. If you think you're a comedian, there's probably an open-mic night at the local comedy club where your repartee might be more appreciated.

10. **Don't drink too much – at least, not until after the quiz**. A drunk with a mic in his hand who thinks he's funny almost certainly isn't, and questions are easier to understand when they're not being slurred. Save your Shane MacGowan impersonation for karaoke night.

11. **Tailor your questions to your audience**. If you're at a genteel tavern full of nice middle-aged folks, they're probably not that familiar with the Marilyn Manson songbook. Likewise, if it's a rock bar, don't overdo the Celine Dion and Westlife excerpts. Obvious, but so many overlook this point.

12. **Don't believe what you read (unless it's in a reputable reference book such as this one, of course)**. Magazines and newspapers, especially the tabloids, often exaggerate or misinterpret pop chart facts.

13. **Try to apply some imagination when setting the questions and deciding the format of your quiz**. Endless questions simply asking who had a hit with (fill in name of song) soon become pretty tedious. If you're going to use excerpts from songs, how about using the choruses – but playing them backwards? You can create your own backwards tapes simply by finding vinyl copies of the records you want to use and winding them backwards on a turntable by hand. Ask what a list of acts have in common – which might be all having had hits with one songwriter's material, or all hailing from the same place. The best and/or most frustrating questions (depending on whether you are asking or answering) are invariably the guess-the-lyric ones. Even the most mighty massively well-known hits provide head-scratchingly difficult questions when a phrase from the song is written down or spoken.

14. **Boring but necessary: ensure that everything you're doing in your quiz is legal**. If you're playing music during your quiz, the venue will need licences from both PPL (Phonographic Performance Ltd) and the PRS (Performing Right Society), so it's a good idea to check.

You can buy ready-made quiz tapes with all the necessary copyright clearance taken care of, but making your own tapes is a legal minefield. In theory, you should contact all the record companies involved with the records you're copying in order to

get their permission to copy snippets of their music on to a blank cassette or CD. Having got a full set of positive responses, you should then get a licence from the MCPS (Mechanical Copyright Protection Society), granting you permission to transfer the music from its original source to your tape or CD. The current cost of a licence to copy less than 30 minutes of music is £17.63, assuming that you're not planning to make more than 100 copies. For details on the audio copyright laws, contact MCPS-PRS Alliance Licensing Services.

Further potential difficulties surface if you're planning to include a picture round. It's illegal to photocopy visual images from record sleeves, magazines or books (including this one!) without the copyright holder's permission.

So do all good quizmasters comply with these regulations? Of course not. Most probably don't even know about some of them. But if you choose to ignore any or all of them, and the copyright authorities raid your quiz, don't blame us.

THE CUSTOMER IS SOMETIMES RIGHT

Being a successful player is a relatively simple matter. Naturally, the first thing you need is a good knowledge of music, but if you haven't got that already, then this book should help a bit.

Beyond that…

1. **Cheats never prosper**. Well, certainly not in quizzes and venues that we've been barred from, which is a likely outcome if you're caught. And anyway, it spoils things for everyone.

2. **If it's a team quiz, try to organise a balanced team with a wide range of musical tastes**. Bands often split up because of musical differences – quiz teams should get together because of them. A family team might work very well in a pop quiz, if Mum and Dad know their Beatles and Bowie and the kids can fill them in on dance and boy bands.

3. **The quizmaster and/or adjudicator's decision is FINAL**. Even if you know they're wrong.

4. **Don't take it too seriously**. It's only questions about rock 'n' roll … we like it.

5. **Whatever you do, don't forget to have fun**.

Many thanks to the readers of The Guinness Book of British Hit Singles who helped in the compilation of this feature. They are: Steve Haberfield who runs a particularly successful and very rewarding weekly quiz at the Coopers Arms, Weston-on-Trent, Derbyshire, Richard M White, Robin Clarke, Derek Christie, Allan Hollings, Andy Brobbin and Andy Gregory.

British Hit Singles

New chart entries in 2000: 846

New singles released in 2000: 6,414

Craig David

Most weeks on chart by any act: 58 – Craig David

Sonique

Most No.1s by any act: 4 – Westlife

Most weeks at No.1: 3 – It Feels So Good - Sonique

Biggest-selling group: Westlife – 1,244,000 singles

Westlife and Mariah Carey

Most weeks on chart by any single: Amazed – Lonestar – 22 weeks (highest position; 21)

Biggest-selling female: Britney Spears – 1,060,000 singles

Britney Spears

Lowest-selling No.1: The Masses Against The Classes – Manic Street Preachers – 142,000

Total No.1 hits: 43 (a new record)

Average first-week sales of a new No.1 – 119,753

Biggest-selling male: Eminem – 1,242,000 singles

Biggest-selling single: Can We Fix It – Bob The Builder – 853,151

Bob The Builder

Statistics 2000

2000 TOP 10 SINGLES
Biggest selling

All topped the chart apart from
'Who Let The Dogs Out' by Baha Men
which peaked at No.2

1.	**CAN WE FIX IT** Bob The Builder	**853,151**
2.	**PURE SHORES** All Saints	**685,343**
3.	**IT FEELS SO GOOD** Sonique	**642,001**
4.	**WHO LET THE DOGS OUT** Baha Men	**617,576**
5.	**ROCK DJ** Robbie Williams	**578,092**
6.	**STAN** Eminem	**544,380**
7.	**TOCA'S MIRACLE** Fragma	**530,742**
8.	**GROOVEJET (IF THIS AIN'T LOVE)** Spiller	**523,242**
9.	**NEVER HAD A DREAM COME TRUE** S Club 7	**491,948**
10.	**FILL ME IN** Craig David	**480,106**

SOURCE: CIN

2000 TOP 10 SINGLES
By weeks on chart and peak chart position

Points awarded: 75 points for a week at No.1, 74 for
each week at No.2, right down to one point for one
week on the final chart position of 75

1.	**AMAZED** Lonestar	**919 pts**
2.	**REACH** S Club 7	**896 pts**
3.	**IT FEELS SO GOOD** Sonique	**886 pts**
4.	**THE REAL SLIM SHADY** Eminem	**856 pts**
5.	**MUSIC** Madonna	**849 pts**
6.	**SANDSTORM** Darude	**848 pts**
7.	**THE BAD TOUCH** The Bloodhound Gang	**832 pts**
8.	**GROOVEJET (IF THIS AIN'T LOVE)** Spiller	**819 pts**
9.	**ROCK DJ** Robbie Williams	**798 pts**
10.	**I'M OUTTA LOVE** Anastacia	**784 pts**

SOURCE: GRS

Pop Review of the Year

January

The year kicks off with **Westlife** still having a dream at the top of the UK singles chart, but there's already trouble in the **Eminem** household. The naughty rapper causes his gran some grief by planning to include a tape of his late Uncle Ronnie on a forthcoming album… **Rene Elizondo**, aka **Mr Janet Jackson**, files for divorce… Domestic disturbance also turns **Mel G** back into **Mel B**, while **Mrs Beckham** adds another level to her hubby's terrace-teasing by announcing that he wears her underwear… **Geri** and **Mel C** share a bill – but not a stage – at a Manchester charity gig… Standing by her man, **Jennifer Lopez** is "surprised and saddened" when – after a seasonal shooting incident – **Puff Daddy** is indicted on weapons charges… **Phil Collins** proves to be king of the jungle at the Golden Globe Awards. **Courtney Love** presents him with the Best Original Song gong for 'You'll Be in My Heart', from Disney's Tarzan.

Confirming UK garage as THE sound of young Britain, DJs the **Dreem Teem** secure a Sunday lunchtime slot on BBC Radio 1… The elder **Gallagher** rubbishes his band's new video for 'Go Let It Out' ("The director decided that he was going to get the singer to work on the idea with him… you don't let the singer have any creative input on anything, because they're useless") but welcomes his new baby daughter Anaïs… The Recording Industry Association of America launches the first of the year's battles against software company **Napster**, whose distribution of MP3 files over the net is portrayed as the moth in many a musical wardrobe… The web waves its wand over EMI too when the label moots a merger with Time Warner, who in turn hook up with net biggies AOL.

Rock rebellion gets the upper hand for a week when **Manic Street Preachers** storm the top slot with 'The Masses Against the Classes', then **Britney** takes over with 'Born to Make You Happy'… Poppy punk pranksters the **Bloodhound Gang** make their last low-key live appearances before notoriety beckons… **Rage Against the Machine** hit Wembley for what will turn out to be Zach de la Rocha's British swan song… Fellow angst-monger Billy Corgan brings his **Smashing Pumpkins** to Britain too, albeit without manager **Sharon "Mrs Ozzy" Osbourne**, who resigns "due to medical reasons: **Billy Corgan** was making me sick"… Former Pumpkins bassist **D'Arcy Wretzsky** heads court-wards after being arrested, as does old hand **Shane MacGowan**.

A bikini babe bursts out of a cake at a **Foo Fighters** gig, much to the embarrassment of blushing birthday boy **Dave Grohl**… **Whitney Houston** suffers some grief when Hawaiian airport security discovers marijuana in her handbag… Rather less surprisingly,

Photo: Angela Lubrano

Another busy year for Britney Spears. Manor house hunting in Gloucestershire, a starring role with Prince William (sadly, in Channel 4 cartoon form only) and, of course, two more UK chart-toppers

Ol' Dirty Bastard begins the year much as he finished the last: by falling asleep in one court appearance, then failing to show up at another… **Dub Jones** of the yakkety-yakking **Coasters** dies on the 15th and the Creation label shuts up shop.

February

Striking gold at the Grammys are **Santana** (nine), **Sting** (two), **Cher**, **Whitney Houston** and **Christina Aguilera**. Cheeky monkey **Eminem** makes off with two, while **Jennifer Lopez**'s outfit inspires more than half a million hits on the Grammy website. It also inspires a hit of a different kind for **Garbage** gobstress **Shirley Manson**, who launches into Lopez with "a beautiful face, but I want to punch it nevertheless"… In more placatory fashion, **Madonna** pays a visit to Lopez to settle rumours of a rift dating from Donatella Versace's New Year's Eve party.

Two of 2000's most enduringly successful singles hit the UK top slot: **Gabrielle**'s 'Rise' and **All Saints**' 'Pure Shores', the year's second-best-selling single… The latter is from the movie The Beach, at whose London premiere Leonardo DiCaprio is reported to have achieved the popular feat of pulling an **Appleton**… In between, **Oasis** return to the top spot with 'Go Let It Out'… **Destiny's Child** begin their biggest year by losing half their staff: LaTavia and LeToya are out, Farrah and Michelle are in… **Geri**'s World Walkabout hits our TV screens as the multimillionairess gets caring and sharing with slum-dwellers in the Philippines and eco-warriors in Wales. Scooter manufacturers Aprilia sue her ex-cohorts after contending that the Spices signed a group sponsorship deal when they knew Ginger was leaving.

Another year of antiques polishing by **The Who** gets under way with the release of their BBC Sessions on Valentine's Day, followed by **Pete Townshend**'s one-off staging of his decades-old 'Lifehouse' at London's Sadler's Wells Theatre… **Lou Reed** dons a theatrical hat too, directing the Edgar Allan Poe-inspired musical Poe-try in Hamburg… Bare-chested love god

> " I resigned due to medical reasons: Billy Corgan was making me sick "
>
> *Sharon Mrs "Ozzy" Osbourne*

D'Angelo returns with the soulful Voodoo album… Boiler-suited brain-bashers **Slipknot** hit the UK gig trail… **Mariah Carey** pays a rare visit to British shores for a fantastic one-off gig at Wembley Arena… **Screamin' Jay Hawkins** stops putting a spell on you when he dies on the 12th… **Doris Kenner-Jackson** of **The Shirelles** dies on the 3rd… **Big Pun** raps his last on the 7th… Cancer claims **Foghat**'s **Dave Peverett** on the same day… Israeli superstar **Ofra Haza** – heard on hits by the **Sisters of Mercy** and **Eric B & Rakim** as well as her own 'Im Nin'alu – dies on the 23rd.

March

Madonna gives a helping hand to her movie The Next Best Thing when 'American Pie' goes one place better than the original and hits the top, and **Chicane** also make No.1, lending a soupçon of street cred to **Bryan Adams** with 'Don't Give Up'… Branded "a fat dancer from Take That" by **Noel Gallagher**, **Robbie Williams** promptly delivers a wreath to the **Oasis** camp, care of the Sun: "RIP. Heard your latest album. With deepest sympathy"… In no way predictably, **Liam Gallagher** threatens to break Robbie's nose and 'Standing on the Shoulder of Giants' enters atop the album chart… **'N Sync** do the same Stateside, albeit with more seismic sales (2.4m): No Strings Attached becomes the fastest-selling album ever.

Excitement in Gloucestershire as **Britney** is reported to have purchased a manor

Eminem in 2000. Constantly controversial, actively aggressive, always interesting

Photo: Pictorial Press

Cheltenham… Mopey **Moby** hit 'Natural Blues' gives the year-old Play album a healthy shove into the best-seller lists, while the soon-to-be superstar revamps his 'Why Does My Heart Feel So Bad?' with **Elton John**… The **Stereophonics** add a youthful veneer to the **Tom Jones** bandwagon as 'Mama Told Me Not to Come' keeps Reload rolling… The **Beckhams**' hairstyles make headlines: while Dave crops his locks, Vic briefly goes blonde… **Pretenders**' protester **Chrissie Hynde** is arrested after an animal rights demo at a Gap store in New York.

The Artist Formerly Known as **Ginger** declines to join her former bandmates to collect an Outstanding Contribution to British Music award at the Brits. **Ms Halliwell**'s show-stopping performance owes much to her raunchy stage entrance between a pair of gigantic sexy legs… The ceremony claims more column inches with well-refreshed **DJ Brandon Block**'s rushing of the stage, **Ali G**'s spectacularly rude introduction of double winner **Macy Gray**, and **Robbie**'s soon-to-be-legendary challenge to the junior **Gallagher**: "Would anybody like to see me fight Liam? Would you pay to come and see it? Liam: hundred grand of your money, hundred grand of my money. We'll get in the ring and we'll have a fight and you can all watch it on TV. What do you think about that?"… And the winners are: **Travis** (Best Group and Best Album), **Robbie** (Best Video and Single for 'She's the One'), **Beth Orton** (Best British Female), **Tom Jones** (Best British Male), **S Club 7** (Best British Newcomer), **Macy Gray** (Best International Female and Newcomer), **Beck** (Best International Male), the **Chemicals** (Best Dance), **TLC** (Best International Group), **Five** (Best Pop Act), **Steps** (Best-Selling Live Act) and Notting Hill (Best Soundtrack)… **Five** premiere their 'We Will Rock You' revamp with **Brian May** and **Roger Taylor**… Tub-thumper Taylor also undergoes laser eye treatment at a London clinic previously patronised by **Mel B**.

A1's high-profile year gets in gear with 'Like a Rose'… **U2** receive the keys to the city of Dublin, celebrating with a four-song performance… Not content with playing God in the recent movie Dogma, **Alanis Morissette** hits the New York stage in feminist play The Vagina Monologues… UK cinemas are briefly overrun by US musicians: **Ice Cube**, **Mark Wahlberg** and video director Spike Jonze join

Boiler-suited brain-bashers Slipknot retained their anonymity throughout their UK tour until famously "exposed" in their dressing room at *TFI Friday* when Lionel Blair was spotted emerging from his diguise

Photo: Roadrunner Records

George Clooney in Three Kings, Cube reappears in Next Friday, and **Courtney Love** stars in the REM-inspired Man on the Moon… Meanwhile, **Madonna** and **Will Smith** win three awards each from the Golden Raspberry Award Foundation, celebrating Worst Achievements in Film for 1999, the 1990s, and the 20th century. The **Fresh Prince** shares brickbats handed out to Wild Wild West, while Her Madgesty earns the Worst Actress of the Century title for classics such as Shanghai Surprise and Four Rooms.

Twenty years of profitable bootlegging come to an end with **Pink Floyd**'s issuing of Is There Anybody Out There? The Wall Live… Back-back-back are **Elastica**, with the underrated The Menace album… Somewhat belatedly, a Los Angeles judge orders **Ol' Dirty Bastard** to undergo psychiatric tests… **Fatboy Slim**'s 'Praise You' is used as a campaign song by Democrat presidential hopeful Al Gore. "Thank God it wasn't the Republicans," quips Mr Cook… Two years after **Bob Geldof** prematurely announced his demise, **Ian Dury** – inventor of the phrase "sex and drugs and rock and roll" – loses a long-fought battle against cancer on the 27th… The man carrying the S&D&R&R mantle into the new millennium has a quiet

> " RIP. Heard your latest album. With deepest sympathy "
>
> ***Robbie Williams to Oasis***

month: **Eminem** collects a couple of hip-hoppy awards and pops up on pals' albums. Bless.

April

Whoops, spoke too soon! Responding to her highly unflattering name-check on Em's imminent 'The Real Slim Shady', **Christina Aguilera** tells MTV: "It's disgusting and offensive and above all it's not true." **Limp Bizkit** leader **Fred Durst**, with whom Aguilera is linked in the lyric, chivalrously announces: "Christina's amazing. I'm really attracted to her, I like her, and I've talked to her a couple of times, and that's that. I haven't had any type of relationship with her, or any type of intercourse with her." Fellow lambastee **Justin Timberlake** of ***N Sync** says: "Christina got it the worst. I feel bad for her." Meanwhile, the Emster gets in gear for the Up In Smoke tour alongside **Ice Cube**, **Snoop Dogg** and his mentor **Dr Dre**.

One-time **Sex Pistols** Svengali **Malcolm McLaren** resigns from the race to become London Mayor… The **Prodigy** lose lanky leg-wiggler **Leeroy Thornhill** – a development that, in the words of **Liam Howlett**, "is obviously not going to affect the music". Leeroy's stock plummets further later in 2000 when fiancée **Sara Cox** sets her sights on **DJ Jon Carter** instead… Techno grandads **Underworld** lose bright young thing **Darren Emerson**… Playing just three hits in three hours, **The Cure** make what could be their final British appearance at Wembley Arena… The same venue isn't graced by **Puff Daddy** on the second of his dates there, a no-show variously blamed on squiffy scheduling and underwhelming ticket sales.

A close encounter of the oyster kind puts **Mariah Carey** in hospital for three days with food poisoning… The mucho-lauded **Doves** release their Lost Souls album, making them indie gods for five seconds between **Travis** and **Coldplay**… **Primal Scream** plug the plaudited Xtrmntr album on a road trip with critical faves **Death In Vegas**… **Mel C** knocks ex-pal **Geri Halliwell** off No.1, as her **Lisa Left-Eye Lopes**-starring 'Never Be the Same Again' displaces 'Bag It Up'. Meanwhile, **Victoria** is reported to have lost a demo of the new Spice album when her luggage is nicked en route from Miami to London, but is

voted the Ultimate Fashion Icon in a poll conducted by Channel 4 and Company magazine.

Westlife score No.1 No.5 with 'Fool Again', succeeded by two of the year's biggies: **Craig David**'s boingy 'Fill Me In' and **Fragma**'s hello-is-it-Ibiza-already anthem 'Toca's Miracle'… Back from Broadway, **Toni Braxton** returns to R&B rudeness with the hit 'He Wasn't Man Enough'… **Richard Ashcroft** bounces back with 'A Song for the Lovers', **Oasis** hit with 'Who Feels Love' and Dad-rock rules with 'He's the Keeper', **Paul Weller**'s contribution to 2000… Grandad-rock is also represented in the Top 3, as **Santana** sails 'Smooth' upwards… In other rave-from-the-grave news, **Robbie** falls foul of folk-rock pioneer **Woody Guthrie**. Seems that **Loudon Wainwright III**'s 'I Am the Way', which inspired His Williamsness' 'Jesus in a Campervan', was itself indebted to Guthrie's 'New York Town' – and Guthrie's publishers want a slice of the pop pie.

A $20,000 reward is offered by **James Brown** for information relating to an arson attack on the Godfather of Soul's office… This month's music-in-movies: **Bono**'s baby The Million Dollar

*N Sync look suitably satisfied with life as their 'No Strings Attached' album becomes the fastest seller ever

Hotel plops into UK cinemas for a brief spell, the **RZA**-scored Ghost Dog wu-tangs screen-wards and American Psycho dissects **Genesis** and **Huey Lewis**… On the small screen, **Oasis** grace a Later special. In real life, they're starting a US tour on which, Sir Noel declares, "We'll share a tour bus for the first time. We'll either come back really close mates… or we'll hate each other"… **Heinz** of the **Tornados** dies on the 7th, as does 'Turn the Beat Around' disco diva **Vicki Sue Robinson** on the 27th…

An Ivor Novello award and two No.1s in 2000 for Craig David. Whoever thought he would "bo" so far?

May

After a rare two-week residency at No.1, **Fragma** are toppled by **Oxide & Neutrino**'s TV Casualty-sampling 'Bound 4 Da Reload'… They're then beaten by **Britney**, who also shoves her boyfriend's band **'N Sync** off the top of the US album chart, with 1.3 million sales of Oops!… I Did It Again… But **Britney**'s highest ever first-week sales for a solo artist are promptly beaten by **Eminem**'s The Marshall Mathers LP, launched at a party where guests **Puff Daddy**, **Jay-Z** and **Aaliyah** are greeted with hanging effigies of **'N Sync**, **Christina Aguilera** and, um, **Britney Spears**… In a similarly loving display, **Noel Gallagher** huffs off Oasis's world tour on the grounds that he can no longer share a stage with his brother. **Paul Weller** associate **Matt Deighton** is promptly promoted to lead guitar… Former friends turned arch enemies **Marilyn Manson** and Nine Inch Nailer **Trent Reznor** kiss and make up. The reunited duo set their sights (in a NIN video) on the likes of **Michael Stipe**, **Mariah Carey** and Limp Bizkit's **Fred Durst** – the latter, inconveniently enough, being an executive at Reznor's record company… **Metallica**'s 'I Disappear' spearheads the Mission: Impossible II soundtrack sales drive… The metallic ones endure derision from fans and bands alike when they succeed in barring 355,000 users from Napster… **Cypress Hill** ride a wave of mainstream rap success as their Skull & Bones album joins **Dr Dre** in the UK chart… Dre, meanwhile, is fighting star wars with George Lucas. The Phantom Menacer objects to a copy of his THX sound signature on the Doc's Chronic 2001 album. Re-released to great effect, **Madison Avenue**'s delicious 'Don't Call Me Baby' hits No.1, followed by

Billie's Britney-cloning 'Day and Night'… With Billie graduating to the Wonderbra league, the young and innocent crown passes to **Charlotte Church**, whose appearance on Oprah confirms her as one of Britain's few Stateside success stories this year (**Sting** and **Sonique** also keep the Union Jack flying)… Whoever thought he would "bo" so far? **Craig David** is among the winners at the Ivor Novello songwriting awards, alongside Travis's **Fran Healy** (songwriter of the year), **Sir Paul McCartney**, **Leiber and Stoller**, **Sir Elton John**, **Madness**, **Robbie Williams** and **Pet Shop Boys**. **Sir Cliff Richard** is thwarted by an ongoing dispute over copyright and credits which prevents attempts to reward 'The Millennium Prayer's best-selling status… Fewer plaudits rain on the **Bloodhound Gang**, although their irresistible 'The Bad Touch' gives the Discovery Channel its second name-check of the year (before 'The Real Slim Shady') and becomes one of the year's chart mainstays and best-sellers (as does **S Club 7**'s anthemic 'Reach').

The Bloodhounds aren't the chart's only comedians, as **Richard Blackwood** revamps his uncle Junior's 'Mama Used to Say' for the smash 'Mama – Who Da Man?'… **Robbie Williams** visits flood-afflicted Mozambique on behalf of Unicef… **Eagles** dude **Don Henley** returns from the wilderness with his Inside Job album… **Emma Bunton**, **Melanie Blatt** and **Shaznay Lewis** check out the return of **Damage**, featuring Em's squeeze **Jade**… Bon-bons a-shaking, **Ricky Martin** hits UK concert halls… **Eminem** pops over for a London gig with **Dr Dre**, gives everyone a good night out and goes home again, having raised no ruckus at all. Someone pinch us, we must be dreaming… There's fisticuffs elsewhere in the capital, however, as **Guy Ritchie** takes exception to a fan of his girlfriend hanging around outside her rented London mansion. Mr Madge-to-be is arrested and charged with suspicion of causing actual bodily harm.

Boo to guns is what they're saying at the Million Mom March in Washington. Among the maternal marchers are **Courtney Love**, **Rickie Lee Jones** and **Emmylou Harris**… **Moby** and **Public Enemy** entertain soggy shufflers at the Homelands festival in windswept Winchester. PE's possibly misled **Flavor Flav** declares: "It's the best thing that can happen for homeless people"… May+movies+music = Honest (which hardly anyone goes to see despite the delights of **All Saints** stars Mel, Nic 'n' Nat), The Virgin Suicides (soundtracked by Air) and The Filth and the Fury (a **Sex Pistols** biopic whose premiere is attended by **Robbie** Rotten, er, Williams)… **Geri** is cast in Brit flick

Therapy as a woman whose counsellor falls for her… The month closes with the deaths of Latin American superstar (and one-time Simpsons guest) **Tito Puente** and soul singer **Johnnie Taylor** on the 31st.

June

Summer's here and the time is right for getting arrested in a Michigan bar brawl. If, obviously, your name is **Slim Shady**. Mrs Shady, **Kimberley Mathers**, helpfully explains: "My husband came up to Hot Rocks to check up on me – why is still unknown to me because if I was to cheat on him it wouldn't be in a neighbourhood bar where he knows I am." Slim had warmed up for that incident by waving a weapon at an employee of arch-enemies **Insane Clown Posse**… The **Eurythmics** warm up for summer with a private gig in London, attended by **Mick Jagger** and **Jerry Hall**… **Nate Dogg** (as in Snoop) reportedly warms up his ex-girlfriend's mother's car. By torching it. He also kidnaps and assaults said ex. An arrest promptly ensues… **The Corrs** headline the Fleadh festival in London, supported by a reformed (if you don't count Feargal) **Undertones**. Not notably Irish popsters **Suzanne Vega** and **Billy Bragg** tag along too.

S Express singer turned DJ turned solo star **Sonique** enjoys a year's best three weeks at No.1 with 'It Feels So Good' which finds itself the subject of a special feature in this edition of The Guinness Book of British Hit Singles… Humpty Dumpty goes on the run in the video for 'Coming Around' by **Travis**, which despite being Byrdsy fails to fly to the top… **Travis** triumph, however, at the over-attended Glastonbury festival, their heartwarming headliner rivalled only by Mr **Bowie** wheeling out the hits. Elsewhere on the weekend's bill, **Leftfield**, **Nine Inch Nails** and the **Chemical Brothers** bring the noise, **Pet Shop Boys** camp it up, **Happy Mondays** bring it down and **Moloko** make madness into music… **Gary Numan** – whose spreading influence this year spawns covers by **Armand Van Helden** and **Nine Inch Nails** – presents a best-of-the-year award to **Moby** at the DanceStar 2000 event in London… The Mobe-man proves you don't have to look like/sound like/slag off **Britney** to have a hit by sailing the beautiful 'Porcelain' into the Top 5.

After endless speculation, **Prince William** celebrates turning 18 by hooking up with **Britney** – in, sadly, fictitious form only,

Photo: Steve Gillett

thanks to a Channel 4 cartoon… La Spears, meanwhile, is runner-up to **Jennifer Lopez** in lad-mag FHM's annual survey of the planet's sexiest women. Also flying the pop flag are **Shania Twain** (6), **Louise** (9), **Mariah Carey** (17), **S Clubbers Rachel** and **Hannah** (18 and 97), **Christina Aguilera** (19), **Andrea Corr** (28), **Stepstresses Claire**, **Lisa** and **Faye** (36-70-72), **Geri** (43), **Natalie Imbruglia** (47), **Emma Bunton** (51), **Dannii** and **Kylie Minogue** (58 and 67), **Nat** 'n' **Nic Appleton** (65 and 78), **Jessica Simpson** (73), **Lisa Left-Eye Lopes** (76) and **Billie** (86) … **Moby**, **Eminem**, **Dr Dre** and **Tom Jones** graciously shuffle round the Top 10 album chart to accommodate Onka's Big Moka by newcomers **Toploader**.

Still claiming that **Boyzone** haven't split up, **Mikey Graham** has a hit with 'You're My Angel' – only to land in hot water with unfortunate statements about cannabis and capital punishment… Dinky diplomats **Daphne & Celeste** wind more critics up with 'U.G.L.Y.'… **Barry White** is impersonated to chart-topping effect on **Black Legend**'s bass-quaking 'You See the Trouble with Me'… Excitement-starved metalheads can buy a **Black Sabbath** best-of (a surprise Top 30 hit), see **Iron Maiden** reunited with **Bruce Dickinson** in London, fly to LA to bid for **Kiss**'s old stage costumes, and visit the cinema to see U-571 starring **Jon Bon Jovi**… Reclusive rocker **Axl Rose** stretches his legs in LA, attending a gig by **Roger Waters**, then jamming with ex-**Guns N' Roses** guitarist **Gilby Clarke** at a Hollywood nightclub… **Ralph Jones** of **Bill Haley's Comets** dies on the 1st… Nine people die in surges during **Pearl Jam**'s set at the Roskilde festival in Denmark. "Our lives will never be the same," announce the band. "But we know that it is nothing compared to the grief of the families and friends of those involved."

David Bowie drew unanimous approval ("didn't he look good and wasn't the coat fantastic") at an over-attended Glastonbury festival

One single that didn't make it into the chart in 2000 was Robbie Williams's 'United' which was available only with Pepsi's exclusive ring-pull collecting offer

collecting ring-pulls... Despite being largely written off by critics, Rob's ol' pals **Oasis** score their third hit of the year with 'Sunday Morning Call'. The nation's stadiums echo to the sound of the reunited albeit hardly reconciled Gallagher brothers... The Gallaghers' old pal **Richard Ashcroft** is sued by his ex-manager for breach of contract... Mere months after her arrival, Farrah Franklin is booted out of **Destiny's Child** for failing to turn up at promo appearances.

Notably failing to make as much of an impact as money men had clearly hoped, **Girl Thing** nonetheless crash the Top 10 with 'Last One Standing'... Proto-Girl Thingers the **Spice Girls** unveil their new album to Virgin sales reps... Showing them how it should be done, **Steps** notch up their 10th hit with 'When I Said Goodbye'/'Summer of Love', and play Hyde Park's Route of Kings ... Looking and sounding fab, **David Bowie** plays a special concert for the BBC, later released as part of his Bowie at the Beeb box-set... Looking and sounding like Marilyn Manson's dad, **Alice Cooper** tours Britain, sporting a "Britney Wants Me ... Dead" T-shirt... Looking and sounding like Ricky from EastEnders, **Sid Owen** takes the Walford reggae vibe to No.14 with 'Good Thing Going'... **Radiohead** return to live service with a London show at the **Scott Walker**-masterminded Meltdown festival... **kd lang** returns to chart duties with the Invincible Summer album.

The summer proves very vincible indeed as rain lashes the Party in the Park in Hyde Park. With one **Backstreet Boy** unavailable for their slot, **Elton John** substitutes as a quasi Backstreet Boy, and from under a canopy of umbrellas most eyes are on a very slinky **Victoria Beckham** – currently everywhere to promote her duet with **Another Level** refugee **Dane Bowers** on **True Steppers**' 'Out of Your Mind'. The show is stolen by soul boys **Craig David** and **Sisqo** (whose 'Thong Song' is THE singalong of the summer)... An appropriately wet 'n' windswept video for 'Yellow' rockets **Coldplay** from obscurity to This Year's Travis... Last year's **Travis** keep the homefires burning by becoming the T in the T in the Park festival... Half a million happy clappers take to the streets of Leeds for the Love Parade, entertained by DJs including **Danny Rampling** and **Judge Jules**.

The year's most unusual bill blesses Guildford Live 2000, headlined by **Motörhead**, **Culture Club** and **Van Morrison**... **Ash** are obliged to entertain disgruntled **Nine Inch Nails** fans when the headliners pull out of a big London gig... **Tina Turner**

July

After June's mischief in Michigan, **Eminem** begins the month in court. Things get no better when his two-month reign atop the US album chart is ended by Now That's What I Call Music 4 – the first 'Now' album to go top – featuring ol' pal **Britney**. Mrs Shady attempts suicide and Top of the Pops declines to show his new video... 'The Real Slim Shady' does, however, top the UK chart, amid a pretty parade of **Kylie** ('Spinning Around'), **The Corrs** ('Breathless') and **Ronan Keating** ('Life Is a Rollercoaster', also the title of his autobiography)... The pretty boy/pomp rock interface is explored on **Five**'s right royal rocking chart-topping remake of 'We Will Rock You' featuring old Queensmen **Brian May** and **Roger Taylor**... The other Queen's Birthday Honours list hands out an OBE to **Lulu** (for services to music) and an MBE to skiffle superstar **Lonnie Donegan** (for an influence that spans the decades to include this year's **Van Morrison** collaboration The Skiffle Sessions – Live In Belfast)... Pepsi goes pop with **Robbie Williams**, who donates the exclusive song 'United' to a CD obtainable only by

The Sun — Wednesday, August 16, 2000 — 30p — www.the-sun.co.uk

OUR BOYS GO IN TO SAVE RUSSIAN CREW
By GEORGE PASCOE-WATSON
Deputy Political Editor

EXCLUSIVE

DESPERATE

Nick... he's still in the house

Big Bruv Nick beats chop from show again

By EMILY SMITH and JOHN PLUNKETT

After countless PR stunts, Posh takes Becks to Oldham Woolies in a last-ditch bid to top charts

— FULL STORY PAGE 7 —

Media coverage of the battle for No.1 reached fever pitch in the week when Spiller and Victoria Beckham's association with True Steppers and Dane Bowers shared first-week sales of more than 383,000

---

fills Wembley Stadium… **Louise** makes a creditable comeback with '2-Faced'… The Bizkit boys hitch their playpen rap-metal to the Mission: Impossible II bandwagon which makes possible the huge hit 'Take a Look Around'… Smokin' in that big boys' room in the sky is **Michael Coda** of **Brownsville Station**, who dies on the 1st… **Sad Café** singer turned Mechanic (as in Mike and the) **Paul Young** dies on the 15th.

August

"**Robbie** and **Geri**: It's Love," announces the Sun – inaccurately, as it turns out ("Geri is a really nice girl who I can't mess about," admits the Robster), but it still maintains his position at the top of the tabloids league… Still claiming that **Boyzone** haven't split up, **Ronan** tops the UK album chart… Recently disentangled from Patsy Kensit, **Liam Gallagher** escorts **Courtney Love** round London, before – in a twist worthy of EastEnders – taking up with Robbie's ex **Nicole**

Appleton… Lourdes "Lola" Ciccone gets a little brother on the 11th. Mum and dad call him Rocco. A brief flap ensues when **Madonna** defends her decision to give birth in the States with "Have you been to hospitals in England?"… Mr **Bowie** becomes Daddy David for the second time… Nearing the end of hip-hop yomp the Up In Smoke tour, **Eminem** finds time to file for divorce and decline the offer of an out-of-court end to an ongoing legal battle with his mom. The two Mrs Mathers promptly add another couple of lawsuits to his burgeoning caseload, and his planned appearance at the Reading and Leeds festivals falls through.

Headliners **Oasis** and **Pulp** do make it to the shows, although most honours go to the stirring **Stereophonics**, with special guest Mr **Tom Jones**… **Travis** and **Richard Ashcroft** headline V2000… Love is in the air atop the UK chart, with **Craig David**'s shag-happy '7 Days', **Mel C**'s trancey 'I Turn to You' and **Spiller**'s ginormous 'Groovejet'… The latter dashes **Victoria Beckham**'s hopes of becoming the fourth chart-topping solo Spice in the most talked-about battle for No.1 since **Blur** beat **Oasis** in 1995. Despite a week of shameless showboating, 'Out of Your Mind', with sales of 181,000, turns out to be big-selling No.2 behind 'Groovejet''s 202,500.

Number one on the hype-o-meter is **Robbie**, whose new album 'Sing When You're Winning' becomes the UK's fastest shifter thus far this year, and whose 'Rock DJ' becomes No.1 single on the back of an audaciously weird lyric and Hellraiserish video… The similarly ghoulish **Slipknot** celebrate their triple win at the Kerrang! magazine awards by chucking chairs around the room. Not to be outdone, Britt Ekland slips on a slice of melon on her way to presenting an award to **Marilyn Manson**… Wembley Stadium goes out with a bang, or rather a Bon, as the **Bon Jovi** boys host the venue's final gigs… Producer and orchestral arranger **Jack Nitzsche** – who has worked with the **Stones**, **Phil Spector** and **Neil Young** – dies on the 25th… **Allman Brothers** bassist **Douglas Allen Woody** is found dead the next day.

September

Two of the year's best videos hit British TVs: the animation-and-**Ali G** extravaganza with which **Madonna** takes 'Music' to numero uno and the excitingly expensive one for 'Take On Me' with which **A1** follow her to the top of the singles chart… **Badly Drawn Boy**'s The Hour of Bewilderbeast beats **Coldplay**, **Death In Vegas**, **Doves**, **Richard Ashcroft**, **Leftfield** and seven others to win this year's Mercury Music Prize… The MTV Video Music Awards add to the groaning mantelpieces of **Eminem** and **'N Sync**, who take home three apiece. Despite the danger of **Eminem** (who performs with a small army of doppelgängers) sharing New York's Radio City Music Hall with so many of his targets, the flap flag is instead raised by **Rage**

Against the Machine bassist **Tim C**'s set-climbing antics (to the embarrassment of soon-to-be-ex-bandmate **Zach de la Rocha**), Napster's **Shawn Fanning** wearing a **Metallica** shirt (to the evident disapproval of **Lars Ulrich**), **Fred Durst**'s duet with **Christina Aguilera** (who complains she is "misunderstood and not taken seriously"), and **Britney**'s rock through the Stones' 'Satisfaction'. "Pretty racy for a mousekateer," notes **Marilyn Manson**, who cameos in 'The Way I Am', the new video by Brit's bud **Eminem**.

Madonna reveals that her favourite flavour of ice cream is "Chocolate Tufutti" and that she and daughter Lourdes "sing **Britney Spears** songs together"… Tents and torment usher in the autumn as **Radiohead** take their marquee show around Britain, while **Bob Dylan** plies his trade in the nation's arenas… $2,500 is the asking price for seats at **Barbra Streisand**'s final concerts in LA and New York… More affordable are tickets for **Melanie C**'s exhaustive UK tour, the success of which outweighs tabloid carping about her love life and figure… The increasingly occasional feat of spending more than a week at No.1 is achieved by successive chart-toppers **Modjo** ('Lady (Hear Me Tonight)') and **Mariah Carey** with **Westlife** ('Against All Odds')… Despite **Vanessa Amorosi**'s efforts to win over 'Absolutely Everybody' at the Sydney Olympics, the gold goes to **Kylie**. The mischievous Minogue, who will go on to complete a storming return to the UK singles chart in 2000, closes the event with **Abba**'s 'Dancing Queen'.

Britain's brightest young popsters **Sugababes** debut with a No.6 single, 'Overload', while indie kids **JJ72** (next year's This Year's Coldplay) crash the album chart Top 20… September celluloid: **Björk**'s starring role attracts a lot of attention, albeit not a lot of cinema-goers, to the musical Dancer in the Dark. **Busta Rhymes** and **Vanessa** 'Save the Best for Last' **Williams** get super-bad in Shaft Returns and **Jennifer Lopez** gets very scary in The Cell… Hits writer **Carl Sigman** signs off on the 26th… **Paula Yates** passes on the 17th. Her funeral is attended by **Bono**, **Annie Lennox**, **Paul Young**, **Jools Holland**, **Rupert Everett** and **Yasmin Le Bon**.

Kylie Minogue racked up four Top 10 singles in 2000 including her first No.1 in more than a decade

Photo: Emi Records/Liz Collins

October

Weird but wonderful, **Radiohead** prove that incomprehensible lyrics and an aversion to melody and single releases are no obstacles to superduperdom: Kid A enters at the top of transatlantic album charts with US first-week sales of 207,000. It is also the first album by a British act to hit the top since July 1997 when The **Prodigy**'s The Fat of the Land made the summit… **Robbie Williams**'s new album debuts in the same week but shifts just 13,400 Stateside… **Celine Dion** and The **Beatles** publish their autobiographies, respectively My Story, My Dream and Anthology… **John Lennon**'s assassin **Mark Chapman** is refused parole by the board at New York's Attica state prison… The Steinway piano on which Lennon composed 'Imagine' is sold for more than $2 million in a transatlantic auction; the buyer a **Mr G Michael**.

All Saints top the chart with 'Black Coffee', before **A-Ha** rise again. After **A1**'s cover of 'Take On Me', **U2** strike a familiar

> ❝ Pretty racy for a mousekateer ❞
>
> *Marilyn Manson on Britney Spears*

chord for owners of 'The Sun Always Shines on TV' with the No.1 'Beautiful Day'. The latter is one of three they play on a New York balcony for hundreds of fans in Times Square… With Michigan prosecutors still on his tail, **Eminem** lays the groundwork for seasonal single 'Stan'. Aiming for a video of 'Thriller'-esque epicness, the Slimster recruits **Devon Sawa**, star of smash hit movie Final Destination, to play him. Devon's declining to comment, on the grounds that he might "end up in his next song", look eminently sensible when Everlast becomes the latest target of the Mathers muck-chucking… At the opening date of the **Em/Limp Bizkit** double-header The Anger Management Tour, fellow diplomat **Fred Durst** describes **Christina Aguilera** as a "bitch"… Equally kind words doubtless fly in the **Steven Kurtz** household, as the manager is sued by his former charge: **Christina Aguilera**.

Canada tries (unsuccessfully) to stop **Eminem** crossing its borders… Not to be outdone, **Kim Mathers** is fined for disorderly conduct… Feathers fly at Q magazine's awards ceremony: **Liam** heckles **Robbie** and **Kylie**… Sopranos star **Dominic Chianese**, aka Uncle Junior, is reported to be working on an album… Channel 4's annual survey of the biggest influences on Britain, the Power 300, includes the **Beckhams** (59), **Madonna** (94), **DJ Pete Tong** (146), Napster's **Shawn Fanning** (189), garage gurus **The Dreem Teem** (211), **David Bowie** (222), **Marshall Mathers** (243) and **George Michael** (267). Reformed rock 'n' roller **Tony Blair** tops the chart… Mr **Bowie** is represented chart-wise by **Samantha Mumba**'s 'Ashes to Ashes'-quoting 'Body II Body'… Plucky **Northern Line** lose their best-looking members, Dan and Zak.

Undeterred by reports of internal dissent, **Steps** 'Stomp' to the top of the chart… Tag teams **Kylie** 'n' **Robbie** and **Whitney** 'n' **Enrique** do Top 10 business with 'Kids' and 'Could I Have This Kiss Forever'… **Robbie** begins a UK tour that had sold out in record time… **Posh** and **Becks** grace the encore at the Manchester date of **Smashing Pumpkins**' farewell tour – sadly in fancy-dress form only, thanks to bassist **Melissa Auf Der Maur** and **leader Billy Corgan**… "A hearty but firm thanks-but-no-thanks" is the response of the George W Bush camp to **Marilyn Manson**'s endorsement of their presidential candidate.

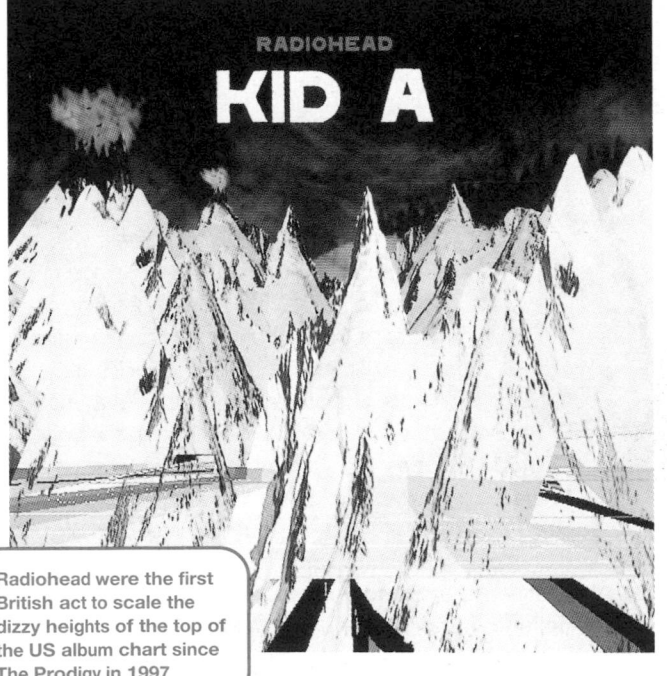

Radiohead were the first British act to scale the dizzy heights of the top of the US album chart since The Prodigy in 1997

"We do not plan a coalition of Cross-Dressing Glam Rockers for Bush anytime soon"… Equally unimpressed is **Don Henley** fan Mary Ann Haley, who gets litigious when the none-too-eagle-eyed ex-Eagle allegedly bops her with a maraca.

Courtney Love takes daughter Frances Bean to her first fashion show. "I've taught her simple and elegant is the way to go," declares the legendarily elegant grungestress… Fellow feisty femme **Pink** gets chart action with 'Most Girls'… **Garth Brooks** celebrates 100 million album sales but mourns his marriage, which finally fails after a decade of hiccups… Marital upheaval fuels the allegedly Jimmy Gulzar-bashing theme of **Mel B**'s solo stab 'Tell Me'… Still claiming that **Boyzone** haven't split up, **Stephen Gately** falls just short of the Top 10 with his 'Billy Elliot' soundtrack cut 'I Believe'… Still claiming that **Guns N' Roses** haven't split up, **Axl Rose** announces plans to tour in 2001, with eccentrically millinered guitarist **Buckethead** in the **Slash**-less line-up… Not claiming that **Spandau Ballet** haven't split up, **Tony Hadley** and co nonetheless celebrate their enduring appeal with a successful Best Of… Not claiming musical differences but blaming a breakdown in "artistic and political" ideals, **Zach de la Rocha** exits **Rage Against the Machine**.

With uncharacteristic toughness, **The Corrs** – no fans of Napster – play a gig for MEPs in Strasbourg in an attempt to persuade the EU to strengthen copyright laws… With uncharacteristic chirpiness, **Blur** pop up all over kids TV to push their Best Of album and daringly uncommercial newie 'Music Is My Radar'… Professor of lurve **Barry White** addresses the Oxford Union Debating Society… **Elton John** plays

❝ That Madonna is one sexy bitch **❞**

Chad Smith, Red Hot Chilli Peppers

Madonna, sporting a "Britney" top at a New York gig and a "Kylie" version at the MTV Awards, sparks off THE fashion item of the winter

21

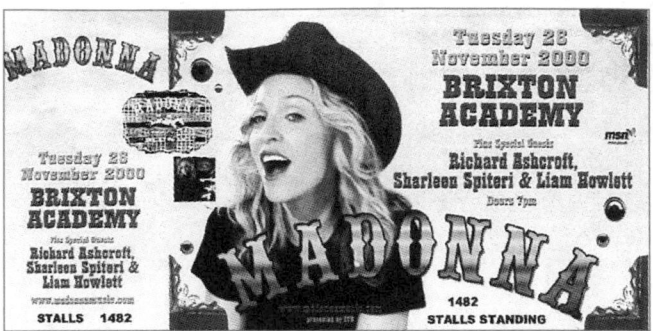

star-studded gigs in New York, rush-released as the One Night Only album… A re-release of This Is **Spinal Tap** aside, R&B vixens rule music-and-movies this month: **Janet Jackson** goes for laughs in Nutty Professor 2 while **Aaliyah** kicks ass in Romeo Must Die.

Cars bassist and composer of the classic 'Drive' **Benjamin Orr** dies on the 3rd, and **Julie London** cries her last river on the 18th, aged 74… Still sexy hot property, the long gone **Jim Morrison** flies again in sampled form on **Fatboy Slim**'s 'Bird of Prey'… The Fatboy's fave of the year, **Azzido de Bass**'s whomping 'Doom's Night', is a hit thanks to a remix by cult club supremo **Timo Maas**… Meanwhile, speculation that Lizard King Mr **Morrison** is to be moved prompts the Père Lachaise cemetery in Paris to declare: "He's here to stay."

November

Having packed a lifetime of lawsuits and superstar squabbling into one year, **Eminem** faces his biggest trauma to date: losing a lyric notebook with a picture of **Britney** on the cover… There's some consolation at the MTV Europe Music Awards where he wins two more statuettes. However, the night belongs to **Madonna**; introduced by **Ali G** to a rapturous reception, she receives two awards and the touchingly worded approval of **Chili Pepper** drummer **Chad Smith**: "That Madonna is one sexy bitch. I'd take her over, like, Britney Spears and Christina Aguilera any day." Madge's "Kylie Minogue" T-shirt, following her "Britney Spears" effort at a one-off New York gig, makes glittery star-endorsing shirts THE fashion item of the winter… Other winners include **Robbie Williams** ("I'd like to thank MTV for my three houses,

my five cars and my supermodel girlfriend. Live the dream."), **All Saints**, **Blink 182**, **Jennifer Lopez**, **Ricky Martin**, **Moby**, the **Bomfunk MCs** and the Burger King-sponsored **Backstreet Boys**.

The BSBs visit six continents in four days to promote their Black and Blue album. Huge sales ensue, albeit not on the axis-shifting scale of ***N Sync**… A cannabis-carrying caricature of Ann Widdecombe is used to promote **UB40**'s 'Light My Fire', much to the Conservative MP's displeasure… Any large-scale music-cred hopes of celebrity chef **Jamie Oliver** come a cropper when his band **Scarlet Division** fail to make the charts with 'Sundial'… With Girl Power having transformed into an anaemic imitation of Destiny's Child, the **Spice Girls** limp to No.1 with 'Holler/Let Love Lead the Way'. **Westlife** strike back with seventh smash 'My Love'. Amid battle-crazed bitching by **Victoria**, the two groups go head to head in an albums-released-on-the-same-day struggle that, to the surprise of precisely no one, sees Coast to Coast lording it over Forever… The latter does, however, do better than **Mel B**'s solo album Hot.

In the fall-out, **Mel C** stops bothering to pretend that the Spices might last into the New Year… The whole débâcle is put into perspective when **Oasis**'s actually-really-good Familiar to Millions live album is roundly trounced by The **Beatles**' 1, as is everything else… **Madonna** manages, in **Kylie Minogue**'s words, to "turn London upside down" with a showcase at Brixton Academy. After support slots by **Richard Ashcroft**, **Sharleen Spiteri** and **Liam Howlett**, her half-hour set is enjoyed by **Kylie**, **Mel C** and **Mick Jagger**, plus millions more on a record-breaking webcast… Wannabe actress **Billie** claims to "really identify" with Anne Frank… Little **LeAnn Rimes**'s Coyote Ugly cut 'Can't Fight the Moonlight' springs Spearsishly to the top of the singles chart... In a High Court battle over managerial fees, **Sir Elton John** admits a somewhat cavalier attitude to finance – entirely justified by his ranking as the UK's fourth-highest earner. Other big wallets in a Mail on Sunday survey are the **Stones**, **George Michael** and **Robbie Williams**… Fancy something "a little bit hippie"? Got $600 to spend? Then **Cher**'s jewellery line, launched this month, is for you… **Britney** tours Britain, while **Noel Gallagher**, **Paul Weller** and **Eddie Vedder** join **The Who** on stage in London… 75-year-old pianist **Russ Conway** dies on the 16th, just two weeks after his last performance.

The 27 UK and US singles included on The Beatles' '1' skyrocketed the Fab Four back to the top of the UK and US album charts. Robbie and Eminem sold massively but neither could match the mega, best of the year, 1.8 million UK sales

December

Christmas. Goodwill to all men. Unless, obviously, you're **Eminem** – whose ongoing dispute with Everlast surfaces in a lyrical suggestion to "Hit him with sticks, bricks, rocks"… On a brighter note, rap's very own Terry and June kiss and make up: "Mrs Mathers is pleased that she and her husband have been able to set their differences aside," announce Kim's lawyers, "particularly for the sake of their daughter Hailie Jade." If she's into kids TV, young Hailie may be the only one in the Mathers home pinning her hopes on a certain hard-hatted chart rival… **Woody Cook** becomes the newest member of the Fatboy family when **Zoë Ball** gives birth at the hospital where **Mel B** and **Victoria** released the Spice sprogs.

S Club 7 take their Children in Need theme 'Never Had a Dream Come True' to No.1 and **Destiny's Child** shrug off a year of shifting line-ups and split rumours with an overdue chart-topper, 'Independent Women', from the Charlie's Angels soundtrack… Hotly tipped at one time for the coveted Christmas No.1 slot, Channel 4's Big Brother winner **Craig Phillips** instead makes it only as far as 14 with 'At This Time of Year'… Angelic **Eminem**'s 'Stan' reigns victorious for one week

before being bested by **Bob the Builder**'s 'Can We Fix It?'. The latter becomes the official Christmas 2000 No.1 and goes on to sell more copies than any other 2000 release. Bob also disappoints **Westlife** in their quest for an eighth consecutive chart-topper, not to mention the many punters who thought them a safe bet with the bookies… **Westlife** do, however, win once again at the Record of the Year show, with 'My Love', and at the Poll Winners Party. Notable losers at the latter include the **Spice Girls**.

Far too late to have much effect on her solo album's uninspiring chart showing, **Mel B** is the subject of a BBC TV documentary … Meanwhile, **Madonna** gets an entire evening devoted to her on Channel 4. She also makes an honest man of **Guy Ritchie**, at Scotland's Skibo Castle. The ceremony is besieged by hundreds of reporters and attended by **Sting** (the couple's matchmaker), **Gwyneth Paltrow** and **Stella McCartney**… Stella's dad confirms his place in the history books as sales of 1 motor into the multimillions, amid industry predictions that it might become the all-time album best-seller. Far-fetched perhaps, but year-end UK sales of The **Beatles**' 27 UK and US chart-toppers total more than 1.8 million and make it the UK's best-selling album in 2000.

'You Make Me Wanna' six-packer **Usher** announces his comeback… Flying in the face of logic, taste and diplomacy, **Keith** and **Shane** of Boyzone cover **Milli Vanilli**'s 'Girl You Know It's True'. Lyrical embellishments include the rhyming of "**Westlife**" with "lowlife" and the prediction "When the lads go out, **Five** better watch out"… Doubtless celebrating Keith and Shane's scrape into the lower reaches of the Top 40, two of **Five** (**Ritchie** and **J**) are detained by police after a bar brawl in Dublin… Re-formed rabble-rousers The **Wonder Stuff** revive the spirit of 92 on a highly successful UK tour… **10,000 Maniacs**' guitarist **Rob Buck** dies on the 19th… **Kirsty MacColl** is killed in a boating accident on the 18th… The **Smashing Pumpkins** cease to be with a four-and-a-half hour show in Chicago. "Ladies and gentlemen," announces **Billy Corgan**, "there is nowhere left to go."

The 886th and final No.1 hit of the 20th century was not Westlife, as predicted by those betting on the 2000 Christmas No.1, but a 9-inch builder called Bob

Anatomy of a Hit Single

Sonique's rollercoaster ride to No.1

Every now and then a song comes out of nowhere to storm the chart summit. Some might have been summer hits in Ibiza which then become hot sounds of the autumn, while others had been the target of a concentrated marketing campaign. But Sonique's "It Feels So Good", which topped the UK chart for three weeks in June 2000, was neither. Its success came through an old-fashioned buzz generated by people who had fallen in love with the record and couldn't get enough of it.

About seven years ago, the 32-year-old DJ and former S Express member had put together a demo of 'It Feels So Good' and then promptly forgot about it. By 1998 she was signed up with Simon Belofsky's Serious Records, whose sister company Serious Artist Management was handling her DJ bookings. Looking for a new song to record, Sonique hunted down her old demo and played it to Belofsky. "Every once in a while you have a moment in this business," he recalls. "The spark was there. Everything was so right about the song. We were both jumping up and down in her front room saying 'This is the one!'."

Belofsky's Serious Records, a relatively new venture, also had a recording facility for its artists at its north London base. He brought in Sonique to record new vocals while he, fellow producer Graham Pleeth (formerly of 80s group Wang Chung) and engineer Chris Allen fleshed out the music. "The track came together almost immediately," says Belofsky. "It took only a few hours to knock it into shape, and six weeks to get the finished version and all the mixes." It was only the third track the studio had recorded.

A promotional campaign was put together for the single's release, which included a low-budget video (costing £20,000) and the use of television and radio pluggers. But it didn't make the playlists of national radio, so it didn't get further than No.24 when it was released on 5 December 1998. Although it pales in comparison with the No.1 spot it reached on its second outing, Belofsky was thrilled with the initial result. "It was fantastic," he

It Feels So Good Timeline

1993
Sonique and Linus Burdick produce demo of 'It Feels So Good'

October 1998
Serious Records b[...] Simon Belofsky a[...] Sonique dig out the tape when looking [...] single release

says. "It was only our third record. We had licensed it to quite a few territories, but when the record was about to blow up the second time round we bought the rights back. Little did they know."

Belofsky himself wasn't to know what was in store for the single over the coming months. It started when an enterprising pair called Conductor and the Cowboy phoned Belofsky to say that they had bootlegged 'It Feels So Good' and would he like to listen to their mix. "Normally I would take them to court, but I loved it," says Belofsky. "It was a breath of fresh air. They got a recording contract out of it." A couple of hundred copies were pressed on to a white label, along with two other remixes. "The remixes added to the buzz," adds Belofsky. "It kept the record alive and in the public eye."

Several thousand copies were exported to America, and the song was eventually picked up by DJ Stan the Man at WFLD in Miami, Florida. Stan the Man, to whom Belofsky admits eternal gratitude, started generating such excitement with it that it wasn't long before the song became a huge hit in the Florida clubs, bars and local radio stations in the late summer of 1999. Within two months, American record labels were on the phone to Belofsky expressing their interest in the song. It was John Dunton of Caffeine Records who convinced Belofsky to license the record in the US to his label. "At that time I thought why not. Let's get some exposure for Sonique in America," says Belofsky. "They're only going to do a few thousand copies. I hadn't really taken that much notice of the buzz that was going on in the States at that moment. So I did the deal with them. Within four days my phone hit meltdown. I was getting calls from every major player in the game."

When Belofsky realised what a hot property Sonique had become, he quickly bought the rights for 'It Feels So Good' back from Caffeine Records. They had paid about $4,000 for them and sold them back for $75,000. Not bad for a month's work.

> **"** I'm very spontaneous. When music's playing I start hearing lyrics **"**

During this time Sonique and Serious Records had not lifted a finger when it came to promoting the record, which still astonishes Belofsky. "Sonique had by this become the world's most successful female DJ and was singing the record over her set," he says. "But as far as personal appearances went, there was nothing. It was all about the record – purely about the music."

As winter 1999 approached, Belofsky found himself in a situation that was both exciting and surreal. Managing directors from three major record labels had ensconced themselves in hotels in London's Park Lane, and Belofsky spent several days walking back from one hotel to another while the price rose rapidly. It started at £150,000 and ended up as what Belofsky describes as a "multi-million-dollar, multi-album deal". He eventually signed a deal with Monty Lipman, chairman of Universal. "They'd offered as much as everybody else, but they rose to the challenge to sign straight away," explains Belofsky. "They had balls."

But one person at Universal wasn't happy. Music industry veteran Jimmy Iovine, who runs Universal offshoot Interscope (home to Dr Dre and Eminem), wanted Sonique on his new Farm Club venture, so there was more haggling within Universal itself. When Belofsky and Sonique were invited to New York to start work on her debut album on 12 December 1999, they were quickly whisked away to Los Angeles where Iovine, as Belofsky says, "had the power to pull people in there and then". Iovine brought in Rick Nowels (who's worked with Mel C and Ronan Keating), Thunderpuss 2000, Gerald Isaacs and DJ/producer BT, and work on the album was done in LA and London at a dizzying speed.

The whole project was completed by 17 January 2000 and the album was released in the US on Valentine's Day. It quickly went gold and 'It Feels So Good' went to No.8 in the main Billboard chart, topped the Billboard dance chart and made a huge impact on US radio airplay as well.

November 1998
Final version of 'It Feels So Good' recorded at Serious studios

5 December 1998
Single released in the UK and reaches No.24

August 1999
Radio DJ Stan the Man at WFLD in Florida gets a copy and makes it a hit there

October/November 1999
'It Feels So Good' reaches the attention of American record companies

December 1999
Deal signed with Universal offshoot Farm Club

By late spring 2000, the British music industry realised that 'It Feels So Good' was just too big to ignore the second time round. Simon Belofsky had a meeting with Radio 1's editor of music policy, Alex Jones-Donelly, who wanted to be responsible for breaking Sonique in the UK. Jones-Donelly had been tracking the song's progress in the US, and knew the time was right for British success. Radio 1 started playing the single during the first week of March 2000 without playlisting it, but a month later it reached the station's C list where it got about four plays every seven days. Within a week it went up to the B list (12 plays a week) and a fortnight later it made the A list (25 plays a week). Two weeks before the record was released for the second time it was on Radio 1's super list, which gave it 35 plays a week.

> " I was gobsmacked the first week we went to No.1. Week two, I was on the floor and now after three weeks I have no words left apart from how proud I am "
>
> *Sonique: June 2000*

With the single's massive airplay, the new promotional campaign went into top gear with major press, TV and radio coverage. A new video was filmed, this time at a cost of $300,000. The single went to No.1 on 4 June 2000, and its three-week stay at the top proved to be a record in a year in which the No.1 song changed on an almost weekly basis.

Because Serious Records was a small independent label when it released 'It Feels So Good' in 1998, Belofsky wasn't in a position to offer Sonique the sort of advance that comes from a major record label. He and Sonique have a profit-sharing deal which still stands. With UK sales of 'It Feels So Good' approaching 700,000 by the end of 2000, it has proved to be a major money-spinner.

When a single makes this much of an impact, it's easy to wonder why it wasn't a hit first time round. Simon Belofsky speculates: "It was probably ahead of its time. We were trying to create a very specific sound, which I believe we've got, and people weren't ready for it."

17 January 2000
Sonique's debut album completed in New York

22 April 2000
Single reaches No.8 in US Billboard chart

29 May 2000
Single re-released in UK and enters at No.1 on 3 June, selling 195,000 in the first week

...
It remains at the top of the chart for three weeks, the longest time a single has held the spot in 2000

December 2000
Sales for the year total 642,000

Top 10 Record-Breaking Facts

Here are some of the biggest facts behind the 25,726 UK hit singles listed in this book

MOST NO.1 HITS: Male – Elvis Presley (17) Female – Madonna (10) Group – Beatles (17)

MOST WEEKS AT NO.1: (18) I Believe – Frankie Laine (in three separate visits)

BIGGEST-SELLING SINGLE: (5.34 million) Candle in the Wind / Something About the Way You Look Tonight 1997 – Elton John (world record sales: 33 million)

Diana Ross

Beatles

MOST HITS: Male – Elvis Presley (130) Female – Diana Ross (77) Group – Shadows (63)

MOST CONSECUTIVE WEEKS AT NUMBER ONE: 16 (Everything I Do) I Do It For You – Bryan Adams

YOUNGEST CHART-TOPPER: Little Jimmy Osmond (9 years, 251 days)

CONSECUTIVE NO.1 HITS FROM DEBUT: Westlife (7)

Commonest title for a hit single: Crazy (17) and I Believe (17)

Westlife

OLDEST CHART-TOPPER: **Louis Armstrong (66 years, 187 days)**

Most weeks on chart: Male – Elvis Presley (1,168) Female – Diana Ross (560) Group – Shadows (770)

Elvis Presley

The 886 Number One Hits

Every single No.1 hit is listed chronologically and in numerical order, with the date, blobs (●●●) indicating the weeks at the top, song, act name, and, for the first time, the writers, facts and stories behind all 886 No.1 hits. For those people anxious to pinpoint what was top of the charts on a particular day, note that the dates given here are, as chart tradition decrees, the end of that song's first whole week at the top. The all-important Christmas No.1 is the last hit listed for each year.

1952

1. 14 Nov ●●●●●●●● HERE IN MY HEART – Al Martino Writers: Pat Genero, Lou Levinson and Bill Borelli. We will never know how long this track was Britain's No.1 single, as it had already been the UK's top seller for several weeks before the NME chart began.

1953

2. 16 Jan ● YOU BELONG TO ME – Jo Stafford Writers: PeeWee King, Redd Stewart and Chilton Price. Paul Weston (Jo Stafford's husband) provided the orchestra and production on this, the first female No.1.

3. 23 Jan ● COMES A-LONG A-LOVE – Kay Starr Writer: Al Sherman. Katherine Starks is the only chart-topper who can claim to have been born on an Indian reservation. The track cost $375.43 to record (a small fortune at the time).

4. 30 Jan ● OUTSIDE OF HEAVEN – Eddie Fisher Writers: Sammy Gallop and Chester Conn. Famously requested by Princess Margaret who attended a performance by Fisher at London's Savoy.

5. 6 Feb ●●●● DON'T LET THE STARS GET IN YOUR EYES – Perry Como Writer: Slim Willet. The song had originally been a country hit for composer Slim Willet as well as for Pat Boone's father-in-law Red Foley, Skeets McDonald and Ray Price.

6. 13 Mar ●●●● SHE WEARS RED FEATHERS – Guy Mitchell Writer: Bob Merrill. This bizarre tale of an English banker's love for a hula-hula girl made only No.19 in the US chart.

7. 10 Apr ● BROKEN WINGS – The Stargazers Writers: John Jerome and Bernard Gunn. The first British act (and the first group) to top the UK charts had the highest-placed version of a song that also charted for Dickie Valentine and Art and Dotty Todd.

8. 17 Apr ● (HOW MUCH IS) THAT DOGGIE IN THE WINDOW – Lita Roza Writer: Bob Merrill. The 27-year-old Liverpudlian hit the top with a cover of Patti Page's original. Lita disliked the song so much she never performed it live on stage.

9. 24 Apr ●●●●●●●●● 3 Jul ●●●●●● 21 Aug ●●● I BELIEVE – Frankie Laine Writers: Erwin Drake, Irvin Graham, Jimmy Shirl and Al Stillman. More weeks at No.1 than any other single in its three chart runs, during which time Queen Elizabeth was crowned and Mount Everest was conquered for the first time.

10. 26 Jun ● I'M WALKING BEHIND YOU – Eddie Fisher featuring Sally Sweetland Writer: Billy Reid. The lyric describes the often married Fisher walking down the aisle as his prospective bride prepares to marry somebody else.

11. 14 Aug ● SONG FROM THE MOULIN ROUGE – Mantovani and his Orchestra Writer: Georges Auric. The first instrumental to top the charts was the theme from the film Moulin Rouge.

12. 11 Sep ●●●●●● LOOK AT THAT GIRL – Guy Mitchell Writer: Bob Merrill. The record that ended 'I Believe''s domination of the 1953 chart year. It made a big impact in the UK but didn't chart in the US.

13. 23 Oct ●● HEY JOE – Frankie Laine Writer: Boudleaux Bryant. Cover of a country No.1 by Carl Smith. Bryant later penned a string of hits for Everly Brothers.

14. 6 Nov ● 11 Dec (equal top) ● ANSWER ME – David Whitfield Writers: Gerhard Winkler and Fred Rauch; English lyrics by Carl Sigman. For the only time in UK chart history, two versions of the same song tied at the top.

15. 13 Nov ●●●●●●●● 11 Dec (equal top) ANSWER ME – Frankie Laine Writers: Gerhard Winkler and Fred Rauch; English lyrics by Carl Sigman. Frankie Laine ended an astonishing year by becoming the first act to have three No.1s, first to make the top spot with consecutive releases, and the record holder for most weeks of a calendar year at No.1 with 27 weeks.

1954

16. 8 Jan ●●●●●●●● OH MEIN PAPA – Eddie Calvert Writers: Paul Burkhard; English lyrics by John Turner and Geoffrey Parsons. A first No.1 for producer Norrie Paramor and the first of dozens of chart-toppers to be recorded at Abbey Road Studios.

17. 12 Mar ●●●●● 23 Apr ● I SEE THE MOON – The Stargazers Writer: Meredith Wilson. The first British act to reach No.1 with their first two chart hits. Member Cliff Adams later achieved success with BBC Radio 2's Sing Something Simple as The Cliff Adams Singers.

18. 16 Apr ● 7 May ●●●●●●●● SECRET LOVE – Doris Day Writers: Paul Francis Webster and Sammy Fain. The song came from the movie Calamity Jane and won a Best Song Oscar for 1953.

19. 30 Apr ● SUCH A NIGHT – Johnnie Ray Writer: Lincoln Chase. This Drifters cover was refused airplay on many US stations; as a result it was not a major US hit for the boy from Oregon who was partially deafened in an accident aged nine.

20. 2 Jul ●●●●●●●●● CARA MIA – David Whitfield with Chorus and Mantovani and his Orchestra Writers: Lee Lange and Tulio Trapani (aka producer Bunny Lewis and arranger Mantovani). Only record by a UK male vocalist to make the US Top 10 in the early 1950s.

21. 10 Sep ● LITTLE THINGS MEAN A LOT – Kitty Kallen Writers: Carl Stultz and Edith Lindermann. Kitty Kallen was the first of the one-hit wonders. Written by a DJ and a 56-year-old journalist, both from Richmond, Virginia.

22. 17 Sep ●●● THREE COINS IN THE FOUNTAIN – Frank Sinatra Writers: Sammy Cahn and Jule Styne. The Academy Award-winning Best Original Song of 1954, from the movie of the same name.

23. 8 Oct ●●●● 19 Nov ● HOLD MY HAND – Don Cornell Writers: Jack Lawrence and Richard Myers. Another song from a movie, 'Hold My Hand' was in Susan Slept Here but was banned by the BBC for the words "kingdom of heaven".

24. 5 Nov ●● MY SON MY SON – Vera Lynn Writers: Bob Howard, Melville Farley and Eddie Calvert. Already a US chart-topper with 'Auf Wiederseh'n Sweetheart' in 1952, wartime radio favourite Vera Lynn had to wait for her first official UK chart-topper.

25. 26 Nov ● THIS OLE HOUSE – Rosemary Clooney Writer: Stuart Hamblen. Also a No.1 for Shakin' Stevens, Hamblen wrote the song on a hunting expedition after discovering the body of an old man in a shack in the wilderness.

26. 3 Dec ●●●●● LET'S HAVE ANOTHER PARTY – Winifred Atwell Writers: Nat D Ayer, Clifford Grey, James W Tate, Ray Henderson, Mort Dixon, Albert Fitz, William Penn, Gus Cahn, Walter Donaldson, Leslie Stuart, Harry Armstrong, Ted Snyder, Leo Wood, Harry Wood. The first black artist and only female instrumentalist to hit the top.

1955

27. 7 Jan ● 21 Jan ●● FINGER OF SUSPICION – Dickie Valentine Writers: Al Lewis and Paul Mann. The first No.1 to be pushed off the top twice by the same record – 'Mambo Italiano'.

28. 14 Jan ● 4 Feb ●● MAMBO ITALIANO – Rosemary Clooney Writer: Bob Merrill. This track was banned by all ABC-owned stations in the US because "it did not reach standards of good taste".

29. 18 Feb ●●● SOFTLY SOFTLY – Ruby Murray Writers: Mark Paul and Pierre Dudan; English lyrics by Paddy Roberts. Belfast girl Ruby Murray was the most successful singer in 1955 with seven Top 10 singles and 80 weeks on the British singles chart.

30. 11 Mar ●●●●●● GIVE ME YOUR WORD – Tennessee Ernie Ford Writers: George Wyle and Irving Taylor. First appeared as the B-side of a minor US hit, 'The River Of No Return'; the sides were reversed for the UK release as the label thought "the British public would like to hear a cowboy sing a plush ballad". Not arf.

31. 29 Apr ●● CHERRY PINK AND APPLE BLOSSOM WHITE – Perez Prado Writer: Louis Guilielmi Louiguy. This instrumental appeared as a theme for the 1955 movie Underwater starring Jane Russell and topped the US chart for 10 weeks.

32. 13 May ●● STRANGER IN PARADISE – Tony Bennett Writers: Robert Wright and George Forrest. Based on a theme from Borodin's 1888 opera Prince Igor, the song was a hit in the 1953 Broadway show Kismet and reached the UK charts in no fewer than six versions.

33. 27 May ●●●● CHERRY PINK AND APPLE BLOSSOM WHITE – Eddie Calvert Writer: Louis Guilielmi Louiguy. The second visit by this five-year-old French tune to the top of the UK charts, and the second No.1 for "the man with the golden trumpet".

34. 24 Jun ●●● UNCHAINED MELODY – Jimmy Young Writers: Alex North and Hy Zaret. With 14 different versions of the song flooding the shops, it was Jimmy Young who beat American Al Hibbler to the top spot. The song has spent 96 weeks on the chart in 10 visits.

35. 15 Jul ●● DREAMBOAT – Alma Cogan Writer: Al Hoffman. Only No.1 for "the girl with the giggle in her voice" the most consistently successful British female singer of the mid-50s.

36. 29 Jul ●●●●●●●●●● ROSE MARIE – Slim Whitman Writers: Rudolf Friml, Otto Harbach and Oscar Hammerstein II. The first left-handed guitarist to top the charts, preceding McCartney and Hendrix. Although an 11-week chart limpet at the summit in the UK, Whitman's 'Rose Marie' failed to make the US Top 20.

37. 14 Oct ●●●● THE MAN FROM LARAMIE – Jimmy Young Writers: Lester Lee and Ned Washington. Scored his second No.1 in three months with the theme song (which Al Martino had recorded unsuccessfully in the US) from a James Stewart western.

22 – Frank Sinatra

Photo: Pictorial Press

38. 11 Nov ●● HERNANDO'S HIDEAWAY – The Johnston Brothers Writers: Richard Adler and Jerry Ross. The song, taken from the musical The Pajama Game, went to No.1 in the week in which co-writer Ross died.

39. 25 Nov ●●● 6 Jan 1956 ●● ROCK AROUND THE CLOCK – Bill Haley and his Comets Writers: Jimmy de Knight (James Myers) and Max C Freedman. The song was originally recorded by Haley as a favour to his manager James Myers. The song took off only when featured in the 1955 Glenn Ford movie Blackboard Jungle and became the world's third best-selling single.

40. 16 Dec ●●● CHRISTMAS ALPHABET – Dickie Valentine Writers: Buddy Kaye and Jules Loman. The first Christmas song to top the charts.

1956

41. 20 Jan ●●●● SIXTEEN TONS – Tennessee Ernie Ford Writer: Merle Travis. The chorus was based on a saying of the writer's father: "Another day older and deeper in debt".

42. 17 Feb ●●●● MEMORIES ARE MADE OF THIS – Dean Martin Writers: Terry Gilkyson, Richard Dehr and Frank Miller. The writers of this Dino classic sang backing vocals under their stage name Easy Riders.

43. 16 Mar ●● 6 Apr ● IT'S ALMOST TOMORROW – The Dreamweavers Writers: Wade Buff and Eugene Adkinson. Buff and Adkinson could find nobody to record their song, so they formed their own group to do so and even paid for the session themselves.

44. 30 Mar ● ROCK AND ROLL WALTZ – Kay Starr with the Hugo Winterhalter Orchestra Writers: Dick Ware and Shorty Allen. Starr, who uniquely started and finished her UK chart career with No.1s, was persuaded, against her better judgement, to record the song at her first RCA session by producer Joe Carlton.

45. 13 Apr ●●● THE POOR PEOPLE OF PARIS – Winifred Atwell Writers: Marguerite Monnot and Rene Rouzaud. The original song had been made popular in France by Edith Piaf before pianist Atwell, a qualified chemist, secured her second UK No.1.

46. 4 May ●●●●●● NO OTHER LOVE – Ronnie Hilton Writers: Richard Rodgers and Oscar Hammerstein II. Hilton's only No.1 was taken from the musical Me and Juliet. Perry Como took it to the top in the US three years earlier.

47. 15 Jun ●●●●● I'LL BE HOME – Pat Boone Writers: Ferdinand Washington and Stan Lewis. A descendant of the American frontiersman Daniel Boone, Pat covered this R&B hit by The Flamingos for his only UK No.1.

48. 20 Jul ●●● WHY DO FOOLS FALL IN LOVE? – The Teenagers featuring Frankie Lymon Writers: Frankie Lymon, Jimmy Merchant and Herman Santiago. The first R&B record to top the charts, it later lent its name to a film of Frankie Lymon's life.

49. 10 Aug ●●●●●● WHATEVER WILL BE WILL BE – Doris Day Writers: Ray Evans and Jay Livingston. Aka 'Que Sera Sera', this No.1 was already half written when a song was requested for Doris Day to sing to her son in Hitchcock's The Man Who Knew Too Much.

50. 21 Sep ●●●● LAY DOWN YOUR ARMS – Anne Shelton Writers: Leon Land and Ake Gerhard. Paddy Roberts, the humourist and songwriter, found a Swedish song called 'Ann-Caroline' and turned it into this saga of a returning soldier.

51. 19 Oct ●●●● A WOMAN IN LOVE – Frankie Laine Writer: Frank Loesser. Taken from Guys and Dolls, this Mitch Miller-produced song was Laine's fourth and final visit to the top.

52. 16 Nov ●●●●●●● JUST WALKIN' IN THE RAIN – Johnnie Ray Writers: Johnny Bragg and Robert S Riley. The song was written and first recorded by The Prisonaires, inmates of Tennessee State Prison, in 1954.

1957

53. 4 Jan ● 18 Jan ● 1 Feb (top equal) ● SINGING THE BLUES – Guy Mitchell Writer: Melvin Endsley. The third chart-topper in a row produced by Mitch Miller became one of the most successful songs in British pop, with Dave Edmunds (No.28), Daniel O'Donnell (No.23) and Tommy Steele (No.1) also charting.

54. 11 Jan ● SINGING THE BLUES – Tommy Steele and the Steelmen Writer: Melvin Endsley. The only act promoted by legendary Larry Parnes to have a No.1, Tommy Steele succeeded while stable mates Marty Wilde, Billy Fury and Joe Brown all stalled at No.2.

55. 25 Jan ● 1 Feb (equal top) ● 8 Feb ●● THE GARDEN OF EDEN – Frankie Vaughan Writer: Denise Norwood. The line "A voice in the garden tells you she is forbidden" attracted censure from some religious circles and caused a partial broadcast ban.

56. 22 Feb ●●●●●●● YOUNG LOVE – Tab Hunter Writers: Carole Joyner and Ric Cartey. Cartey first recorded this but when his version flopped, movie star Hunter's rendition went all the way to the top.

57. 12 Apr ●●●●● CUMBERLAND GAP – Lonnie Donegan Writers: Traditional, arranged by Lonnie Donegan. The King of Skiffle's fifth visit to the Top 10 produced his first of three No.1s.

58. 17 May ● ROCK-A-BILLY – Guy Mitchell Writers: Woody Harris and Eddie V Deane. Mitchell equalled his label mate Frankie Laine's record four No.1s with this tribute to rockabilly – the mid-50s musical style that mixed rock and hillbilly and gave the world Elvis.

59. 24 May ●● BUTTERFLY – Andy Williams Writer: Anthony September (aka Kal Mann and Bernie Lowe). The only Andy Williams release ever to top the charts in either the UK or the US.

60. 7 Jun ●●● YES TONIGHT JOSEPHINE – Johnnie Ray Writers: Winfield Scott and Dorothy Goodman. This was Mitch Miller's 16th No.1 as a producer, but the prototype Elvis was about to be usurped by the real thing.

61. 28 Jun ●● GAMBLIN' MAN / PUTTING ON THE STYLE – Lonnie Donegan Writers: Woody Guthrie and Lonnie Donegan /

79 – Jane Morgan

traditional arranged by Norman Cazden. The first double-sided No.1, and also the first "live" chart-topper.

62. 12 Jul ●●●●●●● ALL SHOOK UP – Elvis Presley Writers: Otis Blackwell and Elvis Presley. Elvis finally hit the top with his 10th hit single. It was the only one of his 17 UK chart-toppers on which he shared a writing credit.

63. 30 Aug ●●●●●●●●● DIANA – Paul Anka Writer: Paul Anka. Canadian Anka was the first teenage solo act to reach the top. Recorded in one take, the single sold more than 10 million copies.

64. 1 Nov ●●● THAT'LL BE THE DAY – The Crickets Writers: Buddy Holly, Jerry Allison and Norman Petty. The title of the song that introduced the UK to Buddy Holly was taken from a phrase used by John Wayne in the movie The Searchers.

65. 22 Nov ●●●●●●● MARY'S BOY CHILD – Harry Belafonte Writer: Jester Hairston. The fastest record so far to reach sales of a million in Britain (six weeks) and the first Christmas song to hit No.1 in two different versions (in 1978 with Boney M).

1958

66. 10 Jan ●● GREAT BALLS OF FIRE – Jerry Lee Lewis Writers: Otis Blackwell and Jack Hammer. With producer Sam Phillips's help, the 23-year-old from Ferriday, Louisiana, recorded arguably the wildest record ever to top the UK charts.

67. 24 Jan ●●● JAILHOUSE ROCK – Elvis Presley Writers: Jerry Leiber and Mike Stoller. This title tune from the third Elvis movie became the first hit to enter at No.1 since the chart began. It was also the first to chalk up advance sales of 250,000.

68. 14 Feb ●● THE STORY OF MY LIFE – Michael Holliday Writers: Burt Bacharach and Hal David. Marty Robbins, Alma Cogan, Dave King and Gary Miller competed with versions of the same song, but Liverpool-born Michael Milne had the most success, giving Burt Bacharach his first No.1.

69. 28 Feb ●●●●●●●● MAGIC MOMENTS – Perry Como Writers: Burt Bacharach and Hal David. Perry Como was the highest-paid performer with the most popular television variety show of the time, and this gave Bacharach his second successive No.1.

70. 25 Apr ●●● WHOLE LOTTA WOMAN – Marvin Rainwater Writer: Marvin Rainwater. Marvin Percy took his mother's Cherokee maiden name when he became a country singer and saw the first of his two hits reach the top in the UK but peak at only No.60 in the US.

71. 16 May ●●●●●● WHO'S SORRY NOW? – Connie Francis Writers: Ted Snyder, Bert Kalmar and Herman Ruby. After nine unsuccessful releases, this single was recorded in the last 20 minutes of what was supposedly her final MGM recording session.

72. 27 Jun ● 4 Jul (equal top) ● ON THE STREET WHERE YOU LIVE – Vic Damone Writers: Alan Jay Lerner and Frederick Loewe. Mitch Miller's 17th and final UK No.1 as producer, from My Fair Lady.

73. 4 Jul (equal top) ● 11 Jul ●●●●●● ALL I HAVE TO DO IS DREAM / CLAUDETTE – Everly Brothers Writers: Felice and Boudleaux Bryant / Roy Orbison. The Bryants claimed to have written their half of this chart-topper in just 15 minutes. The flip side was Roy Orbison's rocking tribute to his wife.

74. 22 Aug ●●●●● WHEN – The Kalin Twins Writers: Jack Reardon and Paul Evans. One-hit wonders Herb and Hal were the only twins to hit the top as a duo and were supported by Cliff Richard on their only UK tour.

75. 26 Sep ●●●●●● CAROLINA MOON / STUPID CUPID – Connie Francis Writers: Benny Davis and Joe Burke / Neil Sedaka and Howard Greenfield. The combination of a revival of an American 20s standard and a rocker penned by newcomer Neil Sedaka gave Francis her second No.1 in three releases.

76. 7 Nov ●●● IT'S ALL IN THE GAME – Tommy Edwards Writers: Charles Gates Dawes and Carl Sigman. Enjoyed three million sales worldwide, was written in 1912 by a Chicago banker who went on to be a US vice-president in 1925. His original tune, 'Melody in A Major', was transformed when Carl Sigman added lyrics almost 40 years later.

77. 28 Nov ●●● HOOTS MON – Lord Rockingham's XI Writer: Harry Robinson. Based on the traditional Scottish folk song 'One Hundred Pipers', 'Hoots Mon' featured the rasping sax of Red Price and writer and musician Benny Green, who, like the rest of the XI, earned just £6 for a single with sales of 500,000.

78. 19 Dec ●●●●● IT'S ONLY MAKE BELIEVE – Conway Twitty Writers: Conway Twitty and Jack Nance. The first song to reach the British Top 10 in four different years when Billy Fury (1964), Glen Campbell (1970) and Child (1978) all took it back to the higher reaches.

1959

79. 23 Jan ● THE DAY THE RAINS CAME – Jane Morgan Writers: Gilbert Becaud; English lyrics by Carl Sigman. In 1958 Jane Morgan recorded the song in French – 'Le Jour Où La Pluie Viendra' – but the decision to record in English pushed this melodramatic ballad to No.1, with the French version on the B-side.

80. 30 Jan ●●● ONE NIGHT / I GOT STUNG – Elvis Presley Writers: Dave Bartholomew and Pearl King / Aaron Schroeder and David Hill. 'One Night', a cleaned-up revival of Smiley Lewis's R&B hit, remained unissued for two years.

81. 20 Feb ●●●● AS I LOVE YOU – Shirley Bassey Writers: Jay Livingston and Ray Evans. Heavy TV exposure broke this song for the girl from Tiger Bay, who has had more hit albums than any female.

82. 20 Mar ● SMOKE GETS IN YOUR EYES – The Platters Writers: Jerome Kern and Otto Harbach. Doo-wop's most successful group scored their only UK No.1 with their French-recorded version of another chart-topper from a musical, 1933's Roberta.

83. 27 Mar ●●●● SIDE SADDLE – Russ Conway Writer: Trevor Stanford. Still the longest-running instrumental No.1. Pianist Russ Conway, originally Trevor Stanford, famously cut off the top of a finger while operating a bread slicer when he was in the Royal Navy.

84. 24 Apr ●●● IT DOESN'T MATTER ANYMORE – Buddy Holly Writer: Paul Anka. Buddy Holly's only solo No.1 recorded three months before his death in an air crash on 3 Feb 1959.

85. 15 May ●●●●● A FOOL SUCH AS I / I NEED YOUR LOVE TONIGHT – Elvis Presley Writers: William Trader / Sid Wayne and Bix Reichner. Produced by Steve Sholes and Chet Atkins and recorded in Nashville, this was a revival of a country hit by Hank Snow whom Elvis supported on tour in 1955.

86. 19 Jun ●● ROULETTE – Russ Conway Writer: Trevor Stanford. The only solo instrumentalist to achieve consecutive No.1 hits, this release was the first to receive a silver disc for sales exceeding 250,000.

87. 3 Jul ●●●● DREAM LOVER – Bobby Darin Writer: Bobby Darin. This was Darin's last teenybop single and made the top in the UK and US before a jazzier style took over.

88. 31 Jul ●●●●●● LIVING DOLL – Cliff Richard and the Drifters Writer: Lionel Bart. Cliff's first million-seller won an Ivor Novello award and the song returned to the top 27 years later in a Comic Relief re-recording with TV comedy quartet The Young Ones.

89. 11 Sep ●●●● ONLY SIXTEEN – Craig Douglas Writer: Barbara Campbell (aka Lou Adler, Herb Alpert and Sam Cooke). Douglas, former Isle of Wight milkman Terence Perkins, beat Sam Cooke's version to the top at the tender age of 18. The youngest UK male soloist to top the chart.

90. 9 Oct ● HERE COMES SUMMER – Jerry Keller Writer: Jerry Keller. Keller wrote this ultimate high school summer song at the age of 22, after spells in The Tulsa Boy Singers, Jack Dalton's Orchestra and nine months as a Tulsa DJ. This was to be his only hit on either side of the pond.

91. 16 Oct ●● MACK THE KNIFE – Bobby Darin Writers: Bertolt Brecht and Kurt Weill; English lyrics by Marc Blitzstein. Translated from 'Moritat' included in The Threepenny Opera, Darin insisted the selection

of the track would succeed when most others, including DJ Dick Clark, thought he was crazy.

92. 30 Oct ●●●●● TRAVELLIN' LIGHT – Cliff Richard and the Shadows Writers: Sid Tepper and Roy C Bennett. The B-side, 'Dynamite', was so popular that it charted for four weeks in its own right, reaching No.16.

93. 4 Dec ●●● (one week equal) WHAT DO YOU WANT – Adam Faith Writer: Les Vandyke. The first of a record-breaking seven successive Top 5s for Faith. The producer was John Burgess and the arranger John Barry.

94. 18 Dec ●●●●●● (one week equal) WHAT DO YOU WANT TO MAKE THOSE EYES AT ME FOR – Emile Ford and the Checkmates Writers: Joseph McCarthy, Howard Johnson and Jimmy Monaco. New version of a 1917 song revived in 1945 by Betty Hutton for her movie Incendiary Blonde. This was the last time two records officially shared the top spot; strangely, both began with the same four words.

1960

95. 29 Jan ● STARRY EYED – Michael Holliday Writers: Earl Shuman and Mort Garson. Holliday was the first Liverpudlian to achieve two No.1 hits. His record was bettered by a Gerry and the Pacemakers hat-trick in October 1963, which coincided with Holliday's death at the age of 37.

96. 5 Feb ●●●● WHY – Anthony Newley Writers: Bob Marcucci and Peter de Angelis. The actor / pop star turned this cover version of Frankie Avalon's US No.1 into the shortest titled chart-topper, until 'If' 15 years later.

97. 10 Mar ● POOR ME – Adam Faith Writer: Les Vandyke. The first No.1 on the Record Retailer chart, which was Britain's first record industry chart and the first Top 50.

98. 17 Mar ●● RUNNING BEAR – Johnny Preston Writer: J P Richardson. The saga of an Indian brave and Little White Dove was recorded with backing vocals by the Big Bopper, who wrote the track, and future country superstar George Jones.

99. 31 Mar ●●●● MY OLD MAN'S A DUSTMAN – Lonnie Donegan Writers: Traditional; new lyrics by Lonnie Donegan, Peter Buchanan and Beverley Thorn. This live comedy record was a cleaned-up version of the raunchy old pub song 'What Do You Think About That?'.

100. 28 Apr ● DO YOU MIND – Anthony Newley Writer: Lionel Bart. After consecutive No.1s with question songs, Newley's chart career started to fade, although his personal fortune was assured by co-writing another question song, 'What Kind Of Fool Am I?'.

101. 5 May ●●●●●●● CATHY'S CLOWN – Everly Brothers Writers: Don and Phil Everly. The duo's biggest hit, achieved after a risky million-dollar switch to Warner Bros. The company's first single topped the chart on both sides of the Atlantic.

102. 23 Jun ●● THREE STEPS TO HEAVEN – Eddie Cochran Writers: Eddie and Bob Cochran. The second posthumous British

No.1. Eddie was killed in a car crash, shortly after recording this prophetic song. Spookily, he was backed by the Crickets, the backing band of the previous posthumous chart-topper, Buddy Holly.

103. 7 Jul ●●● GOOD TIMIN' – Jimmy Jones Writers: Fred Tobias and Clint Ballard Jr. The last in a long line of chart-toppers for the distinctive yellow MGM label, until the Osmonds' five in the 70s.

104. 28 Jul ● 11 Aug ●● PLEASE DON'T TEASE – Cliff Richard and the Shadows Writers: Pete Chester and Bruce Welch. The choice for Cliff's third No.1 was decided by votes from a cross-section of people who were played a selection of songs over tea and biscuits. The majority went for this song penned by Shadow Bruce Welch and Pete (son of comedian Charlie) Chester.

105. 4 Aug ● SHAKIN' ALL OVER – Johnny Kidd and the Pirates Writers: Frederick Heath and Gus Robinson. Innovative British rock and roll classic, penned by lead singer Kidd (Heath) and his manager. The swashbucklingly dressed Pirates lost their frontman when Kidd was killed in a car crash in 1966.

106. 25 Aug ●●●●● APACHE – The Shadows Writer: Jerry Lordan. Lordan, on the same bill as the Shadows, played them the tune on his ukulele. Bert Weedon had already recorded the instrumental but had no release plans and the Shadows made it their first No.1. Danish guitarist Jorgen Ingmann's 'Apache' beat them in the US chart race.

107. 29 Sep ●●● TELL LAURA I LOVE HER – Ricky Valance Writers: Jeff Barry and Ben Raleigh. Banned by the BBC, who tended to ignore any songs that mentioned death, the record found favour with Radio Luxembourg.

108. 20 Oct ●● ONLY THE LONELY – Roy Orbison Writer: Roy Orbison. Reportedly, both Elvis and the Everly Brothers turned down the song before Orbison was forced to release it himself.

109. 3 Nov ●●●●●●●● IT'S NOW OR NEVER – Elvis Presley Writers: Eduardo di Capua, Aaron Shroeder and Wally Gold. Elvis's longest run at the top was with a song that had copyright problems and nearly didn't get a British release as it was adapted from the 1901 Italian song 'O Sole Mio'.

110. 29 Dec ●● I LOVE YOU – Cliff Richard and the Shadows Writer: Bruce Welch. A return to the easy-paced style of 'Living Doll' and 'Travellin' Light', this was Cliff's 10th Top 10 single in two years and allowed him to topple Elvis from the top for the first time.

1961

111. 12 Jan ●● POETRY IN MOTION – Johnny Tillotson Writers: Paul Kauffman and Mike Anthony. The Florida-born country singer's biggest UK hit was written by two New Yorkers. Recordings in both New York and Nashville were completed before the latter became a US, UK and international hit.

112. 26 Jan ●●●● ARE YOU LONESOME TONIGHT? – Elvis Presley Writers: Ray Turk and Lou Handman. A revamped song from 1926 which shot to No.1 thanks in part to the spoken passage beginning with a line inspired by a speech in Shakespeare's As You Like It: "You know, someone said that all the world's a stage".

113. 23 Feb ● SAILOR – Petula Clark Writers: Fini Busch and Werner Scharfenburger. Written by the two Austrian composers, the song was transformed with English lyrics by EMI producer Norman Newell (using the pseudonym David West). Lolita's German version was a bigger hit worldwide.

114. 2 Mar ●●● WALK RIGHT BACK / EBONY EYES – Everly Brothers Writers: Sonny Curtis / John D Loudermilk. The most played track from the Everlys' second double-sided chart-topper was 'Walk Right Back' penned by Sonny Curtis of The Crickets.

115. 23 Mar ●●●●●● WOODEN HEART – Elvis Presley Writers: Bert Kaempfert, Kay Twomey, Fred Wise and Ben Weisman. This adaptation of a German folk song taken from the movie GI Blues gave Elvis his longest consecutive stay, racking up 27 weeks.

116. 4 May ●● BLUE MOON – The Marcels Writers: Richard Rodgers and Lorenz Hart. The Pittsburgh, US, doo-wop quintet took just 10 minutes to record this re-working of a 1935 hit by, among others, Benny Goodman, then Billy Cotton and Henry Hall.

117. 18 May ● ON THE REBOUND – Floyd Cramer Writer: Floyd Cramer. In-demand Nashville pianist (for Elvis and others) Cramer saw this Chet Atkins production become his biggest of three hits that made the UK chart.

118. 25 May ● YOU'RE DRIVING ME CRAZY – The Temperance Seven Writer: Walter Donaldson. Producer George Martin's first No.1 single was recorded by an act best summed up by their publicity: "Formed in 1906 for a season at the Pasadena Coca Rooms in the Balls Pond Road".

119. 1 Jun ●●●● SURRENDER – Elvis Presley Writers: Ernesto and B G De Curtis; English lyrics by Doc Pomus and Mort Shuman. Recorded in Nashville on 30 and 31 Oct 1960, this was another old Italian song ('Torna A Sorrento') from 1911.

100 – Anthony Newley

Photo: Pictorial Press

120. 29 Jun ●●● RUNAWAY – Del Shannon Writers: Del Shannon and Max Crook. The highly distinctive instrumental break in the middle was by Shannon's co-writer Max Crook and was played on a musitron, an early forerunner of the synth.

121. 20 Jul ●● TEMPTATION – Everly Brothers Writers: Nacio Herb Brown and Arthur Freed. Originally performed by Bing Crosby in the 1933 movie Going Hollywood. The brothers' joined the US marines soon after scoring, this, their final UK No.1.

122. 3 Aug ● WELL I ASK YOU – Eden Kane Writer: Les Vandyke. Penned by Adam Faith's hit writer Johnny Worth, who wrote all his hits under this alias.

123. 10 Aug ●●● YOU DON'T KNOW – Helen Shapiro Writers: John Schroeder and Mike Hawker. By reaching No.1, Helen Shapiro became a national celebrity as the schoolgirl with the grown-up voice. She was, at 14 years and 316 days old, the youngest artist to top the UK chart.

124. 31 Aug ●●● 28 Sep ● JOHNNY REMEMBER ME – John Leyton Writer: Geoff Goddard. Produced by great British independent Joe Meek. Managed by Robert Stigwood, the actor / vocalist's track became a hit after he sang it on TV's Harper West One series, in which he played a pop singer.

125. 21 Sep ● REACH FOR THE STARS / CLIMB EV'RY MOUNTAIN – Shirley Bassey Writers: Udo Jurgens; English lyrics by David West / Richard Rodgers and Oscar Hammerstein II. 'Reach for the Stars' was penned by the man who would later win the 1966 Eurovision Song Contest for Austria. The flip side was one of only two chart hits ('Edelweiss' was the other) from The Sound of Music.

126. 5 Oct ● KON-TIKI – The Shadows Writer: Michael Carr. Songwriter Carr (also a film stuntman, cowboy and seaman) wrote such classics as 'South of the Border' and 'Hang Out the Washing on the Siegfried Line'.

127. 12 Oct ● MICHAEL – The Highwaymen Writer: Traditional, arranged by Dave Fisher. Student quintet from the Wesleyan University of Middletown, Connecticut. Leader Dave Fisher's treatment of the Negro spiritual beat Lonnie Donegan's version which peaked at No.6.

128. 19 Oct ●●● WALKIN' BACK TO HAPPINESS – Helen Shapiro Writers: John Schroeder and Mike Hawker. The girl from Bethnal Green left school shortly after this, her third hit, made No.1 and went on to sell a million worldwide.

129. 9 Nov ●●●● LITTLE SISTER / HIS LATEST FLAME – Elvis Presley Writers: Doc Pomus and Mort Shuman. Elvis recorded both sides of his ninth UK No.1 at Nashville sessions on 25 and 26 Jun 1961 to give him his record-breaking fifth No.1 in 12 months.

130. 7 Dec ●●● TOWER OF STRENGTH – Frankie Vaughan Writers: Burt Bacharach and Bob Hilliard. Frankie Vaughan's career was in decline until he recorded this track, which was Bacharach's only No.1 written without Hal David.

131. 28 Dec ●● MOON RIVER – Danny Williams Writers: Henry Mancini and Johnny Mercer. An Oscar-winning song and theme to the Audrey Hepburn movie Breakfast at Tiffany's. Williams was the first South African to reach No.1.

1962

132. 11 Jan ●●●●●● THE YOUNG ONES – Cliff Richard and the Shadows Writers: Sid Tepper and Roy C Bennett. Amassed record advance orders of 524,000 copies, which enabled Cliff's second million-seller to become the first single by a UK act to enter at No.1.

133. 22 Feb ●●●● ROCK-A-HULA BABY / CAN'T HELP FALLING IN LOVE – Elvis Presley Writers: Fred Wise, Ben Weisman and Dolores Fuller / George David Weiss, Hugo Peretti and Luigi Creatore. The King's fourth double-sided chart-topper was taken from Blue Hawaii, his most financially successful movie and biggest-selling soundtrack album.

134. 22 Mar ●●●●●●●● WONDERFUL LAND – The Shadows Writer: Jerry Lordan. The biggest Shadows hit was recorded 12 months previously but not considered chartworthy until a string section was added.

135. 17 May ● NUT ROCKER – B Bumble and the Stingers Writer: Pyotr Ilyich Tchaikovsky. Arranged and produced by Kim Fowley, this was the first time in chart history that one instrumental had replaced another at No.1.

136. 24 May ●●●●● GOOD LUCK CHARM – Elvis Presley Writers: Aaron Schroeder and Wally Gold. The King's sixth and final transatlantic No.1 was the biggest hit of the year in Norway.

137. 28 Jun ●● COME OUTSIDE – Mike Sarne with Wendy Richard Writer: Charles Blackwell. Only the second comedy No.1 so far, the song features roles acted out by Sarne and actress Wendy Richard (later of Are You Being Served? and EastEnders) in a boyfriend / girlfriend situation.

138. 12 Jul ●● I CAN'T STOP LOVING YOU – Ray Charles Writer: Don Gibson. A country ballad written in 1957 which gave Charles, blinded at six and orphaned by 14, his biggest worldwide hit.

139. 26 Jul ●●●●●●● I REMEMBER YOU – Frank Ifield Writers: Johnny Mercer and Victor Scherzinger. The song, from the 1942 movie The Fleet's In, was selected from a box of old sheet music. Ifield's yodelling was the extra element that made it a British million-seller.

140. 13 Sep ●●● SHE'S NOT YOU – Elvis Presley Writers: Doc Pomus, Jerry Leiber and Mike Stoller. Rare collaboration by these three writers. They were asked by Elvis's publisher, Freddy Bienstock, to come up with some new country-flavoured material.

141. 4 Oct ●●●●● TELSTAR – The Tornados Writer: Joe Meek. This instumental track by Billy Fury's backing band was the first single by a UK group to top the US chart.

142. 8 Nov ●●●●● LOVESICK BLUES – Frank Ifield Writers: Irving Mills and Cliff Friend. Hank Williams's version topped the US country chart for 16 weeks in 1949. Frank's release amassed UK advance orders of 200,000.

143. 13 Dec ●●● RETURN TO SENDER – Elvis Presley Writers: Otis Blackwell and Winfield Scott. The first Elvis UK No.1 to feature the saxophone. Recorded at Paramount Studios, Hollywood, and was included in his 11th movie Girls! Girls! Girls!.

1963

144. 3 Jan ●●● THE NEXT TIME / BACHELOR BOY – Cliff Richard and the Shadows Writers: Buddy Kaye and Philip Springer / Bruce Welch and Cliff Richard. The only double-sided Cliff topper was also his only No.1 as a composer. Both songs came from the movie Summer Holiday.

145. 24 Jan ● DANCE ON – Shadows Writers: Valerie and Elaine Murtagh and Ray Adams. The group's fourth chart-topper was composed by The Avons – remember 'Seven Little Girls Sitting in the Back Seat'?

146. 31 Jan ●●● DIAMONDS – Jet Harris and Tony Meehan Writer: Jerry Lordan. After the Shadows replaced Cliff Richard at No.1 they were dethroned by two ex-Shadows. It was the duo's first release; like the Shadows' first No.1, 'Apache', it was penned by Lordan.

147. 21 Feb ●●● THE WAYWARD WIND – Frank Ifield Writers: Stan Labowsky and Herb Newman. The song, which had topped the US chart in 1956 by Gogi Grant, made Frank Ifield the first UK-based artist to score three No.1s with consecutive singles.

148. 14 Mar ●● 4 Apr ● SUMMER HOLIDAY – Cliff Richard and the Shadows Writers: Bruce Welch and Brian Bennett. Title song from Cliff's fourth film was penned by two of his backing band. The song has become Britain's summer's equivalent to winter's 'White Christmas'.

149. 29 Mar ● FOOT TAPPER – Shadows Writers: Hank B Marvin and Bruce Welch. Sixth No.1 for producer Norrie Paramor in five months; he produced six of the last eight chart-toppers and all of the last three.

150. 11 Apr ●●● HOW DO YOU DO IT? – Gerry and the Pacemakers Writer: Mitch Murray. First record by a Liverpool band to top the chart. It was written for Adam Faith and previously had been recorded by The Beatles. It reached the US Top 10 18 months later, one of five of their hits to go Top 20 over the water.

151. 2 May ●●●●●●● FROM ME TO YOU – Beatles Writers: John Lennon and Paul McCartney. Fab Four's first of a record 11 consecutive UK No.1s was also their first song to chart Stateside – although it was a hit there by Del Shannon.

152. 20 June ●●●● I LIKE IT – Gerry and the Pacemakers Writer: Mitch Murray. Third successive No.1 for producer George Martin and manager Brian Epstein. The group was the first act to top the chart with initial two releases.

153. 18 Jul ●● CONFESSIN' – Frank Ifield Writers: Al J Neiburg, Doc Daugherty and Ellis Reynolds. Despite Merseybeat mania, the yodelling star scored his fourth No.1 in a year with a song that had topped charts in 1930 by Guy Lombardo and megaphone-toting idol Rudy Vallee.

154. 1 Aug ● (YOU'RE THE) DEVIL IN DISGUISE – Elvis Presley Writers: Bill Giant, Bernie Baum and Florence Kaye. Only record to top the UK chart in 1963 by an American and the King's last newly recorded No.1 of the decade.

155. 8 Aug ●● SWEETS FOR MY SWEET – Searchers Writers: Doc Pomus and Mort Shuman. The third Liverpool band (first not managed by Brian Epstein) to top the chart did so with an old Drifters song. John Lennon called it "the best disc ever from a Liverpool group".

156. 22 Aug ●●● BAD TO ME – Billy J Kramer and the Dakotas Writers: John Lennon and Paul McCartney. Third Liverpool group produced by George Martin and managed by Brian Epstein to reach No.1 in just four months. The record peaked on Kramer's 20th birthday.

157. 12 Sep ●●●● 28 Nov ●● SHE LOVES YOU – Beatles Writers: John Lennon and Paul McCartney. With record advance orders exceeding 300,000, this was the UK's top seller of the 1960s with sales of more than 1.6 million.

158. 10 Oct ●●● DO YOU LOVE ME – Brian Poole and the Tremeloes Writer: Berry Gordy Jr. First South of England group to reach No.1 in the Merseybeat era clicked with their sixth single, which was written by Motown's owner and first recorded by the label's group The Contours.

159. 31 Oct ●●●● YOU'LL NEVER WALK ALONE – Gerry and the Pacemakers Writers: Richard Rodgers and Oscar Hammerstein II. Gerry Marsden's men became the first act to top the chart with their first three releases – a record not equalled for 20 years. Gerry also fronted a No.1 revival of the song in 1985.

160. 12 Dec ●●●●● I WANT TO HOLD YOUR HAND – Beatles Writers: John Lennon and Paul McCartney. Single broke The Beatles in the US and started British Invasion of US charts. With world sales exceeding 10 million, it was the biggest-selling UK record until 1997.

1964

161. 16 Jan ●● GLAD ALL OVER – Dave Clark Five Writers: Dave Clark and Mike Smith. London group's third release on their third label sold almost a million in the UK, and made them the second British group (after Beatles) to crack the US Top 10 in 1964.

162. 30 Jan ●●● NEEDLES AND PINS – Searchers Writers: Sonny Bono and Jack Nitzsche. The group's biggest transatlantic hit was originally recorded by Jackie DeShannon (as was Searchers' 'When You Walk in the Room') and composed by Bono, of chart-topping Sonny and Cher.

163. 20 Feb ● DIANE – Bachelors Writers: Erno Rapee and Lew Pollack. Easy-listening trio became the first Irish group to reach the top and the first to reach the US Top 10. The composers had penned this and the group's first hit, 'Charmaine', in 1927.

164. 27 Feb ●●● ANYONE WHO HAD A HEART – Cilla Black Writers: Burt Bacharach and Hal David. Liverpool's leading lady topped the first all-British Top 10 (12 Mar) with her version of an American hit by Dionne Warwick.

165. 19 Mar ●● LITTLE CHILDREN – Billy J Kramer and the Dakotas Writers: Mort Shuman and John Leslie McFarland. Group's first single not composed by Lennon and McCartney was their biggest US hit and Shuman's fifth No.1.

166. 2 Apr ●●● CAN'T BUY ME LOVE – Beatles Writers: John Lennon and Paul McCartney. Single broke advance orders record on both sides of the Atlantic by amassing one million in the UK and two in the US. It topped the US chart in two weeks (a record not bettered until 1995) and completed an all-Beatles Top 5.

167. 23 Apr ●● A WORLD WITHOUT LOVE – Peter and Gordon Writers: John Lennon and Paul McCartney. Song rejected by Billy J Kramer took the duo to the top on both sides of the Atlantic. It was the composers' eighth UK No.1 in 14 months and fifth in the US in 22 weeks.

168. 7 May ●● DON'T THROW YOUR LOVE AWAY – Searchers Writers: Jimmy Wisner and Billy Jackson. Group completed hat-trick of chart toppers in nine months, all of which were covers of US songs. This originally was recorded as a throwaway B-side by R&B group The Orlons.

169. 21 May ● JULIET – Four Pennies Writers: Mike Wilsh, Fritz Fryer and Lionel Morton. Self-penned ballad was intended as B-side. Only 1964 No.1 by a UK group not to chart Stateside.

170. 28 May ●●●● YOU'RE MY WORLD – Cilla Black Writers: Umberto Bindi, Gino Paoli and Carl Sigman. Brian Epstein's first female client sold lorra lorra copies of an Italian song that gave lyricist Sigman his fourth No.1.

171. 25 Jun ●● IT'S OVER – Roy Orbison Writers: Roy Orbison and Bill Dees. The "Big O" was the most successful American act in Britain during Beatlemania, and this was the first US-recorded No.1 for 11 months.

166 – Beatles

172. 9 Jul ● HOUSE OF THE RISING SUN – Animals Writers: Traditional, arranged by Alan Price. The four-minute-plus single was the longest No.1 yet. It took just 20 minutes to record, was a transatlantic topper and the first of many Top 10s for producer Mickie Most.

173. 16 Jul ● IT'S ALL OVER NOW – Rolling Stones Writers: Bobby and Shirley Womack. Britain's most popular R&B band's first No.1 was cut at the legendary Chess studios in Chicago. Bobby Womack's group, The Valentinos, had previously recorded the song.

174. 23 Jul ●●● A HARD DAY'S NIGHT – Beatles Writers: John Lennon and Paul McCartney. Title song from their first film shot to the top in the UK and the US where the soundtrack LP sold a record-breaking million copies in four days.

175. 13 Aug ●● DO WAH DIDDY DIDDY – Manfred Mann Writers: Jeff Barry and Ellie Greenwich. British R&B band's first cover version (released earlier by The Exciters) became the seventh UK record to top the transatlantic charts in just eight months.

176. 2 7Aug ●● HAVE I THE RIGHT? – Honeycombs Writers: Ken Howard and Alan Blaikley. Last No.1 produced by Joe Meek was penned by the group's managers and also reached the US Top 10. The act included female drummer Annie "Honey" Lantree.

177. 10 Sep ●● YOU REALLY GOT ME – Kinks Writers: Ray Davies. The group's self-penned third single started a long run of transatlantic successes. This classic rock song has been played more than two million times on US radio.

178. 24 Sep ●● I'M INTO SOMETHING GOOD – Herman's Hermits Writers: Carole King and Gerry Goffin. The Manchester group, fronted by 16-year-old Peter Noone, was extremely popular in the US. Mickie Most-produced version was Goffin and King's only UK No.1.

179. 8 Oct ●● OH PRETTY WOMAN – Roy Orbison Writers: Roy Orbison and Bill Dees. Orbison's only transatlantic No.1 was also a chart-topper around Europe. Song was inspired by his wife, Claudette, who had also inspired an earlier No.1 (see 73).

180. 22 Oct ●●● (THERE'S) ALWAYS SOMETHING THERE TO REMIND ME – Sandie Shaw Writers: Burt Bacharach and Hal David. Eight months after Cilla Black topped the chart with a cover of a Bacharach and David song, this 17-year-old barefoot pop star repeated the feat.

181. 19 Nov ●● BABY LOVE – Supremes Writers: Brian Holland, Lamont Dozier and Eddie Holland. First girl group recording to top the UK chart was one of a record dozen US No.1s for the trio in the 60s. Returned to the UK Top 20 in 1974.

182. 3 Dec ● LITTLE RED ROOSTER – Rolling Stones Writer: Willie Dixon. A song written by the Chess blues legend and earlier recorded by such artists as Sam Cooke, Griffin Brothers and Howlin' Wolf returned the Stones to the summit.

183. 10 Dec ●●●●● I FEEL FINE – Beatles Writers: John Lennon and Paul McCartney. Credited with the first use of feedback guitar, the song had UK advance orders of 750,000 and was the Christmas No.1 on both sides of the Atlantic.

1965

184. 14 Jan ●● YEH YEH – Georgie Fame Writers: Rogers Grant, Pat Patrick and Jon Hendricks. Pioneering British R&B artist initially considered his first No.1 to be "too jazzy" to be a hit.

185. 28 Jan ● GO NOW! – Moody Blues Writers: Larry Banks and Milton Bennett. Midlands R&B band turned progressive rock legends had their only No.1 single with a song penned by ex-doo wop vocalist Banks and first recorded by his wife Bessie.

186. 4 Feb ●● YOU'VE LOST THAT LOVIN' FEELIN' – Righteous Brothers Writers: Phil Spector, Barry Mann and Cynthia Weil. Acclaimed Phil Spector production also reached Top 10 in 1969 and 1990. Only song to receive more than eight million US radio plays.

187. 18 Feb ● TIRED OF WAITING FOR YOU – Kinks Writers: Ray Davies. Group's third successive UK Top 3 entry and third US Top 10 single. Song returned to the Top 10 in 1988 by The Stranglers.

188. 25 Feb ●● I'LL NEVER FIND ANOTHER YOU – Seekers Writers: Tom Springfield. First single by an Australian group to top the chart and first to reach the US Top 5 was penned and produced by a former member of The Springfields.

189. 11 Mar ● IT'S NOT UNUSUAL – Tom Jones Writers: Les Reed and Gordon Mills. Song penned for Sandie Shaw launched Jones's long and lucrative career. The timeless track, which features guitarist Jimmy Page, returned to the Top 20 in 1987.

190. 18 Mar ●●● THE LAST TIME – Rolling Stones Writers: Mick Jagger and Keith Richard. Group's first self-penned hit completed a hat-trick of No.1s and took them into the transatlantic Top 10 for the first time.

191. 8 Apr ● CONCRETE AND CLAY – Unit 4 Plus 2 Writers: Brian Parker and Tommy Moeller. Hypnotic self-penned hit gave Hertfordshire sextet their biggest seller. The song returned to Top 20 in 1976 by Randy Edelman.

192. 15 Apr ● THE MINUTE YOU'RE GONE – Cliff Richard Writers: Jimmy Gately. Cliff's first No.1 minus The Shadows was recorded in Nashville and revived a country chart-topper by Sonny James.

193. 22 Apr ●●● TICKET TO RIDE – Beatles Writers: John Lennon and Paul McCartney. The first single from the group's second film, Help!, extended their record number of consecutive No.1s to seven. During its chart run they were awarded MBEs.

194. 13 May ● KING OF THE ROAD – Roger Miller Writer: Roger Miller. This rare country No.1 oddly won the Grammy for Best Rock and Roll Single. The hobo hymn returned to the Top 10 in 1990 by The Proclaimers.

195. 20 May ● WHERE ARE YOU NOW (MY LOVE) – Jackie Trent Writers: Jackie Trent and Tony Hatch. Produced by Trent's future husband and co-writer Tony Hatch, his fifth No.1 within two years.

196. 27 May ●●● LONG LIVE LOVE – Sandie Shaw Writer: Chris Andrews. Composer / producer Andrews wrote hits for Adam Faith (who discovered Shaw), himself and Sandie, but this was his only No.1.

197. 17 Jun ● **17 Jul** ● CRYING IN THE CHAPEL – Elvis Presley Writer: Artie Glenn. Recorded at the same session as his 1960 No.1 'Surrender'. This song was penned by Glenn and was a big hit in 1953 for several acts including his teenage son Darrell Glenn.

198. 24 Jun ● **8 Jul** ●● I'M ALIVE – Hollies Writer: Clint Ballard Jr. The group's first No.1, and their last for 23 years, was composed by Ballard for Wayne Fontana and the Mindbenders, who had hit with his song 'Game of Love'.

199. 22 Jul ●● MR TAMBOURINE MAN – Byrds Writer: Bob Dylan. First US group to top the UK chart for almost four years. The record put folk / rock on the musical map and was Dylan's first No.1.

200. 5 Aug ●●● HELP! – Beatles Writers: John Lennon and Paul McCartney. Title song from the group's first colour film gave them another transatlantic topper. It was No.1 when they performed their famous New York Shea Stadium show.

201. 26 Aug ●● I GOT YOU BABE – Sonny and Cher Writer: Sonny Bono. The most talked-about new act of 1965 took the world by storm with "the first hippie anthem". It returned to the top in 1985 by UB40.

202. 9 Sep ●● (I CAN'T GET NO) SATISFACTION – Rolling Stones Writers: Mick Jagger and Keith Richard. Classic rock record, which gave the Stones their first transatlantic No.1. It was recorded in America and headed the US chart before its UK release.

203. 23 Sep ● MAKE IT EASY ON YOURSELF – Walker Brothers Writers: Burt Bacharach and Hal David. US teen-targeted trio, who first found fame in the UK, gave Bacharach his sixth No.1 with a song originally recorded by R&B star Jerry Butler.

204. 30 Sep ●●●●● TEARS – Ken Dodd Writers: Billy Uhr and Frank Capano. The year's top seller sold more than a million in the UK and was a hit in 1931, a year before Dodd or his Diddymen were born.

205. 4 Nov ●●● GET OFF OF MY CLOUD – Rolling Stones Writers: Mick Jagger and Keith Richard. Another self-penned, US-recorded, transatlantic topper for the Stones. It was the last of their five successive UK No.1s – a feat previously achieved only by Elvis and The Beatles.

206. 25 Nov ●●● THE CARNIVAL IS OVER – Seekers Writer: Tom Springfield. The group, who spent more time on the UK charts in 1965 than any other act, sold a million copies of this single in Britain alone.

207. 16 Dec ●●●●● DAY TRIPPER / WE CAN WORK IT OUT – Beatles Writers: John Lennon and Paul McCartney. A record third successive Christmas No.1 for The Beatles. In the US, soul greats Otis Redding and Stevie Wonder, respectively, later had hits with these songs.

1966

208. 20 Jan ● KEEP ON RUNNIN' – Spencer Davis Group Writer: Jackie Edwards. Ska star Edwards composed both the No.1 hits for the Birmingham band that introduced the world to 17-year-old-singer / pianist Steve Winwood.

209. 27 Jan ●●● MICHELLE – Overlanders Writers: John Lennon and Paul McCartney. Three days after Tony Hatch produced this Beatles ballad it was on sale, and three weeks later it was No.1.

210. 17 Feb ●●●● THESE BOOTS ARE MADE FOR WALKIN' – Nancy Sinatra Writer: Lee Hazlewood. After more than a dozen flops, Frank's daughter teamed with Duane Eddy's producer for this transatlantic chart-topper.

211. 17 Mar ●●●● THE SUN AIN'T GONNA SHINE ANYMORE – Walker Brothers Writers: Bob Crewe and Bob Gaudio. The first US male trio to top the chart scored their final No.1 with a song previously recorded by Four Seasons leader Frankie Valli.

212. 14 Apr ●● SOMEBODY HELP ME – Spencer Davis Group Writer: Jackie Edwards. Like the group's previous release, the No.1 'Keep On Running', this reggae-rooted track was produced by Island Records' founder Chris Blackwell.

213. 28 Apr ● YOU DON'T HAVE TO SAY YOU LOVE ME – Dusty Springfield Writers: Pino Donaggio, Vito Pallavicini, Vicki Wickham and Simon Napier-Bell. Dusty's only No.1 was an Italian ballad that won the prestigious San Remo Festival in 1965. English lyrics were by Vicki Wickham, the producer of TV's Ready Steady Go.

214. 5 May ●●● PRETTY FLAMINGO – Manfred Mann Writer: Mark Barkan. The group's last single to showcase lead vocalist Paul Jones also featured their short-lived bass player Jack Bruce, who then joined legendary trio Cream.

215. 26 May ● PAINT IT BLACK – Rolling Stones Writers: Mick Jagger and Keith Richard. Macabre song was recorded in Hollywood and featured Brian Jones on sitar. In 1990, this single returned to UK chart and reached No.1 again in Holland.

216. 2 Jun ●●● STRANGERS IN THE NIGHT – Frank Sinatra Writers: Bert Kaempfert, Charlie Singleton and Eddie Snyder. Multi-Grammy-winning record gave "Ol' Blue Eyes" his only transatlantic No.1, and German composer Kaempfert his second of the 1960s.

217. 23 Jun ●● PAPERBACK WRITER – Beatles Writers: John Lennon and Paul McCartney. Released soon after the group's final UK live show at the NME poll winners' concert. Like its seven predecessors it reached the top spot in just two weeks.

228 – Monkees

Photo: Rex features

218. 7 Jul ●● SUNNY AFTERNOON – Kinks Writer: Ray Davies. The distinctive group's third and last chart-topper was also a big success around Europe, and gave them their last US Top 20 hit of the decade.

219. 21 Jul ● GET AWAY – Georgie Fame Writer: Clive Powell. Written as a TV commercial for petrol, this song proved so popular with viewers that Fame released it as a single. It was his only self-penned No.1.

220. 28 Jul ● OUT OF TIME – Chris Farlowe and the Thunderbirds Writers: Mick Jagger and Keith Richard. Only Rolling Stones song to hit the top by another artist. British R&B pioneer Farlowe reached No.1 as England won the World Cup – neither repeated the feat.

221. 4 Aug ●● WITH A GIRL LIKE YOU – Troggs Writers: Reg Presley. Although best remembered for their five-million-selling 'Wild Thing' and the original version of 'Love Is All Around', this self-penned song was The Troggs' only No.1.

222. 18 Aug ●●●● YELLOW SUBMARINE / ELEANOR RIGBY – Beatles Writers: John Lennon and Paul McCartney. The last of a record-shattering 11 successive No.1s was their first topper sung by drummer Ringo Starr. 'Yellow Submarine' gave birth to a full-length animated film.

223. 15 Sep ● ALL OR NOTHING – Small Faces Writers: Steve Marriott and Ronnie Lane. Mod icons were regular chart visitors in the late 60s and clocked up five Top 10 entries including this self-penned No.1.

224. 22 Sep ●●●●● DISTANT DRUMS – Jim Reeves Writer: Cindy Walker. The war song gave the country vocalist his only No.1 two years after his death. Walker was the first solo female songwriter to pen a No.1.

225. 27 Oct ●●● REACH OUT I'LL BE THERE – Four Tops Writers: Brian Holland, Lamont Dozier and Eddie Holland. Timeless Motown classic gave the soulful quartet their only transatlantic No.1. A remixed version made the UK Top 20 in 1988.

226. 17 Nov ●● GOOD VIBRATIONS – Beach Boys Writers: Brian Wilson and Mike Love. Regarded as one of the all-time great pop singles, this track took six months to complete. The group used four studios, 17 sessions and spent a (then) record $50,000.

227. I Dec ●●●●●●● GREEN GREEN GRASS OF HOME – Tom Jones Writer: Claude "Curly" Putnam Jr. Timeless Tom's biggest hit was a cover of a country composition about a man awaiting hanging. A scene in the 1950 film Asphalt Jungle inspired the song.

1967

228. 19 Jan ●●●● I'M A BELIEVER – Monkees Writer: Neil Diamond. Thanks to their Beatles-inspired series, this single shot the made-for-TV group to No.1 on both sides of the Atlantic. In the US it had advance orders of more than a million.

229. 16 Feb ●● THIS IS MY SONG – Petula Clark Writer: Charlie Chaplin. Written by the silent screen legend for the film A Countess in Hong Kong, and produced in America by Ernie (B Bumble) Freeman. Chaplin is the oldest person to compose a No.1.

230. 2 Mar ●●●●●● RELEASE ME (AND LET ME LOVE AGAIN) – Engelbert Humperdinck Writers: Eddie Miller, Robert Yount, Dub Williams and Robert Harris. Humperdinck's first hit came eight years after his recording debut. His revival of this 17-year-old country song spent 56 weeks on the chart and sold more than a million.

231. 13 Apr ●● SOMETHIN' STUPID – Nancy and Frank Sinatra Writer: C Carson Parks. The only father-and-daughter duet to top the chart did so with one of the earliest eight-track recordings.

232. 27 Apr ●●● PUPPET ON A STRING – Sandie Shaw Writers: Bill Martin and Phil Coulter. The first British song to win the Eurovision Song Contest made Shaw the first female to amass three No.1s (a record only bettered in 1987 by Madonna).

233. 18 May ●●● SILENCE IS GOLDEN – Tremeloes Writers: Bob Gaudio and Bob Crewe. A song that started life on the B-side of The Four Seasons' 1964 No.2 'Rag Doll' gave the Essex boys their last transatlantic Top 20 entry.

234. 8 Jun ●●●●●● A WHITER SHADE OF PALE – Procol Harum Writers: Keith Reid and Gary Brooker. Haunting Bach-based song was one of the biggest hits of the "Summer of Love". The single, which sold more than six million worldwide, returned to UK Top 20 in 1972.

235. 19 Jul ●●● ALL YOU NEED IS LOVE – Beatles Writers: John Lennon and Paul McCartney. A worldwide audience of 400 million saw the group introduce this flower power anthem on the first worldwide live TV show, Our World.

236 9 Aug ●●●● SAN FRANCISCO (BE SURE TO WEAR SOME FLOWERS IN YOUR HAIR) – Scott McKenzie Writer: John Phillips. Hippie anthem penned and co-produced by Papa John was turned into a worldwide seven-million-seller by this one-time Monkees reject, who later joined re-formed Mamas and Papas

237. 6 Sep ●●●●● THE LAST WALTZ – Engelbert Humperdinck Writers: Les Reed and Barry Mason. One of most performed British songs of all time sold more than a million copies in the UK alone.

238. 11 Oct ●●●● MASSACHUSETTS – Bee Gees Writers: Barry, Robin and Maurice Gibb. New York-recorded track was first of many No.1s for the group as artist and composers. They had never been to Massachusetts when they wrote it.

239. 8 Nov ●● BABY, NOW THAT I FOUND YOU – Foundations Writers: Tony Macaulay and John McLeod. Multi racial British band not only topped the chart with their first release, but also took it into the US R&B Top 40 – a rare occurrence for a UK recording.

240. 22 Nov ●● LET THE HEARTACHES BEGIN – Long John Baldry Writers: Tony Macaulay and John McLeod. UK writing team made it two No.1s in succession. The 6' 7" singer, whose band once included Elton John and Rod Stewart, was the tallest British chart-topper.

241. 6 Dec ●●●●●●● HELLO GOODBYE – Beatles Writers: John Lennon and Paul McCartney. The group said goodbye to 1967 and hello to 1968 in the top spot. It was their first release after the death of manager Brian Epstein.

1968

242. 24 Jan ● THE BALLAD OF BONNIE & CLYDE – Georgie Fame Writers: Mitch Murray and Peter Callender. Inspired by (but not heard in) the movie Bonnie and Clyde, this gory gangster ditty was the last of Fame's three No.1s and his only US Top 20 entry.

243. 31 Jan ●● EVERLASTING LOVE – Love Affair Writers: Buzz Cason and Mac Gayden. The media had a field day when the teen quartet admitted they didn't play on their chart-topping cover of Robert Knight's US hit.

244. 14 Feb ●● MIGHTY QUINN – Manfred Mann Writer: Bob Dylan. Anthony Quinn's performance in the film The Savage Innocents supposedly inspired Dylan to write the song that gave the group their only No.1 featuring vocalist Mike D'Abo.

245. 28 Feb ●●● CINDERELLA ROCKAFELLA – Esther and Abi Ofarim Writer: Mason Williams. Appearances on the Rolf Harris and Eamonn Andrews TV shows help to rocket the Israeli husband and wife to the top with a novelty song previously recorded unsuccessfully by its composer.

246. 20 Mar ● LEGEND OF XANADU – Dave Dee, Dozy, Beaky, Mick and Tich Writers: Ken Howard and Alan Blaikley. Quirkily named quintet, who always provided original songs and clever productions, had their only No.1 with a whip-cracking classic penned by their managers.

247. 27 Mar ●● LADY MADONNA – Beatles Writers: John Lennon and Paul McCartney. McCartney recorded this track while the other Beatles meditated in India. Weeks after the group grabbed four Grammy awards for Sgt. Pepper, this earned them another gold.

248. 10 Apr ●● CONGRATULATIONS – Cliff Richard Writers: Bill Martin and Phil Coulter. Eurovision runner-up penned by same pair who wrote a previous winner for Sandie Shaw. It gave Cliff his biggest worldwide seller to date.

249. 24 Apr ●●●● WHAT A WONDERFUL WORLD / CABARET – Louis Armstrong Writers: George David Weiss and George Douglas / John Kander and Fred Ebb. Single which made Satchmo the oldest singer to top the UK chart finally reached the Top 40 in his homeland in 1988 – 17 years after his death.

250. 22 May ●●●● YOUNG GIRL – Gary Puckett and the Union Gap Writer: Jerry Fuller. They sold more singles Stateside in 1968 than The Beatles and took this No.1 back into the UK Top 20 in 1974 – three years after they had disbanded.

251. 19 Jun ●● JUMPIN' JACK FLASH – Rolling Stones Writers: Mick Jagger and Keith Richard. A return to their earlier and earthier sound put the Stones on top after a two-year absence. Traffic's producer Jimmy Miller handled the session.

252. 3 Juk ●●● BABY COME BACK – Equals Writer: Eddy Grant. Originally released in 1966, this track took off in the UK only after hitting around Europe. Group member Grant's song returned to the top spot in 1994 by Pato Banton.

253. 24 Jul ● I PRETEND – Des O'Connor Writers: Les Reed and Barry Mason. The popular TV personality had his only No.1 with a song

penned by the team who previously provided chart-toppers for Tom Jones and Engelbert Humperdinck.

254. 31 Jul ●● 21 Aug ● MONY MONY – Tommy James and the Shondells Writers: Bobby Bloom, Richie Cordell, Bo Gentry and Tommy James. Consistently successful US recording group's only UK Top 20 hit was inspired by a sign for the Mutual of New York company.

255. 14 Aug ● FIRE – Crazy World of Arthur Brown Writers: Vincent Crane, Arthur Brown, Peter Ker and Michael Finesilver. One of the world's hottest singles in the summer of 68 was performed by this bizarre British band, whose stage wear influenced Alice Cooper and other shock rockers.

256. 28 Aug ● DO IT AGAIN – Beach Boys Writers: Brian Wilson and Mike Love. Even though the group's surfing singles meant little in Britain, this nostalgic sun-and-surf track gave them their last chart-topper.

257. 4 Sep ● I'VE GOTTA GET A MESSAGE TO YOU – Bee Gees Writers: Barry, Robin and Maurice Gibb. Single which introduced the Brothers Gibb to the US Top 10 was the second song about a man on death row to top chart in the late 60s (see 227).

258. 11 Sep ●● HEY JUDE – Beatles Writers: John Lennon and Paul McCartney. First release on group's Apple label was the longest No.1 to date (7 mins, 10 secs). No single in the 1960s bettered its nine weeks at the top in the US.

259. 25 Sep ●●●●●● THOSE WERE THE DAYS – Mary Hopkin Writers: Gene Raskin and Alexander Vertinski. Apple Records' first female artist dethroned the label's owners at the top. Paul McCartney produced the track which was based on Russian folk song 'Darogoi Dimmoyo'.

260. 6 Nov ● WITH A LITTLE HELP FROM MY FRIENDS – Joe Cocker Writers: John Lennon and Paul McCartney. Third successive No.1 with Beatle connections gave the revered rocker his only chart-topper. Wet Wet Wet returned the song to the top in 1988.

261. 13 Nov ●●●● THE GOOD, THE BAD AND THE UGLY – Hugo Montenegro and his Orchestra Writer: Ennio Morricone. Spaghetti western theme was the first American instrumental single to top the charts for six years. It featured a memorable ocarina introduction by Arthur Smith and grunts from Montenegro himself.

262. 11 Dec ●●● 8 Jan ● LILY THE PINK – Scaffold Writers: John Gorman, Mike McGear and Roger McGough. Paul McCartney's brother Mike was in the trio that had the Christmas No.1 with a song about medicinal compounds. It was the last of producer Norrie Paramor's 27 chart-toppers.

1969

263. 1 Jan ● 15 Jan ●● OB-LA-DI OB-LA-DA – Marmalade Writers: John Lennon and Paul McCartney. The first record by a Scottish group to top the chart featured their version of a reggae-styled song taken from The Beatles' White Album.

264. 29 Jan ● ALBATROSS – Fleetwood Mac Writer: Peter Green. This instrumental nearly became the first single to top the chart on two separate occasions – it returned and peaked at No.2 in 1973, three years after composer / group member Green had left.

265. 5 Feb ● BLACKBERRY WAY – Move Writer: Roy Wood. Psychedelic singalong gave the often controversial Midlands group their fifth successive Top 5 entry and their only No.1.

266. 12 Feb ●● (IF PARADISE IS) HALF AS NICE – Amen Corner Writers: Lucio Battisti and Jack Fishman. First Welsh group to top the chart jumped from 19 to one with an Italian song that started life as 'Il Paradiso Belavista' and had English lyrics by veteran composer Fishman.

267. 26 Feb ●●●● WHERE DO YOU GO TO MY LOVELY – Peter Sarstedt Writer: Peter Sarstedt. The brother and one-time roadie of 1961 chart-topper Eden Kane scored with a continental-sounding song that picked up the prestigious Ivor Novello award for Song of the Year.

268. 26 Mar ●●● I HEARD IT THROUGH THE GRAPEVINE – Marvin Gaye Writers: Norman Whitfield and Barrett Strong. Soul superstar's first major UK solo hit became his only transatlantic No.1. Record returned to the Top 10 in 1986 after being heard in a Levi's commercial.

269. 16 Apr ● ISRAELITES – Desmond Dekker and the Aces Writers: Desmond Dekker and Leslie Kong. Although few could understand all the lyrics, this single was the first reggae No.1 and the first to crack the US Top 10. It returned to the UK Top 10 in 1975.

270. 23 Apr ●●●●●● GET BACK – Beatles with Billy Preston Writers: John Lennon and Paul McCartney. Group's only hit on which they shared artist credits. Surprisingly this retro rocker was the sole track by the group to enter the chart at No.1.

271. 4 Jun ● DIZZY – Tommy Roe Writers: Tommy Roe and Freddy Weller. Regular US hitmaker had his only transatlantic No.1 with this bubblegum classic penned with Paul Revere and the Raiders member Weller. Song returned to No.1 in 1991 courtesy of Vic Reeves.

272. 11 Jun ●●● BALLAD OF JOHN AND YOKO – Beatles Writers: John Lennon and Paul McCartney. Only the composers appeared on this Beatles track about John and Yoko's recent problems. Regarded by some as blasphemous, it was the last of their 17 UK No.1s.

273. 2 Jul ●●● SOMETHING IN THE AIR – Thunderclap Newman Writer: Speedy Keen. The Who's Pete Townshend put this band together and played bass on their self-penned chart-topping debut single. Oddly The Who's own 31 chart entries produced no No.1s.

274. 23 Jul ●●●●● HONKY TONK WOMEN – Rolling Stones Writers: Mick Jagger and Keith Richard. Eighth No.1 for the 1960s' second most successful group. Thirty years later they were still at the top even though they added no more chart-toppers.

275. 30 Aug ●●● IN THE YEAR 2525 (EXORDIUM & TERMINUS) – Zager and Evans Writer: Rick Evans. The act paid $500 for the recording session and originally released this transatlantic topper on their own label.

276. 20 Sep ●●● BAD MOON RISING – Creedence Clearwater Revival Writer: John Fogerty. In their homeland, where they never enjoyed a No.1, this single gave the contemporary rockabilly band the second of five No.2 hits.

277. 11 Oct ● JE T'AIME … MOI NON PLUS – Jane Birkin and Serge Gainsbourg Writer: Serge Gainsbourg. Two weeks after Fontana stopped pressing this record, it moved to No.1 on Major Minor and Gainsbourg became the first Frenchman to top the UK chart.

278 . 18 Oct ● I'LL NEVER FALL IN LOVE AGAIN – Bobbie Gentry Writers: Burt Bacharach and Hal David. Despite the fact that this single did not reach the Top 100 in her homeland, Gentry's recording gave Bacharach his fifth No.1 of the decade.

279. 25 Oct ●●●●●●● SUGAR SUGAR – Archies Writers: Jeff Barry and Andy Kim. These comic book and TV cartoon characters had the world's most successful single of 1969. The mastermind behind the record was Don Kirshner, who gave us The Monkees.

280. 20 Dec ●●●●●● TWO LITTLE BOYS – Rolf Harris Writers: Theodore Morse and Edward Madden. The Swinging Sixties ended with a sentimental turn-of-the-century music hall song at the top. Multi-talented Harris was the first Australian solo artist to achieve a No.1.

1970

281. 31 Jan ●●●●● LOVE GROWS (WHERE MY ROSEMARY GOES) – Edison Lighthouse Writers: Barry Mason and Tony Macaulay. Lead vocalist Tony Burrows also sang on hits by White Plains, Pipkins, Brotherhood of Man, Flowerpot Men, Ivy League and First Class. The single's two-week rise to No.1 was a record for a debut act.

282. 7 Mar ●●● WAND'RIN' STAR – Lee Marvin Writers: Alan Jay Lerner and Frederick Loewe. Noted actor Marvin joined the one-hit wonders club with a song from his film Paint Your Wagon. It sold two million worldwide but flopped in the US.

283. 28 Mar ●●● BRIDGE OVER TROUBLED WATER – Simon and Garfunkel Writer: Paul Simon. Multi-Grammy-winning single was the title track of the 1970s' biggest-selling album.

284. 18 Apr ●● ALL KINDS OF EVERYTHING – Dana Writers: Denny Lindsay and Jackie Smith. Eurovision winner for the 18-year-old who later became a major Irish political figure and MEP.

285. 2 May ●● SPIRIT IN THE SKY – Norman Greenbaum Writer: Norman Greenbaum. Singer who previously recorded as Dr Norman Greenbaum topped the chart with his only hit. Returned to the top courtesy of another Doctor in 1986.

286. 16 May ●●● BACK HOME – England World Cup Squad Writers: Bill Martin and Phil Coulter. The first major football hit was released to tie in with England's defence of their World Cup in Mexico. Composers' previous hits included Cliff's No.1 'Congratulations'.

287. 6 Jun ● YELLOW RIVER – Christie Writer: Jeff Christie. Group's debut hit, which was rejected by The Tremeloes, went on to sell three million worldwide. Song was later used to advertise BT's Yellow Pages.

259 – Mary Hopkin

288. 13 Jun ●●●●●● IN THE SUMMERTIME – Mungo Jerry Writer: Ray Dorset. Seven million people worldwide bought this record which jumped from 13 to one in the UK. It was the first three-track single to top the chart.

289. 1 Aug ●●●●●● THE WONDER OF YOU – Elvis Presley Writer: Baker Knight. The King's first No.1 for more than six years was also the last in his lifetime.

290. 12 Sep ● THE TEARS OF A CLOWN – Smokey Robinson and the Miracles Writer: Henry Cosby, William Robinson and Stevie Wonder. First released and ignored in 1967. UK Motown unearthed it and it gave the group their only No.1.

291. 19 Sep ●●●●●● BAND OF GOLD – Freda Payne Writers: Ron Dunbar and Edith Wayne. First solo female US R&B vocalist to top the UK chart did it with a song about an unconsummated marriage. It was on a label owned by ex-Motown men Holland, Dozier and Holland.

292. 31 Oct ●●● WOODSTOCK – Matthews' Southern Comfort Writer: Joni Mitchell. Although she had to cancel her appearance at Woodstock, Mitchell wrote this about the famous rock festival for Crosby, Stills, Nash and Young who had a US Top 20 hit with a rock version of the song in 1969.

293. 21 Nov ● VOODOO CHILE – Jimi Hendrix Experience Writer: Jimi Hendrix. Bargain price three-track single (included previous hits 'Hey Joe' and 'All Along the Watchtower'), which was released as a tribute soon after Hendrix death, was his only No.1 single.

294. 28 Nov ●●●●●● I HEAR YOU KNOCKING – Dave Edmunds Writers: Dave Bartholomew and Pearl King. Ex-Love Sculpture member jumped from 16 to one with first solo hit, which updated a mid-50s R&B hit by Smiley Lewis. Edmunds name-checks various R&B legends in the middle break.

1971

295. 9 Jan ●●● GRANDAD – Clive Dunn Writers: Herbie Flowers and Kenny Pickett. Relatively youthful Dad's Army actor had his sole hit with the kind of record that could get played only at Christmas.

296. 30 Jan ●●●●● MY SWEET LORD – George Harrison Writer: George Harrison. First solo single by a Beatle to reach No.1. It was later ruled that the song was based on The Chiffons' hit 'He's So Fine'.

297. 6 Mar ●● BABY JUMP – Mungo Jerry Writer: Ray Dorset. The Ray Dorset-fronted group equalled a record set by Gerry and the Pacemakers when they made it two No.1s from their first two releases.

298. 20 Mar ●●●●●● HOT LOVE – T. Rex Writer: Marc Bolan. First chart-topper by one of the early 1970s' most influential groups. Almost overnight Bolan changed from acoustic folkie to teen idol.

299. 1 May ●● DOUBLE BARREL – Dave and Ansil Collins Writer: Winston Riley. First UK No.1 in Britain by a black duo also took the Jamaican reggae duo into the US Top 40 and into the Top 10 around Europe.

300. 15 May ●●●●● KNOCK THREE TIMES – Dawn Writers: Irwin Levine and L Russell Brown. Session singer Tony Orlando and the two girls who made up Dawn did not even meet until after this track (their second Top 10 hit) was recorded.

301. 19 Jun ●●●●● CHIRPY CHIRPY CHEEP CHEEP – Middle of the Road Writer: Lally Scott. Mixed Scottish group, who recorded all their hits in Italy, claim their version of a song first cut by its composer sold 10 million worldwide.

302. 24 Jul ●●●● GET IT ON – T. Rex Writer: Marc Bolan. Year's hottest new act's second No.1 came from their chart-topping Electric Warrior LP. Renamed 'Bang A Gong' in the US, it was their only Top 40 entry there.

303. 21 Aug ●●●● I'M STILL WAITING – Diana Ross Writer: Deke Richards. Motown released the track from her Surrender album because Radio 1's Tony Blackburn raved about it.

304. 18 Sep ●●● HEY GIRL DON'T BOTHER ME – Tams Writer: Ray Whitley. This mid-table US hit from 1964 gave the Atlanta group a surprise UK No.1 thanks to its initial support on the northern soul scene.

305. 9 Oct ●●●●● MAGGIE MAY – Rod Stewart Writers: Rod Stewart and Martin Quittenton. Rod's first hit single and the album it was taken from, Every Picture Tells a Story, simultaneously topped the UK and US chart – an unprecedented feat.

310 – Chicory Tip

Photo: Pictorial Press

306. 13 Nov ●●●● COZ I LUV YOU – Slade Writers: Noddy Holder and Jim Lea. The first of seven successive phonetically spelt titles (including four No.1s) for the Midlands band who had few equals in the 1970s.

307. 11 Dec ●●●● ERNIE (THE FASTEST MILK MAN IN THE WEST) – Benny Hill Writer: Benny Hill. Veteran funny man had the year's Christmas hit with this dairy drama, which also headed the Australian chart by the entertainer who became a US megastar late in life.

1972

308. 8 Jan ●●●● I'D LIKE TO TEACH THE WORLD TO SING – New Seekers Writers: Roger Cook, Roger Greenaway, William Backer and Billy Davis. Most successful advertising jingle in history began as 'I'd Like To Buy the World a Coke' recorded by The Hillside Singers, before The New Seekers had their biggest hit with the song on both sides of the Atlantic.

309. 5 Feb ●● TELEGRAM SAM – T. Rex Writer: Marc Bolan. The band's third No.1 and only release on the T. Rex label, the single revisited the lower reaches of the chart 10 years later.

310. 19 Feb ●●● SON OF MY FATHER – Chicory Tip Writers: Giorgio Moroder, Peter Belotte and Michael Holm. Originally recorded by Moroder himself. First chart-topper to feature a synthesizer, played by studio engineer Chris Thomas.

311. 11 Mar ●●●●● WITHOUT YOU – Nilsson Writers: Peter Ham and Tom Evans. The two writers of this transatlantic No.1 were both from Badfinger, whose own hit 'Day After Day' made the Top 10 in the same month.

312. 15 Apr ●●●●● AMAZING GRACE – The Pipes and Drums and Military Band of the Royal Scots Dragoon Guards Writers: Traditional. The longest-named act ever to top the charts, and the first No.1 to feature bagpipes, this version of 'Amazing Grace' was released only after massive listener reaction on BBC Radio 2.

313. 20 May ●●●● METAL GURU – T. Rex Writer: Marc Bolan. Fourth and last No.1 for Marc Bolan giving him an unlikely record of three chart-toppers on different labels within 10 months.

314. 17 Jun ●● VINCENT – Don McLean Writer: Don McLean. 'American Pie' had stalled at No.2 four months earlier so this was McLean's first chart-topper and one of two about painters. (See 421)

315. 1 July ● TAKE ME BACK 'OME – Slade Writers: Noddy Holder and Jim Lea. Their shortest stay at the top and the shortest stay of any single since Jimi Hendrix 19 months earlier.

316. 8 July ●●●●● PUPPY LOVE – Donny Osmond Writer: Paul Anka. The writer had a US No.1 and a UK No.33 in 1960 with his own song before it gave Donny the first of three No.1s in just over a year.

317. 12 Aug ●●● SCHOOL'S OUT – Alice Cooper Writers: Alice Cooper and Michael Bruce. MPs and outraged parents teamed up to prevent Alice Cooper from touring Britain; the free publicity shot 'School's Out' to the top.

318. 2 Sept ● YOU WEAR IT WELL – Rod Stewart Writers: Rod Stewart and Martin Quittenton. First single release from the No.1 album Never a Dull Moment. Backing him were guitarist and fellow ex-Face Ronnie Wood and drummer Mickey Waller, from his days in Steam Packet.

319. 9 Sept ●●● MAMA WEER ALL CRAZEE NOW – Slade Writers: Noddy Holder, Jim Lea. Had 'Gudbuy To Jane', the follow-up to their second No.1, not peaked at No.2, the Wolverhampton boys would have enjoyed a run of five consecutive chart-toppers.

320. 30 Sept ●● HOW CAN I BE SURE – David Cassidy Writers: Felix Cavaliere and Eddie Brigati. David was a member of The Partridge Family in which his "real" stepmother, Shirley Jones, played his screen mother in the TV show. The song was a US Top 5 hit for the Young Rascals in 1967.

321. 14 Oct ●●●● MOULDY OLD DOUGH – Lieutenant Pigeon Writers: Nigel Fletcher and Robert Woodward. Formerly Staveley Makepeace, they became the only No.1 to feature a mum and son in the line-up. The song was recorded in the front room of Hilda (pianist and mum) and Rob Woodward's house.

322. 11 Nov ●● CLAIR – Gilbert O'Sullivan Writer: Gilbert O'Sullivan. The subject of the song was the young daughter of O'Sullivan's manager (and the record's producer) Gordon Mills, for whom Gilbert babysat.

323. 25 Nov ●●●● MY DING-A-LING – Chuck Berry Writer: Chuck Berry. This transatlantic No.1 and his only UK chart-topper was an entertaining but unrepresentative song recorded as part of the great rock 'n' roller's 1972 live Lanchester Arts Festival gig.

324. 23 Dec ●●●●● LONG HAIRED LOVER FROM LIVERPOOL – Little Jimmy Osmond Writer: Christopher Kingsley. The youngest of Olive and George Osmond's eight sons, Jimmy was, and still is, the youngest chart-topper at nine years, 251 days.

1973

325. 27 Jan ●●●●● BLOCKBUSTER – Sweet Writers: Nicky Chinn and Mike Chapman. One of the early 1970s' most popular groups scored their only No.1 with their sixth Top 20 entry. In Germany, it was one of their eight chart-toppers.

326. 3 Mar ●●●● CUM ON FEEL THE NOIZE – Slade Writers: Noddy Holder and Jim Lea. First of a record-breaking three singles by Slade to enter the UK chart at No.1 in 1973 – a feat not matched for another 20 years.

327. 31 Mar ● THE TWELFTH OF NEVER – Donny Osmond Writers: Jay Livingston and Paul Francis Webster. Donny's fourth successive Top 5 entry, like all its predecessors, was a revival of a previous hit (Cliff Richard in 1964).

328. 7 Apr ●● GET DOWN – Gilbert O'Sullivan Writer: Gilbert O'Sullivan. Less than five months after becoming the first solo Irishman to top the chart, Gilbert repeated the feat. No one would equal this record for another 27 years.

329. 21 Apr ●●●● TIE A YELLOW RIBBON ROUND THE OLD OAK TREE – Dawn Writers: Irwin Levine and L Russell Brown. Based on the true story of a Florida convict, it was most successful single of the year in the UK and US, selling six million copies worldwide.

330. 19 May ●●●● SEE MY BABY JIVE – Wizzard Writer: Roy Wood. Written and produced by the group's flamboyant frontman. This Spector-esque single soon recouped its large recording costs.

331. 16 Jun ● CAN THE CAN – Suzi Quatro Writers: Nicky Chinn and Mike Chapman. When her self-penned debut single 'Rolling Stone' stiffed, bassist / vocalist Suzi teamed with Sweet's production / songwriting duo and started a string of rock hits.

332. 23 Jun ● RUBBER BULLETS – 10cc Writers: Kevin Godley, Lol Creme and Graham Gouldman. After scoring No.2 hits with Wayne Fontana and the Mindbenders, The Mindbenders, Hotlegs and 10cc, member Eric Stewart finally shot to the top spot.

333. 30 Jun ●●● SKWEEZE ME PLEEZE ME – Slade Writers: Noddy Holder and Jim Lea. Another phonetically spelt smash from Slade made them the first British act to have two singles enter at No.1.

334. 21 Jul ● WELCOME HOME – Peters and Lee Writers: Jean-Alphonse Dupré, Stanislas Beldone; English lyrics by Bryan Blackburn. Rolling Stone Charlie Watts's uncle, Lennie Peters, and Di Lee hit the big time after winning on TV's Opportunity Knocks.

335. 28 Jul ●●●● I'M THE LEADER OF THE GANG (I AM) – Gary Glitter Writers: Gary Glitter and Mike Leander. The first of his trio of toppers came with his 12th single. This anthemic stomper was released 13 years after Gary's debut single as Paul Raven.

336. 25 Aug ●●●● YOUNG LOVE – Donny Osmond Writers: Carole Joyner and Ric Cartey. The first chart-topper to be revived and returned to the No.1 slot. Teen idol's version of Tab Hunter's 1957 No.1 jumped from 16 to one.

337. 22 Sep ● ANGEL FINGERS – Wizzard Writer: Roy Wood. Roy Wood became one of only a handful of artists to top the chart in two groups. The second successive No.1 for the ex-Move maestro.

338. 29 Sep ●●●● EYE LEVEL – Simon Park Orchestra Writers: Simon Park and Jack Trombey. The first TV theme to top the chart came from the series Van Der Walk. The 50th No.1 on Columbia had peaked at 42 the previous November.

339. 27 Oct ●●● DAYDREAMER / THE PUPPY SONG – David Cassidy Writers: Terry Dempsey / Harry Nilsson. David performed both sides of this single on the 500th edition of Top of the Pops. Despite the record's UK success it did not chart in the US.

340. 17 Nov ●●●● I LOVE YOU LOVE ME LOVE – Gary Glitter Writers: Gary Glitter and Mike Leander. The only non-Slade single to enter at No.1 in 1973 gave the larger-than-life glam rocker his biggest-selling UK hit.

341. 15 Dec ●●●●● MERRY XMAS EVERYBODY – Slade Writers: Noddy Holder and Jim Lea. Timeless Christmas epic was recorded mid-summer in New York. Also charted in 1980, 81, 82, 83, 84, 85, 86 and 98 and spent longer on the chart than any other Christmas record.

1974

342. 19 Jan ● YOU WON'T FIND ANOTHER FOOL LIKE ME – New Seekers Writers: Tony Macaulay and Geoff Stephens. Rumours that they were about to split were circulating when the group scored their final No.1. Like their predecessors, The Seekers, they scored eight Top 20 singles.

343. 26 Jan ●●●● TIGER FEET – Mud Writers: Nicky Chinn and Mike Chapman. First of Mud's eight successive Top 10 entries jumped from 10 to one and was a smash around Europe.

344. 23 Feb ●● DEVIL GATE DRIVE – Suzi Quatro Writers: Nicky Chinn and Mike Chapman. The second successive No.1 for the writer / production team was covered in the US by previous chart-topper Tommy James, but neither version became a hit there.

345. 9 Mar ● JEALOUS MIND – Alvin Stardust Writer: Peter Shelley. Only No.1 by one of the decade's most popular performers. Like all his six successive Top 20s it was penned and produced by fellow Magnet artist Peter Shelley.

346. 16 Mar ●●● BILLY, DON'T BE A HERO – Paper Lace Writers: Mitch Murray and Peter Callander. Nottingham's merry men found fame after winning on TV talent show Opportunity Knocks. Song was a US No.1 when covered by Bo Donaldson. Paper Lace's follow-up, 'The Night Chicago Died,' was a US chart-topper.

347. 6 Apr ●●●● SEASONS IN THE SUN – Terry Jacks Writers: Jacques Brel; English lyrics by Rod McKuen. Globally successful single was the first No.1 by a Canadian act since 1957. The 1961 French song (recorded in English by Kingston Trio in 1964) was returned to the top in 1999 by Westside.

348. 4 May ●● WATERLOO – Abba Writers: Björn Ulvaeus, Benny Andersson and Stig Anderson. Britain hosted 1974's Eurovision Song Contest, and the winning song launched the most successful Scandinavian act of all time. It was the only winner to reach the US Top 10.

349. 18 May ●●●● SUGAR BABY LOVE – Rubettes Writers: Wayne Bickerton and Tony Waddington. Barry Blue's ex-backing group had a long string of mid-70s European hits; their only No.1, and only US Top 40 entry, featured short-lived member Paul Da Vinci.

350. 15 Jun ● THE STREAK – Ray Stevens Writer: Ray Stevens. Funny man had his biggest worldwide hit with a novelty song about the short-lived "streaking" craze, one of at least 30 streaking singles released Stateside.

351. 22 Jun ● ALWAYS YOURS – Gary Glitter Writers: Mike Leander and Gary Glitter. The last of Glitter's three chart-toppers was penned, as were the others, by the singer and his producer Mike Leander.

352. 29 Jun ●●●● SHE – Charles Aznavour Writers: Charles Aznavour and Herbert Kretzmer. Theme from the TV series The Seven Faces of Woman took just two weeks to reach No.1, and made Aznavour the only French male solo singer to top the UK chart.

353. 27 Jul ●●● ROCK YOUR BABY – George McCrae Writers: Harry W Casey and Richard Finch. Classic dance record sold 10 million worldwide and helped to kickstart the 70s disco craze. George's wife Gwen was supposed to record the track but could not make the session.

354. 17 Aug ●● WHEN WILL I SEE YOU AGAIN – Three Degrees Writers: Kenny Gamble and Leon Huff. Only American female group to top the chart in the 1970s. In the US, it was also their biggest hit, peaking at No.2.

355. 31 Aug ●●● LOVE ME FOR A REASON – The Osmonds Writer: Johnny Bristol. R&B singer Bristol penned and originally recorded the song that gave the Osmonds their only No.1 and Boyzone their first hit 20 years later.

356. 21 Sep ●●● KUNG FU FIGHTING – Carl Douglas Writer: Karl Douglas. Recorded as a throwaway B-side at the end of a session, this track sold 10 million globally and also topped the US chart.

357. 12 Oct ● ANNIE'S SONG – John Denver Writer: John Denver. Despite scoring more than 30 US hits, this ode to his wife was Denver's only UK charter. Song returned to the Top 3 in 1978, played by his RCA label mate James Galway.

358. 19 Oct ● SAD SWEET DREAMER – Sweet Sensation Writer: D E S Parton. Winners on TV's New Faces were produced by the show's panelist Tony "Hatchet Man" Hatch. The R&B group fronted by 16-year-old Marcel King also took the single into the US Top 20.

359. 26 Oct ●●● EVERYTHING I OWN – Ken Boothe Writer: David Gates. Reggae revival of Bread's self-penned 1972 Top 40 entry. Boothe's recording does not mention the title – he sings "anything I own". Song returned to the top by Boy George in 1987.

360. 16 Nov ●●● GONNA MAKE YOU A STAR – David Essex Writer: David Essex. Successful singer / actor and pin-up's third Top 10 hit was his first No.1. Track features bassist Herbie Flowers who wrote earlier chart-topper 'Grandad'.

361. 7 Dec ●● YOU'RE THE FIRST, THE LAST, MY EVERYTHING – Barry White Writers: Barry White, Tony Sepe and Peter Radcliffe. The legendary luv song singer had his first and last No.1 with the first UK release on 20th Century Fox's label.

362. 21 Dec ●●●● LONELY THIS CHRISTMAS – Mud Writers: Nicky Chinn and Mike Chapman. Elvis-orientated Christmas tear-jerker also topped the Benelux charts and was one of the group's seven 1975 chart entries.

1975

363. 18 Jan ● DOWN DOWN – Status Quo Writers: Francis Rossi and Robert Young. Amazingly this headbanger's anthem was the only No.1 from an act with more chart entries than any other group.

364. 25 Jan ● MS GRACE – Tymes Writers: John Hall and Johanna Hall. They headed the US chart in 1963 with 'So Much In Love' but had their biggest UK hit with this record which stalled at No.91 in their homeland.

365. 1 Feb ●●● JANUARY – Pilot Writer: David Paton. First of two successive No.1s for producer Alan Parsons. The flavour-of-the-month Scottish group surprisingly failed to make the Top 30 again.

366. 22 Feb ●● MAKE ME SMILE (COME UP AND SEE ME) – Steve Harley and Cockney Rebel Writer: Steve Harley. For the only time, two successive singles jumped from nine to one. Among the backing vocalists on the act's only No.1 was future chart-topper Tina Charles.

367. 8 Mar ●● IF – Telly Savalas Writer: David Gates. Star of TV's top cop show Kojak gave Bread their second No.1 in five months as composers. One of the few artists to top the chart after his 50th birthday.

368. 22 Mar ●●●●●● BYE BYE BABY – Bay City Rollers Writers: Bob Gaudio and Bob Crewe. Tartan-clad teenybop idols' biggest UK hit was their sixth Top 10 single. It revived a song the Four Seasons had taken into the US Top 20 in 1965.

369. 3 May ●● OH BOY – Mud Writers: Sonny West, Norman Petty and Bill Tilghman. Only Chinn and Chapman-produced No.1 they did not compose, having been a Top 3 hit for The Crickets in 1957.

370. 17 May ●●● STAND BY YOUR MAN – Tammy Wynette Writers: Billy Sherrill and Tammy Wynette. Seven-year-old US hit became the first single by a female country singer to top the chart. Its UK success came two months after she divorced her third husband, singer George Jones.

371. 7 Jun ●●● WHISPERING GRASS – Windsor Davies and Don Estelle Writers: Fred and Doris Fisher. Stars of TV's It Ain't Half Hot Mum had this novelty topper with a carefully cloned revival of the 1940 Ink Spots favourite.

372. 28 Jun ●● I'M NOT IN LOVE – 10cc Writers: Graham Gouldman and Eric Stewart. Once described as the slowest No.1 hit by one of the decade's most regular chart visitors and is regarded by many as a pop masterpiece and has been voted Best Pop Single of All Time.

373. 12 Jul ● TEARS ON MY PILLOW – Johnny Nash Writer: Ernie Smith. American vocalist, who first recorded in 1957, had No.1 reggae hits in the UK and US ('I Can See Clearly Now'). Oddly his sole UK topper missed the US chart.

374. 19 Jul ●●● GIVE A LITTLE LOVE – Bay City Rollers Writers: Johnny Goodison and Phil Wainman. Rollermania was at its height when the Scottish superstars scored their second successive No.1.

375. 09 Aug ● BARBADOS – Typically Tropical Writers: Jeffrey Calvert and Max West. One-off novelty penned, produced and performed by two recording studio engineers. The song returned to the top when re-jigged by The Vengaboys as 'We're Going To Ibiza!' in 1999.

376. 16 Aug ●●● CAN'T GIVE YOU ANYTHING (BUT MY LOVE) – Stylistics Writers: Hugo Peretti, Luigi Creatore and George David Weiss. Biggest hit from the 1970s' most successful US group. Written by the team which penned the twice-topping 'Can't Help Falling In Love', a song Stylistics also hit with the following year.

384 – Slik

377. 6 Sep ●●●● SAILING – Rod Stewart Writer: Gavin Sutherland. Stewart saw his version of the Sutherland Brothers' singalong anthem as "one for the terraces". It returned to the Top 3 in 1976 after it was used in the BBC TV documentary Sailor.

378. 4 Oct ●●● HOLD ME CLOSE – David Essex Writer: David Essex. Second self-composed chart-topper for the teen idol voted Top Male Singer of 1974 in Record Mirror and Disc. Both No.1s were produced by Jeff "War of the Worlds" Wayne.

379. 25 Oct ●● I ONLY HAVE EYES FOR YOU – Art Garfunkel Writers: Harry Warren and Al Dubin. On the day Art's version of this 40-year-old standard topped the UK chart, his ex-partner Paul Simon's No.1 US LP, Still Crazy After All These Years, debuted Stateside.

380. 8 Nov ●● SPACE ODDITY – David Bowie Writer: David Bowie. Ivor Novello-award-winning song, originally penned for never-screened TV film, first reached the Top 5 in 1969, entered the US Top 20 in 1973 and topped the UK chart as a three-track maxi-single.

381. 22 Nov ● D.I.V.O.R.C.E. – Billy Connolly Writers: Billy Connolly, Claude Putnam Jr and Bobby Braddock. Folk singer turned top comedian's parody of country queen Tammy Wynette's tear-jerker proved far more successful than her original record.

382. 29 Nov ●●●●●●●●● BOHEMIAN RHAPSODY – Queen Writer: Freddie Mercury. This six-minute epic, produced by Roy Thomas Baker, was the most successful chart record recorded in the 1970s, the first single to spend nine weeks at the top since 1957 and the first to benefit substantially from video.

1976

383. 31 Jan ●● MAMMA MIA – Abba Writers: Stig Anderson, Björn Ulvaeus and Benny Andersson. The 400th different song to reach the top was the one that finally forced the UK chart door wide open for European acts.

384. 14 Feb ● FOREVER & EVER – Slik Writers: Bill Martin and Phil Coulter. Heavily hyped Scottish band's only major hit was written and produced by the team behind early Bay City Rollers' hits.

385. 21 Feb ●● **DECEMBER '63 (OH WHAT A NIGHT)** – Four Seasons Writers: Bob Gaudio and Judy Parker. Veteran group's sole UK topper (they had three US No.1s before December 1963) spent more than a year on the US chart.

386. 6 Mar ●●● **I LOVE TO LOVE (BUT MY BABY LOVES TO DANCE)** – Tina Charles Writers: Jack Robinson and James Bolden. Second No.1 for Asian-born producer Biddu (after 'Kung Fu Fighting') helped to make this session singer, who sang lead on 5000 Volt's first hit, the UK's leading disco diva of 1976.

387. 27 Mar ●●●●●● **SAVE YOUR KISSES FOR ME** – Brotherhood of Man Writers: Tony Hiller, Martin Lee and Lee Sheridan. The self-penned song broke the scoring record in the Eurovision Song Contest, outsold all Eurovision songs and was No.1 across Europe.

388. 8 May ●●●● **FERNANDO** – Abba Writers: Stig Anderson, Björn Ulvaeus and Benny Andersson. Anti-war song that had first been sung in Swedish on a solo album by group member Frida.

389. 5 Jun ● **NO CHARGE** – J J Barrie Writer: Harlan Howard. Singer / manager (Blue Mink) and ex-comedian joined one-hit wonders thanks to a cover of a US No.1 country hit by Melba Montgomery. It featured female vocals from Joe Brown's wife Vicky.

390. 12 Jun ●●● **COMBINE HARVESTER (BRAND NEW KEY)** – Wurzels Writer: Melanie Safka. Trio turned Melanie's 1972 Top 5 hit into a No.1. It was the second parody topper in seven months.

391. 26 Jun ●●● **YOU TO ME ARE EVERYTHING** – Real Thing Writers: Ken Gold and Micky Denne. First and biggest hit by the most successful British R&B group of the 1970s. In 1986, it became the first single to make the Top 10 in original and remixed forms.

392. 17 Jul ● **THE ROUSSOS PHENOMENON EP** – Demis Roussos Writers: 'Forever and Ever', 'So Dreamy', 'My Friend the Wind' – Stylianos Vlaviano and Robert Costandinos; 'Sing an Ode to Love' – Stylianos Vlaviano, Charalampe Chalkitis and Robert Costandinos. Egyptian-born ex-member of Aphrodite's Child was the first artist to top the chart with an official EP (playing time 14 mins, 44 sec). The tracks were recorded between 1973 and 1976.

393. 24 Jul ●●●●●● **DON'T GO BREAKING MY HEART** – Elton John and Kiki Dee Writers: Ann Orson and Carte Blanche (aka Elton John and Bernie Taupin). Elton finally hit the top with his 14th Top 20 single. He would have to wait another 14 years, and 14 Top 20s, before he achieved a solo No.1.

394. 4 Sep ●●●●●● **DANCING QUEEN** – Abba Writers: Stig Anderson, Benny Andersson and Björn Ulvaeus. Group's third successive chart-topper jumped from 16 to one. It was the quartet's only US No.1 and returned to the UK Top 20 in 1992.

395. 16 Oct ●●●● **MISSISSIPPI** – Pussycat Writer: Werner Theunissen. The septet, which included three sisters, became the first Dutch act to top the chart. It was also the first time one European act replaced another at No.1.

396. 13 Nov ●●● **IF YOU LEAVE ME NOW** – Chicago Writer: Peter Cetera. One of America's most consistently successful groups of the rock era had their first UK Top 5 entry (and only transatlantic topper) with their 11th US Top 10 single.

397. 4 Dec ●●● **UNDER THE MOON OF LOVE** – Showaddywaddy Writers: Tommy Boyce and Curtis Lee. Ex-Springfields member Mike Hurst produced the group's revival of an overlooked 1961 release by Curtis Lee, which gave the chart regulars their only No.1.

398. 25 Dec ●●● **WHEN A CHILD IS BORN (SOLEADO)** – Johnny Mathis Writers: Fred Jay and Di Damicco Ciro. Eighteen years after his first seasonal hit, 'Winter Wonderland', Mathis scored his only No.1 with a Christmas song that had been a European success earlier for German Michael Holm.

1977

399. 15 Jan ●●●● **DON'T GIVE UP ON US** – David Soul Writer: Tony Macaulay. US TV actor, best known as Hutch in Starsky and Hutch, had the year's biggest UK seller and a US No.1 (four months later) with British produced and written song.

400. 12 Feb ● **DON'T CRY FOR ME ARGENTINA** – Julie Covington Writers: Tim Rice and Andrew Lloyd Webber. With sales of just under a million, it was the biggest-selling single by a female at the time. She originally recorded it as 'It's Only Your Lover Returning' before composers / producers amended the title and re-did the vocal.

401. 19 Feb ●●● **WHEN I NEED YOU** – Leo Sayer Writers: Albert Hammond and Carole Bayer Sager. Anglo-American composition was the UK singer's first topper (after three No.2 hits) and his second successive US No.1. It was the first of two UK toppers in a row for producer Richard Perry.

402. 12 Mar ●●● **CHANSON D'AMOUR** – Manhattan Transfer Writer: Wayne Shanklin. Despite failing to chart in the US, this revival of Art and Dotty Todd's 1958 American Top 20 hit gave the multi-Grammy-winning US group their only UK Top 10 entry.

403. 2 Apr ●●●●● **KNOWING ME KNOWING YOU** – Abba Writers: Stig Anderson, Benny Andersson and Björn Ulvaeus. If 'Money Money Money' had reached No.1 this would have been Abba's fourth of seven consecutive toppers. However, it was first of their second trio of successive No.1s.

404. 7 May ●● **FREE** – Deniece Williams Writers: Denise Williams, Hank Redd, Nathan Watts and Susaye Green. Stevie Wonder discovered the singer who topped the UK chart with the first of four Top 10 entries. Earth, Wind and Fire's Maurice White produced it.

405. 21 May ●●●● **I DON'T WANT TO TALK ABOUT IT / FIRST CUT IS THE DEEPEST** – Rod Stewart Writers: Danny Whitten / Cat Stevens. Top side was originally recorded as an album track by Neil Young's group Crazy Horse; sadly, group member / composer Whitten died of a drug overdose before Rod charted with it.

406. 18 Jun ● **LUCILLE** – Kenny Rogers Writers: Roger Bowling and Hal Bynum. Grammy-winning single was the first of his 16 US country No.1 hits for the only country singer to score two UK chart-toppers.

407. 25 Jun ● SHOW YOU THE WAY TO GO – Jacksons Writers: Kenny Gamble and Leon Huff. Only UK No.1 from one of the 1970s' biggest groups came after their Motown days and was written and produced by Motown's main rivals Gamble and Huff.

408. 2 Jul ●●● SO YOU WIN AGAIN – Hot Chocolate Writer: Russ Ballard. Only British act to chart every year of the 1970s had their sole No.1 with one of their few hits not composed by leader Errol Brown.

409. 23 Jul ●●●● I FEEL LOVE – Donna Summer Writers: Giorgio Moroder, Pete Bellotte and Donna Summer. On the day Elvis Presley died, disco diva Summer was enjoying her only No.1 and producer / composer Moroder his second (see 310). A remix returned it to the Top 10 in 1995.

410. 20 Aug ● ANGELO – Brotherhood of Man Writers: Tony Hiller, Martin Lee and Lee Sheridan. This sad saga about poor boy and rich girl dying together in Mexico made the foursome the first UK contest winners to top the chart after Eurovision success.

411. 27 Aug ● FLOAT ON – Floaters Writers: Arnold Ingram, James Mitchell Jr and Marvin Willis. Only No.1 where group members talk about their birth signs gave the Detroit act an entry into One-Hit Wonders Hall of Fame.

412. 3 Sep ●●●●● WAY DOWN – Elvis Presley Writer: Layng Martine Jr. After a slow start, the single rocketed from 42 to four a week after his death. It was the 17th and last No.1 for the most successful artist in chart history.

413. 8 Oct ●●● SILVER LADY – David Soul Writers: Tony Macaulay and Geoff Stephens. Soul was the first singing TV cop to cop two chart-toppers.

414. 29 Oct ● YES SIR I CAN BOOGIE – Baccara Writers: Frank Dostal and Rolf Soja. The first Spanish act and the first female duo ever to reach No.1, stopping the French female duo La Belle Epoque from taking that second record.

415. 5 Nov ●●●● THE NAME OF THE GAME – Abba Writers: Stig Anderson, Benny Andersson and Björn Ulvaeus. On the 25th anniversary of the first chart, one of the most successful acts returned for their sixth No.1. The Beatles and Stones were the only groups with more.

416. 3 Dec ●●●●●●●● MULL OF KINTYRE / GIRLS' SCHOOL – Wings Writers: Paul McCartney and Denny Laine. Outside the Beatles, Paul's first No.1 was the UK's first two million-selling single. In the US, Mull Of Kintyre was considered worthy only of B-side status.

1978

417. 4 Feb ● UPTOWN TOP RANKING – Althia And Donna Writers: Althia Forest, Donna Reid and Errol Thompson. Youngest female duo to reach No.1 did so with a rewrite of the reggae track 'Three Piece Suit' by Trinity. Few non-West Indians understood the lyric, but that did not stop its top of chart ranking.

418. 11 Feb ● FIGARO – Brotherhood of Man Writers: Tony Hiller, Martin Lee and Lee Sheridan. Last of the quartet's trio of toppers told the tale of a foreigner with a six-letter name ending in 'o' – as had their previous No.1 'Angelo'.

419. 18 Feb ●●● TAKE A CHANCE ON ME – Abba Writers: Benny Andersson and Björn Ulvaeus. Group's sixth No.1 in 26 months was only their second single to crack the US Top 3.

420. 11 Mar ●●●● WUTHERING HEIGHTS – Kate Bush Writer: Kate Bush. Unmistakable teenage singer / songwriter reached chart heights with her debut single, inspired by the classic novel by Emily Brontë, with whom Kate Bush shares her birthday.

421. 8 Apr ●●● MATCHSTALK MEN AND MATCHSTALK CATS AND DOGS – Brian and Michael Writer: Michael Coleman. Song inspired by painter L S Lowry gave the duo a No.1 with their only hit. Backed by St Winifred's School Choir, who had their own chart-topper in 1980.

422. 29 Apr ●● NIGHT FEVER – Bee Gees Writers: Barry, Robin and Maurice Gibb. One of many successful songs written, sung and produced by the brothers for the Saturday Night Fever soundtrack which sold a record-breaking 30 million copies worldwide.

423. 13 May ●●●●● RIVERS OF BABYLON / BROWN GIRL IN THE RING – Boney M Writers: Traditional, arranged by Frank Farian and Hans-Georg Mayer. Both sides made independent trips into the Top 3, and in total this record scored 40 chart weeks, becoming only the second single to sell two million in the UK.

424. 17 Jun ●●●●●●●●● YOU'RE THE ONE THAT I WANT – John Travolta and Olivia Newton-John Writer: John Farrar. Written and produced by ex-Shadow Farrar, this million-seller was featured in the enduringly popular movie Grease. It returned to the Top 5 in 1990 (in megamix) and 1998.

425. 19 Aug ●●●●● THREE TIMES A LADY – Commodores Writer: Lionel Richie Jr. Group's Richie was inspired to write this song by a speech his father made about his mother on their wedding anniversary. Its 975,000 sales made it Motown's biggest UK seller.

426. 23 Sep ● DREADLOCK HOLIDAY – 10cc Writers: Eric Stewart and Graham Gouldman. The last of the group's 11 Top 10 entries was based on the holiday experiences of a close friend, Moody Blues member Justin Hayward.

424 – John Travolta and Olivia Newton-John

439 – Tubeway Army

Photo: Pictorial Press

427. 30 Sep ●●●●●●● **SUMMER NIGHTS** – John Travolta and Olivia Newton-John Writers: Warren Casey and Jim Jacobs. This duo released only two singles. Both sold a million in the UK and together they spent 16 weeks at the top. Like its predecessor it came from Grease.

428. 18 Nov ●● **RAT TRAP** – Boomtown Rats Writer: Bob Geldof. First new wave No.1 came from the Irish group that introduced Bob Geldof to the world. Producer Robert John "Mutt" Lange's later hits included many by his wife, Shania Twain.

429. 2 Dec ● **DA YA THINK I'M SEXY** – Rod Stewart Writers: Rod Stewart and Carmen Appice. Rock idol gave his songwriter's royalty to Unicef for disco-directed track which topped charts in 11 countries. The 12" version was reportedly the first 48-track disco mix.

430. 9 Dec ●●●● **MARY'S BOY CHILD – OH MY LORD** – Boney M Writers: Jester Harrison, Frank Farian and Fred Jay. First Christmas song to top the chart twice. Like the 1957 Harry Belafonte hit it sold more than a million in UK, and was their second million-seller of 1978.

1979

431. 6 Jan ●●● **YMCA** – Village People Writers: Jacques Morali, Henri Belodo and Victor Willis. The first gay supergroup was created by Frenchman Jacques Morali and named after the men of Greenwich Village in New York. 'YMCA' shifted 150,000 copies in one day in the UK alone over Christmas.

432. 27 Jan ● **HIT ME WITH YOUR RHYTHM STICK** – Ian Dury and the Blockheads Writers: Ian Dury and Chas Jankel. Produced by co-writer and group member Jankel, this disco-slanted new wave track sold almost a million in the UK and charted three times.

433. 3 Feb ●●●● **HEART OF GLASS** – Blondie Writers: Chris Stein and Deborah Harry. First of three transatlantic No.1s by new wave's foremost female, Debbie Harry, and her group. Producer Mike Chapman had scored previous No.1s with Suzi Quatro and Mud.

434. 3 Mar ●● **TRAGEDY** – Bee Gees Writers: Barry, Maurice and Robin Gibb. Their fifth successive US chart-topper was the last UK No.1 for eight years by the world's biggest-selling group of the late 70s.

435. 17 Mar ●●●● **I WILL SURVIVE** – Gloria Gaynor Writers: Dino Fekaris and Freddie Perren. Timeless disco anthem that started life as a B-side (to 'Substitute') simultaneously topped the UK and US chart and, when remixed, returned to the Top 5 in 1993.

436. 14 Apr ●●●●●● **BRIGHT EYES** – Art Garfunkel Writer: Mike Batt. Art's second solo hit followed its predecessor to No.1. The theme from the animated film Watership Down was a Stateside stiff but sold a million in the UK.

437. 26 May ●●● **SUNDAY GIRL** – Blondie Writer: Chris Stein. No act spent longer at the top, nor in the Top 75, in 1979 than Blondie and no single that year topped the chart faster (two weeks) than this one.

438. 16 Jun ●● **RING MY BELL** – Anita Ward Writer: Frederick Knight. Classic disco single briefly turned Memphis-born schoolteacher into worldwide hit-maker. Composer / producer Knight played all the instruments on the track.

439. 30 Jun ●●●● **ARE 'FRIENDS' ELECTRIC?** – Tubeway Army Writer: Gary Numan. Hit that launched Numan's career combined two songs: a ballad with spoken lyrics and a basic melody riff. Their speedily recorded album Replicas stood simultaneously at No.1.

440. 28 Jul ●●●● **I DON'T LIKE MONDAYS** – Boomtown Rats Writer: Bob Geldof. Controversial single, about San Diego schoolgirl Brenda Spencer who shot and killed 11 children, jumped from 15 to one. It was banned by many US stations.

441. 25 Aug ●●●● **WE DON'T TALK ANYMORE** – Cliff Richard Writer: Alan Tarney. Cliff's only No.1 of the 1970s was also one of only three of his singles to crack the US Top 10. Norrie Paramor, who produced all his earlier No.1s, died as this record headed the chart.

442. 22 Sep ● **CARS** – Gary Numan Writer: Gary Numan. Tubeway Army's leader quickly returned to No.1, and repeated the feat of simultaneously topping single and album chart (The Pleasure Principle). Remixed versions motored up the chart in 1987, 1993 and 1996.

443. 29 Sep ●●● **MESSAGE IN A BOTTLE** – Police Writer: Sting. Seventeen years after its formation, Herb Alpert's A&M label notched up its first No.1 with first of five chart-toppers by Anglo-American trio.

444. 20 Oct ● **VIDEO KILLED THE RADIO STAR** – Buggles Writers: Bruce Woolley, Trevor Horn and Geoff Downes. Track that later launched MTV also launched the chart career of award-winning producer Trevor Horn (previously in the band of No.1 hitmaker Tina Charles).

445. 27 Oct ●●● **ONE DAY AT A TIME** – Lena Martell Writer: Kris Kristofferson. Gospel song, which had been adopted as theme by US Alcoholics Anonymous, gave the singer her only hit after 18 years of recording. It had been a 1974 US country hit for Marilyn Sellars.

446. 17 Nov ●●● WHEN YOU'RE IN LOVE WITH A BEAUTIFUL WOMAN – Dr Hook Writer: Even Stevens. Regular chart entrants, who had already clocked up two No.2s, closed the decade with their sole chart-topper. Group's Dennis Locorriere is one of three eye-patch-wearing vocalists to reach No.1.

447. 8 Dec ● WALKING ON THE MOON – Police Writer: Sting. Second successive No.1 from their chart-topping Reggatta de Blanc album (the first of their five No.1 albums in a row). Last of seven chart-topping songs to mention the moon.

448. 15 Dec ●●●●● ANOTHER BRICK IN THE WALL (PT.2) – Pink Floyd Writer: Roger Waters. Only hit single of the 70s by one of the decade's top album acts. Anthemic children's chorus cry of "we don't need no education" helped to take it to the top around the globe.

1980

449. 19 Jan ●● BRASS IN POCKET – The Pretenders Writers: Chrissie Hynde and James Honeyman-Scott. This single was nearly frozen out during the Christmas period but eventually climbed to the top of the tree after a lengthy 10 weeks on the chart.

450. 2 Feb ●● THE SPECIAL AKA LIVE EP Writers: Jerry Dammers, Lloyd Chalmers, Dimitri Tiomkin, Paul Francis Webster; Sydney Roy Crooks, Jackie Robinson, George Agard; Harry Johnson; Morty Naismith and Roy Ellis. The Specials used their earlier name on this collection which included four revivals of 60s reggae / ska songs.

451. 16 Feb ●● COWARD OF THE COUNTY – Kenny Rogers Writers: Roger Bowling and B E Wheeler. In 1981 Rogers starred in a TV movie based on the lyrics of this hit which made him the only country artist to have two UK No.1s.

452. 1 Mar ●● ATOMIC – Blondie Writers: Chris Stein and Debbie Harry. The third track to be lifted from the Eat to the Beat album, 'Atomic' entered the chart at No.3 and was their third No.1.

453. 15 Mar ● TOGETHER WE ARE BEAUTIFUL – Fern Kinney Writer: Ken Leray. Originally released by its British composer in 1977 without success, this US cover rewarded him with a No.1 and Fern with the coveted title of the first one-hit wonder of the 80s.

454. 22 Mar ●●● GOING UNDERGROUND / DREAMS OF CHILDREN – The Jam Writer: Paul Weller. The Jam's 10th single finally produced their first No.1, the first single to debut at the top since 1973 and the first double A-side to do so.

455. 12 Apr ●● WORKING MY WAY BACK TO YOU – FORGIVE ME GIRL – Detroit Spinners Writer: Sandy Linzer, Denny Randell and Michael Zager. The Spinners were called the Motown Spinners and then the Detroit Spinners in Britain to avoid confusion with the folk singers of the same name.

456. 26 Apr ● CALL ME – Blondie Writer: Giorgio Moroder and Debbie Harry. The best-selling single of 1980 in the US, thanks in part to the production talents of Giorgio Moroder and the song's inclusion in the controversial movie American Gigolo.

457. 3 May ●● GENO – Dexy's Midnight Runners Writers: Kevin Rowland and Al Archer. Kevin Rowland's maverick Midnight Runners'

first smash hit was written about one of his heroes, American artist Geno Washington, who in the mid 1960s led the Ram Jam Band, a UK soul outfit. Geno never made the Top 30 in his own right.

458. 17 May ●● WHAT'S ANOTHER YEAR – Johnny Logan Writer: Shay Healy. This Irish entry in the 25th Eurovision Song Contest was sung by the Australian Logan who was soon granted Irish citizenship. He became the first act to win the contest twice when 'Hold Me Now' went all the way in 1987.

459. 31 May ●●● THEME FROM M*A*S*H (SUICIDE IS PAINLESS) – Mash Writers: Mike Altman and Johnny Mandel. Title track from the film and long-running TV series about a mobile army surgical hospital. This song hit the top a decade after it was recorded and was co-written by the son of the film's director, Robert Altman.

460. 21 Jun ●●● CRYING – Don McLean Writers: Roy Orbison and Joe Melson. After being initially rejected by the record company, it was the rapturous reception the track received on an Israeli TV appearance which led to its eventual release.

461. 12 Jul ●● XANADU – Olivia Newton-John and Electric Light Orchestra. Writer: Jeff Lynne. "The most dreadful, tasteless movie of the decade. Indeed probably of all time," Felix Barker wrote of the Gene Kelly / Olivia Newton-John film of the same name. It gave ELO their only No.1 from 27 Top 40 hits.

462. 26 Jul ●● USE IT UP AND WEAR IT OUT – Odyssey Writers: Sandy Linzer and L Russell Brown. The third American record this year to reach the pop peak in Britain without even penetrating the Top 100 at home (after Fern Kinney and Mash).

463. 9 Aug ●● THE WINNER TAKES IT ALL – Abba Writers: Benny Anderson and Björn Ulvaeus. By the time the group recorded the album 'Super Trouper', from which this track was taken, both romantic partnerships within Abba had come to an end, but this had little effect on their well-oiled hit making machine.

464. 23 Aug ●● ASHES TO ASHES – David Bowie Writer: David Bowie. Eleven years after he was left floating in his tin can in 'Space Oddity' (a UK 1975 No.1), Major Tom returned as "a junkie … hitting an all time low".

465. 6 Sep ● START – The Jam Writer: Paul Weller. This was their ninth hit of the year – more than any other act in 1980 – thanks mainly to a slew of re-issues charting briefly in April.

466. 13 Sep ●● FEELS LIKE I'M IN LOVE – Kelly Marie Writer: Ray Dorset. Dorset was the former lead singer of Mungo Jerry and he originally wrote this hit for his hero Elvis who died before he had a chance to hear it.

467. 27 Sep ●●●● DON'T STAND SO CLOSE TO ME – Police Writer: Sting. The best-selling single of 1980 in the UK, about the attraction between a teacher and his pupil, was the act's third No.1. They were the eighth act to achieve the hat-trick.

468. 25 Oct ●●● WOMAN IN LOVE – Barbra Streisand Writers: Barry and Robin Gibb. Streisand's biggest international hit and only UK No.1 was the first of many hits written by Bee Gees but taken to the top by another artist.

469. 15 Nov ●● THE TIDE IS HIGH – Blondie Writer: John Holt. Blondie reunited with Mike Chapman, the producer of their first three No.1s, for their fifth No.1 – their last for 18 years.

470. 29 Nov ●●● SUPER TROUPER – Abba Writer: Benny Andersson and Björn Ulvaeus. This single, Abba's final chart- topper took their No.1s tally to nine, putting them ahead of the Rolling Stones. No overseas group has beaten the Superswedes' total.

471. 20 Dec ● (JUST LIKE) STARTING OVER – John Lennon Writer: John Lennon. Having previously peaked at No.8, the tragic news of Lennon's murder catapulted this single to No.1 from outside the Top 20 – a leap last achieved by 'Hey Jude' in 1968.

472. 27 Dec ●● THERE'S NO ONE QUITE LIKE GRANDMA – St Winifred's School Choir Writer: Gordon Lorenz. Featured eight-year old lead vocalist Dawn Ralph in the first choir to top the chart. They had previously sung backing vocals on the Brian and Michael No.1 hit 'Matchstalk Men and Matchstalk Cats and Dogs'.

1981

473. 10 Jan ●●●● IMAGINE – John Lennon Writer: John Lennon. Following his murder on 8 Dec, a month later there were three Lennon songs in the Top 5. Winner of BBC's Top Lyric of the Century, this Phil Spector-produced masterpiece was recorded 10 years previously and went to No.6 when originally released in 1975.

474. 7 Feb ●● WOMAN – John Lennon Writer: John Lennon. With this single Lennon equalled a record set by the Beatles when he knocked himself off the top of the charts and completed a hat-trick of No.1s in a record seven weeks.

475. 21 Feb ●●● SHADDAP YOU FACE – Joe Dolce Music Theatre Writer: Joe Dolce. Recorded in character as "Giuseppi", Dolce himself had to shaddap when all his follow-up singles failed to chart. This track famously prevented 'Vienna' by Ultravox from reaching No.1.

476. 14 Mar ●● JEALOUS GUY – Roxy Music Writer: John Lennon. The only words printed on the sleeve of this single were the title, the artist and the phrase "a tribute".

477. 28 Mar ●●●● THIS OLE HOUSE – Shakin' Stevens Writer: Stuart Hamblen. Stevens first heard this classic performed by NRBQ, a US band. A new arrangement and his interpretation gave him his first No.1.

478. 18 Apr ●●● MAKING YOUR MIND UP – Bucks Fizz Writers: Andy Hill and John Danter. The fourth British Eurovision winner (after Sandie Shaw, Brotherhood of Man and Lulu) was a massive hit across Europe.

479. 9 May ●●●●● STAND AND DELIVER – Adam and the Ants Writers: Adam Ant and Marco Pirroni. The act's first No.1 came in a year in which their records racked up a massive total of 91 weeks on the chart.

480. 13 Jun ●● BEING WITH YOU – Smokey Robinson Writer: William "Smokey" Robinson. The success of this single prompted Motown to celebrate Smokey's 25th anniversary in showbiz and gave him his biggest solo hit on either side of the Atlantic.

481. 27 Jun ●● ONE DAY IN YOUR LIFE – Michael Jackson Writers: Sam Brown III and Renee Armand. First released five years previously, this track gave the label its second chart-topper in a row – the only instance of two consecutive Motown No.1s.

482. 11 July ●●● GHOST TOWN – Specials Writer: Jerry Dammers. Even before 'Ghost Town' had made it to the top, Neville Staples, Terry Hall and Lynval Golding had announced their departure to form Fun Boy Three. The Specials reverted to their original name, the Special AKA.

483. 1 Aug ●●●● GREEN DOOR – Shakin' Stevens Writers: Bob Davie and Marvin Moore. Nick Lowe, whom Stuart Coleman met in a pub during recording, flippantly suggested this track. Stevens thought they'd had one too many, but tried it and it became his second No.1.

484. 29 Aug ● JAPANESE BOY – Aneka Writer: Bobby Heatlie. This oriental hit was actually by the Scottish folk singer Mary Sandeman who donned a kimono and a wig and leafed through the phone book to find a name.

485. 5 Sep ●● TAINTED LOVE – Soft Cell Writer: Ed Cobb. Reworking of a northern soul classic by Gloria Jones composed by a member of 50s hitmakers The Four Preps.

486. 19 Sep ●●●● PRINCE CHARMING – Adam and the Ants Writers: Marco Pirroni and Adam Ant. The videos for all the group's hits were based on storyboards by former art student Adam.

487. 17 Oct ●●●● IT'S MY PARTY – Dave Stewart with Barbara Gaskin Writers: Herb Weiner, Wally Gold, John Gluck Jr. A US No.1 for Lesley Gore in 1963. Gaskin and Stewart (not the Eurythmics one) were formerly in Hatfield and the North.

488. 14 Nov ● EVERY LITTLE THING SHE DOES IS MAGIC – Police Writer: Sting. After 'Invisible Sun' was prevented from being shown on British TV due to footage of riots in Northern Ireland in the video, this single was rush-released and entered the charts just four weeks later.

501 – Madness

Photo: Pictorial Press

489. 21 Nov ●● UNDER PRESSURE – Queen and David Bowie Writers: Queen and David Bowie. The second occasion on which two makers of No.1 hits came together to record another No.1. The previous pair was Frank and Nancy Sinatra.

490. 5 Dec ● BEGIN THE BEGUINE (VOLVER A EMPEZAR) – Julio Iglesias Writer: Cole Porter; Spanish lyrics by Julio Iglesias. The first Spaniard to reach the top; the former Real Madrid goalkeeper was described by CBS as the "top-selling male singer in the world".

491. 12 Dec ●●●●● DON'T YOU WANT ME – Human League Writers: Jo Callis, Phil Oakey and Philip Adrian Wright. In a poor year for singles sales, this was its only million-seller. Seven months later it topped the US charts and started the second British Invasion.

1982

492. 16 Jan ●● LAND OF MAKE BELIEVE – Bucks Fizz Writers: Andy Hill and Peter Sinfield. The act's second No.1 ended with a poem read by 11-year-old Abby Kimber, a member of the Mini-Pops children's group.

493. 30 Jan ● OH JULIE – Shakin' Stevens Writer: Shakin' Stevens. Stevens' third No.1 within a year was his first recording with a Cajun flavour. This first self-penned hit was successfully covered in the US by Barry Manilow, among many others.

494. 6 Feb ● THE MODEL / COMPUTER LOVE – Kraftwerk Writers: Ralf Hutter, Karl Bartos and Emil Schulz. This massively influential act was the first German group to top the charts. The single had peaked at 36 seven months earlier.

495. 13 Feb ●●● A TOWN CALLED MALICE / PRECIOUS – The Jam Writer: Paul Weller. EMI objected to the single being available on a studio-recorded 7" and a live 12", feeling that fans were buying both versions and preventing the Stranglers' 'Golden Brown' (on EMI) from reaching No.1.

496. 6 Mar ●●● THE LION SLEEPS TONIGHT – Tight Fit Writers: Hugo Peretti, Luigi Creatore, George David Weiss, Solomon Linda, Paul Campbell. Based on the Zulu folk tune 'Wimoweh', this song had been a hit for The Tokens.

497. 27 Mar ●●● SEVEN TEARS – The Goombay Dance Band Writers: Wolff-Ekkehardt, Stein and Wolfgang Jass. The second German-based act to hit No.1 in the UK after Kraftwerk a few weeks previously, they were the only group to include a fire-eater to reach No.1.

498. 17 Apr ● MY CAMERA NEVER LIES – Bucks Fizz Writers: Andy Hill and Nicola Martin. Eurovision-winning quartet became the first British group to achieve three No.1s in a year since Slade in 1973.

499. 24 Apr ●●● EBONY AND IVORY – Paul McCartney with Stevie Wonder Writer: Paul McCartney. At this stage neither artist had had a solo No.1; this call for racial harmony, recorded in Montserrat, held the No.1 spot in the US for seven weeks.

500. 15 May ●● A LITTLE PEACE – Nicole Writers: Ralph Siegel and Bernd Meinunger. For the third consecutive year the winner of the Eurovision Song Contest also won a place at the top of the British charts. The third German No.1 of the year.

501. 29 May ●● HOUSE OF FUN – Madness Writers: Mike Barson and Lee Thompson. This celebration of a young man's introduction into the wicked adult world was the north London ska band's only No.1.

502. 12 Jun ●● GOODY TWO SHOES – Adam Ant Writers: Adam Ant and Marco Pirroni. The third No.1 to feature the vocals of Stuart Goddard, aka Adam Ant, was the only one of the three to be credited to him alone.

503. 26 Jun ● I'VE NEVER BEEN TO ME – Charlene Writers: Ron Miller and Ken Hirsch. A minor US hit five years earlier, Charlene Duncan is the only white act on Motown to reach No.1.

504. 3 Jul ●● HAPPY TALK – Captain Sensible Writers: Richard Rodgers and Oscar Hammerstein II. This ex-Damned member gave Rodgers and Hammerstein their fifth No.1 and made the biggest ever jump to No.1 – from No.33.

505. 17 Jul ●●● FAME – Irene Cara Writers: Michael Gore and Dean Pitchford. Irene broke into the limelight as Coco Hernandez in the film Fame, but it wasn't until the TV series became a hit in the UK that the theme song followed suit.

506. 7 Aug ●●●● COME ON EILEEN – Dexys Midnight Runners and the Emerald Express Writers: Kevin Rowland, Jimmy Patterson and Kevin Adams. Rowland teamed up with a group of fiddlers for this million-selling, transatlantic chart-topping Celtic soul masterpiece.

507. 4 Sep ●●●● EYE OF THE TIGER – Survivor Writers: Frankie Sullivan and Jim Peterik. Sly Stallone himself commissioned Chicago band Survivor to write the theme for the third instalment in the Rocky series, hence ensuring their, erm, survival.

508. 2 Oct ●●● PASS THE DUTCHIE – Musical Youth Writers: Jackie Mittoo, Fitzroy Simpson and Lloyd Ferguson. This contagious reggae track originally referred to a "kutchie" but was tactfully changed to "dutchie" – a Jamaican cooking pot. Kutchie is a different type of pot altogether.

509. 23 Oct ●●● DO YOU REALLY WANT TO HURT ME – Culture Club Writers: Culture Club. First noticed by ex-Pistols manager Malcolm McLaren and were originally called In Praise of Lemmings, then Sex Gang Children. They won the Best New Act Grammy in 1983.

510. 13 Nov ●●● I DON'T WANT TO DANCE – Eddy Grant Writer: Eddy Grant. This one-man pop machine was based in Barbados where he wrote and produced material for his own label. The third consecutive reggae-oriented No.1.

511. 4 Dec ●● BEAT SURRENDER – The Jam Writer: Paul Weller. The Jam's final single before disbanding was their third to enter at No.1. The trio truly quit at the top and, as this exited the chart, 13 of their previous hits re-entered.

512. 18 Dec ●●●● SAVE YOUR LOVE – Renée and Renato Writers: John and Sue Edward. Hilary Lester, "Renée" on the record, left before the single became a success to be replaced by Val Penny who was drafted in to mime her way through the video in a wig.

1983

513. 15 Jan ●● YOU CAN'T HURRY LOVE – Phil Collins Writers: Brian Holland, Lamont Dozier, Eddie Holland. The first of Collins's two No.1s, both of which were covers, was a version of a Supremes hit and was only the third No.1 for the legendary Motown writing team.

514. 29 Jan ●●● DOWN UNDER – Men At Work Writers: Colin Hay and Ron Strykert. Track about Aussie expats was the first Australian No.1 since Rolf Harris in 1969 and the first No.1 to name-check Vegemite.

515. 19 Feb ●● TOO SHY – Kajagoogoo Writers: Kajagoogoo, lyrics by Limahl and Nick Beggs. Leader Chris Hamill called himself Limahl – an anagram of his surname. The track was produced by Duran Duran's Nick Rhodes before his own band had hit the top.

516. 5 Mar ● BILLIE JEAN – Michael Jackson Writer: Michael Jackson. Another immaculate Quincy Jones production job, 'Billie Jean' was the track that kicked Thriller into the stratosphere. The LP is the biggest seller of all time (45 million-plus copies) but the six singles it produced managed only this one week at pole position between them.

517. 12 Mar ●● TOTAL ECLIPSE OF THE HEART – Bonnie Tyler Writer: Jim Steinman. Gave Meat Loaf mastermind Jim Steinman his first No.1. The only single by a British female to top both the UK and US charts.

518. 26 Mar ●● IS THERE SOMETHING I SHOULD KNOW – Duran Duran Writers: Duran Duran. The band's name was inspired by the villain in Jane Fonda's 1968 movie Barbarella (also the name of a Birmingham club where they gigged). Features the classic lyric "You're about as easy as a nuclear war".

519. 9 Apr ●●● LET'S DANCE – David Bowie Writer: David Bowie. Bowie's 34th UK hit became the only one of his three solo No.1s to duplicate the feat in the US and gave Chic's Nile Rodgers his first No.1 production credit.

520. 30 Apr ●●●● TRUE – Spandau Ballet Writer: Gary Kemp. No.1 the week Top of the Pops celebrated its 1,000th edition, this classic smoocher – the band's only UK chart-topper – became a US No.1 in 1991 when sampled by PM Dawn.

521. 28 May ● CANDY GIRL – New Edition Writers: Maurice Starr and Michael Jonzun. The act's first record and only No.1. The constituent parts (Bobby Brown, Bell Biv Devoe and Ralph Tresvant) went on to have success as individuals.

522. 4 Jun ●●●● EVERY BREATH YOU TAKE – The Police Writer: Sting. Their fifth and final UK No.1, which made Sting the first person to compose five No.1 singles single-handedly.

523. 2 Jul ●●● BABY JANE – Rod Stewart Writers: Rod Stewart and Jay Davis. Four and a half years since 'Da Ya Think I'm Sexy?', the gravel-voiced charmer scored his sixth chart-topper. No UK male has had more solo No.1s.

524. 23 Jul ●●● WHEREVER I LAY MY HAT (THAT'S MY HOME) – Paul Young Writers: Marvin Gaye, Norman Whitfield and Barrett Strong. The Luton lad rose to fame with this cover of the B-side to Marvin Gaye's 'Too Busy Thinkin' 'Bout My Baby', giving Marvin his only UK No.1 composer credit in his lifetime.

525. 13 Aug ●●● GIVE IT UP – KC and the Sunshine Band Writers: Harry Casey and Debra Carter. This single was released while Harry "KC" Casey was recuperating from a serious car crash. The act finally hit the jackpot in the UK nine years after their chart debut.

526. 3 Sep ●●● RED RED WINE – UB40 Writer: Neil Diamond. This was Neil Diamond's first British No.1 as a writer since the Monkees' 'I'm a Believer' 16 years previously, and the first No.1 for the act who had more hits in the 80s than any other group.

527. 24 Sep ●●●●●● KARMA CHAMELEON – Culture Club Writers: Culture Club. Worldwide superstars by this stage, this was their only UK million-seller. Questions were asked about the originality of this Brit award-winning song as some thought it similar to the 1960 Jimmy Jones hit 'Handy Man'.

528. 5 Nov ●●●●● UPTOWN GIRL – Billy Joel Writer: Billy Joel. Joel recorded this as a tribute to the Four Seasons and dedicated it to Christie Brinkley, who appeared in the video and later married him. She then headed downtown when they split in 1994.

529. 10 Dec ●●●●● ONLY YOU – Flying Pickets Writer: Vince Clarke. The first a cappella chart topper, this Christmas No.1 was a revival of the not very old Yazoo No.2.

1984

530. 14 Jan ●● PIPES OF PEACE – Paul McCartney Writer: Paul McCartney. The third Beatle to reach the top solo, this was McCartney's 25th as a writer. This made him the first performer to hit the top spot as a soloist, as part of a duo (with Stevie Wonder), as part of a trio (with Wings), as part of a quartet (the Beatles), and as part of a quintet (the Beatles with Billy Preston).

531. 28 Jan ●●●●● RELAX – Frankie Goes To Hollywood Writers: Peter Gill, Holly Johnson and Mark O'Toole. This slow burner rose to infamy when Radio 1's breakfast DJ Mike Read refused to play the track which led to an all-out BBC primetime and daytime ban, guaranteeing its cult status. Spent more weeks on the UK chart than any other No.1.

532. 3 Mar ●●● 99 RED BALLOONS – Nena Writers: Joern-Uwe Fahrenkrog-Peterson and Carlo Karges; English lyrics by Kevin McAlea. The group's anti-nuclear pop song provided the only instance of a single by the same act reaching the US and UK Top 3 in different languages – the Americans got the original '99 Luftballoons'.

533. 24 Mar ●●●●●● HELLO – Lionel Richie Writer: Lionel Richie. With this release, taken from the year's top-selling album, 'Can't Slow Down', Lionel Brockman Richie Jr became the first American to have transatlantic No.1s both as a soloist and (in the Commodores) as part of a group.

534. 5 May ●●●● THE REFLEX – Duran Duran Writers: Duran Duran. The decision to draft in Chic's production genius Nile Rodgers

540 – Chaka Khan

to remix 'The Reflex' gave them their only transatlantic chart-topper during a run of 10 consecutive UK Top 10 hits.

535 2 Jun ●● WAKE ME UP BEFORE YOU GO-GO – Wham! Writer: George Michael. Their first of four 80s No.1s – a total equalling the Jam's record for a UK act during this period – was the only one to top the US chart too.

536. 16 Jun ●●●●●●●● TWO TRIBES – Frankie Goes To Hollywood Writers: Peter Gill, Holly Johnson and Mark O'Toole. When 'Relax' climbed back up in the charts Frankie became the only group apart from the Beatles and the first act since John Lennon in 1981 to occupy the top two places on the chart. The single's nine-week residency at No.1 was the longest of the 80s.

537. 18 Aug ●●● CARELESS WHISPER – George Michael Writers: George Michael and Andrew Ridgeley. Michael's first No.1 as both writer and producer. The only song where his Wham! partner gets a writing credit was ironically the first released under George's name alone.

538. 8 Sep ●●●●●● I JUST CALLED TO SAY I LOVE YOU – Stevie Wonder Writer: Stevie Wonder. Taken from Stevie's soundtrack to the film The Woman in Red, it gave him both his first British solo No.1, 18 years after his chart debut, and an Oscar to boot.

539. 20 Oct ●● FREEDOM – Wham! Writer: George Michael. Epic released two picture discs of 'Freedom', one George-shaped, one Andrew-shaped. With this release three of the past five No.1s had writer credits for George Michael.

540. 10 Nov ●●● I FEEL FOR YOU – Chaka Khan Writer: Prince. Ending a barren 20-month spell for female artists at the top, the single was aided by three other megastars in black music with writer Prince, Stevie Wonder on harmonica and Grandmaster Melle Mel with the opening rap.

541. 1 Dec ● I SHOULD HAVE KNOWN BETTER – Jim Diamond Writers: Jim Diamond and Graham Lyle. Diamond guaranteed himself a place in pop history when he declared that he hoped his single didn't last longer than a week at the top. This was to make room for 'Do They Know It's Christmas?' which wasn't released in time to take over from Jim. The first Scotsman to top the chart since Billy Connolly in 1975.

542. 8 Dec ● THE POWER OF LOVE – Frankie Goes To Hollywood Writers: Peter Gill, Holly Johnson, Brian Nash and Mark

O'Toole. Frankie concluded their staggering year by equalling the 21-year-old record – set by fellow Liverpudlians Gerry and the Pacemakers – of making No.1 with each of their first three single releases.

543. 15 Dec ●●●●● DO THEY KNOW IT'S CHRISTMAS – Band Aid Writers: Bob Geldof and Midge Ure. The biggest-selling UK single ever at the time, shifting 3,500,000. The project was put together by Geldof in response to the news footage of the famine in Ethiopia, and all royalties went towards the disaster. Performers credited on the landmark charity single are as follows: Adam Clayton, Bono (U2); Phil Collins; Bob Geldof, Johnny Fingers, Simon Crowe, Peter Briquette (Boomtown Rats); David Bowie; Paul McCartney; Holly Johnson (Frankie Goes To Hollywood); Midge Ure, Chris Cross (Ultravox); Simon Le Bon, Nick Rhodes, Andy Taylor, John Taylor, Roger Taylor (Duran Duran); Paul Young; Tony Hadley, Martin Kemp, John Keeble, Gary Kemp, Steve Norman (Spandau Ballet); Glenn Gregory, Martyn Ware (Heaven 17); Francis Rossi, Rick Parfitt (Status Quo); Sting; Jon Moss, Boy George (Culture Club); Marilyn; Keren Woodward, Sarah Dallin and Siobhan Fahey (Bananarama); Jody Watley (Shalamar); Paul Weller (Style Council); Robert "Kool" Bell, James "JT" Taylor, Dennis Thomas (Kool and the Gang); George Michael.

1985

544. 19 Jan ●●● I WANT TO KNOW WHAT LOVE IS – Foreigner Writer: Mick Jones. Writer Mick got his first taste of the music industry working in a record shop, and once worked with French star Johnny Hallyday. The gospel climax was provided by the New Jersey Mass Choir.

545. 9 Feb ●●●● I KNOW HIM SO WELL – Elaine Paige and Barbara Dickson Writers: Tim Rice, Björn Ulvaeus and Benny Andersson. Taken from the musical Chess, this became the all-time best-selling single by a female duo in Britain.

546. 9 Mar ●● YOU SPIN ME RIGHT ROUND (LIKE A RECORD) – Dead or Alive Writers: Dead or Alive. The first of Stock Aitken and Waterman's No.1 production successes and the first No.1 record to mention the word "record". At the time, it was the "slowest" No.1, taking 14 weeks to reach the top.

547. 23 Mar ●●●● EASY LOVER – Philip Bailey (duet with Phil Collins) Writers: Philip Bailey, Phil Collins and Nathan East. Collins co-wrote, produced and played drums on this track which was credited to Bailey (ex-Earth Wind and Fire vocalist) with "duet with Phil Collins" in miniscule print on the label.

548. 20 Apr ●● WE ARE THE WORLD – USA for Africa Writers: Michael Jackson and Lionel Richie. The world's biggest-selling single of the 80s, United Support of Artists for Africa was a direct result of the Band Aid initiative and another step on the road to Live Aid.

549. 4 May ● MOVE CLOSER – Phyllis Nelson Writer: Phyllis Nelson. The first overseas female to write her own No.1. The song resurfaced in 1994 thanks to an advert for a popular anti-perspirant.

550. 11 May ●●●●● 19 – Paul Hardcastle Writers: Paul Hardcastle, William Coutourie, Jonas McCord and Mike Oldfield. The title refers to the average age of American soldiers in the Vietnam War, and was based on samples from a documentary about the conflict.

551. 15 Jun ●● YOU'LL NEVER WALK ALONE – The Crowd
Writers: Richard Rodgers and Oscar Hammerstein II. This charity disc
came about as a result of the fire that destroyed a stand at Bradford
City Football Club, killing more than 50 people. Featuring the vocals of
Gerry Marsden, he became the first singer to appear on different No.1
versions of the same song.

552. 29 Jun ●●●● FRANKIE – Sister Sledge Writer: Joy Denny. The
first sister act to top the UK chart did so with an uncharacteristic pop
ditty with a lyric inspired by Frank Sinatra, which gave Nile Rodgers his
second No.1 production credit.

553. 27 Jul ● THERE MUST BE AN ANGEL (PLAYING WITH MY
HEART) – Eurythmics Writers: Dave Stewart and Annie Lennox. The
only week in pole position for the UK chart's most successful male /
female duo featured Stevie Wonder on harmonica and came nearly two
years after their solitary week at No.1 in the States.

554. 3 Aug ●●●● INTO THE GROOVE – Madonna Writers:
Madonna and Steve Bray. During this disc's run at the top, a
reactivated 'Holiday' spent a week at No.2, making Madonna the only
woman to achieve the 1-2 double.

555. 31 Aug ● I GOT YOU BABE – UB40, guest vocals by Chrissie
Hynde Writer: Sonny Bono. No.1 exactly 20 years after it had topped
the chart for its originators Sonny and Cher. It is also the first instance
of two previous chart-topping acts collaborating on a former No.1 and
taking it back to the top.

556. 7 Sep ●●●● DANCING IN THE STREET – David Bowie and
Mick Jagger Writers: Ivy Hunter, William Stevenson and Marvin Gaye.
Previewed on video at Live Aid, this was the first pairing of previously
charting solo males to create a No.1 single.

570 – Spitting Image

Photo: Pictorial Press

557. 5 Oct ● IF I WAS – Midge Ure Writers: Midge Ure and Danny
Mitchell. Long overdue solo recognition for the man who co-wrote 'Do
They Know It's Christmas?' and just missed the top spot with the
massive 'Vienna' when he was with Ultravox.

558. 12 Oct ●●●●● THE POWER OF LOVE – Jennifer Rush
Writers: Candy de Rouge, Gunther Mende, Jennifer Rush and Mary
Susan Applegate. The only million-seller of 1985 and the biggest-selling
single by a woman (until Whitney Houston smashed the record in 1992)
took 16 weeks on the chart to get to the top spot.

559. 16 Nov ●● A GOOD HEART – Feargal Sharkey Writer: Maria
McKee. The second No.1 of the year produced by David A Stewart
brought the Ulsterman to a far wider audience than he ever reached
with the highly rated Undertones.

560. 30 Nov ●● I'M YOUR MAN – Wham! Writer: George Michael.
With this release they became the first duo to have three No.1s in the
80s and, with the re-issue of 'Last Christmas', the first UK duo to have
simultaneous Top 10 hits.

561. 14 Dec ●● SAVING ALL MY LOVE FOR YOU – Whitney
Houston Writers: Michael Masser and Gerry Goffin. Dionne Warwick's
cousin became a record fourth US female soloist to top the UK chart in
a year with this Marilyn McCoo and Billy Davis Jr cover from 1978.

562. 28 Dec ●● MERRY CHRISTMAS EVERYONE – Shakin'
Stevens Writer: Bob Heatlie. Produced by Dave Edmunds, the release
was delayed so as not to clash with Band Aid the previous year. This
Christmas No.1 and regular Christmas classic was the fourth chart-topper for Stevens, who scored more 80s UK hits (30) than any other act.

1986

563. 11 Jan ●● WEST END GIRLS – Pet Shop Boys Writers: Neil
Tennant and Chris Lowe. After the song's first release in 1984 flopped
and the boys were dropped by their record company, a re-recording
resulted in a transatlantic No.1.

564. 25 Jan ●● THE SUN ALWAYS SHINES ON TV – A-Ha Writer:
Paul Waaktaar. First Norwegian group to top the UK chart. This Alan
Tarney production was his first trip to the top since composing Cliff's
1979 hit 'We Don't Talk Anymore'.

565. 8 Feb ●●●● WHEN THE GOING GETS TOUGH, THE TOUGH
GET GOING – Billy Ocean Writers: Wayne Braithwaite, Barry J
Eastmond, R J "Mutt" Lange and Billy Ocean. Boosted by its inclusion
in the Michael Douglas movie Jewel of the Nile. Boyzone then took it
back to No.1 in 1999.

566. 8 Mar ●●● CHAIN REACTION – Diana Ross Writers: Barry,
Robin and Maurice Gibb. Her first solo visit to No.1 since 1971 still
stands as the record for the longest gap between newly recorded
chart-toppers by a solo female. The sixth No.1 composition by the
brothers Gibb.

567. 29 Mar ●●● LIVING DOLL – Cliff Richard and the Young
Ones, featuring Hank Marvin Writer: Lionel Bart. This first Comic
Relief single paired Cliff and Hank (recreating their roles from the original
1959 No.1) with TV comedy students The Young Ones. This single
made Cliff the first artist to top the charts in four decades.

568. 19 Apr ●●● A DIFFERENT CORNER – George Michael Writer: George Michael. Officially the first solo artist to reach the top spot with his first two releases. Credited with being the first No.1 on which the artist wrote, sang, played, arranged and produced the whole thing single-handedly.

569. 10 May ● ROCK ME AMADEUS – Falco Writers: Rob Bolland, Ferdi Bolland and Falco. The first record by an Austrian act to top the UK chart was a celebration of his fellow countryman, classical composer Wolfgang Amadeus Mozart. The first bilingual No.1 since Julio Iglesias in 1981.

570. 17 May ●●● THE CHICKEN SONG – Spitting Image Writers: Philip Pope, Robert Grant and Doug Naylor. After appearing on the TV political satire show from which the act's name is taken, this attack on the summer holiday hits by Black Lace became the first chart-topper by a non-human British act.

571. 7 Jun ●●● SPIRIT IN THE SKY – Doctor and the Medics Writer: Norman Greenbaum. The first song to be No.1 for two different acts with their first hit and the first No.1 song from the 70s to do it again in the 80s.

572. 28 Jun ●● THE EDGE OF HEAVEN – Wham! Writer: George Michael. Their final release was the first double single to top the chart – the 7" version was available only as a double pack. First UK duo to notch up four No.1s.

573. 12 Jul ●●● PAPA DON'T PREACH – Madonna Writers: Brian Elliott; additional lyrics by Madonna. The pop princess's first transatlantic No.1 was her 10th consecutive UK Top 10 (with a new recording), a record for a female act that she would hold and extend to 32 in 1994.

574. 2 Aug ●●● THE LADY IN RED – Chris de Burgh Writer: Chris de Burgh. Written for his wife, 'The Lady in Red' was de Burgh's first UK Top 40 single after 23 releases and 10 million album sales worldwide. First UK No.1 by an act born in Argentina.

575. 23 Aug ●●● I WANT TO WAKE UP WITH YOU – Boris Gardiner Writer: Ben Peters. The first Jamaican reggae artist to hit No.1 since Althia and Donna (1978) – and the first soloist – had to wait 16 years from his instrumental chart debut for a No.1 hit with his vocal follow-up.

576. 13 Sep ●●●● DON'T LEAVE ME THIS WAY – Communards with Sarah Jane Morris Writers: Kenny Gamble, Leon Huff and Cary Gilbert. Having already given the Three Degrees and the Jacksons their only UK No.1s, the legendary US writing team of Gamble and Huff helped to provide this act with the same service.

577. 11 Oct ● TRUE BLUE – Madonna Writers: Madonna and Stephen Bray. The title track from the year's best-selling album made Madonna the first American female to have three UK No.1s and put her equal first with Sandie Shaw as the women with the most chart-toppers.

578. 18 Oct ●●● EVERY LOSER WINS – Nick Berry Writers: Simon May, Stewart James and Bradley James. Berry played Simon Wicks in TV soap EastEnders, and with this track he achieved the biggest jump for a single on its way to the top (from 66 to No.4) and gave BBC Records its first No.1.

579. 8 Nov ●●●● TAKE MY BREATH AWAY – Berlin Writers: Giorgio Moroder and Tom Whitlock. The Oscar-winning theme tune to the movie Top Gun returned to the chart in early 1988 and again at the end of 1990, giving it a total of 30 weeks on chart.

580. 6 Dec ●● THE FINAL COUNTDOWN – Europe Writer: Joey Tempest. The second group of Swedes to top the chart, Abba's Björn Ulvaeus described their sound as "melodic hard rock… that's the way music should sound today". The track by these former Eurovision entrants sold two million copies worldwide and topped the charts in 13 countries.

581. 20 Dec ● CARAVAN OF LOVE – Housemartins Writers: Ernie Isley, Chris Jasper and Marvin Isley. "A cappella is a musical form, using voices alone which started in the small Northern town of Hull… Power to the people. Respect to the steeple." So say the single's sleevenotes.

582. 27 Dec ●●●● REET PETITE – Jackie Wilson Writers: Berry Gordy and Tyran Carlo. First entered the British charts in 1957. At 29 years and 42 days, this was the slowest journey to No.1 and made Wilson the seventh posthumous chart-topper.

1987

583. 24 Jan ●● JACK YOUR BODY – Steve "Silk" Hurley Writer: Steve "Silk" Hurley. The first house music No.1 and first to register more than half its sales on the 12" format which broke chart rules by exceeding the 25-minute maximum length allowed at the time.

584. 7 Feb ●● I KNEW YOU WERE WAITING (FOR ME) – George Michael and Aretha Franklin Writers: Simon Climie and Denis Morgan. This was the Queen of Soul's first trip to the top of the UK charts, and made George Michael the first person to reach the top as part of two different duos (the first being Wham!).

585. 21 Feb ●●● STAND BY ME – Ben E King Writers: Jerry Loiber, Mike Stoller and Ben E King. With Percy Sledge's 'When a Man Loves a Woman' at No.2, this was the only instance of recordings more than 20 years old holding down the top two positions on the UK chart. Both were re-issued after being included in Levi's jeans commercials.

586. 14 Mar ●● EVERYTHING I OWN – Boy George Writer: David Gates. George now joined the exclusive club of men to top the chart solo and as part of a group with this cover of a Bread song.

587. 28 Mar ● RESPECTABLE – Mel and Kim Writer: Mike Stock, Matt Aitken and Pete Waterman. These former models were the first British sisters to top the UK chart, giving Stock Aitken and Waterman their first No.1 writer credit.

588. 4 Apr ●●● LET IT BE – Ferry Aid Writers: John Lennon and Paul McCartney. The sixth charity No.1, in aid of Zeebrugge ferry disaster victims, was the first Beatles cover to improve on the original's chart placing.

589. 25 Apr ●● LA ISLA BONITA – Madonna Writers: Madonna and Patrick Leonard. With this release, Madonna clinched records for both most No.1s by a female artist (four) – all of which she co-wrote and co-produced – and most Top 10 hits by a woman (14), both records she still holds and keeps increasing.

590. 9 May ●●●● NOTHING'S GONNA STOP US NOW – Starship Writers: Diane Warren and Albert Hammond. From the movie Mannequin, this gave Grace Slick her first trip to the Top 10, at age 47, with the band she joined in 1966 – then named Jefferson Airplane.

591. 6 Jun ●● I WANNA DANCE WITH SOMEBODY (WHO LOVES ME) – Whitney Houston Writers: George Merrill and Shannon Rubicam. As Thatcher secured her third general election victory, Ms Houston scored her second No.1 and Narada Michael Walden a second consecutive No.1 production credit.

592. 20 Jun ●● STAR TREKKIN' – The Firm Writers: Grahame Lister and John O'Connor. This unashamedly novelty hit based its lyrics on Star Trek and boldly went where only 591 records had gone before. Two weeks previously it had entered the chart at No.74, the lowest start for a future No.1.

593. 4 Jul ●●● IT'S A SIN – Pet Shop Boys Writers: Neil Tennant and Chris Lowe. This Hi-NRG stomper had a serious lyric inspired by Tennant's strict Catholic upbringing and a video directed by Derek Jarman.

594. 25 Jul ● WHO'S THAT GIRL – Madonna Writers Madonna and Patrick Leonard. Her fifth No.1 – more than any other 80s act – from the film in which she starred was the first in an unprecedented sequence of consecutive chart-toppers which were movie title songs.

595. 1 Aug ●● LA BAMBA – Los Lobos Writer: Traditional, arranged by Ritchie Valens. This Ritchie Valens revival (from his bio-pic) by the five Spanish-Americans was the first chart-topper sung completely in Spanish.

597 – Rick Astley

Photo: Rex Features / E.Adebari

596. 15 Aug ●● I JUST CAN'T STOP LOVING YOU – Michael Jackson Writer: Michael Jackson. Having topped the chart solo, with his brothers and as part of a larger ensemble (USA for Africa) Jackson had this No.1 duet although his partner, Seidah Garrett, did not receive a label credit.

597. 29 Aug ●●●●● NEVER GONNA GIVE YOU UP – Rick Astley Writers: Mike Stock, Matt Aitken and Pete Waterman. At 800,000 copies this Brit-winning single was the biggest seller of the year giving Manchester lad Astley the first of two US No.1s.

598. 3 Oct ●● PUMP UP THE VOLUME / ANITINA (THE FIRST TIME I SEE SHE DANCE) – M/A/R/R/S Writers: Steven and Martin Young, A R Kane, C J Mackintosh, John Fryer and Dave Darrell / A R Kane and Colourbox. An injunction by Stock Aitken and Waterman over a disputed sample on this track prevented it from being distributed for five days, leaving Rick Astley on top for an extra week.

599. 17 Oct ●●●● YOU WIN AGAIN – Bee Gees Writers: Barry, Robin and Maurice Gibb. With their fifth No.1 the Gibbs became the only group to top the charts in the 60s, 70s and 80s.

600. 14 Nov ●●●● CHINA IN YOUR HAND – T'Pau Writers: Carol Decker and Ron Rogers. Produced by 'Bohemian Rhapsody' mastermind Roy Thomas Baker, this hit failed to chart in the US where their debut single 'Heart And Soul' broke first.

601. 19 Dec ●●●● ALWAYS ON MY MIND – Pet Shop Boys Writers: Mark James, Johnny Christopher, Wayne Thompson. This Elvis cover was commissioned by a TV show called Love Me Tender in which contemporary artists performed versions of Elvis classics.

1988

602. 16 Jan ●● HEAVEN IS A PLACE ON EARTH – Belinda Carlilse Writers: Rick Nowels and Ellen Shipley. Belinda started her chart career with The Go-Go's and then became the first of three successive female soloists to top the UK chart.

603. 30 Jan ●●● I THINK WE'RE ALONE NOW – Tiffany Writer: Ritchie Cordell. After courting much publicity by performing in US shopping malls, her follow-up 'Could've Been' hit No.1 in the States while this sat atop the UK chart, making her the first female to have simultaneous transatlantic chart-toppers with different singles.

604. 20 Feb ●●●●● I SHOULD BE SO LUCKY – Kylie Minogue Writers: Mike Stock, Matt Aitken and Pete Waterman. First Australian female to top the chart did so thanks to regular appearances on TV soap Neighbours and the writing / production assistance of SAW, under whose guidance she would collect a female record-breaking 13 Top 10 hits with her first 13 releases.

605. 26 Mar ●● DON'T TURN AROUND – Aswad Writers: Diane Warren and Albert Hammond. Aswad, which means "black" in Arabic, hit with this second No.1 from the songwriting duo, previously recorded by Kim Goody, Tina Turner and Luther Ingram.

606. 9 Apr ●● HEART – Pet Shop Boys Writers: Neil Tennant and Chris Lowe. Their fourth chart-topper equalled the record for most No.1s by a duo and most by a British act in the 80s. This disc extended their total weeks at the top for the decade to 12.

607. 30 Apr ●● THEME FROM S EXPRESS – S Express Writers: Mark Moore and Pascal Gabriel. With its distinctive "Enjoy this trip… countdown is progressing", this disco-house track sampled Rose Royce's 1979 hit 'Is It Love You're After' and allegedly cost DJ Mark Moore only £250 to put together.

608. 14 May ● PERFECT – Fairground Attraction Writer: Mark E Nevin. This skiffle-flavoured Brit Best Single-winner taken from a Brit-winning album was written by the act's guitarist. Vocalist Eddi Reader went on to win the 1995 Best Female Brit award.

609. 21 May ●●●● WITH A LITTLE HELP FROM MY FRIENDS / SHE'S LEAVING HOME – Wet Wet Wet / Billy Bragg with Cara Tivey Writers: John Lennon and Paul McCartney. Taken from an NME-led charity album of Beatles covers in support of Childline, this double A-side was the first No.1 for all the artists involved. 'With A Little Help…' became the first Beatles original to become a No.1 in two different versions.

610. 18 Jun ● DOCTORIN' THE TARDIS – Timelords Writers: Mike Chapman, Nicky Chinn, Roy Grainer, Gary Glitter, Mike Leander, Timelords. The first instance of consecutive Scottish acts at No.1, The Timelords were the first hit incarnation of the KLF. Their chart-topper included snatches of Sweet, Gary Glitter songs and the Dr Who theme.

611. 25 Jun ●● I OWE YOU NOTHING – Bros Writers: The Brothers (Nicky Graham and Tom Watkins). Although the trio caused mass teen hysteria, this was to be their only No.1 despite eight consecutive Top 10 hits, making Matt and Luke Goss the most successful chart twins after the Bee Gees' Maurice and Robin Gibb.

612. 9 Jul ●●●● NOTHING'S GONNA CHANGE MY LOVE FOR YOU – Glenn Medeiros Writers: Michael Masser, Gerry Goffin. After being discovered in a Hawaiian radio contest, Glenn charted this George Benson cover in the States when he was still 16. Having stiffed on its original UK release in 1987, he finally topped our chart just after his 18th birthday.

613. 6 Aug ●●●●● THE ONLY WAY IS UP – Yazz and the Plastic Population Writers: George Jackson, Johnny Henderson. Having sung on Coldcut's introductory hit they now returned the favour by producing this cover of a 1983 Otis Clay recording.

614. 10 Sep ●● A GROOVY KIND OF LOVE – Phil Collins Writers: Toni Wine and Carole Bayer Sager. Collins won the chart championship on both sides of the Atlantic reviving this 60s track for the movie Buster, in which he played the Great Train Robber of the title, and improving on the Mindbenders' 1966 No.2 version.

615. 24 Sep ●● HE AIN'T HEAVY HE'S MY BROTHER – Hollies Writers: Bob Russell and Bobby Scott. Thanks to its inclusion in a Miller Lite TV ad, this track hit the top 23 years after 'I'm Alive' in 1965, giving the Hollies the longest gap between No.1s for a British act.

616. 8 Oct ● DESIRE – U2 Writers: U2, lyrics by Bono. Named after the American spy plane, these Dubliners had been a major force in the album charts for seven years before they first scored a No.1 single with this rocker taken from their fourth No.1 album 'Rattle And Hum'.

617. 15 Oct ●● ONE MOMENT IN TIME – Whitney Houston Writers: Albert Hammond and John Bettis. This track was recorded for a concept album to tie in with the 1988 Seoul Olympics. Houston earned a silver herself for sales of this single and completed a hat-trick of UK No.1s.

618. 29 Oct ●●● ORINOCO FLOW (SAIL AWAY) – Enya Writers: Enya Brennan and Roma Ryan. The former Clannad vocalist produced, played keyboards and sang on this huge international hit. The first Irish female to hit No.1 since Dana in 1970.

619. 19 Nov ●●● THE FIRST TIME – Robin Beck Writers Gavin Spencer, Tom Anthony and Terry Boyle. After waiting 35 years for the first instance of three consecutive female soloists at the top of the chart, Beck completed the second occurrence in under a year with this Coke ad song.

620. 10 Dec ●●●● MISTLETOE AND WINE – Cliff Richard Writers: Leslie Stewart, Jeremy Paul and Keith Strachan. Cliff's first self-produced single was his 12th No.1 over a span of four decades, his 98th hit on the British singles charts and his first Christmas No.1.

1989

621. 7 Jan ●●● ESPECIALLY FOR YOU – Kylie Minogue and Jason Donovan Writers: Mike Stock, Matt Aitken, Pete Waterman. The Neighbours couple sat at No.2 for four consecutive weeks before hitting the top while Angry Anderson was down at No.3 with their soap characters' wedding song.

622. 28 Jan ●●●● SOMETHING'S GOTTEN HOLD OF MY HEART – Mark Almond with special guest Gene Pitney Writers: Roger Cook and Roger Greenaway. Almond was little known in the US and the record company called Pitney to tell him the record wouldn't be released in the States as young audiences might assume it was a gay love duet. It marks Pitney's first week at No.1 since his chart debut in 1961, the longest wait for a living male artist.

623. 25 Feb ●● BELFAST CHILD – Simple Minds Writers: Traditional; lyrics by Simple Minds. Trevor Horn's sixth No.1 production credit: it lasted 6 mins 39 secs – the longest No.1 since 'Hey Jude'.

624. 11 Mar ●● TOO MANY BROKEN HEARTS – Jason Donovan Writers: Mike Stock, Matt Aitken, Pete Waterman. From the year's best-selling album, 'Ten Good Reasons'. It gave Jason his first solo chart-topper and in its second week at No.1 it was one of three SAW productions in the Top 4.

625. 25 Mar ●●● LIKE A PRAYER – Madonna Writers: Madonna and Patrick Leonard. The controversial video prompted Pepsi to sever its commercial connections with Madonna. This single gave her a total of 14 weeks at No.1 in the 80s, more than any other overseas act.

626. 15 Apr ●●●● ETERNAL FLAME – Bangles Writers: Susanna Hoffs, Billy Steinberg, Tom Kelly. The title referred to the eternal flame burning at Elvis Presley's grave in Memphis. The first by an all-female band (ie vocal and instrumental) to top both the US and UK charts.

627. 13 May ● HAND ON YOUR HEART – Kylie Minogue Writers: Mike Stock, Matt Aitken, Pete Waterman. First of three consecutive No.1s produced by Stock Aitken and Waterman, the first producers to put together such a sequence since George Martin in 1964.

628. 20 May ●●● FERRY 'CROSS THE MERSEY – Christians, Holly Johnson, Paul McCartney, Gerry Marsden and Stock Aitken Waterman. Writer: Gerry Marsden. Raised money for victims of the Hillsborough disaster, and made Gerry Marsden the only person to reach No.1 twice with newly recorded vocals on a song he originally sang (first time as part of The Crowd in 1985).

629. 10 Jun ●● SEALED WITH A KISS – Jason Donovan Writers: Gary Geld, Peter Udell. The writers went on to write for Broadway, notably the musicals Purlie and Shenandoah. Jason became the first overseas act to go straight in at No.1 since Elvis Presley's 'It's Now or Never' in 1960, with this Brian Hyland cover.

630. 24 Jun ●●●● BACK TO LIFE (HOWEVER DO YOU WANT ME) – Soul II Soul featuring Caron Wheeler Writers: Beresford Romeo, Caron Wheeler, Simon Law, Nellee Hooper. This song has the honour of being the fastest-selling 12" single in New York, and was the first No.1 by a UK act to top the US R&B singles chart.

631. 22 Jul ●● YOU'LL NEVER STOP ME LOVING YOU – Sonia Writers: Mike Stock, Matt Aitken, Pete Waterman. The ninth different chart-topping act to be sprinkled with the SAW gold dust, this teenage Scouser made her debut performing on Pete Waterman's Hitman and Her TV show.

632. 5 Aug ●●●●● SWING THE MOOD – Jive Bunny and the Mastermixers Medley produced by: Andy Pickles and Les Hemstock. Despite horrendous licensing problems, this sampled medley of 50s and 60s hits charted worldwide thanks to a cartoon bunny and a Yorkshire duo from the Music Factory DJ mixing service.

633. 9 Sep ●●●●●● RIDE ON TIME – Black Box Writers: Dan Hartman, Daniele Davoli, Marco Limoni, Valerio Semplici. The year's best-selling single from the first No.1 Italian act sampled the vocal from Loleatta Holloway's 'Love Sensation' before Martha Wash re-recorded them.

634. 21 Oct ●●● THAT'S WHAT I LIKE – Jive Bunny and the Mastermixers Medley produced by: Andy Pickles and Les Hemstock. This mix sampled hits as diverse as the theme from Hawaii Five-O and 'Great Balls of Fire'. The third sample-based chart-topper in a row.

635. 11 Nov ●● ALL AROUND THE WORLD – Lisa Stansfield Writers: Lisa Stansfield, Ian Devaney, Andy Morris. This Ivor Novello award-winning song became the first by a white British female to top the US R&B singles chart.

636. 25 Nov ●●● YOU GOT IT (THE RIGHT STUFF) – New Kids on the Block Writer: Maurice Starr. Once Starr's original boy wonders New Edition had made their millions and gone solo he set out to find a white New Edition, and came up with the New Kids from Boston. This single was their first of eight consecutive Top 10 hits.

637. 16 Dec ● LET'S PARTY – Jive Bunny and the Mastermixers Medley Produced by: Andy Pickles and Ian Morgan. With this scourge of the office Christmas party the cartoon bunny managed to complete the fastest No.1 hat-trick in just 20 weeks.

638. 23 Dec ●●● DO THEY KNOW IT'S CHRISTMAS? – Band Aid II Writers: Bob Geldof and Midge Ure. The year's seventh Stock Aitken and Waterman No.1 production was the only 80s song to reach No.1 in two different recordings. Both featured Keren and Sarah from Bananarama.

1990

639. 16 Jan ●● HANGIN' TOUGH – New Kids on the Block Writer: Maurice Starr. This single returned to the top just five weeks after their first No.1 vacated the top spot – the shortest gap between any group's first two No.1s, but was widely reported to be the smallest recorded single week sale for a chart-topper at just under 30,000 copies.

640. 27 Jan ● TEARS ON MY PILLOW – Kylie Minogue Writers: Sylvester Bradford and Al Lewis. Taken from the soundtrack of Kylie's first feature film The Delinquents, this Little Anthony and the Imperials cover was SAW's final, unlucky 13th No.1 production.

641. 3 Feb ●●●● NOTHING COMPARES 2 U – Sinead O'Connor Writer: Prince. This self-produced track was the biggest-selling new release of the year and was Prince's second composition to top the charts. It proved to be O'Connor's only major hit.

642. 3 Mar ●●●● DUB BE GOOD TO ME – Beats International featuring Lindy Layton Writers: Norman Cook, Jimmy Jam and Terry Lewis. This cover of the SOS Band's 'Just Be Good To Me' gave the legendary Jam and Lewis their only UK No.1 writing credit.

643. 31 Mar ●● THE POWER – Snap! Writers: Benito Benites, John "Virgo" Garrett III. Penny Ford was drafted in for vocal duties on the recommendation of Chaka Khan who turned down an opportunity to appear on the track, the first to single in chart history to descend from No.1, to 2 to 3 to 4.

644. 14 Apr ●●●● VOGUE – Madonna Writers: Madonna and Shep Pettibone. Her seventh No.1 which celebrated the immortal style of a roll call of stars (Bette Davis, James Dean, etc). Elvis is the only artist to have had more solo No.1s.

645. 12 May ●●●● KILLER – Adamski Writers: Adam Tinley and Sealhenry Samuel. A classic of the 1988 summer-of-love rave scene, this track proved to be a much better launching pad for the uncredited vocalist Seal than Adamski (Adam Tinley).

646. 9 Jun ●● WORLD IN MOTION – Englandneworder Writers: New Order and Keith Allen. This hot summer soccer soundtrack helped the nation to cheer an England squad on to a World Cup semi-final. Included John Barnes (rap duties) and comedian Keith Allen (backing vocals).

647. 23 Jun ●●●●● SACRIFICE / HEALING HANDS – Elton John Writers: Elton John and Bernie Taupin. After scoring his first No.1 in 1976 in his duet with Kiki Dee, Elton had to wait until 1990 for his first solo chart-topper with this double A-side benefiting Aids charities.

648. 28 Jul ●●●● TURTLE POWER – Partners In Kryme Writers: James P Alpern and Richard A Usher Jr. This track was written for the movie Teenage Mutant Ninja Turtles and PIK became the first one-hit wonders of the 90s.

663 – Chesney Hawkes

649. 25 Aug ●●● ITSY BITSY TEENY WEENY YELLOW POLKA DOT BIKINI – Bombalurina Writers: Lee Pockriss and Paul Vance. Children's TV hero Timmy Mallett covered Brian Hyland's 1960 US No.1 with the longest non-bracketed title to top the chart.

650. 15 Sep ●● THE JOKER – Steve Miller Band Writer: Steve Miller. There was a two-way sales tie for No.1 this week but the chart compilers placed Deee-Lite's 'Groove Is in the Heart' / 'What Is Love' second as 'The Joker' had shown the bigger increase in sales over the week. Hitting the top 16 years and eight months after its original release on the back of a Levi's ad, Miller claimed 'The Joker' took him only half an hour to write.

651. 29 Sep ●●●● SHOW ME HEAVEN – Maria McKee Writers: Joshua Rifkin, Eric Rackin and Maria McKee. The former Lone Justice vocalist was the first woman to compose No.1 hits for herself and another artist (Feargal Sharkey)

652. 27 Oct ● A LITTLE TIME – Beautiful South Writers: Paul Heaton and Dave Rotheray. The act's only No.1 was their first single not to feature Heaton on lead vocals and was supported by a Brit award-winning video.

653. 3 Nov ●●●● UNCHAINED MELODY – Righteous Brothers Writers: Hy Zaret and Alex North. The year's best seller was used in the hit movie Ghost and created the longest gap (see Jimmy Young in 1955) between two No.1 versions of the same song.

654. 1 Dec ●●●● ICE ICE BABY – Vanilla Ice Writers: Vanilla Ice, Earthquake, David Bowie, Queen. US airplay turned this 'Under Pressure'-sampling track from a B-side into an A-side, which entered the UK chart at No.3 – the highest debut by a new act at the time.

655. 29 Dec ● SAVIOUR'S DAY – Cliff Richard Writer: Chris Eaton. His 13th chart-topper and his third Christmas No.1 in a row (including Band Aid II). Cliff became the only act to top the charts in five decades.

1991

656 5 Jan ●● BRING YOUR DAUGHTER... TO THE SLAUGHTER – Iron Maiden Writer: Bruce Dickinson. Clinging to the Top 75 for just five weeks (the shortest for any No.1) Maiden's 23rd hit provided a chart milestone: the last No.1 not available on CD.

657 19 Jan ● SADNESS PART ONE – Enigma Writers: Michael Cretu, Franz Gregorian and David Fairstein. The first No.1 to feature passages sung in Latin was originally called 'Sadeness' (after the Marquis de Sade), but the title was modified in case British fans didn't understand the original pun.

658 26 Jan ● INNUENDO – Queen Writers: Queen. Hitting No.1 for the first time on their own in 15 years, this was the first No.1 hit to spend only two weeks in the Top 10.

659 2 Feb ●● 3AM ETERNAL – KLF featuring Children of the Revolution Writers: Jim Cauty, Bill Drummond and Ricardo Lyte. '3AM…' was originally recorded as part of the soundtrack to the feature film The White Room, which remains unreleased.

660 16 Feb ●●● DO THE BARTMAN – Simpsons Writer: Bryan Loren. Bart's vocals were sung by Nancy Cartwright and although the credited writer sang on and produced the track, it is widely believed the line "If you can do the Bart, you're bad like Michael Jackson" holds the key to the real composer.

661 9 Mar ●● SHOULD I STAY OR SHOULD I GO – The Clash Writers: The Clash. The band's 21st chart entry was a re-issue of a 1982 A-side, their first trip to the Top 10 and No.1 due to a Levi's ad.

662 23 Mar ● THE STONK – Hale and Pace and the Stonkers Writers: Joe Griffiths, Gareth Hale and Norman Pace. The third Comic Relief single was produced by and featured Brian May. Roger Taylor was one of the Stonkers.

663 30 Mar ●●●●● THE ONE AND ONLY – Chesney Hawkes Writer: Nik Kershaw. With a track from the film Buddy's Song, in which he starred with Roger Daltrey, Hawkes became the first chart-topping son of a chart-topping father, namely the Tremeloes' Chip Hawkes.

664 4 May ●●●●● THE SHOOP SHOOP SONG (IT'S IN HIS KISS) – Cher Writer: Rudy Clark. Taken from the end credits of Cher's film Mermaids, this was her first No.1 since the duet with her then husband Sonny Bono in 1965 – giving her the longest gap between appearances on newly recorded No.1 singles for any act.

665 8 Jun ●●● I WANNA SEX YOU UP – Color Me Badd Writer: Dr Freeze. Taken from the soundtrack to New Jack City. The first time that three consecutive chart-toppers had been specifically recorded for films and the first No.1 to mention sex in the title.

666 29 Jun ●● ANY DREAM WILL DO – Jason Donovan Writers: Tim Rice and Andrew Lloyd Webber. Jason became the first person to have a No.1 from a London stage show while still starring in it, in this case Joseph and His Amazing Technicolour Dreamcoat.

667 13 Jul ●●●●●●●●●●●●●●●● (EVERYTHING I DO) I DO IT FOR YOU – Bryan Adams Writers: Bryan Adams, Michael Kamen and Robert John "Mutt" Lange. Adams had never previously entered the Top 10 when this theme from the movie Robin Hood: Prince of Thieves began its 16 weeks at the top – the longest consecutive run at No.1 by any single in UK chart history and the year's top seller, shifting almost two million copies. Michael Kamen originally presented his melody in an early music style, but participation of hard-rock producer Lange ensured that the end product would not be a period piece.

668 2 Nov ● THE FLY – U2 Writers: U2. The second U2 No.1 toppled Adams thanks partly to a record company claim that the single would be available for only three weeks, thus encouraging sales.

669 9 Nov ●● DIZZY – Vic Reeves and the Wonder Stuff Writers: Tommy Roe and Freddy Weller. "It's nice to have a No.1," said Reeves of his cover of Tommy Roe's transatlantic chart-topper. "I can recommend it."

670. 23 Nov ●● BLACK OR WHITE – Michael Jackson Writer: Michael Jackson. Jacko's fourth solo No.1 featured Slash of Guns N' Roses on guitar and his pal Macaulay Culkin miming to Bill Bottrell's rap in the video.

671. 7 Dec ●● DON'T LET THE SUN GO DOWN ON ME – George Michael and Elton John Writers: Elton John and Bernie Taupin. On its initial outing in 1974 this composition was kept off the BBC Radio 1 A-list in its first week of release because it was "too slow".

672. 21 Dec ●●●●● BOHEMIAN RHAPSODY / THESE ARE THE DAYS OF OUR LIVES – Queen Writers: Freddie Mercury / Queen. In the aftermath of Freddie Mercury's death, royalties from this single were donated to the Terrence Higgins Trust. 'Bo Rap', the only recording to top the chart twice with different releases, claimed the Christmas No.1 spot for a second time, making it the only single to top the chart in four different years.

1992

673. 25 Jan ●●●● GOODNIGHT GIRL – Wet Wet Wet Writers: Graeme Clark, Tommy Cunningham, Neil Mitchell, Marti Pellow. Their only original No.1 song marked the band's transition from teen sensation to adult appreciation.

674. 22 Feb ●●●●●●●● STAY – Shakespear's Sister Writers: Siobhan Fahey, Marcella Detroit and Guiot (Dave Stewart). With a name inspired by a 1985 Smiths hit, the first transatlantic female duo to reach No.1 had the longest "stay" at the top for a female duo or group.

675. 18 Apr ●●● DEEPLY DIPPY – Right Said Fred Writers: Richard Fairbrass, Fred Fairbrass and Rob Manzoli. Before topping the US chart earlier in the year with 'I'm Too Sexy', the highlight of the Fairbrass brothers' careers had been a stint in Bob Dylan's backing band.

676. 9 May ●●●●● PLEASE DON'T GO / GAME BOY – KWS Writers: Harry W Casey, Richard Finch / Chris King, Winston Williams.

689 – Ace of Base

Photo: Pictorial Press

The most successful of two competing dance versions of a 1979 KC and the Sunshine Band ballad.

677 13 Jun ●●●●● ABBA-ESQUE (EP) – Erasure Writers: 'Lay All Your Love on Me', 'Take A Chance on Me', 'Voulez-Vous' – Benny Andersson, Björn Ulvaeus; 'S.O.S.' – Benny Andersson, Björn Ulvaeus and Stig Anderson. After more than 20 self-penned hits, this collection of Abba songs gave Erasure their only No.1.

678. 18 Jul ●●● AIN'T NO DOUBT – Jimmy Nail Writers: Guy Pratt, Danny Schogger, Jimmy Nail and Charlie Dore. At 37, the Geordie TV star became the oldest British TV actor to launch a pop career (lengthy in his case) and have a No.1 since Clive Dunn in 1971.

679. 8 Aug ●●●●●● RHYTHM IS A DANCER – SNAP! Writers: Benito Benitez, John "Virgo" Garrett III, Thea Austin, Durron Butler. Turbo B's rap featured one of the most tasteless lines in pop history: "I'm as serious as cancer, when I say: rhythm is a dancer".

680. 19 Sep ●●●● EBENEEZER GOODE – Shamen Writers: Colin Angus, Richard West (Mr C). With its repeated chorus of "Eezer Goode", the band was accused of promoting the illegal drug Ecstasy.

681. 17 Oct ●● SLEEPING SATELLITE – Tasmin Archer Writers: Tasmin Archer, John Beck and John Hughes. The Yorkshire girl's first single hit the top spot in five European countries besides the UK and earned her a Best Newcomer Brit award.

682. 31 Oct ●●● THE END OF THE ROAD – Boyz II Men Writers: L A Reid, Babyface and Daryl Simmons. This single earned the boyz a Grammy award for Best R&B performance for the second year running and topped the chart for 13 weeks in their US homeland.

683. 21 Nov ●● WOULD I LIE TO YOU – Charles and Eddie Writers: Mick Leeson and Peter Vale. This pair became the first black and white male duo to hit No.1 since Paul McCartney and Stevie Wonder 10 years earlier with a rare UK-penned No.1 for a US act.

684. 5 Dec ●●●●●●●●●● I WILL ALWAYS LOVE YOU – Whitney Houston Writer: Dolly Parton. Featured in The Best Little Whorehouse in Texas, Houston's cover appeared in The Bodyguard in which she starred opposite Kevin Costner. It was the longest run at No.1 in the UK by a female artist and the year's best seller at 1.4m.

1993

685. 13 Feb ●●●●● NO LIMIT – 2 Unlimited Writers: Anita Dels, Ray Slijngaard, Phil Wilde and Jean Paul de Coster. First song by a Dutch act to reach No.1 since Pussycat's 'Mississippi'. Band member Kid Ray earned a writer credit for his line "techno techno techno techno".

686. 20 Mar ●● OH CAROLINA – Shaggy Writer: John Folkes. The Jamaican-born former US Marine took this 1960 Folkes Brothers track to No.1 while Snow and Shabba Ranks lined up behind, creating the first reggae-based Top 3.

687. 3 Apr ●●●● YOUNG AT HEART – The Bluebells Writers: Bobby Hodgens and Siobhan Fahey. The band had long since split by the time this Bananarama cover was re-issued after being used in a Volkswagen TV commercial, but they did reunite for Top of the Pops.

688. 1 May ●●● FIVE LIVE (EP) – George Michael and Queen with Lisa Stansfield Writers: 'Somebody to Love' – Freddie Mercury; 'Killer – Papa Was a Rolling Stone' – Seal, Adam Tinley, Norman Whitfield and Barrett Strong; 'These Are the Days of Our Lives' – Queen; 'Calling You' – Bob Telson. Taken from a huge Freddie Mercury tribute concert in support of Aids charities, George Michael was the only person to perform on all four tracks and it was the only release he sanctioned during a three-year squabble with his record company.

689. 22 May ●●● ALL THAT SHE WANTS – Ace of Base Writers: Joker and Buddha. The third Swedish-based act to top the charts in the UK, they were also the first Swedes to have a US No.1 album.

690. 12 Jun ●● (I CAN'T HELP) FALLING IN LOVE WITH YOU – UB40 Writers: Hugo Peretti, Luigi Creatore and George David Weiss. This Elvis No.1 had subsequently revisited the Top 10 with covers from Andy Williams and the Stylistics before UB40 made it their third No.1 cover version.

691. 26 Jun ●●● DREAMS – Gabrielle Writers: Gabrielle and Tim Laws. The original version of 'Dreams' sampled the distinctive guitar introduction to Tracy Chapman's 'Fast Car' but had to be re-recorded when use of the sample was refused.

692. 17 Jul ●●●● PRAY – Take That Writer: Gary Barlow. The first of seven No.1 composer credits for band member Gary Barlow.

693. 14 Aug ●● LIVING ON MY OWN – Freddie Mercury Writer: Freddie Mercury. Two years after Mercury's death his manager responded to demand for fresh material by inviting the Belgian-based production team No More Brothers to re-work this track which had previously peaked at No.50 in 1985.

694. 28 Aug ●●●● MR VAIN – Culture Beat Writers: Steven Lewis, Noise Katzmann and Jay Supreme. The biggest-selling record of the year in Europe, and the first No.1 single not to be made available on 7" vinyl.

695. 25 Sep ●● BOOM! SHAKE THE ROOM – Jazzy Jeff and the Fresh Prince Writers: Will Smith, Lee Haggard, Walter Williams and Ken Mayberry. Contains a sample of 'Funky Worm', written and performed originally by Leroy Bonner, Clarence Satchell, Marshall Jones, Billy "Diamond" Williams, Merv Pierce, Billy Beck and Ralph Middlebrook (The Ohio Players). Rapper turned actor Will Smith's first No.1 in his earlier incarnation as the Fresh Prince.

696. 9 Oct ●● RELIGHT MY FIRE – Take That featuring Lulu Writer: Dan Hartman. Hartman claimed his second No.1 writing credit before his death in 1994 with this cover of his 1979 recording with Loleatta Holloway's original vocal part performed by Lulu, who had a chart career spanning 29 years 148 days – the longest wait of any artist from their first chart entry to reaching the top.

697. 23 Oct ●●●●●●● I'D DO ANYTHING FOR LOVE (BUT I WON'T DO THAT) – Meat Loaf Writer: Jim Steinman. The year's best-selling single, from the year's best-selling album Bat Out of Hell II – Back into Hell, featured UK vocalist Lorraine Crosby, aka Mrs Loud.

698. 11 Dec ● 25 Dec ●● MR BLOBBY – Mr Blobby Writers: Paul Shaw and David Rogers. The infamous Mr Blobby hit the top spot and then reclaimed it after having been usurped by plucky upstarts Take That. The yellow and pink disaster area was the first act to reach No.1 with an eponymous single.

699. 18 Dec ● BABE – Take That Writer: Gary Barlow. With this Mark Owen lead vocal, Take That became the first act to have three consecutive singles debut at No.1.

1994

700. 8 Jan ●● TWIST AND SHOUT – Chaka Demus and Pliers with Jack Radics and Taxi Gang Writers: Bert Berns and Phil Medley. Song previously charted by the Isley Brothers, Brian Poole and the Tremeloes, The Beatles and Salt-N-Pepa. This was the first version to reach No.1.

701. 22 Jan ●●●● THINGS CAN ONLY GET BETTER – D:Ream Writers: Peter Cunnah and Jamie Petrie. This re-issue, which owed much of its popularity to a Paul Oakenfold remix, was subsequently used by New Labour as the soundtrack to their 1997 election campaign.

702. 19 Feb ●●●● WITHOUT YOU – Mariah Carey Writers: Pete Ham and Tom Evans. The first single by a female solo artist to debut at No.1 was a cover of a 1972 transatlantic Nilsson No.1.

703. 19 Mar ●●● DOOP – Doop Writer: Frederick Ridderhof. Widely regarded as the first instrumental to top the chart in more than 20 years, this weird Dutch mix of house and Charleston did in fact feature a vocal repeating the title.

704. 9 Apr ●● EVERYTHING CHANGES – Take That Writers: Gary Barlow, Mike Ward, Eliot Kennedy and Cary Baylis. This extended the group's record to four immediate chart-toppers, and was the first UK No.1 to feature lead vocals by Robbie Williams.

705. 23 Apr ●● THE MOST BEAUTIFUL GIRL IN THE WORLD – Symbol Writer: Symbol. Despite writing No.1 hits for Chaka Khan and Sinead O'Connor, it was not until his 38th new hit that The Artist Formely Known As Prince topped the charts as a performer.

706. 7 May ● THE REAL THING – Tony Di Bart Writers: Lucinda Drayton, Tony Di Bart and Andy Blissett. Having made no impression on the Top 75 in its original form the previous September, the Joy Brothers remixed it to the top spot, while a 2 Unlimited song of the same name hung around the Top 10.

707. 14 May ● INSIDE – Stilskin Writer: Peter Lawlor. One of many No.1s to benefit from a massive Levi's TV campaign, but the first time that a new track was used.

708. 21 May ●● COME ON YOU REDS – Manchester United Football Squad Writers: Francis Rossi, Andy Brown, John Edwards. Manchester United became the first club to complete the League, Cup and Charts treble with a little help from Status Quo.

709. 4 Jun ●●●●●●●●●●●●●●● LOVE IS ALL AROUND – Wet Wet Wet Writer: Reg Presley. The year's biggest seller in the UK, this Troggs' cover had the longest run at No.1 by a British act, and was famously deleted from sale a week before equalling Bryan Adams's 16-week record.

710. 17 Sep ●●●● SATURDAY NIGHT – Whigfield Writers: Larry Pignagnoli and Davide Riva. The blonde bombshell from Denmark was the first artist to make a chart debut at No.1, with a hit that spawned a nationwide dance craze.

711. 15 Oct ●● SURE – Take That Writers: Gary Barlow, Robbie Williams and Mark Owen. This track was the fab five's fifth entry at No.1 in just 15 months and their first self-penned chart-topper.

712. 29 Oct ●●●● BABY COME BACK – Pato Banton Writer: Eddy Grant. A reggae revival of the Equals' 1968 No.1 was written by another No.1 artist and Equals band member.

713. 26 Nov ●● LET ME BE YOUR FANTASY – Baby D Writer: Floyd Dyce. This single hung around the nether regions of the Top 200 for two years before a remix and relaunch took it to the top.

714. 10 Dec ●●●●● STAY ANOTHER DAY – East 17 Writers: Tony Mortimer, Rob Kean and Dominic Hawken. Provided the phenomenally successful boy band with their only No.1 in a nine-year career.

1995

715. 14 Jan ●●● COTTON EYE JOE – Rednex Writers: Jan Ericsson, Oban and Pat Reiniz. A house version of an old country song, the video was banned on many US country TV programmes due to act's "hillbilly" image.

716. 4 Feb ●●●●●●● THINK TWICE – Celine Dion Writers: Andy Hill and Pete Sinfield. The bilingual French-Canadian songstress took a record 16 weeks to reach No.1 with this British-penned million-seller.

717. 25 Mar ● LOVE CAN BUILD A BRIDGE – Cher, Chrissie Hynde and Neneh Cherry with Eric Clapton Writers: Naomi Judd, John Jarvis and Paul Overstreet. A charity single in aid of Comic Relief, the hit revived a US country No.1 by The Judds and gave Eric Clapton his only No.1.

718. 1 Apr ● DON'T STOP (WIGGLE WIGGLE) – Outhere Brothers Writers: Hula Mahone, Craig Simpkins, Keith Mayberry and Aladino. Despite never hitting the Top 40 in the States, this US rap act managed to reach the chart summit twice in the UK.

719. 8 Apr ●●●● BACK FOR GOOD – Take That Writer: Gary Barlow. This was the pop princes' last hit before Robbie Williams went solo and it gave the act their only US hit.

720. 6 May ● SOME MIGHT SAY – Oasis Writer: Noel Gallagher. This track was the band's sixth hit and their first No.1, which went on to re-enter the chart six times.

721. 13 May ● DREAMER – Livin' Joy Writers: Paolo Visnadi and Janice Robinson. The first Italian / American No.1 act with a remixed version of their 1994 Top 20 entry.

722. 20 May ●●●●●●● UNCHAINED MELODY / WHITE CLIFFS OF DOVER – Robson Green and Jerome Flynn Writers: Alex North and Hy Zaret / Walter Kent and Janice Robinson. The TV stars were first UK act to make their chart debut at No.1. They did it with a pair of Righteous Brothers covers.

723. 8 Jul ●●●● BOOM BOOM BOOM – Outhere Brothers Writers: Hula Mahone and Keith Mayberry. The pop / rap duo was the first US act to top UK chart with its first two releases – NKOTB had managed it only when their first release was re-issued.

724. 5 Aug ●●● NEVER FORGET – Take That Writer: Gary Barlow. The band announced they were splitting soon after this hit, which proved to be an appropriate swan song.

725. 26 Aug ●● COUNTRY HOUSE – Blur Writers: Damon Albarn / Blur. This single release beat 'Roll With It' by Oasis in the headline-grabbing Britpop chart battle of the decade.

726. 9 Sep ●● YOU ARE NOT ALONE – Michael Jackson Writer: R Kelly. Jacko's big ballad was the first single to enter US chart at No.1, breaking his previous record set by Scream, which went in at No.5.

727. 23 Sep ● BOOMBASTIC – Shaggy Writer: Orville Burrell, Robert Livingstone and King Floyd. Shaggy is the only Jamaican-born act to score two No.1s. This was the fifth record used in Levi's advert to top the chart.

728. 30 Sep ●●●● FAIRGROUND – Simply Red Writer: Mick Hucknall. Despite massive international success, this was the only chart-topper for Hucknall's soul smoothies, and at the 20th attempt.

729. 28 Oct ●● GANGSTA'S PARADISE – Coolio featuring LV Writers: Artis Ivey Jr, Stevie Wonder, Larry Sanders and Doug Rasheed. Transatlantic No.1 based on Stevie Wonder's 'Pastime Paradise'. Coolio's single was 1995's biggest-selling single worldwide.

730. 11 Nov ●●●● I BELIEVE / UP ON THE ROOF – Robson Green and Jerome Flynn Writers: Ervin Drake, Irvin Graham, Jimmy Shirl and Al Stillman / Gerry Coffin and Carole King. Robson and Jerome returned Frankie Laine's 18-week No.1 'I Believe' to the top, and in so doing became the first act to enter at No.1 with its first two singles.

731. 9 Dec ●●●●●● EARTH SONG – Michael Jackson Writer: Michael Jackson. Jacko's live version on the Brits a few weeks later caused much controversy when Pulp singer Jarvis Cocker objected to the Christ-like nature of Jackson's performance and wiggled his bum at the cameras in protest.

1996

732. 20 Jan ● JESUS TO A CHILD – George Michael Writer: George Michael. George's first solo single for four years and his first solo hit to enter at No.1. It was highest new UK entry in the US chart (No.7) for more than 25 years.

733. 27 Jan ●●●●● SPACEMAN – Babylon Zoo Writer: Jas Mann. Fronted by the eccentric Mann, this track was yet another No.1 supported by a Levi's commercial and sold 400,000 copies in its first week – then a record for a debut chart act.

734. 2 Mar ● DON'T LOOK BACK IN ANGER – Oasis Writer: Noel

Gallagher. The band's only No.1 featuring Noel Gallagher on lead vocals and was the most played track on US college radio in 1997.

735. 9 Mar ●●● HOW DEEP IS YOUR LOVE – Take That Writers: Robin, Barry and Maurice Gibb. The Bee Gees' self-penned US No.1 was the group's last single and eighth chart-topper. They were the first act to have eight singles enter at No.1.

736. 30 Mar ●●● FIRESTARTER – Prodigy Writers: Liam Howlett, Keith Flint, Trevor Horn and Art of Noise. In the month after this hit single (which sampled The Art of Noise's 'Close to the Edit'), eight of the act's previous singles re-charted.

737. 20 Apr ●● RETURN OF THE MACK – Mark Morrison Writer: Mark Morrison. This was a very rare late-1990s US Top 3 single by a UK act, and came from Morrison's five-hit-spawning debut album.

738. 4 May ●●● FASTLOVE – George Michael Writers: George Michael, Patrice Rushen and Fred Washington. This disco-inflected hit owed something to Patrice Rushen's 'Forget Me Nots', as did Will Smith's No.1 'Men In Black'.

739. 25 May ● OOH AAH…JUST A LITTLE BIT – Gina G Writers: Simon Tauber, Steve Rodway. Gina G's hit is the only UK Eurovision Song Contest entry (and the first by a non-British representative) ever to reach the US Top 20.

740. 1 Jun ● 6 Jul ● THREE LIONS (THE OFFICIAL SONG OF THE ENGLAND FOOTBALL TEAM) – Baddiel and Skinner and Lightning Seeds Writers: Ian Broudie, Frank Skinner and David Baddiel. The football anthem written to support England's Euro 96 bid was the first No.1 of its kind not to feature footballers.

741. 8 Jun ●●●● KILLING ME SOFTLY – Fugees Writers: Norman Gimbel, Charles Fox. The top-selling single of the year was originally a US No.1 for Roberta Flack. The single became the first by a US group to debut at No.1 in the UK.

742. 20 Jul ● FOREVER LOVE – Gary Barlow Writer: Gary Barlow. Gary beat Robbie in the race for the first No.1 from an ex-Take That member. It was his seventh No.1 as a composer.

743. 27 Jul ●●●●●●● WANNABE – Spice Girls Writers: Richard Stannard, Matthew Rowe and Spice Girls. The first British all-girl group to top the chart, this would prove to be the biggest worldwide hit for the top UK act of the 1990s.

744. 14 Sep ● FLAVA – Peter Andre Writer: Peter Andre, Andy Whitmore, Wayne Hector and Cee. First of two successive entries at No.1 for the British-born, Australian-bred singer /songwriter.

745. 21 Sep ●● READY OR NOT – Fugees Writers: Wyclef Jean, Pras Michel, Lauryn Hill, William Hart and Thomas Bell. The second No.1 for the US group from their million-selling album The Score. Neither track was released as a single in America.

746. 5 Oct ● BREAKFAST AT TIFFANY'S – Deep Blue Something Writer: Todd David Pipes. The only US rock group since The Crickets (1957) to top the chart with its first self-penned Top 20 entry. The song originally peaked at No.55 two months earlier.

743 – Spice Girls

747. 12 Oct ● SETTING SUN – Chemical Brothers Writers: Ed Simons, Tom Rowlands and Noel Gallagher. Noel sang on the hit which equalled the two-week short-stay record for a No.1 in the Top 10.

748. 19 Oct ● WORDS – Boyzone Writers: Robin, Barry and Maurice Gibb. First No.1 for the top boy band of the 90s revived a 1968 Bee Gees Top 10 entry, the second Bees Gees-penned No.1 of the year.

749. 26 Oct ●● SAY YOU'LL BE THERE – Spice Girls Writers: Spice Girls and Eliot Kennedy. This track sold 350,000 copies in its first week; Sporty, Posh, Ginger, Baby and Scary became the first girl group to score two successive No.1s.

750. 9 Nov ●● WHAT BECOMES OF THE BROKEN HEARTED / SATURDAY NIGHT AT THE MOVIES / YOU'LL NEVER WALK ALONE – Robson Green and Jerome Flynn Writers: James Dean, Paul Riser and William Weatherspoon / Barry Mann and Cynthia Weil / Richard Rodgers and Oscar Hammerstein II. First act to debut at No.1 with its first three singles and the first triple A-side to reach No.1.

751. 23 Nov ●● BREATHE – Prodigy Writers: Liam Howlett, Keith Flint and Maxim. Rave music's No.1 act, with their 11th Top 15 single in a row and their second successive No.1.

752. 7 Dec ● I FEEL YOU – Peter Andre Writers: Peter Andre, Glen Goldsmith, Terry Jones and Oliver Jacobs. Andre was 1996's top male vocalist, achieving his second chart-topper in three months. It was, however, the smallest-selling No.1 of the year.

753. 14 Dec ● A DIFFERENT BEAT – Boyzone Writers: Ronan Keating, Stephen Gately, Shane Lynch, Keith Duffy, Ray Hedges, Larry Brannigan. The first part-penned No.1 for the Irish superstars, it set a record by becoming their second No.1 entry within two months.

754. 21 Dec ● KNOCKIN' ON HEAVEN'S DOOR / THROW THESE GUNS AWAY – Dunblane Writer: Bob Dylan / Edward Christopher and Thomas Millar. Dylan approved changes to the lyrics on a track that gave him his third No.1 as a composer and raised money for the Dunblane tragedy's families.

755. 28 Dec ●●● **2 BECOME 1 – Spice Girls** Writers: Spice Girls, Richard Stannard and Matt Rowe. The last million-selling Christmas hit made it three No.1s from three releases for the group.

1997

756. 18 Jan ● **PROFESSIONAL WIDOW (IT'S GOT TO BE BIG) – Tori Amos** Writer: Tori Amos. This Armand Van Helden remix of Amos's 1996 Top 20 entry was her first No.1 but used only brief vocal snippets from the original.

757. 25 Jan ● **YOUR WOMAN – White Town** Writer: Jyoti Mishra. This song sung by a male vocalist from a female point of view was produced in the Indian-born artist's bedroom. Mishra became the first solo male to make his chart debut at No.1.

758. 1 Feb ● **BEETLEBUM – Blur** Writers: Damon Albarn, Graham Coxon, Alex James and Dave Rowntree. The first No.1 hit recorded in Iceland was the act's last chart-topper of the century and the first No.1 to spend only two weeks in the Top 20.

759. 8 Feb ● **AIN'T NOBODY – LL Cool J** Writers: David Wolinski. Taken from the Beavis & Butt-head movie, this song reached No.1 on its fifth chart run 13 years after Mr Cool J's chart debut.

760. 15 Feb ● **DISCOTHEQUE – U2** Writers: Bono, The Edge, Adam Clayton, Larry Mullen and Simon Pyke. Unusually, this song by Dublin's rock aristocrats topped both US Modern Rock and Club Play charts.

761. 22 Feb ●●● **DON'T SPEAK – No Doubt** Writers: Gwen Stefani and Eric Stefani. With this single, No Doubt became the first US act to debut in the UK chart at No.1, with a track that was not released as a single in the US.

762. 15 Mar ●●● **MAMA / WHO DO YOU THINK YOU ARE – Spice Girls** Writers: Spice Girls, Richard Stannard, Matt Rowe / Spice Girls, Andy Watson and Paul Wilson. This Comic Relief single made the Spice Girls the first act to reach No.1 with their first four singles.

763. 5 Apr ● **BLOCK ROCKIN' BEATS – Chemical Brothers** Writers: Tom Rowlands, Ed Simons and Jesse Weaver. The second successive No.1 entry for the Chems featured an uncredited Schoolly D vocal. They were also the first UK named "brothers" act to top the charts since The Johnstone Brothers in 1955. Neither act were real brothers.

764. 12 Apr ●●● **I BELIEVE I CAN FLY – R Kelly** Writer: R Kelly. The biggest of eight hits from the R album, which amazingly failed to make the Top 20 album chart. It was also the biggest of six hits from the film Space Jam.

765. 3 May ● **BLOOD ON THE DANCE FLOOR – Michael Jackson** Writers: Michael Jackson and Teddy Riley. The troubled self-styled King of Pop's last No.1 of the century (and his seventh solo No.1) failed to reach the US Top 40. Cliff (if you add his hits with the Shadows) and Elvis are the only males to score more solo No.1s.

766. 10 May ● **LOVE WON'T WAIT – Gary Barlow** Writers: Madonna and Shep Pettibone. Barlow's second solo No.1 made him the only act to score 10 No.1s in the 90s. It was the first Madonna-penned topper for seven years and her only No.1 song performed by another act.

767. 17 May ●● **YOU'RE NOT ALONE – Olive** Writers: Tim Kellett and Robin Taylor-Firth. This first charted at No.42 in 1996. Olive were the first UK act to top the chart with a single that previously peaked outside the Top 40.

768. 31 May ● **I WANNA BE THE ONLY ONE – Eternal featuring BeBe Winans** Writers: BeBe Winans and James Lawrence. With the help of US gospel star Winans (his first UK hit), the group achieved their 13th successive Top 15 entry and their only No.1.

769. 07 Jun ●●● **MMMBOP – Hanson** Writers: Isaac, Taylor and Zach Hanson. The first debut single to top UK and US chart simultaneously, the youngest act to earn a platinum disc in the UK and the first family group to reach No.1 with their debut single.

770. 28 Jun ●●● **26 Jul** ●●● **I'LL BE MISSING YOU – Puff Daddy and Faith Evans (featuring 112)** Writer: Sting. This tribute to murdered rapper Notorious B.I.G. is based on a previous Police No.1. Sales of seven million made this the world's biggest-selling rap single and raised $3 million for Biggie's children. It's also the first single to debut at No.1 in both the UK and US.

771. 19 Jul ● **D'YOU KNOW WHAT I MEAN? – Oasis** Writer: Noel Gallagher. The group's third chart-topper sold 371,000 copies in its first week. At 7' 32" it was then the second-longest No.1.

772. 16 Aug ●●●● **MEN IN BLACK – Will Smith** Writers: Will Smith, Patrice Rushen, Terry McFadden and Fred Washington. The first solo No.1 for the artist formerly known as the Fresh Prince wasn't released as single in the US (although it topped airplay charts).

773. 13 Sep ● **THE DRUGS DON'T WORK – Verve** Writer: Richard Ashcroft. The first No.1 to mention drugs in the title was the act's only No.1 single and was soon dethroned by the world's biggest seller.

774. 20 Sep ●●●●● **CANDLE IN THE WIND 1997 / SOMETHING ABOUT THE WAY YOU LOOK TONIGHT – Elton John** Writers: Elton John and Bernie Taupin. The fastest-selling and biggest-selling single of all time with world sales of 33 million in three months. The hit was also a record 28th No.1 for producer George Martin.

772 – Will Smith

775. 25 Oct ● SPICE UP YOUR LIFE – Spice Girls Writers: Spice Girls, Richard Stannard and Matt Rowe. This single made them the first act to earn platinum discs with their first five singles.

776. 1 Nov ●●●● BARBIE GIRL – Aqua Writers: Soren Rasted, Claus Noreen, Rene Dif and Lene Nykstrom. The first Danish-based group to top the chart. At the time its US chart entry at No.7 was the highest for a debuting act.

777. 29 Nov ●● 10 Jan 1998 ● PERFECT DAY – Various Writer: Lou Reed. An all-star BBC charity record in aid of Children In Need and sold 385,000 in its first week. Singers included Lou Reed who originally wrote and recorded the song in 1972.

778. 13 Dec ●● TELETUBBIES SAY EH-OH! – Teletubbies Writers: Andrew McCrorie-Shand, Andrew Davenport. Taken from a TV show aimed at toddlers, this was the characters' only single. It sold more than a million and they were the fifth non-human act to top the chart.

779. 27 Dec ●● TOO MUCH – Spice Girls Writers: Spice Girls, Andy Watkins and Paul Wilson. The first act to score six No.1s in a row since The Beatles in 1964-66.

1998

780. 17 Jan ● NEVER EVER – All Saints Writers: Rickidy Raw and Shaznay Lewis. Sold more copies (770,000) before reaching No.1 than any previous single. This track was in the Top 20 best sellers for both 1997 and 1998.

781. 24 Jan ● ALL AROUND THE WORLD – Oasis Writer: Noel Gallagher. The longest single to top the chart at 9' 38". It gave the group No.1s in four consecutive years.

782. 31 Jan ● YOU MAKE ME WANNA – Usher Writers: Jermaine Dupri, Seal and Usher Raymond. At 18, Usher was the youngest chart-topper to write or co-write his own No.1 since Paul Anka some 40 years earlier.

783. 7 Feb ●● DOCTOR JONES – Aqua Writers: Soren Rasted, Claus Noreen, Rene Dif and Lene Nykstrom. The first Scandinavian act to reach No.1 with its first two releases, a record Abba couldn't match.

784. 21 Feb ● 14 Mar ● MY HEART WILL GO ON – Celine Dion Writers: James Horner and Will Jennings. Second UK million-seller for Celine – a record for a female act. She is joint record holder for the slowest (16 weeks) and fastest (one week) No.1. This single is the only record by a female to enter at No.1 in both the UK and US.

785. 28 Feb ● BRIMFUL OF ASHA – Cornershop Writer: Tjinder Singh. This Norman Cook remix of their earlier No.60 hit was the most played track on radio pre-release, and sold more than 200,000 in its first week.

786. 7 Mar ● FROZEN – Madonna Writer: Madonna and Patrick Leonard. Madge's 40th Top 10 entry came in her 40th year. It gave her her eighth No.1 after an eight-year absence.

787. 21 Mar ●●●●●● IT'S LIKE THAT – Run-DMC vs Jason Nevins Writer: Joseph Simmons, Darryl McDaniels and Lawrence Smith. Remix of rap pioneers' first US hit from 1983 stopped the Spice Girls from scoring their seventh No.1 with 'Stop'.

788. 2 May ● ALL THAT I NEED – Boyzone Writer: Carl Sturken and Evan Rogers. The Irish boy band equalled Gary Glitter's best male chart start with their 11th successive Top 5 entry.

789. 9 May ● 23 May ● UNDER THE BRIDGE / LADY MARMALADE – All Saints Writers: Anthony Kiedis, Michael Balzary, John Frusciante and Chad Smith / Bob Crewe and Kenny Nolan. These were revivals of previous Red Hot Chili Peppers and Labelle hits – both of which missed the Top 10.

790. 16 May ● TURN BACK TIME – Aqua Writers: Soren Rasted, Claus Noreen, Rene Dif and Lene Nykstrom. Third self-penned single made Aqua the first overseas act to have their first three releases reach the top.

791. 30 May ● FEEL IT – Tamperer featuring Maya Writers: Michael Jackson and Jackie Jackson. This hit samples the Jacksons' 1981 Top 10 entry 'Can You Feel It' and was the seventh No.1 penned by Michael Jackson.

792. 6 Jun ●●C'EST LA VIE – B*Witched Writers: B*Witched, Ray Hedges, Tracey Ackerman, Martin Brannigan. The first debut record by a female group or an Irish act to enter at No.1. They are the youngest girl group to reach No.1.

793. 20 Jun ●●● 3 LIONS '98 – Baddiel and Skinner and Lightning Seeds Writers: Ian Broudie, David Baddiel and Frank Skinner. The first song to reach the top twice with amended lyrics by the same act. It sadly failed to inspire the England team in France.

794. 11 Jul ● BECAUSE WE WANT TO – Billie Writer: Dion Rambo, Jacques Richmond, Wendy Page and Jim Marr. At 15 Billie became the youngest female to make her chart debut at No.1.

795. 18 Jul ● FREAK ME – Another Level Writers: Roy Murray and Keith Sweat. The only No.1 by 1998's biggest-selling new UK group had previously been a US chart-topper (and minor UK hit) by Silk.

796. 25 Jul ● DEEPER UNDERGROUND – Jamiroquai Writers: Jason Kay and Toby Smith. It was 13th time lucky – the group's first No.1 with their 13th hit was featured in the film Godzilla. The video reportedly cost $1 million.

797. 1 Aug ●● VIVA FOREVER – Spice Girls Writers: Spice Girls, Richard Stannard and Matt Rowe. The girl power group's seventh No.1 in two years pushed their UK single sales past six million.

798. 15 Aug ●●● NO MATTER WHAT – Boyzone Writers: Andrew Lloyd Webber and Jim Steinman. The first act to see all of their initial dozen singles reach the Top 5. The third No.1 for both composers and winner of the first Record of the Year was the biggest seller ever by an Irish act.

799. 5 Sep ● IF YOU TOLERATE THIS YOUR CHILDREN WILL BE NEXT – Manic Street Preachers Writers: James Dean Bradfield, Sean Moore and Nick Jones. This song equals the record for the longest unbracketed title to top the chart and the act was the first Welsh group to hit the top since Amen Corner in 1969.

800. 12 Sep ● BOOTIE CALL – All Saints Writers: Shaznay Lewis and Karl Gordon. This was the band's third No.1 of the year and marked the 800th chart-topper.

801. 19 Sep ● MILLENNIUM – Robbie Williams Writers: Robbie Williams, Guy Chambers, John Barry and Leslie Bricusse. The ex-Take That star's first No.1 samples 'You Only Live Twice', making it the only James Bond theme to reach the top.

802. 26 Sep ● I WANT YOU BACK – Melanie B featuring Missy Elliott Writers: Missy Elliott, Gerard Thomas and Donald Holmes. The first solo No.1 for a Spice Girl was Elliott's third chart entry in six weeks. This hit gave Mel B her eighth UK No.1 – equalling the female record.

803. 3 Oct 98 ●● ROLLERCOASTER – B*Witched Writers: B*Witched, Ray Hedges, Tracey Ackerman, Martin Brannigan. The first female act and first non-UK act to enter at No.1 with first two releases.

804. 17 Oct ● GIRLFRIEND – Billie Writers: Dion Rambo and Jacques Richmond. She is the youngest artist and the first female soloist to reach No.1 with her first two singles.

805. 24 Oct ● GYM AND TONIC – Spacedust Writers: Spacedust. The smallest-selling No.1 of the year was a cover of Bob Sinclar's 'Gymtonic' which sampled actress / keep-fit guru Jane Fonda.

806. 31 Oct ●●●●●●● BELIEVE – Cher Writers: Brian Higgins, Paul Barry, Steve Torch, Matt Gray, Stuart McLennen and Timothy Powell. Cher extended her No.1 span to a record 33 years two months with the year's top seller. At 52 was (still) the oldest solo female to top the charts.

807. 19 Dec ● TO YOU I BELONG – B*Witched Writers: B*Witched, Ray Hedges, Tracey Ackerman, Martin Brannigan. Their third No.1 of the year with their third release. They are the only female act to debut at No.1 with first three releases.

808. 26 Dec ● GOODBYE – Spice Girls Writers: Spice Girls, Richard Stannard, Matt Rowe. Their eighth No.1 and third Christmas topper in succession. The girls' last release of the decade made them the top-selling singles act of the 90s.

1999

809. 2 Jan ● CHOCOLATE SALTY BALLS (PS I LOVE YOU) – Chef Writer: Trey Parker. The 1970s soul legend Isaac Hayes performed as the voice of Chef in the adult cartoon South Park, scoring his first No.1 22 years after his last hit.

810. 9 Jan ● HEARTBEAT / TRAGEDY – Steps Writers: Jackie James / Barry, Maurice and Robin Gibb. This single spent 30 weeks on the chart and sold more than a million. The double A-side included the Bee Gees' 10th No.1 and their biggest-selling hit as composers.

811. 16 Jan ● PRAISE YOU – Fatboy Slim Writers: Norman Cook and Camille Yarborough. Norman Cook's third No.1 after chart-toppers with Housemartins and Beats International (plus a No.1 remix for Cornershop). At times this was only the UK record in the US Top 100.

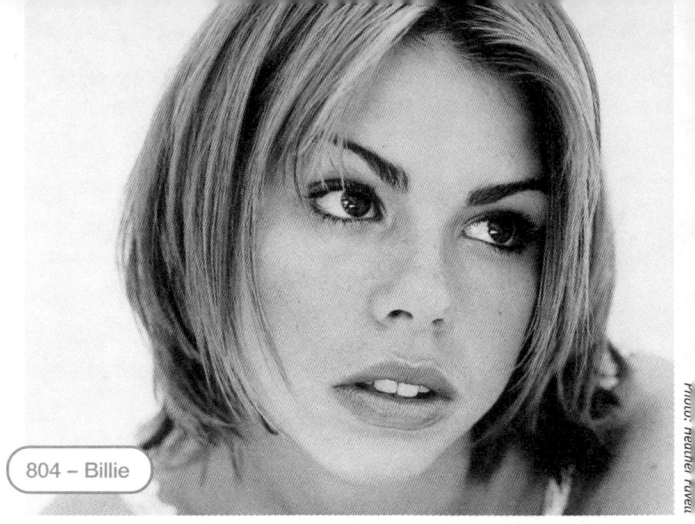

804 – Billie

812. 23 Jan ● A LITTLE BIT MORE – 911 Writer: Bobby Gosh. A revival of a 1976 No.2 hit by Dr Hook, 911's ninth consecutive Top 10 entry was the only one to reach No.1.

813. 30 Jan ● PRETTY FLY (FOR A WHITE GUY) – Offspring Writers: Dexter Holland, Robert John "Mutt" Lange, Joe Elliott and Steve Clark. A record eighth No.1 in eight weeks, this track has been downloaded from the internet a record 22 million times.

814. 6 Feb ● YOU DON'T KNOW ME – Armand Van Helden featuring Duane Harden Writers: Armand Van Helden and Duane Harden. The biggest hit for the US producer who has reportedly mixed more than 60 hit records for other acts including a No.1 for Tori Amos.

815. 13 Feb ● MARIA – Blondie Writer: Jimmy Destri. Fifty-three-year-old Debbie Harry's group extended the record gap between newly recorded No.1s by the same act to 18 years and three months.

816. 20 Feb ● FLY AWAY – Lenny Kravitz Writer: Lenny Kravitz. This Grammy winner was the first TV commercial (Peugeot in UK and Nissan in the US) to reach No.1 for three years.

817. 27 Feb ●● BABY ONE MORE TIME – Britney Spears Writer: Max Martin. The fastest-selling debut single ever – 464,000 copies were sold in the first week. She was the youngest female act to achieve a million-seller in the UK, and this was a record-shattering 12th different No.1 in 12 weeks. Its final UK total soared to 1,445,000.

818. 13 Mar ●● WHEN THE GOING GETS TOUGH – Boyzone Writers: Wayne Braithwaite, Barry Eastmond, Mutt Lange and Billy Ocean. This cover of the 1986 No.1 by Billy Ocean was co-written by Shania Twain's husband Mutt Lange and royalties went to Comic Relief.

819. 27 Mar ● BLAME IT ON THE WEATHERMAN – B*Witched Writers: Ray Hedges, Tracey Ackerman, Martin Brannigan and Andy Caine. B*Witched became the first act to debut at No.1 with their first four releases. It also marked the first time siblings followed each other to No.1 – Keavy and Edele being sisters of Boyzone's Shane.

820. 3 Apr ●● FLAT BEAT – Mr Oizo Writer: Quentin Dupieux. The first French act to reach the top for almost 25 years and the seventh Levi's TV ad track to reach No.1. Advert and video featured puppet Flat Eric.

821. 17 Apr ●● PERFECT MOMENT – Martine McCutcheon
Writers: Wendy Page and Jim Marr. Martine was the third EastEnders regular to score a chart-topper after Wendy Richard (1962) and Nick Berry (1986), and was only female to top the chart after being seen regularly in a soap.

822. 1 May ●● SWEAR IT AGAIN – Westlife Writers: Steve Mac and Wayne Hector. After the last-minute name change from Westside, the Irish act was the first boy band to make its chart debut at No.1. The single also earned them a US gold record.

823. 15 May ● I WANT IT THAT WAY – Backstreet Boys
Writers: Randy Goodrum. The group's first No.1 came with their eighth successive Top 10 entry, which was a record for a US group.

824. 22 May ● YOU NEEDED ME – Boyzone Writers: Randy Goodrum. Their record 15th consecutive Top 5 entry was a revival of a minor UK hit by Anne Murray which had topped the US chart in 1978.

825. 29 May ●● SWEET LIKE CHOCOLATE – Shanks & Bigfoot
Writers: Stephen Meade and Daniel Langsman. The title was a tribute to the act's label, Chocolate Boy, and the track features uncredited vocals by Sharon Woolf. It sold a staggering 74,000 on its first day.

826. 12 Jun ● EVERYBODY'S FREE (TO WEAR SUNSCREEN) – Baz Luhrmann Writers: Tim Cox, Nigel Swanston and Mary Schmich. One of the most unusual No.1s of all time started life as part of a graduation speech by Chicago student Mary Schmich. The first non-rap, spoken-word chart-topper since J J Barrie back in 1976.

827. 19 Jun ● BRING IT ALL BACK – S Club 7 Writers: Elliot Kennedy, Mike Percy, Tim Lever and S Club 7. The much-hyped stars of TV series Miami 7 (shown in 100 countries) entered the chart at No.1 with their debut single. The youthful septet is the biggest vocal group to top the chart.

828. 26 Jun ● BOOM, BOOM, BOOM, BOOM!! – Vengaboys
Writers: Dennis Van Den Driessen and Wessel Van Diepen. Positiva Records' first No.1 from seven dozen hits. The fourth No.1 within six years that had "boom" in its title and the only chart-topper to repeat the same word four times in its title.

829. 03 Jul ●● (9PM) TILL I COME – ATB Writers: Anor Tanneberger, Arcos Ferrerons and Garrido Rivera. First time in 22 years that Continental European acts had back-to-back No.1s. This was the single's fourth chart visit (once on vinyl only and two import versions).

830. 17 Jul ●●● LIVIN' LA VIDA LOCA – Ricky Martin Writers: Robi Rosa and Desmond Child. Transatlantic chart-topper gave composer Child his first No.1 with his 28th hit. Martin was the first Puerto Rican to reach the top.

831. 07 Aug ●● WHEN YOU SAY NOTHING AT ALL – Ronan Keating
Writers: Paul Overstreet and Don Schlitz. Song previously topped the US country chart by the late Keith Whitley (1987) and won a Grammy for Alison Krauss. This recording was featured in the film Notting Hill.

832. 21 Aug ● IF I LET YOU GO – Westlife Writers: Jorgen Elofsson, Per Magnusson and David Kreuger. Fifth of a record seven singles by Irish groups to reach No.1 this year (beating the total of the previous 46 years combined!). It dethroned their co manager, Ronan Keating.

833. 28 Aug ● MI CHICO LATINO – Geri Halliwell Writers: Geri Halliwell, Paul Wilson and Andy Watkins. First of three successive No.1s (a record for a solo female vocalist) for the ex-Spice Girl was another Latin-influenced 1999 hit.

834. 04 Sep ●● MAMBO NO.5 (A LITTLE BIT OF…) – Lou Bega
Writers: Perez Prado, David LuBega and Christian Pletschacher. Worldwide hit which was the flagship of a short-lived mambo revival was an update of a 1950s favourite by previous chart-topper Perez Prado.

835. 18 Sep ● WE'RE GOING TO IBIZA! – Vengaboys Writers: Jeff Calvert and Geraint Hughes. Multinational European-based act made it two No.1s in a row with a slight rewrite of Typically Tropical's 1975 chart-topper 'Barbados'.

836. 25 Sep ●●● BLUE (DA BA DEE) – Eiffel 65 Writers: Massimo Gabutti, Maurizo Lobina and Gianfranco Randone. Third successive European-recorded chart-topper. The Italian trio's first hit was No.1 simultaneously in 10 European countries and sold 500,000 in the UK in just 20 days.

837. 16 Oct ●● GENIE IN A BOTTLE – Christina Aguilera Writers: Steve Kipner, David Frank and Pam Sheyne. Part-British composition took the US teenager to the top on both side of the Atlantic. In the US, part of the lyric was considered "too racy" and was amended.

838. 30 Oct ● FLYING WITHOUT WINGS – Westlife Writers: Steve Mac and Wayne Hector. Like their first two releases this entered at No.1 – no previous act achieved this feat faster. The song was the winner of TV's Record of the Year award.

839. 06 Nov ● KEEP ON MOVIN' – Five Writers: Richard Stannard, Julian Gallagher, Jay Brown, Abs Breen and Sean Conlon. Five's seventh successive Top 10 entry gave the boy band their first No.1. It was the ninth topper that co-writer Stannard (of Spice Girls fame) had produced.

840. 13 Nov ● LIFT ME UP – Geri Halliwell Writers: Geri Halliwell, Paul Wilson, Andy Watkins and Tracey Ackerman. After a much publicised battle for the summit, the ex-Spice Girl beat current group member Emma Bunton to No.1.

841. 20 Nov ● SHE'S THE ONE / IT'S ONLY US – Robbie Williams
Writers: Karl Wallinger / Guy Chambers and Steve Power. A-side was a Brit-winning single and video which revived the World Party track and 'It's Only Us' was used on a FIFA football simulation game.

842. 27 Nov ● KING OF THE CASTLE – Wamdue Project Writer: Chris Brann. Originally released June 1998, it took off thanks to Roy Malone's remix (which Brann was not too keen on). The sixth No.1 of 1999 to chart first on import.

843. 04 Dec ●●● THE MILLENNIUM PRAYER – Cliff Richard
Writers: Traditional, arranged by Paul Field, Stephen Deal, Cliff Richard and Nigel Wright. The first single to climb to No.1 for a record 11 months contained the oldest lyric and tune to top the chart. It extended Cliff's No.1 span to 40 years.

844. 25 Dec ●●●● I HAVE A DREAM / SEASONS IN THE SUN – Westlife Writers: Benny Andersson and Björn Ulvaeus / Jacques

Brel and Rod McKuen. The millennium ended with Westlife becoming the only act since Elvis in 1962 to amass four No.1s in a year. The single coupled an Abba No.2 hit with a previous No.1.

2000

845. 22 Jan ● THE MASSES AGAINST THE CLASSES – Manic Street Preachers Writers: James Dean Bradfield, Sean Moore and Nick Jones. The Welsh rockers, who had the most consecutive Top 40 entries in the 1990s, notched up the first chart-topper of the new millennium.

846. 29 Jan ● BORN TO MAKE YOU HAPPY – Britney Spears Writers: Kristian Lundin and Andreas Carlsson. Second No.1 from the biggest-selling album ever by a teenager returned the youngest US female to enter at No.1 back to the top.

847. 05 Feb ●● RISE – Gabrielle Writers: Bob Dylan, Louise Bobb, Ferdy Under-Hamilton and Ollie Dagois. For the second time in 40 months, Dylan's 'Knockin' on Heaven's Door' was heard on a chart-topper.

848. 19 Feb ● GO LET IT OUT – Oasis Writer: Noel Gallagher. The group's first single for two years was the inaugural release on their own label and the first single featuring their two new members.

849. 26 Feb ●● PURE SHORES – All Saints Writers: Shaznay Lewis and William Orbit. Sales of 685,000 made this second-highest-selling single of 2000. Taken from the film The Beach it was first of two successive soundtrack No.1s for producer William Orbit.

850. 11 Mar ● AMERICAN PIE – Madonna Writers: Don McLean. Her update of this previous No.2 hit by composer McLean gave Madonna her 50th (different) hit and her ninth No.1.

851. 18 Mar ● DON'T GIVE UP – Chicane featuring Bryan Adams Writers: Nick Bracegirdle, Bryan Adams and Ray Hedges. Adam's first No.1 since the record-breaking 'Everything I Do'. He is the only Canadian male to top the chart since 1976.

852. 25 Mar ● BAG IT UP – Geri Halliwell Writers: Geri Halliwell, Paul Wilson and Andy Watkins. Her third successive solo No.1 was also her 10th chart-topper in total – both records for female performers.

853. 01 Apr ● NEVER BE THE SAME AGAIN – Melanie C / Lisa Left Eye Lopes Writers: Melanie Chisholm, Rhett Lawrence, Lisa Lopes and Paul Cruz. Spice Girl replaces ex-Spice Girl at the top. It was Mel C's first No.1 without the rest of the quartet and TLC member Lopes's first.

854. 08 Apr ● FOOL AGAIN – Westlife Writers: Jorgen Elofsson, Per Magnusson and David Kreuger. The fifth Swedish-penned No.1 in a year made the boys the first act to have five UK No.1s with their first five releases.

855. 15 Apr ● FILL ME IN – Craig David Writers: Craig David and Mark Hill. Youngest UK male soloist to top the chart for more than 40 years (since Craig Douglas in 1959) and the youngest to write his own No.1.

856. 22 Apr ●● TOCA'S MIRACLE – Fragma Writers: Ramon Zenker, Dirk Duderstadt, Marco Duderstadt, Victor Imbres and Rob Davies. Combining Fragma's 1999 Top 20 hit 'Toca Me' and Coco's 1997 Top 40 entry 'I Need a Miracle' proved to be a winning idea.

857. 06 May ● BOUND 4 DA RELOAD (CASUALTY) – Oxide & Neutrino Writers: Alex Rivers, Kenneth Freeman and Mark Oseitutu. Teenage production duo's re-working of the theme from the TV series Casualty. Oddly, it did not reach the Top 40 radio airplay chart.

858. 13 May ● OOPS! … I DID IT AGAIN – Britney Spears Writers: Max Martin and Rami Yacoub. Oops she did it again, and became the youngest female artist to clock up three No.1s – a record she held for only two weeks.

859. 20 May ● DON'T CALL ME BABY – Madison Avenue Writers: Cheyne Coates, Andy Van Dorsselaer, Duane Morrison and Guiseppe Chierchia. Six months after peaking at No.30 it re-entered at No.1. It spent 20 weeks in the US Top 100 and reached only 88.

860. 27 May ● DAY & NIGHT – Billie Piper Writers: Elliot Kennedy, Tim Lever, Billie Piper and Mark Cawley. Youngest female to score trio of No.1s did so with the sixth of a record 11 toppers in 2000 to feature solo female vocalists.

861. 3 Jun ●●● IT FEELS SO GOOD – Sonique Writers: Sonia Clarke, Simon Belofsky, Graeme Pleeth and Linus Burdick. No single by a UK female spent longer at No.1 since Kate Bush's 'Wuthering Heights' in 1978.

862. 24 Jun ● YOU SEE THE TROUBLE WITH ME – Black Legend Writers: Barry White and Ray Parker Jr. This massive club hit initially sampled Barry White's 1975 hit. When the walrus of lurve wouldn't give clearance for the sample, the vocal was provided by Elroy "Spoonface" Powell.

863. 1 Jul ● SPINNING AROUND – Kylie Minogue Writers: Ira Shickman, Dinky Bingham, Kara DioGuardi and Paula Abdul. Kylie has had a staggering 25 solo Top 20 hits (out of 26 releases) before this, her first single to enter at No.1.

864. 8 Jul ● THE REAL SLIM SHADY – Eminem Writers: Marshall Mathers, Andre Young and Melvin Bradfield. This track name-checks more popstars than any other No.1, including Dr Dre, Christina Aguilera, Britney Spears, Fred Durst and the man himself, Eminem.

865. 15 Jul ● BREATHLESS – Corrs Writers: Robert John "Mutt" Lange and Corrs. This makes the Corrs the only mixed family group and the first female / male Irish act to hit the top spot.

866. 22 Jul ● LIFE IS A ROLLERCOASTER – Ronan Keating Writers: Rick Nowels and Gregg Alexander. No Irish solo act can better Ronan's two chart-toppers and no Irish artist has appeared on more No.1s.

867. 29 Jul ● WE WILL ROCK YOU – Five and Queen Writers: Brian May, Abs Breen and Jay Brown. Marks the first time the song has ever charted and the first time two groups have combined on a No.1.

868. 5 Aug ● 7 DAYS – Craig David Writers: Craig David, Mark Hill and Darren Hill. Craig was the youngest British male solo artist to top the charts twice. Ironically, it spent just seven days at No.1

869. 12 Aug ● ROCK DJ – Robbie Williams Writers: Robbie Williams, Guy Chambers, Kelvin Andrews, Nelson Pigford and Ekundayo Paris. Based around a Barry White sample, Robbie's 10th topper was the second No.1 to be inspired by the soul legend in just eight weeks.

870. 19 Aug ● I TURN TO YOU – Melanie C Writers: Melanie Chisholm, Rick Nowels and Billy Steinberg. With this hit Mel C became the first female to top the chart as a soloist, in a duo and in a group.

871. 26 Aug ● GROOVEJET (IF THIS AIN'T LOVE) – Spiller Writers: Cristano Spiller, Sophie Ellis-Bextor, Robert Davis, Vince Montana Jr and Ron Walker. The year's fastest-selling No.1 with record-breaking first-week sales of more than 200,000 copies. It stopped Victoria Beckham from reaching No.1 in a hugely hyped chart battle.

872. 2 Sep ● MUSIC – Madonna Writers: Madonna Ciccone and Mirwais Ahmadzai. Madonna's 10th No.1 was one of only two US million-sellers in 2000. Only the Beatles, Elvis and Cliff have had more No.1s.

873. 9 Sep ● TAKE ON ME – A1 Writers: Pal Waaktaar, Mags Furuholmen and Morten Harket. A1 were the first Anglo-Norwegian act to top the charts, achieved with a track which Norway's A-Ha took to No.2 15 years earlier.

874. 16 Sep ●● LADY (HEAR ME TONIGHT) – Modjo Writers: Yann Destagnol, Romain Tranchart, Nile Rodgers and Bernard Edwards. The first French group to top the UK chart, and the first Rodgers and Edwards (Chic) No.1.

875. 30 Sep ●● AGAINST ALL ODDS – Mariah Carey and Westlife Writer: Phil Collins. This version beat the Phil Collins original which peaked at No.2 in 1984. Only Mariah Carey's second UK No.1, neither of which have hit the top in the US – conversely, none of her 15 US No.1s have gone all the way in the UK.

876. 14 Oct ● BLACK COFFEE – All Saints Writers: Tom Nichols, Alexander Soos and Kirsty Elizabeth Roper. All seven All Saints singles to date had reached the Top 10, with five going to No.1. The first single with coffee in the title to make the Top 10.

877. 21 Oct ● BEAUTIFUL DAY – U2 Writers: Adam Clayton, David Evans, Paul Hewson and Larry Mullen. U2's 25th Top 20 hit, 21st Top 10 hit and their fourth No.1 was the sixth Irish single to top the chart in 2000.

878. 28 Oct ● STOMP – Steps Writers: Mark Topham, Karl Twigg and Rita Campbell. Scoring their 150th week on chart with this hit, Steps were the first boy / girl UK group to have two No.1s since Bucks Fizz.

879. 4 Nov ● HOLLER / LET LOVE LEAD THE WAY – Spice Girls Writers: Rodney Jerkins, LeShawn Daniels, Fred Jerkins III and Spice Girls / Same writers plus Harvey Mason Jr. The girls now have more No.1s than the Rolling Stones and Take That. The Beatles are the only group to have amassed more chart-toppers faster.

880. 11 Nov ● MY LOVE – Westlife Writers: Pelle Nylen, Per Magnusson, David Kreuger and Jorgan Elofsson. With No.1s from all of their first seven releases, they surpassed Elvis as the quickest act to accumulate seven No.1s.

881. 18 Nov ● SAME OLD BRAND NEW YOU – A1 Writers: Eric Foster White, Ben Adams, Mark Read and Christian Ingebrigtsen. Track was co-written by the band and Eric White who has written for Whitney Houston among others. First boy band quartet to score two No.1s.

882. 24 Nov ● CAN'T FIGHT THE MOONLIGHT – LeAnn Rimes Writer: Diane Warren. Rimes, who recorded the all-time biggest-selling country single ('How Do I Live?'), is the first country singer to enter the UK chart at No.1. It was Diane Warren's first solely composed No.1.

883. 2 Dec ● INDEPENDENT WOMEN PART 1 – Destiny's Child Writers: Samuel Barnes, Jean Oliver, Cory Rooney and Beyonce Knowles. The first US female trio to top the UK charts since the Three Degrees in 1974, and the first record by an American girl group to top the UK and US chart simultaneously since the Supremes did it with 'Baby Love' exactly 36 years earlier.

884. 9 Dec ● NEVER HAD A DREAM COME TRUE – S CLUB 7 Writers: Cathy Dennis and Simon Ellis. The group is the only TV / pop act to have two No.1s, beating the Partridge Family, the Monkees, the Archies and others. The hit raised money for Children In Need.

885. 16 Dec ● STAN – Eminem Writers: Marshall Mathers, Dido Armstrong and Paul Herman. The only male rapper to score two solo No.1s, and the first No.1 with a boy's name as the title since 'Frankie' by Sister Sledge in 1985.

886. 23 Dec ●● CAN WE FIX IT – Bob the Builder Writer: Mike Joyce. Achieved the year's highest sales (853,000) and was the first record to climb to No.1 since Cliff's 'Millennium Prayer'. Bob's the first builder to reach the Top 10 since Loadsamoney in 1988.

866 – Ronan Keating

Photo: Mark Allan

Top 40 Acts

Here is the Guinness British Hit Singles Top 100 ranked first by the number of weeks any act has racked up in the entire history of the UK singles chart (1952-2000). Where acts tie for a position in our league table by having an identical number of weeks on the chart, we rank one act above another by taking into account their tally of No.1 hits. If this fails to separate the wheat from the pop chaff, then we take into account other peak positions at No.2, then No.3 and so on.

The calculations in this league table have been used throughout the main section of this book (the hit singles: A-Z by artist) which includes, for every act ranked within the Top 500 by weeks on chart, a numbered position within the pop elite.

Regular sharp-eyed readers of Guinness British Hit Singles will note the elevation of the Shadows and Diana Ross into the Top 5 this year. This is not because of a huge revival in the year's chart fortunes for these pop legends, merely a strong feeling that the Shads should be credited with all of the Cliff and the Shadows hits that include their name as the act on the record at the time of the release. Similarly, Diana Ross gets added chart weeks for the hits on which she was name-checked with the Supremes.

	ACT NAME	TOTAL WEEKS ON CHART	NO.1 HITS	TOTAL HITS
1	Elvis PRESLEY	1168	17	130
2	Cliff RICHARD	1142	14	131
3	SHADOWS	770	12	63
4	Elton JOHN	566	4	75
5	Diana ROSS	560	2	77
6	MADONNA	546	10	54
7	Michael JACKSON	480	7	51
8	Rod STEWART	475	6	61
9	BEATLES	456	17	32
10	David BOWIE	477	5	66
11	Frank SINATRA	440	3	38
12	QUEEN	419	6	51
13	Stevie WONDER	415	2	54
14	STATUS QUO	413	1	56
15	Paul McCARTNEY	408	4	51
16	Tom JONES	390	2	41
17	ROLLING STONES	366	8	48
18	BEE GEES	349	5	37
19	Roy ORBISON	345	3	34
20	EVERLY BROTHERS	344	4	30
21	UB40	329	3	47
22	Shirley BASSEY	326	2	31
23	Perry COMO	322	2	26
24	Jim REEVES	322	1	26
25	Lonnie DONEGAN	321	3	30
26	HOLLIES	318	2	32
27	FOUR TOPS	318	1	33
28	OASIS	309	5	17
29	Whitney HOUSTON	308	4	32
30	Pat BOONE	308	1	27
31	SUPREMES	306	1	31
32	PRINCE	305	1	51
33	Donna SUMMER	299	1	42
34	HOT CHOCOLATE	283	1	35
35	Frankie LAINE	281	4	27
36	BEACH BOYS	281	2	32
37	Billy FURY	281	0	29
38	SLADE	279	6	36
39	Shakin' STEVENS	277	4	37
40	MADNESS	268	1	32

The Shadows: Jet Harris, Hank Marvin, Bruce Welch and Tony Meehan. This line-up contributed most to their 770 weeks on chart

Where more than one hit was in the chart simultaneously, each hit counts for one week. A double A-side normally counts as only one single, ie one disc.

Photo: Redferns

Top of the Pops Top 40

BBC TV's Top of the Pops commissioned Guinness British Hit Singles to compile a Top 40 based on every chart since the show began in January 1964. The results shown here are based on chart performance points due to the lack of complete sales data during some years between 1964 and 2000.

The Guinness ranking system points are awarded as follows: 40 points for a week spent at No.1, 39 points for a week spent at No.2, 38 points for a week spent at No.3 and so on, down to one point for a week at No.40.

Free: Highest placed band without a No.1 hit in the Top 40

Pos / Single title / Act name	Peak chart pos	Release years	Points total
1. RELAX - Frankie Goes To Hollywood	(1)	1984,1993	1,210 pts
2. SHE LOVES YOU - Beatles	(1)	1963	948 pts
3. MY WAY – Frank Sinatra	(5)	1969,1970,1971	936 pts
4. I LOVE YOU BECAUSE – Jim Reeves	(5)	1964,1971	920 pts
5. BOHEMIAN RHAPSODY – Queen	(1)	1975,1991	913 pts
6. (EVERYTHING I DO) I DO IT FOR YOU – Bryan Adams	(1)	1991	855 pts
7. LOVE IS ALL AROUND – Wet Wet Wet	(1)	1994	846 pts
8. RIVERS OF BABYLON / BROWN GIRL IN THE RING – Boney M	(1)	1978,1993	827 pts
9. ALBATROSS – Fleetwood Mac	(1)	1968,1973	796 pts
10. THINK TWICE – Celine Dion	(1)	1994	788 pts
11. RELEASE ME – Engelbert Humperdinck	(1)	1967	785 pts
12. THE LAST WALTZ – Engelbert Humperdinck	(1)	1967	770 pts
13. YOU'RE THE ONE THAT I WANT – John Travolta and Olivia Newton-John	(1)	1978,1998	760 pts
14. TEARS – Ken Dodd	(1)	1965	757 pts
15. TIE A YELLOW RIBBON ROUND THE OLD OAK TREE – Dawn featuring Tony Orlando	(1)	1973	756 pts
16. ALL RIGHT NOW – Free	(2)	1970,1973,1991	754 pts
17. IMAGINE – John Lennon	(1)	1975,1980,1999	745 pts
18. AMAZING GRACE – Judy Collins	(5)	1970,1971,1972	729 pts
19. YOUNG GIRL – Gary Puckett and the Union Gap	(1)	1968,1974	721 pts
20. I WILL ALWAYS LOVE YOU – Whitney Houston	(1)	1992,1993	700 pts
21. DISTANT DRUMS – Jim Reeves	(1)	1966	696 pts
22. BLUE MONDAY – New Order	(3)	1983,1988,1995	688 pts
23. YOU'VE LOST THAT LOVIN' FEELIN' – The Righteous Brothers	(1)	1965,1969,1990	684 pts
24. I WON'T FORGET YOU – Jim Reeves	(3)	1964	683 pts
25. SAILING – Rod Stewart	(1)	1975,1976	675 pts
26. SUGAR SUGAR – Archies	(1)	1969	671 pts
27. HOW DO I LIVE – LeAnn Rimes	(7)	1998	666 pts
28. NEVER EVER – All Saints	(1)	1997	641 pts
29. YOU SEXY THING – Hot Chocolate	(2)	1975,1987,1997	640 pts
30. HEARTBEAT / TRAGEDY – Steps	(1)	1998	639 pts

Pos / Single title / Act name	Peak chart pos	Release years	Points total
31. WHAT A WONDERFUL WORLD / CABARET – Louis Armstrong	(1)	1968	633 pts
32. TWO LITTLE BOYS – Rolf Harris	(1)	1969	631 pts
33. CANDLE IN THE WIND 1997 / SOMETHING ABOUT THE WAY YOU LOOK TONIGHT – Elton John	(1)	1997	625 pts
34. LEADER OF THE PACK – Shangri-Las	(3)	1965,1972,1976	623 pts
35. HONEY – Bobby Goldsboro	(2)	1968,1975	620 pts
36. A WHITER SHADE OF PALE – Procol Harum	(1)	1967,1972	618 pts
37. TAKE MY BREATH AWAY (LOVE THEME FROM 'TOP GUN') – Berlin	(1)	1986,1990	613 pts
38. GHOSTBUSTERS – Ray Parker Jr	(2)	1984	611 pts
39. TWO TRIBES – Frankie Goes To Hollywood	(1)	1984,1994,2000	608 pts
40. GREEN GREEN GRASS OF HOME – Tom Jones	(1)	1966	605 pts

Re-entries, re-issues, remixes and re-recordings are all counted provided the original vocal is used and the original artists are credited.

All years listed are for appearances by singles within the UK Top 40.

All singles included have appeared in the UK singles chart since the first Top of the Pops show in January 1964. Any single that appeared in the chart used in the first show carries the full chart history of that single's performance in the weeks before the first show. Chief example of this is 'She Loves You' by The Beatles.

Hit No.15 was also the lead track of Free EP which peaked at No.11 but was not included in our calculations. Hit No.18 was credited to "Union Gap featuring Gary Puckett" on its first chart entry. Hit No.13 was also featured in 'Grease Megamix' which peaked at No.3 but was not included in our calculations here. Hit No.33 does not include points for previous versions of 'Candle in the Wind'.

Chart Trivia – Top 10s

TOP 10 BOND THEMES

What, no 'Diamonds Are Forever', 'Goldfinger' and 'From Russia with Love'? None of these John Barry-composed classics breached the Top 10 in their day, so our 007 chart champions look like this.

Pos	Hit/Act	Weeks on chart/Peak position/Total points		
1.	A VIEW TO A KILL *Duran Duran*	16	2	**102**
2.	WE HAVE ALL THE TIME IN THE WORLD *Louis Armstrong*	13	3	**98**
3.	NOBODY DOES IT BETTER *Carly Simon*	12	7	**79**
4.	LICENCE TO KILL *Gladys Knight*	11	6	**65**
5.	LIVE AND LET DIE *Wings*	14	9	**51**
6.	THE LIVING DAYLIGHTS *A-Ha*	9	5	**49**
7.	FOR YOUR EYES ONLY *Sheena Easton*	13	8	**45**
8.	YOU ONLY LIVE TWICE *Nancy Sinatra*	19	11	**27**
9.	GOLDENEYE *Tina Turner*	9	10	**13**
10.	THE WORLD IS NOT ENOUGH *Garbage*	9	11	**10**

Based on 20 points for one week at No.1, 19 points for one week at No.2 etc.

Duran Duran

TOP 10 SOAPS IN POP

The most successful soaps calculated by the hits associated with their actors are determined by ...

Pos	Soap	Total weeks on chart/Total hits/Charting acts from the soap		
1.	NEIGHBOURS	489	65	7
2.	EASTENDERS	450	61	15
3.	CORONATION STREET	434	61	15
4.	BROOKSIDE	90	9	1
5.	HOME AND AWAY	68	14	2
6.	EMMERDALE	49	10	5
7.	CROSSROADS	35	4	3
8.	PRISONER CELL BLOCK H	19	3	2
9.	HOLLYOAKS	9	2	1
10.	SONS AND DAUGHTERS	3	1	1

TOP 10 HITS BY SOAP STARS

The top songs by stars of soaps screened on British TV are calculated by weeks on chart and highest chart position

Pos	Hit/Act	Weeks on chart/Highest chart position	
1.	PERFECT MOMENT *Martine McCutcheon*	20	1
2.	TORN *Natalie Imbruglia*	17	2
3.	I SHOULD BE SO LUCKY *Kylie Minogue*	16	1
4.	SWEETNESS *Michelle Gayle*	16	4
5.	LOVE ME / TALKING IN YOUR SLEEP *Martine McCutcheon*	16	6
6.	ESPECIALLY FOR YOU *Kylie Minogue and Jason Donovan*	14	1
7.	HILLBILLY ROCK HILLBILLY ROLL *Woolpackers*	14	5
8.	EVERY LOSER WINS *Nick Berry*	13	1
9.	TOO MANY BROKEN HEARTS *Jason Donovan*	13	1
10.	JE NE SAIS PAS POURQUOI *Kylie Minogue*	13	2

Equal peak positions (8 and 9) are ranked by the number of weeks at No.1

Martine McCutcheon

NON-HUMAN TOP 10

Chart calculated by most weeks on chart

1. WOMBLES – 96 weeks

With their policy of "making good use of the things that they find", they have been credited by some with the invention of sampling.

2. SMURFS – 52 weeks

Small, blue and Dutch, their biggest hit was the unimaginatively titled 'The Smurf Song'.

3. TWEETS – 34 weeks

Developed by MI5 interrogation experts as an answer to Chinese water torture, except the torture kicks in after about 30 seconds.

4. TELETUBBIES – 32 weeks

Cuddly aliens who sent 'Teletubbies Say Eh-Oh!' to No.1 in 1997.

5. ARCHIES – 26 weeks

'Sugar Sugar' was No.1 on both sides of the Atlantic for these cartoon teenagers.

6. SIMPSONS – 19 weeks

'Do the Bartman' and 'Deep Deep Trouble' make up the dysfunctional family's chart repertoire.

7. ROLAND RAT SUPERSTAR – 19 weeks

Just pipped for sixth place by The Simpsons, as none of his three hits, on Rodent label, troubled the Top 10.

8. SPITTING IMAGE – 18 weeks

Latex puppets who accumulated their chart tally singing about chickens, out-of-work Santas, and atheist choirs.

9. MR BLOBBY – 16 weeks

Along with Long John Baldry, a contender for tallest UK No.1 act.

10. MUPPETS – 15 weeks

Eight of these weeks on chart are courtesy of Robin the frog's Nick Drake-influenced 'Halfway Down the Stairs', a childhood lament about not fitting in, which puts most of his uncle Kermit's material in the shade.

> *Honourable mentions should go to Jive Bunny, that long-eared scourge of the Christmas party, who didn't sing or play on his hits, and French fashion icon Flat Eric – 'Flat Beat' was actually credited to his human buddy Mr Oizo. Recent chart sensations Mr Hanky, Bob the Builder and Chef need a little more chart action before making an impact on any future list.*

The Archies

TOP 10 SOAP STARS IN POP

Martin Kemp, Bernadette Nolan, Clare Grogan, Wendy Richard and Mike Reid head the list of pop people who charted before soap stardom, but who are the most successful actors turned pop stars? Based on actors appearing in soaps screened on British TV, here is the Top 10 calculated by weeks on chart, total hits and highest chart position.

Pos	Artist	Weeks on chart	Total hits	Peak position
1.	KYLIE MINOGUE	250	32	1
2.	JASON DONOVAN	137	17	1
3.	DANNII MINOGUE	67	13	4
4.	MARTINE McCUTCHEON	56	5	1
5.	MICHELLE GAYLE	52	7	4
6.	CRAIG McLACHLAN	40	8	2
7.	MICHAEL BALL	39	10	2
8.	NATALIE IMBRUGLIA	39	4	2
9.	SEAN MAGUIRE	34	8	14
10.	NICK BERRY	24	3	1

The likes of Peter Noone (Herman's Hermits) and Davey Jones (Monkees) have not had enough solo chart action to merit a place here.

TOP 10 CHRISTMAS HITS

Although 'I Will Always Love You' by Whitney Houston and 'Bohemian Rhapsody' by Queen are the most successful Christmas hits of all time, here are the "real" Christmas singles that actually name-check the festive season in their song titles.

Calculated by weeks at No. 1, 2, 3, 4 and 5

1. DO THEY KNOW IT'S CHRISTMAS? *Band Aid*
2. MERRY XMAS EVERYBODY *Slade*
3. LONELY THIS CHRISTMAS *Mud*
4. CHRISTMAS ALPHABET *Dickie Valentine*
5. DO THEY KNOW IT'S CHRISTMAS? *Band Aid II*
6. MERRY CHRISTMAS EVERYONE *Shakin' Stevens*
7. LAST CHRISTMAS *Wham!*
8. SANTO NATALE (MERRY CHRISTMAS) *David Whitfield*
9. ALL I WANT FOR CHRISTMAS IS YOU *Mariah Carey*
10. I BELIEVE IN FATHER CHRISTMAS *Greg Lake*

Statistically, these are the best, but let's name-check some classics that fell short of the Top 10. 'White Christmas', 'Rockin' Around The Christmas Tree', 'I Wish It Could Be Christmas Every Day' and 'Wonderful Christmas Time' all use the "C" word and are as much a part of the celebrations as turkey and crackers.

The Hits That Never Were

Fans of Guinness British Hit Singles continue to bemoan the omission of a select few milestone tracks and artists from our pages. 'Matrimony' by Gilbert O'Sullivan and lesser known rarities such as Marty Wilde's 'Abergavenny' and Cockney Rebel's 'Sebastian' might be well-loved classics to some, but if they failed to scrape a lowly chart placing or were never even released as a single, then they simply don't make the cut. Here are the biggies that never were.

1966   HEV YEW GOTTA LOIGHT BOY?
The Singing Postman

Allan Smethurst appeared on the same Top of the Pops show as the Rolling Stones. His record also outsold theirs, but only in his native Norfolk. During his period of fame he was a 37-year-old postman earning £12 a week. 'Hev Yew Gotta Loight Boy' included the immortal verse, "Molly Windley, she smokes just loike a chimbley but she's my little nicotine girl". The lyrics helped this chart escapee to win an Ivor Novello award for best novelty song of 1966. Smethurst died aged 73 in 2000, before seeing the completion of his set of republished songs on the Anglian Music label.

1968   TIP-TOE THRU' THE TULIPS WITH ME
Tiny Tim

Rock nutter of the highest order, big-boned Tiny Tim was an idiosyncratic figure missed by literally hundreds of adoring fans. 'Tip-Toe Thru' the Tulips with Me' was a cover of a 1929 Nick Lucas track from the movie musical Gold Diggers of Broadway, and Tim's version reached the US Top 20 in 1968. Born Herbert Khaury (you can see why he changed his name) in 1930, he rose to fame on US TV playing his ukulele on shows such as Rowan and Martin's Laugh-In. His highly moral stance on sexuality earned him serious column inches and he married his sweetheart Miss Vicki on Johnny Carson's Tonight Show. The couple had one daughter, and they called her Tulip.

1971   STAIRWAY TO HEAVEN
Led Zeppelin

Any true Led Head will tell you that Zep were too rock to release singles. Singles are for girls. This didn't stop the heavy rock anthem becoming at one stage the most played song on US rock radio, and certainly the track most budding Jimmy Pages choose to play in guitar shops across the world. The song made it into this book most recently by way of an unlikely cover by Rolf Harris in 1993. Australia's second-finest export (after Kylie, obviously) had never heard the track and performed his rendition with only the sheet music to guide him. He went on to perform his version at Glastonbury, after having received death threats from heavy metal heavies in New Zealand who considered Rolf's unique version of this classic to be sacrilege.

1967   BROWN EYED GIRL
Van Morrison

This Belfast-born member of the Rock and Roll Hall of Fame has produced his fair share of classic recordings, but perhaps the track that really broke him post-Them was this Bert Berns-produced celebration of love in a style redolent of classic black harmony groups. The song which did make the US Top 10 began life as 'Brown Skinned Girl' but evolved into its new form in the vocal booth as Mr Morrison thought it sounded better. Despite press reports to the contrary, Van the Man claims the song wasn't referring to anyone in particular.

1963   PUFF THE MAGIC DRAGON
Peter, Paul and Mary

These Sixties folk popsters did a nice line in Dylan covers and children's songs, the most memorable of which was 'Puff the Magic Dragon' which reached the US No.2 spot in 1963. Written by Peter Yarrow, the track was a doleful ditty about the loss of innocence in the early Sixties and elaborated on an idea by Yarrow's schoolfriend Leonard Lipton. The mythical nature of the lyrics left it open to rampant misinterpretation by mischievous hippies who discovered references in the song to everything from the Vietnam War to marijuana.

The Singing Postman

Photo: Pictorial Press

A–Z by Artist

This section of Guinness British Hit Singles lists every act, from A to ZZ Top, that has ever had a hit on the UK singles chart from 1952 to the end of 2000. A hit is defined as any release that makes the chart even for one week in the bottom position (currently No.75).

DATES OF HITS

When using this section please note that the dates given are for the date of chart entry and not the single's peak position. The date shown is traditionally the week ending date (usually and currently Saturday) when the record hits the chart. As an example, 'Goodbye' by The Spice Girls entered the chart in the week ending 26 December 1998, which means that its first day of chart action was 20 December, also making it the 1998 Christmas No.1.

WHAT DO THE SYMBOLS MEAN?

Information on which singles went straight in at No.1, million-sellers, US No.1s and much more are indicated by the symbols which are explained at the foot of each page. These, together with a list of abbreviations used in the act biographies, are clearly

From A...

Photo: Angela Lubrano

explained in the "How to use this section" instructions on the following page.

RECORD CATALOGUE NUMBERS

Catalogue numbers listed in this book are generally taken from the seven-inch single before January 1993 and CD single after this time.

WHO GETS THE CREDIT?

If a hit appears in an act's list of singles but has a different act name or collaboration with another artist, we acknowledge the fact by using a boxed number footnote, which is explained on the page following.

COLLABORATIONS

All collaborative hits are listed under the entries of both or all the artists credited. So, for example, both Mariah Carey and Westlife entries carry their 2000 collaboration on 'Against All Odds'. There is no separate entry for them as a new act and the weeks that this record spent on the chart are credited to both Mariah Carey and Westlife.

...to ZZ Top

Photo: Pictorial Press

How to Use this Section

This totally fictitious entry illustrates how to understand all the symbols and access all the information you need to know about each single.

Position in the Top 500 acts of all time (calculated by most weeks on chart – see also page 70)

Act name

INDIGO MOOD (466 *Top 500*) *UK male vocal / instrumental band, formed in 1969. Original line-up: Tel "Slowhand" Petitt (g), Dave Whitehead replaced by Steve "Medicine Man" Bailey (d), Alan Davies (v), Les Gray replaced by Steve "Eggy" Randall (b). Hugely popular in Hemel Hempstead, Hertfordshire (99 WEEKS)*

Mini-biography for acts within the Top 500

Total weeks on chart

pos/wks

Peak position / weeks on chart

Indicates a UK Top 10 hit

19 Nov 69 ● **SPANISH EYES** *Guinness World Records 001* ◆ 9   9

UK million seller

22 Apr 70   **UNDERNEATH THE ARCHES** *Guinness World Records 002*......31   4

US No.1

All re-entries indented

2 May 70   **HELLO MARYLOO** *Guinness World Records 002* ▲ 16   7

No.1 hit

12 Sep 70 — **HELLO MARYLOO (re-entry)** *Guinness World Records 002* 39   4

30 Dec 70 ★ **HELLO MARYLOO (re-mix)** *Guinness World Records 003* [1] 1 18

Highest position reached on chart

14 Mar 71 ● **MY WAY (AL'S BIG BALLAD)** *Guinness World Records 004* 7 11

Weeks on chart

Date of chart entry (week ending on a Friday, or more recently a Saturday)

30 Oct 72   **SUMP GREEN / SUITS AND RED** *Guinness World Records 005*..50   1

22 Jul 73   **THE BIRD ON MRS COLETART'S ROOF**
   Guinness World Records 006 [2] 26   7

Refers to numbered footnote

UK entry at No.1

22 Dec 00   **UNCLE EGGY'S BIRTHDAY CAKE** *Eve Records 007* ■ 12   1+

Alternative label credit

[1] Indigo Mood featuring Greenhills Carol [2] Indigo Mood featuring Mrs Gretoli

Still on chart in Jan 2001

Cross-reference: linking act to associated act or acts

See also MANDATE

Label and catalogue number

MINI-BIOGRAPHY ABBREVIATIONS

b. – born, d. – died, b – bass guitar, d – drums, fl – flute, g – guitar, k – keyboard, prc – percussion, prog – programming, s – saxophone, syn – synthesizer, t – trumpet, v – vocals

In this edition, for the first time, the act biographies include the real names of all solo artists and duos scoring a Top 10 hit and the lead vocalists on all chart-toppers.

A

A
UK, male vocal / instrumental group (6 WEEKS) pos/wks

7 Feb 98	FOGHORN *Tycoon TYCD 5*	63	1
11 Apr 98	NUMBER ONE *Tycoon TYCD 6*	47	1
27 Jun 98	SING-A-LONG *Tycoon TYCD 7*	57	1
24 Oct 98	SUMMER ON THE UNDERGROUND *Tycoon TYCD 8*	72	1
5 Jun 99	OLD FOLKS *Tycoon TYCD 9*	54	1
21 Aug 99	I LOVE LAKE TAHOE *Tycoon TYCD 10*	59	1

A1
UK / Norway, male vocal group (58 WEEKS) pos/wks

3 Jul 99	● BE THE FIRST TO BELIEVE *Columbia 6674222*	6	9
11 Sep 99	● SUMMERTIME OF OUR LIVES *Columbia 6678322*	5	6
13 Nov 99	SUMMERTIME OF OUR LIVES (re-entry) *Columbia 6678322*	62	2
20 Nov 99	● EVERYTIME / READY OR NOT *Columbia 6681872*	3	11
4 Mar 00	● LIKE A ROSE *Columbia 6689032*	6	12
9 Sep 00	★ TAKE ON ME *Columbia 6695902* ■	1	10
18 Nov 00	★ SAME OLD BRAND NEW YOU *Columbia 6705202* ■	1	7+
2 Dec 00	TAKE ON ME (re-entry) *Columbia 6695902*	69	1

A PERFECT CIRCLE
US, male vocal / instrumental group (1 WEEK) pos/wks

18 Nov 00	THE HOLLOW *Virgin VUSCD 181*	72	1

A+
US, male rapper - Andre Levins (9 WEEKS) pos/wks

13 Feb 99	● ENJOY YOURSELF *Universal UND 56230*	5	9

A TEENS
Sweden, male / female vocal group (10 WEEKS) pos/wks

4 Sep 99	MAMMA MIA *Stockholm 5613432*	12	5
11 Dec 99	SUPER TROUPER *Stockholm 5615002*	21	5

A vs B
UK, male production duo (1 WEEK) pos/wks

9 May 98	RIPPED IN 2 MINUTES *Positiva CDTIV 89*	49	1

AALIYAH
US, female vocalist - Aaliyah Haughton (43 WEEKS) pos/wks

2 Jul 94	BACK AND FORTH *Jive JIVECD 357*	16	5
15 Oct 94	(AT YOUR BEST) YOU ARE LOVE *Jive JIVECD 359*	27	2
11 Mar 95	AGE AIN'T NOTHING BUT A NUMBER *Jive JIVECD 369*	32	2
13 May 95	DOWN WITH THE CLIQUE *Jive JIVECD 377*	33	2
9 Sep 95	THE THING I LIKE *Jive JIVECD 382*	33	2
3 Feb 96	I NEED YOU TONIGHT *Big Beat A 8130CD* [1]	66	1
24 Aug 96	IF YOUR GIRL ONLY KNEW *Atlantic A 5669CD*	21	2
23 Nov 96	GOT TO GIVE IT UP *Atlantic A 5632CD*	37	2
24 May 97	IF YOUR GIRL ONLY KNEW / ONE IN A MILLION (re-issue) *Atlantic A 5610CD*	15	3
30 Aug 97	4 PAGE LETTER *Atlantic AT 0010CD1*	24	2
22 Nov 97	THE ONE I GAVE MY HEART TO / HOT LIKE FIRE *Atlantic AT 0017CD*	30	2
18 Apr 98	JOURNEY TO THE PAST *Atlantic AT 0026CD*	22	3
12 Sep 98	ARE YOU THAT SOMEBODY? *Atlantic AT 0047CD*	11	4
22 Jul 00	● TRY AGAIN *Virgin VUSCD 167* ▲	5	11

[1] Junior M.A.F.I.A. featuring Aaliyah

ABBA `43` `Top 500`
The most successful Swedish recording act in the UK: Bjorn Ulvaeus (g/v), Benny Andersson (k/v), Agnetha Faltskog (v), and Norwegian Anni-Frid (Frida) Lyngstad (v). 'Waterloo' was the first Scandinavian No.1 in the UK and the biggest ever Eurovision Song Contest-winning hit in the US (252 WEEKS) pos/wks

20 Apr 74	★ WATERLOO *Epic EPC 2240*	1	9
13 Jul 74	RING RING *Epic EPC 2452*	32	5
12 Jul 75	I DO I DO I DO I DO I DO *Epic EPC 3229*	38	6
20 Sep 75	● S. O. S. *Epic EPC 3576*	6	10

13 Dec 75	★ MAMMA MIA *Epic EPC 3790*	1	14
27 Mar 76	★ FERNANDO *Epic EPC 4036*	1	15
21 Aug 76	★ DANCING QUEEN *Epic EPC 4499* ▲	1	15
20 Nov 76	● MONEY MONEY MONEY *Epic EPC 4713*	3	12
26 Feb 77	★ KNOWING ME KNOWING YOU *Epic EPC 4955*	1	13
22 Oct 77	★ THE NAME OF THE GAME *Epic EPC 5750*	1	12
4 Feb 78	★ TAKE A CHANCE ON ME *Epic EPC 5950*	1	10
16 Sep 78	● SUMMER NIGHT CITY *Epic EPC 6595*	5	9
3 Feb 79	● CHIQUITITA *Epic EPC 7030*	2	9
5 May 79	● DOES YOUR MOTHER KNOW *Epic EPC 7316*	4	9
14 Jul 79	● ANGELEYES / VOULEZ-VOUS *Epic EPC 7499*	3	11
20 Oct 79	● GIMME GIMME GIMME (A MAN AFTER MIDNIGHT) *Epic EPC 7914*	3	12
15 Dec 79	● I HAVE A DREAM *Epic EPC 8088*	2	10
2 Aug 80	★ THE WINNER TAKES IT ALL *Epic EPC 8835*	1	10
15 Nov 80	★ SUPER TROUPER *Epic EPC 9089*	1	12
18 Jul 81	● LAY ALL YOUR LOVE ON ME *Epic EPC A13 1456*	7	7
12 Dec 81	● ONE OF US *Epic EPC A 1740*	3	10
20 Feb 82	HEAD OVER HEELS *Epic EPC A 2037*	25	7
23 Oct 82	THE DAY BEFORE YOU CAME *Epic EPC A 2847*	32	6
11 Dec 82	UNDER ATTACK *Epic EPC A 2971*	26	8
12 Nov 83	THANK YOU FOR THE MUSIC *CBS A 3894*	33	6
5 Sep 92	DANCING QUEEN (re-issue) *Polydor PO 231*	16	5

'Lay All Your Love On Me' was available only on 12" vinyl in the UK

ABBACADABRA
UK, male / female vocal / instrumental group (1 WEEK) pos/wks

5 Sep 92	DANCING QUEEN *PWL International PWL 246*	57	1

Russ ABBOT
UK, male vocalist - Russell Roberts (22 WEEKS) pos/wks

6 Feb 82	A DAY IN THE LIFE OF VINCE PRINCE *EMI 5249*	61	1
20 Feb 82	A DAY IN THE LIFE OF VINCE PRINCE (re-entry) *EMI 5249*	75	1
29 Dec 84	● ATMOSPHERE *Spirit FIRE 4*	7	13
13 Jul 85	ALL NIGHT HOLIDAY *Spirit FIRE 6*	20	7

Gregory ABBOTT
US, male vocalist (13 WEEKS) pos/wks

22 Nov 86	● SHAKE YOU DOWN *CBS A 7326* ▲	6	13

ABC `328` `Top 500`
Glossy but witty pop group formed 1980, in Sheffield, South Yorkshire, UK. Led by stylish vocalist Martin Fry b. 9 Mar 1959. First UK group of the 1980s to prise four Top 20 hits off debut album (1982's The Lexicon of Love) and were equally successful Stateside (93 WEEKS) pos/wks

31 Oct 81	TEARS ARE NOT ENOUGH *Neutron NT 101*	19	8
20 Feb 82	● POISON ARROW *Neutron NT 102*	6	11
15 May 82	● THE LOOK OF LOVE *Neutron NT 103*	4	11
4 Sep 82	● ALL OF MY HEART *Neutron NT 104*	5	8
15 Jan 83	THE LOOK OF LOVE (re-entry) *Neutron NT 103*	71	1
5 Nov 83	THAT WAS THEN THIS IS NOW *Neutron NT 105*	18	4
21 Jan 84	S.O.S. *Neutron NT 106*	39	5
10 Nov 84	HOW TO BE A MILLIONAIRE *Neutron NT 107*	49	4
6 Apr 85	BE NEAR ME *Neutron NT 108*	26	4
15 Jun 85	VANITY KILLS *Neutron NT 109*	70	1
16 Jan 86	OCEAN BLUE *Neutron NT 110*	51	3
6 Jun 87	WHEN SMOKEY SINGS *Neutron NT 111*	11	10
5 Sep 87	THE NIGHT YOU MURDERED LOVE *Neutron NT 112*	31	8
28 Nov 87	KING WITHOUT A CROWN *Neutron NT 113*	44	3
27 May 89	ONE BETTER WORLD *Neutron NT 114*	32	4
23 Sep 89	THE REAL THING *Neutron NT 115*	68	1
14 Apr 90	THE LOOK OF LOVE (re-mix) *Neutron NT 116*	68	1
27 Jul 91	LOVE CONQUERS ALL *Parlophone R 6292*	47	2
11 Jan 92	SAY IT *Parlophone R 6298*	42	3
22 Mar 97	STRANGER THINGS *Blatant / Deconstruction 453632*	57	1

The act was a UK, male vocal / instrumental group for first six hits, and a UK / US, male / female vocal / instrumental group for the next four; male duo 87-92 and Martin Fry alone for 'Stranger Things'

Paula ABDUL
US, female vocalist (67 WEEKS) pos/wks

4 Mar 89	● STRAIGHT UP *Siren SRN 111* ▲	3	13
3 Jun 89	FOREVER YOUR GIRL *Siren SRN 112* ▲	24	6
19 Aug 89	KNOCKED OUT *Siren SRN 92*	45	3

UK No.1 ★ UK Top 10 ● Still on chart + UK million seller ◆ UK entry at No.1 ■ US No.1 ▲

2 Dec 89	(IT'S JUST) THE WAY THAT YOU LOVE ME *Siren SRN 101*	74	1
7 Apr 90 ●	OPPOSITES ATTRACT *Siren SRN 124* 1 ▲	2	13
21 Jul 90	KNOCKED OUT (re-mix) *Virgin America VUS 23*	21	5
29 Sep 90	COLD HEARTED *Virgin America VUS 27* ▲	46	3
22 Jun 91 ●	RUSH RUSH *Virgin America VUS 38* ▲	6	11
31 Aug 91	THE PROMISE OF A NEW DAY *Virgin America VUS 44* ▲	52	2
18 Jan 92	VIBEOLOGY *Virgin America VUS 53*	19	6
8 Aug 92	WILL YOU MARRY ME *Virgin America VUS 58*	73	1
17 Jun 95	MY LOVE IS FOR REAL *Virgin America VUSCD 91* 2	28	3

1 Paula Abdul with the Wild Pair 2 Paula Abdul featuring Ofra Haza

ABI UK, male vocalist (2 WEEKS)
pos/wks
| 13 Jun 98 | COUNTING THE DAYS *Kuku CDKUKU 1* | 44 | 2 |

ABIGAIL UK, female vocalist (4 WEEKS)
pos/wks
| 16 Jul 94 | SMELLS LIKE TEEN SPIRIT *Klone CDKLONE 25* | 29 | 4 |

Colonel ABRAMS US, male vocalist (35 WEEKS)
pos/wks
17 Aug 85 ●	TRAPPED *MCA MCA 997*	3	23
7 Dec 85	THE TRUTH *MCA MCA 1022*	53	3
8 Feb 86	I'M NOT GONNA LET YOU (GET THE BEST OF ME) *MCA MCA 1031*	24	7
15 Aug 87	HOW SOON WE FORGET *MCA MCA 1179*	75	2

ABSOLUTE US, male production / instrumental duo (3 WEEKS)
pos/wks
| 18 Jan 97 | I BELIEVE *AM:PM 5820752* 1 | 38 | 2 |
| 14 Mar 98 | CATCH ME *AM:PM 5825032* | 69 | 1 |

1 Absolute featuring Suzanne Palmer

ABSOLUTELY FABULOUS – See PET SHOP BOYS

AC/DC 210 Top 500 Internationally acclaimed Australia-based quintet: Angus Young (g), Malcolm Young (g), Bon Scott (v) (d. 1980), Cliff Williams (b), Phillip Rudd (d). Brian Johnson (ex-Geordie) replaced Scott in 1980. No act has had more hits (28) without a Top 10 than AC/DC (126 WEEKS)
pos/wks
10 Jun 78	ROCK 'N' ROLL DAMNATION *Atlantic K 11142*	24	9
1 Sep 79	HIGHWAY TO HELL *Atlantic K 11321*	56	4
2 Feb 80	TOUCH TOO MUCH *Atlantic K 11435*	29	9
28 Jun 80	DIRTY DEEDS DONE DIRT CHEAP *Atlantic HM 2*	47	3
28 Jun 80	HIGH VOLTAGE (LIVE VERSION) *Atlantic HM 1*	48	3
28 Jun 80	IT'S A LONG WAY TO THE TOP (IF YOU WANNA ROCK 'N' ROLL) *Atlantic HM 3*	55	3
28 Jun 80	WHOLE LOTTA ROSIE *Atlantic HM 4*	36	8
13 Sep 80	YOU SHOOK ME ALL NIGHT LONG *Atlantic K 11600*	38	8
29 Nov 80	ROCK 'N' ROLL AIN'T NOISE POLLUTION *Atlantic K 11630*	15	8
6 Feb 82	LET'S GET IT UP *Atlantic K 11706*	13	6
3 Jul 82	FOR THOSE ABOUT TO ROCK (WE SALUTE YOU) *Atlantic K 11721*	15	6
29 Oct 83	GUNS FOR HIRE *Atlantic A 9774*	37	4
4 Aug 84	NERVOUS SHAKEDOWN *Atlantic A 9651*	35	4
6 Jul 85	DANGER *Atlantic A 9532*	48	4
18 Jan 86	SHAKE YOUR FOUNDATIONS *Atlantic A 9474*	24	5
24 May 86	WHO MADE WHO *Atlantic A 9425*	16	5
30 Aug 86	YOU SHOOK ME ALL NIGHT LONG (re-issue) *Atlantic A 9377*	46	4
16 Jan 88	HEATSEEKER *Atlantic A 9136*	12	6
2 Apr 88	THAT'S THE WAY I WANNA ROCK 'N' ROLL *Atlantic A 9098*	22	5
22 Sep 90	THUNDERSTRUCK *Atco B 8907*	13	5
24 Nov 90	MONEYTALKS *Atco B 8886*	36	3
27 Apr 91	ARE YOU READY *Atco B 8830*	34	3
17 Oct 92	HIGHWAY TO HELL (LIVE) *Atco B 8479*	14	4
6 Mar 93	DIRTY DEEDS DONE DIRT CHEAP (LIVE) *Atco B 6073CD*	68	1
10 Jul 93	BIG GUN *Atco B 8396CD*	23	3
30 Sep 95	HARD AS A ROCK *Atlantic A 4368CD*	33	2
11 May 96	HAIL CAESAR *East West 7559660512*	56	1
15 Apr 00	STIFF UPPER LIP *EMI CDSTIFF 100*	65	1

ACE UK, male vocal / instrumental group (10 WEEKS)
pos/wks
| 9 Nov 74 | HOW LONG *Anchor ANC 1002* | 20 | 10 |

Richard ACE Jamaica, male vocalist (2 WEEKS)
pos/wks
| 2 Dec 78 | STAYIN' ALIVE *Blue Inc. INC 2* | 66 | 2 |

ACE OF BASE 296 Top 500
Swedish pop-reggae outfit comprising three Berggren family members, Linn, b. 31 Oct 1970 (v), Jenny, b. 19 May 1972 (v), Jonas 'Joker', b. 21 Mar 1967 (k) and Ulf 'Buddha' Ekberg, b. 6 Dec 1970 (k) all from Gothenburg. Only Swedish act to top the US album chart with 'The Sign' (titled 'Happy Nation' outside US) in 1994 (100 WEEKS)
pos/wks
8 May 93 ★	ALL THAT SHE WANTS *London 8612702*	1	16
28 Aug 93	WHEEL OF FORTUNE *London 8615452*	20	6
13 Nov 93	HAPPY NATION *London 8619272*	42	3
26 Feb 94 ●	THE SIGN *London ACECD 1* ▲	2	16
11 Jun 94 ●	DON'T TURN AROUND *London ACECD 2*	5	11
15 Oct 94	HAPPY NATION (re-issue) *London 8610972*	40	5
14 Jan 95	LIVING IN DANGER *London ACECD 3*	18	4
11 Nov 95	LUCKY LOVE *London ACECD 4*	20	5
27 Jan 96	BEAUTIFUL LIFE *London ACECD 5*	15	6
25 Jul 98 ●	LIFE IS A FLOWER *London ACECD 7*	5	11
10 Oct 98 ●	CRUEL SUMMER *London ACECD 8*	8	5
19 Dec 98	ALWAYS HAVE, ALWAYS WILL *London ACECD 9*	12	10
17 Apr 99	EVERYTIME IT RAINS *London ACECD 10*	22	4

ACEN UK, male producer (4 WEEKS)
pos/wks
| 8 Aug 92 | TRIP II THE MOON *Production House PNT 042* | 38 | 3 |
| 10 Oct 92 | TRIP II THE MOON (re-mix) *Production House PNT 042RX* | 71 | 1 |

ACES – See Desmond DEKKER and the ACES

Tracy ACKERMAN – See Q

ACT
UK / Germany, male / female vocal / instrumental group (2 WEEKS)
pos/wks
| 23 May 87 | SNOBBERY AND DECAY *ZTT ZTAS 28* | 60 | 2 |

ACT ONE US, male / female vocal / instrumental group (6 WEEKS)
pos/wks
| 18 May 74 | TOM THE PEEPER *Mercury 6008 005* | 40 | 6 |

ADAM and the ANTS 195 Top 500 Warpaint-wearing, colourfully costumed 'Antmusic' innovators: included Stuart (Adam Ant) Goddard (v) and Marco Pirroni (g). The London-based act was 1981's top chart act with nine hits. Also in that year, they amassed 91 chart weeks - a total not bettered until 1996 (130 WEEKS)
pos/wks
2 Aug 80	KINGS OF THE WILD FRONTIER *CBS 8877*	48	5
11 Oct 80 ●	DOG EAT DOG *CBS 9039*	4	16
6 Dec 80 ●	ANTMUSIC *CBS 9352*	2	18
27 Dec 80 ●	YOUNG PARISIANS *Decca F13803*	9	13
24 Jan 81	CARTROUBLE *Do It DUN 10*	33	9
24 Jan 81	ZEROX *Do It DUN 8*	45	9
21 Feb 81 ●	KINGS OF THE WILD FRONTIER (re-entry) *CBS 8877*	2	13
9 May 81 ★	STAND AND DELIVER *CBS A 1065* ■	1	15
12 Sep 81 ★	PRINCE CHARMING *CBS A 1408*	1	12
12 Dec 81	ANT RAP *CBS A 1738*	3	10
27 Feb 82	DEUTSCHER GIRLS *Ego 5*	13	6
13 Mar 82	THE ANTMUSIC EP (THE B-SIDES) *Do It DUN 20*	46	4

Tracks on The Antmusic EP (The B-sides): Friends / Kick / Physical

See also Adam ANT

A.D.A.M. featuring AMY
France, male / female vocal / instrumental duo (11 WEEKS)
pos/wks
| 1 Jul 95 | ZOMBIE *Eternal YZ 951CD* | 16 | 11 |

Arthur ADAMS US, male vocalist (5 WEEKS)
pos/wks
| 24 Oct 81 | YOU GOT THE FLOOR *RCA 146* | 38 | 5 |

UK No.1 ★   UK Top 10 ●   Still on chart +   UK million seller ◆   UK entry at No.1 ■   US No.1 ▲

Bryan ADAMS `54` **Top 500** *Globally successful rock singer / songwriter / guitarist, b. 5 Nov 1959, Kingston, Ontario. He has had more UK hits than any other Canadian artist and was the biggest-selling singles artist in the UK in 1991 (235 WEEKS)*

pos/wks

12 Jan 85	RUN TO YOU *A&M AM 224*	11	12
16 Mar 85	SOMEBODY *A&M AM 236*	35	7
25 May 85	HEAVEN *A&M AM 256* ▲	38	5
10 Aug 85	SUMMER OF '69 *A&M AM 267*	42	7
2 Nov 85	IT'S ONLY LOVE *A&M AM 285* [1]	29	6
21 Dec 85	CHRISTMAS TIME *A & M AM 297*	55	2
22 Feb 86	THIS TIME *A & M AM 295*	41	7
12 Jul 86	STRAIGHT FROM THE HEART *A & M AM 322*	51	3
28 Mar 87	HEAT OF THE NIGHT *A & M ADAM 2*	50	2
20 Jun 87	HEARTS ON FIRE *A & M ADAM 3*	57	3
17 Oct 87	VICTIM OF LOVE *A & M AM 407*	68	2
29 Jun 91	★ (EVERYTHING I DO) I DO IT FOR YOU *A & M AM 789* ◆ ▲	1	24
14 Sep 91	CAN'T STOP THIS THING WE STARTED *A & M AM 612*	12	6
23 Nov 91	THERE WILL NEVER BE ANOTHER TONIGHT *A & M AM 838*	32	3
28 Dec 91	(EVERYTHING I DO) I DO IT FOR YOU (re-entry) *A & M AM 789*	73	1
22 Feb 92	● THOUGHT I'D DIED AND GONE TO HEAVEN *A & M AM 848*	8	7
18 Jul 92	ALL I WANT IS YOU *A & M AM 879*	22	5
26 Sep 92	DO I HAVE TO SAY THE WORDS *A & M AM 0068*	30	3
30 Oct 93	● PLEASE FORGIVE ME *A & M 5804272*	2	16
15 Jan 94	● ALL FOR LOVE *A & M 5804772* [2] ▲	2	13
22 Apr 95	● HAVE YOU EVER REALLY LOVED A WOMAN *A & M 5810282* ▲	4	9
11 Nov 95	ROCK STEADY *Capitol CDCL 763* [3]	50	2
1 Jun 96	● THE ONLY THING THAT LOOKS GOOD ON ME IS YOU *A & M 5813692*	6	7
24 Aug 96	● LET'S MAKE A NIGHT TO REMEMBER *A & M 5815672*	10	8
23 Nov 96	STAR *A & M 5820252*	13	4
8 Feb 97	● I FINALLY FOUND SOMEONE *A & M 5820832* [4]	10	7
19 Apr 97	18 TIL I DIE *A & M 5821852*	22	3
20 Dec 97	BACK TO YOU *A & M 5824752*	18	7
21 Mar 98	I'M READY *A & M 5825352*	20	4
10 Oct 98	ON A DAY LIKE TODAY *Mercury MERCD 516*	13	5
12 Dec 98	● WHEN YOU'RE GONE *A & M 5828212* [5]	3	19
15 May 99	● CLOUD NUMBER 9 *A&M / Mercury 5828492*	6	9
18 Dec 99	THE BEST OF ME *Mercury / A & M 4971952*	47	1
22 Jan 00	THE BEST OF ME (re-entry) *Mercury / A & M 4971952*	55	2
18 Mar 00	★ DON'T GIVE UP *Xtravaganza XTRAV 9CDS* [6] ■	1	14

[1] Bryan Adams and Tina Turner [2] Bryan Adams, Rod Stewart and Sting [3] Bonnie Raitt and Bryan Adams [4] Barbra Streisand and Bryan Adams [5] Bryan Adams featuring Melanie C [6] Chicane featuring Bryan Adams

Cliff ADAMS ORCHESTRA *UK, orchestra (2 WEEKS)*

pos/wks

28 Apr 60	THE LONELY MAN THEME *Pye International 7N 25056*	39	2

Gayle ADAMS *US, female vocalist (1 WEEK)*

pos/wks

26 Jul 80	STRETCHIN' OUT *Epic EPC 8791*	64	1

Marie ADAMS – See Johnny OTIS SHOW

Oleta ADAMS *US, female vocalist (36 WEEKS)*

pos/wks

24 Mar 90	RHYTHM OF LIFE *Fontana OLETA 1*	52	2
3 Nov 90	RHYTHM OF LIFE (re-entry) *Fontana OLETA 1*	56	3
12 Jan 91	● GET HERE *Fontana OLETA 3*	4	12
13 Apr 91	YOU'VE GOT TO GIVE ME ROOM / RHYTHM OF LIFE (re-issue) *Fontana OLETA 4*	49	3
29 Jun 91	CIRCLE OF ONE *Fontana OLETA 5*	73	1
28 Sep 91	DON'T LET THE SUN GO DOWN ON ME *Fontana TRIBO 1*	33	5
25 Apr 92	WOMAN IN CHAINS (re-issue) *Fontana IDEA 16* [1]	57	1
10 Jul 93	I JUST HAD TO HEAR YOUR VOICE *Fontana OLECD 6*	42	3
7 Oct 95	NEVER KNEW LOVE *Fontana OLECD 9*	22	3
16 Dec 95	RHYTHM OF LIFE (re-mix) *Fontana OLECD 10*	38	2
10 Feb 96	WE WILL MEET AGAIN *Mercury OLECD 11*	51	1

[1] Tears For Fears featuring Oleta Adams

The original release of 'Woman in Chains' credited Tears For Fears only

ADAMSKI *UK, male instrumentalist / producer - Adam Tinley (39 WEEKS)*

pos/wks

20 Jan 90	N-R-G *MCA MCA 1386*	12	6
7 Apr 90	★ KILLER *MCA MCA 1400*	1	18
8 Sep 90	● THE SPACE JUNGLE *MCA MCA 1435*	7	8
17 Nov 90	FLASHBACK JACK *MCA MCA 1459*	46	2
9 Nov 91	NEVER GOIN' DOWN / BORN TO BE ALIVE *MCA MCS 1578* [1]	51	2
4 Apr 92	GET YOUR BODY *MCA MCS 1613* [2]	68	1
4 Jul 92	BACK TO FRONT *MCA MCS 1644*	63	1
11 Jul 98	ONE OF THE PEOPLE *ZTT ZTT 101CD* [3]	56	1

[1] Adamski featuring Jimi Polo / Adamski featuring Soho [2] Adamski featuring Nina Hagen [3] Adamski's Thing

Featured vocalist on 'Killer' was Seal

ADDAMS and GEE *UK, male instrumental duo (1 WEEK)*

pos/wks

20 Apr 91	CHUNG KUO (REVISITED) *Debut DEBT 3108*	72	1

ADDIS BLACK WIDOW *US, male rap duo (2 WEEKS)*

pos/wks

3 Feb 96	INNOCENT *Mercury Black Vinyl MBVCD 1*	42	2

ADDRISI BROTHERS *US, male vocal duo (3 WEEKS)*

pos/wks

6 Oct 79	GHOST DANCER *Scotti Brothers K 11361*	57	3

ADEVA *US, female vocalist - Patricia Daniels (66 WEEKS)*

pos/wks

14 Jan 89	RESPECT *Cooltempo COOL 179*	17	9
25 Mar 89	MUSICAL FREEDOM (MOVING ON UP) *Cooltempo COOL 182*	22	8
12 Aug 89	WARNING *Cooltempo COOL 185*	17	8
21 Oct 89	I THANK YOU *Cooltempo COOL 192*	17	7
16 Dec 89	BEAUTIFUL LOVE *Cooltempo COOL 195*	57	5
28 Apr 90	TREAT ME RIGHT *Cooltempo COOL 200*	62	2
6 Apr 91	RING MY BELL *Cooltempo COOL 224* [2]	20	5
19 Oct 91	IT SHOULD'VE BEEN ME *Cooltempo COOL 236*	48	3
29 Feb 92	DON'T LET IT SHOW ON YOUR FACE *Cooltempo COOL 248*	34	4
6 Jun 92	UNTIL YOU COME BACK TO ME *Cooltempo COOL 254*	45	3
17 Oct 92	I'M THE ONE FOR YOU *Cooltempo COOL 264*	51	2
11 Dec 93	RESPECT (re-mix) *Network NWKCD 79*	65	1
27 May 95	TOO MANY FISH *Virgin America VUSCD 89* [3]	34	2
18 Nov 95	WHADDA U WANT (FROM ME) *Virgin America VUSCD 98* [3]	36	2
6 Apr 96	DO WATCHA DO *Avex UK AVEXCD 24* [4]	54	1
4 May 96	I THANK YOU (re-mix) *Cooltempo CDCOOLS 318*	37	2
12 Apr 97	DO WATCHA DO (re-mix) *Distinctive DISNCD 28* [4]	60	1
26 Jul 97	WHERE IS THE LOVE? / THE WAY THAT YOU FEEL *Distinctive DISNCD 31*	54	1

[1] Paul Simpson featuring Adeva [2] Monie Love vs Adeva [3] Frankie Knuckles featuring Adeva [4] Hyper Go Go and Adeva

ADICTS *UK, male vocal / instrumental group (1 WEEK)*

pos/wks

14 May 83	BAD BOY *Razor RZS 104*	75	1

ADIEMUS *UK, male instrumental duo (2 WEEKS)*

pos/wks

14 Oct 95	ADIEMUS *Venture VEND 4*	48	2

Larry ADLER – See Kate BUSH

ADONIS featuring 2 PUERTO RICANS, A BLACK MAN AND A DOMINICAN *US, male vocal / instrumental group (4 WEEKS)*

pos/wks

13 Jun 87	DO IT PROPERLY ('NO WAY BACK') / NO WAY BACK *London LON 136*	47	4

ADRENALIN M.O.D. *UK, male instrumental / production group (5 WEEKS)*

pos/wks

8 Oct 88	O-O-O *MCA RAGAT 2*	49	5

ADULT NET
UK / US, male / female vocal / instrumental group (2 WEEKS) pos/wks

10 Jun 89	**WHERE WERE YOU** *Fontana BRX 2*	66 2

ADVENTURES *UK, male vocal / instrumental group (24 WEEKS)* pos/wks

15 Sep 84	**ANOTHER SILENT DAY** *Chrysalis CHS 2000*	71 2
1 Dec 84	**SEND MY HEART** *Chrysalis CHS 2001*	62 4
13 Jul 85	**FEEL THE RAINDROPS** *Chrysalis AD 1*	58 3
9 Apr 88	**BROKEN LAND** *Elektra EKR 69*	20 10
2 Jul 88	**DROWNING IN THE SEA OF LOVE** *Elektra EKR 76*	44 4
13 Jun 92	**RAINING ALL OVER THE WORLD** *Polydor PO 211*	68 1

ADVENTURES OF STEVIE V
UK, male / female production group (22 WEEKS) pos/wks

21 Apr 90 ●	**DIRTY CASH** *Mercury MER 311*	2 13
29 Sep 90	**BODY LANGUAGE** *Mercury MER 331*	29 5
2 Mar 91	**JEALOUSY** *Mercury MER 337*	58 3
27 Sep 97	**DIRTY CASH** (re-mix) *Avex Trax AVEXCDX 57*	69 1

ADVERTS
UK, male / female vocal / instrumental group (11 WEEKS) pos/wks

27 Aug 77	**GARY GILMORE'S EYES** *Anchor ANC 1043*	18 7
4 Feb 78	**NO TIME TO BE 21** *Bright BR 1*	34 4

AEROSMITH ⟨377 **Top 500**⟩ *Godfathers of contemporary heavy rock scene, formed 1970 New Hampshire, US. Multi-platinum album act's UK success came only after front men Steven Tyler (v) and Joe Perry (g) teamed with rappers Run DMC on 'Walk This Way' (1986). Group's first US No.1 single (1998) came 25 years after chart debut (85 WEEKS)* pos/wks

17 Oct 87	**DUDE (LOOKS LIKE A LADY)** *Geffen GEF 29*	45 5
16 Apr 88	**ANGEL** *Geffen GEF 34*	69 2
9 Sep 89	**LOVE IN AN ELEVATOR** *Geffen GEF 63*	13 8
24 Feb 90	**DUDE (LOOKS LIKE A LADY)** (re-issue) *Geffen GEF 72*	20 5
14 Apr 90	**RAG DOLL** *Geffen GEF 76*	42 4
1 Sep 90	**THE OTHER SIDE** *Geffen GEF 79*	46 2
10 Apr 93	**LIVIN' ON THE EDGE** *Geffen GFSTD 35*	19 4
3 Jul 93	**EAT THE RICH** *Geffen GFSTD 46*	34 3
30 Oct 93	**CRYIN'** *Geffen GFSTD 56*	17 6
18 Dec 93	**AMAZING** *Geffen GFSTD 63*	57 3
2 Jul 94	**SHUT UP AND DANCE** *Geffen GFSTD 75*	24 4
20 Aug 94	**SWEET EMOTION** *Columbia 6604492*	74 1
5 Nov 94	**CRAZY / BLIND MAN** *Geffen GFSTD 80*	23 4
8 Mar 97	**FALLING IN LOVE (IS HARD ON THE KNEES)** *Columbia 6640752*	22 4
21 Jun 97	**HOLE IN MY SOUL** *Columbia 66645012*	29 2
27 Dec 97	**PINK** *Columbia 6648722*	38 2
12 Sep 98 ●	**I DON'T WANT TO MISS A THING** *Columbia 6664082* ▲	4 20
26 Jun 99	**PINK** (re-issue) *Columbia 6675342*	13 6

AFRICAN BUSINESS
Italy, male vocal / instrumental group (1 WEEK) pos/wks

17 Nov 90	**IN ZAIRE** *Urban URB 64*	73 1

AFRO CELT SOUND SYSTEM
UK / Ireland / France / Guinea, male vocal / instrumental group (1 WEEK) pos/wks

29 Apr 00	**RELEASE** *Realworld RWSCD 10*	71 1

AFRO MEDUSA
UK, male production duo and Spain, female vocalist (2 WEEKS) pos/wks

28 Oct 00	**PASILDA** *Rulin RULIN 6CDS*	31 2

AFTER 7 *US, male vocal group (3 WEEKS)* pos/wks

3 Nov 90	**CAN'T STOP** *Virgin America VUS 31*	54 3

AFTER THE FIRE
UK, male vocal / instrumental group (12 WEEKS) pos/wks

9 Jun 79	**ONE RULE FOR YOU** *CBS 7025*	40 6
8 Sep 79	**LASER LOVE** *CBS 7769*	62 2
9 Apr 83	**DER KOMMISSAR** *CBS A 2399*	47 4

AFTERNOON BOYS – See Steve WRIGHT

AFTERSHOCK *US, male vocal / instrumental duo (8 WEEKS)* pos/wks

21 Aug 93	**SLAVE TO THE VIBE** *Virgin America VUSCD 75*	11 8

AGE OF CHANCE
UK, male / female vocal / instrumental group (13 WEEKS) pos/wks

17 Jan 87	**KISS** *Fon AGE 5*	50 6
30 May 87	**WHO'S AFRAID OF THE BIG BAD NOISE!** *Fon VS 962*	65 2
20 Jan 90	**HIGHER THAN HEAVEN** *Virgin VS 1228*	53 5

AGE OF LOVE
Italy, male instrumental / production duo (6 WEEKS) pos/wks

5 Jul 97	**THE AGE OF LOVE - THE REMIXES** *React CDREACT 100*	17 4
19 Sep 98	**AGE OF LOVE** *React CDREACT 135*	38 2

AGENT 00 *UK, male production duo (1 WEEK)* pos/wks

7 Mar 98	**THE MAGNIFICENT** *Inferno CDFERN 002*	65 1

AGENT PROVOCATEUR
UK, male / female vocal / production group (1 WEEK) pos/wks

22 Mar 97	**AGENT DAN** *Epic AGENT 3CD*	49 1

AGNELLI & NELSON *Ireland, male DJ duo (12 WEEKS)* pos/wks

15 Aug 98	**EL NINO** *Xtravaganza 0091575 EXT*	21 4
11 Sep 99	**EVERYDAY** *Xtravaganza XTRAV 2CDS*	17 4
17 Jun 00	**EMBRACE** *Xtravaganza XTRAV 11CDS*	35 2
9 Sep 00	**HUDSON STREET** *Xtravaganza XTRAV 13CDS*	29 2

Christina AGUILERA *US, female vocalist (51 WEEKS)* pos/wks

11 Sep 99	**GENIE IN A BOTTLE (IMPORT)** *RCA 701062*	50 5
16 Oct 99 ★	**GENIE IN A BOTTLE** *RCA 74321705482* ■ ▲	1 19
26 Feb 00 ●	**WHAT A GIRL WANTS** *RCA 74321737522* ▲	3 13
22 Jul 00	**I TURN TO YOU** *RCA 74321765472*	19 6
11 Nov 00 ●	**COME ON OVER BABY (ALL I WANT IS YOU)** *RCA 74321799912* ▲	8 8+

A-HA ⟨191 **Top 500**⟩ *Norway's biggest-selling act: Morten Harket (v), Pal Waaktaar (g), Magna Furuholmen (k). This globally popular teen-targeted trio was noted for its innovative videos and stage shows (133 WEEKS)* pos/wks

28 Sep 85 ●	**TAKE ON ME** *Warner Bros. W 9006* ▲	2 19
28 Dec 85 ★	**THE SUN ALWAYS SHINES ON TV** *Warner Bros. W 8846*	1 12
5 Apr 86 ●	**TRAIN OF THOUGHT** *Warner Bros. W 8736*	8 8
14 Jun 86 ●	**HUNTING HIGH AND LOW** *Warner Bros. W 6663*	5 10
4 Oct 86 ●	**I'VE BEEN LOSING YOU** *Warner Bros. W 8594*	8 7
6 Dec 86 ●	**CRY WOLF** *Warner Bros. W 8500*	5 9
28 Feb 87	**MANHATTAN SKYLINE** *Warner Bros. W 8405*	13 6
4 Jul 87 ●	**THE LIVING DAYLIGHTS** *Warner Bros. W 8305*	5 9
26 Mar 88 ●	**STAY ON THESE ROADS** *Warner Bros. W 7936*	5 6
18 Jun 88	**THE BLOOD THAT MOVES THE BODY** *Warner Bros. W 7840*	25 4
27 Aug 88	**TOUCHY!** *Warner Bros. W 7749*	11 7
3 Dec 88	**YOU ARE THE ONE** *Warner Bros. W 7636*	13 10
13 Oct 90	**CRYING IN THE RAIN** *Warner Bros. W 9547*	13 7
15 Dec 90	**I CALL YOUR NAME** *Warner Bros. W 9462*	44 5
26 Oct 91	**MOVE TO MEMPHIS** *Warner Bros. W 0070*	47 2
5 Jun 93	**DARK IS THE NIGHT** *Warner Bros. W 0175CD*	19 4
18 Sep 93	**ANGEL** *Warner Bros. W 0195CD*	41 3
26 Mar 94	**SHAPES THAT GO TOGETHER** *Warner Bros. W 0236CD*	27 3
3 Jun 00	**SUMMER MOVED ON** *WEA WEA 275CD*	33 2

AHMAD US, male rapper (2 WEEKS)

		pos/wks	
9 Jul 94	BACK IN THE DAY *Giant 74321212042*	64	2

AIDA Holland, male production duo (1 WEEK)

		pos/wks	
19 Feb 00	FAR AND AWAY *48K / Perfecto SPECT 03CDS*	58	1

AIR
France, male instrumental / production duo - Benoit Dunkel, Nicolas Godin (12 WEEKS)

		pos/wks	
21 Feb 98	SEXY BOY *Virgin VSCDT 1672*	13	4
16 May 98	KELLY WATCH THE STARS *Virgin VSCDT 1690*	18	3
21 Nov 98	ALL I NEED *Virgin VSCDT 1702*	29	3
26 Feb 00	PLAYGROUND LOVE *Virgin VSCDT 1764* 1	25	2

1 Sung by Gordon Tracks

AIR SUPPLY
UK / Australia, male vocal / instrumental group (17 WEEKS)

		pos/wks	
27 Sep 80	ALL OUT OF LOVE *Arista ARIST 362*	11	11
2 Oct 82	EVEN THE NIGHTS ARE BETTER *Arista ARIST 474*	44	4
20 Nov 93	GOODBYE *Giant 74321153462*	66	4

AIRHEAD UK, male vocal / instrumental group (10 WEEKS)

		pos/wks	
5 Oct 91	FUNNY HOW *Korova KOW 47*	57	3
21 Dec 91	COUNTING SHEEP *Korova KOW 48*	35	5
7 Mar 92	RIGHT NOW *Korova KOW 49*	50	2

AIRSCAPE
Belgium / Holland, male instrumental / production group. Leader Johann Gielen (5 WEEKS)

		pos/wks	
9 Aug 97	PACIFIC MELODY *Multiply CDMULTY 22*	27	2
29 Aug 98	AMAZON CHANT *Xtravaganza 0091605 EXT*	46	1
4 Dec 99	L'ESPERANZA *Xtravaganza EXTRAV 7CD*	33	2

See also BLUE BAMBOO; CUBIC 22; TRANSFORMER 2

Laurel AITKEN and the UNITONE
Jamaica / Cuba, male vocal / instrumental group (3 WEEKS)

		pos/wks	
17 May 80	RUDI GOT MARRIED *I-Spy SEE 6*	60	3

AKA UK, male vocal group (2 WEEKS)

		pos/wks	
12 Oct 96	WARNING *RCA 74321360662*	43	2

Jewel AKENS US, male / vocalist (8 WEEKS)

		pos/wks	
25 Mar 65	THE BIRDS AND THE BEES *London HLN 9954*	29	8

AKIN UK, female vocal duo (1 WEEK)

		pos/wks	
14 Jun 97	STAY RIGHT HERE *WEA WEA 117CD*	60	1

ALABAMA 3 UK, male vocal / instrumental group (3 WEEKS)

		pos/wks	
22 Nov 97	SPEED AT THE SOUND OF LONELINESS *Elemental ELM 42CDS 1721*	72	1
11 Apr 98	AIN'T GOIN' TO GOA *Elemental ELM 45CDS1*	40	2

ALANA – See MK

ALARM UK, male vocal / instrumental group (64 WEEKS)

		pos/wks	
24 Sep 83	68 GUNS *IRS PFP 1023*	17	7
21 Jan 84	WHERE WERE YOU HIDING WHEN THE STORM BROKE *IRS IRS 101*	22	6
31 Mar 84	THE DECEIVER *IRS IRS 103*	51	4
3 Nov 84	THE CHANT HAS JUST BEGUN *IRS IRS 104*	48	4
2 Mar 85	ABSOLUTE REALITY *IRS ALARM 1*	35	6
28 Sep 85	STRENGTH *IRS IRM 104*	40	4
18 Jan 86	SPIRIT OF '76 *IRS IRM 109*	22	5
26 Apr 86	KNIFE EDGE *IRS IRM 112*	43	3
17 Oct 87	RAIN IN THE SUMMERTIME *IRS IRM 144*	18	5

		pos/wks	
12 Dec 87	RESCUE ME *IRS IRM 150*	48	2
20 Feb 88	PRESENCE OF LOVE (LAUGHERNE) *IRS IRM 155*	44	3
16 Sep 89	SOLD ME DOWN THE RIVER *IRS EIRS 123*	43	3
4 Nov 89	A NEW SOUTH WALES / THE ROCK *IRS EIRS 129*	31	5
3 Feb 90	LOVE DON'T COME EASY *IRS EIRS 134*	48	3
27 Oct 90	UNSAFE BUILDING 1990 *IRS ALARM 2*	54	2
13 Apr 91	RAW *IRS ALARM 3*	51	2

'A New South Wales' features Morriston Orpheus Male Voice Choir

Morris ALBERT
Brazil, male vocalist - Morris Kaisermann (10 WEEKS)

		pos/wks	
27 Sep 75 ●	FEELINGS *Decca F 13591*	4	10

ALBERTA Sierra Leone, female vocalist (3 WEEKS)

		pos/wks	
26 Dec 98	YOYO BOY *RCA 74321640602*	48	3

ALBERTO Y LOS TRIOS PARANOIAS
UK, male vocal / instrumental group (5 WEEKS)

		pos/wks	
23 Sep 78	HEADS DOWN NO NONSENSE MINDLESS BOOGIE *Logo GO 323*	47	5

Al ALBERTS – See FOUR ACES

ALBION Holland, male producer - Ferry Corsten (1 WEEK)

		pos/wks	
3 Jun 00	AIR 2000 *Platipus PLATCD 73*	59	1

See also SYSTEM F; VERACOCHA; MOONMAN; GOURYELLA; Ferry CORSTEN

ALCATRAZ US, male instrumental / production duo (4 WEEKS)

		pos/wks	
17 Feb 96	GIV ME LUV *AM:PM 5814332*	12	4

ALDA Iceland, female vocalist - Alda Olafsdottir (14 WEEKS)

		pos/wks	
29 Aug 98 ●	REAL GOOD TIME *Wildstar CDWILD 7*	7	7
26 Dec 98	GIRLS NIGHT OUT *Wildstar CDWILD 10*	20	7

Cali ALEMAN – See Tito PUENTE Jr and the LATIN RHYTHM featuring Tito PUENTE, INDIA and Cali ALEMAN

ALENA Jamaica, female vocalist (5 WEEKS)

		pos/wks	
13 Nov 99	TURN IT AROUND *Wonderboy WBOYD 16*	14	5

ALESSI US, male vocal duo - Billy & Bobby Alessi (11 WEEKS)

		pos/wks	
11 Jun 77 ●	OH LORI *A & M AMS 7289*	8	11

ALEX PARTY
Italy / UK, male / female vocal / instrumental group. Leader Paolo Visnadi (28 WEEKS)

		pos/wks	
18 Dec 93	SATURDAY NIGHT PARTY *Cleveland City Imports CCICD 17000*	49	6
28 May 94	SATURDAY NIGHT PARTY (READ MY LIPS) (re-entry) *Cleveland City Imports CCICD 17000*	29	4
18 Feb 95 ●	DON'T GIVE ME YOUR LIFE *Systematic SYSCD 7*	2	13
18 Nov 95	WRAP ME UP *Systematic SYSCD 22*	17	3
19 Oct 96	READ MY LIPS (re-mix) *Systematic SYSCD 30*	28	2

'Read My Lips' in 1996 is a remix of the first hit with added vocals

See also LIVIN' JOY

ALEXIA Italian, female vocalist - Alessia Aquilani (15 WEEKS)

		pos/wks	
21 Mar 98 ●	UH LA LA LA *Dance Pool ALEX 1CD*	10	9
13 Jun 98	GIMME LOVE *Dance Pool ALEX 2CDZ*	17	4
10 Oct 98	THE MUSIC I LIKE *Dance Pool ALEX 3CD*	31	2

ALFI and HARRY
US, male vocalist / instumentalist - David Seville under two false names (5 WEEKS)

		pos/wks	
23 Mar 56	TROUBLE WITH HARRY *London HLU 8242*	15	5

See also David SEVILLE; CHIPMUNKS

John ALFORD *UK, male vocalist (12 WEEKS)*

		pos/wks	
17 Feb 96	SMOKE GETS IN YOUR EYES *Love This LUVTHISCD 7*	13	5
25 May 96 ●	BLUE MOON / ONLY YOU *Love This LUVTHISCD 9*	9	4
23 Nov 96	IF / KEEP ON RUNNING *Love This LUVTHISCD 15*	24	3

ALI *UK, male vocalist (2 WEEKS)*

		pos/wks	
23 May 98	LOVE LETTERS *Wild Card 5698092*	63	1
24 Oct 98	FEELIN' YOU *Wild Card 5676992*	63	1

Tatyana ALI *US, female vocalist (18 WEEKS)*

		pos/wks	
14 Nov 98 ●	DAYDREAMIN' *Epic 6665462*	6	5
13 Feb 99 ●	BOY YOU KNOCK ME OUT *MJJ / Epic 6669372* [1]	3	8
15 May 99	BOY YOU KNOCK ME OUT (re-entry) *MJJ / Epic 6669372* [1]	69	1
19 Jun 99	EVERYTIME *Epic / MJJ 674742*	20	4

[1] Tatyana Ali featuring Will Smith

ALI and FRAZIER *UK, female vocal duo (4 WEEKS)*

		pos/wks	
7 Aug 93	UPTOWN TOP RANKING *Arista 74321158842*	33	4

ALIBI *UK, male vocal duo (2 WEEKS)*

		pos/wks	
15 Feb 97	I'M NOT TO BLAME *Urgent 74321434762*	51	1
7 Feb 98	HOW MUCH I FEEL *Urgent 74321548472*	58	1

ALICE DEEJAY
Holland, male / female production / vocal group (46 WEEKS)

		pos/wks	
31 Jul 99 ●	BETTER OFF ALONE *Positiva CDTIV 113* [1]	2	16
4 Dec 99 ●	BACK IN MY LIFE *Positiva CDTIV 121*	4	15
15 Jul 00 ●	WILL I EVER *Positiva CDTIV 134*	7	10
21 Oct 00	THE LONELY ONE *Positiva CDTIV 145*	16	5

[1] DJ Jurgen Presents Alice Deejay

ALICE IN CHAINS
US, male vocal / instrumental group (14 WEEKS)

		pos/wks	
23 Jan 93	WOULD *Columbia 6588882*	19	3
20 Mar 93	THEM BONES *Columbia 6590902*	26	3
5 Jun 93	ANGRY CHAIR *Columbia 6593652*	33	2
23 Oct 93	DOWN IN A HOLE *Columbia 6597512*	36	2
11 Nov 95	GRIND *Columbia 6626232*	23	2
10 Feb 96	HEAVEN BESIDE YOU *Columbia 6628935*	35	2

ALIEN VOICES
UK, male producer - Andros Georgiou (2 WEEKS)

		pos/wks	
26 Dec 98	LAST CHRISTMAS *Wildstar CDWILD 15* [1]	54	2

[1] Alien Voices featuring the Three Degrees

See also Andy G's STARSKY & HUTCH ALL STARS; BOOGIE BOX HIGH

ALISHA *US, female vocalist (2 WEEKS)*

		pos/wks	
25 Jan 86	BABY TALK *Total Control TOCO 6*	67	2

ALISHA'S ATTIC *UK, female vocal duo (42 WEEKS)*

		pos/wks	
3 Aug 96	I AM I FEEL *Mercury AATCD 1*	14	10
2 Nov 96	ALISHA RULES THE WORLD *Mercury AATCD 2*	12	6
15 Mar 97	INDESTRUCTIBLE *Mercury AATCD 3*	12	6
12 Jul 97	AIR WE BREATHE *Mercury AATCD 4*	12	6
19 Sep 98	THE INCIDENTALS *Mercury AATCD 5*	13	7
9 Jan 99	WISH I WERE YOU *Mercury AATCD 6*	29	5
17 Apr 99	BARBARELLA *Mercury AATCD 7*	34	2

ALL ABOUT EVE
UK, female / male vocal / instrumental group (47 WEEKS)

		pos/wks	
31 Oct 87	IN THE CLOUDS *Mercury EVEN 5*	47	5
23 Jan 88	WILD HEARTED WOMAN *Mercury EVEN 6*	33	4
9 Apr 88	EVERY ANGEL *Mercury EVEN 7*	30	5
30 Jul 88 ●	MARTHA'S HARBOUR *Mercury EVEN 8*	10	8
12 Nov 88	WHAT KIND OF FOOL *Mercury EVEN 9*	29	4

		pos/wks	
30 Sep 89	ROAD TO YOUR SOUL *Mercury EVEN 10*	37	4
16 Dec 89	DECEMBER *Mercury EVEN 11*	34	5
28 Apr 90	SCARLET *Mercury EVEN 12*	34	2
15 Jun 91	FAREWELL MR SORROW *Mercury EVEN 14*	36	2
10 Aug 91	STRANGE WAY *Vertigo EVEN 15*	50	3
19 Oct 91	THE DREAMER *Vertigo EVEN 16*	41	2
10 Oct 92	PHASED (EP) *MCA MCS 1688*	38	2
28 Nov 92	SOME FINER DAY *MCA MCS 1706*	57	1

Tracks on Phased (EP): Phased / Mine / Infra Red / Ascent-Descent

ALL BLUE *UK, male vocal duo (1 WEEK)*

		pos/wks	
21 Aug 99	PRISONER *WEA WEA 213CD1*	73	1

ALL-4-ONE *US, male vocal group (23 WEEKS)*

		pos/wks	
2 Apr 94	SO MUCH IN LOVE *Atlantic A 7261CD*	60	1
18 Jun 94 ●	I SWEAR *Atlantic A 7255CD* ▲	2	18
19 Nov 94	SO MUCH IN LOVE (re-mix) *Atlantic A 7216CD*	49	2
15 Jul 95	I CAN LOVE YOU LIKE THAT *Atlantic A 8193CD*	33	2

ALL SAINTS [310 *Top 500*] *From All Saints Road, London, a cooler, R&B motivated vocal girl group in the wake of The Spice Girls. Melanie Blatt b. 25 Mar 1975, London, Shaznay Lewis b. 14 Oct 1975, London, Nicole Appleton b. 7 Oct 1974, London, Natalie Appleton b. 14 May 1973, Canada. Crowned Best Breakthrough Artists in the 1998 MTV Europe Music Awards (96 WEEKS)*

		pos/wks	
6 Sep 97 ●	I KNOW WHERE IT'S AT *London LONCD 398*	4	8
22 Nov 97 ★	NEVER EVER *London LONCD 407* ◆	1	24
9 May 98 ★	UNDER THE BRIDGE / LADY MARMALADE *London LONCD 408* ■	1	14
12 Sep 98 ★	BOOTIE CALL *London LONCD 415* ■	1	11
5 Dec 98 ●	WAR OF NERVES *London LONCD 421*	7	11
26 Feb 00 ★	PURE SHORES *London LONCD 444* ■	1	16
14 Oct 00 ★	BLACK COFFEE *London LONCD 454* ■	1	12+

THE ALL SEEING I
UK male vocal / instrumental group (17 WEEKS)

		pos/wks	
28 Mar 98	BEAT GOES ON *ffrr FCD 334*	11	7
23 Jan 99 ●	WALK LIKE A PANTHER '98 *ffrr FCD 351* [1]	10	7
18 Sep 99	1ST MAN IN SPACE *ffrr FCD 370*	28	3

[1] The All Seeing I featuring Tony Christie

'Walk Like A Panther '98' written by the group and Jarvis Cocker. Vocals by Tony Christie who had previously recorded a different song with the same title.

ALL STAR CHOIR – See Donna SUMMER

ALL-STARS – See Louis ARMSTRONG

ALL-STARS – See Junior WALKER and the ALL-STARS

ALL SYSTEMS GO
UK, male vocal / instrumental group (2 WEEKS)

		pos/wks	
18 Jun 88	POP MUZIK *Unique NIQ 03*	63	2

Richard ALLAN *UK, male vocalist (1 WEEK)*

		pos/wks	
24 Mar 60	AS TIME GOES BY *Parlophone R 4634*	44	1

Steve ALLAN *UK, male vocalist (2 WEEKS)*

		pos/wks	
27 Jan 79	TOGETHER WE ARE BEAUTIFUL *Creole CR 164*	67	1
10 Feb 79	TOGETHER WE ARE BEAUTIFUL (re-entry) *Creole CR 164*	70	1

Donna ALLEN *US, female vocalist (27 WEEKS)*

		pos/wks	
18 Apr 87 ●	SERIOUS *Portrait 650744 7*	8	12
3 Jun 89 ●	JOY AND PAIN *BCM BCM 257*	10	10
21 Jan 95	REAL *Epic 6610992*	34	2
11 Oct 97	SATURDAY *AM:PM 5823752* [1]	29	3

[1] East 57th Street featuring Donna Allen

UK No.1 ★   UK Top 10 ●   Still on chart +   UK million seller ◆   UK entry at No.1 ■   US No.1 ▲

Keith ALLEN – See BLACK GRAPE; Joe STRUMMER; FAT LES

ALLISONS
UK, male vocal duo - John Alford & Bob Day (27 WEEKS)   pos/wks

23 Feb 61	● ARE YOU SURE *Fontana H 294*....................	2	16
18 May 61	WORDS *Fontana H 304*....................	34	5
15 Feb 62	LESSONS IN LOVE *Fontana H 362*....................	30	6

ALLNIGHT BAND *UK, male instrumental group (3 WEEKS)*   pos/wks

| 3 Feb 79 | THE JOKER (THE WIGAN JOKER) *Casino Classics CC 6* .... | 50 | 3 |

ALLURE *US, female vocal group (8 WEEKS)*   pos/wks

| 14 Jun 97 | HEAD OVER HEELS *Epic 6645942* [1] .... | 18 | 3 |
| 10 Jan 98 | ALL CRIED OUT *Epic 6652715* [2] .... | 12 | 5 |

[1] Allure featuring NAS [2] Allure featuring 112

ALMIGHTY *UK, male vocal / instrumental group (22 WEEKS)*   pos/wks

30 Jun 90	WILD AND WONDERFUL *Polydor PO 75*....................	50	2
2 Mar 91	FREE 'N' EASY *Polydor PO 127*	35	2
11 May 91	DEVIL'S TOY *Polydor PO 144*	36	2
29 Jun 91	LITTLE LOST SOMETIMES *Polydor PO 151*	42	2
3 Apr 93	ADDICTION *Polydor PZCD 261*	38	2
29 May 93	OUT OF SEASON *Polydor PZCD 266*	41	2
30 Oct 93	OVER THE EDGE *Polydor PZCD 298*	38	2
24 Sep 94	WRENCH *Chrysalis CDCHS 5014*	26	2
14 Jan 95	JONESTOWN MIND *Chrysalis CDCHS 5017*	26	3
16 Mar 96	ALL SUSSED OUT *Chrysalis CDCHS 5030*	28	2
25 May 96	DO YOU UNDERSTAND *Raw Power RAWX 1022*	38	1

Marc ALMOND (248 Top 500) *Distinctive vocalist who first found fame fronting chart regulars Soft Cell, b. 9 Jul, 1957, Southport, UK. His only No.1 also gave co-vocalist Gene Pitney his first British chart-topper and sold more than one million copies in Europe alone (112 WEEKS)*   pos/wks

2 Jun 83	BLACK HEART *Some Bizarre BZS 19* [1]	49	3
2 Jun 84	THE BOY WHO CAME BACK *Some Bizarre BZS 23*	52	5
1 Sep 84	YOU HAVE *Some Bizarre BZS 24*	57	3
20 Apr 85	● I FEEL LOVE (MEDLEY) *Forbidden Fruit BITE 4* [2]	3	12
24 Aug 85	STORIES OF JOHNNY *Some Bizarre BONK 1*	23	5
26 Oct 85	LOVE LETTER *Some Bizarre BONK 2*	68	3
4 Jan 86	THE HOUSE IS HAUNTED (BY THE ECHO OF YOUR LAST GOODBYE) *Some Bizarre GLOW 1*	55	3
7 Jun 86	A WOMAN'S STORY *Some Bizarre GLOW 2* [3]	41	5
18 Oct 86	RUBY RED *Some Bizarre GLOW 3*	47	3
14 Feb 87	MELANCHOLY ROSE *Some Bizarre GLOW 4*	71	1
3 Sep 88	TEARS RUN RINGS *Parlophone R 6186*	26	7
5 Nov 88	BITTER SWEET *Some Bizarre R 6194*	40	3
14 Jan 89	★ SOMETHING'S GOTTEN HOLD OF MY HEART *Parlophone R 6201* [4]	1	12
8 Apr 89	ONLY THE MOMENT *Parlophone R 6210*	45	2
3 Mar 90	A LOVER SPURNED *Some Bizarre R 6229*	29	4
19 May 90	THE DESPERATE HOURS *Some Bizarre R 6252*	45	2
23 Mar 91	SAY HELLO WAVE GOODBYE '91 (re-recording) *Mercury SOFT 1* [5]	38	3
18 May 91	● TAINTED LOVE (re-issue) *Mercury SOFT 2* [5]	5	8
28 Sep 91	JACKY *Some Bizarre YZ 610*	17	6
11 Jan 92	MY HAND OVER MY HEART *Some Bizarre YZ 633*....................	33	5
25 Apr 92	● THE DAYS OF PEARLY SPENCER *Some Bizarre YZ 638*...........	4	7
27 Mar 93	WHAT MAKES A MAN A MAN (LIVE) *Some Bizarre YZ 720CD*	60	2
13 May 95	ADORED AND EXPLORED *Some Bizarre MERCD 431*..............	25	3
29 Jul 95	THE IDOL *Some Bizarre MERCD 437*....................	44	1
30 Dec 95	CHILD STAR *Some Bizarre MERCD 450*	41	1
28 Dec 96	YESTERDAY HAS GONE *EMI Premier CDPRESX 13* [6]	58	1
11 Jan 97	YESTERDAY HAS GONE (re-entry) *EMI Premier CDPRESX 13* [6]	69	1

[1] Marc and the Mambas [2] Bronski Beat and Marc Almond [3] Marc Almond and the Willing Sinners [4] Marc Almond featuring special guest star Gene Pitney [5] Soft Cell / Marc Almond [6] PJ Proby and Marc Almond featuring the My Life Story Orchestra

I Feel Love medley comprises: I Feel Love / Love to Love You Baby / Johnny Remember Me. 'Say Hello Wave Goodbye' 1991 is a re-recording of a Soft Cell hit

ALOOF *UK, male vocal / instrumental group (6 WEEKS)*   pos/wks

19 Sep 92	ON A MISSION *Cowboy RODEO 5*....................	64	1
18 May 96	WISH YOU WERE HERE ... *East West EW 038CD*	61	1
30 Nov 96	ONE NIGHT STAND *East West EW 067CD*....................	30	2
1 Mar 97	WISH YOU WERE HERE ... (re-mix) *East West EW 083CD1*....................	43	1
29 Aug 98	WHAT I MISS THE MOST *East West EW 179CD1*	70	1

Herb ALPERT (273 Top 500) *Leader of the US's biggest-selling instrumental act, The Tijuana Brass, b. 31 Mar 1935, Los Angeles. Multi-talented trumpet-toting star, whose band had four albums simultaneously in the US Top 10 in the mid-1960s. He sold his A&M label for $300 million in 1989 and its publishing company for $350 million in 2000 (106 WEEKS)*   pos/wks

3 Jan 63	THE LONELY BULL *Stateside SS 138* [1]	22	9
9 Dec 65	● SPANISH FLEA *Pye International 7 N 25335* [2]	3	20
24 Mar 66	TIJUANA TAXI *Pye International 7 N 25352* [2]	37	4
27 Apr 67	CASINO ROYALE *A & M AMS 700* [2]	27	14
3 Jul 68	● THIS GUY'S IN LOVE WITH YOU *A & M AMS 727* ▲	3	16
26 Mar 69	THIS GUY'S IN LOVE WITH YOU (re-entry) *A & M AMS 727*	47	1
9 Apr 69	THIS GUY'S IN LOVE WITH YOU (2nd re-entry) *A & M AMS 727*	49	1
7 May 69	THIS GUY'S IN LOVE WITH YOU (3rd re-entry) *A & M AMS 727*	50	1
18 Jun 69	WITHOUT HER *A & M AMS 755* [2]	36	5
12 Dec 70	JERUSALEM *A & M AMS 810* [2]	47	1
2 Jan 71	JERUSALEM (re-entry) *A & M AMS 810* [2]	42	2
13 Oct 79	RISE *A & M AMS 7465* ▲	13	13
19 Jan 80	ROTATION *A & M AMS 7500*	46	3
21 Mar 87	KEEP YOUR EYE ON ME *Breakout USA 602*	19	9
6 Jun 87	DIAMONDS *Breakout USA 605*....................	27	7

[1] Tijuana Brass [2] Herb Alpert and the Tijuana Brass

Alpert provides vocals on 'This Guy's in Love With You' and 'Without Her'. Janet Jackson provides uncredited vocals on 'Diamonds'

ALPHA-BETA – See Izhar COHEN and the ALPHA-BETA

ALPHAVILLE
Germany, male vocal / instrumental group (13 WEEKS)   pos/wks

| 18 Aug 84 | ● BIG IN JAPAN *WEA Int. X9505* .... | 8 | 13 |

Gerald ALSTON *US, male vocalist (1 WEEK)*   pos/wks

| 15 Apr 89 | ACTIVATED *RCA ZB 42681* .... | 73 | 1 |

ALTERED IMAGES
UK, male / female vocal / instrumental group (60 WEEKS)   pos/wks

28 Mar 81	DEAD POP STARS *Epic EPC A 1023*....................	67	2
26 Sep 81	● HAPPY BIRTHDAY *Epic EPC A 1522*....................	2	17
12 Dec 81	● I COULD BE HAPPY *Epic EPC A 1834*	7	12
27 Mar 82	SEE THOSE EYES *Epic EPC A 2198*	11	7
22 May 82	PINKY BLUE *Epic EPC A 2426*	35	6
19 Mar 83	● DON'T TALK TO ME ABOUT LOVE *Epic EPC A 3083*	7	7
28 May 83	BRING ME CLOSER *Epic EPC A 3398*	29	6
16 Jul 83	LOVE TO STAY *Epic EPC A 3582*	46	3

ALTERN 8
UK, male instrumental / production duo - Mark Archer & Chris Peat (34 WEEKS)   pos/wks

13 Jul 91	INFILTRATE 202 *Network NWK 24*	28	7
16 Nov 91	● ACTIV 8 (COME WITH ME) *Network NWK 34*	3	9
8 Feb 92	FREQUENCY *Network NWKT 37*	41	1
11 Apr 92	● EVAPOR 8 *Network NWK 38*	6	6
4 Jul 92	HYPNOTIC ST-8 *Network NWK 49*	16	4
10 Oct 92	SHAME *Network NWKTEN 56* [1]	74	1
12 Dec 92	BRUTAL-8-E *Network NWK 59*	43	5
3 Jul 93	EVERYBODY *Network NWKCD 73*	58	1

[1] Altern 8 vs Evelyn King

ALTHIA and DONNA
Jamaica, female vocal duo – Althia Forest and Donna Reid
(11 WEEKS) pos/wks
24 Dec 77 ★ UPTOWN TOP RANKING *Lightning LIG 506* **1** 11

ALVIN and the CHIPMUNKS – See CHIPMUNKS

ALY-US *US, male vocal / instrumental group (2 WEEKS)* pos/wks
21 Nov 92 FOLLOW ME *Cooltempo COOL 266* **43** 2

Shola AMA *UK, female vocalist – Mathurin Campbell (50 WEEKS)* pos/wks
19 Apr 97 ● YOU MIGHT NEED SOMEBODY
WEA WEA 097CD1 ....**4** 14
30 Aug 97 ● YOU'RE THE ONE I LOVE *WEA WEA 121CD1* **3** 8
29 Nov 97 WHO'S LOVING MY BABY *WEA WEA 145CD1* **13** 7
21 Feb 98 MUCH LOVE *WEA WEA 154CD1* **17** 3
11 Apr 98 SOMEDAY I'LL FIND YOU / I'VE BEEN TO A
MARVELLOUS PARTY *EMI CDTCB 001* [1] **28** 3
17 Apr 99 ● TABOO *WEA WEA 203CD* [2] **10** 8
6 Nov 99 STILL BELIEVE *WEA WEA 239CD1* **26** 3
29 Apr 00 IMAGINE *WEA WEA 252 CD* **24** 4

[1] Shola Ama and Craig Armstrong / Divine Comedy [2] Glamma Kid featuring
Shola Ama

Eddie AMADOR *US, male DJ / producer (5 WEEKS)* pos/wks
24 Oct 98 HOUSE MUSIC *Pukka CDPUKKA 18* **37** 2
22 Jan 00 RISE *Defected DEFECT 9CDS* **19** 3

AMAR *UK, female vocalist / instrumentalist – Amar Nagi (1 WEEK)* pos/wks
9 Sep 00 SOMETIMES IT SNOWS IN APRIL
Blanco Y Negro NEG 129CD **48** 1

AMAZULU
UK, female / male vocal / instrumental group (57 WEEKS) pos/wks
6 Jul 85 EXCITABLE *Island IS 201* **12** 13
23 Nov 85 DON'T YOU JUST KNOW IT *Island IS 233* **15** 11
15 Mar 86 THE THINGS THE LONELY DO *Island IS 267* **43** 6
31 May 86 ● TOO GOOD TO BE FORGOTTEN
Island IS 284 ....**5** 13
13 Sep 86 MONTEGO BAY *Island IS 293* **16** 9
10 Oct 87 MONY MONY *EMI EM 32* **38** 5

AMBASSADOR *Holland, male DJ / production group (1 WEEK)* pos/wks
12 Feb 00 ONE OF THESE DAYS *Platipus PLATCD 69* **67** 1

AMBASSADORS OF FUNK featuring MC MARIO
UK, male DJ and rapper – Simon Harris and Einstein (8 WEEKS) pos/wks
31 Oct 92 ● SUPERMARIOLAND *Living Beat SMASH 23* **8** 8

See also Simon HARRIS

AMBER *Holland, female vocalist – Marie Cremers (2 WEEKS)* pos/wks
24 Jun 00 SEXUAL *Substance SUBS 2CDS* **34** 2

AMEN CORNER
UK, male vocal / instrumental group – lead vocal Andy Fairweather-Low
(67 WEEKS) pos/wks
26 Jul 67 GIN HOUSE BLUES *Deram DM 136* **12** 10
11 Oct 67 WORLD OF BROKEN HEARTS *Deram DM 151* **24** 6
17 Jan 68 ● BEND ME SHAPE ME *Deram DM 172* **3** 12
31 Jul 68 ● HIGH IN THE SKY *Deram DM 197* **6** 13
29 Jan 69 ★ (IF PARADISE IS) HALF AS NICE
Immediate IM 073 ....**1** 11
25 Jun 69 ● HELLO SUZIE *Immediate IM 081* **4** 10
14 Feb 76 (IF PARADISE IS) HALF AS NICE (re-issue)
Immediate IMS 103 ....**34** 5

See also FAIR WEATHER; Andy FAIRWEATHER-LOW

AMEN UK *UK, male / female vocal / production group (6 WEEKS)* pos/wks
8 Feb 97 PASSION *Feverpitch CDFVR 1015* **15** 4
28 Jun 97 PEOPLE OF LOVE *Feverpitch CDFVR 18* **36** 2

AMERICA *US, male vocal / instrumental group (20 WEEKS)* pos/wks
18 Dec 71 HORSE WITH NO NAME *Warner Bros. K 16128* **49** 2
8 Jan 72 ● HORSE WITH NO NAME (re-entry)
Warner Bros. K 16128 ▲ **3** 11
25 Nov 72 VENTURA HIGHWAY *Warner Bros. K 16219* **43** 4
6 Nov 82 YOU CAN DO MAGIC *Capitol CL 264* **59** 3

AMERICAN BREED
US, male vocal / instrumental group (6 WEEKS) pos/wks
7 Feb 68 BEND ME SHAPE ME *Stateside SS 2078* **24** 6

AMERICAN MUSIC CLUB
US, male vocal / instrumental group (4 WEEKS) pos/wks
24 Apr 93 JOHNNY MATHIS' FEET *Virgin VSCDG 1445* **58** 2
10 Sep 94 WISH THE WORLD AWAY *Virgin VSCDX 1512* **46** 2

AMES BROTHERS *US, male vocal group (6 WEEKS)* pos/wks
4 Feb 55 ● THE NAUGHTY LADY OF SHADY LANE *HMV B 10800* **6** 6
This release was 'With Hugo Winterhalter & his Orchestra'

AMIL – See JAY-Z

AMIRA *US, female vocalist (3 WEEKS)* pos/wks
13 Dec 97 MY DESIRE *VC VCRD 27* **51** 1
8 Aug 98 MY DESIRE (re-mix) *VC Recordings VCRD 36* **46** 2

AMNESIA – See Frank'o MOIRAGHI featuring AMNESIA

Cherie AMORE *France, female vocalist (2 WEEKS)* pos/wks
15 Apr 00 I DON'T WANT NOBODY (TELLIN' ME WHAT TO DO)
Eternal / WEA WEA 262CD **33** 2

Vanessa AMOROSI *Australia, female vocalist (10 WEEKS)* pos/wks
23 Sep 00 ● ABSOLUTELY EVERYBODY *Mercury 1582972* **7** 10

AMOS *UK, male vocalist / rapper / producer (12 WEEKS)* pos/wks
3 Sep 94 ONLY SAW TODAY - INSTANT KARMA *Positiva CDTIV 16* **48** 2
25 Mar 95 LET LOVE SHINE *Positiva CDTIV 24* **31** 2
7 Oct 95 CHURCH OF FREEDOM *Positiva CDTIV 38* **54** 1
12 Oct 96 STAMP! *Positiva CDTIV 65* **11** 5
31 May 97 ARGENTINA *Positiva CDTIV 74* [1] **30** 2

[1] Jeremy Healy + Amos

Tori AMOS *US, female vocalist / instrumentalist (64 WEEKS)* pos/wks
23 Nov 91 SILENT ALL THESE YEARS *East West YZ 618* **51** 3
1 Feb 92 CHINA *East West YZ 7531* **51** 2
21 Mar 92 WINTER *East West A 7504* **25** 4
20 Jun 92 CRUCIFY *East West A 7479* **15** 6
22 Aug 92 SILENT ALL THESE YEARS (re-issue)
East West A 7433 ....**26** 4
22 Jan 94 ● CORNFLAKE GIRL *East West A 7281CD* **4** 6
19 Mar 94 ● PRETTY GOOD YEAR *East West A 7263CD* **7** 4
28 May 94 PAST THE MISSION *East West YZ 7257CD* **31** 3
15 Oct 94 GOD *East West A 7251CD* **44** 2
13 Jan 96 CAUGHT A LITE SNEEZE *East West A 5524CD1* ...**20** 3
23 Mar 96 TALULA *East West A 8512CD1* **22** 2
3 Aug 96 HEY JUPITER / PROFESSIONAL WIDOW *East West A 5494CD* **20** 9
9 Nov 96 BLUE SKIES *Perfecto PERF 130CD1* [1] **26** 2
11 Jan 97 ★ PROFESSIONAL WIDOW (IT'S GOT TO BE BIG) (re-mix)
East West A 5450CD **1** 10
2 May 98 SPARK *Atlantic AT 0031CD* **16** 3
13 Nov 99 GLORY OF THE 80'S *Atlantic AT 0077CD1* **46** 1

[1] BT featuring Tori Amos

UK No.1 ★   UK Top 10 ●   Still on chart +   UK million seller ◆   UK entry at No.1 ■   US No.1 ▲

AMOURE *UK, male production duo - Rod Edwards and Nick Magnus* (2 WEEKS)

		pos/wks
27 May 00	**IS THAT YOUR FINAL ANSWER? (WHO WANTS TO BE A MILLIONAIRE - THE SINGLE)** *Celador MILLION 2* 33	2

AMPS *US, male / female vocal / instrumental group (1 WEEK)*

		pos/wks
21 Oct 95	**TIPP CITY** *4AD BAD 5015CD* 61	1

AMY – See A.D.A.M. featuring AMY

ANASTACIA *US, female vocalist - Anastacia Newkirk (14 WEEKS)*

		pos/wks
30 Sep 00	● **I'M OUTTA LOVE** *Epic 6695782* 6	14+

AND WHY NOT? *UK, male vocal / instrumental group (18 WEEKS)*

		pos/wks
14 Oct 89	**RESTLESS DAYS (SHE CRIES OUT LOUD)** *Island IS 426* 38	7
13 Jan 90	**THE FACE** *Island IS 444* 13	8
21 Apr 90	**SOMETHING YOU GOT** *Island IS 452* 39	3

... AND YOU WILL KNOW US BY THE TRAIL OF THE DEAD *US, male vocal / instrumental group (1 WEEK)*

		pos/wks
11 Nov 00	**MISTAKES AND REGRETS** *Domino RUG 114CD* 69	1

Angry ANDERSON *Australia, male vocalist (13 WEEKS)*

		pos/wks
19 Nov 88	● **SUDDENLY** *Food For Thought YUM 113* 3	13

Carl ANDERSON *US, male vocalist (4 WEEKS)*

		pos/wks
8 Jun 85	**BUTTERCUP** *Streetwave KHAN 45* 49	4

Carleen ANDERSON *US, female vocalist (17 WEEKS)*

		pos/wks
12 Feb 94	**NERVOUS BREAKDOWN** *Circa YRCDG 112* 27	4
28 May 94	**MAMA SAID** *Circa YRCD 114* 26	4
13 Aug 94	**TRUE SPIRIT** *Circa YRCD 118* 24	3
14 Jan 95	**LET IT LAST** *Circa YRCD 119* 16	3
7 Feb 98	**MAYBE I'M AMAZED** *Circa YRCD 120* 24	2
25 Apr 98	**WOMAN IN ME** *Circa YRCD 129* 74	1

See also BRAND NEW HEAVIES

Gillian ANDERSON – See HAL featuring Gillian ANDERSON

John ANDERSON BIG BAND *UK, big band (5 WEEKS)*

		pos/wks
21 Dec 85	**GLENN MILLER MEDLEY** *Modern GLEN 1* 63	2
11 Jan 86	**GLENN MILLER MEDLEY (re-entry)** *Modern GLEN 1* 61	3

Glenn Miller Medley comprises the following tracks: In the Mood / American Patrol / Little Brown Jug / Pennsylvania 65000

Laurie ANDERSON *US, female vocalist / multi-instrumentalist (6 WEEKS)*

		pos/wks
17 Oct 81	● **O SUPERMAN** *Warner Bros. K 17870* 2	6

Leroy ANDERSON and his POPS CONCERT ORCHESTRA *US, orchestra (4 WEEKS)*

		pos/wks
28 Jun 57	**FORGOTTEN DREAMS** *Brunswick 05485* 28	1
12 Jul 57	**FORGOTTEN DREAMS (re-entry)** *Brunswick 05485* 30	1
6 Sep 57	**FORGOTTEN DREAMS (2nd re-entry)** *Brunswick 05485* 24	2

Lynn ANDERSON *US, female vocalist (20 WEEKS)*

		pos/wks
20 Feb 71	● **ROSE GARDEN** *CBS 5360* 3	20

Moira ANDERSON *UK, female vocalist (2 WEEKS)*

		pos/wks
27 Dec 69	**THE HOLY CITY** *Decca F 12989* 43	2

ANDERSON BRUFORD WAKEMAN HOWE *UK, male vocal / instrumental group (2 WEEKS)*

		pos/wks
24 Jun 89	**BROTHER OF MINE** *Arista 112379* 63	2

See also YES

Peter ANDRE 〔385 **Top 500**〕 *Australian-raised teen-dream vocalist with six-pack stomach, b. 27 Feb 1973, Middlesex, UK. Chart-topping debut album, Natural, included platinum single 'Mysterious Girl' and two UK No.1s. However, his ventures into more mature R&B-flava'd tracks proved less accessible to his previously large fan base (83 WEEKS)*

		pos/wks
10 Jun 95	**TURN IT UP** *Mushroom D 1000* 64	1
16 Sep 95	**MYSTERIOUS GIRL** *Mushroom D 11921* 53	2
16 Mar 96	**ONLY ONE** *Mushroom D 1307* 16	3
13 Apr 96	**ONLY ONE (re-entry)** *Mushroom D 1307* 69	1
1 Jun 96	● **MYSTERIOUS GIRL (re-issue)** *Mushroom D 2000* [1] 2	18
14 Sep 96	★ **FLAVA** *Mushroom D 2003* ■ 1	9
7 Dec 96	★ **I FEEL YOU** *Mushroom D 1521* ■ 1	9
1 Mar 97	**I FEEL YOU (re-entry)** *Mushroom D 1521* 65	1
8 Mar 97	● **NATURAL** *Mushroom DX 1577* 6	8
15 Mar 97	**I FEEL YOU (2nd re-entry)** *Mushroom D 1521* 74	1
10 May 97	**NATURAL (re-entry)** *Mushroom DX 1577* 58	1
24 May 97	**NATURAL (2nd re-entry)** *Mushroom DX 1577* 68	2
9 Aug 97	● **ALL ABOUT US** *Mushroom MUSH 5CD* 3	8
1 Nov 97	**ALL ABOUT US (re-entry)** *Mushroom MUSH 5CD* 75	1
8 Nov 97	● **LONELY** *Mushroom MUSH 16CD* 6	5
3 Jan 98	**LONELY (re-entry)** *Mushroom MUSH 16CD* 68	4
24 Jan 98	**ALL NIGHT ALL RIGHT** *Mushroom MUSH 21CD* [2] 16	4
25 Jul 98	● **KISS THE GIRL** *Mushroom MUSH 34CDSX* 9	5

[1] Peter Andre featuring Bubbler Ranx [2] Peter Andre featuring Warren G

Chris ANDREWS *UK, male vocalist (36 WEEKS)*

		pos/wks
7 Oct 65	● **YESTERDAY MAN** *Decca F 12236* 3	15
2 Dec 65	**TO WHOM IT CONCERNS** *Decca F 22285* 13	10
14 Apr 66	**SOMETHING ON MY MIND** *Decca F 22365* 45	1
28 Apr 66	**SOMETHING ON MY MIND (re-entry)** *Decca F 22365* 41	2
2 Jun 66	**WHATCHA GONNA DO NOW** *Decca F 22404* 40	4
25 Aug 66	**STOP THAT GIRL** *Decca F 22472* 36	4

Eamonn ANDREWS *Ireland, male vocalist (3 WEEKS)*

		pos/wks
20 Jan 56	**THE SHIFTING WHISPERING SANDS (PARTS 1 & 2)** *Parlophone R 4106* 18	3

Hit is credited: 'with Ron Goodwin and his Orchestra and Chorus'

ANEKA *UK, female vocalist - Mary Sandeman (16 WEEKS)*

		pos/wks
8 Aug 81	★ **JAPANESE BOY** *Hansa HANSA 5* 1	12
7 Nov 81	**LITTLE LADY** *Hansa HANSA 8* 50	4

Dave ANGEL *UK, male DJ / producer (1 WEEK)*

		pos/wks
2 Aug 97	**TOKYO STEALTH FIGHTER** *Fourth & Broadway BRCD 355* 58	1

Simone ANGEL *Holland, female vocalist (1 WEEK)*

		pos/wks
13 Nov 93	**LET THIS FEELING** *A & M 5803652* 60	1

ANGELETTES *UK, female vocal group (5 WEEKS)*

		pos/wks
13 May 72	**DON'T LET HIM TOUCH YOU** *Decca F 13284* 35	5

ANGELHEART *UK, female producer (2 WEEKS)*

		pos/wks
6 Apr 96	**COME BACK TO ME** *Hi-Life 5776312* [1] 68	1
22 Mar 97	**I'M STILL WAITING** *Hi-Life 5735452* [2] 74	1

[1] Angelheart featuring Rochelle Harris [2] Angelheart featuring Aletia Bourne

ANGELIC *UK, male / female production / vocal duo (10 WEEKS)*

		pos/wks
17 Jun 00	**IT'S MY TURN** *Serious MCSTD 40235* 11	10

ANGELIC UPSTARTS
UK, male vocal / instrumental group (30 WEEKS)

			pos/wks
21 Apr 79	I'M AN UPSTART *Warner Bros. K 17354*	**31**	8
11 Aug 79	TEENAGE WARNING *Warner Bros. K 17426*	**29**	6
3 Nov 79	NEVER 'AD NOTHIN' *Warner Bros. K 17476*	**52**	4
9 Feb 80	OUT OF CONTROL *Warner Bros. K 17558*	**58**	3
22 Mar 80	WE GOTTA GET OUT OF THIS PLACE *Warner Bros. K 17576*	**65**	2
2 Aug 80	LAST NIGHT ANOTHER SOLDIER *Zonophone Z 7*	**51**	4
7 Feb 81	KIDS ON THE STREET *Zonophone Z 16*	**57**	3

Bobby ANGELO and the TUXEDOS
UK, male vocal / instrumental group (6 WEEKS)

			pos/wks
10 Aug 61	BABY SITTIN' *HMV POP 892*	**30**	6

ANGELS *US, female vocal group (1 WEEK)*

			pos/wks
3 Oct 63	MY BOYFRIEND'S BACK *Mercury AMT 1211* ▲	**50**	1

ANGELS OF LIGHT – See PSYCHIC TV

ANGELWITCH *UK, male vocal / instrumental group (1 WEEK)*

			pos/wks
7 Jun 80	SWEET DANGER *EMI 5064*	**75**	1

ANIMAL
US, male puppet vocal and instrumental - drums (3 WEEKS)

			pos/wks
23 Jul 94	WIPE OUT *BMG Kidz 74321219532*	**38**	3

ANIMAL NIGHTLIFE
UK, male / female vocal / instrumental group (22 WEEKS)

			pos/wks
13 Aug 83	NATIVE BOY (UPTOWN) *Innervision A3584*	**60**	3
18 Aug 84	MR SOLITAIRE *Island IS 193*	**25**	12
6 Jul 85	LOVE IS JUST THE GREAT PRETENDER *Island IS 200*	**28**	6
5 Oct 85	PREACHER, PREACHER *Island IS 245*	**67**	1

ANIMALHOUSE *UK, male vocal / instrumental group (1 WEEK)*

			pos/wks
15 Jul 00	READY TO RECEIVE *Boilerhouse / Arista 74321771072*	**61**	1

ANIMALS `151` `Top 500`
Groundbreaking Newcastle band: Eric Burdon (v), Alan Price (k), Brian 'Chas' Chandler (b) (d. 1996), Hilton Valentine (g), John Steel (d). They were the first hit act produced by Mickie Most and, after The Tornados and The Beatles, the third UK group to top the US singles chart (147 WEEKS)

			pos/wks
16 Apr 64	BABY LET ME TAKE YOU HOME *Columbia DB 7247*	**21**	8
25 Jun 64	★ HOUSE OF THE RISING SUN *Columbia DB 7301* ▲ ◆	**1**	12
17 Sep 64	● I'M CRYING *Columbia DB 7354*	**8**	10
4 Feb 65	● DON'T LET ME BE MISUNDERSTOOD *Columbia DB 7445*	**3**	9
8 Apr 65	● BRING IT ON HOME TO ME *Columbia DB 7539*	**7**	11
15 Jul 65	● WE GOTTA GET OUT OF THIS PLACE *Columbia DB 7639*	**2**	12
28 Oct 65	● IT'S MY LIFE *Columbia DB 7741*	**7**	11
17 Feb 66	INSIDE - LOOKING OUT *Decca F 12332*	**12**	8
2 Jun 66	● DON'T BRING ME DOWN *Decca F 12407*	**6**	8
27 Oct 66	HELP ME GIRL *Decca F 12502* [1]	**14**	10
15 Jun 67	WHEN I WAS YOUNG *MGM 1340* [2]	**45**	3
6 Sep 67	GOOD TIMES *MGM 1344* [2]	**20**	11
18 Oct 67	● SAN FRANCISCAN NIGHTS *MGM 1359* [2]	**7**	10
14 Feb 68	SKY PILOT *MGM 1373* [2]	**40**	3
15 Jan 69	RING OF FIRE *MGM 1461* [2]	**35**	5
7 Oct 72	HOUSE OF THE RISING SUN (re-issue) *RAK RR 1*	**25**	6
18 Sep 82	HOUSE OF THE RISING SUN (re-entry of re-issue) *RAK RR 1*	**11**	10

[1] Eric Burdon and session musicians billed as The Animals [2] Eric Burdon and The Animals

ANIMOTION
US / UK, male / female vocal / instrumental group (12 WEEKS)

			pos/wks
11 May 85	● OBSESSION *Mercury PH 34*	**5**	12

Paul ANKA `186` `Top 500`
Celebrated Canadian singer / songwriter. b. 30 Jul 1941, Ottawa. He topped the UK and US charts aged 16 and was the youngest transatlantic chart regular of the 1950s. He also penned big hits for Buddy Holly, Tom Jones, Donny Osmond and 'My Way' for Frank Sinatra (134 WEEKS)

			pos/wks
9 Aug 57	★ DIANA *Columbia DB 3980* ◆ ▲	**1**	25
8 Nov 57	● I LOVE YOU, BABY *Columbia DB 4022*	**3**	15
8 Nov 57	TELL ME THAT YOU LOVE ME *Columbia DB 4022*	**25**	2
31 Jan 58	● YOU ARE MY DESTINY *Columbia DB 4063*	**6**	13
30 May 58	CRAZY LOVE *Columbia DB 4110*	**26**	1
26 Sep 58	MIDNIGHT *Columbia DB 4172*	**26**	1
30 Jan 59	● (ALL OF A SUDDEN) MY HEART SINGS *Columbia DB 4241*	**10**	13
10 Jul 59	● LONELY BOY *Columbia DB 4324* ▲	**3**	17
30 Oct 59	● PUT YOUR HEAD ON MY SHOULDER *Columbia DB 4355*	**7**	12
26 Feb 60	IT'S TIME TO CRY *Columbia DB 4390*	**28**	1
31 Mar 60	PUPPY LOVE *Columbia DB 4434*	**33**	4
14 Apr 60	IT'S TIME TO CRY (re-entry) *Columbia DB 4390*	**47**	1
5 May 60	PUPPY LOVE (re-entry) *Columbia DB 4434*	**37**	3
15 Sep 60	HELLO YOUNG LOVERS *Columbia DB 4504*	**44**	1
15 Mar 62	LOVE ME WARM AND TENDER *RCA 1276*	**19**	11
26 Jul 62	A STEEL GUITAR AND A GLASS OF WINE *RCA 1292*	**41**	4
28 Sep 74	● (YOU'RE) HAVING MY BABY *United Artists UP 35713* [1] ▲	**6**	10

[1] Paul Anka featuring Odia Coates

ANOTHER LEVEL `399` `Top 500`
Soulful, teen-targeted UK pop vocal group; Dane Bowers, Wayne Williams, Mark Baron, Bobak Kianoush. Credible quartet, who have had hits with top US rap stars TQ, Jay-Z and Ghostface Killah, were nominated for a Brit award in 1999 but split in 2000 (81 WEEKS)

			pos/wks
28 Feb 98	● BE ALONE NO MORE *Northwestside 74321551982*	**6**	9
18 Jul 98	★ FREAK ME *Northwestside 74321582362* ■	**1**	12
7 Nov 98	● GUESS I WAS A FOOL *Northwestside 74321621202*	**5**	13
23 Jan 99	● I WANT YOU FOR MYSELF *Northwestside 7432164632* [1]	**2**	8
10 Apr 99	● BE ALONE NO MORE *Northwestside 74321658472* [2]	**11**	9
12 Jun 99	● FROM THE HEART *Northwestside 74321673012*	**6**	10
28 Aug 99	FROM THE HEART (re-entry) *Northwestside 74321673012*	**74**	1
4 Sep 99	● SUMMERTIME *Northwestside 74321694672* [3]	**7**	7
13 Nov 99	● BOMB DIGGY *Northwestside 74321712212*	**6**	12

[1] Another Level / Ghostface Killah [2] Another Level featuring Jay-Z [3] Another Level Featuring TQ

ANOUCHKA – See Terry HALL

Adam ANT `500` `Top 500`
Innovative and flamboyant pop idol. b. Stuart Goddard, 3 Nov 1954, London. He left Adam and The Ants at their peak and immediately topped UK chart and scored first ever US hit. Later made his mark as an actor (69 WEEKS)

			pos/wks
22 May 82	★ GOODY TWO SHOES *CBS A 2367*	**1**	11
18 Sep 82	● FRIEND OR FOE *CBS A 2736*	**9**	8
27 Nov 82	DESPERATE BUT NOT SERIOUS *CBS A 2892*	**33**	7
29 Oct 83	● PUSS 'N BOOTS *CBS A 3614*	**5**	11
10 Dec 83	STRIP *CBS A 3589*	**41**	6
22 Sep 84	APOLLO 9 *CBS A 4719*	**13**	8
13 Jul 85	VIVE LE ROCK *CBS A 6367*	**50**	4
17 Feb 90	ROOM AT THE TOP *MCA MCA 1387*	**13**	7
28 Apr 90	CANT SET RULES ABOUT LOVE *MCA MCA 1404*	**47**	2
11 Feb 95	WONDERFUL *EMI CDEMS 366*	**32**	3
3 Jun 95	GOTTA BE A SIN *EMI CDEMS 379*	**48**	2

See also ADAM and the ANTS

ANT & DEC `408` `Top 500`
Newcastle-born child actors turned TV presenters. Geordie jokers Anthony McPartlin and Declan Donnelly (aka PJ & Duncan) initially recorded under their character aliases from the children's TV series Byker Grove. They scored impressive 12 Top 20 entries within three years (81 WEEKS)

			pos/wks
18 Dec 93	TONIGHT I'M FREE *Telstar CDSTAS 2706*	**62**	3
23 Apr 94	WHY ME *Telstar CDSTAS 2719*	**27**	4

23 Jul 94 ●	LET'S GET READY TO RHUMBLE *XSrhythm CDANT 1* 9	11
8 Oct 94	IF I GIVE YOU MY NUMBER *XSrhythm CDANT 2* **15**	7
3 Dec 94	ETERNAL LOVE *XSrhythm CDANT 3*.........................**12**	9
25 Feb 95	OUR RADIO ROCKS *XSrhythm CDANT 4*...................**15**	5
29 Jul 95	STUCK ON U *XSrhythm CDANT 5*..........................**15**	5
14 Oct 95	U KRAZY KATZ *XSrhythm CDANT 6*.......................**15**	4
2 Dec 95	PERFECT *Telstar CDANT 7*................................**16**	7
20 Mar 96	STEPPING STONE *Telstar CDANT 8*.....................**11**	5
24 Aug 96 ●	BETTER WATCH OUT *Telstar CDANT 9*.................**10**	4
23 Nov 96	WHEN I FALL IN LOVE *Telstar CDANT 10*...............**12**	8
15 Mar 97 ●	SHOUT *Telstar CDDEC 11*...............................**10**	5
10 May 97	FALLING *Telstar CDDEC 12*.............................**14**	4

All hits up to and including 20 Mar 96 credited to PJ & Duncan

ANTARCTICA *Australia, male producer – Steve Gibbs (2 WEEKS)* pos/wks

29 Jan 00	RETURN TO REALITY *React CDREACT 173*................**53**	1
8 Jul 00	ADRIFT (CAST YOUR MIND) *React CDREACT 172* **72**	1

Mark ANTHONI – See FIRE ISLAND

Billie ANTHONY
UK, female vocalist – Philomena Brown (16 WEEKS) pos/wks

15 Oct 54 ●	THIS OLE HOUSE *Columbia DB 3519* **4**	16

This release was 'With Eric Jupp & his Orchestra'

Marc ANTHONY *US, male vocalist (3 WEEKS)* pos/wks

13 Nov 99	I NEED TO KNOW *Columbia 6683612* **28**	3

See also Louie VEGA and Marc ANTHONY

Miki ANTHONY *UK, male vocalist (7 WEEKS)* pos/wks

3 Feb 73	IF IT WASN'T FOR THE REASON THAT I LOVE YOU *Bell 1275*......**27**	7

Ray ANTHONY & His ORCHESTRA *US, orchestra (2 WEEKS)* pos/wks

4 Dec 53 ●	DRAGNET *Capitol CL 13983* **7**	1
8 Jan 54	DRAGNET (re-entry) *Capitol CL 13983* **11**	1

Richard ANTHONY *France, male vocalist (15 WEEKS)* pos/wks

12 Dec 63	WALKING ALONE *Columbia DB 7133* **37**	5
2 Apr 64	IF I LOVED YOU *Columbia DB 7235* **48**	1
23 Apr 64	IF I LOVED YOU (re-entry) *Columbia DB 7235* **18**	9

ANTHRAX *US, male vocal / instrumental group (37 WEEKS)* pos/wks

28 Feb 87	I AM THE LAW *Island IS LAW 1* **32**	5
27 Jun 87	INDIANS *Island IS 325*.......................................**44**	4
5 Dec 87	I'M THE MAN *Island IS 338*..................................**20**	6
10 Sep 88	MAKE ME LAUGH *Island IS 379*............................**26**	3
18 Mar 89	ANTI-SOCIAL *Island IS 409*..................................**44**	3
1 Sep 90	IN MY WORLD *Island IS 470*.................................**29**	2
5 Jan 91	GOT THE TIME *Island IS 476*................................**16**	4
6 Jul 91	BRING THE NOISE *Island IS 490* [1] **14**	5
8 May 93	ONLY *Elektra EKR 166CD*....................................**36**	3
11 Sep 93	BLACK LODGE *Elektra EKR 171CD*.........................**53**	2

[1] Anthrax featuring Chuck D

ANTI-NOWHERE LEAGUE
UK, male vocal / instrumental group (10 WEEKS) pos/wks

23 Jan 82	STREETS OF LONDON *WXYZ ABCD 1*.......................**48**	5
20 Mar 82	I HATE . . . PEOPLE *WXYZ ABCD 2*.........................**46**	3
3 Jul 82	WOMAN *WXYZ ABCD 4*......................................**72**	1

ANTI-PASTI – See EXPLOITED

ANTICAPPELLA
Italy / UK, male / female vocal / instrumental group (12 WEEKS) pos/wks

16 Nov 91	231 *PWL Continental PWL 205*................................**24**	4
18 Apr 92	EVERY DAY *PWL Continental PWL 220*......................**45**	2

25 Jun 94	MOVE YOUR BODY *Media MCSTD 1980* [1] **21**	3
1 Apr 95	EXPRESS YOUR FREEDOM *Media MCSTD 2048*..........**31**	2
25 May 96	231 / MOVE YOUR BODY (re-mix) *Media MCSTD 40037* **54**	1

[1] Anticappella featuring MC Fixx It

ANTONIA – See BOMB THE BASS

ANTS – See ADAM and the ANTS

ANUNA – See Bill WHELAN featuring ANUNA and the RTE CONCERT ORCHESTRA

APACHE INDIAN *UK, male vocalist – Steven Kapur (33 WEEKS)* pos/wks

28 Nov 92	FE' REAL *Ten TEN 416* [1] **33**	3
2 Jan 93	ARRANGED MARRIAGE *Island CID 544*...................**16**	6
27 Mar 93	CHOK THERE *Island CID 555*...............................**30**	4
14 Aug 93 ●	NUFF VIBES (EP) *Island CID 560* **5**	10
22 Oct 93	MOVIN' ON *Island CID 580*..................................**48**	2
7 May 94	WRECKX SHOP *MCA MCSTD 1969* [2] **26**	2
11 Feb 95	MAKE WAY FOR THE INDIAN *Island CID 586* [3] **29**	2
22 Apr 95	RAGGAMUFFIN GIRL *Island CID 606* [4] **31**	2
29 Mar 97	LOVIN' (LET ME LOVE YOU) *Coalition COLA 002CD*.......**53**	1
18 Oct 97	REAL PEOPLE *Coalition COLA 019CD*......................**66**	1

[1] Maxi Priest featuring Apache Indian [2] Wreckx-N-Effect featuring Apache Indian [3] Apache Indian and Tim Dog [4] Apache Indian with Frankie Paul

The listed flip side of 'Fe' Real' was 'Just Wanna Know' by Maxi Priest. Tracks on Nuff Vibes (EP): Boom Shack a Lak / Fun / Caste System / Warning

APHEX TWIN
UK, male instrumentalist / producer – Richard James (12 WEEKS) pos/wks

9 May 92	DIGERIDOO *R&S RSUK 12* **55**	2
27 Nov 93	ON *Warp WAP 39CD* **32**	3
8 Apr 95	VENTOLIN *Warp WAP 60CD* **49**	1
26 Oct 96	GIRL / BOY (EP) *Warp WAP 78CD* **64**	1
18 Oct 97	COME TO DADDY *Warp WAP 94CD* **36**	2
3 Apr 99	WINDOWLICKER *Warp WAP 105CD* **16**	3

Tracks on Girl / Boy (EP): Girl / Boy Song / Milkman / Inkey $ / Beatles Under My Carpet. The EP was incorrectly listed in the chart and, because of its length, should have been considered an album

See also POLYGON WINDOW

APHRODITE'S CHILD
Greece, male vocal / instrumental group (7 WEEKS) pos/wks

6 Nov 68	RAIN AND TEARS *Mercury MF 1039* **29**	7

APOLLO FOUR FORTY
UK, male instrumental / production group (50 WEEKS) pos/wks

22 Jan 94	ASTRAL AMERICA *Stealth Sonic SSXCD 2* [1] **36**	2
5 Nov 94	LIQUID COOL *Stealth Sonic SSXCD 3* [1] **35**	2
25 Mar 95	(DON'T FEAR) THE REAPER *Stealth Sonic SSXCD 4* [1] **35**	2
27 Jul 96	KRUPA *Stealth Sonic SSXCD 5*.............................**23**	4
28 Sep 96	KRUPA (re-entry) *Stealth Sonic SSXCD 5* **24**	4
15 Feb 97 ●	AIN'T TALKIN' 'BOUT DUB *Stealth Sonic SSXCDX 6* **7**	7
5 Jul 97	RAW POWER *Stealth Sonic SSXCD 7* **32**	3
11 Jul 98	RENDEZ-VOUS '98 *Epic 6661102* [2] **12**	6
8 Aug 98 ●	LOST IN SPACE *Stealth Sonic SSX 9CD* **4**	9
28 Aug 99 ●	STOP THE ROCK *Epic SSX 10CD* **10**	6
27 Nov 99	HEART GO BOOM *Epic SSX 11CD*..........................**57**	1
9 Dec 00	CHARLIE'S ANGELS 2000 *Epic SSX 13CD*..................**29**	4+

[1] Apollo 440 [2] Jean-Michel Jarre and Apollo 440

APOLLO Presents HOUSE OF VIRGINISM
Sweden, male instrumentalist and Sweden, male vocal / instrumental group (1 WEEK) pos/wks

17 Feb 96	EXCLUSIVE *Logic 74321324102* **67**	1

Fiona APPLE *US, female vocalist (2 WEEKS)* pos/wks

26 Feb 00	FAST AS YOU CAN *Columbia 6689962* **33**	2

Kim APPLEBY UK, female vocalist (31 WEEKS)

		pos/wks
3 Nov 90 ●	DON'T WORRY *Parlophone R 6272*	2 10
9 Feb 91 ●	G.L.A.D. *Parlophone R 6281*	10 6
29 Jun 91	MAMA *Parlophone R 6291*	19 8
19 Oct 91	IF YOU CARED *Parlophone R 6297*	44 3
31 Jul 93	LIGHT OF THE WORLD *Parlophone CDR 6352*	41 2
13 Nov 93	BREAKAWAY *Parlophone CDR 6362*	56 1
12 Nov 94	FREE SPIRIT *Parlophone CDR 6397*	51 1

See also MEL and KIM

APPLEJACKS
UK, male / female vocal / instrumental group (29 WEEKS)

		pos/wks
5 Mar 64 ●	TELL ME WHEN *Decca F 11833*	7 13
11 Jun 64	LIKE DREAMERS DO *Decca F 11916*	20 11
15 Oct 64	THREE LITTLE WORDS *Decca F 11981*	23 5

APPLES UK, male vocal / instrumental group (1 WEEK)

		pos/wks
23 Mar 91	EYE WONDER *Epic 6566717*	75 1

Charlie APPLEWHITE US, male vocalist (1 WEEK)

		pos/wks
23 Sep 55	BLUE STAR (THE MEDIC THEME) *Brunswick 05416*	20 1

This release was 'With Victor Young & Chorus'

Helen APRIL – See John DUMMER and Helen APRIL

APRIL WINE Canada, male vocal / instrumental group (9 WEEKS)

		pos/wks
15 Mar 80	I LIKE TO ROCK *Capitol CL 16121*	41 5
11 Apr 81	JUST BETWEEN YOU AND ME *Capitol CL 16184*	52 4

AQUA `371` `Top 500` Scandinavian Europop act: Claus Noreen b. 5 Jun 1970, Denmark, Soren Rasted b 13 Jun 1969, Denmark, fronted by the flame-haired Lene Nystrom b. 2 Oct 1973, Norway and the bald-headed Rene Dif b. 17 Oct 1967, Denmark. 'Barbie Girl' was a global smash and their debut album Aquarium sold more than 14 million worldwide (85 WEEKS)

		pos/wks
25 Oct 97 ★	BARBIE GIRL *Universal UMD 80413* ◆	1 24
7 Feb 98 ★	DOCTOR JONES *Universal UMD 80457* ■	1 14
25 Apr 98	BARBIE GIRL (re-entry) *Universal UMD 80413*	66 2
16 May 98 ★	TURN BACK TIME *Universal UMD 80490* ■	1 10
1 Aug 98 ●	MY OH MY *Universal UMD 85058*	6 9
17 Oct 98	MY OH MY (re-entry) *Universal UMD 85058*	66 2
26 Dec 98	GOOD MORNING SUNSHINE *Universal UMD 85086*	18 7
26 Feb 00 ●	CARTOON HEROES *Universal MCSTD 40226*	7 9
13 May 00	CARTOON HEROES (re-entry) *Universal MCSTD 40226*	73 2
10 Jun 00	AROUND THE WORLD *Universal MCSTD 40234*	26 6

AQUA MARINA – See FAB

AQUARIAN DREAM
US, male / female vocal / instrumental group (1 WEEK)

		pos/wks
24 Feb 79	YOU'RE A STAR *Elektra LV 7*	67 1

ARAB STRAP UK, male vocal / instrumental duo (3 WEEKS)

		pos/wks
13 Sep 97	THE GIRLS OF SUMMER (EP) *Chemikal CHEM 017CD*	74 1
4 Apr 98	HERE WE GO / TRIPPY *Chemikal CHEM 20CD*	48 1
10 Oct 98	(AFTERNOON) SOAPS *Chemikal CHEM 27CD*	74 1

Tracks on The Girls of Summer (EP): Hey! Fever / Girls of Summer / The Beautiful Barmaids of Dundee / One Day After School

ARCADIA UK, male vocal / instrumental group (13 WEEKS)

		pos/wks
26 Oct 85 ●	ELECTION DAY *Odeon NSR 1*	7 7
25 Jan 86	THE PROMISE *Odeon NSR 2*	37 4
26 Jul 86	THE FLAME *Odeon NSR 3*	58 2

Arcadia was Duran Duran sideline band featuring Simon Le Bon, Nick Rhodes and Roger Taylor

See also DURAN DURAN

Tasmin ARCHER UK, female vocalist (37 WEEKS)

		pos/wks
12 Sep 92 ★	SLEEPING SATELLITE *EMI EM 233*	1 15
2 Jan 93	SLEEPING SATELLITE (re-entry) *EMI EM 233*	67 2
20 Feb 93	IN YOUR CARE *EMI CDEMS 260*	16 6
29 May 93	LORDS OF THE NEW CHURCH *EMI CDEM 266*	26 4
21 Aug 93	ARIENNE *EMI CDEM 275*	30 4
8 Jan 94	SHIPBUILDING *EMI CDEM 302*	40 4
23 Mar 96	ONE MORE GOOD NIGHT WITH THE BOYS *EMI CDEM 401*	45 2

ARCHIES
US, male / female cartoon vocal group - Lead vocal Ron Dante (26 WEEKS)

		pos/wks
11 Oct 69 ★	SUGAR SUGAR *RCA 1872* ▲	1 26

ARCHITECHS featuring NANA
UK, male production duo and female vocalist (13 WEEKS)

		pos/wks
7 Oct 00 ●	BODY GROOVE *Go. Beat / Polydor GOBCD33*	3 13+

Jann ARDEN Canada, female vocalist (2 WEEKS)

		pos/wks
13 Jul 96	INSENSITIVE *A & M 5812652*	40 2

Tina ARENA Australia, female vocalist (32 WEEKS)

		pos/wks
15 Apr 95 ●	CHAINS *Columbia 6611255*	6 11
12 Aug 95	HEAVEN HELP MY HEART *Columbia 6620975*	25 5
2 Dec 95	SHOW ME HEAVEN *Columbia 6626975*	29 3
3 Aug 96	SORRENTO MOON (I REMEMBER) *Columbia 6635435*	22 4
27 Jun 98	WHISTLE DOWN THE WIND *Really Useful 5672192*	24 5
24 Oct 98	IF I WAS A RIVER *Columbia 6665605*	43 2
13 Mar 99	BURN *Columbia 6667442*	47 1
20 May 00	LIVE FOR THE ONE I LOVE *Columbia 6691332*	63 1

ARGENT UK, male vocal / instrumental group (27 WEEKS)

		pos/wks
4 Mar 72 ●	HOLD YOUR HEAD UP *Epic EPC 7786*	5 12
10 Jun 72	TRAGEDY *Epic EPC 85115*	34 7
24 Mar 73	GOD GAVE ROCK AND ROLL TO YOU *Epic EPC 1243*	18 8

See also SAN JOSE featuring Rodriguez ARGENTINA; SILSOE

ARIEL Argentina, male DJ / producer - Ariel Belloso (6 WEEKS)

		pos/wks
27 Mar 93	LET IT SLIDE *Deconstruction 74321134512*	57 2
21 Jun 97	DEEP (I'M FALLING DEEPER) *Wonderboy WBOYD 005*	47 1
17 Jun 00	A9 *Essential Recordings ESCD 15*	28 3

ARIZONA Featuring ZEITIA
UK, male production / instrumental duo & female vocalist (1 WEEK)

		pos/wks
12 Mar 94	I SPECIALIZE IN LOVE *Union City UCRCD 27*	74 1

Ship's Company and Royal Marine Band of HMS ARK ROYAL
UK, male choir and marine band (6 WEEKS)

		pos/wks
23 Dec 78	THE LAST FAREWELL *BBC RESL 61*	46 6

ARKARNA
UK, male vocal / instrumental / production group (3 WEEKS)

		pos/wks
25 Jan 97	HOUSE ON FIRE *WEA WEA 088CD1*	33 2
2 Aug 97	SO LITTLE TIME *WEA WEA 108CD1*	46 1

Joan ARMATRADING UK, female vocalist (53 WEEKS)

		pos/wks
16 Oct 76 ●	LOVE AND AFFECTION *A & M AMS 7249*	10 9
23 Feb 80	ROSIE *A & M AMS 7506*	49 5
14 Jun 80	ME MYSELF I *A & M AMS 7527*	21 11
6 Sep 80	ALL THE WAY FROM AMERICA *A & M AMS 7552*	54 3
12 Sep 81	I'M LUCKY *A & M AMS 8163*	46 5
16 Jan 82	NO LOVE *A & M AMS 8179*	50 5
19 Feb 83	DROP THE PILOT *A & M AMS 8306*	11 10
16 Mar 85	TEMPTATION *A & M AM 238*	65 2
26 May 90	MORE THAN ONE KIND OF LOVE *A & M AM 561*	75 1
23 May 92	WRAPPED AROUND HER *A & M AM 877*	56 2

UK No.1 ★   UK Top 10 ●   Still on chart +   UK million seller ◆   UK entry at No.1 ■   US No.1 ▲

ARMIN
Holland, male DJ producer (4 WEEKS)

		pos/wks
14 Feb 98	**BLUE FEAR** *Xtravaganza 0091485 EXT* 45 1
12 Feb 00	**COMMUNICATION** *AM:PM CDAMPM 129* 18 3

ARMOURY SHOW
UK, male vocal / instrumental group (6 WEEKS)

		pos/wks
25 Aug 84	**CASTLES IN SPAIN** *Parlophone R 6079* 69 2
26 Jan 85	**WE CAN BE BRAVE AGAIN** *Parlophone R 6087* 66 1
17 Jan 87	**LOVE IN ANGER** *Parlophone R 6149* 63 3

Craig ARMSTRONG – See Shola AMA

Louis ARMSTRONG 325 Top 500
Best known jazz artist of the 20th century, b. 4 Aug 1901, New Orleans, USA, (not 4 Jul 1900 according to previous claims by the man himself). This groundbreaking, trumpet-toting gravel-voiced vocalist, known as 'Satchmo', d. 6 Jul 1971. He is the oldest performer to top either the UK or US charts. (93 WEEKS)

		pos/wks
19 Dec 52 ●	**TAKES TWO TO TANGO** *Brunswick 04995* 6 10
13 Apr 56 ●	**THEME FROM THE THREEPENNY OPERA** *Philips PB 574* 1 ......8 11
15 Jun 56	**TAKE IT SATCH (EP)** *Philips BBE 12035* 1 ......29 1
13 Jul 56	**THE FAITHFUL HUSSAR** *Philips PB 604* 1 ......27 2
6 Nov 59	**MACK THE KNIFE** *Philips PB 967* 1 ......24 1
4 Jun 64 ●	**HELLO DOLLY** *London HLR 9878* ▲ 4 14
7 Feb 68 ★	**WHAT A WONDERFUL WORLD / CABARET** *HMV POP 1615* 1 29
26 Jun 68	**SUNSHINE OF LOVE** *Stateside SS 2116* 41 7
16 Apr 88	**WHAT A WONDERFUL WORLD (re-issue)** *A & M AM 435* 53 5
19 Nov 94 ●	**WE HAVE ALL THE TIME IN THE WORLD** *EMI CDEM 357* 3 11
18 Mar 95	**WE HAVE ALL THE TIME IN THE WORLD (re-entry)** *EMI CDEM 357* 66 2

1 Louis Armstrong with his All-Stars

Take It Satch (EP) tracks: Tiger Rag / Mack the Knife / The Faithful Hussar / Back O'Town Blues. 'Mack the Knife' is a re-issue of 'Theme From Threepenny Opera' under a different title. 'Cabaret' was not listed with 'What a Wonderful World' until 14 Feb 1968

ARMY OF LOVERS
Sweden / France, male / female vocal / group (12 WEEKS)

		pos/wks
17 Aug 91	**CRUCIFIED** *Ton Son Ton WOK 2007* 47 5
28 Dec 91	**OBSESSION** *Ton Son Ton WOK 2009* 67 1
15 Feb 92	**CRUCIFIED (re-issue)** *Ton Son Ton WOK 2017* 31 5
18 Apr 92	**RIDE THE BULLET** *Ton Son Ton WOK 2018* 67 1

ARNEE and the TERMINATERS
UK, male vocal / instrumental group (7 WEEKS)

		pos/wks
24 Aug 91 ●	**I'LL BE BACK** *Epic 6574177* 5 7

ARNIE'S LOVE
US, male / female vocal / instrumental group (3 WEEKS)

		pos/wks
26 Nov 83	**I'M OUT OF YOUR LIFE** *Streetwave WAVE 9* 67 3

David ARNOLD – See Nina PERSSON and David ARNOLD; BJORK; David McALMONT; PROPELLERHEADS

Eddy ARNOLD
US, male vocalist (21 WEEKS)

		pos/wks
17 Feb 66 ●	**MAKE THE WORLD GO AWAY** *RCA 1496* 8 17
26 May 66	**I WANT TO GO WITH YOU** *RCA 1519* 49 1
9 Jun 66	**I WANT TO GO WITH YOU (re-entry)** *RCA 1519* 46 2
28 Jul 66	**IF YOU WERE MINE MARY** *RCA 1529* 49 1

PP ARNOLD
US, female vocalist (37 WEEKS)

		pos/wks
4 May 67	**FIRST CUT IS THE DEEPEST** *Immediate IM 047* 18 10
2 Aug 67	**THE TIME HAS COME** *Immediate IM 055* 47 2
24 Jan 68	**(IF YOU THINK YOU'RE) GROOVY** *Immediate IM 061* 41 4
10 Jul 68	**ANGEL OF THE MORNING** *Immediate IM 067* 29 11
24 Sep 88	**BURN IT UP** *Rhythm King LEFT 27* 1 ......14 10

1 Beatmasters with PP Arnold

ARPEGGIO
US, male / female vocal group (3 WEEKS)

		pos/wks
31 Mar 79	**LOVE AND DESIRE (PART 1)** *Polydor POSP 40* 63 3

ARRESTED DEVELOPMENT
US, male / female vocal / instrumental / rap group (39 WEEKS)

		pos/wks
16 May 92	**TENNESSEE** *Cooltempo COOL 253* 46 4
11 Jul 92	**TENNESSEE (re-entry)** *Cooltempo COOL 253* 54 3
24 Oct 92 ●	**PEOPLE EVERYDAY** *Cooltempo COOL 265* 2 14
9 Jan 93 ●	**MR WENDAL / REVOLUTION** *Cooltempo CDCOOL 288* 4 9
3 Apr 93	**TENNESSEE (re-issue)** *Cooltempo CDCOOL 270* 18 6
28 May 94	**EASE MY MIND** *Cooltempo CDCOOL 293* 33 3

Steve ARRINGTON
US, male vocalist (19 WEEKS)

		pos/wks
27 Apr 85 ●	**FEEL SO REAL** *Atlantic A 9576* 5 10
6 Jul 85	**DANCIN' IN THE KEY OF LIFE** *Atlantic A 9534* 21 8
7 Sep 85	**DANCIN' IN THE KEY OF LIFE (re-entry)** *Atlantic A 9534* 75 1

ARRIVAL
UK, male / female vocal / instrumental group (20 WEEKS)

		pos/wks
10 Jan 70 ●	**FRIENDS** *Decca F 12986* 8 9
6 Jun 70	**I WILL SURVIVE** *Decca F 13026* 16 11

ARROLA – See RUFF DRIVERZ

ARROW
Montserrat, male vocalist (15 WEEKS)

		pos/wks
28 Jul 84	**HOT HOT HOT** *Cooltempo ARROW 1* 59 5
13 Jul 85	**LONG TIME** *London LON 70* 30 7
3 Sep 94	**HOT HOT HOT (re-mix)** *The Hit Label HLC 7* 38 3

ARROWS
US / UK, male vocal / instrumental group (16 WEEKS)

		pos/wks
25 May 74 ●	**A TOUCH TOO MUCH** *RAK 171* 8 9
1 Feb 75	**MY LAST NIGHT WITH YOU** *RAK 189* 25 7

ARSENAL FC
UK, male football team vocal group (16 WEEKS)

		pos/wks
8 May 71	**GOOD OLD ARSENAL** *Pye 7N 45067* 1 ......16 7
15 May 93	**SHOUTING FOR THE GUNNERS** *London LONCD 342* 2 ......34 3
23 May 98 ●	**HOT STUFF** *Grapevine AFCCD 1* 9 5
3 Jun 00	**ARSENAL NUMBER ONE / OUR GOAL** *Grapevine CDGPS280* 46 1

1 Arsenal FC First Team Squad 2 Arsenal FA Cup Squad featuring Tippa Irie and Peter Hunnigale

ART COMPANY
Holland, male vocal / instrumental group (11 WEEKS)

		pos/wks
26 May 84	**SUSANNA** *Epic A 4174* 12 11

ART OF NOISE
UK, male / female instrumental / production group (65 WEEKS)

		pos/wks
24 Nov 84 ●	**CLOSE (TO THE EDIT)** *ZTT ZTPS 01* 8 19
13 Apr 85	**MOMENTS IN LOVE / BEAT BOX** *ZTT ZTPS 02* 51 4
9 Nov 85	**LEGS** *China WOK 5* 69 1
22 Mar 86 ●	**PETER GUNN** *China WOK 6* 1 ......8 9
21 Jun 86	**PARANOIMIA** *China WOK 9* 2 ......12 9
18 Jul 87	**DRAGNET** *China WOK 14* 60 4
29 Oct 88 ●	**KISS** *China CHINA 11* 3 ......5 7
12 Aug 89	**YEBO** *China CHINA 18* 4 ......63 3
16 Jun 90	**ART OF LOVE** *China CHINA 23* 67 1
11 Jan 92	**INSTRUMENTS OF DARKNESS (ALL OF US ARE ONE PEOPLE)** *China WOK 2012* 45 5
29 Feb 92	**SHADES OF PARANOIMIA** *China WOK 2014* 53 2
26 Jun 99	**METAFORCE** *ZTT ZTT 129CD* 53 1

1 Art of Noise featuring Duane Eddy 2 Art of Noise featuring Max Headroom 3 Art of Noise featuring Tom Jones 4 Art of Noise featuring Mahlathini and the Mahotella Queens

ART OF TRANCE
UK, male instrumentalist / producer (3 WEEKS) pos/wks

31 Oct 98	**MADAGASCAR** *Platipus PLAT 43CD* 69 1
7 Aug 99	**MADAGASCAR (re-mix)** *Platipus PLAT 58CD* 48 2

ARTEMESIA
Holland, male producer - Patrick Prinz (4 WEEKS)

		pos/wks	
15 Apr 95	**BITS + PIECES** *Hooj Choons HOOJ 31CD*	**46**	2
23 Sep 95	**BITS + PIECES (re-entry)** *Hooj Choons HOOJ 31CD*	**75**	1
12 Aug 00	**BITS AND PIECES (re-mix)** *Tidy Trax TIDT 141CD*	**51**	1

See also ETHICS; MOVIN' MELODIES; SUBLIMINAL CUTS

ARTFUL DODGER
UK, male production / instrumental duo - Mark Hill and Peter Devereux (45 WEEKS)

		pos/wks	
11 Dec 99 ●	**RE-REWIND THE CROWD SAY BO SELECTA** *Public Demand / Relentless RELENT 1CDS* 1	**2**	17
4 Mar 00 ●	**MOVIN TOO FAST** *Locked On XL LOX 117CD* 2	**2**	11
10 Jun 00	**MOVIN TOO FAST (re-entry)** *Locked On XL LOX 117CD* 2	**64**	1
15 Jul 00 ●	**WOMAN TROUBLE** *Public Demand / ffrr FCD 380* 3	**6**	10
25 Nov 00 ●	**PLEASE DON'T TURN ME ON** *Public Demand / ffrr FCD 388* 4	**4**	6+

1 Artful Dodger featuring Craig David 2 Artful Dodger & Romina Johnson 3 Artful Dodger and Robbie Craig featuring Craig David 4 Artful Dodger Featuring Lifford

Neil ARTHUR *UK, male vocalist (2 WEEKS)*

		pos/wks	
5 Feb 94	**I LOVE I HATE** *Chrysalis CDCHSS 5005*	**50**	2

ARTIST – See PRINCE

ARTISTS UNITED AGAINST APARTHEID
International, male / female vocal / instrumental charity assembly (8 WEEKS)

		pos/wks	
23 Nov 85	**SUN CITY** *Manhattan MT 7*	**21**	8

ASAP *UK, male vocal / instrumental group (4 WEEKS)*

		pos/wks	
14 Oct 89	**SILVER AND GOLD** *EMI EM 107*	**60**	2
3 Feb 90	**DOWN THE WIRE** *EMI EM 131*	**67**	2

ASCENSION
UK, male / female vocal / DJ / production group (3 WEEKS)

		pos/wks	
5 Jul 97	**SOMEONE** *Perfecto PERF 141CD*	**55**	1
15 Jul 00	**SOMEONE (re-mix)** *Code Blue BLU 011CD1*	**43**	2

ASH
Ireland, male (+ female after 1996) vocal / instrumental group (34 WEEKS)

		pos/wks	
1 Apr 95	**KUNG FU** *Infectious INFECT 21CD*	**57**	1
12 Aug 95	**GIRL FROM MARS** *Infectious INFECT 24CD*	**11**	5
21 Oct 95	**ANGEL INTERCEPTOR** *Infectious INFECT 27CD*	**14**	4
27 Apr 96 ●	**GOLDFINGER** *Infectious INFECT 39CD*	**5**	5
6 Jul 96 ●	**OH YEAH** *Infectious INFECT 41CD*	**6**	7
28 Sep 96	**OH YEAH (re-entry)** *Infectious INFECT 41CD*	**69**	1
25 Oct 97 ●	**A LIFE LESS ORDINARY** *Infectious INFECT 50CD*	**10**	5
3 Oct 98	**JESUS SAYS** *Infectious INFECT 59CD*	**15**	4
5 Dec 98	**WILD SURF** *Infectious INFECT 61CDS*	**31**	2

ASH – See QUENTIN and ASH

ASHA *Italy, female vocalist (2 WEEKS)*

		pos/wks	
8 Jul 95	**JJ TRIBUTE** *Ffrreedom TABCD 228*	**38**	2

ASHAYE *UK, male vocalist (3 WEEKS)*

		pos/wks	
15 Oct 83	**MICHAEL JACKSON MEDLEY** *Record Shack SOHO 10*	**45**	3

Tracks on medley: Don't Stop Til You Get Enough / Wanna Be Startin' Something / Shake Your Body Down to the Ground / Blame It on the Boogie

Richard ASHCROFT *UK, male vocalist (18 WEEKS)*

		pos/wks	
15 Apr 00 ●	**A SONG FOR THE LOVERS** *Hut / Virgin HUTCD 128*	**3**	10
24 Jun 00	**MONEY TO BURN** *Hut / Virgin HUTCD 136*	**17**	4

		pos/wks	
1 Jul 00	**A SONG FOR THE LOVERS (re-entry)** *Hut / Virgin HUTCD 128*	**61**	1
23 Sep 00	**C'MON PEOPLE (WE'RE MAKING IT NOW)** *Hut / Virgin HUTCD 138*	**21**	3

See also VERVE

John ASHER *UK, male vocalist (6 WEEKS)*

		pos/wks	
15 Nov 75	**LET'S TWIST AGAIN** *Creole CR 112*	**14**	6

ASHFORD and SIMPSON *US, male / female vocal duo - Nickolas Ashford & Valerie Simpson (22 WEEKS)*

		pos/wks	
18 Nov 78	**IT SEEMS TO HANG ON** *Warner Bros. K 17237*	**48**	4
5 Jan 85 ●	**SOLID** *Capitol CL 345*	**3**	15
20 Apr 85	**BABIES** *Capitol CL 355*	**56**	3

ASHTON, GARDNER AND DYKE
UK, male vocal / instrumental group (14 WEEKS)

		pos/wks	
16 Jan 71 ●	**THE RESURRECTION SHUFFLE** *Capitol CL 15665*	**3**	14

ASIA *UK, male vocal / instrumental group (13 WEEKS)*

		pos/wks	
3 Jul 82	**HEAT OF THE MOMENT** *Geffen GEF A2494*	**46**	5
18 Sep 82	**ONLY TIME WILL TELL** *Geffen GEF A2228*	**54**	3
13 Aug 83	**DON'T CRY** *Geffen A 3580*	**33**	5

ASIA BLUE *UK, female vocal group (2 WEEKS)*

		pos/wks	
27 Jun 92	**ESCAPING** *Atomic WNR 882*	**50**	2

ASIAN DUB FOUNDATION
UK, male vocal / instrumental group (7 WEEKS)

		pos/wks	
21 Feb 98	**FREE SATPAL RAM** *ffrr FCD 326*	**56**	1
2 May 98	**BUZZIN'** *ffrr FCD 335*	**31**	2
4 Jul 98	**BLACK WHITE** *ffrr FCD 337*	**52**	1
18 Mar 00	**REAL GREAT BRITAIN** *ffrr FCD 376*	**41**	2
3 Jun 00	**NEW WAY, NEW LIFE** *ffrr FCD 378*	**49**	1

ASSEMBLY *UK, male vocal / instrumental group (10 WEEKS)*

		pos/wks	
12 Nov 83 ●	**NEVER NEVER** *Mute TINY 1*	**4**	10

See also ERASURE

ASSOCIATES *UK, male vocal / instrumental group (47 WEEKS)*

		pos/wks	
20 Feb 82 ●	**PARTY FEARS TWO** *Associates ASC 1*	**9**	10
8 May 82	**CLUB COUNTRY** *Associates ASC 2*	**13**	10
7 Aug 82	**LOVE HANGOVER / 18 CARAT LOVE AFFAIR** *Associates ASC 3*	**21**	8
16 Jun 84	**THOSE FIRST IMPRESSIONS** *WEA YZ 6*	**43**	6
1 Sep 84	**WAITING FOR THE LOVEBOAT** *WEA YZ 16*	**53**	4
19 Jan 85	**BREAKFAST** *WEA YZ 28*	**49**	6
17 Sep 88	**HEART OF GLASS** *WEA YZ 310*	**56**	3

'18 Carat Love Affair' listed until 28 Aug only. Act was duo on 1982 hits

ASSOCIATION *US, male vocal / instrumental group (8 WEEKS)*

		pos/wks	
22 May 68	**TIME FOR LIVING** *Warner Bros. WB 7195*	**23**	8

Rick ASTLEY (332 **Top 500**) *Soulful-voiced pop vocalist . b. 6 Feb 1966, Warrington, UK. Brit award-winning, US chart- topping debut hit was 1987's best-selling UK single. No British male can match his seven consecutive (mostly Stock, Aitken Waterman produced) Top 10 hits in the 1980s (91 WEEKS)*

		pos/wks	
8 Aug 87 ★	**NEVER GONNA GIVE YOU UP** *RCA PB 41447* ▲	**1**	18
31 Oct 87 ●	**WHENEVER YOU NEED SOMEBODY** *RCA PB 41567*	**3**	12
12 Dec 87 ●	**WHEN I FALL IN LOVE / MY ARMS KEEP MISSING YOU** *RCA PB 41683*	**2**	10
27 Feb 88 ●	**TOGETHER FOREVER** *RCA PB 41817* ▲	**2**	9
24 Sep 88 ●	**SHE WANTS TO DANCE WITH ME** *RCA PB 42189*	**6**	10
26 Nov 88 ●	**TAKE ME TO YOUR HEART** *RCA PB 42573*	**8**	10
11 Feb 89 ●	**HOLD ME IN YOUR ARMS** *RCA PB 42615*	**10**	8

UK No.1 ★ UK Top 10 ● Still on chart + UK million seller ◆ UK entry at No.1 ■ US No.1 ▲

Date	Title	pos/wks	
26 Jan 91 ●	CRY FOR HELP *RCA PB 44247*	7	7
30 Mar 91	MOVE RIGHT OUT *RCA PB 44407*	58	2
29 Jun 91	NEVER KNEW LOVE *RCA PB 44737*	70	1
4 Sep 93	THE ONES YOU LOVE *RCA 74321160142*	48	2
13 Nov 93	HOPELESSLY *RCA 74321175642*	33	2

Before 9 Jan 1988, 'When I Fall in Love' was listed by itself. After that date 'My Arms Keep Missing You' was the side listed

ASTRO TRAX *UK, male / female vocal / production trio (1 WEEK)* pos/wks

24 Oct 98	THE ENERGY (FEEL THE VIBE) *Satellite 74321622052*	74	1

ASWAD `410` `Top 500` *Seminal reggae outfit formed 1975 London, UK. Featured former child actor Brinsley Forde (v), b. 1952, Guyana. They signed to Island in 1976, topped the chart with an old Tina Turner B-side and followed it into the Top 20 with a Bucks Fizz B-side (80 WEEKS)* pos/wks

3 Mar 84	CHASING FOR THE BREEZE *Island IS 160*	51	3
6 Oct 84	54-46 (WAS MY NUMBER) *Island IS 170*	70	3
27 Feb 88 ★	DON'T TURN AROUND *Mango IS 341*	1	12
21 May 88	GIVE A LITTLE LOVE *Mango IS 358*	11	8
24 Sep 88	SET THEM FREE *Mango IS 383*	70	2
1 Apr 89	BEAUTY'S ONLY SKIN DEEP *Mango MNG 105*	31	6
22 Jul 89	ON AND ON *Mango MNG 708*	25	8
18 Aug 90	NEXT TO YOU *Mango MNG 753*	24	6
17 Nov 90	SMILE *Mango MNG 767* [1]	53	2
30 Mar 91	TOO WICKED (EP) *Mango MNG 771*	61	2
31 Jul 93	HOW LONG *Polydor PZCD 252* [2]	31	5
9 Oct 93	DANCEHALL MOOD *Bubblin' CDBUBB 1*	48	2
18 Jun 94 ●	SHINE *Bubblin' CDBUBB 3*	5	14
17 Sep 94	WARRIORS *Bubblin' CDBUBB 4*	33	3
18 Feb 95	YOU'RE NO GOOD *Bubblin' CDBUBB 5*	35	3
5 Aug 95	IF I WAS *Bubblin' CDBUBB 6*	58	1

[1] Aswad featuring Sweetie Irie [2] Yazz and Aswad

Tracks on Too Wicked (EP): Best of My Love / Warrior Re-Charge / Fire / I Shot The Sheriff

AT THE DRIVE-IN
US, male vocal / instrumental group (2 WEEKS) pos/wks

19 Aug 00	ONE ARMED SCISSOR *Grand Royal GR 091CD*	64	1
16 Dec 00	ROLODEX PROPAGANDA *Grand Royal / Virgin VUSCD 189*	54	1

Gali ATARI – See MILK AND HONEY featuring Gali ATARI

ATB *Germany, male producer - Andre Tanneberger (46 WEEKS)* pos/wks

13 Mar 99	(9PM) TILL I COME *Ministry of Sound DATA 1*	68	1
22 May 99	(9PM) TILL I COME (German import) *Club Tools CLU 66066*	72	3
19 Jun 99	(9PM) TILL I COME (Australian import) *Dancenet DNET 131*	63	1
19 Jun 99	(9PM) TILL I COME (German import) (re-entry) *Club Tools CLU 66066*	47	1
3 Jul 99 ★	(9PM) TILL I COME *Sound of Ministry MOSCDS 132* ■	1	15
9 Oct 99	DON'T STOP (IMPORT) *Club Tools CLU 66406*	61	2
23 Oct 99 ●	DON'T STOP *Sound of Ministry MOSCDS 134*	3	9
1 Jan 00	DON'T STOP (re-entry) *Sound of Ministry MOSCDS 134*	48	4
25 Mar 00 ●	KILLER *Sound of Ministry MOSCDS 138*	4	8
17 Jun 00	KILLER (re-entry) *Sound of Ministry MOSCDS 138*	74	1

A.T.F.C. presents ONEPHATDEEVA
UK, male producer - Aydin Hasirci (8 WEEKS) pos/wks

30 Oct 99	IN AND OUT OF MY LIFE *Defected DEFECT 8CDS*	11	5
16 Sep 00	BAD HABIT *Defected DFECT 19CDS* [1]	17	3

[1] A.T.F.C. Presents Onephatdeeva Featuring Lisa Millett

ATGOC *Italy, male instrumentalist / producer (2 WEEKS)* pos/wks

21 Nov 98	REPEATED LOVE *Wonderboy WBOYD 012*	38	2

Chet ATKINS *US, male instrumentalist - guitar (2 WEEKS)* pos/wks

17 Mar 60	TEENSVILLE *RCA 1174*	46	1
5 May 60	TEENSVILLE (re-entry) *RCA 1174*	49	1

ATLANTA RHYTHM SECTION
US, male vocal / instrumental group (4 WEEKS) pos/wks

27 Oct 79	SPOOKY *Polydor POSP 74*	48	4

ATLANTIC OCEAN *Holland, male instrumental duo (14 WEEKS)* pos/wks

19 Feb 94	WATERFALL *Eastern Bloc BLOCCD 001*	22	6
2 Jul 94	BODY IN MOTION *Eastern Bloc BLOCCD 009*	15	4
26 Nov 94	MUSIC IS A PASSION *Eastern Bloc BLOCCDX 017*	59	1
30 Nov 96	WATERFALL (re-mix) *Eastern Bloc BLOC 104CD*	21	3

ATLANTIC STARR
US, male / female vocal / instrumental group (48 WEEKS) pos/wks

9 Sep 78	GIMME YOUR LOVIN' *A & M AMS 7380*	66	3
29 Jun 85	SILVER SHADOW *A & M AM 260*	41	6
7 Sep 85	ONE LOVE *A & M AM 273*	58	4
15 Mar 86 ●	SECRET LOVERS *A & M AM 307*	10	12
24 May 86	IF YOUR HEART ISN'T IN IT *A & M AM 319*	48	4
13 Jun 87 ●	ALWAYS *Warner Bros. W 8455* ▲	3	14
12 Sep 87	ONE LOVER AT A TIME *Warner Bros. W 8327*	57	3
27 Aug 94	EVERYBODY'S GOT SUMMER *Arista 74321228072*	36	2

ATLANTIS vs AVATAR
UK, male production group featuring female vocalist - Miriam Stockley (2 WEEKS) pos/wks

28 Oct 00	FIJI *Inferno CDFERN 34*	52	2

Natacha ATLAS – See Jean-Michel JARRE

ATMOSFEAR *UK, male instrumental group (7 WEEKS)* pos/wks

17 Nov 79	DANCING IN OUTER SPACE *MCA 543*	46	7

ATOMIC KITTEN *UK, female vocal group (26 WEEKS)* pos/wks

11 Dec 99 ●	RIGHT NOW *Innocent SINCD 15*	10	9
8 Apr 00 ●	SEE YA *Innocent SINCD 17*	6	6
1 Jul 00	SEE YA (re-entry) *Innocent SINCD 17*	74	1
15 Jul 00 ●	I WANT YOUR LOVE *Innocent SINCD 18*	10	5
21 Oct 00 ●	FOLLOW ME *Innocent SINCD 22*	20	5

ATOMIC ROOSTER
UK, male vocal / instrumental group (25 WEEKS) pos/wks

6 Feb 71	TOMORROW NIGHT *B & C CB 131*	11	12
10 Jul 71 ●	THE DEVIL'S ANSWER *B & C CB 157*	4	13

ATTRACTIONS – See Elvis COSTELLO

Winifred ATWELL `229` `Top 500` *The 'Queen of the Ivories' (and Elton John's early idol) b. 27 Apr 1914, Trinidad, d. 28 Feb 1983. Britain's all-time top female instrumentalist, who earned a couple of gold discs for her popular party medleys and hosted a very successful TV series in 1957 (117 WEEKS)* pos/wks

12 Dec 52	BRITANNIA RAG *Decca F 10015*	11	1
9 Jan 53 ●	BRITANNIA RAG (re-entry) *Decca F 10015*	5	5
15 May 53	CORONATION RAG *Decca F 10110*	12	1
29 May 53 ●	CORONATION RAG (re-entry) *Decca F 10110*	5	5
25 Sep 53	FLIRTATION WALTZ *Decca F 10161*	12	1
9 Oct 53 ●	FLIRTATION WALTZ (re-entry) *Decca F 10161*	10	1
6 Nov 53	FLIRTATION WALTZ (2nd re-entry) *Decca F 10161*	12	1
4 Dec 53 ●	LET'S HAVE A PARTY *Philips PB 213*	2	9
23 Jul 54 ●	RACHMANINOFF'S 18TH VARIATION ON A THEME BY PAGANINI (THE STORY OF THREE LOVES) *Philips PB 234*	9	7
1 Oct 54	RACHMANINOFF'S 18TH VARIATION ON A THEME BY PAGANINI (THE STORY OF THREE LOVES) (re-entry) *Philips PB 234*	19	2
26 Nov 54	LET'S HAVE A PARTY (re-entry) *Philips PB 213*	14	6

26 Nov 54 ★	LET'S HAVE ANOTHER PARTY *Philips PB 268*....................	1	8
4 Nov 55 ●	LET'S HAVE A DING DONG *Decca F 10634*	3	10
16 Mar 56 ★	POOR PEOPLE OF PARIS *Decca F 10681*	1	16
18 May 56	PORT AU PRINCE *Decca F 10727* [1]	18	6
20 Jul 56	LEFT BANK *Decca F 10762*	14	7
26 Oct 56 ●	MAKE IT A PARTY *Decca F 10796*	7	12
22 Feb 57	LET'S ROCK 'N' ROLL *Decca F 10852*	28	2
15 Mar 57	LET'S ROCK 'N' ROLL (re-entry) *Decca F 10852*	24	2
6 Dec 57 ●	LET'S HAVE A BALL *Decca F 10956*	4	6
7 Aug 59	SUMMER OF THE SEVENTEENTH DOLL		
	Decca F 11143	24	2
27 Nov 59 ●	PIANO PARTY *Decca F 11183*	10	7

[1] Winifred Atwell and Frank Chacksfield

Various hits listed above were medleys as follows: Let's Have a Party: If You Knew Suzie / The More We Are Together / That's My Weakness Now / Knees Up Mother Brown / Daisy Bell / Boomps A Daisy / She Was One Of The Early Birds / Three O'Clock In The Morning. Let's Have Another Party: Somebody Stole My Gal / I Wonder Where My Baby Is Tonight / When The Red Red Robin / Bye Bye Blackbird / Sheik Of Araby / Another Little Drink / Lilly Of Laguna / Honeysuckle and The Bee / Broken Doll / Nellie Dean. Let's Have a Ding Dong: Ain't She Sweet / Oh Johnny Oh Johnny Oh / Oh You Beautiful Doll / Yes We Have No Bananas / Happy Days Are Here Again / I'm Forever Blowing Bubbles / I'll Be Your Sweetheart / If These Lips Could Only Speak / Who's Taking You Home Tonight. Make It a Party: Who Were You With Last Night / Hello Hello Who's Your Lady Friend / Yes Sir That's My Baby / Don't Dilly Dally On the Way / Beer Barrel Polka / After the Ball / Peggy O'Neil / Meet Me Tonight in Dreamland / I Belong To Glasgow / Down at the Old Bull and Bush. Let's Rock 'n' Roll: Singin' The Blues / Green Door / See You Later Alligator / Shake Rattle and Roll / Rock Around the Clock / Razzle Dazzle. Let's Have a Ball: Music Music Music / This Ole House / Heartbreaker / Woody Woodpecker / Last Train to San Fernando / Bring a Little Water Sylvie / Puttin' On The Style / Don't You Rock Me Daddy-O. Piano Party: Baby Face / Comin' Thru' The Rye / Annie Laurie / Little Brown Jug / Let Him Go Let Him Tarry / Put Your Arms Around Me Honey / I'll Be With You in Apple Blossom Time / Shine On Harvest Moon / Blue Skies / I'll Never Say 'Never Again' Again / I'll See You In My Dreams.

AUDIOWEB *UK, male vocal / instrumental group (12 WEEKS)*

pos/wks

14 Oct 95	SLEEPER *Mother MUMCD 69*	74	1
9 Mar 96	YEAH *Mother MUMCD 72*	73	1
15 Jun 96	INTO MY WORLD *Mother MUMCD 76*	42	1
19 Oct 96	SLEEPER (re-mix) *Mother MUMCD 78*	50	2
15 Feb 97	BANKROBBER *Mother MUMCD 85*	19	2
24 May 97	FAKER *Mother MUMCD 91*	70	1
25 Apr 98	POLICEMAN SKANK ... (THE STORY OF MY LIFE)		
	Mother MUMCD 100	21	2
4 Jul 98	PERSONAL FEELING *Mother MUMCD 104*	65	1
20 Feb 99	TEST THE THEORY *Mother MUMCD 110*	56	1

Brian AUGER – See Julie DRISCOLL, Brian AUGER and the TRINITY

AURA – See POPPERS presents AURA

AURORA *UK, male production duo - aka Dive (12 WEEKS)*

pos/wks

5 Jun 99	HEAR YOU CALLING *Additive 12AD 040*	71	1
5 Feb 00	HEAR YOU CALLING (re-issue) *Positiva CDTIV 124*	17	4
23 Sep 00 ●	ORDINARY WORLD *Positiva CDTIV 139* [1]	5	7

[1] Aurora Featuring Naimee Coleman

See also DIVE

AURRA *US, male / female vocal / instrumental group (18 WEEKS)*

pos/wks

4 May 85	LIKE I LIKE IT *10 TEN 45*	51	5
19 Apr 86	YOU AND ME TONIGHT *10 TEN 71*	12	8
21 Jun 86	LIKE I LIKE IT (re-issue) *10 TEN 126*	43	5

Adam AUSTIN *UK, male vocalist (1 WEEK)*

pos/wks

13 Feb 99	CENTERFOLD *Media PSRCA 0107*	41	1

David AUSTIN *UK, male vocalist (3 WEEKS)*

pos/wks

21 Jul 84	TURN TO GOLD *Parlophone R 6068*	68	3

Patti AUSTIN *US, female vocalist (11 WEEKS)*

pos/wks

12 Feb 83	BABY COME TO ME *Qwest K 15005* [1] ▲	11	10
5 Sep 92	I'LL KEEP YOUR DREAMS ALIVE *Ammi AMMI 101* [2]	68	1

[1] Patti Austin and James Ingram [2] George Benson and Patti Austin

AUTECHRE *UK, male instrumental duo (1 WEEK)*

pos/wks

7 May 94	BASSCAD *Warp WAP 44CD*	56	1

AUTEURS *UK, male / female vocal / instrumental group (9 WEEKS)*

pos/wks

27 Nov 93	LENNY VALENTINO *Hut HUTCD 36*	41	2
23 Apr 94	CHINESE BAKERY *Hut HUTDX 41*	42	2
6 Jan 96	BACK WITH THE KILLER AGAIN *Hut HUTCD 65*	45	3
24 Feb 96	LIGHT AIRCRAFT ON FIRE *Hut HUTCD 66*	58	1
3 Jul 99	THE RUBETTES *Hut HUTCD 113*	66	1

AUTUMN *UK, male vocal / instrumental group (6 WEEKS)*

pos/wks

16 Oct 71	MY LITTLE GIRL *Pye 7N 45090*	37	6

Peter AUTY and the SINFONIA OF LONDON conducted by Howard BLAKE *UK, male vocalist with UK orchestra (9 WEEKS)*

pos/wks

14 Dec 85	WALKING IN THE AIR *Stiff LAD 1*	42	5
19 Dec 87	WALKING IN THE AIR (re-issue) *CBS GA 3950*	37	4

See also DIGITAL DREAM BABY

Frankie AVALON *US, male vocalist (15 WEEKS)*

pos/wks

10 Oct 58	GINGERBREAD *HMV POP 517*	30	1
24 Apr 59	VENUS *HMV POP 603* ▲	16	6
22 Jan 60	WHY *HMV POP 688* ▲	20	4
28 Apr 60	DON'T THROW AWAY ALL THOSE TEARDROPS *HMV POP 727*	37	4

AVALON BOYS – See LAUREL and HARDY with the AVALON BOYS featuring Chill WILLS

AVERAGE WHITE BAND

UK, male vocal / instrumental vocal group (47 WEEKS)

pos/wks

22 Feb 75 ●	PICK UP THE PIECES *Atlantic K 10489* ▲	6	9
26 Apr 75	CUT THE CAKE *Atlantic K 10605*	31	4
9 Oct 76	QUEEN OF MY SOUL *Atlantic K 10825*	23	7
28 Apr 79	WALK ON BY *RCA XC 1087*	46	5
25 Aug 79	WHEN WILL YOU BE MINE *RCA XB 1096*	49	5
26 Apr 80	LET'S GO ROUND AGAIN PT.1 *RCA AWB 1*	12	11
26 Jul 80	FOR YOU FOR LOVE *RCA AWB 2*	46	4
26 Mar 94	LET'S GO ROUND AGAIN (re-mix) *The Hit Label HLC 5*	56	2

Kevin AVIANCE *US, male vocalist (1 WEEK)*

pos/wks

13 Jun 98	DIN DA DA *Distinctive DISNCD 42*	65	1

AVONS *UK, male / female vocal trio (22 WEEKS)*

pos/wks

13 Nov 59 ●	SEVEN LITTLE GIRLS SITTING IN THE BACK SEAT		
	Columbia DB 4363	3	13
7 Jul 60	WE'RE ONLY YOUNG ONCE *Columbia DB 4461*	49	1
21 Jul 60	WE'RE ONLY YOUNG ONCE (re-entry)		
	Columbia DB 4461	45	1
27 Oct 60	FOUR LITTLE HEELS *Columbia DB 4522*	45	2
1 Dec 60	FOUR LITTLE HEELS (re-entry) *Columbia DB 4522*	49	1
26 Jan 61	RUBBER BALL *Columbia DB 4569*	30	4

AWESOME *UK, male vocal group (2 WEEKS)*

pos/wks

8 Nov 97	RUMOURS *Universal MCSTD 40145*	58	1
21 Mar 98	CRAZY *Universal MCSTD 40195*	63	1

AWESOME 3

UK, male / female vocal / instrumental group (8 WEEKS)

pos/wks

8 Sep 90	HARD UP *A & M AM 591*	55	3
3 Oct 92	DON'T GO *Citybeat CBE 1271*	75	1

UK No.1 ★   UK Top 10 ●   Still on chart +   UK million seller ◆   UK entry at No.1 ■   US No.1 ▲

		pos/wks
4 Jun 94	**DON'T GO (re-mix)** *Citybeat CBX 771CD*	**45** 2
26 Oct 96	**DON'T GO (2nd) (re-mix)** *XL XLS 78CD* [1]	**27** 2

[1] Awesome 3 featuring Julie McDermott

Hoyt AXTON *US, male vocalist (4 WEEKS)*
		pos/wks
7 Jun 80	**DELLA AND THE DEALER** *Young Blood YB 82*	**48** 4

AXUS *UK, male / female vocal / production duo (1 WEEK)*
		pos/wks
26 Sep 98	**ABACUS (WHEN I FALL IN LOVE)** *INCcredible INCRL 8CD*	**62** 1

Roy AYERS
US, male vocalist / instrumentalist - vibraphone (13 WEEKS)
		pos/wks
21 Oct 78	**GET ON UP, GET ON DOWN** *Polydor AYERS 7*	**41** 4
13 Jan 79	**HEAT OF THE BEAT** *Polydor POSP 16* [1]	**43** 5
2 Feb 80	**DON'T STOP THE FEELING** *Polydor STEP 6*	**56** 3
16 May 98	**EXPANSIONS** *Soma Recordings SOMA 65CDS* [2]	**68** 1

[1] Roy Ayers and Wayne Henderson [2] Scott Grooves featuring Roy Ayers

AYLA *Germany, male producer - Ingo Kunzi (3 WEEKS)*
		pos/wks
4 Sep 99	**AYLA** *Positiva CDTIV 117*	**22** 3

AZ *US, male rapper - Anthony Cruz (1 WEEK)*
		pos/wks
30 Mar 96	**SUGARHILL** *Cooltempo CDCOOL 315*	**67** 1

AZ YET *US, male vocal group (10 WEEKS)*
		pos/wks
1 Mar 97	**LAST NIGHT** *LaFace 74321423202*	**21** 3
21 Jun 97	● **HARD TO SAY I'M SORRY** *LaFace 74321481482* [1]	**7** 7

[1] AZ YET featuring Peter Cetera

Charles AZNAVOUR *France, male vocalist (29 WEEKS)*
		pos/wks
22 Sep 73	**THE OLD FASHIONED WAY** *Barclay BAR 20*	**50** 1
20 Oct 73	**THE OLD FASHIONED WAY (re-entry)** *Barclay BAR 20*	**38** 12
22 Jun 74	★ **SHE** *Barclay BAR 26*	**1** 14
27 Jul 74	**THE OLD FASHIONED WAY (2nd re-entry)** *Barclay BAR 20*	**47** 1

AZTEC CAMERA `461` `Top 500`
Sensitive, tuneful pop band formed 1980, and centred around teenage singer / songwriter Roddy Frame, b. 29 Jan 1964, East Kilbride, Scotland. Album Love was among nominations for Best British Album at 1989 Brit awards (74 WEEKS)
		pos/wks
19 Feb 83	**OBLIVIOUS** *Rough Trade RT 122*	**47** 6
4 Jun 83	**WALK OUT TO WINTER** *Rough Trade RT 132*	**64** 4
5 Nov 83	**OBLIVIOUS (re-issue)** *WEA AZTEC 1*	**18** 11
1 Sep 84	**ALL I NEED IS EVERYTHING / JUMP** *WEA AC 1*	**34** 6
13 Feb 88	**HOW MEN ARE** *WEA YZ 168*	**25** 9
23 Apr 88	● **SOMEWHERE IN MY HEART** *WEA YZ 181*	**3** 14
6 Aug 88	**WORKING IN A GOLDMINE** *WEA YZ 199*	**31** 5
8 Oct 88	**DEEP AND WIDE AND TALL** *WEA YZ 154*	**55** 3
7 Jul 90	**THE CRYING SCENE** *WEA YZ 492*	**70** 3
6 Oct 90	**GOOD MORNING BRITAIN** *WEA YZ 521* [1]	**19** 8
18 Jul 92	**SPANISH HORSES** *WEA YZ 688*	**52** 3
1 May 93	**DREAM SWEET DREAMS** *WEA YZ 740CD1*	**67** 2

[1] Aztec Camera and Mick Jones

'Jump' listed only from 22 Sep to end of chart run

AZTEC MYSTIC – See DJ ROLANDO AKA AZTEC MYSTIC

AZURE *Italy / US, male / female vocal / DJ duo (1 WEEK)*
		pos/wks
25 Apr 98	**MAMA USED TO SAY** *Inferno CDFERN 005*	**56** 1

AZYMUTH *Brazil, male instrumental group (8 WEEKS)*
		pos/wks
12 Jan 80	**JAZZ CARNIVAL** *Milestone MRC 101*	**19** 8

Bob AZZAM & His ORCHESTRA
Egypt, singing orchestra (14 WEEKS)
		pos/wks
26 May 60	**MUSTAPHA** *Decca F 21235*	**23** 14

B B and Q BAND
US, male vocal / instrumental group (15 WEEKS)
		pos/wks
18 Jul 81	**ON THE BEAT** *Capitol CL 202*	**41** 5
6 Jul 85	**GENIE** *Cooltempo COOL 110* [1]	**40** 4
20 Sep 86	**(I'M A) DREAMER** *Cooltempo COOL 132*	**35** 5
17 Oct 87	**RICOCHET** *Cooltempo COOL 154*	**71** 1

[1] Brooklyn Bronx and Queens

Derek B *UK, male rapper (15 WEEKS)*
		pos/wks
27 Feb 88	**GOODGROOVE** *Music of Life 7NOTE 12*	**16** 6
7 May 88	**BAD YOUNG BROTHER** *Tuff Audio DRKB 1*	**16** 6
2 Jul 88	**WE'VE GOT THE JUICE** *Tuff Audio DRKB 2*	**56** 3

Eric B and RAKIM *US, male DJ / rap duo (26 WEEKS)*
		pos/wks
7 Nov 87	**PAID IN FULL** *Fourth & Broadway BRW 78*	**15** 6
20 Feb 88	**MOVE THE CROWD** *Fourth & Broadway BRW 88*	**53** 2
12 Mar 88	**I KNOW YOU GOT SOUL** *Cooltempo COOL 146*	**13** 6
2 Jul 88	**FOLLOW THE LEADER** *MCA MCA 1256*	**21** 5
19 Nov 88	**THE MICROPHONE FIEND** *MCA MCA 1300*	**74** 1
12 Aug 89	**FRIENDS** *MCA MCA 1352* [1]	**21** 6

[1] Jody Watley with Eric B and Rakim

B-15 PROJECT featuring Crissy D & Lady G
UK / Jamaica, male production duo and female vocalists (10 WEEKS)
		pos/wks
17 Jun 00	● **GIRLS LIKE US** *Ministry of Sound RELENT 3CDS*	**7** 8
19 Aug 00	**GIRLS LIKE US (re-entry)** *Ministry of Sound RELENT 3CDS*	**56** 2

B-52's *US, male / female vocal / instrumental group (61 WEEKS)*
		pos/wks
11 Aug 79	**ROCK LOBSTER** *Island WIP 6506*	**37** 5
9 Aug 80	**GIVE ME BACK MY MAN** *Island WIP 6579*	**61** 3
7 May 83	**(SONG FOR A) FUTURE GENERATION** *Island IS 107*	**63** 2
10 May 86	**ROCK LOBSTER / PLANET CLAIRE (re-issue)** *Island BFT 1*	**12** 7
3 Mar 90	● **LOVE SHACK** *Reprise W 9917*	**2** 13
19 May 90	**ROAM** *Reprise W 9827*	**17** 7
18 Aug 90	**CHANNEL Z** *Reprise W 9737*	**61** 2
20 Jun 92	**GOOD STUFF** *Reprise W 0109*	**21** 6
12 Sep 92	**TELL IT LIKE IT T-I-IS** *Reprise W 0130*	**61** 3
9 Jul 94	● **(MEET) THE FLINTSTONES** *MCA MCSTD 1986* [1]	**3** 12
30 Jan 99	**LOVE SHACK 99** *Reprise W 0461CD*	**66** 1

[1] BC-52's

'Planet Claire' listed only from 17 May 1986

Howie B *UK male instrumentalist / producer (4 WEEKS)*
		pos/wks
19 Jul 97	**ANGELS GO BALD: TOO** *Polydor 5711672*	**36** 2
18 Oct 97	**SWITCH** *Polydor 5717112*	**62** 1
11 Apr 98	**TAKE YOUR PARTNER BY THE HAND** *Polydor 5693272* [1]	**74** 1

[1] Howie B featuring Robbie Robertson

JAZZIE B – See Maxi PRIEST; SOUL II SOUL

Jon B *US, male vocalist (2 WEEKS)*
		pos/wks
17 Oct 98	**THEY DON'T KNOW** *Epic 6663975*	**32** 2

Lisa B *US, female vocalist (9 WEEKS)*
		pos/wks
12 Jun 93	**GLAM** *ffrr FCD 210*	**49** 2
25 Sep 93	**FASCINATED** *ffrr FCD 218*	**35** 3
8 Jan 94	**YOU AND ME** *ffrr FCD 226*	**39** 4

Lorna B *UK, female vocalist (6 WEEKS)*

			pos/wks	
28 Jan 95	DO YOU WANNA PARTY *Steppin' Out SPONCD 2* [1]		36	3
1 Apr 95	SWEET DREAMS *Steppin' Out SPONCD 3* [1]		37	2
15 Mar 97	FEELS SO GOOD *Avex UK AVEXCD 53*		69	1

[1] DJ Scott featuring Lorna B

Melanie B *UK, female vocalist - Melanie Brown (24 WEEKS)*

			pos/wks	
26 Sep 98	★ I WANT YOU BACK *Virgin VSCDT 1716* [1] ■		1	9
10 Jul 99	WORD UP *Virgin VSCDT 1735* [2]		14	7
25 Sep 99	WORD UP (re-entry) *Virgin VSCDT 1735* [2]		71	1
7 Oct 00	● TELL ME *Virgin VSCDT 1777*		4	7

[1] Melanie B featuring Missy 'Misdemeanor' Elliott [2] Melanie G

For 1999 hits Melanie B became Melanie G

See also SPICE GIRLS

Sandy B *US, female vocalist (8 WEEKS)*

			pos/wks	
20 Feb 93	FEEL LIKE SINGIN' *Nervous SANCD 1*		60	1
18 May 96	MAKE THE WORLD GO ROUND *Champion CHAMPCD 322*		73	1
24 May 97	MAKE THE WORLD GO ROUND (re-mix)			
	Champion CHAMPCD 327		35	2
8 Nov 97	AIN'T NO NEED TO HIDE *Champion CHAMPCD 331*		60	1
28 Feb 98	MAKE THE WORLD GO ROUND (2nd) (re-mix)			
	Champion CHAMPCD 333		20	3

Stevie B *US, male vocalist - Steven Hill (9 WEEKS)*

			pos/wks	
23 Feb 91	● BECAUSE I LOVE YOU (THE POSTMAN SONG)			
	Polydor PO 126 ▲		6	9

Tairrie B *US, female rapper (2 WEEKS)*

			pos/wks	
1 Dec 90	MURDER SHE WROTE *MCA MCA 1455*		71	2

B BUMBLE and the STINGERS
US, male instrumental group (26 WEEKS)

			pos/wks	
19 Apr 62	★ NUT ROCKER *Top Rank JAR 611*		1	15
3 Jun 72	NUT ROCKER (re-issue) *Stateside SS 2203*		19	11

B REAL / BUSTA RHYMES / COOLIO / LL COOL J / METHOD MAN
US, male rappers (6 WEEKS)

			pos/wks	
5 Apr 97	● HIT 'EM HIGH (MONSTARS' ANTHEM)			
	Atlantic A 5449CD		8	6

B-CREW *US, female vocal group (1 WEEK)*

			pos/wks	
20 Sep 97	PARTAY FEELING *Positiva CDTIV 78*		45	1

B-MOVIE *UK, male vocal / instrumental group (7 WEEKS)*

			pos/wks	
18 Apr 81	REMEMBRANCE DAY *Deram DM 437*		61	3
27 Mar 82	NOWHERE GIRL *Some BizarrJDDe BZZ 8*		67	4

B-TRIBE
Spain, male / female vocal / instrumental group (4 WEEKS)

			pos/wks	
25 Sep 93	!FIESTA FATAL! *East West YZ 770CD*		64	4

B*WITCHED (370 Top 500) *Ireland's most successful female group, Edele and Keavy Lynch, Sinead O'Carroll and Lindsay Armaou. Youngest girl group to top chart, who sold more than one million of debut album in US and were first act to enter at No.1 with first four singles (85 WEEKS)*

			pos/wks	
6 Jun 98	★ C'EST LA VIE *Glow Worm / Epic 6660532* ■		1	19
3 Oct 98	★ ROLLERCOASTER *Glow Worm / Epic 6664752* ■		1	15
19 Dec 98	★ TO YOU I BELONG *Glow Worm / Epic 6667712* ■		1	12
27 Mar 99	★ BLAME IT ON THE WEATHERMAN			
	Glow Worm / Epic 6670335 ■		1	9
27 Mar 99	TO YOU I BELONG (re-entry)			
	Glow Worm / Epic 6667712		64	2
16 Oct 99	● JESSE HOLD ON *Glow Worm / Epic 6679612*		4	10
18 Dec 99	I SHALL BE THERE *Glow Worm / Epic 683332* [1]		13	9
8 Jan 00	JESSE HOLD ON (re-entry) *Glow Worm / Epic 6679612*		60	2
8 Apr 00	JUMP DOWN *Glow Worm / Epic 6691282*		16	5
27 May 00	JUMP DOWN (re-entry) *Glow Worm / Epic 6691282*		62	2

[1] B*witched featuring Ladysmith Black Mambazo

BABE INSTINCT *UK, female vocal group (2 WEEKS)*

			pos/wks	
16 Jan 99	DISCO BABES FROM OUTER SPACE *Positiva CDTIV 103*		21	2

Alice BABS *Sweden, female vocalist (1 WEEK)*

			pos/wks	
15 Aug 63	AFTER YOU'VE GONE *Fontana TF 409*		43	1

BABY BUMPS
UK, male / female vocal / instrumental duo (6 WEEKS)

			pos/wks	
8 Aug 98	BURNING *Delirious DELICD 10*		17	4
26 Feb 00	I GOT THIS FEELING *Sound of Ministry MOSCDS 137*		22	2

BABY D *UK, male / female vocal / instrumental group (45 WEEKS)* pos/wks

18 Dec 93	DESTINY *Production House PNC 057*		69	1
23 Jul 94	CASANOVA *Production House PNC 065*		67	1
19 Nov 94	★ LET ME BE YOUR FANTASY *Systematic SYSCD 4*		1	14
3 Jun 95	● (EVERYBODY'S GOT TO LEARN SOMETIME) I NEED YOUR			
	LOVING *Systematic SYSCD 11*		3	12
13 Jan 96	● SO PURE *Systematic SYSCD 21*		3	7
6 Apr 96	TAKE ME TO HEAVEN *Systematic SYSCD 26*		15	5
2 Sep 00	LET ME BE YOUR FANTASY (re-mix) *Systematic SYSCD 35*		16	5

BABY DC Featuring IMAJIN
US, male rapper - Derrick Coleman Jr. and vocal group (1 WEEK) pos/wks

24 Apr 99	BOUNCE, ROCK, SKATE, ROLL *Jive 0522142*		45	1

BABY FORD *UK, male instrumentalist - keyboards (16 WEEKS)* pos/wks

10 Sep 88	OOCHY KOOCHY *Rhythm King 7BFORD 1*		58	6
24 Dec 88	CHIKKI CHIKKI AHH AHH *Rhythm King 7BFORD 2*		75	1
7 Jan 89	CHIKKI CHIKKI AHH AHH (re-entry)			
	Rhythm King 7BFORD 2		54	3
17 Jun 89	CHILDREN OF THE REVOLUTION *Rhythm King 7BFORD 4*		53	4
17 Feb 90	BEACH BUMP *Rhythm King 7BFORD 6*		68	2

BABY JUNE *UK, male vocalist - Tim Hegarty (1 WEEK)* pos/wks

15 Aug 92	HEY! WHAT'S YOUR NAME *Arista 115271*		75	1

BABY O *US, male / female vocal / instrumental group (5 WEEKS)* pos/wks

26 Jul 80	IN THE FOREST *Calibre CAB 505*		46	5

BABY ROOTS *UK, male vocalist (1 WEEK)* pos/wks

1 Aug 92	ROCK ME BABY *ZYX ZYX 68027*		71	1

BABYBIRD *UK, male vocalist / instrumentalist (35 WEEKS)* pos/wks

10 Aug 96	GOODNIGHT *Echo ECSCD 24*		28	2
12 Oct 96	● YOU'RE GORGEOUS *Echo ECSD 26*		3	16
1 Feb 97	CANDY GIRL *Echo ECSCD 31*		14	3
17 May 97	CORNERSHOP *Echo ECSCD 33*		37	2
9 May 98	BAD OLD MAN *Echo ECSCD 60*		31	2
22 Aug 98	IF YOU'LL BE MINE *Echo ECSCX 65*		28	4
27 Feb 99	BACK TOGETHER *Echo ECSCD 73*		22	3
25 Mar 00	THE F-WORD *Echo ECSCD 92*		35	2
3 Jun 00	OUT OF SIGHT *Echo ECSCD 97*		58	1

BABYFACE *US, male vocalist - Kenneth Edmonds (23 WEEKS)* pos/wks

9 Jul 94	ROCK BOTTOM *Epic 6601832*		50	4
1 Oct 94	WHEN CAN I SEE YOU *Epic 6606592*		35	3
9 Nov 96	THIS IS FOR THE LOVER IN YOU *Epic 6639352*		12	5
8 Mar 97	EVERYTIME I CLOSE MY EYES *Epic 6642492*		13	4
19 Jul 97	● HOW COME, HOW LONG *Epic 6646202* [1]		10	5
25 Oct 97	SUNSHINE *Northwestside 74321528702* [2]		25	2

[1] Babyface featuring Stevie Wonder [2] Jay-Z featuring Babyface and Foxy Brown

BABYLON ZOO
UK, male vocalist / multi-instrumentalist - Jas Mann (20 WEEKS)

		pos/wks
27 Jan 96 ★	SPACEMAN *EMI CDEM 416* ◆ ■	...1 14
27 Apr 96	ANIMAL ARMY *EMI CDEM 425*	...17 3
5 Oct 96	THE BOY WITH THE X-RAY EYES *EMI CDEMS 440*	...32 2
6 Feb 99	ALL THE MONEY'S GONE *EMI CDEM 519*	...46 1

BABYS
US / UK, male vocal / instrumental group (3 WEEKS)

21 Jan 78	ISN'T IT TIME *Chrysalis CHS 2173*	...45 3

BACCARA
Spain, female vocal duo - Maria Mendiola & Mayte Mateos (25 WEEKS)

		pos/wks
17 Sep 77 ★	YES SIR I CAN BOOGIE *RCA PB 5526*	...1 16
14 Jan 78 ●	SORRY I'M A LADY *RCA PB 5555*	...8 9

Burt BACHARACH
US, orchestra and chorus (12 WEEKS)

		pos/wks
20 May 65 ●	TRAINS AND BOATS AND PLANES *London HL 9968*	...4 11
1 May 99	TOLEDO *Mercury 8709652* [1]	...72 1

[1] Elvis Costello / Burt Bacharach

BACHELORS (99 Top 500)
Irish vocal / instrumental trio, who were one of the few popular non-rock groups of the 1960s: brothers Declan and Con Cluskey and John Stokes. This Dublin act had hits on both sides of the Atlantic with revivals of popular pre-rock ballads (187 WEEKS)

		pos/wks
24 Jan 63 ●	CHARMAINE *Decca F 11559*	...6 19
4 Jul 63	FARAWAY PLACES *Decca F 11666*	...36 3
29 Aug 63	WHISPERING *Decca F 11712*	...18 10
23 Jan 64 ★	DIANE *Decca F 11799*	...1 19
19 Mar 64 ●	I BELIEVE *Decca F 11857*	...2 17
4 Jun 64 ●	RAMONA *Decca F 11910*	...4 13
13 Aug 64 ●	I WOULDN'T TRADE YOU FOR THE WORLD *Decca F 11949*	...4 16
3 Dec 64 ●	NO ARMS CAN EVER HOLD YOU *Decca F 12034*	...7 12
1 Apr 65	TRUE LOVE FOR EVER MORE *Decca F 12108*	...34 6
20 May 65 ●	MARIE *Decca F 12156*	...9 12
28 Oct 65	IN THE CHAPEL IN THE MOONLIGHT *Decca F 12256*	...27 10
6 Jan 66	HELLO DOLLY *Decca F 12309*	...38 4
17 Mar 66 ●	THE SOUND OF SILENCE *Decca F 12351*	...3 13
7 Jul 66	CAN I TRUST YOU *Decca F 12417*	...26 7
1 Dec 66	WALK WITH FAITH IN YOUR HEART *Decca F 22523*	...22 9
6 Apr 67	OH HOW I MISS YOU *Decca F 22592*	...30 8
5 Jul 67	MARTA *Decca F 22634*	...20 9

Randy BACHMAN – See BUS STOP; BACHMAN-TURNER OVERDRIVE

Tal BACHMAN
Canadian, male vocalist / guitarist (2 WEEKS)

		pos/wks
30 Oct 99	SHE'S SO HIGH *Columbia 6679932*	...30 2

BACHMAN-TURNER OVERDRIVE
Canada, male vocal / instrumental group (18 WEEKS)

		pos/wks
16 Nov 74 ●	YOU AIN'T SEEN NOTHING YET *Mercury 6167 025* ▲	...2 12
1 Feb 75	ROLL ON DOWN THE HIGHWAY *Mercury 6167 071*	...22 6

See also Randy BACHMAN

BACK TO THE PLANET
UK, male / female vocal / instrumental group (2 WEEKS)

		pos/wks
10 Apr 93	TEENAGE TURTLES *Parallel LLLCD 3*	...52 1
4 Sep 93	DAYDREAM *Parallel LLLCD 8*	...52 1

BACKBEAT BAND
US, male vocal / instrumental group (5 WEEKS)

		pos/wks
26 Mar 94	MONEY *Virgin VSCDX 1489*	...48 3
23 Apr 94	MONEY (re-entry) *Virgin VSCDX 1489*	...73 1
14 May 94	PLEASE MR POSTMAN *Virgin VSCDX 1502*	...69 1

BACKBEAT DISCIPLES – See Arthur BAKER

BACKROOM BOYS – See Frank IFIELD

BACKSTREET BOYS (168 Top 500)
American 'boy band' vocal quintet (Brian Littrell, Nick Carter, AJ McLean, Howie Dorough, Kevin Richardson) created teen hysteria in Europe before becoming 1999's top-selling act in their homeland. Twelve consecutive UK Top 10s is most by any US band (142 WEEKS)

		pos/wks
28 Oct 95	WE'VE GOT IT GOIN' ON *Jive JIVECD 386*	...54 1
16 Dec 95	I'LL NEVER BREAK YOUR HEART *Jive JIVECD 389*	...42 3
1 Jun 96	GET DOWN (YOU'RE THE ONE FOR ME) *Jive JIVECD 394*	...14 8
24 Aug 96 ●	WE'VE GOT IT GOIN' ON (re-issue) *Jive JIVECD 400*	...3 7
16 Nov 96 ●	I'LL NEVER BREAK YOUR HEART (re-issue) *Jive JIVERCD 406*	...8 8
18 Jan 97 ●	QUIT PLAYING GAMES (WITH MY HEART) *Jive JIVECD 409*	...2 10
29 Mar 97 ●	ANYWHERE FOR YOU *Jive JIVECD 416*	...4 6
31 May 97	ANYWHERE FOR YOU (re-entry) *Jive JIVECD 416*	...72 1
14 Jun 97	ANYWHERE FOR YOU (2nd re-entry) *Jive JIVECD 416*	...70 1
2 Aug 97 ●	EVERYBODY (BACKSTREET'S BACK) *Jive JIVECD 426*	...3 11
11 Oct 97 ●	AS LONG AS YOU LOVE ME *Jive JIVECD 434*	...3 19
14 Feb 98 ●	ALL I HAVE TO GIVE *Jive JIVECD 445*	...2 12
15 May 99 ★	I WANT IT THAT WAY *Jive 0523392* ■	...1 14
30 Oct 99 ●	LARGER THAN LIFE *Jive 0550562*	...5 14
26 Feb 00	SHOW ME THE MEANING OF BEING LONELY (IMPORT) *Jive IMPORT 9250082*	...66 1
4 Mar 00 ●	SHOW ME THE MEANING OF BEING LONELY *Jive 9250082*	...3 9
3 Jun 00	SHOW ME THE MEANING OF BEING LONELY (re-entry) *Jive 9250082*	...51 2
24 Jun 00 ●	THE ONE *Jive 9250662*	...8 7
9 Sep 00	THE ONE (re-entry) *Jive 9250662*	...75 1
18 Nov 00 ●	SHAPE OF MY HEART *Jive 9251442*	...4 7+

BAD ANGEL – See BOOTH and the BAD ANGEL

BAD BOYS INC
UK, male vocal group (31 WEEKS)

		pos/wks
14 Aug 93	DON'T TALK ABOUT LOVE *A & M 5803412*	...19 5
2 Oct 93	WHENEVER YOU NEED SOMEONE *A & M 5804032*	...26 3
11 Dec 93	WALKING ON AIR *A & M 5804692*	...24 6
21 May 94 ●	MORE TO THIS WORLD *A & M 5806072*	...8 7
23 Jul 94	TAKE ME AWAY (I'LL FOLLOW YOU) *A & M 5806912*	...15 6
17 Sep 94	LOVE HERE I COME *A & M 5807752*	...26 4

BAD COMPANY
UK, male vocal / instrumental group (23 WEEKS)

		pos/wks
1 Jun 74	CAN'T GET ENOUGH *Island WIP 6191*	...15 8
22 Mar 75	GOOD LOVIN' GONE BAD *Island WIP 6223*	...31 6
30 Aug 75	FEEL LIKE MAKIN' LOVE *Island WIP 6242*	...20 9

BAD ENGLISH
UK / US, male vocal / instrumental group (3 WEEKS)

		pos/wks
25 Nov 89	WHEN I SEE YOU SMILE *Epic 655347 1* ▲	...61 3

BAD HABIT BOYS
Germany, male production duo (1 WEEK)

		pos/wks
1 Jul 00	WEEKEND *Inferno CDFERN 28*	...41 1

BAD MANNERS (256 Top 500)
Good-time ska band fronted by shaven-headed Buster Bloodvessel (b. Douglas Trendle, 6 Sep 1958, London). Spent more weeks on UK chart in 1980 (45) than anyone bar Madness. Even after the hits, they remained a popular live attraction (111 WEEKS)

		pos/wks
1 Mar 80	NE-NE NA-NA NA-NA NU-NU *Magnet MAG 164*	...28 14
14 Jun 80	LIP UP FATTY *Magnet MAG 175*	...15 14
27 Sep 80 ●	SPECIAL BREW *Magnet MAG 180*	...3 13
6 Dec 80	LORRAINE *Magnet MAG 181*	...21 12
28 Mar 81	JUST A FEELING *Magnet MAG 187*	...13 9
27 Jun 81 ●	CAN CAN *Magnet MAG 190*	...3 13
26 Sep 81 ●	WALKING IN THE SUNSHINE *Magnet MAG 197*	...10 9
21 Nov 81	BUONA SERA *Magnet MAG 211*	...34 9
1 May 82	GOT NO BRAINS *Magnet MAG 216*	...44 5
31 Jul 82 ●	MY GIRL LOLLIPOP (MY BOY LOLLIPOP) *Magnet MAG 232*	...9 7
30 Oct 82	SAMSON AND DELILAH *Magnet MAG 236*	...58 3
14 May 83	THAT'LL DO NICELY *Magnet MAG 243*	...49 3

BAD NEWS *UK, male vocal group (5 WEEKS)*   pos/wks
12 Sep 87	**BOHEMIAN RHAPSODY** *EMI EM 24*	**44** 5

BAD RELIGION *US, male vocal / instrumental group (2 WEEKS)*   pos/wks
11 Feb 95	**21ST CENTURY (DIGITAL BOY)** *Columbia 6611435*	**41** 2

BAD SEEDS – See Nick CAVE and the BAD SEEDS

BAD YARD CLUB – See David MORALES

Angelo BADALAMENTI – See ORBITAL

Wally BADAROU
France, male instrumentalist - keyboards (6 WEEKS)   pos/wks
19 Oct 85	**CHIEF INSPECTOR** *Fourth & Broadway BRW 37*	**46** 6

BADDIEL and SKINNER and THE LIGHTNING SEEDS
UK, male vocal group - David Baddiel, Frank Skinner (Christopher Collins) and Ian Broudie (28 WEEKS)   pos/wks
1 Jun 96	★ **THREE LIONS (THE OFFICIAL SONG OF THE ENGLAND FOOTBALL TEAM)** *Epic 6632732* ■	**1** 15
20 Jun 98	★ **3 LIONS '98** *Epic 6660982* ■	**1** 13

BADFINGER *UK, male vocal / instrumental group (34 WEEKS)*   pos/wks
10 Jan 70	● **COME AND GET IT** *Apple 20*	**4** 11
9 Jan 71	● **NO MATTER WHAT** *Apple 31*	**5** 12
29 Jan 72	● **DAY AFTER DAY** *Apple 40*	**10** 11

BADLY DRAWN BOY
UK, male vocalist / producer / instrumentalist - Damon Gough (7 WEEKS)   pos/wks
4 Sep 99	**ONCE AROUND THE BLOCK** *Twisted Nerve / XL Recordings TNXL 003CD*	**46** 2
17 Jun 00	**ANOTHER PEARL** *Twisted Nerve / XL Recordings TNXL 004CD*	**41** 1
16 Sep 00	**DISILLUSION** *Twisted Nerve / XL Recordings TNXL 005CD*	**26** 2
25 Nov 00	**ONCE AROUND THE BLOCK (re-issue)** *Twisted Nerve / XL Recordings TNXL 009CD*	**27** 2

BADMAN *UK, male producer - Julian Brettle (3 WEEKS)*   pos/wks
2 Feb 91	**MAGIC STYLE** *Citybeat CBE 759*	**61** 3

Erykah BADU *US, female vocalist (13 WEEKS)*   pos/wks
19 Apr 97	**ON & ON** *Universal UND 561117*	**12** 4
14 Jun 97	**NEXT LIFETIME** *Universal UND 56132*	**30** 3
29 Nov 97	**APPLE TREE** *Universal UND 56150*	**47** 1
11 Jul 98	**ONE** *Elektra E 3833CD1* [1]	**23** 3
6 Mar 99	**YOU GOT ME** *MCA MCSTD 48110* [2]	**31** 2

[1] Busta Rhymes featuring Erykah Badu [2] Roots featuring Erykah Badu

Joan BAEZ *US, female vocalist (47 WEEKS)*   pos/wks
6 May 65	**WE SHALL OVERCOME** *Fontana TF 564*	**26** 10
8 Jul 65	● **THERE BUT FOR FORTUNE** *Fontana TF 587*	**8** 12
2 Sep 65	**IT'S ALL OVER NOW BABY BLUE** *Fontana TF 604*	**22** 8
23 Dec 65	**FAREWELL ANGELINA** *Fontana TF 639*	**35** 3
20 Jan 66	**FAREWELL ANGELINA (re-entry)** *Fontana TF 639*	**49** 1
28 Jul 66	**PACK UP YOUR SORROWS** *Fontana TF 727*	**50** 1
9 Oct 71	● **THE NIGHT THEY DROVE OLD DIXIE DOWN** *Vanguard VS 35138*	**6** 12

BAHA MEN *Bahamas, male vocal group (12 WEEKS)*   pos/wks
14 Oct 00	● **WHO LET THE DOGS OUT** *Edel 0115425 ERE*	**2** 12+

Carol BAILEY *UK, female vocalist (2 WEEKS)*   pos/wks
25 Feb 95	**FEEL IT** *Multiply CDMULTY 3*	**41** 2

Philip BAILEY *US, male vocalist (20 WEEKS)*   pos/wks
9 Mar 85	★ **EASY LOVER** *CBS A 4915* [1]	**1** 12
18 May 85	**WALKING ON THE CHINESE WALL** *CBS A 6202*	**34** 8

[1] Philip Bailey (duet with Phil Collins)

See also EARTH WIND AND FIRE

Merril BAINBRIDGE *Australia, female vocalist (1 WEEK)*   pos/wks
7 Dec 96	**MOUTH** *Gotham 74321431012*	**51** 1

Adrian BAKER *UK, male vocalist (8 WEEKS)*   pos/wks
19 Jul 75	● **SHERRY** *Magnet MAG 34*	**10** 8

See also GIDEA PARK

Anita BAKER *US, female vocalist (22 WEEKS)*   pos/wks
15 Nov 86	**SWEET LOVE** *Elektra EKR 44*	**13** 10
31 Jan 87	**CAUGHT UP IN THE RAPTURE** *Elektra EKR 49*	**51** 5
8 Oct 88	**GIVING YOU THE BEST THAT I GOT** *Elektra EKR 79*	**55** 3
30 Jun 90	**TALK TO ME** *Elektra EKR 111*	**68** 2
17 Sep 94	**BODY & SOUL** *Elektra EKR 190CD*	**48** 2

Arthur BAKER
US, male producer / multi-instrumentalist (7 WEEKS)   pos/wks
20 May 89	**IT'S YOUR TIME** *Breakout USA 654* [1]	**64** 2
21 Oct 89	**THE MESSAGE IS LOVE** *Breakout USA 668* [2]	**38** 5

[1] Arthur Baker featuring Shirley Lewis [2] Arthur Baker and the Backbeat Disciples featuring Al Green

See also Wally JUMP Jr and the CRIMINAL ELEMENT

Hylda BAKER and Arthur MULLARD
UK, female / male comedy duo (6 WEEKS)   pos/wks
9 Sep 78	**YOU'RE THE ONE THAT I WANT** *Pye 7N 46121*	**22** 6

George BAKER SELECTION
Holland, male / female vocal / instrumental group (10 WEEKS)   pos/wks
6 Sep 75	● **PALOMA BLANCA** *Warner Bros. K 16541*	**10** 10

BALAAM AND THE ANGEL
UK, male vocal / instrumental group (2 WEEKS)   pos/wks
29 Mar 86	**SHE KNOWS** *Virgin VS 842*	**70** 2

Long John BALDRY *UK, male vocalist (36 WEEKS)*   pos/wks
8 Nov 67	★ **LET THE HEARTACHES BEGIN** *Pye 7N 17385*	**1** 13
28 Aug 68	**WHEN THE SUN COMES SHININ' THRU** *Pye 7N 17593*	**29** 7
23 Oct 68	**MEXICO** *Pye 7N 17563*	**15** 8
29 Jan 69	**IT'S TOO LATE NOW** *Pye 7N 17664*	**21** 8

BALEARIC BILL *UK / Belgium, DJ / production trio (2 WEEKS)*   pos/wks
2 Oct 99	**DESTINATION SUNSHINE** *Xtravaganza XTRAV 3CDS*	**36** 2

Edward BALL *UK, male vocalist (2 WEEKS)*   pos/wks
20 Jul 96	**THE MILL HILL SELF HATE CLUB** *Creation CRESCD 233* ...	**57** 1
22 Feb 97	**LOVE IS BLUE** *Creation CRESCD 244*	**59** 1

Kenny BALL and his JAZZMEN (182 **Top 500**) *Top UK trad jazz-band leader. b. 22 May 1930, Essex. His Dixieland band was at the forefront of the early 1960s jazz revival. Their biggest hit, 'Midnight in Moscow', reached runner-up spot on both sides of the Atlantic (136 WEEKS)*   pos/wks
23 Feb 61	**SAMANTHA** *Pye Jazz Today 7NJ 2040*	**13** 15
11 May 61	**I STILL LOVE YOU ALL** *Pye Jazz 7NJ 2042*	**24** 6
31 Aug 61	**SOMEDAY (YOU'LL BE SORRY)** *Pye Jazz 7NJ 2047*	**28** 6
9 Nov 61	● **MIDNIGHT IN MOSCOW** *Pye Jazz 7NJ 2049*	**2** 21
15 Feb 62	● **MARCH OF THE SIAMESE CHILDREN** *Pye Jazz 7NJ 2051* ..	**4** 13
17 May 62	● **THE GREEN LEAVES OF SUMMER** *Pye Jazz 7NJ 2054*	**7** 14
23 Aug 62	**SO DO I** *Pye Jazz 7NJ 2056*	**14** 8

		pos/wks
18 Oct 62	THE PAY OFF *Pye Jazz 7NJ 2061*	**23** 6
17 Jan 63 ●	SUKIYAKI *Pye Jazz 7NJ 2062*	**10** 13
25 Apr 63	CASABLANCA *Pye Jazz 7NJ 2064*	**21** 11
13 Jun 63	RONDO *Pye Jazz 7NJ 2065*	**24** 8
22 Aug 63	ACAPULCO 1922 *Pye Jazz 7NJ 2067*	**27** 6
11 Jun 64	HELLO DOLLY *Pye Jazz 7NJ 2071*	**30** 7
19 Jul 67	WHEN I'M SIXTY FOUR *Pye 7N 17348*	**43** 2

Michael BALL *UK, male vocalist (39 WEEKS)* pos/wks

28 Jan 89 ●	LOVE CHANGES EVERYTHING *Really Useful RUR 3*	**2** 14
28 Oct 89	THE FIRST MAN YOU REMEMBER *Really Useful RUR 6* [1]	**68** 2
10 Aug 91	IT'S STILL YOU *Polydor PO 160*	**58** 2
25 Apr 92	ONE STEP OUT OF TIME *Polydor PO 206*	**20** 7
12 Dec 92	IF I CAN DREAM (EP) *Polydor PO 248*	**51** 1
26 Dec 92	IF I CAN DREAM (EP) (re-entry) *Polydor PO 248*	**68** 1
11 Sep 93	SUNSET BOULEVARD *Polydor PZCD 293*	**72** 1
30 Jul 94	FROM HERE TO ETERNITY *Columbia 6606905*	**36** 3
17 Sep 94	THE LOVERS WE WERE *Columbia 6607972*	**63** 2
9 Dec 95	THE ROSE *Columbia 6614535*	**42** 4
17 Feb 96	(SOMETHING INSIDE) SO STRONG *Columbia 6629005*	**40** 2

[1] Michael Ball and Diana Morrison

Tracks on If I Can Dream (EP): If I Can Dream / You Don't Have to Say You Love Me / Always on My Mind / Tell Me There's a Heaven

BALTIMORA *Ireland, male vocalist - Jimmy McShane (12 WEEKS)* pos/wks

10 Aug 85 ●	TARZAN BOY *Columbia DB 9102*	**3** 12

Charli BALTIMORE *US, female rapper (4 WEEKS)* pos/wks

1 Aug 98	MONEY *Epic 6662272*	**12** 4

BAM BAM *US, male vocalist / instrumentalist (2 WEEKS)* pos/wks

19 Mar 88	GIVE IT TO ME *Serious 7OUS 10*	**65** 2

Afrika BAMBAATAA
US, male DJ / producer / rapper - Kevin Donovan (32 WEEKS) pos/wks

28 Aug 82	PLANET ROCK *21 POSP 497* [1]	**53** 3
10 Mar 84	RENEGADES OF FUNK *Tommy Boy AFR 1* [1]	**30** 4
1 Sep 84	UNITY (PART 1 – THE THIRD COMING) *Tommy Boy AFR 2* [2]	**49** 5
27 Feb 88	RECKLESS *EMI EM 41* [3]	**17** 8
12 Oct 91	JUST GET UP AND DANCE *EMI USA MT 100*	**45** 3
17 Oct 98	GOT TO GET UP *Multiply CDMULTY 42*	**22** 4
18 Sep 99 ●	AFRIKA SHOX *Hard Hands HAND 057CD1* [4]	**7** 5

[1] Afrika Bambaataa and the Soul Sonic Force [2] Afrika Bambaataa and James Brown [3] Afrika Bambaataa and Family featuring UB40 [4] Leftfield / Bambaataa

BAMBOO *UK, male producer - Andrew Livingstone (12 WEEKS)* pos/wks

17 Jan 98 ●	BAMBOOGIE *VC Recordings VCRD 29*	**2** 10
4 Jul 98	THE STRUTT *VC Recordings VCRD 35*	**36** 2

BANANARAMA (86) **Top 500** Britain's most charted female group:
Sarah Dallin, Keren Woodward, Siobhan Fahey. The London-based trio were also best sellers in the USA, where 'Venus' topped the chart. Fahey, who married Eurythmic Dave Stewart, left in 1988 to form Shakespears Sister and was replaced by Jacqui O'Sullivan (202 WEEKS) pos/wks

13 Feb 82 ●	IT AIN'T WHAT YOU DO IT'S THE WAY THAT YOU DO IT *Chrysalis CHS 2570* [1]	**4** 10
10 Apr 82 ●	REALLY SAYING SOMETHING *Deram NANA 1* [2]	**5** 10
3 Jul 82 ●	SHY BOY *London NANA 2*	**4** 11
4 Dec 82	CHEERS THEN *London NANA 3*	**45** 7
26 Feb 83 ●	NA NA HEY HEY KISS HIM GOODBYE *London NANA 4*	**5** 10
9 Jul 83 ●	CRUEL SUMMER *London NANA 5*	**8** 10
3 Mar 84 ●	ROBERT DE NIRO'S WAITING *London NANA 6*	**3** 11
26 May 84	ROUGH JUSTICE *London NANA 7*	**23** 7
24 Nov 84	HOTLINE TO HEAVEN *London NANA 8*	**58** 2
24 Aug 85	DO NOT DISTURB *London NANA 9*	**31** 6
31 May 86 ●	VENUS *London NANA 10* ▲	**8** 13
16 Aug 86	MORE THAN PHYSICAL *London NANA 11*	**41** 5
14 Feb 87	TRICK OF THE NIGHT *London NANA 12*	**32** 5
11 Jul 87	I HEARD A RUMOUR *London NANA 13*	**14** 9
10 Oct 87 ●	LOVE IN THE FIRST DEGREE *London NANA 14*	**3** 12
9 Jan 88	I CAN'T HELP IT *London NANA 15*	**20** 6
9 Apr 88 ●	I WANT YOU BACK *London NANA 16*	**5** 10
24 Sep 88	LOVE, TRUTH AND HONESTY *London NANA 17*	**23** 8
19 Nov 88	NATHAN JONES *London NANA 18*	**15** 9
25 Feb 89 ●	HELP *London LON 222* [3]	**3** 9
10 Jun 89	CRUEL SUMMER (re-mix) *London NANA 19*	**19** 6
28 Jul 90	ONLY YOUR LOVE *London NANA 21*	**27** 4
5 Jan 91	PREACHER MAN *London NANA 23*	**20** 6
20 Apr 91	LONG TRAIN RUNNING *London NANA 24*	**30** 5
29 Aug 92	MOVIN' ON *London NANA 25*	**24** 5
28 Nov 92	LAST THING ON MY MIND *London NANA 26*	**71** 2
20 Mar 93	MORE MORE MORE *London NACPD 27*	**24** 4

[1] Fun Boy Three and Bananarama [2] Bananarama with Fun Boy Three [3] Bananarama / La Na Nee Nee Noo Loo

The listed flip side of 'Love in the First Degree' was 'Mr Sleaze' by Stock Aitken Waterman. Act was a duo for last three hits

BAND *Canada / US, male vocal / instrumental group (18 WEEKS)* pos/wks

18 Sep 68	THE WEIGHT *Capitol CL 15559*	**21** 9
4 Apr 70	RAG MAMA RAG *Capitol CL 15629*	**16** 9

BAND AID
International, male / female vocal / instrumental charity assembly (26 WEEKS) pos/wks

15 Dec 84 ★	DO THEY KNOW IT'S CHRISTMAS? *Mercury FEED 1* ◆ ■	**1** 13
7 Dec 85 ●	DO THEY KNOW IT'S CHRISTMAS? (re-entry) *Mercury FEED 1*	**3** 7
23 Dec 89 ★	DO THEY KNOW IT'S CHRISTMAS? *PWL/Polydor FEED 2* [1] ■	**1** 6

[1] Band Aid II

BAND AID: Adam Clayton, Bono (U2); Bob Geldof, Johnny Fingers, Simon Crowe, Peter Briquette (Boomtown Rats); David Bowie; Paul McCartney; Holly Johnson (Frankie Goes To Hollywood); Midge Ure, Chris Cross (Ultravox); Simon Le Bon, Nick Rhodes, Andy Taylor, John Taylor, Roger Taylor (Duran Duran); Paul Young; Tony Hadley, Martin Kemp, John Keeble, Gary Kemp, Steve Norman (Spandau Ballet); Martyn Ware, Glenn Gregory (Heaven 17); Sting; Boy George, Jon Moss (Culture Club); Marilyn; Keren Woodward, Sarah Dallin, Siobhan Fahey (Bananarama); Jody Watley (Shalamar); Paul Weller; Robert 'Kool' Bell, James Taylor, Dennis Thomas (Kool and the Gang); George Michael.
BAND AID II: Bananarama, Big Fun, Bros, Cathy Dennis, D Mob, Jason Donovan, Kevin Godley, Glen Goldsmith, Kylie Minogue, The Pasadenas, Chris Rea, Cliff Richard, Jimmy Somerville, Sonia, Lisa Stansfield, Technotronic, Wet Wet Wet

BAND AKA *US, male vocal / instrumental group (12 WEEKS)* pos/wks

15 May 82	GRACE *Epic EPC A 2376*	**41** 5
5 Mar 83	JOY *Epic EPC A 3145*	**24** 7

BAND OF GOLD
Holland, male / female vocal / instrumental group (11 WEEKS) pos/wks

14 Jul 84	LOVE SONGS ARE BACK AGAIN (MEDLEY) *RCA 428*	**24** 11

BAND OF THIEVES – See Luke GOSS and the BAND OF THIEVES

BANDERAS *UK, female vocal / instrumental duo (16 WEEKS)* pos/wks

23 Feb 91	THIS IS YOUR LIFE *London LON 290*	**16** 10
15 Jun 91	SHE SELLS *London LON 298*	**41** 6

BANDWAGON – See Johnny JOHNSON and the BANDWAGON

Honey BANE *UK, female vocalist (8 WEEKS)* pos/wks

24 Jan 81	TURN ME ON TURN ME OFF *Zonophone Z 15*	**37** 5
18 Apr 81	BABY LOVE *Zonophone Z 19*	**58** 3

BANG *UK, male vocal duo (2 WEEKS)* pos/wks

6 May 89	YOU'RE THE ONE *RCA PB 42715*	**74** 2

UK No.1 ★   UK Top 10 ●   Still on chart +   UK million seller ◆   UK entry at No.1 ■   US No.1 ▲

BANGLES `317` **Top 500** *Melodic pop-rock quartet formed 1981, Los Angeles, California, USA. Comprised Susanna Hoffs (v), sisters Vicki (g) and Debbi Peterson (d) and Michael Steele (b). Split 1989, having become most successful all-female band in chart history, then reformed for a tour in 2000 (94 WEEKS)*

		pos/wks
15 Feb 86 ●	MANIC MONDAY *CBS A 6796*	.......2 12
26 Apr 86	IF SHE KNEW WHAT SHE WANTS *CBS A 7062*	.....31 7
5 Jul 86	GOING DOWN TO LIVERPOOL *CBS A 7255*	......56 3
13 Sep 86 ●	WALK LIKE AN EGYPTIAN *CBS 650071 7* ▲	.......3 19
10 Jan 87	WALKING DOWN YOUR STREET *CBS BANGS 1*	.....16 6
18 Apr 87	FOLLOWING *CBS BANGS 2*	.......55 3
6 Feb 88	HAZY SHADE OF WINTER *Def Jam BANGS 3*	.....11 10
5 Nov 88	IN YOUR ROOM *CBS BANGS 4*	......35 6
18 Feb 89 ★	ETERNAL FLAME *CBS BANGS 5* ▲	.......1 18
10 Jun 89	BE WITH YOU *CBS BANGS 6*	......23 8
14 Oct 89	I'LL SET YOU FREE *CBS BANGS 7*	.......74 1
9 Jun 90	WALK LIKE AN EGYPTIAN (re-issue) *CBS BANGS 8*	.......73 1

Tony BANKS – See FISH

BANNED *UK, male vocal / instrumental group (6 WEEKS)*

		pos/wks
17 Dec 77	LITTLE GIRL *Harvest HAR 5145*	.......36 6

BANSHEES – See SIOUXSIE and the BANSHEES

Buju BANTON *Jamaica, male vocalist (1 WEEK)*

		pos/wks
7 Aug 93	MAKE MY DAY *Mercury BUJCD 2*	.......72 1

Pato BANTON *UK, male vocalist - Patrick Murray (37 WEEKS)*

		pos/wks
1 Oct 94 ★	BABY COME BACK *Virgin VSCDT 1522*	.......1 18
11 Feb 95	THIS COWBOY SONG *A & M 5809652* [1]	.....15 6
8 Apr 95	BUBBLING HOT *Virgin VSCDT 1530* [2]	.....15 7
20 Jan 96	SPIRITS IN THE MATERIAL WORLD *MCA MCSTD 2113* [3]	.....36 2
27 Jul 96	GROOVIN' *IRS CDEIRS 195* [4]	.....14 4

[1] Sting featuring Pato Banton [2] Pato Banton with Ranking Roger [3] Pato Banton with Sting [4] Pato Banton and the Reggae Revolution

The sleeve of 'Baby Come Back' credits Ali and Robin Campbell

BAR CODES featuring Alison BROWN
UK, male / female vocal group (1 WEEK)

		pos/wks
17 Dec 94	SUPERMARKET SWEEP *Blanca Casa BC 101CD*	.......72 1

BAR-KAYS *US, male vocal / instrumental group (15 WEEKS)*

		pos/wks
23 Aug 67	SOUL FINGER *Stax 601 014*	.......33 7
22 Jan 77	SHAKE YOUR RUMP TO THE FUNK *Mercury 6167 417*	.....41 4
12 Jan 85	SEXOMATIC *Club JAB 10*	.......51 4

Chris BARBER'S JAZZ BAND
UK, male jazz band, Chris Barber - trombone (30 WEEKS)

		pos/wks
13 Feb 59 ●	PETITE FLEUR *Pye Nixa NJ 2026*	.......3 22
31 Jul 59	PETITE FLEUR (re-entry) *Pye Nixa NJ 2026*	.....22 2
9 Oct 59	LONESOME (SI TU VOIS MA MERE) *Columbia DB 4333* [1]	.....27 2
4 Jan 62	REVIVAL *Columbia SCD 2166*	.......50 2
1 Feb 62	REVIVAL (re-entry) *Columbia SCD 2166*	.......43 2

[1] Chris Barber featuring Monty Sunshine

BARBRA and NEIL – See Barbra STREISAND; Neil DIAMOND

BARCLAY JAMES HARVEST
UK, male vocal / instrumental group (9 WEEKS)

		pos/wks
2 Apr 77	LIVE (EP) *Polydor 2229 198*	.......49 1
16 Apr 77	LIVE (EP) (re-entry) *Polydor 2229 198*	.......49 1
26 Jan 80	LOVE ON THE LINE *Polydor POSP 97*	.......63 2
22 Nov 80	LIFE IS FOR LIVING *Polydor POSP 195*	.......61 3
21 May 83	JUST A DAY AWAY *Polydor POSP 585*	.......68 2

Tracks on Live (EP): Rock 'n' Roll Star / Medicine Man (Parts 1 & 2)

BARDO *UK, male / female vocal duo - Sally Ann Triplett & Stephen Fischer (8 WEEKS)*

		pos/wks
10 Apr 82 ●	ONE STEP FURTHER *Epic EPC A2265*	.......2 8

BAREFOOT MAN *Germany, male vocalist (7 WEEKS)*

		pos/wks
5 Dec 98	BIG PANTY WOMAN *Plaza PZACD 082*	.......21 7

BARENAKED LADIES
Canada, male vocal / instrumental group (12 WEEKS)

		pos/wks
20 Feb 99 ●	ONE WEEK *Reprise W 468CD* ▲	.......5 8
15 May 99	IT'S ALL BEEN DONE *Reprise W 476CD*	.....28 2
24 Jul 99	CALL AND ANSWER *Reprise W498CD1*	.....52 1
11 Dec 99	BRIAN WILSON *Reprise W 511CD1*	.......73 1

BARKIN BROTHERS featuring Johnnie FIORI
UK, male production group and US female vocalist (2 WEEKS)

		pos/wks
15 Apr 00	GONNA CATCH YOU *Brothers Organisation BRUVCD 15*	.....51 2

Gary BARLOW *UK, male vocalist (47 WEEKS)*

		pos/wks
20 Jul 96 ★	FOREVER LOVE *RCA 74321397922* ■	.......1 16
10 May 97 ★	LOVE WON'T WAIT *RCA 74321470842* ■	.......1 7
26 Jul 97	LOVE WON'T WAIT (re-entry) *RCA 74321470842*	.....64 1
26 Jul 97	SO HELP ME GIRL *RCA 74321501202*	.....11 7
9 Aug 97	LOVE WON'T WAIT (2nd re-entry) *RCA 74321470842*	.....67 1
20 Sep 97	SO HELP ME GIRL (re-entry) *RCA 74321501202*	.....64 4
15 Nov 97 ●	OPEN ROAD *RCA 74321518292*	.......7 5
17 Jul 99	STRONGER *RCA 74321682002*	.....16 4
9 Oct 99	FOR ALL THAT YOU WANT *RCA 74321701012*	.....24 2

See also TAKE THAT

Gary BARNACLE – See BIG FUN; SONIA

BARNBRACK *UK, male vocal / instrumental group (7 WEEKS)*

		pos/wks
16 Mar 85	BELFAST *Homespun HS 092*	.......45 7

Jimmy BARNES – See INXS

Richard BARNES *UK, male vocalist (10 WEEKS)*

		pos/wks
23 May 70	TAKE TO THE MOUNTAINS *Philips BF 1840*	.......35 6
24 Oct 70	GO NORTH *Philips 6006 039*	.......49 1
7 Nov 70	GO NORTH (re-entry) *Philips 6006 039*	.......38 3

BARRACUDAS
UK / US, male vocal / instrumental group (6 WEEKS)

		pos/wks
16 Aug 80	SUMMER FUN *Zonophone Z 5*	.......37 6

Wild Willy BARRETT – See John OTWAY and Wild Willy BARRETT

Amanda BARRIE and Johnny BRIGGS
UK, female / male vocal duo (3 WEEKS)

		pos/wks
16 Dec 95	SOMETHING STUPID *EMI Premier CDEMS 411*	.......35 3

The listed flip side of 'Something Stupid' was 'Always Look on the Bright Side of Life' by the Coronation Street Cast

J.J. BARRIE *Canada, male vocalist - Barrie Authors (11 WEEKS)*

		pos/wks
24 Apr 76 ★	NO CHARGE *Power Exchange PX 209*	.......1 11

Featured vocalist is Vicki Brown

Ken BARRIE *UK, male vocalist (15 WEEKS)*

		pos/wks
10 Jul 82	POSTMAN PAT *Post Music PP 001*	.......44 8
25 Dec 82	POSTMAN PAT (re-entry) *Post Music PP 001*	.......54 3
24 Dec 83	POSTMAN PAT (2nd re-entry) *Post Music PP 001*	.......59 4

BARRON KNIGHTS `320` **Top 500** *Britain's princes of pop parody, formed Leighton Buzzard, UK, fronted by Duke D'Mond (b. Richard Palmer).*

Group's humorous hit medleys proved popular in the 1960s and 1970s and helped to stop pop music taking itself too seriously (94 WEEKS) pos/wks

9 Jul 64 ●	CALL UP THE GROUPS *Columbia DB 7317* [1]	3	13
22 Oct 64	COME TO THE DANCE *Columbia DB 7375* [1]	42	2
25 Mar 65 ●	POP GO THE WORKERS *Columbia DB 7525* [1]	5	13
16 Dec 65 ●	MERRY GENTLE POPS *Columbia DB 7780* [1]	9	7
1 Dec 66	UNDER NEW MANAGEMENT *Columbia DB 8071* [1]	15	4
23 Oct 68	AN OLYMPIC RECORD *Columbia DB 8485*	35	4
29 Oct 77 ●	LIVE IN TROUBLE *Epic EPC 5752*	7	10
2 Dec 78 ●	A TASTE OF AGGRO *Epic EPC 6829*	3	10
8 Dec 79	FOOD FOR THOUGHT *Epic EPC 8011*	46	6
4 Oct 80	THE SIT SONG *Epic EPC 8994*	44	4
6 Dec 80	NEVER MIND THE PRESENTS *Epic EPC 9070*	17	8
5 Dec 81	BLACKBOARD JUMBLE *CBS A 1795*	52	5
19 Mar 83	BUFFALO BILL'S LAST SCRATCH *Epic EPC A 3208*	49	3

[1] The Barron Knights with Duke D'Mond

Joe BARRY *US, male vocalist (1 WEEK)* pos/wks

24 Aug 61	I'M A FOOL TO CARE *Mercury AMT 1149*	49	1

Len BARRY *US, male vocalist - Leonard Borisoff (24 WEEKS)* pos/wks

4 Nov 65 ●	1-2-3 *Brunswick 05942*	3	14
13 Jan 66 ●	LIKE A BABY *Brunswick 05949*	10	10

John BARRY ORCHESTRA (423) Top 500 *Early UK rock 'n' roll bandleader, who arranged Adam Faith's hits and found global fame writing film scores (including many for James Bond), b. Jonathan Barry Prendergast, 3 Nov 1933, York, UK. This Oscar and Grammy winner received an OBE in 1999 (78 WEEKS)* pos/wks

5 Mar 60 ●	HIT AND MISS *Columbia DB 4414* [1]	10	12
28 Apr 60	BEAT FOR BEATNIKS *Columbia DB 4446*	40	2
9 Jun 60	HIT AND MISS (re-entry) *Columbia DB 4414* [1]	45	1
14 Jul 60	NEVER LET GO *Columbia DB 4480*	49	1
18 Aug 60	BLUEBERRY HILL *Columbia DB 4480*	34	3
8 Sep 60	WALK DON'T RUN *Columbia DB 4505* [1]	49	1
22 Sep 60	WALK DON'T RUN (re-entry) *Columbia DB 4505* [1]	11	13
8 Dec 60	BLACK STOCKINGS *Columbia DB 4554* [1]	27	9
2 Mar 61	THE MAGNIFICENT SEVEN *Columbia DB 4598* [1]	48	1
16 Mar 61	THE MAGNIFICENT SEVEN (re-entry) *Columbia DB 4598* [1]	45	2
6 Apr 61	THE MAGNIFICENT SEVEN (2nd re-entry) *Columbia DB 4598* [1]	60	1
8 Jun 61	THE MAGNIFICENT SEVEN (3rd re-entry) *Columbia DB 4598* [1]	47	1
26 Apr 62	CUTTY SARK *Columbia DB 4806* [1]	35	2
1 Nov 62 ●	JAMES BOND THEME *Columbia DB 4898*	13	11
21 Nov 63	FROM RUSSIA WITH LOVE *Ember S 181*	44	1
19 Dec 63	FROM RUSSIA WITH LOVE (re-entry) *Ember S 181*	39	2
11 Dec 71	THE PERSUADERS *CBS 7469* [2]	13	15

[1] John Barry Seven [2] John Barry

Michael BARRYMORE *UK, male vocalist (4 WEEKS)* pos/wks

16 Dec 95	TOO MUCH FOR ONE HEART *EMI CDEM 412*	25	4

Bart & Homer – See SIMPSONS

Lionel BART *UK, male vocalist (3 WEEKS)* pos/wks

25 Nov 89	HAPPY ENDINGS (GIVE YOURSELF A PINCH) *EMI EM 121*	...68	1
23 Dec 89	HAPPY ENDINGS (GIVE YOURSELF A PINCH) (re-entry) *EMI EM 121*	71	2

BAS NOIR *US, female vocal duo (1 WEEK)* pos/wks

11 Feb 89	MY LOVE IS MAGIC *10 TEN 257*	73	1

Rob BASE and DJ E-Z ROCK *US, male rap / DJ duo (19 WEEKS)* pos/wks

16 Apr 88	IT TAKES TWO *Citybeat CBE 724*	24	6
14 Jan 89	GET ON THE DANCE FLOOR *Supreme SUPE 139*	14	7
4 Mar 89	IT TAKES TWO (re-entry) *Citybeat CBE 724*	49	3
22 Apr 89	JOY AND PAIN *Supreme SUPE 143*	47	3

BASEMENT BOYS *US, male production group (1 WEEK)* pos/wks

23 Feb 91	IS IT LOVE *Eternal YZ 509* [1]	71	1

[1] Basement Boys present Ultra Nate

BASEMENT JAXX *UK, male DJ / producer duo - Simon Ratcliffe & Felix Buxton (30 WEEKS)* pos/wks

31 May 97	FLY LIFE *Multiply CDMULTY 21*	19	3
1 May 99 ●	RED ALERT *XL Recordings XLS 100CD*	5	10
14 Aug 99 ●	RENDEZ-VU *XL Recordings XLS 110CD*	4	8
6 Nov 99	JUMP 'N SHOUT *XL Recordings XLS 116CD*	12	5
15 Apr 00	BINGO BANGO *XL Recordings XLS 120CD*	13	4

BASIA *Poland, female vocalist (9 WEEKS)* pos/wks

23 Jan 88	PROMISES *Epic BASH 4*	48	4
28 May 88	TIME AND TIDE *Epic BASH 5*	61	3
14 Jan 95	DRUNK ON LOVE *Epic 6611582*	41	2

Count BASIE – See Frank SINATRA

Toni BASIL *US, female vocalist - Antonia Basilotta (16 WEEKS)* pos/wks

6 Feb 82 ●	MICKEY *Radialchoice TIC 4* ▲	2	12
1 May 82	NOBODY *Radialchoice TIC 2*	52	4

Olav BASOSKI *Holland, male producer (1 WEEK)* pos/wks

26 Aug 00	OPIUM SCUMBAGZ *Defected DFECT 20CDS*	56	1

Alfie BASS – See Michael MEDWIN, Bernard BRESSLAW, Alfie BASS and Leslie FYSON

Fontella BASS *US, female vocalist (15 WEEKS)* pos/wks

2 Dec 65	RESCUE ME *Chess CRS 8023*	11	10
20 Jan 66	RECOVERY *Chess CRS 8027*	32	5

BASS BOYZ *UK, male producer - James Sammon (1 WEEK)* pos/wks

28 Sep 96	GUNZ AND PIANOZ *Polydor 5753432*	74	1

See also PIANOMAN

BASS BUMPERS *Germany / UK, male / female vocal / instrumental group (4 WEEKS)* pos/wks

25 Sep 93	RUNNIN' *Vertigo VERCD 78*	68	1
5 Feb 94	THE MUSIC'S GOT ME *Vertigo VERCD 84*	25	3

BASS JUMPERS *Holland, male producer and female vocalist (1 WEEK)* pos/wks

13 Feb 99	MAKE UP YOUR MIND *Pepper 0530112*	44	1

BASS-O-MATIC *UK, male multi-instrumentalist / producer - William Orbit (19 WEEKS)* pos/wks

12 May 90	IN THE REALM OF THE SENSES *Virgin VS 1265*	66	3
1 Sep 90 ●	FASCINATING RHYTHM *Virgin VS 1274*	9	11
22 Dec 90	EASE ON BY *Virgin VS 1295*	61	4
3 Aug 91	FUNKY LOVE VIBRATIONS *Virgin VS 1355*	71	1

See also William ORBIT

Shirley BASSEY (22) Top 500 *Internationally acclaimed vocalist and cabaret entertainer. b. 8 Jan 1937, Cardiff, Wales. With 30 hit singles (spanning a record 42-year period for a female) and 35 hit albums, she is Britain's most successful female chart artist. Honoured with a damehood in 2000 (326 WEEKS)* pos/wks

15 Feb 57 ●	THE BANANA BOAT SONG *Philips PB 668*	8	10
23 Aug 57	FIRE DOWN BELOW *Philips PB 723*	30	1
6 Sep 57	YOU YOU ROMEO *Philips PB 723*	29	2
19 Dec 58	AS I LOVE YOU *Philips PB 845*	27	2
26 Dec 58 ●	KISS ME, HONEY HONEY, KISS ME *Philips PB 860*	3	17
9 Jan 59 ★	AS I LOVE YOU (re-entry) *Philips PB 845*	1	17

UK No.1 ★   UK Top 10 ●   Still on chart +   UK million seller ◆   UK entry at No.1 ■   US No.1 ▲

		pos/wks
31 Mar 60	WITH THESE HANDS *Columbia DB 4421*	38 2
21 Apr 60	WITH THESE HANDS (re-entry) *Columbia DB 4421*	31 2
12 May 60	WITH THESE HANDS (2nd re-entry) *Columbia DB 4421*	41 2
4 Aug 60 ●	AS LONG AS HE NEEDS ME *Columbia DB 4490*	2 30
11 May 61 ●	YOU'LL NEVER KNOW *Columbia DB 4643*	6 17
27 Jul 61 ★	REACH FOR THE STARS / CLIMB EV'RY MOUNTAIN *Columbia DB 4685*	1 16
23 Nov 61 ●	I'LL GET BY *Columbia DB 4737*	10 8
23 Nov 61	REACH FOR THE STARS / CLIMB EV'RY MOUNTAIN (re-entry) *Columbia DB 4685*	40 2
15 Feb 62	TONIGHT *Columbia DB 4777*	21 8
26 Apr 62	AVE MARIA *Columbia DB 4816*	31 4
31 May 62	FAR AWAY *Columbia DB 4836*	24 13
30 Aug 62 ●	WHAT NOW MY LOVE *Columbia DB 4882*	5 17
28 Feb 63	WHAT KIND OF FOOL AM I? *Columbia DB 4974*	47 2
26 Sep 63	I (WHO HAVE NOTHING) *Columbia DB 7113*	6 20
23 Jan 64	MY SPECIAL DREAM *Columbia DB 7185*	32 7
9 Apr 64	GONE *Columbia DB 7248*	36 5
15 Oct 64	GOLDFINGER *Columbia DB 7360*	21 9
20 May 65	NO REGRETS *Columbia DB 7535*	39 4
11 Oct 67	BIG SPENDER *United Artists UP 1192*	21 15
20 Jun 70 ●	SOMETHING *United Artists UP 35125*	4 21
2 Jan 71	THE FOOL ON THE HILL *United Artists UP 35156*	48 1
23 Jan 71	SOMETHING (re-entry) *United Artists UP 35125*	50 1
27 Mar 71	(WHERE DO I BEGIN) LOVE STORY *United Artists UP 35194*	34 9
7 Aug 71	FOR ALL WE KNOW *United Artists UP 35267*	46 1
21 Aug 71 ●	FOR ALL WE KNOW (re-entry) *United Artists UP 35267*	6 23
15 Jan 72	DIAMONDS ARE FOREVER *United Artists UP 35293*	38 6
3 Mar 73 ●	NEVER NEVER NEVER *United Artists UP 35490*	8 18
14 Jul 73	NEVER NEVER NEVER (re-entry) *United Artists UP 35490*	48 1
22 Aug 87	THE RHYTHM DIVINE *Mercury MER 253* [1]	54 2
16 Nov 96	'DISCO' LA PASSIONE *East West EW 072CD* [2]	41 1
20 Dec 97	HISTORY REPEATING *Wall of Sound WALLD 036* [3]	19 7
23 Oct 99	WORLD IN UNION *Universal TV 4669402* [4]	35 3

[1] Yello featuring Shirley Bassey [2] Chris Rea and Shirley Bassey [3] Propellerheads featuring Miss Shirley Bassey [4] Shirley Bassey / Bryn Terfel

BASSHEADS
UK, male / female vocal / instrumental group (19 WEEKS) pos/wks

16 Nov 91 ●	IS THERE ANYBODY OUT THERE *Deconstruction R 6303*	5 8
30 May 92	BACK TO THE OLD SCHOOL *Deconstruction R 6310*	12 4
28 Nov 92	WHO CAN MAKE ME FEEL GOOD *Deconstruction R 6326*	38 2
28 Aug 93	START A BRAND NEW LIFE (SAVE ME) *Deconstruction CDR 6353*	49 2
15 Jul 95	IS THERE ANYBODY OUT THERE (re-mix) *Deconstruction 74321293882*	24 3

BASSTOY *US, male / female vocal / instrumental duo (1 WEEK)* pos/wks

27 May 00	RUNNIN *Neo NEOCD 029*	62 1

BATES *Germany, male vocal / instrumental group (1 WEEK)* pos/wks

3 Feb 96	BILLIE JEAN *Virgin International DINSD 151*	67 1

Mike BATT with the NEW EDITION
UK, male vocalist with male / female vocal group (8 WEEKS) pos/wks

16 Aug 75 ●	SUMMERTIME CITY *Epic EPC 3460*	4 8

See also WOMBLES

BAUHAUS *UK, male / instrumental group (35 WEEKS)* pos/wks

18 Apr 81	KICK IN THE EYE *Beggars Banquet BEG 54*	59 3
4 Jul 81	THE PASSION OF LOVERS *Beggars Banquet BEG 59*	56 4
6 Mar 82	KICK IN THE EYE (EP) *Beggars Banquet BEG 74*	45 4
19 Jun 82	SPIRIT *Beggars Banquet BEG 79*	42 5
9 Oct 82	ZIGGY STARDUST *Beggars Banquet BEG 83*	15 7
22 Jan 83	LAGARTIJA NICK *Beggars Banquet BEG 88*	44 4
9 Apr 83	SHE'S IN PARTIES *Beggars Banquet BEG 91*	26 6
29 Oct 83	THE SINGLES 1981-83 *Beggars Banquet BEG 100E*	52 4

Tracks on Kick in the Eye (EP): Kick in the Eye (Searching for Satori) / Harry / Earwax. The Singles 1981-83 was an EP: The Passion of Lovers / Kick In The Eye etc

Les BAXTER *US, orchestra and chorus (9 WEEKS)* pos/wks

13 May 55 ●	UNCHAINED MELODY *Capitol CL 14257*	10 9

BAY CITY ROLLERS (233 Top 500) *Tartan teen sensations from Edinburgh: Leslie McKeown (v), Eric Faulkner (g), Stuart Wood (g), Alan Longmuir (b), Derek Longmuir (d). They were the first of many acts heralded as 'Biggest Group Since The Beatles' and one of the most screamed-at teeny-bopper acts of the 70s (116 WEEKS)* pos/wks

18 Sep 71 ●	KEEP ON DANCING *Bell 1164*	9 13
9 Feb 74 ●	REMEMBER (SHA-LA-LA) *Bell 1338*	6 12
27 Apr 74 ●	SHANG-A-LANG *Bell 1355*	2 10
27 Jul 74 ●	SUMMERLOVE SENSATION *Bell 1369*	3 10
12 Oct 74 ●	ALL OF ME LOVES ALL OF YOU *Bell 1382*	4 10
8 Mar 75 ★	BYE BYE BABY *Bell 1409*	1 16
12 Jul 75 ★	GIVE A LITTLE LOVE *Bell 1425*	1 9
22 Nov 75 ●	MONEY HONEY *Bell 1461*	3 9
10 Apr 76 ●	LOVE ME LIKE I LOVE YOU *Bell 1477*	4 9
11 Sep 76 ●	I ONLY WANNA BE WITH YOU *Bell 1493*	4 9
7 May 77	IT'S A GAME *Arista 108*	16 6
30 Jul 77	YOU MADE ME BELIEVE IN MAGIC *Arista 127*	34 3

BBC CONCERT ORCHESTRA, BBC SYMPHONY CHORUS cond. Stephen JACKSON
UK, orchestra, chorus and conductor (3 WEEKS) pos/wks

22 Jun 96	ODE TO JOY (FROM BEETHOVEN'S SYMPHONY NO.9) *Virgin VSCDT 1591*	36 3

BBE *France / Italy, male instrumental group (20 WEEKS)* pos/wks

28 Sep 96 ●	SEVEN DAYS AND ONE WEEK *Positiva CDTIV 67*	3 9
29 Mar 97 ●	FLASH *Positiva CDTIV 73*	5 5
14 Feb 98	DESIRE *Positiva CDTIV 87*	19 3
30 May 98	DEEPER LOVE (SYMPHONIC PARADISE) *Positiva CDTIV 93*	19 3

BBG *UK, male vocal / instrumental group (10 WEEKS)* pos/wks

28 Apr 90	SNAPPINESS *Urban URB 54* [1]	28 5
11 Aug 90	SOME KIND OF HEAVEN *Urban URB 59*	65 2
23 Mar 96	LET THE MUSIC PLAY *MCA MCSTD 40029* [2]	46 1
18 May 96	SNAPPINESS (re-mix) *Hi-Life 5762972*	50 1
5 Jul 97	JUST BE TONIGHT *Hi-Life 5738972* [2]	45 1

[1] BBG featuring Dina Taylor [2] BBG featuring Erin

BBM *UK, male vocal / instrumental group (2 WEEKS)* pos/wks

6 Aug 94	WHERE IN THE WORLD *Virgin VSCD 1495*	57 2

BBMAK *UK, male vocal group (2 WEEKS)* pos/wks

28 Aug 99	BACK HERE *Telstar CDSTAS 3053*	37 2

BC-52's – See B-52's

BE BOP DELUXE
UK, male vocal / instrumental group (13 WEEKS) pos/wks

21 Feb 76	SHIPS IN THE NIGHT *Harvest HAR 5104*	23 8
13 Nov 76	HOT VALVES (EP) *Harvest HAR 5117*	36 5

Tracks on Hot Valves (EP): Maid in Heaven / Blazing Apostles / Jet Silver and the Dolls of Venus / Bring Back the Spark

See also Bill NELSON

BEACH BOYS (36 Top 500) *California family band famous for their harmonies. The most successful and consistently popular US group of the rock era: Brian Wilson (b/k/v), Mike Love (v), Carl Wilson (g/v) (d. 1998), Al Jardine (g/v), Dennis Wilson (d/v) (d. 1983) (281 WEEKS)* pos/wks

1 Aug 63	SURFIN' USA *Capitol CL 15305*	34 7
9 Jul 64 ●	I GET AROUND *Capitol CL 15350* ▲	7 13
29 Oct 64	WHEN I GROW UP (TO BE A MAN) *Capitol CL 15361*	44 2
19 Nov 64	WHEN I GROW UP (TO BE A MAN) (re-entry) *Capitol CL 15361*	27 5
21 Jan 65	DANCE DANCE DANCE *Capitol CL 15370*	24 6

UK No.1 ★   UK Top 10 ●   Still on chart +   UK million seller ◆   UK entry at No.1 ■   US No.1 ▲

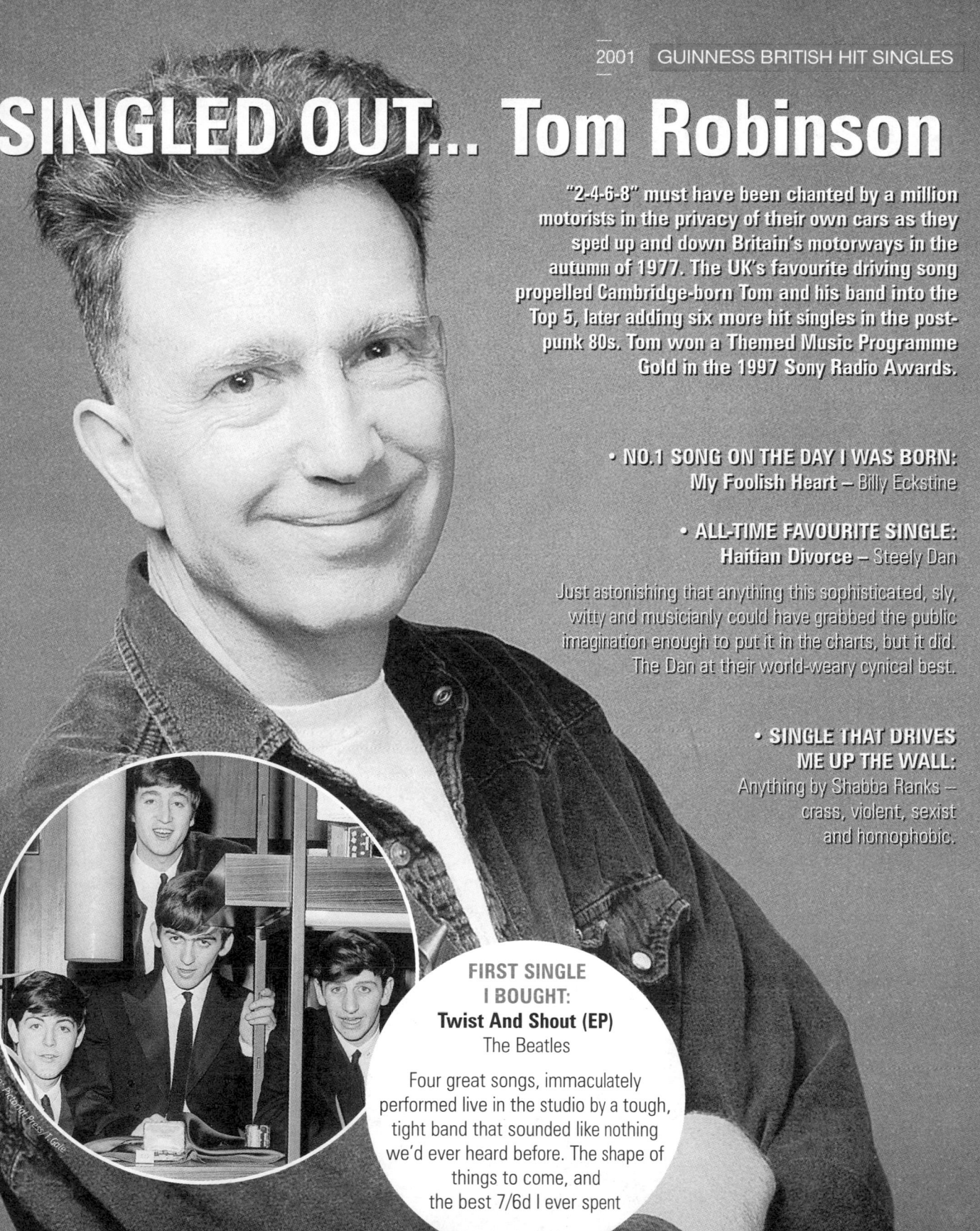

SINGLED OUT... Tom Robinson

"2-4-6-8" must have been chanted by a million motorists in the privacy of their own cars as they sped up and down Britain's motorways in the autumn of 1977. The UK's favourite driving song propelled Cambridge-born Tom and his band into the Top 5, later adding six more hit singles in the post-punk 80s. Tom won a Themed Music Programme Gold in the 1997 Sony Radio Awards.

• **NO.1 SONG ON THE DAY I WAS BORN:**
My Foolish Heart – Billy Eckstine

• **ALL-TIME FAVOURITE SINGLE:**
Haitian Divorce – Steely Dan

Just astonishing that anything this sophisticated, sly, witty and musicianly could have grabbed the public imagination enough to put it in the charts, but it did. The Dan at their world-weary cynical best.

• **SINGLE THAT DRIVES ME UP THE WALL:**
Anything by Shabba Ranks – crass, violent, sexist and homophobic.

FIRST SINGLE I BOUGHT:
Twist And Shout (EP)
The Beatles

Four great songs, immaculately performed live in the studio by a tough, tight band that sounded like nothing we'd ever heard before. The shape of things to come, and the best 7/6d I ever spent

SINGLED OUT...
Dolly Parton

Dolly has written and released more hit singles than you can shake a lil' ol' mountain stick at. Her country / pop writing skills are best displayed on the Whitney Houston interpretation of Dolly's 'I Will Always Love You' which, as the most successful UK Christmas No.1, racked up 29 weeks on the chart – a staggering 10 of which were spent in the top spot.

- **NO.1 ON THE US CHART THE DAY I WAS BORN:**
  Let It Snow! Let It Snow! Let It Snow!
  Vaughn Monroe and His Orchestra

- **ALL-TIME FAVOURITE SINGLE:**
  I always say different things to this question depending when I'm asked, but the one I think of most often is **Sometimes When We Touch** (Dan Hill). I also love **The Wind Beneath My Wings** by Bette Midler.

FIRST SINGLE I BOUGHT:
I WANT TO HOLD YOUR HAND – The Beatles

We'd had records before, because my uncle bought them for us, but I really wanted this one and saved up for it

Photo: Pictorial Press

3 Jun 65	HELP ME RHONDA *Capitol CL 15392* ▲	27	10
2 Sep 65	CALIFORNIA GIRLS *Capitol CL 15409*	26	8
17 Feb 66 ●	BARBARA ANN *Capitol CL 15432*	3	10
21 Apr 66 ●	SLOOP JOHN B *Capitol CL 15441*	2	15
28 Jul 66 ●	GOD ONLY KNOWS *Capitol CL 15459*	2	14
3 Nov 66 ★	GOOD VIBRATIONS *Capitol CL 15475* ▲	1	13
4 May 67 ●	THEN I KISSED HER *Capitol CL 15502*	4	11
23 Aug 67 ●	HEROES AND VILLAINS *Capitol CL 15510*	8	9
22 Nov 67	WILD HONEY *Capitol CL 15521*	29	6
17 Jan 68	DARLIN' *Capitol CL 15527*	11	14
8 May 68	FRIENDS *Capitol CL 15545*	25	7
24 Jul 68 ★	DO IT AGAIN *Capitol CL 15554*	1	14
25 Dec 68	BLUEBIRDS OVER THE MOUNTAIN *Capitol CL 15572*	33	5
26 Feb 69 ●	I CAN HEAR MUSIC *Capitol CL 15584*	10	13
11 Jun 69 ●	BREAK AWAY *Capitol CL 15598*	6	11
16 May 70 ●	COTTONFIELDS *Capitol CL 15640*	5	17
3 Mar 73	CALIFORNIA SAGA - CALIFORNIA *Reprise K 14232*	37	5
3 Jul 76	GOOD VIBRATIONS (re-issue) *Capitol CL 15875*	18	7
10 Jul 76	ROCK AND ROLL MUSIC *Reprise K 14440*	36	4
31 Mar 79	HERE COMES THE NIGHT *Caribou CRB 7204*	37	8
16 Jun 79 ●	LADY LYNDA *Caribou CRB 7427*	6	11
29 Sep 79	SUMAHAMA *Caribou CRB 7846*	45	4
29 Aug 81	BEACH BOYS MEDLEY *Capitol CL 213*	47	4
22 Aug 87	WIPEOUT *Urban URB 5* [1]	2	12
19 Nov 88	KOKOMO *Elektra EKR 85* ▲	25	9
2 Jun 90	WOULDN'T IT BE NICE *Capitol CL 579*	58	1
29 Jun 91	DO IT AGAIN (re-issue) *Capitol EMCT 1*	61	2
2 Mar 96	FUN FUN FUN *PolyGram TV 5762972* [2]	24	4

[1] Fat Boys and the Beach Boys [2] Status Quo with the Beach Boys

Walter BEASLEY *US, male vocalist (3 WEEKS)*

		pos/wks	
23 Jan 88	I'M SO HAPPY *Urban URB 14*	70	3

BEASTIE BOYS *US, male rap group (59 WEEKS)*

		pos/wks	
28 Feb 87	(YOU GOTTA) FIGHT FOR YOUR RIGHT (TO PARTY) *Def Jam 650418 7*	11	11
30 May 87	NO SLEEP TILL BROOKLYN *Def Jam BEAST 1*	14	7
18 Jul 87 ●	SHE'S ON IT *Def Jam BEAST 2*	10	8
3 Oct 87	GIRLS / SHE'S CRAFTY *Def Jam BEAST 3*	34	4
11 Apr 92	PASS THE MIC *Capitol 12CL 653*	47	2
4 Jul 92	FROZEN METAL HEAD (EP) *Capitol 12CL 665*	55	1
9 Jul 94	GET IT TOGETHER / SABOTAGE *Capitol CDCL 716*	19	4
26 Nov 94	SURE SHOT *Capitol CDCL 726*	27	3
4 Jul 98 ●	INTERGALACTIC *Grand Royal CDCL 803*	5	7
7 Nov 98	BODY MOVIN' *Grand Royal CDCL 809*	15	4
16 Jan 99	BODY MOVIN' (re-entry) *Grand Royal CDCL 809*	69	1
29 May 99	REMOTE CONTROL / 3 MCS & 1 DJ *Grand Royal CDCL 812*	21	3
18 Dec 99	ALIVE *Grand Royal CDCL 818*	28	4

Tracks on Frozen Metal Head (EP): Jimmy James / Jimmy James (Original) / Drinkin' Wine / The Blue Nun

BEAT (331) Top 500 *Birmingham, UK-based band, who married ska and new wave influences, formed 1978; Dave Wakeling (v/g), Ranking Roger (v), Andy Cox (g) and David Steele (b). After 1983 break-up, former two launched General Public and latter pair formed Fine Young Cannibals (92 WEEKS)*

		pos/wks	
8 Dec 79 ●	TEARS OF A CLOWN / RANKING FULL STOP *2 Tone CHSTT 6*	6	11
23 Feb 80 ●	HANDS OFF - SHE'S MINE *Go Feet FEET 1*	9	9
3 May 80 ●	MIRROR IN THE BATHROOM *Go Feet FEET 2*	4	9
16 Aug 80	BEST FRIEND / STAND DOWN MARGARET (DUB) *Go Feet FEET 3*	22	9
13 Dec 80 ●	TOO NICE TO TALK TO *Go Feet FEET 4*	7	11
18 Apr 81	DROWNING / ALL OUT TO GET YOU *Go Feet FEET 6*	22	8
20 Jun 81	DOORS OF YOUR HEART *Go Feet FEET 9*	33	6
5 Dec 81	HIT IT *Go Feet FEET 11*	70	2
17 Apr 82	SAVE IT FOR LATER *Go Feet FEET 333*	47	4
18 Sep 82	JEANETTE *Go Feet FEET 15*	45	3
4 Dec 82	I CONFESS *Go Feet FEET 16*	54	3
30 Apr 83 ●	CAN'T GET USED TO LOSING YOU *Go Feet FEET 17*	3	11
2 Jul 83	ACKEE 1-2-3 *Go Feet FEET 18*	54	4
27 Jan 96	MIRROR IN THE BATHROOM (re-mix) *Go Feet 74321232062*	44	2

BEAT SYSTEM *UK, male vocal / instrumental group (3 WEEKS)*

		pos/wks	
3 Mar 90	WALK ON THE WILD SIDE *Fourth & Broadway BRW 163*	63	2
18 Sep 93	TO A BRIGHTER DAY (O' HAPPY DAY) *ffrr FCD 217*	70	1

BEATCHUGGERS
Denmark, male producer - Michael Linde (2 WEEKS)

		pos/wks	
18 Nov 00	FOREVER MAN (HOW MANY TIMES) *ffrr FCD 386* [1]	26	2

[1] Beatchuggers featuring Eric Clapton

BEATLES (9) Top 500 *World's most successful group. John Lennon (v/g) b. 9 Oct, 1940, Liverpool, d. 8 Dec 1980, New York, Paul McCartney (v/b) b. 18 Jun 1942, Liverpool, George Harrison (v/g) b. 24 Feb 1943, Liverpool, Ringo Starr (Richard Starkey) (v/d) b. 7 Jul 1940, Liverpool. Legendary group, who changed the face of popular music. Achievements include: most No.1 singles and albums in the UK and US. Within three months of their US chart debut in 1964, they held all the Top 5 single chart places, had a record 14 simultaneous entries on Billboard Top 100 and had the two top-selling albums. During those 12 weeks they earned six gold singles and sold four million albums. Their album Sgt. Pepper's Lonely Hearts Club Band is the biggest-seller ever in the UK, and group is No.1 all time US best-selling album act. They split in 1970, since when Lennon, McCartney and Harrison have all had No.1 singles (Starr reached No. 2). In 1996, double album Anthology sold 10 million worldwide in only four weeks. 2000's 1 collection is the world's fastest selling album ever with 13.5 million in first month and was the top-selling album of 2000 in the UK. The Beatles, who were awarded MBEs in 1965, have sold an estimated one billion records. (456 WEEKS)*

		pos/wks	
11 Oct 62	LOVE ME DO *Parlophone R 4949* ▲	17	18
17 Jan 63 ●	PLEASE PLEASE ME *Parlophone R 4983*	2	18
18 Apr 63 ★	FROM ME TO YOU *Parlophone R 5015*	1	21
6 Jun 63	MY BONNIE *Polydor NH 66833* [1]	48	1
29 Aug 63 ★	SHE LOVES YOU *Parlophone R 5055* ◆ ▲	1	31
5 Dec 63 ★	I WANT TO HOLD YOUR HAND *Parlophone R 5084* ◆ ▲	1	21
26 Mar 64 ★	CAN'T BUY ME LOVE *Parlophone R 5114* ◆ ▲	1	14
9 Apr 64	SHE LOVES YOU (re-entry) *Parlophone R 5055*	42	2
14 May 64	I WANT TO HOLD YOUR HAND (re-entry) *Parlophone R 5084*	48	1
11 Jun 64	AIN'T SHE SWEET *Polydor 52 317*	29	6
9 Jul 64	CAN'T BUY ME LOVE (re-entry) *Parlophone R 5114*	47	1
16 Jul 64 ★	A HARD DAY'S NIGHT *Parlophone R 5160* ▲	1	13
3 Dec 64 ★	I FEEL FINE *Parlophone R 5200* ◆ ▲	1	13
15 Apr 65 ★	TICKET TO RIDE *Parlophone R 5265* ▲	1	12
29 Jul 65 ★	HELP! *Parlophone R 5305* ▲	1	14
9 Dec 65 ★	DAY TRIPPER / WE CAN WORK IT OUT *Parlophone R 5389* ◆ ▲	1	12
16 Jun 66 ★	PAPERBACK WRITER *Parlophone R 5452* ▲	1	11
11 Aug 66 ★	YELLOW SUBMARINE / ELEANOR RIGBY *Parlophone R 5493*	1	13
23 Feb 67 ●	PENNY LANE / STRAWBERRY FIELDS FOREVER *Parlophone R 5570*	2	11
12 Jul 67 ★	ALL YOU NEED IS LOVE *Parlophone R 5620* ▲	1	13
29 Nov 67 ★	HELLO GOODBYE *Parlophone R 5655* ▲	1	12
13 Dec 67 ●	MAGICAL MYSTERY TOUR (DOUBLE EP) *Parlophone SMMT/MMT 1*	2	12
20 Mar 68 ★	LADY MADONNA *Parlophone R 5675*	1	8
4 Sep 68 ★	HEY JUDE *Apple R 5722* ▲	1	16
23 Apr 69 ★	GET BACK *Apple R 5777* [2] ■ ▲	1	17
4 Jun 69 ★	BALLAD OF JOHN AND YOKO *Apple R 5786*	1	14
8 Nov 69 ●	SOMETHING / COME TOGETHER *Apple R 5814* ▲	4	12
14 Mar 70 ●	LET IT BE *Apple R 5833* ▲	2	9
24 Oct 70	LET IT BE (re-entry) *Apple R 5833*	43	1
13 Mar 76 ●	YESTERDAY *Apple R 6013* ▲	8	7
27 Mar 76	HEY JUDE *Apple R 5722*	12	7
27 Mar 76	PAPERBACK WRITER (re-entry) *Parlophone R 5452*	23	5
3 Apr 76	GET BACK (re-entry) *Apple R 5777* [2]	28	5
3 Apr 76	STRAWBERRY FIELDS FOREVER (re-entry) *Parlophone R 5570*	32	3
10 Apr 76	HELP! (re-entry) *Parlophone R 5305*	37	3
10 Jul 76	BACK IN THE USSR *Parlophone R 6016*	19	6
7 Oct 78	SGT. PEPPER'S LONELY HEARTS CLUB BAND - WITH A LITTLE HELP FROM MY FRIENDS *Parlophone R 6022*	63	3

		pos	wks
5 Jun 82 ●	BEATLES MOVIE MEDLEY *Parlophone R 6055*......	10	9
16 Oct 82 ●	LOVE ME DO (re-entry) *Parlophone R 4949*......	4	7
22 Jan 83	PLEASE PLEASE ME (re-entry) *Parlophone R 4983*.....	29	4
23 Apr 83	FROM ME TO YOU (re-entry) *Parlophone R 5015*	40	4
3 Sep 83	SHE LOVES YOU (2nd re-entry) *Parlophone R 5055*.....	45	3
26 Nov 83	I WANT TO HOLD YOUR HAND (2nd re-entry) *Parlophone R 5084*......	62	2
31 Mar 84	CAN'T BUY ME LOVE (2nd re-entry) *Parlophone R 5114*......	53	2
21 Jul 84	A HARD DAY'S NIGHT (re-entry) *Parlophone R 5160*......	52	2
8 Dec 84	I FEEL FINE (re-entry) *Parlophone R 5200*	65	1
20 Apr 85	TICKET TO RIDE (re-entry) *Parlophone R 5265*......	70	2
30 Aug 86	YELLOW SUBMARINE / ELEANOR RIGBY (re-entry) *Parlophone R 5493*......	63	1
28 Feb 87	PENNY LANE (re-entry) / STRAWBERRY FIELDS FOREVER (2nd re-entry) *Parlophone R 5570*......	65	2
18 Jul 87	ALL YOU NEED IS LOVE (re-entry) *Parlophone R 5620*......	47	3
5 Dec 87	HELLO GOODBYE (re-entry) *Parlophone R 5655*......	63	1
26 Mar 88	LADY MADONNA (re-entry) *Parlophone R 5675*......	67	1
10 Sep 88	HEY JUDE (2nd re-entry) *Apple R 5722*	52	2
22 Apr 89	GET BACK (2nd re-entry) *Apple R 5777* [2]	74	1
17 Oct 92	LOVE ME DO (2nd re-entry) *Parlophone R 4949*......	53	1
1 Apr 95 ●	BABY IT'S YOU *Apple CDR 6406*......	7	6
8 Jul 95	BABY IT'S YOU (re-entry) *Apple CDR 6406*......	71	1
16 Dec 95 ●	FREE AS A BIRD *Apple CDR 6422*	2	8
16 Mar 96 ●	REAL LOVE *Apple CDR 6425*	4	7

[1] Tony Sheridan and the Beatles [2] Beatles with Billy Preston

Tracks on Magical Mystery Tour (EP): Magical Mystery Tour / Your Mother Should Know / I Am the Walrus / Fool on the Hill / Flying / Blue Jay Way

See also Paul McCARTNEY; Ringo STARR; John LENNON; George HARRISON

BEATMASTERS *UK, male / female production group (47 WEEKS)* pos/wks

9 Jan 88 ●	ROK DA HOUSE *Rhythm King LEFT 11* [1]......	5	11
24 Sep 88	BURN IT UP *Rhythm King LEFT 27* [2]	14	10
22 Apr 89 ●	WHO'S IN THE HOUSE *Rhythm King LEFT 31* [3]	8	9
12 Aug 89 ●	HEY DJ - I CAN'T DANCE (TO THAT MUSIC YOU'RE PLAYING) / SKA TRAIN *Rhythm King LEFT 34* [4]	7	11
2 Dec 89	WARM LOVE *Rhythm King LEFT 37* [5]	51	2
21 Sep 91	BOULEVARD OF BROKEN DREAMS *Rhythm King 6573617*......	62	1
16 May 92	DUNNO WHAT IT IS (ABOUT YOU) *Rhythm King 6580017* [6]	43	3

[1] Beatmasters featuring the Cookie Crew [2] Beatmasters with PP Arnold [3] Beatmasters featuring Merlin [4] Beatmasters featuring Betty Boo [5] Beatmasters featuring Claudia Fontaine [6] Beatmasters featuring Elaine Vassell

BEATRICE – See Mike KOGLIN

BEATS INTERNATIONAL
UK, male / female vocal / instrumental group - leader Norman Cook (30 WEEKS) pos/wks

10 Feb 90 ★	DUB BE GOOD TO ME *Go.Beat GOD 39* [1]	1	13
12 May 90 ●	WON'T TALK ABOUT IT *Go.Beat GOD 43*......	9	7
15 Sep 90	BURUNDI BLUES *Go.Beat GOD 45*......	51	3
2 Mar 91	ECHO CHAMBER *Go.Beat GOD 51*......	60	2
21 Sep 91	THE SUN DOESN'T SHINE *Go.Beat GOD 59*	66	2
23 Nov 91	IN THE GHETTO *Go.Beat GOD 64*	44	3

[1] Beats International featuring Lindy Layton

See also FREAKPOWER; PIZZAMAN; Norman COOK; FATBOY SLIM; MIGHTY DUB KATZ; HOUSEMARTINS

BEAUTIFUL PEOPLE
UK, male instrumental / sampling group (1 WEEK) pos/wks

28 May 94	IF 60S WERE 90S *Essential ESSX 2037*......	74	1

BEAUTIFUL SOUTH (145) Top 500 Ex-Housemartins Paul Heaton (v/g) and Dave Hemingway (v) (from the beautiful north of England) formed the

band that featured Briana Corrigan (v) (replaced by Jacqui Abbot in 1994). Heaton and Dave Rotheray (g) write the witty and ironic songs
(150 WEEKS) pos/wks

3 Jun 89 ●	SONG FOR WHOEVER *Go! Discs GOD 32*	2	11
23 Sep 89 ●	YOU KEEP IT ALL IN *Go! Discs GOD 35*	8	8
2 Dec 89	I'LL SAIL THIS SHIP ALONE *Go! Discs GOD 38*	31	8
6 Oct 90 ★	A LITTLE TIME *Go! Discs GOD 47*	1	14
8 Dec 90	MY BOOK *Go! Discs GOD 48*	43	6
16 Mar 91	LET LOVE SPEAK UP ITSELF *Go! Discs GOD 53*	51	2
11 Jan 92	OLD RED EYES IS BACK *Go! Discs GOD 66*	22	6
14 Mar 92	WE ARE EACH OTHER *Go! Discs GOD 71*	30	3
13 Jun 92	BELL BOTTOMED TEAR *Go! Discs GOD 78*	16	5
26 Sep 92	36D *Go! Discs GOD 88*	46	2
12 Mar 94	GOOD AS GOLD *Go! Discs GODCD 110*	23	5
4 Jun 94	EVERYBODY'S TALKIN' *Go! Discs GODCD 113*	12	8
3 Sep 94	PRETTIEST EYES *Go! Discs GODCD 119*	37	3
12 Nov 94	ONE LAST LOVE SONG *Go! Discs GODCD 122*	14	5
18 Nov 95	PRETENDERS TO THE THRONE *Go! Discs GODCD 134*	18	4
12 Oct 96 ●	ROTTERDAM *Go! Discs GODCD 155*	5	9
14 Dec 96 ●	DON'T MARRY HER *Go! Discs GODCD 158*	8	10
29 Mar 97	BLACKBIRD ON THE WIRE *Go! Discs 5821252*	23	5
5 Jul 97	LIARS' BAR *Go! Discs 5822492*	43	1
3 Oct 98 ●	PERFECT 10 *Go! Discs 5664832*	2	14
19 Dec 98	DUMB *Go! Discs 5667532*	16	7
13 Mar 99	DUMB *Go! Discs 5667532*	72	1
20 Mar 99	HOW LONG'S A TEAR TAKE TO DRY? *Go! Discs 8708212*	12	6
10 Jul 99	THE TABLE *Go! Discs 5621652*	47	2
7 Oct 00	CLOSER THAN MOST *Go! Discs / Mercury 5629672*	22	4
23 Dec 00	THE RIVER / JUST CHECKIN' *Go! Discs / Mercury 5727552*	59	1

BEAVIS and BUTT-HEAD – See CHER

Gilbert BECAUD *France, male vocalist (12 WEEKS)* pos/wks

29 Mar 75 ●	A LITTLE LOVE AND UNDERSTANDING *Decca F 13537*......	10	12

BECK *US, male vocalist (27 WEEKS)* pos/wks

5 Mar 94	LOSER *Geffen GFSTD 67*	15	6
29 Jun 96	WHERE IT'S AT *Geffen GFSTD 22156*	35	2
16 Nov 96	DEVIL'S HAIRCUT *Geffen GFSTD 22183*	22	2
8 Mar 97	THE NEW POLLUTION *Geffen GFSTD 22205*	14	5
24 May 97	SISSYNECK *Geffen GFSTD 22253*	30	2
8 Nov 97	DEADWEIGHT *Geffen GFSTD 22293*	23	3
19 Dec 98	TROPICALIA *Geffen GFSTD 22365*	39	2
20 Nov 99	SEXX LAWS *Geffen 4971812*	27	3
8 Apr 00	MIXED BIZNESS *Geffen 4973002*	34	2

Jeff BECK *UK, male vocalist / instrumentalist - guitar (57 WEEKS)* pos/wks

23 Mar 67	HI-HO SILVER LINING *Columbia DB 8151*	14	14
2 Aug 67	TALLYMAN *Columbia DB 8227*	30	3
28 Feb 68	LOVE IS BLUE *Columbia DB 8359*	23	7
9 Jul 69	GOO GOO BARABAJAGAL (LOVE IS HOT) *Pye 7N 17778* [1]	12	9
4 Nov 72	HI-HO SILVER LINING (re-issue) *RAK RR 3*	17	11
5 May 73	I'VE BEEN DRINKING *RAK RR 4* [2]	27	6
9 Oct 82	HI-HO SILVER LINING (re-entry of re-issue) *RAK RR 3*	62	4
7 Mar 92	PEOPLE GET READY *Epic 6577567* [2]	49	3

[1] Donovan with the Jeff Beck Group [2] Jeff Beck and Rod Stewart

Robin BECK *US, female vocalist (13 WEEKS)* pos/wks

22 Oct 88 ★	THE FIRST TIME *Mercury MER 270*	1	13

Peter BECKETT – See Barry GRAY ORCHESTRA

Victoria BECKHAM – See SPICE GIRLS; TRUE STEPPERS

BEDAZZLED *UK, male vocal / instrumental group (1 WEEK)* pos/wks

4 Jul 92	SUMMER SONG *Columbia 6581627*	73	1

BEDLAM *UK, male DJ production duo (1 WEEK)* pos/wks

6 Feb 99	DA-FORCE *Playola 0091695 PLA*	68	1

UK No.1 ★   UK Top 10 ●   Still on chart +   UK million seller ◆   UK entry at No.1 ■   US No.1 ▲

BEDLAM AGO GO UK, male vocal / instrumental group (1 WEEK) pos/wks
| 4 Apr 98 | SEASON NO. 5 *Sony S2 BDLM 2CD* | 57 | 1 |

BEDROCK
UK, male / female vocal / instrumental group (9 WEEKS) pos/wks
1 Jun 96	FOR WHAT YOU DREAM OF *Stress CDSTR 23* [1]	25	3
12 Jul 97	SET IN STONE / FORBIDDEN ZONE *Stress CDSTR 80*	71	1
6 Nov 99	HEAVEN SCENT *Bedrock BEDRCDS 001*	35	3
8 Jul 00	VOICES *Bedrock BEDRCDS 005*	44	2

[1] Bedrock Featuring KYO

BEDROCKS UK, male vocal / instrumental group (7 WEEKS) pos/wks
| 18 Dec 68 | OB-LA-DI OB-LA-DA *Columbia DB 8516* | 20 | 7 |

Celi BEE and the BUZZY BUNCH
US, male / female vocal / instrumental group (1 WEEK) pos/wks
| 17 Jun 78 | HOLD YOUR HORSES BABE *TK TKR 6032* | 72 | 1 |

BEE GEES [18] Top 500 *All-time top family recording act. Group nucleus: British-born and Australian-raised Barry, Robin and Maurice Gibb. Among other achievements, they have composed 10 UK No.1s, and in 1978 penned four consecutive US chart-toppers (349 WEEKS)* pos/wks
27 Apr 67	NEW YORK MINING DISASTER 1941 *Polydor 56 161*	12	10
12 Jul 67	TO LOVE SOMEBODY *Polydor 56 178*	50	1
26 Jul 67	TO LOVE SOMEBODY (re-entry) *Polydor 56 178*	41	4
20 Sep 67	★ MASSACHUSETTS *Polydor 56 192*	1	17
22 Nov 67	● WORLD *Polydor 56 220*	9	16
31 Jan 68	● WORDS *Polydor 56 229*	8	10
27 Mar 68	JUMBO / THE SINGER SANG HIS SONG *Polydor 56 242*	25	7
7 Aug 68	● I'VE GOTTA GET A MESSAGE TO YOU *Polydor 56 273*	1	15
19 Feb 69	● FIRST OF MAY *Polydor 56 304*	6	11
4 Jun 69	TOMORROW TOMORROW *Polydor 56 331*	23	8
16 Aug 69	● DON'T FORGET TO REMEMBER *Polydor 56 343*	2	15
28 Mar 70	I.O.I.O. *Polydor 56 377*	49	1
5 Dec 70	LONELY DAYS *Polydor 2001 104*	33	9
29 Jan 72	MY WORLD *Polydor 2058 185*	16	9
22 Jul 72	● RUN TO ME *Polydor 2058 255*	9	10
28 Jun 75	● JIVE TALKIN' *RSO 2090 160* ▲	5	11
31 Jul 76	● YOU SHOULD BE DANCING *RSO 2090 195* ▲	5	10
13 Nov 76	LOVE SO RIGHT *RSO 2090 207*	41	4
29 Oct 77	● HOW DEEP IS YOUR LOVE *RSO 2090 259* ▲	3	15
4 Feb 78	● STAYIN' ALIVE *RSO 2090 267* ▲	4	12
15 Apr 78	★ NIGHT FEVER *RSO 002* ▲	1	20
13 May 78	STAYIN' ALIVE (re-entry) *RSO 2090 267*	63	6
25 Nov 78	● TOO MUCH HEAVEN *RSO 25* ▲	3	13
17 Feb 79	★ TRAGEDY *RSO 27* ▲	1	10
14 Apr 79	LOVE YOU INSIDE OUT *RSO 31* ▲	13	9
5 Jan 80	SPIRITS (HAVING FLOWN) *RSO 52*	16	7
17 Sep 83	SOMEONE BELONGING TO SOMEONE *RSO 96*	49	4
26 Sep 87	★ YOU WIN AGAIN *Warner Bros. W 8351*	1	15
12 Dec 87	E.S.P. *Warner Bros. W 8139*	51	5
15 Apr 89	ORDINARY LIVES *Warner Bros. W 7523*	54	3
24 Jun 89	ONE *Warner Bros. W 2916*	71	1
2 Mar 91	● SECRET LOVE *Warner Bros. W 0014*	5	11
21 Aug 93	PAYING THE PRICE OF LOVE *Polydor PZCD 284*	23	5
27 Nov 93	● FOR WHOM THE BELL TOLLS *Polydor PZCD 299*	4	14
16 Apr 94	HOW TO FALL IN LOVE PART 1 *Polydor PZDD 311*	30	4
1 Mar 97	● ALONE *Polydor 5735272*	5	9
21 Jun 97	I COULD NOT LOVE YOU MORE *Polydor 5712232*	14	3
8 Nov 97	STILL WATERS (RUN DEEP) *Polydor 5718892*	18	3
18 Jul 98	● IMMORTALITY *Epic 6661682* [1]	5	12

[1] Celine Dion with Bee Gees

See also Robin GIBB; Barry GIBB

BEENIE MAN
Jamaica, male vocalist / toaster / rapper - Moses David (16 WEEKS) pos/wks
| 20 Sep 97 | DANCEHALL QUEEN *Island Jamaica IJCD 2018* | 70 | 1 |
| 7 Mar 98 | ● WHO AM I *Greensleeves GRECD 588* | 10 | 5 |

| 8 Aug 98 | FOUNDATION *Shocking Vibes SVJCDS1* | 69 | 1 |
| 4 Mar 00 | ● MONEY *Parlophone Rhythm Series CDRHYTHM 27* [1] | 5 | 9 |

[1] Jamelia featuring Beenie Man

BEF Featuring Lalah Hathaway
US male production group featuring female vocalist (5 WEEKS) pos/wks
| 27 Jul 91 | FAMILY AFFAIR *Ten TEN 369* | 37 | 5 |

Lou BEGA *Germany, male vocalist - David Lubega (21 WEEKS)* pos/wks
7 Aug 99	MAMBO NO.5 (A LITTLE BIT OF ...) (IMPORT) *Ariola 74321658012*	31	4
4 Sep 99	★ MAMBO NO.5 (A LITTLE BIT OF ...) *RCA 74321696722* ■	1	15
18 Dec 99	I GOT A GIRL *RCA 74321720642*	55	2

BEGGAR and CO
UK, male vocal / instrumental group (15 WEEKS) pos/wks
| 7 Feb 81 | (SOMEBODY) HELP ME OUT *Ensign ENY 201* | 15 | 10 |
| 12 Sep 81 | MULE (CHANT NO 2) *RCA 130* | 37 | 5 |

BEGINNING OF THE END
US, male vocal / instrumental group (6 WEEKS) pos/wks
| 23 Feb 74 | FUNKY NASSAU *Atlantic K 10021* | 31 | 6 |

BEIJING SPRING *UK, female vocal duo (5 WEEKS)* pos/wks
| 23 Jan 93 | I WANNA BE IN LOVE AGAIN *MCA MCSTD 1709* | 43 | 3 |
| 8 May 93 | SUMMERLANDS *MCA MCSTD 1761* | 53 | 2 |

BEL CANTO *UK, male vocal / instrumental group (1 WEEK)* pos/wks
| 14 Oct 95 | WE'VE GOT TO WORK IT OUT *Good Groove CDGG 2* | 65 | 1 |

Harry BELAFONTE [355] Top 500 *Singer / actor, civil rights campaigner and driving force behind USA for Africa b. 1 Mar 1927, New York, US. Started transatlantic calypso craze in 1957 when his LP, Calypso, topped US chart for 31 weeks. Became Unicef goodwill ambassador in 1987 (87 WEEKS)* pos/wks
1 Mar 57	● BANANA BOAT SONG *HMV POP 308* [1]	2	18
14 Jun 57	● ISLAND IN THE SUN *RCA 1007*	3	25
6 Sep 57	SCARLET RIBBONS *HMV POP 360* [2]	18	6
1 Nov 57	★ MARY'S BOY CHILD *RCA 1022*	1	12
22 Aug 58	LITTLE BERNADETTE *RCA 1072* [3]	16	7
28 Nov 58	● MARY'S BOY CHILD (re-entry) *RCA 1022* ◆	10	6
12 Dec 58	SON OF MARY *RCA 1084*	18	4
11 Dec 59	MARY'S BOY CHILD (2nd re-entry) *RCA 1022*	30	1
21 Sep 61	HOLE IN THE BUCKET *RCA 1247* [4]	32	2
12 Oct 61	HOLE IN THE BUCKET (re-entry) *RCA 1247* [4]	34	6

[1] Harry Belafonte With Tony Scott's Orchestra & Chorus & Millard Thomas, Guitar [2] Harry Belafonte and Millard Thomas [3] Belafonte [4] Harry Belafonte and Odetta

BELL and JAMES *US, male vocal duo (3 WEEKS)* pos/wks
| 31 Mar 79 | LIVIN' IT UP (FRIDAY NIGHT) *A & M AMS 7424* | 68 | 1 |
| 14 Apr 79 | LIVIN' IT UP (FRIDAY NIGHT) (re-entry) *A & M AMS 7424* | 59 | 2 |

Archie BELL and the DRELLS
US, male vocal / instrumental group (33 WEEKS) pos/wks
7 Oct 72	HERE I GO AGAIN *Atlantic K 10210*	11	10
27 Jan 73	THERE'S GONNA BE A SHOWDOWN *Atlantic K 10263*	36	5
8 May 76	SOUL CITY WALK *Philadelphia International PIR 4250*	13	10
11 Jun 77	EVERYBODY HAVE A GOOD TIME *Philadelphia International PIR 5179*	43	4
28 Jun 86	DON'T LET LOVE GET YOU DOWN *Portrait A 7254*	49	4

BELL BIV DEVOE *US, male vocal group (29 WEEKS)* pos/wks
| 30 Jun 90 | POISON *MCA MCA 1414* | 19 | 11 |
| 22 Sep 90 | DO ME *MCA MCA 1440* | 56 | 3 |

15 Aug 92	●	THE BEST THINGS IN LIFE ARE FREE		
		Perspective PERSS 7400 [1]	**2**	13
9 Oct 93		SOMETHING IN YOUR EYES *MCA MCSTD 1934*	**60**	2

[1] Luther Vandross and Janet Jackson with special guests BBD and Ralph Tresvant

BELL BOOK & CANDLE
Germany, male / female vocal / instrumental group (1 WEEK) pos/wks

17 Oct 98		RESCUE ME *Logic 74321616882*	**63**	1

Freddie BELL and the BELLBOYS
US, male vocal / instrumental group (10 WEEKS) pos/wks

28 Sep 56	●	GIDDY-UP-A-DING-DONG *Mercury MT 122*	**4**	10

BELLAMY BROTHERS
US, male vocal duo - Howard & David Bellamy (29 WEEKS) pos/wks

17 Apr 76	●	LET YOUR LOVE FLOW *Warner Bros. K 16690* ▲	**7**	12
21 Aug 76		SATIN SHEETS *Warner Bros. K 16775*	**43**	3
11 Aug 79	●	IF I SAID YOU HAVE A BEAUTIFUL BODY WOULD YOU HOLD IT AGAINST ME *Warner Bros. K 17405*	**3**	14

BELLBOYS – See Freddie BELL and the BELLBOYS

Maggie BELL
UK, female vocalist (12 WEEKS) pos/wks

15 Apr 78		HAZELL *Swansong SSK 19412*	**37**	3
13 May 78		HAZELL (re-entry) *Swansong SSK 19412*	**74**	1
17 Oct 81		HOLD ME *Swansong BAM 1* [1]	**11**	8

[1] BA Robertson and Maggie Bell

William BELL
US, male vocalist - William Yarborough (22 WEEKS) pos/wks

29 May 68		TRIBUTE TO A KING *Stax 601 038*	**31**	7
20 Nov 68	●	PRIVATE NUMBER *Stax 101* [1]	**8**	14
26 Apr 86		HEADLINE NEWS *Absolute LUTE 1*	**70**	1

[1] Judy Clay and William Bell

BELLATRIX
Iceland, male / female vocal / instrumental group (1 WEEK) pos/wks

16 Sep 00		JEDI WANNABE *Fierce Panda NING 101CD*	**65**	1

BELLE & SEBASTIAN
UK, male / female vocal / instrumental group (8 WEEKS) pos/wks

24 May 97		DOG ON WHEELS *Jeepster JPRCDS 001*	**59**	1
9 Aug 97		LAZY LINE PAINTER JANE *Jeepster JPRCDS 002*	**41**	2
25 Oct 97		3... 6... 9 SECONDS OF LIGHT (EP) *Jeepster JPRCDS 003*	**32**	2
3 Jun 00		LEGAL MAN *Jeepster JPRCD 018*	**15**	3

Tracks on 3... 6... 9 Seconds of Light (EP): A Century of Fakers / Le Pastie de la Bourgeoisie / Beautiful / Put The Book Back On The Shelf

BELLE and the DEVOTIONS
UK, female vocal group (8 WEEKS) pos/wks

21 Apr 84		LOVE GAMES *CBS A 4332*	**11**	8

Regina BELLE
US, female vocalist (13 WEEKS) pos/wks

21 Oct 89		GOOD LOVIN' *CBS 655230*	**73**	1
11 Dec 93		A WHOLE NEW WORLD (ALADDIN'S THEME) *Columbia 6599002* [1] ▲	**12**	12

[1] Regina Belle and Peabo Bryson

BELLE STARS
UK, female vocal / instrumental group (42 WEEKS) pos/wks

5 Jun 82		IKO IKO *Stiff BUY 150*	**35**	6
17 Jul 82		THE CLAPPING SONG *Stiff BUY 155*	**11**	9
16 Oct 82		MOCKINGBIRD *Stiff BUY 159*	**51**	3
15 Jan 83	●	SIGN OF THE TIMES *Stiff BUY 167*	**3**	11
16 Apr 83		SWEET MEMORY *Stiff BUY 174*	**22**	9
13 Aug 83		INDIAN SUMMER *Stiff BUY 185*	**52**	3
14 Jul 84		80s ROMANCE *Stiff BUY 200*	**71**	1

BELLINI
Germany, male vocal / production group (7 WEEKS) pos/wks

27 Sep 97	●	SAMBA DE JANEIRO *Virgin DINSD 165*	**8**	7

Louis BELLSON – See Duke ELLINGTON

BELLY
US, male / female vocal / instrumental group (9 WEEKS) pos/wks

23 Jan 93		FEED THE TREE *4AD BAD 3001CD*	**32**	3
10 Apr 93		GEPETTO *4AD BAD 2018CD*	**49**	2
4 Feb 95		NOW THEY'LL SLEEP *4AD BAD 5003CD*	**28**	2
22 Jul 95		SEAL MY FATE *4AD BAD 5007CD*	**35**	2

BELMONTS – See DION

BELOUIS SOME
UK, male vocalist (26 WEEKS) pos/wks

27 Apr 85		IMAGINATION *Parlophone R 6097*	**50**	7
18 Jan 86		IMAGINATION (re-issue) *Parlophone R 1986*	**17**	10
12 Apr 86		SOME PEOPLE *Parlophone R 6130*	**33**	7
16 May 87		LET IT BE WITH YOU *Parlophone R 6154*	**53**	2

BELOVED
UK, male / female vocal / instrumental duo (47 WEEKS) pos/wks

21 Oct 89		THE SUN RISING *WEA YZ 414*	**26**	7
27 Jan 90		HELLO *WEA YZ 426*	**19**	7
24 Mar 90		YOUR LOVE TAKES ME HIGHER *East West YZ 463*	**39**	3
9 Jun 90		TIME AFTER TIME *East West YZ 482*	**46**	4
10 Nov 90		IT'S ALRIGHT NOW *East West YZ 541*	**48**	3
23 Jan 93	●	SWEET HARMONY *East West YZ 709CD*	**8**	10
10 Apr 93		YOU'VE GOT ME THINKING *East West YZ 738CD*	**23**	4
14 Aug 93		OUTERSPACE GIRL *East West YZ 726CD*	**38**	2
30 Mar 96		SATELLITE *East West EW 034CD*	**19**	3
10 Aug 96		EASE THE PRESSURE *East West EW 058CD*	**43**	2
30 Aug 97		THE SUN RISING (re-issue) *East West EW 122CD1*	**31**	2

Act was male only before 1993

BELTRAM
US, male producer - Joey Beltram (4 WEEKS) pos/wks

28 Sep 91		ENERGY FLASH (EP) *R&S RSUK 3*	**52**	2
7 Dec 91		THE OMEN *R&S RSUK 7* [1]	**53**	2

[1] Program 2 Beltram

Tracks on Energy Flash (EP): Energy Flash / Psycho Bass / My Sound / Sub-Base Experience

Pat BENATAR
US, female vocalist (53 WEEKS) pos/wks

21 Jan 84		LOVE IS A BATTLEFIELD *Chrysalis CHS 2747*	**49**	5
12 Jan 85		WE BELONG *Chrysalis CHS 2821*	**22**	9
23 Mar 85		LOVE IS A BATTLEFIELD (re-issue) *Chrysalis PAT 1*	**17**	10
15 Jun 85		SHADOWS OF THE NIGHT *Chrysalis PAT 2*	**50**	4
19 Oct 85		INVINCIBLE (THEME FROM 'THE LEGEND OF BILLIE JEAN') *Chrysalis PAT 3*	**53**	3
15 Feb 86		SEX AS A WEAPON *Chrysalis PAT 4*	**67**	3
2 Jul 88		ALL FIRED UP *Chrysalis PAT 5*	**19**	10
1 Oct 88		DON'T WALK AWAY *Chrysalis PAT 6*	**42**	5
14 Jan 89		ONE LOVE *Chrysalis PAT 7*	**59**	3
30 Oct 93		SOMEBODY'S BABY *Chrysalis CDCHS 5001*	**48**	1

David BENDETH
Canada, male vocalist and multi-instrumentalist (5 WEEKS) pos/wks

8 Sep 79		FEEL THE REAL *Sidewalk SID 113*	**44**	5

BENELUX and Nancy DEE
Belgium / Holland / Luxembourg, female vocal group (4 WEEKS) pos/wks

25 Aug 79		SWITCH *Scope SC 4*	**52**	4

Eric BENET
US, male vocalist (5 WEEKS) pos/wks

22 Mar 97		SPIRITUAL THANG *Warner Bros. W 0390CD*	**62**	1
1 May 99		GEORGY PORGY *Warner Bros. W478CD2* [1]	**28**	3
5 Feb 00		WHY YOU FOLLOW ME *Warner Bros. W491CD*	**48**	1

[1] Eric Benet featuring Faith Evans

Nigel BENN – See PACK featuring Nigel BENN

BENNET UK, male vocal / instrumental group (3 WEEKS)
pos/wks
22 Feb 97	MUM'S GONE TO ICELAND *Roadrunner RR 22853*	34	2
3 May 97	SOMEONE ALWAYS GETS THERE FIRST *Roadrunner RR 22983*	69	1

Boyd BENNETT and his ROCKETS
US, male vocalist and male vocal / instrumental group (2 WEEKS)
pos/wks
23 Dec 55	SEVENTEEN *Parlophone R 4063*	16	2

Chris BENNETT – See MUNICH MACHINE

Cliff BENNETT and the REBEL ROUSERS
UK, male vocal / instrumental group (23 WEEKS)
pos/wks
1 Oct 64 ●	ONE WAY LOVE *Parlophone R 5173*	9	9
4 Feb 65	I'LL TAKE YOU HOME *Parlophone R 5229*	42	3
11 Aug 66 ●	GOT TO GET YOU INTO MY LIFE *Parlophone R 5489*	6	11

Peter E BENNETT with the CO-OPERATION CHOIR
UK, male vocalist and choir (1 WEEK)
pos/wks
7 Nov 70	THE SEAGULL'S NAME WAS NELSON *RCA 1991*	45	1

Tony BENNETT
US, male vocalist - Anthony Benedetto (61 WEEKS)
pos/wks
15 Apr 55 ★	STRANGER IN PARADISE *Philips PB 420*	1	16
16 Sep 55	CLOSE YOUR EYES *Philips PB 445*	18	1
13 Apr 56	COME NEXT SPRING *Philips PB 537*	29	1
5 Jan 61	TILL *Philips PB 1079*	35	2
18 Jul 63	THE GOOD LIFE *CBS AAG 153*	27	13
6 May 65	IF I RULED THE WORLD *CBS 201735*	40	5
27 May 65	I LEFT MY HEART IN SAN FRANCISCO *CBS 201730*	46	2
30 Sep 65	I LEFT MY HEART IN SAN FRANCISCO (re-entry) *CBS 201730*	40	5
9 Dec 65	I LEFT MY HEART IN SAN FRANCISCO (2nd re-entry) *CBS 201730*	25	7
23 Dec 65	THE VERY THOUGHT OF YOU *CBS 202021*	21	9

Gary BENSON UK, male vocalist (8 WEEKS)
pos/wks
9 Aug 75	DON'T THROW IT ALL AWAY *State STAT 10*	20	8

George BENSON (167 Top 500) *Grammy-winning guitarist / vocalist, b. 22 Mar 1943, Pennsylvania, US. This one-time child prodigy topped the US chart in 1976 with the triple-platinum album Breezin'. He was also a major live attraction in Britain during the 1980s (143 WEEKS)*
pos/wks
25 Oct 75	SUPERSHIP *CTI CTSP 002*	30	6
4 Jun 77	NATURE BOY *Warner Bros. K 16921*	26	6
24 Sep 77	THE GREATEST LOVE OF ALL *Arista 133*	27	7
31 Mar 79	LOVE BALLAD *Warner Bros. K 17333*	29	9
26 Jul 80 ●	GIVE ME THE NIGHT *Warner Bros. K 17673*	7	10
4 Oct 80 ●	LOVE X LOVE *Warner Bros. K 17699*	10	8
7 Feb 81	WHAT'S ON YOUR MIND *Warner Bros. K 17748*	45	5
19 Sep 81	LOVE ALL THE HURT AWAY *Arista ARIST 428* [2]	49	3
14 Nov 81	TURN YOUR LOVE AROUND *Warner Bros. K 17877*	29	11
23 Jan 82	NEVER GIVE UP ON A GOOD THING *Warner Bros. K 17902*	14	10
21 May 83	LADY LOVE ME (ONE MORE TIME) *Warner Bros. W 9614*	11	10
16 Jul 83	FEEL LIKE MAKIN' LOVE *Warner Bros. W 9551*	28	5
24 Sep 83 ●	IN YOUR EYES *Warner Bros. W 9487*	7	10
17 Dec 83	INSIDE LOVE (SO PERSONAL) *WEA Int. W 9427*	57	5
19 Jan 85	20 / 20 *Warner Bros. W 9120*	29	9
20 Apr 85	BEYOND THE SEA (LA MER) *Warner Bros. W 9014*	60	3
16 Aug 86	KISSES IN THE MOONLIGHT *Warner Bros. W 8640*	60	4
29 Nov 86	SHIVER *Warner Bros. W 8523*	19	9
14 Feb 87	TEASER *Warner Bros. W 8437*	45	4
27 Aug 88	LET'S DO IT AGAIN *Warner Bros. W 7780*	56	3
5 Sep 92	I'LL KEEP YOUR DREAMS ALIVE *Ammi AMMI 101* [3]	68	1
11 Jul 98	SEVEN DAYS *MCA MCSTD 48083* [4]	22	3

[1] George 'Bad' Benson [2] Aretha Franklin and George Benson [3] George Benson and Patti Austin [4] Mary J Blige featuring George Benson

BENTLEY RHYTHM ACE UK, male instrumental duo (7 WEEKS)
pos/wks
6 Sep 97	BENTLEY'S GONNA SORT YOU OUT ! *Parlophone CDRS 6476*	17	4
27 May 00	THEME FROM GUTBUSTER *Parlophone CDRS 6537*	29	2
2 Sep 00	HOW'D I DO DAT *Parlophone CDRS 6543*	57	1

Brook BENTON US, male vocalist (18 WEEKS)
pos/wks
10 Jul 59	ENDLESSLY *Mercury AMT 1043*	28	2
6 Oct 60	KIDDIO *Mercury AMT 1109*	42	3
3 Nov 60	KIDDIO (re-entry) *Mercury AMT 1109*	41	3
16 Feb 61	FOOLS RUSH IN *Mercury AMT 1121*	50	1
13 Jul 61	BOLL WEEVIL SONG *Mercury AMT 1148*	30	9

BENZ UK, male rap / vocal group (9 WEEKS)
pos/wks
16 Dec 95	BOOM ROCK SOUL *Hacktown 74321329652*	62	2
16 Mar 96	URBAN CITY GIRL *Hacktown 74321348732*	31	3
25 May 96	MISS PARKER *Hacktown 74321377292*	35	2
29 Mar 97	IF I REMEMBER *Hendricks CDBENZ 1*	59	1
9 Aug 97	ON A SUN-DAY *Hendricks CDBENZ 2*	73	1

Ingrid BERGMAN – See Dooley WILSON

BERLIN US, male / female vocal / instrumental group - lead vocal Terri Nunn (39 WEEKS)
pos/wks
25 Oct 86 ★	TAKE MY BREATH AWAY (LOVE THEME FROM 'TOP GUN') *CBS A 7320* ▲	1	15
17 Jan 87	YOU DON'T KNOW *Mercury MER 237*	39	6
14 Mar 87	LIKE FLAMES *Mercury MER 240*	47	3
20 Feb 88	TAKE MY BREATH AWAY (LOVE THEME FROM 'TOP GUN') (re-entry) *CBS A 7320*	52	3
13 Oct 90 ●	TAKE MY BREATH AWAY (re-issue) *CBS 656361 7*	3	12

Elmer BERNSTEIN US, orchestra (11 WEEKS)
pos/wks
18 Dec 59 ●	STACCATO'S THEME *Capitol CL 15101*	4	10
10 Mar 60	STACCATO'S THEME (re-entry) *Capitol CL 15101*	40	1

Leonard BERNSTEIN, ORCHESTRA and CHORUS
US, male conductor, orchestra and chorus (4 WEEKS)
pos/wks
2 Jul 94	AMERICA – WORLD CUP THEME 1994 *Deutsche Grammophon USACD 1*	44	4

BERRI UK, female vocalist - Beverley Sleight (22 WEEKS)
pos/wks
26 Nov 94	THE SUNSHINE AFTER THE RAIN *Ffrreedom TABCD 223* [1]	26	6
2 Sep 95 ●	THE SUNSHINE AFTER THE RAIN (re-mix) *Ffrreedom TABCD 232*	4	11
2 Dec 95	SHINE LIKE A STAR *Ffrreedom TABCD 239*	20	5

[1] New Atlantic / U4EA featuring Berri

LaKiesha BERRI US, female vocalist (1 WEEK)
pos/wks
5 Jul 97	LIKE THIS AND LIKE THAT *Adept ADPTCD 7*	54	1

Chuck BERRY (334 Top 500) *First guitar-playing rock star, b. 18 Oct 1926, Missouri, US. Often called rock 'n' roll's premier poet and most influential instrumentalist. 'Duck walking' legend was among first acts inducted into Rock and Roll Hall of Fame (91 WEEKS)*
pos/wks
21 Jun 57	SCHOOL DAY *Columbia DB 3951*	24	2
12 Jul 57	SCHOOL DAY (re-entry) *Columbia DB 3951*	24	2
25 Apr 58	SWEET LITTLE SIXTEEN *London HLM 8585*	16	5
11 Jul 63	GO GO GO *Pye International 7N 25209*	38	6
10 Oct 63 ●	LET IT ROCK / MEMPHIS TENNESSEE *Pye International 7N 25218*	6	13
19 Dec 63	RUN RUDOLPH RUN *Pye International 7N 25228*	36	6
13 Feb 64	NADINE (IS IT YOU) *Pye International 7N 25236*	27	6
2 Apr 64	NADINE (IS IT YOU) (re-entry) *Pye International 7N 25236*	43	1
7 May 64 ●	NO PARTICULAR PLACE TO GO *Pye International 7N 25242*	3	12

20 Aug 64	YOU NEVER CAN TELL	
	Pye International 7N 25257	23 8
14 Jan 65	PROMISED LAND *Pye International 7N 25285*	26 6
28 Oct 72 ★	MY DING-A-LING *Chess 6145 019* ▲	1 17
3 Feb 73	REELIN' AND ROCKIN' *Chess 6145 020*	18 7

Dave BERRY `445` `Top 500` *Unique charismatic performer b. Dave Grundy, 6 Feb 1941, Sheffield, UK. Major European star, whose 'This Strange Effect' is among Holland's biggest sellers. Stage act influenced Alvin Stardust, and several punk bands acknowledge him as an inspiration (76 WEEKS)* pos/wks

19 Sep 63	MEMPHIS TENNESSEE *Decca F 11734* [1]	19 13
9 Jan 64	MY BABY LEFT ME *Decca F 11803* [1]	41 1
23 Jan 64	MY BABY LEFT ME (re-entry) *Decca F 11803* [1]	37 8
30 Apr 64	BABY IT'S YOU *Decca F 11876*	24 4
6 Aug 64 ●	THE CRYING GAME *Decca F 11937*	5 12
26 Nov 64	ONE HEART BETWEEN TWO *Decca F 12020*	41 2
25 Mar 65 ●	LITTLE THINGS *Decca F 12103*	5 12
22 Jul 65	THIS STRANGE EFFECT *Decca F 12188*	37 6
30 Jun 66 ●	MAMA *Decca F 12435*	5 16

[1] Dave Berry and the Cruisers

Mike BERRY *UK, male vocalist (51 WEEKS)* pos/wks

12 Oct 61	TRIBUTE TO BUDDY HOLLY *HMV POP 912* [1]	24 6
3 Jan 63 ●	DON'T YOU THINK IT'S TIME *HMV POP 1105* [1]	6 12
11 Apr 63	MY LITTLE BABY *HMV POP 1142* [1]	34 7
2 Aug 80 ●	THE SUNSHINE OF YOUR SMILE *Polydor 2059 261*	9 12
29 Nov 80	IF I COULD ONLY MAKE YOU CARE	
	Polydor POSP 202	37 9
5 Sep 81	MEMORIES *Polydor POSP 287*	55 5

[1] Mike Berry & the Outlaws

Nick BERRY *UK, male vocalist (24 WEEKS)* pos/wks

4 Oct 86 ★	EVERY LOSER WINS *BBC RESL 204*	1 11
27 Dec 86	EVERY LOSER WINS (re-entry) *BBC RESL 204*	72 2
13 Jun 92 ●	HEARTBEAT *Columbia 6581517*	2 8
31 Oct 92	LONG LIVE LOVE *Columbia 6587597*	47 3

Adele BERTEI – See JELLYBEAN

BEST COMPANY *UK, male vocal duo (1 WEEK)* pos/wks

27 Mar 93	DON'T YOU FORGET ABOUT ME *ZYX ZYX 69468*	65 1

BEST SHOT *UK, male rap group (2 WEEKS)* pos/wks

5 Feb 94	UNITED COLOURS *East West YZ 795CD*	64 2

Martin BETTINGHAUS – See Timo MAAS

BEVERLEY SISTERS *UK, female vocal group (34 WEEKS)* pos/wks

27 Nov 53	I SAW MOMMY KISSING SANTA CLAUS	
	Philips PB 188	11 1
11 Dec 53 ●	I SAW MOMMY KISSING SANTA CLAUS (re-entry)	
	Philips PB 188	6 4
13 Apr 56	WILLIE CAN *Decca F 10705*	23 4
1 Feb 57	I DREAMED *Decca F 10832*	24 2
13 Feb 59 ●	LITTLE DRUMMER BOY *Decca F 11107*	6 13
20 Nov 59	LITTLE DONKEY *Decca F 11172*	14 7
23 Jun 60	GREEN FIELDS *Columbia DB 4444*	48 1
7 Jul 60	GREEN FIELDS (re-entry) *Columbia DB 4444*	29 2

Frankie BEVERLY – See MAZE featuring Frankie BEVERLY

BEYOND *UK, male vocal / instrumental group (1 WEEK)* pos/wks

21 Sep 91	RAGING EP *Harvest HARS 530*	68 1

Tracks on Raging (EP): Great Indifference / Nail / Eve of My Release

BG THE PRINCE OF RAP *Germany, male rapper (2 WEEKS)* pos/wks

18 Jan 92	TAKE CONTROL OF THE PARTY *Columbia 6576330*	71 2

BIBLE *UK, male vocal / instrumental group (8 WEEKS)* pos/wks

20 May 89	GRACELAND *Chrysalis BIB 4*	51 4
26 Aug 89	HONEY BE GOOD *Ensign BIB 5*	54 4

BIBLE OF DREAMS – See Johnny PANIC and the BIBLE OF DREAMS

BIDDU *UK, orchestra (13 WEEKS)* pos/wks

2 Aug 75	SUMMER OF '42 *Epic EPC 3318*	14 8
17 Apr 76	RAIN FOREST *Epic EPC 4084*	39 4
11 Feb 78	JOURNEY TO THE MOON *Epic EPC 5910*	41 1

BIG APPLE BAND – See Walter MURPHY and the BIG APPLE BAND

BIG AUDIO DYNAMITE *UK / US, male vocal / instrumental group (27 WEEKS)* pos/wks

22 Mar 86	E=MC2 *CBS A 6963*	11 9
7 Jun 86	MEDICINE SHOW *CBS A 7181*	29 5
18 Oct 86	C'MON EVERY BEATBOX *CBS 650147*	51 3
21 Feb 87	V THIRTEEN *CBS BAAD 2*	49 5
28 May 88	JUST PLAY MUSIC *CBS BAAD 4*	51 3
12 Nov 94	LOOKING FOR A SONG *Columbia 6610182* [1]	68 2

[1] Big Audio

BIG BAD HORNS – See LITTLE ANGELS

BIG BAM BOO *UK / Canada, male vocal / instrumental duo (2 WEEKS)* pos/wks

28 Jan 89	SHOOTING FROM MY HEART *MCA MCA 1281*	61 2

BIG BASS vs Michelle NARINE *Canada, male production group & female vocalist (1 WEEK)* pos/wks

2 Sep 00	WHAT YOU DO *Stonebridge / Edel 0110965ERE*	67 1

BIG BEN *UK, clock (2 WEEKS)* pos/wks

1 Jan 00	MILLENNIUM CHIMES *London BIGONE 2000*	53 2

BIG BEN BANJO BAND *UK, instrumental group (6 WEEKS)* pos/wks

10 Dec 54 ●	LET'S GET TOGETHER NO.1 *Columbia DB 3549*	6 4
9 Dec 55	LET'S GET TOGETHER AGAIN *Columbia DB 3676*	19 1
30 Dec 55	LET'S GET TOGETHER AGAIN (re-entry)	
	Columbia DB 3676	18 1

These hits were both medleys as follows: Let's Get Together No.1: I'm Just Wild About Harry / April Showers / Rock-a-Bye Your Baby / Swanee / Darktown Strutters Ball / For Me and My Gal / Oh You Beautiful Doll / Yes Sir That's My Baby / Let's Get Together

BIG BOPPER *US, male vocalist (8 WEEKS)* pos/wks

26 Dec 58	CHANTILLY LACE *Mercury AMT 1002*	30 1
9 Jan 59	CHANTILLY LACE (re-entry) *Mercury AMT 1002*	12 7

BIG BOSS STYLUS presents RED VENOM *UK, male production duo and male rapper - Mike Neilson (1 WEEK)* pos/wks

31 Jul 99	LET'S GET IT ON *All Around the World CDGLOBE 195*	72 1

BIG C – See Alex WHITCOMBE & BIG C

BIG COUNTRY `291` `Top 500` *Distinctive folk-influenced rock quartet from Dunfermline, Scotland: Stuart Adamson (v/g, ex-Skids), Bruce Watson (g), Tony Butler (b), Mark Brzezicki (d). These frequent early-1980s chart visitors achieved five Top 10 albums including the 1984 No.1 Steeltown (103 WEEKS)* pos/wks

26 Feb 83 ●	FIELDS OF FIRE (400 MILES) *Mercury COUNT 2*	10 12
28 May 83	IN A BIG COUNTRY *Mercury COUNT 3*	17 7
3 Sep 83 ●	CHANCE *Mercury COUNT 4*	9 9
21 Jan 84 ●	WONDERLAND *Mercury COUNT 5*	8 8
29 Sep 84	EAST OF EDEN *Mercury MER 175*	17 6
1 Dec 84	WHERE THE ROSE IS SOWN *Mercury MER 185*	29 7

UK No.1 ★   UK Top 10 ●   Still on chart +   UK million seller ◆   UK entry at No.1 ■   US No.1 ▲

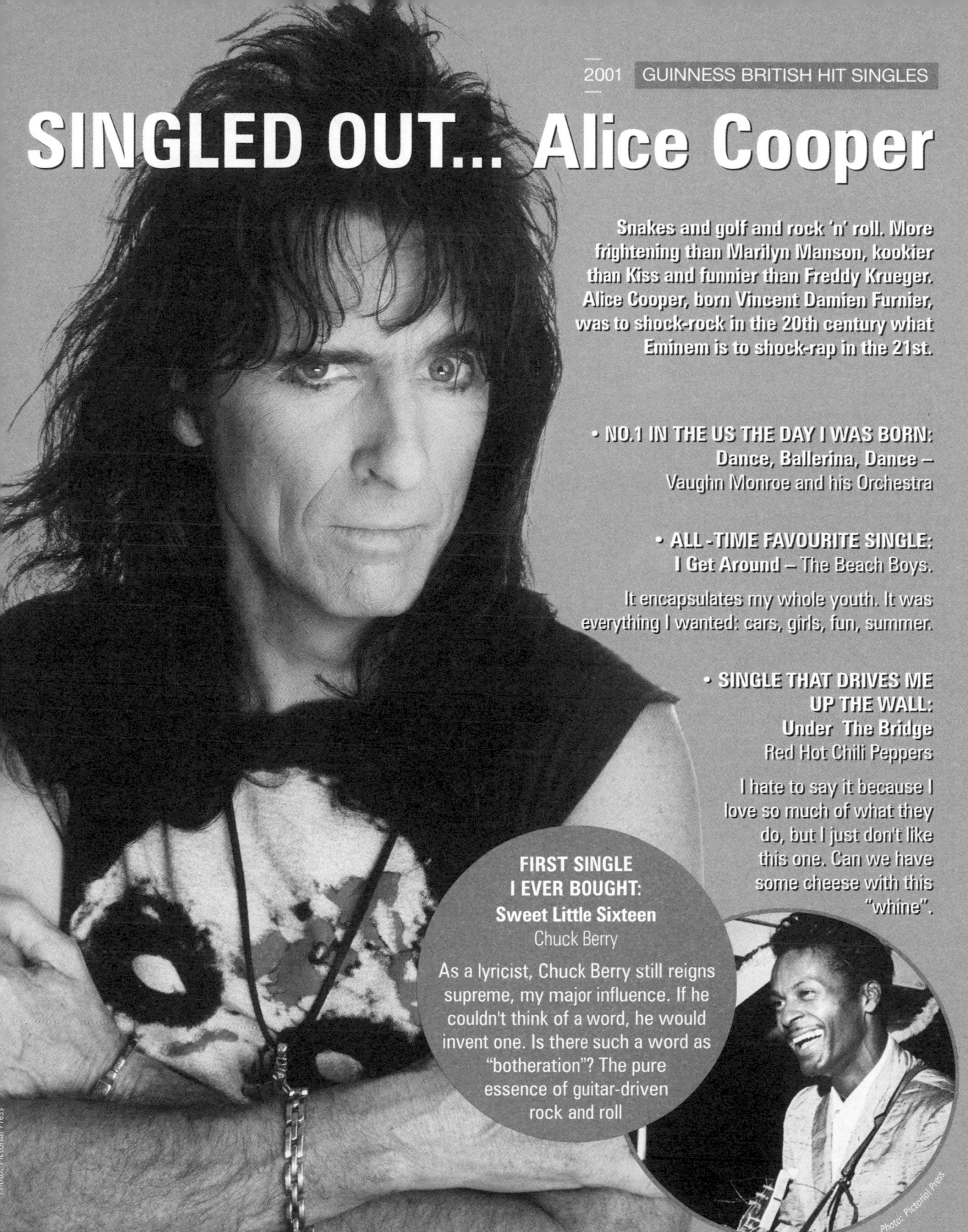

SINGLED OUT... Alice Cooper

Snakes and golf and rock 'n' roll. More frightening than Marilyn Manson, kookier than Kiss and funnier than Freddy Krueger. Alice Cooper, born Vincent Damien Furnier, was to shock-rock in the 20th century what Eminem is to shock-rap in the 21st.

• NO.1 IN THE US THE DAY I WAS BORN:
Dance, Ballerina, Dance —
Vaughn Monroe and his Orchestra

• ALL - TIME FAVOURITE SINGLE:
I Get Around — The Beach Boys.

It encapsulates my whole youth. It was everything I wanted: cars, girls, fun, summer.

• SINGLE THAT DRIVES ME UP THE WALL:
Under The Bridge
Red Hot Chili Peppers

I hate to say it because I love so much of what they do, but I just don't like this one. Can we have some cheese with this "whine".

FIRST SINGLE I EVER BOUGHT:
Sweet Little Sixteen
Chuck Berry

As a lyricist, Chuck Berry still reigns supreme, my major influence. If he couldn't think of a word, he would invent one. Is there such a word as "botheration"? The pure essence of guitar-driven rock and roll

Photo: Pictorial Press

Photo: Pictorial Press

19 Jan 85	JUST A SHADOW *Mercury BCO 8*	**26**	4
12 Apr 86 ●	LOOK AWAY *Mercury BIGC 1*	**7**	8
21 Jun 86	THE TEACHER *Mercury BIGC 2*	**28**	4
20 Sep 86	ONE GREAT THING *Mercury BIGC 3*	**19**	6
29 Nov 86	HOLD THE HEART *Mercury BIGC 4*	**55**	2
20 Aug 88	KING OF EMOTION *Mercury BIGC 5*	**16**	5
1 Oct 88	KING OF EMOTION (re-entry) *Mercury BIGC 5*...	**74**	1
5 Nov 88	BROKEN HEART (THIRTEEN VALLEYS)		
	Mercury BIGC 6	**47**	4
4 Feb 89	PEACE IN OUR TIME *Mercury BIGC 7*	**39**	3
12 May 90	SAVE ME *Mercury BIGC 8*	**41**	3
21 Jul 90	HEART OF THE WORLD *Mercury BIGC 9*.......	**50**	2
31 Aug 91	REPUBLICAN PARTY REPTILE (EP)		
	Vertigo BIC 1	**37**	2
19 Oct 91	BEAUTIFUL PEOPLE *Vertigo BIC 2*	**72**	1
13 Mar 93	ALONE *Compulsion CDPULSS 4*	**24**	3
1 May 93	SHIPS (WHERE WERE YOU)		
	Compulsion CDPULSS 6	**29**	3
10 Jun 95	I'M NOT ASHAMED *Transatlantic TRAX 1009*...	**69**	1
9 Sep 95	YOU DREAMER *Transatlantic TRAD 1012*	**68**	1
21 Aug 99	FRAGILE THING *Track TRACK 0004A* [1]	**69**	1

[1] Big Country featuring Eddi Reader

Tracks on Republican Party Reptile (EP): Republican Party Reptile / Comes a Time / You Me and the Truth

BIG DADDY *US, male rapper (8 WEEKS)*
			pos/wks
9 Mar 85	DANCING IN THE DARK *Making Waves SURF 1033*	**21**	8

BIG DADDY KANE *US, male rapper (6 WEEKS)*
			pos/wks
13 May 89	RAP SUMMARY / WRATH OF KANE		
	Cold Chillin' W 2973	**52**	2
26 Aug 89	SMOOTH OPERATOR *Cold Chillin' W 2804* ...	**65**	1
13 Jan 90	AIN'T NO STOPPIN' US NOW		
	Cold Chillin' W 2635	**44**	3

BIG DISH *UK, male vocal / instrumental group (5 WEEKS)*
			pos/wks
12 Jan 91	MISS AMERICA *East West YZ 529*	**37**	5

BIG FAMILY – See JT and the BIG FAMILY

BIG FUN *UK, male vocal group (33 WEEKS)*
			pos/wks
12 Aug 89 ●	BLAME IT ON THE BOOGIE *Jive JIVE 217* ...	**4**	11
25 Nov 89 ●	CAN'T SHAKE THE FEELING *Jive JIVE 234* ...	**8**	9
17 Mar 90	HANDFUL OF PROMISES *Jive JIVE 243*	**21**	6
23 Jun 90	YOU'VE GOT A FRIEND *Jive CHILD 90* [1] ...	**14**	6
4 Aug 90	HEY THERE LONELY GIRL *Jive JIVE 251* ...	**62**	1

[1] Big Fun and Sonia featuring Gary Barnacle

BIG MOUNTAIN
US, male / female vocal / instrumental group (15 WEEKS)
			pos/wks
4 Jun 94 ●	BABY I LOVE YOUR WAY *RCA 74321198062* ...	**2**	14
24 Sep 94	SWEET SENSUAL LOVE *Giant 74321234642*...	**51**	1

BIG PUN – See Jennifer LOPEZ

BIG ROLL BAND – See Zoot MONEY and the BIG ROLL BAND

BIG RON
UK, male producer - Aaron Gilbert (aka Jules Verne) (1 WEEK)
			pos/wks
11 Mar 00	LET THE FREAK *48k SPECT 06CDS*...............	**57**	1

BIG ROOM GIRL featuring Darryl PANDY *UK, male production / instrumental duo (aka Rhythm Masters) and US, male vocalist (2 WEEKS)*
			pos/wks
20 Feb 99	RAISE YOUR HANDS *VC Recordings VCRD 44* ...	**40**	2

See also RHYTHM MASTERS

BIG SOUND – See Simon DUPREE and the BIG SOUND

BIG SOUND AUTHORITY *UK, male / female vocal / instrumental group (12 WEEKS)*
			pos/wks
19 Jan 85	THIS HOUSE (IS WHERE YOUR LOVE STANDS) *Source BSA 1* ...	**21**	9
8 Jun 85	A BAD TOWN *Source BSA 2*	**54**	3

BIG SUPREME *UK, male vocal group (5 WEEKS)*
			pos/wks
20 Sep 86	DON'T WALK *Polydor POSP 809*	**58**	3
14 Mar 87	PLEASE YOURSELF *Polydor POSP 840*	**64**	2

BIG THREE *UK, vocal / instrumental group (17 WEEKS)*
			pos/wks
11 Apr 63	SOME OTHER GUY *Decca F 11614*	**37**	7
11 Jul 63	BY THE WAY *Decca F 11689*	**22**	10

BIG TIME CHARLIE *UK, male DJ / production duo (4 WEEKS)*
			pos/wks
23 Oct 99	ON THE RUN *Inferno CDFERN 18*	**22**	2
18 Mar 00	MR DEVIL *Inferno CDFERN 24* [1]	**39**	2

[1] Big Time Charlie Featuring Soozy Q

Barry BIGGS *Jamaica, male vocalist (46 WEEKS)*
			pos/wks
28 Aug 76	WORK ALL DAY *Dynamic DYN 101*	**38**	5
4 Dec 76 ●	SIDESHOW *Dynamic DYN 118*	**3**	16
23 Apr 77	YOU'RE MY LIFE *Dynamic DYN 127*	**36**	4
9 Jul 77	THREE RING CIRCUS *Dynamic DYN 128* ...	**22**	8
15 Dec 79	WHAT'S YOUR SIGN GIRL *Dynamic DYN 150*...	**55**	7
20 Jun 81	WIDE AWAKE IN A DREAM *Dynamic DYN 10*...	**44**	6

Ronald BIGGS – See SEX PISTOLS

Ivor BIGGUN *UK, male vocalist (15 WEEKS)*
			pos/wks
2 Sep 78	WINKER'S SONG (MISPRINT) *Beggars Banquet BOP 1* [1] ...	**22**	12
12 Sep 81	BRAS ON 45 (FAMILY VERSION) *Dead Badger BOP 6* [2] ...	**50**	3

[1] Ivor Biggun and the Red Nosed Burglars [2] Ivor Biggun and the D Cups

BILBO *UK, male vocal / instrumental group (7 WEEKS)*
			pos/wks
26 Aug 78	SHE'S GONNA WIN *Lightning LIG 548*	**42**	7

Mr Acker BILK and his PARAMOUNT JAZZ BAND
115 **Top 500** First UK act to top US chart in 1960s, b. 28 Jan 1929, Somerset, UK. Band leader / clarinettist / vocalist was at forefront of UK trad-jazz revival. 'Stranger on the Shore' spent more than one year on chart and was voted No.1 Instrumental of 1962 in the US. Made an MBE in the 2001 honours list *(171 WEEKS)*
			pos/wks
22 Jan 60 ●	SUMMER SET *Columbia DB 4382*	**5**	19
9 Jun 60	GOODNIGHT SWEET PRINCE *Melodisc MEL 1547*...	**50**	1
18 Aug 60	WHITE CLIFFS OF DOVER *Columbia DB 4492* ...	**30**	9
8 Dec 60 ●	BUONA SERA *Columbia DB 4544*	**7**	18
13 Jul 61 ●	THAT'S MY HOME *Columbia DB 4673*	**7**	17
2 Nov 61	STARS AND STRIPES FOREVER / CREOLE JAZZ		
	Columbia SCD 2155	**22**	10
30 Nov 61 ●	STRANGER ON THE SHORE *Columbia DB 4750* [1] ◆ ▲ ...	**2**	55
15 Mar 62	FRANKIE AND JOHNNY *Columbia DB 4795* ...	**42**	2
26 Jul 62	GOTTA SEE BABY TONIGHT *Columbia SCD 2176*...	**24**	9
27 Sep 62	LONELY *Columbia DB 4897* [1]	**14**	11
24 Jan 63	A TASTE OF HONEY *Columbia DB 4949* [1] ...	**16**	9
21 Aug 76 ●	ARIA *Pye 7N 45607* [2]	**5**	11

[1] Mr Acker Bilk with the Leon Young String Chorale [2] Acker Bilk, his Clarinet and Strings

BILL *UK, male vocalist (1 WEEK)*
			pos/wks
23 Oct 93	CAR BOOT SALE *Mercury MINCD 1*...............	**73**	1

BILLIE – See H20; Billie PIPER

BIMBO JET
France, male / female vocal / instrumental group (10 WEEKS)
			pos/wks
26 Jul 75	EL BIMBO *EMI 2317*...............................	**12**	10

UK No.1 ★ UK Top 10 ● Still on chart + UK million seller ◆ UK entry at No.1 ■ US No.1 ▲

BINARY FINARY UK, male production duo (9 WEEKS) — pos/wks

Date	Title	pos	wks
10 Oct 98	**1998** *Positiva CDTIV 98*	24	3
28 Aug 99	**1999** *Positiva CDTIV 118*	11	6

Umberto BINDI Italy, male vocalist (1 WEEK) — pos/wks

Date	Title	pos	wks
10 Nov 60	**IL NOSTRO CONCERTO** *Oriole CB 1577*	47	1

BINI & MARTINI Italy, male production duo (1 WEEK) — pos/wks

Date	Title	pos	wks
4 Mar 00	**HAPPINESS (MY VISION IS CLEAR)** *Azuli AZNYCDX 113*	53	1

BIOHAZARD US, male vocal / instrumental group (4 WEEKS) — pos/wks

Date	Title	pos	wks
9 Jul 94	**TALES FROM THE HARD SIDE** *Warner Bros. W 0254CD*	47	2
20 Aug 94	**HOW IT IS** *Warner Bros. W 0259CD*	62	2

La BIONDA Italy, male / female vocal group (4 WEEKS) — pos/wks

Date	Title	pos	wks
7 Oct 78	**ONE FOR YOU ONE FOR ME** *Philips 6198 227*	54	4

BIOSPHERE
Norway, male instrumentalist - Ger Jenssen, keyboards (2 WEEKS) pos/wks

Date	Title	pos	wks
29 Apr 95	**NOVELTY WAVES** *Apollo APOLLO 20CDX*	51	2

BIRDLAND UK, male vocal / instrumental group (7 WEEKS) — pos/wks

Date	Title	pos	wks
1 Apr 89	**HOLLOW HEART** *Lazy LAZY 13*	70	1
8 Jul 89	**PARADISE** *Lazy LAZY 14*	70	1
3 Feb 90	**SLEEP WITH ME** *Lazy LAZY 17*	32	3
22 Sep 90	**ROCK 'N' ROLL NIGGER** *Lazy LAZY 20*	47	1
2 Feb 91	**EVERYBODY NEEDS SOMEBODY** *Lazy LAZY 24*	44	1

BIRDS UK, male vocal / instrumental group (1 WEEK) — pos/wks

Date	Title	pos	wks
27 May 65	**LEAVING HERE** *Decca F 12140*	45	1

Jane BIRKIN and Serge GAINSBOURG
UK / France, female / male vocal duo (34 WEEKS) — pos/wks

Date	Title	pos	wks
30 Jul 69 ●	**JE T'AIME . . . MOI NON PLUS** *Fontana TF 1042*	2	11
4 Oct 69 ★	**JE T'AIME . . . MOI NON PLUS (re-issue)** *Major Minor MM 645*	1	14
7 Dec 74	**JE T'AIME . . . MOI NON PLUS (2nd re-issue)** *Antic K 11511*	31	9

BIS UK, male / female vocal / instrumental group (9 WEEKS) — pos/wks

Date	Title	pos	wks
30 Mar 96	**THE SECRET VAMPIRE SOUNDTRACK (EP)** *Chemikal Underground CHEM 003CD*	25	2
22 Jun 96	**BIS VS THE DIY CORPS (EP)** *Teen-C SKETCH 001CD*	45	1
9 Nov 96	**ATOM POWERED ACTION (EP)** *Wiiija WIJ 55CD*	54	1
15 Mar 97	**SWEET SHOP AVENGERZ** *Wiiija WIJ 67CD*	46	1
10 May 97	**EVERYBODY THINKS THAT THEY'RE GOING TO GET THEIRS** *Wiiija WIJ 69CD*	64	1
14 Nov 98	**EURODISCO** *Wiiija WIJ 86CD*	37	2
27 Feb 99	**ACTION AND DRAMA** *Wiiija WIJ 95CD*	50	1

Tracks on The Secret Vampire Soundtrack (EP): Kandy Pop / Secret Vampires / Teen-C Power / Diska. Tracks on Bis vs The DIY Corps (EP): This Is Fake DIY / Burn the Suit / Dance to the Disco Beat. Tracks on Atom Powered Action (EP): Starbright Boy / Wee Love / Team Theme / Cliquesuck

Elvin BISHOP US, male instrumentalist - guitar (4 WEEKS) — pos/wks

Date	Title	pos	wks
15 May 76	**FOOLED AROUND AND FELL IN LOVE** *Capricorn 2089 024*	34	4

Hit has vocal (uncredited) by Mickey Thomas

BITI – See DEGREES OF MOTION featuring BITI

BIZARRE INC
UK, male / female vocal / instrumental group (49 WEEKS) — pos/wks

Date	Title	pos	wks
16 Mar 91	**PLAYING WITH KNIVES** *Vinyl Solution STORM 25R*	43	5
14 Sep 91	**SUCH A FEELING** *Vinyl Solution STORM 32S*	13	9
23 Nov 91 ●	**PLAYING WITH KNIVES (re-issue)** *Vinyl Solution STORM 38S*	4	8
3 Oct 92 ●	**I'M GONNA GET YOU** *Vinyl Solution STORM 46S* [1]	3	12
2 Jan 93	**I'M GONNA GET YOU (re-entry)** *Vinyl Solution STORM 46S* [1]	72	1
27 Feb 93	**TOOK MY LOVE** *Vinyl Solution STORM 60CD* [1]	19	5
23 Mar 96	**KEEP THE MUSIC STRONG** *Some Bizarre MERCD 451*	33	2
6 Jul 96	**SURPRISE** *Some Bizarre MERCD 462*	21	3
14 Sep 96	**GET UP SUNSHINE STREET** *Some Bizarre MERCD 471*	45	2
13 Mar 99	**PLAYING WITH KNIVES (re-mix)** *Vinyl Solution VC01CD1*	30	2

[1] Bizarre Inc featuring Angie Brown

BIZZ NIZZ US / Belgium, male / female vocal / instrumental group
(11 WEEKS) — pos/wks

Date	Title	pos	wks
31 Mar 90 ●	**DON'T MISS THE PARTYLINE** *Cooltempo COOL 203*	7	11

BIZZI UK, male vocalist (1 WEEK) — pos/wks

Date	Title	pos	wks
6 Dec 97	**BIZZI'S PARTY** *Parlophone Rhythm CDRHYTHM 7*	62	1

BJÖRK
Captivating, eccentric, uncompromising, female singer / songwriter, b. Björk Gudmundsdottir, 21 Nov 1965, Reykjavik, Iceland. Formerly a member of The Sugarcubes, artist was double Brits winner in 1994 (Best International Female and Best International Newcomer) (69 WEEKS) pos/wks

Date	Title	pos	wks
27 Apr 91	**OOOPS** *ZTT ZANG 19* [1]	42	3
19 Jun 93	**HUMAN BEHAVIOUR** *One Little Indian 112 TP7CD*	36	2
4 Sep 93	**VENUS AS A BOY** *One Little Indian 122 TP7CD*	29	4
23 Oct 93	**PLAY DEAD** *Island CID 573* [2]	12	6
4 Dec 93	**BIG TIME SENSUALITY** *One Little Indian 132 TP7CD*	17	8
19 Mar 94	**VIOLENTLY HAPPY** *One Little Indian 142 TP7CD*	13	4
6 May 95 ●	**ARMY OF ME** *One Little Indian 162 TP7CD*	10	5
26 Aug 95	**ISOBEL** *One Little Indian 172 TP7CD*	23	3
25 Nov 95 ●	**IT'S OH SO QUIET** *One Little Indian 182 TP7CD*	4	15
24 Feb 96 ●	**HYPERBALLAD** *One Little Indian 192 TP7CD*	8	4
9 Nov 96	**POSSIBLY MAYBE** *One Little Indian 193 TP7CD*	13	3
1 Mar 97	**I MISS YOU** *One Little Indian 194 TP7CDL*	36	2
20 Dec 97	**BACHELORETTE** *One Little Indian 212 TP7CD*	21	5
17 Oct 98	**HUNTER** *One Little Indian 222 TP7CD*	44	1
12 Dec 98	**ALARM CALL** *One Little Indian 232 TP7CDL*	33	4
19 Jun 99	**ALL IS FULL OF LOVE** *One Little Indian 242 TP7CD*	24	2

[1] 808 State featuring Björk [2] Björk and David Arnold

BJORN AGAIN
Australia, male / female vocal / instrumental group (8 WEEKS) — pos/wks

Date	Title	pos	wks
24 Oct 92	**ERASURE-ISH (A LITTLE RESPECT / STOP!)** *M & G MAGS 32*	25	3
12 Dec 92	**SANTA CLAUS IS COMING TO TOWN** *M & G MAGS 35*	55	4
27 Nov 93	**FLASHDANCE ... WHAT A FEELING** *M & G MAGCD 50*	65	1

BLACK UK, male vocalist - Colin Vearncombe (35 WEEKS) — pos/wks

Date	Title	pos	wks
27 Sep 86	**WONDERFUL LIFE** *Ugly Man JACK 71*	72	1
27 Jun 87 ●	**SWEETEST SMILE** *A & M AM 394*	8	10
22 Aug 87 ●	**WONDERFUL LIFE** *A & M AM 402*	8	9
16 Jan 88	**PARADISE** *A & M AM 422*	38	3
24 Sep 88	**THE BIG ONE** *A & M AM 468*	54	4
21 Jan 89	**NOW YOU'RE GONE** *A & M AM 491*	66	2
4 May 91	**FEEL LIKE CHANGE** *A & M AM 780*	56	2
15 Jun 91	**HERE IT COMES AGAIN** *A & M AM 753*	70	1
5 Mar 94	**WONDERFUL LIFE (re-issue)** *PolyGram TV 5805552*	42	3

'Wonderful Life' on A & M is a re-recording. It was re-issued on PolyGram TV in 1994

Cilla BLACK (93 Top 500)
Undoubtedly one of Britain's favourite female vocalists / entertainers this century, b. Priscilla White, 27 May, 1943, Liverpool. After handing in her Top 20 season ticket, she has become an award-winning and extremely popular TV presenter (194 WEEKS) — pos/wks

Date	Title	pos	wks
17 Oct 63	**LOVE OF THE LOVED** *Parlophone 5065*	35	6
6 Feb 64 ★	**ANYONE WHO HAD A HEART** *Parlophone R 5101*	1	17
7 May 64 ★	**YOU'RE MY WORLD** *Parlophone R 5133*	1	17
6 Aug 64 ●	**IT'S FOR YOU** *Parlophone R 5162*	7	10
14 Jan 65 ●	**YOU'VE LOST THAT LOVIN' FEELIN'** *Parlophone R 5225*	2	9

UK No.1 ★ UK Top 10 ● Still on chart + UK million seller ◆ UK entry at No.1 ■ US No.1 ▲

BLACK MAGIC US, male producer - Lil' Louis (2 WEEKS)

		pos/wks
1 Jun 96	FREEDOM (MAKE IT FUNKY) Positiva CDTIV 51	41 2

See also LIL' LOUIS

BLACK RIOT US, male producer (3 WEEKS)

		pos/wks
3 Dec 88	WARLOCK / A DAY IN THE LIFE Champion CHAMP 75	68 3

'A Day in the Life' listed only from 17 Dec 1988

BLACK ROB US, male rapper - Robert Ross (2 WEEKS)

		pos/wks
12 Aug 00	WHOA Puff Daddy / Arista 74321782732	44 2

BLACK SABBATH `493` `Top 500` Macabre Birmingham, UK-based
seminal rock outfit first fronted by the inimitable Ozzy (John) Osbourne (v)
and Tommy Iommi (g). Later vocalists include Ronnie James Dio and Ian
Gillan. Voted Best Band in the World and Act of the Millennium in Kerrang!
magazine in 1999 (70 WEEKS)

		pos/wks
29 Aug 70 ●	PARANOID Vertigo 6059 010	4 18
3 Jun 78	NEVER SAY DIE Vertigo SAB 001	21 8
14 Oct 78	HARD ROAD Vertigo SAB 002	33 4
5 Jul 80	NEON KNIGHTS Vertigo SAB 3	22 9
16 Aug 80	PARANOID (re-issue) Nems BSS 101	14 12
6 Dec 80	DIE YOUNG Vertigo SAB 4	41 7
7 Nov 81	MOB RULES Vertigo SAB 5.	46 4
13 Feb 82	TURN UP THE NIGHT Vertigo SAB 6	37 5
15 Apr 89	HEADLESS CROSS IRS EIRS 107	62 1
13 Jun 92	TV CRIMES IRS EIRSP 178	33 2

Group UK only for first three hits and re-issue of 'Paranoid'

BLACK SHEEP US, male rap duo (1 WEEK)

		pos/wks
19 Nov 94	WITHOUT A DOUBT Mercury MERCD 417	60 1

BLACK SLATE UK / Jamaica, male vocal / instrumental group (15 WEEKS)

		pos/wks
20 Sep 80 ●	AMIGO Ensign ENY 42	9 9
6 Dec 80	BOOM BOOM Ensign ENY 47	51 6

BLACK UHURU Jamaica, male vocal / instrumental group (9 WEEKS)

		pos/wks
8 Sep 84	WHAT IS LIFE? Island IS 150	56 6
31 May 86	THE GREAT TRAIN ROBBERY Real Authentic Sound RAS 7018	62 3

Band of the BLACK WATCH UK, military band (22 WEEKS)

		pos/wks
30 Aug 75 ●	SCOTCH ON THE ROCKS Spark SRL 1128	8 14
13 Dec 75	DANCE OF THE CUCKOOS (THE 'LAUREL AND HARDY' THEME) Spark SRL 1135	37 8

Tony BLACKBURN UK, male vocalist (7 WEEKS)

		pos/wks
24 Jan 68	SO MUCH LOVE MGM 1375	31 4
26 Mar 69	IT'S ONLY LOVE MGM 1467	42 3

BLACKBYRDS US, male vocal / instrumental group (6 WEEKS)

		pos/wks
31 May 75	WALKING IN RHYTHM Fantasy FTC 114	23 6

BLACKFOOT US, male vocal / instrumental group (5 WEEKS)

		pos/wks
6 Mar 82	DRY COUNTY Atco K 11686	43 4
18 Jun 83	SEND ME AN ANGEL Atco B 9880	66 1

J BLACKFOOT US, male vocalist (4 WEEKS)

		pos/wks
17 Mar 84	TAXI Allegiance ALES 2	48 4

BLACKFOOT SUE
UK, male vocal / instrumental group (15 WEEKS)

		pos/wks
12 Aug 72 ●	STANDING IN THE ROAD Jam 13	4 10
16 Dec 72	SING DON'T SPEAK Jam 29	36 5

BLACKGIRL US, female vocal group (3 WEEKS)

		pos/wks
16 Jul 94	90s GIRL RCA 74321217882	23 3

BLACKHEARTS – See Joan JETT and the BLACKHEARTS

Honor BLACKMAN – See Patrick MacNEE and Honor BLACKMAN

BLACKNUSS
Sweden, male / female vocal / instrumental group (1 WEEK)

		pos/wks
28 Jun 97	DINAH Arista 74321479762	56 1

BLACKOUT UK, male production / instrumental duo (1 WEEK)

		pos/wks
27 Mar 99	GOTTA HAVE HOPE Multiply CDMULTY 47	46 1

Bill BLACK'S COMBO
US, male instrumentalist - bass (8 WEEKS)

		pos/wks
8 Sep 60	WHITE SILVER SANDS London HLU 9090	50 1
3 Nov 60	DON'T BE CRUEL London HLU 9212	32 7

BLACKSTREET US, male vocal group (63 WEEKS)

		pos/wks
19 Jun 93	BABY BE MINE MCA MCSTD 1772 [1]	37 3
13 Aug 94	BOOTI CALL Interscope A 8250CD	56 1
11 Feb 95	U BLOW MY MIND Interscope A 8222CD	39 2
27 May 95	JOY Interscope A 8195CD	56 2
19 Oct 96 ●	NO DIGGITY Interscope IND 95003 [2] ▲	9 7
8 Mar 97	GET ME HOME Def Jam DEFCD 32 [3]	11 5
26 Apr 97 ●	DON'T LEAVE ME Interscope IND 95534	6 10
27 Sep 97 ●	FIX Interscope IND 97521	7 5
13 Dec 97	(MONEY CAN'T) BUY ME LOVE Interscope IND 95563	18 6
27 Jun 98	THE CITY IS MINE Northwestside 74321588012 [4]	38 2
12 Dec 98 ●	TAKE ME THERE Interscope IND 95620 [5]	7 9
17 Apr 99	GIRLFRIEND / BOYFRIEND Interscope IND 95640 [6]	11 7
10 Jul 99	GET READY Puff Daddy / Arista 74321682602 [7]	32 4

[1] BLACKstreet featuring Teddy Riley [2] BLACKstreet featuring Dr Dre [3] Foxy
Brown featuring BLACKstreet [4] Jay-Z featuring BLACKstreet [5] BLACKstreet and
Mya featuring Mase & Blinky Blink [6] BLACKstreet with Janet [7] Mase featuring
BLACKstreet

BLACKWELLS US, male vocal group (2 WEEKS)

		pos/wks
18 May 61	LOVE OR MONEY London HLW 9334	46 2

Richard BLACKWOOD UK, male rapper (16 WEEKS)

		pos/wks
17 Jun 00 ●	MAMA - WHO DA MAN? East West MICKY 01CD1	3 7
16 Sep 00 ●	1.2.3.4. GET WITH THE WICKED East West MICKY 05CD1	10 6
25 Nov 00	SOMEONE THERE FOR ME Hopefield / East West MICKY 06CD	23 3

BLAGGERS I.T.A. UK, male vocal / instrumental group (7 WEEKS) pos/wks

		pos/wks
12 Jun 93	STRESSS Parlophone CDITA 1	56 2
9 Oct 93	OXYGEN Parlophone CDITA 2	51 2
8 Jan 94	ABANDON SHIP Parlophone CDITA 3	48 3

BLAHZAY BLAHZAY US, male rap duo (1 WEEK)

		pos/wks
2 Mar 96	DANGER Mercury Black Vinyl MBVCD 2	56 1

Vivian BLAINE US, female vocalist (1 WEEK)

		pos/wks
10 Jul 53	BUSHEL AND A PECK Brunswick 05100	12 1

BLAIR – See Terry HALL

BLAIR UK, male vocalist (5 WEEKS)

		pos/wks
2 Sep 95	HAVE FUN GO MAD Mercury MERCD 443	37 3
6 Jan 96	LIFE Mercury MERCD 447	44 2

Peter BLAKE UK, male vocalist (4 WEEKS)

		pos/wks
8 Oct 77	LIPSMACKIN' ROCK 'N' ROLLIN' Pepper UP 36295	40 4

BLAME UK, male instrumental / production duo (2 WEEKS) pos/wks

11 Apr 92	**MUSIC TAKES YOU** *Moving Shadow SHADOW 11*	48	2

BLAMELESS UK, male vocal / instrumental group (5 WEEKS) pos/wks

4 Nov 95	**TOWN CLOWNS** *China WOKCD 2046*	56	1
23 Mar 96	**BREATHE (A LITTLE DEEPER)** *China WOKCD 2070*	27	3
1 Jun 96	**SIGNS...** *China WOKCD 2077*	49	1

BLANCMANGE `484` `Top 500` Electronic pop duo with penchant for Eastern rhythms, formed 1981 Blackburn, Lancashire, UK, split 1987. Comprised Neil Arthur (v/g), Stephen Luscombe (k). 'The Day Before You Came' was the first Abba hit to reach a higher position as a cover (71 WEEKS) pos/wks

17 Apr 82	**GOD'S KITCHEN / I'VE SEEN THE WORD** *London BLANC 1*	65	2
31 Jul 82	**FEEL ME** *London BLANC 2*	46	5
30 Oct 82 ●	**LIVING ON THE CEILING** *London BLANC 3*	7	14
19 Feb 83	**WAVES** *London BLANC 4*	19	9
7 May 83 ●	**BLIND VISION** *London BLANC 5*	10	8
26 Nov 83	**THAT'S LOVE, THAT IT IS** *London BLANC 6*	33	8
14 Apr 84 ●	**DON'T TELL ME** *London BLANC 7*	8	10
21 Jul 84	**THE DAY BEFORE YOU CAME** *London BLANC 8*	22	8
7 Sep 85	**WHAT'S YOUR PROBLEM?** *London BLANC 9*	40	5
10 May 86	**I CAN SEE IT** *London BLANC 11*	71	2

Billy BLAND US, male vocalist (10 WEEKS)

19 May 60	**LET THE LITTLE GIRL DANCE** *London HL 9096*	15	10

BLANK & JONES Germany, production duo (5 WEEKS) pos/wks

26 Jun 99	**CREAM** *Devia DVNT 31CDS*	24	3
27 May 00	**AFTER LOVE** *Nebula NEBCDS 3*	57	1
30 Sep 00	**THE NIGHTFLY** *Nebula NEBCD 010*	55	1

BLAQUE IVORY US, female vocal group (3 WEEKS) pos/wks

3 Jul 99	**808** *Columbia 6674962*	31	3

BLAST featuring VDC
Italy, male / female vocal / instrumental group (5 WEEKS) pos/wks

18 Jun 94	**CRAYZY MAN** *UMM MCSTD 1982*	22	3
12 Nov 94	**PRINCES OF THE NIGHT** *UMM MCSTD 2011*	40	2

BLEACHIN' UK, male vocal / instrumental group (4 WEEKS) pos/wks

22 Jul 00	**PEAKIN'** *Boiler House / Arista 74321774812*	32	3
2 Sep 00	**PEAKIN' (re-entry)**		
	Boiler House / Arista 74321774812	70	1

BLESSID UNION OF SOULS
US, male vocal / instrumental group (6 WEEKS) pos/wks

27 May 95	**I BELIEVE** *EMI CDEM 374*	29	5
23 Mar 96	**LET ME BE THE ONE** *EMI CDEM 387*	74	1

BLESSING UK, male vocal / instrumental group (13 WEEKS) pos/wks

11 May 91	**HIGHWAY 5** *MCA MCS 1509*	42	6
18 Jan 92	**HIGHWAY 5 (re-mix)** *MCA MCS 1603*	30	6
19 Feb 94	**SOUL LOVE** *MCA MCSTD 1940*	73	1

Mary J. BLIGE `376` `Top 500` Original queen of hip hop and soul, b. 11 Jan 1971, Atlanta, Georgia, US. Transatlantic chart regular since platinum-selling debut album, What's The 411? (1992). Recorded with numerous top acts including Elton John, Puff Daddy, Eric Clapton, Lauryn Hill and Aretha Franklin (85 WEEKS) pos/wks

28 Nov 92	**REAL LOVE** *Uptown MCS 1721*	68	2
27 Feb 93	**REMINISCE** *Uptown MCSTD 1731*	31	4
12 Jun 93	**YOU REMIND ME** *Uptown MCSTD 1770*	48	3
28 Aug 93	**REAL LOVE (re-mix)** *Uptown MCSTD 1922*	26	4
4 Dec 93	**YOU DON'T HAVE TO WORRY** *Uptown MCSTD 1948*	36	2
14 May 94	**MY LOVE** *Uptown MCSTD 1972*	29	3

10 Dec 94	**BE HAPPY** *Uptown MCSTD 2033*	30	4
15 Apr 95	**I'M GOIN' DOWN** *Uptown MCSTD 2053*	12	4
29 Jul 95 ●	**I'LL BE THERE FOR YOU - YOU'RE ALL I NEED TO GET BY** *Def Jam DEFDX 11* 1	10	5
30 Sep 95	**MARY JANE (ALL NIGHT LONG)** *Uptown MCSTD 2088*	17	4
16 Dec 95	**(YOU MAKE ME FEEL LIKE A) NATURAL WOMAN** *Uptown MCSTD 2108*	23	3
30 Mar 96	**NOT GON' CRY** *Arista 74321358252*	39	2
1 Mar 97	**CAN'T KNOCK THE HUSTLE** *Northwestside 74321447192* 2	30	2
17 May 97	**LOVE IS ALL WE NEED** *Uptown MCSTD 48053*	15	4
16 Aug 97 ●	**EVERYTHING** *MCA MCSTD 48059*	6	9
29 Nov 97	**MISSING YOU** *MCA MCSTD 48071*	19	3
3 Jan 98	**MISSING YOU (re-entry)** *MCA MCSTD 48071*	72	1
31 Jan 98	**MISSING YOU (2nd re-entry)** *MCA MCSTD 48071*	74	1
11 Jul 98	**SEVEN DAYS** *MCA MCSTD 48083* 3	22	3
13 Mar 99 ●	**AS** *Epic 6670122* 4	4	10
21 Aug 99	**ALL THAT I CAN SAY** *MCA MCSTD 40215*	29	3
11 Dec 99	**DEEP INSIDE** *MCA MCSTD 40224*	42	1
29 Apr 00	**GIVE ME YOU** *MCA MCSTD 40230*	19	4
16 Dec 00 ●	**911** *Columbia 6706122* 5	9	3+

1 Method Man featuring Mary J Blige 2 Jay-Z featuring Mary J Blige 3 Mary J Blige featuring George Benson 4 George Michael and Mary J Blige 5 Wyclef Jean featuring Mary J Blige

BLIND MELON US, male vocal / instrumental group (13 WEEKS) pos/wks

12 Jun 93	**TONES OF HOME** *Capitol CDCL 687*	62	2
11 Dec 93	**NO RAIN** *Capitol CDCL 699*	17	6
9 Jul 94	**CHANGE** *Capitol CDCL 717*	35	3
5 Aug 95	**GALAXIE** *Capitol CDCLS 755*	37	2

BLINK Ireland, male vocal / instrumental group (1 WEEK) pos/wks

16 Jul 94	**HAPPY DAY** *Lime CDR 6385*	57	1

BLINK 182 US, male vocal / instrumental group (18 WEEKS) pos/wks

2 Oct 99	**WHAT'S MY AGE AGAIN?** *MCA MCSTD 40219*	38	2
25 Mar 00 ●	**ALL THE SMALL THINGS** *MCA MCSTD 40223*	2	10
8 Jul 00	**WHAT'S MY AGE AGAIN? (re-issue)** *MCA MCSZD 40219*	17	6

BLINKY BLINK – See BLACKSTREET

BLOCKHEADS – See Ian DURY and the BLOCKHEADS

BLOCKSTER UK / Italy, male production group (11 WEEKS) pos/wks

16 Jan 99 ●	**YOU SHOULD BE ...** *Sound of Ministry MOSCDS 128*	3	9
24 Jul 99	**GROOVELINE** *Sound of Ministry MOSCDS 131*	18	2

Kristine BLOND Denmark, female vocalist (5 WEEKS) pos/wks

11 Apr 98	**LOVE SHY** *Reverb BNOISE 1CD*	22	3
11 Nov 00	**LOVE SHY (re-mix)** *Relentless RELENT 4CDS*	28	2

BLONDIE `118` `Top 500` Influential New York-based quintet, fronted by ex-Bunny Girl Deborah Harry (v) (b. 1 Jul 1945, Miami) and fiancé Chris Stein (g). Few acts were more popular internationally 1978-1981, and no other US act in the 1980s matched their three No.1s (169 WEEKS) pos/wks

18 Feb 78 ●	**DENIS** *Chrysalis CHS 2204*	2	14
6 May 78 ●	**(I'M ALWAYS TOUCHED BY YOUR) PRESENCE DEAR** *Chrysalis CHS 2217*	10	9
26 Aug 78	**PICTURE THIS** *Chrysalis CHS 2242*	12	11
11 Nov 78 ●	**HANGING ON THE TELEPHONE** *Chrysalis CHS 2266*	5	12
27 Jan 79 ★	**HEART OF GLASS** *Chrysalis CHS 2275* ◆ ▲	1	12
19 May 79 ★	**SUNDAY GIRL** *Chrysalis CHS 2320*	1	13
29 Sep 79 ●	**DREAMING** *Chrysalis CHS 2350*	2	8
24 Nov 79	**UNION CITY BLUE** *Chrysalis CHS 2400*	13	10
23 Feb 80 ★	**ATOMIC** *Chrysalis CHS 2410*	1	9
12 Apr 80 ★	**CALL ME** *Chrysalis CHS 2414* ▲	1	9
8 Nov 80 ★	**THE TIDE IS HIGH** *Chrysalis CHS 2465* ▲	1	12
24 Jan 81 ●	**RAPTURE** *Chrysalis CHS 2485* ▲	5	8
8 May 82	**ISLAND OF LOST SOULS** *Chrysalis CHS 2608*	11	9
24 Jul 82	**WAR CHILD** *Chrysalis CHS 2624*	39	4
3 Dec 88	**DENIS (re-mix)** *Chrysalis CHS 3328*	50	3

Date	Title	Label	pos	wks
11 Feb 89	CALL ME (re-mix) *Chrysalis CHS 3342*		61	2
10 Sep 94	ATOMIC (re-mix) *Chrysalis CDCHS 5013*		19	4
8 Jul 95	HEART OF GLASS (re-mix) *Chrysalis CSCHS 5023*		15	3
28 Oct 95	UNION CITY BLUE (re-mix) *Chrysalis CDCHS 5027*		31	2
13 Feb 99	★ MARIA *Beyond 74321645632* ■		1	12
12 Jun 99	NOTHING IS REAL BUT THE GIRL *Beyond 74321669472*		26	3

See also Deborah HARRY

BLOOD SWEAT AND TEARS
US / Canada, male vocal / instrumental group (6 WEEKS)   pos/wks

30 Apr 69	YOU'VE MADE ME SO VERY HAPPY *CBS 4116*	35	6

BLOODHOUND GANG
US, male vocal / instrumental group (21 WEEKS)   pos/wks

23 Aug 97	WHY'S EVERYBODY ALWAYS PICKIN' ON ME? *Geffen GFSTD 22252*	56	1
15 Apr 00	● THE BAD TOUCH *Geffen 4972672*	4	14
2 Sep 00	THE BALLAD OF CHASEY LAIN *Geffen 4973812*	15	6

Male / female act for 1997 debut hit

BLOODSTONE *US, male vocal / instrumental group (4 WEEKS)*   pos/wks

18 Aug 73	NATURAL HIGH *Decca F 13382*	40	4

Bobby BLOOM *US, male vocalist (24 WEEKS)*   pos/wks

29 Aug 70	● MONTEGO BAY *Polydor 2058 051*	3	14
12 Dec 70	MONTEGO BAY (re-entry) *Polydor 2058 051*	42	3
9 Jan 71	HEAVY MAKES YOU HAPPY *Polydor 2001 122*	31	5
9 Jan 71	MONTEGO BAY (2nd re-entry) *Polydor 2058 051*	47	2

BLOOMSBURY SET
UK, male vocal / instrumental group (3 WEEKS)   pos/wks

25 Jun 83	HANGING AROUND WITH THE BIG BOYS *Stiletto STL 13*	56	3

Tanya BLOUNT *US, female vocalist (1 WEEK)*   pos/wks

11 Jun 94	I'M GONNA MAKE YOU MINE *Polydor PZCD 315*	69	1

Kurtis BLOW *US, male rapper (23 WEEKS)*   pos/wks

15 Dec 79	CHRISTMAS RAPPIN' *Mercury BLOW 7*	30	6
11 Oct 80	THE BREAKS *Mercury BLOW 8*	47	4
16 Mar 85	PARTY TIME (THE GO-GO EDIT) *Club JAB 12*	67	1
15 Jun 85	SAVE YOUR LOVE (FOR NUMBER 1) *Club JAB 14* [1]	66	2
18 Jan 86	IF I RULED THE WORLD *Club JAB 26*	24	8
8 Nov 86	I'M CHILLIN' *Club JAB 42*	64	2

[1] René and Angela featuring Kurtis Blow

BLOW MONKEYS *UK, male vocal / instrumental group (46 WEEKS)*
pos/wks

1 Mar 86	DIGGING YOUR SCENE *RCA PB 40599*	12	10
17 May 86	WICKED WAYS *RCA MONK 2*	60	2
31 Jan 87	● IT DOESN'T HAVE TO BE THIS WAY *RCA MONK 4*	5	8
28 Mar 87	OUT WITH HER *RCA MONK 5*	30	6
30 May 87	(CELEBRATE) THE DAY AFTER YOU *RCA MONK 6* [1]	52	2
15 Aug 87	SOME KIND OF WONDERFUL *RCA MONK 7*	67	1
6 Aug 88	THIS IS YOUR LIFE *RCA PB 42149*	70	2
8 Apr 89	THIS IS YOUR LIFE (re-mix) *RCA PB 42695*	32	5
15 Jul 89	CHOICE? *RCA PB 42885* [2]	22	6
14 Oct 89	SLAVES NO MORE *RCA PB 43201* [2]	73	2
26 May 90	SPRINGTIME FOR THE WORLD *RCA PB 43623*	69	2

[1] Blow Monkeys with Curtis Mayfield [2] Blow Monkeys featuring Sylvia Tella

BLU PETER *UK, male DJ / producer (1 WEEK)*   pos/wks

21 Mar 98	TELL ME WHAT YOU WANT / JAMES HAS KITTENS *React CDREACT 285*	70	1

BLUE *UK, male vocal / instrumental group (8 WEEKS)*   pos/wks

30 Apr 77	GONNA CAPTURE YOUR HEART *Rocket ROKN 522*	18	8

Babbity BLUE *UK, female vocalist (2 WEEKS)*   pos/wks

11 Feb 65	DON'T MAKE ME (FALL IN LOVE WITH YOU) *Decca F 12053*	48	2

Barry BLUE *UK, male vocalist - Barry Green (48 WEEKS)*   pos/wks

28 Jul 73	● (DANCING) ON A SATURDAY NIGHT *Bell 1295*	2	15
3 Nov 73	● DO YOU WANNA DANCE *Bell 1336*	7	12
2 Mar 74	SCHOOL LOVE *Bell 1345*	11	9
3 Aug 74	MISS HIT AND RUN *Bell 1364*	26	7
26 Oct 74	HOT SHOT *Bell 1379*	23	5

See also CRY SISCO!

BLUE ADONIS featuring LIL' MISS MAX
Belgium, male production duo, female vocalist (3 WEEKS)   pos/wks

17 Oct 98	DISCO COP *Serious SERR 002CD*	27	3

BLUE AEROPLANES
UK, male / female vocal / instrumental group (3 WEEKS)   pos/wks

17 Feb 90	JACKET HANGS *Ensign ENY 628*	72	1
26 May 90	. . . AND STONES *Ensign ENY 632*	63	2

BLUE AMAZON
UK, male production duo / female vocalist (2 WEEKS)   pos/wks

17 May 97	AND THEN THE RAIN FALLS *Sony S2 BAS 301 CD*	53	1
1 Jul 00	BREATHE *Subversive SUB 61D*	73	1

BLUE BAMBOO
Belgium, male producer - Johan Gielen (4 WEEKS)   pos/wks

3 Dec 94	ABC AND D . . . *Escapade CDJAPE 6*	23	4

See also AIRSCAPE; CUBIC 22; TRANSFORMER 2

BLUE BOY *UK, male producer - Alexis Blackmore (16 WEEKS)*   pos/wks

1 Feb 97	● REMEMBER ME *Pharm CDPHARM 1*	8	13
23 Aug 97	SANDMAN *Sidewalk CDSWALK 001*	25	3

BLUE FEATHER
Holland, male vocal / instrumental group (4 WEEKS)   pos/wks

3 Jul 82	LET'S FUNK TONIGHT *Mercury MER 109*	50	4

BLUE FLAMES – See Georgie FAME

BLUE GRASS BOYS – See Johnny DUNCAN and the BLUE GRASS BOYS

BLUE HAZE *UK, male vocal / instrumental group (6 WEEKS)*   pos/wks

18 Mar 72	SMOKE GETS IN YOUR EYES *A & M AMS 891*	32	6

BLUE JEANS – See Bob B SOXX and the BLUE JEANS

BLUE MELONS
UK, male / female vocal / instrumental group (1 WEEK)   pos/wks

8 Jun 96	DO WAH DIDDY DIDDY *Fundamental FUNDCD 1*	70	1

BLUE MERCEDES
UK, male vocal / instrumental duo (18 WEEKS)   pos/wks

10 Oct 87	I WANT TO BE YOUR PROPERTY *MCA BONA 1*	23	11
13 Feb 88	SEE WANT MUST HAVE *MCA BONA 2*	57	2
23 Jul 88	LOVE IS THE GUN *MCA BONA 3*	46	5

BLUE MINK 〔389 Top 500〕 *UK based session musician supergroup with writers Roger Cook and Roger Greenaway providing the classic pop songs for group members Roger Cook (v), Madeline Bell b. 23 Jul 1942,*

Newark, New Jersey, US (v), Roger Coulam (k), Herbie Flowers (b), Barry Morgan (d). Greenaway received OBE in 2001 (83 WEEKS)   pos/wks

15 Nov 69 ●	MELTING POT *Philips BF 1818*	3	15
28 Mar 70 ●	GOOD MORNING FREEDOM *Philips BF 1838*	10	10
19 Sep 70	OUR WORLD *Philips 6006 042*	17	9
29 May 71 ●	BANNER MAN *Regal Zonophone RZ 3034*	3	14
11 Nov 72	STAY WITH ME *Regal Zonophone RZ 3064*	11	13
17 Feb 73	STAY WITH ME (re-entry) *Regal Zonophone RZ 3064*	43	2
3 Mar 73	BY THE DEVIL (I WAS TEMPTED) *EMI 2007*	26	9
23 Jun 73 ●	RANDY *EMI 2028*	9	11

BLUE NILE
UK, male vocal / instrumental group (4 WEEKS)   pos/wks

30 Sep 89	THE DOWNTOWN LIGHTS *Linn LKS 3*	67	1
29 Sep 90	HEADLIGHTS ON THE PARADE *Linn LKS 4*	72	1
19 Jan 91	SATURDAY NIGHT *Linn LKS 5*	50	2

BLUE OYSTER CULT
US, male vocal / instrumental group (14 WEEKS)   pos/wks

20 May 78	(DON'T FEAR) THE REAPER *CBS 6333*	16	14

BLUE PEARL
UK / US, male / female vocal / instrumental group (29 WEEKS)   pos/wks

7 Jul 90 ●	NAKED IN THE RAIN *Big Life BLR 23*	4	13
3 Nov 90	LITTLE BROTHER *Big Life BLR 32*	31	5
11 Jan 92	(CAN YOU) FEEL THE PASSION *Big Life BLR 67*	14	6
25 Jul 92	MOTHER DAWN *Big Life BLR 73*	50	2
27 Nov 93	FIRE OF LOVE *Logic 74321170292* [1]	71	1
4 Jul 98	NAKED IN THE RAIN '98 (re-recording) *Malarky MLKD 7*	22	2

[1] Jungle High with Blue Pearl

BLUE RONDO A LA TURK
UK, male vocal / instrumental group (9 WEEKS)   pos/wks

14 Nov 81	ME AND MR SANCHEZ *Virgin VS 463*	40	4
13 Mar 82	KLACTOVEESEDSTEIN *Diable Noir VS 476*	50	5

BLUE ZOO
UK, male vocal / instrumental group (17 WEEKS)   pos/wks

12 Jun 82	I'M YOUR MAN *Magnet MAG 224*	55	3
16 Oct 82	CRY BOY CRY *Magnet MAG 234*	13	10
28 May 83	I JUST CAN'T (FORGIVE AND FORGET) *Magnet MAG 241*	60	4

BLUEBELLS
UK, male vocal / instrumental group (49 WEEKS)   pos/wks

12 Mar 83	CATH *London LON 20*	62	2
9 Jul 83	SUGAR BRIDGE (IT WILL STAND) *London LON 27*	72	1
24 Mar 84	I'M FALLING *London LON 45*	11	12
23 Jun 84 ●	YOUNG AT HEART *London LON 49*	8	12
1 Sep 84	CATH (re-issue) *London LON 54*	38	7
9 Feb 85	ALL I AM (IS LOVING YOU) *London LON 58*	58	3
27 Mar 93 ★	YOUNG AT HEART (re-issue) *London LONCD 338*	1	12

BLUENOTES – See Harold MELVIN and the BLUENOTES

BLUES BAND
UK, male vocal / instrumental group (2 WEEKS)   pos/wks

12 Jul 80	BLUES BAND (EP) *Arista BOOT 2*	68	2

Tracks on Blues Band (EP): Maggie's Farm / Ain't it Tuff / Diddy Wah Diddy / Back Door Man

BLUES BROTHERS
US, male vocal duo (8 WEEKS)   pos/wks

7 Apr 90	EVERYBODY NEEDS SOMEBODY TO LOVE *East West A7591*	12	8

For the first two weeks, the flip side of 'Everybody Needs Somebody to Love' - 'Think' by Aretha Franklin - was listed

BLUETONES
UK, male vocal / instrumental group (41 WEEKS)   pos/wks

17 Jun 95	ARE YOU BLUE OR ARE YOU BLIND *Superior Quality BLUE 001CD*	31	2
14 Oct 95	BLUETONIC *Superior Quality BLUE 002CD*	19	3
3 Feb 96 ●	SLIGHT RETURN *Superior Quality BLUE 003CD*	2	8

11 May 96 ●	CUT SOME RUG / CASTLE ROCK *Superior Quality BLUE 005CD*	7	5
20 Jul 96	CUT SOME RUG / CASTLE ROCK (re-entry) *Superior Quality BLUE 005CD*	73	1
28 Sep 96 ●	MARBLEHEAD JOHNSON *Superior Quality BLUE 006CD*	7	6
21 Feb 98 ●	SOLOMON BITES THE WORM *Superior Quality BLUED 007*	10	3
9 May 98	IF ... *Superior Quality BLUED 009*	13	5
8 Aug 98	SLEAZY BED TRACK *Superior Quality BLUED 010*	35	2
4 Mar 00	KEEP THE HOME FIRES BURNING *Superior Quality BLUED 012*	13	3
20 May 00	AUTOPHILIA *Superior Quality BLUED 013*	18	3

Colin BLUNSTONE
UK, male vocalist (29 WEEKS)   pos/wks

12 Feb 72	SAY YOU DON'T MIND *Epic EPC 7765*	15	9
11 Nov 72	I DON'T BELIEVE IN MIRACLES *Epic EPC 8434*	31	6
17 Feb 73	HOW COULD WE DARE TO BE WRONG *Epic EPC 1197*	45	2
14 Mar 81	WHAT BECOMES OF THE BROKEN HEARTED *Stiff BROKEN 1* [1]	13	10
29 May 82	TRACKS OF MY TEARS *PRT 7P 236*	60	2

[1] Dave Stewart. Guest vocals: Colin Blunstone

See also ARGENT; Neil MacARTHUR; ZOMBIES

BLUR (196 *Top 500*) *Prime movers of Britpop: Damon Albarn (v/k), Graham Coxon (g), Alex James (b), Dave Rowntree (d). They won a record four Brit awards in 1995, and their first No.1 caused a media storm when it outpaced 'Roll With It' by Britpop rivals Oasis (130 WEEKS)*   pos/wks

27 Oct 90	SHE'S SO HIGH *Food FOOD 26*	48	3
27 Apr 91 ●	THERE'S NO OTHER WAY *Food FOOD 29*	8	8
10 Aug 91	BANG *Food FOOD 31*	24	4
11 Apr 92	POPSCENE *Food FOOD 37*	32	2
1 May 93	FOR TOMORROW *Food CDFOODS 40*	28	4
10 Jul 93	CHEMICAL WORLD *Food CDFOODS 45*	28	4
16 Oct 93	SUNDAY SUNDAY *Food CDFOOD 46*	26	3
19 Mar 94 ●	GIRLS AND BOYS *Food CDFOODS 47*	5	7
11 Jun 94	TO THE END *Food CDFOODS 50*	16	5
3 Sep 94 ●	PARKLIFE *Food CDFOOD 53*	10	7
19 Nov 94	END OF A CENTURY *Food CDFOOD 56*	19	3
26 Aug 95 ★	COUNTRY HOUSE *Food CDFOODS 63* ■	1	11
9 Sep 95	COUNTRY HOUSE *Food FOODS 63*	57	1
25 Nov 95 ●	THE UNIVERSAL *Food CDFOODS 69*	5	9
24 Feb 96 ●	STEREOTYPES *Food CDFOOD 73*	7	5
11 May 96 ●	CHARMLESS MAN *Food CDFOOD 77*	5	6
1 Feb 97 ★	BEETLEBUM *Food CDFOODS 89* ■	1	5
19 Apr 97 ●	SONG 2 *Food CDFOODS 93*	2	5
26 Apr 97	BEETLEBUM (re-entry) *Food CDFOODS 89*	59	2
28 Jun 97 ●	ON YOUR OWN *Food CDFOOD 98*	5	5
27 Sep 97	MOR *Food CDFOOD 107*	15	3
6 Mar 99 ●	TENDER *Food CDFOODS 117*	2	10
10 Jul 99	COFFEE + TV *Food CDFOODS 122*	11	7
27 Nov 99	NO DISTANCE LEFT TO RUN *Food CDFOOD 123*	14	3
22 Jan 00	NO DISTANCE LEFT TO RUN (re-entry) *Food CDFOOD 123*	65	1
28 Oct 00 ●	MUSIC IS MY RADAR *Food / Parlophone CDFOODS 135*	10	7

Chart rules allow for a maximum of three formats; the 7-inch of 'Country House', already available on 2 CDs and cassette, was therefore listed separately

BMR Featuring FELICIA
Germany, male producer – Michi Lange featuring female vocalist (2 WEEKS)   pos/wks

1 May 99	CHECK IT OUT (EVERYBODY) *AM:PM CDAMPM 120*	29	2

BMU
US / UK, male vocal group (2 WEEKS)   pos/wks

18 Feb 95	U WILL KNOW *Mercury MERCD 420*	23	2

BOB and EARL
US, male vocal duo - Bobby Relf and Earl Nelson (13 WEEKS)   pos/wks

12 Mar 69 ●	HARLEM SHUFFLE *Island WIP 6053*	7	13

BOB and MARCIA
Jamaica, male / female vocal duo - Bob Andy and Marcia Griffiths (25 WEEKS)

		pos/wks
14 Mar 70	● YOUNG GIFTED AND BLACK *Harry J HJ 6605*	**5** 12
5 Jun 71	PIED PIPER *Trojan TR 7818*	**11** 13

BOB THE BUILDER
UK, male silicone puppet building contractor - Neil Morrissey (3 WEEKS)

		pos/wks
16 Dec 00	★ CAN WE FIX IT *BBC Music WMSS 60372*..........	**1** 3+

BOBBYSOCKS
Norway / Sweden, female vocal duo (4 WEEKS)

		pos/wks
25 May 85	LET IT SWING *RCA PB 40127*	**44** 4

Su Su BOBIEN – See MASS SYNDICATE featuring Su Su BOBIEN

Andrea BOCELLI
Italy, male vocalist (24 WEEKS)

		pos/wks
24 May 97	● TIME TO SAY GOODBYE (CON TE PARTIRO) *Coalition COLA 003CD* [1]	**2** 14
25 Sep 99	CANTO DELLA TERRA *Polydor / Sugar 5613192*	**25** 4
18 Dec 99	AVE MARIA *Philips 4644852*	**65** 1
1 Jul 00	CANTO DELLA TERRA (re-entry) *Polydor / Sugar 5613192*..........	**24** 5

[1] Sarah Brightman and Andrea Bocelli

Karen BODDINGTON and Mark WILLIAMS
Australia, female / male vocal duo (1 WEEK)

		pos/wks
2 Sep 89	HOME AND AWAY *First Night SCORE 19*	**73** 1

BODY COUNT
US, male rap / instrumental group (4 WEEKS)

		pos/wks
8 Oct 94	BORN DEAD *Rhyme Syndicate SYNDG 4*	**28** 2
17 Dec 94	NECESSARY EVIL *Virgin VSCDX 1529*	**45** 2

See also ICE-T

BODYSNATCHERS
UK, female vocal / instrumental group (12 WEEKS)

		pos/wks
15 Mar 80	LET'S DO ROCK STEADY *2 Tone CHSTT 9*..........	**22** 9
19 Jul 80	EASY LIFE *2 Tone CHSTT 12*..........	**50** 3

Humphrey BOGART – See Dooley WILSON

Hamilton BOHANNON
US, male vocalist / instrumentalist - drums (38 WEEKS)

		pos/wks
15 Feb 75	SOUTH AFRICAN MAN *Brunswick BR 16*	**22** 8
24 May 75	● DISCO STOMP *Brunswick BR 19*	**6** 12
5 Jul 75	FOOT STOMPIN' MUSIC *Brunswick BR 21*	**23** 6
6 Sep 75	HAPPY FEELING *Brunswick BR 24*	**49** 3
26 Aug 78	LET'S START THE DANCE *Mercury 6167 700*..........	**56** 4
13 Feb 82	LET'S START TO DANCE AGAIN *London HL 10582*..........	**49** 5

BOILING POINT
US, male vocal / instrumental group (6 WEEKS)

		pos/wks
27 May 78	LET'S GET FUNKTIFIED *Bang BANG 1312*	**41** 6

Marc BOLAN – See T. REX

CJ BOLLAND
Belgium, male producer (10 WEEKS)

		pos/wks
5 Oct 96	SUGAR IS SWEETER *Internal LIECD 35*	**11** 5
17 May 97	THE PROPHET *ffrr FCD 300*	**19** 3
3 Jul 99	IT AIN'T GONNA BE ME *Essential Recordings ESCD 5*..........	**35** 2

See also RAVESIGNAL III

Michael BOLTON 246 Top 500
Soulful rock balladeer / songwriter who initially recorded under his real name, Michael Bolotin (b. 26 Feb 1953, Connecticut, US), and fronted recording groups The Nomads and Blackjack (113 WEEKS)

		pos/wks
17 Feb 90	● HOW AM I SUPPOSED TO LIVE WITHOUT YOU *CBS 655397 7* ◆	**3** 10
28 Apr 90	● HOW CAN WE BE LOVERS *CBS 655918 7*	**10** 10
21 Jul 90	WHEN I'M BACK ON MY FEET AGAIN *CBS 656077 7*..........	**44** 5
20 Apr 91	LOVE IS A WONDERFUL THING *Columbia 6567717*	**23** 8
27 Jul 91	TIME LOVE AND TENDERNESS *Columbia 6569897*..........	**28** 7
9 Nov 91	● WHEN A MAN LOVES A WOMAN *Columbia 6574887* ▲	**8** 9
8 Feb 92	STEEL BARS *Columbia 6577257*	**17** 6
9 May 92	MISSING YOU NOW *Columbia 6579917* [1]	**28** 4
31 Oct 92	TO LOVE SOMEBODY *Columbia 6584557*	**16** 6
26 Dec 92	DRIFT AWAY *Columbia 6588657*	**18** 5
13 Mar 93	REACH OUT I'LL BE THERE *Columbia 6588972*	**37** 4
13 Nov 93	SAID I LOVED YOU BUT I LIED *Columbia 6598762*..........	**15** 8
26 Feb 94	SOUL OF MY SOUL *Columbia 6601772*	**32** 3
14 May 94	LEAN ON ME *Columbia 6604132*	**14** 7
9 Sep 95	● CAN I TOUCH YOU ... THERE *Columbia 6624385*	**6** 9
2 Dec 95	A LOVE SO BEAUTIFUL *Columbia 6627092*	**27** 5
16 Mar 96	SOUL PROVIDER *Columbia 6629812*..........	**35** 3
8 Nov 97	THE BEST OF LOVE / GO THE DISTANCE *Columbia 6652802*..........	**14** 4

[1] Michael Bolton featuring Kenny G

BOMB THE BASS
UK, male producer - Tim Simenon (50 WEEKS)

		pos/wks
20 Feb 88	● BEAT DIS *Mister-ron DOOD 1*	**2** 9
27 Aug 88	● MEGABLAST / DON'T MAKE ME WAIT *Mister-ron DOOD 2* [1]	**6** 9
26 Nov 88	● SAY A LITTLE PRAYER *Rhythm King DOOD 3* [2]	**10** 10
27 Jul 91	● WINTER IN JULY *Rhythm King 6572757*	**7** 9
9 Nov 91	THE AIR YOU BREATHE *Rhythm King 6575387*	**52** 3
2 May 92	KEEP GIVING ME LOVE *Rhythm King 6579887*	**62** 2
1 Oct 94	BUG POWDER DUST *Stoned Heights BRCD 300* [3]	**24** 3
17 Dec 94	DARKHEART *Stoned Heights BRCD 305* [4]	**35** 3
1 Apr 95	1 TO 1 RELIGION *Stoned Heights BRCD 313* [5]	**53** 1
16 Sep 95	SANDCASTLES *Fourth & Broadway BRCD 324* [6]	**54** 1

[1] Bomb The Bass featuring Merlin and Antonia / Bomb The Bass featuring Lorraine and Lose [2] Bomb the Bass featuring Maureen [3] Bomb The Bass featuring Justin Warfield [4] Bomb The Bass featuring Spikey Tee [5] Bomb The Bass featuring Carlton [6] Bomb The Bass featuring Bernard Fowler

See also ANTONIA

BOMBALURINA
UK, male / female vocal group (20 WEEKS) pos/wks

28 Jul 90	★ ITSY BITSY TEENY WEENY YELLOW POLKA DOT BIKINI *Carpet CRPT 1*	**1** 13
24 Nov 90	SEVEN LITTLE GIRLS SITTING IN THE BACKSEAT *Carpet CRPT 2* [1]	**18** 7

[1] Bombalurina featuring Timmy Mallett

BOMBERS
Canada, male / female vocal / instrumental group (10 WEEKS) pos/wks

5 May 79	(EVERYBODY) GET DANCIN' *Flamingo FM 1*	**37** 7
18 Aug 79	LET'S DANCE *Flamingo FM 4*	**58** 3

BOMFUNK MC'S
Finland, male DJ / rap duo - Raymond Ebanks and DJ Gismo (17 WEEKS) pos/wks

5 Aug 00	● FREESTYLER *Dancepool DPS 2CD*..........	**2** 12
2 Dec 00	UP ROCKING BEATS *INCredible 6706132*..........	**11** 5+

BON JOVI 82 Top 500
Globally popular New Jersey band: Jon Bon Jovi (v), Richie Sambora (g), David Bryan (k), Alec John Such (b), Tico Torres (d). The UK's biggest-selling album act of 1994. Estimated 75 million albums sold worldwide (206 WEEKS) pos/wks

31 Aug 85	HARDEST PART IS THE NIGHT *Vertigo VER 22*	**68** 1
9 Aug 86	YOU GIVE LOVE A BAD NAME *Vertigo VER 26* ▲	**14** 10
25 Oct 86	● LIVIN' ON A PRAYER *Vertigo VER 28* ▲	**4** 15
11 Apr 87	WANTED DEAD OR ALIVE *Vertigo JOV 1*	**13** 7
15 Aug 87	NEVER SAY GOODBYE *Vertigo JOV 2*	**21** 5
24 Sep 88	BAD MEDICINE *Vertigo JOV 3* ▲	**17** 7
10 Dec 88	BORN TO BE MY BABY *Vertigo JOV 4*	**22** 7
29 Apr 89	I'LL BE THERE FOR YOU *Vertigo JOV 5* ▲	**18** 7
26 Aug 89	LAY YOUR HANDS ON ME *Vertigo JOV 6*	**18** 6
9 Dec 89	LIVING IN SIN *Vertigo JOV 7*	**35** 6

Date		Title	pos	wks
24 Oct 92	★	KEEP THE FAITH *Jambco JOV 8*	5	6
23 Jan 93		BED OF ROSES *Jambco JOVCD 9*	13	6
15 May 93	●	IN THESE ARMS *Jambco JOVCD 10*	9	7
7 Aug 93		I'LL SLEEP WHEN I'M DEAD *Jambco JOVCD 11*	17	5
2 Oct 93		I BELIEVE *Jambco JOVCD 12*	11	6
26 Mar 94	●	DRY COUNTY *Jambco JOVCD 13*	9	6
24 Sep 94	●	ALWAYS *Jambco JOVCD 14*	2	18
17 Dec 94	●	PLEASE COME HOME FOR CHRISTMAS *Jambco JOVCD 16*	7	6
25 Feb 95	●	SOMEDAY I'LL BE SATURDAY NIGHT *Jambco JOVDD 15*	7	7
4 Mar 95		PLEASE COME HOME FOR CHRISTMAS (re-entry) *Jambco JOVCD 16*	46	4
10 Jun 95	●	THIS AIN'T A LOVE SONG *Mercury JOVCD 17*	6	9
30 Sep 95	●	SOMETHING FOR THE PAIN *Mercury JOVCD 18*	8	7
25 Nov 95	●	LIE TO ME *Mercury JOVCD 19*	10	8
9 Mar 96	●	THESE DAYS *Mercury JOVCD 20*	7	6
6 Jul 96	●	HEY GOD *Mercury JOVCD 21*	13	5
10 Apr 99	●	REAL LIFE *Reprise W 479CD*	21	5
3 Jun 00	●	IT'S MY LIFE *Mercury 5627682*	3	13
9 Sep 00	●	SAY IT ISN'T SO *Mercury 5688972*	10	6
18 Nov 00		SAY IT ISN'T SO (re-entry) *Mercury 5688972*	73	1
9 Dec 00	●	THANK YOU FOR LOVING ME *Mercury 5727302*	12	4+

See also Jon BON JOVI

Jon BON JOVI *US, male vocalist/instrumentalist - John Bongiovi Jr*
(27 WEEKS)

Date		Title	pos	wks
4 Aug 90		BLAZE OF GLORY *Vertigo JBJ 1* ▲	13	8
10 Nov 90		MIRACLE *Vertigo JBVJ 2*	29	5
14 Jun 97	●	MIDNIGHT IN CHELSEA *Mercury MERCD 488*	4	7
30 Aug 97	●	QUEEN OF NEW ORLEANS *Mercury MERCD 493*	10	4
15 Nov 97		JANIE, DON'T TAKE YOUR LOVE TO TOWN *Mercury 5749872*	13	3

See also BON JOVI

Ronnie BOND *UK, male vocalist (5 WEEKS)*

Date		Title	pos	wks
31 May 80		IT'S WRITTEN ON YOUR BODY *Mercury MER 13*	52	5

Gary 'US' BONDS *US, male vocalist - Gary Anderson*
(39 WEEKS)

Date		Title	pos	wks
19 Jan 61		NEW ORLEANS *Top Rank JAR 527* [1]	16	11
20 Jul 61	●	QUARTER TO THREE *Top Rank JAR 575* [1] ▲	7	13
30 May 81		THIS LITTLE GIRL *EMI America EA 122*	43	6
22 Aug 81		JOLE BLON *EMI America EA 127*	51	3
31 Oct 81		IT'S ONLY LOVE *EMI America EA 128*	43	3
17 Jul 82		SOUL DEEP *EMI America EA 140*	59	3

[1] US Bonds

BONE *UK, male vocal / instrumental duo (1 WEEK)*

Date		Title	pos	wks
2 Apr 94		WINGS OF LOVE *Deconstruction 74321176282*	55	1

BONE THUGS-N-HARMONY *US, male rap group (22 WEEKS)*

Date		Title	pos	wks
4 Nov 95		1ST OF THA MONTH *Epic 6625172*	32	2
10 Aug 96	●	THA CROSSROADS *Epic 6635502* ▲	8	11
9 Nov 96		1ST OF THA MONTH (re-issue) *Epic 6638505*	15	4
15 Feb 97		DAYS OF OUR LIVEZ *East West A 3982CD*	37	2
26 Jul 97		LOOK INTO MY EYES *Epic 6647862*	16	3

Elbow BONES and the RACKETEERS *US, male group leader and female backing group (9 WEEKS)*

Date		Title	pos	wks
14 Jan 84		A NIGHT IN NEW YORK *EMI America EA 165*	33	9

BONEY M [120] [Top 500] *Internationally successful West Indian vocal group: Bobby Farrell, Marcia Barrett, Liz Mitchell, Maisie Williams. This German-based quartet was assembled by producer Frank Farian (later behind controversial duo Milli Vanilli) (169 WEEKS)*

Date		Title	pos	wks
18 Dec 76	●	DADDY COOL *Atlantic K 10827*	6	13
12 Mar 77	●	SUNNY *Atlantic K 10892*	3	10
25 Jun 77	●	MA BAKER *Atlantic K 10965*	2	13
29 Oct 77	●	BELFAST *Atlantic K 11020*	8	13
29 Apr 78	★	RIVERS OF BABYLON / BROWN GIRL IN THE RING *Atlantic/Hansa K 11120* ◆	1	40
7 Oct 78	●	RASPUTIN *Atlantic/Hansa K 11192*	2	10
2 Dec 78	★	MARY'S BOY CHILD - OH MY LORD *Atlantic/Hansa K 11221* ◆	1	8
3 Mar 79	●	PAINTER MAN *Atlantic/Hansa K 11255*	10	6
28 Apr 79	●	HOORAY HOORAY IT'S A HOLI-HOLIDAY *Atlantic/Hansa K 11279*	3	9
11 Aug 79		GOTTA GO HOME / EL LUTE *Atlantic/Hansa K 11351*	12	11
15 Dec 79		I'M BORN AGAIN *Atlantic/Hansa K 11410*	35	7
26 Apr 80		MY FRIEND JACK *Atlantic/Hansa K 11463*	57	5
14 Feb 81		CHILDREN OF PARADISE *Atlantic/Hansa K 11637*	66	2
21 Nov 81		WE KILL THE WORLD (DON'T KILL THE WORLD) *Atlantic/Hansa K 11689*	39	5
24 Dec 88		MEGAMIX / MARY'S BOY CHILD (re-mix) *Ariola 111947*	52	3
5 Dec 92	●	BONEY M MEGAMIX *Arista 74321125127*	7	9
17 Apr 93		BROWN GIRL IN THE RING (re-mix) *Arista 74321137052*	38	3
8 May 99		MA BAKER - SOMEBODY SCREAM *Logic 74321653872* [1]	22	2

[1] Boney M vs Horny United

'Brown Girl in the Ring' listed with 'Rivers of Babylon' only from 5 Aug 1978, peaking at No.2. 'El Lute' listed with 'Gotta Go Home' only from 29 Sep 1979. The 1988 and 1992 megamixes are different

Graham BONNET *UK, male vocalist (15 WEEKS)*

Date		Title	pos	wks
21 Mar 81	●	NIGHT GAMES *Vertigo VER 1*	6	11
13 Jun 81		LIAR *Vertigo VER 2*	51	4

Graham BONNEY *UK, male vocalist (8 WEEKS)*

Date		Title	pos	wks
24 Mar 66		SUPERGIRL *Columbia DB 7843*	19	8

BONO *Ireland, male vocalist (25 WEEKS)*

Date		Title	pos	wks
25 Jan 86		IN A LIFETIME *RCA PB 40535* [1]	20	5
10 Jun 89		IN A LIFETIME (re-issue) *RCA PB 42873* [1]	17	7
4 Dec 93	●	I'VE GOT YOU UNDER MY SKIN *Island CID 578* [2]	4	9
9 Apr 94		IN THE NAME OF THE FATHER *Island CID 593* [3]	46	2
23 Oct 99		NEW DAY *Columbia 6682122* [4]	23	2

[1] Clannad featuring Bono [2] Frank Sinatra with Bono [3] Bono and Gavin Friday [4] Wyclef Jean featuring Bono

I've Got You Under My Skin was the listed B-side of 'Stay (Faraway So Close)' by U2.

See also U2

BONZO DOG DOO-DAH BAND
UK, male vocal / instrumental group (14 WEEKS)

Date		Title	pos	wks
6 Nov 68	●	I'M THE URBAN SPACEMAN *Liberty LBF 15144*	5	14

Betty BOO *UK, female rapper - Alison Clarkson (55 WEEKS)*

Date		Title	pos	wks
12 Aug 89	●	HEY DJ - I CAN'T DANCE (TO THAT MUSIC YOU'RE PLAYING) / SKA TRAIN *Rhythm King LEFT 34* [1]	7	11
19 May 90	●	DOIN' THE DO *Rhythm King LEFT 39*	7	12
11 Aug 90	●	WHERE ARE YOU BABY *Rhythm King LEFT 43*	3	10
1 Dec 90		24 HOURS *Rhythm King LEFT 45*	25	8
8 Aug 92		LET ME TAKE YOU THERE *WEA YZ 677*	12	8
3 Oct 92		I'M ON MY WAY *WEA YZ 693*	44	3
10 Apr 93		HANGOVER *WEA YZ 719CD*	50	3

[1] Beatmasters featuring Betty Boo

BOO RADLEYS *UK, male vocal / instrumental group (27 WEEKS)*

Date		Title	pos	wks
20 Jun 92		DOES THIS HURT / BOO! FOREVER *Creation CRE 128*	67	1
23 Oct 93		WISH I WAS SKINNY *Creation 169*	75	1
12 Feb 94		BARNEY (. . . & ME) *Creation CRESCD 178*	48	2
11 Jun 94		LAZARUS *Creation CRESCD 187*	50	2
11 Mar 95	●	WAKE UP BOO! *Creation CRESCD 191*	9	8
13 May 95		FIND THE ANSWER WITHIN *Creation CRESCD 202*	37	3
29 Jul 95		IT'S LULU *Creation CRESCD 211*	25	2

7 Oct 95	FROM THE BENCH AT BELVIDERE *Creation CRESCD 214* **24**	2
17 Aug 96	WHAT'S IN THE BOX (SEE WATCHA GOT)	
	Creation CRESCD 220 ....**25**	2
19 Oct 96	C'MON KIDS *Creation CRESCD 236* **18**	2
1 Feb 97	RIDE THE TIGER *Creation CRESCD 248X* **38**	1
17 Oct 98	FREE HUEY *Creation CRESCD 299X*........**54**	1

BOO-YAA T.R.I.B.E. *US, male rap group (6 WEEKS)* pos/wks

30 Jun 90	PSYKO FUNK *Fourth & Broadway BRW 179* **43**	3
6 Nov 93	ANOTHER BODY MURDERED *Epic 6597942* [1] **26**	3

[1] Faith No More and Boo-Yaa T.R.I.B.E.

BOOGIE BOX HIGH *UK, male vocal / instrumental group - leader Andros Georgiou (11 WEEKS)* pos/wks

4 Jul 87	● JIVE TALKIN' *Hardback 7BOSS 4* **7**	11

See also ALIEN VOICES Featuring THREE DEGREES; Andy G's STARSKY & HUTCH ALL STARS

BOOGIE DOWN PRODUCTIONS
US, male rap / production duo (2 WEEKS) pos/wks

4 Jun 88	MY PHILOSOPHY / STOP THE VIOLENCE *Jive JIVEX 170* **69**	2

BOOKER T & the MG's
US, male instrumental group (43 WEEKS) pos/wks

11 Dec 68	SOUL LIMBO *Stax 102* **30**	9
7 May 69	● TIME IS TIGHT *Stax 119* **4**	18
30 Aug 69	SOUL CLAP '69 *Stax 127* **35**	4
15 Dec 79	● GREEN ONIONS *Atlantic K 10109* **7**	12

BOOM – See Boris DLUGOSCH presents BOOOM

BOOM BOOM ROOM
UK, male vocal / instrumental group (1 WEEK) pos/wks

8 Mar 86	HERE COMES THE MAN *Fun After All FUN 101* **74**	1

Taka BOOM – See Joey NEGRO

BOOMTOWN RATS 213 Top 500 New-wave group named after a band in a Woody Guthrie novel. Fronted by charismatic Bob Geldof (b. 5 Oct 1954, Dublin), who was later knighted for organising Live Aid. This punk-inspired outfit achieved five Top 10s within 18 months (123 WEEKS) pos/wks

27 Aug 77	LOOKING AFTER NO. 1 *Ensign ENY 4* **11**	9
19 Nov 77	MARY OF THE 4TH FORM *Ensign ENY 9* **15**	9
15 Apr 78	SHE'S SO MODERN *Ensign ENY 13* **12**	11
17 Jun 78	● LIKE CLOCKWORK *Ensign ENY 14* **6**	13
14 Oct 78	★ RAT TRAP *Ensign ENY 16* **1**	15
21 Jul 79	★ I DON'T LIKE MONDAYS *Ensign ENY 30* **1**	12
17 Nov 79	DIAMOND SMILES *Ensign ENY 33* **13**	10
26 Jan 80	● SOMEONE'S LOOKING AT YOU *Ensign ENY 34* **4**	9
22 Nov 80	● BANANA REPUBLIC *Mercury BONGO 1* **3**	11
31 Jan 81	THE ELEPHANT'S GRAVEYARD (GUILTY) *Mercury BONGO 2* **26**	6
12 Dec 81	NEVER IN A MILLION YEARS *Mercury MER 87* **62**	4
20 Mar 82	HOUSE ON FIRE *Mercury MER 91* **24**	8
18 Feb 84	TONIGHT *Mercury MER 154* **73**	1
19 May 84	DRAG ME DOWN *Mercury MER 163* **50**	3
2 Jul 94	I DON'T LIKE MONDAYS (re-issue) *Vertigo VERCD 87* **38**	2

See also Bob GELDOF

Clint BOON EXPERIENCE
UK, male / female vocal / instrumental group (3 WEEKS) pos/wks

6 Nov 99	WHITE NO SUGAR *Artful CDARTFUL 32* **61**	1
5 Feb 00	BIGGEST HORIZON *Artful CDARTFUL 33* **70**	1
5 Aug 00	DO WHAT YOU DO (EARWORM SONG) *Artful CDARTFUL 34* **63**	1

Daniel BOONE *UK, male vocalist (25 WEEKS)* pos/wks

14 Aug 71	DADDY DON'T YOU WALK SO FAST	
	Penny Farthing PEN 764 ....**17**	15

1 Apr 72	BEAUTIFUL SUNDAY *Penny Farthing PEN 781* **48**	1
15 Apr 72	BEAUTIFUL SUNDAY (re-entry)	
	Penny Farthing PEN 781 ....**21**	9

Debby BOONE *US, female vocalist (2 WEEKS)* pos/wks

24 Dec 77	YOU LIGHT UP MY LIFE *Warner Bros. K 17043* ▲ **48**	2

Pat BOONE 30 Top 500 Major rival to Elvis in late 1950s, b. 1 Jun 1934, Florida. This clean-cut vocalist was voted the World's Outstanding Male Singer in the UK in 1957. He was seldom absent from the UK or US charts during the early rock 'n' roll years (308 WEEKS) pos/wks

18 Nov 55	● AIN'T THAT A SHAME *London HLD 8173* **7**	9
27 Apr 56	★ I'LL BE HOME *London HLD 8253* **1**	22
27 Jul 56	LONG TALL SALLY *London HLD 8291* **27**	3
17 Aug 56	I ALMOST LOST MY MIND *London HLD 8303* **14**	7
24 Aug 56	LONG TALL SALLY (re-entry) *London HLD 8291* **18**	4
7 Dec 56	● FRIENDLY PERSUASION *London HLD 8346* **3**	21
11 Jan 57	AIN'T THAT A SHAME (re-entry)	
	London HLD 8173 ....**22**	2
11 Jan 57	I'LL BE HOME (re-entry) *London HLD 8253* **19**	2
1 Feb 57	● DON'T FORBID ME *London HLD 8370* **2**	16
26 Apr 57	WHY BABY WHY *London HLD 8404* **17**	7
5 Jul 57	● LOVE LETTERS IN THE SAND *London HLD 8445* ▲ **2**	21
27 Sep 57	● REMEMBER YOU'RE MINE / THERE'S A GOLDMINE IN THE SKY *London HLD 8479* **5**	18
6 Dec 57	● APRIL LOVE *London HLD 8512* ▲ **7**	23
13 Dec 57	WHITE CHRISTMAS *London HLD 8520* **29**	1
4 Apr 58	● A WONDERFUL TIME UP THERE *London HLD 8574 (A)* **2**	17
11 Apr 58	● IT'S TOO SOON TO KNOW *London HLD 8574 (B)* **7**	12
27 Jun 58	● SUGAR MOON *London HLD 8640* **6**	12
29 Aug 58	IF DREAMS CAME TRUE *London HLD 8675* **16**	11
5 Dec 58	GEE BUT IT'S LONELY *London HLD 8739* **30**	1
16 Jan 59	I'LL REMEMBER TONIGHT *London HLD 8775* **28**	1
6 Feb 59	I'LL REMEMBER TONIGHT (re-entry)	
	London HLD 8775 ....**21**	1
20 Feb 59	I'LL REMEMBER TONIGHT (2nd re-entry)	
	London HLD 8775 ....**18**	7
10 Apr 59	WITH THE WIND AND THE RAIN IN YOUR HAIR	
	London HLD 8824 ....**21**	3
22 May 59	FOR A PENNY *London HLD 8855* **28**	3
26 Jun 59	FOR A PENNY (re-entry) *London HLD 8855* **19**	6
31 Jul 59	'TWIXT TWELVE AND TWENTY *London HLD 8910* **18**	6
18 Sep 59	'TWIXT TWELVE AND TWENTY (re-entry)	
	London HLD 8910 ....**26**	1
23 Jun 60	WALKING THE FLOOR OVER YOU *London HLD 9138* **40**	2
14 Jul 60	WALKING THE FLOOR OVER YOU (re-entry)	
	London HLD 9138 ....**46**	1
4 Aug 60	WALKING THE FLOOR OVER YOU (2nd re-entry)	
	London HLD 9138 ....**39**	2
6 Jul 61	MOODY RIVER *London HLD 9350* ▲ **18**	10
7 Dec 61	● JOHNNY WILL *London HLD 9461* **4**	13
15 Feb 62	I'LL SEE YOU IN MY DREAMS *London HLD 9504* **27**	9
24 May 62	QUANDO QUANDO QUANDO *London HLD 9543* **41**	4
12 Jul 62	● SPEEDY GONZALES *London HLD 9573* **2**	19
15 Nov 62	THE MAIN ATTRACTION *London HLD 9620* **12**	11

'There's a Goldmine in the Sky' was listed only for the week of 27 Sep 1957. It peaked at No.23. 'A Wonderful Time Up There' and 'It's Too Soon To Know' were both on the same single release

BOOT ROOM BOYZ – See LIVERPOOL FC

Duke BOOTEE – See GRANDMASTER FLASH, Melle MEL and the FURIOUS FIVE

BOOTH and the BAD ANGEL
UK / US, male vocal / instrumental duo (4 WEEKS) pos/wks

22 Jun 96	I BELIEVE *Fontana BBCD 1* **25**	3
11 Jul 98	FALL IN LOVE WITH ME *Mercury MERCD 503* **57**	1

Ken BOOTHE *Jamaica, male vocalist (22 WEEKS)* pos/wks

21 Sep 74	★ EVERYTHING I OWN *Trojan TR 7920* **1**	12
14 Dec 74	CRYING OVER YOU *Trojan TR 7944* **11**	10

BOOTHILL FOOT-TAPPERS
UK, male / female vocal / instrumental group (3 WEEKS) pos/wks

14 Jul 84	GET YOUR FEET OUT OF MY SHOES *Go! Discs TAP 1*	64	3

BOOTSY'S RUBBER BAND
US, male vocal / instrumental group (3 WEEKS) pos/wks

8 Jul 78	BOOTZILLA *Warner Bros. K 17196*	43	3

BOOTZILLA ORCHESTRA – See Malcolm McLAREN

BOSS *US, male producer - David Morales (1 WEEK)* pos/wks

27 Aug 94	CONGO *Cooltempo CDCOOL 296*	54	1

See also BAD YARD CLUB; David MORALES

BOSTON *US, male vocal / instrumental group (13 WEEKS)* pos/wks

29 Jan 77	MORE THAN A FEELING *Epic EPC 4658*	22	8
7 Oct 78	DON'T LOOK BACK *Epic EPC 6653*	43	5

Eve BOSWELL *Hungary, female vocalist - Eva Keleti (13 WEEKS)* pos/wks

30 Dec 55 ●	PICKIN' A CHICKEN *Parlophone R 4082* [1]	9	7
2 Mar 56	PICKIN' A CHICKEN (re-entry)		
	Parlophone R 4082 [1]	16	3
6 Apr 56	PICKIN' A CHICKEN (2nd re-entry)		
	Parlophone R 4082 [1]	20	3

[1] 'with Glen Somers and his Orchestra'

Judy BOUCHER *St Vincent, female vocalist (23 WEEKS)* pos/wks

4 Apr 87 ●	CAN'T BE WITH YOU TONIGHT *Orbitone OR 721*	2	14
4 Jul 87	YOU CAUGHT MY EYE *Orbitone OR 722*	18	9

Peter BOUNCER – See SHUT UP AND DANCE

BOUNCING CZECKS
UK, male vocal / instrumental group (1 WEEK) pos/wks

29 Dec 84	I'M A LITTLE CHRISTMAS CRACKER *RCA 463*	72	1

BOUNTY KILLER
Jamaica, male rapper - Rodney Price (1 WEEK) pos/wks

27 Feb 99	IT'S A PARTY *Edel 0066135 BLA*	65	1

BOURGEOIS TAGG
US, male vocal / instrumental duo (6 WEEKS) pos/wks

6 Feb 88	I DON'T MIND AT ALL *Island IS 353*	35	6

BOURGIE BOURGIE
UK, male vocal / instrumental group (4 WEEKS) pos/wks

3 Mar 84	BREAKING POINT *MCA BOU 1*	48	4

Toby BOURKE with George MICHAEL
UK male vocalists (4 WEEKS) pos/wks

7 Jun 97 ●	WALTZ AWAY DREAMING *Aegean AECD 01*	10	4

Aletia BOURNE – See ANGELHEART

BOW WOW WOW *UK / Burma, female / male vocal / instrumental group (54 WEEKS)* pos/wks

26 Jul 80	C30, C60, C90, GO *EMI 5088*	34	7
6 Dec 80	YOUR CASSETTE PET *EMI WOW 1*	58	6
28 Mar 81	W.O.R.K. (N.O. NAH NO NO MY DADDY DON'T)		
	EMI 5153	62	3
15 Aug 81	PRINCE OF DARKNESS *RCA 100*	58	4
7 Nov 81	CHIHUAHUA *RCA 144*	51	4
30 Jan 82 ●	GO WILD IN THE COUNTRY *RCA 175*	7	13
1 May 82	SEE JUNGLE (JUNGLE BOY) / TV SAVAGE *RCA 220*	45	3
5 Jun 82 ●	I WANT CANDY *RCA 238*	9	8

31 Jul 82	LOUIS QUATORZE *RCA 263*	66	2
12 Mar 83	DO YOU WANNA HOLD ME *RCA 314*	47	4

Your Cassette Pet listed as Louis Quatorze on 6 Dec 1980 only. Tracks on Your Cassette Pet (available only as a cassette) are: Louis Quatorze / Gold He Said / Umo-Sex-Al Apache / I Want My Baby On Mars / Sexy Eiffel Towers / Giant Sized Baby Thing / Fools Rush In / Radio G String. RCA 263 is disc version of track on EMI WOW 1 Cassette

BOWA featuring MALA
US, male / female vocal / instrumental duo (1 WEEK) pos/wks

7 Dec 91	DIFFERENT STORY *Dead Dead Good GOOD 8*	64	1

Dane BOWERS – See TRUE STEPPERS

David BOWIE ⟨10⟩ Top 500
Chameleon-like singer / songwriter / entertainer b. David Jones 8 Jan 1947, Brixton, London. Noted for his changes of character and fashion, he became Ziggy Stardust, Aladdin Sane and The Thin White Duke. His striking appearance was enhanced by an unfortunate school playground incident that changed the colour of one of his blue eyes to green when stabbed by a compass. Voted most influential artist in an NME poll in 2000. Among his many accolades and awards, for both recording and songwriting, is the 1996 Brit Award for Outstanding Contribution to British Music. (He is the only act to reject induction into the Rock And Roll Hall Of Fame.) No UK act can better the 10 albums he charted with simultaneously in the Top 100 in 1983, and no British male can match his eight No.1 albums. This often sampled performer has starred in movies, acted on Broadway, painted and recorded music with many of the world's leading acts. In 1999 he released the first virtual album and became the first major act to make a full album available for download, releasing the first enhanced CD single (1995) and being the first singer / songwriter to go to the stock market selling interest in his back catalogue, raising $55 million in the process. (447 WEEKS) pos/wks

6 Sep 69	SPACE ODDITY *Philips BF 1801*	48	1
20 Sep 69 ●	SPACE ODDITY (re-entry) *Philips BF 1801*	5	13
24 Jun 72	STARMAN *RCA 2199*	10	11
16 Sep 72	JOHN I'M ONLY DANCING *RCA 2263*	12	10
9 Dec 72 ●	THE JEAN GENIE *RCA 2302*	2	13
14 Apr 73 ●	DRIVE-IN SATURDAY *RCA 2352*	3	10
30 Jun 73 ●	LIFE ON MARS *RCA 2316*	3	13
15 Sep 73 ●	THE LAUGHING GNOME *Deram DM 123*	6	12
20 Oct 73 ●	SORROW *RCA 2424*	3	15
23 Feb 74 ●	REBEL REBEL *RCA LPBO 5009*	5	7
20 Apr 74	ROCK 'N' ROLL SUICIDE *RCA LPBO 5021*	22	7
22 Jun 74	DIAMOND DOGS *RCA APBO 0293*	21	6
28 Sep 74 ●	KNOCK ON WOOD *RCA 2466*	10	6
1 Mar 75	YOUNG AMERICANS *RCA 2523*	18	7
2 Aug 75	FAME *RCA 2579* ▲	17	8
11 Oct 75 ★	SPACE ODDITY (re-issue) *RCA 2593*	1	10
29 Nov 75 ●	GOLDEN YEARS *RCA 2640*	8	10
22 May 76	TVC 15 *RCA 2682*	33	4
19 Feb 77 ●	SOUND AND VISION *RCA PB 0905*	3	11
15 Oct 77	HEROES *RCA PB 1121*	24	8
21 Jan 78	BEAUTY AND THE BEAST *RCA PB 1190*	39	3
2 Dec 78	BREAKING GLASS (EP) *RCA BOW 1*	54	7
5 May 79 ●	BOYS KEEP SWINGING *RCA BOW 2*	7	10
21 Jul 79	DJ *RCA BOW 3*	29	5
15 Dec 79	JOHN I'M ONLY DANCING (AGAIN) (1975) / JOHN I'M ONLY DANCING (1972) *RCA BOW 4*	12	8
1 Mar 80	ALABAMA SONG *RCA BOW 5*	23	5
16 Aug 80 ★	ASHES TO ASHES *RCA BOW 6*	1	10
1 Nov 80 ●	FASHION *RCA BOW 7*	5	12
10 Jan 81	SCARY MONSTERS (AND SUPER CREEPS) *RCA BOW 8*	20	6
28 Mar 81	UP THE HILL BACKWARDS *RCA BOW 9*	32	6
14 Nov 81 ★	UNDER PRESSURE *EMI 5250* [1]	1	11
28 Nov 81	WILD IS THE WIND *RCA BOW 10*	24	10
6 Mar 82	BAAL'S HYMN (EP) *RCA BOW 11*	29	5
10 Apr 82 ●	CAT PEOPLE (PUTTING OUT FIRE) *MCA 770*	26	6
27 Nov 82 ●	PEACE ON EARTH - LITTLE DRUMMER BOY *RCA BOW 12* [2]	3	8
26 Mar 83 ★	LET'S DANCE *EMI America EA 152* ▲	1	14
11 Jun 83 ●	CHINA GIRL *EMI America EA 157*	2	8
24 Sep 83 ●	MODERN LOVE *EMI America EA 158*	2	8

UK No.1 ★ UK Top 10 ● Still on chart + UK million seller ◆ UK entry at No.1 ■ US No.1 ▲

SINGLED OUT...Gavin Rossdale

Bush may not have chalked up many weeks on the UK chart but lead singer and guitarist Gavin Rossdale's multi-million-selling, stadium-touring track record in the US makes Robbie and Liam look like mere herbaceous borders in the garden of pop.

- **NO.1 ON THE UK SINGLES CHART THE DAY I WAS BORN:**
Massachusetts – Bee Gees

- **ALL-TIME FAVOURITE SINGLE:**
Jamming – Bob Marley and the Wailers

Photo: Pictorial Press

FIRST SINGLE I EVER BOUGHT:

Wild Is The Wind
David Bowie

5 Nov 83	WHITE LIGHT, WHITE HEAT *RCA 372*	46	3
22 Sep 84 ●	BLUE JEAN *EMI America EA 181*	6	8
8 Dec 84	TONIGHT *EMI America EA 187*	53	4
9 Feb 85	THIS IS NOT AMERICA (THE THEME FROM 'THE FALCON		
	AND THE SNOWMAN') *EMI America EA 190* [3]	14	7
8 Jun 85	LOVING THE ALIEN *EMI America EA 195*	19	6
27 Jul 85	LOVING THE ALIEN (re-entry) *EMI America EA 195*	67	1
7 Sep 85 ★	DANCING IN THE STREET *EMI America EA 204* [4] ■	1	12
15 Mar 86 ●	ABSOLUTE BEGINNERS *Virgin VS 838*	2	9
21 Apr 86	UNDERGROUND *Virgin VS 216*	21	6
8 Nov 86	WHEN THE WIND BLOWS *Virgin VS 906*	44	4
4 Apr 87	DAY-IN DAY-OUT *EMI America EA 230*	17	6
27 Jun 87	TIME WILL CRAWL *EMI America EA 237*	33	4
29 Aug 87	NEVER LET ME DOWN *EMI America EA 239*	34	6
7 Apr 90	FAME (re-mix) *EMI-USA FAME 90*	28	4
22 Aug 92	REAL COOL WORLD *Warner Bros. W 0127*	53	1
27 Mar 93 ●	JUMP THEY SAY *Arista 74321139422*	9	6
12 Jun 93	BLACK TIE WHITE NOISE *Arista 74321148682* [5]	36	2
23 Oct 93	MIRACLE GOODNIGHT *Arista 74321162262*	40	2
4 Dec 93	BUDDHA OF SUBURBIA *Arista 74321177052* [6]	35	3
23 Sep 95	THE HEART'S FILTHY LESSON *RCA 74321307032*	35	2
2 Dec 95	STRANGERS WHEN WE MEET / THE MAN WHO SOLD THE		
	WORLD (LIVE) *RCA 74321329402*	39	2
2 Mar 96	HALLO SPACEBOY *RCA 74321353842*	12	4
8 Feb 97	LITTLE WONDER *RCA 74321452072*	14	3
26 Apr 97	DEAD MAN WALKING *RCA 74321475852*	32	2
30 Aug 97	SEVEN YEARS IN TIBET *RCA 74321512542*	61	1
21 Feb 99	I CAN'T READ *Velvet ZYX 87578*	73	1
2 Oct 99	THURSDAY'S CHILD *Virgin VSCDT 1753*	16	3
18 Dec 99	UNDER PRESSURE (re-mix) *Parlophone CDQUEEN 28* [1]	14	7
5 Feb 00	SURVIVE *Virgin VSCDT 1767*	28	2
29 Jul 00	SEVEN *Virgin VSCDT 1776*	32	2

[1] Queen and David Bowie [2] David Bowie and Bing Crosby [3] David Bowie and the Pat Metheny Group [4] David Bowie and Mick Jagger [5] David Bowie featuring Al B Sure! [6] David Bowie featuring Lenny Kravitz

Tracks on Breaking Glass (EP): Breaking Glass / Art Decade / Ziggy Stardust. All three versions of 'John I'm Only Dancing' are different. Tracks on Baal's Hymn (EP): Baal's Hymn / The Drowned Girl / Remembering Marie / The Dirty Song / Ballad of the Adventurers

George BOWYER *UK, male vocalist (2 WEEKS)* pos/wks

22 Aug 98	GUARDIANS OF THE LAND *Boys BYSCD 01*	33	2

BOX TOPS *US, male vocal / instrumental group (33 WEEKS)* pos/wks

13 Sep 67 ●	THE LETTER *Stateside SS 2044* ▲	5	12
20 Mar 68	CRY LIKE A BABY *Bell 1001*	15	12
23 Aug 69	SOUL DEEP *Bell 1068*	22	9

BOY GEORGE *UK, male vocalist - George O'Dowd (46 WEEKS)* pos/wks

7 Mar 87 ★	EVERYTHING I OWN *Virgin BOY 100*	1	9
6 Jun 87	KEEP ME IN MIND *Virgin BOY 101*	29	4
18 Jul 87	SOLD *Virgin BOY 102*	24	5
21 Nov 87	TO BE REBORN *Virgin BOY 103*	13	7
5 Mar 88	LIVE MY LIFE *Virgin BOY 105*	62	2
18 Jun 88	NO CLAUSE 28 *Virgin BOY 106*	57	3
8 Oct 88	DON'T CRY *Virgin BOY 107*	60	2
4 Mar 89	DON'T TAKE MY MIND ON A TRIP *Virgin BOY 108*	68	2
19 Sep 92	THE CRYING GAME *Spaghetti CIAO 6*	22	4
12 Jun 93	MORE THAN LIKELY *Gee Street GESCD 49* [1]	40	3
1 Apr 95	FUNTIME *Virgin VSCDG 1538*	45	2
1 Jul 95	IL ADORE *Virgin VSCDX 1543*	50	2
21 Oct 95	SAME THING IN REVERSE *Virgin VSCDT 1561*	56	1

[1] PM Dawn featuring Boy George

See also CULTURE CLUB

BOY MEETS GIRL *US, male / female vocal duo - Shannon Rubicam and George Merrill (13 WEEKS)* pos/wks

3 Dec 88 ●	WAITING FOR A STAR TO FALL *RCA PB 49519*	9	13

BOY WUNDA – See PROGRESS presents the BOY WUNDA

Jimmy BOYD *US, male vocalist (22 WEEKS)* pos/wks

8 May 53 ●	TELL ME A STORY *Philips PB 126* [1]	5	15
11 Sep 53	TELL ME A STORY (re-entry) *Philips PB 126* [1]	12	1
27 Nov 53 ●	I SAW MOMMY KISSING SANTA CLAUS *Columbia DB 3365* ▲	3	6

[1] Jimmy Boyd - Frankie Laine

Jacqueline BOYER *France, female vocalist (2 WEEKS)* pos/wks

28 Apr 60	TOM PILLIBI *Columbia DB 4452*	33	2

BOYS *US, male vocal group (5 WEEKS)* pos/wks

12 Nov 88	DIAL MY HEART *Motown ZB 42245*	61	2
29 Sep 90	CRAZY *Motown ZB 44037*	57	3

BOYSTOWN GANG *US, male / female vocal group (20 WEEKS)* pos/wks

22 Aug 81	AIN'T NO MOUNTAIN HIGH ENOUGH - REMEMBER ME		
	(MEDLEY) *WEA DICK 1*	46	6
31 Jul 82 ●	CAN'T TAKE MY EYES OFF YOU *ERC 101*	4	11
9 Oct 82	SIGNED SEALED DELIVERED (I'M YOURS) *ERC 102*	50	3

BOYZ – See HEAVY D and the BOYZ

BOYZ II MEN (402) Top 500 *R&B vocal harmony quartet formed 1988 in Philadelphia (brothers Nathan and Wanya Morris, Shawn Stockman, Michael McCary) were Motown's biggest sellers in the 1990s. The Beatles are the only group to have spent longer at the top of the US chart (81 WEEKS)* pos/wks

5 Sep 92 ●	END OF THE ROAD *Motown TMG 1411* ▲	1	21
19 Dec 92	MOTOWNPHILLY *Motown TMG 1402*	23	6
27 Feb 93	IN THE STILL OF THE NITE (I'LL REMEMBER)		
	Motown TMGCD 1415	27	4
3 Sep 94 ●	I'LL MAKE LOVE TO YOU *Motown TMGCD 1431* ▲	5	12
26 Nov 94	ON BENDED KNEE *Motown TMGCD 1433* ▲	20	3
24 Dec 94	I'LL MAKE LOVE TO YOU (re-entry) *Motown TMGCD 1431*	57	3
22 Apr 95	THANK YOU *Motown TMGCD 1438*	26	3
8 Jul 95	WATER RUNS DRY *Motown TMGCD 1443*	24	3
9 Dec 95 ●	ONE SWEET DAY *Columbia 6626035* [1] ▲	6	11
20 Jan 96	HEY LOVER *Def Jam DEFCD 14* [2]	17	4
20 Sep 97 ●	4 SEASONS OF LONELINESS *Motown 8606992* ▲	10	6
6 Dec 97	A SONG FOR MAMA *Motown 8607372*	34	2
25 Jul 98	CAN'T LET HER GO *Motown 8607952*	23	3

[1] Mariah Carey and Boyz II Men [2] LL Cool J featuring Boyz II Men

BOYZONE (73) Top 500 *Irish 'boy band' vocal quintet who became international teen idols: Ronan Keating, Stephen Gately, Mikey Graham, Keith Duffy, Shane Lynch. They achieved the best ever start to a UK singles career with 16 consecutive Top 5 singles (213 WEEKS)* pos/wks

10 Dec 94 ●	LOVE ME FOR A REASON *Polydor 8512802*	2	13
29 Apr 95 ●	KEY TO MY LIFE *Polydor PZCD 342*	3	8
12 Aug 95 ●	SO GOOD *Polydor 5797732*	3	6
25 Nov 95 ●	FATHER AND SON *Polydor 5775762*	2	16
9 Mar 96 ●	COMING HOME NOW *Polydor 5775702*	4	9
19 Oct 96 ★	WORDS *Polydor 5755372* ■	1	14
14 Dec 96 ★	A DIFFERENT BEAT *Polydor 5732052* ■	1	10
1 Mar 97	A DIFFERENT BEAT (re-entry) *Polydor 5732052*	74	1
15 Mar 97	A DIFFERENT BEAT (2nd re-entry) *Polydor 5732052*	62	4
22 Mar 97 ●	ISN'T IT A WONDER *Polydor 5735472*	2	7
17 May 97	ISN'T IT A WONDER (re-entry) *Polydor 5735472*	44	7
2 Aug 97 ●	PICTURE OF YOU *Polydor 5713112*	2	18
6 Dec 97 ●	BABY CAN I HOLD YOU / SHOOTING STAR *Polydor 5691672*	2	14
2 May 98 ★	ALL THAT I NEED *Polydor 5698732* ■	1	10
18 Jul 98	ALL THAT I NEED (re-entry) *Polydor 5698732*	49	4
15 Aug 98 ★	NO MATTER WHAT *Polydor 5675672* ◆ ■	1	15
5 Dec 98 ●	I LOVE THE WAY YOU LOVE ME *Polydor 5631992*	2	13
13 Mar 99 ★	WHEN THE GOING GETS TOUGH *Polydor 5699132* ■	1	14
22 May 99 ★	YOU NEEDED ME *Polydor 5639332* ■	1	12
17 Jul 99	WHEN THE GOING GETS TOUGH (re-entry) *Polydor 5699132*	57	2
28 Aug 99	YOU NEEDED ME (re-entry) *Polydor 5639332*	60	3
4 Dec 99 ●	EVERY DAY I LOVE YOU *Polydor 5615802*	3	13

Shooting Star was in fact a solo by Stephen Gately, from the movie 'Hercules'

See also Ronan KEATING; Stephen GATELY; Mikey GRAHAM

UK No.1 ★   UK Top 10 ●   Still on chart +   UK million seller ◆   UK entry at No.1 ■   US No.1 ▲

SINGLED OUT... Rick Wakeman

The former Strawbs and Yes keyboard wizard was responsible for one of the more over-the-top rock star initiatives when staging and performing in The Myths and Legends of King Arthur and the Knights of the Round Table, with a 50-piece orchestra, on ice, at The Empire Pool, Wembley. He now suffers from an aversion to the Honeycombs' 1964 chart-topping classic but has first-hand experience of why Bowie's first No.1 is so exceptional.

- **NO.1 SONG ON THE DAY I WAS BORN:**
  Lavender Blue – Burl Ives

- **FIRST SINGLE BOUGHT:**
  Have A Drink On Me – Lonnie Donegan

- **SINGLE THAT DRIVES ME UP THE WALL:**
  Have I The Right – The Honeycombs

ALL-TIME
FAVOURITE
SINGLE:
Space Oddity
David Bowie

... and not just because
I played on it!

Photo: Pictorial Press

BRAD US, male vocal / instrumental group (1 WEEK)

		pos/wks
26 Jun 93	20TH CENTURY Epic 6592482	64 1

Scott BRADLEY UK, male vocalist (1 WEEK)

		pos/wks
15 Oct 94	ZOOM Hidden Agenda HIDDCD 1	61 1

Paul BRADY UK, male vocalist (1 WEEK)

		pos/wks
13 Jan 96	THE WORLD IS WHAT YOU MAKE IT Mercury PBCD 5	67 1

Billy BRAGG UK, male vocalist (51 WEEKS)

		pos/wks
16 Mar 85	BETWEEN THE WARS (EP) Go! Discs AGOEP 1	15 6
28 Dec 85	DAYS LIKE THESE Go! Discs GOD 8	43 5
28 Jun 86	LEVI STUBBS' TEARS Go! Discs GOD 12	29 6
15 Nov 86	GREETINGS TO THE NEW BRUNETTE Go! Discs GOD 15 [1]	58 2
14 May 88 ★	SHE'S LEAVING HOME Childline CHILD 1 [2]	1 11
10 Sep 88	WAITING FOR THE GREAT LEAP FORWARDS Go! Discs GOD 23	52 3
8 Jul 89	WON'T TALK ABOUT IT Go.Beat GOD 33 [3]	29 6
6 Jul 91	SEXUALITY Go! Discs GOD 56	27 5
7 Sep 91	YOU WOKE UP MY NEIGHBOURHOOD Go! Discs GOD 60	54 2
29 Feb 92	ACCIDENT WAITING TO HAPPEN (EP) Go! Discs GOD 67	33 3
31 Aug 96	UPFIELD Cooking Vinyl FRYCD 051	46 1
17 May 97	THE BOY DONE GOOD Cooking Vinyl FRYCD 064	55 1

[1] Billy Bragg with Johnny Marr and Kirsty MacColl [2] Billy Bragg with Cara Tivey [3] Norman Cook featuring Billy Bragg

Tracks on Between the Wars (EP): Between the Wars / Which Side Are You On / World Turned Upside Down / It Says Here. Tracks on Accident Waiting to Happen (EP): Accident Waiting to Happen / Revolution / Sulk / The Warmest Room. 'She's Leaving Home' was listed with the flip side 'With a Little Help from My Friends' by Wet Wet Wet. 'Won't Talk About It' was listed with the flip side 'Blame It on the Bassline' by Norman Cook featuring MC Wildski

BRAIDS US, female vocal duo (3 WEEKS)

		pos/wks
2 Nov 96	BOHEMIAN RHAPSODY Atlantic A 5640CD	21 3

BRAIN BASHERS
UK, male / female DJ / production duo (1 WEEK)

		pos/wks
1 Jul 00	DO IT NOW Tidy Trax TIDY 137 CD	64 1

BRAINBUG Italy, male producer – Alberto Bertapelle (7 WEEKS)

		pos/wks
3 May 97	NIGHTMARE Positiva CDTIV 76	11 5
22 Nov 97	BENEDICTUS / NIGHTMARE Positiva CDTIV 86	24 2

BRAINCHILD
Germany, male producer – Matthias Hoffmann (2 WEEKS)

		pos/wks
30 Oct 99	SYMMETRY C Multiply CDMULTY 55	31 2

Wilfrid BRAMBELL and Harry H CORBETT
UK, male vocal TV comedy duo (12 WEEKS)

		pos/wks
28 Nov 63	AT THE PALACE (PARTS 1 & 2) Pye 7N 15588	25 12

Bekka BRAMLETT – See Joe COCKER

BRAN VAN 3000
Canada, male / female vocal / instrumental group (13 WEEKS)

		pos/wks
6 Jun 98	DRINKING IN L.A. Capitol CDCL 802	34 2
21 Aug 99 ●	DRINKING IN L.A. (re-issue) Capitol CDCL 811	3 11

BRAND NEW HEAVIES
UK / US, male / female vocal / instrumental group (68 WEEKS)

		pos/wks
5 Oct 91	NEVER STOP ffrr F 165	43 3
15 Feb 92	DREAM COME TRUE ffrr F 180	24 4
18 Apr 92	ULTIMATE TRUNK FUNK (EP) ffrr F 185	19 6
1 Aug 92	DON'T LET IT GO TO YOUR HEAD ffrr BNH 1	24 4
19 Dec 92	STAY THIS WAY ffrr BNH 2	40 5
26 Mar 94	DREAM ON DREAMER ffrr BNHCD 3	15 4
11 Jun 94	BACK TO LOVE ffrr BNHCD 4	23 4
13 Aug 94	MIDNIGHT AT THE OASIS ffrr BNHCD 5	13 6
5 Nov 94	SPEND SOME TIME ffrr BNHCD 6	26 4
11 Mar 95	CLOSE TO YOU ffrr BNHCD 7	38 3
12 Apr 97	SOMETIMES ffrr BNHCD 8	11 5
28 Jun 97	YOU ARE THE UNIVERSE ffrr GNHCD 9	21 4
18 Oct 97 ●	YOU'VE GOT A FRIEND London BNHCD 10	9 8
10 Jan 98	SHELTER London BNHCD 11	31 4
11 Sep 99	SATURDAY NITE London BNHCD 12	35 2
29 Jan 00	APPARENTLY NOTHING ffrr BNHCD 13	32 2

The first 10 hits are credited 'featuring N'Dea Davenport' on either the sleeve or the label. Tracks on Ultimate Trunk Funk (EP): Never Stop / Stay This Way / Mr Tanaka. BNH 2 is a re-mixed version of the track on the Ultimate Trunk Funk EP. Carleen Anderson replaced vocalist Siedah Garrett in 1999

Johnny BRANDON UK, male vocalist (12 WEEKS)

		pos/wks
11 Mar 55 ●	TOMORROW Polygon P 1131 [1]	8 6
29 Apr 55	TOMORROW (re-entry) Polygon P 1131 [1]	16 2
1 Jul 55	DON'T WORRY Polygon P 1163	18 4

[1] Johnny Brandon with the Phantoms and the Norman Warren Music

BRANDY US, female vocalist – Brandy Norwood (52 WEEKS)

		pos/wks
10 Dec 94	I WANNA BE DOWN Atlantic A7217CD	44 3
3 Jun 95	I WANNA BE DOWN (re-mix) Atlantic A 7186CD	36 3
3 Feb 96	SITTIN' UP IN MY ROOM Arista 74321344012	30 4
6 Jun 98 ●	THE BOY IS MINE Atlantic AT 0036CD [1] ▲	2 20
10 Oct 98 ●	TOP OF THE WORLD Atlantic AT 0046CD [2]	2 8
12 Dec 98	HAVE YOU EVER? Atlantic AT 0058CD ▲	13 8
9 Jan 99	TOP OF THE WORLD (re-entry) Atlantic AT 0046CD [2]	61 1
19 Jun 99	ALMOST DOESN'T COUNT Atlantic AT0068CD1	15 5

[1] Brandy and Monica [2] Brandy featuring Mase

Laura BRANIGAN US, female vocalist (33 WEEKS)

		pos/wks
18 Dec 82 ●	GLORIA Atlantic K 11759	6 13
7 Jul 84 ●	SELF CONTROL Atlantic A 9676	5 17
6 Oct 84	THE LUCKY ONE Atlantic A 9636	56 3

BRASS CONSTRUCTION
US, male vocal / instrumental group (35 WEEKS)

		pos/wks
3 Apr 76	MOVIN' United Artists UP 36090	23 6
5 Feb 77	HA CHA CHA (FUNKTION) United Artists UP 36205	37 5
26 Jan 80	MUSIC MAKES YOU FEEL LIKE DANCING United Artists UP 615	39 6
28 May 83	WALKIN' THE LINE Capitol CL 292	47 3
16 Jul 83	WE CAN WORK IT OUT Capitol CL 299	70 2
7 Jul 84	PARTYLINE Capitol CL 335	56 4
27 Oct 84	INTERNATIONAL Capitol CL 341	70 2
9 Nov 85	GIVE AND TAKE Capitol CL 377	62 3
28 May 88	MOVIN' 1988 (re-mix) Syncopate SY 11	24 4

BRAT UK, male vocalist – Roger Kitter (8 WEEKS)

		pos/wks
10 Jul 82	CHALK DUST - THE UMPIRE STRIKES BACK Hansa SMASH 1	19 8

BRAVADO
UK, male / female vocal / instrumental group (3 WEEKS)

		pos/wks
18 Jun 94	HARMONICA MAN Peach PEACHCD 5	37 3

BRAVO ALL STARS
UK / US, male / female vocal / instrumental group (2 WEEKS)

		pos/wks
29 Aug 98	LET THE MUSIC HEAL YOUR SOUL Edel 0039335 ERE	36 2

Artists featured: Backstreet Boys, Aaron Carter, Scooter, 'N Sync, Caught in the Act, The Boyz, Blumchen, Gil, Squeezer, Mr President, Touche, R'N'G and the Moffatts

Alan BRAXE & Fred FALKE
France, male production duo (3 WEEKS)

		pos/wks
25 Nov 00	INTRO Vulture / Credence CDCRED 006	35 3

UK No.1 ★   UK Top 10 ●   Still on chart +   UK million seller ◆   UK entry at No.1 ■   US No.1 ▲

Dhar BRAXTON US, female vocalist (8 WEEKS)

			pos/wks
31 May 86	JUMP BACK (SET ME FREE) Fourth & Broadway BRW 47	32	8

Toni BRAXTON (387) Top 500 Sultry, sexy soul / R&B vocalist, b. 7 Oct 1968, Maryland, US, who won Best New Artist Grammy in 1993 and was one of America's top selling pop and R&B artists of the 1990s. Her biggest hits have been ballads from the pens of top writers Babyface, Diane Warren, R Kelly and Rodney Jerkins (83 WEEKS)

			pos/wks
18 Sep 93	ANOTHER SAD LOVE SONG LaFace 74321163502	51	2
15 Jan 94 ●	BREATHE AGAIN LaFace 74321185442	2	12
2 Apr 94	ANOTHER SAD LOVE SONG (re-issue) LaFace 74321196682	15	8
9 Jul 94	YOU MEAN THE WORLD TO ME LaFace 74321214702	30	5
3 Dec 94	LOVE SHOULDA BROUGHT YOU HOME LaFace 74321249412	33	3
13 Jul 96 ●	YOU'RE MAKIN' ME HIGH LaFace 74321395402 ▲	7	11
2 Nov 96 ●	UN-BREAK MY HEART LaFace 74321410632 ▲	2	19
24 May 97 ●	I DON'T WANT TO LaFace 74321468612	9	8
8 Nov 97	HOW COULD AN ANGEL BREAK MY HEART LaFace 74321531982 [1]	22	4
29 Apr 00 ●	HE WASN'T MAN ENOUGH LaFace 74321757852	5	11

[1] Toni Braxton with Kenny G

BRAXTONS US, female vocal group (7 WEEKS)

			pos/wks
1 Feb 97	SO MANY WAYS Atlantic A 5469CD	32	2
29 Mar 97	THE BOSS Atlantic A 5441CD	31	3
19 Jul 97	SLOW FLOW Atlantic AT 0001CD	26	2

BREAD US, male vocal / instrumental group (46 WEEKS)

			pos/wks
1 Aug 70 ●	MAKE IT WITH YOU Elektra 2101 010 ▲	5	14
15 Jan 72	BABY I'M A WANT YOU Elektra K 12033	14	10
29 Apr 72	EVERYTHING I OWN Elektra K 12041	32	6
30 Sep 72	THE GUITAR MAN Elektra K 12066	16	9
25 Dec 76	LOST WITHOUT YOUR LOVE Elektra K 12241	27	7

BREAK MACHINE US, male vocal group (32 WEEKS)

			pos/wks
4 Feb 84 ●	STREET DANCE Record Shack SOHO 13	3	14
12 May 84 ●	BREAKDANCE PARTY Record Shack SOHO 20	9	8
14 Jul 84	BREAKDANCE PARTY (re-entry) Record Shack SOHO 20	65	2
11 Aug 84	ARE YOU READY? Record Shack SOHO 24	27	8

BREAKBEAT ERA
UK, male / female drum and bass trio (5 WEEKS)

			pos/wks
18 Jul 98	BREAKBEAT ERA XL Recordings XLS 95CD	38	2
21 Aug 99	ULTRA - OBSCENE XL Recordings XLS 107CD	48	2
11 Mar 00	BULLITPROOF XL Recordings XLS 115CD	65	1

BREAKFAST CLUB
US, male vocal / instrumental group (3 WEEKS)

			pos/wks
27 Jun 87	RIGHT ON TRACK MCA MCA 1146	54	3

BREATHE UK, male vocal / instrumental group (27 WEEKS)

			pos/wks
30 Jul 88 ●	HANDS TO HEAVEN Siren SRN 68	4	12
22 Oct 88	JONAH Siren SRN 95	60	3
3 Dec 88	HOW CAN I FALL Siren SRN 102	48	7
11 Mar 89	DON'T TELL ME LIES Siren SRN 109	45	5

Freddy BRECK Germany, male vocalist (4 WEEKS)

			pos/wks
13 Apr 74	SO IN LOVE WITH YOU Decca F 13481	44	4

BRECKER BROTHERS
US, male vocal / instrumental group (5 WEEKS)

			pos/wks
4 Nov 78	EAST RIVER Arista ARIST 211	34	5

BREEDERS
US / UK, female / male vocal / instrumental group (6 WEEKS)

			pos/wks
18 Apr 92	SAFARI (EP) 4AD BAD 2003	69	1
21 Aug 93	CANNONBALL (EP) 4AD BAD 3011CD	40	3

6 Nov 93	DIVINE HAMMER 4AD BAD 3017CD		59	1
23 Jul 94	HEAD TO TOE (EP) 4AD BADD 4012		68	1

Tracks on Safari (EP): Do You Love Me Now / Don't Call Home / Safari / So Sad About Us. Tracks on Cannonball (EP): Cannonball / Cro-Aloha / Lord of the Thighs / 900. Tracks on Head to Toe (EP): Head to Toe / Shocker In Gloom Town / Freed Pig
See also THROWING MUSES; PIXIES

BREEKOUT KREW US, male vocal duo (3 WEEKS)

			pos/wks
24 Nov 84	MATT'S MOOD London LON 59	51	3

Ann BREEN Ireland, female vocalist (2 WEEKS)

			pos/wks
19 Mar 83	PAL OF MY CRADLE DAYS Homespun HS 052	69	1
7 Jan 84	PAL OF MY CRADLE DAYS (re-entry) Homespun HS 052	74	1

BRENDON UK, male vocalist (9 WEEKS)

			pos/wks
19 Mar 77	GIMME SOME Magnet MAG 80	14	9

Maire BRENNAN Ireland, female vocalist (12 WEEKS)

			pos/wks
16 May 92	AGAINST THE WIND RCA PB 45399	64	2
5 Jun 99 ●	SALTWATER Xtravaganza XTRAV 1CDS [1]	6	10

[1] Chicane featuring Maire Brennan of Clannad

Rose BRENNAN Ireland, female vocalist (9 WEEKS)

			pos/wks
7 Dec 61	TALL DARK STRANGER Philips PB 1193	31	9

Walter BRENNAN US, male vocalist (3 WEEKS)

			pos/wks
28 Jun 62	OLD RIVERS Liberty LIB 55436	38	3

Tony BRENT UK, male vocalist - Reginald Bretagne (52 WEEKS)

			pos/wks
19 Dec 52 ●	WALKIN' TO MISSOURI Columbia DB 3147	9	2
2 Jan 53 ●	MAKE IT SOON Columbia DB 3187	9	4
9 Jan 53 ●	WALKIN' TO MISSOURI (re-entry) Columbia DB 3147	7	5
23 Jan 53	GOT YOU ON MY MIND Columbia DB 3226	12	1
13 Mar 53 ●	MAKE IT SOON (re-entry) Columbia DB 3187	9	3
30 Nov 56	CINDY, OH CINDY Columbia DB 3844	16	6
8 Feb 57	CINDY, OH CINDY (re-entry) Columbia DB 3844	30	1
28 Jun 57	DARK MOON Columbia DB 3950	17	14
28 Feb 58	THE CLOUDS WILL SOON ROLL BY Columbia DB 4066	24	3
9 May 58	THE CLOUDS WILL SOON ROLL BY (re-entry) Columbia DB 4066	20	2
5 Sep 58	GIRL OF MY DREAMS Columbia DB 4177	16	7
24 Jul 59	WHY SHOULD I BE LONELY Columbia DB 4304	24	4

Bernard BRESSLAW UK, male actor (11 WEEKS)

			pos/wks
5 Sep 58 ●	MAD PASSIONATE LOVE HMV POP 522	6	11

See also Michael MEDWIN, Bernard BRESSLAW, Alfie BASS and Leslie FYSON

Teresa BREWER US, female vocalist - Theresa Breuer (53 WEEKS)

			pos/wks
11 Feb 55 ●	LET ME GO LOVER Vogue/Coral Q 72043 [1]	9	10
13 Apr 56 ●	A TEAR FELL Vogue/Coral Q 72146	2	15
13 Jul 56 ●	A SWEET OLD FASHIONED GIRL Vogue/Coral Q 72172	3	15
10 May 57	NORA MALONE Vogue/Coral Q 72224	26	2
23 Jun 60	HOW DO YOU KNOW IT'S LOVE Coral Q 72396	21	11

[1] Teresa Brewer with The Lancers

BRIAN and MICHAEL UK, male vocal duo - Brian Burke and Michael Coleman (19 WEEKS)

			pos/wks
25 Feb 78 ★	MATCHSTALK MEN AND MATCHSTALK CATS AND DOGS Pye 7N 46035	1	19

BRICK US, male vocal / instrumental group (4 WEEKS)

			pos/wks
5 Feb 77	DAZZ Bang 004	36	4

UK No.1 ★ UK Top 10 ● Still on chart + UK million seller ◆ UK entry at No.1 ■ US No.1 ▲

Edie BRICKELL and the NEW BOHEMIANS *US, female / male vocal / instrumental group (10 WEEKS)* pos/wks

4 Feb 89	WHAT I AM *Geffen GEF 49*	31	7
27 May 89	CIRCLE *Geffen GEF 51*	74	1
1 Oct 94	GOOD TIMES *Geffen GFSTD 78* [1]	40	2

[1] Edie Brickell

Alicia BRIDGES *US, female vocalist (11 WEEKS)* pos/wks

11 Nov 78	I LOVE THE NIGHT LIFE (DISCO ROUND) *Polydor 2066 936*	32	10
8 Oct 94	I LOVE THE NIGHT LIFE (DISCO ROUND) (re-mix) *Mother MUMCD 57*	61	1

Johnny BRIGGS – See Amanda BARRIE and Johnny BRIGGS

BRIGHOUSE AND RASTRICK BRASS BAND
UK, male brass band (13 WEEKS) pos/wks

12 Nov 77 ●	THE FLORAL DANCE *Transatlantic BIG 548*	2	13

Bette BRIGHT *UK, female vocalist (5 WEEKS)* pos/wks

8 Mar 80	HELLO I AM YOUR HEART *Korova KOW 3*	50	5

Sarah BRIGHTMAN (301 **Top 500**) *Multi-faceted Hot Gossip dancer turned pop and classical star, b. 14 Aug 1960, Hertfordshire, UK. Singer / actress, and ex-wife of Andrew Lloyd Webber. 'Time To Say Goodbye' was biggest selling single in Germany (2.5 million) (98 WEEKS)* pos/wks

11 Nov 78 ●	I LOST MY HEART TO A STARSHIP TROOPER *Ariola/Hansa AHA 527* [1]	6	14
7 Apr 79	THE ADVENTURES OF THE LOVE CRUSADER *Ariola/Hansa AHA 538* [2]	53	5
30 Jul 83	HIM *Polydor POSP 625* [3]	55	4
23 Mar 85 ●	PIE JESU *HMV WEBBER 1* [4]	3	8
11 Jan 86 ●	THE PHANTOM OF THE OPERA *Polydor POSP 800* [5]	7	10
4 Oct 86 ●	ALL I ASK OF YOU *Polydor POSP 802* [6]	3	16
10 Jan 87 ●	WISHING YOU WERE SOMEHOW HERE AGAIN *Polydor POSP 803*	7	11
11 Jul 92	AMIGOS PARA SIEMPRE (FRIENDS FOR LIFE) *Really Useful RUR 10* [7]	11	11
24 May 97 ●	TIME TO SAY GOODBYE (CON TE PARTIRO) *Coalition COLA 003CD* [8]	2	14
23 Aug 97	WHO WANTS TO LIVE FOREVER *Coalition COLA 014CD*	45	1
6 Dec 97	JUST SHOW ME HOW TO LOVE YOU *Coalition COLA 035CD* [9]	54	2
14 Feb 98	STARSHIP TROOPERS *Coalition COLA 040CD* [10]	58	1
13 Feb 99	EDEN *Coalition COLA 065CD*	68	1

[1] Sarah Brightman and Hot Gossip [2] Sarah Brightman and the Starship Troopers [3] Sarah Brightman and the London Philharmonic [4] Sarah Brightman and Paul Miles-Kingston [5] Sarah Brightman and Steve Harley [6] Cliff Richard and Sarah Brightman [7] José Carreras and Sarah Brightman [8] Sarah Brightman and Andrea Bocelli [9] Sarah Brightman and the LSO featuring José Cura [10] United Citizen Federation featuring Sarah Brightman

The listed flip side of 'Wishing You Were Somehow Here Again' was 'The Music of the Night' by Michael Crawford. COLA 040CD is a dance re-mix of AHA 527

BRIGHTON AND HOVE ALBION FC
UK, male football team vocalists (2 WEEKS) pos/wks

28 May 83	THE BOYS IN THE OLD BRIGHTON BLUE *Energy NRG 2*	65	2

BRILLIANT
UK, male / female vocal / instrumental group (13 WEEKS) pos/wks

19 Oct 85	IT'S A MAN'S MAN'S MAN'S WORLD *Food FOOD 5*	58	5
22 Mar 86	LOVE IS WAR *Food FOOD 6*	64	4
2 Aug 86	SOMEBODY *Food FOOD 7*	67	4

Danielle BRISEBOIS *US, female vocalist (1 WEEK)* pos/wks

9 Sep 95	GIMME LITTLE SIGN *Epic 6610782*	75	1

Johnny BRISTOL *US, male vocalist (16 WEEKS)* pos/wks

24 Aug 74 ●	HANG ON IN THERE BABY *MGM 2006 443*	3	11
19 Jul 80	MY GUY - MY GIRL (MEDLEY) *Atlantic / Hansa K 11550* [1]	39	5

[1] Amii Stewart and Johnny Bristol

BRIT PACK *UK, Ireland, male vocal group (2 WEEKS)* pos/wks

12 Feb 00	SET ME FREE *When! WENX 2000*	41	2

BRITS – See VARIOUS ARTISTS (MONTAGES)

BROCK LANDARS *UK, male vocal / production duo (2 WEEKS)* pos/wks

11 Jul 98	S.M.D.U. *Parlophone CDBLUE 001*	49	2

BROKEN ENGLISH
UK, male vocal / instrumental group (13 WEEKS) pos/wks

30 May 87	COMIN' ON STRONG *EMI EM 5*	18	10
3 Oct 87	LOVE ON THE SIDE *EMI EM 55*	69	3

BRONSKI BEAT (421 **Top 500**) *Electronic dance trio formed 1984 London, UK; Steve Bronski (k), Larry Steinbachek (k) and the plaintive falsetto of Jimmy Somerville (v), who left in 1985 for The Communards (replaced by John Foster). First openly gay hit pop group, split in 1989 (78 WEEKS)* pos/wks

2 Jun 84 ●	SMALLTOWN BOY *Forbidden Fruit BITE 1*	3	13
22 Sep 84 ●	WHY? *Forbidden Fruit BITE 2*	6	10
1 Dec 84	IT AIN'T NECESSARILY SO *Forbidden Fruit BITE 3*	16	11
20 Apr 85 ●	I FEEL LOVE (MEDLEY) *Forbidden Fruit BITE 4* [1]	3	12
30 Nov 85 ●	HIT THAT PERFECT BEAT *Forbidden Fruit BITE 6*	3	14
29 Mar 86	COME ON, COME ON *Forbidden Fruit BITE 7*	20	7
1 Jul 89 ●	CHA CHA HEELS *Arista 112331* [2]	32	7
2 Feb 91	SMALLTOWN BOY (re-mix) *London LON 287* [3]	32	4

[1] Bronski Beat and Marc Almond [2] Eartha Kitt and Bronski Beat [3] Jimmy Somerville with Bronski Beat

Tracks on medley: I Feel Love / Love to Love You Baby / Johnny Remember Me

Jet BRONX and the FORBIDDEN
UK, male vocal / instrumental group (1 WEEK) pos/wks

17 Dec 77	AIN'T DOIN' NOTHIN' *Lightning LIG 50*	49	1

BROOK BROTHERS
UK, male vocal duo - Geoff and Ricky Brook (35 WEEKS) pos/wks

30 Mar 61 ●	WARPAINT *Pye 7N 15333*	5	14
24 Aug 61	AIN'T GONNA WASH FOR A WEEK *Pye 7N 15369*	13	10
25 Jan 62	HE'S OLD ENOUGH TO KNOW BETTER *Pye 7N 15409*	37	1
16 Aug 62	WELCOME HOME BABY *Pye 7N 15453*	33	6
21 Feb 63	TROUBLE IS MY MIDDLE NAME *Pye 7N 15498*	38	4

Bruno BROOKES – See Liz KERSHAW and Bruno BROOKES

BROOKLYN BOUNCE *Germany, male production duo, and male / female vocal group (1 WEEK)* pos/wks

30 May 98	THE MUSIC'S GOT ME *Club Tools 0064795 CLU*	67	1

BROOKLYN, BRONX and QUEENS – See B B and Q BAND

Elkie BROOKS (337 **Top 500**) *Husky-voiced female vocalist, professional at age 15, b. Elaine Bookbinder, 25 Feb 1945, Salford, UK. Blues, jazz then rock phases (in Vinegar Joe with Robert Palmer) followed by a solo career which featured an impressive 20-year run of 15 hit albums from 1977 (91 WEEKS)* pos/wks

2 Apr 77 ●	PEARL'S A SINGER *A & M AMS 7275*	8	9
20 Aug 77 ●	SUNSHINE AFTER THE RAIN *A & M AMS 7306*	10	9
25 Feb 78	LILAC WINE *A & M AMS 7333*	16	7
3 Jun 78	ONLY LOVE CAN BREAK YOUR HEART *A & M AMS 7353*	43	5
11 Nov 78	DON'T CRY OUT LOUD *A & M AMS 7395*	12	11

5 May 79	THE RUNAWAY *A & M AMS 7428*....................	**50**	5
16 Jan 82	FOOL IF YOU THINK IT'S OVER *A & M AMS 8187*.........	**17**	10
1 May 82	OUR LOVE *A & M AMS 8214*	**43**	5
17 Jul 82	NIGHTS IN WHITE SATIN *A & M AMS 8235*	**33**	5
22 Jan 83	GASOLINE ALLEY *A & M AMS 8305*	**52**	5
22 Nov 86 ●	NO MORE THE FOOL *Legend LM 4*	**5**	16
4 Apr 87	BREAK THE CHAIN *Legend LM 8*	**55**	3
11 Jul 87	WE'VE GOT TONIGHT *Legend LM 9*.........	**69**	1

Garth BROOKS *US, male vocalist (15 WEEKS)*

		pos/wks	
1 Feb 92	SHAMELESS *Capitol CL 646*...............	**71**	1
22 Jan 94	THE RED STROKES / AIN'T GOING DOWN		
	Liberty CDCLS 704	**13**	5
16 Apr 94	STANDING OUTSIDE THE FIRE *Liberty CDCL 712*	**28**	4
18 Feb 95	THE DANCE / FRIENDS IN LOW PLACES		
	Capitol CDCL 735....................	**36**	3
17 Feb 96	SHE'S EVERY WOMAN *Capitol CDCL 767*	**55**	1
13 Nov 99	LOST IN YOU *Capitol CDCL 814*	**70**	1

Mel BROOKS *US, male actor / rapper (10 WEEKS)*

		pos/wks	
18 Feb 84	TO BE OR NOT TO BE (THE HITLER RAP)		
	Island IS 158	**12**	10

Meredith BROOKS
US, female vocal / instrumentalist (13 WEEKS)

		pos/wks	
2 Aug 97 ●	BITCH *Capital CDCL 790*..................	**6**	10
6 Dec 97	I NEED *Capital CDCLS 794*	**28**	2
7 Mar 98	WHAT WOULD HAPPEN *Capital CDCL 798*..........	**49**	1

Norman BROOKS *Canada, male vocalist (1 WEEK)*

		pos/wks	
12 Nov 54	A SKY BLUE SHIRT AND A RAINBOW TIE *London L 1228*	**17**	1

BROS (382) **Top 500** Top teen appeal act; photogenic twins Matt Goss (v) and Luke Goss (d), b. 29 Sep 1968, London, UK, and Craig Logan (b) - who left in 1989. Sold out tours, broke sales records, created hysteria and won Brits Best Newcomer of 1988 award (84 WEEKS)

		pos/wks	
5 Dec 87	WHEN WILL I BE FAMOUS *CBS ATOM 2*	**62**	2
9 Jan 88 ●	WHEN WILL I BE FAMOUS (re-entry) *CBS ATOM 2*	**2**	13
19 Mar 88 ●	DROP THE BOY *CBS ATOM 3*	**2**	10
10 Jun 88 ★	I OWE YOU NOTHING *CBS ATOM 4*	**1**	11
17 Sep 88 ●	I QUIT *CBS ATOM 5*	**4**	8
3 Dec 88 ●	CAT AMONG THE PIGEONS / SILENT NIGHT *CBS ATOM 6*........	**2**	8
29 Jul 89 ●	TOO MUCH *CBS ATOM 7*	**2**	7
7 Oct 89 ●	CHOCOLATE BOX *CBS ATOM 8*	**9**	6
16 Dec 89 ●	SISTER *CBS ATOM 9*	**10**	6
10 Mar 90	MADLY IN LOVE *CBS ATOM 10*	**14**	4
13 Jul 91	ARE YOU MINE *Columbia 6569707*	**12**	5
21 Sep 91	TRY *Columbia 6574047*	**27**	4

Act was duo for last six hits

BROTHER BEYOND
UK, male vocal / instrumental group (58 WEEKS)

		pos/wks	
4 Apr 87	HOW MANY TIMES *EMI EMI 5591*..........	**62**	3
8 Aug 87	CHAIN-GANG SMILE *Parlophone R 6160*	**57**	3
23 Jan 88	CAN YOU KEEP A SECRET *Parlophone R 6174*	**56**	4
30 Jul 88 ●	THE HARDER I TRY *Parlophone R 6184*	**2**	14
5 Nov 88 ●	HE AIN'T NO COMPETITION *Parlophone R 6193*	**6**	10
21 Jan 89	BE MY TWIN *Parlophone R 6195*	**14**	6
1 Apr 89	CAN YOU KEEP A SECRET (re-mix) *Parlophone R 6197*.........	**22**	5
28 Oct 89	DRIVE ON *Parlophone R 6233*	**39**	4
9 Dec 89	WHEN WILL I SEE YOU AGAIN *Parlophone R 6239*......	**43**	5
10 Apr 90	TRUST *Parlophone R 6245*	**53**	2
19 Jan 91	THE GIRL I USED TO KNOW *Parlophone R 6265*	**48**	2

BROTHER BROWN featuring FRANK'EE *Denmark, male DJ / production duo (4 WEEKS)*

		pos/wks	
2 Oct 99	UNDER THE WATER *ffrr FCD 367*	**18**	4

BROTHER LOVE – See PRATT and McCLAIN with BROTHERLOVE

BROTHERHOOD *UK, male rap group (1 WEEK)*

		pos/wks	
27 Jan 96	ONE SHOT / NOTHING IN PARTICULAR *Bite It BHOODD 3*	**55**	1

BROTHERHOOD OF MAN (303) **Top 500** Triple chart-topping UK vocal group formed by producer / composer Tony Hiller, which originally featured Tony Burrows (Edison Lighthouse, White Plains, etc.). Their 2 boy 2 girl line-up in 1976 broke voting record for Eurovision Song Contest and had contest's biggest selling UK hit (97 WEEKS)

		pos/wks	
14 Feb 70 ●	UNITED WE STAND *Deram DM 284* *Deram DM 298*.........	**10**	9
4 Jul 70	WHERE ARE YOU GOING TO MY LOVE *Deram DM 298*.........	**22**	10
13 Mar 76 ★	SAVE YOUR KISSES FOR ME *Pye 7N 45569* ◆	**1**	16
19 Jun 76	MY SWEET ROSALIE *Pye 7N 45602*.........	**30**	7
26 Feb 77 ●	OH BOY (THE MOOD I'M IN) *Pye 7N 45656*	**8**	12
9 Jul 77 ★	ANGELO *Pye 7N 45699*	**1**	12
14 Jan 78 ★	FIGARO *Pye 7N 46037*............	**1**	11
27 May 78	BEAUTIFUL LOVER *Pye 7N 46071*	**15**	12
30 Sep 78	MIDDLE OF THE NIGHT *Pye 7N 46117*.........	**41**	6
3 Jul 82	LIGHTNING FLASH *EMI 5309*	**67**	2

BROTHERS *UK, male vocal group (9 WEEKS)*

		pos/wks	
29 Jan 77 ●	SING ME *Bus Stop Bus 1054*	**8**	9

BROTHERS FOUR *US, male vocal group (2 WEEKS)*

		pos/wks	
23 Jun 60	GREENFIELDS *Philips PB 1009*	**49**	1
7 Jul 60	GREENFIELDS (re-entry) *Philips PB 1009*	**40**	1

BROTHERS GRIMM – See JAZZ and the BROTHERS GRIMM

BROTHERS IN RHYTHM
UK, male instrumental / production duo (12 WEEKS)

		pos/wks	
16 Mar 91	SUCH A GOOD FEELING *Fourth & Broadway BRW 228*	**64**	2
14 Sep 91	SUCH A GOOD FEELING (re-issue)		
	Fourth & Broadway BRW 228 210	**14**	8
30 Apr 94	FOREVER AND A DAY *Stress CDSTR 36* [1]	**51**	2

[1] Brothers in Rhythm present Charvoni

BROTHERS JOHNSON *US, male vocal / instrumental duo - George and Louis Johnson (34 WEEKS)*

		pos/wks	
9 Jul 77	STRAWBERRY LETTER 23 *A & M AMS 7297*	**35**	5
2 Sep 78	AIN'T WE FUNKIN' NOW *A & M AMS 7379*	**43**	6
4 Nov 78	RIDE-O-ROCKET *A & M AMS 7400*	**50**	4
23 Feb 80 ●	STOMP *A & M AMS 7509*	**6**	12
31 May 80	LIGHT UP THE NIGHT *A & M AMS 7526*	**47**	4
25 Jul 81	THE REAL THING *A & M AMS 8149*	**50**	3

BROTHERS LIKE OUTLAW featuring Alison EVELYN
UK, male / female vocal group (1 WEEK)

		pos/wks	
23 Jan 93	GOOD VIBRATIONS *Gee Street GESCD 44*	**74**	1

Edgar BROUGHTON BAND
UK, male vocal / instrumental group (10 WEEKS)

		pos/wks	
18 Apr 70	OUT DEMONS OUT *Harvest HAR 5015*	**39**	5
23 Jan 71	APACHE DROPOUT *Harvest HAR 5032*	**49**	1
6 Feb 71	APACHE DROPOUT (re-entry) *Harvest HAR 5032*	**35**	2
13 Mar 71	APACHE DROPOUT (2nd re-entry) *Harvest HAR 5032*	**35**	1
27 Mar 71	APACHE DROPOUT (3rd re-entry) *Harvest HAR 5032*	**33**	1

Alison BROWN – See BAR CODES featuring Alison BROWN

Angie BROWN – See BIZARRE INC; MOTIV 8

Bobby BROWN (216) **Top 500** Energetic swingbeat superstar, b. 5 Feb 1969, Massachusetts, who married Whitney Houston in 1992. He joined a re-formed New Edition in 1996, the vocal group in which he topped the chart with 'Candy Girl' as a 14-year-old (123 WEEKS)

		pos/wks	
6 Aug 88	DON'T BE CRUEL *MCA MCA 1268*	**42**	7
17 Dec 88 ●	MY PREROGATIVE *MCA MCA 1299* ▲	**6**	17

25 Mar 89	DON'T BE CRUEL (re-issue) MCA MCA 1310	13	8
20 May 89 ●	EVERY LITTLE STEP MCA MCA 1338	6	9
15 Jul 89 ●	ON OUR OWN (FROM GHOSTBUSTERS II) MCA MCA 1350	4	9
23 Sep 89	ROCK WIT'CHA MCA MCA 1367	33	6
25 Nov 89	RONI MCA MCA 1384	21	7
9 Jun 90	THE FREE STYLE MEGA-MIX MCA MCA 1421	14	7
30 Jun 90	SHE AIN'T WORTH IT London LON 265 [1] ▲	12	9
22 Aug 92	HUMPIN' AROUND MCA MCS 1680	19	6
17 Oct 92	GOOD ENOUGH MCA MCS 1704	41	4
19 Jun 93	THAT'S THE WAY LOVE IS MCA MCSTD 1783	56	2
22 Jan 94	SOMETHING IN COMMON MCA MCSTD 1957 [2]	16	5
25 Jun 94	TWO CAN PLAY THAT GAME MCA MCSTD 1973	38	3
1 Apr 95 ●	TWO CAN PLAY THAT GAME (re-entry) MCA MCSTD 1973	3	12
8 Jul 95 ●	HUMPIN' AROUND (re-mix) MCA MCSTD 2073	8	4
14 Oct 95	MY PREROGATIVE (re-mix) MCA MCSTD 2094	17	3
3 Feb 96	EVERY LITTLE STEP (re-mix) MCA MCSTD 48004	25	2
22 Nov 97	FEELIN' INSIDE MCA MCSTD 48067	40	1

[1] Glenn Medeiros featuring Bobby Brown [2] Bobby Brown and Whitney Houston

Carl BROWN – See DOUBLE TROUBLE

Crazy World of Arthur BROWN
UK, male vocal / instrumental group (14 WEEKS)   pos/wks

| 26 Jun 68 ★ | FIRE Track 604 022 | 1 | 14 |

Dennis BROWN Jamaica, male vocalist (18 WEEKS)   pos/wks

3 Mar 79	MONEY IN MY POCKET Lightning LV 5	14	9
3 Jul 82	LOVE HAS FOUND ITS WAY A & M AMS 8226	47	6
11 Sep 82	HALFWAY UP HALFWAY DOWN A & M AMS 8250	56	3

Diana BROWN and Barrie K SHARPE
UK, female / male vocal duo (11 WEEKS)   pos/wks

2 Jun 90	THE MASTERPLAN ffrr F 133	39	6
1 Sep 90	SUN WORSHIPPERS (POSITIVE THINKING) ffrr F 144	61	2
23 Mar 91	LOVE OR NOTHING ffrr F 152	71	1
27 Jun 92	EATING ME ALIVE ffrr F 190	53	2

Errol BROWN UK, male vocalist (13 WEEKS)   pos/wks

4 Jul 87	PERSONAL TOUCH WEA YZ 130	25	8
28 Nov 87	BODY ROCKIN' WEA YZ 162	51	2
14 Feb 98	IT STARTED WITH A KISS EMI CDHOT 101 [1]	18	3

[1] Hot Chocolate featuring Errol Brown

See also HOT CHOCOLATE

Foxy BROWN US, female rapper - Jennifer Hylton (22 WEEKS)   pos/wks

21 Sep 96	TOUCH ME TEASE ME Def Jam DEFCD 18 [1]	26	3
8 Mar 97	GET ME HOME Def Jam DEFCD 32 [2]	11	5
10 May 97	AIN'T NO PLAYA Northwestside 74321474842 [3]	31	2
21 Jun 97 ●	I'LL BE Def Jam 5710432 [4]	9	5
11 Oct 97	BIG BAD MAMMA Def Jam 5749792 [5]	12	3
25 Oct 97	SUNSHINE Northwestside 74321528702 [6]	25	2
13 Mar 99	HOT SPOT Def Jam 8708352	31	2

[1] Case featuring Foxy Brown [2] Foxy Brown featuring BLACKstreet [3] Jay-Z featuring Foxy Brown [4] Foxy Brown featuring Jay-Z [5] Foxy Brown featuring Dru Hill [6] Jay-Z featuring Babyface and Foxy Brown

Gloria D. BROWN US, female vocalist (3 WEEKS)   pos/wks

| 8 Jun 85 | THE MORE THEY KNOCK, THE MORE I LOVE YOU 10 TEN 52 | 57 | 3 |

Horace BROWN US, male vocalist (7 WEEKS)   pos/wks

25 Feb 95	TASTE YOUR LOVE Uptown MCSTD 2026	58	1
18 May 96	ONE FOR THE MONEY Motown 8605232	12	4
12 Oct 96	THINGS WE DO FOR LOVE Motown 8605712	27	2

Ian BROWN UK, male vocal / instrumentalist (26 WEEKS)   pos/wks

24 Jan 98 ●	MY STAR Polydor 5719872	5	4
4 Apr 98	CORPSES Polydor 5696552	14	4
20 Jun 98	CAN'T SEE ME Polydor 5440452	21	3
20 Feb 99 ●	BE THERE Mo Wax MW 108CD1 [1]	8	6
6 Nov 99	LOVE LIKE A FOUNTAIN Polydor 5615162	23	3
19 Feb 00 ●●	DOLPHINS WERE MONKEYS Polydor 5616372	5	4
17 Jun 00	GOLDEN GAZE Polydor 5618442	29	2

[1] Unkle featuring Ian Brown

See also STONE ROSES

James BROWN ⟨285⟩ [Top 500] 'Soul Brother No.1', b. 3 May 1928, South Carolina, US. The most charted R&B performer of all time has influenced numerous musical styles since the mid-1950s. Only Elvis Presley has enjoyed more US Pop chart entries (104 WEEKS)   pos/wks

23 Sep 65	PAPA'S GOT A BRAND NEW BAG London HL 9990 [1]	25	7
24 Feb 66	I GOT YOU Pye International 7N 25350 [1]	29	6
16 Jun 66	IT'S A MAN'S MAN'S MAN'S WORLD Pye International 7N 25371 [1]	13	9
10 Oct 70	GET UP I FEEL LIKE BEING A SEX MACHINE Polydor 2001 071	32	7
27 Nov 71	HEY AMERICA Mojo 2093 006	47	3
18 Sep 76	GET UP OFFA THAT THING Polydor 2066 687	22	6
29 Jan 77	BODY HEAT Polydor 2066 763	36	4
10 Jan 81	RAPP PAYBACK (WHERE IZ MOSES?) RCA 28	39	5
2 Jul 83	BRING IT ON . . . BRING IT ON Sonet SON 2258	45	4
1 Sep 84	UNITY (PART 1 – THE THIRD COMING) Tommy Boy AFR 2 [2]	49	5
27 Apr 85	FROGGY MIX Boiling Point FROG 1	50	3
1 Jun 85	GET UP I FEEL LIKE BEING A SEX MACHINE (re-issue) Boiling Point POSP 751	47	5
25 Jan 86 ●	LIVING IN AMERICA Scotti Brothers A 6701	5	10
1 Mar 86	GET UP I FEEL LIKE BEING A SEX MACHINE (re-entry of re-issue) Boiling Point POSP 751	46	4
18 Oct 86	GRAVITY Scotti Brothers 650059 7	65	2
30 Jan 88	SHE'S THE ONE Urban URB 13	45	3
23 Apr 88	THE PAYBACK MIX Urban URB 17	12	6
4 Jun 88	I'M REAL Scotti Brothers JSB 1 [3]	31	4
23 Jul 88	I GOT YOU (I FEEL GOOD) (re-issue) A & M AM 444	52	3
16 Nov 91	GET UP (I FEEL LIKE BEING A) SEX MACHINE (2nd re-issue) Polydor PO 185	69	2
24 Oct 92	I GOT YOU (I FEEL GOOD) (re-mix) FBI FBI 9 [4]	72	1
17 Apr 93	CAN'T GET ANY HARDER Polydor PZCD 262	59	2
17 Apr 99	FUNK ON AH ROLL Inferno / Eagle EAGXA 073	40	2
22 Apr 00	FUNK ON AH ROLL (re-mix) Eagle EAGXS 127	63	1

[1] James Brown and the Famous Flames [2] Afrika Bambaataa and James Brown [3] James Brown featuring Full Force [4] James Brown vs Dakeyne

'Froggy Mix' is a medley of 12 James Brown songs. The listed flip side of 'I Got You (I Feel Good)' was 'Nowhere to Run' by Martha Reeves and the Vandellas

Jennifer BROWN Sweden, female vocalist (1 WEEK)   pos/wks

| 1 May 99 | TUESDAY AFTERNOON RCA 74321604092 | 57 | 1 |

Joanne BROWN – See Tony OSBORNE SOUND

Jocelyn BROWN ⟨441⟩ [Top 500] Super session singer from North Carolina who relocated to New York, b. 25 Nov 1950. She has sung backing vocals for such acts as John Lennon, Bruce Springsteen, Luther Vandross, Diana Ross and Bob Dylan and has had UK hits with ten separate recording acts. (76 WEEKS)   pos/wks

21 Apr 84	SOMEBODY ELSE'S GUY Fourth & Broadway BRW 5	13	9
22 Sep 84	I WISH YOU WOULD Fourth & Broadway BRW 14	51	1
15 Mar 86	LOVE'S GONNA GET YOU Warner Bros. W 8889	70	1
29 Jun 91 ●	ALWAYS THERE Talkin Loud TLK 10 [1]	6	9
14 Sep 91	SHE GOT SOUL A & M AM 819 [2]	57	3
7 Dec 91 ●	DON'T TALK JUST KISS Tug SNOG 2 [3]	3	11
20 Mar 93	TAKE ME UP A & M AMCD 210 [4]	61	1
11 Jun 94	NO MORE TEARS (ENOUGH IS ENOUGH) Ding Dong 74321209032 [5]	13	7
8 Oct 94	GIMME ALL YOUR LOVIN' Ding Dong 74321231322 [5]	22	3
13 Jul 96 ●	KEEP ON JUMPIN' Manifesto FESCD 11 [6]	8	6

10 May 97		IT'S ALRIGHT, I FEEL IT! *Talkin Loud TLCD 22* [7]	26	2
12 Jul 97	●	SOMETHING GOIN' ON *Manifesto FESCD 25* [6]	5	10
25 Oct 97		I AM THE BLACK GOLD OF THE SUN *Talkin Loud TLCD 26* [7]	31	2
22 Nov 97		HAPPINESS *Sony S3 KAMCD 2* [8]	45	1
2 May 98		FUN *INCredible INCRL 2CD* [9]	33	2
29 Aug 98		AIN'T NO MOUNTAIN HIGH ENOUGH *INCredible INCRL 7CD*	35	2
27 Mar 99		I BELIEVE *Playola 0091705 PLA* [2]	62	1
3 Jul 99		IT'S ALL GOOD *INCredible INCRL 14CD*	54	1
11 Mar 00		BELIEVE *Defected DFECT 14CD3* [10]	45	2

[1] Incognito featuring Jocelyn Brown [2] Jamestown featuring Jocelyn Brown [3] Right Said Fred. Guest vocals: Jocelyn Brown [4] Sonic Surfers featuring Jocelyn Brown [5] Jocelyn Brown and Kym Mazelle [6] Todd Terry featuring Martha Wash and Jocelyn Brown [7] Nuyorican Soul featuring Jocelyn Brown [8] Kamasutra featuring Jocelyn Brown [9] Da Mob featuring Jocelyn Brown [10] Ministers De La Funk featuring Jocelyn Brown

See also Todd TERRY PROJECT

Joe BROWN and the BRUVVERS (330 Top 500) *Chirpy Cockney singer / guitarist, b. 13 May 1941, Lincolnshire, UK. Joe was one of the original artists managed by early rock impresario Larry Parnes. Voted Top UK Vocal Personality in 1962 NME Poll. (92 WEEKS)*

				pos/wks
17 Mar 60		DARKTOWN STRUTTERS BALL *Decca F 11207*	34	6
26 Jan 61		SHINE *Pye 7N 15322* [1]	33	1
11 Jan 62		WHAT A CRAZY WORLD WE'RE LIVING IN *Piccadilly 7N 35024*	37	2
17 May 62	●	A PICTURE OF YOU *Piccadilly 7N 35047*	2	19
13 Sep 62		YOUR TENDER LOOK *Piccadilly 7N 35058*	31	6
15 Nov 62	●	IT ONLY TOOK A MINUTE *Piccadilly 7N 35082*	6	13
7 Feb 63	●	THAT'S WHAT LOVE WILL DO *Piccadilly 7N 35106*	3	14
21 Feb 63		IT ONLY TOOK A MINUTE (re-entry) *Piccadilly 7N 35082*	50	1
27 Jun 63		NATURE'S TIME FOR LOVE *Piccadilly 7N 35129*	26	6
26 Sep 63		SALLY ANN *Piccadilly 7N 35138*	28	9
29 Jun 67		WITH A LITTLE HELP FROM MY FRIENDS *Pye 7N 17339* [1]	32	4
14 Apr 73		HEY MAMA *Ammo AMO 101* [1]	33	6

[1] Joe Brown

Karen BROWN – See DJ's RULE

Kathy BROWN *US, female vocalist (1 WEEK)*

				pos/wks
10 Apr 99		JOY *Azuli AZNYCDX 094*	63	1

See also PRAXIS

Miquel BROWN *US, female vocalist (7 WEEKS)*

				pos/wks
18 Feb 84		HE'S A SAINT, HE'S A SINNER *Record Shack SOHO 15*	68	4
24 Aug 85		CLOSE TO PERFECTION *Record Shack SOHO 48*	63	3

Peter BROWN *US, male vocalist (9 WEEKS)*

				pos/wks
11 Feb 78		DO YA WANNA GET FUNKY WITH ME *TK TKR 6009*	43	4
17 Jun 78		DANCE WITH ME *TK TKR 6027*	57	5

Polly BROWN *UK, female vocalist (5 WEEKS)*

				pos/wks
14 Sep 74		UP IN A PUFF OF SMOKE *GTO GT 2*	43	5

Roy 'Chubby' BROWN
UK, male comedian - Royston Vasey (22 WEEKS)

				pos/wks
13 May 95		LIVING NEXT DOOR TO ALICE (WHO THE F**K IS ALICE) *N.O.W. CDWAG 245* [1]	64	2
12 Aug 95	●	LIVING NEXT DOOR TO ALICE (WHO THE F**K IS ALICE) (re-entry) *N.O.W. CDWAG 245* [1]	3	17
21 Dec 96		ROCKIN' GOOD CHRISTMAS *PolyStar 5732612*	51	3

[1] Smokie featuring Roy 'Chubby' Brown

Sam BROWN *UK, female vocalist (35 WEEKS)*

				pos/wks
11 Jun 88		STOP *A & M AM 440*	52	3
4 Feb 89	●	STOP (re-entry) *A & M AM 440*	4	12
13 May 89		CAN I GET A WITNESS *A & M AM 509*	15	7
3 Mar 90		WITH A LITTLE LOVE *A & M AM 539*	44	4

5 May 90		KISSING GATE *A & M AM 549*	23	8
26 Aug 95		JUST GOOD FRIENDS *Dick Bros. DDICK 014CD1* [1]	63	1

[1] Fish featuring Sam Brown

Sharon BROWN *US, female vocalist (11 WEEKS)*

				pos/wks
17 Apr 82		I SPECIALIZE IN LOVE *Virgin VS 494*	38	9
26 Feb 94		I SPECIALIZE IN LOVE (re-mix) *Deep Distraxion OILYCD 025*	62	2

BROWN SAUCE *UK, male / female vocal group (12 WEEKS)*

				pos/wks
12 Dec 81		I WANNA BE A WINNER *BBC RESL 101*	15	12

BROWN SUGAR – See SEX CLUB featuring BROWN SUGAR

Duncan BROWNE *UK, male vocalist (8 WEEKS)*

				pos/wks
19 Aug 72		JOURNEY *RAK 135*	23	6
22 Dec 84		THEME FROM 'THE TRAVELLING MAN' *Towerbell TOW 64*	68	2

Jackson BROWNE *US, male vocalist (14 WEEKS)*

				pos/wks
1 Jul 78		STAY *Asylum K 13128*	12	11
18 Oct 86		IN THE SHAPE OF A HEART *Elektra EKR 42*	66	2
25 Jun 94		EVERYWHERE I GO *Elektra EKR 184CD1*	67	1

Ronnie BROWNE – See SCOTTISH RUGBY TEAM with Ronnie BROWNE

Tom BROWNE *US, male instrumentalist - trumpet (24 WEEKS)*

				pos/wks
19 Jul 80	●	FUNKIN' FOR JAMAICA (N.Y.) *Arista ARIST 357*	10	11
25 Oct 80		THIGHS HIGH (GRIP YOUR HIPS AND MOVE) *Arista ARIST 367*	45	5
30 Jan 82		FUNGI MAMA (BEBOPAFUNKADISCOLYPSO) *Arista ARIST 450*	58	4
11 Jan 92		FUNKIN' FOR JAMAICA (re-mix) *Arista 114998*	45	4

BROWNS *US, male / female vocal group - Jim Ed, Maxine and Bonnie Brown (13 WEEKS)*

				pos/wks
18 Sep 59	●	THE THREE BELLS *RCA 1140* ▲	6	13

BROWNSTONE *US, female vocal group (24 WEEKS)*

				pos/wks
1 Apr 95	●	IF YOU LOVE ME *MJJ 6614135*	8	12
15 Jul 95		GRAPEVYNE *MJJ 6620942*	16	4
23 Sep 95		I CAN'T TELL YOU WHY *MJJ 6623775*	27	4
17 May 97		5 MILES TO EMPTY *Epic 6640962*	12	4
27 Sep 97		KISS AND TELL *Epic 6649852*	21	2

BROWNSVILLE STATION
US, male vocal / instrumental group (6 WEEKS)

				pos/wks
2 Mar 74		SMOKIN' IN THE BOYS' ROOM *Philips 6073 834*	27	6

Dave BRUBECK QUARTET
US, male instrumental group (30 WEEKS)

				pos/wks
26 Oct 61	●	TAKE FIVE *Fontana H 339*	6	15
8 Feb 62		IT'S A RAGGY WALTZ *Fontana H 352*	36	3
17 May 62		UNSQUARE DANCE *CBS AAG 102*	14	12

Tommy BRUCE and the BRUISERS
UK, male vocal / instrumental group (21 WEEKS)

				pos/wks
26 May 60	●	AIN'T MISBEHAVIN' *Columbia DB 4453*	3	16
8 Sep 60		BROKEN DOLL *Columbia DB 4498*	36	4
22 Feb 62		BABETTE *Columbia DB 4776* [1]	50	2

[1] Tommy Bruce

Claudia BRUCKEN *Germany, female vocalist (2 WEEKS)*

				pos/wks
11 Aug 90		ABSOLUT(E) *Island IS 471*	71	1
16 Feb 91		KISS LIKE ETHER *Island IS 479*	63	1

BRUISERS *UK, male instrumental group (7 WEEKS)*

				pos/wks
8 Aug 63		BLUE GIRL *Parlophone R 5042*	31	6
26 Sep 63		BLUE GIRL (re-entry) *Parlophone R 5042*	47	1

Frank BRUNO *UK, male vocalist (4 WEEKS)* pos/wks

23 Dec 95	EYE OF THE TIGER *RCA 74321336282*	28	4

BRUNO and LIZ – See Liz KERSHAW and Bruno BROOKES

Tyrone BRUNSON *US, male instrumentalist - bass (5 WEEKS)* pos/wks

25 Dec 82	THE SMURF *Epic EPC A 3024*	52	5

BRUVVERS – See Joe BROWN and the BRUVVERS

Dora BRYAN *UK, female actress (6 WEEKS)* pos/wks

5 Dec 63	ALL I WANT FOR CHRISTMAS IS A BEATLE *Fontana TF 427*	20	6

Kelle BRYAN *UK, female vocalist (4 WEEKS)* pos/wks

2 Oct 99	HIGHER THAN HEAVEN *1st Avenue / Mercury MERCD 522*	14	4

See also ETERNAL

Anita BRYANT *US, female vocalist (6 WEEKS)* pos/wks

26 May 60	PAPER ROSES *London HLL 9144*	49	1
30 Jun 60	PAPER ROSES (re-entry) *London HLL 9144*	45	1
14 Jul 60	PAPER ROSES (2nd re-entry) *London HLL 9144*	24	2
6 Oct 60	MY LITTLE CORNER OF THE WORLD *London HLL 9171*	48	2

Peabo BRYSON *US, male vocalist (35 WEEKS)* pos/wks

20 Aug 83	● TONIGHT I CELEBRATE MY LOVE *Capitol CL 302* [1] ●	2	13
16 May 92	● BEAUTY AND THE BEAST *Epic 6576607* [2] ●	9	7
17 Jul 93	BY THE TIME THIS NIGHT IS OVER *Arista 74321157142* [3]	56	3
11 Dec 93	A WHOLE NEW WORLD (ALADDIN'S THEME) *Columbia 6599002* [4] ▲	12	12

[1] Peabo Bryson and Roberta Flack [2] Celine Dion and Peabo Bryson [3] Kenny G with Peabo Bryson [4] Regina Belle and Peabo Bryson

BT *US, male producer - Brian Transeau (25 WEEKS)* pos/wks

18 Mar 95	EMBRACING THE SUNSHINE *East West YZ 895CD*	34	2
16 Sep 95	LOVING YOU MORE *Perfecto PERF 110CD* [1]	28	2
10 Feb 96	LOVING YOU MORE (re-mix) *Perfecto PERF 117CD* [1]	14	3
9 Nov 96	BLUE SKIES *Perfecto PERF 130CD1* [2]	26	2
19 Jul 97	FLAMING JUNE *Perfecto PERF 145CD1*	19	4
29 Nov 97	LOVE, PEACE & GREASE *Perfecto PERF 153CD1*	41	1
10 Jan 98	FLAMING JUNE (re-mix) *Perfecto PERF 157CD1*	28	4
18 Apr 98	REMEMBER *Perfecto PERF 160CD1*	27	2
21 Nov 98	GODSPEED *Renaissance RENCD 002*	54	1
9 Oct 99	MERCURY AND SOLACE *Headspace HEDSCD 001*	38	2
24 Jun 00	DREAMING *Headspace HEDSCD 002* [3]	38	2

[1] BT featuring Vincent Covello [2] BT featuring Tori Amos [3] BT featuring Kirsty Hawkshaw

BT EXPRESS *US, male instrumental / vocal group (11 WEEKS)* pos/wks

29 Mar 75	EXPRESS *Pye International 7N 25674*	34	6
26 Jul 80	DOES IT FEEL GOOD / GIVE UP THE FUNK (LET'S DANCE) *Calibre CAB 503*	52	4
23 Apr 94	EXPRESS (re-mix) *PWL International PWCD 285*	67	1

BUBBLEROCK – See Jonathan KING

Catherine BUCHANAN – See JELLYBEAN

Roy BUCHANAN *US, male instrumentalist - guitar (3 WEEKS)* pos/wks

31 Mar 73	SWEET DREAMS *Polydor 2066 307*	40	3

BUCKETHEADS *US, male producer - Kenny Gonzalez (16 WEEKS)* pos/wks

4 Mar 95	● THE BOMB! (THESE SOUNDS FALL INTO MY MIND) *Positiva CDTIV 33*	5	13
20 Jan 96	GOT MYSELF TOGETHER *Positiva CDTIV 48*	12	3

Lindsey BUCKINGHAM *US, male vocalist (7 WEEKS)* pos/wks

16 Jan 82	TROUBLE *Mercury MER 85*	31	7

See also FLEETWOOD MAC

Jeff BUCKLEY *US, male vocalist (3 WEEKS)* pos/wks

27 May 95	LAST GOODBYE *Columbia 6620422*	54	2
6 Jun 98	EVERYBODY HERE WANTS YOU *Columbia 6657912*	43	1

BUCKS FIZZ (144 Top 500) *Cheryl Baker, Mike Nolan, Jay Aston (replaced by Shelley Preston in 1985) and Bobby G (Gubby). Formed for the 1981 Eurovision Song Contest, they were the last UK winners for 16 years (150 WEEKS)* pos/wks

28 Mar 81	★ MAKING YOUR MIND UP *RCA 56*	1	12
6 Jun 81	PIECE OF THE ACTION *RCA 88*	12	9
15 Aug 81	ONE OF THOSE NIGHTS *RCA 114*	20	10
28 Nov 81	★ THE LAND OF MAKE BELIEVE *RCA 163*	1	16
27 Mar 82	★ MY CAMERA NEVER LIES *RCA 202*	1	8
19 Jun 82	● NOW THOSE DAYS ARE GONE *RCA 241*	8	9
27 Nov 82	● IF YOU CAN'T STAND THE HEAT *RCA 300*	10	11
12 Mar 83	RUN FOR YOUR LIFE *RCA FIZ 1*	14	7
18 Jun 83	● WHEN WE WERE YOUNG *RCA 342*	10	8
1 Oct 83	LONDON TOWN *RCA 363*	34	6
17 Dec 83	RULES OF THE GAME *RCA 380*	57	6
25 Aug 84	TALKING IN YOUR SLEEP *RCA FIZ 2*	15	9
27 Oct 84	GOLDEN DAYS *RCA FIZ 3*	42	4
29 Dec 84	I HEAR TALK *RCA FIZ 4*	34	8
22 Jun 85	YOU AND YOUR HEART SO BLUE *RCA PB 40233*	43	4
14 Sep 85	MAGICAL *RCA PB 40367*	57	3
7 Jun 86	● NEW BEGINNING (MAMBA SEYRA) *Polydor POSP 794*	8	10
30 Aug 86	LOVE THE ONE YOU'RE WITH *Polydor POSP 813*	47	3
15 Nov 86	KEEP EACH OTHER WARM *Polydor POSP 835*	45	4
5 Nov 88	HEART OF STONE *RCA PB 42035*	50	3

BUCKSHOT LEFONQUE
US, male vocal / instrumental group (1 WEEK) pos/wks

6 Dec 97	ANOTHER DAY *Columbia 6653762*	65	1

Roy BUDD *UK, male instrumentalist - piano (1 WEEK)* pos/wks

10 Jul 99	GET CARTER *Cinephile CINX 1003*	68	1

BUDGIE *UK, male vocal / instrumental group (2 WEEKS)* pos/wks

3 Oct 81	KEEPING A RENDEZVOUS *RCA BUDGIE 3*	71	2

BUFFALO G *Ireland, female vocal / rap duo (4 WEEKS)* pos/wks

10 Jun 00	WE'RE REALLY SAYING SOMETHING *Epic 6694182*	17	3
8 Jul 00	WE'RE REALLY SAYING SOMETHING (re-entry) *Epic 6694182*	74	1

BUFFALO TOM *US, male vocal / instrumental group (5 WEEKS)* pos/wks

23 Oct 99	● GOING UNDERGROUND *Ignition IGNSCD 16*	6	5

Listed flip side was 'Carnation' by Liam Gallagher and Steve Cradock.

BUG KANN and the PLASTIC JAM
UK, male / female vocal / instrumental group (2 WEEKS) pos/wks

31 Aug 91	MADE IN TWO MINUTES *Optimum Dance BKPJ 1S* [1]	70	1
26 Feb 94	MADE IN 2 MINUTES (re-mix) *PWL International PWCD 286*	64	1

[1] Bug Kann and Plastic Jam featuring Patti Low and Doogie

BUGGLES *UK, male vocal / instrumental duo - Trevor Horn and Geoff Downes (28 WEEKS)* pos/wks

22 Sep 79	★ VIDEO KILLED THE RADIO STAR *Island WIP 6524*	1	11
26 Jan 80	THE PLASTIC AGE *Island WIP 6540*	16	8
5 Apr 80	CLEAN CLEAN *Island WIP 6584*	38	5
8 Nov 80	ELSTREE *Island WIP 6624*	55	4

James BULLER *UK, male vocalist (1 WEEK)* pos/wks

6 Mar 99	CAN'T SMILE WITHOUT YOU *BBC Music WMSS 60092*	51	1

UK No.1 ★ UK Top 10 ● Still on chart + UK million seller ◆ UK entry at No.1 ■ US No.1 ▲

Silvah BULLET – See Jonny L

BUMP UK, male instrumental / production duo (5 WEEKS) — pos/wks

| 4 Jul 92 | I'M RUSHING *Good Boy EDGE7 1* | 40 | 4 |
| 11 Nov 95 | I'M RUSHING (re-mix) *Deconstruction 74321320692* | 45 | 1 |

BUMP & FLEX UK, male / female vocal / production duo (1 WEEK) — pos/wks

| 23 May 98 | LONG TIME COMING *Heat Recordings HEATCD 014* | 73 | 1 |

BUNKER KRU – See HARLEQUIN 4s / BUNKER KRU

BUNNYMEN – See ECHO and the BUNNYMEN

Emma BUNTON – See SPICE GIRLS; TIN TIN OUT

Eric BURDON – See ANIMALS

Geoffrey BURGON UK, orchestra (4 WEEKS) — pos/wks

| 26 Dec 81 | BRIDESHEAD THEME *Chrysalis CHS 2562* | 48 | 4 |

Keni BURKE US, male vocalist (4 WEEKS) — pos/wks

| 27 Jun 81 | LET SOMEBODY LOVE YOU *RCA 93* | 59 | 3 |
| 18 Apr 92 | RISIN' TO THE TOP *RCA PB 49103* | 70 | 1 |

Hank C BURNETTE
Sweden, male multi-instrumentalist (8 WEEKS) — pos/wks

| 30 Oct 76 | SPINNING ROCK BOOGIE *Sonet SON 2094* | 21 | 8 |

Johnny BURNETTE US, male vocalist (48 WEEKS) — pos/wks

29 Sep 60 ●	DREAMIN' *London HLG 9172*	5	16
12 Jan 61 ●	YOU'RE SIXTEEN *London HLG 9254*	3	12
13 Apr 61	LITTLE BOY SAD *London HLG 9315*	12	12
10 Aug 61	GIRLS *London HLG 9388*	37	5
17 May 62	CLOWN SHOES *Liberty LIB 55416*	35	3

Rocky BURNETTE US, male vocalist (7 WEEKS) — pos/wks

| 17 Nov 79 | TIRED OF TOEIN' THE LINE *EMI 2992* | 58 | 7 |

Jerry BURNS UK, female vocalist (1 WEEK) — pos/wks

| 25 Apr 92 | PALE RED *Columbia 6579467* | 64 | 1 |

Ray BURNS UK, male vocalist (19 WEEKS) — pos/wks

| 11 Feb 55 ● | MOBILE *Columbia DB 3563* [1] | 4 | 13 |
| 26 Aug 55 | THAT'S HOW A LOVE SONG WAS BORN *Columbia DB 3640* [2] | 14 | 6 |

[1] Ray Burns With Eirc Jupp and His Orchestra [2] Ray Burns with the Coronets

Malandra BURROWS UK, female vocalist (10 WEEKS) — pos/wks

1 Dec 90	JUST THIS SIDE OF LOVE *Yorkshire Television DALE 1*	11	8
18 Oct 97	CARNIVAL IN HEAVEN *Warner.esp WESP 001CD*	49	1
29 Aug 98	DON'T LEAVE ME *Warner.esp WESP 004CD*	54	1

Jenny BURTON US, female vocalist (2 WEEKS) — pos/wks

| 30 Mar 85 | BAD HABITS *Atlantic A 9583* | 68 | 2 |

BURUNDI STEIPHENSON BLACK Burundi, drummers and chanters
with orchestral additions by Mike Steiphenson of France
(14 WEEKS) — pos/wks

| 13 Nov 71 | BURUNDI BLACK *Barclay BAR 3* | 31 | 14 |

BUS 75 – See WHALE

BUS STOP UK, male production group (19 WEEKS) — pos/wks

23 May 98 ●	KUNG FU FIGHTING *All Around the World CDGLOBE 173* [1]	8	11
24 Oct 98	YOU AIN'T SEEN NOTHIN' YET *All Around the World CDGLOBE 187* [2]	22	4
10 Apr 99	JUMP *All Around the World CDGLOBE 186*	23	3
7 Oct 00	GET IT ON *All Around the World CDGLOBE 225* [3]	59	1

[1] Bus Stop featuring Carl Douglas [2] Bus Stop featuring Randy Bachman [3] Bus Stop featuring T. Rex

Lou BUSCH US, orchestra and chorus (17 WEEKS) — pos/wks

| 27 Jan 56 ● | ZAMBESI *Capitol CL 14504* | 2 | 17 |

See also Joe 'Fingers' CARR

BUSH UK, male vocal / instrumental group (13 WEEKS) — pos/wks

8 Jun 96	MACHINEHEAD *Interscope IND 95505*	48	2
1 Mar 97 ●	SWALLOWED *Interscope IND 95528*	7	5
7 Jun 97	GREEDY FLY *Interscope IND 95536*	22	2
1 Nov 97	BONE DRIVEN *Interscope IND 95553*	49	1
4 Dec 99	THE CHEMICALS BETWEEN US *Trauma / Polydor 4972222*	46	1
18 Mar 00	WARM MACHINE *Trauma / Polydor 4972752*	45	1
3 Jun 00	LETTING THE CABLES SLEEP *Trauma / Polydor 4973352*	51	1

Kate BUSH ⟨122 Top 500⟩ Unmistakable singer / songwriter with
operatic vocal ability, b. 30 Jul 1958, Kent. Discovered by Dave Gilmour of
Pink Floyd. First British female to top the singles chart with a self-composed
song and the first to have a UK No.1 album (168 WEEKS) — pos/wks

11 Feb 78 ★	WUTHERING HEIGHTS *EMI 2719*	1	12
13 May 78	WUTHERING HEIGHTS (re-entry) *EMI 2719*	75	1
10 Jun 78 ●	MAN WITH THE CHILD IN HIS EYES *EMI 2806*	6	11
11 Nov 78	HAMMER HORROR *EMI 2887*	44	6
17 Mar 79	WOW *EMI 2911*	14	10
15 Sep 79 ●	ON STAGE (EP) *EMI MIEP 2991*	10	9
26 Apr 80	BREATHING *EMI 5058*	16	7
5 Jul 80 ●	BABOOSHKA *EMI 5085*	5	10
4 Oct 80	ARMY DREAMERS *EMI 5106*	16	9
6 Dec 80	DECEMBER WILL BE MAGIC AGAIN *EMI 5121*	29	7
11 Jul 81	SAT IN YOUR LAP *EMI 5201*	11	7
7 Aug 82	THE DREAMING *EMI 5296*	48	3
17 Aug 85 ●	RUNNING UP THAT HILL *EMI KB 1*	3	11
26 Oct 85	CLOUDBUSTING *EMI KB 2*	20	5
1 Mar 86	HOUNDS OF LOVE *EMI KB 3*	18	5
10 May 86	THE BIG SKY *EMI KB 4*	37	3
1 Nov 86 ●	DON'T GIVE UP *Virgin PGS 2* [1]	9	11
8 Nov 86	EXPERIMENT IV *EMI KB 5*	23	4
30 Sep 89	THE SENSUAL WORLD *EMI EM 102*	12	5
2 Dec 89	THIS WOMAN'S WORK *EMI EM 119*	25	5
10 Mar 90	LOVE AND ANGER *EMI EM 134*	38	3
7 Dec 91	ROCKET MAN (I THINK IT'S GOING TO BE A LONG LONG TIME) *Mercury TRIBO 2*	12	8
18 Sep 93	RUBBERBAND GIRL *EMI CDEM 280*	12	5
27 Nov 93	MOMENTS OF PLEASURE *EMI CDEM 297*	26	3
16 Apr 94	THE RED SHOES *EMI CDEMS 316*	21	3
30 Jul 94	THE MAN I LOVE *Mercury MERCD 408* [2]	27	2
19 Nov 94	AND SO IS LOVE *EMI CDEMS 355*	26	2

[1] Peter Gabriel and Kate Bush [2] Kate Bush and Larry Adler

Tracks on On Stage (EP): Them Heavy People / Don't Push Your Foot on the
Heartbreak / James and the Cold Gun / L'Amour Looks Something Like You

BUSTER UK, male vocal / instrumental group (1 WEEK) — pos/wks

| 19 Jun 76 | SUNDAY *RCA 2678* | 49 | 1 |

Bernard BUTLER UK, male vocal / instrumentalist (21 WEEKS) — pos/wks

27 May 95 ●	YES *Hut HUTCD 53* [1]	8	8
4 Nov 95	YOU DO *Hut HUTDG 57* [1]	17	4
17 Jan 98	STAY *Creation CRESCD 281*	12	4
28 Mar 98	NOT ALONE *Creation CRESCD 289*	27	3
27 Jun 98	A CHANGE OF HEART *Creation CRESCD 297*	45	1
23 Oct 99	YOU MUST GO ON *Creation CRESCD 324*	44	1

[1] McAlmont and Butler

See also SUEDE

Jonathan BUTLER
South Africa, male vocalist / instrumentalist - guitar (18 WEEKS) pos/wks

25 Jan 86	IF YOU'RE READY (COME GO WITH ME) *Jive JIVE 109* [1]	**30** 7
8 Aug 87	LIES *Jive JIVE 141*	**18** 11

[1] Ruby Turner featuring Jonathan Butler

BUTTERSCOTCH *UK, male vocal group (11 WEEKS)*
pos/wks

2 May 70	DON'T YOU KNOW *RCA 1937*	**17** 11

BUTTHOLE SURFERS
US, male vocal / instrumental group (1 WEEK) pos/wks

5 Oct 96	PEPPER *Capitol CDCL 778*	**59** 1

BUZZCOCKS *UK, male vocal / instrumental group (53 WEEKS)*
pos/wks

18 Feb 78	WHAT DO I GET *United Artists UP 36348*	**37** 3
13 May 78	I DON'T MIND *United Artists UP 36386*	**55** 2
15 Jul 78	LOVE YOU MORE *United Artists UP 36433*	**34** 6
23 Sep 78	EVER FALLEN IN LOVE (WITH SOMEONE YOU SHOULDN'T'VE) *United Artists UP 36455*	**12** 11
25 Nov 78	PROMISES *United Artists UP 36471*	**20** 10
10 Mar 79	EVERYBODY'S HAPPY NOWADAYS *United Artists UP 36499*	**29** 6
21 Jul 79	HARMONY IN MY HEAD *United Artists UP 36541*	**32** 6
25 Aug 79	SPIRAL SCRATCH (EP) *New Hormones ORG 1*	**31** 6
6 Sep 80	ARE EVERYTHING / WHY SHE'S A GIRL FROM THE CHAINSTORE *United Artists BP 365*	**61** 3

Tracks on Spiral Scratch (EP): Breakdown / Time's Up / Boredom / Friends of Mine. Sleeve of EP (not the label) credits 'Buzzcocks with Howard Devoto. 'Why She's a Girl from the Chainstore' listed from 13 Sep 1980

BUZZY BUNCH – See Celi BEE and the BUZZY BUNCH

BVSMP *US, male rap / vocal group (12 WEEKS)*
pos/wks

23 Jul 88	● I NEED YOU *Debut DEBT 3044*	**3** 12

BY ALL MEANS *US, male vocal group (2 WEEKS)*
pos/wks

18 Jun 88	I SURRENDER TO YOUR LOVE *Fourth & Broadway BRW 102*	**65** 2

Max BYGRAVES ⟨194 ▮Top 500▮⟩ *One of Britain's best-loved entertainers, b. 16 Oct, 1922, London. The comedian / singer / songwriter was the only British male on the first UK singles chart. He had five Top 20 'sing-a-long' hit albums in just 15 months of the 1970s (131 WEEKS)* pos/wks

14 Nov 52	COWPUNCHER'S CANTATA *HMV B 10250*	**11** 1
2 Jan 53	● COWPUNCHER'S CANTATA (re-entry) *HMV B 10250*	**8** 1
23 Jan 53	● COWPUNCHER'S CANTATA (2nd re-entry) *HMV B 10250*	**6** 5
6 Mar 53	● COWPUNCHER'S CANTATA (3rd re-entry) *HMV B 10250*	**10** 1
14 May 54	● (THE GANG THAT SANG) HEART OF MY HEART *HMV B 10654*	**7** 8
10 Sep 54	● GILLY GILLY OSSENFEFFER KATZENELLEN BOGEN BY THE SEA *HMV B 10734*	**7** 7
5 Nov 54	GILLY GILLY OSSENFEFFER KATZENELLEN BOGEN BY THE SEA (re-entry) *HMV B 10734*	**20** 1
21 Jan 55	MISTER SANDMAN *HMV B 10801*	**16** 1
18 Nov 55	● MEET ME ON THE CORNER *HMV POP 116*	**2** 11
17 Feb 56	THE BALLAD OF DAVY CROCKETT *HMV POP 153*	**20** 1
25 May 56	OUT OF TOWN *HMV POP 164*	**18** 7
5 Apr 57	HEART *HMV F 10862* [1]	**14** 8
2 May 58	● YOU NEED HANDS / TULIPS FROM AMSTERDAM *Decca F 11004* [2]	**3** 25
22 Aug 58	LITTLE TRAIN / GOTTA HAVE RAIN *Decca F 11046*	**28** 2
2 Jan 59	MY UKELELE *Decca F 11077*	**19** 4
18 Dec 59	● JINGLE BELL ROCK *Decca F 11176*	**7** 4
10 Mar 60	● FINGS AIN'T WOT THEY USED T'BE *Decca F 11214*	**5** 15
28 Jul 60	CONSIDER YOURSELF *Decca F 11251*	**50** 1
1 Jun 61	BELLS OF AVIGNON *Decca F 11350*	**36** 5
19 Feb 69	YOU'RE MY EVERYTHING *Pye 7N 17705*	**50** 1
5 Mar 69	YOU'RE MY EVERYTHING (re-entry) *Pye 7N 17705*	**34** 3
6 Oct 73	DECK OF CARDS *Pye 7N 45276*	**13** 15
9 Dec 89	WHITE CHRISTMAS *Parkfield PMS 5012*	**71** 4

[1] Max Bygraves With Malcolm Lockyer and his Orchestra [2] Max Bygraves with the Clark Bros and both sides with Eric Rodgers and his Orchestra

Cowpuncher's Cantata is a medley with the following songs: Cry of the Wild Goose / Riders in the Sky / Mule Train / Jezebel. 'Tulips From Amsterdam' was listed with 'You Need Hands' from 9 May 1958

BYKER GROOOVE! *UK, female vocal group (3 WEEKS)*
pos/wks

24 Dec 94	LOVE YOUR SEXY . . . !! *Groove GROVD 01*	**48** 3

Charlie BYRD – See Stan GETZ

Debra BYRD – See Barry MANILOW

Donald BYRD *US, male instrumentalist - trumpet (6 WEEKS)*
pos/wks

26 Sep 81	LOVING YOU / LOVE HAS COME AROUND *Elektra K 12559*	**41** 6

Gary BYRD and the GB EXPERIENCE *US, male rapper and male / female vocal / instrumental group (9 WEEKS)*
pos/wks

23 Jul 83	● THE CROWN *Motown TMGT 1312*	**6** 9

BYRDS *US, male vocal / instrumental group (52 WEEKS)*
pos/wks

17 Jun 65	★ MR. TAMBOURINE MAN *CBS 201765* ▲	**1** 14
12 Aug 65	● ALL I REALLY WANT TO DO *CBS 201796*	**4** 10
11 Nov 65	TURN! TURN! TURN! *CBS 202008* ▲	**26** 8
5 May 66	EIGHT MILES HIGH *CBS 202067*	**24** 9
5 Jun 68	YOU AIN'T GOIN' NOWHERE *CBS 3411*	**45** 3
13 Feb 71	CHESTNUT MARE *CBS 5322*	**19** 8

Edward BYRNES & Connie STEVENS
US, male / female vocal duo (8 WEEKS) pos/wks

5 May 60	KOOKIE KOOKIE (LEND ME YOUR COMB) *Warner Bros. WB 5*	**27** 8

See also Connie STEVENS

BYSTANDERS *UK, male vocal / instrumental group (1 WEEK)*
pos/wks

9 Feb 67	98.6 *Piccadilly 7N 35363*	**45** 1

C & C MUSIC FACTORY / CLIVILLES & COLE *US, male instrumental / production duo featuring male / female vocalists / rappers (53 WEEKS)* pos/wks

15 Dec 90	● GONNA MAKE YOU SWEAT (EVERYBODY DANCE NOW) *CBS 6564540* [1] ▲	**3** 12
30 Mar 91	HERE WE GO *Columbia 6567557* [1]	**20** 7
6 Jul 91	● THINGS THAT MAKE YOU GO HMMM... *Columbia 6566907* [1]	**4** 11
23 Nov 91	JUST A TOUCH OF LOVE (EVERYDAY) *Columbia 6575247* [2]	**31** 3
18 Jan 92	PRIDE (IN THE NAME OF LOVE) *Columbia 6577017* [3]	**15** 5
14 Mar 92	A DEEPER LOVE *Columbia 6578497* [3]	**15** 5
3 Oct 92	KEEP IT COMIN' (DANCE TILL YOU CAN'T DANCE NO MORE) *Columbia 6584307* [4]	**34** 3
27 Aug 94	DO YOU WANNA GET FUNKY *Columbia 6607622* [5]	**27** 3
18 Feb 95	I FOUND LOVE / TAKE A TOKE *Columbia 6612112* [6]	**26** 2
11 Nov 95	I'LL ALWAYS BE AROUND *MCA MCSTD 40001* [5]	**42** 2

[1] C & C Music Factory (featuring Freedom Williams) [2] C & C Music Factory featuring Zelma Davis [3] Clivilles and Cole [4] C & C Music Factory featuring Q Unique and Deborah Cooper [5] C & C Music Factory [6] C & C Music Factory / C & C Music Factory featuring Martha Wash

C.J. & CO *US, male vocal / instrumental group (2 WEEKS)* pos/wks

30 Jul 77	**DEVIL'S GUN** *Atlantic K 10956*	43	2

Melanie C *UK, female vocalist - Melanie Chisholm (68 WEEKS)* pos/wks

12 Dec 98 ●	**WHEN YOU'RE GONE** *A & M 5828212* [1]	3	19
9 Oct 99 ●	**GOIN' DOWN** *Virgin VSCDT 1744*	4	4
13 Nov 99	**GOIN' DOWN** (re-entry) *Virgin VSCDT 1744*	64	2
4 Dec 99 ●	**NORTHERN STAR** *Virgin VSCDT 1748*	4	11
1 Apr 00 ★	**NEVER BE THE SAME AGAIN** *Virgin VSCDT 1762* [2] ■	1	14
22 Jul 00	**NEVER BE THE SAME AGAIN** (re-entry) *Virgin VSCDT 1762* [2]	70	2
19 Aug 00 ★	**I TURN TO YOU** *Virgin VSCDT 1772* ■	1	12
9 Dec 00	**IF THAT WERE ME** *Virgin VSCDT 1786*	18	4+

[1] Bryan Adams featuring Melanie C [2] Melanie C / Lisa 'Left Eye' Lopes

See also SPICE GIRLS

Roy C *US, male vocalist - Roy C Hammond (24 WEEKS)* pos/wks

21 Apr 66 ●	**SHOTGUN WEDDING** *Island WI 273*	6	11
25 Nov 72 ●	**SHOTGUN WEDDING** (re-issue) *UK 19*	8	13

ÇA VA ÇA VA *UK, male vocal / instrumental group (8 WEEKS)* pos/wks

18 Sep 82	**WHERE'S ROMEO** *Regard RG 103*	49	5
19 Feb 83	**BROTHER BRIGHT** *Regard RG 105*	65	3

Montserrat CABALLE – See Freddie MERCURY

CABANA *Brazil, male / female vocal / instrumental duo (1 WEEK)* pos/wks

15 Jul 95	**BAILANDO CON LOBOS** *Hi-Life 5792512*	65	1

CABARET VOLTAIRE *UK, male vocal / instrumental group (8 WEEKS)* pos/wks

18 Jul 87	**DON'T ARGUE** *Parlophone R 6157*	69	2
4 Nov 89	**HYPNOTISED** *Parlophone R 6227*	66	2
12 May 90	**KEEP ON** *Parlophone R 6250*	55	2
18 Aug 90	**EASY LIFE** *Parlophone R 6261*	61	2

CABLE *UK, male vocal / instrumental group (2 WEEKS)* pos/wks

14 Jun 97	**FREEZE THE ATLANTIC** *Infectious INFECT 38CD*	44	2

Albert CABRERA – See David MORALES

CACIQUE *UK, male / female vocal / instrumental group (1 WEEK)* pos/wks

1 Jun 85	**DEVOTED TO YOU** *Diamond Duel DISC 1*	69	1

CACTUS WORLD NEWS *Ireland, male vocal / instrumental group (7 WEEKS)* pos/wks

8 Feb 86	**YEARS LATER** *MCA MCA 1024*	59	3
26 Apr 86	**WORLDS APART** *MCA MCA 1040*	58	3
20 Sep 86	**THE BRIDGE** *MCA MCA 1080*	74	1

CADETS with Eileen READ *Ireland, male / female vocal group (1 WEEK)* pos/wks

3 Jun 65	**JEALOUS HEART** *Pye 7N 15852*	42	1

Susan CADOGAN *UK, female vocalist (19 WEEKS)* pos/wks

5 Apr 75 ●	**HURT SO GOOD** *Magnet MAG 23*	4	12
19 Jul 75	**LOVE ME BABY** *Magnet MAG 36*	22	7

Athena CAGE – See Keith SWEAT

Al CAIOLA *US, orchestra, Al Caiola - guitar (6 WEEKS)* pos/wks

15 Jun 61	**THE MAGNIFICENT SEVEN** *HMV POP 889*	34	6

CAKE *US, male vocal / instrumental group (6 WEEKS)* pos/wks

22 Mar 97	**THE DISTANCE** *Capricorn 5742212*	22	3

31 May 97	**I WILL SURVIVE** *Capricorn 5744712*	29	2
1 May 99	**NEVER THERE** *Capricorn 8708112*	66	1

CALIBRE CUTS – See VARIOUS ARTISTS (MONTAGES)

CALIFORNIA SUNSHINE *Israel / Italy, male / female DJ / production group (1 WEEK)* pos/wks

16 Aug 97	**SUMMER '89** *Perfecto PERF 143CD*	56	1

CALL *US, male vocal / instrumental group (6 WEEKS)* pos/wks

30 Sep 89	**LET THE DAY BEGIN** *MCA MCA 1362*	42	6

Terry CALLIER *US, male vocalist (4 WEEKS)* pos/wks

13 Dec 97	**BEST BIT (EP)** *Heavenly HVN 72CD* [1]	36	3
23 May 98	**LOVE THEME FROM SPARTACUS** *Talkin' Loud TLCD 32*	57	1

[1] Beth Orton featuring Terry Callier

Eddie CALVERT (409 Top 500) *'The Man with the Golden Trumpet', b. 13 Mar 1922, Lancashire, UK, d. 7 Aug 1978, South Africa. First British instrumentalist to achieve two No.1s and first to earn US gold disc. 'Oh Mein Papa' spent nine weeks at the top - a record for an instrumental (80 WEEKS)* pos/wks

18 Dec 53 ★	**OH MEIN PAPA** *Columbia DB 3337*	1	21
8 Apr 55 ★	**CHERRY PINK AND APPLE BLOSSOM WHITE** *Columbia DB 3581*	1	21
13 May 55	**STRANGER IN PARADISE** *Columbia DB 3594*	14	4
29 Jul 55 ●	**JOHN AND JULIE** *Columbia DB 3624*	6	11
9 Mar 56	**ZAMBESI** *Columbia DB 3747*	18	1
23 Mar 56	**ZAMBESI** (re-entry) *Columbia DB 3747*	13	6
7 Feb 58 ●	**MANDY (LA PANSE)** *Columbia DB 3956*	9	14
20 Jun 58	**LITTLE SERENADE** *Columbia DB 4105*	28	2

Donnie CALVIN – See ROCKER'S REVENGE featuring Donnie CALVIN

CAMEO *US, male vocal / instrumental group (66 WEEKS)* pos/wks

31 Mar 84	**SHE'S STRANGE** *Club JAB 2*	37	8
13 Jul 85	**ATTACK ME WITH YOUR LOVE** *Club JAB 16*	65	5
14 Sep 85	**SINGLE LIFE** *Club JAB 21*	15	10
7 Dec 85	**SHE'S STRANGE** (re-issue) *Club JAB 25*	22	8
22 Mar 86	**A GOODBYE** *Club JAB 28*	65	2
30 Aug 86 ●	**WORD UP** *Club JAB 38*	3	13
29 Nov 86	**CANDY** *Club JAB 43*	27	9
25 Apr 87	**BACK AND FORTH** *Club JAB 49*	11	9
17 Oct 87	**SHE'S MINE** *Club JAB 57*	35	4
29 Oct 88	**YOU MAKE ME WORK** *Club JAB 70*	74	1

Andy CAMERON *UK, male vocalist (8 WEEKS)* pos/wks

4 Mar 78 ●	**ALLY'S TARTAN ARMY** *Klub 03*	6	8

CAM'RON featuring MASE *US, male rappers (4 WEEKS)* pos/wks

19 Sep 98	**HORSE AND CARRIAGE** *Epic 6662612*	12	4

Tony CAMILLO'S BAZUKA *US, male instrumental / vocal group (5 WEEKS)* pos/wks

31 May 75	**DYNOMITE (PART 1)** *A & M AMS 7168*	28	5

CAMISRA *UK, male DJ / producer - 'Tall Paul' Newman (12 WEEKS)* pos/wks

21 Feb 98 ●	**LET ME SHOW YOU** *VC Recordings VCRD 31*	5	8
11 Jul 98	**FEEL THE BEAT** *VC Recordings VCRD 39*	32	2
22 May 99	**CLAP YOUR HANDS** *VC Recordings VCRD 49*	34	2

See also PARTIZAN; ESCRIMA; TALL PAUL; GRIFTERS

CAMOUFLAGE featuring MYSTI *UK, male / female vocal / instrumental group (3 WEEKS)* pos/wks

24 Sep 77	**BEE STING** *State STAT 58*	48	3

CAMP LO US, male rap duo (1 WEEK)

		pos/wks
16 Aug 97	LUCHINI AKA (THIS IS IT) *ffrr FCD 305*	74 1

CAMPAG VELOCET
UK, male female vocal / instrumental group (1 WEEK)

		pos/wks
19 Feb 00	VITO SATAN *Pias Recordings PIASX 010CD*	75 1

Ali CAMPBELL UK, male vocalist (18 WEEKS)

		pos/wks
20 May 95 ●	THAT LOOK IN YOUR EYE *Kuff KUFFDG 1*	5 10
26 Aug 95	LET YOUR YEAH BE YEAH *Kuff KUFFD 2*	25 4
9 Dec 95	SOMETHIN' STUPID *Kuff KUFFDG 5* [1]	30 4

[1] Ali and Kibibi Campbell

See also Pato BANTON; UB40

Danny CAMPBELL and SASHA
UK, male vocalist and male DJ / producer (1 WEEK)

		pos/wks
31 Jul 93	TOGETHER *ffrr FCD 212*	57 1

See also SASHA

Don CAMPBELL – See GENERAL SAINT

Ellie CAMPBELL UK, female vocalist (4 WEEKS)

		pos/wks
3 Apr 99	SWEET LIES *Jive / Eastern Bloc 0519222*	42 1
14 Aug 99	SO MANY WAYS *Jive / Eastern Bloc 0519362*	26 3

Ethna CAMPBELL UK, female vocalist (11 WEEKS)

		pos/wks
27 Dec 75	THE OLD RUGGED CROSS *Philips 6006 475*	33 11

Ian CAMPBELL FOLK GROUP
UK, male vocal / instrumental group (5 WEEKS)

		pos/wks
11 Mar 65	THE TIMES THEY ARE A-CHANGIN' *Transatlantic SP 5*	42 2
1 Apr 65	THE TIMES THEY ARE A-CHANGIN' (re-entry) *Transatlantic SP 5*	47 1
15 Apr 65	THE TIMES THEY ARE A-CHANGIN' (2nd re-entry) *Transatlantic SP 5*	46 2

Glen CAMPBELL `302 Top 500`
Top session guitarist and singer who became one of the 1960s biggest selling Country and Easy Listening artists, b. 22 Apr 1936, Arkansas, US. Other notable credits include: part-time member of The Beach Boys and vocalist with The Crickets (98 WEEKS)

		pos/wks
29 Jan 69 ●	WICHITA LINEMAN *Ember EMBS 261*	7 13
7 May 69	GALVESTON *Ember EMBS 263*	14 10
6 Dec 69 ●	ALL I HAVE TO DO IS DREAM *Capitol CL 15619* [1]	3 14
7 Feb 70	TRY A LITTLE KINDNESS *Capitol CL 15622*	45 2
9 May 70 ●	HONEY COME BACK *Capitol CL 15638*	4 19
26 Sep 70	EVERYTHING A MAN COULD EVER NEED *Capitol CL 15653*	32 5
21 Nov 70 ●	IT'S ONLY MAKE BELIEVE *Capitol CL 15663*	4 14
27 Mar 71	DREAM BABY *Capitol CL 15674*	39 3
4 Oct 75 ●	RHINESTONE COWBOY *Capitol CL 15824* ▲	4 12
26 Mar 77	SOUTHERN NIGHTS *Capitol CL 15907* ▲	28 6

[1] Bobbie Gentry and Glen Campbell

Jo Ann CAMPBELL US, female vocalist (3 WEEKS)

		pos/wks
8 Jun 61	MOTORCYCLE MICHAEL *HMV POP 873*	41 3

Junior CAMPBELL UK, male vocalist (18 WEEKS)

		pos/wks
14 Oct 72 ●	HALLELUJAH FREEDOM *Deram DM 364*	10 9
2 Jun 73	SWEET ILLUSION *Deram DM 387*	15 9

Kibibi CAMPBELL – See Ali CAMPBELL

Naomi CAMPBELL UK, female vocalist (3 WEEKS)

		pos/wks
24 Sep 94	LOVE AND TEARS *Epic 6608352*	40 3

Pat CAMPBELL Ireland, male vocalist (5 WEEKS)

		pos/wks
15 Nov 69	THE DEAL *Major Minor MM 648*	31 5

Stan CAMPBELL UK, male vocalist (3 WEEKS)

		pos/wks
6 Jun 87	YEARS GO BY *WEA YZ 127*	65 3

Tevin CAMPBELL US, male vocalist (2 WEEKS)

		pos/wks
18 Apr 92	TELL ME WHAT YOU WANT ME TO DO *Qwest W 0102*	63 2

CAN Germany, male vocal / instrumental group (10 WEEKS)

		pos/wks
28 Aug 76	I WANT MORE *Virgin VS 153*	26 10

CANDIDO US, male multi-instrumentalist (3 WEEKS)

		pos/wks
18 Jul 81	JINGO *Excalibur EXC 102*	55 3

CANDLEWICK GREEN
UK, male vocal / instrumental duo (8 WEEKS)

		pos/wks
23 Feb 74	WHO DO YOU THINK YOU ARE *Decca F 13480*	21 8

CANDY FLIP UK, male vocal / instrumental duo - Rick Peel and Danny 'Dizzy' Deo (14 WEEKS)

		pos/wks
17 Mar 90 ●	STRAWBERRY FIELDS FOREVER *Debut DEBT 3092*	3 10
14 Jul 90	THIS CAN BE REAL *Debut DEBT 3099*	60 4

CANDY GIRLS
UK, male / female instrumental / production duo (10 WEEKS)

		pos/wks
30 Sep 95	FEE FI FO FUM *VC VCRD 1* [1]	23 4
24 Feb 96	WHAM BAM *VC VCRD 6* [1]	20 4
7 Dec 96	I WANT CANDY *Feverpitch CDFVR 1013* [2]	30 2

[1] Candy Girls featuring Sweet Pussy Pauline [2] Candy Girls featuring Valerie Malcolm

CANDYLAND UK, male vocal / instrumental group (1 WEEK)

		pos/wks
9 Mar 91	FOUNTAIN O' YOUTH *Non Fiction YES 4*	72 1

CANDYSKINS UK, male vocal / instrumental group (4 WEEKS)

		pos/wks
19 Oct 96	MRS HOOVER *Ultimate TOPP 051CD*	65 1
8 Feb 97	MONDAY MORNING *Ultimate TOPP 055CD*	34 2
3 May 97	HANG MYSELF ON YOU *Ultimate TOPP 059CD*	65 1

CANIBUS US, male rapper (3 WEEKS)

		pos/wks
27 Jun 98	SECOND ROUND K.O. *Universal UND 56198*	35 2
10 Oct 98	HOW COME *Interscope IND 95598* [1]	52 1

[1] Youssou N'Dour and Canibus

CANNED HEAT US, male vocal / instrumental group (41 WEEKS)

		pos/wks
24 Jul 68 ●	ON THE ROAD AGAIN *Liberty LBS 15090*	8 15
1 Jan 69	GOING UP THE COUNTRY *Liberty LBF 15169*	19 10
17 Jan 70 ●	LET'S WORK TOGETHER *Liberty LBF 15302*	2 15
11 Jul 70	SUGAR BEE *Liberty LBF 15350*	49 1

Freddy CANNON
US, male vocalist - Freddy Picariello (53 WEEKS)

		pos/wks
14 Aug 59	TALLAHASSEE LASSIE *Top Rank JAR 135*	17 8
1 Jan 60 ●	WAY DOWN YONDER IN NEW ORLEANS *Top Rank JAR 247*	3 17
5 Mar 60	CALIFORNIA HERE I COME *Top Rank JAR 309*	25 2
17 Mar 60	INDIANA *Top Rank JAR309*	42 1
24 Mar 60	CALIFORNIA HERE I COME (re-entry) *Top Rank JAR 309*	46 1
19 May 60	THE URGE *Top Rank JAR 369*	18 10
20 Apr 61	MUSKRAT RAMBLE *Top Rank JAR 548*	32 5
28 Jun 62	PALISADES PARK *Stateside SS 101*	20 9

Jim CAPALDI UK, male vocalist (17 WEEKS)

		pos/wks
27 Jul 74	IT'S ALL UP TO YOU *Island WIP 6198*	27 6
25 Oct 75 ●	LOVE HURTS *Island WIP 6246*	4 11

UK No.1 ★ UK Top 10 ● Still on chart + UK million seller ◆ UK entry at No.1 ■ US No.1 ▲

SINGLED OUT... Jimmy Osmond

Still the youngest human being ever to top the chart, Little Jimmy (as he was, way back when he was your 'Long Haired Lover From Liverpool') is now manager of The Osmonds and released his first album in 26 years in spring 2001.

• **NO.1 ON THE UK SINGLES CHART THE DAY I WAS BORN:** **How Do You Do It?** – Gerry and the Pacemakers

• **FIRST SINGLE I BOUGHT:** **Superstition** – Stevie Wonder

• **ALL-TIME FAVOURITE SINGLE:** **Get Over It** – The Eagles

SINGLE THAT DRIVES ME UP THE WALL:

Muskrat Love
Captain and Tennille

Photo: F.Costello/Redferns

CAPERCAILLIE
UK, male / female vocal / instrumental group (3 WEEKS) pos/wks

23 May 92	**A PRINCE AMONG ISLANDS (EP)**		
	Survival ZB 45393	39	2
17 Jun 95	**DARK ALAN (AILEIN DUINN)** *Survival SURCD 55*	65	1

Tracks on A Prince Among Islands (EP): Coisich a Ruin (Walk My Beloved) / Fagail Bhearnaraid (Leaving Bernaray) / The Lorn Theme / Gun Teann Mi Ris Na Ruinn Tha Seo (Remembrance)

CAPPADONNA – See WU-TANG CLAN

CAPPELLA
Catchy dance / pop makers essentially consisted of Italian composer / instrumentalist / producer Gianfranco Bortolotti, until he brought in Londoners Rodney Bishop and Kelly Overett as full-time vocalists in 1993. Allison Jordan replaced Overett in 1995. Only Italian act to score four UK Top 10s (68 WEEKS) pos/wks

9 Apr 88	**PUSH THE BEAT / BAUHAUS** *Fast Globe FGL 1*	60	2
6 May 89	**HELYOM HALIB** *Music Man MMPS 7004*	11	9
23 Sep 89	**HOUSE ENERGY REVENGE**		
	Music Man MMPS 7009	73	1
27 Apr 91	**EVERYBODY** *ffrr F158*	66	1
18 Jan 92	**TAKE ME AWAY** *PWL Continental PWL 210* [1]	25	5
3 Apr 93 ●	**U GOT 2 KNOW** *Internal Dance IDC 1*	6	11
14 Aug 93	**U GOT 2 KNOW (re-mix)**		
	Internal Dance IDCR 2	43	3
23 Oct 93 ●	**U GOT 2 LET THE MUSIC** *Internal Dance IDC 3*	2	12
19 Feb 94 ●	**MOVE ON BABY** *Internal Dance IDC 4*	7	7
18 Jun 94 ●	**U & ME** *Internal Dance IDCC 6*	10	7
15 Oct 94	**MOVE IT UP / BIG BEAT** *Internal Dance IDC 7*	16	6
16 Sep 95	**TELL ME THE WAY** *Systematic SYSCD 17*	17	3
6 Sep 97	**BE MY BABY** *Nukleuz PSNC 0072*	53	1

[1] Cappella featuring Loleatta Holloway

See also 49ers

CAPRICCIO
UK, production duo (2 WEEKS) pos/wks

27 Mar 99	**EVERYBODY GET UP** *Defected DEFECT 2CDS*	44	2

CAPRICE
US, female vocalist (3 WEEKS) pos/wks

4 Sep 99	**OH YEAH** *Virgin VSCDT 1745*	24	3

CAPRICORN
Belgium, male DJ (1 WEEK) pos/wks

29 Nov 97	**20 HZ (NEW FREQUENCIES)** *R&S RS 97126CD*	73	1

Tony CAPSTICK and the CARLTON MAIN / FRICKLEY COLLIERY BAND
UK, male vocalist and male instrumental band (8 WEEKS) pos/wks

21 Mar 81 ●	**THE SHEFFIELD GRINDER / CAPSTICK COMES HOME**		
	Dingles SID 27	3	8

CAPTAIN BEAKY – See Keith MICHELL

CAPTAIN HOLLYWOOD PROJECT
US / Germany, male / female vocal / instrumental group (31 WEEKS) pos/wks

22 Sep 90	**I CAN'T STAND IT** *BCM BCMR 395* [1]	7	10
24 Nov 90	**ARE YOU DREAMING** *BCM BCM 07504* [1]	17	10
27 Mar 93	**ONLY WITH YOU** *Pulse 8 CDLOSE 40*	67	1
6 Nov 93	**MORE AND MORE** *Pulse 8 CDLOSE 50*	23	5
5 Feb 94	**IMPOSSIBLE** *Pulse 8 CDLOSE 54*	29	3
11 Jun 94	**ONLY WITH YOU (re-issue)** *Pulse 8 CDLOSE 62*	61	1
1 Apr 95	**FLYING HIGH** *Pulse 8 CDLOSE 82*	58	1

[1] Twenty 4 Seven featuring Captain Hollywood

CAPTAIN SENSIBLE
UK, male vocalist - Ray Burns (31 WEEKS) pos/wks

26 Jun 82 ★	**HAPPY TALK** *A & M CAP 1*	1	8
14 Aug 82	**WOT** *A & M CAP 2*	26	7
24 Mar 84 ●	**GLAD IT'S ALL OVER / DAMNED ON 45** *A & M CAP 6*	6	10
28 Jul 84	**THERE ARE MORE SNAKES THAN LADDERS** *A & M CAP 7*	57	5
10 Dec 94	**THE HOKEY COKEY** *Have A Nice Day CDHOKEY 1*	71	1

CAPTAIN and TENNILLE
US, male instrumentalist / keyboards and female vocalist - Daryl Dragon and Toni Tennille (24 WEEKS) pos/wks

2 Aug 75	**LOVE WILL KEEP US TOGETHER** *A & M AMS 7165* ▲	32	5
24 Jan 76	**THE WAY I WANT TO TOUCH YOU** *A & M AMS 7203*	28	6
4 Nov 78	**YOU NEVER DONE IT LIKE THAT** *A & M AMS 7384*	63	3
16 Feb 80 ●	**DO THAT TO ME ONE MORE TIME** *Casablanca CAN 175* ▲	7	10

Irene CARA
US, female vocalist (33 WEEKS) pos/wks

3 Jul 82 ★	**FAME** *RSO 90*	1	16
4 Sep 82	**OUT HERE ON MY OWN** *RSO 66*	58	3
4 Jun 83 ●	**FLASHDANCE . . . WHAT A FEELING**		
	Casablanca CAN 1016 ▲	2	14

CARAMBA
Sweden, male vocalist / multi-instrumentalist dog impersonator - Michael Tretow (6 WEEKS) pos/wks

12 Nov 83	**FEDORA (I'LL BE YOUR DAWG)** *Billco BILL 101*	56	6

CARAVELLES
UK, female vocal duo - Lois Wilkinson and Andrea Simpson (13 WEEKS) pos/wks

8 Aug 63 ●	**YOU DON'T HAVE TO BE A BABY TO CRY** *Decca F 11697*	6	13

CARDIGANS
Sweden, male / female vocal / instrumental group (66 WEEKS) pos/wks

17 Jun 95	**CARNIVAL** *Trampolene PZCD 345*	72	1
30 Sep 95	**SICK AND TIRED** *Stockholm 5773112*	34	3
2 Dec 95	**CARNIVAL (re-entry)** *Trampolene PZCD 345*	35	2
17 Feb 96	**RISE AND SHINE** *Trampolene 5778252*	29	2
21 Sep 96	**LOVEFOOL** *Stockholm 5752952*	21	4
7 Dec 96	**BEEN IT** *Stockholm 5759672*	56	1
3 May 97 ●	**LOVEFOOL (re-issue)** *Stockholm 5710502*	2	13
6 Sep 97	**YOUR NEW CUCKOO** *Stockholm 5716632*	35	2
17 Oct 98 ●	**MY FAVOURITE GAME** *Stockholm 5679912*	14	18
6 Mar 99 ●	**ERASE / REWIND** *Stockholm 5635332*	7	9
24 Jul 99	**HANGING AROUND** *Stockholm 5612682*	17	4
25 Sep 99 ●	**BURNING DOWN THE HOUSE** *Gut CDGUT 26* [1]	7	7

[1] Tom Jones and The Cardigans

CARE
UK, male vocal / instrumental duo (4 WEEKS) pos/wks

12 Nov 83	**FLAMING SWORD** *Arista KBIRD 2*	48	4

Mariah CAREY
49 **Top 500** *Record-shattering vocalist / songwriter, b. 27 Mar 1970, New York. Since her 1990 chart debut she has sold more than 115 million albums worldwide and has topped the US singles chart 15 times - only Elvis Presley has spent longer at the top (245 WEEKS)* pos/wks

4 Aug 90 ●	**VISION OF LOVE** *CBS 6559320* ▲	9	12
10 Nov 90	**LOVE TAKES TIME** *CBS 6563647* ▲	37	8
26 Jan 91	**SOMEDAY** *Columbia 6565837* ▲	38	5
1 Jun 91	**THERE'S GOT TO BE A WAY** *Columbia 6569317*	54	3
5 Oct 91	**EMOTIONS** *Columbia 6574037* ▲	17	9
11 Jan 92	**CAN'T LET GO** *Columbia 6576627*	20	7
18 Apr 92	**MAKE IT HAPPEN** *Columbia 6579417*	17	5
27 Jun 92 ●	**I'LL BE THERE** *Columbia 6581377* ▲	2	9
21 Aug 93 ●	**DREAMLOVER** *Columbia 6594445* ▲	9	10
6 Nov 93 ●	**HERO** *Columbia 6598122* ▲	7	15
19 Feb 94 ★	**WITHOUT YOU** *Columbia 6599192*	1	14
18 Jun 94 ●	**ANYTIME YOU NEED A FRIEND** *Columbia 6603542*	8	10
17 Sep 94 ●	**ENDLESS LOVE** *Epic 6608062* [1]	3	10
10 Dec 94 ●	**ALL I WANT FOR CHRISTMAS IS YOU** *Columbia 6610702*	2	7
7 Jan 95	**ENDLESS LOVE (re-entry)** *Epic 6608062* [1]	70	2
4 Feb 95	**ENDLESS LOVE (2nd re-entry)** *Epic 6608062* [1]	55	4
11 Mar 95	**ALL I WANT FOR CHRISTMAS IS YOU (re-entry)**		
	Columbia 6610702	59	1
23 Sep 95 ●	**FANTASY** *Columbia 6624952* ▲	4	11
9 Dec 95 ●	**ONE SWEET DAY** *Columbia 6626035* [2] ▲	6	11
17 Feb 96 ●	**OPEN ARMS** *Columbia 6629772*	4	6
22 Jun 96 ●	**ALWAYS BE MY BABY** *Columbia 6633345* ▲	3	10
6 Sep 97 ●	**HONEY** *Columbia 6650192* ▲	3	8
13 Dec 97	**BUTTERFLY** *Columbia 6653365*	22	6
13 Jun 98 ●	**MY ALL** *Columbia 6660592* ▲	4	8

UK No.1 ★   UK Top 10 ●   Still on chart +   UK million seller ◆   UK entry at No.1 ■   US No.1 ▲

19 Dec 98 ●	WHEN YOU BELIEVE *Columbia 6667522* 3	4	11
27 Mar 99	WHEN YOU BELIEVE (re-entry) *Columbia 6667522* 3	68	2
10 Apr 99	I STILL BELIEVE *Columbia 6670732*	16	7
6 Nov 99 ●	HEARTBREAKER *Columbia 6683012* 4 ▲	5	13
11 Mar 00 ●	THANK GOD I FOUND YOU *Columbia 6690582* 5 ▲	10	9
20 May 00	THANK GOD I FOUND YOU (re-entry) *Columbia 6690582* 5	71	1
30 Sep 00 ★	AGAINST ALL ODDS *Columbia 6698872* 6 ■	1	11

1 Luther Vandross and Mariah Carey 2 Mariah Carey and Boyz II Men 3 Mariah Carey and Whitney Houston 4 Mariah Carey featuring Jay-Z 5 Mariah Carey featuring Joe and 98° 6 Mariah Carey & Westlife

Although he is uncredited, 'I'll Be There' is a duet with Trey Lorenz

CARL – See CLUBHOUSE

Belinda CARLISLE 158 Top 500
Lead vocalist of the first really successful all-girl rock group, The Go-Gos; b. 17 Aug 1958, Hollywood. She married the son of British-born film star James Mason in 1992 and her career fared even better in the UK than in her homeland (145 WEEKS) pos/wks

12 Dec 87 ★	HEAVEN IS A PLACE ON EARTH *Virgin VS 1036* ▲	1	14
27 Feb 88 ●	I GET WEAK *Virgin VS 1046*	10	9
7 May 88 ●	CIRCLE IN THE SAND *Virgin VS 1074*	4	11
6 Aug 88	MAD ABOUT YOU *IRS IRM 118*	67	3
10 Sep 88	WORLD WITHOUT YOU *Virgin VS 1114*	34	6
10 Dec 88	LOVE NEVER DIES... *Virgin VS 1150*	54	5
7 Oct 89 ●	LEAVE A LIGHT ON *Virgin VS 1210*	4	10
9 Dec 89	LA LUNA *Virgin VS 1230*	38	6
24 Feb 90	RUNAWAY HORSES *Virgin VS 1244*	40	5
26 May 90	VISION OF YOU *Virgin VS 1264*	41	4
13 Oct 90 ●	(WE WANT) THE SAME THING *Virgin VS 1219*	6	10
22 Dec 90	SUMMER RAIN *Virgin VS 1323*	23	10
20 Apr 91	VISION OF YOU (re-entry) *Virgin VS 1264*	71	1
28 Sep 91	LIVE YOUR LIFE BE FREE *Virgin VS 1370*	12	7
16 Nov 91	DO YOU FEEL LIKE I FEEL *Virgin VS 1383*	29	4
11 Jan 92	HALF THE WORLD *Virgin VS 1388*	35	4
29 Aug 92	LITTLE BLACK BOOK *Virgin VS 1428*	28	5
25 Sep 93	BIG SCARY ANIMAL *Virgin VSCDT 1472*	12	6
27 Nov 93	LAY DOWN YOUR ARMS *Virgin VSCDG 1476*	27	6
13 Jul 96 ●	IN TOO DEEP *Chrysalis CDCHS 5033*	6	7
21 Sep 96 ●	ALWAYS BREAKING MY HEART *Chrysalis CDCHS 5037*	8	6
30 Nov 96	LOVE IN THE KEY OF C *Chrysalis CDCHS 5044*	20	3
1 Mar 97	CALIFORNIA *Chrysalis CDCHSS 5047*	31	2
27 Nov 99	ALL GOD'S CHILDREN *Virgin VSCDT 1756*	66	1

Bob CARLISLE US, male vocalist (2 WEEKS) pos/wks
| 30 Aug 97 | BUTTERFLY KISSES *Jive JIVECD 249* | 56 | 2 |

Sara CARLSON – See MANIC MCs featuring Sara CARLSON

CARLTON UK, male vocalist (3 WEEKS) pos/wks
| 16 Feb 91 | LOVE AND PAIN *Smith & Mighty SNM 4* | 56 | 2 |
| 1 Apr 95 | 1 TO 1 RELIGION *Stoned Heights BRCD 313* 1 | 53 | 1 |

1 Bomb The Bass featuring Carlton

Carl CARLTON US, male vocalist (8 WEEKS) pos/wks
| 18 Jul 81 | SHE'S A BAD MAMA JAMA (SHE'S BUILT, SHE'S STACKED) *20th Century TC 2488* | 34 | 8 |

Larry CARLTON – See Mike POST

CARLTON MAIN / FRICKLEY COLLIERY BAND – See Tony CAPSTICK and the CARLTON MAIN / FRICKLEY COLLIERY BAND

CARMEL UK, female / male vocal / instrumental group (19 WEEKS) pos/wks
6 Aug 83	BAD DAY *London LON 29*	15	9
11 Feb 84	MORE, MORE, MORE *London LON 44*	23	7
14 Jun 86	SALLY *London LON 90*	60	3

Eric CARMEN US, male vocalist (7 WEEKS) pos/wks
| 10 Apr 76 | ALL BY MYSELF *Arista 42* | 12 | 7 |

Jean CARN – See Bobby M featuring Jean CARN

Kim CARNEGIE UK, female vocalist (1 WEEK) pos/wks
| 19 Jan 91 | JAZZ RAP *Best ZB 44085* | 73 | 1 |

Kim CARNES US, female vocalist (15 WEEKS) pos/wks
9 May 81 ●	BETTE DAVIS EYES *EMI America EA 121* ▲	10	9
8 Aug 81	DRAW OF THE CARDS *EMI America EA 125*	49	4
9 Oct 82	VOYEUR *EMI America EA 143*	68	2

CARNIVAL featuring RIP vs RED RAT
UK, male production duo, and Jamaica, male vocalist (1 WEEK) pos/wks
| 12 Sep 98 | ALL OF THE GIRLS (ALL AI-DI GIRL DEM) *Pepper 0530072* | 51 | 1 |

See also RIP PRODUCTIONS

Renato CAROSONE and his SEXTET
Italy, male vocalist and instrumental backing group (1 WEEK) pos/wks
| 4 Jul 58 | TORERO - CHA CHA CHA *Parlophone R 4433* | 25 | 1 |

Mary-Chapin CARPENTER US, female vocalist (6 WEEKS) pos/wks
20 Nov 93	HE THINKS HE'LL KEEP HER *Columbia 6598632*	71	1
7 Jan 95	ONE COOL REMOVE *Columbia 6611342* 1	40	3
3 Jun 95	SHUT UP AND KISS ME *Columbia 6613675*	35	2

1 Shawn Colvin with Mary-Chapin Carpenter

CARPENTERS 113 Top 500
All-time biggest-selling brother / sister duo: Karen Carpenter (v/d) (d. 4 Feb 1983), Richard Carpenter (k/v). This Connecticut couple was among the world's most popular pop / MOR acts of the 1970s before Karen's tragic anorexia-associated death (173 WEEKS) pos/wks

5 Sep 70 ●	(THEY LONG TO BE) CLOSE TO YOU *A & M AMS 800* ▲	6	18
9 Jan 71	WE'VE ONLY JUST BEGUN *A & M AMS 813*	28	7
18 Sep 71	SUPERSTAR / FOR ALL WE KNOW *A & M AMS 864*	18	13
1 Jan 72	MERRY CHRISTMAS DARLING *A & M AME 601*	45	1
23 Sep 72 ●	I WON'T LAST A DAY WITHOUT YOU / GOODBYE TO LOVE *A & M AMS 7023*	9	16
7 Jul 73 ●	YESTERDAY ONCE MORE *A & M AMS 7073*	2	17
20 Oct 73 ●	TOP OF THE WORLD *A & M AMS 7086* ▲	5	18
2 Mar 74	JAMBALAYA (ON THE BAYOU) / MR GUDER *A & M AMS 7098*	12	11
8 Jun 74	I WON'T LAST A DAY WITHOUT YOU (re-issue) *A & M AMS 7111*	32	5
18 Jan 75 ●	PLEASE MR POSTMAN *A & M AMS 7141* ▲	2	12
19 Apr 75 ●	ONLY YESTERDAY *A & M AMS 7159*	7	10
30 Aug 75	SOLITAIRE *A & M AMS 7187*	32	5
20 Dec 75	SANTA CLAUS IS COMIN' TO TOWN *A & M AMS 7144*	37	4
27 Mar 76	THERE'S A KIND OF HUSH (ALL OVER THE WORLD) *A & M AMS 7219*	22	6
3 Jul 76	I NEED TO BE IN LOVE *A & M AMS 7238*	36	5
8 Oct 77 ●	CALLING OCCUPANTS OF INTERPLANETARY CRAFT (THE RECOGNISED ANTHEM OF WORLD CONTACT DAY) *A & M AMS 7318*	9	9
11 Feb 78	SWEET SWEET SMILE *A & M AMS 7327*	40	4
22 Oct 83	MAKE BELIEVE IT'S YOUR FIRST TIME *A & M AM 147*	60	3
8 Dec 90	MERRY CHRISTMAS DARLING / (THEY LONG TO BE) CLOSE TO YOU (re-issue) *A & M AM 716*	25	5
13 Feb 93	RAINY DAYS AND MONDAYS *A & M AMCD 0180*	63	2
24 Dec 94	TRYIN' TO GET THE FEELING AGAIN *A & M 5807612*	44	2

'I Won't Last a Day Without You' AMS 7023 listed by itself 23 Sep 1972 at No.49. 'Goodbye to Love', the other side, listed by itself from 30 Sep 1972, until the end of the record's chart run. 'Mr Guder' listed with 'Jambalaya' from 16 Mar 1974, until the end of the chart run

Pearl CARR and Teddy JOHNSON
UK, female / male vocal duo (19 WEEKS) pos/wks
| 20 Mar 59 | SING LITTLE BIRDIE *Columbia DB 4275* | 12 | 8 |
| 6 Apr 61 | HOW WONDERFUL TO KNOW *Columbia DB 4603* | 23 | 11 |

Dick CARR – See Slim DUSTY

Joe 'Fingers' CARR US, male instrumentalist - piano, Lou Busch under a false name (5 WEEKS)

		pos/wks
29 Jun 56	**PORTUGUESE WASHERWOMAN** Capitol CL 14587	**20** 5

See also Lou BUSCH

Linda CARR US, female vocalist (12 WEEKS)

		pos/wks
12 Jul 75	**HIGHWIRE** Chelsea 2005 025 [1]	**15** 8
5 Jun 76	**SOLD MY ROCK 'N' ROLL (GAVE IT FOR FUNKY SOUL)** Spark SRL 1139 [2]	**36** 4

[1] Linda Carr and the Love Squad [2] Linda and the Funky Boys

Suzi CARR US, female vocalist (1 WEEK)

		pos/wks
8 Oct 94	**ALL OVER ME** Cowboy RODEO 947CD	**45** 1

Valerie CARR US, female vocalist (2 WEEKS)

		pos/wks
4 Jul 58	**WHEN THE BOYS TALK ABOUT THE GIRLS** Columbia DB 4131	**29** 1
18 Jul 58	**WHEN THE BOYS TALK ABOUT THE GIRLS (re-entry)** Columbia DB 4131	**30** 1

Vikki CARR US, female vocalist - Florencia Bisenta De Casillas Martinez Cardona (26 WEEKS)

		pos/wks
1 Jun 67 ●	**IT MUST BE HIM (SEUL SUR SON ETOILE)** Liberty LIB 55917	**2** 20
30 Aug 67	**THERE I GO** Liberty LBF 15022	**50** 1
12 Mar 69	**WITH PEN IN HAND** Liberty LBF 15166	**43** 1
26 Mar 69	**WITH PEN IN HAND (re-entry)** Liberty LBF 15166	**39** 2
30 Apr 69	**WITH PEN IN HAND (2nd re-entry)** Liberty LBF 15166	**40** 2

Raffaella CARRA Italy, female vocalist (12 WEEKS)

		pos/wks
15 Apr 78 ●	**DO IT DO IT AGAIN** Epic EPC 6094	**9** 12

Paul CARRACK UK, male vocalist (18 WEEKS)

		pos/wks
16 May 87	**WHEN YOU WALK IN THE ROOM** Chrysalis CHS 3109	**48** 5
18 Mar 89	**DON'T SHED A TEAR** Chrysalis CHS 3164	**60** 3
6 Jan 96	**EYES OF BLUE** IRS CDEIRS 192	**40** 4
6 Apr 96	**HOW LONG** IRS CDEIRS 193	**32** 5
24 Aug 96	**EYES OF BLUE (re-mix)** IRS CDEIRS 194	**45** 1

CARRAPICHO – See CHILLI featuring CARRAPICHO

Josë CARRERAS Spain, male vocalist (19 WEEKS)

		pos/wks
11 Jul 92	**AMIGOS PARA SIEMPRE (FRIENDS FOR LIFE)** Really Useful RUR 10 [1]	**11** 11
30 Jul 94	**LIBIAMO / LA DONNA E MOBILE** Teldec YZ 843CD [2]	**21** 4
25 Jul 98	**YOU'LL NEVER WALK ALONE** Decca 4607982 [3]	**35** 4

[1] JosÈ Carreras and Sarah Brightman [2] JosÈ Carreras featuring Placido Domingo and Luciano Pavarotti with Mehta [3] JosÈ Carreras, Placido Domingo and Luciano Pavarotti with Mehta

Tia CARRERE US, female vocalist (6 WEEKS)

		pos/wks
30 May 92	**BALLROOM BLITZ** Reprise W 0105	**26** 6

Jim CARREY Canada, male vocalist (3 WEEKS)

		pos/wks
21 Jan 95	**CUBAN PETE** Columbia 6606625	**31** 3

CARRIE US / UK, male vocal / instrumental group (2 WEEKS)

		pos/wks
14 Mar 98	**MOLLY** Island CID 687	**56** 1
9 May 98	**CALIFORNIA SCREAMIN'** Island CID 694	**55** 1

Dina CARROLL (309) Top 500 Brit award-winning Best Female Vocalist of 1994 b. 21 Aug 1968, Newmarket, UK. Soul / dance vocalist's So Close was the biggest-selling debut album by a British female artist in the 1990s, and she was the only UK woman to have two simultaneous Top 10 singles that decade (in 1993) (97 WEEKS)

		pos/wks
2 Feb 91 ●	**IT'S TOO LATE** Mercury ITM 3 [1]	**8** 14
15 Jun 91	**NAKED LOVE (JUST SAY YOU WANT ME)** Mercury ITM 4 [2]	**39** 3
11 Jul 92	**AIN'T NO MAN** A & M AM 0001	**16** 8
10 Oct 92	**SPECIAL KIND OF LOVE** A & M AM 0088	**16** 5
5 Dec 92	**SO CLOSE** A & M AM 0101	**20** 8
27 Feb 93	**THIS TIME** A & M AMCD 0184	**23** 6
15 May 93	**EXPRESS** A & M 5802632	**12** 6
16 Oct 93 ●	**DON'T BE A STRANGER** A & M 5803892	**3** 13
11 Dec 93 ●	**THE PERFECT YEAR** A & M 5804812	**5** 11
28 Sep 96 ●	**ESCAPING** Mercury DCCD 1	**3** 8
21 Dec 96	**ONLY HUMAN** Mercury DCCD 2	**33** 4
24 Oct 98	**ONE, TWO, THREE** 1st Avenue MERCD 514	**16** 4
24 Jul 99	**WITHOUT LOVE** Manifesto / First Avenue FESCD 57	**13** 7

[1] Quartz introducing Dina Carroll [2] Quartz and Dina Carroll

Ron CARROLL – See SUPERFUNK

Ronnie CARROLL Ireland, male vocalist - Ronald Cleghorn (50 WEEKS)

		pos/wks
27 Jul 56	**WALK HAND IN HAND** Philips PB 605	**13** 8
29 Mar 57	**THE WISDOM OF A FOOL** Philips PB 667	**20** 2
31 Mar 60	**FOOTSTEPS** Philips PB 1004	**36** 3
22 Feb 62	**RING A DING GIRL** Philips PB 1222	**46** 3
2 Aug 62 ●	**ROSES ARE RED** Philips 326532 BF	**3** 16
15 Nov 62	**IF ONLY TOMORROW** Philips 326550 BF	**33** 4
7 Mar 63 ●	**SAY WONDERFUL THINGS** Philips 326574 BF	**6** 14

Jasper CARROTT UK, male comedian / vocalist - Bob Davies (15 WEEKS)

		pos/wks
16 Aug 75 ●	**FUNKY MOPED / MAGIC ROUNDABOUT** DJM DJS 388	**5** 15

CARS US, male vocal / instrumental group (51 WEEKS)

		pos/wks
11 Nov 78 ●	**MY BEST FRIEND'S GIRL** Elektra K 12301	**3** 10
17 Feb 79	**JUST WHAT I NEEDED** Elektra K 12312	**17** 10
28 Jul 79	**LET'S GO** Elektra K 12371	**51** 4
5 Jun 82	**SINCE YOU'RE GONE** Elektra K 13177	**37** 4
29 Sep 84 ●	**DRIVE** Elektra E 9706	**5** 11
3 Aug 85 ●	**DRIVE (re-entry)** Elektra E 9706	**4** 12

Aaron CARTER US, male vocalist (29 WEEKS)

		pos/wks
29 Nov 97 ●	**CRUSH ON YOU** Ultra Pop 0099605 ULT	**9** 8
7 Feb 98 ●	**CRAZY LITTLE PARTY GIRL** Ultra Pop 0099645 ULT	**7** 6
28 Mar 98	**I'M GONNA MISS YOU FOREVER** Ultra Pop 0099725 ULT	**24** 5
4 Jul 98	**SURFIN' USA** Ultra Pop 0099805 ULT	**18** 5
16 Sep 00	**I WANT CANDY** Jive 9250892	**31** 3
28 Oct 00	**AARON'S PARTY (COME GET IT)** Jive 9251272	**51** 2

Clarence CARTER US, male vocalist (13 WEEKS)

		pos/wks
10 Oct 70 ●	**PATCHES** Atlantic 2091 030	**2** 13

CARTER - THE UNSTOPPABLE SEX MACHINE UK, male vocal / instrumental duo (46 WEEKS)

		pos/wks
26 Jan 91	**BLOODSPORTS FOR ALL** Rough Trade R 20112687	**48** 2
22 Jun 91	**SHERIFF FATMAN** Big Cat USM 1	**23** 7
26 Oct 91	**AFTER THE WATERSHED** Big Cat USM 2	**11** 5
11 Jan 92	**RUBBISH** Big Cat USM 3	**14** 5
25 Apr 92 ●	**THE ONLY LIVING BOY IN NEW CROSS** Big Cat USM 4	**7** 5
4 Jul 92	**DO RE ME SO FAR SO GOOD** Chrysalis USM 5	**22** 3
28 Nov 92	**THE IMPOSSIBLE DREAM** Chrysalis USM 6	**21** 3
4 Sep 93	**LEAN ON ME I WON'T FALL OVER** Chrysalis CDUSM 7	**16** 3
16 Oct 93	**LENNY AND TERENCE** Chrysalis CDUSM 8	**40** 2
12 Mar 94	**GLAM ROCK COPS** Chrysalis CDUSM 10	**24** 3
19 Nov 94	**LET'S GET TATTOOS** Chrysalis CDUSMS 30	**30** 3

4 Feb 95		THE YOUNG OFFENDER'S MUM *Chrysalis CDUSMS 12*	34	3
30 Sep 95		BORN ON THE 5TH OF NOVEMBER *Chrysalis CDUSM 13*	35	2

CARTER TWINS *Ireland, male vocal duo (1 WEEK)*　　　pos/wks

8 Mar 97		THE TWELFTH OF NEVER / TOO RIGHT TO BE *RCA 74321453082*	61	1

Junior CARTIER *UK, male producer - Jon Carter (1 WEEK)*　　pos/wks

6 Nov 99		WOMEN BEAT THEIR MEN *Nucamp CAMPD 3X*	70	1

CARTOONS
Denmark, male / female vocal / instrumental group (30 WEEKS)　pos/wks

3 Apr 99	●	WITCH DOCTOR *Flex / EMI CDTOONS 001*	2	13
19 Jun 99	●	DOODAH! *Flex / EMI CDTOON 002*	7	11
4 Sep 99		AISY WAISY *Flex / EMI CDTOONS 003*	16	5
16 Oct 99		DOODAH! (re-entry) *Flex / EMI CDTOON 002*	73	1

Sam CARTWRIGHT – See VOLCANO

CARVELLS
UK, male vocalist / instrumentalist - Alan Carvell (4 WEEKS)　pos/wks

26 Nov 77		THE L.A. RUN *Creole CR 143*	31	4

CASCADES *US, male vocal group (16 WEEKS)*　　　pos/wks

28 Feb 63	●	RHYTHM OF THE RAIN *Warner Bros. WB 88*	5	16

CASE – See Foxy BROWN

Ed CASE *UK, male producer - Edward Makromallies (2 WEEKS)*　pos/wks

21 Oct 00		SOMETHING IN YOUR EYES *Red Rose CDRRROSE 003*	38	2

Natalie CASEY *UK, female vocalist (1 WEEK)*　　　pos/wks

7 Jan 84		CHICK CHICK CHICKEN *Polydor CHICK 1*	72	1

Johnny CASH *US, male vocalist (59 WEEKS)*　　　pos/wks

3 Jun 65		IT AIN'T ME BABE *CBS 201760*	28	8
6 Sep 69	●	A BOY NAMED SUE *CBS 4460*	4	19
23 May 70		WHAT IS TRUTH *CBS 4934*	21	11
15 Apr 72	●	A THING CALLED LOVE *CBS 7797* [1]	4	13
22 Jul 72		A THING CALLED LOVE (re-entry) *CBS 7797* [1]	48	1
3 Jul 76		ONE PIECE AT A TIME *CBS 4287* [2]	32	7

[1] Johnny Cash with the Evangel Temple Choir [2] Johnny Cash with the Tennessee Three

Pat CASH – See John McENROE and Pat CASH with the FULL METAL RACKETS

CA$HFLOW *US, male vocal / instrumental group (8 WEEKS)*　pos/wks

24 May 86		MINE ALL MINE / PARTY FREAK *Club JAB 30*	15	8

CASHMERE *US, male vocal / instrumental group (11 WEEKS)*　pos/wks

19 Jan 85		CAN I *Fourth & Broadway BRW 19*	29	8
23 Mar 85		WE NEED LOVE *Fourth & Broadway BRW 22*	52	3

CASINO *UK, male vocal / production group (2 WEEKS)*　pos/wks

17 May 97		SOUND OF EDEN *Worx WORXCD 005*	52	1
10 Jul 99		ONLY YOU *Pow! CDPOW 006*	72	1

CASINOS *US, male vocal group (7 WEEKS)*　　　pos/wks

23 Feb 67		THEN YOU CAN TELL ME GOODBYE *President PT 123*	28	7

David CASSIDY 262 **Top 500** Top teen idol of 1970s, b. 12 Apr 1950, New York. This photogenic singer / actor first found fame via the TV series The Partridge Family. His UK chart career took off as his US sales slowed down *(109 WEEKS)*　　　pos/wks

8 Apr 72	●	COULD IT BE FOREVER / CHERISH *Bell 1224*	2	17
16 Sep 72	★	HOW CAN I BE SURE *Bell 1258*	1	11
25 Nov 72		ROCK ME BABY *Bell 1268*	11	9
24 Mar 73	●	I AM A CLOWN / SOME KIND OF A SUMMER *Bell MABEL 4*	3	12
13 Oct 73	★	DAYDREAMER / THE PUPPY SONG *Bell 1334*	1	15
11 May 74	●	IF I DIDN'T CARE *Bell 1350*	9	8
27 Jul 74		PLEASE PLEASE ME *Bell 1371*	16	8
5 Jul 75		I WRITE THE SONGS / GET IT UP FOR LOVE *RCA 2571*	11	8
25 Oct 75		DARLIN' *RCA 2622*	16	8
23 Feb 85	●	THE LAST KISS *Arista ARIST 589*	6	9
11 May 85		ROMANCE (LET YOUR HEART GO) *Arista ARIST 620*	54	6

See also PARTRIDGE FAMILY

CASSIUS *France / DJ production duo - Philippe Zdar and Hubert Blanc-Francart (12 WEEKS)*　　　pos/wks

23 Jan 99	●	CASSIUS 1999 *Virgin DINSD 177*	7	7
15 May 99		FEELING FOR YOU *Virgin DINSD 181*	16	4
20 Nov 99		LA MOUCHE *Virgin DINSD 188*	53	1

CAST *UK, male vocal / instrumental group (54 WEEKS)*　pos/wks

15 Jul 95		FINETIME *Polydor 5795072*	17	4
30 Sep 95		ALRIGHT *Polydor 5799272*	13	4
20 Jan 96	●	SANDSTORM *Polydor 5778732*	8	5
30 Mar 96	●	WALKAWAY *Polydor 5762852*	9	7
26 Oct 96	●	FLYING *Polydor 5754772*	4	5
5 Apr 97	●	FREE ME *Polydor 5736512*	7	6
21 Jun 97		FREE ME (re-entry) *Polydor 5736512*	64	1
28 Jun 97	●	GUIDING STAR *Polydor 5711732*	9	6
13 Sep 97	●	LIVE THE DREAM *Polydor 5716852*	7	5
15 Nov 97		I'M SO LONELY *Polydor 5690592*	14	3
8 May 99	●	BEAT MAMA *Polydor 5635932*	9	5
7 Aug 99		MAGIC HOUR *Polydor 5612272*	28	3

CAST FROM CASUALTY
UK, male / female vocal group (6 WEEKS)　　　pos/wks

14 Mar 98	●	EVERLASTING LOVE *Warner.esp WESP 003CD*	5	6

CAST OF THE NEW ROCKY HORROR SHOW
UK, male / female vocal group (1 WEEK)　　　pos/wks

12 Dec 98		THE TIMEWARP *Damn It Janet DAMJAN 1CD*	57	1

Roy CASTLE *UK, male vocalist (3 WEEKS)*　　　pos/wks

22 Dec 60		LITTLE WHITE BERRY *Philips PB 1087*	40	3

CASUALS *UK, male vocal / instrumental group (26 WEEKS)*　pos/wks

14 Aug 68	●	JESAMINE *Decca F 22784*	2	18
4 Dec 68		TOY *Decca F 22852*	30	8

CAT *UK, male vocalist (4 WEEKS)*　　　pos/wks

23 Oct 93		TONGUE TIED *EMI CDEM 286*	17	4

CATATONIA
UK, male / female vocal / instrumental group (46 WEEKS)　pos/wks

3 Feb 96		SWEET CATATONIA *Blanco Y Negro NEG 85CD*	61	1
4 May 96		LOST CAT *Blanco Y Negro NEG 88CD1*	41	1
7 Sep 96		YOU'VE GOT A LOT TO ANSWER FOR *Blanco Y Negro NEG 93CD1*	35	2
30 Nov 96		BLEED *Blanco Y Negro NEG 97CD1*	46	1
18 Oct 97		I AM THE MOB *Blanco Y Negro NEG 107CD*	40	2
31 Jan 98	●	MULDER AND SCULLY *Blanco Y Negro NEG 109CD*	3	10
2 May 98	●	ROAD RAGE *Blanco Y Negro NEG 112CD*	5	8
1 Aug 98		STRANGE GLUE *Blanco Y Negro NEG 113CD*	11	6
7 Nov 98		GAME ON *WEA NEG 114CD*	33	2
10 Apr 99	●	DEAD FROM THE WAIST DOWN *Blanco Y Negro NEG 115CD1*	7	8
24 Jul 99		LONDINIUM *Blanco Y Negro NEG 117CD*	20	3
13 Nov 99		KARAOKE QUEEN *Blanco Y Negro NEG 119CD*	36	2

CATCH *UK, male vocal / instrumental group (1 WEEK)*　pos/wks

17 Nov 90		FREE (C'MON) *ffrr F 147*	70	1

CATCH UK, male vocal instrumental group (6 WEEKS)

		pos/wks	
11 Oct 97	BINGO *Virgin VSCDT 1656*	23	4
21 Feb 98	DIVE IN *Virgin VSCDT 1665*	44	2

CATHERINE WHEEL
UK, male vocal / instrumental group (12 WEEKS)

		pos/wks	
23 Nov 91	BLACK METALLIC (EP) *Fontana CW 1*	68	1
8 Feb 92	BALLOON *Fontana CW 2*	59	1
18 Apr 92	I WANT TO TOUCH YOU *Fontana CW 3*	35	2
9 Jan 93	30TH CENTURY MAN *Fontana CWCD 4*	47	2
10 Jul 93	CRANK *Fontana CWCD 5*	66	1
16 Oct 93	SHOW ME MARY *Fontana CWCDA 6*	62	1
5 Aug 95	WAYDOWN *Fontana CWCD 7*	67	1
13 Dec 97	DELICIOUS *Chrysalis CDCHS 5071*	53	1
28 Feb 98	MA SOLITUDA *Chrysalis CDCHS 5077*	53	1
2 May 98	BROKEN NOSE *Chrysalis CDCHS 5086*	48	1

Tracks on Black Metallic (EP): Black Metallic / Crawling Over Me / Let Me Down Again / Saccharine

Lorraine CATO UK, female vocalist (3 WEEKS)

		pos/wks	
6 Feb 93	HOW CAN YOU TELL ME IT'S OVER *Columbia 6587662*	46	2
3 Aug 96	I WAS MADE TO LOVE YOU *MCA MCSTD 40055*	41	1

CATS UK, male instrumental group (2 WEEKS)

		pos/wks	
9 Apr 69	SWAN LAKE *BAF 1*	48	1
21 May 69	SWAN LAKE (re-entry) *BAF 1*	50	1

CATS UK UK, female vocal group (8 WEEKS)

		pos/wks	
6 Oct 79	LUTON AIRPORT *WEA K 18075*	22	8

Nick CAVE and the BAD SEEDS Australia / Germany, male vocal / instrumental group (10 WEEKS)

		pos/wks	
11 Apr 92	STRAIGHT TO YOU / JACK THE RIPPER *Mute MUTE 140*	68	1
12 Dec 92	WHAT A WONDERFUL WORLD *Mute MUTE 151* [1]	72	1
9 Apr 94	DO YOU LOVE ME *Mute CDMUTE 160*	68	1
14 Oct 95	WHERE THE WILD ROSES GROW *Mute CDMUTE 185* [2]	11	4
9 Mar 96	HENRY LEE *Mute CDMUTE 189* [3]	36	1
22 Feb 97	INTO MY ARMS *Mute CDMUTE 192*	53	1
31 May 97	(ARE YOU) THE ONE THAT I'VE BEEN… *Mute CDMUTE 206*	67	1

[1] Nick Cave and Shane McGowan [2] Nick Cave and Kylie Minogue [3] Nick Cave and the Bad Seeds and P J Harvey

CAVEMAN UK, male rap group (2 WEEKS)

		pos/wks	
9 Mar 91	I'M READY *Profile PROF 330*	65	2

CCS UK, male vocal / instrumental group (55 WEEKS)

		pos/wks	
31 Oct 70	WHOLE LOTTA LOVE *RAK 104*	13	13
27 Feb 71	WALKIN' *RAK 109*	7	16
4 Sep 71 ●	TAP TURNS ON THE WATER *RAK 119*	5	13
4 Mar 72	BROTHER *RAK 126*	25	8
4 Aug 73	BAND PLAYED THE BOOGIE *RAK 154*	36	5

CECIL UK, male vocal / instrumental group (2 WEEKS)

		pos/wks	
25 Oct 97	HOSTAGE IN A FROCK *Parlophone CDRS 6471*	68	1
28 Mar 98	THE MOST TIRING DAY *Parlophone CDR 6490*	69	1

CELEDA US, female vocalist (5 WEEKS)

		pos/wks	
5 Sep 98	MUSIC IS THE ANSWER (DANCIN' AND PRANCIN) *Twisted UK TWCD 10038* [1]	36	3
12 Jun 99	BE YOURSELF *Twisted UK TWCD 10049*	61	1
23 Oct 99	MUSIC IS THE ANSWER (DANCIN' AND PRANCIN) *Twisted UK TWCD 10052* [2]	50	1

[1] Danny Tenaglia and Celeda [2] Celeda with Danny Tenaglia

CELETIA UK, female vocalist (3 WEEKS)

		pos/wks	
11 Apr 98	REWIND *Big Life BLRD 142*	29	2
8 Aug 98	RUNAWAY SKIES *Big Life BLRD 144*	66	1

CENTORY US, male rapper (1 WEEK)

		pos/wks	
17 Dec 94	POINT OF NO RETURN *EMI CDEM 354*	67	1

CENTRAL LINE UK, male vocal / instrumental group (30 WEEKS) pos/wks

		pos/wks	
31 Jan 81	(YOU KNOW) YOU CAN DO IT *Mercury LINE 7*	67	3
15 Aug 81	WALKING INTO SUNSHINE *Mercury MER 78*	42	10
30 Jan 82	DON'T TELL ME *Mercury MER 90*	55	3
20 Nov 82	YOU'VE SAID ENOUGH *Mercury MER 117*	58	3
22 Jan 83	NATURE BOY *Mercury MER 131*	21	8
11 Jun 83	SURPRISE SURPRISE *Mercury MER 133*	48	3

CERRONE France, male producer / multi-instrumentalist - Jean-Marc Cerrone (21 WEEKS)

		pos/wks	
5 Mar 77	LOVE IN C MINOR *Atlantic K 10895*	31	4
29 Jul 78 ●	SUPERNATURE *Atlantic K 11089*	8	12
13 Jan 79	JE SUIS MUSIC *CBS 6918*	39	4
10 Aug 96	SUPERNATURE (re-mix) *Encore CDCOR 013*	66	1

A CERTAIN RATIO
UK, male vocal / instrumental group (3 WEEKS)

		pos/wks	
16 Jun 90	WON'T STOP LOVING YOU *A & M ACR 540*	55	3

Peter CETERA US, male vocalist (20 WEEKS)

		pos/wks	
2 Aug 86 ●	GLORY OF LOVE *Full Moon W 8662* ▲	3	13
21 Jun 97 ●	HARD TO SAY I'M SORRY *La Face 74321481482* [1]	7	7

[1] Az Yet featuring Peter Cetera

See also CHICAGO

Frank CHACKSFIELD UK, orchestra (41 WEEKS)

		pos/wks	
3 Apr 53 ●	LITTLE RED MONKEY *Parlophone R 3658* [1]	10	3
22 May 53 ●	TERRY'S THEME FROM 'LIMELIGHT' *Decca F 10106*	2	24
12 Feb 54 ●	EBB TIDE *Decca F 10122*	9	2
24 Feb 56	IN OLD LISBON *Decca F 10689*	15	4
18 May 56	PORT AU PRINCE *Decca F 10727* [2]	18	6
31 Aug 56	DONKEY CART *Decca F 10743*	26	2

[1] Frank Chacksfield's Tunesmiths, featuring Jack Jordan - clavioline [2] Winifred Atwell and Frank Chacksfield

CHAIRMEN OF THE BOARD (432 Top 500) Superior 70s soul group fronted by distinctive singer / songwriter Norman (General) Johnson, b. 23 May 1944, Virginia, US. Detroit-based quartet, who recorded on Holland, Dozier and Holland's Invictus label, are regarded as legends by US 'Beach' (vintage soul) music fans (77 WEEKS)

		pos/wks	
22 Aug 70 ●	GIVE ME JUST A LITTLE MORE TIME *Invictus INV 501*	3	13
14 Nov 70 ●	YOU'VE GOT ME DANGLING ON A STRING *Invictus INV 504*	5	13
20 Feb 71	EVERYTHING'S TUESDAY *Invictus INV 507*	12	9
15 May 71	PAY TO THE PIPER *Invictus INV 511*	34	7
4 Sep 71	CHAIRMAN OF THE BOARD *Invictus INV 516*	48	2
15 Jul 72	WORKING ON A BUILDING OF LOVE *Invictus INV 519*	20	8
7 Oct 72	ELMO JAMES *Invictus INV 524*	21	7
16 Dec 72	I'M ON MY WAY TO A BETTER PLACE *Invictus INV 527*	38	1
6 Jan 73	I'M ON MY WAY TO A BETTER PLACE (re-entry) *Invictus INV 527*	30	5
23 Jun 73	FINDERS KEEPERS *Invictus INV 530*	21	9
13 Sep 86	LOVERBOY *EMI EMI 5585* [1]	56	3

[1] Chairmen of the Board featuring General Johnson

CHAKACHAS
Belgium, male / female vocal / instrumental group (8 WEEKS)

		pos/wks	
11 Jan 62	TWIST TWIST *RCA 1264*	48	1
27 May 72	JUNGLE FEVER *Polydor 2121 064*	29	7

George CHAKIRIS US, male vocalist (1 WEEK)

		pos	wks
2 Jun 60	HEART OF A TEENAGE GIRL *Triumph RGM 1010*	49	1

CHAKKA BOOM BANG
Holland, male instrumental / production group (1 WEEK)

		pos	wks
20 Jan 96	TOSSING AND TURNING *Hooj Choons HOOJCD 39*	57	1

CHAKRA *UK, male / female vocal / instrumental group (5 WEEKS)* pos/wks

		pos	wks
18 Jan 97	I AM *WEA WEA 091CD*	24	2
23 Aug 97	HOME *WEA WEA 116CD2*	46	1
23 Oct 99	LOVE SHINES THROUGH *WEA WEA 227CD*	67	1
26 Aug 00	HOME (re-mix) *WEA WEA 266CD*	47	1

Sue CHALONER *UK, female vocalist (1 WEEK)*

		pos	wks
22 May 93	MOVE ON UP *Pulse 8 CDLOSE 41*	64	1

Richard CHAMBERLAIN *US, male actor (36 WEEKS)*

		pos	wks
7 Jun 62	THEME FROM 'DR. KILDARE' (THREE STARS WILL SHINE TONIGHT) *MGM 1160*	12	10
1 Nov 62	LOVE ME TENDER *MGM 1173*	15	11
21 Feb 63	HI-LILI HI-LO *MGM 1189*	20	9
18 Jul 63	TRUE LOVE *MGM 1205*	30	6

CHAMELEON *UK, male vocal / instrumental group (2 WEEKS)*

		pos	wks
18 May 96	THE WAY IT IS *Stress CDSTR 65*	34	2

CHAMELEONS – See LORI and the CHAMELEONS

CHAMPAIGN
US, male / female vocal / instrumental group (13 WEEKS)

		pos	wks
9 May 81 ●	HOW 'BOUT US *CBS A 1046*	5	13

CHAMPIONSHIP LEGEND – See RAZE

CHAMPS *US, male instrumental group (10 WEEKS)*

		pos	wks
4 Apr 58 ●	TEQUILA *London HLU 8580* ▲	5	9
17 Mar 60	TOO MUCH TEQUILA *London HLH 9052*	49	1

CHAMPS BOYS *France, male instrumental group (6 WEEKS)*

		pos	wks
19 Jun 76	TUBULAR BELLS *Philips 6006 519*	41	6

CHANCE – See SUNKIDS featuring CHANCE

Gene CHANDLER *US, male vocalist (29 WEEKS)*

		pos	wks
5 Jun 68	NOTHING CAN STOP ME *Soul City SC 102*	41	4
3 Feb 79	GET DOWN *20th Century BTC 1040*	11	11
1 Sep 79	WHEN YOU'RE NUMBER 1 *20th Century TC 2411*	43	5
28 Jun 80	DOES SHE HAVE A FRIEND *20th Century TC 2451*	28	9

CHANELLE *US, female vocalist (9 WEEKS)*

		pos	wks
11 Mar 89	ONE MAN *Cooltempo COOL 183*	16	8
10 Dec 94	ONE MAN (re-mix) *Deep Distraxion OILYCD 031*	50	1

CHANGE *US, male / female vocal / instrumental group (43 WEEKS)* pos/wks

		pos	wks
28 Jun 80	A LOVER'S HOLIDAY / GLOW OF LOVE *WEA K 79141*	14	8
6 Sep 80	SEARCHING *WEA K 79156*	11	10
2 Jun 84	CHANGE OF HEART *WEA YZ 7*	17	10
11 Aug 84	YOU ARE MY MELODY *WEA YZ 14*	48	4
16 Mar 85	LET'S GO TOGETHER *Cooltempo COOL 107*	37	7
25 May 85	OH WHAT A FEELING *Cooltempo COOL 109*	56	2
13 Jul 85	MUTUAL ATTRACTION *Cooltempo COOL 111*	60	2

See also Luther VANDROSS

CHANGING FACES *US, female vocal duo - Cassandra Lucas and Charisse Rose (12 WEEKS)*

		pos	wks
24 Sep 94	STROKE YOU UP *Big Beat A 8251CD*	43	3
26 Jul 97 ●	G.H.E.T.T.O.U.T. *Atlantic AT 0003CD*	10	5
1 Nov 97	I GOT SOMEBODY ELSE *Atlantic AT 0014CD*	42	1
4 Apr 98	TIME AFTER TIME *Atlantic AT 0027CD*	35	2
1 Aug 98	SAME TEMPO *A&M 5826952*	53	1

Bruce CHANNEL *US, male vocalist (28 WEEKS)*

		pos	wks
22 Mar 62 ●	HEY! BABY *Mercury AMT 1171* ▲	2	12
26 Jun 68	KEEP ON *Bell 1010*	12	16

CHANNEL X
Belgium, male / female vocal / instrumental group (1 WEEK)

		pos	wks
14 Dec 91	GROOVE TO MOVE *PWL Continental PWL 209*	67	1

CHANSON *US, male / female vocal group (7 WEEKS)*

		pos	wks
13 Jan 79	DON'T HOLD BACK *Ariola ARO 140*	33	7

CHANTAL – See MOONMAN

CHANTAYS *US, male instrumental group (14 WEEKS)*

		pos	wks
18 Apr 63	PIPELINE *London HLD 9696*	16	14

CHANTER SISTERS *UK, female vocal group (5 WEEKS)*

		pos	wks
17 Jul 76	SIDE SHOW *Polydor 2058 735*	43	5

CHAOS *UK, male vocal group (2 WEEKS)*

		pos	wks
3 Oct 92	FAREWELL MY SUMMER LOVE *Arista 74321116397*	55	2

Harry CHAPIN *US, male vocalist (5 WEEKS)*

		pos	wks
11 May 74	W.O.L.D. *Elektra K 12133*	34	5

Simone CHAPMAN – See ILLEGAL MOTION featuring Simone CHAPMAN

Tracy CHAPMAN *US, female vocalist (15 WEEKS)*

		pos	wks
11 Jun 88 ●	FAST CAR *Elektra EKR 73*	5	12
30 Sep 89	CROSSROADS *Elektra EKR 95*	61	3

CHAPTERHOUSE *UK, male vocal / instrumental group (3 WEEKS)* pos/wks

		pos	wks
30 Mar 91	PEARL *Dedicated STONE 003*	67	1
12 Oct 91	MESMERISE *Dedicated HOUSE 001*	60	2

CHAQUITO
UK, male arranger / conductor - Johnny Gregory (1 WEEK)

		pos	wks
27 Oct 60	NEVER ON SUNDAY *Fontana H 265*	50	1

CHARLATANS (472 Top 500) *North country boys from Northwich who came to prominence as part of the 'Madchester' scene, Tim Burgess (v) b. 30 May 1968, Manchester, UK, and Rob Collins (k) b. 23 Feb 1963, d. 23 Jul 1996. Act has six Top 10 albums including three No.1s (72 WEEKS)* pos/wks

		pos	wks
2 Jun 90 ●	THE ONLY ONE I KNOW *Situation Two SIT 70T*	9	9
22 Sep 90	THEN *Situation Two SIT 74T*	12	5
9 Mar 91	OVER RISING *Situation Two SIT 76*	15	5
17 Aug 91	INDIAN ROPE *Dead Dead Good GOOD 1T*	57	1
9 Nov 91	ME. IN TIME *Situation Two SIT 84*	28	3
7 Mar 92	WEIRDO *Situation Two SIT 88*	19	4
18 Jul 92	TREMELO SONG (EP) *Situation Two SIT 97T*	44	2
5 Feb 94	CAN'T GET OUT OF BED *Beggars Banquet BBQ 27CD*	24	3
19 Mar 94	I NEVER WANT AN EASY LIFE IF ME AND HE WERE EVER TO GET THERE *Beggars Banquet BBQ 31CD*	38	1
2 Jul 94	JESUS HAIRDO *Beggars Banquet BBQ 32CD1*	48	2
7 Jan 95	CRASHIN' IN *Beggars Banquet BBQ 44CD*	31	2
27 May 95	JUST LOOKIN' / BULLET COMES *Beggars Banquet BBQ 55CD*	32	3
26 Aug 95	JUST WHEN YOU'RE THINKIN' THINGS OVER *Beggars Banquet BBQ 60CD*	12	3

7 Sep 96 ●	**ONE TO ANOTHER** *Beggars Banquet BBQ 301CD*	3 6
5 Apr 97 ●	**NORTH COUNTRY BOY** *Beggars Banquet BBQ 309CD*	4 5
21 Jun 97 ●	**HOW HIGH** *Beggars Banquet BBQ 312CD*	6 5
21 Jun 97	**NORTH COUNTRY BOY (re-entry)** *Beggars Banquet BBQ 309CD*	74 1
1 Nov 97	**TELLIN' STORIES** *Beggars Banquet BBQ 318CD*	16 3
16 Oct 99	**FOREVER** *Universal MCSTD 40220*	12 3
18 Dec 99	**MY BEAUTIFUL FRIEND** *Universal MCSTD 40225*	31 3
27 May 00	**IMPOSSIBLE** *Universal MCSTD 40231*	15 3

Tracks on Tremelo Song (EP): Tremelo Song / Happen to Die / Normality Swing

CHARLENE *US, female vocalist - Charlene Duncan (12 WEEKS)* pos/wks

15 May 82 ★	**I'VE NEVER BEEN TO ME** *Motown TMG 1260*	1 12

Don CHARLES *UK, male vocalist (5 WEEKS)* pos/wks

22 Feb 62	**WALK WITH ME MY ANGEL** *Decca F 11424*	39 5

Ray CHARLES (198 Top 500) *Rock era's first 'genius', b. Ray Charles Robinson, 23 Sep 1930, Georgia. This blind singer / songwriter / pianist and band leader had a US chart career spanning six decades. In 1994 he received a prestigious National Medal of Arts from US President Clinton (130 WEEKS)* pos/wks

1 Dec 60	**GEORGIA ON MY MIND** *HMV POP 792* ▲	47 1
15 Dec 60	**GEORGIA ON MY MIND (re-entry)** *HMV POP 792*	24 7
19 Oct 61	**HIT THE ROAD JACK** *HMV POP 935* ▲	6 12
14 Jun 62 ★	**I CAN'T STOP LOVING YOU** *HMV POP 1034* ▲	1 17
13 Sep 62 ●	**YOU DON'T KNOW ME** *HMV POP 1064*	9 13
13 Dec 62	**YOUR CHEATING HEART** *HMV POP 1099*	13 8
28 Mar 63	**DON'T SET ME FREE** *HMV POP 1133*	37 3
16 May 63 ●	**TAKE THESE CHAINS FROM MY HEART** *HMV POP 1161*	5 20
12 Sep 63	**NO ONE** *HMV POP 1202*	35 7
31 Oct 63	**BUSTED** *HMV POP 1221*	21 10
24 Sep 64	**NO ONE TO CRY TO** *HMV POP 1333*	38 3
21 Jan 65	**MAKIN' WHOOPEE** *HMV POP 1383*	42 4
10 Feb 66	**CRYIN' TIME** *HMV POP 1502*	50 1
21 Apr 66	**TOGETHER AGAIN** *HMV POP 1519*	48 1
5 Jul 67	**HERE WE GO AGAIN** *HMV POP 1595*	38 1
19 Jul 67	**HERE WE GO AGAIN (re-entry)** *HMV POP 1595*	45 2
20 Dec 67	**YESTERDAY** *Stateside SS 2071*	44 4
31 Jul 68	**ELEANOR RIGBY** *Stateside SS 2120*	36 9
13 Jan 90	**I'LL BE GOOD TO YOU** *Qwest W 2697* [1]	21 7

[1] Quincy Jones featuring Ray Charles and Chaka Khan

See also INXS

Suzette CHARLES *US, female vocalist (2 WEEKS)* pos/wks

21 Aug 93	**FREE TO LOVE AGAIN** *RCA 74321158372*	58 2

Tina CHARLES *UK, female vocalist (63 WEEKS)* pos/wks

7 Feb 76 ★	**I LOVE TO LOVE (BUT MY BABY LOVES TO DANCE)** *CBS 3937*	1 12
1 May 76	**LOVE ME LIKE A LOVER** *CBS 4237*	31 7
21 Aug 76 ●	**DANCE LITTLE LADY DANCE** *CBS 4480*	6 13
4 Dec 76 ●	**DR LOVE** *CBS 4779*	4 10
14 May 77	**RENDEZVOUS** *CBS 5174*	27 6
29 Oct 77	**LOVE BUG - SWEETS FOR MY SWEET (MEDLEY)** *CBS 5680*	26 4
11 Mar 78	**I'LL GO WHERE YOUR MUSIC TAKES ME** *CBS 6062*	27 8
30 Aug 86	**I LOVE TO LOVE (re-mix)** *DMC DECK 1*	67 3

CHARLES and EDDIE *US, male vocal duo - Charles Pettigrew and Eddie Chacon (30 WEEKS)* pos/wks

31 Oct 92 ★	**WOULD I LIE TO YOU** *Capitol CL 673*	1 17
20 Feb 93	**N.Y.C. (CAN YOU BELIEVE THIS CITY)** *Capitol CDCL 681*	33 5
22 May 93	**HOUSE IS NOT A HOME** *Capitol CDCLS 688*	29 4
13 May 95	**24-7-365** *Capitol CDCLS 747*	38 4

Dick CHARLESWORTH and his CITY GENTS *UK, male jazz band group, Dick Charlesworth - clarinet (1 WEEK)* pos/wks

4 May 61	**BILLY BOY** *Top Rank JAR 558*	43 1

CHARLOTTE *UK, female vocalist (4 WEEKS)* pos/wks

12 Mar 94	**QUEEN OF HEARTS** *Big Life BLRD 106*	54 1
2 May 98	**BE MINE** *Parlophone Rhythm CDRHYTHM 10*	59 1
29 May 99	**SKIN** *Parlophone Rhythm Series CDRHYTHM 20*	56 1
4 Sep 99	**SOMEDAY** *Parlophone Rhythm Series CDRHYTHM 23*	74 1

CHARME *US, male / female vocal group (2 WEEKS)* pos/wks

17 Nov 84	**GEORGY PORGY** *RCA 464*	68 2

CHARO and the SALSOUL ORCHESTRA *US, female vocalist and orchestra (4 WEEKS)* pos/wks

29 Apr 78	**DANCE A LITTLE BIT CLOSER** *Salsoul SSOL 101*	44 4

CHARVONI – See BROTHERS IN RHYTHM

CHAS and DAVE *UK, male vocal / instrumental duo - Chas Hodges and Dave Peacock (66 WEEKS)* pos/wks

11 Nov 78	**STRUMMIN'** *EMI 2874* [1]	52 3
26 May 79	**GERTCHA** *EMI 2947*	20 8
1 Sep 79	**THE SIDEBOARD SONG (GOT MY BEER IN THE SIDEBOARD HERE)** *EMI 2986*	55 3
29 Nov 80 ●	**RABBIT** *Rockney 9*	8 11
12 Dec 81	**STARS OVER 45** *Rockney KOR 12*	21 8
13 Mar 82 ●	**AIN'T NO PLEASING YOU** *Rockney KOR 14*	2 11
17 Jul 82	**MARGATE** *Rockney KOR 15*	46 4
19 Mar 83	**LONDON GIRLS** *Rockney KOR 17*	63 3
3 Dec 83	**MY MELANCHOLY BABY** *Rockney KOR 21*	51 6
3 May 86 ●	**SNOOKER LOOPY** *Rockney POT 147* [2]	6 9

[1] Chas and Dave with Rockney [2] Matchroom Mob with Chas and Dave

See also TOTTENHAM HOTSPUR FA CUP FINAL SQUAD

Tara CHASE – See Sonny JONES featuring Tara CHASE

CHEAP TRICK *US, male vocal / instrumental group (14 WEEKS)* pos/wks

5 May 79	**I WANT YOU TO WANT ME** *Epic EPC 7258*	29 9
2 Feb 80	**WAY OF THE WORLD** *Epic EPC 8114*	73 2
31 Jul 82	**IF YOU WANT MY LOVE** *Epic EPC A 2406*	57 3

Oliver CHEATHAM *US, male vocalist (5 WEEKS)* pos/wks

2 Jul 83	**GET DOWN SATURDAY NIGHT** *MCA 828*	38 5

CHECK 1-2 – See Craig McLACHLAN

Chubby CHECKER (250 Top 500) *The 'King of the Twist', b. Ernest Evans, 3 Oct 1941, South Carolina, US. This rotund vocalist helped to make the Twist the most popular dance of the rock era. 'The Twist' was the only single to top the US chart on two separate occasions (112 WEEKS)* pos/wks

22 Sep 60	**THE TWIST** *Columbia DB 4503* ▲	49 1
6 Oct 60	**THE TWIST (re-entry)** *Columbia DB 4503*	44 1
30 Mar 61	**PONY TIME** *Columbia DB 4591* ▲	27 6
17 Aug 61	**LET'S TWIST AGAIN** *Columbia DB 4691*	37 3
28 Dec 61 ●	**LET'S TWIST AGAIN (re-entry)** *Columbia DB 4691*	2 27
11 Jan 62	**THE TWIST (2nd re-entry)** *Columbia DB 4503* ▲	14 10
5 Apr 62	**SLOW TWISTIN'** *Columbia DB 4808*	23 8
19 Apr 62	**TEACH ME TO TWIST** *Columbia DB 4802* [1]	45 1
9 Aug 62	**DANCIN' PARTY** *Columbia DB 4876*	19 13
23 Aug 62	**LET'S TWIST AGAIN (2nd re-entry)** *Columbia DB 4691*	46 1
13 Sep 62	**LET'S TWIST AGAIN (3rd re-entry)** *Columbia DB 4691*	49 3
1 Nov 62	**LIMBO ROCK** *Cameo Parkway P 849*	32 10
20 Dec 62	**JINGLE BELL ROCK** *Cameo Parkway C 205* [1]	40 3
31 Oct 63	**WHAT DO YA SAY** *Cameo Parkway P 806*	37 4
29 Nov 75 ●	**LET'S TWIST AGAIN / THE TWIST (re-issue)** *London HLU 10512*	5 10
18 Jun 88 ●	**THE TWIST (YO, TWIST)** *Urban URB 20* [2]	2 11

[1] Chubby Checker and Bobby Rydell [2] Fat Boys and Chubby Checker

CHECKMATES – See Emile FORD and the CHECKMATES

CHECKMATES LTD.
US, male vocal / instrumental group (8 WEEKS) pos/wks

15 Nov 69	**PROUD MARY** *A & M AMS 769*		.30	8

Judy CHEEKS *US, female vocalist (15 WEEKS)* pos/wks

13 Nov 93	**SO IN LOVE (THE REAL DEAL)** *Positiva CDTIV 6*		.27	3
7 May 94	**REACH** *Positiva CDTIV 12*		.17	4
4 Mar 95	**THIS TIME / RESPECT** *Positiva CDTIV 28*		.23	2
17 Jun 95	**YOU'RE THE STORY OF MY LIFE / AS LONG AS YOU'RE GOOD TO ME** *Positiva CDTIV 34*		.30	3
13 Jan 96	**REACH (re-mix)** *Positiva CDTIV 42*		.22	3

CHEETAHS *UK, male vocal / instrumental group (6 WEEKS)* pos/wks

1 Oct 64	**MECCA** *Philips BF 1362*		.36	3
21 Jan 65	**SOLDIER BOY** *Philips BF 1383*		.39	3

CHEF *US, male cartoon vocalist - Isaac Hayes (13 WEEKS)* pos/wks

26 Dec 98 ★	**CHOCOLATE SALTY BALLS (PS I LOVE YOU)** *Columbia 6667985*		.1	13

CHELSEA FC *UK, male football team vocalists (22 WEEKS)* pos/wks

26 Feb 72 ●	**BLUE IS THE COLOUR** *Penny Farthing PEN 782*		.5	12
14 May 94	**NO ONE CAN STOP US NOW** *RCA 74321210452*		.23	3
17 May 97	**BLUE DAY** *WEA WEA 112CD* [1]		.22	5
27 May 00	**BLUE TOMORROW** *Telstar TV CFCCD 2000*		.22	2

[1] Suggs & Co featuring Chelsea Team

CHEMICAL BROTHERS *UK, male instrumental / production duo - Tom Rowlands and Ed Simons (47 WEEKS)* pos/wks

17 Jun 95	**LEAVE HOME** *Junior Boy's Own CHEMSD 1*		.17	4
9 Sep 95	**LIFE IS SWEET** *Junior Boy's Own CHEMSD 2*		.25	3
27 Jan 96	**LOOPS OF FURY (EP)** *Junior Boy's Own CHEMSD 3*		.13	2
12 Oct 96 ★	**SETTING SUN** *Junior Boy's Own CHEMSD 4* ■		.1	7
5 Apr 97 ★	**BLOCK ROCKIN' BEATS** *Virgin CHEMSD 5* ■		.1	6
28 Jun 97	**BLOCK ROCKIN' BEATS (re-entry)** *Virgin CHEMSD 5*		.69	1
20 Sep 97	**ELEKTROBANK** *Virgin CHEMSD 6*		.17	4
12 Jun 99 ●	**HEY BOY HEY GIRL** *Virgin CHEMSD 8*		.3	10
14 Aug 99 ●	**LET FOREVER BE** *Virgin CHEMSD 9*		.9	7
23 Oct 99	**OUT OF CONTROL** *Virgin CHEMSD 10*		.21	4

Tracks on Loops of Fury (EP): Loops of Fury / (The Best Part of) Breaking Up / Get Upon It Like This / Chemical Beats. Uncredited vocal on 'Setting Sun' by Noel Gallagher

CHEQUERS *UK, male vocal / instrumental group (10 WEEKS)* pos/wks

18 Oct 75	**ROCK ON BROTHER** *Creole CR 111*		.21	5
28 Feb 76	**HEY MISS PAYNE** *Creole CR 116*		.32	5

CHER `69` `Top 500` *Perennially popular vocalist, b. Cherilyn LaPierre, 20 May 1946, California. She was half of the most successful husband/wife duo ever, Sonny and Cher, and had an equally stunning run of solo smashes. At the age of 52 she is the oldest female solo singer to top the chart (219 WEEKS)* pos/wks

19 Aug 65 ●	**ALL I REALLY WANT TO DO** *Liberty LIB 66114*		.9	10
31 Mar 66 ●	**BANG BANG (MY BABY SHOT ME DOWN)** *Liberty LIB 66160*		.3	12
4 Aug 66	**I FEEL SOMETHING IN THE AIR** *Liberty LIB 12034*		.43	2
22 Sep 66	**SUNNY** *Liberty LIB 12083*		.32	5
6 Nov 71 ●	**GYPSYS TRAMPS AND THIEVES** *MCA MU 1142* ▲		.4	13
16 Feb 74	**DARK LADY** *MCA 101* ▲		.36	3
16 Mar 74	**DARK LADY (re-entry)** *MCA 101*		.45	1
19 Dec 87 ●	**I FOUND SOMEONE** *Geffen GEF 31*		.5	10
2 Apr 88	**WE ALL SLEEP ALONE** *Geffen GEF 35*		.47	5
2 Sep 89 ●	**IF I COULD TURN BACK TIME** *Geffen GEF 59*		.6	14
13 Jan 90	**JUST LIKE JESSE JAMES** *Geffen GEF 69*		.11	11
7 Apr 90	**HEART OF STONE** *Geffen GEF 75*		.43	5
11 Aug 90	**YOU WOULDN'T KNOW LOVE** *Geffen GEF 77*		.55	3
13 Apr 91 ★	**THE SHOOP SHOOP SONG (IT'S IN HIS KISS)** *Epic 6566737*		.1	15
13 Jul 91 ●	**LOVE AND UNDERSTANDING** *Geffen GFS 5*		.10	8
12 Oct 91	**SAVE UP ALL YOUR TEARS** *Geffen GFS 11*		.37	5
7 Dec 91	**LOVE HURTS** *Geffen GFS 16*		.43	5
18 Apr 92	**COULD'VE BEEN YOU** *Geffen GFS 19*		.31	4
14 Nov 92	**OH NO NOT MY BABY** *Geffen GFS 29*		.33	4
16 Jan 93	**MANY RIVERS TO CROSS** *Geffen GFSTD 31*		.37	3
6 Mar 93	**WHENEVER YOU'RE NEAR** *Geffen GFSTD 32*		.72	1
15 Jan 94	**I GOT YOU BABE** *Geffen GFSTD 64* [1]		.35	3
18 Mar 95 ★	**LOVE CAN BUILD A BRIDGE** *London COCD 1* [2]		.1	8
28 Oct 95	**WALKING IN MEMPHIS** *WEA WEA 021CD1*		.11	7
20 Jan 96 ●	**ONE BY ONE** *WEA WEA 032CD*		.7	9
27 Apr 96	**NOT ENOUGH LOVE IN THE WORLD** *WEA WEA 052CD*		.31	2
17 Aug 96	**THE SUN AIN'T GONNA SHINE ANYMORE** *WEA WEA 071CD*		.26	3
31 Oct 98 ★	**BELIEVE** *WEA WEA 175CD* ◆ ■ ▲		.1	26
6 Mar 99 ●	**STRONG ENOUGH** *WEA WEA 201CD1*		.5	10
8 May 99	**BELIEVE (re-entry)** *WEA WEA 175CD*		.59	2
19 Jun 99	**ALL OR NOTHING** *WEA WEA 212CD1*		.12	7
6 Nov 99	**DOVE L'AMORE** *WEA WEA 230CD1*		.21	3

[1] Cher with Beavis and Butt-Head [2] Cher, Chrissie Hynde and Neneh Cherry with Eric Clapton

See also SONNY and CHER; MEAT LOAF

CHERI *Canada, female vocal duo (9 WEEKS)* pos/wks

19 Jun 82	**MURPHY'S LAW** *Polydor POSP 459*		.13	9

CHEROKEES *UK, male vocal / instrumental group (5 WEEKS)* pos/wks

3 Sep 64	**SEVEN DAFFODILS** *Columbia DB 7341*		.33	5

CHERRELLE *US, female vocalist - Cheryl Norton (26 WEEKS)* pos/wks

28 Dec 85 ●	**SATURDAY LOVE** *Tabu A 6829* [1]		.6	11
1 Mar 86	**WILL YOU SATISFY?** *Tabu A 6927*		.57	3
6 Feb 88	**NEVER KNEW LOVE LIKE THIS** *Tabu 6513827* [2]		.26	7
6 May 89	**AFFAIR** *Tabu 654673 7*		.67	2
24 Mar 90	**SATURDAY LOVE (re-mix)** *Tabu 6558007* [1]		.55	2
2 Aug 97	**BABY COME TO ME** *One World OWECD 1* [2]		.56	1

[1] Cherrelle with Alexander O'Neal [2] Alexander O'Neal featuring Cherrelle

Don CHERRY *US, male vocalist (11 WEEKS)* pos/wks

10 Feb 56 ●	**BAND OF GOLD** *Philips PB 549*		.6	11

Eagle-Eye CHERRY *Sweden, male vocalist (28 WEEKS)* pos/wks

4 Jul 98 ●	**SAVE TONIGHT** *Polydor 5695952*		.6	13
14 Nov 98 ●	**FALLING IN LOVE AGAIN** *Polydor 5630252*		.8	8
20 Mar 99	**PERMANENT TEARS** *Polydor 5636752*		.43	1
29 Apr 00	**ARE YOU STILL HAVING FUN** *Polydor 5618032*		.21	4
11 Nov 00	**LONG WAY AROUND** *Polydor 5677812* [1]		.48	2

[1] Eagle-Eye Cherry featuring Neneh Cherry

Neneh CHERRY `300` `Top 500` *Sassy strident rapper-singer, b.10 Mar 1964, Stockholm, Sweden, raised in New York and relocated to UK early 1980s. Stepdaughter of jazz trumpeter Don Cherry and sister of Eagle-Eye Cherry. Winner of 1990 Best New Female award in Rolling Stone and at the Brits (98 WEEKS)* pos/wks

10 Dec 88 ●	**BUFFALO STANCE** *Circa YR 21*		.3	13
20 May 89 ●	**MANCHILD** *Circa YR 30*		.5	10
12 Aug 89	**KISSES ON THE WIND** *Circa YR 33*		.20	6
23 Dec 89	**INNA CITY MAMMA** *Circa YR 42*		.31	7
29 Sep 90	**I'VE GOT YOU UNDER MY SKIN** *Circa YR 53*		.25	5
3 Oct 92	**MONEY LOVE** *Circa YR 83*		.23	4
16 Jan 93	**BUDDY X** *Circa YRCD 98*		.35	3
25 Jun 94 ●	**7 SECONDS** *Columbia 6605082* [1]		.3	21
24 Dec 94	**7 SECONDS (re-entry)** *Columbia 6605082* [1]		.54	4
18 Mar 95 ★	**LOVE CAN BUILD A BRIDGE** *London COCD 1* [2]		.1	8
3 Aug 96 ●	**WOMAN** *Hut HUTCD 70*		.9	7
14 Dec 96	**KOOTCHI** *Hut HUTDG 75*		.38	2
22 Feb 97	**FEEL IT** *Hut HUTCD 79*		.68	1
6 Nov 99	**BUDDY X 99** *4 Liberty LIBTCD 33* [3]		.15	5
11 Nov 00	**LONG WAY AROUND** *Polydor 5677812* [4]		.48	2

[1] Youssou N'Dour (featuring Neneh Cherry) [2] Cher, Chrissie Hynde and Neneh Cherry with Eric Clapton [3] Dreem Teem vs Neneh Cherry [4] Eagle-Eye Cherry featuring Neneh Cherry

CHI-LITES (349) Top 500 *Supreme soft-soul vocal quartet from Chicago, fronted by Eugene Record, b.23 Dec 1940, Illinois, US, who originally formed group with Marshall Thompson as the Hi-Lites. Record also produced and wrote the vast majority of their many transatlantic hits. (89 WEEKS)*

		pos/wks
28 Aug 71	(FOR GOD'S SAKE) GIVE MORE POWER TO THE PEOPLE	
	MCA MU 1138..	**32** 6
15 Jan 72 ●	HAVE YOU SEEN HER *MCA MU 1146*................	**3** 12
27 May 72 ●	OH GIRL *MCA MU 1156* ▲	**14** 9
23 Mar 74 ●	HOMELY GIRL *Brunswick BR 9*	**13** 13
20 Jul 74	I FOUND SUNSHINE *Brunswick BR 12*..............	**35** 5
2 Nov 74 ●	TOO GOOD TO BE FORGOTTEN *Brunswick BR 13*	**10** 11
21 Jun 75 ●	HAVE YOU SEEN HER / OH GIRL (re-issue) *Brunswick BR 20* 5	9
13 Sep 75 ●	IT'S TIME FOR LOVE *Brunswick BR 25*..............	**5** 10
31 Jul 76 ●	YOU DON'T HAVE TO GO *Brunswick BR 34*	**3** 11
13 Aug 83	CHANGING FOR YOU *R & B RBS 215*..................	**61** 3

CHIC (344) Top 500 *Acclaimed groundbreaking funk-disco collective, formed 1976, New York City by Nile Rodgers (g), b. 19 Sep 1952 and Bernard Edwards (b), b. 31 Oct 1952; d. 18 Apr 1996, who became one of the top songwriter / production teams of the '80s. 'Good Times' was sampled on first rap hit, 'Rapper's Delight', by Sugarhill Gang (90 WEEKS)*

		pos/wks
26 Nov 77 ●	DANCE DANCE DANCE (YOWSAH YOWSAH YOWSAH)	
	Atlantic K 11038..	**6** 12
1 Apr 78 ●	EVERYBODY DANCE *Atlantic K 11097*	**9** 11
18 Nov 78 ●	LE FREAK *Atlantic K 11209* ▲	**7** 16
24 Feb 79 ●	I WANT YOUR LOVE *Atlantic LV 16*	**4** 11
30 Jun 79 ●	GOOD TIMES *Atlantic K 11310* ▲	**5** 11
13 Oct 79	MY FORBIDDEN LOVER *Atlantic K 11385*	**15** 8
8 Dec 79	MY FEET KEEP DANCING *Atlantic K 11415*.......	**21** 9
12 Mar 83	HANGIN' *Atlantic A 9898*...................................	**64** 1
19 Sep 87	JACK LE FREAK *Atlantic A 9198*	**19** 6
14 Jul 90	MEGACHIC - CHIC MEDLEY *East West A 7949*	**58** 2
15 Feb 92	CHIC MYSTIQUE *Warner Bros. W 0083*	**48** 3

CHICAGO (401) Top 500 *Pioneering jazz-rock group included Peter Cetera (v / b) b. 13 Sep 1944. Group relocated from city of the same name to California, US, in 1967. Released longest numerical sequence of album titles (majority going platinum in the US) - the most recent being Chicago 26 (1999) (81 WEEKS)*

		pos/wks
10 Jan 70 ●	I'M A MAN *CBS 4715* [1]	**8** 11
18 Jul 70	25 OR 6 TO 4 *CBS 5076*	**7** 13
9 Oct 76 ★	IF YOU LEAVE ME NOW *CBS 4603* ▲	**1** 16
5 Nov 77	BABY WHAT A BIG SURPRISE *CBS 5672*	**41** 3
21 Aug 82 ●	HARD TO SAY I'M SORRY *Full Moon K 79301* ▲	**4** 15
27 Oct 84 ●	HARD HABIT TO BREAK *Full Moon W 9214*	**8** 13
26 Jan 85	YOU'RE THE INSPIRATION *Warner Bros. W 9126*	**14** 10

[1] Chicago Transit Authority

See also Peter CETERA

CHICANE *UK, male producer - Nick Bracegirdle (48 WEEKS)*

		pos/wks
21 Dec 96	OFFSHORE *Xtravaganza 0091005*	**14** 7
14 Jun 97	SUNSTROKE *Xtravaganza 0091125*...................	**21** 3
13 Sep 97	OFFSHORE '97 (re-mix) *Xtravaganza 0091255 EXT* [1]	**17** 4
20 Dec 97	LOST YOU SOMEWHERE *Xtravaganza 0091415*..........	**35** 3
10 Oct 98	STRONG IN LOVE *Xtravaganza 0091675EXT* [2]	**32** 2
5 Jun 99 ●	SALTWATER *Xtravaganza XTRAV 1CDS* [3]........	**6** 10
18 Mar 00 ★	DON'T GIVE UP *Xtravaganza XTRAV 9CDS* [4] ■	**1** 14
22 Jul 00	NO ORDINARY MORNING / HALCYON	
	Xtravaganza XTRAV 12CDS	**28** 3
28 Oct 00	AUTUMN TACTICS *Xtravaganza XTRAV 17CDS*	**44** 2

[1] Chicane with Power Circle [2] Chicane featuring Mason [3] Chicane featuring Maire Brennan of Clannad [4] Chicane featuring Bryan Adams

Chicane are Disco Citizens under another name

CHICKEN SHACK
UK, male / female vocal / instrumental group (19 WEEKS)

		pos/wks
7 May 69	I'D RATHER GO BLIND *Blue Horizon 57-3153*	**14** 13
6 Sep 69	TEARS IN THE WIND *Blue Horizon 57-3160*..............	**29** 6

CHICKEN SHED THEATRE
UK, youth theatre company (6 WEEKS)

		pos/wks
27 Dec 97	I AM IN LOVE WITH THE WORLD *Columbia 6654172*	**15** 6

CHICORY TIP *UK, male vocal / instrumental group (34 WEEKS)*

		pos/wks
29 Jan 72 ★	SON OF MY FATHER *CBS 7737*...........................	**1** 13
20 May 72	WHAT'S YOUR NAME *CBS 8021*.........................	**13** 8
31 Mar 73	GOOD GRIEF CHRISTINA *CBS 1258*	**17** 13

CHIEFTAINS *Ireland, male vocal / instrumental group (4 WEEKS)*

		pos/wks
18 Mar 95	HAVE I TOLD YOU LATELY THAT I LOVE YOU	
	RCA 74321271702 [1]	**71** 1
12 Jun 99	I KNOW MY LOVE *RCA Victor 74321670622* [2]	**37** 3

[1] Chieftains with Van Morrison [2] Chieftains featuring The Corrs

CHIFFONS *US, female vocal group (40 WEEKS)*

		pos/wks
11 Apr 63	HE'S SO FINE *Stateside SS 172* ▲	**16** 12
18 Jul 63	ONE FINE DAY *Stateside SS 202*	**29** 6
26 May 66	SWEET TALKIN' GUY *Stateside SS 512*	**31** 8
18 Mar 72 ●	SWEET TALKIN' GUY (re-issue) *London HL 10271*	**4** 14

CHILD *UK, male vocal / instrumental group (22 WEEKS)*

		pos/wks
29 Apr 78	WHEN YOU WALK IN THE ROOM *Ariola Hansa AHA 511* 38	5
22 Jul 78 ●	IT'S ONLY MAKE BELIEVE *Ariola Hansa AHA 522*........	**10** 12
28 Apr 79	ONLY YOU (AND YOU ALONE) *Ariola Hansa AHA 536*..........	**33** 5

Jane CHILD *Canada, female vocalist (8 WEEKS)*

		pos/wks
12 May 90	DON'T WANNA FALL IN LOVE *Warner Bros. W 9817*..........	**22** 8

CHILDLINERS
UK / Australia, male / female vocal group (6 WEEKS)

		pos/wks
16 Dec 95 ●	THE GIFT OF CHRISTMAS *London LONCD 376*	**9** 6

CHILDREN FOR RWANDA *UK, male / female choir (2 WEEKS)*

		pos/wks
10 Sep 94	LOVE CAN BUILD A BRIDGE *East West YZ 849CD*........	**57** 2

CHILDREN OF THE NIGHT
UK, male vocalist / producer (2 WEEKS)

		pos/wks
26 Nov 88	IT'S A TRIP (TUNE IN, TURN ON, DROP OUT) *Jive JIVE 189*	**52** 2

CHILDREN OF THE REVOLUTION – See KLF

Toni CHILDS *US, female vocalist (4 WEEKS)*

		pos/wks
25 Mar 89	DON'T WALK AWAY *A & M AM 462*	**53** 4

CHILI HI FLY *Australia, male DJ / production duo (2 WEEKS)*

		pos/wks
18 Mar 00	IS IT LOVE? *Ministry Of Sound MOSCDS 141*	**37** 2

CHILL FAC-TORR
US, male vocal / instrumental group (8 WEEKS)

		pos/wks
2 Apr 83	TWIST (ROUND 'N' ROUND) *Phillyworld PWS 109*	**37** 8

CHILLI featuring CARRAPICHO *US / Ghana / Brazil, male / female vocal / instrumental group (1 WEEK)*

		pos/wks
20 Sep 97	TIC, TIC TAC *Arista 74321511332*	**59** 1

CHIMES *UK, male / female vocal / instrumental group (28 WEEKS)*

		pos/wks
19 Aug 89	1-2-3 *CBS 655166 7*...	**60** 3
2 Dec 89	HEAVEN *CBS 655432 7*	**66** 2
6 Jan 90	HEAVEN (re-entry) *CBS 655432 7*	**69** 3
19 May 90 ●	I STILL HAVEN'T FOUND WHAT I'M LOOKING FOR	
	CBS CHIM 1	**6** 9
28 Jul 90	TRUE LOVE *CBS CHIM 2*	**48** 3
29 Sep 90	HEAVEN (re-issue) *CBS CHIM 3*	**24** 6
1 Dec 90	LOVE COMES TO MIND *CBS CHIM 4*	**49** 2

UK No.1 ★ UK Top 10 ● Still on chart + UK million seller ◆ UK entry at No.1 ■ US No.1 ▲

CHIMIRA South Africa, female vocalist (1 WEEK)
pos/wks

6 Dec 97	SHOW ME HEAVEN *Neoteric NRDCD 11*	70	1

CHINA BLACK UK, male vocal / instrumental duo - Errol Reid and Simon Fung (35 WEEKS)
pos/wks

16 Jul 94 ●	SEARCHING *Wild Card CARDD 7*	4	16
29 Oct 94	STARS *Wild Card CARDD 9*	19	7
17 Dec 94	SEARCHING (re-entry) *Wild Card CARDD 7*	54	4
11 Feb 95	ALMOST SEE YOU (SOMEWHERE) *Wild Card CARDW 15*	31	2
3 Jun 95	SWING LOW SWEET CHARIOT *PolyGram TV SWLOW 2* [1]	15	6

[1] Ladysmith Black Mambazo featuring China Black

CHINA CRISIS UK, male vocal / instrumental group (66 WEEKS)
pos/wks

7 Aug 82	AFRICAN AND WHITE *Inevitable INEV 011*	45	5
22 Jan 83	CHRISTIAN *Virgin VS 562*	12	9
21 May 83	TRAGEDY AND MYSTERY *Virgin VS 587*	46	6
15 Oct 83	WORKING WITH FIRE AND STEEL *Virgin VS 620*	48	5
14 Jan 84 ●	WISHFUL THINKING *Virgin VS 647*	9	8
10 Mar 84	HANNA HANNA *Virgin VS 665*	44	3
30 Mar 85	BLACK MAN RAY *Virgin VS 752*	14	9
1 Jun 85	KING IN A CATHOLIC STYLE (WAKE UP) *Virgin VS 765*	19	9
7 Sep 85	YOU DID CUT ME *Virgin VS 799*	54	3
8 Nov 86	ARIZONA SKY *Virgin VS 898*	47	4
24 Jan 87	BEST KEPT SECRET *Virgin VS 926*	36	5

CHINA DRUM UK, male vocal / instrumental group (4 WEEKS)
pos/wks

2 Mar 96	CAN'T STOP THESE THINGS *Mantra MNT 8CD*	65	1
20 Apr 96	LAST CHANCE *Mantra MNT 10CD*	60	1
9 Aug 97	FICTION OF LIFE *Mantra MNT 21CD*	65	1
27 Sep 97	SOMEWHERE ELSE *Mantra MNT 022CD1*	74	1

Jonny CHINGAS US, male instrumentalist (6 WEEKS)
pos/wks

19 Feb 83	PHONE HOME *CBS A 3121*	43	6

CHIPMUNKS US, chipmunk vocal trio (12 WEEKS)
pos/wks

24 Jul 59	RAGTIME COWBOY JOE *London HLU 8916* [1]	11	8
19 Dec 92	ACHY BREAKY HEART *Epic 6588837* [2]	53	3
14 Dec 96	MACARENA *Sony Wonder 6639981* [3]	65	1

[1] David Seville and the Chipmunks [2] Alvin and the Chipmunks featuring Billy Ray Cyrus [3] Los Del Chipmunks

The Chipmunk characters were created by David Seville, who died in 1972. His son resurrected the act in 1980

See also David SEVILLE

CHIPPENDALES UK / US, male vocal group (4 WEEKS)
pos/wks

31 Oct 92	GIVE ME YOUR BODY *XSrhythm XSR 3*	28	4

George CHISHOLM – See JOHNSTON BROTHERS

CHOO CHOO PROJECT
US, male / female production / instrumental vocal duo (3 WEEKS)
pos/wks

15 Jan 00	HAZIN' & PHAZIN' *Defected DEFECT 10CDS*	21	3

See also Harry 'Choo Choo' ROMERO presents INAYA DAY

CHOPS-EMC + EXTENSIVE
UK, male instrumental group and rapper (1 WEEK)
pos/wks

8 Aug 92	ME' ISRAELITES *Faze 2 FAZE 6*	60	1

CHORDETTES US, female vocal group (25 WEEKS)
pos/wks

17 Dec 54	MR SANDMAN *Columbia DB 3553* ▲	11	8
31 Aug 56 ●	BORN TO BE WITH YOU *London HLA 8302*	8	9
18 Apr 58 ●	LOLLIPOP *London HLD 8584*	6	8

CHORDS UK, male vocal / instrumental group (17 WEEKS)
pos/wks

6 Oct 79	NOW IT'S GONE *Polydor 2059 141*	63	2
2 Feb 80	MAYBE TOMORROW *Polydor POSP 101*	40	5
26 Apr 80	SOMETHING'S MISSING *Polydor POSP 146*	55	3
12 Jul 80	THE BRITISH WAY OF LIFE *Polydor 2059 258*	54	3
18 Oct 80	IN MY STREET *Polydor POSP 185*	50	4

CHRIS and JAMES
UK, male instrumental / production duo (3 WEEKS)
pos/wks

17 Sep 94	CALM DOWN (BASS KEEPS PUMPIN') *Stress 12STR 38*	74	1
4 Nov 95	FOX FORCE FIVE *Stress CDSTR 61*	71	1
7 Nov 98	CLUB FOR LIFE '98 *Stress CDSTR 85*	66	1

Neil CHRISTIAN UK, male vocalist (10 WEEKS)
pos/wks

7 Apr 66	THAT'S NICE *Strike JH 301*	14	10

Roger CHRISTIAN UK, male vocalist (3 WEEKS)
pos/wks

30 Sep 89	TAKE IT FROM ME *Island IS 427*	63	3

CHRISTIANS (383 Top 500) Soul / gospel-influenced UK pop group: vocalist brothers Russell, Roger (who went solo in 1986) and Garry Christian plus Henry Priestman (k/v). In1974, the brothers appeared on TV talent show Opportunity Knocks. Their self-titled debut album went double platinum (84 WEEKS)
pos/wks

31 Jan 87	FORGOTTEN TOWN *Island IS 291*	22	11
13 Jun 87	HOOVERVILLE (THEY PROMISED US THE WORLD) *Island IS 326*	21	10
26 Sep 87	WHEN THE FINGERS POINT *Island IS 335*	34	7
5 Dec 87	IDEAL WORLD *Island IS 347*	14	13
23 Apr 88	BORN AGAIN *Island IS 365*	25	7
15 Oct 88 ●	HARVEST FOR THE WORLD *Island IS 395*	8	7
20 May 89 ★	FERRY 'CROSS THE MERSEY *PWL PWL 41* [1] ■	1	7
23 Dec 89	WORDS *Island IS 450*	18	8
7 Apr 90	I FOUND OUT *Island IS 453*	56	2
15 Sep 90	GREENBANK DRIVE *Island IS 466*	63	2
5 Sep 92	WHAT'S IN A WORD *Island IS 536*	33	5
14 Nov 92	FATHER *Island IS 543*	55	2
6 Mar 93	THE BOTTLE *Island CID 549*	39	3

[1] Christians, Holly Johnson, Paul McCartney, Gerry Marsden and Stock Aitken Waterman

CHRISTIE UK, male vocal / instrumental group (37 WEEKS)
pos/wks

2 May 70 ★	YELLOW RIVER *CBS 4911*	1	22
10 Oct 70	SAN BERNADINO *CBS 5169*	49	1
24 Oct 70 ●	SAN BERNADINO (re-entry) *CBS 5169*	7	13
25 Mar 72	IRON HORSE *CBS 7747*	47	1

David CHRISTIE France, male vocalist (12 WEEKS)
pos/wks

14 Aug 82 ●	SADDLE UP *KR KR 9*	9	12

John CHRISTIE Australia, male vocalist (6 WEEKS)
pos/wks

25 Dec 76	HERE'S TO LOVE (AULD LANG SYNE) *EMI 2554*	24	6

Lou CHRISTIE US, male vocalist - Lugee Sacco (35 WEEKS)
pos/wks

24 Feb 66	LIGHTNIN' STRIKES *MGM 1297* ▲	11	8
28 Apr 66	RHAPSODY IN THE RAIN *MGM 1308*	37	2
13 Sep 69 ●	I'M GONNA MAKE YOU MINE *Buddah 201 057*	2	17
27 Dec 69	SHE SOLD ME MAGIC *Buddah 201 073*	25	8

Tony CHRISTIE UK, male vocalist - Tony Fitzgerald (54 WEEKS)
pos/wks

9 Jan 71	LAS VEGAS *MCA MK 5058*	21	9
8 May 71 ●	I DID WHAT I DID FOR MARIA *MCA MK 5064*	2	17
20 Nov 71	IS THIS THE WAY TO AMARILLO *MCA MKS 5073*	18	13
10 Feb 73	AVENUES AND ALLEYWAYS *MCA MKS 5101*	37	4

17 Jan 76	DRIVE SAFELY DARLIN' *MCA 219*	35	4
23 Jan 99 ●	WALK LIKE A PANTHER '98 *ffrr FCD 351* [1]	10	7

[1] The All Seeing I featuring Tony Christie

'Walk Like A Panther '98' written by the group and Jarvis Cocker. Vocals by Tony Christie who had previously recorded a different song with the same title.

Shawn CHRISTOPHER *US, female vocalist (10 WEEKS)*   pos/wks

4 May 91	ANOTHER SLEEPLESS NIGHT *Arista 114186*	50	4
21 Mar 92	DON'T LOSE THE MAGIC *Arista 115097*	30	5
2 Jul 94	MAKE MY LOVE *BTB BTBCD 502*	57	1

CHUCKS *UK, male / female vocal group (7 WEEKS)*   pos/wks

24 Jan 63	LOO-BE-LOO *Decca F 11569*	22	7

CHUMBAWAMBA
UK, male / female vocal / instrumental group (31 WEEKS)   pos/wks

18 Sep 93	ENOUGH IS ENOUGH *One Little Indian 79 TP7CD* [1]	56	2
4 Dec 93	TIMEBOMB *One Little Indian 89 TP7CD*	59	1
23 Aug 97 ●	TUBTHUMPING *EMI CDEM 486*	2	20
31 Jan 98 ●	AMNESIA *EMI CDEM 498*	10	5
13 Jun 98	TOP OF THE WORLD (OLE, OLE, OLE) *EMI CDEM 511*	21	3

[1] Chumbawamba and Credit to the Nation

Chubby CHUNKS *UK, male instrumentalist / producer (2 WEEKS)* pos/wks

4 Jun 94	TESTAMENT 4 *Cleveland City CLECD 13017* [1]	52	1
29 May 99	I'M TELLIN YOU (re-mix) *Cleveland City CLECD 13052* [2]	61	1

[1] Chubby Chunks Volume II [2] Chubby Chunks featuring Kim Ruffin

CHUPITO *Spain, male vocalist (2 WEEKS)*   pos/wks

23 Sep 95	AMERICAN PIE *Eternal WEA 018CD*	54	2

Charlotte CHURCH *UK, female vocalist (4 WEEKS)*   pos/wks

25 Dec 99	JUST WAVE HELLO *Sony Classical 6685312*	34	4

CHYNA – See INCOGNITO

CICA – See PQM featuring CICA

CICERO *UK, male vocalist (12 WEEKS)*   pos/wks

18 Jan 92	LOVE IS EVERYWHERE *Spaghetti CIAO 3*	19	8
18 Apr 92	THAT LOVING FEELING *Spaghetti CIAO 4*	46	3
1 Aug 92	HEAVEN MUST HAVE SENT YOU BACK *Spaghetti CIAO 5*	70	1

CINDERELLA *US, male vocal / instrumental group (7 WEEKS)*   pos/wks

6 Aug 88	GYPSY ROAD *Vertigo VER 40*	54	2
4 Mar 89	DON'T KNOW WHAT YOU GOT *Vertigo VER 43*	54	2
17 Nov 90	SHELTER ME *Vertigo VER 51*	55	2
27 Apr 91	HEARTBREAK STATION *Vertigo VER 53*	63	1

CINDY and the SAFFRONS *UK, female vocal group (3 WEEKS)* pos/wks

15 Jan 83	PAST, PRESENT AND FUTURE *Stiletto STL 9*	56	3

CINERAMA *UK, male / female vocal / instrumental duo (1 WEEK)* pos/wks

18 Jul 98	KERRY KERRY *Cooking Vinyl FRYCD 072*	71	1

Gigliola CINQUETTI *Italy, female vocalist (27 WEEKS)*   pos/wks

23 Apr 64	NON HO L'ETA PER AMARTI *Decca F 21882*	17	17
4 May 74 ●	GO (BEFORE YOU BREAK MY HEART) *CBS 2294*	8	10

CIRCA featuring DESTRY
UK, male production group and US, male vocalist (1 WEEK)   pos/wks

27 Nov 99	SUN SHINING DOWN *Inferno CDFERN 22*	70	1

CIRCUIT *UK, male / female vocal / instrumental group (3 WEEKS)* pos/wks

20 Jul 91	SHELTER ME *Cooltempo COOL 237*	44	2
1 Apr 95	SHELTER ME (re-issue) *Pukka CDPUKA 2*	50	1

CIRRUS *UK, male vocal group (1 WEEK)*   pos/wks

30 Sep 78	ROLLIN' ON *Jet 123*	62	1

CITY BOY *UK, male vocal / instrumental group (20 WEEKS)*   pos/wks

8 Jul 78 ●	5-7-0-5 *Vertigo 6059 207*	8	12
28 Oct 78	WHAT A NIGHT *Vertigo 6059 211*	39	5
15 Sep 79	THE DAY THE EARTH CAUGHT FIRE *Vertigo 6059 238*	67	3

CITY GENTS – See Dick CHARLESWORTH and his CITY GENTS

Gary CLAIL ON-U SOUND SYSTEM
UK, male vocal / instrumental group (19 WEEKS)   pos/wks

14 Jul 90	BEEF *RCA PB 49265* [1]	64	2
30 Mar 91 ●	HUMAN NATURE *Perfecto PB 44401*	10	9
8 Jun 91	ESCAPE *Perfecto PB 44563*	44	3
14 Nov 92	WHO PAYS THE PIPER *Perfecto 74321117017*	31	3
22 May 93	THESE THINGS ARE WORTH FIGHTING FOR *Perfecto 74321147222*	45	2

[1] Gary Clail

See also PRIMAL SCREAM

CLAIRE and FRIENDS
UK, female vocalist and young male / female friends (11 WEEKS) pos/wks

7 Jun 86	IT'S 'ORRIBLE BEING IN LOVE (WHEN YOU'RE 8 1/2) *BBC RESL 189*	13	11

CLANNAD *Ireland, male / female vocal group (29 WEEKS)*   pos/wks

6 Nov 82 ●	THEME FROM HARRY'S GAME *RCA 292*	5	10
2 Jul 83	NEW GRANGE *RCA 340*	65	1
12 May 84	ROBIN (THE HOODED MAN) *RCA HOOD 1*	42	5
25 Jan 86	IN A LIFETIME *RCA PB 40535* [1]	20	5
10 Jun 89	IN A LIFETIME (re-issue) *RCA PB 42873* [1]	17	7
10 Aug 91	BOTH SIDES NOW *MCA MCS 1546* [2]	74	1

[1] Clannad featuring Bono [2] Clannad and Paul Young

Jimmy CLANTON *US, male vocalist (1 WEEK)*   pos/wks

21 Jul 60	ANOTHER SLEEPLESS NIGHT *Top Rank JAR 382*	50	1

Eric CLAPTON (146 Top 500) *Rock guitar player, b. Eric Clapp, 30 Mar 1945, Surrey. Prior to long and lucrative solo career he recorded with hitmakers The Yardbirds, Cream, Blind Faith and Derek and the Dominoes. Multi-Grammy-winning singer-guitarist and mega-grossing live performer (150 WEEKS)*   pos/wks

20 Dec 69	COMIN' HOME *Atlantic 584 308* [1]	16	9
12 Aug 72 ●	LAYLA *Polydor 2058 130* [2]	7	11
27 Jul 74 ●	I SHOT THE SHERIFF *RSO 2090 132* ▲	9	9
10 May 75	SWING LOW SWEET CHARIOT *RSO 2090 158*	19	9
16 Aug 75	KNOCKIN' ON HEAVEN'S DOOR *RSO 2090 166*	38	4
24 Dec 77	LAY DOWN SALLY *RSO 2090 264*	39	6
21 Oct 78	PROMISES *RSO 21*	37	7
6 Mar 82 ●	LAYLA (re-issue) *RSO 87* [2]	4	10
5 Jun 82	I SHOT THE SHERIFF (re-issue) *RSO 88*	64	2
23 Apr 83	THE SHAPE YOU'RE IN *Duck W 9701*	75	1
16 Mar 85	FOREVER MAN *Warner Bros. W 9069*	51	4
4 Jan 86	EDGE OF DARKNESS *BBC RESL 178* [3]	65	3
17 Jan 87	BEHIND THE MASK *Duck W 8461*	15	11
20 Jun 87	TEARING US APART *Duck W 8299* [4]	56	3
27 Jan 90	BAD LOVE *Duck W 2644*	25	7
14 Apr 90	NO ALIBIS *Duck W 2981*	53	3
16 Nov 91	WONDERFUL TONIGHT (LIVE) *Duck W 0069*	30	7
8 Feb 92	TEARS IN HEAVEN *Reprise W 0081*	50	3
7 Mar 92 ●	TEARS IN HEAVEN (re-entry) *Reprise W 0081*	5	9
1 Aug 92	RUNAWAY TRAIN *Rocket EJS 29* [5]	31	4
29 Aug 92	IT'S PROBABLY ME *A & M AM 883* [6]	30	5

UK No.1 ★ UK Top 10 ● Still on chart + UK million seller ◆ UK entry at No.1 ■ US No.1 ▲

		pos	wks
3 Oct 92	LAYLA (ACOUSTIC) (re-recording) *Duck W 0134*	45	3
15 Oct 94	MOTHERLESS CHILD *Duck W 0271CD*	63	1
18 Mar 95 ★	LOVE CAN BUILD A BRIDGE *London COCD 1* [7]	1	8
20 Jul 96	CHANGE THE WORLD *Reprise W 0358CD*	18	5
4 Apr 98	MY FATHER'S EYES *Duck W 0443CD*	33	2
4 Jul 98	CIRCUS *Duck W 0447CD*	39	2
18 Nov 00	FOREVER MAN (HOW MANY TIMES) *ffrr FCD 386* [8]	26	2

[1] Delaney and Bonnie and Friends featuring Eric Clapton [2] Derek and the Dominoes [3] Eric Clapton featuring Michael Kamen [4] Eric Clapton and Tina Turner [5] Elton John and Eric Clapton [6] Sting with Eric Clapton [7] Cher, Chrissie Hynde and Neneh Cherry with Eric Clapton [8] Beatchuggers featuring Eric Clapton

CLARISSA – See DJ VISAGE featuring CLARISSA

Dave CLARK FIVE (111) Top 500
Beat Boom superstars from Tottenham, London: Dave Clark (d), Mike Smith (v/k), Lenny Davidson (g), Denis Payton (s), Rick Huxley (g). In the first years of the 'British Invasion', this foot-stomping quintet was second only to The Beatles in the US (174 WEEKS)

		pos	wks
3 Oct 63	DO YOU LOVE ME *Columbia DB 7112*	30	6
21 Nov 63 ★	GLAD ALL OVER *Columbia DB 7154*	1	19
20 Feb 64 ●	BITS AND PIECES *Columbia DB 7210*	2	11
28 May 64 ●	CAN'T YOU SEE THAT SHE'S MINE *Columbia DB 7291*	10	11
13 Aug 64	THINKING OF YOU BABY *Columbia DB 7335*	26	6
22 Oct 64	ANYWAY YOU WANT IT *Columbia DB 7377*	25	5
14 Jan 65	EVERYBODY KNOWS *Columbia DB 7453*	37	4
11 Mar 65	REELIN' AND ROCKIN' *Columbia DB 7503*	24	8
27 May 65	COME HOME *Columbia DB 7580*	16	8
15 Jul 65 ●	CATCH US IF YOU CAN *Columbia DB 7625*	5	11
11 Nov 65	OVER AND OVER *Columbia DB 7744* ▲	45	4
19 May 66	LOOK BEFORE YOU LEAP *Columbia DB 7909*	50	1
16 Mar 67	YOU GOT WHAT IT TAKES *Columbia DB 8152*	28	8
1 Nov 67 ●	EVERYBODY KNOWS *Columbia DB 8286*	2	14
28 Feb 68	NO ONE CAN BREAK A HEART LIKE YOU *Columbia DB 8342*	28	4
18 Sep 68 ●	RED BALLOON *Columbia DB 8465*	7	11
27 Nov 68	LIVE IN THE SKY *Columbia DB 8505*	39	6
25 Oct 69	PUT A LITTLE LUV IN YOUR HEART *Columbia DB 8624*	31	4
6 Dec 69 ●	GOOD OLD ROCK 'N' ROLL *Columbia DB 8638*	7	12
7 Mar 70 ●	EVERYBODY GET TOGETHER *Columbia DB 8660*	8	8
4 Jul 70	HERE COMES SUMMER *Columbia DB 8689*	44	3
7 Nov 70	MORE GOOD OLD ROCK 'N' ROLL *Columbia DB 8724*	34	6
1 May 93	GLAD ALL OVER (re-issue) *EMI CDEMCT 9*	37	3

'Everybody Knows' on DB 7453 and 'Everybody Knows' on DB 8286 are two different songs. The two Rock 'n' Roll titles are medleys as follows: Good Old Rock 'n' Roll / Sweet Little Sixteen / Long Tall Sally / Whole Lotta Shakin' Goin' On / Blue Suede Shoes / Lucille / Reelin' and Rockin' / Memphis Tennessee. More Good Old Rock 'n' Roll Music / Blueberry Hill / Good Golly Miss Molly / My Blue Heaven / Keep a Knockin' / Loving You / One Night / Lawdy Miss Clawdy

Dee CLARK *US, male vocalist (9 WEEKS)*

		pos	wks
2 Oct 59	JUST KEEP IT UP *London HL 8915*	26	1
11 Oct 75	RIDE A WILD HORSE *Chelsea 2005 037*	16	8

Gary CLARK *UK, male vocalist (8 WEEKS)*

		pos	wks
30 Jan 93	WE SAIL ON THE STORMY WATERS *Circa YRCDX 93*	34	4
3 Apr 93	FREEFLOATING *Circa YRCDX 94*	50	3
19 Jun 93	MAKE A FAMILY *Circa YRCDX 105*	70	1

Loni CLARK *US, female vocalist (6 WEEKS)*

		pos	wks
5 Jun 93	RUSHING *A & M 5802862*	37	2
22 Jan 94	U *A & M 5804752*	28	3
17 Dec 94	LOVE'S GOT ME ON A TRIP SO HIGH *A & M 5808872*	59	1

Petula CLARK (47) Top 500
Britain's most consistently successful female vocalist, b. 15 Nov 1931, Surrey. Before her 34-year chart span, she starred in movies and was voted Britain's Top TV Personality. First UK female to win a Grammy and be named Top Female Vocalist of the Year in the US in 1966 (247 WEEKS)

		pos	wks
11 Jun 54	THE LITTLE SHOEMAKER *Polygon P 1117*	12	1

		pos	wks
25 Jun 54 ●	THE LITTLE SHOEMAKER (re-entry) *Polygon P 1117*	7	9
18 Feb 55	MAJORCA *Polygon P 1146*	12	4
25 Mar 55	MAJORCA (re-entry) *Polygon P 1146*	18	1
25 Nov 55 ●	SUDDENLY THERE'S A VALLEY *Pye Nixa N 15013*	7	10
26 Jul 57 ●	WITH ALL MY HEART *Pye Nixa N 15096*	4	18
15 Nov 57 ●	ALONE *Pye Nixa N 15112*	8	12
28 Feb 58	BABY LOVER *Pye Nixa N 15126*	12	7
26 Jan 61 ★	SAILOR *Pye 7N 15324*	1	15
13 Apr 61	SOMETHING MISSING *Pye 7N 15337*	44	1
13 Jul 61 ●	ROMEO *Pye 7N 15361*	3	15
16 Nov 61 ●	MY FRIEND THE SEA *Pye 7N 15389*	7	13
8 Feb 62	I'M COUNTING ON YOU *Pye 7N 15407*	41	2
28 Jun 62	YA YA TWIST *Pye 7N 15448*	14	11
20 Sep 62	YA YA TWIST (re-entry) *Pye 7N 15448*	45	2
2 May 63	CASANOVA / CHARIOT *Pye 7N 15522*	39	7
12 Nov 64 ●	DOWNTOWN *Pye 7N 15722* ▲	2	15
11 Mar 65	I KNOW A PLACE *Pye 7N 15772*	17	8
12 Aug 65	YOU BETTER COME HOME *Pye 7N 15864*	44	3
14 Oct 65	ROUND EVERY CORNER *Pye 7N 15945*	43	3
4 Nov 65	YOU'RE THE ONE *Pye 7N 15991*	23	9
10 Feb 66 ●	MY LOVE *Pye 7N 17038* ▲	4	9
21 Apr 66	A SIGN OF THE TIMES *Pye 7N 17071*	49	1
30 Jun 66 ●	I COULDN'T LIVE WITHOUT YOUR LOVE *Pye 7N 17133*	6	11
2 Feb 67 ★	THIS IS MY SONG *Pye 7N 17258*	1	14
25 May 67	DON'T SLEEP IN THE SUBWAY *Pye 7N 17325*	12	11
13 Dec 67	THE OTHER MAN'S GRASS (IS ALWAYS GREENER) *Pye 7N 17416*	20	9
6 Mar 68	KISS ME GOODBYE *Pye 7N 17466*	50	1
30 Jan 71	THE SONG OF MY LIFE *Pye 7N 45026*	41	1
13 Feb 71	THE SONG OF MY LIFE (re-entry) *Pye 7N 45026*	32	11
15 Jan 72	I DON'T KNOW HOW TO LOVE HIM *Pye 7N 45112*	47	1
29 Jan 72	I DON'T KNOW HOW TO LOVE HIM (re-entry) *Pye 7N 45112*	49	1
19 Nov 88 ●	DOWNTOWN (re-mix) *PRT PYS 19*	10	11

Roland CLARK – See Armand VAN HELDEN

Dave CLARKE *UK, male producer (6 WEEKS)*

		pos	wks
30 Sep 95	RED THREE: THUNDER / STORM *Deconstruction 74321306992*	45	2
3 Feb 96	SOUTHSIDE *Bush 74321335382*	34	2
15 Jun 96	NO ONE'S DRIVING *Bush 74321380162*	37	2

John Cooper CLARKE *UK, male vocalist (3 WEEKS)*

		pos	wks
10 Mar 79	GIMMIX! PLAY LOUD *Epic EPC 7009*	39	3

Rick CLARKE *UK, male vocalist (2 WEEKS)*

		pos	wks
30 Apr 88	I'LL SEE YOU ALONG THE WAY *WA WA 1*	63	2

Sharon D CLARKE – See FPI PROJECT; SERIOUS ROPE

Julian CLARY – See JOAN COLLINS FAN CLUB

CLASH (184) Top 500
Leading lights of the UK punk rock explosion: Joe Strummer (b. John Mellor) (v/g), Mick Jones (g/v), Paul Simonon (b), Topper Headon (d). Their third LP, London Calling (first released 1979), was voted Best Album of the 1980s by Rolling Stone magazine (135 WEEKS)

		pos	wks
2 Apr 77	WHITE RIOT *CBS 5058*	38	3
8 Oct 77	COMPLETE CONTROL *CBS 5664*	28	2
4 Mar 78	CLASH CITY ROCKERS *CBS 5834*	35	4
24 Jun 78	(WHITE MAN) IN HAMMERSMITH PALAIS *CBS 6383*	32	7
2 Dec 78	TOMMY GUN *CBS 6788*	19	10
3 Mar 79	ENGLISH CIVIL WAR (JOHNNY COMES MARCHING HOME) *CBS 7082*	25	6
19 May 79	THE COST OF LIVING (EP) *CBS 7324*	22	8
15 Dec 79	LONDON CALLING *CBS 8087*	11	10
9 Aug 80	BANKROBBER *CBS 8323*	12	10
6 Dec 80	THE CALL UP *CBS 9339*	40	6
24 Jan 81	HITSVILLE UK *CBS 9480*	56	4
25 Apr 81	THE MAGNIFICENT SEVEN *CBS 1133*	34	5
28 Nov 81	THIS IS RADIO CLASH *CBS A 1797*	47	1
1 May 82	KNOW YOUR RIGHTS *CBS A 2309*	43	3

26 Jun 82	ROCK THE CASBAH *CBS A 2429*	**30**	10
25 Sep 82	SHOULD I STAY OR SHOULD I GO / STRAIGHT TO HELL		
	CBS A 2646	**17**	9
12 Oct 85	THIS IS ENGLAND *CBS A 6122*	**24**	5
12 Mar 88	I FOUGHT THE LAW *CBS CLASH 1*	**29**	5
7 May 88	LONDON CALLING (re-issue) *CBS CLASH 2*	**46**	3
21 Jul 90	RETURN TO BRIXTON *CBS 656072 7*	**57**	2
2 Mar 91	★ SHOULD I STAY OR SHOULD I GO (re-issue)		
	Columbia 6566677	**1**	9
13 Apr 91	ROCK THE CASBAH (re-issue) *Columbia 6568147*	**15**	6
8 Jun 91	LONDON CALLING (re-issue)		
	Columbia 6569467	**64**	2

Tracks on The Cost of Living (EP): I Fought the Law / Groovy Times / Gates of the West / Capital Radio. CBS CLASH 1 is a re-issue of a track from The Cost of Living (EP)

CLASS ACTION featuring Chris WILTSHIRE
US, female vocal group (3 WEEKS) pos/wks

| 7 May 83 | WEEKEND *Jive JIVE 35* | **49** | 3 |

CLASSICS IV *US, male vocal / instrumental group (1 WEEK)* pos/wks

| 28 Feb 68 | SPOOKY *Liberty LBS 15051* | **46** | 1 |

CLASSIX NOUVEAUX
UK, male vocal / instrumental group (34 WEEKS) pos/wks

28 Feb 81	GUILTY *Liberty BP 388*	**43**	7
16 May 81	TOKYO *Liberty BP 397*	**67**	3
8 Aug 81	INSIDE OUTSIDE *Liberty BP 403*	**45**	5
7 Nov 81	NEVER AGAIN (THE DAYS TIME ERASED)		
	Liberty BP 406	**44**	4
13 Mar 82	IS IT A DREAM *Liberty BP 409*	**11**	9
29 May 82	BECAUSE YOU'RE YOUNG *Liberty BP 411*	**43**	4
30 Oct 82	THE END ... OR THE BEGINNING *Liberty BP 414*	**60**	2

CLAWFINGER
Norway / Sweden, male vocal / instrumental group (1 WEEK) pos/wks

| 19 Mar 94 | WARFAIR *East West YZ 804CD1* | **54** | 1 |

Judy CLAY – See William BELL

Adam CLAYTON and Larry MULLEN
Ireland, male instrumental duo (12 WEEKS) pos/wks

| 15 Jun 96 | ● THEME FROM MISSION: IMPOSSIBLE *Mother MUMCD 75* | **7** | 12 |

See also U2

Merry CLAYTON *US, female vocalist (1 WEEK)* pos/wks

| 21 May 88 | YES *RCA PB 49563* | **70** | 1 |

CLAYTOWN TROUPE
UK, male vocal / instrumental group (3 WEEKS) pos/wks

| 16 Jun 90 | WAYS OF LOVE *Island IS 464* | **57** | 2 |
| 14 Mar 92 | WANTED IT ALL *EMI USA MT 102* | **74** | 1 |

Johnny CLEGG and SAVUKA
UK / South Africa, male vocal / instrumental group (1 WEEK) pos/wks

| 16 May 87 | SCATTERLINGS OF AFRICA *EMI EMI 5605* | **75** | 1 |

CLEOPATRA *UK, female vocal group - Cleopatra, Zainam and Yonah Higgins (31 WEEKS)* pos/wks

14 Feb 98	● CLEOPATRA'S THEME *WEA WEA 133CD*	**3**	10
16 May 98	● LIFE AIN'T EASY *WEA WEA 159CD1*	**4**	7
22 Aug 98	● I WANT YOU BACK *WEA WEA 172CD1*	**4**	7
6 Mar 99	A TOUCH OF LOVE *WEA WEA 199CD1*	**24**	4
29 Jul 00	COME AND GET ME *WEA WEA 216CD1*	**29**	3

CLICK *US, male rap group (1 WEEK)* pos/wks

| 29 Jun 96 | SCANDALOUS *Jive JIVECD 393* | **54** | 1 |

Jimmy CLIFF
Jamaica, male vocalist - James Chambers (33 WEEKS) pos/wks

25 Oct 69	● WONDERFUL WORLD BEAUTIFUL PEOPLE *Trojan TR 690*	**6**	13
14 Feb 70	VIETNAM *Trojan TR 7722*	**47**	1
28 Feb 70	VIETNAM (re-entry) *Trojan TR 7722*	**46**	2
8 Aug 70	● WILD WORLD *Island WIP 6087*	**8**	12
19 Mar 94	I CAN SEE CLEARLY NOW *Columbia 6601982*	**23**	5

Buzz CLIFFORD *US, male vocalist (13 WEEKS)* pos/wks

| 2 Mar 61 | BABY SITTIN' BOOGIE *Fontana H 297* | **17** | 13 |

Linda CLIFFORD *US, female vocalist (12 WEEKS)* pos/wks

| 10 Jun 78 | IF MY FRIENDS COULD SEE ME NOW *Curtom K 17163* | **50** | 5 |
| 5 May 79 | BRIDGE OVER TROUBLED WATER *RSO 30* | **28** | 7 |

CLIMAX BLUES BAND
UK, male vocal / instrumental group (9 WEEKS) pos/wks

| 9 Oct 76 | ● COULDN'T GET IT RIGHT *BTM SBT 105* | **10** | 9 |

CLIMIE FISHER *UK, male vocal / instrumental duo - Simon Climie and Rob Fisher (44 WEEKS)* pos/wks

5 Sep 87	LOVE CHANGES (EVERYTHING) *EMI EM 15*	**67**	2
12 Dec 87	● RISE TO THE OCCASION *EMI EM 33*	**10**	11
12 Mar 88	● LOVE CHANGES (EVERYTHING) (re-mix) *EMI EM 47*	**2**	12
21 May 88	THIS IS ME *EMI EM 58*	**22**	5
20 Aug 88	I WON'T BLEED FOR YOU *EMI EM 66*	**35**	4
24 Dec 88	LOVE LIKE A RIVER *EMI EM 81*	**22**	7
23 Sep 89	FACTS OF LOVE *EMI EM 103*	**50**	3

Simon CLIMIE *UK, male vocalist (2 WEEKS)* pos/wks

| 19 Sep 92 | SOUL INSPIRATION *Epic 6582837* | **60** | 2 |

See also CLIMIE FISHER

Patsy CLINE *US, female vocalist (17 WEEKS)* pos/wks

26 Apr 62	SHE'S GOT YOU *Brunswick 05866*	**43**	1
29 Nov 62	HEARTACHES *Brunswick 05878*	**31**	5
8 Dec 90	CRAZY *MCA MCA 1465*	**14**	11

CLINIC *UK, male vocal / instrumental group (2 WEEKS)* pos/wks

| 22 Apr 00 | THE RETURN OF EVIL BILL *Domino RUG 093CD* | **70** | 1 |
| 4 Nov 00 | THE SECOND LINE *Domino RUG 116CD* | **56** | 1 |

George CLINTON *US, male vocalist (10 WEEKS)* pos/wks

4 Dec 82	LOOPZILLA *Capitol CL 271*	**57**	5
26 Apr 86	DO FRIES GO WITH THAT SHAKE *Capitol CL 402*	**57**	2
27 Aug 94	BOP GUN (ONE NATION) *Fourth & Broadway BRCD 308* [1]	**22**	3

[1] Ice Cube featuring George Clinton

CLIVILLES & COLE – See C & C MUSIC FACTORY / CLIVILLES & COLE

CLOCK (492 Top 500) *UK instrumental production duo Stu Allan and Pete Pritchard featured various rappers / vocalists before Lorna Saunders fronted the act from 1998. A talent for updating dancefloor hits resulted in more 1990s charted revivals (8) than any other act (70 WEEKS)* pos/wks

30 Oct 93	HOLDING ON *Media MRLCD 007*	**66**	1
21 May 94	THE RHYTHM *Media MCSTD 1971*	**28**	2
10 Sep 94	KEEP THE FIRES BURNING *Media MCSTD 1998*	**36**	3
4 Mar 95	● AXEL F / KEEP PUSHIN' *Media MCSTD 2041*	**7**	9
1 Jul 95	● WHOOMPH! (THERE IT IS) *Media MCSTD 2059*	**4**	9
26 Aug 95	● EVERYBODY *Media MCSTD 2077*	**6**	5
18 Nov 95	IN THE HOUSE *Media MCSTD 40005*	**23**	3
24 Feb 96	HOLDING ON 4 U (re-mix) *Media MCSTD 40019*	**27**	2
7 Sep 96	OH WHAT A NIGHT *Power Station MCSTD 40057*	**13**	10
22 Mar 97	● IT'S OVER *Media MCSTD 40100*	**10**	5
18 Oct 97	U SEXY THING *Media MCSTD 40138*	**11**	9
17 Jan 98	THAT'S THE WAY (I LIKE IT) *Media MCSTD 40148*	**11**	4
11 Jul 98	ROCK YOUR BODY *Media MCSTD 40160*	**30**	3

28 Nov 98	BLAME IT ON THE BOOGIE *Media MCSTD 40191*	16 4
31 Jul 99	SUNSHINE DAY *Media MCSTD 40208*	58 1

Rosemary CLOONEY 397 Top 500

Top 50s female vocalist and 90s Grammy-nominated granny, b. 23, May 1928, Kentucky, US. Award-winning balladeer and jazz song stylist was at the forefront of first Mambo craze in mid-1950s. Sampled on original Shaft 1999 recording '(Mucho Mambo) Sway' which has appeared on a number of compilation albums (81 WEEKS)

pos/wks

14 Nov 52 ●	HALF AS MUCH *Columbia DB 3129*	3 9
5 Feb 54 ●	MAN *Philips PB 220*	7 5
8 Oct 54 ★	THIS OLE HOUSE *Philips PB 336* ▲	1 18
17 Dec 54 ★	MAMBO ITALIANO *Philips PB 382* 1	1 16
20 May 55 ●	WHERE WILL THE DIMPLE BE? *Philips PB 428* 2	6 13
30 Sep 55 ●	HEY THERE *Philips PB 494* ▲	4 11
29 Mar 57	MANGOS *Philips PB 671*	25 2
26 Apr 57	MANGOS (re-entry) *Philips PB 671*	17 7

1 Rosemary Clooney and the Mellomen 2 Rosemary Clooney & The Mellomen

From 19 Feb 1954, other side of 'Man', 'Woman', by Jose Ferrer was also credited

CLOUD *UK, male instrumental group (1 WEEK)*

pos/wks

31 Jan 81	ALL NIGHT LONG / TAKE IT TO THE TOP *UK Champagne FUNK 1*	72 1

CLOUT *South Africa, female vocal / instrumental group (15 WEEKS)*

pos/wks

17 Jun 78 ●	SUBSTITUTE *Carrere EMI 2788*	2 15

CLS *US, male vocal / production duo (1 WEEK)*

pos/wks

30 May 98	CAN YOU FEEL IT *Satellite 74321580162*	46 1

CLUB NOUVEAU

US, male / female vocal / instrumental group (12 WEEKS)

pos/wks

21 Mar 87 ●	LEAN ON ME *King Jay W 8430* ▲	3 12

CLUB 69

Austria / US, male / female vocal / instrumental duo (6 WEEKS)

pos/wks

5 Dec 92	LET ME BE YOUR UNDERWEAR *ffrr F 204*	33 5
14 Nov 98	ALRIGHT *Twisted UK TWCD 10039* 1	70 1

1 Club 69 featuring Suzanne Palmer

CLUBHOUSE *Italy, male vocal / instrumental group (40 WEEKS)*

pos/wks

23 Jul 83	DO IT AGAIN - BILLIE JEAN (MEDLEY) *Island IS 132*	11 6
3 Dec 83	SUPERSTITION - GOOD TIMES (MEDLEY) *Island IS 147*	59 3
1 Jul 89	I'M A MAN - YE KE YE KE (MEDLEY) *Music Man MMPS 7003*	69 3
20 Apr 91	DEEP IN MY HEART *ffrr F 157*	59 2
22 Jun 91	DEEP IN MY HEART (re-entry) *ffrr F 157*	55 2
4 Sep 93	LIGHT MY FIRE *PWL Continental PWCD 272* 1	59 1
13 Nov 93	LIGHT MY FIRE (re-entry) *PWL Continental PWCD 272* 1	45 5
25 Dec 93	LIGHT MY FIRE (2nd re-entry) *PWL Continental PWCD 272* 1	53 6
30 Apr 94 ●	LIGHT MY FIRE (re-mix) *PWL Continental PWCD 288* 1	7 8
23 Jul 94	LIVING IN THE SUNSHINE *PWL Continental PWCD 309* 1	21 3
11 Mar 95	NOWHERE LAND *PWL International PWCD 318* 1	56 1

1 Clubhouse featuring Carl

CLUBZONE

UK / Germany, male vocal / instrumental group (1 WEEK)

pos/wks

19 Nov 94	HANDS UP *Logic 74321236982*	50 1

CLUELESS *US, male / female vocal / production group (1 WEEK)*

pos/wks

5 Apr 97	DON'T SPEAK *ZYX ZYX 660738*	61 1

Jeremy CLYDE – See Chad STUART and Jeremy CLYDE

CLYDE VALLEY STOMPERS

UK, male instrumental group (8 WEEKS)

pos/wks

9 Aug 62	PETER AND THE WOLF *Parlophone R 4928*	25 8

Co Co – See FRAGMA

CO-CO *UK, male / female vocal / instrumental group (7 WEEKS)*

pos/wks

22 Apr 78	BAD OLD DAYS *Ariola Hansa AHA 513*	13 7

CO-OPERATION CHOIR – See Peter E BENNETT with the CO-OPERATION CHOIR

COAST TO COAST

UK, male vocal / instrumental group (22 WEEKS)

pos/wks

31 Jan 81 ●	(DO) THE HUCKLEBUCK *Polydor POSP 214*	5 15
23 May 81	LET'S JUMP THE BROOMSTICK *Polydor POSP 249*	28 7

COASTERS *US, male vocal group (32 WEEKS)*

pos/wks

27 Sep 57	SEARCHIN' *London HLE 8450*	30 1
15 Aug 58	YAKETY YAK *London HLE 8665*	12 8
27 Mar 59 ●	CHARLIE BROWN *London HLE 8819*	6 12
30 Oct 59	POISON IVY *London HLE 8938*	15 7
9 Apr 94	SORRY BUT I'M GONNA HAVE TO PASS *Rhino A 4519CD*	41 4

Odia COATES – See Paul ANKA

Luis COBOS featuring Placido DOMINGO *Spain, male orchestra conductor and Spain, male vocalist (2 WEEKS)*

pos/wks

16 Jun 90	NESSUN DORMA FROM 'TURANDOT' *Epic 656005 7*	59 2

Eddie COCHRAN 342 Top 500

Legendary rock 'n' roll singer / songwriter and guitarist b. 3 Oct 1938, Oklahoma, US, d. 17 Apr 1960, Wiltshire, UK. Distinctive and influential 'teen rebel' rocker (90 WEEKS)

pos/wks

7 Nov 58	SUMMERTIME BLUES *London HLU 8702*	18 6
13 Mar 59 ●	C'MON EVERYBODY *London HLU 8792*	6 13
16 Oct 59	SOMETHIN' ELSE *London HLU 8944*	22 3
22 Jan 60	HALLELUJAH I LOVE HER SO *London HLW 9022*	28 1
5 Feb 60	HALLELUJAH I LOVE HER SO (re-entry) *London HLW 9022*	22 3
12 May 60 ★	THREE STEPS TO HEAVEN *London HLG 9115*	1 15
6 Oct 60	SWEETIE PIE *London HLG 9196*	38 3
3 Nov 60	LONELY *London HLG 9196*	41 1
15 Jun 61	WEEKEND *London HLG 9362*	15 16
30 Nov 61	JEANNIE, JEANNIE, JEANNIE *London HLG 9460*	31 4
25 Apr 63	MY WAY *Liberty LIB 10088*	23 10
24 Apr 68	SUMMERTIME BLUES (re-issue) *Liberty LBF 15071*	34 8
13 Feb 88	C'MON EVERYBODY (re-issue) *Liberty EDDIE 501*	14 7

Tom COCHRANE *Canada, male vocalist (2 WEEKS)*

pos/wks

27 Jun 92	LIFE IS A HIGHWAY *Capitol CL 660*	62 2

COCK ROBIN *US, male / female vocal / instrumental group (12 WEEKS)*

pos/wks

31 May 86	THE PROMISE YOU MADE *CBS A 6764*	28 12

Joe COCKER 347 Top 500

Throaty emotive pop / rock singer b. 20 May 1944, Sheffield, UK, whose first single was released in 1964. 'Up Where We Belong' won both Oscar and Grammy awards for the vocalist, who was still scoring Top 20 albums across Europe in 2000 (89 WEEKS)

pos/wks

22 May 68	MARJORINE *Regal-Zonophone RZ 3006*	48 1
2 Oct 68 ★	WITH A LITTLE HELP FROM MY FRIENDS *Regal-Zonophone RZ 3013*	1 13
27 Sep 69 ●	DELTA LADY *Regal-Zonophone RZ 3024*	10 11
4 Jul 70	THE LETTER *Regal-Zonophone RZ 3027*	39 6
26 Sep 81	I'M SO GLAD I'M STANDING HERE TODAY *MCA 741* 1	61 3
15 Jan 83 ●	UP WHERE WE BELONG *Island WIP 6830* 2 ▲	7 13
14 Nov 87	UNCHAIN MY HEART *Capitol CL 465*	46 4
13 Jan 90	WHEN THE NIGHT COMES *Capitol CL 535*	65 2

7 Mar 92	(ALL I KNOW) FEELS LIKE FOREVER		
	Capitol CL 645 ....**25**	5
9 May 92	NOW THAT THE MAGIC HAS GONE Capitol CL 657 ....**28**	6
4 Jul 92	UNCHAIN MY HEART (re-issue) Capitol CL 664 ....**17**	6
21 Nov 92	WHEN THE NIGHT COMES (re-issue) Capitol CL 674 ....**61**	3
13 Aug 94	THE SIMPLE THINGS Capitol CDCLS 722 ....**17**	5
22 Oct 94	TAKE ME HOME Capitol CDCLS 729 [3] **41**	3
17 Dec 94	LET THE HEALING BEGIN Capitol CDCLS 727 ....**32**	5
23 Sep 95	HAVE A LITTLE FAITH Capitol CDCLS 744 ....**67**	2
12 Oct 96	DON'T LET ME BE MISUNDERSTOOD		
	Parlophone CDCLS 779 ....**53**	1

[1] Crusaders, featured vocalist Joe Cocker [2] Joe Cocker and Jennifer Warnes [3] Joe Cocker featuring Bekka Bramlett

COCKEREL CHORUS
UK, male Tottenham Hotspur Football Club Supporters vocal group (12 WEEKS) pos/wks

| 24 Feb 73 | NICE ONE CYRIL Youngblood YB 1017 ....**14** | 12 |

COCKNEY REBEL – See Steve HARLEY and COCKNEY REBEL

COCKNEY REJECTS
UK, male vocal / instrumental group (22 WEEKS) pos/wks

1 Dec 79	I'M NOT A FOOL EMI 5008 ....**65**	2
16 Feb 80	BADMAN EMI 5035 ....**65**	3
26 Apr 80	THE GREATEST COCKNEY RIPOFF Zonophone Z 2 ....**21**	7
17 May 80	I'M FOREVER BLOWING BUBBLES Zonophone Z 4 ....**35**	5
12 Jul 80	WE CAN DO ANYTHING Zonophone Z 6 ....**65**	2
25 Oct 80	WE ARE THE FIRM Zonophone Z 10 ....**54**	3

COCO *UK, female vocalist (2 WEEKS)* pos/wks

| 8 Nov 97 | I NEED A MIRACLE Positiva CDTIV 81 ....**39** | 2 |

COCONUTS *US, female vocal group (3 WEEKS)* pos/wks

| 11 Jun 83 | DID YOU HAVE TO LOVE ME LIKE YOU DID | | |
| | EMI America EA 156 ....**60** | 3 |

See also Kid CREOLE and the COCONUTS

COCTEAU TWINS
UK, male / female vocal / instrumental group (25 WEEKS) pos/wks

28 Apr 84	PEARLY-DEWDROPS' DROPS 4AD 405 ....**29**	5
30 Mar 85	AIKEA-GUINEA 4AD AD 501 ....**41**	3
23 Nov 85	TINY DYNAMITE (EP) 4AD BAD 510 ....**52**	2
7 Dec 85	ECHOES IN A SHALLOW BAY (EP) 4AD BAD 511 ....**65**	1
25 Oct 86	LOVE'S EASY TEARS 4AD AD 610 ....**53**	1
8 Sep 90	ICEBLINK LUCK 4AD AD 0011 ....**38**	3
2 Oct 93	EVANGELINE Fontana CTCD 1 ....**34**	2
18 Dec 93	WINTER WONDERLAND / FROSTY THE SNOWMAN		
	Fontana COCCD 1 ....**58**	1
26 Feb 94	BLUEBEARD Fontana CTCD 2 ....**33**	2
7 Oct 95	TWINLIGHTS (EP) Fontana CTCD 3 ....**59**	1
4 Nov 95	OTHERNESS (EP) Fontana CTCD 4 ....**59**	1
30 Mar 96	TISHBITE Fontana CTCD 5 ....**34**	2
20 Jul 96	VIOLAINE Fontana CTCD 6 ....**56**	1

Tracks on Tiny Dynamite (EP): Pink Orange Red / Ribbed and Veined / Plain Tiger / Sultitan Itan. Tracks on Echoes in a Shallow Bay (EP): Great Spangled Fritillary / Melonella / Pale Clouded White / Eggs and Their Shells. Tracks on Twinlights (EP): Golden-Vein / Half-Gifts / Pink Orange Red / Rilkean Heart. Tracks On Otherness (EP): Cherry Coloured Funk / Feet Like Fins / Seekers Who Are Lovers / Violaine

C.O.D *US, male vocal / instrumental group (2 WEEKS)* pos/wks

| 14 May 83 | IN THE BOTTLE Streetwave WAVE 2 ....**54** | 2 |

CODE RED *UK, male vocal group (7 WEEKS)* pos/wks

6 Jul 96	I GAVE YOU EVERYTHING Polydor 5763992 ....**50**	1
16 Nov 96	THIS IS OUR SONG Polydor 5756332 ....**59**	1
14 Jun 97	CAN WE TALK... Polydor 5710992 ....**29**	2
9 Aug 97	IS THERE SOMEONE OUT THERE? Polydor 5714652 ......**34**	2
4 Jul 98	WHAT WOULD YOU DO IF...? Polydor 569932 ....**55**	1

COFFEE *US, female vocal group (13 WEEKS)* pos/wks

| 27 Sep 80 | CASANOVA De-Lite MER 38 ....**13** | 10 |
| 6 Dec 80 | SLIP AND DIP / I WANNA BE WITH YOU De-Lite DE 1 ......**57** | 3 |

Alma COGAN 258 **Top 500** *Very popular 1950s radio, TV and recording star, b. 19 May 1932, d. 26 Oct 1966. The singer, who was renowned for her glamour and was known as the 'gal with the giggle in her voice', was the youngest English female to top the chart in the 1950s (110 WEEKS)* pos/wks

19 Mar 54 ●	BELL BOTTOM BLUES HMV B 10653 ....**4**	9
27 Aug 54	LITTLE THINGS MEAN A LOT HMV B 10717 ....**11**	2
8 Oct 54	LITTLE THINGS MEAN A LOT (re-entry) HMV B 10717 ....**19**	1
22 Oct 54	LITTLE THINGS MEAN A LOT (2nd re-entry)		
	HMV B 10717 ....**18**	2
3 Dec 54 ●	I CAN'T TELL A WALTZ FROM A TANGO HMV B 10786 ......**6**	11
27 May 55 ★	DREAMBOAT HMV B 10872 ....**1**	16
23 Sep 55	THE BANJO'S BACK IN TOWN HMV B 10917 (A) **17**	1
14 Oct 55	GO ON BY HMV B 10917 (B) **16**	4
16 Dec 55	TWENTY TINY FINGERS HMV POP 129(A) **17**	1
23 Dec 55 ●	NEVER DO A TANGO WITH AN ESKIMO HMV POP 129(B) **6**	5
30 Mar 56	WILLIE CAN HMV POP 187 [1] **13**	8
13 Jul 56	THE BIRDS AND THE BEES HMV POP 223 ....**25**	4
10 Aug 56	WHY DO FOOLS FALL IN LOVE HMV POP 223 ....**22**	3
2 Nov 56	IN THE MIDDLE OF THE HOUSE HMV POP 261 ....**26**	1
23 Nov 56	IN THE MIDDLE OF THE HOUSE (re-entry)		
	HMV POP 261 ....**20**	3
18 Jan 57	YOU ME AND US HMV POP 284 ....**18**	6
29 Mar 57	WHATEVER LOLA WANTS HMV POP 317 ....**26**	2
31 Jan 58	THE STORY OF MY LIFE HMV POP 433 ....**25**	2
14 Feb 58	SUGARTIME HMV POP 450 ....**16**	10
2 May 58	SUGARTIME (re-entry) HMV POP 450 ....**30**	1
23 Jan 59	LAST NIGHT ON THE BACK PORCH HMV POP 573 ....**27**	2
18 Dec 59	WE GOT LOVE HMV POP 670 ....**26**	4
12 May 60	DREAM TALK HMV POP 728 ....**48**	1
11 Aug 60	TRAIN OF LOVE HMV POP 760 ....**27**	5
20 Apr 61	COWBOY JIMMY JOE Columbia DB 4607 ....**37**	6

[1] Alma Cogan with Desmond Lane - Penny Whistle

Shaye COGAN *US, female vocalist (1 WEEK)* pos/wks

| 24 Mar 60 | MEAN TO ME MGM 1063 ....**40** | 1 |

Izhar COHEN and the ALPHA-BETA
Israel, male / female vocal group (7 WEEKS) pos/wks

| 13 May 78 | A BA NI BI Polydor 2001 781 ....**20** | 7 |

Marc COHN *US, male vocalist (15 WEEKS)* pos/wks

25 May 91	WALKING IN MEMPHIS Atlantic A 7747 ....**66**	4
10 Aug 91	SILVER THUNDERBIRD Atlantic A 7657 ....**54**	3
12 Oct 91	WALKING IN MEMPHIS (re-issue) Atlantic A 7585 ....**22**	5
29 May 93	WALK THROUGH THE WORLD Atlantic A 7340CD **37**	3

COLA BOY *UK, male / female vocal / instrumental duo - Andrew Midgely and Janey Lee Grace (7 WEEKS)* pos/wks

| 6 Jul 91 ● | 7 WAYS TO LOVE Arista 114526 ....**8** | 7 |

COLD JAM featuring GRACE
US, male / female vocal / instrumental group (2 WEEKS) pos/wks

| 28 Jul 90 | LAST NIGHT A DJ SAVED MY LIFE Big Wave BWR 39 ....**64** | 2 |

COLDCUT *UK, male production duo - Matt Black and Jonathan Moore (38 WEEKS)* pos/wks

20 Feb 88 ●	DOCTORIN' THE HOUSE Ahead of Our Time CCUT 27 [1] **6**	9
10 Sep 88	STOP THIS CRAZY THING Ahead of Our Time CCUT 4 [2] **21**	7
25 Mar 89	PEOPLE HOLD ON Ahead of Our Time CCUT 5 [3] **11**	9
3 Jun 89	MY TELEPHONE Ahead of Our Time CCUT 6 ....**52**	1
16 Dec 89	COLDCUT'S CHRISTMAS BREAK		
	Ahead of Our Time CCUT 7 ....**67**	3
26 May 90	FIND A WAY Ahead of our Time CCUT 8 [4] **52**	2

UK No.1 ★ UK Top 10 ● Still on chart + UK million seller ◆ UK entry at No.1 ■ US No.1 ▲

4 Sep 93	DREAMER *Arista 74321156642*	54	2
22 Jan 94	AUTUMN LEAVES *Arista 74321171052*	50	2
16 Aug 97	MORE BEATS & PIECES *Ninja Tune ZENCDS 58*	37	2

[1] Coldcut featuring Yazz and the Plastic Population [2] Coldcut featuring Junior Reid and the Ahead of Our Time Orchestra [3] Coldcut featuring Lisa Stansfield [4] Coldcut featuring Queen Latifah

COLDPLAY *UK, male vocal / instrumental group (23 WEEKS)*
		pos	wks
18 Mar 00	SHIVER *Parlophone CDR 6536*	35	3
8 Jul 00 ●	YELLOW *Parlophone CDR 6538*	4	11
4 Nov 00 ●	TROUBLE *Parlophone CDR 6549*	10	9

Andy COLE *UK, male vocalist / footballer (1 WEEK)*
		pos	wks
18 Sep 99	OUTSTANDING *WEA WEA 224CD*	68	1

Cozy COLE *US, male instrumentalist - drums (1 WEEK)*
		pos	wks
5 Dec 58	TOPSY (PARTS 1 AND 2) *London HL 8750*	29	1

George COLE – See Dennis WATERMAN

Lloyd COLE *UK, male vocalist (62 WEEKS)*
		pos	wks
26 May 84	PERFECT SKIN *Polydor COLE 1* [1]	71	1
9 Jun 84	PERFECT SKIN (re-entry) *Polydor COLE 1* [1]	26	8
25 Aug 84	FOREST FIRE *Polydor COLE 2* [1]	41	6
17 Nov 84	RATTLESNAKES *Poldor COLE 3* [1]	65	1
14 Sep 85	BRAND NEW FRIEND *Polydor COLE 4* [1]	19	8
9 Nov 85	LOST WEEKEND *Polydor COLE 5* [1]	17	7
18 Jan 86	CUT ME DOWN *Polydor COLE 6* [1]	38	4
3 Oct 87	MY BAG *Polydor COLE 7* [1]	46	4
9 Jan 88	JENNIFER SHE SAID *Polydor COLE 8* [1]	31	5
23 Apr 88	FROM THE HIP (EP) *Polydor COLE 9* [1]	59	2
3 Feb 90	NO BLUE SKIES *Polydor COLE 11*	42	4
7 Apr 90	DON'T LOOK BACK *Polydor COLE 12*	59	3
31 Aug 91	SHE'S A GIRL AND I'M A MAN *Polydor COLE 14*	55	2
25 Sep 93	SO YOU'D LIKE TO SAVE THE WORLD *Fontana VIBE D1*	72	1
16 Sep 95	LIKE LOVERS DO *Fontana LCDD 1*	24	3
2 Dec 95	SENTIMENTAL FOOL *Fontana LCDD 2*	73	1

[1] Lloyd Cole and the Commotions

Tracks on From the Hip (EP): From the Hip / Please / Lonely Mile / Love Your Wife

MJ COLE *UK, male producer - Matt Coleman (16 WEEKS)*
		pos	wks
23 May 98	SINCERE *AM:PM 5826912*	38	2
6 May 00 ●	CRAZY LOVE *Talkin Loud TLCD 59*	10	7
12 Aug 00	SINCERE (re-mix) *Talkin Loud TLCD 60*	13	5
2 Dec 00	HOLD ON TO ME *Talkin Loud TLCD 62* [1]	35	2

[1] MJ Cole featuring Elizabeth Troy

Nat 'King' COLE (51) Top 500
One of the 20th century's most distinctive song stylists, b. 17 Mar 1917, Alabama, d. 15 Feb 1965. His 41-year chart span is proof that the highly regarded vocalist's recordings are timeless *(240 WEEKS)*
		pos	wks
14 Nov 52 ●	SOMEWHERE ALONG THE WAY *Capitol CL 13774*	3	7
19 Dec 52 ●	BECAUSE YOU'RE MINE *Capitol CL 13811*	6	2
2 Jan 53	FAITH CAN MOVE MOUNTAINS *Capitol CL 13811*	11	1
16 Jan 53	FAITH CAN MOVE MOUNTAINS (re-entry) *Capitol CL 13811*	12	1
23 Jan 53 ●	BECAUSE YOU'RE MINE (re-entry) *Capitol CL 13811*	10	1
6 Feb 53 ●	FAITH CAN MOVE MOUNTAINS (2nd re-entry) *Capitol CL 13811*	10	1
13 Feb 53	BECAUSE YOU'RE MINE (2nd re-entry) *Capitol CL 13811*	11	1
24 Apr 53 ●	PRETEND *Capitol CL 13878*	2	18
14 Aug 53 ●	CAN'T I *Capitol CL 13937*	9	3
18 Sep 53 ●	CAN'T I (re-entry) *Capitol CL 13937*	6	4
18 Sep 53 ●	MOTHER NATURE AND FATHER TIME *Capitol CL 13912*	7	7
30 Oct 53 ●	CAN'T I (2nd re-entry) *Capitol CL 13937*	10	1
16 Apr 54 ●	TENDERLY *Capitol CL 14061*	10	1
10 Sep 54 ●	SMILE *Capitol CL 14149*	2	14
8 Oct 54 ●	MAKE HER MINE *Capitol CL 14149*	11	2
25 Feb 55 ●	A BLOSSOM FELL *Capitol CL 14235*	3	10
26 Aug 55	MY ONE SIN *Capitol CL 14327*	18	1
16 Sep 55	MY ONE SIN (re-entry) *Capitol CL 14327*	17	1
27 Jan 56 ●	DREAMS CAN TELL A LIE *Capitol CL 14513*	10	9
11 May 56	TOO YOUNG TO GO STEADY *Capitol CL 14573*	8	14
14 Sep 56	LOVE ME AS THOUGH THERE WERE NO TOMORROW *Capitol CL 14621*	24	2
5 Oct 56	LOVE ME AS THOUGH THERE WERE NO TOMORROW (re-entry) *Capitol CL 14621*	11	13
19 Apr 57 ●	WHEN I FALL IN LOVE *Capitol CL 14709*	2	20
5 Jul 57	WHEN ROCK 'N ROLL CAME TO TRINIDAD *Capitol CL 14733*	28	1
18 Oct 57	MY PERSONAL POSSESSION *Capitol CL 14765*	21	2
25 Oct 57	STARDUST *Capitol CL 14787*	24	2
29 May 59	YOU MADE ME LOVE YOU *Capitol CL 15017*	22	3
4 Sep 59	MIDNIGHT FLYER *Capitol CL 15056*	27	1
18 Sep 59	MIDNIGHT FLYER (re-entry) *Capitol CL 15056*	23	3
12 Feb 60	TIME AND THE RIVER *Capitol CL 15111*	29	1
26 Feb 60	TIME AND THE RIVER (re-entry) *Capitol CL 15111*	23	2
31 Mar 60	TIME AND THE RIVER (2nd re-entry) *Capitol CL 15111*	47	1
26 May 60 ●	THAT'S YOU *Capitol CL 15129*	10	8
10 Nov 60	JUST AS MUCH AS EVER *Capitol CL 15163*	18	10
2 Feb 61	THE WORLD IN MY ARMS *Capitol CL 15178*	36	10
16 Nov 61	LET TRUE LOVE BEGIN *Capitol CL 15224*	29	10
22 Mar 62	BRAZILIAN LOVE SONG *Capitol CL 15241*	34	4
31 May 62	THE RIGHT THING TO SAY *Capitol CL 15250*	42	4
19 Jul 62	LET THERE BE LOVE *Capitol CL 15257* [1]	11	14
27 Sep 62 ●	RAMBLIN' ROSE *Capitol CL 15270*	5	14
20 Dec 62	DEAR LONELY HEARTS *Capitol CL 15280*	37	3
12 Dec 87 ●	WHEN I FALL IN LOVE (re-issue) *Capitol CL 15975*	4	7
14 Dec 91	THE CHRISTMAS SONG *Capitol CL 641*	69	2
19 Mar 94	LET'S FACE THE MUSIC AND DANCE *EMI CDEM 312*	30	3

[1] Nat 'King' Cole with George Shearing

See also Natalie COLE

Natalie COLE (361) Top 500
Daughter of legendary Nat 'King 'Cole who has a 20-year Grammy-winning span of her own, b. 6 Feb 1950, Los Angeles, US. 'Unforgettable' in 1991 was an electronically recorded duet with her late father. Nat and Natalie are the only dad and daughter who both have No.1 US albums *(87 WEEKS)*
		pos	wks
11 Oct 75	THIS WILL BE *Capitol CL 15834*	32	5
8 Aug 87	JUMP START *Manhattan MT 22*	44	8
26 Mar 88 ●	PINK CADILLAC *Manhattan MT 35*	5	12
25 Jun 88	EVERLASTING *Manhattan MT 46*	28	6
20 Aug 88	JUMP START (re-issue) *Manhattan MT 50*	36	5
26 Nov 88	I LIVE FOR YOUR LOVE *Manhattan MT 57*	23	14
15 Apr 89 ●	MISS YOU LIKE CRAZY *EMI-USA MT 63*	2	15
22 Jul 89	REST OF THE NIGHT *EMI-USA MT 69*	56	2
16 Dec 89	STARTING OVER AGAIN *EMI-USA MT 77*	56	4
21 Apr 90	WILD WOMEN DO *EMI-USA MT 81*	16	7
22 Jun 91	UNFORGETTABLE *Elektra EKR 128.*	19	8
16 May 92	THE VERY THOUGHT OF YOU *Elektra EKR 147*	71	1

Paula COLE *US, female vocalist (9 WEEKS)*
		pos	wks
28 Jun 97	WHERE HAVE ALL THE COWBOYS GONE? *Warner Bros. W 0406CD*	15	8
1 Aug 98	I DON'T WANT TO WAIT *Warner Bros. W 0422CD*	43	1

Naimee COLEMAN – See AURORA

COLETTE – See SISTER BLISS

John Ford COLEY – See ENGLAND DAN and John Ford COLEY

COLLAGE
US / Canada / Philippines, male vocal / instrumental group (5 WEEKS) pos/wks
21 Sep 85	ROMEO WHERE'S JULIET? *MCA MCA 1006*	46	5

COLLAPSED LUNG
UK, male vocal / instrumental group (8 WEEKS) pos/wks
22 Jun 96	LONDON TONIGHT / EAT MY GOAL *Deceptive BLUFF 029CD*	31	3
30 May 98	EAT MY GOAL (re-issue) *Deceptive BLUFF 060CD*	18	5

Dave and Ansil COLLINS
Jamaica, male vocal / instrumental duo (27 WEEKS)   pos/wks

Date	Title	pos	wks
27 Mar 71	★ DOUBLE BARREL *Technique TE 901*	1	15
26 Jun 71	● MONKEY SPANNER *Technique TE 914* [1]	7	12

[1] Dave and Ansel Collins

Edwyn COLLINS *UK, male vocalist / instrumentalist (25 WEEKS)* pos/wks

Date	Title	pos	wks
11 Aug 84	PALE BLUE EYES *Swamplands SWP 1*	72	2
12 Nov 94	EXPRESSLY (EP) *Setanta ZOP 001CD1*	42	3
17 Jun 95	● A GIRL LIKE YOU (re-issue) *Setanta ZOP 003CD*	4	14
2 Mar 96	KEEP ON BURNING *Setanta ZOP 004CD1*	45	2
2 Aug 97	THE MAGIC PIPER (OF LOVE) *Setanta SETCDA 041*	32	3
18 Oct 97	ADIDAS WORLD *Setanta SETCDB 045*	71	1

The only track on all formats of Expressly (EP) was 'A Girl Like You'

See also ORANGE JUICE

Felicia COLLINS – See LUKK featuring Felicia COLLINS

Jeff COLLINS *UK, male vocalist (8 WEEKS)* pos/wks

Date	Title	pos	wks
18 Nov 72	ONLY YOU *Polydor 2058 287*	40	8

Judy COLLINS (369 Top 500) *Distinctive folk / pop singer born 1 May 1939, Washington, US, and raised in Colorado. 'Both Sides Now' was the first Joni Mitchell composition to chart and 'Amazing Grace' spent longer on the chart than any other single by a female artist (86 WEEKS)* pos/wks

Date	Title	pos	wks
17 Jan 70	BOTH SIDES NOW *Elektra EKSN 45043*	14	11
5 Dec 70	● AMAZING GRACE *Elektra 2101 020*	5	32
24 Jul 71	AMAZING GRACE (re-entry) *Elektra 2101 020*	48	1
4 Sep 71	AMAZING GRACE (2nd re-entry) *Elektra 2101 020*	40	7
20 Nov 71	AMAZING GRACE (3rd re-entry) *Elektra 2101 020*	50	1
18 Dec 71	AMAZING GRACE (4th re-entry) *Elektra 2101 020*	48	2
22 Apr 72	AMAZING GRACE (5th re-entry) *Elektra 2101 020*	20	19
9 Sep 72	AMAZING GRACE (6th re-entry) *Elektra 2101 020*	46	2
23 Dec 72	AMAZING GRACE (7th re-entry) *Elektra 2101 020*	49	3
17 May 75	● SEND IN THE CLOWNS *Elektra K 12177*	6	8

Michelle COLLINS *UK, female vocalist (3 WEEKS)* pos/wks

Date	Title	pos	wks
27 Feb 99	SUNBURN *BBC Music WMSS 60082*	28	3

Phil COLLINS (62 Top 500) *Continually popular singer / songwriter (b. 31 Jan 1951, London) who simultaneously fronted Genesis (until 1996) and managed a successful solo career. Only members of The Beatles have appeared on more UK No.1 albums (226 WEEKS)* pos/wks

Date	Title	pos	wks
17 Jan 81	● IN THE AIR TONIGHT *Virgin VS102*	2	10
7 Mar 81	I MISSED AGAIN *Virgin VS 402*	14	8
30 May 81	IF LEAVING ME IS EASY *Virgin VS 423*	17	8
23 Oct 82	THRU' THESE WALLS *Virgin VS 524*	56	2
4 Dec 82	★ YOU CAN'T HURRY LOVE *Virgin VS 531*	1	16
19 Mar 83	DON'T LET HIM STEAL YOUR HEART AWAY *Virgin VS 572*	45	5
7 Apr 84	● AGAINST ALL ODDS (TAKE A LOOK AT ME NOW) *Virgin VS 674* ▲	2	14
26 Jan 85	SUSSUDIO *Virgin VS 736* ▲	12	9
9 Mar 85	★ EASY LOVER *CBS A 4915* [1]	1	12
13 Apr 85	● ONE MORE NIGHT *Virgin VS 755* ▲	4	9
27 Jul 85	TAKE ME HOME *Virgin VS 777*	19	9
23 Nov 85	● SEPARATE LIVES *Virgin VS 818* [2] ▲	4	13
18 Jun 88	IN THE AIR TONIGHT (re-mix) *Virgin VS 102*	4	9
3 Sep 88	★ A GROOVY KIND OF LOVE *Virgin VS 1117* ▲	1	13
26 Nov 88	● TWO HEARTS *Virgin VS 1141* ▲	6	11
4 Nov 89	● ANOTHER DAY IN PARADISE *Virgin VS 1234* ▲	2	11
27 Jan 90	● I WISH IT WOULD RAIN DOWN *Virgin VS 1240*	7	9
28 Apr 90	SOMETHING HAPPENED ON THE WAY TO HEAVEN *Virgin VS 1251*	15	7
28 Jul 90	THAT'S JUST THE WAY IT IS *Virgin VS 1277*	26	5
6 Oct 90	HANG IN LONG ENOUGH *Virgin VS 1300*	34	3
8 Dec 90	DO YOU REMEMBER (LIVE) *Virgin VS 1305*	57	5
15 May 93	HERO *Atlantic A 7360*	56	3
30 Oct 93	● BOTH SIDES OF THE STORY *Virgin VSCDT 1500*	7	5
1 Jan 94	BOTH SIDES OF THE STORY (re-entry) *Virgin VSCDT 1500*	61	1
15 Jan 94	EVERYDAY *Virgin VSCDT 1505*	15	5
7 May 94	WE WAIT AND WE WONDER *Virgin VSCDT 1510*	45	2
5 Oct 96	● DANCE INTO THE LIGHT *Face Value EW 066CD*	9	4
14 Dec 96	IT'S IN YOUR EYES *Face Value EW 076CD1*	30	4
12 Jul 97	WEAR MY HAT *Face Value EW 113CD*	43	2
7 Nov 98	TRUE COLORS *Virgin VSCDT 1715*	26	4
6 Nov 99	YOU'LL BE IN MY HEART *Edel / Walt Disney 0100735 DNY*	17	6

[1] Philip Bailey (duet with Phil Collins) [2] Phil Collins and Marilyn Martin

See also GENESIS

Rodger COLLINS *US, male vocalist (6 WEEKS)* pos/wks

Date	Title	pos	wks
3 Apr 76	YOU SEXY SUGAR PLUM (BUT I LIKE IT) *Fantasy FTC 132*	22	6

Willie COLLINS *US, male vocalist (4 WEEKS)* pos/wks

Date	Title	pos	wks
28 Jun 86	WHERE YOU GONNA BE TONIGHT? *Capitol CL 410*	46	4

Willie COLON *US, male vocalist (7 WEEKS)* pos/wks

Date	Title	pos	wks
28 Jun 86	SET FIRE TO ME *A & M AM 330*	41	7

COLOR ME BADD *US, male vocal group (31 WEEKS)* pos/wks

Date	Title	pos	wks
18 May 91	★ I WANNA SEX YOU UP *Giant W 0036*	1	14
3 Aug 91	● ALL 4 LOVE *Giant W 0053* ▲	5	10
12 Oct 91	I ADORE MI AMOR *Giant W 0067* ▲	44	2
9 Nov 91	I ADORE MI AMOR (re-issue) *Giant W 0076*	59	2
22 Feb 92	HEARTBREAKER *Giant W 0078*	58	1
20 Nov 93	TIME AND CHANCE *Giant 74321168992*	62	1
16 Apr 94	CHOOSE *Giant 74321199432*	65	1

COLORADO *UK, female vocal group (3 WEEKS)* pos/wks

Date	Title	pos	wks
21 Oct 78	CALIFORNIA DREAMIN' *Pinnacle PIN 67*	45	3

COLOUR FIELD *UK, male vocal / instrumental group (18 WEEKS)* pos/wks

Date	Title	pos	wks
21 Jan 84	THE COLOUR FIELD *Chrysalis COLF 1*	43	4
28 Jul 84	TAKE *Chrysalis COLF 2*	70	1
26 Jan 85	THINKING OF YOU *Chrysalis COLF 3*	12	10
13 Apr 85	CASTLES IN THE AIR *Chrysalis COLF 4*	51	3

COLOUR GIRL *UK, female vocalist - Rebecca Skingley (4 WEEKS)* pos/wks

Date	Title	pos	wks
11 Mar 00	CAN'T GET USED TO LOSING YOU *4 Liberty LIBT CD037*	31	3
9 Sep 00	JOYRIDER (YOU'RE PLAYING WITH FIRE) *4 Liberty LIBT CD039*	51	1

COLOURS featuring EMMANUEL & ESKA
UK, male instrumentalist / producer and female vocalist (1 WEEK) pos/wks

Date	Title	pos	wks
27 Feb 99	WHAT U DO *Inferno CDFERN 12*	51	1

COLUMBO featuring OOE *UK, male production duo (1 WEEK)* pos/wks

Date	Title	pos	wks
15 May 99	ROCKABILLY BOB *V2 / Milkgems VVR 5006903*	59	1

Shawn COLVIN *US, female vocalist (11 WEEKS)* pos/wks

Date	Title	pos	wks
27 Nov 93	I DON'T KNOW WHY *Columbia 6598272*	62	1
12 Feb 94	ROUND OF BLUES *Columbia 6594282*	73	1
3 Sep 94	EVERY LITTLE THING HE DOES IS MAGIC *Columbia 6607742*	65	1
7 Jan 95	ONE COOL REMOVE *Columbia 6611342* [1]	40	3
12 Aug 95	I DON'T KNOW WHY (re-issue) *Columbia 6622725*	52	1
15 Mar 97	GET OUT OF THIS HOUSE *Columbia 6638522*	70	1
30 May 98	SUNNY CAME HOME *Columbia 6648022*	29	3

[1] Shawn Colvin with Mary-Chapin Carpenter

COMETS – See Bill HALEY and his COMETS

COMING OUT CREW *US, male / female vocal duo (1 WEEK)* pos/wks

Date	Title	pos	wks
18 Mar 95	FREE, GAY AND HAPPY *Out on Vinyl CDOOV 002*	50	1

UK No.1 ★   UK Top 10 ●   Still on chart +   UK million seller ◆   UK entry at No.1 ■   US No.1 ▲

COMMANDER TOM
Germany, male producer - Tom Weyer (1 WEEK) pos/wks

| 23 Dec 00 | EYE BEE M *Tripoli Trax TTRAX 069CD*........ | 75 | 1 |

COMMENTATORS
UK, male impressionist - Rory Bremner (7 WEEKS) pos/wks

| 22 Jun 85 | N-N-NINETEEN NOT OUT *Oval 100*........ | 13 | 7 |

COMMITMENTS
Ireland, male / female vocal / instrumental group (1 WEEK) pos/wks

| 30 Nov 91 | MUSTANG SALLY *MCA MCS 1598*........ | 63 | 1 |

COMMODORES `219` `Top 500`
Top-notch US R&B combo: Lionel Richie (v/k), William King (t), Thomas McClary (g), Milan Williams (var), Ronald LaPread (b), Walter Orange (d). They were among the 1970s' biggest-selling groups, but lost ground when songwriter Richie went solo in 1982 (121 WEEKS) pos/wks

24 Aug 74	MACHINE GUN *Tamla Motown TMG 902*........	20	11
23 Nov 74	THE ZOO (THE HUMAN ZOO) *Tamla Motown TMG 924*	44	2
2 Jul 77 ●	EASY *Motown TMG 1073*........	9	10
8 Oct 77	SWEET LOVE / BRICK HOUSE *Motown TMG 1086*........	32	6
11 Mar 78	TOO HOT TO TROT / ZOOM *Motown TMG 1096*........	38	4
24 Jun 78	FLYING HIGH *Motown TMG 1111*........	37	7
5 Aug 78 ★	THREE TIMES A LADY *Motown TMG 1113* ▲........	1	14
25 Nov 78	JUST TO BE CLOSE TO YOU *Motown TMG 1127*........	62	4
25 Aug 79 ●	SAIL ON *Motown TMG 1155*........	8	10
3 Nov 79 ●	STILL *Motown TMG 1166* ▲........	4	11
19 Jan 80	WONDERLAND *Motown TMG 1172*........	40	4
1 Aug 81	LADY (YOU BRING ME UP) *Motown TMG 1238*........	56	5
21 Nov 81	OH NO *Motown TMG 1245*........	44	3
26 Jan 85 ●	NIGHTSHIFT *Motown TMG 1371*........	3	14
11 May 85	ANIMAL INSTINCT *Motown ZB 40097*........	74	1
25 Oct 86	GOIN' TO THE BANK *Polydor POSPA 826*........	43	4
13 Aug 88	EASY (re-issue) *Motown ZB 41793*	15	11

Group was US / UK for 1985 and 1986 hits

COMMON
US, male rapper - Rasheed Lynn (2 WEEKS) pos/wks

| 8 Nov 97 | REMINDING ME (OF SEF) *Relativity 6560762* [1] .... | 59 | 1 |
| 14 Oct 00 | THE LIGHT / THE 6TH SENSE *MCA MCSTD 40237*........ | 56 | 1 |

[1] Common featuring Chantay Savage

COMMOTIONS – See Lloyd COLE

COMMUNARDS `438` `Top 500`
Controversial but melodic pop duo consisted of Bronski Beat's Jimmy Somerville (v) b. 22 Jun 1961, Glasgow, Scotland, and Richard Coles (k), b. 23 Jun 1962, Northampton, UK. Their No.1 cover marked the song's third Top 20 reading within a decade (76 WEEKS) pos/wks

12 Oct 85	YOU ARE MY WORLD *London LON 77*........	30	8
24 May 86	DISENCHANTED *London LON 89*........	29	5
23 Aug 86 ★	DON'T LEAVE ME THIS WAY *London LON 103* [1]	1	14
29 Nov 86 ●	SO COLD THE NIGHT *London LON 110*........	8	10
21 Feb 87	YOU ARE MY WORLD (87) (re-mix) *London LON 123*	21	4
12 Sep 87	TOMORROW *London LON 143*........	23	7
7 Nov 87 ●	NEVER CAN SAY GOODBYE *London LON 158*	4	11
20 Feb 88	FOR A FRIEND *London LON 166*........	28	7
11 Jun 88	THERE'S MORE TO LOVE *London LON 173*........	20	8

[1] Communards with Sarah Jane Morris

Perry COMO `23` `Top 500`
One of the century's most enduring entertainers, b. 18 May 1912, Pennsylvania. This easy-on-the-ear relaxed balladeer launched his career in 1933, collected 150 US chart entries, hosted an Emmy-winning TV series, and continued to score hits past the age of 60 (322 WEEKS) pos/wks

16 Jan 53 ★	DON'T LET THE STARS GET IN YOUR EYES *HMV B 10400* [1] ▲........	1	15
4 Jun 54 ●	WANTED *HMV B 10691* ▲........	4	14
25 Jun 54 ●	IDLE GOSSIP *HMV B 10667*........	3	15

1 Oct 54	WANTED (re-entry) *HMV B 10691*........	18	1
10 Dec 54	PAPA LOVES MAMBO *HMV B 10776*........	16	1
30 Dec 55	TINA MARIE *HMV POP 103*........	24	1
27 Apr 56	JUKE BOX BABY *HMV POP 191*........	22	6
25 May 56 ●	HOT DIGGITY *HMV POP 212*........	4	13
21 Sep 56 ●	MORE *HMV POP 240*........	10	11
28 Sep 56	GLENDORA *HMV POP 240*........	18	6
14 Dec 56	MORE (re-entry) *HMV POP 240*........	29	1
7 Feb 58 ★	MAGIC MOMENTS *RCA 1036*........	1	17
7 Mar 58 ●	CATCH A FALLING STAR *RCA 1036*........	9	10
9 May 58 ●	KEWPIE DOLL *RCA 1055*........	9	7
30 May 58	I MAY NEVER PASS THIS WAY AGAIN *RCA 1062*........	15	8
5 Sep 58	MOON TALK *RCA 1071*........	17	11
7 Nov 58 ●	LOVE MAKES THE WORLD GO ROUND *RCA 1086*........	6	14
21 Nov 58	MANDOLINS IN THE MOONLIGHT *RCA 1086*........	13	12
27 Feb 59 ●	TOMBOY *RCA 1111*........	10	12
10 Jul 59	I KNOW *RCA 1126*........	13	16
26 Feb 60 ●	DELAWARE *RCA 1170*........	3	13
10 May 62	CATERINA *RCA 1283*........	37	4
14 Jun 62	CATERINA (re-entry) *RCA 1283*........	45	2
30 Jan 71 ●	IT'S IMPOSSIBLE *RCA 2043*........	4	23
15 May 71	I THINK OF YOU *RCA 2075*........	14	11
21 Apr 73 ●	AND I LOVE YOU SO *RCA 2346*........	3	31
25 Aug 73 ●	FOR THE GOOD TIMES *RCA 2402*........	7	27
8 Dec 73	WALK RIGHT BACK *RCA 2432*........	33	10
12 Jan 74	AND I LOVE YOU SO (re-entry) *RCA 2346*........	40	4
25 May 74	I WANT TO GIVE *RCA LPBO 7518*........	31	6

[1] Perry Como with the Ramblers

COMPAGNONS DE LA CHANSON
France, male vocal group (3 WEEKS) pos/wks

| 9 Oct 59 | THE THREE BELLS (THE JIMMY BROWN SONG) *Columbia DB 4358*........ | 27 | 1 |
| 23 Oct 59 | THE THREE BELLS (THE JIMMY BROWN SONG) (re-entry) *Columbia DB 4358*........ | 21 | 2 |

COMSAT ANGELS
UK, male vocal / instrumental group (2 WEEKS) pos/wks

| 21 Jan 84 | INDEPENDENCE DAY *Jive JIVE 54*........ | 75 | 1 |
| 4 Feb 84 | INDEPENDENCE DAY (re-entry) *Jive JIVE 54*........ | 71 | 1 |

CON FUNK SHUN
US, male vocal / instrumental group (2 WEEKS) pos/wks

| 19 Jul 86 | BURNIN' LOVE *Club JAB 32*........ | 68 | 2 |

CONCEPT
US, male vocalist / instrumentalist - keyboards (6 WEEKS) pos/wks

| 14 Dec 85 | MR DJ *Fourth & Broadway BRW 40*........ | 27 | 6 |

CONDUCTOR & THE COWBOY
UK, male production duo (2 WEEKS) pos/wks

| 20 May 00 | FEELING THIS WAY *Serious SERR 016CD*........ | 35 | 2 |

CONFEDERATES – See Elvis COSTELLO

CONGREGATION *UK, male / female choir (14 WEEKS)* pos/wks

| 27 Nov 71 ● | SOFTLY WHISPERING I LOVE YOU *Columbia DB 8830*........ | 4 | 14 |

CONGRESS
UK, male / female vocal / instrumental group (4 WEEKS) pos/wks

| 26 Oct 91 | 40 MILES *Inner Rhythm 7HEART 01*........ | 26 | 4 |

Arthur CONLEY *US, male vocalist (15 WEEKS)* pos/wks

| 27 Apr 67 ● | SWEET SOUL MUSIC *Atlantic 584 083*........ | 7 | 14 |
| 10 Apr 68 | FUNKY STREET *Atlantic 583 175*........ | 46 | 1 |

CONNELLS
US, male vocal / instrumental group (11 WEEKS) pos/wks

12 Aug 95	74-75 *TVT LONCD 369*	14	8
16 Mar 96	74-75 (re-entry) *TVT LONCD 369*	21	3

Harry CONNICK Jr
US, male vocalist (11 WEEKS) pos/wks

25 May 91	RECIPE FOR LOVE / IT HAD TO BE YOU *Columbia 6568907*	32	6
3 Aug 91	WE ARE IN LOVE *Columbia 6572847*	62	2
23 Nov 91	BLUE LIGHT RED LIGHT (SOMEONE'S THERE) *Columbia 6575367*	54	3

Billy CONNOLLY
UK, male comedian / vocalist / instrumentalist (31 WEEKS) pos/wks

1 Nov 75	★ D.I.V.O.R.C.E. *Polydor 2058 652*	1	10
17 Jul 76	NO CHANCE (NO CHARGE) *Polydor 2058 748*	24	5
25 Aug 79	IN THE BROWNIES *Polydor 2059 160*	38	7
9 Mar 85	SUPER GRAN *Stiff BUY 218*	32	9

CONQUERING LION
UK, male vocal group (1 WEEK) pos/wks

8 Oct 94	CODE RED *Mango CIDM 821*	53	1

Leena CONQUEST and HIP HOP FINGER
US, female vocalist (1 WEEK) pos/wks

18 Jun 94	BOUNDARIES *BOUNDARIES*	67	1

Jess CONRAD
UK, male vocalist (13 WEEKS) pos/wks

30 Jun 60	CHERRY PIE *Decca F 1123*	39	1
26 Jan 61	MYSTERY GIRL *Decca F 11315*	44	1
9 Feb 61	MYSTERY GIRL (re-entry) *Decca F 11315*	18	9
11 Oct 62	PRETTY JENNY *Decca F 11511*	50	2

CONSORTIUM
UK, male vocal group (9 WEEKS) pos/wks

12 Feb 69	ALL THE LOVE IN THE WORLD *Pye 7N 17635*	22	9

Ann CONSUELO – See SUBTERRANIA featuring Ann CONSUELO

CONTOURS
US, male vocal group (6 WEEKS) pos/wks

24 Jan 70	JUST A LITTLE MISUNDERSTANDING *Tamla Motown TMG 723*	31	6

CONTRABAND
Germany / US, male / female vocal / instrumental group (2 WEEKS) pos/wks

20 Jul 91	ALL THE WAY FROM MEMPHIS *Impact American EM 195*	65	2

CONTROL
UK, male / female vocal / instrumental group (5 WEEKS) pos/wks

2 Nov 91	DANCE WITH ME *All around the World GLOBE 105*	17	5

CONVERT
Belgium, male instrumental / production duo (7 WEEKS) pos/wks

11 Jan 92	NIGHTBIRD *A & M AM 845*	39	4
29 May 93	ROCKIN' TO THE RHYTHM *A & M 5802532*	42	2
31 Jan 98	NIGHTBIRD (re-issue) *Wonderboy WBOYD 008*	45	1

CONWAY BROTHERS
US, male vocal group (10 WEEKS) pos/wks

22 Jun 85	TURN IT UP *10 TEN 57*	11	10

Russ CONWAY `107` **Top 500**
Popular pianist and composer. b. Trevor Stanford, 2 Sep 1925, Bristol, d. 2000. Against the trends of the day this MOR piano player was the UK's top-selling artist in 1959 (178 WEEKS) pos/wks

29 Nov 57	PARTY POPS *Columbia DB 4031*	24	5
29 Aug 58	GOT A MATCH *Columbia DB 4166*	30	1
28 Nov 58	● MORE PARTY POPS *Columbia DB 4204*	10	7
23 Jan 59	THE WORLD OUTSIDE *Columbia DB 4234*	24	1
20 Feb 59	★ SIDE SADDLE *Columbia DB 4256*	1	30
6 Mar 59	THE WORLD OUTSIDE (re-entry) *Columbia DB 4234*	24	3
15 May 59	★ ROULETTE *Columbia DB 4298*	1	19

21 Aug 59	● CHINA TEA *Columbia DB 4337*	5	13
13 Nov 59	● SNOW COACH *Columbia DB 4368*	7	9
20 Nov 59	● MORE AND MORE PARTY POPS *Columbia DB 4373*	5	8
5 Mar 60	ROYAL EVENT *Columbia DB 4418*	15	7
21 Apr 60	FINGS AIN'T WOT THEY USED T'BE *Columbia DB 4422*	47	1
19 May 60	LUCKY FIVE *Columbia DB 4457*	14	9
29 Sep 60	PASSING BREEZE *Columbia DB 4508*	16	10
24 Nov 60	EVEN MORE PARTY POPS *Columbia DB 4535*	27	9
19 Jan 61	PEPE *Columbia DB 4564*	19	9
25 May 61	PABLO *Columbia DB 4649*	45	2
24 Aug 61	SAY IT WITH FLOWERS *Columbia DB 4665* [1]	23	10
30 Nov 61	● TOY BALLOONS *Columbia DB 4738*	7	11
22 Feb 62	LESSON ONE *Columbia DB 4784*	21	7
29 Nov 62	ALWAYS YOU AND ME *Columbia DB 4934*	33	4
3 Jan 63	ALWAYS YOU AND ME (re-entry) *Columbia DB 4934*	35	3

[1] Dorothy Squires and Russ Conway

'Always You and Me' featured Russ Conway talking as well as playing piano. Several of the discs were medleys as follows: Party Pops: When You're Smiling / I'm Looking over a Four-Leafed Clover / When You Wore a Tulip / Row Row Row / For Me and My Girl / Shine on Harvest Moon / By the Light of the Silvery Moon / Side By Side. More Party Pops: Music Music Music / If You Were the Only Girl in the World / Nobody's Sweetheart / Yes Sir That's My Baby / Some of these Days / Honeysuckle and the Bee / Hello Hello Who's Your Lady Friend / Shanty in Old Shanty Town. More and More Party Pops: Sheik of Araby / Who Were You With Last Night / Any Old Iron / Tiptoe Through the Tulips / If You Were the Only Girl in the World / When I Leave the World Behind. Even More Party Pops: Ain't She Sweet / I Can't Give You Anything But Love / Yes We Have No Bananas / I May Be Wrong / Happy Days And Lonely Nights / Glad Rag Doll

Martin COOK – See Richard DENTON and Martin COOK

Norman COOK
UK, male producer / multi-instrumentalist (10 WEEKS) pos/wks

8 Jul 89	WON'T TALK ABOUT IT / BLAME IT ON THE BASSLINE *Go.Beat GOD 33* [1]	29	6
21 Oct 89	FOR SPACIOUS LIES *Go.Beat GOD 37* [2]	48	4

[1] Norman Cook featuring Billy Bragg / Norman Cook featuring MC Wildski [2] Norman Cook featuring Lester

See also FATBOY SLIM; FREAKPOWER; MIGHTY DUB KATZ; PIZZAMAN; BEATS INTERNATIONAL; HOUSEMARTINS

Peter COOK
UK, male comedian / vocalist (15 WEEKS) pos/wks

17 Jun 65	GOODBYE-EE *Decca F 12158* [1]	18	10
15 Jul 65	THE BALLAD OF SPOTTY MULDOON *Decca F 12182*	34	5

[1] Peter Cook and Dudley Moore

Brandon COOKE featuring Roxanne SHANTE
UK, male producer and US, female rapper (3 WEEKS) pos/wks

29 Oct 88	SHARP AS A KNIFE *Club JAB 73*	45	3

See also Roxanne SHANTE

Sam COOKE `395` **Top 500**
Gospel great turned soul superstar. b. 22 Jan 1931, Mississippi, US, d. 11 Dec 1964. Former leader of the Soul Stirrers and transatlantic hitmaker. Acclaimed singer / songwriter who influenced many R&B and pop vocalists including Otis Redding and Rod Stewart (82 WEEKS) pos/wks

17 Jan 58	YOU SEND ME *London HLU 8506* ▲	29	1
14 Aug 59	ONLY SIXTEEN *HMV POP 642*	23	4
7 Jul 60	WONDERFUL WORLD *HMV POP 754*	27	8
29 Sep 60	● CHAIN GANG *RCA 1202*	9	11
27 Jul 61	● CUPID *RCA 1242*	7	14
8 Mar 62	TWISTIN' THE NIGHT AWAY *RCA 1277*	6	14
16 May 63	ANOTHER SATURDAY NIGHT *RCA 1341*	23	12
5 Sep 63	FRANKIE AND JOHNNY *RCA 1361*	30	6
22 Mar 86	● WONDERFUL WORLD (re-issue) *RCA PB 49871*	2	11
10 May 86	ANOTHER SATURDAY NIGHT (re-issue) *RCA PB 49849*	75	1

COOKIE CREW UK, female rap duo (31 WEEKS) pos/wks

9 Jan 88 ●	ROK DA HOUSE Rhythm King LEFT 11 [1]	5	11
7 Jan 89	BORN THIS WAY (LET'S DANCE) ffrr FFR 19	23	5
1 Apr 89	GOT TO KEEP ON ffrr FFR 25	17	9
15 Jul 89	COME AND GET SOME ffrr F 110	42	3
27 Jul 91	SECRETS (OF SUCCESS) ffrr F159 [2]	53	3

[1] Beatmasters featuring the Cookie Crew [2] Cookie Crew featuring Danny D

COOKIES US, female vocal group (1 WEEK) pos/wks

10 Jan 63	CHAINS London HLU 9634	50	1

COOL DOWN ZONE
UK, male / female vocal / instrumental group (4 WEEKS) pos/wks

30 Jun 90	HEAVEN KNOWS 10 TEN 309	52	4

COOL JACK Italy, male instrumental / production duo (1 WEEK) pos/wks

9 Nov 96	JUS' COME AM:PM 5819892	44	1

COOL, the FAB, and the GROOVY present Quincy JONES UK, male production duo, US, male band, and US male producer / instrumentalist (1 WEEK) pos/wks

1 Aug 98	SOUL BOSSA NOVA Manifesto FESCD 48	47	1

Rita COOLIDGE US, female vocalist (24 WEEKS) pos/wks

25 Jun 77 ●	WE'RE ALL ALONE A & M AMS 7295	6	13
15 Oct 77	(YOUR LOVE HAS LIFTED ME) HIGHER AND HIGHER A & M AMS 7315	49	1
29 Oct 77	(YOUR LOVE HAS LIFTED ME) HIGHER AND HIGHER (re-entry) A & M AMS 7315	48	1
4 Feb 78	WORDS A & M AMS 7330	25	8
25 Jun 83	ALL TIME HIGH A & M AM 007	75	1

COOLIO US, male rapper - Artis Ivey Jr (62 WEEKS) pos/wks

23 Jul 94	FANTASTIC VOYAGE Tommy Boy TB 0617CD	41	2
15 Oct 94	I REMEMBER Tommy Boy TBXCD 635	73	1
28 Oct 95 ★	GANGSTA'S PARADISE Tommy Boy MCSTD 2104 [1] ◆ ■ ▲	1	20
20 Jan 96 ●	TOO HOT Tommy Boy TBCD 718	9	6
6 Apr 96	1234 (SUMPIN' NEW) Tommy Boy TBCD 7721	13	7
17 Aug 96	IT'S ALL THE WAY LIVE (NOW) Tommy Boy TBCD 7731	34	2
5 Apr 97 ●	HIT EM HIGH (THE MONSTARS' ANTHEM) Atlantic A 5449CD [2]	8	6
7 Jun 97	THE WINNER Atlantic A 5433CD	53	1
19 Jul 97 ●	C U WHEN U GET THERE Tommy Boy TBCD 785 [3]	3	12
11 Oct 97	OOH LA LA Tommy Boy TBCD 799	14	5

[1] Coolio featuring LV [2] B Real / Busta Rhymes / Coolio / LL Cool J / Method Man [3] Coolio featuring 40 Thevz

COOLNOTES
UK, male / female vocal / instrumental group (28 WEEKS) pos/wks

18 Aug 84	YOU'RE NEVER TOO YOUNG Abstract Dance AD 1	42	5
17 Nov 84	I FORGOT Abstract Dance AD 2	63	2
23 Mar 85	SPEND THE NIGHT Abstract Dance AD 3	11	9
13 Jul 85	IN YOUR CAR Abstract Dance AD 4	13	9
19 Oct 85	HAVE A GOOD FOREVER Abstract Dance AD 5	73	1
17 May 86	INTO THE MOTION Abstract Dance AD 8	66	2

COOLY'S HOT BOX – See Roger SANCHEZ

Alice COOPER (281 Top 500) The alter ego of shock-rock vocalist Vincent Furnier, b. 4 Feb 1948, Detroit, US. Transatlantic chart-topper whose group was voted World's Top Band in 1972 in UK. Renowned for onstage shock-horror theatrics (104 WEEKS) pos/wks

15 Jul 72 ★	SCHOOL'S OUT Warner Bros. K 16188	1	12
7 Oct 72 ●	ELECTED Warner Bros. K 16214	4	10
10 Feb 73 ●	HELLO HURRAY Warner Bros. K 16248	6	12
21 Apr 73 ●	NO MORE MR NICE GUY Warner Bros. K 16262	10	10
19 Jan 74	TEENAGE LAMENT 74 Warner Bros. K 16345	12	7

21 May 77	(NO MORE) LOVE AT YOUR CONVENIENCE Warner Bros. K 16935	44	2
23 Dec 78	HOW YOU GONNA SEE ME NOW Warner Bros. K 17270	61	6
6 Mar 82	SEVEN AND SEVEN IS (live version) Warner Bros. K 17924	62	3
8 May 82	FOR BRITAIN ONLY / UNDER MY WHEELS Warner Bros. K 17940	66	2
18 Oct 86	HE'S BACK (THE MAN BEHIND THE MASK) MCA MCA 1090	61	2
9 Apr 88	FREEDOM MCA MCA 1241	50	3
29 Jul 89 ●	POISON Epic 655061 7	2	11
7 Oct 89	BED OF NAILS Epic ALICE 3	38	5
2 Dec 89	HOUSE OF FIRE Epic ALICE 4	65	2
22 Jun 91	HEY STOOPID Epic 656983 7	21	6
5 Oct 91	LOVE'S A LOADED GUN Epic 6574387	38	3
6 Jun 92	FEED MY FRANKENSTEIN Epic 6580927	27	3
28 May 94	LOST IN AMERICA Epic 6603472	22	3
23 Jul 94	IT'S ME Epic 6605632	34	2

For the first five hits, 'Alice Cooper' was the name of the entire group, not just of the lead vocalist

Deborah COOPER – See C & C MUSIC FACTORY / CLIVILLES & COLE

Tommy COOPER UK, male comedian / vocalist (3 WEEKS) pos/wks

29 Jun 61	DON'T JUMP OFF THE ROOF DAD Palette PG 9019	40	2
20 Jul 61	DON'T JUMP OFF THE ROOF DAD (re-entry) Palette PG 9019	50	1

Julian COPE UK, male vocalist (59 WEEKS) pos/wks

19 Nov 83	SUNSHINE PLAYROOM Mercury COPE 1	64	1
31 Mar 84	THE GREATNESS AND PERFECTION OF LOVE Mercury MER 155	52	5
27 Sep 86	WORLD SHUT YOUR MOUTH Island IS 290	19	9
17 Jan 87	TRAMPOLENE Island IS 305	31	6
11 Apr 87	EVE'S VOLCANO (COVERED IN SIN) Island IS 318	41	5
24 Sep 88	CHARLOTTE ANNE Island IS 380	35	6
21 Jan 89	5 O'CLOCK WORLD Island IS 399	42	4
24 Jun 89	CHINA DOLL Island IS 406	53	2
9 Feb 91	BEAUTIFUL LOVE Island IS 483	32	6
20 Apr 91	EAST EASY RIDER Island IS 492	51	3
3 Aug 91	HEAD Island IS 497	57	2
8 Aug 92	WORLD SHUT YOUR MOUTH (re-issue) Island IS 534	44	3
17 Oct 92	FEAR LOVES THIS PLACE Island IS 545	42	2
12 Aug 95	TRY TRY TRY Echo ECSCD 11	24	3
27 Jul 96	I COME FROM ANOTHER PLANET BABY Echo ECSCD 22	34	2
5 Oct 96	PLANETARY SIT-IN (EVERY GIRL HAS YOUR NAME) Echo ECSCD 25	34	1

Imani COPPOLA US, female vocalist / instrumentalist (3 WEEKS) pos/wks

28 Feb 98	LEGEND OF A COWGIRL Columbia 6656015	32	3

Harry H CORBETT – See Wilfrid BRAMBELL and Harry H CORBETT

Frank CORDELL UK, orchestra (4 WEEKS) pos/wks

24 Aug 56	SADIE'S SHAWL HMV POP 229	29	2
16 Feb 61	BLACK BEAR HMV POP 824	44	2

Louise CORDET UK, female vocalist (13 WEEKS) pos/wks

5 Jul 62	I'M JUST A BABY Decca F 11476	13	13

Chris CORNELL US, male vocalist (1 WEEK) pos/wks

23 Oct 99	CAN'T CHANGE ME A&M 4971732	62	1

See also SOUNDGARDEN

Don CORNELL US, male vocalist - Luigi Varlaro (23 WEEKS) pos/wks

3 Sep 54 ★	HOLD MY HAND Vogue Q 2013	1	21
22 Apr 55	STRANGER IN PARADISE Vogue Q 72073	19	2

Lynn CORNELL UK, female vocalist (9 WEEKS) pos/wks

20 Oct 60	NEVER ON SUNDAY Decca F 11277	30	9

SINGLED OUT...
Davina McCall

Brit Awards host and presenter of probably the most talked-about TV show in 2000, 'Big Brother', Davina's music collection does not include anything by The Tweets.

- **NO.1 ON THE UK SINGLES CHART THE DAY I WAS BORN:**
  Massachusetts – Bee Gees

- **ALL-TIME FAVOURITE SINGLE:**
  Sugarhill Rap – The Sugarhill Gang

  [Don't you mean Rapper's Delight? – Ed]

  Still sounds great. Been sampled endlessly by bands ... I spent weeks and weeks learning all the words.

- **SINGLE THAT DRIVES ME UP THE WALL:**
  The Birdie Song – The Tweets

  Yuck. It makes me want to vomit.

FIRST SINGLE I EVER BOUGHT:

Oliver's Army
Elvis Costello

I think Elvis C is king. It was one of those must-have records. Heard it on the radio and had to go and get it straight away. I only just had enough money!

Photos: Pictorial Press

CORNERSHOP UK, male vocal / instrumental duo (16 WEEKS)

			pos/wks
30 Aug 97	BRIMFUL OF ASHA Wiiija WIJ 75CD	60	1
28 Feb 98 ★	BRIMFUL OF ASHA (re-mix) Wiiija WIJ 81CD ■	1	12
16 May 98	SLEEP ON THE LEFT SIDE Wiiija WIJ 80CD	23	3

Charlotte CORNWELL – See Julie COVINGTON, Rula LENSKA, Charlotte CORNWELL and Sue JONES-DAVIES

Hugh CORNWELL
UK, male vocalist / instrumentalist - guitar (3 WEEKS)

			pos/wks
24 Jan 87	FACTS + FIGURES Virgin VS 922	61	2
7 May 88	ANOTHER KIND OF LOVE Virgin VS 945	71	1

See also STRANGLERS

CO-RO featuring TARLISA
Germany, male / female vocal / production group (1 WEEK)

			pos/wks
12 Dec 92	BECAUSE THE NIGHT ZYX ZYX 68227	61	1

CORONA Brazil, male producer and female vocalist - Francesco Bontempi and Olga De Souza (44 WEEKS)

			pos/wks
10 Sep 94 ●	THE RHYTHM OF THE NIGHT WEA YZ 837CD1	2	14
31 Dec 94	THE RHYTHM OF THE NIGHT (re-entry) WEA YZ 837CD1	55	4
8 Apr 95 ●	BABY BABY Eternal YZ 919CD	5	8
22 Jul 95 ●	TRY ME OUT Eternal YZ 955CD	6	10
23 Dec 95	I DON'T WANNA BE A STAR Eternal WEA 029CD	22	6
22 Feb 97	MEGAMIX Eternal WEA 092CD	36	2

CORONATION STREET CAST featuring Bill WADDINGTON
UK, male / female vocal group (3 WEEKS)

			pos/wks
16 Dec 95	ALWAYS LOOK ON THE BRIGHT SIDE OF LIFE EMI Premier CDEMS 411	35	3

The listed flip side of 'Always Look on the Bright Side of Life' was 'Something Stupid' by Amanda Barrie and Johnny Briggs

CORONETS UK, male / female vocal group (7 WEEKS)

			pos/wks
26 Aug 55	THAT'S HOW A LOVE SONG WAS BORN Columbia DB 3640 [1]	14	6
25 Nov 55	TWENTY TINY FINGERS Columbia DB 3671	20	1

[1] Ray Burns with the Coronets

Briana CORRIGAN UK, female vocalist (2 WEEKS)

			pos/wks
11 May 96	LOVE ME NOW East West EW 041CD1	48	2

See also BEAUTIFUL SOUTH

CORRS (386 Top 500)
Internationally successful Irish sisters and brother group: Andrea, Caroline, Sharon and Jim Corr. Quartet, which has sold more than five million albums in UK, was voted Best International Group at the 1996 Brit awards. 'Talk On Corners' was top UK album in 1998 (83 WEEKS)

			pos/wks
17 Feb 96	RUNAWAY Atlantic A 5727CD	49	2
7 Dec 96	RUNAWAY (re-entry) Atlantic A 5727CD	60	1
1 Feb 97	LOVE TO LOVE YOU / RUNAWAY (re-issue) Atlantic A 5621CD	62	1
25 Oct 97	ONLY WHEN I SLEEP Atlantic AT 0015CD	58	1
20 Dec 97	I NEVER LOVED YOU ANYWAY Atlantic AT 0018CD	43	2
28 Mar 98	WHAT CAN I DO Atlantic AT 0029CD	53	1
16 May 98 ●	DREAMS Atlantic AT 0032CD	6	10
29 Aug 98 ●	WHAT CAN I DO (re-mix) Atlantic AT 0044CD	3	11
28 Nov 98 ●	SO YOUNG Atlantic AT 0057CD1	6	13
27 Feb 99 ●	RUNAWAY (re-mix) Atlantic AT 0062CD	2	11
12 Jun 99	I KNOW MY LOVE RCA Victor 74321670622 [1]	37	3
11 Dec 99	RADIO Atlantic AT 0079CD	18	1
15 Jul 00 ★	BREATHLESS Atlantic AT 0084CD ■	1	13
11 Nov 00	IRRESISTIBLE Atlantic AT 0089CD	20	5

[1] Chieftains featuring The Corrs

Ferry CORSTEN – See SYSTEM F; VERACOCHA; ALBION; GOURYELLA; MOONMAN

Vladimir COSMA Hungary, orchestra (1 WEEK)

			pos/wks
14 Jul 79	DAVID'S SONG (MAIN THEME FROM 'KIDNAPPED') Decca FR 13841	64	1

COSMIC BABY Germany, male producer (1 WEEK)

			pos/wks
26 Feb 94	LOOPS OF INFINITY Logic 74321191432	70	1

COSMOS UK, male production / instrumental duo (1 WEEK)

			pos/wks
18 Sep 99	SUMMER IN SPACE Island Blue PFACD 3	49	1

Don COSTA US, orchestra (10 WEEKS)

			pos/wks
13 Oct 60	NEVER ON SUNDAY London HLT 9195	27	9
22 Dec 60	NEVER ON SUNDAY (re-entry) London HLT 9195	41	1

Elvis COSTELLO (106 Top 500)
Acclaimed singer / songwriter, b. Declan McManus, 25 Aug 1955, Liverpool. He emerged during punk explosion of 1976, but was soon accepted as a mainstream artist. Has clocked up 12 US Top 40 albums (179 WEEKS)

			pos/wks
5 Nov 77	WATCHING THE DETECTIVES Stiff BUY 20	15	11
11 Mar 78	(I DON'T WANT TO GO TO) CHELSEA Radar ADA 3 [1]	16	10
13 May 78	PUMP IT UP Radar ADA 10 [1]	24	10
28 Oct 78	RADIO RADIO Radar ADA 24 [1]	29	7
10 Feb 79 ●	OLIVER'S ARMY Radar ADA 31 [1]	2	12
12 May 79	ACCIDENTS WILL HAPPEN Radar ADA 35 [1]	28	8
16 Feb 80 ●	I CAN'T STAND UP FOR FALLING DOWN F. Beat XX 1	4	8
12 Apr 80	HI FIDELITY F. Beat XX 3	30	5
7 Jun 80	NEW AMSTERDAM F. Beat XX 5	36	4
20 Dec 80	CLUBLAND F. Beat XX 12	60	4
3 Oct 81 ●	A GOOD YEAR FOR THE ROSES F. Beat XX 17	6	11
12 Dec 81	SWEET DREAMS F. Beat XX 19	42	8
10 Apr 82	I'M YOUR TOY F. Beat XX 21 [2]	51	3
19 Jun 82	YOU LITTLE FOOL F. Beat XX 26	52	3
31 Jul 82	MAN OUT OF TIME F. Beat XX 28	58	2
25 Sep 82	FROM HEAD TO TOE F. Beat XX 30	43	4
11 Dec 82	PARTY PARTY A & M AMS 8267 [3]	48	6
11 Jun 83	PILLS AND SOAP Imp IMP 001 [4]	16	4
9 Jul 83	EVERYDAY I WRITE THE BOOK F. Beat XX 32	28	8
17 Sep 83	LET THEM ALL TALK F. Beat XX 33	59	2
28 Apr 84	PEACE IN OUR TIME Imposter TRUCE 1 [4]	48	3
16 Jun 84	I WANNA BE LOVED / TURNING THE TOWN RED F. Beat XX 35	25	6
25 Aug 84	THE ONLY FLAME IN TOWN F. Beat XX 37	71	2
4 May 85	GREEN SHIRT F. Beat ZB 40085	71	1
18 May 85	GREEN SHIRT (re-entry) F. Beat ZB 40085	68	1
1 Feb 86	DON'T LET ME BE MISUNDERSTOOD F. Beat ZB 40555 [5]	33	4
30 Aug 86	TOKYO STORM WARNING Imp IMP 007	73	1
4 Mar 89	VERONICA Warner Bros. W 7558	31	6
20 May 89	BABY PLAYS AROUND (EP) Warner Bros. W 2949	65	1
4 May 91	THE OTHER SIDE OF SUMMER Warner Bros. W 0025	43	4
5 Mar 94	SULKY GIRL Warner Bros. W 0234CD [1]	22	3
30 Apr 94	13 STEPS LEAD DOWN Warner Bros. W 0245CD [1]	59	1
26 Nov 94	LONDON'S BRILLIANT PARADE Warner Bros. W 0270CD1 [1]	48	2
11 May 96	IT'S TIME Warner Bros. W 0348CD [1]	58	1
1 May 99	TOLEDO Mercury 8709652 [6]	72	1
31 Jul 99	SHE Mercury MERCD 521	19	8
9 Oct 99	SHE (re-entry) Mercury MERCD 521	57	2

[1] Elvis Costello and the Attractions [2] Elvis Costello and the Attractions with the Royal Philharmonic Orchestra [3] Elvis Costello and the Attractions with the Royal Horn Guards [4] Imposter [5] The Costello Show featuring the Confederates [6] Elvis Costello / Burt Bacharach

Tracks on Baby Plays Around (EP): Baby Plays Around / Poisoned Rose / Almost Blue / My Funny Valentine

COTTAGERS – See Tony REES and the COTTAGERS

Billy COTTON and his BAND UK, male bandleader / vocalist, with band and chorus (25 WEEKS)

			pos/wks
1 May 53 ●	IN A GOLDEN COACH (THERE'S A HEART OF GOLD) Decca F 10058 [1]	3	10

SINGLED OUT... Chris Rea

No surprise that ace guitarist Chris Rea chooses hits that reflect his own love affair with the instrument. The gravel-voiced six-string stalwart counts Ry Cooder and Joe Walsh among his inspirations, in addition to Hank, Eric and Pete who are name-checked here.

•**NO.1 SONG ON THE THE DAY I WAS BORN:**
The Tennessee Waltz – Patti Page

•**FIRST SINGLE I EVER BOUGHT:**
FBI – The Shadows

The sound of the guitars and the general atmosphere blew me away.

•**SINGLE THAT DRIVES ME UP THE WALL:**
Let Me Entertain You – Robbie Williams

It sounds too too much like the Who. I'm surprised Pete Townshend didn't complain!

ALL-TIME FAVOURITE SINGLE:
Badge – Cream

It was the first single of that kind, way ahead of everyone else. It incorporated a "live" sound approach, with two separate parts. Eric's playing was unique compared with anything else around

Photo: Pictorial Press

Photo: Pictorial Press

CRAIG UK, male vocalist (2 WEEKS)

		pos/wks
23 Dec 00	AT THIS TIME OF YEAR *WEA WEA 321CD*..................................14 2+	

Robbie CRAIG – See ARTFUL DODGER

Floyd CRAMER US, male instrumentalist - piano (24 WEEKS)

		pos/wks
13 Apr 61	★ ON THE REBOUND *RCA 1231* 1 14	
20 Jul 61	SAN ANTONIO ROSE *RCA 1241* 36 8	
23 Aug 62	HOT PEPPER *RCA 1301* 46 2	

CRAMPS US, male / female vocal / instrumental group (4 WEEKS) pos/wks

9 Nov 85	CAN YOUR PUSSY DO THE DOG? *Big Beat NS 110* 68 1	
10 Feb 90	BIKINI GIRLS WITH MACHINE GUNS *Enigma ENV 17* 35 3	

CRANBERRIES
Ireland, male / female vocal / instrumental group (50 WEEKS) pos/wks

27 Feb 93	LINGER *Island CID 556* 74 1	
12 Feb 94	LINGER (re-issue) *Island CID 559* 14 11	
7 May 94	DREAMS *Island CIDX 594* 27 5	
1 Oct 94	ZOMBIE *Island CID 600* 14 6	
3 Dec 94	ODE TO MY FAMILY *Island CIDX 601* 26 6	
11 Mar 95	I CAN'T BE WITH YOU *Island CID 605* 23 5	
12 Aug 95	RIDICULOUS THOUGHTS *Island CID 616*.....................20 3	
20 Apr 96	SALVATION *Island CID 633* 13 5	
13 Jul 96	FREE TO DECIDE *Island CID 637* 33 3	
17 Apr 99	PROMISES *Island US / Mercury 5725912* 13 4	
17 Jul 99	ANIMAL INSTINCT *Island US / Mercury 5621972* 54 1	

Les CRANE US, male vocalist (14 WEEKS)

		pos/wks
19 Feb 72	● DESIDERATA *Warner Bros. K 16119*...........................7 14	

Whitfield CRANE – See ICE-T; MOTORHEAD

CRANES UK, male / female vocal / instrumental group (2 WEEKS) pos/wks

25 Sep 93	JEWEL *Dedicated CRANE 007CD*.................................29 1	
3 Sep 94	SHINING ROAD *Dedicated CRANE 008CD1*.......................57 1	

CRASH TEST DUMMIES
Canada, male / female vocal / instrumental group (20 WEEKS) pos/wks

23 Apr 94	● MMM MMM MMM MMM *RCA 74321201512*............................2 11	
16 Jul 94	AFTERNOONS & COFFEESPOONS *RCA 74321219622*...............23 5	
15 Apr 95	THE BALLAD OF PETER PUMPKINHEAD *RCA 74321276772* [1] 30 4	

[1] Crash Test Dummies featuring Ellen Reid

Beverley CRAVEN UK, female vocalist (33 WEEKS)

		pos/wks
20 Apr 91	● PROMISE ME *Epic 6559437*..3 13	
20 Jul 91	HOLDING ON *Epic 6565507* 32 7	
5 Oct 91	WOMAN TO WOMAN *Epic 6574647* 40 5	
7 Dec 91	MEMORIES *Epic 6576617* 68 2	
25 Sep 93	LOVE SCENES *Epic 6595952*............................34 4	
20 Nov 93	MOLLIE'S SONG *Epic 6598132* 61 2	

Billy CRAWFORD US, male vocalist (2 WEEKS)

		pos/wks
10 Oct 98	URGENTLY IN LOVE *V2 VVR 5003063* 48 2	

Jimmy CRAWFORD UK, male vocalist (11 WEEKS)

		pos/wks
8 Jun 61	LOVE OR MONEY *Columbia DB 4633*...........................49 1	
16 Nov 61	I LOVE HOW YOU LOVE ME *Columbia DB 4717* 18 10	

Michael CRAWFORD
UK, male vocalist - Michael Dumble-Smith (14 WEEKS) pos/wks

10 Jan 87	● THE MUSIC OF THE NIGHT *Polydor POSP 803*...................7 11	
15 Jan 94	THE MUSIC OF THE NIGHT *Columbia 6597382* [1] 54 3	

[1] Barbra Streisand (duet with Michael Crawford)

The flip side of POSP 803 - 'Wishing You Were Somehow Here Again' by Sarah
Brightman - was also listed

Randy CRAWFORD (451) **Top 500** *Soulful jazz-slanted song stylist - b.*
18 Feb 1952, Georgia, US. Has surprisingly proved more successful in
Europe than her homeland, where she has yet to crack the pop Top 100.
Winner of Brit's Best Female Artist award in 1982 (75 WEEKS) pos/wks

21 Jun 80	LAST NIGHT AT DANCELAND *Warner Bros. K 17631*.........61 2	
30 Aug 80	● ONE DAY I'LL FLY AWAY *Warner Bros. K 17680*...............2 11	
30 May 81	YOU MIGHT NEED SOMEBODY *Warner Bros. K 17803* 11 13	
8 Aug 81	RAINY NIGHT IN GEORGIA *Warner Bros. K 17840*..........18 9	
31 Oct 81	SECRET COMBINATION *Warner Bros. K 17872*...............48 3	
30 Jan 82	IMAGINE *Warner Bros. K 17906* 60 1	
13 Feb 82	IMAGINE (re-entry) *Warner Bros. K 17906* 75 1	
5 Jun 82	ONE HELLO *Warner Bros. K 17948* 48 4	
19 Feb 83	HE REMINDS ME *Warner Bros. K 17970* 65 2	
8 Oct 83	NIGHT LINE *Warner Bros. W 9530* 51 4	
29 Nov 86	● ALMAZ *Warner Bros. W 8583* 4 17	
18 Jan 92	DIAMANTE *London LON 313* [1] 44 7	
15 Nov 97	GIVE ME THE NIGHT *WEA WEA 142CD*......................60 1	

[1] Zucchero with Randy Crawford

See also CRUSADERS

Robert CRAY BAND
US, male vocal / instrumental group (5 WEEKS) pos/wks

20 Jun 87	RIGHT NEXT DOOR (BECAUSE OF ME) *Mercury CRAY 3*.........50 4	
20 Apr 96	BABY LEE *Silvertone ORECD 81* [1] 65 1	

[1] John Lee Hooker with Robert Cray

CRAZY ELEPHANT US, male vocal group (13 WEEKS) pos/wks

21 May 69	GIMME GIMME GOOD LOVIN' *Major Minor MM 609*.............12 13	

CRAZYHEAD UK, male vocal / instrumental group (4 WEEKS) pos/wks

16 Jul 88	TIME HAS TAKEN ITS TOLL ON YOU *Food FOOD 12*.............65 2	
25 Feb 89	HAVE LOVE, WILL TRAVEL (EP) *Food SGE 2025* 68 2	

Tracks on Have Love, Will Travel (EP): Have Love Will Travel / Out on a Limb (Live) /
Baby Turpentine (Live) / Snake Eyes (Live)

CREAM UK, male vocal / instrumental group (59 WEEKS) pos/wks

20 Oct 66	WRAPPING PAPER *Reaction 591 007* 34 6	
15 Dec 66	I FEEL FREE *Reaction 591 011* 11 12	
8 Jun 67	STRANGE BREW *Reaction 591 015* 17 9	
5 Jun 68	ANYONE FOR TENNIS (THE SAVAGE SEVEN THEME)	
	Polydor 56 258 ....40 3	
9 Oct 68	SUNSHINE OF YOUR LOVE *Polydor 56 286* 25 7	
15 Jan 69	WHITE ROOM *Polydor 56 300* 28 8	
9 Apr 69	BADGE *Polydor 56 315* 18 10	
28 Oct 72	BADGE (re-issue) *Polydor 2058 285* 42 4	

See also Eric CLAPTON

CREATION UK, male vocal / instrumental group (3 WEEKS) pos/wks

7 Jul 66	MAKING TIME *Planet PLF 116* 49 1	
3 Nov 66	PAINTER MAN *Planet PLF 119* 36 2	

CREATURES
UK, male / female vocal / instrumental group (27 WEEKS) pos/wks

3 Oct 81	MAD EYED SCREAMER *Polydor POSPD 354* 24 7	
23 Apr 83	MISS THE GIRL *Wonderland SHE 1*........................21 7	
16 Jul 83	RIGHT NOW *Wonderland SHE 2*............................14 10	
14 Oct 89	STANDING THERE *Wonderland SHE 17*......................53 2	
27 Mar 99	SAY *Sioux SIOUX 6CD* 72 1	

See also SIOUXSIE and the BANSHEES

CREDIT TO THE NATION UK, male rap group (11 WEEKS) pos/wks

22 May 93	CALL IT WHAT YOU WANT *One Little Indian 94 TP7CD* 57 3	
18 Sep 93	ENOUGH IS ENOUGH *One Little Indian 79 TP7CD* [1] 56 2	
12 Mar 94	TEENAGE SENSATION *One Little Indian 124 TP7CD*...........24 3	
14 May 94	SOWING THE SEEDS OF HATRED	
	One Little Indian 134 TP7CD...........................72 1	

UK No.1 ★   UK Top 10 ●   Still on chart +   UK million seller ◆   UK entry at No.1 ■   US No.1 ▲

| 22 Jul 95 | LIAR LIAR *One Little Indian 144 TP7CD* | 60 | 1 |
| 12 Sep 98 | TACKY LOVE SONG *Chrysalis CDCHS 5097* | 60 | 1 |

[1] Chumbawamba and Credit to the Nation

CREED *US, male vocal / instrumental group (1 WEEK)*
pos/wks
| 15 Jan 00 | HIGHER *Epic 6683152* | 47 | 1 |

CREEDENCE CLEARWATER REVIVAL (319 Top 500) *Internationally successful combo who cleverly created original songs with 50s rock 'n' roll feel, fronted by John Fogerty b. 28 May 1945, California, US. Voted World's Top Group in UK Polls 1970/71 (beating The Beatles and The Rolling Stones) (94 WEEKS)*
pos/wks
28 May 69 ●	PROUD MARY *Liberty LBF 15223*	8	13
16 Aug 69 ★	BAD MOON RISING *Liberty LBF 15230*	1	15
15 Nov 69	GREEN RIVER *Liberty LBF 15250*	19	11
14 Feb 70	DOWN ON THE CORNER *Liberty LBF 15283*	31	6
4 Apr 70 ●	TRAVELLIN' BAND *Liberty LBF 15310*	8	12
20 Jun 70 ●	UP AROUND THE BEND *Liberty LBF 15354*	3	12
4 Jul 70	TRAVELLIN' BAND (re-entry) *Liberty LBF 15310*	46	1
5 Sep 70	LONG AS I CAN SEE THE LIGHT *Liberty LBF 15384*	20	9
20 Mar 71	HAVE YOU EVER SEEN THE RAIN *Liberty LBF 15440*	36	6
24 Jul 71	SWEET HITCH-HIKER *United Artists UP 35261*	36	8
2 May 92	BAD MOON RISING (re-issue) *Epic 6580047*	71	1

Kid CREOLE and the COCONUTS
US, male vocalist and female vocal group (58 WEEKS)
pos/wks
13 Jun 81	ME NO POP I *Ze WIP 6711* [1]	32	7
15 May 82 ●	I'M A WONDERFUL THING, BABY *Ze WIP 6756*	4	11
24 Jul 82	STOOL PIGEON *Ze WIP 6793*	7	9
9 Oct 82 ●	ANNIE I'M NOT YOUR DADDY *Ze WIP 6801*	2	8
11 Dec 82	DEAR ADDY *Ze WIP 6840*	29	7
10 Sep 83	THERE'S SOMETHING WRONG IN PARADISE *Island IS 130*	35	5
19 Nov 83	THE LIFEBOAT PARTY *Island IS 142*	49	4
14 Apr 90	THE SEX OF IT *CBS 655698 7*	29	5
10 Apr 93	I'M A WONDERFUL THING BABY (re-mix) *Island CID 551*	60	2

[1] Kid Creole and the Coconuts present Coati Mundi

See also COCONUTS

CRESCENDO *UK / US, male / female vocal / instrumental duo (5 WEEKS)*
pos/wks
| 23 Dec 95 | ARE YOU OUT THERE *ffrr FCD 270* | 20 | 5 |

CREW CUTS *Canada, male vocal group (29 WEEKS)*
pos/wks
| 1 Oct 54 | SH-BOOM *Mercury MB 3140* ▲ | 12 | 9 |
| 15 Apr 55 ● | EARTH ANGEL *Mercury MB 3202* | 4 | 20 |

Bernard CRIBBINS *UK, male actor (29 WEEKS)*
pos/wks
15 Feb 62 ●	HOLE IN THE GROUND *Parlophone R 4869*	9	13
5 Jul 62 ●	RIGHT SAID FRED *Parlophone R 4923*	10	10
13 Dec 62	GOSSIP CALYPSO *Parlophone R 4961*	25	6

CRICKETS (305 Top 500) *Band that originally featured Buddy Holly formed in Lubbock, Texas, US, best known members being Jerry Allison (d), Joe B. Mauldin (b) and Sonny Curtis (g/v). Without Buddy they recorded original versions of Top 10 hits 'I Fought The Law', 'Someone Someone', 'When You Ask About Love' and 'More Than I Can Say' (97 WEEKS)*
pos/wks
27 Sep 57 ★	THAT'LL BE THE DAY *Vogue Coral Q 72279* ▲	1	14
27 Dec 57 ●	OH BOY *Coral Q 72298*	3	15
10 Jan 58	THAT'LL BE THE DAY (re-entry) *Vogue Coral Q 72279*	29	1
14 Mar 58 ●	MAYBE BABY *Coral Q 72307*	4	10
25 Jul 58	THINK IT OVER *Coral Q 72329*	11	7
24 Apr 59	LOVE'S MADE A FOOL OF YOU *Coral Q 72365*	26	1
8 May 59	LOVE'S MADE A FOOL OF YOU (re-entry) *Coral Q 72365*	30	1
15 Jan 60	WHEN YOU ASK ABOUT LOVE *Coral Q 72382*	27	1
12 May 60	MORE THAN I CAN SAY *Coral Q 72395*	42	1
26 May 60	BABY MY HEART *Coral Q 72395*	33	4
21 Jun 62 ●	DON'T EVER CHANGE *Liberty LIB 55441*	5	13
24 Jan 63	MY LITTLE GIRL *Liberty LIB 10067*	17	9

6 Jun 63	DON'T TRY TO CHANGE ME *Liberty LIB 10092*	37	4
14 May 64	YOU'VE GOT LOVE *Coral Q 72472* [1]	40	6
2 Jul 64	(THEY CALL HER) LA BAMBA *Liberty LIB 55696*	21	10

[1] Buddy Holly and the Crickets

Although not credited on the records, Buddy Holly was featured on the first four hits

CRIMINAL ELEMENT ORCHESTRA – See Wally JUMP Jr and the CRIMINAL ELEMENT

CRISPY AND COMPANY
US, male vocal / instrumental group (11 WEEKS)
pos/wks
| 16 Aug 75 | BRAZIL *Creole CR 109* | 26 | 5 |
| 27 Dec 75 | GET IT TOGETHER *Creole CR 114* | 21 | 6 |

CRITTERS *US, male vocal / instrumental group (5 WEEKS)*
pos/wks
| 30 Jun 66 | YOUNGER GIRL *London HL 10047* | 38 | 5 |

Tony CROMBIE and his ROCKETS *UK, male vocal / instrumental group, Tony Crombie - drums (2 WEEKS)*
pos/wks
| 19 Oct 56 | TEACH YOU TO ROCK / SHORT'NIN' BREAD *Columbia DB 3822* | 25 | 2 |

Bing CROSBY (308 Top 500) *The King of the Crooners. Bing released 2,500 tracks, 299 of which reached the US Top 20 with estimated sales of more than 300,000,000. b. 3 May 1903, Washington, US, d.14 Oct 1977, Spain. 'White Christmas' (the most charted single in the USA) is the No.2 all-time best-seller (97 WEEKS)*
pos/wks
14 Nov 52 ●	ISLE OF INNISFREE *Brunswick 04900*	3	12
5 Dec 52 ●	ZING A LITTLE ZONG *Brunswick 04981* [1]	10	2
19 Dec 52 ●	SILENT NIGHT *Brunswick 03929*	8	2
19 Mar 54 ●	CHANGING PARTNERS *Brunswick 05244*	10	1
2 Apr 54 ●	CHANGING PARTNERS (re-entry) *Brunswick 05244*	9	1
23 Apr 54	CHANGING PARTNERS (2nd re-entry) *Brunswick 05244*	11	1
7 Jan 55	COUNT YOUR BLESSINGS *Brunswick 05339*	18	1
21 Jan 55	COUNT YOUR BLESSINGS (re-entry) *Brunswick 05339*	11	2
29 Apr 55	STRANGER IN PARADISE *Brunswick 05410*	17	2
27 Apr 56	IN A LITTLE SPANISH TOWN *Brunswick 05543*	22	3
23 Nov 56 ●	TRUE LOVE *Capitol CL 14645* [2]	4	27
24 May 57 ●	AROUND THE WORLD *Brunswick 05674*	5	15
9 Aug 75	THAT'S WHAT LIFE IS ALL ABOUT *United Artists UP 35852*	41	4
3 Dec 77 ◆	WHITE CHRISTMAS *MCA 111*	5	7
27 Nov 82 ●	PEACE ON EARTH - LITTLE DRUMMER BOY *RCA BOW 12* [3]	3	8
17 Dec 83	TRUE LOVE (re-issue) *Capitol CL 315* [2]	70	3
21 Dec 85	WHITE CHRISTMAS (re-issue) *MCA BING 1*	69	2
19 Dec 98	WHITE CHRISTMAS (2nd re-issue) *MCA MCSRD 48105*	29	4

[1] Bing Crosby and Jane Wyman [2] Bing Crosby and Grace Kelly [3] David Bowie and Bing Crosby

David CROSBY featuring Phil COLLINS
US / UK, male vocalist / instrumentalists (3 WEEKS)
pos/wks
| 15 May 93 | HERO *Atlantic A 7360* | 56 | 3 |

See also CROSBY, STILLS, NASH and YOUNG; Phil COLLINS

CROSBY, STILLS, NASH and YOUNG
US / UK / Canada, male vocal / instrumental group (12 WEEKS)
pos/wks
| 16 Aug 69 | MARRAKESH EXPRESS *Atlantic 584 283* [1] | 17 | 9 |
| 21 Jan 89 | AMERICAN DREAM *Atlantic A 9003* | 55 | 3 |

[1] Crosby, Stills and Nash

See also Stephen STILLS; Neil YOUNG; David CROSBY Featuring Phil COLLINS

CROSS *UK / US, male vocal / instrumental group (1 WEEK)*
pos/wks
| 17 Oct 87 | COWBOYS AND INDIANS *Virgin VS 1007* | 74 | 1 |

UK No.1 ★ UK Top 10 ● Still on chart + UK million seller ◆ UK entry at No.1 ■ US No.1 ▲

Christopher CROSS
US, male vocalist - Christopher Geppert (27 WEEKS) pos/wks

19 Apr 80	RIDE LIKE THE WIND *Warner Bros. K 17582*..............................69	1
14 Feb 81	SAILING *Warner Bros. K 17695* ▲ 48	6
17 Oct 81	ARTHUR'S THEME (BEST THAT YOU CAN DO) *Warner Bros. K 17847* ▲ 56	4
9 Jan 82 ●	ARTHUR'S THEME (BEST THAT YOU CAN DO) (re-entry) *Warner Bros. K 17847*..........................7	11
5 Feb 83	ALL RIGHT *Warner Bros. W 9843* 51	5

Sheryl CROW `435` `Top 500`
Multi-Grammy-winning pop singer / songwriter born 11 Feb 1962, Missouri, US. The one-time backing singer for Michael Jackson and George Harrison became first US female soloist to score six UK hits off debut LP (1993's Tuesday Night Music Club) (77 WEEKS) pos/wks

18 Jun 94	LEAVING LAS VEGAS *A & M 5806472* 66	1
5 Nov 94 ●	ALL I WANNA DO *A & M 5808452* 4	13
11 Feb 95	STRONG ENOUGH *A & M 5809212*..33	4
27 May 95	CAN'T CRY ANYMORE *A & M 5810552*..................................33	3
29 Jul 95	RUN BABY RUN *A & M 5811492*..24	4
11 Nov 95	WHAT I CAN DO FOR YOU *A & M 5812292* 43	1
21 Sep 96 ●	IF IT MAKES YOU HAPPY *A & M 5819032* 9	6
30 Nov 96	EVERYDAY IS A WINDING ROAD *A & M 5820232*................12	6
29 Mar 97	HARD TO MAKE A STAND *A & M 5821492* 22	3
12 Jul 97 ●	A CHANGE WOULD DO YOU GOOD *A & M 5822092* 8	5
18 Oct 97	HOME *A & M 0440312* 25	2
13 Dec 97	TOMORROW NEVER DIES *A & M 5824572* 12	9
12 Sep 98 ●	MY FAVORITE MISTAKE *Polydor 5827632*................................9	6
5 Dec 98	THERE GOES THE NEIGHBORHOOD *A&M 5828092* 19	7
6 Mar 99	ANYTHING BUT DOWN *A&M / Polydor 5828272* 19	4
11 Sep 99	SWEET CHILD O' MINE *Columbia 6678882*...........................30	3

CROWD
International, male / female vocal / instrumental charity assembly (11 WEEKS) pos/wks

1 Jun 85 ★	YOU'LL NEVER WALK ALONE *Spartan BRAD 1* 1	11

CROWDED HOUSE
New Zealand / Australia, male vocal / instrumental group (64 WEEKS) pos/wks

6 Jun 87	DON'T DREAM IT'S OVER *Capitol CL 438* 27	8
22 Jun 91	CHOCOLATE CAKE *Capitol CL 618*..69	2
2 Nov 91	FALL AT YOUR FEET *Capitol CL 626* 17	7
29 Feb 92 ●	WEATHER WITH YOU *Capitol CL 643* 7	9
20 Jun 92	FOUR SEASONS IN ONE DAY *Capitol CL 655* 26	5
26 Sep 92	IT'S ONLY NATURAL *Capitol CL 661* 24	4
2 Oct 93	DISTANT SUN *Capitol CDCLS 697* 19	6
20 Nov 93	NAILS IN MY FEET *Capitol CDCLS 701* 22	4
19 Feb 94	LOCKED OUT *Capitol CDCLS 707* 12	4
11 Jun 94	FINGERS OF LOVE *Capitol CDCLS 715* 25	3
24 Sep 94	PINEAPPLE HEAD *Capitol CDCLS 723* 27	3
22 Jun 96	INSTINCT *Capitol CDCLS 774* 12	4
17 Aug 96	NOT THE GIRL YOU THINK YOU ARE *Capitol CDCLS 776* 20	3
9 Nov 96	DON'T DREAM IT'S OVER (re-issue) *Capitol CDCL 780*........25	2

See also FINN; Neil FINN; Tim FINN

CROWN HEIGHTS AFFAIR
US, male vocal / instrumental group (34 WEEKS) pos/wks

19 Aug 78	GALAXY OF LOVE *Mercury 6168 801* 24	10
11 Nov 78	I'M GONNA LOVE YOU FOREVER *Mercury 6168 803* 47	4
14 Apr 79	DANCE LADY DANCE *Mercury 6168 804*..............................44	4
3 May 80 ●	YOU GAVE ME LOVE *De-Lite MER 9* 10	12
9 Aug 80	YOU'VE BEEN GONE *De-Lite MER 28* 44	4

Julee CRUISE
US, female vocalist (14 WEEKS) pos/wks

10 Nov 90 ●	FALLING *Warner Bros. W 9544* 7	11
2 Mar 91	ROCKIN' BACK INSIDE MY HEART *Warner Bros. W 0004* 66	2
11 Sep 99	IF I SURVIVE *Distinctive DISNCD 55* [1] 52	1

[1] Hybrid featuring Julee Cruise

CRUISERS – See Dave BERRY

CRUSADERS
US, male vocal / instrumental group (16 WEEKS) pos/wks

18 Aug 79 ●	STREET LIFE *MCA 513* 5	11
26 Sep 81	I'M SO GLAD I'M STANDING HERE TODAY *MCA 741* [1] 61	3
7 Apr 84	NIGHT LADIES *MCA MCA 853* 55	2

[1] Crusaders, featured vocalist Joe Cocker

Vocalist on 'Street Life' was Randy Crawford, though uncredited

CRUSH
UK, female vocal duo (3 WEEKS) pos/wks

24 Feb 96	JELLYHEAD *Telstar CDSTAS 2809* 50	2
3 Aug 96	LUV'D UP *Telstar CDSTAS 2833* 45	1

Bobby CRUSH
UK, male instrumentalist - piano (4 WEEKS) pos/wks

4 Nov 72	BORSALINO *Philips 6006 248*..37	4

CRW
Italy, male producer - Mauro Picotto (6 WEEKS) pos/wks

26 Feb 00	I FEEL LOVE *VC Recordings VCRD 63*....................................15	4
25 Nov 00	LOVIN' *VC Recordings VCRD 77*...49	2

See also Mauro PICOTTO

CRY BEFORE DAWN
Ireland, male vocal / instrumental group (2 WEEKS) pos/wks

17 Jun 89	WITNESS FOR THE WORLD *Epic GONE 3*..............................67	2

CRY OF LOVE
US, male / female vocal / instrumental group (1 WEEK) pos/wks

15 Jan 94	BAD THING *Columbia 6600462*...60	1

CRY SISCO!
UK, male producer - Barry Blue (9 WEEKS) pos/wks

2 Sep 89	AFRO DIZZI ACT *Escape AWOL 1*...42	8
20 Jan 90	AFRO DIZZI ACT (re-entry) *Escape AWOL 1*...........................70	1

See also Barry BLUE

CRYIN' SHAMES
UK, male vocal / instrumental group (7 WEEKS) pos/wks

31 Mar 66	PLEASE STAY *Decca F 12340*..26	7

CRYPT-KICKERS – See Bobby 'Boris' PICKETT and the CRYPT-KICKERS

CRYSTAL METHOD
US, male instrumental duo (4 WEEKS) pos/wks

11 Oct 97	(CAN YOU) TRIP LIKE I DO *Epic 6650862* [1] 39	2
7 Mar 98	KEEP HOPE ALIVE *Sony S2 CM 3CD*.....................................71	1
8 Aug 98	COMIN' BACK *Sony S2 CM 4CD*...73	1

[1] Filter and The Crystal Method

CRYSTAL PALACE
UK, male football team vocalists (2 WEEKS) pos/wks

12 May 90	GLAD ALL OVER / WHERE EAGLES FLY *Parkfield PMS 5019*................50	2

CRYSTALS
US, female vocal group (54 WEEKS) pos/wks

22 Nov 62	HE'S A REBEL *London HLU 9611* ▲ 19	13
20 Jun 63 ●	DA DOO RON RON *London HLU 9732* 5	16
19 Sep 63 ●	THEN HE KISSED ME *London HLU 9773* 2	14
5 Mar 64	I WONDER *London HLU 9852*...36	3
19 Oct 74	DA DOO RON RON (re-issue) *Warner Spector K 19010*........15	8

CSILLA
Hungary, female vocalist (1 WEEK) pos/wks

13 Jul 96	MAN IN THE MOON *Worx WORXCD 001* 69	1

CUBAN BOYS
UK, male / female production group (9 WEEKS) pos/wks

25 Dec 99 ●	COGNOSCENTI VS INTELLIGENTSIA *EMI CDCUBAN 001* 4	7
19 Feb 00	COGNOSCENTI VS INTELLIGENTSIA (re-entry) *EMI CDCUBAN 001* 58	2

UK No.1 ★   UK Top 10 ●   Still on chart +   UK million seller ◆   UK entry at No.1 ■   US No.1 ▲

CUBIC 22 *Belgium, male instrumental / production duo (7 WEEKS)*

		pos/wks
22 Jun 91	NIGHT IN MOTION *XL XLS 20*	15 7

See also AIRSCAPE; BLUE BAMBOO; TRANSFORMER 2

CUD *UK, male vocal / instrumental group (16 WEEKS)*

		pos/wks
19 Oct 91	OH NO WON'T DO (EP) *A & M AMB 829*	49 2
28 Mar 92	THROUGH THE ROOF *A & M AM 857*	44 2
30 May 92	RICH AND STRANGE *A & M AM 871*	24 3
15 Aug 92	PURPLE LOVE BALLOON *A & M AM 0024*	27 3
10 Oct 92	ONCE AGAIN *A & M AM 0081*	45 1
12 Feb 94	NEUROTICA *A & M 5805172*	37 2
2 Apr 94	STICKS AND STONES *A & M 5805472*	68 1
3 Sep 94	ONE GIANT LOVE *A & M 5807292*	52 2

Tracks on Oh No Won't Do (EP): Oh No Won't Do / Profession / Ariel / Price of Love

CUFFLINKS *US, male vocal group (30 WEEKS)*

		pos/wks
29 Nov 69 ●	TRACY *MCA MU 1101*	4 16
14 Mar 70 ●	WHEN JULIE COMES AROUND *MCA MU 1112*	10 14

CULT 413 Top 500
UK gothic rock stars who became US heavy rock heroes previously recorded as Southern Death Cult and Death Cult. West Yorkshire band's constant members Ian Astbury (v) and Billy Duffy (g). Group, who relocated to US in 1988, topped UK album chart with hits collection in 1993 (80 WEEKS)

		pos/wks
22 Dec 84	RESURRECTION JOE *Beggars Banquet BEG 122*	74 2
25 May 85	SHE SELLS SANCTUARY *Beggars Banquet BEG 135*	15 17
28 Sep 85	SHE SELLS SANCTUARY (re-entry) *Beggars Banquet BEG 135*	61 2
5 Oct 85	RAIN *Beggars Banquet BEG 147*	17 8
30 Nov 85	REVOLUTION *Beggars Banquet BEG 152*	30 7
28 Feb 87	LOVE REMOVAL MACHINE *Beggars Banquet BEG 182*	18 7
2 May 87	LIL' DEVIL *Beggars Banquet BEG 188*	11 7
22 Aug 87	WILD FLOWER (DOUBLE SINGLE) *Beggars Banquet BEG 195D*	24 2
29 Aug 87	WILD FLOWER *Beggars Banquet BEG 195*	30 4
1 Apr 89	FIRE WOMAN *Beggars Banquet BEG 228*	15 4
8 Jul 89	EDIE (CIAO BABY) *Beggars Banquet BEG 230*	32 5
18 Nov 89	SUN KING / EDIE (CIAO BABY) (re-issue) *Beggars Banquet BEG 235*	39 2
10 Mar 90	SWEET SOUL SISTER *Beggars Banquet BEG 241*	42 4
14 Sep 91	WILD HEARTED SON *Beggars Banquet BEG 255*	40 2
29 Feb 92	HEART OF SOUL *Beggars Banquet BEG 260*	51 1
30 Jan 93	SHE SELLS SANCTUARY (re-mix) *Beggars Banquet BEG 253CD*	15 4
8 Oct 94	COMING DOWN *Beggars Banquet BBQ 40CD*	50 1
7 Jan 95	STAR *Beggars Banquet BBQ 45CD*	65 1

Tracks on double single: Wild Flower / Love Trooper / Outlaw (live) / Horse Nation (live)

CULT JAM – See LISA LISA

CULTURE BEAT *UK / US / Germany, male / female vocal / instrumental group (46 WEEKS)*

		pos/wks
3 Feb 90	CHERRY LIPS (DER ERDBEERMUND) *Epic 6556337*	55 3
7 Aug 93 ★	MR VAIN *Epic 6594682*	1 15
6 Nov 93 ●	GOT TO GET IT *Epic 6597212*	4 11
15 Jan 94 ●	ANYTHING *Epic 6600252*	5 8
2 Apr 94	WORLD IN YOUR HANDS *Epic 6602292*	20 4
27 Jan 96	INSIDE OUT *Epic 6626562*	32 2
15 Jun 96	CRYING IN THE RAIN *Epic 6633582*	29 2
28 Sep 96	TAKE ME AWAY *Epic 6637552*	52 1

CULTURE CLUB 224 Top 500
Internationally successful London-based quartet, whose flamboyant lead singer, Boy George (b. George O'Dowd, 14 Jun 1961, Kent), attracted considerable media attention. In 1984, they won both Brit (Best Group) and Grammy Awards (Best New Artist). Original members re-formed in 1998 (119 WEEKS)

		pos/wks
18 Sep 82 ★	DO YOU REALLY WANT TO HURT ME *Virgin VS 518*	1 18
27 Nov 82 ●	TIME (CLOCK OF THE HEART) *Virgin VS 558*	3 12

		pos/wks
9 Apr 83 ●	CHURCH OF THE POISON MIND *Virgin VS 571*	2 9
17 Sep 83 ★	KARMA CHAMELEON *Virgin VS 612* ◆ ▲	1 20
10 Dec 83 ●	VICTIMS *Virgin VS 641*	3 10
24 Mar 84 ●	IT'S A MIRACLE *Virgin VS 662*	4 9
6 Oct 84 ●	THE WAR SONG *Virgin VS 694*	2 8
1 Dec 84	THE MEDAL SONG *Virgin VS 730*	32 4
5 Jan 85	THE MEDAL SONG (re-entry) *Virgin VS 730*	74 1
15 Mar 86 ●	MOVE AWAY *Virgin VS 845*	7 7
31 May 86	GOD THANK YOU WOMAN *Virgin VS 861*	31 5
31 Oct 98 ●	I JUST WANNA BE LOVED *Virgin VSCDT 1710*	4 10
7 Aug 99	YOUR KISSES ARE CHARITY *Virgin VSCDT 1736*	25 4
27 Nov 99	COLD SHOULDER / STARMAN *Virgin VSCDT 1758*	43 2

See also BOY GEORGE

Smiley CULTURE *UK, male vocalist (13 WEEKS)*

		pos/wks
15 Dec 84	POLICE OFFICER *Fashion FAD 7012*	12 10
6 Apr 85	COCKNEY TRANSLATION *Fashion FAD 7028*	71 1
13 Sep 86	SCHOOLTIME CHRONICLE *Polydor POSP 815*	59 2

LARRY CUNNINGHAM and the MIGHTY AVONS
Ireland, male vocal / instrumental group (11 WEEKS)

		pos/wks
10 Dec 64	TRIBUTE TO JIM REEVES *King KG 1016*	40 8
25 Feb 65	TRIBUTE TO JIM REEVES (re-entry) *King KG 1016*	46 3

CUPID'S INSPIRATION
UK, male vocal / instrumental group (19 WEEKS)

		pos/wks
19 Jun 68 ●	YESTERDAY HAS GONE *Nems 56 3500*	4 11
2 Oct 68	MY WORLD *Nems 56 3702*	33 8

José CURA – See Sarah BRIGHTMAN

CURE 161 Top 500
Goth rock giants: Robert Smith (v/g), Lol Tolhurst (k), Simon Gallup (b), Porl Thompson (g), Boris Williams (d), who went from UK cult heroes to stadium-packing supergroup. Voted Best Group at 1991 Brit Awards (144 WEEKS)

		pos/wks
12 Apr 80	A FOREST *Fiction FICS 10*	31 8
4 Apr 81	PRIMARY *Fiction FICS 12*	43 6
17 Oct 81	CHARLOTTE SOMETIMES *Fiction FICS 14*	44 4
24 Jul 82	HANGING GARDEN *Fiction FICS 15*	34 4
27 Nov 82	LET'S GO TO BED *Fiction FICS 17*	44 4
8 Jan 83	LET'S GO TO BED (re-entry) *Fiction FICS 17*	75 1
9 Jul 83	THE WALK *Fiction FICS 18*	12 8
29 Oct 83 ●	THE LOVE CATS *Fiction FICS 19*	7 11
7 Apr 84	THE CATERPILLAR *Fiction FICS 20*	14 7
27 Jul 85	IN BETWEEN DAYS *Fiction FICS 22*	15 10
21 Sep 85	CLOSE TO ME *Fiction FICS 23*	24 8
3 May 86	BOYS DON'T CRY *Fiction FICS 24*	22 6
18 Apr 87	WHY CAN'T I BE YOU *Fiction FICS 25*	21 6
4 Jul 87	CATCH *Fiction FICS 26*	27 6
17 Oct 87	JUST LIKE HEAVEN *Fiction FICS 27*	29 5
20 Feb 88	HOT HOT HOT!!! *Fiction FICSX 28*	45 3
22 Apr 89 ●	LULLABY *Fiction FICS 29*	5 6
2 Sep 89	LOVESONG *Fiction FICS 30*	18 6
31 Mar 90	PICTURES OF YOU *Fiction FICS 34*	24 6
29 Sep 90	NEVER ENOUGH *Fiction FICS 35*	13 5
3 Nov 90	CLOSE TO ME (re-mix) *Fiction FICS 36*	13 5
28 Mar 92 ●	HIGH *Fiction FICS 39*	8 3
11 Apr 92	HIGH (re-mix) *Fiction FICSX 41*	44 1
23 May 92 ●	FRIDAY I'M IN LOVE *Fiction FICS 42*	6 7
17 Oct 92	A LETTER TO ELISE *Fiction FICS 46*	28 2
4 May 96	THE 13TH *Fiction 5764692*	15 2
29 Jun 96	MINT CAR *Fiction FISCD 52*	31 2
14 Dec 96	GONE *Fiction FICD 53*	60 1
29 Nov 97	WRONG NUMBER *Fiction FICD 54*	62 1

CURIOSITY *UK, male vocal / instrumental group (58 WEEKS)*

		pos/wks
13 Dec 86 ●	DOWN TO EARTH *Mercury CAT 2* [1]	3 18
4 Apr 87	ORDINARY DAY *Mercury CAT 3* [1]	11 7

20 Jun 87	● MISFIT *Mercury CAT 4* [1]	7	9
19 Sep 87	FREE *Mercury CAT 5* [1]	56	2
16 Sep 89	NAME AND NUMBER *Mercury CAT 6*	14	9
25 Apr 92	● HANG ON IN THERE BABY *RCA PB 45377*	3	10
29 Aug 92	I NEED YOUR LOVIN' *RCA 74321111377*	47	2
30 Oct 93	GIMME THE SUNSHINE *RCA 74321168602*	73	1

[1] Curiosity Killed the Cat

CURLS – See Paul EVANS

Chantal CURTIS *France, female vocalist (3 WEEKS)*
pos/wks
14 Jul 79	GET ANOTHER LOVE *Pye 7P 5003*	51	3

TC CURTIS *Jamaica, male vocalist / instrumentalist (4 WEEKS)*
pos/wks
23 Feb 85	YOU SHOULD HAVE KNOWN BETTER *Hot Melt VS 754*	50	4

CURVE *UK, male / female vocal / instrumental duo (14 WEEKS)*
pos/wks
16 Mar 91	THE BLINDFOLD (EP) *Anxious ANX 27*	68	1
25 May 91	COAST IS CLEAR *Anxious ANX 30*	34	3
9 Nov 91	CLIPPED *Anxious ANX 35*	36	2
7 Mar 92	FAIT ACCOMPLI *Anxious ANXT 36*	22	3
18 Jul 92	HORROR HEAD (EP) *Anxious ANXT 38*	31	2
4 Sep 93	BLACKERTHREETRACKER (EP) *Anxious ANXCD 42*	39	2
16 May 98	COMING UP ROSES *Universal UND 80489*	51	1

Tracks on The Blindfold (EP): Ten Little Girls / I Speak Your Every Word / Blindfold / No Escape from Heaven. Tracks on Horror Head (EP): Horror Head / Falling Free / Mission from God / Today Is Not the Day. Only track available on all formats of Blackerthreetracker (EP): Missing Link

CURVED AIR
UK, male / female vocal / instrumental group (12 WEEKS)
pos/wks
7 Aug 71	● BACK STREET LUV *Warner Bros. K 16092*	4	12

CUT 'N' MOVE
Denmark, male / female vocal / instrumental group (4 WEEKS)
pos/wks
2 Oct 93	GIVE IT UP *EMI CDEM 273*	61	2
9 Sep 95	I'M ALIVE *EMI CDEM 375*	49	2

Frankie CUTLASS *US, male rapper (1 WEEK)*
pos/wks
5 Apr 97	THE CYPHER: PART 3 *Epic 6641445*	59	1

Adge CUTLER – See WURZELS

CUTTING CREW
UK / Canada, male vocal / instrumental group (37 WEEKS)
pos/wks
16 Aug 86	● (I JUST) DIED IN YOUR ARMS *Siren SIREN 21* ▲	4	12
25 Oct 86	I'VE BEEN IN LOVE BEFORE *Siren SIREN 29*	31	9
10 Jan 87	I'VE BEEN IN LOVE BEFORE (re-entry) *Siren SIREN 29*	70	1
7 Mar 87	ONE FOR THE MOCKINGBIRD *Siren SIREN 40*	52	5
21 Nov 87	I'VE BEEN IN LOVE BEFORE (re-mix) *Siren SRN 29*	24	8
22 Jul 89	(BETWEEN A) ROCK AND A HARD PLACE *Siren SRN 108*	66	2

CYBERSONIK *US, male instrumentalist / producers (1 WEEK)*
pos/wks
10 Nov 90	TECHNARCHY *Champion CHAMP 264*	73	1

CYGNUS X *Germany, male producer - A.C. Bousten (2 WEEKS)*
pos/wks
11 Mar 00	THE ORANGE THEME *Hooj Choons HOOJ 88CD*	43	2

Johnny CYMBAL *Canada, male vocalist (10 WEEKS)*
pos/wks
14 Mar 63	MR BASS MAN *London HLR 9682*	24	10

CYPRESS HILL *US, male rap group (41 WEEKS)*
pos/wks
31 Jul 93	INSANE IN THE BRAIN *Ruff House 6595332*	32	4
2 Oct 93	WHEN THE SH.. GOES DOWN *Ruff House 6596702*	19	4
11 Dec 93	I AIN'T GOIN' OUT LIKE THAT *Ruff House 6596902*	15	7
26 Feb 94	INSANE IN THE BRAIN (re-issue) *Ruff House 6601762*	21	4
7 May 94	LICK A SHOT *Ruff House 6603192*	20	3
7 Oct 95	THROW YOUR SET IN THE AIR *Ruff House 6623542*	15	3
17 Feb 96	ILLUSIONS *Columbia 6629052*	23	2
10 Oct 98	TEQUILA SUNRISE *Columbia 6664935*	23	2
10 Apr 99	DR GREENTHUMB *Columbia 6671202*	34	2
26 Jun 99	INSANE IN THE BRAIN *INCredible INCRL 17CD* [1]	19	3
29 Apr 00	(RAP) SUPERSTAR / (ROCK) SUPERSTAR *Columbia 669264 2*	13	5
16 Sep 00	HIGHLIFE / CAN'T GET THE BEST OF ME *Columbia 6697892*	35	2

[1] Jason Nevins vs Cypress Hill

Billy Ray CYRUS *US, male vocalist (18 WEEKS)*
pos/wks
25 Jul 92	● ACHY BREAKY HEART *Mercury MER 373*	3	10
10 Oct 92	COULD'VE BEEN ME *Mercury MER 378*	24	4
28 Nov 92	THESE BOOTS ARE MADE FOR WALKIN' *Mercury MER 384*	63	1
19 Dec 92	ACHY BREAKY HEART *Epic 6588837* [1]	53	3

[1] Alvin and the Chipmunks featuring Billy Ray Cyrus

CZR featuring DELANO
US, male production group & US male vocalist (1 WEEK)
pos/wks
30 Sep 00	I WANT YOU *Credence CDCRED 002*	57	1

D

Chuck D *US, male rapper (6 WEEKS)*
pos/wks
6 Jul 91	BRING THE NOISE *Island IS 490* [1]	14	5
26 Oct 96	NO *Mercury MERCD 476*	55	1

[1] Anthrax featuring Chuck D

Crissy D – See B15 Project featuring Crissy D & Lady G

Danny D – See COOKIE CREW

Dimples D *US, female rapper (10 WEEKS)*
pos/wks
17 Nov 90	SUCKER DJ *FBI FBI 11*	17	10

Longsy D *UK, male instrumentalist / producer (7 WEEKS)*
pos/wks
4 Mar 89	THIS IS SKA *Big One VBIG 13*	56	7

Nikki D *US, female rapper (6 WEEKS)*
pos/wks
6 May 89	MY LOVE IS SO RAW *Def Jam 6548987* [1]	34	5
30 Mar 91	DADDY'S LITTLE GIRL *Def Jam 6567347*	75	1

[1] Alyson Williams featuring Nikki D

Vicky D *US, female vocalist (6 WEEKS)*
pos/wks
13 Mar 82	THIS BEAT IS MINE *Virgin VS 486*	42	6

D.O.S.E. featuring Mark E Smith
UK, male production group and UK male vocalist (1 WEEK)
pos/wks
23 Mar 96	PLUG MYSELF IN *Coliseum TOGA 001CD1*	50	1

D:REAM 459 Top 500
Uplifting pop / dance act featuring Ulster-born Peter Cunnah (v) and Scotsman Al Mackenzie (k) who left 1993. 'Things Can Only Get Better'(first three-time top 30 entrant in the 1990s) used as theme for Labour Party's 1997 general election campaign (74 WEEKS)
pos/wks
4 Jul 92	U R THE BEST THING *FXU FXU 3*	72	1
30 Jan 93	THINGS CAN ONLY GET BETTER *Magnet MAG 1010CD*	24	5
24 Apr 93	U R THE BEST THING (re-issue) *Magnet MAG 1011CD*	19	8
31 Jul 93	UNFORGIVEN *Magnet MAG 1016CD*	29	3

UK No.1 ★ UK Top 10 ● Still on chart + UK million seller ◆ UK entry at No.1 ■ US No.1 ▲

DALE SISTERS US, female vocal group (6 WEEKS)

		pos/wks	
23 Nov 61	MY SUNDAY BABY *Ember S 140*	36	6

DALI'S CAR UK, male vocal / instrumental duo (2 WEEKS)

		pos/wks	
3 Nov 84	THE JUDGEMENT IS THE MIRROR *Paradox DOX 1*	66	2

Roger DALTREY UK, male vocalist (46 WEEKS)

		pos/wks	
14 Apr 73 ●	GIVING IT ALL AWAY *Track 2094 110*	5	11
4 Aug 73	I'M FREE *Ode ODS 66302*	13	10
14 May 77	WRITTEN ON THE WIND *Polydor 2121 319*	46	2
2 Aug 80	FREE ME *Polydor 2001 980*	39	6
11 Oct 80	WITHOUT YOUR LOVE *Polydor POSP 181*	55	4
3 Mar 84	WALKING IN MY SLEEP *WEA U 9686*	56	3
5 Oct 85	AFTER THE FIRE *10 TEN 69*	50	5
8 Mar 86	UNDER A RAGING MOON *10 TEN 81*	43	5

See also WHO

DAMAGE UK, male vocal group (44 WEEKS)

		pos/wks	
20 Jul 96	ANYTHING *Big Life BLRD 129*	68	1
12 Oct 96	LOVE II LOVE *Big Life BLRD 131*	12	6
14 Dec 96 ●	FOREVER *Big Life BLRD 132*	6	9
22 Mar 97 ●	LOVE GUARANTEED *Big Life BLRDA 133*	7	6
17 May 97 ●	WONDERFUL TONIGHT *Big Life BLRDA 134*	3	8
14 Jun 97	LOVE GUARANTEED (re-entry) *Big Life BLRDA 133*	73	1
9 Aug 97	LOVE LADY *Big Life BLRDB 137*	33	2
1 Jul 00 ●	GHETTO ROMANCE *Cooltempo CDCOOL 347*	7	7
28 Oct 00	RUMOURS *Cooltempo CDCOOLS 352*	22	4

Carolina DAMAS – See SUENO LATINO

Bobby D'AMBROSIO US, male DJ / producer (3 WEEKS)

		pos/wks	
2 Aug 97	MOMENT OF MY LIFE *Ministry of Sound MOSCDS 1* [1]	23	3

[1] Bobby D'Ambrosio Featuring Michelle Weeks

DAMIAN UK, male vocalist - Damian Davis (26 WEEKS)

		pos/wks	
26 Dec 87	THE TIME WARP 2 *Jive JIVE 160*	51	6
27 Aug 88	THE TIME WARP 2 (re-issue) *Jive JIVE 182*	64	3
19 Aug 89 ●	THE TIME WARP (re-mix) *Jive JIVE 209*	7	13
16 Dec 89	WIG WAM BAM *Jive JIVE 236*	49	4

'The Time Warp' is a re-mix of 'The Time Warp 2'

DAMNED (433 Top 500) Anarchic stalwarts of the UK punk rock scene: Dave Vanian (v), Brian James (g), Captain Sensible (b) and Rat Scabies (d). London-based band released first UK punk single 'New Rose' (1976) and album Damned, Damned, Damned (1977) (77 WEEKS)

		pos/wks	
5 May 79	LOVE SONG *Chiswick CHIS 112*	20	8
20 Oct 79	SMASH IT UP *Chiswick CHIS 116*	35	5
1 Dec 79	I JUST CAN'T BE HAPPY TODAY *Chiswick CHIS 120*	46	5
4 Oct 80	HISTORY OF THE WORLD (PART 1) *Chiswick CHIS 135*	51	4
28 Nov 81	FRIDAY 13TH (EP) *Stale One TRY 1*	50	4
10 Jul 82	LOVELY MONEY *Bronze BRO 149*	42	4
9 Jun 84	THANKS FOR THE NIGHT *Damned DAMNED 1*	43	4
30 Mar 85	GRIMLY FIENDISH *MCA GRIM 1*	21	7
22 Jun 85	THE SHADOW OF LOVE *MCA GRIM 2*	25	8
21 Sep 85	IS IT A DREAM *MCA GRIM 3*	34	4
8 Feb 86 ●	ELOISE *MCA GRIM 4*	3	9
19 Apr 86	ELOISE (re-entry) *MCA GRIM 4*	72	1
22 Nov 86	ANYTHING *MCA GRIM 5*	32	4
7 Feb 87	GIGOLO *MCA GRIM 6*	29	3
25 Apr 87	ALONE AGAIN OR *MCA GRIM 7*	27	6
28 Nov 87	IN DULCE DECORUM *MCA GRIM 8*	72	1

Tracks on Friday 13th (EP): Disco Man / Limit Club / Billy Bad Breaks / Citadel

Kenny DAMON US, male vocalist (1 WEEK)

		pos/wks	
19 May 66	WHILE I LIVE *Mercury MF 907*	48	1

Vic DAMONE US, male vocalist - Vito Farinola (22 WEEKS)

		pos/wks	
6 Dec 57	AN AFFAIR TO REMEMBER *Philips PB 745*	29	1
31 Jan 58	AN AFFAIR TO REMEMBER (re-entry) *Philips PB 745*	30	1
9 May 58 ★	ON THE STREET WHERE YOU LIVE *Philips PB 819*	1	17
1 Aug 58	THE ONLY MAN ON THE ISLAND *Philips PB 837*	24	3

DAN-I UK, male vocalist (9 WEEKS)

		pos/wks	
10 Nov 79	MONKEY CHOP *Island WIP 6520*	30	9

Richie DAN UK, male DJ / producer - Richard Gittens (3 WEEKS)

		pos/wks	
12 Aug 00	CALL IT FATE *Pure Silk CDPSR 1*	34	3

DANA (449 Top 500) Petite teenager won Eurovision Song Contest for Ireland with her first hit in 1970. Born Rosemary Brown (later Scallon), 30 Aug 1951, London, UK. Winning debut hit sold more than two million and was a hit in Europe, Australia and South Africa. Ran for Irish presindency in 1997 (75 WEEKS)

		pos/wks	
4 Apr 70 ★	ALL KINDS OF EVERYTHING *Rex R 11054*	1	15
25 Jul 70	ALL KINDS OF EVERYTHING (re-entry) *Rex R 11054*	47	1
13 Feb 71	WHO PUT THE LIGHTS OUT *Rex R 11062*	14	11
25 Jan 75 ●	PLEASE TELL HIM THAT I SAID HELLO *GTO GT 6*	8	14
13 Dec 75 ●	IT'S GONNA BE A COLD COLD CHRISTMAS *GTO GT 45*	4	6
6 Mar 76	NEVER GONNA FALL IN LOVE AGAIN *GTO GT 55*	31	4
16 Oct 76	FAIRYTALE *GTO GT 66*	13	16
31 Mar 79	SOMETHING'S COOKIN' IN THE KITCHEN *GTO GT 243*	44	5
15 May 82	I FEEL LOVE COMIN' ON *Creole CR 32*	66	3

DANA INTERNATIONAL Israel, female vocalist (4 WEEKS)

		pos/wks	
27 Jun 98	DIVA *Dance Pool DANA 1CD*	11	4

DANCE CONSPIRACY UK, male instrumental / production duo (1 WEEK)

		pos/wks	
3 Oct 92	DUB WAR *XL XLT 34*	72	1

DANCE FLOOR VIRUS Italy, male vocal / instrumental group (2 WEEKS)

		pos/wks	
21 Oct 95	MESSAGE IN A BOTTLE *Epic 6623742*	49	2

DANCE 2 TRANCE Germany, male instrumental / production duo (8 WEEKS)

		pos/wks	
24 Apr 93	P.OWER OF A.MERICAN N.ATIVES *Logic 74321139582*	25	4
24 Jul 93	TAKE A FREE FALL *Logic 74321153602*	36	3
4 Feb 95	WARRIOR *Logic 74321257722*	56	1

Evan DANDO – See Kirsty MacCOLL; LEMONHEADS

DANDY WARHOLS US, male / female vocal / instrumental group (11 WEEKS)

		pos/wks	
28 Feb 98	EVERY DAY SHOULD BE A HOLIDAY *Capitol CDCL 797*	29	2
2 May 98	NOT IF YOU WERE THE LAST JUNKIE ON EARTH *Capitol CDCL 800*	13	4
8 Aug 98	BOYS BETTER *Capitol CDCLS 805*	36	2
10 Jun 00	GET OFF *Capitol CDCLS 821*	38	2
9 Sep 00	BOHEMIAN LIKE YOU *Capitol CDCLS 823*	42	1

DANDYS UK, male vocal / instrumental group (2 WEEKS)

		pos/wks	
14 Mar 98	YOU MAKE ME WANT TO SCREAM *Artificial ATFCD 3*	71	1
30 May 98	ENGLISH COUNTRY GARDEN *Artificial ATFCD 4*	57	1

D'ANGELO US, male vocalist (11 WEEKS)

		pos/wks	
28 Oct 95	BROWN SUGAR *Cooltempo CDCOOL 307*	24	3
2 Mar 96	COLD WORLD *Geffen GFSTD 22114* [1]	40	2
2 Mar 96	CRUISIN' *Cooltempo CDCOOL 316*	31	2
15 Jun 96	LADY *Cooltempo CDCOOLS 323*	21	2
22 May 99	BREAK UPS 2 MAKE UPS *Def Jam 8709272* [2]	33	2

[1] Genius / GZA featuring D'Angelo [2] Method Man featuring D'Angelo

UK No.1 ★ UK Top 10 ● Still on chart + UK million seller ◆ UK entry at No.1 ■ US No.1 ▲

SINGLED OUT... Suzi Quatro

Queen of Britain's glam rock boom, Susan Kay Quatrocchio racked up 122 weeks on the UK chart in less than a decade. Detroit born and now based in the UK, she is currently broadcasting to the nation via her regular show on BBC Radio 2.

• NO.1 ON THE US CHART ON THE DAY I WAS BORN:
The Third Man Theme – Anton Karas

• ALL-TIME FAVOURITE SINGLE:
When I Fall In Love – Nat "King" Cole

My favourite single is one that means so much to me I want it played at my funeral! It's Nat "King" Cole's 'When I Fall in Love'. Why? I think it says everything there is to say about love, and that's a big subject with me. I think love should be for ever.

• SINGLE THAT DRIVES ME UP THE WALL:
None, really – nothing I can think of off hand.

FIRST SINGLE I BOUGHT:
You Must Have Been A Beautiful Baby – Bobby Darin

I heard it, I liked it and it was the first time my Dad gave me some pocket money to go buy it

DANGER DANGER
US, male vocal / instrumental group (5 WEEKS) pos/wks

8 Feb 92	MONKEY BUSINESS *Epic 6577517*	42	2
28 Mar 92	I STILL THINK ABOUT YOU *Epic 6578387*	46	2
13 Jun 92	COMIN' HOME *Epic 6581337*	75	1

Charlie DANIELS BAND
US, male vocal / instrumental group (10 WEEKS) pos/wks

22 Sep 79	THE DEVIL WENT DOWN TO GEORGIA *Epic EPC 7737*	14	10

Johnny DANKWORTH *UK, male orchestral / group leader / instrumentalist - alto sax (33 WEEKS)* pos/wks

22 Jun 56 ●	EXPERIMENTS WITH MICE *Parlophone R 4185*	7	12
23 Feb 61 ●	AFRICAN WALTZ *Columbia DB 4590*	9	21

Dannii – See Dannii MINOGUE

DANNY and the JUNIORS *US, male vocal group (19 WEEKS)* pos/wks

17 Jan 58 ●	AT THE HOP *HMV POP 436* ▲	3	14
10 Jul 76	AT THE HOP (re-issue) *ABC 4123*	39	5

DANNY WILSON
UK, male vocal / instrumental group (28 WEEKS) pos/wks

22 Aug 87	MARY'S PRAYER *Virgin VS 934*	42	7
2 Apr 88 ●	MARY'S PRAYER (re-entry) *Virgin VS 934*	3	11
17 Jun 89	THE SECOND SUMMER OF LOVE *Virgin VS 1186*	23	9
16 Sep 89	NEVER GONNA BE THE SAME *Virgin VS 1203*	69	1

DANSE SOCIETY *UK, male vocal / instrumental group (5 WEEKS)* pos/wks

27 Aug 83	WAKE UP *Society SOC 5*	61	3
5 Nov 83	HEAVEN IS WAITING *Society SOC 6*	60	2

Steven DANTE *UK, male vocalist (16 WEEKS)* pos/wks

26 Sep 87	THE REAL THING *Chrysalis CHS 3167* [1]	13	10
9 Jul 88	I'M TOO SCARED *Cooltempo DANTE 1*	34	6

[1] Jellybean featuring Steven Dante

Tonja DANTZLER *US, female vocalist (1 WEEK)* pos/wks

17 Dec 94	IN AND OUT OF MY LIFE *ffrr FCD 246*	66	1

DANY – See DOUBLE DEE featuring DANY

DANZIG *US, male vocal / instrumental group (1 WEEK)* pos/wks

14 May 94	MOTHER *American MOMDD 1*	62	1

DAPHNE *US, female vocalist (1 WEEK)* pos/wks

9 Dec 95	CHANGE *Stress CDSTR 54*	71	1

DAPHNE & CELESTE *US, female vocal duo - Daphne DeConcetto & Celeste Cruz (28 WEEKS)* pos/wks

5 Feb 00	OOH STICK YOU! *Universal MCSTD 40209*	8	12
17 Jun 00	UGLY *Universal MCSTD 40232*	18	12
2 Sep 00	SCHOOL'S OUT *Universal MCSTD 40238*	12	4

Terence Trent D'ARBY (431 Top 500) *US pop / soul singer, b. 15 Mar 1962, New York, US. Success came after relocating to UK. Multi-million-selling, Grammy-winning debut album, Introducing the Hardline, was worldwide hit. Winner of 1988 Brit award for Best International Newcomer (77 WEEKS)* pos/wks

14 Mar 87 ●	IF YOU LET ME STAY *CBS TRENT 1*	7	13
20 Jun 87 ●	WISHING WELL *CBS TRENT 2* ▲	4	11
10 Oct 87	DANCE LITTLE SISTER (PART ONE) *CBS TRENT 3*	20	7
9 Jan 88 ●	SIGN YOUR NAME *CBS TRENT 4*	2	10
20 Jan 90	TO KNOW SOMEONE DEEPLY IS TO KNOW SOMEONE SOFTLY *CBS TRENT 6*	55	3
17 Apr 93	DO YOU LOVE ME LIKE YOU SAY *Columbia 6590732*	14	6
19 Jun 93	DELICATE *Columbia 6593312* [1]	14	6

28 Aug 93	SHE KISSED ME *Columbia 6595922*	16	7
20 Nov 93	LET HER DOWN EASY *Columbia 6598642*	18	7
8 Apr 95	HOLDING ON TO YOU *Columbia 6614235*	20	6
5 Aug 95	VIBRATOR *Columbia 6622585*	57	1

[1] Terence Trent D'Arby featuring Des'ree

Richard DARBYSHIRE *UK, male vocalist (7 WEEKS)* pos/wks

20 Aug 88	COMING BACK FOR MORE *Chrysalis JEL 4* [1]	41	3
24 Jul 93	THIS I SWEAR *Dome CDDOME 1003*	50	3
12 Feb 94	WHEN ONLY LOVE WILL DO *Dome CDDOME 1008*	54	1

[1] Jellybean featuring Richard Darbyshire

DARE *UK, male vocal / instrumental group (7 WEEKS)* pos/wks

29 Apr 89	THE RAINDANCE *A & M AM 483*	62	2
29 Jul 89	ABANDON *A & M AM 519*	71	1
10 Aug 91	WE DON'T NEED A REASON *A & M AM 755*	52	2
5 Oct 91	REAL LOVE *A & M AM 824*	67	1

Matt DAREY *UK, male producer / instrumentalist (9 WEEKS)* pos/wks

9 Oct 99	LIBERATION (TEMPTATION - FLY LIKE AN EAGLE) *Incentive CENT 1CDS* [1]	19	3
22 Apr 00	FROM RUSSIA WITH LOVE *Liquid Asset ASSET CD003* [2]	40	2
15 Jul 00	BEAUTIFUL *Incentive CENT 7CDS* [3]	21	4

[1] Matt Darey presents Mash Up [2] Matt Darey Presents DSP [3] Matt Darey's Mash Up Presents Marcella Woods

See also SUNBURST; MELT featuring LITTLE MS MARCIE

Bobby DARIN (129 Top 500) *Singer / songwriter / actor and multi-instrumentalist who had pop, rock, R&B, country and MOR hits, b. Walden Robert Cassotto, 14 May 1936, New York, d. 20 Dec 1973. This Grammy winner was posthumously inducted into the Rock and Roll Hall of Fame in 1990 (161 WEEKS)* pos/wks

1 Aug 58	SPLISH SPLASH *London HLE 8666*	28	1
15 Aug 58	SPLISH SPLASH (re-entry) *London HLE 8666*	18	6
9 Jan 59	QUEEN OF THE HOP *London HLE 8737*	24	2
29 May 59 ★	DREAM LOVER *London HLE 8867*	1	19
25 Sep 59 ★	MACK THE KNIFE *London HLK 8939* ▲	1	16
22 Jan 60	MACK THE KNIFE (re-entry) *London HLK 8939*	30	1
29 Jan 60 ●	LA MER (BEYOND THE SEA) *London HLK 9034*	8	10
10 Mar 60	MACK THE KNIFE (2nd re-entry) *London HLK 8939*	50	1
31 Mar 60 ●	CLEMENTINE *London HLK 9086*	8	12
21 Apr 60	LA MER (BEYOND THE SEA) (re-entry) *London HLK 9034*	40	2
30 Jun 60	BILL BAILEY *London HLK 9142*	36	1
14 Jul 60	BILL BAILEY (re-entry) *London HLK 9142*	34	1
16 Mar 61 ●	LAZY RIVER *London HLK 9303*	2	13
6 Jul 61	NATURE BOY *London HLK 9375*	24	7
12 Oct 61 ●	YOU MUST HAVE BEEN A BEAUTIFUL BABY *London HLK 9429*	10	11
26 Oct 61	COME SEPTEMBER *London HLK 9407* [1]	50	1
21 Dec 61 ●	MULTIPLICATION *London HLK 9474*	5	13
19 Jul 62 ●	THINGS *London HLK 9575*	2	17
4 Oct 62	IF A MAN ANSWERS *Capitol CL 15272*	24	6
29 Nov 62	BABY FACE *London HLK 9624*	40	4
25 Jul 63	EIGHTEEN YELLOW ROSES *Capitol CL 15306*	37	4
13 Oct 66 ●	IF I WERE A CARPENTER *Atlantic 584 051*	9	12
14 Apr 79	DREAM LOVER / MACK THE KNIFE (re-issue) *Lightning LIG 9017*	64	1

[1] Bobby Darin Orchestra

DARK STAR *UK, male vocal / instrumental group (6 WEEKS)* pos/wks

26 Jun 99	ABOUT 3AM *Harvest CDEM 545*	50	1
15 Jan 00	GRACEADELICA *Harvest CDEMS 556*	25	3
13 May 00	I AM THE SUN *Harvest CDEMS 566*	31	2

DARKMAN *UK, male rapper (7 WEEKS)* pos/wks

14 May 94	YABBA DABBA DOO *Wild Card CARDD 6*	49	2
20 Aug 94	WHO'S THE DARKMAN *Wild Card CARDD 8*	46	2
3 Dec 94	YABBA DABBA DOO (re-issue) *Wild Card CARDD 11*	37	2
21 Oct 95	BRAND NEW DAY *Wild Card 5771892*	74	1

DARLING BUDS
UK, male / female vocal / instrumental group (20 WEEKS)   pos/wks

8 Oct 88	BURST *Epic BLOND 1*	50	5
7 Jan 89	HIT THE GROUND *CBS BLOND 2*	27	5
25 Mar 89	LET'S GO ROUND THERE *CBS BLOND 3*	49	4
22 Jul 89	YOU'VE GOT TO CHOOSE *CBS BLOND 4*	45	3
2 Jun 90	TINY MACHINE *CBS BLOND 5*	60	2
12 Sep 92	SURE THING *Epic 6582157*	71	1

Guy DARRELL *UK, male vocalist (13 WEEKS)*   pos/wks

| 18 Aug 73 | I'VE BEEN HURT *Santa Ponsa PNS 4* | 12 | 13 |

James DARREN *US, male vocalist (25 WEEKS)*   pos/wks

11 Aug 60	BECAUSE THEY'RE YOUNG *Pye International 7N 25059*	29	7
14 Dec 61	GOODBYE CRUEL WORLD *Pye International 7N 25116*	28	9
29 Mar 62	HER ROYAL MAJESTY *Pye International 7N 25125*	36	3
21 Jun 62	CONSCIENCE *Pye International 7N 25138*	30	6

DARTS `231` `Top 500`
Britain's best-known doo-wop vocal group; line-up included Den Hegarty, Griff Fender, Rita Ray and Bob Fish. The popular London-based eight-piece band had three successive No.2 hits with revivals of early US rock 'n' roll and R&B songs *(117 WEEKS)*   pos/wks

5 Nov 77 ●	DADDY COOL / THE GIRL CAN'T HELP IT *Magnet MAG 100*	6	13
28 Jan 78 ●	COME BACK MY LOVE *Magnet MAG 110*	2	12
6 May 78 ●	BOY FROM NEW YORK CITY *Magnet MAG 116*	2	13
5 Aug 78 ●	IT'S RAINING *Magnet MAG 126*	2	11
11 Nov 78	DON'T LET IT FADE AWAY *Magnet MAG 134*	18	11
10 Feb 79 ●	GET IT *Magnet MAG 140*	10	9
21 Jul 79 ●	DUKE OF EARL *Magnet MAG 147*	6	11
20 Oct 79	CAN'T GET ENOUGH OF YOUR LOVE *Magnet MAG 156*	43	6
1 Dec 79	REET PETITE *Magnet MAG 160*	51	7
31 May 80	LET'S HANG ON *Magnet MAG 174*	11	14
6 Sep 80	PEACHES *Magnet MAG 179*	66	3
29 Nov 80	WHITE CHRISTMAS / SH-BOOM (LIFE COULD BE A DREAM) *Magnet MAG 184*	48	7

DARUDE *Finland, male producer - Ville Virtanen (21 WEEKS)*   pos/wks

| 24 Jun 00 ● | SANDSTORM *Neo NEOCD 033* | 3 | 15 |
| 25 Nov 00 ● | FEEL THE BEAT *Neo NEOCD 045* | 5 | 6+ |

DAS EFX *US, male production / rap duo (5 WEEKS)*   pos/wks

| 7 Aug 93 | CHECK YO SELF *Fourth & Broadway BRCD 283* [1] | 36 | 4 |
| 25 Apr 98 | RAP SCHOLAR *East West E 3853CD* [2] | 42 | 1 |

[1] Ice Cube featuring Das EFX [2] Das EFX featuring Redman

N'dea DAVENPORT *US, female vocalist (3 WEEKS)*   pos/wks

| 11 Sep 93 | TRUST ME *Cooltempo CDCOOL 278* [1] | 34 | 2 |
| 20 Jun 98 | BRING IT ON *Gee Street VVR5002033* | 52 | 1 |

[1] Guru featuring N'Dea Davenport

N'dea Davenport was vocalist on the first 10 Brand New Heavies hits

See also BRAND NEW HEAVIES; GURU

Anne-Marie DAVID *France, female vocalist (9 WEEKS)*   pos/wks

| 28 Apr 73 | WONDERFUL DREAM *Epic EPC 1446* | 13 | 9 |

Craig DAVID *UK, male vocalist (61 WEEKS)*   pos/wks

11 Dec 99 ●	RE-REWIND THE CROWD SAY BO SELECTA *Public Demand / Relentless RELENT 1CDS* [1]	2	17
15 Apr 00 ★	FILL ME IN *Wildstar CDWILD 28* ■	1	14
15 Jul 00 ●	WOMAN TROUBLE *Public Demand / ffrr FCD 380* [2]	6	10
5 Aug 00 ★	7 DAYS *Wildstar CDWILD 30* ■	1	14
18 Nov 00	7 DAYS (re-entry) *Wildstar CDWILD 30*	74	1
2 Dec 00 ●	WALKING AWAY *Wildstar CDWILD 35*	3	5+

[1] Artful Dodger featuring Craig David [2] Artful Dodger and Robbie Craig featuring Craig David

FR DAVID *France, male vocalist - Robert Fitoussi (13 WEEKS)*   pos/wks

| 2 Apr 83 ● | WORDS *Carrere CAR 248* | 2 | 12 |
| 18 Jun 83 | MUSIC *Carrere CAR 282* | 71 | 1 |

David DEVANT & HIS SPIRIT WIFE
UK, male vocal / instrumental group (2 WEEKS)   pos/wks

| 5 Apr 97 | GINGER *Rhythm King KIND 4CD* | 54 | 1 |
| 21 Jun 97 | THIS IS FOR REAL *Rhythm King KIND 5CD* | 61 | 1 |

DAVID and JONATHAN
UK, male vocal duo - Roger Greenaway & Roger Cook (22 WEEKS)   pos/wks

| 13 Jan 66 | MICHELLE *Columbia DB 7800* | 11 | 6 |
| 7 Jul 66 ● | LOVERS OF THE WORLD UNITE *Columbia DB 7950* | 7 | 16 |

See also BLUE MINK; PIPKINS

Jim DAVIDSON *UK, male vocalist (4 WEEKS)*   pos/wks

| 27 Dec 80 | WHITE CHRISTMAS / TOO RISKY *Scratch SCR 001* | 52 | 4 |

Paul DAVIDSON *Jamaica, male vocalist (10 WEEKS)*   pos/wks

| 27 Dec 75 ● | MIDNIGHT RIDER *Tropical ALO 56* | 10 | 10 |

Dave DAVIES *UK, male vocalist (17 WEEKS)*   pos/wks

| 19 Jul 67 ● | DEATH OF A CLOWN *Pye 7N 17356* | 3 | 10 |
| 6 Dec 67 | SUSANNAH'S STILL ALIVE *Pye 7N 17429* | 20 | 7 |

See also KINKS

Windsor DAVIES and Don ESTELLE
UK, male comedy / vocal duo (16 WEEKS)   pos/wks

| 17 May 75 ★ | WHISPERING GRASS *EMI 2290* | 1 | 12 |
| 25 Oct 75 | PAPER DOLL *EMI 2361* | 41 | 4 |

Billie DAVIS *UK, female vocalist - Carol Hedges (33 WEEKS)*   pos/wks

30 Aug 62	WILL I WHAT *Parlophone R 4932* [1]	18	10
7 Feb 63 ●	TELL HIM *Decca F 11572*	10	12
30 May 63	HE'S THE ONE *Decca F 11658*	40	3
9 Oct 68	I WANT YOU TO BE MY BABY *Decca F 12823*	33	8

[1] Mike Sarne with Billie Davis

Billy DAVIS Jr – See Marilyn McCOO and Billy DAVIS Jr

Darlene DAVIS *US, female vocalist (5 WEEKS)*   pos/wks

| 7 Feb 87 | I FOUND LOVE *Serious 70US 1* | 55 | 5 |

John DAVIS and the MONSTER ORCHESTRA
US, male vocal / instrumental group (2 WEEKS)   pos/wks

| 10 Feb 79 | AIN'T THAT ENOUGH FOR YOU *Miracle M 2* | 70 | 2 |

Mac DAVIS *US, male vocalist (22 WEEKS)*   pos/wks

| 4 Nov 72 | BABY DON'T GET HOOKED ON ME *CBS 8250* ▲ | 29 | 6 |
| 15 Nov 80 | IT'S HARD TO BE HUMBLE *Casablanca CAN 210* | 27 | 16 |

Richie DAVIS – See SHUT UP AND DANCE

Roy DAVIS Jr featuring Peven EVERETT
US, male producer, male vocalist (4 WEEKS)   pos/wks

| 1 Nov 97 | GABRIEL *XL XLS 88CD* | 22 | 4 |

Ruth DAVIS – See Bo KIRKLAND and Ruth DAVIS

Sammy DAVIS Jr *US, male vocalist (37 WEEKS)*   pos/wks

29 Jul 55	SOMETHING'S GOTTA GIVE *Brunswick LAT 8296*	19	2
19 Aug 55	SOMETHING'S GOTTA GIVE (re-entry) *Brunswick LAT 8296*	11	5
9 Sep 55 ●	LOVE ME OR LEAVE ME *Brunswick 05428*	8	6

30 Sep 55	THAT OLD BLACK MAGIC *Brunswick 05450*	16	1
7 Oct 55	HEY THERE *Brunswick 05469*	19	1
4 Nov 55	LOVE ME OR LEAVE ME (re-entry) *Brunswick 05428*	18	2
20 Apr 56	IN A PERSIAN MARKET *Brunswick 05518*	28	1
28 Dec 56	ALL OF YOU *Brunswick 05629*	28	1
16 Jun 60	HAPPY TO MAKE YOUR ACQUAINTANCE *Brunswick 05830* [1]	46	1
22 Mar 62	WHAT KIND OF FOOL AM I? / GONNA BUILD A MOUNTAIN *Reprise R 20048*	26	8
13 Dec 62	ME AND MY SHADOW *Reprise R 20128* [2]	20	7
7 Feb 63	ME AND MY SHADOW (re-entry) *Reprise R 20128* [2]	47	2

[1] Sammy Davis Jr. and Carmen McRae [2] Frank Sinatra and Sammy Davis Jr

Skeeter DAVIS *US, female vocalist (13 WEEKS)* pos/wks

| 14 Mar 63 | END OF THE WORLD *RCA 1328* | 18 | 13 |

Spencer DAVIS GROUP (477 | Top 500)
Big selling Birmingham (UK) band; Spencer Davis (v/g), Peter York (d) and brothers Muff (b) and Steve Winwood (v/g/k). Both No.1s penned by reggae artist Jackie Edwards. Teenager Steve Winwood left 1967, and continued hit run with Blind Faith, Traffic and as soloist (71 WEEKS) pos/wks

5 Nov 64	I CAN'T STAND IT *Fontana TF 499*	47	3
25 Feb 65	EVERY LITTLE BIT HURTS *Fontana TF 530*	43	2
18 Mar 65	EVERY LITTLE BIT HURTS (re-entry) *Fontana TF 530*	41	1
10 Jun 65	STRONG LOVE *Fontana TF 571*	50	1
24 Jun 65	STRONG LOVE (re-entry) *Fontana TF 571*	44	3
2 Dec 65	★ KEEP ON RUNNING *Fontana TF 632*	1	14
24 Mar 66	★ SOMEBODY HELP ME *Fontana TF 679*	1	10
1 Sep 66	WHEN I COME HOME *Fontana TF 739*	12	9
3 Nov 66	● GIMME SOME LOVING *Fontana TF 762*	2	12
26 Jan 67	● I'M A MAN *Fontana TF 785*	9	7
9 Aug 67	TIME SELLER *Fontana TF 854*	30	5
10 Jan 68	MR SECOND CLASS *United Artists UP 1203*	35	4

T L DAVIS – See FULL MONTY ALLSTARS featuring T.J. DAVIS

Zelma DAVIS – See C & C MUSIC FACTORY / CLIVILLES & COLE

DAVIS PINCKNEY PROJECT – See GO GO LORENZO and the DAVIS PINCKNEY PROJECT

DAWN (264 | Top 500)
Top-notch vocal trio fronted by one-time teenage hitmaker Tony Orlando (b. Michael Cassavitis, 3 Apr 1944, New York) and including Telma Hopkins and Joyce Vincent. Their 'Tie a Yellow Ribbon' was the top single of 1973 in both the UK and the US (109 WEEKS) pos/wks

16 Jan 71	● CANDIDA *Bell 1118*	9	11
10 Apr 71	★ KNOCK THREE TIMES *Bell 1146* ▲	1	27
31 Jul 71	● WHAT ARE YOU DOING SUNDAY *Bell 1169* [1]	3	12
10 Mar 73	★ TIE A YELLOW RIBBON ROUND THE OLD OAK TREE *Bell 1287* [1] ▲	1	39
4 Aug 73	SAY, HAS ANYBODY SEEN MY SWEET GYPSY ROSE *Bell 1322* [1]	12	15
5 Jan 74	TIE A YELLOW RIBBON ROUND THE OLD OAK TREE (re-entry) *Bell 1287* [1]	41	1
9 Mar 74	WHO'S IN THE STRAWBERRY PATCH WITH SALLY *Bell 1343* [2]	37	4

[1] Dawn featuring Tony Orlando [2] Tony Orlando and Dawn

Julie DAWN – See Cyril STAPLETON and his ORCHESTRA

Liz DAWN – See Joe LONGTHORNE

DAWN OF THE REPLICANTS
UK, male vocal / instrumental group (2 WEEKS) pos/wks

| 7 Feb 98 | CANDLEFIRE *East West EW 147CD1* | 52 | 1 |
| 4 Apr 98 | HOGWASH FARM (THE DIESEL HANDS EP) *East West EW 157CD* | 65 | 1 |

Tracks on Hogwash Farm (The Diesel Hands EP): Hogwash Farm (re-built) / Night Train to Lichtenstein / The Duchess of Surin / Crow Valley

Dana DAWSON *US, female vocalist (14 WEEKS)* pos/wks

15 Jul 95	● 3 IS FAMILY *EMI CDEM 378*	9	8
28 Oct 95	GOT TO GIVE ME LOVE *EMI CDEM 392*	27	2
4 May 96	SHOW ME *EMI CDEMS 423*	28	3
20 Jul 96	HOW I WANNA BE LOVED *EMI CDEMS 432*	42	1

Bobby DAY *US, male vocalist (2 WEEKS)* pos/wks

| 7 Nov 58 | ROCKIN' ROBIN *London HL 8726* | 29 | 2 |

Darren DAY *UK, male vocalist (7 WEEKS)* pos/wks

8 Oct 94	YOUNG GIRL *Bell 74321231082*	42	2
8 Jun 96	SUMMER HOLIDAY MEDLEY *RCA 74321384472*	17	4
9 May 98	HOW CAN I BE SURE ? *Eastcoast DDCD 001*	71	1

Doris DAY (154 | Top 500)
The Fifties' favourite singer / actress, b. Doris Kappelhoff, 3 Apr 1924, Cincinnati. The No.1 female movie star of that era, she also had numerous British hits (not to mention 25 US bestsellers) before the UK chart first started (146 WEEKS) pos/wks

14 Nov 52	● SUGARBUSH *Columbia DB 3123* [1]	8	2
21 Nov 52	● MY LOVE AND DEVOTION *Columbia DB 3157*	10	2
5 Dec 52	● SUGARBUSH (re-entry) *Columbia DB 3123* [1]	8	6
3 Apr 53	MA SAYS, PA SAYS *Columbia DB 3242* [2]	12	1
17 Apr 53	FULL TIME JOB *Columbia DB 3242* [2]	11	1
24 Jul 53	● LET'S WALK THAT-A-WAY *Philips PB 157* [2]	4	14
2 Apr 54	★ SECRET LOVE *Philips PB 230* ▲	1	29
27 Aug 54	● THE BLACK HILLS OF DAKOTA *Philips PB 287*	7	8
1 Oct 54	● IF I GIVE MY HEART TO YOU *Philips PB 325* [3]	4	11
8 Apr 55	● READY, WILLING AND ABLE *Philips PB 402*	7	9
9 Sep 55	LOVE ME OR LEAVE ME *Philips PB 479*	20	1
21 Oct 55	I'LL NEVER STOP LOVING YOU *Philips PB 497*	17	2
25 Nov 55	I'LL NEVER STOP LOVING YOU (re-entry) *Philips PB 497*	19	1
29 Jun 56	★ WHATEVER WILL BE, WILL BE (QUE SERA, SERA) *Philips PB 586*	1	22
13 Jun 58	A VERY PRECIOUS LOVE *Philips PB 799*	16	11
15 Aug 58	EVERYBODY LOVES A LOVER *Philips PB 843*	25	3
26 Sep 58	EVERYBODY LOVES A LOVER (re-entry) *Philips PB 843*	27	1
12 Mar 64	● MOVE OVER DARLING *CBS AAG 183*	8	16
18 Apr 87	MOVE OVER DARLING (re-issue) *CBS LEGS 1*	45	6

[1] Doris Day and Frankie Laine [2] Doris Day and Johnnie Ray [3] Doris Day With The Mellowmen

Inaya DAY *US, female vocalist (3 WEEKS)* pos/wks

| 22 May 99 | JUST CAN'T GET ENOUGH *AM:PM CDAMPM 121* [1] | 39 | 2 |
| 7 Oct 00 | FEEL IT *Positiva CDTIV 141* | 51 | 1 |

[1] Harry 'Choo Choo' Romero presents Inaya Day

DAY ONE *UK, male vocal / instrumental duo (1 WEEK)* pos/wks

| 13 Nov 99 | I'M DOIN' FINE *Melankolic / Virgin SADD6* | 68 | 1 |

Patti DAY *US, female vocalist (1 WEEK)* pos/wks

| 9 Dec 89 | RIGHT BEFORE MY EYES *Debut DEBT 3080* | 69 | 1 |

DAYEENE *Sweden, female vocal duo (1 WEEK)* pos/wks

| 17 Jul 99 | AND IT HURTS *Pukka CDPUKKA 20* | 63 | 1 |

Taylor DAYNE
US, female vocalist - Leslie Wundermann (54 WEEKS) pos/wks

23 Jan 88	● TELL IT TO MY HEART *Arista 109616*	3	13
19 Mar 88	● PROVE YOUR LOVE *Arista 109830*	8	10
11 Jun 88	I'LL ALWAYS LOVE YOU *Arista 111536*	41	7
18 Nov 89	WITH EVERY BEAT OF MY HEART *Arista 112760*	53	2
14 Apr 90	I'LL BE YOUR SHELTER *Arista 112996*	43	5
4 Aug 90	LOVE WILL LEAD YOU BACK *Arista 113277* ▲	69	1
3 Jul 93	CAN'T GET ENOUGH OF YOUR LOVE *Arista 74321147852*	14	8
16 Apr 94	I'LL WAIT *Arista 74321203472*	29	3

UK No.1 ★   UK Top 10 ●   Still on chart +   UK million seller ◆   UK entry at No.1 ■   US No.1 ▲

4 Feb 95	ORIGINAL SIN (THEME FROM 'THE SHADOW')		
	Arista 74321223462	63	1
18 Nov 95	SAY A PRAYER Arista 74321324292	58	1
13 Jan 96	TELL IT TO MY HEART (re-mix) Arista 74321335962	23	3

DAYTON US, male vocal group (1 WEEK)   pos/wks

10 Dec 83	THE SOUND OF MUSIC Capitol CL 318	75	1

DAZZ BAND US, male vocal / instrumental group (12 WEEKS)   pos/wks

3 Nov 84	LET IT ALL BLOW Motown TMG 1361	12	12

DBM Germany, male / female vocal / instrumental group (3 WEEKS)
pos/wks

12 Nov 77	DISCO BEATLEMANIA Atlantic K 11027	45	3

D, B, M and T UK, male vocal / instrumental group (8 WEEKS)   pos/wks

1 Aug 70	MR PRESIDENT Fontana 6007 022	33	8

See also Dave DEE, DOZY, BEAKY, MICK and TICH

D BO GENERAL – See URBAN SHAKEDOWN

Darryl D'BONNEAU – See Barbara TUCKER

D'BORA US, female vocalist (4 WEEKS)   pos/wks

14 Sep 91	DREAM ABOUT YOU Polydor PO 161	75	1
1 Jul 95	GOING ROUND Vibe MCSTD 2055	40	2
30 Mar 96	GOOD LOVE REAL LOVE Music Plant MCSTD 40023	58	1

Nino DE ANGELO Germany, male vocalist (5 WEEKS)   pos/wks

21 Jul 84	GUARDIAN ANGEL Carrere CAR 335	57	5

DE BOS Holland, male DJ / producer (1 WEEK)   pos/wks

25 Oct 97	ON THE RUN Jive JIVECD 433	51	1

Chris DE BURGH ⟨479⟩ Top 500 Son of a diplomat, Irish singer /
songwriter b. Christopher John Davidson, 15 Oct 1948, Argentina. The first
act to enter the Swiss album chart at No.1, he will, despite his international
album sales success, be for ever remembered for the 1986 million-selling
No.1 hit he wrote for and about his wife (71 WEEKS)   pos/wks

23 Oct 82	DON'T PAY THE FERRYMAN A & M AMS 8256	48	5
12 May 84	HIGH ON EMOTION A & M AM 190	44	5
12 Jul 86	★ THE LADY IN RED A & M AM 331	1	14
20 Sep 86	FATAL HESITATION A & M AM 346	44	4
13 Dec 86	A SPACEMAN CAME TRAVELLING / THE BALLROOM OF ROMANCE A & M AM 365	40	5
21 Feb 87	THE LADY IN RED (re-entry) A & M AM 331	74	1
12 Dec 87	THE SIMPLE TRUTH (A CHILD IS BORN) A & M AM 427	69	2
2 Jan 88	THE SIMPLE TRUTH (A CHILD IS BORN) (re-entry) A & M AM 427	55	1
29 Oct 88	● MISSING YOU A & M AM 474	3	12
7 Jan 89	TENDER HANDS A & M AM 486	43	6
14 Oct 89	THIS WAITING HEART A & M AM 528	59	3
25 May 91	THE SIMPLE TRUTH (A CHILD IS BORN) (re-issue) A & M RELF 1	36	2
11 Apr 92	SEPARATE TABLES A & M AM 863	30	4
21 May 94	BLONDE HAIR BLUE JEANS A & M 5805932	51	1
9 Dec 95	THE SNOWS OF NEW YORK A & M 5813132	60	1
27 Sep 97	SO BEAUTIFUL A & M 5823932	29	4
18 Sep 99	WHEN I THINK OF YOU A&M / Mercury 4971302	59	1

DE CASTRO SISTERS Cuba, female vocal group (1 WEEK)   pos/wks

11 Feb 55	TEACH ME TONIGHT London HL 8104	20	1

DE-CODE featuring Beverli SKEETE UK, male / female vocal /
instrumental group (1 WEEK)   pos/wks

18 May 96	WONDERWALL / SOME MIGHT SAY Neoteric NRCD 2	69	1

Etienne DE CRECY France, male DJ / producer (1 WEEK)   pos/wks

28 Mar 98	PRIX CHOC REMIXES Different DIF 007CD	60	1

DE FUNK Featuring F45
Italy / UK male production / vocal group (1 WEEK)   pos/wks

25 Sep 99	PLEASURE LOVE INCredible INCS 3CD	49	1

Lennie DE ICE UK, male producer (1 WEEK)   pos/wks

17 Apr 99	WE ARE I. E. Distinctive DISNCD 50	61	1

DE LA SOUL US, male rap group (62 WEEKS)   pos/wks

8 Apr 89	ME MYSELF AND I Big Life BLR 7	22	8
8 Jul 89	SAY NO GO Big Life BLR 10	18	7
21 Oct 89	EYE KNOW Big Life BLR 13	14	7
23 Dec 89	● THE MAGIC NUMBER / BUDDY Big Life BLR 14	7	8
24 Mar 90	MAMA GAVE BIRTH TO THE SOUL CHILDREN Gee Street GEE 26 [1]	14	7
27 Apr 91	● RING RING RING (HA HA HEY) Big Life BLR 42	10	7
3 Aug 91	A ROLLER SKATING JAM NAMED 'SATURDAYS' Big Life BLR 55	22	5
23 Nov 91	KEEPIN' THE FAITH Big Life BLR 64	50	2
18 Sep 93	BREAKADAWN Big Life BLRD 103	39	3
2 Apr 94	FALLIN' Epic 6602622 [2]	59	1
29 Jun 96	STAKES IS HIGH Tommy Boy TBCD 7730	55	1
8 Mar 97	4 MORE Tommy Boy TBCD 7779A [3]	52	1
22 Jul 00	OOOH Tommy Boy TBCD 2102 [4]	29	2
11 Nov 00	ALL GOOD Tommy Boy TBCD 2154B [5]	33	3

[1] Queen Latifah + De La Soul [2] Teenage Fanclub and De La Soul [3] De La Soul
featuring Zhané [4] De La Soul featuring Redman [5] De La Soul featuring Chaka Khan

'Buddy' listed only until Jan 6 1990, peaking at No. 8

See also JUNGLE BROTHERS

Donna DE LORY US, female vocalist (1 WEEK)   pos/wks

24 Jul 93	JUST A DREAM MCA MCSTD 1750	71	1

Vincent DE MOOR Holland, male producer (1 WEEK)   pos/wks

16 Aug 97	FLOWTATION XL XLS 89CD	54	1

Lynsey DE PAUL
UK, female vocalist - Lynsey Rubin (54 WEEKS)   pos/wks

19 Aug 72	● SUGAR ME MAM 81	5	11
2 Dec 72	GETTING A DRAG MAM 88	18	8
27 Oct 73	WON'T SOMEBODY DANCE WITH ME MAM 109	14	7
8 Jun 74	OOH I DO Warner Bros. K 16401	25	6
2 Nov 74	● NO HONESTLY Jet 747	7	11
22 Mar 75	MY MAN AND ME Jet 750	40	4
26 Mar 77	ROCK BOTTOM Polydor 2058 859 [1]	19	7

[1] Lynsey De Paul and Mike Moran

Tullio DE PISCOPO Italy, male vocalist (4 WEEKS)   pos/wks

28 Feb 87	STOP BAJON . . . PRIMAVERA Greyhound GREY 9	58	4

Rebecca DE RUVO Sweden, female vocalist (1 WEEK)   pos/wks

1 Oct 94	I CAUGHT YOU OUT Arista 74321230782	72	1

Teri DE SARIO US, female vocalist (5 WEEKS)   pos/wks

2 Sep 78	AIN'T NOTHING GONNA KEEP ME FROM YOU Casablanca CAN 128	52	5

Stephanie DE SYKES
UK, female vocalist - Stephanie Ryton (17 WEEKS)   pos/wks

20 Jul 74	● BORN WITH A SMILE ON MY FACE Bradley's BRAD 7409 [1]	2	10
19 Apr 75	WE'LL FIND OUR DAY Bradley's BRAD 7509	17	7

[1] Stephanie De Sykes with Rain

William DE VAUGHN US, male vocalist (10 WEEKS)

		pos/wks	
6 Jul 74	BE THANKFUL FOR WHAT YOU'VE GOT *Chelsea 2005 002*	31	5
20 Sep 80	BE THANKFUL FOR WHAT YOU'VE GOT (re-recording) *EMI 5101*	44	5

Tony DE VIT UK, male DJ / producer (11 WEEKS)

		pos/wks	
4 Mar 95	BURNING UP *Icon ICONCD 001*	25	3
12 Aug 95	HOOKED *Labello Dance LAD 18CD* [1]	28	2
9 Sep 95	TO THE LIMIT *X:Plode BANG 1CD*	44	2
30 May 96	I'LL BE THERE *Labello Dance LAD 25CD1* [1]	37	2
28 Oct 00	DAWN *Tidy Trax TIDY 140CD*	56	2

[1] 99th Floor Elevators featuring Tony De Vit

DEACON BLUE (256 Top 500) Scottish sextet with fervent following, led by singer / songwriter Ricky Ross (v) and featuring his wife Lorraine McIntosh (v). Named after the Steely Dan song, they achieved five Top 5 albums, including the million-selling When the World Knows Your Name (111 WEEKS)

		pos/wks	
23 Jan 88	DIGNITY *CBS DEAC 4*	31	8
9 Apr 88	WHEN WILL YOU MAKE MY TELEPHONE RING *CBS DEAC 5*	34	7
16 Jul 88	CHOCOLATE GIRL *CBS DEAC 6*	43	7
15 Oct 88 ●	REAL GONE KID *CBS DEAC 7*	8	13
4 Mar 89	WAGES DAY *CBS DEAC 8*	18	6
20 May 89	FERGUS SINGS THE BLUES *CBS DEAC 9*	14	6
16 Sep 89	LOVE AND REGRET *CBS DEAC 10*	28	5
6 Jan 90	QUEEN OF THE NEW YEAR *CBS DEAC 11*	21	5
25 Aug 90 ●	FOUR BACHARACH AND DAVID SONGS (EP) *CBS DEAC 12*	2	9
25 May 91	YOUR SWAYING ARMS *Columbia 6568937*	23	4
27 Jul 91 ●	TWIST AND SHOUT *Columbia 6573027*	10	9
12 Oct 91	CLOSING TIME *Columbia 6575027*	42	3
14 Dec 91	COVER FROM THE SKY *Columbia 6576737*	31	4
28 Nov 92	YOUR TOWN *Columbia 6587867*	14	8
13 Feb 93	WILL WE BE LOVERS *Columbia 6589732*	31	4
24 Apr 93	ONLY TENDER LOVE *Columbia 6591842*	22	4
17 Jul 93	HANG YOUR HEAD *Columbia 6594602*	21	3
2 Apr 94	I WAS RIGHT AND YOU WERE WRONG *Columbia 6602222*	32	3
28 May 94	DIGNITY *Columbia 6604485*	20	3

Tracks on Four Bacharach and David Songs (EP): I'll Never Fall in Love Again / The Look of Love / Message to Michael / Are You There (With Another Girl). 'Dignity' in 1994 was the original recording of the song first issued in 1987 when it failed to chart

DEAD DRED UK, male instrumental / production duo (2 WEEKS)

		pos/wks	
5 Nov 94	DRED BASS *Moving Shadow SHADOW 50CD*	60	2

DEAD END KIDS
UK, male vocal / instrumental group (10 WEEKS)

		pos/wks	
26 Mar 77 ●	HAVE I THE RIGHT *CBS 4972*	6	10

DEAD KENNEDYS
US, male vocal / instrumental group (9 WEEKS)

		pos/wks	
1 Nov 80	KILL THE POOR *Cherry Red CHERRY 16*	49	3
30 May 81	TOO DRUNK TO FUCK *Cherry Red CHERRY 24*	36	6

DEAD OR ALIVE (485 Top 500) Alternative rock / dance group formed 1980, Liverpool, UK, who became notorious for flamboyant singer Pete Burns, b. 5 Aug 1959. 'You Spin Me Round', which took 15 weeks to reach the top, was first UK No.1 produced by the hit machine of Stock Aitken & Waterman (70 WEEKS)

		pos/wks	
24 Mar 84	THAT'S THE WAY (I LIKE IT) *Epic A 4271*	22	9
1 Dec 84 ★	YOU SPIN ME ROUND (LIKE A RECORD) *Epic A 4861*	1	23
20 Apr 85	LOVER COME BACK TO ME *Epic A 6086*	11	8
29 Jun 85	IN TOO DEEP *Epic A 6360*	14	8
21 Sep 85	MY HEART GOES BANG (GET ME TO THE DOCTOR) *Epic A 6571*	23	6
20 Sep 86	BRAND NEW LOVER *Epic A 650075 7*	31	4
10 Jan 87	SOMETHING IN MY HOUSE *Epic BURNS 1*	12	7
4 Apr 87	HOOKED ON LOVE *Epic BURNS 2*	69	2
3 Sep 88	TURN ROUND AND COUNT 2 TEN *Epic BURNS 4*	70	1
22 Jul 89	COME HOME WITH ME BABY *Epic BURNS 5*	62	2

DEAD PREZ US, male rap duo (2 WEEKS)

		pos/wks	
13 Mar 00	HIP HOP *Epic 6689862*	41	2

DEADLY SINS
UK / Italy, male vocal / instrumental duo (2 WEEKS)

		pos/wks	
30 Apr 94	WE ARE GOING ON DOWN *Ffrreedom TABCD 220*	45	2

Hazell DEAN (482 Top 500) Exuberant pop-dance singer, b. 27 Oct 1958, Essex, UK, who started recording in 1976. Became associated with frenetic Hi-NRG dance boom of the 1980s. Many of her hits were produced by Stock Aitken & Waterman including their first Top 10 entry, 'Whatever I Do' (71 WEEKS)

		pos/wks	
18 Feb 84	EVERGREEN / JEALOUS LOVE *Proto ENA 114*	63	3
21 Apr 84 ●	SEARCHIN' (I GOTTA FIND A MAN) *Proto ENA 109*	6	15
28 Jul 84 ●	WHATEVER I DO (WHEREVER I GO) *Proto ENA 119*	4	11
3 Nov 84	BACK IN MY ARMS (ONCE AGAIN) *Proto ENA 122*	41	4
2 Mar 85	NO FOOL (FOR LOVE) *Proto ENA 123*	41	5
12 Oct 85	THEY SAY IT'S GONNA RAIN *Parlophone R 6107*	58	4
2 Apr 88 ●	WHO'S LEAVING WHO *EMI EM 45*	4	11
25 Jun 88	MAYBE (WE SHOULD CALL IT A DAY) *EMI EM 62*	15	6
24 Sep 88	TURN IT INTO LOVE *EMI EM 71*	21	7
26 Aug 89	LOVE PAINS *Lisson DOLE 12*	48	4
23 Mar 91	BETTER OFF WITHOUT YOU *Lisson DOLE 19*	72	1

Jimmy DEAN US, male vocalist - Seth Ward (17 WEEKS)

		pos/wks	
26 Oct 61 ●	BIG BAD JOHN *Philips PB 1187* ▲	2	13
8 Nov 62	LITTLE BLACK BOOK *CBS AAG 122*	33	4

Letitia DEAN and Paul MEDFORD
UK, female / male vocal duo (7 WEEKS)

		pos/wks	
25 Oct 86	SOMETHING OUTA NOTHING *BBC RESL 203*	12	7

DEANNA – See David MORALES

DEAR JON
UK, female / male vocal / instrumental group (1 WEEK)

		pos/wks	
22 Apr 95	ONE GIFT OF LOVE *MDMC DEVCS 2*	68	1

DEATH IN VEGAS UK, male instrumental / production duo - Richard Fearless & Tim Holmes (8 WEEKS)

		pos/wks	
2 Aug 97	DIRT *Concrete HARD 27CD*	61	1
1 Nov 97	ROCCO *Concrete HARD 29CD*	51	1
12 Feb 00 ●	AISHA *Concrete HARD 43CD*	9	4
6 May 00	DIRGE *Concrete HARD 44CD*	24	2

DeBARGE US, male / female vocal group (17 WEEKS)

		pos/wks	
6 Apr 85 ●	RHYTHM OF THE NIGHT *Gordy TMG 1376*	4	14
21 Sep 85	YOU WEAR IT WELL *Gordy ZB 40345* [1]	54	3

[1] El DeBarge with DeBarge

See also El DeBARGE; Chico DeBARGE

Chico DeBARGE US, male vocalist (1 WEEK)

		pos/wks	
14 Mar 98	IGGIN' ME *Universal UND 56170*	50	1

See also DeBARGE

El DeBARGE US, male vocalist (3 WEEKS)

		pos/wks	
28 Jun 86	WHO'S JOHNNY ('SHORT CIRCUIT' THEME) *Gordy ELD 1*	60	2
31 Mar 90	SECRET GARDEN *Qwest W 9992* [1]	67	1

[1] Quincy Jones featuring Al B Sure!, James Ingram, El DeBarge and Barry White

See also DeBARGE

Diana DECKER US, female vocalist (10 WEEKS)

		pos/wks	
23 Oct 53 ●	POPPA PICCOLINO *Columbia DB 3325*	2	8
8 Jan 54 ●	POPPA PICCOLINO (re-entry) *Columbia DB 3325*	5	2

Dave DEE UK, male vocalist (4 WEEKS)

			pos/wks
14 Mar 70	MY WOMAN'S MAN Fontana TF 1074	42	4

See also Dave DEE, DOZY, BEAKY, MICK and TICH

Dave DEE, DOZY, BEAKY, MICK and TICH `170` `Top 500`
Quirkily named UK quintet was very popular in late 1960s: Dave Dee (David Harman) (v), Dozy (Trevor Davies) (b), Beaky (John Dymond) (g), Mick (Michael Wilson) (d), Tich (Ian Amey) (g). Catchy productions and ultra-commercial songs (penned by managers Howard and Blaikley) ensured string of hits (141 WEEKS)

			pos/wks
23 Dec 65	YOU MAKE IT MOVE Fontana TF 630	26	8
3 Mar 66 ●	HOLD TIGHT Fontana TF 671	4	17
9 Jun 66 ●	HIDEAWAY Fontana TF 711	10	11
15 Sep 66 ●	BEND IT Fontana TF 746	2	12
8 Dec 66 ●	SAVE ME Fontana TF 775	3	10
9 Mar 67	TOUCH ME TOUCH ME Fontana TF 798	13	9
18 May 67 ●	OKAY! Fontana TF 830	4	11
11 Oct 67 ●	ZABADAK! Fontana TF 873	3	14
14 Feb 68 ★	LEGEND OF XANADU Fontana TF 903	1	12
3 Jul 68 ●	LAST NIGHT IN SOHO Fontana TF 953	8	11
2 Oct 68	WRECK OF THE ANTOINETTE Fontana TF 971	14	9
5 Mar 69	DON JUAN Fontana TF 1000	23	9
14 May 69	SNAKE IN THE GRASS Fontana TF 1020	23	8

Jazzy DEE US, male rapper / instrumentalist (5 WEEKS)

			pos/wks
5 Mar 83	GET ON UP Laurie LRS 101	53	5

Joey DEE and the STARLITERS
US, male vocal / instrumental group (8 WEEKS)

			pos/wks
8 Feb 62	PEPPERMINT TWIST Columbia DB 4758 ▲	33	8

Kiki DEE `415` `Top 500`
First white UK artist to secure a recording deal with Tamla Motown, b. Pauline Matthews, 6 Mar 1947, Bradford. Vocalist, much respected by her peers, who achieved an Olivier Award nomination in 1989 for her acting skills demonstrated in Willy Russell's West End stage hit 'Blood Brothers' (79 WEEKS)

			pos/wks
10 Nov 73	AMOUREUSE Rocket PIG 4	13	13
7 Sep 74	I'VE GOT THE MUSIC IN ME Rocket PIG 12 [1]	19	8
12 Apr 75	(YOU DONT KNOW) HOW GLAD I AM Rocket PIG 16 [1]	33	4
3 Jul 76 ★	DON'T GO BREAKING MY HEART Rocket ROKN 512 [2] ▲	1	14
11 Sep 76	LOVING AND FREE / AMOUREUSE (re-issue) Rocket ROKN 515	13	8
19 Feb 77	FIRST THING IN THE MORNING Rocket ROKN 520	32	5
11 Jun 77	CHICAGO Rocket ROKN 526	28	4
21 Feb 81	STAR Ariola ARO 251	13	10
23 May 81	PERFECT TIMING Ariola ARO 257	66	3
20 Nov 93 ●	TRUE LOVE Rocket EJSCX 32 [2]	2	10

[1] Kiki Dee Band [2] Elton John and Kiki Dee

On 18 Sep, 25 Sep and 2 Oct 1976, 'Loving and Free' was listed by itself. 'Chicago' was one side of a double-sided chart entry, the other being 'Bite Your Lip (Get Up and Dance)' by Elton John

Nancy DEE – See BENELUX and Nancy DEE

DEEE-LITE US / Russia / Japan, male / female vocal / instrumental group (30 WEEKS)

			pos/wks
18 Aug 90 ●	GROOVE IS IN THE HEART / WHAT IS LOVE Elektra EKR 114	2	13
24 Nov 90	POWER OF LOVE / DEEE-LITE THEME Elektra EKR 117	25	7
23 Feb 91	HOW DO YOU SAY . . . LOVE / GROOVE IS IN THE HEART (re-mix) Elektra EKR 118	52	2
27 Apr 91	GOOD BEAT / RIDING ON THROUGH Elektra EKR 122	53	3
13 Jun 92	RUNAWAY Elektra EKR 148	45	3
30 Jul 94	PICNIC IN THE SUMMERTIME Elektra EKR 186CD1	43	2

'What Is Love' listed only from 25 Aug 1990

DEEJAY PUNK-ROC US, male DJ / producer (5 WEEKS)

			pos/wks
21 Mar 98	DEAD HUSBAND Independiente ISOM 9MS	71	1
9 May 98	MY BEATBOX Independiente ISOM 12MS	43	1
8 Aug 98	FAR OUT Independiente ISOM 17MS	43	2
20 Feb 99	ROC-IN-IT Independiente ISOM 21MS [1]	59	1

[1] Deejay Punk-Roc vs Onyx

DEEJAY SVEN – See MC MIKER 'G' and Deejay SVEN

Carol DEENE UK, female vocalist (25 WEEKS)

			pos/wks
26 Oct 61	SAD MOVIES (MAKE ME CRY) HMV POP 922	44	3
25 Jan 62	NORMAN HMV POP 973	24	8
5 Jul 62	JOHNNY GET ANGRY HMV POP 1027	32	4
23 Aug 62	SOME PEOPLE HMV POP 1058	25	10

DEEP BLUE UK, male producer – Sean O'Keefe (2 WEEKS)

			pos/wks
16 Apr 94	HELICOPTER TUNE Moving Shadow SHADOW 41CD	68	2

DEEP BLUE SOMETHING
US, male vocal / instrumental group (17 WEEKS)

			pos/wks
6 Jul 96	BREAKFAST AT TIFFANY'S Interscope IND 80032	55	2
21 Sep 96 ★	BREAKFAST AT TIFFANY'S (re-entry) Interscope IND 80032	1	12
7 Dec 96	JOSEY Interscope IND 95518	27	3

DEEP C UK, male / female vocal / instrumental group (3 WEEKS)

			pos/wks
19 Jan 91	AFRICAN REIGN M & G MAGS 4	75	1
8 Jun 91	CHILL TO THE PANIC M & G MAGS 10	73	2

DEEP CREED '94
US, male producer – Armand van Helden (1 WEEK)

			pos/wks
7 May 94	CAN U FEEL IT Eastern Bloc BLOCCD 005	59	1

DEEP DISH Iran, male instrumental / production duo (4 WEEKS)

			pos/wks
26 Oct 96	STAY GOLD Deconstruction 74321418222	41	1
1 Nov 97	STRANDED Deconstruction 74321512232	60	1
3 Oct 98	THE FUTURE OF THE FUTURE (STAY GOLD) Deconstruction 74321616252 [1]	31	2

[1] Deep Dish with Everything but the Girl

DEEP FEELING UK, male vocal / instrumental group (5 WEEKS)

			pos/wks
25 Apr 70	DO YOU LOVE ME Page One POF 165	45	1
9 May 70	DO YOU LOVE ME (re-entry) Page One POF 165	34	4

DEEP FOREST France, male instrumental duo – Eric Mouquet & Michael Sanchez (14 WEEKS)

			pos/wks
5 Feb 94 ●	SWEET LULLABY Columbia 6599242	10	6
21 May 94	DEEP FOREST Columbia 6604115	20	4
23 Jul 94	SAVANNA DANCE Columbia 6606355	28	2
24 Jun 95	MARTA'S SONG Columbia 6621402	26	2

DEEP PURPLE `372` `Top 500`
Long-running legendary heavy rock group. London band's ever-changing line-up ensured many spin-off groups, among them Rainbow (founded by ex-guitarist Ritchie Blackmore), Whitesnake (featuring ex-vocalist David Coverdale) and Gillan (started by ex-vocalist Ian Gillan) (85 WEEKS)

			pos/wks
15 Aug 70 ●	BLACK NIGHT Harvest HAR 5020	2	21
27 Feb 71 ●	STRANGE KIND OF WOMAN Harvest HAR 5033	8	12
13 Nov 71	FIREBALL Harvest HAR 5045	15	13
1 Apr 72	NEVER BEFORE Purple PUR 102	35	6
16 Apr 77	SMOKE ON THE WATER Purple PUR 132	21	7
15 Oct 77	NEW LIVE AND RARE (EP) Purple PUR 135	31	4
7 Oct 78	NEW LIVE AND RARE II (EP) Purple PUR 137	45	3
2 Aug 80	BLACK NIGHT (re-issue) Harvest HAR 5210	43	6
1 Nov 80	NEW LIVE AND RARE VOLUME 3 EP Harvest SHEP 101	48	3
26 Jan 85	PERFECT STRANGERS Polydor POSP 719	48	3
15 Jun 85	KNOCKING AT YOUR BACK DOOR / PERFECT STRANGERS Polydor POSP 749	68	1
18 Jun 88	HUSH Polydor PO 4	62	2
20 Oct 90	KING OF DREAMS RCA PB 49247	70	1

UK No.1 ★   UK Top 10 ●   Still on chart +   UK million seller ◆   UK entry at No.1 ■   US No.1 ▲

| 2 Mar 91 | LOVE CONQUERS ALL *RCA PB 49225* | 57 | 2 |
| 24 Jun 95 | BLACK NIGHT (re-mix) *EMI CDEM 382* | 66 | 1 |

Tracks on New Live and Rare (EP): Black Night (Live) / Painted Horse / When a Blind Man Cries. New Live and Rare II (EP): Burn (Edited Version) / Coronarias Redig / Mistreated (Interpolating Rock Me Baby). New Live and Rare Volume 3 (EP): Smoke on the Water / Bird Has Flown / Grabsplatter

DEEP RIVER BOYS *US, male vocal group (1 WEEK)*
pos/wks
| 7 Dec 56 | THAT'S RIGHT *HMV POP 263* | 29 | 1 |

Scotti DEEP *US, male producer / instrumentalist (1 WEEK)*
pos/wks
| 15 Mar 97 | BROOKLYN BEATS *Xtravaganza 0090095* | 67 | 1 |

Rick DEES and his CAST OF IDIOTS *US, male vocalist with male / female vocal / instrumental group (9 WEEKS)*
pos/wks
| 18 Sep 76 ● | DISCO DUCK (PART ONE) *RSO 2090 204* ▲ | 6 | 9 |

DEETAH *Chile, female vocalist (10 WEEKS)*
pos/wks
| 26 Sep 98 | RELAX *ffrr FCDP 345* | 11 | 8 |
| 1 May 99 | EL PARAISO RICO *ffrr FCD 356* | 39 | 2 |

DEF LEPPARD (251 Top 500) *Mainstream UK rock stalwarts who wooed US before their homeland: Joe Elliott (v), Phil Collen (g from 1983), Steve Clark (g) (d. 1991), Rick Savage (b), Rick Allen (d). In US achieved feat of two consecutive albums selling more than eight million (112 WEEKS)*
pos/wks
17 Nov 79	WASTED *Vertigo 6059 247*	61	3
23 Feb 80	HELLO AMERICA *Vertigo LEPP 1*	45	4
5 Feb 83	PHOTOGRAPH *Vertigo VER 5*	66	3
27 Aug 83	ROCK OF AGES *Vertigo VER 6*	41	4
1 Aug 87 ●	ANIMAL *Bludgeon Riffola LEP 1*	6	9
19 Sep 87	POUR SOME SUGAR ON ME		
	Bludgeon Riffola LEP 2	18	6
28 Nov 87	HYSTERIA *Bludgeon Riffola LEP 3*	26	5
9 Jan 88	HYSTERIA (re-entry) *Bludgeon Riffola LEP 3*	74	1
9 Apr 88	ARMAGEDDON IT *Bludgeon Riffola LEP 4*	20	5
16 Jul 88	LOVE BITES *Bludgeon Riffola LEP 5* ▲	11	8
11 Feb 89	ROCKET *Bludgeon Riffola LEP 6*	15	7
28 Mar 92 ●	LET'S GET ROCKED *Bludgeon Riffola DEF 7*	2	7
27 Jun 92	MAKE LOVE LIKE A MAN *Bludgeon Riffola LEP 7*	12	5
12 Sep 92	HAVE YOU EVER NEEDED SOMEONE SO BAD		
	Bludgeon Riffola LEP 8	16	5
30 Jan 93	HEAVEN IS *Bludgeon Riffola LEPCD 9*	13	5
1 May 93	TONIGHT *Bludgeon Riffola LEPCD 10*	34	3
18 Sep 93	TWO STEPS BEHIND *Bludgeon Riffola LEPCD 12*	32	4
15 Jan 94	ACTION *Bludgeon Riffola LEPCD 13*	14	5
14 Oct 95 ●	WHEN LOVE AND HATE COLLIDE		
	Bludgeon Riffola LEPCD 14	2	10
4 May 96	SLANG *Bludgeon Riffola LEPCD 15*	17	5
13 Jul 96	WORK IT OUT *Bludgeon Riffola LEPCD 16*	22	3
28 Sep 96	ALL I WANT IS EVERYTHING		
	Bludgeon Riffola LEPCD 17	38	2
30 Nov 96	BREATHE A SIGH *Bludgeon Riffola LEPCD 18*	43	1
24 Jul 99	PROMISES *Bludgeon Riffola 5621362*	41	1
9 Oct 99	GOODBYE *Bludgeon Riffola 5622892*	54	1

DEFINITION OF SOUND *UK, male rap duo (25 WEEKS)*
pos/wks
9 Mar 91	WEAR YOUR LOVE LIKE HEAVEN *Circa YR 61*	17	9
1 Jun 91	NOW IS TOMORROW *Circa YR 66*	46	4
8 Feb 92	MOIRA JANE'S CAFE *Circa YR 80*	34	4
19 Sep 92	WHAT ARE YOU UNDER *Circa YR 95*	68	1
14 Nov 92	CAN I GET OVER *Circa YR 97*	61	2
20 May 95	BOOM BOOM *Fontana DOSCD 1*	59	1
2 Dec 95	PASS THE VIBES *Fontana DOSCD 2*	23	3
24 Feb 96	CHILD *Fontana DOSCD 3*	48	1

DEFTONES *US, male vocal / instrumental group (4 WEEKS)*
pos/wks
21 Mar 98	MY OWN SUMMER (SHOVE IT) *Maverick W 0432CD*	29	2
11 Jul 98	BE QUIET AND DRIVE (FAR AWAY) *Maverick W 0445CD*	50	1
26 Aug 00	CHANGE (IN THE HOUSE OF FLIES) *Maverick W531CD*	53	1

DEGREES OF MOTION featuring BITI
US, female vocal group (21 WEEKS)
pos/wks
25 Apr 92	DO YOU WANT IT RIGHT NOW *ffrr F 184*	31	5
18 Jul 92	SHINE ON *ffrr F 192* [1]	43	3
7 Nov 92	SOUL FREEDOM - FREE YOUR SOUL *ffrr FX 201*	64	1
19 Mar 94 ●	SHINE ON (re-mix) *ffrr FCD 229*	8	8
25 Jun 94	DO YOU WANT IT RIGHT NOW (re-mix) *ffrr FCD 236*	26	4

[1] Degrees of Motion featuring Biti with Kit West

DEJA *US, male / female vocal duo (1 WEEK)*
pos/wks
| 29 Aug 87 | SERIOUS *10 TEN 132* | 75 | 1 |

DEJA VU *UK, male vocal / instrumental duo (1 WEEK)*
pos/wks
| 5 Feb 94 | WHY WHY WHY *Cowboy CDRODEO 941* | 57 | 1 |

Desmond DEKKER and the ACES (478 Top 500) *First reggae act to top UK chart, leader b. Desmond Dacres, 16 Jul 1942, Kingston, Jamaica. Winner of Jamaican 'King of Bluebeat' award five times between 1963-69. Despite obscure patois lyric, 'Israelites' reached Top 10 in UK (twice) and US (71 WEEKS)*
pos/wks
12 Jul 67	007 *Pyramid PYR 6004*	14	11
19 Mar 69 ★	ISRAELITES *Pyramid PYR 6058*	1	14
25 Jun 69 ●	IT MIEK *Pyramid PYR 6068*	7	11
2 Jul 69	ISRAELITES (re-entry) *Pyramid PYR 6058*	45	1
10 Jan 70	PICKNEY GAL *Pyramid PYR 6078*	42	3
22 Aug 70 ●	YOU CAN GET IT IF YOU REALLY WANT		
	Trojan TR 7777 [1]	2	15
10 May 75 ●	ISRAELITES (re-recording) *Cactus CT 57* [1]	10	9
30 Aug 75	SING A LITTLE SONG *Cactus CT 73* [1]	16	7

[1] Desmond Dekker

DEL AMITRI *Stylish soft rock band whose name is Greek for 'from the womb'. Core members Justin Currie (v,b) and Iain Harvie (g) formed band in Glasgow, Scotland, 1983. 'Roll To Me' was one of the few UK records to reach US Top 10 in late 1990s (69 WEEKS)*
pos/wks
19 Aug 89	KISS THIS THING GOODBYE *A & M AM 515*	59	2
13 Jan 90	NOTHING EVER HAPPENS *A & M AM 536*	11	9
24 Mar 90	KISS THIS THING GOODBYE (re-issue) *A & M AM 551*	43	4
16 Jun 90	MOVE AWAY JIMMY BLUE *A & M AM 555*	36	6
3 Nov 90	SPIT IN THE RAIN *A & M AM 589*	21	6
9 May 92	ALWAYS THE LAST TO KNOW *A & M AM 870*	13	7
11 Jul 92	BE MY DOWNFALL *A & M AM 884*	30	4
12 Sep 92	JUST LIKE A MAN *A & M AM 0057*	25	4
23 Jan 93	WHEN YOU WERE YOUNG *A & M AMCD 0132*	20	3
18 Feb 95	HERE AND NOW *A & M 5809692*	21	4
29 Apr 95	DRIVING WITH THE BRAKES ON *A & M 5810072*	18	4
8 Jul 95	ROLL TO ME *A & M 5811312*	22	4
28 Oct 95	TELL HER THIS *A & M 5812172*	32	2
21 Jun 97	NOT WHERE IT'S AT *A & M 5822532*	21	3
6 Dec 97	SOME OTHER SUCKER'S PARADE *A&M 5824352*	46	1
13 Jun 98	DON'T COME HOME TOO SOON *A&M 5827052*	15	4
5 Sep 98	CRY TO BE FOUND *A&M MERCD 513*	40	2

DE'LACY
US, male / female vocal / instrumental group (16 WEEKS)
pos/wks
2 Sep 95 ●	HIDEAWAY *Slip 'N' Slide 74321310472*	9	10
31 Aug 96	THAT LOOK *Slip 'N' Slide 74321398322*	19	4
14 Feb 98	HIDEAWAY 1998 (re-mix) *Slip 'N'Slide 74321561052*	21	2

DELAGE *UK, female vocal group (2 WEEKS)*
pos/wks
| 15 Dec 90 | ROCK THE BOAT *PWL / Polydor PO 113* | 63 | 2 |

DELAKOTA *UK, male vocal / instrumental duo (3 WEEKS)*
pos/wks
18 Jul 98	THE ROCK *Go.Beat GOBCD 10*	60	1
19 Sep 98	C'MON CINCINNATI *Go.Beat GOBCD 11* [1]	55	1
13 Feb 99	555 *Go.Beat GOBCD 14*	42	1

[1] Delakota featuring Rose Smith

UK No.1 ★   UK Top 10 ●   Still on chart +   UK million seller ◆   UK entry at No.1 ■   US No.1 ▲

DELANEY and BONNIE and FRIENDS featuring Eric CLAPTON
US, male / female vocal duo and instrumental group (9 WEEKS)   pos/wks

20 Dec 69	COMIN' HOME *Atlantic 584 308*	**16** 9

See also Eric CLAPTON

DELANO – See CZR featuring DELANO

DELEGATION *UK, male vocal / instrumental group (7 WEEKS)*   pos/wks

23 Apr 77	WHERE IS THE LOVE (WE USED TO KNOW) *State STAT 40*	**22** 6
20 Aug 77	YOU'VE BEEN DOING ME WRONG *State STAT 55*	**49** 1

DELERIUM *Canada, male production duo (14 WEEKS)*   pos/wks

12 Jun 99	SILENCE *Nettwerk 398152*	**73** 1
5 Feb 00	HEAVEN'S EARTH *Nettwerk 331032*	**44** 1
14 Oct 00 ●	SILENCE (re-mix) *Nettwerk 331072*	**3** 12+

Sarah McLachlan provide vocals on Silence (re-mix) but was not credited on label

DELFONICS *US, male vocal group (23 WEEKS)*   pos/wks

10 Apr 71	DIDN'T I (BLOW YOUR MIND THIS TIME) *Bell 1099*	**43** 1
24 Apr 71	DIDN'T I (BLOW YOUR MIND THIS TIME) (re-entry) *Bell 1099* ...	**22** 8
10 Jul 71	LA-LA MEANS I LOVE YOU *Bell 1165*	**19** 10
16 Oct 71	READY OR NOT HERE I COME *Bell 1175*	**41** 4

DELGADOS
UK, male / female vocal / instrumental group (2 WEEKS)   pos/wks

23 May 98	PULL THE WIRES FROM THE WALL *Chemikal CHEM 023CD* ..	**69** 1
3 Jun 00	AMERICAN TRILOGY *Chemical Underground CHEM 039CD* ...	**61** 1

DELIRIOUS? *UK, male vocal / instrumental group (13 WEEKS)*   pos/wks

1 Mar 97	WHITE RIBBON DAY *Furious? CDFURY 1*	**41** 2
17 May 97	DEEPER *Furious? CDFURY 2*	**20** 3
26 Jul 97	PROMISE *Furious? CDFURY 3*	**20** 2
15 Nov 97	DEEPER (EP) *Furious? CXFURY 4*	**36** 2
27 Mar 99	SEE THE STAR *Furious? CDFURY 5*	**16** 2
4 Mar 00	IT'S OK *Furious? CDFURY 6*	**18** 2

Tracks on Deeper (EP): Deeper / Summer of Love / Touch / Sanctify

'DELIVERANCE' SOUNDTRACK *US, male instrumental duo - Eric Weissberg on banjo and Steve Mandell on guitar (7 WEEKS)*   pos/wks

31 Mar 73	DUELLING BANJOS *Warner Bros. K 16223*	**17** 7

DELLS *US, male vocal group (9 WEEKS)*   pos/wks

16 Jul 69	I CAN SING A RAINBOW - LOVE IS BLUE (MEDLEY) *Chess CRS 8099*	**15** 9

DELRONS – See REPARATA and the DELRONS

DELTA – See David MORALES; Crystal WATERS

DELUXE *US, female vocalist (1 WEEK)*   pos/wks

18 Mar 89	JUST A LITTLE MORE *Unyque UNQ 5*	**74** 1

DEM 2 *UK, male production duo (2 WEEKS)*   pos/wks

24 Oct 98	DESTINY *Locked On LOX 101CD*	**58** 2

DEMETREUS – See Christian FALK featuring DEMETREUS

DEMOLITION MAN – See PRIZNA featuring DEMOLITION MAN

D'EMPRESS – See 187 LOCKDOWN

Chaka DEMUS and PLIERS *Jamaica, male vocal duo (55 WEEKS)* pos/wks

12 Jun 93 ●	TEASE ME *Mango CIDM 806*	**3** 15
18 Sep 93 ●	SHE DON'T LET NOBODY *Mango CIDM 810*	**4** 10
18 Dec 93 ★	TWIST AND SHOUT *Mango CIDM 814* [1]	**1** 13
12 Mar 94	MURDER SHE WROTE *Mango CIDM 812*	**27** 4
18 Jun 94	I WANNA BE YOUR MAN *Mango CIDM 817*	**19** 6
27 Aug 94	GAL WINE *Mango CIDM 818*	**20** 4
1 Apr 95	TWIST AND SHOUT (re-entry) *Mango CIDM 814* [1]	**67** 1
31 Aug 96	EVERY KINDA PEOPLE *Island Jamaica IJCD 2005*	**47** 1
30 Aug 97	EVERY LITTLE THING SHE DOES IS MAGIC *Virgin VSCDT 1654*	**51** 1

[1] Chaka Demus and Pliers featuring Jack Radics and Taxi Gang

Terry DENE *UK, male vocalist (20 WEEKS)*   pos/wks

7 Jun 57	A WHITE SPORT COAT *Decca F 10895*	**18** 6
19 Jul 57	START MOVIN' *Decca F 10914*	**15** 8
26 Jul 57	A WHITE SPORT COAT (re-entry) *Decca F 10895*	**30** 1
16 May 58	STAIRWAY OF LOVE *Decca F 11016*	**16** 5

DENISE and JOHNNY *UK, male / female vocal duo - Denise Van Outen & Johnny Vaughan (12 WEEKS)*   pos/wks

26 Dec 98 ●	ESPECIALLY FOR YOU *RCA 74321644722*	**3** 10
10 Apr 99	ESPECIALLY FOR YOU (re-entry) *RCA 74321644722*	**53** 2

Cathy DENNIS *UK, female vocalist (68 WEEKS)*   pos/wks

21 Oct 89	C'MON AND GET MY LOVE *ffrr F 117* [1]	**15** 10
7 Apr 90	THAT'S THE WAY OF THE WORLD *ffrr F 132* [1]	**48** 3
4 May 91 ●	TOUCH ME (ALL NIGHT LONG) *Polydor CATH 3*	**5** 10
20 Jul 91	JUST ANOTHER DREAM *Polydor CATH 2*	**13** 7
5 Oct 91	TOO MANY WALLS *Polydor CATH 4*	**17** 7
7 Dec 91	EVERYBODY MOVE *Polydor CATH 5*	**25** 8
29 Aug 92	YOU LIED TO ME *Polydor CATH 6*	**34** 4
21 Nov 92	IRRESISTIBLE *Polydor CATH 7*	**24** 6
6 Feb 93	FALLING *Polydor CATHD 8*	**32** 2
12 Feb 94	WHY *ffrr FCD 227* [1]	**23** 3
10 Aug 96	WEST END PAD *Polydor 5752812*	**25** 2
1 Mar 97	WATERLOO SUNSET *Polydor 5759612*	**11** 5
21 Jun 97	WHEN DREAMS TURN TO DUST *Polydor 5711852*	**43** 1

[1] D Mob with Cathy Dennis

Jackie DENNIS *UK, male vocalist (10 WEEKS)*   pos/wks

14 Mar 58 ●	LA DEE DAH *Decca F 10992*	**4** 9
27 Jun 58	PURPLE PEOPLE EATER *Decca F 11033*	**29** 1

Stefan DENNIS *Australia, male vocalist (8 WEEKS)*   pos/wks

6 May 89	DON'T IT MAKE YOU FEEL GOOD *Sublime LIME 105*	**16** 7
7 Oct 89	THIS LOVE AFFAIR *Sublime LIME 113*	**67** 1

DENNISONS *UK, male vocal / instrumental group (13 WEEKS)*   pos/wks

15 Aug 63	BE MY GIRL *Decca F 11691*	**46** 6
7 May 64	WALKIN' THE DOG *Decca F 11880*	**36** 7

Richard DENTON and Martin COOK *UK, male orchestra leaders - instrumental duo, guitar and keyboards (7 WEEKS)*   pos/wks

15 Apr 78	THEME FROM 'THE HONG KONG BEAT' *BBC RESL 52*	**25** 7

John DENVER
US, male vocalist - Henry Deutschendorf (22 WEEKS)   pos/wks

17 Aug 74 ★	ANNIE'S SONG *RCA APBO 0295* ▲	**1** 13
12 Dec 81	PERHAPS LOVE *CBS A 1905* [1]	**46** 9

[1] Placido Domingo with John Denver

Karl DENVER   `208` **Top 500**   *Versatile Scottish singer with multi-octave vocal range, b. Angus McKenzie, 16 Dec 1934, Glasgow (d. 21 Dec 1998). This unique artist, whose yodel-laced style added colour and contrast to the charts, reached the Top 20 with his first five singles (127 WEEKS)*   pos/wks

22 Jun 61 ●	MARCHETA *Decca F 11360*	**8** 20
19 Oct 61 ●	MEXICALI ROSE *Decca F 11395*	**8** 11
25 Jan 62 ●	WIMOWEH *Decca F 11420*	**4** 17

		pos/wks
22 Feb 62 ●	NEVER GOODBYE *Decca F 11431*	9 18
7 Jun 62	A LITTLE LOVE A LITTLE KISS *Decca F 11470*	19 10
20 Sep 62	BLUE WEEKEND *Decca F 11505*	33 5
21 Mar 63	CAN YOU FORGIVE ME *Decca F 11608*	32 8
13 Jun 63	INDIAN LOVE CALL *Decca F 11674*	32 8
22 Aug 63	STILL *Decca F 11720*	13 15
5 Mar 64	MY WORLD OF BLUE *Decca F 11828*	29 6
4 Jun 64	LOVE ME WITH ALL YOUR HEART *Decca F 11905*	37 6
9 Jun 90	LAZYITIS - ONE ARMED BOXER *Factory FAC 2227* [1]	46 3

[1] Happy Mondays and Karl Denver

DENZIE – See MONSTA BOY featuring DENZIE

DEODATO
US, male multi-instrumentalist - Eumir Deodato (9 WEEKS) pos/wks

5 May 73 ●	ALSO SPRACH ZARATHUSTRA (2001) *Creed Taylor CTI 4000*	7 9

DEPARTMENT S
UK, male vocal / instrumental group (13 WEEKS) pos/wks

4 Apr 81	IS VIC THERE? *Demon D 1003*	22 10
11 Jul 81	GOING LEFT RIGHT *Stiff BUY 118*	55 3

DEPECHE MODE (63 Top 500) *Consistently successful synth-led Essex band: Dave Gahan (v), Martin Gore (syn), Andy Fletcher (b, syn), Vince Clarke (syn - replaced 1982 by Alan Wilder). One of the world's best-selling groups, who reached the Top 10 UK albums with first dozen releases (226 WEEKS)* pos/wks

4 Apr 81	DREAMING OF ME *Mute MUTE 013*	57 4
13 Jun 81	NEW LIFE *Mute MUTE 014*	11 15
19 Sep 81 ●	JUST CAN'T GET ENOUGH *Mute MUTE 016*	8 10
13 Feb 82 ●	SEE YOU *Mute MUTE 018*	6 10
8 May 82	THE MEANING OF LOVE *Mute MUTE 022*	12 8
28 Aug 82	LEAVE IN SILENCE *Mute BONG 1*	18 10
12 Feb 83	GET THE BALANCE RIGHT *Mute 7BONG 2*	13 8
23 Jul 83 ●	EVERYTHING COUNTS *Mute 7BONG 3*	6 11
1 Oct 83	LOVE IN ITSELF *Mute 7BONG 4*	21 7
24 Mar 84 ●	PEOPLE ARE PEOPLE *Mute 7BONG 5*	4 10
1 Sep 84 ●	MASTER AND SERVANT *Mute 7BONG 6*	9 9
10 Nov 84	SOMEBODY / BLASPHEMOUS RUMOURS *Mute 7BONG 7*	16 6
11 May 85	SHAKE THE DISEASE *Mute BONG 8*	18 9
28 Sep 85	IT'S CALLED A HEART *Mute BONG 9*	18 4
22 Feb 86	STRIPPED *Mute BONG 10*	15 5
26 Apr 86	A QUESTION OF LUST *Mute BONG 11*	28 5
23 Aug 86	A QUESTION OF TIME *Mute BONG 12*	17 6
9 May 87	STRANGELOVE *Mute BONG 13*	16 5
5 Sep 87	NEVER LET ME DOWN AGAIN *Mute BONG 14*	22 4
9 Jan 88	BEHIND THE WHEEL *Mute BONG 15*	21 5
28 May 88	LITTLE 15 (IMPORT) *Mute LITTLE 15*	60 2
25 Feb 89	EVERYTHING COUNTS *Mute BONG 16*	22 7
9 Sep 89	PERSONAL JESUS *Mute BONG 17*	13 8
17 Feb 90 ●	ENJOY THE SILENCE *Mute BONG 18*	6 9
19 May 90	POLICY OF TRUTH *Mute BONG 19*	16 6
29 Sep 90	WORLD IN MY EYES *Mute BONG 20*	17 6
27 Feb 93 ●	I FEEL YOU *Mute CDBONG 21*	8 7
8 May 93	WALKING IN MY SHOES *Mute CDBONG 22*	14 4
25 Sep 93 ●	CONDEMNATION *Mute CDBONG 23*	9 4
22 Jan 94 ●	IN YOUR ROOM *Mute CDBONG 24*	8 4
15 Feb 97 ●	BARREL OF A GUN *Mute CDBONG 25*	4 4
12 Apr 97 ●	IT'S NO GOOD *Mute CDBONG 26*	5 5
28 Jun 97	HOME *Mute CDBONG 27*	23 4
1 Nov 97	USELESS *Mute CDBONG 28*	28 2
19 Sep 98	ONLY WHEN I LOSE MYSELF *Mute CDBONG 29*	17 3

'BONG 16' is a live version of 'BONG 3'

DEPTH CHARGE
UK, male producer - Jonathan Kane (1 WEEK) pos/wks

29 Jul 95	LEGEND OF THE GOLDEN SNAKE *DC DC 01CD*	75 1

DER DRITTE RAUM
Germany, male producer - Andreas Kruger (1 WEEK) pos/wks

4 Sep 99	HALE BOPP *Additive 12AD 042*	75 1

DEREK and the DOMINOES – See Eric CLAPTON

DESIDERIO
UK, Holland, male production duo / female vocalist (1 WEEK) pos/wks

3 Jun 00	STARLIGHT *Code Blue BLU 010CD*	57 1

Kevin DESIMONE – See Barry MANILOW

DESIRELESS *France, female vocalist (19 WEEKS)* pos/wks

31 Oct 87	VOYAGE VOYAGE *CBS DESI 1*	53 6
14 May 88 ●	VOYAGE VOYAGE (re-mix) *CBS DESI 2*	5 13

DESIYA featuring Melissa YIANNAKOU
UK, male / female vocal / instrumental duo (1 WEEK) pos/wks

1 Feb 92	COMIN' ON STRONG *Black Market 12MKT 2*	74 1

DESKEE *UK, male instrumentalist (3 WEEKS)* pos/wks

3 Feb 90	LET THERE BE HOUSE *Big One VBIG 19*	52 2
8 Sep 90	DANCE, DANCE *Big One VBIG 22*	74 1

DES'REE (473 Top 500) *Gospel / folk-tinged soul singer, b. Des'ree Weekes 30 Nov 1968, London, UK, who in 1999 picked up Brit award for Best Female and World Music Award for Top UK Act. 'You Gotta Be' was only single to reach UK Top 20 three times in the 1990s and 'Life' was among Europe's biggest sellers in 1998 (72 WEEKS)* pos/wks

31 Aug 91	FEEL SO HIGH *Dusted Sound 6573667*	51 5
11 Jan 92	FEEL SO HIGH (re-issue) *Dusted Sound 6576897*	13 7
21 Mar 92	MIND ADVENTURES *Dusted Sound 6578637*	43 3
27 Jun 92	WHY SHOULD I LOVE YOU *Dusted Sound 6580917*	44 3
19 Jun 93	DELICATE *Columbia 6593312* [1]	14 6
9 Apr 94	YOU GOTTA BE *Dusted Sound 6601342*	20 7
18 Jun 94	I AIN'T MOVIN' *Dusted Sound 6604672*	44 3
3 Sep 94	LITTLE CHILD *Dusted Sound 6604515*	69 1
11 Mar 95	YOU GOTTA BE (re-mix) *Dusted Sound 6613215*	14 8
20 Jun 98 ●	LIFE *Sony S2 6659302*	8 15
7 Nov 98	WHAT'S YOUR SIGN? *Sony S2 6665162*	19 4
3 Apr 99 ●	YOU GOTTA BE (2nd re-mix) *Dusted Sound / Sony S2 6668935*	10 8
16 Oct 99	AIN'T NO SUNSHINE *Universal Music TV 1564332* [2]	42 2

[1] Terence Trent D'Arby featuring Des'ree [2] Ladysmith Black Mambazo featuring Des'ree

DESTINY'S CHILD
US, female vocal trio - lead vocal Beyoncé Knowles (62 WEEKS) pos/wks

28 Mar 98 ●	NO, NO, NO *Columbia 6656592*	5 8
11 Jul 98	WITH ME *Columbia 6661472*	19 3
7 Nov 98	SHE'S GONE *Columbia 6664915* [1]	24 3
23 Jan 99	GET ON THE BUS *East West E 3780CD* [2]	15 5
24 Jul 99 ●	BILLS, BILLS, BILLS *Columbia 6676902* ▲	6 9
30 Oct 99	BUG A BOO *Columbia 6681882*	9 7
8 Apr 00 ●	SAY MY NAME *Columbia 6691882* ▲	3 11
29 Jul 00 ●	JUMPIN' JUMPIN' *Columbia 6696292*	5 11
2 Dec 00 ★	INDEPENDENT WOMEN PART 1 *Columbia 6705932* ■ ▲	1 5+

[1] Matthew Marsden featuring Destiny's Child [2] Destiny's Child featuring Timbaland

DESTRY – See CIRCA featuring DESTRY; ZOO EXPERIENCE featuring DESTRY

Marcella DETROIT *US, female vocalist (16 WEEKS)* pos/wks

12 Mar 94	I BELIEVE *London LONCD 347*	11 8
14 May 94	AIN'T NOTHING LIKE THE REAL THING *London LONCD 350* [1]	24 4
16 Jul 94	I'M NO ANGEL *London LOCDP 351*	33 4

[1] Marcella Detroit and Elton John

DETROIT EMERALDS *US, male vocal group (44 WEEKS)* pos/wks

10 Feb 73 ●	FEEL THE NEED IN ME *Janus 6146 020*	4 15
5 May 73	YOU WANT IT YOU GOT IT *Westbound 6146 103*	12 9

UK No.1 ★   UK Top 10 ●   Still on chart +   UK million seller ◆   UK entry at No.1 ■   US No.1 ▲

11 Aug 73		I THINK OF YOU *Westbound 6146 104*........................**27** 9	
18 Jun 77		FEEL THE NEED (re-recording) *Atlantic K 10945* **12** 11	

DETROIT GRAND PU BAHS
US, male production / vocal group (3 WEEKS)   pos/wks

8 Jul 00		SANDWICHES *Jive Electro 9230252* **29** 3	

DETROIT SPINNERS `325` `Top 500`
Detroit-based R&B quintet known as The Spinners in US. Lead singers included G C Cameron, Phillippe Wynne (died on stage 1984) and John Edwards. Group, who unusually fared better after leaving Motown, have a 33-year US Top 40 span (93 WEEKS)   pos/wks

14 Nov 70		IT'S A SHAME *Tamla Motown TMG 755* [1] **20** 11
21 Apr 73		COULD IT BE I'M FALLING IN LOVE *Atlantic K 10283* **11** 11
29 Sep 73 ●		GHETTO CHILD *Atlantic K 10359* **7** 10
19 Oct 74		THEN CAME YOU *Atlantic K 10495* [2] ▲ **29** 6
11 Sep 76		THE RUBBERBAND MAN *Atlantic K 10807* **16** 11
29 Jan 77		WAKE UP SUSAN *Atlantic K 10799* **29** 6
7 May 77		COULD IT BE I'M FALLING IN LOVE (EP)
		Atlantic K 10935....**32** 3
23 Feb 80 ★		WORKING MY WAY BACK TO YOU -
		FORGIVE ME GIRL - (MEDLEY) *Atlantic K 11432* **1** 14
10 May 80		BODY LANGUAGE *Atlantic K 11392* **40** 7
28 Jun 80 ●		CUPID - I'VE LOVED YOU FOR A LONG TIME (MEDLEY)
		Atlantic K 11498....**4** 10
24 Jun 95		I'LL BE AROUND *Cooltempo CDCOOL 306* [3] **30** 4

[1] Motown Spinners [2] Dionne Warwick & the Detroit Spinners [3] Rappin' 4-Tay featuring the Spinners

Tracks on Could It Be I'm Falling in Love (EP): Could It Be I'm Falling in Love / You're Throwing a Good Love Away / Games People Play / Lazy Susan

DETROIT WHEELS – See Mitch RYDER and the DETROIT WHEELS

DEUCE *UK, male / female vocal group (23 WEEKS)*   pos/wks

21 Jan 95		CALL IT LOVE *London LONCD 355* **11** 10
22 Apr 95 ●		I NEED YOU *London LONCD 365* **10** 5
19 Aug 95		ON THE BIBLE *London LONCD 368.*.............................**13** 6
29 Jun 96		NO SURRENDER *Love This LUVTHISCD 10* **29** 2

dEUS *Belgium, male vocal / instrumental group (7 WEEKS)*   pos/wks

11 Feb 95		HOTEL LOUNGE (BE THE DEATH OF ME) *Island CID 603* **55** 1
13 Jul 96		THEME FROM TURNPIKE (EP) *Island CID 630* **68** 1
19 Oct 96		LITTLE ARITHMETICS *Island CID 643* **44** 2
15 Mar 97		ROSES *Island CID 645* **56** 1
24 Apr 99		INSTANT STREET *Island CID 742* **49** 1
3 Jul 99		SISTER DEW *Island CID 750* **62** 1

Tracks on Theme from Turnpike EP: Theme from Turnpike / Worried About Satan / Overflow / My Little Contessa

Sidney DEVINE *UK, male vocalist (1 WEEK)*   pos/wks

1 Apr 78		SCOTLAND FOREVER *Philips SCOT 1* **48** 1

DEVO *US, male vocal / instrumental group (23 WEEKS)*   pos/wks

22 Apr 78		(I CAN'T ME GET NO) SATISFACTION *Stiff BOY 1.*.......**41** 8
13 May 78		JOCKO HOMO *Stiff DEV 1* **62** 3
12 Aug 78		BE STIFF *Stiff BOY 2* **71** 1
2 Sep 78		COME BACK JONEE *Virgin VS 223.*...............................**60** 4
22 Nov 80		WHIP IT *Virgin VS 383.*..**51** 7

Sheila B DEVOTION *France, female vocalist (33 WEEKS)*   pos/wks

11 Mar 78		SINGIN' IN THE RAIN PART 1 *Carrere EMI 2751* **11** 13
22 Jul 78		YOU LIGHT MY FIRE *Carrere EMI 2828* **44** 6
24 Nov 79		SPACER *Carrere CAR 128.*...**18** 14

Some copies of Spacer credited Sheila & B Devotion

DEVOTIONS – See BELLE and the DEVOTIONS

Howard DEVOTO – See BUZZCOCKS; MAGAZINE

DEXY'S MIDNIGHT RUNNERS `322` `Top 500`
Maverick Birmingham UK-based post-punk group who split up in 1987. Led throughout radical personnel and stylistic changes by Kevin Rowland (v/g), b 17 Aug 1953. 'Come On Eileen', was the top selling UK single of 1982 (93 WEEKS)   pos/wks

19 Jan 80		DANCE STANCE *Oddball Productions R 6028* **40** 6
22 Mar 80 ★		GENO *Late Night Feelings R 6033* **1** 14
12 Jul 80 ●		THERE THERE MY DEAR *Late Night Feelings R 6038*.......**7** 9
21 Mar 81		PLAN B *Parlophone R 6046* **58** 2
11 Jul 81		SHOW ME *Mercury DEXYS 6* **16** 9
20 Mar 82		THE CELTIC SOUL BROTHERS *Mercury DEXYS 8* [1] **45** 4
3 Jul 82 ★		COME ON EILEEN *Mercury DEXYS 9* [2] ◆ ▲ **1** 17
2 Oct 82 ●		JACKIE WILSON SAID (I'M IN HEAVEN WHEN YOU
		SMILE) *Mercury DEXYS 10* [2] **5** 7
4 Dec 82		LET'S GET THIS STRAIGHT (FROM THE START) / OLD
		Mercury DEXYS 11 [2] **17** 9
2 Apr 83		THE CELTIC SOUL BROTHERS *Mercury DEXYS 12* [2] **20** 6
22 Nov 86		BECAUSE OF YOU *Mercury BRUSH 1* **13** 10

[1] Dexy's Midnight Runners with the Emerald Express [2] Kevin Rowland and Dexy's Midnight Runners

DEXYS 12 is a different version from DEXYS 8

Tony DI BART *UK, male vocalist (19 WEEKS)*   pos/wks

9 Apr 94 ★		THE REAL THING *Cleveland City Blues CCBCD 15001* **1** 12
20 Aug 94		DO IT *Cleveland City Blues CCBCD 15003* **21** 4
20 May 95		WHY DID YA *Cleveland City Blues CCBCD 15004* **46** 1
2 Mar 96		TURN YOUR LOVE AROUND
		Cleveland City Blues CCBCD 15006............................**66** 1
17 Oct 98		THE REAL THING (re-mix) *Cleveland City CLECD 13050*..........**51** 1

Gregg DIAMOND BIONIC BOOGIE
US, male / female vocal group (3 WEEKS)   pos/wks

20 Jan 79		CREAM (ALWAYS RISES TO THE TOP) *Polydor POSP 18* **61** 3

Jim DIAMOND *UK, male vocalist (30 WEEKS)*   pos/wks

3 Nov 84 ★		I SHOULD HAVE KNOWN BETTER *A & M AM 220* **1** 13
2 Feb 85		I SLEEP ALONE AT NIGHT *A & M AM 229.*.....................**72** 1
18 May 85		REMEMBER I LOVE YOU *A & M AM 247* **42** 5
22 Feb 86 ●		HI HO SILVER *A & M AM 296* **5** 11

See also PhD

Neil DIAMOND `221` `Top 500`
World-renowned singer / guitarist / songwriter, b. Noah Kaminsky, 24 Jan 1941, Brooklyn, US. First found international fame as writer of 'I'm a Believer' (Monkees), before going on to become one of world's most popular live artists and biggest-selling album acts (121 WEEKS)   pos/wks

7 Nov 70 ●		CRACKLIN' ROSIE *Uni UN 529* ▲....................................**3** 17
20 Feb 71 ●		SWEET CAROLINE *Uni UN 531* ▲...................................**8** 11
8 May 71 ●		I AM . . . I SAID *Uni UN 532* **4** 12
13 May 72		SONG SUNG BLUE *Uni UN 538* ▲...............................**14** 13
14 Aug 76		IF YOU KNOW WHAT I MEAN *CBS 4398* **35** 4
23 Oct 76		BEAUTIFUL NOISE *CBS 4601* **13** 9
24 Dec 77		DESIREE *CBS 5869* **39** 6
25 Nov 78 ●		YOU DON'T BRING ME FLOWERS *CBS 6803* [1] ▲..........**5** 12
3 Mar 79		FOREVER IN BLUE JEANS *CBS 7047* **16** 12
15 Nov 80		LOVE ON THE ROCKS *Capitol CL 16173* **17** 12
14 Feb 81		HELLO AGAIN *Capitol CL 16176.*..................................**51** 4
20 Nov 82		HEARTLIGHT *CBS A 2814.*...**47** 7
21 Nov 92		MORNING HAS BROKEN *Columbia 6588267* **36** 2

[1] Barbra and Neil

Barbra was Barbra Streisand

DIAMOND HEAD *UK, male vocal / instrumental group (2 WEEKS)* pos/wks

11 Sep 82		IN THE HEAT OF THE NIGHT *MCA DHM 102.*...................**67** 2

DIAMONDS *Canada / US, male vocal group (17 WEEKS)*   pos/wks

31 May 57 ●		LITTLE DARLIN' *Mercury MT 148* **3** 17

DIANA – See Diana ROSS

DICK and DEEDEE US, male / female vocal duo (3 WEEKS)
pos/wks

| 26 Oct 61 | THE MOUNTAIN'S HIGH London HLG 9408 | 37 | 3 |

Charles DICKENS UK, male vocalist (8 WEEKS)
pos/wks

| 1 Jul 65 | THAT'S THE WAY LOVE GOES Pye 7N 15887 | 37 | 8 |

Gwen DICKEY US, female vocalist (13 WEEKS)
pos/wks

27 Jan 90	CAR WASH Swanyard SYR 7	72	2
2 Jul 94	AIN'T NOBODY (LOVES ME BETTER) X-clusive XCLU 010CD [1]	21	4
14 Feb 98	WISHING ON A STAR Northwestside 74321554632 [2]	13	4
31 Oct 98	CAR WASH (re-recording) MCA MCSTD 48096 [3]	18	3

[1] KWS and Gwen Dickey [2] Jay-Z featuring Gwen Dickey [3] Rose Royce featuring Gwen Dickey

See also ROSE ROYCE

Neville DICKIE UK, male instrumentalist - piano (10 WEEKS)
pos/wks

| 25 Oct 69 | ROBIN'S RETURN Major Minor MM 644 | 33 | 7 |
| 20 Dec 69 | ROBIN'S RETURN (re-entry) Major Minor MM 644 | 43 | 3 |

DICKIES US, male vocal / instrumental group (28 WEEKS)
pos/wks

16 Dec 78	SILENT NIGHT A & M AMS 7403	47	4
21 Apr 79 ●	BANANA SPLITS (TRA LA LA SONG) A & M AMS 7431	7	8
21 Jul 79	PARANOID A & M AMS 7368	45	6
15 Sep 79	NIGHTS IN WHITE SATIN A & M AMS 7469	39	5
16 Feb 80	FAN MAIL A & M AMS 7504	57	3
19 Jul 80	GIGANTOR A & M AMS 7544	72	2

Bruce DICKINSON UK, male vocalist (23 WEEKS)
pos/wks

28 Apr 90	TATTOOED MILLIONAIRE EMI EM 138	18	5
23 Jun 90	ALL THE YOUNG DUDES EMI EM 142	23	5
25 Aug 90	DIVE! DIVE! DIVE! EMI EM 151	45	2
4 Apr 92 ●	(I WANT TO BE) ELECTED London LON 319 [1]	9	5
28 May 94	TEARS OF THE DRAGON EMI CDEM 322	28	2
8 Oct 94	SHOOT ALL THE CLOWNS EMI CDEMS 341	37	2
13 Apr 96	BACK FROM THE EDGE Raw Power RAWX 1012	68	1
3 May 97	ACCIDENT OF BIRTH Raw Power RAWX 1042	54	1

[1] Mr. Bean and Smear Campaign featuring Bruce Dickinson

See also IRON MAIDEN

Barbara DICKSON UK, female vocalist (49 WEEKS)
pos/wks

17 Jan 76 ●	ANSWER ME RSO 2090 174	9	7
26 Feb 77	ANOTHER SUITCASE IN ANOTHER HALL MCA 266	18	7
19 Jan 80	CARAVAN SONG Epic EPC 8103	41	7
15 Mar 80	JANUARY FEBRUARY Epic	11	10
14 Jun 80	IN THE NIGHT Epic EPC 8593	48	2
5 Jan 85 ★	I KNOW HIM SO WELL RCA CHESS 3 [1]	1	16

[1] Elaine Paige and Barbara Dickson

DICTATORS US, male vocal / instrumental group (2 WEEKS)
pos/wks

| 17 Sep 77 | SEARCH AND DESTROY Asylum K 13091 | 49 | 1 |
| 1 Oct 77 | SEARCH AND DESTROY (re-entry) Asylum K 13091 | 50 | 1 |

Bo DIDDLEY US, male vocalist / instrumentalist - guitar (10 WEEKS)
pos/wks

| 10 Oct 63 | PRETTY THING Pye International 7N 25217 | 34 | 6 |
| 18 Mar 65 | HEY GOOD LOOKIN' Chess 8000 | 39 | 4 |

DIDDY UK, male producer (3 WEEKS)
pos/wks

| 19 Feb 94 | GIVE ME LOVE Positiva CDTIV 8 | 52 | 1 |
| 12 Jul 97 | GIVE ME LOVE (re-mix) Feverpitch CDFVR 19 | 23 | 2 |

DIESEL PARK WEST UK, male vocal / instrumental group (15 WEEKS)
pos/wks

4 Feb 89	ALL THE MYTHS ON SUNDAY Food FOOD 17	66	2
1 Apr 89	LIKE PRINCES DO Food FOOD 19	58	3
5 Aug 89	WHEN THE HOODOO COMES Food FOOD 20	62	2
18 Jan 92	FALL TO LOVE Food FOOD 35	48	3
21 Mar 92	BOY ON TOP OF THE NEWS Food FOOD 36	58	2
5 Sep 92	GOD ONLY KNOWS Food FOOD 39	57	3

DIFFERENT GEAR Vs POLICE UK / Italy, male production group & UK / US male vocal / instrumental trio (3 WEEKS)
pos/wks

| 5 Aug 00 | WHEN THE WORLD IS RUNNING DOWN Pagan PAGAN039CDS | 28 | 3 |

DIFFORD and TILBROOK UK, male vocal / instrumental duo (2 WEEKS)
pos/wks

| 30 Jun 84 | LOVE'S CRASHING WAVES A & M AM 193 | 57 | 2 |

See also SQUEEZE

DIGABLE PLANETS US, male / female vocal / instrumental group (2 WEEKS)
pos/wks

| 13 Feb 93 | REBIRTH OF SLICK (COOL LIKE DAT) Pendulum EKR 159CD | 67 | 2 |

DIGITAL DREAM BABY UK, male producer - Steven Teear (4 WEEKS)
pos/wks

| 14 Dec 91 | WALKING IN THE AIR Columbia 6576067 | 49 | 4 |

Hit is a dance re-mix of 'Walking in the Air' by vocalist Peter Auty

See also Peter AUTY and the SINFONIA OF LONDON conducted by Howard BLAKE

DIGITAL EXCITATION Belgium, male producer - Frank de Wulf (2 WEEKS)
pos/wks

| 29 Feb 92 | PURE PLEASURE R&S RSUK 10 | 37 | 2 |

DIGITAL ORGASM Belgium, male / female vocal / instrumental group (14 WEEKS)
pos/wks

7 Dec 91	RUNNING OUT OF TIME Dead Dead Good GOOD 009	16	9
18 Apr 92	STARTOUCHERS DDG International GOOD 13	31	3
25 Jul 92	MOOG ERUPTION DDG International GOOD 17	62	2

DIGITAL UNDERGROUND US, male rap group (4 WEEKS)
pos/wks

| 16 Mar 91 | SAME SONG Big Life BLR 40 | 52 | 4 |

DILEMMA Italy, male instrumental / production group (1 WEEK)
pos/wks

| 6 Apr 96 | IN SPIRIT ffrr FCD 274 | 42 | 1 |

Ricky DILLARD – See Farley 'Jackmaster' FUNK

D'INFLUENCE UK, male / female vocal / instrumental group (10 WEEKS)
pos/wks

20 Jun 92	GOOD LOVER East West A 8573 [1]	46	2
27 Mar 93	GOOD LOVER (re-mix) East West America A 8439CD [1]	61	1
24 Jun 95	MIDNITE East West A 4418CD [2]	58	1
16 Aug 97	HYPNOTIZE Echo ECSCD 41	33	2
11 Oct 97	MAGIC Echo ECSCD 45	45	1
5 Sep 98	ROCK WITH YOU Echo ECSCD 56	30	3

[1] D-Influence [2] D*Influence

Paolo DINI – See FPI PROJECT

Mark DINNING US, male vocalist (4 WEEKS)
pos/wks

| 10 Mar 60 | TEEN ANGEL MGM 1053 ▲ | 37 | 3 |
| 7 Apr 60 | TEEN ANGEL (re-entry) MGM 1053 | 42 | 1 |

DINOSAUR JR. *US, male vocal / instrumental group (13 WEEKS)*

		pos/wks
2 Feb 91	THE WAGON *Blanco Y Negro NEG 48*	49 2
14 Nov 92	GET ME *Blanco Y Negro NEG 60*	44 1
30 Jan 93	START CHOPPIN' *Blanco Y Negro NEG 61CD*	20 3
12 Jun 93	OUT THERE *Blanco Y Negro NEG 63CD*	44 2
27 Aug 94	FEEL THE PAIN *Blanco Y Negro NEG 74CD*	25 3
11 Feb 95	I DON'T THINK SO *Blanco Y Negro NEG 77CD*	67 1
5 Apr 97	TAKE A RUN AT THE SUN *Blanco Y Negro NEG 103CD*	53 1

DINOSAURS – See Terry DACTYL and the DINOSAURS

DIO *UK / US, male vocal / instrumental group (22 WEEKS)*

		pos/wks
20 Aug 83	HOLY DIVER *Vertigo DIO 1*	72 2
29 Oct 83	RAINBOW IN THE DARK *Vertigo DIO 2*	46 3
11 Aug 84	WE ROCK *Vertigo DIO 3*	42 3
29 Sep 84	MYSTERY *Vertigo DIO 4*	34 4
10 Aug 85	ROCK 'N' ROLL CHILDREN *Vertigo DIO 5*	26 6
2 Nov 85	HUNGRY FOR HEAVEN *Vertigo DIO 6*	72 1
17 May 86	HUNGRY FOR HEAVEN (re-issue) *Vertigo DIO 7*	56 2
1 Aug 87	I COULD HAVE BEEN A DREAMER *Vertigo DIO 8*	69 1

DION *US, male vocalist - Dion DiMucci (35 WEEKS)*

		pos/wks
26 Jun 59	A TEENAGER IN LOVE *London HLU 8874* [1]	28 2
19 Jan 61	LONELY TEENAGER *Top Rank JAR 521*	47 1
2 Nov 61	RUNAROUND SUE *Top Rank JAR 586* ▲	11 9
15 Feb 62	● THE WANDERER *HMV POP 971*	10 12
22 May 76	THE WANDERER (re-issue) *Philips 6146 700*	16 9
19 Aug 89	KING OF THE NEW YORK STREET *Arista 112556*	74 2

[1] Dion and the Belmonts

Celine DION ⟨60 Top 500⟩ *French-Canadian vocalist who won the 1988 Eurovision Song Contest (for Switzerland), b. 30 Mar 1968, Quebec. She has sold a reported 130 million albums worldwide and is the only female with two UK million-selling singles (230 WEEKS)*

		pos/wks
16 May 92	● BEAUTY AND THE BEAST *Epic 6576607* [1]	9 7
4 Jul 92	IF YOU ASKED ME TO *Epic 6581927*	60 2
14 Nov 92	LOVE CAN MOVE MOUNTAINS *Epic 6587787*	46 2
26 Dec 92	IF YOU ASKED ME TO (re-entry) *Epic 6581927*	57 2
3 Apr 93	WHERE DOES MY HEART BEAT NOW *Epic 6563265*	72 1
29 Jan 94	● THE POWER OF LOVE *Epic 6597992* ▲	4 10
23 Apr 94	MISLED *Epic 6602922*	40 3
22 Oct 94	★ THINK TWICE *Epic 6606422* ◆	1 31
20 May 95	● ONLY ONE ROAD *Epic 6613535*	8 8
9 Sep 95	● TU M'AIMES ENCORE (TO LOVE ME AGAIN) *Epic 6624255*	7 9
2 Dec 95	● MISLED (re-issue) *Epic 6626495*	15 6
2 Mar 96	● FALLING INTO YOU *Epic 6629795*	10 10
1 Jun 96	● BECAUSE YOU LOVED ME (THEME FROM 'UP CLOSE AND PERSONAL') *Epic 6632382* ▲	5 16
5 Oct 96	● IT'S ALL COMING BACK TO ME NOW *Epic 6637112*	3 14
21 Dec 96	● ALL BY MYSELF *Epic 6640622*	6 10
15 Mar 97	ALL BY MYSELF (re-entry) *Epic 6640622*	58 1
28 Jun 97	CALL THE MAN *Epic 6646922*	11 6
15 Nov 97	● TELL HIM *Epic 6653052* [2]	3 15
20 Dec 97	THE REASON *Epic 6653812*	11 8
21 Feb 98	★ MY HEART WILL GO ON *Epic 6655472* ◆ ■ ▲	1 20
18 Jul 98	● IMMORTALITY *Epic 6661682* [3]	5 12
28 Nov 98	● I'M YOUR ANGEL *Epic 6666282* [4] ▲	3 13
10 Jul 99	TREAT HER LIKE A LADY *Epic 6675522*	29 3
11 Dec 99	THAT'S THE WAY IT IS *Epic 6684622*	12 11
8 Apr 00	THE FIRST TIME EVER I SAW YOUR FACE *Epic 6691942*	19 6
10 Jun 00	THE FIRST TIME EVER I SAW YOUR FACE (re-entry) *Epic 6691942*	74 1

[1] Celine Dion and Peabo Bryson [2] Barbra Streisand and Celine Dion [3] Celine Dion with Bee Gees [4] Celine Dion and R Kelly

KATHRYN DION – See 2 FUNKY 2 starring Kathryn DION

DIONNE *Canada, female vocalist (2 WEEKS)*

		pos/wks
23 Sep 89	COME GET MY LOVIN' *Citybeat CBC 745*	69 2

Wasis DIOP Featuring Lena FIAGBE *Senegal, male producer featuring UK, female vocalist (2 WEEKS)*

		pos/wks
10 Feb 96	AFRICAN DREAM *Mercury MERCD 453*	44 2

DIRE STRAITS ⟨227 Top 500⟩ *Multi- Brit- and Grammy- award-winning group led by vocalist / lead guitarist / songwriter Mark Knopfler, b. 12 Aug 1949, Glasgow. This London-based band, whose world tours attracted millions, is among the Top 5 album-selling acts in the UK. Knopfler was honoured with an MBE in 2000 and shortly afterwards, had a dinosaur named after him (119 WEEKS)*

		pos/wks
10 Mar 79	● SULTANS OF SWING *Vertigo 6059 206*	8 11
28 Jul 79	LADY WRITER *Vertigo 6059 230*	51 6
17 Jan 81	● ROMEO AND JULIET *Vertigo MOVIE 1*	8 11
4 Apr 81	SKATEAWAY *Vertigo MOVIE 2*	37 5
10 Oct 81	TUNNEL OF LOVE *Vertigo MUSIC 3*	54 3
4 Sep 82	● PRIVATE INVESTIGATIONS *Vertigo DSTR 1*	2 8
22 Jan 83	TWISTING BY THE POOL *Vertigo DSTR 2*	14 7
18 Feb 84	LOVE OVER GOLD (LIVE) / SOLID ROCK (LIVE) *Vertigo DSTR 6*	50 3
20 Apr 85	SO FAR AWAY *Vertigo DSTR 9*	20 6
6 Jul 85	● MONEY FOR NOTHING *Vertigo DSTR 10* ▲	4 16
26 Oct 85	BROTHERS IN ARMS *Vertigo DSTR 11*	16 13
11 Jan 86	● WALK OF LIFE *Vertigo DSTR 12*	2 11
3 May 86	YOUR LATEST TRICK *Vertigo DSTR 13*	26 6
5 Nov 88	SULTANS OF SWING (re-issue) *Vertigo DSTR 15*	62 1
31 Aug 91	CALLING ELVIS *Vertigo DSTR 16*	21 4
2 Nov 91	HEAVY FUEL *Vertigo DSTR 17*	55 2
29 Feb 92	ON EVERY STREET *Vertigo DSTR 18*	42 2
27 Jun 92	THE BUG *Vertigo DSTR 19*	67 1
22 May 93	ENCORES (EP) *Vertigo DSCD 20*	31 3

Tracks on Encores (EP): Your Latest Trick / The Bug / Solid Rock / Local Hero (Wild Theme)

See also Mark KNOPFLER

DIRECKT *UK, male instrumental / production duo (2 WEEKS)*

		pos/wks
13 Aug 94	TWO FATT GUITARS (REVISITED) *UFG UFG 7CD*	36 2

DIRECT DRIVE *UK, male / female vocal / instrumental group (3 WEEKS)*

		pos/wks
26 Jan 85	ANYTHING *Polydor POSP 728*	67 2
4 May 85	A.B.C. (FALLING IN LOVE'S NOT EASY) *Boiling Point POSP 742*	75 1

DIRTY ROTTEN SCOUNDRELS – See Lisa STANSFIELD

DISCHARGE *UK, male vocal / instrumental group (3 WEEKS)*

		pos/wks
24 Oct 81	NEVER AGAIN *Clay CLAY 6*	64 3

DISCO ANTHEM *Holland, male producer - Lex van Coeverden (2 WEEKS)*

		pos/wks
18 Jun 94	SCREAM *Sweat MCSTD 1977*	47 2

DISCO CITIZENS *UK, male instrumental / production duo (5 WEEKS)*

		pos/wks
22 Jul 95	RIGHT HERE RIGHT NOW *Deconstruction 74321293872*	40 2
12 Apr 97	FOOTPRINT *Xtravaganza 0091115*	34 2
4 Jul 98	NAGASAKI BADGER *Xtravaganza 0091595 EXT*	56 1

See also CHICANE

DISCO EVANGELISTS *UK, male instrumental / production group (2 WEEKS)*

		pos/wks
8 May 93	DE NIRO *Positiva CDTIV 2*	59 2

DISCO TEX and the SEX-O-LETTES *US, male vocalist / female vocal group (22 WEEKS)*

		pos/wks
23 Nov 74	● GET DANCING *Chelsea 2005 013*	8 12
26 Apr 75	● I WANNA DANCE WIT CHOO *Chelsea 2005 024* [1]	6 10

[1] Disco Tex and the Sex-O-Lettes featuring Sir Montl Rock III

UK No.1 ★   UK Top 10 ●   Still on chart +   UK million seller ◆   UK entry at No.1 ■   US No.1 ▲

DISPOSABLE HEROES OF HIPHOPRISY
US, male rap / instrumental duo (7 WEEKS)   pos/wks

4 Apr 92	**TELEVISION THE DRUG OF THE NATION**		
	Fourth & Broadway BRW 241	**57**	2
30 May 92	**LANGUAGE OF VIOLENCE** *Fourth & Broadway 12BRW 248*	**68**	1
19 Dec 92	**TELEVISION THE DRUG OF THE NATION** (re-entry)		
	Fourth & Broadway BRW 241	**44**	4

Sacha DISTEL *France, male vocalist (27 WEEKS)*   pos/wks

10 Jan 70	**RAINDROPS KEEP FALLING ON MY HEAD**		
	Warner Bros. WB 7345	**50**	1
24 Jan 70 ●	**RAINDROPS KEEP FALLING ON MY HEAD** (re-entry)		
	Warner Bros. WB 7345	**10**	20
27 Jun 70	**RAINDROPS KEEP FALLING ON MY HEAD** (2nd		
	re-entry) *Warner Bros. WB 7345*	**43**	4
1 Aug 70	**RAINDROPS KEEP FALLING ON MY HEAD** (3rd		
	re-entry) *Warner Bros. WB 7345*	**47**	1
15 Aug 70	**RAINDROPS KEEP FALLING ON MY HEAD** (4th		
	re-entry) *Warner Bros. WB 7345*	**44**	1

DIVA *Norway, female vocal duo (2 WEEKS)*   pos/wks

7 Oct 95	**THE SUN ALWAYS SHINES ON TV** *East West YZ 947CD*	**53**	1
20 Jul 96	**EVERYBODY (MOVE YOUR BODY)** *East West EW 035CD*	**44**	1

DIVA SURPRISE Featuring Georgia JONES *US / Spain, male production duo and US, female vocalist (2 WEEKS)*   pos/wks

14 Nov 98	**ON THE TOP OF THE WORLD** *Positiva CDTIV 100*	**29**	2

DIVE *UK, male production duo - Sacha Collisson and Simon Greenaway (1 WEEK)*   pos/wks

21 Feb 98	**BOOGIE** *WEA WEA 147CD1*	**35**	1

Hit featured vocalist Nasreen Shah

See also AURORA

DIVERSIONS
UK, male / female vocal / instrumental group (3 WEEKS)   pos/wks

20 Sep 75	**FATTIE BUM BUM** *Gull GULS 18*	**34**	3

DIVINE *US, male vocalist (24 WEEKS)*   pos/wks

15 Oct 83	**LOVE REACTION**		
	Design Communication DES 4	**65**	2
14 Jul 84	**YOU THINK YOU'RE A MAN** *Proto ENA 118*	**16**	10
20 Oct 84	**I'M SO BEAUTIFUL** *Proto ENA 121*	**52**	2
27 Apr 85	**WALK LIKE A MAN** *Proto ENA 125*	**23**	7
20 Jul 85	**TWISTIN' THE NIGHT AWAY** *Proto ENA 127*	**47**	3

DIVINE *US, female vocal group (1 WEEK)*   pos/wks

16 Oct 99	**LATELY** *Mushroom / Red Ant RA 002CDS*	**52**	1

DIVINE COMEDY
UK, male vocalist / instrumentalist - Neil Hannon (33 WEEKS)   pos/wks

29 Jun 96	**SOMETHING FOR THE WEEKEND**		
	Setanta SETCD 26	**14**	5
24 Aug 96	**BECOMING MORE LIKE ALFIE** *Setanta SETCD 27*	**27**	2
16 Nov 96	**THE FROG PRINCESS** *Setanta SETCD 32*	**15**	2
22 Mar 97	**EVERYBODY KNOWS (EXCEPT YOU)**		
	Setanta SETCDA 038	**14**	4
11 Apr 98	**SOMEDAY I'LL FIND YOU / I'VE BEEN TO A**		
	MARVELLOUS PARTY *EMI CDTCB 001* [1]	**28**	3
26 Sep 98	**GENERATION SEX** *Setanta SETCDA 050*	**19**	3
28 Nov 98	**THE CERTAINTY OF CHANCE**		
	Setanta SETCDA 067	**49**	1
6 Feb 99 ●	**NATIONAL EXPRESS** *Setanta SETCDA 069*	**8**	7
21 Aug 99	**THE POP SINGER'S FEAR OF THE POLLEN COUNT**		
	Setanta SETCDA 070	**17**	4
13 Nov 99	**GIN SOAKED BOY** *Setanta SETCDA 071*	**38**	2

[1] Shola Ama and Craig Armstrong / Divine Comedy

DIVINYLS *Australia, male / female vocal / instrumental duo (12 WEEKS)*   pos/wks

18 May 91 ●	**I TOUCH MYSELF** *Virgin America VUS 36*	**10**	12

DIXIE CHICKS *US, female vocal group (6 WEEKS)*   pos/wks

3 Jul 99	**THERE'S YOUR TROUBLE** *Epic 6675162*	**26**	5
6 Nov 99	**READY TO RUN** *Epic 6682472*	**53**	1

DIXIE CUPS *US, female vocal group (16 WEEKS)*   pos/wks

18 Jun 64	**CHAPEL OF LOVE** *Pye International 7N 25245* ▲	**22**	8
13 May 65	**IKO IKO** *Red Bird RB 10024*	**23**	8

DIZZY HEIGHTS *UK, male rapper (4 WEEKS)*   pos/wks

18 Dec 82	**CHRISTMAS RAPPING** *Polydor WRAP 1*	**49**	4

DJ ALIGATOR PROJECT
Denmark, male producer - Aliasghar Movasat (1 WEEK)   pos/wks

7 Sep 00	**THE WHISTLE SONG** *EMI CDBLOW 001*	**57**	1

DJ BOBO *Switzerland, male producer - Rene Baumann (4 WEEKS)*   pos/wks

24 Sep 94	**EVERYBODY** *PWL Continental PWCD 312*	**47**	2
17 Jun 95	**LOVE IS ALL AROUND** *Avex UK AXEXCD 7*	**49**	2

DJ DADO *Italy, male producer - Roberto Gallo (9 WEEKS)*   pos/wks

6 Apr 96 ●	**X-FILES** *ZYX ZYX 8065R8*	**8**	6
14 Mar 98	**COMING BACK** *ffrr TABCD 247*	**63**	1
11 Jul 98	**GIVE ME LOVE**		
	VC Recordings VCRD 37 [1]	**59**	1
8 May 99	**READY OR NOT** *Chemistry CDKEM 006* [2]	**51**	1

[1] DJ Dado vs Michelle Weeks [2] DJ Dado & Simone Jay

DJ DEE KLINE *UK, male DJ / producer - Nick Annand (6 WEEKS)*   pos/wks

3 Jun 00	**I DON'T SMOKE** *East West EW 213CD*	**11**	6

DJ DISCIPLE *US, male DJ / producer (1 WEEK)*   pos/wks

12 Nov 94	**ON THE DANCEFLOOR** *Mother MUMCD 55*	**67**	1

DJ DUKE *US, male producer (7 WEEKS)*   pos/wks

8 Jan 94	**BLOW YOUR WHISTLE** *ffrr FCD 228*	**15**	5
16 Jul 94	**TURN IT UP (SAY YEAH)** *ffrr FCD 235*	**31**	2

DJ E-Z ROCK – See Rob BASE and DJ E-Z ROCK

DJ EMPIRE presents Giorgio MORODER
German, male producer - Alexander Wilkie (1 WEEK)   pos/wks

12 Feb 00	**THE CHASE (re-recording)** *LOGIC 731482*	**46**	1

DJ ERIC *UK, male production trio (3 WEEKS)*   pos/wks

13 Feb 99	**WE ARE LOVE** *Distinctive DISNCD 49*	**37**	2
10 Jun 00	**DESIRE** *Distinctive DISNCD 56*	**67**	1

DJ 'FAST' EDDIE *US, male producer (15 WEEKS)*   pos/wks

11 Apr 87	**CAN U DANCE** *Champion CHAMP 41* [1]	**71**	2
14 Nov 87	**CAN U DANCE (re-entry)** *Champion CHAMP 41* [1]	**67**	2
21 Jan 89	**HIP HOUSE / I CAN DANCE**		
	DJ International DJIN 5	**47**	4
11 Mar 89	**YO YO GET FUNKY** *DJ International DJIN 7*	**54**	3
28 Oct 89	**GIT ON UP** *DJ International 655366 7* [2]	**49**	4

[1] Kenny 'Jammin' Jason and 'Fast' Eddie Smith [2] DJ 'Fast' Eddie featuring Sundance

DJ FLAVOURS *UK, male producer (4 WEEKS)*   pos/wks

11 Oct 97	**YOUR CARESS (ALL I NEED)**		
	All Around the World CDGLOBE 160	**19**	4

DJ HYPE *UK, male producer (1 WEEK)*
		pos/wks
20 Mar 93	**SHOT IN THE DARK** *Suburban Base SUBBASE 20CD*...............63	1

DJ JAZZY JEFF & the FRESH PRINCE – See JAZZY JEFF & the FRESH PRINCE

DJ JEAN *Holland, DJ / producer - Jan Engelaar (11 WEEKS)*
		pos/wks
11 Sep 99	● **THE LAUNCH** *AM:PM CDAMPM 123* 2	11

DJ JURGEN Presents Alice DEEJAY *Holland, male DJ / production group and female vocalist (16 WEEKS)*
		pos/wks
31 Jul 99	● **BETTER OFF ALONE** *Positiva CDTIV 113*...............2	16

See also ALICE DEEJAY

DJ KOOL
US, male rapper / DJ / producer - John Bowman (7 WEEKS)
		pos/wks
22 Feb 97	● **LET ME CLEAR MY THROAT** *American 74321452092* 8	7

DJ KRUSH *Japan, male producer (2 WEEKS)*
		pos/wks
16 Mar 96	**MEISO** *Mo Wax MW 042CD*...............52	1
12 Oct 96	**ONLY THE STRONG SURVIVE** *Mo Wax MW 060CD* 71	1

DJ LUCK & MC NEAT *UK, male DJ / producers - Joel Samuels and Michael Rose (29 WEEKS)*
		pos/wks
25 Dec 99	● **A LITTLE BIT OF LUCK** *Red Rose CORROSLE 1* 9	15
27 May 00	● **MASTERBLASTER 2000** *Red Rose RROSE 002CD* [1] 5	8
7 Oct 00	● **AIN'T NO STOPPIN' US** *Red Rose CDRROSE 004* [1] 8	6

[1] DJ Luck & MC Neat Featuring JJ

DJ MANTA *Holland, male / female DJ / production trio (1 WEEK)*
		pos/wks
9 Oct 99	**HOLDING ON** *AM:PM CDAMPM 125* 47	1

DJ MIKO *Italy, male producer - Quartobaro Manier (10 WEEKS)*
		pos/wks
13 Aug 94	● **WHAT'S UP** *Systematic SYSCD 2* 6	10

DJ MILANO Featuring SAMANTHA FOX
Italy, male DJ / producer and UK, female vocalist (2 WEEKS)
		pos/wks
28 Mar 98	**SANTA MARIA** *All Around the World CDGLOBE 163*...............31	2

See also Samantha FOX

DJ MISJAH and DJ TIM
Holland, male instrumental / production duo (4 WEEKS)
		pos/wks
23 Mar 96	**ACCESS** *Ffrreedom TABCD 240*...............16	3
27 May 00	**ACCESS (re-mix)** *Tripoli Trax TTRAXCD 063* 45	1

DJ POWER *Italy, male producer - Steve Gambaroli (2 WEEKS)*
		pos/wks
7 Mar 92	**EVERYBODY PUMP** *Cooltempo COOL 252*...............46	2

DJ PROFESSOR *Italy, male producer (6 WEEKS)*
		pos/wks
10 Aug 91	**WE GOTTA DO IT** *Fourth & Broadway BRW 225* [1] 57	2
28 Mar 92	**ROCK ME STEADY** *PWL Continental PWL 219*...............49	2
8 Oct 94	**ROCKIN' ME** *Citra CITRA 1CD* [2] 56	1
1 Mar 97	**WALKIN' ON UP** *Nukleuz MCSTD 40098* [3] 64	1

[1] DJ Professor featuring Francesco Zappala [2] Professor [3] DJ PROF-X-OR

DJ QUICKSILVER
Turkey, male DJ / producer - Ohran Terzi (29 WEEKS)
		pos/wks
5 Apr 97	● **BELLISSIMA** *Positiva CDTIV 72* 4	17
6 Sep 97	● **FREE** *Positiva CDTIVS 77* 7	7
21 Feb 98	**PLANET LOVE** *Positiva CDTIV 88*...............12	5

DJ Quik – See TONY TONI TON...

DJ RAP *UK, female vocalist / DJ / producer (5 WEEKS)*
		pos/wks
4 Jul 98	**BAD GIRL** *Higher Ground HIGHS 8CD*...............32	2
17 Oct 98	**GOOD TO BE ALIVE** *Higher Ground HIGHS 14CD*...............36	2
3 Apr 99	**EVERYDAY GIRL** *Higher Ground HIGHS 19CD* 47	1

DJ ROLANDO AKA AZTEC MYSTIC
US, male DJ / producer - Rolando Rocha (2 WEEKS)
		pos/wks
21 Oct 00	**JAGUAR** *430 West 430 WUKTCD1* 43	2

DJ SAKIN & FRIENDS
Germany, DJ / Producer - Sakin Botzkurt (18 WEEKS)
		pos/wks
20 Feb 99	● **PROTECT YOUR MIND (FOR THE LOVE OF A PRINCESS)** *Positiva CDTIV 107* 4	10
8 May 99	**PROTECT YOUR MIND (FOR THE LOVE OF A PRINCESS) (re-entry)** *Positiva CDTIV 107*...............71	1
5 Jun 99	**NOMANSLAND (DAVID'S SONG)** *Positiva CDTIV 112* 14	7

DJ SANDY VS HOUSETRAP
Germany, female DJ / producer & vocalist (2 WEEKS)
		pos/wks
1 Jul 00	**OVERDRIVE** *Positiva CDTIV 133* 32	2

DJ SCOT PROJECT *Germany, male DJ / producer (2 WEEKS)*
		pos/wks
27 Jul 96	**U (I GOT THE FEELING)** *Positiva CDTIV 55* 66	1
14 Feb 98	**Y (HOW DEEP IS YOUR LOVE)** *Perfecto PERF 158CD1* 57	1

DJ SCOTT featuring Lorna B
Scotland, male DJ and female vocalist (5 WEEKS)
		pos/wks
28 Jan 95	**DO YOU WANNA PARTY** *Steppin' Out SPONCD 2* 36	3
1 Apr 95	**SWEET DREAMS** *Steppin' Out SPONCD 3*...............37	2

DJ Doc SCOTT *UK, male producer (2 WEEKS)*
		pos/wks
1 Feb 92	**NHS (EP)** *Absolute 2 ABS 001DJ* 64	2

Tracks on NHS (EP): Surgery / Night Nurse

DJ SEDUCTION *UK, male producer - John Kallum (8 WEEKS)*
		pos/wks
22 Feb 92	**HARDCORE HEAVEN / YOU AND ME** *Ffrreedom TAB 103* 26	5
11 Jul 92	**COME ON** *Ffrreedom TAB 111* 37	3

DJ SHADOW *US, male producer (7 WEEKS)*
		pos/wks
25 Mar 95	**WHAT DOES YOUR SOUL LOOK LIKE** *Mo Wax MW 027CD*...............59	1
14 Sep 96	**MIDNIGHT IN A PERFECT WORLD** *Mo Wax MW 057CD* 54	1
9 Nov 96	**STEM** *Mo Wax MW 058CD*...............74	1
11 Oct 97	**HIGH NOON** *Mo Wax MW 063CD* 22	2
20 Dec 97	**CAMEL BOBSLED RACE** *Mo Wax MW 084CD* 62	1
24 Jan 98	**WHAT DOES YOUR SOUL LOOK LIKE (PART 1)** *Mo Wax MW 087* 54	1

DJ SHORTY – See Lenny FONTANA & DJ SHORTY

DJ SUPREME *UK, male producer - Nick Destri (11 WEEKS)*
		pos/wks
5 Oct 96	**THA WILD STYLE** *Distinctive DISNCD 19* 39	2
3 May 97	**THA WILD STYLE (re-issue)** *Distinctive DISNCD 29* 24	2
6 Dec 97	**ENTER THE SCENE** *Distinctive DISNCD 40* [1] 49	1
21 Feb 98	**THA HORNS OF JERICHO** *All Around the World CDGLOBE 164*...............29	2
16 Jan 99	● **UP TO THE WILDSTYLE** *All Around the World CDGLOBE 170* [2] 10	4

[1] DJ Supreme vs the Rhythm Masters [2] Porn Kings vs DJ Supreme

DJ TAUCHER
German, male DJ / producer - Ralf Armand Beck (1 WEEK)
		pos/wks
8 May 99	**CHILD OF THE UNIVERSE** *Additive 12AD 037* 74	1

DJ TIM – See DJ MISJAH and DJ TIM

DJ VISAGE featuring CLARISSA Denmark / Germany, male DJ / producer / female vocalist (1 WEEK)

		pos/wks
10 Jun 00	THE RETURN (TIME TO SAY GOODBYE) *One Step Music OSMCDS 13* 58	1

DJ ZINC UK, male DJ / producer - Benjamin Pettit (3 WEEKS)

		pos/wks
18 Nov 00	138 TREK *Phaze One PHAZE CDXO3* 27	3

DJAIMIN Switzerland, male producer (2 WEEKS)

		pos/wks
19 Sep 92	GIVE YOU *Cooltempo COOL 262* 45	2

DJH featuring STEFY
Italy, male instrumental / production group (14 WEEKS)

		pos/wks
16 Feb 91	THINK ABOUT . . . *RCA PB 44385* 22	6
13 Jul 91	I LIKE IT *RCA PB 44741* 16	7
19 Oct 91	MOVE YOUR LOVE *RCA PB 44965* [1] 73	1

[1] DJH Stefy

DJPC Belgium, male producer (5 WEEKS)

		pos/wks
26 Oct 91	INSSOMNIAK *Hype 7PUM 005* 62	4
29 Feb 92	INSSOMNIAK (re-issue) *Hype PUMR 005* 64	1

DJ's RULE Canada, male instrumental / production duo (2 WEEKS)

		pos/wks
2 Mar 96	GET INTO THE MUSIC *Distinctive DISNCD 9* 72	1
5 Apr 97	GET INTO THE MUSIC (re-mix) *Distinctive DISNCDD27* [1] 65	1

[1] DJ's Rule featuring Karen Brown

DJUM DJUM – See LEFTFIELD

Boris DLUGOSCH presents BOOOM
Germany / US, male production / female vocal duo (4 WEEKS)

		pos/wks
7 Dec 96	KEEP PUSHIN' *Manifesto FESCD 17* 41	2
13 Sep 97	HOLD YOUR HEAD UP HIGH *Positiva CDTIV 79* 23	2

D'LUX UK, male / female vocal / instrumental group (1 WEEK)

		pos/wks
22 Jun 96	LOVE RESURRECTION *Logic 74321371012* 58	1

D'MENACE UK, male production duo (3 WEEKS)

		pos/wks
8 Aug 98	DEEP MENACE (SPANK) *Inferno CDFERN 8* 20	3

D MOB UK, male producer - Danny D (48 WEEKS)

		pos/wks
15 Oct 88 ●	WE CALL IT ACIEED *ffrr FFR 13* [1] 3	12
3 Jun 89 ●	IT IS TIME TO GET FUNKY *ffrr F 107* [2] 9	10
21 Oct 89	C'MON AND GET MY LOVE *ffrr F 117* [3] 15	10
6 Jan 90 ●	PUT YOUR HANDS TOGETHER *ffrr F 124* [4] 7	8
7 Apr 90	THAT'S THE WAY OF THE WORLD *ffrr F 132* [3] 48	3
12 Feb 94	WHY *ffrr FCD 227* [3] 23	3
3 Sep 94	ONE DAY *ffrr FCDP 239* 41	2

[1] D Mob featuring Gary Haisman [2] D Mob featuring LRS [3] D Mob with Cathy Dennis [4] D Mob featuring Nuff Juice

DMX US, male rapper - Earl Simmons (2 WEEKS)

		pos/wks
15 May 99	SLIPPIN' *Def Jam 8707552* 30	2

DNA UK, male production duo - Neal Slateford & Nick Bett (29 WEEKS)

		pos/wks
28 Jul 90 ●	TOM'S DINER (re-mix) *A & M AM 592* [1] 2	10
18 Aug 90	LA SERENISSIMA *Raw Bass RBASS 006* 34	8
3 Aug 91	REBEL WOMAN *DNA 7DNA 001* [2] 42	4
1 Feb 92	CAN YOU HANDLE IT (re-recording) *EMI EM 219* [3] 17	5
9 May 92	BLUE LOVE (CALL MY NAME) *EMI EM 226* [4] 66	2

[1] DNA featuring Suzanne Vega [2] DNA featuring Jazzi P [3] DNA featuring Sharon Redd [4] DNA featuring Joe Nye

D*NOTE UK, male producer - Matt Winn (2 WEEKS)

		pos/wks
12 Jul 97	WAITING HOPEFULLY *A & M 5822792* 46	1
15 Nov 97	LOST AND FOUND *VC VCRD 25* 59	1

Carl DOBKINS Jr US, male vocalist (1 WEEK)

		pos/wks
31 Mar 60	LUCKY DEVIL *Brunswick 05817* 44	1

Anita DOBSON UK, female vocalist (13 WEEKS)

		pos/wks
9 Aug 86 ●	ANYONE CAN FALL IN LOVE *BBC RESL 191* [1] 4	9
18 Jul 87	TALKING OF LOVE *Parlophone R 6159* 43	4

[1] Anita Dobson featuring the Simon May Orchestra

DR ALBAN Nigeria, male vocalist - Alban Nwapa (28 WEEKS)

		pos/wks
5 Sep 92 ●	IT'S MY LIFE *Logic 115330* 2	12
14 Nov 92	ONE LOVE *Logic 74321108727* 45	2
10 Apr 93	SING HALLELUJAH! *Logic 74321136202* 16	8
26 Mar 94	LOOK WHO'S TALKING *Logic 74321195342* 55	3
13 Aug 94	AWAY FROM HOME *Logic 74321222682* 42	2
29 Apr 95	SWEET DREAMS *Logic 74321251552* [1] 59	1

[1] Swing featuring Dr Alban

DOCTOR and the MEDICS UK, male / female vocal / instrumental group - lead vocal Clive Jackson (25 WEEKS)

		pos/wks
10 May 86 ★	SPIRIT IN THE SKY *IRS IRM 113* 1	15
9 Aug 86	BURN *IRS IRM 119* 29	6
22 Nov 86	WATERLOO *IRS IRM 125* [1] 45	4

[1] Doctor and the Medics featuring Roy Wood

DR DRE US, male rapper - Andre Young (56 WEEKS)

		pos/wks
22 Jan 94	NUTHIN' BUT A 'G' THANG / LET ME RIDE *Death Row A 8328CD* 31	3
3 Sep 94	DRE DAY *Death Row A 8292CD* 59	2
15 Apr 95	NATURAL BORN KILLAZ *Death Row A 8197CD* [1] 45	2
10 Jun 95	KEEP THEIR HEADS RINGIN' *Priority PTYCD 103* 25	4
13 Apr 96 ●	CALIFORNIA LOVE *Death Row DRWCD 3* [2] ▲ 6	8
19 Oct 96 ●	NO DIGGITY *Interscope IND 95003* [3] ▲ 9	7
11 Jul 98	ZOOM *Interscope IND 95594* [4] 15	3
14 Aug 99	GUILTY CONSCIENCE *Interscope IND 4971282* [5] 5	8
25 Mar 00 ●	STILL D.R.E. *Interscope 4972742* [6] 6	10
10 Jun 00 ●	FORGOT ABOUT DRE *Interscope 4973412* [7] 7	9

[1] Dr Dre and Ice Cube [2] 2Pac featuring Dr Dre [3] BLACKstreet featuring Dr Dre [4] Dr Dre and LL Cool J [5] Eminem featuring Dr Dre [6] Dr Dre featuring Snoop Dogg [7] Dr Dre featuring Eminem

DR FEELGOOD UK, male vocal / instrumental group (29 WEEKS)

		pos/wks
11 Jun 77	SNEAKIN' SUSPICION *United Artists UP 36255* 47	3
24 Sep 77	SHE'S A WIND UP *United Artists UP 36304* 34	5
30 Sep 78	DOWN AT THE DOCTOR'S *United Artists UP 36444* 48	5
20 Jan 79 ●	MILK AND ALCOHOL *United Artists UP 36468* 9	9
5 May 79	AS LONG AS THE PRICE IS RIGHT *United Artists YUP 36506* 40	6
8 Dec 79	PUT HIM OUT OF YOUR MIND *United Artists BP 306* 73	1

DR HOOK [280 Top 500] Distinctive group fronted by vocalists Dennis Locorriere and Ray Sawyer: had eight years of regular UK / US hits. Early recordings often featured humorous anarchic Shel Silverstein songs, but this good-time New Jersey act had greater success with later gentler material 104 WEEKS)

		pos/wks
24 Jun 72 ●	SYLVIA'S MOTHER *CBS 7929* [1] 2	13
26 Jun 76 ●	A LITTLE BIT MORE *Capitol CL 15871* 2	14
30 Oct 76 ●	IF NOT YOU *Capitol CL 15885* 5	10
25 Mar 78	MORE LIKE THE MOVIES *Capitol CL 15967* 14	10
22 Sep 79 ★	WHEN YOU'RE IN LOVE WITH A BEAUTIFUL WOMAN *Capitol CL 16039* 1	17
5 Jan 80 ●	BETTER LOVE NEXT TIME *Capitol CL 16112* 8	8
29 Mar 80 ●	SEXY EYES *Capitol CL 16127* 4	9
23 Aug 80	YEARS FROM NOW *Capitol CL 16154* 47	6
8 Nov 80	SHARING THE NIGHT TOGETHER *Capitol CL 16171* 43	4

UK No.1 ★   UK Top 10 ●   Still on chart +   UK million seller ◆   UK entry at No.1 ■   US No.1 ▲

22 Nov 80	GIRLS CAN GET IT *Mercury MER 51*	40	5
1 Feb 92	WHEN YOU'RE IN LOVE WITH A BEAUTIFUL WOMAN (re-issue) *Capitol EMCT 4*	44	4
6 Jun 92	A LITTLE BIT MORE (re-issue) *EMI EMCT 6*	47	4

[1] Dr Hook and the Medicine Show

DR OCTAGON *US, male producer - Keith Thornton (1 WEEK)*
pos/wks
| 7 Sep 96 | BLUE FLOWERS *Mo Wax MW 055CD* | 66 | 1 |

DOCTOR SPIN
UK, male instrumental / production duo (8 WEEKS)
pos/wks
| 3 Oct 92 ● | TETRIS *Carpet CRPT 4* | 6 | 8 |

Ken DODD (58 Top 500) *Seasoned stand-up comedian-cum-balladeer, b. 8 Nov 1929, Liverpool. The tickling-stick-wielding troubadour was one of the most successful Merseyside acts in the mid-1960s, at times enjoying two Top 10 singles simultaneously (233 WEEKS)*
pos/wks
7 Jul 60 ●	LOVE IS LIKE A VIOLIN *Decca F 11248*	8	18
15 Jun 61	ONCE IN EVERY LIFETIME *Decca F 11355*	28	7
10 Aug 61	ONCE IN EVERY LIFETIME (re-entry) *Decca F 11355*	47	1
24 Aug 61	ONCE IN EVERY LIFETIME (2nd re-entry) *Decca F 11355*	31	10
1 Feb 62	PIANISSIMO *Decca F 11422*	21	15
29 Aug 63	STILL *Columbia DB 7094*	35	10
6 Feb 64	EIGHT BY TEN *Columbia DB 7191*	22	11
23 Jul 64	HAPPINESS *Columbia DB 7325*	31	13
26 Nov 64	SO DEEP IS THE NIGHT *Columbia DB 7398*	31	7
2 Sep 65 ★	TEARS *Columbia DB 7659* ◆	1	24
18 Nov 65 ●	THE RIVER (LE COLLINE SONO IN FIORO) *Columbia DB 7750*	3	14
12 May 66 ●	PROMISES *Columbia DB 7914*	6	14
4 Aug 66	MORE THAN LOVE *Columbia DB 7976*	14	11
27 Oct 66	IT'S LOVE *Columbia DB 8031*	36	7
19 Jan 67	LET ME CRY ON YOUR SHOULDER *Columbia DB 8101*	11	10
30 Jul 69	TEARS WON'T WASH AWAY THESE HEARTACHES *Columbia DB 8600*	22	11
5 Dec 70	BROKEN HEARTED *Columbia DB 8725*	15	9
13 Feb 71	BROKEN HEARTED (re-entry) *Columbia DB 8725*	38	1
10 Jul 71	WHEN LOVE COMES ROUND AGAIN (L'ARCA DI NOE) *Columbia DB 8796*	19	16
18 Nov 72	JUST OUT OF REACH (OF MY TWO EMPTY ARMS) *Columbia DB 8947*	29	11
29 Nov 75	(THINK OF ME) WHEREVER YOU ARE *EMI 2342*	21	8
26 Dec 81	HOLD MY HAND *Images IMGS 0002*	44	5

Rory DODD – See Jim STEINMAN

DODGY *UK, male vocal / instrumental group (41 WEEKS)*
pos/wks
8 May 93	LOVEBIRDS *A & M AMCD 0177*	65	2
3 Jul 93	I NEED ANOTHER (EP) *A & M 5803172*	67	2
6 Aug 94	THE MELOD-EP *Bostin 5806772*	53	2
1 Oct 94	STAYING OUT FOR THE SUMMER *Bostin 5807972*	38	2
7 Jan 95	SO LET ME GO FAR *Bostin 5809032*	30	3
11 Mar 95	MAKING THE MOST OF *Bostin 5809892* [1]	22	3
10 Jun 95	STAYING OUT FOR THE SUMMER (re-mix) *Bostin 5810952*	19	5
8 Jun 96	IN A ROOM *A & M 5816252*	12	6
10 Aug 96 ●	GOOD ENOUGH *A & M 5818152*	4	8
16 Nov 96	IF YOU'RE THINKING OF ME *A & M 5819992*	11	4
15 Mar 97	FOUND YOU *A & M 5821332*	19	3
26 Sep 98	EVERY SINGLE DAY *A&M MERCD 512*	32	2

[1] Dodgy with the Kick Horns

Tracks on I Need Another (EP): I Need Another / If I Fall / Hendre DDU. Tracks on The Melod-EP: Melodies Haunt You / The Snake / Don't Go / Summer Fayre

Tim DOG *US, male rapper (3 WEEKS)*
pos/wks
| 29 Oct 94 | BITCH WITH A PERM *Dis-stress DISCD 1* | 49 | 1 |
| 11 Feb 95 | MAKE WAY FOR THE INDIAN *Island CID 586* [1] | 29 | 2 |

[1] Apache Indian and Tim Dog

DOG EAT DOG *US, male vocal / instrumental group (7 WEEKS)*
pos/wks
19 Aug 95	NO FRONTS *Roadrunner RR 23312*	64	1
3 Feb 96 ●	NO FRONTS (re-entry) *Roadrunner RR 23312*	9	5
13 Jul 96	ISMS *Roadrunner RR 23083*	43	1

Nate DOGG – See Warren G

DOGS D'AMOUR
UK, male vocal / instrumental group (15 WEEKS)
pos/wks
4 Feb 89	HOW COME IT NEVER RAINS *China CHINA 13*	44	3
5 Aug 89	SATELLITE KID *China CHINA 17*	26	3
14 Oct 89	TRAIL OF TEARS *China CHINA 20*	47	3
23 Jun 90	VICTIMS OF SUCCESS *China CHINA 24*	36	3
15 Sep 90	EMPTY WORLD *China CHINA 27*	61	2
19 Jun 93	ALL OR NOTHING *China WOKCD 2033*	53	1

Ken DOH *UK, male producer - Michael Devlin (7 WEEKS)*
pos/wks
| 30 Mar 96 ● | NAGASAKI EP (I NEED A LOVER TONIGHT) *ffrr FCD 272* | 7 | 7 |

Joe DOLAN *Ireland, male vocalist (40 WEEKS)*
pos/wks
25 Jun 69 ●	MAKE ME AN ISLAND *Pye 7N 17738*	3	18
1 Nov 69	TERESA *Pye 7N 17833*	20	7
8 Nov 69	MAKE ME AN ISLAND (re-entry) *Pye 7N 17738*	48	1
28 Feb 70	YOU'RE SUCH A GOOD LOOKING WOMAN *Pye 7N 17891*	17	13
17 Sep 77	I NEED YOU *Pye 7N 45702*	43	1

Thomas DOLBY
UK, male vocalist / multi-instrumentalist (51 WEEKS)
pos/wks
3 Oct 81	EUROPA AND THE PIRATE TWINS *Parlophone R 6051*	48	3
14 Aug 82	WINDPOWER *Venice In Peril VIPS 103*	31	8
6 Nov 82	SHE BLINDED ME WITH SCIENCE *Venice In Peril VIPS 104*	49	4
16 Jul 83	SHE BLINDED ME WITH SCIENCE (re-issue) *Venice In Peril VIPS 105*	56	4
21 Jan 84	HYPERACTIVE *Parlophone Odeon R 6065*	17	9
31 Mar 84	I SCARE MYSELF *Parlophone Odeon R 6067*	46	5
16 Apr 88	AIRHEAD *Manhattan MT 38*	53	3
9 May 92	CLOSE BUT NO CIGAR *Virgin VS 1410*	22	5
11 Jul 92	I LOVE YOU GOODBYE *Virgin VS 1417*	36	4
26 Sep 92	SILK PYJAMAS *Virgin VS 1430*	62	2
22 Jan 94	HYPERACTIVE! (re-mix) *Parlophone CDEMCTS 10*	23	4

Joe DOLCE MUSIC THEATRE *US, male vocalist (10 WEEKS)*
pos/wks
| 7 Feb 81 ★ | SHADDAP YOU FACE *Epic EPC 9518* | 1 | 10 |

DOLL *UK, male / female vocal / instrumental group (8 WEEKS)*
pos/wks
| 13 Jan 79 | DESIRE ME *Beggars Banquet BEG 11* | 28 | 8 |

DOLLAR (203 Top 500) *Photogenic teen-targeted UK vocal duo, who were originally one - third of Guys and Dolls: David Van Day and Thereze Bazar. Their Top 10 hits came from writers as diverse as John Lennon / Paul McCartney, Trevor Horn, Erasure and themselves (128 WEEKS)*
pos/wks
11 Nov 78	SHOOTING STAR *Carrere 2871*	14	12
19 May 79	WHO WERE YOU WITH IN THE MOONLIGHT *Carrere CAR 110*	14	12
18 Aug 79 ●	LOVE'S GOTTA HOLD ON ME *Carrere CAR 122*	4	13
24 Nov 79 ●	I WANNA HOLD YOUR HAND *Carrere CAR 131*	9	14
25 Oct 80	TAKIN' A CHANCE ON YOU *WEA K 18353*	62	3
15 Aug 81	HAND HELD IN BLACK AND WHITE *WEA BUCK 1*	19	12
14 Nov 81 ●	MIRROR MIRROR (MON AMOUR) *WEA BUCK 2*	4	17
20 Mar 82	RING RING *Carrere CAR 225*	61	2
27 Mar 82 ●	GIVE ME BACK MY HEART *WEA BUCK 3*	4	9
19 Jun 82	VIDEOTHEQUE *WEA BUCK 4*	17	10
18 Sep 82	GIVE ME SOME KINDA MAGIC *WEA BUCK 5*	34	6
16 Aug 86	WE WALKED IN LOVE *Arista DIME 1*	61	4
26 Dec 87 ●	O L'AMOUR *London LON 146*	7	11
16 Jul 88	IT'S NATURE'S WAY (NO PROBLEM) *London LON 179*	58	3

Placido DOMINGO Spain, male vocalist (28 WEEKS)

			pos/wks
12 Dec 81	PERHAPS LOVE CBS A 1905 [1]	46	9
27 May 89	TILL I LOVED YOU CBS 654843 7 [2]	24	9
16 Jun 90	NESSUN DORMA FROM 'TURANDOT' Epic 656005 7 [3]	59	2
30 Jul 94	LIBIAMO / LA DONNA E MOBILE Teldec YZ 843CD [4]	21	4
25 Jul 98	YOU'LL NEVER WALK ALONE Decca 4607982 [5]	35	4

[1] Placido Domingo with John Denver [2] Placido Domingo and Jennifer Rush [3] Luis Cobos featuring Placido Domingo [4] José Carreras featuring Placido Domingo and Luciano Pavarotti with Mehta [5] José Carreras, Placido Domingo and Luciano Pavarotti with Mehta

DOMINO US, male rapper / vocalist (6 WEEKS)

			pos/wks
22 Jan 94	GETTO JAM Chaos 6600402	33	4
14 May 94	SWEET POTATOE PIE Chaos 6603292	42	2

Fats DOMINO (266 Top 500) Pioneering rock 'n' roll singer / songwriter and pianist. b. 26 Feb 1928, New Orleans. Sold millions of rockin' records in pre-Haley / Presley years and is still among the biggest-selling artists and most successful composers of the rock era (109 WEEKS)

			pos/wks
27 Jul 56	I'M IN LOVE AGAIN London HLU 8280	28	1
17 Aug 56	I'M IN LOVE AGAIN (re-entry) London HLU 8280	12	13
30 Nov 56	BLUEBERRY HILL London HLU 8330	26	1
21 Dec 56 ●	BLUEBERRY HILL (re-entry) London HLU 8330	6	14
25 Jan 57	AIN'T THAT A SHAME London HLU 8173	23	2
1 Feb 57	HONEY CHILE London HLU 8356	29	1
29 Mar 57	BLUE MONDAY London HLP 8377	23	1
19 Apr 57	BLUE MONDAY (re-entry) London HLP 8377	30	1
19 Apr 57	I'M WALKIN' London HLP 8407	19	7
19 Jul 57	VALLEY OF TEARS London HLP 8449	25	1
28 Mar 58	THE BIG BEAT London HLP 8575	20	4
4 Jul 58	SICK AND TIRED London HLP 8628	26	1
22 May 59	MARGIE London HLP 8865	18	5
16 Oct 59	I WANT TO WALK YOU HOME London HLP 8942	14	5
18 Dec 59	BE MY GUEST London HLP 9005	11	8
19 Feb 60	BE MY GUEST (re-entry) London HLP 9005	19	3
17 Mar 60	COUNTRY BOY London HLP 9073	19	11
21 Jul 60	WALKING TO NEW ORLEANS London HLP 9163	19	10
10 Nov 60	THREE NIGHTS A WEEK London HLP 9198	45	2
5 Jan 61	MY GIRL JOSEPHINE London HLP 9244	32	4
27 Jul 61	IT KEEPS RAININ' London HLP 9374	49	1
30 Nov 61	WHAT A PARTY London HLP 9456	43	1
29 Mar 62	JAMBALAYA London HLP 9520	41	1
31 Oct 63	RED SAILS IN THE SUNSET HMV POP 1219	34	6
24 Apr 76	BLUEBERRY HILL (re-issue) United Artists UP 35797	41	5

DON PABLO'S ANIMALS
Italy, male production group (10 WEEKS)

			pos/wks
19 May 90 ●	VENUS Rumour RUMA 18	4	10

DON-E UK, male vocalist (8 WEEKS)

			pos/wks
9 May 92	LOVE MAKES THE WORLD GO ROUND Fourth & Broadway BRW 242	18	6
25 Jul 92	PEACE IN THE WORLD Fourth & Broadway BRW 256	41	1
28 Feb 98	DELICIOUS Mushroom MUSH 20CD [1]	52	1

[1] Deni Hines featuring Don-E

Lonnie DONEGAN (25 Top 500) The 'King of Skiffle'. b. 29 Apr 1931. Glasgow, Scotland. Britain's most successful and influential recording artist before The Beatles. Chalked up 28 successive Top 30 entries, and was the first UK male to score two US Top 10s. Album with Van Morrison and Chris Barber reached Top 20 in 2000 (321 WEEKS)

			pos/wks
6 Jan 56 ●	ROCK ISLAND LINE Decca F 10647 [1]	8	13
13 Apr 56	ROCK ISLAND LINE (re-entry) Decca F 10647 [1]	16	3
20 Apr 56	STEWBALL Pye Nixa N 15036	27	1
27 Apr 56 ●	LOST JOHN / STEWBALL (re-entry) Pye Nixa N 15036	2	17
11 May 56	ROCK ISLAND LINE (2nd re-entry) Decca F 10647 [1]	19	6
6 Jul 56	SKIFFLE SESSION (EP) Pye Nixa NJE 1017	20	2
7 Sep 56 ●	BRING A LITTLE WATER SYLVIE / DEAD OR ALIVE Pye Nixa N 15071	7	12
21 Dec 56	LONNIE DONEGAN SHOWCASE (LP) Pye Nixa NPT 19012	26	3
11 Jan 57	BRING A LITTLE WATER SYLVIE / DEAD OR ALIVE (re-entry) Pye Nixa N 15071	30	1
18 Jan 57 ●	DON'T YOU ROCK ME DADDY-O Pye Nixa N 15080	4	17
5 Apr 57 ★	CUMBERLAND GAP Pye Nixa N 15087	1	12
7 Jun 57 ★	GAMBLIN' MAN / PUTTING ON THE STYLE Pye Nixa N 15093	1	19
11 Oct 57 ●	MY DIXIE DARLING Pye Nixa N 15108	10	15
20 Dec 57	JACK O' DIAMONDS Pye Nixa 7N 15116	14	7
11 Apr 58 ●	GRAND COOLIE DAM Pye Nixa 7N 15129	6	15
11 Jul 58	SALLY DON'T YOU GRIEVE / BETTY BETTY BETTY Pye Nixa 7N 15148	11	7
26 Sep 58	LONESOME TRAVELLER Pye Nixa 7N 15158	28	1
14 Nov 58	LONNIE'S SKIFFLE PARTY Pye Nixa 7N 15165	23	5
21 Nov 58 ●	TOM DOOLEY Pye Nixa 7N 15172	3	14
6 Feb 59 ●	DOES YOUR CHEWING GUM LOSE ITS FLAVOUR Pye Nixa 7N 15181	3	12
8 May 59	FORT WORTH JAIL Pye Nixa 7N 15198	14	5
26 Jun 59 ●	BATTLE OF NEW ORLEANS Pye 7N 15206	2	16
11 Sep 59	SAL'S GOT A SUGAR LIP Pye 7N 15223	13	4
4 Dec 59	SAN MIGUEL Pye 7N 15237	19	4
24 Mar 60 ★	MY OLD MAN'S A DUSTMAN Pye 7N 15256	1	13
26 May 60 ●	I WANNA GO HOME Pye 7N 15267	5	17
25 Aug 60 ●	LORELEI Pye 7N 15275	10	8
24 Nov 60	LIVELY Pye 7N 15312	13	9
8 Dec 60	VIRGIN MARY Pye 7N 15315	27	5
11 May 61 ●	HAVE A DRINK ON ME Pye 7N 15354	8	15
31 Aug 61 ●	MICHAEL ROW THE BOAT / LUMBERED Pye 7N 15371	6	11
18 Jan 62	THE COMANCHEROS Pye 7N 15410	14	10
5 Apr 62 ●	THE PARTY'S OVER Pye 7N 15424	9	12
16 Aug 62	PICK A BALE OF COTTON Pye 7N 15455	11	10

[1] The Lonnie Donegan Skiffle Group

'Stewball' had one week on the chart by itself on 20 Apr 1956. 'Lost John', the other side, replaced it on 27 Apr 1956, but 'Stewball' was given co-billing with 'Lost John' for the weeks of 11, 18 and 25 May 1956, peaking only at No.7. 'Dead or Alive' was not listed with 'Bring a Little Water Sylvie' for the week 7 Sep 1956. 'Putting on the Style' was not listed with 'Gamblin' Man' for the weeks of 7 and 14 Jun 1956. Tracks on Skiffle Session (EP): Railroad Bill / Stockalee / Ballad of Jesse James / Ol' Riley. Tracks on Lonnie Donegan Showcase (LP): Wabash Cannonball / How Long / How Long Blues / Nobody's Child / I Shall Not Be Moved / I'm Alabammy Bound / I'm a Rambling Man / Wreck of the Old '97 / Frankie and Johnny

Tanya DONELLY US, female vocalist / instrumentalist (2 WEEKS)

			pos/wks
30 Aug 97	PRETTY DEEP 4AD BAD 7007CD	55	1
6 Dec 97	THE BRIGHT LIGHT 4AD BAD 7012CD	64	1

Ral DONNER US, male vocalist (10 WEEKS)

			pos/wks
21 Sep 61	YOU DON'T KNOW WHAT YOU'VE GOT (UNTIL YOU LOSE IT) Parlophone R 4820	25	10

DONOVAN (297 Top 500) Acclaimed Celtic singer / songwriter, b. Donovan Leitch, 10 May 1946, Glasgow. Initially dubbed British version of Bob Dylan, he enjoyed massive fame on both sides of the Atlantic in the 'flower power' years of the late 1960s (100 WEEKS)

			pos/wks
25 Mar 65 ●	CATCH THE WIND Pye 7N 15801	4	13
3 Jun 65 ●	COLOURS Pye 7N 15866	4	12
11 Nov 65	TURQUOISE Pye 7N 15984	30	6
8 Dec 66 ●	SUNSHINE SUPERMAN Pye 7N 17241 ▲	2	11
9 Feb 67 ●	MELLOW YELLOW Pye 7N 17267	8	8
25 Oct 67 ●	THERE IS A MOUNTAIN Pye 7N 17403	8	11
21 Feb 68 ●	JENNIFER JUNIPER Pye 7N 17457	5	11
29 May 68 ●	HURDY GURDY MAN Pye 7N 17537	4	10
4 Dec 68	ATLANTIS Pye 7N 17660	23	8
9 Jul 69	GOO GOO BARABAJAGAL (LOVE IS HOT) Pye 7N 17778 [1]	12	9
1 Dec 90	JENNIFER JUNIPER Fontana SYP 1 [2]	68	1

[1] Donovan with the Jeff Beck Group [2] Singing Corner meets Donovan

UK No.1 ★ UK Top 10 ● Still on chart + UK million seller ◆ UK entry at No.1 ■ US No.1 ▲

SINGLED OUT... Joe Brown

One of the few chart artists with a charting daughter – Sam. Lincolnshire-born Joe has not added to his 92 weeks on the UK chart since 1973, but still plays a blinding set to packed venues on a regular basis.

• **NO.1 SONG ON THE DAY I WAS BORN:**
Over The Hill – Joe Loss and his Orchestra

• **ALL-TIME FAVOURITE SINGLE:**
River Deep Mountain High – Ike and Tina Turner

I'm not sure where Ike went to on this record...

• **SINGLE THAT DRIVES ME UP THE WALL:**
Shout – Lulu

Don't get me wrong, I love Lulu – but the first few bars of vocal sound like a Japanese motorbike revving up!

FIRST SINGLE I BOUGHT:
Rock Island Line
Lonnie Donegan

He was Jesus and we were his disciples. (He still thinks he's Jesus!)

Photo: Rex Features

Jason DONOVAN (176) `Top 500`

The top teen idol of the late 1980s, b. 1 Jun 1968, Melbourne. Australian actor-turned-singer, who had impressive array of UK hits after leaving TV soap 'Neighbours'. His debut LP, Ten Good Reasons, was the UK's top-selling album of 1989 (137 WEEKS)

		pos/wks
10 Sep 88 ●	NOTHING CAN DIVIDE US *PWL PWL 17*	5 12
10 Dec 88 ★	ESPECIALLY FOR YOU *PWL PWL 24* [1]	1 14
4 Mar 89 ★	TOO MANY BROKEN HEARTS *PWL PWL 32*	1 13
10 Jun 89 ★	SEALED WITH A KISS *PWL PWL 39* ■	1 10
9 Sep 89 ●	EVERY DAY (I LOVE YOU MORE) *PWL PWL 43*	2 9
9 Dec 89 ●	WHEN YOU COME BACK TO ME *PWL PWL 46*	2 11
7 Apr 90 ●	HANG ON TO YOUR LOVE *PWL PWL 51*	8 7
30 Jun 90	ANOTHER NIGHT *PWL PWL 58*	18 5
1 Sep 90 ●	RHYTHM OF THE RAIN *PWL PWL 60*	9 6
27 Oct 90	I'M DOING FINE *PWL PWL 69*	22 6
18 May 91	RSVP *PWL PWL 80*	17 5
22 Jun 91 ★	ANY DREAM WILL DO *Really Useful RUR 7*	1 12
24 Aug 91 ●	HAPPY TOGETHER *PWL PWL 203*	10 6
7 Dec 91	JOSEPH MEGA REMIX *Really Useful RUR 9* [2]	13 8
18 Jul 92	MISSION OF LOVE *Polydor PO 222*	26 4
28 Nov 92	AS TIME GOES BY *Polydor PO 245*	26 6
7 Aug 93	ALL AROUND THE WORLD *Polydor PZCD 278*	41 3

[1] Kylie Minogue and Jason Donovan [2] Jason Donovan and Original London Cast featuring Linzi Hately, David Easter and Johnny Amobi

DOOBIE BROTHERS
US, male vocal / instrumental group (45 WEEKS)

		pos/wks
9 Mar 74	LISTEN TO THE MUSIC *Warner Bros. K 16208*	29 7
7 Jun 75	TAKE ME IN YOUR ARMS *Warner Bros. K 16559*	29 5
17 Feb 79	WHAT A FOOL BELIEVES *Warner Bros. K 17314* ▲	31 10
5 May 79	WHAT A FOOL BELIEVES (re-entry) *Warner Bros. K 17314*	72 1
14 Jul 79	MINUTE BY MINUTE *Warner Bros. K 17411*	47 4
24 Jan 87	WHAT A FOOL BELIEVES (re-issue) *Warner Bros. W 8451* [1]	57 3
29 Jul 89	THE DOCTOR *Capitol CL 536*	73 2
27 Nov 93 ●	LONG TRAIN RUNNIN' *Warner Bros. W 0217CD*	7 10
14 May 94	LISTEN TO THE MUSIC (re-mix) *Warner Bros. W 0228CD*	37 3

[1] Doobie Brothers featuring Michael McDonald

DOOGIE – See BUG KANN and the PLASTIC JAM

DOOLALLY
UK, male production duo, aka Shanks & Bigfoot (16 WEEKS)

		pos/wks
14 Nov 98	STRAIGHT FROM THE HEART *Locked On LOX 104CD*	20 6
2 Jan 99	STRAIGHT FROM THE HEART (re-entry) *Locked On LOX 104CD*	63 4
7 Aug 99 ●	STRAIGHT FROM THE HEART (re-issue) *Chocolate Boy / Locked On LOX 112CD*	9 6

See also SHANKS & BIGFOOT

DOOLEYS (391) `Top 500`

Largest UK family act to chart (seven members at times); Jim, John, Frank, Kathy, Helen, Anne Dooley plus Anne's husband Bob, and Alan Bogan. (83 WEEKS)

		pos/wks
13 Aug 77	THINK I'M GONNA FALL IN LOVE WITH YOU *GTO GT 95*	13 10
12 Nov 77 ●	LOVE OF MY LIFE *GTO GT 110*	9 11
13 May 78	DON'T TAKE IT LYIN' DOWN *GTO GT 220*	60 3
2 Sep 78	A ROSE HAS TO DIE *GTO GT 229*	11 11
10 Feb 79	HONEY I'M LOST *GTO GT 242*	24 9
16 Jun 79 ●	WANTED *GTO GT 249*	3 14
22 Sep 79 ●	THE CHOSEN FEW *GTO GT 258*	7 11
8 Mar 80	LOVE PATROL *GTO GT 260*	29 7
6 Sep 80	BODY LANGUAGE *GTO GT 276*	46 4
10 Oct 81	AND I WISH *GTO GT 300*	52 3

Val DOONICAN (164) `Top 500`

Popular balladeer and TV host, b. 3 Feb 1928, Waterford, Ireland. This relaxed crooner, who was known for his rocking chair and multi-coloured jumpers, had five successive Top 10 albums in the Swinging Sixties (143 WEEKS)

		pos/wks
15 Oct 64 ●	WALK TALL *Decca F 11982*	3 21
21 Jan 65 ●	THE SPECIAL YEARS *Decca F 12049*	7 12
8 Apr 65	I'M GONNA GET THERE SOMEHOW *Decca F 12118*	25 5
22 Apr 65	THE SPECIAL YEARS (re-entry) *Decca F 12049*	49 1
17 Mar 66 ●	ELUSIVE BUTTERFLY *Decca F 12358*	5 12
3 Nov 66 ●	WHAT WOULD I BE *Decca F 12505*	2 17
23 Feb 67	MEMORIES ARE MADE OF THIS *Decca F 12566*	11 12
25 May 67	TWO STREETS *Decca F 12608*	39 4
18 Oct 67 ●	IF THE WHOLE WORLD STOPPED LOVING *Pye 7N 17396*	3 19
21 Feb 68	YOU'RE THE ONLY ONE *Pye 7N 17465*	37 4
12 Jun 68	NOW *Pye 7N 17534*	43 2
23 Oct 68	IF I KNEW THEN WHAT I KNOW NOW *Pye 7N 17616*	14 13
23 Apr 69	RING OF BRIGHT WATER *Pye 7N 17713*	48 1
4 Dec 71	MORNING *Philips 6006 177*	12 13
10 Mar 73	HEAVEN IS MY WOMAN'S LOVE *Philips 6028 031*	34 6
28 Apr 73	HEAVEN IS MY WOMAN'S LOVE (re-entry) *Philips 6028 031*	47 1

DOOP
Holland, male instrumental duo (12 WEEKS)

		pos/wks
12 Mar 94 ★	DOOP *Citybeat CBE 774CD*	1 12

DOORS
US, male vocal / instrumental group (42 WEEKS)

		pos/wks
16 Aug 67	LIGHT MY FIRE *Elektra EKSN 45014* ▲	49 1
28 Aug 68	HELLO I LOVE YOU *Elektra EKSN 45037* ▲	15 12
16 Oct 71	RIDERS ON THE STORM *Elektra K 12021*	50 1
30 Oct 71	RIDERS ON THE STORM (re-entry) *Elektra K 12021*	22 10
20 Mar 76	RIDERS ON THE STORM (re-issue) *Elektra K 12203*	33 5
3 Feb 79	HELLO I LOVE YOU (re-issue) *Elektra K 12215*	71 2
27 Apr 91	BREAK ON THROUGH *Elektra EKR 121*	64 2
1 Jun 91 ●	LIGHT MY FIRE (re-issue) *Elektra EKR 125*	7 8
10 Aug 91	RIDERS ON THE STORM (2nd re-issue) *Elektra EKR 131*	68 1

D.O.P.
UK, male instrumental / production duo (2 WEEKS)

		pos/wks
3 Feb 96	STOP STARTING TO START STOPPING (EP) *Hi-Life 5779472*	58 1
13 Jul 96	GROOVY BEAT *Hi-Life 5750652*	54 1

Tracks on Stop Starting to Stop Stopping (EP): Gusta / Dance to the House / Can You Feel It / How Do Y'All Feel

DOPE SMUGGLAZ
UK, male DJ / production duo (5 WEEKS)

		pos/wks
5 Dec 98	THE WORD *Mushroom PERFCDS 1*	62 1
7 Aug 99	DOUBLE DOUBLE DUTCH *Perfecto PERF2CDS*	15 4

Charlie DORE
UK, female vocalist (2 WEEKS)

		pos/wks
17 Nov 79	PILOT OF THE AIRWAVES *Island WIP 6526*	66 2

DOROTHY
UK, male instrumental duo (5 WEEKS)

		pos/wks
9 Dec 95	WHAT'S THAT TUNE (DOO DOO DOO DOO DOO-DOO-DOO-DOO-DOO-DOO) *RCA 74321330912*	31 5

Lee DORSEY
US, male vocalist (36 WEEKS)

		pos/wks
3 Feb 66	GET OUT OF MY LIFE WOMAN *Stateside SS 485*	22 7
5 May 66	CONFUSION *Stateside SS 506*	38 6
11 Aug 66 ●	WORKING IN THE COALMINE *Stateside SS 528*	8 11
27 Oct 66 ●	HOLY COW *Stateside SS 552*	6 12

Marc DORSEY
US, male vocalist (1 WEEK)

		pos/wks
19 Jun 99	IF YOU REALLY WANNA KNOW *Jive 0522592*	58 1

Tommy DORSEY ORCHESTRA starring Warren COVINGTON
US, orchestra - Warren Covington, male instrumentalist - trombone (19 WEEKS)

		pos/wks
17 Oct 58 ●	TEA FOR TWO CHA CHA *Brunswick 05757*	3 19

DOUBLE
Switzerland, male vocal / instrumental duo - Kurt Maloo & Felix Haug (10 WEEKS)

		pos/wks
25 Jan 86 ●	THE CAPTAIN OF HER HEART *Polydor POSP 779*	8 9
5 Dec 87	DEVIL'S BALL *Polydor POSP 888*	71 1

UK No.1 ★   UK Top 10 ●   Still on chart +   UK million seller ◆   UK entry at No.1 ■   US No.1 ▲

DOUBLE DEE featuring DANY
Italy, male vocal / instrumental duo (4 WEEKS)   pos/wks

| 1 Dec 90 | FOUND LOVE *Epic 6563766* | 63 | 2 |
| 25 Nov 95 | FOUND LOVE (re-mix) *Sony S3 DANUCD 1* | 33 | 2 |

DOUBLE 99
UK, male instrumental / production duo (9 WEEKS)   pos/wks

| 31 May 97 | RIPGROOVE *Satellite 74321485132* | 31 | 3 |
| 1 Nov 97 | RIPGROOVE (re-mix) *Satellite 74321529322* | 14 | 6 |

See also RIP PRODUCTIONS

007 – See RED RAW featuring 007

DOUBLE SIX
UK, male vocal / instrumental group (2 WEEKS)   pos/wks

| 19 Sep 98 | REAL GOOD *Multiply CDMULTY 39* | 66 | 1 |
| 12 Jun 99 | BREAKDOWN *Multiply CDMULTY 50* | 59 | 1 |

DOUBLE TROUBLE
UK, male instrumental / production duo - Leigh Guest & Michael Menson (35 WEEKS)   pos/wks

27 May 89	JUST KEEP ROCKIN' *Desire WANT 9* [1]	11	12
7 Oct 89 ●	STREET TUFF *Desire WANT 18* [2]	3	14
12 May 90	TALK BACK *Desire WANT 27* [3]	71	1
30 Jun 90	LOVE DON'T LIVE HERE ANYMORE *Desire WANT 32* [4]	21	6
15 Jun 91	RUB-A-DUB *Desire WANT 41*	66	2

[1] Double Trouble and the Rebel MC [2] Rebel MC and Double Trouble [3] Double Trouble featuring Janette Sewell [4] Double Trouble featuring Janette Sewell and Carl Brown

DOUBLE YOU?
Italy, male vocalist - Willie Morales (3 WEEKS)   pos/wks

| 2 May 92 | PLEASE DON'T GO *ZYX ZYX 67487* | 41 | 3 |

Rob DOUGAN
UK, male vocalist / instrumentalist / producer (1 WEEK)   pos/wks

| 4 Apr 98 | FURIOUS ANGELS *Cheeky CHEKCD 025* | 62 | 1 |

Carl DOUGLAS
Jamaica, male vocalist (39 WEEKS)   pos/wks

17 Aug 74 ★	KUNG FU FIGHTING *Pye 7N 45377* ▲	1	13
30 Nov 74	DANCE THE KUNG FU *Pye 7N 45418*	35	5
3 Dec 77	RUN BACK *Pye 7N 46018*	25	10
23 May 98 ●	KUNG FU FIGHTING *All Around the World CDGLOBE 173* [1]	8	11

[1] Bus Stop featuring Carl Douglas

Second listing for Kung Fu Fighting was not a re-mix of the original but Douglas's 1974 hit vocal sampled and used in a new recording by Bus Stop

Carol DOUGLAS
US, female vocalist (4 WEEKS)   pos/wks

| 22 Jul 78 | NIGHT FEVER *Gull GULS 61* | 66 | 4 |

Craig DOUGLAS   249   Top 500
Clean-cut early Sixties teen idol, b. Terence Perkins, 12 Aug 1941, Isle of Wight. Voted Best New Singer of 1959; had eight cover versions among his nine Top 20 entries. He topped the bill on The Beatles' first major stage show (112 WEEKS)   pos/wks

12 Jun 59	A TEENAGER IN LOVE *Top Rank JAR 133*	13	11
7 Aug 59 ★	ONLY SIXTEEN *Top Rank JAR 159*	1	15
22 Jan 60 ●	PRETTY BLUE EYES *Top Rank JAR 268*	4	14
28 Apr 60 ●	THE HEART OF A TEENAGE GIRL *Top Rank JAR 340*	10	9
11 Aug 60	OH! WHAT A DAY *Top Rank JAR 406*	43	1
20 Apr 61 ●	A HUNDRED POUNDS OF CLAY *Top Rank JAR 556*	9	9
29 Jun 61 ●	TIME *Top Rank JAR 569*	9	14
22 Mar 62 ●	WHEN MY LITTLE GIRL IS SMILING *Top Rank JAR 610*	9	13
28 Jun 62 ●	OUR FAVOURITE MELODIES *Columbia DB 4854*	9	10
18 Oct 62	OH LONESOME ME *Decca F 11523*	15	12
28 Feb 63	TOWN CRIER *Decca F 11575*	36	4

DOVE
Ireland, male / female vocal group (2 WEEKS)   pos/wks

| 11 Sep 99 | DON'T DREAM *ZTT 135CD* | 37 | 2 |

DOVES
UK, male vocal / instrumental group (7 WEEKS)   pos/wks

14 Aug 99	HERE IT COMES *Casino CHIP 003CD*	73	1
1 Apr 00	THE CEDAR ROOM *Heavenly HVN 95CD*	33	2
10 Jun 00	CATCH THE SUN *Heavenly HVN 96CD*	32	2
11 Nov 00	THE MAN WHO TOLD EVERYTHING *Heavenly HVN 98CD*	32	2

DOWLANDS
UK, male vocal duo (7 WEEKS)   pos/wks

| 9 Jan 64 | ALL MY LOVING *Oriole CB 1897* | 33 | 7 |

Robert DOWNEY Jr.
US, male vocalist (1 WEEK)   pos/wks

| 30 Jan 93 | SMILE *Epic 6589052* | 68 | 1 |

Don DOWNING
US, male vocalist (10 WEEKS)   pos/wks

| 10 Nov 73 | LONELY DAYS, LONELY NIGHTS *People PEO 102* | 32 | 10 |

Will DOWNING
US, male vocalist (35 WEEKS)   pos/wks

2 Apr 88	A LOVE SUPREME *Fourth & Broadway BRW 90*	14	10
25 Jun 88	IN MY DREAMS *Fourth & Broadway BRW 104*	34	6
1 Oct 88	FREE *Fourth & Broadway BRW 112*	58	5
21 Jan 89	WHERE IS THE LOVE *Fourth & Broadway BRW 122* [1]	19	7
28 Oct 89	TEST OF TIME *Fourth & Broadway BRW 146*	67	2
24 Feb 90	COME TOGETHER AS ONE *Fourth & Broadway BRW 159*	48	4
18 Sep 93	THERE'S NO LIVING WITHOUT YOU *Fourth & Broadway BRCD 278*	67	1

[1] Mica Paris and Will Downing

Lamont DOZIER – See HOLLAND-DOZIER featuring Lamont DOZIER

Charlie DRAKE
UK, male comedian / vocalist - Charles Sprigall (37 WEEKS)   pos/wks

8 Aug 58 ●	SPLISH SPLASH *Parlophone R 4461*	7	11
24 Oct 58	VOLARE *Parlophone R 4478*	28	2
27 Oct 60	MR CUSTER *Parlophone R 4701*	12	12
5 Oct 61	MY BOOMERANG WON'T COME BACK *Parlophone R 4824*	14	11
1 Jan 72	PUCKWUDGIE *Columbia DB 8829*	47	1

DRAMATIS
UK, male vocal / instrumental group (8 WEEKS)   pos/wks

| 5 Dec 81 | LOVE NEEDS NO DISGUISE *Beggars Banquet BEG 60* [1] | 33 | 7 |
| 13 Nov 82 | I CAN SEE HER NOW *Rocket XPRES 83* | 57 | 1 |

[1] Gary Numan and Dramatis

Rusty DRAPER
US, male vocalist (4 WEEKS)   pos/wks

| 11 Aug 60 | MULE SKINNER BLUES *Mercury AMT 1101* | 39 | 4 |

DREAD ZEPPELIN
US, male vocal / instrumental group (3 WEEKS)   pos/wks

| 1 Dec 90 | YOUR TIME IS GONNA COME *IRS DREAD 1* | 59 | 1 |
| 13 Jul 91 | STAIRWAY TO HEAVEN *IRS DREAD 2* | 62 | 2 |

DREADZONE
UK, male instrumental group (15 WEEKS)   pos/wks

6 May 95	ZION YOUTH *Virgin VSCDG 1537*	49	2
29 Jul 95	CAPTAIN DREAD *Virgin VSCDG 1541*	49	2
23 Sep 95	MAXIMUM (EP) *Virgin VSCDT 1555*	56	2
6 Jan 96	LITTLE BRITAIN *Virgin VSCDG 1565*	20	6
30 Mar 96	LIFE LOVE AND UNITY *Virgin VSCDT 1583*	56	1
10 May 97	EARTH ANGEL *Virgin VSCDT 1593*	51	1
26 Jul 97	MOVING ON *Virgin VSCDT 1635*	58	1

Tracks on Maximum (EP): Maximum / Fight the Power 95 / One Way

DREAM ACADEMY
UK, male / female vocal / instrumental group (10 WEEKS)   pos/wks

| 30 Mar 85 | LIFE IN A NORTHERN TOWN *Blanco Y Negro NEG 10* | 15 | 8 |
| 14 Sep 85 | THE LOVE PARADE *Blanco Y Negro NEG 16* | 68 | 2 |

DREAM FREQUENCY UK, male producer - Ian Bland (12 WEEKS) pos/wks

12 Jan 91	LOVE PEACE AND HARMONY Citybeat CBE 756	71	2
25 Jan 92	FEEL SO REAL Citybeat CBE 763 [1]	23	5
25 Apr 92	TAKE ME Citybeat CBE 768	39	3
21 May 94	GOOD TIMES / THE DREAM Citybeat CBE 773CD	67	1
10 Sep 94	YOU MAKE ME FEEL MIGHTY REAL Citybeat CBE 775CD	65	1

[1] Dream Frequency featuring Debbie Sharp

DREAM WARRIORS Canada, male rap group (19 WEEKS) pos/wks

14 Jul 90	WASH YOUR FACE IN MY SINK Fourth & Broadway BRW 183	16	8
24 Nov 90	MY DEFINITION OF A BOOMBASTIC JAZZ STYLE Fourth & Broadway BRW 197	13	8
2 Mar 91	LUDI Fourth & Broadway BRW 206	39	3

DREAMERS – See FREDDIE and the DREAMERS

DREAMHOUSE UK, male vocal / instrumental group (2 WEEKS) pos/wks

| 3 Jun 95 | STAY Chase CDPALACE 1 | 62 | 2 |

DREAMWEAVERS US, male / female vocal group (18 WEEKS) pos/wks

| 10 Feb 56 ★ | IT'S ALMOST TOMORROW Brunswick 05515 | 1 | 18 |

DREEM TEEM UK, male DJ / production trio (9 WEEKS) pos/wks

| 13 Dec 97 | THE THEME 4 Liberty 74321542032 | 34 | 4 |
| 6 Nov 99 | BUDDY X 99 4 Liberty LIBTCD 33 [1] | 15 | 5 |

[1] Dreem Teem vs Neneh Cherry

DRELLS – See Archie BELL and the DRELLS

Eddie DRENNON and B.B.S. UNLIMITED
US, male vocal / instrumental group (6 WEEKS) pos/wks

| 28 Feb 76 | LET'S DO THE LATIN HUSTLE Pye International 7N 25702 | 20 | 6 |

Alan DREW UK, male vocalist (2 WEEKS) pos/wks

| 26 Sep 63 | ALWAYS THE LONELY ONE Columbia DB 7090 | 48 | 2 |

DRIFTERS – See SHADOWS

DRIFTERS (109 Top 500) Ever changing, ever popular US group, founded in 1953 by Clyde McPhatter (d. 1972) and still active today, with erstwhile members including Ben E. King, Johnny Moore (d. 1998) and Rudy Lewis (d. 1964). Inducted into Rock and Roll Hall of Fame in 1988 (176 WEEKS) pos/wks

8 Jan 60	DANCE WITH ME London HLE 8988	17	4
10 Mar 60	DANCE WITH ME (re-entry) London HLE 8988	35	1
3 Nov 60 ●	SAVE THE LAST DANCE FOR ME London HLK 9201 ▲	2	18
16 Mar 61	I COUNT THE TEARS London HLK 9287	28	6
5 Apr 62	WHEN MY LITTLE GIRL IS SMILING London HLK 9522	31	3
10 Oct 63	I'LL TAKE YOU HOME London HLK 9785	37	5
24 Sep 64	UNDER THE BOARDWALK Atlantic AT 4001	45	4
8 Apr 65	AT THE CLUB Atlantic AT 4019	35	7
29 Apr 65	COME ON OVER TO MY PLACE Atlantic AT 4023	40	5
2 Feb 67	BABY WHAT I MEAN Atlantic 584 065	49	1
25 Mar 72	AT THE CLUB Atlantic K 10148	39	1
8 Apr 72 ●	AT THE CLUB / SATURDAY NIGHT AT THE MOVIES (re-entry of re-issue) Atlantic K 10148	3	19
26 Aug 72 ●	COME ON OVER TO MY PLACE (re-issue) Atlantic K 10216	9	11
4 Aug 73 ●	LIKE SISTER AND BROTHER Bell 1313	7	12
15 Jun 74 ●	KISSIN' IN THE BACK ROW OF THE MOVIES Bell 1358	2	13
12 Oct 74 ●	DOWN ON THE BEACH TONIGHT Bell 1381	7	9
8 Feb 75	LOVE GAMES Bell 1396	33	6
6 Sep 75 ●	THERE GOES MY FIRST LOVE Bell 1433	3	12
29 Nov 75 ●	CAN I TAKE YOU HOME LITTLE GIRL Bell 1462	10	10
13 Mar 76	HELLO HAPPINESS Bell 1469	12	8
11 Sep 76	EVERY NITE'S A SATURDAY NIGHT WITH YOU Bell 1491	29	7

| 18 Dec 76 ● | YOU'RE MORE THAN A NUMBER IN MY LITTLE RED BOOK Arista 78 | 5 | 12 |
| 14 Apr 79 | SAVE THE LAST DANCE FOR ME / WHEN MY LITTLE GIRL IS SMILING (re-issue) Lightning LIG 9014 | 69 | 2 |

'Saturday Night at the Movies' received chart credit with 'At the Club' only after the re-issue's return to the chart on 8 Apr 1972

Julie DRISCOLL, Brian AUGER and the TRINITY
UK, female vocalist / male instrumental group (16 WEEKS) pos/wks

| 17 Apr 68 ● | THIS WHEEL'S ON FIRE Marmalade 598 006 | 5 | 16 |

DRIVER 67 UK, male vocalist - Paul Phillips (12 WEEKS) pos/wks

| 23 Dec 78 ● | CAR 67 Logo GO 336 | 7 | 12 |

DRIZABONE
UK / US, male / female vocal / instrumental group (18 WEEKS) pos/wks

22 Jun 91	REAL LOVE Fourth & Broadway BRW 223	16	8
26 Oct 91	CATCH THE FIRE Fourth & Broadway BRW 232	54	2
23 Apr 94	PRESSURE Fourth & Broadway BRCD 264	33	2
15 Oct 94	BRIGHTEST STAR Fourth & Broadway BRCD 293	45	2
4 Mar 95	REAL LOVE (re-recording) Fourth & Broadway BRCD 311	24	4

Frank D'RONE US, male vocalist (6 WEEKS) pos/wks

| 22 Dec 60 | STRAWBERRY BLONDE Mercury AMT 1123 | 24 | 6 |

DRU HILL US, male vocal group (42 WEEKS) pos/wks

15 Feb 97	TELL ME Fourth & Broadway BRCD 342	30	3
10 May 97	IN MY BED Fourth & Broadway BRCD 353	16	3
11 Oct 97	BIG BAD MAMMA Def Jam 5749792 [1]	12	3
6 Dec 97	5 STEPS Island Black Music CID 675	22	3
24 Oct 98 ●	HOW DEEP IS YOUR LOVE Island Black Music CID 725 [2]	9	7
16 Jan 99	HOW DEEP IS YOUR LOVE (re-entry) Island Black Music CID 725 [2]	75	1
6 Feb 99 ●	THESE ARE THE TIMES Island Black Music CID 733	4	6
10 Jul 99 ●	WILD WILD WEST Columbia 6675962 [3] ▲	2	16

[1] Foxy Brown featuring Dru Hill [2] Dru Hill featuring Redman [3] Will Smith featuring Dru Hill - additional vocals Kool Moe Dee

DRUGSTORE
UK / US / Brazil, male / female vocal / instrumental group (5 WEEKS) pos/wks

10 Jun 95	FADER Honey HONCD 7	72	1
2 May 98	EL PRESIDENT Roadrunner RR 22369 [1]	20	3
4 Jul 98	SOBER Roadrunner RR22303	68	1

[1] Additional vocals by Thom Yorke

DRUM CLUB UK, male instrumental / production duo (1 WEEK) pos/wks

| 6 Nov 93 | SOUND SYSTEM Butterfly BFLD 10 | 62 | 1 |

DRUM THEATRE UK, male vocal / instrumental group (8 WEEKS) pos/wks

| 15 Feb 86 | LIVING IN THE PAST Epic A 6798 | 67 | 2 |
| 17 Jan 87 | ELDORADO Epic EMU 1 | 44 | 6 |

DRUPI Italy, male vocalist (12 WEEKS) pos/wks

| 1 Dec 73 | VADO VIA A & M AMS 7083 | 17 | 12 |

DSK
UK, male / female vocal / instrumental / production group (4 WEEKS) pos/wks

| 31 Aug 91 | WHAT WOULD WE DO? / READ MY LIPS Boy's Own BOI 6 | 46 | 3 |
| 22 Nov 97 | WHAT WOULD WE DO (re-mix) Fresh FRSHD 63 | 55 | 1 |

DSM US, male rap group (4 WEEKS) pos/wks

| 7 Dec 85 | WARRIOR GROOVE 10 DAZZ 45-7 | 68 | 4 |

DSP – See Matt DAREY

UK No.1 ★   UK Top 10 ●   Still on chart +   UK million seller ◆   UK entry at No.1 ■   US No.1 ▲

DTI US, male vocal / instrumental group (1 WEEK)
pos/wks
16 Apr 88	**KEEP THIS FREQUENCY CLEAR / KEEP IT CLEAR**		
	Premiere UK ERE 501	**73**	1

DTOX UK, male / female vocal / instrumental group (1 WEEK)
pos/wks
| 21 Nov 92 | **SHATTERED GLASS** *Vitality VITal 1* | **75** | 1 |

John DU CANN UK, male vocalist (6 WEEKS)
pos/wks
| 22 Sep 79 | **DON'T BE A DUMMY** *Vertigo 6059 241* | **33** | 6 |

John DU PREZ – See MODERN ROMANCE

DUB CONSPIRACY – See TRU FAITH & DUB CONSPIRACY

DUB PISTOLS
UK, male vocal / instrumental / production group (1 WEEK)
pos/wks
10 Oct 98	**CYCLONE**		
	Deconstruction HARD 36CD	**63**	1

DUB WAR UK, male vocal / instrumental group (5 WEEKS)
pos/wks
3 Jun 95	**STRIKE IT** *Earache MOSH 138CD*	**70**	1
27 Jan 96	**ENEMY MAKER** *Earache MOSH 147CD*	**41**	2
24 Aug 96	**CRY DIGNITY** *Earache MOSH 163CDD*	**59**	1
29 Mar 97	**MILLION DOLLAR LOVE** *Earache MOSH 170CD1*	**73**	1

DUBLINERS Ireland, male vocal / instrumental group (45 WEEKS)
pos/wks
30 Mar 67	● **SEVEN DRUNKEN NIGHTS** *Major Minor MM 506*	**7**	17
30 Aug 67	**BLACK VELVET BAND** *Major Minor MM 530*	**15**	15
20 Dec 67	**MAIDS WHEN YOU'RE YOUNG NEVER WED AN OLD MAN**		
	Major Minor MM 551	**43**	3
28 Mar 87	● **THE IRISH ROVER** *Stiff BUY 258* [1]	**8**	8
16 Jun 90	**JACK'S HEROES / WHISKEY IN THE JAR**		
	Pogue Mahone YZ 500 [1]	**63**	2

[1] Pogues and the Dubliners

DUBSTAR UK, male / female vocal / instrumental group (26 WEEKS)
pos/wks
8 Jul 95	**STARS** *Food CDFOOD 61*	**40**	3
30 Sep 95	**ANYWHERE** *Food CDFOOD 67*	**37**	3
6 Jan 96	**NOT SO MANIC NOW** *Food CDFOOD 71*	**18**	5
30 Mar 96	**STARS (re-issue)** *Food CDFOODS 75*	**15**	6
3 Aug 96	**ELEVATOR SONG** *Food CDFOOD 80*	**25**	2
19 Jul 97	**NO MORE TALK** *Food CDFOOD 96*	**20**	3
20 Sep 97	**CATHEDRAL PARK** *Food CDFOOD 104*	**41**	1
7 Feb 98	**I WILL BE YOUR GIRLFRIEND** *Food CDFOODS 108*	**28**	2
27 May 00	**I (FRIDAY NIGHT)** *Food CDFOODS 128*	**37**	1

Mary DUFF – See Daniel O'DONNELL

DUFFO Australia, male vocalist (2 WEEKS)
pos/wks
| 24 Mar 79 | **GIVE ME BACK ME BRAIN** *Beggars Banquet BEG 15* | **60** | 2 |

Stephen 'Tin Tin' DUFFY UK, male vocalist (24 WEEKS)
pos/wks
9 Jul 83	**HOLD IT** *Curve X 9763* [1]	**55**	4
2 Mar 85	● **KISS ME** *10 TIN 2*	**4**	11
18 May 85	**ICING ON THE CAKE** *10 TIN 3*	**14**	9

[1] Tin Tin

DUKE UK, male vocalist (6 WEEKS)
pos/wks
25 May 96	**SO IN LOVE WITH YOU** *Encore CDCOR 009*	**66**	1
26 Oct 96	**SO IN LOVE WITH YOU (re-issue)**		
	Pukka CDPUKKA 11	**22**	4
11 Nov 00	**SO IN LOVE WITH YOU (re-mix)**		
	48k / Perfecto SPECT 08CDS	**65**	1

George DUKE US, male vocalist / instrumentalist (6 WEEKS)
pos/wks
| 12 Jul 80 | **BRAZILIAN LOVE AFFAIR** *Epic EPC 8751* | **36** | 6 |

DUKE BAYSEE UK, male vocalist (6 WEEKS)
pos/wks
| 3 Sep 94 | **SUGAR SUGAR** *Bell 74321228702* | **30** | 4 |
| 21 Jan 95 | **DO YOU LOVE ME** *Double Dekker CDDEK 1* | **46** | 2 |

DUKES UK, male vocal duo (13 WEEKS)
pos/wks
| 17 Oct 81 | **MYSTERY GIRL** *WEA K 18867* | **47** | 7 |
| 1 May 82 | **THANK YOU FOR THE PARTY** *WEA K 19136* | **53** | 6 |

Candy DULFER
Holland, female instrumentalist - saxophone (14 WEEKS)
pos/wks
| 24 Feb 90 | ● **LILY WAS HERE** *RCA ZB 43045* [1] | **6** | 12 |
| 4 Aug 90 | **SAXUALITY** *RCA PB 43769* | **60** | 2 |

[1] David A Stewart featuring Candy Dulfer

DUM DUMS UK, male vocal / instrumental group (13 WEEKS)
pos/wks
11 Mar 00	**EVERYTHING** *Good Behavior CDGOOD 1*	**21**	5
8 Jul 00	**CAN'T GET YOU OUT OF MY THOUGHTS**		
	Good Behaviour GDGOOD 2	**18**	5
23 Sep 00	**YOU DO SOMETHING TO ME** *Good Behaviour CDGOLD 3*	**27**	3

Thuli DUMAKUDE South Africa, male vocalist (1 WEEK)
pos/wks
| 2 Jan 88 | **THE FUNERAL (SEPTEMBER 25, 1977)** *MCA MCA 1228* | **75** | 1 |

The listed flip side of 'The Funeral' was 'Cry Freedom' by George Fenton and Jonas Gwangwa

John DUMMER and Helen APRIL
UK, male / female vocal duo (3 WEEKS)
pos/wks
| 28 Aug 82 | **BLUE SKIES** *Speed SPEED 8* | **54** | 3 |

DUNBLANE
UK, male / female vocal / instrumental group (15 WEEKS)
pos/wks
| 21 Dec 96 | ★ **KNOCKIN' ON HEAVEN'S DOOR / THROW THESE GUNS AWAY** *BMG 74321442182* ■ | **1** | 15 |

Johnny DUNCAN and the BLUE GRASS BOYS US, male vocalist and UK, instrumental group (20 WEEKS)
pos/wks
26 Jul 57	● **LAST TRAIN TO SAN FERNANDO** *Columbia DB 3959*	**2**	17
25 Oct 57	**BLUE BLUE HEARTACHES** *Columbia DB 3996*	**27**	1
29 Nov 57	**FOOTPRINTS IN THE SNOW** *Columbia DB 4029*	**27**	1
3 Jan 58	**FOOTPRINTS IN THE SNOW (re-entry)** *Columbia DB 4029*	**28**	1

David DUNDAS UK, male vocalist (14 WEEKS)
pos/wks
| 24 Jul 76 | ● **JEANS ON** *Air CHS 2094* | **3** | 9 |
| 9 Apr 77 | **ANOTHER FUNNY HONEYMOON** *Air CHS 2136* | **29** | 5 |

Erroll DUNKLEY Jamaica, male vocalist (14 WEEKS)
pos/wks
| 22 Sep 79 | **OK FRED** *Scope SC 6* | **11** | 11 |
| 2 Feb 80 | **SIT DOWN AND CRY** *Scope SC 11* | **52** | 3 |

Clive DUNN UK, male actor / vocalist (28 WEEKS)
pos/wks
| 28 Nov 70 | ★ **GRANDAD** *Columbia DB 8726* | **1** | 27 |
| 26 Jun 71 | **GRANDAD (re-entry)** *Columbia DB 8726* | **50** | 1 |

Simon DUPREE and the BIG SOUND
UK, male vocal / instrumental group (16 WEEKS)
pos/wks
| 22 Nov 67 | ● **KITES** *Parlophone R 5646* | **9** | 13 |
| 3 Apr 68 | **FOR WHOM THE BELL TOLLS** *Parlophone R 5670* | **43** | 3 |

DURAN DURAN [67] [Top 500] New Romantics turned teen idols:
Simon Le Bon (v), Nick Rhodes (k), John Taylor (b), Andy Taylor (g), Roger Taylor (d). The Birmingham band's successive Top 10 hits included 'A View to a Kill' the best-selling James Bond theme ever in the UK and the US. The three Taylors were unrelated (222 WEEKS)
pos/wks
| 21 Feb 81 | **PLANET EARTH** *EMI 5137* | **12** | 11 |
| 9 May 81 | **CARELESS MEMORIES** *EMI 5168* | **37** | 7 |

SINGLED OUT...
Phill Jupitus

From Buzzcocks to Blockheads, Mr Jupitus is a big man with big opinions who is always worth listening to.

- **NO.1 ON THE UK SINGLES CHART THE DAY I WAS BORN:**
Good Luck Charm
Elvis Presley

- **FIRST SINGLE I EVER BOUGHT:**
The Streak – Ray Stevens

Bought it for my mother but it was for me really … sorry mum

- **SINGLE THAT DRIVES ME UP THE WALL:**
Boy bands, girl bands but not real bands. I blame the upsurge of karaoke and line-dancing.

ALL-TIME FAVOURITE SINGLE:
Hit Me With Your Rhythm Stick
Ian Dury and the Blockheads

I remember how exciting it was when I first heard it on the radio and going out to try to buy it but it hadn't been released yet

Photo: Rex Features – Tony Larkin

25 Jul 81 ●	GIRLS ON FILM EMI 5206	5	11
28 Nov 81	MY OWN WAY EMI 5254	14	11
15 May 82 ●	HUNGRY LIKE THE WOLF EMI 5295	5	12
21 Aug 82 ●	SAVE A PRAYER EMI 5327	2	9
13 Nov 82 ●	RIO EMI 5346	9	11
26 Mar 83 ★	IS THERE SOMETHING I SHOULD KNOW EMI 5371 ■	1	9
29 Oct 83 ●	UNION OF THE SNAKE EMI 5429	3	7
24 Dec 83	UNION OF THE SNAKE (re-entry) EMI 5429	66	4
4 Feb 84 ●	NEW MOON ON MONDAY EMI DURAN 1	9	7
28 Apr 84 ★	THE REFLEX EMI DURAN 2 ▲	1	14
3 Nov 84 ●	WILD BOYS Parlophone DURAN 3	2	14
18 May 85 ●	A VIEW TO A KILL Parlophone DURAN 007 ▲	2	16
1 Nov 86 ●	NOTORIOUS EMI DDN 45	7	7
3 Jan 87	NOTORIOUS (re-entry) EMI DDN 45	73	1
21 Feb 87	SKIN TRADE EMI TRADE 1	22	6
25 Apr 87	MEET EL PRESIDENTE EMI TOUR 1	24	5
1 Oct 88	I DON'T WANT YOUR LOVE EMI YOUR 1	14	5
7 Jan 89 ●	ALL SHE WANTS IS EMI DD 11	9	5
22 Apr 89	DO YOU BELIEVE IN SHAME EMI DD 12	30	4
16 Dec 89	BURNING THE GROUND EMI DD 13	31	5
4 Aug 90	VIOLENCE OF SUMMER (LOVE'S TAKING OVER) Parlophone DD 14	20	4
17 Nov 90	SERIOUS Parlophone DD 15	48	3
30 Jan 93 ●	ORDINARY WORLD Parlophone CDDDS 16	6	9
10 Apr 93	COME UNDONE Parlophone CDDDS 17	13	8
4 Sep 93	TOO MUCH INFORMATION Parlophone CDDDS 18	35	3
25 Mar 95	PERFECT DAY Parlophone CDDDS 20	28	4
17 Jun 95	WHITE LINES (DON'T DO IT) Parlophone CDDD 19 [1]	17	5
24 May 97	OUT OF MY MIND Virgin VSCDT 1639	21	2
30 Jan 99	ELECTRIC BARBARELLA EMI CDELEC 2000	23	3
10 Jun 00	SOMEONE ELSE NOT ME Hollywood / Edel 0108845 HWR	53	1

[1] Duran Duran featuring Melle Mel and Grandmaster Flash and the Furious Five Group was UK / US from 'Burning the Ground'

See also POWER STATION; ARCADIA

Jimmy DURANTE US, male vocalist (1 WEEK)
		pos/wks
14 Dec 96	MAKE SOMEONE HAPPY Warner Bros. W 0385CD	69	1

Judith DURHAM Australia, female vocalist (5 WEEKS)
		pos/wks
15 Jun 67	OLIVE TREE Columbia DB 8207	33	5

See also SEEKERS

Ian DURY and the BLOCKHEADS
UK, male vocal / instrumental group (56 WEEKS)
		pos/wks
29 Apr 78 ●	WHAT A WASTE Stiff BUY 27	9	12
9 Dec 78 ★	HIT ME WITH YOUR RHYTHM STICK Stiff BUY 38 [1]	1	15
4 Aug 79	REASONS TO BE CHEERFUL (PT. 3) Stiff BUY 50	3	8
30 Aug 80	I WANT TO BE STRAIGHT Stiff BUY 90	22	7
15 Nov 80	SUEPERMAN'S BIG SISTER Stiff BUY 100	51	3
25 May 85	HIT ME WITH YOUR RHYTHM STICK (re-mix) Stiff BUY 214	55	4
26 Oct 85	PROFOUNDLY IN LOVE WITH PANDORA EMI EMI 5534 [2]	45	5
27 Jul 91	HIT ME WITH YOUR RHYTHM STICK (2nd) (re-mix) Flying FLYR 1	73	1
11 Mar 00	DRIP FED FRED Virgin VSCDT 1768 [3]	55	1

[1] Ian and the Blockheads [2] Ian Dury [3] Madness featuring Ian Dury

DUST BROTHERS US, male production duo (1 WEEK)
		pos/wks
11 Dec 99	THIS IS YOUR LIFE Restless 74321713962	60	1

DUST JUNKYS UK, male vocal / instrumental group (5 WEEKS)
		pos/wks
15 Nov 97	(NONSTOPOPERATION) Polydor 5719732	47	2
28 Feb 98	WHAT TIME IS IT? Polydor 5694912	39	2
16 May 98	NOTHIN' PERSONAL Polydor 5699092	62	1

Slim DUSTY
Australia, male vocalist - David Kirkpatrick (15 WEEKS)
		pos/wks
30 Jan 59 ●	A PUB WITH NO BEER Columbia DB 4212 [1]	3	15

[1] Slim Dusty with Dick Carr & His Bushlanders

DUTCH FORCE Holland, male producer - Benno De Goeij (2 WEEKS)
		pos/wks
6 May 00	DEADLINE Inferno CDFERN 27	35	2

Ondrea DUVERN – See HUSTLERS CONVENTION featuring Dave LAUDAT and Ondrea DUVERNEY

DWEEB UK, male / female vocal / instrumental trio (2 WEEKS)
		pos/wks
22 Feb 97	SCOOBY DOO Blanco Y Negro NEG 100CD	63	1
7 Jun 97	OH YEAH, BABY Blanco Y Negro NEG 102CD1	70	1

Sarah DWYER – See LANGE featuring SARAH DWYER

Bob DYLAN (180 Top 500) The most influential folk / rock vocalist / guitarist ever, b. Robert Zimmerman, 24 May 1941, Minnesota, US. The legendary performer, who led the 1960s folk music movement, redefined the term and, indeed, image of the singer / songwriter. He remains one of the biggest-selling album acts of the rock era (137 WEEKS)
		pos/wks
25 Mar 65 ●	TIMES THEY ARE A-CHANGIN' CBS 201751	9	11
29 Apr 65 ●	SUBTERRANEAN HOMESICK BLUES CBS 201753	9	9
17 Jun 65	MAGGIE'S FARM CBS 201781	22	8
19 Aug 65 ●	LIKE A ROLLING STONE CBS 201811	4	12
28 Oct 65 ●	POSITIVELY FOURTH STREET CBS 201824	8	12
27 Jan 66	CAN YOU PLEASE CRAWL OUT YOUR WINDOW CBS 201900	17	5
14 Apr 66	ONE OF US MUST KNOW (SOONER OR LATER) CBS 202053	33	5
12 May 66 ●	RAINY DAY WOMEN NOS. 12 & 35 CBS 202307	7	8
21 Jul 66	I WANT YOU CBS 202258	16	9
14 May 69	I THREW IT ALL AWAY CBS 4219	30	6
13 Sep 69 ●	LAY LADY LAY CBS 4434	5	12
10 Jul 71	WATCHING THE RIVER FLOW CBS 7329	24	9
6 Oct 73	KNOCKIN' ON HEAVEN'S DOOR CBS 1762	14	9
7 Feb 76	HURRICANE CBS 3878	43	4
29 Jul 78	BABY STOP CRYING CBS 6499	13	11
28 Jul 78	IS YOUR LOVE IN VAIN CBS 6718	56	3
20 May 95	DIGNITY Columbia 6620762	33	2
11 Jul 98	LOVE SICK Columbia 6659972	64	1
14 Oct 00	THINGS HAVE CHANGED Columbia 6693792	58	1

DYNAMIX II featuring TOO TOUGH TEE
US, male vocal / instrumental group and rapper (4 WEEKS)
		pos/wks
8 Aug 87	JUST GIVE THE DJ A BREAK Cooltempo COOL 151	50	4

DYNASTY US, male / female vocal / instrumental group (20 WEEKS)
		pos/wks
13 Oct 79	I DON'T WANT TO BE A FREAK (BUT I CAN'T HELP MYSELF) Solar FB 1694	20	13
9 Aug 80	I'VE JUST BEGUN TO LOVE YOU Solar SO 10	51	4
21 May 83	DOES THAT RING A BELL Solar E 9911	53	3

Ronnie DYSON US, male vocalist (6 WEEKS)
		pos/wks
4 Dec 71	WHEN YOU GET RIGHT DOWN TO IT CBS 7449	34	6

Katherine E US, female vocalist (7 WEEKS)
		pos/wks
6 Apr 91	I'M ALRIGHT Dead Dead Good GOOD 2	41	5
18 Jan 92	THEN I FEEL GOOD PWL Continental PWL 13	56	2

Lizz E – See FRESH 4 featuring Lizz E

Sheila E
US, female vocalist / instrumentalist - percussion (9 WEEKS)
		pos/wks
23 Feb 85	THE BELLE OF ST MARK Warner Bros. W 9180	18	9

E-LUSTRIOUS UK, male instrumental / production duo (2 WEEKS)
pos/wks

		pos	wks
15 Feb 92	**DANCE NO MORE** MOS MOS 001T [1]	58	1
2 Jul 94	**IN YOUR DANCE** UFG UFG 6CD	69	1

[1] E-Lustrious featuring Deborah French

E-MALE UK, male vocal / instrumental group (1 WEEK)
pos/wks

		pos	wks
31 Jan 98	**WE ARE E-MALE** East West EW 137CD	44	1

E-MOTION UK, male vocal / instrumental duo (7 WEEKS)
pos/wks

		pos	wks
3 Feb 96	**THE NAUGHTY NORTH AND THE SEXY SOUTH** Soundproof MCSTD 40017	20	3
17 Aug 96	**I STAND ALONE** Soundproof MCSTD 40061	60	1
26 Oct 96	**THE NAUGHTY NORTH AND THE SEXY SOUTH (re-mix)** Soundproof MCSTD 40076	17	3

E-ROTIC Germany / US, male / female vocal / instrumental group (2 WEEKS)
pos/wks

		pos	wks
3 Jun 95	**MAX DON'T HAVE SEX WITH YOUR EX** Stip CDSTIP 2	45	2

E-SMOOVE featuring Latanza WATERS
UK, male production team, and US female vocalist (1 WEEK)
pos/wks

		pos	wks
15 Aug 98	**DEJA VU** AM:PM 5827671	63	1

E-TYPE Sweden, male vocalist (2 WEEKS)
pos/wks

		pos	wks
23 Sep 95	**THIS IS THE WAY** Ffrreedom TABCD 237	53	1
24 Jun 00	**CAMPIONE 2000** Polydor 1580822	58	1

E.U. – See SALT-N-PEPA

E-ZEE POSSEE UK, male / female vocal / instrumental group (16 WEEKS)
pos/wks

		pos	wks
26 Aug 89	**EVERYTHING STARTS WITH AN 'E'** More Protein PROT 1	69	1
20 Jan 90	**LOVE ON LOVE** More Protein PROT 3	59	3
17 Mar 90	**EVERYTHING STARTS WITH AN 'E' (re-entry)** More Protein PROT 1	15	8
30 Jun 90	**THE SUN MACHINE** More Protein PROT 4	62	3
21 Sep 91	**BREATHING IS E-ZEE** More Protein PROT 12 [1]	72	1

[1] E-Zee Possee featuring Tara Newley

E-Z ROLLERS UK, male / female vocal / instrumental group (3 WEEKS)
pos/wks

		pos	wks
24 Apr 99	**WALK THIS LAND** Moving Shadow 130CD1	18	3

EAGLES US, male vocal / instrumental group (51 WEEKS)
pos/wks

		pos	wks
9 Aug 75	**ONE OF THESE NIGHTS** Asylum AYM 543 ▲	23	7
1 Nov 75	**LYIN' EYES** Asylum AYM 548	23	7
6 Mar 76	**TAKE IT TO THE LIMIT** Asylum K 13029	12	7
15 Jan 77	**NEW KID IN TOWN** Asylum K 13069 ▲	20	7
16 Apr 77 ●	**HOTEL CALIFORNIA** Asylum K 13079 ▲	8	10
16 Dec 78	**PLEASE COME HOME FOR CHRISTMAS** Asylum K 13145	30	5
13 Oct 79	**HEARTACHE TONIGHT** Asylum K 12394 ▲	40	5
1 Dec 79	**THE LONG RUN** Elektra K 12404	66	2
13 Jul 96	**LOVE WILL KEEP US ALIVE** Geffen GFSTD 21980	52	1

Robert EARL UK, male vocalist (27 WEEKS)
pos/wks

		pos	wks
25 Apr 58	**I MAY NEVER PASS THIS WAY AGAIN** Philips PB 805	14	13
24 Oct 58	**MORE THAN EVER (COME PRIMA)** Philips PB 867	26	2
21 Nov 58	**MORE THAN EVER (COME PRIMA) (re-entry)** Philips PB 867	28	2
13 Feb 59	**THE WONDERFUL SECRET OF LOVE** Philips PB 891	17	10

Charles EARLAND US, male instrumentalist - keyboards (5 WEEKS)
pos/wks

		pos	wks
19 Aug 78	**LET THE MUSIC PLAY** Mercury 6167 703	46	5

Steve EARLE US, male vocalist / instrumentalist - guitar (7 WEEKS)
pos/wks

		pos	wks
15 Oct 88	**COPPERHEAD ROAD** MCA MCA 1280	45	6
31 Dec 88	**JOHNNY COME LATELY** MCA MCA 1301	75	1

EARLY MUSIC CONSORT directed by David MUNROW
UK, male / female instrumental group (1 WEEK)
pos/wks

		pos	wks
3 Apr 71	**HENRY VIII SUITE (EP)** BBC RESL 1	49	1

Tracks on Henry VIII Suite (EP): Fanfare, Passomezo du Roy, Gaillarde d'Escosse / Pavane, Mille Ducats / Larocque Gaillarde / Allemande / Wedding March, La Mourisque / If Love Now Reigned / Rone, Pourquoi

EARTH WIND AND FIRE (202 | Top 500) Colourful, mystical, Los Angeles-based group noted for flamboyant stage performances. Formed by Maurice White (d/v) and included Philip Bailey (v), Ronnie Laws (s/fl) and Verdine White (b). Few R&B acts outsold them in the late 1970s, when they achieved eight successive US Top 10 albums (128 WEEKS)
pos/wks

		pos	wks
12 Feb 77	**SATURDAY NITE** CBS 4835	17	9
11 Feb 78	**FANTASY** CBS 6056	14	10
13 May 78	**JUPITER** CBS 6267	41	5
29 Jul 78	**MAGIC MIND** CBS 6490	75	1
12 Aug 78	**MAGIC MIND (re-entry)** CBS 6490	54	4
7 Oct 78	**GOT TO GET YOU INTO MY LIFE** CBS 6553	33	7
9 Dec 78 ●	**SEPTEMBER** CBS 6922	3	13
12 May 79 ●	**BOOGIE WONDERLAND** CBS 7292 [1]	4	13
28 Jul 79 ●	**AFTER THE LOVE HAS GONE** CBS 7721	4	10
6 Oct 79	**STAR** CBS 7902	16	8
15 Dec 79	**CAN'T LET GO** CBS 8077	46	7
8 Mar 80	**IN THE STONE** CBS 8252	53	3
11 Oct 80	**LET ME TALK** CBS 8982	29	5
20 Dec 80	**BACK ON THE ROAD** CBS 9377	63	4
7 Nov 81 ●	**LET'S GROOVE** CBS A 1679	3	13
6 Feb 82	**I'VE HAD ENOUGH** CBS A 1959	29	6
5 Feb 83	**FALL IN LOVE WITH ME** CBS A 2927	47	4
7 Nov 87	**SYSTEM OF SURVIVAL** CBS EWF 1	54	3
31 Jul 99	**SEPTEMBER 99 (re-mix)** INCredible INCR 24CD	25	2

[1] Earth Wind and Fire with the Emotions

EARTHLING UK, male vocal / instrumental duo (2 WEEKS)
pos/wks

		pos	wks
14 Oct 95	**ECHO ON MY MIND PART II** Cooltempo CDCOOL 312	61	1
1 Jun 96	**BLOOD MUSIC (EP)** Cooltempo CDCOOL 319	69	1

Tracks on Blood Music (EP): First Transmission / Because the Night / Soup or No Soup / Infinite M

EAST 57th STREET featuring Donna ALLEN
UK, male production trio - US female vocalist (3 WEEKS)
pos/wks

		pos	wks
11 Oct 97	**SATURDAY** AM:PM 5823752	29	3

EAST OF EDEN UK, male instrumental group (12 WEEKS)
pos/wks

		pos	wks
17 Apr 71 ●	**JIG A JIG** Deram DM 297	7	12

EAST 17 (117 | Top 500) London-based singing, rapping and dancing lads with international teen appeal: Tony Mortimer (v/k), Brian Harvey (v), John Hendy (v), Terry Coldwell (v). Bad press and personal problems resulted in main songwriter Mortimer quitting, and a name change to E-17 for their 1998 comeback (170 WEEKS)
pos/wks

		pos	wks
29 Aug 92 ●	**HOUSE OF LOVE** London LON 325	10	9
14 Nov 92	**GOLD** London LON 331	28	4
19 Dec 92	**GOLD (re-entry)** London LON 331	64	4
30 Jan 93 ●	**DEEP** London LOCDP 334	5	10
10 Apr 93	**SLOW IT DOWN** London LONCD 339	13	7
26 Jun 93	**WEST END GIRLS** London LONCD 344	11	7
4 Dec 93 ●	**IT'S ALRIGHT** London LONCD 345	3	14
14 May 94 ●	**AROUND THE WORLD** London LONCD 349	3	13
1 Oct 94 ●	**STEAM** London LONCD 353	7	8
3 Dec 94 ★	**STAY ANOTHER DAY** London LONCD 354	1	15

UK No.1 ★   UK Top 10 ●   Still on chart +   UK million seller ◆   UK entry at No.1 ■   US No.1 ▲

25 Mar 95 ●	LET IT RAIN *London LONCD 363*	**10**	7
6 May 95	STAY ANOTHER DAY (re-entry)		
	London LONCD 354	**64**	1
17 Jun 95	HOLD MY BODY TIGHT *London LONCD 367*	**12**	7
4 Nov 95 ●	THUNDER *London LONCD 373*	**4**	14
10 Feb 96 ●	DO U STILL *London LONCD 379*	**7**	7
10 Aug 96	SOMEONE TO LOVE *London LONCD 385*	**16**	8
2 Nov 96 ●	IF YOU EVER *London LONCD 388* [1]	**2**	15
18 Jan 97 ●	HEY CHILD *London LONCD 390*	**3**	5
14 Nov 98 ●	EACH TIME *Telstar CDSTAS 3017* [2]	**2**	10
13 Mar 99	BETCHA CAN'T WAIT *Telstar CDSTAS 3031* [2]	**12**	5

[1] East 17 featuring Gabrielle [2] E-17

EAST SIDE BEAT *Italy, male vocal / instrumental duo - Carl Fanini and Francesco Petrocchi (18 WEEKS)*
pos/wks
30 Nov 91 ●	RIDE LIKE THE WIND *ffrr F 176*	**3**	11
19 Dec 92	ALIVE AND KICKING *ffrr F 206*	**26**	6
29 May 93	YOU'RE MY EVERYTHING *ffrr FCD 207*	**65**	1

Sheena EASTON 284 Top 500 *Scotland's most successful act Stateside, b. Sheena Orr, 27 Apr 1959, Glasgow. This vocalist was first seen in TV documentary 'The Big Time'. Reached the big time on both sides of the Atlantic and won the Grammy for Best New Artist of 1981 (104 WEEKS)*
pos/wks
5 Apr 80	MODERN GIRL *EMI 5042*	**56**	3
19 Jul 80 ●	9 TO 5 *EMI 5066* ▲	**3**	15
9 Aug 80 ●	MODERN GIRL (re-entry) *EMI 5042*	**8**	12
25 Oct 80	ONE MAN WOMAN *EMI 5114*	**14**	6
14 Feb 81	TAKE MY TIME *EMI 5135*	**44**	5
2 May 81	WHEN HE SHINES *EMI 5166*	**12**	8
27 Jun 81 ●	FOR YOUR EYES ONLY *EMI 5195*	**8**	13
12 Sep 81	JUST ANOTHER BROKEN HEART *EMI 5232*	**33**	8
5 Dec 81	YOU COULD HAVE BEEN WITH ME *EMI 5252*	**54**	3
31 Jul 82	MACHINERY *EMI 5326*	**38**	5
12 Feb 83	WE'VE GOT TONIGHT *Liberty UP 658* [1]	**28**	7
21 Jan 89	THE LOVER IN ME *MCA MCA 1289*	**15**	8
18 Mar 89	DAYS LIKE THIS *MCA MCA 1325*	**43**	3
15 Jul 89	101 *MCA MCA 1348*	**54**	2
18 Nov 89	THE ARMS OF ORION *Warner Bros. W 2757* [2]	**27**	5
9 Dec 00	GIVING UP GIVING IN *Universal MCSTD 40244*	**54**	1

[1] Kenny Rogers and Sheena Easton [2] Prince with Sheena Easton

See also PRINCE

EASTSIDE CONNECTION *US, disco aggregation (3 WEEKS)*
pos/wks
| 8 Apr 78 | YOU'RE SO RIGHT FOR ME *Creole CR 149* | **44** | 3 |

Clint EASTWOOD *US, male actor (2 WEEKS)*
pos/wks
| 7 Feb 70 | I TALK TO THE TREES *Paramount PARA 3004* | **18** | 2 |

This is the flip of 'Wand'rin Star' by Lee Marvin and was listed with Marvin's A-side for two weeks only

Clint EASTWOOD and GENERAL SAINT
UK, male vocal group (8 WEEKS)
pos/wks
| 29 Sep 84 | LAST PLANE (ONE WAY TICKET) *MCA MCA 910* [1] | **51** | 3 |
| 2 Apr 94 | OH CAROL! *Copasetic COPCD 0009* | **54** | 5 |

EASY RIDERS – See Frankie LAINE

EASYBEATS *Australia, male vocal / instrumental group (24 WEEKS)*
pos/wks
| 27 Oct 66 ● | FRIDAY ON MY MIND *United Artists UP 1157* | **6** | 15 |
| 10 Apr 68 | HELLO HOW ARE YOU *United Artists UP 2209* | **20** | 9 |

EAT *UK / US, male / female vocal / instrumental group (1 WEEK)*
pos/wks
| 12 Jun 93 | BLEED ME WHITE *Fiction FICCD 48* | **73** | 1 |

EAT STATIC *UK, male production duo (3 WEEKS)*
pos/wks
| 22 Feb 97 | HYBRID *Planet Dog BARK 024CD* | **41** | 1 |

| 27 Sep 97 | INTERCEPTOR *Planet Dog BARK 030CD* | **44** | 1 |
| 27 Jun 98 | CONTACT... *Planet Dog BARK 033CD* | **67** | 1 |

Cleveland EATON *US, male instrumentalist - keyboards (6 WEEKS)*
pos/wks
| 23 Sep 78 | BAMA BOOGIE WOOGIE *Gull GULS 63* | **35** | 6 |

EAV *Austria, male vocal / instrumental group (4 WEEKS)*
pos/wks
| 27 Sep 86 | BA-BA-BANKROBBERY (ENGLISH VERSION) | | |
| | *Columbia DB 9139* | **63** | 4 |

EAV is short for Erste Allgemeine Verunsicherung

EAZY-E *US, male rapper (3 WEEKS)*
pos/wks
| 6 Jan 96 | JUST TAH LET YOU KNOW *Epic 6628162* | **30** | 3 |

ECHO and the BUNNYMEN 379 Top 500 *Cult alternative rock group originally from Liverpool, UK, who named themselves after their drum machine. Ian McCulloch (v). b. 5 May 1959, frontman of this moody and atmospheric group, went solo 1988. Original line-up regrouped in 1997 (85 WEEKS)*
pos/wks
17 May 80	RESCUE *Korova KOW 1*	**62**	1
18 Apr 81	CROCODILES *Korova ECHO 1*	**37**	4
18 Jul 81	A PROMISE *Korova KOW 15*	**49**	4
29 May 82	THE BACK OF LOVE *Korova KOW 24*	**19**	7
22 Jan 83 ●	THE CUTTER *Korova KOW 26*	**8**	8
16 Jul 83	NEVER STOP *Korova KOW 28*	**15**	7
28 Jan 84 ●	THE KILLING MOON *Korova KOW 32*	**9**	6
21 Apr 84	SILVER *Korova KOW 34*	**30**	5
14 Jul 84	SEVEN SEAS *Korova KOW 35*	**16**	7
19 Oct 85	BRING ON THE DANCING HORSES *Korova KOW 43*	**21**	7
13 Jun 87	THE GAME *WEA YZ 134*	**28**	4
1 Aug 87	LIPS LIKE SUGAR *WEA YZ 144*	**36**	4
20 Feb 88	PEOPLE ARE STRANGE *WEA YZ 175*	**29**	5
2 Mar 91	PEOPLE ARE STRANGE (re-issue) *East West YZ 567*	**34**	4
28 Jun 97 ●	NOTHING LASTS FOREVER *London LOCDP 396*	**8**	6
13 Sep 97	I WANT TO BE THERE WHEN YOU COME *London LONCD 399*	**30**	2
8 Nov 97	DON'T LET IT GET YOU DOWN *London LOCDP 406*	**50**	1
27 Mar 99	RUST *London LONCD 424*	**22**	3

ECHOBEATZ *UK, male DJ / production duo - Dave De Braie and Paul Moody (5 WEEKS)*
pos/wks
| 25 Jul 98 ● | MAS QUE NADA *Eternal WEA 176CD* | **10** | 5 |

ECHOBELLY
UK / Sweden, male / female vocal / instrumental group (16 WEEKS)
pos/wks
2 Apr 94	INSOMNIAC *Fauve FAUV 1CD*	**47**	1
2 Jul 94	I CAN'T IMAGINE THE WORLD WITHOUT ME *Fauve FAUV 2CD*	**39**	2
5 Nov 94	CLOSE...BUT *Fauve FAUV 4CD*	**59**	1
2 Sep 95	GREAT THINGS *Fauve FAUV 5CD*	**13**	3
4 Nov 95	KING OF THE KERB *Fauve FAUV 7CD*	**25**	3
2 Mar 96	DARK THERAPY *Fauve FAUV 8CD*	**20**	3
23 Aug 97	THE WORLD IS FLAT *Epic 6648152*	**31**	2
8 Nov 97	HERE COMES THE BIG RUSH *Epic 6652452*	**56**	1

See also LITHIAM and Sonya MADAN

Billy ECKSTINE *US, male vocalist (48 WEEKS)*
pos/wks
12 Nov 54 ●	NO ONE BUT YOU *MGM 763*	**3**	17
27 Sep 57	PASSING STRANGERS *Mercury MT 164* [1]	**22**	2
13 Feb 59 ●	GIGI *Mercury AMT 1018*	**8**	14
12 Mar 69	PASSING STRANGERS (re-issue) *Mercury MF 1082* [1]	**20**	15

[1] Billy Eckstine and Sarah Vaughan

ECLIPSE *Italy, male producer / instrumentalist - Gianni Bini (4 WEEKS)*
pos/wks
| 14 Aug 99 | MAKES ME LOVE YOU *Azuli AZNYCDX 100* | **25** | 4 |

Silvio ECOMO *Holland, male producer (1 WEEK)*
pos/wks
| 15 Jul 00 | STANDING *Hooj Choons HOOJ 098CD* | **70** | 1 |

EDDIE and the HOT RODS
UK, male vocal / instrumental group (26 WEEKS) pos/wks

11 Sep 76	LIVE AT THE MARQUEE (EP0 *Island IEP 2*	43	5
13 Nov 76	TEENAGE DEPRESSION *Island WIP 6354*	35	4
23 Apr 77	I MIGHT BE LYING *Island WIP 6388*	44	3
13 Aug 77 ●	DO ANYTHING YOU WANNA DO		
	Island WIP 6401 [1]	9	10
21 Jan 78	QUIT THIS TOWN *Island WIP 6411*	36	4

[1] Rods

Tracks on Live at the Marquee (EP): 96 Tears / Get out of Denver / Medley: Gloria / Satisfaction

EDDY
UK, female vocalist (2 WEEKS) pos/wks

| 9 Jul 94 | SOMEDAY *Positiva CDTIV 14* | 49 | 2 |

Duane EDDY and the REBELS (87 Top 500)
Twangy guitar legend. b. 26 Apr 1938, New York. Early rock's No.1 solo instrumentalist assembled a long string of UK and US hit singles and was one of the first rock acts to score on the album charts (201 WEEKS) pos/wks

5 Sep 58	REBEL ROUSER *London HL 8669*	19	10
2 Jan 59	CANNONBALL *London HL 8764*	22	4
19 Jun 59 ●	PETER GUNN *London HLW 8879* [1]	6	10
24 Jul 59	YEP *London HLW 8879*	17	5
4 Sep 59	FORTY MILES OF BAD ROAD *London HLW 8929*	11	9
11 Sep 59	PETER GUNN (re-entry) *London HLW 8879* [1]	27	1
18 Dec 59	SOME KINDA EARTHQUAKE *London HLW 9007*	12	5
19 Feb 60	BONNIE CAME BACK *London HLW 9050*	12	10
28 Apr 60 ●	SHAZAM! *London HLW 9104*	4	13
21 Jul 60 ●	BECAUSE THEY'RE YOUNG *London HLW 9162*	2	18
10 Nov 60	KOMMOTION *London HLW 9225*	13	10
12 Jan 61 ●	PEPE *London HLW 9257*	2	14
20 Apr 61 ●	THEME FROM DIXIE *London HLW 9324*	7	10
22 Jun 61	RING OF FIRE *London HLW 9370*	17	10
14 Sep 61	DRIVIN' HOME *London HLW 9406*	30	4
5 Oct 61	CARAVAN *Parlophone R 4826* [1]	42	3
24 May 62	DEEP IN THE HEART OF TEXAS *RCA 1288* [1]	19	8
23 Aug 62	BALLAD OF PALADIN *RCA 1300* [1]	10	10
8 Nov 62 ●	(DANCE WITH THE) GUITAR MAN *RCA 1316* [2]	4	16
14 Feb 63	BOSS GUITAR *RCA 1329* [2]	27	8
30 May 63	LONELY BOY LONELY GUITAR *RCA 1344* [2]	35	4
29 Aug 63	YOUR BABY'S GONE SURFIN' *RCA 1357* [2]	49	1
8 Mar 75 ●	PLAY ME LIKE YOU PLAY YOUR GUITAR		
	GTO GT 11 [2]	9	9
22 Mar 86 ●	PETER GUNN *China WOK 6* [3]	8	9

[1] Duane Eddy [2] Duane Eddy and the Rebelettes [3] Art of Noise featuring Duane Eddy

EDDY and the SOUL BAND
US, male / female vocal / instrumental group (7 WEEKS) pos/wks

| 23 Feb 85 | THE THEME FROM 'SHAFT' *Club JAB 11* | 13 | 7 |

Randy EDELMAN
US, male vocalist / instrumentalist - piano (18 WEEKS) pos/wks

6 Mar 76	CONCRETE AND CLAY *20th Century BTC 2261*	11	7
18 Sep 76	UPTOWN UPTEMPO WOMAN		
	20th Century BTC 2225	25	7
15 Jan 77	YOU *20th Century BTC 2253*	49	2
17 Jul 82	NOBODY MADE ME *Rocket XPRES 81*	60	2

EDELWEISS
Austria, male / female vocal / instrumental group (10 WEEKS) pos/wks

| 29 Apr 89 ● | BRING ME EDELWEISS *WEA YZ 353* | 5 | 10 |

EDEN
UK / Australia, male / female vocal / instrumental group (2 WEEKS) pos/wks

| 6 Mar 93 | DO U FEEL 4 ME *Logic 74321135422* | 51 | 2 |

Lyn EDEN – See SMOKIN BEATS featuring Lyn EDEN

EDISON LIGHTHOUSE
UK, male vocal / instrumental group, lead vocal Tony Burrows (13 WEEKS) pos/wks

| 24 Jan 70 ★ | LOVE GROWS (WHERE MY ROSEMARY GOES) *Bell 1091* | 1 | 12 |
| 30 Jan 71 | IT'S UP TO YOU PETULA *Bell 1136* | 49 | 1 |

Dave EDMUNDS (324 Top 500)
Former member of one-hit wonders Love Sculpture, b. 15 Apr 1944, Cardiff, Wales. Singer / guitarist and retro-sounding performer / producer's debut solo hit sold three million worldwide. He has produced many top acts including Dion, Everly Brothers, Del Shannon, Status Quo, Shakin' Stevens and Stray Cats (93 WEEKS) pos/wks

21 Nov 70 ★	I HEAR YOU KNOCKING *MAM 1*	1	14
20 Jan 73 ●	BABY I LOVE YOU *Rockfield ROC 1*	8	13
9 Jun 73 ●	BORN TO BE WITH YOU *Rockfield ROC 2*	5	12
2 Jul 77	I KNEW THE BRIDE *Swansong SSK 19411*	26	8
30 Jun 79 ●	GIRLS TALK *Swansong SSK 19418*	4	11
22 Sep 79	QUEEN OF HEARTS *Swansong SSK 19419*	11	9
24 Nov 79	CRAWLING FROM THE WRECKAGE *Swansong SSK 19420*	59	4
9 Feb 80	SINGING THE BLUES *Swansong SSK 19422*	28	8
28 Mar 81	ALMOST SATURDAY NIGHT *Swansong SSK 19424*	58	3
20 Jun 81	THE RACE IS ON *Swansong SSK 19425* [2]	34	6
26 Mar 83	SLIPPING AWAY *Arista ARIST 522*	60	4
7 Apr 90	KING OF LOVE *Capitol CL 568*	68	2

[1] Dave Edmunds' Rockpile [2] Dave Edmunds and the Stray Cats

Alton EDWARDS
Zimbabwe, male vocalist (9 WEEKS) pos/wks

| 9 Jan 82 | I JUST WANNA (SPEND SOME TIME WITH YOU) | | |
| | *Streetwave STRA 1897* | 20 | 9 |

Dennis EDWARDS featuring Siedah GARRETT
US, male / female vocal duo (10 WEEKS) pos/wks

| 24 Mar 84 | DON'T LOOK ANY FURTHER *Gordy TMG 1334* | 45 | 5 |
| 20 Jun 87 | DON'T LOOK ANY FURTHER (re-entry) *Gordy TMG 1334* | 55 | 5 |

Rupie EDWARDS
Jamaica, male vocalist (16 WEEKS) pos/wks

| 23 Nov 74 ● | IRE FEELINGS (SKANGA) *Cactus CT 38* | 9 | 10 |
| 8 Feb 75 | LEGO SKANGA *Cactus CT 51* | 32 | 6 |

Tommy EDWARDS
US, male vocalist (18 WEEKS) pos/wks

| 3 Oct 58 ★ | IT'S ALL IN THE GAME *MGM 989* ▲ | 1 | 17 |
| 7 Aug 59 | MY MELANCHOLY BABY *MGM 1020* | 29 | 1 |

EELS
US, male vocal / instrumental group (21 WEEKS) pos/wks

15 Feb 97 ●	NOVOCAINE FOR THE SOUL *Dreamworks DRMCD 22174*	10	5
17 May 97 ●	SUSAN'S HOUSE *Dreamworks DRMCD 22238*	9	5
13 Sep 97	YOUR LUCKY DAY IN HELL *Dreamworks DRMCD 22277*	35	2
26 Sep 98	LAST STOP: THIS TOWN *Dreamworks DRMCD 22346*	23	3
12 Dec 98	CANCER FOR THE CURE *Dreamworks DRMCD 22373*	60	1
26 Feb 00	MR E'S BEAUTIFUL BLUES *Dreamworks DRMCD 4509762*	11	4
24 Jun 00	FLYSWATTER *Dreamworks DRMCD 4509462*	55	1

EFUA
UK, female vocalist (5 WEEKS) pos/wks

| 3 Jul 93 | SOMEWHERE *Virgin VSCDT 1463* | 42 | 5 |

EGG
UK, male vocal / instrumental group (1 WEEK) pos/wks

| 30 Jan 99 | GETTING AWAY WITH IT *Indochina ID 079CD* | 58 | 1 |

EGGS ON LEGS
UK, male vocalist (1 WEEK) pos/wks

| 23 Sep 95 | COCK A DOODLE DO IT *Avex UK AVEXCD 18* | 42 | 1 |

EGYPTIAN EMPIRE
UK, male producer - Tim Taylor (2 WEEKS) pos/wks

| 24 Oct 92 | THE HORN TRACK *Ffrreedom TAB 115* | 61 | 2 |

EIFFEL 65
Italy, male vocal trio (36 WEEKS) pos/wks

21 Aug 99	BLUE (DA BA DEE) (IMPORT) *Logic 74321688212*	39	5
25 Sep 99 ★	BLUE (DA BA DEE) *Eternal WEA 226CD1* ■	1	21
19 Feb 00 ●	MOVE YOUR BODY *Eternal WEA 255CD1*	3	10

18 WHEELER *UK, male vocal / instrumental group (1 WEEK)* pos/wks

15 Mar 97	**STAY** *Creation CRESCD 249*	**59**	1

EIGHTH WONDER
UK, male / female vocal / instrumental group (25 WEEKS) pos/wks

2 Nov 85	**STAY WITH ME** *CBS A 6594*	**65**	2
20 Feb 88	● **I'M NOT SCARED** *CBS SCARE 1*	**7**	13
25 Jun 88	**CROSS MY HEART** *CBS 651552 7*	**13**	8
1 Oct 88	**BABY BABY** *CBS BABE 1*	**65**	2

808 STATE <small>493 Top 500</small> *Ambient house / UK techno pioneers formed in Manchester by DJ / instrumentalist / producers Graham Massey, Darren Partington, Andrew Barker and, until 1992, Martin Price. A UK dance act clocking up three instrumental Top 10 hits was unheard of at the start of the 1990s (70 WEEKS)* pos/wks

18 Nov 89	● **PACIFIC** *ZTT ZANG 1*	**10**	9
31 Mar 90	**THE EXTENDED PLEASURE OF DANCE (EP)** *ZTT ZANG 2T*	**56**	1
2 Jun 90	● **THE ONLY RHYME THAT BITES** *ZTT ZANG 3* [1]	**10**	10
15 Sep 90	**TUNES SPLITS THE ATOM** *ZTT ZANG 6* [1]	**18**	7
10 Nov 90	● **CUBIK / OLYMPIC** *ZTT ZANG 5*	**10**	10
16 Feb 91	● **IN YER FACE** *ZTT ZANG 14*	**9**	6
27 Apr 91	**OOOPS** *ZTT ZANG 19*	**42**	3
17 Aug 91	**LIFT / OPEN YOUR MIND** *ZTT ZANG 20*	**38**	4
29 Aug 92	**TIME BOMB / NIMBUS** *ZTT ZANG 33*	**59**	1
12 Dec 92	**ONE IN TEN (re-mix)** *ZTT ZANG 39* [3]	**17**	8
30 Jan 93	**PLAN 9** *ZTT ZANG 38CD*	**50**	2
26 Jun 93	**10 X 10** *ZTT ZANG 42CD*	**67**	1
13 Aug 94	**BOMBADIN** *ZTT ZANG 54CD*	**67**	1
29 Jun 96	**BOND** *ZTT ZANG 80CD*	**57**	1
8 Feb 97	**LOPEZ** *ZTT ZANG 87CD*	**20**	2
16 May 98	**PACIFIC / CUBIK (re-mixes)** *ZTT ZTT 98CD1*	**21**	3
6 Mar 99	**THE ONLY RHYME THAT BITES 99** *ZTT ZTT 125CD*	**53**	1

[1] MC Tunes versus 808 State [2] 808 State featuring Björk [3] 808 State vs UB40

Tracks on The Extended Pleasure of Dance (EP): Cobra Bora / Ancodia / Cubik. 'Cubik' is a re-issue of one of the tracks from The Extended Pleasure of Dance (EP). 'Lopez' features the uncredited vocals of James Dean Bradfield, lead singer of the Manic Street Preachers

88.3 – See Lisa MAY

EINSTEIN *UK, male rapper (6 WEEKS)* pos/wks

18 Nov 89	**ANOTHER MONSTERJAM** *ffrr F 116* [1]	**65**	1
15 Dec 90	**TURN IT UP** *Swanyard SYD 9* [2]	**42**	4
24 Aug 96	**THE POWER 96** *Arista 74321398672* [3]	**42**	1

[1] Simon Harris featuring Einstein [2] Technotronic featuring Melissa and Einstein [3] Snap featuring Einstein

See also AMBASSADORS OF FUNK featuring MC MARIO

EL COCO *US, male vocal / instrumental group (4 WEEKS)* pos/wks

14 Jan 78	**COCOMOTION** *Pye International 7N 25761*	**31**	4

EL MARIACHI *US, male producer - Roger Sanchez (2 WEEKS)* pos/wks

9 Nov 96	**CUBA** *ffrr FCD 286*	**38**	2

See also FUNK JUNKEEZ; Roger SANCHEZ

ELASTICA
UK, female / male vocal / instrumental group (12 WEEKS) pos/wks

12 Feb 94	**LINE UP** *Deceptive BLUFF 004CD*	**20**	3
22 Oct 94	**CONNECTION** *Deceptive BLUFF 010CD*	**17**	4
25 Feb 95	**WAKING UP** *Deceptive BLUFF 011CD*	**13**	4
24 Jun 00	**MAD DOG** *Deceptive BLUFF 077CD*	**44**	1

ELATE *UK, male / female vocal / instrumental trio (2 WEEKS)* pos/wks

26 Jul 97	**SOMEBODY LIKE YOU** *VC VCRD 22*	**38**	2

Donnie ELBERT *US, male vocalist (29 WEEKS)* pos/wks

8 Jan 72	● **WHERE DID OUR LOVE GO?** *London HL 10352*	**8**	10
26 Feb 72	**I CAN'T HELP MYSELF** *Avco 6105 009*	**11**	10
29 Apr 72	**LITTLE PIECE OF LEATHER** *London HL 10370*	**27**	9

ELECTRA *UK, male vocal / instrumental group (7 WEEKS)* pos/wks

6 Aug 88	**JIBARO** *ffrr FFR 9*	**54**	3
30 Dec 89	**IT'S YOUR DESTINY / AUTUMN LOVE** *London F 121*	**51**	4

ELECTRAFIXION *UK, male vocal / instrumental group (6 WEEKS)* pos/wks

19 Nov 94	**ZEPHYR** *WEA YZ 865CD*	**47**	2
9 Sep 95	**LOWDOWN** *WEA YZ 977CD*	**54**	2
4 Nov 95	**NEVER** *Spacejunk WEA 022CD*	**58**	1
16 Mar 96	**SISTER PAIN** *Spacejunk WEA 037CD1*	**27**	1

ELECTRASY *UK, male vocal / instrumental group (7 WEEKS)* pos/wks

13 Jun 98	**LOST IN SPACE** *MCA MCSTD 40171*	**60**	1
5 Sep 98	**MORNING AFTERGLOW** *MCA MCSTD 40184*	**19**	4
28 Nov 98	**BEST FRIEND'S GIRL** *MCA MCSXD 40195*	**41**	2

ELECTRIBE 101 *UK / Germany, male / female vocal / instrumental group (15 WEEKS)* pos/wks

28 Oct 89	**TELL ME WHEN THE FEVER ENDED** *Mercury MER 310*	**32**	5
24 Feb 90	**TALKING WITH MYSELF** *Mercury MER 316*	**23**	5
22 Sep 90	**YOU'RE WALKING** *Mercury MER 328*	**50**	3
10 Oct 98	**TALKING WITH MYSELF '98 (re-mix)** *Manifesto FESDD 49*	**39**	2

ELECTRIC LIGHT ORCHESTRA <small>41 Top 500</small> *Groundbreaking and innovative UK group, fronted by multi-talented Jeff Lynne (v/g) from Birmingham and originally included Roy Wood (The Move). Their unique sound, which featured an orchestral string section, helped them to achieve numerous transatlantic hits (255 WEEKS)* pos/wks

29 Jul 72	● **10538 OVERTURE** *Harvest HAR 5053*	**9**	8
27 Jan 73	● **ROLL OVER BEETHOVEN** *Harvest HAR 5063*	**6**	10
6 Oct 73	**SHOWDOWN** *Harvest HAR 5077*	**12**	10
9 Mar 74	**MA-MA-MA-BELLE** *Warner Bros. K 16349*	**22**	8
10 Jan 76	● **EVIL WOMAN** *Jet 764*	**10**	8
3 Jul 76	**STRANGE MAGIC** *Jet 779*	**38**	3
13 Nov 76	● **LIVIN' THING** *Jet UP 36184*	**4**	12
19 Feb 77	● **ROCKARIA!** *Jet UP 36209*	**9**	9
21 May 77	● **TELEPHONE LINE** *Jet UP 36254*	**8**	10
29 Oct 77	**TURN TO STONE** *Jet UP 36313*	**18**	12
28 Jan 78	● **MR BLUE SKY** *Jet UP 36342*	**6**	11
10 Jun 78	● **WILD WEST HERO** *Jet JET 109*	**6**	14
7 Oct 78	● **SWEET TALKIN' WOMAN** *Jet 121*	**6**	9
9 Dec 78	**ELO (EP)** *Jet ELO 1*	**34**	8
19 May 79	● **SHINE A LITTLE LOVE** *Jet 144*	**6**	10
21 Jul 79	● **THE DIARY OF HORACE WIMP** *Jet 150*	**8**	9
1 Sep 79	● **DON'T BRING ME DOWN** *Jet 153*	**3**	9
17 Nov 79	● **CONFUSION / LAST TRAIN TO LONDON** *Jet 166*	**8**	10
24 May 80	**I'M ALIVE** *Jet 179*	**20**	9
21 Jun 80	★ **XANADU** *Jet 185* [1]	**1**	11
2 Aug 80	**ALL OVER THE WORLD** *Jet 195*	**11**	8
22 Nov 80	**DON'T WALK AWAY** *Jet 7004*	**21**	10
1 Aug 81	● **HOLD ON TIGHT** *Jet 7011*	**4**	12
24 Oct 81	**TWILIGHT** *Jet 7015*	**30**	7
9 Jan 82	**TICKET TO THE MOON / HERE IS THE NEWS** *Jet 7018*	**24**	8
18 Jun 83	**ROCK 'N' ROLL IS KING** *Jet A 3500*	**13**	9
3 Sep 83	**SECRET MESSAGES** *Jet A 3720*	**48**	3
1 Mar 86	**CALLING AMERICA** *Epic A 6844*	**28**	7
11 May 91	**HONEST MEN** *Telstar ELO 100* [2]	**60**	1

[1] Olivia Newton-John and Electric Light Orchestra [2] Electric Light Orchestra Part 2
'Here Is the News' listed from 16 Jan 1982. Tracks on ELO (EP): Can't Get You Out of My Head / Strange Magic / Ma-Ma-Ma-Belle / Evil Woman

ELECTRIC PRUNES *US, male vocal / instrumental group (5 WEEKS)* pos/wks

9 Feb 67	**I HAD TOO MUCH TO DREAM LAST NIGHT** *Reprise RS 20532*	**49**	1
11 May 67	**GET ME TO THE WORLD ON TIME** *Reprise RS 20564*	**42**	4

ELECTRIQUE BOUTIQUE
UK / France, male production group (2 WEEKS)   pos/wks

26 Aug 00	REVELATION *Data DATA 14CDS*	37	2

ELECTRONIC
UK, male vocal / instrumental group (36 WEEKS)   pos/wks

16 Dec 89	GETTING AWAY WITH IT *Factory FAC 2577*	12	9
27 Apr 91 ●	GET THE MESSAGE *Factory FAC 2877*	8	7
21 Sep 91	FEEL EVERY BEAT *Factory FAC 3287*	39	4
4 Jul 92 ●	DISAPPOINTED *Parlophone R 6311*	6	5
6 Jul 96	FORBIDDEN CITY *Parlophone CDR 6436*	14	4
28 Sep 96	FOR YOU *Parlophone CDR 6445*	16	2
15 Feb 97	SECOND NATURE *Parlophone CDR 6455*	35	2
24 Apr 99	VIVID *Parlophone CDR 6514*	17	3

ELECTRONICAS
Holland, male instrumental group (8 WEEKS)   pos/wks

19 Sep 81	ORIGINAL BIRD DANCE *Polydor POSP 360*	22	8

ELECTROSET
UK, male instrumental production group (4 WEEKS)   pos/wks

21 Nov 92	HOW DOES IT FEEL *ffrr F 203*	27	3
15 Jul 95	SENSATION *Ffrreedom TABCD 231*	69	1

ELEGANTS
US, male vocal group (2 WEEKS)   pos/wks

26 Sep 58	LITTLE STAR *HMV POP 520* ▲	25	2

ELEMENT FOUR
UK, male production duo – Paul Oakenfold and Andy Gray (9 WEEKS)   pos/wks

9 Sep 00 ●	BIG BROTHER UK TV THEME *Channel 4 Music C4M 00072*	4	9

ELEVATION
UK, male instrumental / production duo (1 WEEK)   pos/wks

23 May 92	CAN YOU FEEL IT *Nova Mute 12NOMU 3*	62	1

ELEVATOR SUITE
UK, male production / instrumental trio (1 WEEK)   pos/wks

12 Aug 00	BACK AROUND *Infectious INFECT 85CDS*	71	1

ELEVATORMAN
UK, male instrumental / production group (4 WEEKS)   pos/wks

14 Jan 95	FUNK AND DRIVE *Wired WIRED 211*	37	3
1 Jul 95	FIRED UP *Wired WIRED 216*	44	1

ELGINS
US, male / female vocal group (20 WEEKS)   pos/wks

1 May 71 ●	HEAVEN MUST HAVE SENT YOU *Tamla Motown TMG 771*	3	13
9 Oct 71	PUT YOURSELF IN MY PLACE *Tamla Motown TMG 787*	28	7

ELIAS and his ZIGZAG JIVE FLUTES
South Africa, male instrumental group (14 WEEKS)   pos/wks

25 Apr 58 ●	TOM HARK *Columbia DB 4109*	2	14

Yvonne ELLIMAN
US, female vocalist (44 WEEKS)   pos/wks

29 Jan 72	I DON'T KNOW HOW TO LOVE HIM *MCA MKS 5077*	47	1
6 Nov 76 ●	LOVE ME *RSO 2090 205*	6	13
7 May 77	HELLO STRANGER *RSO 2090 236*	26	5
13 Aug 77	I CAN'T GET YOU OUT OF MY MIND *RSO 2090 251*	17	13
6 May 78	IF I CAN'T HAVE YOU *RSO 2090 266* ▲	4	12

'I Don't Know How to Love Him' was one of four tracks on a maxi-single, two of which were credited during the disc's one week on the chart. The other track credited was 'Superstar' by Murray Head

Duke ELLINGTON
US, orchestra (4 WEEKS)   pos/wks

5 Mar 54 ●	SKIN DEEP *Philips PB 243* [1]	7	4

[1] Duke Ellington with Louis Bellson (drums)

Lance ELLINGTON
UK, male vocalist (1 WEEK)   pos/wks

21 Aug 93	LONELY (HAVE WE LOST OUR LOVE) *RCA 74321158332*	57	1

Ray ELLINGTON
UK, male vocal / instrumental group (4 WEEKS)   pos/wks

15 Nov 62	THE MADISON *Ember S 102*	41	2
20 Dec 62	THE MADISON (re-entry) *Ember S 102*	36	2

Bern ELLIOTT and the FENMEN
UK, male vocal / instrumental group (22 WEEKS)   pos/wks

21 Nov 63	MONEY *Decca F 11770*	14	13
19 Mar 64	NEW ORLEANS *Decca F 11852*	24	9

Joe ELLIOTT – See Mick RONSON with Joe ELLIOTT

Missy 'Misdemeanor' ELLIOTT
US, female rapper / producer (33 WEEKS)   pos/wks

30 Aug 97	THE RAIN (SUPA DUPA FLY) *East West E 3919 CD*	16	3
29 Nov 97	SOCK IT 2 ME *East West E 3890CD*	33	2
25 Apr 98	BEEP ME 911 *East West E 3859CD*	14	3
22 Aug 98	HIT 'EM WIT DA HEE *East West E3824 CD1* [1]	25	3
22 Aug 98	MAKE IT HOT *East West E 3821 CD* [2]	22	4
26 Sep 98 ★	I WANT YOU BACK *Virgin VSCDT 1716* [3] ■	1	9
21 Nov 98	5 MINUTES *Elektra E 3803CD* [4]	72	1
13 Mar 99	HERE WE COME *Virgin DINSD 179* [5]	43	1
25 Sep 99	ALL N MY GRILL *Elektra E 3742 CD* [6]	20	4
22 Jan 00	HOT BOYZ *Elektra E 7002CD* [7]	18	3

[1] Missy 'Misdemeanor' Elliott featuring Lil' Kim [2] Nicole featuring Missy 'Misdemeanor' Elliott and Mocha [3] Melanie B featuring Missy 'Misdemeanor' Elliott [4] Lil' Mo featuring Missy 'Misdemeanor' Elliott [5] Timbaland / Missy Elliott & Magoo [6] Missy 'Misdemeanor' Elliott featuring MC Solaar [7] Missy 'Misdemeanor' Eliott featuring Nas, Eve & Q Tip

Greg ELLIS – See Reva RICE and Greg ELLIS

Joey B ELLIS
US, male rapper (10 WEEKS)   pos/wks

16 Feb 91	GO FOR IT (HEART AND FIRE) *Capitol CL 601* [1]	20	8
18 May 91	THOUGHT U WERE THE ONE FOR ME *Capitol CL 614*	58	2

[1] Rocky V featuring Joey B Ellis and Tynetta Hare

Shirley ELLIS
US, female vocalist (17 WEEKS)   pos/wks

6 May 65 ●	THE CLAPPING SONG *London HLR 9961*	6	13
8 Jul 78	THE CLAPPING SONG (EP) *MCA MCEP 1*	59	4

Tracks on The Clapping Song (EP): The Clapping Song / Ever See a Diver Kiss His Wife While the Bubbles Bounce Above the Water / The Name Game / The Nitty Gritty. 'The Clapping Song' itself qualifies as a re-issue

ELLIS, BEGGS and HOWARD
UK, male vocal / instrumental group (8 WEEKS)   pos/wks

2 Jul 88	BIG BUBBLES, NO TROUBLES *RCA PB 42089*	59	3
11 Mar 89	BIG BUBBLES, NO TROUBLES (re-entry) *RCA PB 42089*	41	5

ELWOOD
US, male rapper / vocalist Elwood Strickland (1 WEEK)   pos/wks

26 Aug 00	SUNDOWN *Palm Pictures PPCD 70342*	72	1

EMBRACE
UK, male vocal / instrumental group (32 WEEKS)   pos/wks

17 May 97	FIREWORKS (EP) *Hut HUTCD 84*	34	2
19 Jul 97	ONE BIG FAMILY (EP) *Hut HUTCD 86*	21	3
8 Nov 97 ●	ALL YOU GOOD GOOD PEOPLE (EP) *Hut HUTCD 90*	8	4
6 Jun 98 ●	COME BACK TO WHAT YOU KNOW *Hut HUTCD 93*	6	8
29 Aug 98 ●	MY WEAKNESS IS NONE OF YOUR BUSINESS *Hut HUTCD 103*	9	4
13 Nov 99	HOOLIGAN *Hut HUTCD 123*	18	3
25 Mar 00	YOU'RE NOT ALONE *Hut / Virgin HUTCD 126*	14	3
10 Jun 00	SAVE ME *Hut / Virgin HUTCD 133*	29	2
15 Jul 00	SAVE ME (re-entry) *Hut / Virgin HUTCD 133*	67	1
19 Aug 00	I WOULDN'T WANNA HAPPEN TO YOU *Hut / Virgin HUTCD 137*	23	2

Tracks on Fireworks (EP): The Last Gas / Now You're Nobody / Blind / Fireworks. Tracks on One Big Family (EP): One Big Family / Dry Kids / You've Only Got to Stop to Get Better / Butter Wouldn't Melt. Tracks on All You Good Good People (EP): All You Good Good People / You Don't Amount To Anything - This Time / The Way I Do / Free Ride

EMERSON – See SASHA

Keith EMERSON *UK, male instrumentalist - keyboards (5 WEEKS)* pos/wks

10 Apr 76	**HONKY TONK TRAIN BLUES** *Manticore K 13513*	**21** 5

See also EMERSON, LAKE and PALMER

EMERSON, LAKE and PALMER
UK, male instrumental group (13 WEEKS) pos/wks

4 Jun 77 ●	**FANFARE FOR THE COMMON MAN** *Atlantic K 10946*	**2** 13

See also Keith EMERSON; Greg LAKE; ASIA

Dick EMERY *UK, male actor / vocalist (8 WEEKS)* pos/wks

26 Feb 69	**IF YOU LOVE HER** *Pye 7N 17644*	**32** 4
13 Jan 73	**YOU ARE AWFUL** *Pye 7N 45202*	**43** 4

EMF *UK, male vocal / instrumental group (50 WEEKS)* pos/wks

3 Nov 90 ●	**UNBELIEVABLE** *Parlophone R 6273* ▲	**3** 13
2 Feb 91	**I BELIEVE** *Parlophone R 6279*	**6** 7
27 Apr 91	**CHILDREN** *Parlophone R 6288*	**19** 5
31 Aug 91	**LIES** *Parlophone R 6295*	**28** 3
2 May 92	**UNEXPLAINED (EP)** *Parlophone SGE 2026*	**18** 4
19 Sep 92	**THEY'RE HERE** *Parlophone R 6321*	**29** 3
21 Nov 92	**IT'S YOU** *Parlophone R 6327*	**23** 3
25 Feb 95	**PERFECT DAY** *Parlophone CDRS 6401*	**27** 3
8 Jul 95 ●	**I'M A BELIEVER** *Parlophone CDR 6412* [1]	**3** 8
28 Oct 95	**AFRO KING** *Parlophone CDRS 6416*	**51** 1

[1] EMF and Reeves and Mortimer

Tracks on Unexplained (EP): Getting Through / Far From Me / The Same / Search and Destroy

EMILIA *Sweden, female vocalist - Emilia Rydberg (14 WEEKS)* pos/wks

12 Dec 98 ●	**BIG BIG WORLD** *Universal UMD 87190*	**5** 13
1 May 99	**GOOD SIGN** *Universal UMD 87206*	**54** 1

EMINEM *US, male rappper - Marshall Mathers III (56 WEEKS)* pos/wks

10 Apr 99 ●	**MY NAME IS** *Interscope IND 95638*	**2** 11
24 Jul 99	**MY NAME IS (re-entry)** *Interscope IND 95638*	**68** 1
14 Aug 99 ●	**GUILTY CONSCIENCE** *Interscope IND 4971282* [1]	**5** 8
10 Jun 00 ●	**FORGOT ABOUT DRE** *Interscope 4973412* [2]	**7** 9
8 Jul 00 ★	**THE REAL SLIM SHADY** *Interscope 4973792* ■	**1** 15
14 Oct 00 ●	**THE WAY I AM** *Interscope 4974252*	**8** 9
16 Dec 00 ★	**STAN** *Interscope IND 97470* ■	**1** 3+

[1] Eminem featuring Dr Dre [2] Dr Dre featuring Eminem

'Stan' features uncredited vocals by Dido

EMMA *UK, female vocalist (6 WEEKS)* pos/wks

28 Apr 90	**GIVE A LITTLE LOVE BACK TO THE WORLD** *Big Wave BWR 33*	**33** 6

EMMANUEL & ESKA – See COLOURS featuring EMMANUEL & ESKA; EN-CORE featuring Stephen EMMANUEL & ESKA

EMMIE *UK, female vocalist - Emma Norton-Smith (8 WEEKS)* pos/wks

23 Jan 99 ●	**MORE THAN THIS** *Indirect/Manifesto FESCD 52*	**5** 8

AN EMOTIONAL FISH
Ireland, male vocal / instrumental group (5 WEEKS) pos/wks

23 Jun 90	**CELEBRATE** *East West YZ 489*	**46** 5

EMOTIONS *US, female vocal group (28 WEEKS)* pos/wks

10 Sep 77 ●	**BEST OF MY LOVE** *CBS 5555* ▲	**4** 10
24 Dec 77	**I DON'T WANNA LOSE YOUR LOVE** *CBS 5819*	**40** 5
12 May 79 ●	**BOOGIE WONDERLAND** *CBS 7292* [1]	**4** 13

[1] Earth Wind and Fire with the Emotions

EMPIRION *UK, male instrumental / production group (2 WEEKS)* pos/wks

6 Jul 96	**NARCOTIC INFLUENCE** *XL XLS 72CD*	**64** 1
21 Jun 97	**BETA** *XL XLS 77CD*	**75** 1

EN VOGUE `392` `Top 500` *Very Influential post-feminist R&B vocal quartet formed Oakland, California, US; Terry Ellis, Maxine Jones, Dawn Robinson (left 1995) and ex-beauty pageant winner Cindy Herron. Award-winning team blended hip hop and R&B and helped to launch the New Jill Swing movement (83 WEEKS)* pos/wks

5 May 90 ●	**HOLD ON** *East West America 7908*	**5** 11
21 Jul 90	**LIES** *East West America 7893*	**44** 4
4 Apr 92	**MY LOVIN'** *East West America A 8578*	**69** 3
9 May 92 ●	**MY LOVIN' (re-entry)** *East West America A 8578*	**4** 9
15 Aug 92	**GIVING HIM SOMETHING HE CAN FEEL** *East West America A 8524*	**44** 3
7 Nov 92	**FREE YOUR MIND / GIVING HIM SOMETHING HE CAN FEEL (re-issue)** *East West America A 8468*	**16** 8
16 Jan 93	**GIVE IT UP TURN IT LOOSE** *East West America A 8445CD*	**22** 4
10 Apr 93	**LOVE DON'T LOVE YOU** *East West America A 8424CD*	**64** 1
9 Oct 93	**RUNAWAY LOVE** *East West America A 8359CD*	**36** 3
19 Mar 94 ●	**WHATTA MAN** *ffrr FCD 222* [1]	**7** 10
11 Jan 97 ●	**DON'T LET GO (LOVE)** *East West A 3976CD*	**5** 16
14 Jun 97	**WHATEVER** *East West E 3642CD*	**14** 5
6 Sep 97	**TOO GONE, TOO LONG** *East West E 3908CD*	**20** 3
28 Nov 98	**HOLD ON (re-mix)** *East West E 3796 CD*	**53** 1
1 Jul 00	**RIDDLE** *Elektra E 7053CD*	**33** 2

[1] Salt-N-Pepa with En Vogue

EN-CORE featuring Stephen EMMANUEL & ESKA
UK, male producer / female vocalist (2 WEEKS) pos/wks

9 Sep 00	**COOCHY COO** *VC Recordings VCRD 72*	**32** 2

ENCORE *France, female vocalist (4 WEEKS)* pos/wks

14 Feb 98	**LE DISC JOCKEY** *Sum CDSUM 2*	**12** 4

ENERGISE *UK, male vocal / instrumental group (1 WEEK)* pos/wks

16 Feb 91	**REPORT TO THE DANCEFLOOR** *Network NWKT 16*	**69** 1

ENERGY 52 *Germany, male DJ / producer (7 WEEKS)* pos/wks

8 Mar 97	**CAFE DEL MAR** *Hooj Choons HOOJCD 51*	**51** 1
25 Jul 98	**CAFE DEL MAR '98 (re-mix)** *Hooj Choons HOOJ 64CD*	**12** 6

ENERGY ORCHARD
Ireland, male vocal / instrumental group (6 WEEKS) pos/wks

27 Jan 90	**BELFAST** *MCA MCA 1392*	**52** 4
7 Apr 90	**SAILORTOWN** *MCA MCA 1402*	**73** 2

Harry ENFIELD *UK, male comedian / vocalist (7 WEEKS)* pos/wks

7 May 88 ●	**LOADSAMONEY (DOIN' UP THE HOUSE)** *Mercury DOSH 1*	**4** 7

ENGLAND DAN and John Ford COLEY
US, male vocal duo (12 WEEKS) pos/wks

25 Sep 76	**I'D REALLY LOVE TO SEE YOU TONIGHT** *Atlantic K 10810*	**26** 7
23 Jun 79	**LOVE IS THE ANSWER** *Big Tree K 11296*	**45** 5

ENGLAND RUGBY WORLD CUP SQUAD – See UNION featuring the ENGLAND WORLD CUP SQUAD

ENGLAND SISTERS *UK, female vocal group (1 WEEK)* pos/wks

17 Mar 60	**HEARTBEAT** *HMV POP 710*	**33** 1

ENGLAND SUPPORTERS' BAND *UK, male instrumental group (4 WEEKS)* pos/wks

27 Jun 98	**THE GREAT ESCAPE** *V2 VVR 5002163*	**46** 2
24 Jun 00	**THE GREAT ESCAPE 2000 (re-recording)** *V2 VVR 5014293*	**26** 2

ENGLAND UNITED
UK, male / female vocal / instrumental group (11 WEEKS) pos/wks

13 Jun 98 ●	(HOW DOES IT FEEL TO BE) ON TOP OF THE WORLD *London LONCD 414*	9	9
22 Aug 98	(HOW DOES IT FEEL TO BE) ON TOP OF THE WORLD (re-entry) *London LONCD 414*	61	2

ENGLAND WORLD CUP SQUAD
UK, male football team vocalists (46 WEEKS) pos/wks

18 Apr 70 ★	BACK HOME *Pye 7N 17920*	1	16
15 Aug 70	BACK HOME (re-entry) *Pye 7N 17920*	46	1
10 Apr 82 ●	THIS TIME (WE'LL GET IT RIGHT) / ENGLAND WE'LL FLY THE FLAG *England ER 1*	2	13
19 Apr 86	WE'VE GOT THE WHOLE WORLD AT OUR FEET / WHEN WE ARE FAR FROM HOME *Columbia DB 9128*	66	2
21 May 88	ALL THE WAY *MCA GOAL 1* [1]	64	2
2 Jun 90 ★	WORLD IN MOTION . . . *Factory / MCA FAC 2937* [2]	1	12

[1] England Football Team and the 'sound' of Stock, Aitken and Waterman [2] Englandneworder

ENGLAND'S BARMY ARMY
UK, 5,000 male / female vocal cricket supporters (1 WEEK) pos/wks

12 Jun 99	COME ON ENGLAND! *Wildstar CDWILD 20*	45	1

Kim ENGLISH
US, female vocalist (7 WEEKS) pos/wks

23 Jul 94	NITE LIFE *Hi-Life PZCD 323*	35	2
4 Mar 95	TIME FOR LOVE *Hi-Life HICD 8*	48	1
9 Sep 95	I KNOW A PLACE *Hi-Life 5798072*	52	1
30 Nov 96	NITE LIFE (re-mix) *Hi-Life 5755332*	35	2
26 Apr 97	SUPERNATURAL *Hi-Life 5736972*	50	1

Scott ENGLISH
US, male vocalist (10 WEEKS) pos/wks

9 Oct 71	BRANDY *Horse HOSS 7*	12	10

ENIAC – See Tom NOVY

ENIGMA
UK, male / female vocal / instrumental group (15 WEEKS) pos/wks

23 May 81	AIN'T NO STOPPING *Creole CR 9*	11	8
8 Aug 81	I LOVE MUSIC *Creole CR 14*	25	7

ENIGMA
Germany / Romania, male / female vocal / instrumental duo (45 WEEKS) pos/wks

15 Dec 90 ★	SADNESS PART 1 *Virgin International DINS 101*	1	12
30 Mar 91	MEA CULPA PART II *Virgin International DINS 104*	55	2
10 Aug 91	PRINCIPLES OF LUST *Virgin International DINS 110*	59	2
11 Jan 92	THE RIVERS OF BELIEF *Virgin International DINS 112*	68	2
29 Jan 94 ●	RETURN TO INNOCENCE *Virgin International DINSD 123*	3	14
14 May 94	THE EYES OF TRUTH *Virgin International DINSD 126*	21	4
20 Aug 94	AGE OF LONELINESS *Virgin International DINSD 135*	21	5
25 Jan 97	BEYOND THE INVISIBLE *Virgin International DINSD 155*	26	2
19 Apr 97	TNT FOR THE BRAIN *Virgin International DINSD 161*	60	1

ENYA
Ireland, female vocalist / instrumentalist - Eithne Ni Bhraonain (62 WEEKS) pos/wks

15 Oct 88 ★	ORINOCO FLOW *WEA YZ 312*	1	13
24 Dec 88	EVENING FALLS . . . *WEA YZ 356*	20	4
10 Jun 89	STORMS IN AFRICA (PART II) *WEA YZ 368*	41	4
19 Oct 91	CARIBBEAN BLUE *WEA YZ 604*	13	7
7 Dec 91	HOW CAN I KEEP FROM SINGING *WEA YZ 365*	32	5
1 Aug 92 ●	BOOK OF DAYS *WEA YZ 640*	10	6
14 Nov 92	THE CELTS *WEA YZ 705*	29	4
18 Nov 95 ●	ANYWHERE IS *WEA WEA 023CD*	7	12
7 Dec 96	ON MY WAY HOME *WEA WEA 047CD*	26	2
13 Dec 97	ONLY IF... *WEA WEA 143CD*	43	2
25 Nov 00	ONLY TIME *WEA WEA 316CD*	32	3

EON
UK, male producer - Ian Bela (1 WEEK) pos/wks

17 Aug 91	FEAR: THE MINDKILLER *Vinyl Solution STORM 33*	63	1

EPMD – See MANTRONIK

EQUALS (500) Top 500
North London-based pop / reggae band included brothers Derv and Lincoln Gordon and Eddy Grant. Their self-penned No.1 'Baby Come Back' was a hit first in Germany in 1966 and was a No.1 in 1994 by Pato Banton. Grant had a successful solo career in 1980s (69 WEEKS) pos/wks

21 Feb 68	I GET SO EXCITED *President PT 180*	44	4
1 May 68	BABY COME BACK *President PT 135*	50	1
15 May 68 ★	BABY COME BACK (re-entry) *President PT 135*	1	17
21 Aug 68	LAUREL AND HARDY *President PT 200*	35	5
27 Nov 68	SOFTLY SOFTLY *President PT 222*	48	3
2 Apr 69	MICHAEL AND THE SLIPPER TREE *President PT 240*	24	7
30 Jul 69 ●	VIVA BOBBY JOE *President PT 260*	6	14
27 Dec 69	RUB A DUB DUB *President PT 275*	34	7
19 Dec 70 ●	BLACK SKIN BLUE EYED BOYS *President PT 325*	9	11

ERASURE (84) Top 500
UK duo formed by Vince Clarke (k) and Andy Bell (v). After hits with Depeche Mode, Yazoo and The Assembly, this act was Clarke's greatest success, with five albums entering at No.1 (203 WEEKS) pos/wks

5 Oct 85	WHO NEEDS LOVE LIKE THAT *Mute MUTE 40*	55	2
25 Oct 86 ●	SOMETIMES *Mute MUTE 51*	2	17
28 Feb 87	IT DOESN'T HAVE TO BE *Mute MUTE 56*	12	9
30 May 87 ●	VICTIM OF LOVE *Mute MUTE 61*	7	9
3 Oct 87 ●	THE CIRCUS *Mute MUTE 66*	6	10
5 Mar 88 ●	SHIP OF FOOLS *Mute MUTE 74*	6	8
11 Jun 88	CHAINS OF LOVE *Mute MUTE 83*	11	7
1 Oct 88 ●	A LITTLE RESPECT *Mute MUTE 85*	4	10
10 Dec 88 ●	CRACKERS INTERNATIONAL (EP) *Mute MUTE 93*	2	13
30 Sep 89 ●	DRAMA! *Mute MUTE 89*	4	8
9 Dec 89	YOU SURROUND ME *Mute MUTE 99*	15	9
10 Mar 90 ●	BLUE SAVANNAH *Mute MUTE 109*	3	10
2 Jun 90	STAR *Mute MUTE 111*	11	7
29 Jun 91 ●	CHORUS *Mute MUTE 125*	3	9
21 Sep 91 ●	LOVE TO HATE YOU *Mute MUTE 131*	4	9
7 Dec 91	AM I RIGHT (EP) *Mute MUTE 134*	15	6
11 Jan 92	AM I RIGHT EP (re-mix) *Mute L12MUTE 134*	22	3
28 Mar 92 ●	BREATH OF LIFE *Mute MUTE 142*	8	6
13 Jun 92 ★	ABBA-ESQUE (EP) *Mute MUTE 144* ■	1	12
7 Nov 92 ●	WHO NEEDS LOVE (LIKE THAT) (re-mix) *Mute MUTE 150*	10	4
23 Apr 94 ●	ALWAYS *Mute CDMUTE 152*	4	9
30 Jul 94 ●	RUN TO THE SUN *Mute CDMUTE 153*	6	5
3 Dec 94	I LOVE SATURDAY *Mute CDMUTE 166*	20	6
23 Sep 95	STAY WITH ME *Mute CDMUTE 174*	15	4
9 Dec 95	FINGERS AND THUMBS (COLD SUMMER'S DAY) *Mute CDMUTE 178*	20	3
18 Jan 97	IN MY ARMS *Mute CDMUTE 190*	13	4
8 Mar 97	DON'T SAY YOUR LOVE IS KILLING ME *Mute CDMUTE 195*	23	2
21 Oct 00	FREEDOM *Mute CDMUTE 244*	27	2

Tracks on Crackers International (EP): Stop / The Hardest Part / Knocking on Your Door / She Won't Be Home. Tracks on Am I Right (EP): Am I Right / Carry On Clangers / Let It Flow / Waiting for Sex. Tracks on Am I Right (Re-mix EP): Am I Right / Chorus / Love to Hate You / Perfect Stranger. Tracks on Abba-esque (EP): Lay All Your Love on Me / SOS / Take a Chance on Me / Voulez-Vous. 'Take a Chance On Me' credits MC Kinky

See also KINKY

ERIC and the GOOD GOOD FEELING
UK, male / female vocal / instrumental group (1 WEEK) pos/wks

3 Jun 89	GOOD GOOD FEELING *Equinox EQN 1*	73	1

ERIK
UK, female vocalist (5 WEEKS) pos/wks

10 Apr 93	LOOKS LIKE I'M IN LOVE AGAIN *PWL Sanctuary PWCD 252* [1]	46	2
29 Jan 94	GOT TO BE REAL *PWL International PWCD 278*	42	2
1 Oct 94	WE GOT THE LOVE *PWL International PWCD 305*	55	1

[1] Key West featuring Erik

ERIN – See SHUT UP AND DANCE; BBG

UK No.1 ★ UK Top 10 ● Still on chart + UK million seller ◆ UK entry at No.1 ■ US No.1 ▲

EROTIC DRUM BAND
Canada, male / female vocal / instrumental group (3 WEEKS)　　pos/wks

9 Jun 79	LOVE DISCO STYLE *Scope SC 1*	47	3

ERUPTION
US, male / female vocal / instrumental group (21 WEEKS)　　pos/wks

18 Feb 78	●	I CAN'T STAND THE RAIN *Atlantic K 11068* [1]	5	11
21 Apr 79	●	ONE WAY TICKET *Atlantic/Hansa K 11266*	9	10

[1] Eruption featuring Precious Wilson

ESCORTS
UK, male vocal / instrumental group (2 WEEKS)　　pos/wks

2 Jul 64	THE ONE TO CRY *Fontana TF 474*	49	2

ESCRIMA
UK, male producer - Paul Newman (4 WEEKS)　　pos/wks

11 Feb 95	TRAIN OF THOUGHT *Ffrreedom TABCD 225*	36	2
7 Oct 95	DEEPER *Hooj Choons TABCD 236*	27	2

See also TALL PAUL; PARTIZAN; CAMISRA; GRIFTERS

ESKIMOS & EGYPT
UK, male vocal / instrumental group (4 WEEKS)　　pos/wks

13 Feb 93	FALL FROM GRACE *One Little Indian EEF 96CD*	51	2
29 May 93	UK-USA *One Little Indian 99 TP7CD*	52	2

ESPIRITU
UK / France, male / female vocal / instrumental duo (10 WEEKS)　　pos/wks

6 Mar 93	CONQUISTADOR *Heavenly HVN 28CD*	47	2
7 Aug 93	LOS AMERICANOS *Heavenly HVN 33CD*	45	2
20 Aug 94	BONITA MANANA *Columbia 6606925*	50	1
25 Mar 95	ALWAYS SOMETHING THERE TO REMIND ME *WEA YZ 911CD* [1]	14	5

[1] Tin Tin Out featuring Espiritu

ESSENCE
UK, male production group and UK, female vocalist (2 WEEKS)　　pos/wks

21 Mar 98	THE PROMISE *Innocent SINCD 1*	27	2

ESSEX
US, male / female vocal group (5 WEEKS)　　pos/wks

8 Aug 63	EASIER SAID THAN DONE *Columbia DB 7077* ▲	41	5

David ESSEX [90 　Top 500]
Actor / teeny-bop star, b. David Cook, 23 Jul 1947, London. This singer / songwriter was voted No.1 British Male Vocalist (1974) and was a teen idol for more than a decade. Starred in the stage show 'Godspell' and graduated successfully to films (199 WEEKS)　　pos/wks

18 Aug 73	●	ROCK ON *CBS 1693*	3	11
10 Nov 73	●	LAMPLIGHT *CBS 1902*	7	15
11 May 74		AMERICA *CBS 2176*	32	5
12 Oct 74	★	GONNA MAKE YOU A STAR *CBS 2492*	1	17
14 Dec 74	●	STARDUST *CBS 2828*	7	10
5 Jul 75	●	ROLLING STONE *CBS 3425*	5	7
13 Sep 75	★	HOLD ME CLOSE *CBS 3572*	1	10
6 Dec 75		IF I COULD *CBS 3776*	13	8
20 Mar 76		CITY LIGHTS *CBS 4050*	24	4
16 Oct 76		COMING HOME *CBS 4486*	24	6
17 Sep 77		COOL OUT TONIGHT *CBS 5495*	23	6
11 Mar 78		STAY WITH ME BABY *CBS 6063*	45	5
19 Aug 78	●	OH WHAT A CIRCUS *Mercury 6007 185*	3	11
21 Oct 78		BRAVE NEW WORLD *CBS 6705*	55	3
3 Mar 79		IMPERIAL WIZARD *Mercury 6007 202*	32	8
5 Apr 80	●	SILVER DREAM MACHINE (PART 1) *Mercury BIKE 1*	4	11
14 Jun 80		HOT LOVE *Mercury HOT 11*	57	4
26 Jun 82		ME AND MY GIRL (NIGHT-CLUBBING) *Mercury MER 107* ...	13	10
11 Dec 82	●	A WINTER'S TALE *Mercury MER 127*	2	10
4 Jun 83		THE SMILE *Mercury ESSEX 1*	52	4
27 Aug 83	●	TAHITI (FROM 'MUTINY ON THE BOUNTY') *Mercury BOUNT 1*	8	11
26 Nov 83		YOU'RE IN MY HEART *Mercury ESSEX 2*	67	2
17 Dec 83		YOU'RE IN MY HEART (re-entry) *Mercury ESSEX 2*	59	4
23 Feb 85		FALLING ANGELS RIDING *Mercury ESSEX 5*	29	7

18 Apr 87	MYFANWY *Arista RIS 11*	41	7
26 Nov 94	TRUE LOVE WAYS *PolyGram TV TLWCD 2* [1]	38	3

[1] David Essex and Catherine Zeta Jones

Gloria ESTEFAN [104 　Top 500]
Latin music's leading lady, b. Gloria Fajardo, 1 Dec 1957, Cuba. Successes in the dance and MOR fields have pushed her world sales to more than 35 million, with two of the vocalist's albums passing the one-million sales mark in the UK (182 WEEKS)　　pos/wks

16 Jul 88	●	ANYTHING FOR YOU *Epic 651673 7* [1] ▲	10	16
22 Oct 88	●	1-2-3 *Epic 652958 7* [1]	9	9
17 Dec 88		RHYTHM IS GONNA GET YOU *Epic 654514 7* [1]	16	9
31 Dec 88		1-2-3 (re-entry) *Epic 652958 7*	72	1
11 Feb 89	●	CAN'T STAY AWAY FROM YOU *Epic 651444 7* [1]	7	12
15 Jul 89	●	DON'T WANNA LOSE YOU *Epic 655054 0* ▲	6	10
16 Sep 89		OYE MI CANTO (HEAR MY VOICE) *Epic 655287 7*	16	8
25 Nov 89		GET ON YOUR FEET *Epic 655450 7*	23	7
3 Mar 90		HERE WE ARE *Epic 655473 9*	23	6
26 May 90		CUTS BOTH WAYS *Epic 655982 7*	49	5
26 Jan 91		COMING OUT OF THE DARK *Epic 6565747* ▲	25	5
6 Apr 91		SEAL OUR FATE *Epic 6567737*	24	7
8 Jun 91		REMEMBER ME WITH LOVE *Epic 6569687*	22	6
21 Sep 91		LIVE FOR LOVING YOU *Epic 6573827*	33	5
24 Oct 92		ALWAYS TOMORROW *Epic 6583977*	24	4
12 Dec 92	●	MIAMI HIT MIX / CHRISTMAS THROUGH YOUR EYES *Epic 6588377*	8	9
13 Feb 93		I SEE YOUR SMILE *Epic 6589612*	48	2
3 Apr 93		GO AWAY *Epic 6590952*	13	6
3 Jul 93		MI TIERRA *Epic 6593512*	36	3
14 Aug 93		IF WE WERE LOVERS / CON LOS ANOS QUE ME QUEDAN *Epic 6595702*	40	3
18 Dec 93		MONTUNO *Epic 6599972*	55	2
15 Oct 94		TURN THE BEAT AROUND *Epic 6606822*	21	6
3 Dec 94		HOLD ME THRILL ME KISS ME *Epic 6610802*	11	10
18 Feb 95		EVERLASTING LOVE *Epic 6611595*	19	5
18 Mar 95		HOLD ME THRILL ME KISS ME (re-entry) *Epic 6610802* ..	68	1
25 May 96		REACH *Epic 6632642*	15	6
3 Aug 96		REACH (re-entry) *Epic 6632642*	68	1
17 Aug 96		REACH (2nd re-entry) *Epic 6632642*	55	1
24 Aug 96		YOU'LL BE MINE (PARTY TIME) *Epic 6636505*	18	3
14 Dec 96		I'M NOT GIVING YOU UP *Epic 6640222*	28	3
6 Jun 98		HEAVEN'S WHAT I FEEL *Epic 6660042*	17	4
10 Oct 98		OYE *Epic 6664645*	33	2
16 Jan 99		DON'T LET THIS MOMENT END *Epic 6667472*	28	2
8 Jan 00		MUSIC OF MY HEART *Epic 6605272* [2]	34	3

[1] Gloria Estefan and Miami Sound Machine [2] 'N Sync / Gloria Estefan

'Christmas Through Your Eyes' was listed only from 19 Dec 1992

See also MIAMI SOUND MACHINE

Don ESTELLE – See Windsor DAVIES and Don ESTELLE

Deon ESTUS
US, male vocalist / instrumentalist - bass (7 WEEKS)　　pos/wks

25 Jan 86	MY GUY - MY GIRL (MEDLEY) *Sedition EDIT 3310* [1]	63	3
29 Apr 89	HEAVEN HELP ME *Mika MIKA 2*	41	4

[1] Amii Stewart and Deon Estus

ETA
Denmark, male instrumental group (5 WEEKS)　　pos/wks

28 Jun 97	CASUAL SUB (BURNING SPEAR) *East West EW 110CD*	28	3
31 Jan 98	CASUAL SUB (BURNING SPEAR) (re-mix) *East West Dance EW 145CD*	28	2

ETERNAL [187 　Top 500]
London-based vocal group with across-the-board appeal: sisters Easther and Vernett Bennett, Kellé Bryan, Louise Nurding. First all-female act to shift more than one million copies of an album in the UK. Louise left for a successful solo career in 1995 followed by Kellé four years later (134 WEEKS)　　pos/wks

2 Oct 93	●	STAY *EMI CDEM 283*	4	9
15 Jan 94	●	SAVE OUR LOVE *EMI CDEM 296*	8	7
30 Apr 94	●	JUST A STEP FROM HEAVEN *EMI CDEM 311*	8	10
20 Aug 94	●	SO GOOD *EMI CDEMS 339*	13	7

UK No.1 ★   UK Top 10 ●   Still on chart +   UK million seller ◆   UK entry at No.1 ■   US No.1 ▲

Betty EVERETT US, female vocalist (14 WEEKS)

			pos/wks
14 Jan 65	GETTING MIGHTY CROWDED Fontana TF 520	29	7
30 Oct 68	IT'S IN HIS KISS President PT 215	34	7

Kenny EVERETT UK, male vocalist (12 WEEKS)

			pos/wks
12 Nov 77	CAPTAIN KREMMEN (RETRIBUTION) DJM DJS 10810 [1]	32	4
26 Mar 83 ●	SNOT RAP RCA KEN 1	9	8

[1] Kenny Everett and Mike Vickers

Peven EVERETT – See Roy DAVIS Jr featuring Peven EVERETT

EVERLAST US, male vocalist - Erik Schrody (3 WEEKS)

			pos/wks
27 Feb 99	WHAT IT'S LIKE Tommy Boy TBCD 7470	34	2
3 Jul 99	ENDS Tommy Boy TBCD 346	47	1

EVERLY BROTHERS 20 Top 500 Award-winning and extremely influential American brothers Don (g/v) and Phil (g/v) Everly. Achieved long string of transatlantic hits and were among the first acts inducted into the Rock and Roll Hall of Fame in 1986 (344 WEEKS)

			pos/wks
12 Jul 57 ●	BYE BYE LOVE London HLA 8440	6	16
8 Nov 57 ●	WAKE UP LITTLE SUSIE London HLA 8498 ▲	2	13
23 May 58 ★	ALL I HAVE TO DO IS DREAM / CLAUDETTE London HLA 8618 ▲	1	21
12 Sep 58 ●	BIRD DOG London HLA 8685	2	16
23 Jan 59 ●	PROBLEMS London HLA 8781	6	12
22 May 59	TAKE A MESSAGE TO MARY London HLA 8863	29	1
29 May 59	POOR JENNY London HLA 8863	14	11
19 Jun 59	TAKE A MESSAGE TO MARY (re-entry) London HLA 8863	27	1
3 Jul 59	TAKE A MESSAGE TO MARY (2nd re-entry) London HLA 8863	20	8
11 Sep 59 ●	('TIL) I KISSED YOU London HLA 8934	2	15
12 Feb 60	LET IT BE ME London HLA 9039	13	5
31 Mar 60	LET IT BE ME (re-entry) London HLA 9039	26	4
14 Apr 60 ★	CATHY'S CLOWN Warner Bros. WB 1 ▲	1	18
14 Jul 60 ●	WHEN WILL I BE LOVED London HLA 9157	4	16
22 Sep 60 ●	LUCILLE / SO SAD (TO WATCH GOOD LOVE GO BAD) Warner Bros. WB 19	4	15
15 Dec 60	LIKE STRANGERS London HLA 9250	11	10
9 Feb 61 ★	WALK RIGHT BACK / EBONY EYES Warner Bros. WB 33	1	16
15 Jun 61 ★	TEMPTATION Warner Bros. WB 42	1	15
5 Oct 61	MUSKRAT / DON'T BLAME ME Warner Bros. WB 50	20	6
18 Jan 62 ●	CRYIN' IN THE RAIN Warner Bros. WB 56	6	15
17 May 62	HOW CAN I MEET HER Warner Bros. WB 67	12	10
25 Oct 62	NO ONE CAN MAKE MY SUNSHINE SMILE Warner Bros. WB 79	11	11
21 Mar 63	SO IT WILL ALWAYS BE Warner Bros. WB 94	23	11
13 Jun 63	IT'S BEEN NICE Warner Bros. WB 99	26	5
17 Oct 63	THE GIRL SANG THE BLUES Warner Bros. WB 109	25	9
16 Jul 64	FERRIS WHEEL Warner Bros. WB 135	22	10
3 Dec 64	GONE GONE GONE Warner Bros. WB 146	36	7
6 May 65	THAT'LL BE THE DAY Warner Bros. WB 158	30	4
20 May 65 ●	THE PRICE OF LOVE Warner Bros. WB 161	2	14
26 Aug 65	I'LL NEVER GET OVER YOU Warner Bros. WB 5639	35	5
21 Oct 65	LOVE IS STRANGE Warner Bros. WB 5649	11	9
8 May 68	IT'S MY TIME Warner Bros. WB 7192	39	6
22 Sep 84	ON THE WINGS OF A NIGHTINGALE Mercury MER 170	41	9

'All I Have to Do Is Dream' was listed without Claudette for its first week on the chart but, from 30 May 1958, both sides were charted for 20 more weeks. 'Take A Message to Mary' and 'Poor Jenny' were both sides of the same single

Phil EVERLY US, male vocalist (24 WEEKS)

			pos/wks
6 Nov 82	LOUISE Capitol CL 266	47	6
19 Feb 83 ●	SHE MEANS NOTHING TO ME Capitol CL 276 [1]	9	9
10 Dec 94	ALL I HAVE TO DO IS DREAM EMI CDEMS 359 [2]	14	6
25 Feb 95	ALL I HAVE TO DO IS DREAM (re-entry) EMI CDEMS 359 [2]	58	3

[1] Phil Everly and Cliff Richard [2] Cliff Richard and Phil Everly

'All I Have to Do Is Dream' was listed with its flip side 'Miss You Nights' by Cliff Richard

See also EVERLY BROTHERS

EVERTON FOOTBALL CLUB UK, male football team vocalists (8 WEEKS)

			pos/wks
11 May 85	HERE WE GO Columbia DB 9106 [1]	14	5
20 May 95	ALL TOGETHER NOW MDMC DEVCS 3	24	3

[1] Everton 1985

EVERYTHING BUT THE GIRL 319 Top 500 Introspective pop duo formed 1982, Hull, UK; Tracey Thorn (v) b. 26 Sep 1962, Ben Watt (k), b. 6 Dec 1962. Gained greatest popularity after mid-90s conversion to low-key dance music. Remix of 'Missing' was first single to spend an uninterrupted year on the US chart (94 WEEKS)

			pos/wks
12 May 84	EACH AND EVERY ONE Blanco Y Negro NEG 1	28	7
21 Jul 84	MINE Blanco Y Negro NEG 3	58	1
6 Oct 84	NATIVE LAND Blanco Y Negro NEG 6	73	1
2 Aug 86	COME ON HOME Blanco Y Negro NEG 21	44	7
11 Oct 86	DON'T LEAVE ME BEHIND Blanco Y Negro NEG 23	72	2
13 Feb 88	THESE EARLY DAYS Blanco Y Negro NEG 30	75	1
9 Jul 88 ●	I DON'T WANT TO TALK ABOUT IT Blanco Y Negro NEG 34	3	9
27 Jan 90	DRIVING Blanco Y Negro NEG 40	54	2
22 Feb 92	COVERS (EP) Blanco Y Negro NEG 54	13	6
24 Apr 93	THE ONLY LIVING BOY IN NEW YORK (EP) Blanco Y Negro NEG 62CD	42	5
19 Jun 93	I DIDN'T KNOW I WAS LOOKING FOR LOVE (EP) Blanco Y Negro NEG 64CD	72	1
4 Jun 94	ROLLERCOASTER (EP) Blanco Y Negro NEG 69CD	65	1
20 Aug 94	MISSING Blanco Y Negro NEG 71CD	69	1
28 Oct 95 ●	MISSING (re-mix) Blanco Y Negro NEG 84CD	3	22
20 Apr 96 ●	WALKING WOUNDED Virgin VSCDT 1577	6	6
29 Jun 96 ●	WRONG Virgin VSCDT 1589	8	7
5 Oct 96	SINGLE Virgin VSCDT 1600	20	3
7 Dec 96	DRIVING (re-mix) Blanco Y Negro NEG 99CD1	36	2
1 Mar 97	BEFORE TODAY Virgin VSCDT 1624	25	2
3 Oct 98	THE FUTURE OF THE FUTURE (STAY GOLD) Deconstruction 74321616252 [1]	31	2
25 Sep 99	FIVE FATHOMS Virgin VSCDT 1742	27	3
4 Mar 00	TEMPERAMENTAL Virgin VSCDT 1761	72	1

[1] Deep Dish with Everything but the Girl

Tracks on Covers (EP): Love Is Strange / Tougher Than the Rest / Time After Time / Alison. Tracks on The Only Living Boy in New York (EP): The Only Living Boy in New York / Birds / Gabriel / Horses in the Room. Tracks on I Didn't Know I Was Looking For Love (EP): I Didn't Know I Was Looking For Love / My Head Is My Only House Unless It Rains / Political Science / A Piece of My Mind. Tracks on Rollercoaster (EP): Rollercoaster / Straight Back to You / Lights of Te Touan / I Didn't Know I Was Looking For Love (demo)

E'VOKE UK, female vocal duo (6 WEEKS)

			pos/wks
25 Nov 95	RUNAWAY Ffrreedom TABCD 238	30	3
24 Aug 96	ARMS OF LOREN Manifesto FESCD 10	25	3

EVOLUTION UK, male / female vocal / instrumental group (12 WEEKS)

			pos/wks
20 Mar 93	LOVE THING Deconstruction 74321134272	32	2
3 Jul 93	EVERYBODY DANCE Deconstruction 74321152012	19	5
8 Jan 94	EVOLUTIONDANCE PART ONE (EP) Deconstruction 74321171912	52	3
4 Nov 95	LOOK UP TO THE LIGHT Deconstruction 74321318042	55	1
19 Oct 96	YOUR LOVE IS CALLING Deconstruction 74321422872	60	1

Tracks on Evolutiondance Part One (EP): Escape 2 Alcatraz (remix) / Everybody / Don't Stop the Rain

EX PISTOLS UK, male vocal / instrumental group (2 WEEKS)

			pos/wks
2 Feb 85	LAND OF HOPE AND GLORY Virginia PISTOL 76	69	2

EXCITERS US, male / female vocal group (7 WEEKS)

			pos/wks
21 Feb 63	TELL HIM United Artists UP 1011	46	1
4 Oct 75	REACHING FOR THE BEST 20th Century BTC 1005	31	6

EXETER BRAMDEAN BOYS' CHOIR UK, male choir (3 WEEKS) pos/wks

| 18 Dec 93 | REMEMBERING CHRISTMAS | | |
| | Golden Sounds DSCC 1 | 46 | 3 |

EXILE US, male vocal / instrumental group (18 WEEKS) pos/wks

19 Aug 78 ●	KISS YOU ALL OVER RAK 279 ▲	6	12
12 May 79	HOW COULD THIS GO WRONG		
	RAK 293	67	2
12 Sep 81	HEART AND SOUL RAK 333	54	4

EXOTERIX UK, male producer - Duncan Millar (2 WEEKS) pos/wks

| 24 Apr 93 | VOID Positiva CDTIV 1 | 58 | 1 |
| 5 Feb 94 | SATISFY MY LOVE Union UCRCD 26 | 62 | 1 |

EXOTICA featuring Itsy FOSTER
UK / Italy, male / female vocal / instrumental group (1 WEEK) pos/wks

| 16 Sep 95 | THE SUMMER IS MAGIC | | |
| | Polydor 5798392 | 68 | 1 |

EXPLOITED UK, male vocal / instrumental group (13 WEEKS) pos/wks

18 Apr 81	DOGS OF WAR Secret SHH 110	63	4
17 Oct 81	DEAD CITIES Secret SHH 120	31	5
5 Dec 81	DON'T LET 'EM GRIND YOU DOWN		
	Superville EXP 1003 [1]	70	1
8 May 82	ATTACK Secret SHH 130	50	3

[1] Exploited and Anti-Pasti

EXPOSÉ US, female vocal group (1 WEEK) pos/wks

| 28 Aug 93 | I'LL NEVER GET OVER YOU (GETTING OVER ME) | | |
| | Arista 74321158962 | 75 | 1 |

EXPRESS OF SOUND
Italy, male instrumental / production group (1 WEEK) pos/wks

| 2 Nov 96 | REAL VIBRATION (WANT LOVE) | | |
| | Positiva CDTIV 66 | 45 | 1 |

EXPRESSOS
UK, male / female vocal / instrumental group (5 WEEKS) pos/wks

| 21 Jun 80 | HEY GIRL WEA K 18246 | 60 | 3 |
| 14 Mar 81 | TANGO IN MONO WEA K 18431 | 70 | 2 |

EXTENSIVE – See CHOPS-EMC + EXTENSIVE

EXTREME US, male vocal / instrumental group (46 WEEKS) pos/wks

8 Jun 91	GET THE FUNK OUT A & M AM 737	19	7
27 Jul 91 ●	MORE THAN WORDS A & M AM 792 ▲	2	11
12 Oct 91	DECADENCE DANCE A & M AM 773	36	3
23 Nov 91	HOLE HEARTED A & M AM 839	12	7
2 May 92	SONG FOR LOVE A & M AM 698	12	6
5 Sep 92	REST IN PEACE A & M AM 0055	13	5
14 Nov 92	STOP THE WORLD A & M AM 0096	22	2
6 Feb 93	TRAGIC COMIC A & M AMCD 0156	15	4
11 Mar 95	HIP TODAY A & M 5809932	44	1

EYC US, male vocal group (36 WEEKS) pos/wks

11 Dec 93	FEELIN' ALRIGHT MCA MCSTD 1952	16	8
5 Mar 94	THE WAY YOU WORK IT MCA MCSTD 1963	14	7
14 May 94	NUMBER ONE MCA MCSTD 1976	27	5
30 Jul 94	BLACK BOOK MCA MCSTD 1987	13	6
10 Dec 94	ONE MORE CHANCE MCA MCSTD 2025	25	6
23 Sep 95	OOH-AH-AA (I FEEL IT)		
	Gasoline Alley MCSTD 2096	33	2
2 Dec 95	IN THE BEGINNING		
	Gasoline Alley MCSTD 2107	41	2

EYES CREAM Italy, male producer - Agostino Carollo (1 WEEK) pos/wks

| 16 Oct 99 | FLY AWAY (BYE BYE) Accolade CDAC 001 | 53 | 1 |

Adam F UK, male producer (6 WEEKS) pos/wks

| 27 Sep 97 | CIRCLES Positiva CDFJ 002 | 20 | 3 |
| 7 Mar 98 | MUSIC IN MY MIND Positiva CDFJ 003 | 27 | 3 |

F45 – See DE FUNK Featuring F45

F L B – See FAT LARRY'S BAND

F.L.O. – See Rahni HARRIS and F.L.O.

FAB UK, male producers (11 WEEKS) pos/wks

7 Jul 90 ●	THUNDERBIRDS ARE GO Brothers Organisation FAB 1 [1]	5	8
20 Oct 90	THE PRISONER Brothers Organisation FAB 6 [2]	56	2
1 Dec 90	THE STINGRAY MEGAMIX		
	Brothers Organisation FAB 2 [3]	66	1

[1] FAB featuring MC Parker [2] FAB featuring MC Number 6 [3] FAB featuring Aqua Marina

FAB! Ireland, female vocal group (1 WEEK) pos/wks

| 1 Aug 98 | TURN AROUND Break Records BRCX 107 | 59 | 1 |

Shelley FABARES US, female vocalist (4 WEEKS) pos/wks

| 26 Apr 62 | JOHNNY ANGEL Pye International 7N 25132 ▲ | 41 | 4 |

FABIAN US, male vocalist (1 WEEK) pos/wks

| 10 Mar 60 | HOUND DOG MAN HMV POP 695 | 46 | 1 |

LARA FABIAN Belgium, female vocalist (1 WEEK) pos/wks

| 28 Oct 00 | I WILL LOVE AGAIN Columbia 6694062 | 63 | 1 |

FABULOUS BAKER BOYS
UK, male DJ production trio (2 WEEKS) pos/wks

| 15 Nov 97 | OH BOY Multiply CDMULTY 28 | 34 | 2 |

FACE – See David MORALES

FACES UK, male vocal / instrumental group (46 WEEKS) pos/wks

18 Dec 71 ●	STAY WITH ME Warner Bros. K 16136	6	14
17 Feb 73 ●	CINDY INCIDENTALLY Warner Bros. K 16247	2	9
8 Dec 73 ●	POOL HALL RICHARD / I WISH IT WOULD RAIN		
	Warner Bros. K 16341	8	11
7 Dec 74	YOU CAN MAKE ME DANCE SING OR ANYTHING		
	(EVEN TAKE THE DOG FOR A WALK, MEND A FUSE,		
	FOLD AWAY THE IRONING BOARD, OR ANY OTHER		
	DOMESTIC SHORT COMINGS) Warner Bros. K 16494 [1]	12	9
4 Jun 77	THE FACES (EP) Riva 8	41	3

[1] Faces / Rod Stewart

Tracks on The Faces (EP): Memphis / You Can Make Me Dance Sing or Anything / Stay With Me / Cindy Incidentally

See also Rod STEWART

FACTORY OF UNLIMITED RHYTHM Jamaica, male / female vocal / instrumental group (1 WEEK) pos/wks

| 1 Jun 96 | THE SWEETEST SURRENDER Kuff KUFFD 6 | 59 | 1 |

Donald FAGEN US, male vocalist (2 WEEKS) pos/wks

| 3 Jul 93 | TOMORROW'S GIRLS Reprise W 0180CDX | 46 | 2 |

See also STEELY DAN

UK No.1 ★   UK Top 10 ●   Still on chart +   UK million seller ◆   UK entry at No.1 ■   US No.1 ▲

Joe FAGIN *UK, male vocalist (20 WEEKS)* pos/wks

		pos	wks
7 Jan 84 ●	THAT'S LIVIN' ALRIGHT *Towerbell TOW 46*	3	11
5 Apr 86	BACK WITH THE BOYS AGAIN / GET IT RIGHT *Towerbell TOW 84*	53	9

FAIR WEATHER *UK, male vocal / instrumental group (12 WEEKS)* pos/wks

		pos	wks
18 Jul 70 ●	NATURAL SINNER *RCA 1977*	6	12

Fair Weather is led by Andy Fairweather-Low

See also Andy FAIRWEATHER-LOW; AMEN CORNER

Yvonne FAIR *US, female vocalist (11 WEEKS)* pos/wks

		pos	wks
24 Jan 76 ●	IT SHOULD HAVE BEEN ME *Tamla Motown TMG 1013*	5	11

FAIRGROUND ATTRACTION *UK, female / male vocal / instrumental group, lead vocal Eddi Reader (27 WEEKS)* pos/wks

		pos	wks
16 Apr 88 ★	PERFECT *RCA PB 41845*	1	13
30 Jul 88 ●	FIND MY LOVE *RCA PB 42079*	7	10
19 Nov 88	A SMILE IN A WHISPER *RCA PB 42249*	75	1
28 Jan 89	CLARE *RCA PB 42607*	49	3

See also Eddi READER

FAIRPORT CONVENTION
UK, male / female vocal / instrumental group (9 WEEKS) pos/wks

		pos	wks
23 Jul 69	SI TU DOIS PARTIR *Island WIP 6064*	21	8
27 Sep 69	SI TU DOIS PARTIR (re-entry) *Island WIP 6064*	49	1

Andy FAIRWEATHER-LOW *UK, male vocalist (18 WEEKS)* pos/wks

		pos	wks
21 Sep 74 ●	REGGAE TUNE *A & M AMS 7129*	10	8
6 Dec 75 ●	WIDE EYED AND LEGLESS *A & M AMS 7202*	6	10

See also AMEN CORNER; FAIR WEATHER

Adam FAIH 43 Top 500 *Teen-idol vocalist turned top actor, b. Terence Nelhams, 23 Jun 1940, London. Became the first UK artist to lodge initial seven hits in the Top 5 (251 WEEKS)* pos/wks

		pos	wks
20 Nov 59 ★	WHAT DO YOU WANT *Parlophone R 4591*	1	19
22 Jan 60 ★	POOR ME *Parlophone R 4623*	1	17
14 Apr 60 ●	SOMEONE ELSE'S BABY *Parlophone R 4643*	2	13
30 Jun 60 ●	WHEN JOHNNY COMES MARCHING HOME / MADE YOU *Parlophone R 4665*	5	13
15 Sep 60 ●	HOW ABOUT THAT *Parlophone R 4689*	4	14
17 Nov 60 ●	LONELY PUP (IN A CHRISTMAS SHOP) *Parlophone R 4708*	4	11
9 Feb 61 ●	WHO AM I / THIS IS IT! *Parlophone R 4735*	5	14
27 Apr 61	EASY GOING ME *Parlophone R 4766*	12	10
20 Jul 61	DON'T YOU KNOW IT *Parlophone R 4807*	12	10
26 Oct 61 ●	THE TIME HAS COME *Parlophone R 4837*	4	14
18 Jan 62	LONESOME *Parlophone R 4864*	12	9
3 May 62 ●	AS YOU LIKE IT *Parlophone R 4896*	5	15
30 Aug 62 ●	DON'T THAT BEAT ALL *Parlophone R 4930* [1]	8	11
13 Dec 62	BABY TAKE A BOW *Parlophone R 4964*	22	6
31 Jan 63	WHAT NOW *Parlophone R 4990* [1]	31	5
11 Jul 63	WALKIN' TALL *Parlophone R 5039*	23	6
19 Sep 63 ●	THE FIRST TIME *Parlophone R 5061* [2]	5	13
12 Dec 63	WE ARE IN LOVE *Parlophone R 5091* [2]	11	12
12 Mar 64	IF HE TELLS YOU *Parlophone R 5109* [2]	25	9
28 May 64	I LOVE BEING IN LOVE WITH YOU *Parlophone R 5138* [2]	33	6
26 Nov 64	MESSAGE TO MARTHA (KENTUCKY BLUEBIRD) *Parlophone R 5201*	12	11
11 Feb 65	STOP FEELING SORRY FOR YOURSELF *Parlophone R 5235*	23	6
17 Jun 65	SOMEONE'S TAKEN MARIA AWAY *Parlophone R 5289*	34	5
20 Oct 66	CHERYL'S GOIN' HOME *Parlophone R 5516*	46	2

[1] Adam Faith with Johnny Keating and his Orchestra [2] Adam Faith and the Roulettes

Horace FAITH *Jamaica, male vocalist (10 WEEKS)* pos/wks

		pos	wks
12 Sep 70	BLACK PEARL *Trojan TR 7790*	13	10

Percy FAITH *Canada, orchestra (30 WEEKS)* pos/wks

		pos	wks
5 Mar 60 ●	THE THEME FROM 'A SUMMER PLACE' *Philips PB 989* ▲	2	30

FAITH BROTHERS *UK, male vocal / instrumental group (6 WEEKS)* pos/wks

		pos	wks
13 Apr 85	THE COUNTRY OF THE BLIND *Siren SIREN 2*	63	3
6 Jul 85	A STRANGER ON HOME GROUND *Siren SIREN 4*	69	3

FAITH, HOPE AND CHARITY
US, male / female vocal group (4 WEEKS) pos/wks

		pos	wks
31 Jan 76	JUST ONE LOOK *RCA 2632*	38	4

FAITH, HOPE AND CHARITY *UK, female vocal group (3 WEEKS)* pos/wks

		pos	wks
23 Jun 90	BATTLE OF THE SEXES *WEA YZ 480*	53	3

FAITH NO MORE *US, male vocal / instrumental group (65 WEEKS)* pos/wks

		pos	wks
6 Feb 88	WE CARE A LOT *Slash LASH 17*	53	3
10 Feb 90	EPIC *Slash LASH 21*	37	4
14 Apr 90	FROM OUT OF NOWHERE *Slash LASH 24*	23	6
14 Jul 90	FALLING TO PIECES *Slash LASH 25*	41	3
8 Sep 90	EPIC (re-issue) *Slash LASH 26*	25	5
6 Jun 92 ●	MIDLIFE CRISIS *Slash LASH 37*	10	5
15 Aug 92	A SMALL VICTORY *Slash LASH 39*	29	5
12 Sep 92	A SMALL VICTORY (re-mix) *Slash LASHX 40*	55	1
21 Nov 92	EVERYTHING'S RUINED *Slash LASH 43*	28	3
16 Jan 93 ●	I'M EASY / BE AGGRESSIVE *Slash LACDP 44*	3	7
13 Mar 93	I'M EASY / BE AGGRESSIVE (re-entry) *Slash LACDP 44*	75	1
6 Nov 93	ANOTHER BODY MURDERED *Epic 6597942* [1]	26	3
11 Mar 95	DIGGING THE GRAVE *Slash LASCD 51*	16	4
27 May 95	RICOCHET *Slash LASCD 53*	27	2
29 Jul 95	EVIDENCE *Slash LASCD 54*	32	3
31 May 97	ASHES TO ASHES *Slash LASCD 61*	15	3
16 Aug 97	LAST CUP OF SORROW *Slash LASCD 62*	51	1
13 Dec 97	THIS TOWN AIN'T BIG ENOUGH FOR BOTH OF US *Roadrunner RR 22513* [2]	40	2
17 Jan 98	ASHES TO ASHES (re-issue) *Slash LACDP 63*	29	3
7 Nov 98	I STARTED A JOKE *Slash LASCD 65*	49	1

[1] Faith No More and Boo-Yaa T.R.I.B.E. [2] Sparks vs Faith No More

Marianne FAITHFULL *UK, female vocalist (59 WEEKS)* pos/wks

		pos	wks
13 Aug 64 ●	AS TEARS GO BY *Decca F 11923*	9	13
18 Feb 65 ●	COME AND STAY WITH ME *Decca F 12075*	4	13
6 May 65 ●	THIS LITTLE BIRD *Decca F 12162*	6	11
22 Jul 65 ●	SUMMER NIGHTS *Decca F 12193*	10	10
4 Nov 65	YESTERDAY *Decca F 12268*	36	4
9 Mar 67	IS THIS WHAT I GET FOR LOVING YOU *Decca F 22524*	43	2
24 Nov 79	THE BALLAD OF LUCY JORDAN *Island WIP 6491*	48	6

FAITHLESS
UK, male / female vocal / instrumental group (50 WEEKS) pos/wks

		pos	wks
5 Aug 95	SALVA MEA (SAVE ME) *Cheeky CHEKCD 008*	30	2
9 Dec 95	INSOMNIA *Cheeky CHEKCD 010*	27	2
23 Mar 96	DON'T LEAVE *Cheeky CHEKCD 012*	34	2
26 Oct 96 ●	INSOMNIA (re-issue) *Cheeky CHEKCD 017*	3	13
21 Dec 96 ●	SALVA MEA (re-mix) *Cheeky CHEKCD 018*	9	7
26 Apr 97 ●	REVERENCE *Cheeky CHEKCD 019*	10	3
15 Nov 97	DON'T LEAVE (re-mix) *Cheeky CHEKXCD 024*	21	2
5 Sep 98 ●	GOD IS A DJ *Cheeky CHEKCD 028*	6	8
5 Dec 98	TAKE THE LONG WAY HOME *Cheeky CHEKCD 031*	15	6
1 May 99	BRING MY FAMILY BACK *Cheeky CHEKCD 035*	14	5

FALCO *Austria, male vocalist, - Johann Holzel (26 WEEKS)* pos/wks

		pos	wks
22 Mar 86 ★	ROCK ME AMADEUS *A & M AM 278* ▲	1	15
31 May 86 ●	VIENNA CALLING *A & M AM 318*	10	8
2 Aug 86	JEANNY *A & M AM 333*	68	1
27 Sep 86	THE SOUND OF MUSIK *WEA U 8591*	61	2

Christian FALK featuring DEMETREUS
Sweden, male producer & Swedish, male vocalist (3 WEEKS) pos/wks

		pos	wks
26 Aug 00	MAKE IT RIGHT *London LONCD 452*	22	3

Fred FALKE – See Alan BRAXE and Fred FALKE

FALL
UK, vocal / instrumental group - leader Mark E Smith (25 WEEKS) pos/wks

13 Sep 86	MR PHARMACIST *Beggars Banquet BEG 168*	75	1
20 Dec 86	HEY! LUCIANI *Beggars Banquet BEG 176*	59	1
9 May 87	THERE'S A GHOST IN MY HOUSE *Beggars Banquet BEG 187*	30	4
31 Oct 87	HIT THE NORTH *Beggars Banquet BEG 200*	57	5
30 Jan 88	VICTORIA *Beggars Banquet BEG 206*	35	3
26 Nov 88	BIG NEW PRINZ / JERUSALEM (DOUBLE SINGLE) *Beggars Banquet FALL 2/3*	59	2
27 Jan 90	TELEPHONE THING *Cog Sinister SIN 4*	58	1
8 Sep 90	WHITE LIGHTNING *Cog Sinister SIN 6*	56	2
14 Mar 92	FREE RANGE *Cog Sinister SINS 8*	40	1
17 Apr 93	WHY ARE PEOPLE GRUDGEFUL *Permanent CDSPERM 9*	43	1
25 Dec 93	BEHIND THE COUNTER *Permanent CDSPERM 13*	75	1
30 Apr 94	15 WAYS *Permanent CDSPERM 14*	65	1
17 Feb 96	THE CHISELERS *Jet JETSCD 500*	60	1
21 Feb 98	MASQUERADE *Artful CDARTFUL 1*	69	1

Tracks on 'Big New Prinz / Jerusalem' double single: Big New Prinz / Wrong Place
Right Time Number Two / Jerusalem / Acid Priest 2088

See also Mark E SMITH

Harold FALTERMEYER
Germany, male instrumentalist - keyboards (23 WEEKS) pos/wks

23 Mar 85	AXEL F *MCA MCA 949*	62	4
1 Jun 85 ●	AXEL F (re-entry) *MCA MCA 949*	2	18
24 Aug 85	FLETCH THEME *MCA MCA 991*	74	1

Agnetha FALTSKOG *Sweden, female vocalist (12 WEEKS)* pos/wks

28 May 83	THE HEAT IS ON *Epic A 3436*	35	6
13 Aug 83	WRAP YOUR ARMS AROUND ME *Epic A 3622*	44	5
22 Oct 83	CAN'T SHAKE LOOSE *Epic A 3812*	63	1

See also ABBA

Georgie FAME 235 Top 500
Critically acclaimed R&B / jazz vocalist / keyboard player, b. Clive Powell, 26 Jun 1943, Lancashire, UK. One-time rock 'n' roll tour musician, who had a string of Sixties' hits, is still a popular performer, working with contemporaries such as Van Morrison and Bill Wyman (115 WEEKS) pos/wks

17 Dec 64 ★	YEH YEH *Columbia DB 7428* [1]	1	12
4 Mar 65	IN THE MEANTIME *Columbia DB 7494* [1]	22	8
29 Jul 65	LIKE WE USED TO BE *Columbia DB 7633* [1]	33	7
28 Oct 65	SOMETHING *Columbia DB 7727* [1]	23	7
23 Jun 66 ★	GET AWAY *Columbia DB 7946* [1]	1	11
22 Sep 66	SUNNY *Columbia DB 8015*	13	8
22 Dec 66	SITTING IN THE PARK *Columbia DB 8096* [1]	12	10
23 Mar 67	BECAUSE I LOVE YOU *CBS 202587*	15	8
13 Sep 67	TRY MY WORLD *CBS 2945*	37	5
13 Dec 67 ★	BALLAD OF BONNIE AND CLYDE *CBS 3124*	1	13
9 Jul 69	PEACEFUL *CBS 4295*	16	9
13 Dec 69	SEVENTH SON *CBS 4659*	25	7
10 Apr 71	ROSETTA *CBS 7108* [2]	11	10

[1] Georgie Fame and the Blue Flames [2] Fame and Price Together

FAMILY *UK, male vocal / instrumental group (44 WEEKS)* pos/wks

1 Nov 69	NO MULE'S FOOL *Reprise RS 27001*	29	7
22 Aug 70	STRANGE BAND *Reprise RS 27009*	11	12
17 Jul 71 ●	IN MY OWN TIME *Reprise K 14090*	4	13
23 Sep 72	BURLESQUE *Reprise K 14196*	13	12

FAMILY CAT *UK, male vocal / instrumental group (4 WEEKS)* pos/wks

28 Aug 93	AIRPLANE GARDENS / ATMOSPHERIC ROAD *Dedicated FCUK 003CD*	69	1
21 May 94	WONDERFUL EXCUSE *Dedicated 74321208432*	48	1
30 Jul 94	GOLDENBOOK *Dedicated 74321220072*	42	2

FAMILY COOKIN' – See LIMMIE and the FAMILY COOKIN'

FAMILY DOGG *UK, male / female vocal group (14 WEEKS)* pos/wks

28 May 69 ●	WAY OF LIFE *Bell 1055*	6	14

FAMILY FOUNDATION
UK, male / female vocal / instrumental group (4 WEEKS) pos/wks

13 Jun 92	XPRESS YOURSELF *380 PEW 1*	42	4

FAMILY STAND
US, male / female vocal / instrumental group (13 WEEKS) pos/wks

31 Mar 90 ●	GHETTO HEAVEN *East West A 7997*	10	11
17 Jan 98	GHETTO HEAVEN (re-mix) *Perfecto PERF 156CD1*	30	2

FAMILY STONE – See SLY and the FAMILY STONE

FAMOUS FLAMES – See James BROWN

FANTASTIC FOUR *US, male vocal group (4 WEEKS)* pos/wks

24 Feb 79	B.Y.O.F. (BRING YOUR OWN FUNK) *Atlantic LV 14*	62	4

FANTASTICS *US, male vocal group (12 WEEKS)* pos/wks

27 Mar 71 ●	SOMETHING OLD, SOMETHING NEW *Bell 1141*	9	12

FANTASY UFO *UK, male instrumental group (6 WEEKS)* pos/wks

29 Sep 90	FANTASY *XL XLT 15*	56	3
10 Aug 91	MIND BODY SOUL *Strictly Underground YZ 591* [1]	50	3

[1] Fantasy UFO featuring Jay Groove

FAR CORPORATION *UK / US / Germany / Switzerland, male vocal / instrumental group (11 WEEKS)* pos/wks

26 Oct 85 ●	STAIRWAY TO HEAVEN *Arista ARIST 639*	8	11

Don FARDON *UK, male vocalist - Donald Maughn (22 WEEKS)* pos/wks

18 Apr 70	BELFAST BOY *Young Blood YB 1010*	32	5
10 Oct 70 ●	INDIAN RESERVATION *Young Blood YB 1015*	3	17

FARGETTA *Italy / UK male producer (3 WEEKS)* pos/wks

23 Jan 93	MUSIC *Synthetic CDR 6334* [1]	34	2
10 Aug 96	THE MUSIC IS MOVING *Arista 74321381572*	74	1

[1] Fargetta and Anne-Marie Smith

Chris FARLOWE *UK, male vocalist - John Deighton (36 WEEKS)* pos/wks

27 Jan 66	THINK *Immediate IM 023*	49	1
10 Feb 66	THINK (re-entry) *Immediate IM 023*	37	2
23 Jun 66 ★	OUT OF TIME *Immediate IM 035*	1	13
27 Oct 66	RIDE ON BABY *Immediate IM 038*	31	7
16 Feb 67	MY WAY OF GIVING IN *Immediate IM 041*	48	1
29 Jun 67	MOANIN' *Immediate IM 056*	46	2
13 Dec 67	HANDBAGS AND GLADRAGS *Immediate IM 065*	33	6
27 Sep 75	OUT OF TIME (re-issue) *Immediate IMS 101*	44	4

FARM *UK, male vocal / instrumental group (54 WEEKS)* pos/wks

5 May 90	STEPPING STONE / FAMILY OF MAN *Produce MILK 101*	58	4
1 Sep 90 ●	GROOVY TRAIN *Produce MILK 102*	6	10
8 Dec 90 ●	ALL TOGETHER NOW *Produce MILK 103*	4	12
13 Apr 91	SINFUL! *Siren SRN 138* [1]	28	5
4 May 91	DON'T LET ME DOWN *Produce MILK 104*	36	3
24 Aug 91	MIND *Produce MILK 105*	31	4
14 Dec 91	LOVE SEE NO COLOUR *Produce MILK 106*	58	4
4 Jul 92	RISING SUN *Produce MILK 107*	48	3
17 Oct 92	DON'T YOU WANT ME *End Product 6581737*	18	5
2 Jan 93	LOVE SEE NO COLOUR (re-mix) *End Product 6588682*	35	4

[1] Pete Wylie with the Farm

FARMERS BOYS *UK, male vocal / instrumental group (17 WEEKS)* pos/wks

9 Apr 83	MUCK IT OUT *EMI 5380*	48	6
30 Jul 83	FOR YOU *EMI 5401*	66	3
4 Aug 84	IN THE COUNTRY *EMI FAB 2*	44	5
3 Nov 84	PHEW WOW *EMI FAB 3*	59	3

UK No.1 ★ UK Top 10 ● Still on chart + UK million seller ◆ UK entry at No.1 ■ US No.1 ▲

John FARNHAM *Australia, male vocalist (17 WEEKS)* pos/wks

25 Apr 87	● YOU'RE THE VOICE *Wheatley PB 41093*	6	17

Joanne FARRELL *US, female vocalist (2 WEEKS)* pos/wks

24 Jun 95	ALL I WANNA DO *Big Beat A 8194CD*	40	2

Joe FARRELL *US, male instrumentalist - saxophone (4 WEEKS)* pos/wks

16 Dec 78	NIGHT DANCING *Warner Bros. LV 2*	57	4

Dionne FARRIS *US, female vocalist (6 WEEKS)* pos/wks

18 Mar 95	I KNOW *Columbia 6613542*	47	2
27 May 95	I KNOW (re-entry) *Columbia 6613542*	41	3
7 Jun 97	HOPELESS *Columbia 6645165*	42	1

Gene FARROW and G.F. BAND
UK, male vocal / instrumental group (8 WEEKS) pos/wks

1 Apr 78	MOVE YOUR BODY *Magnet MAG 109*	33	5
13 May 78	MOVE YOUR BODY (re-entry) *Magnet MAG 109*	67	1
5 Aug 78	DON'T STOP NOW *Magnet MAG 125*	71	1
19 Aug 78	DON'T STOP NOW (re-entry) *Magnet MAG 125*	74	1

FASCINATIONS *US, female vocal group (6 WEEKS)* pos/wks

3 Jul 71	GIRLS ARE OUT TO GET YOU *Mojo 2092 004*	32	6

FASHION *UK, male vocal / instrumental group (12 WEEKS)* pos/wks

3 Apr 82	STREETPLAYER (MECHANIK) *Arista ARIST 456*	46	5
21 Aug 82	LOVE SHADOW *Arista ARIST 483*	51	5
18 Feb 84	EYE TALK *De Stijl A 4106*	69	2

Susan FASSBENDER *UK, female vocalist (8 WEEKS)* pos/wks

17 Jan 81	TWILIGHT CAFE *CBS 9468*	21	8

'Fast' Eddie SMITH – See DJ 'FAST' EDDIE

FASTBALL *US, male vocal / instrumental trio (5 WEEKS)* pos/wks

3 Oct 98	THE WAY *Polydor 5699472*	21	5

FASTWAY *UK, male vocal / instrumental group (1 WEEK)* pos/wks

2 Apr 83	EASY LIVIN' *CBS A 3196*	74	1

FAT BOYS *US, male rap group (29 WEEKS)* pos/wks

4 May 85	JAIL HOUSE RAP *Sultra U 9123*	63	2
22 Aug 87	● WIPEOUT *Urban URB 5* [1]	2	12
18 Jun 88	● THE TWIST (YO, TWIST) *Urban URB 20* [2]	2	11
5 Nov 88	LOUIE LOUIE *Urban URB 26*	46	4

[1] Fat Boys and the Beach Boys [2] Fat Boys and Chubby Checker

FAT JOE – See Jennifer LOPEZ

FAT LADY SINGS
Ireland, male vocal / instrumental group (2 WEEKS) pos/wks

17 Jul 93	DRUNKARD LOGIC *East West YZ 756CD*	56	2

FAT LARRY'S BAND
US, male vocal / instrumental group (26 WEEKS) pos/wks

2 Jul 77	CENTER CITY *Atlantic K 10951*	31	5
10 Mar 79	BOOGIE TOWN *Fantasy FTC 168* [1]	46	4
18 Aug 79	LOOKING FOR LOVE TONIGHT *Fantasy FTC 179*	46	6
18 Sep 82	● ZOOM *Virgin VS 546*	2	11

[1] F.L.B.

FAT LES *UK, male / female vocal group (22 WEEKS)* pos/wks

20 Jun 98	● VINDALOO *Telstar CDSTAS 2982*	2	12
19 Dec 98	NAUGHTY CHRISTMAS (GOBLIN IN THE OFFICE) *Turtleneck NECKCD 001*	21	5

17 Jun 00	● JERUSALEM *Parlophone CDR 6540* [1]	10	3
5 Aug 00	JERUSALEM (re-entry) *Parlophone CDR 6540* [1]	55	2

[1] Fat Les 2000

FATBACK BAND
US, male vocal / instrumental group (67 WEEKS) pos/wks

6 Sep 75	YUM YUM (GIMME SOME) *Polydor 2066 590*	40	6
6 Dec 75	(ARE YOU READY) DO THE BUS STOP *Polydor 2066 637*	18	10
21 Feb 76	● (DO THE) SPANISH HUSTLE *Polydor 2066 656*	10	7
29 May 76	PARTY TIME *Polydor 2066 682*	41	4
14 Aug 76	NIGHT FEVER *Spring 2066 706*	38	4
12 Mar 77	DOUBLE DUTCH *Spring 2066 777*	31	4
9 Aug 80	BACKSTROKIN' *Spring POSP 149* [1]	41	9
23 Jun 84	I FOUND LOVIN' *Master Mix CHE 8401*	49	4
4 May 85	GIRLS ON MY MIND *Atlantic/Cotillion FBACK 1* [1]	69	2
6 Sep 86	I FOUND LOVIN' (re-issue) *Important TAN 10*	55	5
5 Sep 87	● I FOUND LOVIN' (re-entry) *Master Mix CHE 8401*	7	12

[1] Fatback

FATBOY SLIM *UK, male producer - Norman Cook (53 WEEKS)* pos/wks

3 May 97	GOING OUT OF MY HEAD *Skint SKINT 19CD*	57	1
1 Nov 97	EVERYBODY NEEDS A 303 *Skint SKINT 31CD*	34	2
20 Jun 98	● THE ROCKAFELLER SKANK *Skint SKINT 35CD*	6	10
17 Oct 98	● GANGSTER TRIPPIN' *Skint SKINT 39CD*	3	8
16 Jan 99	★ PRAISE YOU *Skint SKINT 42CD* ■	1	12
1 May 99	BADDER BADDER SCHWING *Eye Q EYEUK 040CD* [1]	34	2
1 May 99	● RIGHT HERE RIGHT NOW *Skint SKINT 46CD*	2	10
28 Oct 00	● SUNSET (BIRD OF PREY) *Skint SKINT 58CD*	9	7
30 Dec 00	SUNSET (BIRD OF PREY) (re-entry) *Skint SKINT 58CD*	70	1+

[1] Freddy Fresh featuring Fatboy Slim

See also Norman COOK; BEATS INTERNATIONAL; MIGHTY DUB KATZ; HOUSEMARTINS; FREAKPOWER; PIZZAMAN; URBAN ALL STARS

FATHER ABRAHAM – See SMURFS

FATHER ABRAPHART and the SMURPS – See Jonathan KING

FATIMA MANSIONS
Ireland, male vocal / instrumental group (11 WEEKS) pos/wks

23 May 92	EVIL MAN *Radioactive SKX 56*	59	1
1 Aug 92	1000% *Radioactive SKX 59*	61	3
19 Sep 92	● (EVERYTHING I DO) I DO IT FOR YOU *Columbia 6583827*	7	6
6 Aug 94	THE LOYALISER *Kitchenware SKCD 67*	58	1

'(Everything I Do) I Do It For You' was listed with 'Theme From M.A.S.H. (Suicide Is Painless)' by Manic Street Preachers

FBI – See REDHEAD KINGPIN and the FBI

FEAR FACTORY *US, male vocal / instrumental group (1 WEEK)* pos/wks

9 Oct 99	CARS *Roadrunner RR 21893*	57	1

Phil FEARON *UK, male vocalist (63 WEEKS)* pos/wks

23 Apr 83	● DANCING TIGHT *Ensign ENY 501* [1]	4	11
30 Jul 83	WAIT UNTIL TONIGHT (MY LOVE) *Ensign ENY 503* [1]	20	8
22 Oct 83	FANTASY REAL *Ensign ENY 507* [2]	41	6
10 Mar 84	● WHAT DO I DO *Ensign ENY 510* [2]	5	10
14 Jul 84	● EVERYBODY'S LAUGHING *Ensign ENY 514* [2]	10	10
15 Jun 85	YOU DON'T NEED A REASON *Ensign ENY 517* [2]	42	4
27 Jul 85	THIS KIND OF LOVE *Ensign ENY 521* [3]	70	3
2 Aug 86	● I CAN PROVE IT *Ensign PF 1*	8	9
15 Nov 86	AIN'T NOTHING BUT A HOUSEPARTY *Ensign PF 2*	60	2

[1] Galaxy featuring Phil Fearon [2] Phil Fearon and Galaxy [3] Phil Fearon and Galaxy featuring Dee Galdes

FEEDER *UK, male vocal / instrumental group (16 WEEKS)* pos/wks

8 Mar 97	TANGERINE *Echo ECSCD 32*	60	1
10 May 97	CEMENT *Echo ECSCX 36*	53	1
23 Aug 97	CRASH *Echo ECSCD 42*	48	1

		pos/wks
18 Oct 97	HIGH *Echo ECSCD 44*	**24** 2
28 Feb 98	SUFFOCATE *Echo ECSCX 52*	**37** 1
3 Apr 99	DAY IN DAY OUT *Echo ECSCD 75*	**31** 2
12 Jun 99	INSOMNIA *Echo ECSCD 77*	**22** 3
21 Aug 99	YESTERDAY WENT TOO SOON *Echo ECSCD 79*	**20** 3
20 Nov 99	PAPERFACES *Echo ECSCD 85*	**41** 2

Wilton FELDER US, male instrumentalist - tenor sax (7 WEEKS)
		pos/wks
1 Nov 80	INHERIT THE WIND *MCA 646*	**39** 5
16 Feb 85	(NO MATTER HOW HIGH I GET) I'LL STILL BE LOOKIN' UP TO YOU *MCA MCA 919* [1]	**63** 2

[1] Featuring Bobby Womack and introducing Alltrina Grayson

Bobby Womack uncredited vocalist on 'Inherit the Wind'

José FELICIANO
US, male vocalist / instrumentalist - guitar (23 WEEKS)
		pos/wks
18 Sep 68 ●	LIGHT MY FIRE *RCA 1715*	**6** 16
18 Oct 69	AND THE SUN WILL SHINE *RCA 1871*	**25** 7

FELIX UK, male producer - Francis Wright (29 WEEKS)
		pos/wks
8 Aug 92 ●	DON'T YOU WANT ME *Deconstruction 74321110507*	**6** 11
24 Oct 92	IT WILL MAKE ME CRAZY *Deconstruction 74321118137*	**11** 6
22 May 93	STARS *Deconstruction 74321147102*	**29** 3
12 Aug 95 ●	DON'T YOU WANT ME (re-mix) *Deconstruction 74321293972*	**10** 5
19 Oct 96	DON'T YOU WANT ME (2nd) (re-mix) *Deconstruction 74321418142*	**17** 4

FELIX DA HOUSECAT – See QWILO & FELIX DA HOUSECAT

Julie FELIX US, female vocalist (19 WEEKS)
		pos/wks
18 Apr 70	IF I COULD (EL CONDOR PASA) *RAK 101*	**19** 11
17 Oct 70	HEAVEN IS HERE *RAK 105*	**22** 8

FELLY – See TECHNOTRONIC

FE-M@IL UK, female vocal group (2 WEEKS)
		pos/wks
5 Aug 00	FLEE FLY FLO *Jive 9250592*	**46** 2

FEMME FATALE
US, male / female vocal / instrumental group (2 WEEKS)
		pos/wks
11 Feb 89	FALLING IN AND OUT OF LOVE *MCA MCA 1309*	**69** 2

FENDERMEN
US, male vocal / instrumental duo - guitars (9 WEEKS)
		pos/wks
18 Aug 60	MULE SKINNER BLUES *Top Rank JAR 395*	**50** 1
1 Sep 60	MULE SKINNER BLUES (re-entry) *Top Rank JAR 395*	**37** 2
29 Sep 60	MULE SKINNER BLUES (2nd re-entry) *Top Rank JAR 395*	**32** 6

FENMEN – See Bern ELLIOTT and the FENMEN

George FENTON and Jonas GWANGWA
UK / South Africa, male instrumental / production duo (1 WEEK)
		pos/wks
2 Jan 88	CRY FREEDOM *MCA MCA 1228*	**75** 1

The listed flip side of 'Cry Freedom' was 'The Funeral' by Thuli Dumakude

Peter FENTON UK, male vocalist (3 WEEKS)
		pos/wks
10 Nov 66	MARBLE BREAKS IRON BENDS *Fontana TF 748*	**46** 3

Shane FENTON and the FENTONES
UK, male vocal / instrumental group (28 WEEKS)
		pos/wks
26 Oct 61	I'M A MOODY GUY *Parlophone R 4827*	**22** 8
1 Feb 62	WALK AWAY *Parlophone R 4866*	**38** 5
5 Apr 62	IT'S ALL OVER NOW *Parlophone R 4883*	**29** 7
12 Jul 62	CINDY'S BIRTHDAY *Parlophone R 4921*	**19** 8

See also FENTONES; Alvin STARDUST

FENTONES UK, male instrumental group (4 WEEKS)
		pos/wks
19 Apr 62	THE MEXICAN *Parlophone R 4899*	**41** 3
27 Sep 62	THE BREEZE AND I *Parlophone R 4937*	**48** 1

See also Shane FENTON and the FENTONES

FERGIE Ireland, male DJ / producer - Robert Ferguson (3 WEEKS)
		pos/wks
9 Sep 00	DECEPTION *Duty Free DF 020CD*	**47** 1
25 Nov 00	HOOVERS & HORNS *Nukleuz NUKC 0185* [1]	**57** 2

[1] Fergie & BK

Sheila FERGUSON US, female vocalist (1 WEEK)
		pos/wks
5 Feb 94	WHEN WILL I SEE YOU AGAIN *XSrhythm CDSTAS 2711*	**60** 1

See also THREE DEGREES

FERKO STRING BAND US, male instrumental group (2 WEEKS)
		pos/wks
12 Aug 55	ALABAMA JUBILEE *London HL 8140*	**20** 2

Luisa FERNANDEZ Spain, female vocalist (8 WEEKS)
		pos/wks
11 Nov 78	LAY LOVE ON YOU *Warner Bros. K 17061*	**31** 8

Pamela FERNANDEZ US, female vocalist (3 WEEKS)
		pos/wks
17 Sep 94	KICKIN' IN THE BEAT *Ore AG 5CD*	**43** 2
3 Jun 95	LET'S START OVER / KICKIN' IN THE BEAT (re-mix) *Ore AG 9CD*	**59** 1

FERRANTE and TEICHER US, male instrumental duo, pianos - Arthur Ferrante and Louis Teicher (18 WEEKS)
		pos/wks
18 Aug 60	THEME FROM 'THE APARTMENT' *London HLT 9164*	**44** 1
9 Mar 61 ●	EXODUS (THEME FROM 'EXODUS') *London HLT 9298 and HMV POP 881*	**6** 17

Exodus (Theme From 'Exodus') available first on London, then on HMV when the US label, United Artists, changed its UK outlet

Jose FERRER
US, male vocalist - Jose Vincente Ferrer Y Centron (3 WEEKS)
		pos/wks
19 Feb 54 ●	WOMAN *Philips PB 220*	**7** 3

'Woman' coupled with 'Man' by Rosemary Clooney

Tony FERRINO UK, male vocalist / comedian Steve Coogan (2 WEEKS)
		pos/wks
23 Nov 96	HELP YOURSELF / BIGAMY AT CHRISTMAS *RCA 74321430302*	**42** 2

FERRY AID
International, male / female charity ensemble (7 WEEKS)
		pos/wks
4 Apr 87 ★	LET IT BE *The Sun AID 1* ■	**1** 7

Bryan FERRY `192` `Top 500` Stylish UK vocalist / songwriter, b. 26 Sep 1945, Tyne and Wear. Sophisticated singer who split his time between solo career and fronting the fashionable and successful group Roxy Music (133 WEEKS)
		pos/wks
29 Sep 73 ●	A HARD RAIN'S GONNA FALL *Island WIP 6170*	**10** 9
25 May 74	THE 'IN' CROWD *Island WIP 6196*	**13** 6
31 Aug 74	SMOKE GETS IN YOUR EYES *Island WIP 6205*	**17** 8
5 Jul 75	YOU GO TO MY HEAD *Island WIP 6234*	**33** 3
12 Jun 76 ●	LET'S STICK TOGETHER (LET'S WORK TOGETHER) *Island WIP 6307*	**4** 10
7 Aug 76 ●	EXTENDED PLAY (EP) *Island IEP 1*	**7** 9
5 Feb 77 ●	THIS IS TOMORROW *Polydor 2001 704*	**9** 9
14 May 77	TOKYO JOE *Polydor 2001 711*	**15** 7
13 May 78	WHAT GOES ON *Polydor POSP 3*	**67** 2
5 Aug 78	SIGN OF THE TIMES *Polydor 2001 798*	**37** 8
11 May 85 ●	SLAVE TO LOVE *EG FERRY 1*	**10** 9
31 Aug 85	DON'T STOP THE DANCE *EG FERRY 2*	**21** 7
7 Dec 85	WINDSWEPT *EG FERRY 3*	**46** 3
29 Mar 86	IS YOUR LOVE STRONG ENOUGH? *EG FERRY 4*	**22** 7

		pos	wks
10 Oct 87	THE RIGHT STUFF *Virgin VS 940*	37	6
13 Feb 88	KISS AND TELL *Virgin VS 1034*	41	5
29 Oct 88	LET'S STICK TOGETHER (re-mix) *EG EGO 44*	12	7
11 Feb 89	THE PRICE OF LOVE (re-mix) *EG EGO 46*	49	3
22 Apr 89	HE'LL HAVE TO GO *EG EGO 48*	63	1
6 Mar 93	I PUT A SPELL ON YOU *Virgin VSCDG 1400*	18	5
29 May 93	WILL YOU LOVE ME TOMORROW *Virgin VSCDG 1455*	23	5
4 Sep 93	GIRL OF MY BEST FRIEND *Virgin VSCDG 1488*	57	2
29 Oct 94	YOUR PAINTED SMILE *Virgin VSCDG 1508*	52	1
11 Feb 95	MAMOUNA *Virgin VSCDG 1528*	57	1

Tracks on Extended Play (EP): Price of Love / Shame Shame Shame / Heart on My Sleeve / It's Only Love

See also ROXY MUSIC

FEVER featuring Tippa IRIE *UK, male production / instrumental group with male vocalist (1 WEEK)*

		pos	wks
8 Jul 95	STAYING ALIVE 95 *Telstar CDSTAS 2776* [1]	48	1

[1] Fever featuring Tippa Irie

Lena FIAGBE *UK, female vocalist (13 WEEKS)*

		pos	wks
24 Jul 93	YOU COME FROM EARTH *Mother MUMCD 42* [1]	69	1
23 Oct 93	GOTTA GET IT RIGHT *Mother MUMCD 44*	20	5
16 Apr 94	WHAT'S IT LIKE TO BE BEAUTIFUL *Mother MUMCD 49*	52	3
25 Jun 94	VISIONS *Mother MUMCD 53*	48	2
10 Feb 96	AFRICAN DREAM *Mercury MERCD 453* [2]	44	2

[1] Lena [2] Wasis Diop featuring Lena Fiagbe

Karel FIALKA *UK, male vocalist / multi-instrumentalist (12 WEEKS)*

		pos	wks
17 May 80	THE EYES HAVE IT *Blueprint BLU 2005*	52	4
5 Sep 87 ●	HEY MATTHEW *IRS IRM 140*	9	8

FIAT LUX *UK, male vocal / instrumental group (4 WEEKS)*

		pos	wks
28 Jan 84	SECRETS *Polydor FIAT 2*	65	3
17 Mar 84	BLUE EMOTION *Polydor FIAT 3*	59	1

FICTION FACTORY *UK, male vocal / instrumental group (11 WEEKS)*

		pos	wks
14 Jan 84 ●	(FEELS LIKE) HEAVEN *CBS A 3996*	6	9
17 Mar 84	GHOST OF LOVE *CBS A 3819*	64	2

FIDDLER'S DRAM *UK, male / female vocal / instrumental group (9 WEEKS)*

		pos	wks
15 Dec 79 ●	DAY TRIP TO BANGOR (DIDN'T WE HAVE A LOVELY TIME) *Dingles SID 211*	3	9

FIDELFATTI featuring RONNETTE *Italy, male producer and female vocalist (1 WEEK)*

		pos	wks
27 Jan 90	JUST WANNA TOUCH ME *Urban URB 46*	65	1

Billy FIELD *Australia, male vocalist (3 WEEKS)*

		pos	wks
12 Jun 82	YOU WEREN'T IN LOVE WITH ME *CBS A 2344*	67	3

Ernie FIELDS *US, orchestra (8 WEEKS)*

		pos	wks
25 Dec 59	IN THE MOOD *London HL 8985*	13	8

Gracie FIELDS *UK, female vocalist - Grace Stansfield (15 WEEKS)*

		pos	wks
31 May 57 ●	AROUND THE WORLD *Columbia DB 3953*	8	8
2 Aug 57	AROUND THE WORLD (re-entry) *Columbia DB 3953*	24	1
6 Nov 59	LITTLE DONKEY *Columbia DB 4360*	30	1
20 Nov 59	LITTLE DONKEY (re-entry) *Columbia DB 4360*	20	5

Richard 'Dimples' FIELDS *US, male vocalist (4 WEEKS)*

		pos	wks
20 Feb 82	I'VE GOT TO LEARN TO SAY NO *Epic EPC A 1918*	56	4

FIELDS OF THE NEPHILIM *UK, male vocal / instrumental group (9 WEEKS)*

		pos	wks
24 Oct 87	BLUE WATER *Situation Two SIT 48*	75	1
4 Jun 88	MOONCHILD *Situation Two SIT 52*	28	3
27 May 89	PSYCHONAUT *Situation Two ST 57*	35	3
4 Aug 90	FOR HER LIGHT *Beggars Banquet BEG 244T*	54	1
24 Nov 90	SUMERLAND (DREAMED) *Beggars Banquet BEG 250*	37	1

FIERCE *UK, female vocal group (23 WEEKS)*

		pos	wks
9 Jan 99	RIGHT HERE RIGHT NOW *Wildstar CDWILD 13*	25	5
15 May 99	DAYZ LIKE THAT *Wildstar CDWILD 19*	11	5
14 Aug 99	SO LONG *Wildstar CDWILD 27*	15	5
12 Feb 00 ●	SWEET LOVE 2K *Wildstar CDWILD 34*	3	8

FIFTH DIMENSION *US, male / female vocal group (21 WEEKS)*

		pos	wks
16 Apr 69	AQUARIUS / LET THE SUNSHINE IN (MEDLEY) *Liberty LBF 15193* ▲	11	12
17 Jan 70	WEDDING BELL BLUES *Liberty LBF 15288* ▲	16	9

53RD & 3RD – See Jonathan KING

52ND STREET *UK, male / female vocal / instrumental group (13 WEEKS)*

		pos	wks
2 Nov 85	TELL ME (HOW IT FEELS) *10 TEN 74*	54	5
11 Jan 86	YOU'RE MY LAST CHANCE *10 TEN 89*	49	4
8 Mar 86	I CAN'T LET YOU GO *10 TEN 114*	57	4

FILTER *US, male vocal / instrumental group (5 WEEKS)*

		pos	wks
11 Oct 97	(CAN YOU) TRIP LIKE I DO *Epic 6650862* [1]	39	2
18 Mar 00	TAKE A PICTURE *Reprise W 515CD*	25	3

[1] Filter and The Crystal Method

FINAL CUT – See TRUE FAITH with FINAL CUT

FINE YOUNG CANNIBALS (407 Top 500) *Politically aware pop / soul trio from Birmingham, UK: Roland Gift (v), ex-Beat members Andy Cox (g) and David Steele (b). Unmistakable vocalist Gift also acted in films, most notably 1989's Scandal. FYC, who were among 1989's biggest selling acts worldwide, won (and returned) two Brit awards in 1990 (81 WEEKS)*

		pos	wks
8 Jun 85 ●	JOHNNY COME HOME *London LON 68*	8	13
9 Nov 85	BLUE *London LON 79*	41	6
11 Jan 86 ●	SUSPICIOUS MINDS *London LON 82*	8	9
12 Apr 86	FUNNY HOW LOVE IS *London LON 88*	58	4
21 Mar 87 ●	EVER FALLEN IN LOVE *London LON 121*	9	10
7 Jan 89 ●	SHE DRIVES ME CRAZY *London LON 199* ▲	5	11
15 Apr 89 ●	GOOD THING *London LON 218* ▲	7	8
19 Aug 89	DON'T LOOK BACK *London LON 220*	34	4
18 Nov 89	I'M NOT THE MAN I USED TO BE *London LON 244*	20	8
24 Feb 90	I'M NOT SATISFIED *London LON 252*	46	3
16 Nov 96	THE FLAME *ffrr LONCD 389*	17	3
11 Jan 97	SHE DRIVES ME CRAZY (re-mix) *ffrr LONCD 391*	36	2

FINITRIBE *UK, male instrumental / production group (2 WEEKS)*

		pos	wks
11 Jul 92	FOREVERGREEN *One Little Indian 74 TP12F*	51	1
19 Nov 94	BRAND NEW *ffrr FCD 247*	69	1

FINK BROTHERS *UK, male vocal / instrumental duo (4 WEEKS)*

		pos	wks
9 Feb 85	MUTANTS IN MEGA CITY ONE *Zarjazz JAZZ 2*	50	4

FINN *New Zealand, male vocal / instrumental duo (5 WEEKS)*

		pos	wks
14 Oct 95	SUFFER NEVER *Parlophone CDRS 6417*	29	3
9 Dec 95	ANGEL'S HEAP *Parlophone CDRS 6421*	41	2

See also CROWDED HOUSE; Neil FINN; Tim FINN

Micky FINN – See URBAN SHAKEDOWN

Neil FINN New Zealand, male vocalist / instrumentalist (3 WEEKS)

			pos/wks
13 Jun 98	SHE WILL HAVE HER WAY Parlophone CDR 6495	26	2
17 Oct 98	SINNER Parlophone CDR 6505	39	1

See also CROWDED HOUSE; FINN

Tim FINN New Zealand, male vocalist (6 WEEKS)

			pos/wks
26 Jun 93	PERSUASION Capitol 6592482	43	3
18 Sep 93	HIT THE GROUND RUNNING Capitol CDCLS 694	50	3

See also CROWDED HOUSE; FINN

Johnnie FIORI – See BARKIN BROTHERS featuring Johnnie FIORI

Elisa FIORILLO US, female vocalist (14 WEEKS)

			pos/wks
28 Nov 87 ●	WHO FOUND WHO Chrysalis CHS JEL 1 [1]	10	10
13 Feb 88	HOW CAN I FORGET YOU Chrysalis ELISA 1	50	4

[1] Jellybean featuring Elisa Fiorillo

FIRE INC – See Jim STEINMAN

FIRE ISLAND
UK, male instrumental / production group (7 WEEKS)

			pos/wks
8 Aug 92	IN YOUR BONES / FIRE ISLAND Boy's Own BOIX 11	66	1
12 Mar 94	THERE BUT FOR THE GRACE OF GOD Junior Boy's Own JBO 18CD [1]	32	3
4 Mar 95	IF YOU SHOULD NEED A FRIEND Junior Boy's Own JBO 26CDS [2]	51	1
11 Apr 98	SHOUT TO THE TOP JBO JNR 5001573 [3]	23	2

[1] Fire Island featuring Love Nelson [2] Fire Island featuring Mark Anthoni [3] Fire Island featuring Loleatta Holloway

See also HELLER & FARLEY PROJECT

FIREBALLS US, male vocal / instrumental group (17 WEEKS)

			pos/wks
27 Jul 61	QUITE A PARTY Pye International 7N 25092	29	9
14 Nov 63	SUGAR SHACK London HLD 9789 [1]	45	4
19 Dec 63	SUGAR SHACK (re-entry) London HLD 9789 [1]	46	4

[1] Jimmy Gilmer and the Fireballs

FIREHOUSE US, male vocal / instrumental group (2 WEEKS)

			pos/wks
13 Jul 91	DON'T TREAT ME BAD Epic 6567807	71	1
19 Dec 92	WHEN I LOOK INTO YOUR EYES Epic 6588347	65	1

FIRM UK, male vocal / instrumental group (21 WEEKS)

			pos/wks
17 Jul 82	ARTHUR DALEY (E'S ALRIGHT) Bark HID 1	14	9
6 Jun 87 ★	STAR TREKKIN' Bark TREK 1	1	12

FIRM featuring Dawn ROBINSON
US, male rap group, and US, female vocalist (3 WEEKS)

			pos/wks
29 Nov 97	FIRM BIZ Columbia 6651612	18	3

FIRST CHOICE US, female vocal group (21 WEEKS)

			pos/wks
19 May 73	ARMED AND EXTREMELY DANGEROUS Bell 1297	16	10
4 Aug 73 ●	SMARTY PANTS Bell 1324	9	11

FIRST CLASS UK, male vocal group (10 WEEKS)

			pos/wks
15 Jun 74	BEACH BABY UK 66	13	10

FIRST EDITION – See Kenny ROGERS

FIRST LIGHT UK, male vocal / instrumental duo (5 WEEKS)

			pos/wks
21 May 83	EXPLAIN THE REASONS London LON 26	65	3
28 Jan 84	WISH YOU WERE HERE London LON 43	71	2

FIRSTBORN Ireland, male producer - Oisin Lunny (1 WEEK)

			pos/wks
19 Jun 99	THE MOOD CLUB Independiente ISOM 28MS	69	1

FISCHER-Z UK, male vocal / instrumental group (7 WEEKS)

			pos/wks
26 May 79	THE WORKER United Artists UP 36509	53	5
3 May 80	SO LONG United Artists BP 342	72	2

FISH UK, male vocalist (20 WEEKS)

			pos/wks
18 Oct 86	SHORT CUT TO SOMEWHERE Charisma CB 426 [1]	75	1
28 Oct 89	STATE OF MIND EMI EM 109	32	3
6 Jan 90	BIG WEDGE EMI EM 125	25	4
17 Mar 90	A GENTLEMAN'S EXCUSE ME EMI EM 135	30	3
28 Sep 91	INTERNAL EXILE Polydor FISHY 1	37	2
11 Jan 92	CREDO Polydor FISHY 2	38	2
4 Jul 92	SOMETHING IN THE AIR Polydor FISHY 3	51	2
16 Apr 94	LADY LET IT LIE Dick Bros. DDICK 3CD1	46	1
1 Oct 94	FORTUNES OF WAR Dick Bros. DDICK 008CD1	67	1
26 Aug 95	JUST GOOD FRIENDS Dick Bros. DDICK 014CD1 [2]	63	1

[1] Fish and Tony Banks [2] Fish featuring Sam Brown

See also MARILLION

FISHBONE US, male vocal / instrumental group (3 WEEKS)

			pos/wks
1 Aug 92	EVERYDAY SUNSHINE / FIGHT THE YOUTH Columbia 6581937	60	2
28 Aug 93	SWIM Columbia 6596252	54	1

Cevin FISHER US, male DJ / producer (7 WEEKS)

			pos/wks
3 Oct 98	THE FREAKS COME OUT Ministry of Sound MOSCDS 127 [1]	34	2
20 Feb 99	(YOU GOT ME) BURNING UP Wonderboy WBOYD 013 [2]	14	4
7 Aug 99	MUSIC SAVED MY LIFE Sm:)e Communications SM 90982	67	1

[1] Cevin Fisher's Big Break [2] Cevin Fisher / Loleatta Holloway

Eddie FISHER (277 Top 500) Leading 1950s heartthrob, b. 10 Aug 1929, Philadelphia. The US's most successful male singer between 1950-1954; accumulated many more UK hits in the pre-chart years. Married Elizabeth Taylor, Debbie Reynolds and Connie Stevens and is father of the actress Carrie Fisher (105 WEEKS)

			pos/wks
2 Jan 53 ★	OUTSIDE OF HEAVEN HMV B 10362	1	16
23 Jan 53	EVERYTHING I HAVE IS YOURS HMV B 10398	12	1
6 Feb 53 ●	EVERYTHING I HAVE IS YOURS (re-entry) HMV B 10398	8	4
1 May 53 ●	DOWNHEARTED HMV B 10450	3	15
1 May 53	OUTSIDE OF HEAVEN (re-entry) HMV B 10362	12	1
22 May 53 ★	I'M WALKING BEHIND YOU HMV B 10564 [1] ▲	1	18
6 Nov 53 ●	WISH YOU WERE HERE HMV B 10564	8	9
22 Jan 54 ●	OH MY PAPA (OH MEIN PAPA) HMV B 10614 ▲	9	1
5 Feb 54	OH MY PAPA (OH MEIN PAPA) (re-entry) HMV B 10614	11	1
26 Feb 54 ●	OH MY PAPA (OH MEIN PAPA) (2nd re-entry) HMV B 10614	10	1
12 Mar 54	OH MY PAPA (OH MEIN PAPA) (3rd re-entry) HMV B 10614	11	1
29 Oct 54	I NEED YOU NOW HMV B 10755 ▲	16	2
19 Nov 54	I NEED YOU NOW (re-entry) HMV B 10755	13	7
21 Jan 55	I NEED YOU NOW (2nd re-entry) HMV B 10755	19	1
18 Mar 55 ●	(I'M ALWAYS HEARING) WEDDING BELLS HMV B 10839	5	11
23 Nov 56 ●	CINDY, OH CINDY HMV POP 273	5	16

[1] Eddie Fisher with Sally Sweetland (soprano)

Mark FISHER featuring Dotty GREEN UK, male instrumentalist - keyboards and female vocalist (2 WEEKS)

			pos/wks
29 Jun 85	LOVE SITUATION Total Control TOCO 3	59	2

Toni FISHER US, female vocalist (1 WEEK)

			pos/wks
12 Feb 60	THE BIG HURT Top Rank JAR 261	30	1

FITS OF GLOOM UK / Italy, male vocal duo (4 WEEKS)

			pos/wks
4 Jun 94	HEAVEN Media MCSTD 1981	47	2
5 Nov 94	THE POWER OF LOVE Media MCSTD 2016 [1]	49	2

[1] Fits of Gloom featuring Lizzy Mack

UK No.1 ★ UK Top 10 ● Still on chart + UK million seller ◆ UK entry at No.1 ■ US No.1 ▲

Ella FITZGERALD *US, female vocalist (29 WEEKS)*

			pos/wks
23 May 58		SWINGIN' SHEPHERD BLUES *HMV POP 486*	15 5
16 Oct 59		BUT NOT FOR ME *HMV POP 657*	25 2
25 Dec 59		BUT NOT FOR ME (re-entry) *HMV POP 657*	29 1
21 Apr 60		MACK THE KNIFE *HMV POP 736*	19 9
6 Oct 60		HOW HIGH THE MOON *HMV POP 782*	46 1
22 Nov 62		DESAFINADO *Verve VS 502*	38 4
27 Dec 62		DESAFINADO (re-entry) *Verve VS 502*	41 2
30 Apr 64		CAN'T BUY ME LOVE *Verve VS 519*	34 5

Scott FITZGERALD
UK, male vocalist - William McPhail (12 WEEKS)

			pos/wks
14 Jan 78	●	IF I HAD WORDS *Pepper UP 36333* [1]	3 10
7 May 88		GO *PRT PYS 10*	52 2

[1] Scott Fitzgerald and Yvonne Keeley and the St Thomas More School Choir

FIVE 254 *Top 500*
Superior all-boy vocal group: Abs Breen, Jay Brown, Sean Conlon, Rich Neville, Scott Robinson. Eponymous debut album sold more than four million worldwide and quintet's self-penned seventh successive Top 10 entry (in two years) took them to the top after three successive No.2s (109 WEEKS)

			pos/wks
13 Dec 97	●	SLAM DUNK (DA FUNK) *RCA 74321537352*	10 9
14 Mar 98	●	WHEN THE LIGHTS GO OUT *RCA 74321562312*	4 9
20 Jun 98	●	GOT THE FEELIN' *RCA 74321584892*	3 13
12 Sep 98	●	EVERYBODY GET UP *RCA 74321613752*	2 12
28 Nov 98	●	UNTIL THE TIME IS THROUGH *RCA 74321632602*	2 12
31 Jul 99	●	IF YA GETTIN' DOWN *RCA 74321689692*	2 12
6 Nov 99	★	KEEP ON MOVIN' *RCA 74321709862* ■	1 17
18 Mar 00	●	DON'T WANNA LET YOU GO *RCA 74321745292*	9 12
29 Jul 00	★	WE WILL ROCK YOU *RCA 74321774022* [1] ■	1 12
4 Nov 00		WE WILL ROCK YOU (re-entry) *RCA 74321774022* [1]	72 1

[1] Five & Queen

FIVE SMITH BROTHERS *UK, male vocal group (1 WEEK)*

			pos/wks
22 Jul 55		I'M IN FAVOUR OF FRIENDSHIP *Decca F 10527*	20 1

FIVE STAR 171 *Top 500*
Britain's best known black family act: Deniece, Doris, Stedman, Lorraine and Delroy Pearson. The Essex-based group became the youngest act to top the LP chart with the UK million seller Silk and Steel. In 1987 they were voted Top British Group in Smash Hits and at Brit Awards (140 WEEKS)

			pos/wks
4 May 85		ALL FALL DOWN *Tent PB 40039*	15 12
20 Jul 85		LET ME BE THE ONE *Tent PB 40193*	18 9
14 Sep 85		LOVE TAKE OVER *Tent PB 40353*	25 9
16 Nov 85		RSVP *Tent PB 40445*	45 5
11 Jan 86	●	SYSTEM ADDICT *Tent PB 40515*	3 11
12 Apr 86	●	CAN'T WAIT ANOTHER MINUTE *Tent PB 40697*	7 10
26 Jul 86		FIND THE TIME *Tent PB 40799*	7 10
13 Sep 86	●	RAIN OR SHINE *Tent PB 40901*	2 11
22 Nov 86		IF I SAY YES *Tent PB 40981*	15 9
7 Feb 87	●	STAY OUT OF MY LIFE *Tent PB 41131*	9 8
18 Apr 87	●	THE SLIGHTEST TOUCH *Tent PB 41265*	4 9
22 Aug 87		WHENEVER YOU'RE READY *Tent PB 41477*	11 6
10 Oct 87		STRONG AS STEEL *Tent PB 41565*	16 7
5 Dec 87		SOMEWHERE SOMEBODY *Tent PB 41661*	23 6
4 Jun 88		ANOTHER WEEKEND *Tent PB 42081*	18 4
6 Aug 88		ROCK MY WORLD *Tent PB 42145*	28 4
17 Sep 88		THERE'S A BRAND NEW WORLD *Tent PB 42235*	61 2
19 Nov 88		LET ME BE YOURS *Tent PB 42343*	51 3
8 Apr 89		WITH EVERY HEARTBEAT *Tent PB 42693*	49 2
10 Mar 90		TREAT ME LIKE A LADY *Tent FIVE 1*	54 2
7 Jul 90		HOT LOVE *Tent FIVE 2*	68 1

FIVE THIRTY *UK, male vocal / instrumental group (4 WEEKS)*

			pos/wks
4 Aug 90		ABSTAIN *East West YZ 530*	75 1
25 May 91		13TH DISCIPLE *East West YZ 577*	67 1
3 Aug 91		SUPERNOVA *East West YZ 594*	75 1
2 Nov 91		YOU (EP *East West YZ 624*	72 1

Tracks on You (EP): You / Cuddly Drug / Slow Train into the Ocean

5000 VOLTS
UK, male / female vocal / instrumental group (18 WEEKS)

			pos/wks
6 Sep 75	●	I'M ON FIRE *Philips 6006 464*	4 9
24 Jul 76	●	DR KISS KISS *Philips 6006 533*	8 9

FIXX *UK, male vocal / instrumental group (8 WEEKS)*

			pos/wks
24 Apr 82		STAND OR FALL *MCA FIXX 2*	54 4
17 Jul 82		RED SKIES *MCA FIXX 3*	57 4

FKW *UK, male vocal / instrumental group (8 WEEKS)*

			pos/wks
2 Oct 93		NEVER GONNA (GIVE YOU UP) *PWL International PWCD 273*	48 2
11 Dec 93		SEIZE THE DAY *PWL International PWCD 279*	45 2
5 Mar 94		JINGO *PWL International PWCD 283*	30 3
4 Jun 94		THIS IS THE WAY *PWL International PWCD 307*	63 1

Roberta FLACK 417 *Top 500*
Groundbreaking, song stylist / pianist, b. 10 Feb 1939, North Carolina, US. Recorded original hit 'Killing Me Softly with His Song' (written about Don McLean) and was the first black female soloist to top the US album chart (First Take - 1972) (79 WEEKS)

			pos/wks
27 May 72		THE FIRST TIME EVER I SAW YOUR FACE *Atlantic K 10161* ▲	14 14
5 Aug 72		WHERE IS THE LOVE *Atlantic K 10202* [1]	29 7
17 Feb 73	●	KILLING ME SOFTLY WITH HIS SONG *Atlantic K 10282* ▲	6 14
24 Aug 74		FEEL LIKE MAKING LOVE *Atlantic K 10467* ▲	34 7
6 May 78		THE CLOSER I GET TO YOU *Atlantic K 11099* [1]	42 4
17 May 80	●	BACK TOGETHER AGAIN *Atlantic K 11481* [1]	3 11
30 Aug 80		DON'T MAKE ME WAIT TOO LONG *Atlantic K 11555*	44 7
20 Aug 83	●	TONIGHT I CELEBRATE MY LOVE *Capitol CL 302* [2]	2 13
29 Jul 89		UH-UH OOH OOH LOOK OUT (HERE IT COMES) *Atlantic A 8941*	72 2

[1] Roberta Flack and Donny Hathaway [2] Peabo Bryson and Roberta Flack

FLAJ – See GETO BOYS featuring FLAJ

FLAMING LIPS *US, male vocal / instrumental group (4 WEEKS)*

			pos/wks
9 Mar 96		THIS HERE GIRAFFE *Warner Bros. W 0335CD*	72 1
26 Jun 99		RACE FOR THE PRIZE *Warner Bros. W 494CD1*	39 2
20 Nov 99		WAITIN' FOR A SUPERMAN *Warner Bros. W 505CD1*	73 1

FLAMINGOS *US, male vocal group (5 WEEKS)*

			pos/wks
4 Jun 69		BOOGALOO PARTY *Philips BF 1786*	26 5

Michael FLANDERS *UK, male vocalist (3 WEEKS)*

			pos/wks
27 Feb 59		LITTLE DRUMMER BOY *Parlophone R 4528* [1]	20 2
17 Apr 59		LITTLE DRUMMER BOY (re-entry) *Parlophone R 4528* [1]	24 1

[1] with the Michael Sammes Singers

FLASH and the PAN
Australia, male vocal / instrumental group (15 WEEKS)

			pos/wks
23 Sep 78		AND THE BAND PLAYED ON (DOWN AMONG THE DEAD MEN) *Ensign ENY 15*	54 4
21 May 83	●	WAITING FOR A TRAIN *Easybeat EASY 1*	7 11

Lester FLATT and Earl SCRUGGS
US, male instrumental duo - banjos (6 WEEKS)

			pos/wks
15 Nov 67		FOGGY MOUNTAIN BREAKDOWN *CBS 3038 and Mercury MF 1007*	39 6

The versions on the two labels were not the same cuts; CBS had a 1965 recording, Mercury a 1949 recording. The chart did not differentiate and listed both together

Fogwell FLAX and the ANKLEBITERS from FREEHOLD JUNIOR SCHOOL *UK, male vocalist and school choir (2 WEEKS)*

			pos/wks
26 Dec 81		ONE NINE FOR SANTA *EMI 5255*	68 2

FLEE-REKKERS *UK, male instrumental group (13 WEEKS)*

			pos/wks
19 May 60		GREEN JEANS *Triumph RGM 1008*	23 13

FLEETWOOD MAC `66` `Top 500` *Record-breaking Anglo-American act.*
Members included: Mick Fleetwood (d), John McVie (b), Peter Green (g), Christine McVie (k/v), Lindsey Buckingham (g/v), Stevie Nicks (v). Grammy-winning album Rumours sold more than 18 million copies in the US alone and has spent longer at the top of the album chart than any other LP (223 WEEKS) pos/wks

10 Apr 68	BLACK MAGIC WOMAN *Blue Horizon 57 3138*	37 7
17 Jul 68	NEED YOUR LOVE SO BAD *Blue Horizon 57 3139*	31 13
4 Dec 68 ★	ALBATROSS *Blue Horizon 57 3145*	1 20
16 Apr 69 ●	MAN OF THE WORLD *Immediate IM 080*	2 14
23 Jul 69	NEED YOUR LOVE SO BAD (re-issue) *Blue Horizon 57 3157*	32 6
13 Sep 69	NEED YOUR LOVE SO BAD (re-entry of re-issue) *Blue Horizon 57 3157*	42 3
4 Oct 69 ●	OH WELL *Reprise RS 27000*	2 16
23 May 70 ●	THE GREEN MANALISHI (WITH THE TWO-PRONG CROWN) *Reprise RS 27007*	10 12
12 May 73 ●	ALBATROSS (re-issue) *CBS 8306*	2 15
13 Nov 76	SAY YOU LOVE ME *Reprise K 14447*	40 4
19 Feb 77	GO YOUR OWN WAY *Warner Bros. K 16872*	38 4
30 Apr 77	DON'T STOP *Warner Bros. K 16930*	32 5
9 Jul 77	DREAMS *Warner Bros. K 16969* ▲	24 9
22 Oct 77	YOU MAKE LOVING FUN *Warner Bros. K 17013*	45 2
11 Mar 78	RHIANNON *Reprise K 14430*	46 3
6 Oct 79 ●	TUSK *Warner Bros. K 17468*	6 10
22 Dec 79	SARA *Warner Bros. K 17533*	37 8
25 Sep 82	GYPSY *Warner Bros. K 17997*	46 3
18 Dec 82 ●	OH DIANE *Warner Bros. FLEET 1*	9 15
4 Apr 87 ●	BIG LOVE *Warner Bros. W 8398*	9 12
11 Jul 87	SEVEN WONDERS *Warner Bros. W 8317*	56 4
26 Sep 87 ●	LITTLE LIES *Warner Bros. W 8291*	5 12
26 Dec 87	FAMILY MAN *Warner Bros. W 8114*	54 5
2 Apr 88 ●	EVERYWHERE *Warner Bros. W 8143*	4 10
18 Jun 88	ISN'T IT MIDNIGHT *Warner Bros. W 7860*	60 2
17 Dec 88	AS LONG AS YOU FOLLOW *Warner Bros. W 7644*	66 3
5 May 90	SAVE ME *Warner Bros. W 9866*	53 3
25 Aug 90	IN THE BACK OF MY MIND *Warner Bros. W 9739*	58 3

Group was UK and male-only up to and including the re-issue of 'Albatross'

FLEETWOODS *US, male / female vocal group (8 WEEKS)* pos/wks

24 Apr 59 ●	COME SOFTLY TO ME *London HLU 8841* ▲	6 8

John '00' FLEMING *UK, male DJ / producer (2 WEEKS)* pos/wks

25 Dec 99	LOST IN EMOTION *React CDREACT 170*	74 1
12 Aug 00	FREE *React CDREACT 186*	61 1

La FLEUR *Holland, male / female vocal / instrumental group (4 WEEKS)* pos/wks

30 Jul 83	BOOGIE NIGHTS *Proto ENA 111*	51 4

FLICKMAN *Italy, male production duo (5 WEEKS)* pos/wks

4 Mar 00	THE SOUND OF BAMBOO *Inferno CDFERN 25*	11 5

K.C. FLIGHTT *US, male rapper (4 WEEKS)* pos/wks

1 Apr 89	PLANET E *RCA PT 49404*	48 4

Dread FLIMSTONE and the NEW TONE AGE FAMILY
US, male vocal / instrumental group (1 WEEK) pos/wks

30 Nov 91	FROM THE GHETTO *Urban URB 87*	66 1

Berni FLINT *UK, male vocalist (11 WEEKS)* pos/wks

19 Mar 77 ●	I DON'T WANT TO PUT A HOLD ON YOU *EMI 2599*	3 10
23 Jul 77	SOUTHERN COMFORT *EMI 2621*	48 1

FLINTLOCK *UK, male vocal / instrumental group (5 WEEKS)* pos/wks

29 May 76	DAWN *Pinnacle P 8419*	30 5

FLIPMODE SQUAD *US, male / female production / rap group (1 WEEK)* pos/wks

31 Oct 98	CHA CHA CHA *Elektra E 3810CD*	54 1

FLOATERS *US, male vocal group (11 WEEKS)* pos/wks

23 Jul 77 ★	FLOAT ON *ABC 4187*	1 11

A FLOCK OF SEAGULLS
UK, male vocal / instrumental group (46 WEEKS) pos/wks

27 Mar 82	I RAN *Jive JIVE 14*	43 6
12 Jun 82	SPACE AGE LOVE SONG *Jive JIVE 17*	34 6
6 Nov 82 ●	WISHING (IF I HAD A PHOTOGRAPH OF YOU) *Jive JIVE 25*	10 12
23 Apr 83	NIGHTMARES *Jive JIVE 33*	53 3
25 Jun 83	TRANSFER AFFECTION *Jive JIVE 41*	38 5
14 Jul 84	THE MORE YOU LIVE, THE MORE YOU LOVE *Jive JIVE 62*	26 11
19 Oct 85	WHO'S THAT GIRL (SHE'S GOT IT) *Jive JIVE 106*	66 3

FLOORPLAY *UK, male instrumental / production duo (1 WEEK)* pos/wks

27 Jan 96	AUTOMATIC *Perfecto PERF 115CD*	50 1

FLOWERED UP *UK, male vocal / instrumental group (17 WEEKS)* pos/wks

28 Jul 90	IT'S ON *Heavenly HVN 3*	54 4
24 Nov 90	PHOBIA *Heavenly HVN 7*	75 1
11 May 91	TAKE IT *London FUP 1*	34 4
17 Aug 91	IT'S ON / EGG RUSH (re-recording) *London FUP 2*	38 3
2 May 92	WEEKENDER *Heavenly HVN 16*	20 5

FLOWERPOT MEN *UK, male vocal group (12 WEEKS)* pos/wks

23 Aug 67 ●	LET'S GO TO SAN FRANCISCO *Deram DM 142*	4 12

Mike FLOWERS POPS
UK, male / female vocal / instrumental group (14 WEEKS) pos/wks

30 Dec 95 ●	WONDERWALL *London LONCD 378*	2 7
13 Apr 96	WONDERWALL (re-entry) *London LONCD 378*	52 2
8 Jun 96	LIGHT MY FIRE / PLEASE RELEASE ME *London LONCD 384*	39 2
28 Dec 96	DON'T CRY FOR ME ARGENTINA *Love This LUVTHIS 16*	30 3

Eddie FLOYD *US, male vocalist (29 WEEKS)* pos/wks

2 Feb 67	KNOCK ON WOOD *Atlantic 584 041*	50 1
2 Mar 67	KNOCK ON WOOD (re-entry) *Atlantic 584 041*	19 17
16 Mar 67	RAISE YOUR HAND *Stax 601 001*	42 3
9 Aug 67	THINGS GET BETTER *Stax 601 016*	31 8

FLUFFY *UK, female vocal / instrumental group (2 WEEKS)* pos/wks

17 Feb 96	HUSBAND *Parkway PARK 006CD*	58 1
5 Oct 96	NOTHING *Virgin VSCDT 1614*	52 1

FLUKE *UK, male instrumental / production group (20 WEEKS)* pos/wks

20 Mar 93	SLID *Circa YRCD 103*	59 1
19 Jun 93	ELECTRIC GUITAR *Circa YRCD 104*	58 1
11 Sep 93	GROOVY FEELING *Circa YRCD 106*	45 3
23 Apr 94	BUBBLE *Circa YRCD 110*	37 2
29 Jul 95	BULLET *Circa YRCD 121*	23 3
16 Dec 95	TOSH *Circa YRCD 122*	32 3
16 Nov 96	ATOM BOMB *Circa YRCD 125*	20 3
31 May 97	ABSURD *Virgin YRCD 126*	25 2
27 Sep 97	SQUIRT *Circa YRCD 127*	46 1

See also LUCKY MONKEYS

FLUSH – See SLADE

FLYING LIZARDS
UK, male / female vocal / instrumental group (16 WEEKS) pos/wks

4 Aug 79 ●	MONEY *Virgin VS 276*	5 10
9 Feb 80	TV *Virgin VS 325*	43 6

UK No.1 ★   UK Top 10 ●   Still on chart +   UK million seller ◆   UK entry at No.1 ■   US No.1 ▲

FLYING PICKETS UK, male vocal group (20 WEEKS) — pos/wks

Date		Title	pos	wks
26 Nov 83	★	ONLY YOU *10 TEN 14*	1	11
21 Apr 84	●	WHEN YOU'RE YOUNG AND IN LOVE *10 TEN 20*	7	8
8 Dec 84		WHO'S THAT GIRL *10 GIRL 1*	71	1

Jerome FLYNN – See ROBSON and JEROME

FM UK, male vocal / instrumental group (11 WEEKS) — pos/wks

Date	Title	pos	wks
31 Jan 87	FROZEN HEART *Portrait DIDGE 1*	64	2
20 Jun 87	LET LOVE BE THE LEADER *Portrait MERV 1*	71	2
5 Aug 89	BAD LUCK *Epic 655031 7*	54	4
7 Oct 89	SOMEDAY (YOU'LL COME RUNNING) *CBS DINK 1*	64	2
10 Feb 90	EVERYTIME I THINK OF YOU *Epic DINK 2*	73	1

FOCUS Holland, male instrumental group (21 WEEKS) — pos/wks

Date		Title	pos	wks
20 Jan 73		HOCUS POCUS *Polydor 2001 211*	20	10
27 Jan 73	●	SYLVIA *Polydor 2001 422*	4	11

FOG US, male DJ / producer (4 WEEKS) — pos/wks

Date	Title	pos	wks
19 Feb 94	BEEN A LONG TIME *Columbia 6601212*	44	2
6 Jun 98	BEEN A LONG TIME (re-mix) *Pukka CDPUKKA 16*	27	2

Dan FOGELBERG US, male vocalist (4 WEEKS) — pos/wks

Date	Title	pos	wks
15 Mar 80	LONGER *Epic EPC 8230*	59	4

Ben FOLDS FIVE
US, male vocal / instrumental group (12 WEEKS) — pos/wks

Date	Title	pos	wks
14 Sep 96	UNDERGROUND *Caroline CDCAR 008*	37	2
1 Mar 97	BATTLE OF WHO COULD CARE LESS *Epic 6642302*	26	3
7 Jun 97	KATE *Epic 6645365*	39	2
18 Apr 98	BRICK *Epic 6656612*	26	3
24 Apr 99	ARMY *Epic 6672182*	28	2

FOLK IMPLOSION US, male vocal / instrumental duo (1 WEEK) — pos/wks

Date	Title	pos	wks
15 Jun 96	NATURAL ONE *London LONCD 382*	45	1

Claudia FONTAINE – See BEATMASTERS

Lenny FONTANA & DJ SHORTY
US, male production duo (2 WEEKS) — pos/wks

Date	Title	pos	wks
4 Mar 00	CHOCOLATE SENSATION *ffrr FCD 375*	39	2

Wayne FONTANA UK, male vocalist (76 WEEKS) — pos/wks

Date		Title	pos	wks
11 Jul 63		HELLO JOSEPHINE *Fontana TF 404* [1]	46	2
28 May 64		STOP LOOK AND LISTEN *Fontana TF 451* [1]	37	4
8 Oct 64	●	UM UM UM UM UM UM *Fontana TF 497* [1]	5	15
4 Feb 65	●	GAME OF LOVE *Fontana TF 535* [1] ▲	2	11
17 Jun 65		JUST A LITTLE BIT TOO LATE *Fontana TF 579* [1]	20	7
30 Sep 65		SHE NEEDS LOVE *Fontana TF 611* [1]	32	6
9 Dec 65		IT WAS EASIER TO HURT HER *Fontana TF 642*	36	6
21 Apr 66		COME ON HOME *Fontana TF 684*	16	12
25 Aug 66		GOODBYE BLUEBIRD *Fontana TF 737*	49	1
8 Dec 66		PAMELA PAMELA *Fontana TF 770*	11	12

[1] Wayne Fontana and the Mindbenders

See also MINDBENDERS

FOO FIGHTERS US, male vocal / instrumental group (32 WEEKS) — pos/wks

Date		Title	pos	wks
1 Jul 95	●	THIS IS A CALL *Roswell CDCL 753*	5	4
16 Sep 95		I'LL STICK AROUND *Roswell CDCL 757*	18	3
2 Dec 95		FOR ALL THE COWS *Roswell CDCL 762*	28	2
6 Apr 96		BIG ME *Roswell CDCL 768*	19	3
10 May 97		MONKEY WRENCH *Roswell CDCLS 788*	12	4
30 Aug 97		EVERLONG *Roswell CDCL 792*	18	3
31 Jan 98		MY HERO *Roswell CDCL 796*	21	2
29 Aug 98		WALKING AFTER YOU; BEACON LIGHT *Elektra E 4100CD* [1]	20	3
30 Oct 99		LEARN TO FLY *RCA 74321706622*	21	3
30 Sep 00		BREAKOUT *RCA 74321790102*	29	3
16 Dec 00		NEXT YEAR *RCA 74321809262*	42	2

[1] Foo Fighters: Ween

FOOL BOONA UK, male DJ / producer - Colin Tevendale (1 WEEK) — pos/wks

Date	Title	pos	wks
10 Apr 99	POPPED!! *Virgin / VC Recordings / Uber Disko VCRD 46*	52	1

FOOL'S GARDEN
Germany, male vocal / instrumental group (4 WEEKS) — pos/wks

Date	Title	pos	wks
25 May 96	LEMON TREE *Encore CDCOR 014*	61	1
3 Aug 96	LEMON TREE (re-issue) *Encore CDCOR 018*	26	3

FOR REAL US, female vocal group (2 WEEKS) — pos/wks

Date	Title	pos	wks
1 Jul 95	YOU DON'T KNOW NOTHIN' *A & M 5811232*	54	1
12 Jul 97	LIKE I DO *Rowdy 74321486582*	45	1

Bill FORBES UK, male vocalist (1 WEEK) — pos/wks

Date	Title	pos	wks
15 Jan 60	TOO YOUNG *Columbia DB 4386*	29	1

FORBIDDEN – See Jet BRONX and the FORBIDDEN

FORCE & STYLES featuring Kelly LLORENNA
UK, male DJ duo (1 WEEK) — pos/wks

Date	Title	pos	wks
25 Jul 98	HEART OF GOLD *Diverse VERSE 2CD*	55	1

FORCE MDs US, male vocal group (9 WEEKS) — pos/wks

Date	Title	pos	wks
12 Apr 86	TENDER LOVE *Tommy Boy IS 269*	23	9

Clinton FORD UK, male vocalist (25 WEEKS) — pos/wks

Date	Title	pos	wks
23 Oct 59	OLD SHEP *Oriole CB 1500*	27	1
17 Aug 61	TOO MANY BEAUTIFUL GIRLS *Oriole CB 1623*	48	1
8 Mar 62	FANLIGHT FANNY *Oriole CB 1706*	22	10
5 Jan 67	RUN TO THE DOOR *Piccadilly 7N 35361*	25	13

Emile FORD and the CHECKMATES (356 | Top 500)
First group to top the chart in the 1960s, fronted by vocalist b. Emile Sweatman 16 Oct 1937, Bahamas. UK-based multi-racial act had five consecutive Top 20 entries - three with updates of oldies. NME readers voted them Best New Act 1960
(87 WEEKS) — pos/wks

Date		Title	pos	wks
30 Oct 59	★	WHAT DO YOU WANT TO MAKE THOSE EYES AT ME FOR *Pye 7N 15225*	1	25
5 Feb 60	●	ON A SLOW BOAT TO CHINA *Pye 7N 15245*	3	14
26 May 60		YOU'LL NEVER KNOW WHAT YOU'RE MISSING ('TIL YOU TRY) *Pye 7N 15268*	12	9
1 Sep 60		THEM THERE EYES *Pye 7N 15282* [1]	18	16
8 Dec 60	●	COUNTING TEARDROPS *Pye 7N 15314*	4	12
2 Mar 61		WHAT AM I GONNA DO *Pye 7N 15331*	33	2
18 May 61		HALF OF MY HEART *Piccadilly 7N 35003* [1]	50	1
22 Jun 61		HALF OF MY HEART (re-entry) *Piccadilly 7N 35003* [1]	42	3
8 Mar 62		I WONDER WHO'S KISSING HER NOW *Piccadilly 7N 35033* [1]	43	1

[1] Emile Ford

Lita FORD UK, female vocalist (7 WEEKS) — pos/wks

Date	Title	pos	wks
17 Dec 88	KISS ME DEADLY *RCA PB 49575*	75	1
20 May 89	CLOSE MY EYES FOREVER *Dreamland PB 49409* [1]	47	3
11 Jan 92	SHOT OF POISON *RCA PB 49145*	63	3

[1] Lita Ford duet with Ozzy Osbourne

Martyn FORD ORCHESTRA UK, orchestra (3 WEEKS) — pos/wks

Date	Title	pos	wks
14 May 77	LET YOUR BODY GO DOWNTOWN *Mountain TOP 26*	38	3

Mary FORD – See Les PAUL and Mary FORD

UK No.1 ★   UK Top 10 ●   Still on chart +   UK million seller ◆   UK entry at No.1 ■   US No.1 ▲

Penny FORD US, female vocalist (7 WEEKS)

			pos/wks
4 May 85	DANGEROUS Total Experience FB 49975 [1]		43 5
29 May 93	DAYDREAMING Columbia 6590592		43 2

[1] Pennye Ford

See also SNAP

Tennessee Ernie FORD US, male vocalist (42 WEEKS)

			pos/wks
21 Jan 55	★ GIVE ME YOUR WORD Capitol CL 14005		1 24
6 Jan 56	★ SIXTEEN TONS Capitol CL 14500 ▲		1 11
13 Jan 56	● THE BALLAD OF DAVY CROCKETT Capitol CL 14506		3 7

Julia FORDHAM UK, female vocalist (32 WEEKS)

			pos/wks
2 Jul 88	HAPPY EVER AFTER Circa YR 15		27 9
25 Feb 89	WHERE DOES THE TIME GO Circa YR 23		41 5
31 Aug 91	I THOUGHT IT WAS YOU Circa YR 69		64 2
18 Jan 92	LOVE MOVES (IN MYSTERIOUS WAYS) Circa YR 73		19 9
30 May 92	I THOUGHT IT WAS YOU (re-mix) Circa YR 90		45 3
30 Apr 94	DIFFERENT TIME DIFFERENT PLACE Circa YRCD 111		41 3
23 Jul 94	I CAN'T HELP MYSELF Circa YRCD 116		62 1

FOREIGNER (419 Top 500) Melodic Anglo-American rock group who amassed six US Top 10 albums. Featured Londoner Mick Jones (g) and New York native Lou Gramm (v). 'Waiting for a Girl Like You' stayed at No.2 in US for record-breaking 10 weeks (78 WEEKS)

			pos/wks
6 May 78	FEELS LIKE THE FIRST TIME Atlantic K 11086		39 6
15 Jul 78	COLD AS ICE Atlantic K 10986		24 10
28 Oct 78	HOT BLOODED Atlantic K 11167		42 3
24 Feb 79	BLUE MORNING BLUE DAY Atlantic K 11236		45 4
29 Aug 81	URGENT Atlantic K 11665		54 4
10 Oct 81	JUKE BOX HERO Atlantic K 11678		48 4
12 Dec 81	● WAITING FOR A GIRL LIKE YOU Atlantic K 11696		8 13
8 May 82	URGENT (re-issue) Atlantic K 11728		45 5
8 Dec 84	★ I WANT TO KNOW WHAT LOVE IS Atlantic A 9596 ▲		1 16
6 Apr 85	THAT WAS YESTERDAY Atlantic A 9571		28 6
22 Jun 85	COLD AS ICE (re-mix) Atlantic A 9539		64 2
19 Dec 87	SAY YOU WILL Atlantic A 9169		71 4
22 Oct 94	WHITE LIE Arista 74321232862		58 1

FORMATIONS US, male vocal group (11 WEEKS)

			pos/wks
31 Jul 71	AT THE TOP OF THE STAIRS Mojo 2027 001		50 1
14 Aug 71	AT THE TOP OF THE STAIRS (re-entry) Mojo 2027 001		28 10

George FORMBY UK, male vocalist / instrumentalist - ukelele (3 WEEKS)

			pos/wks
21 Jul 60	HAPPY GO LUCKY ME / BANJO BOY Pye 7N 15269		40 3

See also 2 IN A TENT

FORREST US, male vocalist - Forrest M Thomas Jr (20 WEEKS)

			pos/wks
26 Feb 83	● ROCK THE BOAT CBS A 3163		4 10
14 May 83	FEEL THE NEED IN ME CBS A 3411		17 8
17 Sep 83	ONE LOVER (DON'T STOP THE SHOW) CBS A 3734		67 2

Sharon FORRESTER Jamaica, female vocalist (1 WEEK)

			pos/wks
11 Feb 95	LOVE INSIDE ffrr FCD 253		50 1

Lance FORTUNE UK, male vocalist - Chris Morris (17 WEEKS)

			pos/wks
19 Feb 60	● BE MINE Pye 7N 15240		4 12
5 May 60	THIS LOVE I HAVE FOR YOU Pye 7N 15260		26 5

FORTUNES UK, male vocal / instrumental group (65 WEEKS)

			pos/wks
8 Jul 65	● YOU'VE GOT YOUR TROUBLES Decca F 12173		2 14
7 Oct 65	● HERE IT COMES AGAIN Decca F 12243		4 14
3 Feb 66	THIS GOLDEN RING Decca F 12321		15 9
11 Sep 71	● FREEDOM COME FREEDOM GO Capitol CL 15693		6 17
29 Jan 72	● STORM IN A TEACUP Capitol CL 15707		7 11

FOSTER and ALLEN Ireland, male vocal duo (47 WEEKS)

			pos/wks
27 Feb 82	A BUNCH OF THYME Ritz RITZ 5		18 11
30 Oct 82	OLD FLAMES Ritz RITZ 028		51 8
19 Feb 83	MAGGIE Ritz RITZ 025		27 9
29 Oct 83	I WILL LOVE YOU ALL MY LIFE Ritz RITZ 056		49 6
30 Jun 84	JUST FOR OLD TIME'S SAKE Ritz RITZ 066		47 6
29 Mar 86	AFTER ALL THESE YEARS Ritz RITZ 106		43 7

Itsy FOSTER – See EXOTICA featuring Itsy FOSTER

FOUNDATIONS West Indies / UK / Sri Lanka, male vocal / instrumental group (57 WEEKS)

			pos/wks
27 Sep 67	★ BABY NOW THAT I'VE FOUND YOU Pye 7N 17366		1 16
24 Jan 68	BACK ON MY FEET AGAIN Pye 7N 17417		18 10
1 May 68	ANY OLD TIME Pye 7N 17503		48 1
15 May 68	ANY OLD TIME (re-entry) Pye 7N 17503		50 1
20 Nov 68	● BUILD ME UP BUTTERCUP Pye 7N 17636		2 15
12 Mar 69	● IN THE BAD BAD OLD DAYS Pye 7N 17702		8 10
13 Sep 69	BORN TO LIVE AND BORN TO DIE Pye 7N 17809		46 3
12 Dec 98	BUILD ME UP BUTTERCUP (re-issue) Castle NEEX 1001		71 1

FOUNTAINS OF WAYNE US, male vocal / instrumental group (7 WEEKS)

			pos/wks
22 Mar 97	RADIATION VIBE Atlantic 7567956262		32 2
10 May 97	SINK TO THE BOTTOM Atlantic A 5612CD		42 1
26 Jul 97	SURVIVAL CAR Atlantic AT 0004CD		53 1
27 Dec 97	I WANT AN ALIEN FOR CHRISTMAS Atlantic AT 0020CD		36 2
20 Mar 99	DENISE Atlantic AT 0053CD		57 1

FOUR ACES US, male vocal group (40 WEEKS)

			pos/wks
30 Jul 54	● THREE COINS IN THE FOUNTAIN Brunswick 05308 [1]		5 5
22 Oct 54	THREE COINS IN THE FOUNTAIN (re-entry) Brunswick 05308 [1]		17 1
7 Jan 55	● MISTER SANDMAN Brunswick 05355 [1]		9 5
20 May 55	STRANGER IN PARADISE Brunswick 05418		6 6
18 Nov 55	● LOVE IS A MANY SPLENDORED THING Brunswick 05480 [1] ▲		2 13
19 Oct 56	A WOMAN IN LOVE Brunswick 05589 [1]		19 3
4 Jan 57	FRIENDLY PERSUASION Brunswick 05623 [1]		29 1
23 Jan 59	THE WORLD OUTSIDE Brunswick 05773		18 6

[1] Four Aces featuring Al Alberts

FOUR BUCKETEERS UK, male / female vocal group (6 WEEKS)

			pos/wks
3 May 80	THE BUCKET OF WATER SONG CBS 8393		26 6

FOUR ESQUIRES US, male vocal group (2 WEEKS)

			pos/wks
31 Jan 58	LOVE ME FOREVER London HLO 8533		23 2

4 HERO UK, male instrumental group (5 WEEKS)

			pos/wks
24 Nov 90	MR KIRK'S NIGHTMARE Reinforced RIVET 1203		73 2
9 May 92	COOKIN' UP YAH BRAIN Reinforced RIVET 1216		59 2
15 Aug 98	STAR CHASERS Talkin' Loud TLCD 36		41 1

400 BLOWS UK, male vocal / instrumental duo (4 WEEKS)

			pos/wks
29 Jun 85	MOVIN' Illuminated ILL 61		54 4

FOUR JAYS – See Billy FURY

FOUR KESTRELS – See Billy FURY

FOUR KNIGHTS US, male vocal group (11 WEEKS)

			pos/wks
4 Jun 54	● (OH BABY MINE) I GET SO LONELY Capitol CL 14076		5 7
30 Jul 54	● (OH BABY MINE) I GET SO LONELY (re-entry) Capitol CL 14076		10 4

FOUR LADS Canada, male vocal group (23 WEEKS)

			pos/wks
19 Dec 52	● FAITH CAN MOVE MOUNTAINS Columbia DB 3154 [1]		7 2
9 Jan 53	● FAITH CAN MOVE MOUNTAINS (re-entry) Columbia DB 3154 [1]		9 1

| 22 Oct 54 ● | RAIN RAIN RAIN *Philips PB 311* [2] | 8 | 16 |
| 28 Apr 60 | STANDING ON THE CORNER *Philips PB 1000* | 34 | 4 |

[1] Johnnie Ray and the Four Lads [2] Frankie Laine and the Four Lads

4 NON BLONDES
US, female / male vocal / instrumental group (19 WEEKS) pos/wks

| 19 Jun 93 ● | WHAT'S UP *Interscope A 8412CD* | 2 | 17 |
| 16 Oct 93 | SPACEMAN *Interscope A 8349CD* | 53 | 2 |

4 OF US *Ireland, male vocal / instrumental group (6 WEEKS)* pos/wks

| 27 Feb 93 | SHE HITS ME *Columbia 6589192* | 35 | 4 |
| 1 May 93 | I MISS YOU *Columbia 6591722* | 62 | 2 |

FOUR PENNIES *UK, male vocal / instrumental group - lead vocal Lionel Morton (56 WEEKS)* pos/wks

16 Jan 64	DO YOU WANT ME TO *Philips BF 1296*	47	1
6 Feb 64	DO YOU WANT ME TO (re-entry) *Philips BF 1296*	49	1
2 Apr 64 ★	JULIET *Philips BF 1322*	1	15
16 Jul 64	I FOUND OUT THE HARD WAY *Philips BF 1349*	14	11
29 Oct 64	BLACK GIRL *Philips BF 1366*	20	12
7 Oct 65	UNTIL IT'S TIME FOR YOU TO GO *Philips BF 1435*	19	11
17 Feb 66	TROUBLE IS MY MIDDLE NAME *Philips BF 1469*	32	5

FOUR PREPS *US, male vocal group (23 WEEKS)* pos/wks

13 Jun 58 ●	BIG MAN *Capitol CL 14873*	2	13
19 Sep 58	BIG MAN (re-entry) *Capitol CL 14873*	22	1
26 May 60	GOT A GIRL *Capitol CL 15128*	28	6
14 Jul 60	GOT A GIRL (re-entry) *Capitol CL 15128*	47	1
2 Nov 61	MORE MONEY FOR YOU AND ME (MEDLEY) *Capitol CL 15217*	39	2

Tracks on medley: Mr Blue / Alley Oop / Smoke Gets in Your Eyes / In This Whole Wide World / A Worried Man / Tom Dooley / A Teenager in Love - all songs feature new lyrics

FOUR SEASONS ⟨342⟩ ⟨Top 500⟩ *No.1 US group of the early 1960s: Frankie Valli (v), Bob Gaudio (k/v), Nick Massi (b/v) (died 2000), Tommy DeVito (g/v). Falsetto-voiced Valli's quartet, the first group to score three US No.1s in succession, has a chart span there of almost 40 years. (151 WEEKS)* pos/wks

4 Oct 62 ●	SHERRY *Stateside SS 122* ▲	8	16
17 Jan 63	BIG GIRLS DON'T CRY *Stateside SS 145* ▲	13	10
28 Mar 63	WALK LIKE A MAN *Stateside SS 169* ▲	12	12
27 Jun 63	AIN'T THAT A SHAME *Stateside SS 194*	38	3
27 Aug 64 ●	RAG DOLL *Philips BF 1347* [1] ▲	2	13
18 Nov 65 ●	LET'S HANG ON *Philips BF 1439* [1]	4	16
31 Mar 66	WORKIN' MY WAY BACK TO YOU *Philips BF 1474* [2]	50	3
2 Jun 66	OPUS 17 (DON'T YOU WORRY 'BOUT ME) *Philips BF 1493* [2]	20	9
29 Sep 66	I'VE GOT YOU UNDER MY SKIN *Philips BF 1511* [2]	12	11
12 Jan 67	TELL IT TO THE RAIN *Philips BF 1538* [2]	37	5
19 Apr 75	NIGHT *Mowest MW 3024* [3]	7	9
20 Sep 75 ●	WHO LOVES YOU *Warner Bros. K 16602*	6	9
31 Jan 76 ★	DECEMBER '63 (OH WHAT A NIGHT) *Warner Bros. K 16688* ▲	1	10
24 Apr 76 ●	SILVER STAR *Warner Bros. K 16742*	3	9
27 Nov 76	WE CAN WORK IT OUT *Warner Bros. K 16845*	34	4
18 Jun 77	RHAPSODY *Warner Bros. K 16932*	37	3
20 Aug 77	DOWN THE HALL *Warner Bros. K 16982*	34	5
29 Oct 88	DECEMBER '63 (OH WHAT A NIGHT) (re-mix) *BR 45277* [3]	49	4

[1] Four Seasons with the sound of Frankie Valli [2] Four Seasons with Frankie Valli [3] Frankie Valli and the Four Seasons

4 STRINGS
Holland, male / female production / vocal duo (2 WEEKS) pos/wks

| 23 Dec 00 | DAY TIME *Island CDAMPM 139* | 48 | 2+ |

4 THE CAUSE *US, male / female vocal group (9 WEEKS)* pos/wks

| 10 Oct 98 | STAND BY ME *RCA 74321622442* | 12 | 9 |

FOUR TOPS ⟨27⟩ ⟨Top 500⟩ *Unmistakable R&B vocal group from Detroit: Levi Stubbs, Renaldo Benson, Lawrence Payton (d. 1997), Abdul Fakir. Legendary Motown act, who performed together for a record 44 years (until Payton's death) and were inducted into the Rock and Roll Hall of Fame in 1990 (318 WEEKS)* pos/wks

1 Jul 65	I CAN'T HELP MYSELF *Tamla Motown TMG 515* ▲	23	9
2 Sep 65	IT'S THE SAME OLD SONG *Tamla Motown TMG 528*	34	8
21 Jul 66	LOVING YOU IS SWEETER THAN EVER *Tamla Motown TMG 568*	21	12
13 Oct 66 ★	REACH OUT I'LL BE THERE *Tamla Motown TMG 579* ▲	1	16
12 Jan 67 ●	STANDING IN THE SHADOWS OF LOVE *Tamla Motown TMG 589*	6	8
30 Mar 67 ●	BERNADETTE *Tamla Motown TMG 601*	8	10
15 Jun 67	SEVEN ROOMS OF GLOOM *Tamla Motown TMG 612*	12	9
11 Oct 67	YOU KEEP RUNNING AWAY *Tamla Motown TMG 623*	26	7
13 Dec 67 ●	WALK AWAY RENEE *Tamla Motown TMG 634*	3	11
13 Mar 68 ●	IF I WERE A CARPENTER *Tamla Motown TMG 647*	7	11
21 Aug 68	YESTERDAY'S DREAMS *Tamla Motown TMG 665*	23	15
13 Nov 68	I'M IN A DIFFERENT WORLD *Tamla Motown TMG 675*	27	13
28 May 69	WHAT IS A MAN *Tamla Motown TMG 698*	16	11
27 Sep 69	DO WHAT YOU GOTTA DO *Tamla Motown TMG 710*	11	11
21 Mar 70 ●	I CAN'T HELP MYSELF (re-issue) *Tamla Motown TMG 732*	10	11
30 May 70 ●	IT'S ALL IN THE GAME *Tamla Motown TMG 736*	5	14
12 Sep 70	IT'S ALL IN THE GAME (re-entry) *Tamla Motown TMG 736*	48	2
3 Oct 70 ●	STILL WATER (LOVE) *Tamla Motown TMG 752*	10	10
19 Dec 70	STILL WATER (LOVE) (re-entry) *Tamla Motown TMG 752*	44	2
1 May 71	JUST SEVEN NUMBERS (CAN STRAIGHTEN OUT MY LIFE) *Tamla Motown TMG 770*	36	5
26 Jun 71	RIVER DEEP MOUNTAIN HIGH *Tamla Motown TMG 777* [1]	11	10
25 Sep 71 ●	SIMPLE GAME *Tamla Motown TMG 785*	3	11
20 Nov 71	YOU GOTTA HAVE LOVE IN YOUR HEART *Tamla Motown TMG 793* [1]	25	10
11 Mar 72	BERNADETTE (re-issue) *Tamla Motown TMG 803*	23	7
5 Aug 72	WALK WITH ME TALK WITH ME DARLING *Tamla Motown TMG 823*	32	6
18 Nov 72	KEEPER OF THE CASTLE *Probe PRO 575*	18	9
10 Nov 73	SWEET UNDERSTANDING LOVE *Probe PRO 604*	29	10
17 Oct 81 ●	WHEN SHE WAS MY GIRL *Casablanca CAN 1005*	3	10
19 Dec 81	DON'T WALK AWAY *Casablanca CAN 1006*	16	11
6 Mar 82	TONIGHT I'M GONNA LOVE YOU ALL OVER *Casablanca CAN 1008*	43	4
26 Jun 82	BACK TO SCHOOL AGAIN *RSO 89*	62	2
23 Jul 88	REACH OUT I'LL BE THERE (re-mix) *Motown ZB 41943*	11	9
17 Sep 88	INDESTRUCTIBLE *Arista 111717* [2]	55	4
3 Dec 88 ●	LOCO IN ACAPULCO *Arista 111850*	7	13
25 Feb 89	INDESTRUCTIBLE *Arista 112074* [2]	30	7

[1] Supremes and the Four Tops [2] Four Tops featuring Smokey Robinson

The original US recording of 'Indestructible' was not issued until after the chart run of the UK-only mix

4MANDU *UK, male vocal group (6 WEEKS)* pos/wks

29 Jul 95	THIS IS IT *Final Vinyl 74321291222*	45	3
17 Feb 96	DO IT FOR LOVE *Arista 74321343902*	45	2
15 Jun 96	BABY DON'T GO *Arista 74321375914*	47	1

FOURMOST *UK, male vocal / instrumental group (64 WEEKS)* pos/wks

12 Sep 63 ●	HELLO LITTLE GIRL *Parlophone R 5056*	9	17
26 Dec 63	I'M IN LOVE *Parlophone R 5078*	17	12
23 Apr 64 ●	A LITTLE LOVING *Parlophone R 5128*	6	13
13 Aug 64	HOW CAN I TELL HER *Parlophone R 5157*	33	4
26 Nov 64	BABY I NEED YOUR LOVIN' *Parlophone R 5194*	24	12
9 Dec 65	GIRLS GIRLS GIRLS *Parlophone R 5379*	33	6

14-18 *UK, male vocalist - Peter Waterman (4 WEEKS)* pos/wks

| 1 Nov 75 | GOODBYE-EE *Magnet MAG 48* | 33 | 4 |

See also STOCK AITKEN WATERMAN

40 THEVZ – See COOLIO

UK No.1 ★ UK Top 10 ● Still on chart + UK million seller ◆ UK entry at No.1 ■ US No.1 ▲

213

45 KING US, male producer - Mark James (6 WEEKS)

		pos	wks
28 Oct 89	THE KING IS HERE / THE 900 NUMBER *Dance Trax DRX 9*	60	5
11 Aug 90	THE KING IS HERE / THE 900 NUMBER (re-entry) *Dance Trax DRX 9*	73	1

49ers Italy, male producer - Gianfranco Bortolotti (27 WEEKS)

		pos	wks
16 Dec 89 ●	TOUCH ME *Fourth & Broadway BRW 157*	3	13
17 Mar 90	DON'T YOU LOVE ME *Fourth & Broadway BRW 167*	12	6
9 Jun 90	GIRL TO GIRL *Fourth & Broadway BRW 174*	31	3
6 Jun 92	GOT TO BE FREE *Fourth & Broadway BRW 255*	46	2
29 Aug 92	THE MESSAGE *Fourth & Broadway BRW 257*	68	1
18 Mar 95	ROCKIN' MY BODY *Media MCSTD 2021* [1]	31	2

[1] 49ers featuring Ann-Marie Smith

See also CAPPELLA

Bernard FOWLER – See BOMB THE BASS

FOX UK / US, male / female vocal / instrumental group (29 WEEKS)

		pos	wks
15 Feb 75 ●	ONLY YOU CAN *GTO GT 8*	3	11
10 May 75	IMAGINE ME IMAGINE YOU *GTO GT 21*	15	8
10 Apr 76 ●	S-S-S-SINGLE BED *GTO GT 57*	4	10

Noosha FOX UK, female vocalist (6 WEEKS)

		pos	wks
12 Nov 77	GEORGINA BAILEY *GTO GT 106*	31	6

Samantha FOX `467` `Top 500`
Former Sun 'Page 3 girl', b. 15 Apr 1966, London, UK, had big hits worldwide - including countries where she wasn't previously known for topless modelling. Only British female to register three Top 10 singles in the UK and US in 1980s (73 WEEKS)

		pos	wks
22 Mar 86 ●	TOUCH ME (I WANT YOUR BODY) *Jive FOXY 1*	3	10
28 Jun 86 ●	DO YA DO YA (WANNA PLEASE ME) *Jive FOXY 2*	10	7
6 Sep 86	HOLD ON TIGHT *Jive FOXY 3*	26	5
13 Dec 86	I'M ALL YOU NEED *Jive FOXY 4*	41	6
30 May 87 ●	NOTHING'S GONNA STOP ME NOW *Jive FOXY 5*	8	9
25 Jul 87	I SURRENDER (TO THE SPIRIT OF THE NIGHT) *Jive FOXY 6*	25	7
17 Oct 87	I PROMISE YOU (GET READY) *Jive FOXY 7*	58	3
19 Dec 87	TRUE DEVOTION *Jive FOXY 8*	62	3
21 May 88	NAUGHTY GIRLS (NEED LOVE TOO) *Jive FOXY 9* [1]	31	5
19 Nov 88	LOVE HOUSE *Jive FOXY 10*	32	6
28 Jan 89	I ONLY WANNA BE WITH YOU *Jive FOXY 11*	16	8
17 Jun 89	I WANNA HAVE SOME FUN *Jive FOXY 12*	63	2
28 Mar 98	SANTA MARIA *All Around the World CDGLOBE 163* [2]	31	2

[1] Samantha Fox featuring Full Force [2] DJ Milano featuring Samantha Fox

See also SOX

Bruce FOXTON UK, male vocalist (9 WEEKS)

		pos	wks
30 Jul 83	FREAK *Arista BFOX 1*	23	5
29 Oct 83	THIS IS THE WAY *Arista BFOX 2*	56	3
21 Apr 84	IT MAKES ME WONDER *Arista BFOX 3*	74	1

See also JAM

Inez FOXX US, female vocalist (8 WEEKS)

		pos	wks
23 Jul 64	HURT BY LOVE *Sue WI 323*	40	3
19 Feb 69	MOCKINGBIRD *United Artists UP 2269* [1]	36	2
19 Mar 69	MOCKINGBIRD (re-entry) *United Artists UP 2269* [1]	33	3

[1] Inez and Charlie Foxx

John FOXX UK, male vocalist (31 WEEKS)

		pos	wks
26 Jan 80	UNDERPASS *Virgin VS 318*	31	8
29 Mar 80	NO ONE DRIVING (DOUBLE SINGLE) *Virgin VS 338*	32	4
19 Jul 80	BURNING CAR *Virgin VS 360*	35	7
8 Nov 80	MILES AWAY *Virgin VS 382*	51	3
29 Aug 81	EUROPE (AFTER THE RAIN) *Virgin VS 393*	40	5
2 Jul 83	ENDLESSLY *Virgin VS 543*	66	3
17 Sep 83	YOUR DRESS *Virgin VS 615*	61	1

Tracks on double single: No One Driving / Glimmer / Mr No / This City

FPI PROJECT
Italy, male instrumental / production group (17 WEEKS)

		pos	wks
9 Dec 89 ●	GOING BACK TO MY ROOTS / RICH IN PARADISE *Rumour RUMAT 9*	9	12
9 Mar 91	EVERYBODY (ALL OVER THE WORLD) *Rumour RUMA 29*	65	3
7 Aug 93	COME ON (AND DO IT) *Synthetic SYNTH 006CD*	59	1
13 Mar 99	EVERYBODY (ALL OVER) (re-mix) *99 North CDNTH 14*	67	1

'Going Back to My Roots' was a vocal track available in two formats and featured either Paolo Dini or Sharon Dee Clarke

FRAGGLES UK / US, puppets from TV series (8 WEEKS)

		pos	wks
18 Feb 84	'FRAGGLE ROCK' THEME *RCA 389*	33	8

FRAGMA Germany / Spain, male / female production / vocal group (23 WEEKS)

		pos	wks
25 Sep 99	TOCA ME *Positiva CDTIV 120* [1]	11	6
22 Apr 00 ★	TOCA'S MIRACLE (re-mix) *Positiva CDTIV 128* ■	1	15
12 Aug 00	TOCA'S MIRACLE (re-entry of re-mix) *Positiva CDTIV 128*	52	2

[1] Vocals by Co Co

Roddy FRAME UK, male vocalist / instrumentalist (2 WEEKS)

		pos	wks
19 Sep 98	REASON FOR LIVING *Independiente ISOM 18MS*	45	2

See also AZTEC CAMERA

Peter FRAMPTON UK, male vocalist (24 WEEKS)

		pos	wks
1 May 76 ●	SHOW ME THE WAY *A & M AMS 7218*	10	12
11 Sep 76	BABY I LOVE YOUR WAY *A & M AMS 7246*	43	5
6 Nov 76	DO YOU FEEL LIKE WE DO *A & M AMS 7260*	39	4
23 Jul 77	I'M IN YOU *A & M AMS 7298*	41	3

Connie FRANCIS `50` `Top 500`
The original Italian-American queen of pop, b. Concetta Franconero, 12 Dec 1938, New Jersey. The most successful international female vocalist of the 1950s and 1960s and the first female solo artist to top the UK album chart (244 WEEKS)

		pos	wks
4 Apr 58 ★	WHO'S SORRY NOW *MGM 975*	1	25
27 Jun 58	I'M SORRY I MADE YOU CRY *MGM 982*	11	10
22 Aug 58 ★	CAROLINA MOON / STUPID CUPID *MGM 985*	1	19
31 Oct 58	I'LL GET BY *MGM 993*	19	6
21 Nov 58	FALLIN' *MGM 993*	20	5
26 Dec 58	YOU ALWAYS HURT THE ONE YOU LOVE *MGM 998*	13	7
13 Feb 59 ●	MY HAPPINESS *MGM 1001*	4	14
29 May 59	MY HAPPINESS (re-entry) *MGM 1001*	30	1
3 Jul 59 ●	LIPSTICK ON YOUR COLLAR *MGM 1018*	3	16
11 Sep 59	PLENTY GOOD LOVIN' *MGM 1036*	18	6
4 Dec 59	AMONG MY SOUVENIRS *MGM 1046*	11	10
17 Mar 60	VALENTINO *MGM 1060*	27	8
19 May 60 ●	MAMA / ROBOT MAN *MGM 1076*	2	19
18 Aug 60 ●	EVERYBODY'S SOMEBODY'S FOOL *MGM 1086* ▲	5	13
3 Nov 60 ●	MY HEART HAS A MIND OF ITS OWN *MGM 1100* ▲	3	15
12 Jan 61	MANY TEARS AGO *MGM 1111*	12	9
16 Mar 61 ●	WHERE THE BOYS ARE / BABY ROO *MGM 1121*	5	14
15 Jun 61	BREAKIN' IN A BRAND NEW BROKEN HEART *MGM 1136*	12	11
14 Sep 61 ●	TOGETHER *MGM 1138*	6	11
14 Dec 61	BABY'S FIRST CHRISTMAS *MGM 1145*	30	4
26 Apr 62	DON'T BREAK THE HEART THAT LOVES YOU *MGM 1157* ▲	39	3
2 Aug 62	VACATION *MGM 1165*	10	9
20 Dec 62	I'M GONNA BE WARM THIS WINTER *MGM 1185*	48	1
10 Jun 65	MY CHILD *MGM 1271*	26	6
20 Jan 66	JEALOUS HEART *MGM 1293*	44	2

Baby Roo listed with 'Where the Boys Are' for first eight weeks only

Jill FRANCIS UK, female vocalist (1 WEEK)

		pos	wks
3 Jul 93	MAKE LOVE TO ME *Glady Wax GW 003CD*	70	1

Claude FRANCOIS France, male vocalist (4 WEEKS)

		pos	wks
10 Jan 76	TEARS ON THE TELEPHONE *Bradley's BRAD 7528*	35	4

Joe FRANK – See HAMILTON, Joe FRANK and REYNOLDS

SINGLED OUT...
Pete Tong

Pete Tong has become a British institution – like Burberry, John Peel and warm lager, his influence is never far away. His Friday Night Essential Selection on Radio 1 is the soundtrack to millions of clubbers' pre-party drinkies. He constantly pushes the envelope: in his time he has broken just about every hot 12-inch that later made the charts and helped to send such underground acts as Basement Jaxx and Daft Punk into the Top 10. He's also an international DJ of some repute, and probably has enough air miles to get to the moon and back.

• NO.1 ON THE UK SINGLES CHART ON THE DAY I WAS BORN:
Please Don't Tease –
Cliff Richard and the Shadows

• FIRST SINGLE I EVER BOUGHT:
Ride a White Swan – T. REX

• SINGLE THAT DRIVES ME UP THE WALL:
Tie a Yellow Ribbon Round the Old Oak Tree –
Dawn featuring Tony Orlando

ALL-TIME FAVOURITE SINGLE:

Say a Little Prayer –
Aretha Franklin

FRANK AND WALTERS
Ireland, male vocal / instrumental group (13 WEEKS)   pos/wks

21 Mar 92		HAPPY BUSMAN *Setanta HOO 2* **49**	2
12 Sep 92		THIS IS NOT A SONG *Setanta HOO 3* **46**	3
9 Jan 93		AFTER ALL *Setanta HOOCD 4* **11**	5
17 Apr 93		FASHION CRISIS HITS NEW YORK *Setanta HOOCD 5* **42**	3

FRANKE *UK, male vocalist - Franke Pharoah (3 WEEKS)*   pos/wks

| 7 Nov 92 | | UNDERSTAND THIS GROOVE *China WOK 2028* ....**60** | 2 |
| 21 May 94 | | LOVE COME HOME *Triangle BLUESCD 001* [1] ....**73** | 1 |

[1] Our Tribe with Franke Pharoah and Kristine W

FRANK'EE – See BROTHER BROWN featuring FRANK'EE

FRANKIE GOES TO HOLLYWOOD (149 Top 500) *Fiercely marketed and controversial Merseyside-based quintet fronted by Holly Johnson (b. 19 Feb 1960, Sudan). First act since Gerry and the Pacemakers to hit No.1 with initial three releases. During July 1984, 'Two Tribes' and 'Relax' held top two places in the chart (147 WEEKS)*   pos/wks

26 Nov 83	★	RELAX *ZTT ZTAS 1* ◆ **1**	48
16 Jun 84	★	TWO TRIBES *ZTT ZTAS 3* ◆ ■ **1**	20
10 Nov 84		TWO TRIBES (re-entry) *ZTT ZTAS 3* **73**	1
1 Dec 84	★	THE POWER OF LOVE *ZTT ZTAS 5* **1**	11
16 Feb 85		RELAX (re-entry) *ZTT ZTAS 1* **58**	4
23 Feb 85		THE POWER OF LOVE (re-entry) *ZTT ZTAS 5* **64**	1
30 Mar 85	●	WELCOME TO THE PLEASURE DOME *ZTT ZTAS 7* **2**	11
6 Sep 86	●	RAGE HARD *ZTT ZTAS 22* **4**	7
22 Nov 86		WARRIORS (OF THE WASTELAND) *ZTT ZTAS 25* **19**	8
7 Mar 87		WATCHING THE WILDLIFE *ZTT ZTAS 26* **28**	4
2 Oct 93	●	RELAX (re-issue) *ZTT FGTH 1CD* **5**	7
20 Nov 93		WELCOME TO THE PLEASURE DOME (re-mix) *ZTT FGTH 2CD* **18**	3
18 Dec 93	●	THE POWER OF LOVE (re-issue) *ZTT FGTH 3CD* **10**	7
26 Feb 94		TWO TRIBES (re-mix) *ZTT FGTH 4CD* **16**	3
1 Jul 00	●	THE POWER OF LOVE (re-mix) *ZTT ZTT 150CD* **6**	6
9 Sep 00		TWO TRIBES (re-mix) *ZTT ZTT 154CD* **17**	3
18 Nov 00		WELCOME TO THE PLEASURE DOME (2nd re-mix) *ZTT 166CD* **45**	1

Aretha FRANKLIN (103 Top 500) *The 'Queen of Soul Music', b. 25 Mar 1942, Tennessee, US. During her five decades of recording this legendary gospel-influenced vocalist has won countless awards and amassed more pop and R&B hits than any other female in her homeland (182 WEEKS)*   pos/wks

8 Jun 67	●	RESPECT *Atlantic 584 115* ▲ **10**	14
23 Aug 67		BABY I LOVE YOU *Atlantic 584 127* **39**	4
20 Dec 67		CHAIN OF FOOLS / SATISFACTION *Atlantic 584 157* ..**43**	2
10 Jan 68		SATISFACTION *Atlantic 584 157* **37**	5
13 Mar 68		SINCE YOU'VE BEEN GONE *Atlantic 584 172* **47**	1
22 May 68		THINK *Atlantic 584 186* **26**	9
7 Aug 68	●	I SAY A LITTLE PRAYER *Atlantic 584 206* **4**	14
22 Aug 70		DON'T PLAY THAT SONG *Atlantic 2091 027* **13**	11
2 Oct 71		SPANISH HARLEM *Atlantic 2091 138* **14**	9
8 Sep 73		ANGEL *Atlantic K 10346* **37**	5
16 Feb 74		UNTIL YOU COME BACK TO ME (THAT'S WHAT I'M GONNA DO) *Atlantic K 10399* **26**	8
6 Dec 80		WHAT A FOOL BELIEVES *Arista ARIST 377* **46**	7
19 Sep 81		LOVE ALL THE HURT AWAY *Arista ARIST 428* [1] **49**	3
4 Sep 82		JUMP TO IT *Arista ARIST 479* **42**	5
23 Jul 83		GET IT RIGHT *Arista ARIST 537* **74**	2
13 Jul 85		FREEWAY OF LOVE *Arista ARIST 624* **68**	3
2 Nov 85	●	SISTERS ARE DOIN' IT FOR THEMSELVES *RCA PB 40339* [2] **9**	11
23 Nov 85		WHO'S ZOOMIN' WHO *Arista ARIST 633* **11**	14
22 Feb 86		ANOTHER NIGHT *Arista ARIST 657* **54**	6
10 May 86		FREEWAY OF LOVE (re-entry) *Arista ARIST 624* **51**	3
25 Oct 86		JUMPIN' JACK FLASH *Arista ARIST 678* **58**	3
31 Jan 87	★	I KNEW YOU WERE WAITING (FOR ME) *Epic DUET 1* [3] ▲ ...**1**	9
14 Mar 87		JIMMY LEE *Arista RIS 6* **46**	4
6 May 89		THROUGH THE STORM *Arista 112185* [4] **41**	3
9 Sep 89		IT ISN'T, IT WASN'T, IT AIN'T NEVER GONNA BE *Arista 112545* [5] **29**	5
7 Apr 90		THINK *East West A 7951* **31**	2
27 Jul 91		EVERYDAY PEOPLE *Arista 114420* **69**	1

12 Feb 94	●	A DEEPER LOVE *Arista 74321187022* **5**	7
25 Jun 94		WILLING TO FORGIVE *Arista 74321213342* **17**	7
9 May 98		A ROSE IS STILL A ROSE *Arista 74321569742* **22**	4
26 Sep 98		HERE WE GO AGAIN *Arista 74321612742* **68**	1

[1] Aretha Franklin and George Benson [2] Eurythmics and Aretha Franklin [3] Aretha Franklin and George Michael [4] Aretha Franklin and Elton John [5] Aretha Franklin and Whitney Houston

'Think' on East West is a re-recording. It was the flip side of 'Everybody Needs Somebody to Love' by Blues Brothers and was listed for the first two weeks of that record's run

Erma FRANKLIN *US, female vocalist (10 WEEKS)*   pos/wks

| 10 Oct 92 | ● | (TAKE A LITTLE) PIECE OF MY HEART *Epic 6583847* ....**9** | 10 |

Rodney FRANKLIN *US, male instrumentalist - piano (9 WEEKS)*   pos/wks

| 19 Apr 80 | ● | THE GROOVE *CBS 8529* ....**7** | 9 |

Chevelle FRANKLYN / BEENIE MAN
Jamaica, female / male vocalists (1 WEEK)   pos/wks

| 20 Sep 97 | | DANCEHALL QUEEN *Island Jamaica IJCD 2018* ....**70** | 1 |

See also BEENIE MAN

FRANTIC FIVE – See Don LANG

FRANTIQUE *US, female vocal group (12 WEEKS)*   pos/wks

| 11 Aug 79 | ● | STRUT YOUR FUNKY STUFF *Philadelphia Int. PIR 7728* ....**10** | 12 |

Elizabeth FRASER – See COCTEAU TWINS; MASSIVE ATTACK; Ian McCULLOCH; FUTURE SOUND OF LONDON

Wendy FRASER – See Patrick SWAYZE featuring Wendy FRASER

FRASH *UK, male vocal / instrumental group (1 WEEK)*   pos/wks

| 18 Feb 95 | | HERE I GO AGAIN *PWL International FLIPCD 1* ....**69** | 1 |

FRAZIER CHORUS
UK, male / female vocal / instrumental group (14 WEEKS)   pos/wks

4 Feb 89		DREAM KITCHEN *Virgin VS 1145* **57**	3
15 Apr 89		TYPICAL! *Virgin VS 1174* **53**	2
15 Jul 89		SLOPPY HEART *Virgin VS 1192* **73**	1
9 Jun 90		CLOUD 8 *Virgin VS 1252* **52**	3
25 Aug 90		NOTHING *Virgin VS 1284* **51**	3
16 Feb 91		WALKING ON AIR *Virgin VS 1330* **60**	2

FREAKPOWER
UK / Canada, male vocal / instrumental group (20 WEEKS)   pos/wks

16 Oct 93		TURN ON TUNE IN COP OUT *Fourth & Broadway BRCD 284* **29**	5
26 Feb 94		RUSH *Fourth & Broadway BRCD 291* **62**	2
18 Mar 95	●	TURN ON TUNE IN COP OUT (re-issue) *Fourth & Broadway BRCD 317* **3**	9
8 Jun 96		NEW DIRECTION *Fourth & Broadway BRCD 331* **60**	1
9 May 98		NO WAY *Deconstruction 74321578572* **29**	3

See also Norman COOK; BEATS INTERNATIONAL; PIZZAMAN; FATBOY SLIM; MIGHTY DUB KATZ; HOUSEMARTINS

FREAKY REALISTIC
UK / Japan, male / female vocal / instrumental group (3 WEEKS)   pos/wks

| 3 Apr 93 | | KOOCHIE RYDER *Realism FRECD 2* ....**52** | 2 |
| 3 Jul 93 | | LEONARD NIMOY *Realism FRECD 3* ....**71** | 1 |

FREAKYMAN
Holland, male producer - Andre Van Den Bosch (1 WEEK)   pos/wks

| 27 Sep 97 | | DISCOBUG '97 *Xtravaganza 0091285 EXT* ....**68** | 1 |

Stan FREBERG
US, male vocalist (5 WEEKS) pos/wks

19 Nov 54	SH-BOOM *Capitol CL 14187* [1]	15	2
27 Jul 56	ROCK ISLAND LINE / HEARTBREAK HOTEL		
	Capitol CL 14608 [2]	24	1
10 Aug 56	ROCK ISLAND LINE / HEARTBREAK HOTEL (re-entry)		
	Capitol CL 14608 [2]	29	1
12 May 60	THE OLD PAYOLA ROLL BLUES *Capitol CL 15122* [3]	40	1

[1] Stan Freberg with the Toads [2] Stan Freberg and his Sniffle Group [3] Stan Freberg with Jesse White

FRED & ROXY
UK, female vocal duo (2 WEEKS) pos/wks

5 Feb 00	SOMETHING FOR THE WEEKEND *Echo ECSCD 81*	36	2

John FRED and the PLAYBOY BAND
US, male vocal / instrumental group (12 WEEKS) pos/wks

3 Jan 68 ●	JUDY IN DISGUISE (WITH GLASSES)		
	Pye International 7N 25442 ▲	3	12

FREDDIE and the DREAMERS (371 Top 500)
Fun beat group fronted and founded by the leaping, laughing Freddie Garrity, b. 14 Nov 1936, Manchester, UK. Immortalised in the 1965 film 'Every Day's a Holiday', which was re-titled 'Seaside Swingers' in the US where they topped the charts with 'I'm Telling You Now' (85 WEEKS) pos/wks

9 May 63 ●	IF YOU GOTTA MAKE A FOOL OF SOMEBODY *Columbia DB 7032*	3	14
8 Aug 63 ●	I'M TELLING YOU NOW *Columbia DB 7086* ▲	2	11
7 Nov 63 ●	YOU WERE MADE FOR ME *Columbia DB 7147*	3	15
20 Feb 64	OVER YOU *Columbia DB 7214*	13	11
14 May 64	I LOVE YOU BABY *Columbia DB 7286*	16	8
16 Jul 64	JUST FOR YOU *Columbia DB 7322*	41	3
5 Nov 64 ●	I UNDERSTAND *Columbia DB 7381*	5	15
22 Apr 65	A LITTLE YOU *Columbia DB 7526*	26	5
4 Nov 65	THOU SHALT NOT STEAL *Columbia DB 7720*	44	3

FREDERICK – See NINA and FREDERICK

Dee FREDRIX
UK, female vocalist (5 WEEKS) pos/wks

27 Feb 93	AND SO I WILL WAIT FOR YOU *East West YZ 725CD*	56	4
3 Jul 93	DIRTY MONEY *East West YZ 750CD*	74	1

FREE (452 Top 500)
Blues-oriented London rock quartet, Paul Rodgers (v), Paul Kossoff (g), Andy Fraser (b) and Simon Kirke (d); split 1973 when Rodgers and Kirke formed Bad Company. 'All Right Now' became first track to reach Top 20 in 70s, 80s and 90s (75 WEEKS) pos/wks

6 Jun 70 ●	ALL RIGHT NOW *Island WIP 6082*	2	16
1 May 71 ●	MY BROTHER JAKE *Island WIP 6100*	4	11
27 May 72	LITTLE BIT OF LOVE *Island WIP 6129*	13	10
13 Jan 73 ●	WISHING WELL *Island WIP 6146*	7	10
21 Jul 73	ALL RIGHT NOW (re-entry) *Island WIP 6082*	15	9
18 Feb 78	FREE (EP) *Island IEP 6*	11	7
23 Oct 82	FREE (EP) (re-entry) *Island IEP 6*	57	3
9 Feb 91 ●	ALL RIGHT NOW (re-mix) *Island IS 486*	8	9

Tracks on Free (EP): All Right Now (long version) / My Brother Jake (re-issue) / Wishing Well (re-issue)

FREE – See QUEEN; Wyclef JEAN; Pras MICHEL; QUEEN LATIFAH

FREE SPIRIT
UK, male / female vocal duo (1 WEEK) pos/wks

13 May 95	NO MORE RAINY DAYS *Columbia 6612822*	68	1

FREEEZ
UK, male vocal / instrumental group (48 WEEKS) pos/wks

7 Jun 80	KEEP IN TOUCH *Calibre CAB 103*	49	3
7 Feb 81 ●	SOUTHERN FREEEZ *Beggars Banquet BEG 51* [1]	8	11
18 Apr 81	FLYING HIGH *Beggars Banquet BEG 55*	35	5
18 Jun 83 ●	I.O.U. *Beggars Banquet BEG 96*	2	15
1 Oct 83	POP GOES MY LOVE *Beggars Banquet BEG 98*	26	6
17 Jan 87	I.O.U. (re-mix) *Citybeat CBE 709* [2]	23	6
30 May 87	SOUTHERN FREEZ (re-mix) *Total Control TOCO 14* [1]	63	2

[1] Freeez featuring Ingrid Mansfield Allman [2] Freeez featuring John Rocca

FREEFALL featuring Jan JOHNSTON
UK / Australia, male DJ / production duo and female vocalist (3 WEEKS) pos/wks

28 Nov 98	SKYDIVE *Stress CDSTR 89*	75	1
22 Jul 00	SKYDIVE (re-mix) *Renaissance Recordings RENCDS 002*	43	2

FREEFALL featuring PSYCHOTROPIC
UK / US, male instrumental / production group (1 WEEK) pos/wks

27 Jul 91	FEEL SURREAL *ffrr FX 160*	63	1

FREEHOLD JUNIOR SCHOOL – See Fogwell FLAX and the ANKLEBITERS from FREEHOLD JUNIOR SCHOOL

FREESTYLERS
UK, male instrumental / vocal group (5 WEEKS) pos/wks

7 Feb 98	B-BOY STANCE *Freskanova FND 7* [1]	23	3
14 Nov 98	WARNING *Freskanova FND 14* [2]	68	1
24 Jul 99	HERE WE GO *Freskanova FND 19*	45	1

[1] Freestylers featuring Tenor Fly [2] Freestylers featuring Navigator

FREIHEIT
Germany, male vocal / instrumental group (9 WEEKS) pos/wks

17 Dec 88	KEEPING THE DREAM ALIVE *CBS 652989 7*	14	9

FRENCH AFFAIR
France, male production duo / female vocalist (3 WEEKS) pos/wks

16 Sep 00	MY HEART GOES BOOM *Arista 74321 780562*	44	3

Deborah FRENCH – See E-LUSTRIOUS

Nicki FRENCH
UK, female vocalist (18 WEEKS) pos/wks

15 Oct 94	TOTAL ECLIPSE OF THE HEART *Bags of Fun BAGSCD 1*	54	1
14 Jan 95 ●	TOTAL ECLIPSE OF THE HEART (re-entry)		
	Bags of Fun BAGSCD 1	5	12
22 Apr 95	FOR ALL WE KNOW *Bags of Fun BAGSCD 4*	42	2
15 Jul 95	DID YOU EVER REALLY LOVE ME *Love This LUVTHISCD 2*	55	1
27 May 00	DON'T PLAY THAT SONG AGAIN *RCA 74321764572*	34	2

Doug E FRESH and the GET FRESH CREW
US, male rap / DJ group (11 WEEKS) pos/wks

9 Nov 85 ●	THE SHOW *Cooltempo COOL 116*	7	11

FRESH 4 featuring Lizz E
UK, male DJ / production group and female vocalist (9 WEEKS) pos/wks

7 Oct 89 ●	WISHING ON A STAR *10 TEN 287*	10	9

Freddy FRESH
US, male producer - Frederick Schmid (3 WEEKS) pos/wks

1 May 99	BADDER BADDER SCHWING *Eye Q EYEUK 040CD* [1]	34	2
31 Jul 99	WHAT IT IS *Eye Q EYEUK 043CD*	63	1

[1] Freddy Fresh featuring Fatboy Slim

FRESH PRINCE – See JAZZY JEFF & the FRESH PRINCE

FRESHIES
UK, male vocal / instrumental group (3 WEEKS) pos/wks

14 Feb 81	I'M IN LOVE WITH THE GIRL ON A CERTAIN		
	MANCHESTER MEGASTORE CHECKOUT DESK *MCA 670*	54	3

Matt FRETTON
UK, male vocalist (5 WEEKS) pos/wks

11 Jun 83	IT'S SO HIGH *Chrysalis MATT 1*	50	5

FREUR
UK, male vocal / instrumental group (4 WEEKS) pos/wks

23 Apr 83	DOOT DOOT *CBS A 3141*	59	4

Glenn FREY
US, male vocalist (20 WEEKS) pos/wks

2 Mar 85	THE HEAT IS ON *MCA MCA 941*	12	12
22 Jun 85	SMUGGLER'S BLUES *BBC RESL 170*	22	8

See also EAGLES

FRIDA Norway, female vocalist (12 WEEKS)

		pos/wks
21 Aug 82	I KNOW THERE'S SOMETHING GOING ON Epic EPC A2603	43 7
17 Dec 83	TIME Epic A 3983 [1]	45 5

[1] Frida and BA Robertson

See also ABBA

Gavin FRIDAY – See BONO

Ralph FRIDGE Germany, male producer - Ralf Fritsch (4 WEEKS)

		pos/wks
24 Apr 99	PARADISE Additive 12AD 036	68 1
8 Apr 00	ANGEL Incentive CENT 6CDS	20 3

Dean FRIEDMAN US, male vocalist (22 WEEKS)

		pos/wks
3 Jun 78	WOMAN OF MINE Lifesong LS 401	52 5
23 Sep 78 ●	LUCKY STARS Lifesong LS 402	3 10
18 Nov 78	LYDIA Lifesong LS 403	31 7

FRIENDS AGAIN UK, male vocal / instrumental group (3 WEEKS)

		pos/wks
4 Aug 84	THE FRIENDS AGAIN EP Mercury FA 1	59 3

Tracks on The Friends Again EP: Lullaby On Board / Wand You Wave / Thank You for Being an Angel

FRIENDS OF MATTHEW
UK, male / female vocal / instrumental group (1 WEEK)

		pos/wks
10 Jul 99	OUT THERE Serious SERR 007CD	61 1

FRIGID VINEGAR UK, male rap / production duo (1 WEEK)

		pos/wks
21 Aug 99	DOGMONAUT 2000 (IS THERE ANYONE OUT THERE?) Gut CDGUT 27	53 1

FRIJID PINK US, male vocal / instrumental group (16 WEEKS)

		pos/wks
28 Mar 70 ●	HOUSE OF THE RISING SUN Deram DM 288	4 16

Robert FRIPP – See David SYLVIAN

Jane FROMAN US, female vocalist (4 WEEKS)

		pos/wks
17 Jun 55	I WONDER Capitol CL 14254	14 4

FRONT 242 Belgium / US, male vocal / instrumental group (1 WEEK)

		pos/wks
1 May 93	RELIGION RRE RRE 106CD	46 1

Christian FRY UK, male vocalist (3 WEEKS)

		pos/wks
14 Nov 98	YOU GOT ME Mushroom MUSH 33CDS	45 2
3 Apr 99	WON'T YOU SAY Mushroom MUSH 46CDS	48 1

FUGEES US vocal / rap trio of Wyclef Jean, Pras Michel (both of Haitian descent) and Lauryn Hill, who all had solo success after becoming the first hip hop / R&B group to score four consecutive Top 3 singles. Neither of their two No.1s were released as singles in US. 'Killing Me Softly' was UK's top-selling single in 1996. (65 WEEKS)

		pos/wks
6 Apr 96	FU-GEE-LA Columbia 6630662	21 5
8 Jun 96 ★	KILLING ME SOFTLY Columbia 6633435 ◆ ■	1 20
14 Sep 96 ★	READY OR NOT Columbia 6637215	1 12
30 Nov 96 ●	NO WOMAN, NO CRY Columbia 6639925	2 9
15 Mar 97 ●	RUMBLE IN THE JUNGLE Mercury 5740692	3 8
28 Jun 97	WE TRYING TO STAY ALIVE Columbia 6646815 [1]	13 5
6 Sep 97	THE SWEETEST THING Columbia 6649785 [2]	18 4
27 Sep 97	GUANTANAMERA Columbia 6650852 [3]	25 2

[1] Wyclef Jean & The Refugee Allstars [2] Refugee Camp Allstars featuring Lauryn Hill [3] Wyclef Jean and The Refugee Allstars

See also Lauryn HILL; Wyclef JEAN; Pras MICHEL

FULL CIRCLE US, male vocal group (5 WEEKS)

		pos/wks
7 Mar 87	WORKIN' UP A SWEAT EMI America EA 229	41 5

FULL FORCE US, male vocal / instrumental group (37 WEEKS)

		pos/wks
4 May 85	I WONDER IF I TAKE YOU HOME CBS A 6057 [1]	53 6
3 Aug 85	I WONDER IF I TAKE YOU HOME (re-entry) CBS A 6057 [1]	12 11
21 Dec 85 ●	ALICE I WANT YOU JUST FOR ME CBS A 6640	9 11
21 May 88	NAUGHTY GIRLS (NEED LOVE TOO) Jive FOXY 9 [2]	31 5
4 Jun 88	I'M REAL Scotti Brothers JSB 1 [3]	31 4

[1] Lisa Lisa and Cult Jam with Full Force [2] Samantha Fox featuring Full Force [3] James Brown featuring Full Force

FULL INTENTION
UK, male instrumental / production group (7 WEEKS)

		pos/wks
6 Apr 96	AMERICA (I LOVE AMERICA) Stress CDSTR 56	32 2
10 Aug 96	UPTOWN DOWNTOWN Stress CDSTR 67	61 1
26 Jul 97	SHAKE YOUR BODY (DOWN TO THE GROUND) Sugar Daddy CDSTR 82	34 2
22 Nov 97	AMERICA (I LOVE AMERICA) (re-mix) Sugar Daddy CDSTRX 56	56 1
6 Jun 98	YOU ARE SOMEBODY Sugar Daddy CDSD 001	75 1

See also SEX-O-SONIQUE; HUSTLERS CONVENTION featuring Dave LAUDAT and Ondrea DUVERNEY

FULL METAL RACKETS – See John McENROE and Pat CASH with the FULL METAL RACKETS

FULL MONTY ALLSTARS featuring TJ DAVIS
UK, male vocal / instrumental group (1 WEEK)

		pos/wks
27 Jul 96	BRILLIANT FEELING Arista 74321380902	72 1

Bobby FULLER FOUR
US, male vocal / instrumental group (4 WEEKS)

		pos/wks
14 Apr 66	I FOUGHT THE LAW London HL 10030	33 4

FUN BOY THREE [490] [Top 500] Multi-racial genre-hopping pop trio formed after fragmentation of Coventry band The Specials. Split after 1983 US tour. Singer Terry Hall has had hits as a soloist and as part of five bands (Specials, FB3, Colour Field, Vegas and Terry, Blair and Anouchka) (70 WEEKS)

		pos/wks
7 Nov 81	THE LUNATICS (HAVE TAKEN OVER THE ASYLUM) Chrysalis CHS 2563	20 12
13 Feb 82 ●	IT AIN'T WHAT YOU DO IT'S THE WAY THAT YOU DO IT Chrysalis CHS 2570 [1]	4 10
10 Apr 82 ●	REALLY SAYING SOMETHING Deram NANA 1 [2]	5 10
8 May 82	THE TELEPHONE ALWAYS RINGS Chrysalis CHS 2609	17 9
31 Jul 82	SUMMERTIME Chrysalis CHS 2629	18 8
15 Jan 83	THE MORE I SEE (THE LESS I BELIEVE) Chrysalis CHS 2664	68 1
5 Feb 83 ●	TUNNEL OF LOVE Chrysalis CHS 2678	10 10
30 Apr 83 ●	OUR LIPS ARE SEALED Chrysalis FUNB 1	7 10

[1] Fun Boy Three and Bananarama [2] Bananarama with Fun Boy Three

See also SPECIALS

FUN LOVIN' CRIMINALS US, male vocal / rap / instrumental trio (24 WEEKS)

		pos/wks
8 Jun 96	THE GRAVE AND THE CONSTANT Chrysalis CDCHS 5031	72 1
17 Aug 96	SCOOBY SNACKS Chrysalis CDCHS 5034	22 3
16 Nov 96	THE FUN LOVIN' CRIMINAL Chrysalis CDCHS 5040	26 3
29 Mar 97	KING OF NEW YORK Chrysalis CDCHS 5049	28 3
5 Jul 97	I'M NOT IN LOVE / SCOOBY SNACKS Chrysalis CDCHS 5060	12 5
15 Aug 98	LOVE UNLIMITED Chrysalis CDCHS 5096	18 4
17 Oct 98	BIG NIGHT OUT Chrysalis CDCHSS 5101	29 2
8 May 99	KOREAN BODEGA Chrysalis CDCHS 5108	15 3

Farley 'Jackmaster' FUNK
US, male producer - Farley Williams (16 WEEKS)

		pos/wks
23 Aug 86 ●	LOVE CAN'T TURN AROUND DJ International LON 105	10 12

			pos/wks
11 Feb 89	**AS ALWAYS** *Champion CHAMP 90* [1]	.....**49**	2
14 Dec 96	**LOVE CAN'T TURN AROUND** *4 Liberty LIBTCD 27* [2]	.....**40**	2

[1] Farley 'Jackmaster' Funk featuring Ricky Dillard [2] Farley 'Jackmaster' Funk with Darryl Pandy.

'Love Can't Turn Around' in 1996 is a re-recording

FUNK JUNKEEZ
US, male DJ / producer - Roger Sanchez (1 WEEK) pos/wks

21 Feb 98	**GOT FUNK** *Evocative EVOKE 1CDS*	.....**57**	1

See also EL MARIACHI; Roger SANCHEZ

FUNK MASTER
UK, male / female vocal / instrumental group (12 WEEKS) pos/wks

18 Jun 83	● **IT'S OVER** *Master Funk Records 7MP 004*	.....**8**	12

FUNKADELIC *US, male vocal / instrumental group (13 WEEKS)* pos/wks

9 Dec 78	● **ONE NATION UNDER A GROOVE (PART 1)** *Warner Bros. K 17246...*	**9**	12
21 Aug 99	**MOTHERSHIP RECONNECTION** *Virgin DINSD 185* [1]	.....**55**	1

[1] Scott Grooves featuring Parliament / Funkadelic

FUNKAPOLITAN *UK, male vocal / instrumental group (7 WEEKS)* pos/wks

22 Aug 81	**AS THE TIME GOES BY** *London LON 001*	.....**41**	7

FUNKDOOBIEST *US, male rap group (6 WEEKS)* pos/wks

11 Dec 93	**WOPBABALUBOP** *Immortal 6597112*	.....**37**	4
5 Mar 94	**BOW WOW WOW** *Immortal 6594052*	.....**34**	2

FUNKSTAR DE LUXE *Denmark, male producer / instrumentalist - Matt Ottesen (18 WEEKS)* pos/wks

25 Sep 99	● **SUN IS SHINING** *Club Tools / Edel 0066895 CLU* [1]	.....**3**	10
22 Jan 00	**RAINBOW COUNTRY** *Club Tools 0067225CLU* [1]	.....**11**	6
13 May 00	**WALKIN IN THE NAME** *Club Tools 0067375 CLU* [2]	.....**42**	1
25 Nov 00	**PULL UP TO THE BUMPER** *Club Tools 0120375 CLU* [3]	.....**60**	1

[1] Bob Marley vs Funkstar De Luxe [2] Funkstar De Luxe vs Terry Maxx [3] Grace Jones vs Funkstar De Luxe

FUNKY BOYS – See Linda CARR

FUNKY BUNCH – See MARKY MARK and the FUNKY BUNCH

FUNKY CHOAD featuring Nick SKITZ *Australia / Italy, male production duo and Australia, male vocalist (1 WEEK)* pos/wks

29 Aug 98	**THE ULTIMATE** *ffrr FCD 341*	.....**51**	1

FUNKY GREEN DOGS
US, male / female vocal / production group (6 WEEKS) pos/wks

12 Apr 97	**FIRED UP!** *Twisted UK TWCD 10016*	.....**17**	3
28 Jun 97	**THE WAY** *Twisted UK TWCD 10026*	.....**43**	1
20 Jun 98	**UNTIL THE DAY** *Twisted UK TWCD 10034*	.....**75**	1
27 Feb 99	**BODY** *Twisted UK TWCD 110041*	.....**46**	1

FUNKY POETS *US, male vocal group (1 WEEK)* pos/wks

7 May 94	**BORN IN THE GHETTO** *Epic 6603522*	.....**72**	1

FUNKY WORM
UK, male / female vocal / instrumental group (14 WEEKS) pos/wks

30 Jul 88	**HUSTLE! (TO THE MUSIC . . .)** *Fon FON 15*	.....**13**	8
26 Nov 88	**THE SPELL!** *Fon FON 16*	.....**61**	3
20 May 89	**U + ME = LOVE** *Fon FON 19*	.....**46**	3

FUREYS *Ireland, male vocal group (14 WEEKS)* pos/wks

10 Oct 81	**WHEN YOU WERE SWEET SIXTEEN** *Ritz RITZ 003* [1]	.....**14**	11
3 Apr 82	**I WILL LOVE YOU (EV'RY TIME WHEN WE ARE GONE)** *Ritz RITZ 012*	.....**54**	3

[1] Fureys with Davey Arthur

FURIOUS FIVE – See GRANDMASTER FLASH, Melle MEL and the FURIOUS FIVE

FURNITURE
UK, male / female vocal / instrumental group (10 WEEKS) pos/wks

14 Jun 86	**BRILLIANT MIND** *Stiff BUY 251*	.....**21**	10

Billy FURY 〈 37 | Top 500 〉
Early British rock 'n' roll star, b. Ronald Wycherley, 17 Apr 1941, Liverpool, d. 28 Jan 1983. Scored more hits in the 1960s than fellow Liverpudlians The Beatles, and spent 281 weeks on chart but without ever without reaching No.1 (281 WEEKS) pos/wks

27 Feb 59	**MAYBE TOMORROW** *Decca F 11102*	.....**22**	3
27 Mar 59	**MAYBE TOMORROW (re-entry)** *Decca F 11102*	.....**18**	6
26 Jun 59	**MARGO** *Decca F 11128*	.....**28**	1
10 Mar 60	● **COLETTE** *Decca F 11200*	.....**9**	10
26 May 60	**THAT'S LOVE** *Decca F 11237* [1]	.....**19**	11
22 Sep 60	**WONDROUS PLACE** *Decca F 11267*	.....**25**	9
19 Jan 61	**A THOUSAND STARS** *Decca F 11311*	.....**14**	10
27 Apr 61	**DON'T WORRY** *Decca F 11334* [2]	.....**40**	2
11 May 61	● **HALFWAY TO PARADISE** *Decca F 11349*	.....**3**	23
7 Sep 61	● **JEALOUSY** *Decca F 11384*	.....**2**	12
14 Dec 61	● **I'D NEVER FIND ANOTHER YOU** *Decca F 11409*	.....**5**	15
15 Mar 62	**LETTER FULL OF TEARS** *Decca F 11437*	.....**32**	6
3 May 62	● **LAST NIGHT WAS MADE FOR LOVE** *Decca F 11458*	.....**4**	16
19 Jul 62	● **ONCE UPON A DREAM** *Decca F 11485*	.....**7**	13
25 Oct 62	**BECAUSE OF LOVE** *Decca F 11508*	.....**18**	14
14 Feb 63	● **LIKE I'VE NEVER BEEN GONE** *Decca F11582*	.....**3**	15
16 May 63	● **WHEN WILL YOU SAY I LOVE YOU** *Decca F 11655*	.....**3**	12
25 Jul 63	● **IN SUMMER** *Decca F 11701*	.....**5**	11
3 Oct 63	**SOMEBODY ELSE'S GIRL** *Decca F 11744*	.....**18**	7
2 Jan 64	**DO YOU REALLY LOVE ME TOO** *Decca F 11792*	.....**13**	10
30 Apr 64	**I WILL** *Decca F 11888*	.....**14**	12
23 Jul 64	● **IT'S ONLY MAKE BELIEVE** *Decca F 11939*	.....**10**	10
14 Jan 65	**I'M LOST WITHOUT YOU** *Decca F 12048*	.....**16**	10
22 Jul 65	● **IN THOUGHTS OF YOU** *Decca F 12178*	.....**9**	11
16 Sep 65	**RUN TO MY LOVIN' ARMS** *Decca F 12230*	.....**25**	7
10 Feb 66	**I'LL NEVER QUITE GET OVER YOU** *Decca F 12325*	.....**35**	5
4 Aug 66	**GIVE ME YOUR WORD** *Decca F 12459*	.....**27**	7
4 Sep 82	**LOVE OR MONEY** *Polydor POSP 488*	.....**57**	5
13 Nov 82	**DEVIL OR ANGEL** *Polydor POSP 528*	.....**58**	4
4 Jun 83	**FORGET HIM** *Polydor POSP 558*	.....**59**	4

[1] Billy Fury with the Four Jays [2] Billy Fury with the Four Kestrels

FUSED *Sweden, male instrumental / production duo / female vocalist (1 WEEK)* pos/wks

20 Mar 99	**THIS PARTY SUCKS!** *Columbia 6669302*	.....**64**	1

FUTURE BREEZE *Germany, male production duo - Markus Boehme and Martin Hensing (1 WEEK)* pos/wks

6 Sep 97	**WHY DON'T YOU DANCE WITH ME** *AM:PM 5823312*	.....**50**	1

FUTURE FORCE
UK / US, male / female vocal / instrumental duo (1 WEEK) pos/wks

17 Aug 96	**WHAT YOU WANT** *AM:PM 5816592*	.....**47**	1

FUTURE SOUND OF LONDON
UK, male instrumental / production duo (22 WEEKS) pos/wks

23 May 92	**PAPUA NEW GUINEA** *Jumpin' & Pumpin' TOT 17*	.....**22**	6
6 Nov 93	**CASCADE** *Virgin VSCDT 1478*	.....**27**	3
30 Jul 94	**EXPANDER** *Jumpin' & Pumpin' CDSTOT 37*	.....**72**	1
13 Aug 94	**LIFEFORMS** *Virgin VSCDT 1484*	.....**14**	3
27 May 95	**FAR-OUT SON OF LUNG AND THE RAMBLINGS OF A MADMAN** *Virgin VSCDT 1540*	.....**22**	3
26 Oct 96	**MY KINGDOM** *Virgin VSCDT 1605*	.....**13**	3
12 Apr 97	**WE HAVE EXPLOSIVE** *Virgin VSCDX 1616*	.....**12**	3

[1] F.S.O.L. vocals by Elizabeth Fraser

FUZZBOX – See WE'VE GOT A FUZZBOX AND WE'RE GONNA USE IT

Leslie FYSON – See Michael MEDWIN, Bernard BRESSLAW, Alfie BASS and Leslie FYSON

G

Andy G's STARSKY & HUTCH ALL STARS
UK, male producer (1 WEEK) pos/wks

3 Oct 98	STARSKY & HUTCH - THE THEME *Virgin VSCDT 1708*	51	1

Bobby G *UK, male vocalist (12 WEEKS)* pos/wks

1 Dec 84	BIG DEAL *BBC RESL 151*	75	1
15 Dec 84	BIG DEAL (re-entry) *BBC RESL 151*	65	5
19 Oct 85	BIG DEAL (2nd re-entry) *BBC RESL 151*	46	6

See also BUCKS FIZZ

Dario G *UK, male DJ / production trio (33 WEEKS)* pos/wks

27 Sep 97 ●	SUNCHYME *Eternal WEA 130CD*	2	18
20 Jun 98 ●	CARNAVAL DE PARIS *Eternal WEA 162CD*	5	9
12 Sep 98	SUNMACHINE *Eternal WEA 173CD*	17	4
25 Mar 00	VOICES *Eternal WEA 256CD*	37	2

Gina G *Australia, female vocalist - Gina Gardiner (51 WEEKS)* pos/wks

6 Apr 96 ★	OOH AAH...JUST A LITTLE BIT *Eternal WEA 041CD*	1	23
21 Sep 96	OOH AAH...JUST A LITTLE BIT (re-entry) *Eternal WEA 041CD*	62	1
5 Oct 96	OOH AAH...JUST A LITTLE BIT (2nd re-entry) *Eternal WEA 041CD*	64	1
9 Nov 96 ●	I BELONG TO YOU *Eternal WEA 081CD*	6	11
22 Mar 97 ●	FRESH! *Eternal WEA 095CD*	6	7
7 Jun 97	TI AMO *Eternal WEA 107CD1*	11	5
6 Sep 97	GIMME SOME LOVE *Eternal WEA 101CD1*	25	2
15 Nov 97	EVERY TIME I FALL *Eternal WEA 134CD*	52	1

Hurricane G – See PUFF DADDY

Kenny G *US, male instrumentalist - saxophone (26 WEEKS)* pos/wks

21 Apr 84	HI! HOW YA DOIN'? *Arista ARIST 561*	70	3
30 Aug 86	WHAT DOES IT TAKE (TO WIN YOUR LOVE) *Arista ARIST 672*	64	2
4 Jul 87	SONGBIRD *Arista RIS 18*	22	7
9 May 92	MISSING YOU NOW *Columbia 6579917* [1]	28	4
24 Apr 93	FOREVER IN LOVE *Arista 74321145552*	47	3
17 Jul 93	BY THE TIME THIS NIGHT IS OVER *Arista 74321157142* [2]	56	3
8 Nov 97	HOW COULD AN ANGEL BREAK MY HEART *LaFace 74321531982* [3]	22	4

[1] Michael Bolton featuring Kenny G [2] Kenny G with Peabo Bryson [3] Toni Braxton with Kenny G

G-CLEFS *US, male vocal group (12 WEEKS)* pos/wks

30 Nov 61	I UNDERSTAND *London HLU 9433*	17	12

Warren G *US, male rapper - Warren Griffin (59 WEEKS)* pos/wks

23 Jul 94 ●	REGULATE *Death Row A 8290CD* [1]	5	14
12 Nov 94	THIS DJ *RAL RALCD 1*	12	5
31 Dec 94	THIS DJ (re-entry) *RAL RALCD 1*	68	2
25 Mar 95	DO YOU SEE *RAL RALCD 3*	29	2
23 Nov 96 ●	WHAT'S LOVE GOT TO DO WITH IT *Interscope IND 97008* [2]	2	12
22 Feb 97 ●	I SHOT THE SHERIFF *Mercury DEFCD 31*	2	8
31 May 97	SMOKIN' ME OUT *Def Jam 5744432* [3]	14	5
10 Jan 98	PRINCE IGOR *Def Jam 5749652* [4]	15	7
24 Jan 98	ALL NIGHT ALL RIGHT *Mushroom MUSH 21CD* [5]	16	4

[1] Warren G and Nate Dogg [2] Warren G featuring Adina Howard [3] Warren G featuring Ron Isley [4] Warren G featuring Sissel [5] Peter Andre featuring Warren G

G NATION featuring ROSIE *UK, male production duo - Jake Moses and Mark Smith - and UK, female vocalist (1 WEEK)* pos/wks

9 Aug 97	FEEL THE NEED *Cooltempo CDCOOL 327*	58	1

G.O.S.H. *UK, male / female charity ensemble (11 WEEKS)* pos/wks

28 Nov 87	THE WISHING WELL *MBS GOSH 1*	22	11

Eric GABLE *US, male vocalist (1 WEEK)* pos/wks

19 Mar 94	PROCESS OF ELIMINATION *Epic 6602282*	63	1

Peter GABRIEL (252 Top 500) *Award-winning singer / songwriter, b. 13 Feb 1950, Surrey, UK. Fronted Genesis until 1975, when replaced by Phil Collins. He broke through internationally with 'Sledgehammer', which also made him a video innovator. He is the driving force behind the Womad festival and is a tireless Amnesty International supporter (112 WEEKS)* pos/wks

9 Apr 77	SOLSBURY HILL *Charisma CB 301*	13	9
9 Feb 80 ●	GAMES WITHOUT FRONTIERS *Charisma CB 354*	4	11
10 May 80	NO SELF CONTROL *Charisma CB 360*	33	6
23 Aug 80	BIKO *Charisma CB 370*	38	3
25 Sep 82	SHOCK THE MONKEY *Charisma SHOCK 1*	58	5
9 Jul 83	I DON'T REMEMBER *Charisma GAB 1*	62	3
2 Jun 84	WALK THROUGH THE FIRE *Virgin VS 689*	69	3
26 Apr 86 ●	SLEDGEHAMMER *Virgin PGS 1* ▲	4	16
1 Nov 86 ●	DON'T GIVE UP *Virgin PGS 2* [1]	9	11
28 Mar 87	BIG TIME *Charisma PGS 3*	13	7
11 Jul 87	RED RAIN *Charisma PGS 4*	46	3
21 Nov 87	BIKO (LIVE) *Charisma PGS 6*	49	6
3 Jun 89	SHAKING THE TREE *Virgin VS 1167* [2]	61	3
22 Dec 90	SOLSBURY HILL / SHAKING THE TREE (re-issue) *Virgin VS 1322* [3]	57	4
19 Sep 92	DIGGING IN THE DIRT *Realworld PGS 7*	24	4
16 Jan 93 ●	STEAM *Realworld PGSDG 8*	10	7
3 Apr 93	BLOOD OF EDEN *Realworld PGSDG 9*	43	4
25 Sep 93	KISS THAT FROG *Realworld PGSDG 10*	46	3
25 Jun 94	LOVETOWN *Epic 6604802*	49	2
3 Sep 94	SW LIVE (EP) *Realworld PGSCD 11*	39	2

[1] Peter Gabriel and Kate Bush [2] Youssou N'Dour and Peter Gabriel [3] Peter Gabriel / Youssou N'Dour and Peter Gabriel

Tracks available on all formats of SW Live (EP): Red Rain / San Jacinto. 'Red Rain' is a live version of his 1987 hit

GABRIELLE (218 Top 500) *Eyepatch-wearing soul / pop vocalist, born Louisa Gabrielle Bobb, 16 May 1970, London, UK. Broke record for highest chart debut when 'Dreams' entered at No.2. Voted Best British Newcomer at 1994 Brit Awards and Best British Female Vocalist in 1997 (121 WEEKS)* pos/wks

19 Jun 93 ★	DREAMS *Go.Beat GODCD 99*	1	15
2 Oct 93 ●	GOING NOWHERE *Go.Beat GODCD 106*	9	7
11 Dec 93	I WISH *Go.Beat GODCD 108*	26	5
26 Feb 94	BECAUSE OF YOU *Go.Beat GODCD 109*	24	5
24 Feb 96 ●	GIVE ME A LITTLE MORE TIME *Go.Beat GODCD 139*	5	18
22 Jun 96	FORGET ABOUT THE WORLD *Go.Beat GODCD 146*	23	5
5 Oct 96	IF YOU REALLY CARED *Go.Beat GODCD 153*	15	5
2 Nov 96 ●	IF YOU EVER *London LONCD 388* [1]	2	15
1 Feb 97 ●	WALK ON BY *Go.Beat GODCD 159*	7	8
9 Oct 99 ●	SUNSHINE *Go.Beat GOBCD 23*	9	8
5 Feb 00 ★	RISE *Go.Beat / Polydor GOBCD 25* ■	1	15
17 Jun 00 ●	WHEN A WOMAN *Go.Beat / Polydor GOBCD 27*	6	8
4 Nov 00	SHOULD I STAY *Go.Beat / Polydor GOBCD 32*	13	7

[1] East 17 featuring Gabrielle

Yvonne GAGE *US, female vocalist (4 WEEKS)* pos/wks

16 Jun 84	DOIN' IT IN A HAUNTED HOUSE *Epic A 4519*	45	4

Danni'elle GAHA *Australia, female vocalist (7 WEEKS)* pos/wks

1 Aug 92	STUCK IN THE MIDDLE *Epic 6581247*	68	2
27 Feb 93	DO IT FOR LOVE *Epic 6584612*	52	2
12 Jun 93	SECRET LOVE *Epic 6592212*	41	3

Billy and Sarah GAINES *US, male / female vocal duo (1 WEEK)* pos/wks

14 Jun 97	**I FOUND SOMEONE** *Expansion CDEXP 27*	**48**	1

Rosie GAINES *US, female vocalist (15 WEEKS)* pos/wks

11 Nov 95	**I WANT U** *Motown 8604852*	**70**	1
31 May 97 ●	**CLOSER THAN CLOSE** *Big Bang CDBBANG 1*	**4**	12
29 Nov 97	**I SURRENDER** *Big Bang CDBBANG 2*	**39**	2

Serge GAINSBOURG – See Jane BIRKIN and Serge GAINSBOURG

GALA *Italy, female vocalist - Gala Rizzatto (24 WEEKS)* pos/wks

19 Jul 97 ●	**FREED FROM DESIRE** *Big Life BLRD 135*	**2**	14
6 Dec 97	**LET A BOY CRY** *Big Life BLRD 140*	**11**	8
22 Aug 98	**COME INTO MY LIFE** *Big Life BLRD 147*	**38**	2

GALAXY – See Phil FEARON

Dee GALDES – See Phil FEARON

Eve GALLAGHER *UK, female vocalist (8 WEEKS)* pos/wks

1 Dec 90	**LOVE COME DOWN** *More Protein PROT 6*	**61**	3
29 Dec 90	**LOVE COME DOWN (re-entry)** *More Protein PROT 6*	**68**	1
15 Apr 95	**YOU CAN HAVE IT ALL** *Cleveland City CLECD 13023*	**43**	2
28 Oct 95	**LOVE COME DOWN (re-recording)** *Cleveland City CLECD 13028*	**57**	1
6 Jul 96	**HEARTBREAK** *React CDREACT 78* [1]	**44**	1

[1] Mrs Wood featuring Eve Gallagher

Liam GALLAGHER – See OASIS; BUFFALO TOM

GALLAGHER and LYLE *UK, male vocal / instrumental duo - Benny Gallagher and Graham Lyle (27 WEEKS)* pos/wks

28 Feb 76 ●	**I WANNA STAY WITH YOU** *A & M AMS 7211*	**6**	9
22 May 76 ●	**HEART ON MY SLEEVE** *A & M AMS 7227*	**6**	10
11 Sep 76	**BREAKAWAY** *A & M AMS 7245*	**35**	4
29 Jan 77	**EVERY LITTLE TEARDROP** *A & M AMS 7274*	**32**	4

Patsy GALLANT *Canada, female vocalist (9 WEEKS)* pos/wks

10 Sep 77 ●	**FROM NEW YORK TO LA** *EMI 2620*	**6**	9

GALLIANO
UK, male / female vocal / instrumental group (14 WEEKS) pos/wks

30 May 92	**SKUNK FUNK** *Talkin Loud TLK 23*	**41**	2
1 Aug 92	**PRINCE OF PEACE** *Talkin Loud TLK 24*	**47**	3
10 Oct 92	**JUS' REACH (RECYCLED)** *Talkin Loud TLK 29*	**66**	2
28 May 94	**LONG TIME GONE** *Talkin Loud TLKCD 48*	**15**	3
30 Jul 94	**TWYFORD DOWN** *Talkin Loud TLKCD 49*	**37**	2
27 Jul 96	**EASE YOUR MIND** *Talkin Loud TLCD 10*	**45**	2

James GALWAY *UK, male instrumentalist - flute (13 WEEKS)* pos/wks

27 May 78 ●	**ANNIE'S SONG** *RCA Red Seal RB 5085*	**3**	13

GAMBAFREAKS *Italy, male production duo (2 WEEKS)* pos/wks

12 Sep 98	**INSTANT REPLAY** *Evocative EVOKE 7CDS* [1]	**57**	1
13 May 00	**DOWN DOWN DOWN** *Azuli AZNYCDX 116*	**57**	1

[1] Gambafreaks featuring Paco Rivaz

GANG OF FOUR *UK, male vocal / instrumental group (5 WEEKS)* pos/wks

16 Jun 79	**AT HOME HE'S A TOURIST** *EMI 2956*	**58**	3
22 May 82	**I LOVE A MAN IN UNIFORM** *EMI 5299*	**65**	2

GANG STARR *US, male rap group (8 WEEKS)* pos/wks

13 Oct 90	**JAZZ THING** *CBS 356377 7*	**66**	2
23 Feb 91	**TAKE A REST** *Cooltempo COOL 230*	**63**	1
25 May 91	**LOVESICK** *Cooltempo COOL 234*	**50**	3
13 Jun 92	**2 DEEP** *Cooltempo COOL 256*	**67**	2

GANT *UK, production duo - Julian Jonah and Danny Harrison (1 WEEK)* pos/wks

27 Dec 97	**SOUND BWOY BURIAL / ALL NIGHT LONG** *Positiva CDTIV 85*	**67**	1

GAP BAND (396 Top 500) *Soul / funk / disco outfit from Tulsa, Oklahoma, US, featuring brothers Charlie, Ronnie and Robert Wilson. Named after Greenwood, Archer and Pine - three streets in their hometown. First British hit launched a 'rowing-boat' craze on UK dancefloors (82 WEEKS)* pos/wks

12 Jul 80 ●	**OOPS UP SIDE YOUR HEAD** *Mercury MER 22*	**6**	14
27 Sep 80	**PARTY LIGHTS** *Mercury MER 37*	**30**	8
27 Dec 80	**BURN RUBBER ON ME (WHY YOU WANNA HURT ME)** *Mercury MER 52*	**22**	11
11 Apr 81	**HUMPIN'** *Mercury MER 63*	**36**	6
27 Jun 81	**YEARNING FOR YOUR LOVE** *Mercury MER 73*	**47**	4
5 Jun 82	**EARLY IN THE MORNING** *Mercury MER 97*	**55**	3
19 Feb 83	**OUTSTANDING** *Total Experience TE 001*	**68**	2
31 Mar 84	**SOMEDAY** *Total Experience TE 5*	**17**	8
23 Jun 84	**JAMMIN' IN AMERICA** *Total Experience TE 6*	**64**	2
13 Dec 86 ●	**BIG FUN** *Total Experience FB 49779*	**4**	12
14 Mar 87	**HOW MUSIC CAME ABOUT (BOP B DA B DA DA)** *Total Experience FB 49755*	**61**	2
11 Jul 87	**OOPS UPSIDE YOUR HEAD (re-mix)** *Club JAB 54*	**20**	8
18 Feb 89	**I'M GONNA GIT YOU SUCKA** *Arista 112016*	**63**	2

GARBAGE
US / UK, male / female vocal / instrumental group (57 WEEKS) pos/wks

19 Aug 95	**SUBHUMAN** *Mushroom D 1138*	**50**	1
30 Sep 95	**ONLY HAPPY WHEN IT RAINS** *Mushroom D 1199*	**29**	3
2 Dec 95	**QUEER** *Mushroom D 1237*	**13**	4
23 Mar 96 ●	**STUPID GIRL** *Mushroom D 1271*	**4**	7
23 Nov 96 ●	**MILK** *Mushroom D 1494* [1]	**10**	7
18 Jan 97	**MILK (re-entry)** *Mushroom D 1494* [1]	**74**	1
9 May 98	**PUSH IT** *Mushroom MUSH 28CDS*	**9**	5
18 Jul 98	**I THINK I'M PARANOID** *Mushroom MUSH 35CDS*	**9**	5
17 Oct 98	**SPECIAL** *Mushroom MUSH 39CDS*	**15**	4
6 Feb 99 ●	**WHEN I GROW UP** *Mushroom MUSH 43CDS*	**9**	7
5 Jun 99	**YOU LOOK SO FINE** *Mushroom MUSH 49CDS*	**19**	4
27 Nov 99	**THE WORLD IS NOT ENOUGH** *Radioactive RAXTD 40*	**11**	9

[1] Garbage featuring Tricky

Adam GARCIA *Australia, male vocalist (5 WEEKS)* pos/wks

16 May 98	**NIGHT FEVER** *Polydor 5697972*	**15**	5

Scott GARCIA featuring MC STYLES
UK, male producer and UK, male rapper (3 WEEKS) pos/wks

1 Nov 97	**A LONDON THING** *Connected CDCONNECT 1*	**29**	3

Boris GARDINER
Jamaica, male vocalist / instrumentalist (38 WEEKS) pos/wks

17 Jan 70	**ELIZABETHAN REGGAE** *Duke DU 39*	**48**	1
31 Jan 70	**ELIZABETHAN REGGAE (re-entry)** *Duke DU 39*	**14**	13
26 Jul 86 ★	**I WANT TO WAKE UP WITH YOU** *Revue REV 733*	**1**	15
4 Oct 86	**YOU'RE EVERYTHING TO ME** *Revue REV 735*	**11**	8
27 Dec 86	**THE MEANING OF CHRISTMAS** *Revue REV 740*	**69**	1

The first copies of 'Elizabethan Reggae', an instrumental, were printed with the label incorrectly crediting Byron Lee as the performer. The charts for the first entry, and the first four weeks of the re-entry, all reprinted this error. All charts and discs printed after 28 Feb 1970 gave Boris Gardiner the credit he deserved

Paul GARDINER *UK, male instrumentalist - bass (4 WEEKS)* pos/wks

25 Jul 81	**STORMTROOPER IN DRAG** *Beggars Banquet BEG 61*	**49**	4

Uncredited vocalist is Gary Numan

Art GARFUNKEL *US, male vocalist (37 WEEKS)* pos/wks

13 Sep 75 ★	**I ONLY HAVE EYES FOR YOU** *CBS 3575*	**1**	11
3 Mar 79 ★	**BRIGHT EYES** *CBS 6947* ◆	**1**	19
7 Jul 79	**SINCE I DON'T HAVE YOU** *CBS 7371*	**38**	7

See also SIMON and GARFUNKEL

24 Dec 83	I AM WHAT I AM (FROM 'LA CAGE AUX FOLLES')		
	Chrysalis CHS 2765	13	12
26 Jun 93 ●	I WILL SURVIVE (re-mix) *Polydor PZCD 270*	5	10
3 Jun 00	LAST NIGHT *Logic 74321738082*	67	1

GAZ *US, male vocal / instrumental group (4 WEEKS)*

		pos/wks	
24 Feb 79	SING SING *Salsoul SSOL 116*	60	4

GAZZA *UK, male vocalist - Paul Gascoigne (14 WEEKS)*

		pos/wks	
10 Nov 90 ●	FOG ON THE TYNE (REVISITED) *Best ZB 44083* [1]	2	9
22 Dec 90	GEORDIE BOYS (GAZZA RAP) *Best ZB 44229*	31	5

[1] Gazza and Lindisfarne

GBH *UK, male vocal / instrumental group (5 WEEKS)*

		pos/wks	
6 Feb 82	NO SURVIVORS *Clay CLAY 8*	63	2
20 Nov 82	GIVE ME FIRE *Clay CLAY 16*	69	3

J GEILS BAND *US, male vocal / instrumental group (20 WEEKS)*

		pos/wks	
9 Jun 79	ONE LAST KISS *EMI America AM 507*	74	1
13 Feb 82 ●	CENTERFOLD *EMI America EA 135* ▲	3	9
10 Apr 82	FREEZE-FRAME *EMI America EA 134*	27	7
26 Jun 82	ANGEL IN BLUE *EMI America EA 138*	55	3

Bob GELDOF *Ireland, male vocalist (15 WEEKS)*

		pos/wks	
1 Nov 86	THIS IS THE WORLD CALLING *Mercury BOB 101*	25	5
21 Feb 87	LOVE LIKE A ROCKET *Mercury BOB 102*	61	3
23 Jun 90	THE GREAT SONG OF INDIFFERENCE		
	Mercury BOB 104	15	6
7 May 94	CRAZY *Vertigo VERCX 85*	65	1

See also BOOMTOWN RATS

GEM – See OUR TRIBE / ONE TRIBE

GEMINI *UK, male vocal duo (7 WEEKS)*

		pos/wks	
30 Sep 95	EVEN THOUGH YOU BROKE MY HEART *EMI CDEMS 391*	40	3
10 Feb 96	STEAL YOUR LOVE AWAY *EMI CDEMS 407*	37	2
29 Jun 96	COULD IT BE FOREVER *EMI CDEMS 426*	38	2

GEMS FOR JEM *UK, male instrumental / production duo (2 WEEKS)*

		pos/wks	
6 May 95	LIFTING ME HIGHER *Box 21 CDSBOKS 3*	28	2

GENE *UK, male vocal / instrumental group (22 WEEKS)*

		pos/wks	
13 Aug 94	BE MY LIGHT BE MY GUIDE *Costermonger COST 002CD*	54	1
12 Nov 94	SLEEP WELL TONIGHT *Costermonger COST 003CD*	36	2
4 Mar 95	HAUNTED BY YOU *Costermonger COST 004CD*	32	2
22 Jul 95	OLYMPIAN *Costermonger COST 005CD*	18	2
13 Jan 96	FOR THE DEAD *Costermonger COST 006CD*	14	3
2 Nov 96	FIGHTING FIT *Costermonger COST 009CD*	22	2
1 Feb 97	WE COULD BE KINGS *Polydor COSCD 10*	17	2
10 May 97	WHERE ARE THEY NOW? *Polydor COSCD 11*	22	2
9 Aug 97	SPEAK TO ME SOMEONE *Polydor COSCD 12*	30	2
27 Feb 99	AS GOOD AS IT GETS *Polydor COSCD 14*	23	2
24 Apr 99	FILL HER UP *Polydor COSCD 15*	36	2

GENE AND JIM ARE INTO SHAKES
UK, male vocal / instrumental duo (2 WEEKS)

		pos/wks	
19 Mar 88	SHAKE! (HOW ABOUT A SAMPLING GENE)		
	Rough Trade RT 216	68	2

GENE LOVES JEZEBEL
UK, male vocal / instrumental group (7 WEEKS)

		pos/wks	
29 Mar 86	SWEETEST THING *Beggars Banquet BEG 156*	75	1
14 Jun 86	HEARTACHE *Beggars Banquet BEG 161*	71	2
5 Sep 87	THE MOTION OF LOVE *Beggars Banquet BEG 192*	56	3
5 Dec 87	GORGEOUS *Beggars Banquet BEG 202*	68	1

GENERAL DEGREE – See Richie STEPHENS

GENERAL LEVY *UK, male vocalist (13 WEEKS)*

		pos/wks	
4 Sep 93	MONKEY MAN *ffrr FCD 214*	75	1
18 Jun 94	INCREDIBLE *Renk RENK 42 CD* [1]	39	3
10 Sep 94 ●	INCREDIBLE (re-mix) *Renk CD RENK 44* [1]	8	9

[1] M-Beat featuring General Levy

GENERAL PUBLIC *UK, male vocal / instrumental group (4 WEEKS)*

		pos/wks	
10 Mar 84	GENERAL PUBLIC *Virgin VS 659*	60	3
2 Jul 94	I'LL TAKE YOU THERE *Epic 6605532*	73	1

See also BEAT

GENERAL SAINT *UK, male vocalist (9 WEEKS)*

		pos/wks	
29 Sep 84	LAST PLANE (ONE WAY TICKET) *MCA MCA 910* [1]	51	3
2 Apr 94	OH CAROL! *Copasetic COPCD 0009* [1]	54	5
6 Aug 94	SAVE THE LAST DANCE FOR ME *Copasetic COPCD 12* [2]	75	1

[1] Clint Eastwood and General Saint [2] General Saint featuring Don Campbell

GENERATION X *UK, male vocal / instrumental group (31 WEEKS)*

		pos/wks	
17 Sep 77	YOUR GENERATION *Chrysalis CHS 2165*	36	4
11 Mar 78	READY STEADY GO *Chrysalis CHS 2207*	47	3
20 Jan 79	KING ROCKER *Chrysalis CHS 2261*	11	9
7 Apr 79	VALLEY OF THE DOLLS *Chrysalis CHS 2310*	23	7
30 Jun 79	FRIDAY'S ANGELS *Chrysalis CHS 2330*	62	2
18 Oct 80	DANCING WITH MYSELF *Chrysalis CHS 2444* [1]	62	2
24 Jan 81	DANCING WITH MYSELF (EP) *Chrysalis CHS 2488* [1]	60	4

[1] Gen X

Tracks on Dancing With Myself (EP): Dancing With Myself / Untouchables / Rock On / King Rocker

See also Billy IDOL

GENERATOR *Holland, male producer - Robert Smit (1 WEEK)*

		pos/wks	
23 Oct 99	WHERE ARE YOU NOW? *Tidy Trax TIDY 130CD*	60	1

GENESIS 「102」 Top 500 *Perennially popular UK group. Stalwart members are Tony Banks (k) and Mike Rutherford (g); others included Peter Gabriel (v), Phil Collins (v/d), Steve Hackett (g). These progressive 1970s rockers became a major act in the 1980s and had 10 consecutive Top 3 albums (187 WEEKS)*

		pos/wks	
6 Apr 74	I KNOW WHAT I LIKE (IN YOUR WARDROBE)		
	Charisma CB 224	21	7
26 Feb 77	YOUR OWN SPECIAL WAY *Charisma CB 300*	43	3
28 May 77	SPOT THE PIGEON (EP) *Charisma GEN 001*	14	7
11 Mar 78 ●	FOLLOW YOU FOLLOW ME *Charisma CB 309*	7	13
8 Jul 78	MANY TOO MANY *Charisma CB 315*	43	5
15 Mar 80 ●	TURN IT ON AGAIN *Charisma CB 356*	8	10
17 May 80	DUCHESS *Charisma CB 363*	46	5
13 Sep 80	MISUNDERSTANDING *Charisma CB 369*	42	5
22 Aug 81 ●	ABACAB *Charisma CB 388*	9	8
31 Oct 81	KEEP IT DARK *Charisma CB 391*	33	4
13 Mar 82	MAN ON THE CORNER *Charisma CB 393*	41	5
22 May 82 ●	3 X 3 (EP) *Charisma GEN 1*	10	8
3 Sep 83 ●	MAMA *Virgin / Charisma MAMA 1*	4	10
12 Nov 83	THAT'S ALL *Charisma / Virgin TATA 1*	16	11
11 Feb 84	ILLEGAL ALIEN *Charisma / Virgin AL1*	46	3
10 Mar 84	ILLEGAL ALIEN (re-entry) *Charisma / Virgin AL1*	70	1
31 May 86	INVISIBLE TOUCH *Virgin GENS 1* ▲	15	8
30 Aug 86	IN TOO DEEP *Virgin GENS 2*	19	9
22 Nov 86	LAND OF CONFUSION *Virgin GENS 3*	14	12
14 Mar 87	TONIGHT TONIGHT TONIGHT *Virgin GENS 4*	18	6
20 Jun 87	THROWING IT ALL AWAY *Virgin GENS 5*	22	8
2 Nov 91 ●	NO SON OF MINE *Virgin GENS 6*	6	6
4 Jan 92	NO SON OF MINE (re-entry) *Virgin GENS 6*	70	1
11 Jan 92	I CAN'T DANCE *Virgin GENS 7*	7	9
18 Apr 92	HOLD ON MY HEART *Virgin GENS 8*	16	5
25 Jul 92	JESUS HE KNOWS ME *Virgin GENS 9*	20	7
21 Nov 92 ●	INVISIBLE TOUCH (LIVE) *Virgin GENS 10*	7	4
20 Feb 93	TELL ME WHY *Virgin GENDG 11*	40	3
27 Sep 97	CONGO *Virgin GENSD 12*	29	2

13 Dec 97	**SHIPWRECKED** *Virgin GENDX14*	**54**	1
7 Mar 98	**NOT ABOUT US** *Virgin GENSD 15*	**66**	1

Tracks on Spot the Pigeon (EP): Match of the Day / Pigeons / Inside and Out. Tracks on 3 x 3 (EP): Paperlate / You Might Recall / Me and Virgil

See also MIKE and the MECHANICS; Phil COLLINS; Steve HACKETT; FISH; Peter GABRIEL

Lee A GENESIS – See Bob SINCLAR

GENEVA *UK, male vocal / instrumental group (9 WEEKS)*　pos/wks
26 Oct 96	**NO ONE SPEAKS** *Nude NUD 22CD*	**32**	2
8 Feb 97	**INTO THE BLUE** *Nude NUD 25CD*	**26**	2
31 May 97	**TRANQUILIZER** *Nude NUD 28 CD1*	**24**	2
16 Aug 97	**BEST REGRETS** *Nude NUD 31CD1*	**38**	1
27 Nov 99	**DOLLARS IN THE HEAVENS** *Nude NUD 46CD1*	**59**	1
11 Mar 00	**IF YOU HAVE TO GO** *Nude NUD 49CD1*	**69**	1

GENEVIEVE *France, female vocalist (1 WEEK)*　pos/wks
5 May 66	**ONCE** *CBS 202061*	**43**	1

GENIUS / GZA featuring D'ANGELO *(2 WEEKS)*　pos/wks
2 Mar 96	**COLD WORLD** *Geffen GFSTD 22114*	**40**	2

Bobbie GENTRY *US, female vocalist - Roberta Streeter (48 WEEKS)*　pos/wks
13 Sep 67	**ODE TO BILLY JOE** *Capitol CL 15511* ▲	**13**	11
30 Aug 69	★ **I'LL NEVER FALL IN LOVE AGAIN** *Capitol CL 15606*	**1**	19
6 Dec 69	● **ALL I HAVE TO DO IS DREAM** *Capitol CL 15619* [1]	**3**	14
21 Feb 70	**RAINDROPS KEEP FALLIN' ON MY HEAD** *Capitol CL 15626*	**40**	4

[1] Bobbie Gentry and Glen Campbell

GEORDIE *UK, male vocal / instrumental group (35 WEEKS)*　pos/wks
2 Dec 72	**DON'T DO THAT** *Regal Zonophone RZ 3067*	**32**	7
17 Mar 73	● **ALL BECAUSE OF YOU** *EMI 2008*	**6**	13
16 Jun 73	**CAN YOU DO IT** *EMI 2031*	**13**	9
25 Aug 73	**ELECTRIC LADY** *EMI 2048*	**32**	6

Robin GEORGE *UK, male vocalist / instrumentalist - guitar (2 WEEKS)*　pos/wks
27 Apr 85	**HEARTLINE** *Bronze BRO 191*	**68**	2

Sophia GEORGE *Jamaica, female vocalist (11 WEEKS)*　pos/wks
7 Dec 85	● **GIRLIE GIRLIE** *Winner WIN 01*	**7**	11

GEORGIA SATELLITES
US, male vocal / instrumental group (8 WEEKS)　pos/wks
7 Feb 87	**KEEP YOUR HANDS TO YOURSELF** *Elektra EKR 50*	**69**	1
16 May 87	**BATTLESHIP CHAINS** *Elektra EKR 58*	**44**	4
21 Jan 89	**HIPPY HIPPY SHAKE** *Elektra EKR 86*	**63**	3

GEORGIE PORGIE *US, male producer (3 WEEKS)*　pos/wks
12 Aug 95	**EVERYBODY MUST PARTY** *Vibe MCSTD 2068*	**61**	1
4 May 96	**TAKE ME HIGHER** *Music Plant MCSTD 40031*	**61**	1
26 Aug 00	**LIFE GOES ON** *Neo NEOCD 039*	**54**	1

GEORGIO *US, male vocalist (3 WEEKS)*　pos/wks
20 Feb 88	**LOVER'S LANE** *Motown ZB 41611*	**54**	3

Danyel GERARD *France, male vocalist (12 WEEKS)*　pos/wks
18 Sep 71	**BUTTERFLY** *CBS 7454*	**11**	12

GERIDEAU *US, male vocalist (2 WEEKS)*　pos/wks
27 Aug 94	**BRING IT ALL BACK 2 LUV** *Fruittree FTREE 10CD*	**65**	1
4 Jul 98	**MASQUERADE** *Inferno CDFERN7*	**63**	1

See also PROJECT featuring GERIDEAU

GERRY and the PACEMAKERS (237 Top 500) *Record-breaking*
Merseybeat band: Gerry Marsden (v/g), Les Chadwick (b), Les McGuire (p), Freddie Marsden (d). Second Liverpool group to chart (after The Beatles), but first to reach No.1 and first act ever to top UK chart with their initial three singles (114 WEEKS)　pos/wks
14 Mar 63	★ **HOW DO YOU DO IT?** *Columbia DB 4987*	**1**	18
30 May 63	★ **I LIKE IT** *Columbia DB 7041*	**1**	15
10 Oct 63	★ **YOU'LL NEVER WALK ALONE** *Columbia DB 7126*	**1**	19
16 Jan 64	● **I'M THE ONE** *Columbia DB 7189*	**2**	15
16 Apr 64	● **DON'T LET THE SUN CATCH YOU CRYING** *Columbia DB 7268*	**6**	11
3 Sep 64	**IT'S GONNA BE ALL RIGHT** *Columbia DB 7353*	**24**	7
17 Dec 64	● **FERRY ACROSS THE MERSEY** *Columbia DB 7437*	**8**	13
25 Mar 65	**I'LL BE THERE** *Columbia DB 7504*	**15**	9
18 Nov 65	**WALK HAND IN HAND** *Columbia DB 7738*	**29**	7

GET FRESH CREW – See Doug E FRESH and the GET FRESH CREW

GET READY *UK, male vocal group (1 WEEK)*　pos/wks
3 Jun 95	**WILD WILD WEST** *Mega GACXCD 2698*	**65**	1

GETO BOYS featuring FLAJ *US, male rap group (1 WEEK)*　pos/wks
11 May 96	**THE WORLD IS A GHETTO** *Virgin America VUSCD 104*	**49**	1

Stan GETZ *US, male instrumentalist - tenor sax (29 WEEKS)*　pos/wks
8 Nov 62	**DESAFINADO** *HMV POP 1061* [1]	**11**	13
23 Jul 64	**THE GIRL FROM IPANEMA (GAROTA DE IPANEMA)** *Verve VS 520* [2]	**29**	10
25 Aug 84	**THE GIRL FROM IPANEMA (re-issue)** *Verve IPA 1* [3]	**55**	6

[1] Stan Getz and Charlie Byrd [2] Stan Getz and Joao Gilberto [3] Astrud Gilberto

The re-issue of 'The Girl From Ipanema' was credited only to Astrud Gilberto, the vocalist, even though it was exactly the same recording as the original hit

Amanda GHOST *UK, female vocalist (1 WEEK)*　pos/wks
8 Apr 00	**IDOL** *Warner Brothers W 518CD*	**63**	1

GHOST DANCE *UK, male vocal / instrumental group (2 WEEKS)*　pos/wks
17 Jun 89	**DOWN TO THE WIRE** *Chrysalis CHS 3376*	**66**	2

GHOSTFACE KILLAH
US, male rapper - Dennis Coles (13 WEEKS)　pos/wks
12 Jul 97	**ALL THAT I GOT IS YOU** *Epic 6646842*	**11**	4
23 Jan 99	● **I WANT YOU FOR MYSELF** *Northwestside 74321643632* [1]	**2**	8
4 Nov 00	**MISS FAT BOOTY - PART II** *Rawkus RWK 282CD* [2]	**64**	1

[1] Another Level / Ghostface Killah [2] Mos Def featuring Ghostface Killah

Andy GIBB *UK, male vocalist (30 WEEKS)*　pos/wks
25 Jun 77	**I JUST WANNA BE YOUR EVERYTHING** *RSO 2090 237* ▲	**26**	7
13 May 78	**SHADOW DANCING** *RSO 001* ▲	**42**	6
12 Aug 78	● **AN EVERLASTING LOVE** *RSO 015*	**10**	10
27 Jan 79	**(OUR LOVE) DON'T THROW IT ALL AWAY** *RSO 26*	**32**	7

Barry GIBB – See BEE GEES; Barbra STREISAND

Robin GIBB *UK, male vocalist (21 WEEKS)*　pos/wks
9 Jul 69	● **SAVED BY THE BELL** *Polydor 56-337*	**2**	16
15 Nov 69	**SAVED BY THE BELL (re-entry)** *Polydor 56-337*	**49**	1
7 Feb 70	**AUGUST OCTOBER** *Polydor 56-371*	**45**	3
11 Feb 84	**ANOTHER LONELY NIGHT IN NEW YORK** *Polydor POSP 668*	**71**	1

See also BEE GEES

Steve GIBBONS BAND
UK, male vocal / instrumental group (14 WEEKS)　pos/wks
6 Aug 77	**TULANE** *Polydor 2058 889*	**12**	10
13 May 78	**EDDY VORTEX** *Polydor 2059 017*	**56**	4

Georgia GIBBS US, female vocalist (2 WEEKS)   pos/wks

| 22 Apr 55 | TWEEDLE DEE *Mercury MB 3196* | 20 | 1 |
| 13 Jul 56 | KISS ME ANOTHER *Mercury MT 110* | 24 | 1 |

Debbie GIBSON `496` `Top 500` *First female to write, sing and produce a US No.1 single on her own, b. 31 Aug 1970, New York, US. America's top female singer of 1988 was the first teenage female to top US singles and album chart simultaneously. As Deborah Gibson, she moved successfully into stage musicals in early 1990s. (70 WEEKS)*   pos/wks

26 Sep 87	ONLY IN MY DREAMS *Atlantic A 9322*	54	5
23 Jan 88 ●	SHAKE YOUR LOVE *Atlantic A 9187*	7	8
19 Mar 88	ONLY IN MY DREAMS (re-entry) *Atlantic A 9322*	11	7
7 May 88	OUT OF THE BLUE *Atlantic A 9091*	19	7
9 Jul 88 ●	FOOLISH BEAT *Atlantic A 9059* ▲	9	9
15 Oct 88	STAYING TOGETHER *Atlantic A 9020*	53	2
28 Jan 89	LOST IN YOUR EYES *Atlantic A 8970* ▲	34	7
29 Apr 89	ELECTRIC YOUTH *Atlantic A 8919*	14	8
19 Aug 89	WE COULD BE TOGETHER *Atlantic A 8896*	22	8
9 Mar 91	ANYTHING IS POSSIBLE *Atlantic A 7735*	51	2
3 Apr 93	SHOCK YOUR MAMA *Atlantic A 7386CD*	74	1
24 Jul 93	YOU'RE THE ONE THAT I WANT *Epic 6595222* [1]	13	6

[1] Craig McLachlan and Debbie Gibson

Don GIBSON US, male vocalist (16 WEEKS)   pos/wks

| 31 Aug 61 | SEA OF HEARTBREAK *RCA 1243* | 14 | 13 |
| 1 Feb 62 | LONESOME NUMBER ONE *RCA 1272* | 47 | 3 |

Wayne GIBSON UK, male vocalist (13 WEEKS)   pos/wks

| 3 Sep 64 | KELLY *Pye 7N 15680* | 48 | 2 |
| 23 Nov 74 | UNDER MY THUMB *Pye Disco Demand DDS 2001* | 17 | 11 |

GIBSON BROTHERS Martinique, male vocal / instrumental group (54 WEEKS)   pos/wks

10 Mar 79	CUBA *Island WIP 6483*	41	9
21 Jul 79 ●	OOH! WHAT A LIFE *Island WIP 6503*	10	12
17 Nov 79 ●	QUE SERA MI VIDA (IF YOU SHOULD GO) *Island WIP 6525*	5	11
23 Feb 80	CUBA / BETTER DO IT SALSA (re-issue) *Island WIP 6561*	12	9
12 Jul 80	MARIANA *Island WIP 6617*	11	10
9 Jul 83	MY HEART'S BEATING WILD (TIC TAC TIC TAC) *Stiff BUY 184*	56	3

GIDEA PARK
UK, male vocal / instrumentalist - Adrian Baker (19 WEEKS)   pos/wks

| 4 Jul 81 | BEACH BOY GOLD *Stone SON 2162* | 11 | 13 |
| 12 Sep 81 | SEASONS OF GOLD *Polo POLO 14* | 28 | 6 |

GIFTED UK, male instrumentalist (1 WEEK)   pos/wks

| 23 Aug 97 | DO I *Perfecto PERF 140CD* | 60 | 1 |

GIGOLO AUNTS US, male vocal / instrumental group (4 WEEKS)   pos/wks

| 23 Apr 94 | MRS WASHINGTON *Fire BLAZE 68CD* | 74 | 1 |
| 13 May 95 | WHERE I FIND MY HEAVEN *Fire BLAZE 87CD* | 29 | 3 |

Astrud GILBERTO – See Stan GETZ

Joao GILBERTO – See Stan GETZ

Donna GILES US, female vocalist (4 WEEKS)   pos/wks

| 13 Aug 94 | AND I'M TELLING YOU I'M NOT GOING *Ore AG 4CD* | 43 | 2 |
| 10 Feb 96 | AND I'M TELLING YOU I'M NOT GOING (re-issue) *Ore AGR 4CD* | 27 | 2 |

Johnny GILL US, male vocalist (12 WEEKS)   pos/wks

23 Feb 91	WRAP MY BODY TIGHT *Motown ZB 44271*	57	1
28 Nov 92	SLOW AND SEXY *Epic 6587727* [1]	17	7
17 Jul 93	THE FLOOR *Motown TMGCD 1416*	53	1
29 Jan 94	A CUTE SWEET LOVE ADDICTION *Motown TMGCD 1420*	46	2

[1] Shabba Ranks featuring Johnny Gill

Vince GILL – See Amy GRANT; Barbra STREISAND

GILLAN UK, male vocal / instrumental group (46 WEEKS)   pos/wks

14 Jun 80	SLEEPIN' ON THE JOB *Virgin VS 355*	55	3
4 Oct 80	TROUBLE *Virgin VS 377*	14	6
14 Feb 81	MUTUALLY ASSURED DESTRUCTION *Virgin VSK 103*	32	5
21 Mar 81	NEW ORLEANS *Virgin VS 406*	17	10
20 Jun 81	NO LAUGHING IN HEAVEN *Virgin VS 425*	31	6
10 Oct 81	NIGHTMARE *Virgin VS 441*	36	6
23 Jan 82	RESTLESS *Virgin VS 465*	25	7
4 Sep 82	LIVING FOR THE CITY *Virgin VS 519*	50	3

GILLETTE – See 20 FINGERS

Stuart GILLIES UK, male vocalist (10 WEEKS)   pos/wks

| 31 Mar 73 | AMANDA *Philips 6006 293* | 13 | 10 |

Jimmy GILMER – See FIREBALLS

James GILREATH US, male vocalist (10 WEEKS)   pos/wks

| 2 May 63 | LITTLE BAND OF GOLD *Pye International 7N 25190* | 29 | 10 |

Jim GILSTRAP US, male vocalist (11 WEEKS)   pos/wks

| 15 Mar 75 ● | SWING YOUR DADDY *Chelsea 2005 021* | 4 | 11 |

Gordon GILTRAP
UK, male instrumentalist - guitar (10 WEEKS)   pos/wks

| 14 Jan 78 | HEARTSONG *Electric WOT 19* | 21 | 7 |
| 28 Apr 79 | FEAR OF THE DARK *Electric WOT 29* [1] | 58 | 3 |

[1] Gordon Giltrap Band

GIN BLOSSOMS
US, male vocal / instrumental group (12 WEEKS)   pos/wks

5 Feb 94	HEY JEALOUSY *Fontana GINCD 3*	24	5
16 Apr 94	FOUND OUT ABOUT YOU *Fontana GINCD 4*	40	3
10 Feb 96	TIL I HEAR IT FROM YOU *A & M 5812272*	39	2
27 Apr 96	FOLLOW YOU DOWN *A & M 5815512*	30	2

GINGERBREADS – See GOLDIE and the GINGERBREADS

GINUWINE US, male rapper - Elgin Lumpkin (22 WEEKS)   pos/wks

25 Jan 97	PONY *Epic 6641282*	16	6
24 May 97	TELL ME DO U WANNA *Epic 6645272*	16	3
6 Sep 97 ●	WHEN DOVES CRY *Epic 6649245*	10	5
14 Mar 98	HOLLER *Epic 6653372*	13	4
13 Mar 99 ●	WHAT'S SO DIFFERENT? *Epic 6670522*	10	4

GIPSY KINGS
France, male vocal / instrumental group (2 WEEKS)   pos/wks

| 3 Sep 94 | HITS MEDLEY *Columbia 6606022* | 53 | 2 |

Martine GIRAULT UK, female vocalist (7 WEEKS)   pos/wks

29 Aug 92	REVIVAL *ffrr FX 195*	53	2
30 Jan 93	REVIVAL (re-issue) *ffrr FCD 205*	37	3
28 Oct 95	BEEN THINKING ABOUT YOU *RCA 74321316142*	63	1
1 Feb 97	REVIVAL (re-mix) *RCA 74321432162*	61	1

GIRL UK, male vocal / instrumental group (3 WEEKS)   pos/wks

| 12 Apr 80 | HOLLYWOOD TEASE *Jet 176* | 50 | 3 |

GIRL THING UK / Holland, female vocal group (13 WEEKS)   pos/wks

1 Jul 00 ●	LAST ONE STANDING *RCA 74321762412*	8	8
9 Sep 00	LAST ONE STANDING (re-entry) *RCA 74321762412*	65	2
18 Nov 00	GIRLS ON TOP *RCA 74321801162*	25	3

GIRLFRIEND Australia, female vocal group (6 WEEKS)   pos/wks

| 30 Jan 93 | TAKE IT FROM ME *Arista 74321114252* | 47 | 4 |
| 15 May 93 | GIRL'S LIFE *Arista 74321138452* | 68 | 2 |

UK No.1 ★   UK Top 10 ●   Still on chart +   UK million seller ◆   UK entry at No.1 ■   US No.1 ▲

GIRLSCHOOL *UK, female vocal / instrumental group (25 WEEKS)* pos/wks

2 Aug 80		RACE WITH THE DEVIL *Bronze BRO 100*	49	6
21 Feb 81	●	ST VALENTINE'S DAY MASSACRE (EP) *Bronze BRO 116* [1]	5	8
11 Apr 81		HIT AND RUN *Bronze BRO 118*	32	6
11 Jul 81		C'MON LET'S GO *Bronze BRO 126*	42	3
3 Apr 82		WILDLIFE (EP) *Bronze BRO 144*	58	2

[1] Motörhead and Girlschool (also known as Headgirl)

Tracks on St Valentine's Day Massacre (EP): Please Don't Touch / Emergency / Bomber. Tracks on Wildlife (EP): Don't Call It Love / Wildlife / Don't Stop

Junior GISCOMBE – See JUNIOR

GITTA
Denmark / Italy, male / female vocal / instrumental group (1 WEEK) pos/wks

19 Aug 00	NO MORE TURNING BACK *Pepper 9230302*	54	1

GLADIATORS – See NERO and the GLADIATORS

GLADIATORS *UK, male / female vocal group (1 WEEK)* pos/wks

30 Nov 96	THE BOYS ARE BACK IN TOWN *RCA 74321417002*	70	1

GLAM *Italy, male instrumental / production group (2 WEEKS)* pos/wks

1 May 93	HELL'S PARTY *Six6 SIXCD 001*	42	2

GLAM METAL DETECTIVES *UK, male / female vocal group (2 WEEKS)* pos/wks

11 Mar 95	EVERYBODY UP! *ZTT ZANG 62CD*	29	2

GLAMMA KID
UK, male vocalist / rapper - Iyael Constable (24 WEEKS) pos/wks

21 Nov 98		FASHION '98 *WEA WEA 179CD*	49	1
17 Apr 99	●	TABOO *WEA WEA 203CD* [1]	10	8
27 Nov 99	●	WHY *WEA WEA 229 CD1*	10	10
2 Sep 00		BILLS 2 PAY *WEA WEA 268CD*	17	4
14 Oct 00		BILLS 2 PAY (re-entry) *WEA WEA 268CD*	69	1

[1] Glamma Kid featuring Shola Ama

GLASS TIGER *Canada, male vocal / instrumental group (18 WEEKS)* pos/wks

18 Oct 86	DON'T FORGET ME (WHEN I'M GONE) *Manhattan MT 13*	29	9
31 Jan 87	SOMEDAY *Manhattan MT 17*	66	2
26 Oct 91	MY TOWN *EMI EM 212*	33	7

'My Town' features the uncredited vocals of Rod Stewart

Mayson GLEN ORCHESTRA – See Paul HENRY and the Mayson GLEN ORCHESTRA

GLENN and CHRIS *UK, male footballers / vocal duo - Glenn Hoddle and Chris Waddle (8 WEEKS)* pos/wks

18 Apr 87	DIAMOND LIGHTS *Record Shack KICK 1*	12	8

GLITTER BAND *UK, male vocal / instrumental group (60 WEEKS)* pos/wks

23 Mar 74	●	ANGEL FACE *Bell 1348*	4	10
3 Aug 74	●	JUST FOR YOU *Bell 1368*	10	8
19 Oct 74	●	LET'S GET TOGETHER AGAIN *Bell 1383*	8	8
18 Jan 75	●	GOODBYE MY LOVE *Bell 1395*	2	9
12 Apr 75	●	THE TEARS I CRIED *Bell 1416*	8	8
9 Aug 75		LOVE IN THE SUN *Bell 1437*	15	8
28 Feb 76	●	PEOPLE LIKE YOU AND PEOPLE LIKE ME *Bell 1471*	5	9

See also Gary GLITTER

Gary GLITTER `116` `Top 500` *Glitter rock giant, b. Paul Gadd, 8 May 1940, Oxfordshire, UK. Started recording in 1960 (as Paul Raven), and was first act to put first 11 hits into the Top 10. This singer / songwriter remained a popular live performer until jailed in 1999 (170 WEEKS)* pos/wks

10 Jun 72	●	ROCK AND ROLL (PARTS 1 & 2) *Bell 1216*	2	15
23 Sep 72	●	I DIDN'T KNOW I LOVED YOU (TILL I SAW YOU ROCK'N' ROLL) *Bell 1259*	4	11
20 Jan 73	●	DO YOU WANNA TOUCH ME? (OH YEAH) *Bell 1280*	2	11
7 Apr 73	●	HELLO HELLO I'M BACK AGAIN *Bell 1299*	2	14
21 Jul 73	★	I'M THE LEADER OF THE GANG (I AM) *Bell 1321*	1	12
17 Nov 73	★	I LOVE YOU LOVE ME LOVE *Bell 1337* ◆ ■	1	14
30 Mar 74	●	REMEMBER ME THIS WAY *Bell 1349*	3	8
15 Jun 74	★	ALWAYS YOURS *Bell 1359*	1	9
23 Nov 74	●	OH YES! YOU'RE BEAUTIFUL *Bell 1391*	2	10
3 May 75	●	LOVE LIKE YOU AND ME *Bell 1423*	10	6
21 Jun 75	●	DOING ALRIGHT WITH THE BOYS *Bell 1429*	6	7
8 Nov 75		PAPA OOM MOW MOW *Bell 1451*	38	5
13 Mar 76		YOU BELONG TO ME *Bell 1473*	40	5
22 Jan 77		IT TAKES ALL NIGHT LONG *Arista 85*	25	6
16 Jul 77		A LITTLE BOOGIE WOOGIE IN THE BACK OF MY MIND *Arista 112*	31	5
20 Sep 80		GARY GLITTER (EP) *GTO GT 282*	57	3
10 Oct 81		AND THEN SHE KISSED ME *Bell BELL 1497*	39	5
5 Dec 81		ALL THAT GLITTERS *Bell BELL 1498*	48	5
23 Jun 84		DANCE ME UP *Arista ARIST 570*	25	5
1 Dec 84	●	ANOTHER ROCK AND ROLL CHRISTMAS *Arista ARIST 592*	7	7
10 Oct 92		AND THE LEADER ROCKS ON *EMI EM 252*	58	2
21 Nov 92		THROUGH THE YEARS *EMI EM 256*	49	3
16 Dec 95		HELLO HELLO I'M BACK AGAIN (AGAIN!) *Carlton Sounds 3036000192*	50	2

'Rock and Roll Part 1' not listed with 'Part 2' for weeks of 10 and 17 Jun 1972. Tracks on Gary Glitter (EP): I'm the Leader of the Gang (I Am) / Rock and Roll (Part 2) / Hello Hello I'm Back Again / Do You Wanna Touch Me? (Oh Yeah). All were re-issues. 'Hello Hello I'm Back Again (Again!)' in 1995 is a re-recording

GLOBAL COMMUNICATION
UK, male instrumental / production duo (1 WEEK) pos/wks

11 Jan 97	THE WAY / THE DEEP *Dedicated GLOBA 002CD*	51	1

GLOVE *UK, male vocal / instrumental group (3 WEEKS)* pos/wks

20 Aug 83	LIKE AN ANIMAL *Wonderland SHE 3*	52	3

See also SIOUXSIE and the BANSHEES

GLOWORM *UK / US, male vocal / instrumental group (17 WEEKS)* pos/wks

6 Feb 93		I LIFT MY CUP *Pulse 8 CDLOSE 37*	20	4
14 May 94	●	CARRY ME HOME *Go.Beat GODCD 112*	9	11
6 Aug 94		I LIFT MY CUP (re-issue) *Pulse 8 CDLOSE 67*	46	2

GO GO LORENZO and the DAVIS PINCKNEY PROJECT
US, male vocal / instrumental group (8 WEEKS) pos/wks

6 Dec 86	YOU CAN DANCE (IF YOU WANT TO) *Boiling Point POSP 836*	46	8

GO-GO's *US, female vocal / instrumental group (10 WEEKS)* pos/wks

15 May 82	OUR LIPS ARE SEALED *IRS GDN 102*	47	6
26 Jan 91	COOL JERK *IRS AM 712*	60	1
18 Feb 95	THE WHOLE WORLD LOST ITS HEAD *IRS CDEIRS 190*	29	3

See also Belinda CARLISLE

GO WEST `379` `Top 500` *Songwriting duo specialising in radio-friendly white soul sounds; Peter Cox (v) and Richard Drummie (g/k/v). Best Newcomers at the 1986 Brit awards had US Top 10 hit with 'King of Wishful Thinking', from the soundtrack of Pretty Woman. (85 WEEKS)* pos/wks

23 Feb 85	●	WE CLOSE OUR EYES *Chrysalis CHS 2850*	5	14
11 May 85		CALL ME *Chrysalis GOW 1*	12	10
3 Aug 85		GOODBYE GIRL *Chrysalis GOW 2*	25	7
23 Nov 85		DON'T LOOK DOWN - THE SEQUEL *Chrysalis GOW 3*	13	10
29 Nov 86		TRUE COLOURS *Chrysalis GOW 4*	48	7
9 May 87		I WANT TO HEAR IT FROM YOU *Chrysalis GOW 5*	43	3
12 Sep 87		THE KING IS DEAD *Chrysalis GOW 6*	67	2
28 Jul 90		THE KING OF WISHFUL THINKING *Chrysalis GOW 8*	18	10
17 Oct 92		FAITHFUL *Chrysalis GOW 9*	13	6
16 Jan 93		WHAT YOU WON'T DO FOR LOVE *Chrysalis CDGOWS 10*	15	5
27 Mar 93		STILL IN LOVE *Chrysalis CDGOWS 11*	43	3
2 Oct 93		TRACKS OF MY TEARS *Chrysalis CDGOWS 12*	16	5
4 Dec 93		WE CLOSE OUR EYES (re-mix) *Chrysalis CDGOWS 13*	40	3

UK No.1 ★   UK Top 10 ●   Still on chart +   UK million seller ◆   UK entry at No.1 ■   US No.1 ▲

GOATS US, male rap group (2 WEEKS)

		pos/wks
29 May 93	AAAH D YAAA / TYPICAL AMERICAN Ruff House 6593032	53 2

'Typical American' listed only from 5 Jun 1993, peaking at No.65

GOD MACHINE US, male vocal / instrumental group (2 WEEKS)

		pos/wks
30 Jan 93	HOME Fiction FICCD 47	65 2

GODIEGO Japan / US, male vocal / instrumental group (11 WEEKS)

		pos/wks
15 Oct 77	THE WATER MARGIN BBC RESL 50	37 4
16 Feb 80	GANDHARA BBC RESL 66	56 7

'The Water Margin' is the English version of the song, which shared chart credit with the Japanese language version by Pete Mac Jr

GODLEY and CREME UK, male vocal / instrumental duo - Kevin Godley and Lol Creme (36 WEEKS)

		pos/wks
12 Sep 81 ●	UNDER YOUR THUMB Polydor POSP 322	3 11
21 Nov 81 ●	WEDDING BELLS Polydor POSP 369	7 11
30 Mar 85	CRY Polydor POSP 732	19 11
16 Aug 86	CRY (re-entry) Polydor POSP 732	66 3

See also 10 CC

GOD'S PROPERTY US, male / female gospel choir (1 WEEK)

		pos/wks
22 Nov 97	STOMP B-rite Music IND 95559	60 1

Andrew GOLD
US, male vocalist / instrumentalist - piano (36 WEEKS)

		pos/wks
2 Apr 77	LONELY BOY Asylum K 13076	11 9
25 Mar 78 ●	NEVER LET HER SLIP AWAY Asylum K 13112	5 13
24 Jun 78	HOW CAN THIS BE LOVE Asylum K 13126	19 10
14 Oct 78	THANK YOU FOR BEING A FRIEND Asylum K 13135	42 4

GOLD BLADE UK, male vocal / instrumental group (1 WEEK)

		pos/wks
22 Mar 97	STRICTLY HARDCORE Ultimate TOPP 056CD	64 1

Brian and Tony GOLD – See RED DRAGON with Brian and Tony GOLD

GOLDBUG UK, male / female vocal / instrumental group (5 WEEKS)

		pos/wks
27 Jan 96 ●	WHOLE LOTTA LOVE Acid Jazz JAZID 125CD	3 5

GOLDEN EARRING
Holland, male vocal / instrumental group (16 WEEKS)

		pos/wks
8 Dec 73 ●	RADAR LOVE Track 2094 116	7 13
8 Oct 77	RADAR LOVE Polydor 2121 335	44 3

The 8 Oct 1977 version of Radar Love credits Golden Earring 'Live'

GOLDEN GIRLS UK, male producer / instrumentalist (3 WEEKS)

		pos/wks
3 Oct 98	KINETIC Distinctive DISNCD 46	38 2
4 Dec 99	KINETIC '99 (re-mix) Distinctive DISNCD 59	56 1

GOLDENSCAN UK, male DJ / production duo (1 WEEK)

		pos/wks
11 Nov 00	SUNRISE VC Recordings VCRD 79	52 1

GOLDIE UK, male vocal / instrumental group (11 WEEKS)

		pos/wks
27 May 78 ●	MAKING UP AGAIN Bronze BRO 50	7 11

GOLDIE UK, male producer - Clifford Price (16 WEEKS)

		pos/wks
3 Dec 94	INNER CITY LIFE ffrr FCD 251 [1]	49 2
9 Sep 95	ANGEL ffrr FCD 266	41 3
11 Nov 95	INNER CITY LIFE (re-mix) ffrr FCD 267	39 2
1 Nov 97	DIGITAL ffrr FCD 316 [2]	13 3
24 Jan 98	TEMPERTEMPER ffrr FCD 325 [2]	13 4
18 Apr 98	BELIEVE ffrr FCD 332	36 2

[1] Goldie presents Metalheadz [2] Goldie featuring KRS One

GOLDIE and the GINGERBREADS
US, female vocal / instrumental group (5 WEEKS)

		pos/wks
25 Feb 65	CAN'T YOU HEAR MY HEART BEAT? Decca F 12070	25 5

Bobby GOLDSBORO US, male vocalist (47 WEEKS)

		pos/wks
17 Apr 68 ●	HONEY United Artists UP2215 ▲	2 15
4 Aug 73 ●	SUMMER (THE FIRST TIME) United Artists UP35558	9 10
3 Aug 74	HELLO SUMMERTIME United Artists UP35705	14 10
29 Mar 75 ●	HONEY (re-issue) United Artists UP35633	2 12

Glen GOLDSMITH UK, male vocalist (24 WEEKS)

		pos/wks
7 Nov 87	I WON'T CRY Reproduction PB 41493	34 7
12 Mar 88	DREAMING Reproduction PB 41711	12 11
11 Jun 88	WHAT YOU SEE IS WHAT YOU GET Reproduction PB 42075	33 5
3 Sep 88	SAVE A LITTLE BIT Reproduction PB 42147	73 1

GOMEZ UK, male vocal / instrumental group (13 WEEKS)

		pos/wks
11 Apr 98	78 STONE WOBBLE Hut HUTCD 95	44 1
13 Jun 98	GET MYSELF ARRESTED Hut HUTCD 97	45 1
12 Sep 98	WHIPPIN' PICCADILLY Hut HUTCD 105	35 3
10 Jul 99	BRING IT ON Hut HUTCD 112	21 3
11 Sep 99	RHYTHM & BLUES ALIBI Hut HUTCD 114	18 3
27 Nov 99	WE HAVEN'T TURNED AROUND Hut HUTCD 117	38 2

Leroy GOMEZ – See SANTA ESMERALDA and Leroy GOMEZ

GOMPIE Holland, male vocal / instrumental group (12 WEEKS)

		pos/wks
20 May 95	ALICE (WHO THE X IS ALICE) (LIVING NEXT DOOR TO ALICE) Habana HABSCD 5	34 5
2 Sep 95	ALICE (WHO THE X IS ALICE) (LIVING NEXT DOOR TO ALICE) (re-entry) Habana HABSCD 5	17 7

GONZALEZ UK / US, male vocal / instrumental group (11 WEEKS)

		pos/wks
31 Mar 79	HAVEN'T STOPPED DANCING YET Sidewalk SID 102	15 11

GOO GOO DOLLS US, male vocal / instrumental trio (4 WEEKS)

		pos/wks
1 Aug 98	IRIS Reprise W 0449CD	50 1
27 Mar 99	SLIDE Edel / Hollywood / Third Rail 0102035 HWR	43 1
17 Jul 99	IRIS (re-issue) Hollywood 0102485 HWR	26 2

GOOD GIRLS US, female vocal group (1 WEEK)

		pos/wks
24 Jul 93	JUST CALL ME Motown TMGCD 1417	75 1

GOODBYE MR MACKENZIE
UK, male / female vocal / instrumental group (13 WEEKS)

		pos/wks
20 Aug 88	GOODBYE MR MACKENZIE Capitol CL 501	62 2
11 Mar 89	THE RATTLER Capitol CL 522	37 6
29 Jul 89	GOODWILL CITY / I'M SICK OF YOU Capitol CL 538	49 2
21 Apr 90	LOVE CHILD Parlophone R 6247	52 2
23 Jun 90	BLACKER THAN BLACK Parlophone R 6257	61 1

GOODFELLAZ US, male vocal trio (2 WEEKS)

		pos/wks
10 May 97	SUGAR HONEY ICE TEA Wild Card 5736132	25 2

GOODIES UK, male comedy / vocal group (38 WEEKS)

		pos/wks
7 Dec 74 ●	THE INBETWEENIES / FATHER CHRISTMAS DO NOT TOUCH ME Bradley's BRAD 7421	7 9
15 Mar 75 ●	FUNKY GIBBON / SICK MAN BLUES Bradley's BRAD 7504	4 10
21 Jun 75	BLACK PUDDING BERTHA (THE QUEEN OF NORTHERN SOUL) Bradley's BRAD 7517	19 7
27 Sep 75	NAPPY LOVE / WILD THING Bradley's BRAD 7524	21 6
13 Dec 75	MAKE A DAFT NOISE FOR CHRISTMAS Bradley's BRAD 7533	20 6

Cuba GOODING US, male vocalist (2 WEEKS)

		pos/wks
19 Nov 83	HAPPINESS IS JUST AROUND THE BEND London LON 41	72 2

GOODMEN
Holland, male instrumental / production duo - Rene Terhorst and Gaston Steenkist (19 WEEKS) — pos/wks

			pos	wks
7 Aug 93		**GIVE IT UP** *Fresh Fruit TABCD 118*	23	5
9 Oct 93	●	**GIVE IT UP (re-entry)** *Fresh Fruit TABCD 118*	5	14

See also JARK PRONGO

Ron GOODWIN
UK, orchestra (24 WEEKS) — pos/wks

			pos	wks
15 May 53	●	**TERRY'S THEME FROM 'LIMELIGHT'** *Parlophone R 3686*	3	23
28 Oct 55		**BLUE STAR (THE MEDIC THEME)** *Parlophone R 4074*	20	1

See also Eamonn ANDREWS

GOODY GOODY
US, female vocal duo (5 WEEKS) — pos/wks

			pos	wks
2 Dec 78		**NUMBER ONE DEE JAY** *Atlantic LV 3*	55	5

GOOMBAY DANCE BAND
Germany / Montserrat, male / female vocal / instrumental group (16 WEEKS) — pos/wks

			pos	wks
27 Feb 82	★	**SEVEN TEARS** *Epic EPC A 1242*	1	12
15 May 82		**SUN OF JAMAICA** *Epic EPC A 2345*	50	4

GOONS
UK, male comedy / vocal group (30 WEEKS) — pos/wks

			pos	wks
29 Jun 56	●	**I'M WALKING BACKWARDS FOR CHRISTMAS / BLUEBOTTLE BLUES** *Decca F 10756*	4	10
14 Sep 56	●	**BLOODNOK'S ROCK 'N' ROLL CALL / YING TONG SONG** *Decca E 10780*	3	10
21 Jul 73	●	**YING TONG SONG (re-issue)** *Decca F 13414*	9	10

'Bluebottle Blues' listed only from 13 Jul 1956. It peaked at No.5

Lonnie GORDON
US, female vocalist (23 WEEKS) — pos/wks

			pos	wks
24 Jun 89		**(I'VE GOT YOUR) PLEASURE CONTROL** *ffrr F 106* [1]	60	3
27 Jan 90	●	**HAPPENIN' ALL OVER AGAIN** *Supreme SUPE 159*	4	10
11 Aug 90		**BEYOND YOUR WILDEST DREAMS** *Supreme SUPE 167*	48	2
17 Nov 90		**IF I HAVE TO STAND ALONE** *Supreme SUPE 181*	68	1
4 May 91		**GONNA CATCH YOU** *Supreme SUPE 185*	32	5
7 Oct 95		**LOVE EVICTION** *X:Plode BANG 2CD*	32	2

[1] Simon Harris featuring Lonnie Gordon

Lesley GORE
US, female vocalist (20 WEEKS) — pos/wks

			pos	wks
20 Jun 63	●	**IT'S MY PARTY** *Mercury AMT 1205* ▲	9	12
24 Sep 64		**MAYBE I KNOW** *Mercury MF 829*	20	8

GORKY'S ZYGOTIC MYNCI
UK, male / female vocal / instrumental group (7 WEEKS) — pos/wks

			pos	wks
9 Nov 96		**PATIO SONG** *Fontana GZMCD 1*	41	1
29 Mar 97		**DIAMOND DEW** *Fontana GZMCD 2*	42	1
21 Jun 97		**YOUNG GIRLS & HAPPY ENDINGS / DARK NIGHT** *Fontana GZMCD 3*	49	1
6 Jun 98		**SWEET JOHNNY** *Fontana GZMCD 4*	60	1
29 Aug 98		**LET'S GET TOGETHER (IN OUR MINDS)** *Fontana GZMCD 5*	43	1
2 Oct 99		**SPANISH DANCE TROUPE** *Mantra / Beggars Banquet MNT 47CD*	47	1
4 Mar 00		**POODLE ROCKIN'** *Mantra / Beggars Banquet MNT 52CD*	52	1

Eydie GORME
US, female vocalist (33 WEEKS) — pos/wks

			pos	wks
24 Jan 58		**LOVE ME FOREVER** *HMV POP 432*	21	5
21 Jun 62	●	**YES MY DARLING DAUGHTER** *CBS AAG 105*	10	9
31 Jan 63		**BLAME IT ON THE BOSSA NOVA** *CBS AAG 131*	32	6
22 Aug 63	●	**I WANT TO STAY HERE** *CBS AAG 163* [1]	3	13

[1] Steve and Eydie

Luke GOSS and the BAND OF THIEVES
UK, male vocal / instrumental group (3 WEEKS) — pos/wks

			pos	wks
12 Jun 93		**SWEETER THAN THE MIDNIGHT RAIN** *Sabre CDSAB 1*	52	2
21 Aug 93		**GIVE ME ONE MORE CHANCE** *Sabre CDSAB 2*	68	1

See also BROS

Matt GOSS
UK, male vocalist (5 WEEKS) — pos/wks

			pos	wks
26 Aug 95		**THE KEY** *Atlas 5811532*	40	2
27 Apr 96		**IF YOU WERE HERE TONIGHT** *Atlas 5762932*	23	3

See also BROS

Nigel GOULDING – See Abigail MEAD and Nigel GOULDING

Graham GOULDMAN
UK, male vocalist (4 WEEKS) — pos/wks

			pos	wks
23 Jun 79		**SUNBURN** *Mercury SUNNY 1*	52	4

See also 10 CC

GOURYELLA
Holland, male production duo (11 WEEKS) — pos/wks

			pos	wks
10 Jul 99		**GOURYELLA** *Code Blue BLU 001CD*	15	7
4 Dec 99		**WALHALLA** *Code Blue BLU 006CD*	27	2
23 Dec 00		**TENSHI** *Code Blue BLUE 017CD*	45	2

See also MOONMAN; Ferry CORSTEN; SYSTEM F; VERACOCHA

GQ
US, male vocal / instrumental group (6 WEEKS) — pos/wks

			pos	wks
10 Mar 79		**DISCO NIGHTS (ROCK FREAK)** *Arista ARIST 245*	42	6

GRACE
UK, female vocalist - Dominique Atkins (24 WEEKS) — pos/wks

			pos	wks
8 Apr 95	●	**NOT OVER YET** *Perfecto PERF 104CD*	6	8
23 Sep 95		**I WANT TO LIVE** *Perfecto PERF 109CD*	30	2
24 Feb 96		**SKIN ON SKIN** *Perfecto PERF 116CD*	21	3
1 Jun 96		**DOWN TO EARTH** *Perfecto PERF 120CD*	20	2
28 Sep 96		**IF I COULD FLY** *Perfecto PERF 127CD*	29	2
3 May 97		**HAND IN HAND** *Perfecto PERF 129CD*	38	1
26 Jul 97		**DOWN TO EARTH (re-mix)** *Perfecto PERF 142CD1*	29	2
14 Aug 99		**NOT OVER YET 99** *Code Blue BLU 004CD1* [1]	16	4

[1] Planet Perfecto featuring Grace

GRACE BROTHERS
UK, male instrumental duo (1 WEEK) — pos/wks

			pos	wks
20 Apr 96		**ARE YOU BEING SERVED** *EMI Premier PRESCD 1*	51	1

Charlie GRACIE
US, male vocalist - Charlie Graci (41 WEEKS) — pos/wks

			pos	wks
19 Apr 57		**BUTTERFLY** *Parlophone R 4290*	12	8
14 Jun 57	●	**FABULOUS** *Parlophone R 4313*	8	16
23 Aug 57		**I LOVE YOU SO MUCH IT HURTS / WANDERIN' EYES** *London HLU 8467*	14	2
6 Sep 57	●	**WANDERIN' EYES** *London HLU 8467*	6	12
6 Sep 57		**I LOVE YOU SO MUCH IT HURTS** *London HLU 8467*	20	2
10 Jan 58		**COOL BABY** *London HLU 8521*	26	1

'I Love You So Much It Hurts' and 'Wanderin' Eyes' were listed together for two weeks, then listed separately for a further two and 12 weeks respectively

Eve GRAHAM – See NEW SEEKERS

Jaki GRAHAM (453 | Top 500)
Britain's foremost black female vocalist of the 1980s, b. 15 Sep 1956, Birmingham, UK, who was first introduced to the public via a duet with ex-Linx vocalist David Grant. One-time UB40 backing vocalist, who helped to open doors for other UK female soul singers (75 WEEKS) — pos/wks

			pos	wks
23 Mar 85	●	**COULD IT BE I'M FALLING IN LOVE** *Chrysalis GRAN 6* [1]	5	11
29 Jun 85	●	**ROUND AND ROUND** *EMI JAKI 4*	9	11
31 Aug 85		**HEAVEN KNOWS** *EMI JAKI 5*	59	3
16 Nov 85		**MATED** *EMI JAKI 6* [1]	20	10
3 May 86	●	**SET ME FREE** *EMI JAKI 7*	7	12
9 Aug 86		**BREAKING AWAY** *EMI JAKI 8*	16	8
15 Nov 86		**STEP RIGHT UP** *EMI JAKI 9*	15	12
9 Jul 88		**NO MORE TEARS** *EMI JAKI 12*	60	2
24 Jun 89		**FROM NOW ON** *EMI JAKI 15*	73	2
16 Jul 94		**AIN'T NOBODY** *Pulse 8 CDLOSE 64*	44	2
4 Feb 95		**YOU CAN COUNT ON ME** *Avex UK AVEXCD 1*	62	1
8 Jul 95		**ABSOLUTE E-SENSUAL** *Avex UK AVEXCD 5*	69	1

[1] David Grant and Jaki Graham

UK No.1 ★   UK Top 10 ●   Still on chart +   UK million seller ◆   UK entry at No.1 ■   US No.1 ▲

Larry GRAHAM
US, male vocalist / instumentalist - bass (4 WEEKS) pos/wks

Date	Title	Pos	Wks
3 Jul 82	SOONER OR LATER *Warner Bros. K 17925*	54	4

Mikey GRAHAM
Ireland, male vocalist (5 WEEKS) pos/wks

Date	Title	Pos	Wks
10 Jun 00	YOU'RE MY ANGEL *Public PR 001CDS*	13	5

See also BOYZONE

Ron GRAINER ORCHESTRA
UK, orchestra (7 WEEKS) pos/wks

Date	Title	Pos	Wks
9 Dec 78	A TOUCH OF VELVET A STING OF BRASS *Casino Classics CC 5*	60	7

GRAM'MA FUNK – See GROOVE ARMADA; ILLICIT featuring GRAM'MA FUNK

GRAND FUNK RAILROAD
US, male vocal / instrumental group (1 WEEK) pos/wks

Date	Title	Pos	Wks
6 Feb 71	INSIDE LOOKING OUT *Capitol CL 15668*	40	1

GRAND PLAZ
UK, male instrumental / production group (4 WEEKS) pos/wks

Date	Title	Pos	Wks
8 Sep 90	WOW WOW - NA NA *Urban URB 60*	41	4

GRAND PRIX
UK, male vocal / instrumental group (1 WEEK) pos/wks

Date	Title	Pos	Wks
27 Feb 82	KEEP ON BELIEVING *RCA 162*	75	1

GRAND PUBA
US, male rapper - Maxwell Dixon (6 WEEKS) pos/wks

Date	Title	Pos	Wks
13 Jan 96	WHY YOU TREAT ME SO BAD *Virgin VSCDT 1566* [1]	11	5
30 Mar 96	WILL YOU BE MY BABY *GHQ 74321339092* [2]	53	1

[1] Shaggy featuring Grand Puba [2] Infiniti featuring Grand Puba

GRANDAD ROBERTS AND HIS SON ELVIS
UK, male vocal duo (1 WEEK) pos/wks

Date	Title	Pos	Wks
20 Jun 98	MEAT PIE SAUSAGE ROLL *WEA WEA 160CD*	67	1

GRANDADDY
US, male vocal / instrumental group (1 WEEK) pos/wks

Date	Title	Pos	Wks
2 Sep 00	HEWLETT'S DAUGHTER *V2 VVR 5014333*	71	1

GRANDMASTER FLASH, Melle MEL and the FURIOUS FIVE
365 **Top 500** *Pioneering rap act who led the genre into more serious subjects. New York act fronted by Grandmaster Flash (Joseph Saddler) and Melle Mel (Melvin Glover). 'White Lines' took a record 23 weeks to make the Top 10 (87 WEEKS)* pos/wks

Date	Title	Pos	Wks
28 Aug 82 ●	THE MESSAGE *Sugarhill SHL 117* [1]	8	9
22 Jan 83	MESSAGE II (SURVIVAL) *Sugarhill SH 119* [2]	74	2
19 Nov 83	WHITE LINES (DON'T DON'T DO IT) *Sugarhill SH 130* [3]	60	3
11 Feb 84 ●	WHITE LINES (DON'T DON'T DO IT) (re-entry) *Sugarhill SH 130* [3]	7	38
30 Jun 84	BEAT STREET BREAKDOWN *Atlantic A 9659* [4]	42	7
22 Sep 84	WE DON'T WORK FOR FREE *Sugarhill SH 136* [4]	45	4
24 Nov 84	WHITE LINES (DON'T DON'T DO IT) (2nd re-entry) *Sugarhill SH 130* [3]	75	1
15 Dec 84 ●	STEP OFF (PART 1) *Sugarhill SH 139* [4]	8	12
5 Jan 85	WHITE LINES (DON'T DON'T DO IT) (3rd re-entry) *Sugarhill SH 130* [3]	73	1
16 Feb 85	SIGN OF THE TIMES *Elektra E 9677* [5]	72	1
16 Mar 85	PUMP ME UP *Sugarhill SH 141* [4]	45	6
8 Jan 94	WHITE LINES (DON'T DO IT) (re-mix) *WGAF WGAFCD 103* [3]	59	3

[1] Grandmaster Flash and the Furious Five [2] Melle Mel and Duke Bootee [3] Grandmaster and Melle Mel [4] Grandmaster Melle Mel and the Furious Five [5] Grandmaster Flash

See also DURAN DURAN

GRANDMIXER DST
US, male DJ / producer - Derek Howells (3 WEEKS) pos/wks

Date	Title	Pos	Wks
24 Dec 83	CRAZY CUTS *Island IS 146*	73	2
14 Jan 84	CRAZY CUTS (re-entry) *Island IS 146*	71	1

GRANGE HILL CAST
UK, male / female vocal charity assembly (6 WEEKS) pos/wks

Date	Title	Pos	Wks
19 Apr 86 ●	JUST SAY NO *BBC RESL 183*	5	6

Gerri GRANGER
US, female vocalist (3 WEEKS) pos/wks

Date	Title	Pos	Wks
30 Sep 78	I GO TO PIECES (EVERYTIME) *Casino Classics CC3*	50	3

Amy GRANT
US, female vocalist (39 WEEKS) pos/wks

Date	Title	Pos	Wks
11 May 91 ●	BABY BABY *A & M AM 727* ▲	2	13
3 Aug 91	EVERY HEARTBEAT *A & M AM 783*	25	7
2 Nov 91	THAT'S WHAT LOVE IS FOR *A & M AM 666*	60	3
15 Feb 92	GOOD FOR ME *A & M AM 810*	60	1
13 Aug 94	LUCKY ONE *A & M 5807322*	60	1
22 Oct 94	SAY YOU'LL BE MINE *A & M 5808292*	41	2
24 Jun 95	BIG YELLOW TAXI *A & M 5809972*	20	10
14 Oct 95	HOUSE OF LOVE *A & M 5812332* [1]	46	2

[1] Amy Grant with Vince Gill

Andrea GRANT
UK, female vocalist (1 WEEK) pos/wks

Date	Title	Pos	Wks
14 Nov 98	REPUTATIONS (JUST BE GOOD TO ME) *WEA WEA 192CD*	75	1

Boysie GRANT – See Ezz RECO and the LAUNCHERS with Boysie GRANT

David GRANT
UK, male vocalist (59 WEEKS) pos/wks

Date	Title	Pos	Wks
30 Apr 83	STOP AND GO *Chrysalis GRAN 1*	19	9
16 Jul 83 ●	WATCHING YOU WATCHING ME *Chrysalis GRAN 2*	10	13
8 Oct 83	LOVE WILL FIND A WAY *Chrysalis GRAN 3*	24	6
26 Nov 83	ROCK THE MIDNIGHT *Chrysalis GRAN 4*	46	4
23 Mar 85 ●	COULD IT BE I'M FALLING IN LOVE *Chrysalis GRAN 6* [1]	5	11
16 Nov 85	MATED *EMI JAKI 6* [1]	20	10
1 Aug 87	CHANGE *Polydor POSP 871*	55	4
12 May 90	KEEP IT TOGETHER *Fourth & Broadway BRW 169*	56	2

[1] David Grant and Jaki Graham

Eddy GRANT
318 **Top 500** *Former lead guitarist and songwriter for successful multi-racial UK group The Equals, b. 5 Mar 1948, Plaisance, Guyana. Left group 1972, went into production and formed own label, Ice. Million seller 'Electric Avenue' reached No.2 in US (94 WEEKS)* pos/wks

Date	Title	Pos	Wks
2 Jun 79	LIVING ON THE FRONT LINE *Ensign ENY 26*	11	11
15 Nov 80 ●	DO YOU FEEL MY LOVE *Ensign ENY 45*	8	11
4 Apr 81	CAN'T GET ENOUGH OF YOU *Ensign ENY 207*	13	10
25 Jul 81	I LOVE YOU, YES I LOVE YOU *Ensign ENY 216*	37	6
16 Oct 82 ★	I DON'T WANNA DANCE *Ice ICE 56*	1	15
15 Jan 83 ●	ELECTRIC AVENUE *Ice ICE 57*	2	9
19 Mar 83	LIVING ON THE FRONT LINE / DO YOU FEEL MY LOVE (re-issue) *Mercury MER 135*	47	4
23 Apr 83	WAR PARTY *Ice ICE 58*	42	4
29 Oct 83	TILL I CAN'T TAKE LOVE NO MORE *Ice ICE 60*	42	7
19 May 84	ROMANCING THE STONE *Ice ICE 61*	52	3
23 Jan 88 ●	GIMME HOPE JO'ANNA *Ice ICE 78701*	7	12
27 May 89	WALKING ON SUNSHINE *Blue Wave R 6217*	63	2

Gogi GRANT
US, female vocalist - Audrey Arinsberg (11 WEEKS) pos/wks

Date	Title	Pos	Wks
29 Jun 56 ●	THE WAYWARD WIND *London HLB 8282* ▲	9	11

Julie GRANT
UK, female vocalist (17 WEEKS) pos/wks

Date	Title	Pos	Wks
3 Jan 63	UP ON THE ROOF *Pye 7N 15483*	33	3
28 Mar 63	COUNT ON ME *Pye 7N 15508*	24	9
24 Sep 64	COME TO ME *Pye 7N 15684*	31	5

Rudy GRANT
Guyana, male vocalist (3 WEEKS) pos/wks

Date	Title	Pos	Wks
14 Feb 81	LATELY *Ensign ENY 202*	58	3

GRAPEFRUIT
UK, male vocal / instrumental group (19 WEEKS) pos/wks

Date	Title	Pos	Wks
14 Feb 68	DEAR DELILAH *RCA 1656*	21	9
14 Aug 68	C'MON MARIANNE *RCA 1716*	31	10

GRASS-SHOW
Sweden, male vocal / instrumental group (2 WEEKS) · pos/wks

		pos	wks
22 Mar 97	**1962** *Food CDFOOD 90*	53	1
23 Aug 97	**OUT OF THE VOID** *Food CDFOOD 103*	75	1

GRAVEDIGGAZ
US, male rap group (6 WEEKS) · pos/wks

		pos	wks
11 Mar 95	**SIX FEET DEEP (EP)** *Gee Street GESCD 62*	64	1
5 Aug 95	**THE HELL (EP)** *Fourth & Broadway BRCD 326* [1]	12	3
24 Jan 98	**THE NIGHT THE EARTH CRIED** *Gee Street GEE 5001013*	44	1
25 Apr 98	**UNEXPLAINED** *Gee Street GEE 5001623*	48	1

[1] Tricky vs the Gravediggaz

Tracks on Six Feet Deep (EP): Bang Your Head / Mommy / Suicide. Tracks on The Hell EP: Hell Is Round the Corner / Hell Is Round the Corner (remix) / Psychosis / Tonite Is a Special Nite

David GRAY
UK, male vocalist (19 WEEKS) · pos/wks

		pos	wks
4 Dec 99	**PLEASE FORGIVE ME** *IHT IHTCDS 003*	72	1
1 Jul 00 ●	**BABYLON** *IHT / East West EW 215CD1*	5	12
28 Oct 00	**PLEASE FORGIVE ME (re-issue)** *IHT / East West EW 219CD*	18	6

Dobie GRAY
US, male vocalist (11 WEEKS) · pos/wks

		pos	wks
25 Feb 65	**THE IN CROWD** *London HL 9953*	25	7
27 Sep 75	**OUT ON THE FLOOR** *Black Magic BM 107*	42	4

Dorian GRAY
UK, male vocalist (7 WEEKS) · pos/wks

		pos	wks
27 Mar 68	**I'VE GOT YOU ON MY MIND** *Parlophone R 5667*	36	7

Les GRAY
UK, male vocalist (5 WEEKS) · pos/wks

		pos	wks
26 Feb 77	**A GROOVY KIND OF LOVE** *Warner Bros. K 16883*	32	5

See also MUD

Macy GRAY
US, female vocalist - Natalie McIntyre (35 WEEKS) · pos/wks

		pos	wks
3 Jul 99	**DO SOMETHING** *Epic 6675932*	51	1
9 Oct 99 ●	**I TRY** *Epic 6681832*	6	22
25 Mar 00	**STILL** *Epic 6689822*	18	7
20 May 00	**STILL (re-entry)** *Epic 6689822*	65	2
5 Aug 00	**WHY DIDN'T YOU CALL ME** *Epic 6696682*	38	2
26 Aug 00	**WHY DIDN'T YOU CALL ME (re-entry)** *Epic 6696682*	74	1

Barry GRAY ORCHESTRA
UK, orchestra (8 WEEKS) · pos/wks

		pos	wks
11 Jul 81	**THUNDERBIRDS** *PRT 7P 216*	61	2
14 Jun 86	**JOE 90 (THEME) / CAPTAIN SCARLET THEME** *PRT 7PX 354* [1]	53	6

[1] Barry Gray Orchestra with Peter Beckett - keyboards

Alltrinna GRAYSON – See Wilton FELDER

GREAT WHITE
US, male vocal / instrumental group (5 WEEKS) · pos/wks

		pos	wks
24 Feb 90	**HOUSE OF BROKEN LOVE** *Capitol CL 562*	44	2
16 Feb 91	**CONGO SQUARE** *Capitol CL 605*	62	1
7 Sep 91	**CALL IT ROCK 'N' ROLL** *Capitol CL 625*	67	2

Buddy GRECO
US, male vocalist (8 WEEKS) · pos/wks

		pos	wks
7 Jul 60	**LADY IS A TRAMP** *Fontana H 225*	26	8

GREED featuring Ricardo DA FORCE
UK, male instrumental duo and UK, male rapper (2 WEEKS) · pos/wks

		pos	wks
18 Mar 95	**PUMP UP THE VOLUME** *Stress CDSTR 49*	51	2

GREEDIES
Ireland / UK / US, male vocal / instrumental group (5 WEEKS) · pos/wks

		pos	wks
15 Dec 79	**A MERRY JINGLE** *Vertigo GREED 1*	28	5

Al GREEN
Seventies soul superstar, b. 13 Apr 1946, Arkansas, US. Acclaimed singer / songwriter, who had seven successive million-selling singles Stateside. He returned to gospel music in the 1980s, winning a handful of Grammy Awards in this genre (68 WEEKS) · pos/wks

		pos	wks
9 Oct 71 ●	**TIRED OF BEING ALONE** *London HL 10337*	4	13
8 Jan 72 ●	**LET'S STAY TOGETHER** *London HL 10348* ▲	7	12
20 May 72	**LOOK WHAT YOU DONE FOR ME** *London HL 10369*	44	4
19 Aug 72	**I'M STILL IN LOVE WITH YOU** *London HL 10382*	35	5
16 Nov 74	**SHA-LA-LA (MAKE ME HAPPY)** *London HL 10470*	20	11
15 Mar 75	**L.O.V.E.** *London HL 10482*	24	8
3 Dec 88	**PUT A LITTLE LOVE IN YOUR HEART** *A & M AM 484* [1]	28	8
21 Oct 89	**THE MESSAGE IS LOVE** *Breakout USA 668* [2]	38	5
2 Oct 93	**LOVE IS A BEAUTIFUL THING** *Arista 74321162692*	56	2

[1] Annie Lennox and Al Green [2] Arthur Baker and the Backbeat Disciples featuring Al Green

Dotty GREEN – See Mark FISHER featuring Dotty GREEN

Jesse GREEN
Jamaica, male vocalist (26 WEEKS) · pos/wks

		pos	wks
7 Aug 76	**NICE AND SLOW** *EMI 2492*	17	12
18 Dec 76	**FLIP** *EMI 2564*	26	8
11 Jun 77	**COME WITH ME** *EMI 2615*	29	6

Robson GREEN and Jerome FLYNN – See ROBSON and JEROME

GREEN DAY
US, male vocal / instrumental group (39 WEEKS) · pos/wks

		pos	wks
20 Aug 94	**BASKET CASE** *Reprise W 0257CD*	55	2
29 Oct 94	**WELCOME TO PARADISE** *Reprise W 0269CDX*	20	3
28 Jan 95 ●	**BASKET CASE (re-issue)** *Reprise W 0279CD*	7	6
18 Mar 95	**LONGVIEW** *Reprise W 0278CD*	30	3
20 May 95	**WHEN I COME AROUND** *Reprise W 0294CD*	27	3
7 Oct 95	**GEEK STINK BREATH** *Reprise W 0320CD*	16	3
6 Jan 96	**STUCK WITH ME** *Reprise W 0327CD*	24	3
6 Jul 96	**BRAIN STEW / JADED** *Reprise W 0339CD*	28	2
11 Oct 97	**HITCHIN' A RIDE** *Reprise W 0424CD*	25	2
31 Jan 98	**TIME OF YOUR LIFE (GOOD RIDDANCE)** *Reprise W 0430CD1*	11	5
9 May 98	**REDUNDANT** *Reprise W 0438CD1*	27	2
30 Sep 00	**MINORITY** *Reprise W 532CD*	18	3
23 Dec 00	**WARNING** *Reprise W 548CD1*	27	2+

GREEN JELLY
US, male vocal / instrumental group (15 WEEKS) · pos/wks

		pos	wks
5 Jun 93 ●	**THREE LITTLE PIGS** *Zoo 74321151422*	5	8
14 Aug 93	**ANARCHY IN THE UK** *Zoo 74321159052*	27	3
25 Dec 93	**I'M THE LEADER OF THE GANG** *Arista 74321174892* [1]	25	4

[1] Hulk Hogan with Green Jelly

Norman GREENBAUM
US, male vocalist (20 WEEKS) · pos/wks

		pos	wks
21 Mar 70 ★	**SPIRIT IN THE SKY** *Reprise RS 20885*	1	20

Lorne GREENE
Canada, male actor / vocalist (8 WEEKS) · pos/wks

		pos	wks
17 Dec 64	**RINGO** *RCA 1428* ▲	22	8

Lee GREENWOOD
US, male vocalist (6 WEEKS) · pos/wks

		pos	wks
19 May 84	**THE WIND BENEATH MY WINGS** *MCA 877*	49	6

Iain GREGORY
UK, male vocalist (2 WEEKS) · pos/wks

		pos	wks
4 Jan 62	**CAN'T YOU HEAR THE BEAT OF A BROKEN HEART** *Pye 7N 15397*	39	2

Johnny GREGORY – See CHAQUITO; Russ HAMILTON

Band of the GRENADIER GUARDS – See ST JOHN'S COLLEGE SCHOOL CHOIR and the Band of the GRENADIER GUARDS

UK No.1 ★ UK Top 10 ● Still on chart + UK million seller ◆ UK entry at No.1 ■ US No.1 ▲

GREYHOUND *Jamaica, male vocal / instrumental group (33 WEEKS)* pos/wks

26 Jun 71 ●	BLACK AND WHITE *Trojan TR 7820* 6 13	
8 Jan 72 ●	MOON RIVER *Trojan TR 7848* 12 11	
25 Mar 72	I AM WHAT I AM *Trojan TR 7853* 20 9	

GRID *UK, male instrumental / production duo - Richard Norris and Dave Ball (47 WEEKS)* pos/wks

7 Jul 90	FLOATATION *East West YZ 475* 60 2	
29 Sep 90	A BEAT CALLED LOVE *East West YZ 498* 64 4	
25 Jul 92	FIGURE OF 8 *Virgin VSTG 1421* 50 3	
3 Oct 92	HEARTBEAT *Virgin VST 1427* 72 4	
13 Mar 93	CRYSTAL CLEAR *Virgin VSCDT 1442* 27 4	
30 Oct 93	TEXAS COWBOYS *Deconstruction 74321167762* 21 3	
4 Jun 94 ●	SWAMP THING *Deconstruction 74321205842* 3 17	
17 Sep 94	ROLLERCOASTER *Deconstruction 74321230772* 19 4	
3 Dec 94	TEXAS COWBOYS (re-issue) *Deconstruction 74321244032* 17 6	
23 Sep 95	DIABLO *Deconstruction 74321308402* 32 2	

Zaine GRIFF *New Zealand, male vocalist (6 WEEKS)* pos/wks

16 Feb 80	TONIGHT *Automatic K 17547* 54 3	
31 May 80	ASHES AND DIAMONDS *Automatic K 17610* 68 3	

Billy GRIFFIN *US, male vocalist (12 WEEKS)* pos/wks

8 Jan 83	HOLD ME TIGHTER IN THE RAIN *CBS A 2935* 17 9	
14 Jan 84	SERIOUS *CBS A 4053* 64 3	

See also MIRACLES

Clive GRIFFIN *UK, male vocalist (5 WEEKS)* pos/wks

24 Jun 89	HEAD ABOVE WATER *Mercury STEP 4* 60 2	
11 May 91	I'LL BE WAITING *Mercury STEP 6* 56 3	

Roni GRIFFITH *US, female vocalist (4 WEEKS)* pos/wks

30 Jun 84	(THE BEST PART OF) BREAKING UP *Making Waves SURF 101* 63 4	

GRIFTERS *UK, male production duo - Paul Newman and Brandon Block (1 WEEK)* pos/wks

20 Feb 99	FLASH *Duty Free DF 004CD* 63 1	

See also TALL PAUL; ESCRIMA; CAMISRA; PARTIZAN

GRIMETHORPE COLLIERY BAND – See Peter SKELLERN

Jay GROOVE – See FANTASY UFO

GROOVE ARMADA
UK, male production / instrumental duo (13 WEEKS) pos/wks

8 May 99	IF EVERYBODY LOOKED THE SAME *Pepper 0530292* 25 2	
7 Aug 99	AT THE RIVER *Pepper 0530062* 19 5	
27 Nov 99	I SEE YOU BABY *Pepper 9230002* [1] 17 4	
15 Jan 00	I SEE YOU BABY (re-entry) *Pepper 9230002* [1] 70 2	

[1] Groove Armada featuring Gram'ma Funk

GROOVE CONNEKTION 2
UK, male producer / instrumentalist (1 WEEK) pos/wks

11 Apr 98	CLUB LONELY *XL Recordings XLT 94CD* 54 1	

GROOVE CORPORATION
UK / Italy, male / female vocal / instrumental group (1 WEEK) pos/wks

16 Apr 94	RAIN *Six6 SIXCD 109* 71 1	

GROOVE GANG – See DAFFY DUCK featuring the GROOVE GANG

GROOVE GENERATION featuring Leo SAYER
UK, male production group (3 WEEKS) pos/wks

8 Aug 98	YOU MAKE ME FEEL LIKE DANCING *Brothers Org. CDBRUV 8* 32 3	

GROOVE THEORY *UK, male vocal / instrumental duo (3 WEEKS)* pos/wks

18 Nov 95	TELL ME *Epic 6623882* 31 3	

GROOVERIDER *UK, male DJ / producer (3 WEEKS)* pos/wks

26 Sep 98	RAINBOWS OF COLOUR *Higher Ground HIGHS 13CD* 40 2	
19 Jun 99	WHERE'S JACK THE RIPPER *Higher Ground HIGHS 20CD* 61 1	

Scott GROOVES *US, male DJ / producer (3 WEEKS)* pos/wks

16 May 98	EXPANSIONS *Soma Recordings SOMA 65CDS* [1] 68 1	
28 Nov 98	MOTHERSHIP RECONNECTION *Soma Recordings SOMA 71CDS* 55 1	
21 Aug 99	MOTHERSHIP RECONNECTION *Virgin DINSD 185* [2] 55 1	

[1] Scott Grooves featuring Roy Ayers [2] Scott Grooves featuring Parliament / Funkadelic

Henry GROSS *US, male vocalist (4 WEEKS)* pos/wks

28 Aug 76	SHANNON *Life Song ELS 45002* 32 4	

GROUND LEVEL
Australia, male instrumental / production group (2 WEEKS) pos/wks

30 Jan 93	DREAMS OF HEAVEN *Faze 2 CDFAZE 14* 54 2	

GROUP THERAPY *US, male rap group (1 WEEK)* pos/wks

30 Nov 96	EAST COAST / WEST COAST KILLAS *Interscope IND 95516* 51 1	

Boring Bob GROVER – See PIRANHAS

GSP *UK, male instrumental / production duo (3 WEEKS)* pos/wks

3 Oct 92	THE BANANA SONG *Yoyo YOYO 1* 37 3	

GTO *UK, male / female instrumental / production duo (7 WEEKS)* pos/wks

4 Aug 90	PURE *Cooltempo COOL 218* 57 3	
7 Sep 91	LISTEN TO THE RHYTHM FLOW / BULLFROG *React REACT 7001* 72 2	
2 May 92	ELEVATION *React REACT 4* 59 2	

GTO are also Tricky Disco and Technohead

See also TECHNOHEAD; TRICKY DISCO

GUESS WHO *Canada, male vocal / instrumental group (14 WEEKS)* pos/wks

16 Feb 67	HIS GIRL *King KG 1044* 45 1	
9 May 70	AMERICAN WOMAN *RCA 1943* 45 2	
30 May 70	AMERICAN WOMAN (re-entry) *RCA 1943* ▲ 19 11	

GUN *UK, male vocal / instrumental trio (11 WEEKS)* pos/wks

20 Nov 68 ●	RACE WITH THE DEVIL *CBS 3734* 8 11	

GUN *UK, male vocal / instrumental group (46 WEEKS)* pos/wks

1 Jul 89	BETTER DAYS *A & M AM 505* 33 9	
16 Sep 89	MONEY (EVERYBODY LOVES HER) *A & M AM 520* 73 2	
11 Nov 89	INSIDE OUT *A & M AM 531* 57 2	
10 Feb 90	TAKING ON THE WORLD *A & M AM 541* 50 3	
14 Jul 90	SHAME ON YOU *A & M AM 573* 33 4	
14 Mar 92	STEAL YOUR FIRE *A & M AM 851* 24 4	
2 May 92	HIGHER GROUND *A & M AM 869* 48 2	
4 Jul 92	WELCOME TO THE REAL WORLD *A & M AM 885* 43 2	
9 Jul 94 ●	WORD UP *A & M 5806672* 8 7	
24 Sep 94	DON'T SAY IT'S OVER *A & M 5807572* 19 3	
25 Feb 95	THE ONLY ONE *A & M 5809552* 29 3	
15 Apr 95	SOMETHING WORTHWHILE *A & M 5810452* 39 2	
26 Apr 97	CRAZY YOU *A & M 5821932* [1] 21 2	
12 Jul 97	MY SWEET JANE *A & M 5822792* [1] 51 1	

[1] G.U.N.

GUNS N' ROSES `269` `Top 500`

Often controversial Los Angeles-based band. Best known line-up included W Axl Rose (b. William Bailey) (v). Slash (b. Saul Hudson) (g). Izzy Stradlin (b. Jeffrey Isbell) (g). The only act to hold the top two album spots in both the UK and the US on the week of releasing both records: Use Your Illusion 1 and 2 in 1991 (107 WEEKS)

		pos	wks
3 Oct 87	WELCOME TO THE JUNGLE *Geffen GEF 30*	67	2
20 Aug 88	SWEET CHILD O' MINE *Geffen GEF 43* ▲	24	8
29 Oct 88	WELCOME TO THE JUNGLE / NIGHTRAIN (re-issue) *Geffen GEF 47*	24	5
18 Mar 89 ●	PARADISE CITY *Geffen GEF 50*	6	9
3 Jun 89 ●	SWEET CHILD O' MINE (re-issue) *Geffen GEF 55*	6	9
1 Jul 89 ●	PATIENCE *Geffen GEF 56*	10	7
2 Sep 89	NIGHTRAIN (re-issue) *Geffen GEF 60*	17	5
13 Jul 91 ●	YOU COULD BE MINE *Geffen GFS 6*	3	10
21 Sep 91 ●	DON'T CRY *Geffen GFS 9*	8	4
21 Dec 91 ●	LIVE AND LET DIE *Geffen GFS 17*	5	7
7 Mar 92 ●	NOVEMBER RAIN *Geffen GFS 18*	4	5
23 May 92 ●	KNOCKIN' ON HEAVEN'S DOOR *Geffen GFS 21*	2	9
21 Nov 92 ●	YESTERDAYS / NOVEMBER RAIN (re-issue) *Geffen GFS 27*	8	9
29 May 93	THE CIVIL WAR (EP) *Geffen GFSTD 43*	11	3
20 Nov 93 ●	AIN'T IT FUN *Geffen GFSTD 62*	9	3
4 Jun 94 ●	SINCE I DON'T HAVE YOU *Geffen GFSTD 70*	10	6
14 Jan 95 ●	SYMPATHY FOR THE DEVIL *Geffen GFSTD 86*	9	6

The re-issue of 'November Rain' was listed only from 28 Nov 1992. Tracks on The Civil War (EP): Civil War / Garden of Eden / Dead Horse / Interview

GURU US, male rapper / producer - Keith Allam (12 WEEKS)

		pos	wks
11 Sep 93	TRUST ME *Cooltempo CDCOOL 278* [1]	34	2
13 Nov 93	NO TIME TO PLAY *Cooltempo CDCOOL 282* [2]	25	3
19 Aug 95	WATCH WHAT YOU SAY *Cooltempo CDCOOL 308* [3]	28	3
18 Nov 95	FEEL THE MUSIC *Cooltempo CDCOOLS 313*	34	2
13 Jul 96	LIVIN' IN THIS WORLD / LIFESAVER *Cooltempo CDCOOL 320*	61	1
16 Dec 00	KEEP YOUR WORRIES *Virgin VUSCD 177* [4]	57	1

[1] Guru featuring N'Dea Davenport [2] Guru featuring DC Lee [3] Guru featuring Chaka Khan [4] Guru's Jazzmatazz featuring Angie Stone

GURU JOSH UK, male producer - Paul Walden (14 WEEKS)

		pos	wks
24 Feb 90 ●	INFINITY *Deconstruction PB 43475*	5	10
16 Jun 90	WHOSE LAW (IS IT ANYWAY) *Deconstruction PB 43647*	26	4

Adrian GURVITZ UK, male vocalist (16 WEEKS)

		pos	wks
30 Jan 82 ●	CLASSIC *RAK 339*	8	13
12 Jun 82	YOUR DREAM *RAK 343*	61	3

GUS GUS
Iceland, male / female vocal / instrumental group (3 WEEKS)

		pos	wks
21 Feb 98	POLYESTERDAY *4AD BAD 8002CD*	55	1
13 Mar 99	LADYSHAVE *4AD BAD 9001CD*	64	1
24 Apr 99	STARLOVERS *4AD BADD 9004CD*	62	1

GUSTO US, male producer - Edward Green (8 WEEKS)

		pos	wks
2 Mar 96 ●	DISCO'S REVENGE *Manifesto FESCD 6*	9	5
7 Sep 96	LET'S ALL CHANT *Manifesto FESCD 13*	21	3

Gwen GUTHRIE US, female vocalist (25 WEEKS)

		pos	wks
19 Jul 86 ●	AIN'T NOTHING GOIN' ON BUT THE RENT *Boiling Point POSP 807*	5	12
11 Oct 86	(THEY LONG TO BE) CLOSE TO YOU *Boiling Point POSP 822*	25	7
14 Feb 87	GOOD TO GO LOVER / OUTSIDE IN THE RAIN *Boiling Point POSP 841*	37	4
4 Sep 93	AIN'T NOTHIN' GOIN' ON BUT THE RENT (re-mix) *Polydor PZCD 276*	42	2

GUY US, male vocal group (4 WEEKS)

		pos	wks
4 May 91	HER *MCA MCS 1575*	58	4

A GUY CALLED GERALD
UK, male producer - Gerald Simpson (23 WEEKS)

		pos	wks
8 Apr 89	VOODOO RAY *Rham! RS 804*	55	8
24 Jun 89	VOODOO RAY (re-entry) *Rham! RS 804*	12	10
16 Dec 89	FX / EYES OF SORROW *Subscape AGCG 1*	52	5

GUYS and DOLLS UK, male / female vocal group (33 WEEKS)

		pos	wks
1 Mar 75 ●	THERE'S A WHOLE LOT OF LOVING *Magnet MAG 20*	2	11
17 May 75	HERE I GO AGAIN *Magnet MAG 30*	33	5
21 Feb 76 ●	YOU DON'T HAVE TO SAY YOU LOVE ME *Magnet MAG 50*	5	8
6 Nov 76	STONEY GROUND *Magnet MAG 76*	38	4
13 May 78	ONLY LOVING DOES IT *Magnet MAG 115*	42	5

Jonas GWANGWA – See George FENTON and Jonas GWANGWA

GYRES UK, male vocal / instrumental group (2 WEEKS)

		pos	wks
13 Apr 96	POP COP *Sugar SUGA 9CD*	71	1
6 Jul 96	ARE YOU READY *Sugar SUGA 11CD*	71	1

H

HABIT UK, male vocal / instrumental group (2 WEEKS)

		pos	wks
30 Apr 88	LUCY *Virgin VS 1063*	56	2

Steve HACKETT
UK, male vocalist / instrumentalist - guitar (2 WEEKS)

		pos	wks
2 Apr 83	CELL 151 *Charisma CELL 1*	66	2

See also GENESIS

HADDAWAY
Trinidad and Tobago, male vocalist - Nester Haddaway (52 WEEKS)

		pos	wks
5 Jun 93 ●	WHAT IS LOVE *Logic 74321148502*	2	15
25 Sep 93 ●	LIFE *Logic 74321164212*	6	9
18 Dec 93 ●	I MISS YOU *Logic 74321181522*	9	14
2 Apr 94 ●	ROCK MY HEART *Logic 74321194122*	9	9
24 Jun 95	FLY AWAY *Logic 74321286942*	20	3
23 Sep 95	CATCH A FIRE *Logic 74321306652*	39	2

Tony HADLEY UK, male vocalist (9 WEEKS)

		pos	wks
7 Mar 92	LOST IN YOUR LOVE *EMI EM 222*	42	4
29 Aug 92	FOR YOUR BLUE EYES ONLY *EMI EM 234*	67	2
16 Jan 93	GAME OF LOVE *EMI CDEM 254*	72	1
10 May 97	DANCE WITH ME *VC VCRD 17* [1]	35	2

[1] Tin Tin Out featuring Tony Hadley

See also SPANDAU BALLET

Sammy HAGAR
US, male vocalist / instrumentalist - guitar (15 WEEKS)

		pos	wks
15 Dec 79	THIS PLANET'S ON FIRE / SPACE STATION NO. 5 *Capitol CL 16114*	52	5
16 Feb 80	I'VE DONE EVERYTHING FOR YOU *Capitol CL 16120*	36	5
24 May 80	HEARTBEAT / LOVE OR MONEY *Capitol RED 1*	67	2
16 Jan 82	PIECE OF MY HEART *Geffen GEFA 1884*	67	1
30 Jan 82	PIECE OF MY HEART (re-entry) *Geffen GEFA 1884*	67	2

See also VAN HALEN; MONTROSE

Paul HAIG UK, male vocalist (3 WEEKS)

		pos	wks
28 May 83	HEAVEN SENT *Island IS 111*	74	3

UK No.1 ★   UK Top 10 ●   Still on chart +   UK million seller ◆   UK entry at No.1 ■   US No.1 ▲

HAIRCUT 100 UK, male vocal / instrumental group (47 WEEKS)

		pos/wks
24 Oct 81	● FAVOURITE SHIRTS (BOY MEETS GIRL) Arista CLIP 1	4 14
30 Jan 82	● LOVE PLUS ONE Arista CLIP 2	3 12
10 Apr 82	● FANTASTIC DAY Arista CLIP 3	9 9
21 Aug 82	● NOBODY'S FOOL Arista CLIP 4	9 7
6 Aug 83	PRIME TIME Polydor HC 1	46 5

Curtis HAIRSTON US, male vocalist (16 WEEKS)

		pos/wks
15 Oct 83	I WANT YOU (ALL TONIGHT) RCA 368	44 5
27 Apr 85	I WANT YOUR LOVIN' (JUST A LITTLE BIT) London LON 66	13 7
6 Dec 86	CHILLIN' OUT Atlantic A 9335	57 4

Gary HAISMAN – See D MOB

HAL featuring Gillian ANDERSON
UK, male producers and US, female vocalist (3 WEEKS)

		pos/wks
24 May 97	EXTREMIS Virgin VSCDT 1636	23 3

HALE and PACE and the STONKERS UK, male comedy duo - Gareth Hale and Norman Pace, and backing group (7 WEEKS)

		pos/wks
9 Mar 91	★ THE STONK London LON 296	1 7

Bill HALEY and his COMETS (91 Top 500) Original 'King of Rock 'n' Roll', b. 6 Jul 1925, Detroit, d. 9 Feb 1981. The kiss-curl hairstyled frontman introduced rock to the world via a string of mid-1950s smashes, including 'Rock Around the Clock', the only record to return to the Top 20 on five occasions (199 WEEKS)

		pos/wks
17 Dec 54	● SHAKE RATTLE AND ROLL Brunswick 05338	4 14
7 Jan 55	ROCK AROUND THE CLOCK Brunswick 05317	17 2
15 Apr 55	MAMBO ROCK Brunswick 05405	14 2
14 Oct 55	★ ROCK AROUND THE CLOCK (re-entry) Brunswick 05317◆ ▲	1 17
30 Dec 55	● ROCK-A-BEATIN' BOOGIE Brunswick 05509	4 9
9 Mar 56	● SEE YOU LATER ALLIGATOR Brunswick 05530	7 13
25 May 56	● THE SAINTS ROCK 'N ROLL Brunswick 05565	5 24
17 Aug 56	● ROCKIN' THROUGH THE RYE Brunswick 05582	3 18
14 Sep 56	RAZZLE DAZZLE Brunswick 05453	13 8
21 Sep 56	● ROCK AROUND THE CLOCK (2nd re-entry) Brunswick 05317	5 11
21 Sep 56	SEE YOU LATER ALLIGATOR (re-entry) Brunswick 05530	12 8
9 Nov 56	● RIP IT UP Brunswick 05615	4 18
9 Nov 56	ROCK 'N ROLL STAGE SHOW (LP) Brunswick LAT 8139	30 1
23 Nov 56	RUDY'S ROCK Brunswick 05616	30 1
14 Dec 56	ROCK AROUND THE CLOCK (3rd re-entry) Brunswick 05317	24 2
14 Dec 56	RUDY'S ROCK (re-entry) Brunswick 05616	26 4
4 Jan 57	ROCK AROUND THE CLOCK (4th re-entry) Brunswick 05317	25 2
4 Jan 57	ROCKIN' THROUGH THE RYE (re-entry) Brunswick 05582	19 5
25 Jan 57	ROCK AROUND THE CLOCK (5th re-entry) Brunswick 05317	22 2
1 Feb 57	ROCK THE JOINT London HLF 8371	20 4
8 Feb 57	● DON'T KNOCK THE ROCK Brunswick 05640	7 8
3 Apr 68	ROCK AROUND THE CLOCK (re-issue) MCA MU 1013	20 11
16 Mar 74	ROCK AROUND THE CLOCK (2nd re-issue) MCA 128	12 10
25 Apr 81	HALEY'S GOLDEN MEDLEY MCA 694	50 5

Tracks on Rock 'n' Roll Stage Show (LP): Calling All Comets / Rockin' Through the Rye / A Rockin' Little Tune / Hide and Seek / Hey There Now / Goofin' Around / Hook Line and Sinker / Rudy's Rock / Choo Choo Ch'Boogie / Blue Comets Rock / Hot Dog Buddy Buddy / Tonight's the Night. Occasionally, some of the 'Rock Around the Clock' labels billed the song as '(We're Gonna) Rock Around the Clock'

Aaron HALL US, male vocalist (3 WEEKS)

		pos/wks
13 Jun 92	DON'T BE AFRAID MCA MCS 1632	56 2
23 Oct 93	GET A LITTLE FREAKY WITH ME MCA MCSTD 1936	66 1

Audrey HALL Jamaica, female vocalist (20 WEEKS)

		pos/wks
25 Jan 86	ONE DANCE WON'T DO Germain DG7-1985	20 11
5 Jul 86	SMILE Germain DG 15	14 9

Daryl HALL US, male vocalist (26 WEEKS)

		pos/wks
2 Aug 86	DREAMTIME RCA HALL 1	28 8
25 Sep 93	I'M IN A PHILLY MOOD Epic 6595555	59 2
8 Jan 94	STOP LOVING ME STOP LOVING YOU Epic 6599982	30 6
26 Mar 94	I'M IN A PHILLY MOOD (re-entry) Epic 6595555	52 2
14 May 94	HELP ME FIND A WAY TO YOUR HEART Epic 6604102	70 1
2 Jul 94	GLORYLAND Mercury MERCD 404 [1]	36 4
10 Jun 95	WHEREVER WOULD I BE Columbia 6620592 [2]	44 3

[1] Daryl Hall and the Sounds of Blackness [2] Dusty Springfield and Daryl Hall

Daryl HALL and John OATES (384 Top 500) White, soul-influenced US duo: Daryl Hall (v), b. 11 Oct 1948, Philadelphia and John Oates (g) b. 7 Apr 1949, New York. Met at university in 1967, eventually becoming the most successful duo in US singles chart history, with 16 Top 10s and six No.1s (84 WEEKS)

		pos/wks
16 Oct 76	SHE'S GONE Atlantic K 10828	42 4
14 Jun 80	RUNNING FROM PARADISE RCA RUN 1	41 6
20 Sep 80	YOU'VE LOST THAT LOVIN' FEELIN' RCA 1	55 3
15 Nov 80	KISS ON MY LIST RCA 15 ▲	33 8
23 Jan 82	● I CAN'T GO FOR THAT (NO CAN DO) RCA 172 ▲	8 10
10 Apr 82	PRIVATE EYES RCA 134 ▲	32 7
30 Oct 82	● MANEATER RCA 290 ▲	6 11
22 Jan 83	ONE ON ONE RCA 305	63 3
30 Apr 83	FAMILY MAN RCA 323	15 7
12 Nov 83	SAY IT ISN'T SO RCA 375	69 3
10 Mar 84	ADULT EDUCATION RCA 396	63 2
20 Oct 84	OUT OF TOUCH RCA 449 ▲	48 5
9 Feb 85	METHOD OF MODERN LOVE RCA 472	21 8
22 Jun 85	OUT OF TOUCH RCA PB 49967	62 3
21 Sep 85	A NIGHT AT THE APOLLO LIVE! RCA PB 49935 [1]	58 2
29 Sep 90	SO CLOSE Arista 113600 [2]	69 1
26 Jan 91	EVERYWHERE I LOOK Arista 113980	74 1

[1] Daryl Hall and John Oates featuring David Ruffin and Eddie Kendrick [2] Hall and Oates

'A Night at the Apollo Live!' is a medley of 'The Way You Do the Things You Do' and 'My Girl'

Lynden David HALL UK, male vocal / instrumentalist (12 WEEKS)

		pos/wks
25 Oct 97	SEXY CINDERELLA Cooltempo CDCOOL 328	45 2
14 Mar 98	DO I QUALIFY? Cooltempo CDCOOLS 331	26 2
4 Jul 98	CRESCENT MOON Cooltempo CDCOOL 333	45 1
31 Oct 98	SEXY CINDERELLA (re-issue) Cooltempo CDCOOLS 340	17 3
11 Mar 00	FORGIVE ME Cooltempo CDCOOLS 346	30 2
27 May 00	SLEEPING WITH VICTOR Cooltempo CDCOOL 348	49 1
23 Sep 00	LET'S DO IT AGAIN Cooltempo CDCOOL 351	69 1

Pam HALL Jamaica, female vocalist (4 WEEKS)

		pos/wks
16 Aug 86	DEAR BOOPSIE Bluemountain BM 027	54 4

Terry HALL UK, male vocalist (6 WEEKS)

		pos/wks
11 Nov 89	MISSING Chrysalis CHS 3381	75 1
27 Aug 94	FOREVER J Anxious ANX 1024CDX	67 1
12 Nov 94	SENSE Anxious ANX 1027CD	54 2
28 Oct 95	CHASING A RAINBOW Anxious ANX 1033CD1	62 1
14 Jun 97	BALLAD OF A LANDLORD Southsea Bubble CDBUBBLE 1	50 1

The sleeve, not the label, of 'Missing' credits Terry, Blair and Anouchka

See also FUN BOY THREE; SPECIALS

Toni HALLIDAY – See LEFTFIELD; Paul VAN DYK

Geri HALLIWELL UK, female vocalist (54 WEEKS)

		pos/wks
22 May 99	● LOOK AT ME EMI CDEM 542	2 12
28 Aug 99	LOOK AT ME (re-entry) EMI CDEM 542	60 2
28 Aug 99	★ MI CHICO LATINO EMI CDEM 548■	1 13
13 Nov 99	★ LIFT ME UP EMI CDEM 554■	1 15
4 Mar 00	LIFT ME UP (re-entry) EMI CDEM 554	62 1
25 Mar 00	★ BAG IT UP EMI CDEMS 560■	1 11

See also SPICE GIRLS

UK No.1 ★ UK Top 10 ● Still on chart + UK million seller ◆ UK entry at No.1 ■ US No.1 ▲

HALO JAMES UK, male vocal / instrumental group (24 WEEKS)

			pos/wks
7 Oct 89		WANTED *Epic HALO 1*	45 5
23 Dec 89 ●		COULD HAVE TOLD YOU SO *Epic HALO 2*	6 12
17 Mar 90		BABY *Epic HALO 3*	43 4
19 May 90		MAGIC HOUR *Epic HALO 4*	59 3

George HAMILTON IV US, male vocalist (13 WEEKS)

		pos/wks
7 Mar 58	WHY DON'T THEY UNDERSTAND *HMV POP 429*	22 9
18 Jul 58	I KNOW WHERE I'M GOING *HMV POP 505*	29 1
8 Aug 58	I KNOW WHERE I'M GOING (re-entry) *HMV POP 505*	23 3

Lynne HAMILTON Australia, female vocalist (11 WEEKS)

		pos/wks
29 Apr 89 ●	ON THE INSIDE (THEME FROM 'PRISONER CELL BLOCK H') *A1 A1 311*	3 11

Russ HAMILTON UK, male vocalist - Ronald Hulme (26 WEEKS)

		pos/wks
24 May 57 ●	WE WILL MAKE LOVE *Oriole CB 1359*	2 20
27 Sep 57	WEDDING RING *Oriole CB 1388* [1]	20 6

[1] Russ Hamilton with Johnny Gregory and his Orchestra with the Tonettes

HAMILTON, Joe FRANK and REYNOLDS US, male vocal group (6 WEEKS)

		pos/wks
13 Sep 75	FALLIN' IN LOVE *Pye International 7N 25690*	33 6

Marvin HAMLISCH US, male instrumentalist - piano (13 WEEKS)

		pos/wks
30 Mar 74	THE ENTERTAINER *MCA 121*	25 13

HAMMER
World's top rap star of early 1990s (as MC Hammer), b. Stanley Burrell, 30 Mar 1963, California, US. Album Please Hammer Don't Hurt 'Em, which cost just $10,000 to record, was the biggest-selling rap album in the US, with world sales exceeding 15 million (68 WEEKS)

			pos/wks
9 Jun 90 ●	U CAN'T TOUCH THIS *Capitol CL 578* [1]		3 16
6 Oct 90 ●	HAVE YOU SEEN HER *Capitol CL 590* [1]		8 7
8 Dec 90 ●	PRAY *Capitol CL 599* [1]		8 10
23 Feb 91	HERE COMES THE HAMMER *Capitol CL 610* [1]		15 5
1 Jun 91	YO!! SWEETNESS *Capitol CL 616* [1]		16 5
20 Jul 91	(HAMMER HAMMER) THEY PUT ME IN THE MIX *Capitol CL 607* [1]		20 4
26 Oct 91	2 LEGIT 2 QUIT *Capitol CL 636*		60 2
21 Dec 91 ●	ADDAMS GROOVE *Capitol CL 642*		4 9
21 Mar 92	DO NOT PASS ME BY *Capitol CL 650*		14 6
12 Mar 94	IT'S ALL GOOD *RCA 74321188612*		52 2
13 Aug 94	DON'T STOP *RCA 74321220012*		72 1
3 Jun 95	STRAIGHT TO MY FEET *Priority PTYCD 102* [2]		57 1

[1] MC Hammer [2] Hammer featuring Deion Saunders

Jan HAMMER
Czech Republic, male instrumentalist - keyboards (26 WEEKS)

		pos/wks
12 Oct 85 ●	MIAMI VICE THEME *MCA MCA 1000* ▲	5 8
19 Sep 87 ●	CROCKETT'S THEME *MCA MCA 1193*	2 12
1 Jun 91	CROCKETT'S THEME (re-issue) *MCA MCS 1541*	47 6

Albert HAMMOND UK, male vocalist (11 WEEKS)

		pos/wks
30 Jun 73	FREE ELECTRIC BAND *Mums 1494*	19 11

Beres HAMMOND – See Maxi PRIEST

Herbie HANCOCK
US, male vocalist / instrumentalist - keyboards (41 WEEKS)

		pos/wks
26 Aug 78	I THOUGHT IT WAS YOU *CBS 6530*	15 9
3 Feb 79	YOU BET YOUR LOVE *CBS 7010*	18 10
30 Jul 83 ●	ROCKIT *CBS A 3577*	8 12
8 Oct 83	AUTODRIVE *CBS A 3802*	33 4
21 Jan 84	FUTURE SHOCK *CBS A 4075*	54 3
4 Aug 84	HARDROCK *CBS A 4616*	65 3

HANDBAGGERS
UK, male / female vocal / instrumental group (1 WEEK)

		pos/wks
15 Jun 96	U FOUND OUT *Tidy Trax TIDY 104CD*	55 1

HANDLEY FAMILY UK, male / female vocal group (7 WEEKS)

		pos/wks
7 Apr 73	WAM BAM *GL 100*	30 7

HANI US, male DJ / producer (1 WEEK)

		pos/wks
11 Mar 00	BABY WANTS TO RIDE *Neo NEO CD025*	70 1

Jayn HANNA UK, female vocalist (2 WEEKS)

		pos/wks
13 Apr 96	LOVELIGHT (RIDE ON A LOVE TRAIN) *VC VCRD 10*	42 1
1 Feb 97	LOST WITHOUT YOU *VC VCRD 16*	44 1

HANNAH UK, female vocalist - Hannah Waddingham (2 WEEKS)

		pos/wks
21 Oct 00	OUR KIND OF LOVE *Telstar CDSTAS 3149*	41 2

HANNAH – See MAN WITH NO NAME

HANNAH and her SISTERS – See Hannah JONES

HANOI ROCKS
Finland / UK, male vocal / instrumental group (2 WEEKS)

		pos/wks
7 Jul 84	UP AROUND THE BEND *CBS A 4513*	61 2

HANSON US, male vocal / instrumental group (47 WEEKS)

		pos/wks
7 Jun 97 ★	MMMBOP *Mercury 5745012* ■ ▲	1 13
13 Sep 97 ●	WHERE'S THE LOVE *Mercury 5749032*	4 9
22 Nov 97 ●	I WILL COME TO YOU *Mercury 5680672*	5 9
28 Mar 98	WEIRD *Mercury 5685412*	19 5
4 Jul 98	THINKING OF YOU *Mercury 5688132*	23 6
5 Sep 98	THINKING OF YOU (re-entry) *Mercury 5688132*	69 1
29 Apr 00	IF ONLY *Mercury 5627502*	15 4

HAPPENINGS US, male vocal group (14 WEEKS)

		pos/wks
18 May 67	I GOT RHYTHM *Stateside SS 2013*	28 9
16 Aug 67	MY MAMMY *Pye International 7N 25501 and BT Puppy BTS 45530*	34 5

Pye gave the US BT Puppy label its own identification halfway through the success of 'My Mammy'

HAPPY CLAPPERS
UK, male / female vocal / instrumental group (19 WEEKS)

		pos/wks
3 Jun 95	I BELIEVE *Shindig SHIN 4CD*	21 3
26 Aug 95	HOLD ON *Shindig SHIN 7CD*	27 2
18 Nov 95 ●	I BELIEVE (re-issue) *Shindig SHIN 9CD*	7 8
15 Jun 96	CAN'T HELP IT *Coliseum TOGA 004CD*	18 3
21 Dec 96	NEVER AGAIN *Coliseum TOGA 012CD*	49 1
22 Nov 97	I BELIEVE 97 *Coalition COLA 027CD*	28 2

HAPPY MONDAYS
UK, male vocal / instrumental group (53 WEEKS)

		pos/wks
30 Sep 89	WFL *Factory FAC 2327*	68 2
25 Nov 89	MADCHESTER RAVE ON (EP) *Factory FAC 2427*	19 14
7 Apr 90 ●	STEP ON *Factory FAC 2727*	5 11
9 Jun 90	LAZYITIS - ONE ARMED BOXER *Factory FAC 2227* [1]	46 3
20 Oct 90 ●	KINKY AFRO *Factory FAC 3027*	5 7
9 Mar 91	LOOSE FIT *Factory FAC 3127*	17 7
30 Nov 91	JUDGE FUDGE *Factory FAC 3327*	24 3
19 Sep 92	STINKIN THINKIN *Factory FAC 3627*	31 3
21 Nov 92	SUNSHINE AND LOVE *Factory FAC 3727*	62 1
22 May 99	THE BOYS ARE BACK IN TOWN *London LONCD 432*	24 2

[1] Happy Mondays and Karl Denver

Tracks on Madchester Rave On (EP): Hallelujah / Holy Ghost / Clap Your Hands / Rave On

See also BLACK GRAPE

Paul HARDCASTLE *UK, male producer (66 WEEKS)*

		pos/wks	
7 Apr 84	YOU'RE THE ONE FOR ME – DAYBREAK – AM *Total Control TOCO 1*	**41**	4
28 Jul 84	GUILTY *Total Control TOCO 2*	**55**	3
22 Sep 84	RAIN FOREST *Bluebird BR 8*	**41**	5
17 Nov 84	EAT YOUR HEART OUT *Cooltempo COOL 102*	**59**	4
4 May 85 ★	19 *Chrysalis CHS 2860*	**1**	16
15 Jun 85	RAIN FOREST (re-issue) *Bluebird / 10 BR 15*	**53**	4
9 Nov 85	JUST FOR MONEY *Chrysalis CASH 1*	**19**	5
1 Feb 86 ●	DON'T WASTE MY TIME *Chrysalis PAUL 1* [1]	**8**	11
21 Jun 86	FOOLIN' YOURSELF *Chrysalis PAUL 2*	**51**	3
11 Oct 86	THE WIZARD *Chrysalis PAUL 3*	**15**	6
9 Apr 88	WALK IN THE NIGHT *Chrysalis PAUL 4*	**54**	3
4 Jun 88	40 YEARS *Chrysalis PAUL 5*	**53**	2

[1] Paul Hardcastle featuring Carol Kenyon

'Just for Money' features the voices of Laurence Olivier, Bob Hoskins, Ed O'Ross and Alan Talbot, who are credited on the sleeve only

See also SILENT UNDERDOG

HARDCORE RHYTHM TEAM
UK, male vocal / production group (1 WEEK)

		pos/wks	
14 Mar 92	HARDCORE – THE FINAL CONFLICT *Furious FRUT 001*	**69**	1

Duane HARDEN – See Armand VAN HELDEN; POWERHOUSE

HARDFLOOR
Germany, male instrumental / production group (6 WEEKS)

		pos/wks	
26 Dec 92	HARDTRANCE ACPERIENCE *Harthouse UK HARTUK 1*	**56**	4
10 Apr 93	TRANCESCRIPT *Harthouse UK HARTUK 5CD*	**72**	1
25 Oct 97	ACPERIENCE (re-mix) *Eye-q EYEUK 018CD1*	**60**	1

Tim HARDIN *US, male vocalist (1 WEEK)*

		pos/wks	
5 Jan 67	HANG ON TO A DREAM *Verve VS 1504*	**50**	1

Carolyn HARDING – See PROSPECT PARK / Carolyn HARDING

Mike HARDING *UK, male comedian (8 WEEKS)*

		pos/wks	
2 Aug 75	ROCHDALE COWBOY *Rubber ADUB 3*	**22**	8

Françoise HARDY *France, female vocalist (26 WEEKS)*

		pos/wks	
25 Jun 64	TOUS LES GARÇONS ET LES FILLES *Pye 7N 15653*	**36**	7
7 Jan 65	ET MEME *Pye 7N 15740*	**31**	4
25 Mar 65	ALL OVER THE WORLD *Pye 7N 15802*	**16**	15

Tynetta HARE – See Joey B ELLIS

NIKI HARIS – See SNAP

Morten HARKET *Norway, male vocalist (1 WEEK)*

		pos/wks	
19 Aug 95	A KIND OF CHRISTMAS CARD *Warner Bros. W 0304CD*	**53**	1

See also A-HA

HARLEM COMMUNITY CHOIR – See John LENNON

HARLEQUIN 4s / BUNKER KRU *US, male / female vocal / instrumental group with UK, male production duo (4 WEEKS)*

		pos/wks	
19 Mar 88	SET IT OFF *Champion CHAMP 64*	**55**	4

Steve HARLEY and COCKNEY REBEL (499 Top 500) *Distinctive singer / songwriter b. Steven Nice, 27, Feb 1951, London, UK, fronted band until he went solo in 1977. His self-penned No.1, 'Make Me Smile' returned to the Top 40 in 1995 after being used in a Carlsberg TV commercial (69 WEEKS)*

		pos/wks	
11 May 74 ●	JUDY TEEN *EMI 2128* [1]	**5**	11
10 Aug 74 ●	MR SOFT *EMI 2191* [1]	**8**	9
8 Feb 75 ★	MAKE ME SMILE (COME UP AND SEE ME) *EMI 2263*	**1**	9
7 Jun 75	MR RAFFLES (MAN IT WAS MEAN) *EMI 2299*	**13**	6
31 Jul 76 ●	HERE COMES THE SUN *EMI 2505* [2]	**10**	7
6 Nov 76	LOVE'S A PRIMA DONNA *EMI 2539* [2]	**41**	4
20 Oct 79	FREEDOM'S PRISONER *EMI 2994* [2]	**58**	3
13 Aug 83	BALLERINA (PRIMA DONNA) *Stiletto STL 14* [2]	**51**	5
11 Jan 86 ●	THE PHANTOM OF THE OPERA *Polydor POSP 800* [3]	**7**	10
25 Apr 92	MAKE ME SMILE (COME UP AND SEE ME) (re-issue) *EMI EMCT 5* [2]	**46**	2
30 Dec 95	MAKE ME SMILE (COME UP AND SEE ME) (2nd re-issue) *EMI CDHARLEY 1*	**33**	3

[1] Cockney Rebel [2] Steve Harley [3] Sarah Brightman and Steve Harley

HARLEY QUINNE *UK, male vocal group (8 WEEKS)*

		pos/wks	
14 Oct 72	NEW ORLEANS *Bell 1255*	**19**	8

HARMONIX *UK, male producer - Hamish Brown (2 WEEKS)*

		pos/wks	
30 Mar 96	LANDSLIDE *Deconstruction 74321330762*	**28**	2

HARMONY GRASS *UK, male vocal / instrumental group (7 WEEKS)*

		pos/wks	
29 Jan 69	MOVE IN A LITTLE CLOSER *RCA 1772*	**24**	7

Ben HARPER *US, male vocalist / instrumentalist (1 WEEK)*

		pos/wks	
4 Apr 98	FADED *Virgin VUSCD 134*	**54**	1

Charlie HARPER *UK, male vocalist (1 WEEK)*

		pos/wks	
19 Jul 80	BARMY LONDON ARMY *Gem GEMS 35*	**68**	1

HARPERS BIZARRE *US, male vocal group (13 WEEKS)*

		pos/wks	
30 Mar 67	59TH STREET BRIDGE SONG (FEELING GROOVY) *Warner Bros. WB 5890*	**34**	7
4 Oct 67	ANYTHING GOES *Warner Bros. WB 7063*	**33**	6

HARPO *Sweden, male vocalist (6 WEEKS)*

		pos/wks	
17 Apr 76	MOVIE STAR *DJM DJS 400*	**24**	6

T HARRINGTON – See Rahni HARRIS and F.L.O.

Anita HARRIS *UK, female vocalist (50 WEEKS)*

		pos/wks	
29 Jun 67 ●	JUST LOVING YOU *CBS 2724*	**6**	30
11 Oct 67	PLAYGROUND *CBS 2991*	**46**	3
24 Jan 68	ANNIVERSARY WALTZ *CBS 3211*	**21**	9
14 Aug 68	DREAM A LITTLE DREAM OF ME *CBS 3637*	**33**	8

Emmylou HARRIS *US, female vocalist (6 WEEKS)*

		pos/wks	
6 Mar 76	HERE THERE AND EVERYWHERE *Reprise K 14415*	**30**	6

Jet HARRIS *UK, male instrumentalist - bass (18 WEEKS)*

		pos/wks	
24 May 62	BESAME MUCHO *Decca F 11466*	**22**	7
16 Aug 62	MAIN TITLE THEME FROM 'MAN WITH THE GOLDEN ARM' *Decca F 11488*	**12**	11

See also Jet HARRIS and Tony MEEHAN; SHADOWS

Major HARRIS *US, male vocalist (9 WEEKS)*

		pos/wks	
9 Aug 75	LOVE WON'T LET ME WAIT *Atlantic K 10585*	**37**	7
5 Nov 83	ALL MY LIFE *London LON 37*	**61**	2

Max HARRIS *UK, orchestra (10 WEEKS)*

		pos/wks	
1 Dec 60	GURNEY SLADE *Fontana H 282*	**11**	10

Rahni HARRIS and F.L.O.
US, male instrumental group (7 WEEKS)

		pos/wks	
16 Dec 78	SIX MILLION STEPS (WEST RUNS SOUTH) *Mercury 6007 198*	**43**	7

Hit has credit 'vocals by T Harrington and O Rasbury'

Richard HARRIS *Ireland, male actor (18 WEEKS)*

pos/wks

Date	Title	pos	wks
26 Jun 68 ●	MACARTHUR PARK *RCA 1699*	4	12
8 Jul 72	MACARTHUR PARK (re-issue) *Probe GFF 101*	38	6

Rochelle HARRIS – See ANGELHEART

Rolf HARRIS `426` `Top 500` *Lovable Australian musician, artist and presenter b. 30 Mar 1930, can lay claim to having some of the unlikeliest hits in the history of the UK charts. His only No.1 was a song written in 1903 by Theodore F Morse and Edward Madden and was the final chart-topper of the 60s (77 WEEKS)*

pos/wks

Date	Title	pos	wks
21 Jul 60 ●	TIE ME KANGAROO DOWN SPORT *Columbia DB 4483* [1]	9	13
25 Oct 62 ●	SUN ARISE *Columbia DB 4888*	3	16
28 Feb 63	JOHNNY DAY *Columbia DB 4979*	44	2
16 Apr 69	BLUER THAN BLUE *Columbia DB 8553*	30	8
22 Nov 69 ★	TWO LITTLE BOYS *Columbia DB 8630*	1	24
20 Jun 70	TWO LITTLE BOYS (re-entry) *Columbia DB 8630*	50	1
13 Feb 93 ●	STAIRWAY TO HEAVEN *Vertigo VERCD 73*	7	6
1 Jun 96	BOHEMIAN RHAPSODY *Living Beat LBECD 41*	50	1
25 Oct 97	SUN ARISE (re-recording) *EMI CDROO 001*	26	3
14 Oct 00	FINE DAY *Tommy Boy TBCD 2155*	24	3

[1] Rolf Harris with his wobble board and The Rhythm Spinners

Ronnie HARRIS *UK, male vocalist (3 WEEKS)*

pos/wks

Date	Title	pos	wks
24 Sep 54	THE STORY OF TINA *Columbia DB 3499*	12	3

Sam HARRIS *US, male vocalist (2 WEEKS)*

pos/wks

Date	Title	pos	wks
9 Feb 85	HEARTS ON FIRE / OVER THE RAINBOW *Motown TMG 1370*	67	2

Simon HARRIS *UK, male / DJ producer (17 WEEKS)*

pos/wks

Date	Title	pos	wks
19 Mar 88	BASS (HOW LOW CAN YOU GO) *ffrr FFR 4*	12	6
29 Oct 88	HERE COMES THAT SOUND *ffrr FFR 12*	38	4
24 Jun 89	(I'VE GOT YOUR) PLEASURE CONTROL *ffrr F 106* [1]	60	3
18 Nov 89	ANOTHER MONSTERJAM *ffrr F 116* [2]	65	1
10 Mar 90	RAGGA HOUSE (ALL NIGHT LONG) *Living Beat 7SMASH 9* [3]	56	3

[1] Simon Harris featuring Lonnie Gordon [2] Simon Harris featuring Einstein [3] Simon Harris featuring Daddy Freddy

See also AMBASSADORS OF FUNK featuring MC MARIO

Jet HARRIS and Tony MEEHAN *UK, male instrumental duo - bass and drums (39 WEEKS)*

pos/wks

Date	Title	pos	wks
10 Jan 63 ★	DIAMONDS *Decca F 11563*	1	13
25 Apr 63 ●	SCARLETT O'HARA *Decca F 11644*	2	13
5 Sep 63 ●	APPLEJACK *Decca F 11710*	4	13

See also Jet HARRIS; Tony MEEHAN COMBO; SHADOWS

Keith HARRIS and ORVILLE *UK, male ventriloquist vocalist with feathered dummy (20 WEEKS)*

pos/wks

Date	Title	pos	wks
18 Dec 82 ●	ORVILLE'S SONG *BBC RESL 124*	4	11
24 Dec 83	COME TO MY PARTY *BBC RESL 138* [1]	44	4
14 Dec 85	WHITE CHRISTMAS *Columbia DB 9121*	40	5

[1] Keith Harris and Orville with Dippy

George HARRISON `393` `Top 500` *Former Beatles guitarist, much inspired by Eastern musicians, born 24 Feb 1943, Liverpool UK. First ex-Beatle to score a solo UK No.1 single, and only act in history to make UK and US Top 5 with back-to back triple albums (82 WEEKS)*

pos/wks

Date	Title	pos	wks
23 Jan 71 ★	MY SWEET LORD *Apple R 5884* ▲	1	17
14 Aug 71 ●	BANGLA DESH *Apple R 5912*	10	9
2 Jun 73 ●	GIVE ME LOVE (GIVE ME PEACE ON EARTH) *Apple R 5988* ▲	8	10
21 Dec 74	DING DONG *Apple R 6002*	38	5
11 Oct 75	YOU *Apple R 6007*	38	5
10 Mar 79	BLOW AWAY *Dark Horse K 17327*	51	5
23 May 81	ALL THOSE YEARS AGO *Dark Horse K 17807*	13	7

Date	Title	pos	wks
24 Oct 87 ●	GOT MY MIND SET ON YOU *Dark Horse W 8178* ▲	2	14
6 Feb 88	WHEN WE WAS FAB *Dark Horse W 8131*	25	7
25 Jun 88	THIS IS LOVE *Dark Horse W 7913*	55	3

Noel HARRISON *UK, male vocalist (14 WEEKS)*

pos/wks

Date	Title	pos	wks
26 Feb 69 ●	WINDMILLS OF YOUR MIND *Reprise RS 20758*	8	14

Deborah HARRY *US, female vocalist (52 WEEKS)*

pos/wks

Date	Title	pos	wks
1 Aug 81	BACKFIRED *Chrysalis CHS 2526* [1]	32	6
15 Nov 86 ●	FRENCH KISSIN' IN THE USA *Chrysalis CHS 3066* [1]	8	10
28 Feb 87	FREE TO FALL *Chrysalis CHS 3093* [1]	46	4
9 May 87	IN LOVE WITH LOVE *Chrysalis CHS 3128* [1]	45	5
7 Oct 89	I WANT THAT MAN *Chrysalis CHS 3369*	13	10
2 Dec 89	BRITE SIDE *Chrysalis CHS 3452*	59	4
31 Mar 90	SWEET AND LOW *Chrysalis CHS 3491*	57	3
5 Jan 91	WELL DID YOU EVAH! *Chrysalis CHS 3646* [2]	42	4
3 Jul 93	I CAN SEE CLEARLY NOW *Chrysalis CDCHSS 4900*	23	4
18 Sep 93	STRIKE ME PINK *Chrysalis CDCHSS 5000*	46	2

[1] Debbie Harry [2] Deborah Harry and Iggy Pop

See also BLONDIE

HARRY J ALL STARS *Jamaica, male instrumental group (25 WEEKS)*

pos/wks

Date	Title	pos	wks
25 Oct 69 ●	LIQUIDATOR *Trojan TR 675*	9	20
29 Mar 80	LIQUIDATOR (re-issue) *Trojan TRO 9063*	42	5

Re-issue of 'Liquidator' coupled with re-issue of 'Long Shot Kick De Bucket' by The Pioneers

Richard HARTLEY / Michael REED ORCHESTRA *UK, male instrumentalist - synthesizer, orchestra (10 WEEKS)*

pos/wks

Date	Title	pos	wks
25 Feb 84 ●	THE MUSIC OF TORVILL AND DEAN (EP) *Safari SKATE 1*	9	10

Tracks on EP: Bolero / Capriccio Espagnole Opus 34 (Nos. 4 and 5) by Richard Hartley; Barnum on Ice / Discoskate by the Michael Reed Orchestra

Dan HARTMAN *US, male vocalist (34 WEEKS)*

pos/wks

Date	Title	pos	wks
21 Oct 78 ●	INSTANT REPLAY *Blue Sky SKY 6706*	8	15
13 Jan 79	THIS IS IT *Blue Sky SKY 6999*	17	8
18 May 85	SECOND NATURE *MCA MCA 957*	66	2
24 Aug 85	I CAN DREAM ABOUT YOU *MCA MCA 988*	12	8
1 Apr 95	KEEP THE FIRE BURNIN' *Columbia 6611552* [1]	49	1

[1] Dan Hartman starring Loleatta Holloway

Alex HARVEY BAND – See SENSATIONAL Alex HARVEY BAND

Brian HARVEY – See TRUE STEPPERS; EAST 17

HARVEY DANGER *US, male vocal / instrumental group (1 WEEK)*

pos/wks

Date	Title	pos	wks
1 Aug 98	FLAGPOLE SITTA *Slash LASCD 64*	57	1

P J HARVEY *UK, female vocalist - Polly Jean Harvey (19 WEEKS)*

pos/wks

Date	Title	pos	wks
29 Feb 92	SHEELA-NA-GIG *Too Pure PURE 008*	69	1
1 May 93	50 FT QUEENIE *Island CID 538*	27	2
17 Jul 93	MAN-SIZE *Island CID 569*	42	2
18 Feb 95	DOWN BY THE WATER *Island CID 607*	38	2
22 Jul 95	C'MON BILLY *Island CID 614*	29	2
28 Oct 95	SEND HIS LOVE TO ME *Island CID 610*	34	2
9 Mar 96	HENRY LEE *Mute CDMUTE 189* [1]	36	1
23 Nov 96	THAT WAS MY VEIL *Island CID 648*	75	1
26 Sep 98	A PERFECT DAY ELISE *Island CID 718*	25	2
23 Jan 99	THE WIND *Island CID 730*	29	2
25 Nov 00	GOOD FORTUNE *Island CID 769*	41	2

[1] Nick Cave and the Bad Seeds and P J Harvey

For the first three hits P J Harvey was the name of the entire group, not just the lead singer

Steve HARVEY UK, male vocalist (6 WEEKS)

		pos/wks
28 May 83	SOMETHING SPECIAL *London LON 25*	46 4
29 Oct 83	TONIGHT *London LON 36*	63 2

David HASSELHOFF US, male vocalist (2 WEEKS)

		pos/wks
13 Nov 93	IF I COULD ONLY SAY GOODBYE *Arista 74321172262*	35 2

Tony HATCH UK, orchestra (1 WEEK)

		pos/wks
4 Oct 62	OUT OF THIS WORLD *Pye 7N 15460*	50 1

Juliana HATFIELD US, female vocalist / instrumetalist (2 WEEKS)

		pos/wks
11 Sep 93	MY SISTER *Mammoth YZ 767CD* [1]	71 1
18 Mar 95	UNIVERSAL HEART-BEAT *East West YZ 916CD*	65 1

[1] Juliana Hatfield Three

Donny HATHAWAY – See Roberta FLACK

Lalah HATHAWAY US, female vocalist (10 WEEKS)

		pos/wks
1 Sep 90	HEAVEN KNOWS *Virgin America VUS 28*	66 2
2 Feb 91	BABY DON'T CRY *Virgin America VUS 35*	54 3
27 Jul 91	FAMILY AFFAIR *Ten TEN 369*	37 5

HAVANA UK, male instrumental / production group (1 WEEK)

		pos/wks
6 Mar 93	ETHNIC PRAYER *Limbo LIMBO 007CD*	71 1

Nic HAVERSON UK, male vocalist (3 WEEKS)

		pos/wks
30 Jan 93	HEAD OVER HEELS *Telstar CDHOH 1*	48 3

Chesney HAWKES UK, male vocalist (25 WEEKS)

		pos/wks
23 Feb 91	★ THE ONE AND ONLY *Chrysalis CHS 3627*	1 16
22 Jun 91	I'M A MAN NOT A BOY *Chrysalis CHS 3708*	27 5
28 Sep 91	SECRETS OF THE HEART *Chrysalis CHS 3681*	57 3
29 May 93	WHAT'S WRONG WITH THIS PICTURE *Chrysalis CDCHS 3969*	63 1

Screamin' Jay HAWKINS US, male vocalist (3 WEEKS)

		pos/wks
3 Apr 93	HEART ATTACK AND VINE *Columbia 6591092*	42 3

Sophie B HAWKINS US, female vocalist (37 WEEKS)

		pos/wks
4 Jul 92	DAMN I WISH I WAS YOUR LOVER *Columbia 6581077*	14 9
12 Sep 92	CALIFORNIA HERE I COME *Columbia 6583177*	53 3
6 Feb 93	I WANT YOU *Columbia 6587772*	49 2
13 Aug 94	RIGHT BESIDE YOU *Columbia 6606915*	13 12
26 Nov 94	DON'T DON'T TELL ME NO *Columbia 6610152*	36 5
11 Mar 95	AS I LAY ME DOWN *Columbia 6612125*	24 6

Edwin HAWKINS SINGERS
US, male / female vocal group (13 WEEKS)

		pos/wks
21 May 69	● OH HAPPY DAY *Buddah 201 048*	2 12
23 Aug 69	OH HAPPY DAY (re-entry) *Buddah 201 048*	43 1

Kirsty HAWKSHAW – See BT

HAWKWIND
UK, male vocal / instrumental group with female dancer (28 WEEKS)

		pos/wks
1 Jul 72	● SILVER MACHINE *United Artists UP 35381*	3 15
11 Aug 73	URBAN GUERRILLA *United Artists UP 35566*	39 3
21 Oct 78	SILVER MACHINE (re-entry) *United Artists UP 35381*	34 5
19 Jul 80	SHOT DOWN IN THE NIGHT *Bronze BRO 98*	59 3
15 Jan 83	SILVER MACHINE (2nd re-entry) *United Artists UP 35381*	67 2

Bill HAYES US, male vocalist (9 WEEKS)

		pos/wks
6 Jan 56	● THE BALLAD OF DAVY CROCKETT *London HLA 8220* [1] ▲	2 9

[1] with Archie Bleyer's Orchestra

Isaac HAYES US, male vocalist / multi-instrumentalist (35 WEEKS)

		pos/wks
4 Dec 71	● THEME FROM 'SHAFT' *Stax 2025 069* ▲	4 12
3 Apr 76	● DISCO CONNECTION *ABC 4100* [1]	10 9
26 Dec 98	★ CHOCOLATE SALTY BALLS (PS I LOVE YOU) *Columbia 6667985* [2]	1 13
30 Sep 00	THEME FROM SHAFT (re-recording) *LaFace / Arista 74321792582*	53 1

[1] Isaac Hayes Movement [2] Chef

HAYSI FANTAYZEE UK, male / female vocal duo (25 WEEKS)

		pos/wks
24 Jul 82	JOHN WAYNE IS BIG LEGGY *Regard RG 100*	11 10
13 Nov 82	HOLY JOE *Regard RG 104*	51 3
22 Jan 83	SHINY SHINY *Regard RG 106*	16 10
25 Jun 83	SISTER FRICTION *Regard RG 108*	62 2

Justin HAYWARD UK, male vocalist (20 WEEKS)

		pos/wks
25 Oct 75	● BLUE GUITAR *Threshold TH 21* [1]	8 7
8 Jul 78	● FOREVER AUTUMN *CBS 6368*	5 13

[1] Justin Hayward and John Lodge

See also MOODY BLUES

Leon HAYWOOD US, male vocalist (11 WEEKS)

		pos/wks
15 Mar 80	DON'T PUSH IT, DON'T FORCE IT *20th Century Fox TC 2443*	12 11

HAYWOODE UK, female vocalist (31 WEEKS)

		pos/wks
17 Sep 83	A TIME LIKE THIS *CBS A 3651*	48 7
29 Sep 84	I CAN'T LET YOU GO *CBS A 4664*	63 4
13 Apr 85	ROSES *CBS A 6069*	65 3
5 Oct 85	GETTING CLOSER *CBS A 6582*	67 2
21 Jun 86	ROSES (re-issue) *CBS A 7224*	11 11
13 Sep 86	I CAN'T LET YOU GO (re-issue) *CBS 650076 7*	50 4

Ofra HAZA Israel, female vocalist (12 WEEKS)

		pos/wks
30 Apr 88	IM NIN'ALU *WEA YZ 190*	15 8
17 Jun 95	MY LOVE IS FOR REAL *Virgin America VUSCD 91* [1]	28 3
3 Apr 99	BABYLON *Warner Esp. WESP 006CD1* [2]	65 1

[1] Paula Abdul featuring Ofra Haza [2] Black Dog featuring Ofra Haza

Lee HAZLEWOOD – See Nancy SINATRA

Murray HEAD UK, male vocalist (15 WEEKS)

		pos/wks
29 Jan 72	SUPERSTAR *MCA MMKS 5077*	47 1
10 Nov 84	ONE NIGHT IN BANGKOK *RCA CHESS 1*	12 13
16 Feb 85	ONE NIGHT IN BANGKOK (re-entry) *RCA CHESS 1*	74 1

'Superstar' was one of four tracks on a maxi single, two of which were credited during the disc's one week on the chart. The other track credited was 'I Don't Know How to Love Him' by Yvonne Elliman

Roy HEAD US, male vocalist (5 WEEKS)

		pos/wks
4 Nov 65	TREAT HER RIGHT *Vocalion V-P 9248*	30 5

HEADBANGERS UK, male vocal / instrumental group (3 WEEKS)

		pos/wks
10 Oct 81	STATUS ROCK *Magnet MAG 206*	60 3

HEADBOYS UK, male vocal / instrumental group (8 WEEKS)

		pos/wks
22 Sep 79	THE SHAPE OF THINGS TO COME *RSO 40*	45 8

HEADGIRL – See MOTORHEAD; GIRLSCHOOL

Max HEADROOM – See ART OF NOISE

HEADS UK, male instrumental group (4 WEEKS)

		pos/wks
21 Jun 86	AZTEC LIGHTNING (THEME FROM BBC WORLD CUP GRANDSTAND) *BBC RESL 184*	45 4

HEADS with Shaun RYDER
US / UK, male / female vocal / instrumental group (1 WEEK) pos/wks

9 Nov 96	DON'T TAKE MY KINDNESS FOR WEAKNESS		
	Radioactive MCSTD 48024	**60**	1

Heads are Talking Heads minus lead singer David Byrne

See also TALKING HEADS

HEADSWIM *UK, male vocal / instrumental group (5 WEEKS)* pos/wks

25 Feb 95	CRAWL *Epic 6612252*	**64**	1
14 Feb 98	TOURNIQUET *Epic 6650442*	**30**	3
16 May 98	BETTER MADE *Epic 6658402*	**42**	1

Jeremy HEALY and AMOS
UK, male production / vocal duo (7 WEEKS) pos/wks

12 Oct 96	STAMP! *Positiva CDTIV 65*	**11**	5
31 May 97	ARGENTINA *Positiva CDTIV 74*	**30**	2

Imogen HEAP – See URBAN SPECIES

HEAR 'N' AID *International, male / female vocal / instrumental charity assembly (6 WEEKS)* pos/wks

19 Apr 86	STARS *Vertigo HEAR 1*	**26**	6

HEART (442 *Top 500*) *Giants of Stateside AOR, who first tasted success in Canada and are regarded as key players on the Seattle music scene. Fronted by Californian-born Wilson sisters Ann (v/g/f) b. 19 Jun 1951 and Nancy (g/v) b. 16 Mar 1954. UK chart career began a full decade after US debut (76 WEEKS)* pos/wks

29 Mar 86	THESE DREAMS *Capitol CL 394* ▲	**62**	4
13 Jun 87 ●	ALONE *Capitol CL 448* ▲	**3**	16
19 Sep 87	WHO WILL YOU RUN TO *Capitol CL 457*	**30**	7
12 Dec 87	THERE'S THE GIRL *Capitol CL 473*	**34**	7
5 Mar 88 ●	NEVER / THESE DREAMS (re-issue) *Capitol CL 482*	**8**	9
14 May 88	WHAT ABOUT LOVE *Capitol CL 487*	**14**	6
22 Oct 88	NOTHIN' AT ALL *Capitol CL 507*	**38**	3
24 Mar 90 ●	ALL I WANNA DO IS MAKE LOVE TO YOU *Capitol CL 569*	**8**	13
28 Jul 90	I DIDN'T WANT TO NEED YOU *Capitol CL 580*	**47**	3
17 Nov 90	STRANDED *Capitol CL 595*	**60**	1
14 Sep 91	YOU'RE THE VOICE *Capitol CLS 624*	**56**	2
20 Nov 93	WILL YOU BE THERE (IN THE MORNING) *Capitol CDCLS 700*	**19**	4

HEARTBEAT *UK, male / female vocal / instrumental group (5 WEEKS)* pos/wks

24 Oct 87	TEARS FROM HEAVEN *Priority P 17*	**32**	4
23 Apr 88	THE WINNER *Priority P 19*	**70**	1

HEARTBEAT COUNTRY *UK, male vocalist - Bill Maynard (1 WEEK)* pos/wks

31 Dec 94	HEARTBEAT *MMM MMM 01CD*	**75**	1

HEARTBREAKERS – See Tom PETTY and the HEARTBREAKERS; Stevie NICKS

HEARTISTS *Italy, male DJ / production trio (5 WEEKS)* pos/wks

9 Aug 97	BELO HORIZONTI *VC VCRD 23*	**42**	3
31 Jan 98	BELO HORIZONTI (re-mix) *VC VCRD 28*	**40**	2

Ted HEATH *UK, orchestra (56 WEEKS)* pos/wks

16 Jan 53	VANESSA *Decca F 9983*	**11**	1
3 Jul 53 ●	HOT TODDY *Decca F 10093*	**6**	11
23 Oct 53	DRAGNET *Decca F 10176*	**12**	1
27 Nov 53 ●	DRAGNET (re-entry) *Decca F 10176*	**9**	1
11 Dec 53	DRAGNET (2nd re-entry) *Decca F 10176*	**11**	1
15 Jan 54	DRAGNET (3rd re-entry) *Decca F 10176*	**11**	1
5 Feb 54	DRAGNET (4th re-entry) *Decca F 10176*	**12**	1
12 Feb 54 ●	SKIN DEEP *Decca F 10246*	**9**	3
6 Jul 56	THE FAITHFUL HUSSAR *Decca F 10746*	**18**	9
14 Mar 58 ●	SWINGIN' SHEPHERD BLUES *Decca F 11000*	**3**	14
11 Apr 58	TEQUILA *Decca F 11003*	**21**	6
4 Jul 58	TOM HARK *Decca F 11025*	**24**	2
5 Oct 61	SUCU SUCU *Decca F 11392*	**36**	4
9 Nov 61	SUCU SUCU (re-entry) *Decca F 11392*	**47**	1

HEATWAVE (411 *Top 500*) *Internationally successful UK-based soul / disco band formed Germany 1973 by brothers Johnnie and Keith Wilder (Ohio, US). Group's keyboard player and main songwriter, UK-born Rod Temperton, later penned many hits including several for Michael Jackson (80 WEEKS)* pos/wks

22 Jan 77 ●	BOOGIE NIGHTS *GTO GT 77*	**2**	14
7 May 77	TOO HOT TO HANDLE / SLIP YOUR DISC TO THIS *GTO GT 91*	**15**	11
14 Jan 78	THE GROOVE LINE *GTO GT 115*	**12**	8
3 Jun 78	MIND BLOWING DECISIONS *GTO GT 226*	**12**	11
4 Nov 78 ●	ALWAYS AND FOREVER / MIND BLOWING DECISIONS (re-mix) *GTO GT 236*	**9**	14
26 May 79	RAZZLE DAZZLE *GTO GT 248*	**43**	5
17 Jan 81	GANGSTERS OF THE GROOVE *GTO GT 285*	**19**	8
21 Mar 81	JITTERBUGGIN' *GTO GT 290*	**34**	7
1 Sep 90	MIND BLOWING DECISIONS (re-recording) *Brothers Organisation HW 1*	**65**	2

HEAVEN 17 (360 *Top 500*) *Politically astute electronic pop trio from Sheffield, UK: Martyn Ware (k), Ian Craig Marsh (k) (both previously in Human League) and Glenn Gregory (v). Act, named after a fictional band in cult film A Clockwork Orange, reunited and played first ever gigs in 1997 (87 WEEKS)* pos/wks

21 Mar 81	(WE DON'T NEED THIS) FASCIST GROOVE THANG *Virgin VS 400*	**45**	5
5 Sep 81	PLAY TO WIN *Virgin VS 433*	**46**	7
14 Nov 81	PENTHOUSE AND PAVEMENT *Virgin VS 455*	**57**	3
30 Oct 82	LET ME GO *Virgin VS 532*	**41**	6
16 Apr 83 ●	TEMPTATION *Virgin VS 570*	**2**	13
25 Jun 83 ●	COME LIVE WITH ME *Virgin VS 607*	**5**	11
10 Sep 83	CRUSHED BY THE WHEELS OF INDUSTRY *Virgin VS 628*	**17**	7
1 Sep 84	SUNSET NOW *Virgin VS 708*	**24**	6
27 Oct 84	THIS IS MINE *Virgin VS 722*	**23**	7
19 Jan 85	. . . (AND THAT'S NO LIE) *Virgin VS 740*	**52**	5
17 Jan 87	TROUBLE *Virgin VS 920*	**51**	3
21 Nov 92 ●	TEMPTATION (re-mix) *Virgin VS 1446*	**4**	11
27 Feb 93	(WE DON'T NEED THIS) FASCIST GROOVE THANG *Virgin VSCDT 1451*	**40**	2
10 Apr 93	PENTHOUSE AND PAVEMENT (re-mix) *Virgin VSCDT 1457*	**54**	1

Carol Kenyon is the uncredited vocalist on 'Temptation'. 'Fascist Groove Thang' in 1993 is a re-recording

HEAVY D and the BOYZ
Jamaica / US, male rap / vocal duo (28 WEEKS) pos/wks

6 Dec 86	MR BIG STUFF *MCA MCA 1106*	**61**	8
15 Jul 89	WE GOT OUR OWN THANG *MCA MCA 23942*	**69**	2
6 Jul 91 ●	NOW THAT WE FOUND LOVE *MCA MCS 1550*	**2**	12
28 Sep 91	IS IT GOOD TO YOU *MCA MCS 1564*	**46**	3
8 Oct 94	THIS IS YOUR NIGHT *MCA MCSTD 2010*	**30**	3

HEAVY PETTIN' *UK, male vocal / instrumental group (2 WEEKS)* pos/wks

17 Mar 84	LOVE TIMES LOVE *Polydor HEP 3*	**69**	2

HEAVY STEREO *UK, male vocal / instrumental group (4 WEEKS)* pos/wks

22 Jul 95	SLEEP FREAK *Creation CRESCD 203*	**46**	1
28 Oct 95	SMILER *Creation CRESCD 213*	**46**	1
10 Feb 96	CHINESE BURN *Creation CRESCD 218*	**45**	1
24 Aug 96	MOUSE IN A HOLE *Creation CRESCD 230*	**53**	1

HEAVY WEATHER *US, male vocalist - Peter Lee (1 WEEK)* pos/wks

29 Jun 96	LOVE CAN'T TURN AROUND *Pukka CDPUKKA 6*	**56**	1

Bobby HEBB *US, male vocalist (15 WEEKS)* pos/wks

8 Sep 66	SUNNY *Philips BF 1503*	**12**	9
19 Aug 72	LOVE LOVE LOVE *Philips 6051 023*	**32**	6

UK No.1 ★ UK Top 10 ● Still on chart + UK million seller ◆ UK entry at No.1 ■ US No.1 ▲

HED BOYS
UK, male instrumental / production duo - Dave Lee and Andrew Livingstone (6 WEEKS)   pos/wks

| 6 Aug 94 | GIRLS + BOYS *Deconstruction 74321223322* | 21 | 4 |
| 4 Nov 95 | GIRLS + BOYS (re-mix) *Deconstruction 74321322032* | 36 | 2 |

See also Joey Negro, Raven Maize, Phaze II and Li Kwan

HEDGEHOPPERS ANONYMOUS
UK, male vocal / instrumental group (12 WEEKS)   pos/wks

| 30 Sep 65 | ● IT'S GOOD NEWS WEEK *Decca F 12241* | 5 | 12 |

HEFNER
UK, male vocal / instrumental group (2 WEEKS)   pos/wks

| 26 Aug 00 | GOOD FRUIT *Too Pure PURE 108CDS* | 50 | 1 |
| 14 Oct 00 | THE GREEDY UGLY PEOPLE *Too Pure PURE 111CDS* | 64 | 1 |

Neal HEFTI
US, male orchestra (4 WEEKS)   pos/wks

| 9 Apr 88 | BATMAN THEME *RCA PB 49571* | 55 | 4 |

Den HEGARTY
UK, male vocalist (2 WEEKS)   pos/wks

| 31 Mar 79 | VOODOO VOODOO *Magnet MAG 143* | 73 | 2 |

See also DARTS

Anita HEGERLAND – See Mike OLDFIELD

HEINZ
UK, male vocalist - Heinz Burt (35 WEEKS)   pos/wks

8 Aug 63	● JUST LIKE EDDIE *Decca F 11693*	5	15
28 Nov 63	COUNTRY BOY *Decca F 11768*	26	9
27 Feb 64	YOU WERE THERE *Decca F 11831*	26	8
15 Oct 64	QUESTIONS I CAN'T ANSWER *Columbia DB 7374*	39	2
18 Mar 65	DIGGIN' MY POTATOES *Columbia DB 7482* [1]	49	1

[1] Heinz and the Wild Boys

HELICOPTER
UK, male instrumental / production duo (4 WEEKS)   pos/wks

| 27 Aug 94 | ON YA WAY *Helicopter TIG 007CD* | 32 | 2 |
| 22 Jun 96 | ON YA WAY (re-mix) *Systematic SYSCD 27* | 37 | 2 |

HELIOCENTRIC WORLD
UK, male / female vocal group (2 WEEKS)   pos/wks

| 14 Jan 95 | WHERE'S YOUR LOVE BEEN *Talkin Loud TLKCD 51* | 71 | 2 |

HELIOTROPIC featuring Verna V
UK, male production duo (2 WEEKS)   pos/wks

| 16 Oct 99 | ALIVE *Multiply CDMULTY 52* | 33 | 2 |

HELLER & FARLEY PROJECT
UK, male instrumental / production duo (7 WEEKS)   pos/wks

| 24 Feb 96 | ULTRA FLAVA *AM:PM 5814372* | 22 | 3 |
| 28 Dec 96 | ULTRA FLAVA (re-mix) *AM:PM 5820552* | 32 | 4 |

Pete HELLER
UK, male DJ / producer (7 WEEKS)   pos/wks

| 15 May 99 | BIG LOVE *Essential Recordings ESCD 4* | 12 | 7 |

HELLO
UK, male vocal / instrumental group (21 WEEKS)   pos/wks

| 9 Nov 74 | ● TELL HIM *Bell 1377* | 6 | 12 |
| 18 Oct 75 | ● NEW YORK GROOVE *Bell 1438* | 9 | 9 |

HELLOWEEN
US, male vocal / instrumental group (7 WEEKS)   pos/wks

27 Aug 88	DR STEIN *Noise International 7HELLO 1*	57	3
12 Nov 88	I WANT OUT *Noise International 7HELLO 2*	69	2
2 Mar 91	KIDS OF THE CENTURY *EMI EM 178*	56	2

Bobby HELMS
US, male vocalist (7 WEEKS)   pos/wks

29 Nov 57	MY SPECIAL ANGEL *Brunswick 05721* [1]	22	3
21 Feb 58	NO OTHER BABY *Brunswick 05730*	30	1
1 Aug 58	JACQUELINE *Brunswick 05748* [1]	20	3

[1] Bobby Helms with the Anita Kerr Singers

Jimmy HELMS
US, male vocalist (10 WEEKS)   pos/wks

| 24 Feb 73 | ● GONNA MAKE YOU AN OFFER YOU CAN'T REFUSE *Cube BUG 27* | 8 | 10 |

HELTAH SKELTAH and ORIGINOO GUNN CLAPPAZ as the FABULOUS FIVE
US, male rap / vocal / production group (1 WEEK)   pos/wks

| 1 Jun 96 | BLAH *Priority PTYCD 117* | 60 | 1 |

Eddie HENDERSON
US, male instrumentalist - trumpet (6 WEEKS)   pos/wks

| 28 Oct 78 | PRANCE ON *Capitol CL 16015* | 44 | 6 |

Joe 'Mr Piano' HENDERSON
UK, male instrumentalist – piano (23 WEEKS)   pos/wks

3 Jun 55	SING IT WITH JOE *Polygon P 1167*	14	4
2 Sep 55	SING IT AGAIN WITH JOE *Polygon P 1184*	18	3
25 Jul 58	TRUDIE *Pye Nixa N 15147*	14	12
24 Oct 58	TRUDIE (re-entry) *Pye Nixa N 15147*	23	2
23 Oct 59	TREBLE CHANCE *Pye 7N 15224*	28	1
24 Mar 60	OOH! LA! LA! *Pye 7N 15257*	46	1

First two hits are medleys as follows: Sing It with Joe: Margie / I'm Nobody's Sweetheart / Somebody Stole My Gal / Moonlight Bay / By the Light of the Silvery Moon / Cuddle Up a Little Closer. Sing It Again With Joe: Put Your Arms Around Me Honey / Ain't She Sweet / When You're Smiling / Shine on Harvest Moon / My Blue Heaven / Show Me the Way to Go Home

Wayne HENDERSON – See Roy AYERS

Billy HENDRIX
Germany, male producer - Sharam Jey (2 WEEKS)   pos/wks

| 12 Sep 98 | THE BODY SHINE (EP) *Hooj Choons HOOJ 65CD* | 55 | 2 |

Tracks on The Body Shine (EP): The Body Shine / Funky Shine / Colour Systems Inc's Amber Dub / Timewriter re-mix

Jimi HENDRIX EXPERIENCE ⟨ 358 | Top 500 ⟩
Guitar ace and hugely influential 20th-century icon, b. Johnny Allen Hendrix, 27 Nov 1942, Seattle, US, renamed James Marshall Hendrix, d. 18 Sep 1970, London. After being 'discovered' and then managed by Animals' bassist Chas Chandler, the left-handed guitarist and vocalist formed The Jimi Hendrix Experience, featuring Mitch Mitchell (d) and Noel Redding (b). His timeless appeal consistently generates annual global album sales of around three million (87 WEEKS)   pos/wks

5 Jan 67	● HEY JOE *Polydor 56 139*	6	10
23 Mar 67	● PURPLE HAZE *Track 604 001*	3	14
11 May 67	● THE WIND CRIES MARY *Track 604 004*	6	11
30 Aug 67	BURNING OF THE MIDNIGHT LAMP *Track 604 007*	18	9
23 Oct 68	● ALL ALONG THE WATCHTOWER *Track 604 025*	5	11
16 Apr 69	CROSSTOWN TRAFFIC *Track 604 029*	37	3
7 Nov 70	★ VOODOO CHILE *Track 2095 001*	1	13
30 Oct 71	GYPSY EYES / REMEMBER *Track 2094 010*	35	5
12 Feb 72	JOHNNY B GOODE *Polydor 2001 277* [1]	35	5
21 Apr 90	CROSSTOWN TRAFFIC (re-issue) *Polydor PO 71* [1]	61	3
20 Oct 90	ALL ALONG THE WATCHTOWER (EP) *Polydor PO 100* [1]	52	3

[1] Jimi Hendrix

Tracks on All Along the Watchtower (EP): All Along the Watchtower / Voodoo Chile / Hey Joe (re-issues)

Nona HENDRYX
US, female vocalist (2 WEEKS)   pos/wks

| 16 May 87 | WHY SHOULD I CRY *EMI America EA 234* | 60 | 2 |

Don HENLEY
US, male vocalist (30 WEEKS)   pos/wks

12 Feb 83	DIRTY LAUNDRY *Asylum E 9894*	59	3
9 Feb 85	THE BOYS OF SUMMER *Geffen A 4945*	12	10
29 Jul 89	THE END OF THE INNOCENCE *Geffen GEF 57*	48	5
3 Oct 92	SOMETIMES LOVE JUST AIN'T ENOUGH *MCA MCS 1692* [1]	22	6
18 Jul 98	BOYS OF SUMMER (re-issue) *Geffen GFSTD 22350*	12	6

[1] Patty Smyth with Don Henley

See also EAGLES

SINGLED OUT... Jimmy Nail

The Geordie actor and singer / songwriter has a hit singles career that includes 73 weeks on chart, spanning more than 13 years.

- **NO.1 ON THE UK SINGLES CHART THE DAY I WAS BORN:**
  I See The Moon – The Stargazers

- **ALL-TIME FAVOURITE SINGLE:**
  Heroes – David Bowie

  It's like the advert, "Does exactly what it says on the tin". It somehow manages to sound heroic.

- **SINGLE THAT DRIVES ME UP THE WALL:**
  I can't think of any.

FIRST SINGLE I BOUGHT:
All Along The Watchtower – Jimi Hendrix

I'd love to have bought all kinds of other stuff before then [1970], but that was the first time I had any money to spend

Photo: Rex Features – D Hoffman

Photo: Rex Features

Clarence 'Frogman' HENRY US, male vocalist (35 WEEKS)

		pos/wks
4 May 61 ●	BUT I DO Pye International 7N 25078	3 19
13 Jul 61 ●	YOU ALWAYS HURT THE ONE YOU LOVE Pye International 7N 25089	6 12
21 Sep 61	LONELY STREET / WHY CAN'T YOU Pye International 7N 25108	42 2
17 Jul 93	(I DON'T KNOW WHY) BUT I DO (re-issue) MCA MCSTD 1797	65 2

Kevin HENRY – See LA MIX

Paul HENRY and the Mayson GLEN ORCHESTRA
UK, male vocalist / orchestra (2 WEEKS)

		pos/wks
14 Jan 78	BENNY'S THEME Pye 7N 46027	39 2

Pauline HENRY UK, female vocalist (21 WEEKS)

		pos/wks
18 Sep 93	TOO MANY PEOPLE Sony S2 6595942	38 2
6 Nov 93	FEEL LIKE MAKING LOVE Sony S2 6597972	12 7
29 Jan 94	CAN'T TAKE YOUR LOVE Sony S2 6599902	30 2
21 May 94	WATCH THE MIRACLE START Sony S2 6602772	54 1
30 Sep 95	SUGAR FREE Sony S2 6624362	57 2
23 Dec 95	LOVE HANGOVER Sony S2 6626132	37 3
24 Feb 96	NEVER KNEW LOVE LIKE THIS Sony S2 6629382 [1]	40 2
1 Jun 96	HAPPY Sony S2 6630692	46 1

[1] Pauline Henry featuring Wayne Marshall

Pierre HENRY France, male instrumentalist (1 WEEK)

		pos/wks
4 Oct 97	PSYCHE ROCK Hi-Life 4620312	58 1

HEPBURN UK, female vocal / instrumental group (15 WEEKS)

		pos/wks
29 May 99 ●	I QUIT Columbia 6674012	8 7
28 Aug 99	BUGS Columbia 6677382	14 5
19 Feb 00	DEEP DEEP DOWN Columbia 6683382	16 3

HERD UK, male vocal / instrumental group (35 WEEKS)

		pos/wks
13 Sep 67 ●	FROM THE UNDERWORLD Fontana TF 856	6 13
20 Dec 67	PARADISE LOST Fontana TF 887	15 9
10 Apr 68 ●	I DON'T WANT OUR LOVING TO DIE Fontana TF 925	5 13

HERMAN'S HERMITS (76 Top 500) Manchester quintet fronted by teenage vocalist Peter Noone, b. 5 Nov 1947, whose US popularity in the mid-1960s rivalled The Beatles. This band sold more than 40 million records and at times had three singles simultaneously in the US Top 20 (211 WEEKS)

		pos/wks
20 Aug 64 ★	I'M INTO SOMETHING GOOD Columbia DB 7338	1 15
19 Nov 64	SHOW ME GIRL Columbia DB 7408	19 9
18 Feb 65 ●	SILHOUETTES Columbia DB 7475	3 12
29 Apr 65 ●	WONDERFUL WORLD Columbia DB 7546	7 9
2 Sep 65	JUST A LITTLE BIT BETTER Columbia DB 7670	15 9
23 Dec 65 ●	A MUST TO AVOID Columbia DB 7791	6 11
24 Mar 66	YOU WON'T BE LEAVING Columbia DB 7861	20 7
23 Jun 66	THIS DOOR SWINGS BOTH WAYS Columbia DB 7947	18 7
6 Oct 66 ●	NO MILK TODAY Columbia DB 8012	7 11
1 Dec 66	EAST WEST Columbia DB 8076	37 7
9 Feb 67 ●	THERE'S A KIND OF HUSH Columbia DB 8123	7 11
17 Jan 68	I CAN TAKE OR LEAVE YOUR LOVING Columbia DB 8327	11 9
1 May 68	SLEEPY JOE Columbia DB 8404	12 10
17 Jul 68 ●	SUNSHINE GIRL Columbia DB 8446	8 14
18 Dec 68 ●	SOMETHING'S HAPPENING Columbia DB 8504	6 15
23 Apr 69 ●	MY SENTIMENTAL FRIEND Columbia DB 8563	2 12
8 Nov 69	HERE COMES THE STAR Columbia DB 8626	33 9
7 Feb 70 ●	YEARS MAY COME, YEARS MAY GO Columbia DB 8656	7 11
2 May 70	YEARS MAY COME, YEARS MAY GO (re-entry) Columbia DB 8656	45 1
23 May 70	BET YER LIFE I DO RAK 102	22 10
14 Nov 70	LADY BARBARA RAK 106 [1]	13 12

[1] Peter Noone and Herman's Hermits

See also Peter NOONE

HERNANDEZ UK, male vocalist (3 WEEKS)

		pos/wks
15 Apr 89	ALL MY LOVE Epic HER 1	58 3

Patrick HERNANDEZ Guadeloupe, male vocalist (14 WEEKS)

		pos/wks
16 Jun 79 ●	BORN TO BE ALIVE Gem GEM 4	10 14

HERREYS Sweden, male vocal group (3 WEEKS)

		pos/wks
26 May 84	DIGGI LOO-DIGGI LEY Panther PAN 5	46 3

Kristin HERSH US, female vocalist (3 WEEKS)

		pos/wks
22 Jan 94	YOUR GHOST 4AD BAD 4001CD	45 2
16 Apr 94	STRINGS 4AD BAD 4006CD	60 1

Nick HEYWARD UK, male vocalist (65 WEEKS)

		pos/wks
19 Mar 83	WHISTLE DOWN THE WIND Arista HEY 1	13 8
4 Jun 83	TAKE THAT SITUATION Arista HEY 2	11 10
24 Sep 83	BLUE HAT FOR A BLUE DAY Arista HEY 3	14 8
3 Dec 83	ON A SUNDAY Arista HEY 4	52 5
2 Jun 84	LOVE ALL DAY Arista HEY 5	31 6
3 Nov 84	WARNING SIGN Arista HEY 6	25 8
5 Jan 85	WARNING SIGN (re-entry) Arista HEY 6	72 1
8 Jun 85	LAURA Arista HEY 8	45 4
10 May 86	OVER THE WEEKEND Arista HEY 9	43 5
10 Sep 88	YOU'RE MY WORLD Warner Bros. W 7758	67 2
21 Aug 93	KITE Epic 6594882	44 2
16 Oct 93	HE DOESN'T LOVE YOU LIKE I DO Epic 6597282	58 2
30 Sep 95	THE WORLD Epic 6623845	47 2
13 Jan 96	ROLLERBLADE Epic 6627912	37 2

See also HAIRCUT 100

HHC UK, male DJ / production duo (1 WEEK)

		pos/wks
19 Apr 97	WE'RE NOT ALONE Perfecto PERF 138CD	44 1

HI-FIVE US, male vocal group (8 WEEKS)

		pos/wks
1 Jun 91	I LIKE THE WAY (THE KISSING GAME) Jive JIVE 271 ▲	43 6
24 Oct 92	SHE'S PLAYING HARD TO GET Jive JIVE 316	55 2

HI-GATE UK, male production duo - Julius (Judge Jules) O'Riordan and Paul Masterson and female vocalist (11 WEEKS)

		pos/wks
29 Jan 00 ●	PITCHIN' (IN EVERY DIRECTION) Incentice CENT 3CD	6 6
26 Aug 00	I CAN HEAR VOICES / CANED AND UNABLE Incentive CENT 9 CDS	12 5

HI GLOSS US, disco aggregation (13 WEEKS)

		pos/wks
8 Aug 81	YOU'LL NEVER KNOW Epic EPC A 1387	12 13

HI-LUX UK, male instrumental / production duo (3 WEEKS)

		pos/wks
18 Feb 95	FEEL IT Cheeky CHEKCD 006	41 2
2 Sep 95	NEVER FELT THIS WAY / FEEL IT (re-issue) Champion CHAMPCD 319	58 1

HI POWER Germany, male rap group (1 WEEK)

		pos/wks
1 Sep 90	CULT OF SNAP / SIMBA GROOVE Rumour RUMAT 24	73 1

HI-TEK 3 featuring YA KID K
Belgium, male / female vocal / instrumental group (10 WEEKS)

		pos/wks
3 Feb 90	SPIN THAT WHEEL Brothers Organisation BORG 1	69 3
29 Sep 90	SPIN THAT WHEEL (TURTLES GET REAL) (re-issue) Brothers Organisation BORG 16	15 7

See also TECHNOTRONIC

HI TENSION UK, male vocal / instrumental group (23 WEEKS)

		pos/wks
6 May 78	HI TENSION Island WIP 6422	13 12
12 Aug 78 ●	BRITISH HUSTLE / PEACE ON EARTH Island WIP 6446	8 11

'Peace on Earth' credited with 'British Hustle' from 2 Sep 1978 to end of record's chart run

UK No.1 ★ UK Top 10 ● Still on chart + UK million seller ◆ UK entry at No.1 ■ US No.1 ▲

Al HIBBLER US, male vocalist (17 WEEKS) — pos/wks

Date	Title	pos	wks
13 May 55 ●	UNCHAINED MELODY Brunswick 05420	2	17

Hinda HICKS UK, female vocalist (15 WEEKS) — pos/wks

Date	Title	pos	wks
7 Mar 98	IF YOU WANT ME Island CID 689	25	3
16 May 98	YOU THINK YOU OWN ME Island CID 700	19	4
15 Aug 98	I WANNA BE YOUR LADY Island CID 709	14	5
24 Oct 98	TRULY Island CID 721	31	2
14 Oct 00	MY REMEDY Island CID 765	61	1

Bertie HIGGINS US, male vocalist (4 WEEKS) — pos/wks

Date	Title	pos	wks
5 Jun 82	KEY LARGO Epic EPC A 2168	60	4

HIGH UK, male vocal group (11 WEEKS) — pos/wks

Date	Title	pos	wks
25 Aug 90	UP AND DOWN London LON 272	53	4
27 Oct 90	TAKE YOUR TIME London LON 280	56	2
12 Jan 91	BOX SET GO London LONG 286	28	3
6 Apr 91	MORE . . . London LON 297	67	2

HIGH FIDELITY UK, male vocal / instrumental group (1 WEEK) — pos/wks

Date	Title	pos	wks
25 Jul 98	LUV DUP Plastique FAKE 03CDS	70	1

HIGH NUMBERS UK, male vocal / instrumental group (4 WEEKS) — pos/wks

Date	Title	pos	wks
5 Apr 80	I'M THE FACE Back Door DOOR 4	49	4

The High Numbers were an early incarnation of the Who

HIGH SOCIETY UK, male vocal / instrumental group (4 WEEKS) — pos/wks

Date	Title	pos	wks
15 Nov 80	I NEVER GO OUT IN THE RAIN Eagle ERS 002	53	4

HIGHLY LIKELY UK, male vocal / instrumental group (4 WEEKS) — pos/wks

Date	Title	pos	wks
21 Apr 73	WHATEVER HAPPENED TO YOU ('LIKELY LADS' THEME) BBC RESL 10	35	4

HIGHWAYMEN US, male vocal group (18 WEEKS) — pos/wks

Date	Title	pos	wks
7 Sep 61 ★	MICHAEL HMV POP 910 ▲	1	14
7 Dec 61	GYPSY ROVER HMV POP 948	41	3
11 Jan 62	GYPSY ROVER (re-entry) HMV POP 948	43	1

HIJACK UK, male rap group (3 WEEKS) — pos/wks

Date	Title	pos	wks
6 Jan 90	THE BADMAN IS ROBBIN' Rhyme Syndicate 655517 7	56	3

Benny HILL UK, male comedian / vocalist (43 WEEKS) — pos/wks

Date	Title	pos	wks
16 Feb 61	GATHER IN THE MUSHROOMS Pye 7N 15327	12	8
1 Jun 61	TRANSISTOR RADIO Pye 7N 15359	24	6
16 May 63	HARVEST OF LOVE Pye 7N 15520	20	8
13 Nov 71 ★	ERNIE (THE FASTEST MILKMAN IN THE WEST) Columbia DB 8833	1	17
30 May 92	ERNIE (THE FASTEST MILKMAN IN THE WEST) (re-issue) EMI ERN 1	29	4

Chris HILL UK, male vocalist / DJ / producer (14 WEEKS) — pos/wks

Date	Title	pos	wks
6 Dec 75 ●	RENTA SANTA Philips 6006 491	10	7
4 Dec 76 ●	BIONIC SANTA Philips 6006 551	10	7

Dan HILL Canada, male vocalist (13 WEEKS) — pos/wks

Date	Title	pos	wks
18 Feb 78	SOMETIMES WHEN WE TOUCH 20th Century BTC 2355	46	1
4 Mar 78	SOMETIMES WHEN WE TOUCH (re-entry) 20th Century BTC 2355	13	12

Faith HILL US, female vocalist (14 WEEKS) — pos/wks

Date	Title	pos	wks
14 Nov 98	THIS KISS Warner Brothers W463CD	13	11
17 Apr 99	LET ME LET GO Warner Bros. W473CD	72	1
20 May 00	BREATHE WEA WEA 520CD	33	2

Lauryn HILL US, female vocalist (35 WEEKS) — pos/wks

Date	Title	pos	wks
6 Sep 97	THE SWEETEST THING Columbia 6649785 [1]	18	4
27 Dec 97	ALL MY TIME World Entertainment OWECD 2 [2]	57	1
3 Oct 98 ●	DOO WOP (THAT THING) Ruffhouse 6665152 ▲	3	7
27 Feb 99 ●	EX-FACTOR Columbia / Ruffhouse 6669452	4	9
22 May 99	EX-FACTOR (re-entry) Columbia / Ruffhouse 6669452	67	1
10 Jul 99	EVERYTHING IS EVERYTHING Columbia / Ruffhouse 6675742	19	6
11 Dec 99	TURN YOUR LIGHTS DOWN LOW Columbia 6684362 [3]	15	7

[1] Refugee Camp Allstars featuring Lauryn Hill [2] Paid + Live featuring Lauryn Hill [3] Bob Marley featuring Lauryn Hill

See also FUGEES

Lonnie HILL US, male vocalist (4 WEEKS) — pos/wks

Date	Title	pos	wks
22 Mar 86	GALVESTON BAY 10 TEN 111	51	4

Roni HILL US, female vocalist (4 WEEKS) — pos/wks

Date	Title	pos	wks
7 May 77	YOU KEEP ME HANGIN' ON - STOP IN THE NAME OF LOVE (MEDLEY)	36	4

Vince HILL (335 Top 500) Easy listening balladeer, b. 16 Apr 1937, Coventry, UK. Member of critically acclaimed Raindrops (with Jackie Lee and composer Johnny Worth) and regularly heard on 'live' radio before starting 60s chart run (91 WEEKS) — pos/wks

Date	Title	pos	wks
7 Jun 62	THE RIVER'S RUN DRY Piccadilly 7N 35043	49	1
28 Jun 62	THE RIVER'S RUN DRY (re-entry) Piccadilly 7N 35043	41	1
6 Jan 66	TAKE ME TO YOUR HEART AGAIN Columbia DB 7781	13	11
17 Mar 66	HEARTACHES Columbia DB 7852	28	5
2 Jun 66	MERCI CHERI Columbia DB 7924	36	6
9 Feb 67 ●	EDELWEISS Columbia DB 8127	2	17
11 May 67	ROSES OF PICARDY Columbia DB 8185	13	11
27 Sep 67	LOVE LETTERS IN THE SAND Columbia DB 8268	23	9
26 Jun 68	IMPORTANCE OF YOUR LOVE Columbia DB 8414	32	12
12 Feb 69	DOESN'T ANYBODY KNOW MY NAME? Columbia DB 8515	50	1
25 Oct 69	LITTLE BLUE BIRD Columbia DB 8616	42	1
25 Sep 71	LOOK AROUND Columbia DB 8804	12	16

HILLMAN MINX UK / France, male / female vocal group (1 WEEK) — pos/wks

Date	Title	pos	wks
5 Sep 98	I'VE HAD ENOUGH Mercury MERCD 509	72	1

HILLTOPPERS US, male vocal group (30 WEEKS) — pos/wks

Date	Title	pos	wks
27 Jan 56 ●	ONLY YOU London HLD 8221	3	22
10 Aug 56	ONLY YOU (re-entry) London HLD 8221	24	1
14 Sep 56	TRYIN' London HLD 8298	30	1
5 Apr 57	MARIANNE London HLD 8381	20	2
26 Apr 57	MARIANNE (re-entry) London HLD 8381	23	4

Ronnie HILTON (181 Top 500) Favourite 1950s balladeer, b. Adrian Hill, 26 Jan 1926, Hull, UK. Despite the rise of rock 'n' roll, he amassed a formidable selection of best-sellers, albeit mainly with cover versions (the customary UK practice in the 1950s) (136 WEEKS) — pos/wks

Date	Title	pos	wks
26 Nov 54 ●	I STILL BELIEVE HMV B 10785	3	14
10 Dec 54	VENI VIDI VICI HMV B 10785	12	8
11 Mar 55 ●	A BLOSSOM FELL HMV B 10808	10	5
26 Aug 55	STARS SHINE IN YOUR EYES HMV B 10901	13	7
11 Nov 55	THE YELLOW ROSE OF TEXAS HMV B 10924	15	2
10 Feb 56	YOUNG AND FOOLISH HMV POP 154	17	1
24 Feb 56	YOUNG AND FOOLISH (re-entry) HMV POP 154	20	1
9 Mar 56	YOUNG AND FOOLISH (2nd re-entry) HMV POP 154	19	1
20 Apr 56 ★	NO OTHER LOVE HMV POP 198	1	14
29 Jun 56 ●	WHO ARE WE HMV POP 221	6	12
21 Sep 56	A WOMAN IN LOVE HMV POP 248	30	1
9 Nov 56	TWO DIFFERENT WORLDS HMV POP 274	13	13
24 May 57 ●	AROUND THE WORLD HMV POP 338	4	18
2 Aug 57	WONDERFUL! WONDERFUL! HMV POP 364	27	2
21 Feb 58	MAGIC MOMENTS HMV POP 446	22	2
18 Apr 58	I MAY NEVER PASS THIS WAY AGAIN HMV POP 468 [1]	30	1
2 May 58	I MAY NEVER PASS THIS WAY AGAIN (re-entry) HMV POP 468 [1]	30	1

UK No.1 ★   UK Top 10 ●   Still on chart +   UK million seller ◆   UK entry at No.1 ■   US No.1 ▲

6 Jun 58	I MAY NEVER PASS THIS WAY AGAIN (2nd re-entry)		
	HMV POP 468 [1]	27	1
9 Jan 59	THE WORLD OUTSIDE HMV POP 559 [1]	18	6
21 Aug 59	THE WONDER OF YOU HMV POP 638	22	3
21 May 64	DON'T LET THE RAIN COME DOWN HMV POP 1291	21	10
11 Feb 65	A WINDMILL IN OLD AMSTERDAM HMV POP 1378	23	13

[1] Ronnie Hilton with the Michael Sammes Singers

HINDSIGHT UK, male vocal / instrumental group (3 WEEKS)

		pos/wks	
5 Sep 87	LOWDOWN Circa YR 5	62	3

Deni HINES Australia, female vocalist (6 WEEKS)

		pos/wks	
14 Jun 97	IT'S ALRIGHT Mushroom D 1593	35	2
20 Sep 97	I LIKE THE WAY Mushroom MUSH 7CDX	37	2
28 Feb 98	DELICIOUS Mushroom MUSH 20CD [1]	52	1
23 May 98	JOY Mushroom MUSH 30CDS	47	1

[1] Deni Hines featuring Don-E

Gregory HINES – See Luther VANDROSS

HIPSWAY UK, male vocal / instrumental group (21 WEEKS)

		pos/wks	
13 Jul 85	THE BROKEN YEARS Mercury MER 193	72	3
14 Sep 85	ASK THE LORD Mercury MER 195	72	1
22 Feb 86	THE HONEYTHIEF Mercury MER 212	17	9
10 May 86	ASK THE LORD (re-recording) Mercury LORD 1	50	5
20 Sep 86	LONG WHITE CAR Mercury MER 230	55	2
1 Apr 89	YOUR LOVE Mercury MER 279	66	1

HISTORY featuring Q-TEE
UK, male production duo and female rapper (2 WEEKS)

		pos/wks	
10 Feb 96	GIMME THAT BODY Heavenly HVN 48CD	40	2

Carol HITCHCOCK Australia, female vocalist (5 WEEKS)

		pos/wks	
30 May 87	GET READY A & M AM 391	56	5

HITHOUSE Holland, male producer - Peter Slaghuis (13 WEEKS)

		pos/wks	
5 Nov 88	JACK TO THE SOUND OF THE UNDERGROUND		
	Supreme SUPE 137	14	12
19 Aug 89	MOVE YOUR FEET TO THE RHYTHM OF THE BEAT		
	Supreme SUPE 149	69	1

HITMAN HOWIE TEE – See REAL ROXANNE

Helen HOBSON – See Cliff RICHARD

Edmund HOCKRIDGE Canada, male vocalist (18 WEEKS)

		pos/wks	
17 Feb 56 ●	YOUNG AND FOOLISH Nixa N 15039	10	7
13 Apr 56	YOUNG AND FOOLISH (re-entry) Nixa N 15039	28	1
4 May 56	YOUNG AND FOOLISH (2nd re-entry) Nixa N 15039	26	1
11 May 56	NO OTHER LOVE Nixa N 15048	24	2
1 Jun 56	NO OTHER LOVE (re-entry) Nixa N 15048	29	1
15 Jun 56	NO OTHER LOVE (2nd re-entry) Nixa N 15048	30	1
31 Aug 56	BY THE FOUNTAINS OF ROME Pye Nixa N 15063	17	5

Eddie HODGES US, male vocalist (10 WEEKS)

		pos/wks	
28 Sep 61	I'M GONNA KNOCK ON YOUR DOOR		
	London HLA 9369	37	6
9 Aug 62	MADE TO LOVE (GIRLS GIRLS GIRLS)		
	London HLA 9576	37	4

Roger HODGSON – See SUPERTRAMP

Susanna HOFFS US, female vocalist (8 WEEKS)

		pos/wks	
2 Mar 91	MY SIDE OF THE BED Columbia 6565547	44	4
11 May 91	UNCONDITIONAL LOVE Columbia 6567827	65	2
19 Oct 96	ALL I WANT London LONCD 387	32	2

See also BANGLES

Hulk HOGAN with GREEN JELLY US, male wrestler /
vocalist and US, male vocal / instrumental group (4 WEEKS)

		pos/wks	
25 Dec 93	I'M THE LEADER OF THE GANG Arista 74321174892	25	4

HOLE US, female / male vocal / instrumental group (15 WEEKS)

		pos/wks	
17 Apr 93	BEAUTIFUL SON City Slang EFA 0491603	54	1
9 Apr 94	MISS WORLD City Slang EFA 049362	64	1
15 Apr 95	DOLL PARTS Geffen GFSTD 91	16	3
29 Jul 95	VIOLET Geffen GFSTD 94	17	2
12 Sep 98	CELEBRITY SKIN Geffen GFSTD 22345	19	4
30 Jan 99	MALIBU Geffen GFSTD 22369	22	2
10 Jul 99	AWFUL Geffen INTDE 97098	42	2

HOLE IN ONE Holland, male DJ / producer (2 WEEKS)

		pos/wks	
15 Feb 97	LIFE'S TOO SHORT Manifesto FESCD 21	36	2

HOLLAND-DOZIER featuring Lamont DOZIER
US, male vocal duo (5 WEEKS)

		pos/wks	
28 Oct 72	WHY CAN'T WE BE LOVERS Invictus INV 525	29	5

Jennifer HOLLIDAY US, female vocalist (6 WEEKS)

		pos/wks	
4 Sep 82	AND I'M TELLING YOU I'M NOT GOING Geffen GEF A 2644	32	6

Michael HOLLIDAY UK, male vocalist - Norman Milne (65 WEEKS)

		pos/wks	
30 Mar 56	NOTHIN' TO DO Columbia DB 3746	20	1
27 Apr 56	NOTHIN' TO DO (re-entry) Columbia DB 3746	23	2
15 Jun 56	THE GAL WITH THE YALLER SHOES		
	Columbia DB 3783	13	3
22 Jun 56	HOT DIGGITY (DOG ZIGGITY BOOM) Columbia DB 3783	14	5
3 Aug 56	HOT DIGGITY (DOG ZIGGITY BOOM) / THE GAL WITH		
	THE YALLER SHOES Columbia DB 3783	17	3
5 Oct 56	TEN THOUSAND MILES Columbia DB 3813	24	3
17 Jan 58 ★	THE STORY OF MY LIFE Columbia DB 4058	1	15
14 Mar 58	IN LOVE Columbia DB 4087	26	3
16 May 58 ●	STAIRWAY OF LOVE Columbia DB 4121	3	13
11 Jul 58	I'LL ALWAYS BE IN LOVE WITH YOU Columbia DB 4155	27	1
1 Jan 60 ★	STARRY EYED Columbia DB 4378 [1]	1	12
14 Apr 60	SKYLARK Columbia DB 4437	39	3
1 Sep 60	LITTLE BOY LOST Columbia DB 4475	50	1

[1] Michael Holliday with the Michael Sammes Singers

When 'Hot Diggity (Dog Ziggity Boom) / Gal With the Yaller Shoes' re-entered the chart on 3 Aug 1956, 'Hot Diggity (Dog Ziggity Boom)' was listed by itself on 3 Aug and 10 Aug. Both sides were listed on 17 Aug - 'Gal With the Yaller Shoes' peaking at No.25

HOLLIES 26 Top 500 Distinctive, influential and well-respected
Manchester group: Allan Clarke (v), Graham Nash (g), Tony Hicks (g), Eric Haydock (b), Bobby Elliott (d). They were among the most regular chart visitors of the 1960s, and their No.1s span 23 years (318 WEEKS)

		pos/wks	
30 May 63	(AIN'T THAT) JUST LIKE ME Parlophone R 5030	25	10
29 Aug 63	SEARCHIN' Parlophone R 5052	12	14
21 Nov 63 ●	STAY Parlophone R 5077	8	16
27 Feb 64 ●	JUST ONE LOOK Parlophone R 5104	2	13
21 May 64 ●	HERE I GO AGAIN Parlophone R 5137	4	12
17 Sep 64 ●	WE'RE THROUGH Parlophone R 5178	7	11
28 Jan 65 ●	YES I WILL Parlophone R 5232	9	13
27 May 65 ★	I'M ALIVE Parlophone R 5287	1	14
2 Sep 65 ●	LOOK THROUGH ANY WINDOW Parlophone R 5322	4	11
9 Dec 65	IF I NEEDED SOMEONE Parlophone R 5392	20	9
24 Feb 66 ●	I CAN'T LET GO Parlophone R 5409	2	10
23 Jun 66 ●	BUS STOP Parlophone R 5469	5	9
13 Oct 66 ●	STOP STOP STOP Parlophone R 5508	2	12
16 Feb 67 ●	ON A CAROUSEL Parlophone R 5562	4	11
1 Jun 67 ●	CARRIE-ANNE Parlophone R 5602	3	11
27 Sep 67	KING MIDAS IN REVERSE Parlophone R 5637	18	8
27 Mar 68 ●	JENNIFER ECCLES Parlophone R 5680	7	11
2 Oct 68	LISTEN TO ME Parlophone R 5733	11	11
5 Mar 69 ●	SORRY SUZANNE Parlophone R 5765	3	12
4 Oct 69 ●	HE AIN'T HEAVY, HE'S MY BROTHER Parlophone R 5806	3	15

18 Apr 70 ●	I CAN'T TELL THE BOTTOM FROM THE TOP *Parlophone R 5837*	7 10
3 Oct 70	GASOLINE ALLEY BRED *Parlophone R 5862*	14 7
22 May 71	HEY WILLY *Parlophone R 5905*	22 7
26 Feb 72	THE BABY *Polydor 2058 199*	26 4
2 Sep 72	LONG COOL WOMAN IN A BLACK DRESS *Parlophone R 5939* 32 8	
13 Oct 73	THE DAY THAT CURLY BILLY SHOT DOWN CRAZY SAM MCGHEE *Polydor 2058 403*	24 6
9 Feb 74 ●	THE AIR THAT I BREATHE *Polydor 2058 435*	2 13
14 Jun 80	SOLDIER'S SONG *Polydor 2059 246*	58 3
29 Aug 81	HOLLIEDAZE (MEDLEY) *EMI 5229*	28 7
3 Sep 88 ★	HE AIN'T HEAVY, HE'S MY BROTHER (re-issue) *EMI EM 74*.......1 11	
3 Dec 88	THE AIR THAT I BREATHE (re-issue) *EMI EM 80*	60 5
20 Mar 93	THE WOMAN I LOVE *EMI CDEM 264*	42 2

Loleatta HOLLOWAY US, female vocalist (21 WEEKS) pos/wks

31 Aug 91	GOOD VIBRATIONS *Interscope A 8764* [1]	14 7
18 Jan 92	TAKE ME AWAY *PWL Continental PWL 210* [2]	25 5
26 Mar 94	STAND UP *Six6 SIXCD 111*	68 1
1 Apr 95	KEEP THE FIRE BURNIN' *Columbia 6611552* [3]	49 1
11 Apr 98	SHOUT TO THE TOP *JBO JNR 5001573* [4]	23 2
20 Feb 99	(YOU GOT ME) BURNING UP *Wonderboy WBOYD 013* [5] ..	14 4
25 Nov 00	DREAMIN' *Defected DFECT 22CDS*	59 1

[1] Marky Mark and the Funky Bunch featuring Loleatta Holloway [2] Cappella featuring Loleatta Holloway [3] Dan Hartman starring Loleatta Holloway [4] Fire Island featuring Loleatta Holloway [5] Cevin Fisher / Loleatta Holloway

HOLLOWAY & CO. US, male producer - Nicky Holloway (1 WEEK) pos/wks

21 Aug 99	I'LL DO ANYTHING - TO MAKE YOU MINE *INCredible INCS 2CD*	58 1

Buddy HOLLY (97) Top 500 Highly respected and exceptionally influential singer / songwriter, b. Charles Hardin Holley, 7 Sep 1936, Texas, US, d. 3 Feb 1959 (aka 'the day the music died'). Despite a relatively brief career, his records and songs are still frequently heard around the globe (190 WEEKS) pos/wks

6 Dec 57 ●	PEGGY SUE *Coral Q 72293*	6 17
14 Mar 58	LISTEN TO ME *Coral Q 72288*	16 2
20 Jun 58 ●	RAVE ON *Coral Q 72325*	5 14
29 Aug 58	EARLY IN THE MORNING *Coral Q 72333*	17 4
16 Jan 59	HEARTBEAT *Coral Q 72346*	30 1
27 Feb 59 ★	IT DOESN'T MATTER ANYMORE *Coral Q 72360*	1 21
31 Jul 59	MIDNIGHT SHIFT *Brunswick 05800*	26 3
11 Sep 59	PEGGY SUE GOT MARRIED *Coral Q 72376*	13 10
28 Apr 60	HEARTBEAT (re-issue) *Coral Q 72392*	30 3
26 May 60	TRUE LOVE WAYS *Coral Q 72397*	25 7
20 Oct 60	LEARNIN' THE GAME *Coral Q 72411*	36 3
26 Jan 61	WHAT TO DO *Coral Q 72419*	34 6
6 Jul 61	BABY I DON'T CARE / VALLEY OF TEARS *Coral Q 72432* 12 14	
15 Mar 62	LISTEN TO ME (re-issue) *Coral Q 72449*	48 1
13 Sep 62	REMINISCING *Coral Q 72455*	17 11
14 Mar 63 ●	BROWN-EYED HANDSOME MAN *Coral Q 72459*	3 17
6 Jun 63 ●	BO DIDDLEY *Coral Q 72463*	4 12
5 Sep 63 ●	WISHING *Coral Q 72466*	10 11
19 Dec 63	WHAT TO DO (re-recording) *Coral Q 72469*	27 8
14 May 64	YOU'VE GOT LOVE *Coral Q 72472* [1]	40 6
10 Sep 64	LOVE'S MADE A FOOL OF YOU *Coral Q 72475*	39 6
3 Apr 68	PEGGY SUE / RAVE ON (re-issue) *MCA MU 1012*	32 9
10 Dec 88	TRUE LOVE WAYS (re-issue) *MCA MCA 1302*	65 4

[1] Buddy Holly and the Crickets

Buddy Holly's version of 'Love's Made a Fool of You' is not the same version as the Crickets' hit of 1959, on which Holly did not appear. 'Valley of Tears' was not listed together with 'Baby I Don't Care' until 13 Jul 1961

HOLLY and the IVYS
UK, male / female vocal / instrumental group (4 WEEKS) pos/wks

19 Dec 81	CHRISTMAS ON 45 *Decca SANTA 1*	40 4

HOLLYWOOD ARGYLES US, male vocal group (10 WEEKS) pos/wks

21 Jul 60	ALLEY OOP *London HLU 9146* ▲	24 10

HOLLYWOOD BEYOND UK, male group (14 WEEKS) pos/wks

12 Jul 86 ●	WHAT'S THE COLOUR OF MONEY? *WEA YZ 76*	7 10
20 Sep 86	NO MORE TEARS *WEA YZ 81*	47 4

Eddie HOLMAN US, male vocalist (13 WEEKS) pos/wks

19 Oct 74 ●	(HEY THERE) LONELY GIRL *ABC 4012*	4 13

David HOLMES UK, male producer (8 WEEKS) pos/wks

6 Apr 96	GONE *Go! Discs GODCD 140*	75 1
23 Aug 97	GRITTY SHAKER *Go.Beat GOBCD 2*	53 1
10 Jan 98	DON'T DIE JUST YET *Go.Beat GOLCD 6*	33 3
4 Apr 98	MY MATE PAUL *Go.Beat GOBCD 8*	39 2
19 Aug 00	69 POLICE *Go.Beat / Polydor GOBCD 30*	53 1

Rupert HOLMES US, male vocalist (14 WEEKS) pos/wks

12 Jan 80	ESCAPE (THE PINA COLADA SONG) *Infinity INF 120* ▲ 23 7	
22 Mar 80	HIM *MCA 565*	31 7

John HOLT Jamaica, male vocalist (14 WEEKS) pos/wks

14 Dec 74 ●	HELP ME MAKE IT THROUGH THE NIGHT *Trojan TR 7909*.........6 14	

Nichola HOLT UK, female vocalist (1 WEEK) pos/wks

21 Oct 00	THE GAME *RCA 74321798992*	72 1

A HOMEBOY, a HIPPIE and a FUNKI DREDD
UK, male vocal / instrumental group (9 WEEKS) pos/wks

13 Oct 90	TOTAL CONFUSION *Tam Tam 7TTT 031*	56 3
29 Dec 90	FREEDOM *Tam Tam 7TTT 039*	68 4
8 Jan 94	HERE WE GO AGAIN *Polydor PZCD 302*	57 2

HONDY Italy, female vocalist (2 WEEKS) pos/wks

12 Apr 97	HONDY (NO ACCESS) *Manifesto FESCD 20*	26 2

HONEYBUS UK, male vocal / instrumental group (12 WEEKS) pos/wks

20 Mar 68 ●	I CAN'T LET MAGGIE GO *Deram DM 182*	8 12

HONEYCOMBS UK, male / female vocal / instrumental group - lead vocal Dennis D'Ell (Dalziel) (39 WEEKS) pos/wks

23 Jul 64 ★	HAVE I THE RIGHT *Pye 7N 15664*	1 15
22 Oct 64	IS IT BECAUSE *Pye 7N 15705*	38 6
29 Apr 65	SOMETHING BETTER BEGINNING *Pye 7N 15827*	39 4
5 Aug 65	THAT'S THE WAY *Pye 7N 15890*	12 14

HONEYCRACK UK, male vocal / instrumental group (9 WEEKS) pos/wks

4 Nov 95	SITTING AT HOME *Epic 6625382*	42 2
24 Feb 96	GO AWAY *Epic 6628642*	41 2
11 May 96	KING OF MISERY *Epic 6631472*	32 2
20 Jul 96	SITTING AT HOME (re-issue) *Epic 6635032*	32 2
16 Nov 96	ANYWAY *EG EGO 52A*	67 1

HONEYDRIPPERS
UK / US, male vocal / instrumental group (3 WEEKS) pos/wks

2 Feb 85	SEA OF LOVE *Es Paranza YZ 33*	56 3

See also Robert PLANT

HONEYZ UK / France, female vocal trio (53 WEEKS) pos/wks

5 Sep 98 ●	FINALLY FOUND *1st Avenue / Mercury HNZCD 1*	4 12
19 Dec 98 ●	END OF THE LINE *1st Avenue / Mercury HNZCD 2*	5 12
24 Apr 99	END OF THE LINE (re-entry) *1st Avenue / Mercury HNZCD 2*	64 2
24 Apr 99 ●	LOVE OF A LIFETIME *1st Avenue / Mercury HNZCD 3*	9 9
23 Oct 99 ●	NEVER LET YOU DOWN *1st Avenue / Mercury HNZCD 4* 7 6	
11 Mar 00 ●	WON'T TAKE IT LYING DOWN *1st Avenue / Mercury HNZCD 5*......7 7	
13 May 00	WON'T TAKE IT LYING DOWN (re-entry) *1st Avenue / Mercury HNZCD 5*	72 1

UK No.1 ★   UK Top 10 ●   Still on chart +   UK million seller ◆   UK entry at No.1 ■   US No.1 ▲

28 Oct 00	NOT EVEN GONNA TRIP *1st Avenue / Mercury HNZCD 7*	24	3
25 Nov 00	NOT EVEN GONNA TRIP (re-entry)		
	1st Avenue / Mercury HNZCD 7	68	1

HONKY *UK, male vocal / instrumental group (5 WEEKS)*
pos/wks

30 Oct 93	THE HONKY DOODLE DAY EP *ZTT ZANG 45CD*	61	1
19 Feb 94	THE WHISTLER *ZTT ZANG 48CD*	41	2
20 Apr 96	HIP HOP DON'T YA DROP *Higher Ground HIGHS 1CD*	70	1
10 Aug 96	WHAT'S GOIN DOWN *Higher Ground HIGHS 2CD*	49	1

Tracks on The Honky Doodle Day EP: KKK (Boom Boom Tra La La La) / Honky Doodle Dub / Chains

HONKY *UK, male vocal / instrumental group (5 WEEKS)*
pos/wks

| 28 May 77 | JOIN THE PARTY *Creole CR 137* | 28 | 5 |

Frank HOOKER and POSITIVE PEOPLE
US, male / female vocal / instrumental group (4 WEEKS)
pos/wks

| 5 Jul 80 | THIS FEELIN' *DJM DJS 10947* | 48 | 4 |

John Lee HOOKER *US, male vocalist (23 WEEKS)*
pos/wks

11 Jun 64	DIMPLES *Stateside SS 297*	23	10
24 Oct 92	BOOM BOOM *Pointblank POB 3*	16	5
16 Jan 93	BOOGIE AT RUSSIAN HILL *Pointblank POBDX 4*	53	2
15 May 93	GLORIA *Exile VANCD 11* [1]	31	3
11 Feb 95	CHILL OUT (THINGS GONNA CHANGE) *Pointblank POBD 10*	45	2
20 Apr 96	BABY LEE *Silvertone ORECD 81* [2]	65	1

[1] Van Morrison and John Lee Hooker [2] John Lee Hooker with Robert Cray

HOOTERS *US, male vocal / instrumental group (9 WEEKS)*
pos/wks

| 21 Nov 87 | SATELLITE *CBS 651168 7* | 22 | 9 |

HOOTIE & THE BLOWFISH
US, male vocal / instrumental group (6 WEEKS)
pos/wks

25 Feb 95	HOLD MY HAND *Atlantic A 7230CD*	50	3
27 May 95	LET HER CRY *Atlantic A 7188CD*	75	1
4 May 96	OLD MAN AND ME (WHEN I GET TO HEAVEN) *Atlantic A 5513CD*	57	1
7 Nov 98	I WILL WAIT *Atlantic AT 0048CD*	57	1

HOPE A.D. *UK, male producer - David Hope (1 WEEK)*
pos/wks

| 4 Jun 94 | TREE FROG *Sun-Up SUN 003CD* | 73 | 1 |

See also MIND OF KANE

Mary HOPKIN (456   Top 500) *Propelled to stardom from TV talent show 'Opportunity Knocks' witnessed by Twiggy who recommended the Welsh singer (b. 3 May 1950) to Paul McCartney. The Beatle produced 'Those Were the Days', originally a Russian folk song, which ironically knocked 'Hey Jude' from the No.1 spot. (74 WEEKS)*
pos/wks

4 Sep 68	★ THOSE WERE THE DAYS *Apple 2*	1	21
2 Apr 69	● GOODBYE *Apple 10*	2	14
31 Jan 70	● TEMMA HARBOUR *Apple 22*	6	11
28 Mar 70	● KNOCK KNOCK WHO'S THERE *Apple 26*	2	14
31 Oct 70	THINK ABOUT YOUR CHILDREN *Apple 30*	19	7
2 Jan 71	THINK ABOUT YOUR CHILDREN (re-entry) *Apple 30*	46	2
31 Jul 71	LET MY NAME BE SORROW *Apple 34*	46	1
20 Mar 76	IF YOU LOVE ME *Good Earth GD 2*	32	4

Anthony HOPKINS *UK, male actor / vocalist (1 WEEK)*
pos/wks

| 27 Dec 86 | DISTANT STAR *Juice AA 5* | 75 | 1 |

Nick HORNBY – See PRETENDERS

Bruce HORNSBY and the RANGE
US, male vocal / instrumental group (15 WEEKS)
pos/wks

2 Aug 86	THE WAY IT IS *RCA PB 49805* ▲	15	10
25 Apr 87	MANDOLIN RAIN *RCA PB 49769*	70	1
28 May 88	THE VALLEY ROAD *RCA PB 49561*	44	4

HORNY UNITED – See BONEY M

HORSE *UK, female / male vocal / instrumental group (10 WEEKS)*
pos/wks

24 Nov 90	CAREFUL *Capitol CL 587*	52	3
21 Aug 93	SHAKE THIS MOUNTAIN *Oxygen GASPD 7*	52	2
23 Oct 93	GOD'S HOME MOVIE *Oxygen GASXD 10*	56	1
15 Jan 94	CELEBRATE *Oxygen GASPD 11*	49	2
5 Apr 97	CAREFUL (re-mix) *Stress CDSTRX 79*	44	2

Johnny HORTON *US, male vocalist (15 WEEKS)*
pos/wks

| 26 Jun 59 | BATTLE OF NEW ORLEANS *Philips PB 932* ▲ | 16 | 4 |
| 19 Jan 61 | NORTH TO ALASKA *Philips PB 1062* | 23 | 11 |

HOT BLOOD *France, male instrumental group (5 WEEKS)*
pos/wks

| 9 Oct 76 | SOUL DRACULA *Creole CR 132* | 32 | 5 |

HOT BUTTER *US, male instrumental group (19 WEEKS)*
pos/wks

| 22 Jul 72 | ● POPCORN *Pye International 7N 25583* | 5 | 16 |
| 23 Dec 72 | POPCORN (re-entry) *Pye International 7N 25583* | 50 | 3 |

HOT CHOCOLATE (34   Top 500) *London-based band who were chart regulars throughout the 1970s and 1980s. Group founders were West Indian-born Errol Brown (v) and Tony Wilson (b/v). The act had at least one hit every year between 1970 and 1984. 'You Sexy Thing' was the only song to make the Top 10 in the 70s, 80s and 90s (283 WEEKS)*
pos/wks

15 Aug 70	● LOVE IS LIFE *RAK 103*	6	12
6 Mar 71	YOU COULD HAVE BEEN A LADY *RAK 110*	22	9
28 Aug 71	● I BELIEVE (IN LOVE) *RAK 118*	8	11
28 Oct 72	YOU'LL ALWAYS BE A FRIEND *RAK 139*	23	8
14 Apr 73	● BROTHER LOUIE *RAK 149*	7	10
18 Aug 73	RUMOURS *RAK 157*	44	3
16 Mar 74	● EMMA *RAK 168*	3	10
30 Nov 74	CHERI BABE *RAK 188*	31	9
24 May 75	DISCO QUEEN *RAK 202*	11	7
9 Aug 75	● A CHILD'S PRAYER *RAK 212*	7	10
8 Nov 75	● YOU SEXY THING *RAK 221*	2	12
20 Mar 76	DON'T STOP IT NOW *RAK 230*	11	8
26 Jun 76	MAN TO MAN *RAK 238*	14	8
21 Aug 76	HEAVEN IS IN THE BACK SEAT OF MY CADILLAC *RAK 240*	25	8
18 Jun 77	★ SO YOU WIN AGAIN *RAK 259*	1	11
26 Nov 77	● PUT YOUR LOVE IN ME *RAK 266*	10	9
4 Mar 78	EVERY 1'S A WINNER *RAK 272*	12	11
2 Dec 78	I'LL PUT YOU TOGETHER AGAIN *RAK 286*	13	11
19 May 79	MINDLESS BOOGIE *RAK 292*	46	5
28 Jul 79	GOING THROUGH THE MOTIONS *RAK 296*	53	4
3 May 80	● NO DOUBT ABOUT IT *RAK 310*	2	11
19 Jul 80	ARE YOU GETTING ENOUGH OF WHAT MAKES YOU HAPPY *RAK 318*	17	7
13 Dec 80	LOVE ME TO SLEEP *RAK 324*	50	5
30 May 81	YOU'LL NEVER BE SO WRONG *RAK 331*	52	4
17 Apr 82	● GIRL CRAZY *RAK 341*	7	11
10 Jul 82	● IT STARTED WITH A KISS *RAK 344*	5	12
25 Sep 82	CHANCES *RAK 350*	32	5
7 May 83	● WHAT KINDA BOY YOU LOOKING FOR (GIRL) *RAK 357*	10	9
17 Sep 83	TEARS ON THE TELEPHONE *RAK 363*	37	5
4 Feb 84	I GAVE YOU MY HEART (DIDN'T I) *RAK 369*	13	10
17 Jan 87	● YOU SEXY THING (re-mix) *EMI 5592*	10	10
4 Apr 87	EVERY 1'S A WINNER (re-mix) *EMI 5607*	69	2
6 Mar 93	IT STARTED WITH A KISS (re-issue) *EMI CDEMCTS 7*	31	5
22 Nov 97	● YOU SEXY THING (re-issue) *EMI CDHOT 100*	6	8
14 Feb 98	IT STARTED WITH A KISS (2nd re-issue) *EMI CDHOT 101* [1]	18	3

[1] Hot Chocolate featuring Errol Brown

HOT GOSSIP – See Sarah BRIGHTMAN

HOT HOUSE
UK, male / female vocal / instrumental group (3 WEEKS)
pos/wks

| 14 Feb 87 | DON'T COME TO STAY *Deconstruction CHEZ 1* | 74 | 1 |
| 24 Sep 88 | DON'T COME TO STAY (re-issue) *Deconstruction PB 42233* | 70 | 2 |

HOT STREAK US, male vocal / instrumental group (8 WEEKS)

		pos/wks
10 Sep 83	BODY WORK *Polydor POSP 642*	19 8

HOTHOUSE FLOWERS Ireland, male vocal / instrumental group (36 WEEKS)

		pos/wks
14 May 88	DON'T GO *London LON 174*	11 8
23 Jul 88	I'M SORRY *London LON 187*	53 3
12 May 90	GIVE IT UP *London LON 258*	30 5
28 Jul 90	I CAN SEE CLEARLY NOW *London LON 269*	23 7
20 Oct 90	MOVIES *London LON 276*	68 2
13 Feb 93	EMOTIONAL TIME *London LONCD 335*	38 4
8 May 93	ONE TONGUE *London LOCDP 340*	45 3
19 Jun 93	ISN'T IT AMAZING *London LOCDP 343*	46 2
27 Nov 93	THIS IS IT (YOUR SOUL) *London LONCD 346*	67 1
16 May 98	YOU CAN LOVE ME NOW *London LONCD 410* ...	65 1

HOTLEGS UK, male vocal / instrumental group (14 WEEKS)

		pos/wks
4 Jul 70 ●	NEANDERTHAL MAN *Fontana 6007 019*	2 14

HOTSHOTS UK, male vocal group (15 WEEKS)

		pos/wks
2 Jun 73 ●	SNOOPY VS THE RED BARON *Mooncrest MOON 5*	4 15

Steven HOUGHTON UK, male vocalist (22 WEEKS)

		pos/wks
29 Nov 97 ●	WIND BENEATH MY WINGS *RCA 74321529272*	3 15
7 Mar 98	TRULY *RCA 74321558552*	23 5
2 May 98	TRULY (re-entry) *RCA 74321558552*	72 2

A HOUSE Ireland, male vocal / instrumental group (8 WEEKS)

		pos/wks
13 Jun 92	ENDLESS ART *Setanta AHOU 1*	46 3
8 Aug 92	TAKE IT EASY ON ME *Setanta AHOU 2*	55 2
25 Jun 94	WHY ME *Setanta CDAHOU 4*	52 1
1 Oct 94	HERE COME THE GOOD TIMES *Setanta CDAHOUS 5* ...	37 2

HOUSE ENGINEERS UK, male vocal / instrumental duo (2 WEEKS)

		pos/wks
5 Dec 87	GHOST HOUSE *Syncopate SY 8*	69 2

HOUSE OF LOVE UK, male vocal / instrumental group (21 WEEKS)

		pos/wks
22 Apr 89	NEVER *Fontana HOL 1*	41 2
18 Nov 89	I DON'T KNOW WHY I LOVE YOU *Fontana HOL 2*	41 3
3 Feb 90	SHINE ON *Fontana HOL 3*	20 4
7 Apr 90	BEATLES AND THE STONES *Fontana HOL 4*	36 4
26 Oct 91	THE GIRL WITH THE LONELIEST EYES *Fontana HOL 5* ...	58 1
2 May 92	FEEL *Fontana HOL 6*	45 3
27 Jun 92	YOU DON'T UNDERSTAND *Fontana HOL 7*	46 3
5 Dec 92	CRUSH ME *Fontana HOL 810*	67 1

HOUSE OF PAIN US, male rap group (24 WEEKS)

		pos/wks
10 Oct 92	JUMP AROUND *Ruffness XLS 32*	32 4
22 May 93 ●	JUMP AROUND / TOP O' THE MORNING TO YA (re-issue) *Ruffness XL 43CD*	8 7
23 Oct 93	SHAMROCKS AND SHENANIGANS / WHO'S THE MAN *Ruffness XLS 46CD*	23 4
16 Jul 94	ON POINT *Ruffness XLS 52CD*	19 3
12 Nov 94	IT AIN'T A CRIME *Ruffness XLS 55CD1*	37 2
1 Jul 95	OVER THERE (I DON'T CARE) *Ruffness XLS 61CD1*	20 3
5 Oct 96	FED UP *Tommy Boy TBCD 7744*	68 1

HOUSE OF VIRGINISM Sweden, male vocal / instrumental group (6 WEEKS)

		pos/wks
20 Nov 93	I'LL BE THERE FOR YOU (DOYA DODODO DOYA) *ffrr FCD 221*	29 3
30 Jul 94	REACHIN *ffrr FCD 238*	35 2
17 Feb 96	EXCLUSIVE *Logic 74321324102*	67 1

HOUSE TRAFFIC Italy / UK, male / female vocal / production duo (3 WEEKS)

		pos/wks
4 Oct 97	EVERY DAY OF MY LIFE *Logic 74321249442*	24 3

HOUSEMARTINS UK, male vocal / instrumental group fronted by Norman Cook (b) and Paul Heaton (v) (59 WEEKS)

		pos/wks
8 Mar 86	SHEEP *Go! Discs GOD 9*	54 3
5 Apr 86	SHEEP (re-entry) *Go! Discs GOD 9*	71 1
7 Jun 86 ●	HAPPY HOUR *Go! Discs GOD 11*	3 13
4 Oct 86	THINK FOR A MINUTE *Go! Discs GOD 13*	18 8
6 Dec 86 ★	CARAVAN OF LOVE *Go! Discs GOD 16*	1 11
23 May 87	FIVE GET OVER EXCITED *Go! Discs GOD 18*	11 6
5 Sep 87	ME AND THE FARMER *Go! Discs GOD 19*	15 5
21 Nov 87	BUILD *Go! Discs GOD 21*	15 8
23 Apr 88	THERE IS ALWAYS SOMETHING THERE TO REMIND ME *Go! Discs GOD 22*	35 4

HOUSEMASTER BOYZ and the RUDE BOY OF HOUSE US, male vocal / instrumental group (14 WEEKS)

		pos/wks
9 May 87	HOUSE NATION *Magnetic Dance MAGD 1*	48 6
12 Sep 87 ●	HOUSE NATION (re-entry) *Magnetic Dance MAGD 1* ...	8 8

HOUSETRAP – See DJ SANDY VS HOUSETRAP

Thelma HOUSTON US, female vocalist (22 WEEKS)

		pos/wks
5 Feb 77	DON'T LEAVE ME THIS WAY *Motown TMG 1060* ▲	13 8
27 Jun 81	IF YOU FEEL IT *RCA 77*	48 4
1 Dec 84	YOU USED TO HOLD ME SO TIGHT *MCA MCA 932*	49 8
21 Jan 95	DON'T LEAVE ME THIS WAY (re-recording) *Dynamo DYND 001* ...	35 2

Whitney HOUSTON 〔29 Top 500〕 Multi-award-winning, record-shattering vocalist b. 9 Aug 1963, New Jersey, US. She recorded the second biggest selling UK single by a female, and scored a record seven successive No.1s in the US. Her UK album sales amount to more than seven million and worldwide exceed 100 million (308 WEEKS)

		pos/wks
16 Nov 85 ★	SAVING ALL MY LOVE FOR YOU *Arista ARIST 640* ▲	1 16
25 Jan 86	HOLD ME *Asylum EKR 32* [1]	44 5
25 Jan 86 ●	HOW WILL I KNOW *Arista ARIST 656* ▲	5 12
12 Apr 86 ●	GREATEST LOVE OF ALL *Arista ARIST 658* ▲	8 11
23 May 87 ★	I WANNA DANCE WITH SOMEBODY (WHO LOVES ME) *Arista RIS 1* ▲	1 16
22 Aug 87	DIDN'T WE ALMOST HAVE IT ALL *Arista RIS 31* ▲ ...	14 8
14 Nov 87 ●	SO EMOTIONAL *Arista RIS 43* ▲	5 11
12 Mar 88	WHERE DO BROKEN HEARTS GO *Arista 109793* ▲ ...	14 8
28 May 88 ●	LOVE WILL SAVE THE DAY *Arista 111516*	10 7
24 Sep 88 ★	ONE MOMENT IN TIME *Arista 111613*	1 12
9 Sep 89	IT ISN'T, IT WASN'T, IT AIN'T NEVER GONNA BE *Arista 112545* [2]	29 5
20 Oct 90 ●	I'M YOUR BABY TONIGHT *Arista 113594* ▲	5 9
22 Dec 90	ALL THE MAN THAT I NEED *Arista 114000* ▲ ...	13 10
29 Dec 90	I'M YOUR BABY TONIGHT (re-entry) *Arista 113594* ...	69 1
6 Jul 91	MY NAME IS NOT SUSAN *Arista 114510*	29 5
28 Sep 91	I BELONG TO YOU *Arista 114727*	54 2
14 Nov 92 ★	I WILL ALWAYS LOVE YOU *Arista 74321120657* ◆ ▲ ...	1 23
20 Feb 93 ●	I'M EVERY WOMAN *Arista 74321131502*	4 11
24 Apr 93 ●	I HAVE NOTHING *Arista 74321146142*	3 10
31 Jul 93	RUN TO YOU *Arista 74321153332*	15 6
6 Nov 93	QUEEN OF THE NIGHT *Arista 74321169302*	14 5
18 Dec 93	I WILL ALWAYS LOVE YOU (re-entry) *Arista 74321120657* ...	25 6
22 Jan 94	SOMETHING IN COMMON *MCA MCSTD 1957* [3] ...	16 5
18 Nov 95	EXHALE (SHOOP SHOOP) *Arista 74321332472* ...	11 9
24 Feb 96	COUNT ON ME *Arista 74321345842* [4]	12 6
21 Dec 96	STEP BY STEP *Arista 74321449332*	13 13
29 Mar 97	I BELIEVE IN YOU AND ME *Arista 74321468602* ...	16 5
19 Dec 98 ●	WHEN YOU BELIEVE *Columbia 6667522* [5] ...	4 11
6 Mar 99 ●	IT'S NOT RIGHT (BUT IT'S OK) *Arista 74321652402* ...	3 15
27 Mar 99	WHEN YOU BELIEVE (re-entry) *Columbia 6667522* [5] ...	68 1
3 Jul 99 ●	MY LOVE IS YOUR LOVE *Arista 74321672862* ...	2 12
11 Dec 99	I LEARNED FROM THE BEST *Arista 74321723992* ...	19 11

UK No.1 ★   UK Top 10 ●   Still on chart +   UK million seller ◆   UK entry at No.1 ■   US No.1 ▲

17 Jun 00	●	IF I TOLD YOU THAT Arista 74321766282 [6]	......	9	9
26 Aug 00		IF I TOLD YOU THAT (re-entry) Arista 74321766282 [6]	....	51	2
14 Oct 00	●	COULD I HAVE THIS KISS FOREVER Arista 74321795992 [7]	...	7	8
30 Dec 00		HEARTBREAK HOTEL Arista 74321820572 [8]	....	26	1+

[1] Teddy Pendergrass with Whitney Houston [2] Aretha Franklin & Whitney Houston [3] Bobby Brown & Whitney Houston [4] Whitney Houston & CeCe Winans [5] Mariah Carey & Whitney Houston [6] Whitney Houston / George Michael [7] Whitney Houston & Enrique Iglesias [8] Whitney Houston featuring Faith Evans & Kelly Price

Adina HOWARD US, female vocalist (16 WEEKS)
pos/wks

4 Mar 95		FREAK LIKE ME East West A 4473CD	....	67	1
6 May 95		FREAK LIKE ME (re-entry) East West A 4473CD	......	33	3
23 Nov 96	●	WHAT'S LOVE GOT TO DO WITH IT Interscope IND 97008 [1]	....	2	12

[1] Warren G featuring Adina Howard

Billy HOWARD UK, male comedian / vocalist (12 WEEKS)
pos/wks

| 13 Dec 75 | ● | KING OF THE COPS Penny Farthing PEN 892 | .... | 6 | 12 |

Miki HOWARD US, female vocalist (2 WEEKS)
pos/wks

| 26 May 90 | | UNTIL YOU COME BACK (THAT'S WHAT I'M GONNA DO) East West 7935 | | 67 | 2 |

Nick HOWARD Australia, male vocalist (1 WEEK)
pos/wks

| 21 Jan 95 | | EVERYBODY NEEDS SOMEBODY Bell 74321220942 | .... | 64 | 1 |

Robert HOWARD – See Kym MAZELLE

HOWLIN' WOLF US, male vocalist - Chester Burnette (5 WEEKS) pos/wks

| 4 Jun 64 | | SMOKESTACK LIGHTNIN' Pye International 7N 25244 | .... | 42 | 5 |

H20 US / Switzerland, male / female vocal / instrumental group (4 WEEKS)
pos/wks

| 14 Sep 96 | | NOBODY'S BUSINESS AM:PM 5818832 [1] | .... | 19 | 3 |
| 30 Aug 97 | | SATISFIED (TAKE ME HIGHER) AM:PM 5823252 | ...... | 66 | 1 |

[1] H20 featuring Billie

H 20 UK, male vocal / instrumental group (16 WEEKS)
pos/wks

| 21 May 83 | | DREAM TO SLEEP RCA 330 | .... | 17 | 10 |
| 13 Aug 83 | | JUST OUTSIDE OF HEAVEN RCA 349 | ...... | 38 | 6 |

Al HUDSON US, male vocalist (22 WEEKS)
pos/wks

9 Sep 78		DANCE, GET DOWN (FEEL THE GROOVE) / HOW DO YOU DO ABC 4229		57	4
15 Sep 79		YOU CAN DO IT MCA 511 [1]	....	15	10
8 Dec 79		MUSIC MCA 542 [1]	....	56	6
29 Jun 85		LET'S TALK MCA 972 [2]	....	64	2

[1] Al Hudson and the Partners [2] One Way featuring Al Hudson

Lavine HUDSON UK, female vocalist (3 WEEKS)
pos/wks

| 21 May 88 | | INTERVENTION Virgin VS 1067 | .... | 57 | 3 |

HUDSON-FORD UK, male vocal / instrumental duo - Richard Hudson and John Ford (20 WEEKS)
pos/wks

18 Aug 73	●	PICK UP THE PIECES A & M AMS 7078	....	8	9
16 Feb 74		BURN BABY BURN A & M AMS 7096	....	15	9
29 Jun 74		FLOATING IN THE WIND A & M AMS 7116	....	35	2

See also MONKS

HUE AND CRY
UK, male vocal / instrumental duo - Pat and Greg Kane (59 WEEKS) pos/wks

13 Jun 87	●	LABOUR OF LOVE Circa YR 4	....	6	16
19 Sep 87		STRENGTH TO STRENGTH Circa YR 6	....	46	5
30 Jan 88		I REFUSE Circa YR 8	....	47	3

22 Oct 88		ORDINARY ANGEL Circa YR 18	....	42	6
28 Jan 89		LOOKING FOR LINDA Circa YR 24	....	15	9
6 May 89		VIOLENTLY (EP) Circa YR 29	....	21	6
30 Sep 89		SWEET INVISIBILITY Circa YR 37	....	55	3
25 May 91		MY SALT HEART Circa YR 64	....	47	3
3 Aug 91		LONG TERM LOVERS OF PAIN (EP) Circa YR 71	....	48	3
11 Jul 92		PROFOUNDLY YOURS Fidelity FIDEL 1	....	74	1
13 Mar 93		LABOUR OF LOVE (re-mix) Circa HUESCD 1	....	25	4

Tracks on Violently (EP): Violently / The Man with the Child In His Eyes / Calamity John. Tracks on Long Term Lovers of Pain (EP): Long Term Lovers of Pain / Heart of Saturday Night / Remembrance and Gold / Stars Crash Down

HUES CORPORATION US, male / female vocal group (16 WEEKS)
pos/wks

| 27 Jul 74 | ● | ROCK THE BOAT RCA APBO 0232 ▲ | .... | 6 | 10 |
| 19 Oct 74 | | ROCKIN' SOUL RCA PB 10066 | .... | 24 | 6 |

HUFF & HERB UK, male DJ / production duo (4 WEEKS)
pos/wks

| 6 Dec 97 | | FEELING GOOD Planet 3 GXY 2018CD | .... | 31 | 3 |
| 7 Nov 98 | | FEELING GOOD '98 (re-mix) Planet 3 GXY 2020CD | .... | 69 | 1 |

HUFF AND PUFF
UK, male instrumental / production duo (4 WEEKS)
pos/wks

| 2 Nov 96 | | HELP ME MAKE IT Skyway SKYWCD 4 | .... | 31 | 2 |
| 21 Jun 97 | | HELP ME MAKE IT (re-mix) Skyway SKYWCD 8 | .... | 37 | 2 |

David HUGHES UK, male vocalist (1 WEEK)
pos/wks

| 21 Sep 56 | | BY THE FOUNTAINS OF ROME Philips PB 606 | .... | 27 | 1 |

HUGO and LUIGI US, orchestra and chorus (2 WEEKS)
pos/wks

| 24 Jul 59 | | LA PLUME DE MA TANTE RCA 1127 | .... | 29 | 2 |

HUMAN LEAGUE [134] Top 500 Early-1980s UK pop sensation. Fronted by Phil Oakey (b. 2 Oct 1955, Sheffield) (v/syn) and joined in 1980 by vocalists Joanne Catherall and Susanne Sulley. The group, which also topped the US chart, won Best Newcomers at the 1982 Brit Awards (155 WEEKS)
pos/wks

3 May 80		HOLIDAY 80 (DOUBLE SINGLE) Virgin SV 105	....	56	5
21 Jun 80		EMPIRE STATE HUMAN Virgin VS 351	....	62	2
28 Feb 81		BOYS AND GIRLS Virgin VS 395	....	48	4
2 May 81		THE SOUND OF THE CROWD Virgin VS 416	....	12	10
8 Aug 81	●	LOVE ACTION (I BELIEVE IN LOVE) Virgin VS 435	....	3	13
10 Oct 81	●	OPEN YOUR HEART Virgin VS 453	....	6	9
5 Dec 81	★	DON'T YOU WANT ME Virgin VS 466 ◆ ▲	....	1	13
9 Jan 82	●	BEING BOILED EMI FAST 4	....	6	9
6 Feb 82		HOLIDAY 80 (DOUBLE SINGLE) (re-entry) Virgin SV 105	....	46	5
20 Nov 82	●	MIRROR MAN Virgin VS 522	....	2	10
23 Apr 83	●	(KEEP FEELING) FASCINATION Virgin VS 569	....	2	9
5 May 84		THE LEBANON Virgin VS 672	....	11	6
23 Jun 84		THE LEBANON (re-entry) Virgin VS 672	....	75	1
30 Jun 84		LIFE ON YOUR OWN Virgin VS 688	....	16	6
17 Nov 84		LOUISE Virgin VS 723	....	13	10
23 Aug 86	●	HUMAN Virgin VS 880 ▲	....	8	8
22 Nov 86		I NEED YOUR LOVING Virgin VS 900	....	72	1
15 Oct 88		LOVE IS ALL THAT MATTERS Virgin VS 1025	....	41	5
18 Aug 90		HEART LIKE A WHEEL Virgin VS 1262	....	29	5
7 Jan 95	●	TELL ME WHEN East West YZ 882CD1	....	6	9
18 Mar 95		ONE MAN IN MY HEART East West YZ 904CD1	....	13	8
17 Jun 95		FILLING UP WITH HEAVEN East West YZ 944CD1	....	36	2
28 Oct 95		DON'T YOU WANT ME (re-mix) Virgin VSCDT 1557	....	16	3
20 Jan 96		STAY WITH ME TONIGHT East West EW 020CD	....	40	2

Tracks on double single: Being Boiled / Marianne / Rock and Roll - Nightclubbing / Dancevision

HUMAN NATURE Australia, male vocal group (2 WEEKS)
pos/wks

| 10 May 97 | | WISHES Epic 6644485 | .... | 44 | 1 |
| 30 Aug 97 | | WHISPER YOUR NAME Epic 6649465 | .... | 53 | 1 |

UK No.1 ★   UK Top 10 ●   Still on chart +   UK million seller ◆   UK entry at No.1 ■   US No.1 ▲

HUMAN RESOURCE
Holland, male instrumental / production group (14 WEEKS) pos/wks

| 14 Sep 91 | DOMINATOR *R&S RSUK 4* | 36 | 7 |
| 21 Dec 91 | THE COMPLETE DOMINATOR (re-mix) *R&S RSUK 4X* | 18 | 7 |

HUMANOID
UK, male producer (13 WEEKS) pos/wks

26 Nov 88	STAKKER HUMANOID *Westside WSR 12*	17	8
22 Apr 89	SLAM *Westside WSR 14*	54	2
8 Aug 92	STAKKER HUMANOID (re-issue) *Jumpin' + Pumpin' TOT 27*	40	3

HUMATE
Germany, male production trio (4 WEEKS) pos/wks

| 30 Jan 99 | LOVE STIMULATION *Deviant DVNT 22CDS* | 18 | 4 |

HUMBLE PIE
UK, male vocal / instrumental group (10 WEEKS) pos/wks

| 23 Aug 69 ● | NATURAL BORN BUGIE *Immediate IM 082* | 4 | 10 |

Engelbert HUMPERDINCK 〔52 *Top 500*〕
Internationally popular cabaret entertainer and easy-on-the-ear vocalist, b. Arnold Dorsey, 2 May 1936, Madras, India. After a slow career start, an unlikely name change helped him to become one of the biggest-earning performers of the 1960s. This Vegas veteran was the UK's biggest-selling artist of 1967 and has reportedly amassed a personal fortune of £100m. (239 WEEKS) pos/wks

26 Jan 67 ★	RELEASE ME *Decca F 12541* ◆	1	56
25 May 67 ●	THERE GOES MY EVERYTHING *Decca F 12610*	2	29
23 Aug 67 ★	THE LAST WALTZ *Decca F 12655* ◆	1	27
10 Jan 68 ●	AM I THAT EASY TO FORGET *Decca F 12722*	3	13
24 Apr 68 ●	A MAN WITHOUT LOVE *Decca F 12770*	2	15
25 Sep 68 ●	LES BICYCLETTES DE BELSIZE *Decca F 12834*	5	15
5 Feb 69 ●	THE WAY IT USED TO BE *Decca F 12879*	3	14
9 Aug 69	I'M A BETTER MAN (FOR HAVING LOVED YOU) *Decca F 12957*	15	13
15 Nov 69 ●	WINTER WORLD OF LOVE *Decca F 12980*	7	13
30 May 70	MY MARIE *Decca F 13032*	31	7
12 Sep 70	SWEETHEART *Decca F 13068*	22	6
31 Oct 70	SWEETHEART (re-entry) *Decca F 13068*	50	1
11 Sep 71	ANOTHER TIME ANOTHER PLACE *Decca F 13212*	13	12
4 Mar 72	TOO BEAUTIFUL TO LAST *Decca F 13281*	14	10
20 Oct 73	LOVE IS ALL *Decca F 13443*	44	4
17 Nov 73	LOVE IS ALL (re-entry) *Decca F 13443*	45	1
30 Jan 99	QUANDO QUANDO QUANDO *The Hit Label HLC 15*	40	3
6 May 00	HOW TO WIN YOUR LOVE *Universal TV 8822682*	59	1

Peter HUNNIGALE – See ARSENAL FC

Geraldine HUNT
Canada, female vocalist (5 WEEKS) pos/wks

| 25 Oct 80 | CAN'T FAKE THE FEELING *Champagne FIZZ 501* | 44 | 5 |

Lisa HUNT – See LOVESTATION

Marsha HUNT
US, female vocalist (3 WEEKS) pos/wks

| 21 May 69 | WALK ON GILDED SPLINTERS *Track 604 030* | 46 | 2 |
| 2 May 70 | KEEP THE CUSTOMER SATISFIED *Track 604 037* | 41 | 1 |

Tommy HUNT
US, male vocalist (17 WEEKS) pos/wks

11 Oct 75	CRACKIN' UP *Spark SRL 1132*	39	5
21 Aug 76	LOVING ON THE LOSING SIDE *Spark SRL 1146*	28	9
4 Dec 76	ONE FINE MORNING *Spark SRL 1148*	44	3

Alfonzo HUNTER
US, male rap / instrumentalist (2 WEEKS) pos/wks

| 22 Feb 97 | JUST THE WAY *Cooltempo CDCOOL 326* | 38 | 2 |

HUNTER featuring Ruby TURNER
UK, male gladiator / vocalist and UK, female vocalist (1 WEEK) pos/wks

| 9 Dec 95 | SHAKABOOM! *Telstar HUNTCD 1* | 64 | 1 |

Ian HUNTER
UK, male vocalist (10 WEEKS) pos/wks

| 3 May 75 | ONCE BITTEN TWICE SHY *CBS 3194* | 14 | 10 |

See also MOTT THE HOOPLE

Tab HUNTER
US, male vocalist - Arthur Kelm (30 WEEKS) pos/wks

8 Feb 57 ★	YOUNG LOVE *London HLD 8380* ▲	1	18
12 Apr 57 ●	99 WAYS *London HLD 8410*	5	11
5 Jul 57	99 WAYS (re-entry) *London HLD 8410*	29	1

Terry HUNTER
US, male DJ / producer (1 WEEK) pos/wks

| 26 Jul 97 | HARVEST FOR THE WORLD *Delirious DELICD 4* | 48 | 1 |

HURLEY & TODD
UK / South Africa, male production duo (2 WEEKS) pos/wks

| 29 Apr 00 | SUNSTORM *Multiply CDMULTY 58* | 38 | 2 |

Steve 'Silk' HURLEY
US, male producer (9 WEEKS) pos/wks

| 10 Jan 87 ★ | JACK YOUR BODY *DJ International LON 117* | 1 | 9 |

HURRICANE – See PUFF DADDY

HURRICANE #1
UK, male vocal / instrumental group (17 WEEKS) pos/wks

10 May 97	STEP INTO MY WORLD *Creation CRESCD 253*	29	2
5 Jul 97	JUST ANOTHER ILLUSION *Creation CRESCD 264*	35	2
6 Sep 97	CHAIN REACTION *Creation CRESCD 271*	30	2
1 Nov 97	STEP INTO MY WORLD (re-mix) *Creation CRESCD 276*	19	3
21 Feb 98	ONLY THE STRONGEST WILL SURVIVE *Creation CRERSCD 285*	19	6
24 Oct 98	RISING SIGN *Creation CRESCD 303*	47	1
3 Apr 99	THE GREATEST HIGH *Creation CRESCD 309*	43	1

HURRICANES – See JOHNNY and the HURRICANES

Phil HURTT
US, male vocalist (5 WEEKS) pos/wks

| 11 Nov 78 | GIVING IT BACK *Fantasy FTC 161* | 36 | 5 |

HUSTLERS CONVENTION featuring Dave LAUDAT and Ondrea DUVERNEY
UK, male instrumental / production duo (1 WEEK) pos/wks

| 20 May 95 | DANCE TO THE MUSIC *Stress CDSTR 53* | 71 | 1 |

See also SEX-O-SONIQUE; FULL INTENTION

Willie HUTCH
US, male vocalist (8 WEEKS) pos/wks

| 4 Dec 82 | IN AND OUT *Motown TMG 1285* | 51 | 7 |
| 6 Jul 85 | KEEP ON JAMMIN' *Motown ZB 40173* | 73 | 1 |

June HUTTON
US, female vocalist (7 WEEKS) pos/wks

| 7 Aug 53 ● | SAY YOU'RE MINE AGAIN *Capitol CL 13918* [1] | 10 | 3 |
| 4 Sep 53 ● | SAY YOU'RE MINE AGAIN (re-entry) *Capitol CL 13918* [1] | 6 | 4 |

[1] June Hutton and Axel Stordahl with the Boys Next Door

HWA featuring SONIC THE HEDGEHOG
UK, male producer - Jeremy Healy (6 WEEKS) pos/wks

| 5 Dec 92 | SUPERSONIC *Internal Affairs KGB 008* | 33 | 6 |

HYBRID
UK, male production trio (4 WEEKS) pos/wks

10 Jul 99	FINISHED SYMPHONY *Distinctive DISNCD 52*	58	1
11 Sep 99	IF I SURVIVE *Distinctive DISNCD 55* [1]	52	1
3 Jun 00	KID 2000 *Virgin / EMI VTS CD2* [2]	32	2

[1] Hybrid featuring Julee Cruise [2] Hybrid featuring Chrissie Hynde

Brian HYLAND 〔473 *Top 500*〕
Successful teen-targeted vocalist, b. 12 Nov 1943, New York, US. First hit the top in the US while still at high school, and teen separation saga, 'Sealed with a Kiss', reached UK Top 10 twice. Both these songs were later UK No.1s by Bombalurina and Jason Donovan respectively (72 WEEKS) pos/wks

7 Jul 60 ●	ITSY BITSY TEENY WEENY YELLOW POLKA DOT BIKINI *London HLR 9161* ▲	8	13
20 Oct 60	FOUR LITTLE HEELS *London HLR 9203*	29	6
10 May 62 ●	GINNY COME LATELY *HMV POP 1013*	5	15
2 Aug 62 ●	SEALED WITH A KISS *HMV POP 1051*	3	15

UK No.1 ★   UK Top 10 ●   Still on chart +   UK million seller ◆   UK entry at No.1 ■   US No.1 ▲

8 Nov 62	WARMED OVER KISSES *HMV POP 1079*.................28	6
27 Mar 71	GYPSY WOMAN *Uni UN 530*.................45	1
10 Apr 71	GYPSY WOMAN (re-entry) *Uni UN 530*.................42	5
28 Jun 75 ●	SEALED WITH A KISS (re-issue) *ABC 4059*.................7	11

Sheila HYLTON *Jamaica, female vocalist (12 WEEKS)* pos/wks

| 15 Sep 79 | BREAKFAST IN BED *United Artists BP 304* ....57 | 5 |
| 17 Jan 81 | THE BED'S TOO BIG WITHOUT YOU *Island WIP 6671* ....35 | 7 |

Phyllis HYMAN *US, female vocalist (9 WEEKS)* pos/wks

| 16 Feb 80 | YOU KNOW HOW TO LOVE ME *Arista ARIST 323*.................47 | 6 |
| 12 Sep 81 | YOU SURE LOOK GOOD TO ME *Arista ARIST 424* ....56 | 3 |

Dick HYMAN TRIO
US, male instrumentalist trio - Dick Hyman, keyboards (10 WEEKS) pos/wks

| 16 Mar 56 ● | THEME FROM 'THE THREEPENNY OPERA' *MGM 890*.................9 | 10 |

Chrissie HYNDE *US, female vocalist / instrumentalist (38 WEEKS)* pos/wks

3 Aug 85 ★	I GOT YOU BABE *DEP International DEP20* [1] 1	13
18 Jun 88 ●	BREAKFAST IN BED *DEP International DEP29* [1] 6	11
12 Oct 91	SPIRITUAL HIGH (STATE OF INDEPENDENCE) *Arista114528* [2] ...66	2
23 Jan 93	SPIRITUAL HIGH (STATE OF INDEPENDENCE) (re-mix) *Arista 74321 127712* [2] 47	2
18 Mar 95 ★	LOVE CAN BUILD A BRIDGE *London CO CD1* [3] 1	8
3 Jun 00	KID 2000 *Virgin / EMI VTS CD2* [4] 32	2

[1] UB40 featuring Chrissie Hynde [2] Moodswings featuring Chrissie Hynde [3] Cher, Chrissie Hynde and Neneh Cherry with Eric Clapton [4] Hybrid featuring Chrissie Hynde

See also PRETENDERS

HYPER GO GO *UK, male instrumental / production duo (15 WEEKS)* pos/wks

22 Aug 92	HIGH *Deconstruction 74321110497* 30	5
31 Jul 93	NEVER LET GO *Positiva CDTIV 3* 45	3
5 Feb 94	RAISE *Positiva CDTIV 9* 36	2
26 Nov 94	IT'S ALRIGHT *Positiva CDTIV 20* 49	1
6 Apr 96	DO WATCHA DO *Avex UK AVEXCD 24* [1] 54	1
12 Oct 96	HIGH (re-mix) *Distinctive DISNCD 24* 32	2
12 Apr 97	DO WATCHA DO (re-mix) *Distinctive DISNCD 28* [1] 60	1

[1] Hyper Go Go and Adeva

HYPERLOGIC *UK, male instrumental / production duo (3 WEEKS)* pos/wks

| 29 Jul 95 | ONLY ME *Systematic SYSCD 15*.................35 | 2 |
| 9 May 98 | ONLY ME (re-mix) *Tidy Trax TIDY 113CD1* ....48 | 1 |

HYPERSTATE *UK, male / female vocal / instrumental duo (1 WEEK)* pos/wks

| 6 Feb 93 | TIME AFTER TIME *M & G MAGCD 34* ....71 | 1 |

HYPNOTIST *UK, male producer - Caspar Pound (5 WEEKS)* pos/wks

| 28 Sep 91 | THE HOUSE IS MINE *Rising High RSN 4*.................65 | 2 |
| 21 Dec 91 | THE HARDCORE EP *Rising High RSN 13* ....68 | 3 |

Tracks on The Hardcore EP: Hardcore U Know the Score / The Ride / Night of the Livin' E Heads / God of the Universe

HYSTERIC EGO *UK, male producer - Rob White (8 WEEKS)* pos/wks

31 Aug 96	WANT LOVE *WEA WEA 070CD*.................28	4
21 Jun 97	MINISTRY OF LOVE *WEA WEA 094CD*.................39	2
28 Feb 98	WANT LOVE - THE REMIXES *WEA WEA 150CD*.................46	1
13 Feb 99	TIME TO GET BACK *WEA WEA 198CD*.................50	1

HYSTERICS *UK, male vocal / instrumental group (5 WEEKS)* pos/wks

| 12 Dec 81 | JINGLE BELLS LAUGHING ALL THE WAY *Record Delivery KA 5* ....44 | 5 |

HYSTERIX *UK, male / female vocal / instrumental group (4 WEEKS)* pos/wks

| 7 May 94 | MUST BE THE MUSIC *Deconstruction 74321207362* ....40 | 3 |
| 18 Feb 95 | EVERYTHING *Deconstruction 74321236882* ....65 | 1 |

I-LEVEL *UK, male vocal / instrumental group (9 WEEKS)* pos/wks

| 16 Apr 83 | MINEFIELD *Virgin VS 563*.................52 | 6 |
| 18 Jun 83 | TEACHER *Virgin VS 595*.................56 | 3 |

Janis IAN *US, female vocalist (10 WEEKS)* pos/wks

| 17 Nov 79 | FLY TOO HIGH *CBS 7936*.................44 | 7 |
| 28 Jun 80 | THE OTHER SIDE OF THE SUN *CBS 8611* ....44 | 3 |

ICE CUBE *US, male rapper - O'Shea Jackson (23 WEEKS)* pos/wks

27 Mar 93	IT WAS A GOOD DAY *Fourth & Broadway BRCD 270*.................27	4
7 Aug 93	CHECK YO SELF *Fourth & Broadway BRCD 283* [1] 36	4
11 Sep 93	WICKED *Fourth & Broadway BRCD 282* 62	1
18 Dec 93	REALLY DOE *Fourth & Broadway BRCD 302* 66	1
26 Mar 94	YOU KNOW HOW WE DO IT *Fourth & Broadway BRCD 303* 41	3
27 Aug 94	BOP GUN (ONE NATION) *Fourth & Broadway BRCD 308* [2] 22	3
24 Dec 94	YOU KNOW HOW WE DO IT (re-entry) *Fourth & Broadway BRCD 303*.................46	2
11 Mar 95	HAND OF THE DEAD BODY *Virgin America VUSCD 88* [3] 41	2
15 Apr 95	NATURAL BORN KILLAZ *Death Row A 8197CD* [4] 45	2
22 Mar 97	THE WORLD IS MINE *Jive JIVECD 419* 60	1

[1] Ice Cube featuring Das EFX [2] Ice Cube featuring George Clinton [3] Scarface featuring Ice Cube [4] Dr Dre and Ice Cube

ICE MC *UK, male rapper - Ian Campbell (5 WEEKS)* pos/wks

6 Aug 94	THINK ABOUT THE WAY (BOM DIGI DIGI BOM...) *WEA YZ 829CD*.................42	2
8 Apr 95	IT'S A RAINY DAY *Eternal YZ 902CD* 73	1
14 Sep 96	BOM DIGI BOM (THINK ABOUT THE WAY) (re-issue) *Eternal WEA 073CD*.................38	2

ICE-T *US, male rapper - Tracy Morrow (29 WEEKS)* pos/wks

18 Mar 89	HIGH ROLLERS *Sire W 7574*.................63	2
17 Feb 90	YOU PLAYED YOURSELF *Sire W 9994*.................64	2
29 Sep 90	SUPERFLY 1990 *Capitol CL 586* [1] 48	3
8 May 93	I AIN'T NEW TA THIS *Rhyme Syndicate SYNDD 1* 62	2
18 Dec 93	THAT'S HOW I'M LIVIN' *Rhyme Syndicate SYNDD 2*.................21	6
9 Apr 94	GOTTA LOTTA LOVE *Rhyme Syndicate SYNDD 3*.................24	4
10 Dec 94	BORN TO RAISE HELL *Fox 74321230152* [2] 47	2
1 Jun 96	I MUST STAND *Rhyme Syndicate SYNDD 5*.................23	3
7 Dec 96	THE LANE *Rhyme Syndicate SYNDD 6* 18	5

[1] Curtis Mayfield and Ice-T [2] Motorhead / Ice-T / Whitfield Crane

ICEBERG SLIMM *UK, male rapper (2 WEEKS)* pos/wks

| 7 Oct 00 | NURSERY RHYMES *Polydor 5877632* ....37 | 2 |

ICEHOUSE
New Zealand, male vocal / instrumental group (28 WEEKS) pos/wks

5 Feb 83	HEY LITTLE GIRL *Chrysalis CHS 2670*.................17	10
23 Apr 83	STREET CAFE *Chrysalis COOL 1* 62	4
3 May 86	NO PROMISES *Chrysalis CHS 2978*.................72	1
29 Aug 87	CRAZY *Chrysalis CHS 3156*.................74	1
13 Feb 88	CRAZY (re-entry) *Chrysalis CHS 3156*.................38	8
14 May 88	ELECTRIC BLUE *Chrysalis CHS 3239* 53	4

ICICLE WORKS *UK, male vocal / instrumental group - lead vocal Ian McNabb (28 WEEKS)* pos/wks

24 Dec 83	LOVE IS A WONDERFUL COLOUR *Beggars Banquet BEG 99*......15	8
10 Mar 84	BIRDS FLY (WHISPER TO A SCREAM) / IN THE CAULDRON OF LOVE *Beggars Banquet BEG 108*.................53	4
26 Jul 86	UNDERSTANDING JANE *Beggars Banquet BEG 160* 52	3

4 Oct 86	WHO DO YOU WANT FOR YOUR LOVE		
	Beggars Banquet BEG 172..................	**54**	4
14 Feb 87	EVANGELINE *Beggars Banquet BEG 181*.............	**53**	4
30 Apr 88	LITTLE GIRL LOST *Beggars Banquet BEG 215*	**59**	4
17 Mar 90	MOTORCYCLE RIDER *Epic WORKS 100*.............	**73**	1

ICON *UK, male / female vocal / instrumental duo (1 WEEK)*   pos/wks

15 Jun 96	TAINTED LOVE *Eternal WEA 057CD*.............	**51**	1

IDEAL *UK, male producer - Jon Da Silva (2 WEEKS)*   pos/wks

6 Aug 94	HOT *Cleveland City CLECD 13019*..................	**49**	2

IDEAL U.S. – See LIL' MO

IDES OF MARCH *US, male vocal / instrumental group (9 WEEKS)*   pos/wks

6 Jun 70	VEHICLE *Warner Bros. WB 7378*	**31**	9

Eric IDLE featuring Richard WILSON
UK, male actors / vocalists (3 WEEKS)   pos/wks

17 Dec 94	ONE FOOT IN THE GRAVE *Victa CDVICTA 1*	**50**	3

IDLEWILD *UK, male vocal / instrumental group (15 WEEKS)*   pos/wks

9 May 98	A FILM FOR THE FUTURE *Food CDFOOD 111*	**53**	1
25 Jul 98	EVERYONE SAYS YOU'RE SO FRAGILE *Food CDFOOD 113*	**47**	1
24 Oct 98	I'M A MESSAGE *Food CDFOOD 114*.............	**41**	1
13 Feb 99	WHEN I ARGUE I SEE SHAPES *Food CDFOOD 116*	**19**	2
2 Oct 99	LITTLE DISCOURAGE *Food CDFOOD 124*	**24**	2
8 Apr 00	ACTUALLY IT'S DARKNESS *Food CDFOOD127*	**23**	3
24 Jun 00	THESE WOODEN IDEAS *Food CDFOOD 132*	**32**	3
28 Oct 00	ROSEABILITY *Food CDFOOD 134*	**38**	2

Billy IDOL 276 *Top 500* *Snarling rock 'n' roll rebel of the 1980s. Former vocalist of punk rock hitmakers Generation X, b. William Broad, 30 Nov 1955, Middlesex, UK. He had his greatest success in the US, where four singles reached the Top 10 and 'Mony Mony' reached No.1 (106 WEEKS)*   pos/wks

11 Sep 82	HOT IN THE CITY *Chrysalis CHS 2625*	**58**	4
24 Mar 84	REBEL YELL *Chrysalis IDOL 2*	**62**	2
30 Jun 84	EYES WITHOUT A FACE *Chrysalis IDOL 3*.........	**18**	11
29 Sep 84	FLESH FOR FANTASY *Chrysalis IDOL 4*	**54**	3
13 Jul 85 ●	WHITE WEDDING *Chrysalis IDOL 5*.........	**6**	15
14 Sep 85 ●	REBEL YELL (re-issue) *Chrysalis IDOL 6*	**6**	12
4 Oct 86	TO BE A LOVER *Chrysalis IDOL 8*	**22**	8
7 Mar 87	DON'T NEED A GUN *Chrysalis IDOL 9*.........	**26**	5
13 Jun 87	SWEET SIXTEEN *Chrysalis IDOL 10*	**17**	9
3 Oct 87 ●	MONY MONY *Chrysalis IDOL 11* ▲	**7**	10
16 Jan 88	HOT IN THE CITY (re-mix) *Chrysalis IDOL 12*	**13**	9
13 Aug 88	CATCH MY FALL *Chrysalis IDOL 13*.........	**63**	3
28 Apr 90	CRADLE OF LOVE *Chrysalis IDOL 14*	**34**	4
11 Aug 90	L.A. WOMAN *Chrysalis IDOL 15*	**70**	2
22 Dec 90	PRODIGAL BLUES *Chrysalis IDOL 16*	**47**	4
26 Jun 93	SHOCK TO THE SYSTEM *Chrysalis CDCHS 3994*	**30**	3
10 Sep 94	SPEED *Fox 74321223472*.........	**47**	2

Frank IFIELD 128 *Top 500* *Early 60s superstar. b. 30 Nov 1937, Coventry, UK, and raised in Australia. This pop vocalist / yodeller had four No.1s in 12 months with revivals of US standards. Unlike many of his early 1960s UK contemporaries, his records also did well internationally (162 WEEKS)* pos/wks

19 Feb 60	LUCKY DEVIL *Columbia DB 4399*.........	**22**	5
7 Apr 60	LUCKY DEVIL (re-entry) *Columbia DB 4399*.........	**33**	2
29 Sep 60	GOTTA GET A DATE *Columbia DB 4496*.........	**49**	1
5 Jul 62 ★	I REMEMBER YOU *Columbia DB 4856* ◆	**1**	28
25 Oct 62 ★	LOVESICK BLUES *Columbia DB 4913*.........	**1**	17
24 Jan 63 ★	THE WAYWARD WIND *Columbia DB 4960*.........	**1**	13
11 Apr 63 ●	NOBODY'S DARLIN' BUT MINE *Columbia DB 7007*.........	**4**	16
27 Jun 63 ★	CONFESSIN' *Columbia DB 7062*.........	**1**	16
17 Oct 63	MULE TRAIN *Columbia DB 7131*	**22**	6
9 Jan 64 ●	DON'T BLAME ME *Columbia DB 7184*.........	**8**	13
23 Apr 64	ANGRY AT THE BIG OAK TREE *Columbia DB 7263*	**25**	8
23 Jul 64	I SHOULD CARE *Columbia DB 7319*	**33**	3

1 Oct 64	SUMMER IS OVER *Columbia DB 7355*.........	**25**	6
19 Aug 65	PARADISE *Columbia DB 7655*	**26**	9
23 Jun 66	NO ONE WILL EVER KNOW *Columbia DB 7940*	**25**	4
8 Dec 66	CALL HER YOUR SWEETHEART *Columbia DB 8078*	**24**	11
7 Dec 91	THE YODELLING SONG *EMI 7YODEL 1* 1	**40**	4

1 Frank Ifield featuring the Backroom Boys

Enrique IGLESIAS *Spain, male vocalist (19 WEEKS)*   pos/wks

11 Sep 99 ●	BAILAMOS *Interscope IND 97131* ▲	**4**	9
18 Dec 99	RHYTHM DIVINE *Interscope 4972242*	**45**	2
14 Oct 00 ●	COULD I HAVE THIS KISS FOREVER *Arista 74321795992* 1	**7**	8

1 Whitney Houston and Enrique Iglesias

Julio IGLESIAS 448 *Top 500* *Spain's most successful vocalist of all time with reported world sales of more than 225 million albums: b. 23 Sep 1943, Madrid. Suave singer was still adding to his hits and awards in late 1990s, when son Enrique also became a leading Latin recording artist (75 WEEKS)* pos/wks

24 Oct 81 ★	BEGIN THE BEGUINE (VOLVER A EMPEZAR)		
	CBS A 1612.........	**1**	14
6 Mar 82 ●	QUIEREME MUCHO (YOURS) *CBS A 1939*	**3**	9
9 Oct 82	AMOR *CBS A 2801*	**32**	7
9 Apr 83	HEY! *CBS JULIO 1*	**31**	7
7 Apr 84	TO ALL THE GIRLS I'VE LOVED BEFORE *CBS A 4252* 1	**17**	10
7 Jul 84	ALL OF YOU *CBS A 4522* 2	**43**	8
6 Aug 88 ●	MY LOVE *CBS JULIO 2* 3	**5**	11
4 Jun 94	CRAZY *Columbia 6603695*	**43**	3
27 Aug 94	CRAZY (re-entry) *Columbia 6603695*	**50**	2
26 Nov 94	FRAGILE *Columbia 6610192*	**53**	2
31 Dec 94	FRAGILE (re-entry) *Columbia 6610192*	**66**	2

1 Julio Iglesias and Willie Nelson 2 Julio Iglesias and Diana Ross 3 Julio Iglesias featuring Stevie Wonder

IGNORANTS *UK, male vocal duo (3 WEEKS)*   pos/wks

25 Dec 93	PHAT GIRLS *Spaghetti CIOCD 8*.........	**59**	3

ILLEGAL MOTION featuring Simone CHAPMAN
UK, male / female vocal / instrumental duo (1 WEEK)   pos/wks

9 Oct 93	SATURDAY LOVE *Arista 74321163032*.........	**67**	1

ILLICIT featuring GRAM'MA FUNK
UK, male producer featuring US, female vocalist (1 WEEK)   pos/wks

2 Sep 00	CHEEKY ARMADA *Yola YOLACDX 01*.........	**72**	1

IMAANI *UK, female vocalist (7 WEEKS)*   pos/wks

9 May 98	WHERE ARE YOU *EMI CDEM 510*	**15**	7

IMAGINATION 278 *Top 500* *Distinctive London-based trio, who created a unique blend of soul and dance music: Leee John (v), Ashley Ingram (v/k), Errol Kennedy (d). One of the most original British acts of the early 1980s, they were fronted by a charismatic and flamboyant lead singer (105 WEEKS)* pos/wks

16 May 81 ●	BODY TALK *R & B RBS 201*	**4**	18
5 Sep 81	IN AND OUT OF LOVE *R & B RBS 202*	**16**	9
14 Nov 81	FLASHBACK *R & B RBS 206*.........	**16**	13
6 Mar 82 ●	JUST AN ILLUSION *R & B RBS 208*	**2**	11
26 Jun 82 ●	MUSIC AND LIGHTS *R & B RBS 210*	**5**	9
25 Sep 82	IN THE HEAT OF THE NIGHT *R & B RBS 211*	**22**	8
11 Dec 82	CHANGES *R & B RBS 213*	**31**	8
4 Jun 83	LOOKING AT MIDNIGHT *R & B RBS 214*	**29**	7
5 Nov 83	NEW DIMENSIONS *R & B RBS 216*	**56**	3
26 May 84	STATE OF LOVE *R & B RBS 218*	**67**	2
24 Nov 84	THANK YOU MY LOVE *R & B RBS 219*	**22**	15
16 Jan 88	INSTINCTUAL *RCA PB 41697*	**62**	2

IMAJIN *US, male vocal group (7 WEEKS)*   pos/wks

27 Jun 98	SHORTY (YOU KEEP PLAYIN' WITH MY MIND)		
	Jive 0521212 1	**22**	3
20 Feb 99	NO DOUBT *Jive 0521772*	**42**	2

24 Apr 99	**BOUNCE, ROCK, SKATE, ROLL** *Jive 0522142* [2]	**45**	1
12 Feb 00	**FLAVA** *Jive 9250012*	**64**	1

[1] Imajin featuring Keith Murray [2] Baby DC featuring Imajin

See also RUFF DRIVERZ

Natalie IMBRUGLIA *Australia, female vocalist (39 WEEKS)* pos/wks

8 Nov 97 ●	**TORN** *RCA 74321527982*	**2**	17
14 Mar 98 ●	**BIG MISTAKE** *RCA 74321566782*	**2**	10
6 Jun 98	**WISHING I WAS THERE** *RCA 74321585062*	**19**	5
17 Oct 98 ●	**SMOKE** *RCA 74321621942*	**5**	7

IMMACULATE FOOLS
UK, male vocal / instrumental group (4 WEEKS) pos/wks

26 Jan 85	**IMMACULATE FOOLS** *A & M AM 227*	**51**	4

IMMATURE featuring SMOOTH
US, male vocal group and US, female vocalist (2 WEEKS) pos/wks

16 Mar 96	**WE GOT IT** *MCA MCSTD 48009*	**26**	2

IMPALAS *US, male vocal group (1 WEEK)* pos/wks

21 Aug 59	**SORRY (I RAN ALL THE WAY HOME)** *MGM 1015*	**28**	1

IMPEDANCE *UK, male producer - Daniel Haydon (4 WEEKS)* pos/wks

11 Nov 89	**TAINTED LOVE** *Jumpin' & Pumpin' TOT 4*	**54**	4

IMPERIAL DRAG *UK, male vocal / instrumental group (1 WEEK)* pos/wks

12 Oct 96	**BOY OR A GIRL** *Columbia 6632992*	**54**	1

IMPERIAL TEEN
US, male / female vocal / instrumental group (1 WEEK) pos/wks

7 Sep 96	**YOU'RE ONE** *Slash LASCD 57*	**69**	1

See also FAITH NO MORE

IMPERIALS *US, male vocal group (9 WEEKS)* pos/wks

24 Dec 77	**WHO'S GONNA LOVE ME** *Power Exchange PX 266*	**17**	9

IMPOSTER – See Elvis COSTELLO

IMPRESSIONS *US, male vocal group (10 WEEKS)* pos/wks

22 Nov 75	**FIRST IMPRESSIONS** *Curtom K 16638*	**16**	10

IN CROWD *UK, male vocal / instrumental group (1 WEEK)* pos/wks

20 May 65	**THAT'S HOW STRONG MY LOVE IS** *Parlophone R 5276*	**48**	1

IN TUA NUA
Ireland, male / female vocal / instrumental group (2 WEEKS) pos/wks

14 May 88	**ALL I WANTED** *Virgin VS 1072*	**69**	2

INAURA *UK, male vocal / instrumental group (1 WEEK)* pos/wks

18 May 96	**COMA AROMA** *EMI CDEM 421*	**57**	1

INCANTATION *UK, male instrumental group (12 WEEKS)* pos/wks

4 Dec 82	**CACHARPAYA (ANDES PUMPSA DAESI)** *Beggars Banquet BEG 84*	**12**	12

INCOGNITO
UK, male / female vocal / instrumental group (38 WEEKS) pos/wks

15 Nov 80	**PARISIENNE GIRL** *Ensign ENY 44*	**73**	2
29 Jun 91 ●	**ALWAYS THERE** *Talkin Loud TLK 10* [1]	**6**	9
14 Sep 91	**CRAZY FOR YOU** *Talkin Loud TLK 14* [2]	**59**	2
6 Jun 92	**DON'T YOU WORRY 'BOUT A THING** *Talkin Loud TLK 21*	**19**	6
15 Aug 92	**CHANGE** *Talkin Loud TLK 26*	**52**	2
21 Aug 93	**STILL A FRIEND OF MINE** *Talkin Loud TLKCD 42*	**47**	2

20 Nov 93	**GIVIN' IT UP** *Talkin Loud TLKCD 44*	**43**	2
12 Mar 94	**PIECES OF A DREAM** *Talkin Loud TLKCD 46*	**35**	2
27 May 95	**EVERYDAY** *Talkin Loud TLKCD 55*	**23**	3
5 Aug 95	**I HEAR YOUR NAME** *Talkin Loud TLKCD 56*	**42**	3
11 May 96	**JUMP TO MY LOVE / ALWAYS THERE (re-recording)** *Talkin Loud TLCD 7*	**29**	3
26 Oct 96	**OUT OF THE STORM** *Talkin Loud TLCD 14*	**57**	1
10 Apr 99	**NIGHTS OVER EGYPT** *Talkin Loud TLCD 40*	**56**	1

[1] Incognito featuring Jocelyn Brown [2] Incognito featuring Chyna

INCUBUS *US male vocal / instrumental group (1 WEEK)* pos/wks

20 May 00	**PARDON ME** *Epic 6693462*	**61**	1

INDEEP *US, male / female vocal / rap duo (11 WEEKS)* pos/wks

22 Jan 83	**LAST NIGHT A DJ SAVED MY LIFE** *Sound of New York SNY 1*	**13**	9
14 May 83	**WHEN BOYS TALK** *Sound of New York SNY 3*	**67**	2

INDIA *US, female vocalist (14 WEEKS)* pos/wks

26 Feb 94	**LOVE AND HAPPINESS (YEMAYA Y OCHUN)** *Cooltempo CDCOOL 287* [1]	**50**	2
5 Aug 95	**I CAN'T GET NO SLEEP** *A & M 5811412*	**44**	2
16 Mar 96	**OYE COMO VA** *Media MCSTD 40013*	**36**	2
8 Feb 97	**RUNAWAY** *Talkin Loud TLCD20*	**24**	4
19 Jul 97	**OYE COMO VA (re-issue)** *Nukleuz MCSTD 40120*	**56**	1
31 Jul 99	**TO BE IN LOVE** *Defected DEFECT 5CDS* [3]	**23**	3

[1] River Ocean featuring India [2] Nuyorican Soul featuring India [3] MAW presents India

INDIAN VIBES *UK, male vocal / instrumental group (2 WEEKS)* pos/wks

24 Sep 94	**MATHAR** *Virgin International DINSD 136*	**68**	1
2 May 98	**MATHAR (re-mix)** *VC Recordings VCRD 32*	**52**	1

INDO *US, female vocal duo (3 WEEKS)* pos/wks

18 Apr 98	**R U SLEEPING** *Satellite 74321568212*	**31**	3

INDUSTRY STANDARD *UK, male DJ / production duo (3 WEEKS)* pos/wks

10 Jan 98	**VOLUME 1 (WHAT YOU WANT WHAT YOU NEED)** *Satellite 74321543742*	**34**	3

INFINITI – See GRAND PUBA

INGRAM *US, male vocal / instrumental group (2 WEEKS)* pos/wks

11 Jun 83	**SMOOTHIN' GROOVIN'** *Streetwave WAVE 3*	**56**	2

James INGRAM *US, male vocalist (42 WEEKS)* pos/wks

12 Feb 83	**BABY COME TO ME** *Qwest K 15005* [1] ▲	**11**	10
18 Feb 84	**YAH MO B THERE** *Qwest W 9394* [2]	**44**	5
7 Apr 84	**YAH MO B THERE (re-entry)** *Qwest W 9394* [2]	**69**	3
12 Jan 85	**YAH MO B THERE (2nd re-entry)** *Qwest W 9394* [2]	**12**	8
11 Jul 87 ●	**SOMEWHERE OUT THERE** *MCA MCA 1132* [3]	**8**	13
31 Mar 90	**SECRET GARDEN** *Qwest W 9992* [4]	**67**	1
16 Apr 94	**THE DAY I FALL IN LOVE** *Columbia 6600282* [5]	**64**	1

[1] Patti Austin and James Ingram [2] James Ingram with Michael McDonald [3] Linda Ronstadt and James Ingram [4] Quincy Jones featuring Al B Sure!, James Ingram, El DeBarge and Barry White [5] Dolly Parton and James Ingram

The second re-entry of W 9394 was a re-mix with the same catalogue number

INK SPOTS *US, male vocal group (4 WEEKS)* pos/wks

29 Apr 55 ●	**MELODY OF LOVE** *Parlophone R 3977*	**10**	4

John INMAN *UK, male actor / vocalist (6 WEEKS)* pos/wks

25 Oct 75	**ARE YOU BEING SERVED SIR** *DJM DJS 602*	**39**	6

INMATES *UK, male vocal / instrumental group (9 WEEKS)* pos/wks

8 Dec 79	**THE WALK** *Radar ADA 47*	**36**	9

INNER CIRCLE
Jamaica, male vocal / instrumental group (35 WEEKS)

pos/wks

24 Feb 79	EVERYTHING IS GREAT *Island WIP 6472*	37	8
12 May 79	STOP BREAKING MY HEART *Island WIP 6488*	50	3
31 Oct 92	SWEAT (A LA LA LA LA LONG) *Magnet 9031776802*	43	5
1 May 93 ●	SWEAT (A LA LA LA LA LONG) (re-entry) *Magnet 9031776802*	3	14
31 Jul 93	BAD BOYS *Magnet MAG 1017CD*	52	3
10 Sep 94	GAMES PEOPLE PLAY *Magnet MAG 1026CD*	67	2

INNER CITY (404 ＿Top 500) *House act from Detroit, US, formed by New York-born producer and club DJ Kevin Saunderson, b. 9 May 1964 which featured distinctive vocalist Paris Grey. Quickly became first house act to reach UK Top 10 with initial three hits (81 WEEKS)*

pos/wks

3 Sep 88 ●	BIG FUN *10 TEN 240* [1]	8	14
10 Dec 88 ●	GOOD LIFE *10 TEN 249*	4	12
22 Apr 89 ●	AIN'T NOBODY BETTER *10 TEN 252*	10	7
29 Jul 89	DO YOU LOVE WHAT YOU FEEL *10 TEN 273*	16	7
18 Nov 89	WATCHA GONNA DO WITH MY LOVIN' *10 TEN 290*	12	9
13 Oct 90	THAT MAN (HE'S ALL MINE) *10 TEN 334*	42	4
23 Feb 91	TILL WE MEET AGAIN *Ten TEN 337*	47	2
7 Dec 91	LET IT REIGN *Ten TEN 392*	51	2
4 Apr 92	HALLELUJAH '92 *Ten TEN 398*	22	4
13 Jun 92	PENNIES FROM HEAVEN *Ten TEN 405*	24	4
12 Sep 92	PRAISE *Ten TENX 408*	59	2
27 Feb 93	TILL WE MEET AGAIN (re-mix) *Ten TENCD 414*	55	1
14 Aug 93	BACK TOGETHER AGAIN *Six6 SIXCD 104*	49	1
5 Feb 94	DO YA *Six6 SIXCD 107*	44	2
9 Jul 94	SHARE MY LIFE *Six6 SIXCD 114*	62	1
10 Feb 96	YOUR LOVE *Six6 SIXCD 127*	28	2
5 Oct 96	DO ME RIGHT *Six6 SIXXCD 2*	47	1
6 Feb 99 ●	GOOD LIFE (BUENA VIDA) (re-recording) *Pias Recordings PIASX 002CD*	10	6

[1] Inner City featuring Kevin Saunderson

INNER SANCTUM *Canada, male producer - Steve Bolton (1 WEEK)* pos/wks

| 23 May 98 | HOW SOON IS NOW *Malarky MLKD 6* | 75 | 1 |

INNERZONE ORCHESTRA *US, male producer - Carl Craig (1 WEEK)* pos/wks

| 28 Sep 96 | BUG IN THE BASSBIN *Mo Wax MW 049CD* | 68 | 1 |

INNOCENCE *UK, male / female vocal / instrumental group (33 WEEKS)* pos/wks

3 Mar 90	NATURAL THING *Cooltempo COOL 201*	16	7
21 Jul 90	SILENT VOICE *Cooltempo COOL 212*	37	5
13 Oct 90	LET'S PUSH IT *Cooltempo COOL 220*	25	6
8 Dec 90	A MATTER OF FACT *Cooltempo COOL 223*	37	7
30 Mar 91	REMEMBER THE DAY *Cooltempo COOL 226*	56	2
20 Jun 92	I'LL BE THERE *Cooltempo COOL 255*	26	3
3 Oct 92	ONE LOVE IN MY LIFETIME *Cooltempo COOL 263*	40	2
21 Nov 92	BUILD *Cooltempo COOL 267*	72	1

INSANE CLOWN POSSE *US, male rap duo (2 WEEKS)* pos/wks

| 17 Jan 98 | HALLS OF ILLUSION *Island CID 685* | 56 | 1 |
| 6 Jun 98 | HOKUS POKUS *Island CIDX 705* | 53 | 1 |

INSPIRAL CARPETS *UK, male vocal / instrumental group (50 WEEKS)* pos/wks

18 Nov 89	MOVE *Cow DUNG 6*	49	2
17 Mar 90	THIS IS HOW IT FEELS *Cow DUNG 7*	14	8
30 Jun 90	SHE COMES IN THE FALL *Cow DUNG 10*	27	6
17 Nov 90	ISLAND HEAD (EP) *Cow DUNG 11*	21	4
30 Mar 91	CARAVAN *Cow DUNG 13*	30	5
22 Jun 91	PLEASE BE CRUEL *Cow DUNG 15*	50	2
29 Feb 92	DRAGGING ME DOWN *Cow DUNG 16*	12	5
30 May 92	TWO WORLDS COLLIDE *Cow DUNG 17*	32	2
19 Sep 92	GENERATIONS *Cow DUNG 18T*	28	3
14 Nov 92	BITCHES BREW *Cow DUNG 20T*	36	2
5 Jun 93	HOW IT SHOULD BE *Cow DUNG 22CD*	49	1
22 Jan 94	SATURN 5 *Cow DUNG 23CD*	20	4
5 Mar 94	I WANT YOU *Cow DUNG 24CD* [1]	18	3

| 7 May 94 | UNIFORM *Cow DUNG 26CD* | 51 | 1 |
| 16 Sep 95 | JOE *Cow DUNG 27CD* | 37 | 2 |

[1] Inspiral Carpets featuring Mark E Smith

Tracks on Island Head (EP): Biggest Mountain / Gold Top / Weakness / I'll Keep It In Mind

INSPIRATIONAL CHOIR *US, male / female choir (11 WEEKS)* pos/wks

| 22 Dec 84 | ABIDE WITH ME *Epic A 4997* | 44 | 5 |
| 14 Dec 85 | ABIDE WITH ME (re-issue) *Portrait A 4997* | 36 | 6 |

Label credits the Royal Choral Society

INSTANT FUNK *US, male vocal / instrumental group (5 WEEKS)* pos/wks

| 20 Jan 79 | GOT MY MIND MADE UP *Salsoul SSOL 114* | 46 | 5 |

INTASTELLA
UK, male / female vocal / instrumental group (6 WEEKS) pos/wks

25 May 91	DREAM SOME PARADISE *MCA MCS 1520*	69	1
24 Aug 91	PEOPLE *MCA MCS 1559*	74	2
16 Nov 91	CENTURY *MCA MCS 1585*	70	2
23 Sep 95	THE NIGHT *Planet 3 GXY 2005CD*	60	1

INTELLIGENT HOODLUM *US, male rapper (3 WEEKS)* pos/wks

| 6 Oct 90 | BACK TO REALITY *A & M AM 598* | 55 | 3 |

INTERACTIVE
Germany, male instrumental / production group (4 WEEKS) pos/wks

| 13 Apr 96 | FOREVER YOUNG *Ffrreedom TABCD 235* | 28 | 4 |

INTRUDERS *US, male vocal group (21 WEEKS)* pos/wks

13 Apr 74	I'LL ALWAYS LOVE MY MAMA *Philadelphia International PIR 2159*	32	7
6 Jul 74	WIN PLACE OR SHOW (SHE'S A WINNER) *Philadelphia International PIR 2212*	14	9
22 Dec 84	WHO DO YOU LOVE? *Streetwave KHAN 34*	65	5

INVADERS OF THE HEART – See Jah WOBBLE'S INVADERS of the HEART

INVISIBLE GIRLS – See Pauline MURRAY and the INVISIBLE GIRLS

INVISIBLE MAN *UK, male producer - Graham Mew (1 WEEK)* pos/wks

| 17 Apr 99 | GIVE A LITTLE LOVE *Serious SERR 006CD* | 48 | 1 |

INXS (220 ＿Top 500) *Stadium-packing rock sextet led by Australian Michael Hutchence (b. 12 Jan 1962, Sydney; d. 22 Nov 1997). Both Hutchence and group won Brit awards in 1991, and the video for their US chart-topper, 'Need You Tonight' won five MTV awards in 1988 (121 WEEKS)*

pos/wks

19 Apr 86	WHAT YOU NEED *Mercury INXS 5*	51	6
28 Jun 86	LISTEN LIKE THIEVES *Mercury INXS 6*	46	7
30 Aug 86	KISS THE DIRT (FALLING DOWN THE MOUNTAIN) *Mercury INXS 7*	54	3
24 Oct 87	NEED YOU TONIGHT *Mercury INXS 8* ▲	58	3
9 Jan 88	NEW SENSATION *Mercury INXS 9*	25	6
12 Mar 88	DEVIL INSIDE *Mercury INXS 10*	47	5
25 Jun 88	NEVER TEAR US APART *Mecury INXS 11*	24	7
12 Nov 88 ●	NEED YOU TONIGHT (re-issue) *Mercury INXS 12*	2	11
8 Apr 89	MYSTIFY *Mercury INXS 13*	14	7
15 Sep 90	SUICIDE BLONDE *Mercury INXS 14*	11	6
8 Dec 90	DISAPPEAR *Mercury INXS 15*	21	8
26 Jan 91	GOOD TIMES *Atlantic A 7751* [1]	18	8
30 Mar 91	BY MY SIDE *Mercury INXS 16*	42	4
13 Jul 91	BITTER TEARS *Mercury INXS 17*	30	3
2 Nov 91	SHINING STAR (EP) *Mercury INXS 18*	27	3
18 Jul 92	HEAVEN SENT *Mercury INXS 19*	31	3
5 Sep 92	BABY DON'T CRY *Mercury INXS 20*	20	5
14 Nov 92	TASTE IT *Mercury INXS 23*	21	4
13 Feb 93	BEAUTIFUL GIRL *Mercury INXCD 24*	23	5
23 Oct 93	THE GIFT *Mercury INXCD 25*	11	4
11 Dec 93	PLEASE (YOU GOT THAT . . .) *Mercury INXCD 26*	50	3

UK No.1 ★   UK Top 10 ●   Still on chart +   UK million seller ◆   UK entry at No.1 ■   US No.1 ▲

22 Oct 94	THE STRANGEST PARTY (THESE ARE THE TIMES)				
	Mercury INXCD 27			**15**	5
22 Mar 97	ELEGANTLY WASTED Mercury INXCD 28			**20**	4
7 Jun 97	EVERYTHING Mercury INXDD 29			**71**	1

[1] Jimmy Barnes and INXS

Tracks on Shining Star (EP): Shining Star / Send a Message (Live) / Faith in Each Other (Live) / Bitter Tears (Live). Although uncredited, 'Please (You Got That...)' is a duet with Ray Charles

Sweetie IRIE – See ASWAD; SCRITTI POLITTI

Tippa IRIE UK, male vocalist (14 WEEKS) pos/wks

22 Mar 86	HELLO DARLING Greensleeves / UK Bubblers TIPPA 4	**22**	7
19 Jul 86	HEARTBEAT Greensleeves / UK Bubblers TIPPA 5	**59**	3
15 May 93	SHOUTING FOR THE GUNNERS London LONCD 342 [1]	**34**	3
8 Jul 95	STAYING ALIVE 95 Telstar CDSTAS 2776 [2]	**48**	1

[1] Arsenal FA Cup Squad featuring Tippa Irie and Peter Hunnigale [2] Fever featuring Tippa Irie

IRON MAIDEN (137 Top 500) Legendary London-based group named after a medieval torture device. Lead vocalists have included Paul Di'Anno and Blaze Bayley, but it was with frontman Bruce Dickinson that they enjoyed a period as arguably the world's top metal band (154 WEEKS) pos/wks

23 Feb 80	RUNNING FREE EMI 5032	**34**	5
7 Jun 80	SANCTUARY EMI 5065	**29**	5
8 Nov 80	WOMEN IN UNIFORM EMI 5105	**35**	4
14 Mar 81	TWILIGHT ZONE / WRATH CHILD EMI 5145	**31**	5
27 Jun 81	PURGATORY EMI 5184	**52**	3
26 Sep 81	MAIDEN JAPAN EMI 5219	**43**	4
20 Feb 82 ●	RUN TO THE HILLS EMI 5263	**7**	10
15 May 82	THE NUMBER OF THE BEAST EMI 5287	**18**	8
23 Apr 83	FLIGHT OF ICARUS EMI 5378	**11**	6
2 Jul 83	THE TROOPER EMI 5397	**12**	7
18 Aug 84	2 MINUTES TO MIDNIGHT EMI 5849	**11**	6
3 Nov 84	ACES HIGH EMI 5502	**20**	5
5 Oct 85	RUNNING FREE (LIVE) EMI 5532	**19**	5
14 Dec 85	RUN TO THE HILLS (LIVE) EMI 5542	**26**	6
6 Sep 86	WASTED YEARS EMI 5583	**18**	4
22 Nov 86	STRANGER IN A STRANGE LAND EMI 5589	**22**	4
27 Dec 86	STRANGER IN A STRANGE LAND (re-entry) EMI 5589	**71**	2
26 Mar 88 ●	CAN I PLAY WITH MADNESS EMI EM 49	**3**	6
13 Aug 88 ●	THE EVIL THAT MEN DO EMI EM 64	**5**	6
19 Nov 88 ●	THE CLAIRVOYANT EMI EM 79	**6**	8
18 Nov 89 ●	INFINITE DREAMS EMI EM 117	**6**	5
30 Dec 89	INFINITE DREAMS (re-entry) EMI EM 117	**74**	1
22 Sep 90 ●	HOLY SMOKE EMI EM 153	**3**	4
5 Jan 91 ★	BRING YOUR DAUGHTER . . . TO THE SLAUGHTER		
	EMI EMPD 171 ■	**1**	5
25 Apr 92 ●	BE QUICK OR BE DEAD EMI EM 229	**2**	4
11 Jul 92	FROM HERE TO ETERNITY EMI EMS 240	**21**	4
13 Mar 93 ●	FEAR OF THE DARK (LIVE) EMI CDEMS 263	**8**	3
16 Oct 93 ●	HALLOWED BE THY NAME (LIVE) EMI CDEM 288	**9**	3
7 Oct 95 ●	MAN ON THE EDGE EMI CDEMS 398	**10**	3
21 Sep 96	VIRUS EMI CDEM 443	**16**	3
21 Mar 98	THE ANGEL AND THE GAMBLER EMI CDEM 507	**18**	3
20 May 00 ●	THE WICKER MAN EMI CDEMS 568	**9**	4
4 Nov 00	OUT OF THE SILENT PLANET EMI CDEM 576	**20**	3

IRONHORSE Canada, male vocal / instrumental group (3 WEEKS) pos/wks

5 May 79	SWEET LUI-LOUISE Scotti Brothers K 11271	**60**	3

Big Dee IRWIN US, male vocalist - Difosco Erwin (17 WEEKS) pos/wks

21 Nov 63 ●	SWINGING ON A STAR Colpix PX 11010	**7**	17

Single was a vocal duet by Big Dee Irwin and Little Eva (uncredited)

Chris ISAAK US, male vocalist (22 WEEKS) pos/wks

24 Nov 90 ●	WICKED GAME London LON 279	**10**	10
2 Feb 91	BLUE HOTEL Reprise W 0005	**17**	7
3 Apr 93	CAN'T DO A THING (TO STOP ME) Reprise W 0161CD	**36**	3
10 Jul 93	SAN FRANCISCO DAYS Reprise W 0182CD	**62**	1

2 Oct 99	BABY DID A BAD BAD THING Reprise W 503CD	**44**	1

ISHA-D UK, male / female vocal / instrumental duo (4 WEEKS) pos/wks

22 Jul 95	STAY (TONIGHT)		
	Cleveland City Blues CCBCD 15005	**28**	3
5 Jul 97	STAY (re-issue) Satellite 74321498212	**58**	1

Ronald ISLEY – See ISLEY BROTHERS; Rod STEWART; R KELLY; Warren G

ISLEY BROTHERS (267 Top 500) Cincinnati brothers who have had five decades of US hits: Ronald, O'Kelly (d. 1986) and Rudolph Isley. These influential singers / songwriters / producers and label-owners penned pop anthem 'Shout', and have remained at cutting edge of R&B for 40 years (108 WEEKS) pos/wks

25 Jul 63	TWIST AND SHOUT Stateside SS 112	**42**	1
28 Apr 66	THIS OLD HEART OF MINE Tamla Motown TMG 555	**47**	1
1 Sep 66	I GUESS I'LL ALWAYS LOVE YOU		
	Tamla Motown TMG 572	**45**	2
23 Oct 68 ●	THIS OLD HEART OF MINE (re-entry)		
	Tamla Motown TMG 555	**3**	16
15 Jan 69	I GUESS I'LL ALWAYS LOVE YOU (re-issue)		
	Tamla Motown TMG 683	**11**	9
16 Apr 69 ●	BEHIND A PAINTED SMILE		
	Tamla Motown TMG 693	**5**	12
25 Jun 69	IT'S YOUR THING Major Minor MM 621	**30**	5
30 Aug 69	PUT YOURSELF IN MY PLACE		
	Tamla Motown TMG 708	**13**	11
22 Sep 73	THAT LADY Epic EPC 1704	**14**	9
19 Jan 74	HIGHWAYS OF MY LIFE Epic EPC 1980	**25**	8
25 May 74	SUMMER BREEZE Epic EPC 2244	**16**	8
10 Jul 76 ●	HARVEST FOR THE WORLD Epic EPC 4369	**10**	8
13 May 78	TAKE ME TO THE NEXT PHASE Epic EPC 6292	**50**	4
3 Nov 79	IT'S A DISCO NIGHT (ROCK DON'T STOP)		
	Epic EPC 7911	**14**	11
16 Jul 83	BETWEEN THE SHEETS Epic A 3513	**52**	3

ISLEY JASPER ISLEY US, male vocal / instrumental group (5 WEEKS) pos/wks

23 Nov 85	CARAVAN OF LOVE Epic A 6612	**52**	5

ISOTONIK UK, male producer - Chris Paul (9 WEEKS) pos/wks

11 Jan 92	DIFFERENT STROKES Ffrreedom TAB 101	**12**	5
2 May 92	EVERYWHERE I GO / LET'S GET DOWN		
	Ffrreedom TAB 108	**25**	4

'Let's Get Down' listed only from 9 May 1992

See also Chris PAUL

IT BITES UK, male vocal / instrumental group (21 WEEKS) pos/wks

12 Jul 86 ●	CALLING ALL THE HEROES Virgin VS 872	**6**	12
18 Oct 86	WHOLE NEW WORLD Virgin VS 896	**54**	3
23 May 87	THE OLD MAN AND THE ANGEL Virgin VS 941	**72**	1
13 May 89	STILL TOO YOUNG TO REMEMBER Virgin VS 1184	**66**	3
24 Feb 90	STILL TOO YOUNG TO REMEMBER (re-issue)		
	Virgin VS 1238	**60**	2

IT'S IMMATERIAL UK, male vocal / instrumental group (10 WEEKS) pos/wks

12 Apr 86	DRIVING AWAY FROM HOME (JIM'S TUNE)		
	Siren SIREN 15	**18**	7
2 Aug 86	ED'S FUNKY DINER (FRIDAY NIGHT, SATURDAY MORNING) Siren SIREN 24	**65**	3

ITTY BITTY BOOZY WOOZY
Holland, male instrumental / production duo (2 WEEKS) pos/wks

25 Nov 95	TEMPO FIESTA (PARTY TIME) Systematic SYSCD 23	**34**	2

Duo also known as Klubbheads

Burl IVES US, male vocalist (25 WEEKS) pos/wks

25 Jan 62 ●	A LITTLE BITTY TEAR Brunswick 05863	**9**	15
17 May 62	FUNNY WAY OF LAUGHIN' Brunswick 05868	**29**	10

IVY LEAGUE *UK, male vocal group (31 WEEKS)*   pos/wks

4 Feb 65	●	FUNNY HOW LOVE CAN BE *Piccadilly 7N 35222*	**8** 9
6 May 65		THAT'S WHY I'M CRYING *Piccadilly 7N 35228*	**22** 8
24 Jun 65	●	TOSSING AND TURNING *Piccadilly 7N 35251*	**3** 13
14 Jul 66		WILLOW TREE *Piccadilly 7N 35326*	**50** 1

IZIT *UK, male / female vocal / instrumental group (3 WEEKS)*   pos/wks

2 Dec 89	STORIES *ffrr F 122*	**52** 3

J

Ray J *US, male vocalist (1 WEEK)*   pos/wks

17 Oct 98	THAT'S WHY I LIE *Atlantic AT 0049CD*	**71** 1

J PAC *UK, male vocal / instrumental duo (2 WEEKS)*   pos/wks

22 Jul 95	ROCK 'N' ROLL (DOLE) *East West YZ 953CD*	**51** 2

JA RULE – See JAY-Z

JACK 'N' CHILL *UK, male instrumental group (21 WEEKS)*   pos/wks

6 Jun 87		THE JACK THAT HOUSE BUILT *Oval / 10 / Virgin TEN 174*	**48** 5
9 Jan 88	●	THE JACK THAT HOUSE BUILT (re-entry) *Oval / 10 / Virgin TEN 174*	**6** 11
9 Jul 88		BEATIN' THE HEAT *10 TEN 234*	**42** 5

Terry JACKS *Canada, male vocalist (21 WEEKS)*   pos/wks

23 Mar 74	★	SEASONS IN THE SUN *Bell 1344* ◆	**1** 12
29 Jun 74	●	IF YOU GO AWAY *Bell 1362*	**8** 9

See also POPPY FAMILY

Chad JACKSON
UK, male DJ / producer - Mark Chadwick (10 WEEKS)   pos/wks

2 Jun 90	●	HEAR THE DRUMMER (GET WICKED) *Big Wave BWR 36*	**3** 10

Dee D JACKSON *UK, female vocalist - Deirdre Cozier (14 WEEKS)*   pos/wks

22 Apr 78	●	AUTOMATIC LOVER *Mercury 6007 171*	**4** 9
2 Sep 78		METEOR MAN *Mercury 6007 182*	**48** 5

Freddie JACKSON *US, male vocalist (31 WEEKS)*   pos/wks

23 Nov 85	YOU ARE MY LADY *Capitol CL 379*	**49** 4
22 Feb 86	ROCK ME TONIGHT (FOR OLD TIME'S SAKE) *Capitol CL 358*	**18** 9
11 Oct 86	TASTY LOVE *Capitol CL 428*	**73** 1
7 Feb 87	HAVE YOU EVER LOVED SOMEBODY *Capitol CL 437*	**33** 6
9 Jul 88	NICE 'N' SLOW *Capitol CL 502*	**56** 2
15 Oct 88	CRAZY (FOR ME) *Capitol CL 510*	**41** 3
5 Sep 92	ME AND MRS JONES *Capitol CL 668*	**32** 5
15 Jan 94	MAKE LOVE EASY *RCA 74321179162*	**70** 1

Gisele JACKSON *US, female vocalist (1 WEEK)*   pos/wks

30 Aug 97	LOVE COMMANDMENTS *Manifesto FESCD 28*	**54** 1

Janet JACKSON `41` **Top 500** *Multi-award-winning, record-breaking vocalist / performer, b. 16 May 1966, Indiana, US. Although not an overnight sensation, the youngest of the talented Jackson family became one of the world's biggest-selling recording artists and has amassed a staggering collection of gold albums and singles (256 WEEKS)*   pos/wks

22 Mar 86	●	WHAT HAVE YOU DONE FOR ME LATELY *A & M AM 308*	**3** 14
31 May 86		NASTY *A & M AM 316*	**19** 9
9 Aug 86	●	WHEN I THINK OF YOU *A & M AM 337* ▲	**10** 10

1 Nov 86		CONTROL *A & M AM 359*	**42** 5
21 Mar 87	●	LET'S WAIT AWHILE *Breakout USA 601*	**3** 10
13 Jun 87		PLEASURE PRINCIPLE *Breakout USA 604*	**24** 5
14 Nov 87		FUNNY HOW TIME FLIES (WHEN YOU'RE HAVING FUN) *A&M Breakout USA 613*	**59** 2
2 Sep 89	●	MISS YOU MUCH *Breakout USA 663* ▲	**22** 5
4 Nov 89		RHYTHM NATION *Breakout USA 673*	**23** 5
27 Jan 90		COME BACK TO ME *Breakout USA 681*	**20** 7
31 Mar 90		ESCAPADE *Breakout USA 684* ▲	**17** 7
7 Jul 90		ALRIGHT *A & M USA 693*	**20** 5
8 Sep 90		BLACK CAT *A & M AM 587* ▲	**15** 6
27 Oct 90		LOVE WILL NEVER DO (WITHOUT YOU) *A & M AM 700* ▲	**34** 4
15 Aug 92	●	THE BEST THINGS IN LIFE ARE FREE *Perspective PERSS 7400* [1]	**2** 13
8 May 93	●	THAT'S THE WAY LOVE GOES *Virgin VSCDG 1460* ▲	**2** 10
31 Jul 93		IF *Virgin VSCDT 1474*	**14** 7
20 Nov 93	●	AGAIN *Virgin VSCDG 1481* ▲	**6** 11
12 Mar 94		BECAUSE OF LOVE *Virgin VSCDG 1488*	**19** 4
18 Jun 94		ANY TIME ANY PLACE *Virgin VSCDT 1501*	**13** 5
26 Nov 94		YOU WANT THIS *Virgin VSCDT 1519*	**14** 3
18 Mar 95	●	WHOOPS NOW / WHAT'LL I DO *Virgin VSCDT 1533*	**9** 8
10 Jun 95	●	SCREAM *Epic 6620222* [2]	**3** 12
24 Jun 95		SCREAM (re-mix) *Epic 6621277* [2]	**43** 2
23 Sep 95	●	RUNAWAY *A & M 5811972*	**6** 7
2 Dec 95		SCREAM (re-entry) *Epic 6620222* [2]	**72** 1
16 Dec 95	●	THE BEST THINGS IN LIFE ARE FREE (re-mix) *A & M 5813092* [3]	**7** 7
6 Apr 96		TWENTY FOREPLAY *A & M 5815112*	**22** 4
4 Oct 97	●	GOT 'TIL IT'S GONE *Virgin VSCDG 1666* [4]	**6** 9
13 Dec 97	●	TOGETHER AGAIN *Virgin VSCDG 1670*	**4** 19
4 Apr 98	●	I GET LONELY *Virgin VSCDT 1683* [5]	**5** 7
27 Jun 98		GO DEEP *Virgin VSCDT 1680*	**13** 5
19 Dec 98		EVERY TIME *Virgin VSCDT 1720*	**46** 1
17 Apr 99		GIRLFRIEND / BOYFRIEND *Interscope IND 95640* [6]	**11** 7
1 May 99	●	WHAT'S IT GONNA BE?! *Elektra E3762CD1* [7]	**6** 7
19 Aug 00	●	DOESN'T REALLY MATTER *Def Soul 5629152* ▲	**5** 11

[1] Luther Vandross and Janet Jackson with special guests BBD and Ralph Tresvant [2] Michael Jackson and Janet Jackson [3] Luther Vandross and Janet Jackson [4] Janet featuring Q-Tip and Joni Mitchell [5] Janet featuring BLACKstreet [6] BLACKstreet with Janet [7] Busta Rhymes Featuring Janet

See also Herb ALPERT

Jermaine JACKSON *US, male vocalist (43 WEEKS)*   pos/wks

10 May 80	●	LET'S GET SERIOUS *Motown TMG 1183*	**8** 11
26 Jul 80		BURNIN' HOT *Motown TMG 1194*	**32** 6
30 May 81		YOU LIKE ME DON'T YOU *Motown TMG 1222*	**41** 5
12 May 84		SWEETEST SWEETEST *Arista JJK 1*	**52** 4
27 Oct 84		WHEN THE RAIN BEGINS TO FALL *Arista ARIST 584* [1]	**68** 2
16 Feb 85	●	DO WHAT YOU DO *Arista ARIST 609*	**6** 13
21 Oct 89		DON'T TAKE IT PERSONAL *Arista 112634*	**69** 2

[1] Jermaine Jackson and Pia Zadora

See also JACKSONS

Joe JACKSON *UK, male vocalist (49 WEEKS)*   pos/wks

4 Aug 79	IS SHE REALLY GOING OUT WITH HIM? *A & M AMS 7459*	**13** 9
12 Jan 80	IT'S DIFFERENT FOR GIRLS *A & M AMS 7493*	**5** 9
4 Jul 81	JUMPIN' JIVE *A & M AMS 8145* [1]	**43** 5
8 Jan 83	STEPPIN' OUT *A & M AMS 8262*	**6** 8
12 Mar 83	BREAKING US IN TWO *A & M AM 101*	**59** 4
28 Apr 84	HAPPY ENDING *A & M AM 186*	**58** 3
7 Jul 84	BE MY NUMBER TWO *A & M AM 200*	**70** 2
7 Jun 86	LEFT OF CENTER *A & M AM 320* [2]	**32** 9

[1] Joe Jackson's Jumpin' Jive [2] Suzanne Vega featuring Joe Jackson

UK No.1 ★   UK Top 10 ●   Still on chart +   UK million seller ◆   UK entry at No.1 ■   US No.1 ▲

Michael JACKSON `7` `Top 500` *The self-proclaimed "King of Pop" b. 29 Aug 1958, Indiana, US, is arguably the best known living musical entertainer. The youngest vocalist (age 11, fronting the Jackson Five) to top the US singles chart, he was also the first artist to enter that chart at No.1 (with 'You Are Not Alone'). In 1991 he became the first US act to enter the UK chart at No.1 since Elvis Presley in 1960 (whose daughter, Lisa Marie, he married in 1994). This outstanding, innovative singer / songwriter and performer has broken countless other records for his singles, albums, videos and tours. 'Thriller' is the world's biggest-selling record with global sales of more than 47 million, including an unbeaten 26 million in the US. It topped the US album chart for an unprecedented 37 weeks and had a record 12 Grammy nominations. Also on the album front, 'Bad' was the first LP to enter both the UK and US chart at No.1; 'History' sold more copies in its first week than any previous double album, and 'Dangerous' sold a staggering 10 million world-wide in its first month. Both 'Thriller' and 'Bad' have sold more than 3 million copies in the UK. Jackson, whose private life and physical appearance have attracted much media attention, was the first entertainer to earn more than $100 million in a year, and the first to receive an award for selling at least 100 million albums outside of the US (480 WEEKS)* pos/wks

			pos	wks
12 Feb 72	●	GOT TO BE THERE *Tamla Motown TMG 797*	5	11
20 May 72	●	ROCKIN' ROBIN *Tamla Motown TMG 816*	3	14
19 Aug 72	●	AIN'T NO SUNSHINE *Tamla Motown TMG 826*	8	11
25 Nov 72	●	BEN *Tamla Motown TMG 834* ▲	7	14
18 Nov 78		EASE ON DOWN THE ROAD *MCA 396* [1]	45	4
15 Sep 79	●	DON'T STOP 'TIL YOU GET ENOUGH *Epic EPC 7763* ▲	3	12
24 Nov 79	●	OFF THE WALL *Epic EPC 8045*	7	10
9 Feb 80	●	ROCK WITH YOU *Epic EPC 8206* ▲	7	9
3 May 80	●	SHE'S OUT OF MY LIFE *Epic EPC 8384*	3	9
26 Jul 80		GIRLFRIEND *Epic EPC 8782*	41	5
23 May 81	★	ONE DAY IN YOUR LIFE *Motown TMG 976*	1	14
1 Aug 81		WE'RE ALMOST THERE *Motown TMG 977*	46	4
6 Nov 82	●	THE GIRL IS MINE *Epic EPC A 2729* [2]	8	9
15 Jan 83		THE GIRL IS MINE (re-entry) *Epic EPC A 2729* [2]	75	1
29 Jan 83	★	BILLIE JEAN *Epic EPC A 3084* ▲	1	15
9 Apr 83	●	BEAT IT *Epic EPC A 3258* ▲	3	12
11 Jun 83	●	WANNA BE STARTIN' SOMETHIN' *Epic EPC A 3427*	8	9
23 Jul 83		HAPPY (LOVE THEME FROM 'LADY SINGS THE BLUES') *Tamla Motown TMG 986*	52	3
15 Oct 83	●	SAY SAY SAY *Parlophone R 6062* [3] ▲	2	15
19 Nov 83	●	THRILLER *Epic A 3643*	10	18
31 Mar 84		P.Y.T. (PRETTY YOUNG THING) *Epic A 4136*	11	8
2 Jun 84	●	FAREWELL MY SUMMER LOVE *Motown TMG 1342*	7	12
11 Aug 84		GIRL YOU'RE SO TOGETHER *Motown TMG 1355*	33	8
8 Aug 87	★	I JUST CAN'T STOP LOVING YOU *Epic 650202 7* ▲	1	9
26 Sep 87	●	BAD *Epic 651155 7* ▲	3	11
5 Dec 87	●	THE WAY YOU MAKE ME FEEL *Epic 651275 7* ▲	3	10
20 Feb 88		MAN IN THE MIRROR *Epic 651388 7* ▲	21	5
28 May 88		GET IT *Motown ZB 41883* [4]	37	4
16 Jul 88	●	DIRTY DIANA *Epic 651546 7* ▲	4	8
10 Sep 88		ANOTHER PART OF ME *Epic 652844 7*	15	6
26 Nov 88	●	SMOOTH CRIMINAL *Epic 653026 7*	8	10
25 Feb 89	●	LEAVE ME ALONE *Epic 654672 7*	2	9
15 Jul 89		LIBERIAN GIRL *Epic 654947 0*	13	6
23 Nov 91	★	BLACK OR WHITE *Epic 6575987* ■ ▲	1	10
18 Jan 92		BLACK OR WHITE (re-mix) *Epic 6577316*	14	4
15 Feb 92	●	REMEMBER THE TIME / COME TOGETHER *Epic 6577747*	3	8
2 May 92	●	IN THE CLOSET *Epic 6580187*	8	6
25 Jul 92	●	WHO IS IT *Epic 6581797*	10	7
12 Sep 92		JAM *Epic 6583607*	13	5
5 Dec 92	●	HEAL THE WORLD *Epic 6584887*	2	15
27 Feb 93	●	GIVE IN TO ME *Epic 6590692*	2	9
10 Jul 93	●	WILL YOU BE THERE *Epic 6592222*	9	8
18 Dec 93		GONE TOO SOON *Epic 6599762*	33	5
10 Jun 95	●	SCREAM *Epic 6620222* [5]	3	12
24 Jun 95		SCREAM (re-mix) *Epic 6621277* [5]	43	2
2 Sep 95	★	YOU ARE NOT ALONE *Epic 6623102* ▲	1	15
2 Dec 95		SCREAM (re-entry) *Epic 6620222* [5]	72	1
9 Dec 95	★	EARTH SONG *Epic 6626955* ◆ ■	1	17
20 Apr 96	●	THEY DON'T CARE ABOUT US *Epic 6629502*	4	12
3 Aug 96		THEY DON'T CARE ABOUT US (re-entry) *Epic 6629502*	66	1
17 Aug 96		THEY DON'T CARE ABOUT US (2nd re-entry) *Epic 6629502*	66	1
24 Aug 96	●	WHY *Epic 6629502* [6]	2	9
16 Nov 96	●	STRANGER IN MOSCOW *Epic 6637872*	4	10
1 Mar 97		STRANGER IN MOSCOW (re-entry) *Epic 6637872*	69	1
3 May 97	★	BLOOD ON THE DANCEFLOOR *Epic 6644625* ■	1	9
19 Jul 97	●	HISTORY / GHOSTS *Epic 6647962*	5	8

[1] Diana Ross and Michael Jackson [2] Michael Jackson and Paul McCartney [3] Paul McCartney and Michael Jackson [4] Stevie Wonder and Michael Jackson [5] Michael Jackson and Janet Jackson [6] 3T featuring Michael Jackson

The sleeve of 'I Just Can't Stop Loving You' credits Siedah Garrett but the label does not. 'Come Together' was listed only from 7 Mar 1992. It peaked at No.10

Mick JACKSON *UK, male vocalist (16 WEEKS)* pos/wks

			pos	wks
30 Sep 78		BLAME IT ON THE BOOGIE *Atlantic K 11102*	15	8
3 Feb 79		WEEKEND *Atlantic K 11224*	38	8

Millie JACKSON *US, female vocalist (8 WEEKS)* pos/wks

			pos	wks
18 Nov 72		MY MAN A SWEET MAN *Mojo 2093 022*	50	1
10 Mar 84		I FEEL LIKE WALKIN' IN THE RAIN *Sire W 9348*	55	2
15 Jun 85		ACT OF WAR *Rocket EJS 8* [1]	32	5

[1] Elton John and Millie Jackson

JACKSON SISTERS *US, female vocal group (2 WEEKS)* pos/wks

			pos	wks
20 Jun 87		I BELIEVE IN MIRACLES *Urban URB 4*	72	2

Stonewall JACKSON *US, male vocalist (2 WEEKS)* pos/wks

			pos	wks
17 Jul 59		WATERLOO *Philips PB 941*	24	2

Tony JACKSON – See Q

Tony JACKSON and the VIBRATIONS
UK, male vocal / instrumental group (3 WEEKS) pos/wks

			pos	wks
8 Oct 64		BYE BYE BABY *Pye 7N 15685*	38	3

See also SEARCHERS

Wanda JACKSON *US, female vocalist (11 WEEKS)* pos/wks

			pos	wks
1 Sep 60		LET'S HAVE A PARTY *Capitol CL 15147*	32	8
26 Jan 61		MEAN MEAN MAN *Capitol CL 15176*	46	1
9 Feb 61		MEAN MEAN MAN (re-entry) *Capitol CL 15176*	40	2

JACKSONS `55` `Top 500` *One of the world's biggest-selling and most popular groups: brothers Jackie, Tito, Jermaine, Marlon and solo superstar Michael Jackson, with Randy joining in 1977. The Indiana quintet topped the US chart with their first four hits, and have reportedly sold more than 100 million records (235 WEEKS)* pos/wks

			pos	wks
31 Jan 70	●	I WANT YOU BACK *Tamla Motown TMG 724* [1] ▲	2	13
16 May 70	●	ABC *Tamla Motown TMG 738* [1] ▲	8	11
1 Aug 70	●	THE LOVE YOU SAVE *Tamla Motown TMG 746* [1] ▲	7	9
21 Nov 70	●	I'LL BE THERE *Tamla Motown TMG 758* [1] ▲	4	16
10 Apr 71		MAMA'S PEARL *Tamla Motown TMG 769*	25	7
17 Jul 71		NEVER CAN SAY GOODBYE *Tamla Motown TMG 778* [1]	33	7
11 Nov 72	●	LOOKIN' THROUGH THE WINDOWS *Tamla Motown TMG 833* [1]	9	11
23 Dec 72		SANTA CLAUS IS COMING TO TOWN *Tamla Motown TMG 837* [1]	43	3
17 Feb 73	●	DOCTOR MY EYES *Tamla Motown TMG 842* [1]	9	10
9 Jun 73		HALLELUJAH DAY *Tamla Motown TMG 856* [1]	20	9
8 Sep 73		SKYWRITER *Tamla Motown TMG 865* [1]	25	8
9 Apr 77		ENJOY YOURSELF *Epic EPC 5063*	42	4
4 Jun 77	★	SHOW YOU THE WAY TO GO *Epic EPC 5266*	1	10
13 Aug 77		DREAMER *Epic EPC 5458*	22	9
5 Nov 77		GOIN' PLACES *Epic EPC 5732*	26	7
11 Feb 78		EVEN THOUGH YOU'VE GONE *Epic EPC 5919*	31	4
23 Sep 78	●	BLAME IT ON THE BOOGIE *Epic EPC 6683*	8	12
3 Feb 79		DESTINY *Epic EPC 6983*	39	6
24 Mar 79	●	SHAKE YOUR BODY (DOWN TO THE GROUND) *Epic EPC 7181*	4	12
25 Oct 80		LOVELY ONE *Epic EPC 9302*	29	6
13 Dec 80		HEARTBREAK HOTEL *Epic EPC 9391*	44	6

SINGLED OUT...
Craig David

Southampton's finest struck gold with his wholly British take on nu-soul, equally happy dropping vocals over a two-step beat or an R&B groove. Citing Terence Trent D'Arby, Michael Jackson and Stevie Wonder as influences, and with superstars such as Puff Daddy and Jennifer Lopez buzzing his pager with offers of a rendezvous, the boy wonder looks as if he'll succeed where Robbie failed in the US – Brits or no Brits.

FIRST SINGLE I EVER BOUGHT:
Leave Me Alone – Michael Jackson

- **NUMBER ONE ON THE UK SINGLES CHART THE DAY I WAS BORN:**
  Stand And Deliver – Adam and the Ants

- **ALL-TIME FAVOURITE SINGLE:**
  Nice And Slow – Usher

28 Feb 81	●	CAN YOU FEEL IT *Epic EPC 9554*	6	15
4 Jul 81	●	WALK RIGHT NOW *Epic EPC A 1294*	7	11
7 Jul 84		STATE OF SHOCK *Epic A 4431* [2]	14	8
8 Sep 84		TORTURE *Epic A 4675*	26	6
16 Apr 88	●	I WANT YOU BACK (re-mix) *Motown ZB 41913* [3]	8	9
13 May 89		NOTHIN' (THAT COMPARES 2 U) *Epic 654808 7*	33	6

[1] Jackson Five [2] Jacksons, lead vocals Mick Jagger and Michael Jackson [3] Michael Jackson with the Jackson Five

JACKY – See Jackie LEE

JACQUELINE – See MACK VIBE featuring JACQUELINE

JADA – See SKIP RAIDERS featuring JADA

JADE *US, female vocal group (28 WEEKS)* pos/wks

20 Mar 93	●	DON'T WALK AWAY *Giant W 0160CD*	7	8
3 Jul 93		I WANNA LOVE YOU *Giant 74321151662*	13	7
18 Sep 93		ONE WOMAN *Giant 74321165122*	22	5
5 Feb 94		ALL THRU THE NITE *Giant 74321187552*	32	3
11 Feb 95		EVERY DAY OF THE WEEK *Giant 74321260242*	19	5

JADE 4 U – See Praga KHAN

JAGGED EDGE *UK, male vocal / instrumental group (2 WEEKS)* pos/wks

15 Sep 90		YOU DON'T LOVE ME *Polydor PO 97*	66	2

Mick JAGGER *UK, male vocalist (42 WEEKS)* pos/wks

14 Nov 70		MEMO FROM TURNER *Decca F 13067*	32	5
7 Jul 84		STATE OF SHOCK *Epic A 4431* [1]	14	8
16 Feb 85		JUST ANOTHER NIGHT *CBS A 4722*	32	6
7 Sep 85	★	DANCING IN THE STREET *EMI America EA 204* [2] ■	1	12
12 Sep 87		LET'S WORK *CBS 651028 7*	31	7
6 Feb 93		SWEET THING *Atlantic A 7410CD*	24	4

[1] Jacksons, lead vocals Mick Jagger and Michael Jackson [2] David Bowie and Mick Jagger

See also ROLLING STONES

JAGS *UK, male vocal / instrumental group (11 WEEKS)* pos/wks

8 Sep 79		BACK OF MY HAND *Island WIP 6501*	17	10
2 Feb 80		WOMAN'S WORLD *Island WIP 6531*	75	1

JALN BAND
UK / Jamaica, male vocal / instrumental group (17 WEEKS) pos/wks

11 Sep 76		DISCO MUSIC (I LIKE IT) *Magnet MAG 73*	21	9
27 Aug 77		I GOT TO SING *Magnet MAG 97*	40	4
1 Jul 78		GET UP *Magnet MAG 118*	53	4

JAM `83` `Top 500` *Influential and extremely popular punk-based Mod trio from Surrey: Paul Weller (v/g), Bruce Foxton (b), Rick Buckler (d). They hold the record for the most simultaneous Top 75 singles with 13 (all reactivated by their 1982 dissolution) (205 WEEKS)* pos/wks

7 May 77		IN THE CITY *Polydor 2058 866*	40	6
23 Jul 77		ALL AROUND THE WORLD *Polydor 2058 903*	13	8
5 Nov 77		THE MODERN WORLD *Polydor 2058 945*	36	4
11 Mar 78		NEWS OF THE WORLD *Polydor 2058 995*	27	5
26 Aug 78		DAVID WATTS / 'A' BOMB IN WARDOUR STREET *Polydor 2059 054*	25	8
21 Oct 78		DOWN IN THE TUBE STATION AT MIDNIGHT *Polydor POSP 8*	15	7
17 Mar 79		STRANGE TOWN *Polydor POSP 34*	15	9
25 Aug 79		WHEN YOU'RE YOUNG *Polydor POSP 69*	17	7
3 Nov 79	●	THE ETON RIFLES *Polydor POSP 83*	3	12
22 Mar 80	★	GOING UNDERGROUND / DREAMS OF CHILDREN *Polydor POSP 113* ■	1	9
26 Apr 80		ALL AROUND THE WORLD (re-entry) *Polydor 2058 903*	43	3
26 Apr 80		DAVID WATTS / 'A' BOMB IN WARDOUR STREET (re-entry) *Polydor 2059 054*	54	3
26 Apr 80		IN THE CITY (re-entry) *Polydor 2058 866*	40	4
26 Apr 80		NEWS OF THE WORLD (re-entry) *Polydor 2058 995*	53	3
26 Apr 80		STRANGE TOWN (re-entry) *Polydor POSP 34*	44	4
26 Apr 80		THE MODERN WORLD (re-entry) *Polydor 2058 945*	52	3
23 Aug 80	★	START! *Polydor 2059 266*	1	8
7 Feb 81		THAT'S ENTERTAINMENT (IMPORT) *Metronome 0030 364*	21	7
6 Jun 81	●	FUNERAL PYRE *Polydor POSP 257*	4	6
24 Oct 81	●	ABSOLUTE BEGINNERS *Polydor POSP 350*	4	6
13 Feb 82	★	TOWN CALLED MALICE / PRECIOUS *Polydor POSP 400* ■	1	8
3 Jul 82	●	JUST WHO IS THE FIVE O'CLOCK HERO *Polydor 2059 504*	8	5
18 Sep 82	●	THE BITTEREST PILL (I EVER HAD TO SWALLOW) *Polydor POSP 505*	2	7
4 Dec 82	★	BEAT SURRENDER *Polydor POSP 540* ■	1	9
22 Jan 83		ALL AROUND THE WORLD (2nd re-entry) *Polydor 2058 903*	38	4
22 Jan 83		DAVID WATTS / 'A' BOMB IN WARDOUR STREET (2nd re-entry) *Polydor 2059 054*	50	4
22 Jan 83		DOWN IN THE TUBE STATION AT MIDNIGHT (re-entry) *Polydor POSP 8*	30	6
22 Jan 83		GOING UNDERGROUND / DREAMS OF CHILDREN (re-entry) *Polydor POSP 113*	21	6
22 Jan 83		IN THE CITY (2nd re-entry) *Polydor 2058 866*	47	4
22 Jan 83		NEWS OF THE WORLD (2nd re-entry) *Polydor 2058 995*	39	4
22 Jan 83		STRANGE TOWN (2nd re-entry) *Polydor POSP 34*	42	5
22 Jan 83		THE MODERN WORLD (2nd re-entry) *Polydor 2058 945*	51	4
22 Jan 83		WHEN YOU'RE YOUNG (re-entry) *Polydor POSP 69*	53	4
29 Jan 83		THAT'S ENTERTAINMENT *Polydor POSP 482*	60	3
5 Feb 83		START! (re-entry) *Polydor 2059 266*	62	2
5 Feb 83		THE ETON RIFLES (re-entry) *Polydor POSP 83*	54	3
5 Feb 83		TOWN CALLED MALICE / PRECIOUS (re-entry) *Polydor POSP 400*	73	1
29 Jun 91		THAT'S ENTERTAINMENT (re-issue) *Polydor PO 155*	57	2
11 Oct 97		THE BITTEREST PILL (I EVER HAD TO SWALLOW) (re-issue) *Polydor 5715992*	30	2

See also Paul WELLER; Bruce FOXTON

JAM & SPOON featuring PLAVKA *Germany, male / female vocal / instrumental group - Jam El Mar & Mark Spoon (24 WEEKS)* pos/wks

2 May 92		TALES FROM A DANCEOGRAPHIC OCEAN (EP) *R&S RSUK 14* [1]	49	1
6 Jun 92		THE COMPLETE STELLA (re-mix) *R&S RSUK 14X* [1]	66	2
26 Feb 94		RIGHT IN THE NIGHT (FALL IN LOVE WITH MUSIC) *Epic 6600822*	31	4
24 Sep 94		FIND ME (ODYSSEY TO ANYOONA) *Epic 6608082*	37	3
10 Jun 95	●	RIGHT IN THE NIGHT (FALL IN LOVE WITH MUSIC) (re-issue) *Epic 6620182*	10	8
16 Sep 95		FIND ME (ODYSSEY TO ANYOONA) (re-issue) *Epic 6623242*	22	3
25 Nov 95		ANGEL (LADADI O-HEYO) *Epic 6626382*	26	2
30 Aug 97		KALEIDOSCOPE SKIES *Epic 6647614*	48	1

[1] Jam and Spoon

Tracks on Tales From a Danceographic Ocean (EP): Stella / Keep on Movin' / My First Fantastic FF. 'The Complete Stella' is a re-mix of a track from the EP

See also TOKYO GHETTO PUSSY; STORM

JAM MACHINE *Italy / US, male vocal / instrumental group (1 WEEK)* pos/wks

23 Dec 89		EVERYDAY *Deconstruction PB 43299*	68	1

JAM ON THE MUTHA
UK, male vocal / instrumental group (2 WEEKS) pos/wks

11 Aug 90		HOTEL CALIFORNIA *M & G MAGS 3*	62	2

JAM TRONIK
Germany, male / female vocal / instrumental group (7 WEEKS) pos/wks

24 Mar 90		ANOTHER DAY IN PARADISE *Debut DEBT 3093*	19	7

JAMAICA UNITED *Jamaica, male vocal ensemble (1 WEEK)* pos/wks

4 Jul 98		RISE UP *Columbia 6660522*	54	1

JAMELIA
UK, female vocalist - Jamelia Davis (18 WEEKS)

			pos/wks
31 Jul 99	I DO *Parlophone Rhythm Series CDRHYTHM 21*	...36	2
4 Mar 00 ●	MONEY *Parlophone Rhythm Series CDRYTHM 27* [1]	...5	9
24 Jun 00	CALL ME *Parlophone Rhythm Series CDRHYTHM 28*	...11	5
21 Oct 00	BOY NEXT DOOR		
	Parlophone Rhythm Series CDRHYTHM 29	...42	2

[1] Jamelia featuring Beenie Man

JAMES (368) **Top 500**
Anthemic indie pop band formed 1982 in Manchester, UK, by mainstays Tim Booth (v) and Larry Gott (g). After several hitless years, critically acclaimed releases and record company changes, they became one of the most consistently successful acts of the 1990s (86 WEEKS)

			pos/wks
12 May 90	HOW WAS IT FOR YOU *Fontana JIM 5*	...32	3
7 Jul 90	COME HOME *Fontana JIM 6*	...32	4
8 Dec 90	LOSE CONTROL *Fontana JIM 7*	...38	5
30 Mar 91 ●	SIT DOWN *Fontana JIM 8*	...2	10
30 Nov 91 ●	SOUND *Fontana JIM 9*	...9	7
1 Feb 92	BORN OF FRUSTRATION *Fontana JIM 10*	...13	6
4 Apr 92	RING THE BELLS *Fontana JIM 11*	...37	2
18 Jul 92	SEVEN (EP) *Fontana JIM 12*	...46	2
11 Sep 93	SOMETIMES *Fontana JIMCD 13*	...18	4
13 Nov 93	LAID *Fontana JIMCD 14*	...25	4
2 Apr 94	JAM J / SAY SOMETHING *Fontana JIMCD 15*	...24	4
22 Feb 97 ●	SHE'S A STAR *Fontana JIMCD 16*	...9	5
3 May 97	TOMORROW *Fontana JIMCD 17*	...12	3
5 Jul 97	WALTZING ALONG *Fontana JIMCD 18*	...23	4
21 Mar 98	DESTINY CALLING *Fontana JIMCD 19*	...17	4
6 Jun 98	RUNAGROUND *Fontana JIMCD 20*	...29	2
21 Nov 98 ●	SIT DOWN (re-mix) *Fontana JIMCD 21*	...7	7
31 Jul 99	I KNOW WHAT I'M HERE FOR *Mercury JIMCD22*	...22	5
16 Oct 99	JUST LIKE FRED ASTAIRE *Mercury JIMCD 23*	...17	3
25 Dec 99	WE'RE GOING TO MISS YOU *Mercury JIMCD 24*	...48	2

Tracks on Seven (EP): Seven / Goalie's Ball / William Burroughs / Still Alive. 'Say Something' listed with 'Jam J' only for first two weeks of record's run

JAMES – See CHRIS and JAMES

Dick JAMES
UK, male vocalist (13 WEEKS)

			pos/wks
20 Jan 56	ROBIN HOOD *Parlophone R 4117*	...14	8
18 May 56	ROBIN HOOD / BALLAD OF DAVY CROCKETT (re-entry)		
	Parlophone R 4117	...29	1
11 Jan 57	GARDEN OF EDEN *Parlophone R 4255*	...18	4

'Robin Hood' is with Stephen James and his Chums

Etta JAMES
US, female vocalist - Jamesetta Hawkins (7 WEEKS)

			pos/wks
10 Feb 96 ●	I JUST WANT TO MAKE LOVE TO YOU *MCA MCSTD 48003*	...5	7

Freddie JAMES
Canada, male vocalist (3 WEEKS)

			pos/wks
24 Nov 79	GET UP AND BOOGIE *Warner Bros. K 17478*	...54	3

Joni JAMES
US, female vocalist (2 WEEKS)

			pos/wks
6 Mar 53	WHY DON'T YOU BELIEVE ME *MGM 582* ▲	...11	1
30 Jan 59	THERE MUST BE A WAY *MGM 1002*	...24	1

Rick JAMES
US, male vocalist (30 WEEKS)

			pos/wks
8 Jul 78	YOU AND I *Motown TMG 1110*	...46	7
7 Jul 79	I'M A SUCKER FOR YOUR LOVE		
	Motown TMG 1146 [1]	...43	8
6 Sep 80	BIG TIME *Motown TMG 1198*	...41	6
4 Jul 81	GIVE IT TO ME BABY *Motown TMG 1229*	...47	3
12 Jun 82	STANDING ON THE TOP (PART 1) *Motown TMG 1263* [2]	...53	3
3 Jul 82	DANCE WIT' ME *Motown TMG 1266*	...53	3

[1] Teena Marie, co-lead vocals Rick James [2] Temptations featuring Rick James

Sonny JAMES
US, male vocalist (8 WEEKS)

			pos/wks
30 Nov 56	THE CAT CAME BACK *Capitol CL 14635*	...30	1
8 Feb 57	YOUNG LOVE *Capitol CL 14683*	...11	7

Wendy JAMES
UK, female vocalist (4 WEEKS)

			pos/wks
20 Feb 93	THE NAMELESS ONE *MCA MCSTD 1732*	...34	3
17 Apr 93	LONDON'S BRILLIANT *MCA MCSTD 1763*	...62	1

JAMES BOYS
UK, male vocal duo (6 WEEKS)

			pos/wks
19 May 73	OVER AND OVER *Penny Farthing PEN 806*	...39	6

Jimmy JAMES and the VAGABONDS
UK, male vocal / instrumental group (25 WEEKS)

			pos/wks
11 Sep 68	RED RED WINE *Pye 7N 17579*	...36	8
24 Apr 76	I'LL GO WHERE YOUR MUSIC TAKES ME *Pye 7N 45585*	...23	8
17 Jul 76 ●	NOW IS THE TIME *Pye 7N 45606*	...5	9

Tommy JAMES and the SHONDELLS
US, male vocal / instrumental group (25 WEEKS)

			pos/wks
21 Jul 66	HANKY PANKY *Roulette RK 7000* ▲	...38	7
5 Jun 68 ★	MONY MONY *Major Minor MM 567*	...1	18

JAMESTOWN Featuring JOCELYN BROWN
US, male instrumentalist / producer - Kent Brainerd and US, female vocalist (1 WEEK)

			pos/wks
27 Mar 99	I BELIEVE *Playola 0091705 PLA*	...62	1

JAMIROQUAI (265) **Top 500**
One of world's biggest-selling acts of the late 1990s features headdress-wearing vocalist Jay Kay, b. 30 Dec 1969, Manchester, UK. Group, whose videos have also earned numerous accolades, sold seven million copies of 1996 album Travelling Without Moving and 1999 album Synkronized topped many European charts (109 WEEKS)

			pos/wks
31 Oct 92	WHEN YOU GONNA LEARN *Acid Jazz JAZID 46*	...52	2
20 Feb 93	WHEN YOU GONNA LEARN (re-entry) *Acid Jazz JAZID 46*	...69	1
13 Mar 93 ●	TOO YOUNG TO DIE *Sony S2 6590112*	...10	7
5 Jun 93	BLOW YOUR MIND *Sony S2 6592972*	...12	6
14 Aug 93	EMERGENCY ON PLANET EARTH *Sony S2 6595782*	...32	3
25 Sep 93	WHEN YOU GONNA LEARN (re-issue) *Sony S2 6596952*	...28	3
8 Oct 94	SPACE COWBOY *Sony S2 6608512*	...17	5
19 Nov 94	HALF THE MAN *Sony S2 6610032*	...15	8
1 Jul 95 ●	STILLNESS IN TIME *Sony S2 6620255*	...9	5
1 Jun 96	DO U KNOW WHERE YOU'RE COMING FROM		
	Renk CDRENK 63 [1]	...12	5
31 Aug 96 ●	VIRTUAL INSANITY *Sony S2 6636132*	...3	11
7 Dec 96 ●	COSMIC GIRL *Sony S2 6638292*	...6	10
10 May 97 ●	ALRIGHT *Sony S2 6643252*	...6	5
13 Dec 97	HIGH TIMES *Sony S2 6653702*	...20	6
25 Jul 98 ★	DEEPER UNDERGROUND *Sony S2 6662182* ■	...1	11
5 Jun 99 ●	CANNED HEAT *Sony S2 6673022*	...4	10
25 Sep 99	SUPERSONIC *Sony S2 6678392*	...22	4
11 Dec 99	KING FOR A DAY *Sony S2 6679732*	...20	7

[1] M-Beat featuring Jamiroquai

JAMMERS
US, male vocal / instrumental group (2 WEEKS)

			pos/wks
29 Jan 83	BE MINE TONIGHT *Salsoul Sal 101*	...65	2

JAN and DEAN
US, male vocal duo (18 WEEKS)

			pos/wks
24 Aug 61	HEART AND SOUL *London HLH 9395*	...24	8
15 Aug 63	SURF CITY *Liberty LIB 55580* ▲	...26	10

JAN and KJELD
Denmark, male vocal duo (4 WEEKS)

			pos/wks
21 Jul 60	BANJO BOY *Ember S 101*	...36	4

JANE'S ADDICTION
US, male vocal / instrumental group (4 WEEKS)

			pos/wks
23 Mar 91	BEEN CAUGHT STEALING *Warner Bros. W 0011*	...34	3
1 Jun 91	CLASSIC GIRL *Warner Bros. W 0031*	...60	1

Horst JANKOWSKI
Germany, male instrumentalist - piano (18 WEEKS)

			pos/wks
29 Jul 65 ●	A WALK IN THE BLACK FOREST *Mercury MF 861*	...3	18

UK No.1 ★ UK Top 10 ● Still on chart + UK million seller ◆ UK entry at No.1 ■ US No.1 ▲

Samantha JANUS
UK, female vocalist (3 WEEKS) pos/wks

11 May 91	A MESSAGE TO YOUR HEART		
	Hollywood HWD 104	30	3

Philip JAP
UK, male vocalist (8 WEEKS) pos/wks

31 Jul 82	SAVE US *A & M AMS 8217*	53	4
25 Sep 82	TOTAL ERASURE *A & M JAP 1*	41	4

JAPAN `407` `Top 500`
Rock quintet who subsequently became New Romantic figureheads fronted by David Sylvian (v), b. David Batt, 23 Feb 1958, London, UK, who later recorded critically acclaimed solo work. Group folded in 1982, but full line-up briefly reconvened as Rain Tree Crow in 1991 (81 WEEKS) pos/wks

18 Oct 80	GENTLEMEN TAKE POLAROIDS *Virgin VS 379*	60	2
9 May 81	THE ART OF PARTIES *Virgin VS 409*	48	5
19 Sep 81	QUIET LIFE *Hansa HANSA 6*	19	9
7 Nov 81	VISIONS OF CHINA *Virgin VS 436*	32	12
23 Jan 82	EUROPEAN SON *Hansa HANSA 10*	31	6
20 Mar 82 ●	GHOSTS *Virgin VS 472*	5	8
22 May 82	CANTONESE BOY *Virgin VS 502*	24	6
3 Jul 82 ●	I SECOND THAT EMOTION *Hansa HANSA 12*	9	11
9 Oct 82	LIFE IN TOKYO *Hansa HANSA 17*	28	6
20 Nov 82	NIGHT PORTER *Virgin VS 554*	29	9
12 Mar 83	ALL TOMORROW'S PARTIES *Hansa HANSA 18*	38	4
21 May 83	CANTON (LIVE) *Virgin VS 581*	42	3

See also RAIN TREE CROW

JARK PRONGO
Holland, production duo (1 WEEK) pos/wks

3 Apr 99	MOVIN' THRU YOUR SYSTEM *Hooj Choons HOOJ 72CD*	58	1

See also GOODMEN

Jean-Michel JARRE
France, male instrumentalist / producer (40 WEEKS) pos/wks

27 Aug 77 ●	OXYGENE PART IV *Polydor 2001 721*	4	9
20 Jan 79	EQUINOXE PART 5 *Polydor POSP 20*	45	5
23 Aug 86	FOURTH RENDEZ-VOUS *Polydor POSP 788*	65	4
5 Nov 88	REVOLUTIONS *Polydor PO 25*	52	2
7 Jan 89	LONDON KID *Polydor PO 32* [1]	52	3
7 Oct 89	OXYGENE PART IV (re-mix) *Polydor PO 55*	65	2
26 Jun 93	CHRONOLOGIE PART 4 *Polydor POCS 274*	55	2
30 Oct 93	CHRONOLOGIE PART 4 (re-mix) *Polydor POCS 274*	56	1
22 Mar 97	OXYGENE 8 *Epic 6643232*	17	3
5 Jul 97	OXYGENE 10 *Epic 6647152*	21	3
11 Jul 98	RENDEZ-VOUS '98 *Epic 6661102* [2]	12	6
26 Feb 00	C'EST LA VIE *Epic 6689302* [3]	40	1

[1] Jean-Michel Jarre featuring Hank Marvin [2] Jean-Michel Jarre and Apollo 440 [3] Jean-Michel Jarre featuring Natacha Atlas

Al JARREAU
US, male vocalist (30 WEEKS) pos/wks

26 Sep 81	WE'RE IN THIS LOVE TOGETHER		
	Warner Bros. K 17849	55	4
14 May 83	MORNIN' *WEA U9929*	28	6
16 Jul 83	TROUBLE IN PARADISE *WEA Int. U9871*	36	5
24 Sep 83	BOOGIE DOWN *WEA U9814*	63	3
16 Nov 85	DAY BY DAY *Polydor POSP 770* [1]	53	3
5 Apr 86	THE MUSIC OF GOODBYE (LOVE THEME FROM 'OUT OF AFRICA') *MCA MCA 1038* [2]	75	1
7 Mar 87 ●	'MOONLIGHTING' THEME *WEA U8407*	8	8

[1] Shakatak featuring Al Jarreau [2] Melissa Manchester and Al Jarreau

Kenny 'Jammin' JASON and DJ 'FAST' Eddie SMITH
US, male DJ / production duo (4 WEEKS) pos/wks

11 Apr 87	CAN U DANCE *Champion CHAMP 41*	71	2
14 Nov 87	CAN U DANCE (re-entry) *Champion CHAMP 41*	67	2

JAVELLS featuring Nosmo KING
UK, male / female vocal group (8 WEEKS) pos/wks

9 Nov 74	GOODBYE NOTHING TO SAY *Pye Disco Demand DDS 2003*	26	8

Peter JAY and the JAYWALKERS
UK, male instrumental group, Peter Jay - drums (11 WEEKS) pos/wks

8 Nov 62	CAN CAN 62 *Decca F 11531*	31	11

Simone JAY – See DJ DADO

JAYDEE
Holland, male DJ / producer (3 WEEKS) pos/wks

20 Sep 97	PLASTIC DREAMS *R&S RS 97117CD*	18	3

OLLIE JAYE – See JON THE DENTIST Vs Ollie JAYE

JAYHAWKS
US, male / female vocal / instrumental group (1 WEEK) pos/wks

15 Jul 95	BAD TIME *American 74321291632*	70	1

JAY-Z
US, male rapper - Shawn Carter (66 WEEKS) pos/wks

1 Mar 97	CAN'T KNOCK THE HUSTLE		
	Northwestside 74321447192 [1]	30	2
10 May 97	AIN'T NO PLAYA *Northwestside 74321474842* [2]	31	2
21 Jun 97 ●	I'LL BE *Def Jam 75710432* [3]	9	5
23 Aug 97	WHO YOU WIT *Qwest W 0411CD*	65	1
25 Oct 97	SUNSHINE *Northwestside 74321528702* [4]	25	2
14 Feb 98	WISHING ON A STAR *Northwestside 74321554632* [5]	13	4
27 Jun 98	THE CITY IS MINE *Northwestside 74321588012* [6]	38	2
12 Dec 98 ●	HARD KNOCK LIFE (GHETTO ANTHEM)		
	Northwestside 74321635332	2	11
13 Mar 99	CAN I GET A... *Def Jam 5668472* [7]	24	3
10 Apr 99	BE ALONE NO MORE *Northwestside 74321658472* [8]	11	9
19 Jun 99	LOBSTER & SCRIMP *Virgin DINSD 186* [9]	48	1
6 Nov 99 ●	HEARTBREAKER *Columbia 6683012* ▲	5	13
4 Dec 99	WHAT YOU THINK OF THAT *Def Jam 8708292* [11]	58	1
26 Feb 00	ANYTHING *Def Jam 5626502*	18	4
24 Jun 00	BIG PIMPIN' *Def Jam 5627742*	29	3
16 Dec 00	I JUST WANNA LOVE U (GIVE IT 2 ME) *Def Jam 5727462*	17	3+

[1] Jay-Z featuring Mary J Blige [2] Jay-Z featuring Foxy Brown [3] Foxy Brown featuring Jay-Z [4] Jay-Z featuring Babyface and Foxy Brown [5] Jay-Z featuring Gwen Dickey [6] Jay-Z featuring BLACKstreet [7] Jay-Z featuring Amil & Ja Rule [8] Another Level featuring Jay-Z [9] Timbaland featuring Jay-Z [10] Mariah Carey featuring Jay-Z [11] Memphis BLEEK featuring Jay-Z

JAZZ and the BROTHERS GRIMM
UK, male vocal / instrumental group (2 WEEKS) pos/wks

9 Jul 88	(LET'S ALL GO BACK) DISCO NIGHTS *Ensign ENY 616*	57	2

JAZZY JEFF & the FRESH PRINCE
US, male rap / DJ duo - Jeff Townes & Will Smith (49 WEEKS) pos/wks

4 Oct 86	GIRLS AIN'T NOTHING BUT TROUBLE		
	Champion Champ 18 [1]	21	8
3 Aug 91 ●	SUMMERTIME *Jive JIVECD 279* [1]	8	8
9 Nov 91	RING MY BELL *Jive JIVECD 288* [1]	53	2
11 Sep 93 ★	BOOM! SHAKE THE ROOM *Jive JIVECD 335*	1	13
20 Nov 93	I'M LOOKING FOR THE ONE (TO BE WITH ME)		
	Jive JIVECD 345	24	4
19 Feb 94	CAN'T WAIT TO BE WITH YOU *Jive JIVECD 348*	29	4
4 Jun 94	TWINKLE TWINKLE (I'M NOT A STAR)		
	Jive JIVECD 354	62	2
6 Aug 94	SUMMERTIME (re-entry) *Jive JIVECD 279* [1]	29	4
2 Dec 95	BOOM! SHAKE THE ROOM (re-mix) *Jive JIVECD 387*	40	2
11 Jul 98	LOVELY DAZE *Jive 0518902* [1]	37	2

[1] DJ Jazzy Jeff and the Fresh Prince

See also Will SMITH

JAZZY M
UK, male DJ / producer - Michael Connelly (2 WEEKS) pos/wks

21 Oct 00	JAZZIN' THE WAY YOU KNOW *Perfecto PERF 08CDS*	47	2

JB's ALL STARS
UK, male / female vocal / instrumental group (4 WEEKS) pos/wks

11 Feb 84	BACKFIELD IN MOTION *RCA Victor RCA 384*	48	4

JC *UK, male producer (1 WEEK)* — pos/wks

7 Feb 98	**SO HOT** *East West EW 146CD*	**74**	1

JC 001 *UK, male rapper (4 WEEKS)* — pos/wks

24 Apr 93	**NEVER AGAIN** *Anxious ANX 1012CD*	**67**	2
26 Jun 93	**CUPID** *Anxious ANX 1014CD*	**56**	2

JD – See SNOOP DOGGY DOGG

JDS *Italy / UK, male DJ / production duo - Julian Napolitano and Darren Pearce (2 WEEKS)* — pos/wks

27 Sep 97	**NINE WAYS** *ffrr FCD 310*	**61**	1
23 May 98	**LONDON TOWN** *Jive 0530042*	**49**	1

Norma JEAN – See Romina JOHNSON

Wyclef JEAN *US, male vocalist / rapper / producer (35 WEEKS)* — pos/wks

28 Jun 97	**WE TRYING TO STAY ALIVE** *Columbia 6646815* [1]	**13**	5
27 Sep 97	**GUANTANAMERA** *Columbia 6650852* [2]	**25**	2
16 May 98 ●	**GONE TILL NOVEMBER** *Columbia 6658712*	**3**	9
14 Nov 98 ●	**ANOTHER ONE BITES THE DUST** *Dreamworks DRMCD 22364* [3]	**5**	6
23 Oct 99	**NEW DAY** *Columbia 6682122* [4]	**23**	2
16 Sep 00 ●	**IT DOESN'T MATTER** *Columbia 6697782* [5]	**3**	8
16 Dec 00 ●	**911** *Columbia 6706122* [6]	**9**	3+

[1] Wyclef Jean & The Refugee Allstars [2] Wyclef Jean and The Refugee Allstars [3] Queen with Wyclef Jean featuring Pras and Free [4] Wyclef Jean featuring Bono [5] Wyclef Jean featuring The Rock and Melky Sedeck [6] Wyclef Jean featuring Mary J Blige

See also FUGEES

JEFFERSON *UK, male vocalist (8 WEEKS)* — pos/wks

9 Apr 69	**COLOUR OF MY LOVE** *Pye 7N 17706*	**22**	8

JEFFERSON STARSHIP – See STARSHIP

Garland JEFFREYS *US, male vocalist (1 WEEK)* — pos/wks

8 Feb 92	**HAIL HAIL ROCK 'N' ROLL** *RCA PB 49171*	**72**	1

JELLYBEAN *US, male producer - John Benitez (47 WEEKS)* — pos/wks

1 Feb 86	**SIDEWALK TALK** *EMI America EA 210* [1]	**47**	4
26 Sep 87	**THE REAL THING** *Chrysalis CHS 3167* [2]	**13**	10
28 Nov 87 ●	**WHO FOUND WHO** *Chrysalis CHS JEL 1* [3]	**10**	10
12 Dec 87	**JINGO** *Chrysalis JEL 2*	**12**	10
12 Mar 88	**JUST A MIRAGE** *Chrysalis JEL 3* [4]	**13**	10
20 Aug 88	**COMING BACK FOR MORE** *Chrysalis JEL 4* [5]	**41**	3

[1] Jellybean featuring Catherine Buchanan [2] Jellybean featuring Steven Dante [3] Jellybean featuring Elisa Fiorillo [4] Jellybean featuring Adele Bertei [5] Jellybean featuring Richard Darbyshire

JELLYFISH *US, male vocal / instrumental group (20 WEEKS)* — pos/wks

26 Jan 91	**THE KING IS HALF UNDRESSED** *Charisma CUSS 1*	**39**	6
27 Apr 91	**BABY'S COMING BACK** *Charisma CUSS 2*	**51**	4
3 Aug 91	**THE SCARY-GO-ROUND EP** *Charisma CUSS 3*	**49**	3
26 Oct 91	**I WANNA STAY HOME** *Charisma CUSS 4*	**59**	2
1 May 93	**THE GHOST AT NUMBER ONE** *Charisma CUSDG 10*	**43**	3
17 Jul 93	**NEW MISTAKE** *Charisma CUSDG 11*	**55**	2

Tracks on The Scary-Go-Round EP: Now She Knows She's Wrong / Bedspring Kiss / She Still Loves Him (Live) / Baby's Coming Back (Live)

JERU THE DAMAJA *US, male rapper (1 WEEK)* — pos/wks

7 Dec 96	**YA PLAYIN YASELF** *ffrr FCD 289*	**67**	1

JESSICA *Sweden, female vocalist (1 WEEK)* — pos/wks

20 Mar 99	**HOW WILL I KNOW (WHO YOU ARE)** *Jive 0522412*	**47**	1

JESUS AND MARY CHAIN *UK, male vocal / instrumental group (59 WEEKS)* — pos/wks

2 Mar 85	**NEVER UNDERSTAND** *Blanco Y Negro NEG 8*	**47**	4
8 Jun 85	**YOU TRIP ME UP** *Blanco Y Negro NEG 13*	**55**	3
12 Oct 85	**JUST LIKE HONEY** *Blanco Y Negro NEG 17*	**45**	3
26 Jul 86	**SOME CANDY TALKING** *Blanco Y Negro NEG 19*	**13**	5
2 May 87 ●	**APRIL SKIES** *Blanco Y Negro NEG 24*	**8**	6
15 Aug 87	**HAPPY WHEN IT RAINS** *Blanco Y Negro NEG 25*	**25**	5
7 Nov 87	**DARKLANDS** *Blanco Y Negro NEG 29*	**33**	4
9 Apr 88	**SIDEWALKING** *Blanco Y Negro NEG 32*	**30**	3
23 Sep 89	**BLUES FROM A GUN** *Blanco Y Negro NEG 41*	**32**	2
18 Nov 89	**HEAD ON** *Blanco Y Negro NEG 42*	**57**	2
8 Sep 90	**ROLLERCOASTER (EP)** *Blanco Y Negro NEG 45*	**46**	2
15 Feb 92 ●	**REVERENCE** *Blanco Y Negro NEG 55*	**10**	4
14 Mar 92	**FAR GONE AND OUT** *Blanco Y Negro NEG 56*	**23**	3
4 Jul 92	**ALMOST GOLD** *Blanco Y Negro NEG 57*	**41**	2
10 Jul 93	**SOUND OF SPEED (EP)** *Blanco Y Negro NEG 66CD*	**30**	2
30 Jul 94	**SOMETIMES ALWAYS** *Blanco Y Negro NEG 70CD*	**22**	3
22 Oct 94	**COME ON** *Blanco Y Negro NEG 73CD1*	**52**	2
17 Jun 95	**I HATE ROCK 'N' ROLL** *Blanco Y Negro NEG 81CD*	**61**	1
18 Apr 98	**CRACKING UP** *Creation CRESCD 292*	**35**	2
30 May 98	**ILOVEROCKNROLL** *Creation CRESCD 296*	**38**	1

Tracks on Rollercoaster (EP): Rollercoaster / Silverblade / Lowlife / Tower of Song.
Tracks on Sound of Speed (EP): Snakedriver / Something I Can't Have / Write Record Release Blues / Little Red Rooster

JESUS JONES *UK, male vocal / instrumental group (52 WEEKS)* — pos/wks

25 Feb 89	**INFO-FREAKO** *Food FOOD 18*	**42**	3
8 Jul 89	**NEVER ENOUGH** *Food FOOD 21*	**42**	3
23 Sep 89	**BRING IT ON DOWN** *Food FOOD 22*	**46**	3
7 Apr 90	**REAL REAL REAL** *Food FOOD 24*	**19**	8
6 Oct 90	**RIGHT HERE RIGHT NOW** *Food FOOD 25*	**31**	4
12 Jan 91 ●	**INTERNATIONAL BRIGHT YOUNG THING** *Food FOOD 27*	**7**	7
2 Mar 91	**WHO WHERE WHY** *Food FOOD 28*	**21**	7
20 Jul 91	**RIGHT HERE RIGHT NOW (re-issue)** *Food FOOD 30*	**31**	4
9 Jan 93 ●	**THE DEVIL YOU KNOW** *Food CDPERV 1*	**10**	5
10 Apr 93	**THE RIGHT DECISION** *Food CDPERV 2*	**36**	3
10 Jul 93	**ZEROES & ONES** *Food CDFOODS 44*	**30**	3
14 Jun 97	**THE NEXT BIG THING** *Food CDFOOD 95*	**49**	1
16 Aug 97	**CHEMICAL #1** *Food CDFOOD 102*	**71**	1

JESUS LIZARD *US, male vocal / instrumental group (2 WEEKS)* — pos/wks

6 Mar 93	**PUSS** *Touch And Go TG 83CD*	**12**	2

The listed flip side of 'Puss' was 'Oh, the Guilt' by Nirvana

JESUS LOVES YOU *UK, male vocalist - Boy George (18 WEEKS)* — pos/wks

11 Nov 89	**AFTER THE LOVE** *More Protein PROT 2*	**68**	1
23 Feb 91	**BOW DOWN MISTER** *More Protein PROT 8*	**27**	8
8 Jun 91	**GENERATIONS OF LOVE** *More Protein PROT 10*	**35**	8
12 Dec 92	**SWEET TOXIC LOVE** *Virgin VS 1449*	**65**	1

JETHRO TULL *UK, male vocal / instrumental group (68 WEEKS)* — pos/wks

1 Jan 69	**LOVE STORY** *Island WIP 6048*	**29**	8
14 May 69 ●	**LIVING IN THE PAST** *Island WIP 6056*	**3**	14
1 Nov 69 ●	**SWEET DREAM** *Chrysalis WIP 6070*	**7**	11
24 Jan 70 ●	**TEACHER / THE WITCH'S PROMISE** *Chrysalis WIP 6077*	**4**	9
18 Sep 71	**LIFE IS A LONG SONG / UP THE POOL** *Chrysalis WIP 6106*	**11**	8
11 Dec 76	**RING OUT SOLSTICE BELLS (EP)** *Chrysalis CXP 2*	**28**	6
15 Sep 84	**LAP OF LUXURY** *Chrysalis TULL 1*	**70**	2
16 Jan 88	**SAID SHE WAS A DANCER** *Chrysalis TULL 4*	**55**	4
21 Mar 92	**ROCKS ON THE ROAD** *Chrysalis TULLX 7*	**47**	3
22 May 93	**LIVING IN THE (SLIGHTLY MORE RECENT) PAST** *Chrysalis CDCHSS 3970*	**32**	3

Tracks on Ring Out Solstice Bells (EP): Ring Out Solstice Bells / March the Mad Scientist / The Christmas Song / Pan Dance. 'Living in the (Slightly More Recent) Past' is a live version of the original

JETS *UK, male vocal / instrumental group (38 WEEKS)* — pos/wks

Date	Title	pos	wks
22 Aug 81	SUGAR DOLL *EMI 5211*	55	3
31 Oct 81	YES TONIGHT JOSEPHINE *EMI 5247*	25	11
6 Feb 82	LOVE MAKES THE WORLD GO ROUND *EMI 5262*	21	9
24 Apr 82	THE HONEYDRIPPER *EMI 5289*	58	3
9 Oct 82	SOMEBODY TO LOVE *EMI 5342*	56	3
6 Aug 83	BLUE SKIES *EMI 5405*	53	3
17 Dec 83	ROCKIN' AROUND THE CHRISTMAS TREE *PRT 7P 297*	62	4
13 Oct 84	PARTY DOLL *PRT JETS 2*	72	2

JETS *US, male / female vocal / instrumental group (19 WEEKS)* — pos/wks

Date	Title	pos	wks
31 Jan 87 ●	CRUSH ON YOU *MCA MCA 1048*	5	13
25 Apr 87	CURIOSITY *MCA MCA 1119*	41	4
28 May 88	ROCKET 2 U *MCA MCA 1226*	69	2

Joan JETT and the BLACKHEARTS *US, female vocalist with male vocal / instrumental group (21 WEEKS)* — pos/wks

Date	Title	pos	wks
24 Apr 82 ●	I LOVE ROCK `N' ROLL *Epic EPC A 2152* ▲	4	10
10 Jul 82	CRIMSON AND CLOVER *Epic EPC A 2485*	60	3
20 Aug 88	I HATE MYSELF FOR LOVING YOU *London LON 195*	46	6
31 Mar 90	DIRTY DEEDS *Chrysalis CHS 3518* [1]	69	1
19 Feb 94	I LOVE ROCK & ROLL (re-issue) *Reprise W 0232CD*	75	1

[1] Joan Jett

JEWEL *US, female vocalist / instrumentalist - guitar (8 WEEKS)* — pos/wks

Date	Title	pos	wks
14 Jun 97	WHO WILL SAVE YOUR SOUL *Atlantic A 8514CD*	52	1
9 Aug 97	YOU WERE MEANT FOR ME *Atlantic A 5463CD*	53	1
22 Nov 97	YOU WERE MEANT FOR ME (re-entry) *Atlantic A 5463CD*	32	2
21 Nov 98	HANDS *Atlantic AT 0055CD*	41	2
26 Jun 99	DOWN SO LONG *Atlantic AT 0069CD*	38	2

JEZ & CHOOPIE *UK / Israel, male DJ / production duo (2 WEEKS)* — pos/wks

Date	Title	pos	wks
21 Mar 98	YIM *Multiply CDMULTY 31*	36	2

JHELISA *US, female vocalist (1 WEEK)* — pos/wks

Date	Title	pos	wks
1 Jul 95	FRIENDLY PRESSURE *Dorado DOR 040CD*	75	1

JIGSAW *UK, male vocal / instrumental group (16 WEEKS)* — pos/wks

Date	Title	pos	wks
1 Nov 75 ●	SKY HIGH *Splash CP1 1*	9	11
6 Aug 77	IF I HAVE TO GO AWAY *Splash CP 11*	36	5

JILTED JOHN *UK, male vocalist - Graham Fellows (12 WEEKS)* — pos/wks

Date	Title	pos	wks
12 Aug 78 ●	JILTED JOHN *EMI International INT 567*	4	12

JIMMY THE HOOVER
UK, male / female vocal / instrumental group (8 WEEKS) — pos/wks

Date	Title	pos	wks
25 Jun 83	TANTALISE (WO WO EE YEH YEH) *Innervision A 3406*	18	8

JINGLE BELLES *US / UK, female vocal group (4 WEEKS)* — pos/wks

Date	Title	pos	wks
17 Dec 83	CHRISTMAS SPECTRE *Passion PASH 14*	37	4

JINNY *Italy, female vocalist (16 WEEKS)* — pos/wks

Date	Title	pos	wks
29 Jun 91	KEEP WARM *Virgin VS 1356*	68	3
22 May 93	FEEL THE RHYTHM *Logic 401633001022*	74	1
15 Jul 95	KEEP WARM (re-mix) *Multiply CDMULTY 5*	11	8
16 Dec 95	WANNA BE WITH YOU *Multiply CDMULTY 8*	30	4

JIVE BUNNY and the MASTERMIXERS *UK, male DJ / production duo - Andy Pickles and Les Hemstock (68 WEEKS)* — pos/wks

Date	Title	pos	wks
15 Jul 89 ★	SWING THE MOOD *Music Factory Dance MFD 001*	1	19
14 Oct 89 ★	THAT'S WHAT I LIKE *Music Factory Dance MFD 002*	1	12
16 Dec 89 ★	LET'S PARTY *Music Factory Dance MFD 003* ■	1	6
17 Mar 90 ●	THAT SOUNDS GOOD TO ME *Music Factory Dance MFD 004*	4	6
25 Aug 90 ●	CAN CAN YOU PARTY *Music Factory Dance MFD 007*	8	6
17 Nov 90	LET'S SWING AGAIN *Music Factory Dance MFD 009*	19	5
22 Dec 90	THE CRAZY PARTY MIXES *Music Factory Dance MFD 010*	13	5
23 Mar 91	OVER TO YOU JOHN (HERE WE GO AGAIN) *Music Factory Dance MFD 012*	28	5
20 Jul 91	HOT SUMMER SALSA *Music Factory Dance MFD 013*	43	2
23 Nov 91	ROCK 'N' ROLL DANCE PARTY *Music Factory Dance MFD 015*	48	2

See also Liz KERSHAW and Bruno BROOKES

JJ *UK, male / female vocal / instumental duo (3 WEEKS)* — pos/wks

Date	Title	pos	wks
9 Feb 91	IF THIS IS LOVE *Columbia 6566097*	55	3

See JJ DJ LUCK & MC NEAT

JJ72 *Ireland, male / female vocal / instrumental group (7 WEEKS)* — pos/wks

Date	Title	pos	wks
3 Jun 00	LONG WAY SOUTH *Lakota LAK 0015CD*	68	1
26 Aug 00	OXYGEN *Lakota LAK 0016CD*	23	3
4 Nov 00	OCTOBER SWIMMER *Lakota LAK 0018CD*	29	3

JKD BAND *UK, male vocal / instrumental group (4 WEEKS)* — pos/wks

Date	Title	pos	wks
1 Jul 78	DRAGON POWER *Satril SAT 132*	58	4

JM SILK *US, male / instrumental duo (6 WEEKS)* — pos/wks

Date	Title	pos	wks
25 Oct 86	I CAN'T TURN AROUND *RCA PB 49793*	62	3
7 Mar 87	LET THE MUSIC TAKE CONTROL *RCA PB 49767*	47	3

JMD – See TYREE

JO BOXERS *UK, male vocal / instrumental group (33 WEEKS)* — pos/wks

Date	Title	pos	wks
19 Feb 83 ●	BOXER BEAT *RCA BOXX 1*	3	15
21 May 83 ●	JUST GOT LUCKY *RCA BOXX 2*	7	9
13 Aug 83	JOHNNY FRIENDLY *RCA BOXX 3*	31	8
12 Nov 83	JEALOUS LOVE *RCA BOXX 4*	72	1

JO JO GUNNE *US, male vocal / instrumental group (12 WEEKS)* — pos/wks

Date	Title	pos	wks
25 Mar 72 ●	RUN RUN RUN *Asylum AYM 501*	6	12

JOAN COLLINS FAN CLUB
UK, male vocalist - Julian Clary (3 WEEKS) — pos/wks

Date	Title	pos	wks
18 Jun 88	LEADER OF THE PACK *10 TEN 227*	60	3

John Paul JOANS *UK, male vocalist (7 WEEKS)* — pos/wks

Date	Title	pos	wks
19 Dec 70	MAN FROM NAZARETH *RAK 107*	41	3
16 Jan 71	MAN FROM NAZARETH (re-entry) *RAK 107*	25	4

JOCASTA *UK, male vocal / instrumental group (2 WEEKS)* — pos/wks

Date	Title	pos	wks
15 Feb 97	GO *Epic 6641415*	50	1
3 May 97	CHANGE ME *Epic 6643902*	60	1

JOCKMASTER B.A. – See MAD JOCKS featuring JOCKMASTER B.A.

JOCKO *US, male rapper - DJ Jocko Henderson (3 WEEKS)* — pos/wks

Date	Title	pos	wks
23 Feb 80	RHYTHM TALK *Philadelphia International PIR 8222*	56	3

JODE featuring YO-HANS
UK, male / female vocal duo featuring male yo-yo expert (2 WEEKS) — pos/wks

Date	Title	pos	wks
19 Dec 98	WALK...(THE DOG) LIKE AN EGYPTIAN *Logic 74321640332*	48	2

JODECI *US, male vocal group (19 WEEKS)* — pos/wks

Date	Title	pos	wks
16 Jan 93	CHERISH *Uptown MCSTD 1726*	56	2
11 Dec 93	CRY FOR YOU *Uptown MCSTD 1951*	56	1
16 Jul 94	FEENIN' *Uptown MCSTD 1984*	18	3
28 Jan 95	CRY FOR YOU (re-issue) *Uptown MCSTD 2039*	20	3
24 Jun 95	FREEK 'N YOU *Uptown MCSTD 2072*	17	5
9 Dec 95	LOVE U 4 LIFE *Uptown MCSTD 2105*	23	3
25 May 96	GET ON UP *MCA MCSTD 48010*	20	2

UK No.1 ★   UK Top 10 ●   Still on chart +   UK million seller ◆   UK entry at No.1 ■   US No.1 ▲

JODIE *Australia, female vocalist (1 WEEK)* pos/wks

25 Feb 95	**ANYTHING YOU WANT** *Mercury MERCD 423*	47	1

JOE *US, male vocalist - Joseph Thomas (32 WEEKS)* pos/wks

22 Jan 94	**I'M IN LUV** *Mercury JOECD 1*	22	4
25 Jun 94	**THE ONE FOR ME** *Mercury JOECD 2*...........................	34	2
22 Oct 94	**ALL OR NOTHING** *Mercury JOECD 3*...........................	56	1
27 Apr 96	**ALL THE THINGS (YOUR MAN WON'T DO)** *Island CID 634* 34		3
14 Jun 97	**DON'T WANNA BE A PLAYER** *Jive JIVECD 410*	16	3
27 Sep 97	**THE LOVE SCENE** *Jive JIVECD 430*	22	2
10 Jan 98	**GOOD GIRLS** *Jive JIVECD 442*	29	3
22 Aug 98	**NO ONE ELSE COMES CLOSE** *Jive 0521682*...............	41	2
31 Oct 98	**ALL THAT I AM** *Jive 0518532*.....................................	52	1
11 Mar 00 ●	**THANK GOD I FOUND YOU** *Columbia 6690582* [1] ▲ 10		9
20 May 00	**THANK GOD I FOUND YOU (re-entry)** *Columbia 6690582* [1] 71		1
15 Jul 00	**TREAT HER LIKE A LADY** *Jive 9250772*.......................	60	1

[1] Mariah Carey featuring Joe and 98 Degrees

JOE PUBLIC *US, male rap group (5 WEEKS)* pos/wks

11 Jul 92	**LIVE AND LEARN** *Columbia 6575267*	43	4
28 Nov 92	**I'VE BEEN WATCHIN'** *Columbia 6587657*	75	1

Billy JOEL (156 **Top 500**) *Platinum-plated singer / songwriter / pianist, b. 9 May 1949, Long Island, US. This relatively youthful Grammy Living Legend Award recipient was first artist to have five albums pass the seven million mark Stateside. (146 WEEKS)* pos/wks

11 Feb 78	**JUST THE WAY YOU ARE** *CBS 5872*............................	19	9
24 Jun 78	**MOVIN' OUT (ANTHONY'S SONG)** *CBS 6412*...............	35	6
2 Dec 78	**MY LIFE** *CBS 6821*	12	15
28 Apr 79	**UNTIL THE NIGHT** *CBS 7242*	50	3
12 Apr 80	**ALL FOR LEYNA** *CBS 8325*..	40	4
9 Aug 80	**IT'S STILL ROCK AND ROLL TO ME** *CBS 8753* ▲........14		11
15 Oct 83 ★	**UPTOWN GIRL** *CBS A 3775*...	1	17
10 Dec 83 ●	**TELL HER ABOUT IT** *CBS A 3655* ▲	4	10
18 Feb 84 ●	**AN INNOCENT MAN** *CBS A 4142*	8	10
28 Apr 84	**THE LONGEST TIME** *CBS A 4280*................................	25	8
23 Jun 84	**LEAVE A TENDER MOMENT ALONE / GOODNIGHT SAIGON** *CBS A 4521*..	29	7
22 Feb 86	**SHE'S ALWAYS A WOMAN / JUST THE WAY YOU ARE (re-issue)** *CBS A 6862*..	53	1
20 Sep 86	**A MATTER OF TRUST** *CBS 650057 7*	52	4
30 Sep 89 ●	**WE DIDN'T START THE FIRE** *CBS JOEL 1* ▲	7	10
16 Dec 89	**LENINGRAD** *CBS JOEL 3*	53	4
10 Mar 90	**I GO TO EXTREMES** *CBS JOEL 2*	70	2
29 Aug 92	**ALL SHOOK UP** *Columbia 6583437*	27	4
31 Jul 93 ●	**THE RIVER OF DREAMS** *Columbia 6595432*................	3	14
23 Oct 93	**ALL ABOUT SOUL** *Columbia 6597362*.........................	32	4
26 Feb 94	**NO MAN'S LAND** *Columbia 6599202*............................	50	3

'Goodnight Saigon' listed only from 30 Jun, 1984

JOHANN *Germany, male producer - Johann Bley (1 WEEK)* pos/wks

16 Mar 96	**NEW KICKS** *Perfecto PERF 118CD*	54	1

Angela JOHN – See José PADILLA featuring Angela JOHN

Elton JOHN (4 **Top 500**) *Flamboyant singer / songwriter / pianist, b. Reginald Dwight, 25 Mar 1947, Pinner, Middlesex, UK. Almost as famous for his outrageous wardrobe as his music, Elton was the biggest-selling pop act of the 1970s, and has sold more albums in the UK and US than any British male singer, with total worldwide sales exceeding 150 million. He is the only British act to enter the US singles chart at No.1 and also recorded the first two albums to enter the US chart at No.1. He holds the record for headlining appearances at New York's Madison Square Garden. Elton, twice Chairman of Watford Football Club, is the only act to chart every year from 1971 - 1999 in the UK and US. His Greatest Hits album has sold over 15 million in the US and has topped the US Adult Contemporary chart a record 16 times. 'Candle In The Wind 1997' (which he performed at the funeral of Diana, Princess of Wales) topped the chart in almost every country. In the UK it sold more than five*

million in six weeks and in the US had record advance orders of 8.7 million (and total sales in excess of 11 million). It also spent a staggering three years in the Canadian Top 20, which included 45 weeks at No.1. It is the world's biggest-selling single, with sales of 33 million in three months. His lyric writing partners have included, most influentially, Bernie Taupin and, more recently, Sir Tim Rice. He became Sir Elton John in 1998 (566 WEEKS) pos/wks

23 Jan 71 ●	**YOUR SONG** *DJM DJS 233*	7	12
22 Apr 72 ●	**ROCKET MAN (I THINK IT'S GOING TO BE A LONG LONG TIME)** *DJM DJX 501*..	2	13
9 Sep 72	**HONKY CAT** *DJM DJS 269*	31	6
4 Nov 72 ●	**CROCODILE ROCK** *DJM DJS 271* ▲	5	14
20 Jan 73	**DANIEL** *DJM DJS 275*..	4	9
7 Jul 73	**SATURDAY NIGHT'S ALRIGHT FOR FIGHTING** *DJM DJX 502*....7		9
29 Sep 73 ●	**GOODBYE YELLOW BRICK ROAD** *DJM DJS 285*..........	6	16
8 Dec 73	**STEP INTO CHRISTMAS** *DJM DJS 290*	24	7
2 Mar 74	**CANDLE IN THE WIND** *DJM DJS 297*	11	9
1 Jun 74	**DON'T LET THE SUN GO DOWN ON ME** *DJM DJS 302* 16		8
14 Sep 74	**THE BITCH IS BACK** *DJM DJS 322*	15	7
23 Nov 74 ●	**LUCY IN THE SKY WITH DIAMONDS** *DJM DJS 340* ▲ 10		10
8 Mar 75	**PHILADELPHIA FREEDOM** *DJM DJS 354* [1] ▲	12	9
28 Jun 75	**SOMEONE SAVED MY LIFE TONIGHT** *DJM DJS 385*	22	5
4 Oct 75	**ISLAND GIRL** *DJM DJS 610* ▲	14	8
20 Mar 76 ●	**PINBALL WIZARD** *DJM DJS 652*...................................	7	7
3 Jul 76 ★	**DON'T GO BREAKING MY HEART** *Rocket ROKN 512* [2] ▲ 1		14
25 Sep 76	**BENNIE AND THE JETS** *DJM DJS 10705* ▲	37	5
13 Nov 76	**SORRY SEEMS TO BE THE HARDEST WORD** *Rocket ROKN 517*....11		10
26 Feb 77	**CRAZY WATER** *Rocket ROKN 521*	27	6
11 Jun 77	**BITE YOUR LIP (GET UP AND DANCE)** *Rocket ROKN 526*....28		4
15 Apr 78	**EGO** *Rocket ROKN 538*	34	6
21 Oct 78	**PART TIME LOVE** *Rocket XPRES 1*	15	13
16 Dec 78 ●	**SONG FOR GUY** *Rocket XPRES 5*................................	4	10
12 May 79	**ARE YOU READY FOR LOVE** *Rocket XPRES 13*...........	42	6
24 May 80	**LITTLE JEANNIE** *Rocket XPRES 32*	33	9
23 Aug 80	**SARTORIAL ELOQUENCE** *Rocket XPRES 41*...............	44	5
21 Mar 81	**I SAW HER STANDING THERE** *DJM DJS 10965* [3]	40	4
23 May 81	**NOBODY WINS** *Rocket XPRES 54*	42	5
27 Mar 82 ●	**BLUE EYES** *Rocket XPRES 71*	8	10
12 Jun 82	**EMPTY GARDEN** *Rocket XPRES 77*	51	4
30 Apr 83 ●	**I GUESS THAT'S WHY THEY CALL IT THE BLUES** *Rocket XPRES 91*..	5	15
30 Jul 83 ●	**I'M STILL STANDING** *Rocket EJS 1*..............................	4	11
15 Oct 83	**KISS THE BRIDE** *Rocket EJS 2*....................................	20	7
10 Dec 83	**COLD AS CHRISTMAS** *Rocket EJS 3*	33	6
26 May 84	**SAD SONGS (SAY SO MUCH)** *Rocket PH 7*	7	12
11 Aug 84 ●	**PASSENGERS** *Rocket EJS 5*.......................................	5	11
20 Oct 84	**WHO WEARS THESE SHOES** *Rocket EJS 6*	50	3
2 Mar 85	**BREAKING HEARTS (AIN'T WHAT IT USED TO BE)** *Rocket EJS 7*	59	3
15 Jun 85	**ACT OF WAR** *Rocket EJS 8* [4]	32	5
12 Oct 85 ●	**NIKITA** *Rocket EJS 9*..	3	13
9 Nov 85	**THAT'S WHAT FRIENDS ARE FOR** *Arista ARIST 638* [5] 16		9
7 Dec 85	**WRAP HER UP** *Rocket EJS 10*.....................................	12	10
1 Mar 86	**CRY TO HEAVEN** *Rocket EJS 11*.................................	47	4
4 Oct 86	**HEARTACHE ALL OVER THE WORLD** *Rocket EJS 12* 45		4
29 Nov 86	**SLOW RIVERS** *Rocket EJS 13* [6]	44	8
20 Jun 87	**FLAMES OF PARADISE** *CBS 6508657* [7]	59	3
16 Jan 88 ●	**CANDLE IN THE WIND** *Rocket EJS 15*	5	11
4 Jun 88	**I DON'T WANNA GO ON WITH YOU LIKE THAT** *Rocket EJS 16* 30		8
3 Sep 88	**TOWN OF PLENTY** *Rocket EJS 17*	74	1
6 May 89	**THROUGH THE STORM** *Arista 112185* [8]	41	3
26 Aug 89	**HEALING HANDS** *Rocket EJS 19*.................................	45	5
4 Nov 89	**SACRIFICE** *Rocket EJS 20*..	55	3
9 Jun 90 ★	**SACRIFICE / HEALING HANDS (re-issue)** *Rocket EJS 22*...........1		15
18 Aug 90	**CLUB AT THE END OF THE STREET / WHISPERS** *Rocket EJS 23*	47	3
20 Oct 90	**YOU GOTTA LOVE SOMEONE** *Rocket EJS 24*	33	4
15 Dec 90	**EASIER TO WALK AWAY** *Rocket EJS 25*	67	1
29 Dec 90	**EASIER TO WALK AWAY (re-entry)** *Rocket EJS 25*...............	63	1
7 Dec 91 ★	**DON'T LET THE SUN GO DOWN ON ME** *Epic 6576467* [9] ■ ▲ ..1		10
6 Jun 92	**THE ONE** *Rocket EJS 28*	10	8
1 Aug 92	**RUNAWAY TRAIN** *Rocket EJS 29* [10]	31	4
7 Nov 92	**THE LAST SONG** *Rocket EJS 30*.................................	21	4
22 May 93	**SIMPLE LIFE** *Rocket EJSCD 31*	44	2

20 Nov 93 ●	TRUE LOVE *Rocket EJSCX 32* [2]	2	10
26 Feb 94 ●	DON'T GO BREAKING MY HEART *Rocket EJRCD 33* [11]	7	7
14 May 94	AIN'T NOTHING LIKE THE REAL THING *London LONCD 350* [12]	24	4
9 Jul 94	CAN YOU FEEL THE LOVE TONIGHT *Mercury EJCD 34*	14	9
8 Oct 94 ●	CIRCLE OF LIFE *Rocket EJSCD 35*	11	12
4 Mar 95	BELIEVE *Rocket EJSCD 36*	15	7
20 May 95	MADE IN ENGLAND *Rocket EJSCD 37*	18	5
3 Feb 96	PLEASE *Rocket EJSCD 40*	33	3
14 Dec 96 ●	LIVE LIKE HORSES *Rocket LLHDD 1* [13]	9	6
20 Sep 97 ★	CANDLE IN THE WIND 1997 / SOMETHING ABOUT THE WAY YOU LOOK TONIGHT *Rocket PTCD 1* ◆ ■ ▲	1	24
14 Feb 98	RECOVER YOUR SOUL *Rocket EJSCD 42*	16	3
13 Jun 98	IF THE RIVER CAN BEND *Rocket EJSDD 43*	32	2
6 Mar 99 ●	WRITTEN IN THE STARS *Mercury EJSCD 45* [14]	10	7
22 May 99	WRITTEN IN THE STARS (re-entry) *Mercury EJSCD 45* [14]	63	1

[1] Elton John Band [2] Elton John and Kiki Dee [3] Elton John Band featuring John Lennon and the Muscle Shoals Horns [4] Elton John and Millie Jackson [5] Dionne Warwick and Friends featuring Elton John, Stevie Wonder and Gladys Knight [6] Elton John and Cliff Richard [7] Jennifer Rush and Elton John [8] Aretha Franklin and Elton John [9] George Michael and Elton John [10] Elton John and Eric Clapton [11] Elton John with RuPaul [12] Marcella Detroit and Elton John [13] Elton John and Luciano Pavarotti [14] Elton John and LeAnn Rimes

'Bite Your Lip (Get Up and Dance)' was one side of a double-sided chart entry, the other being 'Chicago' by Kiki Dee. 'Wrap Her Up' features George Michael as uncredited co-vocalist. 'Candle in the Wind' 1988 was a live recording

Robert JOHN *US, male vocalist (13 WEEKS)* pos/wks
17 Jul 68	IF YOU DON'T WANT MY LOVE *CBS 3436*	42	5
20 Oct 79	SAD EYES *EMI American EA 101* ▲	31	8

JOHNNA *US, female vocalist (3 WEEKS)* pos/wks
10 Feb 96	DO WHAT YOU FEEL *PWL International PWL 323CD*	43	2
11 May 96	IN MY DREAMS *PWL International PWL 325CD*	66	1

JOHNNY and CHARLEY *Spain, male vocal duo (1 WEEK)* pos/wks
14 Oct 65	LA YENKA *Pye International 7N 25326*	49	1

JOHNNY and the HURRICANES (353) Top 500
Internationally successful instrumental quintet formed 1957, Ohio, US. Featured saxophonist Johnny Paris (born Pocisk) and organist Paul Tesluk. Specialised in rocking retreads of old standards. The Beatles supported them in Hamburg in Dec 1962 (88 WEEKS) pos/wks
9 Oct 59 ●	RED RIVER ROCK *London HL 8948*	3	16
25 Dec 59	REVEILLE ROCK *London HL 9017*	14	5
17 Mar 60 ●	BEATNIK FLY *London HLI 9072*	8	11
16 Jun 60 ●	DOWN YONDER *London HLX 9134*	8	11
29 Sep 60 ●	ROCKING GOOSE *London HLX 9190*	3	20
2 Mar 61	JA-DA *London HLX 9289*	14	9
6 Jul 61	OLD SMOKEY / HIGH VOLTAGE *London HLX 9378*	24	8

JOHNNY CORPORATE *US, male production duo (2 WEEKS)* pos/wks
28 Oct 00	SUNDAY SHOUTIN' *Defected DFECT 21CDS*	45	2

JOHNNY HATES JAZZ
UK, male vocal / instrumental group (45 WEEKS) pos/wks
11 Apr 87 ●	SHATTERED DREAMS *Virgin VS 948*	5	14
29 Aug 87	I DON'T WANT TO BE A HERO *Virgin VS 1000*	11	10
21 Nov 87	TURN BACK THE CLOCK *Virgin VS 1017*	12	11
27 Feb 88	HEART OF GOLD *Virgin VS 1045*	19	7
9 Jul 88	DON'T SAY IT'S LOVE *Virgin VS 1081*	48	3

JOHNSON *UK, male / female vocal / instrumental duo (1 WEEK)* pos/wks
27 Mar 99	SAY YOU LOVE ME *Higher Ground HIGHS 18CD*	56	1

Andreas JOHNSON *Sweden, male vocalist (12 WEEKS)* pos/wks
5 Feb 00 ●	GLORIOUS *WEA WEA 254CD*	4	11
27 May 00	THE GAMES WE PLAY *WEA WEA 264*	41	1

Bryan JOHNSON *UK, male vocalist (11 WEEKS)* pos/wks
10 Mar 60	LOOKING HIGH HIGH HIGH *Decca F 11213*	20	11

Carey JOHNSON *Australia, male vocalist (8 WEEKS)* pos/wks
25 Apr 87	REAL FASHION REGGAE STYLE *Oval TEN 170*	19	8

Denise JOHNSON *UK, female vocalist (4 WEEKS)* pos/wks
24 Aug 91	DON'T FIGHT IT FEEL IT *Creation CRE 110* [1]	41	2
14 May 94	RAYS OF THE RISING SUN *Magnet MAG 1022CD*	45	2

[1] Primal Scream featuring Denise Johnson

Don JOHNSON *US, male vocalist (12 WEEKS)* pos/wks
18 Oct 86	HEARTBEAT *Epic 650064 7*	46	5
5 Nov 88	TILL I LOVED YOU (LOVE THEME FROM 'GOYA') *CBS BARB 2* [1]	16	7

[1] Barbra Streisand and Don Johnson

General JOHNSON – See CHAIRMEN OF THE BOARD

Holly JOHNSON *UK, male vocalist (38 WEEKS)* pos/wks
14 Jan 89 ●	LOVE TRAIN *MCA MCA 1306*	4	11
1 Apr 89 ●	AMERICANOS *MCA MCA 1323*	4	11
20 May 89 ★	FERRY 'CROSS THE MERSEY *PWL PWL 41* [1] ■	1	7
24 Jun 89	ATOMIC CITY *MCA MCA 1342*	18	4
30 Sep 89	HEAVEN'S HERE *MCA MCA 1365*	62	2
1 Dec 90	WHERE HAS LOVE GONE *MCA MCA 1460*	73	1
25 Dec 99	THE POWER OF LOVE *Pleasure Dome PLDCD 1005*	56	2

[1] Christians, Holly Johnson, Paul McCartney, Gerry Marsden and Stock Aitken Waterman

See also FRANKIE GOES TO HOLLYWOOD

Howard JOHNSON *US, male vocalist (6 WEEKS)* pos/wks
4 Sep 82	KEEPIN' LOVE NEW / SO FINE *A & M USA 1221*	45	6

'Keepin' Love New' listed 4 Sep 1982 only

Johnny JOHNSON and the BANDWAGON
US, male vocal group (50 WEEKS) pos/wks
16 Oct 68 ●	BREAKIN' DOWN THE WALLS OF HEARTACHE *Direction 58-3670* [1]	4	15
5 Feb 69	YOU *Direction 58-3923* [1]	34	4
28 May 69	LET'S HANG ON *Direction 58-4180* [1]	36	6
25 Jul 70	SWEET INSPIRATION *Bell 1111*	10	12
24 Oct 70	SWEET INSPIRATION (re-entry) *Bell 1111*	46	1
28 Nov 70 ●	BLAME IT ON THE PONY EXPRESS *Bell 1128*	7	12

[1] Bandwagon

Kevin JOHNSON *Australia, male vocalist (6 WEEKS)* pos/wks
11 Jan 75	ROCK 'N ROLL (I GAVE YOU THE BEST YEARS OF MY LIFE) *UK UKR 84*	23	6

Laurie JOHNSON *UK, orchestra (14 WEEKS)* pos/wks
28 Sep 61 ●	SUCU SUCU *Pye 7N 15383*	9	12
17 May 97	THEME FROM 'THE PROFESSIONALS' *Virgin VSCDT 1643* [1]	36	2

[1] Laurie Johnson's London Big Band

LJ JOHNSON *US, male vocalist (6 WEEKS)* pos/wks
7 Feb 76	YOUR MAGIC PUT A SPELL ON ME *Philips 6006 492*	27	6

Lou JOHNSON *US, male vocalist (2 WEEKS)* pos/wks
26 Nov 64	MESSAGE TO MARTHA *London HL 9929*	36	2

Marv JOHNSON US, male vocalist (39 WEEKS) pos/wks

12 Feb 60 ●	YOU GOT WHAT IT TAKES London HLT 9013	**7**	16
5 May 60	I LOVE THE WAY YOU LOVE London HLT 9109	**35**	3
11 Aug 60	AIN'T GONNA BE THAT WAY London HLT 9165	**50**	1
22 Jan 69 ●	I'LL PICK A ROSE FOR MY ROSE Tamla Motown TMG 680	**10**	11
25 Oct 69	I MISS YOU BABY Tamla Motown TMG 713	**25**	8

Orlando JOHNSON – See SECCHI featuring Orlando JOHNSON

Paul JOHNSON US, male producer / instrumentalist (8 WEEKS) pos/wks

25 Sep 99 ●	GET GET DOWN Defected DEFECT 7CDS	**5**	8

Paul JOHNSON UK, male vocalist (7 WEEKS) pos/wks

21 Feb 87	WHEN LOVE COMES CALLING CBS PJOHN 1	**52**	5
25 Feb 89	NO MORE TOMORROWS CBS PJOHN 7	**67**	2

Puff JOHNSON US, female vocalist (6 WEEKS) pos/wks

18 Jan 97	OVER AND OVER Columbia 6640345	**20**	4
12 Apr 97	FOREVER MORE Work 644075	**29**	2

Romina JOHNSON UK female vocalist (13 WEEKS) pos/wks

4 Mar 00 ●	MOVIN TOO FAST Locked On XL LOX 117CD [1]	**2**	11
10 Jun 00	MOVIN TOO FAST (re-entry) Locked On XL LOX 117CD [1]	**64**	1
17 Jun 00	MY FORBIDDEN LOVER 51 Lexington CDLEX 1 [2]	**59**	1

[1] Artful Dodger & Romina Johnson [2] Romina Johnson Featuring Luci Martin & Norma Jean

Teddy JOHNSON – See Pearl CARR and Teddy JOHNSON

JOHNSTON BROTHERS UK, male vocal group - leader Johnny Johnston (Reine) (33 WEEKS) pos/wks

3 Apr 53 ●	OH, HAPPY DAY Decca F 10071	**4**	8
5 Nov 54	WAIT FOR ME, DARLING Decca F 10362 [1]	**18**	1
21 Jan 55	HAPPY DAYS AND LONELY NIGHTS Decca F 10389	**14**	2
7 Oct 55 ★	HERNANDO'S HIDEAWAY Decca F 10608	**1**	13
30 Dec 55 ●	JOIN IN AND SING AGAIN Decca F 10636 [2]	**9**	1
13 Apr 56	NO OTHER LOVE Decca F 10721	**22**	1
30 Nov 56	IN THE MIDDLE OF THE HOUSE Decca F 10781	**27**	1
7 Dec 56	JOIN IN AND SING (NO. 3) Decca F 10814	**30**	1
28 Dec 56	JOIN IN AND SING (NO.3) (re-entry) Decca F 10814	**24**	1
8 Feb 57	GIVE HER MY LOVE Decca F 10828	**27**	1
19 Apr 57	HEART Decca F 10860	**23**	3

[1] Joan Regan with the Johnston Brothers [2] Johnson Brothers & The George Chisholm Sour-Note Six

The following two hits were medleys: Join In and Sing Again: Sheik of Araby / Yes Sir That's My Baby / California Here I Come / Some of These Days / Charleston / Margie. Join In and Sing (No.3): Coal Black Morning / When You're Smiling / Alexander's Ragtime Band / Sweet Sue Just You / When You Wore a Tulip / If You Were the Only Girl in the World.

Bruce JOHNSTON US, male instrumentalist - keyboards (4 WEEKS) pos/wks

27 Aug 77	PIPELINE CBS 5514	**33**	4

Jan JOHNSTON – See FREEFALL featuring Jan JOHNSTON; SUBMERGE featuring Jan JOHNSTON; TOMSKI

Sabrina JOHNSTON US, female vocalist (19 WEEKS) pos/wks

7 Sep 91 ●	PEACE East West YZ 616	**8**	10
7 Dec 91	FRIENDSHIP East West YZ 637	**58**	4
11 Jul 92	I WANNA SING East West YZ 661	**46**	2
3 Oct 92	PEACE (re-mix) Epic 6584377	**35**	2
13 Aug 94	SATISFY MY LOVE Champion CHAMPCD 311	**62**	1

The listed flipside of 'Peace' (re-mix) was 'Gypsy Woman' (re-mix) by Crystal Waters

JOJO – See 2PAC; K-CI & JOJO

James JOLIS – See Barry MANILOW

JOLLY BROTHERS Jamaica, male vocal / instrumental group (7 WEEKS) pos/wks

28 Jul 79	CONSCIOUS MAN United Artists UP 36415	**46**	7

JOLLY ROGER UK, male instrumentalist / producer (12 WEEKS) pos/wks

10 Sep 88	ACID MAN 10 TEN 236	**23**	12

JOMALSKI – See WILDCHILD

JOMANDA US, female vocal group (10 WEEKS) pos/wks

22 Apr 89	MAKE MY BODY ROCK RCA PB 42749	**44**	3
29 Jun 91	GOT A LOVE FOR YOU Giant W 0040	**43**	4
11 Sep 93	I LIKE IT Big Beat A 8377CD	**67**	1
13 Nov 93	NEVER Big Beat A 8347CD	**40**	2

JON and VANGELIS UK, male vocalist and Greece, male multi-instrumentalist - Jon Anderson and Evangelos Papathanassiou (28 WEEKS) pos/wks

5 Jan 80 ●	I HEAR YOU NOW Polydor POSP 96	**8**	11
12 Dec 81 ●	I'LL FIND MY WAY HOME Polydor JV 1	**6**	13
30 Jul 83	HE IS SAILING Polydor JV 4	**61**	2
18 Aug 84	STATE OF INDEPENDENCE Polydor JV 5	**67**	2

See also VANGELIS

JON OF THE PLEASED WIMMIN UK, male DJ / Producer (5 WEEKS) pos/wks

18 Feb 95	PASSION Perfecto YZ 884CD	**27**	3
6 Apr 96	GIVE ME STRENGTH Perfecto PERF 119CD	**30**	2

JON THE DENTIST Vs Ollie JAYE UK, male DJs / producers (2 WEEKS) pos/wks

24 Jul 99	IMAGINATION Tidy Trax TIDY 126CD	**72**	1
10 Jun 00	FEEL SO GOOD Tidy Trax TIDY 135CD	**72**	1

JONAH Holland, male production group (4 WEEKS) pos/wks

22 Jul 00	SSSST (LISTEN) VC Recordings VCRD 69	**25**	4

Aled JONES UK, male vocalist (24 WEEKS) pos/wks

20 Jul 85	MEMORY BBC RESL 175	**42**	4
30 Nov 85 ●	WALKING IN THE AIR HMV ALED 1	**5**	11
14 Dec 85	PICTURES IN THE DARK Virgin VS 836 [1]	**50**	6
20 Dec 86	A WINTER STORY HMV ALED 2	**51**	3

[1] Mike Oldfield featuring Aled Jones, Anita Hegerland and Barry Palmer

Barbara JONES Jamaica, female vocalist (7 WEEKS) pos/wks

31 Jan 81	JUST WHEN I NEEDED YOU MOST Sonet SON 2221	**31**	7

Catherine Zeta JONES UK, female vocalist (9 WEEKS) pos/wks

19 Sep 92	FOR ALL TIME Columbia 6583547	**36**	5
26 Nov 94	TRUE LOVE WAYS PolyGram TV TLWCD 2 [1]	**38**	3
1 Apr 95	IN THE ARMS OF LOVE Wow! WOWCD 7101	**72**	1

[1] David Essex and Catherine Zeta Jones

Donell JONES US, male vocalist (18 WEEKS) pos/wks

15 Feb 97	KNOCKS ME OFF MY FEET LaFace 74321458502	**58**	1
22 Jan 00 ●	U KNOW WHAT'S UP LaFace 74321722752	**2**	11
20 May 00	SHORTY (GOT HER EYES ON ME) Laface 74321748902	**19**	3
2 Dec 00	TRUE STEP TONIGHT Nulife 74321811312 [1]	**25**	3

[1] True Steppers featuring Brian Harvey and Donell Jones

Georgia JONES – See PLUX featuring Georgia JONES; DIVA SURPRISE Featuring Georgia JONES

Grace JONES
US, female vocalist (46 WEEKS) — pos/wks

Date	Title	pos	wks
26 Jul 80	PRIVATE LIFE *Island WIP 6629*	17	8
20 Jun 81	PULL UP TO THE BUMPER *Island WIP 6696*	53	4
30 Oct 82	THE APPLE STRETCHING / NIPPLE TO THE BOTTLE *Island WIP 6779*	50	4
9 Apr 83	MY JAMAICAN GUY *Island IS 103*	56	3
12 Oct 85	SLAVE TO THE RHYTHM *ZTT IS 206*	12	8
18 Jan 86	PULL UP TO THE BUMPER / LA VIE EN ROSE (re-issue) *Island IS 240*	12	9
1 Mar 86	LOVE IS THE DRUG *Island IS 266*	35	4
15 Nov 86	I'M NOT PERFECT (BUT I'M PERFECT FOR YOU) *Manhattan MT 15*	56	3
7 May 94	SLAVE TO THE RHYTHM (re-mix) *Zance ZANG 50CD1* [1]	28	2
25 Nov 00	PULL UP TO THE BUMPER *Club Tools 0120375 CLU* [1]	60	1

[1] Grace Jones vs Funkstar De Luxe

'La Vie En Rose' was listed only from 1 Feb 1986

Hannah JONES
US, female vocalist (9 WEEKS) — pos/wks

Date	Title	pos	wks
14 Sep 91	BRIDGE OVER TROUBLED WATER *Dance Pool 6565467* [1]	21	8
30 Jan 93	KEEP IT ON *TMRC CDTMRC 7*	67	1

[1] PJB featuring Hannah and her Sisters

Howard JONES
287 | Top 500 | Accomplished singer / songwriter, b. 23 Feb 1955, Southampton, UK, who was a regular chart visitor in the mid-1980s with his brand of synth-based pop. Jones, who was equally popular in the US, appeared at Live Aid (103 WEEKS) — pos/wks

Date	Title	pos	wks
17 Sep 83	● NEW SONG *WEA HOW 1*	3	12
26 Nov 83	● WHAT IS LOVE *WEA HOW 2*	2	15
14 Jan 84	NEW SONG (re-entry) *WEA HOW 1*	60	3
18 Feb 84	HIDE AND SEEK *WEA HOW 3*	12	9
26 May 84	● PEARL IN THE SHELL *WEA HOW 4*	7	10
11 Aug 84	● LIKE TO GET TO KNOW YOU WELL *WEA HOW 5*	4	12
9 Feb 85	● THINGS CAN ONLY GET BETTER *WEA HOW 6*	6	8
20 Apr 85	● LOOK MAMA *WEA HOW 7*	10	6
29 Jun 85	LIFE IN ONE DAY *WEA HOW 8*	14	7
15 Mar 86	NO ONE IS TO BLAME *WEA HOW 9*	16	7
4 Oct 86	ALL I WANT *WEA HOW 10*	35	4
29 Nov 86	YOU KNOW I LOVE YOU...DON'T YOU? *WEA HOW 11*	43	3
21 Mar 87	A LITTLE BIT OF SNOW *WEA HOW 12*	70	1
4 Mar 89	EVERLASTING LOVE *WEA HOW 13*	62	3
11 Apr 92	LIFT ME UP *East West HOW 15*	52	3

Janie JONES
UK, female vocalist (3 WEEKS) — pos/wks

Date	Title	pos	wks
27 Jan 66	WITCHES' BREW *HMV POP 1495*	46	3

Jimmy JONES
US, male vocalist (47 WEEKS) — pos/wks

Date	Title	pos	wks
17 Mar 60	● HANDY MAN *MGM 1051*	3	21
16 Jun 60	★ GOOD TIMIN' *MGM 1078*	1	15
18 Aug 60	HANDY MAN (re-entry) *MGM 1051*	32	3
8 Sep 60	I JUST GO FOR YOU *MGM 1091*	35	4
17 Nov 60	READY FOR LOVE *MGM 1103*	46	1
30 Mar 61	I TOLD YOU SO *MGM 1123*	33	3

Juggy JONES
US, male multi-instrumentalist (4 WEEKS) — pos/wks

Date	Title	pos	wks
7 Feb 76	INSIDE AMERICA *Contempo CS 2080*	39	4

Kelly JONES – See MANCHILD featuring Kelly JONES

Lavinia JONES
South Africa, female vocalist (2 WEEKS) — pos/wks

Date	Title	pos	wks
18 Feb 95	SING IT TO YOU (DEE-DOOB-DEE-DOO) *Virgin International DINDG 142*	45	2

Mick JONES – See AZTEC CAMERA; CLASH

Oran 'Juice' JONES
US, male vocalist (14 WEEKS) — pos/wks

Date	Title	pos	wks
15 Nov 86	● THE RAIN *Def Jam A 7303*	4	14

Paul JONES
UK, male vocalist - Paul Pond (34 WEEKS) — pos/wks

Date	Title	pos	wks
6 Oct 66	● HIGH TIME *HMV POP 1554*	4	15
19 Jan 67	● I'VE BEEN A BAD BAD BOY *HMV POP 1576*	5	9
23 Aug 67	THINKIN' AIN'T FOR ME *HMV POP 1602*	47	1
13 Sep 67	THINKIN' AIN'T FOR ME (re-entry) *HMV POP 1602*	32	7
5 Feb 69	AQUARIUS *Columbia DB 8514*	45	2

See also MANFRED MANN; BLUES BAND

Quincy JONES
US, male producer / instrumentalist - keyboards (42 WEEKS) — pos/wks

Date	Title	pos	wks
29 Jul 78	STUFF LIKE THAT *A & M AMS 7367*	34	9
11 Apr 81	AI NO CORRIDA (I-NO-KO-REE-DA) *A & M AMS 8109* [1]	14	10
20 Jun 81	RAZZAMATAZZ *A & M AMS 8140*	11	9
5 Sep 81	BETCHA' WOULDN'T HURT ME *A & M AMS 8157*	52	3
13 Jan 90	I'LL BE GOOD TO YOU *Qwest W 2697* [2]	21	7
31 Mar 90	SECRET GARDEN *Qwest W 9992* [3]	67	1
14 Sep 96	STOMP *Qwest W 0372CD* [4]	28	2
1 Aug 98	SOUL BOSSA NOVA *Manifesto FESCD 48*	47	1

[1] Quincy Jones featuring Dune [2] Quincy Jones featuring Ray Charles and Chaka Khan [3] Quincy Jones featuring Al B Sure!, James Ingram, El DeBarge and Barry White [4] Quincy Jones featuring Melle Mel, Coolio, Yo-Yo, Shaquille O'Neal, The Luniz

Uncredited vocals on 'Stuff Like That' were by Ashford and Simpson and Chaka Khan, and on 'Razzamatazz' and 'Betcha' Wouldn't Hurt Me' by Patti Austin

Rickie Lee JONES
US, female vocalist (9 WEEKS) — pos/wks

Date	Title	pos	wks
23 Jun 79	CHUCK E.'S IN LOVE *Warner Bros. K 17390*	18	9

Shirley JONES – See PARTRIDGE FAMILY

Sonny JONES featuring Tara CHASE
Germany, male vocalist and Canada, female rapper (2 WEEKS) — pos/wks

Date	Title	pos	wks
7 Oct 00	FOLLOW YOU FOLLOW ME *Logic 74321772892*	42	2

Tammy JONES
UK, female vocalist (10 WEEKS) — pos/wks

Date	Title	pos	wks
26 Apr 75	● LET ME TRY AGAIN *Epic EPC 3211*	5	10

Tom JONES
16 | Top 500 | Continually popular vocalist who has remained an international headliner for four decades. b. Thomas Woodward, 7 Jun 1940, South Wales. This long-time sex symbol was the top British solo singer of the 1960s on both sides of Atlantic. His 1999 Album 'Reload' was his biggest-selling UK album ever and was a top 10 hit in many other countries (390 WEEKS) — pos/wks

Date	Title	pos	wks
11 Feb 65	★ IT'S NOT UNUSUAL *Decca F 12062*	1	14
6 May 65	ONCE UPON A TIME *Decca F 12121*	32	4
8 Jul 65	WITH THESE HANDS *Decca F 12191*	13	11
12 Aug 65	WHAT'S NEW PUSSYCAT *Decca F 12203*	11	10
13 Jan 66	THUNDERBALL *Decca F 12292*	35	4
19 May 66	ONCE THERE WAS A TIME / NOT RESPONSIBLE *Decca F 12390*	18	9
18 Aug 66	THIS AND THAT *Decca F 12461*	44	3
10 Nov 66	★ GREEN GREEN GRASS OF HOME *Decca F 22511* ◆	1	22
16 Feb 67	● DETROIT CITY *Decca F 22555*	8	10
13 Apr 67	● FUNNY FAMILIAR FORGOTTEN FEELINGS *Decca F 12599*	7	15
26 Jul 67	● I'LL NEVER FALL IN LOVE AGAIN *Decca F 12639*	2	25
22 Nov 67	● I'M COMING HOME *Decca F 12693*	2	16
28 Feb 68	● DELILAH *Decca F 12747*	2	17
17 Jul 68	● HELP YOURSELF *Decca F 12812*	5	26
27 Nov 68	A MINUTE OF YOUR TIME *Decca F 12854*	14	15
14 May 69	LOVE ME TONIGHT *Decca F 12924*	9	12
13 Dec 69	● WITHOUT LOVE *Decca F 12990*	10	11
14 Mar 70	WITHOUT LOVE (re-entry) *Decca F 12990*	49	1
18 Apr 70	● DAUGHTER OF DARKNESS *Decca F 13013*	5	15
15 Aug 70	I (WHO HAVE NOTHING) *Decca F 13061*	16	9
17 Oct 70	I (WHO HAVE NOTHING) (re-entry) *Decca F 13061*	47	3
16 Jan 71	SHE'S A LADY *Decca F 13113*	13	9
27 Mar 71	SHE'S A LADY (re-entry) *Decca F 13113*	47	1
5 Jun 71	PUPPET MAN *Decca F 13183*	49	1
19 Jun 71	PUPPET MAN (re-entry) *Decca F 13183*	50	1

23 Oct 71	●	TILL Decca F 13236	2	15
1 Apr 72	●	THE YOUNG NEW MEXICAN PUPPETEER Decca F 13298	6	12
14 Apr 73		LETTER TO LUCILLE Decca F 13393	31	8
7 Sep 74		SOMETHING 'BOUT YOU BABY I LIKE Decca F 13550	36	5
16 Apr 77		SAY YOU'LL STAY UNTIL TOMORROW EMI 2583	40	3
18 Apr 87	●	A BOY FROM NOWHERE Epic OLE 1	2	12
30 May 87		IT'S NOT UNUSUAL (re-issue) Decca F 103	17	8
2 Jan 88		I WAS BORN TO BE ME Epic OLE 4	61	1
29 Oct 88	●	KISS China CHINA 11 [1]	5	7
29 Apr 89		MOVE CLOSER Jive JIVE 203	49	3
26 Jan 91		COULDN'T SAY GOODBYE Dover ROJ 10	51	2
16 Mar 91		CARRYING A TORCH Dover ROJ 12	57	2
4 Jul 92		DELILAH (re-issue) The Hit Label TOM 10	68	2
6 Feb 93		ALL YOU NEED IS LOVE Childline CHILDCD 93	19	4
5 Nov 94		IF I ONLY KNEW ZTT ZANG 59CD	11	9
25 Sep 99	●	BURNING DOWN THE HOUSE Gut CDGUT 26 [2]	7	7
18 Dec 99		BABY, IT'S COLD OUTSIDE Gut CDGUT 29 [3]	17	7
18 Mar 00	●	MAMA TOLD ME NOT TO COME Gut CDGUT 031 [4]	4	7
20 May 00	●	SEX BOMB Gut CDGUT 33 [5]	3	10
18 Nov 00		YOU NEED LOVE LIKE I DO GUT CDGUT 36 [6]	24	3

[1] Art of Noise featuring Tom Jones [2] Tom Jones and The Cardigans [3] Tom Jones and Cerys Matthews [4] Tom Jones and Stereophonics [5] Tom Jones & Mousse T [6] Tom Jones and Heather Small

Sue JONES-DAVIES – See Julie COVINGTON, Rula LENSKA, Charlotte CORNWELL and Sue JONES-DAVIES

JONESTOWN US, male vocal duo (1 WEEK)
pos/wks
13 Jun 98	SWEET THANG Universal UMD 70376	49	1

Alison JORDAN UK, female vocalist (4 WEEKS)
pos/wks
9 May 92	BOY FROM NEW YORK CITY Arista 74321100427	23	4

Dick JORDAN UK, male vocalist (4 WEEKS)
pos/wks
17 Mar 60	HALLELUJAH I LOVE HER SO Oriole CB 1534	47	1
9 Jun 60	LITTLE CHRISTINE Oriole CB 1548	39	3

Jack JORDAN – See Frank CHACKSFIELD

Montell JORDAN US, male vocalist (21 WEEKS)
pos/wks
13 May 95	THIS IS HOW WE DO IT Def Jam DEFCD 07 ▲	11	8
2 Sep 95	SOMETHIN' 4 DA HONEYZ Def Jam DEFCD 10	15	4
19 Oct 96	I LIKE Def Jam DEFCD 19 [1]	24	3
23 May 98	LET'S RIDE Def Jam 5686912 [2]	25	2
8 Apr 00	GET IT ON TONITE Def Soul 5627222	15	4

[1] Montell Jordan featuring Slick Rick [2] Montell Jordan featuring Master P & Silkk the Shocker

Ronny JORDAN UK, male instrumentalist - guitar (7 WEEKS)
pos/wks
1 Feb 92	SO WHAT! Antilles ANN 14	32	4
25 Sep 93	UNDER YOUR SPELL Island CID 565	72	1
15 Jan 94	TINSEL TOWN Island CID 566	64	1
28 May 94	COME WITH ME Island CID 584	63	1

David JOSEPH UK, male vocalist (21 WEEKS)
pos/wks
26 Feb 83	YOU CAN'T HIDE (YOUR LOVE FROM ME) Island IS 101	13	9
28 May 83	LET'S LIVE IT UP (NITE PEOPLE) Island IS 116	26	5
18 Feb 84	JOYS OF LIFE Island IS 153	61	2
31 May 86	EXPANSIONS '86 (EXPAND YOUR MIND) Fourth & Broadway BRW 48 [1]	58	5

[1] Chris Paul featuring David Joseph

Martyn JOSEPH UK, male vocalist (10 WEEKS)
pos/wks
20 Jun 92	DOLPHINS MAKE ME CRY Epic 6581347	34	4
12 Sep 92	WORKING MOTHER Epic 6582937	65	1
9 Jan 93	PLEASE SIR Epic 6588552	45	3
3 Jun 95	TALK ABOUT IT IN THE MORNING Epic 6613342	43	2

JOURNEY US, male vocal / instrumental group (9 WEEKS)
pos/wks
27 Feb 82	DON'T STOP BELIEVIN' CBS A 1728	62	4
11 Sep 82	WHO'S CRYING NOW CBS A 2725	46	5

Ruth JOY UK, female vocalist (3 WEEKS)
pos/wks
26 Aug 89	DON'T PUSH IT MCA RJOY 1	66	2
22 Feb 92	FEEL MCA MCS 1574	67	1

JOY DIVISION UK, male vocal / instrumental group (24 WEEKS)
pos/wks
28 Jun 80	LOVE WILL TEAR US APART Factory FAC 23	13	9
29 Oct 83	LOVE WILL TEAR US APART (re-entry) Factory FAC 23	19	7
18 Jun 88	ATMOSPHERE Factory FAC 2137	34	5
17 Jun 95	LOVE WILL TEAR US APART (re-mix) London YOJCD 1	19	3

JOY STRINGS
UK, male / female vocal / instrumental group (11 WEEKS)
pos/wks
27 Feb 64	IT'S AN OPEN SECRET Regal-Zonophone RZ 501	32	7
17 Dec 64	A STARRY NIGHT Regal-Zonophone RZ 504	35	4

JOYRIDER UK, male vocal / instrumental group (4 WEEKS)
pos/wks
27 Jul 96	RUSH HOUR Paradox PDOXD 012	22	3
28 Sep 96	ALL GONE AWAY A & M 5819552	54	1

JT and the BIG FAMILY
Italy, male / female vocal / instrumental group (8 WEEKS)
pos/wks
3 Mar 90	●	MOMENTS IN SOUL Champion CHAMP 237	7	8

JT PLAYAZ UK, male production team (4 WEEKS)
pos/wks
5 Apr 97	JUST PLAYIN' Pukka CDJTP 1	30	3
2 May 98	LET'S GET DOWN MCA MCSTD 40161	64	1

JTQ UK, male instrumental group (6 WEEKS)
pos/wks
3 Apr 93	LOVE THE LIFE Big Life BLRD 93 [1]	34	3
3 Jul 93	SEE A BRIGHTER DAY Big Life BLRDA 97 [1]	49	2
25 Feb 95	LOVE WILL KEEP US TOGETHER Acid Jazz JAZID 112CD [2]	63	1

[1] JTQ with Noel McKoy [2] JTQ featuring Alison Limerick

JUDAS PRIEST UK, male vocal / instrumental group (51 WEEKS)
pos/wks
20 Jan 79	TAKE ON THE WORLD CBS 6915	14	10
12 May 79	EVENING STAR CBS 7312	53	4
29 Mar 80	LIVING AFTER MIDNIGHT CBS 8379	12	7
7 Jun 80	BREAKING THE LAW CBS 8644	12	6
23 Aug 80	UNITED CBS 8897	26	8
21 Feb 81	DON'T GO CBS 9520	51	3
25 Apr 81	HOT ROCKIN' CBS A 1153	60	3
21 Aug 82	YOU'VE GOT ANOTHER THING COMIN' CBS A 2611	66	2
21 Jan 84	FREEWHEEL BURNIN' CBS A 4054	42	3
23 Apr 88	JOHNNY B. GOODE Atlantic A 9114	64	2
15 Sep 90	PAINKILLER CBS 656273 7	74	1
23 Mar 91	A TOUCH OF EVIL Columbia 6565897	58	1
24 Apr 93	NIGHT CRAWLER Columbia 6590972	63	1

JUDGE DREAD `314` `Top 500` Humorous white 'rude' reggae performer named after a Prince Buster track, and whose first hits were inspired by Buster's single 'Big Five', b. Alex Hughes, 1944. d. (on stage at Canterbury) 13 Mar 1998. All his hits were judged unsuitable for radio play (95 WEEKS)
pos/wks
26 Aug 72		BIG SIX Big Shot BI 608	11	27
9 Dec 72	●	BIG SEVEN Big Shot BI 613	8	18
21 Apr 73		BIG EIGHT Big Shot BI 619	14	10
5 Jul 75	●	JE T'AIME (MOI NON PLUS) Cactus CT 65	9	9
27 Sep 75		BIG TEN Cactus CT 77	14	7
6 Dec 75		CHRISTMAS IN DREADLAND / COME OUTSIDE Cactus CT 80	14	7
8 May 76		THE WINKLE MAN Cactus CT 90	35	4
28 Aug 76		Y VIVA SUSPENDERS Cactus CT 99	27	4
2 Apr 77		5TH ANNIVERSARY (EP) Cactus CT 98	31	4
14 Jan 78		UP WITH THE COCK / BIG PUNK Cactus CT 110	49	1

UK No.1 ★ UK Top 10 ● Still on chart + UK million seller ◆ UK entry at No.1 ■ US No.1 ▲

16 Dec 78 HOKEY COKEY / JINGLE BELLS *EMI 2881* **59** 4

Tracks on 5th Anniversary (EP): Jamaica Jerk (Off) / Bring Back the Skins / End of the World / Big Everything. Y Viva Suspenders was listed, additionally, with Confessions Of A Bouncer in its second week on the chart

JUICE *Denmark, female vocal trio (3 WEEKS)*   pos/wks
18 Apr 98 BEST DAYS *Chrysalis CDCHS 5081* **28** 2
22 Aug 98 I'LL COME RUNNIN' *Chrysalis CDCHS 5090*................**48** 1

JUICY *US, male / female vocal duo (5 WEEKS)*   pos/wks
22 Feb 86 SUGAR FREE *Epic A 6917* **45** 5

JUICY LUCY *UK, male vocal / instrumental group (17 WEEKS)*   pos/wks
7 Mar 70 WHO DO YOU LOVE *Vertigo V 1* **14** 12
10 Oct 70 PRETTY WOMAN *Vertigo 6059 015* **45** 2
31 Oct 70 PRETTY WOMAN (re-entry) *Vertigo 6059 015* **44** 3

Thomas JULES-STOCK *UK, male vocalist (1 WEEK)*   pos/wks
15 Aug 98 DIDN'T I TELL YOU TRUE *Mercury MERCD 501* **59** 1

JULIA and COMPANY *US, male / female vocal group (10 WEEKS)* pos/wks
3 Mar 84 BREAKIN' DOWN (SUGAR SAMBA) *London LON 46*......**15** 8
23 Feb 85 I'M SO HAPPY *Next Plateau LON 61* **56** 2

JULUKA *UK / South Africa, male / female vocal / instrumental group (4 WEEKS)*   pos/wks
12 Feb 83 SCATTERLINGS OF AFRICA *Safari ZULU 1* **44** 4

JUMP *UK, male instrumental group (1 WEEK)*   pos/wks
1 Mar 97 FUNKATARIUM *Heat Recordings HEATCD 005* **56** 1

Wally JUMP Jr and the CRIMINAL ELEMENT
US, male producer - Arthur Baker (19 WEEKS)   pos/wks
28 Feb 87 TURN ME LOOSE *London LON 126* **60** 2
5 Sep 87 PUT THE NEEDLE TO THE RECORD *Cooltempo COOL 150* [1] ..**63** 3
12 Dec 87 TIGHTEN UP - I JUST CAN'T STOP DANCING
            Breakout USA 621 ....**24** 7
19 Mar 88 PRIVATE PARTY *Breakout USA 624* **57** 3
6 Oct 90 EVERYBODY (RAP) *Deconstruction PB 44701* [2] **30** 4

[1] Criminal Element Orchestra [2] Criminal Element Orchestra and Wendell Williams

JUMPING JACKS – See Danny PEPPERMINT and the JUMPING JACKS

Rosemary JUNE *US, female vocalist (9 WEEKS)*   pos/wks
23 Jan 59 (I'LL BE WITH YOU) IN APPLE BLOSSOM TIME
            Pye International 7N 25005 ....**14** 9

JUNGLE BOOK *US, male / female vocal group (8 WEEKS)*   pos/wks
8 May 93 THE JUNGLE BOOK GROOVE *Hollywood HWCD 128*................**14** 8

JUNGLE BROTHERS *US, male rap duo (35 WEEKS)*   pos/wks
22 Oct 88 I'LL HOUSE YOU *Gee Street GEE 003* [1] **22** 5
18 Mar 89 BLACK IS BLACK / STRAIGHT OUT OF THE JUNGLE
            Gee Street GEE 15 ....**72** 1
31 Mar 90 WHAT 'U' WAITIN' '4' *Eternal W 9865* **35** 5
21 Jul 90 DOIN' OUR OWN DANG *Eternal W 9754* **33** 6
19 Jul 97 BRAIN *Gee Street GEE 5000388* **52** 1
29 Nov 97 JUNGLE BROTHER *Gee Street GEE 5000493* **56** 1
9 May 98 JUNGLE BROTHER (re-entry) *Gee Street GEE 5000493* **18** 4
11 Jul 98 I'LL HOUSE YOU '98 (re-mix) *Gee Street FCD 338*...........**26** 5
28 Nov 98 BECAUSE I GOT IT LIKE THAT *Gee Street GEE 5003593* **32** 2
10 Jul 99 V.I.P. *Gee Street / V2 GEE 5007953* **33** 3
6 Nov 99 GET DOWN *Gee Street / V2 GEE 5010153* **52** 1
25 Mar 00 FREAKIN' YOU *Gee Street GEE 5008808* **70** 1

[1] Richie Rich meets the Jungle Brothers

'Doin' Our Own Dang' features the uncredited De La Soul and Monie Love

JUNGLE HIGH With BLUE PEARL *UK / Germany, male production / instrumental duo and UK / US, male / female vocal / instrumental group (1 WEEK)*   pos/wks
27 Nov 93 FIRE OF LOVE *Logic 74321170292* [1] **71** 1

[1] Jungle High with Blue Pearl

JUNIOR *UK, male vocalist - Norman Giscombe (57 WEEKS)*   pos/wks
24 Apr 82 ● MAMA USED TO SAY *Mercury MER 98* **7** 13
10 Jul 82 TOO LATE *Mercury MER 112* **20** 9
25 Sep 82 LET ME KNOW / I CAN'T HELP IT *Mercury MER 116*........**53** 3
23 Apr 83 COMMUNICATION BREAKDOWN *Mercury MER 134* **57** 3
8 Sep 84 SOMEBODY *London LON 50* **64** 2
9 Feb 85 DO YOU REALLY (WANT MY LOVE) *London LON 60* **47** 4
30 Nov 85 OH LOUISE *London LON 75* **74** 3
4 Apr 87 ● ANOTHER STEP (CLOSER TO YOU) *MCA KIM 5* [1] **6** 11
25 Aug 90 STEP OFF *MCA MCA 1432* **63** 3
15 Aug 92 THEN CAME YOU *MCA MCS 1676* [2] **32** 5
31 Oct 92 ALL OVER THE WORLD *MCA MCS 1691* [2] **74** 1

[1] Kim Wilde and Junior [2] Junior Giscombe

JUNIOR JACK *Italy, male producer - Vito Lucente (3 WEEKS)*   pos/wks
16 Dec 00 MY FEELING *Defected DFECT 24CDS* ....**31** 3+

JUNIOR M.A.F.I.A. *US, male / female rap ensemble (2 WEEKS)*   pos/wks
3 Feb 96 I NEED YOU TONIGHT *Big Beat A 8130CD* [1] **66** 1
19 Oct 96 GETTIN' MONEY *Big Beat A 5674CD* **63** 1

[1] Junior M.A.F.I.A. featuring Aaliyah

JUNIORS – See DANNY and the JUNIORS

JUNKIE XL *Holland, male producer / vocal duo - Tom Holkenborg and Patrick Tilon (1 WEEK)*   pos/wks
22 Jul 00 ZEROTONINE *Manifesto FESCD71*.............................**63** 1

JUNO REACTOR *UK / Germany, male production duo (1 WEEK)*   pos/wks
8 Feb 97 JUNGLE HIGH *Perfecto PERF 133CD* **45** 1

JURASSIC 5 *US, male rap group (4 WEEKS)*   pos/wks
25 Jul 98 JAYOU *Pan PAN 018CD* **56** 1
24 Oct 98 CONCRETE SCHOOLYARD *Pan PAN 020CD* **35** 3

Christopher JUST *Austria, male producer (2 WEEKS)*   pos/wks
13 Dec 97 I'M A DISCO DANCER *Slut Trax SLUT 001CD*.................**72** 1
6 Feb 99 I'M A DISCO DANCER (re-mix)
            XL Recordings XLS 105CD **69** 1

JUST LUIS *Australia, male vocalist (3 WEEKS)*   pos/wks
14 Oct 95 AMERICAN PIE *Pro-Activ CDPTV 1* **31** 2
17 Feb 96 AMERICAN PIE (re-entry) *Pro-Activ CDPTV 1* **70** 1

Jimmy JUSTICE *UK, male vocalist - James Little (35 WEEKS)*   pos/wks
29 Mar 62 ● WHEN MY LITTLE GIRL IS SMILING *Pye 7N 15421* **9** 13
14 Jun 62 ● AIN'T THAT FUNNY *Pye 7N 15443* **8** 11
23 Aug 62 SPANISH HARLEM *Pye 7N 15457* **20** 11

JUSTIFIED ANCIENTS OF MU MU
UK, male production duo (6 WEEKS)   pos/wks
9 Nov 91 ● IT'S GRIM UP NORTH *KLF Communications JAMS 028* **10** 5
4 Jan 92 IT'S GRIM UP NORTH (re-entry)
            KLF Communications JAMS 028................................**67** 1

See also KLF; 2K; 1300 DRUMS featuring the UNJUSTIFIED ANCIENTS OF MU

JUSTIN *UK, male vocalist (13 WEEKS)*   pos/wks
22 Aug 98 THIS BOY *Virgin STCDT 1* **34** 2
16 Jan 99 OVER YOU *Virgin STCDT 2* **11** 4

Ini KAMOZE *Jamaica, male vocalist (15 WEEKS)* pos/wks
7 Jan 95 ●	HERE COMES THE HOTSTEPPER *Columbia 6610472* ▲	4	15

KANDI *US, female vocalist - Kandi Burruss (8 WEEKS)* pos/wks
11 Nov 00 ●	DON'T THINK I'M NOT *Columbia 6705102*	9	8+

KANDIDATE *UK, male vocal / instrumental group (28 WEEKS)* pos/wks
19 Aug 78	DON'T WANNA SAY GOODNIGHT *RAK 280*	47	6
17 Mar 79	I DON'T WANNA LOSE YOU *RAK 289*	11	12
4 Aug 79	GIRLS GIRLS GIRLS *RAK 295*	34	7
22 Mar 80	LET ME ROCK YOU *RAK 306*	58	3

Eden KANE 〔466 **Top 500**〕 *Last teen idol before The Beatles, b. Richard Sarstedt, 29 Mar 1942, Delhi, India. Stylish pop beat singer who, like Adam Faith, had many of his hits penned for him by Johnny Worth. Brothers Peter and Robin Sarstedt also had Top 3 entries (73 WEEKS)* pos/wks
1 Jun 61 ★	WELL I ASK YOU *Decca F 11353*	1	21
14 Sep 61 ●	GET LOST *Decca F 11381*	10	11
18 Jan 62 ●	FORGET ME NOT *Decca F 11418*	3	14
10 May 62 ●	I DON'T KNOW WHY *Decca F 11460*	7	13
30 Jan 64 ●	BOYS CRY *Fontana TF 438*	8	14

KANE GANG *UK, male vocal / instrumental group (37 WEEKS)* pos/wks
19 May 84	SMALLTOWN CREED *Kitchenware SK 11*	60	2
7 Jul 84	CLOSEST THING TO HEAVEN *Kitchenware SK 15*	12	11
10 Nov 84	RESPECT YOURSELF *Kitchenware SK 16*	21	10
26 Jan 85	RESPECT YOURSELF (re-entry) *Kitchenware SK 16*	75	1
9 Mar 85	GUN LAW *Kitchenware SK 20*	53	4
27 Jun 87	MOTORTOWN *Kitchenware SK 30*	45	5
16 Apr 88	DON'T LOOK ANY FURTHER *Kitchenware SK 33*	52	4

KANSAS *US, male vocal / instrumental group (7 WEEKS)* pos/wks
1 Jul 78	CARRY ON WAYWARD SON *Kirshner KIR 4932*	51	7

Mory KANTE *Guinea, male vocalist (14 WEEKS)* pos/wks
23 Jul 88	YEKE YEKE *London LON 171*	29	9
11 Mar 95	YEKE YEKE (re-mix) *Ffrreedom TABCD 226*	25	3
30 Nov 96	YEKE YEKE (2nd) (re-mix) *ffrr FCD 288*	28	2

KAOMA
France, male / female vocal / instrumental group (20 WEEKS) pos/wks
21 Oct 89 ●	LAMBADA *CBS 655011 7*	4	18
27 Jan 90	DANCANDO LAMBADA *CBS 655235 7*	62	2

KAOTIC CHEMISTRY
UK, male instrumental / production group (1 WEEK) pos/wks
31 Oct 92	LSD (EP) *Moving Shadow SHADOW 20*	68	1

Tracks on LSD (EP): Space Cakes / LSD / Illegal Substances / Drumtrip II

KARIN – See UNIQUE 3

KARIYA *US, female vocalist (9 WEEKS)* pos/wks
8 Jul 89	LET ME LOVE YOU FOR TONIGHT *Sleeping Bag SBUK 4*	44	6
21 Oct 89	LET ME LOVE YOU FOR TONIGHT (re-entry) *Sleeping Bag SBUK 4*	57	3

Mick KARN *UK, male instrumentalist (6 WEEKS)* pos/wks
9 Jul 83	AFTER A FASHION *Musicfest FEST 1* [1]	39	4
17 Jan 87	BUOY *Virgin VS 910* [2]	63	2

[1] Midge Ure and Mick Karn [2] Mick Karn featuring David Sylvian

KARTOON KREW *US, rap / instrumental group (6 WEEKS)* pos/wks
7 Dec 85	INSPECTOR GADGET *Champion CHAMP 6*	58	6

KASENETZ-KATZ SINGING ORCHESTRAL CIRCUS
US, male vocal / instrumental group (15 WEEKS) pos/wks
20 Nov 68	QUICK JOEY SMALL (RUN JOEY RUN) *Buddah 201 022*	19	15

KATCHA *UK, male DJ / producer (1 WEEK)* pos/wks
21 Aug 99	TOUCHED BY GOD *Hooj Choons HOOJ 77CD*	57	1

KATRINA and the WAVES
US / UK, female / male vocal / instrumental group (34 WEEKS) pos/wks
4 May 85 ●	WALKING ON SUNSHINE *Capitol CL 354*	8	12
5 Jul 86	SUN STREET *Capitol CL 407*	22	9
8 Jun 96	WALKING ON SUNSHINE (re-issue) *EMI Premier PRESCD 2*	53	1
10 May 97 ●	LOVE SHINE A LIGHT *Eternal WEA 106CD1*	3	12

KAVANA *UK, male vocalist - Anthony Kavanagh (26 WEEKS)* pos/wks
11 May 96	CRAZY CHANCE *Nemesis NMSD 1*	35	3
24 Aug 96	WHERE ARE YOU *Nemesis NMSD 2*	26	2
11 Jan 97 ●	I CAN MAKE YOU FEEL GOOD *Nemesis NMSDX 3*	8	5
19 Apr 97 ●	MFEO *Nemesis NMSD 4*	8	4
13 Sep 97	CRAZY CHANCE 97 (re-recording) *Nemesis NMSD 5*	16	3
29 Aug 98	SPECIAL KIND OF SOMETHING *Virgin VSCDT 1704*	13	4
12 Dec 98	FUNKY LOVE *Virgin VSCDT 1711*	32	2
9 Jan 99	FUNKY LOVE (re-entry) *Virgin VSCDT 1711*	73	1
20 Mar 99	WILL YOU WAIT FOR ME *Virgin VSCDT 1726*	29	2

Niamh KAVANAGH *Ireland, female vocalist (5 WEEKS)* pos/wks
12 Jun 93	IN YOUR EYES *Arista 74321154152*	24	5

KAWALA *UK, male vocal / instrumental / production group (1 WEEK)* pos/wks
26 Feb 00	HUMANISTIC *Pepper 9230022*	68	1

Janet KAY *UK, female vocalist - Janet Bogle (24 WEEKS)* pos/wks
9 Jun 79 ●	SILLY GAMES *Scope SC 2*	2	14
11 Aug 90	SILLY GAMES *Arista 113452* [1]	22	7
11 Aug 90	SILLY GAMES (re-mix) *Music Factory Dance MFD 006*	62	3

[1] Lindy Layton featuring Janet Kay

Danny KAYE *US, male vocalist - David Kuminsky (10 WEEKS)* pos/wks
27 Feb 53 ●	WONDERFUL COPENHAGEN *Brunswick 05023*	5	10

With Gordon Jenkins and his Orchestra and Chorus

KAYE SISTERS *UK, female vocal group (45 WEEKS)* pos/wks
25 May 56	IVORY TOWER *HMV POP 209* [1]	20	5
1 Nov 57 ●	GOT-TA HAVE SOMETHING IN THE BANK, FRANK *Philips PB 751* [2]	8	11
3 Jan 58	SHAKE ME I RATTLE / ALONE *Philips PB 752*	27	1
1 May 59 ●	COME SOFTLY TO ME *Philips PB 913* [2]	9	9
7 Jul 60 ●	PAPER ROSES *Philips PB 1024*	7	19

[1] Three Kayes [2] Frankie Vaughan and the Kaye Sisters

KAYESTONE *UK, male DJ / production duo (1 WEEK)* pos/wks
29 Jul 00	ATMOSPHERE *Distinctive DISNCD 62*	55	1

KC and the SUNSHINE BAND 〔282 **Top 500**〕 *Red-hot disco act from Florida, US, fronted by KC (b. Harry Wayne Casey, 31 Jan 1951, Florida) and including co-writer / producer Richard Finch (b). Internationally successful group whose wall-to-wall late 1970s hits included five US No.1s (104 WEEKS)* pos/wks
17 Aug 74 ●	QUEEN OF CLUBS *Jayboy BOY 88*	7	12
23 Nov 74	SOUND YOUR FUNKY HORN *Jayboy BOY 83*	17	9
29 Mar 75	GET DOWN TONIGHT *Jayboy BOY 93* ▲	21	9
2 Aug 75 ●	THAT'S THE WAY (I LIKE IT) *Jayboy BOY 99* ▲	4	10
22 Nov 75	I'M SO CRAZY ('BOUT YOU) *Jayboy BOY 101*	34	3
17 Jul 76	(SHAKE SHAKE SHAKE) SHAKE YOUR BOOTY *Jayboy BOY 110* ▲	22	8

11 Dec 76	KEEP IT COMIN' LOVE *Jayboy BOY 112*.........................**31**	8
30 Apr 77	I'M YOUR BOOGIE MAN *TK XB 2167* ▲.........................**41**	4
6 May 78	BOOGIE SHOES *TK TKR 6025*.........................**34**	5
22 Jul 78	IT'S THE SAME OLD SONG *TK TKR 6037* **47**	5
8 Dec 79 ●	PLEASE DON'T GO *TK TKR 7558* ▲.........................**3**	12
16 Jul 83 ★	GIVE IT UP *Epic EPC A 3017*.........................**1**	14
24 Sep 83	(YOU SAID) YOU'D GIMME SOME MORE *Epic A 2760*.........................**41**	3
11 May 91	THAT'S THE WAY I LIKE IT (re-mix)	
	Music Factory Dance M7FAC 2 ....**59**	2

KÉ *US, male vocalist (1 WEEK)*
pos/wks
13 Apr 96	STRANGE WORLD *Venture 74321349412* **73**	1

Johnny KEATING *UK, orchestra (14 WEEKS)*
pos/wks
1 Mar 62 ●	THEME FROM 'Z CARS' (JOHNNY TODD) *Piccadilly 7N 35032* **8**	14

Ronan KEATING *Ireland, male vocalist (36 WEEKS)*
pos/wks
7 Aug 99 ★	WHEN YOU SAY NOTHING AT ALL	
	Polydor 5612902 ■ **1**	15
27 Nov 99	WHEN YOU SAY NOTHING AT ALL (re-entry)	
	Polydor 5612902 ....**75**	1
1 Jan 00	WHEN YOU SAY NOTHING AT ALL (2nd re-entry)	
	Polydor 5612902 ....**66**	1
22 Jul 00 ★	LIFE IS A ROLLERCOASTER *Polydor 5619362* ■ **1**	14
2 Dec 00 ●	THE WAY YOU MAKE ME FEEL *Polydor 5878852*.........................**6**	5+

See also BOYZONE

Kevin KEEGAN *UK, male vocalist (6 WEEKS)*
pos/wks
9 Jun 79	HEAD OVER HEELS IN LOVE *EMI 2965* **31**	6

Yvonne KEELEY – See Scott FITZGERALD

Nelson KEENE *UK, male vocalist (5 WEEKS)*
pos/wks
25 Aug 60	IMAGE OF A GIRL *HMV POP 771* **37**	4
29 Sep 60	IMAGE OF A GIRL (re-entry) *HMV POP 771* **45**	1

KEITH *US, male vocalist (8 WEEKS)*
pos/wks
26 Jan 67	98.6 *Mercury MF 955* **24**	7
16 Mar 67	TELL ME TO MY FACE *Mercury MF 968* **50**	1

KEITH 'N' SHANE *Ireland, male vocal duo (2 WEEKS)*
pos/wks
23 Dec 00	GIRL YOU KNOW IT'S TRUE *Polydor 5879462* **36**	2+

See also BOYZONE

KELIS *US, female vocalist - Kelis Rogers (27 WEEKS)*
pos/wks
26 Feb 00	CAUGHT OUT THERE (IMPORT) *Virgin 8965102CD*.........................**52**	1
4 Mar 00 ●	CAUGHT OUT THERE *Virgin VUSCD 158*.........................**4**	10
20 May 00	CAUGHT OUT THERE (re-entry)	
	Virgin VUSCD 158 ....**64**	2
17 Jun 00	GOOD STUFF *Virgin VUSCD 164*.........................**19**	5
8 Jul 00	GOT YOUR MONEY *Elektra E 7077CD* [1] **11**	8
21 Oct 00	GET ALONG WITH YOU *Virgin VUSCD 174* **51**	1

[1] Ol' Dirty Bastard featuring Kelis

Jerry KELLER *US, male vocalist (14 WEEKS)*
pos/wks
28 Aug 59 ★	HERE COMES SUMMER *London HLR 8890*.........................**1**	14

Frank KELLY *Ireland, male vocalist (5 WEEKS)*
pos/wks
24 Dec 83	CHRISTMAS COUNTDOWN *Ritz RITZ 062*.........................**26**	4
29 Dec 84	CHRISTMAS COUNTDOWN (re-entry)	
	Ritz RITZ 062 ....**54**	1

Frankie KELLY *US, male vocalist / instrumentalist (2 WEEKS)*
pos/wks
2 Nov 85	AIN'T THAT THE TRUTH *10 TEN 87* **65**	2

Grace KELLY – See Bing CROSBY

Keith KELLY *UK, male vocalist (5 WEEKS)*
pos/wks
5 May 60	TEASE ME *Parlophone R 4640* **46**	1
19 May 60	TEASE ME (re-entry) *Parlophone R 4640* **27**	3
18 Aug 60	LISTEN LITTLE GIRL *Parlophone R 4676* **47**	1

R KELLY 159 Top 500 *Phenomenally successful R&B vocalist, b. 8 Jan 1971, Chicago, US, whose writing and production skills are constantly in demand by other top artists. Married chart star Aaliyah in 1994. Amazingly, 1998 album R yielded seven Top 20 hits but never reached the Top 20 itself (144 WEEKS)*
pos/wks
9 May 92	SHE'S GOT THAT VIBE *Jive JIVET 292* [1] **57**	2
20 Nov 93	SEX ME *Jive JIVECD 346* [1] **75**	1
14 May 94	YOUR BODY'S CALLIN' *Jive JIVECD 353*.........................**19**	4
3 Sep 94	SUMMER BUNNIES *Jive JIVECD 358*.........................**23**	3
22 Oct 94 ●	SHE'S GOT THAT VIBE (re-issue) *Jive JIVECD 364* **3**	13
21 Jan 95 ●	BUMP 'N' GRIND *Jive JIVECD 368* ▲.........................**8**	9
6 May 95	THE 4 PLAY EPS *Jive JIVECD 376* **23**	3
11 Nov 95	YOU REMIND ME OF SOMETHING *Jive JIVECD 388*.........................**24**	3
2 Mar 96	DOWN LOW (NOBODY HAS TO KNOW)	
	Jive JIVECD 392 [2] **23**	3
22 Jun 96	THANK GOD IT'S FRIDAY *Jive JIVECD 395*.........................**14**	4
29 Mar 97 ★	I BELIEVE I CAN FLY *Jive JIVECD 415*.........................**1**	17
19 Jul 97 ●	GOTHAM CITY *Jive JIVECD 428*.........................**9**	8
18 Jul 98 ●	BE CAREFUL *Jive 0521452* [3] **7**	6
5 Sep 98	BE CAREFUL (re-entry) *Jive 0521452* [3] **75**	1
26 Sep 98	HALF ON A BABY *Jive 0521802* **16**	4
14 Nov 98	HOME ALONE *Jive 0522392* [4] **17**	4
28 Nov 98 ●	I'M YOUR ANGEL *Epic 6666282* [5] ▲.........................**3**	13
31 Jul 99	DID YOU EVER THINK *Jive 0523612*.........................**20**	5
16 Oct 99	IF I COULD TURN BACK THE HANDS OF TIME (IMPORT)	
	Jive 0523182.........................**57**	2
30 Oct 99 ●	IF I COULD TURN BACK THE HANDS OF TIME	
	Jive 0523182.........................**2**	19
19 Feb 00	SATISFY YOU (IMPORT)	
	Bad Boy / Arista 792832 [6] **73**	1
4 Mar 00	SATISFY YOU (IMPORT) (re-entry)	
	Bad Boy / Arista 792832 [6] **73**	1
11 Mar 00 ●	SATISFY YOU *Bad Boy / Arista 74321745592* [7] **8**	8
22 Apr 00	ONLY THE LOOT CAN MAKE ME HAPPY	
	Jive 9250282.........................**24**	3
21 Oct 00	I WISH *Jive 9251262* **12**	6

[1] R Kelly and Public Announcement [2] R Kelly featuring Ronald Isley [3] Sparkle featuring R Kelly [4] R Kelly featuring Keith Murray [5] Celine Dion and R Kelly [6] Puff Daddy featuring R. Kelly [7] Puff Daddy featuring R Kelly

The 4 Play EP was available on 2 CDs, each featuring 'Your Body's Callin'' and three further tracks

See also PUBLIC ANNOUNCEMENT

Roberta KELLY *US, female vocalist (3 WEEKS)*
pos/wks
21 Jan 78	ZODIACS *Oasis/Hansa 3* **48**	1
4 Feb 78	ZODIACS (re-entry) *Oasis/Hansa 3* **44**	2

KELLY FAMILY
Ireland, male / female vocal / instrumental group (1 WEEK)
pos/wks
21 Oct 95	AN ANGEL *EMI CDEM 390* **69**	1

Johnny KEMP *Barbados, male vocalist (1 WEEK)*
pos/wks
27 Aug 88	JUST GOT PAID *CBS 651470 7* **68**	1

Tara KEMP *US, female vocalist (2 WEEKS)*
pos/wks
20 Apr 91	HOLD YOU TIGHT *Giant W 0020* **69**	2

Graham KENDRICK *UK, male vocalist (4 WEEKS)*
pos/wks
9 Sep 89	LET THE FLAME BURN BRIGHTER *Power P 30*.........................**55**	4

Eddie KENDRICKS *US, male vocalist (20 WEEKS)*
pos/wks
3 Nov 73	KEEP ON TRUCKIN' *Tamla Motown TMG 873* ▲ **18**	14

UK No.1 ★   UK Top 10 ●   Still on chart +   UK million seller ◆   UK entry at No.1 ■   US No.1 ▲

16 Mar 74	**BOOGIE DOWN** *Tamla Motown TMG 888*	**39**	4
21 Sep 85	**A NIGHT AT THE APOLLO LIVE!** *RCA PB 49935* [1]	**58**	2

[1] Daryl Hall and John Oates featuring David Ruffin and Eddie Kendrick

A Night at the Apollo Live! is a medley of 'The Way You Do the Things You Do' and 'My Girl'. Kendricks dropped the 's' from his name for last hit

See also TEMPTATIONS

KENICKIE *UK, female / male vocal / instrumental group (13 WEEKS)* pos/wks
14 Sep 96	**PUNKA** *Emidisc CDDISC 001*	**43**	2
16 Nov 96	**MILLIONAIRE SWEEPER** *Emidisc CDDISC 002*	**60**	1
11 Jan 97	**IN YOUR CAR** *Emidisc CDDISC 005*	**24**	3
3 May 97	**NIGHTLIFE** *Emidisc CDDISC 006*	**27**	3
5 Jul 97	**PUNKA (re-issue)** *Emidisc CDDISC 007*	**38**	2
6 Jun 98	**I WOULD FIX YOU** *EMI CDEM 513*	**36**	2
22 Aug 98	**STAY IN THE SUN** *EMI CDEMS 520*	**43**	1

Jane KENNAWAY and STRANGE BEHAVIOUR
UK, female vocalist, male instrumental group (3 WEEKS) pos/wks
24 Jan 81	**I.O.U.** *Deram DM 436*	**65**	3

Brian KENNEDY *Ireland, male vocalist (8 WEEKS)* pos/wks
22 Jun 96	**A BETTER MAN** *RCA 74321382642*	**28**	3
21 Sep 96	**LIFE, LOVE AND HAPPINESS** *RCA 74321409921*	**27**	3
5 Apr 97	**PUT THE MESSAGE IN THE BOX** *RCA 74321462272*	**37**	2

Kevin KENNEDY *UK, male vocalist (1 WEEK)* pos/wks
24 Jun 00	**BULLDOG NATION** *D2m 74321759742*	**70**	1

KENNY *Ireland, male vocalist (16 WEEKS)* pos/wks
3 Mar 73	**HEART OF STONE** *RAK 144*	**11**	13
30 Jun 73	**GIVE IT TO ME NOW** *RAK 153*	**38**	3

KENNY *UK, male vocal / instrumental group (39 WEEKS)* pos/wks
7 Dec 74	● **THE BUMP** *RAK 186*	**3**	15
8 Mar 75	● **FANCY PANTS** *RAK 196*	**4**	9
7 Jun 75	**BABY I LOVE YOU OK** *RAK 207*	**12**	7
16 Aug 75	● **JULIE ANN** *RAK 214*	**10**	8

Gerard KENNY *US, male vocalist (21 WEEKS)* pos/wks
9 Dec 78	**NEW YORK, NEW YORK** *RCA PB 5117*	**43**	8
21 Jun 80	**FANTASY** *RCA PB 5256*	**65**	1
5 Jul 80	**FANTASY (re-entry)** *RCA PB 5256*	**34**	5
18 Feb 84	**THE OTHER WOMAN, THE OTHER MAN** *Impression IMS 3*	**69**	4
4 May 85	**NO MAN'S LAND** *WEA YZ 38*	**56**	3

KENT *Sweden, male vocal / instrumental group (1 WEEK)* pos/wks
13 Mar 99	**747** *RCA 74321645912*	**61**	1

Klark KENT *US, male vocalist / multi-instrumentalist – Stewart Copeland (4 WEEKS)* pos/wks
26 Aug 78	**DON'T CARE** *A & M AMS 7376*	**48**	4

See also POLICE

Carol KENYON – See Paul HARDCASTLE; HEAVEN 17; RAPINATION

KERBDOG *Ireland, male vocal / instrumental group (5 WEEKS)* pos/wks
12 Mar 94	**DRY RISER** *Vertigo VERCC 83*	**60**	1
6 Aug 94	**DUMMY CRUSHER** *Vertigo VERCD 86*	**37**	2
12 Oct 96	**SALLY** *Fontana KERCD 2*	**69**	1
29 Mar 97	**MEXICAN WAVE** *Fontana KERCD 3*	**49**	1

ANITA KERR SINGERS – See Bobby HELMS

KERRI and MICK *Australia, female / male vocal duo (3 WEEKS)* pos/wks
28 Apr 84	**'SONS AND DAUGHTERS' THEME** *A1 A1 286*	**68**	3

KERRI-ANN *Ireland, female vocalist (1 WEEK)* pos/wks
8 Aug 98	**DO YOU LOVE ME BOY?** *Raglan Road 5671012*	**58**	1

Liz KERSHAW and Bruno BROOKES
UK, male / female vocal duo (3 WEEKS) pos/wks
2 Dec 89	**IT TAKES TWO BABY** *Spartan CIN 101* [1]	**53**	2
1 Dec 90	**LET'S DANCE** *Jive BRUNO 1* [2]	**54**	1

[1] Liz Kershaw, Bruno Brookes, Jive Bunny and Londonbeat [2] Bruno and Liz and the Radio 1 DJ Posse

See also JIVE BUNNY and the MASTERMIXERS; LONDONBEAT

Nik KERSHAW (348) **Top 500** *One time jazz-funk guitarist whose melodic pop repertoire made him a mid-1980s teen idol, b. 1 Mar 1958, Bristol, UK. His 50 weeks on singles chart in 1984 beat all other soloists. He appeared at Live Aid, and penned hits for Let Loose, The Hollies and a No.1 for Chesney Hawkes (89 WEEKS)* pos/wks
19 Nov 83	**I WON'T LET THE SUN GO DOWN ON ME** *MCA MCA 816*	**47**	5
28 Jan 84	● **WOULDN'T IT BE GOOD** *MCA NIK 2*	**4**	14
14 Apr 84	**DANCING GIRLS** *MCA NIK 3*	**13**	9
16 Jun 84	● **I WON'T LET THE SUN GO DOWN ON ME (re-issue)** *MCA NIK 4*	**2**	13
15 Sep 84	**HUMAN RACING** *MCA NIK 5*	**19**	7
17 Nov 84	● **THE RIDDLE** *MCA NIK 6*	**3**	11
16 Mar 85	● **WIDE BOY** *MCA NIK 7*	**9**	8
3 Aug 85	● **DON QUIXOTE** *MCA NIK 8*	**10**	7
30 Nov 85	**WHEN A HEART BEATS** *MCA NIK 9*	**27**	7
11 Oct 86	**NOBODY KNOWS** *MCA NIK 10*	**44**	3
13 Dec 86	**RADIO MUSICOLA** *MCA NIK 11*	**43**	2
4 Feb 89	**ONE STEP AHEAD** *MCA NIK 12*	**55**	1
27 Feb 99	**SOMEBODY LOVES YOU** *Eagle EAGXA 023*	**70**	1
7 Aug 99	**SOMETIMES** *Wall of Sound WALLD 054* [1]	**56**	1

[1] Les Rythmes Digitales featuring Nik Kershaw

KEVIN and PERRY – See PRECOCIOUS BRATS featuring KEVIN and PERRY

KEVIN THE GERBIL *UK, male gerbil vocalist (6 WEEKS)* pos/wks
4 Aug 84	**SUMMER HOLIDAY** *Magnet RAT 3*	**50**	6

KEY WEST – See ERIK

KEYNOTES – See Dave KING

Chaka KHAN (307) **Top 500** *Powerful and influential soul diva b. Yvette Stevens, 23 Mar 1953, Illinois, US. Fronted funk troupe Rufus for six years, went solo 1978. Prince-penned 'I Feel For You' was first UK No.1 to feature rap elements (courtesy of Grandmaster Melle Mel) (97 WEEKS)* pos/wks
2 Dec 78	**I'M EVERY WOMAN** *Warner Bros. K 17269*	**11**	13
31 Mar 84	● **AIN'T NOBODY** *Warner Bros. RCK 1* [1]	**8**	12
20 Oct 84	★ **I FEEL FOR YOU** *Warner Bros. W 9209*	**1**	16
19 Jan 85	**THIS IS MY NIGHT** *Warner Bros. W 9097*	**14**	6
20 Apr 85	**EYE TO EYE** *Warner Bros. W 9009*	**16**	7
12 Jul 86	**LOVE OF A LIFETIME** *Warner Bros. W 8671*	**52**	4
21 Jan 89	**IT'S MY PARTY** *Warner Bros. W 7678*	**71**	2
6 May 89	● **I'M EVERY WOMAN (re-mix)** *Warner Bros. W 2963*	**8**	8
8 Jul 89	● **AIN'T NOBODY (re-mix)** *Warner Bros. W 2880* [1]	**6**	9
7 Oct 89	**I FEEL FOR YOU (re-mix)** *Warner Bros. W 2764*	**45**	2
13 Jan 90	**I'LL BE GOOD TO YOU** *Qwest W 2697* [2]	**21**	7
28 Mar 92	**LOVE YOU ALL MY LIFETIME** *Warner Bros. W 0087*	**49**	3
17 Jul 93	**DON'T LOOK AT ME THAT WAY** *Warner Bros. W 0192CD*	**73**	1
19 Aug 95	**WATCH WHAT YOU SAY** *Cooltempo CDCOOL 308* [3]	**28**	3
1 Mar 97	**NEVER MISS THE WATER** *Reprise W 1393CD* [4]	**59**	1
11 Nov 00	**ALL GOOD** *Tommy Boy TBCD 2154B* [5]	**33**	3

[1] Rufus and Chaka Khan [2] Quincy Jones featuring Ray Charles and Chaka Khan [3] Guru featuring Chaka Khan [4] Chaka Khan featuring Me'Shell Ndegeocello [5] De La Soul featuring Chaka Khan

See also Quincy JONES

Praga KHAN Belgium, male producer (8 WEEKS)
pos/wks

| 4 Apr 92 | **FREE YOUR BODY / INJECTED WITH A POISON** Profile PROFT 347 [1] | 16 | 6 |
| 11 Jul 92 | **RAVE ALERT** Profile PROF 369 | 39 | 2 |

[1] Praga Khan featuring Jade 4 U

Mary KIANI UK, female vocalist (15 WEEKS)
pos/wks

12 Aug 95	**WHEN I CALL YOUR NAME** Mercury MERCD 440	18	4
23 Dec 95	**I GIVE IT ALL TO YOU / I IMAGINE** Mercury MERCD 449	35	4
27 Apr 96	**LET THE MUSIC PLAY** Mercury MERCD 456	19	3
18 Jan 97	**100%** Mercury MERCD 469	23	3
21 Jun 97	**WITH OR WITHOUT YOU** Mercury MERCD 487	46	1

KICK HORNS – See DODGY

KICK SQUAD
UK / Germany, male vocal / instrumental group (2 WEEKS)
pos/wks

| 10 Nov 90 | **SOUND CLASH (CHAMPION SOUND)** Kickin KICK 2 | 59 | 2 |

KICKING BACK with TAXMAN UK, male / female vocal / instrumental duo with male rapper (8 WEEKS)
pos/wks

| 17 Mar 90 | **DEVOTION** 10 TEN 297 | 47 | 4 |
| 7 Jul 90 | **EVERYTHING** 10 TEN 307 | 54 | 4 |

KICKS LIKE A MULE UK, male instrumental / production duo - Nick Halkes & Richard Russell (6 WEEKS)
pos/wks

| 1 Feb 92 ● | **THE BOUNCER** Tribal Bass TRIBE 3S | 7 | 6 |

K.I.D. Antilles, male / female vocal / instrumental group (4 WEEKS)
pos/wks

| 28 Feb 81 | **DON'T STOP** EMI 5143 | 49 | 4 |

KID 'N' PLAY US, male rap duo (7 WEEKS)
pos/wks

18 Jul 87	**LAST NIGHT** Cooltempo COOL 148	71	1
26 Mar 88	**DO THIS MY WAY** Cooltempo COOL 164	48	3
17 Sep 88	**GITTIN' FUNKY** Cooltempo COOL 168	55	3

KID ROCK US, male vocalist / rapper - Bob Ritchie (6 WEEKS)
pos/wks

| 23 Oct 99 | **COWBOY** Atlantic AT 0076CD | 36 | 2 |
| 9 Sep 00 | **AMERICAN BAD ASS** Atlantic AT 0085CD | 25 | 4 |

KID UNKNOWN UK, male producer - Paul Fitzpatrick (1 WEEK)
pos/wks

| 2 May 92 | **NIGHTMARE** Warp WAP 20CD | 64 | 1 |

Carol KIDD featuring Terry WAITE UK, female / male vocal duo (3 WEEKS)
pos/wks

| 17 Oct 92 | **WHEN I DREAM** The Hit Label HLS 1 | 58 | 3 |

Johnny KIDD and the PIRATES UK, male vocal / instrumental group (62 WEEKS)
pos/wks

12 Jun 59	**PLEASE DON'T TOUCH** HMV POP 615 [1]	26	3
17 Jul 59	**PLEASE DON'T TOUCH (re-entry)** HMV POP 615 [1]	25	2
12 Feb 60	**YOU GOT WHAT IT TAKES** HMV POP 698	25	3
16 Jun 60 ★	**SHAKIN' ALL OVER** HMV POP 753	1	19
6 Oct 60	**RESTLESS** HMV POP 790	22	7
13 Apr 61	**LINDA LU** HMV POP 853	47	1
10 Jan 63	**SHOT OF RHYTHM AND BLUES** HMV POP 1088	48	1
25 Jul 63 ●	**I'LL NEVER GET OVER YOU** HMV POP 1173	4	15
28 Nov 63	**HUNGRY FOR LOVE** HMV POP 1228	20	10
30 Apr 64	**ALWAYS AND EVER** HMV POP 1269	46	1

[1] Johnny Kidd

KIDS FROM 'FAME' US, male / female vocal group (36 WEEKS)
pos/wks

14 Aug 82 ●	**HI-FIDELITY** RCA 254 [1]	5	10
2 Oct 82 ●	**STARMAKER** RCA 280	3	10
11 Dec 82	**MANNEQUIN** RCA 299 [2]	50	6
9 Apr 83	**FRIDAY NIGHT (LIVE VERSION)** RCA 320	13	10

[1] Kids from Fame featuring Valerie Landsberg [2] Kids from Fame featuring Gene Anthony Ray

Greg KIHN BAND US, male vocal / instrumental group (2 WEEKS)
pos/wks

| 23 Apr 83 | **JEOPARDY** Beserkley E 9847 | 63 | 2 |

KILLAH PRIEST US, male rapper (1 WEEK)
pos/wks

| 7 Feb 98 | **ONE STEP** Geffen GFSTD 22318 | 45 | 1 |

KILLING JOKE UK, male vocal / instrumental group (48 WEEKS)
pos/wks

23 May 81	**FOLLOW THE LEADERS** Malicious Damage EGMDS 101	55	5
20 Mar 82	**EMPIRE SONG** Malicious Damage EGO 4	43	4
30 Oct 82	**BIRDS OF A FEATHER** EG EGO 10	64	2
25 Jun 83	**LET'S ALL (GO TO THE FIRE DANCES)** EG EGO 11	51	3
15 Oct 83	**ME OR YOU?** EG EGO 14	57	1
7 Apr 84	**EIGHTIES** EG EGO 16	60	5
21 Jul 84	**A NEW DAY** EG EGO 17	56	2
2 Feb 85	**LOVE LIKE BLOOD** EG EGO 20	16	9
30 Mar 85	**KINGS AND QUEENS** EG EGO 21	58	3
16 Aug 86	**ADORATIONS** EG EGO 27	42	6
18 Oct 86	**SANITY** EG EGO 30	70	1
7 May 94	**MILLENNIUM** Butterfly BFLD 12	34	2
16 Jul 94	**PANDEMONIUM** Butterfly BFLD 17	28	3
4 Feb 95	**JANA** Butterfly BFLDA 21	54	1
23 Mar 96	**DEMOCRACY** Butterfly BFLDA 33	39	1

Andy KIM Canada, male vocalist (12 WEEKS)
pos/wks

| 24 Aug 74 ● | **ROCK ME GENTLY** Capitol CL 15787 ▲ | 2 | 12 |

KINANE Ireland, female vocalist (4 WEEKS)
pos/wks

18 May 96	**ALL THE LOVER I NEED** Coliseum TOGA 003CD	59	1
21 Sep 96	**THE WOMAN IN ME** Coliseum TOGA 007CD [1]	73	1
16 May 98	**HEAVEN** Coalition COLA 047CD	49	1
22 Aug 98	**SO FINE** Coalition COLA 055CD1	63	1

[1] Bianca Kinane

KING UK / Ireland, male vocal / instrumental group (44 WEEKS)
pos/wks

12 Jan 85 ●	**LOVE AND PRIDE** CBS A 4988	2	14
23 Mar 85	**WON'T YOU HOLD MY HAND NOW** CBS A 6094	24	8
17 Aug 85 ●	**ALONE WITHOUT YOU** CBS A 6308	8	9
19 Oct 85	**THE TASTE OF YOUR TEARS** CBS A 6618	11	9
11 Jan 86	**TORTURE** CBS A 6761	23	4

See also Paul KING

KING ADORA UK, male vocal / instrumental group (1 WEEK)
pos/wks

| 4 Nov 00 | **SMOULDER** Superior Quality / A&M RQSD 010CD | 62 | 1 |

Albert KING – See Gary MOORE

BB KING US, male vocalist / instrumentalist - guitar (10 WEEKS)
pos/wks

| 15 Apr 89 ● | **WHEN LOVE COMES TO TOWN** Island IS 411 [1] | 6 | 7 |
| 18 Jul 92 | **SINCE I MET YOU BABY** Virgin VS 1423 [2] | 59 | 3 |

[1] U2 with BB King [2] Gary Moore and BB King

Ben E. KING US, male vocalist - Benjamin Nelson (35 WEEKS)
pos/wks

2 Feb 61	**FIRST TASTE OF LOVE** London HLK 9258	27	11
22 Jun 61	**STAND BY ME** London HLK 9358	50	1
6 Jul 61	**STAND BY ME (re-entry)** London HLK 9358	27	6
5 Oct 61	**AMOR AMOR** London HLK 9416	38	4
14 Feb 87 ★	**STAND BY ME (re-issue)** Atlantic A 9361	1	11
4 Jul 87	**SAVE THE LAST DANCE FOR ME** Manhattan MT 25	69	2

See also DRIFTERS

Carole KING *US, female vocalist - Carole Klein (29 WEEKS)* pos/wks

20 Sep 62 ●	IT MIGHT AS WELL RAIN UNTIL SEPTEMBER	
	London HLU 9591 ....**3** 13	
7 Aug 71 ●	IT'S TOO LATE *A & M AMS 849* ▲ **6** 12	
28 Oct 72	IT MIGHT AS WELL RAIN UNTIL SEPTEMBER (re-issue)	
	London HL 10391 ....**43** 4	

Dave KING *UK, male vocalist (29 WEEKS)* pos/wks

17 Feb 56 ●	MEMORIES ARE MADE OF THIS *Decca F 10684* [1] **5** 15	
13 Apr 56	YOU CAN'T BE TRUE TO TWO *Decca F 10720* [1] **11** 9	
21 Dec 56	CHRISTMAS AND YOU *Decca F 10791*.........................**23** 2	
24 Jan 58	THE STORY OF MY LIFE *Decca F 10973*.......................**20** 3	

[1] Dave King featuring The Keynotes

Denis KING – See STUTZ BEARCATS and the Denis KING ORCHESTRA; KING BROTHERS

Diana KING *Jamaica, female vocalist (22 WEEKS)* pos/wks

8 Jul 95 ●	SHY GUY *Columbia 6621682* **2** 13	
28 Oct 95	AIN'T NOBODY *Columbia 6625495*.....................**13** 5	
1 Nov 97	I SAY A LITTLE PRAYER *Columbia 6651472*............**17** 4	

Evelyn 'Champagne' KING (447 Top 500) *Bubbly soul / disco vocalist b. 29 Jun 1960, New York , US. Groundbreaking debut hit 'Shame' was the biggest selling transatlantic 12-inch single at the time. It earned her a US gold record and a silver disc in the UK despite failing to reach the Top 30 (76 WEEKS)* pos/wks

13 May 78	SHAME *RCA PC 1122* **39** 23	
3 Feb 79	I DON'T KNOW IF IT'S RIGHT *RCA PB 1386* **67** 2	
27 Jun 81	I'M IN LOVE *RCA 95* [1] **27** 11	
26 Sep 81	IF YOU WANT MY LOVIN' *RCA 131* [1] **43** 6	
28 Aug 82 ●	LOVE COME DOWN *RCA 249* [1] **7** 13	
20 Nov 82	BACK TO LOVE *RCA 287* [1] **40** 4	
19 Feb 83	GET LOOSE *RCA 315* [1] **45** 5	
9 Nov 85	YOUR PERSONAL TOUCH *RCA PB 49915* **37** 5	
29 Mar 86	HIGH HORSE *RCA PB 49891* **55** 3	
23 Jul 88	HOLD ON TO WHAT YOU'VE GOT *Manhattan MT 49* **47** 3	
10 Oct 92	SHAME (re-mix) *Network NWKTEN 56* [2] **74** 1	

[1] Evelyn King [2] Altern 8 vs Evelyn King

Jonathan KING (204 Top 500) *King of the pseudonyms. b. 6 Dec 1944, London, UK. A multi-faceted pop maestro who masterminded numerous hits and helped Britain to win the Eurovision Song Contest in 1997. He also helped to guide the early careers of Genesis, Bay City Rollers and 10cc (128 WEEKS)* pos/wks

29 Jul 65 ●	EVERYONE'S GONE TO THE MOON *Decca F 12187* **4** 11	
10 Jan 70	LET IT ALL HANG OUT *Decca F 12988* **26** 7	
16 Jan 71	IT'S THE SAME OLD SONG *B & C CB 139* [1] **19** 9	
3 Apr 71	SUGAR SUGAR *RCA 2064* [2] **12** 14	
29 May 71	LAZY BONES *Decca F 13177* **23** 8	
20 Nov 71	HOOKED ON A FEELING *Decca F 13241* **23** 10	
5 Feb 72	FLIRT *Decca F 13276* **22** 9	
14 Oct 72 ●	LOOP DI LOVE *UK 7* [3] **4** 13	
26 Jan 74	(I CAN'T GET NO) SATISFACTION *UK 53* [4] **29** 5	
6 Sep 75 ●	UNA PALOMA BLANCA *UK 105*........................**5** 11	
20 Sep 75	CHICK-A-BOOM (DON'T YA JES LOVE IT) *UK 2012 002* [5] ...**36** 4	
7 Feb 76	IN THE MOOD *UK 121* [6] **46** 3	
26 Jun 76 ●	IT ONLY TAKES A MINUTE *UK 135* [7] **9** 9	
7 Oct 78	ONE FOR YOU ONE FOR ME *GTO GT 237* **29** 6	
16 Dec 78	LICK A SMURP FOR CHRISTMAS (ALL FALL DOWN)	
	Petrol GAS 1 / Magnet MAG 139 [8] **58** 4	
16 Jun 79	YOU'RE THE GREATEST LOVER	
	UK International INT 586 ....**67** 2	
3 Nov 79	GLORIA *Ariola ARO 198* **65** 3	

[1] Weathermen [2] Sakkarin [3] Shag [4] Bubblerock [5] 53rd and 3rd featuring the Sound of Shag [6] Sound 9418 [7] One Hundred Ton and a Feather [8] Father Abraphart and the Smurps

Nosmo KING – See JAVELLS featuring Nosmo KING

Paul KING *UK, male vocalist (3 WEEKS)* pos/wks

2 May 87	I KNOW *CBS PKING 1* **59** 3	

See also KING

Solomon KING *US, male vocalist (28 WEEKS)* pos/wks

3 Jan 68 ●	SHE WEARS MY RING *Columbia DB 8325* **3** 18	
1 May 68	WHEN WE WERE YOUNG *Columbia DB 8402* **21** 10	

KING BEE *UK, male rapper (6 WEEKS)* pos/wks

26 Jan 91	MUST BEE THE MUSIC *Columbia 6565827* **44** 4	
23 Mar 91	BACK BY DOPE DEMAND *First Bass 7RUFF 6X*.........**61** 2	

KING BROTHERS (462 Top 500) *Britain's top male group before The Beatles; brothers Denis (v/p), Michael (v/g) and Tony (v/b) King from Essex, UK. Poll-winning MOR-slanted trio made first of many TV appearances in 1953 (when Denis was 14). Denis became one of UK's top TV theme writers (74 WEEKS)* pos/wks

31 May 57 ●	A WHITE SPORT COAT *Parlophone R 4310*.............**6** 14	
9 Aug 57	IN THE MIDDLE OF AN ISLAND *Parlophone R 4338* **19** 13	
6 Dec 57	WAKE UP LITTLE SUSIE *Parlophone R 4367* **22** 3	
31 Jan 58	PUT A LIGHT IN THE WINDOW *Parlophone R 4389* **29** 1	
14 Feb 58	PUT A LIGHT IN THE WINDOW (re-entry)	
	Parlophone R 4389 ....**28** 1	
28 Feb 58	PUT A LIGHT IN THE WINDOW (2nd re-entry)	
	Parlophone R 4389 ....**25** 2	
14 Apr 60 ●	STANDING ON THE CORNER *Parlophone R 4639* **4** 11	
28 Jul 60	MAIS OUI *Parlophone R 4672* **16** 10	
12 Jan 61	DOLL HOUSE *Parlophone R 4715* **21** 8	
2 Mar 61	76 TROMBONES *Parlophone R 4737* **19** 11	

KING KURT *UK, male vocal / instrumental group (16 WEEKS)* pos/wks

15 Oct 83	DESTINATION ZULULAND *Stiff BUY 189* **36** 6	
28 Apr 84	MACK THE KNIFE *Stiff BUY 199* **55** 4	
4 Aug 84	BANANA BANANA *Stiff BUY 206* **54** 4	
15 Nov 86	AMERICA *Polydor KURT 1* **73** 1	
2 May 87	THE LAND OF RING DANG DO *Polydor KURT 2* **67** 1	

KING SUN-D'MOET *US, male rap / DJ duo (3 WEEKS)* pos/wks

11 Jul 87	HEY LOVE *Flame MELT 5* **66** 3	

Tony KING – See Kylie MINOGUE

KING TRIGGER
UK, male / female vocal / instrumental group (4 WEEKS) pos/wks

14 Aug 82	THE RIVER *Chrysalis CHS 2623* **57** 4	

KINGDOM COME *US, male vocal / instrumental group (2 WEEKS)* pos/wks

16 Apr 88	GET IT ON *Polydor KCS 1* **75** 1	
6 May 89	DO YOU LIKE IT *Polydor KCS 3* **73** 1	

KINGMAKER *UK, male vocal / instrumental group (22 WEEKS)* pos/wks

18 Jan 92	IDIOTS AT THE WHEEL (EP) *Scorch SCORCH 3* **30** 3	
23 May 92	EAT YOURSELF WHOLE *Scorch SCORCHG 5* **15** 3	
31 Oct 92	ARMCHAIR ANARCHIST *Scorch SCORCHG 6* **47** 2	
8 May 93	10 YEARS ASLEEP *Scorch CDSCORCHS 8* **15** 4	
19 Jun 93	QUEEN JANE *Scorch CDSCORS 9* **29** 4	
30 Oct 93	SATURDAY'S NOT WHAT IT USED TO BE	
	Scorch CDSCORCH 10...............................**63** 1	
15 Apr 95	YOU AND I WILL NEVER SEE THINGS EYE TO EYE	
	Scorch CDSCORCHS 11 ....**33** 3	
3 Jun 95	IN THE BEST POSSIBLE TASTE (PART 2)	
	Scorch CDSCORCHS 12 ....**41** 2	

Tracks on Idiots at the Wheel (EP): Really Scrape the Sky / Revelation / Every Teenage Suicide / Strip Away

KINGS OF SWING ORCHESTRA *Australia, orchestra (5 WEEKS)* pos/wks

1 May 82	SWITCHED ON SWING *Philips Swing 1*..................**48** 5	

KINGSMEN US, male vocal / instrumental group (7 WEEKS) pos/wks

30 Jan 64	LOUIE LOUIE *Pye International 7N 25231*	26 7

KINGSTON TRIO US, male vocal / instrumental group (15 WEEKS) pos/wks

21 Nov 58 ●	TOM DOOLEY *Capitol CL 14951* ▲	5 14
4 Dec 59	SAN MIGUEL *Capitol CL 15073*	29 1

KINKS ⟨71⟩ **Top 500** Well-respected and innovative London band, who
had few equals in the 1960s: Ray Davies (v/g), Dave Davies (g), Pete Quaife (b),
Mick Avory (d). Ray Davies, regarded as one of rock's premier songwriters,
remains active over 35 years after the group's first hit (215 WEEKS) pos/wks

13 Aug 64 ★	YOU REALLY GOT ME *Pye 7N 15673*	1 12
29 Oct 64 ●	ALL DAY AND ALL OF THE NIGHT *Pye 7N 15714*	2 14
21 Jan 65 ★	TIRED OF WAITING FOR YOU *Pye 7N 15759*	1 10
25 Mar 65	EVERYBODY'S GONNA BE HAPPY *Pye 7N 15813*	17 8
27 May 65 ●	SET ME FREE *Pye 7N 15854*	9 11
5 Aug 65 ●	SEE MY FRIEND *Pye 7N 15919*	10 9
2 Dec 65 ●	TILL THE END OF THE DAY *Pye 7N 15981*	8 12
3 Mar 66 ●	DEDICATED FOLLOWER OF FASHION *Pye 7N 17064*	4 11
9 Jun 66 ★	SUNNY AFTERNOON *Pye 7N 17125*	1 13
24 Nov 66 ●	DEAD END STREET *Pye 7N 17222*	5 11
11 May 67 ●	WATERLOO SUNSET *Pye 7N 17321*	2 11
18 Oct 67 ●	AUTUMN ALMANAC *Pye 7N 17400*	3 11
17 Apr 68	WONDERBOY *Pye 7N 17468*	36 5
17 Jul 68	DAYS *Pye 7N 17573*	12 10
16 Apr 69	PLASTIC MAN *Pye 7N 17724*	31 4
10 Jan 70	VICTORIA *Pye 7N 17865*	33 4
4 Jul 70 ●	LOLA *Pye 7N 17961*	2 14
12 Dec 70 ●	APEMAN *Pye 7N 45016*	5 14
27 May 72	SUPERSONIC ROCKET SHIP *RCA 2211*	16 8
27 Jun 81	BETTER THINGS *Arista ARIST 415*	46 5
6 Aug 83	COME DANCING *Arista ARIST 502*	12 9
15 Oct 83	DON'T FORGET TO DANCE *Arista ARIST 524*	58 3
15 Oct 83	YOU REALLY GOT ME (re-issue) *PRT KD1*	47 4
18 Jan 97	THE DAYS EP *When! WENX 1016*	35 2

Tracks on The Days EP: Days / You Really Got Me / Dead End Street / Lola

KINKY UK, female rapper (1 WEEK) pos/wks

24 Aug 96	EVERYBODY *Feverpitch CDFVR 1009*	71 1

See also ERASURE

KINKY MACHINE UK, male vocal / instrumental group (4 WEEKS) pos/wks

6 Mar 93	SUPERNATURAL GIVER *Lemon LEMON 006CD*	70 1
29 May 93	SHOCKAHOLIC *Oxygen GASPD 5*	70 1
14 Aug 93	GOING OUT WITH GOD *Oxygen GASPD 9*	74 1
2 Jul 94	10 SECOND BIONIC MAN *Oxygen GASPD 14*	66 1

Fern KINNEY US, female vocalist - Fern Kinney-Lewis (11 WEEKS) pos/wks

16 Feb 80 ★	TOGETHER WE ARE BEAUTIFUL *WEA K 79111*	1 11

KINSHASA BAND – See Johnny WAKELIN

Kathy KIRBY UK, female vocalist (54 WEEKS) pos/wks

15 Aug 63	DANCE ON *Decca F 11682*	11 13
7 Nov 63 ●	SECRET LOVE *Decca F 11759*	4 18
20 Feb 64 ●	LET ME GO LOVER *Decca F 11832*	10 11
7 May 64	YOU'RE THE ONE *Decca F 11892*	17 9
4 Mar 65	I BELONG *Decca F 12087*	36 3

Bo KIRKLAND and Ruth DAVIS
US, male / female vocal duo (9 WEEKS) pos/wks

4 Jun 77	YOU'RE GONNA GET NEXT TO ME *EMI International INT 532*	12 9

KISS US, male vocal / instrumental group (57 WEEKS) pos/wks

30 Jun 79	I WAS MADE FOR LOVIN' YOU *Casablanca CAN 152*	50 7
20 Feb 82	A WORLD WITHOUT HEROES *Casablanca KISS 002*	55 3
30 Apr 83	CREATURES OF THE NIGHT *Casablanca KISS 4*	34 4

29 Oct 83	LICK IT UP *Vertigo KISS 5*	31 5
8 Sep 84	HEAVEN'S ON FIRE *Vertigo VER 12*	43 3
9 Nov 85	TEARS ARE FALLING *Vertigo KISS 6*	57 2
3 Oct 87 ●	CRAZY CRAZY NIGHTS *Vertigo KISS 7*	4 9
5 Dec 87	REASON TO LIVE *Vertigo KISS 8*	33 7
10 Sep 88	TURN ON THE NIGHT *Vertigo KISS 9*	41 3
18 Nov 89	HIDE YOUR HEART *Vertigo KISS 10*	59 2
31 Mar 90	FOREVER *Vertigo KISS 11*	65 2
11 Jan 92 ●	GOD GAVE ROCK AND ROLL TO YOU II *Interscope A 8696*	4 8
9 May 92	UNHOLY *Mercury KISS 12*	26 2

KISS AMC UK, female rap duo (5 WEEKS) pos/wks

1 Jul 89	A BIT OF . . . *Syncopate SY 29*	58 2
19 Aug 89	A BIT OF U2 (re-entry) *Syncopate SY 29*	58 2
3 Feb 90	MY DOCS *Syncopate XAMC 1*	66 1

Before the re-entry of 'A Bit of U2', copyright problems meant that the disc was
unable to be given its full title

KISSING THE PINK
UK, male / female vocal / instrumental group (14 WEEKS) pos/wks

5 Mar 83	LAST FILM *Magnet KTP 3*	19 14

Mac and Katie KISSOON
Trinidad / UK, male / female vocal duo (33 WEEKS) pos/wks

19 Jun 71	CHIRPY CHIRPY CHEEP CHEEP *Young Blood YB 1026*	41 1
18 Jan 75 ●	SUGAR CANDY KISSES *Polydor 2058 531*	3 10
3 May 75 ●	DON'T DO IT BABY *State STAT 4*	9 8
30 Aug 75	LIKE A BUTTERFLY *State STAT 9*	18 9
15 May 76	THE TWO OF US *State STAT 21*	46 5

Kevin KITCHEN UK, male vocalist (3 WEEKS) pos/wks

20 Apr 85	PUT MY ARMS AROUND YOU *China WOK 1*	64 3

Eartha KITT US, female vocalist (34 WEEKS) pos/wks

1 Apr 55 ●	UNDER THE BRIDGES OF PARIS *HMV B 10647*	7 9
10 Jun 55	UNDER THE BRIDGES OF PARIS (re-entry) *HMV B 10647*	20 1
3 Dec 83	WHERE IS MY MAN *Record Shack SOHO 11*	36 11
7 Jul 84	I LOVE MEN *Record Shack SOHO 21*	50 3
12 Apr 86	THIS IS MY LIFE *Record Shack SOHO 61*	73 1
1 Jul 89	CHA CHA HEELS *Arista 112331* [1]	32 7
5 Mar 94	IF I LOVE YA THEN I NEED YA IF I NEED YA THEN I WANT YOU AROUND *RCA 74321190342*	43 2

[1] Eartha Kitt and Bronski Beat

KITTIE Canada, female vocal / instrumental group (2 WEEKS) pos/wks

25 Mar 00	BRACKISH *Epic 6691292*	46 1
22 Jul 00	CHARLOTTE *Epic 6696222*	60 1

KLAXONS Belgium, male vocal / instrumental group (6 WEEKS) pos/wks

10 Dec 83	THE CLAP CLAP SOUND *PRT 7P 290*	45 6

KLEEER US, male / female vocal / instrumental group (10 WEEKS) pos/wks

17 Mar 79	KEEEP YOUR BODY WORKING *Atlantic LV 21*	51 6
14 Mar 81	GET TOUGH *Atlantic 11560*	49 4

KLESHAY UK, female vocal trio (5 WEEKS) pos/wks

19 Sep 98	REASONS *Epic KLE 1CD*	33 2
20 Feb 99	RUSH *Epic KLE 2CD*	19 3

KLF UK, male vocal / instrumental duo - Bill Drummond and Jimmy Cauty
(51 WEEKS) pos/wks

11 Aug 90 ●	WHAT TIME IS LOVE (LIVE AT TRANCENTRAL) *KLF Communications KLF 004* [1]	5 12
19 Jan 91 ★	3 AM ETERNAL *KLF Communications KLF 005* [1]	1 11
4 May 91 ●	LAST TRAIN TO TRANCENTRAL *KLF Communications KLF 008*	2 9

SINGLED OUT... Paul Weller

Revered by mods from St Albans to San Francisco, Paul started his glittering chart career as the angry young man who led the Jam, one of the seminal late 70s UK groups. He has since matured like a fine burgundy into a prolific solo performer with a string of great albums including Heavy Soul, Stanley Road and Heliocentric.

• NO.1 ON THE UK SINGLES CHART THE DAY I WAS BORN:
Who's Sorry Now - Connie Francis

• ALL-TIME FAVOURITE SINGLE:
Strawberry Fields Forever - Beatles

• SINGLE THAT DRIVES ME UP THE WALL:
Most do

FIRST SINGLE
I EVER BOUGHT:
Wonderboy
The Kinks

Photo: Hulton Archive

John KONGOS
South Africa, male vocalist / multi-instrumentalist (25 WEEKS) pos/wks

22 May 71	●	HE'S GONNA STEP ON YOU AGAIN *Fly BUG 8*	4	14
20 Nov 71	●	TOKOLOSHE MAN *Fly BUG 14*	4	11

KOOL and the GANG ⬭81 Top 500
One of the most consistently successful R&B acts, hailing from New Jersey and including Robert 'Kool' Bell (b) and James 'JT' Taylor (v). The band spent 10 years as top US R&B stars before starting their impressive run of international hits (207 WEEKS) pos/wks

27 Oct 79	●	LADIES NIGHT *Mercury KOOL 7*	9	12
19 Jan 80		TOO HOT *Mercury KOOL 8*	23	8
12 Jul 80		HANGIN' OUT *De-Lite KOOL 9*	52	4
1 Nov 80	●	CELEBRATION *De-Lite KOOL 10* ▲	7	13
21 Feb 81		JONES VS JONES / SUMMER MADNESS *De-Lite KOOL 11*	17	11
30 May 81		TAKE IT TO THE TOP *De-Lite DE 2*	15	9
31 Oct 81		STEPPIN' OUT *De-Lite DE 4*	12	13
19 Dec 81	●	GET DOWN ON IT *De-Lite DE 5*	3	12
6 Mar 82		TAKE MY HEART (YOU CAN HAVE IT IF YOU WANT IT) *De-Lite DE 6*	29	7
7 Aug 82		BIG FUN *De-Lite DE 7*	14	8
16 Oct 82	●	OOH LA LA LA (LET'S GO DANCIN') *De-Lite DE 9*	6	9
4 Dec 82		HI DE HI, HI DE HO *De-Lite DE 14*	29	8
10 Dec 83		STRAIGHT AHEAD *De-Lite DE 15*	15	10
11 Feb 84	●	JOANNA / TONIGHT *De-Lite DE 16*	2	11
14 Apr 84	●	(WHEN YOU SAY YOU LOVE SOMEBODY) IN THE HEART *De-Lite DE 17*	7	8
24 Nov 84	●	FRESH *De-Lite DE 18*	11	12
9 Feb 85		MISLED *De-Lite DE 19*	28	5
11 May 85	●	CHERISH *De-Lite DE 20*	4	22
2 Nov 85		EMERGENCY *De-Lite DE 21*	50	3
22 Nov 86		VICTORY *Club JAB 44*	67	2
20 Dec 86		VICTORY (re-entry) *Club JAB 44*	30	10
21 Mar 87		STONE LOVE *Club JAB 47*	45	4
31 Dec 88		CELEBRATION (re-mix) *Club JAB 78*	56	5
6 Jul 91		GET DOWN ON IT (re-mix) *Mercury MER 346*	69	1

'Jones vs Jones' and 'Summer Madness' were labelled as A and B sides with 'Funky Stuff' and 'Hollywood Swinging' as the C and D sides of a two disc release

KOOL ROCK STEADY – See TYREE

KOON + STEPHENSON – See WESTBAM

KORGIS *UK, male vocal / instrumental duo (27 WEEKS)* pos/wks

23 Jun 79		IF I HAD YOU *Rialto TREB 103*	13	12
24 May 80	●	EVERYBODY'S GOT TO LEARN SOMETIME *Rialto TREB 115*	5	12
30 Aug 80		IF IT'S ALRIGHT WITH YOU BABY *Rialto TREB 118*	56	3

KORN *US, male vocal / instrumental group (14 WEEKS)* pos/wks

19 Oct 96		NO PLACE TO HIDE *Epic 6638452*	26	2
15 Feb 97		A.D.I.D.A.S. *Epic 6642042*	22	2
7 Jun 97		GOOD GOD *Epic 6646585*	25	2
22 Aug 98		GOT THE LIFE *Epic 6663912*	23	2
8 May 99		FREAK ON A LEASH *Epic 6672522*	24	2
12 Feb 00		FALLING AWAY FROM ME *Epic 6688692*	24	2
3 Jun 00		MAKE ME BAD *Epic 6694332*	25	2

KOSHEEN *UK, male production duo and female vocalist (1 WEEK)* pos/wks

17 Jun 00		EMPTY SKIES / HIDE U *Moksha Recordings MOKSHA 05CD*	73	1

KP & ENVYI *US, female vocal / rap duo (4 WEEKS)* pos/wks

13 Jun 98		SWING MY WAY *East West E 3849 CD*	14	4

KRAFTWERK ⬭469 Top 500
Acclaimed German band who greatly influenced dance and rock music. Founder members were multi-instrumentalists / vocalists Ralf Hutter and Florian Schneider. 'The Model' was first German record to top UK chart. Hip Hop's pioneers acknowledge their debt to this seminal electronic group (72 WEEKS) pos/wks

10 May 75		AUTOBAHN *Vertigo 6147 012*	11	9
28 Oct 78		NEON LIGHTS *Capitol CL 15998*	53	3
9 May 81		POCKET CALCULATOR *EMI 5175*	39	6
11 Jul 81		COMPUTER LOVE / THE MODEL *EMI 5207*	36	8
26 Dec 81	★	COMPUTER LOVE / THE MODEL (re-entry) *EMI 5207*	1	13
20 Feb 82		SHOWROOM DUMMIES *EMI 5272*	25	5
6 Aug 83		TOUR DE FRANCE *EMI 5413*	22	8
25 Aug 84		TOUR DE FRANCE (re-entry) *EMI 5413*	24	11
1 Jun 91		THE ROBOTS *EMI EM 192*	20	4
2 Nov 91		RADIOACTIVITY *EMI EM 201*	43	2
23 Oct 99		TOUR DE FRANCE (re-issue) *EMI 8874210*	61	1
18 Mar 00		EXPO 2000 *EMI CDEM 562*	27	2

Billy J KRAMER and the DAKOTAS ⬭477 Top 500
Another successful Brian Epstein-managed and George Martin-produced group, led by well-groomed photogenic vocalist, b. William H. Ashton, 19 Aug 1943, Lancashire, UK. Winners of Melody Maker Best Newcomer of 1963 poll. Had most of their hits penned by Lennon and McCartney (71 WEEKS) pos/wks

2 May 63	●	DO YOU WANT TO KNOW A SECRET? *Parlophone R 5023*	2	15
1 Aug 63	★	BAD TO ME *Parlophone R 5049*	1	14
7 Nov 63	●	I'LL KEEP YOU SATISFIED *Parlophone R 5073*	4	13
27 Feb 64	★	LITTLE CHILDREN *Parlophone R 5105*	1	13
23 Jul 64	●	FROM A WINDOW *Parlophone R 5156*	10	8
20 May 65		TRAINS AND BOATS AND PLANES *Parlophone R 5285*	12	8

KRANKIES *UK, male / female vocal duo (6 WEEKS)* pos/wks

7 Feb 81		FAN'DABI'DOZI *Monarch MON 21*	71	1
7 Mar 81		FAN'DABI'DOZI (re-entry) *Monarch MON 21*	46	5

Lenny KRAVITZ *US, male vocalist (68 WEEKS)* pos/wks

2 Jun 90		MR CABDRIVER *Virgin America VUS 20*	58	2
4 Aug 90		LET LOVE RULE *Virgin America VUS 26*	39	4
30 Mar 91		ALWAYS ON THE RUN *Virgin America VUS 34*	41	3
15 Jun 91		IT AIN'T OVER TIL IT'S OVER *Virgin America VUS 43*	11	8
14 Sep 91		STAND BY MY WOMAN *Virgin America VUS 45*	55	3
20 Mar 93	●	ARE YOU GONNA GO MY WAY *Virgin America VUSDG 65*	4	11
22 May 93		BELIEVE *Virgin America VUSCD 72*	30	5
28 Aug 93		HEAVEN HELP *Virgin America VUSDG 73*	20	7
4 Dec 93		BUDDHA OF SUBURBIA *Arista 74321177052* [1]	35	3
4 Dec 93		IS THERE ANY LOVE IN YOUR HEART *Virgin America VUSDG 76*	52	2
9 Sep 95		ROCK AND ROLL IS DEAD *Virgin America VUSCD 93*	22	3
23 Dec 95		CIRCUS *Virgin America VUSCD 96*	54	2
2 Mar 96		CAN'T GET YOU OFF MY MIND *Virgin America VUSCD 100*	54	2
16 May 98		IF YOU CAN'T SAY NO *Virgin VUSCD 130*	48	2
10 Oct 98		I BELONG TO YOU *Virgin VUSCD 138*	75	1
20 Feb 99	★	FLY AWAY *Virgin VUSCD 141* ■	1	10

[1] David Bowie featuring Lenny Kravitz

KRAZE *US, male / female vocal / instrumental group (6 WEEKS)* pos/wks

22 Oct 88		THE PARTY *MCA MCA 1288*	29	5
17 Jun 89		LET'S PLAY HOUSE *MCA MCA 1337*	71	1

KREUZ *UK, male vocal group (1 WEEK)* pos/wks

8 Jul 95		PARTY ALL NIGHT *Diesel DES 004C*	75	1

Chantal KREVIAZUK *Canada, female vocalist (1 WEEK)* pos/wks

6 Mar 99		LEAVING ON A JET PLANE *Epic 6666272*	59	1

KREW-KATS *UK, male instrumental group (10 WEEKS)* pos/wks

9 Mar 61		TRAMBONE *HMV POP 840*	33	9
18 May 61		TRAMBONE (re-entry) *HMV POP 840*	49	1

KRIS KROSS
US, male rap duo - Chris Kelly anf Chris Smith (22 WEEKS) pos/wks

30 May 92	●	JUMP *Ruff House 6578547* ▲	2	8
25 Jul 92		WARM IT UP *Ruff House 6582187*	16	6
17 Oct 92		I MISSED THE BUS *Ruff House 6583927*	57	1
19 Dec 92		IT'S A SHAME *Ruff House 6588587*	31	5
11 Sep 93		ALRIGHT *Ruff House 6595652*	47	2

SINGLED OUT... Frank Skinner

Surprisingly, none of fun-time Frankie's Singled Out selection reflects his great love of both Elvis P and Elvis C, although some of the inspiration for his part in the 'Three Lions' No.1 is plain to see.

- **NO.1 ON THE UK SINGLES CHART THE DAY I WAS BORN:**

  The Garden Of Eden – Frankie Vaughan and **Singing The Blues** – Tommy Steele

  [A rare two-way tie that week]

- **FIRST SINGLE I EVER BOUGHT:**

  Back Home – 1970 England World Cup squad

  Who would have thought that 26 years later...

- **SINGLE THAT DRIVES ME UP THE WALL:**

  Imagine – John Lennon

ALL-TIME FAVOURITE SINGLE:

Showroom Dummies
Kraftwerk

Photo: Pictorial Press

Photo: Rex Features

LA TREC – See SASH!

LaBELLE
US, female vocal group – lead vocal Patti LaBelle (9 WEEKS)   pos/wks

22 Mar 75	LADY MARMALADE (VOULEZ-VOUS COUCHER AVEC MOI CE SOIR?) *Epic EPC 2852* ▲	17 9

See also Patti LaBELLE

Patti LaBELLE *US, female vocalist – Patricia Holt (21 WEEKS)*   pos/wks

3 May 86 ●	ON MY OWN *MCA MCA 1045* [1] ▲	2 13
2 Aug 86	OH, PEOPLE *MCA MCA 1075*	26 6
3 Sep 94	THE RIGHT KINDA LOVER *MCA MCSTD 1995*	50 2

[1] Patti LaBelle and Michael McDonald

See also LaBELLE

LADIES CHOICE *UK, male vocal / instrumental group (4 WEEKS)* pos/wks

25 Jan 86	FUNKY SENSATION *Sure Delight SD 01*	41 4

LADY G – See B15 Project featuring Crissy D & Lady G

LADY J – See RAZE

LADY OF RAGE *US, female rapper (1 WEEK)*   pos/wks

8 Oct 94	AFRO PUFFS *Interscope A 8288CD*	72 1

LADY SAW – See M DUBS featuring LADY SAW

LADYSMITH BLACK MAMBAZO
South Africa, male vocal group (26 WEEKS)   pos/wks

3 Jun 95	SWING LOW SWEET CHARIOT *PolyGram TV SWLOW 2* [1]	15 6
3 Jun 95	WORLD IN UNION '95 *PolyGram TV RUGBY 2* [2]	47 5
15 Nov 97	INKANYEZI NEZAZI (THE STAR AND THE WISEMAN) *A & M 5823892*	33 3
11 Jul 98	THE STAR AND THE WISEMAN (re-issue) *AM:PM 5825692*	63 1
16 Oct 99	AIN'T NO SUNSHINE *Universal Music TV 1564332* [3]	42 2
18 Dec 99	I SHALL BE THERE *Glow Worm / Epic 6683332* [4]	13 9

[1] Ladysmith Black Mambazo featuring China Black [2] Ladysmith Black Mambazo featuring PJ Powers [3] Ladysmith Black Mambazo featuring Des'ree [4] B*witched featuring Ladysmith Black Mambazo

LAGUNA *Italy, male DJ / production duo (2 WEEKS)*   pos/wks

1 Nov 97	SPILLER FROM RIO (DO IT EASY) *Positiva CDTIV 83*	40 2

LAID BACK *Denmark, male vocal / instrumental duo (4 WEEKS)*   pos/wks

5 May 90	BAKERMAN *Arista 112356*	44 4

LAIN – See WOOKIE

Cleo LAINE *UK, female vocalist – Clementina Campbell (14 WEEKS)* pos/wks

29 Dec 60	LET'S SLIP AWAY *Fontana H 269*	42 1
14 Sep 61 ●	YOU'LL ANSWER TO ME *Fontana H 326*	5 13

Frankie LAINE [35] [Top 500] Powerful-voiced No.1 hitmaker of the pre-rock years, b. Frank Lovecchio, 30 Mar 1913, Chicago, US. He spent an unequalled 27 weeks at the top of the UK chart in 1953, including a record 18 by 'I Believe'. At one time had three singles in the Top 5 (281 WEEKS)   pos/wks

14 Nov 52 ●	HIGH NOON (DO NOT FORSAKE ME) *Columbia DB 3113*	7 7
14 Nov 52 ●	SUGARBUSH *Columbia DB 3123* [1]	8 2
5 Dec 52 ●	SUGARBUSH (re-entry) *Columbia DB 3123* [1]	8 6
20 Mar 53	THE GIRL IN THE WOOD *Columbia DB 2907*	11 1
3 Apr 53 ★	I BELIEVE *Philips PB 117*	1 36
8 May 53 ●	TELL ME A STORY *Philips PB 126* [2]	5 15
4 Sep 53 ●	WHERE THE WINDS BLOW *Philips PB 167*	2 12
11 Sep 53	TELL ME A STORY (re-entry) *Philips PB 126* [2]	12 1
16 Oct 53 ★	HEY JOE *Philips PB 172*	1 8
30 Oct 53 ★	ANSWER ME *Philips PB 196*	1 17

8 Jan 54 ●	BLOWING WILD *Philips PB 207*	2 12
26 Mar 54 ●	GRANADA *Philips PB 242*	10 1
9 Apr 54 ●	GRANADA (re-entry) *Philips PB 242*	9 1
16 Apr 54 ●	THE KID'S LAST FIGHT *Philips PB 258*	3 10
13 Aug 54 ●	MY FRIEND *Philips PB 316*	3 15
8 Oct 54 ●	THERE MUST BE A REASON *Philips PB 306*	9 9
22 Oct 54 ●	RAIN RAIN RAIN *Philips PB 311* [3]	8 16
11 Mar 55 ●	IN THE BEGINNING *Philips PB 404*	20 1
24 Jun 55 ●	COOL WATER *Philips PB 465* [4]	2 22
15 Jul 55 ●	STRANGE LADY IN TOWN *Philips PB 478*	6 13
11 Nov 55	HUMMING BIRD *Philips PB 498*	16 1
25 Nov 55 ●	HAWKEYE *Philips PB 519*	7 8
20 Jan 56 ●	SIXTEEN TONS *Philips PB 539* [4]	10 3
4 May 56	HELL HATH NO FURY *Philips PB 585*	28 1
7 Sep 56 ★	A WOMAN IN LOVE *Philips PB 617*	1 21
28 Dec 56	MOONLIGHT GAMBLER *Philips PB 638*	13 12
29 Mar 57	MOONLIGHT GAMBLER (re-entry) *Philips PB 638*	28 1
26 Apr 57	LOVE IS A GOLDEN RING *Philips PB 676* [5]	19 5
4 Oct 57	GOOD EVENING FRIENDS / UP ABOVE MY HEAD I HEAR MUSIC IN THE AIR *Philips PB 708* [6]	25 4
13 Nov 59 ●	RAWHIDE *Philips PB 965*	6 17
31 Mar 60	RAWHIDE (re-entry) *Philips PB 965*	41 2
11 May 61	GUNSLINGER *Philips PB 1135*	50 1

[1] Doris Day and Frankie Laine [2] Jimmy Boyd – Frankie Laine [3] Frankie Laine and the Four Lads [4] Frankie Laine with the Mellomen [5] Frankie Laine and the Easy Riders [6] Frankie Laine and Johnnie Ray

Greg LAKE *UK, male vocalist (12 WEEKS)*   pos/wks

6 Dec 75 ●	I BELIEVE IN FATHER CHRISTMAS *Manticore K 13511*	2 7
25 Dec 82	I BELIEVE IN FATHER CHRISTMAS (re-entry) *Manticore K 13511*	72 3
24 Dec 83	I BELIEVE IN FATHER CHRISTMAS (2nd re-entry) *Manticore K 13511*	65 2

See also EMERSON, LAKE and PALMER

LAMB *UK, male / female vocal / production duo (4 WEEKS)*   pos/wks

29 Mar 97	GORECKI *Fontana LAMCD 4*	30 2
3 Apr 99	B LINE *Fontana LAMCD 5*	52 1
22 May 99	ALL IN YOUR HANDS *Fontana LAMCD 6*	71 1

Annabel LAMB *UK, female vocalist (7 WEEKS)*   pos/wks

27 Aug 83	RIDERS ON THE STORM *A & M AM 131*	27 7

LAMBCHOP *US, male / female vocal / instramental group (1 WEEK)* pos/wks

20 May 00	UP WITH PEOPLE *City Slang 201592*	66 1

LAMBRETTAS *UK, male vocal / instrumental group (24 WEEKS)*   pos/wks

1 Mar 80 ●	POISON IVY *Rocket XPRESS 25*	7 12
24 May 80	D-A-A-ANCE *Rocket XPRESS 33*	12 8
23 Aug 80	ANOTHER DAY (ANOTHER GIRL) *Rocket XPRESS 36*	49 4

LANCASTRIANS *UK, male vocal / instrumental group (2 WEEKS)*   pos/wks

24 Dec 64	WE'LL SING IN THE SUNSHINE *Pye 7N 15732*	47 2

Major LANCE *US, male vocalist (2 WEEKS)*   pos/wks

13 Feb 64	UM UM UM UM UM UM *Columbia DB 7205*	40 2

LANCERS – See Teresa BREWER

Valerie LANDSBERG – See KIDS FROM 'FAME'

LANDSCAPE *UK, male vocal / instrumental group (20 WEEKS)*   pos/wks

28 Feb 81 ●	EINSTEIN A GO-GO *RCA 22*	5 13
23 May 81	NORMAN BATES *RCA 60*	40 7

Desmond LANE – See Alma COGAN; Cyril STAPLETON and his ORCHESTRA

Ronnie LANE and SLIM CHANCE
UK, male vocalist and male instrumental group (12 WEEKS) pos/wks

12 Jan 74	HOW COME *GM GMS 011*	11	8
15 Jun 74	THE POACHER *GM GMS 024*	36	4

See also SMALL FACES

Don LANG *UK, male vocalist - Gordon Langhorn (18 WEEKS)* pos/wks

4 Nov 55	CLOUDBURST *HMV POP 115*	16	2
2 Dec 55	CLOUDBURST (re-entry) *HMV POP 115*	18	1
13 Jan 56	CLOUDBURST (2nd re-entry) *HMV POP 115*	20	1
5 Jul 57	SCHOOL DAY *HMV POP 350* [1]	26	2
23 May 58 ●	WITCH DOCTOR *HMV POP 488* [1]	5	11
10 Mar 60	SINK THE BISMARCK *HMV POP 714*	43	1

[1] Don Lang and his Frantic Five

kd LANG *Canada, female vocalist (25 WEEKS)* pos/wks

16 May 92	CONSTANT CRAVING *Sire W 0100*	52	4
22 Aug 92	CRYING *Virgin America VUS 63* [1]	13	6
27 Feb 93	CONSTANT CRAVING (re-issue) *Sire W 0157CD*	15	8
1 May 93	THE MIND OF LOVE *Sire W 0170CD1*	72	1
26 Jun 93	MISS CHATELAINE *Sire W 0181CDX*	68	2
11 Dec 93	JUST KEEP ME MOVING *Sire W 0227CD*	59	1
30 Sep 95	IF I WERE YOU *Sire W 0319CD*	53	1
18 May 96	YOU'RE OK *Warner Bros. W 0332CD*	44	2

[1] Roy Orbison (duet with kd Lang)

Thomas LANG *UK, male vocalist (3 WEEKS)* pos/wks

30 Jan 88	THE HAPPY MAN *Epic VOW 4*	67	3

LANGE featuring SARAH DWYER
UK, male producer - Stuart Langelann (1 WEEK) pos/wks

19 Jun 99	I BELIEVE *Additive 12 AD039*	68	1

LANTERNS *UK, male / female vocal / instrumental trio (1 WEEK)* pos/wks

6 Feb 99	HIGHRISE TOWN *Columbia 6665712*	50	1

Mario LANZA *US, male vocalist - Alfredo Cocozza (32 WEEKS)* pos/wks

14 Nov 52 ●	BECAUSE YOU'RE MINE *HMV DA 2017*	3	24
4 Feb 55	DRINKING SONG *HMV DA 2065*	13	1
18 Feb 55	I'LL WALK WITH GOD *HMV DA 2062*	18	1
22 Apr 55	SERENADE *HMV DA 2065*	19	1
6 May 55	I'LL WALK WITH GOD (re-entry) *HMV DA 2062*	20	1
6 May 55	SERENADE (re-entry) *HMV DA 2065*	15	2
14 Sep 56	SERENADE *HMV DA 2085*	25	1
12 Oct 56	SERENADE (re-entry) *HMV DA 2085*	29	1

DA 2065 and DA 2085 are two different songs

LAPTOP
US, male vocalist / instrumentalist - Jesse Hartman (1 WEEK) pos/wks

12 Jun 99	NOTHING TO DECLARE *Island CID 744*	74	1

Julius LAROSA *US, male vocalist (9 WEEKS)* pos/wks

4 Jul 58	TORERO *RCA 1063*	15	9

LA's *UK, male vocal / instrumental group (20 WEEKS)* pos/wks

14 Jan 89	THERE SHE GOES *Go! Discs GOLAS 2*	59	4
15 Sep 90	TIMELESS MELODY *Go! Discs GOLAS 4*	57	2
3 Nov 90	THERE SHE GOES (re-issue) *Go! Discs GOLAS 5*	13	9
16 Feb 91	FEELIN' *Go! Discs GOLAS 6*	43	3
10 May 97	FEVER PITCH THE EP *Blanco Y Negro NEG 104CD* [1]	65	1
2 Oct 99	THERE SHE GOES (2nd re-issue) *Polydor 5614032*	65	1

[1] Pretenders, La's, Orlando, Nick Hornby

Lisa LASHES *UK, female DJ / producer (1 WEEK)* pos/wks

8 Jul 00	UNBELIEVABLE *Tidy Trax TIDY 138CD*	63	1

James LAST BAND *Germany, male orchestra (4 WEEKS)* pos/wks

3 May 80	THE SEDUCTION (LOVE THEME) *Polydor PD 2071*	48	4

LAST RHYTHM
Italy, male instrumental / production group (1 WEEK) pos/wks

14 Sep 96	LAST RHYTHM *Stress CDSTR 76*	62	1

LATANZA WATERS – See E-SMOOVE featuring Latanza WATERS

LATE SHOW *UK, male vocal / instrumental group (6 WEEKS)* pos/wks

3 Mar 79	BRISTOL STOMP *Decca F 13822*	40	6

LATIN QUARTER
UK, male / female vocal / instrumental group (10 WEEKS) pos/wks

18 Jan 86	RADIO AFRICA *Rockin' Horse RH 102*	19	9
18 Apr 87	NOMZAMO (ONE PEOPLE ONE CAUSE) *Rockin' Horse RH 113*	73	1

LATIN RHYTHM – See Tito PUENTE Jr and the LATIN RHYTHM featuring Tito
PUENTE, INDIA and Cali ALEMAN

LATIN THING
Canada / Spain, male / female vocal / instrumental group (1 WEEK) pos/wks

13 Jul 96	LATIN THING *Faze 2 CDFAZE 33*	41	1

Gino LATINO *Italy, male producer (7 WEEKS)* pos/wks

20 Jan 90	WELCOME *ffrr F 126*	17	7

LATINO RAVE – See VARIOUS ARTISTS (MONTAGES)

LATOUR *US, male vocalist / producer (7 WEEKS)* pos/wks

8 Jun 91	PEOPLE ARE STILL HAVING SEX *Polydor PO 147*	15	7

Stacy LATTISAW *US, female vocalist (14 WEEKS)* pos/wks

14 Jun 80 ●	JUMP TO THE BEAT *Atlantic / Cotillion K 11496*	3	11
30 Aug 80	DYNAMITE *Atlantic K 11554*	51	3

Dave LAUDAT – See HUSTLERS CONVENTION featuring Dave LAUDAT and Ondrea
DUVERNEY

LAUNCHERS – See Ezz RECO and the LAUNCHERS with Boysie GRANT

Cyndi LAUPER (286 Top 500) *Flamboyant and versatile singer /
songwriter, b. 20 Jun 1953, New York, US. Her debut album, She's So
Unusual (1983), spawned four Top 5 US singles, and she won a Grammy for
Best New Artist of 1984 (easily outpacing her major female rival, Madonna)
(103 WEEKS)* pos/wks

14 Jan 84 ●	GIRLS JUST WANT TO HAVE FUN *Portrait A 3943*	2	12
24 Mar 84	TIME AFTER TIME *Portrait A 4290* ▲	54	4
16 Jun 84 ●	TIME AFTER TIME (re-entry) *Portrait A 4290*	3	13
1 Sep 84	SHE BOP *Portrait A 4620*	46	5
17 Nov 84	ALL THROUGH THE NIGHT *Portrait A 4849*	64	1
20 Sep 86	TRUE COLOURS *Portrait 650026 7* ▲	12	11
27 Dec 86	CHANGE OF HEART *Portrait CYNDI 1*	74	1
10 Jan 87	CHANGE OF HEART (re-entry) *Portrait CYNDI 1*	67	1
28 Mar 87	WHAT'S GOING ON *Portrait CYN 1*	57	3
20 May 89 ●	I DROVE ALL NIGHT *Epic CYN 4*	7	12
5 Aug 89	MY FIRST NIGHT WITHOUT YOU *Epic CYN 5*	53	4
30 Dec 89	HEADING WEST *Epic CYN 6*	68	1
6 Jun 92	THE WORLD IS STONE *Epic 6579707*	15	7
13 Nov 93	THAT'S WHAT I THINK *Epic 6598782*	31	4
8 Jan 94	WHO LET IN THE RAIN *Epic 6590392*	32	4
17 Sep 94 ●	HEY NOW (GIRLS JUST WANT TO HAVE FUN) *Epic 6608072*	4	13
11 Feb 95	I'M GONNA BE STRONG *Epic 6611962*	37	2
26 Aug 95	COME ON HOME *Epic 6614255*	39	2
1 Feb 97	YOU DON'T KNOW *Epic 6641845*	27	2

'Hey Now (Girls Just Want to Have Fun)' is a re-recording of her first hit

SINGLED OUT...
Lorraine Kelly

Gorgeous presenter and columnist, "wee" Lorraine Kelly was exposed to Cliff and the Shads in her very early days but, as a teenager, clearly didn't have a picture of fellow Scot Leslie McKeown on her bedroom wall.

- **NO.1 ON THE UK SINGLES CHART THE DAY I WAS BORN:**
Travellin' Light –
Cliff Richard and The Shadows

- **FIRST SINGLE I EVER BOUGHT:**
School's Out – Alice Cooper

I hated David Cassidy, The Osmonds and the Bay City Rollers. I adored Alice – a refreshing antidote to all that sugar!

- **SINGLE THAT DRIVES ME UP THE WALL:**
Long Haired Lover From Liverpool –
Little Jimmy Osmond

Yuck! A truly evil song.

ALL-TIME FAVOURITE SINGLE:
Constant Craving
kd lang

Sublime! Runner-up? 'Close to Me' by The Cure

LAUREL and HARDY *UK, male vocal / instrumental duo (2 WEEKS)* pos/wks

2 Apr 83	CLUNK CLINK *CBS A 3213*	65	2

LAUREL and HARDY with the AVALON BOYS featuring Chill WILLS
UK / US, male vocal duo Stan Laurel and Oliver Hardy with US, male vocal group (10 WEEKS) pos/wks

22 Nov 75 ●	THE TRAIL OF THE LONESOME PINE *United Artists UP 36026*	2	10

LAURNEA *US, female vocalist (2 WEEKS)* pos/wks

12 Jul 97	DAYS OF YOUTH *Epic 6646932*	36	2

Lauren LAVERNE – See MINT ROYALE

Joanna LAW *UK, female vocalist (8 WEEKS)* pos/wks

7 Jul 90	FIRST TIME EVER *Citybeat CBE 752*	67	3
14 Sep 96	THE GIFT *Deconstruction 74321401912* [1]	15	5

[1] Way Out West featuring Miss Joanna Law

Joanna's contribution to 'The Gift' is a sample from 'First Time Ever'

Steve LAWLER *UK, male DJ / producer (1 WEEK)* pos/wks

11 Nov 00	RISE 'IN *Bedrock BEDRCDS 008*	50	1

Billy LAWRENCE – See RAMPAGE featuring Billy LAWRENCE

Joey LAWRENCE *US, male vocalist (15 WEEKS)* pos/wks

26 Jun 93	NOTHIN' MY LOVE CAN'T FIX *EMI CDEM 271*	13	7
28 Aug 93	I CAN'T HELP MYSELF *EMI CDEM 277*	27	4
30 Oct 93	STAY FOREVER *EMI CDEM 289*	41	3
19 Sep 98	NEVER GONNA CHANGE MY MIND *Curb CUBC 34*	49	1

Lee LAWRENCE *UK, male vocalist - Leon Siroto (10 WEEKS)* pos/wks

20 Nov 53	CRYING IN THE CHAPEL *Decca F 10177*	11	1
11 Dec 53 ●	CRYING IN THE CHAPEL (re-entry) *Decca F 10177*	7	5
2 Dec 55	SUDDENLY THERE'S A VALLEY *Columbia DB 3681*	19	1
16 Dec 55	SUDDENLY THERE'S A VALLEY (re-entry) *Columbia DB 3681*	14	3

Both releases by Lee Lawrence With Ray Martin and his Orchestra

Sophie LAWRENCE *UK, female vocalist (7 WEEKS)* pos/wks

3 Aug 91	LOVE'S UNKIND *IQ ZB 44821*	21	7

Steve LAWRENCE *US, male vocalist - Sidney Leibowitz (27 WEEKS)* pos/wks

21 Apr 60 ●	FOOTSTEPS *HMV POP 726*	4	13
18 Aug 60	GIRLS GIRLS GIRLS *London HLT 9166*	49	1
22 Aug 63 ●	I WANT TO STAY HERE *CBS AAG 163* [1]	3	13

[1] Steve and Eydie

Lindy LAYTON *UK, female vocalist (28 WEEKS)* pos/wks

10 Feb 90 ★	DUB BE GOOD TO ME *Go. Beat GOD 39* [1]	1	13
11 Aug 90	SILLY GAMES *Arista 113452* [2]	22	7
26 Jan 91	ECHO MY HEART *Arista 113845*	42	2
31 Aug 91	WITHOUT YOU (ONE AND ONE) *Arista 114636*	71	2
24 Apr 93	WE GOT THE LOVE *PWL International PWCD 250*	38	3
30 Oct 93	SHOW ME *PWL International PWCD 275*	47	1

[1] Beats International featuring Lindy Layton [2] Lindy Layton featuring Janet Kay

Peter LAZONBY *UK, male DJ / producer (1 WEEK)* pos/wks

10 Jun 00	SACRED CYCLES *Hooj Choons HOOJ 93CD*	49	1

Doug LAZY *US, male rapper (9 WEEKS)* pos/wks

15 Jul 89	LET IT ROLL *Atlantic A 8866* [1]	27	5
4 Nov 89	LET THE RHYTHM PUMP *Atlantic A 8784*	45	3
26 May 90	LET THE RHYTHM PUMP (re-mix) *East West A 7919*	63	1

[1] Raze presents Doug Lazy

LCD *UK, male production group (9 WEEKS)* pos/wks

27 Jun 98	ZORBA'S DANCE *Virgin VSCDT 1693*	20	5
9 Oct 99	ZORBA'S DANCE (re-issue) *Virgin VSCDT 1757*	22	4

Keith LE BLANC – See Malcolm X

LE CLICK *Sweden / US, male / female vocal duo (2 WEEKS)* pos/wks

30 Aug 97	CALL ME *Logic 74321509672*	38	2

Kele LE ROC *UK, female vocalist - Kelly Biggs (15 WEEKS)* pos/wks

31 Oct 98 ●	LITTLE BIT OF LOVIN' *1st Avenue / Wild Card / Polydor 5672812*	8	7
27 Mar 99 ●	MY LOVE *1st Avenue / Wild Card / Polydor 5636112*	8	7
30 Sep 00	THINKING OF YOU *Telstar CDSTAS 3136* [1]	70	1

[1] Curtis Lynch Jr featuring Kele Le Roc & Red Rat

Vicky LEANDROS *Greece, female vocalist (29 WEEKS)* pos/wks

8 Apr 72 ●	COME WHAT MAY *Philips 6000 049*	2	16
23 Dec 72	THE LOVE IN YOUR EYES *Philips 6000 081*	48	3
20 Jan 73	THE LOVE IN YOUR EYES (re-entry) *Philips 6000 081*	40	4
7 Apr 73	THE LOVE IN YOUR EYES (2nd re-entry) *Philips 6000 081*	46	1
7 Jul 73	WHEN BOUZOUKIS PLAYED *Philips 6000 111*	44	2
28 Jul 73	WHEN BOUZOUKIS PLAYED (re-entry) *Philips 6000 111*	45	3

Denis LEARY *US, male vocalist (2 WEEKS)* pos/wks

13 Jan 96	ASSHOLE *A & M 5813352*	58	2

LED ZEPPELIN *UK, male vocal / instrumental group (2 WEEKS)* pos/wks

13 Sep 97	WHOLE LOTTA LOVE *Atlantic ATT00 13CD*	21	2

See also Robert PLANT

Angel LEE *UK, female vocalist (1 WEEK)* pos/wks

3 Jun 00	WHAT'S YOUR NAME? *WEA WEA 258CD*	39	1

Ann LEE *UK, female vocalist - Annerley Gordon (21 WEEKS)* pos/wks

11 Sep 99	2 TIMES (IMPORT) *ZYX ZYX 90188*	57	2
16 Oct 99 ●	2 TIMES *Systematic SYSCD 31*	2	16
4 Mar 00	VOICES *Systematic SYSCD 32*	27	3

Brenda LEE [77] **Top 500** *Biggest-selling teenage female vocalist of the early rock years; b. Brenda Tarpley, 11 Dec 1944, Georgia, US. 'Little Miss Dynamite', who first recorded aged 11, had back-to-back UK / US hits in the early 1960s. She was inducted into the Country Music Hall of Fame in 1997 (210 WEEKS)* pos/wks

17 Mar 60	SWEET NOTHIN'S *Brunswick 05819*	45	1
7 Apr 60 ●	SWEET NOTHIN'S (re-entry) *Brunswick 05819*	4	18
30 Jun 60	I'M SORRY *Brunswick 05833* ▲	12	16
20 Oct 60	I WANT TO BE WANTED *Brunswick 05839* ▲	31	6
19 Jan 61	LET'S JUMP THE BROOMSTICK *Brunswick 05823*	12	15
6 Apr 61	EMOTIONS *Brunswick 05847*	45	1
20 Jul 61	DUM DUM *Brunswick 05854*	22	8
16 Nov 61	FOOL NUMBER ONE *Brunswick 05860*	38	3
8 Feb 62	BREAK IT TO ME GENTLY *Brunswick 05864*	46	2
5 Apr 62 ●	SPEAK TO ME PRETTY *Brunswick 05867*	3	12
21 Jun 62 ●	HERE COMES THAT FEELING *Brunswick 05871*	5	12
13 Sep 62	IT STARTED ALL OVER AGAIN *Brunswick 05876*	15	11
29 Nov 62 ●	ROCKIN' AROUND THE CHRISTMAS TREE *Brunswick 05880*	6	7
17 Jan 63 ●	ALL ALONE AM I *Brunswick 05882*	7	17
28 Mar 63 ●	LOSING YOU *Brunswick 05886*	10	16
18 Jul 63	I WONDER *Brunswick 05891*	14	9
31 Oct 63 ●	SWEET IMPOSSIBLE YOU *Brunswick 05896*	28	6
9 Jan 64 ●	AS USUAL *Brunswick 05899*	5	15
9 Apr 64	THINK *Brunswick 05903*	26	8
10 Sep 64	IS IT TRUE *Brunswick 05915*	17	8
10 Dec 64	CHRISTMAS WILL BE JUST ANOTHER LONELY DAY *Brunswick 05921*	29	5
4 Feb 65	THANKS A LOT *Brunswick 05927*	41	2
29 Jul 65	TOO MANY RIVERS *Brunswick 05936*	22	12

Byron LEE – See Boris GARDINER

Curtis LEE *US, male vocalist (2 WEEKS)*

		pos/wks
31 Aug 61	PRETTY LITTLE ANGEL EYES *London HLX 9397*	**47** 1
14 Sep 61	PRETTY LITTLE ANGEL EYES (re-entry) *London HLX 9397*	**48** 1

DC LEE *UK, female vocalist - Diane Sealey (20 WEEKS)*

		pos/wks
9 Nov 85 ●	SEE THE DAY *CBS A 6570*	**3** 12
8 Mar 86	COME HELL OR WATERS HIGH *CBS A 6869*	**46** 5
13 Nov 93	NO TIME TO PLAY *Cooltempo CDCOOL 282* [1]	**25** 3

[1] Guru featuring DC Lee

See also STYLE COUNCIL

Garry LEE and SHOWDOWN
Canada, male vocal / instrumental group (3 WEEKS)

		pos/wks
31 Jul 93	THE RODEO SONG *Party Dish VCD 101*	**44** 3

Jackie LEE *UK, female vocalist (31 WEEKS)*

		pos/wks
10 Apr 68 ●	WHITE HORSES *Philips BF 1674* [1]	**10** 14
2 Jan 71	RUPERT *Pye 7N 45003*	**14** 17

[1] Jacky

Leapy LEE *UK, male vocalist - Lee Graham (28 WEEKS)*

		pos/wks
21 Aug 68 ●	LITTLE ARROWS *MCA MU 1028*	**2** 21
20 Dec 69	GOOD MORNING *MCA MK 5021*	**47** 1
10 Jan 70	GOOD MORNING (re-entry) *MCA MK 5021*	**29** 6

Peggy LEE *US, female vocalist - Norma Jean Egstrom (29 WEEKS)*

		pos/wks
24 May 57 ●	MR WONDERFUL *Brunswick 05671*	**5** 13
15 Aug 58 ●	FEVER *Capitol CL 14902*	**5** 11
23 Mar 61	TILL THERE WAS YOU *Capitol CL 15184*	**40** 1
6 Apr 61	TILL THERE WAS YOU (re-entry) *Capitol CL 15184*	**30** 3
22 Aug 92	FEVER (re-issue) *Capitol PEG 1*	**75** 1

Toney LEE *US, male vocalist (4 WEEKS)*

		pos/wks
29 Jan 83	REACH UP *TMT TMT 2*	**64** 4

Tracey LEE *US, male vocalist (1 WEEK)*

		pos/wks
19 Jul 97	THE THEME *Universal UND 56133*	**51** 1

LEEDS UNITED FC *UK, male football team vocalists (13 WEEKS)*

		pos/wks
29 Apr 72 ●	LEEDS UNITED *Chapter One SCH 168*	**10** 10
25 Apr 92	LEEDS LEEDS LEEDS *Q Music LUFC 2*	**61** 1
9 May 92	LEEDS LEEDS LEEDS (re-entry) *Q Music LUFC 2*	**54** 2

Carol LEEMING – See STAXX featuring Carol LEEMING

Raymond LEFEVRE *France, orchestra (2 WEEKS)*

		pos/wks
15 May 68	SOUL COAXING *Major Minor MM 559*	**46** 2

LEFTFIELD *UK, male instrumental / production duo - Neil Barnes and Paul Daley (23 WEEKS)*

		pos/wks
12 Dec 92	SONG OF LIFE *Hard Hands HAND 002T*	**59** 1
13 Nov 93	OPEN UP *Hard Hands HAND 009CD* [1]	**13** 5
25 Mar 95	ORIGINAL *Hard Hands HAND 18CD* [2]	**18** 3
5 Aug 95	THE AFRO-LEFT EP *Hard Hands HAND 23CD* [3] ★	**22** 3
20 Jan 96	RELEASE THE PRESSURE *Hard Hands HAND 29CD*	**13** 3
18 Sep 99 ●	AFRIKA SHOX *Hard Hands HAND 057CD1* [4]	**7** 5
11 Dec 99	DUSTED *Hard Hands HAND 058CD1* [5]	**28** 2
22 Jan 00	DUSTED (re-entry) *Hard Hands HAND 058CD1* [5]	**75** 1

[1] Leftfield Lydon [2] Leftfield Halliday [3] Leftfield featuring Djum Djum [4] Leftfield / Bambaataa [5] Leftfield / Roots Manuva

Tracks on The Afro-Left EP: Afro-Left / Afro Ride / Afro Central / Afro Sol

LEGEND B *Germany, male production duo (1 WEEK)*

		pos/wks
22 Feb 97	LOST IN LOVE *Perfecto PERF 132CD*	**45** 1

LEILANI *UK, female vocalist (7 WEEKS)*

		pos/wks
6 Feb 99	MADNESS THING *ZTT ZTT 124CD*	**19** 4
12 Jun 99	DO YOU WANT ME? *ZTT ZTT 134CD*	**40** 2
3 Jun 00	FLYING ELVIS *ZTT ZTT 145CD*	**73** 1

Paul LEKAKIS *US, male vocalist (4 WEEKS)*

		pos/wks
30 May 87	BOOM BOOM (LET'S GO BACK TO MY ROOM) *Champion CHAMP 43*	**60** 4

LEMON PIPERS *US, male vocal / instrumental group (16 WEEKS)*

		pos/wks
7 Feb 68 ●	GREEN TAMBOURINE *Pye International 7N 25444* ▲	**7** 11
1 May 68	RICE IS NICE *Pye International 7N 25454*	**41** 5

LEMON TREES *UK, male vocal / instrumental group (9 WEEKS)*

		pos/wks
26 Sep 92	LOVE IS IN YOUR EYES *Oxygen GASP 1*	**75** 1
7 Nov 92	THE WAY I FEEL *Oxygen GASP 2*	**62** 2
13 Feb 93	LET IT LOOSE *Oxygen GASPD 3*	**55** 2
17 Apr 93	CHILD OF LOVE *Oxygen GASPD 4*	**55** 3
3 Jul 93	I CAN'T FACE THE WORLD *Oxygen GASPD 6*	**52** 1

LEMONHEADS *US / Australia, male vocal / instrumental group, lead vocal - Evan Dando (26 WEEKS)*

		pos/wks
17 Oct 92	IT'S A SHAME ABOUT RAY *Atlantic A 7423*	**70** 1
5 Dec 92	MRS ROBINSON / BEIN' AROUND *Atlantic A 7401*	**19** 9
6 Feb 93	CONFETTI / MY DRUG BUDDY *Atlantic A 7430CD*	**44** 2
10 Apr 93	IT'S A SHAME ABOUT RAY (re-issue) *Atlantic A 5764CD*	**31** 3
16 Oct 93	INTO YOUR ARMS *Atlantic A 7302CD*	**14** 4
27 Nov 93	IT'S ABOUT TIME *Atlantic A 7296CD*	**57** 2
14 May 94	BIG GAY HEART *Atlantic A 7259CD*	**55** 2
28 Sep 96	IF I COULD TALK I'D TELL YOU *Atlantic A 5561CD*	**39** 2
14 Dec 96	IT'S ALL TRUE *Atlantic A 5635CD*	**61** 1

LEN *Canada, male / female DJ / vocal group (15 WEEKS)*

		pos/wks
18 Dec 99 ●	STEAL MY SUNSHINE *Columbia 6685062*	**8** 13
10 Jun 00	CRYPTIK SOULS CREW *Columbia 6693832*	**28** 2

LENA – See Lena FIAGBE

John LENNON `92` `Top 500`
One of the century's greatest musical talents, b. 9 Oct 1940, Liverpool, d. 8 Dec 1980. World-famous singer / songwriter who, together with Paul McCartney, fronted The Beatles and penned their hits. Three of his singles topped the UK chart in the two months after his murder in New York (197 WEEKS)

		pos/wks
9 Jul 69 ●	GIVE PEACE A CHANCE *Apple 13* [1]	**2** 13
1 Nov 69	COLD TURKEY *Apple APPLES 1001* [1]	**14** 8
21 Feb 70	INSTANT KARMA *Apple APPLES 1003* [2]	**5** 9
20 Mar 71 ●	POWER TO THE PEOPLE *Apple R 5892* [3]	**7** 9
9 Dec 72 ●	HAPPY XMAS (WAR IS OVER) *Apple R 5970* [4]	**4** 8
24 Nov 73	MIND GAMES *Apple R 5994*	**26** 9
19 Oct 74	WHATEVER GETS YOU THROUGH THE NIGHT *Apple R 5998* [5] ▲	**36** 4
4 Jan 75	HAPPY XMAS (WAR IS OVER) (re-entry) *Apple R 5970* [4]	**48** 1
8 Feb 75	#9 DREAM *Apple R 6003*	**23** 8
3 May 75	STAND BY ME *Apple R 6005*	**30** 7
1 Nov 75 ●	IMAGINE *Apple R 6009*	**6** 11
8 Nov 80 ★	(JUST LIKE) STARTING OVER *Geffen K 79186* ▲	**1** 15
20 Dec 80 ●	HAPPY XMAS (WAR IS OVER) (2nd re-entry) *Apple 5970* [4]	**2** 9
27 Dec 80 ★	IMAGINE (re-entry) *Apple R 6009* ◆	**1** 13
24 Jan 81	GIVE PEACE A CHANCE (re-entry) *Apple 13* [1]	**33** 5
24 Jan 81 ★	WOMAN *Geffen K 79195*	**1** 11
21 Mar 81	I SAW HER STANDING THERE *DJM DJS 10965* [6]	**40** 4
4 Apr 81	WATCHING THE WHEELS *Geffen K 79207*	**30** 6
19 Dec 81	HAPPY XMAS (WAR IS OVER) (3rd re-entry) *Apple R 5970* [4]	**28** 5
20 Nov 82	LOVE *Parlophone R 6059*	**41** 7
25 Dec 82	HAPPY XMAS (WAR IS OVER) (4th re-entry) *Apple R 5970* [4]	**56** 3
21 Jan 84 ●	NOBODY TOLD ME *Ono Music / Polydor POSP 700*	**6** 6

UK No.1 ★   UK Top 10 ●   Still on chart +   UK million seller ◆   UK entry at No.1 ■   US No.1 ▲

17 Mar 84	BORROWED TIME *Polydor POSP 701*	32 6
30 Nov 85	JEALOUS GUY *Parlophone R 6117*	65 2
10 Dec 88	IMAGINE / JEALOUS GUY / HAPPY XMAS (WAR IS OVER) (re-issue) *Parlophone R 6199*	45 5
25 Dec 99 ●	IMAGINE (re-issue) *Parlophone CDR 6534*	3 11
18 Mar 00	IMAGINE (re-entry of re-issue) *Parlophone CDR 6534*	42 2

1 Plastic Ono Band 2 Lennon, Ono and the Plastic Ono Band 3 John Lennon / Plastic Ono Band 4 John and Yoko and the Plastic Ono Band with the Harlem Community Choir 5 John Lennon with the Plastic Ono Nuclear Band 6 Elton John Band featuring John Lennon and the Muscle Shoals Horns

See also BEATLES

Julian LENNON *UK, male vocalist (47 WEEKS)* pos/wks

6 Oct 84 ●	TOO LATE FOR GOODBYES *Charisma JL 1*	6 11
15 Dec 84	VALOTTE *Charisma JL 2*	55 6
9 Mar 85	SAY YOU'RE WRONG *Charisma JL 3*	75 1
7 Dec 85	BECAUSE *EMI 5538*	40 7
11 Mar 89	NOW YOU'RE IN HEAVEN *Virgin VS 1154*	59 3
24 Aug 91 ●	SALTWATER *Virgin VS 1361*	6 13
30 Nov 91	HELP YOURSELF *Virgin VS 1379*	53 2
25 Apr 92	GET A LIFE *Virgin VS 1398*	56 3
23 May 98	DAY AFTER DAY *Music From Another JULIAN 4CD*	66 1

Annie LENNOX *Innovative, groundbreaking singer / songwriter who has remained consistently successful around the globe. b. 25 Dec 1954, Aberdeen, Scotland. Former frontwoman of The Tourists and Eurythmics, who has won more BRIT awards than any other performer (68 WEEKS)* pos/wks

3 Dec 88	PUT A LITTLE LOVE IN YOUR HEART *A & M AM 484* 1	28 8
28 Mar 92 ●	WHY *RCA PB 45317*	5 8
6 Jun 92	PRECIOUS *RCA 74321100257*	23 5
22 Aug 92 ●	WALKING ON BROKEN GLASS *RCA 74321107227*	8 8
31 Oct 92	COLD *RCA 74321116902*	26 4
13 Feb 93 ●	LITTLE BIRD / LOVE SONG FOR A VAMPIRE *RCA 74321133832*	3 12
18 Feb 95 ●	NO MORE 'I LOVE YOU'S *RCA 74321257162*	2 12
10 Jun 95	A WHITER SHADE OF PALE *RCA 74321284822*	16 6
30 Sep 95	WAITING IN VAIN *RCA 74321316132*	31 3
9 Dec 95	SOMETHING SO RIGHT *RCA 74321332392* 2	44 2

1 Annie Lennox and Al Green 2 Annie Lennox featuring Paul Simon

See also EURYTHMICS

Rula LENSKA – See Julie COVINGTON, Rula LENSKA, Charlotte CORNWELL and Sue JONES-DAVIES

Phillip LEO *UK, male vocalist (3 WEEKS)* pos/wks

23 Jul 94	SECOND CHANCE *EMI CDEM 327*	57 2
25 Mar 95	THINKING ABOUT YOUR LOVE *EMI CDEM 358*	64 1

LES RYTHMES DIGITALES *UK, male DJ / producer - Jacques Lu Cont (Stuart Price) (3 WEEKS)* pos/wks

25 Apr 98	MUSIC MAKES YOU LOSE CONTROL *Wall of Sound WALLD 037*	69 1
7 Aug 99	SOMETIMES *Wall of Sound WALLD 054* 1	56 1
30 Oct 99	JACQUES YOUR BODY (MAKE ME SWEAT) *Wall of Sound WALLD 060*	60 1

1 Les Rythmes Digitales featuring Nik Kershaw

LeSHAUN – See LL COOL J

LESS THAN JAKE *US, male vocal / instrumental group (1 WEEK)* pos/wks

5 Aug 00	ALL MY BEST FRIENDS ARE METALHEADS *Golf CDSHOLE 027*	51 1

LESTER – See Norman COOK

Ketty LESTER *US, female vocalist - Revoyda Frierson (16 WEEKS)* pos/wks

19 Apr 62 ●	LOVE LETTERS *London HLN 9527*	4 12
19 Jul 62	BUT NOT FOR ME *London HLN 9574*	45 4

LET LOOSE *UK, male vocal / instrumental group (62 WEEKS)* pos/wks

24 Apr 93	CRAZY FOR YOU *Vertigo VERCD 74*	44 3
9 Apr 94	SEVENTEEN *Mercury MERCD 400*	44 2
25 Jun 94 ●	CRAZY FOR YOU (re-issue) *Mercury MERCD 402*	2 20
22 Oct 94	SEVENTEEN (re-mix) *Mercury MERCD 406*	11 6
24 Dec 94	CRAZY FOR YOU (re-entry of re-issue) *Mercury MERCD 402*	46 4
7 Jan 95	SEVENTEEN (re-entry of re-mix) *Mercury MERCD 406*	47 3
28 Jan 95	ONE NIGHT STAND *Mercury MERCD 419*	12 6
29 Apr 95 ●	BEST IN ME *Mercury MERCD 428*	8 5
4 Nov 95	EVERYBODY SAY EVERYBODY DO *Mercury MERCD 446*	29 3
13 Jan 96	EVERYBODY SAY EVERYBODY DO (re-entry) *Mercury MERCD 446*	71 1
22 Jun 96 ●	MAKE IT WITH YOU *Mercury MERCD 464*	7 6
7 Sep 96	TAKE IT EASY *Mercury MERCD 472*	25 2
16 Nov 96	DARLING BE HOME SOON *Mercury MERCD 475*	65 1

Gerald LETHAN – See WALL OF SOUND featuring Gerald LETHAN

LETTERMEN *US, male vocal group (3 WEEKS)* pos/wks

23 Nov 61	THE WAY YOU LOOK TONIGHT *Capitol CL 15222*	36 3

LEVEL 42 (108 Top 500) *Critically acclaimed Isle of Wight / Hong Kong / London band: Mark King (v/b), Boon Gould (g), Mike Lindup (k/v), Phil Gould (d). Boasting a world-class bass player in King, they went from Brit-funk cult heroes to international stardom (177 WEEKS)* pos/wks

30 Aug 80	LOVE MEETING LOVE *Polydor POSP 170*	61 4
18 Apr 81	LOVE GAMES *Polydor POSP 234*	38 6
8 Aug 81	TURN IT ON *Polydor POSP 286*	57 6
14 Nov 81	STARCHILD *Polydor POSP 343*	47 4
8 May 82	ARE YOU HEARING (WHAT I HEAR)? *Polydor POSP 396*	49 4
2 Oct 82	WEAVE YOUR SPELL *Polydor POSP 500*	43 4
15 Jan 83	THE CHINESE WAY *Polydor POSP 538*	24 8
16 Apr 83	OUT OF SIGHT, OUT OF MIND *Polydor POSP 570*	41 4
30 Jul 83 ●	THE SUN GOES DOWN (LIVING IT UP) *Polydor POSP 622*	10 12
22 Oct 83	MICRO KID *Polydor POSP 643*	37 5
1 Sep 84	HOT WATER *Polydor POSP 697*	18 9
3 Nov 84	THE CHANT HAS BEGUN *Polydor POSP 710*	41 5
21 Sep 85 ●	SOMETHING ABOUT YOU *Polydor POSP 759*	6 17
7 Dec 85	LEAVING ME NOW *Polydor POSP 776*	15 11
26 Apr 86 ●	LESSONS IN LOVE *Polydor POSP 790*	3 13
14 Feb 87 ●	RUNNING IN THE FAMILY *Polydor POSP 842*	6 10
25 Apr 87 ●	TO BE WITH YOU AGAIN *Polydor POSP 855*	10 7
12 Sep 87 ●	IT'S OVER *Polydor POSP 900*	10 8
12 Dec 87	CHILDREN SAY *Polydor POSP 911*	22 6
3 Sep 88	HEAVEN IN MY HANDS *Polydor PO 14*	12 5
29 Oct 88	TAKE A LOOK *Polydor PO 24*	32 4
21 Jan 89	TRACIE *Polydor PO 34*	25 5
28 Oct 89	TAKE CARE OF YOURSELF *Polydor PO 58*	39 3
17 Aug 91	GUARANTEED *RCA PB 44745*	17 4
19 Oct 91	OVERTIME *RCA PB 44997*	62 2
18 Apr 92	MY FATHER'S SHOES *RCA PB 45271*	55 1
26 Feb 94	FOREVER NOW *RCA 74321190272*	19 4
30 Apr 94	ALL OVER YOU *RCA 74321205662*	26 2
6 Aug 94	LOVE IN A PEACEFUL WORLD *RCA 74321220332*	31 3

LEVELLERS *UK, male vocal / instrumental group (56 WEEKS)* pos/wks

21 Sep 91	ONE WAY *China WOK 2008*	51 2
7 Dec 91	FAR FROM HOME *China WOK 2010*	71 1
23 May 92	15 YEARS (EP) *China WOKX 2020*	11 5
10 Jul 93	BELARUSE *China WOK 2034*	12 5
30 Oct 93	THIS GARDEN *China WOKCD 2039*	12 4
14 May 94	JULIE (EP) *China WOKCD 2042*	17 3
12 Aug 95	HOPE ST *China WOKCD 2059*	12 5
14 Oct 95	FANTASY *China WOKCD 2067*	16 3
23 Dec 95	JUST THE ONE *China WOKCD 2076* 1	12 8
20 Jul 96	EXODUS - LIVE *China WOKCD 2082*	24 2
9 Aug 97	WHAT A BEAUTIFUL DAY *China WOKCD 2088*	13 5
18 Oct 97	CELEBRATE *China WOKCD 2089*	28 2
20 Dec 97	DOG TRAIN *China WOKCD 2090*	24 5
14 Mar 98	TOO REAL *China WOKCD 2091*	46 1

SINGLED OUT... Ian Hunter

Frontman for the fantastically named Mott the Hoople (taken from the title of a novel by Willard Manus), Hunter was obviously inspired by Bob Dylan – as can be seen below – in music and in his permanent wearing of shades and corkscrew hair.

- **NO.1 SONG ON THE DAY I WAS BORN:**
  Deep Purple – Ambrose and his Orchestra

- **ALL-TIME FAVOURITE SINGLE:**
  Like A Rolling Stone – Bob Dylan

  Some of Dylan's stuff would be up there, this one particularly.

- **SINGLE THAT DRIVES ME UP THE WALL:**
  There isn't one. We're all in the same boat. I don't really hate anything – it clouds your judgement. And since I don't listen to the radio I haven't noticed anything recently.

FIRST SINGLE I BOUGHT:
Whole Lotta Shakin' Goin' On – Jerry Lee Lewis

It wasn't a No.1 but it deserved to be! At first I thought it was by Jerry Lewis the comedian; the Atlantic was very wide in those days. But then I saw this guy with the vertical striped jacket and the panel shoes and all that. I thought it was incredible.

Photo:Rex Features - D. Hoffman

			pos/wks
24 Oct 98	**BOZOS** *China WOKCD 2096*	**44**	2
6 Feb 99	**ONE WAY (re-recording)** *China WOKCD 2102*	**33**	2
9 Sep 00	**HAPPY BIRTHDAY REVOLUTION**		
	China EW218CD	**57**	1

[1] Levellers, special guest Joe Strummer

Tracks on 15 Years (EP): 15 Years / Dance Before the Storm / The River Flow (Live) / Plastic Jeezus. Tracks on Julie (EP): Julie / English Civil War / Lowlands of Holland / 100 Years of Solitude

LEVERT US, male vocal group (10 WEEKS)
			pos/wks
22 Aug 87 ●	**CASANOVA** *Atlantic A 9217*	**9**	10

LEVERT SWEAT GILL US, male vocal group (7 WEEKS)
			pos/wks
14 Mar 98	**MY BODY** *East West E 3857CD*	**21**	3
6 Jun 98	**CURIOUS** *East West E 3842CD*	**23**	4
12 Sep 98	**DOOR #1** *East West E 3817CD*	**45**	2

Hank LEVINE US, orchestra (4 WEEKS)
			pos/wks
21 Dec 61	**IMAGE** *HMV POP 947*	**45**	4

LEVITICUS UK, male producer (1 WEEK)
			pos/wks
25 Mar 95	**BURIAL** *ffrr FCD 255*	**66**	1

Barrington LEVY Jamaica, male vocalist (11 WEEKS)
			pos/wks
2 Feb 85	**HERE I COME** *London LON 62*	**41**	4
15 Jun 91	**TRIBAL BASE** *Desire WANT 44* [1]	**20**	6
24 Sep 94	**WORK** *MCA MCSTD 2003*	**65**	1

[1] Rebel MC featuring Tenor Fly and Barrington Levy

Jona LEWIE UK, male vocalist - John Lewis (20 WEEKS)
			pos/wks
10 May 80	**YOU'LL ALWAYS FIND ME IN THE KITCHEN AT PARTIES**		
	Stiff BUY 73	**16**	9
29 Nov 80 ●	**STOP THE CAVALRY** *Stiff BUY 104*	**3**	11

On some copies first title was simply 'Kitchen at Parties'

See also Terry DACTYL and the DINOSAURS

CJ LEWIS UK, male vocalist (32 WEEKS)
			pos/wks
23 Apr 94 ●	**SWEETS FOR MY SWEET** *Black Market BMITD 017*	**3**	13
23 Jul 94 ●	**EVERYTHING IS ALRIGHT (UPTIGHT)**		
	Black Market BMITD 019	**10**	7
8 Oct 94 ●	**BEST OF MY LOVE** *Black Market BMITD 021*	**13**	6
17 Dec 94	**DOLLARS** *Black Market BMITD 023*	**34**	4
9 Sep 95	**R TO THE A** *Black Market BMITD 030*	**34**	2

Danny J LEWIS UK, male producer (2 WEEKS)
			pos/wks
20 Jun 98	**SPEND THE NIGHT** *Locked On LOX 98CD*	**29**	2

Darlene LEWIS US, female vocalist (4 WEEKS)
			pos/wks
16 Apr 94	**LET THE MUSIC (LIFT YOU UP)**		
	KMS/Eastern Bloc KMSCD 10	**16**	4

All formats of 'Let the Music Lift You Up' featured versions by Loveland featuring Rachel McFarlane and also by Darlene Lewis

Dee LEWIS UK, female vocalist (5 WEEKS)
			pos/wks
18 Jun 88	**BEST OF MY LOVE** *Mercury DEE 3*	**47**	5

Donna LEWIS UK, female vocalist (16 WEEKS)
			pos/wks
7 Sep 96 ●	**I LOVE YOU ALWAYS FOREVER** *Atlantic A 5495CD*	**5**	14
8 Feb 97	**WITHOUT LOVE** *Atlantic A 5468CD*	**39**	2

Gary LEWIS and the PLAYBOYS
US, male vocal / instrumental group (7 WEEKS)
			pos/wks
8 Feb 75	**MY HEART'S SYMPHONY** *United Artists UP 35780*	**36**	7

Huey LEWIS and the NEWS
US, male vocal / instrumental group (66 WEEKS)
			pos/wks
27 Oct 84	**IF THIS IS IT** *Chrysalis 2829*	**39**	6
31 Aug 85	**THE POWER OF LOVE** *Chrysalis HUEY 1* ▲	**11**	10
23 Nov 85	**HEART AND SOUL (EP)** *Chrysalis HUEY 2*	**61**	4
8 Feb 86 ●	**THE POWER OF LOVE / DO YOU BELIEVE IN LOVE**		
	(re-issue) *Chrysalis HUEY 3*	**9**	12
10 May 86	**THE HEART OF ROCK AND ROLL** *Chrysalis HUEY 4*	**49**	3
23 Aug 86	**STUCK WITH YOU** *Chrysalis HUEY 5* ▲	**12**	12
6 Dec 86	**HIP TO BE SQUARE** *Chrysalis HUEY 6*	**41**	8
21 Mar 87	**SIMPLE AS THAT** *Chrysalis HUEY 7*	**47**	5
16 Jul 88	**PERFECT WORLD** *Chrysalis HUEY 10*	**48**	4

Tracks on Heart and Soul (EP): Heart and Soul / Hope You Love Me Like You Say You Do / Heart of Rock and Roll / Buzz Buzz Buzz. 'Do You Believe in Love' listed only from 15 Feb 1986

Jerry LEWIS US, male vocalist (8 WEEKS)
			pos/wks
8 Feb 57	**ROCK-A-BYE YOUR BABY (WITH A DIXIE MELODY)**		
	Brunswick 05636	**12**	7
5 Apr 57	**ROCK-A-BYE YOUR BABY (WITH A DIXIE MELODY)**		
	(re-entry) *Brunswick 05636*	**22**	1

Jerry Lee LEWIS US, male vocalist/instrumentalist (68 WEEKS)
			pos/wks
27 Sep 57 ●	**WHOLE LOTTA SHAKIN' GOIN' ON**		
	London HLS 8457	**8**	10
20 Dec 57 ★	**GREAT BALLS OF FIRE** *London HLS 8529*	**1**	12
27 Dec 57	**WHOLE LOTTA SHAKIN' GOIN' ON (re-entry)**		
	London HLS 8457	**26**	1
11 Apr 58 ●	**BREATHLESS** *London HLS 8592*	**8**	7
23 Jan 59	**HIGH SCHOOL CONFIDENTIAL** *London HLS 8780*	**12**	6
1 May 59	**LOVIN' UP A STORM** *London HLS 8840*	**28**	1
9 Jun 60	**BABY BABY BYE BYE** *London HLS 9131*	**47**	1
4 May 61 ●	**WHAT'D I SAY** *London HLS 9335*	**10**	12
3 Aug 61	**WHAT'D I SAY (re-entry)** *London HLS 9335*	**49**	2
6 Sep 62	**SWEET LITTLE SIXTEEN** *London HLS 9584*	**38**	5
14 Mar 63	**GOOD GOLLY MISS MOLLY** *London HLS 9688*	**31**	6
6 May 72	**CHANTILLY LACE** *Mercury 6052 141*	**33**	5

Linda LEWIS UK, female vocalist (31 WEEKS)
			pos/wks
2 Jun 73	**ROCK-A-DOODLE-DOO** *Raft RA 18502*	**15**	11
12 Jul 75 ●	**IT'S IN HIS KISS** *Arista 17*	**6**	8
17 Apr 76	**BABY I'M YOURS** *Arista 43*	**33**	6
2 Jun 79	**I'D BE SURPRISINGLY GOOD FOR YOU**		
	Ariola ARO 166	**40**	5
19 Aug 00	**REACH OUT** *Skint SKINT 54CD* [1]	**61**	1

[1] Midfield General featuring Linda Lewis

Ramsey LEWIS US, male instrumentalist - piano (8 WEEKS)
			pos/wks
15 Apr 72	**WADE IN THE WATER** *Chess 6145 004*	**31**	8

Shirley LEWIS – See Arthur BAKER

John LEYTON ⟨485 Top 500⟩ The sometime actor was a top teen idol in early 1960s, b. 17, Feb 1939, Essex, UK. Leyton is best remembered for Joe Meek-produced debut hit which charted after he performed it in TV series Harpers West One (playing a pop singer). Starred in several Hollywood movies in late 1960s (70 WEEKS)
			pos/wks
3 Aug 61 ★	**JOHNNY REMEMBER ME** *Top Rank JAR 577*	**1**	15
5 Oct 61 ●	**WILD WIND** *Top Rank JAR 585*	**2**	10
28 Dec 61	**SON THIS IS SHE** *HMV POP 956*	**15**	10
15 Mar 62	**LONE RIDER** *HMV POP 992*	**40**	5
3 May 62	**LONELY CITY** *HMV POP 1014*	**14**	11
23 Aug 62	**DOWN THE RIVER NILE** *HMV POP 1054*	**42**	3
21 Feb 63	**CUPBOARD LOVE** *HMV POP 1122*	**22**	12
18 Jul 63	**I'LL CUT YOUR TAIL OFF** *HMV POP 1175*	**50**	1
8 Aug 63	**I'LL CUT YOUR TAIL OFF (re-entry)**		
	HMV POP 1175	**36**	2
20 Feb 64	**MAKE LOVE TO ME** *HMV POP 1264* [1]	**49**	1

[1] John Leyton and the LeRoys

LEYTON BUZZARDS
UK, male vocal / instrumental group (5 WEEKS)   pos/wks

3 Mar 79	**SATURDAY NIGHT (BENEATH THE PLASTIC PALM TREES)**		
	Chrysalis CHS 2288	53	5

LFO *UK, male instrumental group (15 WEEKS)*   pos/wks

14 Jul 90	**LFO** *Warp WAP 5*	12	10
6 Jul 91	**WE ARE BACK / NURTURE** *Warp 7WAP 14*	47	3
1 Feb 92	**WHAT IS HOUSE (EP)** *Warp WAP 17*	62	2

Tracks on What Is House (EP): Tan Ta Ra / Mashed Potato / What Is House / Syndrome

LIBERACE *US, male instrumentalist - piano (2 WEEKS)*   pos/wks

17 Jun 55	**UNCHAINED MELODY** *Philips PB 430*	20	1
19 Oct 56	**I DON'T CARE** *Columbia DB 3834*	28	1

'I Don't Care' featured Liberace as vocalist too

LIBERATION *UK, male instrumental / production duo (3 WEEKS)*   pos/wks

24 Oct 92	**LIBERATION** *ZYX ZYX 68657*	28	3

LIBIDO *Norway, male vocal / instrumental group (1 WEEK)*   pos/wks

31 Jan 98	**OVERTHROWN** *Fire BLAZE 119CD*	53	1

LIBRA presents TAYLOR
US, male / female production / vocal trio (3 WEEKS)   pos/wks

26 Oct 96	**ANOMALY - CALLING YOUR NAME** *Platipus PLATCD 24*	71	1
18 Mar 00	**ANOMALY - CALLING YOUR NAME (re-mix)**		
	Platipus PLATCD 56	43	2

LICK THE TINS
UK, male / female vocal / instrumental group (8 WEEKS)   pos/wks

29 Mar 86	**CAN'T HELP FALLING IN LOVE** *Sedition EDIT 3308*	42	8

Oliver LIEB
Germany, male producer (1 WEEK)   pos/wks

30 Sep 00	**METROPOLIS** *Duty Free DF 019CD*	72	1

See also LSG

Ben LIEBRAND *Holland, male DJ / producer (2 WEEKS)*   pos/wks

9 Jun 90	**PULS(T)AR** *Epic LIEB 1*	68	2

LIEUTENANT PIGEON
UK, male / female instrumental group (29 WEEKS)   pos/wks

16 Sep 72	★ **MOULDY OLD DOUGH** *Decca F 13278*	1	19
16 Dec 72	**DESPERATE DAN** *Decca F 13365*	17	10

LIFFORD – See ARTFUL DODGER

LIGHT OF THE WORLD
UK, male vocal / instrumental group (25 WEEKS)   pos/wks

14 Apr 79	**SWINGIN'** *Ensign ENY 22*	45	5
14 Jul 79	**MIDNIGHT GROOVIN'** *Ensign ENY 29*	72	1
18 Oct 80	**LONDON TOWN** *Ensign ENY 43*	41	5
17 Jan 81	**I SHOT THE SHERIFF** *Ensign ENY 46*	40	5
28 Mar 81	**I'M SO HAPPY / TIME** *Ensign MER 64*	35	6
21 Nov 81	**RIDE THE LOVE TRAIN** *EMI 5242*	49	3

LIGHTER SHADE OF BROWN *US, male vocal duo (3 WEEKS)*   pos/wks

9 Jul 94	**HEY DJ** *Mercury MERCD 401*	33	3

Gordon LIGHTFOOT *Canada, male vocalist (26 WEEKS)*   pos/wks

19 Jun 71	**IF YOU COULD READ MY MIND** *Reprise RS 20974*	30	9
3 Aug 74	**SUNDOWN** *Reprise K 14327* ▲	33	7
15 Jan 77	**THE WRECK OF THE EDMUND FITZGERALD** *Reprise K 14451*	40	4
16 Sep 78	**DAYLIGHT KATY** *Warner Bros. K 17214*	41	6

Terry LIGHTFOOT and his NEW ORLEANS JAZZMEN
UK, vocalist / instrumentalist - clarinet - and male band (17 WEEKS)   pos/wks

7 Sep 61	**TRUE LOVE** *Columbia DB 4696*	33	4
23 Nov 61	**KING KONG** *Columbia SCD 2165*	29	12
3 May 62	**TAVERN IN THE TOWN** *Columbia DB 4822*	49	1

LIGHTFORCE *Germany, male production duo (1 WEEK)*   pos/wks

28 Oct 00	**JOIN ME** *Slinky Music SLINKY 004CD*	53	1

LIGHTHOUSE FAMILY `444` **Top 500** *Smooth, easy-on-the-ear pop / soul duo formed in Newcastle-upon-Tyne, UK; Nigerian-born Tunde Baiyewu (v) and Londoner Paul Tucker (k). After slow start, debut album Ocean Drive (1995) sold more than 1.6 million in UK and made a name for them in Europe (76 WEEKS)*   pos/wks

27 May 95	**LIFTED** *Wild Card CARDW 17*	61	2
14 Oct 95	**OCEAN DRIVE** *Wild Card 5797072*	34	3
10 Feb 96	● **LIFTED (re-issue)** *Wild Card 5779432*	4	10
1 Jun 96	**OCEAN DRIVE (re-issue)** *Wild Card 5766192*	11	8
21 Sep 96	**GOODBYE HEARTBREAK** *Wild Card 5753492*	14	6
21 Dec 96	**LOVING EVERY MINUTE** *Wild Card 5731012*	20	7
11 Oct 97	● **RAINCLOUD** *Wild Card 5717932*	6	7
10 Jan 98	● **HIGH** *Polydor 5691492*	4	14
27 Jun 98	● **LOST IN SPACE** *Polydor 5670592*	6	8
10 Oct 98	**QUESTION OF FAITH** *Wild Card 5673932*	21	5
9 Jan 99	**POSTCARD FROM HEAVEN** *Wild Card 5633952*	24	6

LIGHTNING SEEDS `299` **Top 500** *Conceived as a 'perfect pop' studio project by producer and group veteran Ian Broudie (v/g) 4 Aug 1958, Liverpool, UK. England's most popular footballing anthem, 'Three Lions', became first song to top the charts twice with the same lyrics (98 WEEKS)*   pos/wks

22 Jul 89	**PURE** *Ghetto GTG 4*	16	8
14 Mar 92	**THE LIFE OF RILEY** *Virgin VS 1402*	28	6
30 May 92	**SENSE** *Virgin VS 1414*	31	5
20 Aug 94	**LUCKY YOU** *Epic 6606282*	43	2
14 Jan 95	**CHANGE** *Epic 6609865*	13	6
15 Apr 95	**MARVELLOUS** *Epic 6614265*	24	5
22 Jul 95	**PERFECT** *Epic 6621792*	18	5
21 Oct 95	**LUCKY YOU (re-issue)** *Epic 6625182*	15	6
9 Mar 96	**READY OR NOT** *Epic 6629672*	20	4
1 Jun 96	★ **THREE LIONS (THE OFFICIAL SONG OF THE ENGLAND FOOTBALL TEAM)** *Epic 6632732* ■ [1]	1	15
2 Nov 96	**WHAT IF...** *Epic 6638635*	14	3
11 Jan 97	**WHAT IF... (re-entry)** *Epic 6638635*	64	1
18 Jan 97	**SUGAR COATED ICEBERG** *Epic 6640432*	12	4
26 Apr 97	● **YOU SHOWED ME** *Epic 6643282*	8	5
13 Dec 97	**WHAT YOU SAY** *Epic 6653572*	41	5
20 Jun 98	★ **3 LIONS '98** *Epic 6660982* ■ [1]	1	13
27 Nov 99	**LIFE'S TOO SHORT** *Epic 6681502*	27	3
22 Jan 00	**LIFE'S TOO SHORT (re-entry)** *Epic 6681502*	73	1
18 Mar 00	**SWEETEST SOUL SENSATIONS** *Epic 6689422*	67	1

[1] Baddiel and Skinner and the Lightning Seeds

LIL' KIM *US, female vocalist - Kimberly Jones (21 WEEKS)*   pos/wks

26 Apr 97	**NO TIME** *Atlantic A 5594CD* [1]	45	1
5 Jul 97	**CRUSH ON YOU** *Atlantic AT 0002CD*	36	2
16 Aug 97	**NOT TONIGHT** *Atlantic AT 0007CD*	11	5
25 Oct 97	**CRUSH ON YOU (re-entry)** *Atlantic AT 0002CD*	23	3
22 Aug 98	**HIT 'EM WIT DA HEE** *East West E3824 CD1* [2]	25	3
5 Feb 00	**NOTORIOUS B.I.G.** *Puff Daddy / Arista 747321737312* [3]	16	5
2 Sep 00	**NO MATTER WHAT THEY SAY** *Atlantic 7567846972*	35	2

[1] Lil' Kim featuring Puff Daddy [2] Missy 'Misdemeanor' Elliott featuring Lil' Kim
[3] Notorious B.I.G. featuring Puff Daddy and Lil' Kim

LIL' LOUIS *US, male producer - Louis Burns (21 WEEKS)*   pos/wks

29 Jul 89	● **FRENCH KISS** *ffrr FX 115*	2	11
13 Jan 90	**I CALLED U** *ffrr F 123*	16	6
26 Sep 92	**SAVED MY LIFE** *ffrr FX 197* [1]	74	1
12 Aug 00	**HOW'S YOUR EVENING SO FAR** *ffrr FCD 384* [2]	23	3

[1] Lil' Louis and the World [2] Josh Wink and Lil' Louis

See also BLACK MAGIC

LIL' MISS MAX – See BLUE ADONIS featuring LIL' MISS MAX

LIL' MO US, female vocalist (4 WEEKS)
pos/wks

21 Nov 98	**5 MINUTES** Elektra E 3803CD [1]	**72** 1
23 Sep 99	**WHATEVER** Virgin VUSCD 172 [2]	**31** 3

[1] Lil' Mo featuring Missy 'Misdemeanor' Elliott [2] Ideal U.S. featuring Lil' Mo

LIL' MO' YIN YANG US, male instrumental / production duo - Erick 'More' Morillo and 'Little Louie Vega (2 WEEKS)
pos/wks

9 Mar 96	**REACH** Multiply CDMULTY 9	**28** 2

See also Erick 'More' MORILLO presents RAW; REEL 2 REAL

LILY – See MAXIMA featuring LILY

LILYS US, male vocal / instrumental group (4 WEEKS)
pos/wks

21 Feb 98	**A NANNY IN MANHATTAN** Che CHE 77CD	**16** 4

LIMAHL UK, male vocalist - Chris Hamill (25 WEEKS)
pos/wks

5 Nov 83	**ONLY FOR LOVE** EMI LML 1	**16** 7
7 Jan 84	**ONLY FOR LOVE** (re-entry) EMI LML 1	**75** 1
2 Jun 84	**TOO MUCH TROUBLE** EMI LML 2	**64** 3
13 Oct 84 ●	**NEVER ENDING STORY** EMI LML 3	**4** 14

See also KAJAGOOGOO

Alison LIMERICK UK, female vocalist (39 WEEKS)
pos/wks

30 Mar 91	**WHERE LOVE LIVES** Arista 144208	**27** 8
12 Oct 91	**COME BACK (FOR REAL LOVE)** Arista 114530	**53** 2
21 Dec 91	**MAGIC'S BACK (THEME FROM 'THE GHOSTS OF OXFORD STREET)** RCA PB 45223 [1]	**42** 4
29 Feb 92	**MAKE IT ON MY OWN** Arista 114996	**16** 6
18 Jul 92	**GETTIN' IT RIGHT** Arista 74321102867	**57** 2
28 Nov 92	**HEAR MY CALL** Arista 115337	**73** 1
8 Jan 94	**TIME OF OUR LIVES** Arista 74321180332	**36** 4
19 Mar 94	**LOVE COME DOWN** Arista 74321191952	**36** 2
25 Feb 95	**LOVE WILL KEEP US TOGETHER** Acid Jazz JAZID 112CD [2]	**63** 1
6 Jul 96 ●	**WHERE LOVE LIVES** (re-mix) Arista 74321381592	**9** 6
14 Sep 96	**MAKE IT ON MY OWN** (re-mix) Arista 74321407812	**30** 2
23 Aug 97	**PUT YOUR FAITH IN ME** MBA XES 9001	**42** 1

[1] Malcolm McLaren featuring Alison Limerick [2] JTQ featuring Alison Limerick

LIMIT Holland, male vocal / instrumental duo (8 WEEKS)
pos/wks

5 Jan 85	**SAY YEAH** Portrait A 4808	**17** 8

LIMMIE and the FAMILY COOKIN'
US, male / female vocal group (28 WEEKS)
pos/wks

21 Jul 73 ●	**YOU CAN DO MAGIC** Avco 6105 019	**3** 13
20 Oct 73	**DREAMBOAT** Avco 6105 025	**31** 5
6 Apr 74 ●	**A WALKIN' MIRACLE** Avco 6105 027	**6** 10

LIMP BIZKIT US, male vocal / instrumental group (19 WEEKS)
pos/wks

15 Jul 00 ●	**TAKE A LOOK AROUND (THEME FROM 'MI:2')** Interscope 4973682	**3** 13
11 Nov 00	**MY GENERATION** Interscope IND 97448	**15** 6

Bob LIND US, male vocalist (10 WEEKS)
pos/wks

10 Mar 66 ●	**ELUSIVE BUTTERFLY** Fontana TF 670	**5** 9
26 May 66	**REMEMBER THE RAIN** Fontana TF 702	**46** 1

LINDA and the FUNKY BOYS – See Linda CARR

LINDISFARNE UK, male vocal / instrumental group (55 WEEKS)
pos/wks

26 Feb 72 ●	**MEET ME ON THE CORNER** Charisma CB 173	**5** 11
13 May 72 ●	**LADY ELEANOR** Charisma CB 153	**3** 11
23 Sep 72	**ALL FALL DOWN** Charisma CB 191	**34** 5
3 Jun 78 ●	**RUN FOR HOME** Mercury 6007 177	**10** 15
7 Oct 78	**JUKE BOX GYPSY** Mercury 6007 187	**56** 4
10 Nov 90 ●	**FOG ON THE TYNE (REVISITED)** Best ZB 44083 [1]	**2** 9

[1] Gazza and Lindisfarne

LINER UK, male vocal / instrumental group (6 WEEKS)
pos/wks

10 Mar 79	**KEEP REACHING OUT FOR LOVE** Atlantic K 11235	**49** 3
26 May 79	**YOU AND ME** Atlantic K 11285	**44** 3

Andy LING UK, male producer (1 WEEK)
pos/wks

13 May 00	**FIXATION** Hooj Choons HOOJ 094CD	**55** 1

Laurie LINGO and the DIPSTICKS UK, male vocal duo - DJs Dave Lee Travis and Paul Burnett (7 WEEKS)
pos/wks

17 Apr 76 ●	**CONVOY G.B.** State STAT 23	**4** 7

LINK US, male rapper (1 WEEK)
pos/wks

7 Nov 98	**WHATCHA GONE DO?** Relativity 6666055	**48** 1

LINOLEUM UK, male / female vocal / instrumental group (1 WEEK)
pos/wks

12 Jul 97	**MARQUIS** Lino Vinyl LINO 004CD1	**73** 1

LINX UK, male vocal / instrumental duo - David Grant and Peter Martin (45 WEEKS)
pos/wks

20 Sep 80	**YOU'RE LYING** Chrysalis CHS 2461	**15** 10
7 Mar 81 ●	**INTUITION** Chrysalis CHS 2500	**7** 11
13 Jun 81	**THROW AWAY THE KEY** Chrysalis CHS 2519	**21** 9
5 Sep 81	**SO THIS IS ROMANCE** Chrysalis CHS 2546	**15** 9
21 Nov 81	**CAN'T HELP MYSELF** Chrysalis CHS 2565	**55** 3
10 Jul 82	**PLAYTHING** Chrysalis CHS 2621	**48** 3

LIONROCK UK, male producer - Justin Robertson (14 WEEKS)
pos/wks

5 Dec 92	**LIONROCK** Deconstruction 74321124381	**63** 1
8 May 93	**PACKET OF PEACE** Deconstruction 74321144372	**32** 3
23 Oct 93	**CARNIVAL** Deconstruction 74321164862	**34** 2
27 Aug 94	**TRIPWIRE** Deconstruction 74321204702	**44** 1
6 Apr 96	**STRAIGHT AT YER HEAD** Deconstruction 74321342972	**33** 2
27 Jul 96	**FIRE UP THE SHOESAW** Deconstruction 74321382652	**43** 1
14 Mar 98	**RUDE BOY ROCK** Concrete HARD 31CD	**20** 3
30 May 98	**SCATTER & SWING** Concrete HARD 35CD	**54** 1

LIPPS INC US, male / female vocal / instrumental group (13 WEEKS)
pos/wks

17 May 80 ●	**FUNKYTOWN** Casablanca CAN 194 ▲	**2** 13

LIQUID UK, male producer - Eamon Downes (20 WEEKS)
pos/wks

21 Mar 92	**SWEET HARMONY** XL XLS 28	**15** 6
5 Sep 92	**THE FUTURE MUSIC (EP)** XL XLT 33	**59** 2
20 Mar 93	**TIME TO GET UP** XL XLS 40CD	**46** 2
8 Jul 95	**SWEET HARMONY / ONE LOVE FAMILY (re-mix)** XL XLS 65CD	**14** 6
21 Oct 95	**CLOSER** XL XLS 66CD	**47** 2
25 Jul 98	**STRONG** Higher Ground HIGHS 7CD	**59** 1
21 Oct 00	**ORLANDO DAWN** Xtravaganza XTRAV 16CDS	**53** 1

Tracks on The Future Music (EP): Liquid Is Liquid / Music / House (Is a Feeling) / The Year 3000. On the first two hits act also included Shane Heneghan

LIQUID CHILD Germany, male production duo (2 WEEKS)
pos/wks

23 Oct 99	**DIVING FACES** Essential Recordings ESCD 9	**25** 2

LIQUID GOLD
UK, male / female vocal / instrumental group (46 WEEKS)
pos/wks

2 Dec 78	**ANYWAY YOU DO IT** Creole CR 159	**41** 7
23 Feb 80	**DANCE YOURSELF DIZZY** Polo POLO 1	**2** 14
31 May 80	**SUBSTITUTE** Polo POLO 4	**8** 9
1 Nov 80	**THE NIGHT THE WINE AND THE ROSES** Polo 6	**32** 7

| 28 Mar 81 | DON'T PANIC *Polo POLO 8*.................................... | 42 | 5 |
| 21 Aug 82 | WHERE DID WE GO WRONG *Polo POLO 23* .... | 56 | 4 |

LIQUID OXYGEN *US, male producer (2 WEEKS)* — pos/wks

| 28 Apr 90 | THE PLANET DANCE (MOVE YA BODY) | | |
| | *Champion CHAMP 242* .... | 56 | 2 |

LISA LISA *US, female vocalist (32 WEEKS)* — pos/wks

4 May 85	I WONDER IF I TAKE YOU HOME *CBS A 6057* [1]	53	6
3 Aug 85	I WONDER IF I TAKE YOU HOME (re-entry)		
	CBS A 6057 [1]	12	11
31 Oct 87	LOST IN EMOTION *CBS 651036 7* [2] ▲	58	4
13 Jul 91	LET THE BEAT HIT 'EM *Columbia 6572867* [2]	17	6
24 Aug 91	LET THE BEAT HIT 'EM PART 2		
	Columbia 6573747	49	2
26 Mar 94	SKIP TO MY LU *Chrysalis CDCHS 5006*	34	3

[1] Lisa Lisa and Cult Jam with Full Force [2] Lisa Lisa and Cult Jam

LISA MARIE – See Malcolm McLAREN

LISA MARIE EXPERIENCE *UK, male instrumental / production duo -
Dean Marriot and Neil Hynde (15 WEEKS)* — pos/wks

27 Apr 96	● KEEP ON JUMPIN' *ffrr FCD 271*	7	10
20 Jul 96	KEEP ON JUMPIN' (re-entry) *ffrr FCD 271*	61	3
10 Aug 96	DO THAT TO ME *Positiva CDTIV 57*	33	2

LIT *US, male vocal / instrumental group (7 WEEKS)* — pos/wks

26 Jun 99	MY OWN WORST ENEMY *RCA 74321669992*...........	16	4
25 Sep 99	ZIP - LOCK *RCA 74321701852*	60	1
19 Aug 00	OVER MY HEAD *Capitol 8889532*	37	2

LITHIAM and Sonya MADAN
US, male producer and UK, female vocalist (2 WEEKS) — pos/wks

| 1 Mar 97 | RIDE A ROCKET *ffrr FCD 293* .... | 40 | 2 |

Sonya Madan is lead singer of Echobelly

See also ECHOBELLY

De Etta LITTLE and Nelson PIGFORD
US, female / male vocal duo (5 WEEKS) — pos/wks

| 13 Aug 77 | YOU TAKE MY HEART AWAY *United Artists UP 36257* .... | 35 | 5 |

LITTLE ANGELS *UK, male vocal / instrumental group (41 WEEKS)* — pos/wks

4 Mar 89	BIG BAD EP *Polydor LTLEP 2*............................	74	1
24 Feb 90	KICKING UP DUST *Polydor LTL 5*	46	4
12 May 90	RADICAL YOUR LOVER *Polydor LTL 6* [1]	34	4
4 Aug 90	SHE'S A LITTLE ANGEL *Polydor LTL 7*..................	21	3
2 Feb 91	BONEYARD *Polydor LTL 8*	33	4
30 Mar 91	PRODUCT OF THE WORKING CLASS *Polydor LTL 9*	40	2
1 Jun 91	YOUNG GODS *Polydor LTL 10*	34	2
20 Jul 91	I AIN'T GONNA CRY *Polydor LTL 11*	26	3
7 Nov 92	TOO MUCH TOO YOUNG *Polydor LTL 12*	22	3
9 Jan 93	WOMANKIND *Polydor LTLCD 13*	12	5
24 Apr 93	SOAPBOX *Polydor LTLCD 14*	33	4
25 Sep 93	SAIL AWAY *Polydor LTLCD 15*	45	3
9 Apr 94	TEN MILES HIGH *Polydor LTLCD 16*	18	3

[1] Little Angels featuring the Big Bad Horns

Tracks on Big Bad EP: She's a Little Angel / Don't Waste My Time / Better Than the Rest / Sex in Cars

LITTLE ANTHONY and the IMPERIALS
US, male vocal group (4 WEEKS) — pos/wks

| 31 Jul 76 | BETTER USE YOUR HEAD *United Artists UP 36141*.................. | 42 | 4 |

LITTLE BENNY and the MASTERS *US, male rapper / instrumentalist -
trumpet - and male instrumental group (7 WEEKS)* — pos/wks

| 2 Feb 85 | WHO COMES TO BOOGIE *Bluebird 10 BR 13* .... | 33 | 7 |

LITTLE CAESAR *UK, male vocalist (3 WEEKS)* — pos/wks

| 9 Jun 90 | THE WHOLE OF THE MOON *A1 EAU 1*................... | 68 | 3 |

LITTLE EVA *US, female vocalist - Eva Boyd (45 WEEKS)* — pos/wks

6 Sep 62	● THE LOCO-MOTION *London HL 9581* ▲	2	17
3 Jan 63	KEEP YOUR HANDS OFF MY BABY *London HLU 9633*	30	5
7 Mar 63	LET'S TURKEY TROT *London HLU 9687*	13	12
29 Jul 72	THE LOCO-MOTION (re-entry) *London HL 9581*	11	11

See also Big Dee IRWIN

LITTLE LOUIE – See Louie VEGA and Marc ANTHONY

LITTLE MS MARCIE – See MELT featuring LITTLE MS MARCIE

LITTLE RICHARD 234 Top 500 *Frantic, no-holds-barred rock 'n' roll
singer / songwriter and piano-pounder, b. Richard Penniman, 5 Dec 1935,
Georgia, US. This legendary performer's wild vocals and unrestrained stage
show influenced many later stars. Both The Beatles and The Rolling Stones
supported him on tour (116 WEEKS)* — pos/wks

14 Dec 56	RIP IT UP *London HLO 8336*...........................	30	1
8 Feb 57	● LONG TALL SALLY *London HLO 8366*	3	16
22 Feb 57	TUTTI FRUTTI *London HLO 8366*	29	1
8 Mar 57	SHE'S GOT IT *London HLO 8382*	15	7
15 Mar 57	● THE GIRL CAN'T HELP IT *London HLO 8382*	9	11
24 May 57	SHE'S GOT IT (re-entry) *London HLO 8382*	28	2
28 Jun 57	● LUCILLE *London HLO 8446*	10	9
13 Sep 57	JENNY JENNY *London HLO 8470*	11	5
29 Nov 57	KEEP A KNOCKIN' *London HLO 8509*	21	7
28 Feb 58	● GOOD GOLLY MISS MOLLY *London HLU 8560*	8	9
11 Jul 58	OOH! MY SOUL *London HLO 8647*	30	1
25 Jul 58	OOH! MY SOUL (re-entry) *London HLO 8647*	22	3
2 Jan 59	● BABY FACE *London HLU 8770*	2	15
3 Apr 59	BY THE LIGHT OF THE SILVERY MOON		
	London HLU 8831	17	5
5 Jun 59	KANSAS CITY *London HLU 8868*	26	5
11 Oct 62	HE GOT WHAT HE WANTED *Mercury AMT 1189*	38	4
4 Jun 64	BAMA LAMA BAMA LOO *London HL 9896*	20	7
2 Jul 77	GOOD GOLLY MISS MOLLY / RIP IT UP		
	Creole CR 140	37	4
14 Jun 86	GREAT GOSH A'MIGHTY ! (IT'S A MATTER OF TIME)		
	MCA MCA 1049	62	2
25 Oct 86	OPERATOR *WEA YZ 89*	67	2

The 1977 versions of 'Good Golly Miss Molly' and 'Rip It Up' on Creole are re-recordings

LITTLE STEVEN
US, male vocalist / instrumentalist - guitar (3 WEEKS) — pos/wks

| 23 May 87 | BITTER FRUIT *Manhattan MT 21* .... | 66 | 3 |

LITTLE T – See REBEL MC

LITTLE TONY *Italy, male vocalist (3 WEEKS)* — pos/wks

| 15 Jan 60 | TOO GOOD *Decca F 11190*............................. | 19 | 3 |

LIVE *US, male vocal / instrumental group (13 WEEKS)* — pos/wks

18 Feb 95	I ALONE *Radioactive RAXTD 13*	48	4
1 Jul 95	SELLING THE DRAMA *Radioactive RAXTD 17*	30	2
7 Oct 95	ALL OVER YOU *Radioactive RAXTD 20*	48	1
13 Jan 96	LIGHTNING CRASHES *Radioactive RAXTD 23*	33	2
15 Mar 97	LAKINI'S JUICE *Radioactive RAD 49023*	29	2
12 Jul 97	FREAKS *Radioactive RAXTD 29*	60	1
5 Feb 00	THE DOLPHIN'S CRY *Radioactive RAXTD 39*	62	1

LIVE REPORT *UK, male vocal / instrumental group (1 WEEK)* — pos/wks

| 20 May 89 | WHY DO I ALWAYS GET IT WRONG *Brouhaha CUE 7* ..... | 73 | 1 |

LIVERPOOL EXPRESS
UK, male vocal / instrumental group (26 WEEKS) — pos/wks

| 26 Jun 76 | YOU ARE MY LOVE *Warner Bros. K 16743* .... | 11 | 9 |

UK No.1 ★   UK Top 10 ●   Still on chart +   UK million seller ◆   UK entry at No.1 ■   US No.1 ▲

16 Oct 76	HOLD TIGHT *Warner Bros. K 16799*	**46**	2
18 Dec 76	EVERY MAN MUST HAVE A DREAM *Warner Bros. K 16854*	**17**	11
4 Jun 77	DREAMIN' *Warner Bros. K 16933*	**40**	4

LIVERPOOL FC *UK, male football team vocalists (21 WEEKS)* pos/wks

28 May 77	WE CAN DO IT (EP) *State STAT 50*	**15**	4
23 Apr 83	LIVERPOOL (WE'RE NEVER GONNA...) / LIVERPOOL (ANTHEM) *Mean MEAN 102*	**54**	4
17 May 86	SITTING ON THE TOP OF THE WORLD *Columbia DB 9116*	**50**	2
14 May 88 ●	ANFIELD RAP (RED MACHINE IN FULL EFFECT) *Virgin LFC 1*	**3**	6
18 May 96 ●	PASS AND MOVE (IT'S THE LIVERPOOL GROOVE) *Telstar LFCCD 96* [1]	**4**	5

[1] Liverpool FC and the Boot Room Boyz

Tracks on We Can Do It (EP): We Can Do It / Liverpool Lou / We Shall Not Be Moved / You'll Never Walk Alone

LIVIN' JOY *US / Italy, male / female vocal / instrumental group - leader Paolo Visnadi (44 WEEKS)* pos/wks

3 Sep 94	DREAMER *Undiscovered MCSTD 1993*	**18**	6
13 May 95 ★	DREAMER (re-mix) *Undiscovered MCSTD 2056* ■	**1**	11
15 Jun 96 ●	DON'T STOP MOVIN' *Undiscovered MCSTD 40041*	**5**	14
2 Nov 96 ●	FOLLOW THE RULES *Undiscovered MCSTD 40081*	**9**	5
5 Apr 97	WHERE CAN I FIND LOVE *Undiscovered MCSTD 40108*	**12**	4
23 Aug 97	DEEP IN YOU *Universal MCSTD 40136*	**17**	4

See also ALEX PARTY

LIVING COLOUR *US, male vocal / instrumental group (22 WEEKS)* pos/wks

27 Oct 90	TYPE *Epic LCL 7*	**75**	1
2 Feb 91	LOVE REARS ITS UGLY HEAD *Epic 6565937*	**12**	11
1 Jun 91	SOLACE OF YOU *Epic 6569087*	**33**	5
26 Oct 91	CULT OF PERSONALITY *Epic 6575357*	**67**	2
20 Feb 93	LEAVE IT ALONE *Epic 6589762*	**34**	2
17 Apr 93	AUSLANDER *Epic 6591732*	**53**	1

LIVING IN A BOX *UK, male vocal / instrumental group (62 WEEKS)* pos/wks

4 Apr 87 ●	LIVING IN A BOX *Chrysalis LIB 1*	**5**	13
13 Jun 87	SCALES OF JUSTICE *Chrysalis LIB 2*	**30**	6
26 Sep 87	SO THE STORY GOES *Chrysalis LIB 3* [1]	**34**	8
30 Jan 88	LOVE IS THE ART *Chrysalis LIB 4*	**45**	4
18 Feb 89 ●	BLOW THE HOUSE DOWN *Chrysalis LIB 5*	**10**	9
10 Jun 89	GATECRASHING *Chrysalis LIB 6*	**36**	6
23 Sep 89 ●	ROOM IN YOUR HEART *Chrysalis LIB 7*	**5**	13
30 Dec 89	DIFFERENT AIR *Chrysalis LIB 8*	**64**	1
13 Jan 90	DIFFERENT AIR (re-entry) *Chrysalis LIB 8*	**57**	2

[1] Living in a Box featuring Bobby Womack

Dandy LIVINGSTONE *Jamaica, male vocalist (19 WEEKS)* pos/wks

2 Sep 72	SUZANNE BEWARE OF THE DEVIL *Horse HOSS 16*	**14**	11
13 Jan 73	BIG CITY / THINK ABOUT THAT *Horse HOSS 25*	**26**	8

LL COOL J (439 Top 500) *With a moniker abbreviated from Ladies Love Cool James, this whizz kid was born James Todd Smith, 18 Jun 1968, New York, US. The first solo rap act to score a UK Top 10 hit with 'I Need Love', which was also the first successful rap 'ballad', he has also amassed a record 8 US No.1 rap hits. (76 WEEKS)*

4 Jul 87	I'M BAD *Def Jam 650856 7*	**71**	1
12 Sep 87 ●	I NEED LOVE *Def Jam 651101 7*	**8**	10
21 Nov 87	GO CUT CREATOR GO *Def Jam LLCJ 1*	**66**	2
13 Feb 88	GOING BACK TO CALI / JACK THE RIPPER *Def Jam LLCJ 2*	**37**	4
10 Jun 89	I'M THAT TYPE OF GUY *Def Jam LLCJ 3*	**43**	5
1 Dec 90	AROUND THE WAY GIRL / MAMA SAID KNOCK YOU OUT *Def Jam 6564470*	**41**	4
9 Mar 91	AROUND THE WAY GIRL (re-mix) *Columbia 6564470*	**36**	4
10 Apr 93	HOW I'M COMIN' *Def Jam 6591692*	**37**	2
20 Jan 96	HEY LOVER *Def Jam DEFCD 14* [1]	**17**	4
1 Jun 96	DOIN' IT *Def Jam DEFCD 15* [2]	**15**	3
5 Oct 96 ●	LOUNGIN' *Def Jam DEFCD 30*	**7**	8

8 Feb 97 ★	AIN'T NOBODY *Geffen GFSTD 22195* ■	**1**	9
5 Apr 97 ●	HIT EM HIGH (THE MONSTARS' ANTHEM) *Atlantic A 5449CD* [3]	**8**	6
1 Nov 97 ●	PHENOMENON *Def Jam 5681172*	**9**	5
28 Mar 98 ●	FATHER *Def Jam 5685292*	**10**	5
11 Jul 98	ZOOM *Interscope IND 95594* [4]	**15**	3
5 Dec 98	INCREDIBLE *Jive 0522102* [5]	**52**	1

[1] LL Cool J featuring Boyz II Men [2] LL Cool J, guest vocals by LeShaun [3] B Real / Busta Rhymes / Coolio / LL Cool J / Method Man [4] Dr Dre and LL Cool J [5] Keith Murray featuring LL Cool J

'Jack the Ripper' listed only from 20 Feb 1988

LLAMA FARMERS *UK, male / female vocal / instrumental group (2 WEEKS)* pos/wks

6 Feb 99	BIG WHEELS *Beggars Banquet BBQ 333CD*	**67**	1
15 May 99	GET THE KEYS AND GO *Beggars Banquet BBQ 335CD*	**74**	1

Kelly LLORENNA *UK, female vocalist (7 WEEKS)* pos/wks

7 May 94	SET YOU FREE *All around the World CDGLOBE 124* [1]	**39**	4
24 Feb 96	BRIGHTER DAY *Pukka CDPUKKA 5*	**43**	2
25 Jul 98	HEART OF GOLD *Diverse VERSE 2CD* [2]	**55**	1

[1] N-Trance featuring Kelly Llorenna [2] FORCE + STYLES featuring Kelly Llorenna

See also N-TRANCE

Don LLOYDIE – See SOUNDMAN and Don LLOYDIE with Elisabeth TROY

LNR *US, male vocal / instrumental duo (2 WEEKS)* pos/wks

3 Jun 89	WORK IT TO THE BONE *Kool Kat KOOL 501*	**64**	2

LO FIDELITY ALLSTARS *UK, male vocal / instrumental group (5 WEEKS)* pos/wks

11 Oct 97	DISCO MACHINE GUN *Skint SKINT 30CD*	**50**	1
2 May 98	VISION INCISION *Skint SKINT 33CD*	**30**	2
28 Nov 98	BATTLEFLAG *Skint SKINT 38CD* [1]	**36**	2

[1] Lo Fidelity Allstars featuring Pigeonhed

LOBO *US, male vocalist - Kent LaVoie (25 WEEKS)* pos/wks

19 Jun 71 ●	ME AND YOU AND A DOG NAMED BOO *Philips 6073 801*	**4**	14
8 Jun 74 ●	I'D LOVE YOU TO WANT ME *UK 68*	**5**	11

LOBO *Holland, male vocalist - Imrich Lobo (11 WEEKS)* pos/wks

25 Jul 81 ●	THE CARIBBEAN DISCO SHOW *Polydor POSP 302*	**8**	11

Tone LOC *US, male rapper - Anthony Smith (19 WEEKS)* pos/wks

11 Feb 89	WILD THING / LOC'ED AFTER DARK *Fourth & Broadway BRW 121*	**21**	8
20 May 89	FUNKY COLD MEDINA / ON FIRE *Fourth & Broadway BRW 129*	**13**	9
5 Aug 89	I GOT IT GOIN' ON *Fourth & Broadway BRW 140*	**55**	2

LOCK 'N' LOAD *Holland, male DJ / production duo - Francis Rooijen and Nilz Pijpers (11 WEEKS)* pos/wks

15 Apr 00 ●	BLOW YA MIND *Pepper 9230162*	**6**	10
1 Jul 00	BLOW YA MIND (re-entry) *Pepper 9230162*	**69**	1

Hank LOCKLIN *US, male vocalist (41 WEEKS)* pos/wks

11 Aug 60 ●	PLEASE HELP ME, I'M FALLING *RCA 1188*	**9**	19
15 Feb 62	FROM HERE TO THERE TO YOU *RCA 1273*	**44**	3
15 Nov 62	WE'RE GONNA GO FISHIN' *RCA 1305*	**18**	11
5 May 66	I FEEL A CRY COMING ON *RCA 1510*	**29**	8

LOCKSMITH *US, male vocal / instrumental group (6 WEEKS)* pos/wks

23 Aug 80	UNLOCK THE FUNK *Arista ARIST 364*	**42**	6

LOCOMOTIVE
UK, male vocal / instrumental group (8 WEEKS)

		pos/wks
16 Oct 68	RUDI'S IN LOVE *Parlophone R 5718*	**25** 8

John LODGE – See Justin HAYWARD; MOODY BLUES

LODGER
UK, male / female vocal / instrumental group (2 WEEKS)

		pos/wks
2 May 98	I'M LEAVING *Island CID 693*	**40** 2

Lisa LOEB and NINE STORIES
US, female / male vocal / instrumental group (17 WEEKS)

		pos/wks
3 Sep 94 ●	STAY (I MISSED YOU) *RCA 74321212522* ▲	**6** 15
16 Sep 95	DO YOU SLEEP *Geffen GFSTD 96*	**45** 2

Nils LOFGREN
US, male vocalist / instrumentalist - guitar (3 WEEKS)

		pos/wks
8 Jun 85	SECRETS IN THE STREET *Towerbell TOW 68*	**53** 3

Johnny LOGAN
Ireland, male vocalist - Sean Sherrard (24 WEEKS)

		pos/wks
3 May 80 ★	WHAT'S ANOTHER YEAR *Epic EPC 8572*	**1** 8
23 May 87 ●	HOLD ME NOW *Epic LOG 1*	**2** 11
22 Aug 87	I'M NOT IN LOVE *Epic LOG 2*	**51** 5

Kenny LOGGINS
US, male vocalist (21 WEEKS)

		pos/wks
28 Apr 84 ●	FOOTLOOSE *CBS A 4101* ▲	**6** 10
1 Nov 86	DANGER ZONE *CBS A 7188*	**45** 11

LOLA
US, female vocalist (1 WEEK)

		pos/wks
28 Mar 87	WAX THE VAN *Syncopate SY 1*	**65** 1

LOLLY
UK, female vocalist - Anna Klumby (44 WEEKS)

		pos/wks
10 Jul 99 ●	VIVA LA RADIO *Polydor 5639492*	**6** 9
18 Sep 99 ●	MICKEY *Polydor 5613682*	**4** 10
4 Dec 99 ●	BIG BOYS DON'T CRY / ROCKIN' ROBIN *Polydor 5615552*	**10** 9
6 May 00	PER SEMPRE AMORE (FOREVER IN LOVE) *Polydor 5617882*	**11** 8
8 Jul 00	PER SEMPRE AMORE (FOREVER IN LOVE) (re-entry) *Polydor 5617882*	**63** 2
9 Sep 00	GIRLS JUST WANNA HAVE FUN *Polydor 5619762*	**14** 6

Alain LOMBARD – See Mady MESPLE and Danielle MILLET with the PARIS OPERA-COMIQUE ORCHESTRA conducted by Alain LOMBARD

LONDON BOYS
UK, male vocal duo (46 WEEKS)

		pos/wks
10 Dec 88	REQUIEM *WEA YZ 345*	**59** 6
1 Apr 89 ●	REQUIEM (re-entry) *WEA YZ 345*	**4** 15
1 Jul 89 ●	LONDON NIGHTS *WEA YZ 393*	**2** 9
16 Sep 89	HARLEM DESIRE *WEA YZ 415*	**17** 7
2 Dec 89	MY LOVE *WEA YZ 433*	**46** 6
16 Jun 90	CHAPEL OF LOVE *East West YZ 458*	**75** 1
19 Jan 91	FREEDOM *East West YZ 554*	**54** 2

LONDON COMMUNITY GOSPEL CHOIR – See Sal SOLO

Julie LONDON
US, female vocalist (3 WEEKS)

		pos/wks
5 Apr 57	CRY ME A RIVER *London HLU 8240*	**22** 3

Laurie LONDON
UK, male vocalist (12 WEEKS)

		pos/wks
8 Nov 57	HE'S GOT THE WHOLE WORLD IN HIS HANDS *Parlophone R 4359*	**12** 12

With Geoff Love his Orchestra and Chorus

LONDON PHILHARMONIC ORCHESTRA – See Cliff RICHARD

LONDON STRING CHORALE
UK, orchestra / choir (13 WEEKS)

		pos/wks
15 Dec 73	GALLOPING HOME *Polydor 2058 280*	**49** 3
19 Jan 74	GALLOPING HOME (re-entry) *Polydor 2058 280*	**31** 10

LONDON SYMPHONY ORCHESTRA
UK, orchestra (5 WEEKS)

		pos/wks
6 Jan 79	THEME FROM 'SUPERMAN' (MAIN TITLE) *Warner Bros. K 17292*	**32** 5

Orchestra conducted by John Williams

LONDONBEAT
UK / US, male vocal group (45 WEEKS)

		pos/wks
26 Nov 88	9 AM (THE COMFORT ZONE) *Anxious ANX 008*	**19** 10
18 Feb 89	FAILING IN LOVE AGAIN *Anxious ANX 007*	**60** 2
1 Sep 90 ●	I'VE BEEN THINKING ABOUT YOU *Anxious ANX 14* ▲	**2** 13
24 Nov 90	A BETTER LOVE *Anxious ANX 21*	**52** 5
2 Mar 91	NO WOMAN NO CRY *Anxious ANX 25*	**64** 2
20 Jul 91	A BETTER LOVE (re-issue) *Anxious ANX 32*	**23** 6
27 Jun 92	YOU BRING ON THE SUN *Anxious ANX 37*	**32** 4
24 Oct 92	THAT'S HOW I FEEL ABOUT YOU *Anxious ANX 40*	**69** 1
8 Apr 95	I'M JUST YOUR PUPPET ON A . . . (STRING) *Anxious 74321270982*	**55** 1
20 May 95	COME BACK *Anxious 74321226682*	**69** 1

See also Liz KERSHAW and Bruno BROOKES

LONE JUSTICE
US, female / male vocal / instrumental group (4 WEEKS)

		pos/wks
7 Mar 87	I FOUND LOVE *Geffen GEF 18*	**45** 4

LONESTAR
US, male vocal / instrumental group (24 WEEKS)

		pos/wks
15 Apr 00	AMAZED *BMG / Grapevine 74321742582* ▲	**21** 22
7 Sep 00	SMILE *BMG / Grapevine 74321786132*	**55** 2

Shorty LONG
US, male vocalist (7 WEEKS)

		pos/wks
17 Jul 68	HERE COMES THE JUDGE *Tamla Motown TMG 663*	**30** 7

LONG AND THE SHORT
UK, male vocal / instrumental group (8 WEEKS)

		pos/wks
10 Sep 64	THE LETTER *Decca F 11964*	**35** 5
24 Dec 64	CHOC ICE *Decca F 12043*	**49** 3

LONG RYDERS
US, male vocal / instrumental group (4 WEEKS)

		pos/wks
5 Oct 85	LOOKING FOR LEWIS AND CLARK *Island IS 237*	**59** 4

LONGPIGS
UK, male vocal / instrumental group (17 WEEKS)

		pos/wks
22 Jul 95	SHE SAID *Mother MUMCD 66*	**67** 1
28 Oct 95	JESUS CHRIST *Mother MUMCD 68*	**61** 1
17 Feb 96	FAR *Mother MUMCD 71*	**37** 2
13 Apr 96	ON AND ON *Mother MUMCD 74*	**16** 3
22 Jun 96	SHE SAID (re-issue) *Mother MUMCD 77*	**16** 4
5 Oct 96	LOST MYSELF *Mother MUMCD 82*	**22** 3
9 Oct 99	BLUE SKIES *Mother MUMCD 113*	**21** 2
18 Dec 99	THE FRANK SONATA *Mother MUMCD 114*	**57** 1

Joe LONGTHORNE
UK, male vocalist (6 WEEKS)

		pos/wks
30 Apr 94	YOUNG GIRL *EMI CDEM 310*	**61** 2
10 Dec 94	PASSING STRANGERS *EMI CDEM 362* [1]	**34** 4

[1] Joe Longthorne and Liz Dawn

LONYO
UK, male vocalist / producer - Lonyo Engele (7 WEEK)

		pos/wks
8 Jul 00 ●	SUMMER OF LOVE *Riverhorse RIVH CD3* [1]	**8** 7

[1] Lonyo – Comme Çi Comme Ça

LOOK
UK, male vocal / instrumental group (15 WEEKS)

		pos/wks
20 Dec 80 ●	I AM THE BEAT *MCA 647*	**6** 12
29 Aug 81	FEEDING TIME *MCA 736*	**50** 3

LOOP DA LOOP
UK, male producer - Nick Dresti (4 WEEKS)

		pos/wks
7 Jun 97	GO WITH THE FLOW *Manifesto FESCD 24*	**47** 1
20 Feb 99	HAZEL *Manifesto FESCD 53*	**20** 3

LOOSE ENDS (446) Top 500 *Soul / disco trio formed in London; Carl McIntosh (v/g), Jane Eugene (v) and Steve Nichol (k) - the latter two leaving in 1990. First UK group to top US R&B chart - achieved this feat with US-produced 'Hangin' on a String' and 'Slow Down' (76 WEEKS)*

		pos/wks	
25 Feb 84	TELL ME WHAT YOU WANT *Virgin VS 658*	74	1
28 Apr 84	EMERGENCY (DIAL 999) *Virgin VS 677*	41	6
21 Jul 84	CHOOSE ME (RESCUE ME) *Virgin VS 697*	59	3
23 Feb 85	HANGIN' ON A STRING (CONTEMPLATING) *Virgin VS 748*	13	13
11 May 85	MAGIC TOUCH *Virgin VS 761*	16	7
27 Jul 85	GOLDEN YEARS *Virgin VS 795*	59	4
14 Jun 86	STAY A LITTLE WHILE, CHILD *Virgin VS 819*	52	5
20 Sep 86	SLOW DOWN *Virgin VS 884*	27	7
29 Nov 86	NIGHTS OF PLEASURE *Virgin VS 919*	42	7
4 Jun 88	MR BACHELOR *Virgin VS 1080*	50	4
25 Aug 90	DON'T BE A FOOL *10 TEN 312*	13	9
17 Nov 90	LOVE'S GOT ME *10 TEN 330*	40	4
20 Jun 92	HANGIN' ON A STRING (re-mix) *Ten TEN 406*	25	5
5 Sep 92	MAGIC TOUCH (re-mix) *Ten TEN 409*	75	1

Lisa LOPES – See Melanie C; TLC

Jennifer LOPEZ *US, female vocalist (31 WEEKS)*

		pos/wks	
3 Jul 99 ●	IF YOU HAD MY LOVE *Columbia 6675772* ▲	4	13
13 Nov 99	WAITING FOR TONIGHT *Columbia 6683072*	5	12
1 Apr 00	FEELIN' SO GOOD *Columbia 6691972* [1]	15	6

[1] Jennifer Lopez featuring Big Pun & Fat Joe

Trini LOPEZ *US, male vocalist (37 WEEKS)*

		pos/wks	
12 Sep 63 ●	IF I HAD A HAMMER *Reprise R 20198*	4	17
12 Dec 63	KANSAS CITY *Reprise R 20236*	35	5
12 May 66	I'M COMING HOME CINDY *Reprise R 20455*	28	5
6 Apr 67	GONNA GET ALONG WITHOUT YA NOW *Reprise R 20547*	41	5
19 Dec 81	TRINI TRAX *RCA 154*	59	5

LO-PRO – See X-PRESS 2

LORD ROCKINGHAM'S XI *UK, male / female instrumental group, leader Harry Robinson (21 WEEKS)*

		pos/wks	
24 Oct 58 ★	HOOTS MON *Decca F 11059*	1	17
6 Feb 59	WEE TOM *Decca F 11104*	16	3
25 Sep 93	HOOTS MON (re-issue) *Decca 8820982*	60	1

LORD TANAMO *Trinidad and Tobago, male vocalist (2 WEEKS)*

		pos/wks	
1 Dec 90	I'M IN THE MOOD FOR LOVE *Mooncrest MOON 1009*	58	2

LORD TARIQ and Peter GUNZ *US, male vocal / rap duo (3 WEEKS)*

		pos/wks	
2 May 98	DEJA VU (UPTOWN BABY) *Columbia 6658722*	21	3

Jerry LORDAN *UK, male vocalist (15 WEEKS)*

		pos/wks	
8 Jan 60	I'LL STAY SINGLE *Parlophone R 4588*	26	2
26 Feb 60	WHO COULD BE BLUER *Parlophone R 4627*	16	9
10 Mar 60	I'LL STAY SINGLE (re-entry) *Parlophone R 4588*	41	1
19 May 60	WHO COULD BE BLUER (re-entry) *Parlophone R 4627*	45	1
2 Jun 60	SING LIKE AN ANGEL *Parlophone R 4653*	36	2

Traci LORDS *US, female vocalist (1 WEEK)*

		pos/wks	
7 Oct 95	FALLEN ANGEL *Radioactive RAXTD 18*	72	1

Sophia LOREN – See Peter SELLERS

Trey LORENZ *US, male vocalist (5 WEEKS)*

		pos/wks	
21 Nov 92	SOMEONE TO HOLD *Epic 6587857*	65	2
30 Jan 93	PHOTOGRAPH OF MARY *Epic 6589542*	38	3

See also Mariah CAREY

LORI and the CHAMELEONS *UK, female / male vocal / instrumental group (1 WEEK)*

		pos/wks	
8 Dec 79	TOUCH *Sire SIR 4025*	70	1

LORRAINE – See BOMB THE BASS

LOS BRAVOS *Spain / Germany, male vocal / instrumental group (24 WEEKS)*

		pos/wks	
30 Jun 66 ●	BLACK IS BLACK *Decca F 22419*	2	13
8 Sep 66	I DON'T CARE *Decca F 22484*	16	11

LOS DEL CHIPMUNKS – See CHIPMUNKS

LOS DEL MAR featuring Wil VELOZ *Cuba / Canada, male vocal / instrumental group (7 WEEKS)*

		pos/wks	
8 Jun 96	MACARENA *Pulse 8 CDLOSE 101*	66	2
6 Jul 96	MACARENA (re-entry) *Pulse 8 CDLOSE 101*	43	5

LOS DEL RIO *Spain, male vocal / instrumental duo - Antonio Monge and Rafael Perdigones (19 WEEKS)*

		pos/wks	
1 Jun 96	MACARENA *RCA 74321345372* ▲	64	1
13 Jul 96 ●	MACARENA (re-entry) *RCA 74321345372*	2	18

LOS INDIOS TABAJARAS *Brazil, male instrumental guitar duo - Natalicio and Antenor Lima (17 WEEKS)*

		pos/wks	
31 Oct 63 ●	MARIA ELENA *RCA 1365*	5	17

LOS LOBOS *US, male vocal / instrumental group - lead vocal David Hildago (24 WEEKS)*

		pos/wks	
6 Apr 85	DON'T WORRY BABY / WILL THE WOLF SURVIVE *London LASH 4*	57	4
18 Jul 87 ★	LA BAMBA *Slash LASH 13* ▲	1	11
26 Sep 87	COME ON LET'S GO *Slash LASH 14*	18	9

LOS UMBRELLOS *Denmark, male / female vocal trio (2 WEEKS)*

		pos/wks	
3 Oct 98	NO TENGO DINERO *Virgin VUSCD 139*	33	2

Joe LOSS *UK, orchestra (53 WEEKS)*

		pos/wks	
29 Jun 61	WHEELS CHA CHA *HMV POP 880*	21	21
19 Oct 61	SUCU SUCU *HMV POP 937*	40	1
29 Mar 62	THE MAIGRET THEME *HMV POP 995*	20	10
1 Nov 62	MUST BE MADISON *HMV POP 1075*	20	13
5 Nov 64	MARCH OF THE MODS *HMV POP 1351*	35	4
24 Dec 64	MARCH OF THE MODS (re-entry) *HMV POP 1351*	31	4

LOST *UK, male / instrumental / production duo (1 WEEK)*

		pos/wks	
22 Jun 91	TECHNO FUNK *Perfecto PT 44560*	75	1

LOST BOYZ *US, male rap group (2 WEEKS)*

		pos/wks	
2 Nov 96	MUSIC MAKES ME HIGH *Universal MCSTD 48015*	42	1
12 Jul 97	LOVE, PEACE & NAPPINESS *Universal UND 56131*	57	1

LOST TRIBE *UK, male production duo (3 WEEKS)*

		pos/wks	
11 Sep 99	GAMEMASTER *Hooj Choons HOOJ 81CD*	24	3

LOST WITNESS *UK, male production duo and female vocalist (10 WEEKS)*

		pos/wks	
29 May 99	HAPPINESS HAPPENING *Ministry of Sound MOSCDS 129*	18	4
18 Sep 99	RED SUN RISING *Ministry of Sound MOSCDS 133*	22	3
16 Dec 00	7 COLOURS *Data DATA 15CDS*	28	3

LOTUS EATERS *UK, male vocal / instrumental duo (16 WEEKS)*

		pos/wks	
2 Jul 83	FIRST PICTURE OF YOU *Sylvan SYL 1*	15	12
8 Oct 83	YOU DON'T NEED SOMEONE NEW *Sylvan SYL 2*	53	4

Bonnie LOU *US, female vocalist - Bonnie Lou Kath (10 WEEKS)* pos/wks
5 Feb 54 ●	TENNESSEE WIG WALK *Parlophone R 3730*	**4** 10

Lippy LOU *UK, female rapper (2 WEEKS)* pos/wks
22 Apr 95	LIBERATION *More Protein PROCD 105*	**57** 2

Louchie LOU and Michie ONE
UK, female rap duo - Louise Gold and Michelle Charles (36 WEEKS) pos/wks
29 May 93 ●	SHOUT *ffrr FCD 211*	**7** 8
14 Aug 93	SOMEBODY ELSE'S GUY *ffrr FCD 216*	**54** 2
26 Aug 95	GET DOWN ON IT *China WOKCD 2054*	**58** 1
13 Apr 96 ●	CECILIA *WEA WEA 042CD1* [1]	**4** 17
15 Jun 96	GOOD SWEET LOVIN' *Indochina ID 050CD*	**34** 2
24 Aug 96	CECILIA (re-entry) *WEA WEA 042CD1* [1]	**65** 1
7 Sep 96	CECILIA (2nd re-entry) *WEA WEA 042CD1* [1]	**59** 1
21 Sep 96	NO MORE ALCOHOL *WEA WEA 065CD1* [1]	**24** 4

[1] Suggs featuring Louchie Lou and Michie One

LOUD *UK, male vocal / instrumental group (2 WEEKS)* pos/wks
28 Mar 92	EASY *China WOK 2016*	**67** 2

John D LOUDERMILK *US, male vocalist (10 WEEKS)* pos/wks
4 Jan 62	THE LANGUAGE OF LOVE *RCA 1269*	**13** 10

Louie LOUIE *US, male vocalist (5 WEEKS)* pos/wks
19 Dec 92	THE THOUGHT OF IT *Hardback YZ 724*	**34** 5

LOUISE *UK, female vocalist - Louise Nurding (69 WEEKS)* pos/wks
7 Oct 95 ●	LIGHT OF MY LIFE *EMI CDEMS 397*	**8** 8
16 Mar 96	IN WALKED LOVE *EMI CDEMS 413*	**17** 6
8 Jun 96 ●	NAKED *EMI CDEMS 431*	**5** 8
31 Aug 96 ●	UNDIVIDED LOVE *EMI CDEM 441*	**5** 6
30 Nov 96 ●	ONE KISS FROM HEAVEN *EMI CDEM 454*	**9** 7
4 Oct 97 ●	ARMS AROUND THE WORLD *EMI CDEM 490*	**4** 7
29 Nov 97 ●	LET'S GO ROUND AGAIN *EMI CDEM 500*	**10** 9
4 Apr 98 ●	ALL THAT MATTERS *1st Avenue CDEM 506*	**11** 5
20 Jun 98	ALL THAT MATTERS (re-entry) *1st Avenue CDEM 506*	**73** 1
29 Jul 00 ●	2 FACED *1st Avenue / EMI CDEMS 570*	**3** 8
11 Nov 00	BEAUTIFUL INSIDE *1st Avenue / EMI CDEMS 575*	**13** 4

See also ETERNAL

Darlene LOVE *US, female vocalist (5 WEEKS)* pos/wks
19 Dec 92	ALL ALONE ON CHRISTMAS *Arista 7432112476*	**31** 4
1 Jan 94	ALL ALONE ON CHRISTMAS (re-entry) *Arista 7432112476*	**72** 1

Geoff LOVE – See MANUEL and his MUSIC OF THE MOUNTAINS; Laurie LONDON

Helen LOVE
UK, male / female vocal / instrumental group (2 WEEKS) pos/wks
20 Sep 97	DOES YOUR HEART GO BOOM *Che CHE 72CD*	**71** 1
19 Sep 98	LONG LIVE THE UK MUSIC SCENE *Che CHE 82CD*	**65** 1

Monie LOVE *UK, female rapper (51 WEEKS)* pos/wks
4 Feb 89	I CAN DO THIS *Cooltempo COOL 177*	**37** 4
24 Jun 89	GRANDPA'S PARTY *Cooltempo COOL 184*	**16** 9
14 Jul 90	MONIE IN THE MIDDLE *Cooltempo COOL 210*	**46** 3
22 Sep 90	IT'S A SHAME (MY SISTER) *Cooltempo COOL 219* [1]	**12** 8
1 Dec 90	DOWN TO EARTH *Cooltempo COOL 222*	**31** 6
6 Apr 91	RING MY BELL *Cooltempo COOL 224* [2]	**20** 5
25 Jul 92	FULL TERM LOVE *Cooltempo COOL 258*	**34** 4
13 Mar 93	BORN 2 B.R.E.E.D. *Cooltempo CDCOOL 269*	**18** 5
12 Jun 93	IN A WORD OR 2 / THE POWER *Cooltempo CDCOOL 273*	**33** 3
21 Aug 93	NEVER GIVE UP *Cooltempo CDCOOL 276*	**41** 2
22 Apr 00	SLICE OF DA PIE *Relentless RELENT 2CDS*	**29** 2

[1] Monie Love featuring True Image [2] Monie Love vs Adeva

LOVE AFFAIR *UK, male vocal / instrumental group - lead vocal Steve Ellis (56 WEEKS)* pos/wks
3 Jan 68 ★	EVERLASTING LOVE *CBS 3125*	**1** 12
17 Apr 68 ●	RAINBOW VALLEY *CBS 3366*	**5** 13
11 Sep 68 ●	A DAY WITHOUT LOVE *CBS 3674*	**6** 12
19 Feb 69	ONE ROAD *CBS 3994*	**16** 9
16 Jul 69 ●	BRINGING ON BACK THE GOOD TIMES *CBS 4300*	**9** 10

LOVE AND MONEY
UK, male vocal / instrumental group (23 WEEKS) pos/wks
24 May 86	CANDYBAR EXPRESS *Mercury MONEY 1*	**56** 4
25 Apr 87	LOVE AND MONEY *Mercury MONEY 4*	**68** 4
17 Sep 88	HALLELUIAH MAN *Fontana MONEY 5*	**63** 4
14 Jan 89	STRANGE KIND OF LOVE *Fontana MONEY 6*	**45** 5
25 Mar 89	JOCELYN SQUARE *Fontana MONEY 7*	**51** 4
16 Nov 91	WINTER *Fontana MONEY 9*	**52** 2

LOVE BITE *Italy, male / female production / vocal group (1 WEEK)* pos/wks
7 Oct 00	TAKE YOUR TIME *AM:PM CDAMPM134*	**56** 1

LOVE CITY GROOVE *UK, male / female vocal / rap / instrumental group (11 WEEKS)* pos/wks
8 Apr 95 ●	LOVE CITY GROOVE *Planet 3 GXY 2003CD*	**7** 11

LOVE CONNECTION
Italy / Germany, male / female vocal / production group (1 WEEK) pos/wks
2 Dec 00	THE BOMB *Multiply CDMULTY 63*	**53** 1

LOVE DECADE
UK, male / female vocal / instrumental group (14 WEEKS) pos/wks
6 Jul 91	DREAM ON (IS THIS A DREAM) *All Around the World GLOBE 100*	**52** 2
23 Nov 91	SO REAL *All Around the World GLOBE 106*	**14** 7
11 Apr 92	I FEEL YOU *All Around the World GLOBE 107*	**34** 3
6 Feb 93	WHEN THE MORNING COMES *All Around the World CDGLOBE 114*	**69** 1
17 Feb 96	IS THIS A DREAM *All Around the World CDGLOBE 132*	**39** 1

'Is This a Dream' in 1996 is a re-recording

LOVE DECREE *UK, male vocal / instrumental group (4 WEEKS)* pos/wks
16 Sep 89	SOMETHING SO REAL (CHINHEADS THEME) *Ariola 112642*	**61** 4

LOVE / HATE *US, male vocal / instrumental group (4 WEEKS)* pos/wks
30 Nov 91	EVIL TWIN *Columbia 6575967*	**59** 1
4 Apr 92	WASTED IN AMERICA *Columbia 6578897*	**38** 3

LOVE INC *UK, male vocal / production duo (3 WEEKS)* pos/wks
9 Feb 91	LOVE IS THE MESSAGE *Love EVOL 1*	**59** 3

LOVE NELSON – See FIRE ISLAND

LOVE REACTION – See ZODIAC MINDWARP and the LOVE REACTION

LOVE SCULPTURE *UK, instrumental group (14 WEEKS)* pos/wks
27 Nov 68 ●	SABRE DANCE *Parlophone R 5744*	**5** 14

See also Dave EDMUNDS

LOVE SQUAD – See Linda CARR

A LOVE SUPREME *UK, male vocal / instrumental group (2 WEEKS)* pos/wks
17 Apr 99	NIALL QUINN'S DISCO PANTS *A Love Supreme / Cherry Red CDVINNIE 3*	**59** 2

UK No.1 ★   UK Top 10 ●   Still on chart +   UK million seller ◆   UK entry at No.1 ■   US No.1 ▲

LOVE TO INFINITY
UK, male / female vocal / instrumental group (4 WEEKS)   pos/wks

24 Jun 95	KEEP LOVE TOGETHER *Mushroom D 00467*	38	2
18 Nov 95	SOMEDAY *Mushroom D 1143*	75	1
3 Aug 96	PRAY FOR LOVE *Mushroom D 1213*	69	1

LOVE TRIBE *US, male / female vocal / instrumental duo (3 WEEKS)*   pos/wks

| 29 Jun 96 | STAND UP *AM:PM 5816272* | 23 | 3 |

LOVE UNLIMITED *US, female vocal group (19 WEEKS)*   pos/wks

| 17 Jun 72 | WALKIN' IN THE RAIN WITH THE ONE I LOVE *Uni UN 539* | 14 | 10 |
| 25 Jan 75 | IT MAY BE WINTER OUTSIDE (BUT IN MY HEART IT'S SPRING) *20th Century BTC 2149* | 11 | 9 |

LOVE UNLIMITED ORCHESTRA *US, orchestra (10 WEEKS)*   pos/wks

| 2 Feb 74 | ● LOVE'S THEME *Pye International 7N 25635* ▲ | 10 | 10 |

Vikki LOVE – See JUNGLE BROTHERS; NUANCE featuring Vikki LOVE

LOVEBUG STARSKI *US, male rapper (9 WEEKS)*   pos/wks

| 31 May 86 | AMITYVILLE (THE HOUSE ON THE HILL) *Epic A 7182* | 12 | 9 |

LOVEDEEJAY AKEMI – See YOSH presents LOVEDEEJAY AKEMI

LOVEHAPPY
US / UK, male / female vocal / instrumental group (3 WEEKS)   pos/wks

| 18 Feb 95 | MESSAGE OF LOVE *MCA MCSTD 2040* | 37 | 2 |
| 20 Jul 96 | MESSAGE OF LOVE (re-mix) *MCA MCSTD 40052* | 70 | 1 |

Bill LOVELADY *UK, male vocalist (10 WEEKS)*   pos/wks

| 18 Aug 79 | REGGAE FOR IT NOW *Charisma CB 337* | 12 | 10 |

LOVELAND featuring the voice of Rachel McFARLANE
UK, male / female vocal / instrumental group (15 WEEKS)   pos/wks

16 Apr 94	LET THE MUSIC (LIFT YOU UP) *KMS/Eastern Bloc KMSCD 10*	16	4
5 Nov 94	(KEEP ON) SHINING / HOPE (NEVER GIVE UP) *Eastern Bloc BLOCCD 016*	37	2
14 Jan 95	I NEED SOMEBODY *Eastern Bloc BLOCCD 019*	21	3
10 Jun 95	DON'T MAKE ME WAIT *Eastern Bloc BLOC 20CD*	22	3
2 Sep 95	THE WONDER OF LOVE *Eastern Bloc BLOC 22CD*	53	1
11 Nov 95	I NEED SOMEBODY (re-mix) *Eastern Bloc BLOC 23CD*	38	2

All formats of 'Let the Music (Lift You Up)' featured versions by Loveland featuring Rachel McFarlane and also by Darlene Lewis

LOVER SPEAKS *UK, male vocal / instrumental duo (5 WEEKS)*   pos/wks

| 16 Aug 86 | NO MORE 'I LOVE YOU'S' *A & M AM 326* | 58 | 5 |

Michael LOVESMITH *US, male vocalist (1 WEEK)*   pos/wks

| 5 Oct 85 | AIN'T NOTHIN' LIKE IT *Motown ZB 40369* | 75 | 1 |

LOVESTATION
UK, male / female vocal / instrumental group (21 WEEKS)   pos/wks

13 Mar 93	SHINE ON ME *RCA 743211337912* [1]	71	1
13 Nov 93	BEST OF MY LOVE *Fresh FRSHD 1*	73	1
18 Mar 95	LOVE COME RESCUE ME *Fresh FRSHD 22*	42	2
1 Aug 98	TEARDROPS *Fresh FRSHD 65*	14	6
5 Dec 98	SENSUALITY *Fresh FRSHD 71*	16	7
5 Feb 00	TEARDROPS (re-mix) *Fresh FRSHD 79*	24	4

[1] Lovestation featuring Lisa Hunt

Lene LOVICH *US, female vocalist - Lili Premilovich (38 WEEKS)*   pos/wks

17 Feb 79	● LUCKY NUMBER *Stiff BUY 42*	3	11
12 May 79	SAY WHEN *Stiff BUY 46*	19	10
20 Oct 79	BIRD SONG *Stiff BUY 53*	39	7
29 Mar 80	WHAT WILL I DO WITHOUT YOU *Stiff BUY 69*	58	3

| 14 Mar 81 | NEW TOY *Stiff BUY 97* | 53 | 5 |
| 27 Nov 82 | IT'S YOU ONLY YOU (MEIN SCHMERZ) *Stiff BUY 164* | 68 | 2 |

LOVIN' SPOONFUL
US / Canada, male vocal / instrumental group (33 WEEKS)   pos/wks

14 Apr 66	● DAYDREAM *Pye International 7N 25361*	2	13
14 Jul 66	● SUMMER IN THE CITY *Kama Sutra KAS 200* ▲	8	11
5 Jan 67	NASHVILLE CATS *Kama Sutra KAS 204*	26	7
9 Mar 67	DARLING BE HOME SOON *Kama Sutra KAS 207*	44	2

LOVINDEER *Jamaica, male vocalist (3 WEEKS)*   pos/wks

| 27 Sep 86 | MAN SHORTAGE *TSOJ TS 1* | 69 | 3 |

Gary LOW *Italy, male vocalist (3 WEEKS)*   pos/wks

| 8 Oct 83 | I WANT YOU *Savoir Faire FAIS 004* | 52 | 3 |

Patti LOW – See BUG KANN and the PLASTIC JAM

Jim LOWE and the HIGH FIVES
US, male vocal / instrumental group (9 WEEKS)   pos/wks

| 26 Oct 56 | ● THE GREEN DOOR *London HLD 8317* | 8 | 9 |

Nick LOWE *UK, male vocalist (27 WEEKS)*   pos/wks

11 Mar 78	● I LOVE THE SOUND OF BREAKING GLASS *Radar ADA 1*	7	8
9 Jun 79	CRACKIN' UP *Radar ADA 34*	34	5
25 Aug 79	CRUEL TO BE KIND *Radar ADA 43*	12	11
26 May 84	HALF A BOY HALF A MAN *F. Beat XX 34*	53	3

LOWGOLD *UK, male vocal / instrumental group (1 WEEK)*   pos/wks

| 30 Sep 00 | BEAUTY DIES YOUNG *Nude NUD 52CD* | 67 | 1 |

LOWRELL *US, male vocalist (9 WEEKS)*   pos/wks

| 24 Nov 79 | MELLOW MELLOW RIGHT ON *AVI AVIS 108* | 37 | 9 |

LRS – See D MOB

L7 *US, female vocal / instrumental group (18 WEEKS)*   pos/wks

4 Apr 92	PRETEND WE'RE DEAD *Slash LASH 34*	21	7
30 May 92	EVERGLADE *Slash LASH 36*	27	3
12 Sep 92	MONSTER *Slash LASH 38*	33	3
28 Nov 92	PRETEND WE'RE DEAD (re-issue) *Slash LASH 42*	50	3
9 Jul 94	ANDRES *Slash LASCD 48*	34	2

LSG *Germany, male DJ / producer - Oliver Lieb (1 WEEK)*   pos/wks

| 10 May 97 | NETHERWORLD *Hooj Choons HOOJCD 52* | 63 | 1 |

LTD *US, male vocal / instrumental group (3 WEEKS)*   pos/wks

| 9 Sep 78 | HOLDING ON (WHEN LOVE IS GONE) *A & M AMS 7378* | 70 | 3 |

LUCAS *Denmark, male vocalist (4 WEEKS)*   pos/wks

| 6 Aug 94 | LUCAS WITH THE LID OFF *WEA YZ 832CD* | 37 | 4 |

Carrie LUCAS *US, female vocalist (6 WEEKS)*   pos/wks

| 16 Jun 79 | DANCE WITH YOU *Solar FB 1482* | 40 | 6 |

Tammy LUCAS – See Teddy RILEY

LUCIANA *UK, female vocalist (5 WEEKS)*   pos/wks

23 Apr 94	GET IT UP FOR LOVE *Chrysalis CDCHS 5008*	55	2
6 Aug 94	IF YOU WANT *Chrysalis CDCHS 5009*	47	2
5 Nov 94	WHAT GOES AROUND / ONE MORE RIVER *Chrysalis CDCHS 5015*	67	1

LUCID UK, male / female vocal / instrumental group (15 WEEKS)

		pos	wks
8 Aug 98 ●	I CAN'T HELP MYSELF ffrr FCD 339	7	8
27 Feb 99	CRAZY ffrr / Delirious / Indirect FCD 355	14	5
16 Oct 99	STAY WITH ME TILL DAWN ffrr FCD 368	25	2

LUCKY MONKEYS UK, male instrumental group (1 WEEK)

		pos	wks
9 Nov 96	BJANGO Hi-Life 5757132	50	1

See also FLUKE

LUCY PEARL US, male / female vocal trio (6 WEEKS)

		pos	wks
29 Jul 00	DANCE TONIGHT Virgin VSCDT 1775	36	2
25 Nov 00	DON'T MESS WITH MY MAN Virgin VSCDT 1778	20	4

Baz LUHRMANN Australia, male producer (16 WEEKS)

		pos	wks
12 Jun 99 ★	EVERYBODY'S FREE (TO WEAR SUNSCREEN) EMI CDBAZ 001 ■	1	16

Uncredited vocals by actor Lee Perry

Robin LUKE US, male vocalist (6 WEEKS)

		pos	wks
17 Oct 58	SUSIE DARLIN' London HLD 8676	24	3
21 Nov 58	SUSIE DARLIN' (re-entry) London HLD 8676	23	1
5 Dec 58	SUSIE DARLIN' (2nd re-entry) London HLD 8676	23	2

LUKK featuring Felicia COLLINS
US, male / female vocal / instrumental group (1 WEEK)

		pos	wks
28 Sep 85	ON THE ONE Important TAN 6	72	1

LULU ⟨110⟩ Top 500 One of Scotland's best-known female vocalists, b. Marie Lawrie, 3 Nov 1948, Strathclyde. She scored her first hit aged 15, had a US chart-topper ('To Sir With Love') aged 18, won the Eurovision Song Contest aged 20, and finally reached No.1 aged 44 (175 WEEKS)

		pos	wks
14 May 64 ●	SHOUT Decca F 11884 [1]	7	13
12 Nov 64	HERE COMES THE NIGHT Decca F 12017	50	1
17 Jun 65 ●	LEAVE A LITTLE LOVE Decca F 12169	8	11
2 Sep 65	TRY TO UNDERSTAND Decca F 12214	25	8
13 Apr 67 ●	THE BOAT THAT I ROW Columbia DB 8169	6	11
29 Jun 67	LET'S PRETEND Columbia DB 8221	11	11
8 Nov 67	LOVE LOVES TO LOVE LOVE Columbia DB 8295	32	6
28 Feb 68 ●	ME THE PEACEFUL HEART Columbia DB 8358	9	9
5 Jun 68	BOY Columbia DB 8425	15	7
6 Nov 68 ●	I'M A TIGER Columbia DB 8500	9	13
12 Mar 69 ●	BOOM BANG-A-BANG Columbia DB 8550	2	13
22 Nov 69	OH ME OH MY (I'M A FOOL FOR YOU BABY) Atco 226008	47	2
26 Jan 74 ●	THE MAN WHO SOLD THE WORLD Polydor 2001 490	3	9
19 Apr 75	TAKE YOUR MAMA FOR A RIDE Chelsea 2005 022	37	4
12 Dec 81	I COULD NEVER MISS YOU (MORE THAN I DO) Alfa ALFA 1700	62	4
16 Jan 82	I COULD NEVER MISS YOU (MORE THAN I DO) (re-entry) Alfa ALFA 1700	63	1
19 Jul 86 ●	SHOUT Jive LULU1 / Decca SHOUT 1	8	11
30 Jan 93	INDEPENDENCE Dome CDDOME 1001	11	5
3 Apr 93	I'M BACK FOR MORE Dome CDDOME 1002 [2]	27	5
4 Sep 93	LET ME WAKE UP IN YOUR ARMS Dome CDDOME 1005	51	2
9 Oct 93 ★	RELIGHT MY FIRE RCA 74321167722 [3] ■	1	14
27 Nov 93	HOW 'BOUT US Dome CDDOME 1007	46	3
27 Aug 94	GOODBYE BABY AND AMEN Dome CDDOME 1011	40	2
26 Nov 94	EVERY WOMAN KNOWS Dome CDDOME 1013	44	2
29 May 99	HURT ME SO BAD Rocket / Mercury 5726132	42	2
8 Jan 00	BETTER GET READY Mercury 5625852	59	1
18 Mar 00	WHERE THE POOR BOYS DANCE Mercury 1568452	24	5

[1] Lulu and the Luvvers [2] Lulu and Bobby Womack [3] Take That featuring Lulu

The newly recorded 'Shout' entered the chart on 19 Jul 1986, and the next week the original Decca version by Lulu and the Luvvers also charted. For all subsequent weeks Gallup amalgamated both versions under one entry and we have added an extra week on chart for the 'double week' to take account of this

Bob LUMAN US, male vocalist (21 WEEKS)

		pos	wks
8 Sep 60 ●	LET'S THINK ABOUT LIVING Warner Bros. WB 18	6	18
15 Dec 60	WHY WHY BYE BYE Warner Bros. WB 28	46	1
4 May 61	THE GREAT SNOWMAN Warner Bros. WB 37	49	2

LUMINAIRE – See Jonathan PETERS presents LUMINAIRE

LUNIZ US, male rap duo - Jerrold 'Yukmouth' Ellis Jr and Garrick 'Knumbskull' Husbands (18 WEEKS)

		pos	wks
17 Feb 96 ●	I GOT 5 ON IT Virgin America VUSCD 101	3	13
11 May 96	PLAYA HATA Virgin America VUSCD 103	20	3
31 Oct 98	I GOT 5 ON IT (re-mix) Virgin VCRD 41	28	2

LUPINE HOWL UK, male vocal / instrumental group (1 WEEK)

		pos	wks
22 Jan 00	VAPORIZER Vinyl Hiss VHISSCD 001	68	1

LURKERS UK, male vocal / instrumental group (11 WEEKS)

		pos	wks
3 Jun 78	AIN'T GOT A CLUE Beggars Banquet BEG 6	45	3
5 Aug 78	I DON'T NEED TO TELL HER Beggars Banquet BEG 9	49	4
3 Feb 79	JUST THIRTEEN Beggars Banquet BEG 14	66	2
9 Jun 79	OUT IN THE DARK / CYANIDE Beggars Banquet BEG 19	72	1
17 Nov 79	NEW GUITAR IN TOWN Beggars Banquet BEG 28	72	1

LUSCIOUS JACKSON US, female vocal / instrumental group (5 WEEKS)

		pos	wks
18 Mar 95	DEEP SHAG / CITYSONG Capitol CDCL 739	69	1
21 Oct 95	HERE Capitol CDCL 758	59	1
12 Apr 97	NAKED EYE Capitol CDCL 786	25	2
3 Jul 99	LADYFINGERS Grand Royal / Parlophone CDCL 813	43	1

LUSH UK, female / male vocal / instrumental group (19 WEEKS)

		pos	wks
10 Mar 90	MAD LOVE (EP) 4AD BAD 003	55	1
27 Oct 90	SWEETNESS AND LIGHT 4AD BAD 0013	47	2
19 Oct 91	NOTHING NATURAL 4AD AD 1016	43	2
11 Jan 92	FOR LOVE (EP) 4AD BAD 2001	35	2
11 Jun 94	DESIRE LINES 4AD BAD 4010CD	60	1
11 Jun 94	HYPOCRITE 4AD BAD 4008CD	52	2
20 Jan 96	SINGLE GIRL 4AD BAD 6001CD	21	3
9 Mar 96	LADYKILLERS 4AD BAD 6002CD	22	3
27 Jul 96	500 (SHAKE BABY SHAKE) 4AD BAD 6009CD	21	3

Tracks on Mad Love (EP): De-Luxe / Leaves Me Cold / Downer / Thoughtforms. Tracks on For Love (EP): For Love / Starlust / Outdoor Miner / Astronaut

LUSTRAL UK, male DJ / production duo - Ricky Simmons and Steve Jones (3 WEEKS)

		pos	wks
18 Oct 97	EVERYTIME Hooj Choons HOOJCD 55	60	1
4 Dec 99	EVERYTIME (re-mix) Hooj Choons HOOJ 83CD	30	2

LUVVERS – See LULU

LV US, male vocalist - Larry Sanders (25 WEEKS)

		pos	wks
28 Oct 95 ★	GANGSTA'S PARADISE Tommy Boy MCSTD 2104 [1] ◆ ■ ▲	1	20
23 Dec 95	THROW YOUR HANDS UP / GANGSTA'S PARADISE Tommy Boy TBCD 699	24	4
4 May 96	I AM LV Tommy Boy TBCD 7724	64	1

[1] Coolio featuring LV

The version of 'Gangsta's Paradise' coupled with 'Throw Your Hands Up' is a re-recorded version without Coolio's vocals

Annabella LWIN Burma, female vocalist (1 WEEK)

		pos	wks
28 Jan 95	DO WHAT YOU DO Sony S2 6611235	61	1

LWS Italy, male instrumental group (1 WEEK)

		pos	wks
29 Oct 94	GOSP Transworld TRANNY 4CD	65	1

UK No.1 ★   UK Top 10 ●   Still on chart +   UK million seller ◆   UK entry at No.1 ■   US No.1 ▲

John LYDON UK, male vocalist (1 WEEK)

			pos/wks	
2 Aug 97	SUN *Virgin VUSCD 122*		42	1

See also PUBLIC IMAGE LTD; SEX PISTOLS; LEFTFIELD

Frankie LYMON and the TEENAGERS
US, male vocal group (38 WEEKS)

			pos/wks	
29 Jun 56	★ WHY DO FOOLS FALL IN LOVE *Columbia DB 3772* [1]		1	16
29 Mar 57	I'M NOT A JUVENILE DELINQUENT *Columbia DB 3878*		12	7
12 Apr 57	● BABY BABY *Columbia DB 3878*		4	12
20 Sep 57	GOODY GOODY *Columbia DB 3983*		24	3

[1] Teenagers featuring Frankie Lymon

Des LYNAM featuring WIMBLEDON CHORAL SOCIETY
UK, male vocalist / TV presenter with Choir (3 WEEKS)

			pos/wks	
12 Dec 98	IF - READ TO FAURE'S 'PAVANE' *BBC Worldwide WMSS 60062*		45	3

Curtis LYNCH Jr. featuring Kele LE ROC & RED RAT UK, male
producer, UK female vocalist and Jamaica male vocalist (1 WEEK)

			pos/wks	
30 Sep 00	THINKING OF YOU *Telstar CDSTAS3136*		70	1

Kenny LYNCH UK, male vocalist (59 WEEKS)

			pos/wks	
30 Jun 60	MOUNTAIN OF LOVE *HMV POP 751*		33	3
13 Sep 62	PUFF *HMV POP 1057*		33	5
25 Oct 62	PUFF (re-entry) *HMV POP 1057*		46	1
6 Dec 62	● UP ON THE ROOF *HMV POP 1090*		10	12
20 Jun 63	● YOU CAN NEVER STOP ME LOVING YOU *HMV POP 1165*		10	14
16 Apr 64	STAND BY ME *HMV POP 1280*		39	7
27 Aug 64	WHAT AM I TO YOU *HMV POP 1321*		37	4
1 Oct 64	WHAT AM I TO YOU (re-entry) *HMV POP 1321*		44	2
17 Jun 65	I'LL STAY BY YOU *HMV POP 1430*		29	7
20 Aug 83	HALF THE DAY'S GONE AND WE HAVEN'T EARNT A PENNY *Satril SAT 510*		50	4

Cheryl LYNN US, female vocalist (2 WEEKS)

			pos/wks	
8 Sep 84	ENCORE *Streetwave KHAN 23*		68	2

Patti LYNN UK, female vocalist (5 WEEKS)

			pos/wks	
10 May 62	JOHNNY ANGEL *Fontana H 391*		37	5

Tami LYNN US, female vocalist (20 WEEKS)

			pos/wks	
22 May 71	● I'M GONNA RUN AWAY FROM YOU *Mojo 2092 001*		4	14
3 May 75	I'M GONNA RUN AWAY FROM YOU (re-issue) *Contempo Raries CS 9026*		36	6

Vera LYNN UK, female vocalist - Vera Walsh (46 WEEKS)

			pos/wks	
14 Nov 52	● AUF WIEDERSEHEN SWEETHEART *Decca F 9927* ▲		10	1
14 Nov 52	● FORGET-ME-NOT *Decca F 9985*		7	1
14 Nov 52	● THE HOMING WALTZ *Decca F 9959*		9	3
28 Nov 52	● FORGET-ME-NOT (re-entry) *Decca F 9985*		5	5
5 Jun 53	THE WINDSOR WALTZ *Decca F 10092*		11	1
15 Oct 54	★ MY SON, MY SON *Decca F 10372* [1]		1	14
8 Jun 56	WHO ARE WE *Decca F 10715*		30	1
26 Oct 56	A HOUSE WITH LOVE IN IT *Decca F 10799*		17	13
15 Mar 57	THE FAITHFUL HUSSAR (DON'T CRY MY LOVE) *Decca F 10846*		29	2
21 Jun 57	TRAVELLIN' HOME *Decca F 10903*		20	5

[1] Vera Lynn with Frank Weir, his saxophone, his Orchestra and Chorus

Jeff LYNNE UK, male vocalist (4 WEEKS)

			pos/wks	
30 Jun 90	EVERY LITTLE THING *Reprise W 9799*		59	4

See also ELECTRIC LIGHT ORCHESTRA

Shelby LYNNE US, female vocalist (1 WEEK)

			pos/wks	
29 Apr 00	LEAVIN' *Mercury 5627372*		73	1

Philip LYNOTT Ireland, male vocalist (36 WEEKS)

			pos/wks	
5 Apr 80	DEAR MISS LONELY HEARTS *Vertigo SOLO 1*		32	6
21 Jun 80	KING'S CALL *Vertigo SOLO 2*		35	6
21 Mar 81	YELLOW PEARL *Vertigo SOLO 3*		56	3
26 Dec 81	YELLOW PEARL (re-entry) *Vertigo SOLO 3*		14	9
18 May 85	● OUT IN THE FIELDS *10 TEN 49* [1]		5	10
24 Jan 87	KING'S CALL (re-mix) *Vertigo LYN 1*		68	2

[1] Gary Moore and Phil Lynott

See also THIN LIZZY

LYNYRD SKYNYRD
US, male vocal / instrumental group (21 WEEKS)

			pos/wks	
11 Sep 76	SWEET HOME ALABAMA / DOUBLE TROUBLE *MCA 251*		31	4
22 Dec 79	SWEET HOME ALABAMA / DOUBLE TROUBLE (re-entry) *MCA 251*		43	8
19 Jun 82	SWEET HOME ALABAMA / DOUBLE TROUBLE (2nd re-entry) *MCA 251*		21	9

Sweet Home Alabama / Double Trouble was the chart listing for what was also alternatively listed as the Freebird EP for the two re-entries

Barbara LYON US, female vocalist (12 WEEKS)

			pos/wks	
24 Jun 55	STOWAWAY *Columbia DB 3619*		12	8
21 Dec 56	LETTER TO A SOLDIER *Columbia DB 3865*		27	4

LYTE FUNKIE ONES US, male vocal / rap group (17 WEEKS)

			pos/wks	
22 May 99	CAN'T HAVE YOU *Logic 74321649152*		54	1
18 Sep 99	SUMMER GIRLS *Logic 74321701152*		16	7
5 Feb 00	● GIRL ON TV *Logic 74321717582*		6	9

Humphrey LYTTELTON BAND
UK, male jazz band, Humphrey Lyttelton - trumpet (6 WEEKS)

			pos/wks	
13 Jul 56	BAD PENNY BLUES *Parlophone R 4184*		19	6

M

M UK, male vocalist / multi-instrumentalist - Robin Scott (39 WEEKS)

			pos/wks	
7 Apr 79	● POP MUZIK *MCA 413* ▲		2	14
8 Dec 79	MOONLIGHT AND MUZAK *MCA 541*		33	9
15 Mar 80	THAT'S THE WAY THE MONEY GOES *MCA 570*		45	5
22 Nov 80	OFFICIAL SECRETS *MCA 650*		64	2
10 Jun 89	POP MUZIK (re-mix) *Freestyle FRS 1*		15	9

M and O BAND UK, male vocal / instrumental group (6 WEEKS)

			pos/wks	
28 Feb 76	LET'S DO THE LATIN HUSTLE *Creole CR 120*		16	6

M-BEAT UK, male producer - Marlon Hart (24 WEEKS)

			pos/wks	
18 Jun 94	INCREDIBLE *Renk RENK 42CD* [1]		39	3
10 Sep 94	● INCREDIBLE (re-mix) *Renk CDRENK 44* [1]		8	9
17 Dec 94	SWEET LOVE *Renk CDRENK 49* [2]		18	7
1 Jun 96	DO U KNOW WHERE YOU'RE COMING FROM *Renk CDRENK 63* [3]		12	5

[1] M-Beat featuring General Levy [2] M-Beat featuring Nazlyn [3] M-Beat featuring Jamiroquai

Bobby M featuring Jean CARN
US, male / female vocal / instrumental duo (3 WEEKS)

			pos/wks	
29 Jan 83	LET'S STAY TOGETHER *Gordy TMG 1288*		53	3

M DUBS featuring LADY SAW
UK / Jamaica, male producer / female vocalist (1 WEEK) pos/wks
16 Dec 00	**BUMP N GRIND (I AM FEELING HOT TONIGHT)**		
	Telstar CDSTAS 3129 ....**59**	1

M + M
Canada, male / female vocal duo (4 WEEKS) pos/wks
28 Jul 84	**BLACK STATIONS WHITE STATIONS** *RCA 426*..........................**46**	4

See also MARTHA and the MUFFINS

M PEOPLE (179 | Top 500)
Clubland favourites turned pop soul sophisticates: Heather Small (v), backed by Paul Heard and Mike Pickering (both k/prog). In 1994 this Manchester act was voted Best British Dance Act at the Brits and won the Mercury Music Prize for their LP Elegant Slumming (137 WEEKS) pos/wks
26 Oct 91	**HOW CAN I LOVE YOU MORE** *Deconstruction PB 44855*..........**29**	9
7 Mar 92	**COLOUR MY LIFE** *Deconstruction PB 45241* **35**	4
18 Apr 92	**SOMEDAY** *Deconstruction PB 45369* [1] **38**	3
10 Oct 92	**EXCITED** *Deconstruction 74321116337* **29**	5
6 Feb 93 ●	**HOW CAN I LOVE YOU MORE (re-mix)**	
	Deconstruction 74321130232 ....**8**	8
26 Jun 93 ●	**ONE NIGHT IN HEAVEN** *Deconstruction 74321151852* **6**	11
25 Sep 93 ●	**MOVING ON UP** *Deconstruction 74321166162* **2**	11
4 Dec 93 ●	**DON'T LOOK ANY FURTHER** *Deconstruction 74321177112* **9**	10
12 Mar 94 ●	**RENAISSANCE** *Deconstruction 74321194132*....................**5**	7
17 Sep 94	**ELEGANTLY AMERICAN: ONE NIGHT IN HEAVEN / MOVING**	
	ON UP (EP) (re-mixes) *Deconstruction 74321231882*......**31**	2
19 Nov 94 ●	**SIGHT FOR SORE EYES** *Deconstruction 74321245472*..........**6**	9
4 Feb 95 ●	**OPEN YOUR HEART** *Deconstruction 74321261532*.............**9**	7
24 Jun 95 ●	**SEARCH FOR THE HERO** *Deconstruction 74321287962* **9**	7
14 Oct 95	**LOVE RENDEZVOUS** *Deconstruction 74321319282* **32**	4
25 Nov 95	**ITCHYCOO PARK** *Deconstruction 74321330732* **11**	8
4 Oct 97 ●	**JUST FOR YOU** *BMG 74321523002*............................**8**	7
6 Dec 97	**FANTASY ISLAND** *BMG 74321542932* **33**	8
28 Feb 98	**FANTASY ISLAND (re-entry)** *BMG 74321542932*..............**69**	1
28 Mar 98 ●	**ANGEL STREET** *M People 74321564182* **8**	6
7 Nov 98	**TESTIFY** *M People 74321621742*..............................**12**	6
13 Feb 99	**DREAMING** *M People 74321645352*...........................**13**	4

[1] M People with Heather Small

M3
UK, male / female production / vocal trio (2 WEEKS) pos/wks
30 Oct 99	**BAILAMOS** *Inferno CDFERN 21* **40**	2

M2M
Norway, female vocal / instrumental duo (6 WEEKS) pos/wks
1 Apr 00	**DON'T SAY YOU LOVE ME** *Atlantic AT 0081CD*..............**16**	6

Timo MAAS
Germany, male DJ / producer (3 WEEKS) pos/wks
1 Apr 00	**DER SCHIEBER** *48k / Perfecto SPECT 07CDS* **50**	1
30 Sep 00	**UBIK** *Perfecto PERF 10CDS* [1] **33**	2

[1] Timo Mass featuring Martin Bettinghaus

MAC BAND featuring the McCAMPBELL BROTHERS
US, male vocal group (17 WEEKS) pos/wks
18 Jun 88 ●	**ROSES ARE RED** *MCA MCA 1264*...............................**8**	13
10 Sep 88	**STALEMATE** *MCA MCA 1271* **40**	4

'Stalemate' credits the McCampbell Brothers on the sleeve only, not on the label

Pete MAC Jr
US, male vocalist (4 WEEKS) pos/wks
15 Oct 77	**THE WATER MARGIN** *BBC RESL 50* **37**	4

This is the Japanese version of the song which shared chart credit with the English language version by Godiego

See also GODIEGO

Keith MAC PROJECT
UK, male / female vocal / instrumental group (1 WEEK) pos/wks
25 Jun 94	**DE DAH DAH (SPICE OF LIFE)** *Public Demand PPDCD 3* **66**	1

Scott MAC – See SIGNUM

David McALMONT
UK, male vocalist (17 WEEKS) pos/wks
27 May 95 ●	**YES** *Hut HUTCD 53* [1] **8**	8
4 Nov 95	**YOU DO** *Hut HUTDG 57* [1] **17**	4
27 Apr 96	**HYMN** *Blanco Y Negro NEG 87CD* [2] **65**	1
9 Aug 97	**LOOK AT YOURSELF** *Hut HUTCD 87* **40**	2
22 Nov 97	**DIAMONDS ARE FOREVER** *East West EW 141CD* [3] **39**	2

[1] McAlmont and Butler [2] Ultramarine featuring David McAlmont [3] David McAlmont / David Arnold

Neil MacARTHUR
UK, male vocalist (5 WEEKS) pos/wks
5 Feb 69	**SHE'S NOT THERE** *Deram DM 225* **34**	5

Neil MacArthur is Colin Blunstone under a pseudonym

David MacBETH
UK, male vocalist (4 WEEKS) pos/wks
30 Oct 59	**MR BLUE** *Pye 7N 15231* **18**	4

Nicko McBRAIN
UK, male vocalist / instrumentalist - drums (1 WEEK) pos/wks
13 Jul 91	**RHYTHM OF THE BEAST** *EMI NICK 01*.........................**72**	1

Frankie McBRIDE
Ireland, male vocalist (15 WEEKS) pos/wks
9 Aug 67	**FIVE LITTLE FINGERS** *Emerald MD 1081* **19**	15

Dan McCAFFERTY
UK, male vocalist (3 WEEKS) pos/wks
13 Sep 75	**OUT OF TIME** *Mountain TOP 1* **41**	3

CW McCALL
US, male vocalist - William Fries (10 WEEKS) pos/wks
14 Feb 76 ●	**CONVOY** *MGM 2006 560* ▲ **2**	10

David McCALLUM
UK, male actor / vocalist (4 WEEKS) pos/wks
14 Apr 66	**COMMUNICATION** *Capitol CL 15439* **32**	4

McCAMPBELL BROTHERS – See MAC BAND featuring the McCAMPBELL BROTHERS

Linda McCARTNEY
US, female vocalist (7 WEEKS) pos/wks
28 Aug 71	**BACK SEAT OF MY CAR** *Apple R 5914* [1] **39**	5
21 Nov 98	**WIDE PRAIRIE** *Parlophone CDR 6510* **74**	1
6 Feb 99	**THE LIGHT COMES FROM WITHIN** *Parlophone CDR 6513* **56**	1

[1] Paul and Linda McCartney

See also Paul McCARTNEY

Paul McCARTNEY (15 | Top 500)
Pop's most successful singer / songwriter, b. 18 Jun 1942, Liverpool, UK. The Guinness Book of World Records presented the ex-Beatle with a unique Rhodium record to honour outstanding sales achievements. He also received a Lifetime Achievement Grammy (1990), a knighthood (1997) and has reportedly amassed a personal fortune of £500m (408 WEEKS) pos/wks
22 Feb 71 ●	**ANOTHER DAY** *Apple R 5889* **2**	12
28 Aug 71	**BACK SEAT OF MY CAR** *Apple R 5914* [1] **39**	5
26 Feb 72	**GIVE IRELAND BACK TO THE IRISH** *Apple R 5936* [2] **16**	8
27 May 72 ●	**MARY HAD A LITTLE LAMB** *Apple R 5949* [2] **9**	11
9 Dec 72 ●	**HI HI HI / C MOON** *Apple R 5973* [2] **5**	13
7 Apr 73 ●	**MY LOVE** *Apple R 5985* [3] ▲ **9**	11
9 Jun 73 ●	**LIVE AND LET DIE** *Apple R 5987* [2] **9**	13
15 Sep 73	**LIVE AND LET DIE (re-entry)** *Apple R 5987* [2] **49**	1
3 Nov 73	**HELEN WHEELS** *Apple R 5993* [3] **12**	12
2 Mar 74	**JET** *Apple R 5996* [3] **7**	9
6 Jul 74 ●	**BAND ON THE RUN** *Apple R 5997* [3] ▲ **3**	11
9 Nov 74	**JUNIOR'S FARM** *Apple R 5999* [3] **16**	10
31 May 75 ●	**LISTEN TO WHAT THE MAN SAID** *Capitol R 6006* [2] ▲...........**6**	8
18 Oct 75	**LETTING GO** *Capitol R 6008* [2] **41**	3
15 May 76 ●	**SILLY LOVE SONGS** *Parlophone R 6014* [2] ▲ **2**	11
7 Aug 76 ●	**LET 'EM IN** *Parlophone R 6015* [2] **2**	10
19 Feb 77	**MAYBE I'M AMAZED** *Parlophone R 6017* [2] **28**	5
19 Nov 77 ★	**MULL OF KINTYRE / GIRLS' SCHOOL** *Capitol R 6018* [2] ◆ **1**	17
1 Apr 78 ●	**WITH A LITTLE LUCK** *Parlophone R 6019* [2] ▲ **5**	9
1 Jul 78	**I'VE HAD ENOUGH** *Parlophone R 6020* [2] **42**	7

9 Sep 78		LONDON TOWN *Parlophone R 6021* [2]	60	4
7 Apr 79	●	GOODNIGHT TONIGHT *Parlophone R 6023* [2]	5	10
16 Jun 79		OLD SIAM SIR *MPL R 6026* [2]	35	6
1 Sep 79		GETTING CLOSER / BABY'S REQUEST *R 6027* [2]	60	3
1 Dec 79		WONDERFUL CHRISTMAS TIME *Parlophone R 6029*	6	8
19 Apr 80	●	COMING UP *Parlophone R 6035* ▲	2	9
21 Jun 80	●	WATERFALLS *Parlophone R 6037*	9	8
10 Apr 82	★	EBONY AND IVORY *Parlophone 6054* [4] ▲	1	10
3 Jul 82		TAKE IT AWAY *Parlophone R 6056*	15	10
9 Oct 82		TUG OF WAR *Parlophone R 6057*	53	3
6 Nov 82	●	THE GIRL IS MINE *Epic EPC A 2729* [5]	8	9
15 Jan 83		THE GIRL IS MINE (re-entry) *Epic EPC A 2729* [5]	75	1
15 Oct 83	●	SAY SAY SAY *Parlophone R 6062* [6] ▲	2	15
17 Dec 83	★	PIPES OF PEACE *Parlophone R 6064*	1	12
6 Oct 84	●	NO MORE LONELY NIGHTS (BALLAD) *Parlophone R 6080*	2	15
24 Nov 84	●	WE ALL STAND TOGETHER *Parlophone R 6086* [7]	3	13
30 Nov 85		SPIES LIKE US *Parlophone R 6118*	13	10
21 Dec 85		WE ALL STAND TOGETHER (re-entry) *Parlophone R 6086* [7]	32	5
26 Jul 86		PRESS *Parlophone R 6133*	25	8
13 Dec 86		ONLY LOVE REMAINS *Parlophone R 6148*	34	5
28 Nov 87	●	ONCE UPON A LONG AGO *Parlophone R 6170*	10	7
20 May 89	★	FERRY 'CROSS THE MERSEY *PWL PWL 41* [8] ■ ▲	1	7
20 May 89		MY BRAVE FACE *Parlophone R 6213*	18	5
29 Jul 89		THIS ONE *Parlophone R 6223*	18	6
25 Nov 89		FIGURE OF EIGHT *Parlophone R 6235*	42	3
17 Feb 90		PUT IT THERE *Parlophone R 6246*	32	2
20 Oct 90		BIRTHDAY *Parlophone R 6271*	29	3
8 Dec 90		ALL MY TRIALS *Parlophone CDR 6278*	35	5
9 Jan 93		HOPE OF DELIVERANCE *Parlophone CDR 6330*	18	6
6 Mar 93		C'MON PEOPLE *Parlophone CDRS 6338*	41	3
10 May 97		YOUNG BOY *Parlophone CDRS 6462*	19	3
19 Jul 97		THE WORLD TONIGHT *Parlophone CDR 6472*	23	2
27 Dec 97		BEAUTIFUL NIGHT *Parlophone CDR 6489*	25	4
6 Nov 99		NO OTHER BABY / BROWN EYED HANDSOME MAN *Parlophone CDR 6527*	42	2

[1] Paul and Linda McCartney [2] Wings [3] Paul McCartney and Wings [4] Paul McCartney with Stevie Wonder [5] Michael Jackson and Paul McCartney [6] Paul McCartney and Michael Jackson [7] Paul McCartney and the Frog Chorus [8] Christians, Holly Johnson, Paul McCartney, Gerry Marsden and Stock Aitken Waterman

R 6027 credits no label at all, although the number is a Parlophone one

See also BEATLES

Kirsty MacCOLL *UK, female vocalist (65 WEEKS)* pos/wks

13 Jun 81		THERE'S A GUY WORKS DOWN THE CHIPSHOP SWEARS HE'S ELVIS *Polydor POSP 250*	14	9
19 Jan 85	●	A NEW ENGLAND *Stiff BUY 216*	7	10
15 Nov 86		GREETINGS TO THE NEW BRUNETTE *Go! Discs GOD 15* [1]	58	2
5 Dec 87	●	FAIRYTALE OF NEW YORK *Pogue Mahone NY 7* [2]	2	9
8 Apr 89		FREE WORLD *Virgin KMA 1*	43	6
1 Jul 89		DAYS *Virgin KMA 2*	12	9
25 May 91		WALKING DOWN MADISON *Virgin VS 1348*	23	7
17 Aug 91		MY AFFAIR *Virgin VS 1354*	56	2
14 Dec 91		FAIRYTALE OF NEW YORK (re-issue) *PM YZ 628* [2]	36	5
4 Mar 95		CAROLINE *Virgin VSCDX 1517*	58	2
24 Jun 95		PERFECT DAY *Virgin VSCDT 1552* [3]	75	1
29 Jul 95		DAYS (re-issue) *Virgin VSCDT 1558*	42	3

[1] Billy Bragg with Johnny Marr and Kirsty MacColl [2] Pogues featuring Kirsty MacColl [3] Kirsty MacColl and Evan Dando

Marilyn McCOO and Billy DAVIS Jr
US, female / male vocal duo (9 WEEKS) pos/wks

19 Mar 77	●	YOU DON'T HAVE TO BE A STAR (TO BE IN MY SHOW) *ABC 4147* ▲	7	9

Van McCOY *US, orchestra (36 WEEKS)* pos/wks

31 May 75	●	THE HUSTLE *Avco 6105 038* [1] ▲	3	12
1 Nov 75		CHANGE WITH THE TIMES *Avco 6105 042*	36	4
12 Feb 77		SOUL CHA CHA *H & L 6105 065*	34	6
9 Apr 77	●	THE SHUFFLE *H & L 6105 076*	4	14

[1] Van McCoy with the Soul City Symphony

McCOYS *US, male vocal / instrumental group (18 WEEKS)* pos/wks

2 Sep 65	●	HANG ON SLOOPY *Immediate IM 001* ▲	5	14
16 Dec 65		FEVER *Immediate IM 021*	44	4

George McCRAE *US, male vocalist (62 WEEKS)* pos/wks

29 Jun 74	★	ROCK YOUR BABY *Jayboy BOY 85* ▲	1	14
5 Oct 74	●	I CAN'T LEAVE YOU ALONE *Jayboy BOY 90*	9	9
14 Dec 74		YOU CAN HAVE IT ALL *Jayboy BOY 92*	23	9
22 Mar 75		SING A HAPPY SONG *Jayboy BOY 95*	38	4
19 Jul 75		IT'S BEEN SO LONG *Jayboy BOY 100*	4	11
18 Oct 75		I AIN'T LYIN' *Jayboy BOY 105*	12	7
24 Jan 76		HONEY I *Jayboy BOY 107*	33	4
25 Feb 84		ONE STEP CLOSER (TO LOVE) *President PT 522*	57	4

Gwen McCRAE *US, female vocalist (5 WEEKS)* pos/wks

30 Apr 88		ALL THIS LOVE THAT I'M GIVING *Flame MELT 7*	63	2
13 Feb 93		ALL THIS LOVE I'M GIVING (re-recording) *KTDA CDKTDA 2* [1]	36	3

[1] Music and Mystery featuring Gwen McCrae

McCRARYS *US, male / female vocal group (4 WEEKS)* pos/wks

31 Jul 82		LOVE ON A SUMMER NIGHT *Capitol CL 251*	52	4

Mindy McCREADY *US, female vocalist (3 WEEKS)* pos/wks

1 Aug 98		OH ROMEO *BNA 74321597242*	41	3

Ian McCULLOCH *UK, male vocalist (14 WEEKS)* pos/wks

15 Dec 84		SEPTEMBER SONG *Korova KOW 40*	51	5
2 Sep 89		PROUD TO FALL *WEA YZ 417*	51	4
12 May 90		CANDLELAND (THE SECOND COMING) *East West YZ 452* [1]	75	2
22 Feb 92		LOVER LOVER LOVER *East West YZ 643*	47	4

[1] Ian McCulloch featuring Elizabeth Fraser

See also ECHO and the BUNNYMEN

Martine McCUTCHEON *UK, female vocalist (56 WEEKS)* pos/wks

18 Nov 95		ARE YOU MAN ENOUGH *Avex UK AVEX CD 14* [1]	62	1
17 Apr 99	★	PERFECT MOMENT *Innocent SINCD 7* ■	1	15
14 Aug 99		PERFECT MOMENT (re-entry) *Innocent SINCD 7*	59	5
11 Sep 99	●	I'VE GOT YOU *Innocent SINCD 12*	6	10
4 Dec 99	●	TALKING IN YOUR SLEEP / LOVE ME *Innocent SINCD 14*	6	16
4 Nov 00	●	I'M OVER YOU *Innocent SINCD 20*	2	9+

[1] Uno Clio featuring Martine McCutcheon

Gene McDANIELS *US, male vocalist (2 WEEKS)* pos/wks

16 Nov 61		TOWER OF STRENGTH *London HLG 9448*	49	1
30 Nov 61		TOWER OF STRENGTH (re-entry) *London HLG 9448*	49	1

Julie McDERMOTT – See THIRD DIMENSION featuring Julie McDERMOTT; AWESOME 3

Charles McDEVITT SKIFFLE GROUP featuring Nancy WHISKEY
UK, male / female vocal / instrumental group (20 WEEKS) pos/wks

12 Apr 57	●	FREIGHT TRAIN *Oriole CB 1352*	5	17
14 Jun 57		GREENBACK DOLLAR *Oriole CB 1371*	28	1
5 Jul 57		GREENBACK DOLLAR (re-entry) *Oriole CB 1371*	30	1
20 Sep 57		FREIGHT TRAIN (re-entry) *Oriole CB 1352*	27	1

Jane McDONALD *UK, female vocalist (7 WEEKS)* pos/wks

26 Dec 98	●	CRUISE INTO CHRISTMAS MEDLEY *Focus Music Int CDFM 2*	10	7

Michael McDONALD
US, male vocalist / instrumentalist (48 WEEKS) pos/wks

18 Feb 84		YAH MO B THERE *Qwest W 9394* [1]	44	5
7 Apr 84		YAH MO B THERE (re-entry) *Qwest W 9394* [1]	69	3
12 Jan 85		YAH MO B THERE (2nd re-entry) *Qwest W 9394* [1]	12	8
3 May 86	●	ON MY OWN *MCA MCA 1045* [2] ▲	2	13

26 Jul 86	I KEEP FORGETTIN' *Warner Bros K 17992*	**43** 6
6 Sep 86	SWEET FREEDOM *MCA MCA 1073*	**12** 10
24 Jan 87	WHAT A FOOL BELIEVES (re-issue)	
	Warner Bros. W 8451 [3]	**57** 3

[1] James Ingram with Michael McDonald [2] Patti LaBelle and Michael McDonald [3] Doobie Brothers featuring Michael McDonald

The 1985 entry of 'Yah Mo B There' is a re-mix of the original hit with the same catalogue number

See also DOOBIE BROTHERS

Carrie McDOWELL *US, female vocalist (3 WEEKS)* pos/wks
26 Sep 87	UH UH NO NO CASUAL SEX *Motown ZV 41501*	**68** 3

John McENROE and Pat CASH with the FULL METAL RACKETS
US / Australia, male vocal / instrumental duo with UK backing group (1 WEEK) pos/wks
13 Jul 91	ROCK 'N' ROLL *Music for Nations KUT 141*	**66** 1

Reba McENTIRE *US, female vocalist (1 WEEK)* pos/wks
19 Jun 99	DOES HE LOVE YOU *MCA Nashville MCSTD 55569*	**62** 1

MACEO & THE MACKS
US male vocal / instrumental group (5 WEEKS) pos/wks
16 May 87	CROSS THE TRACK (WE BETTER GO BACK) *Urban URBX1*	**54** 5

McFADDEN and WHITEHEAD *US, male vocal duo - Gene McFadden and John Whitehead (10 WEEKS)* pos/wks
19 May 79	● AIN'T NO STOPPIN' US NOW	
	Philadelphia International PIR 7365	**5** 10

Rachel McFARLANE *UK, female vocalist (2 WEEKS)* pos/wks
1 Aug 98	LOVER *Multiply CDMULTY 37*	**38** 2

See also LOVELAND featuring the voice of Rachel McFARLANE

Bobby McFERRIN *US, male vocalist (15 WEEKS)* pos/wks
24 Sep 88	● DON'T WORRY BE HAPPY *Manhattan MT 56* ▲	**2** 11
17 Dec 88	THINKIN' ABOUT YOUR BODY *Manhattan BLUE 6*	**46** 4

McGANNS *UK, male vocal trio (4 WEEKS)* pos/wks
14 Nov 98	JUST MY IMAGINATION *Coalition COLA 062CD*	**59** 1
6 Feb 99	A HEARTBEAT AWAY *Coalition COLA 069CD*	**42** 3

Mike McGEAR *UK, male vocalist (4 WEEKS)* pos/wks
5 Oct 74	LEAVE IT *Warner Bros. K 16446*	**36** 4

Maureen McGOVERN *US, female vocalist (8 WEEKS)* pos/wks
5 Jun 76	THE CONTINENTAL *20th Century BTC 2222*	**16** 8

Shane MacGOWAN *UK, male vocalist (9 WEEKS)* pos/wks
12 Dec 92	WHAT A WONDERFUL WORLD *Mute MUTE 151* [1]	**72** 1
3 Sep 94	THE CHURCH OF THE HOLY SPOOK *ZTT ZANG 57CD* [2]	**74** 1
15 Oct 94	THAT WOMAN'S GOT ME DRINKING	
	ZTT ZANG 56CD [2]	**34** 3
29 Apr 95	HAUNTED *ZTT ZANG 65CD* [3]	**30** 2
20 Apr 96	MY WAY *ZTT ZANG 79CD*	**29** 2

[1] Nick Cave and Shane McGowan [2] Shane MacGowan and the Popes [3] Shane MacGowan and Sinead O'Connor

See also POGUES

Ewan McGREGOR – See PF PROJECT featuring Ewan McGREGOR

Freddie McGREGOR *Jamaica, male vocalist (16 WEEKS)* pos/wks
27 Jun 87	● JUST DON'T WANT TO BE LONELY *Germain DG 24*	**9** 11
19 Sep 87	THAT GIRL (GROOVY SITUATION) *Polydor POSP 884*	**47** 5

Mary MacGREGOR *US, female vocalist (10 WEEKS)* pos/wks
19 Feb 77	● TORN BETWEEN TWO LOVERS *Ariola America AA 111* ▲	**4** 10

McGUINNESS FLINT
UK, male vocal / instrumental group (26 WEEKS) pos/wks
21 Nov 70	● WHEN I'M DEAD AND GONE *Capitol CL 15662*	**2** 14
1 May 71	● MALT AND BARLEY BLUES *Capitol CL 15682*	**5** 12

Barry McGUIRE *US, male vocalist (13 WEEKS)* pos/wks
9 Sep 65	● EVE OF DESTRUCTION *RCA 1469* ▲	**3** 13

McGUIRE SISTERS *US, female vocal group (24 WEEKS)* pos/wks
1 Apr 55	NO MORE *Vogue Coral Q 72050*	**20** 1
15 Jul 55	SINCERELY *Vogue Coral Q 72050* ▲	**14** 4
1 Jun 56	DELILAH JONES *Vogue Coral Q 72161*	**24** 2
14 Feb 58	SUGARTIME *Coral Q 72305*	**14** 6
1 May 59	MAY YOU ALWAYS *Coral Q 72356*	**15** 10
17 Jul 59	MAY YOU ALWAYS (re-entry) *Coral Q 72356*	**28** 1

MACHEL *Trinidad, male vocal (2 WEEKS)* pos/wks
14 Sep 96	COME DIG IT *London LONCD 386*	**56** 2

MACHINE HEAD *UK, male vocal / instrumental group (4 WEEKS)* pos/wks
27 May 95	OLD *Roadrunner RR 23403*	**43** 2
6 Dec 97	TAKE MY SCARS *Roadrunner RR 22573*	**73** 1
18 Dec 99	FROM THIS DAY *Roadrunner RR 21383*	**74** 1

Craig MACK *US, male rapper (5 WEEKS)* pos/wks
12 Nov 94	FLAVA IN YA EAR *Bad Boy 74321242582*	**57** 2
1 Apr 95	GET DOWN *Puff Daddy 74321263402*	**54** 1
7 Jun 97	SPIRIT *Perspective 5822312* [1]	**35** 2

[1] Sound of Blackness featuring Craig Mack

Lizzy MACK *UK, female vocalist (3 WEEKS)* pos/wks
5 Nov 94	THE POWER OF LOVE *Media MCSTD 2016* [1]	**49** 2
4 Nov 95	DON'T GO *Power Station MCSTD 40004*	**52** 1

[1] Fits of Gloom featuring Lizzy Mack

Lonnie MACK *US, male instrumentalist - guitar (3 WEEKS)* pos/wks
14 Apr 79	MEMPHIS *Lightning LIG 9011*	**47** 3

'Memphis' was coupled with 'Let's Dance' by Chris Montez as a double A-side

MACK VIBE featuring JACQUELINE
US, male / female vocal / instrumental duo (1 WEEK) pos/wks
4 Feb 95	I CAN'T LET YOU GO *MCA MCSTD 20020*	**53** 1

Maria McKEE *US, female vocalist (23 WEEKS)* pos/wks
15 Sep 90	★ SHOW ME HEAVEN *Epic 656303 7*	**1** 14
26 Jan 91	BREATHE *Geffen GFS 1*	**59** 1
1 Aug 92	SWEETEST CHILD *Geffen GFS 23*	**45** 4
22 May 93	I'M GONNA SOOTHE YOU *Geffen GFSTD 39*	**35** 3
18 Sep 93	I CAN'T MAKE IT ALONE *Geffen GFSTD 53*	**74** 1

Kenneth McKELLAR *UK, male vocalist (4 WEEKS)* pos/wks
10 Mar 66	A MAN WITHOUT LOVE *Decca F 12341*	**30** 4

Terence McKENNA – See SHAMEN

Gisele MacKENZIE
Canada, female vocalist - Gisele LeFleche (6 WEEKS) pos/wks
17 Jul 53	SEVEN LONELY DAYS *Capitol CL 13920*	**12** 1
31 Jul 53	SEVEN LONELY DAYS (re-entry) *Capitol CL 13920*	**11** 1
21 Aug 53	● SEVEN LONELY DAYS (2nd re-entry) *Capitol CL 13920*	**6** 4

UK No.1 ★   UK Top 10 ●   Still on chart +   UK million seller ◆   UK entry at No.1 ■   US No.1 ▲

Scott McKENZIE US, male vocalist - Philip Blondheim (18 WEEKS) pos/wks

		pos	wks
12 Jul 67 ★	SAN FRANCISCO (BE SURE TO WEAR SOME FLOWERS IN YOUR HAIR) CBS 2816	1	17
1 Nov 67	LIKE AN OLD TIME MOVIE CBS 3009 [1]	50	1

[1] The Voice of Scott McKenzie

Ken MACKINTOSH UK, orchestra (9 WEEKS) pos/wks

		pos	wks
15 Jan 54	THE CREEP HMV BD 1295	12	1
29 Jan 54 ●	THE CREEP (re-entry) HMV BD 1295	10	1
7 Feb 58	RAUNCHY HMV POP 426	19	6
10 Mar 60	NO HIDING PLACE HMV POP 713	45	1

Brian McKNIGHT US, male vocalist (4 WEEKS) pos/wks

		pos	wks
6 Jun 98	ANYTIME Motown 8607752	48	2
3 Oct 98	YOU SHOULD BE MINE Motown 8608412	36	2

Vivienne McKONE UK, female vocalist (5 WEEKS) pos/wks

		pos	wks
25 Jul 92	SING (OOH-EE-OOH) ffrr F 183	47	4
31 Oct 92	BEWARE ffrr F 202	69	1

McKOY UK, male / female vocal group (2 WEEKS) pos/wks

		pos	wks
6 Mar 93	FIGHT Rightrack CDTUM 1	54	2

Noel McKOY – See JTQ; McKOY

Craig McLACHLAN Australia, male vocalist (40 WEEKS) pos/wks

		pos	wks
16 Jun 90 ●	MONA Epic 655784 7 [1]	2	11
4 Aug 90	AMANDA Epic 656170 7 [1]	19	6
10 Nov 90	I ALMOST FELT LIKE CRYING Epic 656310 7 [1]	50	3
23 May 92	ONE REASON WHY Epic 6580677	29	6
14 Nov 92	ON MY OWN Epic 6584677	59	2
24 Jul 93	YOU'RE THE ONE THAT I WANT Epic 6595222 [2]	13	6
25 Dec 93	GREASE Epic 6600242	44	4
8 Jul 95	EVERYDAY MDMC DEVCS 6 [3]	65	2

[1] Craig McLachlan and Check 1-2 [2] Craig McLachlan and Debbie Gibson [3] Craig McLachlan and the Culprits

Sarah McLACHLAN
Canada, female vocalist / instrumentalist (17 WEEKS) pos/wks

		pos	wks
3 Oct 98	ADIA Arista 74321613902	18	5
14 Oct 00 ●	SILENCE (re-mixes) Nettwerk 331072 [1]	3	12+

[1] Delerium featuring Sarah McLachlan

Tommy McLAIN US, male vocalist (1 WEEK) pos/wks

		pos	wks
8 Sep 66	SWEET DREAMS London HL 10065	49	1

Malcolm McLAREN UK, male vocalist (65 WEEKS) pos/wks

		pos	wks
4 Dec 82 ●	BUFFALO GALS Charisma MALC 1 [1]	9	12
26 Feb 83	SOWETO Charisma MALC 2	32	5
2 Jul 83 ●	DOUBLE DUTCH Charisma MALC 3	3	13
17 Dec 83	DUCK FOR THE OYSTER Charisma MALC 4	54	5
1 Sep 84	MADAM BUTTERFLY (UN BEL DI VEDREMO) Charisma MALC 5	13	9
27 May 89	WALTZ DARLING Epic WALTZ 2 [3]	31	8
19 Aug 89	SOMETHING'S JUMPIN' IN YOUR SHIRT Epic WALTZ 3 [4]	29	7
25 Nov 89	HOUSE OF THE BLUE DANUBE Epic WALTZ 4 [3]	73	1
21 Dec 91	MAGIC'S BACK (THEME FROM 'THE GHOSTS OF OXFORD STREET') RCA PB 45223 [5]	42	4
3 Oct 98	BUFFALO GALS STAMPEDE (re-mix of first hit) Virgin VSCDT 1717 [6]	65	1

[1] Malcolm McLaren and the World's Famous Supreme Team [2] Malcolm McLaren and the McLarenettes [3] Malcolm McLaren and the Bootzilla Orchestra [4] Malcolm McLaren and the Bootzilla Orchestra featuring Lisa Marie [5] Malcolm McLaren featuring Alison Limerick [6] Malcolm McLaren and the World's Famous Supreme Team plus Rakim and Roger Sanchez

Bitty McLEAN UK, male vocalist (50 WEEKS) pos/wks

		pos	wks
31 Jul 93 ●	IT KEEP RAININ' (TEARS FROM MY EYES) Brilliant CDBRIL 1	2	15
30 Oct 93	PASS IT ON Brilliant CDBRIL 2	35	3
15 Jan 94 ●	HERE I STAND Brilliant CDBRIL 3	10	6
9 Apr 94 ●	DEDICATED TO THE ONE I LOVE Brilliant CDBRIL 4	6	10
6 Aug 94	WHAT GOES AROUND Brilliant CDBRIL 5	36	3
8 Apr 95	OVER THE RIVER Brilliant CDBRIL 9	27	4
17 Jun 95	WE'VE ONLY JUST BEGUN Brilliant CDBRIL 10	23	5
30 Sep 95	NOTHING CAN CHANGE THIS LOVE Brilliant CDBRIL 11	55	2
27 Jan 96	NATURAL HIGH Brilliant CDBRIL 12	63	1
5 Oct 96	SHE'S ALRIGHT Kuff KUFFD 9	53	1

Don McLEAN Singer / songwriter b. 2 Oct 1945, New York, US. The 8.5-minute 'American Pie' is one of the all-time great rock era records. The track, which starts in mono and ends in stereo, was US top single in 1972. The song finally topped the chart when revived by Madonna in 2000. No.1 song 'Killing Me Softly' was written about him (68 WEEKS)

		pos	wks
22 Jan 72 ●	AMERICAN PIE United Artists UP 35325 ▲	2	16
13 May 72 ★	VINCENT United Artists UP 35359	1	15
14 Apr 73	EVERYDAY United Artists UP 35519	38	5
10 May 80 ★	CRYING EMI 5051	1	14
17 Apr 82	CASTLES IN THE AIR EMI 5258	47	8
5 Oct 91	AMERICAN PIE (re-issue) Liberty EMCT 3	12	10

Jackie McLEAN US, male instrumentalist - alto sax (4 WEEKS) pos/wks

		pos	wks
7 Jul 79	DR. JACKYLL AND MISTER FUNK RCA PB 1575	53	4

Phil McLEAN US, male vocalist (4 WEEKS) pos/wks

		pos	wks
18 Jan 62	SMALL SAD SAM Top Rank JAR 597	34	4

Ian McNABB UK, male vocalist (6 WEEKS) pos/wks

		pos	wks
23 Jan 93	IF LOVE WAS LIKE GUITARS This Way Up WAY 233	67	1
2 Jul 94	YOU MUST BE PREPARED TO DREAM This Way Up WAY 3199 [1]	54	1
17 Sep 94	GO INTO THE LIGHT This Way Up WAY 3699	66	2
27 Apr 96	DON'T PUT YOUR SPELL ON ME This Way Up WAY 5033	72	1
6 Jul 96	MERSEYBEAST This Way Up WAY 5266	74	1

[1] Ian McNabb featuring Ralph Molina and Billy Talbot

See also ICICLE WORKS

Lutricia McNEAL US, female vocalist (43 WEEKS) pos/wks

		pos	wks
29 Nov 97 ●	AIN'T THAT JUST THE WAY Wildstar CXSTAS 2907	6	18
23 May 98 ●	STRANDED Wildstar CXSTAS 2973	3	12
26 Sep 98 ●	SOMEONE LOVES YOU HONEY Wildstar CDWILD 9	9	7
19 Dec 98	THE GREATEST LOVE YOU'LL NEVER KNOW Wildstar CDWILD 11	17	6

Patrick MacNEE and Honor BLACKMAN UK, male / female vocal duo (7 WEEKS) pos/wks

		pos	wks
1 Dec 90 ●	KINKY BOOTS Deram KINKY 1	5	7

Rita MacNEIL Canada, female vocalist (10 WEEKS) pos/wks

		pos	wks
6 Oct 90	WORKING MAN Polydor PO 98	11	10

Clyde McPHATTER US, male vocalist (1 WEEK) pos/wks

		pos	wks
24 Aug 56	TREASURE OF LOVE London HLE 8293	27	1

Carmen McRAE – See Sammy DAVIS Jr

Ralph McTELL UK, male vocalist - Ralph May (18 WEEKS) pos/wks

		pos	wks
7 Dec 74 ●	STREETS OF LONDON Reprise K 14380	2	12
20 Dec 75	DREAMS OF YOU Warner Bros. K 16648	36	6

UK No.1 ★ UK Top 10 ● Still on chart + UK million seller ◆ UK entry at No.1 ■ US No.1 ▲

MAD COBRA featuring Richie STEPHENS
Jamaica / UK, male vocal duo (2 WEEKS) pos/wks

15 May 93		LEGACY *Columbia 6592852* [1]		64 2

[1] Mad Cobra featuring Richie Stephens

MAD JOCKS featuring JOCKMASTER B.A.
UK, male vocal / instrumental group (9 WEEKS) pos/wks

19 Dec 87		JOCK MIX 1 *Debut DEBT 3037*		46 5
18 Dec 93		PARTY FOUR (EP) *SMP CDSSKM 24*		57 4

Tracks on Party Four (EP): No Lager / Here We Go Again / Jock Party Mix / Jock Jak Mix

MAD MOSES *US, male DJ / producer - 'Mad' Mitch Moses (1 WEEK)* pos/wks

16 Aug 97		PANTHER PARTY *Hi-Life 5744932*		50 1

MAD STUNTMAN – See REEL 2 REAL

Sonya MADAN – See LITHIAM and Sonya MADAN

MADASUN *UK, female vocal group (13 WEEKS)* pos/wks

11 Mar 00		DON'T YOU WORRY *V2 VVR 5011523*		14 6
27 May 00		WALKING ON WATER *V2 VVR 5012418*		14 4
2 Sep 00		FEEL GOOD *V2 VVR 5012983*		29 3

Danny MADDEN *US, male vocalist (2 WEEKS)* pos/wks

14 Jul 90		THE FACTS OF LIFE *Eternal YZ 473*		72 2

MADDER ROSE
US, male / female vocal / instrumental group (2 WEEKS) pos/wks

26 Mar 94		PANIC ON *Atlantic A 8301CD*		65 1
16 Jul 94		CAR SONG *Seed A 7256CD*		68 1

MADDOG – See STRETCH 'N' VERN present MADDOG

MADE IN LONDON *UK / Norway, female vocal group (6 WEEKS)* pos/wks

13 May 00		DIRTY WATER *RCA 74321746192*		15 5
9 Sep 00		SHUT YOUR MOUTH *RCA 74321772602*		74 1

MADISON AVENUE *Australia, male producer - Andy Van Dorsselaer, and female vocalist - Cheyne Coates (23 WEEKS)* pos/wks

13 Nov 99		DON'T CALL ME BABY *VC Recordings VCRD 56*		30 4
29 Jan 00		DON'T CALL ME BABY (re-entry) *VC Recordings VCRD 56*		74 1
19 Feb 00		DON'T CALL ME BABY (2nd re-entry) *VC Recordings VCRD 56*		70 1
20 May 00	★	DON'T CALL ME BABY (re-issue) *VC Recordings VCRD 64*■		1 12
21 Oct 00	●	WHO THE HELL ARE YOU *VC Recordings VCRD 70*		10 5

MADNESS (40 Top 500) *London-based band whose ska-rooted 'nutty' sound earned them a huge haul of hits. This good-time septet fronted by Graham 'Suggs' McPherson (b. 13 Jan 1961) spent more weeks on the chart in the 1980s than any other group (268 WEEKS)* pos/wks

1 Sep 79		THE PRINCE *2 Tone TT 3*		16 11
10 Nov 79	●	ONE STEP BEYOND *Stiff BUY 56*		7 14
5 Jan 80	●	MY GIRL *Stiff BUY 62*		3 10
5 Apr 80	●	WORK REST AND PLAY (EP) *Stiff BUY 71*		6 8
13 Sep 80	●	BAGGY TROUSERS *Stiff BUY 84*		3 20
22 Nov 80	●	EMBARRASSMENT *Stiff BUY 102*		4 12
24 Jan 81	●	THE RETURN OF THE LOS PALMAS SEVEN *Stiff BUY 108*		7 11
25 Apr 81	●	GREY DAY *Stiff BUY 112*		4 10
26 Sep 81	●	SHUT UP *Stiff BUY 126*		7 9
5 Dec 81	●	IT MUST BE LOVE *Stiff BUY 134*		4 12
20 Feb 82		CARDIAC ARREST *Stiff BUY 140*		14 10
22 May 82	★	HOUSE OF FUN *Stiff BUY 146*		1 9
24 Jul 82	●	DRIVING IN MY CAR *Stiff BUY 153*		4 8
27 Nov 82	●	OUR HOUSE *Stiff BUY 163*		5 13
19 Feb 83	●	TOMORROW'S (JUST ANOTHER DAY) / MADNESS (IS ALL IN THE MIND) *Stiff BUY 169*		8 9
20 Aug 83	●	WINGS OF A DOVE *Stiff BUY 181*		2 10
5 Nov 83	●	THE SUN AND THE RAIN *Stiff BUY 192*		5 10
11 Feb 84		MICHAEL CAINE *Stiff BUY 196*		11 8
2 Jun 84		ONE BETTER DAY *Stiff BUY 201*		17 7
31 Aug 85		YESTERDAY'S MEN *Zarjazz JAZZ 5*		18 7
26 Oct 85		UNCLE SAM *Zarjazz JAZZ 7*		21 11
1 Feb 86		SWEETEST GIRL *Zarjazz JAZZ 8*		35 6
8 Nov 86		(WAITING FOR) THE GHOST TRAIN *Zarjazz JAZZ 9*		18 7
3 Jan 87		(WAITING FOR) THE GHOST TRAIN (re-entry) *Zarjazz JAZZ 9*		74 1
19 Mar 88	●	I PRONOUNCE YOU *Virgin VS 1054* [1]		44 4
15 Feb 92	●	IT MUST BE LOVE (re-issue) *Virgin VS 1405*		6 9
25 Apr 92		HOUSE OF FUN (re-issue) *Virgin VS 1413*		40 3
8 Aug 92		MY GIRL (re-issue) *Virgin VS 1425*		27 4
28 Nov 92		THE HARDER THEY COME *Go! Discs GOD 93*		44 3
27 Feb 93		NIGHT BOAT TO CAIRO *Virgin VSCDT 1447*		56 2
31 Jul 99	●	LOVESTRUCK *Virgin VSCDT 1737*		10 7
6 Nov 99		JOHNNY THE HORSE *Virgin VSCDT 1740*		44 2
11 Mar 00		DRIP FED FRED *Virgin VSCDT 1768* [2]		55 1

[1] The Madness [2] Madness featuring Ian Dury

Tracks on Work Rest and Play (EP): Night Boat to Cairo / Deceives the Eye / The Young and the Old / Don't Quote Me on That. 'Night Boat to Cairo' in 1993 is a re-issue of a track from the Work Rest and Play EP

MADONNA (6 Top 500) *The most successful female chart act of all time in the UK and US, with world sales in excess of 130 million records, b. Madonna Ciccone, 16 Aug 1958, Michigan. Continually groundbreaking and trend setting, this often controversial artist has amassed an unequalled 35 consecutive UK Top 10 singles (includes 2 re-entries, a remix and a re-issue) and an unbeatable tally of Top 5 entries. She has also had more UK No.1 singles and albums than any other female soloist, and at one time held the top two slots on the singles chart (1985). Her accumulated UK Top 10 entries are more than The Beatles and Rolling Stones combined, and her album 'The Immaculate Collection' has sold almost 3 million copies in the UK alone. In the US, the multi-award winning singer holds the female record for 27 consecutive Top 20 entries and 16 successive Top 5s plus a dozen No.1s - 10 of which she wrote. Madonna has produced more No.1s than any female, played to packed stadiums around the globe and starred in several successful films. Her 2000 album, 'Music', topped the chart in 26 countries and shipped five million albums (546 WEEKS)* pos/wks

14 Jan 84	●	HOLIDAY *Sire W 9405*		6 11
17 Mar 84		LUCKY STAR *Sire W 9522*		14 9
2 Jun 84		BORDERLINE *Sire W 9260*		56 4
17 Nov 84	●	LIKE A VIRGIN *Sire W 9210* ▲		3 18
2 Mar 85	●	MATERIAL GIRL *Sire W 9083*		3 10
8 Jun 85	●	CRAZY FOR YOU *Geffen A 6323* ▲		2 15
27 Jul 85	★	INTO THE GROOVE *Sire W 8934*		1 14
3 Aug 85	●	HOLIDAY (re-entry) *Sire W 9405*		2 10
21 Sep 85	●	ANGEL *Sire W 8881*		5 9
12 Oct 85	●	GAMBLER *Geffen A 6585*		4 11
7 Dec 85	●	DRESS YOU UP *Sire W 8848*		5 11
4 Jan 86		GAMBLER (re-entry) *Geffen A 6585*		61 1
25 Jan 86		BORDERLINE (re-entry) *Sire W 9260*		2 9
26 Apr 86	●	LIVE TO TELL *Sire W 8717* ▲		2 12
28 Jun 86	★	PAPA DON'T PREACH *Sire W 8636* ▲		1 14
4 Oct 86	★	TRUE BLUE *Sire W 8550*		1 15
13 Dec 86	●	OPEN YOUR HEART *Sire W 8480* ▲		4 9
4 Apr 87	★	LA ISLA BONITA *Sire W 8378*		1 11
18 Jul 87	★	WHO'S THAT GIRL *Sire W 8341* ▲		1 10
19 Sep 87	●	CAUSING A COMMOTION *Sire W 8224*		4 9
12 Dec 87	●	THE LOOK OF LOVE *Sire W 8115*		9 7
18 Mar 89	★	LIKE A PRAYER *Sire W 7539* ▲		1 12
3 Jun 89	●	EXPRESS YOURSELF *Sire W 2948*		5 10
16 Sep 89	●	CHERISH *Sire W 2883*		3 8
16 Dec 89	●	DEAR JESSIE *Sire W 2668*		5 9
7 Apr 90	★	VOGUE *Sire W 9851* ▲		1 14
21 Jul 90	●	HANKY PANKY *Sire W 9789*		2 9
8 Dec 90	●	JUSTIFY MY LOVE *Sire W 9000* ▲		2 10
2 Mar 91	●	CRAZY FOR YOU (re-mix) *Sire W 0008*		2 8
13 Apr 91	●	RESCUE ME *Sire W 0024*		3 8
8 Jun 91	●	HOLIDAY (re-issue) *Sire W 0037*		5 7
25 Jul 92	●	THIS USED TO BE MY PLAYGROUND *Sire W 0122* ▲		3 9

17 Oct 92 ●	EROTICA *Maverick W 0138*	3	8
12 Dec 92 ●	DEEPER AND DEEPER *Maverick W 0146*	6	9
9 Jan 93	EROTICA (re-entry) *Maverick W 0138*	65	1
6 Mar 93 ●	BAD GIRL *Maverick W 0145CD*	10	7
3 Apr 93 ●	FEVER *Maverick W 0168CD*	6	6
31 Jul 93 ●	RAIN *Maverick W 0190CD*	7	8
2 Apr 94 ●	I'LL REMEMBER *Maverick W 0240CD*	7	8
8 Oct 94 ●	SECRET *Maverick W 0268CD*	5	9
17 Dec 94	TAKE A BOW *Maverick W 0278CD* ▲	16	9
25 Feb 95 ●	BEDTIME STORY *Maverick W 0285CD*	4	8
6 May 95	BEDTIME STORY (re-entry) *Maverick W 0285CD*	66	1
26 Aug 95 ●	HUMAN NATURE *Maverick W 0300CD*	8	5
4 Nov 95 ●	YOU'LL SEE *Maverick W 0324CD*	5	13
6 Jan 96	OH FATHER *Maverick W 0326CD*	16	6
23 Mar 96	ONE MORE CHANCE *Maverick W 0337CD*	11	4
2 Nov 96 ●	YOU MUST LOVE ME *Warner Bros. W 0378CD*	10	4
28 Dec 96 ●	DON'T CRY FOR ME ARGENTINA *Warner Bros. W 0384CD*	3	12
4 Jan 97	YOU MUST LOVE ME (re-entry) *Warner Bros. W 0378CD*	75	1
18 Jan 97	YOU MUST LOVE ME (2nd re-entry) *Warner Bros. W 0378CD*	71	1
29 Mar 97 ●	ANOTHER SUITCASE IN ANOTHER HALL *Warner Bros. W 0388CD*	7	5
7 Mar 98 ★	FROZEN *Maverick W 0433CD* ■	1	13
9 May 98 ●	RAY OF LIGHT *Maverick W 0444CD*	2	9
18 Jul 98	RAY OF LIGHT (re-entry) *Maverick W 0444CD*	75	1
5 Sep 98 ●	DROWNED WORLD (SUBSTITUTE FOR LOVE) *Maverick W 0453CD1*	10	5
5 Dec 98 ●	THE POWER OF GOODBYE / LITTLE STAR *Maverick W 459CD*	6	9
13 Mar 99 ●	NOTHING REALLY MATTERS *Maverick W 471CD*	7	8
5 Jun 99	NOTHING REALLY MATTERS (re-entry) *Maverick W 471CD*	75	1
19 Jun 99 ●	BEAUTIFUL STRANGER *Maverick W 495CD*	2	16
11 Mar 00 ★	AMERICAN PIE *Maverick W 519CD* ■	1	12
17 Jun 00	AMERICAN PIE (re-entry) *Maverick W 519CD*	68	2
2 Sep 00 ★	MUSIC *Maverick W 537CD1* ■ ▲	1	18+
9 Dec 00 ●	DON'T TELL ME *Maverick W 547CD1*	4	4+

MAGAZINE *UK, male vocal / instrumental group, lead vocal – Howard Devoto (7 WEEKS)* pos/wks

11 Feb 78	SHOT BY BOTH SIDES *Virgin VS 200*	41	4
26 Jul 80	SWEET HEART CONTRACT *Virgin VS 368*	54	3

MAGIC AFFAIR
US / Germany, male / female vocal / instrumental group (8 WEEKS) pos/wks

4 Jun 94	OMEN III *EMI CDEM 317*	17	4
27 Aug 94	GIVE ME ALL YOUR LOVE *EMI CDEM 340*	30	2
5 Nov 94	IN THE MIDDLE OF THE NIGHT *EMI CDEM 349*	38	2

MAGIC LADY *US, female vocal duo (3 WEEKS)* pos/wks

14 May 88	BETCHA CAN'T LOSE (WITH MY LOVE) *Motown ZB 42003*	58	3

MAGIC LANTERNS *UK, male vocal / instrumental group (3 WEEKS)* pos/wks

7 Jul 66	EXCUSE ME BABY *CBS 202094*	46	1
28 Jul 66	EXCUSE ME BABY (re-entry) *CBS 202094*	44	1
11 Aug 66	EXCUSE ME BABY (2nd re-entry) *CBS 202094*	46	1

MAGNUM *UK, male vocal / instrumental group (26 WEEKS)* pos/wks

22 Mar 80	MAGNUM (DOUBLE SINGLE) *Jet 175*	47	6
12 Jul 86	LONELY NIGHT *Polydor POSP 798*	70	2
19 Mar 88	DAYS OF NO TRUST *Polydor POSP 910*	32	4
7 May 88	START TALKING LOVE *Polydor POSP 920*	22	4
2 Jul 88	IT MUST HAVE BEEN LOVE *Polydor POSP 930*	33	4
23 Jun 90	ROCKIN' CHAIR *Polydor PO 88*	27	4
25 Aug 90	HEARTBROKE AND BUSTED *Polydor PO 94*	49	2

Tracks on double single: Invasion / Kingdom of Madness / All of My Life / Great Adventure

MAGOO *UK, male vocal / instrumental group (1 WEEK)* pos/wks

4 Apr 98	BLACK SABBATH / SWEET LEAF *Fierce Panda NING 47CD* [1]	60	1

[1] Magoo : Mogwai

MAGOO – See TIMBALAND; Missy 'Misdemeanor' ELLIOTT

Sean MAGUIRE *UK, male vocalist (34 WEEKS)* pos/wks

20 Aug 94	SOMEONE TO LOVE *Parlophone CDR 6390*	14	7
5 Nov 94	TAKE THIS TIME *Parlophone CDR 6395*	27	4
31 Dec 94	TAKE THIS TIME (re-entry) *Parlophone CDR 6395*	74	1
25 Mar 95	SUDDENLY *Parlophone CDR 6403*	18	5
24 Jun 95	NOW I'VE FOUND YOU *Parlophone CDLEEPYS 1*	22	3
18 Nov 95	YOU TO ME ARE EVERYTHING *Parlophone CDR 6420*	16	3
25 May 96	GOOD DAY *Parlophone CDR 6432*	12	4
3 Aug 96	DON'T PULL YOUR LOVE *Parlophone CDR 6440*	14	4
29 Mar 97	TODAY'S THE DAY *Parlophone CDR 6459*	27	3

Siobhan MAHER – See OCEANIC

MAHLATHINI and the MAHOTELLA QUEENS – See ART OF NOISE

MAI TAI *Guyana, female vocal group (30 WEEKS)* pos/wks

25 May 85 ●	HISTORY *Virgin VS 773*	8	13
3 Aug 85 ●	BODY AND SOUL *Virgin VS 801*	9	13
15 Feb 86	FEMALE INTUITION *Virgin VS 844*	54	4

MAIN INGREDIENT *US, male vocal group (7 WEEKS)* pos/wks

29 Jun 74	JUST DON'T WANT TO BE LONELY *RCA APBO 0205*	27	7

MAISONETTES *UK, male / female vocal group (12 WEEKS)* pos/wks

11 Dec 82 ●	HEARTACHE AVENUE *Ready Steady Go! RSG 1*	7	12

Raven MAIZE *UK, male vocalist / producer – Dave Lee (1 WEEK)* pos/wks

5 Aug 89	FOREVER TOGETHER *Republic LIC 014*	67	1

See also Joey NEGRO, HED BOYS, PHASE II, LI KWAN

MAKADOPOULOS and his GREEK SERENADERS
Greece, male vocal / instrumental group (14 WEEKS) pos/wks

20 Oct 60	NEVER ON SUNDAY *Palette PG 9005*	36	14

MAKAVELI *US, male rapper – 2Pac (Tupac Shakur) (8 WEEKS)* pos/wks

12 Apr 97 ●	TO LIVE & DIE IN LA *Interscope IND 95529*	10	4
9 Aug 97	TOSS IT UP *Interscope IND 95521*	15	3
14 Feb 98	HAIL MARY *Interscope IND 95575*	43	1

See also 2PAC

Jack E MAKOSSA *Kenya, male producer (5 WEEKS)* pos/wks

12 Sep 87	THE OPERA HOUSE *Champion CHAMP 50*	48	5

MALA – See BOWA featuring MALA

MALAIKA *US, female vocalist (1 WEEK)* pos/wks

31 Jul 93	GOTTA KNOW (YOUR NAME) *A & M 5802732*	68	1

Carl MALCOLM *Jamaica, male vocalist (8 WEEKS)* pos/wks

13 Sep 75 ●	FATTIE BUM BUM *UK 108*	8	8

Valerie MALCOLM – See CANDY GIRLS

Timmy MALLETT – See BOMBALURINA

MAMA CASS *US, female vocalist – Ellen Cohen (27 WEEKS)* pos/wks

14 Aug 68	DREAM A LITTLE DREAM OF ME *RCA 1726*	11	12
16 Aug 69 ●	IT'S GETTING BETTER *Stateside SS 8021*	8	15

See also MAMAS and the PAPAS

MAMAS and the PAPAS (482 Top 500) Folk-rock harmony quartet
who helped to make California the focal point of mid-60s music; singer /
songwriter John Phillips and wife Michelle, Canadian Dennis Doherty and
(Mama) Cass Elliot (d. 1974). Quartet split in 1968 with Cass becoming solo
hitmaker and Michelle an actress (71 WEEKS)

			pos/wks	
28 Apr 66		CALIFORNIA DREAMIN' *RCA 1503*	23	9
12 May 66	●	MONDAY MONDAY *RCA 1516* ▲	3	13
28 Jul 66		I SAW HER AGAIN *RCA 1533*	11	11
9 Feb 67		WORDS OF LOVE *RCA 1564*	47	3
6 Apr 67	●	DEDICATED TO THE ONE I LOVE *RCA 1576*	2	17
26 Jul 67	●	CREEQUE ALLEY *RCA 1613*	9	11
2 Aug 97	●	CALIFORNIA DREAMIN' (re-issue) *MCA MCSTD 48058*	9	7

See also MAMA CASS

MAMBAS – See Marc ALMOND

Cheb MAMI – See STING

A MAN CALLED ADAM
UK, male / female vocal / instrumental group (4 WEEKS)

		pos/wks	
29 Sep 90	BAREFOOT IN THE HEAD *Big Life BLR 28*	70	2
20 Oct 90	BAREFOOT IN THE HEAD (re-entry) *Big Life BLR 28*	60	2

MAN TO MAN *US, male vocal / instrumental duo (19 WEEKS)*

			pos/wks	
13 Sep 86		MALE STRIPPER *Bolts BOLTS 4* [1]	64	3
3 Jan 87		MALE STRIPPER (re-entry) *Bolts BOLTS 4* [1]	63	1
7 Feb 87	●	MALE STRIPPER (2nd re-entry) *Bolts BOLTS 4* [1]	4	12
4 Jul 87		I NEED A MAN / ENERGY IS EUROBEAT *Bolts BOLTS 5*	43	3

[1] Man 2 Man meet Man Parrish

MAN WITH NO NAME
UK, male producer - Martin Freeland (6 WEEKS)

		pos/wks	
30 Sep 95	FLOOR-ESSENCE *Perfecto PERF 108CD*	68	1
20 Jan 96	PAINT A PICTURE *Perfecto PERF 114CD* [1]	42	2
12 Oct 96	TELEPORT / SUGAR RUSH *Perfecto PERF 126CD*	55	1
2 May 98	VAVOOM! *Perfecto PERF 159CD1*	43	1
18 Jul 98	THE FIRST DAY (HORIZON) *Perfecto PERF 164CD*	72	1

[1] Man with No Name featuring Hannah

Melissa MANCHESTER – See Al JARREAU

MANCHESTER UNITED FOOTBALL CLUB
UK, male football team vocalists (56 WEEKS)

			pos/wks	
8 May 76		MANCHESTER UNITED *Decca F 13633*	50	1
21 May 83		GLORY GLORY MAN UNITED *EMI 5390*	13	5
18 May 85	●	WE ALL FOLLOW MAN UNITED *Columbia DB 9107*	10	5
19 Jun 93		UNITED (WE LOVE YOU)		
		Living Beat LBECD 026 [1]	37	2
30 Apr 94	★	COME ON YOU REDS *PolyGram TV MANU 2*	1	15
13 May 95	●	WE'RE GONNA DO IT AGAIN		
		PolyGram TV MANU 952 [2]	6	6
4 May 96	●	MOVE MOVE MOVE (THE RED TRIBE)		
		Music Collection MANUCD 1 [3]	6	11
3 Aug 96		MOVE MOVE MOVE (THE RED TRIBE) (re-entry)		
		Music Collection MANUCD 1 [3]	50	4
29 May 99		LIFT IT HIGH (ALL ABOUT BELIEF)		
		Music Collection MANUCD 4 [4]	11	6
21 Aug 99		LIFT IT HIGH (ALL ABOUT BELIEF) (re-entry)		
		Music Collection MANUCD 4 [4]	75	1

[1] Manchester United and the Champions [2] Manchester United Football Squad featuring Stryker [3] 1996 Manchester United FA Cup Squad [4] 1999 Manchester United Squad

MANCHILD featuring Kelly JONES
UK, male production duo / male vocalist (1 WEEK)

		pos/wks	
16 Sep 00	THE CLICHES ARE TRUE *One Little Indian 176 TP7CD*	60	1

See also STEREOPHONICS

Henry MANCINI *US, orchestra / chorus (23 WEEKS)*

		pos/wks	
7 Dec 61	MOON RIVER *RCA 1256*	46	2
28 Dec 61	MOON RIVER (re-entry) *RCA 1256*	44	1
24 Sep 64	HOW SOON *RCA 1414*	10	12
25 Mar 72	THEME FROM 'CADE'S COUNTY' *RCA 2182*	42	1
11 Feb 84	MAIN THEME FROM 'THE THORN BIRDS'		
	Warner Bros. 9677	23	7

Steve MANDELL – See 'DELIVERANCE' SOUNDTRACK

MANFRED MANN (70 Top 500) One of the most regular chart
entrants of the 1960s: Manfred Mann (k), Mike Vickers (g), Tom McGuinness
(b), Mike Hugg (d), Paul Jones (v) - Jones was replaced by Mike D'Abo in
1966. They were the first group from the south of England to top the US
charts during 1964's so-called 'British Invasion' (217 WEEKS)

			pos/wks	
23 Jan 64	●	5-4-3-2-1 *HMV POP 1252*	5	13
16 Apr 64		HUBBLE BUBBLE TOIL AND TROUBLE *HMV POP 1282*	11	8
16 Jul 64	★	DO WAH DIDDY DIDDY *HMV POP 1320* ▲	1	14
15 Oct 64	●	SHA LA LA *HMV POP 1346*	3	12
14 Jan 65	●	COME TOMORROW *HMV POP 1381*	4	9
15 Apr 65		OH NO NOT MY BABY *HMV POP 1413*	11	10
16 Sep 65	●	IF YOU GOTTA GO GO NOW *HMV POP 1466*	2	12
21 Apr 66	★	PRETTY FLAMINGO *HMV POP 1523*	1	12
7 Jul 66		YOU GAVE ME SOMEBODY TO LOVE *HMV POP 1541*	36	4
4 Aug 66	●	JUST LIKE A WOMAN *Fontana TF 730*	10	10
27 Oct 66	●	SEMI-DETACHED SUBURBAN MR JAMES *Fontana TF 757*	2	12
30 Mar 67	●	HA HA SAID THE CLOWN *Fontana TF 812*	4	11
25 May 67		SWEET PEA *Fontana TF 828*	36	4
24 Jan 68	★	MIGHTY QUINN *Fontana TF 897*	1	11
12 Jun 68	●	MY NAME IS JACK *Fontana TF 943*	8	11
18 Dec 68	●	FOX ON THE RUN *Fontana TF 985*	5	12
30 Apr 69	●	RAGAMUFFIN MAN *Fontana TF 1013*	8	11
8 Sep 73	●	JOYBRINGER *Vertigo 6059 083* [1]	9	10
28 Aug 76	●	BLINDED BY THE LIGHT *Bronze BRO 29* [1] ▲	6	10
20 May 78	●	DAVY'S ON THE ROAD AGAIN *Bronze BRO 52* [1]	6	12
17 Mar 79		YOU ANGEL YOU *Bronze BRO 68* [1]	54	5
7 Jul 79		DON'T KILL IT CAROL *Bronze BRO 77* [1]	45	4

[1] Manfred Mann's Earth Band

MANHATTAN TRANSFER (470 Top 500) Multi-faceted four-part
harmony vocal group formed New York, US, 1969, whose recordings include
songs from the 1930s to 80s. Their nostalgic sound earned them 10 Grammy
awards, although, oddly, their No.1 hit did not chart in US (72 WEEKS)

			pos/wks	
7 Feb 76		TUXEDO JUNCTION *Atlantic K 10670*	24	6
5 Feb 77	★	CHANSON D'AMOUR *Atlantic K 10886*	1	13
28 May 77		DON'T LET GO *Atlantic K 10930*	32	6
18 Feb 78		WALK IN LOVE *Atlantic K 11075*	48	1
4 Mar 78		WALK IN LOVE (re-entry) *Atlantic K 11075*	12	11
20 May 78		ON A LITTLE STREET IN SINGAPORE *Atlantic K 11136*	20	9
16 Sep 78		WHERE DID OUR LOVE GO / JE VOULAIS TE DIRE (QUE		
		JE T'ATTENDS) *Atlantic K 11182*	40	4
23 Dec 78		WHO WHAT WHEN WHERE WHY *Atlantic K 11233*	49	6
17 May 80		TWILIGHT ZONE - TWILIGHT TONE (MEDLEY)		
		Atlantic K 11476	25	8
21 Jan 84		SPICE OF LIFE *Atlantic A 9728*	19	8

MANHATTANS *US, male vocal group (31 WEEKS)*

			pos/wks	
19 Jun 76	●	KISS AND SAY GOODBYE *CBS 4317* ▲	4	11
2 Oct 76	●	HURT *CBS 4562*	4	11
23 Apr 77		IT'S YOU *CBS 5093*	43	3
26 Jul 80		SHINING STAR *CBS 8824*	45	4
6 Aug 83		CRAZY *CBS A 3578*	63	2

M.A.N.I.C. *UK, male vocal / production duo (1 WEEK)*

		pos/wks	
18 Apr 92	I'M COMIN' HARDCORE *Union City UCRT 2*	60	1

MANIC MCs featuring Sara CARLSON
UK, male production duo and female vocalist (5 WEEKS)

		pos/wks	
12 Aug 89	MENTAL *RCA PB 43037*	30	5

UK No.1 ★ UK Top 10 ● Still on chart + UK million seller ◆ UK entry at No.1 ■ US No.1 ▲

MANIC STREET PREACHERS `201` `Top 500`

Best-selling Welsh act of the 1990s; James Dean Bradfield (v/g), Nicky Wire (b), Sean Moore (d) and Richey Edwards (v/g - missing and presumed dead since 1995). Won trophies for the Best British Group and Best Album at the 1997 and 1999 Brit Awards (128 WEEKS)

		pos/wks
25 May 91	YOU LOVE US *Heavenly HVN 10*	62 2
10 Aug 91	STAY BEAUTIFUL *Columbia 6573377*	40 3
9 Nov 91	LOVE'S SWEET EXILE / REPEAT *Columbia 6575827*	26 3
1 Feb 92	YOU LOVE US (re-issue) *Columbia 6577247*	16 4
28 Mar 92	SLASH 'N' BURN *Columbia 6578737*	20 4
13 Jun 92	MOTORCYCLE EMPTINESS *Columbia 6580837*	17 6
19 Sep 92 ●	THEME FROM M.A.S.H. (SUICIDE IS PAINLESS) *Columbia 6583827*	7 6
21 Nov 92	LITTLE BABY NOTHING *Columbia 6587967*	29 3
12 Jun 93	FROM DESPAIR TO WHERE *Columbia 6593372*	25 4
31 Jul 93	LA TRISTESSE DURERA (SCREAM TO A SIGH) *Columbia 6594772*	22 5
2 Oct 93	ROSES IN THE HOSPITAL *Columbia 6597272*	15 3
12 Feb 94	LIFE BECOMING A LANDSLIDE *Columbia 6600702*	36 2
11 Jun 94	FASTER / PCP *Epic 6604472*	16 3
13 Aug 94	REVOL *Epic 6606862*	22 3
15 Oct 94	SHE IS SUFFERING *Epic 6608952*	25 3
27 Apr 96 ●	A DESIGN FOR LIFE *Epic 6630705*	2 10
27 Jul 96	A DESIGN FOR LIFE (re-entry) *Epic 6630705*	71 1
3 Aug 96 ●	EVERYTHING MUST GO *Epic 6634685*	5 6
12 Oct 96 ●	KEVIN CARTER *Epic 6637752*	9 4
14 Dec 96 ●	AUSTRALIA *Epic 6640442*	7 7
13 Sep 97	LITTLE BABY NOTHING (re-issue) *Epic MANIC 6CD*	50 1
13 Sep 97	LOVE'S SWEET EXILE (re-issue) *Epic MANIC 2CD*	55 1
13 Sep 97	MOTORCYCLE EMPTINESS (re-issue) *Epic MANIC 5CD*	41 1
13 Sep 97	SLASH 'N' BURN (re-issue) *Epic MANIC 4CD*	54 1
13 Sep 97	STAY BEAUTIFUL (re-issue) *Epic MANIC 1CD*	52 1
13 Sep 97	YOU LOVE US (2nd re-issue) *Epic MANIC 3CD*	49 1
5 Sep 98 ★	IF YOU TOLERATE THIS YOUR CHILDREN WILL BE NEXT *Epic 6663452* ■	1 10
5 Dec 98	IF YOU TOLERATE THIS YOUR CHILDREN WILL BE NEXT (re-entry) *Epic 6663452*	69 1
12 Dec 98	THE EVERLASTING *Epic 6666862*	11 8
20 Mar 99 ●	YOU STOLE THE SUN FROM MY HEART *Epic 6669532*	5 8
17 Jul 99	TSUNAMI *Epic 6674112*	11 5
22 Jan 00 ★	THE MASSES AGAINST THE CLASSES *Epic 6685302* ■	1 6
1 Apr 00	THE MASSES AGAINST THE CLASSES (re-entry) *Epic 6685302*	70 1

The listed flipside of 'Theme From M.A.S.H. (Suicide Is Painless)' was '(Everything I Do) I Do It For You' by Fatima Mansions

Barry MANILOW `183` `Top 500`

Middle-of-the-road superstar, b. Barry Pincus, 17 Jun 1946, Brooklyn, US. This crowd-pulling singer / songwriter / pianist with a vast and loyal following on both sides of the Atlantic has sold in excess of 50 million albums (136 WEEKS)

		pos/wks
22 Feb 75	MANDY *Arista 1* ▲	11 9
6 May 78	CAN'T SMILE WITHOUT YOU *Arista 176*	43 7
29 Jul 78	SOMEWHERE IN THE NIGHT / COPACABANA (AT THE COPA) *Arista 196*	42 10
23 Dec 78	COULD IT BE MAGIC *Arista ARIST 229*	25 10
8 Nov 80	LONELY TOGETHER *Arista ARIST 373*	21 13
7 Feb 81	I MADE IT THROUGH THE RAIN *Arista ARIST 384*	37 6
11 Apr 81	BERMUDA TRIANGLE *Arista ARIST 406*	15 9
26 Sep 81	LET'S HANG ON *Arista ARIST 429*	12 11
12 Dec 81	THE OLD SONGS *Arista ARIST 443*	48 8
20 Feb 82	IF I SHOULD LOVE AGAIN *Arista ARIST 453*	66 2
17 Apr 82	STAY *Arista ARIST 464* [1]	23 8
16 Oct 82 ●	I WANNA DO IT WITH YOU *Arista ARIST 495*	8 8
4 Dec 82	I'M GONNA SIT RIGHT DOWN AND WRITE MYSELF A LETTER *Arista ARIST 503*	36 7
25 Jun 83	SOME KIND OF FRIEND *Arista ARIST 516*	48 2
27 Aug 83	YOU'RE LOOKING HOT TONIGHT *Arista ARIST 542*	47 6
10 Dec 83	READ 'EM AND WEEP *Arista ARIST 551*	17 7
8 Apr 89	PLEASE DON'T BE SCARED *Arista 112186*	35 5
10 Apr 93	COPACABANA (AT THE COPA) (re-mix) *Arista 74321136912*	22 4
20 Nov 93	COULD IT BE MAGIC (re-recording) *Arista 74321174882*	36 3
6 Aug 94	LET ME BE YOUR WINGS *EMI CDEM 336* [2]	73 1

[1] Barry Manilow featuring Kevin Desimone and James Jolis [2] Barry Manilow and Debra Byrd

ARIST 464 was available as both a live and studio recording.

MANIX
UK, male / female vocal / instrumental group (6 WEEKS)

		pos/wks
23 Nov 91	MANIC MINDS *Reinforced RIVET 1209*	63 2
7 Mar 92	OBLIVION (HEAD IN THE CLOUDS) (EP) *Reinforced RIVET 1212*	43 3
8 Aug 92	RAINBOW PEOPLE *Reinforced RIVET 1221*	57 1

Tracks on Oblivion (Head in the Clouds) (EP): Oblivion (Head in the Clouds) / Never Been to Belgium (Gotta Rush) / I Can't Stand It / You Held My Hand

MANKEY
UK, male producer - Andy Manston (1 WEEK)

		pos/wks
16 Nov 96	BELIEVE IN ME *Frisky DISKY 3*	74 1

MANKIND
UK, male instrumental group (12 WEEKS)

		pos/wks
25 Nov 78	DR WHO *Pinnacle PIN 71*	25 12

Aimee MANN
US, female vocalist (9 WEEKS)

		pos/wks
31 Oct 87	TIME STAND STILL *Vertigo RUSH 13* [1]	42 3
28 Aug 93	I SHOULD'VE KNOWN *Imago 72787250432*	55 2
20 Nov 93	STUPID THING *Imago 72787250432*	47 2
5 Mar 94	I SHOULD'VE KNOWN (re-issue) *Imago 72787250602*	45 2

[1] Rush with Aimee Mann

Johnny MANN SINGERS
US, male / female vocal group (13 WEEKS)

		pos/wks
12 Jul 67 ●	UP, UP AND AWAY *Liberty LIB 55972*	6 13

MANSUN
UK, male vocal / instrumental group (42 WEEKS)

		pos/wks
6 Apr 96	ONE (EP) *Parlophone CDR 6430*	37 2
15 Jun 96	TWO (EP) *Parlophone CDR 6437*	32 2
21 Sep 96	STRIPPER VICAR *Parlophone CDR 6447*	19 3
17 Dec 96	WIDE OPEN SPACE *Parlophone CDR 6453*	15 4
15 Feb 97 ●	SHE MAKES MY NOSE BLEED *Parlophone CDR 6453*	9 5
10 May 97	TAXLOSS *Parlophone CDRS 6465*	15 3
18 Oct 97 ●	CLOSED FOR BUSINESS *Parlophone CDRS6482*	10 3
11 Jul 98 ●	LEGACY (EP) *Parlophone CDR 6497*	7 4
5 Sep 98	BEING A GIRL (PART ONE) (EP) *Parlophone CDR 6503*	13 3
7 Nov 98	NEGATIVE *Parlophone CDR 6508*	27 2
13 Feb 99	SIX *Parlophone CDR 6511*	16 3
12 Aug 00 ●	I CAN ONLY DISAPOINT U *Parlophone CDR 6544*	8 5
18 Nov 00	ELECTRIC MAN *Parlophone CDR 6550*	23 2

Tracks on One (EP): Egg Shaped Fred / Ski Jump Nose / Lemonade Secret Drinker / Thief. Tracks on Two (EP): Take It Easy Chicken / Drastic Sturgeon / The Greatest Pain / Moronica. Tracks on Legacy (EP): Legacy / Railings / Check Under the Bed / Can't Afford to Die. Tracks on Being a Girl (Part One) (EP): Being A Girl / I Care / Been Here Before / Hideout / Railings

MANTOVANI
UK, orchestra - leader: Annunzio Paolo Mantovani (52 WEEKS)

		pos/wks
19 Dec 52 ●	WHITE CHRISTMAS *Decca F 10017*	6 3
29 May 53 ★	THE SONG FROM THE MOULIN ROUGE *Decca F 10094*	1 21
23 Oct 53 ●	SWEDISH RHAPSODY *Decca F 10168*	2 17
13 Nov 53 ●	THE SONG FROM THE MOULIN ROUGE (re-entry) *Decca F 10094*	10 1
4 Dec 53	THE SONG FROM THE MOULIN ROUGE (2nd re-entry) *Decca F 10094*	12 1
26 Feb 54	SWEDISH RHAPSODY (re-entry) *Decca F 10168*	12 1
11 Feb 55	LONELY BALLERINA *Decca F 10395*	16 3
18 Mar 55	LONELY BALLERINA (re-entry) *Decca F 10395*	18 1
31 May 57	AROUND THE WORLD *Decca F 10888*	20 4

See also David WHITFIELD

MANTRONIK vs EPMD US, male vocalist / instrumentalist / producer – Curtis Mantronik, and US, male rap / DJ duo (1 WEEK)

		pos/wks	
15 Aug 98	STRICTLY BUSINESS Parlophone CDR 6502	43	1

MANTRONIX
US / Jamaica, male vocal / instrumental duo (48 WEEKS)

		pos/wks	
22 Feb 86	LADIES 10 TEN 116	55	4
17 May 86	BASSLINE 10 TEN 118	34	6
7 Feb 87	WHO IS IT 10 TEN 137	40	6
4 Jul 87	SCREAM (PRIMAL SCREAM) 10 TEN 169	46	4
30 Jan 88	SING A SONG (BREAK IT DOWN) 10 TEN 206	61	2
12 Mar 88	SIMPLE SIMON (YOU GOTTA REGARD) 10 TEN 217	72	2
6 Jan 90 ●	GOT TO HAVE YOUR LOVE Capitol CL 559 [1]	4	11
12 May 90 ●	TAKE YOUR TIME Capitol CL 573 [1]	10	7
2 Mar 91	DON'T GO MESSIN' WITH MY HEART Capitol CL 608	22	5
22 Jun 91	STEP TO ME (DO ME) Capitol CL 613	59	1

[1] Mantronix featuring Wondress

MANUEL and his MUSIC OF THE MOUNTAINS
UK, orchestra, leader Geoff Love (31 WEEKS)

		pos/wks	
28 Aug 59	THE HONEYMOON SONG Columbia DB 4323	29	2
25 Sep 59	THE HONEYMOON SONG (re-entry) Columbia DB 4323	22	5
6 Nov 59	THE HONEYMOON SONG (2nd re-entry) Columbia DB 4323	27	2
13 Oct 60	NEVER ON SUNDAY Columbia DB 4515	29	10
13 Oct 66	SOMEWHERE MY LOVE Columbia DB 7969	42	2
31 Jan 76 ●	RODRIGO'S GUITAR CONCERTO DE ARANJUEZ (THEME FROM 2ND MOVEMENT) EMI 2383	3	10

MARATHON
Germany / UK, male vocal / instrumental group (3 WEEKS)

		pos/wks	
25 Jan 92	MOVIN' Ten TEN 395	36	3

MARAUDERS UK, male vocal / instrumental group (4 WEEKS)

		pos/wks	
8 Aug 63	THAT'S WHAT I WANT Decca F 11695	48	1
22 Aug 63	THAT'S WHAT I WANT (re-entry) Decca F 11695	43	3

MARBLES
UK, male vocal duo – Graham Bonnet and Trevor Garden (18 WEEKS)

		pos/wks	
25 Sep 68 ●	ONLY ONE WOMAN Polydor 56 272	5	12
26 Mar 69	THE WALLS FELL DOWN Polydor 56 310	28	6

MARC and the MAMBAS – See Marc ALMOND

MARC et CLAUDE Germany, male DJ / production trio (10 WEEKS)

		pos/wks	
21 Nov 98	LA Positiva CDTIV 104	28	3
22 Jul 00	I NEED YOUR LOVIN' (LIKE THE SUNSHINE) Positiva CDTIV 136	12	7

MARCELS
US, male vocal group – lead vocal: Cornelius Harp (17 WEEKS)

		pos/wks	
13 Apr 61 ★	BLUE MOON Pye International 7N 25073 ▲	1	13
8 Jun 61	SUMMERTIME Pye International 7N 25083	46	4

Little Peggy MARCH US, female vocalist (7 WEEKS)

		pos/wks	
12 Sep 63	HELLO HEARTACHE GOODBYE LOVE RCA 1362	29	7

MARCO POLO Italy, male instrumental / production duo (1 WEEK)

		pos/wks	
8 Apr 95	A PRAYER TO THE MUSIC Hi-Life HICD 7	65	1

MARCY PLAYGROUND
US, male vocal / instrumental trio (3 WEEKS)

		pos/wks	
18 Apr 98	SEX AND CANDY EMI CDEM 508	29	3

MARDI GRAS UK, male vocal / instrumental group (9 WEEKS)

		pos/wks	
5 Aug 72	TOO BUSY THINKING 'BOUT MY BABY Bell 1226	19	9

MARIA – See Maria NAYLER

Kelly MARIE UK, female vocalist (36 WEEKS)

		pos/wks	
2 Aug 80 ★	FEELS LIKE I'M IN LOVE Calibre PLUS 1	1	16
18 Oct 80	LOVING JUST FOR FUN Calibre PLUS 4	21	7
7 Feb 81	HOT LOVE Calibre PLUS 5	22	10
30 May 81	LOVE TRIAL Calibre PLUS 7	51	3

Rose MARIE Ireland, female vocalist (5 WEEKS)

		pos/wks	
19 Nov 83	WHEN I LEAVE THE WORLD BEHIND A1 284	75	1
3 Dec 83	WHEN I LEAVE THE WORLD BEHIND (re-entry) A1 284	63	2
24 Dec 83	WHEN I LEAVE THE WORLD BEHIND (2nd re-entry) A1 284	66	2

Teena MARIE US, female vocalist – Mary Brockert (28 WEEKS)

		pos/wks	
7 Jul 79	I'M A SUCKER FOR YOUR LOVE Motown TMG 1146 [1]	43	8
31 May 80 ●	BEHIND THE GROOVE Motown TMG 1185	6	10
11 Oct 80	I NEED YOUR LOVIN' Motown TMG 1203	28	6
26 Mar 88	OOO LA LA LA Epic 651423 7	74	2
10 Nov 90	SINCE DAY ONE Epic 656429 7	69	2

[1] Teena Marie, co-lead vocals Rick James

MARILLION (288 Top 500) Progressive rock group formed in Buckinghamshire and originally named after Tolkien's novel, Silmarillion. They reached their height of popularity between 1981 and 1988, when fronted by Scottish vocalist / songwriter Fish (b. Derek Dick, 25 Apr 1958) (103 WEEKS)

		pos/wks	
20 Nov 82	MARKET SQUARE HEROES EMI 5351	60	2
12 Feb 83	HE KNOWS YOU KNOW EMI 5362	35	4
16 Apr 83	MARKET SQUARE HEROES (re-entry) EMI 5351	53	6
18 Jun 83	GARDEN PARTY EMI 5393	16	5
11 Feb 84	PUNCH AND JUDY EMI MARIL 1	29	4
12 May 84	ASSASSING EMI MARIL 2	22	5
18 May 85 ●	KAYLEIGH EMI MARIL 3	2	14
7 Sep 85 ●	LAVENDER EMI MARIL 4	5	9
30 Nov 85	HEART OF LOTHIAN EMI MARIL 5	29	6
23 May 87 ●	INCOMMUNICADO EMI MARIL 6	6	5
25 Jul 87	SUGAR MICE EMI MARIL 7	22	5
7 Nov 87	WARM WET CIRCLES EMI MARIL 8	22	4
26 Nov 88	FREAKS (LIVE) EMI MARIL 9	24	3
9 Sep 89	HOOKS IN YOU Capitol MARIL 10	30	3
9 Dec 89	UNINVITED GUEST EMI MARIL 11	53	2
14 Apr 90	EASTER EMI MARIL 12	34	2
8 Jun 91	COVER MY EYES (PAIN AND HEAVEN) EMI MARIL 13	34	4
3 Aug 91	NO ONE CAN EMI MARIL 14	33	4
5 Oct 91	DRY LAND EMI MARIL 15	34	2
23 May 92	SYMPATHY EMI MARIL 16	17	3
1 Aug 92	NO ONE CAN (re-issue) EMI MARIL 17	26	4
26 Mar 94	THE HOLLOW MAN EMI CDEMS 307	30	2
7 May 94	ALONE AGAIN IN THE LAP OF LUXURY EMI CDEMS 318	53	3
10 Jun 95	BEAUTIFUL EMI CDMARILS 18	29	2

See also FISH

MARILYN UK, male vocalist – Peter Robinson (26 WEEKS)

		pos/wks	
5 Nov 83 ●	CALLING YOUR NAME Mercury MAZ 1	4	12
11 Feb 84	CRY AND BE FREE Mercury MAZ 2	31	6
21 Apr 84	YOU DON'T LOVE ME Mercury MAZ 3	40	7
13 Apr 85	BABY U LEFT ME (IN THE COLD) Mercury MAZ 4	70	1

MARILYN MANSON
US, male vocal / instrumental group (13 WEEKS)

		pos/wks	
7 Jun 97	THE BEAUTIFUL PEOPLE Interscope IND 95541	18	3
20 Sep 97	TOURNIQUET Interscope IND 95552	28	2
21 Nov 98	THE DOPE SHOW Interscope IND 95610	12	3
26 Jun 99	ROCK IS DEAD Maverick W 486CD	23	2
18 Nov 00	DISPOSABLE TEENS Nothing 4974372	12	3

Marino MARINI and his QUARTET
Italy, male vocalist and instrumental group (23 WEEKS)

		pos/wks	
3 Oct 58	VOLARE Durium DC 16632 (A)	13	7
10 Oct 58 ●	COME PRIMA Durium DC 16632 (B)	2	14

UK No.1 ★   UK Top 10 ●   Still on chart +   UK million seller ◆   UK entry at No.1 ■   US No.1 ▲

20 Mar 59	CIAO CIAO BAMBINA *Durium DC 16636*	25	1
3 Apr 59	CIAO CIAO BAMBINA (re-entry) *Durium DC 16636*	24	1

MARION *UK, male vocal / instrumental group (9 WEEKS)* pos/wks

25 Feb 95	SLEEP *London LONCD 360*	53	1
13 May 95	TOYS FOR BOYS *London LONCD 366*	57	1
21 Oct 95	LET'S ALL GO TOGETHER *London LONCD 371*	37	2
3 Feb 96	TIME *London LONCD 377*	29	2
30 Mar 96	SLEEP (re-mix) *London LONCD 381*	17	2
7 Mar 98	MIYAKO HIDEAWAY *London LONCD 403*	45	1

MARK 'OH *Germany, male producer - Marko Albrecht (3 WEEKS)* pos/wks

6 May 95	TEARS DON'T LIE *Systematic SYSCD 9*	24	3

Pigmeat MARKHAM *US, male vocalist (8 WEEKS)* pos/wks

17 Jul 68	HERE COMES THE JUDGE *Chess CRS 8077*	19	8

Biz MARKIE *US, male rapper (2 WEEKS)* pos/wks

26 May 90	JUST A FRIEND *Cold Chillin' W 9823*	55	2

Yannis MARKOPOULOS *Greece, orchestra (8 WEEKS)* pos/wks

17 Dec 77	WHO PAYS THE FERRYMAN *BBC RESL 51*	11	8

Guy MARKS *US, male vocalist (8 WEEKS)* pos/wks

13 May 78	LOVING YOU HAS MADE ME BANANAS *ABC 4211*	25	8

MARKY MARK and the FUNKY BUNCH
US, male / female vocal / rap / instrumental group (14 WEEKS) pos/wks

31 Aug 91	GOOD VIBRATIONS *Interscope A 8764* [1]	14	7
2 Nov 91	WILDSIDE *Interscope A 8674*	42	3
12 Dec 92	YOU GOTTA BELIEVE *Interscope A 8480*	54	4

[1] Marky Mark and the Funky Bunch featuring Loleatta Holloway

Ziggy MARLEY and the MELODY MAKERS *Jamaica, male / female vocal / instrumental group (11 WEEKS)* pos/wks

11 Jun 88	TOMORROW PEOPLE *Virgin VS 1049*	22	10
23 Sep 89	LOOK WHO'S DANCING *Virgin America VUS 5*	65	1

Bob MARLEY and the WAILERS (123 Top 500) *Legendary, globally successful Jamaican group. Varying line-up included Bob Marley b. 6 Apr 1945, Jamaica, d. 11 May 1981 Miami, (v/g). Peter Tosh b. 19 Oct 1944, Jamaica, d. 11 Sep, Jamaica, 1987(v/g), Bunny Wailer (v/prc). Their compilation, Legend, is the biggest-selling reggae album in the UK and the USA with combined sales of more than 12 million. (167 WEEKS)* pos/wks

27 Sep 75	NO WOMAN NO CRY *Island WIP 6244*	22	7
25 Jun 77	EXODUS *Island WIP 6390*	14	9
10 Sep 77	WAITING IN VAIN *Island WIP 6402*	27	6
10 Dec 77 ●	JAMMING / PUNKY REGGAE PARTY *Island WIP 6410*	9	12
25 Feb 78 ●	IS THIS LOVE *Island WIP 6420*	9	9
10 Jun 78	SATISFY MY SOUL *Island WIP 6440*	21	10
20 Oct 79	SO MUCH TROUBLE IN THE WORLD *Island WIP 6510*	56	4
21 Jun 80 ●	COULD YOU BE LOVED *Island WIP 6610*	5	12
13 Sep 80	THREE LITTLE BIRDS *Island WIP 6641*	17	9
13 Jun 81 ●	NO WOMAN NO CRY (re-entry) *Island WIP 6244*	8	11
7 May 83 ●	BUFFALO SOLDIER *Island/Tuff Gong IS 108*	4	12
21 Apr 84 ●	ONE LOVE - PEOPLE GET READY *Island IS 169*	5	11
23 Jun 84	WAITING IN VAIN (re-issue) *Island IS 180*	31	7
8 Dec 84	COULD YOU BE LOVED (re-issue) *Island IS 210*	71	2
18 May 91	ONE LOVE - PEOPLE GET READY (re-issue) *Tuff Gong TGX 1*	42	3
19 Sep 92 ●	IRON LION ZION *Tuff Gong TGX 2*	5	9
28 Nov 92	WHY SHOULD I / EXODUS *Tuff Gong TGX 3*	42	3
2 Jan 93	WHY SHOULD I / EXODUS (re-entry) *Tuff Gong TGX 3*	75	1
20 May 95	KEEP ON MOVING *Tuff Gong TGXCD 4*	17	4
8 Jun 96	WHAT GOES AROUND COMES AROUND *Anansi ANACS 002*	42	1
25 Sep 99 ●	SUN IS SHINING *Club Tools / Edel 0066895 CLU* [1]	3	10
11 Dec 99	TURN YOUR LIGHTS DOWN LOW *Columbia 6684362* [2]	15	7
22 Jan 00	RAINBOW COUNTRY *Club Tools 0067225CLU* [1]	11	6
24 Jun 00	JAMMIN' *Tuff Gong TGXCD 9* [3]	42	2

[1] Bob Marley Vs Funkstar De Luxe [2] Bob Marley featuring Lauryn Hill [3] Bob Marley featuring MC Lyte

'Exodus' on Tuff Gong TGX 3 listed with 'Why Should I' only from 5 Dec, 1992, and is a different version from the Island hit. It peaked at No.53

Lene MARLIN
Norway, female vocalist - Lene Marlin Pederson (17 WEEKS) pos/wks

11 Mar 00 ●	SITTING DOWN HERE *Virgin DINSD 183*	5	11
16 Sep 00	UNFORGIVABLE SINNER *Virgin DINSD 202*	13	6

MARLO *UK, male vocal / instrumental group (1 WEEK)* pos/wks

24 Jul 99	HOW DO I KNOW? *Polydor 5611362*	56	1

MARMALADE (197 Top 500) *The first Scottish group to top the chart: included Dean Ford (v), Junior Campbell (g/p/v), Alan Whitehead (d). This pop quintet, who first recorded as Dean Ford and The Gaylords, had a large late-1960s teen following (130 WEEKS)* pos/wks

22 May 68 ●	LOVIN' THINGS *CBS 3412*	6	13
23 Oct 68	WAIT FOR ME MARIANNE *CBS 3708*	30	5
4 Dec 68 ★	OB-LA-DI OB-LA-DA *CBS 3892*	1	20
11 Jun 69 ●	BABY MAKE IT SOON *CBS 4287*	9	13
20 Dec 69 ●	REFLECTIONS OF MY LIFE *Decca F 12982*	3	12
18 Jul 70 ●	RAINBOW *Decca F 13035*	3	14
27 Mar 71	MY LITTLE ONE *Decca F 13135*	15	11
4 Sep 71 ●	COUSIN NORMAN *Decca F 13214*	6	11
27 Nov 71	BACK ON THE ROAD *Decca F 13251*	35	7
22 Jan 72	BACK ON THE ROAD (re-entry) *Decca F 13251*	50	1
1 Apr 72 ●	RADANCER *Decca F 13297*	6	12
21 Feb 76 ●	FALLING APART AT THE SEAMS *Target TGT 105*	9	11

MARMION
Spain / Holland, male instrumental / production duo (2 WEEKS) pos/wks

18 May 96	SCHONEBERG *Hooj Choons HOOJCD 43*	53	1
14 Feb 98	SCHONEBERG (re-mix) *ffrr FCD 324*	56	1

Johnny MARR – See Billy BRAGG; Kirsty MacCOLL; ELECTRONIC; SMITHS

MARRADONA *UK, male DJ / production group (5 WEEKS)* pos/wks

26 Feb 94	OUT OF MY HEAD *Peach PWCD 282*	38	3
26 Jul 97	OUT OF MY HEAD 97 (re-mix) *Soopa SPCD 1*	39	2

M/A/R/R/S *UK, male instrumental / production group (14 WEEKS)* pos/wks

5 Sep 87 ★	PUMP UP THE VOLUME / ANITINA (THE FIRST TIME I SEE SHE DANCE) *4AD AD 70*	1	14

The B-side of this record was listed on the chart at the record company's request without evidence of consumer interest

Gerry MARSDEN – See CHRISTIANS; Holly JOHNSON; Paul McCARTNEY; STOCK AITKEN WATERMAN; GERRY and the PACEMAKERS

Matthew MARSDEN *UK, male vocalist (10 WEEKS)* pos/wks

11 Jul 98	THE HEART'S LONE DESIRE *Columbia 6661152*	13	7
7 Nov 98	SHE'S GONE *Columbia 6664915* [1]	24	3

[1] Matthew Marsden featuring Destiny's Child

Stevie MARSH *UK, female vocalist (4 WEEKS)* pos/wks

4 Dec 59	THE ONLY BOY IN THE WORLD *Decca F 11181*	29	2
25 Dec 59	THE ONLY BOY IN THE WORLD (re-entry) *Decca F 11181*	24	2

MARSHA – See SHAGGY

MARSHALL HAIN *UK, male / female vocal / instrumental duo - Julian Marshall & Kit Hain (19 WEEKS)* pos/wks

3 Jun 78 ●	DANCING IN THE CITY *Harvest HAR 5157*	3	15
14 Oct 78	COMING HOME *Harvest HAR 5168*	39	4

Joy MARSHALL
UK, female vocalist (2 WEEKS) pos/wks

23 Jun 66	THE MORE I SEE YOU *Decca F 12422*	34	2

Keith MARSHALL
UK, male vocalist (10 WEEKS) pos/wks

4 Apr 81	ONLY CRYING *Arrival PIK 2*	12	10

Wayne MARSHALL
UK, male vocalist (7 WEEKS) pos/wks

1 Oct 94	OOH AAH (G-SPOT) *Soultown SOULCDS 322*	29	3
3 Jun 95	SPIRIT *Soultown SOULCDS 00352*	58	1
24 Feb 96	NEVER KNEW LOVE LIKE THIS *Sony S2 6629382* [1]	40	2
7 Dec 96	G SPOT (re-mix) *MBA INTER 9006*	50	1

[1] Pauline Henry featuring Wayne Marshall

MARTAY Featuring ZZ TOP
UK, female rapper - Melone McKenzy and US, male vocal / instrumental trio (2 WEEKS) pos/wks

16 Oct 99	GIMME ALL YOUR LOVIN' 2000 *Riverhorse RIVHCD 2*	28	2

Lena MARTELL
UK, female vocalist - Helen Thomson (18 WEEKS) pos/wks

29 Sep 79	★ ONE DAY AT A TIME *Pye 7N 46021*	1	18

MARTHA and the MUFFINS
Canada, female / male vocal / instrumental group (10 WEEKS) pos/wks

1 Mar 80	● ECHO BEACH *Dindisc DIN 9*	10	10

M + M are Martha and a Muffin

See also M + M

MARTHA and the VANDELLAS – See Martha REEVES and the VANDELLAS

MARTIKA
US, female vocalist - Marta Marrera (57 WEEKS) pos/wks

29 Jul 89	● TOY SOLDIERS *CBS 655049 7* ▲	5	11
14 Oct 89	● I FEEL THE EARTH MOVE *CBS 655294 7*	7	14
13 Jan 90	MORE THAN YOU KNOW *CBS 655526 7*	15	7
17 Mar 90	WATER *CBS 655731 7*	59	3
17 Aug 91	● LOVE . . . THY WILL BE DONE *Columbia 6573137*	9	9
30 Nov 91	MARTIKA'S KITCHEN *Columbia 6575687*	17	10
22 Feb 92	COLOURED KISSES *Columbia 6577097*	41	3

Billie Ray MARTIN
Germany, female vocalist - Birgit Dieckmann (20 WEEKS) pos/wks

19 Nov 94	YOUR LOVING ARMS *Magnet MAG 1028CD*	38	3
20 May 95	● YOUR LOVING ARMS (re-mix) *Magnet MAG 1031CD*	6	10
2 Sep 95	RUNNING AROUND TOWN *Magnet MAG 1035CD*	29	2
6 Jan 96	IMITATION OF LIFE *Magnet MAG 1040CD*	29	3
6 Apr 96	SPACE OASIS *Magnet MAG 1042CD*	66	1
21 Aug 99	HONEY *React CDREACT 129*	54	1

Dean MARTIN `127` **Top 500**
Acclaimed vocalist / entertainer / film actor and cabaret performer, b. Dino Crocetti, 7 Jun 1917, Ohio, d. 25 Dec 1995. He first found fame partnering Jerry Lewis (1946-56), and had a long and successful solo career. He was a member of Frank Sinatra's 'Rat Pack' and had an impressive 46-year chart span (163 WEEKS) pos/wks

18 Sep 53	● KISS *Capitol CL 13893*	9	1
2 Oct 53	● KISS (re-entry) *Capitol CL 13893*	5	7
22 Jan 54	● THAT'S AMORE *Capitol CL 14008*	2	11
1 Oct 54	● SWAY *Capitol CL 14138*	6	7
22 Oct 54	HOW DO YOU SPEAK TO AN ANGEL *Capitol CL 14150*	15	2
19 Nov 54	HOW DO YOU SPEAK TO AN ANGEL (re-entry) *Capitol CL 14150*	17	4
28 Jan 55	● NAUGHTY LADY OF SHADY LANE *Capitol CL 14226*	5	10
4 Feb 55	MAMBO ITALIANO *Capitol CL 14227*	14	2
25 Feb 55	● LET ME GO LOVER *Capitol CL 14226*	3	9
1 Apr 55	● UNDER THE BRIDGES OF PARIS *Capitol CL 14255*	6	8
10 Feb 56	★ MEMORIES ARE MADE OF THIS *Capitol CL 14523* ▲	1	16
2 Mar 56	YOUNG AND FOOLISH *Capitol CL 14519*	20	1
27 Apr 56	INNAMORATA *Capitol CL 14507*	21	3

22 Mar 57	THE MAN WHO PLAYS THE MANDOLINO *Capitol CL 14690*	21	2
13 Jun 58	● RETURN TO ME *Capitol CL 14844*	2	22
29 Aug 58	● VOLARE *Capitol CL 14910*	2	14
27 Aug 64	EVERYBODY LOVES SOMEBODY *Reprise R 20281* ▲	11	13
12 Nov 64	THE DOOR IS STILL OPEN TO MY HEART *Reprise R 20307*	42	4
5 Feb 69	● GENTLE ON MY MIND *Reprise RS 23343*	2	23
30 Aug 69	GENTLE ON MY MIND (re-entry) *Reprise RS 23343*	49	1
22 Jun 96	THAT'S AMORE (re-issue) *EMI Premier PRESCD 3*	43	2
21 Aug 99	SWAY (re-issue) *Capitol CDSWAY 001*	66	1

Juan MARTIN
Spain, male instrumentalist - guitar (7 WEEKS) pos/wks

28 Jan 84	● LOVE THEME FROM 'THE THORN BIRDS' *WEA X 9518*	10	7

Linda MARTIN
Ireland, female vocalist (2 WEEKS) pos/wks

30 May 92	WHY ME *Columbia 6581317*	59	2

Luci MARTIN – See Romina JOHNSON

Marilyn MARTIN – See Phil COLLINS

Ray MARTIN
UK, orchestra (11 WEEKS) pos/wks

14 Nov 52	● BLUE TANGO *Columbia DB 3051*	8	1
28 Nov 52	● BLUE TANGO (re-entry) *Columbia DB 3051*	10	3
4 Dec 53	● SWEDISH RHAPSODY *Columbia DB 3346*	10	1
18 Dec 53	● SWEDISH RHAPSODY (re-entry) *Columbia DB 3346*	4	3
15 Jun 56	THE CAROUSEL WALTZ *Columbia DB 3771*	28	1
3 Aug 56	THE CAROUSEL WALTZ (re-entry) *Columbia DB 3771*	24	2

See also Lee LAWRENCE

Ricky MARTIN
Puerto Rico, male vocalist - Enrique Morales (53 WEEKS) pos/wks

20 Sep 97	● (UN, DOS, TRES) MARIA *Columbia 6649595*	6	6
11 Jul 98	THE CUP OF LIFE *Columbia 6661502*	29	3
17 Jul 99	★ LIVIN' LA VIDA LOCA *Columbia 6676402* ■ ▲	1	17
20 Nov 99	SHAKE YOUR BON-BON *Columbia 6683412*	12	9
29 Apr 00	● PRIVATE EMOTION *Columbia 6692692* [1]	9	9
4 Nov 00	SHE BANGS *Columbia 6705422*	3	9+

[1] Ricky Martin featuring Meja

Tony MARTIN
US, male vocalist - Alvin Morris Jr. (28 WEEKS) pos/wks

22 Apr 55	● STRANGER IN PARADISE *HMV B 10849*	6	13
13 Jul 56	● WALK HAND IN HAND *HMV POP 222*	2	15

Both with Hugo Winterhalter's Orchestra and Chorus

Vince MARTIN – See TARRIERS

Wink MARTINDALE
US, male vocalist (41 WEEKS) pos/wks

4 Dec 59	DECK OF CARDS *London HLD 8962*	18	5
15 Jan 60	DECK OF CARDS (re-entry) *London HLD 8962*	28	2
31 Mar 60	DECK OF CARDS (2nd re-entry) *London HLD 8962*	45	1
18 Apr 63	● DECK OF CARDS (3rd re-entry) *London HLD 8962*	5	21
20 Oct 73	DECK OF CARDS (re-issue) *Dot DOT 109*	22	12

Al MARTINO `356` **Top 500**
Big-voiced balladeer b. Alfred Cini, 7 Oct 1927, Philadelphia, US. First release topped US chart and was first ever UK No.1. After a few lean years, returned to become one of the 1960s top-selling Easy Listening acts in the US (87 WEEKS) pos/wks

14 Nov 52	★ HERE IN MY HEART *Capitol CL 13779* ▲	1	18
21 Nov 52	★ TAKE MY HEART *Capitol CL 13769*	9	1
30 Jan 53	● NOW *Capitol CL 13835*	3	12
10 Jul 53	● RACHEL *Capitol CL 13879*	10	4
11 Sep 53	RACHEL (re-entry) *Capitol CL 13879*	12	1
4 Jun 54	WANTED *Capitol CL 14128*	12	1
18 Jun 54	● WANTED (re-entry) *Capitol CL 14128*	4	14
1 Oct 54	● THE STORY OF TINA *Capitol CL 14163*	10	8
1 Oct 54	WANTED (2nd re-entry) *Capitol CL 14128*	17	1
23 Sep 55	THE MAN FROM LARAMIE *Capitol CL 14343*	19	2

UK No.1 ★   UK Top 10 ●   Still on chart +   UK million seller ◆   UK entry at No.1 ■   US No.1 ▲

MARVELETTES / MARX ... (left column)

28 Oct 55	THE MAN FROM LARAMIE (re-entry) *Capitol CL 14343* **20**	1
31 Mar 60	SUMMERTIME *Top Rank JAR 312* **49**	1
29 Aug 63	I LOVE YOU BECAUSE *Capitol CL 15300* **48**	1
22 Aug 70	SPANISH EYES *Capitol CL 15430* **49**	1
14 Jul 73 ●	SPANISH EYES (re-entry) *Capitol CL 15430* **5**	21

MARVELETTES *US, female vocal group (10 WEEKS)* pos/wks

15 Jun 67	WHEN YOU'RE YOUNG AND IN LOVE	
	Tamla Motown TMG 609 ......**13**	10

MARVIN and TAMARA *UK, male / female vocal duo (9 WEEKS)* pos/wks

7 Aug 99	GROOVE MACHINE *Epic 6675582* **11**	5
25 Dec 99	NORTH, SOUTH, EAST, WEST *Epic 6684902* **44**	4

Hank MARVIN *UK, male vocalist / instrumentalist, guitar - Brian Rankin (36 WEEKS)* pos/wks

13 Sep 69 ●	THROW DOWN A LINE *Columbia DB 8615* [1] **7**	9
21 Feb 70	JOY OF LIVING *Columbia DB 8657* [1] **25**	8
6 Mar 82	DON'T TALK *Polydor POSP 420* **49**	4
22 Mar 86 ★	LIVING DOLL *WEA YZ 65* [2] **1**	11
7 Jan 89	LONDON KID *Polydor PO 32* [3] **52**	3
17 Oct 92	WE ARE THE CHAMPIONS *PolyGram TV PO 229* [4] **66**	1

[1] Cliff and Hank [2] Cliff Richard and the Young Ones featuring Hank B Marvin [3] Jean-Michel Jarre featuring Hank Marvin [4] Hank Marvin featuring Brian May

See also SHADOWS

Lee MARVIN *US, male actor / vocalist (23 WEEKS)* pos/wks

7 Feb 70 ★	WAND'RIN' STAR *Paramount PARA 3004* **1**	18
20 Jun 70	WAND'RIN' STAR (re-entry) *Paramount PARA 3004* **42**	3
15 Aug 70	WAND'RIN' STAR (2nd re-entry) *Paramount PARA 3004* **47**	2

'I Talk to the Trees' by Clint Eastwood, the flip side of 'Wand'rin' Star', was listed with 'Wand'rin' Star' for 7 Feb 1970, and 14 Feb 1970 only

MARVIN THE PARANOID ANDROID *UK, robot (4 WEEKS)* pos/wks

16 May 81	MARVIN *Polydor POSP 261* **53**	4

Richard MARX (450 Top 500) *Child jingle singer-turned session singer turned singer / songwriter. b. 16 Sep 1962, Chicago, US. He scored 12 consecutive Top 20 entries in the US (first six hits in the Top 3) and sold more than 15 million albums. Married Cynthia Rhodes, lead singer of Animotion. Produced and wrote for 'N Sync in 2000 (75 WEEKS)* pos/wks

27 Feb 88	SHOULD'VE KNOWN BETTER *Manhattan MT 32* **50**	5
14 May 88	ENDLESS SUMMER NIGHTS *Manhattan MT 39* **50**	3
17 Jun 89	SATISFIED *EMI-USA MT 64* ▲ **52**	4
2 Sep 89 ●	RIGHT HERE WAITING *EMI-USA MT 72* ▲ **2**	10
11 Nov 89	ANGELIA *EMI-USA MT 74* **45**	4
24 Mar 90	TOO LATE TO SAY GOODBYE *EMI-USA MT 80* **38**	3
7 Jul 90	CHILDREN OF THE NIGHT *EMI-USA MT 84* **54**	2
1 Sep 90	ENDLESS SUMMER NIGHTS / HOLD ON TO THE NIGHTS (re-issue) *EMI-USA MT 89* ▲ **60**	2
19 Oct 91	KEEP COMING BACK *Capitol CL 634* **55**	2
9 May 92 ●	HAZARD *Capitol CL 654* **3**	15
29 Aug 92	TAKE THIS HEART *Capitol CL 667* **13**	6
28 Nov 92	CHAINS AROUND MY HEART *Capitol CL 676* **29**	6
29 Jan 94	NOW AND FOREVER *Capitol CDCLS 703* **13**	6
30 Apr 94	SILENT SCREAM *Capitol CDCLS 714* **32**	4
13 Aug 94	THE WAY SHE LOVES ME *Capitol CDCL 721* **38**	3

MARXMAN *UK / Ireland, rap / instrumental group (5 WEEKS)* pos/wks

6 Mar 93	ALL ABOUT EVE *Talkin Loud TLKCD 35* **28**	4
1 May 93	SHIP AHOY *Talkin Loud TLKCD 39* **64**	1

Sinead O'Connor provides uncredited vocals on 'Ship Ahoy'

MARY JANE GIRLS *US, female vocal group (11 WEEKS)* pos/wks

25 Jun 83	ALL NIGHT LONG *Gordy TMG 1309* **13**	9
8 Oct 83	BOYS *Gordy TMG 1315* **74**	1
18 Feb 95	ALL NIGHT LONG (re-mix) *Motown TMGCD 1436* **51**	1

MARY MARY *US, female vocal duo - Erica and Tina Atkins (14 WEEKS)* pos/wks

10 Jun 00 ●	SHACKLES (PRAISE YOU) *Columbia 6694202* **5**	12
18 Nov 00	I SINGS *Columbia 6699742* **32**	2

Carolyne MAS *US, female vocalist (2 WEEKS)* pos/wks

2 Feb 80	QUOTE GOODBYE QUOTE *Mercury 6167 873* **71**	2

MASE *US, male rapper - Mason Betha (53 WEEKS)* pos/wks

29 Mar 97	CAN'T NOBODY HOLD ME DOWN *Arista 74321464552* [1] ▲ **19**	4
9 Aug 97 ●	MO MONEY MO PROBLEMS *Puff Daddy 74321492492* [2] **6**	10
27 Dec 97 ●	FEEL SO GOOD *Puff Daddy 74321526442* **10**	8
18 Apr 98	WHAT YOU WANT *Puff Daddy74321578772* [3] **15**	5
19 Sep 98	HORSE AND CARRIAGE *Epic 6662612* [4] **12**	4
10 Oct 98 ●	TOP OF THE WORLD *Atlantic AT 0046CD* [5] **2**	8
12 Dec 98 ●	TAKE ME THERE *Interscope IND 95620* [6] **7**	9
9 Jan 99	TOP OF THE WORLD (re-entry) *Atlantic AT 0046CD* [5] **61**	1
10 Jul 99	GET READY *Puff Daddy / Arista 74321682602* [7] **32**	4

[1] Puff Daddy featuring Mase [2] Notorious B.I.G. featuring Puff Daddy and Mase [3] Mase featuring Total [4] Cam'ron featuring Mase [5] Brandy featuring Mase [6] BLACKstreet and Mya featuring Mase & Blinky Blink [7] Mase featuring BLACKstreet

MASH *US, male vocal / instrumental group (12 WEEKS)* pos/wks

10 May 80 ★	THEME FROM M*A*S*H* (SUICIDE IS PAINLESS) *CBS 8536* **1**	12

MASH! *UK / US, male vocal group (3 WEEKS)* pos/wks

21 May 94	U DON'T HAVE TO SAY U LOVE ME *React CDREACT 37* **37**	2
4 Feb 95	LET'S SPEND THE NIGHT TOGETHER *Playa CDXPLAYA 2* **66**	1

MASH UP – See Matt DAREY

MASON – See CHICANE

Barbara MASON *US, female vocalist (5 WEEKS)* pos/wks

21 Jan 84	ANOTHER MAN *Streetwave KHAN 3* **45**	5

Glen MASON *UK, male vocalist (7 WEEKS)* pos/wks

28 Sep 56	GLENDORA *Parlophone R 4203* **28**	2
16 Nov 56	GREEN DOOR *Parlophone R 4244* **24**	5

Mary MASON *UK, female vocalist (6 WEEKS)* pos/wks

8 Oct 77	ANGEL OF THE MORNING - ANY WAY THAT YOU WANT ME (MEDLEY) *Epic EPC 5552* **27**	6

MASQUERADE *UK, male / female vocal group (10 WEEKS)* pos/wks

11 Jan 86	ONE NATION *Streetwave KHAN 59* **54**	6
5 Jul 86	(SOLUTION TO) THE PROBLEM	
	Streetwave KHAN 67 ......**65**	2
26 Jul 86	(SOLUTION TO) THE PROBLEM (re-entry)	
	Streetwave KHAN 67 ......**64**	2

MASS ORDER *US, male vocal / instrumental duo (5 WEEKS)* pos/wks

14 Mar 92	LIFT EVERY VOICE (TAKE ME AWAY)	
	Columbia 6577487 ......**35**	3
23 May 92	LET'S GET HAPPY *Columbia 6580737* **45**	2

MASS PRODUCTION *US, male vocal / instrumental group (7 WEEKS)* pos/wks

12 Mar 77	WELCOME TO OUR WORLD (OF MERRY MUSIC)	
	Atlantic K 10898 ......**44**	3
17 May 80	SHANTE *Atlantic K 11475* **59**	4

MASS SYNDICATE featuring Su Su BOBIEN *US, male producer, and US, female vocalist (1 WEEK)* pos/wks

24 Oct 98	YOU DON'T KNOW *ffrr FCD 347* **71**	1

Zeitia MASSIAH *UK, female vocalist (2 WEEKS)*   pos/wks

| 12 Mar 94 | I SPECIALIZE IN LOVE *Union City UCRCD 27* | 74 | 1 |
| 24 Sep 94 | THIS IS THE PLACE *Virgin VSCDT 1511* | 62 | 1 |

MASSIEL *Spain, female vocalist (4 WEEKS)*   pos/wks

| 24 Apr 68 | LA LA LA *Philips BF 1667* | 35 | 4 |

MASSIVE ATTACK
UK, male / female vocal / instrumental group (42 WEEKS)   pos/wks

23 Feb 91	UNFINISHED SYMPATHY *Wild Bunch WBRS 2* [1]	13	9
8 Jun 91	SAFE FROM HARM *Wild Bunch WBRS 3*	25	6
22 Feb 92	MASSIVE ATTACK (EP) *Wild Bunch WBRS 4*	27	4
29 Oct 94	SLY *Wild Bunch WBRDX 5*	24	4
21 Jan 95	PROTECTION *Wild Bunch WBRX 6* [2]	14	4
1 Apr 95	KARMACOMA *Wild Bunch WBRX 7*	28	4
19 Jul 97	RISINGSON *Circa WBRX 8*	11	3
9 May 98 ●	TEARDROP *Virgin WBRX 9*	10	6
25 Jul 98	ANGEL *Virgin WBRX 10*	30	2

[1] Massive [2] Massive Attack featuring Tracey Thorn

Tracks on Massive Attack (EP): Hymn of the Big Wheel / Home of the Whale / Be Thankful / Any Love. Teardrop features an uncredited vocal by Elizabeth Fraser from the Cocteau Twins.

MASSIVO featuring TRACY
UK, male / female vocal / instrumental group (11 WEEKS)   pos/wks

| 26 May 90 | LOVING YOU *Debut DEBT 3097* | 25 | 11 |

MASTER P – See Montell JORDAN

MASTER SINGERS *UK, male vocal group (7 WEEKS)*   pos/wks

| 14 Apr 66 | HIGHWAY CODE *Parlophone R 5428* | 25 | 6 |
| 17 Nov 66 | WEATHER FORECAST *Parlophone R 5523* | 50 | 1 |

MASTERMIXERS – See JIVE BUNNY and the MASTERMIXERS

MASTERS AT WORK present INDIA
US, male production / instrumental duo, female vocalist (5 WEEKS)   pos/wks

| 5 Aug 95 | I CAN'T GET NO SLEEP *A & M 5811412* | 44 | 2 |
| 31 Jul 99 | TO BE IN LOVE *Defected DEFECT 5CDS* [1] | 23 | 3 |

[1] MAW presents India

Sammy MASTERS *US, male vocalist (5 WEEKS)*   pos/wks

| 9 Jun 60 | ROCKIN' RED WING *Warner Bros. WB 10* | 36 | 5 |

MATCH *UK, male vocal / instrumental group (3 WEEKS)*   pos/wks

| 16 Jun 79 | BOOGIE MAN *Flamingo FM 2* | 48 | 3 |

MATCHBOX *UK, male vocal / instrumental group (66 WEEKS)*   pos/wks

3 Nov 79	ROCKABILLY REBEL *Magnet MAG 155*	18	12
19 Jan 80	BUZZ BUZZ A DIDDLE IT *Magnet MAG 157*	22	8
10 May 80	MIDNITE DYNAMOS *Magnet MAG 169*	14	12
27 Sep 80 ●	WHEN YOU ASK ABOUT LOVE *Magnet MAG 191*	4	12
29 Nov 80	OVER THE RAINBOW - YOU BELONG TO ME (MEDLEY)	15	11
4 Apr 81	BABES IN THE WOOD *Magnet MAG 193*	46	6
1 Aug 81	LOVE'S MADE A FOOL OF YOU *Magnet MAG 194*	63	3
29 May 82	ONE MORE SATURDAY NIGHT *Magnet MAG 223*	63	2

MATCHBOX 20 *US, male vocal / instrumental group (3 WEEKS)*   pos/wks

| 11 Apr 98 | PUSH *Atlantic AT 0021CD* | 38 | 2 |
| 4 Jul 98 | 3 AM *Atlantic AT 0034CD* | 64 | 1 |

MATCHROOM MOB – See CHAS and DAVE

Mireille MATHIEU *France, female vocalist (7 WEEKS)*   pos/wks

| 13 Dec 67 | LA DERNIERE VALSE *Columbia DB 8323* | 26 | 7 |

Johnny MATHIS (178) [Top 500] *Legendary MOR vocal superstar, b. 30 Sep 1935, San Francisco, US. Frank Sinatra and Elvis Presley are the only males with more hit albums in the US, where his greatest hits album charted for almost 10 years - a record for a solo performer (137 WEEKS)*   pos/wks

23 May 58	TEACHER, TEACHER *Fontana H 130*	27	5
26 Sep 58 ●	A CERTAIN SMILE *Fontana H 142*	4	16
19 Dec 58	WINTER WONDERLAND *Fontana H 165*	17	3
7 Aug 59 ●	SOMEONE *Fontana H 199*	6	15
27 Nov 59	THE BEST OF EVERYTHING *Fontana H 218*	30	1
29 Jan 60	MISTY *Fontana H 219*	12	9
24 Mar 60	YOU ARE BEAUTIFUL *Fontana H 234*	38	8
14 Apr 60	MISTY (re-entry) *Fontana H 219*	46	2
26 May 60	YOU ARE BEAUTIFUL (re-entry) *Fontana H 234*	46	1
28 Jul 60	STARBRIGHT *Fontana H 254*	47	2
6 Oct 60 ●	MY LOVE FOR YOU *Fontana H 267*	9	18
4 Apr 63	WHAT WILL MARY SAY *CBS AAG 135*	49	1
25 Jan 75 ●	I'M STONE IN LOVE WITH YOU *CBS 2653*	10	12
13 Nov 76 ★	WHEN A CHILD IS BORN (SOLEADO) *CBS 4599*	1	12
25 Mar 78 ●	TOO MUCH TOO LITTLE TOO LATE *CBS 6164* [1] ▲	3	14
29 Jul 78	YOU'RE ALL I NEED TO GET BY *CBS 6483* [1]	45	6
11 Aug 79	GONE GONE GONE *CBS 7730*	15	10
26 Dec 81	WHEN A CHILD IS BORN *CBS S 1758* [2]	74	2

[1] Johnny Mathis and Deniece Williams [2] Johnny Mathis and Gladys Knight

Ivan MATIAS *US, male vocalist (1 WEEK)*   pos/wks

| 6 Apr 96 | SO GOOD (TO COME HOME TO) / I'VE HAD ENOUGH *Arista 74321345072* | 69 | 1 |

MATT BIANCO
UK, male / female vocal / instrumental group (65 WEEKS)   pos/wks

11 Feb 84	GET OUT OF YOUR LAZY BED *WEA BIANCO 1*	15	8
14 Apr 84	SNEAKING OUT THE BACK DOOR / MATT'S MOOD *WEA YZ 3*	44	7
10 Nov 84	HALF A MINUTE *WEA YZ 26*	23	10
2 Mar 85	MORE THAN I CAN BEAR *WEA YZ 34*	50	7
5 Oct 85	YEH YEH *WEA YZ 46*	13	10
1 Mar 86	JUST CAN'T STAND IT *WEA YZ 62*	66	2
14 Jun 86	DANCING IN THE STREET *WEA YZ 72*	64	3
4 Jun 88	DON'T BLAME IT ON THAT GIRL / WAP-BAM-BOOGIE *WEA YZ 188*	11	13
27 Aug 88	GOOD TIMES *WEA YZ 302*	55	3
4 Feb 89	NERVOUS / WAP-BAM-BOOGIE (re-mix) *WEA YZ 328*	59	2

'Matt's Mood' credited only from 5 May 1984. Act was a UK / Poland, male / female vocal / instrumental group on first five hits

Al MATTHEWS *US, male vocalist (8 WEEKS)*   pos/wks

| 23 Aug 75 | FOOL *CBS 3429* | 16 | 8 |

Cerys MATTHEWS – See Tom JONES; CATATONIA; SPACE

John MATTHEWS – See UNDERCOVER

MATTHEWS SOUTHERN COMFORT *UK, male vocal / instrumental group - lead vocalist: Ian Mathews (18 WEEKS)*   pos/wks

| 26 Sep 70 ★ | WOODSTOCK *Uni UNS 526* | 1 | 18 |

MATUMBI *UK, male vocal / instrumental group (7 WEEKS)*   pos/wks

| 29 Sep 79 | POINT OF VIEW *Matumbi RIC 101* | 35 | 7 |

Susan MAUGHAN *UK, female vocalist (25 WEEKS)*   pos/wks

11 Oct 62 ●	BOBBY'S GIRL *Philips 326544 BF*	3	19
14 Feb 63	HAND A HANDKERCHIEF TO HELEN *Philips 326562 BF*	41	3
9 May 63	SHE'S NEW TO YOU *Philips 326586 BF*	45	3

MAUREEN *UK, female vocalist - Maureen Walsh (22 WEEKS)*   pos/wks

| 26 Nov 88 ● | SAY A LITTLE PRAYER *Rhythm King DOOD 3* [1] | 10 | 10 |

UK No.1 ★   UK Top 10 ●   Still on chart +   UK million seller ◆   UK entry at No.1 ■   US No.1 ▲

			pos/wks	
16 Jun 90	THINKING OF YOU *Urban URB 55*		11	9
12 Jan 91	WHERE HAS ALL THE LOVE GONE *Urban URB 65*		51	3

[1] Bomb the Bass featuring Maureen

Some copies of 'Thinking of You' are credited to the fuller name of Maureen Walsh

Paul MAURIAT *France, orchestra (14 WEEKS)*

			pos/wks	
21 Feb 68	LOVE IS BLUE (L'AMOUR EST BLEU) *Philips BF 1637* ▲		12	14

MAVERICKS *US, male vocal / instrumental group (23 WEEKS)*

			pos/wks	
2 May 98 ●	DANCE THE NIGHT AWAY			
	MCA Nashville MCSTD 48081		4	18
26 Sep 98	I'VE GOT THIS FEELING *MCA Nashville MCSTD 48095*		27	4
5 Jun 99	SOMEONE SHOULD TELL HER			
	MCA Nashville MCSTD 55567		45	1

MAW – See MASTERS AT WORK

MAX Q *Australia, male vocal / instrumental duo (3 WEEKS)*

			pos/wks	
17 Feb 90	SOMETIMES *Mercury MXQ 2*		53	3

MAX WEBSTER *Canada, male vocal / instrumental group (3 WEEKS)* pos/wks

19 May 79	PARADISE SKIES *Capitol CL 16079*		43	3

MAXIM *UK, male producer / vocalist - Keith Palmer (3 WEEKS)* pos/wks

10 Jun 00	CARMEN QUEASY *XL Recordings XLS 119CD*		33	2
23 Sep 00	SCHEMING *XL Recordings XLS 121CD*		53	1

See also PRODIGY

MAXIMA featuring LILY
UK / Spain, male / female vocal / instrumental duo (2 WEEKS) pos/wks

14 Aug 93	IBIZA *Yo! Yo! CDLILY 1*		55	2

MAXWELL *US, male vocalist (10 WEEKS)*

			pos/wks	
11 May 96	...TIL THE COPS COME KNOCKIN' *Columbia 6631792*		63	1
24 Aug 96	ASCENSION NO ONE'S GONNA LOVE YOU SO DON'T EVER			
	WONDER *Columbia 6636265*		39	3
1 Mar 97	SUMTHIN' SUMTHIN' THE MANTRA *Columbia 6638642*		27	3
24 May 97	ASCENSION DON'T EVER WONDER (re-issue)			
	Columbia 6645952		28	3

MAXX *UK / Sweden / Germany, male / female vocal / instrumental group (24 WEEKS)* pos/wks

21 May 94 ●	GET-A-WAY *Pulse 8 CDLOSE 59*		4	12
6 Aug 94 ●	NO MORE (I CAN'T STAND IT) *Pulse 8 CDLOSE 66*		8	8
29 Oct 94	YOU CAN GET IT *Pulse 8 CDLOSE 75*		21	3
22 Jul 95	I CAN MAKE YOU FEEL LIKE *Pulse 8 CDLOSE 88*		56	1

Terry MAXX – See FUNKSTAR DE LUXE

Billy MAY *US, orchestra (10 WEEKS)*

			pos/wks	
27 Apr 56 ●	MAIN TITLE THEME FROM 'MAN WITH THE GOLDEN ARM'			
	Capitol CL 14551		9	10

Brian MAY *UK, male vocalist / instrumentalist - guitar (33 WEEKS)* pos/wks

5 Nov 83	STAR FLEET *EMI 5436* [1]		65	3
7 Dec 91 ●	DRIVEN BY YOU *Parlophone R 6304*		6	9
5 Sep 92 ●	TOO MUCH LOVE WILL KILL YOU *Parlophone R 6320*		5	9
17 Oct 92	WE ARE THE CHAMPIONS *PolyGram TV PO 229* [2]		66	1
21 Nov 92	BACK TO THE LIGHT *Parlophone R 6329*		19	4
19 Jun 93	RESURRECTION *Parlophone CDRS 6351* [3]		23	3
18 Dec 93	LAST HORIZON *Parlophone CDR 6371*		51	2
6 Jun 98	THE BUSINESS *Parlophone CDR 6498*		51	1
12 Sep 98	WHY DON'T WE TRY AGAIN *Parlophone CDR 6504*		44	1

[1] Brian May and Friends [2] Hank Marvin featuring Brian May [3] Brian May with Cozy Powell

See also QUEEN

Lisa MAY *UK, female vocalist (2 WEEKS)*

			pos/wks	
15 Jul 95	WISHING ON A STAR *Urban Gorilla UG 3CD* [1]		61	1
14 Sep 96	THE CURSE OF VOODOO RAY *Fontana VOOCD 1*		64	1

[1] 88.3 featuring Lisa MAY

Mary MAY *UK, female vocalist (1 WEEK)*

			pos/wks	
27 Feb 64	ANYONE WHO HAD A HEART *Fontana TF 440*		49	1

Shernette MAY *UK, female vocalist (1 WEEK)*

			pos/wks	
6 Jun 98	ALL THE MAN THAT I NEED *Virgin VSCDT 1691*		50	1

Simon MAY *UK, male vocalist (21 WEEKS)*

			pos/wks	
9 Oct 76 ●	SUMMER OF MY LIFE *Pye 7N 45627*		7	8
21 May 77	WE'LL GATHER LILACS - ALL MY LOVING (MEDLEY)			
	Pye 7N 45688		49	1
4 Jun 77	WE'LL GATHER LILACS - ALL MY LOVING (MEDLEY)			
	(re-entry) *Pye 7N 45688*		50	1
26 Oct 85	HOWARD'S WAY *BBC RESL 174* [1]		21	11

[1] Simon May Orchestra

See also Anita DOBSON; Marti WEBB

MAYA – See TAMPERER featuring MAYA

Curtis MAYFIELD *US, male vocalist (18 WEEKS)*

			pos/wks	
31 Jul 71	MOVE ON UP *Buddah 2011 080*		12	10
2 Dec 78	NO GOODBYES *Atlantic LV 1*		65	2
30 May 87	(CELEBRATE) THE DAY AFTER YOU *RCA MONK 6* [1]		52	2
29 Sep 90	SUPERFLY 1990 *Capitol CL 586* [2]		48	3

[1] Blow Monkeys with Curtis Mayfield [2] Curtis Mayfield and Ice-T

MAYTALS *Jamaica, male vocal / instrumental group (4 WEEKS)* pos/wks

25 Apr 70	MONKEY MAN *Trojan TR 7711*		50	1
9 May 70	MONKEY MAN (re-entry) *Trojan TR 7711*		47	3

MAYTE *US, female vocalist (1 WEEK)*

			pos/wks	
18 Nov 95	IF EYE LOVE U 2 NIGHT *NPG 0061635*		67	1

MAZE featuring Frankie BEVERLY
US, male vocal / instrumental group (14 WEEKS) pos/wks

20 Jul 85	TOO MANY GAMES *Capitol CL 363*		36	7
23 Aug 86	I WANNA BE WITH YOU *Capitol CL 421*		55	3
27 May 89	JOY AND PAIN *Capitol CL 531* [1]		57	4

[1] Maze

Kym MAZELLE *US, female vocalist - Kimberley Grigsby (66 WEEKS)* pos/wks

12 Nov 88	USELESS (I DON'T NEED YOU NOW) *Syncopate SY 18*		53	3
14 Jan 89 ●	WAIT *RCA PB 42595* [1]		7	10
25 Mar 89	GOT TO GET YOU BACK *Syncopate SY 25*		29	4
7 Oct 89	LOVE STRAIN *Syncopate SY 30*		52	3
20 Jan 90	WAS THAT ALL IT WAS *Syncopate SY 32*		33	6
26 May 90	USELESS (I DON'T NEED YOU NOW) (re-mix)			
	Syncopate SY 36		48	2
24 Nov 90	MISSING YOU *Ten TEN 345* [2]		22	7
25 May 91	NO ONE CAN LOVE YOU MORE THAN ME			
	Parlophone R 6287		62	2
26 Dec 92	LOVE ME THE RIGHT WAY *Arista 74321128097* [3]		22	10
11 Jun 94	NO MORE TEARS (ENOUGH IS ENOUGH)			
	Ding Dong 74321209032		13	7
8 Oct 94	GIMME ALL YOUR LOVIN' *Ding Dong 74321231322* [4]		22	3
23 Dec 95	SEARCHING FOR THE GOLDEN EYE *Eternal WEA 027CD* [5]		40	3
28 Sep 96	LOVE ME THE RIGHT WAY (re-mix) *Logic 74321404442* [3]		55	1
16 Aug 97	YOUNG HEARTS RUN FREE *EMI CDEM 488*		20	4
19 Feb 00	TRULY *Island Blue PFACD 4* [6]		55	1

[1] Robert Howard and Kym Mazelle [2] Soul II Soul featuring Kym Mazelle [3] Rapination and Kym Mazelle [4] Jocelyn Brown and Kym Mazelle [5] Motiv 8 and Kym Mazelle [6] Peshay featuring Kym Mazelle

MAZZY STAR US, male / female vocal / instrumental duo (3 WEEKS)   pos/wks

| 27 Aug 94 | FADE INTO YOU Capitol CDCL 720 | 48 | 1 |
| 2 Nov 96 | FLOWERS IN DECEMBER Capitol CDCL 781 | 40 | 2 |

MC DUKE UK, male rapper (1 WEEK)   pos/wks

| 11 Mar 89 | I'M RIFFIN (ENGLISH RASTA) Music of Life 7NOTE 25 | 75 | 1 |

MC ERIC – See TECHNOTRONIC

MC FIXX IT – See ANTICAPPELLA

MC HAMMER – See HAMMER

MC KIE – See TEEBONE featuring MC KIE and MC SPARKS

MC LETHAL UK, male producer (1 WEEK)   pos/wks

| 14 Nov 92 | THE RAVE DIGGER Network NWKT 60 | 66 | 1 |

MC LYTE US, female rapper - Lana Moorer (16 WEEKS)   pos/wks

15 Jan 94	RUFFNECK Atlantic A 8336CD	67	1
29 Jun 96	KEEP ON KEEPIN' ON East West A 4287CD [1]	39	2
18 Jan 97	COLD ROCK A PARTY East West A 3975CD	15	4
19 Apr 97	KEEP ON KEEPIN' ON (re-issue) East West A 3950CD1 [1]	27	2
5 Sep 98	I CAN'T MAKE A MISTAKE Elektra E 3813CD	46	1
19 Dec 98	IT'S ALL YOURS East West E 3789CD [2]	36	4
24 Jun 00	JAMMIN' Tuff Gong TGXCD 9 [3]	42	2

[1] MC Lyte featuring Xscape [2] MC Lyte featuring Gina Thompson [3] Bob Marley featuring MC Lyte

MC MARIO – See AMBASSADORS OF FUNK featuring MC MARIO

MC MIKEE FREEDOM – See NOMAD

MC MIKER 'G' and Deejay SVEN Holland, male vocal / instrumental rap duo - Lucien Witteveen AND Sven Van Veen (7 WEEKS)   pos/wks

| 6 Sep 86 ● | HOLIDAY RAP Debut DEBT 3008 | 6 | 7 |

MC NEAT – See DJ LUCK & MC NEAT

MC NOISE – See LOVE INC

MC NUMBER 6 – See FAB

MC PARKER – See FAB

M.C.R.B. – See SUNSHIP featuring MCRB

MC SAR – See REAL McCOY

MC SKAT KAT and the STRAY MOB
US, male cartoon feline rap / vocal group (2 WEEKS)   pos/wks

| 9 Nov 91 | SKAT STRUT Virgin America VUS 51 | 64 | 2 |

MC SOLAAR – See URBAN SPECIES; Missy 'Misdemeanor' ELLIOTT

MC SPARKS – See TEEBONE featuring MC KIE and MC SPARKS

MC SPY-D + FRIENDS
UK, male / female vocal / instrumental group (2 WEEKS)   pos/wks

| 11 Mar 95 | THE AMAZING SPIDER-MAN Parlophone CDR 6404 | 37 | 2 |

MC STYLES – See Scott GARCIA featuring MC STYLES

MC TUNES UK, male rapper - Nicholas Lockett (19 WEEKS)   pos/wks

2 Jun 90 ●	THE ONLY RHYME THAT BITES ZTT ZANG 3 [1]	10	10
15 Sep 90	TUNES SPLITS THE ATOM ZTT ZANG 6 [1]	18	7
1 Dec 90	PRIMARY RHYMING ZTT ZANG 10	67	1
6 Mar 99	THE ONLY RHYME THAT BITES 99 ZTT ZTT 125CD [1]	53	1

[1] MC Tunes versus 808 State

MC WILDSKI UK, male rapper (10 WEEKS)   pos/wks

| 8 Jul 89 | BLAME IT ON THE BASSLINE Go.Beat GOD 33 [1] | 29 | 6 |
| 3 Mar 90 | WARRIOR Arista 112956 | 49 | 4 |

[1] Norman Cook featuring MC Wildski

'Blame It on the Bassline' was listed with 'Won't Talk About It' by Norman Cook featuring Billy Bragg

M-D-EMM UK, male producer - Mark Ryder (3 WEEKS)   pos/wks

| 22 Feb 92 | GET DOWN Strictly Underground 7STUR 13 | 55 | 2 |
| 30 May 92 | MOVE YOUR FEET Strictly Underground STUR 15 | 67 | 1 |

ME AND YOU featuring WE THE PEOPLE BAND Jamaica / UK, male / female vocal / instrumental group (9 WEEKS)   pos/wks

| 28 Jul 79 | YOU NEVER KNOW WHAT YOU'VE GOT Laser LAS 8 | 31 | 9 |

ME ME ME UK, male vocal / instrumental group (4 WEEKS)   pos/wks

| 17 Aug 96 | HANGING AROUND Indolent DUFF 005CD | 19 | 4 |

Abigail MEAD and Nigel GOULDING UK / US, female / male producers - Vivian Kubrick & Nigel Goulding (10 WEEKS)   pos/wks

| 26 Sep 87 ● | FULL METAL JACKET (I WANNA BE YOUR DRILL INSTRUCTOR) Warner Bros. W 8187 | 2 | 10 |

MEAT BEAT MANIFESTO UK, male production duo (1 WEEK)   pos/wks

| 20 Feb 93 | MINDSTREAM Play It Again Sam BIAS 232CD | 55 | 1 |

MEAT LOAF 155 Top 500 Larger-than-life vocalist / actor; b. Marvin Lee Aday, 27 Sep 1948, Dallas, US. His collaborations with producer / songwriter Jim Steinman resulted in some of rock's finest recordings. His album Bat Out of Hell sold more than 25 million copies and spent more than nine years in total in the UK chart (146 WEEKS)   pos/wks

20 May 78	YOU TOOK THE WORDS RIGHT OUT OF MY MOUTH Epic EPC 5980	33	8
19 Aug 78	TWO OUT OF THREE AIN'T BAD Epic EPC 6281	32	8
10 Feb 79	BAT OUT OF HELL Epic EPC 7018	15	7
26 Sep 81	I'M GONNA LOVE HER FOR BOTH OF US Epic EPCA 1580	62	3
28 Nov 81 ●	DEAD RINGER FOR LOVE Epic EPCA 1697	5	17
28 May 83	IF YOU REALLY WANT TO Epic A 3357	59	2
24 Sep 83	MIDNIGHT AT THE LOST AND FOUND Epic A 3748	17	8
14 Jan 84	RAZOR'S EDGE Epic A 4080	41	3
6 Oct 84	MODERN GIRL Arista ARIST 585	17	9
22 Dec 84	NOWHERE FAST Arista ARIST 600	67	4
23 Mar 85	PIECE OF THE ACTION Arista ARIST 603	47	5
30 Aug 86	ROCK 'N' ROLL MERCENARIES Arista ARIST 666 [1]	31	6
22 Jun 91	DEAD RINGER FOR LOVE (re-issue) Epic 6569827	53	2
27 Jun 92	TWO OUT OF THREE AIN'T BAD (re-issue) Epic 6574917	69	1
9 Oct 93 ★	I'D DO ANYTHING FOR LOVE (BUT I WON'T DO THAT) Virgin VSCDT 1443 ▲	1	19
18 Dec 93 ●	BAT OUT OF HELL (re-issue) Epic 6600062	8	9
19 Feb 94	ROCK AND ROLL DREAMS COME THROUGH Virgin VSCDT 1479	11	7
7 May 94	OBJECTS IN THE REAR VIEW MIRROR MAY APPEAR CLOSER THAN THEY ARE Virgin VSCDT 1492	26	4
28 Oct 95 ●	I'D LIE FOR YOU (AND THAT'S THE TRUTH) Virgin VSCDT 1563	2	11
27 Jan 96 ●	NOT A DRY EYE IN THE HOUSE Virgin VSCDT 1567	7	6
27 Apr 96	RUNNIN' FOR THE RED LIGHT (I GOTTA LIFE) Virgin VSCDX 1582	21	3
17 Apr 99	IS NOTHING SACRED Virgin VSCDT 1734 [2]	15	4

[1] Meat Loaf featuring John Parr [2] Meat Loaf featuring Patti Russo

'Dead Ringer for Love' features Cher as uncredited co-vocalist. 'I'd Do Anything For Love (But I Won't Do That) features uncredited vocals by Lorraine Crosby (aka Mrs Loud)

MECHANICS – See MIKE and the MECHANICS

MECO US, orchestra - led by Meco Monardo (9 WEEKS)   pos/wks

| 1 Oct 77 ● | STAR WARS THEME - CANTINA BAND RCA XB 1028 ▲ | 7 | 9 |

UK No.1 ★   UK Top 10 ●   Still on chart +   UK million seller ◆   UK entry at No.1 ■   US No.1 ▲

Glenn MEDEIROS US, male vocalist (26 WEEKS)

		pos/wks
18 Jun 88 ★	NOTHING'S GONNA CHANGE MY LOVE FOR YOU *London LON 184*	**1** 13
3 Sep 88	LONG AND LASTING LOVE (ONCE IN A LIFETIME) *London LON 202*	**42** 4
30 Jun 90	SHE AIN'T WORTH IT *London LON 265* [1] ▲	**12** 9

[1] Glenn Medeiros featuring Bobby Brown

Paul MEDFORD – See Letitia DEAN and Paul MEDFORD

MEDICINE HEAD UK, male vocal / instrumental duo - John Fiddler and Peter Hope Evans (37 WEEKS)

		pos/wks
26 Jun 71	(AND THE) PICTURES IN THE SKY *Dandelion DAN 7003*	**22** 8
5 May 73 ●	ONE AND ONE IS ONE *Polydor 2001 432*	**3** 13
4 Aug 73	RISING SUN *Polydor 2058 389*	**11** 9
9 Feb 74	SLIP AND SLIDE *Polydor 2058 436*	**22** 7

MEDICINE SHOW – See DR HOOK

Bill MEDLEY US, male vocalist (29 WEEKS)

		pos/wks
31 Oct 87 ●	(I'VE HAD) THE TIME OF MY LIFE *RCA PB 49625* [1] ▲	**6** 12
27 Aug 88	HE AIN'T HEAVY, HE'S MY BROTHER *Scotti Brothers PO 10*	**25** 6
15 Dec 90 ●	(I'VE HAD) THE TIME OF MY LIFE (re-entry) *RCA PB 49625* [1]	**8** 11

[1] Bill Medley and Jennifer Warnes

See also RIGHTEOUS BROTHERS

MEDWAY US, male producer - Jesse Skeens (1 WEEK)

		pos/wks
29 Apr 00	FAT BASTARD *Hooj Choons HOOJ 92CD*	**69** 1

Michael MEDWIN, Bernard BRESSLAW, Alfie BASS and Leslie FYSON UK, male actor / vocalists (9 WEEKS)

		pos/wks
30 May 58 ●	THE SIGNATURE TUNE OF 'THE ARMY GAME' *HMV POP 490*	**5** 9

See also Bernard BRESSLAW

MEECHIE US, female vocalist (1 WEEK)

		pos/wks
2 Sep 95	YOU BRING ME JOY *Vibe MCSTD 2069*	**74** 1

Tony MEEHAN COMBO
UK, male instrumental group, Tony Meehan - drums (4 WEEKS)

		pos/wks
16 Jan 64	SONG OF MEXICO *Decca F 11801*	**39** 4

See also Jet HARRIS and Tony MEEHAN; SHADOWS

MEEKER UK, female vocal / production duo (1 WEEK)

		pos/wks
26 Feb 00	SAVE ME *Underwater H20 009 CD*	**60** 1

MEGA CITY FOUR UK, male vocal / instrumental group (7 WEEKS)

		pos/wks
19 Oct 91	WORDS THAT SAY *Big Life MEGA 2*	**66** 1
8 Feb 92	STOP (EP) *Big Life MEGA 3*	**36** 2
16 May 92	SHIVERING SAND *Big Life MEGA 4*	**35** 2
1 May 93	IRON SKY *Big Life MEGAD 5*	**48** 1
17 Jul 93	WALLFLOWER *Big Life MEGAD 6*	**69** 1

Tracks on Stop (EP): Stop / Desert Song / Back to Zero / Overlap

MEGABASS – See VARIOUS ARTISTS (MONTAGES)

MEGADETH US, male vocal / instrumental group (32 WEEKS)

		pos/wks
19 Dec 87	WAKE UP DEAD *Capitol CL 476*	**65** 2
27 Feb 88	ANARCHY IN THE UK *Capitol CL 480*	**45** 3
21 May 88	MARY JANE *Capitol CL 489*	**46** 2
13 Jan 90	NO MORE MR. NICE GUY *SBK SBK 4*	**13** 6
29 Sep 90	HOLY WARS . . . THE PUNISHMENT DUE *Capitol CLP 588*	**24** 3
16 Mar 91	HANGAR 18 *Capitol CLS 604*	**26** 4
27 Jun 92	SYMPHONY OF DESTRUCTION *Capitol CLS 662*	**15** 3

24 Oct 92	SKIN O' MY TEETH *Capitol CLP 669*	**13**	3
29 May 93	SWEATING BULLETS *Capitol CDCL 682*	**26**	3
7 Jan 95	TRAIN OF CONSEQUENCES *Capitol CDCL 730*	**22**	3

MEGAMAN – See OXIDE & NEUTRINO

MEHTA – See JosÈ CARRERAS

MEJA Sweden, female vocalist - Meja Beckman (14 WEEKS)

		pos/wks
24 Oct 98	ALL 'BOUT THE MONEY *Columbia 6665662*	**12** 5
29 Apr 00 ●	PRIVATE EMOTION *Columbia 6692692* [1]	**9** 9

[1] Ricky Martin featuring Meja

MEKON featuring Roxanne SHANTE
UK, male producer (John Gosling) and US, female rapper (1 WEEK) pos/wks

		pos/wks
23 Sep 00	WHAT'S GOING ON *Wall of Sound WALD 064*	**43** 1

MEL and KIM – See Mel SMITH; Kim WILDE

MEL and KIM
UK, female vocal duo - Mel and Kim Appleby (51 WEEKS)

		pos/wks
20 Sep 86 ●	SHOWING OUT (GET FRESH AT THE WEEKEND) *Supreme SUPE 107*	**3** 19
7 Mar 87 ★	RESPECTABLE *Supreme SUPE 111*	**1** 15
11 Jul 87 ●	F.L.M. *Supreme SUPE 113*	**7** 10
27 Feb 88 ●	THAT'S THE WAY IT IS *Supreme SUPE 117*	**10** 7

See also Kim APPLEBY

Melle MEL – See GRANDMASTER FLASH, Melle MEL and the FURIOUS FIVE

George MELACHRINO ORCHESTRA UK, orchestra (9 WEEKS) pos/wks

		pos/wks
12 Oct 56	AUTUMN CONCERTO *HMV B 10958*	**18** 9

MELANIE US, female vocalist - Melanie Safka (35 WEEKS)

		pos/wks
26 Sep 70 ●	RUBY TUESDAY *Buddah 2011 038*	**9** 14
9 Jan 71	RUBY TUESDAY (re-entry) *Buddah 2011 038*	**43** 1
16 Jan 71	WHAT HAVE THEY DONE TO MY SONG MA *Buddah*	**39** 1
1 Jan 72 ●	BRAND NEW KEY *Buddah 2011 105* ▲	**4** 12
16 Feb 74	WILL YOU LOVE ME TOMORROW *Neighbourhood NBH 9*	**37** 5
24 Sep 83	EVERY BREATH OF THE WAY *Neighbourhood HOOD NB1*	**70** 2

MELKY SEDECK
US, male / female vocal / instrumental duo (9 WEEKS)

		pos/wks
8 May 99	RAW *MCA MCSTD 48107*	**50** 1
16 Sep 00 ●	IT DOESN'T MATTER *Columbia 6697782* [1]	**3** 8

[1] Wyclef Jean featuring The Rock and Melky Sedeck

John Cougar MELLENCAMP US, male vocalist (18 WEEKS)

		pos/wks
23 Oct 82	JACK AND DIANE *Riva RIVA 37* [1] ▲	**25** 8
1 Feb 86	SMALL TOWN *Riva JCM 5*	**53** 4
10 May 86	R.O.C.K. IN THE U.S.A. *Riva JCM 6*	**67** 3
3 Sep 94	WILD NIGHT *Mercury MERCD 409* [2]	**34** 3

[1] John Cougar [2] John Mellencamp featuring Me'Shell Ndegeocello

MELLOMEN – See Rosemary CLOONEY; Frankie LAINE; Doris DAY

Will MELLOR UK, male vocalist (9 WEEKS)

		pos/wks
28 Feb 98 ●	WHEN I NEED YOU *Unity UNITY 017RCD*	**5** 6
27 Jun 98	NO MATTER WHAT I DO *Jive 0540012*	**23** 3

MELLOW TRAX
Germany, male producer - Christian Schwarnweber (2 WEEKS) pos/wks

		pos/wks
14 Oct 00	OUTTA SPACE *Substance SUBS 3CDS*	**41** 2

MELODIANS Jamaica, male vocal / instrumental group (1 WEEK) pos/wks

		pos/wks
10 Jan 70	SWEET SENSATION *Trojan TR 695*	**41** 1

MESSIAH
UK, male instrumental / production group (13 WEEKS) pos/wks

			pos	wks
20 Jun 92	TEMPLE OF DREAMS *Kickin KICK 12S*		20	5
26 Sep 92	I FEEL LOVE *Kickin KICK 22S* [1]		19	5
27 Nov 93	THUNDERDOME *WEA YZ 790CD1*		29	3

[1] Messiah featuring Precious Wilson

METAL GURUS
UK, male vocal / instrumental group (2 WEEKS) pos/wks

			pos	wks
8 Dec 90	MERRY XMAS EVERYBODY *Mercury GURU 1*		55	2

METALHEADZ – See GOLDIE

METALLICA
US / Denmark, male vocal / instrumental group (59 WEEKS) pos/wks

			pos	wks
22 Aug 87	THE $5.98 EP - GARAGE DAYS RE-REVISITED *Vertigo METAL 112*		27	4
3 Sep 88	HARVESTER OF SORROW *Vertigo METAL 212*		20	3
22 Apr 89	ONE *Vertigo METAL 5*		13	7
10 Aug 91 ●	ENTER SANDMAN *Vertigo METAL 7*		5	4
9 Nov 91	THE UNFORGIVEN *Vertigo METAL 8*		15	4
2 May 92 ●	NOTHING ELSE MATTERS *Vertigo METAL 10*		6	6
31 Oct 92	WHEREVER I MAY ROAM *Vertigo METAL 9*		25	4
20 Feb 93	SAD BUT TRUE *Vertigo METCD 11*		20	3
1 Jun 96 ●	UNTIL IT SLEEPS *Vertigo METCD 12*		5	4
28 Sep 96	HERO OF THE DAY *Vertigo METCD 13*		17	4
7 Dec 96	MAMA SAID *Vertigo METCD 14*		19	2
22 Nov 97	THE MEMORY REMAINS *Vertigo METCD 15*		13	3
7 Mar 98	THE UNFORGIVEN II *Vertigo METDD 17*		15	4
4 Jul 98	FUEL *Vertigo METCD 16*		31	2
27 Feb 99	WHISKEY IN THE JAR *Vertigo METCD 19*		29	2
12 Aug 00	I DISAPPEAR *Hollywood 0113875 HWR*		35	3

Tracks on The $5.98 EP: Garage Days Re-Revisited : Helpless / Crash Course in Brain Surgery / The Small Hours / Last Caress / Green Hell

METEORS
UK, male vocal / instrumental group (2 WEEKS) pos/wks

			pos	wks
26 Feb 83	JOHNNY REMEMBER ME *ID EYE 1*		66	2

Pat METHENY GROUP – See David BOWIE

METHOD MAN
US, male rapper - Clifford Smith (14 WEEKS) pos/wks

			pos	wks
29 Apr 95	RELEASE YO' SELF *Def Jam DEFCD 6*		46	1
29 Jul 95 ●	I'LL BE THERE FOR YOU - YOU'RE ALL I NEED TO GET BY *Def Jam DEFCD 11* [1]		10	5
5 Apr 97 ●	HIT EM HIGH (THE MONSTARS' ANTHEM) *Atlantic A 5449CD* [2]		8	6
22 May 99	BREAK UPS 2 MAKE UPS *Def Jam 8709272* [3]		33	2

[1] Method Man featuring Mary J Blige [2] B Real / Busta Rhymes / Coolio / LL Cool J / Method Man [3] Method Man featuring D'Angelo

MEZZOFORTE
Iceland, male instrumental group (10 WEEKS) pos/wks

			pos	wks
5 Mar 83	GARDEN PARTY *Steinar STE 705*		17	9
11 Jun 83	ROCKALL *Steinar STE 710*		75	1

MFSB
US, orchestra (18 WEEKS) pos/wks

			pos	wks
27 Apr 74	TSOP (THE SOUND OF PHILADELPHIA) *Philadelphia International PIR 2289* [1] ▲		22	9
26 Jul 75	SEXY *Philadelphia International PIR 3381*		37	5
31 Jan 81	MYSTERIES OF THE WORLD *Sound of Philadelphia PIR 9501*		41	4

[1] MFSB featuring the Three Degrees

MG's – See BOOKER T and the MG's

MIAMI SOUND MACHINE (476 Top 500)
Groundbreaking Latin combo formed by percussionist Emilio Estefan and fronted by wife Gloria, who achieved worldwide fame after they started recording in English. Miami honoured them by renaming a street Miami Sound Machine Boulevard. Gloria Went on to become one of world's top selling female artists. (72 WEEKS) pos/wks

			pos	wks
11 Aug 84 ●	DR BEAT *Epic A 4614*		6	14
17 May 86	BAD BOY *Epic A 6537*		16	11
16 Jul 88 ●	ANYTHING FOR YOU *Epic 651673 7* [1] ▲		10	16
22 Oct 88 ●	1-2-3 *Epic 652958 7* [1]		9	9
17 Dec 88 ●	RHYTHM IS GONNA GET YOU *Epic 654514 7* [1]		16	9
31 Dec 88	1-2-3 (re-entry) *Epic 652958 7* [1]		72	1
11 Feb 89 ●	CAN'T STAY AWAY FROM YOU *Epic 651 444 7* [1]		7	12

[1] Gloria Estefan and Miami Sound Machine

See also Gloria ESTEFAN

George MICHAEL (45 Top 500)
Previously half of internationally celebrated duo Wham!, b. Georgios Panayiotou, 25 Jun 1963, London, UK. This multi-talented, award-winning singer / songwriter / producer / arranger and instrumentalist has successfully made the difficult transition from teeny-bopper hero to world-renowned solo star (249 WEEKS) pos/wks

			pos	wks
4 Aug 84 ★	CARELESS WHISPER *Epic A 4603* ◆ ▲		1	17
5 Apr 86 ★	A DIFFERENT CORNER *Epic A 7033*		1	10
31 Jan 87 ★	I KNEW YOU WERE WAITING (FOR ME) *Epic DUET 2* [1] ▲		1	11
13 Jun 87 ●	I WANT YOUR SEX *Epic LUST 1*		3	10
24 Oct 87 ●	FAITH *Epic EMU 3* ▲		2	12
9 Jan 88	FATHER FIGURE *Epic EMU 4* ▲		11	6
23 Apr 88 ●	ONE MORE TRY *Epic EMU 5* ▲		8	7
16 Jul 88	MONKEY *Epic EMU 6* ▲		13	6
3 Dec 88	KISSING A FOOL *Epic EMU 7*		18	6
25 Aug 90 ●	PRAYING FOR TIME *Epic GEO 1* ▲		6	7
27 Oct 90	WAITING FOR THAT DAY *Epic GEO 2*		23	5
15 Dec 90	FREEDOM *Epic GEO 3*		28	6
16 Feb 91	HEAL THE PAIN *Epic 6566477*		31	4
30 Mar 91	COWBOYS AND ANGELS *Epic 6567747*		45	3
7 Dec 91 ★	DON'T LET THE SUN GO DOWN ON ME *Epic 6576467* [2] ■ ▲		1	10
13 Jun 92	TOO FUNKY *Epic 6580587*		4	9
1 May 93 ★	FIVE LIVE (EP) *Parlophone CDRS 6340* [3] ■		1	11
24 Jul 93	FIVE LIVE (EP) (re-entry) *Parlophone CDRS 6340* [3]		74	1
20 Jan 96 ★	JESUS TO A CHILD *Virgin VSCDG 1571* ■		1	10
20 Apr 96	JESUS TO A CHILD (re-entry) *Virgin VSCDG 1571*		68	1
4 May 96	JESUS TO A CHILD (2nd re-entry) *Virgin VSCDG 1571*		65	2
4 May 96 ★	FASTLOVE *Virgin VSCDG 1579* ■		1	14
31 Aug 96 ●	SPINNING THE WHEEL *Virgin VSCDG 1595*		2	12
1 Feb 97 ●	OLDER / I CAN'T MAKE YOU LOVE ME *Virgin VSCDG 1626*		3	8
12 Apr 97	OLDER / I CAN'T MAKE YOU LOVE ME (re-entry) *Virgin VSCDG 1626*		70	1
10 May 97 ●	STAR PEOPLE '97 *Virgin VSCDG 1641*		2	9
7 Jun 97 ●	WALTZ AWAY DREAMING *Aegean AECD 01* [4]		10	4
19 Jul 97	STAR PEOPLE '97 (re-entry) *Virgin VSCDG 1641*		59	4
20 Sep 97 ●	YOU HAVE BEEN LOVED / THE STRANGEST THING '97 *Virgin VSCD 1570*		2	8
31 Oct 98 ●	OUTSIDE *Epic 6665625*		2	14
13 Feb 99	OUTSIDE (re-entry) *Epic 6665625*		61	2
13 Mar 99 ●	AS *Epic 6670122* [5]		4	10
17 Jun 00 ●	IF I TOLD YOU THAT *Arista 74321766282* [6]		9	9
26 Aug 00	IF I TOLD YOU THAT (re-entry) *Arista 74321766282* [6]		51	2

[1] Aretha Franklin and George Michael [2] George Michael and Elton John [3] George Michael and Queen with Lisa Stansfield [4] Toby Bourke with George Michael [5] George Michael and Mary J Blige [6] Whitney Houston / George Michael

Tracks on Five Live (EP): Somebody to Love / These Are the Days of Our Lives / Calling You / Papa Was a Rolling Stone - Killer (medley). The first track on the EP features Queen, the second Queen and Lisa Stansfield

See also Lisa MOORISH; Elton JOHN

MICHAELA
UK, female vocalist (6 WEEKS) pos/wks

			pos	wks
2 Sep 89	H-A-P-P-Y RADIO *London H 1*		62	4
28 Apr 90	TAKE GOOD CARE OF MY HEART *London WAC 90*		66	2

Lisa MICHAELIS – See Frankie KNUCKLES

Pras MICHEL
US, male rapper / producer - Prakazrel Michael (33 WEEKS) pos/wks

			pos	wks
27 Jun 98 ●	GHETTO SUPASTAR (THAT IS WHAT YOU ARE) *Interscope IND 95593* [1]		2	17

7 Nov 98 ●	BLUE ANGELS *Ruffhouse 6666215* [2]	6 10
14 Nov 98 ●	ANOTHER ONE BITES THE DUST *Dreamworks DRMCD 22364* [3]	5 6

[1] Pras Michel featuring Ol' Dirty Bastard introducing Mya [2] Pras [3] Queen with Wyclef Jean featuring Pras and Free

MICHELE – See KING BEE

Keith MICHELL *Australia, male vocalist (25 WEEKS)*
		pos/wks
27 Mar 71	I'LL GIVE YOU THE EARTH (TOUS LES BATEAUX, TOUS LES OISEAUX) *Spark SRL 1046*	43 1
17 Apr 71	I'LL GIVE YOU THE EARTH (TOUS LES BATEAUX, TOUS LES OISEAUX) (re-entry) *Spark SRL 1046*	30 10
26 Jan 80 ●	CAPTAIN BEAKY / WILFRED THE WEASEL *Polydor POSP 106*	5 10
29 Mar 80	THE TRIAL OF HISSING SID *Polydor HISS 1* [1]	53 4

[1] Keith Michell, Captain Beaky and his Band

MICHELLE *Trinidad, female vocalist (1 WEEK)*
		pos/wks
8 Jun 96	STANDING HERE ALL ALONE *Positiva CDTIV 54*	69 1

Yvette MICHELLE *US, female vocalist (3 WEEKS)*
		pos/wks
5 Apr 97	I'M NOT FEELING YOU *Loud 74321465222*	36 3

Lloyd MICHELS – See MISTURA featuring Lloyd MICHELS

MICK and PAT – See PAT and MICK

MICROBE *UK, male vocalist (7 WEEKS)*
		pos/wks
14 May 69	GROOVY BABY *CBS 4158*	29 7

MICRODISNEY *Ireland, male vocal / instrumental group (3 WEEKS)*
		pos/wks
21 Feb 87	TOWN TO TOWN *Virgin VS 927*	55 3

MIDDLE OF THE ROAD (437 Top 500) *Scottish vocal / instrumental pop quartet who re-located to Italy and were extremely successful across Europe. Fronted by sole female Sally Carr (Sarah Young) b. 28 Mar 1945, Glasgow. First hit reportedly sold close to 10 million copies worldwide (76 WEEKS)*
		pos/wks
5 Jun 71 ★	CHIRPY CHIRPY CHEEP CHEEP *RCA 2047*	1 34
4 Sep 71 ●	TWEEDLE DEE TWEEDLE DUM *RCA 2110*	2 17
11 Dec 71 ●	SOLEY SOLEY *RCA 2151*	5 12
25 Mar 72	SACRAMENTO *RCA 2184*	49 1
8 Apr 72	SACRAMENTO (re-entry) *RCA 2184*	23 6
29 Jul 72	SAMSON AND DELILAH *RCA 2237*	26 6

MIDDLESBROUGH FC featuring Bob MORTIMER and Chris REA *UK, male football team / vocal group (1 WEEK)*
		pos/wks
24 May 97	LET'S DANCE *Magnet EW 112CD*	44 1

MIDFIELD GENERAL featuring LINDA LEWIS *UK, male producer - Damian Harris, and UK, female vocalist (1 WEEK)*
		pos/wks
19 Aug 00	REACH OUT *Skint SKINT 54CD*	61 1

MIDGET *UK, male vocal / instrumental group (2 WEEKS)*
		pos/wks
31 Jan 98	ALL FALL DOWN *Radarscope TINYCDS 6X*	57 1
18 Apr 98	INVISIBLE BALLOON *Radarscope TINYCDS 7*	66 1

MIDI XPRESS *UK, male vocal / instrumental duo (1 WEEK)*
		pos/wks
11 May 96	CHASE *Labello Dance LAD 26CD*	73 1

Bette MIDLER *US, female vocalist (27 WEEKS)*
		pos/wks
17 Jun 89 ●	WIND BENEATH MY WINGS *Atlantic A 8972* ▲	5 12
13 Oct 90	FROM A DISTANCE *Atlantic A 7820*	45 5
15 Jun 91 ●	FROM A DISTANCE (re-entry) *Atlantic A 7820*	6 9
5 Dec 98	MY ONE TRUE FRIEND *Warner Brothers W 460CD*	58 1

MIDNIGHT COWBOY SOUNDTRACK *US, orchestra (4 WEEKS)*
		pos/wks
8 Nov 80	MIDNIGHT COWBOY *United Artists UP 634*	47 4

MIDNIGHT OIL *Australia, male vocal / instrumental group (32 WEEKS)*
		pos/wks
23 Apr 88	BEDS ARE BURNING *Sprint OIL 1*	48 5
2 Jul 88	THE DEAD HEART *Sprint OIL 2*	68 2
25 Mar 89 ●	BEDS ARE BURNING (re-issue) *Sprint OIL 3*	6 13
1 Jul 89	THE DEAD HEART (re-issue) *Sprint OIL 4*	62 4
10 Feb 90	BLUE SKY MINE *CBS OIL 5*	66 2
17 Apr 93	TRUGANINI *Columbia 6590492*	29 4
3 Jul 93	MY COUNTRY *Columbia 6593702*	66 1
6 Nov 93	IN THE VALLEY *Columbia 6598492*	60 1

MIDNIGHT STAR *US, male / female vocal / instrumental group (26 WEEKS)*
		pos/wks
23 Feb 85	OPERATOR *Solar MCA 942*	66 2
28 Jun 86	HEADLINES *Solar MCA 1065*	16 8
4 Oct 86 ●	MIDAS TOUCH *Solar MCA 1096*	8 10
7 Feb 87	ENGINE NO.9 *Solar MCA 1117*	64 3
2 May 87	WET MY WHISTLE *Solar MCA 1127*	60 3

MIDNITE BAND – See Tony RALLO and the MIDNITE BAND

MIGHTY AVENGERS *UK, male vocal / instrumental group (2 WEEKS)*
		pos/wks
26 Nov 64	SO MUCH IN LOVE *Decca F 11962*	46 2

MIGHTY AVONS – See LARRY CUNNINGHAM and the MIGHTY AVONS

MIGHTY DUB KATZ *UK, male producer - Norman Cook (5 WEEKS)*
		pos/wks
7 Dec 96	JUST ANOTHER GROOVE *ffrr FCD 287*	43 1
2 Aug 97	MAGIC CARPET RIDE *ffrr FCD 306*	24 4

See also Norman COOK; BEATS INTERNATIONAL; HOUSEMARTINS; FATBOY SLIM; PIZZAMAN; FREAKPOWER

MIGHTY LEMON DROPS *UK, male vocal / instrumental group (7 WEEKS)*
		pos/wks
13 Sep 86	THE OTHER SIDE OF YOU *Blue Guitar AZUR 1*	67 2
18 Apr 87	OUT OF HAND *Blue Guitar AZUR 4*	66 3
23 Jan 88	INSIDE OUT *Blue Guitar AZUR 6*	74 2

MIGHTY MIGHTY BOSSTONES *US, male vocal / instrumental group (6 WEEKS)*
		pos/wks
25 Apr 98	THE IMPRESSION THAT I GET *Mercury 5748432*	12 5
27 Jun 98	THE RASCAL KING *Mercury 5661092*	63 1

MIGHTY MORPH'N POWER RANGERS *US, male / female vocal group (13 WEEKS)*
		pos/wks
17 Dec 94 ●	POWER RANGERS *RCA 74321253022*	3 9
25 Feb 95	POWER RANGERS (re-entry) *RCA 74321253022*	57 2
25 Mar 95	POWER RANGERS (2nd re-entry) *RCA 74321253022*	65 1
8 Apr 95	POWER RANGERS (3rd re-entry) *RCA 74321253022*	74 1

MIGHTY WAH – See WAH!

MIGIL FIVE *UK, male vocal / instrumental group (20 WEEKS)*
		pos/wks
19 Mar 64 ●	MOCKINGBIRD HILL *Pye 7N 15597*	10 13
4 Jun 64	NEAR YOU *Pye 7N 15645*	31 7

MIG29 *Italy, male instrumental / production group (2 WEEKS)*
		pos/wks
22 Feb 92	MIG29 *Champion CHAMP 292*	62 2

MIKAELA – See SUPERCAR

MIKE *UK, male producer - Mark Jolley (2 WEEKS)*
		pos/wks
19 Nov 94	TWANGLING THREE FINGERS IN A BOX *Pukka CDMIKE 100*	40 2

UK No.1 ★   UK Top 10 ●   Still on chart +   UK million seller ◆   UK entry at No.1 ■   US No.1 ▲

MIKE and the MECHANICS
UK, male vocal / instrumental group (67 WEEKS)   pos/wks

15 Feb 86		SILENT RUNNING (ON DANGEROUS GROUND) *WEA U 8908* ..21	9
31 May 86		ALL I NEED IS A MIRACLE *WEA U 8765*	...53 4
14 Jan 89	●	THE LIVING YEARS *WEA U 7717* ▲	..2 11
16 Mar 91		WORD OF MOUTH *Virgin VS 1345*	.13 10
15 Jun 91		A TIME AND PLACE *Virgin VS 1351*	.58 3
8 Feb 92		EVERYBODY GETS A SECOND CHANCE *Virgin VS 1396*	...56 4
25 Feb 95		OVER MY SHOULDER *Virgin VSCDT 1526*	.12 9
17 Jun 95		A BEGGAR ON A BEACH OF GOLD *Virgin VSCDT 1535*	...33 5
2 Sep 95		ANOTHER CUP OF COFFEE *Virgin VSCDT 1554*	.51 4
17 Feb 96		ALL I NEED IS A MIRACLE (re-mix) *Virgin VSCDT 1576*	.27 4
1 Jun 96		SILENT RUNNING (re-issue) *Virgin VSCDT 1585*	.61 1
5 Jun 99		NOW THAT YOU'VE GONE *Virgin VSCDT 1732*	.35 2
28 Aug 99		WHENEVER I STOP *Virgin VSCDT 1743*	.73 1

See also GENESIS

MIKI and GRIFF *UK, female / male vocal duo (25 WEEKS)*   pos/wks

2 Oct 59	HOLD BACK TOMORROW *Pye 7N 15213*	...26	2
13 Oct 60	ROCKIN' ALONE *Pye 7N 15296*	...44	3
1 Feb 62	LITTLE BITTY TEAR *Pye 7N 15412*	.16	13
22 Aug 63	I WANNA STAY HERE *Pye 7N 15555*	.23	7

John MILES *UK, male vocalist / multi-instrumentalist (30 WEEKS)*   pos/wks

18 Oct 75		HIGH FLY *Decca F 13595*	...17 6
20 Mar 76	●	MUSIC *Decca F 13627*	..3 9
16 Oct 76		REMEMBER YESTERDAY *Decca F 13667*	...32 5
18 Jun 77	●	SLOW DOWN *Decca F 13709*	.10 10

Robert MILES
Italy, male instrumentalist, keyboards - Roberto Concina (48 WEEKS)   pos/wks

24 Feb 96	●	CHILDREN *Deconstruction 74321348322*	..2 18
8 Jun 96	●	FABLE *Deconstruction 74321382622*	..7 7
3 Aug 96		FABLE (re-entry) *Deconstruction 74321382622*	.71 1
31 Aug 96		FABLE (2nd re-entry) *Deconstruction 74321382622*	.69 1
16 Nov 96	●	ONE & ONE *Deconstruction 74321427692* 1	..3 17
29 Nov 97		FREEDOM *Deconstruction 74321536952* 2	.15 4

1 Robert Miles featuring Maria Nayler 2 Robert Miles featuring Kathy Sledge

June MILES-KINGSTON – See Jimmy SOMERVILLE

Paul MILES-KINGSTON – See Sarah BRIGHTMAN

MILK AND HONEY featuring Gali ATARI
Israel, male / female vocal / instrumental group (8 WEEKS)   pos/wks

14 Apr 79	●	HALLELUJAH *Polydor 2001 870*	..5 8

MILK INCORPORATED
Belgium, male / female vocal / production group (3 WEEKS)   pos/wks

28 Feb 98	GOOD ENOUGH (LA VACHE) *Malarky MLKD 5*	...23 3

MILL GIRLS – See Billy COTTON and his BAND

MILLA *US, female vocalist (1 WEEK)*   pos/wks

18 Jun 94	GENTLEMAN WHO FELL *SBK CDSBK 49*	...65 1

Frankie MILLER *UK, male vocalist (32 WEEKS)*   pos/wks

4 Jun 77		BE GOOD TO YOURSELF *Chrysalis CHS 2147*	...27 6
14 Oct 78	●	DARLIN' *Chrysalis CHS 2255*	..6 15
20 Jan 79		WHEN I'M AWAY FROM YOU *Chrysalis CHS 2276*	...42 5
21 Mar 92		CALEDONIA *MCS MCS 2001*	...45 6

Gary MILLER *UK, male vocalist - Neville Williams (35 WEEKS)*   pos/wks

21 Oct 55		THE YELLOW ROSE OF TEXAS *Nixa N 15004*	.13 5
13 Jan 56	●	ROBIN HOOD *Nixa N 15020*	.10 6
11 Jan 57		GARDEN OF EDEN *Pye Nixa N 15070*	.14 6
1 Mar 57		GARDEN OF EDEN (re-entry) *Pye Nixa N 15070*	...27 1

19 Jul 57		WONDERFUL, WONDERFUL *Pye Nixa N 15094*	...29 1
17 Jan 58		THE STORY OF MY LIFE *Pye Nixa N 15120*	.14 6
21 Dec 61		THERE GOES THAT SONG AGAIN / THE NIGHT IS YOUNG *Pye 7N 15404*	...29 9
1 Mar 62		THERE GOES THAT SONG AGAIN (re-entry) *Pye 7N 15404*	...48 1

'The Night Is Young' listed with 'There Goes That Song Again' only for weeks 21 and 28 Dec 1961 and 4 Jan 1962. It peaked at No.32

Glenn MILLER *US, orchestra, Glenn Miller - trombone (9 WEEKS)*   pos/wks

12 Mar 54		MOONLIGHT SERENADE *HMV BD 5942*	.12 1
24 Jan 76		MOONLIGHT SERENADE (re-issue) / LITTLE BROWN JUG / IN THE MOOD *RCA 2644*	.13 8

Jody MILLER *US, female vocalist (1 WEEK)*   pos/wks

21 Oct 65	HOME OF THE BRAVE *Capitol CL 15415*	.49 1

Leza MILLER – See Sergio MENDES

Mitch MILLER *US, orchestra and chorus (13 WEEKS)*   pos/wks

7 Oct 55	●	THE YELLOW ROSE OF TEXAS *Philips PB 505* ▲	..2 13

Ned MILLER *US, male vocalist (22 WEEKS)*   pos/wks

14 Feb 63	●	FROM A JACK TO A KING *London HL 9658*	..2 21
18 Feb 65		DO WHAT YOU DO DO WELL *London HL 9937*	...48 1

Roger MILLER *US, male vocalist (42 WEEKS)*   pos/wks

18 Mar 65	★	KING OF THE ROAD *Philips BF 1397*	..1 15
3 Jun 65		ENGINE ENGINE NO. 9 *Philips BF 1416*	...33 5
21 Oct 65		KANSAS CITY STAR *Philips BF 1437*	...48 1
16 Dec 65		ENGLAND SWINGS *Philips BF 1456*	...45 1
6 Jan 66		ENGLAND SWINGS (re-entry) *Philips BF 1456*	.13 7
27 Mar 68		LITTLE GREEN APPLES *Mercury MF 1021*	.19 10
2 Apr 69		LITTLE GREEN APPLES (re-entry) *Mercury MF 1021*	...48 1
7 May 69		LITTLE GREEN APPLES (2nd re-entry) *Mercury MF 1021*	...39 2

Steve MILLER BAND
US, male vocal / instrumental group (36 WEEKS)   pos/wks

23 Oct 76		ROCK 'N ME *Mercury 6078 804* ▲	.11 9
19 Jun 82	●	ABRACADABRA *Mercury STEVE 3* ▲	..2 11
4 Sep 82		KEEPS ME WONDERING WHY *Mercury STEVE 4*	...52 3
11 Aug 90	★	THE JOKER *Capitol CL 583* ▲	..1 13

Suzi MILLER and the JOHNSTON BROTHERS
UK, female vocalist and male vocal group (2 WEEKS)   pos/wks

21 Jan 55	HAPPY DAYS AND LONELY NIGHTS *Decca F 10389*	.14 2

Lisa MILLETT – See SHEER BRONZE featuring Lisa MILLETT; A.T.F.C. presents ONEPHATDEEVA

MILLI VANILLI *France / Germany, male duo - Rob Pilatus and Fabrice Morvan (50 WEEKS)*   pos/wks

1 Oct 88	●	GIRL YOU KNOW IT'S TRUE *Cooltempo COOL 170*	..3 13
17 Dec 88		BABY DON'T FORGET MY NUMBER *Cooltempo COOL 178* ▲	.16 11
22 Jul 89		BLAME IT ON THE RAIN *Cooltempo COOL 180* ▲	...53 5
30 Sep 89	●	GIRL I'M GONNA MISS YOU *Cooltempo COOL 191* ▲	..2 15
2 Dec 89		BLAME IT ON THE RAIN (re-entry) *Cooltempo COOL 180*	...52 5
10 Mar 90		ALL OR NOTHING *Cooltempo COOL 199*	.74 1

MILLICAN and NESBITT *UK, male vocal duo (14 WEEKS)*   pos/wks

1 Dec 73		VAYA CON DIOS *Pye 7N 45310*	...20 11
18 May 74		FOR OLD TIME'S SAKE *Pye 7N 45357*	...38 3

MILLIE *Jamaica, female vocalist - Millie Small (33 WEEKS)*   pos/wks

12 Mar 64	●	MY BOY LOLLIPOP *Fontana TF 449*	..2 18
25 Jun 64		SWEET WILLIAM *Fontana TF 479*	...30 9
11 Nov 65		BLOODSHOT EYES *Fontana TF 617*	...48 1
25 Jul 87		MY BOY LOLLIPOP (re-issue) *Island WIP 6574*	...46 5

MILLIONAIRE HIPPIES
UK, male producer - Danny Rampling (4 WEEKS) pos/wks

| 18 Dec 93 | I AM THE MUSIC HEAR ME! *Deconstruction 74321175432* | 52 | 3 |
| 10 Sep 94 | C'MON *Deconstruction 74321229372* | 59 | 1 |

MILLS BROTHERS *US, male vocal group (1 WEEK)* pos/wks

| 9 Jan 53 | ● THE GLOW WORM *Brunswick 05007* | 10 | 1 |

With Hal McIntyre and his Orchestra

Garry MILLS *UK, male vocalist (31 WEEKS)* pos/wks

7 Jul 60	● LOOK FOR A STAR *Top Rank JAR 336*	7	14
20 Oct 60	TOP TEEN BABY *Top Rank JAR 500*	24	12
22 Jun 61	I'LL STEP DOWN *Decca F 11358*	39	5

Hayley MILLS *UK, female vocalist (11 WEEKS)* pos/wks

| 19 Oct 61 | LET'S GET TOGETHER *Decca F 21396* | 17 | 11 |

Stephanie MILLS *US, female vocalist (33 WEEKS)* pos/wks

18 Oct 80	● NEVER KNEW LOVE LIKE THIS BEFORE *20th Century TC 2460*	4	14
23 May 81	TWO HEARTS *20th Century TC 2492* [1]	49	5
15 Sep 84	THE MEDICINE SONG *Club JAB 8*	29	9
5 Sep 87	(YOU'RE PUTTIN') A RUSH ON ME *MCA MCA 1187*	62	2
1 May 93	NEVER DO YOU WRONG *MCA MCSTD 1767*	57	2
10 Jul 93	ALL DAY ALL NIGHT *MCA MCSTD 1778*	68	1

[1] Stephanie Mills featuring Teddy Pendergrass

Warren MILLS *Zambia, male vocalist (1 WEEK)* pos/wks

| 28 Sep 85 | SUNSHINE *Jive JIVE 99* | 74 | 1 |

MILLTOWN BROTHERS
UK, male vocal / instrumental group (16 WEEKS) pos/wks

2 Feb 91	WHICH WAY SHOULD I JUMP *A & M AM 711*	38	5
13 Apr 91	HERE I STAND *A & M AM 758*	41	4
6 Jul 91	APPLE GREEN *A & M AM 787*	43	4
22 May 93	TURN OFF *A & M 5802692*	55	1
17 Jul 93	IT'S ALL OVER NOW BABY BLUE *A & M 5803332*	48	2

CB MILTON *Holland, male vocalist (5 WEEKS)* pos/wks

21 May 94	IT'S A LOVING THING *Logic 74321208062*	49	2
25 Mar 95	IT'S A LOVING THING (re-mix) *Logic 74321267212*	34	2
19 Aug 95	HOLD ON *Logic 74321292112*	62	1

Garnet MIMMS and TRUCKIN' CO
US, male vocalist and male instrumental group (1 WEEK) pos/wks

| 25 Jun 77 | WHAT IT IS *Arista 109* | 44 | 1 |

MIND OF KANE *UK, male producer - David Hope (1 WEEK)* pos/wks

| 27 Jul 91 | STABBED IN THE BACK *Deja Vu DJV 007* | 64 | 1 |

See also HOPE A.D.

MINDBENDERS `416` `Top 500`
UK, male vocal / instrumental group (79 WEEKS) pos/wks

11 Jul 63	HELLO JOSEPHINE *Fontana TF 404* [1]	46	2
28 May 64	STOP LOOK AND LISTEN *Fontana TF 451* [1]	37	4
8 Oct 64	● UM UM UM UM UM UM *Fontana TF 497* [1]	5	15
4 Feb 65	● GAME OF LOVE *Fontana TF 535* [1] ▲	2	11
17 Jun 65	JUST A LITTLE BIT TOO LATE *Fontana TF 579* [1]	20	7
30 Sep 65	SHE NEEDS LOVE *Fontana TF 611* [1]	32	6
13 Jan 66	● A GROOVY KIND OF LOVE *Fontana TF 644*	2	14
5 May 66	CAN'T LIVE WITH YOU (CAN'T LIVE WITHOUT YOU) *Fontana TF 697*	28	7
25 Aug 66	ASHES TO ASHES *Fontana TF 731*	14	9
20 Sep 67	THE LETTER *Fontana TF 869*	42	4

[1] Wayne Fontana and The Mindbenders

See also Wayne FONTANA

MINDS OF MEN
UK, male / female vocal / instrumental group (1 WEEK) pos/wks

| 22 Jun 96 | BRAND NEW DAY *Perfecto PERF 121CD* | 41 | 1 |

Sal MINEO *US, male vocalist (11 WEEKS)* pos/wks

| 12 Jul 57 | START MOVIN' *Philips PB 707* | 16 | 11 |

Marcello MINERBI *Italy, orchestra (16 WEEKS)* pos/wks

| 22 Jul 65 | ● ZORBA'S DANCE *Durium DRS 54001* | 6 | 16 |

MINI POPS *UK, male / female vocal group (2 WEEKS)* pos/wks

| 26 Dec 87 | SONGS FOR CHRISTMAS '87 (EP) *Bright BULB 9* | 39 | 2 |

Tracks on Songs for Christmas '87 (EP): Thanks for Giving Us Christmas / The Man in Red / Christmas Time Around the World / Shine On

MINIMAL FUNK 2 *Italy, male production duo (1 WEEK)* pos/wks

| 18 Jul 98 | THE GROOVY THANG *Cleveland City CLECD 13046* | 65 | 1 |

MINISTERS DE LA FUNK featuring Jocelyn BROWN
US, male production trio and US, female vocalist (2 WEEKS) pos/wks

| 11 Mar 00 | BELIEVE *Defected DFECT 14CDS* | 45 | 2 |

MINISTRY *US, male vocal / instrumental group (3 WEEKS)* pos/wks

| 8 Aug 92 | NWO *Sire W 0125TE* | 49 | 1 |
| 6 Jan 96 | THE FALL *Warner Bros. W 0328CD* | 53 | 2 |

MINK DE VILLE *US, male vocal / instrumental group (9 WEEKS)* pos/wks

| 6 Aug 77 | SPANISH STROLL *Capitol CLX 103* | 20 | 9 |

MINKY *UK, male producer - Gary Dedman (1 WEEK)* pos/wks

| 30 Oct 99 | THE WEEKEND HAS LANDED *Offbeat OFFCD 1001* | 70 | 1 |

Liza MINNELLI *US, female vocalist (15 WEEKS)* pos/wks

12 Aug 89	● LOSING MY MIND *Epic ZEE 1*	6	7
7 Oct 89	DON'T DROP BOMBS *Epic ZEE 2*	46	3
25 Nov 89	SO SORRY I SAID *Epic ZEE 3*	62	2
3 Mar 90	LOVE PAINS *Epic ZEE 4*	41	3

Dannii MINOGUE *Australia, female vocalist (67 WEEKS)* pos/wks

30 Mar 91	● LOVE AND KISSES *MCA MCS 1529*	8	8
18 May 91	SUCCESS *MCA MCS 1538*	11	7
27 Jul 91	● JUMP TO THE BEAT *MCA MCS 1556*	8	6
19 Oct 91	BABY LOVE *MCA MCS 1580*	14	6
14 Dec 91	I DON'T WANNA TAKE THIS PAIN *MCA MCS 1600*	40	5
1 Aug 92	SHOW YOU THE WAY TO GO *MCA MCS 1671*	30	3
12 Dec 92	LOVE'S ON EVERY CORNER *MCA MCSR 1723*	44	4
17 Jul 93	● THIS IS IT *MCA MCSTD 1790*	10	8
2 Oct 93	THIS IS THE WAY *MCA MCSTD 1935*	27	3
11 Jun 94	GET INTO YOU *Mushroom D 11751*	36	2
23 Aug 97	● ALL I WANNA DO *Eternal WEA 119CD* [1]	4	8
1 Nov 97	EVERYTHING I WANTED *Eternal WEA 137CD* [1]	15	4
28 Mar 98	DISREMEMBRANCE *Eternal WEA 153CD* [1]	21	3

[1] Dannii

Kylie MINOGUE `46` `Top 500` Biggest-selling female vocalist of the late 1980s, b. 28 May 1968, Melbourne. The Australian actress turned singer has had the best ever female chart career start with 13 successive Top 10 entries, and was also the youngest woman to top the album chart (248 WEEKS) pos/wks

23 Jan 88	★ I SHOULD BE SO LUCKY *PWL PWL 8*	1	16
14 May 88	● GOT TO BE CERTAIN *PWL PWL 12*	2	12
6 Aug 88	● THE LOCO-MOTION *PWL PWL 14*	2	11
22 Oct 88	● JE NE SAIS PAS POURQUOI *PWL PWL 21*	2	13
10 Dec 88	★ ESPECIALLY FOR YOU *PWL PWL 24* [1]	1	14
6 May 89	★ HAND ON YOUR HEART *PWL PWL 35*	1	11
5 Aug 89	● WOULDN'T CHANGE A THING *PWL PWL 42*	2	9
4 Nov 89	● NEVER TOO LATE *PWL PWL 45*	4	10

UK No.1 ★   UK Top 10 ●   Still on chart +   UK million seller ◆   UK entry at No.1 ■   US No.1 ▲

20 Jan 90 ★	TEARS ON MY PILLOW *PWL PWL 47*	1	8
12 May 90 ●	BETTER THE DEVIL YOU KNOW *PWL PWL 56*	2	10
3 Nov 90 ●	STEP BACK IN TIME *PWL PWL 64*	4	8
2 Feb 91 ●	WHAT DO I HAVE TO DO *PWL PWL 72*	6	8
1 Jun 91 ●	SHOCKED *PWL PWL 81*	6	7
7 Sep 91	WORD IS OUT	16	5
2 Nov 91 ●	IF YOU WERE WITH ME NOW *PWL PWL 208* [2]	4	7
30 Nov 91	KEEP ON PUMPIN' IT *PWL PWL 207* [3]	49	1
25 Jan 92 ●	GIVE ME JUST A LITTLE MORE TIME *PWL PWL 212*	2	8
25 Apr 92	FINER FEELINGS *PWL International PWL 227*	11	6
22 Aug 92	WHAT KIND OF FOOL (HEARD IT ALL BEFORE) *PWL International PWL 241*	14	5
28 Nov 92	CELEBRATION *PWL International PWL 257*	20	7
10 Sep 94 ●	CONFIDE IN ME *Deconstruction 74321227482*	2	9
26 Nov 94	PUT YOURSELF IN MY PLACE *Deconstruction 74321246572*	11	9
22 Jul 95	WHERE IS THE FEELING *Deconstruction 74321293612*	16	3
14 Oct 95	WHERE THE WILD ROSES GROW *Mute CDMUTE 185* [4]	11	4
20 Sep 97	SOME KIND OF BLISS *Deconstruction 74321517252*	22	5
6 Dec 97	DID IT AGAIN *Deconstruction 74321535702*	14	6
21 Mar 98	BREATHE *Deconstruction 74321570132*	14	4
31 Oct 98	GBI *Arthrob ART 021CD* [5]	63	1
1 Jul 00 ★	SPINNING AROUND *Parlophone CDRS 6542* ■	1	11
23 Sep 00 ●	ON A NIGHT LIKE THIS *Parlophone CDRS 6546*	2	7
21 Oct 00 ●	KIDS *Chrysalis CDCHS 5119* [6]	2	11+
23 Dec 00 ●	PLEASE STAY *Parlophone CDRS 6551*	10	2+

[1] Kylie Minogue and Jason Donovan [2] Kylie Minogue and Keith Washington [3] Visionmasters with Tony King and Kylie Minogue [4] Nick Cave and Kylie Minogue [5] Towa Tei featuring Kylie Minogue [6] Robbie Williams / Kylie Minogue

Morris MINOR and the MAJORS
UK, male vocal / rap group (11 WEEKS)   pos/wks

19 Dec 87 ●	STUTTER RAP (NO SLEEP 'TIL BEDTIME) *10 TEN 203*	4	11

Sugar MINOTT *Jamaica, male vocalist (16 WEEKS)*   pos/wks

28 Mar 81 ●	GOOD THING GOING (WE'VE GOT A GOOD THING GOING) *RCA 58*	4	12
17 Oct 81	NEVER MY LOVE *RCA 138*	52	4

MINT CONDITION *US, male vocal group (3 WEEKS)*   pos/wks

21 Jun 97	WHAT KIND OF MAN WOULD I BE *Wild Card 5710492*	38	2
4 Oct 97	LET ME BE THE ONE *Wild Card 5717132*	63	1

MINT JULEPS *UK, female vocal group (7 WEEKS)*   pos/wks

22 Mar 86	ONLY LOVE CAN BREAK YOUR HEART *Stiff BUY 241*	62	2
30 May 87	EVERY KINDA PEOPLE *Stiff BUY 257*	58	5

MINT ROYALE *UK, male production duo (5 WEEKS)*   pos/wks

5 Feb 00	DON'T FALTER *Faith & Hope FHCD 014* [1]	15	4
6 May 00	TAKE IT EASY *Faith & Hope FHCD 016*	66	1

[1] Mint Royale featuring Lauren Laverne

MINTY *Australia, female vocalist - Angela Kelly (1 WEEK)*   pos/wks

23 Jan 99	I WANNA BE FREE *Virgin VSCDT 1728*	67	1

MIRACLES (400 Top 500) *Motown's first US Top 10 act were fronted, between 1955-1972, by Smokey Robinson who wrote and produced hits for many Motown acts including this quartet. (81 WEEKS)* pos/wks

24 Feb 66	GOING TO A GO-GO *Tamla Motown TMG 547*	44	5
22 Dec 66	(COME 'ROUND HERE) I'M THE ONE YOU NEED *Tamla Motown TMG 584*	45	2
27 Dec 67	I SECOND THAT EMOTION *Tamla Motown TMG 631* [1]	27	11
3 Apr 68	IF YOU CAN WANT *Tamla Motown TMG 648* [1]	50	1
7 May 69 ●	TRACKS OF MY TEARS *Tamla Motown TMG 696* [1]	9	13
1 Aug 70 ★	THE TEARS OF A CLOWN *Tamla Motown TMG 745* [1] ▲	1	14
30 Jan 71	(COME 'ROUND HERE) I'M THE ONE YOU NEED (re-issue) *Tamla Motown TMG 761* [1]	13	9
5 Jun 71	I DON'T BLAME YOU AT ALL *Tamla Motown TMG 774* [1]	11	10

10 Jan 76 ●	LOVE MACHINE *Tamla Motown TMG 1015* ▲	3	10
2 Oct 76	THE TEARS OF A CLOWN (re-issue) *Tamla Motown TMG 1048* [1]	34	6

[1] Smokey Robinson & the Miracles

See also Smokey ROBINSON and the MIRACLES

MIRAGE *UK, male vocal / instrumental group (35 WEEKS)*   pos/wks

14 Jan 84	GIVE ME THE NIGHT *Passion PASH 15* [1]	49	4
9 May 87 ●	JACK MIX II / III *Debut DEBT 3022*	4	11
25 Jul 87	SERIOUS MIX *Debut DEBT 3028*	42	4
7 Nov 87 ●	JACK MIX IV *Debut DEBT 3035*	8	10
27 Feb 88	JACK MIX VII *Debut DEBT 3042*	50	3
2 Jul 88	PUSH THE BEAT *Debut DEBT 3050*	67	2
11 Nov 89	LATINO HOUSE *Debut DEBT 3085*	70	1

[1] Mirage featuring Roy Gayle

'Jack Mix III' listed with 'Jack Mix II' only from 6 Jun 1987

Danny MIRROR *Holland, male vocalist - Eddy Ouwens (9 WEEKS)*   pos/wks

17 Sep 77 ●	I REMEMBER ELVIS PRESLEY (THE KING IS DEAD) *Sonet SON 2121*	4	9

MIRRORBALL
UK, male production duo and female vocalist (5 WEEKS)   pos/wks

13 Feb 99	GIVEN UP *Multiply CDMULTY 46*	12	4
24 Jun 00	BURNIN' *Multiply CDMULTY 56*	47	1

MIRWAIS *France, male producer - Mirwais Ahmadzais (3 WEEKS)*   pos/wks

20 May 00	DISCO SCIENCE *Epic 6693102*	68	1
23 Dec 00	NAIVE SONG *Epic 6706922*	50	2

MISHKA *Bermuda, male vocalist (2 WEEKS)*   pos/wks

15 May 99	GIVE YOU ALL THE LOVE *Creation CRESCD 311*	34	2

MISS JANE *UK, female vocalist (1 WEEK)*   pos/wks

30 Oct 99	IT'S A FINE DAY *G1 Recordings G 1001CD*	62	1

MISS X *UK, female vocalist - Joyce Blair (6 WEEKS)*   pos/wks

1 Aug 63	CHRISTINE *Ember S 175*	37	6

MISSION *UK, male vocal / instrumental group (58 WEEKS)*   pos/wks

14 Jun 86	SERPENTS KISS *Chapter 22 CHAP 6*	70	3
26 Jul 86	GARDEN OF DELIGHT / LIKE A HURRICANE *Chapter 22 CHAP 7*	49	4
18 Oct 86	STAY WITH ME *Mercury MYTH 1*	30	4
17 Jan 87	WASTELAND *Mercury MYTH 2*	11	6
14 Mar 87	SEVERINA *Mercury MYTH 3*	25	5
13 Feb 88	TOWER OF STRENGTH *Mercury MYTH 4*	12	7
23 Apr 88	BEYOND THE PALE *Mercury MYTH 6*	32	4
13 Jan 90	BUTTERFLY ON A WHEEL *Mercury MYTH 8*	12	4
10 Mar 90	DELIVERANCE *Mercury MYTH 9*	27	4
2 Jun 90	INTO THE BLUE *Mercury MYTH 10*	32	3
17 Nov 90	HANDS ACROSS THE OCEAN *Mercury MYTH 11*	28	2
25 Apr 92	NEVER AGAIN *Mercury MYTH 12*	34	3
20 Jun 92	LIKE A CHILD AGAIN *Mercury MYTH 13*	30	2
17 Oct 92	SHADES OF GREEN *Vertigo MYTH 14*	49	2
8 Jan 94	TOWER OF STRENGTH (re-mix) *Vertigo MYTCD 15*	33	3
26 Mar 94	AFTERGLOW *Vertigo MYTCD 16*	53	1
4 Feb 95	SWOON *Neverland HOOKCD 002*	73	1

MISS JONES *US, female vocalist / songwriter (1 WEEK)*   pos/wks

10 Oct 98	2 WAY STREET *Motown 8608572*	49	1

MISTA E *UK, male producer - Damon Rochefort (5 WEEKS)*   pos/wks

10 Dec 88	DON'T BELIEVE THE HYPE *Urban URB 28*	41	5

SINGLED OUT...
Judge Jules

A legendary figure in UK clubland, house god Judge Jules is now a chart star in his own right with Hi-Gate. His diary is full of club bookings which see him flying to and fro across the Atlantic and his Radio 1 show is still unmissable listening for the club cognoscenti.

- **NO.1 ON THE UK SINGLES CHART THE DAY I WAS BORN:**
Tears – Ken Dodd

- **ALL-TIME FAVOURITE SINGLE:**
Golden Brown – The Stranglers

- **SINGLE THAT DRIVES ME UP THE WALL:**
Summertime – Jazzy Jeff and The Fresh Prince

FIRST SINGLE I EVER BOUGHT:

Big Yellow Taxi
Joni Mitchell

MISTURA featuring Lloyd MICHELS *US, male instrumental group, Lloyd Michels - trumpet (10 WEEKS)* pos/wks

| 15 May 76 | | THE FLASHER *Route RT 30* | **23** 10 |

Des MITCHELL *UK / Belgium, male DJ / production trio (5 WEEKS)* pos/wks

| 29 Jan 00 | ● | (WELCOME) TO THE DANCE *Code Blue BLUE 0087CD1* | **5** 5 |

Guy MITCHELL `125` `Top 500` *Extremely popular pre-rock vocalist, b. Al Cernik, 27 Feb 1927, Detroit, US, d. 1 Jul 1999. He appeared on the first and last charts of the 1950s, and was one of most consistently successful singers and performers of that decade (164 WEEKS)* pos/wks

14 Nov 52	●	FEET UP! *Philips PB 3151*	**2** 10
13 Feb 53	★	SHE WEARS RED FEATHERS *Columbia DB 3238*	**1** 15
24 Apr 53	●	PRETTY LITTLE BLACK-EYED SUSIE *Columbia DB 3255*	**2** 11
12 Jun 53		SHE WEARS RED FEATHERS (re-entry) *Columbia DB 3238*	**12** 1
28 Aug 53	★	LOOK AT THAT GIRL *Philips PB 162*	**1** 14
6 Nov 53	●	CHICKA BOOM *Philips PB 178*	**5** 9
18 Dec 53	●	CLOUD LUCKY SEVEN *Philips BBL 7265*	**2** 16
15 Jan 54	●	CHICKA BOOM (re-entry) *Philips PB 178*	**4** 6
19 Feb 54	●	THE CUFF OF MY SHIRT *Philips PB 225*	**9** 1
26 Feb 54		SIPPIN' SODA *Philips PB 210*	**11** 1
19 Mar 54		THE CUFF OF MY SHIRT (re-entry) *Philips PB 225*	**12** 1
2 Apr 54		THE CUFF OF MY SHIRT (2nd re-entry) *Philips PB 225*	**11** 1
30 Apr 54	●	A DIME AND A DOLLAR *Philips PB 248*	**8** 1
14 May 54	●	A DIME AND A DOLLAR (re-entry) *Philips PB 248*	**8** 4
7 Dec 56	★	SINGING THE BLUES *Philips PB 650* ▲	**1** 22
15 Feb 57	●	KNEE DEEP IN THE BLUES *Philips PB 669*	**3** 12
26 Apr 57	★	ROCK-A-BILLY *Philips PB 685*	**1** 14
26 Jul 57		IN THE MIDDLE OF A DARK DARK NIGHT / SWEET STUFF *Philips PB 712*	**27** 2
23 Aug 57		IN THE MIDDLE OF A DARK DARK NIGHT / SWEET STUFF (re-entry) *Philips PB 712*	**25** 2
11 Oct 57		CALL ROSIE ON THE PHONE *Philips PB 743*	**17** 6
27 Nov 59		HEARTACHES BY THE NUMBER *Philips PB 964* ▲	**26** 2
18 Dec 59	●	HEARTACHES BY THE NUMBER (re-entry) *Philips PB 964*	**5** 13

Joni MITCHELL *Canada, female vocalist - Roberta Anderson (24 WEEKS)* pos/wks

| 13 Jun 70 | | BIG YELLOW TAXI *Reprise RS 20906* | **11** 15 |
| 4 Oct 97 | ● | GOT 'TIL IT'S GONE *Virgin VSCDG 1666* [1] | **6** 9 |

[1] Janet featuring Q-Tip and Joni Mitchell

VSCDG 1666 uses samples from RS 20906

Willie MITCHELL *US, male instrumentalist - guitar (3 WEEKS)* pos/wks

| 24 Apr 68 | | SOUL SERENADE *London HLU 10186* | **43** 1 |
| 11 Dec 76 | | THE CHAMPION *London HL 10545* | **47** 2 |

MIX FACTORY *UK, male / female vocal / instrumental group (2 WEEKS)* pos/wks

| 30 Jan 93 | | TAKE ME AWAY (PARADISE) *All Around The World CDGLOBE 120* | **51** 2 |

MIXMASTER *Italy, male producer - Daniele Davoli (10 WEEKS)* pos/wks

| 4 Nov 89 | ● | GRAND PIANO *BCM BCM 344* | **9** 10 |

MIXTURES *Australia, male vocal / instrumental group (21 WEEKS)* pos/wks

| 16 Jan 71 | ● | THE PUSHBIKE SONG *Polydor 2058 083* | **2** 21 |

Hank MIZELL *US, male vocalist (13 WEEKS)* pos/wks

| 20 Mar 76 | ● | JUNGLE ROCK *Charly CS 1005* | **3** 13 |

MK *US, male producer - Mark Kinchen (3 WEEKS)* pos/wks

| 4 Feb 95 | | ALWAYS *Activ CDTV 3* [1] | **69** 1 |
| 27 May 95 | | BURNING *Activ CDTVR 6* | **44** 2 |

[1] MK featuring Alana

Alana appears on both hits, although she is credited only on the first

MN8 *UK / Trinidad, male vocal group (38 WEEKS)* pos/wks

4 Feb 95	●	I'VE GOT A LITTLE SOMETHING FOR YOU *Columbia 6608802*	**2** 13
29 Apr 95	●	IF YOU ONLY LET ME IN *Columbia 6613252*	**6** 7
15 Jul 95	●	HAPPY *Columbia 6622192*	**8** 7
4 Nov 95		BABY IT'S YOU *Columbia 6624522*	**22** 2
6 Jan 96		BABY IT'S YOU (re-entry) *Columbia 6624522*	**59** 1
24 Feb 96		PATHWAY TO THE MOON *Columbia 6629212*	**25** 2
31 Aug 96		TUFF ACT TO FOLLOW *Columbia 6635345*	**15** 3
26 Oct 96		DREAMING *Columbia 6638302*	**21** 3

MNO *Belgium, male instrumental / production group (2 WEEKS)* pos/wks

| 28 Sep 91 | | GOD OF ABRAHAM *A & M AM 820* | **66** 2 |

MOBILES *UK, male / female vocal / instrumental group (14 WEEKS)* pos/wks

| 9 Jan 82 | ● | DROWNING IN BERLIN *Rialto RIA 3* | **9** 10 |
| 27 Mar 82 | | AMOUR AMOUR *Rialto RIA 5* | **45** 4 |

MOBO ALLSTARS
UK / US, male / female vocal / instrumental group (3 WEEKS) pos/wks

| 26 Dec 98 | | AIN'T NO STOPPING US NOW *PolyGram TV 5632302* | **47** 3 |

Artists featured include: Another Level, Shola Ama, Kelle Bryan, Celetia, Cleopatra, Damage, Des'ree, D'Influence, E17, Michelle Gayle, Glamma Kid, Lynden David Hall, Hinda Hicks, Honeyz, Kle'Shay, Kele Le Roc, Beverley Knight, Tony Momrelle, Nine Yards, Mica Paris, Karen Ramirez, Connor Reeves, Roachford, 7th Son, Byron Stingily, Truce, Soundproof, Ultimate Kaos

MOBY *US, male producer - Richard Hall (63 WEEKS)* pos/wks

27 Jul 91		GO *Outer Rhythm FOOT 15*	**46** 3
19 Oct 91	●	GO (re-entry) *Outer Rhythm FOOT 15*	**10** 7
3 Jul 93		I FEEL IT *Equinox AXISCD 001*	**38** 3
11 Sep 93		MOVE *Mute CDMUTE 158*	**21** 5
28 May 94		HYMN *Mute CDMUTE 161*	**31** 2
29 Oct 94		FEELING SO REAL *Mute CDMUTE 173*	**30** 2
25 Feb 95		EVERY TIME YOU TOUCH ME *Mute CDMUTE 176*	**28** 3
1 Jul 95		INTO THE BLUE *Mute CDMUTE 179A*	**34** 2
7 Sep 96		THAT'S WHEN I REACH FOR MY REVOLVER *Mute CDMUTE 184*	**50** 1
15 Nov 97	●	JAMES BOND THEME *Mute CDMUTE 210*	**8** 7
10 Jan 98		JAMES BOND THEME (re-entry) *Mute CDMUTE 210*	**74** 1
5 Sep 98		HONEY *Mute CDMUTE 218*	**33** 2
8 May 99		RUN ON *Mute CDMUTE 221*	**33** 2
24 Jul 99		BODYROCK *Mute CDMUTE 225*	**38** 2
23 Oct 99		WHY DOES MY HEART FEEL SO BAD *Mute CDMUTE 230*	**16** 4
18 Mar 00		NATURAL BLUES *Mute CDMUTE 251*	**11** 6
24 Jun 00	●	PORCELAIN *Mute CDMUTE 252*	**5** 6
28 Oct 00		WHY DOES MY HEART FEEL SO BAD (re-issue) *Mute CDMUTE 255*	**17** 5

MOCA – See David MORALES

MOCHA – See Missy 'Misdemeanor' ELLIOTT; Nicole RAY

MOCK TURTLES
UK, male / female vocal / instrumental group (15 WEEKS) pos/wks

| 9 Mar 91 | | CAN YOU DIG IT? *Siren SRN 136* | **18** 11 |
| 29 Jun 91 | | AND THEN SHE SMILES *Siren SRN 139* | **44** 4 |

MODERN LOVERS – See Jonathan RICHMAN and the MODERN LOVERS

MODERN ROMANCE `436` `Top 500` *Latin-tinged London pop group which evolved out of new wave band The Leyton Buzzards. Lead singer Geoff Deane, who was replaced in 1982 by Michael J Mullins, later became a top TV scriptwriter (Birds of a Feather, Chef!, Babes in the Wood) (77 WEEKS)* pos/wks

15 Aug 81		EVERYBODY SALSA *WEA K 18815*	**12** 10
7 Nov 81	●	AY AY AY AY MOOSEY *WEA K 18883*	**10** 12
30 Jan 82		QUEEN OF THE RAPPING SCENE (NOTHING EVER GOES THE WAY YOU PLAN) *WEA K 18928*	**37** 8
14 Aug 82		CHERRY PINK AND APPLE BLOSSOM WHITE *WEA K 19245* [1]	**15** 8
13 Nov 82		BEST YEARS OF OUR LIVES *WEA ROM 1*	**4** 13

SINGLED OUT...
Mark Radcliffe

Much-loved BBC Radio 1 DJ funster and Shirehorse Mark Radcliffe does not share the same musical taste as his daughter, who has yet to groove – as she inevitably will – to 'Milk and Alcohol'.

- **NO.1 ON THE UK SINGLES CHART THE DAY I WAS BORN:**
  On The Street Where You Live – Vic Damone

- **ALL-TIME FAVOURITE SINGLE:**
  Torn between:
  Hole In My Shoe – Traffic
  Tracks Of My Tears – Smokey Robinson & The Miracles
  Do Anything You Wanna Do – Eddie and the Hot Rods
  Heroes – David Bowie

  If really pushed I would have to go for Traffic – all you need to know about British psychedelia in two and a half minutes!

- **SINGLE THAT DRIVES ME UP THE WALL:**
  Anything by Sting or Westlife obviously! But, probably **Blue (Da Ba Dee)** by **Eiffel 65** which my daughter (aged 12) plays constantly. I'll convert her to Dr Feelgood one day.

FIRST SINGLE I EVER BOUGHT:
I'd like to think it was 'Virginia Plain' by Roxy Music, although that might have been the second. I've got an awful feeling the first was actually...

The Pushbike Song
The Mixtures!

Photo: Pictorial Press

UK No.1 ★   UK Top 10 ●   Still on chart +   UK million seller ◆   UK entry at No.1 ■   US No.1 ▲

MONICA
US, female vocalist - Monica Arnold (37 WEEKS) pos/wks

29 Jul 95	DON'T TAKE IT PERSONAL (JUST ONE OF DEM DAYS)			
	Arista 74321301452	.........**32**	3
17 Feb 96	LIKE THIS AND LIKE THAT *Rowdy 74321344222*	........**33**	2
8 Jun 96	BEFORE YOU WALK OUT OF MY LIFE *Rowdy 74321374042*	.....**22**	3
24 May 97	FOR YOU I WILL *Atlantic A 5437CD*	.......**27**	2
6 Jun 98 ●	THE BOY IS MINE *Atlantic AT 0036 CD* [1] ▲	......**2**	20
17 Oct 98 ●	THE FIRST NIGHT *Rowdy 74321619342* ▲	......**6**	6
4 Sep 99	ANGEL OF MINE *Arista 74321692892* ▲	.....**55**	1

[1] Brandy and Monica

MONIFAH
US, female vocalist (2 WEEKS) pos/wks

30 Jan 99	TOUCH IT *Universal UND 56218*	.........**29**	2

TS MONK
US, male / female vocal / instrumental group (6 WEEKS) pos/wks

7 Mar 81	BON BON VIE *Mirage K 11653*	.........**63**	2
25 Apr 81	CANDIDATE FOR LOVE *Mirage K 11648*	.........**58**	4

MONKEES (293) **Top 500**
The world's top act of 1967: Davy Jones (v/g). Mike Nesmith (v/g), Peter Tork (v/k), Mickey Dolenz (v/d). This Anglo-American quartet was hand-picked for a Beatles-style TV series, which helped to rocket them, albeit briefly, to the top (101 WEEKS) pos/wks

5 Jan 67 ★	I'M A BELIEVER *RCA 1560* ▲	......**1**	17
26 Jan 67	LAST TRAIN TO CLARKSVILLE *RCA 1547* ▲	.....**23**	7
6 Apr 67 ●	A LITTLE BIT ME A LITTLE BIT YOU *RCA 1580*	.....**3**	12
22 Jun 67 ●	ALTERNATE TITLE *RCA 1604*	.....**2**	12
16 Aug 67	PLEASANT VALLEY SUNDAY *RC 1620*	.....**11**	8
15 Nov 67 ●	DAYDREAM BELIEVER *RCA 1645* ▲	.....**5**	17
27 Mar 68	VALLERI *RCA 1673*	.....**12**	8
26 Jun 68	DW WASHBURN *RCA 1706*	.....**17**	6
26 Mar 69	TEARDROP CITY *RCA 1802*	.....**46**	1
25 Jun 69	SOMEDAY MAN *RCA 1824*	.....**47**	1
15 Mar 80	THE MONKEES EP *Arista ARIST 326*	.....**33**	9
18 Oct 86	THAT WAS THEN, THIS IS NOW *Arista ARIST 673*	.....**68**	1
1 Apr 89	THE MONKEES EP *Arista 112157*	.....**62**	2

Tracks on Arista 326 EP: I'm a Believer / Daydream Believer / Last Train to Clarksville / A Little Bit Me a Little Bit You. Tracks on Arista 112157 EP: Daydream Believer / Monkees Theme / Last Train to Clarksville

MONKEY MAFIA
UK, male vocal / instrumental / DJ / production group (3 WEEKS) pos/wks

10 Aug 96	WORK MI BODY *Heavenly HVN 53CD* [1]	.....**75**	1
7 Jun 97	15 STEPS (EP) *Heavenly HVN 67CD*	.....**67**	1
2 May 98	LONG AS I CAN SEE THE LIGHT *Heavenly HVN 84CD*	.....**51**	1

[1] Monkey Mafia featuring Patra

Tracks on 15 Steps (EP): Lion in the Hall / Krash the Decks: Slaughter the Vinyl / Metro Love / Beats in the Hall

MONKS
UK, male vocal / instrumental duo (9 WEEKS) pos/wks

21 Apr 79	NICE LEGS SHAME ABOUT HER FACE *Carrere CAR 104*	.....**19**	9

The Monks were Hudson-Ford under a different name

MONO
UK, male / female vocal / instrumental duo (1 WEEK) pos/wks

2 May 98	LIFE IN MONO *Echo ECSCD 64*	.....**60**	1

Matt MONRO (207) **Top 500**
Superior British balladeer, b. Terence Parsons, 1 Dec 1932, London, d. 7 Feb 1985. This Sinatra-styled vocalist, who was re-named by hitmaker Winifred Atwell, had few MOR equals in the 1960s. In 1961, Billboard magazine named him Top International Act and Most Promising Male Singer (127 WEEKS) pos/wks

15 Dec 60 ●	PORTRAIT OF MY LOVE *Parlophone R 4714*	.....**3**	16
9 Mar 61 ●	MY KIND OF GIRL *Parlophone R 4755*	.....**5**	12
18 May 61	WHY NOT NOW / CAN THIS BE LOVE *Parlophone R 4775*	.....**24**	9
28 Sep 61	GONNA BUILD A MOUNTAIN *Parlophone R 4819*	.....**44**	3
8 Feb 62 ●	SOFTLY AS I LEAVE YOU *Parlophone R 4868*	.....**10**	18
14 Jun 62	WHEN LOVE COMES ALONG *Parlophone R 4911*	.....**46**	3
8 Nov 62	MY LOVE AND DEVOTION *Parlophone R 4954*	.....**29**	5

14 Nov 63	FROM RUSSIA WITH LOVE *Parlophone R 5068*	.....**20**	13
17 Sep 64 ●	WALK AWAY *Parlophone R 5171*	.....**4**	20
24 Dec 64	FOR MAMA *Parlophone R 5215*	.....**36**	4
25 Mar 65	WITHOUT YOU *Parlophone R 5251*	.....**37**	4
21 Oct 65 ●	YESTERDAY *Parlophone R 5348*	.....**8**	12
24 Nov 73	AND YOU SMILED *EMI 2091*	.....**28**	8

Gerry MONROE
UK, male vocalist (57 WEEKS) pos/wks

23 May 70 ●	SALLY *Chapter One CH 122*	.....**4**	20
19 Sep 70	CRY *Chapter One CH 128*	.....**38**	5
14 Nov 70 ●	MY PRAYER *Chapter One CH 132*	.....**9**	12
17 Apr 71	IT'S A SIN TO TELL A LIE *Chapter One CH 144*	.....**13**	12
21 Aug 71	LITTLE DROPS OF SILVER *Chapter One CH 152*	.....**37**	6
12 Feb 72	GIRL OF MY DREAMS *Chapter One CH 159*	.....**43**	2

Hollis P MONROE
Canada, male producer (1 WEEK) pos/wks

24 Apr 99	I'M LONELY *City Beat CBE 778CD*	.....**51**	1

MONSOON
UK, male / female vocal / instrumental group (12 WEEKS) pos/wks

3 Apr 82	EVER SO LONELY *Mobile Suit Corp CORP 2*	.....**12**	9
5 Jun 82	SHAKTI (THE MEANING OF WITHIN)		
	Mobile Suit Corp CORP 4	.....**41**	3

MONSTA BOY featuring DENZIE
UK, male production / vocal instrumental duo (3 WEEKS) pos/wks

7 Oct 00	SORRY (I DIDN'T KNOW) *Locked On LOX 125CD*	.....**25**	3

MONSTER MAGNET
US, male vocal / instrumental group (6 WEEKS) pos/wks

29 May 93	TWIN EARTH *A & M 5802812*	.....**67**	1
18 Mar 95	NEGASONIC TEENAGE WARHEAD		
	A & M 5809812	.....**49**	1
6 May 95	DOPES TO INFINITY *A & M 5810332*	.....**58**	1
23 Jan 99	POWERTRIP *A&M 5828232*	.....**39**	2
6 Mar 99	SPACE LORD *A&M 5632752*	.....**45**	1

MONTAGE
UK, female vocal trio (1 WEEK) pos/wks

15 Feb 97	THERE AIN'T NOTHIN' LIKE THE LOVE *Wildcard 5733172*	.....**64**	1

MONTANA SEXTET
US, male / instrumental group (1 WEEK) pos/wks

15 Jan 83	HEAVY VIBES *Virgin VS 560*	.....**59**	1

MONTANO vs THE TRUMPET MAN
UK, male production / instrumental duo (1 WEEK) pos/wks

18 Sep 99	ITZA TRUMPET THING *Serious SERR 010CD*	.....**46**	1

Hugo MONTENEGRO
US, orchestra (26 WEEKS) pos/wks

11 Sep 68 ★	THE GOOD THE BAD AND THE UGLY *RCA 1727*	.....**1**	24
8 Jan 69	HANG 'EM HIGH *RCA 1771*	.....**50**	1
19 Mar 69	THE GOOD THE BAD AND THE UGLY (re-entry) *RCA 1727*	.....**48**	1

Chris MONTEZ
US, male vocalist - Ezekiel Montanez (61 WEEKS) pos/wks

4 Oct 62 ●	LET'S DANCE *London HLU 9596*	.....**2**	18
17 Jan 63 ●	SOME KINDA FUN *London HLU 9650*	.....**10**	9
30 Jun 66 ●	THE MORE I SEE YOU		
	Pye International 7N 25369	.....**3**	13
22 Sep 66	THERE WILL NEVER BE ANOTHER YOU		
	Pye International 7N 25381	.....**37**	4
14 Oct 72 ●	LET'S DANCE (re-issue) *London HLU 10205*	.....**9**	14
14 Apr 79	LET'S DANCE (2nd re-issue) *Lightning LIG 9011*	.....**47**	3

The second re-issue of 'Let's Dance' on Lightning was coupled with 'Memphis' by Lonnie Mack as a double A-side

MONTROSE
US, male vocal / instrumental group (2 WEEKS) pos/wks

28 Jun 80	SPACE STATION NO.5 / GOOD ROCKIN' TONIGHT		
	WB HM 9	.....**71**	2

MONTROSE AVENUE
UK, male vocal / instrumental group (4 WEEKS)   pos/wks

28 Mar 98	**WHERE DO I STAND?** *Columbia 6656072*	38	2
20 Jun 98	**SHINE** *Columbia 6660012*	58	1
17 Oct 98	**START AGAIN** *Columbia 6664255*	59	1

MONTY PYTHON *UK, male comedy group (9 WEEKS)*   pos/wks

5 Oct 91	● **ALWAYS LOOK ON THE BRIGHT SIDE OF LIFE** *Virgin PYTH 1*	3	9

MONYAKA *US / Jamaica, male vocal / instrumental group (8 WEEKS)*   pos/wks

10 Sep 83	**GO DEH YAKA (GO TO THE TOP)** *Polydor POSP 641*	14	8

MOOD *UK, male vocal / instrumental group (10 WEEKS)*   pos/wks

6 Feb 82	**DON'T STOP** *RCA 171*	59	4
22 May 82	**PARIS IS ONE DAY AWAY** *RCA 211*	42	5
30 Oct 82	**PASSION IN DARK ROOMS** *RCA 276*	74	1

MOODSWINGS / CHRISSIE HYNDE *UK male / instrumental group and US, female vocalist / instrumentalist (4 WEEKS)*   pos/wks

12 Oct 91	**SPIRITUAL HIGH (STATE OF INDEPENDENCE)** *Arista 114528*	66	2
23 Jan 93	**SPIRITUAL HIGH (STATE OF INDEPENDENCE) (re-mix)** *Arista 74321127712*	47	2

See also PRETENDERS

MOODY BLUES   `239` `Top 500` *Long-lived and internationally popular cosmic rock quintet from Birmingham, UK: line-up has included Denny Laine (v/g), Ray Thomas (fl/v), Mike Pinder. (k/v), Graeme Edge (d), Justin Hayward (v/g) and John Lodge (b/v). This album-oriented act has sold more than 50 million records worldwide (114 WEEKS)*   pos/wks

10 Dec 64	★ **GO NOW** *Decca F 12022*	1	14
4 Mar 65	**I DON'T WANT TO GO ON WITHOUT YOU** *Decca F 12095*	33	9
10 Jun 65	**FROM THE BOTTOM OF MY HEART** *Decca F 12166*	22	9
18 Nov 65	**EVERYDAY** *Decca F 12266*	44	2
27 Dec 67	**NIGHTS IN WHITE SATIN** *Deram DM 161*	19	11
7 Aug 68	**VOICES IN THE SKY** *Deram DM 196*	27	10
4 Dec 68	**RIDE MY SEE-SAW** *Deram DM 213*	42	1
2 May 70	● **QUESTION** *Threshold TH 4*	2	12
6 May 72	**ISN'T LIFE STRANGE** *Threshold TH 9*	13	10
2 Dec 72	● **NIGHTS IN WHITE SATIN (re-entry)** *Deram DM 161*	9	11
10 Feb 73	**I'M JUST A SINGER (IN A ROCK 'N' ROLL BAND)** *Threshold TH 13*	36	4
10 Nov 79	**NIGHTS IN WHITE SATIN (2nd re-entry)** *Deram DM 161*	14	12
20 Aug 83	**BLUE WORLD** *Threshold TH 30*	35	5
25 Jun 88	**I KNOW YOU'RE OUT THERE SOMEWHERE** *Polydor POSP 921*	52	4

Michael MOOG *US, male producer - Michael de Medici (2 WEEKS)* pos/wks

11 Dec 99	**THAT SOUND** *ffrr FCD 374*	32	2

MOOGWAI *Switzerland / Holland production duo (1 WEEK)*   pos/wks

6 May 00	**VIOLA** *Platipus PLATCD 71*	55	1

MOONMAN *Holland, male DJ / producer - Ferry Corsten (4 WEEKS)* pos/wks

9 Aug 97	**DON'T BE AFRAID** *Heat Recordings HEATCD 009*	60	1
27 Nov 99	**DON'T BE AFRAID '99 (re-mix)** *Heat Recordings HEATCD 022*	41	2
7 Oct 00	**GALAXIA** *Heat Recordings HEATCD 025* `1`	50	1

`1` Moonman featuring Chantal

See also Ferry CORSTEN; VERACOCHA; GOURYELLA; SYSTEM F

MOONTREKKERS *UK, male instrumental group (1 WEEK)*   pos/wks

2 Nov 61	**NIGHT OF THE VAMPIRE** *Parlophone R 4814*	50	1

Chante MOORE *US, female vocalist (4 WEEKS)*   pos/wks

20 Mar 93	**LOVE'S TAKEN OVER** *MCA MCSTD 1744*	54	3
4 Mar 95	**FREE / SAIL ON** *MCA MCSTD 2042*	69	1

Dorothy MOORE *US, female vocalist (24 WEEKS)*   pos/wks

19 Jun 76	● **MISTY BLUE** *Contempo CS 2087*	5	12
16 Oct 76	**FUNNY HOW TIME SLIPS AWAY** *Contempo CS 2092*	38	3
15 Oct 77	**I BELIEVE YOU** *Epic EPC 5573*	20	9

Dudley MOORE – See Peter COOK

Gary MOORE   `290` `Top 500` *Noted blues guitarist, b. 4 Apr 1952, Belfast. Played in early 1970s Irish band Skid Row (with Phil Lynott) as well as Thin Lizzy and Colosseum II, before successfully launching his solo career (103 WEEKS)*   pos/wks

21 Apr 79	● **PARISIENNE WALKWAYS** *MCA 419*	8	11
21 Jan 84	**HOLD ON TO LOVE** *10 TEN 13*	65	3
11 Aug 84	**EMPTY ROOMS** *10 TEN 25*	51	5
18 May 85	● **OUT IN THE FIELDS** *10 TEN 49* `1`	5	10
27 Jul 85	**EMPTY ROOMS (re-issue)** *10 TEN 58*	23	8
20 Dec 86	**OVER THE HILLS AND FAR AWAY** *10 TEN 134*	20	8
28 Feb 87	**WILD FRONTIER** *10 TEN 159*	35	5
9 May 87	**FRIDAY ON MY MIND** *10 TEN 164*	26	6
29 Aug 87	**THE LONER** *10 TEN 178*	53	5
5 Dec 87	**TAKE A LITTLE TIME (DOUBLE SINGLE)** *10 TEN 190*	75	1
14 Jan 89	**AFTER THE WAR** *Virgin GMS 1*	37	4
18 Mar 89	**READY FOR LOVE** *Virgin GMS 2.*	56	2
24 Mar 90	**OH PRETTY WOMAN** *Virgin VS 1233* `2`	48	3
12 May 90	**STILL GOT THE BLUES (FOR YOU)** *Virgin VS 1267*	31	7
18 Aug 90	**WALKING BY MYSELF** *Virgin VS 1281*	48	5
15 Dec 90	**TOO TIRED** *Virgin VS 1306*	71	1
22 Feb 92	**COLD DAY IN HELL** *Virgin VS 1393*	24	5
9 May 92	**STORY OF THE BLUES** *Virgin VS 1412*	40	4
18 Jul 92	**SINCE I MET YOU BABY** *Virgin VS 1423* `3`	59	3
24 Oct 92	**SEPARATE WAYS** *Virgin VS 1437*	59	1
8 May 93	**PARISIENNE WALKWAYS (re-recording)** *Virgin VSCDX 1456*	32	4
17 Jun 95	**NEED YOUR LOVE SO BAD** *Virgin VSCDG 1546*	48	2

`1` Gary Moore and Phil Lynott `2` Gary Moore featuring Albert King `3` Gary Moore and BB King

'Parisienne Walkways' features uncredited vocals by Phil Lynott. Tracks on double single: Take a Little Time / Out in the Fields / All Messed Up / Thunder Rising

Jackie MOORE *US, female vocalist (5 WEEKS)*   pos/wks

15 Sep 79	**THIS TIME BABY** *CBS 7722*	49	5

Lynsey MOORE – See RAMSEY and FEN featuring Lynsey MOORE

Mandy MOORE *US, female vocalist (18 WEEKS)*   pos/wks

6 May 00	● **CANDY** *Epic 6693452*	6	13
19 Aug 00	**I WANNA BE WITH YOU** *Epic 6695922*	21	5

Mark MOORE – See S EXPRESS

Melba MOORE *US, female vocalist - Melba Hill (29 WEEKS)*   pos/wks

15 May 76	● **THIS IS IT** *Buddah BDS 443*	9	8
26 May 79	**PICK ME UP I'LL DANCE** *Epic EPC 7234*	48	5
9 Oct 82	**LOVE'S COMIN' AT YA** *EMI America EA 146*	15	8
15 Jan 83	**MIND UP TONIGHT** *Capitol CL 272*	22	6
5 Mar 83	**UNDERLOVE** *Capitol CL 281*	60	2

Ray MOORE *UK, male vocalist (9 WEEKS)*   pos/wks

29 Nov 86	**O' MY FATHER HAD A RABBIT** *Play PLAY 213*	24	7
5 Dec 87	**BOG EYED JOG** *Play PLAY 224*	61	2

Sam MOORE and LOU REED *US, male vocalists (10 WEEKS)*   pos/wks

17 Jan 87	**SOUL MAN** *A & M AM 364*	30	10

See also SAM and DAVE; Lou REED

Tina MOORE US, female vocalist (18 WEEKS)
			pos	wks
30 Aug 97 ●	NEVER GONNA LET YOU GO	Delirious 74321511052	7	15
25 Apr 98	NOBODY BETTER	RCA 74321571612	20	3

Lisa MOORISH UK, female vocalist (11 WEEKS)
			pos	wks
7 Jan 95	JUST THE WAY IT IS	Go.Beat GODCD 123	42	3
19 Aug 95	I'M YOUR MAN	Go.Beat GODCD 128	24	3
3 Feb 96	MR FRIDAY NIGHT	Go.Beat GODCD 137	24	3
18 May 96	LOVE FOR LIFE	Go.Beat GODCD 145	37	2

'I'm Your Man' features the uncredited vocals of George Michael

Angel MORAES US, male producer (2 WEEKS)
			pos	wks
16 Nov 96	HEAVEN KNOWS - DEEP DEEP DOWN	ffrr FCD 282	72	1
17 May 97	I LIKE IT	AM:PM 5871792	70	1

David MORALES US, male DJ / producer (16 WEEKS)
			pos	wks
10 Jul 93	GIMME LUV (EENIE MEENIE MINY MO)	Mercury MERCD 390	37	3
20 Nov 93	THE PROGRAM	Mercury MERCD 396	66	1
24 Aug 96	IN DE GHETTO Manifesto FESCD 12 [1]		35	2
15 Aug 98 ●	NEEDIN' U Manifesto FESCD 46 [2]		8	8
24 Jun 00	HIGHER Azuli AZNYCDX 120 [3]		41	2

[1] David Morales and the Bad Yard Club featuring Crystal Waters and Delta [2] David Morales presents The Face [3] David Morales and Albert Cabrera Present Moca featuring Deanna

See also BOSS; PULSE featuring Antoinette ROBERSON

Mike MORAN – See Lynsey DE PAUL

MORCHEEBA
UK, male / female vocal / instrumental group (12 WEEKS)
			pos	wks
13 Jul 96	TAPE LOOP	Indochina ID 045CD	42	1
5 Oct 96	TRIGGER HIPPIE	Indochina ID 052CD	40	2
15 Feb 97	THE MUSIC THAT WE HEAR (MOOG ISLAND) Indochina ID 054CD		47	1
11 Oct 97	SHOULDER HOLSTER	Indochina ID 064CD	53	1
11 Apr 98	BLINDFOLD	Indochina ID 070CD	56	1
20 Jun 98	LET ME SEE	Indochina ID 076CD	46	1
29 Aug 98	PART OF THE PROCESS	China WOKCD 2097	38	2
5 Aug 00	ROME WASN'T BUILT IN A DAY East West EW 214CD		34	3

MORE UK, male vocal / instrumental group (2 WEEKS)
			pos	wks
14 Mar 81	WE ARE THE BAND	Atlantic K 11561	59	2

MOREL US, male vocalist / producer - Richard Morel (1 WEEK)
			pos	wks
12 Aug 00	TRUE (THE FAGGOT IS YOU)	Hooj Choons HOOJ 097CD	64	1

George MOREL featuring Heather WILDMAN
US, male / female vocal / instrumental duo (2 WEEKS)
			pos	wks
26 Oct 96	LET'S GROOVE	Positiva CDTIV 62	42	2

MORGAN UK, male vocal / instrumental duo (1 WEEK)
			pos	wks
27 Nov 99	MISS PARKER	Source CDSOUR 002	74	1

Derrick MORGAN Jamaica, male vocalist (1 WEEK)
			pos	wks
17 Jan 70	MOON HOP	Crab 32	49	1

Jamie J MORGAN US, male vocalist (6 WEEKS)
			pos	wks
10 Feb 90	WALK ON THE WILD SIDE	Tabu 655596 7	27	6

Jane MORGAN US, female vocalist - Jane Currier (22 WEEKS)
			pos	wks
5 Dec 58 ★	THE DAY THE RAINS CAME	London HLR 8751	1	16
22 May 59	IF ONLY I COULD LIVE MY LIFE AGAIN London HLR 8810		27	1
21 Jul 60	ROMANTICA	London HLR 9120	39	5

Meli'sa MORGAN US, female vocalist (7 WEEKS)
			pos	wks
9 Aug 86	FOOL'S PARADISE	Capitol CL 415	41	5
25 Jun 88	GOOD LOVE	Capitol CL 483	59	2

Ray MORGAN UK, male vocalist (6 WEEKS)
			pos	wks
25 Jul 70	THE LONG AND WINDING ROAD	B & C CB 128	32	6

Erick 'More' MORILLO presents RAW US, male DJ / producer / instrumentalist and female vocalist (1 WEEK)
			pos	wks
4 Feb 95	HIGHER (FEEL IT)	A & M 5809412	74	1

See also LIL MO' YIN YANG

Alanis MORISSETTE Canada, female vocalist (45 WEEKS)
			pos	wks
5 Aug 95	YOU OUGHTA KNOW	Maverick W 0307CD	22	7
28 Oct 95	HAND IN MY POCKET	Maverick W 0312CD	26	3
24 Feb 96	YOU LEARN	Maverick W 0334CD	24	4
20 Apr 96	IRONIC	Maverick W 0343CD	11	9
3 Aug 96 ●	HEAD OVER FEET	Maverick W 0355CD	7	7
7 Dec 96	ALL I REALLY WANT	Maverick W 0382CD	59	1
31 Oct 98 ●	THANK U	Maverick W 0458CD	5	10
13 Mar 99	JOINING YOU	Maverick W 472CD1	28	2
31 Jul 99	SO PURE	Maverick W 492CD1	38	2

Giorgio MORODER
Italy, male instrumentalist - synthesizer (36 WEEKS)
			pos	wks
24 Sep 77	FROM HERE TO ETERNITY Oasis 1 [1]		16	10
17 Mar 79	CHASE	Casablanca CAN 144	48	6
22 Sep 84 ●	TOGETHER IN ELECTRIC DREAMS Virgin VS 713 [2]		3	13
29 Jun 85	GOODBYE BAD TIMES Virgin VS 772 [2]		44	5
11 Jul 98	CARRY ON Almighty CDALMY 120 [3]		65	1
12 Feb 00	THE CHASE (re-recording) Logic 74321732112 [4]		46	1

[1] Giorgio [2] Giorgio Moroder and Phil Oakey [3] Donna Summer and Giorgio Moroder [4] DJ Empire Presents Giorgio Moroder

Ennio MORRICONE Italy, orchestra (12 WEEKS)
			pos	wks
11 Apr 81 ●	CHI MAI (THEME FROM THE TV SERIES `THE LIFE AND TIMES OF DAVID LLOYD GEORGE') BBC RESL 92		2	12

Sarah Jane MORRIS – See COMMUNARDS

Diana MORRISON – See Michael BALL

Dorothy Combs MORRISON – See Edwin HAWKINS SINGERS

Mark MORRISON Talented but notorious R&B singer / songwriter whose brushes with the law made him a regular subject of the tabloids. The singer, who changed his name to Abdul Rahman in 1998, b. 3 May 1972, Leicester, UK, spent several years living in the US. His first album included five Top 10 singles (68 WEEKS)
			pos	wks
22 Apr 95	CRAZY	WEA YZ 907CD	19	4
16 Sep 95	LET'S GET DOWN	WEA WEA 001CD	39	2
16 Mar 96 ★	RETURN OF THE MACK	WEA WEA 040CD	1	23
27 Jul 96 ●	CRAZY (re-mix)	WEA WEA 054CD1	6	8
31 Aug 96	RETURN OF THE MACK (re-entry)	WEA WEA 040CD	60	1
19 Oct 96	CRAZY (re-entry of re-mix)	WEA WEA 054CD1	71	1
19 Oct 96 ●	TRIPPIN'	WEA WEA 079CD1	5	5
21 Dec 96 ●	HORNY	WEA WEA 090CD1	5	9
15 Mar 97 ●	MOAN & GROAN	WEA WEA 096CD1	7	6
20 Sep 97	WHO'S THE MACK!	WEA WEA 128CD1	13	5
4 Sep 99	BEST FRIEND WEA WEA 221CD1 [1]		23	3

[1] Mark Morrison and Conner Reeves

Van MORRISON UK, male vocalist (20 WEEKS)
			pos	wks
20 Oct 79	BRIGHT SIDE OF THE ROAD	Mercury 6001 121	63	3
1 Jul 89	HAVE I TOLD YOU LATELY	Polydor VANS 1	74	1
9 Dec 89	WHENEVER GOD SHINES HIS LIGHT Polydor VANS 2 [1]		20	6
15 May 93	GLORIA Exile VANCD 11 [2]		31	3

18 Mar 95	HAVE I TOLD YOU LATELY THAT I LOVE YOU		
	RCA 74321271702 [3]	71	1
10 Jun 95	DAYS LIKE THIS Exile VANCD 12	65	1
2 Dec 95	NO RELIGION Exile 5775792	54	1
1 Mar 97	THE HEALING GAME Exile 5733912	46	1
6 Mar 99	PRECIOUS TIME Pointblank / Virgin POBD 14	36	2
22 May 99	BACK ON TOP Exile / Pointblank / Virgin POBD 15	69	1

[1] Van Morrison with Cliff Richard [2] Van Morrison and John Lee Hooker [3] Chieftains with Van Morrison

'Have I Told You Lately That I Love You' is a re-recording of his second hit

MORRISSEY (463) Top 500
Witty, often provocative vocalist / lyricist and former frontman of The Smiths, born Steven Morrissey, 22 May 1959, Manchester, UK. The first of 15 successive Top 40 singles entered at No.6, thereby immediately outdoing his previous band's chart peak (74 WEEKS) pos/wks

27 Feb 88	●	SUEDEHEAD HMV POP 1618	5	6
11 Jun 88	●	EVERYDAY IS LIKE SUNDAY HMV POP 1619	9	6
11 Feb 89	●	LAST OF THE FAMOUS INTERNATIONAL PLAYBOYS		
		HMV POP 1620	6	5
29 Apr 89	●	INTERESTING DRUG HMV POP 1621	9	4
25 Nov 89		OUIJA BOARD OUIJA BOARD HMV POP 1622	18	4
5 May 90		NOVEMBER SPAWNED A MONSTER HMV POP 1623	12	4
20 Oct 90		PICCADILLY PALARE HMV POP 1624	18	2
23 Feb 91		OUR FRANK HMV POP 1625	26	3
13 Apr 91		SING YOUR LIFE HMV POP 1626	33	2
27 Jul 91		PREGNANT FOR THE LAST TIME HMV POP 1627	25	4
12 Oct 91		MY LOVE LIFE HMV POP 1628	29	2
9 May 92		WE HATE IT WHEN OUR FRIENDS BECOME SUCCESSFUL		
		HMV POP 1629	17	3
18 Jul 92		YOU'RE THE ONE FOR ME, FATTY HMV POP 1630	19	3
19 Dec 92		CERTAIN PEOPLE I KNOW HMV POP 1631	35	4
12 Mar 94	●	THE MORE YOU IGNORE ME THE CLOSER I GET		
		Parlophone CDR 6372	8	3
11 Jun 94		HOLD ON TO YOUR FRIENDS Parlophone CDR 6383	47	2
20 Aug 94		INTERLUDE Parlophone CDR 6365 [1]	25	2
28 Jan 95		BOXERS Parlophone CDR 6400	23	2
2 Sep 95		DAGENHAM DAVE RCA Victor 7432129802	26	2
9 Dec 95		THE BOY RACER RCA Victor 74321332952	36	2
23 Dec 95		SUNNY Parlophone CDR 6243	42	2
2 Aug 97		ALMA MATTERS Island CID 667	16	3
18 Oct 97		ROY'S KEEN Island CID 671	42	1
10 Jan 98		SATAN REJECTED MY SOUL Island CID 686	39	2

[1] Morrissey and Siouxsie

See also SMITHS

MORRISTON ORPHEUS MALE VOICE CHOIR – See ALARM

Buddy MORROW *US, orchestra (1 WEEK)* pos/wks

20 Mar 53	NIGHT TRAIN HMV B 10347	12	1

Bob MORTIMER – See EMF; MIDDLESBROUGH FC featuring Bob MORTIMER and Chris REA

MOS DEF *US male rapper - Dante Smith (2 WEEKS)* pos/wks

24 Jun 00	UMI SAYS Rawkus RWK 232CD	60	1
4 Nov 00	MISS FAT BOOTY - PART II Rawkus RWK 282CD [1]	64	1

[1] Mos Def featuring Ghostface Killah

Mickie MOST *UK, male vocalist (1 WEEK)* pos/wks

25 Jul 63	MISTER PORTER Decca F 11664	45	1

MOTELS *US / UK, male / female vocal / instrumental group (7 WEEKS)* pos/wks

11 Oct 80	WHOSE PROBLEM? Capitol CL 16162	42	4
10 Jan 81	DAYS ARE O.K. Capitol CL 16149	41	3

Wendy MOTEN *US, female vocalist (13 WEEKS)* pos/wks

5 Feb 94	●	COME IN OUT OF THE RAIN EMI-USA CDMT 105	8	9
14 May 94		SO CLOSE TO LOVE EMI-USA CDMTS 106	35	4

MOTHER *UK, male instrumental / production duo (4 WEEKS)* pos/wks

12 Jun 93	ALL FUNKED UP Bosting BYSNCD 101	34	2
1 Oct 94	GET BACK Six6 SIXT 119	73	1
31 Aug 96	ALL FUNKED UP (re-mix) Six6 SIXXCD 1	66	1

MOTHER'S PRIDE *UK, male DJ / production duo (2 WEEKS)* pos/wks

21 Mar 98	FLORIBUNDA Heat Recordings HEATCD 013	42	1
6 Nov 99	LEARNING TO FLY Devolution DEVR 001CDS	54	1

MOTIV 8 *UK, male producer - Steve Rodway (10 WEEKS)* pos/wks

17 Jul 93	ROCKIN' FOR MYSELF Nuff Respect NUFF 002CD [1]	67	1
7 May 94	ROCKIN' FOR MYSELF (re-mix) WEA YZ 814CD	18	4
21 Oct 95	BREAK THE CHAIN Eternal WEA 010CD	31	2
23 Dec 95	SEARCHING FOR THE GOLDEN EYE Eternal WEA 027CD [2]	40	3

[1] Motiv 8 featuring Angie Brown [2] Motiv 8 and Kym Mazelle

MOTLEY CRÜE *US, male vocal / instrumental group (28 WEEKS)* pos/wks

24 Aug 85	SMOKIN' IN THE BOYS ROOM Elektra EKR 16	71	2
8 Feb 86	HOME SWEET HOME / SMOKIN' IN THE BOYS ROOM		
	(re-issue) Elektra EKR 33	51	3
1 Aug 87	GIRLS GIRLS GIRLS Elektra EKR 59	26	6
16 Jan 88	YOU'RE ALL I NEED / WILD SIDE Elektra EKR 65	23	4
4 Nov 89	DR FEELGOOD Elektra EKR 97	50	2
12 May 90	WITHOUT YOU Elektra EKR 109	39	3
7 Sep 91	PRIMAL SCREAM Elektra EKR 133	32	2
11 Jan 92	HOME SWEET HOME (re-mix) Elektra EKR 136	37	2
5 Mar 94	HOOLIGAN'S HOLIDAY Elektra EKR 180CDX	36	2
19 Jul 97	AFRAID Elektra E 3936 CD1	58	1

'Wild Side' listed only with 'You're All I Need' from 30 Jan 1988. It peaked at No 26

MOTÖRHEAD (405) Top 500
Unashamedly loud mainstays of UK heavy rock formed in 1975 after Lemmy (v/b) (b. Ian Kilmister 24 Dec 1945, Stoke-on-Trent, UK) left Hawkwind. Much-touted in punk circles, they helped to show the way to 1980s heavy metal bands such as Metallica (81 WEEKS) pos/wks

16 Sep 78		LOUIE LOUIE Bronze BRO 60	75	1
30 Sep 78		LOUIE LOUIE (re-entry) Bronze BRO 60	68	1
10 Mar 79		OVERKILL Bronze BRO 67	39	4
14 Apr 79		OVERKILL (re-entry) Bronze BRO 67	57	3
30 Jun 79		NO CLASS Bronze BRO 78	61	4
1 Dec 79		BOMBER Bronze BRO 85	34	7
3 May 80	●	THE GOLDEN YEARS (EP) Bronze BRO 92	8	7
1 Nov 80		ACE OF SPADES Bronze BRO 106	15	12
22 Nov 80		BEER DRINKERS AND HELL RAISERS Big Beat SWT 61	43	4
21 Feb 81	●	ST VALENTINE'S DAY MASSACRE (EP) Bronze BRO 116 [1]	5	8
11 Jul 81	●	MOTÖRHEAD (LIVE) Bronze BRO 124	6	7
3 Apr 82		IRON FIST Bronze BRO 146	29	5
21 May 83		I GOT MINE Bronze BRO 165	46	4
30 Jul 83		SHINE Bronze BRO 167	59	2
1 Sep 84		KILLED BY DEATH Bronze BRO 185	51	2
5 Jul 86		DEAF FOREVER GWR GWR 2	67	1
5 Jan 91		THE ONE TO SING THE BLUES Epic 6565787	45	3
14 Nov 92		'92 TOUR (EP) Epic 6588096	63	1
11 Sep 93		ACE OF SPADES (re-issue) WGAF CDWGAF 101	23	5
10 Dec 94		BORN TO RAISE HELL Fox 74321230152 [2]	47	2

[1] Motörhead and Girlschool (also known as Headgirl) [2] Motörhead / Ice-T / Whitfield Crane

Tracks on The Golden Years (EP): Dead Men Tell No Tales / Too Late Too Late / Leaving Here / Stone Dead Forever. Tracks on St Valentine's Day Massacre (EP): Please Don't Touch / Emergency / Bomber. Tracks on '92 Tour (EP): Hellraiser / You Better Run / Going to Brazil / Ramones

MOTORS *UK, male vocal / instrumental group (29 WEEKS)* pos/wks

24 Sep 77		DANCING THE NIGHT AWAY Virgin VS 186	42	4
10 Jun 78	●	AIRPORT Virgin VS 219	4	13
19 Aug 78		FORGET ABOUT YOU Virgin VS 222	13	9
12 Apr 80		LOVE AND LONELINESS Virgin VS 263	58	3

MOTOWN SPINNERS – See DETROIT SPINNERS

UK No.1 ★   UK Top 10 ●   Still on chart +   UK million seller ◆   UK entry at No.1 ■   US No.1 ▲

MOTT THE HOOPLE
UK, male vocal / instrumental group (55 WEEKS) pos/wks

12 Aug 72	●	ALL THE YOUNG DUDES *CBS 8271*	3	11
16 Jun 73		HONALOOCHIE BOOGIE *CBS 1530*	12	9
8 Sep 73	●	ALL THE WAY FROM MEMPHIS *CBS 1764*	10	8
24 Nov 73	●	ROLL AWAY THE STONE *CBS 1895*	8	12
30 Mar 74		GOLDEN AGE OF ROCK AND ROLL *CBS 2177*	16	7
22 Jun 74		FOXY FOXY *CBS 2439*	33	5
2 Nov 74		SATURDAY GIGS *CBS 2754*	41	3

MOUNT RUSHMORE presents THE KNACK
UK, male production duo / female vocalist (1 WEEK) pos/wks

3 Apr 99		YOU BETTER *Universal MCSTD 40192*	53	1

Nana MOUSKOURI *Greece, female vocalist (11 WEEKS)* pos/wks

11 Jan 86	●	ONLY LOVE *Philips PH 38*	2	11

MOUSSE T
Germany, male producer - Mustafa Gundogdu (27 WEEKS) pos/wks

6 Jun 98	●	HORNY *AM:PM 5826712* [1]	2	17
20 May 00	●	SEX BOMB *Gut CDGUT 33* [2]	3	10

[1] Mousse T vs Hot 'N' Juicy [2] Tom Jones & Mousse T

MOUTH and MACNEAL
Holland, male / female vocal duo (10 WEEKS) pos/wks

4 May 74	●	I SEE A STAR *Decca F 13504*	8	10

MOVE (257 Top 500) *Innovative and influential Birmingham band: included Carl Wayne (v), Roy Wood (v/g). They were the first group heard on BBC Radio 1 ('Flowers in the Rain'), and had eight consecutive Top 20 entries. Wood later moved on to a successful solo career, helped to form ELO and went on to front Wizzard (110 WEEKS)* pos/wks

5 Jan 67	●	NIGHT OF FEAR *Deram DM 109*	2	10
6 Apr 67	●	I CAN HEAR THE GRASS GROW *Deram DM 117*	5	10
6 Sep 67	●	FLOWERS IN THE RAIN *Regal Zonophone RZ3001*	2	13
7 Feb 68	●	FIRE BRIGADE *Regal Zonophone RZ3005*	3	11
25 Dec 68	★	BLACKBERRY WAY *Regal Zonophone RZ3015*	1	12
23 Jul 69		CURLY *Regal Zonophone RZ3021*	12	12
25 Apr 70	●	BRONTOSAURUS *Regal Zonophone RZ3026*	7	10
3 Jul 71		TONIGHT *Harvest HAR 5038*	11	10
23 Oct 71		CHINATOWN *Harvest HAR 5043*	23	8
13 May 72	●	CALIFORNIA MAN *Harvest HAR 5050*	7	14

MOVEMENT *US, male vocal / instrumental group (2 WEEKS)* pos/wks

24 Oct 92		JUMP! *Arista 74321116677*	57	2

MOVEMENT 98 featuring Carroll THOMPSON
UK, male / female vocal / instrumental group (8 WEEKS) pos/wks

19 May 90		JOY AND HEARTBREAK *Circa YR 45*	27	5
15 Sep 90		SUNRISE *Circa YR 51*	58	3

MOVIN' MELODIES
Holland, male producer - Patrick Prinz (3 WEEKS) pos/wks

22 Oct 94		LA LUNA *Effective EFFS 017CD* [1]	64	1
29 Jun 96		INDICA *Hooj Choons HOOJCD 44*	62	1
26 Jul 97		ROLLERBLADE *Movin' Melodies 5822352*	71	1

[1] Movin' Melodies Production

See also ARTEMESIA; ETHICS; SUBLIMINAL CUTS

Alison MOYET (270 Top 500) *After five Top 20 hits with Yazoo, the distinctive, bluesy-voiced vocalist (b. 18 Jun 1961, Essex, UK), nicknamed Alf, enjoyed a string of solo successes. Her biggest hits included revivals of songs made popular by Billie Holiday and Ketty Lester (107 WEEKS)* pos/wks

23 Jun 84	●	LOVE RESURRECTION *CBS A 4497*	10	11
13 Oct 84	●	ALL CRIED OUT *CBS A 4757*	8	11
1 Dec 84		INVISIBLE *CBS A 4930*	21	10

16 Mar 85	●	THAT OLE DEVIL CALLED LOVE *CBS A 6044*	2	10
29 Nov 86	●	IS THIS LOVE? *CBS MOYET 1*	3	16
7 Mar 87	●	WEAK IN THE PRESENCE OF BEAUTY *CBS MOYET 2*	6	10
30 May 87		ORDINARY GIRL *CBS MOYET 3*	43	4
28 Nov 87	●	LOVE LETTERS *CBS MOYET 5*	4	10
6 Apr 91		IT WON'T BE LONG *Columbia 6567577*	50	4
1 Jun 91		WISHING YOU WERE HERE *Columbia 6569397*	72	1
12 Oct 91		THIS HOUSE *Columbia 6575157*	40	5
16 Oct 93		FALLING *Columbia 6595962*	42	3
12 Mar 94		WHISPERING YOUR NAME *Columbia 6601622*	18	7
28 May 94		GETTING INTO SOMETHING *Columbia 6603565*	51	2
22 Oct 94		ODE TO BOY *Columbia 6607952*	59	1
26 Aug 95		SOLID WOOD *Columbia 6623265*	44	2

See also YAZOO

MOZAIC *UK, female vocal group (7 WEEKS)* pos/wks

5 Aug 95		SING IT (THE HALLELUJAH SONG) *Perfecto PERF 106CD*	14	4
10 Aug 96		RAYS OF THE RISING SUN *Perfecto PERF 123CD*	32	2
30 Nov 96		MOVING UP MOVING ON *Perfecto PERF 131CD*	62	1

MR and MRS SMITH
UK, male / female instrumental / production group (1 WEEK) pos/wks

12 Oct 96		GOTTA GET LOOSE *Hooj Choons HOOJCD 46*	70	1

MR BEAN and SMEAR CAMPAIGN featuring Bruce DICKINSON
UK, male comedian - Rowan Atkinson and male vocalist (5 WEEKS) pos/wks

4 Apr 92	●	(I WANT TO BE) ELECTED *London LON 319*	9	5

MR BIG *UK, male vocal / instrumental group (14 WEEKS)* pos/wks

12 Feb 77	●	ROMEO *EMI 2567*	4	10
21 May 77		FEEL LIKE CALLING HOME *EMI 2610*	35	4

MR BIG *US, male vocal / instrumental group (17 WEEKS)* pos/wks

7 Mar 92	●	TO BE WITH YOU *Atlantic A 7514* ▲	3	11
23 May 92		JUST TAKE MY HEART *Atlantic A 7490*	26	4
8 Aug 92		GREEN TINTED SIXTIES MIND *Atlantic A 7468*	72	1
20 Nov 93		WILD WORLD *Atlantic A 7310CD*	59	1

MR BLOBBY
UK, male pink, yellow spotted blob vocalist (16 WEEKS) pos/wks

4 Dec 93	★	MR BLOBBY *Destiny Music CDDMUS 104*	1	12
16 Dec 95		CHRISTMAS IN BLOBBYLAND *Destiny DMUSCD 108*	36	4

MR BLOE *UK, male instrumental group (18 WEEKS)* pos/wks

9 May 70	●	GROOVIN' WITH MR BLOE *DJM DJS 216*	2	18

MR FINGERS *US, male producer - Larry Heard (5 WEEKS)* pos/wks

17 Mar 90		WHAT ABOUT THIS LOVE *ffrr F 131*	74	1
7 Mar 92		CLOSER *MCA MCS 1601*	50	3
23 May 92		ON MY WAY *MCA MCS 1630*	71	1

MR FOOD *UK, male vocalist (3 WEEKS)* pos/wks

9 Jun 90		. . . AND THAT'S BEFORE ME TEA! *Tangible TGB 005*	62	3

MR HANKEY *US, male Xmas excrement vocalist (6 WEEKS)* pos/wks

25 Dec 99	●	MR HANKEY THE CHRISTMAS POO *Columbia 6685582*	4	6

MR JACK *Belgium, male producer - Lucente Vito (2 WEEKS)* pos/wks

25 Jan 97		WIGGLY WORLD *Extravaganza 0090965*	32	2

MR LEE *US, male producer - Leroy Haggard (6 WEEKS)* pos/wks

6 Aug 88		PUMP UP LONDON *Breakout USA 639*	64	2
11 Nov 89		GET BUSY *Jive JIVE 231*	71	1
24 Feb 90		GET BUSY (re-entry) *Jive JIVE 231*	41	3

UK No.1 ★ UK Top 10 ● Still on chart + UK million seller ◆ UK entry at No.1 ■ US No.1 ▲

MR MISTER US, male vocal / instrumental group (22 WEEKS)

			pos/wks
21 Dec 85	● BROKEN WINGS RCA PB 49945 ▲		.4 13
1 Mar 86	KYRIE RCA PB 49927 ▲		.11 9

MR OIZO France, male producer - Quentin Dupieux (15 WEEKS)

			pos/wks
3 Apr 99	★ FLAT BEAT		
	F Communications / Pias Recordings F 104CDUK ■		.1 13
7 Aug 99	FLAT BEAT (re-entry)		
	F Communications / Pias Recordings F 104CDUK		.60 2

MR PRESIDENT Germany, male / female vocal group (13 WEEKS)

			pos/wks
14 Jun 97	● COCO JAMBOO WEA WEA 110CD		.8 11
20 Sep 97	I GIVE YOU MY HEART WEA WEA 126CD		.52 1
25 Apr 98	JOJO ACTION WEA WEA 156CD		.73 1

MR ROY UK, male instrumental / production group (6 WEEKS)

			pos/wks
7 May 94	SOMETHING ABOUT YOU Fresh FRSHD 11		.74 1
21 Jan 95	SAVED Fresh FRSHD 21		.24 4
16 Dec 95	SOMETHING ABOUT U (CAN'T BE BEAT) (re-mix)		
	Fresh FRSHCD 33		.49 1

MR V UK, male producer - Rob Villiers (2 WEEKS)

			pos/wks
6 Aug 94	GIVE ME LIFE Cheeky CHEKCD 005		.40 2

MR VEGAS Jamaica, male vocalist - Clifford Smith (7 WEEKS)

			pos/wks
22 Aug 98	HEADS HIGH Greensleeves GRECD 650		.71 1
13 Nov 99	HEADS HIGH (re-issue)		
	Greensleeves GRECD 785		.16 6

MRS MILLS UK, female instrumentalist - piano (5 WEEKS)

			pos/wks
14 Dec 61	MRS MILLS' MEDLEY Parlophone R 4856		.18 5

Mrs Mills' Medley consisted of the following tunes: I Want to Be Happy / Sheik of Araby / Baby Face / Somebody Stole My Gal / Ma (He's Making Eyes At Me) / Swanee / Ain't She Sweet / California Here I Come

MRS WOOD UK, female producer (6 WEEKS)

			pos/wks
16 Sep 95	JOANNA React CDREACT 066		.40 2
6 Jul 96	HEARTBREAK React CDREACT 78 [1]		.44 1
4 Oct 97	JOANNA (re-mix) React CDREACT 107		.34 2
15 Aug 98	1234 React CDREACT 121		.54 1

[1] Mrs Wood featuring Eve Gallagher

MTUME US, male / female vocal / instrumental group (12 WEEKS)

			pos/wks
14 May 83	JUICY FRUIT Epic A 3424		.34 9
22 Sep 84	PRIME TIME Epic A 4720		.57 3

MUD `172` `Top 500`
Rock 'n' roll-influenced Seventies stars: Les Gray (v), Rob Davis (g/v), Ray Stiles (b/v), Dave Mount (d/v). After joining RAK Records and teaming with writer / producers Nicky Chinn and Mike Chapman, this good-time British band had a noteworthy run of hits, including three No.1s. Davis is now a noted dance music producer and composer (139 WEEKS)

			pos/wks
10 Mar 73	CRAZY RAK 146		.12 12
23 Jun 73	HYPNOSIS RAK 152		.16 13
27 Oct 73	● DYNA-MITE RAK 159		.4 12
19 Jan 74	★ TIGER FEET RAK 166		.1 11
13 Apr 74	● THE CAT CREPT IN RAK 170		.2 9
27 Jul 74	● ROCKET RAK 178		.6 9
30 Nov 74	★ LONELY THIS CHRISTMAS RAK 187		.1 10
15 Feb 75	● THE SECRETS THAT YOU KEEP RAK 194		.3 9
26 Apr 75	★ OH BOY RAK 201		.1 9
21 Jun 75	● MOONSHINE SALLY RAK 208		.10 7
2 Aug 75	ONE NIGHT RAK 213		.32 4
4 Oct 75	● L-L-LUCY Private Stock PVT 41		.10 6
29 Nov 75	● SHOW ME YOU'RE A WOMAN Private Stock PVT 45		.8 8
15 May 76	SHAKE IT DOWN Private Stock PVT 65		.12 8
27 Nov 76	● LEAN ON ME Private Stock PVT 85		.7 9
21 Dec 85	LONELY THIS CHRISTMAS (re-entry) RAK 187		.61 3

MUDHONEY US, male vocal / instrumental group (2 WEEKS)

			pos/wks
17 Aug 91	LET IT SLIDE Subpop SP 15154		.60 1
24 Oct 92	SUCK YOU DRY Reprise W 0137		.65 1

MUDLARKS UK, male / female vocal group (19 WEEKS)

			pos/wks
2 May 58	● LOLLIPOP Columbia DB 4099		.2 9
6 Jun 58	● BOOK OF LOVE Columbia DB 4133		.8 9
27 Feb 59	THE LOVE GAME Columbia DB 4250		.30 1

MUFFINS – See MARTHA and the MUFFINS

Idris MUHAMMAD US, male instrumentalist - drums (3 WEEKS)

			pos/wks
17 Sep 77	COULD HEAVEN EVER BE LIKE THIS		
	Kudu 935		.42 3

Vocal by Frank Floyd

MUKKAA UK, male instrumental / production duo (1 WEEK)

			pos/wks
27 Feb 93	BURUCHACCA Limbo LIMBO 008		.74 1

Maria MULDAUR US, female vocalist (8 WEEKS)

			pos/wks
29 Jun 74	MIDNIGHT AT THE OASIS Reprise K 14331		.21 8

Arthur MULLARD – See Hylda BAKER and Arthur MULLARD

Larry MULLEN – See Adam CLAYTON and Larry MULLEN

Shawn MULLINS US, male vocalist (11 WEEKS)

			pos/wks
6 Mar 99	● LULLABY Columbia 6669592		.9 10
2 Oct 99	WHAT IS LIFE Columbia 6678212		.62 1

MULU UK, male / female vocal / instrumental duo (1 WEEK)

			pos/wks
2 Aug 97	PUSSYCAT Dedicated MULU 003CD1		.50 1

Samantha MUMBA Ireland, female vocalist (22 WEEKS)

			pos/wks
8 Jul 00	● GOTTA TELL YOU		
	Wild Card / Polydor 5618832		.2 12
28 Oct 00	● BODY II BODY		
	Wild Card / Polydor 5877742		.5 10+

Coati MUNDI – See Kid CREOLE and the COCONUTS

MUNDY Ireland, male vocalist (2 WEEKS)

			pos/wks
3 Aug 96	TO YOU I BESTOW Epic MUNDY 1CD		.60 1
5 Oct 96	LIFE'S A CINCH Epic MUNDY 2CD		.75 1

MUNGO JERRY `350` `Top 500`
London-based good-time jug-band, fronted by singer / songwriter Ray Dorset, b. 21 Mar 1946, Middlesex, UK. 'In the Summertime', the first three-track No.1, sold seven million worldwide, and their first two singles topped the chart. Dorset also penned Kelly Marie's No.1, 'Feels Like I'm In Love' (88 WEEKS)

			pos/wks
6 Jun 70	★ IN THE SUMMERTIME Dawn DNX 2502		.1 20
6 Feb 71	BABY JUMP Dawn DNX 2505		.32 1
20 Feb 71	★ BABY JUMP (re-entry) Dawn DNX 2505		.1 12
29 May 71	● LADY ROSE Dawn DNX 2510		.5 12
18 Sep 71	YOU DON'T HAVE TO BE IN THE ARMY TO FIGHT IN THE		
	WAR Dawn DNX 2513		.13 8
22 Apr 72	OPEN UP Dawn DNX 2514		.21 8
7 Jul 73	● ALRIGHT ALRIGHT ALRIGHT Dawn DNS 1037		.3 12
10 Nov 73	WILD LOVE Dawn DNS 1051		.32 5
6 Apr 74	LONG LEGGED WOMAN DRESSED IN BLACK		
	Dawn DNS 1061		.13 9
29 May 99	SUPPORT THE TOON - IT'S YOUR DUTY (EP)		
	Saraja TOONCD 001 [1]		.57 1

[1] Mungo Jerry and Toon Travellers

Tracks on Support the Toon - It's Your Duty (EP): Blaydon Races / Going to Wembley / Bottle of Beer

MUNICH MACHINE *Germany, male instrumental group (8 WEEKS)*

		pos/wks	
10 Dec 77	GET ON THE FUNK TRAIN *Oasis OASIS 2*.................	41	4
4 Nov 78	A WHITER SHADE OF PALE *Oasis OASIS 5* [1]	42	4

[1] Munich Machine introducing Chris Bennett

David MUNROW – See EARLY MUSIC CONSORT directed by David MUNROW

MUPPETS *US, frog fronted puppet ensemble (15 WEEKS)*

		pos/wks	
28 May 77 ●	HALFWAY DOWN THE STAIRS *Pye 7N 45698*	7	8
17 Dec 77	THE MUPPET SHOW MUSIC HALL EP *Pye 7NX 8004*..........	19	7

'Halfway Down the Stairs' is sung by Jerry Nelson as Kermit the Frog's nephew, Robin. Tracks on The Muppet Show Music Hall EP: Don't Dilly Dally On the Way / Waiting at the Church / The Boy in the Gallery / Wotcher (Knocked 'Em in the Old Kent Road)

Lydia MURDOCK *US, female vocalist (9 WEEKS)*

		pos/wks	
24 Sep 83	SUPERSTAR *Korova KOW 30*	14	9

Shirley MURDOCK *US, female vocalist (2 WEEKS)*

		pos/wks	
12 Apr 86	TRUTH OR DARE *Elektra EKR 36*	60	2

Eddie MURPHY – See Shabba RANKS

Noel MURPHY *Ireland, male vocalist (4 WEEKS)*

		pos/wks	
27 Jun 87	MURPHY AND THE BRICKS *Murphy's STACK 1*..........	57	4

Walter MURPHY and the BIG APPLE BAND
US, orchestra (9 WEEKS)

		pos/wks	
10 Jul 76	A FIFTH OF BEETHOVEN *Private Stock PVT 59* ▲	28	9

Anne MURRAY *Canada, female vocalist (40 WEEKS)*

		pos/wks	
24 Oct 70	SNOWBIRD *Capitol CL 15654*	23	17
21 Oct 72	DESTINY *Capitol CL 15734*	41	4
9 Dec 78	YOU NEEDED ME *Capitol CL 16011* ▲	22	14
21 Apr 79	I JUST FALL IN LOVE AGAIN *Capitol CL 16069*	58	2
19 Apr 80	DAYDREAM BELIEVER *Capitol CL 16123*	61	3

Keith MURRAY *US, male rapper (10 WEEKS)*

		pos/wks	
2 Nov 96	THE RHYME *Jive JIVECD 407*	59	1
27 Jun 98	SHORTY (YOU KEEP PLAYIN' WITH MY MIND) *Jive 0521212* [1]	22	3
14 Nov 98	HOME ALONE *Jive 0522392* [2]	17	5
5 Dec 98	INCREDIBLE *Jive 0522102* [3]	52	1

[1] Imajin featuring Keith Murray [2] R Kelly featuring Keith Murray [3] Keith Murray featuring LL Cool J

Pauline MURRAY and the INVISIBLE GIRLS *UK, female vocalist with male (really) vocal / instrumental group (2 WEEKS)*

		pos/wks	
2 Aug 80	DREAM SEQUENCE (ONE) *Illusive IVE 1*	67	2

Ruby MURRAY `240` **Top 500** *Britain's singing sensation of 1955, b. 29 Mar 1935, Belfast, d. 17 Dec 1996. This nasal-sounding 'girl-next-door' vocalist captivated UK audiences in the mid-1950s. She was the first artist to have five simultaneous Top 20 singles (114 WEEKS)*

		pos/wks	
3 Dec 54 ●	HEARTBEAT *Columbia DB 3542*....................	3	16
28 Jan 55 ★	SOFTLY, SOFTLY *Columbia DB 3558*..............	1	22
4 Feb 55 ●	HAPPY DAYS AND LONELY NIGHTS *Columbia DB 3577 (A)*......	6	8
4 Mar 55 ●	LET ME GO LOVER *Columbia DB 3577 (B)*	5	7
18 Mar 55 ●	IF ANYONE FINDS THIS, I LOVE YOU *Columbia DB 3580* [1] ...	4	11
1 Jul 55 ●	EVERMORE *Columbia DB 3617*	3	17
8 Jul 55	SOFTLY, SOFTLY (re-entry) *Columbia DB 3558*........	20	1
14 Oct 55 ●	I'LL COME WHEN YOU CALL *Columbia DB 3643*	6	7
31 Aug 56	YOU ARE MY FIRST LOVE *Columbia DB 3770*.......	16	4
5 Oct 56	YOU ARE MY FIRST LOVE (re-entry) *Columbia DB 3770*	21	1
12 Dec 58	REAL LOVE *Columbia DB 4192*	18	6

		pos/wks	
5 Jun 59 ●	GOODBYE JIMMY, GOODBYE *Columbia DB 4305*	10	13
9 Oct 59	GOODBYE JIMMY, GOODBYE (re-entry) *Columbia DB 4305*	26	1

[1] Ruby Murray with Anne Warren

Junior MURVIN *Jamaica, male vocalist (9 WEEKS)*

		pos/wks	
3 May 80	POLICE AND THIEVES *Island WIP 6539*	23	9

MUSE *UK, male vocal / instrumental group (13 WEEKS)*

		pos/wks	
26 Jun 99	UNO *Mushroom MUSH 50CDS*.................	73	1
18 Sep 99	CAVE *Mushroom MUSH 58CDS*	52	1
4 Dec 99	MUSCLE MUSEUM *Mushroom MUSH 66CDS*	43	2
4 Mar 00	SUNBURN *Mushroom MUSH 68CDS*	22	2
17 Jun 00	UNINTENDED *Mushroom MUSH 72CDS*..........	20	4
21 Oct 00	MUSCLE MUSEUM (re-issue) *Mushroom MUSH 84CDS*	25	3

MUSIC and MYSTERY featuring Gwen McCRAE *(3 WEEKS)*

		pos/wks	
13 Feb 93	ALL THIS LOVE I'M GIVING *KTDA CDKTDA 2*	36	3

MUSIC RELIEF '94
UK, male / female vocal / instrumental group (1 WEEK)

		pos/wks	
5 Nov 94	WHAT'S GOING ON *Jive RWANDACD 1*	70	1

MUSICAL YOUTH *UK, male vocal / instrumental group - lead vocal Dennis Seaton (55 WEEKS)*

		pos/wks	
25 Sep 82 ★	PASS THE DUTCHIE *MCA YOU 1*	1	12
20 Nov 82	YOUTH OF TODAY *MCA YOU 2*	13	9
8 Jan 83	PASS THE DUTCHIE (re-entry) *MCA YOU 1*	65	1
12 Feb 83 ●	NEVER GONNA GIVE YOU UP *MCA YOU 3*.........	6	10
16 Apr 83	HEARTBREAKER *MCA YOU 4*	44	3
9 Jul 83	TELL ME WHY *MCA YOU 5*	33	6
22 Oct 83	007 *MCA YOU 6*	26	6
14 Jan 84	SIXTEEN *MCA YOU 7*	23	8

See also Donna SUMMER

MUSIQUE *US, female vocal group (12 WEEKS)*

		pos/wks	
18 Nov 78	IN THE BUSH *CBS 6791*	16	12

MUSTAFA S – See STAIFFI and his MUSTAFAS

MUTANT DISCO – See PHATS + SMALL

MXM *Italy, male / female vocal / instrumental group (1 WEEK)*

		pos/wks	
2 Jun 90	NOTHING COMPARES 2 U *London LON 267*...............	68	1

MY BLOODY VALENTINE
UK, male / female vocal / instrumental group (5 WEEKS)

		pos/wks	
5 May 90	SOON *Creation CRE 073*	41	3
16 Feb 91	TO HERE KNOWS WHEN *Creation CRE 085*	29	2

MY LIFE STORY
UK, male / female vocal / instrumental group (12 WEEKS)

		pos/wks	
17 Aug 96	12 REASONS WHY I LOVE HER *Parlophone CDR 6442* ...	32	2
9 Nov 96	SPARKLE *Parlophone CDR 6450*	34	2
1 Mar 97	THE KING OF KISSINGDOM *Parlophone CDRS 6457*	35	1
17 May 97	STRUMPET *Parlophone CDR 6464*	27	2
23 Aug 97	DUCHESS *Parlophone CDR 6474*	39	1
19 Jun 99	IT'S A GIRL THING *IT ITR 001*	37	2
30 Oct 99	EMPIRE LINE *IT ITR 003*	58	1
19 Feb 00	WALK / DON'T WALK *IT ITR 007*	48	1

MY VITRIOL *UK, male / female vocal / instrumental group (2 WEEKS)*

		pos/wks	
22 Jul 00	CEMENTED SHOES *Infectious INFECT 89CDS*	65	1
11 Nov 00	PIECES *Infectious INFECT 94CDS*	56	1

MYA – See BLACKSTREET; MASE; Pras MICHEL

Tim MYCROFT – See SOUNDS NICE featuring Tim MYCROFT

Alicia MYERS US, female vocalist (3 WEEKS)

		pos/wks	
1 Sep 84	**YOU GET THE BEST FROM ME (SAY SAY SAY)** *MCA MCA 914*	58	3

Billie MYERS UK, female vocalist (12 WEEKS)

		pos/wks	
11 Apr 98 ●	**KISS THE RAIN** *Universal UND 56182*	4	9
25 Jul 98	**TELL ME** *Universal UND 56201*	28	3

Richard MYHILL UK, male vocalist (9 WEEKS)

		pos/wks	
1 Apr 78	**IT TAKES TWO TO TANGO** *Mercury 6007 167*	17	9

Alannah MYLES Canada, female vocalist (17 WEEKS)

		pos/wks	
17 Mar 90 ●	**BLACK VELVET** *East West A 8742* ▲	2	15
16 Jun 90	**LOVE IS** *East West A 8918*	61	2

Marie MYRIAM France, female vocalist (4 WEEKS)

		pos/wks	
28 May 77	**L'OISEAU ET L'ENFANT** *Polydor 2056 634*	42	4

MYRON US male vocalist (1 WEEK)

		pos/wks	
22 Nov 97	**WE CAN GET DOWN** *Island Black Music CID 677*	74	1

MYSTERIANS – See ? (QUESTION MARK) and the MYSTERIANS

MYSTI – See CAMOUFLAGE featuring MYSTI

MYSTIC MERLIN US, male vocal / instrumental group (9 WEEKS)

		pos/wks	
26 Apr 80	**JUST CAN'T GIVE YOU UP** *Capitol CL 16133*	20	9

MYSTIC 3 UK / Italy, male production group (aka Blockster) (1 WEEK)

		pos/wks	
24 Jun 00	**SOMETHING'S GOIN' ON** *Rulin RULIN 2CDS*	63	1

MYSTICA Israel, male production trio (2 WEEKS)

		pos/wks	
24 Jan 98	**EVER REST** *Perfecto PERF 152CD*	62	1
9 May 98	**AFRICAN HORIZON** *Perfecto PERF 161CD*	59	1

MYSTIKAL US, male rapper - Michael Tyler (4 WEEKS)

		pos/wks	
9 Dec 00	**SHAKE YA ASS** *Jive 9251552*	30	4+

MYTOWN Ireland, male vocal group (2 WEEKS)

		pos/wks	
13 Mar 99	**PARTY ALL NIGHT** *Universal UND 56231*	22	2

N-JOI UK, male instrumental / production group (28 WEEKS)

		pos/wks	
27 Oct 90	**ANTHEM** *Deconstruction PB 44041*	45	5
2 Mar 91	**ADRENALIN (EP)** *Deconstruction PT 44344*	23	5
6 Apr 91 ●	**ANTHEM (re-issue)** *Deconstruction PB 44445*	8	8
22 Feb 92	**LIVE IN MANCHESTER (PARTS 1 + 2)** *Deconstruction PT 45252*	12	5
24 Jul 93	**THE DRUMSTRUCK (EP)** *Deconstruction 74321154832*	33	3
17 Dec 94	**PAPILLON** *Deconstruction 74321252132*	70	1
8 Jul 95	**BAD THINGS** *Deconstruction 74321277292*	57	1

Tracks on Adrenalin (EP): Adrenalin / The Kraken / Rhythm Zone / Phoenix Tracks on The Drumstruck (EP): The Void / Boom Bass / Drumstruck

N'n'G featuring KALLAGHAN
UK, male / female production / vocal group (6 WEEKS)

		pos/wks	
1 Apr 00	**RIGHT BEFORE MY EYES** *Urban Heat UHTCD 003*	12	6

*N SYNC US, male vocal group (53 WEEKS)

		pos/wks	
13 Sep 97	**TEARIN' UP MY HEART** *Arista 74321505152*	40	2
22 Nov 97	**I WANT YOU BACK** *Arista 74321541122*	62	1
27 Feb 99 ●	**I WANT YOU BACK (re-issue)** *Transcontinental / Northwestside 74321646972*	5	8
8 May 99	**I WANT YOU BACK (re-entry of re-issue)** *Transcontinental / Northwestside 74321646972*	62	2
26 Jun 99 ●	**TEARIN' UP MY HEART (re-issue)** *Northwestside / Arista 74321675832*	9	8
11 Sep 99	**TEARIN' UP MY HEART (re-entry of re-issue)** *Northwestside / Arista 74321675832*	73	2
8 Jan 00	**MUSIC OF MY HEART** *Epic 6685272* [1]	34	3
11 Mar 00 ●	**BYE BYE BYE** *Jive 9250202*	3	8
22 Jul 00	**I'LL NEVER STOP** *Jive 9250762*	13	6
16 Sep 00 ●	**IT'S GONNA BE ME** *Jive 9251082* ▲	9	8
2 Dec 00	**THIS I PROMISE YOU** *Jive 9251302*	21	5+

[1] *N Sync / Gloria Estefan

N-TRANCE UK, male production duo - Dale Longworth and Kevin O'Toole (62 WEEKS)

		pos/wks	
7 May 94	**SET YOU FREE** *All Around the World CDGLOBE 124* [1]	39	4
22 Oct 94	**TURN UP THE POWER** *All Around the World CDGLOBE 125*	23	3
14 Jan 95 ●	**SET YOU FREE (re-mix)** *All Around the World CDGLOBE 126*	2	15
16 Sep 95 ●	**STAYIN' ALIVE** *All Around the World CDGLOBE 131* [2]	2	11
24 Feb 96	**ELECTRONIC PLEASURE** *All Around the World CDGLOBE 135*	11	4
5 Apr 97	**D.I.S.C.O.** *All Around the World CDGLOBE 153*	11	6
23 Aug 97	**THE MIND OF THE MACHINE** *All Around the World CDGLOBE 159*	15	4
1 Nov 97 ●	**DA YA THINK I'M SEXY** *All Around the World CDGLOBE 150* [3]	7	10
12 Sep 98	**PARADISE CITY** *All Around the World CDGLOBE 140*	28	3
19 Dec 98	**TEARS IN THE RAIN** *All Around the Globe CDGLOBE 185*	53	1
20 May 00	**SHAKE YA BODY** *All Around the World CDGLOBE 204*	37	1

[1] N-Trance featuring Kelly Llorenna [2] N-Trance featuring Ricardo Da Force [3] N-Trance featuring Rod Stewart

Although she is the vocalist on both versions of 'Set You Free', Kelly Llorenna is credited only on the former. Similarly, Ricardo da Force is the vocalist on both 'Stayin' Alive' and 'Electronic Pleasure'

N-TYCE UK, female vocal group (15 WEEKS)

		pos/wks	
5 Jul 97	**HEY DJ! (PLAY THAT SONG)** *Telstar CDSTAS 2885*	20	2
13 Sep 97	**WE COME TO PARTY** *Telstar CDSTAS 2915*	12	4
28 Feb 98	**TELEFUNKIN'** *Telstar CDSTAS 2944*	16	5
6 Jun 98	**BOOM BOOM** *Telstar CDSTAS 2971*	18	4

Jimmy NAIL ⟨465 Top 500⟩ Singer / songwriter, b. James Michael Aloysius Bradford, 1954, Newcastle, UK, whose R&B mixed with a Geordie 'take' on country provided a flip-side to his acting career which included key characters in both 'Auf Wiedersehen Pet' and 'Spender'. His longest stay on the charts was courtesy of another TV series, 'Crocodile Shoes', in which he combined acting and singing (73 WEEKS)

		pos/wks	
27 Apr 85 ●	**LOVE DON'T LIVE HERE ANYMORE** *Virgin VS 764*	3	11
11 Jul 92 ★	**AIN'T NO DOUBT** *East West YZ 686*	1	12
3 Oct 92	**LAURA** *East West YZ 702*	58	2
26 Nov 94 ●	**CROCODILE SHOES** *East West YZ 867CD*	4	13
11 Feb 95	**COWBOY DREAMS** *East West YZ 878CD*	13	7
11 Mar 95	**CROCODILE SHOES (re-entry)** *East West YZ 867CD*	68	3
8 Apr 95	**CROCODILE SHOES (2nd re-entry)** *East West YZ 867CD*	56	4
6 May 95	**CALLING OUT YOUR NAME** *East West YZ 935CD*	65	1
28 Oct 95	**BIG RIVER** *East West EW 008CD*	18	5
23 Dec 95	**LOVE** *East West EW 018CD*	33	4
3 Feb 96	**BIG RIVER (re-mix)** *East West EW 024CD*	72	2
16 Nov 96	**COUNTRY BOY** *East West EW 070CD*	25	8
21 Nov 98	**THE FLAME STILL BURNS** *London LONCD 420* [1]	47	1

[1] Jimmy Nail with Strange Fruit

NAKATOMI UK, male / female production group (2 WEEKS)

		pos/wks	
7 Feb 98	**CHILDREN OF THE NIGHT** *Peach PCHCD 006*	47	2

UK No.1 ★   UK Top 10 ●   Still on chart +   UK million seller ◆   UK entry at No.1 ■   US No.1 ▲

NAKED EYES UK, male vocal / instrumental duo (3 WEEKS)
pos/wks

23 Jul 83	ALWAYS SOMETHING THERE TO REMIND ME *RCA 348*	59	3

NALIN I.N.C. Germany, male production duo (1 WEEK)
pos/wks

28 Mar 98	PLANET VIOLET *Logic 74321565702*	51	1

See also NALIN & KANE

NALIN & KANE Germany, male DJ / production duo (6 WEEKS)
pos/wks

1 Nov 97	BEACHBALL *ffrr FCD 318*	48	1
3 Oct 98	BEACHBALL (re-mix) *LONDON FCD349*	17	5

See also NALIN I.N.C.

NANA – See ARCHITECHS featuring NANA

NAPOLEON XIV US, male vocalist - Jerry Samuels (10 WEEKS)
pos/wks

4 Aug 66 ●	THEY'RE COMING TO TAKE ME AWAY HA-HAAA! *Warner Bros. WB 5831*	4	10

NARADA – See Narada Michael WALDEN

Michelle NARINE – See BIG BASS vs Michelle NARINE

NAS US, male rapper - Nasir Jones (27 WEEKS)
pos/wks

28 May 94	IT AIN'T HARD TO TELL *Columbia 6604702*	64	1
17 Aug 96	IF I RULED THE WORLD *Columbia 6634022*	12	7
25 Jan 97	STREET DREAMS *Columbia 6641302*	12	4
14 Jun 97	HEAD OVER HEELS *Epic 6645942* [1]	18	3
29 May 99	HATE ME NOW *Columbia 6672562* [2]	14	6
15 Jan 00	NASTRADAMUS *Columbia 6685572*	24	3
22 Jan 00	HOT BOYZ *Elektra E 7002CD* [3]	18	3

[1] Allure featuring NAS [2] Nas featuring Puff Daddy [3] Missy 'Misdemeanor' Eliott featuring Nas, Eve & Q Tip

Johnny NASH `271 Top 500` US singer / songwriter / actor and label co-owner, b. 19 Aug 1940, Texas. This versatile vocalist first charted in his homeland in 1957. After recording in Jamaica in the late 1960s, he helped to popularise reggae on both sides of the Atlantic and introduced the public to Bob Marley's songs (106 WEEKS)
pos/wks

7 Aug 68 ●	HOLD ME TIGHT *Regal Zonophone RZ 3010*	5	16
8 Jan 69	YOU GOT SOUL *Major Minor MM 586*	6	12
2 Apr 69	CUPID *Major Minor MM 603*	6	11
25 Jun 69	CUPID (re-entry) *Major Minor MM 603*	50	1
1 Apr 72	STIR IT UP *CBS 7800*	13	12
24 Jun 72 ●	I CAN SEE CLEARLY NOW *CBS 8113* ▲	5	15
7 Oct 72 ●	THERE ARE MORE QUESTIONS THAN ANSWERS *CBS 8351*	9	9
14 Jun 75 ★	TEARS ON MY PILLOW *CBS 3220*	1	11
11 Oct 75	LET'S BE FRIENDS *CBS 3597*	42	3
12 Jun 76	(WHAT A) WONDERFUL WORLD *Epic EPC 4294*	25	7
9 Nov 85	ROCK ME BABY *2000 AD FED 19*	47	4
15 Apr 89	I CAN SEE CLEARLY NOW (re-mix) *Epic JN 1*	54	5

NASHVILLE TEENS
UK, male vocal / instrumental group (37 WEEKS)
pos/wks

9 Jul 64 ●	TOBACCO ROAD *Decca F 11930*	6	13
22 Oct 64 ●	GOOGLE EYE *Decca F 12000*	10	11
4 Mar 65	FIND MY WAY BACK HOME *Decca F 12089*	34	6
20 May 65	THIS LITTLE BIRD *Decca F 12143*	38	4
3 Feb 66	THE HARD WAY *Decca F 12316*	45	2
24 Feb 66	THE HARD WAY (re-entry) *Decca F 12316*	48	1

NATASHA UK, female vocalist - Natasha England (16 WEEKS)
pos/wks

5 Jun 82 ●	IKO IKO *Towerbell TOW 22*	10	11
4 Sep 82	THE BOOM BOOM ROOM *Towerbell TOW 25*	44	5

Ultra NATÉ US, female vocalist - Ultra Naté Wyche (38 WEEKS)
pos/wks

9 Dec 89	IT'S OVER NOW *Eternal YZ 440*	62	3
23 Feb 91	IS IT LOVE *Eternal YZ 509* [1]	71	1

29 Jan 94	SHOW ME *Warner Bros. W 0219CD*	62	1
14 Jun 97 ●	FREE *AM:PM 5822432*	4	17
24 Jan 98	FREE (re-mix) *AM:PM 5825012*	33	2
18 Apr 98 ●	FOUND A CURE *AM:PM 5826452*	6	7
25 Jul 98	NEW KIND OF MEDICINE *AM:PM 5827492*	14	5
22 Jul 00	DESIRE *AM:PM CDAMPM133*	40	2

[1] Basement Boys present Ultra Naté

NATURAL BORN CHILLERS UK, male production duo (3 WEEKS)
pos/wks

1 Nov 97	ROCK THE FUNKY BEAT *East West EW 138CD1*	30	3

NATURAL BORN GROOVES Belgium, male DJ / production duo - Burn Boon and Jaco van Rijsvijck (3 WEEKS)
pos/wks

2 Nov 96	FORERUNNER *XL XLS 76CD*	64	1
19 Apr 97	GROOVEBIRD *Positiva CDTIV 75*	21	2

NATURAL LIFE UK, male / female vocal / instrumental group (3 WEEKS)
pos/wks

7 Mar 92	NATURAL LIFE *Tribe NLIFE 3*	47	3

NATURAL SELECTION US, male vocal / instrumental duo (2 WEEKS)
pos/wks

9 Nov 91	DO ANYTHING *East West A 8724*	69	2

NATURALS UK, male vocal / instrumental group (9 WEEKS)
pos/wks

20 Aug 64	I SHOULD HAVE KNOWN BETTER *Parlophone R 5165*	24	9

David NAUGHTON US, male vocalist (6 WEEKS)
pos/wks

25 Aug 79	MAKIN' IT *RSO 32*	44	6

NAUGHTY BY NATURE US, male rap group (17 WEEKS)
pos/wks

9 Nov 91	O.P.P. *Big Life BLR 62*	73	1
20 Jun 92	O.P.P. (re-issue) *Big Life BLR 74*	35	3
30 Jan 93	HIP HOP HOORAY *Big Life BLRD 89*	22	3
19 Jun 93	IT'S ON *Big Life BLR 99*	48	2
27 Nov 93	HIP HOP HOORAY (re-mix) *Big Life BLRDA 104*	20	4
29 Apr 95	FEEL ME FLOW *Big Life BLRD 115*	23	3
11 Sep 99	JAMBOREE *Arista 74321692882* [1]	51	1

[1] Naughty By Nature featuring Zhane

NAVIGATOR – See FREESTYLERS

Maria NAYLER UK, female vocalist (26 WEEKS)
pos/wks

9 Mar 96	BE AS ONE *Deconstruction 74321342962* [1]	17	4
16 Nov 96 ●	ONE & ONE *Deconstruction 74321427692* [2]	3	17
7 Mar 98	NAKED AND SACRED *Deconstruction 74321534242*	32	3
5 Sep 98	WILL YOU BE WITH ME / LOVE IS THE GOD *Deconstruction 74321591772*	65	1
27 May 00	ANGRY SKIES *Deconstruction 74321759492*	42	1

[1] Sasha and Maria [2] Robert Miles featuring Maria Nayler

NAZARETH `454 Top 500` Earthy but versatile rock band formed 1969 in Dunfermline, Scotland, who throughout their 30-year career have been led by Dan McCafferty (v). Sole US Top 10 hit, 'Love Hurts', also spent a record-shattering 60 weeks on Norwegian chart (75 WEEKS)
pos/wks

5 May 73 ●	BROKEN DOWN ANGEL *Mooncrest MOON 1*	9	11
21 Jul 73 ●	BAD BAD BOY *Mooncrest MOON 9*	10	9
13 Oct 73	THIS FLIGHT TONIGHT *Mooncrest MOON 14*	11	13
23 Mar 74	SHANGHAI'D IN SHANGHAI *Mooncrest MOON 22*	41	4
14 Jun 75	MY WHITE BICYCLE *Mooncrest MOON 47*	14	8
15 Nov 75	HOLY ROLLER *Mountain TOP 3*	36	4
24 Sep 77	HOT TRACKS (EP) *Mountain NAZ 1*	15	11
18 Feb 78	GONE DEAD TRAIN *Mountain NAZ 002*	49	2
13 May 78	PLACE IN YOUR HEART *Mountain TOP 37*	70	1
27 May 78	PLACE IN YOUR HEART (re-entry) *Mountain TOP 37*	74	1
27 Jan 79	MAY THE SUNSHINE *Mountain NAZ 003*	22	8
28 Jul 79	STAR *Mountain TOP 45*	54	3

Tracks on Hot Tracks (EP): Love Hurts / This Flight Tonight / Broken Down Angel / Hair of the Dog

Me'Shell NDEGEOCELLO
US, female vocalist / instrumentalist - bass (5 WEEKS) pos/wks

12 Feb 94	IF THAT'S YOUR BOYFRIEND (HE WASN'T LAST NIGHT) *Maverick W 0223CD1*	74	1
3 Sep 94	WILD NIGHT *Mercury MERCD 409* [1]	34	3
1 Mar 97	NEVER MISS THE WATER *Reprise W 0393CD* [2]	59	1

[1] John Mellencamp featuring Me'Shell Ndegeocello [2] Chaka Khan featuring Me'Shell Ndegeocello

Youssou N'DOUR *Senegal, male vocalist (35 WEEKS)* pos/wks

3 Jun 89	SHAKING THE TREE *Virgin VS 1167* [1]	61	3
22 Dec 90	SHAKING THE TREE (re-issue) *Virgin VS 1322* [1]	57	4
25 Jun 94 ●	7 SECONDS *Columbia 6605082* [2]	3	21
24 Dec 94	7 SECONDS (re-entry) *Columbia 6605082* [2]	54	4
14 Jan 95	UNDECIDED *Columbia 6609712*	53	2
10 Oct 98	HOW COME *Interscope IND 95598* [3]	52	1

[1] Youssou N'Dour and Peter Gabriel [2] Youssou N'Dour (featuring Neneh Cherry) [3] Youssou N'Dour and Canibus

The re-issue of 'Shaking the Tree' was listed with its flip side, 'Solsbury Hill' by Peter Gabriel

NEARLY GOD
UK, male / female vocal / instrumental group (2 WEEKS) pos/wks

20 Apr 96	POEMS *Durban Poison DPCD 3*	28	2

Terry NEASON *UK, female vocalist (1 WEEK)* pos/wks

25 Jun 94	LIFEBOAT *WEA YZ 830*	72	1

NEBULA II *UK, male instrumental / production group (3 WEEKS)* pos/wks

1 Feb 92	SEANCE / ATHEAMA *Reinforced RIVET 1211*	55	2
16 May 92	FLATLINERS *J4M 12NEBULA 2*	54	1

NED'S ATOMIC DUSTBIN
UK, male vocal / instrumental group (24 WEEKS) pos/wks

14 Jul 90	KILL YOUR TELEVISION *Chapter 22 CHAP 48*	53	2
27 Oct 90	UNTIL YOU FIND OUT *Chapter 22 CHAP 52*	51	2
9 Mar 91	HAPPY *Columbia 6566807*	16	4
21 Sep 91	TRUST *Furtive 6574627*	21	4
10 Oct 92	NOT SLEEPING AROUND *Furtive 6583866*	19	3
5 Dec 92	INTACT *Furtive 6588166*	36	6
25 Mar 95	ALL I ASK OF MYSELF IS THAT I HOLD TOGETHER *Furtive 6613565*	33	2
15 Jul 95	STUCK *Furtive 6620562*	64	1

Joey NEGRO *UK, male producer - Dave Lee (15 WEEKS)* pos/wks

16 Nov 91	DO WHAT YOU FEEL *Ten TEN 391*	36	3
21 Dec 91	REACHIN' *Republic LIC 160* [1]	70	1
18 Jul 92	ENTER YOUR FANTASY (EP) *Ten TEN 397*	35	3
25 Sep 93	WHAT HAPPENED TO THE MUSIC *Virgin VSCD 1466*	51	2
19 Feb 00 ●	MUST BE THE MUSIC *Incentive CENT 4CDS* [2]	8	5
16 Sep 00	SATURDAY *Yola YOLA CDX03* [2]	41	1

[1] Joey Negro presents Phase II [2] Joey Negro featuring Taka Boom

Tracks on Enter Your Fantasy (EP): Love Fantasy / Get Up / Enter Your Mind / Everybody

See also Li KWAN, RAVEN MAIZE, PHAZE II, HED BOYS

neil *UK, male actor/ vocalist - Nigel Planer (10 WEEKS)* pos/wks

14 Jul 84 ●	HOLE IN MY SHOE *WEA YZ 10*	2	10

Vince NEIL *US, male vocalist (1 WEEK)* pos/wks

3 Oct 92	YOU'RE INVITED (BUT YOUR FRIEND CAN'T COME) *Hollywood HWD 123*	63	1

NEJA *Italy, female vocalist (1 WEEK)* pos/wks

26 Sep 98	RESTLESS (I KNOW YOU KNOW) *Panorama CDPAN 1*	47	1

NEK *Italy, male vocalist (1 WEEK)* pos/wks

29 Aug 98	LAURA *Coalition COLA 054CD*	59	1

NELLY *US, male rapper - Cornell Haynes (8 WEEKS)* pos/wks

11 Nov 00 ●	(HOT S**T) COUNTRY GRAMMAR *Universal MCSTD 40242*	7	8+

NELSON *US, male vocal duo (3 WEEKS)* pos/wks

27 Oct 90	(CAN'T LIVE WITHOUT YOUR) LOVE AND AFFECTION *DGC GEF 82* ▲	54	3

Bill NELSON *UK, male vocalist / instrumentalist - guitar and synthesizer (12 WEEKS)* pos/wks

24 Feb 79	FURNITURE MUSIC *Harvest HAR 5176* [1]	59	3
5 May 79	REVOLT INTO STYLE *Harvest HAR 5183* [1]	69	2
5 Jul 80	DO YOU DREAM IN COLOUR? *Cocteau COQ 1*	52	4
13 Jun 81	YOUTH OF NATION ON FIRE *Mercury WILL 2*	73	3

[1] Bill Nelson's Red Noise

See also BE BOP DELUXE

Phyllis NELSON *US, female vocalist (24 WEEKS)* pos/wks

23 Feb 85 ★	MOVE CLOSER *Carrere CAR 337*	1	21
21 May 94	MOVE CLOSER (re-issue) *EMI CDEMCT 9*	34	3

Ricky NELSON `147` `Top 500`
TV star turned teen idol and later singer / songwriter. b. 8 May 1940, New Jersey, d. 31 December, 1985. He was virtually raised on a US radio / TV family show. In the 1950s, he enjoyed sales on a par with Elvis Presley and Pat Boone. Both his father and his two sons also topped the US chart (1935 and 1990) (150 WEEKS) pos/wks

21 Feb 58	STOOD UP *London HLP 8542*	27	1
7 Mar 58	STOOD UP (re-entry) *London HLP 8542*	29	1
22 Aug 58 ●	POOR LITTLE FOOL *London HLP 8670* ▲	4	13
7 Nov 58 ●	SOMEDAY *London HLP 8732 (A)*	9	13
21 Nov 58	I GOT A FEELING *London HLP 8732 (B)*	27	1
28 Nov 58	POOR LITTLE FOOL (re-entry) *London HLP 8670*	28	1
17 Apr 59 ●	IT'S LATE *London HLP 8817 (A)*	3	20
15 May 59	NEVER BE ANYONE ELSE BUT YOU *London HLP 8817 (B)*	19	1
5 Jun 59	NEVER BE ANYONE ELSE BUT YOU (re-entry) *London HLP 8817 (B)*	14	9
4 Sep 59	SWEETER THAN YOU *London HLP 8927 (A)*	19	3
11 Sep 59	JUST A LITTLE TOO MUCH *London HLP 8927 (B)*	11	8
15 Jan 60	I WANNA BE LOVED *London HLP 9021*	30	1
7 Jul 60	YOUNG EMOTIONS *London HLP 9121*	48	1
1 Jun 61 ●	HELLO MARY LOU / TRAVELLIN' MAN *London HLP 9347* ▲	2	18
16 Nov 61	EVERLOVIN' *London HLP 9440* [1]	23	5
29 Mar 62	YOUNG WORLD *London HLP 9524*	19	13
30 Aug 62	TEENAGE IDOL *London HLP 9583* [1]	39	4
17 Jan 63	IT'S UP TO YOU *London HLP 9648* [1]	22	9
17 Oct 63	FOOLS RUSH IN *Brunswick 05895* [1]	12	9
30 Jan 64	FOR YOU *Brunswick 05900* [1]	14	10
21 Oct 72	GARDEN PARTY *MCA MU 1165* [1]	41	4
24 Aug 91	HELLO MARY LOU (GOODBYE HEART) (re-issue) *Liberty EMCT 2*	45	5

[1] Rick Nelson

Sandy NELSON *US, male instrumentalist - drums (42 WEEKS)* pos/wks

6 Nov 59 ●	TEEN BEAT *Top Rank JAR 197*	9	11
5 Feb 60	TEEN BEAT (re-entry) *Top Rank JAR 197*	25	1
14 Dec 61 ●	LET THERE BE DRUMS *London HLP 9466*	3	16
22 Mar 62	DRUMS ARE MY BEAT *London HLP 9521*	30	6
7 Jun 62	DRUMMIN' UP A STORM *London HLP 9558*	39	8

Shara NELSON *UK, female vocalist (23 WEEKS)* pos/wks

24 Jul 93	DOWN THAT ROAD *Cooltempo CDCOOL 275*	19	6
18 Sep 93	ONE GOODBYE IN TEN *Cooltempo CDCOOL 279*	21	5
12 Feb 94	UPTIGHT *Cooltempo CDCOOL 286*	19	5
4 Jun 94	NOBODY *Cooltempo CDCOOL 290*	49	1
10 Sep 94	INSIDE OUT / DOWN THAT ROAD (re-mix) *Cooltempo CDCOOLX 295*	34	3

		pos/wks
16 Sep 95	ROUGH WITH THE SMOOTH *Cooltempo CDCOOL 311*	30 2
5 Dec 98	SENSE OF DANGER *Pagan PAGAN 024CDS* [1]	61 1

[1] Presence featuring Shara Nelson

Shelley NELSON – See TIN TIN OUT

Willie NELSON *US, male vocalist (13 WEEKS)*

		pos/wks
31 Jul 82	ALWAYS ON MY MIND *CBS A 2511*	49 3
7 Apr 84	TO ALL THE GIRLS I'VE LOVED BEFORE *CBS A 4252* [1]	17 10

[1] Julio Iglesias and Willie Nelson

NENA *Germany, female / male vocal / instrumental group - lead vocal Gabriele (Nena) Kerner (14 WEEKS)*

		pos/wks
4 Feb 84	★ 99 RED BALLOONS *Epic A 4074*	1 12
5 May 84	JUST A DREAM *Epic H 3249*	70 2

NERIO'S DUBWORK – See Darryl PANDY

Frances NERO *US, female vocalist (9 WEEKS)*

		pos/wks
13 Apr 91	FOOTSTEPS FOLLOWING ME *Debut DEBT 3109*	17 9

NERO and the GLADIATORS
UK, male instrumental group (6 WEEKS)

		pos/wks
23 Mar 61	ENTRY OF THE GLADIATORS *Decca F 11329*	50 1
6 Apr 61	ENTRY OF THE GLADIATORS (re-entry) *Decca F 11329*	37 4
27 Jul 61	IN THE HALL OF THE MOUNTAIN KING *Decca F 11367*	48 1

Ann NESBY *US, female vocalist (3 WEEKS)*

		pos/wks
21 Dec 96	WITNESS (EP) *AM:PM 5875612*	42 2
17 May 97	HOLD ON (EP) *AM:PM 5822332*	75 1

Tracks on Witness (EP): Can I Get a Witness / (mix) / In the Spirit / I'm Still Wearing Your Name. Tracks on Hold On (EP): Hold On (Mousse T's Uplifting Garage Edit) / Hold On (Mousse T's Hard Soul Remix) / Hold On (Klub Head Mix) / This Weekend (Laidback Mix)

Michael NESMITH *US, male vocalist (6 WEEKS)*

		pos/wks
26 Mar 77	RIO *Island WIP 6373*	28 6

See also MONKEES

NETWORK *UK, male vocal / instrumental group (4 WEEKS)*

		pos/wks
12 Dec 92	BROKEN WINGS *Chrysalis CHS 3923*	46 4

NEVADA *UK, male / female vocal / instrumental group (1 WEEK)*

		pos/wks
8 Jan 83	IN THE BLEAK MID WINTER *Polydor POSP 203*	71 1

Robbie NEVIL *US, male vocalist (24 WEEKS)*

		pos/wks
20 Dec 86	● C'EST LA VIE *Manhattan MT 14*	3 11
2 May 87	DOMINOES *Manhattan MT 19*	26 6
11 Jul 87	WOT'S IT TO YA *Manhattan MT 24*	43 7

Aaron NEVILLE – See Linda RONSTADT; NEVILLE BROTHERS

NEVILLE BROTHERS
US, male vocal / instrumental group (7 WEEKS)

		pos/wks
25 Nov 89	WITH GOD ON OUR SIDE *A & M AM 545*	47 6
7 Jul 90	BIRD ON A WIRE *A & M AM 568*	72 1

Jason NEVINS *US, male DJ / producer (24 WEEKS)*

		pos/wks
21 Feb 98	IT'S LIKE THAT (German import) *Columbia 6652932* [1]	63 3
14 Mar 98	IT'S LIKE THAT (US import) *Columbia 6652932* [1]	65 1
21 Mar 98	★ IT'S LIKE THAT *Sm:)e Communications SM 90652* [1] ◆ ■	1 16
18 Apr 98	IT'S TRICKY *Epidrome EPD 6656982* [1]	74 1
26 Jun 99	INSANE IN THE BRAIN *INCredible INCRL 17CD* [2]	19 3

[1] Run-DMC vs Jason Nevins [2] Jason Nevins vs Cypress Hill

NEW ATLANTIC
UK, male instrumental / production duo (15 WEEKS)

		pos/wks
29 Feb 92	I KNOW *3 Beat 3BT 1*	12 7
3 Oct 92	INTO THE FUTURE *3 Beat 3BT 2* [1]	70 1
13 Feb 93	TAKE OFF SOME TIME *3 Beat 3BTCD 14*	64 1
26 Nov 94	THE SUNSHINE AFTER THE RAIN *Ffrreedom TABCD 223* [2]	26 6

[1] New Atlantic featuring Linda Wright [2] New Atlantic / U4EA featuring Berri
'The Sunshine After the Rain' was re-issued in 1995, credited simply to the vocalist Berri

NEW BOHEMIANS – See Edie BRICKELL and the NEW BOHEMIANS

NEW EDITION *US, male vocal group (36 WEEKS)*

		pos/wks
16 Apr 83	★ CANDY GIRL *London LON 21*	1 13
13 Aug 83	POPCORN LOVE *London LON 31*	43 5
23 Feb 85	MR TELEPHONE MAN *MCA MCA 938*	19 9
15 Apr 89	CRUCIAL *MCA MCA 23934*	70 1
10 Aug 96	HIT ME OFF *MCA MCSTD 48014*	20 4
7 Jun 97	SOMETHING ABOUT YOU *MCA MCSTD 48032*	16 4

See also BELL BIV DEVOE; Ralph TRESVANT; Bobby BROWN; Johnny GILL

NEW GENERATION
UK, male vocal / instrumental group (5 WEEKS)

		pos/wks
26 Jun 68	SMOKEY BLUES AWAY *Spark SRL 1007*	38 5

NEW KIDS ON THE BLOCK ⟨ 338 Top 500 ⟩ *Highest earning boy band of all time; Jordan and Jon Knight, Donnie Wahlberg, Danny Wood, Joey McIntyre. Formed Boston, US, by producer / manager Maurice Starr as pop version of his act New Edition. In 1990, grossed reported $861 million and became first group to score eight UK Top 10 entries in a year (90 WEEKS)*

		pos/wks
16 Sep 89	HANGIN' TOUGH *CBS BLOCK 1*	52 4
11 Nov 89	★ YOU GOT IT (THE RIGHT STUFF) *CBS BLOCK 2*	1 13
6 Jan 90	★ HANGIN' TOUGH (re-issue) *CBS BLOCK 3* ▲	1 9
17 Mar 90	● I'LL BE LOVING YOU (FOREVER) *CBS BLOCK 4* ▲	5 8
12 May 90	● COVER GIRL *CBS BLOCK 5*	4 8
16 Jun 90	● STEP BY STEP *CBS BLOCK 6* ▲	2 7
4 Aug 90	● TONIGHT *CBS BLOCK 7*	3 10
13 Oct 90	● LET'S TRY AGAIN / DIDN'T I BLOW YOUR MIND *CBS BLOCK 8*	8 5
8 Dec 90	● THIS ONE'S FOR THE CHILDREN *CBS BLOCK 9*	9 7
9 Feb 91	GAMES *CBS 6566267*	14 4
18 May 91	CALL IT WHAT YOU WANT *Columbia 6567857*	12 5
14 Dec 91	● IF YOU GO AWAY *Columbia 6576667*	9 5
19 Feb 94	DIRTY DAWG *Columbia 6600362* [1]	27 3
26 Mar 94	NEVER LET YOU GO *Columbia 6602072* [1]	42 2

[1] NKOTB

NEW MODEL ARMY
UK, male vocal / instrumental group (33 WEEKS)

		pos/wks
27 Apr 85	NO REST *EMI NMA 1*	28 5
3 Aug 85	THE ACOUSTICS (EP) *EMI NMA 2*	49 1
30 Nov 85	BRAVE NEW WORLD *EMI NMA 3*	57 1
8 Nov 86	51ST STATE *EMI NMA 4*	71 2
28 Feb 87	POISON STREET *EMI NMA 5*	64 1
26 Sep 87	WHITE COATS (EP) *EMI NMA 6*	50 3
21 Jan 89	STUPID QUESTIONS *EMI NMA 7*	31 3
11 Mar 89	VAGABONDS *EMI NMA 8*	37 3
10 Jun 89	GREEN AND GREY *EMI NMA 9*	37 3
8 Sep 90	GET ME OUT *EMI NMA 10*	34 3
3 Nov 90	PURITY *EMI NMA 11*	61 2
8 Jun 91	SPACE *EMI NMA 12*	39 2
20 Feb 93	HERE COMES THE WAR *Epic 6589352*	25 2
24 Jul 93	LIVING IN THE ROSE (THE BALLADS EP) *Epic 6592492*	51 1

Tracks on The Acoustics EP: Better Than Them / No Sense / Adrenalin / Trust. Tracks on White Coats (EP): White Coats / The Charge / Chinese Whispers / My Country. Tracks on Living in the Rose (The Ballads EP): Living in the Rose / Drummy B / Marry the Sea, Sleepwalking.

NEW MUSIK UK, male vocal / instrumental group (27 WEEKS)
pos/wks

6 Oct 79	STRAIGHT LINES GTO GT 255	53	5
19 Jan 80	LIVING BY NUMBERS GTO GT 261	13	8
26 Apr 80	THIS WORLD OF WATER GTO GT 268	31	7
12 Jul 80	SANCTUARY GTO GT 275	31	7

NEW ORDER `105` `Top 500` Innovative Mancunian group featuring three former members of critically acclaimed Joy Division: Bernard Sumner (v/g), Peter Hook (b), Stephen Morris (d), and augmented by Gillian Gilbert (k). 'Blue Monday' remains the UK's biggest-selling 12-inch single of all time (179 WEEKS)
pos/wks

14 Mar 81	CEREMONY Factory FAC 33	34	5
3 Oct 81	PROCESSION / EVERYTHING'S GONE GREEN Factory FAC 53	38	5
22 May 82	TEMPTATION Factory FAC 63	29	7
19 Mar 83	BLUE MONDAY Factory FAC 73	12	7
13 Aug 83 ●	BLUE MONDAY (re-entry) Factory FAC 73	9	17
3 Sep 83	CONFUSION Factory FAC 93	12	7
7 Jan 84	BLUE MONDAY (2nd re-entry) Factory FAC 73	52	4
28 Apr 84	THIEVES LIKE US Factory FAC 103	18	5
25 May 85	THE PERFECT KISS Factory FAC 123	46	4
9 Nov 85	SUB-CULTURE Factory FAC 133	63	4
29 Mar 86	SHELLSHOCK Factory FAC 143	28	5
27 Sep 86	STATE OF THE NATION Factory FAC 153	30	3
27 Sep 86	THE PEEL SESSIONS (1ST JUNE 1982) Strange Fruit SFPS 001	54	1
15 Nov 86	BIZARRE LOVE TRIANGLE Factory FAC 163	56	2
1 Aug 87 ●	TRUE FAITH Factory FAC 183/7	4	10
19 Dec 87	TOUCHED BY THE HAND OF GOD Factory FAC 1937	20	7
7 May 88 ●	BLUE MONDAY (re-mix) Factory FAC 737	3	11
10 Dec 88	FINE TIME Factory FAC 2237	11	8
11 Mar 89	ROUND AND ROUND Factory FAC 2637	21	7
9 Sep 89	RUN 2 Factory FAC 273	49	2
2 Jun 90 ★	WORLD IN MOTION . . . Factory / MCA FAC 2937 [1]	1	12
17 Apr 93 ●	REGRET Centredate Co. NUOCD 1	4	7
3 Jul 93	RUINED IN A DAY Centredate Co. NUOCD 2	22	4
4 Sep 93	WORLD (THE PRICE OF LOVE) Centredate Co. NUOCD 3	13	5
18 Dec 93	SPOOKY Centredate Co. NUOCD 4	22	4
19 Nov 94 ●	TRUE FAITH (re-mix) Centredate Co. NUOCD 5	9	8
21 Jan 95	NINETEEN63 London NUOCD 6	21	4
5 Aug 95	BLUE MONDAY (2nd) (re-mix) London NUOCD 7	17	4

[1] Englandneworder

Group was male only on first hit. 'Blue Monday' in 1988 is a re-mixed version of the original 1983 hit which was made available on 7-inch for the first time, hence the slight difference in catalogue number. Sales for the re-mix and the original were combined from 7 May 1988 onwards when calculating its chart position

NEW ORLEANS JAZZMEN – See Terry LIGHTFOOT and his NEW ORLEANS JAZZMEN

NEW POWER GENERATION US, male / female vocal / instrumental group (64 WEEKS)
pos/wks

31 Aug 91 ●	GETT OFF Paisley Park W 0056 [1]	4	8
21 Sep 91	CREAM Paisley Park W 0061 [1] ▲	15	7
7 Dec 91	DIAMONDS AND PEARLS Paisley Park W 0075 [1]	25	6
28 Mar 92	MONEY DON'T MATTER 2 NIGHT Paisley Park W 0091 [1]	19	5
27 Jun 92	THUNDER Paisley Park W 0113 [1]	28	3
18 Jul 92 ●	SEXY MF / STROLLIN' Paisley Park W 0123 [1]	4	7
10 Oct 92 ●	MY NAME IS PRINCE Paisley Park W 0132 [1]	7	5
14 Nov 92	MY NAME IS PRINCE (re-mix) Paisley Park W 0142T [1]	51	1
5 Dec 92	7 Paisley Park W 0147 [1]	27	6
13 Mar 93	THE MORNING PAPERS Paisley Park W 0162CD [1]	52	3
1 Apr 95	GET WILD NPG 0061045	19	4
19 Aug 95	THE GOOD LIFE NPG 0061515	29	3
5 Jul 97	THE GOOD LIFE (re-entry) NPG 0061515	15	5
21 Nov 98	COME ON RCA 74321634722	65	1

[1] Prince and the New Power Generation

See also PRINCE

NEW RADICALS US, male vocalist - Gregg Alexander (18 WEEKS)
pos/wks

3 Apr 99 ●	YOU GET WHAT YOU GIVE MCA MCSTD 48111	5	17
25 Sep 99	SOMEDAY WE'LL KNOW MCA MCSTD 40217	48	1

NEW SEEKERS `162` `Top 500` Anglo-Australian vocal group formed by ex-Seeker Keith Potger with Eve Graham, Lyn Paul, Peter Doyle, Paul Layton and Marty Kristian. Hits included a Coca-Cola advertisement and a Eurovision entry. The group sold more than 25 million records worldwide and equalled the eight Top 20 entries by The Seekers (143 WEEKS)
pos/wks

17 Oct 70	WHAT HAVE THEY DONE TO MY SONG MA Philips 6006 027	48	1
31 Oct 70	WHAT HAVE THEY DONE TO MY SONG MA (re-entry) Philips 6006 027	44	1
10 Jul 71 ●	NEVER ENDING SONG OF LOVE Philips 6006 125	2	19
18 Dec 71 ★	I'D LIKE TO TEACH THE WORLD TO SING (IN PERFECT HARMONY) Polydor 2058 184	1	21
4 Mar 72 ●	BEG STEAL OR BORROW Polydor 2058 201	2	13
10 Jun 72 ●	CIRCLES Polydor 2058 242	4	16
2 Dec 72	COME SOFTLY TO ME Polydor 2058 315 [1]	20	11
24 Feb 73	PINBALL WIZARD - SEE ME FEEL ME (MEDLEY) Polydor 2058 338	16	8
7 Apr 73	NEVERTHELESS Polydor 2068 340 [2]	34	5
16 Jun 73	GOODBYE IS JUST ANOTHER WORD Polydor 2058 368	36	5
24 Nov 73 ★	YOU WON'T FIND ANOTHER FOOL LIKE ME Polydor 2058 421 [3]	1	16
9 Mar 74 ●	I GET A LITTLE SENTIMENTAL OVER YOU Polydor 2058 439 [3]	5	9
14 Aug 76	IT'S SO NICE (TO HAVE YOU HOME) CBS 4391	44	4
29 Jan 77	I WANNA GO BACK CBS 4786	25	4
15 Jul 78	ANTHEM (ONE DAY IN EVERY WEEK) CBS 6413	21	10

[1] New Seekers featuring Marty Kristian [2] Eve Graham and the New Seekers [3] New Seekers featuring Lynn Paul

NEW TONE AGE FAMILY – See Dread FLIMSTONE and the NEW TONE AGE FAMILY

NEW VAUDEVILLE BAND UK, male vocal / instrumental group (43 WEEKS)
pos/wks

8 Sep 66 ●	WINCHESTER CATHEDRAL Fontana TF 741 ▲	4	19
26 Jan 67 ●	PEEK-A-BOO Fontana TF 784 [1]	7	11
11 May 67	FINCHLEY CENTRAL Fontana TF 824	11	9
2 Aug 67	GREEN STREET GREEN Fontana TF 853	37	4

[1] New Vaudeville Band featuring Tristram

NEW VISION US, male vocal / instrumental duo (2 WEEKS)
pos/wks

29 Jan 00	(JUST) YOU AND ME AM:PM CDAMPM 128	23	2

NEW WORLD Australia, male vocal / instrumental group (53 WEEKS)
pos/wks

27 Feb 71	ROSE GARDEN RAK 111	15	11
3 Jul 71 ●	TOM TOM TURNAROUND RAK 117	6	15
4 Dec 71	KARA KARA RAK 123	17	13
13 May 72 ●	SISTER JANE RAK 130	9	13
12 May 73	ROOF TOP SINGING RAK 148	50	1

NEW YORK CITY US, male vocal group (11 WEEKS)
pos/wks

21 Jul 73	I'M DOING FINE NOW RCA 2351	20	11

NEW YORK SKYY
US, male / female vocal / instrumental group (2 WEEKS)
pos/wks

16 Jan 82	LET'S CELEBRATE Epic EPC A 1898	71	1
30 Jan 82	LET'S CELEBRATE (re-entry) Epic EPC A 1898	67	1

NEWBEATS US, male vocal group (22 WEEKS)
pos/wks

10 Sep 64	BREAD AND BUTTER Hickory 1269	15	9
23 Oct 71 ●	RUN BABY RUN London HL 10341	10	13

Booker NEWBURY III US, male vocalist (11 WEEKS)
pos/wks

28 May 83 ●	LOVE TOWN Polydor POSP 613	6	8
8 Oct 83	TEDDY BEAR Polydor POSP 637	44	3

Mickey NEWBURY US, male vocalist (5 WEEKS)
pos/wks

1 Jul 72	AMERICAN TRILOGY Elektra K 12047	42	5

NEWCLEUS *US, male rap / instrumental group (6 WEEKS)*

		pos/wks
3 Sep 83	JAM ON REVENGE (THE WIKKI WIKKI SONG) *Beckett BKS 8*	**44** 6

Anthony NEWLEY (199 Top 500) *Acclaimed actor / singer and composer. b. 24 Sep 1931, London, , UK, d. 14 Apr 1999. He appeared in more than 20 films before his singing career started. He was among the most innovative UK acts of the early rock years, before moving into musicals and cabaret (129 WEEKS)*

		pos/wks
1 May 59 ●	I'VE WAITED SO LONG *Decca F 11127*	**3** 15
8 May 59	IDLE ON PARADE (EP) *Decca DFE 6566*	**13** 4
12 Jun 59 ●	PERSONALITY *Decca F 11142*	**6** 12
15 Jan 60 ★	WHY *Decca F 11194*	**1** 17
24 Mar 60 ★	DO YOU MIND *Decca F 11220*	**1** 15
14 Jul 60 ●	IF SHE SHOULD COME TO YOU *Decca F 11254*	**3** 14
24 Nov 60 ●	STRAWBERRY FAIR *Decca F 11295*	**3** 11
16 Mar 61 ●	AND THE HEAVENS CRIED *Decca F 11331*	**6** 12
15 Jun 61	POP GOES THE WEASEL / BEE BOM *Decca F 11362*	**12** 9
3 Aug 61	WHAT KIND OF FOOL AM I? *Decca F 11376*	**36** 8
25 Jan 62	D-DARLING *Decca F 11419*	**25** 6
26 Jul 62	THAT NOISE *Decca F 11486*	**34** 5

'Bee Bom' listed together with 'Pop Goes the Weasel' only for weeks of 15 and 22 Jun 1961. It peaked at No.15. Tracks on Idle on Parade (EP): I've Waited So Long / Idle Rock-a-Boogie / Idle on Parade / Saturday Night Rock-a-Boogie

Tara NEWLEY – See E-ZEE POSSEE

Brad NEWMAN *UK, male vocalist (1 WEEK)*

		pos/wks
22 Feb 62	SOMEBODY TO LOVE *Fontana H 357*	**47** 1

Dave NEWMAN *UK, male vocalist (6 WEEKS)*

		pos/wks
15 Apr 72	THE LION SLEEPS TONIGHT *Pye 7N 45134*	**48** 1
29 Apr 72	THE LION SLEEPS TONIGHT (re-entry) *Pye 7N 45134*	**34** 5

Paul NEWMAN – See CAMISRA; ESCRIMA; PARTIZAN; TALL PAUL; GRIFTERS

NEWS – See Huey LEWIS and the NEWS

NEWS *UK, male vocal / instrumental group (3 WEEKS)*

		pos/wks
29 Aug 81	AUDIO VIDEO *George GEORGE 1*	**52** 3

NEWTON *UK, male vocalist (6 WEEKS)*

		pos/wks
15 Jul 95	SKY HIGH *Bags Of Fun BAGSCD 6*	**56** 2
15 Feb 97	SOMETIMES WHEN WE TOUCH *Dominion CDDMIN 202*	**32** 3
16 Aug 97	DON'T WORRY *Dominion CDDMIN 206*	**61** 1

Juice NEWTON *US, female vocalist (6 WEEKS)*

		pos/wks
2 May 81	ANGEL OF THE MORNING *Capitol CL 16189*	**43** 6

Olivia NEWTON-JOHN (56 Top 500) *Top female vocalist in the US in the 1970s, b. 26 Sep 1948, Cambridge, UK. This photogenic Australian-raised singer / actress has won numerous pop and country awards and was the first female to score one dozen US Top 5 singles (234 WEEKS)*

		pos/wks
20 Mar 71 ●	IF NOT FOR YOU *Pye International 7N 25543*	**7** 11
23 Oct 71 ●	BANKS OF THE OHIO *Pye International 7N 25568*	**6** 17
11 Mar 72	WHAT IS LIFE *Pye International 7N 25575*	**16** 8
13 Jan 73	TAKE ME HOME COUNTRY ROADS *Pye International 7N 25599*	**15** 13
16 Mar 74	LONG LIVE LOVE *Pye International 7N 25638*	**11** 8
12 Oct 74	I HONESTLY LOVE YOU *EMI 2216* ▲	**22** 6
11 Jun 77 ●	SAM *EMI 2616*	**6** 11
20 May 78 ★	YOU'RE THE ONE THAT I WANT *RSO 006* [1] ◆ ▲	**1** 26
16 Sep 78 ★	SUMMER NIGHTS *RSO 18* [1] ◆	**1** 19
4 Nov 78	HOPELESSLY DEVOTED TO YOU *RSO 17*	**2** 11
16 Dec 78	A LITTLE MORE LOVE *EMI 2879*	**4** 12
30 Jun 79	DEEPER THAN THE NIGHT *EMI 2954*	**64** 3
21 Jun 80 ★	XANADU *Jet 185* [2]	**1** 11
23 Aug 80	MAGIC *Jet 196* ▲	**32** 7
25 Oct 80	SUDDENLY *Jet 7002* [3]	**15** 7
10 Oct 81 ●	PHYSICAL *EMI 5234* ▲	**7** 16
16 Jan 82	LANDSLIDE *EMI 5257*	**18** 9
17 Apr 82	MAKE A MOVE ON ME *EMI 5291*	**43** 3
23 Oct 82	HEART ATTACK *EMI 5347*	**46** 4
15 Jan 83	I HONESTLY LOVE YOU (re-issue) *EMI 5360*	**52** 4
12 Nov 83	TWIST OF FATE *EMI 5438*	**57** 2
22 Dec 90 ●	THE GREASE MEGAMIX *Polydor PO 114* [1]	**3** 10
23 Mar 91	GREASE – THE DREAM MIX *PWL / Polydor PO 136* [4]	**47** 2
4 Jul 92	I NEED LOVE *Mercury MER 370*	**75** 1
9 Dec 95	HAD TO BE *EMI CDEMS 410* [5]	**22** 4
25 Jul 98 ●	YOU'RE THE ONE THAT I WANT (re-issue) *Polydor 0441332* [1]	**4** 9

[1] John Travolta & Olivia Newton-John [2] Olivia Newton-John & Electric Light Orchestra [3] Olivia Newton-John & Cliff Richard [4] Frankie Valli, John Travolta & Olivia Newton-John [5] Cliff Richard & Olivia Newton-John

NEXT *US, male vocal trio (8 WEEKS)*

		pos/wks
6 Jun 98	TOO CLOSE *Arista 74321580672* ▲	**24** 3
16 Sep 00	WIFEY *Arista 74321790912*	**19** 5

NEXT OF KIN *UK, male vocal / instrumental group (6 WEEKS)*

		pos/wks
20 Feb 99	24 HOURS FROM YOU *Universal MCSTD 40201*	**13** 4
19 Jun 99	MORE LOVE *Universal MCSTD 40207*	**33** 2

NIAGRA *UK, male / female vocal / DJ / production duo (1 WEEK)*

		pos/wks
27 Sep 97	CLOUDBURST *Freeflow FLOW CD2*	**65** 1

NICE *UK, male instrumental group (15 WEEKS)*

		pos/wks
10 Jul 68	AMERICA *Immediate IM 068*	**21** 15

Paul NICHOLAS *UK, male vocalist - Paul Beuselinck (31 WEEKS)*

		pos/wks
17 Apr 76	REGGAE LIKE IT USED TO BE *RSO 2090 185*	**17** 8
9 Oct 76 ●	DANCING WITH THE CAPTAIN *RSO 2090 206*	**8** 9
4 Dec 76 ●	GRANDMA'S PARTY *RSO 2090 216*	**9** 11
9 Jul 77	HEAVEN ON THE 7TH FLOOR *RSO 2090 249*	**40** 3

Sue NICHOLLS *UK, female vocalist (8 WEEKS)*

		pos/wks
3 Jul 68	WHERE WILL YOU BE *Pye 7N 17565*	**17** 8

Stevie NICKS *US, female vocalist (30 WEEKS)*

		pos/wks
15 Aug 81	STOP DRAGGIN' MY HEART AROUND *WEA K 79231* [1]	**50** 4
25 Jan 86	I CAN'T WAIT *Parlophone R 6110*	**54** 4
29 Mar 86	TALK TO ME *Parlophone R 6124*	**68** 2
6 May 89	ROOMS ON FIRE *EMI EM 90*	**16** 7
12 Aug 89	LONG WAY TO GO *EMI EM 97*	**60** 2
11 Nov 89	WHOLE LOTTA TROUBLE *EMI EM 114*	**62** 2
24 Aug 91	SOMETIMES IT'S A BITCH *EMI EM 203*	**40** 4
9 Nov 91	I CAN'T WAIT (re-issue) *EMI EM 214*	**47** 2
2 Jul 94	MAYBE LOVE *EMI CDEMS 328*	**42** 3

[1] Stevie Nicks with Tom Petty and the Heartbreakers

See also FLEETWOOD MAC

NICOLE *Germany, female vocalist - Nicole Hohloch (10 WEEKS)*

		pos/wks
8 May 82 ★	A LITTLE PEACE *CBS A 2365*	**1** 9
21 Aug 82	GIVE ME MORE TIME *CBS A 2467*	**75** 1

NICOLE *US, female vocalist - Nicole McLeod (9 WEEKS)*

		pos/wks
28 Dec 85	NEW YORK EYES *Portrait A 6805* [1]	**41** 7
26 Dec 92	ROCK THE HOUSE *React 12REACT 12* [2]	**63** 1
6 Jul 96	RUNNIN' AWAY *Ore AG 18CD*	**69** 1

[1] Nicole with Timmy Thomas [2] Source featuring Nicole

NICOLE – See Nicole RAY

NICOLETTE *UK, female vocalist (1 WEEK)*

		pos/wks
23 Dec 95	NO GOVERNMENT *Talkin Loud TLCD 1*	**67** 1

UK No.1 ★   UK Top 10 ●   Still on chart +   UK million seller ◆   UK entry at No.1 ■   US No.1 ▲

NIGHTCRAWLERS featuring John REID
UK, male vocalist / multi-instrumentalist - John Reid (36 WEEKS)   pos/wks

15 Oct 94	PUSH THE FEELING ON *ffrr FCD 245* [1]	22	5
4 Mar 95 ●	PUSH THE FEELING ON (re-mix) *ffrr FCD 257*	3	11
27 May 95 ●	SURRENDER YOUR LOVE *Final Vinyl 74321283982*	7	7
9 Sep 95	DON'T LET THE FEELING GO *Final Vinyl 7432129882*	13	4
20 Jan 96	LET'S PUSH IT *Final Vinyl 74321328142*	23	4
20 Apr 96	SHOULD I EVER (FALL IN LOVE)		
	Arista 74321358072	34	2
27 Jul 96	KEEP ON PUSHING OUR LOVE		
	Arista 74321390422 [2]	30	2
3 Jul 99	NEVER KNEW LOVE *Riverhorse RIVHCD 1* [1]	59	1

[1] Nightcrawlers [2] Nightcrawlers featuring John Reid and Alysha Warren

Maxine NIGHTINGALE *UK, female vocalist (16 WEEKS)*   pos/wks

1 Nov 75 ●	RIGHT BACK WHERE WE STARTED FROM		
	United Artists UP 36015	8	8
12 Mar 77	LOVE HIT ME *United Artists UP 36215*	11	8

NIGHTMARES ON WAX
UK, male production / instrumental group (6 WEEKS)   pos/wks

| 27 Oct 90 | AFTERMATH / I'M FOR REAL *Warp WAP 6* | 38 | 5 |
| 26 Jun 99 | FINER *Warp WAP 123CD* | 63 | 1 |

NIGHTWRITERS *US, male vocal / instrumental duo (2 WEEKS)*   pos/wks

| 23 May 92 | LET THE MUSIC USE YOU *Ffrreedom TABX 112* | 51 | 2 |

NIKKE? NICOLE! *US, female rapper (1 WEEK)*   pos/wks

| 1 Jun 91 | NIKKE DOES IT BETTER *Love EVOL 5* | 73 | 1 |

NILSSON *US, male vocalist - Harry Nilsson (55 WEEKS)*   pos/wks

27 Sep 69	EVERYBODY'S TALKIN' *RCA 1876*	50	1
11 Oct 69	EVERYBODY'S TALKIN' (re-entry) *RCA 1876*	23	9
14 Mar 70	EVERYBODY'S TALKIN' (2nd re-entry) *RCA 1876*	39	5
5 Feb 72 ★	WITHOUT YOU *RCA 2165* ▲	1	20
3 Jun 72	COCONUT *RCA 2214*	42	5
16 Oct 76	WITHOUT YOU (re-issue) *RCA 2733*	22	8
20 Aug 77	ALL I THINK ABOUT IS YOU *RCA PB 9104*	43	3
19 Feb 94	WITHOUT YOU (2nd re-issue) *RCA 74321193092*	47	4

Charlotte NILSSON *Sweden, female vocalist (4 WEEKS)*   pos/wks

| 3 Jul 99 | TAKE ME TO YOUR HEAVEN *Arista 74321686952* | 20 | 4 |

NINA and FREDERICK *Denmark, female / male vocal duo - Baron*
Frederick and Baroness Nina Van Pallandt (29 WEEKS)   pos/wks

18 Dec 59	MARY'S BOY CHILD *Columbia DB 4375*	26	1
10 Mar 60	LISTEN TO THE OCEAN *Columbia DB 4332*	47	1
7 Apr 60	LISTEN TO THE OCEAN (re-entry) *Columbia DB 4332*	46	1
17 Nov 60 ●	LITTLE DONKEY *Columbia DB 4536*	3	10
28 Sep 61	LONGTIME BOY *Columbia DB 4703*	43	3
5 Oct 61	SUCU SUCU *Columbia DB 4632*	23	13

NINE INCH NAILS *US, male vocal / instrumental group fronted by Trent*
Reznor (15 WEEKS)   pos/wks

14 Sep 91	HEAD LIKE A HOLE *TVT IS 484*	45	4
16 Nov 91	SIN *TVT IS 508*	35	2
9 Apr 94	MARCH OF THE PIGS *TVT CID 592*	45	3
18 Jun 94	CLOSER *TVT CIDX 596*	25	3
13 Sep 97	THE PERFECT DRUG *Interscope IND 95542*	43	1
18 Dec 99	WE'RE IN THIS TOGETHER *Island 4971402*	39	2

999 *UK, male vocal / instrumental group (13 WEEKS)*   pos/wks

25 Nov 78	HOMICIDE *United Artists UP 36467*	40	3
27 Oct 79	FOUND OUT TOO LATE *Radar ADA 46*	69	2
16 May 81	OBSESSED *Albion ION 1011*	71	1
18 Jul 81	LIL RED RIDING HOOD *Albion ION 1017*	59	3
14 Nov 81	INDIAN RESERVATION *Albion ION 1023*	51	4

911　316　**Top 500**　*Leading UK 'boy band': Lee Brennan, Jimmy*
Constable, Simon 'Spike' Dawbarn. Vocal trio formed in 1996, when they won
GMTV 'Search for the Next Big Thing' contest. Tally of 10 consecutive Top 10s
is among the best chart runs in history (94 WEEKS)   pos/wks

11 May 96	NIGHT TO REMEMBER *Ginga CDGINGA 1*	38	2
10 Aug 96	LOVE SENSATION *Ginga CDGINGA 2*	21	4
9 Nov 96 ●	DON'T MAKE ME WAIT *Ginga VSCDT 1618*	10	6
4 Jan 97	DON'T MAKE ME WAIT (re-entry) *Ginga VSCDT 1618*	63	2
22 Feb 97 ●	THE DAY WE FIND LOVE *Virgin VSCDT 1619*	4	8
3 May 97 ●	BODYSHAKIN' *Virgin VSCDT 1634*	3	7
12 Jul 97 ●	THE JOURNEY *Virgin VSCDT 1645*	3	7
1 Nov 97 ●	PARTY PEOPLE...FRIDAY NIGHT *Ginga / Virgin VSCDT 1658*	5	7
3 Jan 98	PARTY PEOPLE...FRIDAY NIGHT (re-entry)		
	Ginga / Virgin VSCDT 1658	60	3
4 Apr 98 ●	ALL I WANT IS YOU *Virgin VSCDT 1681*	4	6
20 Jun 98	ALL I WANT IS YOU (re-entry) *Virgin VSCDT 1681*	64	1
4 Jul 98 ●	HOW DO YOU WANT ME TO LOVE YOU? *Ginga VSCDT 1686*	10	7
29 Aug 98	HOW DO YOU WANT ME TO LOVE YOU? (re-entry)		
	Ginga VSCDT 1686	57	2
24 Oct 98 ●	MORE THAN A WOMAN *Virgin VSCDT 1707*	2	9
2 Jan 99	MORE THAN A WOMAN (re-entry) *Virgin VSCDT 1707*	64	4
23 Jan 99 ★	A LITTLE BIT MORE *Virgin VSCDT 1719* ■	1	9
15 May 99 ●	PRIVATE NUMBER *Virgin VSCDT 1730*	3	7
23 Oct 99	WONDERLAND *Virgin VSCDT 1755*	13	2

9.9 *US, female vocal group (3 WEEKS)*   pos/wks

| 6 Jul 85 | ALL OF ME FOR ALL OF YOU *RCA PB 49951* | 53 | 3 |

NINE YARDS *UK, male vocal group (3 WEEKS)*   pos/wks

21 Nov 98	LONELINESS IS GONE *Virgin VSCDT 1696*	70	1
10 Apr 99	MATTER OF TIME *Virgin VSCDT 1723*	59	1
28 Aug 99	ALWAYS FIND A WAY *Virgin VSCDT 1746*	50	1

1910 FRUITGUM CO
US, male vocal / instrumental group (16 WEEKS)   pos/wks

| 20 Mar 68 ● | SIMON SAYS *Pye International 7N 25447* | 2 | 16 |

1927 *Australia, male vocal / instrumental group (6 WEEKS)*   pos/wks

| 22 Apr 89 | THAT'S WHEN I THINK OF YOU *WEA YZ 351* | 46 | 6 |

98° *US, male vocal group (17 WEEKS)*   pos/wks

29 Nov 97	INVISIBLE MAN *Motown 8607092*	66	1
31 Oct 98	TRUE TO YOUR HEART *Motown 8608832* [1]	51	1
13 Mar 99	BECAUSE OF YOU *Motown 8609012*	36	2
11 Mar 00 ●	THANK GOD I FOUND YOU *Columbia 6690582* [2] ▲	10	9
11 Mar 00	THE HARDEST THING *Universal MCSTD 40228*	29	2
20 May 00	THANK GOD I FOUND YOU (re-entry)		
	Columbia 6690582 [2]	71	1
2 Dec 00	GIVE ME JUST ONE MORE NIGHT (UNA NOCHE)		
	Universal MCSTD 40243	61	1

[1] 98° featuring Stevie Wonder [2] Mariah Carey featuring Joe and 98°

99TH FLOOR ELEVATORS *UK, male DJ / production duo (5 WEEKS)* pos/wks

12 Aug 95	HOOKED *Labello Dance LAD 18CD* [1]	28	2
30 May 96	I'LL BE THERE *Labello Dance LAD 25CD1* [1]	37	2
8 Apr 00	HOOKED (re-mix) *Tripoli Trax TTRAX 061CD*	66	1

[1] 99th Floor Elevators featuring Tony De Vit

NIRVANA *UK / Ireland, male vocal / instrumental duo (6 WEEKS)* pos/wks

| 15 May 68 | RAINBOW CHASER *Island WIP 6029* | 34 | 6 |

NIRVANA *US, male vocal / instrumental group (36 WEEKS)* pos/wks

30 Nov 91 ●	SMELLS LIKE TEEN SPIRIT *DGC DGCS 5*	7	6
14 Mar 92 ●	COME AS YOU ARE *DGC DGCS 7*	9	5
25 Jul 92	LITHIUM *DGC DGCS 9*	11	6
12 Dec 92	IN BLOOM *Geffen GFS 34*	28	7
6 Mar 93	OH THE GUILT *Touch And Go TG 83CD*	12	2

UK No.1 ★　　UK Top 10 ●　　Still on chart +　　UK million seller ◆　　UK entry at No.1 ■　　US No.1 ▲

11 Sep 93 ●	HEART-SHAPED BOX *Geffen GFSTD 54*	**5** 5
18 Dec 93	ALL APOLOGIES / RAPE ME *Geffen GFSTD 66*	**32** 5

The listed flip side of 'Oh the Guilt' was 'Puss' by Jesus Lizard

NITRO DELUXE
US, male multi-instrumentalist - Lee Junior (16 WEEKS) pos/wks

14 Feb 87	THIS BRUTAL HOUSE *Cooltempo COOL 142*	**47** 7
13 Jun 87	THIS BRUTAL HOUSE (re-entry) *Cooltempo COOL 142*	**62** 4
6 Feb 88	LET'S GET BRUTAL (re-mix) *Cooltempo COOL*	**24** 5

'Let's Get Brutal' is a re-mixed version of 'This Brutal House'

NITZER EBB
UK, male vocal / instrumental group (3 WEEKS) pos/wks

11 Jan 92	GODHEAD *Mute 1MUTE 135T*	**56** 1
11 Apr 92	ASCEND *Mute 110MUTE 145*	**52** 1
4 Mar 95	KICK IT *Mute LCDMUTE 155*	**75** 1

N.K.O.T.B. – See NEW KIDS ON THE BLOCK

NO AUTHORITY
US, male vocal group (1 WEEK) pos/wks

14 Mar 98	DON'T STOP *EPIC 6655592*	**54** 1

NO DICE
UK, male vocal / instrumental group (2 WEEKS) pos/wks

5 May 79	COME DANCING *EMI 2927*	**65** 2

NO DOUBT
US, male / female vocal / instrumental group - lead vocal Gwen Stefani (39 WEEKS) pos/wks

26 Oct 96	JUST A GIRL *Interscope IND 80034*	**38** 2
22 Feb 97 ★	DON'T SPEAK *Interscope IND 95515* ▪	**1** 18
5 Jul 97 ●	JUST A GIRL (re-issue) *Interscope IND 95539*	**3** 7
4 Oct 97	SPIDERWEBS *Interscope IND 95551*	**16** 3
20 Dec 97	SUNDAY MORNING *Interscope IND 95566*	**50** 3
12 Jun 99	NEW *Higher Ground HIGHS 22CD*	**30** 2
25 Mar 00	EX-GIRLFRIEND *Interscope 4972992*	**23** 3
7 Oct 00	SIMPLE KIND OF LIFE *Interscope 4974162*	**69** 1

NO MERCY
US, male vocal / instrumental group (26 WEEKS) pos/wks

18 Jan 97 ●	WHERE DO YOU GO *Arista 74321401502*	**2** 15
24 May 97 ●	PLEASE DON'T GO *Arista 74321481372*	**4** 7
6 Sep 97	KISS YOU ALL OVER *Arista 7432151452*	**16** 4

NO SWEAT
Ireland, male vocal / instrumental group (5 WEEKS) pos/wks

13 Oct 90	HEART AND SOUL *London LON 274*	**64** 4
2 Feb 91	TEAR DOWN THE WALLS *London LON 257*	**61** 1

NO WAY JOSÉ
US, male instrumental group (6 WEEKS) pos/wks

3 Aug 85	TEQUILA *Fourth & Broadway BRW 28*	**47** 6

NO WAY SIS
UK, male vocal / instrumental group (4 WEEKS) pos/wks

21 Dec 96	I'D LIKE TO TEACH THE WORLD TO SING *EMI CDEM 461*	**27** 4

NOLANS 343 Top 500
Dublin-born singing sisters with considerable MOR / pop appeal. Personnel on most hits: Anne, Maureen, Bernadette, Linda and Coleen Nolan. First European act to win the Grand Prize at the prestigious Tokyo Music Festival (1981) (90 WEEKS) pos/wks

6 Oct 79	SPIRIT BODY AND SOUL *Epic EPC 7796* [1]	**34** 6
22 Dec 79 ●	I'M IN THE MOOD FOR DANCING *Epic EPC 8068*	**3** 15
12 Apr 80	DON'T MAKE WAVES *Epic EPC 8349*	**12** 11
13 Sep 80 ●	GOTTA PULL MYSELF TOGETHER *Epic EPC 8878*	**9** 13
6 Dec 80	WHO'S GONNA ROCK YOU *Epic EPC 9325*	**12** 11
14 Mar 81 ●	ATTENTION TO ME *Epic EPC 9571*	**9** 13
15 Aug 81	CHEMISTRY *Epic EPC A 1485*	**15** 8
20 Feb 82	DON'T LOVE ME TOO HARD *Epic EPC A 1927*	**14** 12
1 Apr 95	I'M IN THE MOOD FOR DANCING (re-recording) *Living Beat LBECD 31*	**51** 1

[1] Nolan Sisters

NOMAD
UK, male / female vocal / instrumental duo - Damon Rochefort and Sharon Dee Clarke (22 WEEKS) pos/wks

2 Feb 91 ●	(I WANNA GIVE YOU) DEVOTION *Rumour RUMA 25* [1]	**2** 10
4 May 91	JUST A GROOVE *Rumour RUMA 33*	**16** 6
28 Sep 91	SOMETHING SPECIAL *Rumour RUMA 35*	**73** 1
25 Apr 92	YOUR LOVE IS LIFTING ME *Rumour RUMA 48*	**60** 2
7 Nov 92	24 HOURS A DAY *Rumour RUMA 60*	**61** 1
25 Nov 95	(I WANNA GIVE YOU) DEVOTION (re-mix) *Rumour RUMACD 75*	**42** 2

[1] Nomad featuring MC Mikee Freedom

NONCHALANT
US, female vocalist (1 WEEK) pos/wks

29 Jun 96	5 O'CLOCK *MCA MCSTD 48011*	**44** 1

Peter NOONE
UK, male vocalist (9 WEEKS) pos/wks

22 May 71	OH YOU PRETTY THING *RAK 114*	**12** 9

See also HERMAN'S HERMITS

NOOTROPIC
UK, male instrumental / production duo (1 WEEK) pos/wks

16 Mar 96	I SEE ONLY YOU *Hi-Life 5779832*	**42** 1

Ken NORDENE – See Billy VAUGHN

Chris NORMAN – See Suzi QUATRO; SMOKIE

NORTH AND SOUTH
UK, male vocal / instrumental group (16 WEEKS) pos/wks

17 May 97 ●	I'M A MAN NOT A BOY *RCA 74321461142*	**7** 5
9 Aug 97	TARANTINO'S NEW STAR *RCA 74321501242*	**18** 5
8 Nov 97	BREATHING *RCA 74321528422*	**27** 2
4 Apr 98	NO SWEAT '98 *RCA 74321562212*	**29** 4

NORTHERN LINE
UK / South Africa, male vocal group (12 WEEKS) pos/wks

9 Oct 99	RUN FOR YOUR LIFE *Global Talent GTR 002CDS1*	**18** 4
11 Mar 00	LOVE ON THE NORTHERN LINE *Global Talent GTR 003CDS1*	**15** 5
17 Jun 00	ALL AROUND THE WORLD *Global Talent GTR 004CDS1*	**27** 3

NORTHERN UPROAR
UK, male vocal / instrumental group (11 WEEKS) pos/wks

21 Oct 95	ROLLERCOASTER / ROUGH BOYS *Heavenly HVN 047CD*	**41** 2
3 Feb 96	FROM A WINDOW / THIS MORNING *Heavenly HVN 051CD*	**17** 3
20 Apr 96	LIVIN' IT UP *Heavenly HVN 52CD*	**24** 2
22 Jun 96	TOWN *Heavenly HVN 54CD*	**48** 1
7 Jun 97	ANY WAY YOU LOOK *Heavenly HVN 70CD*	**36** 2
23 Aug 97	A GIRL I ONCE KNEW *Heavenly HVN 73CD*	**63** 1

NORTHSIDE
UK, male vocal / instrumental group (12 WEEKS) pos/wks

9 Jun 90	SHALL WE TAKE A TRIP / MOODY PLACES *Factory FAC 268*	**50** 5
3 Nov 90	MY RISING STAR *Factory FAC 2987*	**32** 3
1 Jun 91	TAKE 5 *Factory FAC 3087*	**40** 4

Freddie NOTES and the RUDIES
Jamaica, male vocal / instrumental group (2 WEEKS) pos/wks

10 Oct 70	MONTEGO BAY *Trojan TR 7791*	**45** 2

NOTORIOUS B.I.G.
US, male rapper - Christopher Wallace (30 WEEKS) pos/wks

29 Oct 94	JUICY *Bad Boy 74321240102*	**72** 1
1 Apr 95	BIG POPPA *Puff Daddy 74321263102*	**63** 1
15 Jul 95	CAN'T YOU SEE *Tommy Boy TBCD 700* [1]	**43** 2
19 Aug 95	ONE MORE CHANCE / STAY WITH ME *Puff Daddy 74321300782*	**34** 2
3 May 97 ●	HYPNOTIZE *Arista 74321466412* ▲	**10** 4
9 Aug 97 ●	MO MONEY MO PROBLEMS *Puff Daddy 74321492492* [2]	**6** 10
14 Feb 98	SKY'S THE LIMIT *Puff Daddy 74321561992* [3]	**35** 2

| 18 Jul 98 | RUNNIN' *Black Jam BJAM 9005* [4] | 15 | 3 |
| 5 Feb 00 | NOTORIOUS B.I.G *Puff Daddy / Arista 74321737312* [5] | 16 | 5 |

[1] Total featuring the Notorious B.I.G. [2] Notorious B.I.G. featuring Puff Daddy and Mase [3] Notorious B.I.G. featuring 112 [4] 2Pac and Notorious B.I.G. [5] Notorious B.I.G. featuring Puff Daddy and Lil' Kim

NOTTINGHAM FOREST FC with PAPER LACE *UK, football team with male vocal / instrumental group. (6 WEEKS)* pos/wks

| 4 Mar 78 | WE'VE GOT THE WHOLE WORLD IN OUR HANDS *Warner Bros. K 17110* | 24 | 6 |

See also PAPER LACE

Heather NOVA *US, female vocalist (1 WEEK)* pos/wks

| 25 Feb 95 | WALK THIS WORLD *Butterfly BFLD 19* | 69 | 1 |

Nancy NOVA *UK, female vocalist (2 WEEKS)* pos/wks

| 4 Sep 82 | NO NO NO *EMI 5328* | 63 | 2 |

Tom NOVY *Germany, male producer (7 WEEKS)* pos/wks

2 May 98	SUPERSTAR *D:disco 74321569352* [1]	32	3
3 Jun 00	PUMPIN *Positiva CDTIV 132* [1]	19	3
2 Sep 00	I ROCK *Rulin RULIN 3CDS* [2]	55	1

[1] Novy vs Eniac [2] Tom Novy featuring Virginia

NRG *UK, male DJ / production duo (2 WEEKS)* pos/wks

| 29 Mar 97 | NEVER LOST HIS HARDCORE *Top Banana TOPCD 04* | 71 | 1 |
| 12 Dec 98 | NEVER LOST HIS HARDCORE '98 (re-mix) *Top Banana TOPCD 010* | 61 | 1 |

NT GANG *Germany, male vocal / instrumental group (1 WEEK)* pos/wks

| 2 Apr 88 | WAM BAM *Cooltempo COOL 163* | 71 | 1 |

NU-BIRTH *UK, male production duo (2 WEEKS)* pos/wks

| 6 Sep 97 | ANYTIME *XL XLS 85CD* | 48 | 1 |
| 6 Jun 98 | ANYTIME (re-issue) *Locked On LOX 97CD* | 41 | 1 |

NU COLOURS
UK, male / female vocal / instrumental group (11 WEEKS) pos/wks

6 Jun 92	TEARS *Wild Card CARD 1*	55	2
10 Oct 92	POWER *Wild Card CARD 3*	64	1
5 Jun 93	WHAT IN THE WORLD *Wild Card CARDD 4*	57	2
27 Nov 93	POWER (re-mix) *Wild Card CARDD 5*	40	2
25 May 96	DESIRE *Wild Card 5763652*	31	2
24 Aug 96	SPECIAL KIND OF LOVER *Wild Card 5752012*	38	2

NU GENERATION *UK, male producer - Aston Harvey (9 WEEKS)* pos/wks

| 29 Jan 00 | ● IN YOUR ARMS (RESCUE ME) *Concept CDCON 7* | 8 | 8 |
| 21 Oct 00 | NOWHERE TO RUN 2000 *Concept CDCON 16* | 66 | 1 |

NU MATIC *UK, male instrumental / production duo (1 WEEK)* pos/wks

| 8 Aug 92 | SPRING IN MY STEP *XL XLS 31* | 58 | 1 |

NU SHOOZ
US, male / female vocal duo - John Smith and Valerie Day (17 WEEKS) pos/wks

| 24 May 86 | ● I CAN'T WAIT *Atlantic A 9446* | 2 | 14 |
| 26 Jul 86 | POINT OF NO RETURN *Atlantic A 9392* | 48 | 3 |

NU SOUL featuring Kelli RICH
US, male / female vocal / instrumental duo (2 WEEKS) pos/wks

| 13 Jan 96 | HIDE-A-WAY *ffrr FCD 269* | 27 | 2 |

NUANCE featuring Vikki LOVE
US, male / female vocal / instrumental group (3 WEEKS) pos/wks

| 19 Jan 85 | LOVERIDE *Fourth & Broadway BRW 20* | 59 | 3 |

NUBIAN PRINZ – See POWERCUT featuring NUBIAN PRINZ

NUFF JUICE – See D MOB

Gary NUMAN (126 Top 500) *The moody, synthesized sound of London-born Gary Webb (b. 8 Mar 1958) first hit the charts in 1979 under the group name Tubeway Army. Five times chart hit 'Cars' was also basis of Armand Van Helden's Top 20 hit 'Koochy' in 2000 (164 WEEKS)* pos/wks

19 May 79	★ ARE 'FRIENDS' ELECTRIC? *Beggars Banquet BEG 18* [1]	1	16
1 Sep 79	★ CARS *Beggars Banquet BEG 23*	1	11
24 Nov 79	● COMPLEX *Beggars Banquet BEG 29*	6	9
24 May 80	● WE ARE GLASS *Beggars Banquet BEG 35*	5	7
30 Aug 80	● I DIE: YOU DIE *Beggars Banquet BEG 46*	6	7
20 Dec 80	THIS WRECKAGE *Beggars Banquet BEG 50*	20	7
29 Aug 81	● SHE'S GOT CLAWS *Beggars Banquet BEG 62*	6	6
5 Dec 81	LOVE NEEDS NO DISGUISE *Beggars Banquet BEG 68* [2]	33	7
6 Mar 82	MUSIC FOR CHAMELEONS *Beggars Banquet BEG 70*	19	7
19 Jun 82	● WE TAKE MYSTERY (TO BED) *Beggars Banquet BEG 77*	9	4
28 Aug 82	WHITE BOYS AND HEROES *Beggars Banquet BEG 81*	20	4
3 Sep 83	WARRIORS *Beggars Banquet BEG 95*	20	5
22 Oct 83	SISTER SURPRISE *Beggars Banquet BEG 101*	32	3
3 Nov 84	BERSERKER *Numa NU 4*	32	5
22 Dec 84	MY DYING MACHINE *Numa NU 6*	66	1
9 Feb 85	CHANGE YOUR MIND *Polydor POSP 722* [3]	17	8
25 May 85	THE LIVE EP *Numa NUM 7*	27	4
10 Aug 85	YOUR FASCINATION *Numa NU 9*	46	5
21 Sep 85	CALL OUT THE DOGS *Numa NU 11*	49	2
16 Nov 85	MIRACLES *Numa NU 13*	49	3
19 Apr 86	THIS IS LOVE *Numa NU 16*	28	3
28 Jun 86	I CAN'T STOP *Numa NU 17*	27	4
4 Oct 86	NEW THING FROM LONDON TOWN *Numa NU 19* [3]	52	3
6 Dec 86	I STILL REMEMBER *Numa NU 21*	74	1
28 Mar 87	RADIO HEART *GFM GFM 109* [4]	35	6
13 Jun 87	LONDON TIMES *GFM GFM 112* [4]	48	2
19 Sep 87	CARS (E REG MODEL) / ARE 'FRIENDS' ELECTRIC? (re-mix) *Beggars Banquet BEG 199*	16	7
30 Jan 88	NO MORE LIES *Polydor POSP 894* [3]	34	3
1 Oct 88	NEW ANGER *Illegal ILS 1003*	46	2
3 Dec 88	AMERICA *Illegal ILS 1004*	49	1
3 Jun 89	I'M ON AUTOMATIC *Polydor PO 43* [3]	44	2
16 Mar 91	HEART *IRS NUMAN 1*	43	2
21 Mar 92	THE SKIN GAME *Numa NU 23*	68	1
1 Aug 92	MACHINE + SOUL *Numa NUM 124*	72	1
4 Sep 93	CARS (2nd re-mix) *Beggars Banquet BEG 264CD*	53	1
16 Mar 96	CARS (re-issue of re-mix) *PolyGram TV PRMCD 1*	17	4

[1] Tubeway Army [2] Gary Numan and Dramatis [3] Sharpe and Numan [4] Radio Heart featuring Gary Numan

Tracks on The Live EP: Are 'Friends' Electric? / Berserker / Cars / We Are Glass. 'Cars' in 1996 is a re-issue of the 1987 remix

See also Paul GARDINER

NUMBER ONE CUP *US, male vocal / instrumental group (1 WEEK)* pos/wks

| 2 Mar 96 | DIVEBOMB *Blue Rose BRRC 10032* | 61 | 1 |

Jose NUNEZ featuring OCTAHVIA
US, male DJ / producer (2 WEEKS) pos/wks

| 5 Sep 98 | IN MY LIFE *Ministry of Sound MOSCDS 126* | 56 | 1 |
| 5 Jun 99 | HOLD ON *Ministry of Sound MOSCDS 130* | 44 | 1 |

Bobby NUNN *US, male vocalist / multi-instrumentalist (3 WEEKS)* pos/wks

| 4 Feb 84 | DON'T KNOCK IT (UNTIL YOU TRY IT) *Motown TMG 1323* | 65 | 3 |

NUSH *UK, male instrumental / production duo (7 WEEKS)* pos/wks

23 Jul 94	U GIRLS *Blunted Vinyl BLNCDX 006*	58	1
22 Apr 95	MOVE THAT BODY *Blunted Vinyl BLNCD 012*	46	2
16 Sep 95	U GIRLS (LOOK SO SEXY) (re-mix) *Blunted Vinyl BLNCD 13*	15	4

NUT *UK, female vocalist (4 WEEKS)*

		pos/wks
8 Jun 96	**BRAINS** *Epic NUTCD 2* 64 1
21 Sep 96	**CRAZY** *Epic NUTCD 5* 56 1
11 Jan 97	**SCREAM** *Epic NUTCD 6* 43 2

NUTTIN' NYCE *US, female vocal group (2 WEEKS)*

		pos/wks
10 Jun 95	**DOWN 4 WHATEVA** *Jive JIVECD 365* 62 1
12 Aug 95	**FROGGY STYLE** *Jive JIVECD 381* 68 1

NUYORICAN SOUL *US, male DJ / production group (8 WEEKS)*

		pos/wks
8 Feb 97	**RUNAWAY** *Talkin Loud TLCD20* [1] 24 4
10 May 97	**IT'S ALRIGHT, I FEEL IT!** *Talkin Loud TLCD 22* [2] ...26 2
25 Oct 97	**I AM THE BLACK GOLD OF THE SUN** *Talkin Loud TLCD 26* [2] 31 2

[1] Nuyorican Soul featuring India [2] Nuyorican Soul featuring Jocelyn Brown

NWA *US, male rap group (15 WEEKS)*

		pos/wks
9 Sep 89	**EXPRESS YOURSELF** *Fourth & Broadway BRW 144* 50 4
26 May 90	**EXPRESS YOURSELF** (re-entry) *Fourth & Broadway BRW 144* 26 5
1 Sep 90	**GANGSTA, GANGSTA** *Fourth & Broadway BRW 191* 70 1
10 Nov 90	**100 MILES AND RUNNIN'** *Fourth & Broadway BRW 200* 38 3
23 Nov 91	**ALWAYZ INTO SOMETHIN'** *Fourth & Broadway BRW 238* 60 2

NYCC *Germany, male rap trio (6 WEEKS)*

		pos/wks
30 May 98	**FIGHT FOR YOUR RIGHT (TO PARTY)** *Control 0042645 CON* 14 5
19 Sep 98	**CAN YOU FEEL IT (ROCK DA HOUSE)** *Control 0042785 CON* ...68 1

Joe NYE – See DNA

NYLON MOON *Italy, male instrumental duo (2 WEEKS)*

		pos/wks
13 Apr 96	**SKY PLUS** *Positiva CDTIV 50* 43 2

Michael NYMAN *UK, male instrumentalist - piano (2 WEEKS)*

		pos/wks
19 Mar 94	**THE HEART ASKS PLEASURE FIRST / THE PROMISE** *Virgin VEND 3* 60 2

Phil OAKEY – See HUMAN LEAGUE; Giorgio MORODER

OASIS `28` `Top 500` *Peerless Manchester-based, Beatles-influenced band: Liam (v) and Noel (g/v) Gallagher, Gem Archer (g), Andy Bell (b), Alan White (d). Tony McCarroll was replaced by Alan White in 1994. In 1999 Paul 'Bonehead' Arthurs was replaced by Gem Archer and Paul McGuigan was replaced by Andy Bell. The often controversial Britpop group smashed many records including most weeks on the chart in one year (134 in 1996) (309 WEEKS)*

		pos/wks
23 Apr 94	**SUPERSONIC** *Creation CRESCD 176* 31 3
2 Jul 94	**SHAKERMAKER** *Creation CRESCD 182* 11 5
20 Aug 94 ●	**LIVE FOREVER** *Creation CRESCD 185* 10 5
22 Oct 94 ●	**CIGARETTES AND ALCOHOL** *Creation CRESCD 190* 7 6
31 Dec 94	**CIGARETTES AND ALCOHOL** (re-entry) *Creation CRESCD 190* 69 1
31 Dec 94 ●	**WHATEVER** *Creation CRESCD 195* 3 10
6 May 95 ★	**SOME MIGHT SAY** *Creation CRESCD 204* ■ 1 14
13 May 95	**SOME MIGHT SAY** *Creation CRE 204T* 71 1
24 Jun 95	**CIGARETTES AND ALCOHOL** (2nd re-entry) *Creation CRESCD 190* 53 3
24 Jun 95	**LIVE FOREVER** (re-entry) *Creation CRESCD 185* 50 3
24 Jun 95	**SHAKERMAKER** (re-entry) *Creation CRESCD 182* 52 3

		pos/wks
24 Jun 95	**SUPERSONIC** (re-entry) *Creation CRESCD 176* 44 3
24 Jun 95	**WHATEVER** (re-entry) *Creation CRESCD 195* 48 3
26 Aug 95 ●	**ROLL WITH IT** *Creation CRESCD 212* 2 11
26 Aug 95	**SOME MIGHT SAY** (re-entry) *Creation CRESCD 204* 73 1
11 Nov 95 ●	**WONDERWALL** *Creation CRESCD 215* 2 20
25 Nov 95	**WIBBLING RIVALRY (INTERVIEWS WITH NOEL AND LIAM GALLAGHER)** *Fierce Panda NING 12CD* [1] 52 2
9 Dec 95	**WHATEVER** (2nd re-entry) *Creation CRESCD 195* 75 1
30 Dec 95	**CIGARETTES AND ALCOHOL** (3rd re-entry) *Creation CRESCD 190* 58 7
30 Dec 95	**SUPERSONIC** (2nd re-entry) *Creation CRESCD 176* 56 4
30 Dec 95	**WHATEVER** (3rd re-entry) *Creation CRESCD 195* 55 3
6 Jan 96	**LIVE FOREVER** (2nd re-entry) *Creation CRESCD 185* 64 1
6 Jan 96	**ROLL WITH IT** (re-entry) *Creation CRESCD 212* 65 3
6 Jan 96	**SHAKERMAKER** (2nd re-entry) *Creation CRESCD 182* 61 2
6 Jan 96	**SOME MIGHT SAY** (2nd re-entry) *Creation CRESCD 204* 59 3
20 Jan 96	**LIVE FOREVER** (3rd re-entry) *Creation CRESCD 185* 71 2
27 Jan 96	**WHATEVER** (4th re-entry) *Creation CRESCD 195* 61 3
24 Feb 96	**WHATEVER** (5th re-entry) *Creation CRESCD 195* 55 15
2 Mar 96	**CIGARETTES AND ALCOHOL** (4th re-entry) *Creation CRESCD 190* 62 4
2 Mar 96 ★	**DON'T LOOK BACK IN ANGER** *Creation CRESCD 221* ■ 1 16
2 Mar 96	**LIVE FOREVER** (4th re-entry) *Creation CRESCD 185* 74 2
2 Mar 96	**SHAKERMAKER** (3rd re-entry) *Creation CRESCD 182* 74 1
2 Mar 96	**SUPERSONIC** (3rd re-entry) *Creation CRESCD 176* 71 1
16 Mar 96	**SOME MIGHT SAY** (3rd re-entry) *Creation CRESCD 204* 75 1
13 Apr 96	**CIGARETTES AND ALCOHOL** (5th re-entry) *Creation CRESCD 190* 74 2
11 May 96	**CIGARETTES AND ALCOHOL** (6th re-entry) *Creation CRESCD 190* 72 3
17 Aug 96	**WHATEVER** (6th re-entry) *Creation CRESCD 195* 62 4
24 Aug 96	**CIGARETTES AND ALCOHOL** (7th re-entry) *Creation CRESCD 190* 72 1
24 Aug 96	**SOME MIGHT SAY** (4th re-entry) *Creation CRESCD 204* 70 1
24 Aug 96	**WONDERWALL** (re-entry) *Creation CRESCD 215* 60 5
21 Sep 96	**WHATEVER** (7th re-entry) *Creation CRESCD 195* 66 1
16 Nov 96	**CIGARETTES AND ALCOHOL** (8th re-entry) *Creation CRESCD 190* 38 5
16 Nov 96	**DON'T LOOK BACK IN ANGER** (re-entry) *Creation CRESCD 221* 53 5
16 Nov 96	**LIVE FOREVER** (5th re-entry) *Creation CRESCD 185* 42 2
16 Nov 96	**ROLL WITH IT** (2nd re-entry) *Creation CRESCD 212* 55 2
16 Nov 96	**SHAKERMAKER** (4th re-entry) *Creation CRESCD 182* 48 2
16 Nov 96	**SOME MIGHT SAY** (5th re-entry) *Creation CRESCD 204* 40 4
16 Nov 96	**SUPERSONIC** (4th re-entry) *Creation CRESCD 176* 47 2
16 Nov 96	**WHATEVER** (8th re-entry) *Creation CRESCD 195* 34 10
16 Nov 96	**WONDERWALL** (2nd re-entry) *Creation CRESCD 215* 36 9
28 Dec 96	**CIGARETTES AND ALCOHOL** (9th re-entry) *Creation CRESCD 190* 56 3
28 Dec 96	**DON'T LOOK BACK IN ANGER** (2nd re-entry) *Creation CRESCD 221* 53 3
28 Dec 96	**LIVE FOREVER** (6th re-entry) *Creation CRESCD 185* 59 3
28 Dec 96	**SOME MIGHT SAY** (6th re-entry) *Creation CRESCD 204* 58 3
4 Jan 97	**ROLL WITH IT** (3rd re-entry) *Creation CRESCD 212* 62 2
4 Jan 97	**SHAKERMAKER** (5th re-entry) *Creation CRESCD 182* 61 2
4 Jan 97	**SUPERSONIC** (5th re-entry) *Creation CRESCD 176* 63 1
19 Jul 97 ★	**D'YOU KNOW WHAT I MEAN?** *Creation CRESCD 256* ■ 1 18
4 Oct 97 ●	**STAND BY ME** *Creation CRESCD 278* 2 18
24 Jan 98 ★	**ALL AROUND THE WORLD** *Creation CRESCD 282* ■ 1 7
11 Apr 98	**ALL AROUND THE WORLD** (re-entry) *Creation CRESCD 282* 68 2
19 Feb 00 ★	**GO LET IT OUT** *Big Brother RKIDSCD 001* ■ 1 10
29 Apr 00 ●	**WHO FEELS LOVE?** *Big Brother RKIDSCD 003* 4 7
6 May 00	**GO LET IT OUT** (re-entry) *Big Brother RKIDSCD 001* 52 2
1 Jul 00	**WHO FEELS LOVE?** (re-entry) *Big Brother RKIDSCD 003* 70 1
15 Jul 00 ●	**SUNDAY MORNING CALL** *Big Brother RKIDSCD004* 4 6

[1] Oas*s

Chart rules allow for a maximum of three formats; the 12-inch of 'Some Might Say' - already available on CD, 7-inch and cassette - was therefore listed separately

John OATES – See Daryl HALL and John OATES

UK No.1 ★ UK Top 10 ● Still on chart + UK million seller ◆ UK entry at No.1 ■ US No.1 ▲

OBERNKIRCHEN CHILDREN'S CHOIR
Germany, children's choir (26 WEEKS) pos/wks

Date	Title	pos	wks
22 Jan 54	● THE HAPPY WANDERER *Parlophone R 3799*	2	23
9 Jul 54	● THE HAPPY WANDERER (re-entry) *Parlophone R 3799*	8	3

Dermot O'BRIEN *Ireland, male vocalist (2 WEEKS)* pos/wks

Date	Title	pos	wks
20 Oct 66	THE MERRY PLOUGHBOY *Envoy ENV 016*	46	1
3 Nov 66	THE MERRY PLOUGHBOY (re-entry) *Envoy ENV 016*	50	1

Billy OCEAN 139 Top 500
Top British-based R&B singer / songwriter of the 1980s, b. Leslie Charles, 21 Jan 1950, Trinidad. He waited seven years after scoring his first four UK Top 20 hits before accumulating an impressive run of transatlantic successes, which included three US No.1s *(153 WEEKS)* pos/wks

Date	Title	pos	wks
21 Feb 76	● LOVE REALLY HURTS WITHOUT YOU *GTO GT 52*	2	10
10 Jul 76	L.O.D. (LOVE ON DELIVERY) *GTO GT 62*	19	8
13 Nov 76	STOP ME (IF YOU'VE HEARD IT ALL BEFORE) *GTO GT 72*	12	11
19 Mar 77	● RED LIGHT SPELLS DANGER *GTO GT 85*	2	10
1 Sep 79	AMERICAN HEARTS *GTO GT 244*	54	5
19 Jan 80	ARE YOU READY *GTO GT 259*	42	7
13 Oct 84	● CARIBBEAN QUEEN (NO MORE LOVE ON THE RUN) *Jive JIVE 77* ▲	6	14
19 Jan 85	LOVERBOY *Jive JIVE 80*	15	10
11 May 85	● SUDDENLY *Jive JIVE 90*	4	14
17 Aug 85	MYSTERY LADY *Jive JIVE 98*	49	4
25 Jan 86	★ WHEN THE GOING GETS TOUGH, THE TOUGH GET GOING *Jive JIVE 114*	1	13
12 Apr 86	THERE'LL BE SAD SONGS (TO MAKE YOU CRY) *Jive JIVE 117* ▲	12	13
9 Aug 86	LOVE ZONE *Jive JIVE 124*	49	3
11 Oct 86	BITTERSWEET *Jive JIVE 133*	44	4
10 Jan 87	LOVE IS FOREVER *Jive JIVE 134*	34	7
6 Feb 88	● GET OUTTA MY DREAMS GET INTO MY CAR *Jive BOS 1* ▲	3	11
7 May 88	CALYPSO CRAZY *Jive BOS 2*	35	4
6 Aug 88	THE COLOUR OF LOVE *Jive BOS 3*	65	3
6 Feb 93	PRESSURE *Jive BOSCD 6*	55	2

OCEAN COLOUR SCENE
UK, male vocal / instrumental group (57 WEEKS) pos/wks

Date	Title	pos	wks
23 Mar 91	YESTERDAY TODAY *!Phfft FIT 2*	49	1
17 Feb 96	● THE RIVERBOAT SONG *MCA MCSTD 40021*	15	5
6 Apr 96	● YOU'VE GOT IT BAD *MCA MCSTD 40036*	7	4
15 Jun 96	● THE DAY WE CAUGHT THE TRAIN *MCA MCSTD 40046*	4	11
28 Sep 96	● THE CIRCLE *MCA MCSTD 40077*	6	6
28 Jun 97	● HUNDRED MILE HIGH CITY *MCA MCSTD 40133*	4	7
6 Sep 97	● TRAVELLERS TUNE *MCA MCSTD 40144*	5	5
22 Nov 97	● BETTER DAY *MCA MCSTD 40151*	9	5
28 Feb 98	● IT'S A BEAUTIFUL THING *MCA MCSTD 40157*	12	4
4 Sep 99	PROFIT IN PEACE *Island CID 757*	13	5
27 Nov 99	SO LOW *Island CID 759*	34	2
8 Jul 00	JULY / I AM THE NEWS *Island CID 763*	31	2

OCEANIC *UK, male / female vocal / instrumental group (26 WEEKS)* pos/wks

Date	Title	pos	wks
24 Aug 91	● INSANITY *Dead Dead Good GOOD 4*	3	15
30 Nov 91	WICKED LOVE *Dead Dead Good GOOD 5*	25	3
28 Dec 91	WICKED LOVE (re-entry) *Dead Dead Good GOOD 5*	65	2
13 Jun 92	CONTROLLING ME *Dead Dead Good GOOD 14*	14	5
14 Nov 92	IGNORANCE *Dead Dead Good GOOD 22* [1]	72	1

[1] Oceanic featuring Siobhan Maher

Des O'CONNOR 230 Top 500
Entertainer, comedian and MOR vocalist, b. 12 Jan 1932. This London-based all-rounder toured with Buddy Holly and Lonnie Donegan in the 1950s, had a series of hits in the 1960s and has been a top-rated TV star for the past five decades *(117 WEEKS)* pos/wks

Date	Title	pos	wks
1 Nov 67	● CARELESS HANDS *Columbia DB 8275* [1]	6	17
8 May 68	★ I PRETEND *Columbia DB 8397*	1	36
20 Nov 68	● 1-2-3 O'LEARY *Columbia DB 8492*	4	11
7 May 69	DICK-A-DUM-DUM (KING'S ROAD) *Columbia DB 8566*	14	10
29 Nov 69	LONELINESS *Columbia DB 8632*	18	11
14 Mar 70	I'LL GO ON HOPING *Columbia DB 8661*	30	7

Date	Title	pos	wks
26 Sep 70	THE TIPS OF MY FINGERS *Columbia DB 8713*	15	15
8 Nov 86	● THE SKYE BOAT SONG *Tembo TML 119* [2]	10	10

[1] Des O'Connor with the Michael Sammes Singers [2] Roger Whittaker and Des O'Connor

Hazel O'CONNOR *UK, female vocalist (46 WEEKS)* pos/wks

Date	Title	pos	wks
16 Aug 80	● EIGHTH DAY *A & M AMS 7553*	5	11
25 Oct 80	GIVE ME AN INCH *A & M AMS 7569*	41	4
21 Mar 81	● D-DAYS *Albion ION 1009*	10	9
23 May 81	● WILL YOU *A & M AMS 8131*	8	10
1 Aug 81	(COVER PLUS) WE'RE ALL GROWN UP *Albion ION 1018*	41	6
3 Oct 81	HANGING AROUND *Albion ION 1022*	45	3
23 Jan 82	CALLS THE TUNE *A & M AMS 8203*	60	3

Sinead O'CONNOR *Ireland, female vocalist (64 WEEKS)* pos/wks

Date	Title	pos	wks
16 Jan 88	MANDINKA *Ensign ENY 611*	17	9
20 Jan 90	★ NOTHING COMPARES 2 U *Ensign ENY 630* ▲	1	14
21 Jul 90	THE EMPEROR'S NEW CLOTHES *Ensign ENY 633*	31	5
20 Oct 90	THREE BABIES *Ensign ENY 635*	42	4
8 Jun 91	MY SPECIAL CHILD *Ensign ENY 646*	42	3
14 Dec 91	SILENT NIGHT *Ensign ENY 652*	60	4
12 Sep 92	SUCCESS HAS MADE A FAILURE OF OUR HOME *Ensign ENY 656*	18	4
12 Dec 92	DON'T CRY FOR ME ARGENTINA *Ensign ENY 657*	53	4
19 Feb 94	YOU MADE ME THE THIEF OF YOUR HEART *Island CID 588*	42	4
26 Nov 94	THANK YOU FOR HEARING ME *Ensign CDENYS 662*	13	7
29 Apr 95	HAUNTED *ZTT ZANG 65CD* [1]	30	2
26 Aug 95	FAMINE *Ensign CDENY 663*	51	1
17 May 97	GOSPEL OAK (EP) *Chrysalis CDCHS 5051*	28	3
6 Dec 97	THIS IS A REBEL SONG *Columbia 6652992*	60	1

[1] Shane MacGowan and Sinead O'Connor

Tracks on Gospel Oak (EP): This Is to Mother You / I Am Enough for Myself / Petit Poulet / 4 My Love

See also MARXMAN; Jah WOBBLE'S INVADERS of the HEART

OCTAHVIA – See Jose NUNEZ featuring OCTAHVIA

OCTOPUS *UK / France, male vocal / instrumental group (5 WEEKS)* pos/wks

Date	Title	pos	wks
22 Jun 96	YOUR SMILE *Food CDFOOD 78*	42	2
14 Sep 96	SAVED *Food CDFOODS 84*	40	2
23 Nov 96	JEALOUSY *Food CDFOODS 87*	59	1

Alan O'DAY *US, male vocalist (3 WEEKS)* pos/wks

Date	Title	pos	wks
2 Jul 77	UNDERCOVER ANGEL *Atlantic K 10926* ▲	43	3

ODETTA – See Harry BELAFONTE

Daniel O'DONNELL *Ireland, male vocalist (63 WEEKS)* pos/wks

Date	Title	pos	wks
12 Sep 92	I JUST WANT TO DANCE WITH YOU *Ritz RITZ 250P*	20	7
2 Jan 93	THE THREE BELLS *Ritz RITZCD 239*	71	1
8 May 93	THE LOVE IN YOUR EYES *Ritz RITZCD 257*	47	3
7 Aug 93	WHAT EVER HAPPENED TO OLD FASHIONED LOVE *Ritz RITZCD 262*	21	5
16 Apr 94	SINGING THE BLUES *Ritz RITZCD 270*	23	4
26 Nov 94	THE GIFT *Ritz RITZCD 275*	46	3
10 Jun 95	SECRET LOVE *Ritz RITZCD 285* [1]	28	3
9 Mar 96	TIMELESS *Ritz RITZCD 293* [1]	32	3
28 Sep 96	FOOTSTEPS *Ritz RITZCD 300*	25	5
7 Jun 97	THE LOVE SONGS EP *Ritz RITZCD 306*	27	4
11 Apr 98	● GIVE A LITTLE LOVE *Ritz RITZCD 315*	7	5
17 Oct 98	THE MAGIC IS THERE *Ritz RZCD 320*	16	4
20 Mar 99	THE WAY DREAMS ARE *Ritz RZCD 325*	18	3
24 Jul 99	UNO MAS *Ritz RZCD 326*	25	3
18 Dec 99	A CHRISTMAS KISS *Ritz RZCD 330*	20	4
15 Apr 00	LIGHT A CANDLE *Ritz RZCD 335*	23	4
16 Dec 00	MORNING HAS BROKEN *Ritz RZCD 341*	32	3+

[1] Daniel O'Donnell and Mary Duff

Tracks on The Love Songs EP: Save the Last Dance for Me / I Can't Stop Loving You / You're the Only Good Thing / Limerick You're a Lady

ODYSSEY `394` `Top 500` *Soul / disco vocal trio formed in New York, US, by non-natives Lillian and Louise Lopez (from Connecticut) and Manila-born Tony Reynolds (replaced 1978 by Bill McEachern). UK success not mirrored in US, where only their debut hit reached the Top 40 (82 WEEKS)* pos/wks

24 Dec 77	● NATIVE NEW YORKER *RCA PC 1129*	5	11
21 Jun 80	★ USE IT UP AND WEAR IT OUT *RCA PB 1962*	1	12
13 Sep 80	● IF YOU'RE LOOKIN' FOR A WAY OUT *RCA 5*	6	15
17 Jan 81	HANG TOGETHER *RCA 23*	36	7
30 May 81	● GOING BACK TO MY ROOTS *RCA 85*	4	12
19 Sep 81	IT WILL BE ALRIGHT *RCA 128*	43	5
12 Jun 82	● INSIDE OUT *RCA 226*	3	11
11 Sep 82	MAGIC TOUCH *RCA 275*	41	5
17 Aug 85	(JOY) I KNOW IT *Mirror BUTCH 12*	51	4

Esther and Abi OFARIM *Israel, female / male vocal duo - Esther Zaled and Abraham Reichstadt (22 WEEKS)* pos/wks

14 Feb 68	★ CINDERELLA ROCKEFELLA *Philips BF 1640*	1	13
19 Jun 68	ONE MORE DANCE *Philips BF 1678*	13	9

Wiston OFFICE – See Frank K featuring Wiston OFFICE

OFF-SHORE *Germany, male instrumental / production duo - Jens Lissat and Peter Harder (12 WEEKS)* pos/wks

22 Dec 90	● I CAN'T TAKE THE POWER *CBS 6565707*	7	11
17 Aug 91	I GOT A LITTLE SONG *Dance Pool 6568257*	64	1

OFFSPRING *US, male vocal / instrumental group - lead vocal Dexter Holland (42 WEEKS)* pos/wks

25 Feb 95	SELF ESTEEM *Golf CDSHOLE 001*	37	3
19 Aug 95	GOTTA GET AWAY *Out Of Step WOOS 2CDS*	43	2
1 Feb 97	ALL I WANT *Epitaph 64912*	31	2
26 Apr 97	GONE AWAY *Epitaph 64982*	42	1
30 Jan 99	★ PRETTY FLY (FOR A WHITE GUY) *Columbia 666802* ■	1	11
8 May 99	● WHY DON'T YOU GET A JOB? *Columbia 6673542*	2	8
11 Sep 99	THE KIDS AREN'T ALRIGHT *Columbia 6677632*	11	6
4 Dec 99	SHE'S GOT ISSUES *Columbia 6683772*	41	2
18 Nov 00	● ORIGINAL PRANKSTER *Columbia 6699972*	6	7+

OH WELL *Germany, male producer - Ackim Faulker (7 WEEKS)* pos/wks

14 Oct 89	OH WELL *Parlophone R 6236*	28	6
3 Mar 90	RADAR LOVE *Parlophone R 6244*	65	1

OHIO EXPRESS *US, male vocal / instrumental group (15 WEEKS)* pos/wks

5 Jun 68	● YUMMY YUMMY YUMMY *Pye International 7N 25459*	5	15

OHIO PLAYERS *US, male vocal / instrumental group (4 WEEKS)* pos/wks

10 Jul 76	WHO'D SHE COO *Mercury PLAY 001*	43	4

O'JAYS `475` `Top 500` *One of the most consistently successful R&B vocal groups; members included Walter Williams and Eddie Levert (whose sons, Gerald and Sean, are in Levert). Formed in 1958 in Ohio, US, they have had four decades of US R&B hits, many produced and composed by Gamble and Huff (72 WEEKS)* pos/wks

23 Sep 72	BACK STABBERS *CBS 8270*	14	9
3 Mar 73	● LOVE TRAIN *CBS 1181* ▲	9	13
31 Jan 76	I LOVE MUSIC *Philadelphia International PIR 3879*	13	9
12 Feb 77	DARLIN' DARLIN' BABY (SWEET, TENDER, LOVE) *Philadelphia International PIR 4834*	24	6
8 Apr 78	I LOVE MUSIC (re-issue) *Philadelphia International PIR 6093*	36	3
17 Jun 78	USED TA BE MY GIRL *Philadelphia International PIR 6332*	12	12
30 Sep 78	BRANDY *Philadelphia International PIR 6658*	21	9
29 Sep 79	SING A HAPPY SONG *Philadelphia International PIR 7825*	39	6
30 Jul 83	PUT OUR HEADS TOGETHER *Philadelphia International A 3642*	45	5

John O'KANE *UK, male vocalist (4 WEEKS)* pos/wks

9 May 92	STAY WITH ME *Circa YR 88*	41	4

OL' DIRTY BASTARD *US, male rapper - Russell Jones (25 WEEKS)* pos/wks

27 Jun 98	● GHETTO SUPERSTAR (THAT IS WHAT YOU ARE) *Interscope IND 95593* [1]	2	17
8 Jul 00	GOT YOUR MONEY *Elektra E 7077CD* [2]	11	8

[1] Pras Michel featuring Ol' Dirty Bastard introducing Mya [2] Ol' Dirty Bastard featuring Kelis

See also WU-TANG CLAN

OLD SKOOL ORCHESTRA *UK, male DJ / production duo (1 WEEK)* pos/wks

23 Jan 99	B-BOY HUMP *East West EW 186CD1*	55	1

See also STRETCH 'N' VERN present MADDOG

Mike OLDFIELD `245` `Top 500` *Composer / producer / multi-instrumentalist, b. 15 May 1953, Reading, UK. His chart-topping 1973 debut album, Tubular Bells, spent five years on the chart, and the belated Tubular Bells II also reached UK No.1 (1992) (113 WEEKS)* pos/wks

13 Jul 74	MIKE OLDFIELD'S SINGLE (THEME FROM TUBULAR BELLS) *Virgin VS 101*	31	6
20 Dec 75	● IN DULCE JUBILO / ON HORSEBACK *Virgin VS 131*	4	10
27 Nov 76	● PORTSMOUTH *Virgin VS 163*	3	12
23 Dec 78	TAKE 4 (EP) *Virgin VS 238*	72	3
21 Apr 79	GUILTY *Virgin VS 245*	22	8
8 Dec 79	BLUE PETER *Virgin VS 317*	19	9
20 Mar 82	FIVE MILES OUT *Virgin VS 464* [1]	43	5
12 Jun 82	FAMILY MAN *Virgin VS 489* [1]	45	6
28 May 83	● MOONLIGHT SHADOW *Virgin VS 586* [2]	4	17
14 Jan 84	CRIME OF PASSION *Virgin VS 648* [1]	61	3
30 Jun 84	TO FRANCE *Virgin VS 686* [1]	48	7
14 Dec 85	PICTURES IN THE DARK *Virgin VS 836* [3]	50	6
3 Oct 92	● SENTINEL *WEA YZ 698*	10	6
19 Dec 92	TATTOO *WEA YZ 708*	33	5
17 Apr 93	THE BELL *WEA YZ 737CD*	50	2
9 Oct 93	MOONLIGHT SHADOW (re-issue) *Virgin VSCDT 1477*	52	2
17 Dec 94	HIBERNACULUM *WEA YZ 871CD*	47	3
2 Sep 95	LET THERE BE LIGHT *WEA YZ 880CD*	51	1
22 Nov 97	WOMEN OF IRELAND *WEA WEA 093CD*	70	1
24 Apr 99	FAR ABOVE THE CLOUDS *WEA WEA 206CD1*	53	1

[1] Mike Oldfield featuring Maggie Reilly [2] Mike Oldfield with vocals by Maggie Reilly [3] Mike Oldfield featuring Aled Jones, Anita Hegerland and Barry Palmer

Tracks on Take 4 (EP): Portsmouth / In Dulce Jubilo / Wrekorder Wrondo / Sailors Hornpipe. 'The Bell' credits Vivian Stanshall

Sally OLDFIELD *UK, female vocalist (13 WEEKS)* pos/wks

9 Dec 78	MIRRORS *Bronze BRO 66*	19	13

Misty OLDLAND *UK, female vocalist (7 WEEKS)* pos/wks

16 Oct 93	GOT ME A FEELING *Columbia 6597872*	59	2
12 Mar 94	A FAIR AFFAIR (JE T'AIME) *Columbia 6601612*	49	4
9 Jul 94	I WROTE YOU A SONG *Columbia 6603732*	73	1

OLGA *Italy, female vocalist (1 WEEK)* pos/wks

1 Oct 94	I'M A BITCH *UMM UMM 144UKCD*	68	1

OLIVE *UK, male / female vocal / instrumental group - vocal Ruth Ann Boyle (24 WEEKS)* pos/wks

7 Sep 96	YOU'RE NOT ALONE *RCA 74321406272*	42	4
15 Mar 97	MIRACLE *RCA 74321461242*	41	2
17 May 97	★ YOU'RE NOT ALONE (re-issue) *RCA 74321473232* ■	1	13
16 Aug 97	OUTLAW *RCA 74321508372*	14	4
8 Nov 97	MIRACLE (re-mix) *RCA 74321530842*	41	1

OLIVER *US, male vocalist - William Swofford (18 WEEKS)* pos/wks

9 Aug 69	● GOOD MORNING STARSHINE *CBS 4435*	6	16
27 Dec 69	GOOD MORNING STARSHINE (re-entry) *CBS 4435*	39	2

UK No.1 ★   UK Top 10 ●   Still on chart +   UK million seller ◆   UK entry at No.1 ■   US No.1 ▲

Frankie OLIVER UK, male vocalist (1 WEEK)

			pos/wks
7 Jun 97	GIVE HER WHAT SHE WANTS Island Jamaica IJCD 2011	**58**	1

OLLIE and JERRY
US, male vocal duo - Ollie Brown and Jerry Knight (14 WEEKS)

			pos/wks
23 Jun 84 ●	BREAKIN'. . . THERE'S NO STOPPING US Polydor POSP 690	**5**	11
9 Mar 85	ELECTRIC BOOGALOO Polydor POSP 730	**57**	3

OLYMPIC ORCHESTRA UK, orchestra (15 WEEKS)

			pos/wks
1 Oct 83	REILLY Red Bus RBUS 82	**26**	15

OLYMPIC RUNNERS
UK, male vocal / instrumental group (21 WEEKS)

			pos/wks
13 May 78	WHATEVER IT TAKES RCA PC 5078	**61**	2
14 Oct 78	GET IT WHILE YOU CAN Polydor RUN 7	**35**	6
20 Jan 79	SIR DANCEALOT Polydor POSP 17	**35**	6
28 Jul 79	THE BITCH Polydor POSP 63	**37**	7

OLYMPICS US, male vocal group (9 WEEKS)

			pos/wks
3 Oct 58	WESTERN MOVIES HMV POP 528	**12**	8
19 Jan 61	I WISH I COULD SHIMMY LIKE MY SISTER KATE Vogue V 9174	**40**	1

OMAR UK, male vocalist - Omar Hammer (18 WEEKS)

			pos/wks
22 Jun 91	THERE'S NOTHING LIKE THIS Talkin Loud TLK 9	**14**	7
23 May 92	YOUR LOSS MY GAIN Talkin Loud TLK 22	**47**	2
26 Sep 92	MUSIC Talkin Loud TLK 28	**53**	2
23 Jul 94	OUTSIDE / SATURDAY RCA 74321213982	**43**	2
15 Oct 94	KEEP STEPPIN' RCA 74321233682	**57**	1
2 Aug 97	SAY NOTHIN' RCA 74321502872	**29**	2
18 Oct 97	GOLDEN BROWN RCA 74321525422	**37**	2

OMC
New Zealand, male vocalist - Paul Fuemana Lawrence (17 WEEKS) pos/wks

20 Jul 96 ●	HOW BIZARRE Polydor 5776202	**5**	16
18 Jan 97	ON THE RUN Polydor 5732452	**56**	1

OMD – See ORCHESTRAL MANOEUVRES IN THE DARK

ONE UK, male vocal group (2 WEEKS)

			pos/wks
11 Jan 97	ONE MORE CHANCE Mercury MERDD 478	**31**	2

ONE DOVE
UK, male / female vocal / instrumental group (9 WEEKS)

			pos/wks
7 Aug 93	WHITE LOVE Boy's Own BOICD 14	**43**	3
16 Oct 93	BREAKDOWN Boy's Own BOICD 15	**24**	3
15 Jan 94	WHY DON'T YOU TAKE ME Boy's Own BOICD 16	**30**	3

187 LOCKDOWN UK, male production duo - Danny Harrison and Julian Jonah (16 WEEKS)

			pos/wks
15 Nov 97	GUNMAN East West EW 140CD	**16**	4
25 Apr 98 ●	KUNG-FU East West EW 155CD	**9**	5
25 Jul 98	GUNMAN (re-mix) East West EW 176CD	**17**	4
3 Oct 98	THE DON East West EW 180CD	**29**	2
13 Feb 99	ALL 'N' ALL East West EW 194CD [1]	**43**	1

[1] 187 Lockdown (featuring D'Empress)

ONE HUNDRED TON AND A FEATHER – See Jonathan KING

Michie ONE – See Louchie LOU and Michie ONE

112 – See NOTORIOUS B.I.G.; ALLURE; PUFF DADDY

ONE THE JUGGLER
UK, male vocal / instrumental group (1 WEEK)

			pos/wks
19 Feb 83	PASSION KILLER Regard RG 107	**71**	1

1000 CLOWNS US, male / female vocal / rap group (4 WEEKS)

			pos/wks
22 May 99	(NOT THE) GREATEST RAPPER Elektra E 3759CD	**23**	4

ONE TRIBE – See OUR TRIBE / ONE TRIBE

ONE 2 MANY
Norway, male / female vocal / instrumental group (11 WEEKS)

			pos/wks
12 Nov 88	DOWNTOWN A & M AM 476	**65**	4
3 Jun 89	DOWNTOWN (re-issue) A & M AM 456	**43**	7

ONE WAY US, male vocal / instrumental group (8 WEEKS)

			pos/wks
8 Dec 79	MUSIC MCA 542 [1]	**56**	6
29 Jun 85	LET'S TALK MCA 972 [1]	**64**	2

[1] One Way featuring Al Hudson

Alexander O'NEAL `260` `Top 500`
Soulful ex-vocalist with Minneapolis-based Flyte Time (line-up featured star producers Jimmy Jam and Terry Lewis, who worked on most of his hits), b. 15 Nov 1953, Mississippi, US. Co-wrote his biggest hit and clocked up impressive five Top 20 albums between 1985 and 1993 (110 WEEKS) pos/wks

28 Dec 85 ●	SATURDAY LOVE Tabu A 6829 [1]	**6**	11
15 Feb 86	IF YOU WERE HERE TONIGHT Tabu A 6391	**13**	10
5 Apr 86	A BROKEN HEART CAN MEND Tabu A 6244	**53**	4
6 Jun 87	FAKE Tabu 650891 7	**33**	6
31 Oct 87 ●	CRITICIZE Tabu 651211 7	**4**	14
6 Feb 88	NEVER KNEW LOVE LIKE THIS Tabu 651382 7 [2]	**26**	7
25 Feb 89	HEARSAY '89 Tabu 654466 7	**56**	2
28 May 88	THE LOVERS Tabu 6515957	**28**	4
23 Jul 88	(WHAT CAN I SAY) TO MAKE YOU LOVE ME Tabu 652852 7	**27**	5
24 Sep 88	FAKE '88 (re-mix) Tabu 652949 7	**16**	7
10 Dec 88	CHRISTMAS SONG (CHESTNUTS ROASTING ON AN OPEN FIRE) / THANK YOU FOR A GOOD YEAR Tabu 653182 7	**30**	5
2 Sep 89	SUNSHINE Tabu 655191 7	**72**	1
9 Dec 89	HITMIX (OFFICIAL BOOTLEG MEGA-MIX) Tabu 655504 7	**19**	7
24 Mar 90	SATURDAY LOVE (re-mix) Tabu 655680 7 [1]	**55**	2
12 Jan 91	ALL TRUE MAN Tabu 6565717	**18**	6
23 Mar 91	WHAT IS THIS THING CALLED LOVE Tabu 6567317	**53**	2
11 May 91	SHAME ON ME Tabu 6568737	**71**	1
9 May 92	SENTIMENTAL Tabu 6580147	**53**	2
30 Jan 93	LOVE MAKES NO SENSE Tabu AMCD 7708	**28**	6
3 Jul 93	IN THE MIDDLE Tabu 5877152	**32**	3
25 Sep 93	ALL THAT MATTERS TO ME Tabu 6577232	**67**	1
2 Nov 96	LET'S GET TOGETHER EMI Premier PRESCD 11	**38**	2
2 Aug 97	BABY COME TO ME One World OWECD 1 [2]	**56**	1
12 Dec 98	CRITICIZE '98 MIX (re-recording) One World OWECD 3	**51**	1

[1] Cherrelle with Alexander O'Neal [2] Alexander O'Neal featuring Cherrelle

Shaquille O'NEAL US, male rapper (4 WEEKS)

			pos/wks
26 Mar 94	I'M OUTSTANDING Jive JIVECD 349	**70**	1
1 Feb 97	YOU CAN'T STOP THE REIGN Interscope IND 95522	**40**	2
17 Oct 98	THE WAY IT'S GOIN' DOWN (T.W.I.S.M. FOR LIFE) A&M 5827932	**62**	1

ONEPHATDEEVA – See A.T.F.C. presents ONEPHATDEEVA

ONLY ONES UK, male vocal / instrumental group (2 WEEKS)

			pos/wks
1 Feb 92	ANOTHER GIRL - ANOTHER PLANET Columbia 6577507	**57**	2

Yoko ONO Japan, female vocalist (5 WEEKS)

			pos/wks
28 Feb 81	WALKING ON THIN ICE Geffen K 79202	**35**	5

See also John LENNON

ONSLAUGHT UK, male vocal / instrumental group (3 WEEKS)

			pos/wks
6 May 89	LET THERE BE ROCK London LON 224	**50**	3

ONYX US, male rap group (8 WEEKS)

			pos/wks
28 Aug 93	SLAM Columbia 6596302	31	4
27 Nov 93	THROW YA GUNZ Columbia 6598312	34	3
20 Feb 99	ROC-IN-IT Independiente ISOM 21MS [1]	59	1

[1] Deejay Punk-Roc vs Onyx

OO LA LA UK, male vocal / instrumental group (2 WEEKS)

			pos/wks
5 Sep 92	OO…AH…CANTONA North Speed OOAH 1	64	2

OOBERMAN UK, male / female vocal / instrumental group (5 WEEKS)

			pos/wks
8 May 99	BLOSSOMS FALLING Independiente ISOM 26MS	39	2
17 Jul 99	MILLION SUNS Independiente ISOM 30MS	43	1
23 Oct 99	TEARS FROM A WILLOW Independiente ISOM 37MS	63	1
8 Apr 00	SHORLEY WALL Independiente ISOM 41MS	47	1

OOE – See COLUMBO featuring OOE

OPEN ARMS featuring ROWETTA
UK, male / female vocal / instrumental group (1 WEEK)

			pos/wks
15 Jun 96	HEY MR DJ All Around the World CDGLOBE 136	62	1

OPTIMYSTIC UK, male / female vocal group (6 WEEKS)

			pos/wks
17 Sep 94	CAUGHT UP IN MY HEART WEA YZ 841CD	49	3
10 Dec 94	NOTHING BUT LOVE WEA 864CD1	37	2
13 May 95	BEST THING IN THE WORLD WEA YZ 920CD	70	1

OPUS Austria, male vocal / instrumental group (15 WEEKS)

			pos/wks
15 Jun 85 ●	LIVE IS LIFE Polydor POSP 743	6	15

OPUS III UK, male / female vocal / instrumental group (10 WEEKS)

			pos/wks
22 Feb 92 ●	IT'S A FINE DAY PWL International PWL 215	5	8
27 Jun 92	I TALK TO THE WIND PWL International PWL 235	52	1
11 Jun 94	WHEN YOU MADE THE MOUNTAIN PWL International PWCD 302	71	1

ORANGE UK, male vocal / instrumental group (1 WEEK)

			pos/wks
8 Oct 94	JUDY OVER THE RAINBOW Chrysalis CDCHS 5012	73	1

ORANGE JUICE UK, male vocal / instrumental group (34 WEEKS)

			pos/wks
7 Nov 81	L.O.V.E….LOVE Polydor POSP 357	65	2
30 Jan 82	FELICITY Polydor POSP 386	63	3
21 Aug 82	TWO HEARTS TOGETHER / HOKOYO Polydor POSP 470	60	2
23 Oct 82	I CAN'T HELP MYSELF Polydor POSP 522	42	3
19 Feb 83 ●	RIP IT UP Polydor POSP 547	8	11
4 Jun 83	FLESH OF MY FLESH Polydor OJ 4	41	6
25 Feb 84	BRIDGE Polydor OJ 5	67	2
12 May 84	WHAT PRESENCE? Polydor OJ 6	47	4
27 Oct 84	LEAN PERIOD Polydor OJ 7	74	1

See also Edwyn COLLINS

ORB UK, male instrumental / production duo - Dr Alex Paterson and Kris Weston (30 WEEKS)

			pos/wks
15 Jun 91	PERPETUAL DAWN Big Life BLRD 46	61	1
20 Jun 92 ●	BLUE ROOM Big Life BLRT 75	8	6
17 Oct 92	ASSASSIN Big Life BLRT 81	12	5
13 Nov 93 ●	LITTLE FLUFFY CLOUDS Big Life BLRD 98	10	5
5 Feb 94	PERPETUAL DAWN (re-entry) Big Life BLRD 46	18	5
27 May 95	OXBOW LAKES Island CID 609	38	2
8 Feb 97 ●	TOXYGENE Island CID 652	4	4
24 May 97	ASYLUM Island CID 657	20	2

Roy ORBISON [19] [Top 500]
Truly original singer / songwriter, b. 23 Apr 1936, Texas, US, d. 6 Dec 1988. He was the most popular American vocalist in Britain during the 1960s Beat Group period, and his trademark was his dark glasses. He had a hit span of more than 33 years (345 WEEKS)

			pos/wks
28 Jul 60	ONLY THE LONELY London HLU 9149	36	1
11 Aug 60 ★	ONLY THE LONELY (re-entry) London HLU 9149	1	23
27 Oct 60	BLUE ANGEL London HLU 9207	11	16
25 May 61 ●	RUNNING SCARED London HLU 9342 ▲	9	15
21 Sep 61	CRYIN' London HLU 9405	25	9
8 Mar 62 ●	DREAM BABY London HLU 9511	2	14
28 Jun 62	THE CROWD London HLU 9561	40	4
8 Nov 62	WORKIN' FOR THE MAN London HLU 9607	50	1
28 Feb 63 ●	IN DREAMS London HLU 9676	6	23
30 May 63 ●	FALLING London HLU 9727	9	11
19 Sep 63 ●	BLUE BAYOU / MEAN WOMAN BLUES London HLU 9777	3	19
20 Feb 64	BORNE ON THE WIND London HLU 9845	15	10
30 Apr 64 ★	IT'S OVER London HLU 9882	1	18
10 Sep 64 ★	OH PRETTY WOMAN London HLU 9919 ▲	1	18
19 Nov 64 ●	PRETTY PAPER London HLU 9930	6	11
11 Feb 65	GOODNIGHT London HLU 9951	14	9
22 Jul 65	(SAY) YOU'RE MY GIRL London HLU 9978	23	8
9 Sep 65	RIDE AWAY London HLU 9986	34	6
4 Nov 65	CRAWLIN' BACK London HLU 10000	19	9
27 Jan 66	BREAKIN' UP IS BREAKIN' MY HEART London HLU 10015	22	6
7 Apr 66	TWINKLE TOES London HLU 10034	29	5
16 Jun 66	LANA London HLU 10051	15	9
18 Aug 66 ●	TOO SOON TO KNOW London HLU 10067	3	17
1 Dec 66	THERE WON'T BE MANY COMING HOME London HLU 10096	12	9
23 Feb 67	SO GOOD London HL 10113	32	6
24 Jul 68	WALK ON London HLU 10206	39	10
25 Sep 68	HEARTACHE London HLU 10222	44	4
30 Apr 69	MY FRIEND London HLU 10261	35	4
13 Sep 69	PENNY ARCADE London HLU 10285	40	3
11 Oct 69	PENNY ARCADE (re-entry) London HLU 10285	27	11
14 Jan 89 ●	YOU GOT IT Virgin VS 1166	3	10
1 Apr 89	SHE'S A MYSTERY TO ME Virgin VS 1173	27	5
4 Jul 92	I DROVE ALL NIGHT MCA MCS 1652	7	10
22 Aug 92	CRYING Virgin America VUS 63 [1]	13	6
7 Nov 92	HEARTBREAK RADIO Virgin America VUS 68	36	3
13 Nov 93	I DROVE ALL NIGHT (re-issue) Virgin America VUSCD 79	47	2

[1] Roy Orbison (duet with kd Lang)

William ORBIT UK, male producer - William Wainwright (18 WEEKS)

			pos/wks
26 Jun 93	WATER FROM A VINE LEAF Guerilla VSCDT 1465	59	1
18 Dec 99 ●	BARBER'S ADAGIO FOR STRINGS WEA WEA 247 CD	4	13
25 Mar 00	BARBER'S ADAGIO FOR STRINGS (re-entry) WEA WEA 247 CD	69	2
6 May 00	RAVEL'S PAVANE POUR UNE INFANTE DEFUNTE WEA WEA 269CD	31	2

ORBITAL UK, male instrumental duo - Paul and Phil Hartnoll (50 WEEKS)

			pos/wks
24 Mar 90	CHIME ffrr F B5	17	7
22 Sep 90	OMEN ffrr F 145	46	3
19 Jan 91	SATAN ffrr FX 149	31	4
15 Feb 92	MUTATIONS (EP) ffrr FCD 181	24	3
26 Sep 92	RADICCIO (EP) ffrr LIARX 1	37	2
21 Aug 93	LUSH Internal LIECD 7	43	2
24 Sep 94	ARE WE HERE Internal LIECD 15	33	2
27 May 95	BELFAST Volume VOLCD 1	53	1
27 Apr 96	THE BOX Internal LIECD 30	11	4
11 Jan 97 ●	SATAN (re-recording) Internal LIECD 37	3	6
19 Apr 97 ●	THE SAINT ffrr FCD 296	3	7
20 Mar 99	STYLE ffrr FCD 358	13	4
17 Jul 99	NOTHING LEFT ffrr FCD 365	32	2
11 Mar 00	BEACHED ffrr FCD 377 [1]	36	3

[1] Orbital and Angelo Badalamenti

Tracks on Mutations (EP): Chime Crime / Oolaa / Farenheit 3D 3 / Speed Freak. Tracks on Radiccio (EP): Halcyon / The Naked and the Dead / Sunday. The listed flip side of 'Belfast' was 'Innocent X' by Therapy?

ORCHESTRA ON THE HALF SHELL US, male vocal / instrumental group (6 WEEKS)

			pos/wks
15 Dec 90	TURTLE RHAPSODY SBK SBK 17	36	6

UK No.1 ★ UK Top 10 ● Still on chart + UK million seller ◆ UK entry at No.1 ■ US No.1 ▲

ORCHESTRAL MANOEUVRES IN THE DARK `88` `Top 500` *One of the most regular chart visitors of the 1980s had a nucleus of Andy McCluskey (v/syn/b) and Paul Humphries (syn), who left in 1989. This Liverpool-based synthesizer band had numerous international hits including 'Maid of Orleans', which was Germany's biggest seller in 1982 (201 WEEKS)* pos/wks

		pos/wks	
9 Feb 80	RED FRAME WHITE LIGHT *Dindisc DIN 6*	67	2
10 May 80	MESSAGES *Dindisc DIN 15*	13	11
4 Oct 80 ●	ENOLA GAY *Dindisc DIN 22*	8	15
29 Aug 81 ●	SOUVENIR *Dindisc DIN 24*	3	12
24 Oct 81 ●	JOAN OF ARC *Dindisc DIN 36*	5	14
23 Jan 82 ●	MAID OF ORLEANS (THE WALTZ JOAN OF ARC)		
	Dindisc DIN 40	4	10
19 Feb 83	GENETIC ENGINEERING *Virgin VS 527*	20	4
9 Apr 83	TELEGRAPH *Virgin VS 580*	42	4
14 Apr 84 ●	LOCOMOTION *Virgin VS 660*	5	11
16 Jun 84	TALKING LOUD AND CLEAR *Virgin VS 685*	11	10
8 Sep 84	TESLA GIRLS *Virgin VS 705*	21	8
10 Nov 84	NEVER TURN AWAY *Virgin VS 727*	70	2
25 May 85	SO IN LOVE *Virgin VS 766*	27	7
20 Jul 85	SECRET *Virgin VS 796*	34	7
26 Oct 85	LA FEMME ACCIDENT *Virgin VS 811*	42	4
3 May 86	IF YOU LEAVE *Virgin VS 843*	48	4
6 Sep 86	(FOREVER) LIVE AND DIE *Virgin VS 888*	11	10
15 Nov 86	WE LOVE YOU *Virgin VS 911*	54	5
2 May 87	SHAME *Virgin VS 938*	52	3
6 Feb 88	DREAMING *Virgin VS 987*	50	3
2 Jul 88	DREAMING (re-entry) *Virgin VS 987*	60	3
30 Mar 91 ●	SAILING ON THE SEVEN SEAS *Virgin VS 1310*	3	13
6 Jul 91 ●	PANDORA'S BOX *Virgin VS 1331*	7	10
14 Sep 91	THEN YOU TURN AWAY *Virgin VS 1368*	50	4
7 Dec 91	CALL MY NAME *Virgin VS 1380*	50	2
15 May 93	STAND ABOVE ME *Virgin VSCDG 1444*	21	4
17 Jul 93	DREAM OF ME (BASED ON LOVE'S THEME)		
	Virgin VSCDT 1461	24	5
18 Sep 93	EVERYDAY *Virgin VSCDT 1471*	59	2
17 Aug 96	WALKING ON THE MILKY WAY *Virgin VSCDT 1599*	17	5
2 Nov 96	UNIVERSAL *Virgin VSCDT 1606*	55	1
26 Sep 98	THE OMD REMIXES (EP) *Virgin VSCDT 1694*	35	2

Group often known as OMD. Tracks on the OMD Remixes (EP): Enola Gay, Souvenir, Electricity

Raul ORELLANA *Spain, male producer (8 WEEKS)* pos/wks

		pos/wks	
30 Sep 89	THE REAL WILD HOUSE *RCA BCM 322*	29	8

O.R.G.A.N. *Spain, male DJ / producer (2 WEEKS)* pos/wks

		pos/wks	
16 May 98	TO THE WORLD *Multiply CDMULTY 34*	33	2

ORIGIN *UK, male production duo (1 WEEK)* pos/wks

		pos/wks	
12 Aug 00	WIDE EYED ANGEL *Lost Language LOST 001CD*	73	1

ORIGIN UNKNOWN
UK, male instrumental / production duo (1 WEEK) pos/wks

		pos/wks	
13 Jul 96	VALLEY OF THE SHADOWS *Ram RAMM 16CD*	60	1

ORIGINAL *US, male vocal / instrumental duo - Everett Bradley and Walter Taieb (14 WEEKS)* pos/wks

		pos/wks	
14 Jan 95	I LUV U BABY *Ore AG 8CD*	31	3
19 Aug 95 ●	I LUV U BABY (re-mix) *Ore AGR 8CD*	2	9
11 Nov 95	B 2 GETHER *Ore AG 12CD*	29	2

ORIGINOO GUNN CLAPPAZ – See HELTAH SKELTAH and ORIGINOO GUNN CLAPPAZ as the FABULOUS FIVE

ORION
UK, male / female production / vocal / instrumental duo (2 WEEKS) pos/wks

		pos/wks	
7 Oct 00	ETERNITY *Incentive CENT 11CDS*	38	2

ORLANDO – See PRETENDERS

Tony ORLANDO *US, male vocalist - Michael Anthony Orlando Cassavitis (11 WEEKS)* pos/wks

		pos/wks	
5 Oct 61 ●	BLESS YOU *Fontana H 330*	5	11

See also DAWN

ORLONS *US, female / male vocal group (3 WEEKS)* pos/wks

		pos/wks	
27 Dec 62	DON'T HANG UP *Cameo Parkway C 231*	50	1
10 Jan 63	DON'T HANG UP (re-entry)		
	Cameo Parkway C 231	39	2

ORN *UK, male DJ / producer - Omio Nourizadeh (1 WEEK)* pos/wks

		pos/wks	
1 Mar 97	SNOW *Deconstruction 74321447612*	61	1

Beth ORTON *UK, female vocalist (11 WEEKS)* pos/wks

		pos/wks	
1 Feb 97	TOUCH ME WITH YOUR LOVE *Heavenly HVN 64CD*	60	1
5 Apr 97	SOMEONE'S DAUGHTER *Heavenly HVN 65CD*	49	1
14 Jun 97	SHE CRIES YOUR NAME *Heavenly HVN 68CD*	40	2
13 Dec 97	BEST BIT (EP) *Heavenly HVN 72CD* [1]	36	3
13 Mar 99	STOLEN CAR *Heavenly HVN 89CD*	34	2
25 Sep 99	CENTRAL RESERVATION *Heavenly HVN 92CD*	37	2

[1] Beth Orton featuring Terry Callier

Tracks on Best Bit (EP): Best Bit / Skimming Stone / Dolphins / Lean on Me

ORVILLE – See Keith HARRIS and ORVILLE

Jeffrey OSBORNE *US, male vocalist (38 WEEKS)* pos/wks

		pos/wks	
17 Sep 83	DON'T YOU GET SO MAD *A & M AM 140*	54	2
14 Apr 84	STAY WITH ME TONIGHT *A & M AM 188*	18	11
23 Jun 84	ON THE WINGS OF LOVE *A & M AM 198*	11	14
20 Oct 84	DON'T STOP *A & M AM 222*	61	2
26 Jul 86	SOWETO *A & M AM 334*	44	5
6 Sep 86	SOWETO (re-entry) *A & M AM 334*	75	1
15 Aug 87	LOVE POWER *Arista RIS 27* [1]	63	3

[1] Dionne Warwick and Jeffrey Osborne

Joan OSBORNE *US, female vocalist (13 WEEKS)* pos/wks

		pos/wks	
10 Feb 96 ●	ONE OF US *Blue Gorilla JOACD 1*	6	10
8 Jun 96	ST TERESA *Blue Gorilla JOACD 3*	33	3

Tony OSBORNE SOUND *UK, orchestra (3 WEEKS)* pos/wks

		pos/wks	
23 Feb 61	MAN FROM MADRID *HMV POP 827* [1]	50	1
3 Feb 73	THE SHEPHERD'S SONG *Philips 6006 266*	46	2

[1] Tony Osborne Sound featuring Joanne Brown

Ozzy OSBOURNE *UK, male vocalist (42 WEEKS)* pos/wks

		pos/wks	
13 Sep 80	CRAZY TRAIN *Jet 197* [1]	49	4
15 Nov 80	MR CROWLEY *Jet 7003* [1]	46	3
26 Nov 83	BARK AT THE MOON *Epic A 3915*	21	8
2 Jun 84	SO TIRED *Epic A 4452*	20	9
1 Feb 86	SHOT IN THE DARK *Epic A 6859*	20	6
9 Aug 86	THE ULTIMATE SIN / LIGHTNING STRIKES		
	Epic A 7311	72	1
20 May 89	CLOSE MY EYES FOREVER		
	Dreamland PB 49409 [2]	47	3
28 Sep 91	NO MORE TEARS *Epic 6574407*	32	3
30 Nov 91	MAMA I'M COMING HOME *Epic 6576177*	46	2
25 Nov 95	PERRY MASON *Epic 6626395*	23	2
31 Aug 96	I JUST WANT YOU *Epic 6635702*	43	1

[1] Ozzy Osbourne's Blizzard of Ozz [2] Lita Ford duet with Ozzy Osbourne

See also BLACK SABBATH

OSIBISA
Ghana / Nigeria, male vocal / instrumental group (12 WEEKS) pos/wks

		pos/wks	
17 Jan 76	SUNSHINE DAY *Bronze BRO 20*	17	6
5 Jun 76	DANCE THE BODY MUSIC *Bronze BRO 26*	31	6

Donny OSMOND `228` `Top 500` *Teenage teen-idol vocalist, b. 9 Dec 1957, Utah, US. The main focal point of the hitmaking family act The Osmonds, he was one of the most popular pin-ups of the 1970s, and had three solo No.1s before his 16th birthday (118 WEEKS)*

		pos/wks
17 Jun 72 ★	PUPPY LOVE *MGM 2006 104*	1 17
16 Sep 72 ●	TOO YOUNG *MGM 2006 113*	5 12
21 Oct 72	PUPPY LOVE (re-entry) *MGM 2006 104*	45 2
11 Nov 72 ●	WHY *MGM 2006 119*	3 20
23 Dec 72	PUPPY LOVE (2nd re-entry) *MGM 2006 104*	46 3
23 Dec 72	TOO YOUNG (re-entry) *MGM 2006 113*	47 3
27 Jan 73	PUPPY LOVE (3rd re-entry) *MGM 2006 104*	48 1
10 Mar 73 ★	THE TWELFTH OF NEVER *MGM 2006 199*	1 14
18 Aug 73 ★	YOUNG LOVE *MGM 2006 300*	1 10
10 Nov 73 ●	WHEN I FALL IN LOVE *MGM 2006 365*	4 13
9 Nov 74	WHERE DID ALL THE GOOD TIMES GO *MGM 2006 468*	18 10
26 Sep 87	I'M IN IT FOR LOVE *Virgin VS 994*	70 1
6 Aug 88	SOLDIER OF LOVE *Virgin VS 1094*	29 8
12 Nov 88	IF IT'S LOVE THAT YOU WANT *Virgin VS 1140*	70 2
9 Feb 91	MY LOVE IS A FIRE *Capitol CL 600*	64 2

See also Donny and Marie OSMOND; OSMONDS

Donny and Marie OSMOND
US, male / female vocal duo (37 WEEKS)

		pos/wks
3 Aug 74 ●	I'M LEAVING IT (ALL) UP TO YOU *MGM 2006 446*	2 12
14 Dec 74 ●	MORNING SIDE OF THE MOUNTAIN *MGM 2006 474*	5 12
21 Jun 75	MAKE THE WORLD GO AWAY *MGM 2006 523*	18 6
17 Jan 76	DEEP PURPLE *MGM 2006 561*	25 7

See also Donny OSMOND; Marie OSMOND

Little Jimmy OSMOND *US, male vocalist (50 WEEKS)*

		pos/wks
25 Nov 72 ★	LONG HAIRED LOVER FROM LIVERPOOL *MGM 2006 109*	1 24
31 Mar 73 ●	TWEEDLE DEE *MGM 2006 175*	4 13
19 May 73	LONG HAIRED LOVER FROM LIVERPOOL (re-entry) *MGM 2006 109*	41 3
23 Mar 74	I'M GONNA KNOCK ON YOUR DOOR *MGM 2006 389*	11 10

Marie OSMOND *US, female vocalist (15 WEEKS)*

		pos/wks
17 Nov 73 ●	PAPER ROSES *MGM 2006 315*	2 15

See also Donny and Marie OSMOND

OSMOND BOYS *US, male vocal group (6 WEEKS)*

		pos/wks
9 Nov 91	BOYS WILL BE BOYS *Curb 6573847*	65 2
11 Jan 92	SHOW ME THE WAY *Curb 6577227*	60 4

OSMONDS `315` `Top 500` *Top teeny-bop act, brothers Donny, Alan, Wayne, Merrill and Jay Osmond from Utah, US. Polished pop quintet created hysteria wherever they appeared. Osmond family (including Marie and Little Jimmy) had record 13 UK hits in 1973 (94 WEEKS)*

		pos/wks
25 Mar 72	DOWN BY THE LAZY RIVER *MGM 2006 096*	40 5
11 Nov 72 ●	CRAZY HORSES *MGM 2006 142*	2 18
14 Jul 73 ●	GOING HOME *MGM 2006 288*	4 10
27 Oct 73 ●	LET ME IN *MGM 2006 321*	2 14
20 Apr 74	I CAN'T STOP *MCA 129*	12 10
24 Aug 74 ★	LOVE ME FOR A REASON *MGM 2006 458*	1 9
1 Mar 75	HAVING A PARTY *MGM 2006 492*	28 8
24 May 75 ●	THE PROUD ONE *MGM 2006 520*	5 8
15 Nov 75	I'M STILL GONNA NEED YOU *MGM 2006 551*	32 4
30 Oct 76	I CAN'T LIVE A DREAM *Polydor 2066 726*	37 5
23 Sep 95	CRAZY HORSES (re-mix) *Polydor 5793212*	50 1
12 Jun 99	CRAZY HORSES (re-issue of re-mix) *Polydor 5611372*	34 2

See also Donny OSMOND; Donny and Marie OSMOND; Little Jimmy OSMOND; Marie OSMOND

Gilbert O'SULLIVAN `157` `Top 500` *Distinctive Irish singer / songwriter / pianist, b. Raymond O'Sullivan, 1 Dec 1946, Waterford. His unusual image - short trousers, flat cap and pudding-basin haircut - helped to launch the successful international career of the performer voted No.1 UK Male Singer of 1972 (145 WEEKS)*

		pos/wks
28 Nov 70 ●	NOTHING RHYMED *MAM 3*	8 11
3 Apr 71	UNDERNEATH THE BLANKET GO *MAM 13*	40 1
17 Apr 71	UNDERNEATH THE BLANKET GO (re-entry) *MAM 13*	42 3
24 Jul 71	WE WILL *MAM 30*	16 11
27 Nov 71 ●	NO MATTER HOW I TRY *MAM 53*	5 15
4 Mar 72 ●	ALONE AGAIN (NATURALLY) *MAM 66* ▲	3 12
17 Jun 72 ●	OOH-WAKKA-DOO-WAKKA-DAY *MAM 78*	8 11
21 Oct 72 ★	CLAIR *MAM 84*	1 14
17 Mar 73 ★	GET DOWN *MAM 96*	1 13
15 Sep 73	OOH BABY *MAM 107*	18 7
10 Nov 73 ●	WHY OH WHY OH WHY *MAM 111*	6 14
9 Feb 74	HAPPINESS IS ME AND YOU *MAM 114*	19 7
24 Aug 74	A WOMAN'S PLACE *MAM 122*	42 3
14 Dec 74	CHRISTMAS SONG *MAM 124*	12 6
14 Jun 75	I DON'T LOVE YOU BUT I THINK I LIKE YOU *MAM 130*	14 6
27 Sep 80	WHAT'S IN A KISS? *CBS 8929*	19 9
24 Feb 90	SO WHAT *Dover ROJ 3*	70 2

O.T. QUARTET – See OUR TRIBE / ONE TRIBE

OTHER TWO *UK, male / female vocal / instrumental duo (5 WEEKS)* pos/wks

9 Nov 91	TASTY FISH *Factory FAC 3297*	41 3
6 Nov 93	SELFISH *London TWOCD 1*	46 2

Johnny OTIS SHOW *US, band, leader - Jon Veliotes (22 WEEKS)* pos/wks

22 Nov 57 ●	MA (HE'S MAKING EYES AT ME) *Capitol CL 14794* [1]	2 15
10 Jan 58	BYE BYE BABY *Capitol CL 14817* [2]	20 7

[1] Johnny Otis and his orchestra with Marie Adams and the Three Tons of Joy [2] Johnny Otis Show, vocals by Marie Adams and Johnny Otis

OTT *Ireland, male vocal group (18 WEEKS)* pos/wks

1 Mar 97	LET ME IN *Epic 6642052*	12 5
17 May 97	FOREVER GIRL *Epic 6645082*	24 3
23 Aug 97	ALL OUT OF LOVE *Epic 6649152*	11 4
24 Jan 98	THE STORY OF LOVE *Epic OTT 1CD*	11 6

OTTAWAN *France, male / female vocal duo (45 WEEKS)* pos/wks

13 Sep 80 ●	D.I.S.C.O. *Carrere CAR 161*	2 18
13 Dec 80	YOU'RE OK *Carrere CAR 168*	56 6
29 Aug 81 ●	HANDS UP (GIVE ME YOUR HEART) *Carrere CAR 183*	3 15
5 Dec 81	HELP, GET ME SOME HELP! *Carrere CAR 215*	49 6

John OTWAY and Wild Willy BARRETT
UK, male vocal / instrumental duo (12 WEEKS) pos/wks

3 Dec 77	REALLY FREE *Polydor 2058 951*	27 8
5 Jul 80	DK 50-80 *Polydor 2059 250* [1]	45 4

[1] Otway and Barrett

OUI 3 *UK / US / Switzerland, male / female rap / instrumental group (21 WEEKS)* pos/wks

20 Feb 93	FOR WHAT IT'S WORTH *MCA MCSTD 1736*	28 6
24 Apr 93	ARMS OF SOLITUDE *MCA MCSTD 1759*	54 2
17 Jul 93	BREAK FROM THE OLD ROUTINE *MCA MCSTD 1793*	17 6
23 Oct 93	FOR WHAT IT'S WORTH (re-mix) *MCA MCSTD 1941*	26 3
29 Jan 94	FACT OF LIFE *MCA MCSTD 1939*	38 2
27 May 95	JOY OF LIVING *MCA MCSTD 2057*	55 2

OUR DAUGHTER'S WEDDING
US, male vocal / instrumental group (6 WEEKS) pos/wks

1 Aug 81	LAWNCHAIRS *EMI America EA 124*	49 6

UK No.1 ★   UK Top 10 ●   Still on chart +   UK million seller ◆   UK entry at No.1 ■   US No.1 ▲

OUR HOUSE *Australia, male instrumental production duo (1 WEEK)* pos/wks

31 Aug 96	FLOOR SPACE *Perfecto PERF 125CD*	52	1

OUR KID *UK, male vocal group (11 WEEKS)* pos/wks

29 May 76	● YOU JUST MIGHT SEE ME CRY *Polydor 2058 729*	2	11

OUR LADY PEACE *Canada, male vocal / instrumental group (1 WEEK)* pos/wks

15 Jan 00	ONE MAN ARMY *Epic 6688662*	70	1

OUR TRIBE / ONE TRIBE
UK / US, male / female vocal / instrumental group (13 WEEKS) pos/wks

20 Jun 92	WHAT HAVE YOU DONE (IS THIS ALL) *Inner Rhythm HEART 03* [1]	52	2
27 Mar 93	I BELIEVE IN YOU *Ffrreedom TABCD 117* [2]	42	2
30 Apr 94	HOLD THAT SUCKER DOWN *Cheeky CHEKCD 004* [3]	24	3
21 May 94	LOVE COME HOME *Triangle BLUESCD 001* [4]	73	1
13 May 95	HIGH AS A KITE *ffrr FCD 259* [5]	55	1
30 Sep 95	HOLD THAT SUCKER DOWN (re-mix) *Cheeky CHEKCD 009* [3] 26		3
9 Dec 00	HOLD THAT SUCKER DOWN (re-issue) *Champion CHAMPCD 786* [3]	45	1

[1] One Tribe featuring Gem [2] Our Tribe [3] OT Quartet [4] Our Tribe with Franke Pharoah and Kristine W [5] One Tribe featuring Roger

OUT OF MY HAIR *UK, male vocal / instrumental group (1 WEEK)* pos/wks

1 Jul 95	MISTER JONES *RCA 74321267812*	73	1

OUTHERE BROTHERS *US, male rap / vocal duo - Lamar Mahone and Craig Simpkins (50 WEEKS)* pos/wks

18 Mar 95	★ DON'T STOP (WIGGLE WIGGLE) *Eternal YZ 917CD*	1	15
17 Jun 95	★ BOOM BOOM BOOM *Eternal YZ 938CD*	1	15
23 Sep 95	● LA LA LA HEY HEY *Eternal YZ 974CD*	7	7
16 Dec 95	● IF YOU WANNA PARTY *Eternal WEA 030CD* [1]	9	10
25 Jan 97	LET ME HEAR YOU SAY 'OLE OLE' *WEA 089CD*	18	3

[1] Molella featuring the Outhere Brothers

OUTKAST *US, male rap duo (1 WEEK)* pos/wks

23 Dec 00	B.O.B (BOMBS OVER BAGHDAD) *Laface / Arista 74321822942*	61	1

OUTLANDER *Belgium, male producer - Marcos Salon (3 WEEKS)* pos/wks

31 Aug 91	VAMP *R&S RSUK 1*	51	2
7 Feb 98	THE VAMP (REVAMPED) *R&S RS 97113CDX*	62	1

OUTLAWS *UK, male instrumental group (4 WEEKS)* pos/wks

13 Apr 61	SWINGIN' LOW *HMV POP 844*	46	2
8 Jun 61	AMBUSH *HMV POP 877*	43	2

See also Mike BERRY

OUTRAGE *US, male vocalist (2 WEEKS)* pos/wks

11 Mar 95	TALL 'N' HANDSOME *Effective ECFL 001CD*	57	1
23 Nov 96	TALL 'N' HANDSOME (re-mix) *Positiva CDTIV 64*	51	1

OVERLANDERS *UK, male vocal / instrumental group - lead vocal Paul Arnold (10 WEEKS)* pos/wks

13 Jan 66	★ MICHELLE *Pye 7N 17034*	1	10

OVERWEIGHT POOCH featuring Ce Ce PENISTON
US, female rapper and female vocalist (2 WEEKS) pos/wks

18 Jan 92	I LIKE IT *A & M AM 847*	58	2

Mark OWEN *UK, male vocalist (24 WEEKS)* pos/wks

30 Nov 96	● CHILD *RCA 74321424422*	3	11
15 Feb 97	● CLEMENTINE *RCA 74321454982*	3	6
22 Feb 97	CHILD (re-entry) *RCA 74321424422*	45	4
23 Aug 97	I AM WHAT I AM *RCA 74321501222*	29	3

See also TAKE THAT

Reg OWEN *UK, orchestra (10 WEEKS)* pos/wks

27 Feb 59	MANHATTAN SPIRITUAL *Pye International 7N 25009*	20	8
27 Oct 60	OBSESSION *Palette PG 9004*	43	2

Sid OWEN *UK, male vocalist (6 WEEKS)* pos/wks

16 Dec 95	BETTER BELIEVE IT (CHILDREN IN NEED) *Trinity TDM 001CD* [1]	60	1
8 Jul 00	GOOD THING GOING *Mushroom MUSH 74CDS*	14	5

[1] Sid Owen and Patsy Palmer

Robert OWENS *US, male vocalist (4 WEEKS)* pos/wks

7 Dec 91	I'LL BE YOUR FRIEND *Perfecto PB 45161*	75	2
26 Apr 97	I'LL BE YOUR FRIEND (re-mix) *Perfecto PERF 137CD1*	25	2

OXIDE & NEUTRINO *UK, male production / rap duo - Alex Rivers and Mark Oseitutu (12 WEEKS)* pos/wks

6 May 00	★ BOUND 4 DA RELOAD (CASUALTY) *East West OXIDE 01CD1* ■	1	11
30 Dec 00	● NO GOOD 4 ME *East West OXIDE 02CD* [1]	6	1+

[1] Oxide & Neutrino featuring Megaman, Romeo and Lisa Maffia

OZOMATLI *US, male vocal / instrumental group (2 WEEKS)* pos/wks

20 Mar 99	CUT CHEMIST SUITE *Almo Sounds CDALM 62*	58	1
22 May 99	SUPER BOWL SUNDAE *Almo Sounds CDALM 63*	68	1

P J B featuring HANNAH and her SISTERS *Germany, male production group and US female vocalists (8 WEEKS)* pos/wks

14 Sep 91	BRIDGE OVER TROUBLED WATER *Dance Pool 6565467*	21	8

See also Hannah JONES

P J POWERS – See LADYSMITH BLACK MAMBAZO

Jazzi P *UK, female rapper (12 WEEKS)* pos/wks

8 Jul 89	GET LOOSE *Breakout USA 659* [1]	25	6
9 Jun 90	FEEL THE RHYTHM *A&M USA 691*	51	2
3 Aug 91	REBEL WOMAN *DNA 7DNA 001* [2]	42	4

[1] LA Mix featuring Jazzi P [2] DNA featuring Jazzi P

Thom PACE *US, male vocalist (15 WEEKS)* pos/wks

19 May 79	MAYBE *RSO 34*	14	15

PACEMAKERS – See GERRY and the PACEMAKERS

PACIFICA *UK, male production duo (1 WEEK)* pos/wks

31 Jul 99	LOST IN THE TRANSLATION *Wildstar CDWILD 25*	54	1

PACK featuring Nigel BENN
UK, male vocal / instrumental group (2 WEEKS) pos/wks

8 Dec 90	STAND AND FIGHT *IQ ZB 44237*	61	2

PACKABEATS *UK, male instrumental group (1 WEEK)* pos/wks

23 Feb 61	GYPSY BEAT *Parlophone R 4729*	49	1

Jose PADILLA featuring Angela JOHN
Spain, male DJ and UK, female vocalist (1 WEEK) pos/wks

8 Aug 98	WHO DO YOU LOVE *Manifesto FESCD 45*	59	1

PAGANINI TRAXX *Italy, male DJ / producer (1 WEEK)* pos/wks

| 1 Feb 97 | **ZOE** *Sony S3 DANUCD 18X* | 47 | 1 |

Jimmy PAGE *UK, male guitarist (16 WEEKS)* pos/wks

17 Dec 94	**GALLOWS POLE** *Fontana PPCD 2* [1]	35	3
11 Apr 98	**MOST HIGH** *Mercury 5687512* [2]	26	2
1 Aug 98	**COME WITH ME (IMPORT)** *Epic 34K78954* [3]	75	1
8 Aug 98 ●	**COME WITH ME** *Epic 6662842* [3]	2	10

[1] Jimmy Page and Robert Plant [2] Page and Plant [3] Puff Daddy featuring Jimmy Page

See also LED ZEPPELIN

Patti PAGE *US, female vocalist - Clara Ann Fowler (5 WEEKS)* pos/wks

| 27 Mar 53 ● | **(HOW MUCH IS) THAT DOGGIE IN THE WINDOW** *Oriole CB 1156* ▲ | 9 | 5 |

Tommy PAGE *US, male vocalist (3 WEEKS)* pos/wks

| 26 May 90 | **I'LL BE YOUR EVERYTHING** *Sire W 9959* ▲ | 53 | 3 |

Wendy PAGE – See TIN TIN OUT

PAGLIARO *Canada, male vocalist (6 WEEKS)* pos/wks

| 19 Feb 72 | **LOVING YOU AIN'T EASY** *Pye 7N 45111* | 31 | 6 |

PAID & LIVE featuring Lauryn HILL *US, male production duo and female rapper / vocalist (1 WEEK)* pos/wks

| 27 Dec 97 | **ALL MY TIME** *World Entertainment OWECD 2* | 57 | 1 |

Elaine PAIGE *UK, female vocalist - Elaine Bickerstaff (41 WEEKS)* pos/wks

21 Oct 78	**DON'T WALK AWAY TILL I TOUCH YOU** *EMI 2862*	46	5
6 Jun 81 ●	**MEMORY** *Polydor POSP 279*	6	12
30 Jan 82	**MEMORY (re-entry)** *Polydor POSP 279*	67	3
14 Apr 84	**SOMETIMES (THEME FROM 'CHAMPIONS')** *Island IS 174*	72	1
5 Jan 85 ★	**I KNOW HIM SO WELL** *RCA CHESS 3* [1]	1	16
21 Nov 87	**THE SECOND TIME (THEME FROM 'BILITIS')** *WEA YZ 163*	69	1
21 Jan 95	**HYMNE A L'AMOUR (IF YOU LOVE ME)** *WEA YZ 899CD*	68	1
24 Oct 98	**MEMORY (re-recording)** *WEA WEA 197CD*	36	2

[1] Elaine Paige and Barbara Dickson

Hal PAIGE and the WHALERS *US, male vocal / instrumental group (1 WEEK)* pos/wks

| 25 Aug 60 | **GOING BACK TO MY HOME TOWN** *Melodisc MEL 1553* | 50 | 1 |

Jennifer PAIGE *US, female vocalist (13 WEEKS)* pos/wks

| 12 Sep 98 ● | **CRUSH** *EAR 0039425* | 4 | 12 |
| 20 Mar 99 | **SOBER** *EAR / Edel 0044105 ERE* | 68 | 1 |

Orchestre de Chambre Jean-François PAILLARD *France, male conductor and orchestra (3 WEEKS)* pos/wks

| 20 Aug 88 | **THEME FROM 'VIETNAM' (CANON IN D)** *Debut DEBT 3053* | 61 | 3 |

PALE *Ireland, male vocal / instrumental group (2 WEEKS)* pos/wks

| 13 Jun 92 | **DOGS WITH NO TAILS** *A & M AM 866* | 51 | 2 |

PALE FOUNTAINS *UK, male vocal / instrumental group (6 WEEKS)* pos/wks

| 27 Nov 82 | **THANK YOU** *Virgin VS 557* | 48 | 6 |

PALE SAINTS *UK, male / female vocal / instrumental group (1 WEEK)* pos/wks

| 6 Jul 91 | **KINKY LOVE** *4AD AD 1009* | 72 | 1 |

Barry PALMER – See Mike OLDFIELD

Patsy PALMER – See Sid OWEN

Robert PALMER (205) **Top 500** *Grammy-winning UK rock-group veteran, b. 19 Jan 1949, Yorkshire. This vocalist's hottest run of transatlantic hits came after he fronted short-lived Anglo-American supergroup Power Station in 1985. He benefited from some striking award-winning videos featuring an all-female backing band (128 WEEKS)* pos/wks

20 May 78	**EVERY KINDA PEOPLE** *Island WIP 6425*	53	4
7 Jul 79	**BAD CASE OF LOVIN' YOU (DOCTOR DOCTOR)** *Island WIP 6481*	61	2
6 Sep 80	**JOHNNY AND MARY** *Island WIP 6638*	44	8
22 Nov 80	**LOOKING FOR CLUES** *Island WIP 6651*	33	9
13 Feb 82	**SOME GUYS HAVE ALL THE LUCK** *Island WIP 6754*	16	8
2 Apr 83	**YOU ARE IN MY SYSTEM** *Island IS 104*	53	4
18 Jun 83	**YOU CAN HAVE IT (TAKE MY HEART)** *Island IS 121*	66	2
10 May 86 ●	**ADDICTED TO LOVE** *Island IS 270* ▲	5	15
19 Jul 86 ●	**I DIDN'T MEAN TO TURN YOU ON** *Island IS 283*	9	9
1 Nov 86	**DISCIPLINE OF LOVE** *Island IS 242*	68	1
26 Mar 88	**SWEET LIES** *Island IS 352*	58	3
11 Jun 88	**SIMPLY IRRESISTABLE** *EMI EM 61*	44	4
15 Oct 88 ●	**SHE MAKES MY DAY** *EMI EM 65*	6	12
13 May 89	**CHANGE HIS WAYS** *EMI EM 85*	28	7
26 Aug 89	**IT COULD HAPPEN TO YOU** *EMI EM 99*	71	1
3 Nov 90 ●	**I'LL BE YOUR BABY TONIGHT** *EMI EM 167* [1]	6	10
5 Jan 91 ●	**MERCY MERCY ME - I WANT YOU** *EMI EM 173*	9	9
15 Jun 91	**DREAMS TO REMEMBER** *EMI EM 193*	68	1
7 Mar 92	**EVERY KINDA PEOPLE (re-mix)** *Island IS 498*	43	3
17 Oct 92	**WITCHCRAFT** *EMI EM 251*	50	3
9 Jul 94	**GIRL U WANT** *EMI CDEMS 331*	57	2
3 Sep 94	**KNOW BY NOW** *EMI CDEMS 343*	25	5
24 Dec 94	**YOU BLOW ME AWAY** *EMI CDEMS 350*	38	4
14 Oct 95	**RESPECT YOURSELF** *EMI CDEMS 399*	45	2

[1] Robert Palmer and UB40

Suzanne PALMER – See CLUB 69; ABSOLUTE

PAN POSITION *Italy / Venezuela, male instrumental / production group (1 WEEK)* pos/wks

| 18 Jun 94 | **ELEPHANT PAW (GET DOWN TO THE FUNK)** *Positiva CDTIV 13* | 55 | 1 |

PANDORA'S BOX *US, male / female vocal / instrumental group (3 WEEKS)* pos/wks

| 21 Oct 89 | **IT'S ALL COMING BACK TO ME NOW** *Virgin VS 1216* | 51 | 3 |

Darryl PANDY *US, male vocalist (5 WEEKS)* pos/wks

14 Dec 96	**LOVE CAN'T TURN AROUND** *4 Liberty LIBTCD 27* [1]	40	2
20 Feb 99	**RAISE YOUR HANDS** *VC Recordings VCRD 44* [2]	40	2
2 Oct 99	**SUNSHINE & HAPPINESS** *Azuli AZNYCD 103* [3]	68	1

[1] Farley 'Jackmaster' Funk with Darryl Pandy. [2] Big Room Girl featuring Darryl Pandy [3] Darryl Pandy / Nerio's Dubwork

Johnny PANIC and the BIBLE OF DREAMS *UK, male / female vocal / instrumental group (2 WEEKS)* pos/wks

| 2 Feb 91 | **JOHNNY PANIC AND THE BIBLE OF DREAMS** *Fontana PANIC 1* | 70 | 2 |

See also TEARS FOR FEARS

PANTERA *US, male vocal / instrumental group (8 WEEKS)* pos/wks

10 Oct 92	**MOUTH FOR WAR** *Atco A 5845T*	73	1
27 Feb 93	**WALK** *Atco B 6076CD*	35	2
19 Mar 94	**I'M BROKEN** *Atco B 5932CD1*	19	2
22 Oct 94	**PLANET CARAVAN** *East West A 5836CD1*	26	3

PAPER DOLLS *UK, female vocal group (13 WEEKS)* pos/wks

| 13 Mar 68 | **SOMETHING HERE IN MY HEART (KEEPS A-TELLIN' ME NO)** *Pye 7N 17456* | 11 | 13 |

UK No.1 ★   UK Top 10 ●   Still on chart +   UK million seller ◆   UK entry at No.1 ■   US No.1 ▲

PAPER LACE
UK, male vocal / instrumental group - lead vocal Phil Wright
(41 WEEKS)   pos/wks

23 Feb 74 ★	BILLY DON'T BE A HERO *Bus Stop BUS 1014*	1	14
4 May 74 ●	THE NIGHT CHICAGO DIED *Bus Stop BUS 1016* ▲	3	11
24 Aug 74	THE BLACK EYED BOYS *Bus Stop BUS 1019*	11	10
4 Mar 78	WE'VE GOT THE WHOLE WORLD IN OUR HANDS *Warner Bros. K 17110*	24	6

PAPERDOLLS
UK, female vocal group (1 WEEK)   pos/wks

| 12 Sep 98 | GONNA MAKE YOU BLUSH *MCA MCSTD 40175* | 65 | 1 |

PAPPA BEAR featuring VAN DER TOORN
Germany, male rapper, and Holland, male vocalist (1 WEEK)   pos/wks

| 16 May 98 | CHERISH *Universal UMD 70316* | 47 | 1 |

Vanessa PARADIS
France, female vocalist (30 WEEKS)   pos/wks

13 Feb 88 ●	JOE LE TAXI *FA Productions POSP 902*	3	10
10 Oct 92 ●	BE MY BABY *Remark PO 235*	6	15
27 Feb 93	SUNDAY MONDAYS *Remark PZCD 251*	49	4
24 Jul 93	JUST AS LONG AS YOU ARE THERE *Remark PZCD 272*	57	1

PARADISE
UK, male vocal / instrumental group (4 WEEKS)   pos/wks

| 10 Sep 83 | ONE MIND, TWO HEARTS *Priority P 1* | 42 | 4 |

PARADISE LOST
UK, male vocal / instrumental group (3 WEEKS)   pos/wks

20 May 95	THE LAST TIME *Music For Nations CDKUT 165*	60	1
7 Oct 95	FOREVER FAILURE *Music For Nations CDKUT 169*	66	1
28 Jun 97	SAY JUST WORDS *Music For Nations CDKUT 174*	53	1

PARADISE ORGANISATION
UK, male instrumental / production group (1 WEEK)   pos/wks

| 23 Jan 93 | PRAYER TOWER *Cowboy RODEO 13* | 70 | 1 |

PARADOX
UK, male instrumental duo (2 WEEKS)   pos/wks

| 24 Feb 90 | JAILBREAK *Ronin 7R2* | 66 | 2 |

Norrie PARAMOR
UK, orchestra (8 WEEKS)   pos/wks

| 17 Mar 60 | THEME FROM 'A SUMMER PLACE' *Columbia DB 4419* | 36 | 2 |
| 22 Mar 62 | THEME FROM 'Z CARS' *Columbia DB 4789* | 33 | 6 |

PARAMOUNT JAZZ BAND – See Mr Acker BILK and his PARAMOUNT JAZZ BAND

PARAMOUNTS
UK, male vocal / instrumental group (7 WEEKS)   pos/wks

| 16 Jan 64 | POISON IVY *Parlophone R 5093* | 35 | 7 |

PARCHMENT
UK, male / female vocal / instrumental group (5 WEEKS)   pos/wks

| 16 Sep 72 | LIGHT UP THE FIRE *Pye 7N 45178* | 31 | 5 |

PARIS
UK, male / female vocal group (4 WEEKS)   pos/wks

| 19 Jun 82 | NO GETTING OVER YOU *RCA 222* | 49 | 4 |

PARIS
US, male vocalist (2 WEEKS)   pos/wks

| 21 Jan 95 | GUERRILLA FUNK *Priority PTYCD 100* | 38 | 2 |

PARIS ANGELS
UK, male / female vocal / instrumental group (5 WEEKS)   pos/wks

3 Nov 90	SCOPE *Sheer Joy SHEER 0047*	75	1
20 Jul 91	PERFUME *Virgin VS 1360*	55	3
21 Sep 91	FADE *Virgin VS 1365*	70	1

Mica PARIS
UK, female vocalist - Michelle Wallen (63 WEEKS)   pos/wks

7 May 88 ●	MY ONE TEMPTATION *Fourth & Broadway BRW 85*	7	11
30 Jul 88	LIKE DREAMERS DO *Fourth & Broadway BRW 108* [1]	26	5
22 Oct 88	BREATHE LIFE INTO ME *Fourth & Broadway BRW 115*	26	10
21 Jan 89	WHERE IS THE LOVE *Fourth & Broadway BRW 122* [2]	19	7
6 Oct 90	CONTRIBUTION *Fourth & Broadway BRW 188*	33	4
1 Dec 90	SOUTH OF THE RIVER *Fourth & Broadway BRW 199*	50	2
23 Feb 91	IF I LOVE U 2 NITE *Fourth & Broadway BRW 207*	43	3
31 Aug 91	YOUNG SOUL REBELS *Big Life BLR 57*	61	3
3 Apr 93	I NEVER FELT LIKE THIS BEFORE *Fourth & Broadway BRCD 263*	15	5
5 Jun 93	I WANNA HOLD ON TO YOU *Fourth & Broadway BRCD 275*	27	3
7 Aug 93	TWO IN A MILLION *Fourth & Broadway BRCD 285*	51	2
4 Dec 93	WHISPER A PRAYER *Fourth & Broadway BRCD 287*	65	1
8 Apr 95	ONE *Cooltempo CDCOOL 304*	29	4
16 May 98	STAY *Cooltempo CDCOOL 334*	40	2
14 Nov 98	BLACK ANGEL *Cooltempo CDCOOL 341*	72	1

[1] Mica Paris featuring Courtney Pine [2] Mica Paris and Will Downing

PARIS RED
US / Germany, male / female vocal / instrumental duo (2 WEEKS) pos/wks

| 29 Feb 92 | GOOD FRIEND *Columbia 6569417* | 61 | 1 |
| 15 May 93 | PROMISES *Columbia 6592342* | 59 | 1 |

Ryan PARIS
France, male vocalist - Fabio Roscioli (10 WEEKS)   pos/wks

| 3 Sep 83 ● | DOLCE VITA *Carrere CAR 289* | 5 | 10 |

John PARISH and Polly Jean HARVEY
US, male producer / instrumentalist and female vocalist (1 WEEK) pos/wks

| 23 Nov 96 | THAT WAS MY VEIL *Island CID 648* | 75 | 1 |

See also P J HARVEY

Simon PARK
UK, orchestra (24 WEEKS)   pos/wks

| 25 Nov 72 | EYE LEVEL *Columbia DB 8946* ◆ | 41 | 2 |
| 15 Sep 73 ★ | EYE LEVEL (re-entry) *Columbia DB 8946* | 1 | 22 |

Graham PARKER and the RUMOUR
UK, male vocal / instrumental group (16 WEEKS)   pos/wks

19 Mar 77	THE PINK PARKER EP *Vertigo PARK 001*	24	5
22 Apr 78	HEY LORD DON'T ASK ME QUESTIONS *Vertigo PARK 002*	32	7
20 Mar 82	TEMPORARY BEAUTY *RCA PARK 100* [1]	50	4

[1] Graham Parker

Tracks on The Pink Parker EP: Hold Back the Night / (Let Me Get) Sweet on You / White Honey / Soul Shoes

Ray PARKER Jr
US, male vocalist (47 WEEKS)   pos/wks

25 Aug 84 ●	GHOSTBUSTERS *Arista ARIST 580* ▲	2	31
18 Jan 86	GIRLS ARE MORE FUN *Arista ARIST 641*	46	4
3 Oct 87	I DON'T THINK THAT MAN SHOULD SLEEP ALONE *Geffen GEF 27*	13	10
30 Jan 88	OVER YOU *Geffen GEF 33*	65	2

See also RAYDIO

Robert PARKER
US, male vocalist (8 WEEKS)   pos/wks

| 4 Aug 66 | BAREFOOTIN' *Island WI 286* | 24 | 8 |

Sara PARKER
US, female vocalist (2 WEEKS)   pos/wks

| 12 Apr 97 | MY LOVE IS DEEP *Manifesto FESCD 22* | 22 | 2 |

Jimmy PARKINSON
Australia, male vocalist (19 WEEKS)   pos/wks

2 Mar 56 ●	THE GREAT PRETENDER *Columbia DB 3729* ▲	9	13
17 Aug 56	WALK HAND IN HAND *Columbia DB 3775*	30	1
5 Oct 56	WALK HAND IN HAND (re-entry) *Columbia DB 3775*	26	1
9 Nov 56	IN THE MIDDLE OF THE HOUSE *Columbia DB 3833*	26	2
30 Nov 56	IN THE MIDDLE OF THE HOUSE (re-entry) *Columbia DB 3833*	20	2

UK No.1 ★   UK Top 10 ●   Still on chart +   UK million seller ◆   UK entry at No.1 ■   US No.1 ▲

PARKS & WILSON
UK, male production duo – Michael Parks and Michael Wilson (1 WEEK)   pos/wks

9 Sep 00	**FEEL THE DRUM (EP)**		
	Hooj Choons HOOJ 099	71	1

Tracks on Feel The Drum (EP): My Orbit / The Dragon / My Orbit / Drum Parade (No UFOs)

PARLIAMENT – See Scott GROOVES

John PARR
UK, male vocalist (22 WEEKS)   pos/wks

14 Sep 85 ●	**ST ELMO'S FIRE (MAN IN MOTION)**		
	London LON 73 ▲	6	13
18 Jan 86	**NAUGHTY NAUGHTY** *London LON 80*	58	3
30 Aug 86	**ROCK 'N' ROLL MERCENARIES** *Arista ARIST 666* [1]	31	6

[1] Meat Loaf featuring John Parr

Dean PARRISH
US, male vocalist (5 WEEKS)   pos/wks

8 Feb 75	**I'M ON MY WAY** *UK USA 2*	38	5

Man PARRISH
US, male mixer (26 WEEKS)   pos/wks

26 Mar 83	**HIP HOP, BE BOP (DON'T STOP)** *Polydor POSP 575*	41	6
23 Mar 85	**BOOGIE DOWN (BRONX)** *Boiling Point POSP 731*	56	4
13 Sep 86	**MALE STRIPPER** *Bolts BOLTS 4* [1]	64	3
3 Jan 87	**MALE STRIPPER (re-entry)** *Bolts BOLTS 4* [1]	63	1
7 Feb 87 ●	**MALE STRIPPER (2nd re-entry)**		
	Bolts BOLTS 4 [1]	4	12

[1] Man 2 Man meet Man Parrish

Bill PARSONS
US, male vocalist (2 WEEKS)   pos/wks

10 Apr 59	**ALL AMERICAN BOY** *London HL 8798*	22	2

Record erroneously credited to Bill Parsons; actual vocalist is Bobby Bare

Alan PARSONS PROJECT
UK, male vocal / instrumental group (4 WEEKS)   pos/wks

15 Jan 83	**OLD AND WISE** *Arista ARIST 494*	74	1
10 Mar 84	**DON'T ANSWER ME** *Arista ARIST 553*	58	3

PARTIZAN
UK, male DJ / production duo – 'Tall Paul' Newman and Craig Daniel-Yefet (3 WEEKS)   pos/wks

8 Feb 97	**DRIVE ME CRAZY** *Multiply CDMULTY 17*	36	2
6 Dec 97	**KEEP YOUR LOVE** *Multiply CDMULTY 29* [1]	53	1

[1] Partizan featuring Natalie Robb

See also TALL PAUL; ESCRIMA; CAMISRA; GRIFTERS

PARTNERS – See Al HUDSON

PARTNERS IN KRYME
US, male rap duo – James Alpem and Richard Usher (10 WEEKS)   pos/wks

21 Jul 90 ★	**TURTLE POWER** *SBK TURTLE 1*	1	10

David PARTON
UK, male vocalist (9 WEEKS)   pos/wks

15 Jan 77 ●	**ISN'T SHE LOVELY** *Pye 7N 45663*	4	9

Dolly PARTON
US, female vocalist (33 WEEKS)   pos/wks

15 May 76 ●	**JOLENE** *RCA 2675*	7	10
21 Feb 81	**9 TO 5** *RCA 25* ▲	47	5
12 Nov 83 ●	**ISLANDS IN THE STREAM** *RCA 378* [1] ▲	7	15
7 Apr 84	**HERE YOU COME AGAIN** *RCA 395*	75	1
16 Apr 94	**THE DAY I FALL IN LOVE**		
	Columbia 6600282 [2]	64	2

[1] Kenny Rogers and Dolly Parton [2] Dolly Parton and James Ingram

Stella PARTON
US, female vocalist (4 WEEKS)   pos/wks

22 Oct 77	**THE DANGER OF A STRANGER** *Elektra K 12272*	35	4

Don PARTRIDGE
UK, male vocalist / instrumentalist – one-man band (32 WEEKS)   pos/wks

7 Feb 68 ●	**ROSIE** *Columbia DB 8330*	4	12
29 May 68 ●	**BLUE EYES** *Columbia DB 8416*	3	13
19 Feb 69	**BREAKFAST ON PLUTO** *Columbia DB 8538*	26	7

PARTRIDGE FAMILY
US, male / female vocal group (53 WEEKS)   pos/wks

13 Feb 71	**I THINK I LOVE YOU** *Bell 1130* [1] ▲	18	9
26 Feb 72	**IT'S ONE OF THOSE NIGHTS (YES LOVE)** *Bell 1203* [1]	11	11
8 Jul 72 ●	**BREAKING UP IS HARD TO DO** *Bell MABEL 1* [1]	3	13
3 Feb 73 ●	**LOOKING THROUGH THE EYES OF LOVE** *Bell 1278* [2]	9	9
19 May 73 ●	**WALKING IN THE RAIN** *Bell 1293* [2]	10	11

[1] Partridge Family starring Shirley Jones featuring David Cassidy [2] Partridge Family starring David Cassidy

See also David CASSIDY

PARTY ANIMALS
Holland, male instrumental / production duo (3 WEEKS)   pos/wks

1 Jun 96	**HAVE YOU EVER BEEN MELLOW** *Mokum DB 17553*	56	1
19 Oct 96	**HAVE YOU EVER BEEN MELLOW (EP)** *Mokum DB 17413*	43	2

Tracks on Have You Ever Been Mellow (EP): Have You Ever Been Mellow / Hava Naquilla / Aquarius

PARTY FAITHFUL
UK, male / female vocal / instrumental group (1 WEEK)   pos/wks

22 Jul 95	**BRASS: LET THERE BE HOUSE** *Ore AG 10CD*	54	1

PASADENAS
UK, male vocal group (57 WEEKS)   pos/wks

28 May 88 ●	**TRIBUTE (RIGHT ON)** *CBS PASA 1*	5	14
17 Sep 88	**RIDING ON A TRAIN** *CBS PASA 2*	13	9
26 Nov 88	**ENCHANTED LADY** *CBS PASA 3*	31	6
12 May 90	**LOVE THING** *CBS PASA 4*	22	5
14 Jul 90	**REELING** *CBS PASA 5*	75	1
1 Feb 92 ●	**I'M DOING FINE NOW** *Columbia 6577187*	4	10
4 Apr 92	**MAKE IT WITH YOU** *Columbia 6579257*	20	4
6 Jun 92	**I BELIEVE IN MIRACLES** *Columbia 6580567*	34	3
29 Aug 92	**MOVING IN THE RIGHT DIRECTION** *Columbia 6583417*	49	2
21 Nov 92	**LET'S STAY TOGETHER** *Columbia 6587747*	22	3

PASSENGERS
Ireland / UK / Italy, male vocal / instrumental group (9 WEEKS)   pos/wks

2 Dec 95 ●	**MISS SARAJEVO** *Island CID 625*	6	9

PASSION
UK, male vocal / rap group (1 WEEK)   pos/wks

25 Jan 97	**SHARE YOUR LOVE (NO DIGGITY)** *Charm CRTCDS 269*	62	1

PASSIONS
UK, male / female vocal / instrumental group (8 WEEKS)   pos/wks

31 Jan 81	**I'M IN LOVE WITH A GERMAN FILM STAR** *Polydor POSP 222*	25	8

PAT and MICK
UK, male vocal duo – Pat Sharp and Mick Brown (27 WEEKS)   pos/wks

9 Apr 88	**LET'S ALL CHANT / ON THE NIGHT** *PWL PWL 10* [1]	11	9
25 Mar 89 ●	**I HAVEN'T STOPPED DANCING YET** *PWL PWL 33*	9	8
14 Apr 90	**USE IT UP AND WEAR IT OUT** *PWL PWL 55*	22	6
23 Mar 91	**GIMME SOME** *PWL PWL 75*	53	2
15 May 93	**HOT HOT HOT** *PWL International PARKCD 1*	47	2

[1] Mick and Pat

'On the Night' listed only from 4 Jun 1988. It peaked at No.70

PATIENCE and PRUDENCE
US, female vocal duo (8 WEEKS)   pos/wks

2 Nov 56	**TONIGHT YOU BELONG TO ME** *London HLU 8321*	28	3
1 Mar 57	**GONNA GET ALONG WITHOUT YA NOW** *London HLU 8369*	22	4
12 Apr 57	**GONNA GET ALONG WITHOUT YA NOW (re-entry)**		
	London HLU 8369	24	1

PATRA Jamaica, female vocalist (11 WEEKS)
pos/wks

25 Dec 93	FAMILY AFFAIR *Polydor PZCD 304* [1]	18	8
30 Sep 95	PULL UP TO THE BUMPER *Epic 6623942*	50	2
10 Aug 96	WORK MI BODY *Heavenly HVN 53CD* [2]	75	1

[1] Shabba Ranks featuring Patra and Terri & Monica [2] Monkey Mafia featuring Patra

PATRIC UK, male vocalist (2 WEEKS)
pos/wks

| 9 Jul 94 | LOVE ME *Bell 7432125352* .... | 54 | 2 |

Dee PATTEN UK, male DJ / producer (1 WEEK)
pos/wks

| 30 Jan 99 | WHO'S THE BAD MAN? *Higher Ground HIGHS 15CD* .... | 42 | 1 |

Kellee PATTERSON US, female vocalist (7 WEEKS)
pos/wks

| 18 Feb 78 | IF IT DON'T FIT DON'T FORCE IT *EMI International INT 544* ..... | 44 | 7 |

Rahsaan PATTERSON US, male vocalist (2 WEEKS)
pos/wks

| 26 Jul 97 | STOP BY *MCA MCSTD 48055* .... | 50 | 1 |
| 21 Mar 98 | WHERE YOU ARE *MCA MCSTD 48073* .... | 55 | 1 |

Billy PAUL US, male vocalist (44 WEEKS)
pos/wks

13 Jan 73	ME AND MRS JONES *Epic EPC 1055* ▲	12	9
12 Jan 74	THANKS FOR SAVING MY LIFE		
	Philadelphia International PIR 1928	33	6
22 May 76	LET'S MAKE A BABY		
	Philadelphia International PIR 4144	30	5
30 Apr 77	LET 'EM IN		
	Philadelphia International PIR 5143	26	5
16 Jul 77	YOUR SONG		
	Philadelphia International PIR 5391	37	7
19 Nov 77	ONLY THE STRONG SURVIVE		
	Philadelphia International PIR 5699	33	7
14 Jul 79	BRING THE FAMILY BACK		
	Philadelphia International PIR 7456	51	5

Chris PAUL UK, male producer / instrumentalist - guitar (8 WEEKS)
pos/wks

31 May 86	EXPANSIONS '86 (EXPAND YOUR MIND)		
	Fourth & Broadway BRW 48 [1]	58	5
21 Nov 87	BACK IN MY ARMS *Syncopate SY 5*	74	2
13 Aug 88	TURN THE MUSIC UP *Syncopate SY 13*	73	1

[1] Chris Paul featuring David Joseph

See also ISOTONIK

Frankie PAUL – See APACHE INDIAN

Les PAUL and Mary FORD
US, male instrumentalist - guitar, and female vocalist (4 WEEKS)
pos/wks

| 20 Nov 53 | ● VAYA CON DIOS (MAY GOD BE WITH YOU) *Capitol CL 13943* ▲ .... | 7 | 4 |

Lyn PAUL UK, female vocalist (6 WEEKS)
pos/wks

| 28 Jun 75 | IT OUGHTA SELL A MILLION *Polydor 2058 602* .... | 37 | 6 |

See also NEW SEEKERS

Owen PAUL UK, male vocalist - Owen McGee (14 WEEKS)
pos/wks

| 31 May 86 | ● MY FAVOURITE WASTE OF TIME *Epic A 7125* .... | 3 | 14 |

PAUL and PAULA US, male / female vocal duo - Ray Hildebrand and Jill Jackson (31 WEEKS)
pos/wks

14 Feb 63	● HEY PAULA *Philips 304012 BF* ▲	8	12
18 Apr 63	● YOUNG LOVERS *Philips 304016 BF*	9	14
16 May 63	HEY PAULA (re-entry) *Philips 304012 BF*	37	5

Luciano PAVAROTTI Italy, male vocalist (30 WEEKS)
pos/wks

16 Jun 90	● NESSUN DORMA *Decca PAV 03*	2	11
24 Oct 92	MISERERE *London LON 329* [1]	15	4
30 Jul 94	LIBIAMO / LA DONNA E MOBILE *Teldec YZ 843CD* [2] ...	21	4

| 14 Dec 96 | ● LIVE LIKE HORSES *Rocket LLHDD 1* [3] .... | 9 | 6 |
| 25 Jul 98 | YOU'LL NEVER WALK ALONE *Decca 4607982* [4] .... | 35 | 4 |

[1] Zucchero with Luciano Pavarotti [2] JosÈ Carreras featuring Placido Domingo and Luciano Pavarotti with Mehta [3] Elton John and Luciano Pavarotti [4] JosÈ Carreras, Placido Domingo and Luciano Pavarotti with Mehta

PAVEMENT US, male vocal / instrumental group (6 WEEKS)
pos/wks

28 Nov 92	WATERY, DOMESTIC (EP) *Big Cat ABB 38T*	58	1
12 Feb 94	CUT YOUR HAIR *Big Cat ABB 55SCD*	52	1
8 Feb 97	STEREO *Domino RUG 51CD*	48	1
3 May 97	SHADY LANE *Domino RUG 53CD*	40	1
22 May 99	CARROT ROPE *Domino RUG 90CD1*	27	2

Tracks on Watery, Domestic (EP): Texas Never Whispers / Frontwards / Feed 'Em / The Linden Lions / Shoot The Singer (1 Sick Verse)

Rita PAVONE Italy, female vocalist (19 WEEKS)
pos/wks

| 1 Dec 66 | HEART *RCA 1553* .... | 27 | 12 |
| 19 Jan 67 | YOU ONLY YOU *RCA 1561* .... | 21 | 7 |

Freda PAYNE US, female vocalist (30 WEEKS)
pos/wks

5 Sep 70	★ BAND OF GOLD *Invictus INV 502*	1	19
21 Nov 70	DEEPER AND DEEPER *Invictus INV 505*	33	9
27 Mar 71	CHERISH WHAT IS DEAR TO YOU *Invictus INV 509*	46	2

Tammy PAYNE UK, female vocalist (2 WEEKS)
pos/wks

| 20 Jul 91 | TAKE ME NOW *Talkin Loud TLK 12* .... | 55 | 2 |

PEACE BY PIECE UK, male vocal group (2 WEEKS)
pos/wks

| 21 Sep 96 | SWEET SISTER *Blanco Y Negro NEG 94CD* .... | 46 | 1 |
| 25 Apr 98 | NOBODY'S BUSINESS *Blanco Y Negro NEG 110CD1* ...... | 50 | 1 |

Heather PEACE UK, female vocalist (1 WEEK)
pos/wks

| 13 May 00 | THE ROSE *RCA 74321742892* .... | 56 | 1 |

PEACH UK / Belgium, female / male vocal / production group (1 WEEK)
pos/wks

| 17 Jan 98 | ON MY OWN *Mute CDMUTE 215* .... | 69 | 1 |

PEACHES and HERB US, female / male vocal duo - Linda Green and Herbert Feemster (23 WEEKS)
pos/wks

| 20 Jan 79 | SHAKE YOUR GROOVE THING *Polydor 2066 892* .... | 26 | 10 |
| 21 Apr 79 | ● REUNITED *Polydor POSP 43* ▲ .... | 4 | 13 |

Mary PEARCE – See UP YER RONSON featuring Mary PEARCE

PEARL JAM US, male vocal / instrumental group (41 WEEKS)
pos/wks

15 Feb 92	ALIVE *Epic 6575727*	16	6
18 Apr 92	EVEN FLOW *Epic 6578577*	27	3
26 Sep 92	JEREMY *Epic 6582587*	15	4
1 Jan 94	DAUGHTER *Epic 6600202*	18	5
28 May 94	DISSIDENT *Epic 6604415*	14	4
26 Nov 94	● SPIN THE BLACK CIRCLE *Epic 6610362*	10	3
25 Feb 95	NOT FOR YOU *Epic 6612032*	34	2
16 Dec 95	I GOT ID *Epic 6627162*	25	3
17 Aug 96	WHO YOU ARE *Epic 6635392*	18	2
31 Jan 98	GIVEN TO FLY *Epic 6653942*	12	3
23 May 98	WISHLIST *Epic 6657902*	30	2
14 Aug 99	LAST KISS *Epic 6674791*	42	1
13 May 00	NOTHING AS IT SEEMS *Epic 6693742*	22	2
22 Jul 00	LIGHT YEARS *Epic 6696282*	52	1

Natasha PEARL – See TASTE XPERIENCE featuring NATASHA PEARL

PEARLS UK, female vocal duo (24 WEEKS)
pos/wks

27 May 72	THIRD FINGER, LEFT HAND *Bell 1217*	31	6
23 Sep 72	YOU CAME YOU SAW YOU CONQUERED *Bell 1254*	32	5
24 Mar 73	YOU ARE EVERYTHING *Bell 1284*	41	3
1 Jun 74	● GUILTY *Bell 1352*	10	10

UK No.1 ★ UK Top 10 ● Still on chart + UK million seller ◆ UK entry at No.1 ■ US No.1 ▲

Johnny PEARSON
UK, orchestra, Johnny Pearson - piano (15 WEEKS)   pos/wks

18 Dec 71 ●	SLEEPY SHORES *Penny Farthing PEN 778*	8	15

PEBBLES
US, female vocalist - Perri McKissack (17 WEEKS)   pos/wks

19 Mar 88 ●	GIRLFRIEND *MCA MCA 1233*	8	11
28 May 88	MERCEDES BOY *MCA MCA 1248*	42	4
27 Oct 90	GIVING YOU THE BENEFIT *MCA MCA 1448*	73	2

PEDDLERS
UK, male vocal / instrumental group (14 WEEKS)   pos/wks

7 Jan 65	LET THE SUNSHINE IN *Philips BF 1375*	50	1
23 Aug 69	BIRTH *CBS 4449*	17	9
31 Jan 70	GIRLIE *CBS 4720*	34	4

PEE BEE SQUAD
UK, male vocalist - Paul Burnett (3 WEEKS)   pos/wks

5 Oct 85	RUGGED AND MEAN, BUTCH AND ON SCREEN *Project PRO 3*	52	3

Ann PEEBLES
US, female vocalist (3 WEEKS)   pos/wks

20 Apr 74	I CAN'T STAND THE RAIN *London HL 10428*	50	1
4 May 74	I CAN'T STAND THE RAIN (re-entry) *London HL 10428*	41	2

PEECH BOYS
US, male vocal / instrumental group (3 WEEKS)   pos/wks

30 Oct 82	DON'T MAKE ME WAIT *TMT TMT 7001*	49	3

Donald PEERS
UK, male vocalist (27 WEEKS)   pos/wks

18 Dec 68 ●	PLEASE DON'T GO *Columbia DB 8502*	3	18
30 Apr 69	PLEASE DON'T GO (re-entry) *Columbia DB 8502*	38	3
24 Jun 72	GIVE ME ONE MORE CHANCE *Decca F 13302*	36	6

PELE
UK, male / female vocal / instrumental group (3 WEEKS)   pos/wks

15 Feb 92	MEGALOMANIA *M & G MAGS 20*	73	1
13 Jun 92	FAIR BLOWS THE WIND FOR FRANCE *M & G MAGS 24*	62	1
31 Jul 93	FAT BLACK HEART *M & G MAGCD 43*	75	1

Debbie PENDER
US, female vocalist (1 WEEK)   pos/wks

30 May 98	MOVIN' ON *AM:PM 5826492*	41	1

Teddy PENDERGRASS
US, male vocalist (24 WEEKS)   pos/wks

21 May 77	THE WHOLE TOWN'S LAUGHING AT ME *Philadelphia International PIR 5116*	44	3
28 Oct 78	ONLY YOU / CLOSE THE DOOR *Philadelphia International PIR 6713*	41	6
23 May 81	TWO HEARTS *20th Century TC 2492* [1]	49	5
25 Jan 86	HOLD ME *Asylum EKR 32* [2]	44	5
28 May 88	JOY *Elektra EKR 75*	58	3
19 Nov 94	THE MORE I GET THE MORE I WANT *X-clusive XCLU 011CD* [3]	35	2

[1] Stephanie Mills featuring Teddy Pendergrass [2] Teddy Pendergrass with Whitney Houston [3] KWS featuring Teddy Pendergrass

Ce Ce PENISTON
US, female vocalist (53 WEEKS)   pos/wks

12 Oct 91	FINALLY *A & M AM 822*	29	7
11 Jan 92 ●	WE GOT A LOVE THANG *A & M AM 846*	6	8
18 Jan 92	I LIKE IT *A & M AM 847*	58	2
21 Mar 92 ●	FINALLY (re-issue) *A & M AM 858*	2	8
23 May 92 ●	KEEP ON WALKIN' *A & M AM 878*	10	6
5 Sep 92	CRAZY LOVE *A & M AM 0060*	44	3
12 Dec 92	INSIDE THAT I CRIED *A & M AM 0121*	42	2
15 Jan 94	I'M IN THE MOOD *A & M 5804552*	16	4
2 Apr 94	KEEP GIVIN' ME YOUR LOVE *A & M 5805492*	36	2
6 Aug 94	HIT BY LOVE *A & M 5806932*	33	2
13 Sep 97	FINALLY (re-mix) *AM:PM 5823432*	26	5
7 Feb 98	SOMEBODY ELSE'S GUY *AM:PM 5825112*	13	4

Dawn PENN
Jamaica, female vocalist - Dawn Pickering (12 WEEKS)   pos/wks

11 Jun 94 ●	YOU DON'T LOVE ME (NO, NO, NO) *Big Beat A 8295CD*	3	12

Barbara PENNINGTON
US, female vocalist (8 WEEKS)   pos/wks

27 Apr 85	FAN THE FLAME *Record Shack SOHO 37*	62	3
27 Jul 85	ON A CROWDED STREET *Record Shack SOHO 49*	57	5

Tricia PENROSE
UK, female vocalist (2 WEEKS)   pos/wks

7 Dec 96	WHERE DID OUR LOVE GO *RCA 74321428152*	71	1
4 Mar 00	DON'T WANNA BE ALONE *Doop DP 2001CD*	44	1

PENTANGLE
UK, male / female vocal / instrumental group (4 WEEKS)   pos/wks

28 May 69	ONCE I HAD A SWEETHEART *Big T BIG 124*	46	1
14 Feb 70	LIGHT FLIGHT *Big T BIG 128*	43	1
28 Feb 70	LIGHT FLIGHT (re-entry) *Big T BIG 128*	45	2

PENTHOUSE 4
UK, male vocal / instrumental duo (3 WEEKS)   pos/wks

23 Apr 88	BUST THIS HOUSE DOWN *Syncopate SY 10*	56	3

PEOPLES CHOICE
US, male vocal / instrumental group (9 WEEKS)   pos/wks

20 Sep 75	DO IT ANYWAY YOU WANNA *Philadelphia International PIR 3500*	36	5
21 Jan 78	JAM JAM JAM *Philadelphia International PIR 5891*	40	4

Danny PEPPERMINT and the JUMPING JACKS
US, male vocal / instrumental group (8 WEEKS)   pos/wks

18 Jan 62	PEPPERMINT TWIST *London HLL 9478*	26	8

PEPPERS
France, male instrumental group (12 WEEKS)   pos/wks

26 Oct 74 ●	PEPPER BOX *Spark SRL 1100*	6	12

PEPSI and SHIRLIE
UK, female vocal duo - Helen DeMacque and Shirley Holliman (24 WEEKS)   pos/wks

17 Jan 87 ●	HEARTACHE *Polydor POSP 837*	2	12
30 May 87 ●	GOODBYE STRANGER *Polydor POSP 865*	9	7
26 Sep 87	CAN'T GIVE ME LOVE *Polydor POSP 885*	58	3
12 Dec 87	ALL RIGHT NOW *Polydor POSP 896*	50	2

PERCEPTION
UK, male vocal group (2 WEEKS)   pos/wks

7 Mar 92	FEED THE FEELING *Talkin Loud TLK 17*	58	2

The listed flip side of 'Feed the Feeling' was 'Three Times a Maybe' by K-Creative

Lance PERCIVAL
UK, male vocalist (3 WEEKS)   pos/wks

28 Oct 65	SHAME AND SCANDAL IN THE FAMILY *Parlophone R 5335*	37	3

PERFECT DAY
UK, male vocal / instrumental group (4 WEEKS)   pos/wks

21 Jan 89	LIBERTY TOWN *London LON 214*	58	3
1 Apr 89	JANE *London LON 188*	68	1

PERFECT PHASE
Holland, male production duo (7 WEEKS)   pos/wks

25 Dec 99	HORNY HORNS *Positiva CDTIV 123*	21	7

PERFECTLY ORDINARY PEOPLE
UK, male vocal / instrumental group (3 WEEKS)   pos/wks

22 Oct 88	THEME FROM P.O.P. *Urban URB 25*	61	3

PERFECTO ALLSTARZ
UK, male instrumental / production duo - Paul Oakenfold and Steve Osborne (11 WEEKS)   pos/wks

4 Feb 95 ●	REACH UP (PAPA'S GOT A BRAND NEW PIG BAG) *Perfecto YZ 892CD*	6	11

PERFUME
UK, male vocal / instrumental group (1 WEEK)   pos/wks

10 Feb 96	HAVEN'T SEEN YOU *Aromasound AROMA 005CDS*	71	1

UK No.1 ★   UK Top 10 ●   Still on chart +   UK million seller ◆   UK entry at No.1 ■   US No.1 ▲

Emilio PERICOLI *Italy, male vocalist (14 WEEKS)*

		pos/wks
28 Jun 62	AL DI LA *Warner Bros. WB 69*	**30** 14

Carl PERKINS *US, male vocalist (8 WEEKS)*

		pos/wks
18 May 56 ●	BLUE SUEDE SHOES *London HLU 8271*	**10** 8

PERPETUAL MOTION
UK, male instrumental / production group (5 WEEKS)

		pos/wks
2 May 98	KEEP ON DANCIN' (LET'S GO) *Positiva CDTIV 90* ..	**12** 5

Steve PERRY *UK, male vocalist (1 WEEK)*

		pos/wks
4 Aug 60	STEP BY STEP *HMV POP 745*	**41** 1

Nina PERSSON & David ARNOLD *Sweden, female vocalist and UK, male instrumentalist / producer (1 WEEK)*

		pos/wks
29 Apr 00	THEME FROM 'RANDALL & HOPKIRK (DECEASED)' *Island CID 762*	**49** 1

Jon PERTWEE *UK, male vocalist / actor (7 WEEKS)*

		pos/wks
1 Mar 80	WORZEL'S SONG *Decca F 13885*	**33** 7

PESHAY *UK, male DJ / producer - Paul Pesce (3 WEEKS)*

		pos/wks
9 May 98	MILES FROM HOME *Mo Wax MW 092*	**75** 1
17 Jul 99	SWITCH *Island Blue PFACD 1*	**59** 1
19 Feb 00	TRULY *Island Blue PFACD 4* [1]	**55** 1

[1] Peshay featuring Kym Mazelle

PET SHOP BOYS (61) **Top 500** *Critically acclaimed and quintessentially English duo: former assistant editor of Smash Hits, Neil Tennant (v), and Chris Lowe (k). No duo has amassed more chart entries than this act, whose first hit was voted Best British Single at the 1987 Brit Awards (227 WEEKS)*

		pos/wks
23 Nov 85 ★	WEST END GIRLS *Parlophone R 6115* ▲	**1** 15
8 Mar 86	LOVE COMES QUICKLY *Parlophone R 6116*	**19** 9
31 May 86	OPPORTUNITIES (LET'S MAKE LOTS OF MONEY) *Parlophone R 6129*	**11** 8
4 Oct 86 ●	SUBURBIA *Parlophone R 6140*	**8** 9
27 Jun 87 ★	IT'S A SIN *Parlophone R 6158*	**1** 11
22 Aug 87 ●	WHAT HAVE I DONE TO DESERVE THIS *Parlophone R 6163* [1]	**2** 9
24 Oct 87 ●	RENT *Parlophone R 6168*	**8** 7
12 Dec 87 ●	ALWAYS ON MY MIND *Parlophone R 6171*	**1** 11
2 Apr 88 ★	HEART *Parlophone R 6177*	**1** 10
24 Sep 88 ●	DOMINO DANCING *Parlophone R 6190*	**7** 8
26 Nov 88 ●	LEFT TO MY OWN DEVICES *Parlophone R 6198*	**4** 8
8 Jul 89 ●	IT'S ALRIGHT *Parlophone R 6220*	**5** 8
6 Oct 90 ●	SO HARD *Parlophone R 6269*	**4** 6
24 Nov 90	BEING BORING *Parlophone R 6275*	**20** 8
23 Mar 91 ●	WHERE THE STREETS HAVE NO NAME - CAN'T TAKE MY EYES OFF YOU / HOW CAN YOU EXPECT TO BE TAKEN SERIOUSLY *Parlophone R 6285*	**4** 8
8 Jun 91 ●	JEALOUSY *Parlophone R 6283*	**12** 5
26 Oct 91 ●	DJ CULTURE *Parlophone R 6301*	**13** 5
23 Nov 91	DJ CULTURE (re-mix) *Parlophone 12RX 6301*	**40** 2
21 Dec 91	WAS IT WORTH IT *Parlophone R 6306*	**24** 4
12 Jun 93 ●	CAN YOU FORGIVE HER *Parlophone CDR 6348*	**7** 7
18 Sep 93 ●	GO WEST *Parlophone CDR 6356*	**2** 9
11 Dec 93	I WOULDN'T NORMALLY DO THIS KIND OF THING *Parlophone CDR 6370*	**13** 7
16 Apr 94	LIBERATION *Parlophone CDR 6377*	**14** 5
11 Jun 94 ●	ABSOLUTELY FABULOUS *Spaghetti CDR 6382* [2]	**6** 7
10 Sep 94	YESTERDAY WHEN I WAS MAD *Parlophone CDR 6386*	**13** 4
5 Aug 95	PANINARO *Parlophone CDR 6414*	**15** 4
4 May 96 ●	BEFORE *Parlophone CDR 6431*	**7** 5
24 Aug 96 ●	SE A VIDE E (THAT'S THE WAY LIFE IS) *Parlophone CDR 6443*	**8** 8
23 Nov 96	SINGLE *Parlophone CDR 6452*	**14** 3
29 Mar 97 ●	A RED LETTER DAY *Parlophone CDR 6460*	**9** 3
5 Jul 97 ●	SOMEWHERE *Parlophone CDR 6470*	**9** 5

		pos/wks
31 Jul 99	I DON'T KNOW WHAT YOU WANT BUT I CAN'T GIVE IT ANYMORE *Parlophone CDR 6523*	**15** 3
9 Oct 99	NEW YORK CITY BOY *Parlophone CDR 6525*	**14** 4
15 Jan 00 ●	YOU ONLY TELL ME YOU LOVE ME WHEN YOU'RE DRUNK *Parlophone CDR 6533*	**8** 4

[1] Pet Shop Boys and Dusty Springfield [2] Absolutely Fabulous

PETER and GORDON (425) **Top 500** *UK duo: Peter Asher and Gordon Waller. who had transatlantic No.1 with debut single (penned, as were two other hits, by Asher's sister's boyfriend, Paul McCartney). Peter became a highly regarded Grammy-winning producer (77 WEEKS)*

		pos/wks
12 Mar 64 ★	A WORLD WITHOUT LOVE *Columbia DB 7225* ▲	**1** 14
4 Jun 64 ●	NOBODY I KNOW *Columbia DB 7292*	**10** 11
8 Apr 65 ●	TRUE LOVE WAYS *Columbia DB 7524*	**2** 15
24 Jun 65 ●	TO KNOW YOU IS TO LOVE YOU *Columbia DB 7617*	**5** 10
21 Oct 65	BABY I'M YOURS *Columbia DB 7729*	**19** 9
24 Feb 66	WOMAN *Columbia DB 7834*	**28** 7
22 Sep 66	LADY GODIVA *Columbia DB 8003*	**16** 11

PETER, PAUL and MARY
US, male / female vocal / instrumental group (38 WEEKS)

		pos/wks
10 Oct 63	BLOWING IN THE WIND *Warner Bros. WB 104*	**13** 16
16 Apr 64	TELL IT ON THE MOUNTAIN *Warner Bros. WB 127*	**33** 4
15 Oct 64	THE TIMES THEY ARE A-CHANGIN' *Warner Bros. WB 142*	**44** 2
17 Jan 70 ●	LEAVIN' ON A JET PLANE *Warner Bros. WB 7340* ▲	**2** 16

PETERS and LEE *UK, male / female vocal duo - Lennie Peters and Dianne Lee (57 WEEKS)*

		pos/wks
26 May 73 ★	WELCOME HOME *Philips 6006 307*	**1** 24
3 Nov 73	BY YOUR SIDE *Philips 6006 339*	**39** 4
20 Apr 74 ●	DON'T STAY AWAY TOO LONG *Philips 6006 388*	**3** 15
17 Aug 74	RAINBOW *Philips 6006 406*	**17** 7
6 Mar 76	HEY MR MUSIC MAN *Philips 6006 502*	**16** 7

Jonathan PETERS presents LUMINAIRE
US, male DJ / producer (1 WEEK)

		pos/wks
24 Jul 99	FLOWER DUET *Pelican PELID 001*	**75** 1

Ray PETERSON *US, male vocalist (9 WEEKS)*

		pos/wks
4 Sep 59	THE WONDER OF YOU *RCA 1131*	**23** 1
24 Mar 60	ANSWER ME *RCA 1175*	**47** 1
19 Jan 61	CORRINE, CORRINA *London HI X 9246*	**48** 1
2 Feb 61	CORRINE, CORRINA (re-entry) *London HLX 9246*	**41** 6

Tom PETTY and the HEARTBREAKERS
US, male vocal / instrumental group (43 WEEKS)

		pos/wks
25 Jun 77	ANYTHING THAT'S ROCK 'N' ROLL *Shelter WIP 6396*	**36** 3
13 Aug 77	AMERICAN GIRL *Shelter WIP 6403*	**40** 5
15 Aug 81	STOP DRAGGIN' MY HEART AROUND *WEA K 79231* [1]	**50** 4
13 Apr 85	DON'T COME AROUND HERE NO MORE *MCA MCA 926*	**50** 4
13 May 89	I WON'T BACK DOWN *MCA MCA 1334* [2]	**28** 10
12 Aug 89	RUNNIN' DOWN A DREAM *MCA MCA 1359* [2]	**55** 4
25 Nov 89	FREE FALLIN' *MCA MCA 1381* [2]	**64** 2
29 Jun 91	LEARNING TO FLY *MCA MCS 1555*	**46** 4
4 Apr 92	TOO GOOD TO BE TRUE *MCA MCS 1616*	**34** 3
30 Oct 93	SOMETHING IN THE AIR *MCA MCSTD 1945* [2]	**53** 2
12 Mar 94	MARY JANE'S LAST DANCE *MCA MCSTD 1966*	**52** 2

[1] Stevie Nicks with Tom Petty and the Heartbreakers [2] Tom Petty

PF PROJECT featuring Ewan McGREGOR *UK, male production duo - Jamie White and Moussa Clarke and UK, male actor (11 WEEKS)*

		pos/wks
15 Nov 97 ●	CHOOSE LIFE *Positiva CDTIV 84*	**6** 11

PHANTOMS – See Johnny BRANDON

PHARAO *Germany, male / female vocal / instrumental group (2 WEEKS)*

		pos/wks
4 Mar 95	THERE IS A STAR *Epic 6611832*	**43** 2

PHARAOHS – See SAM THE SHAM and the PHARAOHS

PHARCYDE US, male rap group (6 WEEKS)

		pos/wks	
31 Jul 93	PASSIN' ME BY *Atlantic A 8360CD*	55	3
6 Apr 96	RUNNIN' *Go.Beat GODCD 142*	36	2
10 Aug 96	SHE SAID *Go.Beat GODCD 144*	51	1

Franke PHAROAH – See FRANKE

PHASE II – See HED BOYS, LI KWAN, RAVEN MAIZE, JOEY NEGRO

PHAT 'N' PHUNKY UK, male production duo (1 WEEK)

		pos/wks	
14 Jun 97	LET'S GROOVE *Chase CDCHASE 8*	61	1

PHATS & SMALL UK, male DJ / production duo - Jason Hayward and Russell Small (30 WEEKS)

		pos/wks	
10 Apr 99 ●	TURN AROUND *Multiply CDMULTY 49*	2	16
14 Aug 99 ●	FEEL GOOD *Multiply CDMULTY 54*	7	8
4 Dec 99	TONITE *Multiply CDMULTY 57*	11	6

PHATT B Holland, male DJ / producer - Bernsquil Verndoom (1 WEEK)

		pos/wks	
11 Nov 00	AND DA DRUM MACHINE *Nulife / Arista 74321801902*	58	1

PhD UK, male vocal / instrumental duo - Jim Diamond and Tony Hymas (14 WEEKS)

		pos/wks	
3 Apr 82 ●	I WON'T LET YOU DOWN *WEA K 79209*	3	14

Barrington PHELOUNG Australia, male conductor (2 WEEKS)

		pos/wks	
13 Mar 93	'INSPECTOR MORSE' THEME *Virgin VSCDT 1458*	61	2

PHILADELPHIA INTERNATIONAL ALL-STARS
US, male / female vocal / instrumental group (8 WEEKS)

		pos/wks	
13 Aug 77	LET'S CLEAN UP THE GHETTO *Philadelphia International PIR 5451*	34	8

PHILHARMONIA ORCHESTRA, conductor Lorin MAAZEL
UK, orchestra and US, male conductor (7 WEEKS)

		pos/wks	
30 Jul 69	THUS SPAKE ZARATHUSTRA *Columbia DB 8607*	33	7

Chynna PHILLIPS US, female vocalist (1 WEEK)

		pos/wks	
3 Feb 96	NAKED AND SACRED *EMI CDEM 409*	62	1

Esther PHILLIPS US, female vocalist - Esther Mae Jones (8 WEEKS)

		pos/wks	
4 Oct 75 ●	WHAT A DIFFERENCE A DAY MAKES *Kudu 925*	6	8

PHOEBE ONE UK, female rapper (3 WEEKS)

		pos/wks	
12 Dec 98	DOIN' OUR THING / ONE MAN'S BITCH *Mecca Recordings MECX 1020*	59	1
15 May 99	GET ON IT *Mecca Recordings MECX 1026*	38	2

Paul PHOENIX UK, male vocalist (4 WEEKS)

		pos/wks	
3 Nov 79	NUNC DIMITTIS *Different HAVE 20*	56	4

Full artist credit on hit as follows: Paul Phoenix (treble) with Instrumental Ensemble - James Watson (trumpet), John Scott (organ), conducted by Barry Rose

PHOTEK UK, male producer - Rupert Parkes (3 WEEKS)

		pos/wks	
22 Mar 97	NI-TEN-ICHI-RYU (TWO SWORDS TECHNIQUE) *Science QEDCD 2*	37	2
28 Feb 98	MODUS OPERANDI *Virgin QEDCD 6*	66	1

PHOTOS UK, male / female vocal / instrumental group (4 WEEKS)

		pos/wks	
17 May 80	IRENE *Epic EPC 8517*	56	4

PHUNKY PHANTOM UK, male producer (3 WEEKS)

		pos/wks	
16 May 98	GET UP STAND UP *Club For Life DISNCD 44*	27	3

PHUTURE ASSASSINS
UK, male instrumental / production group (1 WEEK)

		pos/wks	
6 Jun 92	FUTURE SOUND (EP) *Suburban Base SUBBASE 010*	64	1

Tracks on Future Sound (EP): Future Sound / African Sanctus / Rydim Come Foward / Freedom Sound

PIA – See Pia ZADORA

Edith PIAF France, female vocalist (15 WEEKS)

		pos/wks	
12 May 60	MILORD *Columbia DC 754*	41	4
3 Nov 60	MILORD (re-entry) *Columbia DC 754*	24	11

PIANOHEADZ US, male DJ / production duo (2 WEEKS)

		pos/wks	
11 Jul 98	IT'S OVER (DISTORTION) *Incredible Music INCRL 3CD*	39	2

PIANOMAN UK, male producer - James Sammon (8 WEEKS)

		pos/wks	
15 Jun 96 ●	BLURRED *Ffrreedom TABCD 243*	6	7
26 Apr 97	PARTY PEOPLE (LIVE YOUR LIFE BE FREE) *3 Beat 3 BTCD1*	43	1

See also BASS BOYZ

Bobby 'Boris' PICKETT and the CRYPT-KICKERS
US, male vocal / instrumental group (13 WEEKS)

		pos/wks	
1 Sep 73 ●	MONSTER MASH *London HLU 10320* ▲	3	13

Wilson PICKETT US, male vocalist (61 WEEKS)

		pos/wks	
23 Sep 65	IN THE MIDNIGHT HOUR *Atlantic AT 4036*	12	11
25 Nov 65	DON'T FIGHT IT *Atlantic AT 4052*	29	8
10 Mar 66	634-5789 *Atlantic AT 4072*	36	5
1 Sep 66	LAND OF 1000 DANCES *Atlantic 584 039*	22	9
15 Dec 66	MUSTANG SALLY *Atlantic 584 066*	28	7
27 Sep 67	FUNKY BROADWAY *Atlantic 584 130*	43	3
11 Sep 68	I'M A MIDNIGHT MOVER *Atlantic 584 203*	38	6
8 Jan 69	HEY JUDE *Atlantic 584 236*	16	9
21 Nov 87	IN THE MIDNIGHT HOUR (re-recording) *Motown ZB 41583*	62	3

PICKETTYWITCH UK, male / female vocal / instrumental group (34 WEEKS)

		pos/wks	
28 Feb 70 ●	THAT SAME OLD FEELING *Pye 7N 17887*	5	14
4 Jul 70	(IT'S LIKE A) SAD OLD KINDA MOVIE *Pye 7N 17951*	16	10
7 Nov 70	BABY I WON'T LET YOU DOWN *Pye 7N 45002*	27	10

Mauro PICOTTO Italy, male producer (8 WEEKS)

		pos/wks	
12 Jun 99	LIZARD (GONNA GET YOU) *VC Recordings VCRD 50*	27	3
20 Nov 99	LIZARD (GONNA GET YA) (re-mix) *VC Recordings VCRD 57*	33	2
15 Jul 00	IGUANA *VC Recordings VCRD 68*	33	3

See also CRW

PIGBAG UK, male instrumental group (20 WEEKS)

		pos/wks	
7 Nov 81	SUNNY DAY *Y Records Y 12*	53	3
27 Feb 82	GETTING UP *Y Records Y 16*	61	3
3 Apr 82 ●	PAPA'S GOT A BRAND NEW PIGBAG *Y Records Y 10*	3	11
10 Jul 82	THE BIG BEAN *Y Records Y 24*	40	3

PIGEONHED – See LO FIDELITY ALLSTARS

Nelson PIGFORD – See De Etta LITTLE and Nelson PIGFORD

PIGLETS UK, female vocal group (12 WEEKS)

		pos/wks	
6 Nov 71 ●	JOHNNY REGGAE *Bell 1180*	3	12

Dick PIKE – See Ruby WRIGHT

P.I.L. – See PUBLIC IMAGE LTD

PILOT UK, male vocal / instrumental group (29 WEEKS)

		pos/wks	
2 Nov 74	MAGIC *EMI 2217*	11	11
18 Jan 75 ★	JANUARY *EMI 2255*	1	10

19 Apr 75	CALL ME ROUND *EMI 2287*	34	4
27 Sep 75	JUST A SMILE *EMI 2338*	31	4

PILTDOWN MEN *US, male instrumental group (36 WEEKS)* pos/wks

8 Sep 60	MACDONALD'S CAVE *Capitol CL 15149*	14	18
12 Jan 61	PILTDOWN RIDES AGAIN *Capitol CL 15175*	14	10
9 Mar 61	GOODNIGHT MRS FLINTSTONE *Capitol CL 15186*	18	8

Courtney PINE *UK, male instrumentalist - saxophone (6 WEEKS)* pos/wks

30 Jul 88	LIKE DREAMERS DO *Fourth & Broadway BRW 108* [1]	26	5
7 Jul 90	I'M STILL WAITING *Mango MNG 749* [2]	66	1

[1] Mica Paris featuring Courtney Pine [2] Courtney Pine featuring Carroll Thompson

PING PING and Al VERLAINE
Belgium, male vocal duo (4 WEEKS) pos/wks

28 Sep 61	SUCU SUCU *Oriole CB 1589*	41	4

PINK *US, female vocalist - Alecia Moore (17 WEEKS)* pos/wks

10 Jun 00	● THERE YOU GO *LaFace / Arista 74321757602*	6	9
30 Sep 00	● MOST GIRLS *La Face / Arista 74321792012*	5	8

PINK FLOYD *UK, male vocal / instrumental group (55 WEEKS)* pos/wks

30 Mar 67	ARNOLD LAYNE *Columbia DB 8156*	20	8
22 Jun 67	● SEE EMILY PLAY *Columbia DB 8214*	6	12
1 Dec 79	★ ANOTHER BRICK IN THE WALL (PART 2) *Harvest HAR 5194* ◆ ▲	1	12
7 Aug 82	WHEN THE TIGERS BROKE FREE *Harvest HAR 5222*	39	5
7 May 83	NOT NOW JOHN *Harvest HAR 5224*	30	4
19 Dec 87	ON THE TURNING AWAY *EMI EM 34*	55	4
25 Jun 88	ONE SLIP *EMI EM 52*	50	3
4 Jun 94	TAKE IT BACK *EMI CDEMS 309*	23	4
29 Oct 94	HIGH HOPES / KEEP TALKING *EMI CDEMS 342*	26	3

PINKEES *UK, male vocal / instrumental group (9 WEEKS)* pos/wks

18 Sep 82	● DANGER GAMES *Creole CR 39*	8	9

PINKERTON'S ASSORTED COLOURS
UK, male vocal / instrumental group (12 WEEKS) pos/wks

13 Jan 66	● MIRROR MIRROR *Decca F 12307*	9	11
21 Apr 66	DON'T STOP LOVIN' ME BABY *Decca F 12377*	50	1

PINKY and PERKY *UK, pork puppet duo (3 WEEKS)* pos/wks

29 May 93	REET PETITE *Telstar CDPIGGY 1*	47	3

PIONEERS *Jamaica, male vocal / instrumental group (34 WEEKS)* pos/wks

18 Oct 69	LONG SHOT KICK DE BUCKET *Trojan TR 672*	21	10
10 Jan 70	LONG SHOT KICK DE BUCKET (re-entry) *Trojan TR 672*	40	1
31 Jul 71	● LET YOUR YEAH BE YEAH *Trojan TR 7825*	5	12
15 Jan 72	GIVE AND TAKE *Trojan TR 7846*	35	6
29 Mar 80	LONG SHOT KICK DE BUCKET (re-issue) *Trojan TRO 9063*	42	5

Re-issue of 'Long Shot Kick De Bucket' coupled with re-issue of Liquidator by Harry J All Stars

Billie PIPER (497 Top 500) *Youngest solo act to debut at No.1, b. 22 Sep 1982, Swindon, UK. One-time 'Smash Hits' model topped the chart at 15. Holds the record for being the only female to score three chart-toppers before her 18th birthday (69 WEEKS)* pos/wks

11 Jul 98	★ BECAUSE WE WANT TO *Innocent SINCD 2* [1] ■	1	12
17 Oct 98	★ GIRLFRIEND *Innocent SINCD 3* [1] ■	1	10
19 Dec 98	● SHE WANTS YOU *Innocent SINDXX 6* [1]	3	11
2 Jan 99	GIRLFRIEND (re-entry) *Innocent SINCD 3* [1]	71	2
13 Mar 99	SHE WANTS YOU (re-entry) *Innocent SINDXX 6* [1]	54	2
3 Apr 99	● HONEY TO THE BEE *Innocent SINCD 8*	3	9
26 Jun 99	HONEY TO THE BEE (re-entry) *Innocent SINCD 8*	70	2
27 May 00	★ DAY & NIGHT *Innocent SINCD 11* ■	1	11

30 Sep 00	● SOMETHING DEEP INSIDE *Innocent SINCD 19*	4	8
23 Dec 00	WALK OF LIFE *Innocent SINCD 23*	25	2+

[1] Billie

PIPKINS
UK, male vocal duo - Roger Greenaway and Tony Burrows (10 WEEKS) pos/wks

28 Mar 70	● GIMME DAT DING *Columbia DB 8662*	6	10

See also BLUE MINK

PIPS – See Gladys KNIGHT and the PIPS

PIRANHAS *UK, male vocal / instrumental group (21 WEEKS)* pos/wks

2 Aug 80	● TOM HARK *Sire SIR 4044*	6	12
16 Oct 82	ZAMBESI *Dakota DAK 6* [1]	17	9

[1] Piranhas featuring Boring Bob Grover

PIRATES – See Johnny KIDD and the PIRATES

PITCH SHIFTER *UK, male vocal / instrumental group (3 WEEKS)* pos/wks

28 Feb 98	GENIUS *Geffen GFSTD 22324*	71	1
26 Sep 98	MICROWAVED *Geffen GFSTD 22348*	54	1
21 Oct 00	DEAD BATTERY *MCA MCSTD 40241*	71	1

Gene PITNEY (74 Top 500) *Leading US performer in the 1960s, b. 17 Feb 1941, Connecticut. This unmistakable vocalist and songwriter had a longer and more impressive track record in the UK than in his homeland. Nonetheless, it took him 28 years to reach No.1 (212 WEEKS)* pos/wks

23 Mar 61	(I WANNA) LOVE MY LIFE AWAY *London HL 9270*	26	11
8 Mar 62	TOWN WITHOUT PITY *HMV POP 952*	32	6
5 Dec 63	● TWENTY FOUR HOURS FROM TULSA *United Artists UP 1035*	5	19
5 Mar 64	● THAT GIRL BELONGS TO YESTERDAY *United Artists UP 1045*	7	12
15 Oct 64	IT HURTS TO BE IN LOVE *United Artists UP 1063*	36	4
12 Nov 64	● I'M GONNA BE STRONG *Stateside SS 358*	2	14
18 Feb 65	● I MUST BE SEEING THINGS *Stateside SS 390*	6	10
10 Jun 65	● LOOKING THROUGH THE EYES OF LOVE *Stateside SS 420*	3	12
4 Nov 65	● PRINCESS IN RAGS *Stateside SS 471*	9	12
17 Feb 66	● BACKSTAGE *Stateside SS 490*	4	10
9 Jun 66	● NOBODY NEEDS YOUR LOVE *Stateside SS 518*	2	13
10 Nov 66	● JUST ONE SMILE *Stateside SS 558*	8	12
23 Feb 67	(IN THE) COLD LIGHT OF DAY *Stateside SS 597*	38	6
15 Nov 67	● SOMETHING'S GOTTEN HOLD OF MY HEART *Stateside SS 2060*	5	13
3 Apr 68	SOMEWHERE IN THE COUNTRY *Stateside SS 2103*	19	9
27 Nov 68	YOURS UNTIL TOMORROW *Stateside SS 2131*	34	7
5 Mar 69	MARIA ELENA *Stateside SS 2142*	25	6
14 Mar 70	A STREET CALLED HOPE *Stateside SS 2164*	37	5
3 Oct 70	SHADY LADY *Stateside SS 2177*	29	4
28 Apr 73	24 SYCAMORE *Pye International 7N 25606*	34	7
2 Nov 74	BLUE ANGEL *Bronze BRO 11*	49	1
16 Nov 74	BLUE ANGEL (re-entry) *Bronze BRO 11*	39	3
14 Jan 89	★ SOMETHING'S GOTTEN HOLD OF MY HEART *Parlophone R 6201* [1]	1	12

[1] Marc Almond featuring special guest star Gene Pitney

Mario PIU *Italy, male DJ / producer (9 WEEKS)* pos/wks

11 Dec 99	● COMMUNICATION (SOMEBODY ANSWER THE PHONE) *Incentive CENT 2CDS*	5	9

PIXIES *US, male / female vocal / instrumental group (13 WEEKS)* pos/wks

1 Apr 89	MONKEY GONE TO HEAVEN *4AD AD 904*	60	3
1 Jul 89	HERE COMES YOUR MAN *4AD AD 909*	54	1
28 Jul 90	VELOURIA *4AD AD 0009*	28	3
10 Nov 90	DIG FOR FIRE *4AD AD 0014*	62	1
8 Jun 91	PLANET OF SOUND *4AD AD 1008*	27	3
4 Oct 97	DEBASER *4AD BAD 7010CD*	23	2

PIZZAMAN *UK, male producer - Norman Cook (18 WEEKS)* pos/wks

27 Aug 94	TRIPPIN' ON SUNSHINE *Cowboy Records CDLOAD 16*	33	2
10 Jun 95	SEX ON THE STREETS *Cowboy Records CDLOAD 24*	24	4

★ UK No.1   ● UK Top 10   + Still on chart   ◆ UK million seller   ■ UK entry at No.1   ▲ US No.1

PM DAWN
US, male vocal / instrumental / rap duo - Attrell and Jarrett Cordes (39 WEEKS)

pos/wks

Date	Title	pos	wks
8 Jun 91	A WATCHER'S POINT OF VIEW (DON'T CHA THINK) *Gee Street GEE 32*	36	5
17 Aug 91 ●	SET ADRIFT ON MEMORY BLISS *Gee Street GEE 33*	3	8
19 Oct 91	PAPER DOLL *Gee Street GEE 35*	49	3
22 Feb 92	REALITY USED TO BE A FRIEND OF MINE *Gee Street GEE 37*	29	4
7 Nov 92	I'D DIE WITHOUT YOU *Gee Street GEE 39*	30	4
13 Mar 93	LOOKING THROUGH PATIENT EYES *Gee Street GESCD 47*	11	7
12 Jun 93	MORE THAN LIKELY *Gee Street GESCD 49* [1]	40	3
30 Sep 95	DOWNTOWN VENUS *Gee Street GESCD 63*	58	2
6 Apr 96	SOMETIMES I MISS YOU SO MUCH *Gee Street GESCD 65*	58	1
31 Oct 98	GOTTA BE...MOVIN' ON UP *Gee Street GEE 5003933* [2]	68	1

[1] PM Dawn featuring Boy George [2] PM Dawn featuring Ky-Mani

POB featuring DJ Patrick REID
UK , male producer - Paul Brogden (1 WEEK)

pos/wks

Date	Title	pos	wks
11 Dec 99	BLUEBOTTLE / FLY *Platipus PLAT 63CD*	74	1

POETS
UK, male vocal / instrumental group (5 WEEKS)

pos/wks

Date	Title	pos	wks
29 Oct 64	NOW WE'RE THRU *Decca F 11995*	31	5

POGUES 489 Top 500
Irish band who presented an aggressive, compelling collision of folk, punk and rock. Led by Shane MacGowan (v/g) b. 25 Dec 1957 and originally named Pogue Mahone (Gaelic for 'kiss my arse'). 'The Irish Rover' was the final Top 20 hit released by legendary Stiff label (70 WEEKS)

pos/wks

Date	Title	pos	wks
6 Apr 85	A PAIR OF BROWN EYES *Stiff BUY 220*	72	2
22 Jun 85	SALLY MACLENNANE *Stiff BUY 224*	51	4
14 Sep 85	DIRTY OLD TOWN *Stiff BUY 229*	62	3
8 Mar 86	POGUETRY IN MOTION (EP) *Stiff BUY 243*	29	6
30 Aug 86	HAUNTED *MCA MCA 1084*	42	4
28 Mar 87 ●	THE IRISH ROVER *Stiff BUY 258* [1]	8	8
5 Dec 87 ●	FAIRYTALE OF NEW YORK *Pogue Mahone NY 7* [2]	2	9
5 Mar 88	IF I SHOULD FALL FROM GRACE WITH GOD *Pogue Mahone PG 1*	58	3
16 Jul 88	FIESTA *Pogue Mahone PG 2*	24	5
17 Dec 88	YEAH YEAH YEAH YEAH YEAH *Pogue Mahone YZ 355*	43	4
8 Jul 89	MISTY MORNING, ALBERT BRIDGE *PM YZ 407*	41	3
16 Jun 90	JACK'S HEROES / WHISKEY IN THE JAR *PM YZ 500* [1]	63	2
15 Sep 90	SUMMER IN SIAM *PM YZ 519*	64	2
21 Sep 91	A RAINY NIGHT IN SOHO *PM YZ 603*	67	1
14 Dec 91	FAIRYTALE OF NEW YORK (re-issue) *PM YZ 628* [2]	36	5
30 May 92	HONKY TONK WOMEN *PM YZ 673*	56	2
21 Aug 93	TUESDAY MORNING *PM YZ 758 CD*	18	5
22 Jan 94	ONCE UPON A TIME *PM YZ 771CD*	66	2

[1] Pogues and the Dubliners [2] Pogues featuring Kirsty MacColl

Tracks on Poguetry in Motion (EP): London Girl / The Body of an American / A Rainy Night in Soho / Planxty Noel Hill

POINT BREAK
UK, male vocal group (21 WEEKS)

pos/wks

Date	Title	pos	wks
9 Oct 99	DO WE ROCK *Eternal WEA 216CD1*	29	2
21 Jan 00 ●	STAND TOUGH *Eternal WEA 248CD1*	7	5
22 Apr 00	FREAKYTIME *Eternal WEA 265CD1*	13	6
5 Aug 00	YOU *Eternal WEA 290CD1*	14	5
2 Dec 00	WHAT ABOUT US *Eternal WEA 314CD1*	24	3

POINTER SISTERS 362 Top 500
Talented sibling vocal quartet formed 1971, Oakland, California, US, whose recordings touched many musical bases. Reduced to trio - June, Anita and Ruth - when Bonnie left in 1978. Soulful sisters surprisingly won a country music Grammy for 'Fairytale' in 1974 (87 WEEKS)

pos/wks

Date	Title	pos	wks
3 Feb 79	EVERYBODY IS A STAR *Planet K 12324*	61	3
17 Mar 79	FIRE *Planet K 12339*	34	8
22 Aug 81	SLOWHAND *Planet K 12530*	10	11
5 Dec 81	SHOULD I DO IT? *Reprise K 12578*	50	5
14 Apr 84 ●	AUTOMATIC *Planet RPS 105*	2	15
23 Jun 84 ●	JUMP (FOR MY LOVE) *Planet RPS 106*	6	10

Date	Title	pos	wks
11 Aug 84	I NEED YOU *Planet RPS 107*	25	9
27 Oct 84	I'M SO EXCITED *Planet RPS 108*	11	11
12 Jan 85	NEUTRON DANCE *Planet RPS 109*	31	7
20 Jul 85	DARE ME *RCA PB 49957*	17	8

POISON
US, male vocal / instrumental group (43 WEEKS)

pos/wks

Date	Title	pos	wks
23 May 87	TALK DIRTY TO ME *Music For Nations KUT 125*	67	1
7 May 88	NOTHIN' BUT A GOOD TIME *Capitol CL 486*	35	3
5 Nov 88	FALLEN ANGEL *Capitol CL 500*	59	1
11 Feb 89	EVERY ROSE HAS ITS THORN *Capitol CL 520* ▲	13	9
29 Apr 89	YOUR MAMA DON'T DANCE *Capitol CL 523*	13	7
23 Sep 89	NOTHIN' BUT A GOOD TIME (re-issue) *Capitol CL 539*	48	3
30 Jun 90	UNSKINNY BOP *Capitol CL 582*	15	7
27 Oct 90	SOMETHING TO BELIEVE IN *Enigma CL 594*	35	4
23 Nov 91	SO TELL ME WHY *Capitol CL 640*	25	2
13 Feb 93	STAND *Capitol CDCL 679*	25	3
24 Apr 93	UNTIL YOU SUFFER SOME (FIRE AND ICE) *Capitol CDCL 685*	32	3

POLECATS
UK, male vocal / instrumental group (18 WEEKS)

pos/wks

Date	Title	pos	wks
7 Mar 81	JOHN I'M ONLY DANCING / BIG GREEN CAR *Mercury POLE 1*	35	8
16 May 81	ROCKABILLY GUY *Mercury POLE 2*	35	6
22 Aug 81	JEEPSTER / MARIE CELESTE *Mercury POLE 3*	53	4

POLICE 138 Top 500
World-famous Anglo-American rock trio: Sting (b. Gordon Sumner) (v/b), Andy Summers (g/v), Stewart Copeland (d/v). These Brit and Grammy award winners were one of the 1980s' most popular acts. They had five successive albums entering the UK chart at No.1 (153 WEEKS)

pos/wks

Date	Title	pos	wks
7 Oct 78	CAN'T STAND LOSING YOU *A & M AMS 7381*	42	5
28 Apr 79	ROXANNE *A & M AMS 7348*	12	9
7 Jul 79 ●	CAN'T STAND LOSING YOU (re-entry) *A & M AMS 7381*	2	11
22 Sep 79 ★	MESSAGE IN A BOTTLE *A & M AMS 7474*	1	11
17 Nov 79	FALL OUT *Illegal IL 001*	47	4
1 Dec 79 ★	WALKING ON THE MOON *A & M AMS 7494*	1	10
16 Feb 80 ●	SO LONELY *A & M AMS 7402*	6	10
14 Jun 80	SIX PACK *A & M AMPP 6001*	17	4
27 Sep 80 ●	DON'T STAND SO CLOSE TO ME *A & M AMS 7564* ■	1	10
13 Dec 80 ●	DE DO DO DO, DE DA DA DA *A & M AMS 7578*	5	8
26 Sep 81 ●	INVISIBLE SUN *A & M AMS 8164*	2	8
24 Oct 81 ★	EVERY LITTLE THING SHE DOES IS MAGIC *A & M AMS 8174*	1	13
12 Dec 81	SPIRITS IN THE MATERIAL WORLD *A & M AMS 8194*	12	8
28 May 83 ★	EVERY BREATH YOU TAKE *A & M AM 117* ▲	1	11
23 Jul 83 ●	WRAPPED AROUND YOUR FINGER *A & M AM 127*	7	7
5 Nov 83	SYNCHRONICITY II *A & M AM 153*	17	4
14 Jan 84	KING OF PAIN *A & M AM 176*	17	5
11 Oct 86	DON'T STAND SO CLOSE TO ME '86 (re-mix) *A & M AM 354*	24	4
13 May 95	CAN'T STAND LOSING YOU (LIVE) *A & M 5810372*	27	2
20 Dec 97	ROXANNE '97 (re-mix) *A & M 5824552* [1]	17	6
5 Aug 00	WHEN THE WORLD IS RUNNING DOWN *Pagan PAGAN 039CDS* [2]	28	3

[1] Sting and The Police [2] Different Gear vs The Police

Six Pack consists of six separate Police singles as follows: The Bed's Too Big Without You / Roxanne / Message in a Bottle / Walking on the Moon / So Lonely / Can't Stand Losing You. The last five titles were re-issues

See also STING; Klark KENT

Su POLLARD
UK, female vocalist (11 WEEKS)

pos/wks

Date	Title	pos	wks
5 Oct 85	COME TO ME (I AM WOMAN) *Rainbow RBR 1*	71	1
1 Feb 86 ●	STARTING TOGETHER *Rainbow RBR 4*	2	10

Jimi POLO
US, male vocalist (5 WEEKS)

pos/wks

Date	Title	pos	wks
9 Nov 91	NEVER GOIN' DOWN *MCA MCS 1578* [1]	51	2
1 Aug 92	EXPRESS YOURSELF *Perfecto 74321101827*	59	2
9 Aug 97	EXPRESS YOURSELF (re-issue) *Perfecto PERF 146CD1*	62	1

[1] Adamski featuring Jimi Polo

The listed flip side of 'Never Goin' Down' was 'Born to Be Alive' by Adamski featuring Soho

POLTERGEIST UK, male producer - Simon Berry (2 WEEKS) pos/wks
6 Jul 96   VICIOUS CIRCLES *Manifesto FESCD 8* **32** 2

See also VICIOUS CIRCLES

Peter POLYCARPOU UK, male vocalist (4 WEEKS) pos/wks
20 Feb 93   LOVE HURTS *Soundtrack Music CDEM 259* **26** 4

POLYGON WINDOW UK, male producer - Richard James (1 WEEK) pos/wks
3 Apr 93   QUOTH *Warp WAP 33CD* **49** 1

See also APHEX TWIN

PONI-TAILS US, female vocal group (14 WEEKS) pos/wks
19 Sep 58 ●   BORN TOO LATE *HMV POP 516* **5** 11
10 Apr 59   EARLY TO BED *HMV POP 596* **26** 3

Brian POOLE and the TREMELOES `340` `Top 500`
Formed 1959 and signed by Decca in preference to the Beatles (auditioned same day). First south of England group to top the chart in Beat Boom era. Poole, b. 2 Nov 1941, Essex, UK, went solo in 1966, and group continues with even more success. Poole's daughters hit in late 90s as Alisha's Attic (90 WEEKS) pos/wks
4 Jul 63 ●   TWIST AND SHOUT *Decca F 11694* **4** 14
12 Sep 63 ★   DO YOU LOVE ME *Decca F 11739* **1** 14
28 Nov 63   I CAN DANCE *Decca F 11771* **31** 8
30 Jan 64 ●   CANDY MAN *Decca F 11823* **6** 13
7 May 64 ●   SOMEONE SOMEONE *Decca F 11893* **2** 17
20 Aug 64   TWELVE STEPS TO LOVE *Decca F 11951* **32** 7
7 Jan 65   THREE BELLS *Decca F 12037* **17** 9
22 Jul 65   I WANT CANDY *Decca F 12197* **25** 8

See also TREMELOES

Glyn POOLE UK, male vocalist (8 WEEKS) pos/wks
20 Oct 73   MILLY MOLLY MANDY *York SYK 565* **35** 8

Iggy POP US, male vocalist - James Jewel Osterburg (28 WEEKS) pos/wks
13 Dec 86 ●   REAL WILD CHILD (WILD ONE) *A & M AM 368* **10** 11
10 Feb 90   LIVIN' ON THE EDGE OF THE NIGHT *Virgin America VUS 18*....**51** 4
13 Oct 90   CANDY *Virgin America VUS 29* **67** 1
5 Jan 91   WELL DID YOU EVAH! *Chrysalis CHS 3646* [1] **42** 4
4 Sep 93   THE WILD AMERICA (EP) *Virgin America VUSCD 74*.....**63** 1
21 May 94   BESIDE YOU *Virgin America VUSCD 77* **47** 2
23 Nov 96   LUST FOR LIFE *Virgin America VUSCD 116*...........**26** 2
7 Mar 98   THE PASSENGER *Virgin VSCDT 1689* **22** 3

[1] Deborah Harry and Iggy Pop

Tracks on The Wild America (EP): Wild America / Credit Card / Come Back Tomorrow / My Angel

POP TOPS Spain, male vocal group (6 WEEKS) pos/wks
9 Oct 71   MAMY BLUE *A & M AMS 859* **35** 6

POP WILL EAT ITSELF
UK, male vocal / instrumental group (43 WEEKS) pos/wks
30 Jan 88   THERE IS NO LOVE BETWEEN US ANYMORE
           Chapter 22 CHAP 20 ....**66** 1
23 Jul 88   DEF CON ONE *Chapter 22 PWEI 001* **63** 4
11 Feb 89   CAN U DIG IT *RCA PB 42621* **38** 4
22 Apr 89   WISE UP! SUCKER *RCA PB 42761* **41** 3
2 Sep 89   VERY METAL NOISE POLLUTION (EP) *RCA PB 42883*........**45** 3
9 Jun 90   TOUCHED BY THE HAND OF CICCIOLINA *RCA PB 43735* **28** 4
13 Oct 90   DANCE OF THE MAD *RCA PB 44023* **32** 2
12 Jan 91   X Y & ZEE *RCA PB 44243* **15** 4
1 Jun 91   92° F *RCA PB 44555* **23** 3
6 Jun 92   KARMADROME / EAT ME DRINK ME LOVE ME
           RCA PB 45467 ....**17** 2
29 Aug 92   BULLETPROOF! *RCA 74321110137* **24** 3
16 Jan 93 ●   GET THE GIRL! KILL THE BADDIES! *RCA 74321128802* **9** 4
16 Oct 93   RSVP / FAMILIUS HORRIBILUS *Infectious INFECT 1CD*..........**27** 2
12 Mar 94   ICH BIN EIN AUSLANDER *Infectious INFECT 4CD*.....................**28** 2
10 Sep 94   EVERYTHING'S COOL *Infectious INFECT 9CD* **23** 2

Tracks on Very Metal Noise Pollution (EP): Def Con 1989 AD including the Twilight Zone / Preaching to the Perverted / PWEI-zation / 92° F

POPES – See Shane MacGOWAN

POPPERS presents AURA
UK, male production trio and UK, female vocalist (1 WEEK) pos/wks
25 Oct 97   EVERY LITTLE TIME *VC VCRD 26* **44** 1

POPPY FAMILY Canada, male / female vocal / instrumental group - Terry Jacks and Susan Peklevits (14 WEEKS) pos/wks
15 Aug 70 ●   WHICH WAY YOU GOIN' BILLY *Decca F 22976* **7** 14

See also Terry JACKS

PORN KINGS UK, male instrumental / production group (9 WEEKS) pos/wks
28 Sep 96   UP TO NO GOOD *All Around the World CDGLOBE 145* **28** 2
21 Jun 97   AMOUR (C'MON) *All Around the World CDGLOBE 152* **17** 3
16 Jan 99 ●   UP TO THE WILDSTYLE
           All Around the World CDGLOBE 170 [1] **10** 4

[1] Porn Kings vs DJ Supreme

PORNO FOR PYROS US, male vocal / instrumental group (2 WEEKS) pos/wks
5 Jun 93   PETS *Warner Bros. W 0177 CD* **53** 2

PORTISHEAD
UK, male / female vocal / instrumental group (20 WEEKS) pos/wks
13 Aug 94   SOUR TIMES *Go.Beat GODCD 116* **57** 1
14 Jan 95   GLORY BOX *Go.Beat GODCD 120* **13** 7
22 Apr 95   SOUR TIMES (re-entry) *Go.Beat GODCD 116* **13** 4
20 Sep 97 ●   ALL MINE *Go.Beat 5715972* **8** 4
22 Nov 97   OVER *Go.Beat 5719932* **25** 2
14 Mar 98   ONLY YOU *Go.Beat 5694752* **35** 2

Gary PORTNOY US, male vocalist (3 WEEKS) pos/wks
25 Feb 84   THEME FROM 'CHEERS' *Starblend CHEER 1* **58** 3

PORTRAIT US, male vocal group (6 WEEKS) pos/wks
27 Mar 93   HERE WE GO AGAIN *Capitol CDCL 683* **37** 3
8 Apr 95   I CAN CALL YOU *Capitol CDCL 740* **61** 1
8 Jul 95   HOW DEEP IS YOUR LOVE *Capitol CDCL 751* **41** 2

PORTSMOUTH SINFONIA UK, orchestra (4 WEEKS) pos/wks
12 Sep 81   CLASSICAL MUDDLEY *Island WIP 6736* **38** 4

Sandy POSEY US, female vocalist (32 WEEKS) pos/wks
15 Sep 66   BORN A WOMAN *MGM 1321* **24** 11
5 Jan 67   SINGLE GIRL *MGM 1330* **15** 13
13 Apr 67   WHAT A WOMAN IN LOVE WON'T DO *MGM 1335* **48** 3
6 Sep 75   SINGLE GIRL (re-issue) *MGM 2006 533* **35** 5

POSIES US, male vocal / instrumental group (1 WEEK) pos/wks
19 Mar 94   DEFINITE DOOR *Geffen GFSTD 68* **67** 1

POSITIVE FORCE US, female vocal duo (9 WEEKS) pos/wks
22 Dec 79   WE GOT THE FUNK *Sugarhill SHL 102* **18** 9

POSITIVE GANG
UK, male / female instrumental / vocal group (5 WEEKS) pos/wks
17 Apr 93   SWEET FREEDOM *PWL Continental PWCD 261*........**34** 4
31 Jul 93   SWEET FREEDOM PART 2 *PWL Continental PWCD 264*.........**67** 1

POSITIVE K US, male rapper (2 WEEKS) pos/wks
15 May 93   I GOT A MAN *Fourth & Broadway BRCD 280* **43** 2

Mike POST US, orchestra (18 WEEKS)

		pos/wks	
9 Aug 75	**AFTERNOON OF THE RHINO**		
	Warner Bros. K 16588 [1]	**48**	1
23 Aug 75	**AFTERNOON OF THE RHINO (re-entry)**		
	Warner Bros. K 16588 [1]	**47**	1
16 Jan 82	**THEME FROM 'HILL STREET BLUES'** *Elektra K 12576* [2]	**25**	11
29 Sep 84	**THE A TEAM** *RCA 443*	**45**	5

[1] Mike Post Coalition [2] Mike Post featuring Larry Carlton

POTTERS UK, male Stoke City football supporters vocal group (2 WEEKS)

		pos/wks	
1 Apr 72	**WE'LL BE WITH YOU** *Pye JT 100*	**34**	2

P.O.V. featuring JADE US, male vocal group and female vocal group (3 WEEKS)

		pos/wks	
5 Feb 94	**ALL THRU THE NITE** *Giant 74321187552*	**32**	3

POWDER UK, male / female vocal / instrumental group (1 WEEK)

		pos/wks	
24 Jun 95	**AFRODISIAC** *Parkway PARK 002CD*	**72**	1

Bryan POWELL UK, male vocalist (3 WEEKS)

		pos/wks	
13 Mar 93	**IT'S ALRIGHT** *Talkin' Loud TLKCD 34*	**73**	1
15 May 93	**I THINK OF YOU** *Talkin' Loud TLKCD 38*	**61**	1
7 Aug 93	**NATURAL** *Talkin' Loud TLKCD 41*	**73**	1

Cozy POWELL UK, male instrumentalist, drums - Colin Flooks (38 WEEKS)

		pos/wks	
8 Dec 73 ●	**DANCE WITH THE DEVIL** *RAK 164*	**3**	15
25 May 74	**THE MAN IN BLACK** *RAK 173*	**18**	8
10 Aug 74 ●	**NA NA NA** *RAK 180*	**10**	10
10 Nov 79	**THEME ONE** *Ariola ARO 189*	**62**	2
19 Jun 93	**RESURRECTION** *Parlophone CDRS 6351* [1]	**23**	3

[1] Brian May with Cozy Powell

Kobie POWELL – See US3

POWER CIRCLE – See CHICANE

POWER OF DREAMS Ireland, male vocal / instrumental group (2 WEEKS)

		pos/wks	
19 Jan 91	**AMERICAN DREAM** *Polydor PO 117*	**74**	1
11 Apr 92	**THERE I GO AGAIN** *Polydor PO 200*	**65**	1

POWER STATION UK / US, male vocal / instrumental group (17 WEEKS)

		pos/wks	
16 Mar 85	**SOME LIKE IT HOT** *Parlophone R 6091*	**14**	8
11 May 85	**GET IT ON** *Parlophone R 6096*	**22**	7
9 Nov 85	**COMMUNICATION** *Parlophone R 6114*	**75**	1
12 Oct 96	**SHE CAN ROCK IT** *Chrysalis CDCHS 5039*	**63**	1

POWERCUT featuring NUBIAN PRINZ US, male vocal / instrumental group (4 WEEKS)

		pos/wks	
22 Jun 91	**GIRLS** *Eternal YZ 570*	**50**	4

POWERHOUSE UK, male production duo (9 WEEKS)

		pos/wks	
20 Dec 97	**RHYTHM OF THE NIGHT** *Satellite 74321522592*	**38**	4
22 May 99	**WHAT YOU NEED** *Defected DEFECT 3CDS* [1]	**13**	5

[1] Powerhouse featuring Duane Harden

POWERPILL UK, male instrumental / production group (3 WEEKS)

		pos/wks	
6 Jun 92	**PAC-MAN** *Ffrreedom TABX 110*	**43**	3

Will POWERS US, female vocalist - Lyn Goldsmith (9 WEEKS)

		pos/wks	
1 Oct 83	**KISSING WITH CONFIDENCE** *Island IS 134*	**17**	9

Hit features uncredited vocals by Carly Simon

PQM featuring CICA US, male producer and female vocalist (1 WEEK)

		pos/wks	
9 Dec 00	**THE FLYING SONG** *Renaissance / Yoshitoshi RENCDS 004*	**68**	1

Perez PRADO Cuba, orchestra (57 WEEKS)

		pos/wks	
25 Mar 55 ★	**CHERRY PINK AND APPLE BLOSSOM WHITE**		
	HMV B 10833 [1] ▲	**1**	17
25 Jul 58 ●	**PATRICIA** *RCA 1067*	**8**	16
10 Dec 94	**GUAGLIONE** *RCA 74321250192* [2]	**41**	6
8 Apr 95	**GUAGLIONE (re-entry)** *RCA 74321250192* [2]	**58**	2
6 May 95 ●	**GUAGLIONE (2nd re-entry)**		
	RCA 74321250192 [2]	**2**	16

[1] Perez 'Prez' Prado and his Orchestra, the King of the Mambo [2] Perez 'Prez' Prado and his Orchestra

PRAISE UK, male / female vocal / instrumental group (7 WEEKS)

		pos/wks	
2 Feb 91 ●	**ONLY YOU** *Epic 6566117*	**4**	7

Uncredited vocals by Miriam Stockley

PRAS – See Pras MICHEL

PRATT and McCLAIN with BROTHERLOVE US, male vocal duo with male instrumental group (6 WEEKS)

		pos/wks	
1 Oct 77	**HAPPY DAYS** *Reprise K 14435*	**31**	6

PRAXIS UK, male / female vocal / instrumental group (5 WEEKS)

		pos/wks	
25 Nov 95	**TURN ME OUT** *Stress CDSTR 40*	**44**	2
20 Sep 97	**TURN ME OUT (TURN TO SUGAR) (re-mix)**		
	ffrr FCD 314 [1]	**35**	3

[1] Praxis featuring Kathy Brown

PRAYING MANTIS UK, male vocal / instrumental group (2 WEEKS)

		pos/wks	
31 Jan 81	**CHEATED** *Arista ARIST 378*	**69**	2

PRECIOUS UK, female vocal group (20 WEEKS)

		pos/wks	
29 May 99 ●	**SAY IT AGAIN** *EMI CDEM 544*	**6**	9
28 Aug 99	**SAY IT AGAIN (re-entry)** *EMI CDEM 544*	**53**	2
1 Apr 00	**REWIND** *EMI CDEM 557*	**11**	5
15 Jul 00	**IT'S GONNA BE MY WAY** *EMI CDEM 569*	**27**	3
25 Nov 00	**NEW BEGINNING** *EMI CDEM 573*	**50**	1

PRECOCIOUS BRATS featuring KEVIN and PERRY UK, male production duo and UK, male / female vocal comedy duo - Harry Enfield and Kathy Burke (4 WEEKS)

		pos/wks	
6 May 00	**BIG GIRL** *Virgin / EMI VTSCD 1*	**16**	4

PREFAB SPROUT UK, male / female vocal / instrumental group (60 WEEKS)

		pos/wks	
28 Jan 84	**DON'T SING** *Kitchenware SK 9*	**62**	2
20 Jul 85	**FARON YOUNG** *Kitchenware SK 22*	**74**	1
9 Nov 85	**WHEN LOVE BREAKS DOWN** *Kitchenware SK 21*	**25**	10
8 Feb 86	**JOHNNY JOHNNY** *Kitchenware SK 24*	**64**	2
13 Feb 88	**CARS AND GIRLS** *Kitchenware SK 35*	**44**	5
30 Apr 88 ●	**THE KING OF ROCK 'N' ROLL** *Kitchenware SK 37*	**7**	10
23 Jul 88	**HEY MANHATTAN!** *Kitchenware SK 38*	**72**	2
18 Aug 90	**LOOKING FOR ATLANTIS** *Kitchenware SK 47*	**51**	3
20 Oct 90	**WE LET THE STARS GO** *Kitchenware SK 48*	**50**	3
5 Jan 91	**JORDAN: THE EP** *Kitchenware SK 49*	**35**	4
13 Jun 92	**THE SOUND OF CRYING** *Kitchenware SK 58*	**23**	5
8 Aug 92	**IF YOU DON'T LOVE ME** *Kitchenware SK 60*	**33**	4
3 Oct 92	**ALL THE WORLD LOVES LOVERS** *Kitchenware SK 62*	**61**	2
9 Jan 93	**LIFE OF SURPRISES** *Kitchenware SKCD 63*	**24**	4
10 May 97	**A PRISONER OF THE PAST** *Columbia SKZD 70*	**30**	4
2 Aug 97	**ELECTRIC GUITARS** *Columbia SKZD 71*	**53**	1

Tracks on Jordan: The EP: Carnival 2000 / The Ice Maiden / One of the Broken / Jordan: The Comeback

---

UK No.1 ★   UK Top 10 ●   Still on chart +   UK million seller ◆   UK entry at No.1 ■   US No.1 ▲

PRELUDE *UK, male / female vocal group (26 WEEKS)*   pos/wks

26 Jan 74	**AFTER THE GOLDRUSH** *Dawn DNS 1052*	21	9
26 Apr 80	**PLATINUM BLONDE** *EMI 5046*	45	7
22 May 82	**AFTER THE GOLDRUSH (re-recording)** *After Hours AFT 02*	28	7
31 Jul 82	**ONLY THE LONELY** *After Hours AFT 06*	55	3

PRESENCE *UK, male / female vocal / production group (2 WEEKS)* pos/wks

5 Dec 98	**SENSE OF DANGER** *Pagan PAGAN 024CDS* 1	61	1
19 Jun 99	**FUTURE LOVE** *Pagan PAGAN 028CDS*	66	1

1 Presence featuring Shara Nelson

PRESIDENT BROWN – See SABRE featuring PRESIDENT BROWN

PRESIDENTS OF THE UNITED STATES OF AMERICA
US, male vocal / instrumental trio (21 WEEKS)   pos/wks

6 Jan 96	**LUMP** *Columbia 6624962*	15	7
20 Apr 96 ●	**PEACHES** *Columbia 6631072*	8	7
20 Jul 96	**DUNE BUGGY** *Columbia 6634892*	15	4
2 Nov 96	**MACH 5** *Columbia 6638812*	29	2
1 Aug 98	**VIDEO KILLED THE RADIO STAR** *Maverick W 0450CD*	52	1

Elvis PRESLEY 1 Top 500

The most important, most influential and most impersonated artist of the 20th century, b. 8 Jan 1935, Mississippi, US, d. 16 Aug 1977. The singer, whose first five US singles failed to reach the pop charts, went from rock'n'roll rebel to Las Vegas veteran and on the way sold more records than any other performer in history. He holds, or has held, almost every chart-related record in the UK and US. No other solo artist of the rock era can match his number of best-selling singles and albums in the UK or US, nor his collection of platinum and gold records. The "King of Rock'n'Roll" was the first artist to enter the UK chart at No.1, and the first to amass advance orders in excess of one million copies for a single. He now has a 42-year span of UK Top 20 albums and also holds the record for most simultaneous UK album chart entries (27 in the Top 100) and held the record for the most entries on the UK single chart (9). The best documented entertainer ever has won hundreds of awards, starred in dozens of successful films, broken numerous box office records in North America (the only continent he ever performed in), made Memphis a major tourist attraction and was the first artist credited with sales of one billion records (20 million of which were reportedly sold the day after his death). (1168 WEEKS)   pos/wks

11 May 56 ●	**HEARTBREAK HOTEL** *HMV POP 182* ▲	2	21
25 May 56 ●	**BLUE SUEDE SHOES** *HMV POP 213*	9	8
13 Jul 56	**I WANT YOU I NEED YOU I LOVE YOU** *HMV POP 235* ▲	25	2
3 Aug 56	**I WANT YOU I NEED YOU I LOVE YOU (re-entry)** *HMV POP 235*	14	9
17 Aug 56	**BLUE SUEDE SHOES (re-entry)** *HMV POP 213*	26	2
21 Sep 56 ●	**HOUND DOG** *HMV POP 249* ▲	2	23
26 Oct 56	**HEARTBREAK HOTEL (re-entry)** *HMV POP 182*	23	1
16 Nov 56 ●	**BLUE MOON** *HMV POP 272 (A)*	9	11
23 Nov 56	**I DON'T CARE IF THE SUN DON'T SHINE** *HMV POP 272 (B)*	29	1
7 Dec 56	**LOVE ME TENDER** *HMV POP 253* ▲	11	9
21 Dec 56	**I DON'T CARE IF THE SUN DON'T SHINE (re-entry)** *HMV POP 272*	23	3
15 Feb 57	**MYSTERY TRAIN** *HMV POP 295*	25	5
8 Mar 57	**RIP IT UP** *HMV POP 305* ▲	27	1
10 May 57 ●	**TOO MUCH** *HMV POP 330* ▲	6	8
14 Jun 57	**ALL SHOOK UP** *HMV POP 359*	24	1
28 Jun 57 ★	**ALL SHOOK UP (re-entry)** *HMV POP 359* ▲	1	20
12 Jul 57 ●	**(LET ME BE YOUR) TEDDY BEAR** *RCA1013* ▲ *(A)*	3	19
12 Jul 57	**TOO MUCH (re-entry)** *HMV POP 330*	26	1
30 Aug 57 ●	**PARALYSED** *HMV POP 378*	8	10
4 Oct 57 ●	**PARTY** *RCA 1020 (A)*	2	15
18 Oct 57	**GOT A LOT O' LIVIN' TO DO** *RCA 1020 (B)*	17	4
1 Nov 57	**LOVING YOU** *RCA 1013 (B)*	24	2
1 Nov 57	**TRYING TO GET TO YOU** *HMV POP 408 (A)*	16	4
8 Nov 57	**LAWDY MISS CLAWDY** *HMV POP 408 (B)*	15	5
15 Nov 57 ●	**SANTA BRING MY BABY BACK (TO ME)** *RCA 1025*	7	8
17 Jan 58	**I'M LEFT, YOU'RE RIGHT, SHE'S GONE** *HMV POP 428*	21	2
24 Jan 58 ★	**JAILHOUSE ROCK** *RCA 1028* ■ ▲	1	14
31 Jan 58	**JAILHOUSE ROCK (EP)** *RCA RCX 106*	18	5
7 Feb 58	**I'M LEFT, YOU'RE RIGHT, SHE'S GONE (re-entry)** *HMV POP 428*	29	1

28 Feb 58 ●	**DON'T** *RCA 1043* ▲	2	11
2 May 58 ●	**WEAR MY RING AROUND YOUR NECK** *RCA 1058*	3	10
25 Jul 58 ●	**HARD HEADED WOMAN** *RCA 1070* ▲	2	11
3 Oct 58 ●	**KING CREOLE** *RCA 1081*	2	15
23 Jan 59 ●	**ONE NIGHT / I GOT STUNG** *RCA 1100*	1	12
24 Apr 59 ★	**(NOW AND THEN THERE'S) A FOOL SUCH AS I / I NEED YOUR LOVE TONIGHT** *RCA 1113*	1	15
24 Jul 59 ●	**A BIG HUNK O' LOVE** *RCA 1136* ▲	4	9
12 Feb 60	**STRICTLY ELVIS (EP)** *RCA RCX 175*	26	1
7 Apr 60 ●	**STUCK ON YOU** *RCA 1187* ▲	3	14
28 Jul 60 ●	**A MESS OF BLUES** *RCA 1194* ▲	2	18
3 Nov 60 ★	**IT'S NOW OR NEVER** *RCA 1207* ◆ ■ ▲	1	19
19 Jan 61 ★	**ARE YOU LONESOME TONIGHT** *RCA 1216* ▲	1	15
9 Mar 61 ★	**WOODEN HEART** *RCA 1226*	1	27
25 May 61 ★	**SURRENDER** *RCA 1227* ▲	1	15
7 Sep 61 ●	**WILD IN THE COUNTRY / I FEEL SO BAD** *RCA 1244*	4	12
2 Nov 61 ★	**(MARIE'S THE NAME) HIS LATEST FLAME / LITTLE SISTER** *RCA 1258*	1	13
1 Feb 62 ★	**ROCK A HULA BABY / CAN'T HELP FALLING IN LOVE** *RCA 1270*	1	20
10 May 62 ★	**GOOD LUCK CHARM** *RCA 1280* ▲	1	17
21 Jun 62	**FOLLOW THAT DREAM (EP)** *RCA RCX 211*	34	2
30 Aug 62 ★	**SHE'S NOT YOU** *RCA 1303*	1	14
29 Nov 62 ★	**RETURN TO SENDER** *RCA 1320*	1	14
28 Feb 63	**ONE BROKEN HEART FOR SALE** *RCA 1337*	12	9
4 Jul 63 ★	**(YOU'RE THE) DEVIL IN DISGUISE** *RCA 1355*	1	12
24 Oct 63	**BOSSA NOVA BABY** *RCA 1374*	13	8
19 Dec 63	**KISS ME QUICK** *RCA 1375*	14	10
12 Mar 64	**VIVA LAS VEGAS** *RCA 1390*	17	12
25 Jun 64 ●	**KISSIN' COUSINS** *RCA 1404*	10	11
20 Aug 64	**SUCH A NIGHT** *RCA 1411*	13	10
29 Oct 64	**AIN'T THAT LOVIN' YOU BABY** *RCA 1422*	15	8
3 Dec 64	**BLUE CHRISTMAS** *RCA 1430*	11	7
11 Mar 65	**DO THE CLAM** *RCA 1443*	19	8
27 May 65 ★	**CRYING IN THE CHAPEL** *RCA 1455*	1	15
11 Nov 65	**TELL ME WHY** *RCA 1489*	15	10
24 Feb 66	**BLUE RIVER** *RCA 1504*	22	7
7 Apr 66	**FRANKIE AND JOHNNY** *RCA 1509*	21	9
7 Jul 66 ●	**LOVE LETTERS** *RCA 1526*	6	10
13 Oct 66	**ALL THAT I AM** *RCA 1545*	18	8
1 Dec 66 ●	**IF EVERY DAY WAS LIKE CHRISTMAS** *RCA 1557*	9	7
9 Feb 67	**INDESCRIBABLY BLUE** *RCA 1565*	21	5
11 May 67	**YOU GOTTA STOP / LOVE MACHINE** *RCA 1593*	38	5
16 Aug 67	**LONG LEGGED GIRL (WITH THE SHORT DRESS ON)** *RCA RCA 1616*	49	2
21 Feb 68	**GUITAR MAN** *RCA 1663*	19	9
15 May 68	**US MALE** *RCA 1688*	15	8
17 Jul 68	**YOUR TIME HASN'T COME YET BABY** *RCA 1714*	22	11
16 Oct 68	**YOU'LL NEVER WALK ALONE** *RCA 1747*	44	3
26 Feb 69	**IF I CAN DREAM** *RCA 1795*	11	10
11 Jun 69 ●	**IN THE GHETTO** *RCA 1831*	2	16
6 Sep 69	**CLEAN UP YOUR OWN BACK YARD** *RCA 1869*	21	7
18 Oct 69	**IN THE GHETTO (re-entry)** *RCA 1831*	50	1
29 Nov 69 ●	**SUSPICIOUS MINDS** *RCA 1900* ▲	2	14
28 Feb 70 ●	**DON'T CRY DADDY** *RCA 1916*	8	11
16 May 70	**KENTUCKY RAIN** *RCA 1949*	21	11
11 Jul 70 ★	**THE WONDER OF YOU** *RCA 1974*	1	20
8 Aug 70	**KENTUCKY RAIN (re-entry)** *RCA 1949*	46	1
14 Nov 70 ●	**I'VE LOST YOU** *RCA 1999*	9	12
9 Jan 71 ●	**YOU DON'T HAVE TO SAY YOU LOVE ME** *RCA 2046*	9	7
23 Jan 71	**THE WONDER OF YOU (re-entry)** *RCA 1974*	47	1
6 Mar 71	**YOU DON'T HAVE TO SAY YOU LOVE ME (re-entry)** *RCA 2046*	35	3
20 Mar 71 ●	**THERE GOES MY EVERYTHING** *RCA 2060*	6	11
15 May 71 ●	**RAGS TO RICHES** *RCA 2084*	9	11
17 Jul 71 ●	**HEARTBREAK HOTEL / HOUND DOG (re-issue)** *RCA Maximillion 2104*	10	12
2 Oct 71 ●	**I'M LEAVIN'** *RCA 2125*	23	9
4 Dec 71 ●	**I JUST CAN'T HELP BELIEVING** *RCA 2158*	6	16
11 Dec 71	**JAILHOUSE ROCK (re-issue)** *RCA Maximillion 2153*	42	5
1 Apr 72 ●	**UNTIL IT'S TIME FOR YOU TO GO** *RCA 2188*	5	9
17 Jun 72 ●	**AMERICAN TRILOGY** *RCA 2229*	8	11
30 Sep 72 ●	**BURNING LOVE** *RCA 2267*	7	9
16 Dec 72 ●	**ALWAYS ON MY MIND** *RCA 2304*	9	13

UK No.1 ★ UK Top 10 ● Still on chart + UK million seller ◆ UK entry at No.1 ■ US No.1 ▲

SINGLED OUT...
Chris Tarrant

The man who tries his best to give away a million pounds every week goes for the chart's big guns with his "favourite" and "first" selections.

•NO.1 SONG ON THE DAY I WAS BORN:
Bless You (For Being An Angel) – The Ink Spots

•ALL - TIME FAVOURITE SINGLE:
I Want To Hold Your Hand – The Beatles

They remain the greatest band of all time. I was going out with a particularly nice girl at the time and sadly, in those days, all we did was hold hands!

•SINGLE THAT DRIVES ME UP THE WALL:
Barbie Girl – Aqua

It is easily the worst record ever made.

FIRST SINGLE
I EVER BOUGHT:

Hound Dog – Elvis Presley

I was a mad keen Elvis fan and used to brush my hair up into a quiff and gyrate my pelvis in front of the mirror, convinced I WAS Elvis. As I was only about 10 at the time, I almost certainly looked ridiculous!

Photo: Redferns/Rb

26 May 73	POLK SALAD ANNIE *RCA 2359*	23	7
11 Aug 73	FOOL *RCA 2393*	15	10
24 Nov 73	RAISED ON ROCK *RCA 2435*	36	7
16 Mar 74	I'VE GOT A THING ABOUT YOU BABY *RCA APBO 0196*	33	5
13 Jul 74	IF YOU TALK IN YOUR SLEEP *RCA APBO 0280*	40	5
16 Nov 74	MY BOY *RCA 2458*	5	13
18 Jan 75 ●	PROMISED LAND *RCA PB 10074*	9	8
24 May 75	T. R. O. U. B. L. E. *RCA 2562*	31	4
29 Nov 75	GREEN GREEN GRASS OF HOME *RCA 2635*	29	7
1 May 76	HURT *RCA 2674*	37	5
4 Sep 76 ●	GIRL OF MY BEST FRIEND *RCA 2729*	9	12
25 Dec 76 ●	SUSPICION *RCA 2768*	9	12
5 Mar 77 ●	MOODY BLUE *RCA PB 0857*	6	9
13 Aug 77 ★	WAY DOWN *RCA PB 0998*	1	13
3 Sep 77	ALL SHOOK UP (re-issue) *RCA PB 2694*	41	2
3 Sep 77	ARE YOU LONESOME TONIGHT (re-issue) *RCA PB 2699*	46	1
3 Sep 77	CRYING IN THE CHAPEL (re-issue) *RCA PB 2708*	43	2
3 Sep 77	IT'S NOW OR NEVER (re-issue) *RCA PB 2698*	39	2
3 Sep 77	JAILHOUSE ROCK (2nd re-issue) *RCA PB 2695*	44	2
3 Sep 77	RETURN TO SENDER (re-issue) *RCA PB 2706*	42	3
3 Sep 77	THE WONDER OF YOU (re-issue) *RCA PB 2709*	48	1
3 Sep 77	WOODEN HEART (re-issue) *RCA PB 2700*	49	1
10 Dec 77 ●	MY WAY *RCA PB 1165*	9	8
24 Jun 78	DON'T BE CRUEL *RCA PB 9265*	24	12
15 Dec 79	IT WON'T SEEM LIKE CHRISTMAS (WITHOUT YOU) *RCA PB 9464*	13	6
30 Aug 80 ●	IT'S ONLY LOVE / BEYOND THE REEF *RCA 4*	3	10
6 Dec 80	SANTA CLAUS IS BACK IN TOWN *RCA 16*	41	6
14 Feb 81	GUITAR MAN (re-master) *RCA 43*	43	4
18 Apr 81	LOVING ARMS *RCA 48*	47	6
13 Mar 82	ARE YOU LONESOME TONIGHT (LIVE) *RCA 196*	25	7
26 Jun 82	THE SOUND OF YOUR CRY *RCA 232*	59	2
5 Feb 83	JAILHOUSE ROCK (re-entry) *RCA 1028*	27	6
7 May 83	BABY I DON'T CARE *RCA 332*	61	3
3 Dec 83	I CAN HELP *RCA 369*	30	9
10 Nov 84	THE LAST FAREWELL *RCA 459*	48	6
19 Jan 85	THE ELVIS MEDLEY *RCA 476*	51	3
10 Aug 85	ALWAYS ON MY MIND (re-recording) *RCA PB 49944*	59	4
11 Apr 87	AIN'T THAT LOVIN' YOU BABY / BOSSA NOVA BABY (re-issue) *RCA ARON 1*	47	5
22 Aug 87	LOVE ME TENDER / IF I CAN DREAM (re-issue) *RCA ARON 2*	56	3
16 Jan 88	STUCK ON YOU (re-issue) *RCA PB 49595*	58	2
17 Aug 91	ARE YOU LONESOME TONIGHT (LIVE) (re-issue) *RCA PB 49177*	68	2
29 Aug 92	DON'T BE CRUEL (re-issue) *RCA 74321110777*	42	2
11 Nov 95	THE TWELFTH OF NEVER *RCA 74321320122*	21	3
18 May 96	HEARTBREAK HOTEL / I WAS THE ONE (2nd re-issue) *RCA 74321336862*	45	1
24 May 97	ALWAYS ON MY MIND (re-issue) *RCA 74321485412*	13	6

Tracks on Jailhouse Rock (EP): Jailhouse Rock / Young and Beautiful / I Want to Be Free / Don't Leave Me Now / Baby I Don't Care. On Strictly Elvis (EP): Old Shep / Any Place Is Paradise / Paralysed / Is It So Strange. On Follow That Dream (EP): Follow That Dream / Angel / What a Wonderful Life / I'm Not the Marrying Kind. On 5 Jul 1962, a note on the Top 50 for that week stated: "Due to difficulties in assessing returns of Follow That Dream EP, it has been decided not to include it in Britain's Top 50. It is of course No.1 in the EP charts." Therefore this EP had only a two-week run on the chart when its sales would certainly have justified a much longer one. 'Beyond the Reef' listed only from 30 Aug to 13 Sep 1980. It peaked at No.7. RCA PB 49177 is a re-issue of RCA 196. 'Can't Help Falling in Love' credited from 1 Mar 1962. Tracks on The Elvis Medley: Jailhouse Rock / Teddy Bear / Hound Dog / Don't Be Cruel / Burning Love / Suspicious Minds. RCA PB 49944 is also an alternate version. 1997 Always On My Mind was re-issue of 1972 hit

PRESSURE DROP *UK, male vocal / instrumental duo (1 WEEK)* pos/wks

21 Mar 98	SILENTLY BAD MINDED *Higher Ground HIGHS6 CD*	53	1

Billy PRESTON
US, male vocalist / instrumentalist - keyboards (51 WEEKS) pos/wks

23 Apr 69 ★	GET BACK *Apple R 5777* [1] ■ ▲	1	17
2 Jul 69	THAT'S THE WAY GOD PLANNED IT *Apple 12*	11	10
16 Sep 72	OUTA SPACE *A & M AMS 7007*	44	3
3 Apr 76	GET BACK (re-entry) *Apple R 5777* [1]	28	5

15 Dec 79 ●	WITH YOU I'M BORN AGAIN *Motown TMG 1159* [2]	2	11
8 Mar 80	IT WILL COME IN TIME *Motown TMG 1175* [2]	47	4
22 Apr 89	GET BACK (2nd re-entry) *Apple R 5777* [1]	74	1

[1] Beatles with Billy Preston [2] Billy Preston and Syreeta

Johnny PRESTON *US, male vocalist - Johnny Courville (45 WEEKS)* pos/wks

12 Feb 60 ★	RUNNING BEAR *Mercury AMT 1079* ▲	1	14
21 Apr 60 ●	CRADLE OF LOVE *Mercury AMT 1092*	2	16
2 Jun 60	RUNNING BEAR (re-entry) *Mercury AMT 1079*	41	1
28 Jul 60	I'M STARTING TO GO STEADY *Mercury AMT 1104*	49	1
11 Aug 60	FEEL SO FINE *Mercury AMT 1104*	18	10
8 Dec 60	CHARMING BILLY *Mercury AMT 1114*	34	1
22 Dec 60	CHARMING BILLY (re-entry) *Mercury AMT 1114*	42	2

Mike PRESTON *UK, male vocalist (33 WEEKS)* pos/wks

30 Oct 59	MR BLUE *Decca F 11167*	12	8
25 Aug 60	I'D DO ANYTHING *Decca F 11255*	23	10
22 Dec 60	TOGETHERNESS *Decca F 11287*	41	5
9 Mar 61	MARRY ME *Decca F 11335*	14	10

PRETENDERS 〔 193 *Top 500* 〕 *Internationally successful, British-based post-punk group with an ever-changing line-up, but with ex-NME journalist Chrissie Hynde (b. 7 Sep 1951, Ohio, US) (v/g) as a common factor. Hynde was briefly married to the lead singer of Simple Minds, Jim Kerr, and had a child with Ray Davies of Kinks (132 WEEKS)* pos/wks

10 Feb 79	STOP YOUR SOBBING *Real ARE 6*	34	9
14 Jul 79	KID *Real ARE 9*	33	7
17 Nov 79 ★	BRASS IN POCKET *Real ARE 11*	1	17
5 Apr 80 ●	TALK OF THE TOWN *Real ARE 12*	8	8
14 Feb 81	MESSAGE OF LOVE *Real ARE 15*	11	7
12 Sep 81	DAY AFTER DAY *Real ARE 17*	45	4
14 Nov 81 ●	I GO TO SLEEP *Real ARE 18*	7	10
2 Oct 82	BACK ON THE CHAIN GANG *Real ARE 19*	17	9
26 Nov 83	2000 MILES *Real ARE 20*	15	9
9 Jun 84	THIN LINE BETWEEN LOVE AND HATE *Real ARE 22*	49	3
11 Oct 86 ●	DON'T GET ME WRONG *Real YZ 85*	10	9
13 Dec 86 ●	HYMN TO HER *Real YZ 93*	8	12
15 Aug 87	IF THERE WAS A MAN *Real YZ 149* [1]	49	6
23 Apr 94 ●	I'LL STAND BY YOU *WEA YZ 815CD*	10	10
2 Jul 94	NIGHT IN MY VEINS *WEA YZ 825CD*	25	5
15 Oct 94	977 *WEA YZ 848CD1*	66	2
14 Oct 95	KID *WEA 014CD*	73	1
10 May 97	FEVER PITCH THE EP *Blanco Y Negro NEG 104CD* [2]	65	1
15 May 99	HUMAN *WEA WEA 207CD*	33	3

[1] Pretenders for 007 [2] Pretenders, La's, Orlando, Nick Hornby

Tracks on Fever Pitch the EP: Goin' Back - Pretenders; There She Goes - LA's; How Can We Hang On to a Dream - Orlando; Football - Neil MacColl; Boo Hewerdine - Nick Hornby. 'Kid' in 1995 is a re-recording

See also Chrissie HYNDE

PRETTY BOY FLOYD *US, male vocal / instrumental group (1 WEEK)* pos/wks

10 Mar 90	ROCK AND ROLL (IS GONNA SET THE NIGHT ON FIRE) *MCA MCA 1393*	75	1

PRETTY THINGS *UK, male vocal / instrumental group (41 WEEKS)* pos/wks

18 Jun 64	ROSALYN *Fontana TF 469*	41	5
22 Oct 64 ●	DON'T BRING ME DOWN *Fontana TF 503*	10	11
25 Feb 65	HONEY I NEED *Fontana TF 537*	13	10
15 Jul 65	CRY TO ME *Fontana TF 585*	28	7
20 Jan 66	MIDNIGHT TO SIX MAN *Fontana TF 647*	46	1
5 May 66	COME SEE ME *Fontana TF 688*	43	5
21 Jul 66	A HOUSE IN THE COUNTRY *Fontana TF 722*	50	1
4 Aug 66	A HOUSE IN THE COUNTRY (re-entry) *Fontana TF 722*	50	1

UK No.1 ★   UK Top 10 ●   Still on chart +   UK million seller ◆   UK entry at No.1 ■   US No.1 ▲

Alan PRICE `364` **Top 500**
One-time leader of The Animals (first called Alan Price Combo), who left in 1965, b. 19 Apr 1942, Durham, UK. Best known for keyboards and vocals but wrote the 1973 Bafta-winning film score for O Lucky Man! and won Most Promising New Actor award in 1975 (87 WEEKS) pos/wks

		pos	wks
31 Mar 66 ●	I PUT A SPELL ON YOU *Decca F 12367* [1]	9	10
14 Jul 66	HI LILI HI LO *Decca F 12442* [1]	11	12
2 Mar 67 ●	SIMON SMITH AND HIS AMAZING DANCING BEAR *Decca F 12570* [1]	4	12
2 Aug 67 ●	THE HOUSE THAT JACK BUILT *Decca F 12641* [1]	4	10
15 Nov 67	SHAME *Decca F 12691* [1]	45	2
31 Jan 68	DON'T STOP THE CARNIVAL *Decca F 12731* [1]	13	8
10 Apr 71	ROSETTA *CBS 7108* [2]	11	10
25 May 74 ●	JARROW SONG *Warner Bros. K 16372*	6	9
29 Apr 78	JUST FOR YOU *Jet UP 36358*	43	7
17 Feb 79	BABY OF MINE / JUST FOR YOU (re-issue) *Jet 135*	32	3
30 Apr 88	CHANGES *Ariola 109911*	54	4

[1] Alan Price Set [2] Fame and Price Together

Kelly PRICE *US, female vocalist (6 WEEKS)* pos/wks

		pos	wks
7 Nov 98	FRIEND OF MINE *Island Black Music CID 723*	25	3
8 May 99	SECRET LOVE *Island Black Music CID 739*	26	2
30 Dec 00	HEARTBREAK HOTEL *Arista 74321820572* [1]	26	1+

[1] Whitney Houston featuring Faith Evans and Kelly Price

Lloyd PRICE *US, male vocalist (36 WEEKS)* pos/wks

		pos	wks
13 Feb 59 ●	STAGGER LEE *HMV POP 580* ▲	7	14
15 May 59	WHERE WERE YOU (ON OUR WEDDING DAY)? *HMV POP 598*	15	6
12 Jun 59 ●	PERSONALITY *HMV POP 626*	9	8
14 Aug 59	PERSONALITY (re-entry) *HMV POP 626*	25	2
11 Sep 59	I'M GONNA GET MARRIED *HMV POP 650*	23	5
21 Apr 60	LADY LUCK *HMV POP 712*	45	1

PRICKLY HEAT *UK, male producer (1 WEEK)* pos/wks

		pos	wks
26 Dec 98	OOOIE, OOOIE, OOOIE *Virgin VSCDT 1727*	57	1

Dickie PRIDE *UK, male vocalist (1 WEEK)* pos/wks

		pos	wks
30 Oct 59	PRIMROSE LANE *Columbia DB 4340*	28	1

Maxi PRIEST `275` **Top 500**
Popular dancehall reggae star, b. Max Elliott, 10 Jun 1960, London, UK. This internationally acclaimed vocalist is the only UK reggae act to top the US chart ('Close to You', 1990). A duet with Roberta Flack, 'Set the Night to Music', also reached the US Top 10 in 1991 (106 WEEKS) pos/wks

		pos	wks
29 Mar 86	STROLLIN' ON *10 TEN 84*	32	9
12 Jul 86	IN THE SPRINGTIME *10 TEN 127*	54	3
8 Nov 86	CRAZY LOVE *10 TEN 135*	67	5
4 Apr 87	LET ME KNOW *10 TEN 156*	49	4
24 Oct 87	SOME GUYS HAVE ALL THE LUCK *10 TEN 198*	12	12
20 Feb 88	HOW CAN WE EASE THE PAIN *10 TEN 207* [1]	41	6
4 Jun 88 ●	WILD WORLD *10 TEN 221*	5	9
27 Aug 88	GOODBYE TO LOVE AGAIN *10 TEN 238*	57	3
9 Jun 90 ●	CLOSE TO YOU *10 TEN 294* ▲	7	10
1 Sep 90	PEACE THROUGHOUT THE WORLD *10 TEN 317* [2]	41	4
1 Dec 90	HUMAN WORK OF ART *10 TEN 328*	75	1
15 Dec 90	HUMAN WORK OF ART (re-entry) *10 TEN 328*	71	3
24 Aug 91	HOUSECALL *Epic 6573477* [3]	31	7
5 Oct 91	THE MAXI PRIEST EP *Ten TEN 343*	62	3
26 Sep 92	GROOVIN' IN THE MIDNIGHT *Ten TEN 412*	50	2
28 Nov 92	JUST WANNA KNOW / FE' REAL *Ten TEN 416* [4]	33	3
20 Mar 93	ONE MORE CHANCE *Ten TENCD 420*	40	3
8 May 93 ●	HOUSECALL (re-mix) *Epic 6592842* [3]	8	8
31 Jul 93	WAITING IN VAIN *GRP MCSTD 1921* [5]	65	2
22 Jun 96	THAT GIRL *Virgin America VUSCD 106* [6]	15	7
21 Sep 96	WATCHING THE WORLD GO BY *Virgin America VUSCD 108*	36	2

[1] Maxi Priest featuring Beres Hammond [2] Maxi Priest featuring Jazzie B [3] Shabba Ranks featuring Maxi Priest [4] Maxi Priest / Maxi Priest featuring Apache Indian [5] Lee Ritenour and Maxi Priest [6] Maxi Priest featuring Shaggy

Tracks on The Maxi Priest EP: Just a Little Bit Longer / Best of Me / Searching / Fever

PRIMA DONNA *UK, male / female vocal group (4 WEEKS)* pos/wks

		pos	wks
26 Apr 80	LOVE ENOUGH FOR TWO *Ariola ARO 221*	48	4

Louis PRIMA *US, male vocalist (1 WEEK)* pos/wks

		pos	wks
21 Feb 58	BUONA SERA *Capitol CL 14841*	25	1

PRIMAL SCREAM *UK, male vocal / instrumental group (49 WEEKS)* pos/wks

		pos	wks
3 Mar 90	LOADED *Creation CRE 070*	16	9
18 Aug 90	COME TOGETHER *Creation CRE 078*	26	6
22 Jun 91	HIGHER THAN THE SUN *Creation CRE 096*	40	2
24 Aug 91	DON'T FIGHT IT FEEL IT *Creation CRE 110* [1]	41	2
8 Feb 92	DIXIE-NARCO (EP) *Creation CRE 117*	11	6
12 Mar 94 ●	ROCKS / FUNKY JAM *Creation CRESCD 129*	7	5
18 Jun 94	JAILBIRD *Creation CRESCD 145*	29	2
10 Dec 94	(I'M GONNA) CRY MYSELF BLIND *Creation CRESCD 183*	49	2
15 Jun 96	THE BIG MAN AND THE SCREAM TEAM MEET THE BARMY ARMY UPTOWN *Creation CRESCD 194* [2]	17	2
17 May 97 ●	KOWALSKI *Creation CRESCD 245*	8	3
28 Jun 97	STAR *Creation CRESCD 263*	16	3
25 Oct 97	BURNING WHEEL *Creation CRESCD 272*	17	2
20 Nov 99	SWASTIKA EYES *Creation CRESCD 326*	22	2
1 Apr 00	KILL ALL HIPPIES *Creation CRESCD 332*	24	2
23 Sep 00	ACCELERATOR *Creation CRESCD 333*	34	1

[1] Primal Scream featuring Denise Johnson [2] Primal Scream, Irvine Welsh and On-U Sound

Tracks on Dixie-Narco (EP): Movin' On Up / Stone My Soul / Carry Me Home / Screamadelica

See also Gary CLAIL ON-U SOUND SYSTEM

PRIME MOVERS *US, male vocal / instrumental group (1 WEEK)* pos/wks

		pos	wks
8 Feb 86	ON THE TRAIL *Island IS 263*	74	1

PRIMITIVE RADIO GODS
US, male vocalist - Chris O'Connor (1 WEEK) pos/wks

		pos	wks
30 Mar 96	STANDING OUTSIDE A BROKEN PHONE BOOTH WITH MONEY IN MY HAND *Columbia 6627692*	74	1

PRIMITIVES
UK, male / female vocal / instrumental group (27 WEEKS) pos/wks

		pos	wks
27 Feb 88 ●	CRASH *Lazy PB 41761*	5	10
30 Apr 88	OUT OF REACH *Lazy PB 42011*	25	4
3 Sep 88	WAY BEHIND ME *Lazy PB 42209*	36	4
29 Jul 89	SICK OF IT *Lazy PB 42947*	24	4
30 Sep 89	SECRETS *Lazy PB 43173*	49	3
3 Aug 91	YOU ARE THE WAY *RCA PB 44481*	58	2

PRINCE `32` **Top 500**
Prolific singer / songwriter / producer / multi-instrumentalist / actor / label and studio owner, b. Prince Rogers Nelson, 7 Jun 1958, Minneapolis, US. This often controversial entertainer has packed stadiums and collected awards worldwide. He has recorded under a variety of monikers including a symbol and "The Artist Formerly Known As Prince" (305 WEEKS) pos/wks

		pos	wks
19 Jan 80	I WANNA BE YOUR LOVER *Warner Bros. K 17537*	41	3
29 Jan 83	1999 *Warner Bros. W 9896*	25	7
30 Apr 83	LITTLE RED CORVETTE *Warner Bros. W 9688*	54	6
26 Nov 83	LITTLE RED CORVETTE (re-issue) *Warner Bros. W 9436*	66	2
30 Jun 84 ●	WHEN DOVES CRY *Warner Bros. W 9286* ▲	4	15
22 Sep 84 ●	PURPLE RAIN *Warner Bros. W 9174* [1]	8	9
8 Dec 84	I WOULD DIE 4 U *Warner Bros. W 9121* [1]	58	6
19 Jan 85	1999 / LITTLE RED CORVETTE (re-issue) *Warner Bros. W 1999*	2	10
23 Feb 85	LET'S GO CRAZY / TAKE ME WITH U *Warner Bros. W 2000* [1] ▲	7	9
25 May 85	PAISLEY PARK *WEA W 9052* [1]	18	10
27 Jul 85	RASPBERRY BERET *WEA W 8929* [1]	25	8
26 Oct 85	POP LIFE *Paisley Park W 8858* [1]	60	2
8 Mar 86 ●	KISS *Paisley Park W 8751* [1] ▲	6	9

14 Jun 86		MOUNTAINS *Paisley Park W 8711* [1]	45	4
16 Aug 86		GIRLS AND BOYS *Paisley Park W 8586* [1]	11	8
1 Nov 86		ANOTHERLOVERHOLENYOHEAD *Paisley Park W 8521* [1]	36	3
14 Mar 87	●	SIGN 'O' THE TIMES *Paisley Park W 8399*	10	9
20 Jun 87		IF I WAS YOUR GIRLFRIEND *Paisley Park W 8334*	20	6
15 Aug 87		U GOT THE LOOK *Paisley Park W 8289*	11	9
28 Nov 87		I COULD NEVER TAKE THE PLACE OF YOUR MAN *Paisley Park W 8288*	29	6
7 May 88	●	ALPHABET STREET *Paisley Park W 7900*	9	6
23 Jul 88		GLAM SLAM *Paisley Park W 7806*	29	4
5 Nov 88		I WISH U HEAVEN *Paisley Park W 7745*	24	5
24 Jun 89	●	BATDANCE *Warner Bros. W 2924* ▲	2	12
9 Sep 89		PARTYMAN *Warner Bros. W 2814*	14	6
18 Nov 89		THE ARMS OF ORION *Warner Bros. W 2757* [2]	27	5
4 Aug 90	●	THIEVES IN THE TEMPLE *Paisley Park W 9751*	7	6
10 Nov 90		NEW POWER GENERATION *Paisley Park W 9525*	26	4
31 Aug 91	●	GETT OFF *Paisley Park W 0056* [3]	4	8
21 Sep 91		CREAM *Paisley Park W 0061* [3] ▲	15	7
7 Dec 91		DIAMONDS AND PEARLS *Paisley Park W 0075* [3]	25	6
28 Mar 92		MONEY DON'T MATTER 2 NIGHT *Paisley Park W 0091* [3]	19	5
27 Jun 92		THUNDER *Paisley Park W 0113* [3]	28	3
18 Jul 92	●	SEXY MF / STROLLIN' *Paisley Park W 0123* [3]	4	7
10 Oct 92	●	MY NAME IS PRINCE *Paisley Park W 0132* [3]	7	5
14 Nov 92		MY NAME IS PRINCE (re-mix) *Paisley Park W 0142T* [3]	51	1
5 Dec 92		7 *Paisley Park W 0147* [3]	27	6
13 Mar 93		THE MORNING PAPERS *Paisley Park W 0162CD* [3]	52	3
16 Oct 93		PEACH *Paisley Park W 0210CD*	14	5
11 Dec 93	●	CONTROVERSY *Paisley Park W 0215CD1*	5	5
9 Apr 94	★	THE MOST BEAUTIFUL GIRL IN THE WORLD *NPG NPG 60155*	1	12
4 Jun 94		THE BEAUTIFUL EXPERIENCE (re-mix) *NPG NPG 60212*	18	3
10 Sep 94		LETITGO *Warner Bros. W 0260CD*	30	4
18 Mar 95		PURPLE MEDLEY *Warner Bros. W 0289CD*	33	2
23 Sep 95		EYE HATE U *Warner Bros. W 0315CD*	20	3
9 Dec 95	●	GOLD *Warner Bros. W 0325CD*	10	9
3 Aug 96		DINNER WITH DELORES *Warner Bros. 9362437422*	36	2
14 Dec 96		BETCHA BY GOLLY WOW *NPG CDEM 463* [4]	11	7
8 Mar 97		THE HOLY RIVER *EMI CDEM 467* [4]	19	3
9 Jan 99	●	1999 (re-issue) *Warner Bros. W 467CD*	10	4
18 Dec 99		1999 (re-entry of re-issue) *Warner Bros. W 467CD*	51	5
26 Feb 00		THE GREATEST ROMANCE EVER SOLD *NPG / Arista 74321745002* [4]	65	1

[1] Prince and the Revolution [2] Prince with Sheena Easton [3] Prince and the New Power Generation [4] The Artist

Although uncredited, Sheena Easton also sings on 'U Got the Look'. 'The Beautiful Experience' was a seven-track CD featuring 'The Most Beautiful Girl in the World' and six further mixes of the track

PRINCE BUSTER *Jamaica, male vocalist (16 WEEKS)*

			pos/wks	
23 Feb 67		AL CAPONE *Blue Beat BB 324*	18	13
4 Apr 98		WHINE AND GRINE *Island CID 691*	21	3

PRINCE CHARLES and the CITY BEAT BAND
US, male vocal / instrumental group (2 WEEKS)

			pos/wks	
22 Feb 86		WE CAN MAKE IT HAPPEN *PRT 7P 348*	56	2

PRINCE NASEEM – See KALEEF

PRINCESS *UK, female vocalist - Desiree Heslop (44 WEEKS)*

			pos/wks	
3 Aug 85	●	SAY I'M YOUR NUMBER ONE *Supreme SUPE 101*	7	12
9 Nov 85		AFTER THE LOVE HAS GONE *Supreme SUPE 103*	28	13
19 Apr 86		I'LL KEEP ON LOVING YOU *Supreme SUPE 105*	16	8
5 Jul 86		TELL ME TOMORROW *Supreme SUPE 106*	34	5
25 Oct 86		IN THE HEAT OF A PASSIONATE MOMENT *Supreme SUPE 109*	74	1
13 Jun 87		RED HOT *Polydor POSP 868*	58	5

PRINCESS IVORI *US, female rapper (2 WEEKS)*

			pos/wks	
17 Mar 90		WANTED *Supreme SUPE 163*	69	2

Patrick PRINZ – See ARTEMESIA; ETHICS; MOVIN' MELODIES; SUBLIMINAL CUTS

Maddy PRIOR – See STATUS QUO; STEELEYE SPAN

PRIVATE LIVES *UK, male vocal / instrumental duo (4 WEEKS)*

			pos/wks	
11 Feb 84		LIVING IN A WORLD (TURNED UPSIDE DOWN) *EMI PRIV 2*	53	4

PRIZNA featuring DEMOLITION MAN
UK, male vocal / instrumental group (2 WEEKS)

			pos/wks	
29 Apr 95		FIRE *Labello Blanco NLBCDX 18*	33	2

PJ PROBY (336) Top 500 *Controversial pony tail-wearing, trouser-splitting teen idol, b. James Marcus Smith, 6 Nov 1938, Texas, US. Mannered vocalist found success after relocating to UK, and adopting Tom Jones (the successful 60s film, not the singer) attire. Voted Brightest Hope of 1964 by Melody Maker readers (91 WEEKS)*

			pos/wks	
28 May 64	●	HOLD ME *Decca F 11904*	3	15
3 Sep 64	●	TOGETHER *Decca F 11967*	8	11
10 Dec 64	●	SOMEWHERE *Liberty LIB 10182*	6	12
25 Feb 65		I APOLOGISE *Liberty LIB 10188*	11	8
8 Jul 65		LET THE WATER RUN DOWN *Liberty LIB 10206*	19	8
30 Sep 65		THAT MEANS A LOT *Liberty LIB 10215*	30	6
25 Nov 65	●	MARIA *Liberty LIB 10218*	8	9
10 Feb 66		YOU'VE COME BACK *Liberty LIB 10223*	25	7
16 Jun 66		TO MAKE A BIG MAN CRY *Liberty LIB 10236*	34	3
27 Oct 66		I CAN'T MAKE IT ALONE *Liberty LIB 10250*	37	5
6 Mar 68		IT'S YOUR DAY TODAY *Liberty LBF 15046*	32	5
28 Dec 96		YESTERDAY HAS GONE *EMI Premier CDPRESX 13* [1]	58	5
11 Jan 97		YESTERDAY HAS GONE (re-entry) *EMI Premier CDPRESX 13* [1]	69	1

[1] PJ Proby and Marc Almond featuring the My Life Story Orchestra

PROCLAIMERS *UK, male vocal / instrumental duo - Charlie and Craig Reid (50 WEEKS)*

			pos/wks	
14 Nov 87		LETTER FROM AMERICA *Chrysalis CHS 3178*	3	10
5 Mar 88		MAKE MY HEART FLY *Chrysalis CLAIM 1*	63	3
27 Aug 88		I'M GONNA BE *Chrysalis CLAIM 2*	11	11
12 Nov 88		SUNSHINE ON LEITH *Chrysalis CLAIM 3*	41	5
11 Feb 89		I'M ON MY WAY *Chrysalis CLAIM 4*	43	4
24 Nov 90		KING OF THE ROAD (EP) *Chrysalis CLAIM 5*	9	8
19 Feb 94		LET'S GET MARRIED *Chrysalis CDCLAIM 6*	21	4
16 Apr 94		WHAT MAKES YOU CRY *Chrysalis CDCLAIMS 7*	38	3
22 Oct 94		THESE ARMS OF MINE *Chrysalis CDCLAIM 8*	51	2

Tracks on King of the Road (EP): King of the Road / Long Black Veil / Lulu Selling Tea / Not Ever

PROCOL HARUM *UK, male vocal / instrumental group - lead vocal Gary Brooker (56 WEEKS)*

			pos/wks	
25 May 67	★	A WHITER SHADE OF PALE *Deram DM 126*	1	15
4 Oct 67	●	HOMBURG *Regal Zonophone RZ 3003*	6	10
24 Apr 68		QUITE RIGHTLY SO *Regal Zonophone RZ 3007*	50	1
18 Jun 69		SALTY DOG *Regal Zonophone RZ 3019*	44	1
2 Jul 69		SALTY DOG (re-entry) *Regal Zonophone RZ 3019*	44	1
16 Jul 69		SALTY DOG (2nd re-entry) *Regal Zonophone RZ 3019*	44	1
22 Apr 72		A WHITER SHADE OF PALE (re-issue) *Fly Magnify ECHO 101*	13	13
5 Aug 72		CONQUISTADOR *Chrysalis CHS 2003*	22	7
23 Aug 75		PANDORA'S BOX *Chrysalis CHS 2073*	16	7

Michael PROCTOR – See URBAN BLUES PROJECT presents Michael PROCTER

PRODIGY (173) Top 500 *Confrontational dance-rock collision masterminded by Liam Howlett (k/prog) and featuring charismatic Keith Flint (v). This act has achieved a run of 12 successive Top 20 singles, while their 1997 album, Fat of the Land, debuted at No.1 in more than 20 countries, including the UK and the US. MC / dancer Maxim went solo in 2000 (139 WEEKS)*

			pos/wks	
24 Aug 91	●	CHARLY *XL XLS 21CD*	3	10
4 Jan 92		EVERYBODY IN THE PLACE (EP) *XL XLS 26CD1*	2	9
26 Sep 92		FIRE / JERICHO *XL XLS 30CD*	11	4
21 Nov 92	●	OUT OF SPACE / RUFF IN THE JUNGLE BIZNESS *XL XLS 35CD*	5	12
17 Apr 93		WIND IT UP (REWOUND) *XL XLS 39CD*	11	7
16 Oct 93	●	ONE LOVE *XL XLS 47CD*	8	6

UK No.1 ★   UK Top 10 ●   Still on chart +   UK million seller ◆   UK entry at No.1 ■   US No.1 ▲

28 May 94	●	NO GOOD (START THE DANCE) XL XLS 51CD	4	12
24 Sep 94		VOODOO PEOPLE XL XLS 54CD	13	5
18 Mar 95		POISON XL XLS 58CD	15	6
30 Mar 96	★	FIRESTARTER XL XLS 70CD ■	1	19
20 Apr 96		CHARLY (re-entry) XL XLS 21CD	66	1
20 Apr 96		FIRE / JERICHO (re-entry) XL XLS 30CD	63	1
20 Apr 96		NO GOOD (START THE DANCE) (re-entry) XL XLS 51CD	57	2
20 Apr 96		OUT OF SPACE / RUFF IN THE JUNGLE BIZNESS (re-entry) XL XLS 35CD	52	2
20 Apr 96		POISON (re-entry) XL XLS 58CD	62	1
20 Apr 96		VOODOO PEOPLE (re-entry) XL XLS 54CD	75	1
20 Apr 96		WIND IT UP (REWOUND) (re-entry) XL XLS 39CD	71	1
27 Apr 96		EVERYBODY IN THE PLACE (EP) (re-entry) XL XLS 26CD1	69	1
23 Nov 96	★	BREATHE XL XLS 80CD ■	1	17
14 Dec 96		FIRESTARTER (re-entry) XL XLS 70CD	54	1
25 Jan 97		FIRESTARTER (2nd re-entry) XL XLS 70CD	53	7
5 Apr 97		BREATHE (re-entry) XL XLS 80CD	71	1
29 Nov 97	●	SMACK MY BITCH UP XL XLS 90CD	8	10

Tracks on Everybody in the Place (EP): Everybody in the Place / Crazy Man / G-Force (Energy Flow) / Rip Up the Sound System

PRODUCT G&B – See SANTANA

PROFESSIONALS *UK, male vocal / instrumental group (4 WEEKS)* pos/wks

| 11 Oct 80 | 1-2-3 Virgin VS 376 | 43 | 4 |

PROFESSOR – See DJ PROFESSOR

PROFESSOR T – See SHUT UP AND DANCE

PROGRAM 2 BELTRAM – See BELTRAM

PROGRESS FUNK *Italy, male production trio (1 WEEK)* pos/wks

| 11 Oct 97 | AROUND MY BRAIN Deconstruction 74321518182 | 73 | 1 |

PROGRESS presents the BOY WUNDA
UK, male DJ / producer - Robert Webster (10 WEEKS) pos/wks

| 18 Dec 99 | ● | EVERYBODY Manifesto FESCD 65 | 7 | 10 |

PROJECT featuring GERIDEAU *US, male vocal / instrumental duo (1 WEEK)* pos/wks

| 27 Aug 94 | BRING IT BACK 2 LUV Fruittree FTREE 10CD | 65 | 1 |

PROJECT 1 *UK, male producer - Mark Williams (3 WEEKS)* pos/wks

| 16 May 92 | ROUGHNECK (EP) Rising High RSN 22 | 49 | 2 |
| 29 Aug 92 | DON GARGON COMIN' Rising High RSN 35 | 64 | 1 |

Tracks on Roughneck (EP): Come My Selector / Can't Take the Heartbreak / Live Vibe 4 (Summer Vibes)

PRONG *US, male vocal / instrumental group (1 WEEK)* pos/wks

| 25 Apr 92 | WHOSE FIST IS THIS ANYWAY EP Epic 6580026 | 58 | 1 |

Tracks on Whose Fist Is This Anyway EP: Prove You Wrong / Hell If I Could / (Get a) Grip (On Yourself) / Prove You Wrong (re-mix)

PROPAGANDA
Germany, male / female vocal / instrumental group (35 WEEKS) pos/wks

17 Mar 84	DR MABUSE ZTT ZTAS 2	27	9
4 May 85	DUEL ZTT ZTAS 8	21	12
10 Aug 85	P MACHINERY ZTT ZTAS 12	50	5
28 Apr 90	HEAVEN GIVE ME WORDS Virgin VS 1245	36	5
8 Sep 90	ONLY ONE WORD Virgin VS 1271	71	4

PROPELLERHEADS *UK, male instrumental / production duo - Alex Gifford and Will White (15 WEEKS)* pos/wks

7 Dec 96	TAKE CALIFORNIA Wall of Sound WALLD 024	69	1
17 May 97	SPYBREAK! Wall of Sound WALLD 029X	40	1
18 Oct 97	●	ON HER MAJESTY'S SECRET SERVICE East West EW 136CD [1]	7	5
20 Dec 97		HISTORY REPEATING Wall of Sound WALLD 036 [2]	19	7
27 Jun 98		BANG ON! Wall of Sound WALLD 039	53	1

[1] Propellerheads / David Arnold [2] Propellerheads featuring Miss Shirley Bassey

PROPHETS OF SOUND
UK, male instrumental / production duo (1 WEEK) pos/wks

| 14 Nov 98 | HIGH Distinctive DISNCD 47 | 73 | 1 |

PROSPECT PARK / Carolyn HARDING
UK, male / female vocal / production duo (1 WEEK) pos/wks

| 8 Aug 98 | MOVIN' ON AM:PM 5827312 | 55 | 1 |

Shaila PROSPERE – See RIMES featuring Shaila PROSPERE

Brian PROTHEROE *UK, male vocalist (6 WEEKS)* pos/wks

| 7 Sep 74 | PINBALL Chrysalis CHS 2043 | 22 | 6 |

Dorothy PROVINE *US, female vocalist (15 WEEKS)* pos/wks

| 7 Dec 61 | DON'T BRING LULU Warner Bros. WB 53 | 17 | 12 |
| 28 Jun 62 | CRAZY WORDS CRAZY TUNE Warner Bros. WB 70 | 45 | 3 |

PSEUDO ECHO
Australia, male vocal / instrumental group (12 WEEKS) pos/wks

| 18 Jul 87 | ● | FUNKY TOWN RCA PB 49705 | 8 | 12 |

PSYCHEDELIC FURS
UK, male vocal / instrumental group (31 WEEKS) pos/wks

2 May 81	DUMB WAITERS CBS A 1166	59	2
27 Jun 81	PRETTY IN PINK CBS A 1327	43	5
31 Jul 82	LOVE MY WAY CBS A 2549	42	6
31 Mar 84	HEAVEN CBS A 4300	29	6
16 Jun 84	GHOST IN YOU CBS A 4470	68	2
23 Aug 86	PRETTY IN PINK (re-recording) CBS A 7242	18	9
9 Jul 88	ALL THAT MONEY WANTS CBS FURS 4	75	1

PSYCHIC TV *UK, male / female vocal / instrumental group (4 WEEKS)* pos/wks

| 26 Apr 86 | GODSTAR Temple TOPY 009 [1] | 67 | 2 |
| 20 Sep 86 | GOOD VIBRATIONS / ROMAN P Temple TOPY 23 | 65 | 2 |

[1] Psychic TV and the Angels of Light

PSYCHOTROPIC – See FREEFALL featuring PSYCHOTROPIC; SALT-N-PEPA

PUBLIC ANNOUNCEMENT
US, male vocal / instrumental group (5 WEEKS) pos/wks

9 May 92	SHE'S GOT THAT VIBE Jive JIVET 292 [1]	57	2
20 Nov 93	SEX ME Jive JIVECD 346 [1]	75	1
4 Jul 98	BODY BUMPIN' (YIPPEE-YI-YO) A & M 5826972	38	2

[1] R Kelly and Public Announcement

See also R KELLY

PUBLIC DEMAND *UK, male vocal group (2 WEEKS)* pos/wks

| 15 Feb 97 | INVISIBLE ZTT ZANG 85CD | 41 | 2 |

PUBLIC DOMAIN *UK, male production / vocal group (5 WEEKS)* pos/wks

| 2 Dec 00 | ● | OPERATION BLADE (BASS IN THE PLACE) Xtravaganza X2H1 CDS | 5 | 5+ |

PUBLIC ENEMY *US, male rap group (53 WEEKS)* pos/wks

21 Nov 87	REBEL WITHOUT A PAUSE Def Jam 651245 7	37	5
2 Jan 88	REBEL WITHOUT A PAUSE (re-entry) Def Jam 651245 7	71	2
9 Jan 88	BRING THE NOISE Def Jam 651335 7	32	5
2 Jul 88	DON'T BELIEVE THE HYPE Def Jam 652833 7	18	5
15 Oct 88	NIGHT OF THE LIVING BASEHEADS Def Jam 6530460	63	2
24 Jun 89	FIGHT THE POWER Motown ZB 42877	29	5

20 Jan 90	WELCOME TO THE TERRORDOME *Def Jam 655476 0*	18	4
7 Apr 90	911 IS A JOKE *Def Jam 655830 7*	41	3
23 Jun 90	BROTHERS GONNA WORK IT OUT *Def Jam 656018 1*	46	2
3 Nov 90	CAN'T DO NUTTIN' FOR YA MAN *Def Jam 656385 7*	53	2
12 Oct 91	CAN'T TRUSS IT *Def Jam 6575307*	22	4
25 Jan 92	SHUT 'EM DOWN *Def Jam 6577617*	21	4
11 Apr 92	NIGHTTRAIN *Def Jam 6578647*	55	2
13 Aug 94	GIVE IT UP *Def Jam DEFCD 1*	18	3
29 Jul 95	SO WATCHA GONNA DO NOW *Def Jam DEFCD 5*	50	1
6 Jun 98	HE GOT GAME *Def Jam 5689852* [1]	16	4
25 Sep 99	DO YOU WANNA GO OUR WAY???		
	Pias Recordings PIASX 005CDX	66	1

[1] Public Enemy featuring Stephen Stills

PUBLIC IMAGE LTD
UK, male vocal / instrumental group (61 WEEKS) pos/wks

21 Oct 78 ●	PUBLIC IMAGE *Virgin VS 228*	9	8
7 Jul 79	DEATH DISCO *Virgin VS 274*	20	7
20 Oct 79	MEMORIES *Virgin VS 299*	60	2
4 Apr 81	FLOWERS OF ROMANCE *Virgin VS 397*	24	7
17 Sep 83 ●	THIS IS NOT A LOVE SONG *Virgin VS 529*	5	10
19 May 84	BAD LIFE *Virgin VS 675*	71	2
1 Feb 86	RISE *Virgin VS 841*	11	8
3 May 86	HOME *Virgin VS 855*	75	1
22 Aug 87	SEATTLE *Virgin VS 988*	47	4
6 May 89	DISAPPOINTED *Virgin VS 1181*	38	5
20 Oct 90	DON'T ASK ME *Virgin VS 1231*	22	5
22 Feb 92	CRUEL *Virgin VS 1390*	49	2

Group often known as P.I.L.

See also John LYDON

Gary PUCKETT – See UNION GAP featuring Gary PUCKETT

Tito PUENTE Jr and the LATIN RHYTHM t.o. featuring Tito PUENTE, INDIA and Cali ALEMAN
US, male / female vocal / instrumental group (3 WEEKS) pos/wks

16 Mar 96	OYE COMO VA *Media MCSTD 40013*	36	2
19 Jul 97	OYE COMA VA (re-mix) *Nukleuz MCSTD 40120*	56	1

PUFF DADDY `341` `Top 500`
World Music Award-winning rapper / songwriter / producer and record label owner, b. Sean Combs 1970, New York, US. Only producer to score three successive US No.1 singles in the 1990s. 'I'll Be Missing You', a tribute to (his discovery) Notorious B.I.G., is the most successful rap single of all time (90 WEEKS) pos/wks

29 Mar 97	CAN'T NOBODY HOLD ME DOWN *Arista 74321464552* [1] ▲	19	4
26 Apr 97	NO TIME *Atlantic A 5594CD* [2]	45	1
28 Jun 97 ★	I'LL BE MISSING YOU *Puff Daddy 74321499102* [3] ◆ ■ ▲	1	21
9 Aug 97	MO MONEY MO PROBLEMS *Puff Daddy 74321492492* [4]	6	10
13 Sep 97	SOMEONE *RCA 74321513942* [5]	34	2
1 Nov 97	BEEN AROUND THE WORLD *Puff Daddy 74321539442* [6]	20	4
3 Jan 98	BEEN AROUND THE WORLD (re-entry)		
	Puff Daddy 74321539442 [6]	56	2
7 Feb 98	IT'S ALL ABOUT THE BENJAMINS		
	Puff Daddy 74321561972 [6]	18	3
1 Aug 98	COME WITH ME (IMPORT) *Epic 34K78954* [7]	75	1
8 Aug 98 ●	COME WITH ME *Epic 6662842* [7]	2	10
1 May 99	ALL NIGHT LONG *Puff Daddy 74321665692* [8]	23	3
29 May 99	HATE ME NOW *Columbia 6672562* [9]	14	6
21 Aug 99	P.E. 2000 *Puff Daddy / Arista 74321694972* [10]	13	4
20 Nov 99	BEST FRIEND *Puff Daddy / Arista 74321712312* [11]	24	4
5 Feb 00	NOTORIOUS B.I.G. *Puff Daddy / Arista 74321737312* [12]	16	5
19 Feb 00	SATISFY YOU (IMPORT) *Bad Boy / Arista 7928322* [13]	73	1
4 Mar 00	SATISFY YOU (IMPORT) (re-entry) *Bad Boy / Arista 7928322* [13]	73	1
11 Mar 00 ●	SATISFY YOU *Bad Boy / Arista 74321745592* [13]	8	8

[1] Puff Daddy featuring Mase [2] Lil' Kim featuring Puff Daddy [3] Puff Daddy and Faith Evans featuring 112 [4] Notorious B.I.G. featuring Puff Daddy and Mase [5] SWV featuring Puff Daddy [6] Puff Daddy and the Family [7] Puff Daddy featuring Jimmy Page [8] Faith Evans featuring Puff Daddy [9] Nas featuring Puff Daddy [10] Puff Daddy featuring Hurricane G [11] Puff Daddy featuring Mario Winans [12] Notorious B.I.G. featuring Puff Daddy and Lil' Kim [13] Puff Daddy featuring R. Kelly

PULP `487` `Top 500`
Jarvis Cocker b. 19 Sep 1963, Sheffield UK, is frontman of Pulp, or was Arabacus Pulp as his band was called in 1978. Through countless line-up changes and modest commercial success, 17 years passed before No.1 album 'Different Class' and a string of Top 10 singles troubled the charts. Cocker's unique brand of wit and wisdom was then exposed to the wider world culminating in the legendary bottom wiggling "protest" at Michael Jackson's 1996 Brit Awards performance (70 WEEKS) pos/wks

27 Nov 93	LIP GLOSS *Island CID 567*	50	2
2 Apr 94	DO YOU REMEMBER THE FIRST TIME *Island CID 574*	33	4
4 Jun 94	THE SISTERS (EP) *Island CID 595*	19	4
3 Jun 95 ●	COMMON PEOPLE *Island CID 613*	2	13
7 Oct 95 ●	MIS-SHAPES / SORTED FOR E'S AND WIZZ		
	Island CID 620	2	8
9 Dec 95 ●	DISCO 2000 *Island CID 623*	7	11
30 Dec 95	MIS-SHAPES / SORTED FOR E'S AND WIZZ (re-entry)		
	Island CID 620	62	3
6 Apr 96 ●	SOMETHING CHANGED *Island CID 632*	10	5
8 Jun 96	SOMETHING CHANGED (re-entry) *Island CID 632*	62	1
22 Jun 96	SOMETHING CHANGED (2nd re-entry) *Island CID 632*	61	1
7 Sep 96	DO YOU REMEMBER THE FIRST TIME (re-entry)		
	Island CID 574	73	1
22 Nov 97 ●	HELP THE AGED *Island CID 679*	8	7
24 Jan 98	HELP THE AGED (re-entry) *Island CID 679*	68	2
28 Mar 98	THIS IS HARDCORE *Island CID 695*	12	4
20 Jun 98	A LITTLE SOUL *Island CID 708*	22	2
19 Sep 98	PARTY HARD *Island CID 719*	29	2

Tracks on The Sisters (EP): Babies / Your Sister's Clothes / Seconds / His 'n' Hers

PULSE featuring Antoinette ROBERSON
US, male / female vocal / production duo (3 WEEKS) pos/wks

25 May 96	THE LOVER THAT YOU ARE *ffrr FCD 278*	22	3

Pulse is David Morales

PURE SUGAR
UK, male / female vocal / instrumental trio (1 WEEK) pos/wks

24 Oct 98	DELICIOUS *Geffen GFSTD 22355*	70	1

PURESSENCE
UK, male vocal / instrumental group (5 WEEKS) pos/wks

23 May 98	THIS FEELING *Island CID 688*	33	2
8 Aug 98	IT DOESN'T MATTER ANYMORE		
	Island CID 703	47	1
21 Nov 98	ALL I WANT *Island CID 722*	39	2

James and Bobby PURIFY
US, male vocal duo (16 WEEKS) pos/wks

24 Apr 76	I'M YOUR PUPPET *Mercury 6167 324*	12	10
7 Aug 76	MORNING GLORY *Mercury 6167 380*	27	6

PURPLE HEARTS
UK, male vocal / instrumental group (5 WEEKS) pos/wks

22 Sep 79	MILLIONS LIKE US *Fiction FICS 003*	57	3
8 Mar 80	JIMMY *Fiction FICS 9*	60	2

PURPLE KINGS
UK, male vocal / instrumental duo (3 WEEKS) pos/wks

15 Oct 94	THAT'S THE WAY YOU DO IT *Positiva CDTIV 21*	26	3

PUSH
Belgium, male producer - Dirk Dierickx (5 WEEKS) pos/wks

15 May 99	UNIVERSAL NATION *Bonzai / Inferno CDFERN 16*	36	2
9 Oct 99	UNIVERSAL NATION '99 (re-mix)		
	Inferno CDFERN 20	35	2
23 Sep 00	TILL WE MEET AGAIN *Inferno CDFERN 29*	46	1

PUSSYCAT
Holland, male / female vocal / instrumental group (30 WEEKS) pos/wks

28 Aug 76 ★	MISSISSIPPI *Sonet SON 2077*	1	22
25 Dec 76	SMILE *Sonet SON 2096*	24	8

PYRAMIDS
Jamaica, male vocal / instrumental group (4 WEEKS) pos/wks

22 Nov 67	TRAIN TOUR TO RAINBOW CITY *President PT 161*	35	4

PYTHON LEE JACKSON
Australia, male vocal / instrumental group (12 WEEKS) pos/wks

| 30 Sep 72 | ● IN A BROKEN DREAM *Youngblood YB 1002* | 3 | 12 |

Uncredited lead vocals by Rod Stewart

Q
UK, male instrumental / production duo (6 WEEKS) pos/wks

| 5 Jun 93 | GET HERE *Arista 74321145972* [1] | 37 | 4 |
| 12 Mar 94 | (EVERYTHING I DO) I DO IT FOR YOU *Bell 74321193062* [2] | 47 | 2 |

[1] Q featuring Tracy Ackerman [2] Q featuring Tony Jackson

Q UNIQUE – See C & C MUSIC FACTORY / CLIVILLES & COLE

QATTARA
UK, male production duo - Andy Cato and Alex Whitcombe (2 WEEKS) pos/wks

| 15 Mar 97 | COME WITH ME *Positiva CDTIV 71* | 31 | 2 |

Q-BASS
UK, male production / instrumental group (1 WEEK) pos/wks

| 8 Feb 92 | HARDCORE WILL NEVER DIE *Suburban Base SUBBASE 007* | 64 | 1 |

Q-CLUB
Italy, male / female vocal / instrumental group (3 WEEKS) pos/wks

| 6 Jan 96 | TELL IT TO MY HEART *Manifesto FESCD 5* | 28 | 3 |

QFX
UK, male vocal / instrumental group (16 WEEKS) pos/wks

6 May 95	FREEDOM (EP) *Epidemic EPICD 004*	41	3
3 Feb 96	EVERYTIME YOU TOUCH ME *Epidemic EPICD 006*	22	4
3 Aug 96	YOU GOT THE POWER *Epidemic EPICD 007*	33	3
18 Jan 97	FREEDOM 2 (re-mix) *Epidemic EPICD 008*	21	4
20 Mar 99	SAY YOU'LL BE MINE *Quality Recordings QUAL 005CD*	34	2

Tracks on Freedom (EP): Freedom / Metropolis / Sianora Baby / The Machine

Q-TEE
UK, female rapper (7 WEEKS) pos/wks

| 21 Apr 90 | AFRIKA *SBK SBK 7008* [1] | 42 | 5 |
| 10 Feb 96 | GIMME THAT BODY *Heavenly HVN 48CD* | 40 | 2 |

[1] History featuring Q-Tee

Q-TEX
UK, male / female vocal / instrumental group (7 WEEKS) pos/wks

9 Apr 94	THE POWER OF LOVE *Stoatin' STOAT 002CD*	65	1
26 Nov 94	BELIEVE *23rd Precinct THIRD 2CD*	41	2
15 Jun 96	LET THE LOVE *23rd Precinct THIRD 4CD*	30	2
30 Nov 96	DO YOU WANT ME *23rd Precinct THIRD 5CD*	48	1
28 Jun 97	POWER OF LOVE '97 (re-mix) *23rd Precinct THIRD 7CD*	49	1

Q-TIP
US, male rapper - John Davis (23 WEEKS) pos/wks

4 Oct 97	● GOT 'TIL IT'S GONE *Virgin VSCDG 1666* [1]	6	9
19 Jun 99	GET INVOLVED *Hollywood 0101185 HWR* [2]	36	2
22 Jan 00	HOT BOYZ *Elektra E7002CD* [3]	18	3
12 Feb 00	BREATHE AND STOP *Arista 74321727062*	12	7
6 May 00	VIVRANT THING *Arista 74321751302*	39	2

[1] Janet featuring Q-Tip and Joni Mitchell [2] Raphael Saadiq and Q-Tip [3] Missy 'Misdemeanor' Elliott featuring Nas, Eve and Q-Tip

See also Janet JACKSON; Joni MITCHELL; Missy 'Misdemeanor' ELLIOTT

QUAD CITY DJs
US, male rap duo (1 WEEK) pos/wks

| 15 Nov 97 | SPACE JAM *Atlantic EW773* | 57 | 1 |

See also TAG TEAM

QUADROPHONIA
Belgium, male instrumental / production group (15 WEEKS) pos/wks

13 Apr 91	QUADROPHONIA *ARS 6567687*	14	9
6 Jul 91	THE WAVE OF THE FUTURE *ARS 6569937*	40	3
21 Dec 91	FIND THE TIME (PART ONE) *ARS 6576260*	41	3

QUADS
UK, male vocal / instrumental group (2 WEEKS) pos/wks

| 22 Sep 79 | THERE MUST BE THOUSANDS *Big Bear BB 23* | 66 | 2 |

QUAKE featuring Marcia RAE
UK, male producer and UK, female vocalist (1 WEEK) pos/wks

| 29 Aug 98 | THE DAY WILL COME *ffrr FCD 344* | 53 | 1 |

QUANTUM JUMP
UK, male vocal / instrumental group (10 WEEKS) pos/wks

| 2 Jun 79 | ● THE LONE RANGER *Electric WOT 33* | 5 | 10 |

QUARTERFLASH
US, male / female vocal / instrumental group (5 WEEKS) pos/wks

| 27 Feb 82 | HARDEN MY HEART *Geffen GEF A 1838* | 49 | 5 |

QUARTZ
UK, male instrumental group (19 WEEKS) pos/wks

17 Mar 90	WE'RE COMIN' AT YA *Mercury ITMR 2* [1]	65	2
2 Feb 91	● IT'S TOO LATE *Mercury ITM 3* [2]	8	14
15 Jun 91	NAKED LOVE (JUST SAY YOU WANT ME) *Mercury ITM 4* [3]	39	3

[1] Quartz featuring Stepz [2] Quartz introducing Dina Carroll [3] Quartz and Dina Carroll

Jakie QUARTZ
France, female vocalist (3 WEEKS) pos/wks

| 11 Mar 89 | A LA VIE, A L'AMOUR *PWL PWL 30* | 55 | 3 |

QUARTZ LOCK featuring Lonnie GORDON
UK, male production / instrumental duo and US, female vocalist (2 WEEKS) pos/wks

| 7 Oct 95 | LOVE EVICTION *X:Plode BANG 2CD* | 32 | 2 |

Suzi QUATRO 217 Top 500
Leather-clad US rock singer / guitarist, b. Suzi Quatrocchio, 3 Jun 1950, Detroit. Thanks partly to ultra-commercial songs and productions by Nicky Chinn and Mike Chapman, she was a regular hitmaker in Europe. In her homeland, however, only 'Stumblin' In' reached the Top 40 (122 WEEKS) pos/wks

19 May 73	★ CAN THE CAN *RAK 150*	1	14
28 Jul 73	● 48 CRASH *RAK 158*	3	9
27 Oct 73	DAYTONA DEMON *RAK 161*	14	13
9 Feb 74	★ DEVIL GATE DRIVE *RAK 167*	1	11
29 Jun 74	TOO BIG *RAK 175*	14	6
9 Nov 74	● THE WILD ONE *RAK 185*	7	10
8 Feb 75	YOUR MAMA WON'T LIKE ME *RAK 191*	31	5
5 Mar 77	TEAR ME APART *RAK 248*	27	6
18 Mar 78	● IF YOU CAN'T GIVE ME LOVE *RAK 271*	4	13
22 Jul 78	THE RACE IS ON *RAK 278*	43	5
11 Nov 78	STUMBLIN' IN *RAK 285* [1]	41	8
20 Oct 79	SHE'S IN LOVE WITH YOU *RAK 299*	11	9
19 Jan 80	MAMA'S BOY *RAK 303*	34	5
5 Apr 80	I'VE NEVER BEEN IN LOVE *RAK 307*	56	5
25 Oct 80	ROCK HARD *Dreamland DLSP 6*	68	2
13 Nov 82	HEART OF STONE *Polydor POSP 477*	60	3

[1] Suzi Quatro and Chris Norman

Finley QUAYE
UK, male vocal / instrumentalist (23 WEEKS) pos/wks

21 Jun 97	SUNDAY SHINING *Epic 6644552*	16	6
13 Sep 97	● EVEN AFTER ALL *Epic 6649712*	10	5
29 Nov 97	IT'S GREAT WHEN WE'RE TOGETHER *Epic 6653382*	29	3
7 Mar 98	YOUR LOVE GETS SWEETER *Epic 6656065*	16	5
15 Aug 98	ULTRA STIMULATION *Epic 6660792*	51	1
23 Sep 00	SPIRITUALIZED *Epic 6698032*	26	3

QUEEN `12` **Top 500** *World-renowned, record-breaking British quartet: Freddie Mercury (v) (d. 1991), Brian May (g/v), John Deacon (b/v), Roger Taylor (d/v). The Beatles are the only group to have more UK Top 10 singles than this act, whose Greatest Hits albums sold 25 million copies worldwide (419 WEEKS)* pos/wks

9 Mar 74 ●	SEVEN SEAS OF RHYE *EMI 2121*	10	10
26 Oct 74 ●	KILLER QUEEN *EMI 2229*	2	12
25 Jan 75	NOW I'M HERE *EMI 2256*	11	7
8 Nov 75 ★	BOHEMIAN RHAPSODY *EMI 2375* ◆	1	17
3 Jul 76 ●	YOU'RE MY BEST FRIEND *EMI 2494*	7	8
27 Nov 76 ●	SOMEBODY TO LOVE *EMI 2565*	2	9
19 Mar 77	TIE YOUR MOTHER DOWN *EMI 2593*	31	4
4 Jun 77	QUEEN'S FIRST EP *EMI 2623*	17	10
22 Oct 77 ●	WE ARE THE CHAMPIONS *EMI 2708*	2	11
25 Feb 78	SPREAD YOUR WINGS *EMI 2757*	34	4
28 Oct 78 ●	BICYCLE RACE / FAT BOTTOMED GIRLS *EMI 2870*	11	12
10 Feb 79 ●	DON'T STOP ME NOW *EMI 2910*	9	12
14 Jul 79	LOVE OF MY LIFE *EMI 2959*	63	2
20 Oct 79 ●	CRAZY LITTLE THING CALLED LOVE *EMI 5001* ▲	2	14
2 Feb 80 ●	SAVE ME *EMI 5022*	11	6
14 Jun 80	PLAY THE GAME *EMI 5076*	14	8
6 Sep 80 ●	ANOTHER ONE BITES THE DUST *EMI 5102* ▲	7	9
6 Dec 80 ●	FLASH *EMI 5126*	10	13
14 Nov 81 ★	UNDER PRESSURE *EMI 5250* `1`	1	11
1 May 82	BODY LANGUAGE *EMI 5293*	25	6
12 Jun 82	LAS PALABRAS DE AMOR *EMI 5316*	17	8
21 Aug 82	BACKCHAT *EMI 5325*	40	4
4 Feb 84 ●	RADIO GAGA *EMI QUEEN 1*	2	9
14 Apr 84 ●	I WANT TO BREAK FREE *EMI QUEEN 2*	3	15
28 Jul 84 ●	IT'S A HARD LIFE *EMI QUEEN 3*	6	9
22 Sep 84	HAMMER TO FALL *EMI QUEEN 4*	13	7
8 Dec 84	THANK GOD IT'S CHRISTMAS *EMI QUEEN 5*	21	6
16 Nov 85 ●	ONE VISION *EMI QUEEN 6*	7	10
29 Mar 86 ●	A KIND OF MAGIC *EMI QUEEN 7*	3	11
21 Jun 86	FRIENDS WILL BE FRIENDS *EMI QUEEN 8*	14	8
27 Sep 86	WHO WANTS TO LIVE FOREVER *EMI QUEEN 9*	24	5
13 May 89 ●	I WANT IT ALL *Parlophone QUEEN 10*	3	7
1 Jul 89 ●	BREAKTHRU' *Parlophone QUEEN 11*	7	7
19 Aug 89	THE INVISIBLE MAN *Parlophone QUEEN 12*	12	6
21 Oct 89	SCANDAL *Parlophone QUEEN 14*	25	4
9 Dec 89	THE MIRACLE *Parlophone QUEEN 15*	21	5
26 Jan 91 ★	INNUENDO *Parlophone QUEEN 16* ■	1	6
25 May 91	HEADLONG *Parlophone QUEEN 18*	14	4
25 May 91	I'M GOING SLIGHTLY MAD *Parlophone QUEEN 17*	22	5
26 Oct 91	THE SHOW MUST GO ON *Parlophone QUEEN 19*	16	5
7 Dec 91	THE SHOW MUST GO ON (re-entry) *Parlophone QUEEN 19*	27	5
21 Dec 91 ★	BOHEMIAN RHAPSODY / THESE ARE THE DAYS OF OUR LIVES (re-issue) *Parlophone QUEEN 20* ◆ ■	1	14
1 May 93 ★	FIVE LIVE (EP) *Parlophone CDRS 6340* `2` ■	1	11
24 Jul 93	FIVE LIVE (EP) (re-entry) *Parlophone CDRS 6340* `2`	74	1
4 Nov 95 ●	HEAVEN FOR EVERYONE *Parlophone CDQUEEN 21*	2	12
23 Dec 95 ●	A WINTER'S TALE *Parlophone CDQUEEN 22*	6	6
9 Mar 96	TOO MUCH LOVE WILL KILL YOU *Parlophone CDQUEEN 23*	15	6
29 Jun 96 ●	LET ME LIVE *Parlophone CDQUEEN 24*	9	4
30 Nov 96	YOU DON'T FOOL ME *Parlophone CDQUEEN 25*	17	4
17 Jan 98	NO ONE BUT YOU / TIE YOUR MOTHER DOWN *Parlophone CDQUEEN 27*	13	4
14 Nov 98 ●	ANOTHER ONE BITES THE DUST *Dreamworks DRMCD 22364* `3`	5	6
18 Dec 99	UNDER PRESSURE (re-mix) *Parlophone CDQUEEN 28* `1`	14	7
29 Jul 00 ★	WE WILL ROCK YOU *RCA 74321774022* `4` ■	1	12
4 Nov 00	WE WILL ROCK YOU (re-entry) *RCA 74321774022* `4`	72	1

`1` Queen and David Bowie `2` George Michael and Queen with Lisa Stansfield `3` Queen with Wyclef Jean featuring Pras and Free `4` Five and Queen

Tracks on Queen's First (EP): Good Old Fashioned Lover Boy / Death on Two Legs (Dedicated to...) / Tenement Funster / White Queen (As it Began). Tracks on Five Live EP: Somebody to Love / These Are the Days of Our Lives / Calling You / Papa Was a Rolling Stone - Killer (medley). Queen appear only on the first two tracks. The first credits George Michael and Queen and the second George Michael with Lisa Stansfield

QUEEN LATIFAH *US, female rapper - Dana Owens (17 WEEKS)* pos/wks

24 Mar 90	MAMA GAVE BIRTH TO THE SOUL CHILDREN *Gee Street GEE 26* `1`	14	7
26 May 90	FIND A WAY *Ahead of our Time CCUT 8* `2`	52	2
31 Aug 91	FLY GIRL *Gee Street GEE 34*	67	1
26 Jun 93	WHAT'CHA GONNA DO *Epic 6593072* `3`	21	4
26 Mar 94	U.N.I.T.Y. *Motown TMGCD 1422*	74	1
12 Apr 97	MR BIG STUFF *Motown 5736572* `4`	31	2

`1` Queen Latifah + De La Soul `2` Coldcut featuring Queen Latifah `3` Shabba Ranks featuring Queen Latifah `4` Queen Latifah, Shades and Free

QUEEN PEN *US, female rapper - Lynise Walters (10 WEEKS)* pos/wks

7 Mar 98	MAN BEHIND THE MUSIC *Interscope IND 95562*	38	2
9 May 98	ALL MY LOVE *Interscope IND 95584* `1`	11	5
5 Sep 98	IT'S TRUE *Interscope IND 95597*	24	3

`1` Queen Pen featuring Eric Williams

QUEENS OF THE STONE AGE *US, male vocal / instrumental group (2 WEEKS)* pos/wks

26 Aug 00	THE LOST ART OF KEEPING A SECRET *Interscope 4973912*	31	2

QUEENSRYCHE *US, male vocal / instrumental group (21 WEEKS)* pos/wks

13 May 89	EYES OF A STRANGER *EMI USA MT 65*	59	1
10 Nov 90	EMPIRE *EMI USA MT 90*	61	1
20 Apr 91	SILENT LUCIDITY *EMI USA MT 94*	34	5
6 Jul 91	BEST I CAN *EMI USA MT 97*	36	3
7 Sep 91	JET CITY WOMAN *EMI USA MT 98*	39	2
8 Aug 92	SILENT LUCIDITY (re-issue) *EMI USA MT 104*	18	4
28 Jan 95	I AM I *EMI CDMT 109*	40	2
25 Mar 95	BRIDGE *EMI CDMT 111*	40	3

QUENCH *Australia, male instrumental / production duo (1 WEEK)* pos/wks

17 Feb 96	DREAMS *Infectious INFECT 3CD*	75	1

QUENTIN and ASH *UK, female vocal duo (3 WEEKS)* pos/wks

6 Jul 96	TELL HIM *East West EW 049CD*	25	3

? (QUESTION MARK) and the MYSTERIANS
US, male vocal / instrumental group (4 WEEKS) pos/wks

17 Nov 66	96 TEARS *Cameo Parkway C428* ▲	37	4

QUESTIONS *UK, male vocal / instrumental group (8 WEEKS)* pos/wks

23 Apr 83	PRICE YOU PAY *Respond KOB 702*	56	3
17 Sep 83	TEAR SOUP *Respond KOB 705*	66	1
10 Mar 84	TUESDAY SUNSHINE *Respond KOB 707*	46	4

QUICK *UK, male vocal / instrumental group (7 WEEKS)* pos/wks

15 May 82	RHYTHM OF THE JUNGLE *Epic EPC A 2013*	41	7

Tommy QUICKLY *UK, male vocalist (8 WEEKS)* pos/wks

22 Oct 64	WILD SIDE OF LIFE *Pye 7N 15708*	33	8

QUIET FIVE *UK, male vocal / instrumental group (3 WEEKS)* pos/wks

13 May 65	WHEN THE MORNING SUN DRIES THE DEW *Parlophone R 5273*	45	1
21 Apr 66	HOMEWARD BOUND *Parlophone R 5421*	44	2

QUIET RIOT *US, male vocal / instrumental group (5 WEEKS)* pos/wks

3 Dec 83	METAL HEALTH / CUM ON FEEL THE NOIZE *Epic A 3968*	45	5

'Cum on Feel the Noize' credited only from 10 Dec 1983

Eimear QUINN *Ireland, female vocalist (2 WEEKS)* pos/wks

15 Jun 96	THE VOICE *Polydor 5768842*	40	2

UK No.1 ★   UK Top 10 ●   Still on chart +   UK million seller ◆   UK entry at No.1 ■   US No.1 ▲

Paul QUINN and EDWYN COLLINS
UK, male vocalists / instrumentalists (2 WEEKS)   pos/wks

11 Aug 84	PALE BLUE EYES *Swamplands SWP 1*	72	2

QUIREBOYS
UK, male vocal / instrumental group (27 WEEKS)   pos/wks

4 Nov 89	7 O'CLOCK *Parlophone R 6230*	36	4
6 Jan 90	HEY YOU *Parlophone R 6241*	14	7
7 Apr 90	I DON'T LOVE YOU ANYMORE *Parlophone R 6248*	24	6
8 Sep 90	THERE SHE GOES AGAIN / MISLED *Parlophone R 6267*	37	4
10 Oct 92	TRAMPS AND THIEVES *Parlophone RS 6323*	41	3
20 Feb 93	BROTHER LOUIE *Parlophone CDR 6335*	31	3

QUIVER – See SUTHERLAND BROTHERS and QUIVER

QUIVVER
UK, male instrumental / production duo (3 WEEKS)   pos/wks

5 Mar 94	SAXY LADY *A & M 5805152*	56	2
18 Nov 95	BELIEVE IN ME *Perfecto PERF 111CD*	56	1

QUO VADIS
UK, male production trio (1 WEEK)   pos/wks

16 Dec 00	SONIC BOOM (LIFE'S TOO SHORT) *Serious SERR 028CD*	49	1

QWILO & FELIX DA HOUSECAT
US, male / female vocal / DJ / production duo (1 WEEK)   pos/wks

6 Sep 97	DIRTY MOTHA *Manifesto FESCD 29*	66	1

Eddie RABBITT
US, male vocalist (14 WEEKS)   pos/wks

27 Jan 79	EVERY WHICH WAY BUT LOOSE *Elektra K 12331*	41	9
28 Feb 81	I LOVE A RAINY NIGHT *Elektra K 12498* ▲	53	5

Steve RACE
UK, male instrumentalist - piano (9 WEEKS)   pos/wks

28 Feb 63	PIED PIPER (THE BEEJE) *Parlophone R 4981*	29	9

RACEY
UK, male vocal / instrumental group (44 WEEKS)   pos/wks

25 Nov 78 ●	LAY YOUR LOVE ON ME *RAK 284*	3	14
31 Mar 79 ●	SOME GIRLS *RAK 291*	2	11
18 Aug 79	BOY OH BOY *RAK 297*	22	9
20 Dec 80	RUNAROUND SUE *RAK 325*	13	10

RACING CARS
UK, male vocal / instrumental group (7 WEEKS)   pos/wks

12 Feb 77	THEY SHOOT HORSES DON'T THEY *Chrysalis CHS 2129*	14	7

RACKETEERS – See Elbow BONES and the RACKETEERS

Jimmy RADCLIFFE
US, male vocalist (2 WEEKS)   pos/wks

4 Feb 65	LONG AFTER TONIGHT IS ALL OVER *Stateside SS 374*	40	2

RADHA KRISHNA TEMPLE
UK, male / female vocal / instrumental group (17 WEEKS)   pos/wks

13 Sep 69	HARE KRISHNA MANTRA *Apple 15*	12	9
28 Mar 70	GOVINDA *Apple 25*	23	8

RADICAL ROB
UK, male producer - Rob McLuan (1 WEEK)   pos/wks

11 Jan 92	MONKEY WAH *R&S RSUK 8*	67	1

Jack RADICS – See Chaka DEMUS and PLIERS; SUPERCAT

RADIO HEART featuring Gary NUMAN
UK, male instrumental group and male vocalist / instrumentalist (8 WEEKS)   pos/wks

28 Mar 87	RADIO HEART *GFM GFM 109*	35	6
13 Jun 87	LONDON TIMES *GFM GFM 112*	48	2

RADIO 1 DJ POSSE – See Liz KERSHAW and Bruno BROOKES

RADIO REVELLERS – See Anthony STEEL and the RADIO REVELLERS

RADIO STARS
UK, male vocal / instrumental group (3 WEEKS)   pos/wks

4 Feb 78	NERVOUS WRECK *Chiswick NS 23*	39	3

RADIOHEAD
UK, male vocal / instrumental group (43 WEEKS)   pos/wks

13 Feb 93	ANYONE CAN PLAY GUITAR *Parlophone CDR 6333*	32	2
22 May 93	POP IS DEAD *Parlophone CDR 6345*	42	2
18 Sep 93 ●	CREEP *Parlophone CDR 6359*	7	6
8 Oct 94	MY IRON LUNG *Parlophone CDR 6394*	24	2
11 Mar 95	HIGH AND DRY / PLANET TELEX *Parlophone CDR 6405*	17	4
27 May 95	FAKE PLASTIC TREES *Parlophone CDR 6411*	20	4
2 Sep 95	JUST *Parlophone CDR 6415*	19	3
3 Feb 96 ●	STREET SPIRIT (FADE OUT) *Parlophone CDR 6419*	5	5
7 Jun 97 ●	PARANOID ANDROID *Parlophone CDODATA S 01*	3	5
6 Sep 97 ●	KARMA POLICE *Parlophone CDODATAS 03*	8	4
24 Jan 98 ●	NO SURPRISES *Parlophone CDODATAS 04*	4	6
4 Apr 98	NO SURPRISES (re-entry) *Parlophone CDODATAS 04*	74	1

RADISH
US, male vocal / instrumental group (3 WEEKS)   pos/wks

30 Aug 97	LITTLE PINK STARS *Mercury MERCD 494*	32	2
15 Nov 97	SIMPLE SINCERITY *Mercury MERCD 498*	50	1

RAE & CHRISTIAN featuring VEBA
UK, male production duo and UK, female vocalist (1 WEEK)   pos/wks

6 Mar 99	ALL I ASK *Grand Central GCCD 120*	67	1

Fonda RAE
US, female vocalist (4 WEEKS)   pos/wks

6 Oct 84	TUCH ME *Streetwave KHAN 28*	49	4

Jesse RAE
UK, male vocalist (2 WEEKS)   pos/wks

11 May 85	OVER THE SEA *Scotland-Video YZ 36*	65	2

Marcia RAE – See QUAKE featuring Marcia RAE

RAF
Italy, male producer - Mauro Picotto (6 WEEKS)   pos/wks

14 Mar 92	WE'VE GOT TO LIVE TOGETHER *PWL Continental PWL 218*	34	3
5 Mar 94	TAKE ME HIGHER *Media MRLCD 0012*	71	1
23 Mar 96	TAKE ME HIGHER (re-mix) *Media MCSTD 40026*	59	1
27 Jul 96	ANGEL'S SYMPHONY *Media MCSTD 40051*	73	1

Gerry RAFFERTY
UK, male vocalist (47 WEEKS)   pos/wks

18 Feb 78 ●	BAKER STREET *United Artists UP 36346*	3	15
26 May 79 ●	NIGHT OWL *United Artists UP 36512*	5	13
18 Aug 79	GET IT RIGHT NEXT TIME *United Artists BP 301*	30	9
22 Mar 80	BRING IT ALL HOME *United Artists BP 340*	54	4
21 Jun 80	ROYAL MILE *United Artists BP 354*	67	2
10 Mar 90	BAKER STREET (re-mix) *EMI EM 132*	53	4

RAGE
UK, male vocal / instrumental group (15 WEEKS)   pos/wks

31 Oct 92 ●	RUN TO YOU *Pulse 8 LOSE 33*	3	11
27 Feb 93	WHY DON'T YOU *Pulse 8 CDLOSE 39*	44	2
15 May 93	HOUSE OF THE RISING SUN *Pulse 8 CDLOSE 43*	41	2

RAGE AGAINST THE MACHINE
US, male vocal / instrumental group (19 WEEKS)   pos/wks

27 Feb 93	KILLING IN THE NAME *Epic 6584922*	25	4
8 May 93	BULLET IN THE HEAD *Epic 6592582*	16	4
4 Sep 93	BOMBTRACK *Epic 6594712*	37	2
13 Apr 96 ●	BULLS ON PARADE *Epic 6631522*	8	3

UK No.1 ★   UK Top 10 ●   Still on chart +   UK million seller ◆   UK entry at No.1 ■   US No.1 ▲

7 Sep 96	PEOPLE OF THE SUN *Epic 6636282*	26	2
6 Nov 99	GUERRILLA RADIO *Epic 6683142*	32	2
15 Apr 00	SLEEP NOW IN THE FIRE *Epic 6691362*	43	2

RAGGA TWINS *UK, male vocal group (10 WEEKS)*
pos/wks

10 Nov 90	ILLEGAL GUNSHOT / SPLIFFHEAD		
	Shut Up and Dance SUAD 7	51	2
6 Apr 91	WIPE THE NEEDLE / JUGGLING		
	Shut Up and Dance SUAD 12S	71	2
6 Jul 91	HOOLIGAN 69 *Shut Up and Dance SUAD 16S*	56	2
7 Mar 92	MIXED TRUTH / BRING UP THE MIC SOME MORE		
	Shut Up and Dance SUAD 27S	65	2
11 Jul 92	SHINE EYE *Shut Up and Dance SUAD 32S* [1]	63	2

[1] Ragga Twins featuring Junior Reid

RAGTIMERS *UK, male instrumental group (8 WEEKS)*
pos/wks

16 Mar 74	THE STING *Pye 7N 45323*	46	1
30 Mar 74	THE STING (re-entry) *Pye 7N 45323*	31	7

RAH BAND *UK, male / female vocal / instrumental group - Richard A and Liz Hewson (50 WEEKS)*
pos/wks

9 Jul 77 ●	THE CRUNCH *Good Earth GD 7*	6	12
1 Nov 80	FALCON *DJM DJS 10954*	35	7
7 Feb 81	SLIDE *DJM DJS 10964*	50	7
1 May 82	PERFUMED GARDEN *KR KR 5*	45	7
9 Jul 83	MESSAGES FROM THE STARS *TMT TMT 5*	42	5
19 Jan 85	ARE YOU SATISFIED? (FUNKA NOVA)		
	RCA RCA 470	70	2
30 Mar 85 ●	CLOUDS ACROSS THE MOON *RCA PB 40025*	6	10

RAHSAAN – See US3

RAILWAY CHILDREN
UK, male vocal / instrumental group (13 WEEKS)
pos/wks

24 Mar 90	EVERY BEAT OF THE HEART *Virgin VS 1237*	68	2
2 Jun 90	MUSIC STOP *Virgin VS 1255*	66	2
20 Oct 90	SO RIGHT *Virgin VS 1289*	68	1
2 Feb 91	EVERY BEAT OF THE HEART (re-entry)		
	Virgin VS 1237	24	6
20 Apr 91	SOMETHING SO GOOD *Virgin VS 1318*	57	2

RAIN – See Stephanie DE SYKES

RAIN TREE CROW *UK, male vocal / instrumental group (1 WEEK)*
pos/wks

30 Mar 91	BLACKWATER *Virgin VS 1340*	62	1

Group is Japan under an assumed name

See also JAPAN

RAINBOW *UK, male vocal / instrumental group (62 WEEKS)*
pos/wks

17 Sep 77	KILL THE KING *Polydor 2066 845*	44	3
8 Apr 78	LONG LIVE ROCK 'N' ROLL		
	Polydor 2066 913	33	3
30 Sep 78	L.A. CONNECTION *Polydor 2066 968*	40	4
15 Sep 79 ●	SINCE YOU'VE BEEN GONE *Polydor POSP 70*	6	10
16 Feb 80 ●	ALL NIGHT LONG *Polydor POSP 104*	5	11
31 Jan 81 ●	I SURRENDER *Polydor POSP 221*	3	10
20 Jun 81	CAN'T HAPPEN HERE *Polydor POSP 251*	20	8
11 Jul 81	KILL THE KING (re-issue) *Polydor POSP 274*	41	4
3 Apr 82	STONE COLD *Polydor POSP 421*	34	4
27 Aug 83	STREET OF DREAMS *Polydor POSP 631*	52	3
5 Nov 83	CAN'T LET YOU GO *Polydor POSP 654*	43	2

RAINBOW COTTAGE
UK, male vocal / instrumental group (4 WEEKS)
pos/wks

6 Mar 76	SEAGULL *Penny Farthing PEN 906*	33	4

RAINMAKERS *US, male vocal / instrumental group (11 WEEKS)*
pos/wks

7 Mar 87	LET MY PEOPLE GO-GO *Mercury MER 238*	18	11

Marvin RAINWATER *US, male vocalist - Marvin Percy (22 WEEKS)*
pos/wks

7 Mar 58 ★	WHOLE LOTTA WOMAN *MGM 974*	1	15
6 Jun 58	I DIG YOU BABY *MGM 980*	19	7

RAISSA *UK, female vocalist - Raissa Khan-Panni (1 WEEK)*
pos/wks

12 Feb 00	HOW LONG DO I GET *Polydor 5616282*	47	1

Bonnie RAITT *US, female vocalist (9 WEEKS)*
pos/wks

14 Dec 91	I CAN'T MAKE YOU LOVE ME *Capitol CL 639*	50	4
9 Apr 94	LOVE SNEAKIN' UP ON YOU *Capitol CDCL 713*	69	1
18 Jun 94	YOU *Capitol CDCLS 718*	31	2
11 Nov 95	ROCK STEADY *Capitol CDCL 763* [1]	50	2

[1] Bonnie Raitt and Bryan Adams

RAJA NEE *US, female vocalist (2 WEEKS)*
pos/wks

4 Mar 95	TURN IT UP *Perspective 5874872*	42	2

RAKIM *US, male rapper - William Griffin (5 WEEKS)*
pos/wks

27 Dec 97	GUESS WHO'S BACK *Universal UND 56151*	32	3
22 Aug 98	STAY A WHILE *Universal UND 56203*	53	1
3 Oct 98	BUFFALO GIRLS STAMPEDE (re-mix) *Virgin VSCDT 1717* [1]	65	1

[1] Malcolm McLaren and the World's Famous Supreme Team plus Rakim and Roger Sanchez

See also Eric B and RAKIM

Tony RALLO and the MIDNITE BAND
France / US, male vocal / instrumental group (8 WEEKS)
pos/wks

23 Feb 80	HOLDIN' ON *Calibre CAB 150*	34	8

Sheryl Lee RALPH *US, female vocalist (2 WEEKS)*
pos/wks

26 Jan 85	IN THE EVENING *Arista ARIST 595*	64	2

RAM JAM *US, male vocal / instrumental group (20 WEEKS)*
pos/wks

10 Sep 77 ●	BLACK BETTY *Epic EPC 5492*	7	12
17 Feb 90	BLACK BETTY (re-mix) *Epic 655430 7*	13	8

RAM JAM BAND – See Geno WASHINGTON and the RAM JAM BAND

RAMBLERS – See Perry COMO

RAMBLERS (from the Abbey Hey Junior School)
UK, children's choir (15 WEEKS)
pos/wks

13 Oct 79	THE SPARROW *Decca F 13860*	11	15

Karen RAMIREZ *UK, female vocalist - Karen Ramelize (15 WEEKS)*
pos/wks

28 Mar 98	TROUBLED GIRL *Manifesto FESCD 31*	50	1
27 Jun 98 ●	LOOKING FOR LOVE *Manifesto FESCD 44*	8	11
21 Nov 98	IF WE TRY *Manifesto FESCD 50*	23	3

RAMONES *US, male vocal / instrumental group (32 WEEKS)*
pos/wks

21 May 77	SHEENA IS A PUNK ROCKER *Sire RAM 001*	22	7
6 Aug 77	SWALLOW MY PRIDE *Sire 6078 607*	36	3
30 Sep 78	DON'T COME CLOSE *Sire SRE 1031*	39	5
8 Sep 79	ROCK 'N' ROLL HIGH SCHOOL *Sire SIR 4021*	67	2
26 Jan 80 ●	BABY I LOVE YOU *Sire SIR 4031*	8	9
19 Apr 80	DO YOU REMEMBER ROCK 'N' ROLL RADIO *Sire SIR 4037*	54	3
10 May 86	SOMEBODY PUT SOMETHING IN MY DRINK / SOMETHING TO BELIEVE IN *Beggars Banquet BEG 157*	69	1
19 Dec 92	POISON HEART *Chrysalis CHS 3917*	69	2

RAMP *UK, male instrumental / production duo (1 WEEK)*
pos/wks

8 Jun 96	ROCK THE DISCOTEK *Loaded LOADCD 30*	49	1

RAMPAGE *UK, male DJ / production group (1 WEEK)*
pos/wks

25 Nov 95	THE MONKEES *Almo Sounds CDALMOS 017*	51	1

UK No.1 ★   UK Top 10 ●   Still on chart +   UK million seller ◆   UK entry at No.1 ■   US No.1 ▲

RAMPAGE featuring Billy LAWRENCE
US male rapper - Roger McNair and US male vocalist (1 WEEK)   pos/wks

18 Oct 97	**TAKE IT TO THE STREETS** *Elektra E 3914CD*	**58**	1

RAMRODS *US, male / female instrumental group (12 WEEKS)*   pos/wks

23 Feb 61	● **RIDERS IN THE SKY** *London HLU 9282*	**8**	12

RAMSEY and FEN featuring Lynsey MOORE
UK, male production duo and female vocalist (1 WEEK)   pos/wks

10 Jun 00	**LOVE BUG** *Nebula VCNEBD 4*	**75**	1

RANCID *US, male vocal / instrumental group (1 WEEK)*   pos/wks

7 Oct 95	**TIME BOMB** *Out Of Step WOOS 8CDS*	**56**	1

RANGE – See Bruce HORNSBY and the RANGE

RANGERS FC *UK, male football team vocalists (2 WEEKS)*   pos/wks

4 Oct 97	**GLASGOW RANGERS (NINE IN A ROW)** *Gers GERSCD 1*	**54**	2

RANK 1 *Holland, male production duo - Piet Bervoets and Benno De Goeij (5 WEEKS)*   pos/wks

15 Apr 00	● **AIRWAVE** *Manifesto FESCD 69*	**10**	5

RANKING ANN – See SCRITTI POLITTI

RANKING ROGER – See Pato BANTON

Shabba RANKS
Jamaica, male vocalist - Rawlston Fernando Gordon (67 WEEKS)   pos/wks

16 Mar 91	**SHE'S A WOMAN** *Virgin VS 1333* [1]	**20**	7
18 May 91	**TRAILER LOAD A GIRLS** *Epic 6568747*	**63**	2
24 Aug 91	**HOUSECALL** *Epic 6573477* [2]	**31**	7
8 Aug 92	**MR LOVERMAN** *Epic 6582517*	**23**	7
28 Nov 92	**SLOW AND SEXY** *Epic 6587727* [3]	**17**	7
6 Mar 93	**I WAS A KING** *Motown TMGCD 1414* [4]	**64**	1
13 Mar 93	● **MR LOVERMAN (re-issue)** *Epic 6590782*	**3**	11
8 May 93	● **HOUSECALL (re-mix)** *Epic 6592842* [2]	**8**	8
26 Jun 93	**WHAT'CHA GONNA DO** *Epic 6593072* [5]	**21**	4
25 Dec 93	**FAMILY AFFAIR** *Polydor PZCD 304* [6]	**18**	8
29 Apr 95	**LET'S GET IT ON** *Epic 6614122*	**22**	3
5 Aug 95	**SHINE EYE GAL** *Epic 6622332* [7]	**46**	2

[1] Scritti Politti featuring Shabba Ranks [2] Shabba Ranks featuring Maxi Priest [3] Shabba Ranks featuring Johnny Gill [4] Eddie Murphy featuring Shabba Ranks [5] Shabba Ranks featuring Queen Latifah [6] Shabba Ranks featuring Patra and Terri & Monica [7] Shabba Ranks (featuring Mykal Rose)

Bubbler RANX – See Peter ANDRE

RAPINATION *Italy, male instrumental / production duo (12 WEEKS)*   pos/wks

26 Dec 92	**LOVE ME THE RIGHT WAY** *Logic 74321128097* [1]	**22**	10
10 Jul 93	**HERE'S MY A** *Logic 74321153092* [2]	**69**	1
28 Sep 96	**LOVE ME THE RIGHT WAY (re-mix)** *Logic 7432140442* [1]	**55**	1

[1] Rapination featuring Kym Mazelle [2] Rapination featuring Carol Kenyon

RAPPIN' 4-TAY *US, male rapper (5 WEEKS)*   pos/wks

24 Jun 95	**I'LL BE AROUND** *Cooltempo CDCOOL 306* [1]	**30**	4
30 Sep 95	**PLAYAZ CLUB** *Cooltempo CDCOOL 310*	**63**	1

[1] Rappin' 4-Tay featuring the Spinners

The Spinners on 'I'll Be Around' are the Detroit Spinners

RARE *UK, male / female vocal / instrumental group (1 WEEK)*   pos/wks

17 Feb 96	**SOMETHING WILD** *Equator AXISCD 011*	**57**	1

RARE BIRD *UK, male vocal / instrumental group (8 WEEKS)*   pos/wks

14 Feb 70	**SYMPATHY** *Charisma CB 120*	**27**	8

O RASBURY – See Rahni HARRIS and F.L.O.

RASHAAN – See US3

Roland RAT SUPERSTAR
UK, male rodent vocalist / rapper (20 WEEKS)   pos/wks

19 Nov 83	**RAT RAPPING** *Rodent RAT 1*	**14**	12
28 Apr 84	**LOVE ME TENDER** *Rodent RAT 2*	**32**	7
2 Mar 85	**NO.1 RAT FAN** *Rodent RAT 4*	**72**	1

RATPACK *UK, male instrumental / production duo (3 WEEKS)*   pos/wks

6 Jun 92	**SEARCHIN' FOR MY RIZLA** *Big Giant BIGT 02*	**58**	3

RATTLES *Germany, male vocal / instrumental group (15 WEEKS)*   pos/wks

3 Oct 70	● **THE WITCH** *Decca F 23058*	**8**	15

RAVESIGNAL III
Belgium, male producer - Christian Bolland (2 WEEKS)   pos/wks

14 Dec 91	**HORSEPOWER** *R&S RSUK 6*	**61**	2

See also CJ BOLLAND

RAW – See Erick 'More' MORILLO presents RAW

RAW SILK *US, female vocal group (12 WEEKS)*   pos/wks

16 Oct 82	**DO IT TO THE MUSIC** *KR KR 14*	**18**	9
10 Sep 83	**JUST IN TIME** *West End WEND 2*	**49**	3

RAW STYLUS *UK, male / female vocal / instrumental duo (1 WEEK)*   pos/wks

26 Oct 96	**BELIEVE IN ME** *Wired WIRED 234*	**66**	1

Lou RAWLS *US, male vocalist (10 WEEKS)*   pos/wks

31 Jul 76	● **YOU'LL NEVER FIND ANOTHER LOVE LIKE MINE** *Philadelphia International PIR 4372*	**10**	10

Gene Anthony RAY – See KIDS FROM 'FAME'

Jimmy RAY *UK, male vocalist (6 WEEKS)*   pos/wks

25 Oct 97	**ARE YOU JIMMY RAY?** *Sony S2 6650125*	**13**	5
14 Feb 98	**GOIN' TO VEGAS** *Sony S2 6654652*	**49**	1

Johnnie RAY   121   Top 500
A sensation in the 1950s, the heart-wrenching vocal delivery of the 'Cry Guy' (b. 10 Jan 1927, Oregon, US, d. 25 Feb 1990) influenced many acts, including Elvis, and Ray was the prime target for teen hysteria in pre-Presley days (168 WEEKS)   pos/wks

14 Nov 52	**WALKING MY BABY BACK HOME** *Columbia DB 3060*	**12**	1
19 Dec 52	● **FAITH CAN MOVE MOUNTAINS** *Columbia DB 3154* [1]	**7**	2
9 Jan 53	● **FAITH CAN MOVE MOUNTAINS (re-entry)** *Columbia DB 3154* [1]	**9**	1
3 Apr 53	**MA SAYS, PA SAYS** *Columbia DB3242* [2] (A)	**12**	1
10 Apr 53	● **SOMEBODY STOLE MY GAL** *Philips PB 123*	**6**	1
17 Apr 53	**FULL TIME JOB** *Columbia DB 3242* [2] (B)	**11**	1
24 Apr 53	● **SOMEBODY STOLE MY GAL (re-entry)** *Philips PB 123*	**6**	4
29 May 53	**SOMEBODY STOLE MY GAL (2nd re-entry)** *Philips PB 123*	**12**	1
24 Jul 53	● **LET'S WALK THAT-A-WAY** *Philips PB 157* [2]	**4**	14
7 Aug 53	**SOMEBODY STOLE MY GAL (3rd re-entry)** *Philips PB 123*	**11**	1
9 Apr 54	★ **SUCH A NIGHT** *Philips PB 244*	**1**	18
8 Apr 55	**IF YOU BELIEVE** *Philips PB 379*	**15**	1
13 May 55	● **IF YOU BELIEVE (re-entry)** *Philips PB 379*	**7**	10
20 May 55	**PATHS OF PARADISE** *Philips PB 441*	**20**	1
7 Oct 55	**HERNANDO'S HIDEAWAY** *Philips PB 495*	**11**	5
14 Oct 55	● **HEY THERE** *Philips PB 495*	**5**	9
28 Oct 55	● **SONG OF THE DREAMER** *Philips PB 516*	**10**	5
17 Feb 56	**WHO'S SORRY NOW** *Philips PB 546*	**17**	2
20 Apr 56	**AIN'T MISBEHAVIN'** *Philips PB 580*	**17**	6
8 Jun 56	**AIN'T MISBEHAVIN' (re-entry)** *Philips PB 580*	**24**	1
12 Oct 56	★ **JUST WALKING IN THE RAIN** *Philips PB 624*	**1**	19
18 Jan 57	**YOU DON'T OWE ME A THING** *Philips PB 655* (A)	**12**	15
8 Feb 57	● **LOOK HOMEWARD ANGEL** *Philips PB 655* (B)	**7**	16

			pos/wks
10 May 57	★	**YES TONIGHT JOSEPHINE** *Philips PB 686*	**1** 16
6 Sep 57		**BUILD YOUR LOVE** *Philips PB 721*.....................	**17** 7
4 Oct 57		**GOOD EVENING FRIENDS / UP ABOVE MY HEAD I HEAR**	
		MUSIC IN THE AIR *Philips PB 708* [3]	**25** 4
4 Dec 59		**I'LL NEVER FALL IN LOVE AGAIN** *Philips PB 952*.......	**26** 4
8 Jan 60		**I'LL NEVER FALL IN LOVE AGAIN** (re-entry)	
		Philips PB 952	**26** 1
5 Feb 60		**I'LL NEVER FALL IN LOVE AGAIN** (2nd re-entry)	
		Philips PB 952	**28** 1

[1] Johnnie Ray and the Four Lads [2] Doris Day and Johnnie Ray [3] Frankie Laine and Johnnie Ray

The chart history of 'You Don't Owe Me a Thing / Look Homeward Angel' is complicated and is as follows: 'You Don't Owe Me a Thing' entered the chart by itself on 18 Jan 1957. On 8 and 15 Feb 1957, 'Look Homeward Angel' was coupled with 'You Don't Owe Me a Thing', but from 22 Feb 1957 the two sides went their individual ways on the chart and were listed separately: 'You Don't Owe Me a Thing' for a further 10 weeks and 'Look Homeward Angel' for a further 14 weeks

Nicole RAY *US, female vocalist (5 WEEKS)*
		pos/wks
22 Aug 98	**MAKE IT HOT** *East West E 3821CD* [1]	**22** 4
5 Dec 98	**I CAN'T SEE** *East West E 3801CD*.................	**55** 1

[1] Nicole featuring Missy 'Misdemeanor' Elliott and Mocha

RAYDIO *US, male vocal / instrumental group (21 WEEKS)*
		pos/wks
8 Apr 78	**JACK AND JILL** *Arista 161*	**11** 12
8 Jul 78	**IS THIS A LOVE THING** *Arista 193*	**27** 9

See also Ray PARKER Jr

RAYVON – See SHAGGY

RAZE *US, male / female vocal / instrumental group (47 WEEKS)*
		pos/wks
1 Nov 86	**JACK THE GROOVE** *Champion CHAMP 23*	**57** 7
3 Jan 87	**JACK THE GROOVE** (re-entry) *Champion CHAMP 23*	**20** 8
28 Feb 87	**LET THE MUSIC MOVE U** *Champion CHAMP 27*........	**57** 3
31 Dec 88	**BREAK 4 LOVE** *Champion CHAMP 67*................	**28** 11
15 Jul 89	**LET IT ROLL** *Atlantic A 8866* [1]	**27** 5
2 Sep 89	**BREAK 4 LOVE** (re-entry) *Champion CHAMP 67*........	**59** 5
27 Jan 90	**ALL 4 LOVE (BREAK 4 LOVE 1990)** *Champion CHAMP 228* [2] ..	**30** 5
10 Feb 90	**CAN YOU FEEL IT / CAN YOU FEEL IT**	
	Champion CHAMP 227 [3]	**62** 1
24 Sep 94	**BREAK 4 LOVE** (re-mix) *Champion CHAMPCD 314*......	**44** 2

[1] Raze presents Doug Lazy [2] Raze featuring Lady J and Secretary of Entertainment [3] Raze / Championship Legend

'Can You Feel It' by Championship Legend is a montage of six Raze tracks

RE-FLEX *UK, male vocal / instrumental group (9 WEEKS)*
		pos/wks
28 Jan 84	**THE POLITICS OF DANCING** *EMI FLEX 2*	**28** 9

Chris REA 〔 223 **Top 500** 〕 One of the most popular UK singer / songwriters of the late 1980s, b. 4 Mar 1951, Middlesbrough. He was already a major European star by the time he finally cracked the UK Top 10 with his 18th chart entry, 'The Road to Hell (Part 2)' (120 WEEKS)
		pos/wks
7 Oct 78	**FOOL (IF YOU THINK IT'S OVER)** *Magnet MAG 111*	**30** 7
21 Apr 79	**DIAMONDS** *Magnet MAG 144*.......................	**44** 3
27 Mar 82	**LOVING YOU** *Magnet MAG 215*.....................	**65** 3
1 Oct 83	**I CAN HEAR YOUR HEARTBEAT** *Magnet MAG 244*........	**60** 2
17 Mar 84	**I DON'T KNOW WHAT IT IS BUT I LOVE IT** *Magnet MAG 255*	**65** 2
30 Mar 85	**STAINSBY GIRLS** *Magnet MAG 276*.................	**26** 10
29 Jun 85	**JOSEPHINE** *Magnet MAG 280*	**67** 2
29 Mar 86	**IT'S ALL GONE** *Magnet MAG 283*..................	**69** 1
31 May 86	**ON THE BEACH** *Magnet MAG 294*	**57** 3
28 Jun 86	**ON THE BEACH** (re-entry) *Magnet MAG 294*	**75** 1
12 Jul 86	**ON THE BEACH** (2nd re-entry) *Magnet MAG 294*	**66** 4
6 Jun 87	**LET'S DANCE** *Magnet MAG 299*	**12** 10
29 Aug 87	**LOVING YOU AGAIN** *Magnet MAG 300*	**47** 4
5 Dec 87	**JOYS OF CHRISTMAS** *Magnet MAG 314*	**67** 1
13 Feb 88	**QUE SERA** *Magnet MAG 318*.......................	**73** 2
13 Aug 88	**ON THE BEACH SUMMER '88** *WEA YZ 195*............	**12** 6
22 Oct 88	**I CAN HEAR YOUR HEARTBEAT** *WEA YZ 320*..........	**74** 2
17 Dec 88	**DRIVING HOME FOR CHRISTMAS (EP)** *WEA YZ 325*......	**53** 3
18 Feb 89	**WORKING ON IT** *WEA YZ 350*......................	**53** 3
14 Oct 89	● **THE ROAD TO HELL (PART 2)** *WEA YZ 431*..........	**10** 9
10 Feb 90	**TELL ME THERE'S A HEAVEN** *East West YZ 455*......	**24** 6
5 May 90	**TEXAS** *East West YZ 468*........................	**69** 1
16 Feb 91	**AUBERGE** *East West YZ 555*......................	**16** 6
6 Apr 91	**HEAVEN** *East West YZ 566*.......................	**57** 2
29 Jun 91	**LOOKING FOR THE SUMMER** *East West YZ 584*	**49** 5
9 Nov 91	**WINTER SONG** *East West YZ 629*..................	**27** 4
24 Oct 92	**NOTHING TO FEAR** *East West YZ 699*	**16** 4
28 Nov 92	**GOD'S GREAT BANANA SKIN** *East West YZ 706*........	**31** 3
30 Jan 93	**SOFT TOP HARD SHOULDER** *East West YZ 710CD*	**53** 2
23 Oct 93	**JULIA** *East West YZ 772CD*......................	**18** 5
12 Nov 94	**YOU CAN GO YOUR OWN WAY** *East West YZ 835CD*	**28** 3
24 Dec 94	**TELL ME THERE'S A HEAVEN** (re-issue)	
	East West YZ 885CD	**70** 1
16 Nov 96	**'DISCO' LA PASSIONE**	
	East West EW 072CD [1]	**41** 1
24 May 97	**LET'S DANCE** *Magnet EW 112CD* [2]	**44** 1

[1] Chris Rea and Shirley Bassey [2] Middlesbrough FC featuring Bob Mortimer and Chris Rea

Both 'On the Beach Summer '88' and 'I Can Hear Your Heartbeat' in 1988 are re-recordings. Tracks on Driving Home for Christmas (EP): Driving Home for Christmas / Footsteps in the Snow / Joys of Christmas / Smile

REACT 2 RHYTHM *UK, male production group (1 WEEK)*
		pos/wks
28 Jun 97	**INTOXICATION** *Jackpot WIN 014CD*................	**73** 1

Eileen READ – See CADETS with Eileen READ

Eddi READER *UK, female vocalist (14 WEEKS)*
		pos/wks
4 Jun 94	**PATIENCE OF ANGELS** *Blanco Y Negro NEG 68CD*......	**33** 5
13 Aug 94	**JOKE (I'M LAUGHING)** *Blanco Y Negro NEG 72CD*	**42** 3
5 Nov 94	**DEAR JOHN** *Blanco Y Negro NEG 75CD1*	**48** 2
22 Jun 96	**TOWN WITHOUT PITY** *Blanco Y Negro NEG 90CD1*	**26** 3
21 Aug 99	**FRAGILE THING** *Track TRACK 0004A* [1]	**69** 1

[1] Big Country featuring Eddi Reader

See also FAIRGROUND ATTRACTION

READY FOR THE WORLD
US, male vocal / instrumental group (8 WEEKS)
		pos/wks
26 Oct 85	**OH SHEILA** *MCA MCA 1005* ▲	**50** 5
14 Mar 87	**LOVE YOU DOWN** *MCA MCA 1110*	**60** 3

REAL EMOTION
UK, male / female vocal / instrumental group (1 WEEK)
		pos/wks
1 Jul 95	**BACK FOR GOOD** *Living Beat LBECD 34*............	**67** 1

REAL McCOY
Germany / US, male / female vocal / instrumental duo (36 WEEKS)
		pos/wks
6 Nov 93	**ANOTHER NIGHT** *Logic 74321173732* [1]	**61** 1
5 Nov 94	● **ANOTHER NIGHT** (re-issue)	
	Logic 74321236992 [1]	**2** 12
28 Jan 95	● **RUN AWAY** *Logic 74321258822* [1]	**6** 10
22 Apr 95	**LOVE AND DEVOTION** *Logic 74321272702* [1]	**11** 8
26 Aug 95	**COME AND GET YOUR LOVE** *Logic 74321301272*	**19** 4
11 Nov 95	**AUTOMATIC LOVER (CALL FOR LOVE)** *Logic 74321325042*.....	**58** 1

[1] (MC Sar &) the Real McCoy

REAL PEOPLE *UK, male vocal / instrumental group (8 WEEKS)*
		pos/wks
16 Feb 91	**OPEN UP YOUR MIND (LET ME IN)** *CBS 6566127*......	**70** 1
20 Apr 91	**THE TRUTH** *Columbia 6567877*	**73** 1
6 Jul 91	**WINDOW PANE (EP)** *Columbia 6569327*.............	**60** 1
11 Jan 92	**THE TRUTH** (re-issue) *Columbia 6576987*	**41** 3
23 May 92	**BELIEVER** *Columbia 6580067*.....................	**38** 2

Tracks on Window Pane (EP): Window Pane / See Through You / Everything Must Change

UK No.1 ★ UK Top 10 ● Still on chart + UK million seller ◆ UK entry at No.1 ■ US No.1 ▲

REAL ROXANNE US, female rapper (10 WEEKS)
pos/wks

		pos	wks
28 Jun 86	BANG ZOOM (LET'S GO GO) Cooltempo COOL 124 [1]	11	9
12 Nov 88	RESPECT Cooltempo COOL 176	71	1

[1] Real Roxanne with Hitman Howie Tee

REAL THING (238 Top 500) Liverpool vocal quartet comprising brothers Chris and Eddie Amoo, Ray Lake and Dave Smith. They were the UK's best-selling black group of the late 1970s, whose biggest hits returned to the Top 10 (when re-mixed) in the 1980s (114 WEEKS)
pos/wks

		pos	wks
5 Jun 76	★ YOU TO ME ARE EVERYTHING Pye International 7N 25709	1	11
4 Sep 76	● CAN'T GET BY WITHOUT YOU Pye 7N 45618	2	10
12 Feb 77	YOU'LL NEVER KNOW WHAT YOU'RE MISSING Pye 7N 45662	16	9
30 Jul 77	LOVE'S SUCH A WONDERFUL THING Pye 7N 45701	33	5
4 Mar 78	WHENEVER YOU WANT MY LOVE Pye 7N 46045	18	9
3 Jun 78	LET'S GO DISCO Pye 7N 46078	39	7
12 Aug 78	RAININ' THROUGH MY SUNSHINE Pye 7N 46113	40	8
17 Feb 79	● CAN YOU FEEL THE FORCE Pye 7N 46147	5	11
21 Jul 79	BOOGIE DOWN (GET FUNKY NOW) Pye 7P 109	33	6
22 Nov 80	SHE'S A GROOVY FREAK Calibre CAB 105	52	4
8 Mar 86	● YOU TO ME ARE EVERYTHING (THE DECADE RE-MIX 76-86) PRT 7P 349	5	12
24 May 86	● CAN'T GET BY WITHOUT YOU (THE SECOND DECADE REMIX) (re-entry) PRT 7P 352	6	13
7 Jun 86	YOU TO ME ARE EVERYTHING (THE DECADE REMIX 76-86) PRT 7P 349	72	1
2 Aug 86	CAN YOU FEEL THE FORCE ('86 REMIX) PRT 7P 358	24	6
25 Oct 86	STRAIGHT TO THE HEART Jive JIVE 129	71	2

REAL TO REEL US, male vocal / instrumental group (2 WEEKS)
pos/wks

		pos	wks
21 Apr 84	LOVE ME LIKE THIS Arista ARIST 565	68	2

REBEL MC UK, male rapper - Mike West (52 WEEKS)
pos/wks

		pos	wks
27 May 89	JUST KEEP ROCKIN' Desire WANT 9 [1]	11	12
7 Oct 89	● STREET TUFF Desire WANT 18 [2]	3	14
31 Mar 90	BETTER WORLD Desire WANT 25	20	6
2 Jun 90	REBEL MUSIC Desire WANT 31	53	2
6 Apr 91	WICKEDEST SOUND Desire WANT 40 [3]	43	6
15 Jun 91	TRIBAL BASE Desire WANT 44 [4]	20	6
31 Aug 91	BLACK MEANING GOOD Desire WANT 47	73	1
21 Mar 92	RICH AH GETTING RICHER Big Life BLR 70 [5]	48	4
8 Aug 92	HUMANITY Big Life BLR 78 [6]	62	1

[1] Double Trouble & the Rebel MC [2] Rebel MC & Double Trouble [3] Rebel MC featuring Tenor Fly [4] Rebel MC featuring Tenor Fly & Barrington Levy [5] Rebel MC introducing Little T [6] Rebel MC featuring Lincoln Thompson

REBEL ROUSERS – See Cliff BENNETT and the REBEL ROUSERS

REBELETTES – See Duane EDDY and the REBELS

REBELS – See Duane EDDY and the REBELS

Ezz RECO and the LAUNCHERS with Boysie GRANT Jamaica, male vocal / instrumental group (4 WEEKS)
pos/wks

		pos	wks
5 Mar 64	KING OF KINGS Columbia DB 7217	44	4

RECOIL UK, male vocal / instrumental group (1 WEEK)
pos/wks

		pos	wks
21 Mar 92	FAITH HEALER Mute MUTE 110	60	1

RED BOX UK, male vocal / instrumental duo - Julian Close and Simon Toulson (28 WEEKS)
pos/wks

		pos	wks
24 Aug 85	● LEAN ON ME (AH-LI-AYO) Sire W 8926	3	14
25 Oct 86	● FOR AMERICA Sire YZ 84	10	12
31 Jan 87	HEART OF THE SUN Sire YZ 100	71	2

RED CAR AND THE BLUE CAR UK, male vocal / instrumental group (4 WEEKS)
pos/wks

		pos	wks
14 Dec 91	HOME FOR CHRISTMAS DAY Virgin VS 1394	44	4

RED DRAGON with Brian and Tony GOLD Jamaica, male vocal group (15 WEEKS)
pos/wks

		pos	wks
30 Jul 94	● COMPLIMENTS ON YOUR KISS Mango CIDM 820	2	13
31 Dec 94	COMPLIMENTS ON YOUR KISS (re-entry) Mango CIDM 820	49	2

RED EYE UK, male instrumental / production duo (1 WEEK)
pos/wks

		pos	wks
3 Dec 94	KUT IT Champion CHAMPCD 315	62	1

RED 5 Germany, male producer - Thomas Kukula (10 WEEKS)
pos/wks

		pos	wks
10 May 97	I LOVE YOU … STOP! Multiply CDMULTY 20	11	5
20 Dec 97	LIFT ME UP Multiply CDMULTY 30	26	5

RED HILL CHILDREN UK, male / female children's choir (2 WEEKS)
pos/wks

		pos	wks
30 Nov 96	WHEN CHILDREN RULE THE WORLD Really Useful 5797262	40	2

RED HOT CHILI PEPPERS US, male vocal / instrumental group (56 WEEKS)
pos/wks

		pos	wks
10 Feb 90	HIGHER GROUND EMI-USA MT 75	55	3
23 Jun 90	TASTE THE PAIN EMI-USA MT 85	29	3
8 Sep 90	HIGHER GROUND (re-issue) EMI-USA MT 88	54	3
14 Mar 92	UNDER THE BRIDGE Warner Bros. W 0084	26	4
15 Aug 92	BREAKING THE GIRL Warner Bros. W 0126	41	3
5 Feb 94	● GIVE IT AWAY Warner Bros. W 0225CD1	9	4
30 Apr 94	UNDER THE BRIDGE (re-issue) Warner Bros. W 0237CD	13	6
2 Sep 95	WARPED Warner Bros. W 0316CD	31	2
21 Oct 95	MY FRIENDS Warner Bros. W 0317CD	29	2
17 Feb 96	AEROPLANE Warner Bros. W 0331CD	11	3
14 Jun 97	● LOVE ROLLERCOASTER Geffen GFSTD 22188	7	8
12 Jun 99	SCAR TISSUE Warner Bros. W 490CD	15	6
4 Sep 99	AROUND THE WORLD Warner Bros. W 500CD1	35	2
12 Feb 00	OTHERSIDE Warner Bros. W 510CD1	33	2
19 Aug 00	CALIFORNICATION Warner Bros W 534CD	16	5

RED JERRY – See WESTBAM

RED RAT – See CARNIVAL featuring RIP vs RED RAT; Curtis LYNCH Jr featuring Kele LE ROC & RED RAT

RED RAW featuring 007 UK, male vocal / instrumental duo (1 WEEK)
pos/wks

		pos	wks
28 Oct 95	OOH LA LA LA Media MCSTD 2065	59	1

RED SNAPPER UK, male vocal / instrumental / production group (1 WEEK)
pos/wks

		pos	wks
21 Nov 98	IMAGE OF YOU Warp WAP 111CD	60	1

RED VENOM – See BIG BOSS STYLUS presents RED VENOM

REDBONE US, male vocal / instrumental group (12 WEEKS)
pos/wks

		pos	wks
25 Sep 71	● WITCH QUEEN OF NEW ORLEANS Epic EPC 7351	2	12

REDD KROSS US, male vocal / instrumental group (4 WEEKS)
pos/wks

		pos	wks
5 Feb 94	VISIONARY This Way Up WAY 2733	75	1
10 Sep 94	YESTERDAY ONCE MORE A & M 5807932	45	2
1 Feb 97	GET OUT OF MYSELF This Way Up WAY 5466	63	1

The listed flip side of 'Yesterday Once More' was 'Superstar' by Sonic Youth

Sharon REDD US, female vocalist (32 WEEKS)
pos/wks

		pos	wks
28 Feb 81	CAN YOU HANDLE IT Epic EPC 9572	31	8
2 Oct 82	NEVER GIVE YOU UP Prelude PRL A2755	20	9
15 Jan 83	IN THE NAME OF LOVE Prelude PRL A2905	31	5
22 Oct 83	LOVE HOW YOU FEEL Prelude A3868	39	5
1 Feb 92	CAN YOU HANDLE IT (re-recording) EMI EM 219 [1]	17	5

[1] DNA featuring Sharon Redd

Otis REDDING `212` `Top 500` *Peerless singer / songwriter, b. 9 Sep 1941, Georgia, US, d. 10 Dec 1967. He was one of the first and most influential Sixties soul stars. He replaced Elvis as the World's Top Male Singer in a Melody Maker poll shortly before his death in a plane crash (124 WEEKS)* pos/wks

		pos	wks
25 Nov 65	MY GIRL *Atlantic AT 4050*	11	16
7 Apr 66	SATISFACTION *Atlantic AT 4080*	33	4
14 Jul 66	MY LOVER'S PRAYER *Atlantic 584 019*	37	6
25 Aug 66	I CAN'T TURN YOU LOOSE *Atlantic 584 030*	29	8
24 Nov 66	FA FA FA FA FA (SAD SONG) *Atlantic 584 049*	23	9
26 Jan 67	TRY A LITTLE TENDERNESS *Atlantic 584 070*	46	4
23 Mar 67	DAY TRIPPER *Stax 601 005*	43	6
4 May 67	LET ME COME ON HOME *Stax 601 007*	48	1
15 Jun 67	SHAKE *Stax 601 011*	28	10
19 Jul 67	TRAMP *Stax 601 012* [1]	18	11
11 Oct 67	KNOCK ON WOOD *Stax 601 021* [1]	35	5
14 Feb 68	MY GIRL (re-issue) *Atlantic 584 092*	36	9
21 Feb 68 ●	(SITTIN' ON) THE DOCK OF THE BAY *Stax 601 031* ▲	3	15
29 May 68	HAPPY SONG *Stax 601 040*	24	5
31 Jul 68	HARD TO HANDLE *Atlantic 584 199*	15	12
9 Jul 69	LOVE MAN *Atco 226 001*	43	3

[1] Otis Redding and Carla Thomas

Helen REDDY *Australia, female vocalist (18 WEEKS)* pos/wks

		pos	wks
18 Jan 75 ●	ANGIE BABY *Capitol CL 15799* ▲	5	10
28 Nov 81	I CAN'T SAY GOODBYE TO YOU *MCA 744*	43	8

REDHEAD KINGPIN and the FBI
US, male rapper - David Guppy (11 WEEKS) pos/wks

		pos	wks
22 Jul 89	DO THE RIGHT THING *10 TEN 271*	13	10
2 Dec 89	SUPERBAD SUPERSLICK *10 TEN 286*	68	1

REDMAN *US, male rapper - Reggie Noble (15 WEEKS)* pos/wks

		pos	wks
25 Apr 98	RAP SCHOLAR *East West E 3853CD* [1]	42	1
30 May 98	MADE IT BACK *Parlophone Rhythm CDRHYTHM 11* [2]	21	3
24 Oct 98 ●	HOW DEEP IS YOUR LOVE *Island Black Music CID 725* [3]	9	7
16 Jan 99	HOW DEEP IS YOUR LOVE (re-entry) *Island Black Music CID 725* [3]	75	1
12 Jun 99	DA GOODNESS *Def Jam 8709232*	52	1
22 Jul 00	OOOH *Tommy Boy TBCD 2102* [4]	29	2

[1] Das EFX featuring Redman [2] Beverley Knight featuring Redman [3] Dru Hill featuring Redman [4] De La Soul featuring Redman

REDNEX *Sweden, male / female vocal / instrumental group (23 WEEKS)* pos/wks

		pos	wks
17 Dec 94 ★	COTTON EYE JOE *Internal Affairs KGBCD 016*	1	16
25 Mar 95	OLD POP IN AN OAK *Internal Affairs KGBD 019*	12	6
21 Oct 95	WILD 'N FREE *Internal Affairs KGBD 024*	55	1

REDS UNITED
UK, male vocal group - 40 Manchester United FC fans (13 WEEKS) pos/wks

		pos	wks
6 Dec 97	SING UP FOR THE CHAMPIONS *Music Collection MANUCDP 2*	12	9
9 May 98	UNITED CALYPSO '98 *Music Collection MANUCDP 3*	33	4

REDSKINS *UK, male vocal / instrumental duo (12 WEEKS)* pos/wks

		pos	wks
10 Nov 84	KEEP ON KEEPIN' ON *Decca F 1*	43	5
22 Jun 85	BRING IT DOWN (THIS INSANE THING) *Decca F 2*	33	5
22 Feb 86	THE POWER IS YOURS *Decca F 3*	59	2

Alex REECE *UK, male producer (7 WEEKS)* pos/wks

		pos	wks
16 Dec 95	FEEL THE SUNSHINE *Blunted Vinyl BLNCD 016*	69	1
11 May 96	FEEL THE SUNSHINE (re-mix) *Fourth & Broadway BRCD 332*	26	3
27 Jul 96	CANDLES *Fourth & Broadway BRCD 333*	33	2
18 Nov 96	ACID LAB *Fourth & Broadway BRCD 344*	64	1

Jimmy REED *US, male vocalist (2 WEEKS)* pos/wks

		pos	wks
10 Sep 64	SHAME SHAME SHAME *Stateside SS 330*	45	2

Lou REED *US, male vocalist - Lou Firbank (19 WEEKS)* pos/wks

		pos	wks
12 May 73 ●	WALK ON THE WILD SIDE *RCA 2303*	10	9
17 Jan 87	SOUL MAN *A & M AM 364* [1]	30	10

[1] Sam Moore and Lou Reed

Dan REED NETWORK
US, male vocal / instrumental group (16 WEEKS) pos/wks

		pos	wks
20 Jan 90	COME BACK BABY *Mercury DRN 2*	51	3
17 Mar 90	RAINBOW CHILD *Mercury DRN 3*	60	3
21 Jul 90	STARDATE 1990 / RAINBOW CHILD (re-issue) *Mercury DRN 4*	39	4
8 Sep 90	LOVER / MONEY *Mercury DRN 5*	45	3
13 Jul 91	MIX IT UP *Mercury MER 345*	49	2
21 Sep 91	BABY NOW I *Mercury MER 352*	65	1

Michael REED ORCHESTRA – See Richard HARTLEY / Michael REED ORCHESTRA

REEF *UK, male vocal / instrumental group (45 WEEKS)* pos/wks

		pos	wks
15 Apr 95	GOOD FEELING *Sony S2 6613602*	24	4
3 Jun 95	NAKED *Sony S2 6620622*	11	5
5 Aug 95	WEIRD *Sony S2 6622772*	19	3
2 Nov 96 ●	PLACE YOUR HANDS *Sony S2 6635712*	6	7
25 Jan 97 ●	COME BACK BRIGHTER *Sony S2 6640972*	8	5
5 Apr 97	CONSIDERATION *Sony S2 6643125*	13	4
2 Aug 97	YER OLD *Sony S2 6647032*	21	3
10 Apr 99	I'VE GOT SOMETHING TO SAY *Sony S2 6669542*	15	6
5 Jun 99	SWEETY *Sony S2 6673732*	46	1
11 Sep 99	NEW BIRD *Sony S2 6678512*	73	1
12 Aug 00	SET THE RECORD STRAIGHT *Sony S2 6695952*	19	5
16 Dec 00	SUPERHERO *Sony S2 66999382*	55	1

REEL 2 REAL *US, male vocal / production duo - Erick Morillo and Mark 'The Mad Stuntman' Quashie (53 WEEKS)* pos/wks

		pos	wks
12 Feb 94 ●	I LIKE TO MOVE IT *Positiva CDTIV 10* [1]	5	20
2 Jul 94 ●	GO ON MOVE *Positiva CDTIV 15* [1]	7	9
1 Oct 94	CAN YOU FEEL IT *Positiva CDTIV 22* [1]	13	5
3 Dec 94	RAISE YOUR HANDS *Positiva CDTIV 27* [1]	14	6
1 Apr 95	CONWAY *Positiva CDTIVS 30* [1]	27	4
6 Jul 96 ●	JAZZ IT UP *Positiva CDTIV 59*	7	7
5 Oct 96	ARE YOU READY FOR SOME MORE *Positiva CDTIV 56*	24	2

[1] Reel 2 Real featuring the Mad Stuntman

See also LIL MO' YIN YANG, ERICK 'MORE' MORILLO

Maureen REES *UK, female (TV learner driver) vocalist (4 WEEKS)* pos/wks

		pos	wks
20 Dec 97	DRIVING IN MY CAR *Eagle EAGXS 014*	49	4

Tony REES and the COTTAGERS *UK, male vocal group (1 WEEK)* pos/wks

		pos	wks
10 May 75	VIVA EL FULHAM *Sonet SON 2059*	46	1

REESE PROJECT
US, male producer - Kevin Saunderson (7 WEEKS) pos/wks

		pos	wks
8 Aug 92	THE COLOUR OF LOVE *Network NWK 51*	52	2
12 Dec 92	I BELIEVE *Network NWKT 63*	74	1
13 Mar 93	SO DEEP *Network NWKCD 68*	54	2
24 Sep 94	THE COLOUR OF LOVE (re-mix) *Network NWKCD 81*	55	1
6 May 95	DIRECT-ME *Network NWKCD 87*	44	1

Conner REEVES *UK, male vocalist (18 WEEKS)* pos/wks

		pos	wks
30 Aug 97	MY FATHER'S SON *Wildstar CDWILD 1*	12	5
22 Nov 97	EARTHBOUND *Wildstar CDWILD 2*	14	4
11 Apr 98	READ MY MIND *Wildstar CXWILD 4*	19	4
3 Oct 98	SEARCHING FOR A SOUL *Wildstar CDWILD 6*	28	2
4 Sep 99	BEST FRIEND *WEA WEA 221CD1* [1]	23	3

[1] Mark Morrison and Conner Reeves

UK No.1 ★   UK Top 10 ●   Still on chart +   UK million seller ◆   UK entry at No.1 ■   US No.1 ▲

Jim REEVES `24` `Top 500` *Internationally acclaimed velvet-voiced vocalist b. 20 Aug 1924, Texas, US, d. 31 Jul 1964. 'Gentleman Jim' had an impressive portfolio of posthumous hits, including a record-breaking eight albums simultaneously on the UK chart three months after his death (322 WEEKS)* pos/wks

24 Mar 60	HE'LL HAVE TO GO *RCA 1168*	36	1
7 Apr 60	HE'LL HAVE TO GO (re-entry) *RCA 1168*	12	30
16 Mar 61	WHISPERING HOPE *RCA 1223*	50	1
23 Nov 61	YOU'RE THE ONLY GOOD THING *RCA 1261*	17	19
28 Jun 62	ADIOS AMIGO *RCA 1293*	23	21
22 Nov 62	I'M GONNA CHANGE EVERYTHING *RCA 1317*	42	2
13 Jun 63 ●	WELCOME TO MY WORLD *RCA 1342*	6	15
17 Oct 63	GUILTY *RCA 1364*	29	7
20 Feb 64 ●	I LOVE YOU BECAUSE *RCA 1385*	5	39
18 Jun 64 ●	I WON'T FORGET YOU *RCA 1400*	3	25
5 Nov 64 ●	THERE'S A HEARTACHE FOLLOWING ME *RCA 1423*	6	13
7 Jan 65	I WON'T FORGET YOU (re-entry) *RCA 1400*	47	1
4 Feb 65 ●	IT HURTS SO MUCH *RCA 1437*	8	10
15 Apr 65	NOT UNTIL THE NEXT TIME *RCA 1446*	13	12
6 May 65	HOW LONG HAS IT BEEN *RCA 1445*	45	5
15 Jul 65	THIS WORLD IS NOT MY HOME *RCA 1412*	22	9
11 Nov 65	IS IT REALLY OVER *RCA 1488*	17	9
18 Aug 66 ★	DISTANT DRUMS *RCA 1537*	1	25
2 Feb 67	I WON'T COME IN WHILE HE'S THERE *RCA 1563*	12	11
26 Jul 67	TRYING TO FORGET *RCA 1611*	33	5
22 Nov 67	I HEARD A HEART BREAK LAST NIGHT *RCA 1643*	38	6
27 Mar 68	PRETTY BROWN EYES *RCA 1672*	33	5
25 Jun 69	WHEN TWO WORLDS COLLIDE *RCA 1830*	17	17
6 Dec 69	BUT YOU LOVE ME DADDY *RCA 1899*	15	16
21 Mar 70	NOBODY'S FOOL *RCA 1915*	32	5
12 Sep 70	ANGELS DON'T LIE *RCA 1997*	44	1
26 Sep 70	ANGELS DON'T LIE (re-entry) *RCA 1997*	32	2
26 Jun 71	I LOVE YOU BECAUSE / HE'LL HAVE TO GO / MOONLIGHT & ROSES (re-issue) *RCA Maximillion 2092*	34	8
19 Feb 72	YOU'RE FREE TO GO *RCA 2174*	48	2

Martha REEVES and the VANDELLAS `378` `Top 500` *Fronted by Martha Reeves, b. 18 Jul 1941, Alabama, US, previously a secretary and backing vocalist for the Motown label. The female trio made their UK Top 20 debut six years after doing the same in the US and were inducted into the Rock and Roll Hall of Fame in 1995 (85 WEEKS)* pos/wks

29 Oct 64	DANCING IN THE STREET *Stateside SS 345* [1]	28	8
1 Apr 65	NOWHERE TO RUN *Tamla Motown TMG 502* [1]	26	8
1 Dec 66	I'M READY FOR LOVE *Tamla Motown TMG 582* [1]	29	8
30 Mar 67	JIMMY MACK *Tamla Motown TMG 599* [1]	21	9
17 Jan 68	HONEY CHILE *Tamla Motown TMG 636*	30	9
15 Jan 69 ●	DANCING IN THE STREET (re-issue) *Tamla Motown TMG 684*	4	12
16 Apr 69	NOWHERE TO RUN (re-issue) *Tamla Motown TMG 694*	42	3
29 Aug 70	JIMMY MACK (re-entry) *Tamla Motown TMG 599* [1]	21	12
13 Feb 71	FORGET ME NOT *Tamla Motown TMG 762*	11	8
8 Jan 72	BLESS YOU *Tamla Motown TMG 794*	33	5
23 Jul 88	NOWHERE TO RUN (2nd re-issue) *A&M AM 444*	52	3

[1] Martha and the Vandellas

The listed flip side of 'Nowhere to Run' in 1988 was 'I Got You (I Feel Good)' by James Brown

Vic REEVES *UK, male comedian / vocalist - Jim Moir (29 WEEKS)* pos/wks

27 Apr 91 ●	BORN FREE *Sense SIGH 710* [1]	6	6
26 Oct 91 ★	DIZZY *Sense SIGH 712* [2]	1	12
14 Dec 91	ABIDE WITH ME *Sense SIGH 713*	47	3
8 Jul 95 ●	I'M A BELIEVER *Parlophone CDR 6412* [3]	3	8

[1] Vic Reeves and the Roman Numerals [2] Vic Reeves and the Wonder Stuff [3] EMF and Reeves and Mortimer

REFUGEE ALLSTARS – See Wyclef JEAN; FUGEES

REFUGEE CAMP ALLSTARS – See Lauryn HILL

Joan REGAN *UK, female vocalist (62 WEEKS)* pos/wks

11 Dec 53 ●	RICOCHET *Decca F 10193* [1]	8	1
8 Jan 54 ●	RICOCHET (re-entry) *Decca F 10193* [1]	9	4
14 May 54 ●	SOMEONE ELSE'S ROSES *Decca F 10257*	5	8
1 Oct 54	IF I GIVE MY HEART TO YOU *Decca F 10373*	20	1
29 Oct 54 ●	IF I GIVE MY HEART TO YOU (re-entry) *Decca F 10373*	3	10
5 Nov 54	WAIT FOR ME, DARLING *Decca F 10362* [2]	18	1
25 Mar 55 ●	PRIZE OF GOLD *Decca F 10432*	6	8
6 May 55	OPEN UP YOUR HEART *Decca F 10474* [3]	19	1
1 May 59 ●	MAY YOU ALWAYS *HMV POP 593*	9	16
5 Feb 60	HAPPY ANNIVERSARY *Pye 7N 15238*	29	1
19 Feb 60	HAPPY ANNIVERSARY (re-entry) *Pye 7N 15238*	29	1
28 Jul 60	PAPA LOVES MAMA *Pye 7N 15278*	29	8
24 Nov 60	ONE OF THE LUCKY ONES *Pye 7N 15310*	47	1
5 Jan 61	IT MUST BE SANTA *Pye 7N 15303*	42	1

[1] Joan Regan with the Squadronaires [2] Joan Regan with the Johnston Brothers [3] Joan and Rusty Regan

REGENTS *UK, male / female vocal / instrumental group (14 WEEKS)* pos/wks

22 Dec 79	7 TEEN *Rialto TREB 111*	11	12
7 Jun 80	SEE YOU LATER *Arista ARIST 350*	55	2

REGGAE BOYZ *Jamaica, male vocal / instrumental group (1 WEEK)* pos/wks

27 Jun 98	KICK IT *Universal MCSTD 40167*	59	1

REGGAE PHILHARMONIC ORCHESTRA *UK, male / female vocal / instrumental group (11 WEEKS)* pos/wks

19 Nov 88	MINNIE THE MOOCHER *Mango IS 378*	35	9
28 Jul 90	LOVELY THING *Mango MNG 742*	71	2

REGGAE REVOLUTION – See Pato BANTON

REGGIE – See TECHNOTRONIC

REGINA *US, female vocalist (3 WEEKS)* pos/wks

1 Feb 86	BABY LOVE *Funkin' Marvellous MARV 01*	50	3

REID *UK, male vocal group (12 WEEKS)* pos/wks

8 Oct 88	ONE WAY OUT *Syncopate SY 16*	66	2
11 Feb 89	REAL EMOTION *Syncopate SY 24*	65	2
15 Apr 89	GOOD TIMES *Syncopate SY 27*	55	6
21 Oct 89	LOVIN' ON THE SIDE *Syncopate REID 1*	71	2

Ellen REID – See CRASH TEST DUMMIES

John REID – See NIGHTCRAWLERS featuring John REID

Junior REID – See COLDCUT; RAGGA TWINS; SOUP DRAGONS

Mike REID *UK, male actor / comedian (10 WEEKS)* pos/wks

22 Mar 75 ●	THE UGLY DUCKLING *Pye 7N 45434*	10	8
24 Apr 99	THE MORE I SEE YOU *Telstar TV CDSTAS 3049* [1]	46	2

[1] Barbara Windsor and Mike Reid

Neil REID *UK, male vocalist (26 WEEKS)* pos/wks

1 Jan 72 ●	MOTHER OF MINE *Decca F 13264*	2	20
8 Apr 72	THAT'S WHAT I WANT TO BE *Decca F 13300*	49	1
22 Apr 72	THAT'S WHAT I WANT TO BE (re-entry) *Decca F 13300*	45	5

Patrick REID – See POB featuring DJ Patrick REID

Maggie REILLY – See Mike OLDFIELD

Keith RELF *UK, male vocalist (1 WEEK)* pos/wks

26 May 66	MR ZERO *Columbia DB 7920*	50	1

R.E.M. `143` `Top 500` "America's Best Rock Band", according to Rolling Stone: Michael Stipe (v), Peter Buck (g), Mike Mills (b), Bill Berry (d). This Georgia group went from the US college circuit to packing stadiums worldwide. In 1996, the award-winning, platinum-album-earning quartet signed an $80 million record deal (151 WEEKS)

		pos/wks
28 Nov 87	THE ONE I LOVE *IRS IRM 46*	51 8
30 Apr 88	FINEST WORKSONG *IRS IRM 161*	50 2
4 Feb 89	STAND *Warner Bros. W 7577*	51 3
3 Jun 89	ORANGE CRUSH *Warner Bros. W 2960*	28 5
12 Aug 89	STAND (re-issue) *Warner Bros. W 2833*	48 2
9 Mar 91	LOSING MY RELIGION *Warner Bros. W 0015*	19 9
18 May 91 ●	SHINY HAPPY PEOPLE *Warner Bros. W 0027*	6 11
17 Aug 91	NEAR WILD HEAVEN *Warner Bros. W 0055*	27 4
21 Sep 91	THE ONE I LOVE (re-issue) *IRS IRM 178*	16 6
16 Nov 91	RADIO SONG *Warner Bros. W 0072*	28 3
14 Dec 91	IT'S THE END OF THE WORLD AS WE KNOW IT *IRS IRM 180*	39 4
3 Oct 92	DRIVE *Warner Bros. W 0136*	11 5
28 Nov 92	MAN ON THE MOON *Warner Bros. W 0143*	18 4
20 Feb 93	THE SIDEWINDER SLEEPS TONITE *Warner Bros. W 0152CD1*	17 6
17 Apr 93 ●	EVERYBODY HURTS *Warner Bros. W 0169CD1*	7 12
24 Jul 93	NIGHTSWIMMING *Warner Bros. W 0184CD*	27 5
11 Dec 93	FIND THE RIVER *Warner Bros. W 0211CD*	54 1
17 Sep 94	WHAT'S THE FREQUENCY, KENNETH *Warner Bros. W 0265CD*	9 7
12 Nov 94	BANG AND BLAME *Warner Bros. W 0275CD*	15 4
4 Feb 95	CRUSH WITH EYELINER *Warner Bros. W 0281CD*	23 3
15 Apr 95 ●	STRANGE CURRENCIES *Warner Bros. W 0290CD*	9 4
29 Jul 95	TONGUE *Warner Bros. W 0308CD*	13 5
31 Aug 96 ●	E-BOW THE LETTER *Warner Bros. W 0369CD*	4 5
2 Nov 96	BITTERSWEET ME *Warner Bros. W 0377CD*	19 2
14 Dec 96	ELECTROLITE *Warner Bros. W 0383CD*	29 2
24 Oct 98 ●	DAYSLEEPER *Warner Bros. W 0455CD*	6 6
19 Dec 98	LOTUS *Warner Bros. W 466CD*	26 5
20 Mar 99 ●	AT MY MOST BEAUTIFUL *Warner Bros. W 477CD*	10 4
5 Feb 00 ●	THE GREAT BEYOND *Warner Bros. W 516CD*	3 10

REMBRANDTS *US, male vocal / instrumental group (28 WEEKS)* pos/wks

		pos/wks
2 Sep 95 ●	I'LL BE THERE FOR YOU (THEME FROM 'FRIENDS') *East West A 4390CD*	3 12
20 Jan 96	THIS HOUSE IS NOT A HOME *East West A 4336CD*	58 1
24 May 97 ●	I'LL BE THERE FOR YOU (THEME FROM 'FRIENDS') (re-entry) *East West A 4390CD*	5 15

RENAISSANCE
UK, male / female vocal / instrumental group (11 WEEKS) pos/wks

		pos/wks
15 Jul 78 ●	NORTHERN LIGHTS *Warner Bros. K 17177*	10 11

RENE and ANGELA *US, male / female vocal duo (15 WEEKS)* pos/wks

		pos/wks
15 Jun 85	SAVE YOUR LOVE (FOR NUMBER 1) *Club JAB 14* [1]	66 2
7 Sep 85	I'LL BE GOOD *Club JAB 18*	22 10
2 Nov 85	SECRET RENDEZVOUS *Champion CHAMP 5*	54 3

[1] René and Angela featuring Kurtis Blow

RENÉ and YVETTE *UK, male / female vocal duo (4 WEEKS)* pos/wks

		pos/wks
22 Nov 86	JE T'AIME (ALLO ALLO) / RENE DMC (DEVASTATING MACHO CHARISMA) *Sedition EDIT 3319*	57 4

Nicole RENEE *US, female vocalist (1 WEEK)* pos/wks

		pos/wks
12 Dec 98	STRAWBERRY *Atlantic AT 0050CD*	55 1

RENÉE and RENATO *UK / Italy, female / male vocal duo - Hilary Lester and Renato Pagliari (22 WEEKS)* pos/wks

		pos/wks
30 Oct 82 ★	SAVE YOUR LOVE *Hollywood HWD 003*	1 16
12 Feb 83	JUST ONE MORE KISS *Hollywood HWD 006*	48 6

RENEGADE SOUNDWAVE
UK, male vocal / instrumental group (7 WEEKS) pos/wks

		pos/wks
3 Feb 90	PROBABLY A ROBBERY *Mute MUTE 102*	38 6
5 Feb 94	RENEGADE SOUNDWAVE *Mute CDMUTE 146*	64 1

REO SPEEDWAGON
US, male vocal / instrumental group (38 WEEKS) pos/wks

		pos/wks
11 Apr 81 ●	KEEP ON LOVING YOU *Epic EPC 9544* ▲	7 14
27 Jun 81	TAKE IT ON THE RUN *Epic EPC A 1207*	19 14
16 Mar 85	CAN'T FIGHT THIS FEELING *Epic A 4880* ▲	16 10

REPARATA and the DELRONS
US, female vocal group (12 WEEKS) pos/wks

		pos/wks
20 Mar 68	CAPTAIN OF YOUR SHIP *Bell 1002*	13 10
18 Oct 75	SHOES *Dart 2066 562* [1]	43 2

[1] Reparata

REPRAZENT – See Roni SIZE / REPRAZENT

REPUBLICA
UK, male / female vocal / instrumental group (18 WEEKS) pos/wks

		pos/wks
27 Apr 96	READY TO GO *Deconstruction 74321326132*	43 2
1 Mar 97	READY TO GO (re-issue) *Deconstruction 74321421332*	13 6
3 May 97 ●	DROP DEAD GORGEOUS *Deconstruction 74321408442*	7 7
3 Oct 98	FROM RUSH HOUR WITH LOVE *Deconstruction 74321610472*	20 3

See also SAFFRON

REST ASSURED *UK, male production trio (7 WEEKS)* pos/wks

		pos/wks
28 Feb 98	TREAT INFAMY *ffrr FCD 333*	14 7

REUNION *US, male vocal group (4 WEEKS)* pos/wks

		pos/wks
21 Sep 74	LIFE IS A ROCK (BUT THE RADIO ROLLED ME) *RCA PB 10056*	33 4

REVILLOS – See REZILLOS

REVIVAL 3000 *UK, male DJ / production trio (1 WEEK)* pos/wks

		pos/wks
1 Nov 97	THE MIGHTY HIGH *Hi-Life 5718092*	47 1

REVOLTING COCKS *US, male vocal / instrumental group (1 WEEK)* pos/wks

		pos/wks
18 Sep 93	DA YA THINK I'M SEXY *Devotion CDDVN 111*	61 1

REVOLUTION – See PRINCE

Debbie REYNOLDS *US, female vocalist (17 WEEKS)* pos/wks

		pos/wks
30 Aug 57 ●	TAMMY *Vogue-Coral Q 72274* ▲	2 17

REYNOLDS GIRLS
UK, female vocal duo - Linda and Aisling Reynolds (12 WEEKS) pos/wks

		pos/wks
25 Feb 89 ●	I'D RATHER JACK *PWL PWL 25*	8 12

Jody REYNOLDS *US, male vocalist (1 WEEK)* pos/wks

		pos/wks
14 Apr 79	ENDLESS SLEEP *Lightning LIG 9015*	66 1

'Endless Sleep' was coupled with 'To Know Him Is to Love Him' by the Teddy Bears as a double A-side

LJ REYNOLDS *US, male vocalist (3 WEEKS)* pos/wks

		pos/wks
30 Jun 84	DON'T LET NOBODY HOLD YOU DOWN *Club JAB 5*	53 3

REZILLOS *UK, male / female vocal / instrumental group (21 WEEKS)* pos/wks

		pos/wks
12 Aug 78	TOP OF THE POPS *Sire SIR 4001*	17 9
25 Nov 78	DESTINATION VENUS *Sire SIR 4008*	43 4
18 Aug 79	I WANNA BE YOUR MAN / I CAN'T STAND MY BABY *Sensible SAB 1*	71 1
1 Sep 79	I WANNA BE YOUR MAN / I CAN'T STAND MY BABY (re-entry) *Sensible SAB 1*	75 1
26 Jan 80	MOTORBIKE BEAT *Dindisc DIN 5* [1]	45 6

[1] Revillos

UK No.1 ★   UK Top 10 ●   Still on chart +   UK million seller ◆   UK entry at No.1 ■   US No.1 ▲

RHC *Belgium, male / female vocal / instrumental duo (1 WEEK)* pos/wks

| 11 Jan 92 | FEVER CALLED LOVE *R&S RSUK 9*.. | 65 | 1 |

RHODA with The SPECIAL A.K.A.
UK, female vocalist and male vocal / instrumental group (5 WEEKS) pos/wks

| 23 Jan 82 | THE BOILER *2 Tone CHSTT 18*.. | 35 | 5 |

See also SPECIALS

Busta RHYMES *US, male rapper - Trevor Smith (51 WEEKS)* pos/wks

11 May 96 ●	WOO-HAH!! GOT YOU ALL IN CHECK		
	Elektra EKR 220CD..	8	7
21 Sep 96	IT'S A PARTY *Elektra EKR 226CD* [1]	23	2
5 Apr 97 ●	HIT EM HIGH (THE MONSTARS' ANTHEM)		
	Atlantic A 5449CD [2]	8	6
3 May 97	DO MY THING *Elektra EKR 235CD*......................................	39	1
18 Oct 97	PUT YOUR HANDS WHERE MY EYES COULD SEE		
	Elektra E 3900CD...	16	3
20 Dec 97	DANGEROUS *Elektra E 3877CD*..	32	4
18 Apr 98 ●	TURN IT UP / FIRE IT UP *Elektra E 3847CD*........................	2	10
11 Jul 98	ONE *Elektra E 3833CD1* [3]	23	3
30 Jan 99 ●	GIMME SOME MORE *Elektra E 3782CD*..............................	5	6
1 May 99 ●	WHAT'S IT GONNA BE?!		
	Elektra E 3762CD1 [4]	6	7
22 Jul 00	GET OUT *Elektra E 7075CD*...	57	1
16 Dec 00	FIRE *East West E 7136*..	60	1

[1] Busta Rhymes featuring Zhane [2] B Real / Busta Rhymes / Coolio / LL Cool J /
Method Man [3] Busta Rhymes featuring Erykah Badu [4] Busta Rhymes featuring Janet

RHYTHIM IS RHYTHIM *US, male production group (1 WEEK)* pos/wks

| 11 Nov 89 | STRINGS OF LIFE *Kool Kat KOOL 509*................................. | 74 | 1 |

RHYTHM BANGERS – See Robbie RIVERA presents RHYTHM BANGERS

RHYTHM ETERNITY
UK, male / female vocal / instrumental group (1 WEEK) pos/wks

| 23 May 92 | PINK CHAMPAGNE *Dead Dead Good GOOD 15T*.................... | 72 | 1 |

RHYTHM FACTOR
US, male / female vocal / instrumental group (2 WEEKS) pos/wks

| 29 Apr 95 | YOU BRING ME JOY | | |
| | *Multiply CDMULTY 4*.. | 53 | 2 |

RHYTHM MASTERS *UK / Malta, male DJ / production duo, aka Big Room*
Girl and Rhythmatic Junkies (2 WEEKS) pos/wks

16 Aug 97	COME ON Y'ALL *Faze 2 CDFAZE 37*..................................	49	1
6 Dec 97	ENTER THE SCENE		
	Distinctive DISNCD 40 [1]	49	1

[1] DJ Supreme vs the Rhythm Masters

See also BIG ROOM GIRL featuring Darryl PANDY; RHYTHMATIC JUNKIES

RHYTHM-N-BASS *UK, male vocal group (4 WEEKS)* pos/wks

| 19 Sep 92 | ROSES *Epic 6582907*.. | 56 | 2 |
| 3 Jul 93 | CAN'T STOP THIS FEELING *Epic 6592002*............................ | 59 | 2 |

RHYTHM OF LIFE
UK, male DJ / producer - Steve Burgess (2 WEEKS) pos/wks

| 13 May 00 | YOU PUT ME IN HEAVEN WITH YOUR TOUCH | | |
| | *Xtravaganza XTRAV 4CDS*.. | 24 | 2 |

RHYTHM ON THE LOOSE
UK, male producer - Geoff Hibbert (2 WEEKS) pos/wks

| 19 Aug 95 | BREAK OF DAWN *Six6 SIXCD 126*..................................... | 36 | 2 |

RHYTHM QUEST *UK, male producer - Mark Hadfield (2 WEEKS)* pos/wks

| 20 Jun 92 | CLOSER TO ALL YOUR DREAMS *Network NWK 40*.................. | 45 | 2 |

RHYTHM SECTION *UK, male vocal / instrumental group (1 WEEK)* pos/wks

| 18 Jul 92 | MIDSUMMER MADNESS (EP) *Rhythm Section RSEC 006*......... | 66 | 1 |

Tracks on Midsummer Madness (EP): Dreamworld / Burnin' Up / Perfect Love 2am /
Perfect Love 8am

RHYTHM SOURCE
UK, male / female vocal / instrumental group (1 WEEK) pos/wks

| 17 Jun 95 | LOVE SHINE *A & M 5810672*... | 74 | 1 |

RHYTHMATIC *UK, male instrumental / production duo (3 WEEKS)* pos/wks

12 May 90	TAKE ME BACK *Network NWK 8*.......................................	74	1
26 May 90	TAKE ME BACK (re-entry) *Network NWK 8*........................	71	1
3 Nov 90	FREQUENCY *Network NWK 13*...	62	1

RHYTHMATIC JUNKIES
UK, male vocal / production group (1 WEEK) pos/wks

| 15 May 99 | THE FEELIN (CLAP YOUR HANDS) | | |
| | *Sound of Ministry RIDE 2CDS*.. | 67 | 1 |

RIALTO *UK, male vocal / instrumental group (8 WEEKS)* pos/wks

8 Nov 97	MONDAY MORNING 5:19 *East West EW 116CD*	37	2
17 Jan 98	UNTOUCHABLE *East West EW 107CD1*...............................	20	3
28 Mar 98	DREAM ANOTHER DREAM *East West EW 156CD1*	39	2
17 Oct 98	SUMMER'S OVER *China WOKCDR 2099*	60	1

Reva RICE and Greg ELLIS
UK, male / female vocal duo (2 WEEKS) pos/wks

| 27 Mar 93 | NEXT TIME YOU FALL IN LOVE *Really Useful RURCD 12*......... | 59 | 2 |

Charlie RICH *US, male vocalist (29 WEEKS)* pos/wks

16 Feb 74 ●	THE MOST BEAUTIFUL GIRL *Epic EPC 1897* ▲	2	14
13 Apr 74	BEHIND CLOSED DOORS *Epic EPC 1539*	16	10
1 Feb 75	WE LOVE EACH OTHER *Epic EPC 2868*	37	5

Kelli RICH – See NU SOUL featuring Kelli RICH

Richie RICH *UK, DJ / producer (16 WEEKS)* pos/wks

16 Jul 88	TURN IT UP *Club JAB 68*...	48	3
22 Oct 88	I'LL HOUSE YOU *Gee Street GEE 003* [1]	22	5
10 Dec 88	MY DJ (PUMP IT UP SOME) *Gee Street GEE 7*	74	1
2 Sep 89	SALSA HOUSE *ffrr F 113*	50	3
9 Mar 91	YOU USED TO SALSA *ffrr F 156* [2]	52	3
29 Mar 97	STAY WITH ME *Castle CATX 1001* [3]	58	1

[1] Richie Rich meets the Jungle Brothers [2] Richie Rich featuring Ralphi Rosario [3]
Richie Rich and Esera Tuaolo

'You Used To Salsa' is a remix of 'Salsa House'

Tony RICH PROJECT
US, male vocalist - Antonio Jeffries (22 WEEKS) pos/wks

4 May 96 ●	NOBODY KNOWS *LaFace 74321356422*	4	17
31 Aug 96	LIKE A WOMAN *LaFace 74321401612*...............................	27	4
14 Dec 96	LEAVIN' *LaFace 74321438382*	52	1

Cliff RICHARD (2 | **Top 500**) *Britain's most successful solo vocalist, b.
Harry Webb, 14 Oct 1940, Lucknow, India. Ex-member of Dick Teague Skiffle
Group was instantly successful, and almost overnight became the UK's No.1
rock'n'roll star despite bad press due to "too sexy" live performances. Many
successes on film, stage, TV, radio and video. He has had hits in every major
market around the globe and was named World's No.1 Artist by Billboard in
1963 (with Elvis second and Shadows third). Between 1959 and 1998, Cliff had
a staggering 34 Top 10 albums including seven No.1s, and had more Top 10
albums in the 1980s than any other artist. He was seen on the first Top of the
Pops and has appeared on the TV show more often than any other artist. He
is one of few performers to top the chart with two different recordings of the
same song (Living Doll). This seemingly ageless entertainer's record
number of 64 Top 10 entries now spans 42 years, and at times he held the*

record for being the youngest (1959) and oldest (1999) British singer to top the singles chart. Cliff, who has sold more than 85 million records worldwide, was awarded the Outstanding Contribution to British Music trophy at the 1989 Brits, received an MBE in 1980 and a knighthood in 1995, and holds the unique achievement of a UK No.1 single in five different decades (1142 WEEKS)

pos/wks

12 Sep 58	MOVE IT *Columbia DB 4178* [1]	.2 17
21 Nov 58 ●	HIGH CLASS BABY *Columbia DB 4203* [1]	.7 10
30 Jan 59	LIVIN' LOVIN' DOLL *Columbia DB 4249* [1]	.20 6
8 May 59 ●	MEAN STREAK *Columbia DB 4290 A* [1]	.10 9
15 May 59	NEVER MIND *Columbia DB 4290 B* [1]	.21 2
10 Jul 59 ★	LIVING DOLL *Columbia DB 4306* [1]	.1 21
9 Oct 59	DYNAMITE *Columbia DB 4351 A* [2]	.16 2
9 Oct 59 ★	TRAVELLIN' LIGHT *Columbia DB 4351 B* [2]	.1 17
30 Oct 59	DYNAMITE (re-entry) *Columbia DB 4351 A* [2]	.21 2
11 Dec 59	LIVING DOLL (re-entry) *Columbia DB 4306* [2]	.26 1
1 Jan 60	LIVING DOLL (2nd re-entry) *Columbia DB 4306* [2]	.28 1
15 Jan 60	EXPRESSO BONGO (EP) *Columbia SEG 7971* [2]	.14 7
22 Jan 60 ●	VOICE IN THE WILDERNESS *Columbia DB 4398* [2]	.2 13
24 Mar 60 ●	FALL IN LOVE WITH YOU *Columbia DB 4431* [2]	.2 15
5 May 60	VOICE IN THE WILDERNESS (re-entry) *Columbia DB 4398* [2]	.36 2
30 Jun 60 ★	PLEASE DON'T TEASE *Columbia DB 4479* [3]	.1 18
22 Sep 60 ●	NINE TIMES OUT OF TEN *Columbia DB 4506* [2]	.3 12
1 Dec 60 ★	I LOVE YOU *Columbia DB 4547* [2]	.1 16
2 Mar 61 ●	THEME FOR A DREAM *Columbia DB 4593* [2]	.3 14
30 Mar 61 ●	GEE WHIZ IT'S YOU *Columbia DC 756* [2]	.4 14
22 Jun 61 ●	A GIRL LIKE YOU *Columbia DB 4667* [2]	.3 14
19 Oct 61 ●	WHEN THE GIRL IN YOUR ARMS IS THE GIRL IN YOUR HEART *Columbia DB 4716*	.3 15
11 Jan 62 ★	THE YOUNG ONES *Columbia DB 4761* [2] ◆ ■	.1 21
10 May 62	I'M LOOKING OUT THE WINDOW / DO YOU WANT TO DANCE *Columbia DB 4828* [4]	.2 17
6 Sep 62 ●	IT'LL BE ME *Columbia DB 4886* [2]	.2 12
6 Dec 62 ★	THE NEXT TIME / BACHELOR BOY *Columbia DB 4950* [2]	.1 18
21 Feb 63 ★	SUMMER HOLIDAY *Columbia DB 4977* [2]	.1 18
9 May 63 ●	LUCKY LIPS *Columbia DB 7034* [2]	.4 15
22 Aug 63 ●	IT'S ALL IN THE GAME *Columbia DB 7089*	.2 13
7 Nov 63 ●	DON'T TALK TO HIM *Columbia DB 7150* [2]	.2 13
6 Feb 64 ●	I'M THE LONELY ONE *Columbia DB 7203* [2]	.8 10
13 Feb 64	DON'T TALK TO HIM (re-entry) *Columbia DB 7150* [2]	.50 1
30 Apr 64 ●	CONSTANTLY *Columbia DB 7272*	.4 13
2 Jul 64 ●	ON THE BEACH *Columbia DB 7305* [2]	.7 13
8 Oct 64 ●	THE TWELFTH OF NEVER *Columbia DB 7372*	.8 11
10 Dec 64 ●	I COULD EASILY FALL *Columbia DB 7420* [2]	.9 11
11 Mar 65 ★	THE MINUTE YOU'RE GONE *Columbia DB 7496*	.1 14
10 Jun 65	ON MY WORD *Columbia DB 7596*	.12 10
19 Aug 65	THE TIME IN BETWEEN *Columbia DB 7660* [2]	.22 8
4 Nov 65 ●	WIND ME UP (LET ME GO) *Columbia DB 7745*	.2 16
24 Mar 66	BLUE TURNS TO GREY *Columbia DB 7866* [2]	.15 9
21 Jul 66 ●	VISIONS *Columbia DB 7968*	.7 12
13 Oct 66 ●	TIME DRAGS BY *Columbia DB 8017* [2]	.10 12
15 Dec 66 ●	IN THE COUNTRY *Columbia DB 8094* [2]	.6 10
16 Mar 67 ●	IT'S ALL OVER *Columbia DB 8150*	.9 10
8 Jun 67	I'LL COME RUNNING *Columbia DB 8210*	.26 8
16 Aug 67 ●	THE DAY I MET MARIE *Columbia DB 8245*	.10 14
15 Nov 67 ●	ALL MY LOVE *Columbia DB 8293*	.6 12
20 Mar 68 ★	CONGRATULATIONS *Columbia DB 8376*	.1 13
26 Jun 68	I'LL LOVE YOU FOREVER TODAY *Columbia DB 8437*	.27 6
25 Sep 68	MARIANNE *Columbia DB 8476*	.22 8
27 Nov 68	DON'T FORGET TO CATCH ME *Columbia DB 8503* [2]	.21 10
26 Feb 69	GOOD TIMES (BETTER TIMES) *Columbia DB 8548*	.12 11
28 May 69 ●	BIG SHIP *Columbia DB 8581*	.8 10
13 Sep 69 ●	THROW DOWN A LINE *Columbia DB 8615* [5]	.7 9
6 Dec 69	WITH THE EYES OF A CHILD *Columbia DB 8641*	.20 11
21 Feb 70	JOY OF LIVING *Columbia DB 8657* [5]	.25 8
6 Jun 70 ●	GOODBYE SAM HELLO SAMANTHA *Columbia DB 8685*	.6 15
5 Sep 70	I AIN'T GOT TIME ANYMORE *Columbia DB 8708*	.21 7
23 Jan 71	SUNNY HONEY GIRL *Columbia DB 8747*	.19 8
10 Apr 71	SILVERY RAIN *Columbia DB 8774*	.27 6
17 Jul 71	FLYING MACHINE *Columbia DB 8797*	.37 7
13 Nov 71	SING A SONG OF FREEDOM *Columbia DB 8836*	.13 12
11 Mar 72	JESUS *Columbia DB 8864*	.35 3

26 Aug 72	LIVING IN HARMONY *Columbia DB 8917*	.12 10
17 Mar 73 ●	POWER TO ALL OUR FRIENDS *EMI 2012*	.4 12
12 May 73	HELP IT ALONG / TOMORROW RISING *EMI 2022*	.29 6
1 Dec 73	TAKE ME HIGH *EMI 2088*	.27 12
18 May 74	(YOU KEEP ME) HANGIN' ON *EMI 2150*	.13 8
7 Feb 76	MISS YOU NIGHTS *EMI 2376*	.15 10
8 May 76 ●	DEVIL WOMAN *EMI 2458*	.9 8
21 Aug 76	I CAN'T ASK FOR ANYTHING MORE THAN YOU *EMI 2499*	.17 8
4 Dec 76	HEY MR DREAM MAKER *EMI 2559*	.31 5
5 Mar 77	MY KINDA LIFE *EMI 2584*	.15 8
16 Jul 77	WHEN TWO WORLDS DRIFT APART *EMI 2633*	.46 3
31 Mar 79	GREEN LIGHT *EMI 2920*	.57 3
21 Jul 79 ★	WE DON'T TALK ANYMORE *EMI 2975*	.1 14
3 Nov 79	HOT SHOT *EMI 5003*	.46 5
2 Feb 80 ●	CARRIE *EMI 5006*	.4 10
16 Aug 80 ●	DREAMIN' *EMI 5095*	.8 10
25 Oct 80	SUDDENLY *Jet 7002* [6]	.15 7
24 Jan 81	A LITTLE IN LOVE *EMI 5123*	.15 8
29 Aug 81 ●	WIRED FOR SOUND *EMI 5221*	.4 9
21 Nov 81 ●	DADDY'S HOME *EMI 5251*	.2 12
17 Jul 82 ●	THE ONLY WAY OUT *EMI 5318*	.10 9
25 Sep 82	WHERE DO WE GO FROM HERE *EMI 5341*	.60 3
4 Dec 82	LITTLE TOWN *EMI 5348*	.11 7
19 Feb 83 ●	SHE MEANS NOTHING TO ME *Capitol CL 276* [7]	.9 9
16 Apr 83 ●	TRUE LOVE WAYS *EMI 5385* [8]	.8 8
4 Jun 83	DRIFTING *DJM SHEIL 1* [9]	.64 2
3 Sep 83	NEVER SAY DIE (GIVE A LITTLE BIT MORE) *EMI 5415*	.15 7
26 Nov 83 ●	PLEASE DON'T FALL IN LOVE *EMI 5437*	.7 9
31 Mar 84	BABY YOU'RE DYNAMITE / OCEAN DEEP *EMI 5457*	.27 6
19 May 84	OCEAN DEEP (re-entry) / BABY YOU'RE DYNAMITE (re-entry) *EMI 5457*	.72 1
3 Nov 84	SHOOTING FROM THE HEART *EMI RICH 1*	.51 4
9 Feb 85	HEART USER *EMI RICH 2*	.46 3
14 Sep 85	SHE'S SO BEAUTIFUL *EMI 5531*	.17 9
7 Dec 85	IT'S IN EVERY ONE OF US *EMI 5537*	.45 6
22 Mar 86 ★	LIVING DOLL *WEA YZ 65* [10]	.1 11
4 Oct 86 ●	ALL I ASK OF YOU *Polydor POSP 802* [11]	.3 16
29 Nov 86	SLOW RIVERS *Rocket EJS 13* [12]	.44 8
20 Jun 87 ●	MY PRETTY ONE *EMI EM 4*	.6 10
29 Aug 87 ●	SOME PEOPLE *EMI EM 18*	.3 10
31 Oct 87	REMEMBER ME *EMI EM 31*	.35 4
13 Feb 88	TWO HEARTS *EMI EM 42*	.34 3
3 Dec 88 ★	MISTLETOE AND WINE *EMI EM 78*	.1 8
10 Jun 89 ●	THE BEST OF ME *EMI EM 92*	.2 7
26 Aug 89 ●	I JUST DON'T HAVE THE HEART *EMI EM 101*	.3 8
14 Oct 89	LEAN ON YOU *EMI EM 105*	.17 6
9 Dec 89	WHENEVER GOD SHINES HIS LIGHT *Polydor VANS 2* [13]	.20 6
24 Feb 90	STRONGER THAN THAT *EMI EM 129*	.14 5
25 Aug 90	SILHOUETTES *EMI EM 152*	.10 7
13 Oct 90	FROM A DISTANCE *EMI EM 155*	.11 6
8 Dec 90 ★	SAVIOUR'S DAY *EMI XMAS 90*	.1 7
14 Sep 91	MORE TO LIFE *EMI EM 205*	.23 5
7 Dec 91 ●	WE SHOULD BE TOGETHER *EMI XMAS 91*	.10 6
11 Jan 92	THIS NEW YEAR *EMI EMS 218*	.30 2
5 Dec 92 ●	I STILL BELIEVE IN YOU *EMI EM 255*	.7 6
27 Mar 93 ●	PEACE IN OUR TIME *EMI CDEM 265*	.8 5
12 Jun 93	HUMAN WORK OF ART *EMI CDEM 267*	.24 4
2 Oct 93	NEVER LET GO *EMI CDEM 281*	.32 3
18 Dec 93	HEALING LOVE *EMI CDEM 294*	.19 5
10 Dec 94	ALL I HAVE TO DO IS DREAM / MISS YOU NIGHTS (re-issue) *EMI CDEM 359* [14]	.14 6
25 Feb 95	ALL I HAVE TO DO IS DREAM / MISS YOU NIGHTS (re-entry of re-issue) *EMI CDEM 359* [14]	.58 3
2 Oct 95	MISUNDERSTOOD MAN *EMI CDEM 394*	.19 3
9 Dec 95	HAD TO BE *EMI CDEM 410* [15]	.22 4
30 Mar 96	THE WEDDING *EMI CDEM 422* [16]	.40 1
25 Jan 97	BE WITH ME ALWAYS *EMI CDEM 453*	.52 1
24 Oct 98 ●	CAN'T KEEP THIS FEELING IN *EMI CDEM 526*	.10 4
7 Aug 99	THE MIRACLE *EMI / Blacknight CDEM 546*	.23 2
27 Nov 99 ★	THE MILLENNIUM PRAYER *Papillon PROMISECD 01*	.1 16

[1] Cliff Richard & the Drifters [2] Cliff Richard & the Shadows [3] Cliff Richard & The Shadows [4] Cliff Richard / The Shadows [5] Cliff & Hank [6] Olivia Newton-John & Cliff Richard [7] Phil Everly & Cliff Richard [8] Cliff Richard with the London

UK No.1 ★   UK Top 10 ●   Still on chart +   UK million seller ◆   UK entry at No.1 ■   US No.1 ▲

Philharmonic Orchestra [9] Sheila Walsh & Cliff Richard [10] Cliff Richard & the Young Ones featuring Hank B Marvin [11] Cliff Richard & Sarah Brightman [12] Elton John & Cliff Richard [13] Van Morrison with Cliff Richard [14] Cliff Richard with Phil Everly/Cliff Richard [15] Cliff Richard & Olivia Newton-John [16] Cliff Richard featuring Helen Hobson

Tracks on Expresso Bongo (EP): Love / A Voice in the Wilderness / The Shrine on the Second Floor / Bongo Blues. 'Bongo Blues' features only The Shadows. 'Bachelor Boy' was listed with 'The Next Time' from 10 Jan 1963. 'Ocean Deep' listed from 28 Apr 1984, onwards. It peaked at No.41

Wendy RICHARD – See Mike SARNE

Lionel RICHIE [112] Top 500
Singer / composer / producer, b. 20 Jun 1949, Alabama, US. Launched a solo career in 1982 after 12 years fronting The Commodores. Arguably the most successful US songwriter of the 1980s, who composed at least one US chart-topper per year for a record eight successive years (174 WEEKS)

			pos/wks
12 Sep 81	●	ENDLESS LOVE *Motown TMG 1240* [1] ▲	7 12
20 Nov 82		TRULY *Motown TMG 1284* ▲	6 11
29 Jan 83		YOU ARE *Motown TMG 1290*	43 7
7 May 83		MY LOVE *Motown TMG 1300*	70 3
1 Oct 83	●	ALL NIGHT LONG (ALL NIGHT) *Motown TMG 1319* ▲	2 16
3 Dec 83	●	RUNNING WITH THE NIGHT *Motown TMG 1324*	9 12
10 Mar 84	★	HELLO *Motown TMG 1330* ▲	1 15
23 Jun 84		STUCK ON YOU *Motown TMG 1341*	12 12
20 Oct 84		PENNY LOVER *Motown TMG 1356*	18 7
16 Nov 85	●	SAY YOU, SAY ME *Motown ZB 40421* ▲	8 11
26 Jul 86	●	DANCING ON THE CEILING *Motown LIO1*	7 11
11 Oct 86		LOVE WILL CONQUER ALL *Motown LIO 2*	45 5
20 Dec 86		BALLERINA GIRL / DEEP RIVER WOMAN *Motown LIO3*	17 8
28 Mar 87		SELA *Motown LIO4*	43 6
9 May 92		DO IT TO ME *Motown TMG 1407*	33 6
22 Aug 92	●	MY DESTINY *Motown TMG 1408*	7 13
28 Nov 92		LOVE OH LOVE *Motown TMG 1413*	52 1
26 Dec 92		LOVE OH LOVE (re-entry) *Motown TMG 1413*	73 1
6 Apr 96		DON'T WANNA LOSE YOU *Mercury MERCD 461*	17 5
23 Nov 96		STILL IN LOVE *Mercury MERCD 477*	66 1
27 Jun 98		CLOSEST THING TO HEAVEN *Mercury 5661312*	26 2
21 Oct 00		ANGEL *Mercury 5726702*	18 5
23 Dec 00		DON'T STOP THE MUSIC *Mercury 5688992*	34 2+

[1] Diana Ross and Lionel Richie

'Deep River Woman' was listed only from 17 Jan 1987. It has the following credit: background vocal 'Alabama'

RICH KIDS *UK, male vocal / instrumental group (5 WEEKS)*

			pos/wks
28 Jan 78		RICH KIDS *EMI 2738*	24 5

Jonathan RICHMAN and the MODERN LOVERS *US, male vocal / instrumental group (27 WEEKS)*

			pos/wks
16 Jul 77		ROADRUNNER *Beserkley BZZ 1*	11 9
29 Oct 77	●	EGYPTIAN REGGAE *Beserkley BZZ 2*	5 14
21 Jan 78		MORNING OF OUR LIVES *Beserkley BZZ 7* [1]	29 4

[1] Modern Lovers

Adam RICKITT *UK, male vocalist (19 WEEKS)*

			pos/wks
26 Jun 99	●	I BREATHE AGAIN *Polydor 5611862*	5 10
16 Oct 99		EVERYTHING MY HEART DESIRES *Polydor 5614392*	15 6
5 Feb 00		BEST THING *Polydor 5616132*	25 3

RICO – See SPECIALS

RIDE *UK, male vocal / instrumental group (22 WEEKS)*

			pos/wks
27 Jan 90		RIDE (EP) *Creation CRE 072T*	71 2
14 Apr 90		PLAY (EP) *Creation CRE 075T*	32 3
29 Sep 90		FALL (EP) *Creation CRE 087T*	34 3
16 Mar 91		TODAY FOREVER EP *Creation CRE 100T*	14 4
15 Feb 92	●	LEAVE THEM ALL BEHIND *Creation CRE 123T*	9 3
25 Apr 92		TWISTERELLA *Creation CRE 150T*	36 2
30 Apr 94		BIRDMAN *Creation CRESCD 155*	38 2

			pos/wks
25 Jun 94		HOW DOES IT FEEL TO FEEL *Creation CRESCD 184*	58 1
8 Oct 94		I DON'T KNOW WHERE IT COMES FROM *Creation CRESCD 189R*	46 1
24 Feb 96		BLACK NITE CRASH *Creation CRESCD 199*	67 1

Tracks on Ride (EP): Chelsea Girl / Drive Blind / All I Can See / Close My Eyes. Tracks on Play (EP): Silver / Furthest Sense / Perfect Time. Tracks on Fall (EP): Like a Daydream / Silver / Furthest Sense / Perfect Time. Tracks on Fall (EP): Dreams Burn Down / Taste / Hear and Now / Nowhere. Tracks on Today Forever (EP): Unfamiliar / Sennen / Beneath / Today

Andrew RIDGELEY *UK, male vocalist (3 WEEKS)*

			pos/wks
31 Mar 90		SHAKE *Epic AJR 1*	58 3

See also WHAM!

Stan RIDGWAY *US, male vocalist (12 WEEKS)*

			pos/wks
5 Jul 86	●	CAMOUFLAGE *IRS IRM 114*	4 12

RIGHEIRA *Italy, male vocal duo (3 WEEKS)*

			pos/wks
24 Sep 83		VAMOS A LA PLAYA *A & M AM 137*	53 3

RIGHT SAID FRED *UK, male vocal / instrumental group. Lead vocal Richard Fairbrass (61 WEEKS)*

			pos/wks
27 Jul 91	●	I'M TOO SEXY *Tug SNOG 1* ▲	2 16
7 Dec 91	●	DON'T TALK JUST KISS *Tug SNOG 2* [1]	3 11
21 Mar 92	★	DEEPLY DIPPY *Tug SNOG 3*	1 14
1 Aug 92		THOSE SIMPLE THINGS / DAYDREAM *Tug SNOG 4*	29 5
27 Feb 93	●	STICK IT OUT *Tug CDCOMIC 1* [2]	4 7
23 Oct 93		BUMPED *Tug CDSNOG 7*	32 4
18 Dec 93		HANDS UP (4 LOVERS) *Tug CDSNOG 8*	60 3
19 Mar 94		WONDERMAN *Tug CDSNOG 9*	55 1

[1] Right Said Fred. Guest vocals: Jocelyn Brown [2] Right Said Fred and Friends

RIGHTEOUS BROTHERS [367] Top 500
Pioneering, influential blue-eyed soul duo, Bill Medley b. 19 Sep 1940, California, US, and Bobby Hatfield b. 10 Aug 1940, Wisconsin, US. 'You've Lost That Lovin' Feelin', has an unsurpassed seven million US radio plays and reached UK Top 10 three times (86 WEEKS)

			pos/wks
14 Jan 65	★	YOU'VE LOST THAT LOVIN' FEELIN' *London HLU 9943* ▲	1 10
12 Aug 65		UNCHAINED MELODY *London HL 9975*	14 12
13 Jan 66		EBB TIDE *London HL 10011*	48 2
14 Apr 66		(YOU'RE MY) SOUL AND INSPIRATION *Verve VS 535* ▲	15 10
10 Nov 66		WHITE CLIFFS OF DOVER *London HL 10086*	21 9
22 Dec 66		ISLAND IN THE SUN *Verve VS 547*	36 5
12 Feb 69	●	YOU'VE LOST THAT LOVIN' FEELIN' (re-issue) *London HL 10241*	10 11
19 Nov 77		YOU'VE LOST THAT LOVIN' FEELIN' (2nd re-issue) *Phil Spector International 2010 022*	42 4
27 Oct 90	★	UNCHAINED MELODY (re-issue) *Verve / Polydor PO 101*	1 14
15 Dec 90	●	YOU'VE LOST THAT LOVIN' FEELIN' / EBB TIDE (3rd re-issue) *Verve / Polydor PO 116*	3 9

Cheryl Pepsii RILEY *US, female vocalist (1 WEEK)*

			pos/wks
28 Jan 89		THANKS FOR MY CHILD *CBS 653153 7*	75 1

Jeannie C RILEY *US, female vocalist (15 WEEKS)*

			pos/wks
16 Oct 68		HARPER VALLEY P.T.A. *Polydor 56748* ▲	12 15

Teddy RILEY *US, male producer (5 WEEKS)*

			pos/wks
21 Mar 92		IS IT GOOD TO YOU *MCA MCS 1611* [1]	53 2
19 Jun 93		BABY BE MINE *MCA MCSTD 1772* [2]	37 3

[1] Teddy Riley featuring Tammy Lucas [2] BLACKstreet featuring Teddy Riley

RIMES featuring Shaila PROSPERE
UK, male rapper - Julian Johnson (1 WEEK)

			pos/wks
22 May 99		IT'S OVER *Universal MCSTD 40199*	51 1

LeAnn RIMES US, female vocalist (59 WEEKS)

pos/wks

Date	Title	pos	wks
7 Mar 98 ●	HOW DO I LIVE Curb CUBCX 30	7	33
12 Sep 98	LOOKING THROUGH YOUR EYES / COMMITMENT Curb CUBC 32	38	2
31 Oct 98	HOW DO I LIVE (re-entry) Curb CUBCX 30	72	1
12 Dec 98	BLUE Curb CUBC 39	23	6
6 Mar 99 ●	WRITTEN IN THE STARS Mercury EJSCD 45 [1]	10	7
22 May 99	WRITTEN IN THE STARS (re-entry) Mercury EJSCD 45 [1]	63	1
18 Dec 99	CRAZY Curb CUBC 52	36	3
25 Nov 00 ★	CAN'T FIGHT THE MOONLIGHT Curb CUBC 58 ■	1	6+

[1] Elton John and LeAnn Rimes

RIMSHOTS US, male / female instrumental / vocal group (5 WEEKS) pos/wks

Date	Title	pos	wks
19 Jul 75	7-6-5-4-3-2-1 (BLOW YOUR WHISTLE) All Platinum 6146 304	26	5

RIO and MARS
France / UK, male / female vocal / instrumental duo (3 WEEKS) pos/wks

Date	Title	pos	wks
28 Jan 95	BOY I GOTTA HAVE YOU Dome CDDOME 1014	43	2
13 Apr 96	BOY I GOTTA HAVE YOU (re-issue) Feverpitch CDFVR 1007	46	1

Miguel RIOS Spain, male vocalist (12 WEEKS) pos/wks

Date	Title	pos	wks
11 Jul 70	SONG OF JOY A & M AMS 790	16	12

Waldo de los RIOS
Argentina, orchestra, leader - Osvaldo Ferraro Guiterrez (16 WEEKS) pos/wks

Date	Title	pos	wks
10 Apr 71 ●	MOZART SYMPHONY NO.40 IN G MINOR K550 1ST MOVEMENT (ALLEGRO MOLTO) A & M AMS 836	5	16

RIP PRODUCTIONS UK, production duo (1 WEEK) pos/wks

Date	Title	pos	wks
29 Nov 97	THE CHANT (WE R) / RIP PRODUCTIONS Satellite 74321534022	58	1

See also DOUBLE 99; CARNIVAL featuring RIP vs RED RAT

Minnie RIPERTON US, female vocalist (10 WEEKS) pos/wks

Date	Title	pos	wks
12 Apr 75 ●	LOVING YOU Epic EPC 3121 ▲	2	10

RISE UK, male production duo - Paul Oakenfold and Steve Osborne
(1 WEEK) pos/wks

Date	Title	pos	wks
3 Sep 94	tHE SINGLE East West YZ 839CD	70	1

RITCHIE FAMILY US, female vocal group (19 WEEKS) pos/wks

Date	Title	pos	wks
23 Aug 75	BRAZIL Polydor 2058 625	41	4
18 Sep 76 ●	THE BEST DISCO IN TOWN Polydor 2058 777	10	9
17 Feb 79	AMERICAN GENERATION Mercury 6007 199	49	6

Lee RITENOUR and Maxi PRIEST
US, male instrumentalist - guitar and UK, male vocalist (2 WEEKS) pos/wks

Date	Title	pos	wks
31 Jul 93	WAITING IN VAIN GRP MCSTD 1921	65	2

Tex RITTER US, male vocalist (14 WEEKS) pos/wks

Date	Title	pos	wks
22 Jun 56 ●	WAYWARD WIND Capitol CL 14581	8	14

Paco RIVAZ – See GAMBAFREAKS

RIVER CITY PEOPLE
UK, male / female vocal / instrumental group (27 WEEKS) pos/wks

Date	Title	pos	wks
12 Aug 89	(WHAT'S WRONG WITH) DREAMING EMI EM 95	70	3
3 Mar 90	WALKING ON ICE EMI EM 130	62	2
30 Jun 90	CARRY THE BLAME / CALIFORNIA DREAMIN' EMI EM 145	13	10
22 Sep 90	(WHAT'S WRONG WITH) DREAMING (re-issue) EMI EM 156	40	2
2 Mar 91	WHEN I WAS YOUNG EMI EM 176	62	2
28 Sep 91	SPECIAL WAY EMI EM 207	44	3
22 Feb 92	STANDING IN THE NEED OF LOVE EMI EM 216	36	4

RIVER DETECTIVES UK, male vocal / instrumental duo (4 WEEKS) pos/wks

Date	Title	pos	wks
29 Jul 89	CHAINS WEA YZ 383	51	4

RIVER OCEAN featuring INDIA
US, male producer (Louie Vega) and female vocalist (2 WEEKS) pos/wks

Date	Title	pos	wks
26 Feb 94	LOVE AND HAPPINESS (YEMAYA Y OCHUN) Cooltempo CDCOOL 287	50	2

See also INDIA; Louie VEGA and Marc ANTHONY

Robbie RIVERA presents RHYTHM BANGERS
US, male production group (7 WEEKS) pos/wks

Date	Title	pos	wks
2 Sep 00	BANG Multiply CDMULTY 64	13	7

Danny RIVERS UK, male vocalist (3 WEEKS) pos/wks

Date	Title	pos	wks
12 Jan 61	CAN'T YOU HEAR MY HEART Decca F 11294	36	3

RM PROJECT UK, production group (1 WEEK) pos/wks

Date	Title	pos	wks
3 Jul 99	GET IT UP Inferno CDFERN 15	49	1

ROACH MOTEL
UK, male instrumental / production group (2 WEEKS) pos/wks

Date	Title	pos	wks
21 Aug 93	AFRO SLEEZE / TRANSATLANTIC Junior Boy's Own JBO 1412	73	1
10 Dec 94	HAPPY BIZZNESS / WILD LUV Junior Boy's Own JBO 24	75	1

ROACHFORD UK, male / female vocal / instrumental group - Andrew
Roachford (61 WEEKS) pos/wks

Date	Title	pos	wks
18 Jun 88	CUDDLY TOY CBS ROA 2	61	4
14 Jan 89 ●	CUDDLY TOY (re-issue) CBS ROA 4	4	9
18 Mar 89	FAMILY MAN CBS ROA 5	25	6
1 Jul 89	KATHLEEN CBS ROA 6	43	5
13 Apr 91	GET READY! Columbia 6567057	22	8
19 Mar 94	ONLY TO BE WITH YOU Columbia 6601562	21	7
18 Jun 94	LAY YOUR LOVE ON ME Columbia 6603722	36	5
20 Aug 94	THIS GENERATION Columbia 6607452	38	4
3 Dec 94	CRY FOR ME Columbia 6610742	46	2
1 Apr 95	I KNOW YOU DON'T LOVE ME Columbia 6612525	42	2
11 Oct 97	THE WAY I FEEL Columbia 6651042	20	4
14 Feb 98	HOW COULD I? (INSECURITY) Columbia 6653462	34	3
11 Jul 98	NAKED WITHOUT YOU Columbia 6659362	53	2

ROB 'N' RAZ featuring Leila K Sweden, male production duo and
female rapper (17 WEEKS) pos/wks

Date	Title	pos	wks
25 Nov 89 ●	GOT TO GET Arista 112696	8	14
17 Mar 90	ROK THE NATION Arista 112971	41	3

Kate ROBBINS and BEYOND UK, female / male vocal / instrumental
group (10 WEEKS) pos/wks

Date	Title	pos	wks
30 May 81 ●	MORE THAN IN LOVE RCA 69	2	10

Marty ROBBINS US, male vocalist - Marty Robinson (32 WEEKS) pos/wks

Date	Title	pos	wks
29 Jan 60	EL PASO Fontana H 233 ▲	19	7
7 Apr 60	EL PASO (re-entry) Fontana H 233	44	1
26 May 60	BIG IRON Fontana H 229	48	1
27 Sep 62 ●	DEVIL WOMAN CBS AAG 114	5	17
17 Jan 63	RUBY ANN CBS AAG 128	24	6

Antoinette ROBERSON – See PULSE featuring Antoinette ROBERSON

Austin ROBERTS US, male vocalist (7 WEEKS) pos/wks

Date	Title	pos	wks
25 Oct 75	ROCKY Private Stock PVT 33	22	7

UK No.1 ★ UK Top 10 ● Still on chart + UK million seller ◆ UK entry at No.1 ■ US No.1 ▲

Joe ROBERTS *UK, male vocalist (17 WEEKS)*

		pos/wks	
28 Aug 93	BACK IN MY LIFE *ffrr FCD 215*............................	**59**	1
29 Jan 94	LOVER *ffrr FCD 220*......................................	**22**	5
14 May 94	BACK IN MY LIFE (re-issue) *ffrr FCD 230*...........	**39**	3
6 Aug 94	ADORE *ffrr FCD 240*....................................	**45**	3
18 Feb 95	YOU ARE EVERYTHING *Columbia 6611755* [1]	**28**	4
24 Feb 96	HAPPY DAYS *Grass Green GRASS 10CD* [2]	**63**	1

[1] Melanie Williams and Joe Roberts [2] Sweet Mercy featuring Joe Roberts

Juliet ROBERTS *UK, female vocalist (29 WEEKS)*

		pos/wks	
31 Jul 93	CAUGHT IN THE MIDDLE *Cooltempo CDCOOL 272*	**24**	6
6 Nov 93	FREE LOVE *Cooltempo CDCOOL 281*	**25**	3
19 Mar 94	AGAIN / I WANT YOU *Cooltempo CDCOOL 285*.........	**33**	3
2 Jul 94	CAUGHT IN THE MIDDLE (re-mix) *Cooltempo CDCOOL 291*..	**14**	5
15 Oct 94	I WANT YOU (re-issue) *Cooltempo CDCOOL 297*	**28**	3
31 Jan 98	SO GOOD / FREE LOVE 98 (re-mix) *Delirious 74321554002*	**15**	4
23 Jan 99	BAD GIRLS / I LIKE *Delirious DELICD 11*	**17**	5

Malcolm ROBERTS *UK, male vocalist (29 WEEKS)*

		pos/wks	
11 May 67	TIME ALONE WILL TELL *RCA 1578*....................	**45**	2
30 Oct 68 ●	MAY I HAVE THE NEXT DREAM WITH YOU *Major Minor MM 581*	**8**	14
12 Feb 69	MAY I HAVE THE NEXT DREAM WITH YOU (re-entry) *Major Minor MM 581*	**45**	1
22 Nov 69	LOVE IS ALL *Major Minor MM 637*	**12**	12

B.A. ROBERTSON *UK, male vocalist (60 WEEKS)*

		pos/wks	
28 Jul 79 ●	BANG BANG *Asylum K 13152*	**2**	12
27 Oct 79 ●	KNOCKED IT OFF *Asylum K 12396*	**8**	12
1 Mar 80	KOOL IN THE KAFTAN *Asylum K 12427*	**17**	12
31 May 80 ●	TO BE OR NOT TO BE *Asylum K 12449*	**9**	11
17 Oct 81	HOLD ME *Swansong BAM 1* [1]	**11**	8
17 Dec 83	TIME *Epic A 3983* [2]	**45**	5

[1] BA Robertson and Maggie Bell [2] Frida and BA Robertson

Don ROBERTSON
S, male instrumentalist - piano and whistle (9 WEEKS)

		pos/wks	
11 May 56 ●	THE HAPPY WHISTLER *Capitol CL 14575*.............	**8**	9

Robbie ROBERTSON *Canada, male vocalist (11 WEEKS)*

		pos/wks	
23 Jul 88	SOMEWHERE DOWN THE CRAZY RIVER *Geffen GEF 40*........	**15**	10
11 Apr 98	TAKE YOUR PARTNER BY THE HAND *Polydor 5693272* [1]	**74**	1

[1] Howie B featuring Robbie Robertson

Ivo ROBIC *Yugoslavia, male vocalist (1 WEEK)*

		pos/wks	
6 Nov 59	MORGEN *Polydor 23923*	**23**	1

Dawn ROBINSON – See FIRM

Floyd ROBINSON *US, male vocalist (9 WEEKS)*

		pos/wks	
16 Oct 59 ●	MAKIN' LOVE *RCA 1146*	**9**	9

Smokey ROBINSON *US, male vocalist (45 WEEKS)*

		pos/wks	
23 Feb 74	JUST MY SOUL RESPONDING *Tamla Motown TMG 883*...........	**35**	6
24 Feb 79	POPS WE LOVE YOU *Motown TMG 1136* [1]	**66**	5
9 May 81 ★	BEING WITH YOU *Motown TMG 1223*	**1**	13
13 Mar 82	TELL ME TOMORROW *Motown TMG 1255*...............	**51**	4
28 Mar 87	JUST TO SEE HER *Motown ZB 41147*	**52**	6
17 Sep 88	INDESTRUCTIBLE *Arista 111717* [2]	**55**	4
25 Feb 89	INDESTRUCTIBLE *Arista 112074* [2]	**30**	7

[1] Diana Ross, Marvin Gaye, Smokey Robinson and Stevie Wonder [2] Four Tops featuring Smokey Robinson

The original US recording of 'Indestructible' was not issued until after the chart run of the UK-only mix

See also Smokey ROBINSON and the MIRACLES, MIRACLES

Smokey ROBINSON and the MIRACLES
US male vocal group (64 WEEKS)

		pos/wks	
27 Dec 67	I SECOND THAT EMOTION *Tamla Motown TMG 631*	**27**	11
3 Apr 68	IF YOU CAN WANT *Tamla Motown TMG 648*	**50**	1
7 May 69 ●	TRACKS OF MY TEARS *Tamla Motown TMG 696*	**9**	13
1 Aug 70 ★	THE TEARS OF A CLOWN *Tamla Motown TMG 745* ▲ ...	**1**	14
30 Jan 71	(COME 'ROUND HERE) I'M THE ONE YOU NEED (re-issue) *Tamla Motown TMG 761*	**13**	9
5 Jun 71	I DON'T BLAME YOU AT ALL *Tamla Motown TMG 774*	**11**	10
2 Oct 76	THE TEARS OF A CLOWN (re-issue) *Tamla Motown TMG 1048*	**34**	6

1976 re-issue of 'The Tears of a Clown' was a double A-side Motown Collector Series release with 'Tracks of My Tears'

See also MIRACLES; Smokey ROBINSON

Tom ROBINSON *UK, male vocalist / instrumentalist (41 WEEKS)* pos/wks

		pos/wks	
22 Oct 77 ●	2-4-6-8 MOTORWAY *EMI 2715* [1]	**5**	9
18 Feb 78	DON'T TAKE NO FOR AN ANSWER *EMI 2749* [1]	**18**	6
13 May 78	UP AGAINST THE WALL *EMI 2787* [1]	**33**	6
17 Mar 79	BULLY FOR YOU *EMI 2916* [1]	**68**	2
25 Jun 83 ●	WAR BABY *Panic NIC 2*............................	**6**	9
12 Nov 83	LISTEN TO THE RADIO: ATMOSPHERICS *Panic NIC 3*...................................	**39**	6
15 Sep 84	RIKKI DON'T LOSE THAT NUMBER *Castaway TR 2*..........	**58**	3

[1] Tom Robinson Band

Vicki Sue ROBINSON *US, female vocalist (1 WEEK)*

		pos/wks	
27 Sep 97	HOUSE OF JOY *Logic 74321511492*.................	**48**	1

ROBO BABE – See SIR KILLALOT vs ROBO BABE

ROBSON and JEROME
UK, male vocal duo - Robson Green and Jerome Flynn (45 WEEKS) pos/wks

		pos/wks	
20 May 95 ★	UNCHAINED MELODY / (THERE'LL BE BLUEBIRDS OVER) THE WHITE CLIFFS OF DOVER *RCA 74321284362* [1] ◆ ■	**1**	16
4 Nov 95	UNCHAINED MELODY / (THERE'LL BE BLUEBIRDS OVER) THE WHITE CLIFFS OF DOVER (re-entry) *RCA 74321284362*	**63**	1
11 Nov 95 ★	I BELIEVE / UP ON THE ROOF *RCA 74321326082* ◆ ■	**1**	14
9 Nov 96 ★	WHAT BECOMES OF THE BROKENHEARTED / SATURDAY NIGHT AT THE MOVIES / YOU'LL NEVER WALK ALONE *RCA 74321424732* ■	**1**	14

[1] Robson Green and Jerome Flynn

ROBYN *Sweden, female vocalist - Robyn Carlsson (14 WEEKS)* pos/wks

		pos/wks	
20 Jul 96	YOU'VE GOT THAT SOMETHIN' *RCA 74321393462*..............	**54**	1
16 Aug 97	DO YOU KNOW (WHAT IT TAKES) *RCA 74321509932*.....	**26**	3
7 Mar 98 ●	SHOW ME LOVE *RCA 74321555032*	**8**	6
30 May 98	DO YOU REALLY WANT ME *RCA 74321582982*.........	**20**	4

John ROCCA – See FREEEZ

ROCHELLE *US, female vocalist (6 WEEKS)*

		pos/wks	
1 Feb 86	MY MAGIC MAN *Warner Bros. W 8838*	**27**	6

ROCK AID ARMENIA
UK, male vocal / instrumental charity ensemble (5 WEEKS) pos/wks

		pos/wks	
16 Dec 89	SMOKE ON THE WATER *Life Aid Armenia ARMEN 001*	**39**	5

ROCK CANDY *UK, male vocal / instrumental group (6 WEEKS)* pos/wks

		pos/wks	
11 Sep 71	REMEMBER *MCA MK 5069*...........................	**32**	6

Chubb ROCK *US, male rapper (1 WEEK)*

		pos/wks	
19 Jan 91	TREAT 'EM RIGHT *Champion CHAMP 272*	**67**	1

ROCK GODDESS
UK, female vocal / instrumental group (5 WEEKS) pos/wks

| 5 Mar 83 | MY ANGEL *A & M AMS 8311*.................................. | 64 | 2 |
| 24 Mar 84 | I DIDN'T KNOW I LOVED YOU (TILL I SAW YOU ROCK `N' ROLL) *A & M AMS 185*.................................. | 57 | 3 |

Sir Monti ROCK III – See DISCO TEX and the SEX-O-LETTES

THE ROCK – See Wyclef JEAN

ROCKER'S REVENGE featuring Donnie CALVIN
US, male / female vocal / instrumental group (20 WEEKS) pos/wks

| 14 Aug 82 ● | WALKING ON SUNSHINE *London LON 11* .... | 4 | 13 |
| 29 Jan 83 | THE HARDER THEY COME *London LON 18* .... | 30 | 7 |

ROCKET FROM THE CRYPT
US, male vocal / instrumental group (7 WEEKS) pos/wks

27 Jan 96	BORN IN 69 *Elemental ELM 32CD*.......................	68	1
13 Apr 96	YOUNG LIVERS *Elemental ELM 33CDS*..................	67	1
14 Sep 96	ON A ROPE *Elemental ELM 38CDS1*....................	12	4
29 Aug 98	LIPSTICK *Elemental ELM 48CDS1*.......................	64	1

ROCKETS – See Tony CROMBIE and his ROCKETS

ROCKFORD FILES
UK, male instrumental / production duo (4 WEEKS) pos/wks

| 11 Mar 95 | YOU SEXY DANCER *Escapade CDJAPE 7* .... | 34 | 3 |
| 6 Apr 96 | YOU SEXY DANCER (re-issue) *Escapade CDJAPE 14* .... | 59 | 1 |

ROCKIN' BERRIES
UK, male vocal / instrumental group (41 WEEKS) pos/wks

1 Oct 64	I DIDN'T MEAN TO HURT YOU *Piccadilly 7N 35197*	43	1
15 Oct 64 ●	HE'S IN TOWN *Piccadilly 7N 35203*	3	13
21 Jan 65	WHAT IN THE WORLD'S COME OVER YOU *Piccadilly 7N 35217*....	23	7
13 May 65 ●	POOR MAN'S SON *Piccadilly 7N 35236*	5	11
26 Aug 65	YOU'RE MY GIRL *Piccadilly 7N 35254*	40	7
6 Jan 66	THE WATER IS OVER MY HEAD *Piccadilly 7N 35270*..........	43	1
20 Jan 66	THE WATER IS OVER MY HEAD (re-entry) *Piccadilly 7N 35270*	50	1

ROCKNEY – See CHAS and DAVE

ROCKSTEADY CREW
US, male / female vocal group (16 WEEKS) pos/wks

| 1 Oct 83 ● | (HEY YOU) THE ROCKSTEADY CREW *Charisma / Virgin RSC 1* ....| 6 | 12 |
| 5 May 84 | UPROCK *Charisma / Virgin RSC 2* .... | 64 | 4 |

ROCKWELL
US, male vocalist - Kennedy Gordy (11 WEEKS) pos/wks

| 4 Feb 84 ● | SOMEBODY'S WATCHING ME *Motown TMG 1331* .... | 6 | 11 |

'Somebody's Watching Me' features uncredited vocal by Michael Jackson

ROCKY V – See Joey B ELLIS

ROCOCO
UK / Italy, male / female vocal / instrumental group (5 WEEKS) pos/wks

| 16 Dec 89 | ITALO HOUSE MIX *Mercury MER 314* .... | 54 | 5 |

RODEO JONES
UK / Grenada, male / female vocal / instrumental group (2 WEEKS) pos/wks

| 30 Jan 93 | NATURAL WORLD *A & M AMCD 0165*...................... | 75 | 1 |
| 3 Apr 93 | SHADES OF SUMMER *A & M AMCD 212*................... | 59 | 1 |

Clodagh RODGERS
Ireland, female vocalist (59 WEEKS) pos/wks

26 Mar 69 ●	COME BACK AND SHAKE ME *RCA 1792*.....................	3	14
9 Jul 69 ●	GOODNIGHT MIDNIGHT *RCA 1852*......................	4	11
4 Oct 69	GOODNIGHT MIDNIGHT (re-entry) *RCA 1852*..............	48	1
8 Nov 69	BILJO *RCA 1891*	22	9
4 Apr 70	EVERYBODY GO HOME THE PARTY'S OVER *RCA 1930*	47	2
20 Mar 71 ●	JACK IN THE BOX *RCA 2066*...........................	4	10
9 Oct 71	LADY LOVE BUG *RCA 2117*	28	12

Jimmie RODGERS
US, male vocalist (37 WEEKS) pos/wks

1 Nov 57	HONEYCOMB *Columbia DB 3986* ▲	30	1
20 Dec 57 ●	KISSES SWEETER THAN WINE *Columbia DB 4052*...........	7	11
28 Mar 58	OH-OH, I'M FALLING IN LOVE AGAIN *Columbia DB 4078*....	18	6
19 Dec 58	WOMAN FROM LIBERIA *Columbia DB 4206*..............	18	6
14 Jun 62 ●	ENGLISH COUNTRY GARDEN *Columbia DB 4847*	5	13

Paul RODGERS
UK, male vocalist (2 WEEKS) pos/wks

| 12 Feb 94 | MUDDY WATER BLUES *Victory ROGCD 1* .... | 45 | 2 |

See also FREE; BAD COMPANY

RODRIGUEZ – See SASH!

RODS – See EDDIE and the HOT RODS

Tommy ROE (457) [Top 500]
One of the 1960s' most successful male solo pop singer / songwriters b. 9 May 1942, Georgia, US. Initially recorded Buddy Holly-influenced 'Sheila' with his group The Satins two years before solo version. Co-wrote twice-chart-topping song 'Dizzy' (74 WEEKS) pos/wks

6 Sep 62 ●	SHEILA *HMV POP 1060* ▲	3	14
6 Dec 62	SUSIE DARLIN' *HMV POP 1092*	37	5
21 Mar 63 ●	THE FOLK SINGER *HMV POP 1138*	4	13
26 Sep 63 ●	EVERYBODY *HMV POP 1207*	9	11
19 Dec 63	EVERYBODY (re-entry) *HMV POP 1207*	49	1
16 Apr 69 ★	DIZZY *Stateside SS 2143* ▲	1	19
23 Jul 69	HEATHER HONEY *Stateside SS 2152*	24	9

ROFO
UK, male instrumental / production duo (3 WEEKS) pos/wks

| 1 Aug 92 | ROFO'S THEME *PWL Continental PWLT 236* .... | 44 | 3 |

ROGER
US, male vocalist - Roger Troutman (8 WEEKS) pos/wks

17 Oct 87	I WANT TO BE YOUR MAN *Reprise W 8229*	61	4
12 Nov 88	BOOM! THERE SHE WAS *Virgin VS 1143*	55	3
13 May 95	HIGH AS A KITE *ffrr FCD 259* [1]	55	1

[1] One Tribe featuring Roger

Julie ROGERS
UK, female vocalist - Julie Rolls (38 WEEKS) pos/wks

13 Aug 64 ●	THE WEDDING *Mercury MF 820* [1]	3	23
10 Dec 64	LIKE A CHILD *Mercury MF 838*	21	9
25 Mar 65	HAWAIIAN WEDDING SONG *Mercury MF 849*............	31	6

[1] Julie Rogers with Johnny Arthey and his Orchestra and Chorus

Kenny ROGERS (263) [Top 500]
Celebrated crossover country vocalist / actor, who was one of the US's top-selling artists of the past 30 years, b. 21 Aug 1938, Houston. This Grammy-winning ex-New Christy Minstrel has collected more than 20 US gold albums and is a household name in many countries (109 WEEKS) pos/wks

18 Oct 69 ●	RUBY DON'T TAKE YOUR LOVE TO TOWN *Reprise RS 20829* [1] ...	2	23
7 Feb 70 ●	SOMETHING'S BURNING *Reprise RS 20888* [1]	8	14
30 Apr 77 ★	LUCILLE *United Artists UP 36242*	1	14
17 Sep 77	DAYTIME FRIENDS *United Artists UP 36289*	39	4
2 Jun 79	SHE BELIEVES IN ME *United Artists UP 36533*	42	7
26 Jan 80 ★	COWARD OF THE COUNTY *United Artists UP 614*..........	1	12
15 Nov 80	LADY *United Artists UP 635* ▲	12	12
12 Feb 83	WE'VE GOT TONIGHT *Liberty UP 658* [2]	28	7
22 Oct 83	EYES THAT SEE IN THE DARK *RCA 358*	61	1
12 Nov 83 ●	ISLANDS IN THE STREAM *RCA 378* [3] ▲	7	15

[1] Kenny Rogers and the First Edition [2] Kenny Rogers and Sheena Easton [3] Kenny Rogers and Dolly Parton

ROKOTTO
UK, male vocal / instrumental group (10 WEEKS) pos/wks

| 22 Oct 77 | BOOGIE ON UP *State STAT 62* .... | 40 | 4 |
| 10 Jun 78 | FUNK THEORY *State STAT 80* .... | 49 | 6 |

ROLLERGIRL *Germany, female vocalist - Nicci Juice (3 WEEKS)*   pos/wks

16 Sep 00	**DEAR JESSIE** *Neo NEOCD 038*	22 3

ROLLING STONES `17` `Top 500` *"World's No.1 rock group": Mick Jagger (v), Keith Richard (g), Brian Jones (g) (d. 1969), Bill Wyman (b), Charlie Watts (d) - Ron Wood (g) joined in 1975. No group has accumulated more UK or US Top 10 albums or grossed more income from touring than this legendary British band (366 WEEKS)*   pos/wks

25 Jul 63	**COME ON** *Decca F 11675*	21 14
14 Nov 63	**I WANNA BE YOUR MAN** *Decca F 11764*	12 16
27 Feb 64 ●	**NOT FADE AWAY** *Decca F 11845*	3 15
2 Jul 64 ★	**IT'S ALL OVER NOW** *Decca F 11934*	1 15
19 Nov 64 ★	**LITTLE RED ROOSTER** *Decca F 12014*	1 12
4 Mar 65 ★	**THE LAST TIME** *Decca F 12104*	1 13
26 Aug 65 ★	**(I CAN'T GET NO) SATISFACTION** *Decca F 12220* ▲	1 12
28 Oct 65 ★	**GET OFF OF MY CLOUD** *Decca F 12263* ▲	1 12
10 Feb 66 ●	**NINETEENTH NERVOUS BREAKDOWN** *Decca F 12331*	2 8
19 May 66 ★	**PAINT IT BLACK** *Decca F 12395* ▲	1 10
29 Sep 66 ●	**HAVE YOU SEEN YOUR MOTHER BABY STANDING IN THE SHADOW** *Decca F 12497*	5 8
19 Jan 67 ●	**LET'S SPEND THE NIGHT TOGETHER / RUBY TUESDAY** *Decca F 12546*	3 10
23 Aug 67 ●	**WE LOVE YOU / DANDELION** *Decca F 12654*	8 8
29 May 68 ★	**JUMPIN' JACK FLASH** *Decca F 12782*	1 11
9 Jul 69 ★	**HONKY TONK WOMEN** *Decca F 12952* ▲	1 17
24 Apr 71 ●	**BROWN SUGAR / BITCH / LET IT ROCK** *Rolling Stones RS 19100* ▲	2 13
3 Jul 71	**STREET FIGHTING MAN** *Decca F 13195*	21 8
29 Apr 72 ●	**TUMBLING DICE** *Rolling Stones RS 19103*	5 8
1 Sep 73 ●	**ANGIE** *Rolling Stones RS 19105* ▲	5 10
3 Aug 74 ●	**IT'S ONLY ROCK AND ROLL** *Rolling Stones RS 19114*	10 7
20 Sep 75	**OUT OF TIME** *Decca F 13597*	45 2
1 May 76 ●	**FOOL TO CRY** *Rolling Stones RS 19121*	6 10
3 Jun 78 ●	**MISS YOU / FARAWAY EYES** *Rolling Stones EMI 2802* ▲	3 13
30 Sep 78	**RESPECTABLE** *Rolling Stones EMI 2861*	23 9
5 Jul 80 ●	**EMOTIONAL RESCUE** *Rolling Stones RSR 105*	9 8
4 Oct 80	**SHE'S SO COLD** *Rolling Stones RSR 106*	33 6
29 Aug 81 ●	**START ME UP** *Rolling Stones RSR 108*	7 9
12 Dec 81	**WAITING ON A FRIEND** *Rolling Stones RSR 109*	50 6
12 Jun 82	**GOING TO A GO GO** *Rolling Stones RSR 110*	26 6
2 Oct 82	**TIME IS ON MY SIDE** *Rolling Stones RSR 111*	62 2
12 Nov 83	**UNDERCOVER OF THE NIGHT** *Rolling Stones RSR 113*	11 9
11 Feb 84	**SHE WAS HOT** *Rolling Stones RSR 114*	42 4
21 Jul 84	**BROWN SUGAR (re-issue)** *Rolling Stones SUGAR 1*	58 2
15 Mar 86	**HARLEM SHUFFLE** *Rolling Stones A 6864*	13 7
2 Sep 89	**MIXED EMOTIONS** *Rolling Stones 655193 7*	36 5
2 Dec 89	**ROCK AND A HARD PLACE** *Rolling Stones 655422 7*	63 4
23 Jun 90	**PAINT IT BLACK (re-issue)** *London LON 264*	61 3
30 Jun 90	**ALMOST HEAR YOU SIGH** *Rolling Stones 656065 7*	31 5
30 Mar 91	**HIGHWIRE** *Rolling Stones 6567567*	29 4
1 Jun 91	**RUBY TUESDAY (LIVE)** *Rolling Stones 6568927*	59 2
16 Jul 94	**LOVE IS STRONG** *Virgin VSCDT 1503*	14 5
8 Oct 94	**YOU GOT ME ROCKING** *Virgin VSCDG 1518*	23 3
10 Dec 94	**OUT OF TEARS** *Virgin VSCDT 1524*	36 4
15 Jul 95	**I GO WILD** *Virgin VSCDX 1539*	29 3
11 Nov 95	**LIKE A ROLLING STONE** *Virgin VSCDT 1562*	12 5
4 Oct 97	**ANYBODY SEEN MY BABY?** *Virgin VSCDT 1653*	22 3
7 Feb 98	**SAINT OF ME** *Virgin VSCDT 1667*	26 2
22 Aug 98	**OUT OF CONTROL** *Virgin VSCDT 1700*	51 1

'Faraway Eyes' was listed from 15 July 1978, with a peak position of 10

ROLLINS BAND *US, male vocal / instrumental group (4 WEEKS)*   pos/wks

12 Sep 92	**TEARING** *Imago 72787250187*	54 2
10 Sep 94	**LIAR / DISCONNECT** *Imago 74321213052*	27 2

ROLLO *UK, male producer - Roland Armstrong (8 WEEKS)*   pos/wks

29 Jan 94	**GET OFF YOUR HIGH HORSE** *Cheeky CHEKCD 003* `1`	43 2
1 Oct 94	**GET OFF YOUR HIGH HORSE (re-entry)** *Cheeky CHEKCD 003* `1`	47 2

10 Jun 95	**LOVE LOVE LOVE - HERE I COME** *Cheeky CHEKCD 007* `2`	32 2
8 Jun 96	**LET THIS BE A PRAYER** *Cheeky CHEKCD 013* `3`	26 2

`1` Rollo Goes Camping `2` Rollo Goes Mystic `3` Rollo Goes Spiritual with Pauline Taylor

ROMAN HOLLIDAY *UK, male vocal / instrumental group (19 WEEKS)*   pos/wks

2 Apr 83	**STAND BY** *Jive JIVE 31*	61 3
2 Jul 83	**DON'T TRY TO STOP IT** *Jive JIVE 39*	14 9
24 Sep 83	**MOTORMANIA** *Jive JIVE 49*	40 7

ROMAN NUMERALS – See Vic REEVES

ROMANTICS – See RUBY and the ROMANTICS

Max ROMEO *Jamaica, male vocalist - Maxie Smith (25 WEEKS)*   pos/wks

28 May 69 ●	**WET DREAM** *Unity UN 503*	10 24
29 Nov 69	**WET DREAM (re-entry)** *Unity UN 503*	50 1

Harry 'Choo Choo' ROMERO presents INAYA DAY *US, male producer and US, female vocalist (2 WEEKS)*   pos/wks

22 May 99	**JUST CAN'T GET ENOUGH** *AM:PM CDAMPM 121*	39 2

See also CHOO CHOO PROJECT

RONALDO'S REVENGE *UK, male production duo (2 WEEKS)*   pos/wks

1 Aug 98	**MAS QUE MANCADA** *AM:PM 5827532*	37 2

See also FULL INTENTION

RONDO VENEZIANO *Italy, orchestra (3 WEEKS)*   pos/wks

22 Oct 83	**LA SERENISSIMA (THEME FROM 'VENICE IN PERIL')** *Ferroway 7 RON 1*	58 3

RONETTES *US, female vocal group (34 WEEKS)*   pos/wks

17 Oct 63 ●	**BE MY BABY** *London HLU 9793*	4 13
9 Jan 64	**BABY I LOVE YOU** *London HLU 9826*	11 14
27 Aug 64	**(THE BEST PART OF) BREAKING UP** *London HLU 9905*	43 3
8 Oct 64	**DO I LOVE YOU** *London HLU 9922*	35 4

RONNETTE – See FIDELFATTI featuring RONNETTE

Mick RONSON with Joe ELLIOTT *UK, male instrumental / vocal duo (1 WEEK)*   pos/wks

7 May 94	**DON'T LOOK DOWN** *Epic 6603582*	55 1

Linda RONSTADT *US, female vocalist (34 WEEKS)*   pos/wks

8 May 76	**TRACKS OF MY TEARS** *Asylum K 13034*	42 3
28 Jan 78	**BLUE BAYOU** *Asylum K 13106*	35 4
26 May 79	**ALISON** *Asylum K 13149*	66 2
11 Jul 87 ●	**SOMEWHERE OUT THERE** *MCA MCA 1132* `1`	8 13
11 Nov 89 ●	**DON'T KNOW MUCH** *Elektra EKR 101* `2`	2 12

`1` Linda Ronstadt and James Ingram `2` Linda Ronstadt featuring Aaron Neville

ROOFTOP SINGERS *US, male / female vocal group (12 WEEKS)*   pos/wks

31 Jan 63 ●	**WALK RIGHT IN** *Fontana 271700 TF* ▲	10 12

ROOTJOOSE *UK, male vocal / instrumental group (3 WEEKS)*   pos/wks

17 May 97	**CAN'T KEEP LIVING THIS WAY** *Rage RAGECD 2*	73 1
2 Aug 97	**MR FIXIT** *Rage RAGECDX 3*	54 1
4 Oct 97	**LONG WAY** *Rage RAGECD 5*	68 1

ROOTS *US, male rap / production group (3 WEEKS)*   pos/wks

3 May 97	**WHAT THEY DO** *Geffen GFSTD 22240*	49 1
6 Mar 99	**YOU GOT ME** *MCA MCSTD 48110* `1`	31 2

`1` Roots featuring Erykah Badu

ROOTS MANUVA – See LEFTFIELD

Ralphi ROSARIO – See Richie RICH

Mykal ROSE – See Shabba RANKS

ROSE OF ROMANCE ORCHESTRA *UK, orchestra (1 WEEK)*
pos/wks

9 Jan 82	TARA'S THEME FROM 'GONE WITH THE WIND' *BBC RESL 108*	71	1

ROSE ROYCE 243 Top 500 *The best-selling nine-piece soul / dance combo from Los Angeles, whose biggest hits featured vocalist Gwen Dickey, started as a backing band for Motown acts and topped the UK album chart with their Greatest Hits collection in 1980 (113 WEEKS)*
pos/wks

25 Dec 76 ●	CAR WASH *MCA 267* ▲	9	12
22 Jan 77	PUT YOUR MONEY WHERE YOUR MOUTH IS *MCA 259*	44	5
2 Apr 77	I WANNA GET NEXT TO YOU *MCA 278*	14	8
24 Sep 77	DO YOUR DANCE *Whitfield K 17006*	30	6
14 Jan 78 ●	WISHING ON A STAR *Warner Bros. K 17060*	3	14
6 May 78	IT MAKES YOU FEEL LIKE DANCIN' *Warner Bros. K 17148*	16	10
16 Sep 78 ●	LOVE DON'T LIVE HERE ANYMORE *Whitfield K 17236*	2	10
3 Feb 79	I'M IN LOVE (AND I LOVE THE FEELING) *Whitfield K 17291*	51	4
17 Nov 79	IS IT LOVE YOU'RE AFTER *Whitfield K 17456*	13	13
8 Mar 80	OOH BOY *Whitfield K 17575*	46	7
21 Nov 81	R.R. EXPRESS *Warner Bros. K 17875*	52	3
1 Sep 84	MAGIC TOUCH *Streetwave KHAN 21*	43	8
6 Apr 85	LOVE ME RIGHT NOW *Streetwave KHAN 39*	60	3
11 Jun 88	CAR WASH / IS IT LOVE YOU'RE AFTER (re-issue) *MCA MCA 1253*	20	7
31 Oct 98	CAR WASH (re-recording) *MCA MCSTD 48096* [1]	18	3

[1] Rose Royce featuring Gwen Dickey

ROSE TATTOO *Australia, male vocal / instrumental group (4 WEEKS)*
pos/wks

11 Jul 81	ROCK 'N' ROLL OUTLAW *Carrere CAR 200*	60	4

Jimmy ROSELLI *US, male vocalist (8 WEEKS)*
pos/wks

5 Mar 83	WHEN YOUR OLD WEDDING RING WAS NEW *A1 282*	51	5
20 Jun 87	WHEN YOUR OLD WEDDING RING WAS NEW (re-issue) *First Night SCORE 9*	52	3

ROSIE – See G NATION featuring ROSIE

Diana ROSS 5 Top 500 *Perennially popular ex-leader of the Supremes, the most successful girl group of all time, b. Diane Earle, 26 Mar 1944, Detroit, US. Ross continued to clock up worldwide hits after leaving trio in 1970 and sang lead on at least one hit every year for a record 33 years (1964-1996). The classy vocalist has also had more albums on the UK chart than any other American female artist. Diana, who starred in the movies 'Lady Sings the Blues' (1972), 'Mahogany' ('76) and 'The Wiz' ('78), moved from Motown to RCA in 1981 for a (female) record $20 million. In 1994, she was the star of the opening ceremony of football's World Cup, and in 1998 was sampled on chart-topping singles by Puff Daddy and Monica. In her homeland this supreme song stylist has clocked-up a staggering 22 Top 5 entries during her career, even though she has not had a major hit there since 1984. She has been inducted into the Soul Train and Songwriters Hall of Fame and was the recipient of a Lifetime Achievement trophy at the World Music Awards in 1996 (560 WEEKS)*
pos/wks

30 Aug 67 ●	REFLECTIONS *Tamla Motown TMG 616* [1]	5	14
29 Nov 67	IN AND OUT OF LOVE *Tamla Motown TMG 632* [1]	13	13
10 Apr 68	FOREVER CAME TODAY *Tamla Motown TMG 650* [1]	28	8
3 Jul 68	SOME THINGS YOU NEVER GET USED TO *Tamla Motown TMG 662* [1]	34	6
20 Nov 68	LOVE CHILD *Tamla Motown TMG 677* [1] ▲	15	14
29 Jan 69 ●	I'M GONNA MAKE YOU LOVE ME *Tamla Motown TMG 685* [2]	3	11
23 Apr 69	I'M GONNA MAKE YOU LOVE ME (re-entry) *Tamla Motown TMG 685* [2]	49	1
23 Apr 69	I'M LIVING IN SHAME *Tamla Motown TMG 695* [1]	14	9
2 Jul 69	I'M LIVING IN SHAME (re-entry) *Tamla Motown TMG 695* [1]	50	1

16 Jul 69	NO MATTER WHAT SIGN YOU ARE *Tamla Motown TMG 704* [1]	37	7
20 Sep 69	I SECOND THAT EMOTION *Tamla Motown TMG 709* [2]	18	8
13 Dec 69	SOMEDAY WE'LL BE TOGETHER *Tamla Motown TMG 721* [1] ▲	13	13
21 Mar 70	WHY (MUST WE FALL IN LOVE) *Tamla Motown TMG 730* [2]	31	7
18 Jul 70	REACH OUT AND TOUCH *Tamla Motown TMG 743*	33	5
12 Sep 70 ●	AIN'T NO MOUNTAIN HIGH ENOUGH *Tamla Motown TMG 751* ▲	6	12
3 Apr 71 ●	REMEMBER ME *Tamla Motown TMG 768*	7	12
31 Jul 71 ★	I'M STILL WAITING *Tamla Motown TMG 781*	1	14
30 Oct 71 ●	SURRENDER *Tamla Motown TMG 792*	10	11
13 May 72	DOOBEDOOD'NDOOBE DOOBEDOOD'NDOOBE *Tamla Motown TMG 812*	12	9
14 Jul 73 ●	TOUCH ME IN THE MORNING *Tamla Motown TMG 861* ▲	9	12
13 Oct 73	TOUCH ME IN THE MORNING (re-entry) *Tamla Motown TMG 861*	50	1
5 Jan 74 ●	ALL OF MY LIFE *Tamla Motown TMG 880*	9	13
23 Mar 74	YOU ARE EVERYTHING *Tamla Motown TMG 890* [3]	5	12
4 May 74	LAST TIME I SAW HIM *Tamla Motown TMG 893*	35	4
20 Jul 74	STOP LOOK LISTEN (TO YOUR HEART) *Tamla Motown TMG 906* [3]	25	8
24 Aug 74	BABY LOVE (re-issue) *Tamla Motown TMG 915* [1]	12	10
28 Sep 74	LOVE ME *Tamla Motown TMG 917*	38	5
29 Mar 75	SORRY DOESN'T ALWAYS MAKE IT RIGHT *Tamla Motown TMG 941*	23	9
3 Apr 76 ●	THEME FROM 'MAHOGANY' (DO YOU KNOW WHERE YOU'RE GOING TO) *Tamla Motown TMG 1010* ▲	5	8
24 Apr 76 ●	LOVE HANGOVER *Tamla Motown TMG 1024* ▲	10	10
10 Jul 76	I THOUGHT IT TOOK A LITTLE TIME *Tamla Motown TMG 1032*	32	5
16 Oct 76	I'M STILL WAITING (re-issue) *Tamla Motown TMG 1041*	41	4
19 Nov 77	GETTIN' READY FOR LOVE *Motown TMG 1090*	23	7
22 Jul 78	LOVIN' LIVIN' AND GIVIN' *Motown TMG 1112*	54	6
18 Nov 78	EASE ON DOWN THE ROAD *MCA 396* [4]	45	4
24 Feb 79	POPS WE LOVE YOU *Motown TMG 1136* [5]	66	5
21 Jul 79	THE BOSS *Motown TMG 1150*	40	7
6 Oct 79	NO ONE GETS THE PRIZE *Motown TMG 1160*	59	3
24 Nov 79	IT'S MY HOUSE *Motown TMG 1169*	32	10
19 Jul 80 ●	UPSIDE DOWN *Motown TMG 1195* ▲	2	12
20 Sep 80 ●	MY OLD PIANO *Motown TMG 1202*	5	9
15 Nov 80	I'M COMING OUT *Motown TMG 1210*	13	10
17 Jan 81	IT'S MY TURN *Motown TMG 1217*	16	8
28 Mar 81	ONE MORE CHANCE *Motown TMG 1227*	49	5
13 Jun 81	CRYIN' MY HEART OUT FOR YOU *Motown TMG 1233*	58	3
12 Sep 81 ●	ENDLESS LOVE *Motown TMG 1240* [6] ▲	7	12
7 Nov 81 ●	WHY DO FOOLS FALL IN LOVE *Capitol CL 226*	4	12
23 Jan 82	TENDERNESS *Motown TMG 1248*	73	1
30 Jan 82	MIRROR MIRROR *Capitol CL 234*	36	5
6 Feb 82	TENDERNESS (re-entry) *Motown TMG 1248*	75	1
29 May 82 ●	WORK THAT BODY *Capitol CL 241*	7	11
7 Aug 82	IT'S NEVER TOO LATE *Capitol CL 256*	41	4
23 Oct 82	MUSCLES *Capitol CL 268*	15	9
15 Jan 83	SO CLOSE *Capitol CL 277*	43	4
23 Jul 83	PIECES OF ICE *Capitol CL 298*	46	3
7 Jul 84	ALL OF YOU *CBS A 4522* [7]	43	8
15 Sep 84	TOUCH BY TOUCH *Capitol CL 337*	47	6
28 Sep 85	EATEN ALIVE *Capitol CL 372*	71	1
25 Jan 86 ★	CHAIN REACTION *Capitol CL 386*	1	17
3 May 86	EXPERIENCE *Capitol CL 400*	47	3
13 Jun 87	DIRTY LOOKS *EMI EM 2*	49	3
8 Oct 88	MR LEE *EMI EM 73*	58	2
26 Nov 88	LOVE HANGOVER (re-mix) *Motown ZB 42307*	75	1
18 Feb 89	STOP! IN THE NAME OF LOVE (re-issue) *Motown ZB 41963* [1]	62	1
6 May 89	WORKIN' OVERTIME *EMI EM 91*	32	5
29 Jul 89	PARADISE *EMI EM 94*	61	2
7 Jul 90	I'M STILL WAITING (re-mix) *Motown ZB 43781*	21	6
30 Nov 91 ●	WHEN YOU TELL ME THAT YOU LOVE ME *EMI EM 217*	2	11
15 Feb 92	THE FORCE BEHIND THE POWER *EMI EM 221*	27	3
20 Jun 92 ●	ONE SHINING MOMENT *EMI EM 239*	10	8
28 Nov 92	IF WE HOLD ON TOGETHER *EMI EM 257*	11	10
13 Mar 93	HEART (DON'T CHANGE MY MIND) *EMI CDEM 261*	31	3
9 Oct 93	CHAIN REACTION (re-issue) *EMI CDEM 290*	20	5

UK No.1 ★   UK Top 10 ●   Still on chart +   UK million seller ◆   UK entry at No.1 ■   US No.1 ▲

11 Dec 93		YOUR LOVE *EMI CDEM 299*	**14**	8
2 Apr 94		THE BEST YEARS OF MY LIFE *EMI CDEM 305*	**28**	4
9 Jul 94		WHY DO FOOLS FALL IN LOVE (re-issue) / I'M COMING OUT (re-mix) *EMI CDEM 332*	**36**	4
2 Sep 95		TAKE ME HIGHER *EMI CDEM 388*	**32**	4
25 Nov 95		I'M GONE *EMI CDEM 402*	**36**	3
17 Feb 96		I WILL SURVIVE *EMI CDEM 415* [8]	**14**	4
21 Dec 96		IN THE ONES YOU LOVE *EMI CDEM 457*	**34**	4
6 Nov 99	●	NOT OVER YOU YET *EMI CDEMS 553*	**9**	6
15 Jan 00		NOT OVER YOU YET (re-entry) *EMI CDEMS 553*	**58**	1

[1] Diana Ross and the Supremes [2] Diana Ross and the Supremes and the Temptations [3] Diana Ross and Marvin Gaye [4] Diana Ross and Michael Jackson [5] Diana Ross, Marvin Gaye, Smokey Robinson and Stevie Wonder [6] Diana Ross and Lionel Richie [7] Julio Iglesias and Diana Ross [8] Diana

See also SUPREMES

Ricky ROSS *UK, male vocalist (3 WEEKS)* pos/wks

18 May 96		RADIO ON *Epic 6631352*	**35**	2
10 Aug 96		GOOD EVENING PHILADELPHIA *Epic 6635335*	**58**	1

See also DEACON BLUE

Francis ROSSI *UK, male vocalist (6 WEEKS)* pos/wks

11 May 85		MODERN ROMANCE (I WANT TO FALL IN LOVE AGAIN) *Vertigo FROS 1* [1]	**54**	4
3 Aug 96		GIVE MYSELF TO LOVE *Virgin VSCDT 1594* [2]	**42**	2

[1] Francis Rossi and Bernard Frost [2] Francis Rossi of Status Quo

See also STATUS QUO

Nini ROSSO *Italy, male instrumentalist - trumpet (14 WEEKS)* pos/wks

26 Aug 65	●	IL SILENZIO *Durium DRS 54000*	**8**	14

David Lee ROTH *US, male vocalist (15 WEEKS)* pos/wks

23 Feb 85		CALIFORNIA GIRLS *Warner Bros. W 9102*	**68**	2
5 Mar 88		JUST LIKE PARADISE *Warner Bros. W 8119*	**27**	7
3 Sep 88		DAMN GOOD / STAND UP *Warner Bros. W 7753*	**72**	1
12 Jan 91		A LIL' AIN'T ENOUGH *Warner Bros. W 0002*	**32**	3
19 Feb 94		SHE'S MY MACHINE *Reprise W 0229CD*	**64**	1
28 May 94		NIGHT LIFE *Reprise W 0249CD*	**72**	1

See also VAN HALEN

ROTTERDAM TERMINATION SOURCE
Holland, male instrumental / production duo (6 WEEKS) pos/wks

7 Nov 92		POING *SEP EDGE 74*	**27**	4
25 Dec 93		MERRY X-MESS *React CDREACT 33*	**73**	2

ROULA – See 20 FINGERS

ROULETTES – See Adam FAITH

Demis ROUSSOS *Greece, male vocalist (44 WEEKS)* pos/wks

22 Nov 75	●	HAPPY TO BE ON AN ISLAND IN THE SUN *Philips 6042 033*	**5**	10
28 Feb 76		CAN'T SAY HOW MUCH I LOVE YOU *Philips 6042 114*	**35**	5
26 Jun 76	★	THE ROUSSOS PHENOMENON (EP) *Philips DEMIS 001*	**1**	12
2 Oct 76	●	WHEN FOREVER HAS GONE *Philips 6042 186*	**2**	10
19 Mar 77		BECAUSE *Philips 6042 245*	**39**	4
18 Jun 77		KYRILA (EP) *Philips Demis 002*	**33**	3

Tracks on The Roussos Phenomenon (EP): Forever and Ever / Sing an Ode to Love / So Dreamy / My Friend the Wind. Tracks on Kyrila (EP): Kyrila / I'm Gonna Fall in Love / I Dig You / Sister Emilyne

ROUTERS *US, male instrumental group (7 WEEKS)* pos/wks

27 Dec 62		LET'S GO *Warner Bros. WB 77*	**32**	7

Maria ROWE *UK, female vocalist (2 WEEKS)* pos/wks

20 May 95		SEXUAL *ffrr FCD 248*	**67**	2

ROWETTA – See OPEN ARMS featuring ROWETTA

Kevin ROWLAND – See DEXY'S MIDNIGHT RUNNERS

John ROWLES *New Zealand, male vocalist (28 WEEKS)* pos/wks

13 Mar 68	●	IF I ONLY HAD TIME *MCA MU 1000*	**3**	18
19 Jun 68		HUSH NOT A WORD TO MARY *MCA MU 1023*	**12**	10

ROXETTE `166` `Top 500` *The most successful Scandinavian act in the US singles chart: Marie Fredriksson (v). Per Gessle (v/g). The duo, who have even appeared on postage stamps in their homeland, can claim total worldwide sales in excess of 40 million (143 WEEKS)* pos/wks

22 Apr 89	●	THE LOOK *EMI EM 87* ▲	**7**	10
15 Jul 89		DRESSED FOR SUCCESS *EMI EM 96*	**48**	5
28 Oct 89		LISTEN TO YOUR HEART *EMI EM 108* ▲	**62**	3
2 Jun 90	●	IT MUST HAVE BEEN LOVE *EMI EM 141* ▲	**3**	14
11 Aug 90	●	LISTEN TO YOUR HEART / DANGEROUS (re-issue) *EMI EM 149*	**6**	9
27 Oct 90		DRESSED FOR SUCCESS (re-issue) *EMI EM 162*	**18**	7
9 Mar 91	●	JOYRIDE *EMI EM 177* ▲	**4**	10
11 May 91		FADING LIKE A FLOWER *EMI EM 190*	**12**	6
7 Sep 91		THE BIG L *EMI EM 204*	**21**	6
23 Nov 91		SPENDING MY TIME *EMI EM 215*	**22**	4
28 Mar 92		CHURCH OF YOUR HEART *EMI EM 227*	**21**	4
1 Aug 92		HOW DO YOU DO! *EMI EM 241*	**13**	7
7 Nov 92		QUEEN OF RAIN *EMI EM 253*	**28**	4
24 Jul 93	●	ALMOST UNREAL *EMI CDEM 268*	**7**	9
18 Sep 93	●	IT MUST HAVE BEEN LOVE (re-issue) *EMI CDEM 285*	**10**	8
26 Mar 94		SLEEPING IN MY CAR *EMI CDEM 314*	**14**	6
4 Jun 94		CRASH! BOOM! BANG! *EMI CDEM 324*	**26**	5
17 Sep 94		FIREWORKS *EMI CDEM 345*	**30**	4
3 Dec 94		RUN TO YOU *EMI CDEM 360*	**27**	6
8 Apr 95		VULNERABLE *EMI CDEM 369*	**44**	2
25 Nov 95		THE LOOK (re-mix) *EMI CDEM 406*	**28**	3
30 Mar 96		YOU DON'T UNDERSTAND ME *EMI CDEM 418*	**42**	2
20 Jul 96		JUNE AFTERNOON *EMI CDEM 437*	**52**	1
20 Mar 99		WISH I COULD FLY *EMI CDEM 537*	**11**	7
9 Oct 99		STARS *EMI CDEM 550*	**56**	1

ROXY MUSIC `135` `Top 500` *Stylish art-rock group regarded as highly influential pioneers. Nucleus of oft-changing group line-up: Bryan Ferry (v), Andy Mackay (sax), Phil Manzanera (g). A major act of its time, this group amassed nine Top 10 albums (155 WEEKS)* pos/wks

19 Aug 72	●	VIRGINIA PLAIN *Island WIP 6144*	**4**	12
10 Mar 73	●	PYJAMARAMA *Island WIP 6159*	**10**	12
17 Nov 73	●	STREET LIFE *Island WIP 6173*	**9**	12
12 Oct 74		ALL I WANT IS YOU *Island WIP 6208*	**12**	8
11 Oct 75	●	LOVE IS THE DRUG *Island WIP 6248*	**2**	10
27 Dec 75		BOTH ENDS BURNING *Island WIP 6262*	**25**	7
22 Oct 77		VIRGINIA PLAIN (re-issue) *Polydor 2001 739*	**11**	6
3 Mar 79		TRASH *Polydor POSP 32*	**40**	6
28 Apr 79	●	DANCE AWAY *Polydor POSP 44*	**2**	14
11 Aug 79	●	ANGEL EYES *Polydor POSP 67*	**4**	11
17 May 80	●	OVER YOU *Polydor POSP 93*	**5**	9
2 Aug 80	●	OH YEAH (ON THE RADIO) *Polydor 2001 972*	**5**	8
8 Nov 80		THE SAME OLD SCENE *Polydor ROXY 1*	**12**	7
21 Feb 81	★	JEALOUS GUY *EG ROXY 2*	**1**	11
3 Apr 82	●	MORE THAN THIS *EG ROXY 3*	**6**	8
19 Jun 82		AVALON *EG ROXY 4*	**13**	6
25 Sep 82		TAKE A CHANCE WITH ME *EG ROXY 5*	**26**	6
27 Apr 96		LOVE IS THE DRUG (re-mix) *EG VSCDT 1580*	**33**	2

See also Bryan FERRY

The Central Band of the ROYAL AIR FORCE, Conductor W/Cdr AE SIMS OBE *UK, military band (1 WEEK)* pos/wks

21 Oct 55		THE DAMBUSTERS MARCH *HMV B 10877*	**18**	1

Billy Joe ROYAL *US, male vocalist (4 WEEKS)* pos/wks

7 Oct 65		DOWN IN THE BOONDOCKS *CBS 201802*	**38**	4

ROYAL GUARDSMEN
US, male vocal / instrumental group (17 WEEKS)　　　pos/wks

19 Jan 67	●	SNOOPY VS THE RED BARON Stateside SS 574	8	13
6 Apr 67		RETURN OF THE RED BARON Stateside SS 2010	37	4

ROYAL HOUSE US, male DJ / producer - Todd Terry (18 WEEKS) pos/wks

10 Sep 88	CAN YOU PARTY Champion CHAMP 79	14	14
7 Jan 89	YEAH! BUDDY Champion CHAMP 91	35	4

ROYAL PHILHARMONIC ORCHESTRA arranged and conducted by Louis CLARK UK, orchestra and conductor (19 WEEKS) pos/wks

25 Jul 81	●	HOOKED ON CLASSICS RCA 109	2	11
24 Oct 81		HOOKED ON CAN-CAN RCA 151	47	3
10 Jul 82		BBC WORLD CUP GRANDSTAND BBC RESL 116	61	3
7 Aug 82		IF YOU KNEW SOUSA (AND FRIENDS) RCA 256	71	2

Louis Clark did not conduct the third hit

See also Elvis COSTELLO

The Pipes and Drums and Military Band of the ROYAL SCOTS DRAGOON GUARDS UK, military band (43 WEEKS) pos/wks

1 Apr 72	★	AMAZING GRACE RCA 2191	1	24
19 Aug 72		HEYKENS SERENADE / THE DAY IS ENDED RCA 2251	30	7
2 Dec 72		LITTLE DRUMMER BOY RCA 2301	13	9
23 Dec 72		AMAZING GRACE (re-entry) RCA 2191	42	3

ROYALLE DELITE US, female vocal group (6 WEEKS) pos/wks

14 Sep 85	(I'LL BE A) FREAK FOR YOU Streetwave KHAN 51	45	6

Lita ROZA UK, female vocalist (18 WEEKS) pos/wks

13 Mar 53	★	(HOW MUCH IS) THAT DOGGIE IN THE WINDOW Decca F 10070	1	11
7 Oct 55		HEY THERE Decca F 10611	17	2
23 Mar 56		JIMMY UNKNOWN Decca F 10679	15	5

ROZALLA Zimbabwe, female vocalist - Rozalla Miller (48 WEEKS) pos/wks

27 Apr 91		FAITH (IN THE POWER OF LOVE) Pulse 8 LOSE 7	65	2
7 Sep 91	●	EVERYBODY'S FREE (TO FEEL GOOD) Pulse 8 LOSE 13	6	11
16 Nov 91		FAITH (IN THE POWER OF LOVE) (re-issue) Pulse 8 LOSE 15	11	6
22 Feb 92		ARE YOU READY TO FLY Pulse 8 LOSE 21	14	6
9 May 92		LOVE BREAKDOWN Pulse 8 LOSE 25	65	2
15 Aug 92		IN 4 CHOONS LATER Pulse 8 LOSE 29	50	2
30 Oct 93		DON'T PLAY WITH ME Pulse 8 CDLOSE 52	50	1
5 Feb 94		I LOVE MUSIC Epic 6598932	18	5
6 Aug 94		THIS TIME I FOUND LOVE Epic 6603742	33	3
29 Oct 94		YOU NEVER LOVE THE SAME WAY TWICE Epic 6609052	16	5
4 Mar 95		BABY Epic 6611955	26	3
31 Aug 96		EVERYBODY'S FREE (re-mix) Pulse 8 CDLOSE 110	30	2

RTE CONCERT ORCHESTRA – See Bill WHELAN featuring ANUNA and the RTE CONCERT ORCHESTRA

RUBBADUBB UK, male / female vocal / instrumental group (1 WEEK) pos/wks

18 Jul 98	TRIBUTE TO OUR ANCESTORS Perfecto PERF 165CD	56	1

RUBETTES Ex-Barry Blue backing band fronted by Alan Williams, b. 22 Dec 1950, Hertfordshire, UK, whose brand of 1970s good-time rock 'n' roll produced a string of European hits. Distinctive falsetto Paul Da Vinci left the group after singing on their three-million-selling debut hit (68 WEEKS) pos/wks

4 May 74	★	SUGAR BABY LOVE Polydor 2058 442	1	10
13 Jul 74		TONIGHT Polydor 2058 499	12	9
16 Nov 74	●	JUKE BOX JIVE Polydor 2058 529	3	12
8 Mar 75	●	I CAN DO IT State STAT 1	7	9
21 Jun 75		FOE-DEE-O-DEE State STAT 7	15	6
22 Nov 75		LITTLE DARLING State STAT 13	30	5
1 May 76		YOU'RE THE REASON WHY State STAT 20	28	4
25 Sep 76		UNDER ONE ROOF State STAT 27	40	3
12 Feb 77	●	BABY I KNOW State STAT 37	10	10

RUBY and the ROMANTICS
US, female / male vocal group (6 WEEKS)　　　pos/wks

28 Mar 63	OUR DAY WILL COME London HLR 9679 ▲	38	6

RUDE BOY OF HOUSE – See HOUSEMASTER BOYZ and the RUDE BOY OF HOUSE

RUDIES – See Freddie NOTES and the RUDIES

RUFF DRIVERZ
UK, male / female vocal / production trio (21 WEEKS)　　　pos/wks

7 Feb 98		DON'T STOP Inferno CDFERN 003	30	2
23 May 98		DEEPER LOVE Inferno CDFERN 006	19	3
24 Oct 98		SHAME Inferno CXFERN 9	51	2
28 Nov 98	●	DREAMING Inferno CXFERN 11 [1]	10	8
24 Apr 99		LA MUSICA Inferno CDFERN 14 [1]	14	4
2 Oct 99		WAITING FOR THE SUN Inferno CDFERN 19	37	2

[1] Ruff Driverz presents Arrola

RUFF ENDZ US, male vocal duo (5 WEEKS) pos/wks

19 Aug 00	NO MORE Epic 6696202	11	5

Frances RUFFELLE UK, female vocalist (6 WEEKS) pos/wks

16 Apr 94	LONELY SYMPHONY Virgin VSCDT 1499	25	6

Bruce RUFFIN
Jamaica, male vocalist - Bernard Downer (23 WEEKS)　　　pos/wks

1 May 71		RAIN Trojan TR 7814	19	11
24 Jun 72	●	MAD ABOUT YOU Rhino RNO 101	9	12

David RUFFIN US, male vocalist (10 WEEKS) pos/wks

17 Jan 76	●	WALK AWAY FROM LOVE Tamla Motown TMG 1017	10	8
21 Sep 85		A NIGHT AT THE APOLLO LIVE! RCA PB 49935 [1]	58	2

[1] Daryl Hall and John Oates featuring David Ruffin and Eddie Kendrick

See also TEMPTATIONS

Jimmy RUFFIN 〔274 Top 500〕 Major Motown hitmaker, b. 7 May 1939, Mississippi, US. After rejecting a job as the lead vocalist of The Temptations (taken by his brother David), he had a handful of UK / US hits (several charting twice). He relocated to the UK, and was in a one-off hit act, Council Collective, a Paul Weller project (106 WEEKS) pos/wks

27 Oct 66	●	WHAT BECOMES OF THE BROKENHEARTED Tamla Motown TMG 577	8	15
9 Feb 67		I'VE PASSED THIS WAY BEFORE Tamla Motown TMG 593	29	7
20 Apr 67		GONNA GIVE HER ALL THE LOVE I'VE GOT Tamla Motown TMG 603	26	6
9 Aug 69		I'VE PASSED THIS WAY BEFORE (re-issue) Tamla Motown TMG 703	33	6
28 Feb 70	●	FAREWELL IS A LONELY SOUND Tamla Motown TMG 726	8	16
4 Jul 70	●	I'LL SAY FOREVER MY LOVE Tamla Motown TMG 740	7	12
17 Oct 70	●	IT'S WONDERFUL (TO BE LOVED BY YOU) Tamla Motown TMG 753	6	14
27 Jul 74	●	WHAT BECOMES OF THE BROKENHEARTED (re-issue) Tamla Motown TMG 911	4	12
2 Nov 74		FAREWELL IS A LONELY SOUND (re-issue) Tamla Motown TMG 922	30	5
16 Nov 74		TELL ME WHAT YOU WANT Polydor 2058 433	39	4
3 May 80	●	HOLD ON TO MY LOVE RSO 57	7	8
26 Jan 85		THERE WILL NEVER BE ANOTHER YOU EMI 5541	68	1

Kim RUFFIN – See Chubby CHUNKS

RUFFNECK featuring YAVAHN US, male production group featuring US female vocalist (5 WEEKS) pos/wks

11 Nov 95	EVERYBODY BE SOMEBODY Positiva CDTIV 46	13	4
7 Sep 96	MOVE YOUR BODY Positiva CDTIV 61	60	1

RUFUS – See Chaka KHAN

RUKMANI – See SNAP

RUMOUR – See Graham PARKER and the RUMOUR

RUMPLE-STILTS-SKIN
US, male / female vocal / instrumental group (4 WEEKS) pos/wks

24 Sep 83	**I THINK I WANT TO DANCE WITH YOU** *Polydor POSP 649*	**51**	4

RUN TINGS *UK, male instrumental / production duo (1 WEEK)* pos/wks

16 May 92	**FIRES BURNING** *Suburban Base SUBBASE 009*	**58**	1

Todd RUNDGREN *US, male vocalist (8 WEEKS)* pos/wks

30 Jun 73	**I SAW THE LIGHT** *Bearsville K 15506*	**36**	6
14 Dec 85	**LOVING YOU'S A DIRTY JOB BUT SOMEBODY'S GOTTA DO IT** *CBS A 6662* [1]	**73**	2

[1] Bonnie Tyler, guest vocals Todd Rundgren

RUN-DMC *US, male rap group (59 WEEKS)* pos/wks

19 Jul 86	**MY ADIDAS / PETER PIPER** *London LON 101*	**62**	2
6 Sep 86 ●	**WALK THIS WAY** *London LON 104*	**8**	10
7 Feb 87	**YOU BE ILLIN'** *Profile LON 118*	**42**	4
30 May 87	**IT'S TRICKY** *Profile LON 130.*	**16**	7
12 Dec 87	**CHRISTMAS IN HOLLIS** *Profile LON 163*	**56**	4
21 May 88	**RUN'S HOUSE** *London LON 177*	**37**	4
2 Sep 89	**GHOSTBUSTERS** *MCA 1360*	**65**	2
1 Dec 90	**WHAT'S IT ALL ABOUT** *Profile PROF 315*	**48**	3
27 Mar 93	**DOWN WITH THE KING** *Profile PROFCD 39*	**69**	2
21 Feb 98	**IT'S LIKE THAT (German import)** *Columbia 6652932* [1]	**63**	3
14 Mar 98	**IT'S LIKE THAT (US import)** *Columbia 6652932* [1]	**65**	1
21 Mar 98 ★	**IT'S LIKE THAT** *Sm:)e Communications SM 90652* [1] ◆ ■....**1**	16
18 Apr 98	**IT'S TRICKY (import)** *Epidrome EPD 6656982* [1] **74**	1

[1] Run-DMC vs Jason Nevins

RUNRIG *UK, male vocal / instrumental group (28 WEEKS)* pos/wks

29 Sep 90	**CAPTURE THE HEART (EP)** *Chrysalis CHS 3594*	**49**	2
7 Sep 91	**HEARTHAMMER (EP)** *Chrysalis CHS 3754*	**25**	4
9 Nov 91	**FLOWER OF THE WEST** *Chrysalis CHS 3805*	**43**	2
6 Mar 93	**WONDERFUL** *Chrysalis CDCHS 3952*	**29**	3
15 May 93	**THE GREATEST FLAME** *Chrysalis CDCHS 3975*	**36**	3
7 Jan 95	**THIS TIME OF YEAR** *Chrysalis CDCHS 5018*	**38**	2
6 May 95	**AN UBHAL AS AIRDE (THE HIGHEST APPLE)** *Chrysalis CDCHS 5021*	**18**	5
4 Nov 95	**THINGS THAT ARE** *Chrysalis CDCHS 5029*	**40**	2
12 Oct 96	**RHYTHM OF MY HEART** *Chrysalis CDCHS 5035*	**24**	2
11 Jan 97	**THE GREATEST FLAME (re-issue)** *Chrysalis CDCHSS 5045*	**30**	3

Tracks on Capture the Heart (EP): Stepping Down the Glory Road / Satellite Flood / Harvest Moon / The Apple Came Down. Tracks on Hearthammer (EP): Hearthammer / Pride of the Summer (Live) / Loch Lomond (Live) / Solus Na Madain

RuPAUL *US, male drag queen vocalist - Rupaul Charles (19 WEEKS)* pos/wks

26 Jun 93	**SUPERMODEL (YOU BETTER WORK)** *Union City UCRD 21*	**39**	4
18 Sep 93	**HOUSE OF LOVE / BACK TO MY ROOTS** *Union City UCRD 23*....	**40**	2
22 Jan 94	**SUPERMODEL / LITTLE DRUMMER BOY (re-mix)** *Union City UCRD 25.*	**61**	2
26 Feb 94 ●	**DON'T GO BREAKING MY HEART** *Rocket EJCD 33* [1]	**7**	7
21 May 94	**HOUSE OF LOVE** *Union City UCRDG 29*	**68**	1
28 Feb 98	**IT'S RAINING MEN…THE SEQUEL** *Logic 74321555412* [2]	**21**	3

[1] Elton John with RuPaul [2] Martha Wash featuring RuPaul

RUSH *Canada, male vocal / instrumental group (43 WEEKS)* pos/wks

11 Feb 78	**CLOSER TO THE HEART** *Mercury RUSH 7*	**36**	3
15 Mar 80	**SPIRIT OF RADIO** *Mercury RADIO 7.*	**13**	7
28 Mar 81	**VITAL SIGNS / A PASSAGE TO BANGKOK** *Mercury VITAL7*......	**41**	4
31 Oct 81	**TOM SAWYER** *Mercury EXIT 7*	**25**	6
4 Sep 82	**NEW WORLD MAN** *Mercury RUSH 8.*	**42**	3
30 Oct 82	**SUBDIVISIONS** *Mercury RUSH 9*	**53**	2
7 May 83	**COUNTDOWN / NEW WORLD MAN (LIVE)** *Mercury RUSH 10* ..	**36**	5
26 May 84	**THE BODY ELECTRIC** *Vertigo RUSH 11*	**56**	3

12 Oct 85	**THE BIG MONEY** *Vertigo RUSH 12*	**46**	3
31 Oct 87	**TIME STAND STILL** *Vertigo RUSH 13* [1]	**42**	3
23 Apr 88	**PRIME MOVER** *Vertigo RUSH 14*	**43**	3
7 Mar 92	**ROLL THE BONES** *Atlantic A 7524*	**49**	1

[1] Rush with Aimee Mann

Donell RUSH *US, male vocalist (1 WEEK)* pos/wks

5 Dec 92	**SYMPHONY** *ID 6587977*	**66**	1

Jennifer RUSH *US, female vocalist (58 WEEKS)* pos/wks

29 Jun 85 ★	**THE POWER OF LOVE** *CBS A 5003* ◆	**1**	32
14 Dec 85	**RING OF ICE** *CBS A 4745*	**14**	10
20 Dec 86	**THE POWER OF LOVE (re-entry)** *CBS A 5003*	**55**	4
20 Jun 87	**FLAMES OF PARADISE** *CBS 650865 7* [1]	**59**	3
27 May 89	**TILL I LOVED YOU** *CBS 654843 7* [2]	**24**	9

[1] Jennifer Rush and Elton John [2] Placido Domingo and Jennifer Rush

Patrice RUSHEN *US, female vocalist (25 WEEKS)* pos/wks

1 Mar 80	**HAVEN'T YOU HEARD** *Elektra K 12414*	**62**	3
24 Jan 81	**NEVER GONNA GIVE YOU UP (WON'T LET YOU BE)** *Elektra K 12494*	**66**	3
24 Apr 82 ●	**FORGET ME NOTS** *Elektra K 13173*	**8**	11
10 Jul 82	**I WAS TIRED OF BEING ALONE** *Elektra K 13184*...............	**39**	5
9 Jun 84	**FEELS SO REAL (WON'T LET GO)** *Elektra E 9742*	**51**	3

RUSSELL *US, male vocalist - Russell Taylor (1 WEEK)* pos/wks

27 May 00	**FOOL FOR LOVE** *Rulin RULIN 1CDS*	**52**	1

Brenda RUSSELL *US, female vocalist (17 WEEKS)* pos/wks

19 Apr 80	**SO GOOD SO RIGHT / IN THE THICK OF IT** *A & M AM 7515*........	**51**	5
12 Mar 88	**PIANO IN THE DARK** *Breakout USA 623*	**23**	12

Patti RUSSO – See MEAT LOAF

RUTH *UK, male vocal / instrumental group (1 WEEK)* pos/wks

12 Apr 97	**I DON'T KNOW** *Arc 5737812*	**66**	1

Paul RUTHERFORD *UK, male vocalist (6 WEEKS)* pos/wks

8 Oct 88	**GET REAL** *Fourth & Broadway BRW 113*	**47**	3
19 Aug 89	**OH WORLD** *Fourth & Broadway BRW 136*	**61**	3

See also FRANKIE GOES TO HOLLYWOOD

RUTHLESS RAP ASSASSINS *UK, male rappers (2 WEEKS)* pos/wks

9 Jun 90	**JUST MELLOW** *Syncopate SY 35*	**75**	1
1 Sep 90	**AND IT WASN'T A DREAM** *Syncopate SY 38*	**75**	1

RUTLES *UK, male vocal group (5 WEEKS)* pos/wks

15 Apr 78	**I MUST BE IN LOVE** *Warner Bros. K 17125*	**39**	3
13 May 78	**I MUST BE IN LOVE (re-entry)** *Warner Bros. K 17125*	**64**	1
16 Nov 96	**SHANGRI-LA** *Virgin America VUSCD 117*	**68**	1

RUTS *UK, male vocal / instrumental group (28 WEEKS)* pos/wks

16 Jun 79 ●	**BABYLON'S BURNING** *Virgin VS 271*	**7**	11
8 Sep 79	**SOMETHING THAT I SAID** *Virgin VS 285*	**29**	5
19 Apr 80	**STARING AT THE RUDE BOYS** *Virgin VS 327*	**22**	8
30 Aug 80	**WEST ONE (SHINE ON ME)** *Virgin VS 370*........................	**43**	4

Barry RYAN *UK, male vocalist - Barry Sapherson (33 WEEKS)* pos/wks

23 Oct 68 ●	**ELOISE** *MGM 1442*	**2**	12
19 Feb 69	**LOVE IS LOVE** *MGM 1464*	**25**	4
4 Oct 69	**HUNT** *Polydor 56 348*	**34**	5
21 Feb 70	**MAGICAL SPIEL** *Polydor 56 370.*	**49**	1
16 May 70	**KITSCH** *Polydor 2001 035*	**37**	6
15 Jan 72	**CAN'T LET YOU GO** *Polydor 2001 256*	**32**	5

See also Paul and Barry RYAN

UK No.1 ★ UK Top 10 ● Still on chart + UK million seller ◆ UK entry at No.1 ■ US No.1 ▲

Marion RYAN UK, female vocalist - Marion Sapherson (11 WEEKS)

		pos/wks
24 Jan 58 ● LOVE ME FOREVER Pye Nixa N 15121		5 11

With the Peter Knight Orchestra and the Beryl Stott Chorus

Paul and Barry RYAN UK, male vocal duo (43 WEEKS)

		pos/wks
11 Nov 65	DON'T BRING ME YOUR HEARTACHES Decca F 12260	13 9
3 Feb 66	HAVE PITY ON THE BOY Decca F 12319	18 6
12 May 66	I LOVE HER Decca F 12391	17 8
14 Jul 66	I LOVE HOW YOU LOVE ME Decca F 12445	21 7
29 Sep 66	HAVE YOU EVER LOVED SOMEBODY Decca F 12494	49 1
8 Dec 66	MISSY MISSY Decca F 12520	43 4
2 Mar 67	KEEP IT OUT OF SIGHT Decca F 12567	30 6
29 Jun 67	CLAIRE Decca F 12633	47 2

See also Barry RYAN

Rebekah RYAN UK, female vocalist (5 WEEKS)

		pos/wks
18 May 96	YOU LIFT ME UP MCA MCSTD 40022	26 3
7 Sep 96	JUST A LITTLE BIT OF LOVE MCA MCSTD 40063	51 1
17 May 97	WOMAN IN LOVE MCA MCSTD 40109	64 1

Bobby RYDELL US, male vocalist - Robert Ridarelli (60 WEEKS)

		pos/wks
10 Mar 60 ●	WILD ONE Columbia DB 4429	7 14
23 Jun 60	WILD ONE (re-entry) Columbia DB 4429	47 1
30 Jun 60	SWINGING SCHOOL Columbia DB 4471	44 1
1 Sep 60	VOLARE Columbia DB 4495	46 1
15 Sep 60	VOLARE (re-entry) Columbia DB 4495	22 5
15 Dec 60	SWAY Columbia DB 4545	12 13
23 Mar 61	GOOD TIME BABY Columbia DB 4600	42 7
19 Apr 62	TEACH ME TO TWIST Columbia DB 4802 [1]	45 1
20 Dec 62	JINGLE BELL ROCK Cameo Parkway C 205 [1]	40 3
23 May 63	FORGET HIM Cameo Parkway C 108	13 14

[1] Chubby Checker and Bobby Rydell

Mitch RYDER and the DETROIT WHEELS
US, male vocal / instrumental group (5 WEEKS)

		pos/wks
10 Feb 66	JENNY TAKE A RIDE Stateside SS 481	44 1
24 Feb 66	JENNY TAKE A RIDE (re-entry) Stateside SS 481	33 4

Shaun RYDER – See BLACK GRAPE; HAPPY MONDAYS; HEADS with Shaun RYDER; Russell WATSON

RYTHM SYNDICATE
US, male vocal / instrumental group (5 WEEKS)

		pos/wks
27 Jul 91	P.A.S.S.I.O.N. Impact American EM 197	58 5

Robin S US, female vocalist - Robin Stone (37 WEEKS)

		pos/wks
16 Jan 93	SHOW ME LOVE Champion CHAMPCD 300	59 4
13 Mar 93 ●	SHOW ME LOVE (re-entry) Champion CHAMPCD 300	6 13
31 Jul 93	LUV 4 LUV Champion CHAMPCD 301	11 7
4 Dec 93	WHAT I DO BEST Champion CHAMPCD 307	43 2
19 Mar 94	I WANT TO THANK YOU Champion CHAMPCD 310	48 1
5 Nov 94	BACK IT UP Champion CHAMPCD 312	43 2
8 Mar 97 ●	SHOW ME LOVE (re-mix) Champion CHAMPCD 326	9 5
12 Jul 97	IT MUST BE LOVE Atlantic A 5596CD	37 2
4 Oct 97	YOU GOT THE LOVE Champion CHAMPCD 330	62 1

S CLUB 7 (455 Top 500) Made-for-TV act (series seen in more than 100 countries) had best start to career of any mixed vocal group with six Top 3 hits from first six releases. Award-winning septet is the largest vocal group ever to top the chart, comprising Jo O'Meara, Tina Barrett, Hannah Spearritt, Rachel Stevens, Paul Cattermole, Bradley McIntosh and Jon Lee (74 WEEKS)

		pos/wks
19 Jun 99 ★	BRING IT ALL BACK Polydor 5610852 ■	1 15
2 Oct 99 ●	S CLUB PARTY Polydor 5614172	2 12
25 Dec 99 ●	TWO IN A MILLION / YOU'RE MY NUMBER ONE Polydor 5615962	2 11
8 Jan 00	S CLUB PARTY (re-entry) Polydor 5614172	68 2
3 Jun 00 ●	REACH Polydor 5618302	2 17
23 Sep 00 ●	NATURAL Polydor 5877602	3 13
9 Dec 00 ★	NEVER HAD A DREAM COME TRUE Polydor 5879032 ■	1 4+

S EXPRESS UK, male / female vocal / instrumental group, fronted by Mark Moore (50 WEEKS)

		pos/wks
16 Apr 88 ★	THEME FROM S-EXPRESS Rhythm King LEFT 21	1 13
23 Jul 88 ●	SUPERFLY GUY Rhythm King LEFT 28	5 9
18 Feb 89 ●	HEY MUSIC LOVER Rhythm King LEFT 30	6 10
16 Sep 89	MANTRA FOR A STATE OF MIND Rhythm King LEFT 35	21 8
15 Sep 90	NOTHING TO LOSE Rhythm King SEXY 01	32 4
30 May 92	FIND 'EM, FOOL 'EM, FORGET 'EM Rhythm King 6580137	43 2
11 May 96	THEME FROM S.EXPRESS (re-mix) Rhythm King SEXY 9CD [1]	14 4

[1] Mark Moore presents S Express

S-J UK, female vocalist (4 WEEKS)

		pos/wks
11 Jan 97	FEVER React CDREACT 93	46 1
24 Jan 98	I FEEL DIVINE React CDREACT 113	30 2
7 Nov 98	SHIVER React CDREACT 138	59 1

Raphael SAADIQ US, male vocalist (4 WEEKS)

		pos/wks
23 Nov 96	STRESSED OUT Jive JIVECD 404 [1]	33 2
19 Jun 99	GET INVOLVED Hollywood 0101185 HWR [2]	36 2

[1] A Tribe Called Quest featuring Faith Evans and Raphael Saadiq [2] Raphael Saadiq and Q-Tip

SABRE featuring PRESIDENT BROWN
Jamaica, male vocal duo (1 WEEK)

		pos/wks
19 Aug 95	WRONG OR RIGHT Greensleeves GRECD 485	71 1

SABRES – See Denny SEYTON and the SABRES

SABRES OF PARADISE UK, male production group (8 WEEKS)

		pos/wks
2 Oct 93	SMOKEBELCH II Sabres of Paradise PT 009CD	55 3
9 Apr 94	THEME Sabres of Paradise PT 014CD	56 3
17 Sep 94	WILMOT Warp WAP 50CD	36 2

SABRINA Italy, female vocalist - Sabrina Salerno (22 WEEKS)

		pos/wks
6 Feb 88	BOYS (SUMMERTIME LOVE) IBIZA IBIZ 1	60 3
11 Jun 88 ●	BOYS (SUMMERTIME LOVE) (re-entry) IBIZA IBIZ 1	3 11
1 Oct 88	ALL OF ME PWL PWL 19	25 7
1 Jul 89	LIKE A YO-YO Videogram DCUP 1	72 1

SACRED SPIRIT Germany, male production trio utilising Native American chants (5 WEEKS)

		pos/wks
15 Apr 95	YEHA-NOHA (WISHES OF HAPPINESS AND PROSPERITY) Virgin VSCDT 1514	71 1
18 Nov 95	WISHES OF HAPPINESS AND PROSPERITY (YEHA-NOHA) (re-issue) Virgin VSC 1568	37 2
16 Mar 96	WINTER CEREMONY (TOR-CHENEY-NAHANA) Virgin VSCDT 1574	45 2

SAD CAFE UK, male vocal / instrumental group (44 WEEKS)

		pos/wks
22 Sep 79 ●	EVERY DAY HURTS RCA PB 5180	3 12
19 Jan 80	STRANGE LITTLE GIRL RCA PB 5202	32 5
15 Mar 80	MY OH MY RCA SAD 3	14 11

UK No.1 ★ UK Top 10 ● Still on chart + UK million seller ◆ UK entry at No.1 ■ US No.1 ▲

21 Jun 80	NOTHING LEFT TOULOUSE *RCA SAD 4*	62	4
27 Sep 80	LA-DI-DA *RCA SAD 5*	41	6
20 Dec 80	I'M IN LOVE AGAIN *RCA SAD 6*	40	6

SADE *UK, female / male vocal / instrumental group, lead vocals - Helen Folasade Adu (68 WEEKS)* pos/wks

25 Feb 84 ●	YOUR LOVE IS KING *Epic A 4137*	6	11
19 May 84	YOUR LOVE IS KING (re-entry) *Epic A 4137*	75	1
26 May 84	WHEN AM I GONNA MAKE A LIVING *Epic A 4437*	36	5
15 Sep 84	SMOOTH OPERATOR *Epic A 4655*	19	10
12 Oct 85	THE SWEETEST TABOO *Epic A 6609*	31	5
11 Jan 86	IS IT A CRIME *Epic A 6742*	49	3
2 Apr 88	LOVE IS STRONGER THAN PRIDE *Epic SADE 1*	44	3
4 Jun 88	PARADISE *Epic SADE 2*	29	7
10 Oct 92	NO ORDINARY LOVE *Epic 6583562*	26	3
28 Nov 92	FEEL NO PAIN *Epic 6588297*	56	2
8 May 93	KISS OF LIFE *Epic 6591162*	44	3
5 Jun 93	NO ORDINARY LOVE (re-entry) *Epic 6583562*	14	8
31 Jul 93	CHERISH THE DAY *Epic 6594812*	53	2
18 Nov 00	BY YOUR SIDE *Epic 6699992*	17	5

Staff Sergeant Barry SADLER *US, male vocalist (8 WEEKS)* pos/wks

24 Mar 66	THE BALLAD OF THE GREEN BERETS *RCA 1506* ▲	24	8

SAFFRON *UK, female vocalist (2 WEEKS)* pos/wks

16 Jan 93	CIRCLES *WEA SAFF 9CD*	60	2

See also REPUBLICA

SAFFRONS – See CINDY and the SAFFRONS

Mike SAGAR *UK, male vocalist (5 WEEKS)* pos/wks

8 Dec 60	DEEP FEELING *HMV POP 819*	44	5

SAGAT *US, male rapper (6 WEEKS)* pos/wks

4 Dec 93	FUNK DAT *ffrr FCD 224*	25	5
3 Dec 94	LUVSTUFF *ffrr FCD 250*	71	1

Carole Bayer SAGER *US, female vocalist (9 WEEKS)* pos/wks

28 May 77 ●	YOU'RE MOVING OUT TODAY *Elektra K 12257*	6	9

Bally SAGOO *UK, male producer / instrumentalist (8 WEEKS)* pos/wks

3 Sep 94	CHURA LIYA *Columbia 6607092*	64	1
22 Apr 95	CHOLI KE PEECHE *Columbia 6613352*	45	1
19 Oct 96	DIL CHEEZ (MY HEART...) *Higher Ground 6634882*	12	3
1 Feb 97	TUM BIN JIYA *Higher Ground 6641372*	21	3

SAILOR *UK, male vocal / instrumental group (24 WEEKS)* pos/wks

6 Dec 75 ●	GLASS OF CHAMPAGNE *Epic EPC 3770*	2	12
27 Mar 76 ●	GIRLS GIRLS GIRLS *Epic EPC 3858*	7	8
19 Feb 77	ONE DRINK TOO MANY *Epic EPC 4804*	35	4

ST ANDREWS CHORALE *UK, church choir (5 WEEKS)* pos/wks

14 Feb 76	CLOUD 99 *Decca F 13617*	31	5

ST CECILIA *UK, male vocal / instrumental group (17 WEEKS)* pos/wks

19 Jun 71	LEAP UP AND DOWN (WAVE YOUR KNICKERS IN THE AIR) *Polydor 2058 104*	12	17

SAINT ETIENNE *UK, male / female vocal / instrumental group lead vocal - Sarah Cracknell (50 WEEKS)* pos/wks

18 May 91	NOTHING CAN STOP US / SPEEDWELL *Heavenly HVN 009*	54	3
7 Sep 91	ONLY LOVE CAN BREAK YOUR HEART / FILTHY *Heavenly HVN 12*	39	4
16 May 92	JOIN OUR CLUB / PEOPLE GET REAL *Heavenly HVN 15*	21	3
17 Oct 92	AVENUE *Heavenly HVN 2312*	40	2
13 Feb 93	YOU'RE IN A BAD WAY *Heavenly HVN 25CD*	12	5

22 May 93	HOBART PAVING / WHO DO YOU THINK YOU ARE *Heavenly HVN 29CD*	23	5
18 Dec 93	I WAS BORN ON CHRISTMAS DAY *Heavenly HVN 36CD* [1]	37	5
19 Feb 94	PALE MOVIE *Heavenly HVN 37CD*	28	3
28 May 94	LIKE A MOTORWAY *Heavenly HVN 40CD*	47	2
1 Oct 94	HUG MY SOUL *Heavenly HVN 42CD*	32	2
11 Nov 95	HE'S ON THE PHONE *Heavenly HVN 50CDR* [2]	11	5
7 Feb 98	SYLVIE *Creation CRESCD 279*	12	3
2 May 98	THE BAD PHOTOGRAPHER *Creation CRESCD 290*	27	2
20 May 00 ●	TELL ME WHY (THE RIDDLE) *Deviant DVNT 36CDS* [3]	7	5
24 Jun 00	HEART FAILED (IN THE BACK OF A TAXI) *Mantra / Beggars Banquet MNT 54CD*	50	1

[1] Saint Etienne co-starring Tim Burgess [2] Saint Etienne featuring Etienne Daho [3] Paul Van Dyk featuring Saint Etienne

See also Sarah CRACKNELL

ST GERMAIN *France, male producer (1 WEEK)* pos/wks

31 Aug 96	ALABAMA BLUES (REVISITED) *F Communications F 050CD*	50	1

Barry ST JOHN *UK, female vocalist (1 WEEK)* pos/wks

9 Dec 65	COME AWAY MELINDA *Columbia DB 7783*	47	1

ST JOHN'S COLLEGE SCHOOL CHOIR and the Band of the GRENADIER GUARDS *UK, school choir and military band (3 WEEKS)* pos/wks

3 May 86	THE QUEEN'S BIRTHDAY SONG *Columbia Q1*	40	3

ST LOUIS UNION *UK, male vocal / instrumental group (10 WEEKS)* pos/wks

13 Jan 66	GIRL *Decca F 12318*	11	10

Crispian ST PETERS *UK, male vocalist - Peter Smith (31 WEEKS)* pos/wks

6 Jan 66 ●	YOU WERE ON MY MIND *Decca F 12287*	2	14
31 Mar 66 ●	PIED PIPER *Decca F 12359*	5	13
15 Sep 66	CHANGES *Decca F 12480*	49	1
29 Sep 66	CHANGES (re-entry) *Decca F 12480*	47	3

ST PHILIPS CHOIR *UK, choir (4 WEEKS)* pos/wks

12 Dec 87	SING FOR EVER *BBC RESL 222*	49	4

ST THOMAS MORE SCHOOL CHOIR – See Scott FITZGERALD

ST WINIFRED'S SCHOOL CHOIR *UK, school choir, lead vocal Dawn Ralph (11 WEEKS)* pos/wks

22 Nov 80 ★	THERE'S NO ONE QUITE LIKE GRANDMA *MFP FP 900*	1	11

Buffy SAINTE-MARIE *Canada, female vocalist (29 WEEKS)* pos/wks

17 Jul 71 ●	SOLDIER BLUE *RCA 2081*	7	18
18 Mar 72	I'M GONNA BE A COUNTRY GIRL AGAIN *Vanguard VRS 35143*	34	5
8 Feb 92	THE BIG ONES GET AWAY *Ensign ENY 650*	39	5
4 Jul 92	FALLEN ANGELS *Ensign ENY 655*	57	1

SAINTS *Australia, male vocal / instrumental group (4 WEEKS)* pos/wks

16 Jul 77	THIS PERFECT DAY *Harvest HAR 5130*	34	4

Kyu SAKAMOTO *Japan, male vocalist (13 WEEKS)* pos/wks

27 Jun 63 ●	SUKIYAKI *HMV POP 1171* ▲	6	13

Ryuichi SAKAMOTO – See David SYLVIAN

SAKKARIN – See Jonathan KING

SALAD *UK / Holland, male / female vocal / instrumental group (5 WEEKS)* pos/wks

11 Mar 95	DRINK THE ELIXIR *Island Red CIRD 104*	66	1
13 May 95	MOTORBIKE TO HEAVEN *Island Red CIRD 106*	42	1

16 Sep 95	GRANITE STATUE Island Red CIRD 108	50	1
26 Oct 96	I WANT YOU Island CID 646	60	1
17 May 97	CARDBOY KING Island CID 654	65	1

SALFORD JETS UK, male vocal / instrumental group (2 WEEKS) pos/wks

| 31 May 80 | WHO YOU LOOKING AT RCA PB 5239 | 72 | 2 |

SALSOUL ORCHESTRA – See CHARO and the SALSOUL ORCHESTRA

SALT TANK UK, male production duo (4 WEEKS) pos/wks

11 May 96	EUGINA Internal LIECD 29	40	2
3 Jul 99	DIMENSION Hooj Choons HOOJ 74CD	52	1
9 Dec 00	EUGINA (re-mix) Lost Language LOST 004CD	58	1

SALT-N-PEPA `214` `Top 500` Rappers Cheryl "Salt" James (b. 28 Mar 1969, Brooklyn, US) and Sandra "Pepa" Denton (b. 9 Nov 1969, Kingston, Jamaica), backed up by DJ Dee Dee "Spinderella Roper, are the most commercially successful female rap troupe of all time (123 WEEKS) pos/wks

26 Mar 88	PUSH IT / I AM DOWN ffrr FFR 2	41	6
25 Jun 88 ●	PUSH IT / TRAMP Champion CHAMP 51 & ffrr FFR 2	2	13
3 Sep 88	SHAKE YOUR THANG (IT'S YOUR THING) ffrr FFR 11 [1]	22	8
12 Nov 88 ●	TWIST AND SHOUT ffrr FFR 16	4	9
14 Apr 90	EXPRESSION ffrr F 127	40	6
25 May 91 ●	DO YOU WANT ME ffrr F 151	5	12
31 Aug 91 ●	LET'S TALK ABOUT SEX ffrr F 162 [2]	2	13
30 Nov 91	YOU SHOWED ME ffrr F 174	15	9
28 Mar 92	EXPRESSION (re-mix) ffrr F 182	23	6
3 Oct 92	START ME UP ffrr F 196	39	3
9 Oct 93	SHOOP ffrr FCD 219	29	3
19 Mar 94 ●	WHATTA MAN ffrr FCD 222 [3]	7	10
28 May 94	SHOOP (re-mix) ffrr FCD 234	13	8
12 Nov 94	NONE OF YOUR BUSINESS ffrr FCD 244	19	4
7 Jan 95	NONE OF YOUR BUSINESS (re-entry) ffrr FCD 244	64	1
21 Dec 96	CHAMPAGNE MCA MCSTD 48025	23	6
29 Nov 97	R U READY ffrr FCDP 322	24	2
11 Dec 99	THE BRICK TRACK VERSUS GITTY UP ffrr FCD 373 [4]	22	4

[1] Salt-N-Pepa featuring EU [2] Salt-N-Pepa featuring Psychotropic [3] Salt-N-Pepa with En Vogue [4] Saltnpepa

'I Am Down' listed only from 2 Apr 1988. The disc re-entered on 25 June when it was made available on Champion with a different flip side. Sales for both discs were amalgamated

SAM and DAVE US, male vocal duo (39 WEEKS) pos/wks

16 Mar 67	SOOTHE ME Stax 601 004	48	2
13 Apr 67	SOOTHE ME (re-entry) Stax 601 004	35	6
1 Nov 67	SOUL MAN Stax 601 023	24	14
13 Mar 68	I THANK YOU Stax 601 030	34	9
29 Jan 69	SOUL SISTER, BROWN SUGAR Atlantic 584 237	15	8

See also Lou REED

SAM THE SHAM and the PHARAOHS
US, male vocal / instrumental group (18 WEEKS) pos/wks

24 Jun 65	WOOLY BULLY MGM 1269	11	15
4 Aug 66	LIL' RED RIDING HOOD MGM 1315	48	1
18 Aug 66	LIL' RED RIDING HOOD (re-entry) MGM 1315	46	2

Richie SAMBORA
US, male vocalist / instrumentalist - guitar (4 WEEKS) pos/wks

7 Sep 91	BALLAD OF YOUTH Mercury MER 350	59	1
7 Mar 98	HARD TIMES COME EASY Mercury 5686972	37	2
1 Aug 98	IN IT FOR LOVE Mercury 5660632	58	1

See also BON JOVI

Mike SAMMES SINGERS UK, male / female vocal group (38 WEEKS) pos/wks

| 15 Sep 66 | SOMEWHERE MY LOVE HMV POP 1546 | 22 | 19 |
| 12 Jul 67 | SOMEWHERE MY LOVE (re-entry) HMV POP 1546 | 14 | 19 |

See also Michael FLANDERS; Des O'CONNOR; Malcolm VAUGHAN; Michael HOLLIDAY; Andy STEWART; Jimmy YOUNG

Dave SAMPSON UK, male vocalist (6 WEEKS) pos/wks

| 19 May 60 | SWEET DREAMS Columbia DB 4449 | 48 | 1 |
| 2 Jun 60 | SWEET DREAMS (re-entry) Columbia DB 4449 | 29 | 5 |

SAMSON UK, male vocal / instrumental group (6 WEEKS) pos/wks

4 Jul 81	RIDING WITH THE ANGELS RCA 67	55	3
24 Jul 82	LOSING MY GRIP Polydor POSP 471	63	2
5 Mar 83	RED SKIES Polydor POSP 554	65	1

SAN JOSE featuring Rodriguez ARGENTINA
UK, male instrumental group (8 WEEKS) pos/wks

| 17 Jun 78 | ARGENTINE MELODY (CANCION DE ARGENTINA) MCA 369 | 14 | 8 |

Rodriguez Argentina is Rod Argent

See also SILSOE; ARGENT

SAN REMO STRINGS US, orchestra (8 WEEKS) pos/wks

| 18 Dec 71 | FESTIVAL TIME Tamla Motown TMG 795 | 39 | 8 |

Junior SANCHEZ featuring DAJAE
US, male DJ / producer and US, female vocalist (2 WEEKS) pos/wks

| 16 Oct 99 | B WITH U Manifesto FESCD 62 | 31 | 2 |

Roger SANCHEZ US, male producer (4 WEEKS) pos/wks

| 20 Feb 99 | I WANT YOUR LOVE Perpetual PERPCDS 001 [1] | 31 | 2 |
| 29 Jan 00 | I NEVER KNEW INCredible INCS 4CDS [2] | 24 | 2 |

[1] Roger Sanchez presents Twilight [2] Roger Sanchez featuring Cooly's Hot Box

See also FUNK JUNKEEZ; EL MARIACHI; Malcolm McLAREN; TRANSATLANTIC SOUL

Chris SANDFORD UK, male vocalist (9 WEEKS) pos/wks

| 12 Dec 63 | NOT TOO LITTLE NOT TOO MUCH Decca F 11778 | 17 | 9 |

SANDPIPERS US, male vocal group (33 WEEKS) pos/wks

15 Sep 66 ●	GUANTANAMERA Pye International 7N 25380	7	17
5 Jun 68	QUANDO M'INNAMORO (A MAN WITHOUT LOVE) A & M AMS 723	33	6
26 Mar 69	KUMBAYA A & M AMS 744	38	1
9 Apr 69	KUMBAYA (re-entry) A & M AMS 744	49	1
27 Nov 76	HANG ON SLOOPY Satril SAT 114	32	8

SANDRA Germany, female vocalist (8 WEEKS) pos/wks

| 17 Dec 88 | EVERLASTING LOVE Siren SRN 85 | 45 | 8 |

Jodie SANDS US, female vocalist (10 WEEKS) pos/wks

| 17 Oct 58 | SOMEDAY (YOU'LL WANT ME TO WANT YOU) HMV POP 533 | 14 | 10 |

Tommy SANDS US, male vocalist (7 WEEKS) pos/wks

| 4 Aug 60 | OLD OAKEN BUCKET Capitol CL 15143 | 25 | 7 |

SANDSTORM US, male producer - Mark Picchiotti (1 WEEK) pos/wks

| 13 May 00 | THE RETURN OF NOTHING Renaissance Recordings RENCDS 001 | 54 | 1 |

Samantha SANG Australia, female vocalist (13 WEEKS) pos/wks

| 4 Feb 78 | EMOTIONS Private Stock PVT 128 | 11 | 13 |

SANTA CLAUS and the CHRISTMAS TREES
UK, male vocal / instrumental group (10 WEEKS) pos/wks

| 11 Dec 82 | SINGALONG-A-SANTA Polydor IVY 1 | 19 | 5 |
| 10 Dec 83 | SINGALONG-A-SANTA AGAIN Polydor IVY 2 | 39 | 5 |

SANTA ESMERALDA and Leroy GOMEZ
US / France, male / female vocal / instrumental group (5 WEEKS) pos/wks

| 12 Nov 77 | DON'T LET ME BE MISUNDERSTOOD Philips 6042 325 | 41 | 5 |

UK No.1 ★ UK Top 10 ● Still on chart + UK million seller ◆ UK entry at No.1 ■ US No.1 ▲

SANTANA US, male vocal / instrumental group (45 WEEKS)
pos/wks

28 Sep 74	SAMBA PA TI *CBS 2561*	27	7
15 Oct 77	SHE'S NOT THERE *CBS 5671*	11	12
25 Nov 78	WELL ALL RIGHT *CBS 6755*	53	3
22 Mar 80	ALL I EVER WANTED *CBS 8160*	57	3
23 Oct 99	SMOOTH *Arista 74321709492* [1] ▲	75	1
1 Apr 00 ●	SMOOTH (re-issue) *Arista 74321748762* [1]	3	10
5 Aug 00 ●	MARIA MARIA *Arista 74321769372* [2] ▲	6	9

[1] Santana featuring Rob Thomas [2] Santana featuring the Product G&B

SANTO and JOHNNY
US, male instrumental duo - steel and electric guitars (5 WEEKS)
pos/wks

| 16 Oct 59 | SLEEP WALK *Pye International 7N 25037* ▲ | 22 | 4 |
| 31 Mar 60 | TEARDROP *Parlophone R 4619* | 50 | 1 |

Mike SARNE UK, male vocalist - Mike Scheuer (43 WEEKS)
pos/wks

10 May 62 ★	COME OUTSIDE *Parlophone R 4902* [1]	1	19
30 Aug 62	WILL I WHAT *Parlophone R 4932* [2]	18	10
10 Jan 63	JUST FOR KICKS *Parlophone R 4974*	22	7
28 Mar 63	CODE OF LOVE *Parlophone R 5010*	29	7

[1] Mike Sarne with Wendy Richard [2] Mike Sarne with Billie Davis

Joy SARNEY UK, female vocalist (6 WEEKS)
pos/wks

| 7 May 77 | NAUGHTY NAUGHTY NAUGHTY *Alaska ALA 2005* | 26 | 6 |

SARR BAND Italy / UK / France, male / female vocal / instrumental group (1 WEEK)
pos/wks

| 16 Sep 78 | MAGIC MANDRAKE *Calendar Day 111* | 68 | 1 |

Peter SARSTEDT UK, male vocalist (25 WEEKS)
pos/wks

| 5 Feb 69 ★ | WHERE DO YOU GO TO MY LOVELY *United Artists UP 2262* | 1 | 16 |
| 4 Jun 69 ● | FROZEN ORANGE JUICE *United Artists UP 35021* | 10 | 9 |

Robin SARSTEDT UK, male vocalist (9 WEEKS)
pos/wks

| 8 May 76 ● | MY RESISTANCE IS LOW *Decca F 13624* | 3 | 9 |

SARTORELLO Italy, male / female vocal / instrumental duo (1 WEEK)
pos/wks

| 10 Aug 96 | MOVE BABY MOVE *Multiply CDMUL 12* | 56 | 1 |

SASH! 242 Top 500 German pop / dance act named after instrumentalist / producer Sascha (aka Sasha) Lappessen, featuring programmers Thomas Alisson and Ralf Kappmeier. First four hits uniquely featured vocals in different languages (French, Spanish, English, Italian) (103 WEEKS)
pos/wks

1 Mar 97 ●	ENCORE UNE FOIS *Multiply CDMULTY 18*	2	15
5 Jul 97 ●	ECUADOR *Multiply CDMULTY 23* [1]	2	12
18 Oct 97 ●	STAY *Multiply CDMULTY 26* [2]	2	14
4 Apr 98 ●	LA PRIMAVERA *Multiply CXMULTY 32*	3	12
15 Aug 98 ●	MYSTERIOUS TIMES *Multiply CXMULTY 40* [3]	2	12
28 Nov 98 ●	MOVE MANIA *Multiply CDMULTY 45* [4]	8	10
3 Apr 99	COLOUR THE WORLD *Multiply CDMULTY 48*	15	6
12 Feb 00 ●	ADELANTE *Multiply CDMULTY 60*	2	10
22 Apr 00 ●	JUST AROUND THE HILL *Multiply CDMULTY 62* [3]	8	7
23 Sep 00 ●	WITH MY OWN EYES *Multiply CDMULTY 67*	10	5

[1] Sash! featuring Rodriguez [2] Sash! featuring La Trec [3] Sash! featuring Tina Cousins [4] Sash! featuring Shannon

SASHA UK, male producer - Alexander Coe (15 WEEKS)
pos/wks

31 Jul 93	TOGETHER *ffrr FCD 212* [1]	57	1
19 Feb 94	HIGHER GROUND *Deconstruction 74321189002* [2]	19	3
27 Aug 94	MAGIC *Deconstruction 74321221862* [2]	32	4
9 Mar 96	BE AS ONE *Deconstruction 74321342962* [3]	17	4
23 Sep 00	SCORCHIO *Arista 74321788222* [4]	23	3

[1] Danny Campbell and Sasha [2] Sasha with Sam Mollison [3] Sasha and Maria [4] Sasha / Emerson

Joe SATRIANI US, male instrumentalist - guitar (1 WEEK)
pos/wks

| 13 Feb 93 | THE SATCH EP *Relativity 6589532* | 53 | 1 |

Tracks on The Satch EP: The Extremist / Cryin / Banana Bongo / Crazy

SATURDAY NIGHT BAND
US, male vocal / instrumental group (9 WEEKS)
pos/wks

| 1 Jul 78 | COME ON DANCE DANCE *CBS 6367* | 16 | 9 |

Deion SAUNDERS – See HAMMER

Kevin SAUNDERSON – See INNER CITY

Chantay SAVAGE US, female vocalist (9 WEEKS)
pos/wks

| 4 May 96 | I WILL SURVIVE *RCA 74321377682* | 12 | 8 |
| 8 Nov 97 | REMINDING ME (OF SEF) *Relativity 6560762* [1] | 59 | 1 |

[1] Common featuring Chantay Savage

Edna SAVAGE UK, female vocalist (1 WEEK)
pos/wks

| 13 Jan 56 | ARRIVEDERCI DARLING *Parlophone R 4097* | 19 | 1 |

SAVAGE GARDEN 313 Top 500 Australian pop vocal / instrumental duo: Daniel Jones and Darren Hayes. Eponymous debut album sold more than 11 million copies and huge critical acclaim followed with a record-breaking 10 Arias at the 1997 Australian music industry awards. (96 WEEKS)
pos/wks

21 Jun 97	I WANT YOU *Columbia 6645452*	11	7
27 Sep 97	TO THE MOON AND BACK *Columbia 6648932*	55	1
28 Feb 98 ●	TRULY MADLY DEEPLY *Columbia 6656022* ▲	4	23
22 Aug 98 ●	TO THE MOON AND BACK (re-issue) *Columbia 6662882*	3	16
12 Dec 98	I WANT YOU '98 (re-mix) *Columbia 6667332*	12	10
10 Jul 99	THE ANIMAL SONG *Columbia 6675882*	16	6
13 Nov 99 ●	I KNEW I LOVED YOU *Columbia 6683102* ▲	10	12
1 Apr 00	CRASH AND BURN *Columbia 6690442*	14	6
29 Jul 00 ●	AFFIRMATION *Columbia 6696882*	8	10
25 Nov 00	HOLD ME *Columbia 6706032*	16	5

Telly SAVALAS US, male actor (12 WEEKS)
pos/wks

| 22 Feb 75 ★ | IF *MCA 174* | 1 | 9 |
| 31 May 75 | YOU'VE LOST THAT LOVIN' FEELIN' *MCA 189* | 47 | 3 |

SAVANNA UK, male vocal group (4 WEEKS)
pos/wks

| 10 Oct 81 | I CAN'T TURN AWAY *R & B RBS 203* | 61 | 4 |

S AVUKA – See Johnny CLEGG and SAVUKA

SAW DOCTORS Ireland, male vocal / instrumental group (9 WEEKS)
pos/wks

12 Nov 94	SMALL BIT OF LOVE *Shamtown SAW 001CD*	24	3
27 Jan 96	WORLD OF GOOD *Shamtown SAW 002CD*	15	3
13 Jul 96	TO WIN JUST ONCE *Shamtown SAW 004CD*	14	2
6 Dec 97	SIMPLE THINGS *Shamtown SAW 006CD*	56	1

SAXON UK, male vocal / instrumental group (61 WEEKS)
pos/wks

22 Mar 80	WHEELS OF STEEL *Carrere CAR 143*	20	11
21 Jun 80	747 (STRANGERS IN THE NIGHT) *Carrere CAR 151*	13	9
28 Jun 80	BACKS TO THE WALL *Carrere HM 6*	64	2
28 Jun 80	BIG TEASER / RAINBOW THEME *Carrere HM 5*	66	2
29 Nov 80	STRONG ARM OF THE LAW *Carrere CAR 170*	63	2
11 Apr 81	AND THE BANDS PLAYED ON *Carrere CAR 180*	12	8
18 Jul 81	NEVER SURRENDER *Carrere CAR 204*	18	6
31 Oct 81	PRINCESS OF THE NIGHT *Carrere CAR 208*	57	3
23 Apr 83	POWER AND THE GLORY *Carrere SAXON 1*	32	5
30 Jul 83	NIGHTMARE *Carrere CAR 284*	50	3
31 Aug 85	BACK ON THE STREETS *Parlophone R 6103*	75	1
29 Mar 86	ROCK 'N' ROLL GYPSY *Parlophone R 6112*	71	1
30 Aug 86	WAITING FOR THE NIGHT *EMI EMI 5575*	66	2
5 Mar 88	RIDE LIKE THE WIND *EMI EM 43*	52	4
30 Apr 88	I CAN'T WAIT ANYMORE *EMI EM 54*	71	1

Al SAXON UK, male vocalist (10 WEEKS)

		pos/wks
16 Jan 59	YOU'RE THE TOP CHA *Fontana H 164*	17 4
28 Aug 59	ONLY SIXTEEN *Fontana H 205*	24 3
22 Dec 60	BLUE-EYED BOY *Fontana H 278*	39 2
7 Sep 61	THERE I'VE SAID IT AGAIN *Piccadilly 7N 35011*	48 1

Leo SAYER (141) Top 500 Distinctive singer / songwriter (b. 21 May 1948, Sussex, UK) who was a top singles and album act on both sides of the Atlantic in the late 1970s. His first seven hits all reached the Top 10 - a feat first achieved by his manager, Adam Faith (151 WEEKS)

		pos/wks
15 Dec 73 ●	THE SHOW MUST GO ON *Chrysalis CHS 2023*	2 13
15 Jun 74 ●	ONE MAN BAND *Chrysalis CHS 2045*	6 9
14 Sep 74 ●	LONG TALL GLASSES *Chrysalis CHS 2052*	4 9
30 Aug 75 ●	MOONLIGHTING *Chrysalis CHS 2076*	2 8
30 Oct 76 ●	YOU MAKE ME FEEL LIKE DANCING *Chrysalis CHS 2119* ▲	2 12
29 Jan 77 ★	WHEN I NEED YOU *Chrysalis CHS 2127* ▲	1 13
9 Apr 77 ●	HOW MUCH LOVE *Chrysalis CHS 2140*	10 8
10 Sep 77	THUNDER IN MY HEART *Chrysalis CHS 2163*	22 8
16 Sep 78 ●	I CAN'T STOP LOVIN' YOU (THOUGH I TRY) *Chrysalis CHS 2240*	6 11
25 Nov 78	RAINING IN MY HEART *Chrysalis CHS 2277*	21 10
5 Jul 80 ●	MORE THAN I CAN SAY *Chrysalis CHS 2442*	2 11
13 Mar 82 ●	HAVE YOU EVER BEEN IN LOVE *Chrysalis CHS 2596*	10 9
19 Jun 82	HEART (STOP BEATING IN TIME) *Chrysalis CHS 2616*	22 10
12 Mar 83	ORCHARD ROAD *Chrysalis CHS 2677*	16 8
15 Oct 83	TILL YOU COME BACK TO ME *Chrysalis LEO 01*	51 3
8 Feb 86	UNCHAINED MELODY *Chrysalis LEO 3*	54 4
13 Feb 93	WHEN I NEED YOU (re-issue) *Chrysalis CDCHS 3926*	65 2
8 Aug 98	YOU MAKE ME FEEL LIKE DANCING *Brothers Org. CDBRUV 8* [1]	32 3

[1] Groove Generation featuring Leo Sayer

Alexei SAYLE UK, male comedian / vocalist (8 WEEKS)

		pos/wks
25 Feb 84	'ULLO JOHN GOT A NEW MOTOR? *Island IS 162*	15 8

SCAFFOLD UK, male vocal group (62 WEEKS)

		pos/wks
22 Nov 67 ●	THANK U VERY MUCH *Parlophone R 5643*	4 12
27 Mar 68	DO YOU REMEMBER *Parlophone R 5679*	34 5
6 Nov 68 ★	LILY THE PINK *Parlophone R 5734*	1 24
1 Nov 69	GIN GAN GOOLIE *Parlophone R 5812*	38 11
24 Jan 70	GIN GAN GOOLIE (re-entry) *Parlophone R 5812*	50 1
1 Jun 74 ●	LIVERPOOL LOU *Warner Bros. K 16400*	7 9

Boz SCAGGS US, male vocalist (31 WEEKS)

		pos/wks
30 Oct 76	LOWDOWN *CBS 4563*	28 4
22 Jan 77 ●	WHAT CAN I SAY *CBS 4869*	10 10
14 May 77	LIDO SHUFFLE *CBS 5136*	13 9
10 Dec 77	HOLLYWOOD *CBS 5836*	33 8

SCANTY SANDWICH
UK, male DJ / producer Richard Marshall (8 WEEKS)

		pos/wks
29 Jan 00 ●	BECAUSE OF YOU *Southern Fried ECB 18CDS*	3 8

SCARFACE US, male rapper - Brad Jordan (6 WEEKS)

		pos/wks
11 Mar 95	HAND OF THE DEAD BODY *Virgin America VUSCD 88* [1]	41 2
5 Aug 95	I SEEN A MAN DIE *Virgin America VUSCD 94*	55 2
5 Jul 97	GAME OVER *Virgin VUSCD 121*	34 2

[1] Scarface featuring Ice Cube

SCARFO UK, male vocal / instrumental group (2 WEEKS)

		pos/wks
19 Jul 97	ALKALINE *Deceptive BLUFF 044CD*	61 1
18 Oct 97	COSMONAUT NO. 7 *Deceptive BLUFF 053CD*	67 1

SCARLET UK, female vocal / instrumental duo (18 WEEKS)

		pos/wks
21 Jan 95	INDEPENDENT LOVE SONG *WEA YZ 820CD*	12 12
29 Apr 95	I WANNA BE FREE (TO BE WITH HIM) *WEA YZ 913CD*	21 4
5 Aug 95	LOVE HANGOVER *WEA YZ 969CD*	54 1
6 Jul 96	BAD GIRL *WEA WEA 046CD*	54 1

SCARLET FANTASTIC
UK, male / female vocal / instrumental group (12 WEEKS)

		pos/wks
3 Oct 87	NO MEMORY *Arista RIS 36*	24 10
23 Jan 88	PLUG ME IN (TO THE CENTRAL LOVE LINE) *Arista 109693*	67 2

SCARLET PARTY UK, male vocal / instrumental group (5 WEEKS) pos/wks

16 Oct 82	101 DAM-NATIONS *Parlophone R 6058*	44 5

SCATMAN JOHN US, male vocalist - John Larkin (19 WEEKS)

		pos/wks
13 May 95 ●	SCATMAN (SKI-BA-BOP-BA-DOP-BOP) *RCA 74321281712*	3 12
2 Sep 95 ●	SCATMAN'S WORLD *RCA 74321289952*	10 7

Michael SCHENKER GROUP
Germany / UK, male vocal / instrumental group (9 WEEKS)

		pos/wks
13 Sep 80	ARMED AND READY *Chrysalis CHS 2455*	53 3
8 Nov 80	CRY FOR THE NATIONS *Chrysalis CHS 2471*	56 3
11 Sep 82	DANCER *Chrysalis CHS 2636*	52 3

Lalo SCHIFRIN
Argentina, male conductor and US, orchestra (11 WEEKS)

		pos/wks
9 Oct 76	JAWS *CTI CTSP 005*	14 9
25 Oct 97	BULLITT *Warner.esp WESP 002CD*	36 2

Peter SCHILLING Germany, male vocalist (6 WEEKS)

		pos/wks
5 May 84	MAJOR TOM (COMING HOME) *PSP/WEA X 9438*	42 5
16 Jun 84	MAJOR TOM (COMING HOME) (re-entry) *PSP/WEA X 9438*	73 1

Phillip SCHOFIELD UK, male vocalist (6 WEEKS)

		pos/wks
5 Dec 92	CLOSE EVERY DOOR *Really Useful RUR 11*	27 6

SCIENTIST UK, male producer - Phil Sebastiane (13 WEEKS)

		pos/wks
6 Oct 90	THE EXORCIST *Kickin KICK 1*	62 3
1 Dec 90	THE EXORCIST (re-mix) *Kickin KICK 1TR*	46 3
15 Dec 90	THE BEE *Kickin KICK 3S*	52 3
26 Jan 91	THE BEE (re-entry) *Kickin KICK 3S*	47 3
11 May 91	SPIRAL SYMPHONY *Kickin KICK 5*	74 1

SCOOCH UK, male / female vocal group (20 WEEKS)

		pos/wks
6 Nov 99	WHEN MY BABY *Accolade CDAC 002*	29 4
22 Jan 00 ●	MORE THAN I NEEDED TO KNOW *Accolade CDAC 003*	5 5
6 May 00	THE BEST IS YET TO COME *Accolade CDAC 004*	12 4
8 Jul 00	THE BEST IS YET TO COME (re-entry) *Accolade CDAC 004*	64 1
5 Aug 00	FOR SURE *Accolade CDAS 005*	15 6

SCOOTER
UK / Germany, male vocal / instrumental group (14 WEEKS)

		pos/wks
21 Oct 95	MOVE YOUR ASS *Club Tools 0061675 CLU*	23 4
17 Feb 96	BACK IN THE UK *Club Tools 0061955 CLU*	18 3
25 May 96	REBEL YELL *Club Tools 0062575 CLU*	30 2
19 Oct 96	I'M RAVING *Club Tools 0063015 CLU*	33 3
17 May 97	FIRE *Club Tools 006005 CLU*	45 2

SCORPIONS Germany, male vocal / instrumental group (35 WEEKS) pos/wks

26 May 79	IS THERE ANYBODY THERE / ANOTHER PIECE OF MEAT *Harvest HAR 5185*	39 4
25 Aug 79	LOVEDRIVE *Harvest HAR 5188*	69 2
31 May 80	MAKE IT REAL *Harvest HAR 5206*	72 2
20 Sep 80	THE ZOO *Harvest HAR 5212*	75 1
3 Apr 82	NO ONE LIKE YOU *Harvest HAR 5219*	65 3
1 May 82	NO ONE LIKE YOU (re-entry) *Harvest HAR 5219*	64 1
17 Jul 82	CAN'T LIVE WITHOUT YOU *Harvest HAR 5221*	63 2
4 Jun 88	RHYTHM OF LOVE *Harvest HAR 5240*	59 2
18 Feb 89	PASSION RULES THE GAME *Harvest 5242*	74 1
1 Jun 91	WIND OF CHANGE *Vertigo VER 54*	53 3
28 Sep 91 ●	WIND OF CHANGE (re-issue) *Vertigo VER 58*	2 9
30 Nov 91	SEND ME AN ANGEL *Vertigo VER 60*	27 3
28 Dec 91	SEND ME AN ANGEL (re-entry) *Vertigo VER 60*	68 2

UK No.1 ★   UK Top 10 ●   Still on chart +   UK million seller ◆   UK entry at No.1 ■   US No.1 ▲

SCOTLAND WORLD CUP SQUAD
UK, male football team vocalists (27 WEEKS)

		pos/wks	
22 Jun 74	EASY EASY *Polydor 2058 452*	20	4
27 May 78 ●	OLE OLA (MULHER BRASILEIRA) *Riva 15* [1]	4	6
1 May 82 ●	WE HAVE A DREAM *WEA K 19145*	5	9
9 Jun 90	SAY IT WITH PRIDE *RCA PB 43791*	45	3
15 Jun 96	PURPLE HEATHER *Warner Bros. W 0354CD* [2]	16	5

[1] Rod Stewart featuring the Scottish World Cup Football Squad [2] Rod Stewart with the Scottish Euro '96 Squad

SCOTT & LEON *UK, male production duo (4 WEEKS)*

		pos/wks	
30 Sep 00	YOU USED TO HOLD ME *AM:PM CDAMPM 137*	19	4

Jack SCOTT *Canada, male vocalist - Jack Scafone Jr (28 WEEKS)*

		pos/wks	
10 Oct 58 ●	MY TRUE LOVE *London HLU 8626*	9	10
25 Sep 59	THE WAY I WALK *London HLL 8912*	30	1
10 Mar 60	WHAT IN THE WORLD'S COME OVER YOU *Top Rank JAR 280*	11	15
2 Jun 60	BURNING BRIDGES *Top Rank JAR 375*	32	2

Jill SCOTT *US, female vocalist (3 WEEKS)*

		pos/wks	
4 Nov 00	GETTIN' IN THE WAY *Epic 6705272*	30	3

Linda SCOTT *US, female vocalist - Linda Sampson (14 WEEKS)*

		pos/wks	
18 May 61 ●	I'VE TOLD EVERY LITTLE STAR *Columbia DB 4638*	7	13
14 Sep 61	DON'T BET MONEY HONEY *Columbia DB 4692*	50	1

Mike SCOTT *UK, male vocalist / instrumentalist (4 WEEKS)*

		pos/wks	
16 Sep 95	BRING 'EM ALL IN *Chrysalis CDCHS 5025*	56	1
11 Nov 95	BUILDING THE CITY OF LIGHT *Chrysalis CDCHS 5026*	60	1
27 Sep 97	LOVE ANYWAY *Chrysalis CDCHS 5064*	50	1
14 Feb 98	RARE, PRECIOUS AND GONE *Chrysalis CDCHSS 5073*	74	1

Millie SCOTT *US, female vocalist (11 WEEKS)*

		pos/wks	
12 Apr 86	PRISONER OF LOVE *Fourth & Broadway BRW 45*	52	4
23 Aug 86	AUTOMATIC *Fourth & Broadway BRW 51*	56	3
21 Feb 87	EV'RY LITTLE BIT *Fourth & Broadway BRW 58*	63	4

Simon SCOTT *UK, male vocalist (8 WEEKS)*

		pos/wks	
13 Aug 64	MOVE IT BABY *Parlophone R 5164*	37	8

Tony SCOTT *Holland, male rapper (6 WEEKS)*

		pos/wks	
15 Apr 89	THAT'S HOW I'M LIVING / THE CHIEF *Champion CHAMP 97* [1]	48	4
10 Feb 90	GET INTO IT / THAT'S HOW I'M LIVING (re-issue) *Champion CHAMP 232*	63	2

[1] Toni Scott

'The Chief' listed only from 22 Apr 1989

SCOTTISH RUGBY TEAM with Ronnie BROWNE
UK, male rugby team vocalists (1 WEEK)

		pos/wks	
2 Jun 90	FLOWER OF SCOTLAND *Greentrax STRAX 1001*	73	1

SCREAMING BLUE MESSIAHS
US / UK, male vocal / instrumental group (6 WEEKS)

		pos/wks	
16 Jan 88	I WANNA BE A FLINTSTONE *WEA YZ 166*	28	6

SCREAMING TREES
US, male vocal / instrumental group (2 WEEKS)

		pos/wks	
6 Mar 93	NEARLY LOST YOU *Epic 6582372*	50	1
1 May 93	DOLLAR BILL *Epic 6591792*	52	1

Tracks on 'Nearly Lost You': E.S.K. / Song of a Baker / Winter Song (acoustic)

SCRITTI POLITTI (422) **Top 500** *Cerebral pop group increasingly influenced by dance and hip hop trends. Formed 1977 by Green Gartside (v/g/k) b. 22 Jun 1956, Cardiff, Wales. US-recorded minor hit, 'Perfect Way', was act's only US Top 20 entry. Legendary jazz trumpeter Miles Davis played on 'Oh Patti' (78 WEEKS)*

		pos/wks	
21 Nov 81	THE SWEETEST GIRL *Rough Trade RT 091*	64	3
22 May 82	FAITHLESS *Rough Trade RT 101*	56	4
7 Aug 82	ASYLUMS IN JERUSALEM / JACQUES DERRIDA *Rough Trade RT 111*	43	5
10 Mar 84 ●	WOOD BEEZ (PRAY LIKE ARETHA FRANKLIN) *Virgin VS 657*	10	12
9 Jun 84	ABSOLUTE *Virgin VS 680*	17	9
17 Nov 84	HYPNOTIZE *Virgin VS 725*	68	2
11 May 85 ●	THE WORD GIRL *Virgin VS 747*	6	12
7 Sep 85	PERFECT WAY *Virgin VS 780*	48	5
7 May 88	OH PATTI (DON'T FEEL SORRY FOR LOVERBOY) *Virgin VS 1006*	13	9
27 Aug 88	FIRST BOY IN THIS TOWN (LOVE SICK) *Virgin VS 1082*	63	3
12 Nov 88	BOOM! THERE SHE WAS *Virgin VS 1143*	55	3
16 Mar 91	SHE'S A WOMAN *Virgin VS 1333* [1]	20	7
3 Aug 91	TAKE ME IN YOUR ARMS AND LOVE ME *Virgin VS 1346* [2]	47	3
31 Jul 99	TINSELTOWN TO THE BOOGIEDOWN *Virgin VSCDT 1731*	46	1

[1] Scritti Politti featuring Shabba Ranks [2] Scritti Politti and Sweetie Irie

Earl SCRUGGS – See Lester FLATT and Earl SCRUGGS

SEA FRUIT *UK, male vocal / instrumental group (1 WEEK)*

		pos/wks	
24 Jul 99	HELLO WORLD *Electric Canyon ECCD 3055*	59	1

SEA LEVEL *US, male instrumental group (4 WEEKS)*

		pos/wks	
17 Feb 79	FIFTY-FOUR *Capricorn POSP 28*	63	4

SEAHORSES *UK, male vocal / instrumental group (26 WEEKS)*

		pos/wks	
10 May 97 ●	LOVE IS THE LAW *Geffen GFSTD 22243*	3	7
26 Jul 97 ●	BLINDED BY THE SUN *Geffen GFSTD 22266*	7	7
11 Oct 97	LOVE ME AND LEAVE ME *Geffen GFSTD 22282*	16	4
13 Dec 97	YOU CAN TALK TO ME *Geffen GFSTD 22297*	15	8

SEAL (488) **Top 500** *Golden-voiced dramatic soul singer b. Sealhenry Samuel, 19 Feb 1963, London, UK. His many awards include Best Male Artist and Best British Video at the 1992 Brits, Variety Club of Great Britain Recording Artist of the Year in 1991, a hat-trick of Ivor Novellos and Grammy nominations in the US where 'Kiss From a Rose' was US No.1 hit single after being heard in 'Batman Forever' film (70 WEEKS)*

		pos/wks	
8 Dec 90 ●	CRAZY *ZTT ZANG 8*	2	15
4 May 91	FUTURE LOVE (EP) *ZTT ZANG 11*	12	6
20 Jul 91	THE BEGINNING *ZTT ZANG 21*	24	6
16 Nov 91 ●	KILLER (EP) *ZTT ZANG 23*	8	8
29 Feb 92	VIOLET *ZTT ZANG 27*	39	2
21 May 94	PRAYER FOR THE DYING *ZTT ZANG 51CD*	14	5
30 Jul 94	KISS FROM A ROSE *ZTT ZANG 52CD1*	20	5
5 Nov 94	NEWBORN FRIEND *ZTT ZANG 58CD*	45	2
15 Jul 95 ●	KISS FROM A ROSE / I'M ALIVE (re-issue) *ZTT ZANG 70CD* ▲	4	13
9 Dec 95	DON'T CRY / PRAYER FOR THE DYING (re-issue) *ZTT ZANG 75CD*	51	2
29 Mar 97	FLY LIKE AN EAGLE *ZTT ZEAL 1CD*	13	5
14 Nov 98	HUMAN BEINGS *Warner Brothers W 464CD*	50	1

Tracks on Future Love (EP): Future Love Paradise / A Minor Groove / Violet. Tracks on Killer (EP): Killer / Hey Joe / Come See What Love Has Done

See also ADAMSKI

SEARCHERS (200) **Top 500** *Merseybeat combo initially tipped to be as big as The Beatles, formed 1960: Mike Pender (v/g), John McNally (g/v), Tony Jackson (v/b) (left 1964 - replaced by Frank Allen), Chris Curtis (d). Unlike The Beatles, however, most of this influential act's early hits were cover versions of US originals (128 WEEKS)*

		pos/wks	
27 Jun 63 ★	SWEETS FOR MY SWEET *Pye 7N 15533*	1	16
10 Oct 63	SWEET NOTHINS *Philips BF 1274*	48	2

UK No.1 ★ UK Top 10 ● Still on chart + UK million seller ◆ UK entry at No.1 ■ US No.1 ▲

393

24 Oct 81	HOLLYWOOD NIGHTS *Capitol CL 223*	49	3
6 Feb 82	WE'VE GOT TONITE *Capitol CL 235*	60	4
9 Apr 83	EVEN NOW *Capitol CL 284*	73	2
28 Apr 95	WE'VE GOT TONIGHT (re-issue) *Capitol CDCL 734*	22	5
29 Apr 95	NIGHT MOVES *Capitol CDCL 741*	45	2
29 Jul 95	HOLLYWOOD NIGHTS (re-issue) *Capitol CDCL 749*	52	1
10 Feb 96	LOCK AND LOAD *Parlophone CDCL 765*	57	1

Capitol CL 223 and CL 235 were live versions of earlier studio hits

SEIKO and Donnie WAHLBERG
Japan / US, female / male vocal duo (5 WEEKS) pos/wks

18 Aug 90	THE RIGHT COMBINATION *Epic 656203 7*	44	5

SELECTER
UK, male / female vocal / instrumental group (28 WEEKS) pos/wks

13 Oct 79 ●	ON MY RADIO *2 Tone CHSTT 4*	8	9
2 Feb 80	THREE MINUTE HERO *2 Tone CHSTT 8*	16	6
29 Mar 80	MISSING WORDS *2 Tone CHSTT 10*	23	8
23 Aug 80	THE WHISPER *Chrysalis CHSS 1*	36	5

Peter SELLERS
UK, male actor (39 WEEKS) pos/wks

2 Aug 57	ANY OLD IRON *Parlophone R 4337*	21	3
6 Sep 57	ANY OLD IRON (re-entry) *Parlophone R 4337*	17	8
10 Nov 60 ●	GOODNESS GRACIOUS ME *Parlophone R 4702* [1]	4	14
12 Jan 61	BANGERS AND MASH *Parlophone R 4724* [1]	22	5
23 Dec 65	A HARD DAY'S NIGHT *Parlophone R 5393*	14	7
27 Nov 93	A HARD DAY'S NIGHT (re-issue) *EMI CDEMS 293*	52	2

[1] Peter Sellers and Sophia Loren

Michael SEMBELLO
US, male vocalist (6 WEEKS) pos/wks

20 Aug 83	MANIAC *Casablanca CAN 1017* ▲	43	6

SEMISONIC
US, male vocal / instrumental group (18 WEEKS) pos/wks

10 Jul 99	SECRET SMILE *MCA MCSTD 40210*	13	11
6 Nov 99	CLOSING TIME *MCA MCSTD 40221*	25	5
1 Apr 00	SINGING IN MY SLEEP *MCA MCSTD 40227*	39	2

SEMPRINI
UK, orchestra (8 WEEKS) pos/wks

16 Mar 61	THEME FROM 'EXODUS' *HMV POP 842*	25	8

SENSATIONAL Alex HARVEY BAND
UK, male vocal / instrumental group (25 WEEKS) pos/wks

26 Jul 75 ●	DELILAH *Vertigo ALEX 001*	7	7
22 Nov 75	GAMBLIN' BAR ROOM BLUES *Vertigo ALEX 002*	38	8
19 Jun 76	THE BOSTON TEA PARTY *Mountain TOP 12*	13	10

SENSELESS THINGS
UK, male vocal / instrumental group (19 WEEKS) pos/wks

22 Jun 91	EVERYBODY'S GONE *Epic 6569807*	73	1
28 Sep 91	GOT IT AT THE DELMAR *Epic 6574497*	50	3
11 Jan 92	EASY TO SMILE *Epic 6576957*	18	4
11 Apr 92	HOLD IT DOWN *Epic 6579267*	19	4
5 Dec 92	HOMOPHOBIC ASSHOLE *Epic 6588337*	52	2
13 Feb 93	PRIMARY INSTINCT *Epic 6589402*	41	2
12 Jun 93	TOO MUCH KISSING *Epic 6592502*	69	1
5 Nov 94	CHRISTINE KEELER *Epic 6609572*	56	1
28 Jan 95	SOMETHING TO MISS *Epic 6611162*	57	1

SENSER
UK, male / female vocal / instrumental group (5 WEEKS) pos/wks

25 Sep 93	THE KEY *Ultimate TOPP 019CD*	47	1
19 Mar 94	SWITCH *Ultimate TOPP 022CD*	39	2
23 Jul 94	AGE OF PANIC *Ultimate TOPP 027CD*	52	1
17 Aug 96	CHARMING DEMONS *Ultimate TOPP 045CD*	42	1

SEPULTURA
Brazil, male vocal / instrumental group (12 WEEKS) pos/wks

2 Oct 93	TERRITORY *Roadrunner RR 23823*	66	2
26 Feb 94	REFUSE-RESIST *Roadrunner RR 23773*	51	2
4 Jun 94	SLAVE NEW WORLD *Roadrunner RR 23745*	46	2

24 Feb 96	ROOTS BLOODY ROOTS *Roadrunner RR 23205*	19	2
17 Aug 96	RATAMAHATTA *Roadrunner RR 23145*	23	2
14 Dec 96	ATTITUDE *Roadrunner RR 22995*	46	2

SERIAL DIVA
UK, male / female production group (3 WEEKS) pos/wks

18 Jan 97	KEEP HOPE ALIVE *Sound Of Ministry SOMCD 26*	57	1
15 May 99	PEARL RIVER *Low Sense SENSECD 24* [1]	32	2

[1] Three 'N One presents Johnny Shaker featuring Serial Diva

SERIOUS DANGER
UK, male producer - Richard Phillips (4 WEEKS) pos/wks

20 Dec 97	DEEPER *Fresh FRSHD 68*	40	3
2 May 98	HIGH NOON *Fresh FRSHD 69*	54	1

SERIOUS INTENTION
US, male vocal / instrumental group (6 WEEKS) pos/wks

16 Nov 85	YOU DON'T KNOW (OH-OH-OH) *Important TAN 8*	75	1
5 Apr 86	SERIOUS *Pow Wow LON 93*	51	5

SERIOUS ROPE
UK, male / female vocal / production group (3 WEEKS) pos/wks

22 May 93	HAPPINESS *Rumour RUMACD 64* [1]	54	2
1 Oct 94	HAPPINESS - YOU MAKE ME HAPPY (re-mix) *Mercury MERCD 407*	70	1

[1] Serious Rope presents Sharon Dee Clarke

SET THE TONE
UK, male vocal / instrumental group (4 WEEKS) pos/wks

22 Jan 83	DANCE SUCKER *Island WIP 6836*	62	2
26 Mar 83	RAP YOUR LOVE *Island IS 110*	67	2

SETTLERS
UK, male / female vocal / instrumental group (5 WEEKS) pos/wks

16 Oct 71	THE LIGHTNING TREE *York SYK 505*	36	5

Brian SETZER ORCHESTRA
US, male vocal / instrumental group (3 WEEKS) pos/wks

3 Apr 99	JUMP JIVE AN' WAIL *Interscope IND 95601*	34	3

Taja SEVELLE
US, female vocalist (13 WEEKS) pos/wks

20 Feb 88 ●	LOVE IS CONTAGIOUS *Paisley Park W 8257*	7	9
14 May 88	WOULDN'T YOU LOVE TO LOVE ME *Paisley Park W 8127*	59	4

7TH HEAVEN
UK, male vocal group (5 WEEKS) pos/wks

14 Sep 85	HOT FUN *Mercury MER 199*	47	5

702
US, female vocal group (10 WEEKS) pos/wks

14 Dec 96	STEELO *Motown 8606072*	41	2
29 Nov 97	NO DOUBT *Motown 8607052*	59	1
7 Aug 99	WHERE MY GIRLS AT? *Motown TMGCD 1500*	22	4
27 Nov 99	YOU DON'T KNOW *Motown TMGCD 1502*	36	3

740 BOYZ
US, male vocal / instrumental duo (1 WEEK) pos/wks

4 Nov 95	SHIMMY SHAKE *MCA MCSTD 40002*	54	1

SEVEN GRAND HOUSING AUTHORITY
UK, male producer - Terence Parker (1 WEEK) pos/wks

23 Oct 93	THE QUESTION *Olympic EL YCD 010*	70	1

7669
US, female rap group (1 WEEK) pos/wks

18 Jun 94	JOY *Motown TMGCD 1429*	60	1

SEVERINE
France, female vocalist (11 WEEKS) pos/wks

24 Apr 71 ●	UN BANC, UN ARBRE, UNE RUE *Philips 6009 135*	9	11

David SEVILLE
US, male vocalist (6 WEEKS)   pos/wks

| 23 May 58 | WITCH DOCTOR London HLU 8619 ▲ | 11 | 6 |

See also ALFI and HARRY; CHIPMUNKS

Janette SEWELL – See DOUBLE TROUBLE

SEX CLUB featuring BROWN SUGAR
US, male / female vocal / instrumental duo (1 WEEK)   pos/wks

| 28 Jan 95 | BIG DICK MAN Club Tools CLU 60775 | 67 | 1 |

SEX-O-LETTES – See DISCO TEX and the SEX-O-LETTES

SEX-O-SONIQUE UK, male production / instrumental duo - Mike Gray and Jon Pearn (3 WEEKS)
pos/wks

| 6 Dec 97 | I THOUGHT IT WAS YOU ffrr FCD 321 | 32 | 3 |

See also FULL INTENTION

SEX PISTOLS `352` `Top 500` Provocative and influential quartet who popularised punk. Formed 1975 in London UK, split 1978: Johnny Rotten (v), Steve Jones (g), Paul Cook (d) and Glen Matlock (b) - replaced 1977 by Sid Vicious (d. 1979). Notorious group reunited for brief, and profitable, Filthy Lucre tour in 1996 (88 WEEKS)
pos/wks

18 Dec 76	ANARCHY IN THE UK EMI 2566	38	4
4 Jun 77 ●	GOD SAVE THE QUEEN Virgin VS 181	2	9
9 Jul 77 ●	PRETTY VACANT Virgin VS 184	6	8
22 Oct 77 ●	HOLIDAYS IN THE SUN Virgin VS 191	8	6
8 Jul 78 ●	NO ONE IS INNOCENT / MY WAY Virgin VS 220 [1]	7	10
3 Mar 79 ●	SOMETHING ELSE / FRIGGIN' IN THE RIGGIN' Virgin VS 240	3	12
7 Apr 79 ●	SILLY THING Virgin VS 256	6	8
30 Jun 79 ●	C'MON EVERYBODY Virgin VS 272	3	9
13 Oct 79	THE GREAT ROCK 'N' ROLL SWINDLE Virgin VS 290	21	6
14 Jun 80	(I'M NOT YOUR) STEPPING STONE Virgin VS 339	21	8
3 Oct 92	ANARCHY IN THE UK (re-issue) Virgin VS 1431	33	3
5 Dec 92	PRETTY VACANT (re-issue) Virgin VS 1448	56	2
27 Jul 96	PRETTY VACANT (LIVE) Virgin America VUSCD 113	18	3

[1] Sex Pistols, punk prayer by Ronald Biggs

The listed flip side of 'Silly Thing' was 'Who Killed Bambi' by Ten Pole Tudor. The listed flip side of 'The Great Rock 'n' Roll Swindle' was 'Rock Around the Clock', also by Ten Pole Tudor

Denny SEYTON and the SABRES
UK, male vocal / instrumental group (1 WEEK)   pos/wks

| 17 Sep 64 | THE WAY YOU LOOK TONIGHT Mercury MF 824 | 48 | 1 |

SFX UK, male instrumental / production duo (3 WEEKS)
pos/wks

| 15 May 93 | LEMMINGS Parlophone CDR 6343 | 51 | 3 |

SHABOOM UK, male instrumental / production group (1 WEEK)
pos/wks

| 31 Jul 99 | SWEET SENSATION WEA WEA 218CD1 | 64 | 1 |

SHACK UK, male vocal / instrumental group (3 WEEKS)
pos/wks

26 Jun 99	COMEDY London LONCD 427	44	1
14 Aug 99	NATALIE'S PARTY London LONCD 436	63	1
11 Mar 00	OSCAR London LONCD 445	67	1

SHADES US, female vocal group (3 WEEKS)
pos/wks

| 12 Apr 97 | MR BIG STUFF Motown 5736572 [1] | 31 | 2 |
| 20 Sep 97 | SERENADE Motown 8606892 | 75 | 1 |

[1] Queen Latifah, Shades and Free

SHADES OF LOVE
US, male instrumental / production duo (1 WEEK)   pos/wks

| 22 Apr 95 | KEEP IN TOUCH (BODY TO BODY) Vicious Muzik MUZCD 102 | 64 | 1 |

SHADES OF RHYTHM
UK, male instrumental / production group (25 WEEKS)   pos/wks

2 Feb 91	HOMICIDE / EXORCIST ZTT ZANG 13	53	3
13 Apr 91	SWEET SENSATION ZTT ZANG 18	54	4
20 Jul 91	THE SOUND OF EDEN ZTT ZANG 22	35	5
30 Nov 91	EXTACY ZTT ZANG 24	16	7
20 Feb 93	SWEET REVIVAL (KEEP IT COMIN') ZTT ZANG 40CD	61	1
11 Sep 93	SOUND OF EDEN (re-issue) ZTT ZANG 44CD	37	3
5 Nov 94	THE WANDERING DRAGON Public Demand PPDCD 5	55	1
21 Jun 97	PSYCHO BASE Coalition CRUM 002CD	57	1

SHADOWS `3` `Top 500` Headliners for five decades and Britain's most successful instrumental group: Hank Marvin (b. Brian Rankin, 28 Oct 1941, Newcastle-upon-Tyne) (g), Bruce Welch (b. Bruce Cripps, 2 Nov 1941, Bognor Regis) (g), 'Jet' Harris (b. Terence Hawkins, 6 Jul 1939, London) (b), Tony Meehan (b. Daniel Meehan, 2 Mar 1943, London) (d), Brian Bennett (b. 9 Feb 1940, London) (d). They began their chart life as The Drifters when backing Cliff Richard and went on to contribute significantly on 35 hits with Cliff. Their main claim to fame is as Britain's most influential and imitated act before the Beatles (770 WEEKS)
pos/wks

12 Sep 58 ●	MOVE IT Columbia DB 4178 [1]	2	17
21 Nov 58 ●	HIGH CLASS BABY Columbia DB 4203 [1]	7	10
30 Jan 59 ●	LIVIN' LOVIN' DOLL Columbia DB 4249 [1]	20	6
8 May 59 ●	MEAN STREAK Columbia DB 4290 A [1]	10	9
15 May 59	NEVER MIND Columbia DB 4290 B [1]	21	2
10 Jul 59 ★	LIVING DOLL Columbia DB 4306 [2]	1	21
9 Oct 59	DYNAMITE Columbia DB 4351 A [2]	16	2
9 Oct 59 ★	TRAVELLIN' LIGHT Columbia DB 4351 B [2]	1	17
30 Oct 59	DYNAMITE (re-entry) Columbia DB 4351 A [2]	21	2
11 Dec 59	LIVING DOLL (re-entry) Columbia DB 4306 [2]	26	1
1 Jan 60	LIVING DOLL (2nd re-entry) Columbia DB 4306 [2]	28	1
15 Jan 60	EXPRESSO BONGO (EP) Columbia SEG 7971 [2]	14	7
22 Jan 60 ●	VOICE IN THE WILDERNESS Columbia DB 4398 [2]	2	13
24 Mar 60 ●	FALL IN LOVE WITH YOU Columbia DB 4431 [2]	2	15
5 May 60	VOICE IN THE WILDERNESS (re-entry) Columbia DB 4398 [2]	36	2
30 Jun 60 ★	PLEASE DON'T TEASE Columbia 4479 [2]	1	18
21 Jul 60 ★	APACHE Columbia DB 4484	1	21
22 Sep 60 ●	NINE TIMES OUT OF TEN Columbia DB 4506 [2]	3	12
10 Nov 60 ●	MAN OF MYSTERY / THE STRANGER Columbia DB 4530	5	15
1 Dec 60 ●	I LOVE YOU Columbia DB 4547 [2]	1	16
9 Feb 61 ●	FBI Columbia DB 4580	6	19
2 Mar 61 ●	THEME FOR A DREAM Columbia DB 4593 [2]	3	14
30 Mar 61 ●	GEE WHIZ IT'S YOU Columbia DC 756 [2]	4	14
11 May 61 ●	FRIGHTENED CITY Columbia DB 4637	3	20
22 Jun 61 ●	A GIRL LIKE YOU Columbia DB 4667 [2]	3	14
7 Sep 61 ★	KON-TIKI Columbia DB 4698	1	10
16 Nov 61 ●	THE SAVAGE Columbia DB 4726	10	8
23 Nov 61	KON-TIKI (re-entry) Columbia DB 4698	37	2
11 Jan 62 ★	THE YOUNG ONES Columbia DB 4761 [2] ◆ ■	1	21
1 Mar 62 ●	WONDERFUL LAND Columbia DB 4790	1	19
10 May 62 ●	I'M LOOKING OUT THE WINDOW / DO YOU WANT TO DANCE Columbia DB 4828 [3]	2	17
2 Aug 62 ●	GUITAR TANGO Columbia DB 4870	4	15
6 Sep 62 ●	IT'LL BE ME Columbia DB 4886 [2]	2	12
6 Dec 62 ★	THE NEXT TIME / BACHELOR BOY Columbia DB 4950 [2]	1	18
13 Dec 62 ●	DANCE ON Columbia DB 4948	1	15
21 Feb 63 ★	SUMMER HOLIDAY Columbia DB 4977 [2]	1	18
7 Mar 63 ★	FOOT TAPPER Columbia DB 4984	1	16
9 May 63 ●	LUCKY LIPS Columbia DB 7034 [2]	4	15
6 Jun 63 ●	ATLANTIS Columbia DB 7047	2	17
19 Sep 63 ●	SHINDIG Columbia DB 7106	6	12
7 Nov 63 ●	DON'T TALK TO HIM Columbia DB 7150 [2]	2	13
5 Dec 63	GERONIMO Columbia DB 7163	11	12
6 Feb 64 ●	I'M THE LONELY ONE Columbia DB 7203 [2]	8	10
13 Feb 64	DON'T TALK TO HIM (re-entry) Columbia DB 7150 [2]	50	1
5 Mar 64	THEME FOR YOUNG LOVERS Columbia DB 7231	12	10
7 May 64 ●	THE RISE AND FALL OF FLINGEL BUNT Columbia DB 7261	5	14
2 Jul 64 ●	ON THE BEACH Columbia DB 7305 [2]	7	13
3 Sep 64	RHYTHM AND GREENS Columbia DB 7342	22	7
3 Dec 64	GENIE WITH THE LIGHT BROWN LAMP Columbia DB 7416	17	10
10 Dec 64 ●	I COULD EASILY FALL Columbia DB 7420 [2]	9	11

UK No.1 ★   UK Top 10 ●   Still on chart +   UK million seller ◆   UK entry at No.1 ■   US No.1 ▲

Date	Title	Catalogue	pos	wks
11 Feb 65	MARY ANNE *Columbia DB 7476*		17	10
10 Jun 65	STINGRAY *Columbia DB 7588*		19	7
5 Aug 65 ●	DON'T MAKE MY BABY BLUE *Columbia DB 7650*		10	10
19 Aug 65	THE TIME IN BETWEEN *Columbia DB 7660* [2]		22	8
25 Nov 65	WAR LORD *Columbia DB 7769*		18	9
17 Mar 66	I MET A GIRL *Columbia DB 7853*		22	9
24 Mar 66	BLUE TURNS TO GREY *Columbia DB 7866* [2]		15	9
7 Jul 66	A PLACE IN THE SUN *Columbia DB 7952*		24	6
13 Oct 66 ●	TIME DRAGS BY *Columbia DB 8017* [2]		10	12
3 Nov 66	THE DREAMS I DREAM *Columbia DB 8034*		42	6
15 Dec 66 ●	IN THE COUNTRY *Columbia DB 8094* [2]		6	10
13 Apr 67	MAROC 7 *Columbia DB 8170*		24	8
27 Nov 68	DON'T FORGET TO CATCH ME *Columbia DB 8503* [2]		21	10
8 Mar 75	LET ME BE THE ONE *EMI 2269*		12	9
16 Dec 78 ●	DON'T CRY FOR ME ARGENTINA *EMI 2890*		5	14
28 Apr 79 ●	THEME FROM THE 'DEER HUNTER' (CAVATINA) *EMI 2939*		9	14
26 Jan 80	RIDERS IN THE SKY *EMI 5027*		12	12
23 Aug 80	EQUINOXE (PART V) *Polydor POSP 148*		50	3
2 May 81	THE THIRD MAN *Polydor POSP 255*		44	4

[1] Cliff Richard & the Drifters [2] Cliff Richard & the Shadows [3] Cliff Richard / The Shadows

All the Shadows hits without Cliff Richard were instrumentals except for 'Mary Anne', 'Don't Make My Baby Blue', 'I Met a Girl', 'The Dreams I Dream' and 'Let Me Be the One'. Tracks on Expresso Bongo (EP): Love / A Voice in the Wilderness / The Shrine on the Second Floor / Bongo Blues. Last track featured Shadows only

See also Cliff RICHARD; Hank MARVIN; Jet HARRIS and Tony MEEHAN

SHAFT
UK, male production duo - Elliot Ireland and Alex Rizzo (18 WEEKS) pos/wks

Date	Title	Catalogue	pos	wks
4 Sep 99 ●	(MUCHO MAMBO) SWAY *Wonderboy WBOYD 015*		2	12
20 May 00	MAMBO ITALIANO *Wounderboy WBDD 017*		12	6

SHAFT *UK, male producer - Mark Pritchard (9 WEEKS)* pos/wks

Date	Title	Catalogue	pos	wks
21 Dec 91 ●	ROOBARB AND CUSTARD *Ffrreedom TAB 100*		7	8
25 Jul 92	MONKEY *Ffrreedom TAB 114*		61	1

SHAG – See Jonathan KING

SHAGGY *Jamaica, male vocalist - Orville Burrell (66 WEEKS)* pos/wks

Date	Title	Catalogue	pos	wks
6 Feb 93 ★	OH CAROLINA *Greensleeves GRECD 361*		1	19
10 Jul 93	SOON BE DONE *Greensleeves GRECD 380*		46	3
8 Jul 95	IN THE SUMMERTIME *Virgin VSCDT 1542* [1]		5	9
23 Sep 95 ★	BOOMBASTIC *Virgin VSCDT 1536* ■		1	12
13 Jan 96	WHY YOU TREAT ME SO BAD *Virgin VSCDT 1566* [2]		11	5
23 Mar 96	SOMETHING DIFFERENT / THE TRAIN IS COMING *Virgin VSCDT 1581* [3]		21	5
22 Jun 96	THAT GIRL *Virgin America VUSCDX 106* [4]		15	7
19 Jul 97 ●	PIECE OF MY HEART *Virgin VSCDT 1647* [5]		7	6

[1] Shaggy featuring Rayvon [2] Shaggy featuring Grand Puba [3] Shaggy featuring Wayne Wonder / Shaggy [4] Maxi Priest featuring Shaggy [5] Shaggy featuring Marsha

SHAH *UK, female vocalist (1 WEEK)* pos/wks

Date	Title	Catalogue	pos	wks
6 Jun 98	SECRET LOVE *Evocative EVOKE 5CDS*		69	1

SHAI *US, male vocal group (6 WEEKS)* pos/wks

Date	Title	Catalogue	pos	wks
19 Dec 92	IF I EVER FALL IN LOVE *MCA MCS 1727*		36	6

SHAKATAK (381 Top 500) *London-based pop / jazz / funk ensemble who were big in Japan. Sound was typified by tinkling piano of Bill Sharpe and Jill Saward's soothing vocals. Sharpe later hit with Gary Numan, while Nigel Wright (k) produced Madonna, Take That, Robson and Jerome, Barbra Streisand and Cliff Richard (85 WEEKS)* pos/wks

Date	Title	Catalogue	pos	wks
8 Nov 80	FEELS LIKE THE RIGHT TIME *Polydor POSP 188*		41	5
7 Mar 81	LIVING IN THE UK *Polydor POSP 230*		52	4
25 Jul 81	BRAZILIAN DAWN *Polydor POSP 282*		48	3
21 Nov 81	EASIER SAID THAN DONE *Polydor POSP 375*		12	17
3 Apr 82 ●	NIGHT BIRDS *Polydor POSP 407*		9	8
19 Jun 82	STREETWALKIN' *Polydor POSP 452*		38	6

Date	Title	Catalogue	pos	wks
4 Sep 82	INVITATIONS *Polydor POSP 502*		24	7
6 Nov 82	STRANGER *Polydor POSP 530*		43	3
4 Jun 83	DARK IS THE NIGHT *Polydor POSP 595*		15	8
27 Aug 83	IF YOU COULD SEE ME NOW *Polydor POSP 635*		49	4
7 Jul 84 ●	DOWN ON THE STREET *Polydor POSP 688*		9	11
15 Sep 84	DON'T BLAME IT ON LOVE *Polydor POSP 699*		55	3
16 Nov 85	DAY BY DAY *Polydor POSP 770* [1]		53	3
24 Oct 87	MR MANIC AND SISTER COOL *Polydor MANIC 1*		56	3

[1] Shakatak featuring Al Jarreau

SHAKESPEAR'S SISTER *UK / US, female vocal / instrumental duo - Siobhan Fahey and Marcella (Detroit) Levy (52 WEEKS)* pos/wks

Date	Title	Catalogue	pos	wks
29 Jul 89 ●	YOU'RE HISTORY *ffrr F 112*		7	9
14 Oct 89	RUN SILENT *ffrr F 119*		54	3
10 Mar 90	DIRTY MIND *ffrr F 128*		71	1
12 Oct 91	GOODBYE CRUEL WORLD *London LON 309*		59	2
25 Jan 92 ★	STAY *London LON 314*		1	16
16 May 92	I DON'T CARE *London LON 318*		7	7
18 Jul 92	GOODBYE CRUEL WORLD (re-issue) *London LON 322*		32	4
7 Nov 92	HELLO (TURN YOUR RADIO ON) *London LON 330*		14	6
27 Feb 93	MY 16TH APOLOGY (EP) *London LONCD 337*		61	1
22 Jun 96	I CAN DRIVE *London LONCD 383*		30	3

Tracks on My 16th Apology (EP): My 16th Apology / Catwoman / Dirty Mind (live re-recording) / Hot Love. From 1996 Shakespear's Sister was essentially just vocalist Siobhan Fahey

See also Marcella DETROIT; BANANARAMA

SHAKY and BONNIE – See Shakin' STEVENS; Bonnie TYLER

SHALAMAR (189 Top 500) *Influential US dance-music vocal trio masterminded by Soul Train TV producer Don Cornelius. Line-up 1979-1983: Jeffrey Daniel, Jody Watley, Howard Hewett. Regarded as fashion icons and trend-setters, they helped to introduce "body-popping" to Britain (134 WEEKS)* pos/wks

Date	Title	Catalogue	pos	wks
14 May 77	UPTOWN FESTIVAL *Soul Train FB 0885*		30	5
9 Dec 78	TAKE THAT TO THE BANK *RCA FB 1379*		20	12
24 Nov 79	THE SECOND TIME AROUND *Solar FB 1709*		45	9
9 Feb 80	RIGHT IN THE SOCKET *Solar SO 2*		44	6
30 Aug 80	I OWE YOU ONE *Solar SO 11*		13	10
28 Mar 81	MAKE THAT MOVE *Solar SO 17*		30	10
27 Mar 82 ●	I CAN MAKE YOU FEEL GOOD *Solar K 12599*		7	11
12 Jun 82	A NIGHT TO REMEMBER *Solar K 13162*		5	12
4 Sep 82 ●	THERE IT IS *Solar K 13194*		5	10
27 Nov 82	FRIENDS *Solar CHUM 1*		12	10
11 Jun 83 ●	DEAD GIVEAWAY *Solar E 9819*		8	10
13 Aug 83	DISAPPEARING ACT *Solar E 9807*		18	8
15 Oct 83	OVER AND OVER *Solar E 9792*		23	6
24 Mar 84	DANCING IN THE SHEETS *CBS A 4171*		41	3
31 Mar 84	DEADLINE USA *MCA MCA 866*		52	3
24 Nov 84	AMNESIA *Solar/MCA SHAL 1*		61	2
2 Feb 85	MY GIRL LOVES ME *MCA SHAL 2*		45	3
26 Apr 86	A NIGHT TO REMEMBER (re-mix) *MCA SHAL 3*		52	4

SHAM ROCK *Ireland, male / female vocal / instrumental group (11 WEEKS)* pos/wks

Date	Title	Catalogue	pos	wks
7 Nov 98	TELL ME MA *Jive 0522352*		13	11

SHAM 69 *UK, male vocal / instrumental group (53 WEEKS)* pos/wks

Date	Title	Catalogue	pos	wks
13 May 78	ANGELS WITH DIRTY FACES *Polydor 2059 023*		19	10
29 Jul 78 ●	IF THE KIDS ARE UNITED *Polydor 2059 050*		9	9
14 Oct 78 ●	HURRY UP HARRY *Polydor POSP 7*		10	8
24 Mar 79	QUESTIONS AND ANSWERS *Polydor POSP 27*		18	9
4 Aug 79 ●	HERSHAM BOYS *Polydor POSP 64*		6	9
27 Oct 79	YOU'RE A BETTER MAN THAN I *Polydor POSP 82*		49	5
12 Apr 80	TELL THE CHILDREN *Polydor POSP 136*		45	3

SHAMEN 427 Top 500

Early and highly influential exponents of techno-rock fusion, The Shamen, named after South American Indian tribesmen, comprise duo Colin Angus and Richard West (Mr C) following the departure of founders Peter Stephenson and Keith McKenzie and the death by drowning of Will Sinnott in 1991 (77 WEEKS)

		pos/wks
7 Apr 90	PRO-GEN *One Little Indian 36 TP7*	55 4
22 Sep 90	MAKE IT MINE *One Little Indian 46 TP7*	42 5
6 Apr 91	HYPERREAL *One Little Indian 48 TP7*	29 5
27 Jul 91 ●	MOVE ANY MOUNTAIN (re-mix) *One Little Indian 52 TP7*	4 10
18 Jul 92	LSI *One Little Indian 68 TP7*	6 8
5 Sep 92 ★	EBENEEZER GOODE *One Little Indian 78 TP7*	1 10
7 Nov 92	BOSS DRUM (re-mix) *One Little Indian 88 TP12*	58 1
7 Nov 92 ●	BOSS DRUM *One Little Indian 88 TP7*	4 7
19 Dec 92 ●	PHOREVER PEOPLE *One Little Indian 98 TP7*	5 10
6 Mar 93	RE: EVOLUTION *One Little Indian 118 TP7CD* [1]	18 2
6 Nov 93	THE SOS (EP) *One Little Indian 108 TP7CD*	14 4
19 Aug 95	DESTINATION ESCHATON *One Little Indian 128 TP7CDL*	15 4
21 Oct 95	TRANSAMAZONIA *One Little Indian 138 TP7CD*	28 2
10 Feb 96	HEAL (THE SEPARATION) *One Little Indian 158 TP7CDL*	31 2
21 Dec 96	MOVE ANY MOUNTAIN '96 (2nd) (re-mix) *One Little Indian 169 TP7CD*	35 3

[1] Shamen with Terence McKenna

'Move Any Mountain' is a re-mix of 'Pro-Gen'. Tracks on The SOS (EP): Comin' On / Make It Mine / Possible Worlds (re-mix)

SHAMPOO *UK, female vocal duo (28 WEEKS)*

		pos/wks
30 Jul 94	TROUBLE *Food CDFOOD 51*	11 12
15 Oct 94	VIVA LA MEGABABES *Food CDFOOD 54*	27 4
18 Feb 95	DELICIOUS *Food CDFOOD 58*	21 4
5 Aug 95	TROUBLE (re-issue) *Food CDFOOD 66*	36 3
13 Jul 96	GIRL POWER *Food CDFOOD 76*	25 4
21 Sep 96	I KNOW WHAT BOYS LIKE *Food CDFOOD 83*	42 1

Jimmy SHAND *UK, male dance band (2 WEEKS)*

		pos/wks
23 Dec 55	BLUEBELL POLKA *Parlophone F 3436*	20 2

Paul SHANE and the YELLOWCOATS *UK, male vocalist with male / female vocal group (5 WEEKS)*

		pos/wks
16 May 81	HI DE HI (HOLIDAY ROCK) *EMI 5180*	36 5

SHANGRI-LAS *US, female vocal group (57 WEEKS)*

		pos/wks
8 Oct 64	REMEMBER (WALKIN' IN THE SAND) *Red Bird RB 10008*	14 13
14 Jan 65	LEADER OF THE PACK *Red Bird RB 10014* ▲	11 9
14 Oct 72 ●	LEADER OF THE PACK (re-issue) *Kama Sutra 2013 024*	3 14
5 Jun 76 ●	LEADER OF THE PACK (2nd re-issue) *Charly CS 1009*	7 11
12 Jun 76 ●	LEADER OF THE PACK (3rd re-issue) *Contempo CS 9032*	7 10

From 19 Jun 1976 until 14 Aug 1976, the last week of the disc's chart run, the Charly and Contempo releases of 'Leader of the Pack' were bracketed together on the chart

SHANICE *US, female vocalist - Shanice Wilson (24 WEEKS)*

		pos/wks
23 Nov 91	I LOVE YOUR SMILE *Motown ZB 44907*	55 4
22 Feb 92 ●	I LOVE YOUR SMILE (re-mix) *Motown TMG 1401*	2 10
14 Nov 92	LOVIN' YOU *Motown TMG 1409*	54 1
16 Jan 93	SAVING FOREVER FOR YOU *Giant W 0148CD*	42 3
13 Aug 94	I LIKE *Motown TMGCD 1427*	49 2
16 Dec 95	IF I NEVER KNEW YOU (LOVE THEME FROM 'POCAHONTAS') *Walt Disney WD 7023CD* [1]	51 4

[1] Jon Secada and Shanice

SHANKS & BIGFOOT *UK, male production duo aka Doolally - Stephen Meade and Daniel Langsman (24 WEEKS)*

		pos/wks
29 May 99 ★	SWEET LIKE CHOCOLATE *Pepper / Jive / Chocolate Boy 0530352* ■	1 15
2 Oct 99	SWEET LIKE CHOCOLATE (re-entry) *Pepper / Jive / Chocolate Boy 0530352*	66 1
29 Jul 00	SING-A-LONG *Pepper 9230232*	12 7
23 Sep 00	SING-A-LONG (re-entry) *Pepper 9230232*	52 1

SHANNON *US, female vocalist - Brenda Shannon Greene (54 WEEKS)*

		pos/wks
19 Nov 83	LET THE MUSIC PLAY *Club LET 1*	51 3
28 Jan 84	LET THE MUSIC PLAY (re-entry) *Club LET 1*	14 12
7 Apr 84	GIVE ME TONIGHT *Club JAB 1*	24 7
30 Jun 84	SWEET SOMEBODY *Club JAB 3*	25 8
20 Jul 85	STRONGER TOGETHER *Club JAB 15*	46 6
6 Dec 97	IT'S OVER LOVE *Manifesto FESCD 37* [1]	16 8
28 Nov 98 ●	MOVE MANIA *Multiply CDMULTY 45* [2]	8 10

[1] Todd Terry presents Shannon [2] Sash! featuring Shannon

Del SHANNON 150 Top 500

Early 1960s chart regular. b. Charles Westover, 30 Dec 1934, Michigan, US. d. 8 Feb 1990. This unmistakable singer / songwriter had a falsetto vocal and he topped both the UK and US charts with the first of his many hits (147 WEEKS)

		pos/wks
27 Apr 61 ★	RUNAWAY *London HLX 9317* ▲	1 22
14 Sep 61 ●	HATS OFF TO LARRY *London HLX 9402*	6 12
7 Dec 61	SO LONG BABY *London HLX 9462*	10 11
15 Mar 62 ●	HEY LITTLE GIRL *London HLX 9515*	2 15
6 Sep 62	CRY MYSELF TO SLEEP *London HLX 9587*	29 6
11 Oct 62 ●	SWISS MAID *London HLX 9609*	2 17
17 Jan 63 ●	LITTLE TOWN FLIRT *London HLX 9653*	4 13
25 Apr 63 ●	TWO KINDS OF TEARDROPS *London HLX 9710*	5 13
22 Aug 63	TWO SILHOUETTES *London HLX 9761*	23 6
24 Oct 63	SUE'S GOTTA BE MINE *London HLU 9800*	21 8
12 Mar 64	MARY JANE *Stateside SS 269*	35 5
30 Jul 64	HANDY MAN *Stateside SS 317*	36 4
14 Jan 65 ●	KEEP SEARCHIN' (WE'LL FOLLOW THE SUN) *Stateside SS 368*	3 11
18 Mar 65	STRANGER IN TOWN *Stateside SS 395*	40 2

Roxanne SHANTE *US, female rapper (11 WEEKS)*

		pos/wks
1 Aug 87	HAVE A NICE DAY *Breakout USA 612*	58 3
4 Jun 88	GO ON GIRL *Breakout USA 633*	55 3
29 Oct 88	SHARP AS A KNIFE *Club JAB 73* [1]	45 3
14 Apr 90	GO ON GIRL (re-mix) *Breakout USA 689*	74 1
23 Sep 00	WHAT'S GOING ON *Wall of Sound WALLD 064* [2]	43 1

[1] Brandon Cooke featuring Roxanne Shante [2] Mekon Featuring Roxanne Shante

Helen SHAPIRO 225 Top 500

Youngest female chart-topper. b. 28 Sep 1946, London. Before she was 16 years old, she amassed four Top 5 hits (including two No.1s) and had been voted Britain's Top Female Singer. She headlined the first UK tour on which The Beatles appeared (as her support act) (119 WEEKS)

		pos/wks
23 Mar 61 ●	DON'T TREAT ME LIKE A CHILD *Columbia DB 4589*	3 20
29 Jun 61 ★	YOU DON'T KNOW *Columbia DB 4670*	1 23
28 Sep 61 ★	WALKIN' BACK TO HAPPINESS *Columbia DB 4715*	1 19
15 Feb 62 ●	TELL ME WHAT HE SAID *Columbia DB 4782*	2 15
3 May 62	LET'S TALK ABOUT LOVE *Columbia DB 4824*	23 7
12 Jul 62 ●	LITTLE MISS LONELY *Columbia DB 4869*	8 11
18 Oct 62	KEEP AWAY FROM OTHER GIRLS *Columbia DB 4908*	40 6
7 Feb 63	QUEEN FOR TONIGHT *Columbia DB 4966*	33 5
25 Apr 63	WOE IS ME *Columbia DB 7026*	35 6
24 Oct 63	LOOK WHO IT IS *Columbia DB 7130*	47 3
23 Jan 64	FEVER *Columbia DB 7190*	38 4

SHARADA HOUSE GANG *Italy, male / female vocal / instrumental group (4 WEEKS)*

		pos/wks
12 Aug 95	KEEP IT UP *Media MCSTD 2071*	36 2
11 May 96	LET THE RHYTHM MOVE YOU *Media MCSTD 40035*	50 1
18 Oct 97	GYPSY BOY, GYPSY GIRL *Gut CXGUT 12*	52 1

SHARKEY *UK, male DJ / producer / instrumentalist - Jonathan Sharkey (1 WEEK)*

		pos/wks
8 Mar 97	REVOLUTIONS (EP) *React CDREACT 95*	53 1

Tracks on Revolutions (EP): Revolution Part One / Revolution Part Two / Revolution Part Two (remix)

UK No.1 ★   UK Top 10 ●   Still on chart +   UK million seller ◆   UK entry at No.1 ■   US No.1 ▲

Feargal SHARKEY *Ireland, male vocalist (58 WEEKS)*

			pos/wks
13 Oct 84	LISTEN TO YOUR FATHER *Zarjazz JAZZ 1*	23	7
29 Jun 85	LOVING YOU *Virgin VS 770*	26	10
12 Oct 85 ★	A GOOD HEART *Virgin VS 808*	1	16
4 Jan 86 ●	YOU LITTLE THIEF *Virgin VS 840*	5	9
5 Apr 86	SOMEONE TO SOMEBODY *Virgin VS 828*	64	3
16 Jan 88	MORE LOVE *Virgin VS 992*	44	5
16 Mar 91	I'VE GOT NEWS FOR YOU *Virgin VS 1294*	12	8

See also UNDERTONES; ASSEMBLY

SHARONETTES *US, female vocal group (8 WEEKS)*

			pos/wks
26 Apr 75	PAPA OOM MOW MOW *Black Magic BM 102*	26	5
12 Jul 75	GOING TO A GO-GO *Black Magic BM 104*	46	3

Debbie SHARP – See DREAM FREQUENCY

Dee Dee SHARP *US, female vocalist (2 WEEKS)*

			pos/wks
25 Apr 63	DO THE BIRD *Cameo Parkway C 244*	46	2

SHARPE and NUMAN – See Gary NUMAN

Rocky SHARPE and the REPLAYS
UK, male / female vocal group (41 WEEKS)

			pos/wks
16 Dec 78	RAMA LAMA DING DONG *Chiswick CHIS 104*	17	10
24 Mar 79	IMAGINATION *Chiswick CHIS 110*	39	6
25 Aug 79	LOVE WILL MAKE YOU FAIL IN SCHOOL *Chiswick CHIS 114* [1]	60	4
9 Feb 80	MARTIAN HOP *Chiswick CHIS 121* [1]	55	4
17 Apr 82	SHOUT SHOUT (KNOCK YOURSELF OUT) *Chiswick DICE 3*	19	9
7 Aug 82	CLAP YOUR HANDS *RAK 345*	54	3
26 Feb 83	IF YOU WANNA BE HAPPY *Polydor POSP 560*	46	5

[1] Rocky Sharpe and the Replays featuring the Top Liners

Barrie K SHARPE – See Diana BROWN and Barrie K SHARPE

Mark SHAW *UK, male vocalist (1 WEEK)*

			pos/wks
17 Nov 90	LOVE SO BRIGHT *EMI EM 161*	54	1

Sandie SHAW (124 Top 500) *Barefoot pop princess of the Sixties, b. Sandra Goodrich, 26 Feb 1947, Essex, UK. This distinctive vocalist, who has a 30-year chart span, was the first UK act to win the Eurovision Song Contest (with 'Puppet on a String' in 1967) (165 WEEKS)*

			pos/wks
8 Oct 64 ★	(THERE'S) ALWAYS SOMETHING THERE TO REMIND ME *Pye 7N 15704*	1	11
10 Dec 64 ●	GIRL DON'T COME *Pye 7N 15743*	3	12
18 Feb 65 ●	I'LL STOP AT NOTHING *Pye 7N 15783*	4	11
13 May 65 ★	LONG LIVE LOVE *Pye 7N 15841*	1	14
23 Sep 65 ●	MESSAGE UNDERSTOOD *Pye 7N 15940*	6	10
18 Nov 65	HOW CAN YOU TELL *Pye 7N 15987*	21	9
27 Jan 66 ●	TOMORROW *Pye 7N 17036*	9	9
19 May 66	NOTHING COMES EASY *Pye 7N 17086*	14	9
8 Sep 66	RUN *Pye 7N 17163*	32	5
24 Nov 66	THINK SOMETIMES ABOUT ME *Pye 7N 17212*	32	4
19 Jan 67	I DON'T NEED ANYTHING *Pye 7N 17239*	50	1
16 Mar 67 ★	PUPPET ON A STRING *Pye 7N 17272*	1	18
12 Jul 67	TONIGHT IN TOKYO *Pye 7N 17346*	21	6
4 Oct 67	YOU'VE NOT CHANGED *Pye 7N 17378*	18	12
7 Feb 68	TODAY *Pye 7N 17441*	27	7
12 Feb 69 ●	MONSIEUR DUPONT *Pye 7N 17675*	6	15
14 May 69	THINK IT ALL OVER *Pye 7N 17726*	42	4
21 Apr 84	HAND IN GLOVE *Rough Trade RT 130*	27	5
14 Jun 86	ARE YOU READY TO BE HEARTBROKEN *Polydor POSP 793*	68	1
12 Nov 94	NOTHING LESS THAN BRILLIANT *Virgin VSCDT 1521*	66	2

Tracy SHAW *UK, female vocalist (1 WEEK)*

			pos/wks
4 Jul 98	HAPPENIN' ALL OVER AGAIN *Recognition CDREC 2*	46	1

Winifred SHAW *US, female vocalist (4 WEEKS)*

			pos/wks
14 Aug 76	LULLABY OF BROADWAY *United Artists UP 36131*	42	4

SHE – See URBAN DISCHARGE featuring SHE

SHE ROCKERS *UK, female rap duo (2 WEEKS)*

			pos/wks
13 Jan 90	JAM IT JAM *Jive JIVE 233*	58	2

George SHEARING *UK, male instrumentalist - piano (15 WEEKS)*

			pos/wks
19 Jul 62	LET THERE BE LOVE *Capitol CL 15257* [1]	11	14
4 Oct 62	BAUBLES, BANGLES AND BEADS *Capitol CL 15269*	49	1

[1] Nat 'King' Cole with George Shearing

Gary SHEARSTON *Australia, male vocalist (8 WEEKS)*

			pos/wks
5 Oct 74 ●	I GET A KICK OUT OF YOU *Charisma CB 234*	7	8

SHED SEVEN *UK, male vocal / instrumental group (46 WEEKS)*

			pos/wks
25 Jun 94	DOLPHIN *Polydor YORCD 2*	28	4
27 Aug 94	SPEAKEASY *Polydor YORCD 3*	24	3
12 Nov 94	OCEAN PIE *Polydor YORCD 4*	33	2
13 May 95	WHERE HAVE YOU BEEN TONIGHT *Polydor YORCD 5*	23	2
27 Jan 96	GETTING BETTER *Polydor 5778912*	14	3
23 Mar 96 ●	GOING FOR GOLD *Polydor 5762152*	8	5
18 May 96	BULLY BOY *Polydor 5765972*	22	3
31 Aug 96	ON STANDBY *Polydor 5752732*	12	4
23 Nov 96	CHASING RAINBOWS *Polydor 5759292*	17	5
14 Mar 98	SHE LEFT ME ON FRIDAY *Polydor 5695412*	11	4
23 May 98	THE HEROES *Polydor 5699172*	18	3
22 Aug 98	DEVIL IN YOUR SHOES (WALKING ALL OVER) *Polydor 5672072*	37	2
5 Jun 99	DISCO DOWN *Polydor 5638752*	13	6

SHEEP ON DRUGS *UK, male vocal / instrumental duo (5 WEEKS)*

			pos/wks
27 Mar 93	15 MINUTES OF FAME *Transglobal CID 564*	44	2
30 Oct 93	FROM A TO H AND BACK AGAIN *Transglobal CID 575*	40	2
14 May 94	LET THE GOOD TIMES ROLL *Transglobal CID 576*	56	1

SHEER BRONZE featuring Lisa MILLETT
UK, male / female vocal / instrumental duo (1 WEEK)

			pos/wks
3 Sep 94	WALKIN' ON *Go.Beat GODCD 115*	63	1

SHEER ELEGANCE *UK, male vocal group (23 WEEKS)*

			pos/wks
20 Dec 75	MILKY WAY *Pye International 7N 25697*	18	10
3 Apr 76 ●	LIFE IS TOO SHORT GIRL *Pye International 7N 25703*	9	9
24 Jul 76	IT'S TEMPTATION *Pye International 7N 25715*	41	4

SHEILA AND B DEVOTION – See Sheila B Devotion

Doug SHELDON *UK, male vocalist (15 WEEKS)*

			pos/wks
9 Nov 61	RUNAROUND SUE *Decca F 11398*	36	3
4 Jan 62	YOUR MA SAID YOU CRIED IN YOUR SLEEP LAST NIGHT *Decca F 11416*	29	6
7 Feb 63	I SAW LINDA YESTERDAY *Decca F 11564*	36	6

Pete SHELLEY *UK, male vocalist (1 WEEK)*

			pos/wks
12 Mar 83	TELEPHONE OPERATOR *Genetic XX1*	66	1

See also BUZZCOCKS

Peter SHELLEY *UK, male vocalist (20 WEEKS)*

			pos/wks
14 Sep 74 ●	GEE BABY *Magnet MAG 12*	4	10
22 Mar 75 ●	LOVE ME LOVE MY DOG *Magnet MAG 22*	3	10

Anne SHELTON *UK, female vocalist - Patricia Sibley (31 WEEKS)*

			pos/wks
16 Dec 55	ARRIVEDERCI DARLING *HMV POP 146*	17	4
13 Apr 56	SEVEN DAYS *Philips PB 567*	20	4
24 Aug 56 ★	LAY DOWN YOUR ARMS *Philips PB 616*	1	14
20 Nov 59	VILLAGE OF ST BERNADETTE *Philips PB 969*	27	1
26 Jan 61 ●	SAILOR *Philips PB 1096*	10	8

SHENA UK, female vocalist (2 WEEKS) pos/wks
2 Aug 97	**LET THE BEAT HIT 'EM** *VC VCRD 24*	**28**	2

Vikki SHEPARD – See SLEAZESISTERS

Vonda SHEPARD US, female vocalist (9 WEEKS) pos/wks
5 Dec 98 ●	**SEARCHIN' MY SOUL** *Epic 6666332*	**10**	9

SHEPHERD SISTERS US, female vocal group (6 WEEKS) pos/wks
15 Nov 57	**ALONE** *HMV POP 411*	**14**	5
3 Jan 58	**ALONE (re-entry)** *HMV POP 411*	**22**	1

SHERBET Australia, male vocal / instrumental group (10 WEEKS) pos/wks
25 Sep 76 ●	**HOWZAT** *Epic EPC 4574*	**4**	10

Tony SHERIDAN and the BEATLES
UK, male vocalist / instrumental group (1 WEEK) pos/wks
6 Jun 63	**MY BONNIE** *Polydor NH 668833*	**48**	1

Allan SHERMAN US, male vocalist (10 WEEKS) pos/wks
12 Sep 63	**HELLO MUDDAH HELLO FADDAH** *Warner Bros. WB 106*	**14**	10

Bobby SHERMAN US, male vocalist (4 WEEKS) pos/wks
31 Oct 70	**JULIE DO YA LOVE ME** *CBS 5144*	**28**	4

SHERRICK US, male vocalist (10 WEEKS) pos/wks
1 Aug 87	**JUST CALL** *Warner Bros. W 8380*	**23**	8
21 Nov 87	**LET'S BE LOVERS TONIGHT** *Warner Bros. W 8146*	**63**	2

Pluto SHERVINGTON Jamaica, male vocalist (20 WEEKS) pos/wks
7 Feb 76 ●	**DAT** *Opal Pal 5*	**6**	8
10 Apr 76	**RAM GOAT LIVER** *Trojan TR 7978*	**43**	4
6 Mar 82	**YOUR HONOUR** *KR KR 4* [1]	**19**	8

[1] Pluto

Holly SHERWOOD US, female vocalist (7 WEEKS) pos/wks
5 Feb 72	**DAY BY DAY** *Bell 1182*	**29**	7

Tony SHEVETON UK, male vocalist (1 WEEK) pos/wks
13 Feb 64	**MILLION DRUMS** *Oriole CB 1895*	**49**	1

SHIMMON & WOOLFSON UK, male DJ / production duo (1 WEEK) pos/wks
10 Jan 98	**WELCOME TO THE FUTURE** *React CDREACT 119*	**69**	1

SHINEHEAD Jamaica, male vocalist (6 WEEKS) pos/wks
3 Apr 93	**JAMAICAN IN NEW YORK** *Elektra EKR 161CD*	**30**	5
26 Jun 93	**LET 'EM IN** *Elektra EKR 168CD*	**70**	1

SHIRELLES US, female vocal group (29 WEEKS) pos/wks
9 Feb 61 ●	**WILL YOU LOVE ME TOMORROW** *Top Rank JAR 540* ▲	**4**	15
31 May 62	**SOLDIER BOY** *HMV POP 1019* ▲	**23**	9
23 May 63	**FOOLISH LITTLE GIRL** *Stateside SS 181*	**38**	5

SHIRLEY and COMPANY US, female vocalist and male vocal / instrumental backing group (9 WEEKS) pos/wks
8 Feb 75 ●	**SHAME SHAME SHAME** *All Platinum 6146 301*	**6**	9

SHIVA UK, male / female vocal / instrumental group (5 WEEKS) pos/wks
13 May 95	**WORK IT OUT** *ffrr FCD 261*	**36**	2
19 Aug 95	**FREEDOM** *ffrr FCD 263*	**18**	3

SHO NUFF US, male vocal / instrumental group (4 WEEKS) pos/wks
24 May 80	**IT'S ALRIGHT** *Ensign ENY 37*	**53**	4

Michelle SHOCKED US, female vocalist (10 WEEKS) pos/wks
8 Oct 88	**ANCHORAGE** *Cooking Vinyl LON 193*	**60**	4
14 Jan 89	**IF LOVE WAS A TRAIN** *Cooking Vinyl LON 212*	**63**	3
11 Mar 89	**WHEN I GROW UP** *Cooking Vinyl LON 219*	**67**	3

SHOCKING BLUE
Holland, male / female vocal / instrumental group (14 WEEKS) pos/wks
17 Jan 70 ●	**VENUS** *Penny Farthing PEN 702* ▲	**8**	11
25 Apr 70	**MIGHTY JOE** *Penny Farthing PEN 713*	**43**	3

Troy SHONDELL US, male vocalist (11 WEEKS) pos/wks
2 Nov 61	**THIS TIME** *London HLG 9432*	**22**	11

SHONDELLS – See Tommy JAMES and the SHONDELLS

SHOOTING PARTY UK, male vocal duo (2 WEEKS) pos/wks
31 Mar 90	**LET'S HANG ON** *Lisson DOLE 15*	**66**	2

SHOWADDYWADDY (79 Top 500) Rock 'n' roll revival octet from Leicester, UK, which included vocalists Dave Bartram and Buddy Gask. At the peak of their career, they had seven successive Top 5 entries with rousing revivals of old US rock 'n' roll songs (209 WEEKS) pos/wks
18 May 74 ●	**HEY ROCK AND ROLL** *Bell 1357*	**2**	14
17 Aug 74	**ROCK 'N' ROLL LADY** *Bell 1374*	**15**	9
30 Nov 74	**HEY MR CHRISTMAS** *Bell 1387*	**13**	8
22 Feb 75	**SWEET MUSIC** *Bell 1403*	**14**	9
17 May 75 ●	**THREE STEPS TO HEAVEN** *Bell 1426*	**2**	11
6 Sep 75 ●	**HEARTBEAT** *Bell 1450*	**7**	7
15 Nov 75	**HEAVENLY** *Bell 1460*	**34**	6
29 May 76	**TROCADERO** *Bell 1476*	**32**	3
6 Nov 76 ★	**UNDER THE MOON OF LOVE** *Bell 1495*	**1**	15
5 Mar 77 ●	**WHEN** *Arista 91*	**3**	11
23 Jul 77 ●	**YOU GOT WHAT IT TAKES** *Arista 126*	**2**	10
5 Nov 77 ●	**DANCIN' PARTY** *Arista 149*	**4**	11
25 Mar 78 ●	**I WONDER WHY** *Arista 174*	**2**	11
24 Jun 78 ●	**A LITTLE BIT OF SOAP** *Arista 191*	**5**	12
4 Nov 78 ●	**PRETTY LITTLE ANGEL EYES** *Arista ARIST 222*	**5**	12
31 Mar 79	**REMEMBER THEN** *Arista 247*	**17**	8
28 Jul 79	**SWEET LITTLE ROCK 'N' ROLLER** *Arista 278*	**15**	9
10 Nov 79	**A NIGHT AT DADDY GEE'S** *Arista 314*	**39**	5
27 Sep 80	**WHY DO LOVERS BREAK EACH OTHER'S HEARTS** *Arista ARIST 359*	**22**	10
29 Nov 80	**BLUE MOON** *Arista ARIST 379*	**32**	9
13 Jun 81	**MULTIPLICATION** *Arista ARIST 416*	**39**	4
28 Nov 81	**FOOTSTEPS** *Bell BELL 1499*	**31**	9
28 Aug 82	**WHO PUT THE BOMP (IN THE BOMP-A-BOMP-A-BOMP)** *RCA 236*	**37**	6

SHOWDOWN – See Garry LEE and SHOWDOWN

SHOWDOWN US, male vocal / instrumental group (3 WEEKS) pos/wks
17 Dec 77	**KEEP DOIN' IT** *State STAT 63*	**41**	3

SHOWSTOPPERS US, male vocal group (25 WEEKS) pos/wks
13 Mar 68	**AIN'T NOTHING BUT A HOUSEPARTY** *Beacon 3-100*	**11**	15
13 Nov 68	**EENY MEENY** *MGM 1436*	**33**	7
30 Jan 71	**AIN'T NOTHING BUT A HOUSEPARTY (re-issue)** *Beacon BEA 100*	**43**	1
13 Feb 71	**AIN'T NOTHING BUT A HOUSEPARTY (re-entry of re-issue)** *Beacon BEA 100*	**33**	1
27 Feb 71	**AIN'T NOTHING BUT A HOUSEPARTY (2nd re-entry of re-issue)** *Beacon BEA 100*	**36**	1

SHRIEKBACK UK, male vocal / instrumental group (4 WEEKS) pos/wks
28 Jul 84	**HAND ON MY HEART** *Arista SHRK 1*	**52**	4

SINGLED OUT...Johnnie Walker

ALL-TIME FAVOURITE SINGLE:

Will You Love Me Tomorrow
The Shirelles

I could go for any of those American 50s / 60s special date, romance records and I love strings on a pop record

It has been a long and winding road for Johnnie Walker from the pirate days of Radio Caroline to his current slot on one of the most popular shows on British radio. His drive-time BBC Radio 2 mix of music and interviews maintains Johnnie Walker's position as a DJ who has adapted to and thrived on the changes in five decades of broadcasting.

•FIRST SINGLE I EVER BOUGHT:
Rip It Up – Little Richard

It was a replacement for one of my older brother Frank's 78s.

•SINGLE THAT DRIVES ME UP THE WALL:
Sunrise, Sunset – Don Arden

Dirgiest and most depressing record I've ever heard. I was forced to play it during the "six plays for £100 days" on Caroline.

SHRINK Holland, male DJ / production trio (4 WEEKS)

		pos/wks
10 Oct 98	NERVOUS BREAKDOWN VC Recordings VCRD42 42	2
19 Aug 00	ARE YOU READY TO PARTY Nulife 74321783772 39	2

SHUT UP AND DANCE
UK, male vocal / production group (14 WEEKS)

		pos/wks
21 Apr 90	£20 TO GET IN Shut Up And Dance SUAD 3 56	3
28 Jul 90	LAMBORGHINI Shut Up And Dance SUAD 4 55	2
8 Feb 92	AUTOBIOGRAPHY OF A CRACKHEAD / THE GREEN MAN Shut Up And Dance SUAD 21 43	2
30 May 92 ●	RAVING I'M RAVING Shut Up And Dance SUAD 30S [1] 2	2
15 Aug 92	THE ART OF MOVING BUTTS Shut Up And Dance SUAD 34S [2] 69	1
1 Apr 95	SAVE IT 'TIL THE MOURNING AFTER Pulse 8 PULS 84CD 25	3
8 Jul 95	I LUV U Pulse 8 PULS 90CD [3] 68	1

[1] Shut Up and Dance featuring Peter Bouncer [2] Shut Up and Dance featuring Erin [3] Shut Up and Dance featuring Richie Davis and Professor T

SHY UK, male vocal / instrumental group (3 WEEKS)

		pos/wks
19 Apr 80	GIRL (IT'S ALL I HAVE) Gallery GA 1 60	3

SHY FX
UK, male instrumentalist / producer Andre Williams (4 WEEKS)

		pos/wks
1 Oct 94	ORIGINAL NUTTAH Sound of Underground SOUR 008CD [1] .39	3
20 Mar 99	BAMBAATA 2012 Ebony EBR 020CD 60	1

[1] UK Apachi with Shy FX

SHYHEIM US, male rapper (1 WEEK)

		pos/wks
8 Jun 96	THIS IZ REAL Noo Trybe VUSCD 105 61	1

SIA Australia, female vocalist - Sia Furler (5 WEEKS)

		pos/wks
3 Jun 00 ●	TAKEN FOR GRANTED Long Lost Brother S 002CD1 10	5

Labi SIFFRE UK, male vocalist (44 WEEKS)

		pos/wks
27 Nov 71	IT MUST BE LOVE Pye International 7N 25572 14	12
25 Mar 72	CRYING LAUGHING LOVING LYING Pye International 7N 25576 .11	9
29 Jul 72	WATCH ME Pye International 7N 25586 29	6
4 Apr 87 ●	(SOMETHING INSIDE) SO STRONG China WOK 12 4	13
21 Nov 87	NOTHIN'S GONNA CHANGE China WOK 16 52	4

SIGNUM Holland, male production duo (2 WEEKS)

		pos/wks
28 Nov 98	WHAT YA GOT 4 ME Tidy Trax TIDY 118CD 70	1
31 Jul 99	COMING ON STRONG Tidy Trax TIDY 128T [1] 66	1

[1] Signum featuring Scott Mac

SIGUE SIGUE SPUTNIK
UK, male vocal / instrumental group (20 WEEKS)

		pos/wks
1 Mar 86 ●	LOVE MISSILE F1-11 Parlophone SSS 1 3	9
7 Jun 86	TWENTY-FIRST CENTURY BOY Parlophone SSS 2 20	5
19 Nov 88	SUCCESS Parlophone SSS 3 31	3
1 Apr 89	DANCERAMA Parlophone SSS 5 50	2
20 May 89	ALBINONI VS STAR WARS Parlophone SSS 4 75	1

SIL Holland, male DJ / production duo (1 WEEK)

		pos/wks
11 Apr 98	WINDOWS '98 Hooj Choons HOOJCD 60 58	1

SILENCERS UK, male vocal / instrumental group (7 WEEKS)

		pos/wks
25 Jun 88	PAINTED MOON RCA HUSH 1 57	4
27 May 89	SCOTTISH RAIN RCA PB 42701 71	2
15 May 93	I CAN FEEL IT RCA 74321147112 62	1

SILENT UNDERDOG
UK, male instrumentalist - Paul Hardcastle (1 WEEK)

		pos/wks
16 Feb 85	PAPA'S GOT A BRAND NEW PIGBAG Kaz KAZ 50 73	1

See also Paul HARDCASTLE

SILJE Norway, female vocalist (6 WEEKS)

		pos/wks
15 Dec 90	TELL ME WHERE YOU'RE GOING EMI EM 159 55	6

SILK US, male vocal group (10 WEEKS)

		pos/wks
24 Apr 93	FREAK ME Elektra EKR 165CD ▲ 46	5
5 Jun 93	GIRL U FOR ME Elektra EKR 167CD 67	2
9 Oct 93	BABY IT'S YOU Elektra EKR 173CD 44	2
26 Feb 94	FREAK ME (re-entry) Elektra EKR 165CD 72	1

SILKIE UK, male / female vocal / instrumental group (6 WEEKS)

		pos/wks
23 Sep 65	YOU'VE GOT TO HIDE YOUR LOVE AWAY Fontana TF 603 28	6

SILKK THE SHOCKER – See Montell JORDAN

SILSOE UK, male instrumentalist - keyboards (4 WEEKS)

		pos/wks
21 Jun 86	AZTEC GOLD CBS A 7231 48	4

'Aztec Gold' was the ITV theme to the 1986 World Cup Finals and was performed by Rod Argent under the name Silsoe

See also SAN JOSE featuring Rodriguez ARGENTINA; ARGENT

Luci SILVAS UK, female vocalist (1 WEEK)

		pos/wks
17 Jun 00	IT'S TOO LATE EMI CDEM 565 62	1

SILVER BULLET UK, male rap / instrumental duo (20 WEEKS)

		pos/wks
2 Sep 89	BRING FORTH THE GUILLOTINE Tam Tam TTT 013 70	1
9 Dec 89	20 SECONDS TO COMPLY Tam Tam 7TTT 019 11	10
3 Mar 90	BRING FORTH THE GUILLOTINE (re-entry) Tam Tam TTT 013 45	5
13 Apr 91	UNDERCOVER ANARCHIST Parlophone R 6284 33	4

SILVER BULLET BAND – See Bob SEGER and the SILVER BULLET BAND

SILVER CITY UK, male / female / instrumental duo (1 WEEK)

		pos/wks
30 Oct 93	LOVE INFINITY Silver City GFJMCD 1 62	1

SILVER CONVENTION
Germany / US, female vocal group (35 WEEKS)

		pos/wks
5 Apr 75	SAVE ME Magnet MAG 26 30	7
15 Nov 75	FLY ROBIN FLY Magnet MAG 43 ▲ 28	8
3 Apr 76 ●	GET UP AND BOOGIE Magnet MAG 55 7	11
19 Jun 76	TIGER BABY / NO NO JOE Magnet MAG 69 41	4
29 Jan 77	EVERYBODY'S TALKIN' 'BOUT LOVE Magnet MAG 81 25	5

SILVER SUN UK, male vocal / instrumental group (13 WEEKS)

		pos/wks
2 Nov 96	LAVA Polydor 5756872 54	1
22 Feb 97	LAST DAY Polydor 5732432 48	1
3 May 97	GOLDEN SKIN Polydor 5738272 32	2
5 Jul 97	JULIA Polydor 5711752 51	1
18 Oct 97	LAVA (re-issue) Polydor 5714242 35	2
20 Jun 98	TOO MUCH, TOO LITTLE, TOO LATE Polydor 5699152 20	4
26 Sep 98	I'LL SEE YOU AROUND Polydor 5674532 26	2

SILVERCHAIR Australia, male vocal / instrumental group (8 WEEKS)

		pos/wks
29 Jul 95	PURE MASSACRE Murmur 6622642 71	1
9 Sep 95	TOMORROW Murmur 6623952 59	2
5 Apr 97	FREAK Murmur 6640765 34	2
19 Jul 97	ABUSE ME Murmur 6647907 40	2
15 May 99	ANA'S SONG Columbia 6673452 45	1

Dooley SILVERSPOON US, male vocalist (3 WEEKS)

		pos/wks
31 Jan 76	LET ME BE THE NUMBER 1 (LOVE OF YOUR LIFE) Seville SEV 1020 44	3

Harry SIMEONE CHORALE US, choir (14 WEEKS)

		pos/wks
13 Feb 59	LITTLE DRUMMER BOY Top Rank JAR 101 13	7
22 Dec 60	ONWARD CHRISTIAN SOLDIERS Ember EMBS 118 35	1

UK No.1 ★   UK Top 10 ●   Still on chart +   UK million seller ◆   UK entry at No.1 ■   US No.1 ▲

			pos/wks
5 Jan 61	**ONWARD CHRISTIAN SOLDIERS** (re-entry)		
	Ember EMBS 118	**38**	1
21 Dec 61	**ONWARD CHRISTIAN SOLDIERS** (2nd re-entry)		
	Ember EMBS 118	**36**	3
20 Dec 62	**ONWARD CHRISTIAN SOLDIERS** (re-issue)		
	Ember EMBS 144	**38**	2

Gene SIMMONS *US, male vocalist (4 WEEKS)*   pos/wks

27 Jan 79	**RADIOACTIVE** *Casablanca CAN 134*	**41**	4

See also KISS

Carly SIMON (443) **Top 500** *First charted in US in 1964 as half of folk duo Simon Sisters with sister Lucy, b. 25 Jun 1945, New York. Winner of 1972's Best New Artist Grammy was married to fellow singer / songwriter James Taylor (1973-1982). Elected to Songwriters Hall of Fame 1994 (76 WEEKS)*   pos/wks

16 Dec 72	● **YOU'RE SO VAIN** *Elektra K 12077* ▲ 3		15
31 Mar 73	**THE RIGHT THING TO DO** *Elektra K 12095*	**17**	9
16 Mar 74	**MOCKINGBIRD** *Elektra K 12134* [1]	**34**	5
6 Aug 77	● **NOBODY DOES IT BETTER** *Elektra K 12261*	**7**	12
21 Aug 82	● **WHY** *WEA K 79300*	**10**	13
24 Jan 87	● **COMING AROUND AGAIN** *Arista ARIST 687*	**10**	12
10 Jun 89	**WHY** (re-issue) *WEA U 7501*	**56**	5
20 Apr 91	**YOU'RE SO VAIN** (re-issue) *Elektra EKR 123*	**41**	5

[1] Carly Simon and James Taylor

See also Will POWERS

Joe SIMON *US, male vocalist (10 WEEKS)*   pos/wks

16 Jun 73	**STEP BY STEP** *Mojo 2093 030*	**14**	10

Paul SIMON (375) **Top 500** *Acclaimed award-winning singer / songwriter b. 13 Oct 1941, New Jersey, US. Recorded under various names in early 1960s before forming top duo Simon and Garfunkel. Married to actress Carrie Fisher (1980-83) and later Edie Brickell, he helped popularise world music (85 WEEKS)*   pos/wks

19 Feb 72	● **MOTHER AND CHILD REUNION** *CBS 7793*	**5**	12
29 Apr 72	**ME AND JULIO DOWN BY THE SCHOOLYARD** *CBS 7964*	**15**	9
16 Jun 73	● **TAKE ME TO THE MARDI GRAS** *CBS 1578*	**7**	11
22 Sep 73	**LOVES ME LIKE A ROCK** *CBS 1700*	**39**	5
10 Jan 76	**50 WAYS TO LEAVE YOUR LOVER** *CBS 3887* ▲	**23**	6
3 Dec 77	**SLIP SLIDIN' AWAY** *CBS 5770*	**36**	5
6 Sep 80	**LATE IN THE EVENING** *Warner Bros. K 17666*	**58**	4
13 Sep 86	● **YOU CAN CALL ME AL** *Warner Bros. W 8667*	**4**	13
13 Dec 86	**THE BOY IN THE BUBBLE** *Warner Bros. W 8509*	**26**	8
6 Oct 90	**THE OBVIOUS CHILD** *Warner Bros. W 9549*	**15**	10
9 Dec 95	**SOMETHING SO RIGHT** *RCA 74321332392* [1]	**44**	2

[1] Annie Lennox featuring Paul Simon

See also SIMON and GARFUNKEL

Ronni SIMON *UK, male vocalist (2 WEEKS)*   pos/wks

13 Aug 94	**B GOOD 2 ME** *Network NWKCD 80*	**73**	1
10 Jun 95	**TAKE YOU THERE** *Network NWKCD 85*	**58**	1

Tito SIMON *Jamaica, male vocalist (4 WEEKS)*   pos/wks

8 Feb 75	**THIS MONDAY MORNING FEELING** *Horse HOSS 57*	**45**	4

SIMON and GARFUNKEL (359) **Top 500** *Ultra successful, folk-rooted duo, Paul Simon and Art Garfunkel, who first charted in US as Tom and Jerry in 1957. Their 'Bridge Over Troubled Water' single and album (Top UK LP of both 1970 and 1971!) regarded as among all-time greatest recordings. In 1968 had three of US Top 5 albums (87 WEEKS)*   pos/wks

24 Mar 66	● **HOMEWARD BOUND** *CBS 202045*	**9**	12
16 Jun 66	**I AM A ROCK** *CBS 202303*	**17**	10
10 Jul 68	● **MRS ROBINSON** *CBS 3443* ▲	**4**	12
8 Jan 69	● **MRS ROBINSON** (EP) *CBS EP 6400*	**9**	5
30 Apr 69	● **THE BOXER** *CBS 4162*	**6**	14
21 Feb 70	★ **BRIDGE OVER TROUBLED WATER** *CBS 4790* ▲	**1**	19
15 Aug 70	**BRIDGE OVER TROUBLED WATER** (re-entry) *CBS 4790*	**45**	1

7 Oct 72	**AMERICA** *CBS 8336*	**25**	7
7 Dec 91	**A HAZY SHADE OF WINTER / SILENT NIGHT - SEVEN**		
	O'CLOCK NEWS *Columbia 6576537*	**30**	6
15 Feb 92	**THE BOXER** (re-issue) *Columbia 6578067*	**75**	1

Tracks on Mrs Robinson (EP): Mrs Robinson / Scarborough Fair - Canticle / Sounds of Silence / April Come She Will. This EP would have stayed more than five weeks on chart had a decision to exclude EPs from chart in Feb 1969 not been taken

See also Paul SIMON; Art GARFUNKEL

SIMONE *US, female vocalist (1 WEEK)*   pos/wks

23 Nov 91	**MY FAMILY DEPENDS ON ME** *Strictly Rhythm A 8678*	**75**	1

Nina SIMONE *US, female vocalist - Eunice Waymon (46 WEEKS)*   pos/wks

5 Aug 65	**I PUT A SPELL ON YOU** *Philips BF 1415*	**49**	1
16 Oct 68	● **AIN'T GOT NO - I GOT LIFE / DO WHAT YOU GOTTA DO**		
	RCA 1743	**2**	18
15 Jan 69	**I PUT A SPELL ON YOU** (re-issue) *Philips BF 1736*	**28**	4
15 Jan 69	● **TO LOVE SOMEBODY** *RCA 1779*	**5**	9
31 Oct 87	● **MY BABY JUST CARES FOR ME** *Charly CYZ 7112*	**5**	11
9 Jul 94	**FEELING GOOD** *Mercury MERCD 403*	**40**	3

'Do What You Gotta Do' was listed only for the first eight weeks of the record's chart run. It peaked at No.7

Victor SIMONELLI presents SOLUTION
US, male producer (1 WEEK)   pos/wks

2 Nov 96	**FEELS SO RIGHT** *Soundproof MCSTD 40068*	**63**	1

SIMPLE MINDS (100) **Top 500** *Most successful Scottish band of the 1980s, fronted by Jim Kerr (b. 9 Jul 1959, Glasgow), who married Chrissie Hynde, lead singer of Pretenders. Five of the quintet's albums entered UK chart at No.1, and world sales topped 30 million (187 WEEKS)*   pos/wks

12 May 79	**LIFE IN A DAY** *Zoom ZUM 10*	**62**	2
23 May 81	**THE AMERICAN** *Virgin VS 410*	**59**	3
15 Aug 81	**LOVE SONG** *Virgin VS 434*	**47**	4
7 Nov 81	**SWEAT IN BULLET** *Virgin VS 451*	**52**	3
10 Apr 82	**PROMISED YOU A MIRACLE** *Virgin VS 488*	**13**	11
28 Aug 82	**GLITTERING PRIZE** *Virgin VS 511*	**16**	11
13 Nov 82	**SOMEONE SOMEWHERE (IN SUMMERTIME)** *Virgin VS 538*	**36**	5
26 Nov 83	**WATERFRONT** *Virgin VS 636*	**13**	10
28 Jan 84	**SPEED YOUR LOVE TO ME** *Virgin VS 649*	**20**	4
24 Mar 84	**UP ON THE CATWALK** *Virgin VS 661*	**27**	5
20 Apr 85	● **DON'T YOU (FORGET ABOUT ME)** *Virgin VS 749* ▲	**7**	11
17 Aug 85	**DON'T YOU (FORGET ABOUT ME)** (re-entry)		
	Virgin VS 749	**61**	8
12 Oct 85	● **ALIVE AND KICKING** *Virgin VS 817*	**7**	9
28 Dec 85	**DON'T YOU (FORGET ABOUT ME)** (2nd re-entry)		
	Virgin VS 749	**74**	1
4 Jan 86	**ALIVE AND KICKING** (re-entry) *Virgin VS 817*	**60**	2
1 Feb 86	● **SANCTIFY YOURSELF** *Virgin SM 1*	**10**	7
15 Feb 86	**DON'T YOU (FORGET ABOUT ME)** (3rd re-entry)		
	Virgin VS 749	**62**	3
15 Mar 86	**DON'T YOU (FORGET ABOUT ME)** (4th re-entry)		
	Virgin VS 749	**68**	1
12 Apr 86	● **ALL THE THINGS SHE SAID** *Virgin VS 860*	**9**	8
14 Jun 86	**ALL THE THINGS SHE SAID** (re-entry) *Virgin VS 860*	**73**	1
15 Nov 86	**GHOSTDANCING** *Virgin VS 907*	**13**	6
3 Jan 87	**GHOSTDANCING** (re-entry) *Virgin VS 907*	**68**	2
20 Jun 87	**PROMISED YOU A MIRACLE** *Virgin SM 2*	**19**	7
18 Feb 89	★ **BELFAST CHILD** *Virgin SMX 3*	**1**	11
22 Apr 89	**THIS IS YOUR LAND** *Virgin SMX4*	**13**	4
29 Jul 89	**KICK IT IN** *Virgin SM 5*	**15**	5
9 Dec 89	**THE AMSTERDAM EP** *Virgin SMX 6*	**18**	6
23 Mar 91	● **LET THERE BE LOVE** *Virgin VS 1332*	**6**	7
25 May 91	**SEE THE LIGHTS** *Virgin VS 1343*	**20**	4
31 Aug 91	**STAND BY LOVE** *Virgin VS 1358*	**13**	4
26 Oct 91	**REAL LIFE** *Virgin VS 1382*	**34**	3
10 Oct 92	● **LOVE SONG / ALIVE AND KICKING** (re-issue)		
	Virgin VS 1440	**6**	6
28 Jan 95	● **SHE'S A RIVER** *Virgin VSCDX 1509*	**9**	5
8 Apr 95	**HYPNOTISED** *Virgin VSCDX 1534*	**18**	5

| 14 Mar 98 | GLITTERBALL *Chrysalis CDCHSS 5078* | 18 | 2 |
| 30 May 98 | WAR BABIES *Chrysalis CDCHS 5088* | 43 | 1 |

The 1987 version of 'Promised You a Miracle' was a live recording. Tracks on The Amsterdam EP: Let It All Come Down / Jerusalem / Sign of the Times

SIMPLICIOUS *US, male vocal group (9 WEEKS)*

		pos/wks
29 Sep 84	LET HER FEEL IT *Fourth & Broadway BRW 13*	65	3
2 Feb 85	LET HER FEEL IT (re-issue) *Fourth & Broadway BRW 18*	34	6

The re-issue of 'Let Her Feel It' was listed with 'Personality' by Eugene Wilde

SIMPLY RED   `72`   **Top 500**

The unmistakable Mick Hucknall (b. 8 Jun 1960, Manchester, UK) quickly became the representative face and voice of this internationally popular outfit. Their Stars album sold more than two million in the UK and was the biggest British seller in 1991 and 1992 (214 WEEKS) pos/wks

15 Jun 85	MONEY'S TOO TIGHT (TO MENTION) *Elektra EKR 9*	13	12
21 Sep 85	COME TO MY AID *Elektra EKR 19*	66	2
16 Nov 85	HOLDING BACK THE YEARS *Elektra EKR 29* ▲	51	4
8 Mar 86	JERICHO *Elektra YZ 63*	53	3
17 May 86 ●	HOLDING BACK THE YEARS (re-issue) *WEA YZ 70*	2	13
9 Aug 86	OPEN UP THE RED BOX *WEA YZ 75*	61	4
14 Feb 87	THE RIGHT THING *WEA YZ 103*	11	10
23 May 87	INFIDELITY *Elektra YZ 114*	31	5
28 Nov 87	EV'RY TIME WE SAY GOODBYE *Elektra YZ 161*	11	9
12 Mar 88	I WON'T FEEL BAD *Elektra YZ 172*	68	3
28 Jan 89	IT'S ONLY LOVE *Elektra YZ 349*	13	8
8 Apr 89 ●	IF YOU DON'T KNOW ME BY NOW *Elektra YZ 377* ▲	2	10
8 Jul 89	A NEW FLAME *WEA YZ 404*	17	8
28 Oct 89	YOU'VE GOT IT *Elektra YZ 424*	46	3
21 Sep 91	SOMETHING GOT ME STARTED *East West YZ 614*	11	8
30 Nov 91 ●	STARS *East West YZ 626*	8	10
8 Feb 92 ●	FOR YOUR BABIES *East West YZ 642*	9	8
2 May 92	THRILL ME *East West YZ 671*	33	5
25 Jul 92	YOUR MIRROR *East West YZ 689*	17	4
21 Nov 92	MONTREUX (EP) *East West YZ 716*	11	10
30 Sep 95 ★	FAIRGROUND *East West EW 001CD1* ■	1	14
16 Dec 95	REMEMBERING THE FIRST TIME *East West EW 015CD1*	22	6
24 Feb 96	NEVER NEVER LOVE *East West EW 029CD1*	18	4
22 Jun 96	WE'RE IN THIS TOGETHER *East West EW 046CD1*	11	4
9 Nov 96 ●	ANGEL *East West EW 074CD1*	4	13
20 Sep 97	NIGHT NURSE *East West EW 129CD1* [1]	13	8
16 May 98 ●	SAY YOU LOVE ME *East West EW 164CD*	7	7
22 Aug 98 ●	THE AIR THAT I BREATHE *East West EW 3821CD*	6	7
12 Dec 98	GHETTO GIRL *East West EW 191CD1*	34	2
30 Oct 99	AIN'T THAT A LOT OF LOVE *East West EW 208CD1*	14	6
19 Feb 00	YOUR EYES *East West EW 212CD1*	26	2

[1] Sly and Robbie featuring Simply Red

Tracks on Montreux (EP): Drowning In My Own Tears / Grandma's Hands / Lady Godiva's Room / Love for Sale

SIMPLY RED AND WHITE
UK, male Sunderland FC supporters vocal group (4 WEEKS) pos/wks

6 Apr 96	DAYDREAM BELIEVER (CHEER UP PETER REID) *Ropery SHAYISGOD 1D*	41	3
4 May 96	DAYDREAM BELIEVER (CHEER UP PETER REID) (re-entry) *Ropery SHAYISGOD 1D*	74	1

SIMPLY SMOOTH *US, male / female vocal group (1 WEEK)* pos/wks

| 17 Oct 98 | LADY (YOU BRING ME UP) *Big Bang CDBANG 07* | 70 | 1 |

Jessica SIMPSON *US, female vocalist (18 WEEKS)* pos/wks

22 Apr 00 ●	I WANNA LOVE YOU FOREVER *Columbia 6691272*	7	9
8 Jul 00	I WANNA LOVE YOU FOREVER (re-entry) *Columbia 6691272*	68	2
15 Jul 00	I THINK I'M IN LOVE WITH YOU *Columbia 6695942*	15	7

Paul SIMPSON featuring ADEVA
US, producer / instrumentalist (8 WEEKS) pos/wks

| 25 Mar 89 | MUSICAL FREEDOM (MOVING ON UP) *Cooltempo CDCOOL 182* | 22 | 8 |

Vida SIMPSON *US, female vocalist (1 WEEK)* pos/wks

| 18 Feb 95 | OOHHH BABY *Hi-Life HICD 6* | 70 | 1 |

SIMPSONS *US, male / female cartoon group - lead vocals Bart Simpson (Nancy Cartwright) (19 WEEKS)* pos/wks

26 Jan 91 ★	DO THE BARTMAN *Geffen GEF 87*	1	12
6 Apr 91 ●	DEEP DEEP TROUBLE *Geffen GEF 88* [1]	7	7

[1] Simpsons featuring Bart and Homer

W/Cdr AE SIMS – See The Central Band of the ROYAL AIR FORCE, Conductor W/Cdr AE SIMS OBE

Joyce SIMS *US, female vocalist (36 WEEKS)* pos/wks

19 Apr 86	ALL AND ALL *London LON 94*	16	10
13 Jun 87	LIFETIME LOVE *London LON 137*	34	6
9 Jan 88 ●	COME INTO MY LIFE *London LON 161*	7	9
23 Apr 88	WALK AWAY *London LON 176*	24	6
17 Jun 89	LOOKING FOR A LOVE *ffrr F 109*	39	4
27 May 95	COME INTO MY LIFE (re-mix) *Club Tools 0060435 CLU*	72	1

Kym SIMS *US, female vocalist (23 WEEKS)* pos/wks

7 Dec 91 ●	TOO BLIND TO SEE IT *Atco B 8667*	5	12
28 Mar 92	TAKE MY ADVICE *Atco B 8591*	13	7
27 Jun 92	A LITTLE BIT MORE *Atco B 8528*	30	3
8 Jun 96	WE GOTTA LOVE *Pulse 8 CDLOSE 104*	58	1

SIN WITH SEBASTIAN
Germany, male vocalist - Sebastian Roth (2 WEEKS) pos/wks

16 Sep 95	SHUT UP (AND SLEEP WITH ME) *Sing Sing 74321253592*	44	1
27 Jan 96	SHUT UP (AND SLEEP WITH ME) (re-mix) *Sing Sing 74321337972*	46	1

Frank SINATRA   `11`   **Top 500**

Legendary entertainer regarded by many as the greatest song stylist of the 20th century, b. 12 Dec 1915, New Jersey, US, d. 14 May 1998. He started out as a member of the Hoboken Four in 1935, and four years later joined the Harry James Band. In 1940, he was the vocalist with the Tommy Dorsey Orchestra and sang on 'I'll Never Smile Again' (1940), the No.1 single on the first ever US chart. Sinatra went solo in 1942 and was an instant success. He was often mobbed by young fans and became the first teen idol. 'Songs For Swingin Lovers' is the only album to reach the UK Top 20 singles chart. It is also one of 26 US gold albums amassed by the influential vocalist who has scored more US Top 10 LPs than any other solo artist. Sinatra, who has won countless awards and polls, was one of the first recipients of a Lifetime Achievement Grammy (1965). My Way (released on Reprise - the label he formed in 1961) holds the longevity record in the UK and no other performer has topped the chart with one of their offspring as he did with daughter Nancy. This timeless legend was still adding to his Top 10 albums in the 1990s and, in the US alone, sold more than 1.5 million albums in the five days after his death (440 WEEKS) pos/wks

9 Jul 54	YOUNG AT HEART *Capitol CL 14064*	12	1
16 Jul 54 ★	THREE COINS IN THE FOUNTAIN *Capitol CL 14120*	1	19
10 Jun 55	YOU MY LOVE *Capitol CL 14240*	13	3
22 Jul 55	YOU MY LOVE (re-entry) *Capitol CL 14240*	17	2
5 Aug 55 ●	LEARNIN' THE BLUES *Capitol CL 14296*	2	13
12 Aug 55	YOU MY LOVE (2nd re-entry) *Capitol CL 14240*	17	2
2 Sep 55	NOT AS A STRANGER *Capitol CL 14326*	18	1
13 Jan 56 ●	LOVE AND MARRIAGE *Capitol CL 14503*	3	8
20 Jan 56 ●	(LOVE IS) THE TENDER TRAP *Capitol CL 14511*	2	9
15 Jun 56	SONGS FOR SWINGING LOVERS (LP) *Capitol LCT 6106*	12	8
22 Nov 57	ALL THE WAY *Capitol CL 14800 (A)*	29	1
29 Nov 57	CHICAGO *Capitol CL 14800 (B)*	25	1
6 Dec 57	ALL THE WAY / CHICAGO (re-entry) *Capitol CL 14800*	21	1
13 Dec 57 ●	ALL THE WAY (2nd re-entry) *Capitol CL 14800*	3	17
7 Feb 58	WITCHCRAFT *Capitol CL 14819*	12	8
14 Nov 58	MR SUCCESS *Capitol CL 14956*	29	1
12 Dec 58	MR SUCCESS (re-entry) *Capitol CL 14956*	25	2
2 Jan 59	MR SUCCESS (2nd re-entry) *Capitol CL 14956*	26	1
10 Apr 59	FRENCH FOREIGN LEGION *Capitol CL 14997*	18	5

15 May 59	COME DANCE WITH ME (LP) *Capitol LCT 6179* [1]	30	1
28 Aug 59	HIGH HOPES *Capitol CL 15052*	28	1
11 Sep 59 ●	HIGH HOPES (re-entry) *Capitol CL 15052*	6	13
10 Mar 60	HIGH HOPES (2nd re-entry) *Capitol CL 15052*	42	1
7 Apr 60	IT'S NICE TO GO TRAV'LING *Capitol CL 15116*	48	1
16 Jun 60	RIVER STAY 'WAY FROM MY DOOR *Capitol CL 15135*	18	9
8 Sep 60	NICE 'N' EASY *Capitol CL 15150*	15	12
24 Nov 60	OL' MACDONALD *Capitol CL 15168*	11	8
20 Apr 61	MY BLUE HEAVEN *Capitol CL 15193*	33	7
28 Sep 61	GRANADA *Reprise R 20010*	15	8
23 Nov 61	THE COFFEE SONG *Reprise R 20035*	39	3
5 Apr 62	EVERYBODY'S TWISTING *Reprise R 20063*	22	12
13 Dec 62	ME AND MY SHADOW *Reprise R 20128* [2]	20	7
7 Feb 63	ME AND MY SHADOW (re-entry) *Reprise R 20128* [2]	47	2
7 Mar 63	MY KIND OF GIRL *Reprise R 20148* [3]	35	6
24 Sep 64	HELLO DOLLY *Reprise R 20351* [3]	47	1
12 May 66 ★	STRANGERS IN THE NIGHT *Reprise R 23052* ▲	1	20
29 Sep 66	SUMMER WIND *Reprise RS 20509*	36	5
15 Dec 66	THAT'S LIFE *Reprise RS 20531*	46	5
23 Mar 67 ★	SOMETHIN' STUPID *Reprise RS 23166* [4] ▲	1	18
23 Aug 67	THE WORLD WE KNEW (OVER AND OVER)		
	Reprise RS 20610	33	11
2 Apr 69 ●	MY WAY *Reprise RS 20817*	5	42
4 Oct 69 ●	LOVE'S BEEN GOOD TO ME *Reprise RS 20852*	8	18
31 Jan 70	MY WAY (re-entry) *Reprise RS 20817*	49	1
28 Feb 70	MY WAY (2nd re-entry) *Reprise RS 20817*	30	5
11 Apr 70	MY WAY (3rd re-entry) *Reprise RS 20817*	33	9
27 Jun 70	MY WAY (4th re-entry) *Reprise RS 20817*	28	21
28 Nov 70	MY WAY (5th re-entry) *Reprise RS 20817*	18	16
6 Mar 71	I WILL DRINK THE WINE *Reprise RS 23487*	16	12
27 Mar 71	MY WAY (6th re-entry) *Reprise RS 20817*	22	19
4 Sep 71	MY WAY (7th re-entry) *Reprise RS 20817*	39	8
1 Jan 72	MY WAY (8th re-entry) *Reprise RS 20817*	50	1
20 Dec 75	I BELIEVE I'M GONNA LOVE YOU *Reprise K 14400*	34	7
9 Aug 80	THEME FROM NEW YORK, NEW YORK *Reprise K 14502*	59	4
22 Feb 86 ●	THEME FROM NEW YORK, NEW YORK (re-entry)		
	Reprise K 14502	4	10
4 Dec 93 ●	I'VE GOT YOU UNDER MY SKIN *Island CID 578* [5]	4	9
16 Apr 94	MY WAY (re-issue) *Reprise W 0163CD*	45	2
30 Jan 99	THEY ALL LAUGHED *Reprise W 469CD*	41	1

[1] Frank Sinatra with Billy May and His Orchestra [2] Frank Sinatra and Sammy Davis Jr [3] Frank Sinatra with Count Basie [4] Nancy Sinatra and Frank Sinatra [5] Frank Sinatra with Bono

Tracks on Songs for Swinging Lovers (LP): You Make Me Feel So Young / It Happened In Monterey / You're Getting to Be a Habit with Me / You Brought a New Kind of Love to Me / Too Marvellous for Words / Old Devil Moon / Pennies from Heaven / Love Is Here to Stay / I've Got You Under My Skin / I Thought About You / We'll Be Together Again / Makin' Whoopee / Swingin' Down the Lane / Anything Goes / How About You. Tracks on Come Dance With Me (LP): Come Dance With Me / Something's Gotta Give / Just in Time / Dancing in the Dark / Too Close for Comfort / I Could Have Danced All Night / Saturday Night Is the Loneliest Night of the Week / Day In Day Out / Cheek to Cheek / Baubles Bangles and Beads / The Song Is You / The Last Dance. 'All the Way' and 'Chicago', Capitol CL 14800, were at first billed separately, then together for one week, then 'All the Way' on its own. 'I've Got You Under My Skin' was the flip side of 'Stay (Faraway So Close)' by U2

Nancy SINATRA `298` `Top 500` *Eldest child of legendary singer, b. 8 Jun 1940, New Jersey, US - days before father Frank's first US Top 10 entry. Was subject of 1945 hit 'Nancy (with the Laughing Eyes)'. 'Somethin' Stupid' is the only father-daughter chart topper (99 WEEKS)* pos/wks

27 Jan 66 ★	THESE BOOTS ARE MADE FOR WALKING *Reprise R 20432* ▲	1	14
28 Apr 66	HOW DOES THAT GRAB YOU DARLIN' *Reprise R 20461*	19	8
19 Jan 67 ●	SUGAR TOWN *Reprise RS 20527*	8	10
23 Mar 67 ★	SOMETHIN' STUPID *Reprise RS 23166* [1] ▲	1	18
5 Jul 67	YOU ONLY LIVE TWICE / JACKSON *Reprise RS 20595* [2]	11	19
8 Nov 67	LADYBIRD *Reprise RS 20629* [3]	47	1
29 Nov 69	HIGHWAY SONG *Reprise RS 20869*	21	10
21 Aug 71 ●	DID YOU EVER *Reprise K 14093* [4]	2	19

[1] Nancy Sinatra and Frank Sinatra [2] Nancy Sinatra / Nancy Sinatra and Lee Hazlewood [3] Nancy Sinatra and Lee Hazlewood [4] Nancy and Lee

'Jackson' listed with 'You Only Live Twice' from 12 Jul 1967

SINCLAIR *UK, male vocalist (8 WEEKS)* pos/wks

21 Aug 93	AIN'T NO CASANOVA *Dome CDDOME 1004*	28	5
26 Feb 94	(I WANNA KNOW) WHY		
	Dome CDDOME 1009	58	2
6 Aug 94	DON'T LIE *Dome CDDOME 1010*	70	1

Bob SINCLAR *France, male DJ / Producer (6 WEEKS)* pos/wks

20 Mar 99	MY ONLY LOVE *East West EW 196CD* [1]	56	1
19 Aug 00 ●	I FEEL FOR YOU		
	Defected DEFECT 18CDS	9	5

[1] Bob Sinclar featuring Lee A Genesis

SINDY *UK, female doll vocalist (1 WEEK)* pos/wks

5 Oct 96	SATURDAY NIGHT *Love This LUVTHISCD 13*	70	1

SINE *US, male / female vocal / instrumental group (9 WEEKS)* pos/wks

10 Jun 78	JUST LET ME DO MY THING *CBS 6351*	33	9

SINFONIA OF LONDON – See Peter AUTY and the SINFONIA OF LONDON conducted by Howard BLAKE

SINGING CORNER Meets DONOVAN
UK, male vocalists (1 WEEK) pos/wks

1 Dec 90	JENNIFER JUNIPER *Fontana SYP 1*	68	1

SINGING DOGS *Denmark, canine vocal group (4 WEEKS)* pos/wks

25 Nov 55	THE SINGING DOGS (MEDLEY)		
	Nixa N 15009	13	4

Medley songs: Pat-a-Cake / Three Blind Mice / Jingle Bells / Oh Susanna

SINGING NUN (Soeur Sourire)
Belgium, female vocalist – Jeanine Deckers (14 WEEKS) pos/wks

5 Dec 63 ●	DOMINIQUE *Philips BF 1293* ▲	7	14

SINGING SHEEP *UK, computerized sheep noises (5 WEEKS)* pos/wks

18 Dec 82	BAA BAA BLACK SHEEP *Sheep BAA 1*	42	5

Maxine SINGLETON *US, female vocalist (3 WEEKS)* pos/wks

2 Apr 83	YOU CAN'T RUN FROM LOVE *Creole CR 50*	57	3

SINITTA `283` `Top 500` *As well as a string of Hi-NRG dance hits, disco diva and Miquel Brown's daughter Sinitta Malone (b. 19 Oct 1966, Washington DC) has starred in several London stage musicals including Mutiny with David Essex and What a Feeling with Luke Goss and Sonia (104 WEEKS)* pos/wks

8 Mar 86	SO MACHO / CRUISING *Fanfare FAN 7*	47	11
28 Jun 86 ●	SO MACHO / CRUISING (re-entry)		
	Fanfare FAN 7	2	17
11 Oct 86	FEELS LIKE THE FIRST TIME		
	Fanfare FAN 8	45	5
25 Jul 87 ●	TOY BOY *Fanfare FAN 12*	4	14
12 Dec 87	G.T.O. *Fanfare FAN 14*	15	9
19 Mar 88 ●	CROSS MY BROKEN HEART *Fanfare FAN 15*	6	9
24 Sep 88	I DON'T BELIEVE IN MIRACLES *Fanfare FAN 16*	22	8
3 Jun 89 ●	RIGHT BACK WHERE WE STARTED FROM		
	Fanfare FAN 18	4	10
7 Oct 89	LOVE ON A MOUNTAIN TOP *Fanfare FAN 21*	20	6
21 Apr 90	HITCHIN' A RIDE *Fanfare FAN 24*	24	6
22 Sep 90	LOVE AND AFFECTION *Fanfare FAN 31*	62	3
4 Jul 92	SHAME SHAME SHAME *Arista 74321100327*	28	4
17 Apr 93	THE SUPREME EP *Arista 74321139592*	49	2

Tracks on The Supreme EP: Where Did Our Love Go / Stop! In the Name of Love / You Can't Hurry Love / Remember Me

SINNAMON *US, male vocal / instrumental group (1 WEEK)* pos/wks

28 Sep 96	I NEED YOU NOW *Worx WORXCD 003*	70	1

SIOUXSIE and the BANSHEES (148 Top 500) Long-running

commercially successful UK punk band included Susan 'Siouxsie' Dallion (v), Steve Severin (b) (also recorded as The Glove), Siouxsie's husband, Peter 'Budgie' Clark (d) (who recorded with Siouxsie as The Creatures) and, at times, Cure front man Robert Smith (g) (150 WEEKS)

			pos/wks
26 Aug 78 ●	HONG KONG GARDEN	Polydor 2059 052	7 10
31 Mar 79	THE STAIRCASE (MYSTERY)	Polydor POSP 9	24 8
7 Jul 79	PLAYGROUND TWIST	Polydor POSP 59	28 6
29 Sep 79	MITTAGEISEN (METAL POSTCARD)	Polydor 2059 151	47 3
15 Mar 80	HAPPY HOUSE	Polydor POSP 117	17 8
7 Jun 80	CHRISTINE	Polydor 2059 249	22 8
6 Dec 80	ISRAEL	Polydor POSP 205	41 8
30 May 81	SPELLBOUND	Polydor POSP 273	22 8
1 Aug 81	ARABIAN KNIGHTS	Polydor POSP 309	32 7
29 May 82	FIRE WORKS	Polydor POSPG 450	22 6
9 Oct 82	SLOWDIVE	Polydor POSP 510	41 4
4 Dec 82	MELT / IL EST NE LE DIVIN ENFANT	Polydor POSP 539	49 5
1 Oct 83 ●	DEAR PRUDENCE	Wonderland SHE 4	3 8
24 Mar 84	SWIMMING HORSES	Wonderland SHE 6	28 4
2 Jun 84	DAZZLE	Wonderland SHE 7	33 3
27 Oct 84	THE THORN EP	Wonderland SHEEP 8	47 3
26 Oct 85	CITIES IN DUST	Wonderland SHE 9	21 6
8 Mar 86	CANDYMAN	Wonderland SHE 10	34 5
17 Jan 87	THIS WHEEL'S ON FIRE	Wonderland SHE 11	14 6
28 Mar 87	THE PASSENGER	Wonderland SHE 12	41 6
25 Jul 87	SONG FROM THE EDGE OF THE WORLD	Wonderland SHE 13	59 3
30 Jul 88	PEEK-A-BOO	Wonderland SHE 14	16 6
8 Oct 88	THE KILLING JAR	Wonderland SHE 15	41 3
3 Dec 88	THE LAST BEAT OF MY HEART	Wonderland SHE 16	44 1
25 May 91	KISS THEM FOR ME	Wonderland SHE 19	32 4
13 Jul 91	SHADOWTIME	Wonderland SHE 20	57 1
25 Jul 92	FACE TO FACE	Wonderland SHE 21	21 4
20 Aug 94	INTERLUDE	Parlophone CDR 6365 [1]	25 2
7 Jan 95	O BABY	Wonderland SHECD 22	34 3
18 Feb 95	STARGAZER	Wonderland SHECD 23	64 1

[1] Morrissey and Siouxsie

Tracks on The Thorn Live EP: Overground / Voices / Placebo Effect / Red Over White

SIR DOUGLAS QUINTET

US, male vocal / instrumental group (10 WEEKS)

			pos/wks
17 Jun 65	SHE'S ABOUT A MOVER	London HLU 9964	15 10

SIR KILLALOT vs ROBO BABE

UK, male robot rapper & female vocalist (1 WEEK)

			pos/wks
30 Dec 00	ROBOT WARS (ANDROID LOVE)	Polydor 5879362	51 1+

SIR MIX-A-LOT US, male rapper (2 WEEKS)

			pos/wks
8 Aug 92	BABY GOT BACK	Def American DEFA 20 ▲	56 2

SIRRON – See PLUS ONE featuring SIRRON

SISQO US, male vocalist - Mark Andrews (28 WEEKS)

			pos/wks
12 Feb 00	GOT TO GET IT	Def Soul 5626442	14 4
22 Apr 00 ●	THONG SONG	Def Soul 5688902	3 14
30 Sep 00 ●	UNLEASH THE DRAGON	Def Soul 5726422	6 7
16 Dec 00	INCOMPLETE	Def Soul 5727542 ▲	13 3+

SISSEL – See Warren G

SISTER BLISS

UK, DJ / producer / instrumentalist - Ayalah Ben-Tovim (9 WEEKS) pos/wks

15 Oct 94	CANTGETAMAN CANTGETAJOB (LIFE'S A BITCH)	Go.Beat GODCD 124 [1]	31 4
15 Jul 95	OH! WHAT A WORLD	Go.Beat GODCD 126 [1]	40 2
29 Jun 96	BADMAN	Junk Dog JDOGCD 1	51 1
7 Oct 00	SISTER SISTER	Multiply CDMULTY 68	34 2

[1] Sister Bliss featuring Collette

SISTER SLEDGE (254 Top 500) Successful US family group from

Philadelphia: Kathy, Debra, Joni and Kim Sledge. They found more fame in the UK than in the US, and recorded some of the best-known disco records with noted producer / songwriters Nile Rodgers and Bernard Edwards (111 WEEKS)

			pos/wks
21 Jun 75	MAMA NEVER TOLD ME	Atlantic K 10619	20 6
17 Mar 79 ●	HE'S THE GREATEST DANCER	Atlantic / Cotillion K 11257	6 11
26 May 79	WE ARE FAMILY	Atlantic / Cotillion K 11293	8 10
11 Aug 79	LOST IN MUSIC	Atlantic / Cotillion K 11337	17 10
19 Jan 80	GOT TO LOVE SOMEBODY	Atlantic / Cotillion K 11404	34 4
28 Feb 81	ALL AMERICAN GIRLS	Atlantic K 11656	41 5
26 May 84	THINKING OF YOU	Cotillion / Atlantic B 9744	11 13
8 Sep 84 ●	LOST IN MUSIC (re-mix)	Cotillion / Atlantic B 9718	4 12
17 Nov 84	WE ARE FAMILY (re-mix)	Cotillion / Atlantic B 9692	33 4
1 Jun 85 ★	FRANKIE	Atlantic A 9547	1 16
31 Aug 85	DANCING ON THE JAGGED EDGE	Atlantic A 9520	50 3
23 Jan 93 ●	WE ARE FAMILY (2nd) (re-mix)	Atlantic A 4508CD	5 8
13 Mar 93	LOST IN MUSIC (2nd) (re-mix)	Atlantic A 4509CD	14 5
12 Jun 93	THINKING OF YOU (re-mix)	Atlantic A 4515CD	17 4

SISTER 2 SISTER Australia, female vocal duo (5 WEEKS)

			pos/wks
22 Apr 00	SISTER	Mushroom MUSH 70CDS	18 4
28 Oct 00	WHAT'S A GIRL TO DO	Mushroom MUSH 76CDS	61 1

SISTERS OF MERCY UK, male / female vocal / instrumental group -

leader Andrew Eldritch (40 WEEKS)

			pos/wks
16 Jun 84	BODY AND SOUL / TRAIN	Merciful Release MR 029	46 3
20 Oct 84	WALK AWAY	Merciful Release MR 033	45 3
9 Mar 85	NO TIME TO CRY	Merciful Release MR 035	63 2
3 Oct 87 ●	THIS CORROSION	Merciful Release MR 39	7 6
27 Feb 88	DOMINION	Merciful Release MR 43	13 6
18 Jun 88	LUCRETIA MY REFLECTION	Merciful Release MR 45	20 4
13 Oct 90	MORE	Merciful Release MR 47	14 4
22 Dec 90	DOCTOR JEEP	Merciful Release MR 51	37 4
2 May 92 ●	TEMPLE OF LOVE	Merciful Release MR 53	3 5
28 Aug 93	UNDER THE GUN	Merciful Release MR 59CDX	19 3

SIVUCA Brazil, male instrumentalist (3 WEEKS)

			pos/wks
28 Jul 84	AIN'T NO SUNSHINE	London LON 51	56 3

SIX BY SEVEN UK, male vocal / instrumental group (1 WEEK)

			pos/wks
9 May 98	CANDLELIGHT	Mantra MNT 34CD	70 1

6 BY SIX UK, male instrumental / production duo (1 WEEK)

			pos/wks
4 May 96	INTO YOUR HEART	Six6 SIXCD 130	51 1

SIX CHIX UK, female vocal group (1 WEEK)

			pos/wks
26 Feb 00	ONLY THE WOMEN KNOW	EMI CDCHIX 001	72 1

666 Holland, male production duo (4 WEEKS)

			pos/wks
25 Nov 00	DEVIL	Echo ECSCD 102	18 4

666 Germany, male / female vocal / instrumental group (1 WEEK)

			pos/wks
3 Oct 98	ALARMA	Danceteria CDDAN 001	58 1

SIXPENCE NONE THE RICHER

US, male / female vocal / instrumental group (17 WEEKS)

			pos/wks
29 May 99 ●	KISS ME	Elektra E 3750CD	4 12
18 Sep 99	THERE SHE GOES	Elektra E 3728CD	14 5

60FT DOLLS UK, male vocal / instrumental group (4 WEEKS)

			pos/wks
3 Feb 96	STAY	Indolent DOLLS 002CD	48 1
11 May 96	TALK TO ME	Indolent DOLLS 003CD	37 1
20 Jul 96	HAPPY SHOPPER	Indolent DOLLS 005CD	38 1
9 May 98	ALISON'S ROOM	Indolent DOLLS 007CD1	61 1

SIZE 9 US, male producer – Josh Wink (4 WEEKS)

		pos/wks
17 Jun 95	I'M READY *Virgin America VUSCD 92* **52** 1	
11 Nov 95	I'M READY (re-issue) *VC VCRD 2* [1] **30** 3	

[1] Josh Wink's Size 9

See also Josh WINK

Roni SIZE / REPRAZENT UK, male producer – Ryan Williams with male / female vocal / instrumental group (13 WEEKS)

		pos/wks
14 Jun 97	SHARE THE FALL *Talkin Loud TLCD 21* **37** 2	
13 Sep 97	HEROES *Talkin Loud TLCD 25* **31** 2	
15 Nov 97	BROWN PAPER BAG *Talkin Loud TLCD 28* **20** 3	
14 Mar 98	WATCHING WINDOWS *Talkin Loud TLCD 31* **28** 2	
7 Oct 00	WHO TOLD YOU *Talkin Loud TLCD 61* **17** 4	

SIZZLA Jamaica, male rapper – Miguel Collins (2 WEEKS)

		pos/wks
17 Apr 99	RAIN SHOWERS *Xterminator EXTCDS 76* **51** 2	

S J – See S-J

SKANDAL UK, male vocal group (1 WEEK)

		pos/wks
14 Oct 00	CHAMPAGNE HIGHWAY *Prestige Management CDGING 1* **53** 1	

SKATALITES Jamaica, male instrumental group (6 WEEKS)

		pos/wks
20 Apr 67	GUNS OF NAVARONE *Island WI 168* **36** 6	

SKEE-LO US, male rapper (10 WEEKS)

		pos/wks
9 Dec 95	I WISH *Wild Card 5777752* **15** 8	
27 Apr 96	TOP OF THE STAIRS *Wild Card 5763352* **38** 2	

Beverli SKEETE – See DE-CODE featuring Beverli SKEETE

Peter SKELLERN UK, male vocalist (24 WEEKS)

		pos/wks
23 Sep 72 ●	YOU'RE A LADY *Decca F 13333* **3** 11	
29 Mar 75	HOLD ON TO LOVE *Decca F 13568* **14** 9	
28 Oct 78	LOVE IS THE SWEETEST THING *Mercury 6008 603* [1] **60** 4	

[1] Peter Skellern featuring Grimethorpe Colliery Band

SKID ROW US, male vocal / instrumental group (27 WEEKS)

		pos/wks
18 Nov 89	YOUTH GONE WILD *Atlantic A 8935* **42** 3	
3 Feb 90	18 AND LIFE *Atlantic A 8883* **12** 6	
31 Mar 90	I REMEMBER YOU *East West A 8886* **36** 4	
15 Jun 91	MONKEY BUSINESS *Atlantic A 7673* **19** 3	
14 Sep 91	SLAVE TO THE GRIND *Atlantic A 7603* **43** 2	
23 Nov 91	WASTED TIME *Atlantic A 7570* **20** 3	
29 Aug 92	YOUTH GONE WILD / DELIVERING THE GOODS (re-issue) *Atlantic A 7444* **22** 4	
18 Nov 95	BREAKIN' DOWN *Atlantic A 7135CD1* **48** 2	

SKIDS UK, male vocal / instrumental group (60 WEEKS)

		pos/wks
23 Sep 78	SWEET SUBURBIA *Virgin VS 227* **70** 1	
7 Oct 78	SWEET SUBURBIA (re-entry) *Virgin VS 227* **71** 2	
4 Nov 78	THE SAINTS ARE COMING *Virgin VS 232* **48** 3	
17 Feb 79 ●	INTO THE VALLEY *Virgin VS 241* **10** 11	
26 May 79	MASQUERADE *Virgin VS 262* **14** 9	
29 Sep 79	CHARADE *Virgin VS 288* **31** 6	
24 Nov 79	WORKING FOR THE YANKEE DOLLAR *Virgin VS 306* **20** 11	
1 Mar 80	ANIMATION *Virgin VS 323* **56** 3	
16 Aug 80	CIRCUS GAMES *Virgin VS 359* **32** 7	
18 Oct 80	GOODBYE CIVILIAN *Virgin VS 373* **52** 4	
6 Dec 80	WOMAN IN WINTER *Virgin VSK 101* **49** 3	

SKIN UK / Germany, male vocal / instrumental group (19 WEEKS)

		pos/wks
25 Dec 93	THE SKIN UP (EP) *Parlophone CDR 6363* **67** 2	
12 Mar 94	HOUSE OF LOVE *Parlophone CDR 6374* **45** 2	
30 Apr 94	MONEY / UNBELIEVABLE *Parlophone CDR 6381* **18** 3	
23 Jul 94	TOWER OF STRENGTH *Parlophone CDR 6387* **19** 3	
15 Oct 94	LOOK BUT DON'T TOUCH (EP) (re-issue) *Parlophone CDRS 6391* **33** 3	
20 May 95	TAKE ME DOWN TO THE RIVER *Parlophone CDR 6409* **26** 2	
23 Mar 96	HOW LUCKY YOU ARE *Parlophone CDR 6426* **32** 2	
18 May 96	PERFECT DAY *Parlophone CDR 6433* **33** 2	

Tracks on The Skin Up (EP): Look But Don't Touch / Shine Your Light / Monkey (re-issue). Tracks on Look But Don't Touch (EP): Look But Don't Touch / Should I Stay or Should I Go / Pump It Up / Monkey.

SKIN UP UK, male producer (9 WEEKS)

		pos/wks
7 Sep 91	IVORY *Love EVOL 4* **48** 3	
14 Mar 92	A JUICY RED APPLE *Love EVOL 11* **32** 4	
18 Jul 92	ACCELERATE *Love EVOL 17* **45** 2	

SKINNER – See LIGHTNING SEEDS

SKINNY UK, male vocal / instrumental / production duo (2 WEEKS)

		pos/wks
11 Apr 98	FAILURE *Cheeky CHEKCD 023* **31** 2	

SKIP RAIDERS featuring JADA
UK, male production duo and female vocalist (1 WEEK)

		pos/wks
15 Jul 00	ANOTHER DAY *Perfecto PERF 4CDS* **46** 1	

SKIPWORTH and TURNER US, male vocal duo (12 WEEKS)

		pos/wks
27 Apr 85	THINKING ABOUT YOUR LOVE *Fourth & Broadway BRW 23* **24** 10	
21 Jan 89	MAKE IT LAST *Fourth & Broadway BRW 118* **60** 2	

Nick SKITZ – See FUNKY CHOAD featuring Nick SKITZ

SKUNK ANANSIE
UK, male / female vocal / instrumental group (41 WEEKS)

		pos/wks
25 Mar 95	SELLING JESUS *One Little Indian 101 TP7CD* **46** 1	
17 Jun 95	I CAN DREAM *One Little Indian 121 TP7CD* **41** 2	
2 Sep 95	CHARITY *One Little Indian 131 TP7CD* **40** 2	
27 Jan 96	WEAK *One Little Indian 141 TP7CD* **20** 5	
27 Apr 96	CHARITY (re-issue) *One Little Indian 151 TP7CD* **20** 5	
28 Sep 96	ALL I WANT *One Little Indian 161 TP7CD* **14** 4	
30 Nov 96	TWISTED (EVERYDAY HURTS) *One Little Indian 171 TP7CD* **26** 4	
1 Feb 97	HEDONISM (JUST BECAUSE YOU FEEL GOOD) *One Little Indian 181TP7CD* **13** 6	
14 Jun 97	BRAZEN 'WEEP' *One Little Indian 191TP7CD1* **11** 5	
13 Mar 99	CHARLIE BIG POTATO *Virgin VSCDT 1725* **17** 3	
22 May 99	SECRETLY *Virgin VSCDT 1733* **16** 4	
7 Aug 99	LATELY *Virgin VSCDT 1738* **33** 2	

SKY UK / Australia, male instrumental group (11 WEEKS)

		pos/wks
5 Apr 80 ●	TOCCATA *Ariola ARO 300* **5** 11	

SKYHOOKS Australia, male vocal / instrumental group (1 WEEK)

		pos/wks
9 Jun 79	WOMEN IN UNIFORM *United Artists UP 36508* **73** 1	

SLACKER UK, male production duo (4 WEEKS)

		pos/wks
26 Apr 97	SCARED *XL XLS 84CD* **36** 2	
30 Aug 97	YOUR FACE *XL XLS 87CD* **33** 2	

SLADE 38 Top 500
Top group of the 1970s: Noddy Holder (v/g), Dave Hill (g), Jimmy Lea (b/p), Don Powell (d). They were the first act to have three singles enter at No.1. All six of the Wolverhampton band's chart-topping stompers were penned by Holder and Lea. Noddy was honoured with an MBE in 2000 (279 WEEKS)

		pos/wks
19 Jun 71	GET DOWN AND GET WITH IT *Polydor 2058 112* **16** 14	
30 Oct 71 ★	COZ I LUV YOU *Polydor 2058 155* **1** 15	
5 Feb 72 ●	LOOK WOT YOU DUN *Polydor 2058 195* **4** 10	
3 Jun 72 ★	TAKE ME BAK 'OME *Polydor 2058 231* **1** 13	
2 Sep 72 ★	MAMA WEER ALL CRAZEE NOW *Polydor 2058 274* **1** 10	
25 Nov 72 ●	GUDBUY T'JANE *Polydor 2058 312* **2** 13	
3 Mar 73 ★	CUM ON FEEL THE NOIZE *Polydor 2058 339* ■ **1** 12	

30 Jun 73 ★	SKWEEZE ME PLEEZE ME *Polydor 2058 377* ■	1	10
6 Oct 73 ●	MY FRIEND STAN *Polydor 2058 407*	2	8
15 Dec 73 ★	MERRY XMAS EVERYBODY *Polydor 2058 422* ◆ ■	1	9
6 Apr 74 ●	EVERYDAY *Polydor 2058 453*	3	7
6 Jul 74 ●	THE BANGIN' MAN *Polydor 2058 492*	3	7
19 Oct 74 ●	FAR FAR AWAY *Polydor 2058 522*	2	6
15 Feb 75	HOW DOES IT FEEL *Polydor 2058 547*	15	7
17 May 75 ●	THANKS FOR THE MEMORY (WHAM BAM THANK YOU MAM)		
	Polydor 2058 585	7	7
22 Nov 75 ●	IN FOR A PENNY *Polydor 2058 663*	...11	8
7 Feb 76 ●	LET'S CALL IT QUITS *Polydor 2058 690*	...11	7
5 Feb 77	GYPSY ROAD HOG *Barn 2014 105*	48	2
29 Oct 77	MY BABY LEFT ME - THAT'S ALL RIGHT *Barn 2014 114*	32	4
18 Oct 80	SLADE ALIVE AT READING '80 (EP) *Cheapskate CHEAP 5*	44	5
27 Dec 80	MERRY XMAS EVERYBODY (re-recording)		
	Cheapskate CHEAP 11 [1]	70	2
31 Jan 81 ●	WE'LL BRING THE HOUSE DOWN *Cheapskate CHEAP 16*	...10	9
4 Apr 81	WHEELS AIN'T COMING DOWN *Cheapskate CHEAP 21*	60	3
19 Sep 81	LOCK UP YOUR DAUGHTERS *RCA 124*	29	8
19 Dec 81	MERRY XMAS EVERYBODY (re-entry) *Polydor 2058 422*	32	4
27 Mar 82	RUBY RED *RCA 191*	51	3
27 Nov 82	(AND NOW - THE WALTZ) C'EST LA VIE *RCA 291*	50	6
25 Dec 82	MERRY XMAS EVERYBODY (2nd re-entry) *Polydor 2058 422*	67	3
19 Nov 83 ●	MY OH MY *RCA 373*	2	11
10 Dec 83	MERRY XMAS EVERYBODY (3rd re-entry) *Polydor 2058 422*	20	5
4 Feb 84 ●	RUN RUNAWAY *RCA 385*	7	10
17 Nov 84	ALL JOIN HANDS *RCA 455*	15	9
15 Dec 84	MERRY XMAS EVERYBODY (4th re-entry)		
	Polydor 2058 422	47	4
26 Jan 85	7 YEAR BITCH *RCA 475*	60	3
23 Mar 85	MYZSTERIOUS MIZSTER JONES *RCA PB 40027*	50	5
30 Nov 85	DO YOU BELIEVE IN MIRACLES *RCA PB 40449*	54	6
21 Dec 85	MERRY XMAS EVERYBODY (re-issue) *Polydor POSP 780*	48	3
27 Dec 86	MERRY XMAS EVERYBODY (re-entry of re-issue)		
	Polydor POSP 780	71	1
21 Feb 87	STILL THE SAME *RCA PB 41137*	73	2
19 Oct 91	RADIO WALL OF SOUND *Polydor PO 180*	21	5
26 Dec 98	MERRY XMAS EVERYBODY '98 (re-mix) *Polydor 5633532* [2]	30	3

[1] Slade and the Reading Choir [2] Slade vs Flush

Tracks on Slade Alive at Reading '80 (EP): When I'm Dancin' I Ain't Fightin' / Born to Be Wild / Somethin' Else / Pistol Packin' Mama / Keep a Rollin'

SLAMM *UK, male vocal / instrumental group (6 WEEKS)*

			pos/wks
17 Jul 93	ENERGIZE *PWL International PWCD 266*	57	2
23 Oct 93	VIRGINIA PLAIN *PWL International PWCD 274*	60	1
22 Oct 94	THAT'S WHERE MY MIND GOES		
	PWL International PWCD 310	68	1
4 Feb 95	CAN'T GET BY *PWL International PWCD 316*	47	2

Luke SLATER *UK, male producer (1 WEEK)*

			pos/wks
16 Sep 00	ALL EXHALE *Novamute CDNOMU 79*	74	1

SLAUGHTER *US, male vocal / instrumental group (2 WEEKS)*

			pos/wks
29 Sep 90	UP ALL NIGHT *Chrysalis CHS 3556*	62	1
2 Feb 91	FLY TO THE ANGELS *Chrysalis CHS 3634*	55	1

SLAVE *US, male vocal / instrumental group (3 WEEKS)*

			pos/wks
8 Mar 80	JUST A TOUCH OF LOVE *Atlantic / Cotillion K 11442*	64	3

SLAYER *US, male vocal / instrumental group (3 WEEKS)*

			pos/wks
13 Jun 87	CRIMINALLY INSANE *Def Jam LON 133*	64	1
26 Oct 91	SEASONS IN THE ABYSS *Def American DEFA 9*	51	1
9 Sep 95	SERENITY IN MURDER *American 74321312482*	50	1

SLEAZESISTERS *UK, male producer - Paul Masterson (3 WEEKS)*

			pos/wks
29 Jul 95	SEX *Pulse 8 CDLOSE 92* [1]	53	1
30 Mar 96	LET'S WHIP IT UP (YOU GO GIRL) *Pulse 8 CDLOSE 102* [1]	46	1
26 Sep 98	WORK IT UP *Logic 74321616622* [2]	74	1

[1] Sleazesisters with Vikki Shepard [2] Sleaze Sisters

Kathy SLEDGE *US, female vocalist (7 WEEKS)*

			pos/wks
16 May 92	TAKE ME BACK TO LOVE AGAIN *Epic 6579837*	62	2
18 Feb 95	ANOTHER STAR *NRC DEACD 002*	54	1
29 Nov 97	FREEDOM *Deconstruction 74321536952* [1]	15	4

[1] Robert Miles featuring Kathy Sledge

See also SISTER SLEDGE

Percy SLEDGE *US, male vocalist (34 WEEKS)*

			pos/wks
12 May 66 ●	WHEN A MAN LOVES A WOMAN *Atlantic 584 001* ▲	4	17
4 Aug 66	WARM AND TENDER LOVE *Atlantic 584 034*	34	7
14 Feb 87 ●	WHEN A MAN LOVES A WOMAN (re-issue) *Atlantic YZ 96*	2	10

SLEEPER
UK, male / female vocal / instrumental group (29 WEEKS)

			pos/wks
21 May 94	DELICIOUS *Indolent SLEEP 003CD*	75	1
21 Jan 95	INBETWEENER *Indolent SLEEP 006CD*	16	4
8 Apr 95	VEGAS *Indolent SLEEP 008CD*	33	3
7 Oct 95	WHAT DO I DO NOW *Indolent SLEEP 009CD1*	14	4
4 May 96 ●	SALE OF THE CENTURY *Indolent SLEEP 011CD*	10	5
13 Jul 96 ●	NICE GUY EDDIE *Indolent SLEEP 013CD*	10	5
5 Oct 96	STATUESQUE *Indolent SLEEP 014CD1*	17	3
4 Oct 97	SHE'S A GOOD GIRL *Indolent SLEEP 015CD*	28	2
6 Dec 97	ROMEO ME *Indolent SLEEP 17CD1*	39	2

SLICK *US, male / female vocal / instrumental group (15 WEEKS)*

			pos/wks
16 Jun 79	SPACE BASS *Fantasy FTC 176*	16	10
15 Sep 79	SEXY CREAM *Fantasy FTC 182*	47	5

Grace SLICK *US, female vocalist (4 WEEKS)*

			pos/wks
24 May 80	DREAMS *RCA PB 9534*	50	4

SLICK RICK – See Montell JORDAN

SLIK
UK, male vocal / instrumental group - lead vocal Midge Ure (18 WEEKS) pos/wks

17 Jan 76 ★	FOREVER AND EVER *Bell 1464*	1	9
8 May 76	REQUIEM *Bell 1478*	24	9

SLIM CHANCE – See Ronnie LANE and SLIM CHANCE

SLIPKNOT *US, male vocal / instrumental group (5 WEEKS)*

			pos/wks
11 Mar 00	WAIT AND BLEED *Roadrunner RR 21125*	27	3
16 Sep 00	SPIT IT OUT *Roadrunner RR20903*	28	2

SLIPSTREEM *UK, male vocal group (7 WEEKS)*

			pos/wks
19 Dec 92	WE ARE RAVING - THE ANTHEM *Boogie Food 7BF 1*	18	7

SLITS *UK, female vocal / instrumental group (3 WEEKS)*

			pos/wks
13 Oct 79	TYPICAL GIRLS / I HEARD IT THROUGH THE GRAPEVINE		
	Island WIP 6505	60	3

PF SLOAN *US, male vocalist (3 WEEKS)*

			pos/wks
4 Nov 65	SINS OF THE FAMILY *RCA 1482*	38	3

SLO-MOSHUN
UK, male instrumental / production duo (4 WEEKS)

			pos/wks
5 Feb 94	BELLS OF NY *Six6 SIXCD 108*	29	3
30 Jul 94	HELP MY FRIEND *Six6 SIXCD 117*	52	1

SLOWDIVE
UK, male / female vocal / instrumental group (2 WEEKS)

			pos/wks
15 Jun 91	CATCH THE BREEZE / SHINE *Creation CRE 112*	52	1
29 May 93	OUTSIDE YOUR ROOM (EP) *Creation CRESCD 119*	69	1

Tracks on Outside Your Room (EP): Outside Your Room / Alison / So Tired / Souvlaki Space Station

UK No.1 ★   UK Top 10 ●   Still on chart +   UK million seller ◆   UK entry at No.1 ■   US No.1 ▲

SL2
UK, male DJ / production duo - Matt "Slipmatt" Nelson and John "Lime" Fernandez (25 WEEKS)

			pos/wks
2 Nov 91		DJS TAKE CONTROL / WAY IN MY BRAIN *XL XLS 24*	**11** 5
4 Jan 92		DJS TAKE CONTROL / WAY IN MY BRAIN (re-entry) *XL XLS 24*	**71** 1
18 Apr 92	●	ON A RAGGA TIP *XL XLS 29*	**2** 11
19 Dec 92		WAY IN MY BRAIN (re-mix) / DRUMBEATS *XL XLS 36*	**26** 6
15 Feb 97		ON A RAGGA TIP '97 (re-mix) *XL XLSR 29CD*	**31** 2

SLY and the FAMILY STONE
US, male / female vocal / instrumental / production group (42 WEEKS)

			pos/wks
10 Jul 68	●	DANCE TO THE MUSIC *Direction 58 3568*	**7** 14
2 Oct 68		M'LADY *Direction 58 3707*	**32** 7
19 Mar 69		EVERYDAY PEOPLE *Direction 58 3938* ▲	**36** 1
9 Apr 69		EVERYDAY PEOPLE (re-entry) *Direction 58 3938*	**37** 4
8 Jan 72		FAMILY AFFAIR *Epic EPC 7632* ▲	**15** 8
15 Apr 72		RUNNIN' AWAY *Epic EPC 7810*	**17** 8

SLY FOX
US, male vocal / instrumental duo - Gary Cooper and Michael Camacho (16 WEEKS)

			pos/wks
31 May 86	●	LET'S GO ALL THE WAY *Capitol CL 403*	**3** 16

SLY and ROBBIE
Jamaica, male vocal / instrumental duo (23 WEEKS)

			pos/wks
4 Apr 87		BOOPS (HERE TO GO) *Fourth & Broadway BRW 61*	**12** 11
25 Jul 87		FIRE *Fourth & Broadway BRW 71*	**60** 4
20 Sep 97		NIGHT NURSE *East West EW 129CD1* [1]	**13** 8

[1] Sly and Robbie featuring Simply Red

SMALL ADS
UK, male vocal / instrumental group (3 WEEKS)

			pos/wks
18 Apr 81		SMALL ADS *Bronze BRO 115*	**63** 3

SMALL FACES (177 Top 500)
Revered London-based mod quartet: Steve Marriott (v/g) (d. 1991), Ronnie Lane (b) (d. 1997), Ian McLagan (k), Kenney Jones (d). Marriott and Lane penned most of the act's UK hits. Further international fame came when Marriott formed Humble Pie and the other members formed The Faces (137 WEEKS)

			pos/wks
2 Sep 65		WHATCHA GONNA DO ABOUT IT? *Decca F 12208*	**14** 12
10 Feb 66	●	SHA LA LA LA LEE *Decca F 12317*	**3** 11
12 May 66	●	HEY GIRL *Decca F 12393*	**10** 9
11 Aug 66	★	ALL OR NOTHING *Decca F 12470*	**1** 12
17 Nov 66	●	MY MIND'S EYE *Decca F 12500*	**4** 11
9 Mar 67		I CAN'T MAKE IT *Decca F 12565*	**26** 7
8 Jun 67		HERE COMES THE NICE *Immediate IM 050*	**12** 10
9 Aug 67	●	ITCHYCOO PARK *Immediate IM 057*	**3** 14
6 Dec 67	●	TIN SOLDIER *Immediate IM 062*	**9** 12
17 Apr 68	●	LAZY SUNDAY *Immediate IM 064*	**2** 11
10 Jul 68		UNIVERSAL *Immediate IM 069*	**16** 11
19 Mar 69		AFTERGLOW OF YOUR LOVE *Immediate IM 077*	**36** 1
13 Dec 75	●	ITCHYCOO PARK (re-issue) *Immediate IMS 102*	**9** 11
20 Mar 76		LAZY SUNDAY (re-issue) *Immediate IMS 106*	**39** 5

Heather SMALL
UK, female vocalist (9 WEEKS)

			pos/wks
20 May 00		PROUD *Arista 74321748902*	**16** 5
19 Aug 00		HOLDING ON *Arista 74321781332*	**58** 1
18 Nov 00		YOU NEED LOVE LIKE I DO *GUT CDGUT 36* [1]	**24** 3

[1] Tom Jones and Heather Small

See also M PEOPLE

SMALLER
UK, male vocal / instrumental group (2 WEEKS)

			pos/wks
28 Sep 96		WASTED *Better BETSCD 006*	**72** 1
29 Mar 97		IS *Better BETSCD 008*	**55** 1

SMART E'S
UK, male instrumental / production group (9 WEEKS)

			pos/wks
11 Jul 92	●	SESAME'S TREET *Suburban Base SUBBASE 12S*	**2** 9

S*M*A*S*H
UK, male vocal / instrumental group (1 WEEK)

			pos/wks
6 Aug 94		(I WANT TO) KILL SOMEBODY *Hi-Rise FLATSCD 5*	**26** 1

SMASH MOUTH
US, male vocal / instrumental group (9 WEEKS)

			pos/wks
25 Oct 97		WALKIN' ON THE SUN *Interscope IND 95555*	**19** 4
31 Jul 99		ALL STAR *Interscope 4971172*	**24** 5

SMASHING PUMPKINS
US, male / female vocal / instrumental group (36 WEEKS)

			pos/wks
5 Sep 92		I AM ONE *Hut HUTT 18*	**73** 1
3 Jul 93		CHERUB ROCK *Hut HUTCD 31*	**31** 2
25 Sep 93		TODAY *Hut HUTCD 37*	**44** 2
5 Mar 94		DISARM *Hut HUTCD 43*	**11** 3
28 Oct 95		BULLET WITH BUTTERFLY WINGS *Hut HUTCD 63*	**20** 3
10 Feb 96		1979 *Hut HUTCD 67*	**16** 3
18 May 96	●	TONIGHT TONIGHT *Hut HUTDX 69*	**7** 6
23 Nov 96		THIRTY THREE *Hut HUTCD 78*	**21** 2
14 Jun 97	●	THE END IS THE BEGINNING IS THE END *Warner Bros. W 0404CD*	**10** 4
23 Aug 97		THE END IS THE BEGINNING IS THE END (re-mix) *Warner Bros. W 0410CD*	**72** 1
30 May 98		AVA ADORE *Hut HUTCD 101*	**11** 4
19 Sep 98		PERFECT *Hut HUTCD 106*	**24** 2
4 Mar 00		STAND INSIDE YOUR LOVE *Hut HUTCD 127*	**23** 2
23 Sep 00		TRY TRY TRY *Hut HUTCD 140*	**73** 1

SMEAR CAMPAIGN – See MR BEAN and SMEAR CAMPAIGN featuring Bruce DICKINSON

SMELLS LIKE HEAVEN
Italy, male producer - Fabio Paras (1 WEEK)

			pos/wks
10 Jul 93		LONDRES STRUTT *Deconstruction 74321154312*	**57** 1

Ann-Marie SMITH
UK, female vocalist (5 WEEKS)

			pos/wks
23 Jan 93		MUSIC *Synthetic CDR 6334* [1]	**34** 2
18 Mar 95		ROCKIN' MY BODY *Media MCSTD 2021* [2]	**31** 2
15 Jul 95		(YOU'RE MY ONE AND ONLY) TRUE LOVE *Media MCSTD 2060*	**46** 1

[1] Fargetta and Anne-Marie Smith [2] 49ers featuring Ann-Marie Smith

Elliott SMITH
US, male vocalist / instrumentalist (3 WEEKS)

			pos/wks
19 Dec 98		WALTZ #2 (XO) *DreamWorks DRMCD 22347*	**52** 1
1 May 99		BABY BRITAIN *DreamWorks DRMDM 50950*	**55** 1
8 Jul 00		SON OF SAM *Dreamworks DRMCD 4509492*	**55** 1

Hurricane SMITH
UK, male vocalist - Norman Smith (35 WEEKS)

			pos/wks
12 Jun 71	●	DON'T LET IT DIE *Columbia DB 8785*	**2** 12
29 Apr 72	●	OH BABE WHAT WOULD YOU SAY? *Columbia DB 8878*	**4** 16
2 Sep 72		WHO WAS IT *Columbia DB 8916*	**23** 7

Jimmy SMITH
US, male instrumentalist - organ (3 WEEKS)

			pos/wks
28 Apr 66		GOT MY MOJO WORKING *Verve VS 536*	**48** 2
19 May 66		GOT MY MOJO WORKING (re-entry) *Verve VS 536*	**48** 1

Keely SMITH
US, female vocalist (10 WEEKS)

			pos/wks
18 Mar 65		YOU'RE BREAKIN' MY HEART *Reprise R 20346*	**14** 10

Mandy SMITH
UK, female vocalist (2 WEEKS)

			pos/wks
20 May 89		DON'T YOU WANT ME BABY *PWL PWL 37*	**59** 2

Mark E SMITH – See FALL; INSPIRAL CARPETS; D.O.S.E.

Mel SMITH
UK, male vocalist (10 WEEKS)

			pos/wks
5 Dec 87	●	ROCKIN' AROUND THE CHRISTMAS TREE *10 TEN 2* [1]	**3** 7
21 Dec 91		ANOTHER BLOOMING CHRISTMAS *Epic 6576877*	**59** 3

[1] Mel and Kim (Kim was Kim Wilde)

Muriel SMITH US, female vocalist (17 WEEKS)

		pos/wks
15 May 53 ●	HOLD ME THRILL ME KISS ME *Philips PB 122*	**3** 17

OC SMITH US, male vocalist (23 WEEKS)

		pos/wks
29 May 68 ●	SON OF HICKORY HOLLER'S TRAMP *CBS 3343*	**2** 15
26 Mar 77	TOGETHER *Caribou CRB 4910*	**25** 8

Patti SMITH GROUP
US, female / male vocal / instrumental group (16 WEEKS)

		pos/wks
29 Apr 78 ●	BECAUSE THE NIGHT *Arista 181*	**5** 12
19 Aug 78	PRIVILEGE (SET ME FREE) *Arista 197*	**72** 1
2 Jun 79	FREDERICK *Arista 264*	**63** 3

Rex SMITH and Rachel SWEET
US, male / female vocalists. (7 WEEKS)

		pos/wks
22 Aug 81	EVERLASTING LOVE *CBS A 1405*	**35** 7

Richard Jon SMITH South Africa, male vocalist (2 WEEKS)

		pos/wks
16 Jul 83	SHE'S THE MASTER OF THE GAME *Jive JIVE 38*	**63** 2

Rose SMITH – See DELAKOTA

Whistling Jack SMITH UK, male whistler (12 WEEKS)

		pos/wks
2 Mar 67 ●	I WAS KAISER BILL'S BATMAN *Deram DM 112*	**5** 12

Will SMITH `295` `Top 500`
Artist formerly known as the Fresh Prince is not only one of the 1990s most successful rap stars, but also a top TV personality and movie actor. b. 25 Sep 1968, Philadelphia, US. Quadruple World Music Award winner (1999) helped to make rap respectable and accessible to all ages (100 WEEKS)

		pos/wks
16 Aug 97 ★	MEN IN BLACK *Columbia 6648682* ■	**1** 16
13 Dec 97	JUST CRUISIN' *Columbia 6653482*	**23** 6
7 Feb 98 ●	GETTIN' JIGGY WIT IT *Columbia 6655605* ▲	**3** 10
1 Aug 98 ●	JUST THE TWO OF US *Columbia 6662092*	**2** 10
5 Dec 98 ●	MIAMI *Columbia 6666782*	**3** 14
13 Feb 99 ●	BOY YOU KNOCK ME OUT *MJJ / Epic 6669372* [1]	**3** 8
15 May 99	BOY YOU KNOCK ME OUT (re-entry) *MJJ / Epic 6669372* [1]	**69** 1
10 Jul 99 ●	WILD WILD WEST *Columbia 6675962* [2] ▲	**2** 16
20 Nov 99 ●	WILL 2K *Columbia 6684452*	**2** 11
25 Mar 00	FREAKIN' IT *Columbia 6691052*	**15** 7
27 May 00	FREAKIN' IT (re-entry) *Columbia 6691052*	**59** 1

[1] Tatyana Ali featuring Will Smith [2] Will Smith featuring Dru Hill - additional vocals Kool Moe Dee

See also JAZZY JEFF & the FRESH PRINCE

SMITHS `279` `Top 500`
Mancunian quartet with loyal fan base: Morrissey (b. Stephen Morrissey) (v), Johnny Marr (g), Andy Rourke (b), Mike Joyce (d). Their achievements include monopolising the Top 3 indie chart placings (Feb 1984) and having seven albums simultaneously in UK chart (Mar 1995) (105 WEEKS)

		pos/wks
12 Nov 83	THIS CHARMING MAN *Rough Trade RT 136*	**25** 12
28 Jan 84	WHAT DIFFERENCE DOES IT MAKE *Rough Trade RT 146*	**12** 9
2 Jun 84 ●	HEAVEN KNOWS I'M MISERABLE NOW *Rough Trade RT 156*	**10** 8
1 Sep 84	WILLIAM, IT WAS REALLY NOTHING *Rough Trade RT 166*	**17** 6
9 Feb 85	HOW SOON IS NOW? *Rough Trade RT 176*	**24** 6
30 Mar 85	SHAKESPEARE'S SISTER *Rough Trade RT 181*	**26** 4
13 Jul 85	THAT JOKE ISN'T FUNNY ANYMORE *Rough Trade RT 186*	**49** 3
5 Oct 85	THE BOY WITH THE THORN IN HIS SIDE *Rough Trade RT 191*	**23** 5
31 May 86	BIG MOUTH STRIKES AGAIN *Rough Trade RT 192*	**26** 4
2 Aug 86	PANIC *Rough Trade RT 193*	**11** 8
1 Nov 86	ASK *Rough Trade RT 194*	**14** 5
7 Feb 87	SHOPLIFTERS OF THE WORLD UNITE *Rough Trade RT 195*	**12** 4
25 Apr 87 ●	SHEILA TAKE A BOW *Rough Trade RT 196*	**10** 5
22 Aug 87	GIRLFRIEND IN A COMA *Rough Trade RT 197*	**13** 5
14 Nov 87	I STARTED SOMETHING I COULDN'T FINISH *Rough Trade RT 198*	**23** 4
19 Dec 87	LAST NIGHT I DREAMT THAT SOMEBODY LOVED ME *Rough Trade RT 200*	**30** 4
15 Aug 92 ●	THIS CHARMING MAN (re-issue) *WEA YZ 0001*	**8** 5
12 Sep 92	HOW SOON IS NOW (re-issue) *WEA YZ 0002*	**16** 4
24 Oct 92	THERE IS A LIGHT THAT NEVER GOES OUT *WEA YZ 0003*	**25** 3
18 Feb 95	ASK (re-issue) *WEA YZ 0004CDX*	**62** 1

SMOKE UK, male vocal / instrumental group (3 WEEKS)

		pos/wks
9 Mar 67	MY FRIEND JACK *Columbia DB 8115*	**45** 3

SMOKE CITY
UK / Brazil, male / female vocal / instrumental group (5 WEEKS)

		pos/wks
12 Apr 97 ●	UNDERWATER LOVE *Jive JIVECD 422*	**4** 5

SMOKED – See Oliver LIEB presents SMOKED

SMOKIE `211` `Top 500`
British group who became European superstars, fronted by easily identifiable vocalist Chris Norman. Especially popular in Germany, many of their hits were penned by Mike Chapman and Nicky Chinn (125 WEEKS)

		pos/wks
19 Jul 75 ●	IF YOU THINK YOU KNOW HOW TO LOVE ME *RAK 206* [1]	**3** 9
4 Oct 75 ●	DON'T PLAY YOUR ROCK 'N ROLL TO ME *RAK 217* [1]	**8** 7
31 Jan 76	SOMETHING'S BEEN MAKING ME BLUE *RAK 227*	**17** 8
25 Sep 76	I'LL MEET YOU AT MIDNIGHT *RAK 241*	**11** 9
4 Dec 76 ●	LIVING NEXT DOOR TO ALICE *RAK 244*	**5** 11
19 Mar 77	LAY BACK IN THE ARMS OF SOMEONE *RAK 251*	**12** 9
16 Jul 77 ●	IT'S YOUR LIFE *RAK 260*	**5** 9
15 Oct 77 ●	NEEDLES AND PINS *RAK 263*	**10** 9
28 Jan 78	FOR A FEW DOLLARS MORE *RAK 267*	**17** 6
20 May 78 ●	OH CAROL *RAK 276*	**5** 13
23 Sep 78	MEXICAN GIRL *RAK 283*	**19** 9
19 Apr 80	TAKE GOOD CARE OF MY BABY *RAK 309*	**34** 7
13 May 95	LIVING NEXT DOOR TO ALICE (WHO THE F**K IS ALICE) *NOW CDWAG 245* [2]	**64** 2
12 Aug 95 ●	LIVING NEXT DOOR TO ALICE (WHO THE F**K IS ALICE) (re-entry) *NOW CDWAG 245* [2]	**3** 17

[1] Smokey [2] Smokie featuring Roy 'Chubby' Brown

'Living Next Door to Alice (Who The F**k Is Alice)' is a re-recorded version of 'Living Next Door to Alice'

SMOKIN BEATS featuring Lyn EDEN
UK, male DJ / production duo and UK, female vocalist (3 WEEKS)

		pos/wks
17 Jan 98	DREAMS *AM:PM 5824711*	**23** 3

SMOKIN' MOJO FILTERS
UK / US, male / female vocal / instrumental charity group (5 WEEKS)

		pos/wks
23 Dec 95	COME TOGETHER (WAR CHILD) *Go! Discs GODCD 136*	**19** 5

SMOOTH US, female vocalist (7 WEEKS)

		pos/wks
22 Jul 95	MIND BLOWIN' *Jive JIVECD 379*	**36** 2
7 Oct 95	IT'S SUMMERTIME (LET IT GET IN YOU) *Jive JIVECD 383*	**46** 1
16 Mar 96	LOVE GROOVE (GROOVE WITH YOU) *Jive JIVECD 390*	**46** 1
16 Mar 96	WE GOT IT *MCA MCSTD 48009* [1]	**26** 2
6 Jul 96	UNDERCOVER LOVER *Jive JIVECD 397*	**41** 1

[1] Immature featuring Smooth

Joe SMOOTH US, male producer (4 WEEKS)

		pos/wks
4 Feb 89	PROMISED LAND *DJ International DJIN 6*	**56** 4

SMOOTH TOUCH US, male instrumental / production duo (1 WEEK)

		pos/wks
2 Apr 94	HOUSE OF LOVE (IN MY HOUSE) *Six6 SIXCD 112*	**58** 1

SMURFS Holland, small blue creatures vocal group (52 WEEKS)

		pos/wks
3 Jun 78 ●	THE SMURF SONG *Decca F 13759* [1]	**2** 17
30 Sep 78	DIPPETY DAY *Decca F 13798*	**13** 12

UK No.1 ★   UK Top 10 ●   Still on chart +   UK million seller ◆   UK entry at No.1 ■   US No.1 ▲

2 Dec 78		CHRISTMAS IN SMURFLAND *Decca F 13819*	.....**19**	7
7 Sep 96	●	I'VE GOT A LITTLE PUPPY *EMI TV CDSMURF 100*	.....**4**	10
21 Dec 96	●	YOUR CHRISTMAS WISH *EMI TV CDSMURF 102*	.....**8**	6

1 Father Abraham and the Smurfs

Patty SMYTH – See Don HENLEY

SNAKEBITE *Italy, male production trio (2 WEEKS)* — pos/wks

| 9 Aug 97 | THE BIT GOES ON *Multiply CDMULTY 22* | .....**25** | 2 |

SNAP ⟨236 Top 500⟩ *German-based producers Benito Benites (b. Michael Munzing) and John Garrett Virgo III (b. Luca Anzilotti) masterminded a string of worldwide dance hits for this act, which featured a host of mostly US vocalists and rappers including Turbo B, Jackie Harris, Penny Ford and Thea Austin (115 WEEKS)* — pos/wks

24 Mar 90	★	THE POWER *Arista 113133*	.....**1**	15
16 Jun 90	●	OOOPS UP *Arista 113296*	.....**5**	12
22 Sep 90	●	CULT OF SNAP *Arista 113596*	.....**8**	7
8 Dec 90	●	MARY HAD A LITTLE BOY *Arista 113831*	.....**8**	10
30 Mar 91	●	SNAP MEGAMIX *Arista 114169*	.....**10**	6
21 Dec 91		THE COLOUR OF LOVE *Arista 114678*	.....**54**	3
4 Jul 92	★	RHYTHM IS A DANCER *Arista 115309*	.....**1**	19
9 Jan 93	●	EXTERMINATE! *Arista 74321106962* 1	.....**2**	11
12 Jun 93	●	DO YOU SEE THE LIGHT (LOOKING FOR) *Arista 74321147622* 1	.....**10**	8
17 Sep 94	●	WELCOME TO TOMORROW *Arista 74321223852* 2	.....**6**	13
14 Jan 95		WELCOME TO TOMORROW (re-entry) *Arista 74321223852* 2	.....**75**	1
1 Apr 95		THE FIRST THE LAST ETERNITY (TIL THE END) *Arista 74321254672* 2	.....**15**	7
28 Oct 95		THE WORLD IN MY HANDS *Arista 74321314792* 2	.....**44**	1
13 Apr 96		RAME *Arista 74321368902* 3	.....**50**	1
24 Aug 96		THE POWER 96 *Arista 74321398672* 4	.....**42**	1

1 Snap featuring Niki Haris 2 Snap featuring Summer 3 Snap featuring Rukmani 4 Snap featuring Einstein

SNEAKER PIMPS
UK, male / female vocal / instrumental group (19 WEEKS) — pos/wks

19 Oct 96		6 UNDERGROUND *Clean Up CUP 023CDS*	.....**15**	4
15 Mar 97		SPIN SPIN SUGAR *Clean Up CUP 033CDS*	.....**21**	3
7 Jun 97	●	6 UNDERGROUND (re-mix) *Clean Up CUP 036CDM*	.....**9**	4
30 Aug 97		POST MODERN SLEAZE *Clean Up CUP 038CDM*	.....**22**	3
7 Feb 98		SPIN SPIN SUGAR (re-mix) *Clean Up CUP 037X*	.....**46**	2
21 Aug 99		LOW FIVE *Clean Up CUP 052CDM*	.....**39**	2
30 Oct 99		TEN TO TWENTY *Clean Up CUP 054CDS*	.....**56**	1

SNIFF 'N' THE TEARS
UK, male vocal / instrumental group (5 WEEKS) — pos/wks

| 23 Jun 79 | | DRIVER'S SEAT *Chiswick CHIS 105* | .....**42** | 5 |

SNOOP DOGGY DOGG
US, male rapper - Calvin Broadus (41 WEEKS) — pos/wks

4 Dec 93		WHAT'S MY NAME? *Death Row A 8337CD*	.....**20**	8
12 Feb 94		GIN AND JUICE *Death Row A 8316CD*	.....**39**	3
20 Aug 94		DOGGY DOGG WORLD *Death Row A 8289CD*	.....**32**	3
14 Dec 96		SNOOP'S UPSIDE YA HEAD *Interscope IND 95520* 1	.....**12**	7
26 Apr 97		WANTED DEAD OR ALIVE *Def Jam 5744052* 2	.....**16**	3
3 May 97		VAPORS *Interscope IND 95530*	.....**18**	2
20 Sep 97		WE JUST WANNA PARTY WITH YOU *Columbia 6649902* 3	.....**21**	2
24 Jan 98		THA DOGGFATHER *Interscope IND 95550*	.....**36**	2
12 Dec 98		COME AND GET WITH ME *Elektra E 3787CD* 4	.....**58**	1
25 Mar 00	●	STILL D.R.E. *Interscope 4972742* 5	.....**6**	10

1 Snoop Doggy Dogg featuring Charlie Wilson 2 2Pac and Snoop Doggy Dogg 3 Snoop Doggy Dogg featuring JD 4 Keith Sweat featuring Snoop Dogg 5 Dr Dre featuring Snoop Dogg

SNOW *Canada, male rapper - Darrin O'Brien (18 WEEKS)* — pos/wks

13 Mar 93	●	INFORMER *East West America A 8436CD* ▲	.....**2**	15
5 Jun 93		GIRL I'VE BEEN HURT *East West America A 8417CD*	.....**48**	2
4 Sep 93		UHH IN YOU *Atlantic A 8378CD*	.....**67**	1

Mark SNOW *US, male instrumentalist - keyboards (15 WEEKS)* — pos/wks

| 30 Mar 96 | ● | THE X-FILES *Warner Bros. W 0341CD* | .....**2** | 15 |

Phoebe SNOW *US, female vocalist (7 WEEKS)* — pos/wks

| 6 Jan 79 | | EVERY NIGHT *CBS 6842* | .....**37** | 7 |

SNOWMAN – See Peter AUTY and the SINFONIA OF LONDON conducted by Howard BLAKE

SNOWMEN *UK, male vocal / instrumental group (12 WEEKS)* — pos/wks

| 12 Dec 81 | | HOKEY COKEY *Stiff ODB 1* | .....**18** | 8 |
| 18 Dec 82 | | XMAS PARTY *Solid STOP 006* | .....**44** | 4 |

SNUG *UK, male vocal / instrumental group (1 WEEK)* — pos/wks

| 18 Apr 98 | | BEATNIK GIRL *WEA WEA 151CDX* | .....**55** | 1 |

SO *UK, male vocal / instrumental group (3 WEEKS)* — pos/wks

| 13 Feb 88 | | ARE YOU SURE *Parlophone R 6173* | .....**62** | 3 |

S.O.A.P. *Denmark, female vocal duo (2 WEEKS)* — pos/wks

| 25 Jul 98 | | THIS IS HOW WE PARTY *Columbia 6661295* | .....**36** | 2 |

SOAPY *UK, male instrumental / production duo (2 WEEKS)* — pos/wks

| 14 Sep 96 | | HORNY AS FUNK *WEA WEA 074CD* | .....**35** | 2 |

Gino SOCCIO *Canada, male instrumentalist - keyboards (5 WEEKS)* — pos/wks

| 28 Apr 79 | | DANCER *Warner Bros. K 17357* | .....**46** | 5 |

SOEUR SOURIRE – See SINGING NUN (Soeur Sourire)

SOFT CELL ⟨268 Top 500⟩ *Successful synth-driven duo from Leeds: Marc Almond (v), David Ball (k). The visually striking pair's revival of Northern soul classic 'Tainted Love' was the Top UK single of 1981 and also broke the longevity record in the US Top 100 (107 WEEKS)* — pos/wks

1 Aug 81	★	TAINTED LOVE *Some Bizzare BZS 2*	.....**1**	16
14 Nov 81	●	BEDSITTER *Some Bizzare BZS 6*	.....**4**	12
9 Jan 82		TAINTED LOVE (re-entry) *Some Bizzare BZS 2*	.....**43**	10
6 Feb 82	●	SAY HELLO WAVE GOODBYE *Some Bizzare BZS 7*	.....**3**	9
29 May 82	●	TORCH *Some Bizzare BZS 9*	.....**2**	9
24 Jul 82		TAINTED LOVE (2nd re-entry) *Some Bizzare BZS 2*	.....**50**	4
21 Aug 82	●	WHAT *Some Bizzare BZS 11*	.....**3**	8
4 Dec 82		WHERE THE HEART IS *Some Bizzare BZS 16*	.....**21**	7
5 Mar 83		NUMBERS / BARRIERS *Some Bizzare BZS 17*	.....**25**	4
24 Sep 83		SOUL INSIDE *Some Bizzare BZS 20*	.....**16**	5
25 Feb 84		DOWN IN THE SUBWAY *Some Bizzare BZS 22*	.....**24**	6
9 Feb 85		TAINTED LOVE (3rd re-entry) *Some Bizzare BZS 2*	.....**43**	6
23 Mar 91		SAY HELLO WAVE GOODBYE '91 (re-recording) *Mercury SOFT 1* 1	.....**38**	3
18 May 91	●	TAINTED LOVE (re-issue) *Mercury SOFT 2* 1	.....**5**	8

1 Soft Cell / Marc Almond

SOHO *UK, male / female vocal / instrumental group (11 WEEKS)* — pos/wks

5 May 90		HIPPY CHICK *Savage 7SAV 106*	.....**67**	1
19 Jan 91	●	HIPPY CHICK (re-entry) *Savage 7SAV 106*	.....**8**	8
9 Nov 91		BORN TO BE ALIVE *MCA MCS 1578* 1	.....**51**	2

1 Adamski featuring Soho

The listed flip side of 'Born to Be Alive' was 'Never Goin' Down' by Adamski featuring Jimi Polo

SOLAR STONE UK, male DJ / production trio (3 WEEKS) pos/wks

| 21 Feb 98 | THE IMPRESSIONS EP *Hooj Choons HOOJCD 57* | 75 | 1 |
| 6 Nov 99 | SEVEN CITIES *Hooj Choons HOOJ 85CD* | 39 | 2 |

The Impressions EP: The Calling / Day By Day / The Calling / Day By Day / So Clear

SOLID GOLD CHARTBUSTERS
UK, male / female production / vocal group (1 WEEK) pos/wks

| 25 Dec 99 | I WANNA 1-2-1 WITH YOU *Virgin VSCDT 1765* | 62 | 1 |

SOLID HARMONIE UK / US, female vocal group (11 WEEKS) pos/wks

31 Jan 98	I'LL BE THERE FOR YOU *Jive JIVECD 437*	18	3
18 Apr 98	I WANT YOU TO WANT ME *Jive JIVECD 452*	16	3
15 Aug 98	I WANNA LOVE YOU *Jive 0521742*	20	4
21 Nov 98	TO LOVE ONCE AGAIN *Jive 0522472*	55	1

SOLO UK, male producer - Stuart Crichton (4 WEEKS) pos/wks

20 Jul 91	RAINBOW (SAMPLE FREE) *Reverb RVBT 003*	59	2
18 Jan 92	COME ON! *Reverb RVBT 008*	75	1
11 Sep 93	COME ON! (re-mix) *Stoatin' STOAT 003CD*	63	1

Sal SOLO UK, male vocalist (13 WEEKS) pos/wks

| 15 Dec 84 | SAN DAMIANO (HEART AND SOUL) *MCA MCA 930* | 15 | 10 |
| 6 Apr 85 | MUSIC AND YOU *MCA MCA 946* [1] | 52 | 3 |

[1] Sal Solo with the London Community Gospel Choir

SOLO U.S. US, male vocal group (3 WEEKS) pos/wks

| 3 Feb 96 | HEAVEN *Perspective 5875212* | 35 | 2 |
| 30 Mar 96 | WHERE DO U WANT ME TO PUT IT *Perspective 5875312* | 45 | 1 |

SOLUTION – See Victor SIMONELLI presents SOLUTION

Jimmy SOMERVILLE UK, male vocalist (53 WEEKS) pos/wks

11 Nov 89	COMMENT TE DIRE ADIEU *London LON 241* [1]	14	9
13 Jan 90 ●	YOU MAKE ME FEEL (MIGHTY REAL) *London LON 249*	5	8
17 Mar 90	READ MY LIPS (ENOUGH IS ENOUGH) *London LON 254*	26	6
3 Nov 90 ●	TO LOVE SOMEBODY *London LON 281*	8	11
2 Feb 91	SMALLTOWN BOY (re-mix) *London LON 287* [2]	32	4
10 Aug 91	RUN FROM LOVE *London LON 301*	52	2
28 Jan 95	HEARTBEAT *London LONCD 358*	24	4
27 May 95	HURT SO GOOD *London LONCD 364*	15	6
28 Oct 95	BY YOUR SIDE *London LONCD 372*	41	2
13 Sep 97	DARK SKY *Gut CXGUT 11*	66	1

[1] Jimmy Somerville featuring June Miles-Kingston [2] Jimmy Somerville with Bronski Beat

See also BRONSKI BEAT; COMMUNARDS

SOMETHIN' FOR THE PEOPLE featuring TRINA and TAMARA
US, male vocal / instrumental group and female vocal duo (1 WEEK) pos/wks

| 7 Feb 98 | MY LOVE IS THE SHHH! *Warner Bros W 0427CD* | 64 | 1 |

SOMORE featuring Damon TRUEITT
US, male production group and male vocalist (2 WEEKS) pos/wks

| 24 Jan 98 | I REFUSE (WHAT YOU WANT) *XL Recordings XLS 93CD* | 21 | 2 |

SONGSTRESS US, male production / vocal duo (1 WEEK) pos/wks

| 27 Feb 99 | SEE LINE WOMAN '99 *Locked On LOX 106CD* | 64 | 1 |

SONIA ⟨ 420 ⟩ Top 500
Bubbly teenage pop performer, b. Sonia Evans, 13 Feb 1971, Liverpool, UK. Singer / actress - the youngest UK female to reach No.1 since Mary Hopkin (1968) - was produced by the hit machine Stock Aitken and Waterman (78 WEEKS) pos/wks

24 Jun 89 ★	YOU'LL NEVER STOP ME LOVING YOU *Chrysalis CHS 3385*	1	13
7 Oct 89	CAN'T FORGET YOU *Chrysalis CHS 3419*	17	6
9 Dec 89 ●	LISTEN TO YOUR HEART *Chrysalis CHS 3465*	10	10
7 Apr 90	COUNTING EVERY MINUTE *Chrysalis CHS 3492*	16	7

23 Jun 90	YOU'VE GOT A FRIEND *Jive CHILD 90* [1]	14	6
25 Aug 90	END OF THE WORLD *Chrysalis/PWL CHS 3557*	18	7
1 Jun 91 ●	ONLY FOOLS (NEVER FALL IN LOVE) *IQ ZB 44613*	10	8
31 Aug 91	BE YOUNG BE FOOLISH BE HAPPY *IQ ZB 44935*	22	5
16 Nov 91	YOU TO ME ARE EVERYTHING *IQ ZB 45121*	13	5
12 Sep 92	BOOGIE NIGHTS *Arista 74321113467*	30	3
1 May 93	BETTER THE DEVIL YOU KNOW *Arista 74321146872*	15	7
30 Jul 94	HOPELESSLY DEVOTED TO YOU *Cockney COCCD 2*	61	1

[1] Big Fun and Sonia featuring Gary Barnacle

SONIC SOLUTION
Belgium, male production duo - CJ Bolland and Steve Cop (1 WEEK) pos/wks

| 4 Apr 92 | BEATSTIME *R&S RSUK 11* | 59 | 1 |

SONIC SURFERS
Holland, male instrumental / production duo (2 WEEKS) pos/wks

| 20 Mar 93 | TAKE ME UP *A & M AMCD 210* [1] | 61 | 1 |
| 30 Jul 94 | DON'T GIVE IT UP *Brilliant CDBRIL 6* | 54 | 1 |

[1] Sonic Surfers featuring Jocelyn Brown

SONIC THE HEDGEHOG – See HWA featuring SONIC THE HEDGEHOG

SONIC YOUTH
US, male / female vocal / instrumental group (14 WEEKS) pos/wks

11 Jul 92	100% *DGC DGCS 11*	28	4
7 Nov 92	YOUTH AGAINST FASCISM *Geffen GFS 26*	52	2
3 Apr 93	SUGAR KANE *Geffen GFSTD 37*	26	3
7 May 94	BULL IN THE HEATHER *Geffen GFSTD 72*	24	2
10 Sep 94	SUPERSTAR *A & M 5807932*	45	2
11 Jul 98	SUNDAY *Geffen GFSTD 22332*	72	1

The listed flip side of 'Superstar' was 'Yesterday Once More' by Redd Kross

SONIQUE UK, female vocalist / DJ - Sonia Clarke (36 WEEKS) pos/wks

13 Jun 98	I PUT A SPELL ON YOU *Serious SERR 001CD*	36	2
5 Dec 98	IT FEELS SO GOOD *Serious SERR 004CD*	24	3
3 Jun 00 ★	IT FEELS SO GOOD (re-mix) *Universal MCSTD 40233* ■	1	17
16 Sep 00 ●	SKY *Universal MCSTD 40240*	2	10
9 Dec 00 ●	I PUT A SPELL ON YOU (re-issue) *Universal MCSTD 40245*	8	4+

SONNY US, male vocalist - Salvatore Bono (11 WEEKS) pos/wks

| 19 Aug 65 ● | LAUGH AT ME *Atlantic AT 4038* | 9 | 11 |

See also SONNY and CHER

SONNY and CHER ⟨ 418 ⟩ Top 500
Most successful US husband-and-wife recording team, Salvatore Bono, b 16 Feb 1935, Michigan, US, d. 5 Jan 1998, Cherilyn LaPierre, b. 20 May 1946, California, US. Married 1963-74 and was the major new act of 1965. Cher became a successful soloist and Sonny was elected mayor of Palm Springs (78 WEEKS) pos/wks

12 Aug 65 ★	I GOT YOU BABE *Atlantic AT 4035* ▲	1	12
16 Sep 65	BABY DON'T GO *Reprise R 20309*	11	9
21 Oct 65	BUT YOU'RE MINE *Atlantic AT 4047*	17	8
17 Feb 66	WHAT NOW MY LOVE *Atlantic AT 4069*	13	11
30 Jun 66	HAVE I STAYED TOO LONG *Atlantic 584 018*	42	3
8 Sep 66 ●	LITTLE MAN *Atlantic 584 040*	4	10
17 Nov 66	LIVING FOR YOU *Atlantic 584 057*	44	4
2 Feb 67	THE BEAT GOES ON *Atlantic 584 078*	29	8
15 Jan 72 ●	ALL I EVER NEED IS YOU *MCA MU 1145*	8	12
22 May 93	I GOT YOU BABE (re-issue) *Epic 6592402*	66	1

See also SONNY; CHER

SON'Z OF A LOOP DA LOOP ERA
UK, male producer - Danny Breaks (4 WEEKS) pos/wks

| 15 Feb 92 | FAR OUT *Suburban Base SUBBASE 008* | 36 | 3 |
| 17 Oct 92 | PEACE + LOVEISM *Suburban Base SUBBASE 14* | 60 | 1 |

SOOZY Q – See BIG TIME CHARLIE

UK No.1 ★   UK Top 10 ●   Still on chart +   UK million seller ◆   UK entry at No.1 ■   US No.1 ▲

SORROWS UK, male vocal / instrumental group (8 WEEKS)

		pos	wks
16 Sep 65	TAKE A HEART *Piccadilly 7N 35260*	21	8

S.O.S. BAND
US, male / female vocal / instrumental group (46 WEEKS)

		pos	wks
19 Jul 80	TAKE YOUR TIME (DO IT RIGHT) PART 1 *Tabu TBU 8564*	51	4
26 Feb 83	GROOVIN' (THAT'S WHAT WE'RE DOIN') *Tabu TBU A3120* ...	72	1
7 Apr 84	JUST BE GOOD TO ME *Tabu A 3626*	13	11
4 Aug 84	JUST THE WAY YOU LIKE IT *Tabu A 4621*	32	7
13 Oct 84	WEEKEND GIRL *Tabu A 4785*	51	5
29 Mar 86	THE FINEST *Tabu A 6997*	17	10
5 Jul 86	BORROWED LOVE *Tabu A 7241*	50	5
2 May 87	NO LIES *Tabu 650444 7*	64	3

David SOUL US, male actor / vocalist- David Solberg (56 WEEKS)

		pos	wks
18 Dec 76	★ DON'T GIVE UP ON US *Private Stock PVT 84* ◆ ▲	1	16
26 Mar 77	● GOING IN WITH MY EYES OPEN *Private Stock PVT 99*	2	8
27 Aug 77	★ SILVER LADY *Private Stock PVT 115*	1	14
17 Dec 77	● LET'S HAVE A QUIET NIGHT IN *Private Stock PVT 130*.....	8	9
27 May 78	IT SURE BRINGS OUT THE LOVE IN YOUR EYES *Private Stock PVT 137*	12	9

Jimmy SOUL US, male vocalist (5 WEEKS)

		pos	wks
11 Jul 63	IF YOU WANNA BE HAPPY *Stateside SS 178* ▲	39	2
15 Jun 91	IF YOU WANNA BE HAPPY (re-issue) *Epic 6569647*	68	3

SOUL ASYLUM US, male vocal / instrumental group (33 WEEKS)

		pos	wks
19 Jun 93	RUNAWAY TRAIN *Columbia 6593902*	37	8
4 Sep 93	SOMEBODY TO SHOVE *Columbia 6596492*	34	3
13 Nov 93	● RUNAWAY TRAIN (re-entry) *Columbia 6593902*	7	11
22 Jan 94	BLACK GOLD *Columbia 6598442*	26	4
26 Mar 94	SOMEBODY TO SHOVE (re-issue) *Columbia 6602245*	32	3
15 Jul 95	MISERY *Columbia 6621092*	30	4
2 Dec 95	JUST LIKE ANYONE *Columbia 6624785*	52	1

SOUL BROTHERS UK, male vocal / instrumental group (3 WEEKS)

		pos	wks
22 Apr 65	I KEEP RINGING MY BABY *Decca F 12116*	42	3

SOUL CITY ORCHESTRA
UK, male instrumental / production group (1 WEEK)

		pos	wks
11 Dec 93	IT'S JURASSIC *London JURCD 1*	70	1

SOUL CITY SYMPHONY – See Van McCOY

SOUL FAMILY SENSATION
UK / US, male / female vocal / instrumental group (4 WEEKS)

		pos	wks
11 May 91	I DON'T EVEN KNOW IF I SHOULD CALL YOU BABY *One Little Indian 47 TP7*	49	4

SOUL FOR REAL US, male vocal group (4 WEEKS)

		pos	wks
8 Jul 95	CANDY RAIN *Uptown MCSTD 2052*	23	2
23 Mar 96	EVERY LITTLE THING I DO *Uptown MCSTD 48005*	31	2

SOUL II SOUL (346 Top 500) Enormously influential dance music
project led by entrepreneurial producer / DJ Jazzie B, b. Beresford Romeo, 16 Jan 1963, London. Act featured Nellee Hooper's innovative arrangements and was fronted by succession of vocalists, most notably Caron Wheeler. Unlike UK contemporaries they were equally successful in US (89 WEEKS)

		pos	wks
21 May 88	FAIRPLAY *10 TEN 228* [1]	63	3
17 Sep 88	FEEL FREE *10 TEN 236* [2]	64	2
18 Mar 89	● KEEP ON MOVING *10 TEN 263* [3]	5	12
10 Jun 89	★ BACK TO LIFE (HOWEVER DO YOU WANT ME) *10 TEN 265* [3] ..1		14
9 Dec 89	● GET A LIFE *10 TEN 284*	3	13
5 May 90	● A DREAM'S A DREAM *10 TEN 300*	6	6
24 Nov 90	MISSING YOU *10 TEN 345* [4]	22	7
4 Apr 92	● JOY *Ten TEN 350*	4	7
13 Jun 92	MOVE ME NO MOUNTAIN *Ten TEN 400* [5]	31	4
26 Sep 92	JUST RIGHT *Ten TEN 410*	38	2

		pos	wks
6 Nov 93	WISH *Virgin VSCDG 1480*	24	4
22 Jul 95	LOVE ENUFF *Virgin VSCDT 1527*	12	6
21 Oct 95	I CARE (SOUL II SOUL) *Virgin VSCDT 1560*	17	4
19 Oct 96	KEEP ON MOVIN' (re-mix) *Virgin VSCDT 1612*	31	2
30 Aug 97	REPRESENT *Island CID 668*	39	2
8 Nov 97	PLEASURE DOME *Island CID 669*	51	1

[1] Soul II Soul featuring Rose Windross [2] Soul II Soul featuring Do'reen [3] Soul II Soul featuring Caron Wheeler [4] Soul II Soul featuring Kym Mazelle [5] Soul II Soul, lead vocals Kofi

SOUL SONIC FORCE – See Afrika BAMBAATAA

S.O.U.L. S.Y.S.T.E.M. introducing Michelle VISAGE
US, male / female vocal / instrumental group (5 WEEKS)

		pos	wks
16 Jan 93	IT'S GONNA BE A LOVELY DAY *Arista 74321125692*	17	5

See also C & C MUSIC FACTORY

SOUL U*NIQUE UK, male / female vocal group (2 WEEKS)

		pos	wks
19 Feb 00	BE MY FRIEND *M&J MAJCD 2*	53	1
29 Jul 00	3IL (THRILL) *M&J MAJCD 3*	66	1

SOULED OUT
Italy / US / UK, male / female vocal / instrumental group (1 WEEK)

		pos	wks
9 May 92	IN MY LIFE *Columbia 6578367*	75	1

SOULSEARCHER
US, male / female production / vocal group (9 WEEKS)

		pos	wks
13 Feb 99	● CAN'T GET ENOUGH *Defected DEFECT 1CDS*	8	7
8 Apr 00	DO IT TO ME AGAIN *Defected DFECT 15CDS*	32	2

SOULWAX Belgium, male vocal / instrumental duo (4 WEEKS)

		pos	wks
25 Mar 00	CONVERSATION INTERCOM *Pias Recordings PIASB 018CD*	65	1
24 Jun 00	MUCH AGAINST EVERYONE'S ADVICE *Pias Recordings PIASB 026CD*	56	1
30 Sep 00	TOO MANY DJ'S *Pias Recordings PIASB 036CD*	40	2

SOUND 5 UK, male vocal / instrumental group (1 WEEK)

		pos	wks
24 Apr 99	ALA KABOO *Gut CDGUT 23*	69	1

SOUND FACTORY
Sweden, male vocal / instrumental duo (1 WEEK)

		pos	wks
5 Jun 93	2 THE RHYTHM *Logic 74321149422*	72	1

SOUND 9418 – See Jonathan KING

SOUND OF ONE featuring GLADEZZ
US, male / female vocal / instrumental duo (1 WEEK)

		pos	wks
20 Nov 93	AS I AM *Cooltempo CDCOOL 280*	65	1

SOUNDGARDEN
US, male vocal / instrumental group (24 WEEKS)

		pos	wks
11 Apr 92	JESUS CHRIST POSE *A & M AM 862*	30	3
20 Jun 92	RUSTY CAGE *A & M AM 874*	41	1
21 Nov 92	OUTSHINED *A & M AM 0102*	50	1
26 Feb 94	SPOONMAN *A & M 5805392*	20	3
30 Apr 94	THE DAY I TRIED TO LIVE *A & M 5805952*	42	2
20 Aug 94	BLACK HOLE SUN *A & M 5807532*	12	5
28 Jan 95	FELL ON BLACK DAYS *A & M 5809472*	24	2
18 May 96	PRETTY NOOSE *A & M 5816202*	14	3
28 Sep 96	BURDEN IN MY HAND *A & M 5818552*	33	2
28 Dec 96	BLOW UP THE OUTSIDE WORLD *A & M 5819862*	40	2

SOUNDMAN and Don LLOYDIE with Elisabeth TROY
UK, male / female vocal / production group (2 WEEKS)

		pos	wks
25 Feb 95	GREATER LOVE *Sound of Underground SOURCD 016*	49	2

SOUNDS INCORPORATED
UK, male instrumental group (11 WEEKS)   pos/wks

23 Apr 64	THE SPARTANS *Columbia DB 7239*	30	6
30 Jul 64	SPANISH HARLEM *Columbia DB 7321*	35	5

SOUNDS NICE featuring Tim MYCROFT
UK, male instrumental group (11 WEEKS)   pos/wks

6 Sep 69	LOVE AT FIRST SIGHT (JE T'AIME . . . MOI NON PLUS) *Parlophone R 5797*	18	11

SOUNDS OF BLACKNESS
US, male / female gospel choir (32 WEEKS)   pos/wks

22 Jun 91	OPTIMISTIC *Perspective PERSS 786*	45	4
28 Sep 91	THE PRESSURE PART 1 *Perspective PERSS 816*	71	1
15 Feb 92	OPTIMISTIC (re-issue) *Perspective PERSS 849*	28	4
25 Apr 92	THE PRESSURE PART 1 (re-mix) *Perspective PERSS 867*	49	2
8 May 93	I'M GOING ALL THE WAY *Perspective 5874252*	27	3
26 Mar 94	I BELIEVE *A & M 5874512*	17	4
2 Jul 94	GLORYLAND *Mercury MERCD 404* [1]	36	4
20 Aug 94	EVERYTHING IS GONNA BE ALRIGHT *A & M 5874672*	29	3
14 Jan 95	I'M GOING ALL THE WAY (re-issue) *A & M 5874832*	14	4
7 Jun 97	SPIRIT *A & M 5822292* [2]	35	2
14 Feb 98	THE PRESSURE (2nd re-mix) *AM:PM 5824872*	46	1

[1] Daryl Hall and the Sounds of Blackness [2] Sounds of Blackness / Craig Mack

SOUNDS ORCHESTRAL *UK, orchestra (18 WEEKS)*   pos/wks

3 Dec 64 ●	CAST YOUR FATE TO THE WIND *Piccadilly 7N 35206*	5	16
8 Jul 65	MOONGLOW *Piccadilly 7N 35248*	43	2

SOUNDSATION *UK, male producer (1 WEEK)*   pos/wks

14 Jan 95	PEACE AND JOY *Ffrreedom TABCD 224*	48	1

SOUNDSCAPE *UK, male DJ / production group (1 WEEK)*   pos/wks

14 Feb 98	DUBPLATE CULTURE *Satellite 74321552002*	61	1

SOUNDSOURCE
Sweden / UK, male instrumental / production group (1 WEEK)   pos/wks

11 Jan 92	TAKE ME UP *ffrr FX 177*	62	1

SOUP DRAGONS *UK, male vocal / instrumental group (23 WEEKS)* pos/wks

20 Jun 87	CAN'T TAKE NO MORE *Raw TV RTV 3*	65	1
5 Sep 87	SOFT AS YOUR FACE *Raw TV RTV 4*	66	2
14 Jul 90 ●	I'M FREE *Raw TV RTV 9* [1]	5	12
20 Oct 90	MOTHER UNIVERSE *Big Life BLR 30*	26	5
11 Apr 92	DIVINE THING *Big Life BLR 68*	53	3

[1] Soup Dragons featuring Junior Reid

SOURCE *UK, male producer - John Truelove (22 WEEKS)*   pos/wks

2 Feb 91 ●	YOU GOT THE LOVE *Truelove TLOVE 7001* [1]	4	11
26 Dec 92	ROCK THE HOUSE *React 12REACT 12* [2]	63	1
1 Mar 97 ●	YOU GOT THE LOVE (re-mix) *React CDREACT 89* [1]	3	8
23 Aug 97	CLOUDS *XL XLS 83CD*	38	2

[1] Source featuring Candi Staton [2] Source featuring Nicole

SOURMASH *UK, male production trio (1 WEEK)*   pos/wks

23 Dec 00	PILGRIMAGE / MESCALITO *Hooj Choons HOOJ 102*	73	1

Joe SOUTH *US, male vocalist - Joe Souter (11 WEEKS)*   pos/wks

5 Mar 69 ●	GAMES PEOPLE PLAY *Capitol CL 15579*	6	11

SOUTH ST. PLAYER
US, male vocalist / producer - Roland Clark (1 WEEK)   pos/wks

2 Sep 00	WHO KEEPS CHANGING YOUR MIND *Cream CREAM 4CD*	49	1

Jeri SOUTHERN *US, female vocalist (3 WEEKS)*   pos/wks

21 Jun 57	FIRE DOWN BELOW *Brunswick 05665*	22	3

SOUTHLANDERS *Jamaica / UK, male vocal group (10 WEEKS)*   pos/wks

22 Nov 57	ALONE *Decca F 10946*	17	10

SOUTHSIDE SPINNERS *Holland, male production duo - Marco Verkuylen and Benjamin Kuyten (7 WEEKS)*   pos/wks

27 May 00 ●	LUVSTRUCK *AM:PM CDAMPM 132*	9	7

SOUVLAKI *UK, male producer - Mark Summers (4 WEEKS)*   pos/wks

15 Feb 97	INFERNO *Wonderboy WBOYD 003*	24	3
8 Aug 98	MY TIME *Wonderboy WBOYD 009*	63	1

SOVEREIGN COLLECTION *UK, orchestra (6 WEEKS)*   pos/wks

3 Apr 71	MOZART 40 *Capitol CL 15676*	27	6

Red SOVINE *US, male vocalist (8 WEEKS)*   pos/wks

13 Jun 81 ●	TEDDY BEAR *Starday SD 142*	4	8

SOX *UK, female vocal / instrumental group - lead vocal Samantha Fox (1 WEEK)*   pos/wks

15 Apr 95	GO FOR THE HEART *Living Beat LBECD 33*	47	1

Bob B SOXX and the BLUE JEANS
US, male / female vocal group (2 WEEKS)   pos/wks

31 Jan 63	ZIP-A-DEE-DOO-DAH *London HLU 9646*	45	2

SPACE *France, male instrumental group (12 WEEKS)*   pos/wks

13 Aug 77 ●	MAGIC FLY *Pye International 7N 25746*	2	12

SPACE *UK, male vocal / instrumental group (51 WEEKS)*   pos/wks

6 Apr 96	NEIGHBOURHOOD *Gut CDGUT 1*	56	1
8 Jun 96	FEMALE OF THE SPECIES *Gut CDGUT 2*	14	10
7 Sep 96 ●	ME AND YOU VERSUS THE WORLD *Gut CDGUT 4*	9	6
2 Nov 96	NEIGHBOURHOOD (re-issue) *Gut CDGUT 5*	11	6
22 Feb 97	DARK CLOUDS *Gut CDGUT 6*	14	4
10 Jan 98 ●	AVENGING ANGELS *Gut CDGUT 16*	6	8
7 Mar 98 ●	THE BALLAD OF TOM JONES *Gut CDGUT 018* [1]	4	8
4 Jul 98	BEGIN AGAIN *Gut CDGUT 19*	21	4
5 Dec 98	THE BAD DAYS (EP) *Gut CDGUT 22*	20	3
8 Jul 00	DIARY OF A WIMP *Gut CDGUT 34*	49	1

[1] Space with Cerys of Catatonia

Tracks on The Bad Days (EP): Bad Days / We Gotta Get Out of This Place / The Unluckiest Man in the World

SPACE BABY *UK, male producer - Matt Darey (1 WEEK)*   pos/wks

8 Jul 95	FREE YOUR MIND *Hooj Choons HOOJ 34CD*	55	1

SPACE BROTHERS *UK, male production duo (19 WEEKS)*   pos/wks

17 May 97	SHINE *Manifesto FESCD 23*	23	3
13 Dec 97	FORGIVEN (I FEEL YOUR LOVE) *Manifesto FESCD 36*	27	7
10 Jul 99	LEGACY (SHOW ME LOVE) *Manifesto FESCD 55*	31	3
9 Oct 99	HEAVEN WILL COME *Manifesto FESCD 61*	25	2
5 Feb 00	SHINE 2000 (re-mix) *Manifesto FESCD 67*	18	4

SPACE KITTENS
UK, male instrumental / production group (1 WEEK)   pos/wks

13 Apr 96	STORM *Hooj Choons HOOJCD 41*	58	1

UK No.1 ★   UK Top 10 ●   Still on chart +   UK million seller ◆   UK entry at No.1 ■   US No.1 ▲

SPACE MANOEVRES
UK, male producer - John Graham (2 WEEKS)   pos/wks

29 Jan 00	STAGE ONE *Hooj Choons HOOJ 79CD*	25	2

SPACE MONKEY *UK, male producer - Paul Goodchild (4 WEEKS)* pos/wks

8 Oct 83	CAN'T STOP RUNNING *Innervision A 3742*	53	4

SPACE RAIDERS *UK, male production trio (1 WEEK)*   pos/wks

28 Mar 98	GLAM RAID *Skint SKINT 32CD*	68	1

SPACE 2000 *UK, male vocal / instrumental duo (1 WEEK)*   pos/wks

12 Aug 95	DO U WANNA FUNK *Wired WIRED 218*	50	1

SPACEDUST *UK, male production duo - Paul Glancey and Duncan Glasson (12 WEEKS)* pos/wks

24 Oct 98 ★	GYM AND TONIC *East West EW 188CD* ■	1	8
9 Jan 99	GYM AND TONIC (re-entry) *East West EW 188CD*	55	2
27 Mar 99	LET'S GET DOWN *East West EW 195CD*	20	2

SPACEHOG *UK, male vocal / instrumental group (8 WEEKS)*   pos/wks

11 May 96	IN THE MEANTIME *Sire 7559643162*	70	1
28 Dec 96	IN THE MEANTIME (re-entry) *Sire 7559643162*	29	6
7 Feb 98	CARRY ON *Sire W 0428CD*	43	1

SPACEMAID *UK, male vocal / instrumental group (1 WEEK)*   pos/wks

5 Apr 97	BABY COME ON *Big Star STARC 105*	70	1

SPAGHETTI SURFERS
UK, male instrumental / production duo (1 WEEK)   pos/wks

22 Jul 95	MISIRLOU (THE THEME TO THE MOTION PICTURE 'PULP FICTION') *Tempo Toons CDTOON 4*	55	1

SPAGNA *Italy, female vocalist - Ivana Spagna (23 WEEKS)*   pos/wks

25 Jul 87 ●	CALL ME *CBS 650279 7*	2	12
17 Oct 87	EASY LADY *CBS 651169 7*	62	3
20 Aug 88	EVERY GIRL AND BOY *CBS SPAG 1*	23	8

SPANDAU BALLET (132 Top 500) *Kilt-clad New Romantic revolutionaries. This London band went on to become smart-suited Top 10 regulars: Tony Hadley (v), Gary Kemp (g), Martin Kemp (b), Steve Norman (g/sax/prc), John Keeble (d). The Kemp brothers later went into the movies and TV, including lead roles in The Krays (1990) and, for Martin, a part in BBC soap EastEnders as Steve Owen (159 WEEKS)* pos/wks

15 Nov 80 ●	TO CUT A LONG STORY SHORT *Reformation CHS 2473*	5	11
24 Jan 81	THE FREEZE *Reformation CHS 2486*	17	8
4 Apr 81 ●	MUSCLEBOUND / GLOW *Reformation CHS 2509*	10	10
18 Jul 81 ●	CHANT NO. 1 (I DON'T NEED THIS PRESSURE ON) *Reformation CHS 2528*	3	10
14 Nov 81	PAINT ME DOWN *Chrysalis CHS 2560*	30	5
30 Jan 82	SHE LOVED LIKE DIAMOND *Chrysalis CHS 2585*	49	4
10 Apr 82 ●	INSTINCTION *Chrysalis CHS 2602*	10	11
2 Oct 82 ●	LIFELINE *Chrysalis CHS 2642*	7	9
12 Feb 83	COMMUNICATION *Reformation CHS 2662*	12	10
23 Apr 83 ★	TRUE *Reformation SPAN 1*	1	12
13 Aug 83 ●	GOLD *Reformation SPAN 2*	2	9
9 Jun 84 ●	ONLY WHEN YOU LEAVE *Reformation SPAN 3*	3	9
18 Aug 84	ONLY WHEN YOU LEAVE (re-entry) *Reformation SPAN 3*	74	1
25 Aug 84 ●	I'LL FLY FOR YOU *Reformation SPAN 4*	9	9
20 Oct 84	HIGHLY STRUNG *Reformation SPAN 5*	15	5
8 Dec 84	ROUND AND ROUND *Reformation SPAN 6*	18	8
26 Jul 86	FIGHT FOR OURSELVES *Reformation A 7264*	15	7
8 Nov 86 ●	THROUGH THE BARRICADES *Reformation SPANS 1*	6	10
14 Feb 87	HOW MANY LIES *Reformation SPANS 2*	34	4
3 Sep 88	RAW *CBS SPANS 3*	47	3
26 Aug 89	BE FREE WITH YOUR LOVE *CBS SPANS 4*	42	4

SPARKLE *US, female vocalist (10 WEEKS)*   pos/wks

18 Jul 98 ●	BE CAREFUL *Jive 0521452* [1]	7	6
5 Sep 98	BE CAREFUL (re-entry) *Jive 0521452* [1]	75	1
7 Nov 98	TIME TO MOVE ON *Jive 0522032*	40	2
28 Aug 99	LOVIN' YOU *Jive 0523450*	65	1

[1] Sparkle featuring R Kelly

SPARKLEHORSE *US, male vocal / instrumental group (2 WEEKS)* pos/wks

31 Aug 96	RAINMAKER *Capitol CDCL 777*	61	1
17 Oct 98	SICK OF GOODBYES *Parlophone CDCLS 808*	57	1

SPARKS (403 Top 500) *Eccentric and distinctive-looking pop / rock group, formed by Californian-born brothers Russell (v), 5 Oct 1953 and Ron Mael (k) 12 Aug 1948. Relocated to UK in 1973 and proved more successful in Europe than in their homeland. Voted Top Newcomers in the 1974 Record Mirror poll (81 WEEKS)* pos/wks

4 May 74 ●	THIS TOWN AIN'T BIG ENOUGH FOR BOTH OF US *Island WIP 6193*	2	10
20 Jul 74 ●	AMATEUR HOUR *Island WIP 6203*	7	9
19 Oct 74	NEVER TURN YOUR BACK ON MOTHER EARTH *Island WIP 6211*	13	7
18 Jan 75	SOMETHING FOR THE GIRL WITH EVERYTHING *Island WIP 6221*	17	7
19 Jul 75	GET IN THE SWING *Island WIP 6236*	27	7
4 Oct 75	LOOKS LOOKS LOOKS *Island WIP 6249*	26	4
21 Apr 79	THE NUMBER ONE SONG IN HEAVEN *Virgin VS 244*	14	12
21 Jul 79 ●	BEAT THE CLOCK *Virgin VS 270*	10	9
27 Oct 79	TRYOUTS FOR THE HUMAN RACE *Virgin VS 289*	45	5
29 Oct 94	WHEN DO I GET TO SING 'MY WAY' *Logic 74321234472*	38	3
11 Mar 95	WHEN I KISS YOU (I HEAR CHARLIE PARKER PLAYING) *Logic 74321264272*	36	2
20 May 95	WHEN DO I GET TO SING 'MY WAY' (re-issue) *Logic 74321274002*	32	2
9 Mar 96	NOW THAT I OWN THE BBC *Logic 74321348672*	60	1
25 Oct 97	THE NUMBER ONE SONG IN HEAVEN (re-recording) *Roadrunner RR 22692*	70	1
13 Dec 97	THIS TOWN AIN'T BIG ENOUGH FOR BOTH OF US *Roadrunner RR 22513* [1]	40	2

[1] Sparks vs Faith No More

Group was a UK / US group for first six hits

SPEAR OF DESTINY
UK, male vocal / instrumental group (43 WEEKS)   pos/wks

21 May 83	THE WHEEL *Epic A 3372*	59	5
21 Jan 84	PRISONER OF LOVE *Epic A 4068*	59	3
14 Apr 84	LIBERATOR *Epic A 4310*	67	2
15 Jun 85	ALL MY LOVE (ASK NOTHING) *Epic A 6333*	61	1
10 Aug 85	COME BACK *Epic A 6445*	55	3
7 Feb 87	STRANGERS IN OUR TOWN *10 TEN 148*	49	4
4 Apr 87	NEVER TAKE ME ALIVE *10 TEN 162*	14	11
25 Jul 87	WAS THAT YOU *10 TEN 173*	55	4
3 Oct 87	THE TRAVELLER *10 TEN 189*	44	4
24 Sep 88	SO IN LOVE WITH YOU *Virgin VS 1123*	36	5

SPEARHEAD *US, male vocal / instrumental group (5 WEEKS)*   pos/wks

17 Dec 94	OF COURSE YOU CAN *Capitol CDCL 733*	74	1
22 Apr 95	HOLE IN THE BUCKET *Capitol CDCL 742*	55	1
15 Jul 95	PEOPLE IN THA MIDDLE *Capitol CDCLS 752*	49	2
15 Mar 97	WHY OH WHY *Capital CDCL 785*	45	1

Billie Jo SPEARS *US, female vocalist (40 WEEKS)*   pos/wks

12 Jul 75 ●	BLANKET ON THE GROUND *United Artists UP 35805*	6	13
17 Jul 76 ◆	WHAT I'VE GOT IN MIND *United Artists UP 36118*	4	13
11 Dec 76	SING ME AN OLD FASHIONED SONG *United Artists UP 36179*	34	9
21 Jul 79	I WILL SURVIVE *United Artists UP 601*	47	5

Britney SPEARS `345` `Top 500`
World's top teenage solo star at turn of century, b. 2 Dec 1982, Louisiana, US. Broke debut-act first-week UK sales record (464,000 for 'Baby One More Time') and is the youngest million-selling female in the history of the UK singles chart. (89 WEEKS)

		pos/wks
27 Feb 99	★ BABY ONE MORE TIME *Jive 0522752* ◆ ■ ▲	1 22
26 Jun 99	● SOMETIMES *Jive 0523202*	3 16
2 Oct 99	(YOU DRIVE ME) CRAZY *Jive 0550582*	5 11
29 Jan 00	★ BORN TO MAKE YOU HAPPY *Jive 9250022* ■	1 12
13 May 00	★ OOPS!...I DID IT AGAIN *Jive 9250542* ■	1 14
26 Aug 00	● LUCKY *Jive 9251022*	5 11
16 Dec 00	● STRONGER *Jive 9251502*	7 3+

SPECIALS `292` `Top 500`
Midlands-based septet who led the early 1980s ska revival and, under Jerry Dammers (k), founded the trailblazing indie label 2 Tone. In 1981, Terry Hall (v), Neville Staples (v) and Lynval Golding (g) broke away to form Fun Boy Three (101 WEEKS)

		pos/wks
28 Jul 79	● GANGSTERS *2 Tone CHSTT 1* [1]	6 12
27 Oct 79	● A MESSAGE TO YOU RUDY / NITE KLUB *2 Tone CHSTT 5* [2]	10 14
26 Jan 80	★ THE SPECIAL A.K.A. LIVE EP *2 Tone CHSTT 7* [1]	1 10
24 May 80	● RAT RACE / RUDE BUOYS OUTA JAIL *2 Tone CHSTT 11*	5 9
20 Sep 80	● STEREOTYPE / INTERNATIONAL JET SET	
	2 Tone CHSTT 13	6 8
13 Dec 80	● DO NOTHING / MAGGIE'S FARM *2 Tone CHSTT 16*	4 11
20 Jun 81	★ GHOST TOWN *2 Tone CHSTT 17*	1 14
23 Jan 82	THE BOILER *2 Tone CHSTT 18* [3]	35 5
3 Sep 83	RACIST FRIEND / BRIGHT LIGHTS	
	2 Tone CHSTT 25 [4]	60 3
17 Mar 84	● NELSON MANDELA *2 Tone CHSTT 26* [4]	9 10
8 Sep 84	WHAT I LIKE MOST ABOUT YOU IS YOUR GIRLFRIEND	
	2 Tone CHSTT 27 [4]	51 4
10 Feb 96	HYPOCRITE *Kuff KUFFD 3*	66 1

[1] Special A.K.A. [2] Specials (featuring Rico+) [3] Rhoda with the Special A.K.A.
[4] Special A.K.A.

Tracks on The Special A.K.A. Live EP: Too Much Too Young / Guns of Navarone / Long Shot Kick De Bucket / The Liquidator / Skinhead Moonstomp. 'Maggie's Farm' listed with 'Do Nothing' only from 10 Jan 1981. Group was male / female for last four hits.

SPECTRUM *UK, male instrumental / production group (1 WEEK)*
		pos/wks
26 Sep 92	TRUE LOVE WILL FIND YOU IN THE END *Silvertone ORE 44*	70 1

Chris SPEDDING
UK, male vocalist / instrumentalist - guitar (8 WEEKS)
		pos/wks
23 Aug 75	MOTOR BIKING *RAK 210*	14 8

SPEECH *US, male vocalist (2 WEEKS)*
		pos/wks
17 Feb 96	LIKE MARVIN GAYE SAID (WHAT'S GOING ON)	
	Cooltempo CDCOOL 314	35 2

SPEEDY *UK, male / female vocal / instrumental group (1 WEEK)*
		pos/wks
9 Nov 96	BOY WONDER *Boiler House! BOIL 2CD*	56 1

SPELLBOUND *India, female vocal duo (1 WEEK)*
		pos/wks
31 May 97	HEAVEN ON EARTH *East West EW 098CD*	73 1

Johnnie SPENCE *UK, orchestra (15 WEEKS)*
		pos/wks
1 Mar 62	THEME FROM 'DR KILDARE'	
	Parlophone R 4872	15 15

Don SPENCER *UK, male vocalist (12 WEEKS)*
		pos/wks
21 Mar 63	FIREBALL *HMV POP 1087*	32 11
13 Jun 63	FIREBALL (re-entry) *HMV POP 1087*	49 1

Tracie SPENCER *US, female vocalist (3 WEEKS)*
		pos/wks
4 May 91	THIS HOUSE *Capitol CL 612*	65 2
6 Nov 99	IT'S ALL ABOUT YOU (NOT ABOUT ME)	
	Parlophone Rhythm Series CDCL 815	65 1

Jon SPENCER BLUES EXPLOSION
US, male vocal / instrumental group (1 WEEK)
		pos/wks
10 May 97	WAIL *Mute CDMUTE 204*	66 1

SPHINX *UK / US, male vocal / instrumental group (2 WEEKS)*
		pos/wks
25 Mar 95	WHAT HOPE HAVE I *Champion CHAMPCD 318*	43 2

SPICE GIRLS `114` `Top 500`
Britain's most successful female vocal group: Geri Halliwell (Ginger Spice - left 1998), Melanie Chisholm (Mel C / Sporty Spice), Emma Bunton (Baby Spice), Victoria Adams - then Beckham (Posh Spice), Melanie Brown (Mel B / Mel G / Scary Spice). The girl-power group who made it a Spiceworld was the first act to put its first six singles at No.1 (171 WEEKS)

		pos/wks
20 Jul 96	★ WANNABE *Virgin VSCDX 1588* ◆ ▲	1 26
26 Oct 96	★ SAY YOU'LL BE THERE *Virgin VSCDT 1601* ■	1 17
28 Dec 96	★ 2 BECOME 1 *Virgin VSCDT 1607* ◆ ■	1 19
15 Mar 97	★ MAMA / WHO DO YOU THINK YOU ARE *Virgin VSCDT 1623* ■	1 15
17 May 97	2 BECOME 1 (re-entry) *Virgin VSCDT 1607*	54 4
25 Oct 97	★ SPICE UP YOUR LIFE *Virgin VSCDT 1660* ■	1 15
27 Dec 97	★ TOO MUCH *Virgin VSCDR 1669* ■	1 15
21 Mar 98	● STOP *Virgin VSCDT 1679*	2 15
11 Jul 98	STOP (re-entry) *Virgin VSCDT 1679*	52 2
1 Aug 98	★ VIVA FOREVER *Virgin VSCDT 1692* ■	1 13
26 Dec 98	★ GOODBYE *Virgin VSCDT 1721* ■	1 21
4 Nov 00	★ HOLLER / LET LOVE LEAD THE WAY *Virgin VSCDT 1788* ■	1 9+

See also Melanie B; Melanie C; TIN TIN OUT; TRUE STEPPERS; GERI HALLIWELL

SPIDER *UK, male vocal / instrumental group (5 WEEKS)*
		pos/wks
5 Mar 83	WHY D'YA LIE TO ME *RCA 313*	65 2
10 Mar 84	HERE WE GO ROCK 'N' ROLL *A & M AM 180*	57 3

SPIKEY TEE – See BOMB THE BASS

SPILLER *Italy / UK, male / female production / vocal duo - Cristiano Spiller and Sophie Ellis-Bextor (19 WEEKS)*
		pos/wks
26 Aug 00	★ GROOVEJET (IF THIS AIN'T LOVE) *Positiva CDTIV 137* ■	1 19+

SPIN CITY *UK / Ireland, male vocal group (3 WEEKS)*
		pos/wks
26 Aug 00	LANDSLIDE *Epic 6696132*	30 3

SPIN DOCTORS *US, male vocal / instrumental group (28 WEEKS)*
		pos/wks
15 May 93	● TWO PRINCES *Epic 6591452*	3 15
14 Aug 93	LITTLE MISS CAN'T BE WRONG *Epic 6584892*	23 5
9 Oct 93	JIMMY OLSEN'S BLUES *Epic 6597582*	40 2
4 Dec 93	WHAT TIME IS IT *Epic 6599552*	56 1
25 Jun 94	CLEOPATRA'S CAT *Epic 6604192*	29 2
30 Jul 94	YOU LET YOUR HEART GO TOO FAST *Epic 6606612*	66 1
29 Oct 94	MARY JANE *Epic 6609772*	55 1
8 Jun 96	SHE USED TO BE MINE *Epic 6632682*	55 1

SPINAL TAP *US / UK, male vocal / instrumental group (3 WEEKS)*
		pos/wks
28 Mar 92	BITCH SCHOOL *MCA MCS 1624*	35 2
2 May 92	THE MAJESTY OF ROCK *MCA MCS 1629*	61 1

SPINNERS – See DETROIT SPINNERS

SPIRAL TRIBE
UK, male / female vocal / instrumental group (2 WEEKS)
		pos/wks
29 Aug 92	BREACH THE PEACE (EP) *Butterfly BLRT 79*	66 1
21 Nov 92	FORWARD THE REVOLUTION *Butterfly BLRT 85*	70 1

Tracks on Breach the Peace (EP): Breach the Peace / Do It / Seven / 25 Minute Warning

SPIRITS *UK, male / female vocal duo (5 WEEKS)*
		pos/wks
19 Nov 94	DON'T BRING ME DOWN *MCA MCSTD 2018*	31 3
8 Apr 95	SPIRIT INSIDE *MCA MCSTD 2045*	39 2

SPIRITUAL COWBOYS – See Dave STEWART

UK No.1 ★ UK Top 10 ● Still on chart + UK million seller ◆ UK entry at No.1 ■ US No.1 ▲

SPIRITUALIZED
UK, male / female vocal / instrumental group (12 WEEKS)   pos/wks

30 Jun 90	ANYWAY THAT YOU WANT ME / STEP INTO THE BREEZE		
	Dedicated ZB 43783	**75**	1
17 Aug 91	RUN *Dedicated SPIRT 002*	**59**	1
25 Jul 92	MEDICATION *Dedicated SPIRT 005T*	**55**	1
23 Oct 93	ELECTRIC MAINLINE		
	Dedicated SPIRT 007CD	**49**	1
4 Feb 95	LET IT FLOW *Dedicated SPIRT 009CD* [1]	**30**	2
9 Aug 97	ELECTRICITY *Dedicated SPIRT 012CD1*	**32**	2
14 Feb 98	I THINK I'M IN LOVE *Dedicated SPIRT 014CD*	**27**	2
6 Jun 98	THE ABBEY ROAD EP		
	Dedicated SPIRT 015CD	**39**	2

[1] Spiritualized Electric Mainline

Tracks on The Abbey Road EP: Come Together / Broken Heart / Broken Heart (instrumental)

SPIRO and WIX *UK, male instrumental duo (2 WEEKS)*   pos/wks

| 10 Aug 96 | TARA'S THEME *EMI Premier PRESCD 4* | **29** | 2 |

SPITTING IMAGE *UK, male / female latex puppets (18 WEEKS)*   pos/wks

10 May 86 ★	THE CHICKEN SONG *Virgin SPIT 1*	**1**	10
26 Jul 86	THE CHICKEN SONG (re-entry) *Virgin SPIT 1*	**67**	1
6 Dec 86	SANTA CLAUS IS ON THE DOLE / FIRST ATHEIST		
	TABERNACLE CHOIR *Virgin VS 921*	**22**	7

SPLINTER *UK, male vocal / instrumental duo (10 WEEKS)*   pos/wks

| 2 Nov 74 | COSTAFINE TOWN *Dark Horse AMS 7135* | **17** | 10 |

SPLIT ENZ
New Zealand / UK, male vocal / instrumental group (15 WEEKS)   pos/wks

16 Aug 80	I GOT YOU *A & M AMS 7546*	**12**	11
23 May 81	HISTORY NEVER REPEATS		
	A & M AMS 8128	**63**	4

A SPLIT SECOND
Belgium / Italy, male instrumental / production group (1 WEEK)   pos/wks

| 14 Dec 91 | FLESH *ffrr FX 178* | **68** | 1 |

SPLODGENESSABOUNDS
UK, male vocal / instrumental group (17 WEEKS)   pos/wks

14 Jun 80 ●	SIMON TEMPLAR / TWO PINTS OF LAGER AND A PACKET		
	OF CRISPS PLEASE *Deram BUM 1*	**7**	8
6 Sep 80	TWO LITTLE BOYS / HORSE *Deram ROLF 1*	**26**	7
13 Jun 81	COWPUNK MEDLUM *Deram BUM 3*	**69**	2

SPOILED & ZIGO *Israel, male DJ / production duo (3 WEEKS)*   pos/wks

| 12 Aug 00 | MORE & MORE *Manifesto FESCD 72* | **31** | 3 |

SPONGE *US, male vocal / instrumental group (1 WEEK)*   pos/wks

| 19 Aug 95 | PLOWED *Work 6623162* | **74** | 1 |

SPOOKY *UK, male vocal / instrumental duo (1 WEEK)*   pos/wks

| 13 Mar 93 | SCHMOO *Guerilla GRRR 45CD* | **72** | 1 |

SPORTY THIEVZ *US, male rap / vocal group (6 WEEKS)*   pos/wks

| 10 Jul 99 | NO PIGEONS | | |
| | *Columbia / Roc-A-Blok / Ruffhouse 6676022* | **21** | 6 |

SPOTNICKS *Sweden, male instrumental group (37 WEEKS)*   pos/wks

14 Jun 62	ORANGE BLOSSOM SPECIAL		
	Oriole CB 1724	**29**	10
6 Sep 62	ROCKET MAN *Oriole CB 1755*	**38**	9
31 Jan 63	HAVA NAGILA *Oriole CB 1790*	**13**	12
25 Apr 63	JUST LISTEN TO MY HEART *Oriole CB 1818*	**36**	6

Dusty SPRINGFIELD `75` **Top 500**
One of Britain's leading female vocalists of the 1960s, b. Mary O'Brien, 16 Apr 1939, London, d. 2 Mar 1999. After leaving The Springfields in 1963, she had numerous transatlantic solo hits, and during the Sixties was regularly voted UK's Top Female Singer (211 WEEKS)   pos/wks

21 Nov 63 ●	I ONLY WANT TO BE WITH YOU *Philips BF 1292*	**4**	18
20 Feb 64	STAY AWHILE *Philips BF 1313*	**13**	10
2 Jul 64 ●	I JUST DON'T KNOW WHAT TO DO WITH MYSELF		
	Philips BF 1348	**3**	12
22 Oct 64 ●	LOSING YOU *Philips BF 1369*	**9**	13
18 Feb 65	YOUR HURTIN' KIND OF LOVE *Philips BF 1396*	**37**	4
1 Jul 65 ●	IN THE MIDDLE OF NOWHERE *Philips BF 1418*	**8**	10
16 Sep 65 ●	SOME OF YOUR LOVIN' *Philips BF 1430*	**8**	12
27 Jan 66	LITTLE BY LITTLE *Philips BF 1466*	**17**	9
31 Mar 66 ★	YOU DON'T HAVE TO SAY YOU LOVE ME *Philips BF 1482*	**1**	13
7 Jul 66 ●	GOING BACK *Philips BF 1502*	**10**	10
15 Sep 66 ●	ALL I SEE IS YOU *Philips BF 1510*	**9**	12
23 Feb 67	I'LL TRY ANYTHING *Philips BF 1553*	**13**	9
25 May 67	GIVE ME TIME *Philips BF 1577*	**24**	6
10 Jul 68 ●	I CLOSE MY EYES AND COUNT TO TEN *Philips BF 1682*	**4**	12
4 Dec 68 ●	SON OF A PREACHER MAN *Philips BF 1730*	**9**	9
20 Sep 69	AM I THE SAME GIRL *Philips BF 1811*	**43**	3
18 Oct 69	AM I THE SAME GIRL (re-entry) *Philips BF 1811*	**46**	1
19 Sep 70	HOW CAN I BE SURE *Philips 6006 045*	**36**	4
20 Oct 79	BABY BLUE *Mercury DUSTY 4*	**61**	5
22 Aug 87 ●	WHAT HAVE I DONE TO DESERVE THIS		
	Parlophone R 6163 [1]	**2**	9
25 Feb 89	NOTHING HAS BEEN PROVED *Parlophone R 6207*	**16**	7
2 Dec 89	IN PRIVATE *Parlophone R 6234*	**14**	10
26 May 90	REPUTATION *Parlophone R 6253*	**38**	6
24 Nov 90	ARRESTED BY YOU *Parlophone R 6266*	**70**	2
30 Oct 93	HEART AND SOUL *Columbia 6598562* [2]	**75**	1
10 Jun 95	WHEREVER WOULD I BE *Columbia 6620592* [3]	**44**	3
4 Nov 95	ROLL AWAY *Columbia 6623682*	**68**	1

[1] Pet Shop Boys and Dusty Springfield [2] Cilla Black with Dusty Springfield [3] Dusty Springfield and Daryl Hall

See also SPRINGFIELDS

Rick SPRINGFIELD *Australia, male vocalist (13 WEEKS)*   pos/wks

| 14 Jan 84 | HUMAN TOUCH / SOULS *RCA RICK 1* | **23** | 7 |
| 24 Mar 84 | JESSIE'S GIRL *RCA RICK 2* ▲ | **43** | 6 |

'Souls' listed only from 11 Feb 1984. It peaked at No.24

SPRINGFIELDS
UK, male / female vocal / instrumental group (66 WEEKS)   pos/wks

31 Aug 61	BREAKAWAY *Philips BF 1168*	**31**	8
16 Nov 61	BAMBINO *Philips BF 1178*	**16**	11
13 Dec 62 ●	ISLAND OF DREAMS *Philips 326557 BF*	**5**	26
28 Mar 63 ●	SAY I WON'T BE THERE *Philips 326577 BF*	**5**	15
25 Jul 63	COME ON HOME *Philips BF 1263*	**31**	6

See also Dusty SPRINGFIELD

Bruce SPRINGSTEEN `160` **Top 500**
'The Boss', b. 23 Sep 1949, New Jersey, US. Singer / songwriter / guitarist / rock superstar, whose legendary stage performances have packed stadiums worldwide. He released the biggest-selling box set, and is one of world's best-selling album artists (144 WEEKS)   pos/wks

22 Nov 80	HUNGRY HEART *CBS 9309*	**44**	4
13 Jun 81	THE RIVER *CBS A 1179*	**35**	6
26 May 84	DANCING IN THE DARK *CBS A 4436*	**28**	7
6 Oct 84	COVER ME *CBS A 4662*	**38**	5
12 Jan 85 ●	DANCING IN THE DARK (re-entry) *CBS A 4436*	**4**	16
23 Mar 85	COVER ME (re-entry) *CBS A 4662*	**16**	8
15 Jun 85 ●	I'M ON FIRE / BORN IN THE USA *CBS A 6342*	**5**	12
3 Aug 85	GLORY DAYS *CBS A 6375*	**17**	6
14 Dec 85 ●	SANTA CLAUS IS COMIN' TO TOWN / MY HOMETOWN		
	CBS A 6773	**9**	5
29 Nov 86	WAR *CBS 650193 7*	**18**	7

Date	Title	Pos	Wks
7 Feb 87	FIRE *CBS 650381 7*	54	2
23 May 87	BORN TO RUN *CBS BRUCE 2*	16	4
3 Oct 87	BRILLIANT DISGUISE *CBS 651141 7*	20	5
12 Dec 87	TUNNEL OF LOVE *CBS 651295 7*	45	4
18 Jun 88	TOUGHER THAN THE REST *CBS BRUCE 3*	13	6
24 Sep 88	SPARE PARTS *CBS BRUCE 4*	32	3
21 Mar 92	HUMAN TOUCH *Columbia 6578727*	11	5
23 May 92	BETTER DAYS *Columbia 6578907*	34	3
25 Jul 92	57 CHANNELS (AND NOTHIN' ON) *Columbia 6581387*	32	4
24 Oct 92	LEAP OF FAITH *Columbia 6583697*	46	3
10 Apr 93	LUCKY TOWN (LIVE) *Columbia 6592282*	48	3
19 Mar 94 ●	STREETS OF PHILADELPHIA *Columbia 6600652*	2	12
22 Apr 95	SECRET GARDEN *Columbia 6612955*	44	3
11 Nov 95	HUNGRY HEART (re-issue) *Columbia 6626252*	28	3
4 May 96	THE GHOST OF TOM JOAD *Columbia 6630315*	26	2
19 Apr 97	SECRET GARDEN (re-issue) *Columbia 6643245*	17	4

SPRINGWATER *UK, male instrumentalist - Phil Cordell (12 WEEKS)* pos/wks

23 Oct 71 ●	I WILL RETURN *Polydor 2058 141*	5	12

SPRINKLER *UK / US, male / female vocal / rap group (2 WEEKS)* pos/wks

11 Jul 98	LEAVE 'EM SOMETHING TO DESIRE *Island CID 706*	45	2

SPYRO GYRA *US, male instrumental group (10 WEEKS)* pos/wks

21 Jul 79	MORNING DANCE *Infinity INF 111*	17	10

SQUADRONAIRES – See Joan REGAN

SQUEEZE (215) [Top 500] *Critically acclaimed London band, which had several UK / US best sellers. Featured noted singer / songwriters Glenn Tilbrook (g/v) and Chris Difford (v/g). Fluctuating line-up included Jools Holland (k) and Paul Carrack (v/k - also of Ace, and Mike and the Mechanics fame) (123 WEEKS)* pos/wks

8 Apr 78	TAKE ME I'M YOURS *A & M AMS 7335*	19	9
10 Jun 78	BANG BANG *A & M AMS 7360*	49	5
18 Nov 78	GOODBYE GIRL *A & M AMS 7398*	63	2
24 Mar 79 ●	COOL FOR CATS *A & M AMS 7426*	2	11
2 Jun 79 ●	UP THE JUNCTION *A & M AMS 7444*	2	11
8 Sep 79	SLAP AND TICKLE *A & M AMS 7466*	24	8
1 Mar 80	ANOTHER NAIL IN MY HEART *A & M AMS 7507*	17	9
10 May 80	PULLING MUSSELS (FROM THE SHELL) *A & M AMS 7523*	44	6
16 May 81	IS THAT LOVE *A & M AMS 8129*	35	8
25 Jul 81	TEMPTED *A & M AMS 8147*	41	5
10 Oct 81 ●	LABELLED WITH LOVE *A & M AMS 8166*	4	10
24 Apr 82	BLACK COFFEE IN BED *A & M AMS 8219*	51	4
23 Oct 82	ANNIE GET YOUR GUN *A & M AMS 8259*	43	4
15 Jun 85	LAST TIME FOREVER *A & M AM 255*	45	5
8 Aug 87	HOURGLASS *A & M AM 400*	16	10
17 Oct 87	TRUST ME TO OPEN MY MOUTH *A & M AM 412*	72	1
25 Apr 92	COOL FOR CATS (re-issue) *A & M AM 860*	62	2
24 Jul 93	THIRD RAIL *A & M 5803372*	39	3
11 Sep 93	SOME FANTASTIC PLACE *A & M 5803792*	73	1
9 Sep 95	THIS SUMMER *A & M 5811912*	36	3
18 Nov 95	ELECTRIC TRAINS *A & M 5812692*	44	2
15 Jun 96	HEAVEN KNOWS *A & M 5816052*	27	2
24 Aug 96	THIS SUMMER (re-mix) *A & M 5818372*	32	2

See also DIFFORD and TILBROOK

Billy SQUIER *US, male vocalist (3 WEEKS)* pos/wks

3 Oct 81	THE STROKE *Capitol CL 214*	52	3

Dorothy SQUIRES *UK, female vocalist (56 WEEKS)* pos/wks

5 Jun 53	I'M WALKING BEHIND YOU *Polygon P 1068*	12	1
24 Aug 61	SAY IT WITH FLOWERS *Columbia DB 4665* [1]	23	10
20 Sep 69	FOR ONCE IN MY LIFE *President PT 267*	24	10
20 Dec 69	FOR ONCE IN MY LIFE (re-entry) *President PT 267*	48	1
21 Feb 70	TILL *President PT 281*	25	10
9 May 70	TILL (re-entry) *President PT 281*	48	1
8 Aug 70	MY WAY *President PT 305*	40	5
19 Sep 70	MY WAY (re-entry) *President PT 305*	34	8
28 Nov 70	MY WAY (2nd re-entry) *President PT 305*	25	10

[1] Dorothy Squires and Russ Conway

STABBS *Finland / US / Cameroon, male instrumental / production group (1 WEEK)* pos/wks

24 Dec 94	JOY AND HAPPINESS *Hi-Life HICD 3*	65	1

STACCATO *UK / Holland, male / female vocal / instrumental duo (1 WEEK)* pos/wks

20 Jul 96	I WANNA KNOW *Multiply CDMULTY 11*	65	1

Jim STAFFORD *US, male vocalist (16 WEEKS)* pos/wks

27 Apr 74	SPIDERS AND SNAKES *MGM 2006 374*	14	8
6 Jul 74	MY GIRL BILL *MGM 2006 423*	20	8

Jo STAFFORD *US, female vocalist (28 WEEKS)* pos/wks

14 Nov 52 ★	YOU BELONG TO ME *Columbia DB 3152* ▲	1	19
19 Dec 52	JAMBALAYA *Columbia DB 3169*	11	2
7 May 54 ●	MAKE LOVE TO ME! *Philips PB 233* ▲	8	1
9 Dec 55	SUDDENLY THERE'S A VALLEY *Philips PB 509*	12	5
3 Feb 56	SUDDENLY THERE'S A VALLEY (re-entry) *Philips PB 509*	19	1

Terry STAFFORD *US, male vocalist (9 WEEKS)* pos/wks

7 May 64	SUSPICION *London HLU 9871*	31	9

STAIFFI and his MUSTAFAS *France, male vocal / instrumental group (1 WEEK)* pos/wks

28 Jul 60	MUSTAFA CHA CHA CHA *Pye International 7N 25057*	43	1

STAKKA BO *Sweden, male rap / DJ duo (12 WEEKS)* pos/wks

25 Sep 93	HERE WE GO *Polydor PZCD 280*	13	8
18 Dec 93	DOWN THE DRAIN *Polydor PZCD 301*	64	4

Frank STALLONE *US, male vocalist (2 WEEKS)* pos/wks

22 Oct 83	FAR FROM OVER *RSO 95*	68	2

STAMFORD BRIDGE *UK, male Chelsea FC supporters vocal group (1 WEEK)* pos/wks

16 May 70	CHELSEA *Penny Farthing PEN 715*	47	1

STAN *UK, male vocal / instrumental duo (3 WEEKS)* pos/wks

31 Jul 93	SUNTAN *Hug CDBUM 1*	40	3

Lisa STANSFIELD (209) [Top 500] *Only UK act to have three US R&B No.1 hits, b. 11 Apr 1966, Lancashire. Like Yazz, she was featured vocalist on a Coldcut single before achieving a No.1 in her own right. This multi-Brit award winner has sold millions of records all around the world (126 WEEKS)* pos/wks

25 Mar 89	PEOPLE HOLD ON *Ahead of Our Time CCUT 5* [1]	11	9
12 Aug 89	THIS IS THE RIGHT TIME *Arista 112512*	13	8
28 Oct 89 ★	ALL AROUND THE WORLD *Arista 112693*	1	14
10 Feb 90 ●	LIVE TOGETHER *Arista 112914*	10	6
12 May 90	WHAT DID I DO TO YOU (EP) *Arista 113168*	25	4
19 Oct 91 ●	CHANGE *Arista 114820*	10	7
21 Dec 91	ALL WOMAN *Arista 115000*	20	8
14 Mar 92	TIME TO MAKE YOU MINE *Arista 115113*	14	8
6 Jun 92	SET YOUR LOVING FREE *Arista 74321100587*	28	4
19 Dec 92	SOMEDAY (I'M COMING BACK) *Arista 74321123567*	10	9
1 May 93 ★	FIVE LIVE (EP) *Parlophone CDRS 6340* [2] ■	1	11
5 Jun 93 ●	IN ALL THE RIGHT PLACES *MCA MCSTD 1780*	8	11
24 Jul 93	FIVE LIVE (EP) (re-entry) *Parlophone CDRS 6340* [2]	74	1
23 Oct 93	SO NATURAL *Arista 74321169132*	15	5
11 Dec 93	LITTLE BIT OF HEAVEN *Arista 74321178202*	32	4
18 Jan 97 ●	PEOPLE HOLD ON (THE BOOTLEG MIXES) *Arista 74321452012* [3]	4	6
22 Mar 97 ●	THE REAL THING *Arista 74321463222*	9	7

UK No.1 ★   UK Top 10 ●   Still on chart +   UK million seller ◆   UK entry at No.1 ■   US No.1 ▲

21 Jun 97	NEVER, NEVER GONNA GIVE YOU UP *Arista 74321490392*	25	3
4 Oct 97	THE LINE *RCA 74321511372*	64	1

[1] Coldcut featuring Lisa Stansfield [2] George Michael and Queen with Lisa Stansfield [3] Lisa Stansfield vs The Dirty Rotten Scoundrels

Tracks on What Did I Do to You (EP): What Did I Do to You / My Apple Heart / Lay Me Down / Something's Happenin'. Tracks on Five Live (EP): Somebody to Love / These Are the Days of Our Lives / Calling You / Papa Was a Rolling Stone - Killer (medley). Lisa Stansfield appears only on the second track

Vivian STANSHALL – See Mike OLDFIELD

STAPLE SINGERS *US, male / female vocal group (14 WEEKS)* pos/wks
10 Jun 72	I'LL TAKE YOU THERE *Stax 2025 110* ▲	30	8
8 Jun 74	IF YOU'RE READY (COME GO WITH ME) *Stax 2025 224*	34	6

Cyril STAPLETON & his ORCHESTRA
UK, orchestra (27 WEEKS) pos/wks
27 May 55	ELEPHANT TANGO *Decca F 10488*	20	2
1 Jul 55	ELEPHANT TANGO (re-entry) *Decca F 10488*	20	1
22 Jul 55	ELEPHANT TANGO (2nd re-entry) *Decca F 10488*	19	1
23 Sep 55 ●	BLUE STAR (THE MEDIC THEME) *Decca F 10559* [1]	2	12
6 Apr 56	THE ITALIAN THEME *Decca F 10703*	18	2
1 Jun 56	THE HAPPY WHISTLER *Decca F 10735* [2]	22	4
19 Jul 57	FORGOTTEN DREAMS *Decca F 10912*	27	5

[1] Cyril Stapleton Orchestra featuring Julie Dawn [2] Cyril Stapleton Orchestra featuring Desmond Lane, penny whistle

STARDUST
France, male / female vocal / instrumental group (3 WEEKS) pos/wks
8 Oct 77	ARIANA *Satril SAT 120*	42	3

STARDUST *France, male vocal / production group (26 WEEKS)* pos/wks
1 Aug 98	MUSIC SOUNDS BETTER WITH YOU (import) *Roule ROULE 305*	55	3
22 Aug 98 ●	MUSIC SOUNDS BETTER WITH YOU *Virgin DINSD 175*	2	23

Alvin STARDUST [226] [Top 500]
Sixties hitmaker who became bill-topping Seventies vocalist, b. Bernard Jewry, 27 Sep 1942, London. After several minor hits as Shane Fenton, he collected a string of smashes as OTT rocker Stardust, and extended his chart span to almost 25 years *(119 WEEKS)* pos/wks
3 Nov 73 ●	MY COO-CA-CHOO *Magnet MAG 1*	2	21
16 Feb 74 ★	JEALOUS MIND *Magnet MAG 5*	1	11
4 May 74 ●	RED DRESS *Magnet MAG 8*	7	8
31 Aug 74 ●	YOU YOU YOU *Magnet MAG 13*	6	10
30 Nov 74	TELL ME WHY *Magnet MAG 19*	16	8
1 Feb 75	GOOD LOVE CAN NEVER DIE *Magnet MAG 21*	11	9
12 Jul 75	SWEET CHEATIN' RITA *Magnet MAG 32*	37	4
5 Sep 81	PRETEND *Stiff BUY 124*	4	10
21 Nov 81	A WONDERFUL TIME UP THERE *Stiff BUY 132*	56	8
5 May 84 ●	I FEEL LIKE BUDDY HOLLY *Chrysalis CHS 2784*	7	11
27 Oct 84 ●	I WON'T RUN AWAY *Chrysalis CHS 2829*	7	13
15 Dec 84	SO NEAR TO CHRISTMAS *Chrysalis CHS 2835*	29	4
23 Mar 85	GOT A LITTLE HEARTACHE *Chrysalis CHS 2856*	55	2

See also Shane FENTON and the FENTONES

STARFIGHTER *Belgium, male producer (3 WEEKS)* pos/wks
5 Feb 00	APACHE *Sound of Ministry MOSCDS 136*	31	3

STARGARD *US, female vocal group (14 WEEKS)* pos/wks
28 Jan 78	THEME FROM 'WHICH WAY IS UP' *MCA 346*	19	7
15 Apr 78	LOVE IS SO EASY *MCA 354*	45	1
9 Sep 78	WHAT YOU WAITING FOR *MCA 382*	39	6

STARGAZERS *UK / Australia, male / female vocal group (68 WEEKS)* pos/wks
13 Feb 53	BROKEN WINGS *Decca F 10047*	11	1
27 Feb 53 ★	BROKEN WINGS (re-entry) *Decca F 10047*	1	11
19 Feb 54 ★	I SEE THE MOON *Decca F 10213*	1	15
9 Apr 54	THE HAPPY WANDERER *Decca F 10259*	12	1
17 Dec 54 ★	THE FINGER OF SUSPICION *Decca F 10394* [1]	1	15
4 Mar 55	SOMEBODY *Decca F 10437*	20	1
3 Jun 55	THE CRAZY OTTO RAG *Decca F 10523*	18	3
9 Sep 55 ●	CLOSE THE DOOR *Decca F 10594*	6	9
11 Nov 55 ●	TWENTY TINY FINGERS *Decca F 10626*	4	11
22 Jun 56	HOT DIGGITY *Decca F 10731*	28	1

[1] Dickie Valentine with the Stargazers

STARGAZERS *UK, male vocal / instrumental group (3 WEEKS)* pos/wks
6 Feb 82	GROOVE BABY GROOVE (EP) *Epic EPC A 1924*	56	3

Tracks on Groove Baby Groove (EP): Groove Baby Groove / Jump Around / La Rock 'n' Roll (Quelques Uns a la Lune) / Red Light Green Light

STARJETS *UK, male vocal / instrumental group (5 WEEKS)* pos/wks
8 Sep 79	WAR STORIES *Epic EPC 7770*	51	5

STARLAND VOCAL BAND
US, male / female vocal group (10 WEEKS) pos/wks
7 Aug 76	AFTERNOON DELIGHT *RCA 2716* ▲	18	10

STARLIGHT *Italy, male instrumental / production group (11 WEEKS)* pos/wks
19 Aug 89 ●	NUMERO UNO *Citybeat CBE 742*	9	11

STARLITERS – See Joey DEE and the STARLITERS

STARPARTY *Holland, male production duo - Ferry Corsten and Robert Smit (2 WEEKS)* pos/wks
26 Feb 00	I'M IN LOVE *Incentive CENT 5CDS*	26	2

See also Ferry CORSTEN; MOONMAN; SYSTEM F; GOURYELLA; VERACOCHA

Edwin STARR [490] [Top 500]
Strong-voiced soul star, b. Charles Hatcher, 21 Jan 1942, Nashville, Tennessee, US, who first recorded in 1957. Relocated to UK in early 1980s after last two UK Top 10s failed to crack US Top 40. 'War' is considered one of the 1970s' most important and influential R&B records (70 WEEKS) pos/wks
12 May 66	STOP HER ON SIGHT (SOS) *Polydor BM 56 702*	35	8
18 Aug 66	HEADLINE NEWS *Polydor 56 717*	39	3
11 Dec 68	STOP HER ON SIGHT (SOS) / HEADLINE NEWS (re-issue) *Polydor 56 753*	11	11
13 Sep 69	25 MILES *Tamla Motown TMG 672*	36	6
24 Oct 70 ●	WAR *Tamla Motown TMG 754* ▲	3	12
20 Feb 71	STOP THE WAR NOW *Tamla Motown TMG 764*	33	1
27 Jan 79 ●	CONTACT *20th Century BTC 2396*	6	12
26 May 79 ●	H.A.P.P.Y. RADIO *RCA TC 2408*	9	11
1 Jun 85	IT AIN'T FAIR *Hippodrome HIP 101*	56	4
30 Oct 93	WAR *Weekend CDWEEK 103* [1]	69	2

[1] Edwin Starr and Shadow

'Headline News' not listed with 'SOS' from 22 Jan 1969 to 19 Feb 1969. It therefore peaked at No.16. 'War' in 1993 was a re-recording and was listed with the flip side 'Wild Thing' by the Troggs and Wolf

See also UTAH SAINTS

Freddie STARR *UK, male vocalist - Fred Smith (14 WEEKS)* pos/wks
23 Feb 74 ●	IT'S YOU *Tiffany 6121 501*	9	10
20 Dec 75	WHITE CHRISTMAS *Thunderbird THE 102*	41	4

Kay STARR *US, female vocalist - Katherine Starks (58 WEEKS)* pos/wks
5 Dec 52 ★	COMES A-LONG A-LOVE *Capitol CL 13808*	1	16
24 Apr 53 ●	SIDE BY SIDE *Capitol CL 13871*	7	4
19 Mar 54 ●	CHANGING PARTNERS *Capitol CL 14050*	4	14
15 Oct 54	AM I A TOY OR TREASURE *Capitol CL 14151*	17	3
12 Nov 54	AM I A TOY OR TREASURE (re-entry) *Capitol CL 14151*	20	1
17 Feb 56 ★	ROCK AND ROLL WALTZ *HMV POP 168* ▲	1	20

UK No.1 ★ UK Top 10 ● Still on chart + UK million seller ◆ UK entry at No.1 ■ US No.1 ▲

Ringo STARR *UK, male vocalist – Richard Starkey (56 WEEKS)*

pos/wks

17 Apr 71	●	IT DON'T COME EASY *Apple R 5898*	4	11
1 Apr 72	●	BACK OFF BOOGALOO *Apple R 5944*	2	10
27 Oct 73	●	PHOTOGRAPH *Apple R 5992* ▲	8	13
23 Feb 74	●	YOU'RE SIXTEEN *Apple R 5995* ▲	4	10
30 Nov 74		ONLY YOU *Apple R 6000*	28	11
6 Jun 92		WEIGHT OF THE WORLD *Private Music 115392*	74	1

See also BEATLES

STARS ON 54 *US, female vocal trio (3 WEEKS)*

pos/wks

| 28 Nov 98 | | IF YOU COULD READ MY MIND *Tommy Boy TBCD 7497* ▲ | 23 | 3 |

STARSHIP *US, female / male vocal / instrumental group (41 WEEKS)* pos/wks

26 Jan 80		JANE *Grunt FB 1750* [1]	21	9
16 Nov 85		WE BUILT THIS CITY *RCA PB 49929* ▲	12	12
8 Feb 86		SARA *RCA FB 49893* ▲	66	3
11 Apr 87	★	NOTHING'S GONNA STOP US NOW *Grunt FB 49757* ▲	1	17

[1] Jefferson Starship

STARSOUND *Holland, producer Jaap Eggermont with male / female session singers (37 WEEKS)*

pos/wks

18 Apr 81	●	STARS ON 45 *CBS A 1102* ▲	2	14
4 Jul 81	●	STARS ON 45 VOL.2 *CBS A 1407*	2	10
19 Sep 81		STARS ON 45 VOL.3 *CBS A 1521*	17	6
27 Feb 82		STARS ON STEVIE *CBS A 2041*	14	7

STARTRAX *UK, male / female vocal group (8 WEEKS)*

pos/wks

| 1 Aug 81 | | STARTRAX CLUB DISCO *Picksy KSY 1001* | 18 | 8 |

STARTURN ON 45 (PINTS) *UK, male vocalist (9 WEEKS)*

pos/wks

| 24 Oct 81 | | STARTURN ON 45 (PINTS) *V Tone V TONE 003* | 45 | 4 |
| 30 Apr 88 | | PUMP UP THE BITTER *Pacific DRINK 1* | 12 | 5 |

STARVATION *Multinational, male / female vocal / instrumental charity assembly (6 WEEKS)*

pos/wks

| 9 Mar 85 | | STARVATION / TAM-TAM POUR L'ETHIOPE *Zarjazz JAZZ 3* | 33 | 6 |

STARVING SOULS *UK, male vocal / instrumental group (1 WEEK)* pos/wks

| 21 Oct 95 | | I BE THE PROPHET *Durban Poison DPCD 1* | 66 | 1 |

STATE OF MIND
UK, male / female vocal / production group (3 WEEKS)

pos/wks

| 18 Apr 98 | | THIS IS IT *Ministry of Sound MOSCDS 123* | 30 | 2 |
| 25 Jul 98 | | TAKE CONTROL *Ministry of Sound MOSCDS 124* | 46 | 1 |

STATLER BROTHERS *US, male vocal group (4 WEEKS)*

pos/wks

| 24 Feb 66 | | FLOWERS ON THE WALL *CBS 201976* | 38 | 4 |

Candi STATON `481` `Top 500` *Child gospel performer turned southern soul star turned disco diva, b. 1943, Alabama, US. Grammy-nominated ex-wife of Clarence Carter, who first found US R&B fame in the late 1960s and last hit in UK after she had returned to gospel music (71 WEEKS)*

pos/wks

29 May 76	●	YOUNG HEARTS RUN FREE *Warner Bros. K 16730*	2	13
18 Sep 76		DESTINY *Warner Bros. K 16806*	41	3
23 Jul 77	●	NIGHTS ON BROADWAY *Warner Bros. K 16972*	6	12
3 Jun 78		HONEST I DO LOVE YOU *Warner Bros. K 17164*	48	5
24 Apr 82		SUSPICIOUS MINDS *Sugarhill SH 112*	31	9
31 May 86		YOUNG HEARTS RUN FREE (re-mix) *Warner Bros. W 8680*	47	5
2 Feb 91		YOU GOT THE LOVE *Truelove TLOVE 7001* [1]	4	11
1 Mar 97	●	YOU GOT THE LOVE (re-mix) *React CDREACT 89* [1]	3	8
17 Apr 99		LOVE ON LOVE *React CDREACT 143*	27	3
7 Aug 99		YOUNG HEARTS RUN FREE (re-recording) *React CDREACT 158*	29	2

[1] Source featuring Candi Staton

STATUS IV *US, male vocal group (3 WEEKS)*

pos/wks

| 9 Jul 83 | | YOU AIN'T REALLY DOWN *TMT TMT 4* | 56 | 3 |

STATUS QUO `14` `Top 500` *Ever popular London boogie band: Francis Rossi (g/v), Rick Parfitt (g/v), Alan Lancaster (b), John Coghlan (d). No group has accumulated more British hits than these head-bangers' heroes, who were chosen to open Live Aid in 1985 (413 WEEKS)*

pos/wks

24 Jan 68	●	PICTURES OF MATCHSTICK MEN *Pye 7N 17449*	7	12
21 Aug 68	●	ICE IN THE SUN *Pye 7N 17581*	8	12
28 May 69	●	ARE YOU GROWING TIRED OF MY LOVE *Pye 7N 17728*	46	2
18 Jun 69		ARE YOU GROWING TIRED OF MY LOVE (re-entry) *Pye 7N 17728*	50	1
2 May 70		DOWN THE DUSTPIPE *Pye 7N 17907*	12	17
7 Nov 70		IN MY CHAIR *Pye 7N 17998*	21	14
13 Jan 73	●	PAPER PLANE *Vertigo 6059 071*	8	11
14 Apr 73		MEAN GIRL *Pye 7N 45229*	20	11
8 Sep 73	●	CAROLINE *Vertigo 6059 085*	5	13
4 May 74	●	BREAK THE RULES *Vertigo 6059 101*	8	8
7 Dec 74	★	DOWN DOWN *Vertigo 6059 114*	1	11
17 May 75	●	ROLL OVER LAY DOWN *Vertigo QUO 13*	9	8
14 Feb 76		RAIN *Vertigo 6059 133*	7	7
10 Jul 76		MYSTERY SONG *Vertigo 6059 146*	11	9
11 Dec 76	●	WILD SIDE OF LIFE *Vertigo 6059 153*	9	12
8 Oct 77	●	ROCKIN' ALL OVER THE WORLD *Vertigo 6059 184*	3	16
2 Sep 78		AGAIN AND AGAIN *Vertigo QUO 1*	13	9
25 Nov 78		ACCIDENT PRONE *Vertigo QUO 2*	36	8
22 Sep 79	●	WHATEVER YOU WANT *Vertigo 6059 242*	4	9
24 Nov 79		LIVING ON AN ISLAND *Vertigo 6059 248*	16	10
11 Oct 80	●	WHAT YOU'RE PROPOSING *Vertigo QUO 3*	2	11
6 Dec 80		LIES / DON'T DRIVE MY CAR *Vertigo QUO 4*	11	10
28 Feb 81	●	SOMETHING 'BOUT YOU BABY I LIKE *Vertigo QUO 5*	9	7
28 Nov 81	●	ROCK 'N' ROLL *Vertigo QUO 6*	8	11
27 Mar 82	●	DEAR JOHN *Vertigo QUO 7*	10	8
12 Jun 82		SHE DON'T FOOL ME *Vertigo QUO 8*	36	5
30 Oct 82		CAROLINE (LIVE AT THE NEC) *Vertigo QUO 10*	13	7
10 Sep 83	●	OL' RAG BLUES *Vertigo QUO 11*	9	8
5 Nov 83		A MESS OF BLUES *Vertigo QUO 12*	15	6
10 Dec 83	●	MARGUERITA TIME *Vertigo QUO 14*	3	11
19 May 84		GOING DOWN TOWN TONIGHT *Vertigo QUO 15*	20	6
27 Oct 84	●	THE WANDERER *Vertigo QUO 16*	7	11
17 May 86	●	ROLLIN' HOME *Vertigo QUO 18*	9	6
26 Jul 86		RED SKY *Vertigo QUO 19*	19	8
4 Oct 86	●	IN THE ARMY NOW *Vertigo QUO 20*	2	14
6 Dec 86		DREAMIN' *Vertigo QUO 21*	15	8
26 Mar 88		AIN'T COMPLAINING *Vertigo QUO 22*	19	6
21 May 88		WHO GETS THE LOVE *Vertigo QUO 23*	34	4
20 Aug 88		RUNNING ALL OVER THE WORLD *Vertigo QUAID 1*	17	6
3 Dec 88	●	BURNING BRIDGES (ON AND OFF AND ON AGAIN) *Vertigo QUO 25*	5	10
28 Oct 89		NOT AT ALL *Vertigo QUO 26*	50	1
29 Sep 90	●	THE ANNIVERSARY WALTZ – PART 1 *Vertigo QUO 28*	2	9
15 Dec 90		THE ANNIVERSARY WALTZ – PART 2 *Vertigo QUO 29*	16	7
7 Sep 91		CAN'T GIVE YOU MORE *Vertigo QUO 30*	37	3
18 Jan 92		ROCK 'TIL YOU DROP *Vertigo QUO 32*	38	3
10 Oct 92		ROADHOUSE MEDLEY (ANNIVERSARY WALTZ PART 25) *Polydor QUO 33*	21	4
6 Aug 94		I DIDN'T MEAN IT *Polydor QUOCD 34*	21	4
22 Oct 94		SHERRI DON'T FAIL ME NOW *Polydor QUOCD 35*	38	2
3 Dec 94		RESTLESS *Polydor QUOCD 36*	39	2
4 Nov 95		WHEN YOU WALK IN THE ROOM *PolyGram TV 5775122*	34	2
2 Mar 96		FUN FUN FUN *PolyGram TV 5762632* [1]	24	4
13 Apr 96		DON'T STOP *PolyGram TV 5766352*	35	2
9 Nov 96		ALL AROUND MY HAT *PolyGram TV 5759452* [2]	47	1
20 Mar 99		THE WAY IT GOES *Eagle EAGXS 075*	39	2
12 Jun 99		LITTLE WHITE LIES *Eagle EAGXS 101*	47	1
2 Oct 99		TWENTY WILD HORSES *Eagle EAGXS 105*	53	1
13 May 00		MONY MONY *Universal TV 1580132*	48	1

[1] Status Quo with the Beach Boys [2] Status Quo with Maddy Prior from Steeleye Span

'Don't Drive My Car' listed from 20 Dec 1980 only. 'Running All Over the World' is a re-recorded version of 'Rockin' All Over the World', with a slightly changed lyric, released to promote the Race Against Time of 28 Aug 1988

STAXX featuring Carol LEEMING
UK, male / female vocal / instrumental group (11 WEEKS)   pos/wks

2 Oct 93	JOY *Champion CHAMPCD 303*	25	6
20 May 95	YOU *Champion CHAMPCD 316*	50	1
13 Sep 97	JOY (re-mix) *Champion CHAMPCD 328*	14	4

STEALER'S WHEEL
UK, male vocal / instrumental group (22 WEEKS)   pos/wks

26 May 73	●	STUCK IN THE MIDDLE WITH YOU *A & M AMS 7036*	8	10
1 Sep 73		EVERYTHING'LL TURN OUT FINE *A & M AMS 7079*	33	6
26 Jan 74		STAR *A & M AMS 7094*	25	6

STEAM
US, male vocal / instrumental group (14 WEEKS)   pos/wks

| 31 Jan 70 | ● | NA NA HEY HEY KISS HIM GOODBYE *Fontana TF 1058* ▲ | 9 | 14 |

STEEL – See UNITONE ROCKERS featuring STEEL

Anthony STEEL and the RADIO REVELLERS
UK, male vocalist / male instrumental group (6 WEEKS)   pos/wks

| 10 Sep 54 | WEST OF ZANZIBAR *Polygon P 1114* | 11 | 6 |

STEEL HORSES – See TRUMAN & WOLFF featuring STEEL HORSES

STEEL PULSE *UK, male vocal / instrumental group (12 WEEKS)*   pos/wks

1 Apr 78	KU KLUX KLAN *Island WIP 6428*	41	4
8 Jul 78	PRODIGAL SON *Island WIP 6449*	35	6
23 Jun 79	SOUND SYSTEM *Island WIP 6490*	71	2

Tommy STEELE [152] **Top 500** *Britain's first homegrown rock 'n' roll star, b. Thomas Hicks, 17 Dec 1936, London. Just four months after his chart debut he was filming his life story. The singer / songwriter / guitarist, who topped the chart before Elvis, starred in many other movies and musicals (147 WEEKS)*   pos/wks

26 Oct 56		ROCK WITH THE CAVEMAN *Decca F 10795* [1]	13	4
30 Nov 56		ROCK WITH THE CAVEMAN (re-entry) *Decca F 10795* [1]	23	1
14 Dec 56	★	SINGING THE BLUES *Decca F 10819* [1]	1	13
15 Feb 57		KNEE DEEP IN THE BLUES *Decca F 10849* [1]	15	9
19 Apr 57		SINGING THE BLUES (re-entry) *Decca F 10819* [1]	24	1
3 May 57		BUTTERFINGERS *Decca F 10877* [1]	25	1
17 May 57	●	BUTTERFINGERS (re-entry) *Decca F 10877* [1]	8	17
17 May 57		SINGING THE BLUES (2nd re-entry) *Decca F 10819* [1]	29	1
16 Aug 57	●	WATER WATER / HANDFUL OF SONGS *Decca F 10923* [1]	5	16
30 Aug 57		SHIRALEE *Decca F 10896* [1]	11	4
22 Nov 57		HEY YOU *Decca F 10941* [1]	28	1
13 Dec 57		WATER WATER / HANDFUL OF SONGS (re-entry) *Decca F 10923* [1]	28	1
7 Mar 58	●	NAIROBI *Decca F 10991*	3	11
25 Apr 58		HAPPY GUITAR *Decca F 10976*	20	5
18 Jul 58		THE ONLY MAN ON THE ISLAND *Decca F 11041* [1]	16	8
14 Nov 58	●	COME ON, LET'S GO *Decca F 11072*	10	13
14 Aug 59		TALLAHASSEE LASSIE *Decca F 11152*	16	4
28 Aug 59		GIVE GIVE GIVE *Decca F 11152*	28	2
25 Sep 59		TALLAHASSEE LASSIE (re-entry) *Decca F 11152*	25	1
4 Dec 59	●	LITTLE WHITE BULL *Decca F 11177*	6	12
10 Mar 60		LITTLE WHITE BULL (re-entry) *Decca F 11177*	30	5
23 Jun 60	●	WHAT A MOUTH *Decca F 11245*	5	11
29 Dec 60		MUST BE SANTA *Decca F 11299*	40	1
17 Aug 61		WRITING ON THE WALL *Decca F 11372*	30	5

[1] Tommy Steele and the Steelmen

'Handful of Songs' listed together with 'Water Water' from week of 23 Aug 1957

STEELEYE SPAN
UK, male / female vocal / instrumental group (18 WEEKS)   pos/wks

| 8 Dec 73 | | GAUDETE *Chrysalis CHS 2007* | 14 | 9 |
| 15 Nov 75 | ● | ALL AROUND MY HAT *Chrysalis CHS 2078* | 5 | 9 |

STEELY DAN *US, male vocal / instrumental group (21 WEEKS)*   pos/wks

30 Aug 75	DO IT AGAIN *ABC 4075*	39	4
11 Dec 76	HAITIAN DIVORCE *ABC 4152*	17	9
29 Jul 78	FM (NO STATIC AT ALL) *MCA 374*	49	4
2 Sep 78	FM (NO STATIC AT ALL) (re-entry) *MCA 374*	75	1
10 Mar 79	RIKKI DON'T LOSE THAT NUMBER *ABC 4241*	58	3

STEFY – See DJH featuring STEFY

Jim STEINMAN *US, male producer (9 WEEKS)*   pos/wks

| 4 Jul 81 | ROCK 'N' ROLL DREAMS COME THROUGH *Epic EPC A 1236* [1] | 52 | 7 |
| 23 Jun 84 | TONIGHT IS WHAT IT MEANS TO BE YOUNG *MCA MCA 889* [2] | 67 | 2 |

[1] Jim Steinman, vocals by Rory Dodd [2] Jim Steinman and Fire Inc

STEINSKI and MASS MEDIA
US, male / female production group (2 WEEKS)   pos/wks

| 31 Jan 87 | WE'LL BE RIGHT BACK *Fourth & Broadway BRW 59* | 63 | 2 |

Mike STEIPHENSON – See BURUNDI STEIPHENSON BLACK

STELLA BROWNE *UK, male production duo (1 WEEK)*   pos/wks

| 20 May 00 | EVERY WOMAN NEEDS LOVE *Perfecto PERF 06* | 55 | 1 |

Doreen STEPHENS – See Billy COTTON and his BAND

Richie STEPHENS *Jamaica, male vocalist (3 WEEKS)*   pos/wks

| 15 May 93 | LEGACY *Columbia 6592852* [1] | 64 | 2 |
| 9 Aug 97 | COME GIVE ME YOUR LOVE *Delirious 74321450442* [2] | 61 | 1 |

[1] Mad Cobra featuring Richie Stephens [2] Richie Stephens and General Degree

Martin STEPHENSON and the DAINTEES
UK, male vocal / instrumental group (7 WEEKS)   pos/wks

8 Nov 86	BOAT TO BOLIVIA *Kitchenware SL 27*	70	2
17 Jan 87	TROUBLE TOWN *Kitchenware SK 13* [1]	58	3
27 Jun 92	BIG SKY NEW LIGHT *Kitchenware SK 57*	71	2

[1] Daintees

STEPPENWOLF
US / Canada, male vocal / instrumental group (14 WEEKS)   pos/wks

11 Jun 69	BORN TO BE WILD *Stateside SS 8017*	30	7
9 Aug 69	BORN TO BE WILD (re-entry) *Stateside SS 8017*	50	2
27 Feb 99	BORN TO BE WILD (re-issue) *MCA MCSTD 48104*	18	5

STEPS [130] **Top 500** *Steptacular pop vocal quintet: Lisa Scott-Lee, Claire Richards, Faye Tozer, Lee Latchford-Evans, Ian Watkins (aka H). One of the late 1990s' most popular teen acts whose 1999 tour was reportedly the biggest pop arena tour ever in the UK, they were the first UK mixed quintet to top the chart twice (159 WEEKS)*   pos/wks

22 Nov 97		5, 6, 7, 8 *Jive JIVECD 438*	14	17
2 May 98	●	LAST THING ON MY MIND *Jive 0518492*	6	14
5 Sep 98	●	ONE FOR SORROW *Jive 0519092*	2	11
21 Nov 98	★	HEARTBEAT / TRAGEDY *Jive 0519142* ◆	1	30
20 Mar 99	●	BETTER BEST FORGOTTEN *Ebul / Jive 0519242*	2	15
10 Jul 99		BETTER BEST FORGOTTEN (re-entry) *Ebul / Jive 0519242*	49	2
24 Jul 99		LOVE'S GOT A HOLD ON MY HEART *Ebul / Jive 0519372*	2	11
23 Oct 99	●	AFTER THE LOVE HAS GONE *Ebul / Jive 0519462*	5	9
23 Oct 99		LOVE'S GOT A HOLD ON MY HEART (re-entry) *Ebul / Jive 0519372*	73	1
25 Dec 99	●	SAY YOU'LL BE MINE / BETTER THE DEVIL YOU KNOW *Ebul / Jive 9201008*	4	17
1 Jan 00		AFTER THE LOVE HAS GONE (re-entry) *Ebul / Jive 0519462*	60	2
15 Apr 00	●	DEEPER SHADE OF BLUE *Ebul / Jive 9201022*	4	9

UK No.1 ★   UK Top 10 ●   Still on chart +   UK million seller ◆   UK entry at No.1 ■   US No.1 ▲

15 Jul 00 ●	WHEN I SAID GOODBYE / SUMMER OF LOVE		
	Ebul / Jive 9201162	5	11
28 Oct 00 ★	STOMP Ebul / Jive 9201212 ■	1	10+

STEREO MC's UK, male / female vocal / rap group (31 WEEKS) pos/wks

29 Sep 90	ELEVATE MY MIND Fourth & Broadway BRW 186	74	1
9 Mar 91	LOST IN MUSIC Fourth & Broadway BRW 198	46	3
26 Sep 92	CONNECTED Fourth & Broadway BRW 262	18	6
5 Dec 92	STEP IT UP Fourth & Broadway BRW 266	12	12
20 Feb 93	GROUND LEVEL Fourth & Broadway BRCD 268	19	5
29 May 93	CREATION Fourth & Broadway BRCD 276	19	4

STEREO NATION UK, male vocal duo (1 WEEK) pos/wks

17 Aug 96	I'VE BEEN WAITING EMI Premier PRESCD 5	53	1

STEREOLAB
UK / France, male / female vocal / instrumental group (6 WEEKS) pos/wks

8 Jan 94	JENNY ONDIOLINE / FRENCH DISCO		
	Duophonic UHF DUHFCD 01	75	1
30 Jul 94	PING PONG Duophonic UHF DUHFCD 04	45	2
12 Nov 94	WOW AND FLUTTER Duophonic UHF DUHFCD 07	70	1
2 Mar 96	CYBELE'S REVERIE Duophonic UHF DUHFCD 10	62	1
13 Sep 97	MISS MODULAR Duophonic DUHFCD 16	60	1

STEREOPHONICS UK, male vocal / instrumental trio (65 WEEKS) pos/wks

29 Mar 97	LOCAL BOY IN THE PHOTOGRAPH V2 SPHD 2	51	1
31 May 97	MORE LIFE IN A TRAMP'S VEST V2 SPHD 4	33	2
23 Aug 97	A THOUSAND TREES V2 VVR 5000443	22	3
8 Nov 97	TRAFFIC V2 VVR 5000948	20	3
21 Feb 98	LOCAL BOY IN THE PHOTOGRAPH (re-issue)		
	V2 VVR 5001263	14	4
21 Nov 98 ●	THE BARTENDER AND THE THIEF V2 VVR 5004653	3	12
6 Mar 99 ●	JUST LOOKING V2 VVR 5005303	4	8
15 May 99 ●	PICK A PART THAT'S NEW V2 VVR 5006778	4	9
29 May 99	JUST LOOKING (re-entry) V2 VVR 5005303	73	1
4 Sep 99	I WOULDN'T BELIEVE YOUR RADIO V2 VVR 5008823	11	6
30 Oct 99	I WOULDN'T BELIEVE YOUR RADIO (re-entry)		
	V2 VVR 5008823	71	1
20 Nov 99	HURRY UP AND WAIT V2 VVR 5009323	11	5
1 Jan 00	HURRY UP AND WAIT (re-entry) V2 VVR 5009323	53	3
18 Mar 00 ●	MAMA TOLD ME NOT TO COME Gut CDGUT 031 [1]	4	7

[1] Tom Jones + The Stereophonics

STETSASONIC US, male rap group (3 WEEKS) pos/wks

24 Sep 88	TALKIN' ALL THAT JAZZ Breakout USA 640	73	2
7 Nov 98	TALKIN ALL THAT JAZZ (re-mix) Tommy Boy TBCD 7310A	54	1

STEVE and EYDIE – See Steve LAWRENCE; Eydie GORME

April STEVENS – See Nino TEMPO and April STEVENS

Cat STEVENS (312 Top 500) Critically acclaimed folk-pop singer / songwriter, b. Steven Georgiou, 21 Jul 1947, London, UK, whose songs have been recorded by many top acts. One of world's biggest album sellers in 1970s. Semi-retired 1979, converted to Islamic faith and changed name to Yusuf Islam. Gave royalties for Boyzone version of 'Father and Son' to charity (96 WEEKS) pos/wks

20 Oct 66	I LOVE MY DOG Deram DM 102	28	7
12 Jan 67 ●	MATTHEW AND SON Deram DM 110	2	10
30 Mar 67 ●	I'M GONNA GET ME A GUN Deram DM 118	6	10
2 Aug 67	A BAD NIGHT Deram DM 140	20	8
20 Dec 67	KITTY Deram DM 156	47	1
27 Jun 70 ●	LADY D'ARBANVILLE Island WIP 6086	8	13
28 Aug 71	MOON SHADOW Island WIP 6092	22	11
1 Jan 72 ●	MORNING HAS BROKEN Island WIP 6121	9	13
9 Dec 72	CAN'T KEEP IT IN Island WIP 6152	13	12
24 Aug 74	ANOTHER SATURDAY NIGHT Island WIP 6206	19	8
2 Jul 77	(REMEMBER THE DAYS OF THE) OLD SCHOOL YARD		
	Island WIP 6387	44	3

Connie STEVENS US, female vocalist - Concetta Ingola (20 WEEKS) pos/wks

5 May 60	KOOKIE KOOKIE (LEND ME YOUR COMB)		
	Warner Bros. WB 5 [1]	27	8
5 May 60 ●	SIXTEEN REASONS Warner Bros. WB 3	9	11
4 Aug 60	SIXTEEN REASONS (re-entry) Warner Bros. WB 3	45	1

[1] Edward Byrnes and Connie Stevens

Ray STEVENS US, male vocalist - Ray Ragsdale (64 WEEKS) pos/wks

16 May 70 ●	EVERYTHING IS BEAUTIFUL CBS 4953 ▲	6	16
13 Mar 71 ●	BRIDGET THE MIDGET (THE QUEEN OF THE BLUES)		
	CBS 7070	2	14
25 Mar 72	TURN YOUR RADIO ON CBS 7634	33	4
25 May 74 ★	THE STREAK Janus 6146 201 ▲	1	12
21 Jun 75 ●	MISTY Janus 6146 204	2	10
27 Sep 75	INDIAN LOVE CALL Janus 6146 205	34	4
5 Mar 77	IN THE MOOD Warner Bros. K 16875	31	4

'In the Mood' features Ray Stevens not as a conventional vocalist, but as a group of chickens

Ricky STEVENS UK, male vocalist (7 WEEKS) pos/wks

14 Dec 61	I CRIED FOR YOU Columbia DB 4739	34	7

Shakin' STEVENS (39 Top 500) Performs and records under a broad umbrella of styles from Rock and Country Blues to cajun, b. Michael Barratt, 4 Mar 1948, Glamorgan, Wales. Shares with the Beatles (60s) and Elton John (70s), the distinction of being the most successful UK singles chart performer of a decade (80s) (277 WEEKS) pos/wks

16 Feb 80	HOT DOG Epic EPC 8090	24	9
16 Aug 80	MARIE MARIE Epic EPC 8725	19	10
28 Feb 81 ★	THIS OLE HOUSE Epic EPC 9555	1	17
2 May 81 ●	YOU DRIVE ME CRAZY Epic A 1165	2	12
25 Jul 81 ★	GREEN DOOR Epic A 1354	1	12
10 Oct 81 ●	IT'S RAINING Epic A 1643	10	9
16 Jan 82 ★	OH JULIE Epic EPC A 1742	1	10
24 Apr 82 ●	SHIRLEY Epic EPC A 2087	6	6
21 Aug 82	GIVE ME YOUR HEART TONIGHT Epic EPC A 2656	11	10
16 Oct 82 ●	I'LL BE SATISFIED Epic EPC A 2846	10	8
11 Dec 82 ●	THE SHAKIN' STEVENS EP Epic SHAKY 1	2	7
23 Jul 83	IT'S LATE Epic A 3565	11	7
5 Nov 83 ●	CRY JUST A LITTLE BIT Epic A 3774	3	12
7 Jan 84 ●	A ROCKIN' GOOD WAY Epic A 4071 [1]	5	9
24 Mar 84 ●	A LOVE WORTH WAITING FOR Epic A 4291	2	10
15 Sep 84 ●	A LETTER TO YOU Epic A 4677	10	8
24 Nov 84 ●	TEARDROPS Epic A 4882	5	9
2 Mar 85	BREAKING UP MY HEART Epic A 6072	14	7
12 Oct 85	LIPSTICK POWDER AND PAINT Epic A 6610	11	9
7 Dec 85 ★	MERRY CHRISTMAS EVERYONE Epic A 6769	1	8
8 Feb 86	TURNING AWAY Epic A 6819	15	7
1 Nov 86	BECAUSE I LOVE YOU Epic SHAKY 2	14	10
20 Dec 86	MERRY CHRISTMAS EVERYONE (re-entry) Epic A 6769	58	3
27 Jun 87	A LITTLE BOOGIE WOOGIE (IN THE BACK OF MY MIND)		
	Epic SHAKY 3	12	10
19 Sep 87	COME SEE ABOUT ME Epic SHAKY 4	24	6
28 Nov 87 ●	WHAT DO YOU WANT TO MAKE THOSE EYES AT ME FOR		
	Epic SHAKY 5	5	8
23 Jul 88	FEEL THE NEED IN ME Epic SHAKY 6	26	5
15 Oct 88	HOW MANY TEARS CAN YOU HIDE Epic SHAKY 7	47	4
10 Dec 88	TRUE LOVE Epic SHAKY 8	23	6
18 Feb 89	JEZEBEL Epic SHAKY 9	58	2
13 May 89	LOVE ATTACK Epic SHAKY 10	28	4
24 Feb 90	I MIGHT Epic SHAKY 11	18	6
12 May 90	YES I DO Epic SHAKY 12	60	2
18 Aug 90	PINK CHAMPAGNE Epic SHAKY 13	59	2
13 Oct 90	MY CUTIE CUTIE Epic SHAKY 14	75	1
15 Dec 90	THE BEST CHRISTMAS OF THEM ALL Epic SHAKY 15	19	4
7 Dec 91	I'LL BE HOME THIS CHRISTMAS Epic 6576507	34	5
10 Oct 92	RADIO Epic 6584367 [2]	37	3

[1] Shaky and Bonnie (Bonnie Tyler) [2] Shaky featuring Roger Taylor

Tracks on The Shakin' Stevens EP: Blue Christmas / Que Sera Sera / Josephine / Lawdy Miss Clawdy

STEVENSON'S ROCKET
UK, male vocal / instrumental group (5 WEEKS)

		pos/wks
29 Nov 75	ALRIGHT BABY *Magnet MAG 47*	**37** 2
20 Dec 75	ALRIGHT BABY (re-entry)	
	Magnet MAG 47	**45** 3

Al STEWART *UK, male vocalist (6 WEEKS)*

		pos/wks
29 Jan 77	YEAR OF THE CAT *RCA 2771*	**31** 6

Amii STEWART *US, female vocalist (61 WEEKS)*

		pos/wks
7 Apr 79 ●	KNOCK ON WOOD *Atlantic / Hansa K 11214* ▲	**6** 12
16 Jun 79 ●	LIGHT MY FIRE / 137 DISCO HEAVEN (MEDLEY)	
	Atlantic / Hansa K 11278	**5** 11
3 Nov 79	JEALOUSY *Atlantic / Hansa K 11386*	**58** 3
19 Jan 80	THE LETTER / PARADISE BIRD *Atlantic / Hansa K 11424*	**39** 4
19 Jul 80	MY GUY - MY GIRL (MEDLEY) *Atlantic / Hansa K 11550* [1]	**39** 5
29 Dec 84	FRIENDS *RCA 471*	**12** 11
17 Aug 85 ●	KNOCK ON WOOD / LIGHT MY FIRE (re-mix)	
	Sedition EDIT 3303	**7** 12
25 Jan 86	MY GUY - MY GIRL (MEDLEY) *Sedition EDIT 3310* [2]	**63** 3

[1] Amii Stewart and Johnny Bristol [2] Amii Stewart and Deon Estus

Andy STEWART *UK, male vocalist (67 WEEKS)*

		pos/wks
15 Dec 60	DONALD WHERE'S YOUR TROOSERS	
	Top Rank JAR 427 [1]	**37** 1
12 Jan 61	A SCOTTISH SOLDIER	
	Top Rank JAR 512	**19** 38
1 Jun 61	THE BATTLE'S O'ER *Top Rank JAR 565* [1]	**28** 13
12 Oct 61	A SCOTTISH SOLDIER (re-entry)	
	Top Rank JAR 512	**43** 2
12 Aug 65	DR FINLAY *HMV POP 1454*	**50** 1
26 Aug 65	DR FINLAY (re-entry) *HMV POP 1454*	**43** 4
9 Dec 89 ●	DONALD WHERE'S YOUR TROOSERS (re-issue)	
	Stone SON 2353 [1]	**4** 8

[1] Andy Stewart with the Michael Sammes Singers

Billy STEWART *US, male vocalist (2 WEEKS)*

		pos/wks
8 Sep 66	SUMMERTIME *Chess CRS 8040*	**39** 2

Dave STEWART *UK, male instrumentalist - keyboards (30 WEEKS)* pos/wks

14 Mar 81	WHAT BECOMES OF THE BROKEN HEARTED	
	Stiff BROKEN 1 [1]	**13** 10
19 Sep 81 ★	IT'S MY PARTY *Stiff BROKEN 2* [2]	**1** 13
13 Aug 83	BUSY DOING NOTHING	
	Broken BROKEN 5 [2]	**49** 4
14 Jun 86	THE LOCOMOTION *Broken BROKEN 8* [2]	**70** 3

[1] Dave Stewart. Guest vocals: Colin Blunstone [2] Dave Stewart with Barbara Gaskin

Dave STEWART *UK, male instrumentalist - guitar (19 WEEKS)* pos/wks

24 Feb 90 ●	LILY WAS HERE *RCA ZB 43045* [1]	**6** 12
18 Aug 90	JACK TALKING *RCA PB 43907* [2]	**69** 2
3 Sep 94	HEART OF STONE *East West YZ 845CD*	**36** 5

[1] David A Stewart featuring Candy Dulfer [2] Dave Stewart and the Spiritual Cowboys

See also EURYTHMICS

Jermaine STEWART *US, male vocalist (42 WEEKS)*

		pos/wks
9 Aug 86 ●	WE DON'T HAVE TO . . . *10 TEN 96*	**2** 14
1 Nov 86	JODY *10 TEN 143*	**50** 4
16 Jan 88 ●	SAY IT AGAIN *10 TEN 188*	**7** 12
2 Apr 88	GET LUCKY *Siren SRN 82*	**13** 9
24 Sep 88	DON'T TALK DIRTY TO ME *Siren SRN 86*	**61** 3

John STEWART *US, male vocalist (6 WEEKS)*

		pos/wks
30 Jun 79	GOLD *RSO 35*	**43** 6

Rod STEWART 8 *Top 500*

World-renowned rock superstar b. 10 Jan 1945, London, UK, of Scottish parents. In the 1960s "Rod The Mod" recorded solo singles for Decca, EMI and Immediate, but is best remembered in that period as a member of the Five Dimensions, Hoochie Coochie Men, Steampacket, Shotgun Express and the Jeff Beck Group. Between 1969 and 1975, the gravel-voiced vocalist fronted The Faces as well as having a successful solo career. Over the past 30 years, Stewart has played to packed stadiums worldwide and amassed a vast collection of platinum and gold albums. In the US, he is one of the top selling UK artists of all time with eight Top 10 albums and 16 Top 10 singles. In Britain, he has scored 21 Top 10 LPs including seven solo No.1s. His writing skills have earned him a Lifetime Ivor Novello Award in the UK, while in the US he has recently been nominated for the prestigious Song Writers Hall of Fame. Stewart, whose love life also attracts much media attention, earned a Grammy Living Legend Award in 1989, Lifetime Achievement trophies from the Brits and World Music Awards and was inducted into the Rock and Roll Hall of Fame in 1994. (475 WEEKS)

		pos/wks
4 Sep 71	REASON TO BELIEVE *Mercury 6052 097*	**19** 2
18 Sep 71 ★	MAGGIE MAY *Mercury 6052 097* ▲	**1** 19
12 Aug 72 ★	YOU WEAR IT WELL *Mercury 6052 171*	**1** 12
18 Nov 72 ●	ANGEL / WHAT MADE MILWAUKEE FAMOUS (HAS MADE A LOSER OUT OF ME) *Mercury 6052 198*	**4** 11
5 May 73	I'VE BEEN DRINKING *RAK RR 4* [1]	**27** 6
8 Sep 73 ●	OH NO NOT MY BABY *Mercury 6052 371*	**6** 9
5 Oct 74 ●	FAREWELL - BRING IT ON HOME TO ME / YOU SEND ME *Mercury 6167 033*	**7** 7
7 Dec 74	YOU CAN MAKE ME DANCE SING OR ANYTHING (EVEN TAKE THE DOG FOR A WALK, MEND A FUSE, FOLD AWAY THE IRONING BOARD, OR ANY OTHER DOMESTIC SHORT COMINGS) *Warner Bros. K 16494* [2]	**12** 9
16 Aug 75 ★	SAILING *Warner Bros. K 16600*	**1** 11
15 Nov 75 ●	THIS OLD HEART OF MINE *Riva 1*	**4** 9
5 Jun 76 ●	TONIGHT'S THE NIGHT *Riva 3*	**5** 9
21 Aug 76 ●	THE KILLING OF GEORGIE *Riva 4*	**2** 10
4 Sep 76 ●	SAILING (re-entry) *Warner Bros. K 16600*	**3** 20
20 Nov 76	GET BACK *Riva 6*	**11** 9
4 Dec 76	MAGGIE MAY (re-issue) *Mercury 6160 006*	**31** 7
23 Apr 77 ★	I DON'T WANT TO TALK ABOUT IT / FIRST CUT IS THE DEEPEST *Riva 7*	**1** 13
15 Oct 77 ●	YOU'RE IN MY HEART *Riva 11*	**3** 10
28 Jan 78 ●	HOT LEGS / I WAS ONLY JOKING *Riva 10*	**5** 8
27 May 78 ●	OLE OLA (MULHER BRASILEIRA) *Riva 15* [3]	**4** 6
18 Nov 78 ★	DA YA THINK I'M SEXY? *Riva 17* ▲	**1** 13
3 Feb 79	AIN'T LOVE A BITCH *Riva 18*	**11** 8
5 May 79	BLONDES (HAVE MORE FUN) *Riva 19*	**63** 3
31 May 80	IF LOVING YOU IS WRONG (I DON'T WANT TO BE RIGHT) *Riva 23*	**23** 9
8 Nov 80	PASSION *Riva 26*	**17** 10
20 Dec 80	MY GIRL *Riva 28*	**32** 7
17 Oct 81 ●	TONIGHT I'M YOURS (DON'T HURT ME) *Riva 33*	**8** 13
12 Dec 81	YOUNG TURKS *Riva 34*	**11** 9
27 Feb 82	HOW LONG *Riva 35*	**41** 4
4 Jun 83 ★	BABY JANE *Warner Bros. W 9608*	**1** 14
27 Aug 83 ●	WHAT AM I GONNA DO (I'M SO IN LOVE WITH YOU) *Warner Bros. W 9564*	**3** 8
10 Dec 83	SWEET SURRENDER *Warner Bros. W 9440*	**23** 9
26 May 84	INFATUATION *Warner Bros. W 9256*	**27** 7
28 Jul 84	SOME GUYS HAVE ALL THE LUCK *Warner Bros. W 9204*	**15** 10
24 May 86	LOVE TOUCH *Warner Bros. W 8668*	**27** 5
5 Jul 86	LOVE TOUCH (re-entry) *Warner Bros. W 8668*	**69** 3
12 Jul 86 ●	EVERY BEAT OF MY HEART *Warner Bros. W 8625*	**2** 9
20 Sep 86	ANOTHER HEARTACHE *Warner Bros. W 8631*	**54** 2
28 Mar 87	SAILING (2nd re-entry) *Warner Bros. K 16600*	**41** 3
28 May 88	LOST IN YOU *Warner Bros. W 7927*	**21** 6
13 Aug 88	FOREVER YOUNG *Warner Bros. W 7796*	**57** 3
6 May 89	MY HEART CAN'T TELL YOU NO *Warner Bros. W 7729* [4]	**49** 4
11 Nov 89	THIS OLD HEART OF MINE *Warner Bros. W 2686* [4]	**51** 3
13 Jan 90 ●	DOWNTOWN TRAIN *Warner Bros. W 2647*	**10** 12
24 Nov 90 ●	IT TAKES TWO *Warner Bros. ROD 1* [5]	**5** 8
16 Mar 91 ●	RHYTHM OF MY HEART *Warner Bros. W 0017*	**3** 11
15 Jun 91 ●	THE MOTOWN SONG *Warner Bros. W 0030*	**10** 8
7 Sep 91	BROKEN ARROW *Warner Bros. W 0059*	**54** 3

UK No.1 ★   UK Top 10 ●   Still on chart +   UK million seller ◆   UK entry at No.1 ■   US No.1 ▲

7 Mar 92	PEOPLE GET READY *Epic 6577567* [1]	.49	3
18 Apr 92	YOUR SONG / BROKEN ARROW (re-issue)		
	Warner Bros. W 0104	.41	4
5 Dec 92 ●	TOM TRAUBERT'S BLUES (WALTZING MATILDA)		
	Warner Bros. W 0144	.6	6
20 Feb 93	RUBY TUESDAY *Warner Bros. W 0158CD*	.11	6
17 Apr 93	SHOTGUN WEDDING *Warner Bros. W 0171CD*	.21	4
26 Jun 93 ●	HAVE I TOLD YOU LATELY		
	Warner Bros. W 0185CD	.5	9
21 Aug 93	REASON TO BELIEVE *Warner Bros. W 0198CD1*	.51	3
18 Dec 93	PEOPLE GET READY *Warner Bros. W 0226CD1*	.45	4
15 Jan 94 ●	ALL FOR LOVE *A & M 5804772* [6] ▲	.2	13
20 May 95	YOU'RE THE STAR *Warner Bros. W 0296CD*	.19	5
19 Aug 95	LADY LUCK *Warner Bros. W 0310CD1*	.56	1
15 Jun 96	PURPLE HEATHER *Warner Bros. W 0354CD* [7]	.16	5
14 Dec 96	IF WE FALL IN LOVE TONIGHT		
	Warner Bros. W 0380CD	.58	1
1 Nov 97 ●	DA YA THINK I'M SEXY?		
	All Around the World CDGLOBE 150 [8]	.7	10
30 May 98	OOH LA LA *Warner Brothers W 0446CD*	.16	5
5 Sep 98	ROCKS *Warner Brothers W 0452CD1*	.55	1
17 Apr 99	FAITH OF THE HEART *Universal UND 56235*	.60	1

[1] Jeff Beck and Rod Stewart [2] Faces / Rod Stewart [3] Rod Stewart featuring the Scottish World Cup Football Squad [4] Rod Stewart featuring Ronald Isley [5] Rod Stewart and Tina Turner [6] Bryan Adams, Rod Stewart and Sting [7] Rod Stewart with the Scottish Euro '96 Squad [8] N-Trance featuring Rod Stewart

'Reason to Believe' and 'People Get Ready' in 1993 were re-recordings. 'Reason to Believe' additionally credits Ronnie Wood on the sleeve

See also GLASS TIGER; PYTHON LEE JACKSON; FACES

STEX *UK, male / female vocal / instrumental group (2 WEEKS)* pos/wks

| 19 Jan 91 | STILL FEEL THE RAIN *Some Bizarre SBZ 7002* | .63 | 2 |

STIFF LITTLE FINGERS

Ireland, male vocal / instrumental group (39 WEEKS) pos/wks

29 Sep 79	STRAW DOGS *Chrysalis CHS 2368*	.44	4
16 Feb 80	AT THE EDGE *Chrysalis CHS 2406*	.15	9
24 May 80	NOBODY'S HERO / TIN SOLDIERS		
	Chrysalis CHS 2424	.36	5
2 Aug 80	BACK TO FRONT *Chrysalis CHS 2447*	.49	4
28 Mar 81	JUST FADE AWAY *Chrysalis CHS 2510*	.47	6
30 May 81	SILVER LINING *Chrysalis CHS 2517*	.68	3
23 Jan 82	LISTEN (EP) *Chrysalis CHS 2580*	.33	6
18 Sep 82	BITS OF KIDS *Chrysalis CHS 2637*	.73	2

Tracks on Listen (EP): That's When Your Blood Bumps / Two Guitars Clash / Listen / Sad-Eyed People

Curtis STIGERS *US, male vocalist (34 WEEKS)* pos/wks

18 Jan 92 ●	I WONDER WHY *Arista 114716*	.5	10
28 Mar 92 ●	YOU'RE ALL THAT MATTERS TO ME		
	Arista 115273	.6	12
11 Jul 92	SLEEPING WITH THE LIGHTS ON		
	Arista 74321102307	.53	4
17 Oct 92	NEVER SAW A MIRACLE *Arista 74321117257*	.34	4
3 Jun 95	THIS TIME *Arista 74321286962*	.28	3
2 Dec 95	KEEP ME FROM THE COLD *Arista 74321319162*	.57	1

Stephen STILLS *US, male vocalist / instrumentalist (8 WEEKS)* pos/wks

13 Mar 71	LOVE THE ONE YOU'RE WITH		
	Atlantic 2091 046	.37	4
6 Jun 98	HE GOT GAME *Def Jam 5689852* [1]	.16	4

[1] Public Enemy featuring Stephen Stills

See also CROSBY, STILLS, NASH and YOUNG

STILTSKIN *UK, male vocal / instrumental group – lead vocal Ray Wilson*
(15 WEEKS) pos/wks

| 7 May 94 ★ | INSIDE *White Water LEV 1CD* | .1 | 13 |
| 24 Sep 94 | FOOTSTEPS *White Water WWRD 2* | .34 | 2 |

STING (140) Top 500

World's best known ex-Police-man, b. Gordon Sumner, 2 Oct 1951, Newcastle, UK. This singer / songwriter / bass player has amassed more solo hits than as frontman of that top-selling trio. As a soloist, he has won both Brit and Grammy awards (152 WEEKS) pos/wks

14 Aug 82	SPREAD A LITTLE HAPPINESS *A & M AMS 8242*	.16	8
8 Jun 85	IF YOU LOVE SOMEBODY SET THEM FREE *A & M AM 258*	.26	7
24 Aug 85	LOVE IS THE SEVENTH WAVE *A & M AM 272*	.41	5
19 Oct 85	FORTRESS AROUND YOUR HEART *A & M AM 286*	.49	3
7 Dec 85	RUSSIANS *A & M AM 292*	.12	11
15 Feb 86	MOON OVER BOURBON STREET *A & M AM 305*	.44	4
1 Mar 86	RUSSIANS (re-entry) *A & M AM 292*	.71	1
7 Nov 87	WE'LL BE TOGETHER *A & M AM 410*	.41	4
20 Feb 88	ENGLISHMAN IN NEW YORK *A & M AM 431*	.51	3
9 Apr 88	FRAGILE *A & M AM 439*	.70	2
11 Aug 90	ENGLISHMAN IN NEW YORK (re-mix) *A & M AM 580*	.15	7
12 Jan 91	ALL THIS TIME *A & M AM 713*	.22	4
9 Mar 91	MAD ABOUT YOU *A & M AM 721*	.56	2
4 May 91	THE SOUL CAGES *A & M AM 759*	.57	1
29 Aug 92	IT'S PROBABLY ME *A & M AM 883* [1]	.30	5
13 Feb 93	IF I EVER LOSE MY FAITH IN YOU *A & M AMCD 0172*	.14	6
24 Apr 93	SEVEN DAYS *A & M 5802232*	.25	4
19 Jun 93	FIELDS OF GOLD *A & M 5803012*	.16	6
4 Sep 93	SHAPE OF MY HEART *A & M 5803532*	.57	1
20 Nov 93	DEMOLITION MAN *A & M 5804512*	.21	4
15 Jan 94 ●	ALL FOR LOVE *A & M 5804772* [2] ▲	.2	13
26 Feb 94	NOTHING 'BOUT ME *A & M 5805292*	.32	3
29 Oct 94 ●	WHEN WE DANCE *A & M 5808612*	.9	7
11 Feb 95	THIS COWBOY SONG *A & M 5809652* [3]	.15	6
20 Jan 96	SPIRITS IN THE MATERIAL WORLD *MCA MCSTD 2113* [4]	.36	2
2 Mar 96	LET YOUR SOUL BE YOUR PILOT *A & M 5813312*	.15	4
11 May 96	YOU STILL TOUCH ME *A & M 5815472*	.27	3
22 Jun 96	LIVE AT TFI FRIDAY EP *A & M 5817652*	.53	2
14 Sep 96	I WAS BROUGHT TO MY SENSES *A & M 5818912*	.31	2
30 Nov 96	I'M SO HAPPY I CAN'T STOP CRYING *A & M 5820312*	.54	1
20 Dec 97	ROXANNE '97 (re-mix) *A & M 5824552* [5]	.17	6
25 Sep 99	BRAND NEW DAY *A&M / Polydor 4971522*	.13	5
29 Jan 00	DESERT SONG *A&M / Mercury 4972402* [6]	.15	6
22 Apr 00	AFTER THE RAIN HAS FALLEN *A&M / Mercury 4973252*	.31	4

[1] Sting with Eric Clapton [2] Bryan Adams, Rod Stewart and Sting [3] Sting featuring Pato Banton [4] Pato Banton with Sting [5] Sting and The Police [6] Sting featuring Cheb Mami

Tracks on Live at TFI Friday (EP): You Still Touch Me / Lithium Sunset / Message in a Bottle

STINGERS – See B BUMBLE and the STINGERS

Byron STINGILY *US, male vocalist (14 WEEKS)* pos/wks

25 Jan 97	GET UP (EVERYBODY) *Manifesto FESCD 19*	.14	5
1 Nov 97	SING A SONG *Manifesto FESCD 35*	.38	2
31 Jan 98	YOU MAKE ME FEEL (MIGHTY REAL)		
	Manifesto FESCD 38	.13	4
13 Jun 98	TESTIFY *Manifesto FESCD 42*	.48	1
12 Feb 00	THAT'S THE WAY LOVE IS *Manifesto FESCD 66*	.32	2

STIX 'N' STONED *UK, male instrumental / production duo (2 WEEKS)* pos/wks

| 20 Jul 96 | OUTRAGEOUS *Positiva CDTIV 52* | .39 | 2 |

STOCK AITKEN WATERMAN *UK, male producers (36 WEEKS)* pos/wks

25 Jul 87	ROADBLOCK *Breakout USA 611*	.13	9
24 Oct 87 ●	MR SLEAZE *London NANA 14*	.3	10
12 Dec 87	PACKJAMMED (WITH THE PARTY POSSE)		
	Breakout USA 620	.41	6
21 May 88	ALL THE WAY *MCA GOAL 1* [1]	.64	2
3 Dec 88	SS PAPARAZZI *PWL PWL 22*	.68	2
20 May 89 ★	FERRY 'CROSS THE MERSEY *PWL PWL 41* [2] ■	.1	7

[1] England Football Team and the 'sound' of Stock, Aitken and Waterman [2] Christians, Holly Johnson, Paul McCartney, Gerry Marsden and Stock Aitken Waterman

The listed flip side of 'Mr Sleaze' was 'Love in the First Degree' by Bananarama

Catherine STOCK *UK, female vocalist (6 WEEKS)*   pos/wks
18 Oct 86	TO HAVE AND TO HOLD *Sierra FED 29*	**17** 6

Miriam STOCKLEY – See PRAISE; ATLANTIS vs AVATAR

Rhet STOLLER *UK, male instrumentalist - guitar (8 WEEKS)*   pos/wks
12 Jan 61	CHARIOT *Decca F 11302*	**26** 8

Morris STOLOFF *US, orchestra (11 WEEKS)*   pos/wks
1 Jun 56 ●	MOONGLOW / THEME FROM PICNIC *Brunswick 05553*	**7** 11

Angie STONE *US, female vocalist (4 WEEKS)*   pos/wks
15 Apr 00	LIFE STORY *Arista 74321748492*	**22** 3
16 Dec 00	KEEP YOUR WORRIES *Virgin VUSCD 177* ☐1	**57** 1

☐1 Guru's Jazzmatazz featuring Angie Stone

R & J STONE *UK / US, male / female vocal duo - Russell and Joanne Stone (9 WEEKS)*   pos/wks
10 Jan 76 ●	WE DO IT *RCA 2616*	**5** 9

STONE ROSES ⟨430 *Top 500*⟩ *'Madchester'. 'Baggy' pioneers who successfully combined rock guitar and acid house attitude, inspiring a massive return to guitar-based bands in northern Britain in the 90s. Ian Brown (v), John Squire (g), Mani (aka Gary Mountfield) (b), Reni (aka Alan Wren) (d/v), all from Manchester. Their eponymous debut album, which peaked no higher than No.19 in 1989, continues to register in the top five of best all-time album surveys (77 WEEKS)*   pos/wks
29 Jul 89	SHE BANGS THE DRUMS *Silvertone ORE 6*	**36** 3
25 Nov 89 ●	WHAT THE WORLD IS WAITING FOR / FOOL'S GOLD *Silvertone ORE 13*	**8** 14
6 Jan 90	SALLY CINNAMON *Revolver REV 36*	**75** 1
20 Jan 90	SALLY CINNAMON (re-entry) *Revolver REV 36*	**46** 4
3 Mar 90 ●	ELEPHANT STONE *Silvertone ORE 1*	**8** 6
17 Mar 90	MADE OF STONE *Silvertone ORE 2*	**20** 4
31 Mar 90	SHE BANGS THE DRUMS (re-entry) *Silvertone ORE 6*	**34** 3
14 Jul 90 ●	ONE LOVE *Silvertone ORE 17*	**4** 7
15 Sep 90	WHAT THE WORLD IS WAITING FOR / FOOL'S GOLD (re-entry) *Silvertone ORE 13*	**22** 5
14 Sep 91	I WANNA BE ADORED *Silvertone ORE 31*	**20** 3
11 Jan 92	WATERFALL *Silvertone ORE 35*	**27** 4
11 Apr 92	I AM THE RESURRECTION *Silvertone ORE 40*	**33** 2
30 May 92	FOOL'S GOLD (re-issue) *Silvertone ORET 13*	**73** 1
3 Dec 94 ●	LOVE SPREADS *Geffen GFSTD 84*	**2** 8
11 Mar 95	TEN STOREY LOVE SONG *Geffen GFSTD 87*	**11** 3
29 Apr 95	FOOL'S GOLD (2nd re-issue) *Silvertone ORECD 71*	**25** 3
11 Nov 95	BEGGING YOU *Geffen GFSTD 22060*	**15** 3
6 Mar 99	FOOL'S GOLD (re-mix) *Jive Electro 0523092*	**25** 3

See also Ian BROWN; SEAHORSES

STONE TEMPLE PILOTS
US, male vocal / instrumental group (11 WEEKS)   pos/wks
27 Mar 93	SEX TYPE THING *Atlantic A 5769CD*	**60** 2
4 Sep 93	PLUSH *Atlantic A 7349CD*	**23** 4
27 Nov 93	SEX TYPE THING (re-issue) *Atlantic A 7293CD*	**55** 2
20 Aug 94	VASOLINE *Atlantic A 5650CD*	**48** 2
10 Dec 94	INTERSTATE LOVE SONG *Atlantic A 7192CD*	**53** 1

STONEBRIDGE McGUINNESS
UK, male vocal / instrumental duo (2 WEEKS)   pos/wks
14 Jul 79	OO-EEH BABY *RCA PB 5163*	**54** 2

STONEFREE *UK, male vocalist (1 WEEK)*   pos/wks
23 May 87	CAN'T SAY 'BYE *Ensign ENY 607*	**73** 1

STONEPROOF *UK, male producer - John Graham (1 WEEK)*   pos/wks
15 May 99	EVERYTHING'S NOT YOU *VC Recordings VCRD 47*	**68** 1

STONKERS – See HALE and PACE and the STONKERS

STOP THE VIOLENCE
US, male / female rap charity ensemble (1 WEEK)   pos/wks
18 Feb 89	SELF DESTRUCTION *Jive BDPST 1*	**75** 1

Axel STORDAHL – See June HUTTON

STORM *UK, male / female vocal / instrumental group (10 WEEKS)*   pos/wks
17 Nov 79	IT'S MY HOUSE *Scope SC 10*	**36** 10

STORM *Germany, male production duo (14 WEEKS)*   pos/wks
29 Aug 98	STORM *Positiva CDTIV 94*	**32** 2
12 Aug 00 ●	TIME TO BURN *Data DATA 16CDS*	**3** 10
23 Dec 00	STORM ANIMAL *Data DATA 20CDS*	**21** 2+

See also TOKYO GHETTO PUSSY; JAM & SPOON featuring PLAVKA

Danny STORM *UK, male vocalist (4 WEEKS)*   pos/wks
12 Apr 62	HONEST I DO *Piccadilly 7N 35025*	**42** 4

Rebecca STORM *UK, female vocalist (13 WEEKS)*   pos/wks
13 Jul 85	THE SHOW (THEME FROM 'CONNIE') *Towerbell TVP 3*	**22** 13

STORYVILLE JAZZ BAND – See Bob WALLIS and his STORYVILLE JAZZ BAND

Izzy STRADLIN'
US, male vocalist / instrumentalist - guitar (2 WEEKS)   pos/wks
26 Sep 92	PRESSURE DROP *Geffen GFS 25*	**45** 2

See also GUNS N' ROSES

Nick STRAKER BAND
UK, male vocal / instrumental group (15 WEEKS)   pos/wks
2 Aug 80	A WALK IN THE PARK *CBS 8525*	**20** 12
15 Nov 80	LEAVING ON THE MIDNIGHT TRAIN *CBS 9088*	**61** 3

Peter STRAKER and the HANDS OF DR TELENY *UK, male vocalist and male vocal / instrumental group (4 WEEKS)*   pos/wks
19 Feb 72	THE SPIRIT IS WILLING *RCA 2163*	**40** 4

STRANGE BEHAVIOUR – See Jane KENNAWAY and STRANGE BEHAVIOUR

STRANGE FRUIT – See Jimmy NAIL

STRANGELOVE *UK, male vocal / instrumental group (8 WEEKS)*   pos/wks
20 Apr 96	LIVING WITH THE HUMAN MACHINES *Food CDFOOD 70*	**53** 1
15 Jun 96	BEAUTIFUL ALONE *Food CDFOOD 81*	**35** 2
19 Oct 96	SWAY *Food CDFOOD 82*	**47** 1
26 Jul 97	THE GREATEST SHOW ON EARTH *Food CDFOODS 97*	**36** 2
11 Oct 97	FREAK *Food CDFOOD 105*	**43** 1
21 Feb 98	ANOTHER NIGHT IN *Food CDFOOD 110*	**46** 1

STRANGLERS ⟨95 *Top 500*⟩ *Most commercially successful and long-lasting group to emerge from the punk / new wave scene: Hugh Cornwell (v/g), Jean-Jacques Burnel (b/v), Dave Greenfield (k), Jet Black (d). This London-based band had at least one hit every year between 1977 and 1992 (194 WEEKS)*   pos/wks
19 Feb 77	(GET A) GRIP (ON YOURSELF) *United Artists UP 36211*	**44** 4
21 May 77 ●	PEACHES / GO BUDDY GO *United Artists UP 36248*	**8** 14
30 Jul 77 ●	SOMETHING BETTER CHANGE / STRAIGHTEN OUT *United Artists UP 36277*	**9** 8
24 Sep 77 ●	NO MORE HEROES *United Artists UP 36300*	**8** 9
4 Feb 78	FIVE MINUTES *United Artists UP 36350*	**11** 9
6 May 78	NICE 'N SLEAZY *United Artists UP 36379*	**18** 8
12 Aug 78	WALK ON BY *United Artists UP 36429*	**21** 8
18 Aug 79	DUCHESS *United Artists BP 308*	**14** 9

		pos/wks	
20 Oct 79	NUCLEAR DEVICE (THE WIZARD OF AUS) *United Artists BP 318*	**36**	4
1 Dec 79	DON'T BRING HARRY (EP) *United Artists STR 1*	**41**	3
22 Mar 80	BEAR CAGE *United Artists BP 344*	**36**	5
7 Jun 80	WHO WANTS THE WORLD *United Artists BP 355*	**39**	4
31 Jan 81	THROWN AWAY *Liberty BP 383*	**42**	4
14 Nov 81	LET ME INTRODUCE YOU TO THE FAMILY *Liberty BP 405*	**42**	3
9 Jan 82 ●	GOLDEN BROWN *Liberty BP 407*	**2**	12
24 Apr 82	LA FOLIE *Liberty BP 410*	**47**	3
24 Jul 82 ●	STRANGE LITTLE GIRL *Liberty BP 412*	**7**	9
8 Jan 83 ●	EUROPEAN FEMALE *Epic EPC A 2893*	**9**	6
26 Feb 83	MIDNIGHT SUMMER DREAM *Epic EPC A 3167*	**35**	4
6 Aug 83	PARADISE *Epic A 3387*	**48**	3
6 Oct 84	SKIN DEEP *Epic A 4738*	**15**	7
1 Dec 84	NO MERCY *Epic A 4921*	**37**	7
16 Feb 85	LET ME DOWN EASY *Epic A 6045*	**48**	4
23 Aug 86	NICE IN NICE *Epic 6500557*	**30**	5
18 Oct 86	ALWAYS THE SUN *Epic SOLAR 1*	**30**	5
13 Dec 86	BIG IN AMERICA *Epic HUGE 1*	**48**	6
7 Mar 87	SHAKIN' LIKE A LEAF *Epic SHEIK 1*	**58**	4
9 Jan 88 ●	ALL DAY AND ALL OF THE NIGHT *Epic VICE 1*	**7**	7
28 Jan 89	GRIP '89 (GET A) GRIP (ON YOURSELF) (re-mix) *EMI EM 84*	**33**	3
17 Feb 90	96 TEARS *Epic TEARS 1*	**17**	6
21 Apr 90	SWEET SMELL OF SUCCESS *Epic TEARS 2*	**65**	2
5 Jan 91	ALWAYS THE SUN (re-mix) *Epic 6564307*	**29**	5
30 Mar 91	GOLDEN BROWN (re-mix) *Epic 6567617*	**68**	2
22 Aug 92	HEAVEN OR HELL *Psycho WOK 2025*	**46**	2

'Go Buddy Go' credited with 'Peaches' from 11 Jun 1977. 'Straighten Out' credited with 'Something Better Change' from 13 Aug 1977. Tracks on Don't Bring Harry (EP): Don't Bring Harry / Wired / Crabs (Live) / In the Shadows (Live)

STRAW *UK, male vocal / instrumental group (3 WEEKS)*

		pos/wks	
6 Feb 99	THE AEROPLANE SONG *WEA WEA 196CD*	**37**	2
24 Apr 99	MOVING TO CALIFORNIA *WEA WEA 205CD1*	**50**	1

STRAWBERRY SWITCHBLADE *UK, female vocal duo - Rose McDowell and Jill Bryson (26 WEEKS)*

		pos/wks	
17 Nov 84 ●	SINCE YESTERDAY *Korova KOW 38*	**5**	17
23 Mar 85	LET HER GO *Korova KOW 39*	**59**	5
21 Sep 85	JOLENE *Korova KOW 42*	**53**	4

STRAWBS *UK, male vocal / instrumental group (27 WEEKS)*

		pos/wks	
28 Oct 72	LAY DOWN *A & M AMS 7035*	**12**	13
27 Jan 73 ●	PART OF THE UNION *A & M AMS 7047*	**2**	11
6 Oct 73	SHINE ON SILVER SUN *A & M AMS 7082*	**34**	3

STRAY CATS *US, male vocal / instrumental group (49 WEEKS)*

		pos/wks	
29 Nov 80 ●	RUNAWAY BOYS *Arista SCAT 1*	**9**	10
7 Feb 81 ●	ROCK THIS TOWN *Arista SCAT 2*	**9**	8
25 Apr 81	STRAY CAT STRUT *Arista SCAT 3*	**11**	10
20 Jun 81	THE RACE IS ON *Swansong SSK 19425* [1]	**34**	4
7 Nov 81	YOU DON'T BELIEVE ME *Arista SCAT 4*	**57**	3
6 Aug 83	(SHE'S) SEXY AND 17 *Arista SCAT 6*	**29**	9
4 Mar 89	BRING IT BACK AGAIN *EMI USA MT 62*	**64**	3

[1] Dave Edmunds and the Stray Cats

STRAY MOB – See MC SKAT KAT and the STRAY MOB

STREETBAND *UK, male vocal / instrumental group (6 WEEKS)*

		pos/wks	
4 Nov 78	TOAST / HOLD ON *Logo GO 325*	**18**	6

See also Paul YOUNG

Barbra STREISAND 136 **Top 500** *The world's best-selling female album artist, b. 24 Apr 1942, Brooklyn, US. This world-renowned MOR vocalist / actress has collected countless awards for her recordings and her stage and film work, and is a recipient of both Grammy Living Legend and Lifetime Achievement awards (155 WEEKS)*

		pos/wks	
20 Jan 66	SECOND HAND ROSE *CBS 202025*	**14**	13
30 Jan 71	STONEY END *CBS 5321*	**46**	1
13 Feb 71	STONEY END (re-entry) *CBS 5321*	**27**	10
30 Mar 74	THE WAY WE WERE *CBS 1915* ▲	**31**	6
9 Apr 77 ●	LOVE THEME FROM 'A STAR IS BORN' (EVERGREEN) *CBS 4855* ▲	**3**	19
25 Nov 78 ●	YOU DON'T BRING ME FLOWERS *CBS 6803* [1] ▲	**5**	12
3 Nov 79 ●	NO MORE TEARS (ENOUGH IS ENOUGH) *Casablanca CAN 174/ CBS 8000* [2] ▲	**3**	13
4 Oct 80 ★	WOMAN IN LOVE *CBS 8966* ▲	**1**	16
6 Dec 80	GUILTY *CBS 9315* [3]	**34**	10
30 Jan 82	COMIN' IN AND OUT OF YOUR LIFE *CBS A 1789*	**66**	3
20 Mar 82	MEMORY *CBS A 1903*	**34**	6
5 Nov 88	TILL I LOVED YOU (LOVE THEME FROM 'GOYA') *CBS BARB 2* [4]	**16**	7
7 Mar 92	PLACES THAT BELONG TO YOU *Columbia 6577947*	**17**	5
5 Jun 93	WITH ONE LOOK *Columbia 6593422*	**30**	3
15 Jan 94	THE MUSIC OF THE NIGHT *Columbia 6597382* [5]	**54**	3
30 Apr 94	AS IF WE NEVER SAID GOODBYE *Columbia 6603572*	**20**	3
8 Feb 97 ●	I FINALLY FOUND SOMEONE *A&M 5820832* [6]	**10**	7
15 Nov 97 ●	TELL HIM *Epic 6653052* [7]	**3**	15
30 Oct 99	IF YOU EVER LEAVE ME *Columbia 6681242* [8]	**26**	3

[1] Barbra and Neil [2] Donna Summer and Barbra Streisand [3] Barbra Streisand and Barry Gibb [4] Barbra Streisand and Don Johnson [5] Barbra Streisand (duet with Michael Crawford) [6] Barbra Streisand and Bryan Adams [7] Barbra Streisand and Celine Dion [8] Barbra Streisand / Vince Gill

Neil was Neil Diamond. 'No More Tears (Enough Is Enough)' was released simultaneously on two different labels, a 7-inch single on Casablanca and a 12-inch on CBS

STRESS *UK, male vocal / instrumental group (1 WEEK)*

		pos/wks	
13 Oct 90	BEAUTIFUL PEOPLE *Eternal YZ 495*	**74**	1

STRETCH *UK, male vocal / instrumental group (9 WEEKS)*

		pos/wks	
8 Nov 75	WHY DID YOU DO IT *Anchor ANC 1021*	**16**	9

STRETCH 'N' VERN present MADDOG *UK, male instrumental / production duo - Stuart Collins and Julian Peake (14 WEEKS)*

		pos/wks	
14 Sep 96 ●	I'M ALIVE *ffrr FCD 284*	**6**	9
9 Aug 97	GET UP! GO INSANE! *ffrr FCD 304*	**17**	5

STRICT INSTRUCTOR *Russia, female vocalist (1 WEEK)*

		pos/wks	
24 Oct 98	STEP-TWO-THREE-FOUR *All Around The World CDGLOBE 155*	**49**	1

STRIKE *UK / Australia, male / female vocal / instrumental group (24 WEEKS)*

		pos/wks	
24 Dec 94	U SURE DO *Fresh FRSHD 19*	**31**	5
1 Apr 95 ●	U SURE DO (re-entry) *Fresh FRSHD 19*	**4**	9
23 Sep 95	THE MORNING AFTER (FREE AT LAST) *Fresh FRSHD 37*	**38**	1
29 Jun 96	INSPIRATION *Fresh FRSHD 45*	**27**	2
16 Nov 96	MY LOVE IS FOR REAL *Fresh FRSHD 46*	**35**	2
31 May 97	I HAVE PEACE *Fresh FRSHCD 58*	**17**	4
25 Sep 99	U SURE DO (re-mix) *Fresh FRSHD 78*	**53**	1

STRIKERS *US, male vocal / instrumental group (5 WEEKS)*

		pos/wks	
6 Jun 81	BODY MUSIC *Epic EPC A 1290*	**45**	5

STRING-A-LONGS *US, male instrumental group (16 WEEKS)*

		pos/wks	
23 Feb 61 ●	WHEELS *London HLU 9278*	**8**	16

STRINGS OF LOVE *Italy, male / female vocal / instrumental group (2 WEEKS)*

		pos/wks	
3 Mar 90	NOTHING HAS BEEN PROVED *Breakout USA 688*	**59**	2

Joe STRUMMER *UK, male vocalist - John Mellor (13 WEEKS)*

		pos/wks	
2 Aug 86	LOVE KILLS *CBS A 7244*	**69**	1

UK No.1 ★   UK Top 10 ●   Still on chart +   UK million seller ◆   UK entry at No.1 ■   US No.1 ▲

| 23 Dec 95 | | JUST THE ONE *China WOKCD 2076* [1] | **12** | 8 |
| 29 Jun 96 | ● | ENGLAND'S IRIE *Radioactive RAXTD 25* [2] | **6** | 4 |

[1] Levellers, special guest Joe Strummer [2] Black Grape featuring Joe Strummer and Keith Allen

See also CLASH

STRYKER – See MANCHESTER UNITED FOOTBALL CLUB

Chad STUART and Jeremy CLYDE
UK, male vocal duo (7 WEEKS) pos/wks

| 28 Nov 63 | YESTERDAY'S GONE *Ember EMB S 180* | **37** | 7 |

STUDIO 2 *Jamaica, male vocalist - Errol Jones (1 WEEK)* pos/wks

| 27 Jun 98 | TRAVELLING MAN *Multiply CDMULTY 35* | **40** | 1 |

STUDIO 45 *Germany, male DJ / production duo (2 WEEKS)* pos/wks

| 20 Feb 99 | FREAK IT! *Azuli AZNYCD 090* | **36** | 2 |

STUMP *UK, male vocal / instrumental group (1 WEEK)* pos/wks

| 13 Aug 88 | CHARLTON HESTON *Ensign ENY 614* | **72** | 1 |

STUTZ BEARCATS and the Denis KING ORCHESTRA
UK, male / female vocal group with orchestra (6 WEEKS) pos/wks

| 24 Apr 82 | THE SONG THAT I SING (THEME FROM 'WE'LL MEET AGAIN') *Multi-Media Tapes MMT 6* | **36** | 6 |

STYLE COUNCIL (289 Top 500) *Eighties chart regulars: Paul Weller (v/g), Mick Talbot (k) and sometimes DC Lee (v - former Wham! backing vocalist and Weller's wife). As with Weller's previous band, The Jam, most of this London act's hits were in their homeland (103 WEEKS)* pos/wks

19 Mar 83	●	SPEAK LIKE A CHILD *Polydor TSC 1*	**4**	8
28 May 83		MONEY GO ROUND (PART 1) *Polydor TSC 2*	**11**	6
13 Aug 83	●	LONG HOT SUMMER / PARIS MATCH *Polydor TSC 3*	**3**	9
20 Aug 83		MONEY GO ROUND (PART 1) (re-entry) *Polydor TSC 2*	**74**	1
19 Nov 83		SOLID BOND IN YOUR HEART *Polydor TSC 4*	**11**	8
18 Feb 84	●	MY EVER CHANGING MOODS *Polydor TSC 5*	**5**	7
26 May 84	●	GROOVIN' (YOU'RE THE BEST THING / BIG BOSS GROOVE) *Polydor TSC 6*	**5**	8
13 Oct 84	●	SHOUT TO THE TOP *Polydor TSC 7*	**7**	8
11 May 85	●	WALLS COME TUMBLING DOWN! *Polydor TSC 8*	**6**	7
6 Jul 85		COME TO MILTON KEYNES *Polydor TSC 9*	**23**	5
28 Sep 85		THE LODGERS *Polydor TSC 10*	**13**	6
5 Apr 86		HAVE YOU EVER HAD IT BLUE *Polydor CINE 1*	**14**	6
17 Jan 87	●	IT DIDN'T MATTER *Polydor TSC 12*	**9**	5
14 Mar 87		WAITING *Polydor TSC 13*	**52**	3
31 Oct 87		WANTED *Polydor TSC 14*	**20**	4
28 May 88		LIFE AT A TOP PEOPLE'S HEALTH FARM *Polydor TSC 15*	**28**	3
23 Jul 88		HOW SHE THREW IT ALL AWAY (EP) *Polydor TSC 16*	**41**	2
18 Feb 89		PROMISED LAND *Polydor TSC 17*	**27**	5
27 May 89		LONG HOT SUMMER 89 (re-mix) *Polydor LHS 1*	**48**	2

'Paris Match' was listed with 'Long Hot Summer' from 3 Sep 1983. It peaked at No.7. Tracks on How She Threw It All Away (EP): How She Threw It All Away / Love the First Time / Long Hot Summer / I Do Like to Be B-Side the A-Side. The version of 'Long Hot Summer' on the EP is a re-recording of their third hit

STYLISTICS (163 Top 500) *Stylish and smooth vocal group from Philadelphia, US, fronted by falsetto-voiced Russell Thompkins Jr (b. 21 Mar 1951), whose UK hits continued after success in their homeland diminished. The quintet's Greatest Hits album topped the UK album chart in 1975 (143 WEEKS)* pos/wks

24 Jun 72		BETCHA BY GOLLY WOW *Avco 6105 011*	**13**	12
4 Nov 72	●	I'M STONE IN LOVE WITH YOU *Avco 6105 015*	**9**	10
17 Mar 73		BREAK UP TO MAKE UP *Avco 6105 020*	**34**	5
30 Jun 73		PEEK-A-BOO *Avco 6105 023*	**35**	6
19 Jan 74	●	ROCKIN' ROLL BABY *Avco 6105 026*	**6**	9
13 Jul 74	●	YOU MAKE ME FEEL BRAND NEW *Avco 6105 028*	**2**	14
19 Oct 74	●	LET'S PUT IT ALL TOGETHER *Avco 6105 032*	**9**	9
25 Jan 75		STAR ON A TV SHOW *Avco 6105 035*	**12**	8

10 May 75	●	SING BABY SING *Avco 6105 036*	**3**	10
26 Jul 75	★	CAN'T GIVE YOU ANYTHING (BUT MY LOVE) *Avco 6105 039*	**1**	11
15 Nov 75	●	NA NA IS THE SADDEST WORD *Avco 6105 041*	**5**	10
14 Feb 76	●	FUNKY WEEKEND *Avco 6105 044*	**10**	7
24 Apr 76	●	CAN'T HELP FALLING IN LOVE *H & L 6105 050*	**4**	7
7 Aug 76	●	16 BARS *H & L 6105 059*	**7**	9
27 Nov 76		YOU'LL NEVER GET TO HEAVEN (EP) *H & L STYL 001*	**24**	9
26 Mar 77		7000 DOLLARS AND YOU *H & L 6105 073*	**24**	7

Tracks on You'll Never Get to Heaven (EP): You'll Never Get to Heaven / Country Living / You Are Beautiful / The Miracle

STYX *US, male vocal / instrumental group (18 WEEKS)* pos/wks

5 Jan 80	●	BABE *A & M AMS 7489* ▲	**6**	10
24 Jan 81		THE BEST OF TIMES *A & M AMS 8102*	**42**	5
18 Jun 83		DON'T LET IT END *A & M AM 120*	**56**	3

SUB SUB *UK, male instrumental / production group (12 WEEKS)* pos/wks

| 10 Apr 93 | ● | AIN'T NO LOVE (AIN'T NO USE) *Rob's CDROB 9* [1] | **3** | 11 |
| 19 Feb 94 | | RESPECT *Rob's CDROB 19* | **49** | 1 |

[1] Sub Sub featuring Melanie Williams

SUBCIRCUS
Denmark / UK, male vocal / instrumental group (2 WEEKS) pos/wks

| 26 Apr 97 | YOU LOVE YOU *Echo ECSCD 34* | **61** | 1 |
| 12 Jul 97 | 86'D *Echo ECSCX 43* | **56** | 1 |

SUBLIME *US, male vocal / instrumental group (1 WEEK)* pos/wks

| 5 Jul 97 | WHAT I GOT *Gasoline Alley MCSTD 48045* | **71** | 1 |

SUBLIMINAL CUTS
Holland, male producer - Patrick Prinz (3 WEEKS) pos/wks

| 15 Oct 94 | LE VOIE LE SOLEIL *XL XLS 53CD* | **69** | 1 |
| 20 Jul 96 | LE VOIE LE SOLEIL (re-mix) *XL XLSR 53CD* | **23** | 2 |

See also ARTEMESIA; ETHICS; MOVIN' MELODIES

SUBMERGE featuring Jan JOHNSTON *US, male producer / instrumentalist and US, female vocalist (2 WEEKS)* pos/wks

| 8 Feb 97 | TAKE ME BY THE HAND *AM:PM 5821012* | **28** | 2 |

SUBSONIC 2 *UK, male rap duo (3 WEEKS)* pos/wks

| 13 Jul 91 | THE UNSUNG HEROES OF HIP HOP *Unity 6577947* | **63** | 3 |

SUBTERRANIA featuring Ann CONSUELO
Sweden, male / female vocal / instrumental duo (1 WEEK) pos/wks

| 5 Jun 93 | DO IT FOR LOVE *Champion CHAMPCD 297* | **68** | 1 |

SUEDE *London-based Britpop pioneers include photogenic frontman Brett Anderson (v) and co-writer Bernard Butler (g) who left 1994. MM's "Best Band In Britain" won the Mercury Music Prize for their 1993 self-titled debut album which sold more than 100,000 in its first week (68 WEEKS)* pos/wks

23 May 92		THE DROWNERS / TO THE BIRDS *Nude NUD 1S*	**49**	2
26 Sep 92		METAL MICKEY *Nude NUD 3S*	**17**	3
6 Mar 93	●	ANIMAL NITRATE *Nude NUD 4CD*	**7**	7
29 May 93		SO YOUNG *Nude NUD 5CD*	**22**	3
26 Feb 94	●	STAY TOGETHER *Nude NUD 9CD*	**3**	6
24 Sep 94		WE ARE THE PIGS *Nude NUD 10CD*	**18**	3
19 Nov 94		THE WILD ONES *Nude NUD 11CD*	**18**	4
11 Feb 95		NEW GENERATION *Nude NUD 12CD1*	**21**	3
11 Mar 95		NEW GENERATION (re-entry) *Nude NUD 12CD1*	**75**	1
10 Aug 96	●	TRASH *Nude NUD 21CD1*	**3**	6
26 Oct 96	●	BEAUTIFUL ONES *Nude NUD 23CD1*	**8**	5
25 Jan 97	●	SATURDAY NIGHT *Nude NUD 24CD1*	**6**	4
19 Apr 97	●	LAZY *Nude NUD 27CD1*	**9**	3
23 Aug 97	●	FILMSTAR *Nude NUD 30CD1*	**9**	4
24 Apr 99	●	ELECTRICITY *Nude NUD 43CD1*	**5**	5
3 Jul 99		SHE'S IN FASHION *Nude NUD 44CD1*	**13**	5

| 18 Sep 99 | EVERYTHING WILL FLOW *Nude NUD 45CD1* | 24 | 2 |
| 20 Nov 99 | CAN'T GET ENOUGH *Nude NUD 47CD1* | 23 | 2 |

SUENO LATINO *Italy, male production duo (6 WEEKS)* pos/wks

| 23 Sep 89 | SUENO LATINO *BCM BCM 323* [1] | 47 | 5 |
| 11 Nov 00 | SUENO LATINO (re-mix) *Distinctive DISNCD 64* | 68 | 1 |

[1] Sueno Latino featuring Carolina Damas

SUGABABES *UK, female vocal group (9 WEEKS)* pos/wks

| 23 Sep 00 ● | OVERLOAD *London LONCD 449* | 6 | 8 |
| 30 Dec 00 | NEW YEAR *London LONCD 455* | 12 | 1+ |

SUGAR *US, male vocal / instrumental group (7 WEEKS)* pos/wks

31 Oct 92	A GOOD IDEA *Creation CRE 143*	65	1
30 Jan 93	IF I CAN'T CHANGE YOUR MIND *Creation CRESCD 149*	30	1
21 Aug 93	TILTED *Creation CRECD 156*	48	1
3 Sep 94	YOUR FAVORITE THING *Creation CRESCD 186*	40	2
29 Oct 94	BELIEVE WHAT YOU'RE SAYING *Creation CRESCD 193*	73	1

SUGAR CANE *US, male / female vocal group (5 WEEKS)* pos/wks

| 30 Sep 78 | MONTEGO BAY *Ariola Hansa AHA 524* | 54 | 5 |

SUGAR RAY *US, male vocal / instrumental group (10 WEEKS)* pos/wks

| 31 Jan 98 | FLY *Atlantic AT 0008CD* | 58 | 1 |
| 29 May 99 ● | EVERY MORNING *Lava / Atlantic AT 0065CD* | 10 | 9 |

SUGARCUBES
Iceland, male / female vocal / instrumental group (22 WEEKS) pos/wks

14 Nov 87	BIRTHDAY *One Little Indian 7TP 7*	65	3
30 Jan 88	COLD SWEAT *One Little Indian 7TP 9*	56	4
16 Apr 88	DEUS *One Little Indian 7TP 10*	51	3
3 Sep 88	BIRTHDAY (re-recording) *One Little Indian 7TP 11*	65	3
16 Sep 89	REGINA *One Little Indian 26TP7*	55	2
11 Jan 92	HIT *One Little Indian 62 TP7*	17	6
3 Oct 92	BIRTHDAY (re-mix) *One Little Indian 104 TP12*	64	1

See also BJORK

SUGARHILL GANG *US, male rap group (16 WEEKS)* pos/wks

1 Dec 79 ●	RAPPER'S DELIGHT *Sugarhill SHL 101*	3	11
11 Sep 82	THE LOVER IN YOU *Sugarhill SH 116*	54	3
25 Nov 89	RAPPER'S DELIGHT (re-mix) *Sugarhill SHRD 0007*	58	2

SUGGS *UK, male vocalist - Graham McPherson (46 WEEKS)* pos/wks

12 Aug 95 ●	I'M ONLY SLEEPING / OFF ON HOLIDAY *WEA YZ 975CD*	7	6
14 Oct 95	CAMDEN TOWN *WEA WEA 019CD*	14	6
16 Dec 95	THE TUNE *WEA WEA 031CD*	33	3
13 Apr 96	CECILIA *WEA WEA 042CD1* [1]	4	17
24 Aug 96	CECILIA (re-entry) *WEA WEA 042CD1* [1]	65	1
7 Sep 96	CECILIA (2nd re-entry) *WEA WEA 042CD1* [1]	59	1
21 Sep 96	NO MORE ALCOHOL *WEA WEA 065CD1* [1]	24	4
17 May 97	BLUE DAY *WEA WEA 112CD* [2]	22	5
5 Sep 98	I AM *WEA WEA 174CD*	38	3

[1] Suggs featuring Louchie Lou and Michie One [2] Suggs & Co featuring Chelsea Team

SULTANA *Italy, male instrumental / production group (1 WEEK)* pos/wks

| 26 Mar 94 | TE AMO *Union City UCRD 28* | 57 | 1 |

SULTANS OF PING *Ireland, male vocal / instrumental group (12 WEEKS)* pos/wks

8 Feb 92	WHERE'S ME JUMPER *Divine ATHY 01* [1]	67	2
9 May 92	STUPID KID *Divine ATHY 02* [1]	67	1
10 Oct 92	VERONICA *Divine ATHY 03* [1]	69	1
9 Jan 93	YOU TALK TOO MUCH *Rhythm King 6588872* [1]	26	3
11 Sep 93	TEENAGE PUNKS *Epic 6595792*	49	2

| 30 Oct 93 | MICHIKO *Epic 6598222* | 43 | 2 |
| 19 Feb 94 | WAKE UP AND SCRATCH ME *Epic 6601122* | 50 | 1 |

[1] Sultans of Ping FC

SUMMER – See SNAP

SUMMER DAZE *UK, male instrumental / production duo (1 WEEK)* pos/wks

| 26 Oct 96 | SAMBA MAGIC *VC VCRD 14* | 61 | 1 |

Donna SUMMER (33) Top 500

"Queen of disco music", b. LaDonna Gaines, 31 Dec 1948, Massachusetts, US. Germany was the launching pad for this diva, who had eight successive US Top 5 singles in the late 1970s. She was also the first female to score three consecutive US No.1 albums (299 WEEKS) pos/wks

17 Jan 76 ●	LOVE TO LOVE YOU BABY *GTO GT 17*	4	9
29 May 76	COULD IT BE MAGIC *GTO GT 60*	40	7
25 Dec 76	WINTER MELODY *GTO GT 76*	27	6
9 Jul 77 ★	I FEEL LOVE *GTO GT 100*	1	11
20 Aug 77 ●	DEEP DOWN INSIDE (THEME FROM 'THE DEEP') *Casablanca CAN 111*	5	10
24 Sep 77	I REMEMBER YESTERDAY *GTO GT 107*	14	7
3 Dec 77 ●	LOVE'S UNKIND *GTO GT 113*	3	13
10 Dec 77 ●	I LOVE YOU *Casablanca CAN 114*	10	9
25 Feb 78	RUMOUR HAS IT *Casablanca CAN 122*	19	8
22 Apr 78	BACK IN LOVE AGAIN *GTO GT 117*	29	7
10 Jun 78	LAST DANCE *Casablanca TGIF 2*	70	1
24 Jun 78	LAST DANCE (re-entry) *Casablanca TGIF 2*	51	8
14 Oct 78 ●	MACARTHUR PARK *Casablanca CAN 131* ▲	5	10
17 Feb 79	HEAVEN KNOWS *Casablanca CAN 141*	34	8
12 May 79	HOT STUFF *Casablanca CAN 151* ▲	11	10
7 Jul 79	BAD GIRLS *Casablanca CAN 155* ▲	14	10
1 Sep 79	DIM ALL THE LIGHTS *Casablanca CAN 162*	29	9
3 Nov 79 ●	NO MORE TEARS (ENOUGH IS ENOUGH) *Casablanca CAN 174 / CBS 8000* [1] ▲	3	13
16 Feb 80	ON THE RADIO *Casablanca NB 2236*	32	6
21 Jun 80	SUNSET PEOPLE *Casablanca CAN 198*	46	5
27 Sep 80	THE WANDERER *Geffen K 79180*	48	6
17 Jan 81	COLD LOVE *Geffen K 79193*	44	3
10 Jul 82	LOVE IS IN CONTROL (FINGER ON THE TRIGGER) *Warner Bros. K 79302*	18	11
6 Nov 82	STATE OF INDEPENDENCE *Warner Bros. K 79344*	14	11
4 Dec 82	I FEEL LOVE (re-mix) *Warner Bros. FEEL 7*	21	10
5 Mar 83	THE WOMAN IN ME *Warner Bros. U 9983*	62	2
18 Jun 83	SHE WORKS HARD FOR THE MONEY *Mercury DONNA 1*	25	8
24 Sep 83	UNCONDITIONAL LOVE *Mercury DONNA 2*	14	12
21 Jan 84	STOP LOOK AND LISTEN *Mercury DONNA 3*	57	2
24 Oct 87	DINNER WITH GERSHWIN *Warner Bros. U 8237*	13	11
23 Jan 88	ALL SYSTEMS GO *WEA U 8122*	54	3
25 Feb 89 ●	THIS TIME I KNOW IT'S FOR REAL *Warner Bros. U 7780*	3	14
27 May 89 ●	I DON'T WANNA GET HURT *Warner Bros. U 7567*	7	9
26 Aug 89	LOVE'S ABOUT TO CHANGE MY HEART *Warner Bros. U 7494*	20	6
25 Nov 89	WHEN LOVE TAKES OVER YOU *Warner Bros. U 7361*	72	1
17 Nov 90	STATE OF INDEPENDENCE (re-issue) *Warner Bros. U 2857*	45	3
12 Jan 91	BREAKAWAY *Warner Bros. U 3308*	49	4
30 Nov 91	WORK THAT MAGIC *Warner Bros. U 5937*	74	1
12 Nov 94	MELODY OF LOVE (WANNA BE LOVED) *Mercury MERCD 418*	21	3
9 Sep 95 ●	I FEEL LOVE *Manifesto FESCD 1*	8	5
6 Apr 96	STATE OF INDEPENDENCE (re-mix) *Manifesto FESCD 7* [2]	13	5
11 Jul 98	CARRY ON *Almighty CDALMY 120* [3]	65	1
30 Oct 99	I WILL GO WITH YOU (CON TE PARTIRO) *Epic 6682092*	44	1

[1] Donna Summer and Barbra Streisand [2] Donna Summer featuring the All Star Choir [3] Donna Summer and Giorgio Moroder

'No More Tears (Enough Is Enough)' was released simultaneously on two different labels, a 7-inch single on Casablanca and a 12-inch on CBS. 'Unconditional Love' features the additional vocals of Musical Youth. 'I Feel Love' in 1995 is a re-recording

Mark SUMMERS *UK, male producer (6 WEEKS)* pos/wks

| 26 Jan 91 | SUMMER'S MAGIC *Fourth & Broadway BRW 205* | 27 | 6 |

SINGLED OUT...
Sonique

The athletic lady DJ and pop star who dominated the summer airwaves with the longest-running No.1 of 2000 loves Donna but hates Blobby.

- **NO.1 ON THE UK SINGLES CHART THE DAY I WAS BORN:**
  I'm Alive – The Hollies

- **ALL-TIME FAVOURITE SINGLE:**
  No Woman No Cry – Bob Marley and the Wailers

- **SINGLE THAT DRIVES ME UP THE WALL:**
  Mr Blobby – Mr Blobby

FIRST SINGLE I EVER BOUGHT:
I Feel Love
Donna Summer

That was the start of my musical experience. It reached a part of me other things didn't reach. I knew then that this is the music I like and I never left

SUNBURST UK, male producer - Matt Darey (1 WEEK)

		pos/wks
8 Jul 00	**EYEBALL (EYEBALL PAUL'S THEME)** Virgin / EMI VTSCD 4	48 1

See also MELT featuring LITTLE MS MARCIE; Matt DAREY

SUNDANCE – See DJ 'FAST' EDDIE

SUNDANCE UK, male production duo (7 WEEKS)

		pos/wks
8 Nov 97	**SUNDANCE** React CDREACT 109	33 2
3 Oct 98	**SUNDANCE '98 (re-mix)** React CDREACTX 136	37 2
27 Feb 99	**THE LIVING DREAM** React CDREACT 134	56 1
5 Feb 00	**WON'T LET THIS FEELING GO** Inferno CDFERN 23	40 2

SUNDAYS UK, male / female vocal / instrumental group (12 WEEKS) pos/wks

11 Feb 89	**CAN'T BE SURE** Rough Trade RT 218	45 5
3 Oct 92	**GOODBYE** Parlophone R 6319	27 2
20 Sep 97	**SUMMERTIME** Parlophone CDRS 6475	15 4
22 Nov 97	**CRY** Parlophone CDR 6487	43 1

SUNDRAGON UK, male vocal / instrumental duo (1 WEEK)

		pos/wks
21 Feb 68	**GREEN TAMBOURINE** MGM 1380	50 1

SUNFIRE US, male vocal / instrumental group (11 WEEKS)

		pos/wks
12 Mar 83	**YOUNG, FREE AND SINGLE** Warner Bros. W 9897	20 11

SUNKIDS featuring CHANCE
US, male production duo and US, female vocalist (2 WEEKS)

		pos/wks
13 Nov 99	**RESCUE ME** AM:PM CDAMPM 126	50 2

SUNNY UK, female vocalist - Sunny Leslie (10 WEEKS)

		pos/wks
30 Mar 74 ●	**DOCTOR'S ORDERS** CBS 2068	7 10

SUNSCREEM
UK, male / female vocal / instrumental group (33 WEEKS)

		pos/wks
29 Feb 92	**PRESSURE** Sony S2 6578017	60 2
18 Jul 92	**LOVE U MORE** Sony S2 6581727	23 6
17 Oct 92	**PERFECT MOTION** Sony S2 6584057	18 5
9 Jan 93	**BROKEN ENGLISH** Sony S2 6589032	13 5
27 Mar 93	**PRESSURE US (re-mix)** Sony S2 6591102	19 5
2 Sep 95	**WHEN** Sony S2 6623222	47 2
18 Nov 95	**EXODUS** Sony S2 6625342	40 2
20 Jan 96	**WHITE SKIES** Sony S2 6627425	25 3
23 Mar 96	**SECRETS** Sony S2 6629342	36 2
6 Sep 97	**CATCH** Pulse-8 CDLOSE 117	55 1

Monty SUNSHINE – See Chris BARBER'S JAZZ BAND

SUNSHINE BAND – See KC and the SUNSHINE BAND

SUNSHIP featuring M.C.R.B.
UK, male producer and male vocalist (1 WEEK)

		pos/wks
1 Apr 00	**CHEQUE ONE-TWO** Filter FILT 044	75 1

SUPER FURRY ANIMALS
UK, male vocal / instrumental group (30 WEEKS)

		pos/wks
9 Mar 96	**HOMETOWN UNICORN** Creation CRESCD 222	47 1
11 May 96	**GOD! SHOW ME MAGIC** Creation CRESCD 231	33 2
13 Jul 96	**SOMETHING 4 THE WEEKEND** Creation CRESCD 235	18 3
12 Oct 96	**IF YOU DON'T WANT ME TO DESTROY YOU** Creation CRESCD 243	18 2
14 Dec 96	**THE MAN DON'T GIVE A FUCK** Creation CRESCD 247	22 2
24 May 97	**HERMANN LOVES PAULINE** Creation CRESCD 252	26 2
26 Jul 97	**THE INTERNATIONAL LANGUAGE OF SCREAMING** Creation CRESCD 269	24 2
4 Oct 97	**PLAY IT COOL** Creation CRESCD 275	27 2
6 Dec 97	**DEMONS** Creation CRESCD 283	27 2
6 Jun 98	**ICE HOCKEY HAIR** Creation CRESCD 288	12 3
22 May 99	**NORTHERN LITES** Creation CRESCD 314	11 4

21 Aug 99	**FIRE IN MY HEART** Creation CRESCD 323	25 3
29 Jan 00	**DO OR DIE** Creation CRESCD 329	20 2

SUPERCAR Italy, male DJ production duo (6 WEEKS)

		pos/wks
13 Feb 99	**TONITE** Pepper 0530202	15 5
21 Aug 99	**COMPUTER LOVE** Pepper 0530392 [1]	67 1

[1] Supercar featuring Mikaela

SUPERCAT Jamaica, male vocalist (5 WEEKS)

		pos/wks
1 Aug 92	**IT FE DONE** Columbia 6582737	66 1
6 May 95	**MY GIRL JOSEPHINE** Columbia 6614702 [1]	22 4

[1] Supercat featuring Jack Radics

SUPERFUNK France, male production trio (2 WEEKS)

		pos/wks
4 Mar 00	**LUCKY STAR** Virgin DINSD 198 [1]	42 1
10 Jun 00	**THE YOUNG MC** Virgin DINSD 206	62 1

[1] Superfunk featuring Ron Carroll

SUPERGRASS UK, male vocal / instrumental group (54 WEEKS) pos/wks

29 Oct 94	**CAUGHT BY THE FUZZ** Parlophone CDR 6396	43 2
18 Feb 95	**MANSIZE ROOSTER** Parlophone CDR 6402	20 3
25 Mar 95	**LOSE IT** Sub Pop SP 281	75 1
13 May 95 ●	**LENNY** Parlophone CDR 6410	10 3
15 Jul 95 ●	**ALRIGHT / TIME** Parlophone CDR 6413	2 10
9 Mar 96 ●	**GOING OUT** Parlophone CDR 6428	5 6
12 Apr 97 ●	**RICHARD III** Parlophone CDR 6461	2 5
21 Jun 97 ●	**SUN HITS THE SKY** Parlophone CDR 6469	10 4
18 Oct 97	**LATE IN THE DAY** Parlophone CDR 6484	18 4
5 Jun 99	**PUMPING ON YOUR STEREO** Parlophone CDR 6518	11 6
21 Aug 99	**PUMPING ON YOUR STEREO (re-entry)** Parlophone CDR 6518	74 1
18 Sep 99 ●	**MOVING** Parlophone CDR 6524	9 5
4 Dec 99	**MARY** Parlophone CDR 6531	36 3
22 Jan 00	**MARY (re-entry)** Parlophone CDR 6531	72 1

SUPERNATURALS UK, male vocal / instrumental group (15 WEEKS) pos/wks

26 Oct 96	**LAZY LOVER** Food CDFOOD 85	34 2
8 Feb 97	**THE DAY BEFORE YESTERDAY'S MAN** Food CDFOODS 88	25 3
26 Apr 97	**SMILE** Food CDFOOD 92	23 2
12 Jul 97	**LOVE HAS PASSED AWAY** Food CDFOOD 99	38 2
25 Oct 97	**PREPARE TO LAND** Food CDFOODS 106	48 1
1 Aug 98	**I WASN'T BUILT TO GET UP** Food CDFOOD 112	25 3
24 Oct 98	**SHEFFIELD SONG** Food CDFOODS 115	45 1
13 Mar 99	**EVEREST** Food CDFOOD 119	52 1

SUPERNOVA UK, male / female vocal / instrumental duo (1 WEEK) pos/wks

11 May 96	**SOME MIGHT SAY** Sing Sing 74321369442	55 1

SUPERSISTER UK, female vocal group (5 WEEKS)

		pos/wks
14 Oct 00	**COFFEE** Gut CDGUT 35	16 5

SUPERSTAR UK, male vocal / instrumental group (2 WEEKS)

		pos/wks
7 Feb 98	**EVERY DAY I FALL APART** Camp Fabulous CFAB 003 CD	66 1
25 Apr 98	**SUPERSTAR** Camp Fabulous CFAB 007CD	49 1

SUPERTRAMP UK / US, male vocal / instrumental group (52 WEEKS)

		pos/wks
15 Feb 75	**DREAMER** A & M AMS 7132	13 10
25 Jun 77	**GIVE A LITTLE BIT** A & M AMS 7293	29 7
31 Mar 79 ●	**THE LOGICAL SONG** A & M AMS 7427	7 11
30 Jun 79 ●	**BREAKFAST IN AMERICA** A & M AMS 7451	9 10
27 Oct 79	**GOODBYE STRANGER** A & M AMS 7481	57 3
30 Oct 82	**IT'S RAINING AGAIN** A & M AMS 8255 [1]	26 11

[1] Supertramp featuring vocals by Roger Hodgson

SINGLED OUT... Keith Allen

Versatile actor and massive chart star, Keith Allen had his biggest personal success (as Fat Les) with 'Vindaloo' and 'Jerusalem' but also featured, in some shape or form, in englandneworder's World Cup classic, Blur's weird but wonderful 'Country House' video and the Black Grape / Joe Strummer collaboration 'England's Irie'.

• **NO.1 ON THE UK SINGLES CHART THE DAY I WAS BORN:**
I Believe – Frankie Laine

• **ALL-TIME FAVOURITE SINGLE:**
Theme From Dr. Owen MD.
[Sleepy Shores – Johnny Pearson]

I bought it the same week as Lou Reed's 'Walk on the Wild Side' and found I played the theme more!

• **SINGLE THAT DRIVES ME UP THE WALL:**
Imagine – John Lennon

The biggest joke on the planet – I hate it!

FIRST SINGLE I BOUGHT:
Baby Love
The Supremes

I loved the melody and the lyrics – simple as that!

SUPREMES (31) [Top 500]

World's most successful female group: Diana Ross, Mary Wilson, Florence Ballard (d. 1976). Before Ross went solo in 1969, this Detroit-based trio had amassed a dozen US No.1s. They were inducted into the Rock and Roll Hall of Fame in 1988 (306 WEEKS)   pos/wks

Date	Title	Pos	Wks
3 Sep 64	● WHERE DID OUR LOVE GO *Stateside SS 327* ▲	3	14
22 Oct 64	★ BABY LOVE *Stateside SS 350* ▲	1	15
21 Jan 65	COME SEE ABOUT ME *Stateside SS 376* ▲	27	6
25 Mar 65	● STOP! IN THE NAME OF LOVE *Tamla Motown TMG 501* ▲	7	12
10 Jun 65	BACK IN MY ARMS AGAIN *Tamla Motown TMG 516* ▲	40	5
9 Dec 65	I HEAR A SYMPHONY *Tamla Motown TMG 543* ▲	50	1
23 Dec 65	I HEAR A SYMPHONY (re-entry) *Tamla Motown TMG 543*	39	4
8 Sep 66	● YOU CAN'T HURRY LOVE *Tamla Motown TMG 575* ▲	3	12
1 Dec 66	● YOU KEEP ME HANGIN' ON *Tamla Motown TMG 585* ▲	8	10
2 Mar 67	LOVE IS HERE AND NOW YOU'RE GONE *Tamla Motown TMG 597* ▲	17	10
11 May 67	● THE HAPPENING *Tamla Motown TMG 607* ▲	6	12
30 Aug 67	● REFLECTIONS *Tamla Motown TMG 616* [1]	5	14
29 Nov 67	IN AND OUT OF LOVE *Tamla Motown TMG 632* [1]	13	13
10 Apr 68	FOREVER CAME TODAY *Tamla Motown TMG 650* [1]	28	8
3 Jul 68	SOME THINGS YOU NEVER GET USED TO *Tamla Motown TMG 662* [1]	34	6
20 Nov 68	LOVE CHILD *Tamla Motown TMG 677* [1] ▲	15	14
29 Jan 69	● I'M GONNA MAKE YOU LOVE ME *Tamla Motown TMG 685* [2]	3	11
23 Apr 69	I'M GONNA MAKE YOU LOVE ME (re-entry) *Tamla Motown TMG 685* [2]	49	1
23 Apr 69	I'M LIVING IN SHAME *Tamla Motown TMG 695* [1]	14	9
2 Jul 69	I'M LIVING IN SHAME (re-entry) *Tamla Motown TMG 695* [1]	50	1
16 Jul 69	NO MATTER WHAT SIGN YOU ARE *Tamla Motown TMG 704* [1]	37	7
20 Sep 69	I SECOND THAT EMOTION *Tamla Motown TMG 709* [2]	18	8
13 Dec 69	SOMEDAY WE'LL BE TOGETHER *Tamla Motown TMG 721* [1] ▲	13	13
21 Mar 70	WHY (MUST WE FALL IN LOVE) *Tamla Motown TMG 730* [2]	31	7
2 May 70	● UP THE LADDER TO THE ROOF *Tamla Motown TMG 735*	6	15
16 Jan 71	● STONED LOVE *Tamla Motown TMG 760*	3	13
26 Jun 71	RIVER DEEP MOUNTAIN HIGH *Tamla Motown TMG 777* [3]	11	10
21 Aug 71	● NATHAN JONES *Tamla Motown TMG 782*	5	11
20 Nov 71	YOU GOTTA HAVE LOVE IN YOUR HEART *Tamla Motown TMG 793* [3]	25	10
4 Mar 72	● FLOY JOY *Tamla Motown TMG 804*	9	10
15 Jul 72	● AUTOMATICALLY SUNSHINE *Tamla Motown TMG 821*	10	9
21 Apr 73	BAD WEATHER *Tamla Motown TMG 847*	37	4
24 Aug 74	BABY LOVE (re-issue) *Tamla Motown TMG 915* [1]	12	10
18 Feb 89	STOP! IN THE NAME OF LOVE (re-issue) *Motown ZB 41963* [1]	62	1

[1] Diana Ross and the Supremes [2] Diana Ross and the Supremes and the Temptations [3] Supremes and the Four Tops

Al B SURE! *US, male vocalist (13 WEEKS)*   pos/wks

Date	Title	Pos	Wks
16 Apr 88	NITE AND DAY *Uptown W 8192*	44	5
30 Jul 88	OFF ON YOUR OWN (GIRL) *Uptown W 7870*	70	2
10 Jun 89	IF I'M NOT YOUR LOVER *Uptown W 2908*	54	3
31 Mar 90	SECRET GARDEN *Qwest W 9992* [1]	67	1
12 Jun 93	BLACK TIE WHITE NOISE *Arista 74321148682* [2]	36	2

[1] Quincy Jones featuring Al B Sure!, James Ingram, El DeBarge and Barry White [2] David Bowie featuring Al B Sure!

SUREAL *UK, male producer and female vocalist (4 WEEKS)*   pos/wks

Date	Title	Pos	Wks
7 Oct 00	YOU TAKE MY BREATH AWAY *Cream CREAM 7CD*	15	4

SURFACE *US, male vocal / instrumental duo (14 WEEKS)*   pos/wks

Date	Title	Pos	Wks
23 Jul 83	FALLING IN LOVE *Salsoul SAL 104*	67	3
23 Jun 84	WHEN YOUR 'EX' WANTS YOU BACK *Salsoul SAL 106*	52	4
28 Feb 87	HAPPY *CBS 650393 7*	56	5
12 Jan 91	THE FIRST TIME *Columbia 6564767* ▲	60	2

SURFACE NOISE *UK, male instrumental group (11 WEEKS)*   pos/wks

Date	Title	Pos	Wks
31 May 80	THE SCRATCH *WEA K 18291*	26	8
30 Aug 80	DANCIN' ON A WIRE *Groove Production GP102*	59	3

SURFARIS *US, male instrumental group (14 WEEKS)*   pos/wks

Date	Title	Pos	Wks
25 Jul 63	● WIPE OUT *London HLD 9751*	5	14

SURPRISE SISTERS *UK, female vocal group (3 WEEKS)*   pos/wks

Date	Title	Pos	Wks
13 Mar 76	LA BOOGA ROOGA *Good Earth GD 1*	38	3

SURVIVOR *US, male vocal / instrumental group - lead vocal Dave Bickler (26 WEEKS)*   pos/wks

Date	Title	Pos	Wks
31 Jul 82	★ EYE OF THE TIGER *Scotti Brothers SCT A 2411* ▲	1	15
1 Feb 86	● BURNING HEART *Scotti Brothers A 6708*	5	11

SUTHERLAND BROTHERS and QUIVER
UK, male vocal / instrumental group (20 WEEKS)   pos/wks

Date	Title	Pos	Wks
3 Apr 76	● ARMS OF MARY *CBS 4001*	5	12
20 Nov 76	SECRETS *CBS 4668*	35	4
2 Jun 79	EASY COME EASY GO *CBS 7121* [1]	50	4

[1] Sutherland Brothers

Pat SUZUKI *US, female vocalist (1 WEEK)*   pos/wks

Date	Title	Pos	Wks
14 Apr 60	I ENJOY BEING A GIRL *RCA 1171*	49	1

Billy SWAN *US, male vocalist (13 WEEKS)*   pos/wks

Date	Title	Pos	Wks
14 Dec 74	● I CAN HELP *Monument MNT 2752* ▲	6	9
24 May 75	DON'T BE CRUEL *Monument MNT 3244*	42	4

SWAN LAKE *US, male producer - Todd Terry (4 WEEKS)*   pos/wks

Date	Title	Pos	Wks
17 Sep 88	IN THE NAME OF LOVE *Champion CHAMP 86*	53	4

SWANS WAY
UK, male / female vocal / instrumental group (12 WEEKS)   pos/wks

Date	Title	Pos	Wks
4 Feb 84	SOUL TRAIN *Exit EXT 3*	20	7
26 May 84	ILLUMINATIONS *Balgier PH 5*	57	5

Patrick SWAYZE featuring Wendy FRASER
US, male / female vocal duo (11 WEEKS)   pos/wks

Date	Title	Pos	Wks
26 Mar 88	SHE'S LIKE THE WIND *RCA PB 49565*	17	11

Keith SWEAT *US, male vocalist (23 WEEKS)*   pos/wks

Date	Title	Pos	Wks
20 Feb 88	I WANT HER *Vintertainment EKR 68*	26	10
14 May 88	SOMETHING JUST AIN'T RIGHT *Vintertainment EKR 72*	55	3
14 May 94	HOW DO YOU LIKE IT *Elektra EKR 185CD*	71	1
22 Jun 96	TWISTED *Elektra 223CD*	39	2
23 Nov 96	JUST A TOUCH *Elektra EKR 227CD*	35	2
3 May 97	NOBODY *Elektra EKR 233CD* [1]	30	2
6 Dec 97	I WANT HER (re-mix) *Elektra E 3887CD*	44	1
12 Dec 98	COME AND GET WITH ME *Elektra E 3787CD* [2]	58	1
27 Mar 99	I'M NOT READY *Elektra E 3767CD*	53	1

[1] Keith Sweat featuring Athena Cage [2] Keith Sweat featuring Snoop Dogg

Michelle SWEENEY *US, female vocalist (1 WEEK)*   pos/wks

Date	Title	Pos	Wks
29 Oct 94	THIS TIME *Big Beat A 8229CD*	57	1

SWEET (131) [Top 500]

Glam-rock giants: Brian Connolly (v) (d. 1997), Andy Scott (g). Steve Priest (b), Mick Tucker (d). The flamboyantly attired UK quartet was very popular in Europe and the US. Despite topping the chart only once, they achieved five No.2 hits (159 WEEKS)   pos/wks

Date	Title	Pos	Wks
13 Mar 71	FUNNY FUNNY *RCA 2051*	13	14
12 Jun 71	● CO-CO *RCA 2087*	2	15
16 Oct 71	ALEXANDER GRAHAM BELL *RCA 2121*	33	5
5 Feb 72	POPPA JOE *RCA 2164*	11	12

UK No.1 ★   UK Top 10 ●   Still on chart +   UK million seller ◆   UK entry at No.1 ■   US No.1 ▲

10 Jun 72 ●	LITTLE WILLY *RCA 2225*	4	14
9 Sep 72 ●	WIG-WAM BAM *RCA 2260*	4	13
13 Jan 73 ★	BLOCKBUSTER *RCA 2305*	1	15
5 May 73 ●	HELL RAISER *RCA 2357*	2	11
22 Sep 73 ●	BALLROOM BLITZ *RCA 2403*	2	9
19 Jan 74 ●	TEENAGE RAMPAGE *RCA LPBO 5004*	2	8
13 Jul 74 ●	THE SIX TEENS *RCA LPBO 5037*	9	7
9 Nov 74	TURN IT DOWN *RCA 2480*	41	2
15 Mar 75 ●	FOX ON THE RUN *RCA 2524*	2	10
12 Jul 75	ACTION *RCA 2578*	15	6
24 Jan 76	LIES IN YOUR EYES *RCA 2641*	35	4
28 Jan 78 ●	LOVE IS LIKE OXYGEN *Polydor POSP 1*	9	9
26 Jan 85	IT'S... IT'S... THE SWEET MIX *Anagram ANA 28*	45	5

It's... It's... the Sweet Mix is a medley of the following songs: Blockbuster / Fox on the Run / Teenage Rampage / Hell Raiser / Ballroom Blitz

Rachel SWEET *US, female vocalist (15 WEEKS)* pos/wks

9 Dec 78	B-A-B-Y *Stiff BUY 39*	35	8
22 Aug 81	EVERLASTING LOVE *CBS A 1405* [1]	35	7

[1] Rex Smith and Rachel Sweet

SWEET DREAMS *UK, male / female vocal duo - Polly Brown and Tony Jackson (12 WEEKS)* pos/wks

20 Jul 74 ●	HONEY HONEY *Bradley's BRAD 7408*	10	12

SWEET DREAMS *UK, male / female vocal group (7 WEEKS)* pos/wks

9 Apr 83	I'M NEVER GIVING UP *Ariola ARO 333*	21	7

SWEET FEMALE ATTITUDE *UK, female vocal duo - Leanne Brown and Catherine Cassidy (16 WEEKS)* pos/wks

15 Apr 00 ●	FLOWERS *WEA WEA 267CD*	2	12
7 Oct 00	8 DAYS A WEEK *WEA WEA 296CD*	43	4

SWEET MERCY featuring Joe ROBERTS *UK, male production / instrumental duo and male vocalist (1 WEEK)* pos/wks

24 Feb 96	HAPPY DAYS *Grass Green GRASS 10CD*	63	1

SWEET PEOPLE *France, male vocal / instrumental group (10 WEEKS)* pos/wks

4 Oct 80 ●	ET LES OISEAUX CHANTAIENT (AND THE BIRDS WERE SINGING) *Polydor POSP 179*	4	8
29 Aug 87	ET LES OISEAUX CHANTAIENT (AND THE BIRDS WERE SINGING) (re-entry) *Polydor POSP 179*	73	2

SWEET PUSSY PAULINE – See CANDY GIRLS

SWEET SENSATION *UK, male vocal group - lead vocal Marcel King (17 WEEKS)* pos/wks

14 Sep 74 ★	SAD SWEET DREAMER *Pye 7N 45385*	1	10
18 Jan 75	PURELY BY COINCIDENCE *Pye 7N 45421*	11	7

SWEET TEE *US, female rapper - Toi Jackson (8 WEEKS)* pos/wks

16 Jan 88	IT'S LIKE THAT Y'ALL / I GOT DA FEELIN' *Cooltempo COOL 160*	31	6
13 Aug 94	THE FEELING *Deep Distraxion OILYCD 029* [1]	32	2

[1] Tin Tin Out featuring Sweet Tee

SWEETBACK *UK, male vocal / instrumental group (1 WEEK)* pos/wks

29 Mar 97	YOU WILL RISE *Epic 6643155*	64	1

SWEETBOX *Germany / US, male / female vocal / production duo - Rosan Roberto and Tina Harris (12 WEEKS)* pos/wks

22 Aug 98 ●	EVERYTHING'S GONNA BE ALRIGHT *RCA 74321606842*	5	12

Sally SWEETLAND – See Eddie FISHER

SWERVEDRIVER *UK, male vocal / instrumental group (3 WEEKS)* pos/wks

10 Aug 91	SANDBLASTED (EP) *Creation CRE 102*	67	1
30 May 92	NEVER LOSE THAT FEELING *Creation CRE 120*	62	1
14 Aug 93	DUEL *Creation CRESCD 136*	60	1

Tracks on Sandblasted (EP): Sandblaster / Flawed / Out / Laze It Up

SWIMMING WITH SHARKS *Germany, female vocal duo (3 WEEKS)* pos/wks

7 May 88	CARELESS LOVE *WEA YZ 173*	63	3

SWING featuring DR ALBAN *US, male rapper and Nigeria, male vocalist (1 WEEK)* pos/wks

29 Apr 95	SWEET DREAMS *Logic 74321251552* [1]	59	1

[1] Swing featuring Dr Alban

SWING 52 *US, male vocal / instrumental group (1 WEEK)* pos/wks

25 Feb 95	COLOR OF MY SKIN *ffrr FCD 256*	60	1

SWING KIDS – See K7

SWING OUT SISTER *UK, male / female vocal / instrumental group (55 WEEKS)* pos/wks

25 Oct 86 ●	BREAKOUT *Mercury SWING 2*	4	14
10 Jan 87 ●	SURRENDER *Mercury SWING 3*	7	8
18 Apr 87	TWILIGHT WORLD *Mercury SWING 4*	32	6
11 Jul 87	FOOLED BY A SMILE *Mercury SWING 5*	43	4
8 Apr 89	YOU ON MY MIND *Fontana SWING 6*	28	9
8 Jul 89	WHERE IN THE WORLD *Fontana SWING 7*	47	4
11 Apr 92	AM I THE SAME GIRL *Fontana SWING 9*	21	6
20 Jun 92	NOTGONNACHANGE *Fontana SWING 10*	49	2
27 Aug 94	LA LA (MEANS I LOVE YOU) *Fontana SWIDD 11*	37	2

act became male / female duo in 1989

SWINGING BLUE JEANS *UK, male vocal / instrumental group (57 WEEKS)* pos/wks

20 Jun 63	IT'S TOO LATE NOW *HMV POP 1170*	30	6
8 Aug 63	IT'S TOO LATE NOW (re-entry) *HMV POP 1170*	46	3
12 Dec 63 ●	HIPPY HIPPY SHAKE *HMV POP 1242*	2	17
19 Mar 64	GOOD GOLLY MISS MOLLY *HMV POP 1273*	11	10
4 Jun 64 ●	YOU'RE NO GOOD *HMV POP 1304*	3	13
20 Jan 66	DON'T MAKE ME OVER *HMV POP 1501*	31	8

SWIRL 360 *US, male vocal duo (1 WEEK)* pos/wks

14 Nov 98	HEY NOW NOW *Mercury 5665352*	61	1

SWITCH *US, male vocal / instrumental group (3 WEEKS)* pos/wks

10 Nov 84	KEEPING SECRETS *Total Experience RCA XE 502*	61	3

SWV *US, female vocal group (43 WEEKS)* pos/wks

1 May 93	I'M SO INTO YOU *RCA 74321144972*	17	6
26 Jun 93	WEAK *RCA 74321153352* ▲	33	3
28 Aug 93 ●	RIGHT HERE *RCA 74321160482*	3	12
26 Feb 94	DOWNTOWN *RCA 74321189012*	19	5
11 Jun 94	ANYTHING *RCA 74321212212*	24	3
25 May 96	YOU'RE THE ONE *RCA 74321383312*	13	3
21 Dec 96	IT'S ALL ABOUT U *RCA 74321442152*	36	5
12 Apr 97	CAN WE *Jive JIVECD 423*	18	4
13 Sep 97	SOMEONE *RCA 74321513942* [1]	34	2

[1] SWV featuring Puff Daddy

SYBIL
US, female vocalist – Sybil Lynch (69 WEEKS)   pos/wks

1 Nov 86	FALLING IN LOVE *Champion CHAMP 22*	68	3
25 Apr 87	LET YOURSELF GO *Champion CHAMP 42*	32	6
29 Aug 87	MY LOVE IS GUARANTEED *Champion CHAMPX 55*	42	5
22 Jul 89	DON'T MAKE ME OVER *Champion CHAMP 213*	59	5
14 Oct 89	DON'T MAKE ME OVER (re-entry) *Champion CHAMP 213*	19	6
27 Jan 90 ●	WALK ON BY *PWL PWL 48*	6	9
21 Apr 90	CRAZY FOR YOU *PWL PWL 53*	71	1
16 Jan 93 ●	THE LOVE I LOST *PWL Sanctuary PWCD 253* [1]	3	13
20 Mar 93 ●	WHEN I'M GOOD AND READY *PWL International PWCD 260*	5	13
26 Jun 93	BEYOND YOUR WILDEST DREAMS *PWL International PWCD 265*	41	2
11 Sep 93	STRONGER TOGETHER *PWL International PWCD 269*	41	2
11 Dec 93	MY LOVE IS GUARANTEED (re-mix) *PWL International PWCD 277*	48	1
9 Mar 96	SO TIRED OF BEING ALONE *PWL International PWL 324CD*	53	1
8 Mar 97	WHEN I'M GOOD AND READY (re-mix) *Next Plateau NP 14183*	66	1
26 Jul 97	STILL A THRILL *Coalition COLA 007CD*	55	1

[1] West End featuring Sybil

SYLK 130
US, male production duo (2 WEEKS)   pos/wks

| 25 Apr 98 | LAST NIGHT A DJ SAVED MY LIFE *Sony S2 SYLK 1CD* | 33 | 2 |

SYLVESTER
US, male vocalist – Sylvester James (45 WEEKS)   pos/wks

19 Aug 78 ●	YOU MAKE ME FEEL (MIGHTY REAL) *Fantasy FTC 160*	8	15
18 Nov 78	DANCE (DISCO HEAT) *Fantasy FTC 163*	29	12
31 Mar 79	I (WHO HAVE NOTHING) *Fantasy FTC 171*	46	5
7 Jul 79	STARS *Fantasy FTC 177*	47	3
11 Sep 82	DO YOU WANNA FUNK *London LON 13* [1]	32	8
3 Sep 83	BAND OF GOLD *London LON 33*	67	2

[1] Sylvester with Patrick Cowley

SYLVIA
US, female vocalist – Sylvia Robinson (11 WEEKS)   pos/wks

| 23 Jun 73 | PILLOW TALK *London HL 10415* | 14 | 11 |

SYLVIA
Sweden, female vocalist – Sylvia Vrethammar (33 WEEKS)   pos/wks

10 Aug 74 ●	Y VIVA ESPANA *Sonet SON 2037*	4	19
4 Jan 75	Y VIVA ESPANA (re-entry) *Sonet SON 2037*	35	9
26 Apr 75	HASTA LA VISTA *Sonet SON 2055*	38	5

David SYLVIAN
UK, male vocalist (36 WEEKS)   pos/wks

7 Aug 82	BAMBOO HOUSES / BAMBOO MUSIC *Virgin VS 510* [1]	30	4
2 Jul 83	FORBIDDEN COLOURS *Virgin VS 601* [2]	16	8
2 Jun 84	RED GUITAR *Virgin VS 633*	17	5
18 Aug 84	THE INK IN THE WELL *Virgin VS 700*	36	3
3 Nov 84	PULLING PUNCHES *Virgin VS 717*	56	2
14 Dec 85	WORDS WITH THE SHAMAN *Virgin VS 835*	72	1
9 Aug 86	TAKING THE VEIL *Virgin VS 815*	53	3
17 Jan 87	BUOY *Virgin VS 910* [3]	63	2
10 Oct 87	LET THE HAPPINESS IN *Virgin VS 1001*	66	1
13 Jun 92	HEARTBEAT (TAINAI KAIKI II) RETURNING TO THE WOMB *Virgin America VUS 57* [4]	58	3
28 Aug 93	JEAN THE BIRDMAN *Virgin VSCDG 1462* [5]	68	2
27 Mar 99	I SURRENDER *Virgin VSCDT 1722*	40	2

[1] Sylvian Sakamoto [2] David Sylvian and Riuichi Sakamoto [3] Mick Karn featuring David Sylvian [4] David Sylvian / Riuichi Sakamoto featuring Ingrid Chavez [5] David Sylvian and Robert Fripp

SYMARIP
UK, male vocal / instrumental group (3 WEEKS)   pos/wks

| 2 Feb 80 | SKINHEAD MOONSTOMP *Trojan TRO 9062* | 54 | 3 |

SYMBOLS
UK, male vocal / instrumental group (15 WEEKS)   pos/wks

| 2 Aug 67 | BYE BYE BABY *President PT 144* | 44 | 3 |
| 3 Jan 68 | BEST PART OF BREAKING UP *President PT 173* | 25 | 12 |

Terri SYMON
UK, female vocalist (1 WEEK)   pos/wks

| 10 Jun 95 | I WANT TO KNOW WHAT LOVE IS *A & M 5810592* | 54 | 1 |

SYMPOSIUM
UK, male vocal / instrumental group (10 WEEKS)   pos/wks

22 Mar 97	FAREWELL TO TWILIGHT *Infectious INFECT 34CD*	25	2
31 May 97	THE ANSWER TO WHY I HATE YOU *Infectious INFECT 37CD*	32	2
30 Aug 97	FAIRWEATHER FRIEND *Infectious INFECT 44CD*	25	3
14 Mar 98	AVERAGE MAN *Infectious INFECT 52CD*	45	1
16 May 98	BURY YOU *Infectious INFECT 55CDS*	41	1
18 Jul 98	BLUE *Infectious INFECT 57CD*	48	1

SYREETA
US, female vocalist – Rita Wright (30 WEEKS)   pos/wks

21 Sep 74	SPINNIN' AND SPINNIN' *Tamla Motown TMG 912*	49	3
1 Feb 75	YOUR KISS IS SWEET *Tamla Motown TMG 933*	12	8
12 Jul 75	HARMOUR LOVE *Tamla Motown TMG 954*	32	4
15 Dec 79 ●	WITH YOU I'M BORN AGAIN *Motown TMG 1159* [1]	2	11
8 Mar 80	IT WILL COME IN TIME *Motown TMG 1175* [1]	47	4

[1] Billy Preston and Syreeta

SYSTEM
US, male vocal / instrumental duo (2 WEEKS)   pos/wks

| 9 Jun 84 | I WANNA MAKE YOU FEEL GOOD *Polydor POSP 685* | 73 | 2 |

SYSTEM F
Holland, male producer – Ferry Corsten (10 WEEKS)   pos/wks

| 3 Apr 99 | OUT OF THE BLUE *Essential Recordings ESCD 1* | 14 | 6 |
| 6 May 00 | CRY *Essential Recordings ESCD 14* | 19 | 4 |

See also Ferry CORSTEN; GOURYELLA; MOONMAN; VERACOCHA; STARPARTY

SYSTEM 7
UK / France, male / female instrumental duo (2 WEEKS)   pos/wks

| 13 Feb 93 | 7:7 EXPANSION *Butterfly BFLD 2* | 39 | 1 |
| 17 Jul 93 | SINBAD QUEST *Butterfly BFLD 8* | 74 | 1 |

T-BOZ
US, female vocalist (1 WEEK)   pos/wks

| 23 Nov 96 | TOUCH MYSELF *LaFace 74321422882* | 48 | 1 |

See also TLC

T-CONNECTION
US, male vocal / instrumental group (27 WEEKS)   pos/wks

18 Jun 77	DO WHAT YOU WANNA DO *TK XC 9109*	11	8
14 Jan 78	ON FIRE *TK TKR 6006*	16	5
10 Jun 78	LET YOURSELF GO *TK TKR 6024*	52	3
24 Feb 79	AT MIDNIGHT *TK TKR 7517*	53	5
5 May 79	SATURDAY NIGHT *TK TKR 7536*	41	6

T-COY – See VARIOUS ARTISTS (EPs and LPs)

T-EMPO
UK, male / female vocal / instrumental group (4 WEEKS)   pos/wks

| 7 May 94 | SATURDAY NIGHT SUNDAY MORNING *ffrr FCD 232* | 19 | 3 |
| 9 Nov 96 | THE LOOK OF LOVE / THE BLUE ROOM *ffrr FCD 281* | 71 | 1 |

T-POWER
UK, male producer – Mark Royal (1 WEEK)   pos/wks

| 13 Apr 96 | POLICE STATE *Sound of Underground TPOWCD 001* | 63 | 1 |

T. REX 53 Top 500
Extremely popular acoustic duo turned electric duo group; singer / songwriter / guitarist Marc Bolan (b. Mark Feld, 30 Sep 1947, London, UK; d. 16 Sep 1977), and Steve Peregrin Took (percussion - replaced by Mickey Finn in 1969). Bolan's glam-rock music and image influenced many later artists (236 WEEKS)   pos/wks

| 8 May 68 | DEBORA *Regal Zonophone RZ 3008* [1] | 34 | 7 |
| 4 Sep 68 | ONE INCH ROCK *Regal Zonophone RZ 3011* [1] | 28 | 7 |

9 Aug 69	KING OF THE RUMBLING SPIRES	
	Regal Zonophone RZ 3022 [1] **44** 1
24 Oct 70 ●	RIDE A WHITE SWAN *Fly BUG 1* **2** 20
27 Feb 71 ★	HOT LOVE *Fly BUG 6* **1** 17
10 Jul 71 ★	GET IT ON *Fly BUG 10* **1** 13
13 Nov 71 ●	JEEPSTER *Fly BUG 16* **2** 15
29 Jan 72 ★	TELEGRAM SAM *T. Rex 101* **1** 12
1 Apr 72 ●	DEBORA / ONE INCH ROCK (re-issue)	
	Magnifly ECHO 102 [1] **7** 10
13 May 72 ★	METAL GURU *EMI MARC 1* **1** 14
16 Sep 72 ●	CHILDREN OF THE REVOLUTION *EMI MARC 2* ...**2** 10
9 Dec 72 ●	SOLID GOLD EASY ACTION *EMI MARC 3* **2** 11
10 Mar 73 ●	20TH CENTURY BOY *EMI MARC 4* **3** 9
16 Jun 73 ●	THE GROOVER *EMI MARC 5* **4** 9
24 Nov 73	TRUCK ON (TYKE) *EMI MARC 6* **12** 11
9 Feb 74	TEENAGE DREAM *EMI MARC 7* [2] **13** 5
13 Jul 74	LIGHT OF LOVE *EMI MARC 8* **22** 5
16 Nov 74	ZIP GUN BOOGIE *EMI MARC 9* **41** 3
12 Jul 75	NEW YORK CITY *EMI MARC 10* **15** 8
11 Oct 75	DREAMY LADY *EMI MARC 11* [3] **30** 5
6 Mar 76	LONDON BOYS *EMI MARC 13* **40** 3
19 Jun 76	I LOVE TO BOOGIE *EMI MARC 14* **13** 9
2 Oct 76	LASER LOVE *EMI MARC 15* **41** 4
2 Apr 77	THE SOUL OF MY SUIT *EMI MARC 16* **42** 3
9 May 81	RETURN OF THE ELECTRIC WARRIOR (EP)	
	Rarn MBSF 001 [4] **50** 4
19 Sep 81	YOU SCARE ME TO DEATH	
	Cherry Red CHERRY 29 [4] **51** 4
27 Mar 82	TELEGRAM SAM (re-entry) *T. Rex 101* **69** 2
18 May 85	MEGAREX *Marc On Wax TANX 1* [2] **72** 2
9 May 87	GET IT ON (re-mix) *Marc On Wax MARC 10* [2] ...**54** 4
24 Aug 91	20TH CENTURY BOY (re-issue) *Marc On Wax MARC 501* [2] ...**13** 8
7 Oct 00	GET IT ON *All Around The World CDGLOBE 225* [5] **59** 1

[1] Tyrannosaurus Rex [2] Marc Bolan and T. Rex [3] T. Rex Disco Party [4] Marc Bolan [5] Bus Stop featuring T. Rex

Tracks on Return of the Electric Warrior (EP): Sing Me a Song / Endless Sleep Extended / The Lilac Hand of Menthol Dan. Megarex is a medley of extracts from the following T. Rex hits: Truck On (Tyke) / The Groover / Telegram Sam / Shock Rock / Metal Guru / 20th Century Boy / Children of the Revolution / Hot Love

T-SHIRT *UK, female vocal duo (1 WEEK)*

		pos/wks
13 Sep 97	YOU SEXY THING *Eternal WEA 122CD*...............**63** 1

T-SPOON
Holland, male / female vocal / instrumental group (15 WEEKS)

		pos/wks
19 Sep 98 ●	SEX ON THE BEACH *Control 0042395 CON*.......**2** 13
23 Jan 99	TOM'S PARTY *Control 0043505 CON* **27** 2

T2 featuring Robin S *US, male production duo (1 WEEK)*

		pos/wks
4 Oct 97	YOU GOT THE LOVE *Champion CHAMPCD 330* **62** 1

TABERNACLE *UK, male instrumental / production group (2 WEEKS)*

		pos/wks
4 Mar 95	I KNOW THE LORD *Good Groove CDGG 1* **62** 1
3 Feb 96	I KNOW THE LORD (re-mix)	
	Good Groove CDGGX 1 ....**55** 1

TACK HEAD *US, male vocal / production / rap group (3 WEEKS)*

		pos/wks
30 Jun 90	DANGEROUS SEX *SBK SBK 7014* **48** 3

TAFFY *UK, female vocalist - Catherine Quaye (14 WEEKS)*

		pos/wks
10 Jan 87 ●	I LOVE MY RADIO (MY DEE JAY'S RADIO)	
	Transglobal TYPE 1 ....**6** 10
18 Jul 87	STEP BY STEP *Transglobal TYPE 5*.................**59** 4

TAG TEAM *US, male rap duo (8 WEEKS)*

		pos/wks
8 Jan 94	WHOOMP! (THERE IT IS) *Club Tools SHXCD 1* ...**34** 5
29 Jan 94	ADDAMS FAMILY (WHOOMP!) *Atlas PZCD 305* ...**53** 1
10 Sep 94	WHOOMP! (THERE IT IS) (re-mix) *Club Tools SHXR 1* ...**48** 2

See also QUAD CITY DJs

TAK TIX *US, male / female vocal / production group (2 WEEKS)*

		pos/wks
20 Jan 96	FEEL LIKE SINGING *A & M 5813212* **33** 2

TAKE 5 *US, male vocal group (4 WEEKS)*

		pos/wks
7 Nov 98	I GIVE *Edel 0039635 ERE*.................................**70** 1
27 Mar 99	NEVER HAD IT SO GOOD *Edel 0039355 ERE*.....**34** 3

TAKE THAT ⟨133 Top 500⟩ *Record-breaking British boy band: Gary Barlow (v), Robbie Williams (v), Jason Orange (v), Howard Donald (v), Mark Owen (v). They were the first artists since The Beatles to score four consecutive chart-toppers, and the first act to release eight singles entering at No.1. Robbie Williams departed in July 1995 and Gary Barlow dissolved the band in Feb 1996 having sold nine million albums and 10 million singles (158 WEEKS)*

		pos/wks
23 Nov 91	PROMISES *RCA PB 45085*...................................**38** 2
8 Feb 92	ONCE YOU'VE TASTED LOVE *RCA PB 45257* **47** 3
6 Jun 92 ●	IT ONLY TAKES A MINUTE *RCA 74321101007* ...**7** 8
15 Aug 92	I FOUND HEAVEN *RCA 74321108137*..............**15** 6
10 Oct 92 ●	A MILLION LOVE SONGS *RCA 74321116307* **7** 9
12 Dec 92 ●	COULD IT BE MAGIC *RCA 74321123137*...........**3** 12
20 Feb 93 ●	WHY CAN'T I WAKE UP WITH YOU *RCA 74321133102* ...**2** 10
17 Jul 93 ★	PRAY *RCA 74321154502* **1** 11
9 Oct 93 ★	RELIGHT MY FIRE *RCA 74321167722* [1] ■ **1** 14
18 Dec 93 ★	BABE *RCA 74321182122* ■ **1** 10
9 Apr 94 ★	EVERYTHING CHANGES *RCA 74321167732* ■ **1** 10
9 Jul 94 ●	LOVE AIN'T HERE ANYMORE *RCA 74321214832* ...**3** 10
15 Oct 94	LOVE AIN'T HERE ANYMORE (re-entry)	
	RCA 74321214832 ....**55** 2
15 Oct 94 ★	SURE *RCA 74321236622* ■ **1** 15
8 Apr 95 ★	BACK FOR GOOD *RCA 74321271462* ■ **1** 13
5 Aug 95 ★	NEVER FORGET *RCA 74321299572* ■ **1** 9
9 Mar 96 ★	HOW DEEP IS YOUR LOVE *RCA 74321355592* ■ ...**1** 13
15 Jun 96	HOW DEEP IS YOUR LOVE (re-entry)	
	RCA 74321355592 ....**71** 1

[1] Take That featuring Lulu

Billy TALBOT – See Ian McNABB

TALK TALK ⟨468 Top 500⟩ *London-based synth-pop band who rapidly evolved into organic, reflective rock group: Mark Hollis (v/g/k), Paul Webb (b) and Lee Harris (d). Act, who had several legal wrangles with label EMI, was also popular in Italy, where they scored four Top 20 singles (73 WEEKS)*

		pos/wks
24 Apr 82	TALK TALK *EMI 5284* **52** 4
24 Jul 82	TODAY *EMI 5314*...**14** 13
13 Nov 82	TALK TALK (re-mix) *EMI 5352*..........................**23** 10
19 Mar 83	MY FOOLISH FRIEND *EMI 5373* **57** 3
14 Jan 84	IT'S MY LIFE *EMI 5443*.......................................**46** 5
7 Apr 84	SUCH A SHAME *EMI 5433* **49** 6
11 Aug 84	DUM DUM GIRL *EMI 5480* **74** 1
18 Jan 86	LIFE'S WHAT YOU MAKE IT *EMI EMI 5540* **16** 9
15 Mar 86	LIVING IN ANOTHER WORLD *EMI EMI 5551* **48** 4
17 May 86	GIVE IT UP *Parlophone R 6131* **59** 3
19 May 90	IT'S MY LIFE (re-issue) *Parlophone R 6254* **13** 9
1 Sep 90	LIFE'S WHAT YOU MAKE IT (re-issue)	
	Parlophone R 6264 ....**23** 6

TALKING HEADS
US / UK, male / female vocal / instrumental group (54 WEEKS)

		pos/wks
7 Feb 81	ONCE IN A LIFETIME *Sire SIR 4048*....................**14** 10
9 May 81	HOUSES IN MOTION *Sire SIR 4050*.....................**50** 3
21 Jan 84	THIS MUST BE THE PLACE *Sire W 9451* **51** 3
3 Nov 84	SLIPPERY PEOPLE *Sire 5504* **68** 2
12 Oct 85 ●	ROAD TO NOWHERE *EMI EMI 5530* **6** 16
8 Feb 86	AND SHE WAS *EMI EMI 5543*.............................**17** 8
6 Sep 86	WILD WILD LIFE *EMI EMI 5567* **43** 4
16 May 87	RADIO HEAD *EMI EM 1* **52** 2
13 Aug 88	BLIND *EMI EM 68*...**59** 3
10 Oct 92	LIFETIME PILING UP *EMI EM 250* **50** 3

See also HEADS with Shaun RYDER

SINGLED OUT...
Irvine Welsh

Back in the early 1990s, Brit Lit was taking over from Brit Pop as the new rock 'n' roll and Irvine Welsh was the baddest new ace in the pack. When Trainspotting was released it was a massive critical and popular success and spawned plays, a movie, and THE soundtrack album of the 90s. Not content with this level of pop culture domination, Mr Welsh teamed up with those other Scottish soul rebels Primal Scream for the unofficial Scottish footie hit, catchily titled 'The Big Man and the Scream Team Meet the Barmy Army Uptown', which scored a Top 20 placing back in 1996.

- **NO.1 ON THE UK SINGLES CHART THE DAY I WAS BORN:**
  It's All In The Game – Tommy Edwards

- **ALL-TIME FAVOURITE SINGLE:**
  God Save The Queen – The Sex Pistols

- **SINGLE THAT DRIVES ME UP THE WALL:**
  Red Red Whine! – UB40

FIRST SINGLE
I EVER BOUGHT:

Jeepster
T. Rex

Photo: Pictorial Press

TALL PAUL UK, male DJ / producer – Paul Newman (7 WEEKS) pos/wks

29 Mar 97	ROCK DA HOUSE *VC VCRD 18*	12	4
29 May 99	BE THERE *Duty Free DF 009CD*	45	1
8 Apr 00	FREEBASE *Duty Free DF 015CD*	43	2

See also CAMISRA; ESCRIMA; PARTIZAN; GRIFTERS; Paul NEWMAN

TAMBA TRIO *Argentina, male vocal / instrumental group (2 WEEKS)* pos/wks

| 18 Jul 98 | MAS QUE NADA *Talkin Loud TLCD 34* | 34 | 2 |

TAMPERER featuring MAYA *Italy, male production duo – Alex Farolfi and Mario Fargetta and female vocalist (38 WEEKS)* pos/wks

25 Apr 98 ★	FEEL IT *Pepper 0530032*	1	17
14 Nov 98 ●	IF YOU BUY THIS RECORD YOUR LIFE WILL BE BETTER *Pepper 0530082*	3	14
12 Feb 00 ●	HAMMER TO THE HEART *Pepper 9230032*	6	5
25 Mar 00	HAMMER TO THE HEART (re-entry) *Pepper 9230032*	68	2

TAMS *US, male vocal group – lead vocal Joseph Pope (31 WEEKS)* pos/wks

14 Feb 70	BE YOUNG, BE FOOLISH, BE HAPPY *Stateside SS 2123*	32	7
31 Jul 71 ★	HEY GIRL DON'T BOTHER ME *Probe PRO 532*	1	17
21 Nov 87	THERE AIN'T NOTHING LIKE SHAGGIN' *Virgin VS 1029*	21	7

Norma TANEGA *US, female vocalist (8 WEEKS)* pos/wks

| 7 Apr 66 | WALKING MY CAT NAMED DOG *Stateside SS 496* | 22 | 8 |

The Children of TANSLEY SCHOOL *UK, children's choir (4 WEEKS)* pos/wks

| 28 Mar 81 | MY MUM IS ONE IN A MILLION *EMI 5151* | 27 | 4 |

Jimmy TARBUCK *UK, male vocalist (2 WEEKS)* pos/wks

| 16 Nov 85 | AGAIN *Safari SAFE 68* | 74 | 1 |
| 30 Nov 85 | AGAIN (re-entry) *Safari SAFE 68* | 68 | 1 |

Lord TARIQ and Peter GUNZ *US, male vocal / rap duo (3 WEEKS)* pos/wks

| 2 May 98 | DEJA VU (UPTOWN BABY) *Columbia 6658722* | 21 | 3 |

TARLISA – See CO-RO featuring TARLISA

Bill TARMEY *UK, male vocalist (9 WEEKS)* pos/wks

3 Apr 93	ONE VOICE *Arista 74321140852*	16	4
19 Feb 94	WIND BENEATH MY WINGS *EMI CDEM 304*	40	3
19 Nov 94	IOU *EMI CDEM 361*	55	2

TARRIERS *US, male vocal / instrumental group (6 WEEKS)* pos/wks

| 14 Dec 56 | CINDY, OH CINDY AND THE BANANA BOAT SONG *London HLN 8340* [1] | 26 | 1 |
| 1 Mar 57 | BANANA BOAT SONG *Columbia DB 3891* | 15 | 5 |

[1] Vince Martin and the Tarriers

TARTAN ARMY *UK, male vocal ensemble (4 WEEKS)* pos/wks

| 6 Jun 98 | SCOTLAND BE GOOD *The Precious JWLCD 33* | 54 | 4 |

A TASTE OF HONEY *US, female vocal duo – Janice Marie Johnson and Hazel Payne (19 WEEKS)* pos/wks

| 17 Jun 78 ● | BOOGIE OOGIE OOGIE *Capitol CL 15988* ▲ | 3 | 16 |
| 18 May 85 | BOOGIE OOGIE OOGIE (re-mix) *Capitol CL 357* | 59 | 3 |

TASTE XPERIENCE featuring Natasha PEARL *UK, male instrumental / production group and UK, female vocalist (1 WEEK)* pos/wks

| 6 Nov 99 | SUMMERSAULT *Manifesto FESCD 64* | 66 | 1 |

TATJANA *Croatia, female vocalist (2 WEEKS)* pos/wks

| 21 Sep 96 | SANTA MARIA *Love This LUVTHISCDX 4* | 40 | 2 |

TAVARES (434 Top 500) *Successful R&B and disco era family group from Massachusetts, US, who started performing in 1963 (when aged 9-15) as Chubby and the Turnpikes; brothers Antone, 'Chubby', Ralph, Feliciano, Arthur Lee and Perry Lee Tavares (77 WEEKS)* pos/wks

10 Jul 76 ●	HEAVEN MUST BE MISSING AN ANGEL *Capitol CL 15876*	4	11
9 Oct 76 ●	DON'T TAKE AWAY THE MUSIC *Capitol CL 15886*	4	10
5 Feb 77	MIGHTY POWER OF LOVE *Capitol CL 15905*	25	6
9 Apr 77 ●	WHODUNIT *Capitol CL 15914*	5	10
2 Jul 77	ONE STEP AWAY *Capitol CL 15930*	16	7
18 Mar 78	THE GHOST OF LOVE *Capitol CL 15968*	29	6
6 May 78 ●	MORE THAN A WOMAN *Capitol CL 15977*	7	11
12 Aug 78	SLOW TRAIN TO PARADISE *Capitol CL 15996*	62	3
22 Feb 86	HEAVEN MUST BE MISSING AN ANGEL (re-mix) *Capitol TAV 1*	12	9
3 May 86	IT ONLY TAKES A MINUTE *Capitol TAV 2*	46	4

TAXMAN – See KICKING BACK with TAXMAN

TAYLOR – See LIBRA presents TAYLOR

Andy TAYLOR *UK, male vocalist (2 WEEKS)* pos/wks

| 20 Oct 90 | LOLA *A & M AM 596* | 60 | 2 |

See also DURAN DURAN

Dina TAYLOR – See BBG

Felice TAYLOR *US, female vocalist (13 WEEKS)* pos/wks

| 25 Oct 67 | I FEEL LOVE COMIN' ON *President PT 155* | 11 | 13 |

James TAYLOR *US, male vocalist (23 WEEKS)* pos/wks

21 Nov 70	FIRE AND RAIN *Warner Bros. WB 6104*	42	3
28 Aug 71 ●	YOU'VE GOT A FRIEND *Warner Bros. WB 16085* ▲	4	15
16 Mar 74	MOCKINGBIRD *Elektra K 12134* [1]	34	5

[1] Carly Simon and James Taylor

James TAYLOR QUARTET – See JTQ

John TAYLOR *UK, male vocalist (4 WEEKS)* pos/wks

| 15 Mar 86 | I DO WHAT I DO . . . THEME FOR '9 1/2 WEEKS' *Parlophone R 6125* | 42 | 4 |

See also DURAN DURAN

Johnnie TAYLOR *US, male vocalist (7 WEEKS)* pos/wks

| 24 Apr 76 | DISCO LADY *CBS 4044* ▲ | 25 | 7 |

JT TAYLOR *US, male vocalist (5 WEEKS)* pos/wks

24 Aug 91	LONG HOT SUMMER NIGHT *MCA MCS 1567*	63	2
30 Nov 91	FEEL THE NEED *MCA MCS 1592*	57	1
18 Apr 92	FOLLOW ME *MCA MCS 1617*	59	2

Pauline TAYLOR *UK, female vocalist (3 WEEKS)* pos/wks

| 8 Jun 96 | LET THIS BE A PRAYER *Cheeky CHEKCD 013* [1] | 26 | 2 |
| 9 Nov 96 | CONSTANTLY WAITING *Cheeky CHEKCD 015* | 51 | 1 |

[1] Rollo Goes Spiritual with Pauline Taylor

R Dean TAYLOR *Canada, male vocalist (48 WEEKS)* pos/wks

19 Jun 68	GOTTA SEE JANE *Tamla Motown TMG 656*	17	12
3 Apr 71 ●	INDIANA WANTS ME *Tamla Motown TMG 763*	2	15
11 May 74 ●	THERE'S A GHOST IN MY HOUSE *Tamla Motown TMG 896*	3	12
31 Aug 74	WINDOW SHOPPING *Polydor 2058 502*	36	5
21 Sep 74	GOTTA SEE JANE (re-issue) *Tamla Motown TMG 918*	41	4

Roger TAYLOR *UK, male vocalist (18 WEEKS)* pos/wks

18 Apr 81	FUTURE MANAGEMENT *EMI 5157*	49	4
16 Jun 84	MAN ON FIRE *EMI 5478*	66	2
10 Oct 92	RADIO *Epic 6584367* [1]	37	3

14 May 94	NAZIS *Parlophone CDR 6379*	22	2
1 Oct 94	FOREIGN SAND *Parlophone CDR 6389* [2]	26	2
26 Nov 94	HAPPINESS *Parlophone CDR 6399*	32	2
10 Oct 98	PRESSURE ON *Parlophone CDR 6507*	45	1
10 Apr 99	SURRENDER *Parlophone CDR 6517*	38	2

[1] Shaky featuring Roger Taylor [2] Roger Taylor and Yoshiki

See also QUEEN

TC *Italy, male instrumental / production duo (5 WEEKS)* — pos/wks

14 Mar 92	BERRY *Union City UCRT 1* [1]	73	1
21 Nov 92	FUNKY GUITAR *Union City UCRT 13* [2]	40	2
10 Jul 93	HARMONY *Union UCRD 20* [3]	51	2

[1] TC 1991 [2] TC 1992 [3] TC 1993

Kiri TE KANAWA *New Zealand, female vocalist (11 WEEKS)* — pos/wks

28 Sep 91 ●	WORLD IN UNION *Columbia 6574817*	4	11

TEACH-IN
Holland, male / female vocal / instrumental group (7 WEEKS) — pos/wks

12 Apr 75	DING-A-DONG *Polydor 2058 570*	13	7

TEAM *UK, male vocal / instrumental group (5 WEEKS)* — pos/wks

1 Jun 85	WICKI WACKY HOUSE PARTY *EMI 5519*	55	5

TEAM DEEP *Belgium, male production duo (1 WEEK)* — pos/wks

17 May 97	MORNINGLIGHT *Multiply CDMULTY 19*	42	1

TEARDROP EXPLODES
UK, male vocal / instrumental group (50 WEEKS) — pos/wks

27 Sep 80	WHEN I DREAM *Mercury TEAR 1*	47	6
31 Jan 81 ●	REWARD *Vertigo TEAR 2*	6	13
2 May 81	TREASON (IT'S JUST A STORY) *Mercury TEAR 3*	18	8
29 Aug 81	PASSIONATE FRIEND *Zoo TEAR 5*	25	10
21 Nov 81	COLOURS FLY AWAY *Mercury TEAR 6*	54	3
19 Jun 82	TINY CHILDREN *Mercury TEAR 7*	44	7
19 Mar 83	YOU DISAPPEAR FROM VIEW *Mercury TEAR 8*	41	3

TEARS FOR FEARS [165 | Top 500] *Bath-based band at the forefront of the mid-1980s 'British Invasion' of the US: Roland Orzabal (v/g/k), Curt Smith (v/b; left in 1991). The first of their two US No.1s, 'Everybody Wants to Rule the World', also won the 1986 Brit award for Best Single. (143 WEEKS)* — pos/wks

2 Oct 82 ●	MAD WORLD *Mercury IDEA 3*	3	16
5 Feb 83 ●	CHANGE *Mercury IDEA 4*	4	9
30 Apr 83 ●	PALE SHELTER *Mercury IDEA 5*	5	8
3 Dec 83	THE WAY YOU ARE *Mercury IDEA 6*	24	8
18 Aug 84	MOTHER'S TALK *Mercury IDEA 7*	14	8
1 Dec 84 ●	SHOUT *Mercury IDEA 8* ▲	4	16
30 Mar 85 ●	EVERYBODY WANTS TO RULE THE WORLD *Mercury IDEA 9* ▲	2	14
22 Jun 85	HEAD OVER HEELS *Mercury IDEA 10*	12	9
31 Aug 85	SUFFER THE CHILDREN *Mercury IDEA 1*	52	4
7 Sep 85	PALE SHELTER (re-issue) *Mercury IDEA 2*	73	2
12 Oct 85	I BELIEVE (A SOULFUL RE-RECORDING) *Mercury IDEA 11*	23	4
22 Feb 86	EVERYBODY WANTS TO RULE THE WORLD (re-entry) *Mercury IDEA 9*	73	1
31 May 86 ●	EVERYBODY WANTS TO RUN THE WORLD *Mercury RACE 1*	5	6
19 Jul 86	EVERYBODY WANTS TO RUN THE WORLD (re-entry) *Mercury RACE 1*	73	1
2 Sep 89 ●	SOWING THE SEEDS OF LOVE *Fontana IDEA 12*	5	9
18 Nov 89	WOMAN IN CHAINS *Fontana IDEA 13*	26	8
3 Mar 90	ADVICE FOR THE YOUNG AT HEART *Fontana IDEA 14* ...	36	4
22 Feb 92	LAID SO LOW (TEARS ROLL DOWN) *Fontana IDEA 17*	17	5
25 Apr 92	WOMAN IN CHAINS (re-issue) *Fontana IDEA 16* [1] ...	57	1
29 May 93	BREAK IT DOWN AGAIN *Mercury IDECD 18*	20	5
31 Jul 93	COLD *Mercury IDECD 19*	72	1

7 Oct 95	RAOUL AND THE KINGS OF SPAIN *Epic 6624765*	31	3
29 Jun 96	GOD'S MISTAKE *Epic 6634185*	61	1

[1] Tears For Fears featuring Oleta Adams

Mercury RACE 1 was a slightly changed version of Mercury IDEA 9, released to promote the Race Against Time of 15 May 1986. Oleta Adams is given no label credit on the original release of 'Woman In Chains'. From 1992 Tears For Fears was essentially a male vocalist / multi-instrumentalist - Roland Orzabal

TECHNICIAN 2 *UK, male instrumental / production group (1 WEEK)* — pos/wks

14 Nov 92	PLAYING WITH THE BOY *MCA MCS 1710*	70	1

TECHNIQUE *UK, female vocal / instrumental duo (2 WEEKS)* — pos/wks

10 Apr 99	SUN IS SHINING *Creation CRESCD 306*	64	1
28 Aug 99	YOU + ME *Creation CRESCD 315*	56	1

TECHNO TWINS *UK, male / female vocal duo (2 WEEKS)* — pos/wks

16 Jan 82	FALLING IN LOVE AGAIN *PRT 7P 224*	75	1
30 Jan 82	FALLING IN LOVE AGAIN (re-entry) *PRT 7P 224*	70	1

TECHNOCAT – See Tom WILSON

TECHNOHEAD *UK, male / female / instrumental duo - Michael Wells and Lee Newman (20 WEEKS)* — pos/wks

3 Feb 96 ●	I WANNA BE A HIPPY *Mokum DB 17703*	6	14
27 Apr 96	HAPPY BIRTHDAY *Mokum DB 17593*	18	5
12 Oct 96	BANANA-NA-NA (DUMB DI DUMB) *Mokum DB 17473* ...	64	1

Technohead, Tricky Disco and GTO are all the same act

See also GTO; TRICKY DISCO

TECHNOTRONIC *Belgium, male producer - Jo Bogaert (66 WEEKS)* — pos/wks

2 Sep 89 ●	PUMP UP THE JAM *Swanyard SYR 4* [1]	2	15
3 Feb 90 ●	GET UP (BEFORE THE NIGHT IS OVER) *Swanyard SYR 8* [2] ...	2	10
7 Apr 90	THIS BEAT IS TECHNOTRONIC *Swanyard SYR 9* [3] ...	14	7
14 Jul 90 ●	ROCKIN' OVER THE BEAT *Swanyard SYR 14* [2]	9	9
6 Oct 90 ●	MEGAMIX *Swanyard SYR 19*	6	8
15 Dec 90	TURN IT UP *Swanyard SYD 9* [4]	42	4
25 May 91	MOVE THAT BODY *ARS 6568377* [5]	12	7
3 Aug 91	WORK *ARS 6573317* [5]	40	4
14 Dec 96	PUMP UP THE JAM (re-mix) *Worx WORXCD 004*	36	2

[1] Technotronic featuring Felly [2] Technotronic featuring Ya Kid K [3] Technotronic featuring MC Eric [4] Technotronic featuring Melissa and Einstein [5] Technotronic featuring Reggie

See also HI-TEK 3 featuring YA KID K

TEDDY BEARS *US, male / female vocal group (17 WEEKS)* — pos/wks

19 Dec 58 ●	TO KNOW HIM IS TO LOVE HIM *London HLN 8733* ▲ ...	2	16
14 Apr 79	TO KNOW HIM IS TO LOVE HIM (re-issue) *Lightning LIG 9015*	66	1

'To Know Him Is to Love Him' re-issue was coupled with 'Endless Sleep' by Jody Reynolds as a double A-side

TEEBONE featuring MC KIE & MC SPARKS *UK, male producer (Leon Thompson) and UK, male rap duo (2 WEEKS)* — pos/wks

5 Aug 00	FLY BI *East West EW 217CD*	43	2

TEENAGE FANCLUB
UK, male vocal / instrumental group (21 WEEKS) — pos/wks

24 Aug 91	STAR SIGN *Creation CRE 105*	44	2
2 Nov 91	THE CONCEPT *Creation CRE 111*	51	1
8 Feb 92	WHAT YOU DO TO ME (EP) *Creation CRE 115*	31	2
26 Jun 93	RADIO *Creation CRESCD 130*	31	2
2 Oct 93	NORMAN 3 *Creation CRESCD 142*	50	1
2 Apr 94	FALLIN' *Epic 6602622* [1]	59	1
8 Apr 95	MELLOW DOUBT *Creation CRESCD 175*	34	2
27 May 95	SPARKY'S DREAM *Creation CRESCD 201*	40	2

2 Sep 95	**NEIL JUNG** Creation CRESCD 210	**62**	1
16 Dec 95	**HAVE LOST IT (EP)** Creation CRESCD 216	**53**	1
12 Jul 97	**AIN'T THAT ENOUGH** Creation CRESCD 228	**17**	3
30 Aug 97	**I DON'T WANT CONTROL OF YOU** Creation CRESCD 238	**43**	1
29 Nov 97	**START AGAIN** Creation CRESCD 280	**54**	1
28 Oct 00	**I NEED DIRECTION** Columbia 6699512	**48**	1

1 Teenage Fanclub and De La Soul

Tracks on What You Do to Me (EP): What You Do to Me / B-Side / Life's a Gas / Filler. Tracks on Have Lost It (EP): 120 Mins / Don't Look Back / Everything Flows / Star Sign. This last track is a re-recorded version of their first hit

TEENAGERS – See Frankie LYMON and the TEENAGERS

Towa TEI featuring Kylie MINOGUE Japan, male DJ / producer and Australia, female vocalist (1 WEEK)
pos/wks

31 Oct 98	**GBI** Athrob ART 021CD	**63**	1

TEKNO TOO UK, male instrumental / production duo (2 WEEKS)
pos/wks

13 Jul 91	**JET-STAR** D-Zone DANCE 012	**56**	2

TELETUBBIES
UK, male / female cuddly alien vocal group (32 WEEKS)
pos/wks

13 Dec 97	★ **TELETUBBIES SAY EH-OH!** BBC Worldwide WMXS 00092 ◆ ■	..1	29
18 Jul 98	**TELETUBBIES SAY EH-OH! (re-entry)** BBC Worldwide WMXS 00092	**66**	2
15 Aug 98	**TELETUBBIES SAY EH-OH! (2nd re-entry)** BBC Worldwide WMXS 00092	**72**	1

TELEVISION US, male vocal / instrumental group (10 WEEKS)
pos/wks

16 Apr 77	**MARQUEE MOON** Elektra K 12252	**30**	4
30 Jul 77	**PROVE IT** Elektra K 12262	**25**	4
22 Apr 78	**FOXHOLE** Elektra K 12287	**36**	2

TELEX Belgium, male vocal / instrumental duo (7 WEEKS)
pos/wks

21 Jul 79	**ROCK AROUND THE CLOCK** Sire SIR 4020	**34**	7

Sylvia TELLA – See BLOW MONKEYS

TEMPERANCE SEVEN UK, male vocal / instrumental band. Lead vocal Paul MacDowell (45 WEEKS)
pos/wks

30 Mar 61	★ **YOU'RE DRIVING ME CRAZY** Parlophone R 4757	..1	16
15 Jun 61	● **PASADENA** Parlophone R 4781	**4**	17
28 Sep 61	**HARD HEARTED HANNAH / CHILI BOM BOM** Parlophone R 4823	**28**	4
7 Dec 61	**CHARLESTON** Parlophone R 4851	**22**	8

'Chili Bom Bom' listed with 'Hard Hearted Hannah' only for the weeks of 12 and 19 Oct 1961

TEMPLE OF THE DOG
US, male vocal / instrumental group (2 WEEKS)
pos/wks

24 Oct 92	**HUNGER STRIKE** A & M AM 0091	**51**	2

Nino TEMPO and April STEVENS
US, male / female vocal duo (19 WEEKS)
pos/wks

7 Nov 63	**DEEP PURPLE** London HLK 9782 ▲	**17**	11
16 Jan 64	**WHISPERING** London HLK 9829	**20**	8

TEMPTATIONS 85 Top 500 The world's most successful R&B vocal group: Eddie Kendricks (d. 1992), Otis Williams, Paul Williams (d. 1973), Melvin Franklin (d. 1995), David Ruffin (d. 1991). The Detroit quintet's biggest UK hit, 'My Girl', was a 27-year-old US No 1. The current line-up of the group is still doing well Stateside (203 WEEKS)
pos/wks

18 Mar 65	**MY GIRL** Stateside SS 378 ▲	**43**	1
1 Apr 65	**IT'S GROWING** Tamla Motown TMG 504	**49**	1
15 Apr 65	**IT'S GROWING (re-entry)** Tamla Motown TMG 504	**45**	1
14 Jul 66	**AIN'T TOO PROUD TO BEG** Tamla Motown TMG 565	**21**	11
6 Oct 66	**BEAUTY IS ONLY SKIN DEEP** Tamla Motown TMG 578	**18**	10

15 Dec 66	**(I KNOW) I'M LOSING YOU** Tamla Motown TMG 587	**19**	9
6 Sep 67	**YOU'RE MY EVERYTHING** Tamla Motown TMG 620	**26**	15
6 Mar 68	**I WISH IT WOULD RAIN** Tamla Motown TMG 641	**45**	1
12 Jun 68	**I COULD NEVER LOVE ANOTHER** Tamla Motown TMG 658	**47**	1
29 Jan 69	● **I'M GONNA MAKE YOU LOVE ME** Tamla Motown TMG 685 1	..3	11
5 Mar 69	● **GET READY** Tamla Motown TMG 688	**10**	9
23 Apr 69	**I'M GONNA MAKE YOU LOVE ME (re-entry)** Tamla Motown TMG 685 1	**49**	1
23 Aug 69	**CLOUD NINE** Tamla Motown TMG 707	**15**	10
20 Sep 69	**I SECOND THAT EMOTION** Tamla Motown TMG 709 1	**18**	8
17 Jan 70	**I CAN'T GET NEXT TO YOU** Tamla Motown TMG 722 ▲	**13**	9
21 Mar 70	**WHY (MUST WE FALL IN LOVE)** Tamla Motown TMG 730 1	**31**	7
13 Jun 70	**PSYCHEDELIC SHACK** Tamla Motown TMG 741	**33**	7
19 Sep 70	● **BALL OF CONFUSION** Tamla Motown TMG 749	..7	12
19 Dec 70	**BALL OF CONFUSION (re-entry)** Tamla Motown TMG 749	**48**	3
22 May 71	● **JUST MY IMAGINATION (RUNNING AWAY WITH ME)** Tamla Motown TMG 773 ▲	..8	16
5 Feb 72	**SUPERSTAR (REMEMBER HOW YOU GOT WHERE YOU ARE)** Tamla Motown TMG 800	**32**	5
15 Apr 72	**TAKE A LOOK AROUND** Tamla Motown TMG 808	**13**	10
13 Jan 73	**PAPA WAS A ROLLIN' STONE** Tamla Motown TMG 839 ▲	**14**	8
29 Sep 73	**LAW OF THE LAND** Tamla Motown TMG 866	**41**	4
12 Jun 82	**STANDING ON THE TOP (PART 1)** Motown TMG 1263 2	**53**	3
17 Nov 84	**TREAT HER LIKE A LADY** Motown TMG 1365	**12**	10
15 Aug 87	**PAPA WAS A ROLLIN' STONE (re-mix)** Motown ZB 41431	**31**	6
6 Feb 88	**LOOK WHAT YOU STARTED** Motown ZB 41733	**63**	2
21 Oct 89	**ALL I WANT FROM YOU** Motown ZB 43233	**71**	1
15 Feb 92	● **MY GIRL (re-issue)** Epic 6576767	..2	10
22 Feb 92	**THE JONES'** Motown TMG 1403	**69**	1

1 Diana Ross and the Supremes and the Temptations 2 Temptations featuring Rick James

10 CC 190 Top 500 Multi-talented Manchester supergroup: Graham Gouldman (previously penned hits for Hollies, Yardbirds and Herman's Hermits), Eric Stewart (ex-Mindbenders, Hotlegs), and Lol Creme and Kevin Godley (both ex-Hotlegs). Godley and Creme went on to have hits as a duo and produced award-winning videos (133 WEEKS)
pos/wks

23 Sep 72	● **DONNA** UK 6	..2	13
19 May 73	★ **RUBBER BULLETS** UK 36	..1	15
25 Aug 73	● **THE DEAN AND I** UK 43	**10**	8
15 Jun 74	● **WALL STREET SHUFFLE** UK 69	**10**	10
14 Sep 74	**SILLY LOVE** UK 77	**24**	7
5 Apr 75	● **LIFE IS A MINESTRONE** Mercury 6008 010	..7	8
31 May 75	★ **I'M NOT IN LOVE** Mercury 6008 014	..1	11
29 Nov 75	● **ART FOR ART'S SAKE** Mercury 6008 017	..5	10
20 Mar 76	● **I'M MANDY FLY ME** Mercury 6008 019	..6	9
11 Dec 76	● **THINGS WE DO FOR LOVE** Mercury 6008 022	..6	11
16 Apr 77	● **GOOD MORNING JUDGE** Mercury 6008 025	..5	12
12 Aug 78	★ **DREADLOCK HOLIDAY** Mercury 6008 035	..1	13
7 Aug 82	● **RUN AWAY** Mercury MER 113	**50**	4
18 Mar 95	**I'M NOT IN LOVE (re-recording)** Avex UK AVEXCD 2	**29**	2

From 'Things We Do For Love' 10 CC were a male vocal / instrumental duo

TEN CITY US, male vocal / instrumental group (21 WEEKS)
pos/wks

21 Jan 89	● **THAT'S THE WAY LOVE IS** Atlantic A 8963	..8	10
8 Apr 89	**DEVOTION** Atlantic A 8916	**29**	4
22 Jul 89	**WHERE DO WE GO** Atlantic A 8864	**60**	1
27 Oct 90	**WHATEVER MAKES YOU HAPPY** Atlantic A 7819	**60**	2
15 Aug 92	**ONLY TIME WILL TELL / MY PEACE OF HEAVEN** East West America A 8516	**63**	2
11 Sep 93	**FANTASY** Columbia 6595042	**45**	2

TEN POLE TUDOR UK, male vocal / instrumental group (40 WEEKS)
pos/wks

7 Apr 79	● **WHO KILLED BAMBI** Virgin VS 256	..6	8
13 Oct 79	**ROCK AROUND THE CLOCK** Virgin VS 290	**21**	6
25 Apr 81	● **SWORDS OF A THOUSAND MEN** Stiff BUY 109	..6	12

UK No.1 ★   UK Top 10 ●   Still on chart +   UK million seller ◆   UK entry at No.1 ■   US No.1 ▲

1 Aug 81	**WUNDERBAR** *Stiff BUY 120*		**16**	9
14 Nov 81	**THROWING MY BABY OUT WITH THE BATHWATER** *Stiff BUY 129*		**49**	5

The listed flip side of 'Who Killed Bambi' was 'Silly Thing' by the Sex Pistols. The listed flip side of 'Rock Around the Clock' was 'The Great Rock 'n' Roll Swindle', also by the Sex Pistols

TEN SHARP *Holland, male vocal / instrumental duo (15 WEEKS)* pos/wks

21 Mar 92	● **YOU** *Columbia 6566647*		**10**	13
20 Jun 92	**AIN'T MY BEATING HEART** *Columbia 6580947*		**63**	2

10,000 MANIACS
US, female / male vocal / instrumental group (7 WEEKS) pos/wks

12 Sep 92	**THESE ARE DAYS** *Elektra EKR 156*		**58**	3
10 Apr 93	**CANDY EVERYBODY WANTS** *Elektra EKR 160CD1*		**47**	3
23 Oct 93	**BECAUSE THE NIGHT** *Elektra EKR 175CD*		**65**	1

TEN YEARS AFTER *UK, male vocal / instrumental group (18 WEEKS)* pos/wks

6 Jun 70	● **LOVE LIKE A MAN** *Deram DM 299*		**10**	18

Danny TENAGLIA *US, male DJ / producer (5 WEEKS)* pos/wks

5 Sep 98	**MUSIC IS THE ANSWER (DANCIN' AND PRANCIN')** *Twisted UK TWCD 10038* [1]		**36**	3
10 Apr 99	**TURN ME ON** *Twisted UK TWCD 10045* [2]		**53**	1
23 Oct 99	**MUSIC IS THE ANSWER (re-mix)** *Twisted UK TWCD 10052* [1]		**50**	1

[1] Danny Tenaglia and Celeda [2] Danny Tenaglia featuring Liz Torres

TENNESSEE THREE – See Johnny CASH

TENOR FLY *UK, male vocalist (17 WEEKS)* pos/wks

6 Apr 91	**WICKEDEST SOUND** *Desire WANT 40* [1]		**43**	6
15 Jun 91	**TRIBAL BASE** *Desire WANT 44* [2]		**20**	6
7 Jan 95	**BRIGHT SIDE OF LIFE** *Mango CIDM 825*		**51**	2
7 Feb 98	**B-BOY STANCE** *Freskanova FND 7* [3]		**23**	3

[1] Rebel MC featuring Tenor Fly [2] Rebel MC featuring Tenor Fly and Barrington Levy [3] Freestylers featuring Tenor Fly

Bryn TERFEL – See Shirley BASSEY

TERMINATERS – See ARNEE and the TERMINATERS

TERRA FIRMA *Italy, male producer - Claudio Giussani (1 WEEK)* pos/wks

18 May 96	**FLOATING** *Platipus PLAT 21CD*		**64**	1

Tammi TERRELL – See Marvin GAYE

TERRORIZE *UK, male producer - Shaun Imrei (6 WEEKS)* pos/wks

2 May 92	**IT'S JUST A FEELING** *Hamster STER 1*		**52**	3
22 Aug 92	**FEEL THE RHYTHM** *Hamster 12STER 2*		**69**	1
14 Nov 92	**IT'S JUST A FEELING (re-issue)** *Hamster STER 8*		**47**	2

TERRORVISION *UK, male vocal / instrumental group (53 WEEKS)* pos/wks

19 Jun 93	**AMERICAN TV** *Total Vegas CDVEGAS 3*		**63**	1
30 Oct 93	**NEW POLICY ONE** *Total Vegas CDVEGAS 4*		**42**	2
8 Jan 94	**MY HOUSE** *Total Vegas CDVEGAS 5*		**29**	4
9 Apr 94	**OBLIVION** *Total Vegas CDVEGAS 6*		**21**	5
25 Jun 94	**MIDDLEMAN** *Total Vegas CDVEGAS 7*		**25**	4
3 Sep 94	**PRETEND BEST FRIEND** *Total Vegas CDVEGAS 8*		**25**	3
29 Oct 94	**ALICE WHAT'S THE MATTER** *Total Vegas CDVEGAS 9*		**24**	4
18 Mar 95	**SOME PEOPLE SAY** *Total Vegas CDVEGAS 10*		**22**	3
2 Mar 96	● **PERSEVERANCE** *Total Vegas CDVEGAS 11*		**5**	4
4 May 96	**CELEBRITY HIT LIST** *Total Vegas CDVEGAS 12*		**20**	3
20 Jul 96	● **BAD ACTRESS** *Total Vegas CDVEGAS 13*		**10**	3
11 Jan 97	**EASY** *Total Vegas CDVEGASS 14*		**12**	4
3 Oct 98	**JOSEPHINE** *EMI CDVEGAS 15*		**23**	2
30 Jan 99	● **TEQUILA** *Total Vegas CDVEGAS 16*		**2**	10
15 May 99	**III WISHES** *Total Vegas CDVEGAS 17*		**42**	1

Helen TERRY *UK, female vocalist (6 WEEKS)* pos/wks

12 May 84	**LOVE LIES LOST** *Virgin VS 678*		**34**	6

Tony TERRY *US, male vocalist (6 WEEKS)* pos/wks

27 Feb 88	**LOVEY DOVEY** *Epic TONY 2*		**44**	6

Todd TERRY PROJECT *US, male producer (33 WEEKS)* pos/wks

12 Nov 88	**WEEKEND** *Sleeping Bag SBUK 1T*		**56**	3
14 Oct 95	**WEEKEND (re-mix)** *Ore AG 13CD*		**28**	3
13 Jul 96	● **KEEP ON JUMPIN'** *Manifesto FESCD 11* [1]		**8**	6
12 Jul 97	● **SOMETHING GOIN' ON** *Manifesto FESCD 25* [1]		**5**	10
6 Dec 97	**IT'S OVER LOVE** *Manifesto FESCD 37* [2]		**16**	8
11 Apr 98	**READY FOR A NEW DAY** *Manifesto FESCD 40* [3]		**20**	2
3 Jul 99	**LET IT RIDE** *Innocent RESTCD 1*		**58**	1

[1] Todd Terry featuring Martha Wash and Jocelyn Brown [2] Todd Terry presents Shannon [3] Todd Terry featuring Martha Wash

TESLA *US, male vocal / instrumental group (1 WEEK)* pos/wks

27 Apr 91	**SIGNS** *Geffen GFS 3*		**70**	1

Joe TEX *US, male vocalist - Joe Arlington (11 WEEKS)* pos/wks

23 Apr 77	● **AIN'T GONNA BUMP NO MORE (WITH NO BIG FAT WOMAN)** *Epic EPC 5035*		**2**	11

TEXAS 244 Top 500
Named after Wim Wenders' 'Paris, Texas' the Scots blues-turned-pop chart mainstays are: Sharleen Spiteri (v), Ally McErlaine (g), Johnny McElhone (b), Eddie Campbell (k), all from Glasgow. Stuart Kerr, Richard Hynde and Mykey Wilson have all contributed on drums with Tony McGovern (g) the most recent recruit to a band now well established among the multi-million-selling album elite (113 WEEKS) pos/wks

4 Feb 89	● **I DON'T WANT A LOVER** *Mercury TEX 1*		**8**	11
6 May 89	**THRILL HAS GONE** *Mercury TEX 2*		**60**	3
5 Aug 89	**EVERYDAY NOW** *Mercury TEX 3*		**44**	5
2 Dec 89	**PRAYER FOR YOU** *Mercury TEX 4*		**73**	1
7 Sep 91	**WHY BELIEVE IN YOU** *Mercury TEX 5*		**66**	1
26 Oct 91	**IN MY HEART** *Mercury TEX 6*		**74**	1
8 Feb 92	**ALONE WITH YOU** *Mercury TEX 7*		**32**	4
25 Apr 92	**TIRED OF BEING ALONE** *Mercury TEX 8*		**19**	6
11 Sep 93	**SO CALLED FRIEND** *Vertigo TEXCD 9*		**30**	3
30 Oct 93	**YOU OWE IT ALL TO ME** *Vertigo TEXCD 10*		**39**	3
12 Feb 94	**SO IN LOVE WITH YOU** *Vertigo TEXCD 11*		**28**	2
18 Jan 97	● **SAY WHAT YOU WANT** *Mercury MERCD 480*		**3**	10
19 Apr 97	● **HALO** *Mercury MERCD 482*		**10**	7
9 Aug 97	● **BLACK EYED BOY** *Mercury MERCD 490*		**5**	6
15 Nov 97	● **PUT YOUR ARMS AROUND ME** *Mercury MERCD 497*		**10**	5
3 Jan 98	**PUT YOUR ARMS AROUND ME (re-entry)** *Mercury MERCD 497*		**75**	1
17 Jan 98	**PUT YOUR ARMS AROUND ME (2nd re-entry)** *Mercury MERCD 497*		**64**	2
21 Mar 98	● **INSANE / SAY WHAT YOU WANT (ALL DAY EVERY DAY) (re-mix)** *Mercury MERCD 499* [1]		**4**	7
1 May 99	● **IN OUR LIFETIME** *Mercury MERCD 517*		**4**	9
28 Aug 99	● **SUMMER SON** *Mercury MERCD 520*		**5**	9
27 Nov 99	**WHEN WE ARE TOGETHER** *Mercury MERCD 525*		**12**	9
14 Oct 00	● **IN DEMAND** *Mercuy MERCD 528*		**6**	8

[1] Texas featuring The Wu-Tang Clan.

'Say What You Want (All Day Every Day)' is a new mix of the hit from 18 Jan 97 with rap by Method Man and The RZA

THAT KID CHRIS *US, male DJ / producer - Chris Staropoli (1 WEEK)* pos/wks

22 Feb 97	**FEEL THA VIBE** *Manifesto FESCD 16*		**52**	1

THAT PETROL EMOTION
UK, male vocal / instrumental group (24 WEEKS) pos/wks

11 Apr 87	**BIG DECISION** *Polydor TPE 1*		**43**	7
11 Jul 87	**DANCE** *Polydor TPE 2*		**64**	2
17 Oct 87	**GENIUS MOVE** *Virgin VS 1002*		**65**	2

		pos/wks
31 Mar 90	**ABANDON** *Virgin VS 1242*	**73** 1
1 Sep 90	**HEY VENUS** *Virgin VS 1290*	**49** 4
9 Feb 91	**TINGLE** *Virgin VS 1312*	**49** 4
27 Apr 91	**SENSITIZE** *Virgin VS 1261*	**55** 4

THE AUDIENCE – See THEAUDIENCE

The THE *UK, male vocalist / multi-instrumentalist - Matt Johnson and backing musicians (52 WEEKS)*

		pos/wks
4 Dec 82	**UNCERTAIN SMILE** *Epic EPC A 2787*	**68** 3
17 Sep 83	**THIS IS THE DAY** *Epic A 3710*	**71** 3
9 Aug 86	**HEARTLAND** *Some Bizarre TRUTH 2*	**29** 10
25 Oct 86	**INFECTED** *Some Bizarre TRUTH 3*	**48** 5
24 Jan 87	**SLOW TRAIN TO DAWN** *Some Bizarre TENSE 1*	**64** 2
23 May 87	**SWEET BIRD OF TRUTH** *Epic TENSE 2*	**55** 2
1 Apr 89	**THE BEAT(EN) GENERATION** *Epic EMU 8*	**18** 5
22 Jul 89	**GRAVITATE TO ME** *Epic EMU 9*	**63** 3
7 Oct 89	**ARMAGEDDON DAYS ARE HERE (AGAIN)** *Epic EMU 10*	**70** 2
2 Mar 91	**SHADES OF BLUE (EP)** *Epic 6557968*	**54** 1
16 Jan 93	**DOGS OF LUST** *Epic 6584572*	**25** 4
17 Apr 93	**SLOW EMOTION REPLAY** *Epic 6590772*	**35** 3
19 Jun 93	**LOVE IS STRONGER THAN DEATH** *Epic 6593712*	**39** 3
15 Jan 94	**DIS-INFECTED (EP)** *Epic 6598112*	**17** 4
4 Feb 95	**I SAW THE LIGHT** *Epic 6610912*	**31** 2

Tracks on Shades of Blue (EP): Jealous of Youth / Another Boy Drowning (Live) / Solitude / Dolphins. Tracks on Dis-Infected (EP): This Was The Day / Dis-Infected / Helpline Operator (sickboy remix) / Dogs of Lust (germicide remix). 'That Was the Day' and 'Dis-Infected' on the (EP) are re-recordings of earlier hits. 'Dogs of Lust' is a re-mix

THEATRE OF HATE *UK, male vocal / instrumental group (9 WEEKS)*

		pos/wks
23 Jan 82	**DO YOU BELIEVE IN THE WESTWORLD** *Burning Rome BRR 2*	**40** 7
29 May 82	**THE HOP** *Burning Rome BRR 3*	**70** 2

THEAUDIENCE

UK, male / female, vocal / instrumental group (5 WEEKS)

		pos/wks
7 Mar 98	**IF YOU CAN'T DO IT WHEN YOU'RE YOUNG, WHEN CAN YOU DO IT?** *Mercury AUDCD 2*	**48** 1
23 May 98	**A PESSIMIST IS NEVER DISAPPOINTED** *Mercury AUDCD 3*	**27** 2
8 Aug 98	**I KNOW ENOUGH (I DON'T GET ENOUGH)** *Elleffe AUCD 4*	**25** 2

THEM *UK, male vocal / instrumental group (23 WEEKS)*

		pos/wks
7 Jan 65	● **BABY PLEASE DON'T GO** *Decca F 12018*	**10** 9
25 Mar 65	● **HERE COMES THE NIGHT** *Decca F 12094*	**2** 12
9 Feb 91	**BABY PLEASE DON'T GO (re-issue)** *London LON 292*	**65** 2

THEN JERICO *UK, male vocal / instrumental group (36 WEEKS)*

		pos/wks
31 Jan 87	**LET HER FALL** *London LON 97*	**65** 3
25 Jul 87	**THE MOTIVE (LIVING WITHOUT YOU)** *London LON 145*	**18** 12
24 Oct 87	**MUSCLE DEEP** *London LON 156*	**48** 4
28 Jan 89	**BIG AREA** *London LON 204*	**13** 7
8 Apr 89	**WHAT DOES IT TAKE** *London LON 223*	**33** 4
12 Aug 89	**SUGAR BOX** *London LON 235*	**22** 6

THERAPY? *UK, male vocal / instrumental group (33 WEEKS)*

		pos/wks
31 Oct 92	**TEETHGRINDER** *A & M AM 0097*	**30** 2
20 Mar 93	● **SHORTSHARPSHOCK (EP)** *A & M AMCD 208*	**9** 4
12 Jun 93	**FACE THE STRANGE EP** *A & M 5803052*	**18** 3
28 Aug 93	**OPAL MANTRA** *A & M 5803612*	**14** 3
29 Jan 94	**NOWHERE** *A & M 5805052*	**18** 4
12 Mar 94	**TRIGGER INSIDE** *A & M 5805352*	**22** 3
11 Jun 94	**DIE LAUGHING** *A & M 5805892*	**29** 2
27 May 95	**INNOCENT X** *Volume VOLCD 1*	**53** 1
3 Jun 95	**STORIES** *A & M 5811052*	**14** 3
29 Jul 95	**LOOSE** *A & M 5811652*	**25** 3
18 Nov 95	**DIANE** *A & M 5812912*	**26** 2

		pos/wks
14 Mar 98	**CHURCH OF NOISE** *A & M 5825392*	**29** 2
30 May 98	**LONELY, CRYIN' ONLY** *A & M 0441212*	**32** 1

Tracks on Shortsharpshock (EP): Screamager / Auto Surgery / Totally Random Man / Accelerator. Tracks on Face the Strange (EP): Turn / Speedball / Bloody Blue / Neckfreak. The listed flip side of 'Innocent X' was 'Belfast' by Orbital

THESE ANIMAL MEN

UK, male vocal / instrumental group (3 WEEKS)

		pos/wks
24 Sep 94	**THIS IS THE SOUND OF YOUTH** *Hi-Rise FLATSCD 7*	**72** 1
8 Feb 97	**LIFE SUPPORT MACHINE** *Hut HUTCD 76*	**62** 1
12 Apr 97	**LIGHT EMITTING ELECTRICAL WAVE** *Hut HUTCD 81*	**72** 1

THEY MIGHT BE GIANTS *US, male vocal / instrumental duo - John Flansburgh and John Linnell (13 WEEKS)*

		pos/wks
3 Mar 90	● **BIRDHOUSE IN YOUR SOUL** *Elektra EKR 104*	**6** 11
2 Jun 90	**ISTANBUL (NOT CONSTANTINOPLE)** *Elektra EKR 110*	**61** 2

THIN LIZZY 〔206 Top 500〕 *Accomplished Irish hard-rock group (which at times included noted guitarists Gary Moore, Snowy White and Midge Ure) was built around distinctive singer / bass guitarist Phil Lynott (d. 1986). After a slow start, they wrote their own chapter in British rock history (128 WEEKS)*

		pos/wks
20 Jan 73	● **WHISKEY IN THE JAR** *Decca F 13355*	**6** 12
29 May 76	● **THE BOYS ARE BACK IN TOWN** *Vertigo 6059 139*	**8** 10
14 Aug 76	**JAILBREAK** *Vertigo 6059 150*	**31** 4
15 Jan 77	**DON'T BELIEVE A WORD** *Vertigo Lizzy 001*	**12** 7
13 Aug 77	**DANCIN' IN THE MOONLIGHT (IT'S CAUGHT ME IN ITS SPOTLIGHT)** *Vertigo 6059 177*	**14** 8
13 May 78	**ROSALIE - COWGIRLS' SONG (MEDLEY)** *Vertigo LIZZY 2*	**20** 13
3 Mar 79	● **WAITING FOR AN ALIBI** *Vertigo LIZZY 003*	**9** 8
16 Jun 79	**DO ANYTHING YOU WANT TO** *Vertigo LIZZY 004*	**14** 9
20 Oct 79	**SARAH** *Vertigo LIZZY 5*	**24** 13
24 May 80	**CHINATOWN** *Vertigo LIZZY 6*	**21** 9
27 Sep 80	● **KILLER ON THE LOOSE** *Vertigo LIZZY 7*	**10** 7
2 May 81	**KILLERS LIVE (EP)** *Vertigo LIZZY 8*	**19** 7
8 Aug 81	**TROUBLE BOYS** *Vertigo LIZZY 9*	**53** 4
6 Mar 82	**HOLLYWOOD (DOWN ON YOUR LUCK)** *Vertigo LIZZY 10*	**53** 3
12 Feb 83	**COLD SWEAT** *Vertigo LIZZY 11*	**27** 5
7 May 83	**THUNDER AND LIGHTNING** *Vertigo LIZZY 12*	**39** 2
6 Aug 83	**THE SUN GOES DOWN** *Vertigo LIZZY 13*	**52** 3
26 Jan 91	**DEDICATION** *Vertigo LIZZY 14*	**35** 3
23 Mar 91	**THE BOYS ARE BACK IN TOWN (re-issue)** *Vertigo LIZZY 15*	**63** 1

Tracks on Killers Live (EP): Bad Reputation / Are You Ready / Dear Miss Lonely Hearts

3RD BASS *US, male rap group (5 WEEKS)*

		pos/wks
10 Feb 90	**THE GAS FACE** *Def Jam 655627 0*	**71** 1
7 Apr 90	**BROOKLYN-QUEENS** *Def Jam 655830 7*	**61** 2
22 Jun 91	**POP GOES THE WEASEL** *Def Jam 6569547*	**64** 2

THIRD DIMENSION featuring Julie McDERMOTT *UK, male / female vocal / instrumental group (2 WEEKS)*

		pos/wks
12 Oct 96	**DON'T GO** *Soundproof MCSTD 40082*	**34** 2

THIRD EYE BLIND *US, male vocal / instrumental group (6 WEEKS)*

		pos/wks
27 Sep 97	**SEMI-CHARMED LIFE** *Elektra E 3907CD*	**33** 5
21 Mar 98	**HOW'S IT GOING TO BE** *Elektra E 3863CD*	**51** 1

3RD STOREE *US, male vocal group (1 WEEK)*

		pos/wks
5 Jun 99	**IF EVER** *Yab Yum / Elektra E 3752CD*	**53** 1

THIRD WORLD

Jamaica, male vocal / instrumental group (53 WEEKS)

		pos/wks
23 Sep 78	**NOW THAT WE'VE FOUND LOVE** *Island WIP 6457*	**10** 9
6 Jan 79	**COOL MEDITATION** *Island WIP 6469*	**17** 10
16 Jun 79	**TALK TO ME** *Island WIP 6496*	**56** 5
6 Jun 81	● **DANCING ON THE FLOOR (HOOKED ON LOVE)** *CBS A 1214*	**10** 15
17 Apr 82	**TRY JAH LOVE** *CBS A 2063*	**47** 6
9 Mar 85	**NOW THAT WE'VE FOUND LOVE (re-issue)** *Island IS 219*	**22** 8

THIRST UK, male vocal / instrumental group (2 WEEKS)

		pos/wks	
6 Jul 91	**THE ENEMY WITHIN** Ten TEN 379	61	2

1300 DRUMS featuring the UNJUSTIFIED ANCIENTS OF MU
UK, male instrumental / production group (4 WEEKS)

		pos/wks	
18 May 96	**OOH! AAH! CANTONA** Dynamo DYND 5	11	4

See also KLF; TIMELORDS; 2K; JUSTIFIED ANCIENTS OF MU MU

THIS ISLAND EARTH
UK, male / female vocal / instrumental group (5 WEEKS)

		pos/wks	
5 Jan 85	**SEE THAT GLOW** Magnet MAG 266	47	5

THIS MORTAL COIL
UK, male / female vocal / instrumental group (3 WEEKS)

		pos/wks	
22 Oct 83	**SONG TO THE SIREN** 4AD AD 310	66	2
12 Nov 83	**SONG TO THE SIREN (re-entry)** 4AD AD 310	75	1

THIS WAY UP UK, male vocal / instrumental duo (2 WEEKS)

		pos/wks	
22 Aug 87	**TELL ME WHY** Virgin VS 954	72	2

THIS YEAR'S BLONDE
UK, male / female vocal / instrumental group (8 WEEKS)

		pos/wks	
10 Oct 81	**PLATINUM POP** Creole CR 19	46	5
14 Nov 87	**WHO'S THAT MIX** Debut DEBT 3034	62	3

BJ THOMAS US, male vocalist (4 WEEKS)

		pos/wks	
21 Feb 70	**RAINDROPS KEEP FALLING ON MY HEAD** Wand WN1 ▲	38	3
2 May 70	**RAINDROPS KEEP FALLING ON MY HEAD (re-entry)** Wand WN1	49	1

Carla THOMAS – See Otis REDDING

Evelyn THOMAS US, female vocalist (29 WEEKS)

		pos/wks	
24 Jan 76	**WEAK SPOT** 20th Century BTC 1014	26	7
17 Apr 76	**DOOMSDAY** 20th Century BTC 1017	41	1
1 May 76	**DOOMSDAY (re-entry)** 20th Century BTC 1017	45	1
21 Apr 84 ●	**HIGH ENERGY** Record Shack SOHO 18	5	17
25 Aug 84	**MASQUERADE** Record Shack SOHO 25	60	3

Jamo THOMAS US, male vocalist (2 WEEKS)

		pos/wks	
26 Feb 69	**I SPY FOR THE FBI** Polydor 56755	48	1
12 Mar 69	**I SPY FOR THE FBI (re-entry)** Polydor 56755	44	1

Kenny THOMAS UK, male vocalist (54 WEEKS)

		pos/wks	
26 Jan 91	**OUTSTANDING** Cooltempo COOL 227	12	10
1 Jun 91 ●	**THINKING ABOUT YOUR LOVE** Cooltempo COOL 235	4	13
5 Oct 91	**BEST OF YOU** Cooltempo COOL 243	11	7
30 Nov 91	**TENDER LOVE** Cooltempo COOL 247	26	6
10 Jul 93	**STAY** Cooltempo CDCOOL 271	22	6
4 Sep 93	**TRIPPIN' ON YOUR LOVE** Cooltempo CDCOOL 277	17	5
6 Nov 93	**PIECE BY PIECE** Cooltempo CDCOOL 283	36	3
14 May 94	**DESTINY** Cooltempo CDCOOL 289	59	1
2 Sep 95	**WHEN I THINK OF YOU** Cooltempo CDCOOL 309	27	3

Lillo THOMAS US, male vocalist (10 WEEKS)

		pos/wks	
27 Apr 85	**SETTLE DOWN** Capitol CL 356	66	2
21 Mar 87	**SEXY GIRL** Capitol CL 445	23	5
30 May 87	**I'M IN LOVE** Capitol CL 450	54	3

Mickey THOMAS – See Elvin BISHOP

Millard THOMAS – See Harry BELAFONTE

Nicky THOMAS Jamaica, male vocalist (14 WEEKS)

		pos/wks	
13 Jun 70 ●	**LOVE OF THE COMMON PEOPLE** Trojan TR 7750	9	14

Rob THOMAS – See MATCHBOX 20; SANTANA

Rufus THOMAS US, male vocalist (12 WEEKS)

		pos/wks	
11 Apr 70	**DO THE FUNKY CHICKEN** Stax 144	18	12

Tasha THOMAS US, female vocalist (3 WEEKS)

		pos/wks	
20 Jan 79	**SHOOT ME (WITH YOUR LOVE)** Atlantic LV 4	59	3

Timmy THOMAS US, male vocalist (20 WEEKS)

		pos/wks	
24 Feb 73	**WHY CAN'T WE LIVE TOGETHER** Mojo 2027 012	12	11
28 Dec 85	**NEW YORK EYES** Portrait A 6805 [1]	41	7
14 Jul 90	**WHY CAN'T WE LIVE TOGETHER (re-mix)** TK TKR 1	54	2

[1] Nicole with Timmy Thomas

THOMAS and TAYLOR US, male / female vocal duo (5 WEEKS)

		pos/wks	
17 May 86	**YOU CAN'T BLAME LOVE** Cooltempo COOL 123	53	5

Amanda THOMPSON – See Lesley GARRETT and Amanda THOMPSON

Carroll THOMPSON – See MOVEMENT 98 featuring Carroll THOMPSON; Courtney PINE

Chris THOMPSON UK, male vocalist (5 WEEKS)

		pos/wks	
27 Oct 79	**IF YOU REMEMBER ME** Planet K 12389	42	5

Gina THOMPSON – See MC LYTE

Lincoln THOMPSON – See REBEL MC

Sue THOMPSON US, female vocalist (9 WEEKS)

		pos/wks	
2 Nov 61	**SAD MOVIES (MAKE ME CRY)** Polydor NH 66967	46	1
16 Nov 61	**SAD MOVIES (MAKE ME CRY) (re-entry)** Polydor NH 66967	48	1
21 Jan 65	**PAPER TIGER** Hickory 1284	50	1
11 Feb 65	**PAPER TIGER (re-entry)** Hickory 1284	30	6

THOMPSON TWINS (259 Top 500) British-based synth-rock trio: Tom Bailey (v/syn), New Zealand-born Alannah Currie (v/prc/s), Joe Leeway (prc). Named after characters in a Tin Tin cartoon, they were joined on stage at Live Aid by Madonna and were at the forefront of second so-called 'British Invasion' (110 WEEKS)

		pos/wks	
6 Nov 82	**LIES** Arista ARIST 486	67	3
29 Jan 83 ●	**LOVE ON YOUR SIDE** Arista ARIST 504	9	12
16 Apr 83 ●	**WE ARE DETECTIVE** Arista ARIST 526	7	9
16 Jul 83	**WATCHING** Arista TWINS 1	33	6
19 Nov 83 ●	**HOLD ME NOW** Arista TWINS 2	4	15
4 Feb 84 ●	**DOCTOR DOCTOR** Arista TWINS 3	3	10
31 Mar 84 ●	**YOU TAKE ME UP** Arista TWINS 4	2	9
7 Jul 84	**SISTER OF MERCY** Arista TWINS 5	11	8
8 Sep 84	**SISTER OF MERCY (re-entry)** Arista TWINS 5	66	1
8 Dec 84	**LAY YOUR HANDS ON ME** Arista TWINS 6	13	9
31 Aug 85	**DON'T MESS WITH DOCTOR DREAM** Arista TWINS 9	15	6
19 Oct 85	**KING FOR A DAY** Arista TWINS 7	22	6
7 Dec 85	**REVOLUTION** Arista TWINS 10	56	3
4 Jan 86	**REVOLUTION (re-entry)** Arista TWINS 10	75	1
21 Mar 87	**GET THAT LOVE** Arista TWINS 12	68	2
11 Apr 87	**GET THAT LOVE (re-entry)** Arista TWINS 12	66	1
15 Oct 88	**IN THE NAME OF LOVE '88** Arista 111808	46	3
28 Sep 91	**COME INSIDE** Warner Bros. W 0058	56	4
25 Jan 92	**THE SAINT** Warner Bros. W 0080	53	2

Tracey THORN – See EVERYTHING BUT THE GIRL; MASSIVE ATTACK

David THORNE US, male vocalist (8 WEEKS)

		pos/wks	
24 Jan 63	**ALLEY CAT SONG** Stateside SS 141	21	8

Ken THORNE UK, orchestra (15 WEEKS)

		pos/wks	
18 Jul 63 ●	**THEME FROM THE FILM 'THE LEGION'S LAST PATROL'** HMV POP 1176	4	15

Trumpet solo by Ray Davies

UK No.1 ★   UK Top 10 ●   Still on chart +   UK million seller ◆   UK entry at No.1 ■   US No.1 ▲

THOSE 2 GIRLS *UK, female vocal duo (4 WEEKS)*

		pos/wks	
5 Nov 94	**WANNA MAKE YOU GO . . . UUH!** *Final Vinyl 74321233782*	**74**	1
4 Mar 95	**ALL I WANT** *Final Vinyl 74321254202*	**36**	3

THOUSAND YARD STARE
UK, male vocal / instrumental group (5 WEEKS)

		pos/wks	
26 Oct 91	**SEASONSTREAM (EP)** *Stifled Aardvark AARD 5T*	**65**	1
8 Feb 92	**COMEUPPANCE** *Stifled Aardvark AARD 007*	**37**	2
11 Jul 92	**SPINDRIFT (EP)** *Stifled Aardvark AARDT 010*	**58**	1
8 May 93	**VERSION OF ME** *Polydor AARDC 012*	**57**	1

Tracks on Seasonstream (EP): O-O AET / Village End / Keepsake / Worse for Wear
Tracks on Spindrift (EP): Wideshire Two / Hand, Son / Happenstance / Mocca Pune

THRASHING DOVES
UK, male vocal / instrumental group (3 WEEKS)

		pos/wks	
24 Jan 87	**BEAUTIFUL IMBALANCE** *A & M TDOVE 1*	**50**	3

THREE AMIGOS *UK, male production trio (6 WEEKS)*

		pos/wks	
3 Jul 99	**LOUIE LOUIE** *Inferno CDFERN 17*	**15**	6

3 COLOURS RED *UK, male vocal / instrumental group (17 WEEKS)* pos/wks

		pos/wks	
18 Jan 97	**NUCLEAR HOLIDAY** *Creation CRESCD 250*	**22**	2
15 Mar 97	**SIXTY MILE SMILE** *Creation CRESCD 254*	**20**	3
10 May 97	**PURE** *Creation CRESCD 265*	**28**	1
12 Jul 97	**COPPER GIRL** *Creation CRESCD 270*	**30**	2
8 Nov 97	**THIS IS MY HOLLYWOOD** *Creation CRESCD 277*	**48**	1
23 Jan 99	**BEAUTIFUL DAY** *Creation CRESCD 308*	**11**	6
29 May 99	**THIS IS MY TIME** *Creation CRESCD 313*	**36**	2

THREE DEGREES `241` `Top 500` *US R&B vocal group, who became top UK stars in the 1970s: Sheila Ferguson, Valerie Holiday, Fayette Pinkney. The trio, tagged by the media as "Prince Charles's favourites", was the first girl group to top the UK chart since The Supremes in 1964 (113 WEEKS)* pos/wks

		pos/wks	
13 Apr 74	**YEAR OF DECISION** *Philadelphia International PIR 2073*	**13**	10
27 Apr 74	**TSOP (THE SOUND OF PHILADELPHIA)** *Philadelphia International PIR 2289* [1] ▲	**22**	9
13 Jul 74	★ **WHEN WILL I SEE YOU AGAIN** *Philadelphia International PIR 2155*	**1**	16
2 Nov 74	**GET YOUR LOVE BACK** *Philadelphia International PIR 2737*	**34**	4
12 Apr 75	● **TAKE GOOD CARE OF YOURSELF** *Philadelphia International PIR 3177*	**9**	9
5 Jul 75	**LONG LOST LOVER** *Philadelphia International PIR 3352*	**40**	4
1 May 76	**TOAST OF LOVE** *Epic EPC 4215*	**36**	4
7 Oct 78	**GIVING UP GIVING IN** *Ariola ARO 130*	**12**	10
13 Jan 79	● **WOMAN IN LOVE** *Ariola ARO 141*	**3**	11
24 Mar 79	**THE RUNNER** *Ariola ARO 154*	**10**	10
23 Jun 79	**THE GOLDEN LADY** *Ariola ARO 170*	**56**	3
29 Sep 79	**JUMP THE GUN** *Ariola ARO 183*	**48**	5
24 Nov 79	● **MY SIMPLE HEART** *Ariola ARO 202*	**9**	11
5 Oct 85	**THE HEAVEN I NEED** *Supreme SUPE 102*	**42**	5
26 Dec 98	**LAST CHRISTMAS** *Wildstar CDWILD 15* [2]	**54**	2

[1] MFSB featuring the Three Degrees [2] Alien Voices featuring the Three Degrees

THREE DOG NIGHT
US, male vocal / instrumental group (23 WEEKS)

		pos/wks	
8 Aug 70	● **MAMA TOLD ME NOT TO COME** *Stateside SS 8052* ▲	**3**	14
29 May 71	**JOY TO THE WORLD** *Probe PRO 523* ▲	**24**	9

THREE DRIVES
Holland, male vocal / instrumental group (5 WEEKS)

		pos/wks	
27 Jun 98	**GREECE 2000** *Hooj Choons HOOJCD 63*	**44**	1
30 Jan 99	**GREECE 2000 (re-mix)** *Hooj Choons HOOJ 70CD*	**12**	4

THREE GOOD REASONS
UK, male vocal / instrumental group (3 WEEKS)

		pos/wks	
10 Mar 66	**NOWHERE MAN** *Mercury MF 899*	**47**	3

3 JAYS *UK, male production / vocal trio (5 WEEKS)*

		pos/wks	
31 Jul 99	**FEELING IT TOO** *Multiply CDMULTY 53*	**17**	5

THREE KAYES – See KAYE SISTERS

THREE 'N ONE *Germany, male production duo (3 WEEKS)*

		pos/wks	
7 Jun 97	**REFLECT** *ffrr FCD 301*	**66**	1
15 May 99	**PEARL RIVER** *Low Sense SENSECD 24* [1]	**32**	2

[1] Three 'N One presents Johnny Shaker featuring Serial Diva

3T *US, male vocal trio (45 WEEKS)*

		pos/wks	
27 Jan 96	● **ANYTHING** *MJJ 6627152*	**2**	14
4 May 96	**24 / 7** *MJJ 6631995*	**11**	7
24 Aug 96	● **WHY** *MJJ 6636482* [1]	**2**	9
7 Dec 96	● **I NEED YOU** *Epic 6639912*	**3**	10
5 Apr 97	● **GOTTA BE YOU** *Epic 6643645* [2]	**10**	5

[1] 3T featuring Michael Jackson [2] 3T: rap by Herbie

THREE TONS OF JOY – See Johnny OTIS SHOW

THROWING MUSES
US, male / female vocal / instrumental group (6 WEEKS)

		pos/wks	
9 Feb 91	**COUNTING BACKWARDS** *4AD AD 1001*	**70**	2
1 Aug 92	**FIREPILE (EP)** *4AD BAD 2012*	**46**	1
24 Dec 94	**BRIGHT YELLOW GUN** *4AD BAD 4018CD*	**51**	2
10 Aug 96	**SHARK** *4AD BAD 6016CD*	**53**	1

Tracks on Firepile (EP): Firepile / Manic Depression / Snailhead / City of the Dead

THS - THE HORN SECTION
US, male / female vocal / instrumental group (3 WEEKS)

		pos/wks	
18 Aug 84	**LADY SHINE (SHINE ON)** *Fourth & Broadway BRW 10*	**54**	3

Harry THUMANN
Germany, male instrumentalist - keyboards (6 WEEKS)

		pos/wks	
21 Feb 81	**UNDERWATER** *Decca F 13901*	**41**	6

See also WONDER DOG

THUNDER *UK, male vocal / instrumental group (52 WEEKS)*

		pos/wks	
17 Feb 90	**DIRTY LOVE** *EMI EM 126*	**32**	4
12 May 90	**BACKSTREET SYMPHONY** *EMI EM 137*	**25**	4
14 Jul 90	**GIMME SOME LOVIN'** *EMI EM 148*	**36**	3
29 Sep 90	**SHE'S SO FINE** *EMI EM 158*	**34**	3
23 Feb 91	**LOVE WALKED IN** *EMI EM 175*	**21**	4
15 Aug 92	**LOW LIFE IN HIGH PLACES** *EMI EM 242*	**22**	5
10 Oct 92	**EVERYBODY WANTS HER** *EMI EM 249*	**36**	4
13 Feb 93	**A BETTER MAN** *EMI CDBETTER 1*	**18**	4
19 Jun 93	**LIKE A SATELLITE (EP)** *EMI CDEM 272*	**28**	2
7 Jan 95	**STAND UP** *EMI CDEM 365*	**23**	4
25 Feb 95	**RIVER OF PAIN** *EMI CDEM 367*	**31**	2
6 May 95	**CASTLES IN THE SAND** *EMI CDEM 372*	**30**	3
23 Sep 95	**IN A BROKEN DREAM** *EMI CDEM 384*	**26**	2
25 Jan 97	**DON'T WAIT UP** *Raw Power RAWX 1020*	**27**	2
5 Apr 97	**LOVE WORTH DYING FOR** *Raw Power RAWX 1043*	**60**	1
7 Feb 98	**THE ONLY ONE** *Eagle EAGXA 016*	**31**	2
27 Jun 98	**PLAY THAT FUNKY MUSIC** *Eagle EAGXS 030*	**39**	2
20 Mar 99	**YOU WANNA KNOW** *Eagle EAGXA 037*	**49**	1

Tracks on Like a Satellite (EP): Like a Satellite / The Damage Is Done / Like a Satellite (LIve) / Gimme Shelter

THUNDERBIRDS – See Chris FARLOWE

THUNDERBUGS *UK / France / Germany, female vocal / instrumental group (15 WEEKS)* pos/wks

		pos/wks	
18 Sep 99	● **FRIENDS FOREVER** *First Avenue / Epic 6676932*	**5**	9
11 Dec 99	**FRIENDS FOREVER (re-entry)** *First Avenue / Epic 6676932*	**71**	1
18 Dec 99	**IT'S ABOUT TIME YOU WERE MINE** *First Avenue / Epic 6683972*	**43**	5

SINGLED OUT...
Graham Fellows

Graham went Top 4 in 1978 as and with **JILTED JOHN** and will surely chart again one day with something from another of his characters, John Shuttleworth.

ALL-TIME FAVOURITE SINGLE:
Something In The Air
Thunderclap Newman

Produced by The Who's Pete Townshend, it has a glorious phased guitar sound that today's producers can only dream about. And it's a brilliant song

- **NO.1 ON THE UK SINGLES CHART THE DAY I WAS BORN:**
(Same day as Morrissey, apparently)
A Fool Such As I / I Need Your Love Tonight – Elvis

- **FIRST SINGLE I EVER BOUGHT:**
Whispering Softly I Love You – The Congregation

At the age of 12 I found the combination of cheesy fuzz guitar licks and church choir intriguing and strangely arousing.

- **SINGLE THAT DRIVES ME UP THE WALL:**
Itsy Bitsy Teeny Weeny Yellow Polka Dot Bikini – Bombalurina

It's teeth-crunchingly dreadful, although admittedly one of Lord Lloyd Webber's more inspired productions.

THUNDERCLAP NEWMAN UK, male vocal / instrumental group. Lead vocal - John "Speedy" Keen (13 WEEKS)

		pos/wks
11 Jun 69 ★	SOMETHING IN THE AIR *Track 604-031*	1 12
27 Jun 70	ACCIDENTS *Track 2094 001*	46 1

THUNDERTHIGHS UK, female vocal group (5 WEEKS)

		pos/wks
22 Jun 74	CENTRAL PARK ARREST *Philips 6006 386*	30 5

Bobby THURSTON US, male vocalist (10 WEEKS)

		pos/wks
29 Mar 80 ●	CHECK OUT THE GROOVE *Epic EPC 8348*	10 10

TIFFANY US, female vocalist - Tiffany Darwish (45 WEEKS)

		pos/wks
16 Jan 88 ★	I THINK WE'RE ALONE NOW *MCA MCA 1211* ▲	1 13
19 Mar 88	COULD'VE BEEN *MCA TIFF 2* ▲	4 9
4 Jun 88	I SAW HIM STANDING THERE *MCA TIFF 3*	8 7
6 Aug 88	FEELINGS OF FOREVER *MCA TIFF 4*	52 2
12 Nov 88	RADIO ROMANCE *MCA TIFF 5*	13 11
11 Feb 89	ALL THIS TIME *MCA TIFF 6*	47 3

TIGER
UK / Ireland, male / female vocal / instrumental group (5 WEEKS)

		pos/wks
31 Aug 96	RACE *Trade 2 TRDCD 004*	37 2
16 Nov 96	MY PUPPET PAL *Trade 2 TRDCD 005*	62 1
22 Feb 97	ON THE ROSE *Trade 2 TRDCD 008*	57 1
22 Aug 98	FRIENDS *Trade 2 TRDCD 013*	72 1

TIGERTAILZ US, male vocal / instrumental group (2 WEEKS)

		pos/wks
24 Jun 89	LOVE BOMB BABY *Music for Nations KUT 132*	75 1
16 Feb 91	HEAVEN *Music for Nations KUT 137*	71 1

TIGHT FIT UK, male / female vocal group (49 WEEKS)

		pos/wks
18 Jul 81 ●	BACK TO THE SIXTIES *Jive JIVE 002*	4 11
26 Sep 81	BACK TO THE SIXTIES PART 2 *Jive JIVE 005*	33 5
23 Jan 82 ★	THE LION SLEEPS TONIGHT *Jive JIVE 9*	1 15
1 May 82 ●	FANTASY ISLAND *Jive JIVE 13*	5 12
31 Jul 82	SECRET HEART *Jive JIVE 20*	41 6

TIJUANA BRASS – See Herb ALPERT

TIK and TOK UK, male vocal duo (2 WEEKS)

		pos/wks
8 Oct 83	COOL RUNNING *Survival SUR 016*	69 2

Tanita TIKARAM UK, female vocalist (31 WEEKS)

		pos/wks
30 Jul 88 ●	GOOD TRADITION *WEA YZ 196*	10 10
22 Oct 88	TWIST IN MY SOBRIETY *WEA YZ 321*	22 8
14 Jan 89	CATHEDRAL SONG *WEA YZ 331*	48 3
18 Mar 89	WORLD OUTSIDE YOUR WINDOW *WEA YZ 363*	58 2
13 Jan 90	WE ALMOST GOT IT TOGETHER *WEA YZ 443*	52 3
9 Feb 91	ONLY THE ONES WE LOVE *East West YZ 558*	69 1
4 Feb 95	I MIGHT BE CRYING *East West YZ 879CD*	64 2
6 Jun 98	STOP LISTENING *Mother MUMCD 102*	67 1
29 Aug 98	I DON'T WANNA LOSE AT LOVE *Mother MUMCD 105*	73 1

TILLMAN + REIS Germany, male production duo (1 WEEK)

		pos/wks
16 Sep 00	BASSFLY *Liquid Asset ASSET CD004*	70 1

Johnny TILLOTSON US, male vocalist (50 WEEKS)

		pos/wks
1 Dec 60 ★	POETRY IN MOTION *London HLA 9231*	1 15
2 Feb 61	JIMMY'S GIRL *London HLA 9275*	50 1
16 Feb 61	JIMMY'S GIRL (re-entry) *London HLA 9275*	43 1
12 Jul 62	IT KEEPS RIGHT ON A HURTIN' *London HLA 9550*	31 10
4 Oct 62	SEND ME THE PILLOW YOU DREAM ON *London HLA 9598*	21 10
27 Dec 62	I CAN'T HELP IT *London HLA 9642*	42 1
10 Jan 63	I CAN'T HELP IT (re-entry) *London HLA 9642*	47 1
24 Jan 63	I CAN'T HELP IT (2nd re-entry) *London HLA 9642*	41 4
9 May 63	OUT OF MY MIND *London HLA 9695*	34 5
14 Apr 79	POETRY IN MOTION (re-issue) *Lightning LIG 9016*	67 2

TILT UK, male instrumental / production group (8 WEEKS)

		pos/wks
2 Dec 95	I DREAM *Perfecto PERF 112CD*	69 1
10 May 97	MY SPIRIT *Perfecto PERF 139CD*	61 1
13 Sep 97	PLACES *Perfecto PERF 149CD*	64 1
7 Feb 98	BUTTERFLY *Perfecto PERF 154CD1* [1]	41 1
27 Mar 99	CHILDREN *Deconstruction 74321648172*	51 1
8 May 99	INVISIBLE *Hooj Choons HOOJ 73CD*	20 2
12 Feb 00	DARK SCIENCE (EP) *Hooj Choons HOOJ 87*	55 1

[1] Tilt featuring Zee

TIMBALAND US, male producer / rapper - Tim Mosley (7 WEEKS)

		pos/wks
23 Jan 99	GET ON THE BUS *East West E3780CD* [1]	15 5
13 Mar 99	HERE WE COME *Virgin DINSD 179* [2]	43 1
19 Jun 99	LOBSTER & SCRIMP *Virgin DINSD 186* [3]	48 1

[1] Destiny's Child featuring Timbaland [2] Timbaland / Missy Elliott & Magoo [3] Timbaland featuring Jay-Z

TIMBUK 3 US, male / female vocal / instrumental duo (7 WEEKS)

		pos/wks
31 Jan 87	THE FUTURE'S SO BRIGHT I GOTTA WEAR SHADES *IRS IRM 126*	21 7

TIME FREQUENCY
UK, male instrumental / production group (33 WEEKS)

		pos/wks
6 Jun 92	REAL LOVE *Jive JIVET 307*	60 1
9 Jun 93	NEW EMOTION *Internal Affairs KGBCD 009*	36 6
12 Jun 93	THE ULTIMATE HIGH / THE POWER ZONE *Internal Affairs KGBD 010*	17 11
6 Nov 93 ●	REAL LOVE (re-mix) *Internal Affairs KGBCD 011*	8 6
1 Jan 94	REAL LOVE (re-entry of re-mix) *Internal Affairs KGBCD 011*	71 2
28 May 94	SUCH A PHANTASY *Internal Affairs KGBD 013*	25 4
8 Oct 94	DREAMSCAPE '94 *Internal Affairs KGBD 015*	32 3

TIME OF THE MUMPH
UK, male producer - Mark Mumford (1 WEEK)

		pos/wks
11 Feb 95	CONTROL *Fresh FRSHD 24*	69 1

TIME UK UK, male vocal / instrumental group (3 WEEKS)

		pos/wks
8 Oct 83	THE CABARET *Red Bus / Aroadia TIM 123*	63 3

TIME ZONE UK / US, male vocal / instrumental duo (9 WEEKS)

		pos/wks
19 Jan 85	WORLD DESTRUCTION *Virgin VS 743*	44 9

TIMEBOX UK, male vocal / instrumental group (4 WEEKS)

		pos/wks
24 Jul 68	BEGGIN' *Deram DM 194*	38 4

TIMELORDS UK, male vocal / instrumental group (9 WEEKS)

		pos/wks
4 Jun 88 ★	DOCTORIN' THE TARDIS *KLF Communications KLF 003*	1 9

See also KLF; JUSTIFIED ANCIENTS OF MU MU; 1300 DRUMS featuring the UNJUSTIFIED ANCIENTS OF MU; 2K

TIMEX SOCIAL CLUB
US, male vocal / instrumental group (9 WEEKS)

		pos/wks
13 Sep 86	RUMORS *Cooltempo COOL 133*	13 9

TIN MACHINE US / UK, male vocal / instrumental group (10 WEEKS)

		pos/wks
1 Jul 89	UNDER THE GOD *EMI-USA MT 68*	51 2
9 Sep 89	TIN MACHINE / MAGGIE'S FARM (LIVE) *EMI-USA MT 73*	48 2
24 Aug 91	YOU BELONG IN ROCK 'N' ROLL *London LON 305*	33 3
2 Nov 91	BABY UNIVERSAL *London LON 310*	48 3

See also David BOWIE

TIN TIN OUT
UK, male instrumental / production duo - Lindsay Edwards and Darren Stokes (42 WEEKS)   pos/wks

13 Aug 94	**THE FEELING**		
	Deep Distraxion OILYCD 029 [1]	**32**	2
25 Mar 95	**ALWAYS SOMETHING THERE TO REMIND ME**		
	WEA YZ 911CD [2]	**14**	5
8 Feb 97	**ALL I WANNA DO** *VC VCRD 15*	**31**	2
10 May 97	**DANCE WITH ME** *VC VCRD 17* [3]	**35**	2
20 Sep 97	**STRINGS FOR YASMIN** *VC VCRD 20*	**31**	3
28 Mar 98 ●	**HERE'S WHERE THE STORY ENDS**		
	VC Recordings VCRD 30 [4]	**7**	10
12 Sep 98	**SOMETIMES** *VC Recordings VCRD 34* [4]	**20**	4
11 Sep 99	**ELEVEN TO FLY** *VC Recordings VCRDX 52* [5]	**26**	2
13 Nov 99 ●	**WHAT I AM** *VC Recordings VCRD 53* [6]	**2**	12

[1] Tin Tin Out featuring Sweet Tee [2] Tin Tin Out featuring Espiritu [3] Tin Tin Out featuring Tony Hadley [4] Tin Tin Out featuring Shelley Nelson [5] Tin Tin Out featuring Wendy Page [6] Tin Tin Out featuring Emma Bunton

TINA – See Tina TURNER

TINDERSTICKS
UK, male vocal / instrumental group (6 WEEKS)   pos/wks

5 Feb 94	**KATHLEEN (EP)** *This Way Up WAY 2833CD*	**61**	1
18 Mar 95	**NO MORE AFFAIRS** *This Way Up WAY 3833*	**58**	1
12 Aug 95	**TRAVELLING LIGHT** *This Way Up WAY 4533*	**51**	1
7 Jun 97	**BATHTIME** *This Way Up WAY 6166*	**38**	1
1 Nov 97	**RENTED ROOMS** *This Way Up WAY 6566*	**56**	1
4 Sep 99	**CAN WE START AGAIN?** *Island CID 756*	**54**	1

Tracks on Kathleen (EP): Kathleen / Summat Moon / A Sweet Sweet Man / E-Type Joe

TINGO TANGO
UK, male instrumental group (2 WEEKS)   pos/wks

21 Jul 90	**IT IS JAZZ** *Champion CHAMP 250*	**68**	2

TINMAN
UK, male producer - Paul Dakeyne (9 WEEKS)   pos/wks

20 Aug 94 ●	**EIGHTEEN STRINGS** *ffrr FCD 242*	**9**	8
3 Jun 95	**GUDVIBE** *ffrr FCD 262*	**49**	1

TINY TIM
US, male vocalist (1 WEEK)   pos/wks

5 Feb 69	**GREAT BALLS OF FIRE** *Reprise RS 20802*	**45**	1

TITANIC
Norway / UK, male instrumental group (12 WEEKS)   pos/wks

25 Sep 71 ●	**SULTANA** *CBS 5365*	**5**	12

TITIYO
Sweden, female vocalist (6 WEEKS)   pos/wks

3 Mar 90	**AFTER THE RAIN** *Arista 112722*	**60**	3
6 Oct 90	**FLOWERS** *Arista 113212*	**71**	1
5 Feb 94	**TELL ME I'M NOT DREAMING** *Arista 74321185622*	**45**	2

Cara TIVEY – See Billy BRAGG

TJR featuring XAVIER
UK, male instrumental / production group (2 WEEKS)   pos/wks

27 Sep 97	**JUST GETS BETTER** *Multiply CDMULTY 25*	**28**	2

TLC   `390` `Top 500`
Multi-award-winning 1990s female trio; Tionne "T-Boz" Watkins, Lisa "Left Eye" Lopes and Rozonda "Chilli" Thomas, formed and managed by fellow R&B hitmaker Pebbles. They have nine US gold singles, and The Supremes are only female group with more US No.1s (83 WEEKS) pos/wks

20 Jun 92	**AIN'T 2 PROUD 2 BEG** *Arista 115265*	**13**	5
22 Aug 92	**BABY-BABY-BABY** *LaFace 74321111297*	**55**	3
24 Oct 92	**WHAT ABOUT YOUR FRIENDS**		
	LaFace 74321118177	**59**	2
21 Jan 95	**CREEP** *LaFace 74321254212* ▲	**22**	4
22 Apr 95	**RED LIGHT SPECIAL** *LaFace 74321273662*	**18**	4
5 Aug 95 ●	**WATERFALLS** *LaFace 74321298812* ▲	**4**	14
4 Nov 95	**DIGGIN' ON YOU** *LaFace 74321319252*	**18**	5
13 Jan 96 ●	**CREEP (re-issue)** *LaFace 7432134042*	**6**	7
3 Apr 99 ●	**NO SCRUBS** *LaFace 74321660952* ▲	**3**	19

28 Aug 99 ●	**UNPRETTY** *LaFace 74321695842* ▲	**6**	11
18 Dec 99	**DEAR LIE** *LaFace 74321724012*	**32**	9

See also T-BOZ; LISA 'LEFT EYE' LOPES

T99
Belgium, male instrumental / production group (10 WEEKS)   pos/wks

11 May 91	**ANASTHASIA** *XL XLS 19*	**14**	6
19 Oct 91	**NOCTURNE** *Emphasis 6574097*	**33**	4

TOADS – See Stan FREBERG

Art and Dotty TODD
US, male / female vocal duo (7 WEEKS)   pos/wks

13 Feb 53 ●	**BROKEN WINGS** *HMV B 10399*	**6**	7

TOGETHER
UK, male vocal / instrumental group (8 WEEKS)   pos/wks

4 Aug 90	**HARDCORE UPROAR** *ffrr F 143*	**12**	8

TOKENS
US, male vocal group (12 WEEKS)   pos/wks

21 Dec 61	**THE LION SLEEPS TONIGHT (WIMOWEH)** *RCA 1263* ▲	**11**	12

TOKYO GHETTO PUSSY
Germany, male instrumental / production duo (4 WEEKS)   pos/wks

16 Sep 95	**EVERYBODY ON THE FLOOR (PUMP IT)** *Epic 6611132*	**26**	2
16 Mar 96	**I KISS YOUR LIPS** *Epic 6623212*	**55**	2

See also JAM & SPOON featuring PLAVKA; STORM

TOL and TOL
Holland, male vocal / instrumental duo (2 WEEKS)   pos/wks

14 Apr 90	**ELENI** *Dover ROJ 5*	**73**	2

TOM TOM CLUB
US, female / male vocal / instrumental group (20 WEEKS)   pos/wks

20 Jun 81 ●	**WORDY RAPPINGHOOD** *Island WIP 6694*	**7**	9
10 Oct 81	**GENIUS OF LOVE** *Island WIP 6735*	**65**	2
7 Aug 82	**UNDER THE BOARDWALK** *Island WIP 6762*	**22**	9

TOMCAT
UK, male vocal / instrumental group (1 WEEK)   pos/wks

14 Oct 00	**CRAZY** *Virgin VSCDT 1785*	**48**	1

Satoshi TOMIIE – See Frankie KNUCKLES

TOMSKI
UK, male producer - Tom Jankiewicz (3 WEEKS)   pos/wks

18 Apr 98	**14 HOURS TO SAVE THE EARTH** *Xtravaganza 0091515 EXT*	**42**	1
12 Feb 00	**LOVE WILL COME** *Xtravaganza XTRAV6CDS* [1]	**31**	2

[1] Tomski featuring Jan Johnston

TONGUE 'N' CHEEK
UK, male / female vocal / instrumental group (28 WEEKS)   pos/wks

27 Feb 88	**NOBODY (CAN LOVE ME)** *Criminal BUS 6* [1]	**59**	6
25 Nov 89	**ENCORE** *Syncopate SY 33*	**41**	4
14 Apr 90	**TOMORROW** *Syncopate SY 34*	**20**	7
4 Aug 90	**NOBODY (re-recording)** *Syncopate SY 37*	**37**	5
19 Jan 91	**FORGET ME NOTS** *Syncopate SY 39*	**26**	6

[1] Tongue In Cheek

TONIGHT
UK, male / vocal / instrumental group (10 WEEKS)   pos/wks

28 Jan 78	**DRUMMER MAN** *Target TDS 1*	**14**	8
20 May 78	**MONEY THAT'S YOUR PROBLEM** *Target TDS 2*	**66**	2

TONY TONI TONÉ
US, male vocal group (12 WEEKS)   pos/wks

30 Jun 90	**OAKLAND STROKE** *Wing WING 7* (1)	**50**	5
9 Mar 91	**IT NEVER RAINS (IN SOUTHERN CALIFORNIA)**		
	Wing WING 10 [1]	**69**	2
4 Sep 93	**IF I HAD NO LOOT** *Polydor PZCD 292*	**44**	3
3 May 97	**LET'S GET DOWN** *Mercury MERCD 485* [2]	**33**	2

[1] Tony! Toni! Toné! [2] Tony Toni Toné featuring DJ Quick

TOO TOUGH TEE – See DYNAMIX II featuring TOO TOUGH TEE

TOON TRAVELLERS – See MUNGO JERRY

TOP UK, male vocal / instrumental group (2 WEEKS)
pos/wks
20 Jul 91	NUMBER ONE DOMINATOR *Island IS 496*	67	2

TOP LINERS – See Rocky SHARPE and the REPLAYS

TOPLOADER UK, male vocal / instrumental group (26 WEEKS)
pos/wks
22 May 99	ACHILLES HEEL *Sony S2 6671612*	64	1
7 Aug 99	LET THE PEOPLE KNOW *Sony S2 6677132*	52	1
4 Mar 00	DANCING IN THE MOONLIGHT *Sony S2 6689412*	19	7
13 May 00 ●	ACHILLES HEEL (re-issue) *Sony S2 6691872*	8	7
2 Sep 00	JUST HOLD ON *Sony S2 6696242*	20	4
25 Nov 00	DANCING IN THE MOONLIGHT (re-issue) *Sony S2 6699852*	11	6+

TOPOL Israel, male vocalist / actor - Chaim Topol (20 WEEKS)
pos/wks
20 Apr 67 ●	IF I WERE A RICH MAN *CBS 202651*	9	20

Mel TORME US, male vocalist (32 WEEKS)
pos/wks
27 Apr 56	MOUNTAIN GREENERY *Vogue / Coral Q 72150*	15	11
27 Jul 56 ●	MOUNTAIN GREENERY (re-entry) *Vogue / Coral Q 72150*	4	13
3 Jan 63	COMING HOME BABY *London HLK 9643*	13	8

TORNADOS UK, male instrumental group (59 WEEKS)
pos/wks
30 Aug 62 ★	TELSTAR *Decca F 11494* ▲	1	25
10 Jan 63 ●	GLOBETROTTER *Decca F 11562*	5	11
21 Mar 63	ROBOT *Decca F 11606*	17	12
6 Jun 63	THE ICE CREAM MAN *Decca F 11662*	18	9
10 Oct 63	DRAGONFLY *Decca F 11745*	41	2

Mitchell TOROK US, male vocalist (19 WEEKS)
pos/wks
28 Sep 56 ●	WHEN MEXICO GAVE UP THE RHUMBA *Brunswick 05586*	6	17
11 Jan 57	RED LIGHT, GREEN LIGHT *Brunswick 05626*	29	1
1 Feb 57	WHEN MEXICO GAVE UP THE RHUMBA (re-entry) *Brunswick 05586*	30	1

Liz TORRES – See Danny TENAGLIA

Emiliana TORRINI Italy, female vocalist (2 WEEKS)
pos/wks
10 Jun 00	EASY *One Little Indian 274 TP7CD*	63	1
9 Sep 00	UNEMPLOYED IN SUMMERTIME *One Little Indian 275 TP7CDL*	63	1

Peter TOSH Jamaica, male vocalist (12 WEEKS)
pos/wks
21 Oct 78	(YOU GOTTA WALK) DON'T LOOK BACK *Rolling Stones 2859*	43	7
2 Apr 83	JOHNNY B GOODE *EMI RIC 115*	48	5

TOTAL US, female vocal group (11 WEEKS)
pos/wks
15 Jul 95	CAN'T YOU SEE *Tommy Boy TBCD 700* [1]	43	2
14 Sep 96	KISSIN' YOU *Arista 74321404172*	29	2
15 Feb 97	DO YOU THINK ABOUT US *Puff Daddy 74321458492*	49	1
18 Apr 98	WHAT YOU WANT *Puff Daddy 74321578772* [2]	15	5
30 Sep 00	I WONDER WHY HE'S THE GREATEST DJ *Tommy Boy TBCD 2100* [3]	68	1

[1] Total featuring the Notorious B.I.G. [2] Mase featuring Total [3] Tony Touch featuring Total

TOTAL CONTRAST UK, male vocal / instrumental duo (22 WEEKS)
pos/wks
3 Aug 85	TAKES A LITTLE TIME *London LON 71*	17	10
19 Oct 85	HIT AND RUN *London LON 76*	41	5
1 Mar 86	THE RIVER *London LON 83*	44	3
10 May 86	WHAT YOU GONNA DO ABOUT IT *London LON 95*	63	4

TOTO US, male vocal / instrumental group (35 WEEKS)
pos/wks
10 Feb 79	HOLD THE LINE *CBS 6784*	14	11
5 Feb 83 ●	AFRICA *CBS A 2510* ▲	3	10
9 Apr 83	ROSANNA *CBS A 2079*	12	8
18 Jun 83	I WON'T HOLD YOU BACK *CBS A 3392*	37	5
18 Nov 95	I WILL REMEMBER *Columbia 6626552*	64	1

TOTO COELO UK, female vocal group (14 WEEKS)
pos/wks
7 Aug 82 ●	I EAT CANNIBALS PART 1 *Radialchoice TIC 10*	8	10
13 Nov 82	DRACULA'S TANGO / MUCHO MACHO *Radialchoice TIC 11*	54	4

TOTTENHAM HOTSPUR FA CUP FINAL SQUAD UK, male football team vocalists (23 WEEKS)
pos/wks
9 May 81 ●	OSSIE'S DREAM (SPURS ARE ON THEIR WAY TO WEMBLEY) *Shelf SHELF 1*	5	8
1 May 82	TOTTENHAM TOTTENHAM *Shelf SHELF 2*	19	7
9 May 87	HOT SHOT TOTTENHAM! *Rainbow RBR 16*	18	5
11 May 91	WHEN THE YEAR ENDS IN 1 *A1 A 1324*	44	3

All hits feature the vocal and instrumental talents of Chas and Dave

Tony TOUCH featuring TOTAL
US, male producer - Anthony Hernandez (1 WEEK)
pos/wks
30 Sep 00	I WONDER WHY HE'S THE GREATEST DJ *Tommy Boy TBCD 2100*	68	1

TOUCH & GO UK, male / female vocal / production group (12 WEEKS)
pos/wks
7 Nov 98 ●	WOULD YOU...? *Oval VVR 5003083*	3	12

TOUCH OF SOUL
UK, male / female vocal / instrumental group (3 WEEKS)
pos/wks
19 May 90	WE GOT THE LOVE *Cooltempo COOL 204*	46	3

TOUR DE FORCE UK, male production trio (1 WEEK)
pos/wks
16 May 98	CATALAN *East West EW 161CD*	71	1

TOURISTS UK, male / female vocal / instrumental group (40 WEEKS)
pos/wks
9 Jun 79	BLIND AMONG THE FLOWERS *Logo GO 350*	52	5
8 Sep 79	THE LONELIEST MAN IN THE WORLD *Logo GO 360*	32	7
10 Nov 79 ●	I ONLY WANT TO BE WITH YOU *Logo GO 370*	4	14
9 Feb 80 ●	SO GOOD TO BE BACK HOME AGAIN *Logo TOUR 1*	8	9
18 Oct 80	DON'T SAY I TOLD YOU SO *RCA TOUR 2*	40	5

TOUTES LES FILLES UK, female vocal group (1 WEEK)
pos/wks
4 Sep 99	THAT'S WHAT LOVE CAN DO *London LONCD 434*	44	1

Carol Lynn TOWNES US, female vocalist (7 WEEKS)
pos/wks
4 Aug 84	99 1/2 *Polydor POSP 693*	47	4
19 Jan 85	BELIEVE IN THE BEAT *Polydor POSP 720*	56	3

Fuzz TOWNSHEND UK, male producer (1 WEEK)
pos/wks
6 Sep 97	HELLO DARLIN *Echo ECSCD 46*	51	1

Pete TOWNSHEND UK, male vocalist (17 WEEKS)
pos/wks
5 Apr 80	ROUGH BOYS *Atco K 11460*	39	6
21 Jun 80	LET MY LOVE OPEN YOUR DOOR *Atco K 11486*	46	6
21 Aug 82	UNIFORMS (CORPS D'ESPRIT) *Atco K 11751*	48	5

See also WHO

TOXIC TWO US, male instrumental / production duo (6 WEEKS)
pos/wks
7 Mar 92	RAVE GENERATOR *PWL International PWL 223*	13	6

TOY - BOX Denmark, male / female vocal duo (2 WEEKS)
pos/wks
18 Sep 99	BEST FRIENDS *Edel 0058245 ERE*	41	2

TOY DOLLS UK, male vocal / instrumental group (12 WEEKS)

		pos/wks
1 Dec 84 ●	NELLIE THE ELEPHANT Volume VOL 11	4 12

TOYAH (363 | Top 500) Visually striking punk / pop vocalist, b. Toyah
Willcox 16 May 1958, Birmingham, UK. Came to prominence through acting - first major role in 1977 movie Jubilee. Married King Crimson guitarist Robert Fripp in 1986. One of first acts to chart regularly with EPs (87 WEEKS) pos/wks

		pos/wks
14 Feb 81 ●	FOUR FROM TOYAH (EP) Safari TOY 1	4 14
16 May 81 ●	I WANT TO BE FREE Safari SAFE 34	8 11
3 Oct 81 ●	THUNDER IN THE MOUNTAINS Safari SAFE 38	4 9
28 Nov 81	FOUR MORE FROM TOYAH (EP) Safari TOY 2	14 9
22 May 82	BRAVE NEW WORLD Safari SAFE 45	21 8
17 Jul 82	IEYA Safari SAFE 28	48 5
9 Oct 82	BE LOUD BE PROUD (BE HEARD) Safari SAFE 52	30 7
24 Sep 83	REBEL RUN Safari SAFE 56	24 5
19 Nov 83	THE VOW Safari SAFE 58	50 5
27 Apr 85	DON'T FALL IN LOVE (I SAID) Portrait A 6160	22 6
29 Jun 85	SOUL PASSING THROUGH SOUL Portrait A 6359	57 3
25 Apr 87	ECHO BEACH EG EGO 31	54 5

Tracks on Four From Toyah (EP): It's a Mystery / Revelations / War Boys / Angels and Demons. Tracks on Four More From Toyah (EP): Good Morning Universe / Urban Tribesman / In the Fairground / The Furious Futures

TOYS US, female vocal group (17 WEEKS)

		pos/wks
4 Nov 65 ●	A LOVER'S CONCERTO Stateside SS 460	5 13
27 Jan 66	ATTACK Stateside SS 483	36 4

T'PAU (428 | Top 500) Shropshire lads and a lass whose No.1 hit in 1987
had the distinction of being the 600th chart-topper. T'Pau (Mr Spock's Vulcan friend in Star Trek) comprised writers Carol Decker (v) and Ron Rogers (g), plus Michael Chetwood (k), Paul Jackson (b), Tim Burgess (d) and Taj Wyzgowski (g) (77 WEEKS) pos/wks

		pos/wks
8 Aug 87 ●	HEART AND SOUL Siren SRN 41	4 13
24 Oct 87 ★	CHINA IN YOUR HAND Siren SRN 64	1 15
30 Jan 88 ●	VALENTINE Siren SRN 69	9 8
2 Apr 88	SEX TALK (LIVE) Siren SRN 80	23 7
25 Jun 88	I WILL BE WITH YOU Siren SRN 87	14 6
1 Oct 88	SECRET GARDEN Siren SRN 93	18 7
3 Dec 88	ROAD TO OUR DREAM Siren SRN 100	42 6
25 Mar 89	ONLY THE LONELY Siren SRN 107	28 6
18 May 91	WHENEVER YOU NEED ME Siren SRN 140	16 6
27 Jul 91	WALK ON AIR Siren SRN 142	62 2
20 Feb 93	VALENTINE (re-issue) Virgin VALEG 1	53 1

TQ US, male rapper - Terrance Quaites (30 WEEKS)

		pos/wks
30 Jan 99 ●	WESTSIDE Epic 6668102	4 9
1 May 99 ●	BYE BYE BABY Epic 6672372	7 7
21 Aug 99	BETTER DAYS Epic 6677532	32 2
4 Sep 99 ●	SUMMERTIME Northwestside 74321694672 [1]	7 7
29 Apr 00	DAILY Epic 6692752	14 5

[1] Another Level featuring TQ

TRACIE UK, female vocalist - Tracie Young (24 WEEKS)

		pos/wks
26 Mar 83 ●	THE HOUSE THAT JACK BUILT Respond KOB 701	9 8
16 Jul 83	GIVE IT SOME EMOTION Respond KOB 704	24 9
14 Apr 84	SOUL'S ON FIRE Respond KOB 708	73 2
9 Jun 84	(I LOVE YOU) WHEN YOU SLEEP Respond KOB 710	59 3
17 Aug 85	I CAN'T LEAVE YOU ALONE Respond SBS 1 [1]	60 2

[1] Tracie Young

Gordon TRACKS – See AIR

TRACY – See MASSIVO featuring TRACY

Jeanie TRACY US, female vocalist (3 WEEKS)

		pos/wks
11 Jun 94	IF THIS IS LOVE Pulse 8 CDLOSE 63	73 1
5 Nov 94	DO YOU BELIEVE IN THE WONDER Pulse 8 CDLOSE 74	57 1
13 May 95	IT'S A MAN'S MAN'S MAN'S WORLD Pulse 8 CDLOSE 89 [1]	73 1

[1] Jeanie Tracy and Bobby Womack

TRAFFIC UK, male vocal / instrumental group (40 WEEKS)

		pos/wks
1 Jun 67 ●	PAPER SUN Island WIP 6002	5 10
6 Sep 67 ●	HOLE IN MY SHOE Island WIP 6017	2 14
29 Nov 67 ●	HERE WE GO ROUND THE MULBERRY BUSH Island WIP 6025	8 12
6 Mar 68	NO FACE, NO NAME, NO NUMBER Island WIP 6030	40 4

TRAMAINE US, female vocalist (2 WEEKS)

		pos/wks
5 Oct 85	FALL DOWN (SPIRIT OF LOVE) A & M AM 281	60 2

TRAMMPS US, male vocal group (55 WEEKS)

		pos/wks
23 Nov 74	ZING WENT THE STRINGS OF MY HEART Buddah BDS 405	29 10
1 Feb 75	SIXTY MINUTE MAN Buddah BDS 415	40 4
11 Oct 75 ●	HOLD BACK THE NIGHT Buddah BDS 437	5 8
13 Mar 76	THAT'S WHERE THE HAPPY PEOPLE GO Atlantic K 10703	35 8
24 Jul 76	SOUL SEARCHIN' TIME Atlantic K 10797	42 3
14 May 77	DISCO INFERNO Atlantic K 10914	16 7
24 Jun 78	DISCO INFERNO (re-issue) Atlantic K 11135	47 10
12 Dec 92	HOLD BACK THE NIGHT Network NWK 65 [1]	30 5

[1] KWS features guest vocal from the Trammps

TRANCESETTERS Holland, male production duo (1 WEEK)

		pos/wks
4 Mar 00	ROACHES Hooj Choons HOOJ 89CD	55 1

TRANS-X
Canada, female / male vocal / instrumental group (9 WEEKS)

		pos/wks
13 Jul 85 ●	LIVING ON VIDEO Boiling Point POSP 650	9 9

TRANSA UK, male DJ / production duo (2 WEEKS)

		pos/wks
30 Aug 97	PROPHASE Perfecto PERF 147CD	65 1
21 Feb 98	ENERVATE Perfecto PERF 155CD	42 1

TRANSATLANTIC SOUL
US, male producer - Roger Sanchez (1 WEEK)

		pos/wks
22 Mar 97	RELEASE YO SELF Deconstruction 74321459102	43 1

TRANSFORMER 2 Belgium / Holland, male / female vocal / instrumental group (1 WEEK)

		pos/wks
24 Feb 96	JUST CAN'T GET ENOUGH Positiva CDTIV 49	45 1

See also AIRSCAPE; BLUE BAMBOO; CUBIC 22

TRANSISTER
UK / US, male / female vocal / instrumental group (1 WEEK)

		pos/wks
28 Mar 98	LOOK WHO'S PERFECT NOW Virgin VSCDT 1678	56 1

TRANSVISION VAMP
UK, female / male vocal / instrumental group (59 WEEKS)

		pos/wks
16 Apr 88	TELL THAT GIRL TO SHUT UP MCA TVV 2	45 3
25 Jun 88 ●	I WANT YOUR LOVE MCA TVV 3	5 13
17 Sep 88	REVOLUTION BABY MCA TVV 4	30 5
19 Nov 88	SISTER MOON MCA TVV 5	41 5
1 Apr 89 ●	BABY I DON'T CARE MCA TVV 6	3 11
10 Jun 89	THE ONLY ONE MCA TVV 7	15 6
5 Aug 89	LANDSLIDE OF LOVE MCA TVV 8	14 5
4 Nov 89	BORN TO BE SOLD MCA TVV 9	22 4
13 Apr 91	(I JUST WANNA) B WITH U MCA TVV 10	30 4
22 Jun 91	IF LOOKS COULD KILL MCA TVV 11	41 3

TRASH UK, male vocal / instrumental group (3 WEEKS)

		pos/wks
25 Oct 69	GOLDEN SLUMBERS / CARRY THAT WEIGHT Apple 17	35 3

TRASH CAN SINATRAS
UK, male vocal / instrumental group (1 WEEK)

		pos/wks
24 Apr 93	HAYFEVER Go! Discs GODCD 98	61 1

UK No.1 ★   UK Top 10 ●   Still on chart +   UK million seller ◆   UK entry at No.1 ■   US No.1 ▲

TRAVEL France, male producer - Laurent Gutbier (2 WEEKS)

		pos/wks
24 Apr 99	BULGARIAN *Tidy Trax TIDY 121CD*	67 2

TRAVELING WILBURYS
UK / US, male vocal / instrumental group (19 WEEKS)

		pos/wks
29 Oct 88	HANDLE WITH CARE *Wilbury W 7732*	21 13
11 Mar 89	END OF THE LINE *Wilbury W 7637*	52 4
30 Jun 90	NOBODY'S CHILD *Wilbury W 9773*	44 2

TRAVIS *UK, male vocal / instrumental group (50 WEEKS)*

		pos/wks
12 Apr 97	U16 GIRLS *Independiente ISOM 1MS*	40 2
28 Jun 97	ALL I WANT TO DO IS ROCK *Independiente ISOM 3MS*	39 2
23 Aug 97	TIED TO THE 90'S *Independiente ISOM 5MS*	30 2
25 Oct 97	HAPPY *Independiente ISOM 6MS*	38 2
11 Apr 98	MORE THAN US (EP) *Independiente ISOM 11MS*	16 3
20 Mar 99	WRITING TO REACH YOU *Independiente ISOM 22MS*	14 5
29 May 99	DRIFTWOOD *Independiente ISOM 27MS*	13 5
14 Aug 99 ●	WHY DOES IT ALWAYS RAIN ON ME? *Independiente ISOM 33MS*	10 8
20 Nov 99 ●	TURN *Independiente ISOM 39MS*	8 11
17 Jun 00 ●	COMING AROUND *Independiente ISOM 45MS*	5 7
12 Aug 00	COMING AROUND (re-entry) *Independiente ISOM 45MS*	55 2
2 Sep 00	COMING AROUND (2nd re-entry) *Independiente ISOM 45MS*	75 1

Tracks on More Than Us (EP): More Than Us / Give Me Some Truth / All I Want to Do Is Rock / Funny Thing

Randy TRAVIS *US, male vocalist (6 WEEKS)*

		pos/wks
21 May 88	FOREVER AND EVER, AMEN *Warner Bros. W 8384*	55 6

John TRAVOLTA `339` `Top 500`
Ever popular actor / singer, b. 18 Feb 1954, New Jersey, US. His influential music-based movies include Saturday Night Fever, Urban Cowboy and Grease, whose retro 50s sound has timeless appeal. One of the few acts with two successive UK million sellers (90 WEEKS)

		pos/wks
20 May 78 ★	YOU'RE THE ONE THAT I WANT *RSO 006* [1] ◆ ▲	1 26
16 Sep 78 ●	SUMMER NIGHTS *RSO 18* [1] ◆	1 19
7 Oct 78 ●	SANDY *Polydor POSP 6*	2 15
2 Dec 78	GREASED LIGHTNIN' *Polydor POSP 14*	11 9
22 Dec 90 ●	THE GREASE MEGAMIX *Polydor PO 114* [1]	3 10
23 Mar 91	GREASE - THE DREAM MIX *PWL / Polydor PO 136* [2]	47 2
25 Jul 98 ●	YOU'RE THE ONE THAT I WANT (re-issue) *Polydor 0441332* [1]	4 9

[1] John Travolta and Olivia Newton-John [2] Frankie Valli, John Travolta and Olivia Newton-John

TREMELOES `68` `Top 500`
Early-1960s backing band who become late-1960s stars: Len "Chip" Hawkes (v/b), Rick West (g), Alan Blakely (g), Dave Munden (d). After supporting Brian Poole on his many hits, this Essex group went on to score even more in their own right. Hawkes is the father of 1991 chart-topper Chesney Hawkes (221 WEEKS)

		pos/wks
4 Jul 63 ●	TWIST AND SHOUT *Decca F 11694*	4 14
12 Sep 63 ★	DO YOU LOVE ME *Decca F 11739*	1 14
28 Nov 63	I CAN DANCE *Decca F 11771*	31 8
30 Jan 64 ●	CANDY MAN *Decca F 11823*	6 13
7 May 64 ●	SOMEONE SOMEONE *Decca F 11893*	2 17
20 Aug 64	TWELVE STEPS TO LOVE *Decca F 11951*	32 7
7 Jan 65	THREE BELLS *Decca F 12037*	17 9
22 Jul 65	I WANT CANDY *Decca F 12197*	25 8
2 Feb 67 ●	HERE COMES MY BABY *CBS 202519*	4 11
27 Apr 67 ★	SILENCE IS GOLDEN *CBS 2723*	1 15
2 Aug 67 ●	EVEN THE BAD TIMES ARE GOOD *CBS 2930*	4 13
8 Nov 67	BE MINE *CBS 3043*	39 2
17 Jan 68 ●	SUDDENLY YOU LOVE ME *CBS 3234*	6 11
8 May 68	HELULE HELULE *CBS 2889*	14 9
18 Sep 68 ●	MY LITTLE LADY *CBS 3680*	6 12
11 Dec 68	I SHALL BE RELEASED *CBS 3873*	29 5
19 Mar 69	HELLO WORLD *CBS 4065*	14 8
1 Nov 69 ●	(CALL ME) NUMBER ONE *CBS 4582*	2 14
21 Mar 70	BY THE WAY *CBS 4815*	35 6
12 Sep 70 ●	ME AND MY LIFE *CBS 5139*	4 18
10 Jul 71	HELLO BUDDY *CBS 7294*	32 7

See also Brian POOLE and the TREMELOES

Jackie TRENT *UK, female vocalist - Yvonne Burgess (17 WEEKS)*

		pos/wks
22 Apr 65 ★	WHERE ARE YOU NOW (MY LOVE) *Pye 7N 15776*	1 11
1 Jul 65	WHEN THE SUMMERTIME IS OVER *Pye 7N 15865*	39 2
2 Apr 69	I'LL BE THERE *Pye 7N 17693*	38 4

Ralph TRESVANT *US, male vocalist (21 WEEKS)*

		pos/wks
12 Jan 91	SENSITIVITY *MCA MCS 1462*	18 8
15 Aug 92 ●	THE BEST THINGS IN LIFE ARE FREE *Perspective PERSS 7400* [1]	2 13

[1] Luther Vandross and Janet Jackson with special guests BBD and Ralph Tresvant

TREVOR & SIMON *UK, male production duo (5 WEEKS)*

		pos/wks
10 Jun 00	HANDS UP *Substance SUBS 1CDS*	12 5

TRI *UK, male vocal / instrumental group (1 WEEK)*

		pos/wks
2 Sep 95	WE GOT THE LOVE *Epic 6623642*	61 1

TRIBAL HOUSE *US, male vocal / instrumental group (2 WEEKS)*

		pos/wks
3 Feb 90	MOTHERLAND-A-FRI-CA *Cooltempo COOL 198*	57 2

Tony TRIBE *Jamaica, male vocalist (2 WEEKS)*

		pos/wks
16 Jul 69	RED RED WINE *Downtown DT 419*	50 1
9 Aug 69	RED RED WINE (re-entry) *Downtown DT 419*	46 1

A TRIBE CALLED QUEST *US, male rap group (18 WEEKS)*

		pos/wks
18 Aug 90	BONITA APPLEBUM *Jive JIVE 256*	47 3
19 Jan 91	CAN I KICK IT *Jive JIVE 265*	15 7
11 Jun 94	OH MY GOD *Jive JIVECD 355*	68 1
13 Jul 96	1NCE AGAIN *Jive JIVECD 399*	34 2
23 Nov 96	STRESSED OUT *Jive JIVECD 404* [1]	33 2
23 Aug 97	THE JAM EP *Jive JIVECD 427*	61 1
29 Aug 98	FIND A WAY *Jive 0518982*	41 2

[1] A Tribe Called Quest featuring Faith Evans and Raphael Saadiq

Tracks on The Jam EP: Jam / Get a Hold / Mardi Gras at Midnight / Same Ol' Thing

TRIBE OF TOFFS *UK, male vocal / instrumental group (5 WEEKS)*

		pos/wks
24 Dec 88	JOHN KETTLEY (IS A WEATHERMAN) *Completely Different DAFT 1*	21 5

TRICKBABY *UK, female vocal / instrumental group (2 WEEKS)*

		pos/wks
12 Oct 96	INDIE-YARN *Logic 74321423152*	47 2

TRICKSTER *UK, male producer (3 WEEKS)*

		pos/wks
4 Apr 98	MOVE ON UP *AM:PM 5825812*	19 3

TRICKY
UK, male vocalist / multi-instrumentalist - Adrian Thaus (29 WEEKS)

		pos/wks
5 Feb 94	AFTERMATH *Fourth & Broadway BRCD 288*	69 1
28 Jan 95	OVERCOME *Fourth & Broadway BRCD 304*	34 3
15 Apr 95	BLACK STEEL *Fourth & Broadway BRCD 320*	28 3
5 Aug 95	THE HELL (EP) *Fourth & Broadway BRCD 326* [1]	12 3
11 Nov 95	PUMPKIN *Fourth & Broadway BRCD 330*	26 2
9 Nov 96	CHRISTIANSANDS *Fourth & Broadway BRCD 340*	36 2
23 Nov 96 ●	MILK *Mushroom D 1494* [2]	10 7
11 Jan 97	TRICKY KID *Fourth & Broadway BRCD 341*	28 2
18 Jan 97	MILK (re-entry) *Mushroom D 1494* [2]	74 1
3 May 97	MAKES ME WANNA DIE *Fourth & Broadway BRCD 348*	29 2
30 May 98	MONEY GREEDY / BROKEN HOMES *Island CID 701*	25 2

21 Aug 99   **FOR REAL** *Island CID 753* **45**   1

[1] Tricky vs the Gravediggaz [2] Garbage featuring Tricky

Tracks on The Hell (EP): Hell Is Round the Corner (original) / Hell Is Round the Corner (Hell and Water mix) / Psychosis / Tonite Is a Special Nite (Chaos mass confusion mix)

TRICKY DISCO *UK, male instrumental / production duo (10 WEEKS)* pos/wks

28 Jul 90	**TRICKY DISCO** *Warp WAP 7*	**14**	8
20 Apr 91	**HOUSE FLY** *Warp 7WAP 11*	**55**	2

GTO, Technohead and Tricky Disco are all the same act

See also GTO; TECHNOHEAD

TRIFFIDS *New Zealand, male vocal / instrumental group (1 WEEK)* pos/wks

6 Feb 88	**A TRICK OF THE LIGHT** *Island IS 350*	**73**	1

TRINA and TAMARA *US, female vocal duo (3 WEEKS)* pos/wks

7 Feb 98	**MY LOVE IS THE SHHH!** *Warner Bros W 0427CD* [1]	**64**	1
12 Jun 99	**WHAT'D YOU COME HERE FOR?** *Columbia 6673382*	**46**	2

[1] Somethin' for the People featuring Trina and Tamara

TRINIDAD OIL COMPANY
Trinidad, male / female vocal / instrumental group (5 WEEKS) pos/wks

21 May 77	**THE CALENDAR SONG** *Harvest HAR 5122*	**34**	5

TRINITY – See Julie DRISCOLL, Brian AUGER and the TRINITY

TRIO *Germany, male vocal / instrumental group (10 WEEKS)* pos/wks

3 Jul 82 ●	**DA DA DA** *Mobile Suit Corporation CORP 5*	**2**	10

TRIPLE X *Italy, male production duo (2 WEEKS)* pos/wks

30 Oct 99	**FEEL THE SAME** *Sound of Ministry MOSCDS 135*	**32**	2

TRIPPING DAISY *US, male vocal / instrumental group (1 WEEK)* pos/wks

30 Mar 96	**PIRANHA** *Island CID 638*	**72**	1

TRIUMPH *Canada, male vocal / instrumental group (2 WEEKS)* pos/wks

22 Nov 80	**I LIVE FOR THE WEEKEND** *RCA 13*	**59**	2

TROGGS (354 | **Top 500**) Earthy Sixties pop quartet fronted by Reg Presley (Ball) b. 12. Jun 1943, Hampshire, UK. 'Wild Thing' topped the US chart and sold more than five million worldwide. The Presley-penned 'Love Is All Around' had a 15-week stay at No.1 in 1994 for Wet Wet Wet (87 WEEKS) pos/wks

5 May 66 ●	**WILD THING** *Fontana TF 689* ▲	**2**	12
14 Jul 66 ★	**WITH A GIRL LIKE YOU** *Fontana TF 717*	**1**	12
29 Sep 66 ●	**I CAN'T CONTROL MYSELF** *Page One POF 001*	**2**	14
15 Dec 66 ●	**ANY WAY THAT YOU WANT ME** *Page One POF 010*	**8**	10
16 Feb 67	**GIVE IT TO ME** *Page One POF 015*	**12**	10
1 Jun 67	**NIGHT OF THE LONG GRASS** *Page One POF 022*	**17**	6
26 Jul 67	**HI HI HAZEL** *Page One POF 030*	**42**	3
18 Oct 67 ●	**LOVE IS ALL AROUND** *Page One POF 040*	**5**	14
28 Feb 68	**LITTLE GIRL** *Page One POF 056*	**37**	4
30 Oct 93	**WILD THING** *Weekend CDWEEK 103* [1]	**69**	2

[1] Troggs and Wolf

'Wild Thing' in 1993 is a re-recording and was listed with the flip side, 'War', by Edwin Starr and Shadow

TRONIKHOUSE *US, male producer - Kevin Saunderson (1 WEEK)* pos/wks

14 Mar 92	**UP TEMPO** *KMS UK KMSUK 1*	**68**	1

TROUBADOURS DU ROI BAUDOUIN
Zaire, male / female vocal group (11 WEEKS) pos/wks

19 Mar 69	**SANCTUS (MISSA LUBA)** *Philips BF 1732*	**28**	6
7 May 69	**SANCTUS (MISSA LUBA) (re-entry)** *Philips BF 1732*	**37**	5

TROUBLE FUNK *US, male vocal / instrumental group (3 WEEKS)* pos/wks

27 Jun 87	**WOMAN OF PRINCIPLE** *Fourth & Broadway BRW 70*	**65**	3

Roger TROUTMAN – See 2PAC

Doris TROY *US, female vocalist (12 WEEKS)* pos/wks

19 Nov 64	**WHATCHA GONNA DO ABOUT IT** *Atlantic AT 4011*	**37**	7
21 Jan 65	**WHATCHA GONNA DO ABOUT IT (re-entry)** *Atlantic AT 4011*	**38**	5

Elisabeth TROY – See SOUNDMAN and Don LLOYDIE with Elisabeth TROY; Y-TRIBE featuring Elisabeth TROY; MJ COLE

TRU FAITH & DUB CONSPIRACY
UK, male production groups (5 WEEKS) pos/wks

9 Sep 00	**FREAK LIKE ME** *Public Demand / Positiva CDTIV 138*	**12**	5

TRUBBLE *UK, female vocalist (5 WEEKS)* pos/wks

26 Dec 98	**DANCING BABY (OOGA-CHAKA)** *Island YYCD 1*	**21**	5

TRUCE *UK, female vocal group (6 WEEKS)* pos/wks

2 Sep 95	**THE FINEST** *Big Life BLRD 118*	**54**	1
30 Mar 96	**CELEBRATION OF LIFE** *Big Life BLRD 126*	**51**	1
29 Nov 97	**NOTHIN' BUT A PARTY** *Big Life BLRD 138*	**71**	1
5 Sep 98	**EYES DON'T LIE** *Big Life BLRD 146*	**20**	3

TRUCKIN' CO – See Garnet MIMMS and TRUCKIN' CO

Andrea TRUE CONNECTION *US, female vocalist, male instrumental backing group (16 WEEKS)* pos/wks

17 Apr 76 ●	**MORE MORE MORE** *Buddah BDS 442*	**5**	10
4 Mar 78	**WHAT'S YOUR NAME WHAT'S YOUR NUMBER** *Buddah BDS 467*	**34**	6

TRUE FAITH with FINAL CUT
US, male / female vocal / instrumental group (4 WEEKS) pos/wks

2 Mar 91	**TAKE ME AWAY** *Network NWK 20*	**51**	4

TRUE IMAGE – See Monie LOVE

TRUE PARTY *UK, male production / vocal group (5 WEEKS)* pos/wks

2 Dec 00	**WHAZZUP** *Positiva CDBUD 001*	**13**	5+

TRUE STEPPERS *UK, male production / instrumental duo - Jonny Linders and Andy Lysandrou (27 WEEKS)* pos/wks

29 Apr 00 ●	**BUGGIN'** *Nulife 74321753342* [1]	**6**	8
26 Aug 00 ●	**OUT OF YOUR MIND** *Nulife 74321782942* [2]	**2**	16
2 Dec 00	**TRUE STEP TONIGHT** *Nulife 74321811312* [3]	**25**	3

[1] True Steppers featuring Dane Bowers [2] True Steppers & Dane Bowers featuring Victoria Beckham [3] True Steppers featuring Brian Harvey & Donell Jones

Damon TRUEITT – See SOMORE featuring DAMON TRUEITT

TRUMAN & WOLFF featuring STEEL HORSES *UK, male production duo, and UK male rap group (1 WEEK)* pos/wks

22 Aug 98	**COME AGAIN** *Multiply CDMULTY 38*	**57**	1

TRUMPET MAN – See MONTANO vs THE TRUMPET MAN

TRUSSEL *US, male vocal / instrumental group (4 WEEKS)* pos/wks

8 Mar 80	**LOVE INJECTION** *Elektra K 12412*	**43**	4

TRUTH *UK, male vocal duo (6 WEEKS)* pos/wks

3 Feb 66	**GIRL** *Pye 7N 17035*	**27**	6

TRUTH UK, male vocal / instrumental group (16 WEEKS)
pos/wks

Date	Title	pos	wks
11 Jun 83	CONFUSION (HITS US EVERY TIME) Formation TRUTH 1	22	7
27 Aug 83	A STEP IN THE RIGHT DIRECTION Formation TRUTH 2	32	7
4 Feb 84	NO STONE UNTURNED Formation TRUTH 3	66	2

TSD UK, female vocal group (2 WEEKS)
pos/wks

Date	Title	pos	wks
17 Feb 96	HEART AND SOUL Avex UK AVEXCD 21	69	1
30 Mar 96	BABY I LOVE YOU Avex UK AVEXCD 34	64	1

Esera TUAOLO – See Richie RICH

TUBES US, male vocal / instrumental group (18 WEEKS)
pos/wks

Date	Title	pos	wks
19 Nov 77	WHITE PUNKS ON DOPE A & M AMS 7323	28	4
28 Apr 79	PRIME TIME A & M AMS 7423	34	10
12 Sep 81	DON'T WANT TO WAIT ANYMORE Capitol CL 208	60	4

TUBEWAY ARMY – See Gary NUMAN

Barbara TUCKER US, female vocalist (12 WEEKS)
pos/wks

Date	Title	pos	wks
5 Mar 94	BEAUTIFUL PEOPLE Positiva CDTIV 11	23	3
26 Nov 94	I GET LIFTED Positiva CDTIV 23	33	2
23 Sep 95	STAY TOGETHER Positiva CDTIV 39	46	1
8 Aug 98	EVERYBODY DANCE (THE HORN SONG) Positiva CDTIV 96	28	2
18 Mar 00	STOP PLAYING WITH MY MIND Positiva CDTIV 127 [1]	17	4

[1] Barbara Tucker featuring Darryl D'Bonneau

Junior TUCKER UK, male vocalist (2 WEEKS)
pos/wks

Date	Title	pos	wks
2 Jun 90	DON'T TEST 10 TEN 299	54	2

Louise TUCKER UK, female vocalist (5 WEEKS)
pos/wks

Date	Title	pos	wks
9 Apr 83	MIDNIGHT BLUE Ariola ARO 289	59	5

Tommy TUCKER US, male vocalist (10 WEEKS)
pos/wks

Date	Title	pos	wks
26 Mar 64	HI-HEEL SNEAKERS Pye 7N 25238	23	10

TUFF JAM UK, male production duo (1 WEEK)
pos/wks

Date	Title	pos	wks
10 Oct 98	NEED GOOD LOVE Locked On LOX 99CD	44	1

Ike and Tina TURNER
US, male / female vocal instrumental duo (44 WEEKS)
pos/wks

Date	Title	pos	wks
9 Jun 66 ●	RIVER DEEP MOUNTAIN HIGH London HL 10046	3	13
28 Jul 66	TELL HER I'M NOT HOME Warner Bros. WB 5753	48	1
27 Oct 66	A LOVE LIKE YOURS London HL 10083	16	10
12 Feb 69	RIVER DEEP MOUNTAIN HIGH (re-issue) London HLU 10242	33	7
8 Sep 73 ●	NUTBUSH CITY LIMITS United Artists UP 35582	4	13

See also Tina TURNER

Ruby TURNER UK, female vocalist (31 WEEKS)
pos/wks

Date	Title	pos	wks
25 Jan 86	IF YOU'RE READY (COME GO WITH ME) Jive JIVE 109 [1]	30	7
29 Mar 86	I'M IN LOVE Jive JIVE 118	61	4
13 Sep 86	BYE BABY Jive JIVE 126	52	3
14 Mar 87	I'D RATHER GO BLIND Jive RTS 1	24	8
16 May 87	I'M IN LOVE (re-issue) Jive RTS 2	57	2
13 Jan 90	IT'S GONNA BE ALRIGHT Jive RTS 7	57	3
5 Feb 94	STAY WITH ME BABY M & G MAGCD 53	39	3
9 Dec 95	SHAKABOOM! Telstar HUNTCD 1 [2]	64	1

[1] Ruby Turner featuring Jonathan Butler [2] Hunter featuring Ruby Turner

Sammy TURNER US, male vocalist (2 WEEKS)
pos/wks

Date	Title	pos	wks
13 Nov 59	ALWAYS London HLX 8963	26	2

Tina TURNER [64] Top 500
Supreme soul singer-cum-rock legend, b. Anna Mae Bullock, 26 Nov 1939, Tennessee, US. After a successful, if stormy, partnership with husband Ike, she reached greater heights as a Grammy-winning soloist (224 WEEKS)
pos/wks

Date	Title	pos	wks
19 Nov 83 ●	LET'S STAY TOGETHER Capitol CL 316	6	13
25 Feb 84	HELP Capitol CL 325	40	6
16 Jun 84 ●	WHAT'S LOVE GOT TO DO WITH IT Capitol CL 334 ▲	3	16
15 Sep 84	BETTER BE GOOD TO ME Capitol CL 338	45	5
17 Nov 84	PRIVATE DANCER Capitol CL 343	26	9
2 Mar 85	I CAN'T STAND THE RAIN Capitol CL 352	57	3
20 Jul 85 ●	WE DON'T NEED ANOTHER HERO (THUNDERDOME) Capitol CL 364	3	12
12 Oct 85	ONE OF THE LIVING Capitol CL 376	55	2
2 Nov 85	IT'S ONLY LOVE A & M AM 285 [1]	29	6
23 Aug 86	TYPICAL MALE Capitol CL 419	33	6
8 Nov 86	TWO PEOPLE Capitol CL 430	43	4
14 Mar 87	WHAT YOU GET IS WHAT YOU SEE Capitol CL 439	30	7
13 Jun 87	BREAK EVERY RULE Capitol CL 452	43	3
20 Jun 87	TEARING US APART Duck W 8299 [2]	56	3
19 Mar 88	ADDICTED TO LOVE (LIVE) Capitol CL 484	71	2
2 Sep 89 ●	THE BEST Capitol CL 543	5	12
18 Nov 89 ●	I DON'T WANNA LOSE YOU Capitol CL 553	8	11
17 Feb 90	STEAMY WINDOWS Capitol CL 560	13	6
11 Aug 90	LOOK ME IN THE HEART Capitol CL 584	31	6
13 Oct 90	BE TENDER WITH ME BABY Capitol CL 593	28	4
24 Nov 90 ●	IT TAKES TWO Warner Bros. ROD 1 [3]	5	8
21 Sep 91	NUTBUSH CITY LIMITS (re-recording) Capitol CL 630	23	5
23 Nov 91	WAY OF THE WORLD Capitol CL 637	13	7
15 Feb 92	LOVE THING Capitol CL 644	29	4
6 Jun 92	I WANT YOU NEAR ME Capitol CL 659	22	4
22 May 93 ●	I DON'T WANNA FIGHT Parlophone CDRS 6346	7	9
28 Aug 93	DISCO INFERNO Parlophone CDR 6357	12	6
30 Oct 93	WHY MUST WE WAIT UNTIL TONIGHT Parlophone CDR 6366	14	4
18 Nov 95 ●	GOLDENEYE Parlophone CDR 0071001	10	9
23 Mar 96	WHATEVER YOU WANT Parlophone CDR 6429	23	6
8 Jun 96	ON SILENT WINGS Parlophone CDR 6434	13	6
27 Jul 96	MISSING YOU Parlophone CDR 6441 [4]	12	5
19 Oct 96	SOMETHING BEAUTIFUL REMAINS Parlophone CDR 6448	27	2
21 Dec 96	IN YOUR WILDEST DREAMS Parlophone CDR 6451 [5]	32	2
30 Oct 99 ●	WHEN THE HEARTACHE IS OVER Parlophone CDR 6529 [4]	10	7
12 Feb 00	WHATEVER YOU NEED Parlophone CDR 6532	27	3

[1] Bryan Adams and Tina Turner [2] Eric Clapton and Tina Turner [3] Rod Stewart and Tina Turner [4] Tina [5] Tina Turner featuring Barry White

See also Ike and Tina TURNER

TURNTABLE ORCHESTRA
US, male vocal / instrumental duo (4 WEEKS)
pos/wks

Date	Title	pos	wks
21 Jan 89	YOU'RE GONNA MISS ME Republic LIC 012	52	4

TURTLES US, male vocal / instrumental group (39 WEEKS)
pos/wks

Date	Title	pos	wks
23 Mar 67	HAPPY TOGETHER London HL 10115 ▲	12	12
15 Jun 67 ●	SHE'D RATHER BE WITH ME London HLU 10135	4	15
30 Oct 68 ●	ELENORE London HL 10223	7	12

TUXEDOS – See Bobby ANGELO and the TUXEDOS

T.W.A. UK, male instrumental / production group (1 WEEK)
pos/wks

Date	Title	pos	wks
16 Sep 95	NASTY GIRLS Mercury MERCD 441	51	1

Shania TWAIN [471] Top 500
Pop and country music queen, b. Eileen Regina Edwards 28 Aug 1965, Ontario, Canada. Self-penned 'Come On Over' album sold more than 30 million, including two million in UK and record-breaking 17 million in US. Her tours in 1999 grossed $36.6 million. (72 WEEKS)
pos/wks

Date	Title	pos	wks
28 Feb 98 ●	YOU'RE STILL THE ONE Mercury 5684932	10	10
13 Jun 98	WHEN Mercury 5661192	18	4
28 Nov 98 ●	FROM THIS MOMENT ON Mercury 5665632	9	8
22 May 99 ●	THAT DON'T IMPRESS ME MUCH Mercury 8708032	3	21
2 Oct 99 ●	MAN! I FEEL LIKE A WOMAN! Mercury 5623242	3	18

		pos/wks
26 Feb 00 ●	**DON'T BE STUPID (YOU KNOW I LOVE YOU)** *Mercury 1721492*	5 9
13 May 00	**DON'T BE STUPID (YOU KNOW I LOVE YOU) (re-entry)** *Mercury 1721492*	60 2

TWEENIES UK, male / female kiddie TV characters (8 WEEKS)
		pos/wks
11 Nov 00 ●	**NUMBER 1** *BBC Music WMSS 60332*	5 8+

TWEETS UK, male feathered vocal / instrumental group (34 WEEKS)
		pos/wks
12 Sep 81 ●	**THE BIRDIE SONG (BIRDIE DANCE)** *PRT 7P 219*	2 23
5 Dec 81	**LET'S ALL SING LIKE THE BIRDIES SING** *PRT 7P 226*	44 6
18 Dec 82	**THE BIRDIE SONG (BIRDIE DANCE) (re-entry)** *PRT 7P 219*	46 5

20 FINGERS US, male instrumental / production duo (14 WEEKS)
		pos/wks
26 Nov 94	**SHORT DICK MAN** *Multiply CDMULT 12* [1]	21 4
30 Sep 95	**LICK IT** *Zyx ZYX 75908* [2]	48 3
30 Sep 95	**SHORT SHORT MAN (re-mix)** *Multiply CXMULTY 7* [1]	11 7

[1] 20 Fingers featuring Gillette [2] 20 Fingers featuring Roula

21ST CENTURY GIRLS
UK, female vocal / instrumental group (4 WEEKS)
		pos/wks
12 Jun 99	**21ST CENTURY GIRLS** *EMI NTNCDS 001*	16 4

TWENTY 4 SEVEN Featuring CAPTAIN HOLLYWOOD
US / Germany, male / female vocal / instrumental group (20 WEEKS)
		pos/wks
22 Sep 90 ●	**I CAN'T STAND IT** *BCM BCMR 395*	7 10
24 Nov 90	**ARE YOU DREAMING** *BCM BCM 07504*	17 10

See also CAPTAIN HOLLYWOOD PROJECT

TWICE AS MUCH UK, male vocal duo (9 WEEKS)
		pos/wks
16 Jun 66	**SITTIN' ON A FENCE** *Immediate IM 033*	25 9

TWIGGY UK, female vocalist (10 WEEKS)
		pos/wks
14 Aug 76	**HERE I GO AGAIN** *Mercury 6007 100*	17 10

TWILIGHT – See Roger SANCHEZ

TWIN HYPE US, male rap duo (2 WEEKS)
		pos/wks
15 Jul 89	**DO IT TO THE CROWD** *Profile PROF 255*	65 2

TWINKLE UK, female vocalist - Lynn Ripley (20 WEEKS)
		pos/wks
26 Nov 64 ●	**TERRY** *Decca F 12013*	4 15
25 Feb 65	**GOLDEN LIGHTS** *Decca F 12076*	21 5

TWISTED SISTER
US, male vocal / instrumental group (28 WEEKS)
		pos/wks
26 Mar 83	**I AM (I'M ME)** *Atlantic A 9854*	18 9
28 May 83	**THE KIDS ARE BACK** *Atlantic A 9827*	32 6
20 Aug 83	**YOU CAN'T STOP ROCK 'N' ROLL** *Atlantic A 9792*	43 4
2 Jun 84	**WE'RE NOT GONNA TAKE IT** *Atlantic A 9657*	58 6
18 Jan 86	**LEADER OF THE PACK** *Atlantic A 9478*	47 3

Conway TWITTY US, male vocalist - Harold Jenkins (36 WEEKS)
		pos/wks
14 Nov 58 ★	**IT'S ONLY MAKE BELIEVE** *MGM 992* ▲	1 15
27 Mar 59	**STORY OF MY LOVE** *MGM 1003*	30 1
21 Aug 59 ●	**MONA LISA** *MGM 1029*	5 14
21 Jul 60	**IS A BLUE BIRD BLUE** *MGM 1082*	43 3
23 Feb 61	**C'EST SI BON** *MGM 1118*	40 3

2 BAD MICE UK, male instrumental / production group (4 WEEKS)
		pos/wks
15 Feb 92	**HOLD IT DOWN** *Moving Shadow SHADOW 14*	70 1
8 Aug 92	**HOLD IT DOWN (re-entry)** *Moving Shadow SHADOW 14*	48 2
7 Sep 96	**BOMBSCARE** *Arista 74321397662*	46 1

TWO COWBOYS Italy, male instrumental / production duo Roberto Sagotto and Maurizio Braccagni (11 WEEKS)
		pos/wks
9 Jul 94 ●	**EVERYBODY GONFI-GON** *3 Beat TABCD 221*	7 11

2 EIVISSA Germany, female vocal duo (6 WEEKS)
		pos/wks
4 Oct 97	**OH LA LA LA** *Club Tools 0063475 CLU*	13 6

2 FOR JOY UK, male instrumental / production duo (3 WEEKS)
		pos/wks
1 Dec 90	**IN A STATE** *Mercury MER 333*	61 1
9 Nov 91	**LET THE BASS KICK** *All Around the World GLOBE 102*	67 2

2 FUNKY 2 starring Kathryn DION
UK, male / female vocal / instrumental group (4 WEEKS)
		pos/wks
6 Nov 93	**BROTHERS AND SISTERS** *Logic 74321170772*	56 2
30 Nov 96	**BROTHERS AND SISTERS (re-mix)** *All Around the World CDGLOBE 138*	36 2

2 HOUSE US, male instrumental / production duo (1 WEEK)
		pos/wks
21 Mar 92	**GO TECHNO** *Atlantic A 7519*	65 1

2 IN A ROOM
US, male vocal duo - Roger Pauletta & Rafael Vargas (15 WEEKS)
		pos/wks
18 Nov 89	**SOMEBODY IN THE HOUSE SAY YEAH!** *Big Life BLR 12*	66 1
26 Jan 91 ●	**WIGGLE IT** *SBK SBK 19*	3 8
6 Apr 91	**SHE'S GOT ME GOING CRAZY** *SBK SBK 23*	54 2
22 Oct 94	**EL TRAGO (THE DRINK)** *Positiva CDTIV 18*	34 2
8 Apr 95	**AHORA ES (NOW IS THE TIME)** *Positiva CDTIV 32*	43 1
17 Aug 96	**GIDDY-UP** *Encore CDCOR 008*	74 1

2 IN A TENT UK, male instrumental / production duo (7 WEEKS)
		pos/wks
17 Dec 94	**WHEN I'M CLEANING WINDOWS (TURNED OUT NICE AGAIN)** *Love This SPONCD 1*	25 5
13 May 95	**BOOGIE WOOGIE BUGLE BOY (DON'T STOP)** *Bald Cat BALDCD 1* [1]	48 1
6 Jan 96	**WHEN I'M CLEANING WINDOWS (TURNED OUT NICE AGAIN) (re-entry)** *Love This SPONCD 1*	62 1

[1] 2 In a Tank

First hit features the vocals of George Formby

2 MAD UK, male vocal / instrumental duo (4 WEEKS)
		pos/wks
9 Feb 91	**THINKING ABOUT YOUR BODY** *Big Life BLR 37*	43 4

TWO MAN SOUND
Belgium, male vocal / instrumental group (7 WEEKS)
		pos/wks
20 Jan 79	**QUE TAL AMERICA** *Miracle M 1*	46 7

TWO MEN, A DRUM MACHINE AND A TRUMPET
UK, male instrumental duo (17 WEEKS)
		pos/wks
9 Jan 88	**I'M TIRED OF GETTING PUSHED AROUND** *London LON 141*	18 8
25 Jun 88	**HEAT IT UP** *Jive JIVE 174* [1]	21 9

[1] Wee Papa Girl Rappers featuring Two Men and a Drum Machine

TWO NATIONS UK, male vocal / instrumental group (1 WEEK)
		pos/wks
20 Jun 87	**THAT'S THE WAY IT FEELS** *10 TEN 168*	74 1

TWO PEOPLE UK, male vocal / instrumental group (2 WEEKS)
		pos/wks
31 Jan 87	**HEAVEN** *Polydor POSP 844*	63 2

2WO THIRD3 UK, male vocal / instrumental group (15 WEEKS)
		pos/wks
19 Feb 94	**HEAR ME CALLING** *Epic 6600642*	48 3
11 Jun 94	**EASE THE PRESSURE** *Epic 6604782*	45 2
8 Oct 94	**I WANT THE WORLD** *Epic 6608542*	20 5
17 Dec 94	**I WANT TO BE ALONE** *Epic 6610852*	29 5

2-4 FAMILY
UK / US / Korea, male / female rap / vocal group (1 WEEK) pos/wks

29 May 99	**LEAN ON ME (WITH THE FAMILY)** *Epic 6670132* **69**	1

2 UNLIMITED 〔247 Top 500〕 *The brainchild of Jean-Paul de Coster and Phil Wilde, fronted by the minimalist vocals / chants / raps of Dutch duo Ray Slijngaard and Anita Dels. Their youth-aimed, infectious dance tracks sold millions around Europe and gave them 11 successive UK Top 20 hits (112 WEEKS)* pos/wks

5 Oct 91	● **GET READY FOR THIS** *PWL Continental PWL 206* **2**	15
25 Jan 92	● **TWILIGHT ZONE** *PWL Continental PWL 211* **2**	10
2 May 92	● **WORKAHOLIC** *PWL Continental PWL 228* **4**	7
15 Aug 92	**THE MAGIC FRIEND** *PWL Continental PWL 240* **11**	7
30 Jan 93	★ **NO LIMIT** *PWL Continental PWCD 256* **1**	16
8 May 93	● **TRIBAL DANCE** *PWL Continental PWCD 262* **4**	11
4 Sep 93	● **FACES** *PWL Continental PWCD 268* **8**	7
20 Nov 93	**MAXIMUM OVERDRIVE** *PWL Continental PWCD 276* **15**	8
19 Feb 94	● **LET THE BEAT CONTROL YOUR BODY** *PWL Continental PWCD 280* **6**	9
21 May 94	● **THE REAL THING** *PWL Continental PWCD 306* **6**	7
1 Oct 94	● **NO ONE** *PWL Continental PWCD 314* **17**	6
25 Mar 95	**HERE I GO** *PWL Continental PWCD 317* **22**	3
21 Oct 95	**DO WHAT'S GOOD FOR ME** *PWL Continental PWL 322CD1* **16**	4
11 Jul 98	**WANNA GET UP** *Big Life BLRD 143* **38**	2

In 1995 both Ray Slijngaard and Anita Dels left the act which was fronted by a Dutch female duo for 'Wanna Get Up'

2K *UK, male production duo (2 WEEKS)* pos/wks

25 Oct 97	***K THE MILLENNIUM** *Blast First BFFP 146CDK* **28**	2

See also KLF; TIMELORDS; JUSTIFIED ANCIENTS OF MU MU; 1300 DRUMS featuring the UNJUSTIFIED ANCIENTS OF MU

2PAC *US, male rapper - Tupac Shakur (52 WEEKS)* pos/wks

13 Apr 96	● **CALIFORNIA LOVE** *Death Row DRWCD 3* [1] ▲ **6**	8
27 Jul 96	**HOW DO YOU WANT IT** *Death Row DRWCD 4* [2] **17**	4
30 Nov 96	**I AIN'T MAD AT CHA** *Death Row DRWCD 5* [2] **13**	9
26 Apr 97	**WANTED DEAD OR ALIVE** *Def Jam 5744052* [3] **16**	3
10 Jan 98	**I WONDER IF HEAVEN GOT A GHETTO** *Jive JIVECD 446* **21**	4
13 Jun 98	**DO FOR LOVE** *Jive 0518512* [4] **12**	4
18 Jul 98	**RUNNIN'** *Black Jam BJAM 9005* [5] **15**	3
28 Nov 98	**HAPPY HOME** *Eagle EAGXS 058* **17**	2
20 Feb 99	**CHANGES** *Jive 0522832* **3**	12
3 Jul 99	**DEAR MAMA** *Jive 0523702* **27**	3

[1] 2Pac featuring Dr Dre [2] 2Pac featuring K-Ci and JoJo [3] 2Pac and Snoop Doggy Dogg [4] 2Pac featuring Eric Williams [5] 2Pac and Notorious B.I.G.

See also MAKAVELI

TYGERS OF PAN TANG
UK, male vocal / instrumental group (15 WEEKS) pos/wks

14 Feb 81	**HELLBOUND** *MCA 672* **48**	3
27 Mar 82	**LOVE POTION NO. 9** *MCA 769* **45**	6
10 Jul 82	**RENDEZVOUS** *MCA 777* **49**	4
11 Sep 82	**PARIS BY AIR** *MCA 790* **63**	2

Bonnie TYLER 〔398 Top 500〕 *Raspy-voiced vocalist b. Gaynor Hopkins, 8 Jun 1953, Swansea, Wales. Made US country Top 10 with 'It's A Heartache', and 'Total Eclipse of the Heart' was the first record by a Welsh artist to top the US pop chart (81 WEEKS)* pos/wks

30 Oct 76	● **LOST IN FRANCE** *RCA 2734* **9**	10
19 Mar 77	**MORE THAN A LOVER** *RCA PB 5008* **27**	6
3 Dec 77	● **IT'S A HEARTACHE** *RCA PB 5057* **4**	12
30 Jun 79	**MARRIED MEN** *RCA PB 5164* **35**	6
19 Feb 83	★ **TOTAL ECLIPSE OF THE HEART** *CBS TYLER 1* ▲ **1**	12
7 May 83	**FASTER THAN THE SPEED OF NIGHT** *CBS A 3338* **43**	4
25 Jun 83	**HAVE YOU EVER SEEN THE RAIN** *CBS A 3517* **47**	3
7 Jan 84	● **A ROCKIN' GOOD WAY** *Epic A 4071* [1] **5**	9
31 Aug 85	● **HOLDING OUT FOR A HERO** *CBS A 4251* **2**	13

14 Dec 85	**LOVING YOU'S A DIRTY JOB BUT SOMEBODY'S GOTTA DO IT** *CBS A 6662* [2] **73**	2
28 Dec 91	**HOLDING OUT FOR A HERO (re-issue)** *Total TYLER 10* **69**	2
27 Jan 96	**MAKING LOVE (OUT OF NOTHING AT ALL)** *East West EW 010CD* **45**	2

[1] Shaky and Bonnie (Bonnie Tyler) [2] Bonnie Tyler, guest vocals Todd Rundgren

TYMES *US, male vocal group. Lead vocal George Williams (41 WEEKS)* pos/wks

25 Jul 63	**SO MUCH IN LOVE** *Cameo Parkway P 871* ▲ **21**	8
15 Jan 69	**PEOPLE** *Direction 58 3903* **16**	10
21 Sep 74	**YOU LITTLE TRUSTMAKER** *RCA 2456* **18**	9
21 Dec 74	★ **MS GRACE** *RCA 2493* **1**	11
17 Jan 76	**GOD'S GONNA PUNISH YOU** *RCA 2626* **41**	3

TYPICALLY TROPICAL *UK, male vocal / instrumental duo - Jeff Calvert and Max West (11 WEEKS)* pos/wks

5 Jul 75	★ **BARBADOS** *Gull GULS 14* **1**	11

TYREE *US, male producer (10 WEEKS)* pos/wks

25 Feb 89	**TURN UP THE BASS** *ffrr FFR 24* [1] **12**	7
6 May 89	**HARDCORE HIP HOUSE** *DJ International DJIN 11* **70**	2
2 Dec 89	**MOVE YOUR BODY** *CBS 655470 7* [2] **72**	1

[1] Tyree featuring Kool Rock Steady [2] Tyree featuring JMD

TYRESE *US, male vocalist (2 WEEKS)* pos/wks

31 Jul 99	**NOBODY ELSE** *RCA 74321688282* **59**	1
25 Sep 99	**SWEET LADY** *RCA 74321700842* **55**	1

TYRREL CORPORATION
UK, male vocal / instrumental duo (9 WEEKS) pos/wks

14 Mar 92	**THE BOTTLE** *Volante TYR 1* **71**	1
15 Aug 92	**GOING HOME** *Volante TYR 2* **58**	2
10 Oct 92	**WAKING WITH A STRANGER / ONE DAY** *Volante TYRS 3* **59**	1
24 Sep 94	**YOU'RE NOT HERE** *Cooltempo CDCOOL 292* **42**	2
14 Jan 95	**BETTER DAYS AHEAD** *Cooltempo CDCOOL 303* **29**	3

TZANT *UK, male rap / instrumental duo (10 WEEKS)* pos/wks

7 Sep 96	**HOT AND WET (BELIEVE IT)** *Logic 74321376832* **36**	2
25 Apr 98	**SOUNDS OF WICKEDNESS** *Logic 74321568842* **11**	6
22 Aug 98	**BOUNCE WITH THE MASSIVE** *Logic 74321602102* **39**	2

Judie TZUKE *UK, female vocalist (10 WEEKS)* pos/wks

14 Jul 79	**STAY WITH ME TILL DAWN** *Rocket XPRES 17* **16**	10

UB40 〔21 Top 500〕 *Reggae's most successful transatlantic group: includes brothers Ali (v/g) and Robin (v/g) Campbell, and Earl Falconer (b). Only three groups can claim more chart hits than this act, named after the number of the UK unemployment benefit form (328 WEEKS)* pos/wks

8 Mar 80	● **KING / FOOD FOR THOUGHT** *Graduate GRAD 6* **4**	13
14 Jun 80	● **MY WAY OF THINKING / I THINK IT'S GOING TO RAIN TODAY** *Graduate GRAD 8* **6**	10
1 Nov 80	● **THE EARTH DIES SCREAMING / DREAM A LIE** *Graduate GRAD 10* **10**	12
23 May 81	**DON'T LET IT PASS YOU BY / DON'T SLOW DOWN** *DEP International DEP 1* **16**	9
8 Aug 81	● **ONE IN TEN** *DEP International DEP 2* **7**	10
13 Feb 82	**I WON'T CLOSE MY EYES** *DEP International DEP 3* **32**	6
15 May 82	**LOVE IS ALL IS ALRIGHT** *DEP International DEP 4* **29**	7
28 Aug 82	**SO HERE I AM** *DEP International DEP 5* **25**	9

UBM *Germany, male / female vocal / instrumental group (1 WEEK)* pos/wks

UCC – See URBAN COOKIE COLLECTIVE

UFO *UK / Germany, male vocal / instrumental group (31 WEEKS)* pos/wks

U4EA featuring BERRI – See NEW ATLANTIC

UGLY KID JOE *US, male vocal / instrumental group (28 WEEKS)* pos/wks

UHF *US, male instrumental / production group (4 WEEKS)* pos/wks

UK *UK, male vocal / instrumental group (2 WEEKS)* pos/wks

UK *Canada / Spain, male vocal / instrumental group (1 WEEK)* pos/wks

UK APACHI with SHY FX *UK, male vocal / instrumental duo (3 WEEKS)* pos/wks

UK MIXMASTERS *UK, male producer - Nigel Wright (15 WEEKS)* pos/wks

UK PLAYERS *UK, male vocal / instrumental group (3 WEEKS)* pos/wks

UK SUBS *UK, male vocal / instrumental group (39 WEEKS)* pos/wks

Tracks on She's Not There / Kicks (EP): She's Not There / Kicks / Victim / The Same Thing

Tracey ULLMAN *UK, female vocalist (49 WEEKS)* pos/wks

ULTIMATE KAOS *UK, male vocal group (28 WEEKS)* pos/wks

ULTRA *UK, male vocal / instrumental group (22 WEEKS)* pos/wks

ULTRA HIGH *UK, male vocalist - Michael McCloud (3 WEEKS)* pos/wks

ULTRACYNIC *UK, male / female vocal / instrumental group (3 WEEKS)* pos/wks

ULTRAMARINE UK, male instrumental duo (4 WEEKS)

		pos/wks
24 Jul 93	**KINGDOM** *Blanco Y Negro NEG 65CD* **46** 2
29 Jan 94	**BAREFOOT (EP)** *Blanco Y Negro NEG 67CD* **61** 1
27 Apr 96	**HYMN** *Blanco Y Negro NEG 87CD* [1] **65** 1

[1] Ultramarine featuring David McAlmont

Tracks on Barefoot (EP): Hooter / The Badger / Urf / Happy Land

ULTRA-SONIC UK, male instrumental / production duo (2 WEEKS)

		pos/wks
3 Sep 94	**OBSESSION** *Clubscene DCSRT 027* **75** 1
21 Sep 96	**DO YOU BELIEVE IN LOVE** *Clubscene DCSRT 070* **47** 1

ULTRASOUND
UK, male / female vocal / instrumental group (5 WEEKS)

		pos/wks
7 Mar 98	**BEST WISHES** *Nude NUD 33CD* **68** 1
13 Jun 98	**STAY YOUNG** *Nude NUD 35CD1* **30** 2
10 Apr 99	**FLOODLIT WORLD** *Nude NUD 41CD1* **39** 2

ULTRAVOX `169` `Top 500` *Groundbreaking British electro-rock quartet: Midge Ure (v/g) (replaced John Foxx in 1979), Billy Currie (k/syn), Chris Cross (b/syn), Warren Cann (d). Ex-Slik and Visage vocalist Ure was a driving force behind Band Aid hits, Live Aid and Nelson Mandela birthday concerts (142 WEEKS)*

		pos/wks
5 Jul 80	**SLEEPWALK** *Chrysalis CHS 2441* **29** 11
18 Oct 80	**PASSING STRANGERS** *Chrysalis CHS 2457* **57** 4
17 Jan 81 ●	**VIENNA** *Chrysalis CHS 2481* **2** 14
28 Mar 81	**SLOW MOTION** *Island WIP 6691* **33** 4
6 Jun 81 ●	**ALL STOOD STILL** *Chrysalis CHS 2522* **8** 10
22 Aug 81	**THE THIN WALL** *Chrysalis CHS 2540* **14** 8
7 Nov 81	**THE VOICE** *Chrysalis CHS 2559* **16** 12
25 Sep 82	**REAP THE WILD WIND** *Chrysalis CHS 2639* **12** 9
27 Nov 82	**HYMN** *Chrysalis CHS 2657* **11** 11
19 Mar 83	**VISIONS IN BLUE** *Chrysalis CHS 2676* **15** 6
4 Jun 83	**WE CAME TO DANCE** *Chrysalis VOX 1* **18** 7
11 Feb 84	**ONE SMALL DAY** *Chrysalis VOX 2* **27** 6
19 May 84 ●	**DANCING WITH TEARS IN MY EYES** *Chrysalis UV 1* **3** 10
7 Jul 84	**LAMENT** *Chrysalis UV 2* **22** 6
4 Aug 84	**DANCING WITH TEARS IN MY EYES (re-entry)** *Chrysalis UV 1* **74** 1
25 Aug 84	**LAMENT (re-entry)** *Chrysalis UV 2* **73** 1
20 Oct 84	**LOVE'S GREAT ADVENTURE** *Chrysalis UV 3* **12** 9
27 Sep 86	**SAME OLD STORY** *Chrysalis UV 4* **31** 4
22 Nov 86	**ALL FALL DOWN** *Chrysalis UV 5* **30** 5
6 Feb 93	**VIENNA (re-issue)** *Chrysalis CDCHSS 3936* **13** 4

UMBOZA UK, male instrumental / production duo (9 WEEKS)

		pos/wks
23 Sep 95	**CRY INDIA** *Positiva CDTIV 43* **19** 4
20 Jul 96	**SUNSHINE** *Positiva CDTIV 47* **14** 5

Piero UMILIANI Italy, orchestra and chorus (8 WEEKS)

		pos/wks
30 Apr 77 ●	**MAH NA MAH NA** *EMI International INT 530* **8** 8

UNATION UK, male / female vocal / instrumental group (3 WEEKS)

		pos/wks
5 Jun 93	**HIGHER AND HIGHER** *MCA MCSTD 1773* **42** 2
7 Aug 93	**DO YOU BELIEVE IN LOVE** *MCA MCSTD 1796* **75** 1

UNBELIEVABLE TRUTH
UK, male vocal / instrumental group (5 WEEKS)

		pos/wks
14 Feb 98	**HIGHER THAN REASON** *Virgin VSCDT 1676* **38** 2
9 May 98	**SOLVED** *Virgin VSCDT 1684* **39** 2
18 Jul 98	**SETTLE DOWN / DUNE SEA** *Virgin VSCDT 1697* **46** 1

UNCANNY ALLIANCE
US, male / female vocal / instrumental duo (5 WEEKS)

		pos/wks
19 Dec 92	**I GOT MY EDUCATION** *A & M AM 0128* **39** 5

UNCLE SAM US, male vocalist (2 WEEKS)

		pos/wks
16 May 98	**I DON'T EVER WANT TO SEE YOU AGAIN** *Epic 6656382* **30** 2

UNDERCOVER UK, male vocal / instrumental group (29 WEEKS)

		pos/wks
15 Aug 92 ●	**BAKER STREET** *PWL International PWL 239* **2** 14
14 Nov 92 ●	**NEVER LET HER SLIP AWAY** *PWL International PWL 255* **5** 11
6 Feb 93	**I WANNA STAY WITH YOU** *PWL International PWCD 258* **28** 3
14 Aug 93	**LOVESICK** *PWL International PWCD 271* [1] **62** 1

[1] Undercover featuring John Matthews

UNDERTAKERS UK, male vocal / instrumental group (1 WEEK)

		pos/wks
9 Apr 64	**JUST A LITTLE BIT** *Pye 7N 15607* **49** 1

UNDERTONES Ireland, male vocal / instrumental group (67 WEEKS)

		pos/wks
21 Oct 78	**TEENAGE KICKS** *Sire SIR 4007* **31** 6
3 Feb 79	**GET OVER YOU** *Sire SIR 4010* **57** 4
28 Apr 79	**JIMMY JIMMY** *Sire SIR 4015* **16** 10
21 Jul 79	**HERE COMES THE SUMMER** *Sire SIR 4022* **34** 6
20 Oct 79	**YOU'VE GOT MY NUMBER (WHY DON'T YOU USE IT?)** *Sire SIR 4024* **32** 6
5 Apr 80 ●	**MY PERFECT COUSIN** *Sire SIR 4038* **9** 10
5 Jul 80	**WEDNESDAY WEEK** *Sire SIR 4042* **11** 9
2 May 81	**IT'S GOING TO HAPPEN!** *Ardeck ARDS 8* **18** 9
25 Jul 81	**JULIE OCEAN** *Ardeck ARDS 9* **41** 5
9 Jul 83	**TEENAGE KICKS (re-issue)** *Ardeck ARDS 1* **60** 2

UNDERWORLD UK, male instrumental / vocal group (41 WEEKS)

		pos/wks
18 Dec 93	**SPIKEE / DOGMAN GO WOOF** *Junior Boy's Own JBO 17CD* **63** 1
25 Jun 94	**DARK AND LONG** *Junior Boy's Own JBO 19CDS* **57** 1
13 May 95	**BORN SLIPPY** *Junior Boy's Own JBO 29CDS* **52** 2
18 May 96	**PEARL'S GIRL** *Junior Boy's Own JBO 38CDS1* **24** 2
13 Jul 96 ●	**BORN SLIPPY (re-mix)** *Junior Boy's Own JBO 44CDS* **2** 16
9 Nov 96	**PEARL'S GIRL (re-issue)** *Junior Boy's Own JBO 45CDS1* **22** 3
28 Dec 96	**BORN SLIPPY (re-entry of re-mix)** *Junior Boy's Own JBO 44CDS* **58** 5
27 Mar 99	**PUSH UPSTAIRS** *Junior Boy's Own JBO 5005443* **12** 4
5 Jun 99	**JUMBO** *Junior Boy's Own JBO 5007193* **21** 2
28 Aug 99	**KING OF SNAKE** *Junior Boy's Own JBO 5008793* **17** 3
2 Sep 00	**COWGIRL** *Juniour Boy's Own JBO 5012513* **24** 2

UNDISPUTED TRUTH US, male / female vocal group (4 WEEKS)

		pos/wks
22 Jan 77	**YOU + ME = LOVE** *Warner Bros. K 16804* **43** 4

U96 Germany, male producer - Alex Christiansen (7 WEEKS)

		pos/wks
29 Aug 92	**DAS BOOT** *M & G MAGS 28* **18** 5
4 Jun 94	**INSIDE YOUR DREAMS** *Logic 74321209722* **44** 1
29 Jun 96	**CLUB BIZARRE** *Urban 5750152* **70** 1

UNION featuring the ENGLAND WORLD CUP SQUAD UK / Holland, male instrumental group with UK rugby team vocalists (7 WEEKS)

		pos/wks
12 Oct 91	**SWING LOW (RUN WITH THE BALL)** *Columbia 6575317* **16** 7

UNION GAP featuring Gary PUCKETT
US, male vocal / instrumental group (47 WEEKS)

		pos/wks
17 Apr 68 ★	**YOUNG GIRL** *CBS 3365* **1** 17
7 Aug 68 ●	**LADY WILLPOWER** *CBS 3551* **5** 16
28 Aug 68	**WOMAN WOMAN** *CBS 3110* [1] **48** 1
15 Jun 74 ●	**YOUNG GIRL (re-issue)** *CBS 8202* [1] **6** 13

[1] Gary Puckett and the Union Gap

UNIQUE US, male / female vocal / instrumental group (7 WEEKS)

		pos/wks
10 Sep 83	**WHAT I GOT IS WHAT YOU NEED** *Prelude A 3707* **27** 7

UNIQUE 3 UK, male rap / DJ group (12 WEEKS)

		pos/wks
4 Nov 89	**THE THEME** *10 TEN 285* **61** 3
14 Apr 90	**MUSICAL MELODY / WEIGHT FOR THE BASS** *10 TEN 298* **29** 5
10 Nov 90	**RHYTHM TAKES CONTROL** *10 TEN 327* [1] **41** 3
16 Nov 91	**NO MORE** *10 TEN 387* **74** 1

[1] Unique 3 featuring Karin

UK No.1 ★ UK Top 10 ● Still on chart + UK million seller ◆ UK entry at No.1 ■ US No.1 ▲

UNIT FOUR PLUS TWO UK, male vocal / instrumental group - lead vocal
Peter Moules (29 WEEKS)   pos/wks

13 Feb 64	GREEN FIELDS *Decca F 11821*	48	2
25 Feb 65 ★	CONCRETE AND CLAY *Decca F 12071*	1	15
13 May 65	YOU'VE NEVER BEEN IN LOVE LIKE THIS BEFORE *Decca F 12144*	14	11
17 Mar 66	BABY NEVER SAY GOODBYE *Decca F 12333*	49	1

UNITED CITIZEN FEDERATION featuring Sarah BRIGHTMAN
UK, male production duo and UK, female vocalist (1 WEEK)   pos/wks

| 14 Feb 98 | STARSHIP TROOPERS *Coalition COLA 040CD* | 58 | 1 |

UNITED KINGDOM SYMPHONY UK, orchestra (4 WEEKS)   pos/wks

| 27 Jul 85 | SHADES (THEME FROM THE CROWN PAINT TELEVISION COMMERCIAL) *Food for Thought YUM 108* | 68 | 4 |

UNITONE – See Laurel AITKEN and the UNITONE

UNITONE ROCKERS featuring STEEL UK, male vocal / instrumental
group (1 WEEK)   pos/wks

| 26 Jun 93 | CHILDREN OF THE REVOLUTION *The Hit Label HLC 4* | 60 | 1 |

UNITY UK, male / female vocal / instrumental group (2 WEEKS)   pos/wks

| 31 Aug 91 | UNITY *Cardiac CNY 6* | 64 | 2 |

UNIVERSAL Australia, male vocal group (6 WEEKS)   pos/wks

| 2 Aug 97 | ROCK ME GOOD *London LONCD 397* | 19 | 4 |
| 18 Oct 97 | MAKE IT WITH YOU *London LONCD 404* | 33 | 2 |

UNJUSTIFIED ANCIENTS OF M U – See 1300 DRUMS featuring the UNJUSTIFIED
ANCIENTS OF MU

UNKLE featuring Ian BROWN US / UK, male DJ / production duo - Josh
Davis and James Lavelle and UK, male vocalist (6 WEEKS)   pos/wks

| 20 Feb 99 ● | BE THERE *Mo Wax MW 108CD1* | 8 | 6 |

UNO CLIO featuring Martine McCUTCHEON
UK, male instrumental group (1 WEEK)   pos/wks

| 18 Nov 95 | ARE YOU MAN ENOUGH *Avex UK AVEXCD 14* | 62 | 1 |

UNTOUCHABLES US, male vocal / instrumental group (16 WEEKS) pos/wks

| 6 Apr 85 | FREE YOURSELF *Stiff BUY 221* | 26 | 11 |
| 27 Jul 85 | I SPY FOR THE FBI *Stiff BUY 227* | 59 | 5 |

UP YER RONSON featuring Mary PEARCE
UK, male / female vocal / instrumental group (7 WEEKS)   pos/wks

5 Aug 95	LOST IN LOVE *Hi-Life 5795572*	27	3
30 Mar 96	ARE YOU GONNA BE THERE *Hi-Life 5763272*	27	2
19 Apr 97	I WILL BE RELEASED *Hi-Life 5737352*	32	2

Phil UPCHURCH COMBO US, male instrumental group, Phil Upchurch -
bass guitar (2 WEEKS)   pos/wks

| 5 May 66 | YOU CAN'T SIT DOWN *Sue WI 4005* | 39 | 2 |

UPSETTERS Jamaica, male instrumental group (15 WEEKS)   pos/wks

| 4 Oct 69 ● | RETURN OF DJANGO / DOLLAR IN THE TEETH *Upsetter US 301* | 5 | 15 |

UPSIDE DOWN UK, male vocal group (16 WEEKS)   pos/wks

20 Jan 96	CHANGE YOUR MIND *World CDWORLD 1A*	11	7
13 Apr 96	EVERY TIME I FALL IN LOVE *World CDWORLD 2A*	18	3
8 Jun 96	EVERY TIME I FALL IN LOVE (re-entry) *World CDWORLD 2A*	71	1

| 29 Jun 96 | NEVER FOUND A LOVE LIKE THIS BEFORE *World CDWORLD 3A* | 19 | 3 |
| 23 Nov 96 | IF YOU LEAVE ME NOW *World CDWORLD 4A* | 27 | 2 |

URBAN ALL STARS UK, male producer (Norman Cook) and US, male /
female vocal / instrumental groups (2 WEEKS)   pos/wks

| 27 Aug 88 | IT BEGAN IN AFRICA *Urban URB 23* | 64 | 2 |

URBAN BLUES PROJECT presents Michael PROCTER
US, male vocal / instrumental group (1 WEEK)   pos/wks

| 10 Aug 96 | LOVE DON'T LIVE *AM:PM 5817932* | 55 | 1 |

URBAN COOKIE COLLECTIVE UK, male / female vocal / instrumental
group (37 WEEKS)   pos/wks

10 Jul 93 ●	THE KEY THE SECRET *Pulse 8 CDLOSE 48*	2	16
13 Nov 93 ●	FEELS LIKE HEAVEN *Pulse 8 CDLOSE 55*	5	9
19 Feb 94	SAIL AWAY *Pulse 8 CDLOSE 56*	18	4
23 Apr 94	HIGH ON A HAPPY VIBE *Pulse 8 CDLOSE 60*	31	3
15 Oct 94	BRING IT ON HOME *Pulse 8 CDLOSE 73*	56	1
27 May 95	SPEND THE DAY *Pulse 8 CDLOSE 85*	59	1
9 Sep 95	REST OF MY LOVE *Pulse 8 CDLOSE 93*	67	1
16 Dec 95	SO BEAUTIFUL *Pulse 8 CDLOSE 100*	68	1
24 Aug 96	THE KEY THE SECRET (re-mix) *Pulse 8 CDLOSE 109* [1]	52	1

[1] UCC

URBAN DISCHARGE featuring SHE
US, male / female vocal / instrumental group (1 WEEK)   pos/wks

| 27 Jan 96 | WANNA DROP A HOUSE (ON THAT BITCH) *MCA MCSTD 40020* | 51 | 1 |

URBAN HYPE UK, male production / instrumental group - Robert Dibden
and Mark Chitty (12 WEEKS)   pos/wks

11 Jul 92 ●	A TRIP TO TRUMPTON *Faze 2 FAZE 5*	6	8
17 Oct 92	THE FEELING *Faze 2 FAZE 10*	67	1
9 Jan 93	LIVING IN A FANTASY *Faze 2 CDFAZE 13*	57	3

URBAN SHAKEDOWN
UK / Italy, male DJ / production duo (8 WEEKS)   pos/wks

27 Jun 92	SOME JUSTICE *Urban Shakedown URBST 1*	23	5
12 Sep 92	BASS SHAKE *Urban Shakedown URBST 2* [1]	59	2
10 Jun 95	SOME JUSTICE (re-recording) *Urban Shakedown URBCD 3* [2]	49	1

[1] Urban Shakedown featuring Mickey Finn [2] Urban Shakedown featuring DBO
General

URBAN SOUL
UK / US, male / female vocal / production group (11 WEEKS)   pos/wks

30 Mar 91	ALRIGHT *Cooltempo COOL 231*	60	4
21 Sep 91	ALRIGHT (re-mix) *Cooltempo COOL 244*	43	3
28 Mar 92	ALWAYS *Cooltempo COOL 251*	41	3
13 Jun 98	LOVE IS SO NICE *VC Recordings VCRD 33*	75	1

URBAN SPECIES UK, male vocal / instrumental group (10 WEEKS) pos/wks

12 Feb 94	SPIRITUAL LOVE *Talkin Loud TLKCD 45*	35	4
16 Apr 94	BROTHER *Talkin Loud TLKCD 47*	40	3
20 Aug 94	LISTEN *Talkin Loud TLKCD 50* [1]	47	2
6 Mar 99	BLANKET *Talkin Loud TLDD 39* [2]	56	1

[1] Urban Species featuring MC Solaar [2] Urban Species featuring Imogen Heap

Midge URE UK, male vocalist (56 WEEKS)   pos/wks

12 Jun 82 ●	NO REGRETS *Chrysalis CHS 2618*	9	10
9 Jul 83	AFTER A FASHION *Musicfest FEST 1* [1]	39	4
14 Sep 85 ★	IF I WAS *Chrysalis URE 1*	1	11
16 Nov 85	THAT CERTAIN SMILE *Chrysalis URE 2*	28	4
8 Feb 86	WASTELANDS *Chrysalis URE 3*	46	3
7 Jun 86	CALL OF THE WILD *Chrysalis URE 4*	27	8

20 Aug 88		ANSWERS TO NOTHING *Chrysalis URE 5*	**49**	4
19 Nov 88		DEAR GOD *Chrysalis URE 6*	**55**	4
17 Aug 91		COLD COLD HEART *Arista 114555*	**17**	7
25 May 96		BREATHE *Arista 74321371172*	**70**	1

[1] Midge Ure and Mick Karn

See also SLIK; ULTRAVOX; RICH KIDS; VISAGE

URGE OVERKILL *US, male vocal / instrumental group (6 WEEKS)* pos/wks

21 Aug 93		SISTER HAVANA *Geffen GFSTD 51*	**67**	1
16 Oct 93		POSITIVE BLEEDING *Geffen GFSTD 57*	**61**	1
19 Nov 94		GIRL YOU'LL BE A WOMAN SOON *MCA MCSTD 2024*	**37**	4

URUSEI YATSURA
UK, male / female vocal / instrumental group (4 WEEKS) pos/wks

22 Feb 97		STRATEGIC HAMLETS *Che CHE 67CD*	**64**	1
28 Jun 97		FAKE FUR *Che CHE 70CD*	**58**	1
21 Feb 98		HELLO TIGER *Che CHE 75CD1*	**40**	1
6 Jun 98		SLAIN BY ELF *Che CHE 80CD1*	**63**	1

US3 *UK, male instrumental / production duo (15 WEEKS)* pos/wks

10 Jul 93		RIDDIM *Blue Note CDCL 686* [1]	**34**	6
25 Sep 93		CANTALOOP *Blue Note CDCL 696* [2]	**23**	5
28 May 94		I GOT IT GOIN' ON *Blue Note CDCL 708* [3]	**52**	2
1 Mar 97		COME ON EVERYBODY (GET DOWN) *Blue Note CDCL 784*	**38**	2

[1] Us3 featuring Tukka Yoot [2] Us3 featuring Rahsaan [3] Us3 featuring Kobie Powell and Rahsaan

USA FOR AFRICA *US, male / female vocal charity ensemble, producer - Quincy Jones (9 WEEKS)* pos/wks

13 Apr 85	★	WE ARE THE WORLD *CBS USAID 1* ▲	**1**	9

Soloists: Lionel Richie, Stevie Wonder, Paul Simon, Kenny Rogers, James Ingram, Tina Turner, Billy Joel, Michael Jackson, Diana Ross, Dionne Warwick, Willie Nelson, Al Jarreau, Bruce Springsteen, Kenny Loggins, Steve Perry, Daryl Hall, Huey Lewis, Cyndi Lauper, Kim Carnes, Bob Dylan, Ray Charles. Also credited: Dan Aykroyd, Harry Belafonte, Lindsey Buckingham, Sheila E, Bob Geldof, John Oates, Jackie Jackson, La Toya Jackson, Marlon Jackson, Randy Jackson, Tito Jackson, Waylon Jennings, The News, Bette Midler, Jeffrey Osborne, The Pointer Sisters, Smokey Robinson

USHER *US, male vocalist - Usher Raymond (19 WEEKS)* pos/wks

18 Mar 95		THINK OF YOU *LaFace 74321269252*	**70**	1
31 Jan 98	★	YOU MAKE ME WANNA... *LaFace 74321560652* ■	**1**	12
2 May 98		NICE & SLOW *LaFace 74321579102* ▲	**24**	5
2 May 98		YOU MAKE ME WANNA... (re-entry) *LaFace 74321560652*	**72**	1

USURA *Italy, male / female vocal / instrumental group (15 WEEKS)* pos/wks

23 Jan 93	●	OPEN YOUR MIND *Deconstruction 74321128042*	**7**	9
10 Jul 93		SWEAT *Deconstruction 74321154602*	**29**	3
6 Dec 97		OPEN YOUR MIND 97 (re-mix) *Malarky MLKD 4* [1]	**21**	3

[1] U.S.U.R.A.

UTAH SAINTS *UK, male instrumental / production duo - Jez Wallace and Tim Garbutt (39 WEEKS)* pos/wks

24 Aug 91	●	WHAT CAN YOU DO FOR ME *ffrr F 164*	**10**	11
6 Jun 92	●	SOMETHING GOOD *ffrr F 187*	**4**	9
8 May 93	●	BELIEVE IN ME *ffrr F 209*	**8**	6
17 Jul 93		I WANT YOU *ffrr FCD 213*	**25**	5
25 Jun 94		I STILL THINK OF YOU *ffrr FCD 225*	**32**	2
2 Sep 95		OHIO *ffrr FCD 264*	**42**	2
5 Feb 00		LOVE SONG *Echo ECSCD 83*	**37**	2
20 May 00		FUNKY MUSIC (SHO NUFF TURNS ME ON) *Echo ECSCD 96* [1]	**23**	2

[1] Uncredited vocal for Edwin Starr

U2 (65) `Top 500` *Giants of contemporary rock: Bono (b. Paul Hewson) (v), The Edge (b. David Evans) (g), Adam Clayton (b), Larry Mullen Jr (d). Stadium-packing, award-winning Irish supergroup, who have smashed countless records for sales and live appearances around the globe (223 WEEKS)* pos/wks

8 Aug 81		FIRE *Island WIP 6679*	**35**	6
17 Oct 81		GLORIA *Island WIP 6733*	**55**	4
3 Apr 82		A CELEBRATION *Island WIP 6770*	**47**	4
22 Jan 83	●	NEW YEARS DAY *Island WIP 6848*	**10**	8
2 Apr 83		TWO HEARTS BEAT AS ONE *Island IS 109*	**18**	5
15 Sep 84	●	PRIDE (IN THE NAME OF LOVE) *Island IS 202*	**3**	11
4 May 85	●	THE UNFORGETTABLE FIRE *Island IS 220*	**6**	6
28 Mar 87	●	WITH OR WITHOUT YOU *Island IS 319* ▲	**4**	11
6 Jun 87	●	I STILL HAVEN'T FOUND WHAT I'M LOOKING FOR *Island IS 328* ▲	**6**	11
12 Sep 87	●	WHERE THE STREETS HAVE NO NAME *Island IS 340*	**4**	6
26 Dec 87		IN GOD'S COUNTRY (IMPORT) *Island 7-99385*	**48**	4
1 Oct 88	★	DESIRE *Island IS 400*	**1**	8
17 Dec 88	●	ANGEL OF HARLEM *Island IS 402*	**9**	6
15 Apr 89	●	WHEN LOVE COMES TO TOWN *Island IS 411* [1]	**6**	7
24 Jun 89	●	ALL I WANT IS YOU *Island IS 422*	**4**	6
2 Nov 91	★	THE FLY *Island IS 500* ■	**1**	5
14 Dec 91		THE FLY (re-entry) *Island IS 500*	**62**	1
4 Jan 92	●	MYSTERIOUS WAYS *Island IS 509*	**13**	7
7 Mar 92	●	ONE *Island IS 515*	**7**	6
20 Jun 92		EVEN BETTER THAN THE REAL THING *Island IS 525*	**12**	7
11 Jul 92	●	EVEN BETTER THAN THE REAL THING (re-mix) *Island REAL U 2*	**8**	7
5 Dec 92		WHO'S GONNA RIDE YOUR WILD HORSES *Island IS 550*	**14**	8
4 Dec 93	●	STAY (FARAWAY, SO CLOSE) *Island CID 578*	**4**	9
17 Jun 95	●	HOLD ME THRILL ME KISS ME KILL ME *Atlantic A 7131CD*	**2**	14
15 Feb 97	★	DISCOTHEQUE *Island CID 649* ■	**1**	9
26 Apr 97	●	STARING AT THE SUN *Island CID 658*	**3**	6
17 May 97		DISCOTHEQUE (re-entry) *Island CID 649*	**72**	2
2 Aug 97	●	LAST NIGHT ON EARTH *Island CID 664*	**10**	4
6 Sep 97		LAST NIGHT ON EARTH (re-entry) *Island CID 664*	**68**	1
4 Oct 97	●	PLEASE *Island CID 673*	**7**	4
20 Dec 97		IF GOD WILL SEND HIS ANGELS *Island CID 684*	**12**	6
31 Oct 98	●	SWEETEST THING *Island CID 727*	**3**	13
21 Oct 00	★	BEAUTIFUL DAY *Island CID 766* ■	**1**	11+

[1] U2 with BB King

'Stay (Faraway, So Close)' was listed with 'I've Got You Under My Skin' by Frank Sinatra with Bono, which was featured on many but not all formats

Verna V – See HELIOTROPIC featuring Verna V

VAGABONDS – See Jimmy JAMES and the VAGABONDS

Ricky VALANCE *UK, male vocalist - David Spencer (16 WEEKS)* pos/wks

25 Aug 60	★	TELL LAURA I LOVE HER *Columbia DB 4493*	**1**	16

Ritchie VALENS *US, male vocalist (5 WEEKS)* pos/wks

6 Mar 59		DONNA *London HL 8803*	**29**	1
1 Aug 87		LA BAMBA *RCA PB 41435*	**49**	4

Caterina VALENTE *France, female vocalist (14 WEEKS)* pos/wks

19 Aug 55	●	THE BREEZE AND I *Polydor BM 6002* [1]	**5**	14

[1] with Werner Muller and the Rias Dance Orchestra

VALENTINE BROTHERS *US, male vocal duo (1 WEEK)* pos/wks

23 Apr 83		MONEY'S TOO TIGHT (TO MENTION) *Energy NRG 1*	**73**	1

Dickie VALENTINE (329) Top 500 *UK's No.1 pre rock 'n' roll heart-throb in the mid 1950s, b. Richard Brice, 4 Nov 1929, London, d. 6 May 1971. Voted Top UK Male Vocalist while singing with the Ted Heath Orchestra and after going solo in 1954 (92 WEEKS)*

pos/wks

Date	Title	pos	wks
20 Feb 53	BROKEN WINGS *Decca F 9954*	12	1
13 Mar 53 ●	ALL THE TIME AND EVERYWHERE *Decca F 10038*	9	3
5 Jun 53 ●	IN A GOLDEN COACH (THERE'S A HEART OF GOLD) *Decca F 10098*	7	1
5 Nov 54	ENDLESS *Decca F 10346*	19	1
17 Dec 54 ●	MR SANDMAN *Decca F 10415*	5	12
17 Dec 54 ★	THE FINGER OF SUSPICION *Decca F 10394* [1]	1	15
18 Feb 55 ●	A BLOSSOM FELL *Decca F 10430*	9	9
29 Apr 55	A BLOSSOM FELL (re-entry) *Decca F 10430*	18	1
3 Jun 55 ●	I WONDER *Decca F 10493*	4	15
25 Nov 55 ★	CHRISTMAS ALPHABET *Decca F 10628*	1	7
16 Dec 55	OLD PI-ANNA RAG *Decca F 10645*	15	1
7 Dec 56 ●	CHRISTMAS ISLAND *Decca F 10798*	8	5
27 Dec 57	SNOWBOUND FOR CHRISTMAS *Decca F 10950*	28	1
13 Mar 59	VENUS *Pye Nixa 7N 15192*	28	1
3 Apr 59	VENUS (re-entry) *Pye Nixa 7N 15192*	25	1
17 Apr 59	VENUS (2nd re-entry) *Pye Nixa 7N 15192*	20	4
22 May 59	VENUS (3rd re-entry) *Pye Nixa 7N 15192*	25	1
19 Jun 59	VENUS (4th re-entry) *Pye Nixa 7N 15192*	28	1
23 Oct 59	ONE MORE SUNRISE (MORGEN) *Pye 7N 15221*	14	8

[1] Dickie Valentine with the Stargazers

Joe VALINO *US, male vocalist (2 WEEKS)*

pos/wks

Date	Title	pos	wks
18 Jan 57	GARDEN OF EDEN *HMV POP 283*	23	2

Frankie VALLI *US, male vocalist - Frankie Castellucio (52 WEEKS)*

pos/wks

Date	Title	pos	wks
12 Dec 70	YOU'RE READY NOW *Philips 320226*	11	13
1 Feb 75 ●	MY EYES ADORED YOU *Private Stock PVT 1* ▲	5	11
21 Jun 75	SWEARIN' TO GOD *Private Stock PVT 21*	31	5
17 Apr 76	FALLEN ANGEL *Private Stock PVT 51*	11	7
26 Aug 78 ▲	GREASE *RSO 012*	3	14
23 Mar 91	GREASE - THE DREAM MIX *PWL / Polydor PO 136* [1]	47	2

[1] Frankie Valli, John Travolta and Olivia Newton-John

See also FOUR SEASONS

Mark VAN DALE with ENRICO
Belgium, male production duo (1 WEEK)

pos/wks

Date	Title	pos	wks
3 Oct 98	WATER WAVE *Club Tools 0065815 CLU*	71	1

David VAN DAY *UK, male vocalist (3 WEEKS)*

pos/wks

Date	Title	pos	wks
14 May 83	YOUNG AMERICANS TALKING *WEA DAY 1*	43	3

See also DOLLAR

VAN DER TOORN – See PAPPA BEAR featuring VAN DER TOORN

George VAN DUSEN *UK, male vocalist (4 WEEKS)*

pos/wks

Date	Title	pos	wks
17 Dec 88	IT'S PARTY TIME AGAIN *Bri-Tone 7BT 001*	43	4

Paul VAN DYK *Germany, male DJ / producer (23 WEEKS)*

pos/wks

Date	Title	pos	wks
17 May 97	FORBIDDEN FRUIT *Deviant DVNT 18CDR*	69	1
15 Nov 97	WORDS *Deviant DVNT 26CDS* [1]	54	1
5 Sep 98	FOR AN ANGEL *Deviant DVT 24CDS*	28	4
20 Nov 99	ANOTHER WAY / AVENUE *Deviant DVNT 35CDS*	13	5
8 Jan 00	ANOTHER WAY / AVENUE (re-entry) *Deviant DVNT 35CDS*	69	2
20 May 00 ●	TELL ME WHY (THE RIDDLE) *Deviant DVNT 36CDS* [2]	7	5
2 Dec 00	WE ARE ALIVE *Deviant DVNT 38CDS*	15	5+

[1] Paul Van Dyk featuring Toni Halliday [2] Paul Van Dyk featuring Saint Etienne

Leroy VAN DYKE *US, male vocalist (20 WEEKS)*

pos/wks

Date	Title	pos	wks
4 Jan 62 ●	WALK ON BY *Mercury AMT 1166*	5	17
26 Apr 62	BIG MAN IN A BIG HOUSE *Mercury AMT 1173*	34	3

Niels VAN GOGH *Germany, male producer (1 WEEK)*

pos/wks

Date	Title	pos	wks
10 Apr 99	PULVERTURM *Logic 74321649192*	75	1

VAN HALEN *US / Holland, male vocal / instrumental group (51 WEEKS)*

pos/wks

Date	Title	pos	wks
28 Jun 80	RUNNIN' WITH THE DEVIL *Warner Bros. HM 10*	52	3
4 Feb 84 ●	JUMP *Warner Bros. W 9384* ▲	7	13
19 May 84	PANAMA *Warner Bros. W 9273*	61	2
5 Apr 86 ●	WHY CAN'T THIS BE LOVE *Warner Bros. W 8740*	8	14
12 Jul 86	DREAMS *Warner Bros. W 8642*	62	2
6 Aug 88	WHEN IT'S LOVE *Warner Bros. W 7816*	28	7
1 Apr 89	FEELS SO GOOD *Warner Bros. W 7565*	63	1
22 Jun 91	POUNDCAKE *Warner Bros. W 0045*	74	1
19 Oct 91	TOP OF THE WORLD *Warner Bros. W 0066*	63	1
27 Mar 93	JUMP (LIVE) *Warner Bros. W 0155CD*	26	3
21 Jan 95	DON'T TELL ME *Warner Bros. W 0280CD*	27	1
1 Apr 95	CAN'T STOP LOVIN' YOU *Warner Bros. W 0288CD*	33	2

Armand VAN HELDEN *US, male DJ / producer (27 WEEKS)*

pos/wks

Date	Title	pos	wks
8 Mar 97	THE FUNK PHENOMENA *ZYX ZYX 8523U8*	38	2
8 Nov 97	ULTRAFUNKULA *ffrr FCD 317*	46	1
6 Feb 99 ★	YOU DON'T KNOW ME *ffrr FCD 357* [1] ■	1	11
1 May 99	FLOWERZ *ffrr FCD 361* [2]	18	5
15 May 99	YOU DON'T KNOW ME (re-entry) *ffrr FCD 357* [1]	72	1
20 May 00 ●	KOOCHY *ffrr FCD 379*	4	7

[1] Armand Van Helden featuring Duane Harden [2] Armand Van Helden featuring Roland Clark

VAN TWIST *Zaire / Belgium, male / female vocal / instrumental group (2 WEEKS)*

pos/wks

Date	Title	pos	wks
16 Feb 85	SHAFT *Polydor POSP 729*	57	2

VANDELLAS – See Martha REEVES and the VANDELLAS

Luther VANDROSS (153) Top 500 *Superior soul singer / songwriter and producer, b. 20 Apr 1951, New York, US. Ex-David Bowie backing vocalist, who fronted chart group Change before embarking on a solo career that earned him 10 successive US platinum albums and a stack of awards (147 WEEKS)*

pos/wks

Date	Title	pos	wks
19 Feb 83	NEVER TOO MUCH *Epic EPC A 3101*	44	6
26 Jul 86	GIVE ME THE REASON *Epic A 7288*	60	3
21 Feb 87	GIVE ME THE REASON (re-issue) *Epic 650216 7*	71	2
28 Mar 87	SEE ME *Epic LUTH 1*	60	4
11 Jul 87	I REALLY DIDN'T MEAN IT *Epic LUTH 3*	16	10
5 Sep 87	STOP TO LOVE *Epic LUTH 2*	24	7
7 Nov 87	SO AMAZING *Epic LUTH 4*	33	6
23 Jan 88	GIVE ME THE REASON (2nd re-issue) *Epic LUTH 5*	26	6
16 Apr 88	I GAVE IT UP (WHEN I FELL IN LOVE) *Epic LUTH 6*	28	5
9 Jul 88	THERE'S NOTHING BETTER THAN LOVE *Epic LUTH 7* [1]	72	1
8 Oct 88	ANY LOVE *Epic LUTH 8*	31	4
4 Feb 89	SHE WON'T TALK TO ME *Epic LUTH 9*	34	4
22 Apr 89	COME BACK *Epic LUTH 10*	53	3
28 Oct 89	NEVER TOO MUCH (re-mix) *Epic LUTH 12*	13	7
6 Jan 90	HERE AND NOW *Epic LUTH 13*	43	3
27 Apr 91	POWER OF LOVE - LOVE POWER *Epic 6568227*	46	5
18 Jan 92	THE RUSH *Epic 6577237*	53	3
15 Aug 92 ●	THE BEST THINGS IN LIFE ARE FREE *Perspective PERSS 7400* [2]	2	13
22 May 93	LITTLE MIRACLES (HAPPEN EVERY DAY) *Epic 6590442*	28	3
18 Sep 93	HEAVEN KNOWS *Epic 6596522*	34	3
4 Dec 93	LOVE IS ON THE WAY *Epic 6599592*	38	2
17 Sep 94 ●	ENDLESS LOVE *Epic 6608062* [3]	3	10
26 Nov 94	LOVE THE ONE YOU'RE WITH *Epic 6610612*	31	4
7 Jan 95	ENDLESS LOVE (re-entry) *Epic 6608062* [3]	70	2
4 Feb 95	ALWAYS AND FOREVER *Epic 6611942*	20	5
4 Feb 95	ENDLESS LOVE (2nd re-entry) *Epic 6608062* [3]	55	4
15 Apr 95	AIN'T NO STOPPING US NOW *Epic 6614242*	22	3
11 Nov 95	POWER OF LOVE - LOVE POWER (re-mix) *Epic 6625902*	31	3
16 Dec 95 ●	THE BEST THINGS IN LIFE ARE FREE (re-mix) *A & M 5813092* [4]	7	7

UK No.1 ★ UK Top 10 ● Still on chart + UK million seller ◆ UK entry at No.1 ■ US No.1 ▲

23 Dec 95	EVERY YEAR EVERY CHRISTMAS Epic 6627762	43	2
12 Oct 96	YOUR SECRET LOVE Epic 6638385	14	5
28 Dec 96	I CAN MAKE IT BETTER Epic 6640632	44	2

1 Luther Vandross, duet with Gregory Hines 2 Luther Vandross and Janet Jackson with special guests BBD and Ralph Tresvant 3 Luther Vandross and Mariah Carey 4 Luther Vandross and Janet Jackson

VANESSA-MAE Singapore, female instrumentalist - violin; Vanessa-Mae Nicholson (20 WEEKS)

		pos/wks	
28 Jan 95	TOCCATA AND FUGUE EMI Classics MAE 8816812	16	10
20 May 95	RED HOT EMI CDMAE 2	37	2
18 Nov 95	CLASSICAL GAS EMI CDEM 404	41	2
26 Oct 96	I'M A DOUN FOR LACK O' JOHNNIE (A LITTLE SCOTTISH FANTASY) EMI CDMAE 3	28	2
25 Oct 97	STORM EMI CDEM 497	54	1
20 Dec 97	I FEEL LOVE EMI CDEM 553	41	2
5 Dec 98	DEVIL'S TRILL / REFLECTION EMI CDEM 530	53	1

VANGELIS Greece, male instrumentalist - keyboards; Evangelos Papathanassiou (25 WEEKS)

		pos/wks	
9 May 81	CHARIOTS OF FIRE - TITLES Polydor POSP 246 ▲	12	10
11 Jul 81	HEAVEN AND HELL, THIRD MOVEMENT (THEME FROM THE BBC-TV SERIES 'THE COSMOS') BBC 1	48	6
24 Apr 82	CHARIOTS OF FIRE - TITLES (re-entry) Polydor POSP 246	41	7
31 Oct 92	CONQUEST OF PARADISE East West YZ 704	60	2

See also JON and VANGELIS

VANILLA UK, female vocal group (10 WEEKS)

		pos/wks	
22 Nov 97	NO WAY NO WAY EMI CDEM 487	75	1
27 Dec 97	NO WAY NO WAY (re-entry) EMI CDEM 487	14	7
23 May 98	TRUE TO US EMI CDEM 509	36	2

VANILLA FUDGE US, male vocal / instrumental group (11 WEEKS)

		pos/wks	
9 Aug 67	YOU KEEP ME HANGIN' ON Atlantic 584 123	18	11

VANILLA ICE US, male rapper - Robert Van Winkle (32 WEEKS)

		pos/wks	
24 Nov 90	★ ICE ICE BABY SBK SBK 18 ▲	1	13
2 Feb 91	PLAY THAT FUNKY MUSIC SBK SBK 20	10	6
30 Mar 91	I LOVE YOU SBK SBK 22	45	5
29 Jun 91	ROLLIN' IN MY 5.0 SBK SBK 27	27	4
10 Aug 91	SATISFACTION SBK SBK 29	22	4

VANITY FARE UK, male vocal / instrumental group (34 WEEKS)

		pos/wks	
28 Aug 68	I LIVE FOR THE SUN Page One POF 075	20	9
23 Jul 69	● EARLY IN THE MORNING Page One POF 142	8	12
27 Dec 69	HITCHIN' A RIDE Page One POF 158	16	13

Joe T VANNELLI PROJECT Italy, male producer (2 WEEKS)

		pos/wks	
17 Jun 95	SWEETEST DAY OF MAY Positiva CDTIV 36	45	2

Randy VANWARMER
US, male vocalist - Randall Van Wormer (11 WEEKS)

		pos/wks	
4 Aug 79	● JUST WHEN I NEEDED YOU MOST Bearsville WIP 6516	8	11

VAPORS UK, male vocal / instrumental group (23 WEEKS)

		pos/wks	
9 Feb 80	● TURNING JAPANESE United Artists BP 334	3	13
5 Jul 80	NEWS AT TEN United Artists BP 345	44	4
11 Jul 81	JIMMIE JONES Liberty BP 401	44	6

VARDIS UK, male vocal / instrumental group (4 WEEKS)

		pos/wks	
27 Sep 80	LET'S GO Logo VAR 1	59	4

Halo VARGAS US, male producer (1 WEEK)

		pos/wks	
9 Dec 00	FUTURE Hooj Choons HOOJ 101CD	67	1

VARIOUS ARTISTS (EPs and LPs) (86 WEEKS)

		pos/wks	
15 Jun 56	CAROUSEL - ORIGINAL SOUNDTRACK (LP) Capitol LCT 6105	27	1
29 Jun 56	● ALL STAR HIT PARADE Decca F 10752	2	9
6 Jul 56	CAROUSEL - ORIGINAL SOUNDTRACK (LP) (re-entry) Capitol LCT 6105	26	1
26 Jul 57	ALL STAR HIT PARADE NO.2 Decca F 10915	15	7
9 Dec 89	THE FOOD CHRISTMAS EP Food FOOD 23	63	1
20 Jan 90	THE FURTHER ADVENTURES OF NORTH (EP) Deconstruction PT 43372	64	2
2 Nov 91	THE APPLE EP Apple APP 1	60	1
11 Jul 92	FOURPLAY (EP) XL XLFP 1	45	2
7 Nov 92	THE FRED EP Heavenly HVN 19	26	3
24 Apr 93	GIMME SHELTER (EP) Food CDORDERA 1	23	4
5 Jun 93	SUBPLATES VOLUME 1 (EP) Suburban Base 24CD	69	1
9 Oct 93	THE TWO TONE EP 2 Tone CHSTT 31	30	3
4 Nov 95	HELP (EP) Go! Discs GODCD 135	51	2
16 Mar 96	NEW YORK UNDERCOVER (EP) Uptown MCSTD 48002	39	1
30 Mar 96	DANGEROUS MINDS (EP) MCA MCSTD 48007	35	1
29 Nov 97	★ PERFECT DAY Chrysalis CDNEED 01 ◆ ■	1	19
18 Apr 98	PERFECT DAY (re-entry) Chrysalis CDNEED 01	68	1
12 Sep 98	THE FULL MONTY-MONSTER MIX RCA Victor 74321602582	62	1
26 Sep 98	TRADE (EP) (DISC 2) Tidy Trax TREP2	75	1
10 Apr 99	● THANK ABBA FOR THE MUSIC Epic ABCD 1 1	4	13
25 Dec 99	IT'S ONLY ROCK 'N' ROLL Universal TV 1566012	19	8
26 Feb 00	IT'S ONLY ROCK 'N' ROLL (re-entry) Universal TV 1566012	67	1
17 Jun 00	PERFECT DAY (re-recording) Chrysalis 8887840	69	1

1 Steps, Tina Cousins, Cleopatra, B*Witched, Billie

Tracks and artists on Carousel are as follows: Carousel Waltz - Orchestra conducted by Alfred Newman; You're a Queer One Julie Jordan - Barbara Ruick and Shirley Jones; Mister Snow - Barbara Ruick; If I Loved You - Shirley Jones and Gordon MacRae; June Is Busting Out All Over - Claramae Turner; Soliloquy - Gordon MacRae; Blow High Blow Low - Cameron Mitchell; When the Children Are Asleep - Robert Rounseville and Barbara Ruick; This Was a Real Nice Clambake - Barbara Ruick, Claramae Turner, Robert Rounseville and Cameron Mitchell; Stonecutters Cut It on Stone (There's Nothing So Bad for a Woman) - Cameron Mitchell; What's the Use of Wonderin' - Shirley Jones; You'll Never Walk Alone - Claramae Turner; If I Loved You - Gordon MacRae; You'll Never Walk Alone - Shirley Jones

Tracks on All Star Hit Parade: Theme from The Threepenny Opera - Winifred Atwell; No Other Love - Dave King; My September Love - Joan Regan; A Tear Fell - Lita Roza; Out of Town - Dickie Valentine; It's Almost Tomorrow - David Whitfield. Tracks on All Star Hit Parade No.2: Around the World - Johnston Brothers; Puttin' On the Style - Billy Cotton; When I Fall In Love - Jimmy Young; A White Sport Coat - Max Bygraves; Freight Train - Beverley Sisters; Butterfly - Tommy Steele. Tracks on The Food Christmas EP: Like Princes Do - Crazyhead; I Don't Want That Kind of Love - Jesus Jones; Info Freako - Diesel Park West. Tracks on The Further Adventures of North (EP): Dream 17 - Annette; Carino 90 - T-Coy; The Way I Feel - Frequency 9; Stop This Thing - Dynasty of Two featuring Rowetta. Tracks on The Apple EP: Those Were the Days - Mary Hopkin; That's the Way God Planned It - Billy Preston; Sour Milk Sea - Jackie Lomax; Come and Get It - Badfinger. Tracks on Fourplay (EP): DJs Unite; Alright - Glide; Be Free - Noisy Factory; True Devotion - EQ. Tracks on The Fred EP: Deeply Dippy - Rockingbirds; Don't Talk Just Kiss -Flowered Up; I'm Too Sexy - Saint Etienne. Gimme Shelter EP was available on all four formats, each featuring an interview with the featured artist plus the following artists performing versions of Gimme Shelter: (cassette) Jimmy Somerville and Voice of the Beehive; Heaven 17; (12") Blue Pearl, 808 State and Robert Owens; Pop Will Eat Itself vs Gary Clail; Ranking Roger and the Mighty Diamonds; (CD) Thunder; Little Angels; Hawkwind and Sam Fox; (2nd CD) Cud with Sandie Shaw; Kingmaker; New Model Army and Tom Jones. Tracks on Subplates Volume 1 (EP): Style Warz - Son'z of a Loop Da Loop Era; Funky Dope Track - Q-Bass; The Chopper - DJ Hype; Look No Further - Run Tings. Tracks on The Two Tone EP: Gangsters - Special AKA; The Prince -Madness; On My Radio - Selecter; Tears of a Clown Beat. Tracks on Help (EP): Lucky - Radiohead; 50ft Queenie (Live) PJ Harvey; Momentum - Guru featuring Big Shug; an untitled piece of incidental music. Tracks on New York Undercover (EP): Tell Me What You Like - Guy; Dom Perignon - Little Shawn; I Miss You - Monifah; Jeeps, Lex Coups, Bimax & Menz - Lost Boys. Tracks on Dangerous Minds (EP): Curiosity - Aaron Hall; Gin & Dance - De Vante; It's Alright - Sista featuring Craig Mack. Artists on Perfect Day are as follows: BBC Symphony Orchestra and Andrew Davis, Bono (U2), Boyzone, Brett Anderson (Suede), Brodsky Quartet, Burning Spear, Courtney Pine, David Bowie, Dr John, Elton John, Emmylou Harris, Evan Dando (Lemonheads), Gabrielle, Heather Small (M People), Huey (Fun Lovin' Criminals), Ian Broudie (Lightning Seeds), Joan Armatrading, Laurie Anderson, Lesley Garrett, Lou Reed, Robert Cray, Shane McGowan, Sheona

White, Skye (Morcheeba), Suzanne Vega, Tammy Wynette, Thomas Allen, Tom Jones, Visual Ministry Orchestra. Tracks on The Full-Monty Monster Mix (medley): You Sexy Thing - Hot Chocolate; Hot Stuff - Donna Summer; You Can Leave Your Hat On - Tom Jones. CD also has a full version of 'You Can Leave Your Hat On' by Tom Jones and 'The Stripper' by David Rose. Tracks on Trade (EP) (disc 2): Put Your House in Order - Steve Thomas; The Dawn - Tony De Vit.

VARIOUS ARTISTS (MONTAGES) (31 WEEKS)

			pos/wks
17 May 80		CALIBRE CUTS *Calibre CAB 502*	75 2
25 Nov 89		DEEP HEAT '89 *Deep Heat DEEP 10*	12 11
3 Mar 90	●	THE BRITS 1990 *RCA PB 43565*	2 7
28 Apr 90		THE SIXTH SENSE *Deep Heat DEEP 12*	49 2
10 Nov 90		TIME TO MAKE THE FLOOR BURN *Megabass MEGAX 1*	16 9

The following tracks are sampled: Calibre Cuts: Big Apples Rock - Black Ivory; Don't Hold Back - Chanson; The River Drive - Jupiter Beyond; Dancing in the Disco - LAX; Mellow Mellow Right On - Lowrell; Pata Pata - Osibisa; I Like It - Players Association; We Got the Funk - Positive Force; Holdin' On - Tony Rallo and the Midnight Band; Can You Feel the Force - Real Thing; Miami Heatwave - Seventh Avenue; Rappers Delight - Sugarhill Gang; Que Tal America - Two Man Sound; Remakes by session musicians: Ain't No Stoppin' Us Now, Bad Girls, We Are Family. Deep Heat '89 (credited to Latino Rave): Pump Up the Jam - Technotronics; Stakker Humanoid - Humanoid; A Day in the Life - Black Riot; Work it to the Bone - LNR; I Can Make U Dance - DJ 'Fast' Eddie; Voodoo Ray - A Guy Called Gerald; Numero Uno - Starlight; Bango (To the Batmobile) - Todd Terry; Break 4 Love - Raze; Don't Scandalize Mine - Sugar Bear. The Brits 1990: Street Tuff - Double Trouble and the Rebel MC; Voodoo Ray - A Guy Called Gerald; Theme From S-Express - S-Express; Hey DJ I Can't Dance to That Music You're Playing - Beatmasters; Eve of the War - Jeff Wayne; Pacific State - 808 State; We Call It Acieed - D Mob; Got to Keep On - Cookie Crew. The Sixth Sense (credited to Latino Rave): Get Up - Technotronic; The Magic Number - De La Soul; G'Ding G'Ding (Do Wanna Wanna) - Anna G; Show 'M the Bass - MC Miker G; Turn It Out (Go Base) - Rob Base; Eve of the War (War of the Worlds) - Project D; Moments In Love - 2 to the Power. Time to Make the Floor Burn (credited to Megabass): Do This My Way - Kid 'N' Play; Street Tuff - Double Trouble and the Rebel MC; Sex 4 Daze - Lake Eerie; Ride On Time - Black Box; Make My Body Rock - Jomanda; Don't Miss the Partyline - Bizz Nizz; Pump Pump It Up - Hypnotek; Big Fun - Inner City; Pump That Body - Mr Lee; Pump Up the Jam - Technotronic; This Beat Is Technotronic - Technotronic; Get Busy - Mr Lee; Touch Me - 49ers; Thunderbirds Are Go - FAB.

Junior VASQUEZ *US, male DJ / producer (5 WEEKS)*

			pos/wks
15 Jul 95		GET YOUR HANDS OFF MY MAN! *Positiva CDTIV 37*	22 3
31 Aug 96		IF MADONNA CALLS *Multiply CDMULTY 13*	24 2

Elaine VASSELL – See BEATMASTERS

VAST *Australia, male vocal / instrumental group (1 WEEK)*

			pos/wks
16 Sep 00		FREE *Mushroom MUSH 79CDS*	55 1

Sven VATH *Germany, male DJ / producer (5 WEEKS)*

			pos/wks
24 Jul 93		L'ESPERANZA *Eye Q YZ 757*	63 2
6 Nov 93		AN ACCIDENT IN PARADISE *Eye Q YZ 778CD*	57 2
22 Oct 94		HARLEQUIN - THE BEAUTY AND THE BEAST *Eye Q YZ 857*	72 1

Frankie VAUGHAN 59 Top 500
High-kicking 50s heart-throb vocalist. b. Frank Abelson, 3 Feb 1928, Liverpool, UK, d. 17 Sep 1999. This variety-show veteran, who received an OBE in 1965 for his charity work, was one of the most popular performers of the 1950s (232 WEEKS)

			pos/wks
29 Jan 54		ISTANBUL (NOT CONSTANTINOPLE) *HMV B 10599* [1]	11 1
28 Jan 55		HAPPY DAYS AND LONELY NIGHTS *HMV B 10783*	12 3
22 Apr 55		TWEEDLE DEE *Philips PB 423*	17 1
2 Dec 55		SEVENTEEN *Philips PB 511*	18 3
3 Feb 56		MY BOY FLAT TOP *Philips PB 544*	20 2
9 Nov 56	●	THE GREEN DOOR *Philips PB 640*	2 15
11 Jan 57	★	THE GARDEN OF EDEN *Philips PB 660*	1 13
4 Oct 57	●	MAN ON FIRE / WANDERIN' EYES *Philips PB 729*	6 12
1 Nov 57	●	GOT-TA HAVE SOMETHING IN THE BANK, FRANK *Philips PB 751* [2]	8 11
20 Dec 57	●	KISSES SWEETER THAN WINE *Philips PB 775*	8 11
7 Mar 58		CAN'T GET ALONG WITHOUT YOU / WE ARE NOT ALONE *Philips PB 793*	11 6
9 May 58	●	KEWPIE DOLL *Philips PB 825*	10 12
1 Aug 58		WONDERFUL THINGS *Philips PB 834*	22 3
12 Sep 58		WONDERFUL THINGS (re-entry) *Philips PB 834*	27 3
10 Oct 58		AM I WASTING MY TIME ON YOU *Philips PB 865*	25 2
9 Jan 59		AM I WASTING MY TIME ON YOU (re-entry) *Philips PB 865*	27 2
30 Jan 59		THAT'S MY DOLL *Philips PB 895*	28 2
1 May 59	●	COME SOFTLY TO ME *Philips PB 913* [2]	9 9
24 Jul 59	●	THE HEART OF A MAN *Philips PB 930*	5 14
18 Sep 59		WALKIN' TALL *Philips PB 931*	28 1
2 Oct 59		WALKIN' TALL (re-entry) *Philips PB 931*	29 1
29 Jan 60		WHAT MORE DO YOU WANT *Philips PB 985*	25 2
22 Sep 60		KOOKIE LITTLE PARADISE *Philips PB 1054*	31 5
27 Oct 60		MILORD *Philips PB 1066*	34 6
9 Nov 61	★	TOWER OF STRENGTH *Philips PB 1195*	1 13
1 Feb 62		DON'T STOP TWIST *Philips PB 1219*	22 7
27 Sep 62		HERCULES *Philips 326542 BF*	42 4
24 Jan 63	●	LOOP-DE-LOOP *Philips 326566 BF*	5 12
20 Jun 63		HEY MAMA *Philips BF 1254*	21 9
4 Jun 64		HELLO DOLLY *Philips BF 1339*	18 11
11 Mar 65		SOMEONE MUST HAVE HURT YOU A LOT *Philips BF 1394*	46 1
23 Aug 67	●	THERE MUST BE A WAY *Columbia DB 8248*	7 21
15 Nov 67		SO TIRED *Columbia DB 8298*	21 9
28 Feb 68		NEVERTHELESS *Columbia DB 8354*	29 5

[1] Frankie Vaughan with the Peter Knight Singers [2] Frankie Vaughan and the Kaye Sisters

Malcolm VAUGHAN 272 Top 500
Arguably the last of the hitmaking big-voiced tenors, b. Malcolm Thomas, 1930, Glamorgan, Wales. He was the straight man in a comedy duo with Kenny Earle, while enjoying his enviable run of UK ballad hits (at the height of the rock 'n' roll explosion) (106 WEEKS)

			pos/wks
1 Jul 55	●	EVERY DAY OF MY LIFE *HMV B 10874*	5 16
27 Jan 56		WITH YOUR LOVE *HMV POP 130* [1]	20 1
10 Feb 56		WITH YOUR LOVE (re-entry) *HMV POP 130* [1]	18 1
2 Mar 56		WITH YOUR LOVE (2nd re-entry) *HMV POP 130* [1]	20 1
26 Oct 56		ST THERESE OF THE ROSES *HMV POP 250*	27 1
16 Nov 56	●	ST THERESE OF THE ROSES (re-entry) *HMV POP 250*	3 19
12 Apr 57		THE WORLD IS MINE *HMV POP 303*	30 1
3 May 57		THE WORLD IS MINE (re-entry) *HMV POP 303*	29 2
10 May 57		CHAPEL OF THE ROSES *HMV POP 325*	13 8
31 May 57		THE WORLD IS MINE (2nd re-entry) *HMV POP 303*	26 1
29 Nov 57	●	MY SPECIAL ANGEL *HMV POP 419*	3 14
21 Mar 58		TO BE LOVED *HMV POP 459* [2]	14 12
17 Oct 58	●	MORE THAN EVER (COME PRIMA) *HMV POP 538* [2]	5 14
27 Feb 59		WAIT FOR ME / WILLINGLY *HMV POP 590*	28 1
13 Mar 59		WAIT FOR ME (re-entry) *HMV POP 590*	13 14

[1] Malcolm Vaughan with the Peter Knight Singers [2] Malcolm Vaughan with the Michael Sammes Singers

Norman VAUGHAN *UK, male vocalist (5 WEEKS)*

			pos/wks
17 May 62		SWINGING IN THE RAIN *Pye 7N 15438*	34 5

Sarah VAUGHAN *US, female vocalist (34 WEEKS)*

			pos/wks
27 Sep 57		PASSING STRANGERS *Mercury MT 164* [1]	22 2
11 Sep 59	●	BROKEN HEARTED MELODY *Mercury AMT 1057*	7 13
29 Dec 60		LET'S / SERENATA *Columbia DB 4542*	37 3
2 Feb 61		LET'S / SERENATA (re-entry) *Columbia DB 4542*	47 1
12 Mar 69		PASSING STRANGERS (re-issue) *Mercury MF 1082* [1]	20 15

[1] Billy Eckstine and Sarah Vaughan

Billy VAUGHN *US, orchestra and chorus (8 WEEKS)*

			pos/wks
27 Jan 56		SHIFTING WHISPERING SANDS PART 1 *London HLD 8205* [1]	20 1
23 Mar 56		THEME FROM 'THE THREEPENNY OPERA' *London HLD 8238*	12 7

[1] Billy Vaughn Orchestra and Chorus, narration by Ken Nordene

VDC – See BLAST featuring VDC

VEBA – See RAE & CHRISTIAN featuring VEBA

Bobby VEE `188` **Top 500** *Early 1960s teen idol, b. Robert Velline, 30 Apr 1943, North Dakota, US. This photogenic, Buddy Holly-influenced teenaged vocalist (whose backing band once included Bob Dylan) was rarely away from the UK or US charts in the pre-Beat Boom years (134 WEEKS)* pos/wks

		pos	wks
19 Jan 61	● RUBBER BALL *London HLG 9255*	4	11
13 Apr 61	● MORE THAN I CAN SAY / STAYING IN *London HLG 9316*	4	16
3 Aug 61	● HOW MANY TEARS *London HLG 9389*	10	13
26 Oct 61	● TAKE GOOD CARE OF MY BABY *London HLG 9438* ▲	3	16
21 Dec 61	● RUN TO HIM *London HLG 9470*	6	15
8 Mar 62	PLEASE DON'T ASK ABOUT BARBARA *Liberty LIB 55419*	29	9
7 Jun 62	● SHARING YOU *Liberty LIB 55451*	10	13
27 Sep 62	A FOREVER KIND OF LOVE *Liberty LIB 10046*	13	19
7 Feb 63	● THE NIGHT HAS A THOUSAND EYES *Liberty LIB 10069*	3	12
20 Jun 63	BOBBY TOMORROW *Liberty LIB 55530*	21	10

'Staying In' listed with 'More Than I Can Say' from 13 Apr to 4 May 1961. It peaked at No.13

Louie VEGA and Marc ANTHONY
US, male vocal / instrumental duo (4 WEEKS) pos/wks

		pos	wks
5 Oct 91	RIDE ON THE RHYTHM *Atlantic A 7602* [1]	71	1
23 May 92	RIDE ON THE RHYTHM (re-issue) *Atlantic A 7486*	70	1
31 Jan 98	RIDE ON THE RHYTHM (re-mix) *Perfecto PERF 151CD1* [2]	36	2

[1] Little Louie Vega and Marc Anthony [2] Little Louie and Mark Anthony

See also LIL MO' YIN YANG

Suzanne VEGA *US, female vocalist (52 WEEKS)* pos/wks

		pos	wks
18 Jan 86	SMALL BLUE THING *A & M AM 294*	65	3
22 Mar 86	MARLENE ON THE WALL *A & M AM 309*	21	9
7 Jun 86	LEFT OF CENTER *A & M AM 320* [1]	32	9
23 May 87	LUKA *A & M VEGA 1*	23	8
18 Jul 87	TOM'S DINER *A & M VEGA 2*	58	3
19 May 90	BOOK OF DREAMS *A & M AM 559*	66	1
28 Jul 90	● TOM'S DINER (re-mix) *A & M AM 592* [2]	2	10
22 Aug 92	IN LIVERPOOL *A & M AM 0029*	52	2
24 Oct 92	99.9°F *A & M AM 0085*	46	2
19 Dec 92	BLOOD MAKES NOISE *A & M AM 0112*	60	3
6 Mar 93	WHEN HEROES GO DOWN *A & M AMCD 0158*	58	1
22 Feb 97	NO CHEAP THRILL *A & M 5818692*	40	1

[1] Suzanne Vega featuring Joe Jackson [2] DNA featuring Suzanne Vega

Tata VEGA *US, female vocalist (4 WEEKS)* pos/wks

		pos	wks
26 May 79	GET IT UP FOR LOVE / I JUST KEEP THINKING ABOUT YOU BABY *Motown TMG 1140*	52	4

VEGAS *UK, male vocal / instrumental duo (10 WEEKS)* pos/wks

		pos	wks
19 Sep 92	POSSESSED *RCA 74321110437*	32	4
28 Nov 92	SHE *RCA 74321124657*	43	4
3 Apr 93	WALK INTO THE WIND *RCA 74321122462*	65	2

Rosie VELA *US, female vocalist (7 WEEKS)* pos/wks

		pos	wks
17 Jan 87	MAGIC SMILE *A & M AM 369*	27	7

Wil VELOZ – See LOS DEL MAR featuring Wil VELOZ

VELVELETTES *US, female vocal group (7 WEEKS)* pos/wks

		pos	wks
31 Jul 71	THESE THINGS WILL KEEP ME LOVING YOU *Tamla Motown TMG 780*	34	7

VELVET UNDERGROUND
UK / US, male / female vocal / instrumental group (1 WEEK) pos/wks

		pos	wks
12 Mar 94	VENUS IN FURS *Sire W 0224CD*	71	1

VELVETS *US, male vocal group (2 WEEKS)* pos/wks

		pos	wks
11 May 61	THAT LUCKY OLD SUN *London HLU 9328*	46	1
17 Aug 61	TONIGHT (COULD BE THE NIGHT) *London HLU 9372*	50	1

VENGABOYS `304` **Top 500** *Hungary / Trinidad / Brazil / Holland, male / female vocal / production dance-pop troupe formed in 1992 by Spanish DJs Danski and Delmundo. In 1996 they added singers / dancers Kim, Robin (replaced by Yorick in 1999), Roy and Denice to front group. First Netherlands-based act to score six successive Top 5 singles, selling more than two million in UK in 12 months (97 WEEKS)* pos/wks

		pos	wks
28 Nov 98	● UP AND DOWN *Positiva CDTIV 105*	4	15
13 Mar 99	● WE LIKE TO PARTY! (THE VENGABUS) *Positiva CDTIV 108*	3	14
26 Jun 99	★ BOOM, BOOM, BOOM, BOOM!! *Positiva CDTIV 114* ■	1	15
11 Sep 99	WE'RE GOING TO IBIZA (IMPORT) *Jive 550422*	69	1
18 Sep 99	★ WE'RE GOING TO IBIZA! *Positiva CDTIV 119* ■	1	12
18 Dec 99	● KISS (WHEN THE SUN DON'T SHINE) *Positiva CDTIV 122*	3	18
11 Mar 00	● SHALALA LALA *Positiva CDTIV 126*	5	10
8 Jul 00	● UNCLE JOHN FROM JAMAICA *Positiva CDTIV 135*	6	7
14 Oct 00	CHEEKAH BOW BOW (THAT COMPUTER SONG) *Positiva CDTIV 142*	19	5

VENT 414 *UK, male vocal / instrumental group (1 WEEK)* pos/wks

		pos	wks
28 Sep 96	FIXER *Polydor 5753292*	71	1

VENTURES *US, male instrumental group (31 WEEKS)* pos/wks

		pos	wks
8 Sep 60	● WALK DON'T RUN *Top Rank JAR 417*	8	13
1 Dec 60	● PERFIDIA *London HLG 9232*	4	13
9 Mar 61	RAM-BUNK-SHUSH *London HLG 9292*	45	1
11 May 61	LULLABY OF THE LEAVES *London HLG 9344*	43	4

VERACOCHA *Holland, male production duo (4 WEEKS)* pos/wks

		pos	wks
15 May 99	CARTE BLANCHE *Positiva CDTIV 110*	22	4

See also Ferry CORSTEN; GOURYELLA; MOONMAN; SYSTEM F

Al VERLAINE – See PING PING and Al VERLAINE

VERNONS GIRLS *UK, female vocal group (31 WEEKS)* pos/wks

		pos	wks
17 May 62	LOVER PLEASE *Decca F 11450*	16	9
23 Aug 62	LOVER PLEASE (re-entry) / YOU KNOW WHAT I MEAN *Decca F 11450*	39	7
6 Sep 62	LOCO-MOTION *Decca F 11495*	47	1
18 Oct 62	YOU KNOW WHAT I MEAN (re-entry) *Decca F 11450*	37	3
15 Nov 62	YOU KNOW WHAT I MEAN (2nd re-entry) *Decca F 11450*	50	1
3 Jan 63	FUNNY ALL OVER *Decca F 11549*	31	8
18 Apr 63	DO THE BIRD *Decca F 11629*	50	1
2 May 63	DO THE BIRD (re-entry) *Decca F 11629*	44	1

'You Know What I Mean' was not coupled with 'Lover Please' on the chart of 23 Aug 1962, but both sides of this record were listed for the following six weeks

VERNON'S WONDERLAND *Germany, male producer – Matthias Hoffmann (1 WEEK)* pos/wks

		pos	wks
25 May 96	VERNON'S WONDERLAND *Eye-Q Classics EYECL 004CD*	59	1

VERTICAL HORIZONS
US, male vocal / instrumental group (2 WEEKS) pos/wks

		pos	wks
26 Aug 00	EVERYTHING YOU WANT *RCA 74321748692* ▲	42	2

VERUCA SALT
US, male / female vocal / instrumental group (5 WEEKS) pos/wks

		pos	wks
2 Jul 94	SEETHER *Scared Hitless FRET 003CD*	61	1
3 Dec 94	SEETHER (re-issue) *Hi-Rise FLATSDG 12*	73	1
4 Feb 95	NUMBER ONE BLIND *Hi-Rise FLATSCD 16*	68	1
22 Feb 97	VOLCANO GIRLS *Outpost OPRCD 22197*	56	1
30 Aug 97	BENJAMIN *Outpost OPRCD 22261*	75	1

VERVE *UK, male vocal / instrumental group (50 WEEKS)* pos/wks

		pos	wks
4 Jul 92	SHE'S A SUPERSTAR *Hut HUT 16*	66	1
22 May 93	BLUE *Hut HUTCD 29*	69	1
13 May 95	THIS IS MUSIC *Hut HUTCD 54*	35	3
24 Jun 95	ON YOUR OWN *Hut HUTCD 55*	28	2

VISIONMASTERS with Tony KING and Kylie MINOGUE *UK, male DJ / production duo, UK male DJ / producer and Australia, female vocalist (1 WEEK)* pos/wks

30 Nov 91	KEEP ON PUMPIN' IT *PWL PWL 207*	**49**	1

VIXEN *US, female vocal / instrumental group (21 WEEKS)* pos/wks

3 Sep 88	EDGE OF A BROKEN HEART *Manhattan MT 48*	**51**	4
4 Mar 89	CRYIN' *EMI Manhattan MT 60*	**27**	4
3 Jun 89	LOVE MADE ME *EMI-USA MT 66*	**36**	4
2 Sep 89	EDGE OF A BROKEN HEART (re-issue) *EMI-USA MT 48*	**59**	2
28 Jul 90	HOW MUCH LOVE *EMI-USA MT 87*	**35**	3
20 Oct 90	LOVE IS A KILLER *EMI-USA MT 91*	**41**	2
16 Mar 91	NOT A MINUTE TOO SOON *EMI-USA MT 93*	**37**	2

VOGGUE *Canada, female vocal duo (6 WEEKS)* pos/wks

18 Jul 81	DANCIN' THE NIGHT AWAY *Mercury MER 76*	**39**	6

VOICE OF THE BEEHIVE
US / UK, male / female vocal / instrumental group (51 WEEKS) pos/wks

14 Nov 87	I SAY NOTHING *London LON 151*	**45**	5
5 Mar 88	I WALK THE EARTH *London LON 169*	**42**	4
14 May 88	DON'T CALL ME BABY *London LON 175*	**15**	10
23 Jul 88	I SAY NOTHING (re-issue) *London LON 190*	**22**	6
22 Oct 88	I WALK THE EARTH (re-issue) *London LON 206*	**46**	4
13 Jul 91	MONSTERS AND ANGELS *London LON 302*	**17**	10
28 Sep 91	I THINK I LOVE YOU *London LON 308*	**25**	6
11 Jan 92	PERFECT PLACE *London LON 312*	**37**	6

VOICES OF LIFE *US, male / female vocal / production duo (2 WEEKS)* pos/wks

21 Mar 98	THE WORD IS LOVE (SAY THE WORD) *AM:PM 5825272*	**26**	2

Sterling VOID *UK, male instrumentalist / vocalist (3 WEEKS)* pos/wks

4 Feb 89	RUNAWAY GIRL / IT'S ALL RIGHT *ffrr FFR 21*	**53**	3

VOLCANO
Norway / UK, male / female vocal / instrumental group (4 WEEKS) pos/wks

23 Jul 94	MORE TO LOVE *Deconstruction 74321221832*	**32**	3
18 Nov 95	THAT'S THE WAY LOVE IS *EXP EXPCD 002* [1]	**72**	1

[1] Volcano with Sam Cartwright

VOYAGE *UK / France, disco aggregation (27 WEEKS)* pos/wks

17 Jun 78	FROM EAST TO WEST / SCOTS MACHINE *GTO GT 224*	**13**	13
25 Nov 78	SOUVENIRS *GTO GT 241*	**56**	7
24 Mar 79	LET'S FLY AWAY *GTO GT 245*	**38**	7

'Scots Machine' credited from 24 Jun 1978 until end of record's chart run

VOYAGER *UK, male vocal / instrumental group (8 WEEKS)* pos/wks

26 May 79	HALFWAY HOTEL *Mountain VOY 001*	**33**	8

VYBE *US, female vocal group (1 WEEK)* pos/wks

7 Oct 95	WARM SUMMER DAZE *Fourth & Broadway BRCD 315*	**60**	1

Kristine W *US, female vocalist - Kristine Weitz (8 WEEKS)* pos/wks

21 May 94	LOVE COME HOME *Triangle BLUESCD 001* [1]	**73**	1
25 Jun 94	FEEL WHAT YOU WANT *Champion CHAMPCD 304*	**33**	3
25 May 96	ONE MORE TRY *Champion CHAMPCD 317*	**41**	1
21 Dec 96	LAND OF THE LIVING *Champion CHAMPCD 324*	**57**	1
5 Jul 97	FEEL WHAT YOU WANT (re-issue) *Champion CHAMPCD 329*	**40**	2

[1] Our Tribe with Franke Pharoah and Kristine W

Bill WADDINGTON – See CORONATION STREET CAST featuring Bill WADDINGTON

Adam WADE *US, male vocalist (6 WEEKS)* pos/wks

8 Jun 61	TAKE GOOD CARE OF HER *HMV POP 843*	**38**	1
22 Jun 61	TAKE GOOD CARE OF HER (re-entry) *HMV POP 843*	**38**	5

WAG YA TAIL *UK, male vocal / instrumental group (1 WEEK)* pos/wks

3 Oct 92	XPAND YA MIND (EXPANSIONS) *PWL International PWL 238*	**49**	1

WAH!
UK, male vocal / instrumental group - leader Pete Wylie (26 WEEKS) pos/wks

25 Dec 82	● THE STORY OF THE BLUES *Eternal JF 1*	**3**	12
19 Mar 83	HOPE (I WISH YOU'D BELIEVE ME) *WEA X 9880*	**37**	5
30 Jun 84	COME BACK *Beggars Banquet BEG 111* [1]	**20**	9

[1] Mighty Wah

See also Pete WYLIE

Donnie WAHLBERG – See SEIKO and Donnie WAHLBERG; NEW KIDS ON THE BLOCK

WAIKIKIS *Belgium, male instrumental group (2 WEEKS)* pos/wks

11 Mar 65	HAWAII TATTOO *Pye International 7N 25286*	**41**	2

WAILERS – See Bob MARLEY and the WAILERS

John WAITE *UK, male vocalist (13 WEEKS)* pos/wks

29 Sep 84	● MISSING YOU *EMI America EA 182* ▲	**9**	11
13 Feb 93	MISSING YOU (re-issue) *Chrysalis CDCHS 3938*	**56**	2

WAITRESSES *US, female vocal group (4 WEEKS)* pos/wks

18 Dec 82	CHRISTMAS WRAPPING *Ze / Island WIP 6821*	**45**	4

Johnny WAKELIN *UK, male vocalist (20 WEEKS)* pos/wks

18 Jan 75	● BLACK SUPERMAN (MUHAMMAD ALI) *Pye 7N 45420* [1]	**7**	10
24 Jul 76	● IN ZAIRE *Pye 7N 45595*	**4**	10

[1] Johnny Wakelin and the Kinshasa Band

Narada Michael WALDEN
US, male vocalist / producer (28 WEEKS) pos/wks

23 Feb 80	TONIGHT I'M ALRIGHT *Atlantic K 11437*	**34**	9
26 Apr 80	● I SHOULDA LOVED YA *Atlantic K 11413*	**8**	9
23 Apr 88	● DIVINE EMOTIONS *Reprise W 7967* [1]	**8**	10

[1] Narada

Gary WALKER *US, male vocalist - Gary Leeds (12 WEEKS)* pos/wks

24 Feb 66	YOU DON'T LOVE ME *CBS 202036*	**26**	6
26 May 66	TWINKIE LEE *CBS 202081*	**26**	6

See also WALKER BROTHERS

John WALKER *US, male vocalist - John Maus (6 WEEKS)* pos/wks

5 Jul 67	ANNABELLA *Philips BF 1593*	**48**	1
19 Jul 67	ANNABELLA (re-entry) *Philips BF 1593*	**24**	5

See also WALKER BROTHERS

Scott WALKER *US, male vocalist - Scott Engel (30 WEEKS)* pos/wks

6 Dec 67	JACKIE *Philips BF 1628*	**22**	9
1 May 68	● JOANNA *Philips BF 1662*	**7**	11
11 Jun 69	LIGHTS OF CINCINNATI *Philips BF 1793*	**13**	10

See also WALKER BROTHERS

Junior WALKER and the ALL-STARS
US, male instrumental / vocal group (59 WEEKS)   pos/wks

18 Aug 66	HOW SWEET IT IS Tamla Motown TMG 571	22	10
2 Apr 69	(I'M A) ROAD RUNNER Tamla Motown TMG 691	12	12
18 Oct 69	WHAT DOES IT TAKE (TO WIN YOUR LOVE) Tamla Motown TMG 712	13	12
26 Aug 72	WALK IN THE NIGHT Tamla Motown TMG 824	16	11
27 Jan 73	TAKE ME GIRL I'M READY Tamla Motown TMG 840	16	9
30 Jun 73	WAY BACK HOME Tamla Motown TMG 857	35	5

WALKER BROTHERS `323` `Top 500` Unrelated US trio, who were top UK teen idols in mid-60s. Members Scott Walker (Engel) (v/b/k), John Walker (Maus) (v/g), Gary Walker (Leeds) (d) all had solo hits after trio split in 1967, with Scott (who first recorded solo in 1957) creating a large cult following (93 WEEKS)   pos/wks

29 Apr 65	LOVE HER Philips BF 1409	20	13
19 Aug 65	★ MAKE IT EASY ON YOURSELF Philips BF 1428	1	14
2 Dec 65	● MY SHIP IS COMING IN Philips BF 1454	3	12
3 Mar 66	★ THE SUN AIN'T GONNA SHINE ANYMORE Philips BF 1473	1	11
14 Jul 66	(BABY) YOU DON'T HAVE TO TELL ME Philips BF 1497	13	8
22 Sep 66	ANOTHER TEAR FALLS Philips BF 1514	12	8
15 Dec 66	DEADLIER THAN THE MALE Philips BF 1537	34	6
9 Feb 67	STAY WITH ME BABY Philips BF 1548	26	6
18 May 67	WALKING IN THE RAIN Philips BF 1576	26	6
17 Jan 76	● NO REGRETS GTO GT 42	7	9

See also Gary WALKER; John WALKER; Scott WALKER

WALL OF SOUND featuring Gerald LETHAN
US, male vocal / instrumental group (1 WEEK)   pos/wks

| 31 Jul 93 | CRITICAL (IF YOU ONLY KNEW) Positiva CDTIV 4 | 73 | 1 |

WALL OF VOODOO US, male vocal / instrumental group (3 WEEKS) pos/wks

| 19 Mar 83 | MEXICAN RADIO Illegal ILS 36 | 64 | 3 |

Jerry WALLACE US, male vocalist (1 WEEK)   pos/wks

| 23 Jun 60 | YOU'RE SINGING OUR LOVE SONG TO SOMEBODY ELSE London HLH 9110 | 46 | 1 |

WALLFLOWERS US, male vocal / instrumental group (1 WEEK) pos/wks

| 12 Jul 97 | ONE HEADLIGHT Interscope IND 95532 | 54 | 1 |

Bob WALLIS and his STORYVILLE JAZZ BAND UK, male jazz band,
Bob Wallis vocalist / instrumentalist - trumpet (7 WEEKS)   pos/wks

| 6 Jul 61 | I'M SHY MARY ELLEN I'M SHY Pye Jazz 7NJ 2043 | 44 | 2 |
| 4 Jan 62 | COME ALONG PLEASE Pye Jazz 7NJ 2048 | 33 | 5 |

Joe WALSH US, male vocalist (15 WEEKS)   pos/wks

| 16 Jul 77 | ROCKY MOUNTAIN WAY (EP) ABC ABE 12002 | 39 | 4 |
| 8 Jul 78 | LIFE'S BEEN GOOD Asylum K 13129 | 14 | 11 |

Tracks on Rocky Mountain Way (EP): Rocky Mountain Way / Turn to Stone / Meadows / Walk Away

Maureen WALSH – See MAUREEN

Sheila WALSH and Cliff RICHARD
UK, female / male vocal duo (2 WEEKS)   pos/wks

| 4 Jun 83 | DRIFTING DJM SHEIL 1 | 64 | 2 |

Steve WALSH UK, male DJ / vocalist (18 WEEKS)   pos/wks

18 Jul 87	I FOUND LOVIN' A1 A1 299	74	1
29 Aug 87	● I FOUND LOVIN' (re-entry) A1 A1 299	9	12
12 Dec 87	LET'S GET TOGETHER TONITE A1 A1 303	74	1
30 Jul 88	AIN'T NO STOPPING US NOW (PARTY FOR THE WORLD) A1 A1 304	44	4

Trevor WALTERS UK, male vocalist (22 WEEKS)   pos/wks

24 Oct 81	LOVE ME TONIGHT Magnet MAG 198	27	8
21 Jul 84	● STUCK ON YOU Sanity IS 002	9	12
1 Dec 84	NEVER LET HER SLIP AWAY Polydor POSP 716	73	2

WAMDUE PROJECT US, male producer - Chris Brann (19 WEEKS) pos/wks

20 Nov 99	KING OF MY CASTLE (IMPORT) Orange ORCDM 53584CD	61	1
27 Nov 99	★ KING OF MY CASTLE AM:PM CDAMPM 127 ■	1	15
25 Mar 00	KING OF MY CASTLE (re-entry) AM:PM CDAMPM 127	74	1
15 Apr 00	YOU'RE THE REASON AM:PM CDAMPM 130	39	2

WANG CHUNG UK, male vocal / instrumental group (12 WEEKS) pos/wks

| 28 Jan 84 | DANCE HALL DAYS Geffen A 3837 | 21 | 12 |

WANNADIES
Sweden, male / female vocal / instrumental group (12 WEEKS)   pos/wks

18 Nov 95	MIGHT BE STARS Indolent DIE 003CD1	51	2
24 Feb 96	HOW DOES IT FEEL Indolent DIE 004CD1	53	1
20 Apr 96	YOU AND ME SONG Indolent DIE 005CD	18	3
7 Sep 96	SOMEONE SOMEWHERE Indolent DIE 006CD	38	1
26 Apr 97	HIT Indolent DIE 009CD1	20	2
5 Jul 97	SHORTY Indolent DIE 010CD1	41	2
4 Mar 00	YEAH RCA 74321745552	56	1

Dexter WANSELL US, male instrumentalist - keyboards (3 WEEKS) pos/wks

| 20 May 78 | ALL NIGHT LONG Philadelphia International PIR 6255 | 59 | 3 |

WAR US / Canada / Denmark, male vocal / instrumental group
(32 WEEKS)   pos/wks

24 Jan 76	LOW RIDER Island WIP 6267	12	7
26 Jun 76	ME AND BABY BROTHER Island WIP 6303	21	7
14 Jan 78	GALAXY MCA 339	14	7
15 Apr 78	HEY SENORITA MCA 359	40	2
10 Apr 82	YOU GOT THE POWER RCA 201	58	4
6 Apr 85	GROOVIN' Bluebird BR 16	43	5

Anita WARD US, female vocalist (11 WEEKS)   pos/wks

| 2 Jun 79 | ★ RING MY BELL TK TKR 7543 ▲ | 1 | 11 |

Chrissy WARD US, female vocalist (2 WEEKS)   pos/wks

| 24 Jun 95 | RIGHT AND EXACT Ore AG 6CD | 62 | 1 |
| 8 Feb 97 | RIGHT AND EXACT (re-mix) Ore AG 21CD | 59 | 1 |

Clifford T WARD UK, male vocalist (16 WEEKS)   pos/wks

| 30 Jun 73 | ● GAYE Charisma CB 205 | 8 | 11 |
| 26 Jan 74 | SCULLERY Charisma CB 221 | 37 | 5 |

Michael WARD UK, male vocalist (13 WEEKS)   pos/wks

| 29 Sep 73 | LET THERE BE PEACE ON EARTH (LET IT BEGIN WITH ME) Philips 6006 340 | 15 | 10 |
| 15 Dec 73 | LET THERE BE PEACE ON EARTH (LET IT BEGIN WITH ME) (re-entry) Philips 6006 340 | 50 | 3 |

Billy WARD and HIS DOMINOES
US, male vocal group (13 WEEKS)   pos/wks

13 Sep 57	STARDUST London HLU 8465	13	11
29 Nov 57	DEEP PURPLE London HLU 8502	30	1
3 Jan 58	STARDUST (re-entry) London HLU 8465	26	1

WARD BROTHERS UK, male vocal / instrumental group (8 WEEKS) pos/wks

| 10 Jan 87 | CROSS THAT BRIDGE Siren SIREN 37 | 32 | 8 |

Justin WARFIELD – See BOMB THE BASS

UK No.1 ★ UK Top 10 ● Still on chart + UK million seller ◆ UK entry at No.1 ■ US No.1 ▲

WARM JETS
UK / Canada, male vocal / instrumental group (4 WEEKS) pos/wks

14 Feb 98	NEVER NEVER *Island WAY 6766*	37	2
25 Apr 98	HURRICANE *Island CID 697*	34	2

WARM SOUNDS *UK, male vocal duo (6 WEEKS)* pos/wks

4 May 67	BIRDS AND BEES *Deram DM 120*	27	6

Toni WARNE *UK, female vocalist (4 WEEKS)* pos/wks

25 Apr 87	BEN *Mint CHEW 110*	50	4

Jennifer WARNES *US, female vocalist (37 WEEKS)* pos/wks

15 Jan 83 ●	UP WHERE WE BELONG *Island WIP 6830* [1] ▲	7	13
25 Jul 87	FIRST WE TAKE MANHATTAN *Cypress PB 49709*	74	1
31 Oct 87 ●	(I'VE HAD) THE TIME OF MY LIFE		
	RCA PB 49625 [2] ▲	6	12
15 Dec 90 ●	(I'VE HAD) THE TIME OF MY LIFE (re-entry)		
	RCA PB 49625 [2]	8	11

[1] Joe Cocker and Jennifer Warnes [2] Bill Medley and Jennifer Warnes

WARP BROTHERS
Germany, male DJ / production group (7 WEEKS) pos/wks

11 Nov 00	PHATT BASS (IMPORT)		
	Dos or Die BMSCDM 40009	75	3
9 Dec 00 ●	PHATT BASS *Nulife / Arista 74321817102* [1]	9	4+

[1] Warp Brothers Vs Aquagen

WARRANT *US, male vocal / instrumental group (7 WEEKS)* pos/wks

17 Nov 90	CHERRY PIE *CBS 6562587*	59	2
9 Mar 91	CHERRY PIE (re-issue) *Columbia 6566867*	35	5

Alysha WARREN *UK, female vocalist (4 WEEKS)* pos/wks

24 Sep 94	I'M SO IN LOVE *Wild Card CARDD 10*	61	1
25 Mar 95	I THOUGHT I MEANT THE WORLD TO YOU		
	Wild Card CARDD 16	40	1
27 Jul 96	KEEP ON PUSHING OUR LOVE		
	Arista 74321390422 [1]	30	2

[1] Nightcrawlers featuring John Reid and Alysha Warren

Ann WARREN – See Ruby MURRAY

Nikita WARREN *Italy, female vocalist (1 WEEK)* pos/wks

13 Jul 96	I NEED YOU *VC VCRD 12*	48	1

WARRIOR *UK, male vocal / production / instrumental duo (4 WEEKS)* pos/wks

21 Oct 00	WARRIOR *Incentive CENT 12CDS*	19	4

Dionne WARWICK (294 Top 500) *Super-stylish soul diva, b. 12 Dec 1940, New Jersey, US, whose classy and unmistakable vocals on songs written by Burt Bacharach and Hal David produced more than 30 US hits for her between 1962 and 1972. She is a cousin of Whitney Houston (101 WEEKS)* pos/wks

13 Feb 64	ANYONE WHO HAD A HEART		
	Pye International 7N 25234	42	3
16 Apr 64 ●	WALK ON BY *Pye International 7N 25241*	9	14
30 Jul 64	YOU'LL NEVER GET TO HEAVEN		
	Pye International 7N 25256	20	8
8 Oct 64	REACH OUT FOR ME *Pye International 7N 25265*	23	7
1 Apr 65	YOU CAN HAVE HIM *Pye International 7N 25290*	37	5
13 Mar 68	VALLEY OF THE DOLLS *Pye International 7N 25445*	28	8
15 May 68 ●	DO YOU KNOW THE WAY TO SAN JOSE		
	Pye International 7N 25457	8	10
19 Oct 74	THEN CAME YOU *Atlantic K 10495* [1] ▲	29	6
23 Oct 82 ●	HEARTBREAKER *Arista ARIST 496*	2	13
11 Dec 82 ●	ALL THE LOVE IN THE WORLD *Arista ARIST 507*	10	10
26 Feb 83	YOURS *Arista ARIST 518*	66	2
28 May 83	I'LL NEVER LOVE THIS WAY AGAIN *Arista ARIST 530*	62	3

9 Nov 85	THAT'S WHAT FRIENDS ARE FOR *Arista ARIST 638* [2]	16	9
15 Aug 87	LOVE POWER *Arista RIS 27* [3]	63	3

[1] Dionne Warwick & the Detroit Spinners [2] Dionne Warwick and Friends featuring Elton John, Stevie Wonder and Gladys Knight [3] Dionne Warwick and Jeffrey Osborne

WAS (NOT WAS) *US, male vocal / instrumental duo - Don Fagenson & David Weiss (58 WEEKS)* pos/wks

3 Mar 84	OUT COME THE FREAKS *Ze / Geffen A 4178*	41	5
18 Jul 87	SPY IN THE HOUSE OF LOVE *Fontana WAS 2*	51	7
3 Oct 87 ●	WALK THE DINOSAUR *Fontana WAS 3*	10	10
6 Feb 88	SPY IN THE HOUSE OF LOVE (re-entry) *Fontana WAS 2*	21	8
7 May 88	OUT COME THE FREAKS (AGAIN) *Fontana WAS 4*	44	3
16 Jul 88	ANYTHING CAN HAPPEN *Fontana WAS 5*	67	3
26 May 90	PAPA WAS A ROLLING STONE *Fontana WAS 7*	12	7
11 Aug 90	HOW THE HEART BEHAVES *Fontana WAS 8*	53	3
23 May 92	LISTEN LIKE THIEVES *Fontana WAS 10*	58	2
11 Jul 92 ●	SHAKE YOUR HEAD *Fontana WAS 11*	4	9
26 Sep 92	SOMEWHERE IN AMERICA (THERE'S A STREET NAMED		
	AFTER MY DAD) *Fontana WAS 12*	57	1

Fontana WAS 4 was a re-recorded version of their first hit. 'Shake Your Head' features uncredited vocals by Ozzy Osbourne and Kim Basinger

Martha WASH *US, female vocalist (34 WEEKS)* pos/wks

28 Nov 92	CARRY ON *RCA 74321125457*	74	1
6 Mar 93	GIVE IT TO YOU *RCA 74321136562*	37	4
10 Jul 93	RUNAROUND / CARRY ON (re-mix) *RCA 74321153702*	49	2
18 Feb 95	I FOUND LOVE *Columbia 6612112* [1]	26	2
13 Jul 96 ●	KEEP ON JUMPIN' *Manifesto FESCD 11* [2]	8	6
12 Jul 97 ●	SOMETHING GOIN' ON *Manifesto FESCD 25* [2]	5	10
25 Oct 97	CARRY ON (2nd) (re-mix) *Delirious DELICD 6*	49	1
28 Feb 98	IT'S RAINING MEN…THE SEQUEL		
	Logic 74321555412 [3]	21	3
11 Apr 98	READY FOR A NEW DAY *Manifesto FESCD 40* [4]	20	2
15 Aug 98	CATCH THE LIGHT *Logic 74321587912*	45	1
3 Jul 99	COME *Logic 74321653942*	64	1
5 Feb 00	IT'S RAINING MEN (re-recording) *Logic 74321726282*	56	1

[1] C & C Music Factory featuring Martha Wash [2] Todd Terry featuring Martha Wash and Jocelyn Brown [3] Martha Wash featuring RuPaul [4] Todd Terry featuring Martha Wash

The listed flip side of 'I Found Love' was 'Take a Toke' by C & C Music Factory

See also WEATHER GIRLS

Dinah WASHINGTON *US, female vocalist (8 WEEKS)* pos/wks

30 Nov 61	SEPTEMBER IN THE RAIN *Mercury AMT 1162*	35	3
18 Jan 62	SEPTEMBER IN THE RAIN (re-entry) *Mercury AMT 1162*	49	1
4 Apr 92	MAD ABOUT THE BOY *Mercury DINAH 1*	41	4

Grover WASHINGTON Jr
US, male instrumentalist - saxophone (7 WEEKS) pos/wks

16 May 81	JUST THE TWO OF US *Elektra K 12514*	34	7

Although uncredited, Bill Withers sings on 'Just the Two of Us'

Keith WASHINGTON – See Kylie MINOGUE

Sarah WASHINGTON *UK, female vocalist (13 WEEKS)* pos/wks

14 Aug 93	I WILL ALWAYS LOVE YOU *Almighty CDALMY 33*	12	7
27 Nov 93	CARELESS WHISPER *Almighty CDALMY 43*	45	2
25 May 96	HEAVEN *AM:PM 5815352*	28	2
12 Oct 96	EVERYTHING *AM:PM 5818872*	30	2

Geno WASHINGTON and the RAM JAM BAND *US, male vocalist, and UK, male instrumental backing group (20 WEEKS)* pos/wks

19 May 66	WATER *Piccadilly 7N 35312*	39	8
21 Jul 66	HI HI HAZEL *Piccadilly 7N 35329*	45	3
25 Aug 66	HI HI HAZEL (re-entry) *Piccadilly 7N 35329*	48	1
6 Oct 66	QUE SERA SERA *Piccadilly 7N 35346*	43	3
2 Feb 67	MICHAEL *Piccadilly 7N 35359*	39	5

SINGLED OUT...
Alice Deejay

Lead singer of addictive Dutch export Alice Deejay, Judy has danced her way to 46 weeks of infectious dance pop in just four releases. The bikini-clad chanteuse began her worldwide plan for club domination in Amsterdam's legendary Roxy Club and has since spread the gospel across the globe.

- **NO.1 ON THE UK SINGLES CHART THE DAY I WAS BORN:**
  Bohemian Rhapsody – Queen

- **FIRST SINGLE I EVER BOUGHT:**
  Control – Janet Jackson

- **SINGLE THAT DRIVES ME UP THE WALL:**
  Everything and anything by Mariah Carey

ALL-TIME FAVOURITE SINGLE:

It's Raining Men
The Weather Girls

W.A.S.P.
US, male vocal / instrumental group (38 WEEKS) pos/wks

31 May 86	WILD CHILD *Capitol CL 388*	71	2
11 Oct 86	95 - NASTY *Capitol CL 432*	70	1
29 Aug 87	SCREAM UNTIL YOU LIKE IT *Capitol CL 458*	32	5
31 Oct 87	I DON'T NEED NO DOCTOR (LIVE) *Capitol CL 469*	31	5
20 Feb 88	LIVE ANIMAL (F**K LIKE A BEAST) *Music For Nations KUT 109*	61	3
4 Mar 89	MEAN MAN *Capitol CL 521*	21	5
27 May 89	THE REAL ME *Capitol CL 534*	23	5
9 Sep 89	FOREVER FREE *Capitol CL 546*	25	5
4 Apr 92	CHAINSAW CHARLIE (MURDERS IN THE NEW MORGUE) *Parlophone RS 6308*	17	2
6 Jun 92	THE IDOL *Parlophone RPD 6314*	41	2
31 Oct 92	I AM ONE *Parlophone 10RG 6324*	56	1
23 Oct 93	SUNSET AND BABYLON *Capitol CDCL 698*	38	2

WATERBOYS
UK / Ireland, male vocal / instrumental group (33 WEEKS) pos/wks

2 Nov 85	THE WHOLE OF THE MOON *Ensign ENY 520*	26	7
14 Jan 89	FISHERMAN'S BLUES *Ensign ENY 621*	32	6
1 Jul 89	AND A BANG ON THE EAR *Ensign ENY 624*	51	4
6 Apr 91 ●	THE WHOLE OF THE MOON (re-issue) *Ensign ENY 642*	3	9
8 Jun 91	FISHERMAN'S BLUES (re-issue) *Ensign ENY 645*	75	1
15 May 93	THE RETURN OF PAN *Geffen GFSTD 42*	24	3
24 Jul 93	GLASTONBURY SONG *Geffen GFSTD 49*	29	3

WATERFRONT
UK, male vocal / instrumental duo (19 WEEKS) pos/wks

15 Apr 89	BROKEN ARROW *Polydor WON 3*	63	2
27 May 89	CRY *Polydor WON 1*	17	13
9 Sep 89	NATURE OF LOVE *Polydor WON 2*	63	4

WATERGATE
Turkey, male DJ / producer - Orhan Terzi (10 WEEKS) pos/wks

| 13 May 00 ● | HEART OF ASIA *Positiva CDTIV 129* | 3 | 10 |

See also DJ QUICKSILVER

Dennis WATERMAN
UK, male vocalist (17 WEEKS) pos/wks

| 25 Oct 80 ● | I COULD BE SO GOOD FOR YOU *EMI 5009* [1] | 3 | 12 |
| 17 Dec 83 | WHAT ARE WE GONNA GET 'ER INDOORS *EMI MIN 101* [2] | 21 | 5 |

[1] Dennis Waterman with the Dennis Waterman Band [2] Dennis Waterman and George Cole

Crystal WATERS
US, female vocalist (35 WEEKS) pos/wks

18 May 91 ●	GYPSY WOMAN (LA DA DEE) *A & M AM 772*	2	10
7 Sep 91	MAKIN' HAPPY *A & M AM 790*	18	6
11 Jan 92	MEGAMIX *A & M AM 843*	39	3
3 Oct 92	GYPSY WOMAN (re-mix) *Epic 6584377*	35	2
23 Apr 94	100% PURE LOVE *A & M 8586692*	15	7
2 Jul 94	GHETTO DAY *A & M 8589592*	40	2
25 Nov 95	RELAX *Manifesto FESCD 4*	37	2
24 Aug 96	IN DE GHETTO *Manifesto FESCD 12* [1]	35	2
19 Apr 97	SAY …IF YOU FEEL ALRIGHT *Mercury 5742912*	45	1

[1] David Morales and the Bad Yard Club featuring Crystal Waters and Delta

The listed flip side of 'Gypsy Woman' (re-mix) was 'Peace' (re-mix) by Sabrina Johnston

Muddy WATERS
US, male vocalist / instrumentalist - guitar (6 WEEKS) pos/wks

| 16 Jul 88 | MANNISH BOY *Epic MUD 1* | 51 | 6 |

Roger WATERS
UK, male vocalist / instrumentalist (8 WEEKS) pos/wks

30 May 87	RADIO WAVES *Harvest EM 6*	74	1
26 Dec 87	THE TIDE IS TURNING (AFTER LIVE AID) *Harvest EM 37*	54	4
5 Sep 92	WHAT GOD WANTS PART 1 *Columbia 6581390*	35	3

Michael WATFORD
US, male vocalist (2 WEEKS) pos/wks

| 26 Feb 94 | SO INTO YOU *East West A 8309CD* | 53 | 2 |

Jody WATLEY
US, female vocalist (35 WEEKS) pos/wks

9 May 87	LOOKING FOR A NEW LOVE *MCA MCA 1107*	13	11
17 Oct 87	DON'T YOU WANT ME *MCA MCA 1198*	55	3
8 Apr 89	REAL LOVE *MCA MCA 1324*	31	7
12 Aug 89	FRIENDS *MCA MCA 1352* [1]	21	6
10 Feb 90	EVERYTHING *MCA MCA 1395*	74	2
11 Apr 92	I'M THE ONE YOU NEED *MCA MCS 1608*	50	3
21 May 94	WHEN A MAN LOVES A WOMAN *MCA MCSTD 1964*	33	2
25 Apr 98	OFF THE HOOK *Atlantic AT 0024CD1*	51	1

[1] Jody Watley with Eric B and Rakim

See also SHALAMAR

Johnny 'Guitar' WATSON
US, male vocalist / instrumentalist - guitar (8 WEEKS) pos/wks

| 28 Aug 76 | I NEED IT *DJM DJS 10694* | 35 | 5 |
| 23 Apr 77 | A REAL MOTHER FOR YA *DJM DJS 10762* | 44 | 3 |

Russell WATSON
UK, male vocalist (3 WEEKS) pos/wks

| 30 Oct 99 | SWING LOW '99 *Decca / Universal TV 4669502* | 38 | 2 |
| 22 Jul 00 | BARCELONA (FRIENDS UNTIL THE END) *Decca 4672772* [1] | 68 | 1 |

[1] Russell Watson & Shaun Ryder

WAVELENGTH
UK, male vocal group (12 WEEKS) pos/wks

| 10 Jul 82 | HURRY HOME *Ariola ARO 281* | 17 | 12 |

WAX
US / UK, male vocal / instrumental duo (16 WEEKS) pos/wks

| 12 Apr 86 | RIGHT BETWEEN THE EYES *RCA PB 40509* | 60 | 5 |
| 1 Aug 87 | BRIDGE TO YOUR HEART *RCA PB 41405* | 12 | 11 |

Anthony WAY
UK, choirboy (2 WEEKS) pos/wks

| 15 Apr 95 | PANIS ANGELICUS *Decca 4481642* | 55 | 2 |

A WAY OF LIFE
US, male / female vocal / instrumental group (3 WEEKS) pos/wks

| 21 Apr 90 | TRIPPIN' ON YOUR LOVE *Eternal YZ 464* | 55 | 3 |

WAY OF THE WEST
UK, male vocal / instrumental group (5 WEEKS) pos/wks

| 25 Apr 81 | DON'T SAY THAT'S JUST FOR WHITE BOYS *Mercury MER 66* | 54 | 5 |

WAY OUT WEST
UK, male instrumental / production duo (13 WEEKS) pos/wks

3 Dec 94	AJARE *Deconstruction 74321243802*	52	1
2 Mar 96	DOMINATION *Deconstruction 74321342822*	38	2
14 Sep 96	THE GIFT *Deconstruction 74321401912* [1]	15	5
30 Aug 97	BLUE *Deconstruction 74321477512*	41	2
29 Nov 97	AJARE (re-mix) *Deconstruction 74321521352*	36	2
9 Dec 00	THE FALL *Wow WOW 005CD*	61	1

[1] Way Out West featuring Miss Joanna Law

Bruce WAYNE
Germany, male DJ / producer (2 WEEKS) pos/wks

| 13 Dec 97 | READY *Logic 74321527012* | 44 | 1 |
| 4 Jul 98 | NO GOOD FOR ME *Logic 74321587052* | 70 | 1 |

Jeff WAYNE
US, orchestra (21 WEEKS) pos/wks

9 Sep 78	EVE OF THE WAR *CBS 6496* [1]	36	8
10 Jul 82	MATADOR *CBS A 2493*	57	3
25 Nov 89 ●	EVE OF THE WAR (re-mix) *CBS 6551267* [1]	3	10

[1] Jeff Wayne's War Of The Worlds

WEATHER GIRLS
US, female vocal duo - Martha Wash & Izora Redman (14 WEEKS) pos/wks

| 27 Aug 83 | IT'S RAINING MEN *CBS A 2924* | 73 | 3 |
| 3 Mar 84 ● | IT'S RAINING MEN (re-entry) *CBS A 2924* | 2 | 11 |

See also Martha WASH

WEATHER PROPHETS
UK, male vocal / instrumental group (2 WEEKS)   pos/wks

28 Mar 87	SHE COMES FROM THE RAIN *Elevation ACID 1*	62 2

WEATHERMEN – See Jonathan KING

Marti WEBB *UK, female vocalist (42 WEEKS)*   pos/wks

9 Feb 80 ●	TAKE THAT LOOK OFF YOUR FACE *Polydor POSP 100*	3 12
19 Apr 80	TELL ME ON A SUNDAY *Polydor POSP 111*	67 2
20 Sep 80	YOUR EARS SHOULD BE BURNING NOW *Polydor POSP 166*	61 4
8 Jun 85 ●	BEN *Starblend STAR 6*	5 11
20 Sep 86	ALWAYS THERE *BBC RESL 190* [1]	13 12
6 Jun 87	I CAN'T LET GO *Rainbow RBR 12*	65 1

[1] Marti Webb and the Simon May Orchestra

Joan WEBER *US, female vocalist (1 WEEK)*   pos/wks

18 Feb 55	LET ME GO LOVER *Philips PB 389* ▲	16 1

WEDDING PRESENT *UK, male vocal / instrumental group (38 WEEKS)* pos/wks

5 Mar 88	NOBODY'S TWISTING YOUR ARM *Reception REC 009*	46 2
1 Oct 88	WHY ARE YOU BEING SO REASONABLE NOW *Reception REC 011*	42 2
7 Oct 89	KENNEDY *RCA PB 43117*	33 3
17 Feb 90	BRASSNECK *RCA PB 43403*	24 3
29 Sep 90	3 SONGS (EP) *RCA PB 44021*	25 4
11 May 91	DALLIANCE *RCA PB 44495*	29 3
27 Jul 91	LOVENEST *RCA PT 44750*	58 1
18 Jan 92	BLUE EYES *RCA PB 45185*	26 2
15 Feb 92	GO-GO DANCER *RCA PB 45183*	20 1
14 Mar 92	THREE *RCA PB 45181*	14 2
18 Apr 92	SILVER SHORTS *RCA PB 45311*	14 1
16 May 92 ●	COME PLAY WITH ME *RCA PB 45313*	10 2
13 Jun 92	CALIFORNIA *RCA PB 45315*	16 1
18 Jul 92	FLYING SAUCER *RCA 74321101157*	22 1
15 Aug 92	BOING! *RCA 74321101177*	19 1
19 Sep 92	LOVE SLAVE *RCA 743211101167*	17 1
17 Oct 92	STICKY *RCA 74321116917*	17 1
14 Nov 92	THE QUEEN OF OUTER SPACE *RCA 74321116927*	23 1
19 Dec 92	NO CHRISTMAS *RCA 74321116937*	25 1
10 Sep 94	YEAH YEAH YEAH YEAH *Island CID 585*	51 2
26 Nov 94	IT'S A GAS *Island CID 591*	71 1
31 Aug 96	2, 3, GO *Cooking Vinyl FRYCD 048*	67 1
25 Jan 97	MONTREAL *Cooking Vinyl FRYCD 053*	40 1

Tracks on 3 Songs (EP): Corduroy / Crawl / Make Me Smile (Come Up and See Me)

Fred WEDLOCK *UK, male vocalist (10 WEEKS)*   pos/wks

31 Jan 81 ●	OLDEST SWINGER IN TOWN *Rocket XPRES 46*	6 10

WEE PAPA GIRL RAPPERS *UK, female rap / vocal duo - Samantha and Sandra Lawrence (27 WEEKS)*   pos/wks

12 Mar 88	FAITH *Jive JIVE 164*	60 4
25 Jun 88	HEAT IT UP *Jive JIVE 174* [1]	21 9
1 Oct 88 ●	WEE RULE *Jive JIVE 185*	6 9
24 Dec 88	SOULMATE *Jive JIVE 193*	45 4
25 Mar 89	BLOW THE HOUSE DOWN *Jive JIVE 197*	65 1

[1] Wee Papa Girl Rappers featuring Two Men and a Drum Machine

Bert WEEDON *UK, male instrumentalist - guitar (38 WEEKS)*   pos/wks

15 May 59 ●	GUITAR BOOGIE SHUFFLE *Top Rank JAR 117*	10 9
20 Nov 59	NASHVILLE BOOGIE *Top Rank JAR 221*	29 2
10 Mar 60	BIG BEAT BOOGIE *Top Rank JAR 300*	37 3
7 Apr 60	BIG BEAT BOOGIE (re-entry) *Top Rank JAR 300*	49 1
9 Jun 60	TWELFTH STREET RAG *Top Rank JAR 360*	47 2
28 Jul 60	APACHE *Top Rank JAR 415*	44 1
11 Aug 60	APACHE (re-entry) *Top Rank JAR 415*	24 3
27 Oct 60	SORRY ROBBIE *Top Rank JAR 517*	28 11
2 Feb 61	GINCHY *Top Rank JAR 537*	35 5
4 May 61	MR GUITAR *Top Rank JAR 559*	47 1

WEEKEND
International, male / female vocal / instrumental group (5 WEEKS)   pos/wks

14 Dec 85	CHRISTMAS MEDLEY / AULD LANG SYNE *Lifestyle XY 1*	47 5

Michelle WEEKS *US, female vocalist (6 WEEKS)*   pos/wks

2 Aug 97	MOMENT OF MY LIFE *Ministry of Sound MOSCDS 1* [1]	23 3
8 Nov 97	DON'T GIVE UP *Ministry of Sound MOSCDS 2*	28 2
11 Jul 98	GIVE ME LOVE *VC Recordings VCRD 37* [2]	59 1

[1] Bobby D'Ambrosio Featuring Michelle Weeks [2] DJ Dado vs Michelle Weeks

WEEN – See FOO FIGHTERS

WEEZER *US, male vocal / instrumental group (12 WEEKS)*   pos/wks

11 Feb 95	UNDONE - THE SWEATER SONG *Geffen GFSTD 85*	35 2
6 May 95	BUDDY HOLLY *Geffen GFSTD 88*	12 7
22 Jul 95	SAY IT AIN'T SO *Geffen GFSTD 95*	37 2
5 Oct 96	EL SCORCHO *Geffen GFSTD 22167*	50 1

Frank WEIR *UK, orchestra (4 WEEKS)*   pos/wks

15 Sep 60	CARIBBEAN HONEYMOON *Oriole CB 1559*	42 4

See also Vera LYNN

WEIRD SCIENCE *UK, male DJ / production duo (1 WEEK)*   pos/wks

1 Jul 00	FEEL THE NEED *Nulife 74321751982*	62 1

Eric WEISSBERG – See 'DELIVERANCE' SOUNDTRACK

Denise WELCH *UK, female vocalist (3 WEEKS)*   pos/wks

4 Nov 95	YOU DON'T HAVE TO SAY YOU LOVE ME / CRY ME A RIVER *Virgin VSCDT 1569*	23 3

Paul WELLER *UK, male vocalist (62 WEEKS)*   pos/wks

18 May 91	INTO TOMORROW *Freedom High FHP 1* [1]	36 3
15 Aug 92	UH HUH OH YEH *Go! Discs GOD 86*	18 5
10 Oct 92	ABOVE THE CLOUDS *Go! Discs GOD 91*	47 2
17 Jul 93	SUNFLOWER *Go! Discs GODCD 102*	16 5
4 Sep 93	WILD WOOD *Go! Discs GODCD 104*	14 3
13 Nov 93	THE WEAVER (EP) *Go! Discs GODCD 107*	18 3
9 Apr 94	HUNG UP *Go! Discs GODCD 111*	11 3
5 Nov 94	OUT OF THE SINKING *Go! Discs GODCD 121*	20 3
6 May 95 ●	THE CHANGINGMAN *Go! Discs GODCD 127*	7 4
22 Jul 95 ●	YOU DO SOMETHING TO ME *Go! Discs GODCD 130*	9 6
30 Sep 95	BROKEN STONES *Go! Discs GODCD 132*	20 4
9 Mar 96	OUT OF THE SINKING *Go! Discs GODCD 143*	16 2
17 Aug 96 ●	PEACOCK SUIT *Go! Discs GODCD 149*	5 5
9 Aug 97	BRUSHED *Island CID 666*	14 3
11 Oct 97	FRIDAY STREET *Island CID 676*	21 2
6 Dec 97	MERMAIDS *Island CID 683*	30 2
14 Nov 98	BRAND NEW START *Island CID 711*	16 3
9 Jan 99	WILDWOOD (re-issue) *Island CID 734*	22 3
2 Sep 00	SWEET PEA, MY SWEET PEA *Island CID 764*	44 1

[1] Paul Weller Movement

Tracks on The Weaver (EP): The Weaver / This Is No Time / Another New Day / Ohio (live). 'Out of the Sinking' in 1996 is a re-recording

See also COUNCIL COLLECTIVE; STYLE COUNCIL; JAM

Brandi WELLS *US, female vocalist (1 WEEK)*   pos/wks

20 Feb 82	WATCH OUT *Virgin VS 479*	74 1

Houston WELLS *UK, male vocalist (10 WEEKS)*   pos/wks

1 Aug 63	ONLY THE HEARTACHES *Parlophone R 5031*	22 10

Mary WELLS *US, female vocalist (25 WEEKS)*   pos/wks

21 May 64 ●	MY GUY *Stateside SS 288* ▲	5 14
30 Jul 64	ONCE UPON A TIME *Stateside SS 316* [1]	50 1
8 Jul 72	MY GUY (re-issue) *Tamla Motown TMG 820*	14 10

[1] Marvin Gaye and Mary Wells

UK No.1 ★   UK Top 10 ●   Still on chart +   UK million seller ◆   UK entry at No.1 ■   US No.1 ▲

Terri WELLS US, female vocalist (9 WEEKS)

			pos/wks
2 Jul 83	YOU MAKE IT HEAVEN Phillyworld PWS 111	53	2
5 May 84	I'LL BE AROUND Phillyworld LON 48	17	7

Alex WELSH UK, male instrumentalist - trumpet (4 WEEKS)

			pos/wks
10 Aug 61	TANSY Columbia DB 4686	45	4

Irvine WELSH – See PRIMAL SCREAM

WENDY and LISA US, female vocal duo (31 WEEKS)

			pos/wks
5 Sep 87	WATERFALL Virgin VS 999	66	4
16 Jan 88	SIDE SHOW Virgin VS 1012	49	5
18 Feb 89	ARE YOU MY BABY Virgin VS 1156	70	3
29 Apr 89	LOLLY LOLLY Virgin VS 1175	64	3
8 Jul 89	SATISFACTION Virgin VS 1194	27	8
18 Nov 89	WATERFALL (re-mix) Virgin VS 1223	69	2
30 Jun 90	STRUNG OUT Virgin VS 1272	44	5
10 Nov 90	RAINBOW LAKE Virgin VS 1280	70	1

WES France, male vocalist (7 WEEKS)

			pos/wks
14 Feb 98	ALANE Epic 6654682	11	6
27 Jun 98	I LOVE FOOTBALL Epic 6660772	75	1

Dodie WEST UK, female vocalist (4 WEEKS)

			pos/wks
14 Jan 65	GOING OUT OF MY HEAD Decca F 12046	39	4

Keith WEST UK, male vocalist (18 WEEKS)

			pos/wks
9 Aug 67 ●	EXCERPT FROM A TEENAGE OPERA Parlophone R 5623	2	15
22 Nov 67	SAM Parlophone R 5651	38	3

Kit WEST – See DEGREES OF MOTION featuring BITI

WEST END featuring SYBIL
UK male production duo featuring US, female vocalist (13 WEEKS)

			pos/wks
16 Jan 93 ●	THE LOVE I LOST PWL Sanctuary PWCD253	3	13

WEST END UK, female vocal group (2 WEEKS)

			pos/wks
19 Aug 95	LOVE RULES RCA 74321292702	44	2

WEST HAM UNITED CUP SQUAD
UK, male football team vocalists (2 WEEKS)

			pos/wks
10 May 75	I'M FOREVER BLOWING BUBBLES Pye 7N 45470	31	2

WEST STREET MOB US, male DJ / producers (3 WEEKS)

			pos/wks
8 Oct 83	BREAK DANCIN'- ELECTRIC BOOGIE Sugarhill SH 128	71	1
22 Oct 83	BREAK DANCIN'- ELECTRIC BOOGIE (re-entry) Sugarhill SH 128	64	2

WESTBAM Germany, male producer (9 WEEKS)

			pos/wks
9 Jul 94	CELEBRATION GENERATION Low Spirit PQCD 5	48	2
19 Nov 94	BAM BAM BAM Low Spirit PZCD 329	57	1
3 Jun 95	WIZARDS OF THE SONIC Urban PZCD 344	32	1
23 Mar 96	ALWAYS MUSIC Low Spirit 5779152 [1]	51	1
13 Jun 98	WIZARDS OF THE SONIC (re-mix) Wonderboy WBOYD 010 [2]	43	2
28 Nov 98	ROOF IS ON FIRE Logic 74321633162	58	1

[1] Westbam / Koon + Stephenson [2] Westbam vs Red Jerry

WESTBAM vs RED JERRY
UK, male producer and Germany, male producer (2 WEEKS)

			pos/wks
13 Jun 98	WIZARDS OF THE SONIC (re-mix) Wonderboy WBOYD 010 [1]	43	2

[1] Westbam vs Red Jerry

WESTLIFE (366) Top 500 Record-shattering Irish boy band: Bryan McFadden, Kian Egan, Mark Freehily, Nicky Byrne and Shane Filan. Only act to reach No.1 with their first seven releases - all entered at the top. They are also first UK-based act to amass four No.1s in a year (86 WEEKS)

			pos/wks
1 May 99 ★	SWEAR IT AGAIN RCA 74321662062 ■	1	12
14 Aug 99	SWEAR IT AGAIN (re-entry) RCA 74321662062	71	1
21 Aug 99 ★	IF I LET YOU GO RCA74321692352 ■	1	11
30 Oct 99 ★	FLYING WITHOUT WINGS RCA 74321709162 ■	1	13
25 Dec 99 ★	I HAVE A DREAM / SEASONS IN THE SUN RCA 74321726012 ■	1	17
8 Apr 00 ★	FOOL AGAIN RCA 74321751562 ■	1	10
1 Jul 00	FOOL AGAIN (re-entry) RCA 74321751562	60	2
30 Sep 00 ★	AGAINST ALL ODDS Columbia 6698872 [1] ■	1	11
11 Nov 00 ★	MY LOVE RCA 74321802792 ■	1	8+
30 Dec 00 ●	WHAT MAKES A MAN RCA 74321826252	2	1+

[1] Mariah Carey & Westlife

Kim WESTON – See Marvin GAYE

WESTWORLD
UK / US, male / female vocal / instrumental group (23 WEEKS)

			pos/wks
21 Feb 87	SONIC BOOM BOY RCA BOOM 1	11	7
2 May 87	BA-NA-NA-BAM-BOO RCA BOOM 2	37	5
25 Jul 87	WHERE THE ACTION IS RCA BOOM 3	54	4
17 Oct 87	SILVERMAC RCA BOOM 4	42	5
15 Oct 88	EVERYTHING GOOD IS BAD RCA PB 42243	72	2

WET WET WET (78) Top 500 Perennially popular Glasgow quartet fronted by vocalist Marti Pellow (b. Mark McLoughlin, 23 Mar 1966). They were voted Best British Newcomers at the 1988 Brit Awards. 'Love Is All Around' holds the record for most weeks at No.1 by a UK act - 15 consecutive weeks (209 WEEKS)

			pos/wks
11 Apr 87 ●	WISHING I WAS LUCKY Precious JEWEL 3	6	14
25 Jul 87 ●	SWEET LITTLE MYSTERY Precious JEWEL 4	5	12
5 Dec 87 ●	ANGEL EYES (HOME AND AWAY) Precious JEWEL 6	5	12
19 Mar 88	TEMPTATION Precious JEWEL 7	12	8
14 May 88 ★	WITH A LITTLE HELP FROM MY FRIENDS Childline CHILD 1	1	11
30 Sep 89 ●	SWEET SURRENDER Precious JEWEL 9	6	8
9 Dec 89	BROKE AWAY Precious JEWEL 10	19	7
10 Mar 90	HOLD BACK THE RIVER Precious JEWEL 11	31	4
11 Aug 90	STAY WITH ME HEARTACHE / I FEEL FINE Precious JEWEL 13	30	4
14 Sep 91	MAKE IT TONIGHT Precious JEWEL 15	37	3
2 Nov 91	PUT THE LIGHT ON Precious JEWEL 16	56	2
4 Jan 92 ★	GOODNIGHT GIRL Precious JEWEL 17	1	11
21 Mar 92	MORE THAN LOVE Precious JEWEL 18	19	5
11 Jul 92	LIP SERVICE (EP) Precious JEWEL 19	15	5
8 May 93	BLUE FOR YOU / THIS TIME (LIVE) Precious JWLCD 20	38	2
6 Nov 93	SHED A TEAR Precious JWLCD 21	22	5
8 Jan 94	COLD COLD HEART Precious JWLCD 22	23	4
21 May 94 ★	LOVE IS ALL AROUND Precious JWLCD 23 ◆	1	37
25 Mar 95 ●	JULIA SAYS Precious JWLDD 24	3	9
17 Jun 95 ●	DON'T WANT TO FORGIVE ME NOW Precious JWLDD 25	7	8
30 Sep 95 ●	SOMEWHERE SOMEHOW Precious JWLDD 26	7	7
2 Dec 95	SHE'S ALL ON MY MIND Precious JWLDD 27	17	7
30 Mar 96	MORNING Precious JWLDD 28	16	4
22 Mar 97 ●	IF I NEVER SEE YOU AGAIN Precious JWLCD 29	3	8
14 Jun 97	STRANGE Precious JWLCD 30	13	4
21 Jun 97	IF I NEVER SEE YOU AGAIN (re-entry) Precious JWLCD 29	72	1
19 Jul 97	STRANGE (re-entry) Precious JWLCD 30	74	1
16 Aug 97 ●	YESTERDAY Precious JWLCD 31	4	6

The listed A-side with 'With a Little Help From My Friends' was 'She's Leaving Home' by Billy Bragg with Cara Tivey. Tracks on Lip Service (EP): Lip Service / High On the Happy Side / Lip Service (Live) / More Than Love (Live)

WE'VE GOT A FUZZBOX AND WE'RE GONNA USE IT
UK, female vocal / instrumental group (39 WEEKS)

			pos/wks
26 Apr 86	XX SEX / RULES AND REGULATIONS Vindaloo UGH 11	41	7
15 Nov 86	LOVE IS THE SLUG Vindaloo UGH 14	31	4

UK No.1 ★   UK Top 10 ●   Still on chart +   UK million seller ◆   UK entry at No.1 ■   US No.1 ▲

7 Feb 87	WHAT'S THE POINT *Vindaloo YZ 101*	51	2
25 Feb 89	INTERNATIONAL RESCUE *WEA YZ 347* [1]	11	10
20 May 89	PINK SUNSHINE *WEA YZ 401* [1]	14	10
5 Aug 89	SELF! *WEA YZ 408* [1]	24	6

[1] Fuzzbox

WHALE
Sweden, male / female vocal / instrumental group (8 WEEKS) pos/wks

19 Mar 94	HOBO HUMPIN' SLOBO BABE *East West YZ 798CD*	46	2
15 Jul 95	I'LL DO YA *Hut HUTDG 51*	53	1
25 Nov 95	HOBO HUMPIN' SLOBO BABE (re-issue) *Hut HUTCD 64*	15	4
4 Jul 98	FOUR BIG SPEAKERS *Hut HUTCD 96* [1]	69	1

[1] Whale featuring Bus 75

WHALERS – See Hal PAIGE and the WHALERS

WHAM! 175 Top 500
Teen-dream duo with a feel-good, pure pop sound: George Michael (v), Andrew Ridgeley (g). They were the only British group to have three chart-toppers in the UK and the US during the 1980s, a feat George later equalled as a solo artist (137 WEEKS) pos/wks

16 Oct 82	● YOUNG GUNS (GO FOR IT) *Innervision IVL A2766*	3	17
15 Jan 83	● WHAM RAP! *Innervision IVL A2442*	8	11
14 May 83	● BAD BOYS *Innervision A 3143*	2	14
30 Jul 83	● CLUB TROPICANA *Innervision A 3613*	4	11
3 Dec 83	CLUB FANTASTIC MEGAMIX *Innervision A 3586*	15	8
26 May 84	★ WAKE ME UP BEFORE YOU GO GO *Epic A 4440* ▲	1	16
13 Oct 84	★ FREEDOM *Epic A 4743*	1	14
15 Dec 84	● LAST CHRISTMAS / EVERYTHING SHE WANTS *Epic A 4949* ◆ ▲	2	13
23 Nov 85	★ I'M YOUR MAN *Epic A 6716*	1	12
14 Dec 85	● LAST CHRISTMAS (re-issue) *Epic WHAM 1*	6	7
21 Jun 86	★ THE EDGE OF HEAVEN / WHERE DID YOUR HEART GO *Epic FIN 1*	1	10
20 Dec 86	● LAST CHRISTMAS (2nd re-issue) *Epic 650269 7*	45	4

'Where Did Your Heart Go' listed only from 2 Aug 1986, peaking at No.28

WHATNAUTS – See MOMENTS

Rebecca WHEATLEY *UK, female vocalist (8 WEEKS)* pos/wks

| 26 Feb 00 | ● STAY WITH ME (BABY) *BBC Music WMSS 60222* | 10 | 7 |
| 13 May 00 | STAY WITH ME (BABY) (re-entry) *BBC Music WMSS 60222* | 71 | 1 |

Caron WHEELER *UK, female vocalist (42 WEEKS)* pos/wks

18 Mar 89	● KEEP ON MOVING *10 TEN 263* [1]	5	12
10 Jun 89	★ BACK TO LIFE (HOWEVER DO YOU WANT ME) *10 TEN 265* [1]	1	14
8 Sep 90	LIVIN' IN THE LIGHT *RCA PB 43939*	14	6
10 Nov 90	UK BLAK *RCA PB 43719*	40	4
9 Feb 91	DON'T QUIT *RCA PB 44259*	53	3
7 Nov 92	I ADORE YOU *Perspective PERSS 7407*	59	2
11 Sep 93	BEACH OF THE WAR GODDESS *EMI CDEM 282*	75	1

[1] Soul II Soul featuring Caron Wheeler

Bill WHELAN featuring ANUNA and the RTE CONCERT ORCHESTRA
Ireland, male composer, male / female choir and orchestra (16 WEEKS) pos/wks

| 17 Dec 94 | ● RIVERDANCE *Son RTEBUACD 1* | 9 | 16 |

WHEN IN ROME *UK, male vocal / instrumental group (3 WEEKS)* pos/wks

| 28 Jan 89 | THE PROMISE *10 TEN 244* | 58 | 3 |

WHIGFIELD *Denmark, female vocalist - Sannia Carlson (52 WEEKS)* pos/wks

17 Sep 94	★ SATURDAY NIGHT *Systematic SYSCD 3* ◆ ■	1	18
10 Dec 94	● ANOTHER DAY *Systematic SYSCD 4*	7	10
10 Jun 95	● THINK OF YOU *Systematic SYSCDP 10*	7	11
9 Sep 95	CLOSE TO YOU *Systematic SYCDP 18*	13	7
16 Dec 95	LAST CHRISTMAS / BIG TIME *Systematic SYSCD 24*	21	5
10 Oct 98	SEXY EYES - REMIXES *ZYX ZYX 8085R8*	68	1

WHIPPING BOY *Ireland, male vocal / instrumental group (4 WEEKS)* pos/wks

14 Oct 95	WE DON'T NEED NOBODY ELSE *Columbia 6622205*	51	1
3 Feb 96	WHEN WE WERE YOUNG *Columbia 6628062*	46	2
25 May 96	TWINKLE *Columbia 6632272*	55	1

Nancy WHISKEY – See Charles McDEVITT SKIFFLE GROUP featuring Nancy WHISKEY

WHISPERS *US, male vocal group (52 WEEKS)* pos/wks

2 Feb 80	● AND THE BEAT GOES ON *Solar SO 1*	2	12
10 May 80	LADY *Solar SO 4*	55	3
12 Jul 80	MY GIRL *Solar SO 8*	26	6
14 Mar 81	● IT'S A LOVE THING *Solar SO 16*	9	11
13 Jun 81	I CAN MAKE IT BETTER *Solar SO 19*	44	5
19 Jan 85	CONTAGIOUS *MCA MCA 937*	56	3
28 Mar 87	AND THE BEAT GOES ON (re-issue) *Solar MCA 1126*	45	4
23 May 87	ROCK STEADY *Solar MCA 1152*	38	6
15 Aug 87	SPECIAL F / X *Solar MCA 1178*	69	2

WHISTLE *US, male rap group (8 WEEKS)* pos/wks

| 1 Mar 86 | ● (NOTHIN' SERIOUS) JUST BUGGIN' *Champion CHAMP 12* | 7 | 8 |

Alex WHITCOMBE & BIG C
UK, male DJ, and UK, male vocalist (1 WEEK) pos/wks

| 23 May 98 | ICE RAIN *Xtravaganza 0091075 EXT* | 44 | 1 |

Barry WHITE 174 Top 500
Seventies soul and disco icon, b. 12 Sep 1944, Texas, USA. This singer / songwriter / pianist / producer / arranger was behind best sellers by Love Unlimited and Love Unlimited Orchestra. Lovingly named the "Walrus of Love", his unmistakable deep voice has been in the charts for four decades (138 WEEKS) pos/wks

9 Jun 73	I'M GONNA LOVE YOU JUST A LITTLE BIT MORE BABY *Pye International 7N 25610*	23	7
26 Jan 74	NEVER NEVER GONNA GIVE YA UP *Pye International 7N 25633*	14	11
17 Aug 74	● CAN'T GET ENOUGH OF YOUR LOVE BABE *Pye International 7N 25661* ▲	8	12
2 Nov 74	★ YOU'RE THE FIRST, THE LAST, MY EVERYTHING *20th Century BTC 2133*	1	14
8 Mar 75	● WHAT AM I GONNA DO WITH YOU *20th Century BTC 2177*	5	8
24 May 75	(FOR YOU) I'LL DO ANYTHING YOU WANT ME TO *20th Century BTC 2208*	20	6
27 Dec 75	● LET THE MUSIC PLAY *20th Century BTC 2265*	9	8
6 Mar 76	● YOU SEE THE TROUBLE WITH ME *20th Century BTC 2277*	2	10
21 Aug 76	BABY, WE BETTER TRY TO GET IT TOGETHER *20th Century BTC 2298*	15	7
13 Nov 76	DON'T MAKE ME WAIT TOO LONG *20th Century BTC 2309*	17	8
5 Mar 77	I'M QUALIFIED TO SATISFY *20th Century BTC 2328*	37	5
15 Oct 77	IT'S ECSTASY WHEN YOU LAY DOWN NEXT TO ME *20th Century BTC 2350*	40	3
16 Dec 78	JUST THE WAY YOU ARE *20th Century BTC 2380*	12	12
24 Mar 79	SHA LA LA MEANS I LOVE YOU *20th Century BTC 1041*	55	6
7 Nov 87	SHO' YOU RIGHT *Breakout USA 614*	14	7
16 Jan 88	NEVER NEVER GONNA GIVE YOU UP (re-mix) *Club JAB 59*	63	2
31 Mar 90	SECRET GARDEN *Qwest W 9992* [1]	67	2
21 Jan 95	PRACTICE WHAT YOU PREACH / LOVE IS THE ICON *A & M 5808992*	20	4
8 Apr 95	I ONLY WANT TO BE WITH YOU *A & M 5810252*	36	2
21 Dec 96	IN YOUR WILDEST DREAMS *Parlophone CDR 6451* [2]	32	3
4 Nov 00	LET THE MUSIC PLAY (re-mix) *Wonderboy WBOYD 020*	45	2

[1] Quincy Jones featuring Al B Sure!, James Ingram, El DeBarge and Barry White [2] Tina Turner featuring Barry White

Chris WHITE *UK, male vocalist (4 WEEKS)* pos/wks

| 20 Mar 76 | SPANISH WINE *Charisma CB 272* | 37 | 4 |

Karyn WHITE *US, female vocalist (38 WEEKS)* pos/wks

5 Nov 88	THE WAY YOU LOVE ME *Warner Bros. W 7773*	42	5
18 Feb 89	SECRET RENDEZVOUS *Warner Bros. W 7562*	52	3
10 Jun 89	SUPERWOMAN *Warner Bros. W 2920*	11	13

9 Sep 89	SECRET RENDEZVOUS (re-issue)		
	Warner Bros. W 2855	22	9
17 Aug 91	ROMANTIC Warner Bros. W 0028 ▲	23	5
18 Jan 92	THE WAY I FEEL ABOUT YOU Warner Bros. W 0073	65	2
24 Sep 94	HUNGAH Warner Bros. W 0264CD	69	1

WHITE PLAINS
UK, male group. Lead vocalist - Tony Burrows (56 WEEKS)   pos/wks

7 Feb 70 ●	MY BABY LOVES LOVIN' Deram DM 280	9	11
18 Apr 70	I'VE GOT YOU ON MY MIND Deram DM 291	17	11
24 Oct 70 ●	JULIE DO YA LOVE ME Deram DM 315	8	14
12 Jun 71	WHEN YOU ARE A KING Deram DM 333	13	11
17 Feb 73	STEP INTO A DREAM Deram DM 371	21	9

Snowy WHITE
UK, male vocalist / instrumentalist - guitar (12 WEEKS)   pos/wks

24 Dec 83 ●	BIRD OF PARADISE Towerbell TOW 42	6	10
28 Dec 85	FOR YOU R4 FOR 3	65	1
18 Jan 86	FOR YOU (re-entry) R4 FOR 3	72	1

Tam WHITE *UK, male vocalist (4 WEEKS)*

15 Mar 75	WHAT IN THE WORLD'S COME OVER YOU RAK 193	36	4

Tony Joe WHITE *US, male vocalist (10 WEEKS)*
pos/wks

6 Jun 70	GROUPIE GIRL Monument MON 1043	22	10

WHITE TOWN *UK, male vocalist / instrumentalist / producer - Jyoti Mishra*
(10 WEEKS)   pos/wks

25 Jan 97 ★	YOUR WOMAN Chrysalis CDCHS 5052 ■	1	9
24 May 97	UNDRESSED Chrysalis CDCHS 5058	57	1

WHITE ZOMBIE *US, male vocal / instrumental group (4 WEEKS)*   pos/wks

20 May 95	MORE HUMAN THAN HUMAN Geffen GFSTD 92	51	2
18 May 96	ELECTRIC HEAD PART 2 (THE ECSTASY)		
	Geffen GFSXD 22140	31	2

WHITE and TORCH *UK, male vocal / instrumental duo (4 WEEKS)*   pos/wks

2 Oct 82	PARADE Chrysalis CHS 2641	54	4

WHITEHEAD BROS *US, male vocal duo (5 WEEKS)*   pos/wks

14 Jan 95	YOUR LOVE IS A 187 Motown TMGCD 1434	32	3
13 May 95	FORGET I WAS A G Motown TMGCD 1441	40	2

WHITEHOUSE
US / UK, male vocal / instrumental / production duo (1 WEEK)   pos/wks

15 Aug 98	AIN'T NO MOUNTAIN HIGH ENOUGH		
	Beautiful Noise BNOISE 2CD	60	1

WHITEOUT *UK, male vocal / instrumental group (2 WEEKS)*   pos/wks

24 Sep 94	DETROIT Silvertone ORECD 66	73	1
18 Feb 95	JACKIE'S RACING Silvertone ORECD 68	72	1

WHITESNAKE   253   Top 500
Leading 1980s British rock group founded by ex-Deep Purple vocalist David Coverdale (b. 22 Sep 1949, North Yorkshire, UK), but with an ever-changing line-up. Whitesnake (1987), their most successful album, shifted more than 10 million copies worldwide (112 WEEKS)   pos/wks

24 Jun 78	SNAKE BITE (EP) EMI International INEP 751 [1]	61	3
10 Nov 79	LONG WAY FROM HOME United Artists BP 324	55	2
26 Apr 80	FOOL FOR YOUR LOVING United Artists BP 352	13	9
12 Jul 80	READY AN' WILLING (SWEET SATISFACTION)		
	United Artists BP 363	43	4
22 Nov 80	AIN'T NO LOVE IN THE HEART OF THE CITY		
	Sunburst/Liberty BP 381	51	4
11 Apr 81	DON'T BREAK MY HEART AGAIN Liberty BP 395	17	9
6 Jun 81	WOULD I LIE TO YOU Liberty BP 399	37	6
6 Nov 82	HERE I GO AGAIN / BLOODY LUXURY Liberty BP 416 ▲	34	10
13 Aug 83	GUILTY OF LOVE Liberty BP 420	31	5

14 Jan 84	GIVE ME MORE TIME Liberty BP 422	29	4
28 Apr 84	STANDING IN THE SHADOW Liberty BP 423	62	2
9 Feb 85	LOVE AIN'T NO STRANGER Liberty BP 424	44	4
28 Mar 87	STILL OF THE NIGHT EMI EMI 5606	16	8
6 Jun 87 ●	IS THIS LOVE EMI EM 3	9	11
31 Oct 87 ●	HERE I GO AGAIN (re-mix) EMI EM 35	9	11
6 Feb 88	GIVE ME ALL YOUR LOVE EMI EM 23	18	6
2 Dec 89	FOOL FOR YOUR LOVING EMI EM 123	43	2
10 Mar 90	THE DEEPER THE LOVE EMI EM 128	35	3
25 Aug 90	NOW YOU'RE GONE EMI EM 150	31	4
6 Aug 94	IS THIS LOVE / SWEET LADY LUCK (re-issue)		
	EMI CDEM 329	25	4
7 Jun 97	TOO MANY TEARS EMI CDEM 471 [2]	46	1

[1] David Coverdale's Whitesnake [2] David Coverdale and Whitesnake

Tracks on Snake Bite (EP): Bloody Mary / Steal Away / Ain't No Love In the Heart of the City / Come On. EM 123 is a re-recording of their third hit

David WHITFIELD   96   Top 500
Most successful UK male singer in the US during the pre-rock years, b. 2 Feb 1925, Yorkshire, d. 16 Jan 1980. This operatic-style tenor had a formidable and predominately female fan following in the 1950s (190 WEEKS)   pos/wks

2 Oct 53 ●	BRIDGE OF SIGHS Decca F 10129	9	1
16 Oct 53 ★	ANSWER ME Decca F 10192	1	13
11 Dec 53	RAGS TO RICHES Decca F 10207 [1]	12	1
8 Jan 54 ●	RAGS TO RICHES (re-entry) Decca F 10207 [1]	3	10
29 Jan 54	ANSWER ME (re-entry) Decca F 10192	12	1
19 Feb 54 ●	THE BOOK Decca F 10242	5	12
28 May 54 ●	THE BOOK (re-entry) Decca F 10242	10	3
18 Jun 54 ★	CARA MIA Decca F 10327	1	25
12 Nov 54 ●	SANTO NATALE (MERRY CHRISTMAS)		
	Decca F 10399	2	10
11 Feb 55 ●	BEYOND THE STARS Decca F 10458	8	9
27 May 55	MAMA Decca F 10515	20	1
24 Jun 55	MAMA (re-entry) Decca F 10515	19	2
8 Jul 55 ●	EV'RYWHERE Decca F 10515 [2]	3	20
29 Jul 55	MAMA (2nd re-entry) Decca F 10515	12	8
25 Nov 55 ●	WHEN YOU LOSE THE ONE YOU LOVE		
	Decca F 10627 [3]	7	11
2 Mar 56	MY SEPTEMBER LOVE Decca F 10690	19	2
23 Mar 56	MY SEPTEMBER LOVE (re-entry) Decca F 10690	18	1
6 Apr 56 ●	MY SEPTEMBER LOVE (2nd re-entry) Decca F 10690	3	20
24 Aug 56	MY SON JOHN Decca F 10769	22	4
31 Aug 56	MY UNFINISHED SYMPHONY Decca F 10769	29	1
7 Sep 56	MY SEPTEMBER LOVE (3rd re-entry) Decca F 10690	25	1
25 Jan 57 ●	THE ADORATION WALTZ Decca F 10833 [2]	9	11
5 Apr 57	I'LL FIND YOU Decca F 10864	28	2
7 Jun 57	I'LL FIND YOU (re-entry) Decca F 10864	27	2
14 Feb 58	CRY MY HEART Decca F 10978 [3]	22	3
16 May 58	ON THE STREET WHERE YOU LIVE Decca F 11018 [4]	16	14
8 Aug 58	THE RIGHT TO LOVE Decca F 11039	30	1
24 Nov 60	I BELIEVE Decca F 11289	49	1

[1] David Whitfield with Stanley Black and his Orchestra [2] David Whitfield with the Roland Shaw Orchestra [3] David Whitfield with chorus and Mantovani and his Orchestra [4] David Whitfield with Cyril Stapleton and his Orchestra

Slim WHITMAN   429   Top 500
Distinctive country vocalist whose yodelling style made him a major 1950s pop star in UK, b. 20 Jan 1924, Florida, US. For 36 years, 'Rose Marie' held the record for most consecutive weeks at the top. At 53 (1977) he was the oldest act to top the chart with a new album. It was Whitman's singing that vanquished the aliens in the movie Mars Attacks! (77 WEEKS)   pos/wks

15 Jul 55 ★	ROSE MARIE London HL 8061	1	19
29 Jul 55 ●	INDIAN LOVE CALL London L 1149	7	12
23 Sep 55	CHINA DOLL London L 1149	15	2
9 Mar 56	TUMBLING TUMBLEWEEDS London HLU 8230	19	2
13 Apr 56	I'M A FOOL London HLU 8252	16	3
11 May 56	I'M A FOOL (re-entry) London HLU 8252	29	1
22 Jun 56	SERENADE London HLU 8287	24	3
27 Jul 56 ●	SERENADE (re-entry) London HLU 8287	8	12
12 Apr 57 ●	I'LL TAKE YOU HOME AGAIN KATHLEEN London HLP 8403	7	13
5 Oct 74	HAPPY ANNIVERSARY United Artists UP 35728	14	10

Roger WHITTAKER `374` **Top 500** *World-renowned vocalist and whistler, b. 22 Mar 1936, Nairobi, Kenya. Easy-listening legend and popular live performer with 10 million albums sold in his home base, Germany (85 WEEKS)*

		pos/wks
8 Nov 69	DURHAM TOWN (THE LEAVIN') *Columbia DB 8613*	**12** 18
11 Apr 70 ●	I DON'T BELIEVE IN IF ANYMORE *Columbia DB 8664*	**8** 18
10 Oct 70	NEW WORLD IN THE MORNING *Columbia DB 8718*	**17** 14
3 Apr 71	WHY *Columbia DB 8752*	**47** 1
2 Oct 71	MAMMY BLUE *Columbia DB 8822*	**31** 10
26 Jul 75 ●	THE LAST FAREWELL *EMI 2294*	**2** 14
8 Nov 86 ●	THE SKYE BOAT SONG *Tembo TML 119* [1]	**10** 10

[1] Roger Whittaker and Des O'Connor

WHO `48` **Top 500** *Legendary live band from London, whose Tommy album (1969) popularised rock opera: Roger Daltrey (v), Pete Townshend (g), John Entwistle (b), Keith Moon (d) (d. 1978). These gold-record collectors have spent five decades breaking both guitars and box-office records (247 WEEKS)*

		pos/wks
18 Feb 65 ●	I CAN'T EXPLAIN *Brunswick 05926*	**8** 13
27 May 65 ●	ANYWAY ANYHOW ANYWHERE *Brunswick 05935*	**10** 12
4 Nov 65 ●	MY GENERATION *Brunswick 05944*	**2** 13
10 Mar 66 ●	SUBSTITUTE *Reaction 591 001*	**5** 13
24 Mar 66	A LEGAL MATTER *Brunswick 05956*	**32** 6
1 Sep 66 ●	I'M A BOY *Reaction 591 004*	**2** 13
1 Sep 66	THE KIDS ARE ALRIGHT *Brunswick 05965*	**41** 2
22 Sep 66	THE KIDS ARE ALRIGHT (re-entry) *Brunswick 05965*	**48** 1
15 Dec 66 ●	HAPPY JACK *Reaction 591 010*	**3** 11
27 Apr 67 ●	PICTURES OF LILY *Track 604 002*	**4** 10
26 Jul 67	THE LAST TIME / UNDER MY THUMB *Track 604 006*	**44** 3
18 Oct 67 ●	I CAN SEE FOR MILES *Track 604 011*	**10** 12
19 Jun 68	DOGS *Track 604 023*	**25** 5
23 Oct 68	MAGIC BUS *Track 604 024*	**26** 6
19 Mar 69 ●	PINBALL WIZARD *Track 604 027*	**4** 13
4 Apr 70	THE SEEKER *Track 604 036*	**19** 11
8 Aug 70	SUMMERTIME BLUES *Track 2094 002*	**38** 4
10 Jul 71 ●	WON'T GET FOOLED AGAIN *Track 2094 009*	**9** 12
23 Oct 71	LET'S SEE ACTION *Track 2094 012*	**16** 12
24 Jun 72 ●	JOIN TOGETHER *Track 2094 102*	**9** 9
13 Jan 73	RELAY *Track 2094 106*	**21** 5
13 Oct 73	5.15 *Track 2094 115*	**20** 6
24 Jan 76 ●	SQUEEZE BOX *Polydor 2121 275*	**10** 9
30 Oct 76 ●	SUBSTITUTE (re-issue) *Polydor 2058 803*	**7** 7
22 Jul 78	WHO ARE YOU *Polydor WHO 1*	**18** 12
28 Apr 79	LONG LIVE ROCK *Polydor WHO 2*	**48** 5
7 Mar 81 ●	YOU BETTER YOU BET *Polydor WHO 004*	**9** 8
9 May 81	DON'T LET GO THE COAT *Polydor WHO 005*	**47** 4
2 Oct 82	ATHENA *Polydor WHO 6*	**40** 4
26 Nov 83	READY STEADY WHO (EP) *Polydor WHO 7*	**58** 2
20 Feb 88	MY GENERATION (re-issue) *Polydor POSP 907*	**68** 2
27 Jul 96	MY GENERATION (2nd re-issue) *Polydor 8546372*	**31** 2

Tracks on Ready Steady Who (EP): Disguises / Circles / Batman / Bucket 'T' / Barbara Ann

See also HIGH NUMBERS

WHODINI *US, male rap / DJ duo (10 WEEKS)*

		pos/wks
25 Dec 82	MAGIC'S WAND *Jive JIVE 28*	**47** 6
17 Mar 84	MAGIC'S WAND (THE WHODINI ELECTRIC EP) *Jive JIVE 61*	**63** 4

Tracks on The Whodini Electric EP: Jive Magic Wand / Nasty Lady / Rap Machine / The Haunted House of Rock

WHOOLIGANZ *US, male rap duo (2 WEEKS)*

		pos/wks
13 Aug 94	PUT YOUR HANDZ UP *Positiva CDTIV 17*	**53** 2

WHOOSH *UK, male production trio (1 WEEK)*

		pos/wks
13 Sep 97	WHOOSH *Wonderboy WBOYD 006*	**72** 1

WHYCLIFFE *UK, male vocalist (2 WEEKS)*

		pos/wks
20 Nov 93	HEAVEN *MCA MCSTD 1944*	**56** 1
2 Apr 94	ONE MORE TIME *MCA MCSTD 1955*	**72** 1

Jane WIEDLIN *US, female vocalist (14 WEEKS)*

		pos/wks
6 Aug 88	RUSH HOUR *Manhattan MT 36*	**12** 11
29 Oct 88	INSIDE A DREAM *Manhattan MT 55*	**64** 3

WIGAN'S CHOSEN FEW *Canada, male vocal / instrumental group and UK crowd chants (11 WEEKS)*

		pos/wks
18 Jan 75 ●	FOOTSEE *Pye Disco Demand DDS 111*	**9** 11

WIGAN'S OVATION *UK, male vocal / instrumental group (19 WEEKS)*

		pos/wks
15 Mar 75	SKIING IN THE SNOW *Spark SRL 1122*	**12** 10
28 Jun 75	PER-SO-NAL-LY *Spark SRL 1129*	**38** 6
29 Nov 75	SUPER LOVE *Spark SRL 1133*	**41** 3

WILCO *US, male vocal / instrumental group (1 WEEK)*

		pos/wks
17 Apr 99	CAN'T STAND IT *Reprise W 475CD1*	**67** 1

Jack WILD *UK, male vocalist (2 WEEKS)*

		pos/wks
2 May 70	SOME BEAUTIFUL *Capitol CL 15635*	**46** 2

WILD BOYS – See HEINZ

WILD CHERRY *US, male vocal / instrumental group (11 WEEKS)*

		pos/wks
9 Oct 76 ●	PLAY THAT FUNKY MUSIC *Epic EPC 4593* ▲	**7** 11

WILD COLOUR
UK, male / female vocal / instrumental group (2 WEEKS)

		pos/wks
14 Oct 95	DREAMS *Perfecto PERF 105CD*	**25** 2

WILD PAIR – See Paula ABDUL

WILD WEEKEND *UK, male vocal / instrumental group (2 WEEKS)*

		pos/wks
29 Apr 89	BREAKIN' UP *Parlophone R 6204*	**74** 1
5 May 90	WHO'S AFRAID OF THE BIG BAD LOVE *Parlophone R 6249*	**70** 1

WILDCHILD *UK, male producer - Roger McKenzie (20 WEEKS)*

		pos/wks
22 Apr 95	LEGENDS OF THE DARK BLACK PART 2 *Hi-Life HICD 9*	**34** 3
21 Oct 95	RENEGADE MASTER (re-issue) *Hi-Life 5771312*	**11** 4
23 Nov 96	JUMP TO MY BEAT *Hi-Life 5757372*	**30** 2
17 Jan 98 ●	RENEGADE MASTER '98 *Hi-Life 5692792*	**3** 10
25 Apr 98	BAD BOY *Polydor 5716072* [1]	**38** 1

[1] Wildchild featuring Jomalski

Although titled differently, first two hits are identical

Eugene WILDE *US, male vocalist (15 WEEKS)*

		pos/wks
13 Oct 84	GOTTA GET YOU HOME TONIGHT *Fourth & Broadway BRW 15*	**18** 9
2 Feb 85	PERSONALITY *Fourth & Broadway BRW 18*	**34** 6

'Personality' was coupled with 'Let Her Feel It' by Simplicious

Kim WILDE `94` **Top 500** *Most charted British female vocalist in the 1980s, b. Kim Smith, 18 Nov 1960, London. Neither Kim or her father, rock 'n' roll star Marty Wilde, managed a UK No.1, but Kim did top the US chart. (194 WEEKS)*

		pos/wks
21 Feb 81 ●	KIDS IN AMERICA *RAK 327*	**2** 13
9 May 81 ●	CHEQUERED LOVE *RAK 330*	**4** 9
1 Aug 81	WATER ON GLASS / BOYS *RAK 334*	**11** 8
14 Nov 81	CAMBODIA *RAK 336*	**12** 12
17 Apr 82	VIEW FROM A BRIDGE *RAK 342*	**16** 7
16 Oct 82	CHILD COME AWAY *RAK 352*	**43** 4
30 Jul 83	LOVE BLONDE *RAK 360*	**23** 8
12 Nov 83	DANCING IN THE DARK *RAK 365*	**67** 2
13 Oct 84	THE SECOND TIME *MCA KIM 1*	**29** 8
8 Dec 84	THE TOUCH *MCA KIM 2*	**56** 3
27 Apr 85	RAGE TO LOVE *MCA KIM 3*	**19** 8
25 Oct 86 ●	YOU KEEP ME HANGIN' ON *MCA KIM 4* ▲	**2** 14
4 Apr 87 ●	ANOTHER STEP (CLOSER TO YOU) *MCA KIM 5* [1]	**6** 11

UK No.1 ★   UK Top 10 ●   Still on chart +   UK million seller ◆   UK entry at No.1 ■   US No.1 ▲

8 Aug 87		SAY YOU REALLY WANT ME *MCA KIM 6*	.29	5
5 Dec 87	●	ROCKIN' AROUND THE CHRISTMAS TREE *10 TEN 2* [2]	.3	7
14 May 88		HEY MISTER HEARTACHE *MCA KIM 7*	.31	5
16 Jul 88	●	YOU CAME *MCA KIM 8*	.3	11
1 Oct 88	●	NEVER TRUST A STRANGER *MCA KIM 9*	.7	9
3 Dec 88	●	FOUR LETTER WORD *MCA KIM 10*	.6	12
4 Mar 89		LOVE IN THE NATURAL WAY *MCA KIM 11*	.32	6
14 Apr 90		IT'S HERE *MCA KIM 12*	.42	4
16 Jun 90		TIME *MCA KIM 13*	.71	3
15 Dec 90		I CAN'T SAY GOODBYE *MCA KIM 14*	.51	3
2 May 92		LOVE IS HOLY *MCA KIM 15*	.16	6
27 Jun 92		HEART OVER MIND *MCA KIM 16*	.34	3
12 Sep 92		WHO DO YOU THINK YOU ARE *MCA KIM 17*	.49	3
10 Jul 93		IF I CAN'T HAVE YOU *MCA KIMTD 18*	.12	8
13 Nov 93		IN MY LIFE *MCA KIMTD 19*	.54	1
14 Oct 95		BREAKIN' AWAY *MCA KIMTD 21*	.43	2
10 Feb 96		THIS I SWEAR *MCA KIMTD 22*	.46	1

[1] Kim Wilde and Junior [2] Mel and Kim (Kim was Kim Wilde)

Marty WILDE (232) *Top 500*

Early British rock 'n' roll singing idol, b. Reginald Smith, 15 Apr 1939, London. Although most of his best-sellers were cover versions (the normal practice at the time), he later penned hits for Lulu, Casuals, Status Quo and many for his daughter, Kim Wilde (117 WEEKS)

pos/wks

11 Jul 58	●	ENDLESS SLEEP *Philips PB 835*	.4	14
6 Mar 59	●	DONNA *Philips PB 902*	.3	16
5 Jun 59	●	A TEENAGER IN LOVE *Philips PB 926*	.2	17
3 Jul 59		DONNA (re-entry) *Philips PB 902*	.25	2
25 Sep 59	●	SEA OF LOVE *Philips PB 959*	.3	12
11 Dec 59	●	BAD BOY *Philips PB 972*	.7	8
10 Mar 60		JOHNNY ROCCO *Philips PB 1002*	.30	4
19 May 60		THE FIGHT *Philips PB 1022*	.47	1
22 Dec 60		LITTLE GIRL *Philips PB 1078*	.16	9
26 Jan 61	●	RUBBER BALL *Philips PB 1101*	.9	9
27 Jul 61		HIDE AND SEEK *Philips PB 1161*	.47	2
9 Nov 61		TOMORROW'S CLOWN *Philips PB 1191*	.33	5
24 May 62		JEZEBEL *Philips PB 1240*	.19	11
25 Oct 62		EVER SINCE YOU SAID GOODBYE *Philips 326546 BF*	.31	7

Matthew WILDER *US, male vocalist (11 WEEKS)*

pos/wks

| 21 Jan 84 | ● | BREAK MY STRIDE *Epic A 3908* | .4 | 11 |

WILDHEARTS *UK, male vocal / instrumental group (24 WEEKS)*

pos/wks

20 Nov 93		TV TAN *Bronze YZ 784CD*	.53	2
19 Feb 94		CAFFEINE BOMB *Bronze YZ 794CD*	.31	3
9 Jul 94		SUCKERPUNCH *Bronze YZ 828CD*	.38	2
28 Jan 95		IF LIFE IS LIKE A LOVE BANK I WANT AN OVERDRAFT / GEORDIE IN WONDERLAND *East West YZ 874CD*	.31	3
6 May 95		I WANNA GO WHERE THE PEOPLE GO *East West YZ 923CD*	.16	3
29 Jul 95		JUST IN LUST *East West YZ 967CD*	.28	2
20 Apr 96		SICK OF DRUGS *Round WILD 1CD*	.14	3
29 Jun 96		RED LIGHT - GREEN LIGHT (EP) *Round WILD 2CD*	.30	2
16 Aug 97		ANTHEM *Mushroom MUSH 6CD*	.21	2
18 Oct 97		URGE *Mushroom MUSH 14CD*	.26	2

Tracks on Red Light - Green Light (EP): Red Light - Green Light / Got It On Tuesday / Do Anything / The British All-American Homeboy Crowd

Sue WILKINSON *UK, female vocalist (8 WEEKS)*

pos/wks

| 2 Aug 80 | | YOU GOTTA BE A HUSTLER IF YOU WANNA GET ON *Cheapskate CHEAP 2* | .25 | 8 |

WILL TO POWER *US, male / female vocal / instrumental duo - Bob Rosenberg & Suzi Carr (18 WEEKS)*

pos/wks

| 7 Jan 89 | ● | BABY I LOVE YOUR WAY - FREEBIRD *Epic 6530947* ▲ | .6 | 9 |
| 22 Dec 90 | | I'M NOT IN LOVE *Epic 6565377* | .29 | 9 |

Alyson WILLIAMS *US, female vocalist (28 WEEKS)*

pos/wks

| 4 Mar 89 | | SLEEP TALK *Def Jam 654656 7* | .17 | 9 |

6 May 89		MY LOVE IS SO RAW *Def Jam 654898 7* [1]	.34	5
19 Aug 89	●	I NEED YOUR LOVIN' *Def Jam 655143 7*	.8	11
18 Nov 89		I SECOND THAT EMOTION *Def Jam 655456 7* [2]	.44	3

[1] Alyson Williams featuring Nikki D [2] Alyson Williams with Chuck Stanley

Andy WILLIAMS (57) *Top 500*

Leading MOR vocalist, who hosted top-rated 1960s TV series, b. 3 Dec 1928, Iowa, US. He left the noted family act The Williams Brothers in 1951 and had an enviable portfolio of smooth UK and US hit singles and albums in the 1950s and 1960s. Had a surprise 1999 re-entry for Music to Watch Girls By following its use in a TV car commercial (234 WEEKS)

pos/wks

19 Apr 57	★	BUTTERFLY *London HLA 8399*	.1	15
21 Jun 57		I LIKE YOUR KIND OF LOVE *London HLA 8437*	.16	10
30 Aug 57		BUTTERFLY (re-entry) *London HLA 8399*	.29	1
14 Jun 62		STRANGER ON THE SHORE *CBS AAG 103*	.30	10
21 Mar 63	●	CAN'T GET USED TO LOSING YOU *CBS AAG 138*	.2	18
27 Feb 64		A FOOL NEVER LEARNS *CBS AAG 182*	.40	4
16 Sep 65	●	ALMOST THERE *CBS 201813*	.2	17
24 Feb 66		MAY EACH DAY *CBS 202042*	.19	8
22 Sep 66		IN THE ARMS OF LOVE *CBS 202300*	.33	7
4 May 67		MUSIC TO WATCH GIRLS BY *CBS 2675*	.33	6
2 Aug 67		MORE AND MORE *CBS 2886*	.45	1
13 Mar 68	●	CAN'T TAKE MY EYES OFF YOU *CBS 3298*	.5	18
7 May 69		HAPPY HEART *CBS 4062*	.47	1
21 May 69		HAPPY HEART (re-entry) *CBS 4062*	.19	9
14 Mar 70	●	CAN'T HELP FALLING IN LOVE *CBS 4818*	.3	17
1 Aug 70		IT'S SO EASY *CBS 5113*	.13	13
7 Nov 70		IT'S SO EASY (re-entry) *CBS 5113*	.49	1
21 Nov 70	●	HOME LOVIN' MAN *CBS 5267*	.7	12
20 Mar 71	●	(WHERE DO I BEGIN) LOVE STORY *CBS 7020*	.4	17
24 Jul 71		(WHERE DO I BEGIN) LOVE STORY (re-entry) *CBS 7020*	.49	1
5 Aug 72		LOVE THEME FROM THE GODFATHER *CBS 8166*	.50	1
2 Sep 72		LOVE THEME FROM THE GODFATHER (re-entry) *CBS 8166*	.44	3
30 Sep 72		LOVE THEME FROM THE GODFATHER (2nd re-entry) *CBS 8166*	.42	5
8 Dec 73	●	SOLITAIRE *CBS 1824*	.4	18
18 May 74		GETTING OVER YOU *CBS 2181*	.35	5
31 May 75		YOU LAY SO EASY ON MY MIND *CBS 3167*	.32	7
6 Mar 76		THE OTHER SIDE OF ME *CBS 3903*	.42	3
27 Mar 99	●	MUSIC TO WATCH GIRLS BY (re-issue) *Columbia 6671322*	.9	6

Andy and David WILLIAMS *US, male vocal duo (5 WEEKS)*

pos/wks

| 24 Mar 73 | | I DON'T KNOW WHY *MCA MUS 1183* | .37 | 5 |

Do not see Andy Williams. This Andy is the nephew of the other Andy

Billy WILLIAMS *US, male vocalist (9 WEEKS)*

pos/wks

| 2 Aug 57 | | I'M GONNA SIT RIGHT DOWN AND WRITE MYSELF A LETTER *Vogue Coral Q 72266* | .22 | 8 |
| 18 Oct 57 | | I'M GONNA SIT RIGHT DOWN AND WRITE MYSELF A LETTER (re-entry) *Vogue Coral Q 72266* | .28 | 1 |

Danny WILLIAMS (460) *Top 500*

Velvet-voiced, British-based easy-listening vocalist; b. 7 Jan 1942, South Africa. Johnny Mathis-styled singer who won the UK 'Moon River' battle was first seen on rock'n'roll TV show 'Drumbeat'. Had US Top 10 hit with 1964 UK flop 'White On White' (74 WEEKS)

pos/wks

25 May 61		WE WILL NEVER BE AS YOUNG AS THIS AGAIN *HMV POP 839*	.44	3
6 Jul 61		THE MIRACLE OF YOU *HMV POP 885*	.41	8
2 Nov 61	★	MOON RIVER *HMV POP 932*	.1	19
18 Jan 62		JEANNIE *HMV POP 968*	.14	14
12 Apr 62	●	WONDERFUL WORLD OF THE YOUNG *HMV POP 1002*	.8	13
5 Jul 62		TEARS *HMV POP 1035*	.22	7
28 Feb 63		MY OWN TRUE LOVE *HMV POP 1112*	.45	3
30 Jul 77		DANCIN' EASY *Ensign ENY 3*	.30	7

Deniece WILLIAMS
US, female vocalist - Deniece Chandler (59 WEEKS) pos/wks

2 Apr 77 ★	FREE *CBS 4978*	1	10
30 Jul 77 ●	THAT'S WHAT FRIENDS ARE FOR *CBS 5432*	8	11
12 Nov 77	BABY BABY MY LOVE'S ALL FOR YOU *CBS 5779*	32	5
25 Mar 78 ●	TOO MUCH TOO LITTLE TOO LATE *CBS 6164* [1] ▲	3	14
29 Jul 78	YOU'RE ALL I NEED TO GET BY *CBS 6483* [1]	45	6
5 May 84 ●	LET'S HEAR IT FOR THE BOY *CBS A 4319* ▲	2	12
4 Aug 84	LET'S HEAR IT FOR THE BOY (re-entry) *CBS A 4319*	75	1

[1] Johnny Mathis and Deniece Williams

Diana WILLIAMS *US, female vocalist (3 WEEKS)* pos/wks

25 Jul 81	TEDDY BEAR'S LAST RIDE *Capitol CL 207*	54	3

Don WILLIAMS *US, male vocalist (16 WEEKS)* pos/wks

19 Jun 76	I RECALL A GYPSY WOMAN *ABC 4098*	13	10
23 Oct 76	YOU'RE MY BEST FRIEND *ABC 4144*	35	6

Eric WILLIAMS – See QUEEN PEN; 2PAC

Freedom WILLIAMS *US, male rapper (31 WEEKS)* pos/wks

15 Dec 90 ●	GONNA MAKE YOU SWEAT (EVERYBODY DANCE NOW) *CBS 6564540* [1] ▲	3	12
30 Mar 91	HERE WE GO *Columbia 6567537* [1]	20	7
6 Jul 91 ●	THINGS THAT MAKE YOU GO HMMM... *Columbia 6566907* [1]	4	11
5 Jun 93	VOICE OF FREEDOM *Columbia 6593342*	62	1

[1] C & C Music Factory (featuring Freedom Williams)

Geoffrey WILLIAMS *UK, male vocalist (8 WEEKS)* pos/wks

11 Apr 92	IT'S NOT A LOVE THING *EMI EM 228*	63	2
22 Aug 92	SUMMER BREEZE *EMI EM 245*	56	3
18 Jan 97	DRIVE *Hands On CDHOR 11*	52	2
19 Apr 97	SEX LIFE *Hands On CDHOR 12*	71	1

Iris WILLIAMS *UK, female vocalist (8 WEEKS)* pos/wks

27 Oct 79	HE WAS BEAUTIFUL (CAVATINA) (THE THEME FROM 'THE DEER HUNTER') *Columbia DB 9070*	18	8

John WILLIAMS *UK, male instrumentalist - guitar (11 WEEKS)* pos/wks

19 May 79	CAVATINA *Cube BUG 80*	13	11

John WILLIAMS
US, orchestra leader with US, orchestra (12 WEEKS) pos/wks

18 Dec 82	THEME FROM 'E.T.' (THE EXTRA-TERRESTRIAL) *MCA 800*	17	10
14 Aug 93	THEME FROM JURASSIC PARK *MCA MCSTD 1927*	45	2

Kenny WILLIAMS *US, male vocalist (7 WEEKS)* pos/wks

19 Nov 77	(YOU'RE) FABULOUS BABE *Decca FR 13731*	35	7

Larry WILLIAMS *US, male vocalist (18 WEEKS)* pos/wks

20 Sep 57	SHORT FAT FANNIE *London HLN 8472*	21	8
17 Jan 58	BONY MORONIE *London HLU 8532*	11	10

Lenny WILLIAMS *US, male vocalist (7 WEEKS)* pos/wks

5 Nov 77	SHOO DOO FU FU OOH *ABC 4194*	38	4
16 Sep 78	YOU GOT ME BURNING *ABC 4228*	67	3

Mark WILLIAMS – See Karen BODDINGTON and Mark WILLIAMS

Mason WILLIAMS *US, male instrumentalist - guitar (13 WEEKS)* pos/wks

28 Aug 68 ●	CLASSICAL GAS *Warner Bros. WB 7190*	9	13

Maurice WILLIAMS and the ZODIACS
US, male vocal group (9 WEEKS) pos/wks

5 Jan 61	STAY *Top Rank JAR 526* ▲	14	9

Melanie WILLIAMS *UK, female vocalist (21 WEEKS)* pos/wks

10 Apr 93 ●	AIN'T NO LOVE (AIN'T NO USE) *Rob's CDROB 9* [1]	3	11
9 Apr 94	ALL CRIED OUT *Columbia 6601872*	60	2
11 Jun 94	EVERYDAY THANG *Columbia 6604712*	38	3
17 Sep 94	NOT ENOUGH *Columbia 6607752*	65	1
18 Feb 95	YOU ARE EVERYTHING *Columbia 6611755* [2]	28	4

[1] Sub Sub featuring Melanie Williams [2] Melanie Williams and Joe Roberts

Robbie WILLIAMS 119 ⬤Top 500 *Former Take That teen idol who became multi-award-winning vocalist and songwriter, b. 13 Feb 1974, Stoke-on-Trent, UK. This energetic and humorous showman was UK's top albums act of 1998 and was nominated for an unprecedented six Brit awards in 1999 (169 WEEKS)* pos/wks

10 Aug 96 ●	FREEDOM *Chrysalis CDFREE 1*	2	10
26 Oct 96	FREEDOM (re-entry) *Chrysalis CDFREE 1*	56	4
26 Apr 97 ●	OLD BEFORE I DIE *Chrysalis CDCHS 5055*	2	9
5 Jul 97	OLD BEFORE I DIE (re-entry) *Chrysalis CDCHS 5055*	72	1
19 Jul 97	OLD BEFORE I DIE (2nd re-entry) *Chrysalis CDCHS 5055*	69	1
26 Jul 97 ●	LAZY DAYS *Chrysalis CDCHS 5063*	8	5
27 Sep 97	SOUTH OF THE BORDER *Chrysalis CDCHS 5068*	14	4
13 Dec 97 ●	ANGELS *Chrysalis CDCHS 5072* ◆	4	20
28 Mar 98 ●	LET ME ENTERTAIN YOU *Chrysalis CDCHS 5080*	3	12
19 Sep 98 ★	MILLENNIUM *Chrysalis CDCHS 5099* ■	1	20
12 Dec 98 ●	NO REGRETS *Chrysalis CDCHS 5100*	4	13
2 Jan 99	ANGELS (re-entry) *Chrysalis CDCHS 5072*	57	4
27 Feb 99	ANGELS (2nd re-entry) *Chrysalis CDCHS 5072*	75	1
20 Mar 99	ANGELS (3rd re-entry) *Chrysalis CDCHS 5072*	75	1
27 Mar 99 ●	STRONG *Chrysalis CDCHS 5107*	4	9
20 Nov 99 ★	SHE'S THE ONE / IT'S ONLY US *Chrysalis CDCHS 5112* ■	1	16
1 Jan 00	ANGELS (4th re-entry) *Chrysalis CDCHS 5072*	71	1
8 Jan 00	MILLENNIUM (re-entry) *Chrysalis CDCHS 5099*	74	1
18 Mar 00	SHE'S THE ONE / IT'S ONLY US (re-entry) *Chrysalis CDCHS 5112*	57	4
12 Aug 00 ★	ROCK DJ *Chrysalis CDCHS 5118* ■	1	17
21 Oct 00 ●	KIDS *Chrysalis CHCHS 5119* [1]	2	11+
16 Dec 00	ROCK DJ (re-entry) *Chrysalis CDCHS 5118*	60	1
23 Dec 00 ●	SUPREME *Chrysalis CDCHS 5120*	4	2+

[1] Robbie Williams / Kylie Minogue

Saul WILLIAMS – See KRUST featuring Saul WILLIAMS

Vanessa WILLIAMS *US, female vocalist (24 WEEKS)* pos/wks

20 Aug 88	THE RIGHT STUFF *Wing WING 3*	71	1
25 Mar 89	DREAMIN' *Wing WING 4*	74	2
19 Aug 89	THE RIGHT STUFF (re-mix) *Wing WINR 3*	62	2
21 Mar 92 ●	SAVE THE BEST FOR LAST *Polydor PO 192* ▲	3	11
8 Apr 95	THE SWEETEST DAYS *Mercury MERCD 422*	41	2
8 Jul 95	THE WAY THAT YOU LOVE *Mercury MERCD 439*	52	1
18 Sep 95	COLOURS OF THE WIND *Walt Disney WD 7677CD*	21	5

Vesta WILLIAMS *US, female vocalist (13 WEEKS)* pos/wks

20 Dec 86	ONCE BITTEN TWICE SHY *A & M AM 362*	14	13

Wendell WILLIAMS *US, male rapper (6 WEEKS)* pos/wks

6 Oct 90	EVERYBODY (RAP) *Deconstruction PB 44701* [1]	30	4
18 May 91	SO GROOVY *Deconstruction PB 44567*	74	2

[1] Criminal Element Orchestra and Wendell Williams

WILLING SINNERS – See Marc ALMOND

Bruce WILLIS *US, male vocalist (30 WEEKS)* pos/wks

7 Mar 87 ●	RESPECT YOURSELF *Motown ZB 41117*	7	10
30 May 87 ●	UNDER THE BOARDWALK *Motown ZB 41349*	2	15
12 Sep 87	SECRET AGENT MAN - JAMES BOND IS BACK *Motown ZB 41437*	43	4
23 Jan 88	COMIN' RIGHT UP *Motown ZB 41453*	73	1

Chill WILLS – See LAUREL and HARDY with the AVALON BOYS featuring Chill WILLS

UK No.1 ★ UK Top 10 ● Still on chart + UK million seller ◆ UK entry at No.1 ■ US No.1 ▲

Viola WILLS US, female vocalist (16 WEEKS)

		pos/wks	
6 Oct 79 ●	GONNA GET ALONG WITHOUT YOU NOW		
	Ariola / Hansa AHA 546 8	10	
15 Mar 86	BOTH SIDES NOW / DARE TO DREAM Streetwave KHAN 66....35	6	

Al WILSON US, male vocalist (5 WEEKS)

		pos/wks	
23 Aug 75	THE SNAKE Bell 1436 41	5	

Charlie WILSON – See SNOOP DOGGY DOGG; GAP BAND

Dooley WILSON US, male vocalist (9 WEEKS)

		pos/wks	
3 Dec 77	AS TIME GOES BY United Artists UP 36331 15	9	

Disc has credit: 'With the voices of Humphrey Bogart and Ingrid Bergman'

Jackie WILSON ⟨306 *Top 500*⟩ One of R&B music's greatest stage performers and most distinctive vocalists, b. 9 Jun 1934, Detroit, US, d. 21 Jan 1984 (after eight years in a semi-comatose state). He influenced Elvis Presley, Michael Jackson and Prince. 'Reet Petite' took a record 29 years, 42 days to reach the top (97 WEEKS)

		pos/wks	
15 Nov 57 ●	REET PETITE Coral Q 72290 6	14	
14 Mar 58	TO BE LOVED Coral Q 72306 27	1	
28 Mar 58	TO BE LOVED (re-entry) Coral Q 72306 23	6	
16 May 58	TO BE LOVED (2nd re-entry) Coral Q 72306 23	1	
15 Sep 60	(YOU WERE MADE FOR) ALL MY LOVE Coral Q 72407 33	6	
3 Nov 60	(YOU WERE MADE FOR) ALL MY LOVE (re-entry)		
	Coral Q 72407 47	1	
22 Dec 60	ALONE AT LAST Coral Q 72412 50	1	
14 May 69	(YOUR LOVE KEEPS LIFTING ME) HIGHER AND HIGHER		
	MCA BAG 2 11	11	
29 Jul 72 ●	I GET THE SWEETEST FEELING MCA MU 1160 9	13	
3 May 75	I GET THE SWEETEST FEELING / (YOUR LOVE KEEPS		
	LIFTING ME) HIGHER AND HIGHER (re-issue)		
	Brunswick BR 18 25	8	
29 Nov 86 ★	REET PETITE (re-issue) SMP SKM 3 1	17	
28 Feb 87 ●	I GET THE SWEETEST FEELING (2nd re-issue) SMP SKM 1 3	11	
4 Jul 87	HIGHER AND HIGHER (2nd re-issue) SMP SKM 10 15	7	

'Higher and Higher' was not listed together with 'I Get the Sweetest Feeling' on Brunswick until 17 May 1975

Mari WILSON UK, female vocalist (34 WEEKS)

		pos/wks	
6 Mar 82	BEAT THE BEAT Compact PINK 2 59	3	
8 May 82	BABY IT'S TRUE Compact PINK 3 42	6	
11 Sep 82 ●	JUST WHAT I ALWAYS WANTED Compact PINK 4 8	10	
13 Nov 82	(BEWARE) BOYFRIEND Compact PINK 5 51	4	
19 Mar 83	CRY ME A RIVER Compact PINK 6 27	7	
11 Jun 83	WONDERFUL Compact PINK 7 47	4	

Meri WILSON US, female vocalist (10 WEEKS)

		pos/wks	
27 Aug 77 ●	TELEPHONE MAN Pye International 7N 25747 6	10	

Mike 'Hitman' WILSON US, male producer (1 WEEK)

		pos/wks	
22 Sep 90	ANOTHER SLEEPLESS NIGHT Arista 113506........................74	1	

Precious WILSON – See ERUPTION; MESSIAH

Tom WILSON UK, male producer (4 WEEKS)

		pos/wks	
2 Dec 95	TECHNOCAT Pukka CDPUKKA 4 [1] 33	3	
16 Mar 96	LET YOUR BODY GO Clubscene DCSRT 050 60	1	

[1] Technocat featuring Tom Wilson

Victoria WILSON JAMES US, female vocalist (1 WEEK)

		pos/wks	
9 Aug 97	REACH 4 THE MELODY Sony S3 VWJCD1........................72	1	

WILSON PHILLIPS US, female vocal group (33 WEEKS)

		pos/wks	
26 May 90 ●	HOLD ON SBK SBK 6 ▲ 6	12	
18 Aug 90	RELEASE ME SBK SBK 11 ▲ 36	5	

		pos/wks	
10 Nov 90	IMPULSIVE SBK SBK 16........................42	3	
11 May 91	YOU'RE IN LOVE SBK SBK 25 ▲ 29	5	
23 May 92	YOU WON'T SEE ME CRY SBK SBK 34 18	5	
22 Aug 92	GIVE IT UP SBK SBK 36 36	3	

WILT Ireland, male vocal / instrumental group (2 WEEKS)

		pos/wks	
8 Apr 00	RADIO DISCO Mushroom MUSH 71CDS 56	1	
8 Jul 00	OPEN ARMS Mushroom MUSH 75CDS 59	1	

Chris WILTSHIRE – See CLASS ACTION featuring Chris WILTSHIRE

WIMBLEDON CHORAL SOCIETY UK, choral group (8 WEEKS)

		pos/wks	
4 Jul 98	WORLD CUP '98 - PAVANE Telstar CDSTAS 2979........................20	5	
12 Dec 98	IF - READ TO FAURE'S 'PAVANE'		
	BBC Worldwide WMSS60062 [1] 45	3	

[1] Des Lynam featuring Wimbledon Choral Society

WIN UK, male vocal / instrumental group (3 WEEKS)

		pos/wks	
4 Apr 87	SUPER POPOID GROOVE Swamplands LON 128........................63	3	

WINANS US, male vocal group (1 WEEK)

		pos/wks	
30 Nov 85	LET MY PEOPLE GO (PART 1) Qwest W 8874........................71	1	

BeBe WINANS – See ETERNAL

CeCe WINANS – See Whitney HOUSTON

Mario WINANS – See PUFF DADDY

WINDJAMMER US, male vocal / instrumental group (12 WEEKS)

		pos/wks	
30 Jun 84	TOSSING AND TURNING MCA MCA 897 18	12	

Rose WINDROSS – See SOUL II SOUL

Barbara WINDSOR & Mike REID
UK, female / male vocal duo (2 WEEKS)

		pos/wks	
24 Apr 99	THE MORE I SEE YOU Telstar CDSTAS 3049........................46	2	

WING AND A PRAYER FIFE AND DRUM CORPS
US, male / female vocal / instrumental group (7 WEEKS)

		pos/wks	
24 Jan 76	BABY FACE Atlantic K 10705 12	7	

WINGER US, male vocal / instrumental group (3 WEEKS)

		pos/wks	
19 Jan 91	MILES AWAY Atlantic A 7802 56	3	

Pete WINGFIELD UK, male vocalist / instrumentalist - piano (7 WEEKS)
pos/wks

		pos/wks	
28 Jun 75 ●	EIGHTEEN WITH A BULLET Island WIP 6231 7	7	

WINGS – See Paul McCARTNEY

Josh WINK US, male producer - Joshua Winkelman (29 WEEKS)

		pos/wks	
6 May 95	DON'T LAUGH XL XLS 62CD [1] 38	2	
21 Oct 95 ●	HIGHER STATE OF CONSCIOUSNESS		
	Manifesto FESCD 3 8	8	
30 Dec 95	HIGHER STATE OF CONSCIOUSNESS (re-entry)		
	Manifesto FESCD 3 60	4	
2 Mar 96	HYPNOTIZIN' XL XLS 71CD [1] 35	2	
27 Jul 96 ●	HIGHER STATE OF CONSCIOUSNESS (re-mix)		
	Manifesto FESCD 9 [1] 7	10	
12 Aug 00	HOW'S YOUR EVENING SO FAR ffrr FCD 384 [2] 23	3	

[1] Winx [2] Josh Wink and Lil' Louis

See also SIZE 9

Edgar WINTER GROUP US, male instrumental group (9 WEEKS) pos/wks

		pos/wks	
26 May 73	FRANKENSTEIN Epic EPC 1440 ▲ 18	9	

Ruby WINTERS US, female vocalist (35 WEEKS)

		pos/wks
5 Nov 77 ●	I WILL Creole CR 141	4 13
29 Apr 78	COME TO ME Creole CR 153	11 12
26 Aug 78	I WON'T MENTION IT AGAIN Creole CR 160	45 5
16 Jun 79	BABY LAY DOWN Creole CR 171	43 5

Steve WINWOOD UK, male vocalist (33 WEEKS)

		pos/wks
17 Jan 81	WHILE YOU SEE A CHANCE Island WIP 6655	45 5
9 Oct 82	VALERIE Island WIP 6818	51 4
28 Jun 86	HIGHER LOVE Island IS 288 ▲	13 9
13 Sep 86	FREEDOM OVERSPILL Island IS 294	69 1
24 Jan 87	BACK IN THE HIGH LIFE AGAIN Island IS 303	53 2
19 Sep 87	VALERIE (re-mix) Island IS 336	19 8
11 Jun 88	ROLL WITH IT Virgin VS 1085 ▲	53 4

See also Spencer DAVIS GROUP

WINX – See Josh WINK

WIRE UK, male vocal / instrumental group (4 WEEKS)

		pos/wks
27 Jan 79	OUTDOOR MINER Harvest HAR 5172	51 3
13 May 89	EARDRUM BUZZ Mute MUTE 87	68 1

WIRED
Holland / Finland, male production / instrumental duo (1 WEEK)

		pos/wks
20 Feb 99	TRANSONIC Future Groove CDFGR 001	73 1

WIRELESS UK, male vocal / instrumental group (2 WEEKS)

		pos/wks
28 Jun 97	I NEED YOU Chrysalis CDCHS 5059	68 1
7 Feb 98	IN LOVE WITH THE FAMILIAR Chrysalis CDCHS 5075	69 1

Norman WISDOM UK, male vocalist (20 WEEKS)

		pos/wks
19 Feb 54 ●	DON'T LAUGH AT ME (CAUSE I'M A FOOL) Columbia DB 3133	3 15
15 Mar 57	THE WISDOM OF A FOOL Columbia DB 3903	13 5

WISDOME Italy, male / female production / vocal group (2 WEEKS)

		pos/wks
11 Mar 00	OFF THE WALL Positiva CDTIV 125	33 2

WISEGUYS UK, male DJ / producer - Theo Keating (13 WEEKS)

		pos/wks
6 Jun 98	OOH LA LA Wall of Sound WALLD 038	55 1
12 Sep 98	START THE COMMOTION Wall of Sound WALLD 044	66 1
5 Jun 99 ●	OOH LA LA (re-issue) Wall of Sound WALLD 038X	2 10
11 Sep 99	START THE COMMOTION (re-issue) Wall of Sound WALLD 059	47 1

Bill WITHERS US, male vocalist (29 WEEKS)

		pos/wks
12 Aug 72	LEAN ON ME A & M AMS 7004 ▲	18 9
14 Jan 78 ●	LOVELY DAY CBS 5773	7 8
25 May 85	OH YEAH! CBS A 6154	60 3
10 Sep 88 ●	LOVELY DAY (re-mix) CBS 6530017	4 9

See also Grover WASHINGTON Jr

WITNESS UK, male vocal / instrumental group (2 WEEKS)

		pos/wks
13 Mar 99	SCARS Island CID 740	71 1
19 Jun 99	AUDITION Island CID 749	71 1

WIX – See SPIRO and WIX

WIZZARD 424 Top 500
Early 1970s chart champs led by extrovert Move and ELO frontman Roy Wood, b. 8 Nov 1946, Birmingham, UK. Big-budget Phil Spector-styled recordings are classics of their era. Wood also had several simultaneous solo successes (77 WEEKS)

		pos/wks
9 Dec 72 ●	BALL PARK INCIDENT Harvest HAR 5062	6 12
21 Apr 73 ★	SEE MY BABY JIVE Harvest HAR 5070	1 17
1 Sep 73 ★	ANGEL FINGERS Harvest HAR 5076	1 10

		pos/wks
8 Dec 73 ●	I WISH IT COULD BE CHRISTMAS EVERYDAY Harvest HAR 5079 [1]	4 9
27 Apr 74 ●	ROCK 'N' ROLL WINTER Warner Bros. K16497	6 7
10 Aug 74	THIS IS THE STORY OF MY LOVE (BABY) Warner Bros. K 16434	34 4
21 Dec 74 ●	ARE YOU READY TO ROCK Warner Bros. K 16497	8 10
19 Dec 81	I WISH IT COULD BE CHRISTMAS EVERYDAY (re-issue) Harvest HAR 5173 [1]	41 4
15 Dec 84	I WISH IT COULD BE CHRISTMAS EVERYDAY (re-entry of re-issue) Harvest HAR 5173 [1]	23 4

[1] Wizzard featuring vocal backing by the Suedettes plus the Stockland Green Bilateral School First Year Choir with additional noises by Miss Snob and Class 3C

Jah WOBBLE'S INVADERS of the HEART
UK, male vocalist / multi-instrumentalist (10 WEEKS)

		pos/wks
1 Feb 92	VISIONS OF YOU Oval OVAL 103	35 5
30 Apr 94	BECOMING MORE LIKE GOD Island CID 571	36 2
25 Jun 94	THE SUN DOES RISE Island CIDX 587	41 3

First hit features the uncredited vocals of Sinead O'Connor

Terry WOGAN Ireland, male vocalist (5 WEEKS)

		pos/wks
7 Jan 78	FLORAL DANCE Philips 6006 592	21 5

WOLF – See TROGGS

WOLFSBANE UK, male vocal / instrumental group (1 WEEK)

		pos/wks
5 Oct 91	EZY Def American DEFA 11	68 1

Bobby WOMACK UK, male vocalist (21 WEEKS)

		pos/wks
16 Jun 84	TELL ME WHY Motown TMG 1339	60 3
5 Oct 85	I WISH HE DIDN'T TRUST ME SO MUCH MCA MCA 994	64 2
26 Sep 87	SO THE STORY GOES Chrysalis LIB 3 [1]	34 8
7 Nov 87	LIVING IN A BOX MCA MCA 1210	70 2
3 Apr 93	I'M BACK FOR MORE Dome CDDOME 1002 [2]	27 5
13 May 95	IT'S A MAN'S MAN'S MAN'S WORLD Pulse 8 CDLOSE 89 [3]	73 1

[1] Living in a Box featuring Bobby Womack [2] Lulu and Bobby Womack [3] Jeanie Tracy and Bobby Womack

See also Wilton FELDER

WOMACK and WOMACK
US, male / female vocal duo - Linda & Cecil Womack (51 WEEKS)

		pos/wks
28 Apr 84	LOVE WARS Elektra E 9799	14 10
30 Jun 84	BABY I'M SCARED OF YOU Elektra E 9733	72 2
6 Dec 86	SOUL LOVE - SOUL MAN Manhattan MT 16	58 6
6 Aug 88 ●	TEARDROPS Fourth & Broadway BRW 101	3 17
12 Nov 88	LIFE'S JUST A BALLGAME Fourth & Broadway BRW 116	32 5
25 Feb 89	CELEBRATE THE WORLD Fourth & Broadway BRW 125	19 8
5 Feb 94	SECRET STAR Warner Bros. W 0222CD [1]	46 3

[1] House of Zekkariyas AKA Womack and Womack

WOMBLES 311 Top 500
Furriest (and possibly the tidiest) act in the Top 500 are natives of Wimbledon Common, London, and come under the musical guidance of songwriter and producer Mike Batt, b. 6 Feb 1950, Southampton, UK (96 WEEKS)

		pos/wks
26 Jan 74 ●	THE WOMBLING SONG CBS 1794	4 23
6 Apr 74 ●	REMEMBER YOU'RE A WOMBLE CBS 2241	3 16
22 Jun 74 ●	BANANA ROCK CBS 2465	9 13
12 Oct 74	MINUETTO ALLEGRETTO CBS 2710	16 9
7 Dec 74 ●	WOMBLING MERRY CHRISTMAS CBS 2842	2 8
10 May 75	WOMBLING WHITE TIE AND TAILS CBS 3266	22 7
9 Aug 75	SUPER WOMBLE CBS 3480	20 6
13 Dec 75	LET'S WOMBLE TO THE PARTY TONIGHT CBS 3794	34 5
21 Mar 98	REMEMBER YOU'RE A WOMBLE (re-issue) Columbia 6656202	13 5

UK No.1 ★   UK Top 10 ●   Still on chart +   UK million seller ◆   UK entry at No.1 ■   US No.1 ▲

| 13 Jun 98 | THE WOMBLING SONG (UNDERGROUND OVERGROUND) (re-issue) *Columbia 6660412* | 27 | 3 |
| 30 Dec 00 | I WISH IT COULD BE A WOMBLING MERRY CHRISTMAS EVERY DAY *Dramatico DRAMCDS 0001* [1] | 22 | 1+ |

[1] Wombles with Roy Wood

Stevie WONDER `13` **Top 500** *Consistently successful multi-Grammy winner, b. Steveland Judkins, 13 May 1950, Michigan, US. He was the youngest singer to top the US album chart (aged 13), and he also recorded Motown's biggest UK seller, 'I Just Called to Say I Love You' (415 WEEKS)*

pos/wks

3 Feb 66	UPTIGHT (EVERYTHING'S ALRIGHT) *Tamla Motown TMG 545*	14	10
18 Aug 66	BLOWIN' IN THE WIND *Tamla Motown TMG 570*	36	5
5 Jan 67	A PLACE IN THE SUN *Tamla Motown TMG 588*	20	5
26 Jul 67 ●	I WAS MADE TO LOVE HER *Tamla Motown TMG 613*	5	15
25 Oct 67	I'M WONDERING *Tamla Motown TMG 626*	22	8
8 May 68	SHOO BE DOO BE DOO DA DAY *Tamla Motown TMG 653*	46	4
18 Dec 68 ●	FOR ONCE IN MY LIFE *Tamla Motown TMG 679*	3	13
19 Mar 69	I DON'T KNOW WHY (I LOVE YOU) *Tamla Motown TMG 690*	14	10
9 Jul 69	I DON'T KNOW WHY (I LOVE YOU) (re-entry) *Tamla Motown TMG 690*	43	1
16 Jul 69 ●	MY CHERIE AMOUR *Tamla Motown TMG 690*	4	15
15 Nov 69 ●	YESTER-ME YESTER-YOU YESTERDAY *Tamla Motown TMG 717*	2	13
28 Mar 70 ●	NEVER HAD A DREAM COME TRUE *Tamla Motown TMG 731*	6	12
18 Jul 70	SIGNED SEALED DELIVERED I'M YOURS *Tamla Motown TMG 744*	15	9
26 Sep 70	SIGNED SEALED DELIVERED I'M YOURS (re-entry) *Tamla Motown TMG 744*	49	1
21 Nov 70	HEAVEN HELP US ALL *Tamla Motown TMG 757*	29	11
15 May 71	WE CAN WORK IT OUT *Tamla Motown TMG 772*	27	7
22 Jan 72	IF YOU REALLY LOVE ME *Tamla Motown TMG 798*	20	7
3 Feb 73	SUPERSTITION *Tamla Motown TMG 841* ▲	11	9
19 May 73 ●	YOU ARE THE SUNSHINE OF MY LIFE *Tamla Motown TMG 852* ▲	7	11
13 Oct 73	HIGHER GROUND *Tamla Motown TMG 869*	29	5
12 Jan 74	LIVING FOR THE CITY *Tamla Motown TMG 881*	15	9
13 Apr 74 ●	HE'S MISSTRA KNOW IT ALL *Tamla Motown TMG 892*	10	9
19 Oct 74	YOU HAVEN'T DONE NOTHIN' *Tamla Motown TMG 921* ▲	30	5
11 Jan 75	BOOGIE ON REGGAE WOMAN *Tamla Motown TMG 928*	12	8
18 Dec 76 ●	I WISH *Motown TMG 1054* ▲	5	10
9 Apr 77 ●	SIR DUKE *Motown TMG 1068* ▲	2	9
10 Sep 77	ANOTHER STAR *Motown TMG 1083*	29	5
24 Feb 79	POPS WE LOVE YOU *Motown TMG 1136* [1]	66	5
24 Nov 79	SEND ONE YOUR LOVE *Motown TMG 1149*	52	3
26 Jan 80	BLACK ORCHID *Motown TMG 1173*	63	3
29 Mar 80	OUTSIDE MY WINDOW *Motown TMG 1179*	52	4
13 Sep 80 ●	MASTERBLASTER (JAMMIN') *Motown TMG 1204*	2	10
27 Dec 80 ●	I AIN'T GONNA STAND FOR IT *Motown TMG 1215*	10	10
7 Mar 81 ●	LATELY *Motown TMG 1226*	3	13
25 Jul 81 ●	HAPPY BIRTHDAY *Motown TMG 1235*	2	11
23 Jan 82	THAT GIRL *Motown TMG 1254*	39	6
10 Apr 82 ★	EBONY AND IVORY *Parlophone R 6054* [2] ▲	1	10
5 Jun 82 ●	DO I DO *Motown TMG 1269*	10	7
25 Sep 82	RIBBON IN THE SKY *Motown TMG 1280*	45	4
25 Aug 84 ★	I JUST CALLED TO SAY I LOVE YOU *Motown TMG 1349* ◆ ▲	1	24
1 Dec 84	LOVE LIGHT IN FLIGHT *Motown TMG 1364*	44	5
29 Dec 84	DON'T DRIVE DRUNK *Motown TMG 1372*	71	1
12 Jan 85	DON'T DRIVE DRUNK (re-entry) *Motown TMG 1372*	62	2
7 Sep 85 ●	PART-TIME LOVER *Motown ZB 40351* ▲	3	12
9 Nov 85	THAT'S WHAT FRIENDS ARE FOR *Arista ARIST 638* [3]	16	9
23 Nov 85	GO HOME *Motown ZB 40501*	67	2
28 Dec 85	I JUST CALLED TO SAY I LOVE YOU (re-entry) *Motown TMG 1349*	64	2
8 Mar 86	OVERJOYED *Motown ZB 40567*	17	8
17 Jan 87	STRANGER ON THE SHORE OF LOVE *Motown WOND 2*	55	3
31 Oct 87	SKELETONS *Motown ZB 41439*	59	3
28 May 88	GET IT *Motown ZB 41883* [4]	37	4
6 Aug 88 ●	MY LOVE *CBS JULIO 2* [5]	5	11
20 May 89	FREE *Motown ZB 42855*	49	5
12 Oct 91	FUN DAY *Motown ZB 44957*	63	1
25 Feb 95	FOR YOUR LOVE *Motown TMGCD 1437*	23	4
22 Jul 95	TOMORROW ROBINS WILL SING *Motown 8603732*	71	1

| 19 Jul 97 ● | HOW COME, HOW LONG *Epic 6646202* [6] | 10 | 5 |
| 31 Oct 98 | TRUE TO YOUR HEART *Motown 8608832* [7] | 51 | 1 |

[1] Diana Ross, Marvin Gaye, Smokey Robinson and Stevie Wonder [2] Paul McCartney with Stevie Wonder [3] Dionne Warwick and Friends featuring Elton John, Stevie Wonder and Gladys Knight [4] Stevie Wonder and Michael Jackson [5] Julio Iglesias featuring Stevie Wonder [6] Babyface featuring Stevie Wonder [7] 98 Degrees featuring Stevie Wonder

Wayne WONDER – See SHAGGY

WONDER DOG
Germany, canine vocalist - Harry Thumann (7 WEEKS) pos/wks

| 21 Aug 82 | RUFF MIX *Flip FLIP 001* | 31 | 7 |

WONDERS *US, male vocal / instrumental group (3 WEEKS)* pos/wks

| 22 Feb 97 | THAT THING YOU DO! *Play-Tone 6640552* | 22 | 3 |

WONDER STUFF *UK, male vocal / instrumental group (66 WEEKS)* pos/wks

30 Apr 88	GIVE GIVE GIVE ME MORE MORE MORE *Polydor GONE 3*	72	2
16 Jul 88	A WISH AWAY *Polydor GONE 4*	43	5
24 Sep 88	IT'S YER MONEY I'M AFTER BABY *Polydor GONE 5*	40	3
11 Mar 89	WHO WANTS TO BE THE DISCO KING? *Polydor GONE 6*	28	3
23 Sep 89	DON'T LET ME DOWN GENTLY *Polydor GONE 7*	19	4
11 Nov 89	GOLDEN GREEN / GET TOGETHER *Polydor GONE 8*	33	3
12 May 90	CIRCLESQUARE *Polydor GONE 10*	20	4
13 Apr 91 ●	THE SIZE OF A COW *Polydor GONE 11*	5	7
25 May 91	CAUGHT IN MY SHADOW *Polydor GONE 12*	18	3
7 Sep 91	SLEEP ALONE *Polydor GONE 13*	43	2
26 Oct 91 ★	DIZZY *Sense SIGH 712* [1]	1	12
25 Jan 92 ●	WELCOME TO THE CHEAP SEATS (EP) *Polydor GONE 14*	8	5
25 Sep 93 ●	ON THE ROPES (EP) *Polydor GONCD 15*	10	4
27 Nov 93	FULL OF LIFE (HAPPY NOW) *Polydor GONCD 16*	28	3
26 Mar 94	HOT LOVE NOW *Polydor GONCD 17*	19	3
10 Sep 94	UNBEARABLE *Polydor GONCD 18*	16	3

[1] Vic Reeves and the Wonder Stuff

Tracks on Welcome to the Cheap Seats (EP): Welcome to the Cheap Seats / Me, My Mom, My Dad and My Brother / Will the Circle Be Unbroken / That's Entertainment. Tracks on On the Ropes (EP): On the Ropes / Professional Disturber of the Peace / Hank and John / Whites

WONDRESS – See MANTRONIX

Brenton WOOD *US, male vocalist - Alfred Smith (14 WEEKS)* pos/wks

| 27 Dec 67 ● | GIMME LITTLE SIGN *Liberty LBF 15021* | 8 | 14 |

Roy WOOD *UK, male vocalist / multi-instrumentalist (42 WEEKS)* pos/wks

11 Aug 73	DEAR ELAINE *Harvest HAR 5074*	18	8
1 Dec 73 ●	FOREVER *Harvest HAR 5078*	8	13
15 Jun 74	GOIN' DOWN THE ROAD *Harvest HAR 5083*	13	7
31 May 75	OH WHAT A SHAME *Jet 754*	13	7
22 Nov 86	WATERLOO *IRS IRM 125* [1]	45	4
23 Dec 95	I WISH IT COULD BE CHRISTMAS EVERYDAY *Woody WOODY 001CD* [2]	59	2
30 Dec 00	I WISH IT COULD BE A WOMBLING MERRY CHRISTMAS EVERY DAY *Dramatico DRAMCDS 0001* [3]	22	1+

[1] Doctor and the Medics featuring Roy Wood [2] Roy Wood Big Band [3] Wombles with Roy Wood

See also WIZZARD; ELECTRIC LIGHT ORCHESTRA; MOVE

WOODENTOPS *UK, male vocal / instrumental group (1 WEEK)* pos/wks

| 11 Oct 86 | EVERYDAY LIVING *Rough Trade RT 178* | 72 | 1 |

Marcella WOODS – See Matt DAREY

Edward WOODWARD *UK, male vocalist (2 WEEKS)* pos/wks

| 16 Jan 71 | THE WAY YOU LOOK TONIGHT *DJM DJS 232* | 50 | 1 |
| 30 Jan 71 | THE WAY YOU LOOK TONIGHT (re-entry) *DJM DJS 232* | 42 | 1 |

UK No.1 ★   UK Top 10 ●   Still on chart +   UK million seller ◆   UK entry at No.1 ■   US No.1 ▲

SINGLED OUT... Melanie C

Most successful Spice Mel C has real pop pedigree as can be seen from the single that was No.1 on the day she was born.

- **NO.1 ON THE UK SINGLES CHART THE DAY I WAS BORN:**
  Bohemian Rhapsody – Queen

- **FIRST SINGLE I EVER BOUGHT:**
  I've never been a singles buyer –
  I prefer to buy albums. So it was probably 'Wannabe'

- **SINGLE THAT DRIVES ME UP THE WALL:**
  Most novelty songs and any Steps song

ALL-TIME FAVOURITE SINGLE:

Sir Duke
Stevie Wonder

Photo: Pictorial Press

WOOKIE UK, male producer / vocalist - Jason Chue (8 WEEKS) pos/wks

		pos	wks
3 Jun 00	WHAT'S GOING ON S2S Recordings S2CD 001	45	1
12 Aug 00 ●	BATTLE S2S Recordings S2SPCD001 [1]	10	7

[1] Wookie Featuring Lain

Sheb WOOLEY US, male vocalist (8 WEEKS) pos/wks

		pos	wks
20 Jun 58	THE PURPLE PEOPLE EATER MGM 981 ▲	12	8

WOOLPACKERS UK, male vocal group (24 WEEKS) pos/wks

		pos	wks
16 Nov 96 ●	HILLBILLY ROCK HILLBILLY ROLL RCA 74321425412	5	14
29 Nov 97	LINE DANCE PARTY RCA 74321512262	25	10

WORKING WEEK
UK, male / female vocal / instrumental group (2 WEEKS) pos/wks

		pos	wks
9 Jun 84	VENCEREMOS - WE WILL WIN Virgin VS 684	64	2

WORLD – See LIL' LOUIS

WORLD OF TWIST
UK, male / female vocal / instrumental group (12 WEEKS) pos/wks

		pos	wks
24 Nov 90	THE STORM Circa YR 55	42	3
5 Jan 91	THE STORM (re-entry) Circa YR 55	74	2
23 Mar 91	SONS OF THE STAGE Circa YR 62	47	3
12 Oct 91	SWEETS Circa YR 72	58	2
22 Feb 92	SHE'S A RAINBOW Circa YR 82	62	2

WORLD PARTY
Ireland / UK, male vocal / instrumental group (29 WEEKS) pos/wks

		pos	wks
14 Feb 87	SHIP OF FOOLS Ensign ENY 606	42	6
16 Jun 90	MESSAGE IN THE BOX Ensign ENY 631	39	6
15 Sep 90	WAY DOWN NOW Ensign ENY 634	66	2
18 May 91	THANK YOU WORLD Ensign ENY 643	68	1
10 Apr 93	IS IT LIKE TODAY Ensign CDENY 658	19	6
10 Jul 93	GIVE IT ALL AWAY Ensign CDENY 659	43	3
2 Oct 93	ALL I GAVE Ensign CDENYS 660	37	3
7 Jun 97	BEAUTIFUL DREAM Chrysalis CDCHS 5053	31	2

WORLD PREMIERE US, male vocal / instrumental group (4 WEEKS) pos/wks

		pos	wks
28 Jan 84	SHARE THE NIGHT Epic A 4133	64	4

WORLD WARRIOR UK, male producer - Simon Harris (1 WEEK) pos/wks

		pos	wks
16 Apr 94	STREET FIGHTER II Living Beat LBECD 27	70	1

See also Simon HARRIS

WORLDS APART UK, male vocal group (17 WEEKS) pos/wks

		pos	wks
27 Mar 93	HEAVEN MUST BE MISSING AN ANGEL Arista 74321139362	29	3
3 Jul 93	WONDERFUL WORLD Arista 74321153402	51	1
25 Sep 93	EVERLASTING LOVE Bell 74321164802	20	4
26 Mar 94	COULD IT BE I'M FALLING IN LOVE Bell 74321189952	15	6
4 Jun 94	BEGGIN' TO BE WRITTEN Bell 74321211982	29	3

WORLD'S FAMOUS SUPREME TEAM
US, male vocal / scratch group (19 WEEKS) pos/wks

		pos	wks
4 Dec 82 ●	BUFFALO GALS Charisma MALC 1 [1]	9	12
25 Feb 84	HEY DJ Charisma TEAM 1	52	5
8 Dec 90	OPERAA HOUSE Virgin VS 1273 [2]	75	1
3 Oct 98	BUFFALO GALS STAMPEDE (Re-mix) Virgin VSCDT 1717 [3]	65	1

[1] Malcolm McLaren and the World's Famous Supreme Team [2] World's Famous Supreme Team Show [3] Malcolm McLaren and the World's Famous Supreme Team plus Rakim and Roger Sanchez

WRECKX-N-EFFECT US, male vocal group (18 WEEKS) pos/wks

		pos	wks
13 Jan 90	JUICY Motown ZB 43295 [1]	29	7
5 Dec 92	RUMP SHAKER MCA MCS 1725	24	7
7 May 94	WRECKX SHOP MCA MCSTD 1969 [2]	26	2
13 Aug 94	RUMP SHAKER (re-issue) MCA MCSTD 1989	40	2

[1] Wrecks-N-Effect [2] Wreckx-N-Effect featuring Apache Indian

Betty WRIGHT US, female vocalist (23 WEEKS) pos/wks

		pos	wks
25 Jan 75	SHOORAH SHOORAH RCA 2491	27	7
19 Apr 75	WHERE IS THE LOVE RCA 2548	25	7
8 Feb 86	PAIN Cooltempo COOL 117	42	6
9 Sep 89	KEEP LOVE NEW Sure Delight SD 11	71	3

Ian WRIGHT UK, male vocalist (2 WEEKS) pos/wks

		pos	wks
28 Aug 93	DO THE RIGHT THING M & G MAGCD 45	43	2

Linda WRIGHT – See NEW ATLANTIC

Ruby WRIGHT US, female vocalist (15 WEEKS) pos/wks

		pos	wks
16 Apr 54 ●	BIMBO Parlophone R 3816	7	4
21 May 54	BIMBO (re-entry) Parlophone R 3816	12	1
22 May 59	THREE STARS Parlophone R 4556	19	10

'Three Stars' is narrated by Dick Pike

Steve WRIGHT UK, male vocalist (10 WEEKS) pos/wks

		pos	wks
27 Nov 82	I'M ALRIGHT RCA 296 [1]	40	6
15 Oct 83	GET SOME THERAPY RCA 362 [2]	75	1
1 Dec 84	THE GAY CAVALIEROS (THE STORY SO FAR) MCA 925	61	3

[1] Young Steve and the Afternoon Boys [2] Steve Wright and the Sisters of Soul

WUBBLE-U UK, male production group (1 WEEK) pos/wks

		pos	wks
7 Mar 98	PETAL Indolent DGOL 003CD1	55	1

WURZELS UK, male vocal / instrumental group (28 WEEKS) pos/wks

		pos	wks
2 Feb 67	DRINK UP THY ZIDER Columbia DB 8081 [1]	45	1
15 May 76 ★	COMBINE HARVESTER (BRAND NEW KEY) EMI 2450	1	13
11 Sep 76 ●	I AM A CIDER DRINKER (PALOMA BLANCA) EMI 2520	3	9
25 Jun 77	FARMER BILL'S COWMAN (I WAS KAISER BILL'S BATMAN) EMI 2637	32	5

[1] Adge Cutler and the Wurzels

WU-TANG CLAN US, male rap / instrumental group (14 WEEKS) pos/wks

		pos	wks
16 Aug 97	TRIUMPH Loud 74321510212 [1]	46	1
21 Mar 98 ●	SAY WHAT YOU WANT / INSANE Mercury MERC 499 [2]	4	7
25 Nov 00 ●	GRAVEL PIT Loud / Epic 67015182	6	6+

[1] Wu-Tang Clan featuring Cappadonna [2] Texas featuring Wu-Tang Clan (rap by Method Man and RZA)

WWF SUPERSTARS US / UK, male wrestling vocalists (15 WEEKS) pos/wks

		pos	wks
12 Dec 92 ●	SLAM JAM Arista 74321124887	4	8
13 Feb 93	SLAM JAM (re-entry) Arista 74321124887	75	1
3 Apr 93	WRESTLEMANIA Arista 74321136832	14	5
10 Jul 93	USA Arista 74321153092 [1]	71	1

[1] WWF Superstars featuring Hacksaw Jim Duggan

Robert WYATT UK, male vocalist (11 WEEKS) pos/wks

		pos	wks
28 Sep 74	I'M A BELIEVER Virgin VS 114	29	5
7 May 83	SHIPBUILDING Rough Trade RT 115	35	6

Michael WYCOFF US, male vocalist (2 WEEKS) pos/wks

		pos	wks
23 Jul 83	(DO YOU REALLY LOVE ME) TELL ME LOVE RCA 348	60	2

Pete WYLIE UK, male vocalist (18 WEEKS) pos/wks

		pos	wks
3 May 86	SINFUL Eternal MDM 7	13	10
13 Sep 86	DIAMOND GIRL Eternal MDM 12	57	3
13 Apr 91	SINFUL! Siren SRN 138 [1]	28	5

[1] Pete Wylie with the Farm

See also WAH!

Bill WYMAN
UK, male vocalist (13 WEEKS)

		pos/wks
25 Jul 81	(SI SI) JE SUIS UN ROCK STAR *A & M AMS 8144*	**14** 9
20 Mar 82	A NEW FASHION *A & M AMS 8209*	**37** 4

See also ROLLING STONES

Jane WYMAN – See Bing CROSBY

Tammy WYNETTE
US, female vocalist - Virginia Wynette Pugh (35 WEEKS)

		pos/wks
26 Apr 75 ★	STAND BY YOUR MAN *Epic EPC 7137*	**1** 12
28 Jun 75	D. I. V. O. R. C. E. *Epic EPC 3361*	**12** 7
12 Jun 76	I DON'T WANNA PLAY HOUSE *Epic EPC 4091*	**37** 4
7 Dec 91 ●	JUSTIFIED AND ANCIENT *KLF Communications KLF 099* [1]	**2** 12

[1] KLF guest vocals: Tammy Wynette

Mark WYNTER ⟨412 Top 500⟩ *Teen-targeted pop singer turned actor, b. Terence Lewis, 29 Jan 1943, Surrey, UK. Boy-next-door type performer, whose hit portfolio contains a mix of revivals and cover versions. Moved into acting and TV presentation work (80 WEEKS)*

		pos/wks
25 Aug 60	IMAGE OF A GIRL *Decca F 11263*	**11** 10
10 Nov 60	KICKING UP THE LEAVES *Decca F 11279*	**24** 10
9 Mar 61	DREAM GIRL *Decca F 11323*	**27** 5
8 Jun 61	EXCLUSIVELY YOURS *Decca F 11354*	**32** 7
4 Oct 62 ●	VENUS IN BLUE JEANS *Pye 7N 15466*	**4** 15
13 Dec 62 ●	GO AWAY LITTLE GIRL *Pye 7N 15492*	**6** 11
6 Jun 63	SHY GIRL *Pye 7N 15525*	**28** 6
14 Nov 63	IT'S ALMOST TOMORROW *Pye 7N 15577*	**12** 12
9 Apr 64	ONLY YOU *Pye 7N 15626*	**38** 4

Malcolm X *US, male orator (4 WEEKS)*

		pos/wks
7 Apr 84	NO SELL OUT *Tommy Boy IS 165*	**60** 4

Hit features credit: 'Music by Keith Le Blanc'

XAVIER – See TJR featuring XAVIER

XAVIER *US, male / female vocal / instrumental group (3 WEEKS)*

		pos/wks
20 Mar 82	WORK THAT SUCKER TO DEATH / LOVE IS ON THE ONE *Liberty UP 651*	**53** 3

XPANSIONS *UK, male producer - Richie Malone (20 WEEKS)*

		pos/wks
6 Oct 90	ELEVATION *Optimism 113683*	**49** 5
23 Feb 91 ●	MOVE YOUR BODY (ELEVATION) *Arista 113 683*	**7** 9
15 Jun 91	WHAT YOU WANT *Arista 114 246* [1]	**55** 2
26 Aug 95	MOVE YOUR BODY (re-mix) *Arista 74321294982* [2]	**14** 4

[1] Xpansions featuring Dale Joyner [2] Xpansions 95

'Move Your Body' is a re-mix of 'Elevation'

X-PRESS 2 *UK, male instrumental / production group (8 WEEKS)*

		pos/wks
5 Jun 93	LONDON X-PRESS *Junior Boy's Own JBO 12*	**59** 1
16 Oct 93	SAY WHAT! *Junior Boy's Own JBO 16CD*	**32** 2
30 Jul 94	ROCK 2 HOUSE / HIP HOUSIN' *Junior Boy's Own JBO 21CD* [1]	**55** 2
9 Mar 96	THE SOUND *Junior Boy's Own JBO 36*	**38** 1
12 Oct 96	TRANZ EURO XPRESS *Junior Boy's Own JBO 42CD*	**45** 1
30 Sep 00	AC / DC *Skint SKINT 57*	**60** 1

[1] X-Press 2 featuring Lo-Pro

X-RAY SPEX
UK, male / female vocal / instrumental group (33 WEEKS)

		pos/wks
29 Apr 78	THE DAY THE WORLD TURNED DAY-GLO *EMI International INT 553*	**23** 8
22 Jul 78	IDENTITY *EMI International INT 563*	**24** 10
4 Nov 78	GERM FREE ADOLESCENCE *EMI International INT 573*	**19** 11
21 Apr 79	HIGHLY INFLAMMABLE *EMI International INT 583*	**45** 4

XSCAPE *US, female vocal group (15 WEEKS)*

		pos/wks
20 Nov 93	JUST KICKIN' IT *Columbia 6598622*	**49** 2
5 Nov 94	JUST KICKIN' IT (re-issue) *Columbia 6608642*	**54** 2
7 Oct 95	FEELS SO GOOD *Columbia 6625022*	**34** 2
27 Jan 96	WHO CAN I RUN TO *Columbia 6628112*	**31** 3
29 Jun 96	KEEP ON KEEPIN' ON *East West A 4287CD* [1]	**39** 2
19 Apr 97	KEEP ON KEEPIN' ON (re-issue) *East West A 3950CD1* [1]	**27** 2
22 Aug 98	THE ARMS OF THE ONE WHO LOVES YOU *Columbia 6662522*	**46** 2

[1] MC Lyte featuring Xscape

X-STATIC *Italy, male / female vocal / instrumental group (2 WEEKS)*
pos/wks

4 Feb 95	I'M STANDING (HIGHER) *Positiva CDTIV 25*	**41** 2

XTC ⟨495 Top 500⟩ *Innovative, intelligent and influential pop band, formed 1977 Swindon, Wiltshire, UK. Throughout long and varied life span mainstays have been songwriters Andy Partridge (v/g) and Colin Moulding (v/b). Highly revered by many later groups, their 1999 album, Apple Venus, reached Top 20 in Japan (70 WEEKS)*

		pos/wks
12 May 79	LIFE BEGINS AT THE HOP *Virgin VS 259*	**54** 4
22 Sep 79	MAKING PLANS FOR NIGEL *Virgin VS 282*	**17** 11
6 Sep 80	GENERALS AND MAJORS / DON'T LOSE YOUR TEMPER *Virgin VS 365*	**32** 8
18 Oct 80	TOWERS OF LONDON *Virgin VS 372*	**31** 5
24 Jan 81	SGT ROCK (IS GOING TO HELP ME) *Virgin VS 384*	**16** 9
23 Jan 82 ●	SENSES WORKING OVERTIME *Virgin VS 462*	**10** 9
27 Mar 82	BALL AND CHAIN *Virgin VS 482*	**58** 4
15 Oct 83	LOVE ON A FARMBOY'S WAGES *Virgin VS 613*	**50** 4
29 Sep 84	ALL YOU PRETTY GIRLS *Virgin VS 709*	**55** 5
28 Jan 89	MAYOR OF SIMPLETON *Virgin VS 1158*	**46** 5
4 Apr 92	THE DISAPPOINTED *Virgin VS 1404*	**33** 5
13 Jun 92	THE BALLAD OF PETER PUMPKINHEAD *Virgin VS 1415*	**71** 1

Y?N-VEE *US, female vocal group (1 WEEK)*

		pos/wks
17 Dec 94	CHOCOLATE *RAL RALCD 2*	**65** 1

Y & T *US, male vocal / instrumental group (4 WEEKS)*

		pos/wks
13 Aug 83	MEAN STREAK *A & M AM 135*	**41** 4

Y-TRIBE featuring Elisabeth TROY *UK, male instrumental / production duo with female vocalist (3 WEEKS)*

		pos/wks
18 Dec 99	ENOUGH IS ENOUGH *Northwest 10 NORTHCD 002*	**49** 2
8 Jan 00	ENOUGH IS ENOUGH (re-entry) *Northwest 10 NORTHCD 002*	**75** 1

YA KID K – See HI-TEK 3 featuring YA KID K; TECHNOTRONIC

Weird Al YANKOVIC *US, male vocalist (8 WEEKS)*

		pos/wks
7 Apr 84	EAT IT *Scotti Bros. / Epic A 4257*	**36** 7
4 Jul 92	SMELLS LIKE NIRVANA *Scotti Bros PO 219*	**58** 1

UK No.1 ★   UK Top 10 ●   Still on chart +   UK million seller ◆   UK entry at No.1 ■   US No.1 ▲

YARBROUGH and PEOPLES US, male / female vocal / instrumental duo - Calvin Yarbrough & Alisa Peoples (20 WEEKS)

		pos/wks
27 Dec 80 ●	DON'T STOP THE MUSIC *Mercury MER 53*	**7** 12
5 May 84	DON'T WASTE YOUR TIME *Total Experience XE 501*	**60** 3
11 Jan 86	GUILTY *Total Experience FB 49905*	**53** 3
5 Jul 86	I WOULDN'T LIE *Total Experience FB 49841*	**61** 2

YARDBIRDS UK, male vocal / instrumental group (62 WEEKS)

		pos/wks
12 Nov 64	GOOD MORNING LITTLE SCHOOLGIRL *Columbia DB 7391*	**44** 4
18 Mar 65 ●	FOR YOUR LOVE *Columbia DB 7499*	**3** 12
17 Jun 65 ●	HEART FULL OF SOUL *Columbia DB 7594*	**2** 13
14 Oct 65 ●	EVIL HEARTED YOU / STILL I'M SAD *Columbia DB 7706*	**3** 10
3 Mar 66 ●	SHAPES OF THINGS *Columbia DB 7848*	**3** 9
2 Jun 66 ●	OVER UNDER SIDEWAYS DOWN *Columbia DB 7928*	**10** 9
27 Oct 66	HAPPENINGS TEN YEARS TIME AGO *Columbia DB 8024*	**43** 5

See also Eric CLAPTON; CREAM

YAVAHN – See RUFFNECK featuring YAVAHN

YAZOO UK, female / male vocal / instrumental duo - Alison Moyet & Vince Clarke (55 WEEKS)

		pos/wks
17 Apr 82 ●	ONLY YOU *Mute MUTE 020*	**2** 14
17 Jul 82 ●	DON'T GO *Mute YAZ 001*	**3** 11
20 Nov 82	THE OTHER SIDE OF LOVE *Mute YAZ 002*	**13** 9
21 May 83 ●	NOBODY'S DIARY *Mute YAZ 003*	**3** 11
8 Dec 90	SITUATION *Mute YAZ 4*	**14** 8
4 Sep 99	ONLY YOU (re-mix) *Mute CDYAZ 5*	**38** 2

See also ASSEMBLY; Alison MOYET; ERASURE

YAZZ 498 Top 500 Pop / dance vocalist, born Yasmin Evans, 19 May 1963, London, UK. After singing on six Top 20 hits the former model took a break to have children, but never found the same success again - even with songs that originally made the Top 20 for Ace, The Korgis, Sugar Minott and Gloria Gaynor (69 WEEKS)

		pos/wks
20 Feb 88 ●	DOCTORIN' THE HOUSE *Ahead of Our Time CCUT 27* [1]	**6** 9
23 Jul 88 ★	THE ONLY WAY IS UP *Big Life BLR 4* [2]	**1** 15
29 Oct 88 ●	STAND UP FOR YOUR LOVE RIGHTS *Big Life BLR 5*	**2** 12
4 Feb 89 ●	FINE TIME *Big Life BLR 6*	**9** 8
29 Apr 89	WHERE HAS ALL THE LOVE GONE *Big Life BLR 8*	**16** 6
23 Jun 90	TREAT ME GOOD *Big Life BLR 24*	**20** 5
28 Mar 92	ONE TRUE WOMAN *Polydor PO 198*	**60** 2
31 Jul 93	HOW LONG *Polydor PZCD 252* [3]	**31** 5
2 Apr 94	HAVE MERCY *Polydor PZCD 309*	**42** 3
9 Jul 94	EVERYBODY'S GOT TO LEARN SOMETIME *Polydor PZCD 316*	**56** 2
28 Sep 96	GOOD THING GOING *East West EW 062CD*	**53** 1
22 Mar 97	NEVER CAN SAY GOODBYE *East West EW 081CD*	**61** 1

[1] Coldcut featuring Yazz and the Plastic Population [2] Yazz and the Plastic Population [3] Yazz and Aswad

Trisha YEARWOOD US, female vocalist (1 WEEK)

		pos/wks
9 Aug 97	HOW DO I LIVE *MCA MCSTD 48064*	**66** 1

YELL! UK, male vocal duo - Paul Varney & Daniel James (8 WEEKS)

		pos/wks
20 Jan 90 ●	INSTANT REPLAY *Fanfare FAN 22*	**10** 8

YELLO Switzerland, male vocal / instrumental duo - Dieter Meier & Boris Blank (42 WEEKS)

		pos/wks
25 Jun 83	I LOVE YOU *Stiff BUY 176*	**41** 4
26 Nov 83	LOST AGAIN *Stiff BUY 191*	**73** 1
9 Aug 86	GOLDRUSH *Mercury MER 218*	**54** 3
22 Aug 87	THE RHYTHM DIVINE *Mercury MER 253* [1]	**54** 4
27 Aug 88 ●	THE RACE *Mercury YELLO 1*	**7** 11
17 Dec 88	TIED UP *Mercury YELLO 2*	**60** 5
25 Mar 89	OF COURSE I'M LYING *Mercury YELLO 3*	**23** 8
22 Jul 89	BLAZING SADDLES *Mercury YELLO 4*	**47** 2
8 Jun 91	RUBBERBANDMAN *Mercury YELLO 5*	**58** 2
5 Sep 92	JUNGLE BILL *Mercury MER 376*	**61** 2

		pos/wks
7 Nov 92	THE RACE / BOSTICH (re-issue) *Mercury MER 382*	**55** 1
15 Oct 94	HOW HOW *Mercury MERCD 414*	**59** 1

[1] Yello featuring Shirley Bassey

YELLOW DOG US / UK, male vocal / instrumental group (13 WEEKS)

		pos/wks
4 Feb 78 ●	JUST ONE MORE NIGHT *Virgin VS 195*	**8** 9
22 Jul 78	WAIT UNTIL MIDNIGHT *Virgin VS 217*	**54** 4

YELLOW MAGIC ORCHESTRA Japan, male instrumental group (11 WEEKS)

		pos/wks
14 Jun 80	COMPUTER GAME (THEME FROM 'THE INVADERS') *A & M AMS 7502*	**17** 11

YELLOWCOATS – See Paul SHANE and the YELLOWCOATS

YES UK / South Africa, male vocal / instrumental group (31 WEEKS)

		pos/wks
17 Sep 77 ●	WONDROUS STORIES *Atlantic K 10999*	**7** 9
26 Nov 77	GOING FOR THE ONE *Atlantic K 11047*	**24** 4
9 Sep 78	DON'T KILL THE WHALE *Atlantic K 11184*	**36** 4
12 Nov 83	OWNER OF A LONELY HEART *Atco B 9817* ▲	**28** 9
31 Mar 84	LEAVE IT *Atco B 9787*	**56** 4
3 Oct 87	LOVE WILL FIND A WAY *Atco A 9449*	**73** 1

Group were UK only for first three hits

See also ANDERSON BRUFORD WAKEMAN HOWE

Melissa YIANNAKOU – See DESIYA featuring Melissa YIANNAKOU

YIN and YAN UK, male vocal duo (5 WEEKS)

		pos/wks
29 Mar 75	IF *EMI 2282*	**25** 5

Dwight YOAKAM US, male vocalist (2 WEEKS)

		pos/wks
10 Jul 99	CRAZY LITTLE THING CALLED LOVE *Reprise W 497CD*	**43** 2

YO-HANS – See JODE

YOMANDA UK, male DJ / producer - Paul Masterson (18 WEEKS)

		pos/wks
24 Jul 99 ●	SYNTH & STRINGS *Manifesto FESCD 59*	**8** 10
11 Mar 00	SUNSHINE *Manifesto FESCD 68*	**16** 6
2 Sep 00	ON THE LEVEL *Manifesto FESCD 73*	**28** 2

Tukka YOOT – See US3

YORK Germany, male production / instrumental duo - Torsten & Jorg Stenzel (17 WEEKS)

		pos/wks
9 Oct 99	THE AWAKENING *Manifesto FESCD 60*	**11** 5
10 Jun 00 ●	ON THE BEACH *Manifesto FESCD 70*	**4** 10
18 Nov 00	FAREWELL TO THE MOON *Manifesto FESCD 76*	**37** 2

YOSH presents LOVEDEEJAY AKEMI Holland, male producer (5 WEEKS)

		pos/wks
29 Jul 95	IT'S WHAT'S UPFRONT THAT COUNTS *Limbo LIMB 46CD*	**69** 1
2 Dec 95	IT'S WHAT'S UPFRONT THAT COUNTS (re-mix) *Limbo LIMB 50CD*	**31** 2
20 Apr 96	THE SCREAMER *Limbo LIMB 54CD*	**38** 2

YOSHIKI – See Roger TAYLOR

YOTHU YINDI Australia, male vocal / instrumental group (1 WEEK)

		pos/wks
15 Feb 92	TREATY *Hollywood HWD 116*	**72** 1

Faron YOUNG US, male vocalist (23 WEEKS)

		pos/wks
15 Jul 72 ●	IT'S FOUR IN THE MORNING *Mercury 6052 140*	**3** 23

Jimmy YOUNG `351` **Top 500**
Distincitve balladeer who became top radio DJ. b. 21 Sep, 1923, Gloucestershire, UK. Converted from record maker to record spinner and remained a star for five decades. First UK artist to reach No.1 with two successive singles (88 WEEKS)   pos/wks

9 Jan 53	FAITH CAN MOVE MOUNTAINS *Decca F 9986*	11	1
21 Aug 53 ●	ETERNALLY *Decca F 10130*	8	9
6 May 55 ★	UNCHAINED MELODY *Decca F 10502*	1	19
16 Sep 55 ●	THE MAN FROM LARAMIE *Decca F 10597*	1	12
23 Dec 55	SOMEONE ON YOUR MIND *Decca F 10640*	13	5
16 Mar 56 ●	CHAIN GANG *Decca F 10694*	9	6
8 Jun 56	WAYWARD WIND *Decca F 10736*	27	1
22 Jun 56	RICH MAN POOR MAN *Decca F 10736*	25	1
28 Sep 56 ●	MORE *Decca F 10774*	4	17
3 May 57	ROUND AND ROUND *Decca F 10875*	30	1
10 Oct 63	MISS YOU *Columbia DB 7119*	15	13
26 Mar 64	UNCHAINED MELODY (re-recording) *Columbia DB 7234*	43	3

'Unchained Melody' on Columbia and 'Round and Round' are with the Michael Sammes Singers

John Paul YOUNG *Australia, male vocalist (16 WEEKS)*   pos/wks

29 Apr 78 ●	LOVE IS IN THE AIR *Ariola ARO 117*	5	13
14 Nov 92	LOVE IS IN THE AIR (re-mix) *Columbia 6587697*	49	3

Karen YOUNG *UK, female vocalist (21 WEEKS)*   pos/wks

6 Sep 69 ●	NOBODY'S CHILD *Major Minor MM 625*	6	21

Karen YOUNG *US, female vocalist (9 WEEKS)*   pos/wks

19 Aug 78	HOT SHOT *Atlantic K 11180*	34	7
24 Feb 79	HOT SHOT (re-issue) *Atlantic LV 8*	75	1
15 Nov 97	HOT SHOT '97 (re-recording) *Distinctive DISNCD 37*	68	1

Neil YOUNG *Canada, male vocalist (22 WEEKS)*   pos/wks

11 Mar 72 ●	HEART OF GOLD *Reprise K 14140* ▲	10	11
6 Jan 79	FOUR STRONG WINDS *Reprise K 14493*	57	4
27 Feb 93	HARVEST MOON *Reprise W 0139CD*	36	3
17 Jul 93	THE NEEDLE AND THE DAMAGE DONE *Reprise W 0191CD*	75	1
30 Oct 93	LONG MAY YOU RUN (LIVE) *Reprise W 0207CD*	71	1
9 Apr 94	PHILADELPHIA *Reprise W 0242CD*	62	2

See also CROSBY, STILLS, NASH and YOUNG

Paul YOUNG `185` **Top 500**
Soulful-sounding pop singer / songwriter (b. 17 Jan 1956, Bedfordshire, UK) who earlier fronted The Q-Tips and chart act Streetband. This multi-Brit Award winner sold seven million copies of his No Parlez album (including more than one million in the UK) (134 WEEKS)   pos/wks

18 Jun 83 ★	WHEREVER I LAY MY HAT (THAT'S MY HOME) *CBS A 3371*	1	15
10 Sep 83 ●	COME BACK AND STAY *CBS A 3636*	4	9
19 Nov 83 ●	LOVE OF THE COMMON PEOPLE *CBS A 3585*	2	13
13 Oct 84 ●	I'M GONNA TEAR YOUR PLAYHOUSE DOWN *CBS A 4786*	9	7
8 Dec 84 ●	EVERYTHING MUST CHANGE *CBS A 4972*	9	11
9 Mar 85 ●	EVERYTIME YOU GO AWAY *CBS A 6300* ▲	4	11
22 Jun 85	TOMB OF MEMORIES *CBS A 6321*	16	7
17 Aug 85	TOMB OF MEMORIES (re-entry) *CBS A 6321*	74	1
4 Oct 86	WONDERLAND *CBS YOUNG 1*	24	5
29 Nov 86	SOME PEOPLE *CBS YOUNG 2*	56	3
7 Feb 87	WHY DOES A MAN HAVE TO BE STRONG *CBS YOUNG 3*	63	2
12 May 90	SOFTLY WHISPERING I LOVE YOU *CBS YOUNG 4*	21	6
7 Jul 90	OH GIRL *CBS YOUNG 5*	25	6
6 Oct 90	HEAVEN CAN WAIT *CBS YOUNG 6*	71	2
12 Jan 91	CALLING YOU *CBS YOUNG 7*	57	2
30 Mar 91 ●	SENZA UNA DONNA (WITHOUT A WOMAN) *London LON 294* [1]	4	12
10 Aug 91	BOTH SIDES NOW *MCA MCS 1546* [2]	74	1
26 Oct 91	DON'T DREAM IT'S OVER *Columbia 6574117*	20	5
25 Sep 93	NOW I KNOW WHAT MADE OTIS BLUE *Columbia 6596412*	14	7
27 Nov 93	HOPE IN A HOPELESS WORLD *Columbia 6598652*	42	3
23 Apr 94	IT WILL BE YOU *Columbia 6602812*	34	4
17 May 97	I WISH YOU LOVE *East West EW 100CD1*	33	2

[1] Zucchero and Paul Young [2] Clannad and Paul Young

Retta YOUNG *US, female vocalist (7 WEEKS)*   pos/wks

24 May 75	SENDING OUT AN S.O.S. *All Platinum 6146 305*	28	7

Tracie YOUNG – See TRACIE

YOUNG and COMPANY *US, male / female vocal / instrumental group (12 WEEKS)*   pos/wks

1 Nov 80	I LIKE (WHAT YOU'RE DOING TO ME) *Excalibur EXC 501*	20	12

YOUNG AND MOODY BAND *UK, male vocal / instrumental group (4 WEEKS)*   pos/wks

10 Oct 81	DON'T DO THAT *Bronze BRO 130*	63	4

YOUNG BLACK TEENAGERS *US, male rap group (3 WEEKS)*   pos/wks

9 Apr 94	TAP THE BOTTLE *MCA MCSTD 1967*	39	3

YOUNG DISCIPLES *UK / US, male / female vocal / instrumental group (17 WEEKS)*   pos/wks

13 Oct 90	GET YOURSELF TOGETHER *Talkin Loud TLK 2*	68	1
23 Feb 91	APPARENTLY NOTHIN' *Talkin Loud TLK 5*	46	4
3 Aug 91	APPARENTLY NOTHIN' (re-entry) *Talkin Loud TLK 5*	13	7
5 Oct 91	GET YOURSELF TOGETHER (re-issue) *Talkin Loud TLK 15*	65	2
5 Sep 92	YOUNG DISCIPLES (EP) *Talkin Loud TLKX 18*	48	3

Tracks on Young Disciples (EP): Move On / Freedom / All I Have In Me / Move On (re-mix)

YOUNGER YOUNGER 28'S *UK, male / female vocal / instrumental group (1 WEEK)*   pos/wks

5 Jun 99	WE'RE GOING OUT *V2 VVR 5006943*	61	1

YOUNG IDEA *UK, male vocal duo - Tony Cox & Douglas MacCrae-Brown (6 WEEKS)*   pos/wks

29 Jun 67 ●	WITH A LITTLE HELP FROM MY FRIENDS *Columbia DB 8205*	10	6

YOUNG MC *US, male rapper - Marvin Young (7 WEEKS)*   pos/wks

15 Jul 89	BUST A MOVE *Delicious Vinyl BRW 137*	73	2
17 Feb 90	PRINCIPAL'S OFFICE *Delicious Vinyl BRW 161*	54	3
17 Aug 91	THAT'S THE WAY LOVE GOES *Capitol CL 623*	65	2

YOUNG OFFENDERS *Ireland, male vocal / instrumental group (1 WEEK)*   pos/wks

7 Mar 98	THAT'S WHY WE LOSE CONTROL *Columbia 6651942*	60	1

YOUNG ONES – See Cliff RICHARD

YOUNG RASCALS *US, male vocal / instrumental group (17 WEEKS)*   pos/wks

25 May 67 ●	GROOVIN' *Atlantic 584 111* ▲	8	13
16 Aug 67	A GIRL LIKE YOU *Atlantic 584 128*	37	4

Leon YOUNG STRING CHORALE – See Mr Acker BILK and his PARAMOUNT JAZZ BAND

Sydney YOUNGBLOOD *US, male vocalist - Sydney Ford (31 WEEKS)*   pos/wks

26 Aug 89 ●	IF ONLY I COULD *Circa YR 34*	3	14
9 Dec 89	SIT AND WAIT *Circa YR 40*	16	8
31 Mar 90	I'D RATHER GO BLIND *Circa YR 43*	44	5
29 Jun 91	HOOKED ON YOU *Circa YR 65*	72	2
20 Mar 93	ANYTHING *RCA 74321138672*	48	2

Y-TRAXX *Belgium, male producer - Frederique De Backer (1 WEEK)*   pos/wks

24 May 97	MYSTERY LAND (EP) *ffrr FCD 292*	63	1

Tracks on Mystery Land (EP): Mystery Land (radio edit) / Trance Piano / Kiss the Sound / Mystery Land

UK No.1 ★   **UK Top 10** ●   **Still on chart** +   **UK million seller** ◆   **UK entry at No.1** ■   **US No.1** ▲

Z FACTOR UK, male DJ / producer - Dave Lee (1 WEEK)
		pos/wks
21 Feb 98	GOTTA KEEP PUSHIN' ffr FCD 329	47 1

See also Joey NEGRO

Z2 UK, male production duo (1 WEEK)
		pos/wks
26 Feb 00	I WANT YOU Platipus PLATCD 67 [1]	61 1

[1] Vocal by Alison Rivers

Helmut ZACHARIAS Germany, orchestra (11 WEEKS)
		pos/wks
29 Oct 64 ●	TOKYO MELODY Polydor NH 52341	9 11

Pia ZADORA US, female vocalist (6 WEEKS)
		pos/wks
27 Oct 84	WHEN THE RAIN BEGINS TO FALL Arista ARIST 584 [1]	68 2
12 Nov 88	DANCE OUT OF MY HEAD Epic 6528867 [2]	65 4

[1] Jermaine Jackson and Pia Zadora [2] Pia

ZAGER and EVANS
US, male vocal duo - Denny Zager & Rick Evans (13 WEEKS)
		pos/wks
9 Aug 69 ★	IN THE YEAR 2525 (EXORDIUM AND TERMINUS) RCA 1860 ▲	1 13

Michael ZAGER BAND
US, male / female vocal / instrumental group (12 WEEKS)
		pos/wks
1 Apr 78 ●	LET'S ALL CHANT Private Stock PVT 143	8 12

Gheorghe ZAMFIR
Romania, male instrumentalist - pipes (9 WEEKS)
		pos/wks
21 Aug 76 ●	(LIGHT OF EXPERIENCE) DOINA DE JALE Epic EPC 4310	4 9

Tommy ZANG US, male vocalist (1 WEEK)
		pos/wks
16 Feb 61	HEY GOOD LOOKING Polydor NH 66957	45 1

ZAPP US, male vocal / instrumental group (6 WEEKS)
		pos/wks
25 Jan 86	IT DOESN'T REALLY MATTER Warner Bros. W 8879	57 3
24 May 86	COMPUTER LOVE (PART 1) Warner Bros. W 8805	64 3

Francesco ZAPPALA Italy, male producer (3 WEEKS)
		pos/wks
10 Aug 91	WE GOTTA DO IT Fourth & Broadway BRW 225 [1]	57 2
2 May 92	NO WAY OUT PWL Continental PWL 230	69 1

[1] DJ Professor featuring Francesco Zappala

Lena ZAVARONI UK, female vocalist (14 WEEKS)
		pos/wks
9 Feb 74 ●	MA HE'S MAKING EYES AT ME Philips 6006 367	10 11
1 Jun 74	PERSONALITY Philips 6006 391	33 3

ZED BIAS UK, male vocal / production group (4 WEEKS)
		pos/wks
15 Jul 00	NEIGHBOURHOOD Locked On / XL Recordings LOX 122CD	25 4

ZEE UK, female vocalist (4 WEEKS)
		pos/wks
6 Jul 96	DREAMTIME Perfecto PERF 122CD	31 2
22 Mar 97	SAY MY NAME Perfecto PERF 135CD	36 1
7 Feb 98	BUTTERFLY Perfecto PERF 154CD1 [1]	41 1

[1] Tilt featuring Zee

ZEPHYRS UK, male vocal / instrumental group (1 WEEK)
		pos/wks
18 Mar 65	SHE'S LOST YOU Columbia DB 7481	48 1

ZERO B UK, male instrumentalist - keyboards (6 WEEKS)
		pos/wks
22 Feb 92	THE EP Ffrreedom TAB 102	32 4
24 Jul 93	RECONNECTION (EP) Internal LIECD 6	54 2

Tracks on The EP: Lock Up / Spinning Wheel / Module / Eclipse. Tracks on Reconnection EP: Lock Up / Lock Up (re-mix) / Ou Est Le Spoon / Love to Be In Love. All three versions of 'Lock Up' are different mixes of the same track

ZERO VU Featuring Lorna B
UK, male / female vocal / production group (1 WEEK)
		pos/wks
15 Mar 97	FEELS SO GOOD Avex UK AVEXCD 53	69 1

ZERO ZERO UK, male instrumental / production duo (1 WEEK)
		pos/wks
10 Aug 91	ZEROXED Kickin KICK 9	71 1

ZHANÉ US, female vocal duo (18 WEEKS)
		pos/wks
11 Sep 93	HEY MR DJ Epic 6596102	26 3
4 Dec 93	HEY MR DJ (re-entry) Epic 6596102	50 2
19 Mar 94	GROOVE THANG Motown TMGCD 1423	34 3
20 Aug 94	VIBE Motown TMGCD 1430	67 1
25 Feb 95	SHAME Jive JIVECD 372	66 1
21 Sep 96	IT'S A PARTY Elektra EKR 226CD [1]	23 2
8 Mar 97	4 MORE Tommy Boy TBCD 7779A [2]	52 1
26 Apr 97	REQUEST LINE Motown 8606452	22 3
30 Aug 97	CRUSH Motown 5716712	44 1
11 Sep 99	JAMBOREE Arista 74321692882 [3]	51 1

[1] Busta Rhymes featuring Zhané [2] De La Soul featuring Zhané [3] Naughty By Nature featuring Zhané

ZIG and ZAG Zog / Ireland, male puppet duo (12 WEEKS)
		pos/wks
24 Dec 94 ●	THEM GIRLS THEM GIRLS RCA 74321251042	5 9
1 Jul 95	HANDS UP! HANDS UP! RCA 74321284392	21 3

ZIGZAG JIVE FLUTES – See ELIAS and his ZIGZAG JIVE FLUTES

ZION TRAIN UK, male / female vocal / instrumental group (1 WEEK)
		pos/wks
27 Jul 96	RISE China WOKCD 2085	61 1

ZODIAC MINDWARP and the LOVE REACTION UK, male / female vocal / instrumental group (11 WEEKS)
		pos/wks
9 May 87	PRIME MOVER Mercury ZOD 1	18 6
14 Nov 87	BACKSEAT EDUCATION Mercury ZOD 2	49 3
2 Apr 88	PLANET GIRL Mercury ZOD 3	63 2

ZODIACS – See Maurice WILLIAMS and the ZODIACS

ZOË UK, female vocalist - Zoë Pollock (22 WEEKS)
		pos/wks
10 Nov 90	SUNSHINE ON A RAINY DAY M & G MAGS 6	53 5
24 Aug 91 ●	SUNSHINE ON A RAINY DAY (re-mix) M & G MAGS 14	4 11
2 Nov 91	LIGHTNING M & G MAGS 18	37 4
29 Feb 92	HOLY DAYS M & G MAGS 21	72 2

ZOMBIE NATION Germany, male production duo - Florian "Splank" Senfter & Emanuel "Mooner" Guenther (15 WEEKS)
		pos/wks
2 Sep 00	KERNKRAFT 400 (IMPORT) TRANSK TRANSK 002	61 1
30 Sep 00 ●	KERNKRAFT 400 Data DATA 11CDS	2 14+

Rob ZOMBIE US, male vocalist (2 WEEKS)
		pos/wks
26 Dec 98	DRAGULA Geffen GFSTD 22367	44 2

ZOMBIES UK, male vocal / instrumental group (16 WEEKS)
		pos/wks
13 Aug 64	SHE'S NOT THERE Decca F 11940	12 11
11 Feb 65	TELL HER NO Decca F 12072	42 5

ZOO EXPERIENCE featuring DESTRY UK, male instrumental group, and US, male vocalist (1 WEEK)
		pos/wks
22 Aug 92	LOVE'S GOTTA HOLD ON ME Cooltempo COOL 261	66 1

ZUCCHERO *Italy, male vocalist / instrumentalist - guitar. Adelmo Fornaciari (24 WEEKS)*

pos/wks

30 Mar 91	● SENZA UNA DONNA (WITHOUT A WOMAN) *London LON 294* [1]	4	12
18 Jan 92	DIAMANTE *London LON 313* [2]	44	7
24 Oct 92	MISERERE *London LON 329* [3]	15	5

[1] Zucchero and Paul Young [2] Zucchero with Randy Crawford [3] Zucchero with Luciano Pavarotti

ZZ TOP (322) **Top 500** *Low-slung guitar driven blues-rock trio formed 1969 in Houston, Texas, US; long-bearded duo Billy Gibbons (v/g) and Dusty Hill (v/b) plus clean-shaven Frank Beard (d). Hugely popular stadium-packing festival headliners in the 1980s. Named to ensure they would be the last act in record racks and hit books (94 WEEKS)*

pos/wks

3 Sep 83	GIMME ALL YOUR LOVIN' *Warner Bros. W 9693*.........................	61	3
26 Nov 83	SHARP DRESSED MAN *Warner Bros. W 9576*...........................	53	3
31 Mar 84	TV DINNERS *Warner Bros. W 9334*..	67	3
6 Oct 84	● GIMME ALL YOUR LOVIN' (re-entry) *Warner Bros. W 9693*....	10	15
15 Dec 84	SHARP DRESSED MAN (re-entry) *Warner Bros. W 9576*....	22	10
23 Feb 85	LEGS *Warner Bros. W 9272*..	16	7
13 Jul 85	SUMMER HOLIDAY (EP) *Warner Bros. W 8946*	51	5
19 Oct 85	SLEEPING BAG *Warner Bros. W 2001*	27	5
15 Feb 86	STAGES *Warner Bros. W 2002*...	43	3
19 Apr 86	ROUGH BOY *Warner Bros. W 2003*	23	9
4 Oct 86	VELCRO FLY *Warner Bros. W 8650*...	54	3
21 Jul 90	DOUBLEBACK *Warner Bros. W 9812*	29	6
13 Apr 91	MY HEAD'S IN MISSISSIPPI *Warner Bros W 0009*.....................	37	5
11 Apr 92	● VIVA LAS VEGAS *Warner Bros. W 0098*	10	7
20 Jun 92	ROUGH BOY (re-issue) *Warner Bros. W 0111*	49	3
29 Jan 94	PINCUSHION *RCA 74321184732*..	15	3
7 May 94	BREAKAWAY *RCA 74321192282*	60	1
29 Jun 96	WHAT'S UP WITH THAT *RCA 74321394822*...............................	58	1
16 Oct 99	GIMME ALL YOUR LOVIN' 2000 *Riverhorse RIVHCD 2* [1]	28	2

[1] Martay featuring ZZ Top

Tracks on Summer Holiday (EP): Tush / Got Me Under Pressure / Beer Drinkers and Hell Raisers / I'm Bad, I'm Nationwide

UK No.1 ★   UK Top 10 ●   Still on chart +   UK million seller ◆   UK entry at No.1 ■   US No.1 ▲

A–Z by Song Title

This section contains an alphabetical index of every hit since 1952 in order of title, act name, highest position the hit reached on the chart and the year(s) in which it charted.

Covers: Different songs with the same title are differentiated by a letter in brackets after the song title: [A], [B], etc. Cover versions of the same song share the same letter. For example, there are seven versions of 'Around the World'. Four of these titles share the letter [A], which indicates that they are all covers of the same song (recorded individually by Bing Crosby, Ronnie Hilton, Gracie Fields and Mantovani). However, the fifth version is followed by the letter [B], which indicates that it is a different song (recorded by East 17). If the original version of a cover was never a chart hit, it will not be listed here.

Non-singles: In most cases, individual titles of songs on EP, LP, medley or megamix singles that made the chart are not listed here, although full track listings are included in the artist entries in the A-Z by artist section.

Most duets list both artists involved (eg 'Don't Let the Sun Go Down on Me' by Elton John and George Michael), but some hits are credited only to the main artist. For example, 'Zing a Little Zong' is credited to Bing Crosby. But if you look up his entry in the A-Z by artist section, a footnote for the hit explains that it was, in fact, a duet with Jane Wyman.

Act names use bold capital letters to indicate where to look them up alphabetically in the A-Z by artist section. Groups, bands, orchestras, and ensembles are alphabetised according to the whole act name, while individual artists are ordered according to their surnames. Therefore, DANNY WILSON is a group and appears under 'D', while Jennifer LOPEZ is an individual and appears under 'L'.

different letters denote that songs are unique; the same letter indicates different versions of the same song

song title

BOOGIE DOWN [A] — Eddie KENDRICKS (39) 74
BOOGIE DOWN [B] — Al JARREAU (63) 83
BOOGIE DOWN (BRONX) — Man PARRISH (56) 85
BOOGIE DOWN (GET FUNKY NOW) —
   REAL THING (33) 79
BOOGIE MAN — MATCH (48) 79
BOOGIE NIGHTS [A] — HEATWAVE (2) 77
BOOGIE NIGHTS [A] — La FLEUR (51) 83
BOOGIE NIGHTS [A] — SONIA (30) 92
BOOGIE ON REGGAE WOMAN —

artist

   Stevie WONDER (12) 75

year of chart entry

highest position reached on chart

bold capital letters are used to indicate where to look for an artist alphabetically in the A-Z by artist section, except where multi-artist collaborations occur

co: Pictorial Press

The Who: 29 songs in this index without a single chart-topper

495

503

527

529

533

543

GUINNESS
WORLD RECORDS™

BRITISH HIT SINGLES

WE NEED YOUR VOTES

You've read the book, now choose your favourite 10 singles from the 25,000 hits to contribute toward the ultimate music fan's Top 100 Singles of all-time.

Contribute to the ultimate Top 100 singles chart by registering your votes and you could win one of 100 exclusive Guinness British Hit Singles T-shirts. This survey will form part of the celebrations leading-up to the 50th anniversary of the UK singles chart in 2002.

Write to us or visit our web site for a form to contribute your Top 10 towards the compiling of the Guinness British Hit Singles Top 100.

The Editor
Guinness British Hit Singles
Guinness World Records
338 Euston Road
London NW1 3BD

www.guinnessworldrecords.com/music

MELANIE C'S FAVOURITE SINGLE IS 'SIR DUKE'
BY STEVIE WONDER. **WHAT'S YOURS?**